Honors Programs & Colleges

3rd Edition

Dr. Joan Digby

The Official Guide of the National Collegiate Honors Council

Australia • Canada • Mexico • Singapore • Spain • United Kingdom • United States

About The Thomson Corporation and Peterson's

With revenues of US$7.2 billion, The Thomson Corporation (www.thomson.com) is a leading global provider of integrated information solutions for business, education, and professional customers. Its Learning businesses and brands (www.thomsonlearning.com) serve the needs of individuals, learning institutions, and corporations with products and services for both traditional and distributed learning.

Peterson's, part of The Thomson Corporation, is one of the nation's most respected providers of lifelong learning online resources, software, reference guides, and books. The Education Supersite℠ at www.petersons.com—the Internet's most heavily traveled education resource—has searchable databases and interactive tools for contacting U.S.-accredited institutions and programs. In addition, Peterson's serves more than 105 million education consumers annually.

For more information, contact Peterson's, 2000 Lenox Drive, Lawrenceville, NJ 08648; 800-338-3282; or find us on the World Wide Web at www.petersons.com/about.

ISBN 0-7689-1068-4

Printed in the United States of America

10 9 8 7 6 5 4 3 2 1 04 03 02

CONTENTS

Acknowledgments

Honors is by nature a cooperative enterprise. This book is a testimony to the cooperation of National Collegiate Honors Council administrators and staff, faculty and students, all of whom believe in the honors venture. As our network grows, so does our guide, and that means I have many more people to thank for contributing information that will help students find the extraordinary programs we offer. I thank you all with pleasure. For graciously sharing their personal insights into particular aspects of honors education, I am especially indebted to my NCHC colleagues: Bernice Braid, Gary Bell, John Grady, Hew Joiner, Ada Long, Bob Spurrier, Ross Wheeler, Rosalie Otero, and Len Zane. I am also grateful to our diverse and flourishing alumni for taking the time to reflect on the value of their honors education.

It takes many people, working behind the scenes to bring a book to life. At NCHC national headquarters, Earl Brown and Gayle Barkesdale provided constant support. At Peterson's, our thoughtful and creative editor, Fern Oram, deserves our sincere, collective appreciation for simplifying a difficult project. I also wish to acknowledge the administration of Long Island University for their continued support of this endeavor. In my own honors program, I wish to thank my dedicated assistant, Tracey Christy, and the students who gave her many hands in preparing the materials for this book: Selin Barlas, Patricia Fletcher, Catherine Gembinski, and Shauntice Plowden. Finally, at home, my husband John—a great lover of books—knows the making of this book better than anyone and has helped me shape and reflect all along the way.

Dr. Joan Digby, Director of the Honors Program,
Long Island University, C.W. Post Campus
President, National Collegiate Honors Council 1999–2000

President's Message

Dr. Rosalie Otero, Director of the Honors Program, University of New Mexico
President, National Collegiate Honors Council, 2001–02

Finding the best college is a major decision. There are many questions to be asked and considered. Which college has a major in which I'm interested? Are the freshmen classes large? What is the campus like? Is there a superior faculty? How much will it cost? These are some of the challenging issues that you face as you search for the best place for you. Most students and their families are concerned about getting the best value for their money. They want a good education that will allow their student to be prepared and competitive in future endeavors, whether in an occupation or graduate and professional schools.

Highly motivated bright students look for colleges and universities that will provide them with a challenging, engaging, and comprehensive education to serve as a foundation for their futures. This book will be particularly useful to you. It provides you with a wealth of information that can help you in your decision. Listed here are colleges and universities that are members of the National Collegiate Honors Council (NCHC). NCHC is an organization of institutions (public, private, four-year, and two-year), faculty members, students, administrators, and others interested in supporting honors education. The mission of NCHC is to cultivate excellence in American undergraduate education by assisting honors programs and colleges to create and enhance opportunities (academic, cultural, and social) for exceptionally able, highly motivated undergraduate students.

Performing underwater research in Australia during the 2001 Summer Biological Diversity Research Program in Australia, sponsored by the University of New Mexico University Honors Program.

Honors programs and honors colleges, although differing in many ways, have in common the offering of rigorous, coherent, and integrative academic experiences and a high degree of student-faculty interaction. Honors programs and honors colleges promote creativity, risk-taking, independence, and critical thinking. So for thousands of dollars less, students can enjoy Ivy-level academic and social privileges in the environment of a small school-but often with the benefit of the facilities of a large research institution.

I received a letter from one of my students who was participating in an NCHC Honors Semester in Greece. Here is just a brief excerpt: "I just returned to Athens from an excursion to Crete. After we arrived in Crete, we took a bus tour to the Allied Cemetery at Souda Bay. What a spectacular place looking over the water and a small island said to have been formed by stranded sirens who had lost their wings. Then we drove to the old town of Rethymno which featured the last remaining hand-made fillo dough shop in Crete." The students climbed Mount Olympus and, of course, visited the many historical sites that, prior to this, had only been pictures in books. As director of our honors program, I had the opportunity to visit a group of students who were studying in Spain last fall. They were delighted to find themselves in such a historically rich culture. One young woman told me in Spanish that the opportunity to study and travel in Spain had changed her life. We also have an exciting biodiversity program in Australia during the summer. Students do field study in Lamington National Park, Kakadu National Park, and Lizard Island. As a result of their intense field study, five of these students have received prestigious Goldwater Fellowships. We had a student who studied opera in Italy, one who worked with flood victims in Honduras, and another who founded the Reef Ranger Project in the Virgin Islands-a project for high school students to learn about and care for the world's coral reefs.

These stories aren't particularly unique to our university or our students. I believe you would hear these kinds of stories from every honors program and honors college in the nation, and you'd also find that curiosity, high energy, extraordinary effort, and uniqueness is typical of all honors students. When you join an honors program, you will find a genuine sense of personality that comes from students and faculty members in the programs. The point I'm making is that after careful consideration about campuses, majors, the climate, residence halls, and friends, you can obtain a superior education by becoming an honors student in any of the institutions listed in this book. The institutions include four-year public and private as well as community colleges across the United States and Puerto Rico. I can guarantee that you can call any of the honors directors, coordinators, or deans of these institutions, and they will be happy to answer your questions.

Honors programs and colleges are designed to provide students with varied educational opportunities. Many honors programs and honors colleges offer lecture series, international educational opportunities, research opportunities, and interdisciplinary courses. Students are encouraged to be active in campus politics, service learning, sports, college newspapers and other publications, and various other campus clubs and organizations. Honors programs and colleges provide an environment that encourages students to experiment and strengthen their individual talents in all areas that include the curricular, cocurricular, and extracurricular experiences of the students. Honors programs and colleges are committed to providing an excellent education not only so that students can be competitive in future jobs, but so that they also will be exemplary citizens in a global society.

Most important, students who participate in an honors program or an honors college join a community. These honors communities provide a sense of belonging and solidarity. Education today is often conceived of as a collection of courses without a coherent integrative dimension as well as something that is designed for and applied to students, rather than a joint process. The honors experience is a community of support in which discoveries are shared and ideas are mutually explored and critiqued. You will find honors programs and honors colleges full of high-energy, unique, and extraordinary students and faculty members.

Equally important is the fact that honors students across the nation are competitive scholars for such prestigious fellowships as the Rhodes, Marshall, and Truman. In addition, they are accepted into competitive graduate and professional schools.

In making your college decision, be sure to add to your list of considerations whether the institutions you are comparing have an honors program or an honors college. And finally, whatever your choice, take advantage of every opportunity. See your education as real life, not as something you have to get through. Chances are most of you will see your 100th birthday. Medical science virtually guarantees it. So you can look forward to a long life. To ensure a successful life, make every effort to realize the most of your education. Make sure that you take risks, see learning as a lifelong endeavor, be versatile, discover your own frontiers, and find a way to make a difference and to leave a mark that is uniquely yours.

Learning to dance the Flamenco during the Fall 2001 Semester in Spain, sponsored by the University of New Mexico Honors Program.

HONORS: AN A+ EDUCATION

Dr. Joan Digby, Director of the Honors Program, Long Island University, C. W. Post Campus
President, National Collegiate Honors Council, 1999–2000

Who are Honors Students?

If you are a strong student filled with ideas, longing for creative expression, and ready to take on career-shaping challenges, then an honors education is just for you. Honors programs and colleges offer some of the finest undergraduate degrees available in American colleges and do it with students in mind. The essence of honors is personal attention, top faculty members, enlightening seminars, illuminating study-travel experiences, research options, career-building internships-all designed to enhance a classic education and prepare you for life achievements. And here's an eye-opening bonus: honors programs and colleges may reward your past academic performance by giving you scholarships that will help you pay for your higher education.

Honors students Gretchen Ringhahl (left), Anne Furuseth (middle), and Elissa Grossel (right) perform in the College of St. Scholastica's production of Richard III. *The three students portrayed Queen Elizabeth, Queen Margaret, and the Duchess of York, respectively.*

Take your choice of institutions: community college, state or private four-year college, or large research university. There are honors opportunities in each. What they share in common is an unqualified commitment to academic excellence. Honors education teaches students to think and write clearly, to be excited by ideas, and to become independent, creative, self-confident learners. It prepares exceptional students for professional choices in every imaginable sphere of life: arts and sciences, engineering, business, health, education, medicine, theater, music, film, journalism, media, law, politics-invent your own professional goal, and honors will guide you to it! There are hundreds of honors programs and honors colleges around the country. Whichever one you choose, you can be sure to enjoy an extraordinarily fulfilling undergraduate education.

Who are you? Perhaps a high school junior making out your first college applications, a community college student seeking to transfer to a four-year college, or possibly a four-year college student doing better than you had expected. You might be an international student, a varsity athlete, captain of the debate team, or second violin in the campus orchestra. Whether you are the first person in your family to attend college or an adult with a grown family seeking a new career, honors might well be right for you. Honors programs admit students with every imaginable background and educational goal.

How does honors satisfy them and give them something special? Read what students in some of our member programs say. Although they refer to particular colleges, their experiences are typical of what students find exciting about honors education on hundreds of campuses around the country.

> "Honors is not just a class or a degree but rather a family that you can count on. I was an out-of-state student, not knowing anyone, and honors helped me [make] the drastic change from high school student to college scholar. Through its educators as well as its students, honors has changed my life for the better."
>
> *Chris Whitford*
> *Business major*
> *University of Maine, Orono*

> "Having interested people who remember my name and monitor my progress made a big difference to me. . .. The crossover of disciplines is amazing. I use notes from philosophy class in botany and ecology. The text in ecology uses terms I studied in botany, and they all refer to Aristotle and algebra. Finishing this program has made it a part of me, and it will alter the outcome of my life."
>
> *Andre Chenault*
> *Tulsa Community College*

"Although the structure of my engineering courses makes involvement in the Honors Program difficult, my honors classes have been the perfect break from my major. Rather than sitting in yet another classroom with 20+ students being told how things are, through honors I get to sit in a classroom with 16 or fewer students and actually discuss the material. Discussion and paper assignments in my honors courses have kept me on my toes."

Colin Smith
Villanova University

"Through engaging discussions and readings in seminars like African Literature and Politics and Literature of the Apocalypse, Christ College has challenged me to examine my view of the world by introducing me to different ideas, cultures, beliefs, and lifestyles."

Gretchen Eelkema
Chemistry and French major
Valparaiso University, Christ College

"I went to an arts high school that allowed me to participate in . . music, theater, and the visual arts. . . I had trouble finding a college that would allow me to create a specialized major (and that would be within my budget!). I gave up and settled on Cal State Fullerton as a temporary solution . . . I was also accepted into their Honors Program and I soon discovered that it was the best thing I could have done. . . . To my surprise [my honors director] was an art professor and was excited to create a major specialized to my interests. Unexpectedly Cal State Fullerton became the perfect school for me, but it could not have come about without the special attention I received in the Honors Program."

Joy Shannon
College of the Arts, California State University, Fullerton

"Required core courses failed to present provocative new ways of viewing the work, which I thought to be an inherent part of a college education. This want for insightful academic challenges led to my enrollment in City's Honors Program. Honors classes like World Civilizations inspired critical thought and scrutiny of both self and the world . . . ."

Géraldo E. Médor
Biochemistry major and premed student
The City College of the City University of New York

". . . have been interested in independent research for a long time, and I was fascinated by the idea of [striking] out on my own to pursue an area of research that really interested me. . . . I am writing two theses concurrently, one in chemistry and one in biology, in order to obtain double degrees."

Sam Ozer
New College of Florida

"Beyond the classroom, living on campus in the Honors Building provided the intellectually stimulating environment I craved. . . . The Honors Program provided a crowd of first-rate students who will go on to achieve much success in their lives. Spending time with so many creative, empowered people has helped me in countless ways."

P. Jay Delaney
B.S. Marketing
Wright State University

Students in Central Michigan University's Honors Program face off against faculty members in the traditional chess challenge.

"This enriching environment encouraged me to study abroad, to present papers at professional conferences, and even to create and then teach a course to fellow honors students. Faculty encouraging students to learn from them and learn with them provided the most important collective experience of my undergraduate career."

Erin McMullen
Class of 2001, Ball State University

"My experience in the Honors College of Hampton University is one of the treasures of my academic career. Honors College deserves enormous credit for helping me to achieve admission to Harvard Law School and realizing success as a law student. I learned how to prepare for exams, how to write well, and how to communicate effectively. . . My current involvement with Harvard's Frederick Douglass moot court team was sparked by my years as an Honors College debater. . . . I am also a student attorney for the Harvard Prison Legal Assistance Project (PLAP). The Honors College experience continues to bear fruit in my academic and professional adventures."

Courtney A. Dunbar
Class of 2000, Hampton University

"Within the environment of a large public university, I truly found my niche in the Honors Program. . . .Now that I have begun my career at the Board of Governors of the Federal Reserve System in Washington, D.C., it is not what I learned from a textbook that is most meaningful. The University of Akron's Honors Program helped me realize that the fundamental purpose of education is becoming a student of life."

Christine N. Thomas
Class of 2001, University of Akron

These portraits don't tell the whole story, but they should give you a sense of what it means to be part of an honors program or honors college. Outside of class, honors students often run track, run the student government, and write the college newspaper. They

At the McDonnell–Barksdale Honors College, University of Mississippi, classes are often held on the deck.

are everywhere on campus: in plays and concerts, in laboratories and libraries, in sororities and fraternities. Some are clear about their majors and professions; others need direction and advice. One of the great strengths of honors programs is that they are nurturing environments that encourage students to be well-rounded and help students make life choices.

What is an Honors Program?

An honors program is a sequence of courses designed specifically to encourage independent and creative learning. Whether you want to attend a large state university or a private one, a small or large four-year college, or your local community college, you can make the decision to join an honors program. For more than half a century, honors education, given definition by the National Collegiate Honors Council, has been an institution on American campuses. Although honors programs have many different designs, there are typical components. In two-year colleges, the programs often concentrate on special versions of general education courses and may have individual capstone projects that come out of the students' special interest. In four-year colleges and universities, honors programs are generally designed for students of almost every major in every college on campus. In some cases, they are given additional prominence as honors colleges. Whether a program or a college, honors is most often structured as a general education or core component followed by advanced courses (often called colloquia or seminars) and a thesis or creative project, which may or may not be in the departmental major. Almost always, honors curriculum is incorporated within whatever number of credits is required of every student for graduation. Honors very rarely requires students to take additional credits. Students who complete an honors program or honors college curriculum frequently receive transcript and diploma notations as well as certificates, medallions, or other citations at graduation ceremonies.

While researching honors programs and colleges, you will begin to see typical patterns of academic programming, and that is where you must choose the program or college best suited to your own needs. In every case, catering to the student as an individual plays a central role in honors course design. Most honors classes are small (under 20 students); most are discussion-oriented, giving students a chance to present their own interpretations of ideas and even teach a part of the course. Many classes are interdisciplinary, which means they are taught by faculty members from two or more departments, providing different perspectives on a subject. All honors classes help students develop and articulate their own perspectives by cultivating both verbal and written style. They help students mature intellectually, preparing them to engage in their own explorations and research. Some programs even extend the options for self-growth to study abroad and internships in science, government, the arts, or business related to the major. Other programs encourage or require community service as part of the honors experience. In every case, honors is an experiential education that deepens classroom learning and extends far beyond.

Despite their individual differences, all honors programs and honors colleges rely on faculty members who enjoy working with bright, independent students. The ideal honors faculty members are open-minded and encouraging master teachers. They want to see their students achieve at their highest capacity, and they are glad to spend time with students in discussions and laboratories, on field trips and at conferences, or online in e-mail. They often influence career decisions, provide inspiring models, and remain friends long after they have served as thesis advisers.

Where are Honors Programs and Honors Colleges Located?

Because honors programs and honors colleges include students from many different departments or colleges, they usually have their own offices and space on campus. Some have their own buildings. Most programs have honors centers or lounges where students gather together for informal conversations, luncheons, discussions, lectures, and special projects.

Many honors students have cultivated strong personal interests that have nothing to do with classes; they may be experts at using the Internet; they may be fine artists or poets, musicians or racing car enthusiasts. Some volunteer in hospitals or do landscape gardening to pay for college. Many work in retail stores and catering. Some inline skate and others collect antique watches. When they get together in honors lounges, there is always an interesting mixture of ideas.

In general, honors provides an environment in which students feel free to talk about their passionate interests and ideas, knowing they will find good listeners and sometimes arguers. There is no end to conversations among honors students. Like many students in honors, you may feel a great relief in finding a sympathetic group that respects your intelligence and creativity. In honors, you can be eccentric, you can be yourself! Some lifelong friendships, even marriages, are the result of social relationships developed in honors programs. Of course you will make other friends in classes, clubs, and elsewhere on campus, even through e-mail! But the honors program will build strong bonds too.

The University of West Florida Honors Program, in cooperation with the Washington Center, sends many students each year to intern in Washington, D.C. Pictured at the Capitol with the group is U.S. Congressman Joe Scarborough.

In the honors center, whether program or college, you will also find the honors director or dean. The honors director often serves as a personal adviser to all of the students in the program. Many programs also have peer counselors and mentors who are upperclass honors students and know the ropes from a student's perspective and experience. Some have specially assigned honors advisers who guide honors students through their degrees, assist in registration, and answer every imaginable question. The honors office area usually is a good place to meet people, ask questions, and solve problems.

Are You Ready for Honors?

Admission to honors programs and honors colleges is generally based on a combination of several factors: high school or previous college grades, SAT or ACT scores, personal essay, and extra-curricular achievements. To stay in honors, students need to maintain a certain GPA (grade point average) and show progress toward the completion of the specific honors program or college requirements. Since you have probably exceeded admissions standards all along, maintaining your GPA will not be as big a problem as it sounds. Your faculty members and your honors director are there to help you succeed in the program. Most honors programs have very low attrition rates, because students enjoy classes and do well. You have every reason to believe that you can make the grade.

Of course, you must be careful about how you budget your time for studying. Honors encourages well-rounded, diversified students, and you should play a sport if you want to, work at the radio station, join the clubs that interest you, or pledge a sorority or fraternity. You might find a job in the food service or library that will help you pay for your car expenses, and that also is reasonable. But remember, each activity takes time, and you must strike a balance that will leave you enough time to do your homework, prepare for seminar discussions, do your research, and do well on exams. Choose the extracurricular activities and work opportunities

At Salem State College, the open door policy of the Honors Program office sometimes makes for friendly crowds.

on campus that attract you, but never let them overshadow your primary purpose-to be a student.

Sometimes even the very best students who apply for honors admissions are frightened by the thought of speaking in front of a group, giving seminar papers, or writing a thesis. But if you understand how the programs work, you will see that there is nothing to be frightened about. The basis of honors is confidence in the student and building the student's self-confidence. Once you are admitted to an honors program, you have already demonstrated your academic achievement in high school or college classes. Once in an honors program, you will learn how to formulate and structure ideas so that you can apply critical judgment to sets of facts and opinions. In small seminar classes, you practice discussion and arguments, so by the time you come to the senior thesis or project, the method is second nature. For most honors students, the senior thesis, performance, or portfolio presentation is the project that gives them the greatest fulfillment and pride. In many honors programs and colleges, students present their work either to other students or to faculty members in their major departments. Students often present their work at regional and national honors conferences. Some students even publish their work jointly with their faculty mentors. These are great achievements, and they come naturally with the training. There is nothing to be afraid of. Just do it! Honors will make you ready for life.

All of the honors programs listed in this guide are members of a large national organization, the National Collegiate Honors Council (NCHC), which has advocated honors education for more than fifty years. NCHC holds meetings every year for honors directors, faculty members, and students. Honors students play a large role in NCHC. They have representatives to cover student issues. Students serve on committees and present papers at the national convention. In fact, in some years there are as many students as faculty members attending the annual meeting-leading discussions, sharing their research, and shaping the future of American honors education. Many honors programs pay all or part of their students' travel, both to the national convention and to regional honors conventions, which also present excellent opportunities for student participation. I hope to meet you there.

In the following pages you will hear from honors educators and officers of the National Collegiate Honors Council, who extend to you their greetings and share their experience.

Alumni Profile

Veronika Gagovic
North Central College
Class of 2001

"I arrived at North Central College in 1997, on a path to becoming a physician. My biochemistry background in Bosnia prepared me for an intellectual challenge, but the Honors Program gave me something that was not covered in the science curriculum—an opportunity to explore myself. History of Ideas classes encouraged sharing ideas and opinions, made me aware of where I stand in relation to current and historical issues, and encouraged me to write. As a result, my senior thesis was not a science paper, but was the first two chapters of my book on the Bosnian Civil War. My self-exploration is continuing in medical school at Loyola–Stritch in Chicago. This is where I realized that knowing myself, my motivations, and my opinions is essential to understanding and helping the patients I will treat and where I realized that the Honors Program helped mold me into a better future physician."

NATIONAL COLLEGIATE HONORS COUNCIL'S BASIC CHARACTERISTICS OF A FULLY DEVELOPED HONORS PROGRAM

No one model of an honors program can be superimposed on all types of institutions; however, there are several characteristics in common. Listed below are those characteristics, although not all are necessary for a program to be fully developed or successful.

1. A fully developed honors program should be carefully set up to accommodate the special needs and abilities of the undergraduate students it is designed to serve. This entails identifying the targeted student population by some clearly articulated set of criteria (e.g., GPA or SAT scores or a written essay). A program with open admission needs to spell out expectations for retention in the program and for satisfactory completion of program requirements.
2. The program should have a mandate from the institutional administration, ideally in the form of a mission statement, clearly stating the objectives and responsibilities of the program and defining its place in both the administrative and academic structure of the institution. This mandate or mission statement should ensure the permanence and stability of the program by guaranteeing an adequate budget and by avoiding the tendency to force the program to depend on temporary or spasmodic dedication of particular faculty members or administrators. In other words, the program should be fully institutionalized so as to build a genuine tradition of excellence.
3. The honors director should report to the chief academic officer of the institution.
4. There should be an honors curriculum featuring special courses, seminars, colloquia and independent study established in harmony with the mission statement and in response to the needs of the program.
5. The program requirements should include a substantial proportion of the participants' undergraduate work, usually in the vicinity of 20-25 percent of their total course work and certainly no less than 15 percent.
6. The program should be so formulated that it relates effectively to all the college work for the degree (e.g., by satisfying general education requirements) and to the area of concentration, departmental specialization, and preprofessional or professional training.
7. The program should be both visible and highly reputed throughout the institution so that it is perceived as providing standards and models of excellence for students and faculty members across the campus.
8. Faculty members participating in the program should be fully identified with the aims of the program. They should be carefully selected on the basis of exceptional teaching skills

and the ability to provide intellectual leadership to able students.

9. The program should occupy suitable quarters constituting an honors center, with such facilities as an honors library, a lounge, reading rooms, personal computers, and appropriate decor.
10. The director or other administrative officer charged with administering the program should work in close collaboration with a committee or council of faculty members representing the colleges and/or departments served by the program.
11. The program should have in place a committee of honors students to serve as liaison with the honors faculty committee or council, who must keep the student group fully informed of the program and elicit their cooperation in evaluation and development. This student group should enjoy as much autonomy as possible while conducting the business of the committee in representing the needs and concerns of all honors students to the administration, and it should also be included in governance, serving on the advisory/policy committee, as well as constituting the group that governs the student association.
12. There should be provisions for special academic counseling of honors students by uniquely qualified faculty and/or staff personnel.
13. The honors program, in distinguishing itself from the rest of the institution, serves as a kind of laboratory within which faculty members can try new ideas. When such efforts are demonstrated to be successful, they may well become institutionalized, thereby raising the general level of education within the college or university for all students. In this connection, the honors curriculum should serve as a prototype for educational practices that can work campuswide in the future.
14. The fully developed honors program must be open to continuous and critical review and be prepared to change in order to maintain its distinctive position of offering distinguished education to the best students in the institution.
15. A fully developed program will emphasize the participatory nature of the honors educational process by adopting such measures as offering opportunities for students to participate in regional and national conferences, honors semesters, international programs, community service, and other forms of experiential education.
16. Fully developed two- and four-year honors programs should have articulation agreements by which honors graduates from two-year colleges can be accepted into four-year honors programs when they meet previously agreed-upon requirements.

National Collegiate Honors Council
PO Box 7017
Radford, Virginia 24142-7017
http://www.radford.edu/~nchc/

Partnerships in Honors Education

Dr. G. Hewett Joiner, Director, Orell Bernard Bell and Sue Floyd Bell Honors Program, Georgia Southern University; President, National Collegiate Honors Council 2000–01

In recent years, the National Collegiate Honors Council (NCHC) has formed a network of partnerships with other educational organizations that opens doors to an array of additional benefits and recognition to students in college honors programs.

NCHC has long-standing cooperative friendships with Phi Beta Kappa (established in 1776, America's oldest academic honorary society recognizes outstanding student scholarship in liberal arts fields), Phi Kappa Phi (recognizes exemplary student academic achievement in all fields of study), Phi Theta Kappa (the national honor society for two-year institutions), and Phi Eta Sigma (the national freshman honor society), growing naturally out of a shared mission of enhancing the education of outstanding college students. Via these associations, NCHC seeks to ensure that students recognize the value that these societies bring and to encourage the establishment of chapters of these societies on campuses where they do not currently exist. In addition to the prestige that selection to these societies lends to students' resumes, membership also opens the door to scholarship support from both local chapters and national organizations.

During 2001, NCHC joined with Phi Beta Kappa, Phi Theta Kappa, and the high school National Honor Society in the newly created Alliance for Educational Excellence. The intent of the alliance is to use the collective strength and influence of our four organizations to defend the value of a broad liberal arts education at all levels against those pressures that promote training, rather than a genuine education. Already the alliance has drawn a national spotlight to this vital set of issues, and it promises to be an effective mechanism for ensuring that the focus of high school and undergraduate collegiate education remains the nurturing of all of the qualities that go into cultivation of educated human beings. By speaking with a single, unified voice on this important issue, the alliance also seeks to ensure that resources-public and private-for the ample support of this concept of education continue to flow in the future.

The annual NCHC Satellite Seminars, which make available special enrichments of the educational experiences of college students across the United States via satellite technology, are now being produced in partnership with Phi Theta Kappa. Each year across the U.S., the Satellite Seminars make available a series of seminars on topics of major significance and high contemporary relevance that are presented by nationally recognized experts. Use of satellite technology brings to all institutions, at a very modest cost, access to and interaction with major scholars. Hundreds of institutions of learning take advantage of the Satellite Seminars annually to add fresh dimensions to the education of their students who would otherwise not have access to them.

NCHC has begun to develop a close working relationship with the Association of Collegiate Honor Societies, a national organization of nearly seventy highly regarded academic honorary societies, including a large number that recognize outstanding student achievement in a wide array of specific fields of study. The aim of this partnership is to cultivate a wider array of opportunities and activities to enrich the education of high-ability college students in institutions of higher learning across the United States. A particular goal of this partnership is promotion of expansion of opportunities for undergraduate research on campuses across the nation.

NCHC enjoys a close and cooperative relationship with the Washington Center for Internships and Academic Seminars and the Fund for American Studies.

Both of these organizations offer the broadening experiences of internships in legislative, governmental, and nonprofit institutions to college students. NCHC's collaboration with the Washington Center and the Fund for American Studies opens the doors to students in all honors programs to many valuable opportunities beyond the standard curriculum.

From its inception in 2000, the newly formed National Association of Fellowship Advisors (NAFA) has had a close working relationship with NCHC. Through its partnership with NAFA, NCHC ensures that honors students are made aware of opportunities for fellowship and scholarship support for graduate and professional study beyond the baccalaureate level-including such major scholarships as Rhodes, Marshall, Truman, and Goldwater—and are aware of the qualifications necessary to compete successfully for the award of such scholarships.

NCHC seeks to add additional dimensions to the education of honors students in all institutions and to advance and enhance the character of collegiate education for all students.

Laredo Community College Honors Program students helped clean and mulch the nature trail by International Bridge II as part of the Dia del Rio, *a binational cleanup effort that draws attention to the importance of cleaning and maintaining the Rio Grande to keep it pollution free.*

Honors Students and Scholarships

Dr. Gary M. Bell, Dean, University Honors College, Texas Tech University

Let's begin with some really good news: Students who are considering an honors program are also the very people most likely to be eligible for scholarship assistance. Funding a college is an important, difficult, and even educational part of being a student. Let's face it, college is expensive! Scholarships provide part of the solution for how to finance your undergraduate career. Honors students are precisely the ones that colleges recruit most eagerly. Good high school students add to the prestige of an institution, and schools typically advertise your decision to attend their institution. Thus, there is an excellent chance that the school of your choice may provide scholarship assistance in order to encourage your enrollment and to enhance their bragging rights.

Another way to view the next four (or more) years you will spend earning your college baccalaureate degree is to think of the learning task as your primary employment. It is therefore helpful to think of a scholarship as part of the salary for undertaking your job of learning. From this perspective, you then have the right, again as a potential honors student, to seek the best pay, or scholarship, possible. One of your first inquiries as you examine a potential college setting is about the type of assistance they might provide given your interests, academic record, and personal history. Talk to a financial aid officer or a scholarship coordinator at the school. At most schools, these are special officers—people specifically employed to assist you in your quest for financial assistance. Virtually all schools also have brochures or publications that list scholarship opportunities at their institution. Get this literature and read it carefully.

In your search for monetary assistance, visit either your local bookstore or your local public library where there are usually books that have several hundred scholarships listed in different categories. These types of books can be economically purchased, and they can also typically be found in the reference section of libraries. The Internet is similarly a useful tool to obtain additional information. Lastly, high school counselors often have keen insight into resources available at colleges, especially the schools in your area. These people are the key point of contact between institutions of higher education and you, the high school graduate. In general, it is not a particularly good practice to use a private company that promises, frequently for a considerable fee, a list of scholarships for which you might be eligible. Such lists are often very broad, and more importantly, you can secure the same results by using available high school, university, and published information.

What do we mean be the word "scholarship" anyway? In the very broadest sense, scholarships consist of outright grants of monetary assistance to eligible students to help them attend college. The money is of course to be applied to tuition or the cost of living while in school. Scholarships do not need to be repaid. They do often carry stringent criteria for maintaining

Hillsboro Community College Honors Institute students, alumni, and professors explore New Mexico on a camping trip.

them, such as the achievement of a certain grade point average, the carrying of a given number of class hours, matriculation in a specific program, or membership in a designated group. Scholarships at many schools may be combined with college work-study programs—where some work is also required. Also be sensitive to the fact that many scholarships can be bundled, that is, put together with other scholarships so that collectively they can provide you with a truly attractive financial aid package. Equally important, scholarships can also be bundled with low-interest loan programs to make the school of your choice financially accessible.

Scholarships generally fall into three major categories. These are need-based scholarships, predicated on your or your family's income; merit-based scholarships, based on your academic and sometimes extracurricular achievements; and association-based scholarships, which are dependent on as many different associations as you can imagine (for instance, your home county, your identification with a particular group, or the company for which a parent may work). The range of reasons for which scholarships are given is almost infinite.

Many schools accommodate students who have financial need. Probably the most widespread of the grant programs are the U.S. government-sponsored Federal Pell Grants and the Federal Supplemental Educational Opportunity Grants, which you might want to explore with the financial aid counselor. Also inquire about state-sponsored grant programs.

Merit-based scholarships can come from a variety of sources—from the university as a whole, individual departments or colleges within the university, or special donors who want to assist worthy students. This fact should be remembered as you meet with financial aid officers, because they know that different opportunities may be available for you as a petroleum engineering, agriculture, accounting, pre–veterinary, or performing arts major. Merit-based scholarships are typically designed to reward the highest performers on such precollege measures as standardized tests (the SAT or ACT) and achievement in high school grades. Since repeated performance on standardized tests often leads to higher scores, it may be financially advantageous for you to take these college admissions tests several times. Practice truly does help and may pay dividends.

Frequently, schools have endowed scholarships (scholarships based on a fund, the principal of which

Andrew McLemore (center), Michigan State University honors student, stars in the University's production of The Marriage of Figaro.

can never be used) given by alumni or others with a particular interest in supporting honors students. Thus, your acceptance to an honors program can carry with it not only enhanced educational benefits, but also substantial monetary assistance. A warning needs to be interjected here, however. If you are joining an honors program only for the financial advantage, you are joining for the wrong reason. Honors education is about broadening your educational experiences, opening an array of academic opportunities, and challenging you to be better than you think you can be. If money is your only incentive in becoming associated with honors, you probably need to look elsewhere for financial assistance.

Inquire quite specifically into each of these three categories of scholarships. The association-based scholarships can sometimes be particularly helpful and quite surprising. Employers of parents, people from specific geographical locations, or organizations (churches, civic groups, special interest clubs, and even family name associations) may have assistance for college students that few know about or even bother to use. Campus scholarship literature is the primary key to unlocking the mysteries of association-based financial assistance (and the other two categories as well), but personal interviews with financial officers are also crucial.

There are several issues to which you must attend as you seek scholarship assistance. Probably the most important is to determine deadlines that apply to a scholarship for which you may be eligible. It always wise to begin your search early, so that your eligibility is not nullified by having applied too late. Most scholarship opportunities require an application form, and it is time well spent to make sure the application is neat, grammatically correct, and logical. Correct spelling is essential. Have someone proofread your application (these are not bad guidelines to follow with your honors application as well-if the honors program of your choice requires an application). Keep in mind that if applications require essays, fewer students typically take the time to complete these essays, giving those students who are willing to write a better chance of winning that particular scholarship. Always be accurate about yourself in these applications, but at the same time, provide the most positive self-portrayal to enhance your chances of being considered. Be sensitive to the fact that most merit-based and association-based scholarships are awarded competitively.

Finally, as soon as your plans become firm, do let the people who offer you assistance know your decision about whether or not you will accept their offer. Too many students simply assume that a scholarship offer means automatic acceptance. This is not the case! In almost all instances, you must send a letter of acknowledgement and acceptance. Nationally, virtually all schools have agreed that students must make up their minds about scholarship (and sometimes school) acceptance no later than May 1. But earlier deadlines may apply.

How do you make the choice of which school to attend? There are many elements to consider, such as reputation, programs offered, courses provided, and the school's success in placing graduates. Visit the prospective school and see if the student profile, the campus amenities, and the atmosphere of the campus fit your needs and aspirations. But above most other factors, it is imperative that you pay attention to cost. Where can you realistically afford to go without incurring the very large debts that could plague you after graduation? In the end, you must choose the college or university that seems best for you and that fits your and your family's budget. Scholarships should play a very big role in your decision-making matrix.

As you undoubtedly know, tuition at private schools is typically higher than tuition at state colleges and universities. Scholarships can narrow this gap. Many private institutions have a great deal of money to spend on scholarship assistance, so you may well find that going to a private college will cost no more than attending a state school. You should note one caution, however. A substantial scholarship from a private school may still leave you with a very large annual bill to cover the difference between the scholarship amount and the actual cost of tuition, fees, and living expenses. When you evaluate a scholarship, therefore, do so by comparing your final projected costs as you consider the expense of which school to attend. Another factor to consider is the length of time for which the school extends scholarship support. Be cautious about the school that promises substantial assistance for the first year-in order to get you there-but then provides little or nothing in the second through the fourth or later years. The most attractive and meaningful scholarships are offered for four to five years.

Incidentally, the scholarship search should never be abandoned once you are enrolled at the school of your choice. There are often a number of opportunities for the enrolled student, especially as you prove your ability and interest in a given field. Also, honors students have been particularly successful in national scholarship competitions, such as the Rhodes, Fulbright, Goldwater, Truman, and Udall. Finally, your earned scholarship may well be applied to study-abroad or the National Collegiate Honors Council (NCHC) Honors Semester programs, so begin to consider early in your college career the benefits that an off-campus experience can bestow upon you.

When considering college funding, low-interest or even interest-free, government-provided educational loans can be available to you, depending on your personal circumstances. Many states also have similar loan provisions available for their citizens. Loans are to be sought only after scholarship possibilities are exhausted, but in the last analysis, your education is probably the best investment you will ever make. Thus, borrowing for your college expenses is both a justifiable and sometimes necessary element in securing that most precious and most enduring of all personal assets, a sound educational background.

Alumni Profile

Delia J. Kerr
Hampton University
Class of 2001

"As a student of the Honors College, I have grasped all required and available opportunities. In my graduate experiences, I use the vast information I have learned from honors seminars on multicultural issues to explain to professors the importance of a multicultural perspective in psychological research. The required community-service hours provided me with needed clinical experience as a rape crisis counselor. My love for this topic and the required internships led me to participation in an internship at a sexual-trauma center. This experience, along with opportunities for conference presentations, classified me as a top candidate for graduate school. The opportunities in Honors College helped to mold me into a well-rounded and top graduate student in my Ph.D. program."

NCHC Honors Program and Honors College Students Recognized as Prestigious Scholarship Winners

Dr. Robert L. Spurrier Jr., Director, The Honors College, Oklahoma State University
President, National Collegiate Honors Council, 1998–99

Honors program and honors college students distinguish themselves in many ways in scholarship, leadership, and service. One particularly impressive measure of distinction is winning a major national or international scholarship competition. Again in 2001, honors students at NCHC institutions won British Marshall, Churchill, Fulbright, Goldwater, Javitts, Mellon, Mitchell, National Defense Science and Engineering, National Science Foundation, Phi Kappa Phi, Rhodes, Rotary, Truman, and Udall Scholarships and Fellowships.

Some of these prestigious awards help defray the cost of undergraduate education while offering students an opportunity to pursue research in their majors, graduate with distinction, and take the next step toward advanced degrees. Others provide generous support for graduate education in the United States and abroad. The NCHC web site provides links to detailed information about many of the major scholarships and fellowships for which honors students have competed successfully http://www.radford.edu/~nchc/other-links.htm.

Our students can best explain the meaning of these awards in their own words. Here is what they have to say about the various ways in which their honors experiences helped them become winners of these prestigious scholarships. We congratulate them, and we offer an invitation to entering students to join an NCHC honors program or honors college and help us continue the tradition of academic excellence across the nation.

"I received a Rhodes Scholarship largely due to my participation in the University of Alabama Honors Program. The professors in the Honors Program are deeply devoted to undergraduate research. The students participating in the Honors Program form a community of the best and brightest students on campus, those committed to academic, social, and service-oriented excellence. The chance to be a part of the University of Alabama Honors Program, an Ivy League school in miniature, was a blessed chance for me. I would hope that all the excelling high school seniors in the country and in the world consider this program."

Bradley Davin Tuggle
University of Alabama
Class of 2001

"MSU's Honors Program has added a humanistic dimension to my major in mathematics. It was my advance calculus class that made me realize that I wanted to become a mathematician, but because of several seminars I have also realized what kind of mathematician I want to be. Reading *Einstein's Dreams* in my freshman honors seminar gave me hope for writing fiction with a scientific bent (not necessarily science fiction) alongside the mathematical proofs I write for my

research. While taking a senior honors seminar in environmental ethics, I became conscious of how I can contribute to the environmental movement, both personally and professionally, through mathematical research. Finally, after being a student fellow for the freshman honors course, I realized that I want to remain connected to young people. Mathematics may seem like an island sometimes, but the Montana State University Honors Program is one of my bridges to the rest of humanity."

Kay Kirkpatrick
Montana State University

Kay Kirkpatrick is a senior mathematician and a recipient of the Goldwater Scholarship. She is also a recent co-winner of the Alice T. Schafer Prize, given to the nation's best female undergraduate mathematics student.

"By providing leadership, service, cultural, and research opportunities, the Honors Program prepared me to apply for a Fullbright Grant to study in Germany. Participation in weekly "brown bags" as a presenter and audience member let me see what other students were doing and broadened my horizons. I took advantage of the Honors Program grant money to support my research and to present it. In addition, the Honors Program gave me information about scholarship and fellowships, while also providing advice in how best to apply for them. I strongly believe that my active participation in the Honors Program was key to my Fullbright Grant receipt."

Louisa R. Seifert
University of Toledo
Class of 2001

"The University of Toledo Honors Program gave me the opportunity to seek a challenging undergraduate education, including both research and leadership positions. With the encouragement of the Honors Program staff, I was able to work on research during my first year, later undertake new research under an NSF grant, travel to national conferences, and receive a Fullbright Scholarship. With the confidence that I developed in my honors classes, I pursued subjects that interested me and approached faculty and staff to support my work in these areas. In short, the University of Toledo Honors Program made my undergraduate career a success."

Jason M. Bechtel
University of Toledo
Class of 2000

Jason and Louisa were married in June of 2001. They left Toledo in September 2001 to travel to Freiburg, Germany, where they are both conducting research under the auspices of Fullbright Grants.

"I came to the UCA Honors College as a young, inexperienced 17 year-old who had left high school a year early to hasten my education beyond the pace of the small rural school I was attending. From the first class reading, Walker Percy's *The Loss of the Creature,* I knew that I had found my place. I will always remember that first semester as the greatest period of personal and intellectual growth in my life. Throughout my tenure at the Honors College, I was allowed the freedom to think and grow in a structured, supportive environment. I learned how to think, how to act, and most importantly, how to participate effectively in the human conversation. The skills and ideas I learned have resulted in recently being awarded a Rhodes Scholarship to study the classics at Oxford. I will forever be indebted to those in the Honors College who aided me in my journey of intellectual and personal growth."

Rhett Martin
University of Central Arkansas
Class of 2002

"Winning the (Morris K.) Udall Scholarship is an honor for me and for a fine academic program taught by admirable faculty. Environmental issues have been personal concerns that also have been central to all that I've learned at MSU, where the land-grant traditions have prepared me to serve our society by preserving and enhancing the best qualities of our natural environment."

Amanda L. Grau
Mississippi State University
Class of 2002

Now, meet some of our other scholars.

Clarion University Honors alumni Michelle Aaron (right) has been awarded a Howard Hughes Medical Fellowship. She's no stranger to national recognition. During her four year at Clarion, she received an honorable mention for the National Defense Science and Engineering Graduate Fellowship, a national Barry M. Goldwater Scholarship, and two off-campus science internships. Michelle is pictured with fellow Goldwater winner Jessica Smith and Dennis Slagle, who received honorable mention.

While studying in the United Kingdom on a Fullbright Grant, Villanova University student Pat Doughery visited Beaumaris, a town on the Island of Anglesey in Wales.

Han Kang, member of UC Irvine's campuswide Honors Program, 2000 Truman Scholar, and member of *USA Today* All-American Academic First Team.

Rudyard Sadleir, 2001 Rhodes Scholar from the University of Illinois at Chicago, is studying paleobiology while at Oxford.

Ebony Antoinette Spikes of Baton Rouge, Louisiana, received a Marshall Scholarship for 2002. She is a senior in the Honors College at Louisiana State University, majoring in biochemistry. After completing her honors research in the spring, she plans to study philosophy, psychology, and physiology at Oxford.

ALUMNI PROFILE

Emin Toro
Palm Beach Atlantic College
Class of 1997

"The practice of law demands not only the understanding of fundamental principles but also the mastery of intricate detail. To render sound legal advice to my clients, I must be able to synthesize existing law, and perhaps more importantly, to apply legal principles to specific facts. In attempting to do this, I rely on the foundational skills I gained as a student in the Frederick M. Supper Honors Program at Palm Beach Atlantic College. The program's integrated approach to the study of the humanities instilled in me a desire to search for overarching principles, while our in-depth study of historical events, literary and artistic works, and philosophical ideas helped me develop the ability to grasp details. The program's rigorous writing requirements encouraged me to learn to express myself clearly and succinctly while at the same time being pushed to develop my own ideas and interests. I look back on my years in the Honors Program with appreciation for the lessons I learned and look forward to continuing to apply those lessons as I work in the legal profession."

HONORS: PROGRAM OR COLLEGE?

Dr. Len Zane, Founding Dean of the Honors College, University of Nevada
President, National Collegiate Honors Council, 1995–96

As you read through this guide, you will notice that colleges and universities house honors in one of two distinct units: program or college. Consequently, it is reasonable to ask how an honors college differs from an honors program. Unfortunately like many questions, the question is easier to formulate than it is to answer.

The more relevant question is "Am I likely to have a better experience being part of an honors college than an honors program?" Part of the answer to that question obviously depends on the differences between the two, but the answer also depends on the structure and strengths of the honors colleges and programs being compared. Furthermore, a positive attribute for one person may be a negative for another. For example, does the program or college have an honors residence, and is the residence mandatory or optional? *Is it better or worse to have participants in honors housed separately?* What are the requirements for graduating with honors? *Are more requirements better than fewer?* How many students participate in honors? *Is large better than small?* These are only a few of the questions that should be considered when comparing honors on one campus with honors on another campus.

Some of the differences alluded to above can be influenced by whether or not an institution has an honors program or honors college. To see how these differences arise, it is valuable to describe some of the general characteristics normally associated with a college or program. At universities, colleges are the primary academic units. Colleges typically house a group of academic departments that share some thematic connection. Colleges employ faculty members, establish requirements for graduation, grant degrees, schedule courses, are led by deans, and operate with a large degree of autonomy. It is more difficult to define a typical program at a college or university because the term program has been used to describe a much broader range of units. For example, looking through my campus directory I can find an Academic Support Program, Asian Studies Program, CCSD/UNLV Cooperative Early Childhood Program, Early Studies Program, and six other programs before reaching the place honors would fall in the alphabetical listing. There are thirteen colleges and thirty programs at the University of Nevada, Las Vegas (UNLV). I have no reason to believe UNLV is atypical with respect to the number or variety of entities called program residing on campus. Consequently, on any given campus, an honors college would have a higher institutional profile than an academically equivalent unit that found itself grouped with the larger, less homogeneous collection of units called programs.

The Barrett Honors College at Arizona State University embraces the diverse and eclectic interests of its students. Senior Gouri Nair is not only an electrical engineering major with an eye toward a career in patent law, but a gifted dancer as well. Gouri dances Bharathanatyam, a classical dance form of her native India that tells spiritual stories from Hindu mythology.

In fact, when I asked deans of other honors colleges to assist me in articulating the differences between college and program, the natural panache associated with being a college was cited by several colleagues as one of the substantive advantages of "collegehood." Ted Estess, Dean of the Honors College at the University of Houston, said it best:

> "The difference between college and program is largely symbolic, which is not to say that symbolic difference is not real and substantial. The principle is this: change the symbols and you change the reality. And the change to honors college, as a symbolic change, is a change of reality. Well, what kind of change? For one thing, it symbolizes a change in the placement of honors education in the internal structure of the university. In the case of the University of Houston, honors is now one of fourteen colleges, not one of several dozen programs. The honors dean is more clearly a part of the upper administrative structure of the university, thereby facilitating negotiations with other departments and colleges. But perhaps it is more externally that the symbolic differences have the greatest impact, first to prospective students and their parents, and then to prospective donors and supporters. To both groups, the change to honors college signifies that the university understands itself as a place where truly outstanding students will be attended to. In having an honors college, the university makes more visible and more public its commitment to meeting the specific academic needs of outstanding students."

Implied in the above description is that the creation of an honors college requires a substantially more serious commitment on the part of the central administration to honors than is necessary for the existence of an honors program. The institutional soul-searching that precedes the metamorphosis of honors from a program to a college increases the profile of honors on campus. That higher profile makes it easier for a dean of an honors college to garner the cooperation of other deans and department chairs to support the mission of honors than it is for a director to get an

University of Texas senior Jaime Rauch captures the silver medal in the 800-meter men's freestyle at the summer Olympic Games in Sydney.

Penn State Schreyer Scholars Dave Goldfarb and Dan Fuchs on a service-learning project in south India. Each year, the Schreyer Honors College sponsors a number of domestic and international service opportunities.

equivalent level of support for an honors program. Consequently, in general and on average, honors colleges will have more resources and support than an honors program and will also typically be larger, with a broader array of accouterments.

Regardless of the setting-honors program or college, large university or small college-honors works best at schools that build honors around preexisting strengths of that particular institution. Those strengths can be exceptionally talented faculty members, particularly strong departments, special housing arrangements, international study programs, strong research areas, etc. My experience at UNLV, and the anecdotal experiences shared with me by colleagues from around the country who are deans of honors colleges, strongly support the notion that honors colleges, because of the relationship of the dean to the central administration and the external community, are more able to weave an institution's strengths into the fabric of the education offered within the honors college. This interplay between perception and reality seen in the honors community is strong support for the common observation that perception is reality. At least for honors colleges, perception often becomes reality, once the campus's central administration commits to an honors college.

As you face the daunting task of selecting the college or university to which you want to entrust your postsecondary education, I offer two thoughts that may lessen your stress. First, as you read, ponder, and attempt to use the self-descriptions in this book, remember that the information presented is empowering and allows you to make a more informed decision. Second, high-quality, challenging, and inspiring education happens on literally hundreds and hundreds of campuses across the country. Unique opportunities of various kinds are available on most campuses. Part of being a good consumer of higher education is learning how to maximize the value of the collegiate experience. Needless to say, those of us involved with honors fervently believe that honors education is the most rewarding path on all campuses. Consequently, the actual selection of a college or university is substantially less important than the zest, ambition, skill, and study habits you bring to the institution selected. Recognizing that as a prospective student, you control, to a surprisingly large degree, the quality of experience that you will have in college shifts the anxiety away from the process of selecting the optimal school to optimizing your experience at the selected school.

Best wishes for a successful conclusion to your search for the right college or university. And more importantly, have a great and memorable undergraduate career highlighted by participation in honors at the school of your choice.

Matthew Steele ('00, Chemical Engineering) reports on his work with Royal Dutch Shell in the Netherlands to Ted Estess, Dean of the Honors College at the University of Houston.

ALUMNI PROFILE

John Rodriguez
Lehman College
Class of 2001

"I've always been a Bronx boy, but back when I was growing up on Gun Hill Road, I never thought of being a poet. It never really seemed like an option back then, not for me, not for any of my friends. But I got into Lehman College and with the help of some really good professors in Lehman's English program, I discovered that I am a poet. They showed me that I could write about the block, about my friends, and that those poems count just as much as any poem by Frost or Sheakespeare—which meant we count, too. With the support of my professors, I've been writing, teaching, and performing poetry all over the city."

As a Parent to Parents

Professor John S. Grady, Director, University Honors Program, La Salle University

Having experienced the college selection process firsthand as a parent of five children, each of whom is a graduate of the La Salle University Honors Program, I can appreciate some of the concerns you might have in assisting your child through this process. Given the intellectual talents your child has demonstrated, the task can be even more formidable. In addition to addressing this challenge as a parent, I have attempted to respond to other parents' concerns during the more than three decades I have served as an honors program director. It is this dual perspective of parent and director that prompted the editor to ask me to address some of these concerns for you. I hope what follows proves to be helpful.

Although each parent has concerns specific to a unique situation, I believe there are four major ones that parents and students have mentioned consistently over the years. They are the fear of taking on too much too soon by participating in an honors program, the reluctance to be labeled elitist, the desire to participate to the fullest in the total undergraduate experience, and a parent's natural desire to be kept informed of the student's progress. Obviously, these fears are not totally unrelated.

Some students will be apprehensive about taking on the challenge that participation in honors presents. They might at times question their ability to compete with some of the most intellectually gifted students on the campus. But if you reflect for a minute and recall their track record, these are students who have established a pattern of willingness to accept academic risks. They have been challenged by the best at every level, and they have succeeded. Quite possibly, one of the factors that contributed significantly to that success was their acceptance of that challenge. Their history is not to be denied, and other things being equal, there is every reason to believe they will continue to excel at this next level.

Cal State Fullerton honors students and faculty members participate in the annual AIDS Walk LA, raising more than $1,000 to provide direct support services to men, women, and children living with HIV/AIDS in Los Angeles county.

No one would deny that different people have been blessed with different talents, and many have some talents that are exceptional. There are differences among individuals, and even though we did not create these differences, we would be remiss if we did not recognize those differences and address them. Colleges and universities have long recognized differences in physical and athletic abilities. Some gifted students participate at one level; others less gifted at a somewhat different level. Is this anything more than the recognition and addressing of different endowments? Should this be any less true when the gifts are intellectual? And if to some a greater measure of talents has been given, should we not provide for the recognition and nurturing of those talents? That some students such as your own possess these intellectual gifts, that they constitute an academic elite, if you will, is simply a fact. One of the purposes of an honors program is to recognize that fact and provide those students with the means necessary to develop their talents. I do not see this as being elitist; I see it as being responsible.

If you examine the structure of most honors programs carefully-and you should-you will recognize that in all cases a student is only part-time in honors.

Typically, an honors program student will be completing core or general education requirements in honors while pursuing major courses and electives in the general curriculum. Such a structure belies identification as separatist, since the vast majority of the student's class time will be outside honors. In fact, one of the spillover benefits of having an honors program on campus is to serve as "yeast" to the larger academic community, encouraging a rising quality on each side of the desk. Rather than encouraging withdrawal from the full undergraduate experience, the honors program student is encouraged to lead in that broader area in endeavors that further develop talents. Ironically, then, the honors program student is of both the full community and the honors community, reaping the varied benefits accruing to full participation in each. Indeed, honors program students have been exceptional at building bridges that unite. Again, in most cases, this has simply been one more extension of a student's prior academic history.

Program Director Charlie Slavin with students and faculty members from the University of Maine at Orono at the National Collegiate Honors Council banquet in Chicago.

For many, a child's advancement to college is the first extended separation from family. As a parent or guardian, we want to be kept informed of progress as well as difficulty; we want to continue to parent. While this can certainly be accomplished, you must be cognizant of limitations imposed by law. Since most college students have reached the age of 18, their right to privacy—including their college activities in and out of the classroom—is protected by law. As a professor and also as an honors program director, I am not permitted to reveal your child's academic, social, or disciplinary records to you without his or her permission. All the more reason as a parent that I want every possible assurance that the environment in which my child will learn, socialize, and grow is a nurturing and caring one, one which addresses the development of the whole person as well as demanding the best of that person. This is what we attempt to create in those communities described as honors.

I would like to conclude, as I began, on a personal note. Having seen more than 1,000 students complete their honors education and move on to successful careers and productive lives has been most rewarding. This has been particularly so in the case of my own children, who often speak about how valuable their honors experience has been in strengthening their values and shaping their careers. There is no doubt in my mind as a parent that the honors program experience was the best possible *in loco parentis.*

Honors: A Community for Life

Dr. Ada Long, Director of the Honors Program, University of Alabama at Birmingham
President, National Collegiate Honors Council, 1994–95

Students who join our Honors Program become members of our academic community not just for the next four years, but in most cases, for life. I suspect the same is true for most honors programs. After our students graduate, they serve as mentors to the students who come after them; participate in frequent reunions; help each other find scholarships, jobs, and housing; provide moral and financial support; and visit the Honors House whenever they're in town or in the neighborhood. This community provides a sense of belonging and stability that helps each student find bearings in an educational environment dedicated to challenge and change.

Many students see college today as putting in time before they get to their "real lives", which they see as life after college. Honors programs are designed for the other kind of students: those who see college as real life, as a place and a time in their lives not just to prepare themselves for a career but to learn about themselves and others, to seek wisdom as well as knowledge, to explore the unknown, and to find what most excites them so that they may maintain this excitement for the rest of their lives. Above all, these students want to find a way to make a difference and to leave a mark that is uniquely theirs.

What I think makes honors programs most honorable is the commitment to honoring the distinct gifts of students within a context of high expectations. And what makes directing an honors program the best job in academia is watching those gifts develop, deepen, and then go to work in the world. Each student who has entered our program has a story that illustrates this process; I will tell just four of them.

Kellie skipped her senior year in high school and started college when she was 16. For an upper-level honors project, she did a study of homelessness that included two weeks of living on the street and in shelters—scaring the daylights out of me and her parents (we all checked on her constantly)—and leading to an extraordinarily moving and informative analysis of the daily lives of homeless women in Birmingham. She received a Truman Scholarship, which funded her last two years at the University of Alabama at Birmingham (UAB) and her master's degree at Johns Hopkins University. Since then, she has worked as a consultant for employment services for the homeless in Washington, D.C., and has traveled all over the world as a labor consultant. She is now in her second year of law school at Georgetown. Kellie helps all our current students who are interested in public service careers, serves as an outside adviser on research projects, and spends every New Year's Eve at my house catching me up on the work she has done in Bulgaria and elsewhere.

*Ada Long with (left to right) UAB Honors Program students Neel Varshney (Rhodes Scholar), Jason Lott (Marshall Scholar), and Kira Martin (*USA Today *All-American Academic First Team).*

I met Cedric when he was a student in my remedial English class. An immensely gifted and original young man, he was struggling to make up for twelve years in a rural Alabama school system. I invited him into the honors program, where he quickly became a favorite of his classmates. When he graduated, he took a test for the management training program at State Farm Insurance. An executive at State Farm called me to say that nobody from Cedric's county had ever performed so well on the test. Cedric married another student in the honors program (she is now a pediatrician), they have two sons, and they are regular visitors at the Honors House.

Katie was an anthropology major at UAB. During the summer, she went to Bali with her adviser to study macaques. She married a fellow honors student, an engineering major, at the Honors House. The two of them moved to New York where Katie had a National Science Foundation Fellowship to study for her Ph.D. at The City University of New York (CUNY). She spent much of her time as a doctoral student studying chimpanzees in Cameroon (her work has been written up in the *New York Times*) while her husband was updating computer hardware for the NOAA at the South Pole. Now she is a post-doc at the NIH, and he is a rocket scientist (for real). Both are regular mentors and research advisers for current students.

Andria joined the honors program after a 25-year career as a mother and retail sales manager. She was locally elected as a student representative on the Honors Council and nationally elected to serve on the Executive Committee of the National Collegiate Honors Council. She became an important mother figure to all the college-aged students in the Honors Program while at the same time doing excellent work within her major field, English. Within weeks of graduating from UAB, she got a job at ***Southern Living,*** where she is now foods editor. Three months ago, she was appointed to the University of Alabama System's Board of Trustees, so she is now my boss as well as close friend. Andria has long served on the Advisory Board of the honors program, has given at least five guest lectures, and has helped numerous students find internships and employment.

Florida International University Honors course students hiking in the Everglades.

Many of our other honors students have become lawyers, doctors, accountants, and virtually every other kind of professional you can think of. When I or any of our students need any kind of service, there's always an alumnus or alumna out there to provide it. Our students past and present—and future—contribute their unique gifts not just to the world at large, but to each other, helping to maintain a community that is always changing but always there as a home base. It is a community that is now global as well as local and that welcomes each new student as an individual and as a member of a shared lifelong support network. Surely this is what education is supposed to be, and it is what honors programs throughout the country foster as their special role in higher education.

Reinventing Urban Culture: A National Collegiate Honors Council Honors Semester

Dr. Bernice Braid, Chair, Honors Semesters Committee, National Collegiate Honors Council
Director, University Honors Program, LIU–Brooklyn
Instructor, City as Text©, New York Honors Semester 2001

Dr. Ross Wheeler, Academic Director, New York Honors Semester
Associate Director, University Honors Program, LIU–Brooklyn

Since 1976, in partnership with a member college, the National Collegiate Honors Council (NCHC) has offered a unique opportunity for immersion learning. In the NCHC Honors Semester, courses from several disciplines tied to a theme especially exciting to explore in a particular site and guided by NCHC's hallmark City as Text©, provide a laboratory for learning, growth, and development unmatched in American higher education. Projects have been undertaken in rural areas: Appalachian Culture, Who Goes Hungry, as examined at the epicenter of the world's food industry in Ames, Iowa; in large cities: Globalization, the Making of International Community, explored in New York City; the new European Union, examined in both the Czech Republic and in Thessaloniki, Greece, seen as a crossroads of culture over time; Crossing Borders, experienced in El Paso; and close examination of conflicted cultures influenced by disparate forces, such as in Mexico, Spain, and Puerto Rico—all adding up to twenty-six years of dynamic curricular opportunities for honors students nationwide.

In fall 2001, the ninth NCHC–Long Island University-Brooklyn Campus cosponsorship produced an in-depth look at urban issues. Reinventing Urban Culture concentrated on ways that major metropolitan

Students in New York Honors Semester on Urban Exploration in New York City.

Boys on Stoop, *by Briana Bassler—Student in the New York Honors Semester, Reinventing Urban Culture. Image from Documenting Community and Public Space class.*

areas, New York City in particular, transform, redefine, and reconfigure themselves to establish their importance as cultural and economic centers. Thirty students from twenty-three schools and seventeen states arrived in New York on September 4 and began their studies in the city's downtown and Wall Street area. September 11 found all of them in Manhattan at Grand Central Station, expecting to spend their morning behind the scenes talking to engineers and architects about the place, its function, its rebirth, and the challenge of mass transit in a congested center like this city. By 11 a.m., with subways and bridges closed, students found themselves among the millions walking anywhere from 10 to 30 miles to reach home, which for this group was in downtown Brooklyn at the Long Island University campus—a very long walk south, past the crash sight, then onto one of three bridges leading to the campus.

The Semester Program was readjusted, sending students out into Queens and Brooklyn until Manhattan had stabilized and students were again able to resume explorations there. It is a mark of their grit, their perseverance, and their determination that they all chose to remain with the Semester and in the city. The September events, however, colored much of the work they did, informing the images they took in their photo-documentary course and serving as backdrop to their examination of public space, urban design, and historic preservation. As several of them remarked, the turn of events following that fateful day made the entire Semester a laboratory experience like no other in the world-an insight confirmed by their daily City as Text© explorations throughout the city. As always in an NCHC Semester, students brought with them every kind of past and future expectation. They left with a sparkle in their eyes readable from miles away, excited as much about their discovery of one another as about the invention of new selves in a new city. As one reported in his *Musings* notebook, "Nowhere is normal here. No two communities are alike. Chinatown is as different from nearby Greenwich Village as Forest Hills Gardens is from Midtown Manhattan. There is no epitome district here. If anything, I'm surprised that I haven't completely come to expect the unexpected here, since that's what it's been so much about-the bizarre, the random, the unexpected."

Embracing the unexpected and acquiring the habit of witnessing, deciphering, recording, was the heart of their own "reinvention". These students made their mark, and have been marked by this extraordinary time in an extraordinary place.

Flags, *by Erica Schultz—Student in the New York Honors Semester, Reinventing Urban Culture. Image from Documenting Community and Public Space class.*

ALUMNI PROFILE

Stella SiWan Cheung
Arizona State University
Class of 1997

"A Woodrow Wilson fellowship, a two-semester internship in family studies, community service, an invaluable honors thesis process, and inspiring mentors—these things come to mind when I am asked about my BHC and ASU undergraduate educational experience. My experiences as a BHC student included volunteering for a police gang unit and working with terminally ill hospice patients. My thesis on early adolescence was the cornerstone of my work today. After I graduated, I utilized my fellowship award to attend the Humphrey Institute of Public Policy at the University of Minnesota, where I received a Masters in Public Affairs. I began doing contract work in program evaluation as a graduate student. Today, this has blossomed into ACET Inc., a consulting business serving the program evaluation needs of multiple universities, foundations, school districts, and community organizations in Minnesota and Wisconsin."

How to Use This Guide

As you get ready to use this guide, it is important to look first at the KEY in the upper right-hand section of each program listing. This will help you identify the programs that are best suited for your consideration.

The number **2** or **4** indicates whether the program is part of a two-year or four-year institution. **Pu** stands for a public or state institution, **Pr** for a private college or university. **G** tells you that the program is a general honors program; **D** indicates that it is departmental. Most of the programs listed in the book are primarily general honors. And honors program can also be **S**mall (under 100 students), **M**edium (100-500 students), or **L**arge (more than 500 students). You will know what size program best suits your personality. Even large honors programs provide a great deal of individual attention. If scholarships are available through the honors program, **Sc** will be listed in the key. Programs that take transfer students have the designation **Tr**. Schools that are categorized as historically black colleges are notated as **HBC**. Programs that have special honors academic advisors are designated **AA;** graduate advisers, **GA;** and/or fellowship advisers, **FA**.

So a key entry that reads: **4 Pr G M Sc Tr AA** tells you that the program is part of a four-year private college or university that offers general honors to a medium-size group of students. Scholarships are available, transfer students are admitted, and there is a special honors academic adviser. A key entry that read **2 Pu G S** indicates a two-year public institution (probably a community college) that grants general honors to a small number of students but does not have money designated for scholarship assistance.

Now you are ready to read through the program descriptions. Each has been written by the program's own director, so it contains an intimate view of the program from the inside. It tells you what the program is like, how long it has been in existence, how many honors students are enrolled, what kind of courses are offered, and what special features constitute student life. Each description includes admissions and participation requirements, so you will know exactly what is expected of you in that particular program. In the second section, **The Campus Context,** you will find a description of the college or university as a whole, including the makeup of the students and faculty. It is important to read that section, since it tells you, among other things, the geography of the institution, the special features that might interest you-such as museums and theaters-as well as the size of its library and range of its computer facilities. Both are important for your independent research. You might also want to know if you could join a fraternity or sorority, play varsity tennis, study abroad, or work in a laboratory. Make sure that the school can also accommodate any particular needs that you might have. Finally, you need to look at the cost of tuition and fees as well as room and board. Whether you choose to live on campus is a personal, as well as a financial, matter. You will see that some honors programs have honors dormitories or dorm wings with study areas and even computer facilities. Some students find that appealing, while others prefer to live within the general mix of dorm students, in an off-campus apartment, or at home with their families.

All of the costs quoted here are the most recent at the time of publication. However, you do need to confirm costs when making your other inquiries. At the same time, you will probably find changes in other figures, such as the exact number of students in an honors program or college, the number of books in a library, or number of computers on campus. Colleges and universities are living institutions, and these figures change often. Use this book as a general guide, and then fine-tune your investigation.

Once you have found a college or university that seems to have everything you think you want, it is a good idea to schedule a visit. You can even make a preliminary visit online. Most honors programs have established World Wide Web home pages, and their addresses are included. Each honors program home page is linked to other online information posted by the institution. You can find out a great deal about potential schools through the Internet even before you visit in person. But if possible, make the trip. Before you spend two or four years at a college or university, you should see it with your own eyes and meet the honors director as well as students and faculty members in the program and in your projected major.

ALUMNI PROFILE

Trina Hofreiter
New College of Florida
Class of 2001

"'Ew . . . what is this?' squeals a student as she pulls an insect out of her net. After I explain the answer, she exclaims, 'Oh, cool!' and runs back into the wetland to find more. Turning 'Ew . . . gross!' into 'Oh, cool!' is just part of my job in environmental education with the Nature Conservancy. Creative thinking, a passion for knowledge, and the confidence to work independently are all crucial skills for this position—skills that I learned at New College. New College recognized and encouraged the unique interests of its students. The College's flexible curriculum allowed me to design my own off-campus study program and gain valuable job experience with research internships. I learned to take charge of my education and incorporate real work experiences into my environmental science degree. Today, I'm using the creative, independent learning skills I learned at New College to build a successful career with the Nature Conservancy."

ABILENE CHRISTIAN UNIVERSITY

4 Pr G M Tr

▼ Honors Program

The Honors Program at Abilene Christian University offers academic enrichment and fellowship for highly motivated students in all majors. It requires no extra courses or fees and can be tailored for students with multiple majors or degrees.

In addition to the stimulating classes, Honors Program students enjoy honors social events, visiting speakers, and early registration privileges. Student representatives attend conferences of the National Collegiate Honors Council and the Great Plains Honors Council. Grants are available for study abroad.

Founded in 1984, the program involves an average of 300 students. Planning is underway to convert it to an honors college.

Participation Requirements: Within the program, students pursue either the University Honors track (four years, 30 semester hours) or the Departmental Honors track (two years, 12 semester hours, aimed at transfers with no previous honors credits). Those who finish the requirements and have a cumulative GPA of at least 3.5 receive a note on their transcript, special recognition at Commencement, and a certificate of achievement.

The University honors track includes 18 hours of freshman and sophomore honors classes. These include special versions of core curriculum courses—history, English, Bible, sciences, communications—as well as honors humanities and the honors seminar in social sciences. All honors classes emphasize breadth, flexibility, and critical thinking. These classes are kept small (limited to honors students) and are taught by selected faculty members. Collaborative learning, study abroad, credit by examination, and other options can help meet this requirement.

At the junior and senior level, the University Honors track stresses professional competence, interdisciplinary thinking, and preparation for graduate study or a career. The upper-division requirement (12 hours) includes 6 hours by honors contract in junior- and senior-level courses and a 3-hour Capstone Project, all of which fit into majors' requirements. Also required are three 1-hour interdisciplinary colloquia. Each colloquium features discussion and a position paper. Topics have included Thinking Postmodern, Science and Religion, China New and Old, and Feminist Thinking. Course credit fits into elective hours. Requirements for departmental honors are the same as the upper-division requirements for University honors.

Admission Process: Admission to the program is guaranteed for students who meet three criteria: a combined SAT score of 1220 or an ACT composite score of 27, a high school GPA of 3.75 or rank in the top 10 percent of class, and a satisfactory personal essay. For details and an online application, students should visit http://www.acu.edu/academics/honors/applic.html. No essay is required for students who have received a National Merit Finalist Scholarship or a Presidential Scholarship from ACU. Applicants whose scores are lower may be granted provisional admission on the basis of high school records or other evidence of high motivation and ability.

Scholarship Availability: The University gives more than $42 million in financial aid, including substantial academic scholarships. Ninety percent of freshmen receive financial aid.

The Campus Context: Abilene Christian University is a four-year, residential, private university accredited by the Southern Association of Colleges and Schools. Rated as one of America's Best Colleges by *U.S. News & World Report,* the University offers 117 bachelor's degree programs. Cooperative programs include nursing, electrical engineering, and criminal justice. Its student population of 4,600 makes it one of the largest universities associated with the Churches of Christ. Abilene, Texas, population 110,000, is located 180 miles west of Dallas. It supports three church-related universities, a junior college, an Air Force base, and a lively cultural district downtown.

Student Body Undergraduate enrollment is 3,950: 48 percent men, 52 percent women. Ethnic distribution is 83 percent white, 4 percent African American, 4 percent Hispanic, 3 percent Asian American, 1 percent Native American/Eskimo, 5 percent international. Residential students constitute 52 percent, commuters 48 percent.

Faculty The total number of faculty members is 303 (201 full-time), of whom 87 percent have terminal degrees. The student-faculty ratio is 19:1.

Key Facilities The library houses 1.7 million volumes (483,000 books and government documents, 1 million microform, 76,500 other). Computer facilities include fiber-optic network and Internet access for all residence halls and offices. There are computer labs in each dormitory. Special labs are available for digital media, business, computer science, and English.

Honorary Societies Phi Eta Sigma and Alpha Chi

Athletics Abilene is in Division II NCAA for women in track and field, softball, volleyball, cross-country, and tennis and for men in football, track and field, basketball, golf, baseball, cross-country, and tennis. There is an active intramural program.

Study Abroad Study-abroad opportunities include yearlong programs in Oxford, England; Montevideo, Uruguay; and cooperative programs in China.

Support Services Facilities for disabled students are plentiful. The library, Campus Center, coliseum, all dorms, and all but one office building are wheelchair accessible; accessible restrooms and drinking fountains are numerous.

Job Opportunities Work opportunities on campus and around town are listed in the Campus Placement Office. The Career Services Office assists students nearing graduation.

Tuition: $11,130 per year ($371 per semester hour) (2001–02)

Room and board: $4840 minimum

Room only: $2200 minimum

Mandatory Fees: $500

Contact: Director: Dr. Chris Willerton, ACU Box 29142, Abilene, Texas 79699-8242; Telephone: 915-674-2728; Fax: 915-674-6581; E-mail: willerton@honors.acu.edu; Web site: http://www.acu.edu/academics/honors/

ADELPHI UNIVERSITY

4 Pr G M Sc Tr AA

▼ The Honors College

The Honors College at Adelphi University provides a community, a curriculum, and a wide array of cocurricular activities for students who are passionate about learning, ambitious in their goals, and committed to the hard work and discipline required for superb achievement. Honors classes have an average size of 18 students. In addition to the regular classes, the Dean and Academic Director offer tutorials for single students or very small groups. Honors students may choose any of the majors in the various departments and schools of the University or may craft an interdisciplinary major of their own.

Honors classes are offered in the honors facility, a building that includes administrative offices, study areas, computer and graphics facilities, and dormitory rooms for those students who wish to reside there. From the first semester, honors classes are taught discussion- or seminar-style, calling upon the students for active participation rather than passive note-taking. Courses are designed by professors to provide significant intellectual challenge and the excitement of interdisciplinary exploration.

Students are encouraged to take advantage of opportunities for research and internships as soon as possible. Individual efforts culminate in the senior thesis, a yearlong project guided by a departmental adviser and the College's Academic Director.

The cocurricular program of the Honors College makes extensive use of the cultural resources offered by New York City. Several times each semester, honors students have the opportunity to attend the opera, plays on and off Broadway, museums, dance, and orchestra at little or no cost. Other honors activities include an on-campus film series with discussions and regular dinners at the Dean's residence (next to the campus), followed by book discussions. The Honors College Foreign Policy Symposium Series provides students with the chance to have lunch with experts in various areas of current interest and to hear presentations on timely topics.

The rigor and range of an honors education provide excellent preparation for graduate and professional study. Recent graduates have been admitted to graduate and professional study at Boston University, Brown, Chicago, Columbia, Cornell, Georgetown, NYU, Pennsylvania, Yale, and a number of major state universities throughout the country.

The Honors College, formally founded in 1995 as an expansion of an honors program begun in 1978, currently includes 240 students.

Participation Requirements: Students who fulfill all the requirements receive an Honors College diploma upon graduation. These requirements include 34 to 46 credits in honors courses that fulfill the University's general education requirements, a senior thesis, and regular attendance at cultural events on or off campus. Students must have a minimum GPA of 3.3 upon graduation.

Admission Process: In the initial screening of applications, a number of criteria are considered: cumulative GPA, class rank (usually top 10 percent), SAT (typically a minimum of 1250, with at least 650 verbal) or ACT (minimum score of 26), evidence of desire to attain an excellent education, and an essay representative of the student's best high school work. No single factor is decisive. Promising applicants are asked to come for an interview with the Dean, the Associate Dean, or one of the professors who teaches in the Honors College. (Applicants unable to visit the campus are interviewed by telephone.)

Scholarship Availability: Honors Scholarships are merit-based. Three levels of scholarship are awarded to honors students. Trustee Scholarships for students with SAT scores above 1350 can cover up to full tuition. Presidential Scholarships for students with SAT scores above 1300 can cover as much as $12,500 a year. Provost awards for students with SAT scores of 1250 or above can cover up to approximately $10,000. Honors students can receive increased scholarships if they qualify for other awards offered at Adelphi, including Service Scholarships and awards for talent and athletics. Other financial assistance, including grants, loans, and part-time employment, is available to qualified students.

The Campus Context: Adelphi University's roots reach back to the founding of the Adelphi Academy in 1863. This academy became Adelphi College in 1895 and Adelphi University in 1963. Today, Adelphi University's colleges and schools include the College of Arts and Sciences, the Gordon F. Derner Institute of Advanced Psychological Studies, the Honors College, the School of Business, the School of Nursing, the School of Social Work, and University College. Degree programs range from the B.A. to the Ph.D. With students from thirty-five states and more than fifty other nations, Adelphi provides a cosmopolitan atmosphere conducive to intellectual questioning, surprise, and growth. Located in the beautiful and serene village of Garden City, Adelphi enjoys the accessibility of New York City, with Manhattan a mere 19 miles from the campus. The cultural riches of New York provide a social complexity and real-world laboratory for students' exploration of the modern world.

Student Body Undergraduate enrollment is 3,099 (2,570 full-time equivalent): 2,151 women and 948 men. In 1999–2000 (the most recent year available), financial aid in the form of scholarships, grants, loans, or work-study was awarded to 2,141 undergraduate students. The ethnic distribution is 66.8 percent white, 15.6 percent black, 3.8 percent Asian, 8.5 percent Hispanic, and .2 percent American Indian. There are 127 international students. Approximately one third of the students are residential. Adelphi's ten Greek-letter fraternities and sororities promote community service and enhance the social life of many students.

Faculty Adelphi's 198 full-time faculty members constitute 54 percent of the total full-time-equivalent faculty members. Seventy-eight percent of the full-time faculty members have terminal degrees. The student-faculty ratio is 13:1.

Key Facilities The fully computerized collection in the University's library includes more than 1.7 million volumes and microformat and audiovisual items. The University's Office of Information Technology provides six general-access computer labs equipped with Pentium PCs, Power PC Macintoshes, UNIX workstations, printers, and scanners.

Athletics Adelphi University students compete in sixteen sports, including men's soccer, golf, cross-country, basketball, baseball, tennis, and lacrosse; women's cross-country, soccer, volleyball, basketball, softball, lacrosse, and tennis; and coed swimming and track. The teams compete at the NCAA Division II level, with the exception of men's soccer, which competes in Division I.

Study Abroad Study abroad is partially supported with Provost's Study Abroad Scholarships and is coordinated through the Office of International Student Services. Adelphi is affiliated with a number of agencies, including the American Institute for Foreign Study, the Council for International Educational Exchange, Denmark's International Study Program, and the Washington International Studies Council.

Support Services The Office of Disability Support Services provides support in a large variety of areas. In addition, Adelphi has a nationally recognized Learning Disabilities Program housed within the School of Education.

Job Opportunities On-campus employment is available both for students qualified through the Federal Work-Study Program and for many other students as well. The Center for Career Development educates students about internship and employment opportunities and helps coordinate internship activities. In addition, various departments and schools at Adelphi have their own internship programs.

Tuition: The tuition for 2001–2002 was $16,100.

Room and Board: Room and board rates for triples to singles with air-conditioning ranged from $6250 to $8400 in 2001–02. Most students are housed in doubles, for which the annual fee was $7020.

Mandatory Fees: The student activity fee for 2001–2002 was $170.

Contact: Dean: Richard Garner, Honors College, 100 Earle Hall, Adelphi University, Garden City, New York 11530; Telephone: 516-877-3800; Fax: 516-877-3803; E-mail: garner@adelphi.edu; Web site: http://academics.adelphi.edu/honcol/

Interpreting the symbols: **2**=two-year college, **4**=four-year college; **Pu**=public or state college, **Pr**=private college; **G**=general honors program; **D**=departmental honors program; **S**=small program (fewer than 100 students), **M**=midsize program (100 to 500 students), **L**=large program (more than 500 students); **Sc**=scholarships available in honors program; **Tr**=transfer students accepted into honors program; **HBC**=historically black college; **AA**=academic advisors; **GA**=graduate advisors; **FA**=fellowship advisors.

Albertus Magnus College

4 Pr C S Tr AA

▼ Honors Program

The Honors Program at Albertus Magnus College is designed to enrich highly motivated students' experiences in the general education program and to provide an opportunity for them to pursue their particular intellectual interests in collaboration with faculty members as they progress through the College. The program is 7 years old and open to approximately 70 students per year. The number of students who participate varies. Students work with an advisor to tailor the program to meet their individual goals. Honors students can choose to take honors courses, develop independent projects, participate in graduate seminars, and pursue honors option work in regular courses. Practica and internships are offered in many areas to well-prepared and highly motivated students. Credit is given for work done outside the classroom in an environment suited to the student's major interest.

The program enables students to work closely with faculty members on a one to one basis and to take small classes that allow for individualized attention and promote intellectual development through collaboration with faculty and peers. The program also regularly sponsors cocurricular activities, such as theater trips and honors luncheons.

The College is sponsored by the members of the Congregation of Dominican Sisters of St. Mary of the Springs.

Participation Requirements: Eligible first-year students complete 13 credits in honors humanities and English courses. To successfully complete the program, students must take four additional 3-credit honors courses. Students not completing the courses in the first-year program for honors credit must take six 3-credit honors courses. All honors students must take two upper-level honors courses that satisfy general education requirements. The other honors courses that students take can be general education or non-general education courses. In addition, honors students are eligible to take graduate courses in the Master of Arts in Liberal Studies program, or opt to take independent study, tutorial, or regular courses where honors course work is assigned in order to complete their honors requirements. To participate in the Honors Program, students must maintain a 3.5 GPA. Those who finish the requirements and have a cumulative GPA of at least 3.7 receive a note on their transcript and a certificate of achievement at the Albertus Magnus College awards banquet.

First-year students are admitted to the Honors Program based upon an evaluation of SAT scores, high school ranking, and placement tests administered by the College. Second semester first-year students, sophomores, juniors, and seniors are eligible to participate in the program by maintaining a 3.5 cumulative grade point average.

Scholarship Availability: Albertus Magnus College seeks to make it possible for every student accepted for admission to attend the College by providing financial assistance to its students. Assistance for meeting the cost of a private education is available in the form of scholarships, grants, loans, and employment.

Each year, Albertus Magnus College awards a variety of merit and need-based scholarships. These scholarships are not offered directly through the Honors Program. Academic scholarships, based on the academic achievement of the entering student, are awarded automatically to qualifying students upon acceptance to the College. These scholarships are then incorporated with other funding based on the student's eligibility.

In addition, students with financial need may be eligible to participate in the Federal Work-Study Program. This program provides for the employment of students on campus. Students are also eligible to participate in the Federal Community Service Work-Study program. This program provides for the employment of students to work off-campus at nonprofit organizations and primarily benefits the community.

The Campus Context: The choice of New Haven as the site of Albertus Magnus College is in harmony with the goals and ideals of the institution. A cosmopolitan city with a continuing tradition as a national educational and cultural center, New Haven, located halfway between New York and Boston, has in recent decades added to its already distinguished reputation by notable new developments in many fields. Its programs in urban and regional planning, social action, and health care have attracted wide and favorable notice. The College has a long tradition of being a center of arts and letters, the city has always offered a variety of opportunities in these fields.

New Haven is a college town, and much activity is planned for the benefit of the students from all of the five area colleges and universities. Lectures and musical performances presented by renowned figures as well as a variety of College sporting events draw large audiences. The city has some of the finest theatres in the country, including the award-winning Long Wharf and Yale Repertory theatres. The Yale Art Gallery, the Yale Center for British Art and British Studies that houses the largest collection of British materials outside England, museums, and movie theatres are equally accessible. *Student Body* Today, Albertus has an enrollment of more than 2,200 students. Approximately 360 are full-time day students. More than 90 percent of its students are enrolled on a full-time basis.

Faculty The total number of full-time faculty members is 34, 78 percent of whom hold doctoral or terminal degrees. Forty-three percent of the part-time faculty members are specialists who broaden the available educational opportunities. The student-faculty ratio is 15:5.1.

Key Facilities Aquinas Hall is the chief academic and administrative building on campus. Classrooms, seminar rooms, computer facilities, offices, lounges, two auditoriums, and academic computer labs and computer classrooms are among the facilities in the building. All classrooms are wired for computer utilization, Internet connections and document projection.

The College library is located in a gracious building, which originally housed the entire College. It contains a collection of more than 100,000 volumes, 650 periodical titles, and nearly 2,000 media titles. The library has five CD-ROM terminals and four provide access to the Internet for computer-assisted literature searching. Microform reader-printers are available for microfilm materials. There is a Media Center where students may use audiovisual materials. The collection has recently been converted to an electronic system.

Honorary Societies: Tau Pi Phi, Kappa Gamma Pi

Athletics The Cosgrove, Marcus, Messer Athletic Center opened in 1989. The indoor sports and recreation center houses a pool, a gymnasium and indoor track, racquetball and volleyball courts, weight and dance rooms, and other facilities. The Center also features soccer and softball fields, an outdoor track, and tennis courts. Sports offerings include tennis, baseball, soccer, softball, basketball, volleyball and cross-country. Albertus Magnus College teams compete as members of the NCAA Division III and the Great Northeast Athletic Conference.

Study Abroad A student may study abroad for one or two semesters and is classified as an enrolled student. The student must notify the Registrar's Office in advance with appropriate paperwork. Arrangements are made through the registrar and Office of Career Services.

Support Services Albertus maintains an Academic Development Center where traditional day students may obtain help in improving their study habits, reading efficiency, writing abilities and mathematical fundamentals. During the year, the center sponsors workshops on methods of developing competency in these skills. The center also provides drop-in services, and tutorial and small-group instruction for students who need assistance. Experienced professionals are available for support for students who are learning disabled.

Job Opportunities Listings of part-time jobs are posted on the bulletin board outside the Career Center. This service keeps students notified of jobs available. The office also keeps an updated file of summer-job listings and volunteer openings.

Tuition: $15,246 (2001–02, day program); $816 per 3-credit course (2001–02, continuing education accelerated degree evening program)

Room and Board: $6908 (2001–02)

Mandatory Fees: More than $600 (2001–02)

Contact: Director: Sean P. O'Connell, 700 Prospect Street, New Haven, Connecticut, 06511; Telephone: 203-773-8548; Fax: 203-773-3117; E-mail: o'connell@albertus.edu

ALBION COLLEGE

4 Pr G M Sc Tr

▼ Honors Institute

The Albion College Honors Institute has been designed to provide an exciting and distinctive variety of academic experiences for highly motivated and talented students. The Institute's mix of discussion-oriented classes, field trips, independent research, and personal attention provides honors students with special challenges and opportunities for growth.

Most students join the Honors Institute right out of high school, although later admission is also possible. Students admitted to the program are high achievers who also possess broad intellectual interests and a strong desire to begin the exciting and challenging process of developing their own independent thinking and research skills.

In each semester of their first two years, honors students take a specially designed, interdisciplinary class. Class size is limited to 15 students, and each seminar emphasizes independent reading, open discussion, and extensive writing. Further, each honors seminar counts toward the College's general education requirements. First- and second-year honors students are also eligible to become Student Research Partners, which allows them to participate in research with an Albion faculty member from the moment they arrive on campus.

In their junior year, honors students begin their own original research or creative project, which culminates in the writing of an honors thesis. Normally, the process starts with participation in a thesis development workshop designed to help students identify a thesis topic, select an adviser, and begin their preliminary research. Research and writing then continue under the close supervision of a faculty thesis adviser, and the thesis is completed during the student's senior year. The Jenkins Prize, awarded at Albion's annual Honors Convocation, recognizes the best senior theses. Albion also provides extensive support for student research and creative projects through its Foundation for Undergraduate Research, Scholarship and Creative Activity (FURSCA). FURSCA helps pay for such things as student research expenses, student travel to specialized libraries and to present their research results at scholarly meetings, and student summer research on campus.

The Honors Institute occupies a newly renovated Honors Center, located in the Old Observatory in the heart of the campus. The center contains a seminar room for honors classes, a study lounge with computers, a thesis library, and social space. Honors students have access to this facility on a 24-hours-a-day basis. Honors students also have unique opportunities to meet in small groups with distinguished speakers when they come to the campus, informally socialize with the honors instructors and students, attend an overnight retreat, and go on field trips to concerts, plays, and museums.

The Honors Institute, which has been in existence for more than twenty-five years, has been expanding its program in recent years. Currently, it admits approximately 65 first-year students each year and has an overall enrollment of about 210 students.

Participation Requirements: Once admitted to the Honors Institute, students complete four specially designed interdisciplinary seminars drawn from the four divisions of the College during their first two years. These classes count toward the College's general education requirements. As juniors, honors students begin an original research or creative project for their honors thesis under the close supervision of their thesis adviser. These projects are completed no later than April 1 of the student's senior year. To graduate with Albion College honors, students must have at least a 3.5 cumulative GPA. Successful completion of the program is recognized at commencement and is also noted on the student's official transcript and diploma.

Admission Process: High school students are recruited on the basis of their high school average, ACT or SAT I scores, an application and an essay, and a personal interview. Most students apply for admission to the Honors Institute during their senior year of high school. The deadline for application is March 1. A limited number of additional students who miss the March 1 deadline are admitted to the Institute at the end of their first or second semester at Albion.

Scholarship Availability: Academic scholarships of various amounts are awarded through the Office of Admissions based on high school academic performance and leadership and service activities. Scholarships are not offered through the Honors Institute. Last year, all incoming honors students were recipients of academic scholarships.

The Campus Context: Founded in 1835, Albion College exemplifies "liberal arts at work" by offering a challenging education that links the arts and sciences with preprofessional preparation. Albion ranks fourth in the nation for the percentage of undergraduate students involved in summer research. It is ranked seventh in *Yahoo! Internet Life's* Most Wired Colleges in the USA ranking and is ranked first of any college or university in Michigan. In addition, 46 percent of Albion's alumni regularly support the College, the highest percentage of all schools in Michigan and among the top forty in the nation.

Albion was the first private college in Michigan to have a chapter of Phi Beta Kappa, the oldest national honor society, founded in 1776. Albion's endowed professional institutes in environmental science, public policy and service, professional management, premedical and health-care studies, honors, and education offer world-class internships and study-abroad opportunities. Albion is among the top eighty-five private liberal arts colleges for the number of alumni who are corporate executives, including top executives and CEOs of *Newsweek,* the Lahey Clinic (Massachusetts), PricewaterhouseCoopers, Dow Corning, the NCAA, NYNEX, and the Federal Accounting Standards Board (FASB). Albion's graduate school placement rate is 98 percent for law, 96 percent for dental, and 89 percent for medical schools, including Harvard, Michigan, Columbia, Northwestern, Notre Dame, Vanderbilt, and Wisconsin.

Albion was the top award winner at the 2001 Michigan Campus Compact, which includes public and private schools in Michigan that are committed to service and volunteerism. A long list of

Interpreting the symbols: **2**=two-year college, **4**=four-year college; **Pu**=public or state college, **Pr**=private college; **G**=general honors program; **D**=departmental honors program; **S**=small program (fewer than 100 students), **M**=midsize program (100 to 500 students), **L**=large program (more than 500 students); **Sc**=scholarships available in honors program; **Tr**=transfer students accepted into honors program; **HBC**=historically black college; **AA**=academic advisors; **GA**=graduate advisors; **FA**=fellowship advisors.

campus organizations includes Model United Nations, Fellowship of Christian Athletes, Canoe Club, Black Student Alliance, Equestrian Club, Medievalist Society, Ecological Awareness Club, and fraternity and sorority service organizations.

Albion College awards the Bachelor of Arts and Bachelor of Fine Arts degrees. Majors include American studies, anthropology and sociology, biology, chemistry, computer science, economics and management, English, French, geological sciences, German, history, international studies, mathematics, mathematics/economics, mathematics/physics, music, philosophy, physical education, physics, political science, psychology, public policy, religious studies, Spanish, speech communication and theater, and visual arts.

Student Body Full-time enrollment totals 1,548: 55 percent women, 45 percent men. Students come from twenty-eight states and territories and nineteen other countries, with 9 percent from out of state and 1 percent international. The ethnic distribution is 85 percent white, 2 percent black, 2 percent Asian American or Pacific Islander, and 1 percent Hispanic. Ninety-nine percent live on campus and can participate in more than 120 student organizations devoted to the arts, community service, leadership, and recreation. About 40 percent of Albion students join one of the eleven national fraternities and sororities on campus. More than 65 percent of students receive need-based financial aid.

Faculty The total number of faculty members is 125, of whom 121 are full-time. Ninety-two percent of the full-time faculty members have terminal degrees. The student-faculty ratio is 12:1.

Key Facilities The Stockwell-Mudd Libraries house approximately 550,000 books and nonprint items and more than 900 current journal subscriptions. The campus computer network, with Internet service, links personal computers in public computer laboratories, classrooms, and science laboratories. All residence hall rooms are equipped with network ports as well. Computer facilities are available free of charge.

Honorary Societies There are several interdisciplinary honorary societies on campus that recognize the achievements of honors and other high-achieving students. These include Phi Beta Kappa, Sigma Xi, Mortar Board, Omicron Delta Kappa, and Alpha Lambda Delta.

Athletics A member of NCAA Division III and the Michigan Intercollegiate Athletic Association, Albion offers the following varsity sports: baseball (men), basketball (men and women), cross-country (men and women), football (men), golf (men and women), soccer (men and women), softball (women), swimming and diving (men and women), tennis (men and women), track and field (men and women), and volleyball (women). The Briton football team has made more NCAA postseason appearances (seven) than any other Division III school in Michigan and won the 1994 Division III national championship. Of particular note is Albion's reputation for recruiting academically talented student-athletes; in addition to dominating Division III football, women's soccer, and men's and women's golf and swimming, members of five varsity teams have earned the highest GPA in the MIAA conference, NCAA Division III, or any division nationwide. An extensive intramural sports program is also offered. Indoor athletics facilities include the Dow Recreation and Wellness Center, featuring flexible court space, tennis courts, a running track, a varsity pool, and a weight-training area.

Study Abroad Albion students increase their knowledge of other cultures and their fluency in other languages through study and internship opportunities in England, Scotland, France, Germany, Spain, Italy, the Czech Republic, Russia, Greece, the Dominican Republic, Mexico, Costa Rica, Honduras, Israel, Kenya, Senegal, South Africa, India, Australia, Japan, South Korea, Hong Kong, and China. Options exist for both a semester and a full academic year of international study. On approved Albion study programs, basic costs are generally no greater than expenses for room, board, and tuition on campus.

Support Services The Developing Skills Center provides assistance with study skills, reading, and writing as well as individualized tutoring in specific subject areas. The Quantitative Skills Center supports students in such areas as mathematics and logic and in using statistical and other software.

Job Opportunities Student researchers may apply for summer fellowships that provide a stipend and equipment funds. In addition, part-time jobs are available in many campus departments. A full-service career center provides interview opportunities and links with corporations, foundations, and alumni referrals around the world.

Tuition: $19,390 per year (2000–01)

Room and Board: $5604

Mandatory Fees: $230

Contact: Honors Director, Albion College, KC #4762, Albion, Michigan 49224-5011; Telephone: 517-629-0614; Fax: 517-629-0428; E-mail: honors@albion.edu; Web site: http://www.albion.edu

ALCORN STATE UNIVERSITY

4 Pu G M Sc Tr

▼ Honors Curriculum Program

The Honors Curriculum Program is designed to challenge and stimulate the intellectual curiosity of highly motivated students. Courses are taught by senior faculty members and generally have an enrollment of 25 or fewer students. The program is coordinated by the Honors Council, which is chaired by the Director of Honors. A corps of academic advisers is available to participants during the academic year. The Honors Student Organization (HSO) provides a forum for student-initiated academic, social, and extracurricular activities. A special honors work center, which contains computers, typewriters, a copy machine, and reference materials, is provided for participants. The program has been in place since 1961 and currently enrolls 180 students.

Participation Requirements: During freshman year, students are grouped into special honors sections of general education courses. During sophomore year, students enroll in a colloquium designed to encourage and develop lively communication that grows out of enriched reading experiences. Sophomore students may also enroll in special honors sections of multisection courses, which are offered in response to student interest and when departmental personnel resources permit. At the upper level, there is an interdisciplinary honors seminar for juniors, which widens the student's outlook while providing an opportunity for some preliminary research in a field of special interest. The senior student engages in a program of study related to a single major field that offers the possibility for guided research, a seminar, independent study, or a special project. Students are provided special assistance in applying for merit scholarships, internships, and special summer research programs,

Students in the program must enroll in at least 3 hours of honors work each semester. Participants must maintain a cumulative GPA of at least 3.5. Students who complete 24 hours or more of honors credit and maintain at least a 3.5 cumulative GPA are recognized as Honors Curriculum Scholars upon graduation. Appropriate citation is made on the Commencement program and on the degree certificate.

Admission Process: Freshmen are selected on the basis of scores on admissions and placement examinations. Students applying after the first semester of the freshman year are selected on the basis of their cumulative average and upon the recommendation of faculty members.

Scholarship Availability: Scholarships are provided to participants through the Admissions Office. Full academic scholarships for incoming freshmen (tuition and room and board) are available on a first-come first-served basis. More than 90 percent of participants hold full academic scholarships. The scholarship is renewable, up to four years, provided the student maintains at least a 3.5 cumulative GPA and remains in good standing with the University.

The Campus Context: Alcorn State University consists of five schools at the undergraduate level: the School of Arts and Sciences, the School of Business, the School of Education and Psychology, the School of Agriculture and Applied Sciences, and the School of Nursing. There are seventeen departments within the five schools. Fifty-three degree programs are offered.

Student Body Undergraduate enrollment is 3,094 (804 men and 2,290 women). Ethnic distribution is 91.8 percent African American, 8 percent white, and .2 percent other. There are international students from eleven countries. Eighty-four percent of the students reside in dormitories. Ninety-two percent of students receive financial aid. There are numerous student organizations, including academic, social, and religious, as well as sororities and fraternities.

Faculty There are 193 full-time faculty members; 72 percent hold terminal degrees. The student-faculty ratio is 16:1.

Key Facilities The newly renovated library houses 257,573 volumes and has 1,046 current periodical subscriptions. There are ten computer laboratories campus-wide (PC- or Mac-based networks). Special facilities include the Honors Dormitory; Oakland Memorial Chapel, 1830 (U.S. Historical Register); Belles Lettres, 1830 (U.S. Historical Register); the Cora S. Balmat School of Nursing (Natchez campus); and the Mathematics and Science Complex.

Athletics In athletics, Alcorn State is NCAA Division I-AA. Varsity sports are football, basketball (men's and women's), track, cross-country, baseball, women's softball, golf, and women's volleyball. Intramural sports activities are coordinated by the Office of Student Activities.

Job Opportunities Campus work opportunities include a college work-study program and limited research assistant positions.

Tuition: $3202 for state residents, $7374 for nonresidents, per year (2001–02)

Room and Board: $3090

Contact: Director: Dr. Donzell Lee, 1000 ASU Drive #175, Alcorn State, Lorman, Mississippi 39095; Telephone: 601-877-6138; Fax: 601-877-6256; E-mail: dlee@lorman.alcorn.edu; Web site: http://www.alcorn.edu

ALFRED UNIVERSITY

4 Pr G M Tr

▼ University Honors Program

It is the Honors Program's mission to enrich Alfred's best undergraduate students' education by providing seminars—all electives—to add a dimension to their lives. In recent years, these courses have considered things of the spirit. Students have studied T'ai Chi, alternative healing, spirituality and the counterculture, and Zen, and one group even attempted a vision quest. Others have focused on music: the evolution of jazz, the blues, opera, Mozart, musical theater, and music video. There have been seminars on superconductivity and lasers, dream theory, the old order Amish, Claudius Caesar, fairy tales, biotechnology and bioethics, the beauty of chess, and the World Wide Web. There have also been many seminars on film—film noir, Shakespeare and Hollywood, horror films, fiction into film, and the silent screen.

There are currently 190 students in honors comprising about 10 percent of the student body. In most years there are 65–70 applicants and three quarters are usually admitted. More than a quarter of the students in honors are National Merit Scholars, and Alfred has a very generous scholarship offer for them.

Nonacademic activities include the traditional Death by Chocolate reception in the fall; a banquet in the spring, featuring rock Cornish game hens and student entertainment; and each April seniors have dinner at the president's house. There are road trips to Rochester four or five times a year: first dinner out at a Greek, Thai, Chinese, or Indian restaurant, then to the theater or a symphony.

Being in honors also opens doors to other things. When trustees visit, for example, and want to have lunch with students, or when admissions is looking for tour guides, or when public relations wants student stringers for the *New York Times*, the expectation is that honors will provide them. In recent years, 2 honors students had their articles printed in the *Times*.

The Honors Program has a motto: Time flies like an arrow; fruit flies like a banana. It is a reminder not to take things too seriously.

Participation Requirements: Honors students are required to take four seminars in their first five semesters. These courses do not substitute for anything else—the idea is to take these classes just for the fun of it. Because they are fun, most students choose to take more than four. The seminars are small (class limit is 15 students), informal (some meet at the Honors House with its comfortable couches and rocking chairs), and, in many cases, student-led. Some are the result of student suggestions. Others, like the vision quest seminar, are experimental.

To graduate in honors, a student must complete four seminars, write a senior thesis, and finish with a 3.2 GPA. Theses vary widely. Students have studied barns, cryptology, vigilantes, and graph theory, among other things. While some theses are essentially research papers, many aren't. One student studied traditional quilting techniques and then made a quilt. Other students have built a unicycling robot, created a stained glass window, and written and illustrated a children's book. Some have given public performances. A few years ago a premed student wrote and performed his own piano concerto. The common thread is a chance to work closely with 3 faculty member mentors on a project that really matters. Theses are bound and become a permanent part of Herrick Library's Special Collections. Honors Program graduates have Alfred University Scholar printed on their transcript and handprinted on their diploma.

Admission Process: The single most important consideration for admission is the high school transcript. SAT I scores are taken seriously, but they only measure performance on one day's test. A high school transcript shows what was achieved over four years, so it is a major consideration. Students who have done well taking a demanding schedule, including AP or college-level courses, are the norm in this program. In fact, the majority of those accepted into honors graduate in the top 5 percent of their class, and virtually all are in the top 10 percent. An academic recommendation is a must, as is an essay. Excerpts from the best essays are published in the honors newsletter, *Sublunary Life*. The deadline for applications is June 1.

Scholarship Availability In 1998–99, University-funded aid provided more than $13 million to undergraduates. Scholarships include the National Merit Scholarship, Presidential Scholarship, Southern Tier Scholarship, the Jonathan Allen Award for Leadership, and department competition scholarships. Approximately 90 percent of undergraduates receive some form of financial aid.

Interpreting the symbols: **2**=two-year college, **4**=four-year college; **Pu**=public or state college, **Pr**=private college; **G**=general honors program; **D**=departmental honors program; **S**=small program (fewer than 100 students), **M**=midsize program (100 to 500 students), **L**=large program (more than 500 students); **Sc**=scholarships available in honors program; **Tr**=transfer students accepted into honors program; **HBC**=historically black college; **AA**=academic advisors; **GA**=graduate advisors; **FA**=fellowship advisors.

The Campus Context: The University is located in a small village 70 miles south of Rochester between the foothills of the Allegheny Mountains and the Finger Lakes Region.

Alfred University is consistently ranked among the top comprehensive universities in the North. It comprises five colleges and schools: Liberal Arts and Sciences, Business, Engineering and Professional Studies, and the New York State College of Ceramics (a SUNY statutory unit), which includes the School of Art and Design and the School of Ceramic Engineering and Sciences. Honors is open to students from all colleges.

Nearly 100 clubs and organizations, including Forest People, WALF radio station, ALANA (African, Latino, Asian, Native American) Team, *Fiat Lux* student newspaper, Women's Issues Coalition, Student Volunteers for Community Action, and Greek life (eight fraternities and four sororities), keep Alfred students active and involved. Theater, music, and dance productions are also popular among students. The Student Activities Board (SAB) brings entertainment to the University, including comedians, bands (both small and large acts), and a weekly coffee house series.

Student Body There are approximately 2,000 undergraduates representing more than forty states and several countries. The men-women ratio is close to 50:50. The ethnic distribution is 90 percent white and 10 percent members of minority groups.

Faculty There are 164 full-time faculty members, 90 percent of whom hold the doctorate or the highest degree in their field. The student-faculty ratio is 12:1, the average class size is 18 students, and teaching is the number one priority of faculty members.

Key Facilities Herrick Memorial Library and the Scholes Library of Ceramics contain more than 330,000 volumes, 1,700 subscriptions, 118,000 microforms, and 158,000 audiovisual materials. Both libraries maintain an Online Public Access Catalog, and both libraries provide online access to other libraries.

The campus is fully wired with network and Internet access in every residence hall room and all offices. The student-computer is 7:1 with open computer labs, residence hall computer rooms, and a laptop-lending program.

The University is set on a 232-acre campus with more than fifty buildings, including an observatory, Powell Campus Center (which includes a theater, dining hall, café, and the Knight Club), Miller Performing Arts Center (individual and group practice rooms and theater), Olin Building (home to business and social sciences), and Harder Hall (art facilities including studio space, galleries, an auditorium, and a kiln room).

Athletics Alfred University sponsors NCAA Division III programs for men and women in basketball, swimming and diving, lacrosse, tennis, soccer, golf, cross-country, and downhill skiing. For women only volleyball and softball are offered and for men only, football. There are club teams in rugby, Nordic skiing, and baseball, and there is also a coed equestrian team. The athletics department is housed in the McLane Physical Education Center. McLane houses a 75-foot-long six-lane pool with a diving area; basketball court; six squash/racquetball courts; and a fitness center with Nautilus equipment, Stairmasters, stationery bicycles, treadmills, and various other exercise equipment. There are tennis courts and an omniturf multipurpose field adjacent to the McLane Center. There are hiking and biking trails on campus, and Brentwood stables are a short trip from campus.

Tuition: $18,498 per year, private colleges; $11,650 per year, non–New York State residents, Ceramics College; $8,450 per year, NYS residents, Ceramics College (1998–99)

Room and Board: $6790

Room Only: $3542

Mandatory Fees: $546

Contact: Director: Dr. Paul Strong, Seidlin Hall, Alfred University, Alfred, New York 14802; Telephone: 607-871-2924/2257; Fax: 609-871-2831; E-mail: fstrongp@bigvax.alfred.edu; Web site: http://www.alfred.edu/

ALLEGANY COLLEGE OF MARYLAND

2 Pu G S Sc Tr

▼ Honors Program

Allegany College of Maryland Honors Program allows academically talented students to take a minimum of 12 hours of honors courses by contract either in their major subjects or in their general electives. The honors contract provides an opportunity for students to participate in the Honors Program who otherwise would not be able to complete the requirements of the Honors Program. Members of the Honors Program are eligible to participate in special activities such as receptions, conferences, cultural affairs, and travel, which are planned by and for the Honors Program students. The students have an Honors Lounge. The 11-year-old program currently enrolls 60 students.

Participation Requirements: Honors students are required to complete a minimum of 12 credit hours of honors course work by contract with a minimum GPA of 3.0 in the contracted honors courses to receive an honors diploma. The students in the Honors Program have the opportunity to work closely with their faculty mentors in the completion of their contracts and gain an enhanced appreciation and knowledge of the course material.

Admission Process: Students are identified at registration as potential honors students. Freshmen are selected each summer for the Honors Program on the basis of their high school GPA or demonstration of special talents or abilities and an interview with the Honors Director and/or members of the Honors Committee. Students currently enrolled at Allegany College of Maryland can apply at any time during the academic year, but the applicants must have at least a 3.5 GPA at Allegany College of Maryland in order to be eligible.

Scholarship Availability: All members of the Honors Program enrolled in one or more honors courses by contract have half of their in-county tuition paid by the Allegany College of Maryland Foundation.

The Campus Context: Allegany Community College was founded in 1961 in Cumberland, Maryland, and has expanded to include three campuses: the main campus at Cumberland, Maryland; the Somerset Campus in Somerset, Pennsylvania; and the Bedford Campus in Everett, Pennsylvania. Allegany College of Maryland is located in scenic western Maryland, about 110 miles from Pittsburgh, Pennsylvania, and about 180 from Washington, D.C.

Student Body The number of undergraduates is 2,551. Most students live within a 30-mile radius of campus. All students commute to campus. There are no traditional fraternities or sororities.

Faculty There are 100 full-time faculty members.

Key Facilities The library houses about 55,500 books and periodicals.

Honorary Societies Phi Theta Kappa

Athletics Allegany College of Maryland provides intercollegiate athletics for men and women as well as a wide range of intramural sports.

Job Opportunities Students are offered a range of work opportunities on campus, including tutoring and work-study.

Tuition: $1920 for area residents, $2480 for state residents, $3792 for nonresidents, per year (1998–99)

Mandatory Fees: $100

Contact: Director: Dr. James D. Stickler, 12401 Willowbrook Road, SE, Cumberland, Maryland 21502-2596; Telephone: 301-784-5256; Fax: 301-784-5012; E-mail: davids@ac.cc.md.us; Web site: http://www.ac.cc.md.us

ALLIANT INTERNATIONAL UNIVERSITY

4 Pr G S Tr

▼ Honors Program

This special program for exceptional students is designed to enhance the University experience by providing meaningful and satisfying interactions with other able and highly motivated students and supportive faculty. It offers small classes that are made up of typically 15 students or less who share a dedication to learning. Opportunities are provided to explore areas of personal interest and participate in developing the courses in the program. The Honors Seminar, taken each term, is a cohort group that engages in a variety of educational, cultural, and recreational activities, such as informal conversations with faculty members from various University departments, visits to area art and other museums, and a behind-the-scenes tour of the San Diego Wild Animal Park. The Honors Seminar also connects members with a faculty mentor who leads the Seminar and, along with the Program Director, is available as a resource throughout the student's University career. Oversight and development of the Honors Program is carried out by the Honors Council, which includes administration, faculty, and student members. The AIU Honors Program began in 1995 and normally has nearly 45 participants.

Participation Requirements: Graduation from the Honors Program requires having a cumulative GPA of 3.5 or better, taking at least seven specially designated honors courses, and participating in an Honors Seminar each term. Honors courses can be chosen from a selection of lower and upper-division general education courses, a capstone Senior Seminar and Senior Project, independent study, and graduate-level work if it is available in the student's major. Honors Program graduates are recognized at commencement ceremonies as University Honors Scholars and that description is recorded on their transcript and diploma. In addition, Honors Scholars wear a red cord along with their graduation robe and any other cords they may have earned and receive a certificate of completion. Students who graduate in good standing with the Honors Program but who have not completed seven or more honors courses are awarded a certificate of participation.

Admission Process: To be admitted to the Honors Program, new first-year students must meet at least one of the following criteria: graduation in the upper 10 percent of their high school class, a minimum high school GPA of 3.6, or a minimum composite score of 1100 on the SAT or 26 on the ACT. Transfer students and those currently enrolled at AIU are eligible to join the program if they meet either of the following requirements: a minimum cumulative college GPA of 3.6, a cumulative college GPA between 3.4 and 3.6, two letters of academic recommendation, a letter describing the applicant's reasons for wanting to belong to the Honors Program, and approval by the Honors Council.

Scholarship Availability: Applicants are usually eligible for substantial merit-based scholarships. These are offered as part of the financial-aid package available to the student and are not administered by the Honors Program.

The Campus Context: Alliant International University was established in 2001 through the combination of United States International University and Alliant University/California School of Professional Psychology. Undergraduate programs are available on the San Diego campus as well as in Mexico City, Mexico and Nairobi, Kenya. The University's mission includes a strong commitment to providing students with a global understanding and a multicultural perspective through both its formal curricula and the experiences of studying, working, and living cooperatively in a racially, ethnically, and culturally diverse environment. AIU is made up of six schools: California School of Professional Psychology, College of Arts and Sciences, College of Organizational Studies, School of Social and Policy Studies, School of Education, and United States International College of Business. Undergraduate and graduate degree programs prepare the University's 6400 students for careers in various liberal arts fields, education, business, and behavioral and social science professions. All the University's programs are accredited by the Western Association of Schools and Colleges.

Student Body For the fall 2001 term, the San Diego undergraduate student body consisted of 532 students. Fifty-six percent were U.S. citizens and 44 percent were international students. Fifty-eight percent of the total undergraduate student population at the San Diego campus was women and 42 percent were men.

Faculty There are 23 full-time and 2 half-time faculty members for the undergraduate programs at the San Diego campus. Ninety percent of faculty members have terminal degrees.

Key Facilities The library houses 130,000 books, a strong periodical collection, and provides online access to several major data bases. In addition to library computers for research, four computer laboratories are available on the San Diego campus, one of which is accessible from 9 a.m. to 10 p.m. during the week, and during daylight hours on the weekend on a walk-in basis. The others can be used by any student when no class is in session. There is a Cyber Café on campus that has six computers available for free use by students. All of the housing suites have free internet connections in each bedroom.

Athletics Interscholastic athletics is represented by NAIA men's and women's teams in soccer, tennis, and cross-country. There is also a women's volleyball program. Several AIU teams have achieved national rankings since 1996 and individual men and women athletes have been awarded All-American status.

Study Abroad International study is readily available at AIU's Kenya and Mexico City campuses. Programs at other international sites can be arranged through the International Student Services Office.

Support Services Services for students with disabilities are provided by a cooperative relationship between Academic Affairs and Student Affairs. The Disabilities Office works to ensure that the University is in compliance with Section 504 of the Rehabilitation Act of 1973 and the Americans with Disabilities Act of 1990.

Job Opportunities Work study positions and ICWO are available. Some students are employed by the campus cafeteria and the bookstore.

Tuition: Undergraduate tuition for 2001–02 was $13,950 for the academic year, not including summer school, and $340 per unit.

Room and Board: $6180 double occupancy per academic year

Mandatory fees: $390 full-time per academic year

Contact: Dr. Oscar Schmiege, Department of Global Liberal Studies, Alliant International University, 10455 Pomerado Road, San Diego, California 92131-1799. Telephone: (858) 635-4620; Fax: (858) 635-4730. E-mail: oschmieg@alliant.edu. Web site: http://www.alliant.edu/honors.

AMERICAN RIVER COLLEGE

2 Pu G S Sc Tr

▼ Honors Program

The American River College (ARC) Honors Program offers small, enriched honors sections of required general education courses

Interpreting the symbols: **2**=two-year college, **4**=four-year college; **Pu**=public or state college, **Pr**=private college; **G**=general honors program; **D**=departmental honors program; **S**=small program (fewer than 100 students), **M**=midsize program (100 to 500 students), **L**=large program (more than 500 students); **Sc**=scholarships available in honors program; **Tr**=transfer students accepted into honors program; **HBC**=historically black college; **AA**=academic advisors; **GA**=graduate advisors; **FA**=fellowship advisors.

to highly motivated, academically talented students, giving them the freedom to work independently and collaboratively with their peers and faculty members who stimulate, challenge, and engage them in a seminar-like environment. There are currently twenty-one of these courses offered across the IGETC areas.

A major element of the program is the transfer agreement between American River College and ten major universities in California. These universities (Chapman University, Occidental University, Pepperdine University, Pitzer College, Pomona College, UC Irvine, UCLA, UC Riverside, UC Santa Cruz, and USC) offer priority admission to students who complete the honors transfer requirements.

Honors students also have the opportunity to be active in Alpha Gamma Sigma (the California Honor Society) and Phi Theta Kappa (the international honor society for two-year colleges).

The Honors Program began in January 1997 and has approximately 95 active students. Enrollment in honors classes is limited to 20 students.

Participation Requirements: To graduate from the Honors Program, students must complete a minimum of 15 units in honors with a minimum GPA of 3.25, as well as any special degree requirements for particular majors and/or four-year institutions. Students who complete the Honors Program requirements at ARC have honors designations at graduation and on their transcripts, thus increasing their chances for scholarships.

Admission Process: The requirements for admission to Honors Program courses are unique for each course. In general, students must have at least a 3.0 cumulative GPA and must have completed English 1A with at least a B.

Scholarship Availability: At present, there is only one scholarship (for an incoming high school student) specifically designated for the Honors Program.

The Campus Context: American River College is a California public two-year community college that was founded in 1955. The campus is located in a suburban setting northeast of Sacramento. American River College is among the ten largest community colleges in the state and is looked upon as a leader in innovative programs and services. It transfers more students to UC Davis and CSU Sacramento than any other community college.

American River College offers a wide variety of programs and services to the community. Its commitment is to define the community in a global sense. Recognizing the diversity of the students' backgrounds, needs, and goals, ARC is committed to evaluating and improving the educational program and services in order to anticipate the challenges of social, economic, and technological changes.

Student Body Total enrollment in the fall of 1998 was 22,961; 56 percent were women; 67 percent were white, non-Hispanic; 33 percent were Hispanic and nonwhite. Nearly 71 percent of the students are 22 years of age or older.

Faculty The total number of faculty members in the fall of 1998 was 896. Of those, 325 were full-time; 571 were part-time. Among the faculty members, terminal degrees include Ph.D.'s, Ed.D.'s, M.B.A.'s, M.F.A.'s, and a D.M.A.

Key Facilities The total number of volumes within the library is 81,000. There are thirty computers for student use in the library and more than 100 for student use in the Learning Resource Center.

Honorary Societies Alpha Gamma Sigma and Phi Theta Kappa

Athletics Men's varsity sports include baseball, basketball, cross-country, football, golf, soccer, swimming, tennis, and track. Women's varsity sports include basketball, cross-country, golf, soccer, softball, swimming, tennis, track, volleyball, and water polo.

Study Abroad American River College participates in the Semester Abroad program for California community colleges.

Support Services A variety of supportive services are available at no additional cost to students with a disability. Specialized counseling services, interpreters for the deaf, tutors, notetakers, readers, test facilitators, and mobility aids are provided upon request. An array of specialized equipment, including adapted computer hardware and software, is offered in an effort to accommodate most educational limitations.

The ARC Learning Resource Center is unique because of the wide range of academic services available to students, along with the latest in high-technology equipment, including more than 100 microcomputers, video monitors, CD-ROM and laser disc players, and listening/language stations—all geared toward convenient and efficient alternative learning styles.

Job Opportunities There are more than 300 students involved in work-study, and 174 students hold internships.

Tuition: $12 per academic unit for California residents (1999–2000)

Contact: Honors Coordinator: Ted Kulp, 4700 College Oak Drive, Sacramento, California 95841; Telephone: 916-484-8426; Fax: 916-484-8880; E-mail: honors@arc.losrios.cc.ca.us

American University

4 Pr G M Sc Tr

▼ University Honors Program

The University Honors Program provides an extra challenge for especially capable students. Those who participate in the program have the chance to involve themselves in honors work throughout their college years. Honors students broaden their horizons through exposure to a combination of traditional and innovative scholarship in a variety of disciplines. In addition, they are asked to explore challenging aspects of their favored field of study and cultivate the skills required to achieve excellence in this area.

The honors classroom resembles a forum, a place where students can share and debate ideas and opinions. Honors classes are consistently small, usually fewer than 20 students, which allows professors and students to have individual interactions with each other. The hallmark of honors courses is discussion and a rigorous examination of ideas and a belief that students are prepared and ready to take scholarship to the next level. Numerous guest lecturers, campuswide presentations, and local events enhance the classroom experience. Innovative, cross-cutting semester-long colloquiums are also offered, including "Oral Histories of the Civil Rights Movement" by NAACP Chair Julian Bond, "Artificial Intelligence" by Oxford's Rom Harre, and "Language in the New Millennium" by Edinburgh Prize winner Naomi Baron. One colloquium, "Campaign 2000" by political communications scholar Lenny Steinhorn, was featured on CNN's *NewsStand* throughout the fall 2000 presidential campaign. Approximately fifty honors classes are offered each semester.

The 20-year-old program currently has approximately 900 students. Graduates have reached the highest levels of government, business, the arts, medicine, law, and community service.

In the past two years, program participants have won the following scholarships: Truman, Fulbright, Boren, Udall, National Dean's List, and Goldwater, among others.

Participation Requirements: Honors students must complete 30 credit hours of their course work (roughly 10 courses) for honors credit. Students must achieve a grade of B or better in honors courses to attain honors credit. The four-year program of honors options draws from courses in the General Education Program and work in individual departments. Early honors work gives students a broad base of knowledge, skills, and understanding, which serves as a foundation for increasingly specialized and in-depth advanced course work in the major and related areas. Students have the option of completing requirements for either

University Honors in the major or general University Honors. They differ only in the number of hours that must be completed in the major. Each student also completes a Capstone, which is a senior thesis or project. Among the hundreds of past Capstones are book-length manuscripts, publishable-quality essays, community service, mathematical models, cutting-edge computer programs, portfolios, films, fiction, poetry, musical composition, and musical performances.

Admission Process: Students are admitted to the University Honors Program in three ways. One way is through the initial admissions process. Approximately 15 percent of the entering freshman class is admitted to the program on the basis of their high school record and SAT scores. Another avenue is through program invitation to current University students. Freshmen and sophomores, including transfer students, who have exceptional college grades may be invited to join the program if their cumulative GPA is higher than 3.75. A third avenue is through self-nomination. Freshmen and sophomores who are enrolled at American University may nominate themselves for admission to the program. Students who nominate themselves must have a cumulative GPA of at least 3.5, complete an application form and personal statement, submit a recommendation from a professor, and be interviewed by the program director. Students who enter the University Honors Program after beginning the freshman year are not required to complete the full 30 hours of honors course work. Rather, credit requirements may be slightly modified to allow the student to graduate on time. Exceptions to the number of required hours reduce lower-level course requirements according to an established formula.

Scholarship Availability: Scholarships are not available through the Honors Program but are available from the Undergraduate Admissions Office to applicants who present excellent academic credentials and leadership skills or creative excellence.

The Campus Context: American University's 84-acre traditional campus is located in a residential neighborhood in northwest Washington, D.C., with easy access to the city's resources for internships, employment, and research. American University is composed of five schools and colleges: the College of Arts and Sciences, the School of International Service, the School of Public Affairs, the School of Communications, and the Kogod School of Business. There are more than seventy undergraduate programs on campus.

Student Body Of the 5,851 full-time undergraduates, 60 percent are women. The ethnic distribution of the undergraduate population is 60 percent white, 5.6 percent African American, 4.5 percent Hispanic, 4.1 percent Asian/Pacific Islander, and .2 percent Native American. International students from more than 120 countries comprise 11 percent of the student body. Sixty percent of the students receive some kind of financial aid. There are sororities and fraternities.

Faculty Of the 489 full-time faculty members, 93 percent have terminal degrees. Forty percent are women. The student-faculty ratio is 14:1.

Key Facilities The campus library houses more than 743,000 volumes. There are computing labs on campus, with both PC and Mac links to Eaglenet, the campus network. There are also studio art, dance, music, and theater facilities and a Foreign Language Resource Center, a Media and Technology Center, and science and computer science laboratories.

Honorary Societies Golden Key, Mortar Board, Phi Beta Kappa, and Alpha Lambda Delta

Athletics There are seventeen NCAA Division I–Patriot League intercollegiate sports available. There is also an extensive intramural sports program. American University has a new state-of-the-art fitness center.

Study Abroad American University's World Capitals Program offers study-abroad programs in Beijing, Berlin, Brussels, Buenos Aires, Copenhagen, Corciano (art in Italy), Jerusalem, London, Madrid, the Mediterranean, Moscow, Paris, Prague, Rome, Santiago, South Africa, and Sydney. Additional study-abroad options exist in the School of International Service and the Kogod School of Business.

Support Services The Office of Disability Support Services offers assistance to disabled students. The campus is 94 percent accessible to those with disabilities. On-campus services include the Academic Support Center, Counseling Center, International Student Services, and LD and ADD services.

Job Opportunities There are numerous work-study positions as well as other job openings on campus and throughout the Washington, D.C., area.

Tuition: $22,116 per year (2001–02)

Room and Board: $5673 double occupancy. Meal plans begin at $995. An extensive selection of honors housing is available.

Mandatory Fees: $365

Contact: Director: Michael Mass, 4400 Massachusetts Avenue, NW, Ward 312, Washington, DC 20016-8119; Telephone: 202-885-6194; Fax: 202-885-7013; E-mail: mmass@american.edu

ANDREWS UNIVERSITY

4 Pr G M Sc Tr

▼ John Nevins Andrews Honors Program

Recognizing its responsibility to challenge its best students, Andrews University established the John Nevins Andrews Honors Program in 1966. In 2000, its curriculum was revised to incorporate a separate general education program, rather than honors sections of typical courses. Currently the honors program enrolls more than 150 undergraduates, and beyond its underlying purpose of encouraging student scholarship and research, the program attempts to enrich its students' social and spiritual interests.

Reflecting suggestions from students, faculty members, and alumni for a curriculum based on the study of original texts, independent research, and writing, SAGES (Scholars=Alternative General Education Studies) provides a series of mostly interdisciplinary courses that reduce general education requirements for the Bachelor of Arts and Bachelor of Science degrees. Following a yearlong introduction to Western civilization and culture, students pursue a series of thematically organized seminars similar to a "Great Books" approach, though broader in sources and subjects.

Led by devoted faculty members who are respected for their teaching as well as for their knowledge, SAGES courses involve wider reading, more writing, and deeper discussion than typical alternatives. They are also designed to maintain certain values: the challenge of learning, friendship with peers, and interaction with instructors.

Because SAGES replaces many lower-division courses, there are significant advantages to admission at the beginning of a college career. However, transfer students with demonstrated academic achievement (GPA greater than 3.4) are invited to apply to SAGES and may receive individual waivers for some specific courses.

The program encourages students to participate in regional and national honors conventions, and all members of the honors program are entitled to audit one course per semester without tuition. Given the Andrews University aim to educate the whole person, students in the honors program sponsor a variety of

Interpreting the symbols: **2**=two-year college, **4**=four-year college; **Pu**=public or state college, **Pr**=private college; **G**=general honors program; **D**=departmental honors program; **S**=small program (fewer than 100 students), **M**=midsize program (100 to 500 students), **L**=large program (more than 500 students); **Sc**=scholarships available in honors program; **Tr**=transfer students accepted into honors program; **HBC**=historically black college; **AA**=academic advisors; **GA**=graduate advisors; **FA**=fellowship advisors.

social and religious events ranging from banquets and drama performances to retreats and canoe trips.

Participation Requirements: Graduation as a John Nevins Andrews Honors Scholar is noted on the diploma and signified in student regalia. Its requirements include a 3.5 GPA overall, completion of the SAGES courses, a senior honors thesis or project, and its presentation to an interdisciplinary audience. The honors thesis is listed in the graduation program.

Admission Process: Members are admitted each spring and summer from applicants with a minimum high school GPA of 3.5 and high ACT or SAT scores. Transfer students and others may also apply. Continuation in the program requires honors course work and a minimum GPA of 3.33.

Scholarship Availability: There are University tuition awards for National Merit Scholars and individuals earning outstanding scores on the ACT or SAT I.

The Campus Context: Founded as Battle Creek College in 1874, the institution became Emmanuel Missionary College after moving to Berrien Springs in 1901. Following the transfer of several graduate programs to the campus, it was renamed Andrews University in 1960 and is the first university sponsored by the Seventh-day Adventist Church. Andrews University is ranked nationally by *U.S. News & World Report.* During the 1990s, a number of students in the sciences received Goldwater scholarships.

There are two colleges on the campus, Arts and Sciences and Technology; two schools, Business and Education; the Division of Architecture; and the Theological Seminary. A total of seventy graduate and undergraduate degree programs are offered. Notable facilities include the archaeological and biological museums; construction will begin shortly on a fine arts center.

Student Body Undergraduate enrollment is 1,500 (out of 2,500 total students), representing most states. International students, who compose about 20 percent of the student population, represent nearly 100 countries. About 50 percent of all undergraduates are white; 25 percent African American; 14 percent, Asian; and 10 percent, Hispanic. There are no fraternities or sororities; roughly half of all undergraduates live in campus dormitories. Eighty-five percent of students receive financial aid.

Faculty Of the 250 faculty members, nearly 90 percent are full-time, and most hold the doctorate or other terminal degree. The student-faculty ratio is 13:1.

Key Facilities The library houses nearly 700,000 volumes. There are sixteen computer labs and more than 300 personal computers for student use. The recently remodeled Forsyth Honors House provides many opportunities for formal and informal student gatherings as well as study.

Athletics Although Andrews University has limited intercollegiate athletics, there are intramural leagues for a variety of sports.

Study Abroad Study-abroad opportunities include Newbold College in England and language programs in Spain, France, and Austria. The University also sponsors affiliated programs on campuses in Africa and the Caribbean. University students participate widely in teaching English and in other international service programs.

Job Opportunities Students find employment in a wide variety of campus jobs, including work-study and the Community Service Assistantship Program.

Tuition: $13,350 per year (2001–02)

Room and Board: $4020 minimum

Mandatory Fees: $326

Contact: Director: Malcolm Russell, Berrien Springs, Michigan 49104-0075; Telephone: 616-471-3297; Fax: 616-471-6236; E-mail: russell@andrews.edu; Web site: http://www.andrews.edu/honors.html

ANGELO STATE UNIVERSITY

4 Pu G S AA

▼ Honors Program

The Honors Program at Angelo State University (ASU) is a collection of courses and opportunities that provide honors students with an enriched educational experience. Key characteristics of the program are an honors lounge in the Porter Henderson Library, access to external speakers, and the opportunity to join the Honors Student Association. The honors lounge contains six computer workstations, a study area, a social area, a conference room, and the honors director's office.

The Honors Program at Angelo State University is intended to provide students with the opportunity to achieve a deeper understanding of course material, be exposed to cultural and intellectual events that broaden their appreciation of the world that surrounds them, develop leadership qualities that help them through their careers and personal lives, and nurture an understanding and appreciation of the diverse needs of society and how their personal service can enhance the quality of life for their family and others. The Honors Program achieves these goals through course offerings and extracurricular activities designed to challenge and enhance the intellectual and personal abilities of honors students.

The 2002–03 academic year is the inaugural year for the Honors Program at ASU. The program anticipates 20 students in the initial year of operation.

Participation Requirements: A listing of the formal courses offered in the program appears below. These requirements result in a total of 30 credit hours of work taken by each honors student. Most of the courses required in the program are honors sections of regularly offered courses. During the last two years, students receive honors credit for two courses within their major discipline. These courses can be standard sections, with the honors student being required to complete additional assignments not given to regular students. Alternatively, these major discipline courses may be special courses, such as individual research. Requirements for the Honors Program include Introduction to Honors Study (2 hours, taken as USTD 1201), History 1301 (3 hours), English 1302 (3 hours), Government 2301 (3 hours), humanities (Great Books Courses, 6 hours total; two courses, including a 3-hour course toward the humanities requirement and a 3-hour course toward the visual and performing arts requirement—art, drama, or music), a lab science course (3 hours), Introduction to Honors Research (2 hours), Honors Seminar (1 hour; this class is open to honors students only during their senior year), and department/major discipline courses (6 hours). In future years of the program, class substitutions will be possible for transfer students or existing students who enter the program after their freshman year. These substitutions will be made on an individual basis and will take into account whether the student meets existing requirements for students entering the program. Students will still have to complete 20 hours in residence.

Students must maintain a minimum 3.25 overall GPA. Students who complete all of these requirements receive a separate designation on their diploma and are recognized at graduation.

Admission Process: Students who meet the criteria below and complete an application form are considered for admission into the Honors Program. Admission into the program is on a rolling basis. To be accepted into the program, freshmen must be in the top 10 percent of their high school class, have a minimum score of 1200 on the SAT or 27 on the ACT, submit an essay of 250 words, and have a solid record of participation in extracurricular activities. To be admitted after the freshman year, students must have a minimum GPA of 3.25, score at least 1200 on the SAT or 27 on the ACT, be in the top 10 percent of their high school class, submit an essay of 250 words, and have a solid record of participation in extracurricular activities.

Scholarship Availability: No formal scholarships are available for honors students at this time; however, students who meet the admission requirements for the Honors Program are eligible to apply for the Carr Academic Scholarship. Information concerning this scholarship and other scholarships may be obtained at http://www.angelo.edu/services/financial_aid/prospective/.

The Campus Context: Angelo State University is located in San Angelo, a city of approximately 100,000. The University has an enrollment of approximately 6,300 students. It is a state-sponsored coeducational institution governed by the Texas State University System. Angelo State University is accredited by the Commission on Colleges of the Southern Association of Colleges and Schools (1866 Southern Lane, Decatur, Georgia 30033-4097; telephone: 404-679-4501) to award associate, baccalaureate, and master's degrees. Angelo State University has one of the nation's largest privately funded scholarship programs, supported by a growing endowment exceeding $55 million.

Student Body Undergraduate enrollment is approximately 6,300. ASU has fifteen honor societies, sixteen academic and professional organizations, six Greek organizations, and nine religious organizations. Student demographics may be viewed at http://www.angelo.edu/pstudent/demographics.htm.

Faculty Angelo State University has 225 full-time faculty members, 67 percent of whom have their terminal degree (Ph.D.).

Key Facilities The total library holdings surpass 1.4 million items in a variety of formats, comprising a collection that compares favorably with the national average for library holdings in colleges and universities offering master's degrees. The Porter Henderson Library contains 80,000 square feet of space, which is to be expanded by the addition of another floor to the library. Library facilities include more than 300 study carrels that are conducive to efficient study and research, large reading and reference rooms, open stacks, an audiovisual center, and a microform reading area. Through the library's interlibrary loan service and cooperative agreements with other libraries, faculty members and students may request additional resources for their personal research and classroom assignments.

One of the campus microcomputer labs is located on the second floor of the library. There are a total of seven microcomputer labs spread across the campus to easily accommodate students.

Athletics ASU is in Division II of the NCAA for football, women's soccer, women's volleyball, cross-country/track, men's and women's basketball, and women's softball. There is also an active intramural and sports club program, including a very successful rugby sports club.

Study Abroad ASU has a growing International Studies Program that offers a variety of study-abroad experiences to qualified students. Information concerning this program may be obtained at http://www.angelo.edu/dept/international_studies/index.htm.

Support Services Angelo State University is committed to the principle that no qualified person shall, on the basis of disability, be excluded from participation in or be denied the benefits of the services, programs, or activities of the University, as required by the Americans with Disabilities Act of 1990. Designated handicapped parking spaces are provided in each parking lot serving a University building. Each building has access ramps and an elevator to provide convenient access to all building activities.

Spaces in Massie Residence Hall for Women, Massie Residence Hall for Men, and the Vanderventer Apartments have been adapted to meet the needs of students in wheelchairs or who have other forms of physical disabilities. Students who need assignment to one of these facilities due to a disability should notify the ASU Housing Office as soon as the decision is made to attend Angelo State.

Job Opportunities Work opportunities on campus and around the city may be found at the Center for Career Development on campus. Career development services are available to both current students and ASU graduates.

Tuition and Fees: $1331 per long semester, based on a 15-credit load (2001)

Room and Board: $2370 with seven-day meal plan (2001)

Contact: Director: Dr. Nick Flynn, Assistant Professor of Biochemistry, Angelo State University, San Angelo, Texas 76909; Telephone: 915-942-2722; Fax: 915-942-2716; E-mail: honors@angelo.edu

APPALACHIAN STATE UNIVERSITY

4 Pu D M Sc Tr

▼ University Honors Program

Honors at Appalachian is more than a collection of courses; it is an approach to learning designed to stimulate active involvement by students in their own education. Critical thinking and analysis are stimulated by free and structured discussions in and outside the classroom. Honors classrooms are lively; honors students are encouraged to excel both by their professors and by their gifted peers. Independent projects frequently allow the student to probe the depths of a topic, with individual professorial encouragement and direction. In honors, faculty and students work together to uncover the challenging questions that the academy pursues. With certain restrictions, some regular courses can be taken on honors contract.

Approximately 350–375 students enroll in twenty-three to twenty-five honors courses offered each semester. About 40 to 50 students graduate each year from departmental, college, or General Honors programs.

Participation Requirements: Honors courses are available in several departments. Most freshman-sophomore departmental honors courses substitute for core curriculum requirements or for popular electives. At the upper-division level, departmental courses permit students to pursue graduation with departmental honors recognition. General Honors offers an elective interdisciplinary program featuring team-taught topical courses for core curriculum credit in the social sciences and humanities. An exceptional cross-disciplinary program is available for qualified juniors and seniors majoring in the College of Business. Most programs require that a student maintain at least a 3.2 GPA (on a 4.0 scale). A generic University Honors Program Graduate designation is awarded to students who take 18 hours of honors classes (at least six of which are outside their major), complete a senior honors project, and maintain at least a 3.4 GPA in honors classes.

Beyond the classroom, the honors program at Appalachian seeks to maintain a stimulating and supportive atmosphere for serious students. Coffey Hall, the coed apartment-style residence hall for up to 105 honors students, houses the office of the Honors Coordinator and provides special facilities for living and learning, including a classroom and lounge. The Appalachian Honors Association (AHA), a student-led organization, provides social and community service activities for honors students. Honors students often take field trips, sometimes to the facilities the University maintains in New York or Washington, D.C. Some attend regional, state, or national honors conferences or study abroad for honors credit.

Interpreting the symbols: **2**=two-year college, **4**=four-year college; **Pu**=public or state college, **Pr**=private college; **G**=general honors program; **D**=departmental honors program; **S**=small program (fewer than 100 students), **M**=midsize program (100 to 500 students), **L**=large program (more than 500 students); **Sc**=scholarships available in honors program; **Tr**=transfer students accepted into honors program; **HBC**=historically black college; **AA**=academic advisors; **GA**=graduate advisors; **FA**=fellowship advisors.

Admission Process: Approximately the top 10 percent of the incoming freshman class (about 250 students) get an automatic invitation into honors upon admission or before summer orientation on the basis of their class rank, high school grades, and SAT I or ACT scores. Others may request in writing to be considered. Students already enrolled are recommended for honors work by faculty members or academic advisers. The number of students admitted is determined in part by the number of available seats.

Scholarship Availability: Appalachian's most prestigious merit-based scholarships are the Chancellor's Scholarships. Each year 25 incoming freshmen are selected for these awards (2001–02 stipend: $4500 per year), which are renewable for four years if a minimum 3.4 GPA is maintained. Chancellor's Scholars must take at least one honors course each semester for their first two years. Many scholars go on to graduate from departmental, college, or General Honors programs.

The Campus Context: Appalachian State University celebrated its centennial in 1999. Founded as Watauga Academy to educate teachers for the mountain area, it grew as a teachers' college and, in 1971, became a member institution of the University of North Carolina system offering a broad range of academic programs. With instruction as its primary mission, the University is committed to excellence in teaching and the fostering of scholarship. It continues to serve its region but also draws students from across the state, nation, and from other countries. Its beautiful mountain setting offers many opportunities for outdoor activities, including skiing and hiking. A major addition to the student union opened in summer 1995. The University serves a largely traditional undergraduate population in a residential environment and also offers a wide selection of graduate programs. Continually seeking innovative ways to deliver instruction, Appalachian is increasing its distance learning, study abroad, and continuing education offerings. Academic offerings include more than 300 major programs and seventeen different undergraduate and master's degrees. Ed.D. is the highest degree awarded.

Appalachian maintains two campuses away from Boone: the New York Loft, a totally refurbished, 4,400-square-foot condominium in the Gramercy Park area, and Appalachian House, which opened in 1977, a four-story townhouse in the heart of the Capitol Hill historic district just a block from the Library of Congress.

Student Body Current enrollment is 12,500; 93 percent undergraduate, 7 percent graduate, and 88 percent from North Carolina.

Faculty Appalachian employs 630 full-time faculty members, 87 percent of whom hold doctoral or first professional degrees. About 272 additional faculty members, 30 percent of the total, are part-time. The student-faculty ratio is 14:1.

Key Facilities The University recently completed construction on an academic support building, a science building, a new steam plant, and a convocation center. Planned growth of the University includes expansion of the library and a living-learning center.

Honorary Societies Phi Eta Sigma, Phi Kappa Phi, Gamma Beta Phi, Alpha Chi, and Omicron Delta Kappa

Athletics The University's Division I program fields ten men's and ten women's varsity teams. Several scholar-athletes participate in varsity sports and in honors. Recreational facilities available to all students include the Quinn Recreation Center, an Outdoor Center, and the Mt. Mitchell Life Fitness Center as well as numerous tennis courts and playing fields.

Study Abroad Appalachian is one of the top ten master's degree-granting institutions in the United States in the number of students participating in study-abroad programs, which can be taken for honors credit.

Tuition: $1222 for state residents, $9144 for nonresidents, per year (2001–02)

Room and Board: $3795

Mandatory Fees: $1208

Contact: Coordinator: Dr. Conrad E. Ostwalt Jr., Coffey Hall, Boone, North Carolina 28608; Telephone: 828-262-2083; Fax: 828-262-2734; E-mail: ostwaltce@appstate.edu

Arcadia University

4 Pr G S Tr

▼ Honors Program

The mission of the Arcadia University Honors Program is to offer intellectually challenging and enriching educational opportunities to highly motivated, talented, and creative students in all majors. The program offers scholars occasions to interact collaboratively and form a sense of community through both on- and off-campus learning activities. Honors courses average 10 students in a class, offering the opportunity to interact with faculty members from a variety of academic departments. Students accepted into the Honors Program are encouraged to study abroad during their academic program. All honors students are invited to go to London during spring break for free, while all other full-time freshmen in good academic standing may attend for $245. The Honors Program was founded in the early 1970s and enhanced and broadened in the fall of 1996. The program presently accommodates 80 students.

Participation Requirements: The Honors Program offers four types of academic activities. The first are honors sections of the freshman writing courses, EN 101: Thought and Expression I and EN 102: Thought and Expression II. The second are Honors Readings (HN 201) and Honors Project (HN 202)—courses that are typically taken during the sophomore year. The third activity involves upper-level courses adapted for honors credit. The fourth type is Honors Colloquia (HN 390), which are investigative seminars addressing open-ended topics. They connect at least two disciplines and blend readings in classic texts with innovative learning styles.

Honors Program students must maintain a GPA of at least 3.25 to remain in good standing. Students who complete the Honors Program requirements have the designation Honors Scholar appear on their transcripts.

Admission Process: Students are accepted into the Honors Program on a rolling basis. Freshman applicants to the University with at least a 1200 SAT I who rank in the top 10 percent of their graduating class are evaluated for acceptance into the program based upon the strength of their admissions application (high school average, rank, essay, recommendations, etc.). Transfer applicants with a minimum transfer GPA of 3.25 are reviewed for acceptance into the program as well. Students seeking to enter the program after being enrolled at Arcadia University may be nominated or may self-nominate for consideration if they have an overall GPA of 3.25 or higher.

Scholarship Availability: All students accepted to Arcadia University are automatically reviewed for scholarships. The University's Distinguished Scholarships range from $2000 a year to full tuition, and Achievement Awards range from $1000 to 6000 a year.

The Campus Context: Set on a beautiful 60-acre former private estate in Glenside, a suburb of Philadelphia, Arcadia University offers urban resources in a countrylike setting. The focal point of the campus is the unique Grey Towers Castle, a National Historic Landmark. A coeducational university founded in 1853, Arcadia offers small, dynamic classes where students' world views can come to life. Arcadia University is dedicated to giving students an education with a global perspective. There are undergraduate majors available in forty subject areas. Majors of study include accounting, fine arts, biology, business, chemistry, communications, computer science, environmental studies (3+2), education, engineering (3+2), English, history, international peace and conflict resolution (4+2), management information systems, mathematics, philosophy, physical therapy (4+3), physician assistant studies (4+2), political science, psychology, sociology, Spanish, theater arts and English, and several preprofessional programs. Specific courses of study lead to a Bachelor of Arts, a Bachelor of Fine Arts, or a Bachelor of Science degree.

Student Body The total population of the University, including graduate and part-time students, is 2,841. The total full-time undergraduate population is 1,322, of whom 70 percent are women and 30 percent are men. Twenty-three percent of the undergraduate population are members of minority groups, and 3 percent are international students. Ninety-four percent of the students receive financial aid.

Faculty The total number of faculty members is 292, of whom 92 are full-time. Eighty-five percent of the faculty members have doctoral or terminal degrees in their fields. The student-faculty ratio is 12:1.

Key Facilities The Atwood Library contains more than 128,456 volumes, 776 periodicals, and 188,921 microforms. Construction has begun on an addition and renovation project that will double the size of Arcadia University's current library. Anticipated completion date is fall 2003. A record and videotape collection is also available for student use. Automated online catalogs and CD-ROM workstations assist students in finding needed items. Six computer laboratories on campus allow students access to word processing, the Internet, and personal e-mail accounts seven days a week. All of the residence halls on campus are wired into the campus network. A card purchased from Computer Services allows students to use their personal computers to access the Internet. Public computers dedicated to e-mail and Web access are located in the Dining Hall Complex.

Honorary Societies Kappa Delta Pi, Phi Alpha Theta, Phi Sigma Tau, Pi Delta Phi, Psi Chi, Sigma Beta Delta, Phi Kappa Phi, and Sigma Zeta

Athletics Arcadia University's Athletic Department takes pride in fielding talented, competitive teams. The University competes in the Pennsylvania Athletic Conference and fields both men's and women's Division III teams. Men on campus have the opportunity to compete in baseball, basketball, cross-country, golf, soccer, swimming, and tennis. Women's sports include basketball, cross-country, field hockey, lacrosse, soccer, softball, swimming, tennis, volleyball, and equestrian. For those not interested in being involved in a team sport, intramural sports are available. The Kuch Center, Arcadia's sports and recreation facility, is home to a six-lane swimming pool, an indoor track, basketball and volleyball courts, an aerobics/dance studio, a training center, a sauna and whirlpool, and seating for 1,500 spectators. Outdoors there are tennis courts and sports fields for students' use.

Study Abroad Arcadia University has been a leader in study abroad since 1948. Arcadia's Center for Education Abroad (CEA) serves more than 1,500 students from 300 North American colleges and universities each year. Through its programs of study in Australia, England, Greece, Ireland, Italy, Mexico, New Zealand, Northern Ireland, Scotland, Spain, and Wales, CEA supports and implements the University's commitment to international education. Students have the opportunity to study overseas for a summer, semester, or full year for about the same cost as remaining on the Glenside campus. CEA provides comprehensive predeparture sessions, on-site orientation, individualized advising, and a wide variety of activities and official academic transcripts on every one of its study-abroad programs. Internships and student teaching experiences are also available overseas.

Support Services The Education Enhancement Center, located in Taylor Hall, provides support services for students with disabilities. Arcadia University complies with the Americans with Disabilities Act of 1990. Students with disabilities are accommodated on an individual basis to best meet their particular needs. The Writing Center, math lab, academic advising, tutoring, and personal counseling are available to students to assist them in their search for excellence.

Job Opportunities Work-study jobs are available on campus, and allocation of funds for each student is based on financial need. Work-study jobs range from student tour guides to office assistants. Internships and cooperative education experiences are available to any student on campus. Academic advisers assist students in finding which internships and co-ops are best for them.

Tuition: $18,390 (2001–02)

Room and Board: $7980

Mandatory Fees: $280

Contact: Director: Melissa Keller, 450 South Easton Road, Glenside, Pennsylvania 19038-3295; Telephone: 877-ARCADIA; Fax: 215-572-4049; E-mail: kellerm@arcadia.edu; Web site: http://www.arcadia.edu

Arizona State University

4 Pu L Sc Tr AA FA

▼ The Barrett Honors College

The Barrett Honors College has the responsibility of organizing the academic resources of the University for the benefit of talented and motivated undergraduates at all three of Arizona State University's campuses—main, west, and east—and in all majors, minors, and certificate programs offered at those campuses. The College establishes standards for admission, curriculum, and graduation through the Honors College, assuring University-wide transferability and quality for honors education.

The goal of the College's curriculum is to develop habits of mind that enable persons to be lifelong learners, creative problem solvers, and participatory citizens in a democratic society. The College emphasizes small classes, generally limited to 20 students; seminar and other engaged modes of learning; and the development of critical reading, discussion, and writing skills. The College appoints faculty members who are responsible for offering the core honors curriculum, but the College otherwise utilizes the instructional and research resources of the University as a whole.

The Barrett Honors College offers students access to all of the human and physical resources of one of the nation's most rapidly rising research universities. Honors College students have access to honors advisers appointed by the College and to faculty advisers in the colleges and departments. Based in the Center Complex, nine buildings that accommodate 850 student residents, the College promotes strong relationships among students, faculty members, and members of the College's administration.

The Honors College's residential space includes classrooms, meeting rooms, a library, a state-of-the-art computing lab, and other student services. Arizona State University has more than 1,700 faculty members, most of whom welcome working with strong undergraduates. Honors College students normally fulfill the requirements for their majors and for graduating through the College without having to take additional hours. The College's courses meet a variety of general studies requirements and course work in the major can be adapted to meet college requirements, including the bachelor's honors thesis or creative project.

Notable upper-division honors programs supporting the College's students are coordinated by the College of Business, which designed one of the first business honors programs in the nation; the College of Nursing, which gives priority placement to Honors College students; the College of Education; and the College of Public Programs. Other professional colleges are designing similar programs.

Interpreting the symbols: **2**=two-year college, **4**=four-year college; **Pu**=public or state college, **Pr**=private college; **G**=general honors program; **D**=departmental honors program; **S**=small program (fewer than 100 students), **M**=midsize program (100 to 500 students), **L**=large program (more than 500 students); **Sc**=scholarships available in honors program; **Tr**=transfer students accepted into honors program; **HBC**=historically black college; **AA**=academic advisors; **GA**=graduate advisors; **FA**=fellowship advisors.

Honors students are strongly encouraged to participate in undergraduate research projects and internships. The staff members work closely with colleges and departments to ensure that appropriate programs are available and that honors students have preferential access to them. Many students participate in multiple internships and research projects. These experiences often provide the foundation for honors theses or creative projects.

The College offers four summer study-abroad programs—in London, Edinburgh, and Dublin; Paris and the Loire Valley; Athens, Rome, and Dubrovnik; and Latin America. The summer study-abroad programs are restricted to honors students and taught exclusively by honors faculty members. The programs are open to any college honors student in the nation, and all the courses carry honors credit.

Students in the Barrett Honors College have established a distinguished record in such scholarship and fellowship competitions as the Rhodes, Marshall, Truman, Goldwater, NSEP, Woodrow Wilson, and Mellon. Since 1990, more than 200 of these fellowships and scholarships have been received by Honors College students.

The Barrett Honors College has been in existence for thirteen years, superseding a 27-year-old honors program. There are currently 2,600 students enrolled, with an entering freshman class of 800.

Participation Requirements: Graduation through the Barrett Honors College requires students to complete HON 171-172 or HON 394 (for transfer students), a bachelor's honors thesis or creative project, 24 additional semester hours of course work for honors credit, and the requirements for a bachelor's degree and to maintain at least a 3.4 GPA (on a 4.0 scale) for work completed at ASU.

All work completed for honors credit is noted as such on the student's transcript. Graduation through the College is acknowledged at the University's Commencement exercises and the College's convocation and is noted on the student's transcript. Students who complete their lower-division work (18 hours of honors course work with a minimum overall GPA of 3.4) also have that noted on their transcript.

Admission Process: Students are admitted to the College as freshmen or may transfer into the College either from within the University or from other institutions at any time during their college career as long as time remains to complete the requirements for graduating through the College. Applicants are evaluated on the basis of their high school GPA (Arizona Board of Regents GPA based on sixteen competency courses), high school class rank, and performance on the SAT I or ACT. Some students possess other talents that contribute to academic leadership and community service. The typical first-year student in the Barrett Honors College has a high school GPA of 3.8, is in the top 6 percent of his or her graduating class, and earns a 28 composite on the ACT or 1300 composite on the SAT I. Transfer students are admitted if they are in good standing in the Honors Program at the institution from which they are transferring or if they have established a minimum 3.5 GPA.

Scholarship Availability: Students are eligible for a wide range of scholarships, including in- and out-of-state partial and full fee and tuition waivers, depending on the student's academic and cocurricular achievements; renewable cash awards for National Merit Semi-Finalists and Finalists and other students whose performance on the SAT I or ACT is especially strong; Gammage Scholarships for National Merit Scholars, worth $3500 per year in addition to the National Merit cash award; Leadership Scholar Scholarships for $1500 per year for up to four years; and the Flinn Scholarship, awarded by the Flinn Foundation to Arizona residents attending an Arizona university.

The Campus Context: Arizona State University has several campuses, each with a number of colleges. On the ASU main campus are the Colleges of Architecture and Environmental Design, Business, Education, Engineering and Applied Sciences, Fine Arts, Honors, Law, Liberal Arts and Sciences, Nursing, and Public Programs. The Graduate School is also located on the main campus. ASU also has a west and an east campus. There are more than 100 undergraduate degree programs.

Student Body Undergraduate enrollment is 29,000; 48 percent men and 52 percent women. Twenty-one percent of the students are members of minority groups, and there are 1,256 international students. The percentage of students receiving financial aid is 53. There are forty-four fraternities and sororities.

Faculty Of the 1,976 faculty members, 1,796 are full-time and 83 percent hold terminal degrees. The student-faculty ratio is 19:1.

Key Facilities Among special and distinguished facilities are the Grady Gammage Auditorium, the Nelson Fine Arts Center, the Computing Commons, the Electron Microscopy Laboratory, the Cancer Research Institute, the Goldwater Center for Engineering Sciences, the Noble Science Library, the Plummer Aquatic Center, and the Student Recreation Complex. The library houses 3,073,717 volumes. The University has 37 computer facilities. In addition to the Computing Commons, computer facilities exist in every college and all residence halls.

Honorary Societies Phi Kappa Phi, Golden Key, Phi Beta Kappa, Alpha Lambda Delta, and Mortar Board

Athletics Arizona State University is a member of the NCAA, Division I, and the Pacific Ten Conference. The University has twenty varsity intercollegiate sports and more than 500 participants. Many students in the Barrett Honors College participate in varsity sports as well as club team sports.

Study Abroad The Barrett Honors College offers four summer study-abroad programs in London, Edinburgh, and Dublin; Paris and the Loire Valley; Athens, Rome, and Dubrovnik; and Latin America. They are restricted to honors students from ASU and other universities throughout the nation. The College also sponsors an exchange program with the University of Edinburgh and has an agreement with St. Catherine's College at Cambridge University that allows a restricted number of its students each year to be full matriculants. In addition, the College, in cooperation with the International Programs Office, offers students a full range of overseas study opportunities either as individuals or in groups. For most programs, students can arrange to receive honors credit. Many students use these opportunities to do work that leads to their honors thesis.

Support Services Disability Resources for Students offers a wide range of support services, including academic and career consultation, referral and coordination with other campus programs, the Access Employment Program and Talking Books, nonstandard testing accommodations, an in-class note taking program, assistance with adapting course materials, alternative print formats, Braille production, tutoring, sign language and oral interpreting, and an intracampus cart transport service.

Job Opportunities More than 6,000 students are employed on campus, and jobs are available in every academic, service, and support unit. More than 50 percent of the students in the Barrett Honors College have some kind of campus employment, including paid internships and research laboratory assignments.

Tuition: $2300 for state residents, $10,300 for nonresidents, per year (2001–02)

Room and Board: $4825

Mandatory Fees: $70

Contact: Dean: Ted Humphrey, PO Box 871612, Tempe, Arizona 85287-1612; Telephone: 480-965-2354; Fax: 480-965-0760; E-mail: ted.humphrey@asu.edu; Web site: http://www.asu.edu/honors/

Arizona Western College

2 Pu G L Sc Tr

▼ University Honors Program

The Honors Program at Arizona Western College (AWC) was established in the 1985–86 academic school year and has 32 members at the present time. It offers three different courses of study that provide intellectual challenges and stimulation for academically talented and highly motivated students, encourage students to probe deeply into various subject areas, promote the synthesis of insights they have gained across the curriculum, and facilitate the sharing of their discoveries with faculty members and fellow students. Long-range goals include fostering a lifelong love of scholarly inquiry and independent thinking, building a sense of leadership and responsibility, and evoking an enhanced self-confidence that will result from having met the challenges offered in the program.

Honors courses enrich the regular curriculum with original source material or current research. Honors students have expanded opportunities for discussion and interaction with faculty members and outside experts in a variety of disciplines.

The deadline for submitting grant applications is March 16.

Scholarship Availability: Honors grant awards are available to students living on or off campus. Stipend recipients can receive tuition, fees, room, board, or partial grant awards. Honors students participate in service activities to the Honors Program. Students applying for an honors grant must qualify in one of three ways: graduate from high school in the upper 10 percent of their class, receive a composite score of at least 21 on the ACT or a composite score of 1000 or better on the SAT I, or complete 12 hours or more of college-level course work with a cumulative GPA of 3.5 or better on a 4.0 scale. All applicants must write a 500- to 750-word essay proposing a project to be completed during their time at AWC. Three letters of recommendation as well as secondary and postsecondary transcripts are also required.

The Campus Context: Arizona Western is a two-year college offering the Associate of Arts, Associate of Applied Science, and Associate of General Studies degrees to 7,201 undergraduates. Sharing a friendly and familiar 560-acre oasis in the desert, Arizona Western College and Northern Arizona University in Yuma provide students a seamless transfer opportunity with the 2+2 program.

Student Body There are 1,542 full-time undergraduates of whom 57.2 percent are women and 5,659 part-time undergraduates of whom 62.5 percent are women. The ethnic distribution of the total undergraduate population is 2 percent African American, 1.5 percent Native American/Alaska Native, 1.5 percent Asian or Pacific Islander, 40.3 percent Hispanic, 52.8 percent white/non-Hispanic, and 1.9 percent unknown. There are 6 international students.

Faculty Of the 99 full-time faculty members, 95 percent have master's degrees.

Key Facilities The College has a 55,000-volume library with Internet access and online library catalogs, a 135-station computer laboratory (open 80 hours a week), six computer classrooms, and eight distance learning classrooms.

Athletics The College offers men's and women's intercollegiate athletics. The men's intercollegiate athletics are football, soccer, basketball, and baseball. The women's intercollegiate athletics are volleyball, basketball, and softball.

Tuition: $900 for state residents, $5268 for nonresidents, per year (1998–99)

Room and Board: $2850 to $3350

Contact: Director: Kirstin Ruth Bratt, P.O. Box 929, Yuma, Arizona 85366-0929; Telephone: 520-344-7685; Fax: 520-344-7730; E-mail: aw_honors@awc.cc.az.us

Arkansas State University

4 Pu G M Sc Tr FA

▼ Honors Program

The Honors Program at Arkansas State University (ASU) aims to transform students over the course of their study of various disciplines to make them active, creative scholars who are fully prepared to contribute their knowledge and skills to the wider world. It offers special opportunities for exceptionally qualified students to develop their abilities to think independently and express their thoughts clearly and forcefully in speech and writing. Students majoring in any department in the University may participate in the program. Honors work supplements regular course work within the student's major field of concentration. It also encourages work that will develop familiarity with the relationships among different academic disciplines.

The honors curriculum includes honors sections of general education courses, honors options (in which an additional component is added to an upper-division course in the major or minor), special-topic honors seminars, honors independent study, and the honors senior thesis. Students in the University Honors Program have additional options for earning honors-caliber credit: they may, with approval, substitute selected upper-level courses for general education courses, claim selected upper-level courses outside the major, and take graduate courses for undergraduate credit as juniors and seniors.

The 21-year-old program currently enrolls about 400 people.

Participation Requirements: Students join the Honors Program by enrolling in honors courses; there is no formal application procedure. Aside from Trustees' Scholars and other students who elect to enroll in the University Honors Program, which requires two honors-caliber courses each year, honors students are not required to complete a set number of honors courses each year. To graduate with honors, students must complete at least 18 hours of honors course work, 9 or more of them at the upper level, and earn a minimum cumulative 3.5 GPA. Transfer students may graduate in honors by either meeting these requirements in full or, if entering with 36 or more hours completed, by taking 15 hours of upper-division honors work; they must also have a minimum 3.5 GPA. Diplomas of those fulfilling these requirements bear the designation "Honors Program." Students in the University Honors Program must maintain at least a 3.5 cumulative GPA and complete at least two honors-caliber courses during each academic year, totalling at least 24 credits in all (at least 12 of them at the upper-division level), including an honors senior thesis; diplomas of graduates fulfilling these requirements bear the designation "University Honors Program." All honors courses are indicated as such on the student's transcript. Students graduating with honors and University honors are recognized at Commencement by blue honors cords and by special designation in the Commencement booklet, which also records honors senior theses.

Scholarship Availability: Residents of Arkansas with a composite ACT score of 30 or above who enroll at Arkansas State University in the fall semester immediately following their graduation from an Arkansas high school are eligible to apply for the Board of Trustees Scholarship. This scholarship provides tuition, general

Interpreting the symbols: **2**=two-year college, **4**=four-year college; **Pu**=public or state college, **Pr**=private college; **G**=general honors program; **D**=departmental honors program; **S**=small program (fewer than 100 students), **M**=midsize program (100 to 500 students), **L**=large program (more than 500 students); **Sc**=scholarships available in honors program; **Tr**=transfer students accepted into honors program; **HBC**=historically black college; **AA**=academic advisors; **GA**=graduate advisors; **FA**=fellowship advisors.

fees, room and board, and a stipend of $1200 per semester for up to eight consecutive semesters as long as the student completes at least 12 hours of course work in the fall and spring semesters and fulfills the requirements of the University Honors Program in which Trustees' Scholars are automatically enrolled. Other honors students may be eligible for the Academic Distinction Scholarship, which provides for full tuition in the fall and spring semesters, or the President's Scholarship, which offers housing and tuition. In addition, two $500 Hazel Deutsch scholarships are awarded each fall to students who have demonstrated outstanding performance in the Honors Program.

The Campus Context: The mission of Arkansas State University is to pursue and share knowledge within a caring community that prepares students in challenging and diverse ways to become more productive global citizens. At its main campus and its partner two-year institutions, ASU provides students with the broad educational foundations that help develop critical analytical and communication skills.

The University's baccalaureate programs, backed by extensive laboratory and library resources and offered by a talented and committed faculty, provide excellent training for graduate and professional school and successful careers. Seventy miles northwest of Memphis and 130 miles northeast of Little Rock, ASU is located in Jonesboro, a thriving city of about 50,000, which serves as the cultural, financial, professional, and retail hub for northeast Arkansas. The ASU campus covers approximately 900 acres. The extensive physical plant, with a replacement value of $304 million, includes thirteen classroom/laboratory facilities, five residence halls, and eleven administrative and services buildings.

There are eight colleges on campus—Agriculture, Arts and Sciences, Business, Communications, Education, Engineering, Fine Arts, and Nursing and Health Professions. Students can enroll in eighty-eight undergraduate programs and sixty-eight graduate programs.

Student Body Undergraduate enrollment is 9,289, 41 percent men and 59 percent women. The ethnic distribution is 84 percent white and 13 percent African American. There are 170 international students. Twenty-one percent of the students live in residence halls; the remaining 79 percent commute. Eighty-two percent of the students receive financial aid. There are twelve fraternities and nine sororities.

Faculty Of the 566 faculty members, 431 are full-time and 86 percent hold terminal degrees. The student-faculty ratio is 20:1.

Key Facilities The Dean B. Ellis Library, the expansion of which was dedicated by President Bill Clinton, holds more than 553,000 volumes. The eight-story tower is the principal focus of the campus. Computer facilities include more than 3,000 PCs on campus, about 500 of which are set aside for students in laboratories, the library, and residence halls. The campus is fully networked and all students are given computer accounts, with Internet access, on request.

Honorary Societies Phi Eta Sigma, Alpha Lambda Delta, Phi Kappa Phi, and Gamma Beta Phi

Athletics ASU is an NCAA Division I institution that fields fifteen teams, including men's and women's basketball, indoor and outdoor track, cross-country, and golf. There are women's teams in tennis, volleyball, and soccer and men's teams in baseball and football.

Study Abroad The Office of International Programs and Services develops an expanding set of partnerships with universities in Europe, the Middle East, and Asia, providing exchanges for ASU students and faculty members. In addition, the Assistant Director of Honors coordinates ASU's participation in the National Student Exchange, through which students can study for a semester or a year and one of more than 170 other U.S. and Canadian colleges and universities.

Support Services The Office of Disability Services coordinates the provision of services to students seeking assistance.

Job Opportunities The Office of Career Services assists eligible students with work-study assignments; most campus units also employ part-time student workers through the Office of Human Resources.

Tuition: $168 per credit hour for state residents, $314 per credit hour for nonresidents

Room and Board: $3200

Mandatory Fees: $70

Contact: Director: Dr. F. David Levenbach; Assistant Director: Dr. Wayne Narey; Post Office Box 2889, State University, Arkansas 72467; Telephone: 870-972-2308; Fax: 870-972-3884; E-mail: honors@astate.edu; Web site: http://www.honors.astate.edu

Armstrong Atlantic State University

4 Pu G M Sc Tr

▼ Honors Program

Founded in 1996, the Honors Program at Armstrong Atlantic State University (AASU) has rapidly developed into a vibrant community of students. The program offers talented and motivated students in every department and program at AASU the chance to take creative, small classes in the place of general education requirements, followed by the opportunity to apply their intellectual curiosity to independent projects and special classes within their majors. Honors courses reflect the creative and student-centered approach to learning that is central to the program's mission. For instance, each student in the Honors Civilization class reports on a different textbook, chemistry students engage in creative laboratory research in their first-year class, government students design their own Web pages that respond to issues of global significance, and ethics students tackle real-world questions of aesthetics, censorship, and racial stereotyping.

The program is largely student directed. Students are responsible for soliciting and evaluating suggestions for new courses, publishing newsletters and Web pages, organizing social events, and reaching out to prospective new students. The Honors Program offers numerous opportunities for students interested in taking leadership positions on campus.

The program also offers its members a number of opportunities beyond the classroom, including a special fall orientation, field trips, and social gatherings. Students are active in rewarding community service projects, including tutoring at-risk students in local middle schools and cleaning the beaches of the isolated barrier islands along the Georgia coast. In addition, AASU honors students have been active participants in regional and national conferences. The center of honors life is the Honors Program classroom and lounge, a comfortable facility with a friendly and collegial atmosphere and some of the most powerful computers on campus. Altogether, the Honors Program creates an atmosphere of learning and camaraderie that lasts throughout the Armstrong years and beyond.

Current enrollment in the Honors Program is about 125.

Participation Requirements: The program consists of two parts: Honors in the Core and Honors in the Major. Honors students complete the Honors in the Core requirement by successfully completing four honors courses at the core curriculum level and earning a B or better in each of these classes. Students complete the Honors in the Major component by completing the requirements specified by the major area and approved by the Honors Committee. These requirements may include a specific course, a research project, a paper, or a performance. Students graduate with honors by completing the Honors in the Core component, completing the Honors in the Major component, and finishing with a minimum GPA of 3.2. The achievement is noted on the diploma, on the college transcript, and with a distinctive certificate presented at graduation. Honors Program graduates also receive one of the traditional Latin honors.

Admission Process: There are two ways to enter the program. Entering students may apply to the Honors Program if they score at least 1100 on the SAT I and graduate with a strong high school record. In addition, continuing students may apply to enter the Honors Program if they have at least a 3.2 overall GPA in University courses and either are enrolled in or have completed an honors course.

Scholarship Availability: Scholarship opportunities at Armstrong have expanded substantially in recent years. Honors students typically receive a large number of these awards, and participation in the Honors Program is considered a positive factor in virtually all scholarship programs. Eighty percent of all students on campus receive some type of financial assistance.

The Campus Context: Armstrong Atlantic State University is located in Savannah, Georgia, one of America's most beautiful cities. Within just a few miles of campus, there are uncrowded beaches, Spanish moss–draped forests, and one of the largest and most significant historic districts in the entire nation.

The University was founded as a two-year college in 1935. It became a four-year school in 1964 and has been growing ever since. The University currently offers more than seventy-five degree programs in the Colleges of Arts and Sciences, Education, and Health Professions and the School of Graduate Studies. The campus reflects substantial investment in higher education in recent years. Technology abounds, and the largest and newest buildings on campus are truly state-of-the-art.

Highlights in AASU academic programs include the Medical Technology Program, one of only two such programs in the University System of Georgia, which currently maintains for its graduates a 100 percent employment rate in the field; the GTREP program, an opportunity for engineering students to earn a degree from the Georgia Institute of Technology in either computer systems engineering or civil and environmental engineering without leaving the Savannah area; and the five-year program in physical therapy, which permits entering freshmen to earn a Master of Science degree in just five years. The College of Education has been named Best in the State by the Georgia Association of Teacher Educators, and its Pathways to Teaching Program has been honored by the leading endowment foundations, national media organizations, and the Vice President of the United States.

Student Body University enrollment is about 5,700 undergraduate and graduate students. The student body is about 30 percent members of minority groups and 70 percent women, with an average age of 26. Student life may include participation in one of the many organizations, including Greek organizations (Delta Sigma Theta, Kappa Gamma Pi, Kappa Alpha Psi, Sigma Kappa Chi), academic clubs (Economics, French, Anthropology, and Political Science), societies (American Chemical, Biological, Student Engineering, or other nationally recognized honors societies), athletics (the crew club is a favorite), and creativity (drama club, student art exhibits, Student Photographic Services, and literary publications).

Faculty Sixty-eight percent of the faculty members have earned their terminal degrees. In 1996–97, AASU math professor Anne Hudson was recognized as Professor of the Year, an award given to only one teacher at all senior colleges and universities in the nation.

Key Facilities Lane Library collections include more than 800,000 books, microforms, and audiovisual materials. Computer facilities are abundant on campus and often are uncrowded. New dormitories, expected to open in time for fall 2000, will dramatically improve facilities available for students from beyond the Savannah region.

Athletics AASU is a member of the Peach Belt Athletic Conference and the NCAA Division II. Men's teams compete in basketball, baseball, tennis, and cross-country; women's teams compete in basketball, softball, tennis, cross-country, and volleyball. Intramural programs are strong, and the Honors Program fields a volleyball team each year.

Study Abroad Through the University System of Georgia, AASU participates in a number of vibrant study-abroad programs. The University actively uses financial aid packages as inducements for students, especially honors students, to participate in study-abroad programs.

Job Opportunities Most Armstrong students have full- or part-time jobs in the community. The Honors Program is an informal clearinghouse for a large number of on-campus jobs and summer internships.

Tuition: $1730 for Georgia residents, $6950 for nonresidents, per year (1998–99)

Room and Board: $4284

Mandatory Fees: $290

Contact: Director: Dr. Mark Finlay, Savannah, Georgia 31419; Telephone: 912-921-5642; Fax: 912-921-5581; E-mail: mark_finlay@mailgate.armstrong.edu; Web site: http://www.honors.armstrong.edu/

AUBURN UNIVERSITY

4 Pu L Sc Tr

▼ University Honors College

The University Honors College at Auburn is part of a long tradition. Swarthmore College established the first honors program in this country in 1922, using as its model the Oxford tutorial system in which small classes of students and faculty members studied the Greek and Latin classics. Other models for honors programs and classes include the Socratic dialogues, the German seminars, and the European guild system.

Drawing on these traditions, the University Honors College offers students capable of academic excellence the advantages of a small school or college in the context of a large university. The College selects 200 entering freshmen each year; these students may be enrolled in any college or school of the University that has undergraduate programs or offerings. Students already enrolled in Auburn can also qualify for the College.

Participation in the Honors College exposes students to a wider range of intellectual and academic experience, gives students the opportunity to form lasting friendships with other students committed to academic excellence, and promotes more rewarding interaction between students and teachers. As a result of their special college experience, honors students have a distinct advantage in their future pursuits, whether they go on to graduate or professional school or go directly into their chosen professions.

Entering freshmen are introduced to the University Honors College through Summer Honors Orientation sessions where introductions to faculty members and fellow students are made and friendships begin. Amenities are provided in our Honors Residence Halls to encourage this interaction as well as to encourage individual intellectual growth. The mentor program, organized by upperclass honors students, further assists new students as

Interpreting the symbols: **2**=two-year college, **4**=four-year college; **Pu**=public or state college, **Pr**=private college; **G**=general honors program; **D**=departmental honors program; **S**=small program (fewer than 100 students), **M**=midsize program (100 to 500 students), **L**=large program (more than 500 students); **Sc**=scholarships available in honors program; **Tr**=transfer students accepted into honors program; **HBC**=historically black college; **AA**=academic advisors; **GA**=graduate advisors; **FA**=fellowship advisors.

they adjust to university life. From their second semester in the College, honors students are given priority at registration to ensure timely progress through their curricula. Most important, honors classes are taught in small sections and are designed to provide in-depth dialogue and interaction between students and faculty members. All honors sections are taught by professorial faculty members.

The staff of the Honors College has the responsibility for identifying and developing students to compete for prestigious national and international scholarships (Rhodes, Marshall, Mellon, Fulbright, Rotary, and others). These scholarships have different requirements ranging from a major emphasis on academic achievement to an emphasis on all-around ability.

The Honors Office is currently located in the Ralph B. Draughon Library and houses the offices of the director, assistant director, and secretary. Broun, Teague, Little, and Harper Halls are the Honors Residence Halls and are located in the Quad. They provide a place for the students to live, learn, and relax together. Computers and reference materials are available in the Honors Student Center, located in the basement of Broun Hall.

The 23-year-old program currently enrolls 630 students.

Participation Requirements: The University Honors College has two divisions. The curriculum of the lower division was developed to provide students with an opportunity for broad, enriching educational experiences and consists of honors sections of the required University core curriculum courses. Completion of these courses (24 hours) is recognized by a Junior Honors Certificate. The curriculum of the upper division consists of upper-level contract courses or reading/thesis courses, which provide opportunities for more focused and in-depth studies in the student's chosen discipline. Completion of these upper-level courses is recognized by a Senior Honors Certificate. Students can participate in either of these programs. Those who complete both programs with a minimum GPA of 3.4 will graduate as University Honors Scholars. This distinction is noted on students' diplomas and transcripts.

Admission Process: Entering freshmen and currently enrolled students who demonstrate the potential for academic excellence are eligible for admission into the University Honors College. Selection of incoming freshmen is based on ACT/SAT I scores (29/1280 minimum), high school GPA (3.5 minimum), and a record of leadership and service. Students currently enrolled at Auburn who have a 3.4 GPA may also be considered for admission.

Scholarship Availability: The Carolyn Brinson Reed Scholarships in the Arts and Humanities, the Raymond E. Sullivan Scholarships, the Compass Bank Scholarship, the Aldridge Honors Scholarship, the Boshell/Daniel Scholarships, the Sloan Y. Bashinsky Sr. Honors Scholarship, the Drummond Company Honors Scholarship, and the Wiatt Honors Scholarship are awarded annually to selected upperclassmen.

The Campus Context: Auburn University is composed of the following thirteen colleges and schools: the College of Agriculture, the College of Business, the College of Education, the College of Engineering, the College of Liberal Arts, the College of Sciences and Mathematics, the College of Veterinary Medicine, the College of Architecture, Design and Construction, the School of Forestry and Wildlife Sciences, the College of Human Sciences, the School of Nursing, the School of Pharmacy, and the Graduate School. There are more than 130 baccalaureate degree programs that are offered. Noteworthy research facilities on campus include the Center for the Arts and Humanities, the Alabama Agricultural Experiment Station, the Material Engineering Lab, the Center for Commercial Development of Space, the Space Power Institute, and the Mises Institute.

The city of Auburn is a small residential area that is often referred to as the loveliest village on the plains. The University and the local community offer that rare blend of mutual support and cooperation evident only in a true university community. Auburn University, chartered in 1856, retains in its nationally designated Auburn University Historic District much of the ambience and richness of that era.

Student Body Undergraduate enrollment is 22,469: 11,629 men and 10,840 women. The ethnic distribution of minority students is 1 percent Native American, 1 percent Hispanic, 7 percent African American, and 1 percent Asian. There are 759 international students. On-campus housing spaces are available for 3,736 students; off-campus living is permitted. Fifty-nine percent of the students receive financial aid. The campus has twenty-nine social fraternities and nineteen sororities.

Faculty Of the 1,254 faculty members, 1,138 are full-time. Ninety-one percent of the full-time faculty members have terminal degrees. The student-faculty ratio is 18:1.

Key Facilities The RBD Library, plus two branches, house more than 2.5 million books, 2.9 million microform titles, more than 19,000 current serials, and thirteen on-line bibliographic series, 1.4 million government documents, 134,000 maps, and 150 current newspapers. There are 600 computers for student use in the computer labs, the library, and the dorms. Access is provided to the campus network, e-mail, the Internet, and the World Wide Web. Computer labs on campus are open 24 hours a day.

Honorary Societies Phi Beta Kappa, Phi Eta Sigma, Lambda Sigma, Phi Kappa Phi, Golden Key, and Mortar Board

Athletics In athletics, Auburn is a member of NCAA Division I in all sports except men's football, which is Division I-A. Intercollegiate sports (some offering scholarships) include baseball and football for men; gymnastics, soccer, softball, and volleyball for women; and basketball, cross-country running, golf, swimming and diving, tennis, and track and field for both men and women. Intramural sports include badminton, basketball, bowling, fencing, football, golf, gymnastics, lacrosse, racquetball, rugby, sailing, soccer, softball, swimming and diving, table tennis, tennis, track and field, volleyball, weight lifting, and wrestling.

Study Abroad Auburn University offers seventy-five study-abroad programs in thirty-eight countries. Most major courses are available and many programs do not require prior knowledge of a foreign language. Students may retain official Auburn student status, apply for financial aid, and arrange for a pre-estimation of overseas credits. Study abroad can now be integrated with Auburn University degrees.

Support Services All students being served by the Program for Students with Disabilities have priority registration, use of the Assistive Technology Lab, and appointments with professional staff on request. Other accommodations may include extended time on exams, permission to tape lectures, enlarged print or braille, textbooks on tape, specialized computer equipment, FM system, removal of structural barriers, class notetakers, use of calculator, spellchecker, modified program requirements, alternative evaluation methods, text telephone (TDD), interpreter services, extra time on assignments, special parking, and/or alternative test format. Accommodations are individually determined and must be supported by disability documentation.

Job Opportunities For student employment on campus, work referrals are supplied through Student Employment Services.

Tuition: $3260 for state residents, $9780 for nonresidents, per year (2001–02)

Room: $1590 minimum

Contact: Director: Dr. Jack W. Rogers Jr., RBD Library, Auburn University, Alabama 36849-5360; Telephone: 334-844-5860; Fax: 334-844-4424; E-mail: honors@mail.auburn.edu; Web site: http://www.auburn.edu/academic/other/honors/au_honors.html

Auburn University Montgomery

4 Pu G M Sc Tr

▼ University Honors Program

The University Honors Program offers challenging, stimulating courses for the academically exceptional student. These courses (often with fewer than 10 students) enhance the educational experience inside and outside the classroom. Honors students also enjoy special registration privileges and take part in field trips and social activities. Recent graduates remark that they found an intellectual home in the Honors Program and that they felt a sense of community as a result of extensive interaction with other academically gifted students. The program was founded in 1981 and currently enrolls approximately 120 students.

Participation Requirements: Students have the choice of two levels of involvement. During their four years at Auburn University Montgomery (AUM), Level 1 students take a total of three Honors Colloquia and three honors courses. In addition, they add 1 hour of honors credit to five existing courses in their major and write a senior thesis. Level 2 students add occasional honors offerings to their curriculum. To remain in the program, students must maintain a minimum 3.5 cumulative GPA. The level of participation is recorded on the student's transcript and acknowledged at commencement.

Admission Process: To be eligible for the Honors Program, an entering freshman must have an ACT score of 27 or above. Students in their sophomore and junior years and transfer students must have earned a cumulative GPA of 3.5 or better. A written application is required of all interested students. Admission decisions are made on an ongoing basis.

Scholarship Availability: Each year, AUM offers three merit-based scholarships on a competitive basis to sophomores, juniors, and seniors in the Honors Program. Incoming freshmen who enroll in the Honors Program compete for two full tuition scholarships.

The Campus Context: Auburn University Montgomery is located on a 500-acre campus in eastern Montgomery, the capital of Alabama. Cultural attractions nearby include the Montgomery Museum of Fine Arts, the Alabama Shakespeare Festival, and numerous concert, jazz, and chamber music venues. Founded in 1967, the University is state-supported, comprehensive, and coed. The University offers twenty-four bachelor's, ten master's, and one doctoral degree programs. There are five schools on campus: the School of Business, the School of Education, the School of Liberal Arts, the School of Nursing, and the School of Sciences.

Student Body Of the 4,577 undergraduates enrolled, 63 percent are women and 37 percent, men. Ninety-seven percent are state residents, 2 percent come from out of state, and 1 percent can be classified as international students. The ethnic distribution is 65 percent white, 31 percent black, 2 percent Asian or Pacific Islander, 1 percent Hispanic, and 1 percent Native American. Seventy percent of undergraduates receive financial aid. Auburn University Montgomery hosts four fraternities and five sororities.

Faculty Of the 348 faculty members, 193 are full-time. Ninety-two percent of the full-time faculty members have terminal degrees. The student-faculty ratio is 18:1.

Key Facilities The library houses approximately 300,000 books, 1,500 periodicals, and 500 CD-ROMs. There are 120 computers on campus for general student use. Computer purchase/lease plans are available. A campuswide network can be accessed. Students can contact faculty members and/or advisers through e-mail. Computers for student use in the computer center, computer labs, the learning resource center, classrooms, and the library provide access to the Internet/World Wide Web and on- and off-campus e-mail addresses. A staffed computer lab on campus (open 8 a.m. to 10:30 p.m.) provides training in the use of computers and software.

Honorary Societies Alpha Epsilon Delta, Alpha Phi Sigma, Kappa Delta Pi, Omicron Delta Epsilon, Omicron Delta Kappa, Phi Alpha Theta, Phi Eta Sigma, Pi Alpha Alpha, Pi Sigma Alpha, Psi Chi, and Sigma Tau Delta

Athletics AUM is a member of NAIA. Intercollegiate athletics are baseball (M), basketball (M/W), soccer (M/W), softball (W), and tennis (M/W). There are intramural programs in badminton, basketball, bowling, football, racquetball, softball, swimming and diving, table tennis (Ping-Pong), tennis, and volleyball.

Study Abroad There are no official AUM study-abroad programs. However, honors students are encouraged to study in another country, and students can enroll for credit in study-abroad programs at other institutions.

Support Services Disabled students find the campus accessible and special facilities available. The Center for Special Services provides professional tutoring, academic advisement, and other support services.

Job Opportunities For student employment on campus and in the local community, work referrals are supplied through the Career Development Center. Work opportunities include work-study, co-op, and numerous research and lab positions. The Career Development Center also assists students nearing graduation.

Tuition: $2442 for state residents, $7326 for nonresidents, per year (1998–99)

Room: $1695 minimum

Mandatory Fees: $60

Contact: Director: Dr. David V. Witkosky, P.O. Box 244023, Montgomery, Alabama 36124-4023; Telephone: 334-244-3371; Fax: 334-244-3391; E-mail: dwitkosk@mickey.aum.edu; Web site: http://www.aum.edu

Augsburg College

4 Pr G M Tr

▼ Honors Program

The Honors Program is designed to provide an enriched program of studies as well as social and cultural activities for accomplished students at the College. Honors students enjoy not only an enriched course of studies but also life in a community of people who share a commitment to scholarship and to each other. Graduation from the program is advantageous for graduate school admission or career placement. Indeed, graduates are routinely placed in the best graduate schools in the the country.

Distinctive to the Honors Program at Augsburg is a computational emphasis that was funded by a National Science Foundation Grant. Students entering the program are required to take an honors version of Computer Science 160. The point of the course is to ensure that Honors Program members are well versed in computing and telecommunications skills. These skills include facility with a variety of applications, a good sense of what computers can and cannot do in solving problems, and an excellent command of information access using resources such as the Internet. Other courses in the program make use of these skills in a lab-oriented sequence exploring literature, writing, history, religion, philosophy, and social and natural science.

The program has been in existence for nearly thirty years and currently enrolls about 120 students in the four years of study. The program admits about 40 freshmen each year and accepts transfers up to the beginning of the junior year.

Interpreting the symbols: **2**=two-year college, **4**=four-year college; **Pu**=public or state college, **Pr**=private college; **G**=general honors program; **D**=departmental honors program; **S**=small program (fewer than 100 students), **M**=midsize program (100 to 500 students), **L**=large program (more than 500 students); **Sc**=scholarships available in honors program; **Tr**=transfer students accepted into honors program; **HBC**=historically black college; **AA**=academic advisors; **GA**=graduate advisors; **FA**=fellowship advisors.

Participation Requirements: The freshman year begins with Honors 100, Believing and Knowing, a general introduction to the liberal arts. This seminar is taught by the director of the program. Students also take HON 160, Introduction to Computing and Communications, so that honors students begin their collegiate careers with crisp computing and Internet skills. In the sophomore year, students take two courses from a comprehensive list of social and natural science courses.

Distinctive to junior and senior honors is a Mini-Seminar program. Worth ¼ credit, seminars are designed to offer topics that usually are not included in traditional courses or to involve students in the cultural or service life of the city. In the senior year, the Mini-Seminar and Monday Forum program is augmented by a Senior Seminar. Last, seniors do a departmental honors project or serve on the Augsburg Honors Review. Students are expected to maintain at least a 3.3 GPA in the freshman year, at least a 3.4 in the sophomore year, and a 3.5 or better in the last two years. Students normally enter the program at the beginning of the freshman year, but it is possible to enter as late as the beginning of the junior year.

Admission Process: An application to the program is available at the program Web page (listed below). Requested information includes high school rank, GPA, standardized test scores, and a brief essay explaining why a student wishes to be in the program. The program is open for application until its quota of 40 freshmen has been met, which usually occurs in early summer.

Scholarship Availability: Scholarships are handled by the Admissions Office at Augsburg. Most notably, the Presidential Scholarship is worth full tuition (up to $17,438 per year). Competition for the Presidential Scholarship begins in February. More than 85 percent of students receive some kind of financial aid.

The Campus Context: Augsburg College is located in the dynamic section of Minneapolis that is near the west bank of the University of Minnesota. Augsburg is a church-related (Lutheran) institution that welcomes persons of all religious and ethnic backgrounds. Augsburg provides the warmth and openness of a small school yet is situated to take advantage of the numerous resources of a large metropolitan area. Of note is Augsburg's Center for Global Education, which is nationally known as a resource for international study and travel.

Student Body About 1,800 undergraduates, representing more than thirty-six states and thirty-eight nations, comprise the day school population. About 55 percent are women and 45 percent are men. Most students live on campus.

Faculty There are 256 faculty members (126 full-time; 83 percent with terminal degrees). The student-faculty ratio is 14:1.

Key Facilities Lindell Library was opened in 1997 and features state-of-the-art computing and communication facilities along with membership in a five-college interlibrary loan system. It houses 204,000 volumes and provides access to 1.3 million volumes.

Athletics Augsburg is a member of the Minnesota Intercollegiate Athletic Conference (MIAC) and NCAA Division III. Augsburg's wrestling and football teams have won national championships and recognition over the last few years.

Study Abroad Study abroad is arranged through the nationally recognized Center for Global Education at Augsburg.

Support Services The C.L.A.S.S. office provides support for students with learning disabilities. Augsburg is now one of the most accessible campuses in the region, with an advanced tunnel/skyway/elevator system that provides access to ten major buildings without going outside.

Job Opportunities Situated in the growing Twin Cities area, Augsburg offers on-campus employment, referrals to abundant off-campus employment, and a wide range of internships in area businesses.

Tuition: $17,438

Room and Board: $5540

Mandatory Fees: $130

Contact: Dr. Larry Crockett, Director, Honors Program, 2211 Riverside Avenue, Minneapolis, Minnesota 55454; Telephone: 651-335-7717; Web site: http://honors.org

AUGUSTA STATE UNIVERSITY

4 Pu G S Tr

▼ University Honors Program

The Honors Program offers superior full-time and part-time students in all fields the opportunity to pursue a program of study that leads to recognition as an Honors Program Graduate. Balancing breadth and depth, the Honors Program includes sections of core courses specifically designed for able and energetic learners, seminars that cross the boundaries of discipline and/or culture, a thesis, the possibility of additional honors work in the major field, and a synthesizing capstone. The Honors Program is not a separate degree program but is designed to augment the course work required for a degree, providing the best learning experience possible for its students and faculty. It encourages students to take advantage of a range of opportunities, from study abroad to cooperative learning to presentations at student and professional conferences. Honors classes differ in kind from other classes. They are usually smaller, enrolling a maximum of 20 students; they involve more interaction with the instructor; and they encourage independent work and collaboration among students and between students and professors. Often, professors in honors courses, who are chosen for their commitment to and excellence in undergraduate teaching, see themselves more as facilitators than as instructors or lecturers. Students take an active role in program design and curriculum planning. A relatively new program (approved February 1997), the Augusta State University (ASU) Honors Program currently enrolls 100 students.

Participation Requirements: Honors Program students complete at least five honors sections of freshman and sophomore courses, two upper-level honors classes (one of which must be interdisciplinary and/or multicultural), and an Honors Program capstone. In their last terms, Honors Program students work independently to design and produce an acceptable honors thesis. Honors theses are bound and housed in Reese Library. To graduate from the Honors Program, a student must have achieved a minimum GPA of 3.3.

Admission Process: Students may seek entry into the Honors Program by submitting to the Director an application form and either a letter of intent in which the students introduce themselves and tell what they will contribute to the Honors Program through their participation or an essay in which they define their personal and professional goals. Entering freshmen who meet one of the following criteria are invited to join the Honors Program and cleared to sign up for honors classes: combined SAT I scores of 1160 or better and a cumulative high school GPA of 3.2 or better or combined SAT I scores of 1100 or higher and a cumulative high school GPA of 3.5 or better. Students already enrolled at ASU are invited to join the Honors Program and cleared to sign up for honors classes if they have completed at least 10 semester hours of academic work at ASU, have an overall GPA of at least 3.4, and are not simultaneously in Learning Support. Transfer students who bring in an unadjusted minimum GPA of 3.4 on at least 10 semester hours of course work from another institution and have SAT I scores at least equivalent to those required of entering ASU freshmen are eligible to apply for admission to the program after they have completed at least 6 semester hours at ASU with an ASU unadjusted GPA of 3.4 or higher.

Scholarship Availability: Honors Program students compete favorably for a variety of partial and full University and departmental scholarships. Georgia residents who meet Honors Program requirements are eligible for HOPE scholarships. Augusta State awards more than $15 million each year in scholarships, grants, and loans.

The Campus Context: A senior unit of the University System of Georgia, Augusta State University shares the technological and innovative resources of the University System, while it maintains roots as unique as the century-old oaks and magnolias on its historic Summerville campus. In 2000, a state-of-the-art science facility opened alongside the thick masonry walls of the Augusta Arsenal buildings that hark back to the Civil War. The first of two new multistory classroom and office facilities will open in 2002. Construction of the second will begin in the same year. The Forest Hills campus houses a physical education/athletic complex, which includes a 3,800-seat arena, playing fields, and an eighteen-hole golf course. ASU is the primary public institution of higher learning in Georgia's second-largest metropolitan area, the Central Savannah River Area. Well known for its dedication to expanding educational opportunities for people of all backgrounds and ages, the University offers a full range of undergraduate degree programs, with graduate work in education, business, and psychology. Augusta, also the home of Paine College, the Medical College of Georgia, and Fort Gordon, is a growing center of business, industry, and culture that supports the Morris Museum of Southern Art; Fort Discovery; the Augusta symphony, opera, and ballet companies; several small theater groups; the Golf Hall of Fame; the Augusta National Golf Course; hockey and minor-league baseball teams; and an arena league football team. It is located on the Savannah River, fewer than 3 hours from Atlanta to the west and Savannah and Charleston to the east.

Student Body ASU has an ethnically diverse student body of approximately 5,400 commuting students, most from Georgia and the Central Savannah River Area. More than fifty-nine countries are represented by the approximately 182 international students. Most students work either full- or part-time; the average age of undergraduates is 24.6.

Faculty Augusta State University employs 195 full-time faculty members; 139 hold doctoral degrees.

Key Facilities Reese Library houses more than 430,000 volumes, including an extensive collection of government documents and more than 1,000 current periodical subscriptions, as well as substantial holdings in CD-ROM databases, microform, and audio and video collections. Interlibrary loan, available to undergraduate students, expands research opportunities. GALILEO, a statewide computerized data system, provides more than 100 additional databases, 10 with full text online. A state-of-the-art computerized writing center supports freshman English and other writing activities across campus. Six computer labs with Internet access are available for student use and supported by campus help lines.

Honorary Societies Phi Kappa Phi

Athletics ASU participates in NCAA Division II athletics in men's and women's team sports—basketball, baseball, softball, cross-country, and volleyball—and in Division I in golf. The University is also a member of the Peach Belt Athletic Conference. Intramural teams include rowing crews and six-time national championship table tennis teams.

Study Abroad Study-abroad programs in most parts of the world are available through the University System of Georgia. Augusta State currently sponsors three programs: an Italian Studies Abroad Program in art and humanities, a summer program in Greece, and a Spanish Summer and Semester Abroad Program in Salamanca.

Support Services The Office of Disability Services provides services and accommodations to ensure a positive college experience for students with disabilities. Many areas on campus are correctly accessible, and there are ongoing efforts to improve campus accessibility in older, less accessible structures.

Job Opportunities The Career Center provides assistance in job placement and career development for all enrolled students. Part-time and co-op employment is available on and off campus.

Tuition: $966 per semester for full-time undergraduate state residents, $81 per credit hour for part-time state residents, $3864 per semester for full-time nonresidents, $322 per credit hour for part-time nonresidents (2001–02)

Mandatory Fees: $94 athletic fee, $40 student services fee, $3 transportation fee, $38 technology fee

Contact: Director: Dr. C. Elizabeth Fanning, 2500 Walton Way, Augusta, Georgia 30904-2200; Telephone: 706-667-4445 or 737-1500; Fax: 706-667-4770; E-mail: cfanning@aug.edu

---

AZUSA PACIFIC UNIVERSITY

4 Pr G M

▼ Honors Program

The Azusa Pacific University Honors Program consists of enriched courses developed for 40 talented and motivated students selected from among applicants in each incoming freshman class. These general studies courses are distinguished by their greater depth, intensity, intellectual rigor, and close student-faculty collaboration. The class enrollment is limited to 15 to 18 students, and the courses are designed by outstanding professors in their fields. In addition to the honors curriculum, the program offers a variety of extracurricular cultural and social activities and international learning experiences. For qualified students who choose to participate, the Honors Program provides a challenge and opportunity: the challenge to perform at their highest levels of excellence and the opportunity to develop their abilities to the fullest.

Total program enrollment is currently 126. The deadline for applying is April 1.

Participation Requirements: To remain in the program, students must maintain at least a 3.3 cumulative GPA. Those students who complete a minimum of 26 semester units of Honors Program credits receive an honors certificate and a diploma distinguishing them as Honors Scholars.

Admission Process: To be considered for admission, potential participants must represent the top 10 percent of incoming freshmen, based on their high school GPA and SAT I or ACT scores. Eligible students are selected for the Honors Program on the basis of academic performance, demonstrated leadership ability, and exemplary character. In addition to completing the usual application and reference forms for admission to Azusa Pacific University, interested students need to complete an Honors Program application and submit one additional reference form from a teacher.

The Honors Program began with the freshman class of 1992. Forty students are selected from each entering freshman class, which limits the enrollment to a maximum of 160 students.

Scholarship Availability: Trustees', President's, and Dean's scholarships are available to honors students but are granted independently through Admissions and Student Financial Services.

The Campus Context: Azusa Pacific University was founded in 1899 as an institution of higher education within the Wesleyan evangelical Christian tradition. The University seeks to advance the work of God in the world through academic excellence in

Interpreting the symbols: **2**=two-year college, **4**=four-year college; **Pu**=public or state college, **Pr**=private college; **G**=general honors program; **D**=departmental honors program; **S**=small program (fewer than 100 students), **M**=midsize program (100 to 500 students), **L**=large program (more than 500 students); **Sc**=scholarships available in honors program; **Tr**=transfer students accepted into honors program; **HBC**=historically black college; **AA**=academic advisors; **GA**=graduate advisors; **FA**=fellowship advisors.

liberal arts and professional programs of higher education that encourage students to develop a Christian perspective of truth and life.

The 73-acre campus is located in the San Gabriel Valley community of Azusa, 26 miles northeast of Los Angeles. The surrounding mountains provide a rugged wilderness-like backdrop to the campus. The location affords its residents easy access to the popular mountain and beach resorts of southern California and all of the cultural attractions of Los Angeles County.

The Bachelor of Arts degree is offered with majors in art, athletic training, biblical studies, biochemistry, biology, business administration, chemistry, Christian ministries, communication studies, computer science, computer information systems, English, history, global studies, liberal studies, mathematics, math/physics, music, natural science, philosophy, physical education, physics, political science, psychology, social science, sociology, Spanish, and theology. The B.S.W. is offered in social work. The Bachelor of Science degree is offered with majors in accounting, applied health, biochemistry, biology, chemistry, computer science, finance, international business, management information systems, marketing, mathematics, nursing, physics, and Web and information technology.

The University is accredited by the Western Association of Schools and Colleges, the National League for Nursing Accrediting Commission, the Council on Social Work Education, the Association of Theological Schools, the Commission on Accreditation in Physical Therapy Education of the American Physical Therapy Association, and the California Commission on Teacher Credentialing and Licensing and confers undergraduate and graduate degrees.

Student Body Undergraduate enrollment is 3,654 (3,581 full-time, 73 part-time). The student body is comprised of 64 percent women, 3.1 percent African American/non-Hispanic, 0.5 percent Native American, 5.6 percent Asian/Pacific Islander, 12.3 percent Hispanic, 75.4 percent white, and 3.1 percent unknown. There are 74 international students. Seventy-one percent of the students receive financial aid. Enrollment in graduate programs is 3,181.

Faculty There are 659 faculty members (256 full-time, 403 part-time). Of the full-time faculty members, 73 percent have terminal degrees. The student-faculty ratio is 16:1.

Key Facilities The libraries include the William V. Marshburn Library, the Hugh and Hazel Darling Library, the Stamps Theological Reference Room, and six center libraries located in LA Center, Menifee, Orange, San Bernardino, San Diego, and Ventura. A unified catalog identifies more than 175,000 volumes, media items, and periodical titles. More than 650,000 microforms include the *New York Times* and Educational Resources Information Center collections. The University network provides access to more than 100 electronic information databases. These electronic systems include indexing and abstracting databases, more than 6,500 full-text journals searchable by the Serials Solutions database, and more than 2,000 electronic books through NetLibrary and the Library of American Civilization. There are fourteen computer centers, including IBM and Macintosh computers.

Honorary Societies Alpha Chi

Athletics In athletics, Azusa Pacific University fields a nationally recognized fourteen-team intercollegiate athletic program as a member of the National Association of Intercollegiate Athletics (NAIA). Men's and women's programs include basketball, cross-country, soccer, tennis, and track and field. Men compete in baseball and football; women compete in softball and volleyball.

Over the past five years, the Cougars have finished in the top ten for the prestigious Sears Director's Cup, which rates the top NAIA athletic programs. Azusa Pacific is also the six-time defending Golden State Athletic Conference (GSAC) All-Sports champion.

Azusa Pacific has captured sixteen NAIA national titles since 1980, including men's track and field in 2001 and football in 1998 and women's soccer in 1998. Azusa Pacific is only one of two Coalition for Christian Colleges and Universities members west of the Rockies to sponsor intercollegiate football. Overall, Cougar men's track and field has garnered thirteen NAIA championships, the most in NAIA history. The men's basketball team has won an unprecedented nine straight GSAC championships and has advanced to the NAIA Tournament eight of the past nine years. In fact, the Cougars advanced all the way to the NAIA Final Four in 1998 and again in 1999. The men's tennis team was the NAIA regional champion in 2001 and has made four consecutive trips to the national tournament. Cougar softball has won three of the past six GSAC championships and finished the 2000 season as the NAIA runner-up. The women's cross-country team finished fourth in the NAIA in 2000 and won the GSAC crown in 2001. Women's tennis, in just its fourth season of intercollegiate competition, has already won a GSAC championship and advanced to back-to-back NAIA Tournaments in 2000 and 2001. The volleyball team, which won the 1980 NAIA title, has made four NAIA Tournament appearances, most recently in 1999.

Study Abroad Several University travel-study programs are offered each year through the Departments of Art, Business, Global Studies, History, Literature, Modern Languages, Religion, and the Honors Program. Honors students may apply to participate in the Oxford Honors Semester, which is a selective program for 45 outstanding students from the 101 institutions affiliated with the CCCU.

Tuition: $15,950 per year (2001–02)

Room and Board: $5200

Mandatory Fees: $242

Contact: Director: Dr. Mel Shoemaker, The Honors Office, Azusa Pacific University, Azusa, California 91702-7000; Telephone: 626-815-6000 Ext. 3481; Fax: 626-815-2023; E-mail: mshoemaker@apu.edu

Baldwin-Wallace College

4 Pr G M

▼ Honors Program

The Honors Program is a series of five or six courses designed to focus on "The Human Experience" and represents the decision of the College to provide academically talented students with special opportunities. The courses in this program are designed to establish interdisciplinary connections, enhance critical thinking and reflection, and provide a seminar-learning format. Classes are generally small and typically include interaction outside of classes. Field trips are frequently a part of such classes as are visits from guests across campus. Entering first-year students have the option of a learning communities residence. Periodic social events attended by honors students and faculty members enhance the sense of community. The Honors Program was founded in 1988 and now has about 150 students.

Participation Requirements: Honors students are selected from among the most highly qualified applicants to Baldwin-Wallace College. Students must take 20 credits of honors courses. The student enters by taking a section of "Enduring Ideas" offered at one of the core academic divisions. They proceed to team-taught interdisciplinary courses with very active learning. The program is completed with a number of options, including courses in humanities, social and natural sciences, or leadership or study abroad. Students must maintain at least a 3.0 GPA in their honors courses. Graduating honors students wear distinguishing cords at the ceremony and their diplomas and transcripts recognize them as honors program students.

Admission Process: Baldwin-Wallace College has a rolling admission policy. However, high school seniors are encouraged to apply between September and March of their senior year. Application requirements include ACT or SAT I scores, a writing sample, teacher recommendation, high school transcript, and a $15 application fee. Candidates for the Conservatory of Music must complete the Audition Portfolio in addition to the college application. The admission committee notifies applicants of a decision approximately one month after all required information and forms are received by the Office of Admission. A personal interview is encouraged but not required.

Nearly 30 percent of the entering freshmen rank in the top decile of their graduating class, while more than 60 percent rank in the top quarter.

Scholarship Availability: Merit scholarships are awarded to all admitted students who have achieved a minimum 3.0 GPA or who rank in the top 30 percent of their high school graduating class. Additional scholarships are awarded competitively based on criteria that include exceptional academic achievement, leadership, writing skills, and community involvement. A limited number of academic discipline–related scholarships are also available.

The Campus Context: "Quality education with a personal touch" is the Baldwin-Wallace College experience. Undergraduate, graduate, conservatory, and evening and weekend students choose B-W because they want an exceptional education rooted in the liberal arts, but with an eye to technology and the future at a small college. Students also choose B-W because they want to be part of a person-centered environment where they are members of a close community and where their personal growth is ensured.

Academic programs at Baldwin-Wallace offer students outstanding preparation for their careers. B-W students grow personally and professionally in the liberal arts–based programs, learning to think creatively and critically and communicate effectively.

B-W offers competitive undergraduate and graduate programs in education and business administration for students who wish to enhance their bachelor's degree. The Lifelong Learning Center makes it easy for students to build a career with weekend and evening courses. B-W also offers noncredit executive and professional programs through its Center for Professional Development. Online registration is available to B-W students. The Career Services Center helps students learn valuable job-finding skills. The College also houses the Conservatory of Music.

Student Body Baldwin-Wallace College's student population is approximately 4,800, of whom 63 percent are women. Approximately 3,800 of the students are undergraduates. B-W has approximately 2,900 full-time undergraduate day students, 820 evening and weekend students, and 890 graduate students. Seventy-nine percent of first-time first-year freshmen live on campus. Ninety-two percent of all first-time first-year freshmen receive some sort of financial aid, while 80 percent of all full-time undergraduate students, including first-time first-year freshmen, receive some sort of aid. Thirty-three other countries are represented. There are six national fraternities and six national sororities on campus.

Faculty There are currently 365 faculty members at Baldwin-Wallace College, 162 of them full-time. Forty-six percent of the faculty members have a terminal degree. The student-faculty ratio is 15:1.

Key Facilities There are currently approximately 200,000 books, serial backfiles, and government documents (titles) that are accessible through Baldwin-Wallace College library's catalog. There are 13,883 current paper and microform serial subscriptions.

B-W has twenty-seven PC labs with 425 PCs available, as well as eighty multimedia classrooms. All residence hall rooms contain one port per student and provide individual access to the Internet, e-mail, and cable television.

Honorary Societies Pi-Gamma-Mu as well as other honorary societies. There are a total of seventeen honor societies available in nearly every field of study.

Athletics Baldwin-Wallace College competes in the challenging ten-team Ohio Athletic Conference. It is the nation's second-oldest NCAA Division III conference and offers collegiate competition in baseball, basketball, cross-country, football, golf, soccer, swimming and diving, tennis, track and field (indoor, outdoor), and wrestling for men and basketball, cross-country, golf, soccer, softball, swimming and diving, tennis, track and field (indoor, outdoor), and volleyball for women.

Study Abroad Honors Program students may take advantage of off-campus opportunities for study through the Explorations option. One option is Baldwin-Wallace College faculty-led study tours, such as Seminar in Europe, Seminar in Ecuador, Discover China, or a USA Study Tour. Students may also choose to spend a semester at a B-W partner university—Edgehill College in England, Australia's University of the Sunshine Coast, Ewha University in Korea—or design their own study-abroad experience.

Support Services Baldwin-Wallace College endeavors to provide reasonable accommodations for every student who has a documented disability.

Job Opportunities Baldwin-Wallace College offers a wide range of internships, field experience, work-study for qualified students, and other work-related programs. The Office of Career Services offers self-assessment, resume consultation, job fairs, graduate school workshops, and student mentoring programs.

Tuition and Fees: Undergraduate, $17,432; Conservatory, $18,884 ((2002–03)

Room and Board: $5242 (Room $3042, Board $2200)

Contact: Dr. Craig Heinicke, Director, Honors Program, Baldwin-Wallace College, 191 East Center Street, Kamm Hall, Berea, Ohio 44017; Telephone: 440-826-2419; Fax: 440-826-3835; E-mail: cheinick@bw.edu; Web site: http://www.bw.edu/academics/honors

---

Ball State University

4 Pu G D L Tr AA

▼ Honors College

...to offer distinctive opportunities for students who show promise of outstanding academic achievement, and to do this so well that our graduates are competitive with the best students of any other college or university.

For more than forty years, honors education at Ball State University has tried to accomplish the above-stated purpose. While this purpose guides all that happens in the Honors College, it does not explain the attitude behind its operations. Honors education is intended to be interdisciplinary, assuming the students' abilities to do rote learning and asking them to do more. Concerns with critical and creative thinking and problem-solving tasks form major components of honors education at Ball State.

Classes and other opportunities are not automatically intended to be more difficult than might be experienced in nonhonors situations, but *are* expected to be different. Honors College is as much an attitude as an administrative unit—it is truly a college within a larger university. The excellent instruction and individual attention of the honors programs create many opportunities for students to enrich their educational pursuits and realize the benefits of a first-rate, small-college atmosphere within a progressive university setting.

Honors students take many of their courses in classes of 25 or fewer students, restricted to honors only. All Honors College students are granted extended privileges in the University's

Interpreting the symbols: **2**=two-year college, **4**=four-year college; **Pu**=public or state college, **Pr**=private college; **G**=general honors program; **D**=departmental honors program; **S**=small program (fewer than 100 students), **M**=midsize program (100 to 500 students), **L**=large program (more than 500 students); **Sc**=scholarships available in honors program; **Tr**=transfer students accepted into honors program; **HBC**=historically black college; **AA**=academic advisors; **GA**=graduate advisors; **FA**=fellowship advisors.

libraries. They have scheduling privileges that help ensure enrollment in desired classes at the times preferred. In addition, honors students have their own residence hall and have academic advisers assigned to work exclusively with them. All incoming freshman honors students receive a Presidential Scholarship worth 50 percent of tuition for eight semesters. The Honors College sponsors a program of Honors Undergraduate Fellowships. Students work in one-to-one partnerships with faculty mentors on research or creative endeavors. Undergraduate Fellows receive $800 for each semester of a fellowship.

Honors College and Departmental Honors graduates receive special recognition during graduation ceremonies and are awarded special diplomas. The designations are also part of the final transcript.

There are 1,450 students in the program.

Participation Requirements: The Honors College offers two types of academic programs. The first, designated University Honors, is applicable to all majors. Students must take a core curriculum of six specially designed University Core Curriculum courses and at least two upper-level colloquia designed specifically for the Honors College. Furthermore, they must complete senior theses or creative projects and finish their undergraduate work with a cumulative GPA of at least a 3.33 (B+). Students completing this program earn the designation Honors College Graduate on their diplomas.

The second program is called Departmental Honors. Students selecting this option usually begin work in the third year, pursuing specialized study in their majors and completing requirements specifically tailored to those majors. The students must also complete theses or creative projects. Grade point requirements are established individually by each department. A number of students complete both University and Departmental Honors programs.

Admission Process: Students with at least a 3.6 GPA in a college-preparatory curriculum in high school and SAT I scores of at least 1180 or ACT composites of 26 or higher are reviewed for admissiom into the Honors College. Other interested students are encouraged to apply. Evaluations are made on the basis of class rank, SAT I or ACT scores, academic background, and personal references. Students interested in the Honors College are expected to have had a thorough college-preparatory sequence, including classes in all the basic disciplines. Transfer students are evaluated individually by the Dean of the College.

Scholarship Availability: Ball State University offers many scholarships. All Honors College students can expect to receive a Presidential Scholarship (half tuition and fees) if their application is submitted in a timely manner. Those with a minimum 3.7 GPA who have at least a 1300 combined score on the SAT I or 29 composite on the ACT are eligible to compete for the Whitinger Scholarship. This competition requires a conversation with a representative of the committee, a spontaneous essay, and an autobiography. In addition, Ball State University sponsors National Merit and National Achievement awards. Information about these and other competitive scholarships can be obtained from the Office of Scholarships and Financial Aid.

The Campus Context: Ball State University includes the following colleges: Applied Sciences and Technology; Architecture and Planning; Business; Communication, Information, and Media; Fine Arts; Sciences and Humanities; and Teachers College. There are fourteen associate degree programs, thirty-one endorsement programs, 155 departmental majors, 134 departmental minors, ninety master's degree programs, three specialist programs, and fourteen doctoral degree programs.

Student Body Undergraduate enrollment is 17,000 (54 percent women). Members of ethnic minority groups constitute 9 percent. There are 152 international students. Forty-two percent of the students live in residence halls; 58 percent are commuters. Seventy-one percent of the students receive financial aid. There are eighteen social fraternities and seventeen sororities.

Faculty Of the 1,100 faculty members, 840 are full-time; 70 percent have terminal degrees. The student-faculty ratio is 14:1.

Key Facilities Among its distinguished facilities, Ball State University has an arena that seats more than 11,000 people for basketball, volleyball, concerts, and speakers and excellent performing arts facilities, including a 3,600-seat auditorium for concerts and Broadway shows. The University has well-developed recreational facilities and programs, including an Institute for Wellness.

The telecommunications building has two radio and two television stations. A television, voice, data, and fiber-optic information system is in place throughout the campus, including residence halls. The Honors College has its own residence halls. The campus is also noted for a world-renowned Human Performance Laboratory.

The library contains 1.4 million volumes and more than 4,000 current periodical titles. There are twenty-six state-of-the-art computer laboratories available to all students as well as an additional forty specialized laboratories. The student-computer ratio is 13:1.

Honorary Societies Golden Key, Mortar Board, Alpha Lambda Delta, and Blue Key

Athletics In athletics, Ball State University is a member of the Mid-American Conference, which competes in the NCAA Division I-A in all sports. Ball State has ten women's and nine men's varsity sports: baseball (men) and softball (women), basketball (men and women), swimming and diving (men and women), volleyball (men and women), track and field—indoor and outdoor (men and women), cross-country (men and women), tennis (men and women), golf (men), football (men), field hockey (women), soccer (women), and gymnastics (women). In addition, there are numerous club sports including soccer, lacrosse, hockey, sky-diving, ultimate frisbee, and equestrian sports.

Study Abroad Ball State University participates in the International Student Exchange Program (ISEP), which currently places students in more than thirty-five countries. In addition, the Honors College sponsors its own programs in London (2), Keele, and Oxford (2), England; Limerick, Ireland; and Paris. Specific colleges or departments regularly initiate specialized programs or tours in countries throughout the world.

Support Services Ball State University is particularly noted for the facilities and support provided for students with handicaps or disabilities. These include note takers and readers; specialized computer facilities; completely accessible buildings, laboratories, and restroom facilities; shuttle buses; and excellent accommodations for traffic and security throughout campus.

Job Opportunities There are numerous opportunities for employment on campus and in the surrounding community. Although these vary by department, many are career-related. The University encourages experiential education and often awards credit for exceptional undertakings in this area.

Tuition: $3924 for state residents, $10,800 for nonresidents, per year (2001–02)

Room and Board: $5100

Contact: James S. Ruebel, Dean of the Honors College, Muncie, Indiana 47306; Telephone: 765-285-1024; Fax: 765-285-2072; E-mail: honors@bsu.edu; Web site: http://www.bsu.edu/honors

Baruch College of the City University of New York

4 Pu G M Sc Tr AA

▼ Baruch College Honors Program

The multifaceted Baruch College Honors Program enables highly motivated, intellectually curious students a chance to pursue an intensive course of study under the guidance of selected professors. Open to all undergraduates who meet the requirements, the program is designed to promote and to recognize participants' initiative, independence, and responsibility. The Baruch College Honors Program is part of a larger City University–wide program called the City University of New York (CUNY) Honors College (Baruch is one of seven CUNY senior college campuses participating in the program).

For the first two years of their program, students (known as University Scholars) in the CUNY Honors College work in cross-campus teams on independent projects related to their current honors college seminar. Designed especially for CUNY Honors College students and limited in size to 20 participants, these four interdisciplinary seminars focus on the arts, history, scientific and technical initiatives, and the economic life of New York City. Participation in the CUNY Honors College also confers many additional benefits, including a special orientation weekend, a free laptop (an Apple IBook), a *New York Times* subscription, special honors study abroad programs (including a summer program), and prestigious internships. A new Cultural Passport Program provides free or discounted access to the cultural riches of New York City, including concerts, opera, theater, and museums—more than fifty of the city's foremost institutions.

To graduate with College-wide honors, students must choose from a wide range of honors courses across Baruch's curricula in business, arts and sciences, and public affairs. Honors courses at Baruch are communication intensive, designed to engage students in the full range of intellectual and practical processes that effective communication requires. These courses may be service, laboratory, or team intensive, allowing for exceptional learning experiences in smaller groups. The curriculum encourages students to analyze and synthesize ideas across disciplines and to find practical applications for acquired knowledge.

To graduate with honors in their discipline, students must maintain a minimum cumulative GPA, satisfy certain department-specific requirements, successfully complete a thesis in a chosen field of study under the guidance of a faculty mentor, and gain approval from the College Honors Committee.

Depending on the student's major area of study, certain course distribution requirements may be imposed. In addition to their course work, honors students participate in cultural and service activities designated by the College Honors Committee. Students pursuing College-wide honors are entitled to a special section of freshman orientation, early registration, and special library privileges. Honors students have the exclusive use of the Irving Weinstein Honors Lounge, a distinguished, wood-paneled room complete with computer terminals and a fireplace, which provides space for program seminars, meetings, and studying.

Baruch students may choose to pursue honors in their discipline, College-wide honors, University-wide honors, or all three. They may also participate in local chapters of interdisciplinary and discipline-specific national honor societies.

By engaging in invigorating classroom discussions and attending exclusive seminars and lectures, all honors students experience the pleasure of keen intellectual activity. By serving their community, they learn the meaning of social responsibility. The ease of access to faculty and alumni mentors as well as bonds with a close-knit peer group create for them an exceptional academic experience.

Approximately 300 students currently participate in Baruch's Honors Program, and enrollment is projected to increase.

Participation Requirements: To maintain good standing in the College-wide honors program, students are required to choose at least ten honors courses and to have a minimum cumulative GPA of 3.3, which later increases to 3.5 in the upper division. Participation in service and cultural activities is also expected. To graduate with honors in their discipline, students must meet GPA, thesis, and other requirements as defined by the different departments. Further details are highlighted in the Baruch College Honors Program Web site.

Admission Process: Minimum high school requirements for early admission to the Baruch College Honors Program for freshmen (which includes entry to the CUNY Honors College) are 1250 on the SAT I and an 89 CAA (in a minimum of 14 academic units, 3 of which are in English and 3 of which are in mathematics). In addition, letters of recommendation and an interview are required. Students already at Baruch or those who have transferred to Baruch from other colleges may apply to the College program as well. They face similarly stringent admission criteria and certain restrictions as to when they may apply.

Scholarship Availability: All scholarships are based on merit. For freshmen, merit is based on the high school academic average, SAT I scores, an evaluation of essays, and letters of recommendation. Continuation of the scholarship is based on academic performance. For students who do not receive scholarships as freshmen, merit is based on the overall GPA and the evaluation of the essays and recommendations.

Freshman students are required to have a minimum high school academic average of 87 and a combined SAT I score of 1200 in addition to an essay, a personal interview, and letters of recommendation. A special group of scholarships require a minimum high school academic average of 90 and a combined SAT I score of 1360 as well as an essay, interview, and recommendations. Scholarships typically cover the cost of tuition, at a minimum.

The Campus Context: Baruch College is one of ten senior colleges of the City University of New York, the largest urban public university in the United States. Throughout a distinguished history dating back more than 150 years, the College's primary mission has been to educate students for effective leadership in the political, social, and economic community through business and administrative programs that are integrated with a comprehensive arts and sciences education.

The College includes three schools. The Zicklin School of Business offers degree programs leading to the B.B.A. for majors in all business disciplines. The Weissman School of Arts and Sciences offers the B.A. degree for majors in fourteen fields, including several innovative majors that combine study in arts and business. The School of Public Affairs offers the B.S. degree in public affairs and in real estate and metropolitan development. These schools collectively offer approximately thirty-five graduate programs.

Located in the historic Park Avenue South/Flatiron district of Manhattan, Baruch offers ready access to a world center of art and culture. Furthermore, students have rare opportunities to learn about the arts from master professionals through exceptional Baruch-specific programs, including the Sidney Mishkin Gallery, the Milt Hinton Jazz Perspectives Workshops, the Sidney Harman Writer-in-Residence program, and the respective residencies of the Classic Stage Company and the Alexander String Quartet.

Student Body Undergraduate enrollment is approximately 12,500 (56 percent women). The ethnic distribution of the student body is 27 percent white, 22 percent African American, 20 percent Hispanic, 23 percent Asian/Pacific Islander, and 8 percent nonresident alien. All students commute to campus. Seventy-three percent of the students receive financial aid. CUNY does not have fraternities and sororities.

Interpreting the symbols: **2**=two-year college, **4**=four-year college; **Pu**=public or state college, **Pr**=private college; **G**=general honors program; **D**=departmental honors program; **S**=small program (fewer than 100 students), **M**=midsize program (100 to 500 students), **L**=large program (more than 500 students); **Sc**=scholarships available in honors program; **Tr**=transfer students accepted into honors program; **HBC**=historically black college; **AA**=academic advisors; **GA**=graduate advisors; **FA**=fellowship advisors.

Faculty Of the 828 faculty members, 416 are full-time and 93.5 percent hold terminal degrees.

Key Facilities Baruch's long-awaited seventeen-floor Vertical campus opened in fall 2001. At almost 800,000 square feet. it is the largest single educational facility in New York State, covering nearly an entire square block. This marvel of urban architecture serves as the campus hub, featuring hundreds of classrooms, research facilities, and faculty and staff offices; a three-level sports and recreation center; a theater and recital space; a television studio; a 500-seat auditorium; a food court; and a bookstore. Its learning infrastructure is replete with contemporary technology, including distance learning facilities, more than thirty computer laboratories, and multimedia instruction and "smart" lecterns in each classroom.

Baruch's state-of-the-art Information and Technology Center houses the William and Anita Newman Library, which offers 415,621 volumes, 4,263 periodicals, more than 2 million microforms, and access to fifty licensed online databases. Roughly 2,000 public-access workstations are currently available campuswide, including 500 in the Baruch Computing and Technology Center.

Honorary Societies Alpha Iota Delta, Beta Alpha Psi, Beta Gamma Sigma, Pi Alpha Alpha, Sigma Iota Epsilon, and Golden Key

Athletics The Office of Intercollegiate Athletics coordinates a program of athletic competition with other collegiate institutions in soccer, volleyball, tennis, basketball, and baseball for men and volleyball, basketball, cross-country, and tennis for women. It also sponsors a coed cheerleading squad. Membership on these teams and this squad is open to all qualified students. The College is a member of the National Collegiate Athletic Association (NCAA) and the Eastern College Athletic Conference (ECAC) as well as other regional and metropolitan athletic conferences. There is also an Office of Intramurals and Recreation, which offers extensive activities. A new recreational and sports complex opened in 2002.

Support Services The campus has an Office of Services for Students with Disabilities that coordinates services and programs to ensure that students with disabilities receive equal benefits from all programs provided by the College. A variety of services and auxiliary aids, such as preadmission interviews, liaison with college departments and outside agencies, counseling, alternate testing arrangements, readers, writers, interpreters, library assistants, notetakers, adaptive equipment, priority registration, and classroom changes, are made available to qualified students with varying disabilities. Support services are also offered to students through the Center for Advisement and Orientation, the Career Development Center, the Department of Student Development and Counseling, the Counseling Center, the Health Care Center, and the International Student Service Center.

Job Opportunities There are extensive employment opportunities on campus. In addition to student aide work, motivated students with good performance records are assured the opportunity to work as peer assistants for faculty members and as tutors in the College's Student Academic Consulting Center, which coordinates supplemental instruction for Baruch students at all levels. Students also are employed in technology laboratories.

Tuition: $3200 for state residents, $6800 for nonresidents, per year (2001–02)

Mandatory Fees: $150 per year

Contact: Director: Dr. Etan Bourkoff, Box A-0506, One Bernard Baruch Way, New York, New York 10010-5585; Telephone: 212-802-3062; Fax: 212-802-3063; E-mail: baruch_honors@baruch.cuny.edu; Web site: http://www.Baruch.cuny.edu/honors

Baylor University

4 Pr G L Tr

▼ Honors Program

Established in 1959, the Honors Program at Baylor enables outstanding students to broaden their intellectual horizons in numerous ways. Through exploring their major fields of study intensely, integrating many areas of knowledge, and applying independent research techniques, Honors Program students form a community of shared learning with one another and with faculty members from all disciplines within the University.

Honors students enroll in special sections of certain required courses. During their freshman and sophomore years, students take 18 hours of these honors sections. These classes are generally smaller, providing increased class participation and discussion, and are taught by senior members of the faculty.

Sophomores and juniors take two semesters of Colloquium, which consists of small informal groups that meet regularly to discuss something as ancient as Homer's *Iliad* or as contemporary as Bauby's *The Diving Bell and the Butterfly*. The wide variety of topics and the creative approaches used within the program make this dimension of the Honors Program one that is often described by students as "simply the best course you will take at Baylor." Whether the issue be White House policy, the actions of Dr. Jack Kevorkian, or the writing style of Jane Austen, the sessions are always thought-provoking and filled with lively debates that expand students' viewpoints far beyond the limits of their academic majors.

Juniors participate in two classes in independent readings that help prepare them for their senior essays. Under the mentorship of a professor, the student will focus on readings in one or two fields of study.

Junior and senior honors students produce an original research project. Recent examples include work in genetics, child psychology, economics, French literature, philosophy, and the arts. To design this project, students work closely with a faculty member who serves as a mentor and adviser to the project. Many honors scholars' theses have been published in national journals or have served as the seedbed for books of national significance.

With approximately 500 undergraduates in the program, the Honors Program at Baylor offers its students memorable classes and approachable professors. In addition, the Student Advisory Council and the Faculty Honors Committee as well as the Honors Program staff are committed to providing rich memories for the students inside and outside the classroom. Therefore, along with the rigorous studies, the Honors Program invites its students to join together in retreats, coffee nights, and countless other gatherings that encourage students to become good friends as well as to develop their individual potential as scholars.

Participation Requirements: To graduate from the Honors Program a student must have at least a 3.2 GPA, both cumulative and in the Honors Program; complete at least 18 hours of honors sections (usually within in the first two years); complete three contracted honors courses, which are designated upper-level courses in the major or related area; and complete 10 hours of Honors Program Courses, including two semesters of Colloquium, 2 contracts for Independent Readings, and 4 hours of course work building toward the completed research essay or significant creative project. Each spring the University holds the Harry and Anna Jeanes Academic Honors Week during which selected honors theses are presented to the community.

Scholarship Availability: Scholarships are granted through the Office of Academic Scholarships and Financial Aid.

The Campus Context: Baylor University consists of nine academic units. At the undergraduate level, students may choose from among 156 baccalaureate programs through the College of Arts and Sciences (one of the first institutions accepted for accreditation by the American Academy for Liberal Education), the Hankamer School of Business, and the Schools of Education, Engineering and Computer Science, Music, and Nursing. At the graduate and professional levels, Baylor also houses the School of Law, Graduate School, and the George W. Truett Theological Seminary. In addition to its broad-based liberal arts curriculum, the University offers the University Scholars Program, Honors Program, and the Baylor Interdisciplinary Core program for motivated students pursuing a greater academic challenge.

Student Body The undergraduate student body at Baylor comprises more than 11,000 students. Approximately 21 percent of these students are members of minority groups and 2 percent are international students. A high percentage of the students live on or near the campus with 33 percent living in the residence halls. Opportunities for involvement and leadership abound in more than 250 chartered student organizations, including social, service, and honor groups. There are eighteen fraternities, fifteen of which are national, and fourteen sororities, twelve of which are national.

Faculty Of the 665 faculty members, 606 are full-time. Eighty percent hold terminal degrees. The student-faculty ratio is 17:1.

Key Facilities The University's eight libraries contain 1.5 million bound volumes, 1.3 million microform pieces, and 1.3 million government documents. Distinctive collections include those in the Armstrong Browning Library, housing unique items related to Robert and Elizabeth Barrett Browning, and The Texas Collection, with extensive Texana materials and oral histories.

Computer facilities include extensive Macintosh and IBM-compatible facilities available on campus. Students have access to terminals in dorms and libraries and in areas such as the Bill Daniel Student Center. Students also have access to e-mail accounts and Internet services.

Honorary Societies Golden Key, Mortar Board, Phi Beta Kappa, Alpha Chi, Alpha Lambda Delta, and Gamma Beta Phi

Athletics The following NCAA Division I athletic programs are available: baseball, basketball (men and women), football, golf (men and women), soccer (women), softball (women), tennis (men and women), track (men and women), and volleyball (women). Numerous intramural sports are also available for students.

Study Abroad Baylor offers thirty-six semester and summer study-abroad programs. Information relating to these opportunities can be obtained through the Office of International Programs.

Support Services The Office of Access and Learning Accommodation (OALA) is available to deal with circumstances associated with disabled student facilities.

Job Opportunities The Office of Academic Scholarships and Financial Aid is available to answer questions relating to work opportunities on campus.

Tuition: $9870 per year (1999–2000)

Room and Board: $4784

Mandatory Fees: $1212

Contact: Honors Coordinator: Elaine Harknett, P. O. Box 97122, Waco, Texas 76798-7122; Telephone: 254-710-1119; Fax: 254-710-3639; E-mail: Elaine_Harknett@Baylor.edu; Web site: http://www.baylor.edu/~Honors/

BELMONT UNIVERSITY

4 Pr G M Tr

▼ Honors Program

The honors program at Belmont University was created to provide an enrichment opportunity for students who have a potential for superior academic performance and who seek added challenge and breadth in their studies. The program is designed to allow students to advance as fast as their ability permits and to encourage a range and depth of learning in their study, in keeping with faculty members' expectations of excellence for honors students.

Students are offered a creative curriculum, flexibility and individualization in the formation of their degree plans, the collegiality of like-minded and equally dedicated peers, and academic and personal support from a tutorial relationship with a faculty member in the student's major field.

The honors curriculum is an alternative general education curriculum core that substitutes for the regular general education core for any baccalaureate degree. The 47 hours include 24 hours of interdisciplinary courses arranged around time frames in the development of Western culture, 8 hours of interdisciplinary math and science, 6 hours of courses outside the usual curriculum, 6 hours of tutorial study with a faculty member in the student's major, and a 3-hour thesis.

Successful completion of Belmont's honors program gives the student the designation of Belmont Scholar at graduation, which is noted orally, in the bulletin, and on the diploma.

There are approximately 125 students in the program, with the entering class limited to 36 students per year. The deadline for applying is February 15.

Admission Process: Students applying to the honors program should have both an outstanding high school record and a composite entrance examination score (ACT or SAT I) predictive of their ability to do honors work. In addition, students submit samples of their writing and are interviewed by the director.

Scholarship Availability: Belmont offers many types of financial awards and scholarships to academically superior students. Many students with these awards are also honors program students, but no financial aid is linked to participation in the program.

The Campus Context: Belmont University is a student-centered institution dedicated to providing students from diverse backgrounds an academically challenging education in a Christian community. Its vision is to be a premier teaching university, bringing together the best of liberal arts and professional education in a consistently caring Christian environment.

There are six schools on campus: the School of Business, the School of Humanities and Education, the School of Music, the School of Nursing, the School of Religion, and the School of Sciences. The University offers a variety of degree programs: the B.A. (twenty-one majors), the B.B.A. (ten majors), the B.F.A. (three majors), the B.M. (eight majors), the B.S. (twenty majors), and the B.S.N. (one major).

Student Body Undergraduate enrollment is approximately 3,000. Approximately 60 percent are women; 31 percent, Tennessee residents; and 3.8 percent, international students.

Faculty There are 192 full-time and 196 part-time faculty members, 65 percent of whom hold terminal degrees.

Key Facilities The 205,000-volume library also maintains subscriptions to more than 1,200 periodicals. Belmont has a Macintosh computer lab in the library, an IBM PC lab in the business school, and a VAX 4400 computing system available on the campus network. Several of the schools have classrooms equipped with computers and several have student labs.

Honorary Societies Alpha Chi, Phi Eta Sigma

Athletics Belmont is a member of NCAA Division I. Competition in men's sports includes baseball, basketball, cross-country, golf, soccer, and tennis. Competition in women's sports includes basketball, cross-country, golf, softball, volleyball, and tennis.

Interpreting the symbols: **2**=two-year college, **4**=four-year college; **Pu**=public or state college, **Pr**=private college; **G**=general honors program; **D**=departmental honors program; **S**=small program (fewer than 100 students), **M**=midsize program (100 to 500 students), **L**=large program (more than 500 students); **Sc**=scholarships available in honors program; **Tr**=transfer students accepted into honors program; **HBC**=historically black college; **AA**=academic advisors; **GA**=graduate advisors; **FA**=fellowship advisors.

Study Abroad Through a wide variety of international study programs, Belmont offers students the opportunity to broaden their education while earning credit hours toward their degrees. These programs, which range in duration from two weeks to a full year, can qualify for financial aid for eligible students, and some scholarship money is available. Currently, programs exist in Great Britain, France, Mexico, the Bahamas, Germany, Russia, China, and Italy.

Tuition: $13,040 per year (2001–02)

Room and Board: $3890 minimum

Mandatory Fees: $250

Contact: Director: Devon Boan, Associate Professor, 1900 Belmont Blvd., Nashville, Tennessee 37212; Telephone: 615-460-6472; E-mail: boand@mail.belmont.edu; Web site: http://www.belmont.edu/honorsprogram/honors.html

BEMIDJI STATE UNIVERSITY

4 Pu D M Tr

▼ Honors Program

The Honors Program provides an opportunity for academically talented students to meet academic challenges as undergraduates at Bemidji State University. The program includes interdisciplinary honors courses and a rigorous honors thesis or project generally undertaken during the junior year in collaboration with a faculty member and under the supervision of the Honors Council.

Honors scholars have more freedom in planning a program of study and thus assume a greater responsibility for designing their education. Such students also have an opportunity to accelerate study in their major. Participation in honors courses allows students to master interdisciplinary relationships in the social sciences, arts, and natural sciences through coordinated study by students and faculty members. Students who fulfill all Honors Program requirements are exempt from the University's normal liberal education requirements. The program is 30 years old and currently enrolls 230 students.

Participation Requirements: During the freshman and sophomore terms, honors scholars are advised by faculty members on the Honors Council. Freshman and sophomore students are notified by mail about areas of specialization. Honors scholars must maintain at least a 3.0 GPA in their college work. Honors scholars must also complete five interdisciplinary honors courses and honors core requirements. The Honors Council considers requests for exemptions on an individual basis. Once honor scholars have declared majors (normally at the end of their sophomore year), honors scholars are advised by the faculty members in their area. They must complete five interdisciplinary honors courses, the honors thesis, and a set of honors core requirements to ensure a broad liberal education. They have the advantage of signing up for courses at the time scheduled for seniors. Students completing the Honors Program receive Honors Program notation on their official transcript and an Honors Program certificate.

Admission Process: High school seniors with superior academic records or college students with a cumulative GPA of 3.25 or above are invited to apply. They must submit a short letter stating their interest in being selected as honors scholars. The number of students admitted each academic year is determined by the number of qualified applications received. Students are appointed to the program on a competitive basis by the Honors Council, the faculty advisers to the Honors Program. Applicants are notified in writing.

The Campus Context: In 1919, Bemidji State Normal School began its first regular school year with 38 students. The school was chartered by the Minnesota State Legislature in response to a growing need for public school teachers, and teacher training was its primary curriculum. Then, in a pattern familiar to American higher education, in 1921 Bemidji Normal became Bemidji State Teachers College, offering a four-year degree. Reflecting ongoing changes in the curriculum, the school was renamed Bemidji State College in 1957. In 1975, in recognition of its growing role as a multipurpose educational institution, it became Bemidji State University. Now, just past its seventy-fifth anniversary, BSU hosts nearly 5,000 undergraduate and graduate students. It offers majors in more than fifty baccalaureate fields of study as well as Master of Arts and Master of Science degrees. Some of its degree programs and research activities are unique to the state. Bemidji Sate University, located on an 83-acre small-town campus, is composed of four colleges and schools: the College of Arts and Letters, the College of Social and Natural Sciences, the College of Professional Studies, and the School of Integrative Studies. The University offers two associate degree programs, forty-four baccalaureate degree programs, and ten graduate degree programs.

Student Body Undergraduate enrollment is 4,310 (54 percent women). The ethnic distribution of the student body is approximately 0.5 percent African American, 0.4 percent Asian American, 4 percent Native American, 0.5 percent Hispanic, 74 percent Caucasian, and 4 percent international. Eighty-eight percent are state residents. Seventy-five percent of students receive financial aid. There are three national fraternities, two national sororities, and one local sorority as well as eighty social organizations on campus.

Faculty Of the 201 undergraduate faculty members, 190 are full-time; 77 percent hold terminal degrees. The student-faculty ratio is 21:1.

Key Facilities The A. C. Clark Library houses 185,000 books, 721,255 microform titles, 1,443 periodicals, and 1,650 records, tapes, and CDs. Computer facilities include more than 300 Macintosh and PC computers that are available to students in the computer center, classrooms, libraries, and dorms. All classrooms, labs, and offices as well as student rooms are linked to the network and have access to e-mail and the Internet.

Athletics Bemidji State is a member of NCAA Division II in all sports except hockey (men and women), which is Division I. Division II sports include baseball (men), basketball (men and women), cross-country (women), football (men), golf (men and women), softball (women), tennis (women), track and field (men and women), and volleyball (women). Intramural sports are broomball, co-rec volleyball, 5-on-5 basketball, flag football, floor hockey, golf tournament, ice hockey, indoor soccer, ultimate frisbee, and wallyball.

Study Abroad The Office of International Studies coordinates study-abroad programs in England/Europe, China, Malaysia, Japan, Sweden, and Ukraine. Students may receive academic credit for participation in international studies programs.

Support Services Students with disabilities are served through the Educational Development Center. Services include notetakers, tutors, academic advising, counseling, testing services, career counseling, study skills, and interpreter services. Most campus buildings are accessible by ramps and tunnels and are equipped with elevators. Handicapped parking is available.

Tuition: $2500 for state residents, $5436 for nonresidents, per year (1998–99); $3780 per year for full-time nonresidents eligible for the Midwest Student Exchange Program, $81.10 per semester credit for eligible part-time students

Room and Board: $3083.50

Mandatory Fees: $220

Contact: Director: Ivy Knoshaug, Hagg-Sauer Hall 357, 1500 Birchmont Drive, NE, Bemidji, Minnesota 56601-2699; Telephone: 218-755-3984; Fax: 218-755-2822; E-mail: iknoshaug@bemidjistate.edu; Web site: http://www.bemidjistate.edu/honors/

Benedict College

2 Pr G M Sc Tr HBC

▼ Honors Scholars Program

The Honors Scholars Program at Benedict College has as its mission to enhance intellectual, cultural, social, spiritual, and career opportunities for highly selective, motivated, enthusiastic, and critically inquisitive students. The Honors Scholars Program attempts to achieve its mission by providing exceptional stimulation and by challenging its participants, thus expanding their global horizons and academic expectations. The goals are aimed at providing opportunities for honors scholars to study, conduct research, and exchange ideas in a challenging and supportive academic environment. The program pursues these goals by supporting and encouraging strong leadership skills and encouraging and promoting active student involvement in the local community and in the international community as well. The program seeks the continued development and refinement of communication and research skills. The honors environment at the College is conducive to rigorous research, which allows the student to produce high-quality papers ready for presentation and publication. In addition to receiving effective teaching and pedagogical experiences, the honor scholars engage in meaningful community service. The program has an active internship placement track record and provides opportunities locally, nationally, and internationally as well. Because the honors scholars are required to apply to graduate and professional schools, the Honors Scholars Program presents a solid foundation for the students to engage in challenging academic experiences through stimulating discussions, critical thinking, free inquiry, and investigation. Begun in 1986, the Honors Scholars Program now has 170 members and is expanding its curriculum and faculty to meet twenty-first century challenges.

Participation Requirements: To graduate with honors, a student must maintain a cumulative GPA of at least 3.2, successfully pass 24 hours of honors courses, serve as a presenter at one national conference, write and defend a senior honors research thesis, and sit for at least one graduate or professional school entrance exam. In addition, honors students are expected to complete one community service project each year and develop and maintain a current resume on file at the Honors House. The honors scholars are also required to participate in campus symposia sponsored by the program. Some honors activities include the Summer Internship Symposium, the Honors Lecture Series, the Honors Induction Ceremony, the Academic Honors Convocation, and the Capstone Ceremony.

Admission Process: As a Historically Black College, Benedict College is dedicated to providing opportunities for those who have traditionally and otherwise been left out of the college arena. Consequently, the College gives serious consideration to every application received. However, each applicant must provide evidence of a reasonable probability of success in college before admission can be granted. All students must submit SAT I or ACT scores and submit further testing if necessary for appropriate placement as may be required.

The Campus Context: Benedict College is composed of the School of Arts and Sciences and the School of Professional Programs. The College offers twenty-two degree programs.

Student Body Undergraduate enrollment is 2,425. Of the student body, 99.8 percent are African American. There are a number of international students. South Carolina residents make up 34 percent of the population. Ninety percent of the students receive financial aid. There are four fraternities and four sororities on campus.

Faculty Of the 183 faculty members, 106 are full-time.

Athletics Intercollegiate athletics for men include football, basketball, golf, tennis, and track. Intercollegiate athletics for women include basketball, softball, track, and volleyball. Benedict is governed by the Eastern Intercollegiate Athletic Conference and the National Association of Intercollegiate Athletics (NAIA).

Study Abroad Benedict College encourages students to participate in international visitation and study-abroad programs. The goal is to broaden the students' cultural perspectives about the global community in addition to expanding their educational experiences. Students are particularly encouraged to participate in study programs that include travel to Africa and other Third World countries. The College has developed an active association with Ghanian officials, and Benedict's students travel there in a summer program called Project Ghana. In addition, Benedict students have participated in the Japanese American Exchange Program.

Support Services The architectural design and physical structure of the campus has been developed to accommodate the needs of the College's handicapped students. In addition, the College has established a support center called BC Cares. The center assists students with disabilities in many areas, including tutoring, academic advisement, and with other special needs.

Job Opportunities Students find a variety of work opportunities on campus through the College's Work-Study Program. In addition, being located near several centers of commerce—near the immediate campus environment, the downtown area, and malls—enables students to find employment off campus as well.

Tuition: $7284 per year (1999–2000)

Room and Board: $4182

Mandatory Fees: $594

Contact: Director: Dr. Ronnie Hopkins, 1600 Harden Street, Columbia, South Carolina 29204; Telephone: 803-253-5413; Fax: 803-253-5184

Bergen Community College

2 Pu G M AA

▼ Honors Program

Bergen Community College (BCC) offers a variety of honors courses in the humanities, social sciences, sciences, and business. The purpose of the program is to challenge and prepare students of superior intellectual ability in smaller-than-average classes taught by university-level faculty members who provide enriched versions of traditional syllabi and stimulating consideration of contemporary issues. The Honors Program seeks faculty members of demonstrated excellence in teaching, often published and involved in current research. It encourages greater student participation in classroom discussion, interdisciplinary and innovative approaches to learning, and individual aspirations. Students benefit not only from a close relationship with honors faculty members and with each other, but also from the recognition of the College and a network of support in seeking transfer to baccalaureate programs.

Founded in 1985, the Honors Program has continued to expand both in size and in the number of courses it offers. In 2001–02, it enrolled students in literature, art history, biology, composition, cultural anthropology, ethics, marketing principles, music

Interpreting the symbols: **2**=two-year college, **4**=four-year college; **Pu**=public or state college, **Pr**=private college; **G**=general honors program; **D**=departmental honors program; **S**=small program (fewer than 100 students), **M**=midsize program (100 to 500 students), **L**=large program (more than 500 students); **Sc**=scholarships available in honors program; **Tr**=transfer students accepted into honors program; **HBC**=historically black college; **AA**=academic advisors; **GA**=graduate advisors; **FA**=fellowship advisors.

appreciation, philosophy, psychology, sociology, statistics, religion, and history. In the future, Bergen hopes to add courses in chemistry, computers, and physics.

Currently there are 156 students enrolled in the Honors Program.

Participation Requirements: Students who complete at least 18 credits in the Honors Program are awarded a special certificate upon graduation, the designation H appears on their transcripts (enabling them more easily to secure admission to more advanced programs and scholarship aid), and public recognition is accorded them at Commencement.

Admission Process: Students are identified after their first semester upon attainment of at least a 3.4 GPA. Future plans are to recruit students directly from high school based upon their grades and an interview with an honors officer during their senior year.

The Campus Context: Bergen Community College offers fifty-nine degree programs in addition to twenty-one certificate programs.

Student Body BCC enrolls a student body of 43 percent men and 57 percent women. The ethnic distribution of the student body is 9 percent Asian/Pacific Islander, 5 percent African American, 15 percent Hispanic, 61 percent white, and 10 percent unknown. There are approximately 350 international students. Twenty-four percent of the students receive financial aid. All of the students commute to campus.

Faculty Of the 700 faculty members, 264 are full-time. Nineteen percent of the total faculty members and 29 percent of full-time faculty members hold terminal degrees. The student-faculty ratio is approximately 19:1.

Key Facilities The library houses more than 140,000 volumes. The computing facility is a mainframe IBM 4381.

Honorary Societies Phi Theta Kappa

Athletics Bergen provides numerous intramural and intercollegiate activities. Intercollegiate sports include women's volleyball and cross-country; men's soccer, basketball, indoor track, baseball, softball, golf, and track and field; and coed tennis. The College is a member of the Garden State Athletic Conference as well as the national Junior College Athletic Association, Region XIX, which consists of schools from New Jersey, eastern Pennsylvania, and Delaware. The College also competes with schools from neighboring New York State and Connecticut. During the past academic year, intramural sports included soccer, volleyball, and basketball. In addition, students and faculty members join together for occasional softball games. The College also makes its athletic facilities available to area groups such as the New Jersey Wave and the YMCA.

Support Services Disabled students can find assistance from the Office of Specialized Services.

Job Opportunities Limited part-time work (up to 20 hours per week) is available.

Tuition: $2048.40 for Bergen County residents, $3887 for out-of-county residents and students on nonimmigrant visas, $4127 for out-of-state residents, per year (2001–02)

Mandatory Fees: From $291 to $1162

Contact: Director: Dr. Anne Maganzini, 400 Paramus Road, Paramus, New Jersey 07652; Telephone: 201-612-5328; E-mail: amaganzini@bergen.edu; Web site: http://www.bergen.edu

Berry College

4 Pr G M Tr

▼ Honors Program

Berry College Honors Program provides students with an opportunity to learn within an intellectually challenging community of peers and instructors. Honors courses familiarize students with works that have been central to past and contemporary intellectual traditions while encouraging them to examine issues or themes from multiple and conflicting perspectives. All honors courses are taught as seminars, which provides an ideal environment for the development of effective communication and critical-thinking skills. Class size is restricted to 15 students, with primary emphasis placed on student initiative in discussion, research, and presentations. The program sponsors a Speakers Series that enables honors students to interact with eminent scholars, thinkers, and writers.

There are currently 100 students in the program.

Participation Requirements: Lower-division course work requirements include satisfactory completion of two 3-credit hour Honors Colloquia (HONORS 201, 202) and at least two Honors Seminars (HONORS 211, 212, 221, 222, 250), for which a student receives a minimum of 6 credit hours. Honors Seminars vary in content and emphasis and are taught in rotation. Recent offerings include Europe between the Wars, Hindu Religious Texts, Foundations of Modern Biology, and Individual and Society: Economic and Literary Perspectives. Lower-division honors courses may be used to fulfill various general education requirements. Upper-division course work includes the satisfactory completion of at least two 3-credit hour honors-designated courses at the 300 or 400 level in the major or minor, to be determined by the student in consultation with his or her adviser and the director of the Honors Program. In addition, the student must complete two honors thesis courses in the major, each of which carries 3 credit hours, and perform satisfactorily in a defense of their Senior Honors Thesis, scheduled during the last semester of the student's residence at Berry College.

Admission Process: Students who wish to be admitted into the Honors Program simply complete an application and, upon acceptance, undertake the appropriate course work. Criteria for entering freshmen are scores of 1200 or higher on the SAT I or 27 or higher on the ACT, a 3.5 high school GPA or higher, and a writing sample. Criteria for enrolled Berry students are a 3.5 GPA or higher on college work completed, a writing sample, and names of two Berry College faculty members for reference.

Scholarship Availability: Berry College offers full-tuition Presidential Scholarships as well as partial-tuition Merit and Academic Scholarships. Many students who receive these awards participate in the Honors Program.

The Campus Context: Founded in 1902 by Martha Berry, Berry College is located on 28,000 acres of forests, fields, lakes, and streams, making it the largest campus in the world and one of the most beautiful. It was originally established as a school for mountain children who were willing to work in exchange for an education, and its founder, Miss Berry, is recognized internationally as a pioneer in American education. Berry College is ideally located in the scenic northwest Georgia mountains next to Rome and is situated midway between Atlanta and Chattanooga. There are fifty undergraduate majors leading to the baccalaureate degree, including liberal arts and sciences, business, and education.

Student Body Of the 1,942 undergraduates, 62 percent are women. The ethnic distribution of the total undergraduate population is 1 percent Hispanic, 2 percent African American, and 1 percent Asian American. International students represent less than 2 percent of the total undergraduate population. Eighty percent of all undergraduates reside on campus. Ninety-seven percent of all new first-year students receive financial aid.

Faculty There are 172 faculty members, 129 full-time and 92 percent with a Ph.D. degree. The student-faculty ratio is 14:1.

Key Facilities The library has 145,316 books, 355,573 microform titles, 1,387 periodicals, 75 CD-ROMs, and 1,788 records, tapes, and CDs. There are 100 computers available on campus, with access to the local area network and the Internet. The student-terminal ratio is 18:1. Access to the network will soon be extended into some student dormitories as well.

Athletics Sports teams compete nationally through the National Association of Intercollegiate Athletics (NAIA) in basketball, soccer, tennis, golf, baseball, and cross-country running. Equestrian, rowing, and bicycling teams also compete nationally.

Study Abroad Berry supports an active study-abroad program. Course work completed overseas is applicable for honors credit with the approval of the Honors Program Director.

Support Services Disabled students find that dormitories and academic buildings are totally accessible.

Job Opportunities The Work Program at Berry currently employs 83 percent of the student population, but, according to the Berry tradition, all students are assured a job on campus. The Bonners Scholar Program and the Founders Work Program are other possibilities for students who wish to help finance their education through work and scholarship.

Tuition: $10,900 per year (1998-99)

Room and Board: $5046

Contact: Director: Dr. Zeynep Tenger, Mt. Berry, Georgia 30149; Telephone: 706-233-4074; Fax: 706-236-9004; E-mail: ztenger@odin.berry.edu

---

Bethel College

4 Pr S Tr

▼ Honors Program

The Honors Program at Bethel College offers selected students the opportunity to work with other highly motivated scholars during their four years at Bethel. It is a broad-based liberal arts program that combines four all-honors classes, individual work with professors of the student's choice in two additional courses, and an ongoing program of social events, cultural activities, speakers, and forum presentations.

The Honors Program is designed to encourage and serve students desiring a challenging academic program consistent with Bethel's long-standing commitment to the integration of faith and learning. This program provides an educational experience that moves from a generalist emphasis in the first two years to a discipline-specific focus in the field of the student's choice in the last two years. The program is designed to provide an enriched educational experience for students with exceptional academic ability, to create a social network for such students, and to enhance their preparation for and admission to graduate school as well as to enhance the general academic environment of the College.

There are currently 87 students enrolled in the program.

Participation Requirements: Begun in the 1995–96 academic year, the program goal is to accept 25 new students each year, with an equal number of men and women.

The program consists of two honors courses in the freshman year, one honors course in the sophomore year, and one honors course in the junior year. Students also take any regularly offered course at the sophomore and junior levels on an honors basis, in which they develop individual contacts with faculty members for an enriched experience in that class. Students complete an Honors Senior Project in their major during the senior year. In addition to the courses, there are monthly Honors Forums that students are expected to attend in all four years.

As honors students are exempt from several standard curriculum requirements, the honors degree requires no more credits than a regular degree and can be completed within a normal workload. Students who complete the Honors Program have an Honors Program Graduate designation added to their transcript along with whatever general academic honors they earn. Such recognition enhances graduate school applications and employment prospects.

Admission Process: A short essay is required along with a brief summary of past accomplishments as described in the application form. Students must commit to two honors courses their freshman year and maintain a minimum GPA of 3.3, rising to at least 3.4 sophomore year and 3.5 thereafter.

The deadline for applying is March 15.

The Campus Context: Bethel College is a four-year, Christian liberal arts college located on 231 wooded acres on the shores of Lake Valentine in suburban Arden Hills, Minnesota, just 10 minutes from both downtown Minneapolis and St. Paul. It offers the B.A., B.S., B.Mus., and B.Mus.Ed. degrees and fifty-seven different majors.

Student Body Undergraduate enrollment is approximately 2,200. About 60 percent of the students receive financial aid.

Faculty There are 215 faculty members; 115 are full-time, and 73 percent have terminal degrees. The student-faculty ratio is 15:1.

Key Facilities Bethel's campus is the newest among Minnesota private colleges, providing state-of-the-art computer technology and scientific equipment and modern classrooms, music practice rooms, and residence halls. The Lundquist Community Life Center, completed in 1994, houses the 1,700-seat Benson Great Hall, one of the finest music performance facilities in the Upper Midwest. Bethel's million-dollar Sports and Recreation Center has one of the nation's fastest tracks and is host to national and international meets throughout the year.

Computer facilities include e-mail accounts; access to the Internet; central computer data storage; access to more than 100 PC, Macintosh, NeXT, and Sun systems, all connected to the campus network; high-speed connections to the campus network from on-campus housing; and access to a HELP desk, staffed during regular lab hours.

Athletics Bethel is affiliated with Division III of the National Collegiate Athletic Association (NCAA) and the Minnesota Intercollegiate Athletic Conference (MIAC) for men and women. Bethel offers sixteen intercollegiate sports: baseball (men), basketball (men and women), cross-country (men and women), football (men), golf (men), hockey (men), soccer (men and women), tennis (men and women), track and field (men and women), softball (women), and volleyball (women). A wide variety of recreational and intramural sports are also available.

Study Abroad Bethel provides students with the opportunity to participate in a number of off-campus extension programs, such as the Latin America Studies Program in Costa Rica; the Hollywood Film Studies Program in Los Angeles; the American Studies Program in Washington, DC; the AuSable Trails Institute for Environmental Studies in Michigan; the England Term in England studying English Literature and Language; the Institute of Holy Land Studies in Jerusalem; exchange programs through the Christian College Consortium; and study programs through the Upper Midwest Associations for Intercultural Education.

Support Services All of the main campus buildings, along with several residence halls, are accessible to disabled persons.

Job Opportunities Bethel offers many opportunities for on-campus employment in a wide variety of areas. Students usually work 5–12 hours per week.

Tuition: $14,720 per year (1998–99)

Room and Board: $5180

Fees: $20

Contact: Director: Dr. Marion Larson, 3900 Bethel Drive, St. Paul, Minnesota 55112-6999; Telephone: 651-638-6299; Fax:

Interpreting the symbols: **2**=two-year college, **4**=four-year college; **Pu**=public or state college, **Pr**=private college; **G**=general honors program; **D**=departmental honors program; **S**=small program (fewer than 100 students), **M**=midsize program (100 to 500 students), **L**=large program (more than 500 students); **Sc**=scholarships available in honors program; **Tr**=transfer students accepted into honors program; **HBC**=historically black college; **AA**=academic advisors; **GA**=graduate advisors; **FA**=fellowship advisors.

651-638-6001; E-mail: m-larson@bethel.edu; Web site: http://www.bethel.edu

BIRMINGHAM-SOUTHERN COLLEGE

4 Pr C S Tr

▼ Honors Program

The Honors Program at Birmingham-Southern College places a heavy influence on interdisciplinary learning. The program provides an alternative approach to meeting the general education goals of the institution through a unique educational curriculum. The importance of viewing issues from many perspectives and of integrating as well as analyzing knowledge is a major focus. The curriculum is designed to foster students' intellectual curiosity beyond their major discipline, as well as to improve their oral and written communication skills and their ability to think and study independently.

Over the years, several small, interdisciplinary seminars have been developed specifically for the program. For example, Connections: Music, Mathematics and Structure in the Liberal Arts finds the math in music theory; Frankenstein meets "Snow White" takes into account cross-cultural studies in German and English romanticism; and Plural America teaches history through the literature of the time period being studied. The program typically offers three to four classes per semester, with class sizes ranging from 5 to 20. The average student-teacher ratio is 12:1.

Faculty involvement in both academic and nonacademic activities is high. Students are continually asking honors faculty members to speak or participate in discussion groups. There is an overall sense of rapport and camaraderie between students and teachers. The faculty members work intimately with senior honors students as sponsors for the students' independent study honors projects. Most professors are available to advise students at any hour, and many maintain contact with their honors students long after graduation.

Birmingham-Southern's Honors Program is more than the classes students take. Reminiscent of the European salons, the program strives to create an intellectual community in which its members can feel free to discuss ideas and concepts not tied to their major studies. Lecture series, book groups, and Provost forums have all been sponsored by the program in the past, with speakers and books chosen by honors students. Likewise, social events are planned according to the students needs and interests. The program provides study-break dinners at least once a month, usually in combination with tickets to one of the many on- and off-campus cultural events, for example, the latest Birmingham-Southern theater production of *Hamlet* or *Amadeus* or directions and discounts to the Birmingham Film Festival.

Honors Program facilities center on the Honors House. Located on Townhouse Row, the Honors House is three stories, complete with a full kitchen and laundry facilities. Furniture and electronic equipment, such as a television, VCR, and computer, are provided by the College. Up to 7 students can reside in the Honors House, alternately all men or all women, but it is open to all honors students for use at all times. In addition, the Honors Program works in conjunction with the International Studies Program, providing international and honors students alike with cooking facilities and a good place to "hang out."

Birmingham-Southern's Honors Program was founded circa 1980; currently, there are approximately 60 students enrolled.

Participation Requirements: The Honors Program component of an honors student's general education currently consists of 5 units of honors seminars and 1 unit of independent study, the Honors Project. Students may take one honors interim project, which counts toward the 5 units of honors seminars. The remaining general education requirements within the student's major field are completed according to the regular curriculum of the College. The specific general education requirements met by honors courses and those met by regular courses varies from student to student, depending on which honors courses the student elects to take. Students must maintain a minimum 3.5 GPA to stay enrolled in the program. Upon graduation from the program, the notation "Honors Program Scholar" is placed on the academic transcripts of graduating students.

Admission Process: The Honors Program at Birmingham-Southern College does not set a minimum GPA or SAT/ACT requirement. The College asks for a report of these figures on the application, but these are not the determining factors of admittance to the program. The application requests basic background, academic, and extracurricular information of the perspective student, as well as three letters of reference (one of which must be from a teacher) and an essay question. The applications are reviewed by the Program Director as well as the graduate assistant and other Honors Program faculty members. Application deadlines are typically in February; students should know by April their admittance status to the program.

Scholarship Availability: There are no scholarships specific to the Honors Program, although exceptional students are invited by the College to participate in Scholarship Day. The scholarships awarded are based on academic achievement and merit. Individual departments also have performance/talent-based funding available.

The Campus Context: Birmingham-Southern College is a four-year collegiate liberal arts institution founded in 1856. It is affiliated with the United Methodist Church. For seven straight years, Birmingham-Southern College has been ranked among the top eighty best national liberal arts colleges in the country by *U.S. News & World Report.* The College also has been ranked by the magazine as the most efficiently operated school in the nation and as one of the top ten best values in America. Located in rolling country on a 197-acre campus in western Birmingham, the College is just 3 miles via I-59 from the downtown business district. Birmingham-Southern College was created through a merger of Southern University (established 1856) and Birmingham College (established 1898). Birmingham-Southern has a number of social fraternities as well as several service organizations and numerous special interest groups. The College's unusual facilities include the Robert R. Meyer Planetarium, the first public planetarium in Alabama, and the College Theatre, which has a three revolve-lift stage system and is the only one of its kind in the nation. Construction is under way for a new state-of-the-art science center, with an expected date of completion in fall 2002.

Birmingham-Southern offers the undergraduate degrees of Bachelor of Arts, Bachelor of Science, Bachelor of Music, Bachelor of Music Education, and Bachelor of Fine Arts.

Student Body Enrollment averages 1,500 students a year, typically 650 men and 880 women. Currently, there are 1,540 students from twenty-three states and seven international countries. The middle 50 percent of last year's freshman class had a range of 990 to 1320 on the SAT and 24 to 29 on the ACT; 46 percent of the enrolled freshmen were in the top 10 percent of their high school class.

Faculty The faculty is composed of 101 full-time and 47 part-time teaching members. Of the full-time members of the faculty, 88 percent hold either a doctoral degree or the highest degree in their fields. In addition to teaching, the faculty's major responsibility is advising students. The average student-faculty ratio is 12:1.

Key Facilities The N. E. Miles Library currently holds 270,296 bound volumes and 51,554 microforms. The College computer facilities include four host computers; a campuswide Ethernet network with 630 college-owned personal computers plus connectivity for student-owned machines in the dormitories; seventeen student laboratory locations containing a total of 285 computers and network shared laser printers; a full-time T1 Internet connection offering access to all members of the College community; and a number of multimedia development locations equipped with an optical scanner, color printer, computer with CD-ROM drive, CD-ROM burner, and appropriate software. All students receive access to an e-mail account and may create a personal World Wide Web page. Birmingham-Southern has been recognized by *Yahoo! Internet Life* magazine as one of the top 100 Most Wired Colleges in the country.

Honorary Societies Phi Eta Sigma, Omicron Delta Kappa, Mortar Board, and Phi Beta Kappa

Athletics Women's sports include basketball, cross-country, golf, rifle, soccer, softball, tennis, and volleyball. Men's sports include baseball, basketball, cross-country, golf, soccer, and tennis. All teams are in the process of moving from the NAIA Division to NCAA Division I. In just three years, Birmingham-Southern headed into the 2001–02 academic year with fourteen varsity sports, outstanding facilities, and highly competitive teams.

Study Abroad Many honors students take a semester abroad. Although not a mandatory part of the honors curriculum, it is supported by the program. All study-abroad work is contracted through Birmingham-Southern's Office of International Programs. Students can choose from many locations across the globe, including Asia—Japan, China, Korea, Vietnam, Singapore, India, Indonesia, and Thailand; Africa—Namibia, South Africa, Egypt, Morocco, Ghana, Tunisia, and Zimbabwe; Europe—England, Ireland, the Netherlands, France, Spain, Germany, Austria, Czech Republic, Italy, Poland, Russia, Belgium, Hungary, and Turkey; the Americas—Canada, Mexico, Brazil, Costa Rica, Argentina, Chile, Cuba, Dominican Republic, and Puerto Rico; and Australia.

Support Services Birmingham-Southern College is an equal opportunity institution equipped to meet the needs of all students. The College strives to aid physically handicapped students in all ways, and alternate testing procedures are available for students with diagnosed learning disabilities.

Job Opportunities Birmingham-Southern College offers two student employment programs that provide work opportunities for students: the Federal Work-Study Program (FWS) and the Birmingham-Southern College Work-Study Program (BSCWS). The rate of pay for both programs is $6 per hour. Students should earn only the amount stipulated in their award letters. FWS awards are need-based; BSCWS awards are not need-based and are usually awarded to students at the request of a faculty or staff member to fill positions such as teaching assistants, lab assistants, and lifeguards.

Tuition: estimated full-time tuition per year, $16,810; part-time tuition per year, $2,802 per unit (2001–02)

Room and Board: residence hall (double occupancy): $3,320; meal plan (average): $2,660

Mandatory Fees: activity fee: $250; computer usage fee: $120; insurance: $235; automobile registration: $5

Contact: Director: Dr. Nancy J. Davis, Box 549037, Birmingham-Southern College, Birmingham, Alabama 35254; Telephone: 205-226-4838; E-mail: njdavis@bsc.edu

BLINN COLLEGE

2 Pu G S Sc Tr

▼ Honors Program

The Blinn College Honors Program began in the fall of 2001. It is designed for students seeking enhanced academic challenges in a stimulating learning environment. The reading- and writing-intensive program gives qualified students the opportunity for more in-depth study than may be possible in the traditional classroom. Currently, honors contracts are available in the following subjects: Biology 1406: general biology I, Biology 1407: general biology II, Geology 1403: physical geology, History 1301: history of the United States I, History 1302: history of the United States II, Government 2305: American government (federal), Government 2306: American government (state), Psychology 2301: general psychology, Psychology 2371: abnormal psychology, Math 1324: mathematics analysis I, Math 2413: calculus I, English 1302: composition and introduction to literature, English 2327: survey of American literature I, English 2328: survey of American literature II, English 2332: survey of world literature I, and English 2333: survey of world literature II. As the program grows, additional offerings will become available. Students should check the program Web site for the most current list of honors offerings. The Blinn College Honors Program is affiliated with the National Collegiate Honors Council, the Great Plains Honors Council, and the Gulf Coast Intercollegiate Honors Council.

Participation Requirements: To be an Honors Program graduate, students must earn 18 hours minimum of honors credit, including at least one course from English, mathematics, social sciences, and natural sciences. Hours may be earned through honors contracts in which students complete activities above the normal course expectations with specially designated faculty mentors, through paired interdisciplinary courses, or through honors classes. Students are limited to 6 hours of honors credit per semester. On their transcripts, students receive an honors designation for each 3 hours of honors credit earned as well as transcript recognition for being an Honors Program graduate. Students also receive special recognition at spring Commencement exercises.

Admission Requirements: To qualify for admission to the program, incoming freshmen must have a minimum of 1200 on the SAT or 27 on the ACT, rank in the top 25 percent of their high school graduating class, and enroll as a full-time student. Current or returning students must have a cumulative 3.5 GPA or higher in all classes; have been a full-time student the previous semester with at least 9 hours from a combination of English, mathematics, social science, or natural science; and have passed the TASP or be exempt from the TASP.

All applicants must submit a completed Honors Program application, separate from the application for admission to Blinn; a 500-word minimum essay that explains why they seek acceptance into the program; and three letters of recommendation, two of which must come from high school or college faculty members that are familiar with the student's academic ability. There is a rolling deadline for submitting an application packet to the Honors Program. Tentative deadlines for each long semester will be posted on the program's Web site.

Scholarship Availability: Students accepted into the Honors Program who successfully meet the conditions for honors credit and who maintain a cumulative 3.5 GPA in all their classes qualify for a $500 scholarship each semester they participate in the program.

The Campus Context: Blinn College, the Junior College District of Washington County, is located in Brenham, Texas, and serves a thirteen-county service area. There are also additional campuses in Bryan and Schulenburg. Founded in 1883 by the Southern German Conference of the Methodist Church, ties to the Methodist Church were broken in 1937 and Blinn became the first county-owned junior college district in Texas.

The home campus is located in Brenham, which has a population of approximately 12,000. Brenham is located in south central Texas, which is 90 miles east of Austin and 70 miles west of

Interpreting the symbols: **2**=two-year college, **4**=four-year college; **Pu**=public or state college, **Pr**=private college; **G**=general honors program; **D**=departmental honors program; **S**=small program (fewer than 100 students), **M**=midsize program (100 to 500 students), **L**=large program (more than 500 students); **Sc**=scholarships available in honors program; **Tr**=transfer students accepted into honors program; **HBC**=historically black college; **AA**=academic advisors; **GA**=graduate advisors; **FA**=fellowship advisors.

Houston. Independence, Washington-on-the-Brazos, and Brenham played major roles in the early development of Texas–socially, politically, and educationally.

Since 1970, Blinn College has offered a full schedule of classes in the Bryan-College Station area. The newest Blinn campus opened in the fall of 1997 in Schulenburg.

Blinn offers students two-year Associate of Arts, Associate of Science, and Associate of Applied Science degrees. The College also offers certificates of competency for those enrolled in certificate programs. The College is divided into ten instructional divisions: applied science, business and computer science, fine arts, health and kinesiology, humanities, mathematics and engineering, parallel studies, social science, and technical and workforce education.

Student Body Total enrollment is more than 12,000 students, with 50 percent women and 50 percent men. As of the fall of 2000, 80 percent of the students were white, 7 percent African American, 9 percent Hispanic, 1 percent Asian, and 1 percent international. The average age of students was 22.

Faculty Blinn has 465 faculty members; 216 are full-time and 249 are part-time or adjunct. The student to faculty ratio is 26:1.

Key Facilities The Blinn College libraries provide materials and services to students and faculty members on all campuses from its locations in Brenham, Bryan, and Schulenburg. The combined collections contain more than 130,000 books and bound periodicals; more than 700 magazines and newspaper subscriptions; thousands of microforms, maps, audiovisuals, electronic resources, and other materials. Internet access at multiple workstations is available at each library location. Across the campuses, students have access to 1,059 computers located in 41 laboratories, including the three libraries.

Honorary Societies Phi Theta Kappa, Mu Alpha Theta, Delta Psi Omega, Psi Beta, Sigma Kappa Delta

Athletics Blinn College offers intercollegiate competition in football, men's and women's basketball, baseball, softball, and volleyball. The college is a member of the National Junior College Athletic Association (NJCAA) and competes in the Region XIV Athletic Conference and the Southwest Junior College Football Conference. The division of health and kinesiology sponsors an intramural athletic program open to all students.

Support Services Students with disabilities may seek support from the Blinn College Office of Disability Services. Students are encouraged to contact this office early in the semester to initiate services. Counseling and advising services are available through Counseling Services with offices located on all three campuses.

Job Opportunities There are numerous opportunities for students to gain employment in various campus departments as student workers. These positions are limited to 20 hours per week. Counseling Services maintains a job listings file of position announcements received from local employers.

Tuition and Fees For full-time students with a minimum of 12 credit hours, tuition is $508 for in-district students, $652 for out-of-district students, and $1624 for non-Texas resident/ international students (2001–02 academic year).

Room and Board $1645 to $2900, depending on residence hall, college apartments, and meal plan selected (Brenham campus only).

Contact: Director: Jeffrey K. Scott, Blinn College, 902 College Avenue, Brenham, Texas 77833; Telephone: 979-830-4414; E-mail: blinnhonors@acmail.blinncol.edu; Web site: http://www.blinncol.edu/honorsprogram/

Bloomsburg University of Pennsylvania

4 Pu G M Sc Tr

▼ University Honors Program

The University Honors Program (UHP) at Bloomsburg University (BU) offers students who have demonstrated exceptional academic talents and achievements an opportunity to reach their full potential as scholars. Listed as a "first-rate honors program" by the *Money Advisor* (1995, Time, Inc.), the program challenges students through specially designed honors courses, providing an alternative to Bloomsburg's general education curriculum. Students select classes from a varying menu of humanities, social science, and math/science courses, followed by a selection of junior-level seminars in areas of special concern (values, diversity, quantitative/analytical, and interdisciplinary studies). Honors classes are small (average size is fewer than 20 students) and are taught by outstanding faculty members who are committed to helping their students achieve intellectual depth, pursue creative discovery, and produce finished scholarly work. Honors faculty members must submit course proposals for review by an Honors Advisory Committee consisting of faculty members, students, and the program director. The core program culminates in a two-semester independent study. The topic or subject area is chosen by the student, and both theses and creative projects are encouraged equally. Students are guided and advised during their Senior Honors Program Project by a faculty mentor of their choice. This amounts to an apprenticeship with a practicing scholar and provides an invaluable experience for the exceptional undergraduate student.

In addition to exceptional classes and specialized, advanced study, the UHP fosters and maintains an active community of scholarly students. Through small classes, class and program trips, social activities, and group-oriented service projects, honors students develop and engage in a rewarding community of like-minded students sharing ideas, working together, and supporting one another in their personal and intellectual endeavors. The students have a self-determined governing body and are deeply involved in helping to shape the Honors Program. Honors students serve as interviewers during recruiting, encourage top-notch faculty members to submit course proposals, design and maintain the Honors Program Web site, plan service and social activities, and serve on the Honors Advisory Committee and their own Honors Executive Board.

Approximately 120 students are enrolled in the UHP. Students and faculty members out of all four colleges (Liberal Arts, Science and Technology, Business, and Professional Studies) participate in the Honors Program at Bloomsburg. The overall program meets the guidelines developed by the National Collegiate Honors Council, of which the program is a member.

Participation Requirements: The honors curriculum is a four-year program that follows the basic structure of the University's general education curriculum. Students are required to take a minimum of 25 credits of honors courses (and may take up to 34), including at least one honors humanities, one honors social science, one honors math/science with a laboratory component, and one 300-level honors seminar plus the 1-credit Introduction to Honors Research and two semesters of Honors Independent Study. Students are placed in Honors Composition in the fall of their freshman year if they test at a certain level of proficiency. Students are also required to participate in at least one service project per year. UHP students must maintain a minimum overall 3.0 QPA. Graduates who successfully complete the program are awarded a bachelor's degree with University Honors. They are individually recognized at the Awards Banquet prior to commencement and receive special honors tassels for their graduation caps and recognition in the commencement program. Each honors course completed is designated on the students' transcripts, as is successful completion of the UHP.

Admission Process: Admission of freshmen to the program is by application. Applicants must have a minimum combined SAT I score of 1100 (neither the verbal nor math score may fall below a 500) and rank in the top 20 percent of their high school class. Students are asked to submit an essay on a topic chosen by the

Honors Advisory Committee, a letter of recommendation from a high school faculty member or counselor, and an example of their best written or creative work. Each student is interviewed by a faculty member and a current honors student. Selection of successful applicants is done by the Honors Advisory Committee based on the criteria listed above. Matriculated and transfer students are admitted on an individual basis. Acceptance is determined based on the student's college or university record, a letter of recommendation from a faculty member, an essay, and a work sample.

Within BU guidelines, the UHP accepts Advanced Placement credits to fulfill the Honors Composition requirement.

Scholarship Availability: The UHP has a two-tiered scholarship program. Each year, the program awards approximately twenty freshman scholarships and about twelve smaller scholarships for students above the freshman year. These are merit scholarships. Small grants are commonly available to students working on their Honors Independent Study projects. BU also has a number of University, college, and departmental merit scholarships available.

The Campus Context: BU is one of fourteen universities in the Pennsylvania State System of Higher Education. More than 7,500 students choose from among sixty-three undergraduate and nineteen graduate degree programs offered through the Colleges of Liberal Arts, Science and Technology, Business, and Professional Studies. The University is located in the town of Bloomsburg, county seat of Columbia County, Pennsylvania. Bloomsburg is a small community (population approximately 12,000) in the heart of the Susquehanna River Valley, about 80 miles northeast of Harrisburg. The town is located within 2 miles of two interchanges for Interstate 80, putting the school within easy access to the amenities of New York, Philadelphia, Harrisburg, and Wilkes-Barre/Scranton. Bloomsburg also has numerous local sites of historical, cultural, and recreational interest, including a well-respected legitimate theater company, the Bloomsburg Theater Ensemble. The UHP is housed in a new suite of offices in lower Luzerne Hall. Facilities include separate offices for the director, secretary, and student assistants. The seminar room has a capacity for up to 30 people and has a digital white board connected to the Internet. There is also a student study room. Luzerne Hall has a dormitory wing for honors students. There is extended-hour access to the Honors Center.

Student Body Undergraduate enrollment is about 6,800; 63 percent of the students are women. The ethnic distribution is 3 percent African American, 1.4 percent Hispanic, .7 percent Asian American, and .3 percent Native American. There are about 50 international students currently enrolled at BU. Forty-five percent of full-time undergraduate students live on campus. Approximately 56 percent of BU students receive financial assistance. There are eleven sororities and fourteen fraternities at Bloomsburg.

Faculty There are 383 full-time instructional faculty members, 70 percent of whom have doctorates.

Key Facilities BU's new 105,000-square-foot Andruss Library opened in May 1998, with study seating for more than 1,000 students and faculty members, stack space for more than 400,000 volumes, 500 public-access connections for personal computers, and up-to-date equipment for viewing more than 1.7 million microfilms in the library's collection. There are computer labs or facilities in most academic buildings, and all residence halls have either a computer lab or in-room access.

Athletics Bloomsburg University has eighteen NCAA Division I and II varsity sports teams—nine each for men and women. Men's sports include basketball, baseball, football, wrestling, soccer, swimming, cross-country, track and field, and tennis. Women field teams in basketball, softball, field hockey, lacrosse, soccer, swimming, cross-country, track and field, and tennis.

Study Abroad There are numerous opportunities available for overseas study, and honors students have special summer opportunities through the State System of Higher Education Summer Honors Program.

Support Services Most of the campus is accessible to physically disabled students. Sign language interpreters, note takers, and other special services are also available for students who require them.

Job Opportunities Work opportunities are available both on and off campus. The SOLVE (Students Organized to Learn Through Volunteerism and Employment) Office is also available to help students find employment opportunities in the local area.

Tuition: $4016 for state residents, $10,040 for nonresidents, per year (2001–02)

Room and Board: $4442 per year (double room)

Mandatory Fees: $976

Contact: Director: Dr. Emeric Schultz, University Honors Program, B12 Luzerne Hall, Bloomsburg University, 400 East Second Street, Bloomsburg, PA 17815; Telephone: 570-389-4713; Fax: 570-389-2049; E-mail: eschultz@bloomu.edu

Boise State University

4 Pu G M Sc Tr

▼ University Honors College

Featuring small classes, interdisciplinary study, and cocurricular activities focusing on the environment, the Honors College at Boise State is designed to enhance a student's academic experience. Along with motivated classmates, students are challenged by honors courses that require a more thorough and rigorous analysis of the material. In addition, students have the opportunity to work closely with advisers who help to identify internship, fellowship, and scholarship options to support their educational and career goals.

Admission to the Honors College is an invitation to a lifetime committed to the wonders of the human mind, heart, and spirit. Each semester students choose from a variety of honors courses, including honors seminars, departmental courses, and colloquia. The basic purpose of the seminars is to bring students (especially freshmen and sophomores) together for informal small-group discussions about specific topics. Departmental honors courses are offered regularly in several departments and sometimes may be used to fulfill general University requirements. Recommended for juniors and seniors, interdisciplinary honors colloquia feature a team-taught exploration of subject areas.

The College currently enrolls 250 students.

Participation Requirements: A cumulative GPA of at least 3.5 is a fixed requirement for retention. Any student whose GPA falls below 3.5 for two consecutive semesters is automatically dropped from the program. Students who do not complete any honors work for two consecutive semesters are withdrawn from the program unless they can demonstrate, to the satisfaction of the Director, continuing progress toward the completion of honors graduation requirements. Exceptions may be only to Admission and Retention requirements, and these rare exceptions are granted by the Honors College Committee of the Faculty Senate upon express written petition by the student justifying the exceptions on the basis of other evidence of academic potential.

To graduate with honors, a student must have 26 honors credits. To graduate with honors from the program, a student must have a cumulative undergraduate GPA of at least 3.5. Students whose

Interpreting the symbols: **2**=two-year college, **4**=four-year college; **Pu**=public or state college, **Pr**=private college; **G**=general honors program; **D**=departmental honors program; **S**=small program (fewer than 100 students), **M**=midsize program (100 to 500 students), **L**=large program (more than 500 students); **Sc**=scholarships available in honors program; **Tr**=transfer students accepted into honors program; **HBC**=historically black college; **AA**=academic advisors; **GA**=graduate advisors; **FA**=fellowship advisors.

cumulative undergraduate GPA is at least 3.75 and whose records of academic and cocurricular activities indicate outstanding performance in both areas may be considered by the Honors College Committee of the Faculty Senate for graduation with Distinguished Honors. Cocurricular activities may include publication of undergraduate work, presentations at regional or national conferences, and outstanding service in the Honors Student Association.

Admission Process: Students are required to have a cumulative GPA of at least 3.5 and score in at least the ninetieth percentile on the combined portion of the ACT or SAT I in order to apply to BSU on the basis of high school graduation. A cumulative GPA of at least 3.5 for a minimum of 15 college credits will be required for all others, including continuing students, transfers, and students whose admission to BSU has not been based upon regular high school graduation and ACT or SAT I scores.

Scholarship Availability: Through the generosity of the estate of Dean and Thelma Brown, BSU offers numerous scholarships. Brown Honors Scholars receive full fees plus room and board worth up to $12,000. Up to ten Brown Honors Residential Scholarships are awarded. Moreover, each of these is renewable for up to a total of four years. Numerous other merit-based scholarships are available.

The Campus Context: Boise State University is composed of eight colleges: the College of Arts and Sciences, the College of Business and Economics, the College of Education, the College of Engineering, the College of Health Science, the Honors College, the College of Social Sciences and Public Affairs, and the College of Technology.

Student Body Undergraduate enrollment is 17,140. The ethnic distribution is 1.1 percent Native American, .9 percent African American, 4.2 percent Hispanic, .7 percent Basque, 85 percent white, 1.2 percent international student, and 2.1 percent Asian/Pacific Islander. Approximately 8 percent of the students live on campus. Fifty percent of continuing students receive some form of aid; 31 percent of aid is distributed as grants, 64 percent as student loans, and 3 percent as jobs. BSU has six social, five professional, and seven academic/honorary fraternities and sororities.

Faculty Of the 896 faculty members, 586 are full-time; 413 faculty members have terminal degrees.

Key Facilities Some of the distinguishing facilities on campus include the Centennial Amphitheatre, an outdoor venue for lectures, concerts, and plays, and the Morrison Center for the Performing Arts, which houses the music department, the theater arts department, a 2,000-seat performance hall, a 200-seat recital hall, and a 200-seat theater.

The Student Union provides facilities for social, recreational, and cultural activities. In addition to a computer store, a quick-copy center, and three dining areas, the Student Union contains a game room, several lounges, the Outdoor Rental Center, the BSU Bookstore, and the Bronco Shop.

The Intramural/Recreation Office and one of BSU's Children's Centers are located in the BSU Pavilion, Idaho's largest multipurpose arena. When not filled with fans of Bronco basketball, gymnastics, or volleyball, the Pavilion is the site of concerts, professional sporting events, and family entertainment. Nearby is Bronco Stadium, with a seating capacity of 30,000.

The library houses 418,00 monograph volumes, 63,000 bound periodicals, 4,800 current periodicals, 128,200 maps, 169,300 government publications, and more than 1 million microfilms. The campus has approximately twenty-two computer labs for student use.

Honorary Societies Phi Kappa Phi and Golden Key

Athletics In the intercollegiate athletic program at Boise State University, students engage in outstanding competition with other universities and colleges of the Western Athletic Conference (WAC). This includes the PAC-10 Athletic Conference and the National Collegiate Athletic Association (NCAA). The University fields men's intercollegiate teams in football, basketball, track, wrestling, tennis, cross-country, and golf. The University also fields women's intercollegiate teams in basketball, track, tennis, cross-country, golf, gymnastics, and volleyball.

Study Abroad Boise State University's Honors College and International Programs are dedicated to providing students with the international skills and experiences required by an increasingly interconnected and complex world. Within Idaho alone, more than 50,000 jobs are the direct result of international exports. In today's global village, BSU honors graduates will be called upon to utilize firsthand international experiences and knowledge of other cultures and second and third languages. International programs provide students with many rich opportunities to gain this highly valued international expertise. Summer, semester, and year-long educational programs are offered in Australia, Chile, Costa Rica, England, France, Germany, Italy, Japan, Mexico, Spain (Basque Country), Thailand, and Quebec, Canada.

Support Services The Student Special Services Office is responsible for providing support services that enable all students with disabilities to participate in BSU's educational programs and activities.

Job Opportunities Included in the many job opportunities available campuswide are both work-study and non-work-study positions.

Tuition: None for state residents, $6000 for nonresidents, per year (2001–02)

Room and Board: $3375 minimum

Fees: $2847

Contact: Director: Dr. Gregory A. Raymond, Driscoll Hall, Boise State University, Boise, Idaho 83725-1125; Telephone: 208-426-1122; Fax: 208-426-1247; E-mail: graymon@boisestate.edu; Web site: http://www.idbsu.edu/honors/

Bowie State University

4 Pu D M Sc Tr GA

▼ Honors College

The Bowie State University Honors College is designed to both challenge and foster intellectual growth of academically talented students. The program has provided a diverse and stimulating educational experience for its honors students and McNair Scholars. Drawing from the rich cultural resources that Bowie State University offers, students are encouraged to confront contemporary issues facing society. BSU has well-motivated and skilled faculty members who constitute the core faculty. Honors faculty members are accomplished authorities in their field, proficient at teaching and motivating students to expand their knowledge across disciplines. Students are advised by faculty members in the student's field of interest. The relatively small size of Bowie State University offers the students close personal attention in their studies.

Students in the Honors College have access to all BSU facilities. They have the benefits of a challenging program and the support of a major university within the Maryland University system. This includes a fully equipped computer laboratory, a fully accredited staff, and a library with nearly a quarter million volumes of information and services.

Honors students must complete 24 honors credits in order to have Honors Scholar on the transcript at graduation. All majors are accepted and honors classes are incorporated into the schedule. Eighteen to twenty honors classes are offered each semester and center on a wide range of studies and disciplines. Students are encouraged to use the honors contract for honors credit in major courses. If an Advanced Placement course covers the same material as an honors course, the AP test score, which meets University standards, can be accepted as a substitute.

The Honors College currently has 223 members.

Participation Requirements: Honors members must have a 3.0 GPA in order to graduate, 24 honors credits, and 150 hours of community service.

Admission Process: Freshmen and transfer students are selected each fall based upon high school performance and SAT scores. A 3.2 GPA and a minimum 1100 SAT score are required of freshmen members. Transfer students must have a 3.0 GPA or higher, 15 completed credit hours, and recommendations from at least 2 instructors.

The Campus Context: Bowie State University was founded in 1865 by the Baltimore Association for the Moral and Educational Improvement of Colored People. For decades, Bowie State College was well-known for its education of teachers in high school and secondary education. In 1988, Bowie State College officially became Bowie State University, reflecting the tremendous growth the school had undertaken. Today, BSU resides on a 187-acre campus conveniently located between the major cities of Annapolis, Baltimore, and Washington, D.C. Bowie still holds to a tradition of education for its racially and culturally diverse student body.

Student Body There are 5,181 undergraduates, 62 percent of whom are women, who are enrolled in nineteen degree programs. The ethnic distribution of the student population is 88 percent African American, 8 percent European American, 1 percent Hispanic, and 1 percent Asian/Pacific Islander. Seventy-five percent of the students are commuters. Sixty-seven percent of the students receive financial aid. There are four fraternities and four sororities.

Faculty Of the 312 faculty members, 155 are full-time; 105 of the full-time faculty members have terminal degrees. The student-faculty ratio is 16:1.

Key Facilities The library houses 233,527 volumes. There are 253 Gateway 2000 computers for instructional and public use in library and academic buildings. In fall 2001, Bowie became the first institution in the U.S. to provide laptop computers to all of its first-time freshmen.

Athletics Bowie State University offers intercollegiate athletic teams in basketball, football, cross-country, track and field, volleyball, and softball. Bowie is a member of the NCAA Division II conference and competes in the CIAA. Bowie athletes, on average, maintain high academic grades and enter college with higher SAT scores than non-athletes. More than half complete academic programs and graduate.

Job Opportunities Students are offered a range of work opportunities on campus, including assistantships and work study.

Tuition: $2941 for state residents, $9023 for nonresidents, per year (2000-01)

Room and Board: $5498

Mandatory Fees: $861

Contact: Interim Dean: Dr. Mary H. McManus, Thurgood Marshall Library, Suite 279D 2nd Floor, 14000 Jericho Park Road, Bowie, Maryland 20715; Telephone: 301-860-4090 or 4091; Fax: 301-860-4089; E-mail: mmcmanus@bowiestate.edu

Bradford College

4 Pr G S Tr

▼ Honors Program

The four-year Bradford Honors Program offers academically advanced and motivated students the opportunity for substantial challenges during their time at Bradford. The program seeks to create a community of scholars who will invigorate both each other and the College as a whole to higher standards of intellectual and creative activity.

The 15-year-old program currently enrolls approximately 40 students.

Participation Requirements: Students entering with at least a 3.25 GPA are automatically eligible to enroll in honors courses. In order to remain in the Honors Program, students must maintain a 3.0 GPA or higher in all honors work and a 3.25 GPA or higher in overall college work. Since the College believes that GPAs are not the only measure of honors capability, the program will allow any student to attempt to join the Honors Program in the freshman year regardless of GPA. In addition, any student with a minimum 2.75 GPA or higher who is not a regular member of the Honors Program may elect to take one honors course during their four years at Bradford if the instructor approves and the topic is of particular interest to the student.

The program is an 18-credit program consisting of a combination of specialized honors seminars, the opportunity for Individual Honors Contracts, and weekend seminars. Students completing the required courses and the 18 credit minimum are designated as Honors Scholars at graduation.

The deadline for applying is February 15.

Scholarship Availability: Bradford College offers many generous financial aid opportunities to its students. The College's financial advising staff is committed to assisting students who attend Bradford through its program of financial assistance based on need and merit. Grants, scholarships, loans, and college work opportunities provide the basis for assistance. In recent years, approximately 80 percent of Bradford students have received financial aid.

The Campus Context: Bradford College comprises an 80-acre campus made up of more than a dozen buildings, a pond, and athletic fields, plus 40 acres of woodland.

Among distinguished facilities are the Dorothy Bell Study Center, which houses the college library, art department, art gallery, music department and studios, and Conover Hall, a multipurpose, 225-seat auditorium; Hasseltine Hall, which houses the Writing Center, Media Center, and Academic Resource Center; Denworth Hall, housing the dance studio and two theatres; Bicknell Chapel; and Kimball Tavern, a historic seventeenth century landmark where the College was founded in 1803.

Student Body The student population comprises 34 percent men and 66 percent women. The ethnic distribution of the student body is 73 percent white, 6 percent African American, 9 percent Asian, and 6 percent Hispanic. There are 115 international students (19 percent). Twenty-seven percent of the students are commuters. During the 1998–99 academic year, nearly thirty clubs and organizations were active on campus.

Faculty Of the 35 full-time faculty members, 83 percent have terminal degrees. The student-faculty ratio is 17:1.

Key Facilities The Bradford library houses 64,000 volumes and 250 periodicals. There is a computer center with full Internet access and e-mail with both IBM and Macintosh computers.

Athletics Club sports add an important dimension to student life. The development of sports and recreational clubs fosters intercollegiate competition in such activities as volleyball, soccer, lacrosse, martial arts, basketball, and softball. The number and types of student clubs depend upon student interest and availability of facilities and equipment.

Study Abroad International study or internships during the summer or a semester in the junior year can provide students with the invaluable experience of life in another culture and, in many

Interpreting the symbols: **2**=two-year college, **4**=four-year college; **Pu**=public or state college, **Pr**=private college; **G**=general honors program; **D**=departmental honors program; **S**=small program (fewer than 100 students), **M**=midsize program (100 to 500 students), **L**=large program (more than 500 students); **Sc**=scholarships available in honors program; **Tr**=transfer students accepted into honors program; **HBC**=historically black college; **AA**=academic advisors; **GA**=graduate advisors; **FA**=fellowship advisors.

instances, the opportunity to improve their knowledge of a second or third language. Bradford College's affiliations with Central College, Beaver College Study Abroad Opportunities, the School for Field Studies, the Council on International Education Exchange, the School for International Training, the American Institute of Foreign Studies, and Boston University's International Internship Programs enables students to study or work in settings around the world while they earn Bradford credit.

Support Services All buildings are accessible to students with disabilities.

Job Opportunities Bradford offers numerous work opportunities through work-study programs.

Tuition: $16,500 per year (1998–99)

Room and Board: $6850

Mandatory Fees: $620

Contact: Director: Dr. Barbara Ann McCahill, 320 South Main Street, Haverhill, Massachusetts 01835-7393; Telephone: 978-372-7161 Ext. 5346; Fax: 978-521-0480

BRENAU UNIVERSITY

4 Pr G S Tr

▼ Women's College Honors Program

The honors program of Brenau University Women's College provides students of proven academic skills and motivation an opportunity to excel in their studies. Striving to combine a variety of innovative and traditional approaches, the honors program is designed to encourage analytical and creative thinking, to foster an awareness of the diversity of opinions in the global community, and, above all, to stimulate a love of learning that will continue throughout a student's lifetime. Grounded in a variety of liberal and professional studies, the program seeks to prepare students for future graduate education and to enrich their professional and personal lives.

Small class size is central to the Women's College honors program. Classes of approximately 15 or fewer students stimulate interactive student-faculty dialogue that often continues outside the classroom as students develop their thinking and assume leadership roles on campus. Honors students are actively encouraged to explore study abroad, internships, and other opportunities at appropriate junctures in their undergraduate careers. The curriculum includes several research options, honors disciplinary and interdisciplinary courses, and an optional two-semester capstone project or thesis.

Founded in 1988, the honors program admits approximately 20 to 25 students annually. Currently, about 65 students are enrolled in the program.

Participation Requirements: In their freshman and sophomore years, honors students begin the first phase of their program by taking at least six honors courses to help fulfill their general education requirements. Students are encouraged to take as many honors courses as their interests and schedules allow, and they may extend these courses into their upper-division years, depending on their majors. As many as twelve of these courses may be taken. A special feature of the freshman and sophomore portion of the program, which is open by invitation to selected students, is the opportunity to develop an independent, guided research project on a topic of interest. Up to four independent research courses may be taken by qualified honors students.

In the junior year, students take an interdisciplinary seminar focusing in depth on various topics, such as Literature and the Environment, Women in the Arts, and the Culture of Historic Preservation. Students completing this second phase of the program graduate with Honors in Liberal Studies.

Students then may choose to complete the honors program with an extended Senior Honors Thesis or Project. Usually this is related to the student's major. This two-semester course, often begun in the spring of the junior year, culminates with the award of High Honors in Liberal Studies.

To graduate with honors or high honors, students must maintain a minimum 3.5 GPA in their honors course work and at least a 3.2 cumulative GPA. These students receive special recognition, a certificate, and an embossed gold seal on their diploma at graduation. Students who maintain a minimum 3.0 GPA may continue in the honors program and be recognized as a Graduate of the honors program if they complete the Junior Seminar.

Admission Process: Admission to the honors program is based on SAT I scores, high school GPA, and other factors. Normally, admission is granted to students with an SAT I score of about 1200 (or equivalent ACT) and a GPA of about 3.5, although students of exceptional promise are considered on a case-by-case basis. No special application to the honors program is needed. Currently enrolled students may apply to the honors program with a minimum 3.5 GPA, and transfer students are welcomed into the program.

Scholarship Availability: Scholarships are available through the Admissions Office, and many honors students receive generous financial aid packages.

The Campus Context: Brenau University is located in Gainesville, Georgia, 50 miles northeast of Atlanta on Lake Lanier. Located in Hall County, the town serves as the primary industrial, agricultural, medical, educational, and cultural center for the northeast Georgia area. The population of the greater Gainesville area is approximately 100,000. Nestled in the foothills of the north Georgia mountains, Gainesville combines the charm of a small, established town with the energy of a community with numerous artistic and cultural events. With equally easy access to Atlanta and the north Georgia mountains, students may choose from a variety of activities to supplement their studies. The campus itself consists of more than fifty buildings located on 57 beautifully kept acres in an attractive residential area of town. Notable facilities include the spacious John S. Burd Performing Arts Center, which opened in 2002; the Simmons Visual Arts Center, home to a fine collection of art from across the centuries; the John W. Jacobs, Jr. Business and Communication Arts Building, which houses Brenau's television and radio studios; and a recently renovated natatorium and gymnasium with state-of-the-art fitness equipment. High-technology classrooms are available in each major academic building to enhance the variety of educational opportunities. The Women's College offers thirty-three academic majors and twelve minors leading to bachelor's degrees. Graduate programs are available in several fields of study.

Student Body Approximately 575 students are enrolled as undergraduates in the Women's College. The ethnic distribution of the College is 10 percent African American, 2 percent Asian American, and 2 percent Hispanic. International students represent 5 percent of the undergraduate population. About 45 percent of these students are residential, and the remainder commute. In the Women's College, about 60 percent of the students receive financial aid. In addition to a number of extracurricular clubs and organizations, there are nine national sororities on campus.

Faculty With 111 faculty members in the Women's College, the school has an enviable student-faculty ratio of 8:1. Nearly 85 percent of the faculty members teaching academic courses are full-time, and, of those, 96 percent hold the terminal degree in their field.

Key Facilities The Brenau Trustee Library houses 103,740 volumes, and students may access additional databases through a well-developed technology infrastructure. In addition to the technology classrooms in the academic buildings, there are five computer labs with more than 120 computers on campus, and all residential housing is connected to the Internet via the campuswide network.

E-mail is provided for all students, who can access the campus intranet and the World Wide Web from their residence halls as well as at other places on campus. The campus intranet allows students the option of checking grades and registering online. A campus-wide technology platform permits faculty members and students to supplement classroom discussion with innovative learning activities.

Honorary Societies Alpha Lambda Delta and Phi Beta Sigma

Athletics Brenau Women's College students may compete nationally through the National Association of Intercollegiate Athletics (NAIA) in tennis, soccer, volleyball, and cross-country. The NAIA currently ranks Brenau's tennis team second in the country, and the team has ranked in the top ten since 1993.

Study Abroad The honors program encourages students to expand their horizons and add global perspectives to their studies by exploring options for study abroad. Recently, several students have returned from various sites in Europe with glowing reports of their experiences.

Support Services At Brenau, 90 percent of the buildings on campus are handicapped accessible. An excellent and thorough program is available for students with a professionally diagnosed learning disability through the Brenau Learning Center.

Job Opportunities A variety of work-study experiences are available for students demonstrating financial need, and many academic programs encourage or require internships that may be remunerated.

Tuition, Room, and Board: $20,100 ($426 per credit hour for commuting students) (2001–02)

Mandatory Fees: $100 for residential students

Contact: Director: Dr. Jay Gaspar, One Centennial Circle, Gainesville, Georgia 30501; Telephone: 770-534-6196; Fax: 770-534-6137; E-mail: jgaspar@lib.brenau.edu

Brevard College

4 Pr G S Tr

▼ Honors Program

The mission of the Brevard College Honors Program is to provide an enriched academic experience for those students who are motivated toward academic success and personal development. The basis of honors education is that honors students should be continually challenged to reach their highest potential as scholars and leaders.

Courses in the Brevard College Honors Program are designed to be stimulating, unique, and challenging. In addition to, or instead of, the typical lecture format, discussion periods and independent learning are part of the classroom environment. This environment includes the classroom and the world at large, through experiential and service-learning activities. Students are encouraged to develop their own ideas within an informed and logical framework, to use creativity and an interdisciplinary approach in problem solving, and to develop into the well-rounded, complete person that is the hallmark of a liberal arts education.

Formed in 2000 to recruit, retain, and assist outstanding students, the Brevard College Honors Program is still in the exciting stages of initial development. The 60 current students in the program are shaping it even as they develop as individuals.

Participation Requirements: Most students enter the program as incoming freshmen or returning sophomores. Students complete four 1-hour seminar courses, four 3-hour subject courses, and a senior project within their major, for a total of 19 semester hours. Those who complete these requirements and maintain a GPA of at least 3.3 are recognized at commencement, on their transcript, and on their diploma.

Admission Process: Incoming freshmen with a high school GPA of at least 3.5 and an SAT score of at least 1100 (ACT score of at least 26) are invited to join. Returning sophomores with a minimum 3.3 GPA are invited to join. An application is required. Applications must be received by April 15 in order to secure honors housing. Later applications are accepted, but housing can not be guaranteed.

Scholarship Availability: The College gives substantial academic scholarships, but not through the Honors Program. These scholarships are awarded through the Financial Aid Office, and inquiries should be directed to that office.

The Campus Context: Brevard College is a four-year, residential, private comprehensive college accredited by the Southern Association of Colleges and Schools. It was rated in 2002 as one of America's best colleges as well as one of the best values among comprehensive colleges by *U.S. News & World Report.* Founded in 1853, it is the oldest college or university in the mountains of North Carolina. The school offers the bachelor's degree in thirteen majors and twenty minors. The Department of Music has received additional accreditation through the National Association of Schools of Music. Brevard College is affiliated with the Western North Carolina Conference of The United Methodist Church. The 120-acre campus lies within the city of Brevard, a town of 6,000, and is within minutes of the Pisgah National Forest and Blue Ridge Parkway, providing many opportunities for experiential learning. The city of Brevard is well known for its popular summer festival at the Brevard Music Center.

Student Body The student body has approximately 700 students from forty-one states and twenty-two other countries. Ethnic distribution is 87 percent white, 8 percent African American, 3 percent international, 2 percent Hispanic, 0.4 percent Native American, and 0.2 percent Asian. Fifty-three percent of the student body are men; 47 percent are women. Sixty-four percent live on campus; 45 percent are in-state. Ninety-five percent of students receive financial aid.

Faculty There are 107 faculty members, 63 of whom are full-time. Of the full-time faculty members, 56 percent hold the terminal degree in their field. The student-faculty ratio is 10:1; 77 percent of classes have fewer than 20 students.

Key Facilities More than 50,000 books and 3,000 audiovisual materials, including compact discs and videos, are housed in the collection of the J. A. Jones Library. The library subscribes to more than 300 periodicals and provides access to thousands of full-text articles through online databases, including NC LIVE. Back files of periodicals and newspapers are available on microfilm or in bound volumes. The online catalog of the Mountain College Library Network provides immediate access to an additional 340,000 books and 3,000 periodicals.

The Information Technology Department provides communication, technical, and support services to Brevard College staff members, faculty members, and student body. The college network consists of high-speed (1 GB) fiber-optic cabling between all academic buildings and residence halls, which provides network, Web, e-mail, and file and print services, as well as direct access to the Internet. The campus network consists of twelve network servers, one HP 9000, several general student labs with both PCs and Macs, special labs for art and music students, multiple terminals in the library, and terminals for faculty and staff member offices.

Honorary Societies Omicron Delta Kappa

Athletics Brevard College has a distinguished and successful history in intercollegiate athletics for both men and women. The

Interpreting the symbols: **2**=two-year college, **4**=four-year college; **Pu**=public or state college, **Pr**=private college; **G**=general honors program; **D**=departmental honors program; **S**=small program (fewer than 100 students), **M**=midsize program (100 to 500 students), **L**=large program (more than 500 students); **Sc**=scholarships available in honors program; **Tr**=transfer students accepted into honors program; **HBC**=historically black college; **AA**=academic advisors; **GA**=graduate advisors; **FA**=fellowship advisors.

College is now a member of the Appalachian Athletic Conference (AAC) of the National Association of Intercollegiate Athletics (NAIA). Approximately one third of the student body participates in intercollegiate athletics. Programs for men and women include basketball, cheerleading, cross-country, indoor and outdoor track and field, and soccer. The College also fields teams in women's softball and volleyball and in men's baseball and golf. Athletic talent scholarships are available in all sports. An active intramural program is also in place.

Study Abroad A unique study-abroad opportunity at Brevard College is the Voice of the Rivers expedition (VOR). Three VOR expeditions have been fielded thus far, in 1997, 1999, and 2001. Each VOR expedition has followed a river from its source to its confluence with an ocean, and students have earned up to a semester of course credit. In addition, faculty-sponsored programs to England, Mexico, Costa Rica, and the Canary Islands have been developed by instructors for class credit in specific disciplines.

Support Services The Learning Enhancement Center is designed to assist all students in the full realization of their academic potential. Services provided include academic counseling, secondary advising, tutor referrals, provision of a distraction-reduced study or test area, note-taking arrangements, and others. The Office for Students with Special Needs and Disabilities assists students with disabilities in obtaining equal access to the educational opportunities available at Brevard College.

Job Opportunities The Career Services Center offers workshops, seminars, and counseling to help students make informed career choices. It actively advertises work and internship opportunities, as well as providing individual career assessment and interpretation. The Center for Service Learning provides a unique partnership with community leaders in service learning, embracing the college motto "Learn in Order to Serve."

Tuition: $11,980 per year (2001-2002)

Room and Board: $5310

Mandatory Fees: $946

Contact: Director: Dr. Jennifer Frick, 400 North Broad Street, Brevard, North Carolina 28712. Telephone: 828-883-8292. Fax: 828-884-3790. E-mail: jefrick@brevard.edu. Web site: http://www.brevard.edu/academics/honors_program/index.html

BREVARD COMMUNITY COLLEGE

2 Pu G M Sc Tr

▼ Honors Program

The Brevard Community College (BCC) Honors Program offers exceptional students an academic program of study to challenge them beyond the rigors of traditional classes. Honors students enjoy an environment of scholarly inquiry, creative interaction, and intellectual stimulation through special courses and enrichment activities.

The program offers honors courses across the curriculum and attracts students seeking both Associate of Arts and Associate of Science degrees.

Honors Program students enjoy small classes (generally 8–15 students), priority registration, an Honors Resource Center (Melbourne Campus), special library privileges, and a special agreement of admission to the University of Central Florida (UCF) Honors College.

Participation Requirements: Students may participate in the Honors Program in two ways: as honors students or as honors affiliates. Honors students work toward an honors diploma by completing 18 credit hours (out of a required 60 hours for an associate degree) of honors courses, participating in at least 20 hours of community service, and completing the Phi Theta Kappa–sponsored leadership course while maintaining a 3.5 GPA. Honors affiliates meet the same admissions requirements as honors students, but participate in the program for access to honors classes. Affiliates may take as many or as few honors courses as they like and are not required to perform community service or take the leadership course. They are, however, required to maintain a 3.5 GPA. Honors students are recognized at graduation, and the transcripts of all participants in the Honors Program show the special designation of honors classes.

Admission Process: To be admitted to the Honors Program, students must meet one of the following requirements: have a high school GPA of 3.5 or above on a 4.0 scale; be in the top 10 percent of their high school graduating class; have an SAT I combined score of at least 1100; have an ACT score of at least 26; have a CPT or FELPT score of 100 or higher on Sentence Skills and 97 or higher in Reading; show a 3.5 cumulative GPA from at least 12 credit hours of college-level work at Brevard; show a 3.5 GPA from no more than 6 credit hours in the case of students transferring from another accredited postsecondary school. All applicants must also present a letter of recommendation by a high school teacher and/or guidance counselor, a Brevard adviser or faculty member, or a faculty member from another college in the case of transfer students.

Scholarship Availability: The Brevard Community College Honors Program offers limited scholarship assistance. Scholarships funded from many other sources are also available to Honors Program students. All scholarships require a separate application and have a variety of criteria.

The Campus Context: Brevard Community College, located in the heart of the nation's space coast, is a two-year, coeducational, publicly supported postsecondary institution. Established in 1960, the College serves the residents of Brevard County, Florida, with four physical campuses, a Spaceport Center located at the Kennedy Space Center, and a recently established Virtual Campus, which offers associate degrees by television and/or the Internet. The College is fully accredited by the Southern Association of Colleges and Schools.

Distinctive facilities supported by or affiliated with Brevard Community College include the Astronaut Memorial Planetarium and Observatory, the historic Cocoa Village Playhouse, the Maxwell C. King Center for the Performing Arts, and the Moore Multicultural Activities Center. Brevard Community College also has its own educational television station, WBCC, which dedicates 100 percent of its broadcasting time to delivering educational programs, telecourses, and general interest programs to more than 1 million central Florida residents.

Student Body Brevard Community College offers Associate of Arts, Associate of Science, and Associate in Applied Science curricula to 13,000 credit-seeking students. In addition, the College offers continuing education to 4,000 students through its programs in continuing workforce education, lifelong learning, and recreation and leisure.

Faculty Of the total faculty at BCC, 221 are full-time and approximately 600 are adjunct faculty members (the number varies from semester to semester).

Key Facilities In addition to the Planetarium, the Playhouse, the Performing Arts Center, and the television station, BCC—in a cooperative effort with the University of Central Florida—is the home of the Clark Maxwell Jr. Lifelong Learning Center, a first-of-its-kind joint-use facility for instruction and service. In addition, BCC and UCF share a joint-use library on the BCC Cocoa campus. The library also houses the special collection of the Florida Solar Energy Center. On each campus, students have access to computer labs, computer-assisted instruction labs, TIE facilities, and "smart" classrooms.

Honorary Society Phi Theta Kappa

Study Abroad Each year, students have the opportunity to earn humanities credit through courses that include overseas travel.

Other disciplines also offer credit courses that include a travel component.

Job Opportunities Employment programs allow students to defray part of the expenses of their education by working part-time. Most positions are located on campus and require 12 hours of work per week.

Tuition: $1507 for Florida residents; $5389 for nonresidents

Contact: Director: Beverly J. Slaughter, Honors Program, 3865 North Wickham Road, Melbourne, Florida 32935; Telephone: 321-632-1111 Ext. 32850; Fax: 321-634-3721; E-mail: slaughterb@brevard.cc.fl.us; Web site: http://www.brevard.cc.fl.us/honors

BRIDGEWATER STATE COLLEGE

4 Pu G D S Tr

▼ Honors Program

The Honors Program at Bridgewater encourages gifted and highly motivated students to reach their highest potential through critical thinking and research. Small classes and close student-faculty relations provide for the vigorous and thorough exchange of ideas, while the program as a whole attempts to create an atmosphere fostering intellectual, artistic, and academic achievement.

Students earn honors credits by taking honors sections of regular courses and/or honors colloquia during their freshman and sophomore years, by completing honors work in certain 300- and 400-level courses during their junior and senior years, and by researching and writing an honors thesis in their senior year.

Students in the program have access throughout the year to the Honors Center on the second floor of Harrington Hall. Designed as a study area and meeting place, the center has large work tables, comfortable chairs, computers, and a lending library. The center subscribes to various periodicals (most notably *The New York Review of Books, The Times Literary Supplement, Commentary, The New Republic,* and *The American Scholar*), and these are readily available to students. The Center is open from 9 a.m. to 5 p.m. Monday through Friday during the academic year.

Each term the program hosts an Honors Dinner featuring a prominent off-campus authority as Guest of Honor and Speaker, and on Wednesdays during the term the program maintains a drop-in lunch table for students and faculty members in Flynn Commons.

The honors experience at Bridgewater may be approached in two ways. All-College Honors, which began in 1982, and Departmental Honors, which began in 1968. Current enrollment for both programs is 108.

Participation Requirements: Each semester, the program offers a wide range of 3-credit honors classes and 1-credit honors colloquia. During their freshman and sophomore years, students in All-College Honors are free to chose whatever they please from these offerings provided they accumulate at least 9 honors credits by the end of their sophomore year. The 3-credit honors courses all satisfy general education requirements; the colloquia, which tend to be more specialized, do not. Students must maintain a minimum 3.3 GPA.

As juniors, All-College Honors students may either enter a departmental honors program or, in consultation with the Honors Director, develop an individualized interdisciplinary honors program. During the junior year, students must complete two upper-division courses on an honors-credit basis by engaging in special advanced work under the instructor's direction. During the senior year, students research and write their honors theses under individual faculty member's supervision. Whether the thesis qualifies the student to graduate with honors is determined by either the relevant departmental honors committee or the student's interdisciplinary honors committee. A minimum of 18 credits is required for All-College Honors: 9 at the freshman/sophomore level, 6 in upper-level courses, and 3 on the thesis.

Emphasizing independent study and research in the major, Departmental Honors programs are currently offered in art; biology; chemistry; communication studies and theater arts; English; foreign languages; history; management; mathematics and computer science; movement arts, health promotion, and leisure studies; philosophy; political science; and psychology. Although GPA requirements vary, most departments require either an overall GPA of at least 3.0 or a minimum 3.3 in the major. Admission to Departmental Honors programs does not require completion of honors courses or honors colloquia at the freshman and sophomore levels.

A minimum of 6 credits of honors course work is required for Departmental Honors as well as a thesis or research project for an additional 3 credits.

All honors work is recorded on students' transcripts, and at commencement distinctive sashes are worn by students graduating with All-College or Departmental Honors.

Admission Process: Incoming freshmen who have SAT I scores of at least 580V and 530M and who graduated in the top 30 percent of their high school class are invited to enter the program as are matriculated students with GPAs of 3.3 or better. In special cases, students who do not meet these criteria are also admitted. Admission is rolling.

Scholarship Availability: Each year the College awards approximately nine renewable merit scholarships, covering tuition and fees, to entering freshmen, but these scholarships do not require participation in the Honors Program.

The Campus Context: Located 28 miles southwest of Boston in a picturesque, rural-turned-suburban New England town, Bridgewater State College has a dual mission: to educate its students while using its intellectual and technological resources to advance the economic and cultural life of the region and the state. Founded in 1840 by Horace Mann as one of the first three "normal" schools in America, Bridgewater today provides a broad array of degree programs through its Schools of Arts and Sciences, Management and Aviation Science, and Education and Allied Studies. One of the newest facilities on the 235-acre campus is the John Joseph Moakley Center for Technological Applications, a 50,000-square-foot facility dedicated to harnessing the power of emerging technologies for teaching and learning.

Student Body Undergraduate enrollment is 7,320; 61 percent of the students are women. Seventy-six percent are traditional (i.e., 24 years old or younger), 6 percent are minority, 2 percent are international, and 74 percent are commuters. The campus has five national fraternities, three national sororities, and two independent fraternities.

Faculty Full-time instructional faculty members number 262, 80 percent of whom hold the highest degrees in their fields. The student-faculty ratio is 22:1.

Key Facilities Maxwell Library holds approximately 500,000 volumes and subscribes to more than 1,500 periodicals and newspapers; there are also extensive microfilm, microfiche, and electronic resources. The entire campus, including offices, classrooms, and residence halls, is wired for voice, video, and data transmission. Through the Moakley Center for Technological Applications, the campus will shortly be connected to Boston and the rest of the world by fiber-optic cable.

Interpreting the symbols: **2**=two-year college, **4**=four-year college; **Pu**=public or state college, **Pr**=private college; **G**=general honors program; **D**=departmental honors program; **S**=small program (fewer than 100 students), **M**=midsize program (100 to 500 students), **L**=large program (more than 500 students); **Sc**=scholarships available in honors program; **Tr**=transfer students accepted into honors program; **HBC**=historically black college; **AA**=academic advisors; **GA**=graduate advisors; **FA**=fellowship advisors.

Honorary Societies Gamma Sigma Alpha, The Order of Omega, and Pi Kappa Delta

Athletics The College fields twenty-two intercollegiate varsity sports teams and is a member of the National Collegiate Athletic Association (NCAA) Division III, the Eastern Collegiate Athletic Conference (ECAC), and the Massachusetts State College Athletic Conference (MASCAC).

Study Abroad Bridgewater has formal student exchange agreements with Acadia University (Nova Scotia, Canada) and Manchester Metropolitan University (England). Through the Quebec/New England Exchange, students can study at more than a dozen institutions including Concordia, Laval, McGill, and Montreal universities, and through the Nova Scotia/New England Exchange, opportunities are available at thirteen additional institutions. During the summer, the College operates a three-week study program offering courses in art, history, literature, and political science/law at Wadham College, Oxford (England).

Support Services The Disability Services Office is committed to making the College's facilities, services, and programs accessible to all students.

Job Opportunities In addition to the Federal Work-Study Program, Bridgewater provides employment opportunities both on and off campus through the Student Employment Center.

Tuition: $1150 for residents, $6450 for nonresidents, per year (1998–99)

Room and board:$4302–$4512

Mandatory Fees: $2383.40

Contact: Director: Dr. Charles C. Nickerson, Honors Center, Harrington Hall, Bridgewater, Massachusetts 02325; Telephone: 508-697-1378; Fax: 508-697-1336; E-mail: cnickerson@bridgew.edu

Brigham Young University

4 Pr G L Tr AA FA

▼ University Honors Program

The Brigham Young University Honors Program was founded in 1960 and is one of the oldest programs of its kind.

Honors education at BYU provides an unusually rich and challenging experience for capable and motivated undergraduate students. Honors education is not merely a more intensive general education or a more strenuous program in a major; rather, it attempts to link the broad university perspective with the specific concentration associated with a major. Students who pursue honors education at BYU are offered the challenge of honors courses that form a part of their general education, as well as an intensive experience in their major. Honors education is open to all capable and motivated students and only requires that students have a formal commitment of intent to graduate with University Honors, register for at least one honors course each semester for the first two years in the program, and maintain a 3.5 GPA.

The most important advantage of enrolling in honors is the opportunity to participate in demanding, high-quality courses taught by some of the University's best professors. In addition, honors provides a stimulating learning environment outside formal course settings. Honors offers a curriculum core consisting of two semesters in civilization and in intensive writing. Beyond this core, honors colloquia, seminars, and departmental honors courses provide a variety of experiences for honors students in the historical development of ideas, cultures, arts, letters, and the sciences. Recent colloquia have included Use and Misuse of Human and Natural Resources: Man's Role in Changing the Face of the Earth, The Pen and the Sword: A Study of Writing About How Human Civilization Seeks Peace and Suffers War, The Daedalus Project, Memoir and Imagination, and Shaping the Modern Mind. Recent seminars have included Women's Issues in the Natural Sciences, Wilderness Writing, and Bioethics.

Students in honors benefit most directly from their association with fellow honors students and with honors faculty members. To encourage interaction among students outside the classroom, special on-campus housing for honors students is available. In addition, honors students also have a center in the Karl G. Maeser Memorial Building, which provides them with a quiet study hall, a commons room for informal meetings and discussion, an advisement center, and classrooms. HSAC, the Honors Student Advisory Council, plans many activities for honors students throughout the semester, including lectures, dances, retreats, and outings. The Honors Program publishes the scholarly work of students in *Insight*, an intellectual journal with an all-student staff. A special series of art exhibitions are sponsored in the Maeser Building.

There are approximately 3,000 committed honors students, with more than 8,000 students participating in some aspect of honors.

Participation Requirements: There are certain requirements for students to graduate with University Honors. Students must take 22 credit hours of honors courses (including some required courses), two semesters of foreign language, and calculus, principles of statistics, or advanced logic; meet with an Honors Program representative for advisement at least once each year; demonstrate familiarity with the Great Works of Literature, Art, Music, Theater, and Film by turning in a portfolio of one-page responses to the works and also submitting a portfolio of work representing each semester of undergraduate study and a one-page description of ongoing service to the community for review by the Honors Deans; submit a proposal for an honors thesis during the junior year; and submit a finished honors thesis and pass a thesis defense with a committee of Honors Deans and faculty members during the senior year.

Scholarship Availability: Though BYU offers a variety of scholarships, the Honors Program itself does not. Most honors students hold, or are eligible for, some kind of scholarship. The Honors Program coordinates information and advisement for many graduate scholarships, grants, and fellowships. Money is available directly from the Honors Program to aid in thesis research.

The Campus Context: There are twelve colleges and schools on campus: the College of Biology and Agriculture; the David O. McKay School of Education; the College of Engineering and Technology; the College of Family, Home, and Social Sciences; the College of Fine Arts and Communications; the College of Humanities; the College of Nursing; the College of Physical and Mathematical Sciences; the College of Health and Human Performance; the J. Rueben Clark Law School; the J. Willard and Alice S. Marriot School of Management; and Graduate Studies. In all, there are 217 degree programs.

Student Body There are approximately 29,000 undergraduates enrolled. The student body is relatively balanced in terms of gender, with approximately 50 percent women and 50 percent men. Ethnic minorities compose 10 percent of the student body, with 0.4 percent African American, 0.5 percent Native American, 3.4 percent Asian and Pacific Islanders, 3 percent Hispanic, and 2.7 percent other. Since BYU is restricted by law from requiring students to provide information about race, these figures are voluntary and may not represent a complete picture. There were 1,781 daytime international students enrolled at BYU during winter semester 2001. Of all the students, 78 percent reside off campus. All BYU students receive tuition subsidization from the LDS Church; 66 percent of these students receive additional financial aid. There are no sororities or fraternities at Brigham Young University.

Faculty There are 2,000 faculty members; 1,589 are full-time. Of the full-time faculty members, 78 percent have doctoral degrees,

40 percent are full professors, 31 percent are associate professors, 25 percent are assistant professors, 3 percent are instructors, and 1 percent have other designations or are on leave. The student-faculty ratio is 15:1.

Key Facilities The University's 638-acre campus includes 121 buildings for the University's academic programs, 81 for administration and physical plant services, and 281 buildings for student housing. Major campus construction projects include the recently completed Ezra Taft Benson Science Building; expansion of the J. Reuben Clark Law Library, the Harold B. Lee Library, and the Dairy Products Lab (BYU Creamery); and renovations to the Eyring Science Center, the Ernest L. Wilkinson Center, and the bookstore. There are more than 3 million volumes in the library. There are many computer facilities.

Honorary Societies Phi Eta Sigma, Phi Kappa Phi, and Golden Key

Athletics BYU has a well-established athletic tradition, repeatedly achieving national rankings and recognition. Its intercollegiate program includes nine men's teams and eleven women's teams. The 2000–01 Mountain West Conference ended a historic season for BYU athletics, as twenty of its twenty-one teams participated in postseason competition and won sixteen of nineteen championships—the most titles BYU has won in a year. As a result of BYU teams' success, the combined Cougar program finished seventeenth in the nation in the 2000–01 Sears Directors' Cup, a national tally of the strength of overall athletic programs administered by the National Association of Collegiate Directors of Athletics (NACDA) and sponsored by Sears. The Cougars have claimed men's national championships in volleyball (1999), football (1984), golf (1981), and outdoor track (1970) as well as two NIT championships in basketball (1966, 1951). BYU has won two women's national titles in cross-country (1997, 1999). BYU's football team has won the WAC championships for eighteen of the past thirty-five years and tied first in the inaugural season of the Mountain West Conference. Other sports have performed on a comparable level. Men's outdoor track has also won eighteen of thirty-five possible championships, and women's volleyball has won nineteen conference titles in twenty-eighty years.

Study Abroad Study-abroad programs are open to students from all majors. Students need not be formally admitted to BYU to participate in study abroad, and BYU credit may be transferred to other institutions. Semester and/or term programs are offered in many countries in Asia, Europe, South and Central America, and Africa. These programs feature intensive studies in such disciplines as the arts, history, government, and language. Specialized study in other fields may also be offered.

Support Services BYU has established the Services for Students with Disabilities Office. The purpose of this office is to assure that students are provided access to University programs. Mobility impaired students are encouraged to seek help in ensuring the accessibility of classes and other facilities. Hearing impaired students may obtain the services of qualified sign language interpreters and TDD communications by contacting this office. A list of volunteer readers is maintained for visually impaired or learning disabled students. BYU also provides services for students with other forms of disability.

Job Opportunities Students are employed all over campus at jobs ranging from research and cafeteria work to secretarial work and grounds maintenance. Full-time students can work as many as 20 hours a week on campus.

Tuition: $2940 minimum for LDS church members, $4600 for nonmembers full-time, per year; $312 part-time, per credit (2000–01)

Room and Board: $4400–$4700

Contact: Associate Dean: J. Scott, 350-C MSRB, Box 22600, Provo, Utah 84602-2600; Telephone: 801-422-5225; Fax: 801-422-5976; E-mail: honors@byu.edu; Web site: http://ucs.byu.edu/gened/honors

BROOKLYN COLLEGE OF THE CITY UNIVERSITY OF NEW YORK

4 Pu G M Tr AA

▼ Honors Academy

The Honors Academy at Brooklyn College, established in 1959 with a grant from the Ford Foundation, federates seven honors programs. Each offers distinctive mentoring and direction, access to the Academy's commons room, honors seminars and colloquia, and honors sections of Brooklyn College's nationally recognized core curriculum. The Honors Academy's balanced interdisciplinary curriculum includes humanities, social sciences, and natural sciences.

Four Honors Academy programs accept students from high school. The CUNY Honors College, a University-wide program, integrates honors offerings at seven City University of New York colleges. The Scholars Program offers a four-year interdisciplinary liberal arts education and is open to matriculated and transfer students up to 48 credits. The B.A.-M.D. Program guarantees entrance to medical school at the State University of New York Health Science Center at Brooklyn. Engineering Honors guarantees entrance to Brooklyn's Polytechnic University to complete a degree in engineering.

The upper-division programs focus on disciplinary study. The Mellon Minority Fellowship prepares students for graduate studies leading to college and university teaching. Dean's List–Honors Research integrates departmental honors with the Honors Academy goals and curriculum. The Senior Colloquium supports Honors Academy students researching and writing a senior thesis. The Honors Academy's unique Special Baccalaureate Degree Program offers Honors Academy membership to exceptional nontraditional students attending classes evenings and weekends.

The Honors Academy at Brooklyn College assumes that honors education is intrinsically collaborative. The Academy encourages students to contribute actively to each other's intellectual growth and educational development. Its commons room provides optimum conditions for students, widely diverse in background and interests, to identify one another, mentor one another, learn informally from one another, and work together. Honors Academy students also contribute to the community at large as peer tutors and as Presidential Ambassadors, representing the College to the interested general public.

Participation Requirements: Honors Academy members take honors sections of core studies courses and interdisciplinary honors seminars. Entering freshmen take two semesters of honors-level instruction in writing and research. The Honors Academy precisely coordinates B.A.-M.D. and Engineering Honors courses with medical school and engineering school requirements. The curricula of two upper-division programs have been designed in cooperation with the foundations that established or sustain them, Ford and Mellon. Dean's List–Honors Research students contract with their major departments for individually tailored programs. Special Baccalaureate students pursue intensive liberal studies in seminars designed to accommodate constraints imposed by work and home.

Interpreting the symbols: **2**=two-year college, **4**=four-year college; **Pu**=public or state college, **Pr**=private college; **G**=general honors program; **D**=departmental honors program; **S**=small program (fewer than 100 students), **M**=midsize program (100 to 500 students), **L**=large program (more than 500 students); **Sc**=scholarships available in honors program; **Tr**=transfer students accepted into honors program; **HBC**=historically black college; **AA**=academic advisors; **GA**=graduate advisors; **FA**=fellowship advisors.

Graduation from all Honors Academy programs requires at least a 3.5 GPA. Graduation from the Scholars Program and Mellon Fellowship requires a senior thesis.

Admission Process: Students apply to the CUNY Honors College, B.A.-M.D., Engineering Honors, and the Scholars Program from high school using the CUNY university honors application form. Application includes SAT I scores, a personal essay, and letters of recommendation. The median combined SAT I score of entering students is currently 1260. Transfer and matriculated students may also enter the Scholars Program with up to 48 credits with faculty recommendation and a minimum 3.5 GPA. Entrance to upper-division programs (Mellon, Dean's List–Honors Research, and Senior Colloquium) requires at least a 3.5 GPA. Acceptance by the Special Baccalaureate Degree Program requires demonstration of exceptional accomplishment without benefit of a college diploma and other indications of academic potential.

Scholarship Availability: The Honors Academy does not make scholarship awards. Brooklyn College currently awards most freshman-entry Honors Academy students a four-year, full-tuition Presidential Scholarship.

The Campus Context: Founded in 1930 as a commuter college, Brooklyn College now enrolls about 14,000 students. The College is situated in the geographic center of New York State's Kings County, the Borough of Brooklyn. As one of the nine undergraduate colleges of the City University of New York, it offers bachelor's and master's degrees in more than thirty disciplines. It comprises, in part, the NEH-endowed Wolfe Institute for the Humanities, a Conservatory of Music, an Institute for the Study of American Music, a Master of Fine Arts in Writing program, the nation's first program in children's studies, a graduate program in health science, and programs in accountancy, computer science, speech therapy, and other areas of professional specialization. Its urban archaeology program leads research throughout New York City. Brooklyn College offers courses through the University's Graduate Center leading to a Ph.D. in diverse disciplines and is affiliated with the University's summer Greek and Latin Institute.

Student Body The Honors Academy's 300 students reflect the Brooklyn College student body at large. About 18 percent are of Asian background, 3 percent Hispanic, 12 percent African American, 63 percent women, 47 percent men. Between 60 and 70 percent of Honors Academy students work off campus, some supporting families and themselves.

Tuition: $3500 for New York State residents, $6800 for nonresidents per year (1998–99)

Contact: Director: Kenneth A. Bruffee, Honors Academy, Brooklyn, New York 11210; Telephone: 718-951-4114; Fax: 718-951-5249; E-mail: kbruffee@brooklyn.cuny.edu

Broome Community College

2 Pu G S Sc

▼ Honors Program

The Honors Program at Broome Community College (BCC) is designed for students whose academic ability and personal motivation are so high that existing College programs may not fully challenge them. The BCC Honors Program provides academic opportunities that enrich the traditional educational experience. These opportunities may include working closely with honors faculty members in both regular and seminar classes, studying with other highly motivated students, conducting advanced research projects, participating in conferences and cultural events, qualifying for study-abroad programs and intercollegiate scholarship opportunities, and receiving assistance in securing internships in research and employment. This year, the program began offering a five-day "exploration" in Washington, D.C.

The Honors Program is open to any student across the campus, but so far primarily students in the liberal arts and sciences division have utilized the program. Other students in programs that emphasize transfer to a four-year institution have also entered the program.

BCC Honors Program courses are known for their smaller class size, emphasis on participatory learning styles and learning community methods, stimulating and dedicated faculty members, and an interdisciplinary focus. The program includes regular courses with an enrichment option, advanced-level seminars, honors-level independent study courses, and honors sections of regular courses. However offered, extensive writing and participation by the student are expected components of any course.

To complete the entire honors curriculum, students must acquire college credits holding an honors designation. These are arranged among two general education honors courses, one honors course in the matriculated major field, one interdisciplinary honors seminar, and one honors-level independent study. The heart of the program is the interdisciplinary honors seminar. In this 4-credit course, a small number of students and 2 honors faculty members engage in intensive study of a designated theme. The theme varies each semester; recent investigations have looked at war and peace in American history and literature, leadership development, and the family as myth, metaphor, and reality. Honors faculty members are presently planning two new seminars centering on the underside of the American dream and on local history and architecture. Another important element of the Honors Program is the enriched option. This creates a negotiated honors level to a regular course and involves close and sustained engagement between the instructor and the individual student.

Participation Requirements: In order to complete the entire Honors Program, students must acquire 14 honors-designated credits with a minimum grade of B. An overall GPA of at least 3.5 is the norm for admission and continuation. In enriched courses, students are expected to solicit the agreement of each professor with whom they wish to work.

Honors Program scholarship recipients receive special recognition at a campuswide awards ceremony each spring. Transcripts are annotated for each successfully completed honors course, and each honors graduate receives a certificate of recognition.

Admission Process: Students apply to the program during the first week of the semester or during the advisement process in the previous semester. High school test scores and current GPA are examined as are two recommendations. Each student must meet with the Honors Director.

Scholarship Availability: Small scholarships may be available, depending on the continuing generosity of donors, the number of students enrolled in the program, and successful progress toward completion of the program.

The Campus Context: Broome Community College, founded in 1946, is a student-centered community of learners dedicated to providing commuter students with ambiance and services comparable to residential campuses. Forty-five degree programs are offered in the liberal arts, business, allied health, and technology. There is a great issues academic theme each year. Individualized career and personal counseling are also offered.

Student Body There are 4,419 total undergraduates, 2,509 enrolled as first-time, first-year students; 367 as transfer students. Seventy-three percent of students enrolled in transfer programs go on to four-year colleges. Thirty percent of the students are part-time, 2 percent are from out-of-state, 16 percent are 25 or older, and 56 percent are women. The College offers many activities, clubs, and organizations to enhance student life.

Faculty There are 333 faculty members, of whom 44 percent are full-time. Twelve percent have terminal degrees, 3 percent are members of minority groups, and 55 percent are women.

Key Facilities There are 300 computer workstations in the library and computer center. Commuter students can connect to the campus network. E-mail accounts are available for all students. There are a computer-aided design and computer-aided manufacturing laboratories.

Athletics The College participates in NJCAA sports. Intercollegiate baseball (M), basketball, cross-country, golf (M), soccer, softball (W), tennis (M), and volleyball (W) are offered as are intramural basketball, cross-country, and volleyball. *Support Services* Services are offered for learning disabled students as well as for visually, hearing, and speech impaired students.

Tuition and fees: $2401 for residents, $4669 for nonresidents (1997–98)

Contact: Director: Professor Margaret Wingate, Department of History, P.O. Box 1017, Binghamton, New York 13902; Telephone: 607-778-5098; Fax: 607-778-5394; E-mail: wingate_g@sunybroome.edu; Web site: http://www.sunybroome.edu

Broward Community College

2 Pu G L Sc Tr

▼ Honors Institute

The Honors Institute is a comprehensive honors program that offers honors classes and Phi Theta Kappa chapters on three campuses. The students strive toward excellence in the four hallmarks of scholarship, leadership, service, and fellowship that are promoted in all Phi Theta Kappa chapters. In addition to the honors curriculum, there are honors extracurricular programs that enrich the students' college experiences. For example, the Brain Bowl Team and Mathematics Team provide opportunities for academic competition and teamwork among the participants. Both teams have won numerous state and national honors. The Brain Bowl Team has won the regional championship for eleven years.

Students are encouraged to achieve through a program of recognition, including nominations to the National Dean's List and Who's Who as well as receptions and a convocation where university scholarships are awarded.

The Honors Institute is a national leader in the percentage of graduates who receive university scholarships. More than 90 percent of all graduates have continued at universities across the country on scholarship.

The Honors Institute is nineteen years old. College-wide, there are more than 600 students enrolled in honors classes.

Participation Requirements: Honors students take a minimum of 18 credits in honors classes, small seminar-type classes that emphasize writing, research, and critical and creative thinking.

Admission Process: Students who graduate in the top 10 percent of their Broward County high school class are eligible for scholarships to the Honors Institute. Other admission criteria include overall GPA, SAT I scores, faculty member recommendations, and interviews. The deadline for applying is March 1.

Scholarship Availability: Most high school students who qualify for the Honors Institute receive scholarships based on high school performance that cover the two years at Broward Community College. Upon graduation from the Honors Institute, almost all students are awarded continuing scholarships to in-state and out-of-state universities.

The Campus Context: Broward Community College is composed of four campuses, three with honors coordinators, classes, and Phi Theta Kappa advisers and chapters. The College offers sixty-four degree programs leading to the A.A. and fifty programs leading to the A.S. as well as twenty certificate programs and six Advanced Technical Certificates.

Distinguishing facilities on campus include a planetarium and allied health service.

Student Body There are 25,000 students are enrolled, of whom 60 percent are women. The student body is equally composed of African American, white, and Hispanic students. There are 6,000 international students. Of the students, approximately 50 percent receive financial aid. Broward has no fraternities or sororities.

Faculty There are 350 full-time and 750 part-time faculty members. Twenty-five percent of the faculty members have terminal degrees. The student-faculty ratio is 25:1.

Key Facilities The University Library (combined Florida International University/Florida Atlantic University, BCC) houses 220,000 volumes. There are six computer facilities, five IBM and one Macintosh.

Honorary Societies Phi Theta Kappa

Athletics Athletics available are swimming, tennis, baseball, basketball, and soccer.

Study Abroad The study-abroad program is extensive with programs located across the globe. Students can spend a semester in Europe or South America. They can go on a two- to four-week seminar study tour to Europe, South America, or the Orient. The College's comprehensive International Program includes study-abroad opportunities in England, Spain, Israel, Mexico, and South America. The Honors Institute offered its first International Study Abroad Program in Ecuador in 1997.

Support Services Students with disabilities are provided with study aids and assistants. All classroom buildings are wheelchair accessible.

Job Opportunities Work opportunities on campus include work-study programs on and off campus, job placement, and work community/scholarships.

Tuition: $1402.50 for state residents, $5266.50 for nonresidents, per year (based on 30 credit hours per year) (2001–02)

Contact: Director: Dr. Irmgard Bocchino, 3501 SW Davie Road, Davie, Florida 33314; Telephone: 954-475-6613; Fax: 954-423-6423

Bryant College

4 Pr G S Tr

▼ Honors Program

The current Honors Program at Bryant College represents an expansion and a new focus for the small program that was previously in place. It is designed to be a community of scholars, excellent students who are interested in a career in business but who also want a strong grounding in the liberal arts. Honors courses are offered in both business subjects and humanities, in small classes (usually 8 to 18 students) taught by the College's best instructors.

Honors Program members may also participate in a variety of off-campus excursions to events of cultural, historical, or business interest, and special on-campus dinners are arranged each semester. Forty-three freshmen are enrolled in the program during this, its first year. An optional honors residence floor is a strong possibility for the future.

Participation Requirements: Students must complete at least eight 3-credit honors courses in order to become Honors Program graduates, recognized at commencement and on transcripts and diplomas. The final course is a capstone course, a seminar that

Interpreting the symbols: **2**=two-year college, **4**=four-year college; **Pu**=public or state college, **Pr**=private college; **G**=general honors program; **D**=departmental honors program; **S**=small program (fewer than 100 students), **M**=midsize program (100 to 500 students), **L**=large program (more than 500 students); **Sc**=scholarships available in honors program; **Tr**=transfer students accepted into honors program; **HBC**=historically black college; **AA**=academic advisors; **GA**=graduate advisors; **FA**=fellowship advisors.

requires an independent, term-long project, supervised by a panel of instructors. Students must achieve a minimum overall GPA of 3.5, with at least a 3.2 in honors courses, to graduate in the program.

Admission Process: Freshman applicants for the Honors Program must have a minimum total SAT I score of 1200 (or equivalent ACT) and must rank in the top 20 percent of their high school class. Students who are not ranked by their high schools need a high school GPA of at least 3.5. Other students may apply to join the program later if they have earned at least a 3.5 GPA during their time at Bryant or another college.

Scholarship Availability: Although the Honors Program does not offer scholarships directly, virtually all Honors Program members receive academic scholarships from the College.

The Campus Context: Bryant College, founded in 1863, is dedicated to preparing students for success in life and business. The College is among the sixteen percent of the nation's business programs accredited by AACSB–The International Association for Management Education. Bryant offers a rich, comprehensive curriculum that requires study in both business and the liberal arts. The emphasis on cross-disciplinary thinking fosters innovative problem-solving skills and a global market perspective.

Students may pursue a Bachelor of Science in business administration degree with concentrations in accounting, applied actuarial mathematics, computer information systems, finance, financial services, management, and marketing. Bachelor of Arts in liberal sciences concentrations include communications, economics, English, history, and international studies. Business students must minor in a liberal arts discipline.

Bryant College is situated on 387 acres in suburban Smithfield, Rhode Island. The secure campus is just 15 minutes from the state capital of Providence, with its restaurants, cafes, theaters, and clubs; 1 hour from Boston; and 3 hours from New York City.

Student Body Total undergraduate enrollment is 2,886 (59 percent men, 41 percent women). Eighty-five percent are enrolled full-time and 15 percent are enrolled part-time. The racial/ethnic breakdown is 86 percent white, 2 percent Hispanic, 2 percent African American, 3 percent Asian, 0.2 percent Native American, 5 percent nonresident alien, and 1 percent unknown. Eighty-seven percent of full-time undergraduates receive some form of financial aid. There are eight national fraternities and four national sororities.

Faculty The total number of undergraduate faculty members is 182, of whom 112 are full-time. Eighty percent of the full-time undergraduate faculty members have terminal degrees. The student-faculty ratio is 18:1.

Key Facilities The Edith M. Hodgson Memorial Library contains 132,716 volumes, 12,831 microform items, and 807 audio and video items.

The Koffler Technology Center contains more than 140 state-of-the-art Pentium personal computers, provided on a high-speed network. The facilities are available for student use to assist in homework studies, classroom assignments, hands-on training, group projects, e-mail access, or for research via the high-speed Internet connection to the World Wide Web. Included in Koffler is the Discovery Lab, where specialized tools such as digital cameras, photographic printers, video capture devices, sound systems, and CD-ROM writers are used to explore applications to create multimedia, Webcasting, and microcomputer systems architecture.

Athletics Bryant is a member of the NCAA Division II, ECAC, Northeast-10, and Eastern Football Conference. Intercollegiate sports include men's and women's basketball, cross-country, golf, soccer, tennis, and indoor and outdoor track; men's lacrosse; women's field hockey and volleyball; baseball, football, and softball. Athletic and recreation facilities available include a 2,700-seat gymnasium; fitness center; tennis courts, squash and racquetball courts, and three multipurpose indoor recreation courts; a 400-meter track; cross-country trails; playing fields for baseball, softball, lacrosse, soccer, football, and field hockey; and a 2,500-seat competition stadium (national grass surface).

Study Abroad Bryant's study-abroad opportunities provide all students with a semester, a summer, or even a full academic year of study in another country. Students have the chance to become proficient in another language, gain a global perspective, and have fun learning while enjoying experiences in a different culture. Students interested in study abroad may select from a variety of programs all over the world. Bryant has established several exchange opportunities and offers sponsored study-abroad programs in most regions of the world through U.S.-based colleges and universities. Study abroad is offered in Japan, Great Britain, Spain, Australia, Canada, France, Germany, Greece, Ireland, Italy, Mexico, Switzerland, Costa Rica, Austria, New Zealand, Korea, Taiwan, Chile, Ecuador, Scotland, Singapore, Russia, China, and Thailand.

Support Services The following services are available for physically disabled students: note-taking services, tape recorders, tutors, reader services, interpreters for hearing-impaired, special transportation, special housing, adaptive equipment, Braille services, and special class scheduling. There is a Writing Center and Learning Center. Academic advising and personal, psychological, religious, and career counseling services are also available.

Job Opportunities Students Employment Services assists students seeking part-time employment to help defray the cost of attending college. Students with college work-study awards and other students who show financial need are given priority for on-campus employment. Students are paid an hourly wage (not less than the current federal minimum) that reflects the skills and experience required to do the job.

Tuition: $15,600 (1998–99)

Room and Board: $6700

Contact: Honors Program Coordinator: Dr. Patricia M. Odell, Smithfield, Rhode Island 02917; Telephone: 401-232-6451; E-mail: podell@bryant.edu

BUTLER UNIVERSITY

4 Pr G M Tr

▼ Honors Program

Butler's Honors Program is a university-wide program that fosters interdisciplinary as well as discipline-specific learning through course work, the honors thesis, and cultural events. In the first half of their study, students from all five colleges take courses together and complete an honors curriculum that draws from more than sixty engaging fields of study. Regardless of course choices, students can always count on individualized faculty mentoring and small, interactive classes. In the remaining semesters, students concentrate on their honors thesis, which offers them the chance to work one-on-one with a faculty mentor and to complete a major project or performance. Thesis topics reflect the students' diversity and imagination, which are the hallmarks of the University's Honors Program.

The course work and thesis are complemented by cultural events, which include field trips, workshops, lectures, artistic readings, and performances. While attending these events, students enjoy interaction with inspiring authors, scholars, and artists. The program is also complemented by the activities of the student-run Honors Society, which sponsors volunteer, philanthropic, and social events.

The Honors Program is further enriched by the efforts of the honors faculty advisers, who are trained to aid the students in pursuing their academic, graduate study, and career goals.

The University's highest two Latin honors (summa and magna cum laude) are reserved exclusively for students who complete the Honors Program.

The program is 31 years old. There are 500 students in the program (15 percent of eligible freshmen accept the invitation to participate).

Admission Process: Participation is voluntary. Incoming students who have graduated in the top 7 percent of their high school classes and who have combined SAT I scores of at least 1280 or composite ACT scores of 29 or better are qualified for consideration. The program then issues invitations based on the students' high school academic records, extracurricular/leadership activities, and application essays. Also invited are Butler students who receive a faculty endorsement, achieve a 3.5 GPA or better, and complete 16 credit hours at the end of their first semester (or 32 credit hours at the end of their first year). Transfer students are eligible to apply.

The Campus Context: Butler University is a coeducational, comprehensive institution committed to education in liberal arts and sciences and professional disciplines. The Colleges of Liberal Arts and Sciences, Business, Education, Fine Arts, and Pharmacy and Health Sciences are situated on a 290-acre residential campus with plenty of green space and recreational areas. There are sixty degree programs offered on campus. Facilities on campus include the Holcomb Botanical Garden, historic Hinkle Fieldhouse, Clowes Memorial Hall for performing arts, Holcomb Observatory and Planetarium, and WTBU Television and WRBU Radio studios.

Student Body Undergraduate enrollment is 3,100; 40 percent are men, 60 percent, women. Nine percent of the students are members of minority groups, and 5 percent are international. Resident students comprise 70 percent of the student population, commuters, 30 percent. Eighty-two percent of the students receive financial aid. There are eight fraternities and eight sororities on campus.

Faculty There are 265 full-time faculty members, of whom 83 percent have terminal degrees. There are no teaching assistants at the University. The student-faculty ratio is 13:1.

Key Facilities The library houses 245,000 volumes. The online library resources are extensive. There are eleven Mac or IBM student computer labs on campus as well as access to a VAX mainframe network and the Internet. The residence halls are wired for ethernet.

Athletics Butler is a member of NCAA Division I and participates in the Midwestern Collegiate Conference, Pioneer Football League, and Great Western Lacrosse League. There are eighteen intercollegiate men's and women's sports as well as intramural and club sports.

Study Abroad Butler's Institute for Study Abroad is one of the largest study-abroad programs in the United States and sends students from American colleges and universities to Australia, Ireland, New Zealand, and England. Additional overseas study opportunities are available through International Student Exchange Program and Butler field seminars. Honors students can fulfill part of their course work through overseas study.

Support Services Accommodation, facilities, and resources for disabled students are available.

Job Opportunities One third of Butler students hold campus employment.

Tuition: $18,940

Room and Board: $6450 (average)

Contact: Director: Scott Swanson, 4600 Sunset Avenue, Indianapolis, Indiana 66208; Telephone: 317-940-9680 or 9302; Fax: 317-940-8815; E-mail: honors@butler.edu; Web site: http://www.butler.edu/honors

California State University, Dominguez Hills

4 Pu G M Sc

▼ University Honors Program

California State University, Dominguez Hills' University Honors Program offers high-achieving students a variety of opportunities for enriching their undergraduate studies. Honors students receive the extra stimulation of a special program while participating in the life of the campus at large. They choose their own level of involvement while meeting and learning in the company of their peers.

All components of the program are designed to provide an atmosphere in which committed students may strive for excellence and further the process of self-discovery: "Education is not preparation for life; education is life itself." (John Dewey)

Honors Program students have priority registration privileges and priority consideration for on-campus student housing.

In general studies courses, highly motivated students work in the atmosphere of specially designated sections of the required general studies courses. Several different courses are offered each semester so that, in two years, students can fulfill a large part of their required courses. The courses are taught by outstanding instructors, who encourage students to participate actively in their own education.

Several kinds of upper-division opportunities are available for honors students. Honors contracts enable a student to have the designation "Honors" appended to a given upper-division course by completing more sophisticated work than the instructor asks of the regularly enrolled students. With this option, the student, with the consent and guidance of the instructor, can undertake honors-level study and receive honors credit in a nonhonors course. The honors work undertaken is in addition to, rather than instead of, the regular course work.

The student and faculty member agree at the beginning of the course on the nature of the work to be done for honors credit (examples might include pretesting lab experiments, making one or more special presentations to the class, or creating an annotated bibliography of materials). This agreement, its rationale, and its means of evaluation are specified on a proposal form submitted to the Honors Program Coordinator by the fifth week of the semester.

Special seminar courses are occasionally offered, in which honors students in a particular field of majors (e.g., School of Management students) focus on a topic of mutual interest.

Honors scholars are upper-division Honors Program students who are eligible to apply as apprentices to faculty members in their fields. Apprentices receive a stipend for working with these faculty members on research or teaching-related activities for a semester.

The senior honors thesis enables students to pursue an original project in an area of their interest (usually within a major), culminating in a substantial written report or other appropriate result. Students work under the guidance of a faculty member in the area of interest. Successful completion of the thesis is noted on the student transcript. Students should inquire at the Honors Program office for guidelines and direction.

Participation Requirements: Eligible students may choose as many honors courses in a given semester as they wish, though a

Interpreting the symbols: **2**=two-year college, **4**=four-year college; **Pu**=public or state college, **Pr**=private college; **G**=general honors program; **D**=departmental honors program; **S**=small program (fewer than 100 students), **M**=midsize program (100 to 500 students), **L**=large program (more than 500 students); **Sc**=scholarships available in honors program; **Tr**=transfer students accepted into honors program; **HBC**=historically black college; **AA**=academic advisors; **GA**=graduate advisors; **FA**=fellowship advisors.

minimum of nine courses (out of a required eighteen) are required for the Certificate of Honors in General Studies. Each honors course is specifically noted on the student's transcript and serves as an advantage when applying to graduate school or for employment. These challenging courses provide the basis for a strong liberal education in any major. Honors sections are identified in the class schedule by the designation "H" after the section. Students who are not already members of the Honors Program must receive special permission from the Honors Program coordinator to enroll, on an exceptional basis, in an honors course. Students must be currently active in the program each semester to enjoy priority registration; this can be accomplished by taking an honors class or doing an honors contract, participating on an honors program committee, or attending honors-sponsored activities.

Admission Process: The program is open to undergraduate students from throughout the University. Eligibility is determined by GPA, SAT I scores, and personal interviews. Application forms are available in the program office, SAC 2121. There is a rolling admission.

Scholarship Availability: First-year and transfer students who are eligible for the honors program qualify for the Presidential Honors Scholarship.

The Campus Context: California State University, Dominguez Hills (CSUDH) is located on the historic Rancho San Pedro, the oldest Spanish land grant in the Los Angeles area. Its 346-acre campus is an urban, comprehensive, public university that serves 12,000 students from the greater Los Angeles area. It has the second-most diverse student body in the country, creating a culturally rich and stimulating learning environment. The campus seeks applicants who are committed to educational excellence and is committed to preparing students for leadership in a global society.

Student Body CSUDH, the most ethnically diverse campus in the CSU, has a nontraditional undergraduate student population of 7,676; 69.5 percent are women. African Americans number 29.4 percent; Latino/Latina students comprise 21.8 percent; Asian Americans (including Pacific Islanders), 12.4 percent; and white, 27.5 percent, 1.5 percent of whom are international. Dominguez Hills is predominantly a commuter campus, but it does have on-campus housing. There are 164 furnished apartments located on the northeast corner of the campus. The complex includes thirty-two 1-bedroom, seventy-two 2-bedroom, and sixty 3-bedroom apartments. There are also recreation and meeting rooms, study lounges, laundries, and a computer lab. On the complex grounds are basketball and volleyball courts, a weight room, and a picnic area. Information on housing may be obtained by contacting the Housing Office (310-243-2228). National fraternities and sororities are on campus.

Faculty The faculty numbers 698 (including statewide nursing faculty members). There are 290 full-time faculty members. Ninety-three percent hold terminal degrees.

Key Facilities The University Library serves student research needs with a faculty of 10 (plus a support staff), a book collection of more than 430,000 volumes, more than 678,000 microfilms, and more than 2,500 periodical subscriptions in addition to computerized database services and cooperative agreements with other libraries. The library also houses the University's archives and has been designated by the Board of Trustees as the repository for historical CSU documents of systemwide significance. Campus facilities are constantly being expanded and upgraded for all students in all disciplines. The equipment, software, facilities, and support provide excellent computer services for students, faculty members, and administrative staff of CSU Dominguez Hills.

Honorary Societies Delta Mu Delta—Epsilon Mu chapter, Phi Kappa Phi, Phi Alpha Alpha, Phi Alpha Theta, Sigma Pi Sigma

Athletics The CSU Dominguez Hills athletic department has built a national reputation for athletic and academic achievement. Toro athletics compete nationally at the National Collegiate Athletic Association (NCAA) Division II level. CSU Dominguez Hills is also a member of the California Collegiate Athletic Association (CCAA), which is recognized nationally as the NCAA Division II "Conference of Champions." CSUDH sponsors twelve intercollegiate teams that serve approximately 200 student-athletes: men's and women's basketball and soccer, men's baseball and golf, and women's volleyball, softball, tennis, cross-country, and indoor and outdoor track and field.

Study Abroad The study-abroad program includes the following countries: Australia, Brazil, Canada, Denmark, France, Germany, Israel, Italy, Japan, Korea, Mexico, New Zealand, Spain, Sweden, Taiwan, United Kingdom, and Zimbabwe.

Job Opportunities Work-study and student assistant positions are available in most campus offices and with support services.

Tuition: $753 per semester (full-time)

Room and Board: $2313 (one bedroom), $1788 (two bedrooms), $2613 (three bedrooms)

Mandatory Fees: Application for admission (nonrefundable), $55; late application fee, $15; student activity fees ($70 fall semester, $65 spring semester); $38 student center fee; $3 health facilities fee; $40 health services fee; $5 instructionally related activity fee

Contact: Dr. Joyce Johnson, Coordinator, University Honors Program, CSU Dominguez Hills, 1000 East Victoria Street, Carson, California 90747; Telephone: 310-243-3974; Fax: 310-516-3495; E-mail: jjohnson@dhvx20.csudh.edu

California State University, Los Angeles

4 Pu G M Sc Tr

▼ General Education Honors Program

The University General Education (GE) Honors Program at California State University, Los Angeles (Cal State LA), provides highly qualified students with diverse, enriched, intellectual activities through a separate general education curriculum. The Honors Program offers special sections of lower-division and upper-division general education courses. The University offers at least seven different General Education Honors Program course sections each quarter and more than twenty-five General Education Honors Program sections each year. The GE Honors Program courses include the following honors courses: English, political science, Spanish, geology, anthropology, philosophy, religious studies, history, art, music, dance, speech, critical thinking, mathematics, sociology, psychology, business, and economics. These sections have lower enrollment (approximately 25 students), are limited to honors students, and are taught by renowned faculty members. Honors Program faculty members often experiment with innovative teaching techniques, which include expanded and challenging course requirements.

The General Education Honors Program coordinates membership with other honors organizations on campus. GE Honors Program students are frequently selected as Cal State LA Phi Kappa Phi Outstanding Freshmen of the Year. Program students receive priority registration privileges. Augmenting the extensive academic part of the GE Honors Program are curriculum-related enrichment opportunities and social events. An annual David Lawrence Memorial Lecture brings creative, cutting-edge faculty members and outside experts to lecture to the Honors Program and campus community. An Annual Honors Preview and Awards Dinner brings honors faculty members, student members (new, returning, and alumni), their families and friends, and campus administrators together for an evening of interaction and networking. It is an opportunity for faculty members to showcase their honors courses for the coming year, for the program to honor the Outstanding Honors Students of the Year, and to present honors faculty members with specially designed awards. Annual receptions are held to recognize the Outstanding Honors Professor of the Year, Graduating Honors Seniors, and Retiring Honors Faculty. These events, along with a quarterly honors newsletter, are planned and sponsored by the GE Honors Club Board of Directors.

General Education Honors Program students remain in the program throughout the four years of their baccalaureate degree programs as long as they remain members in good standing. The University's students are as diverse as the program curriculum. They include entering freshmen with outstanding high school academic records; students entering the University through the Early Entrance Program (EEP) who range in age from 11 to 16 and number approximately 20 new admits per year; and returning students who have actively participated in careers, particularly within the arts, and are coming back to Cal State LA to complete their bachelor's degree. The University's Honors Program creates opportunities for high-potential students and faculty members to establish closer educational and personal relationships and prepare students for participation in the upper-division Departmental Honors Program.

The Cal State LA General Education Honors Program has been in existence since 1978.

There are approximately 350 students retaining active membership in the program each year.

Participation Requirements: To retain active membership in the program, honors students must maintain a minimum cumulative 3.3 GPA, complete a minimum of six general education courses as honors (two per year), and complete 12 hours per year, 4 of which must be for the GE Honors Program or club service. General Education Honors scholarship recipients are required to complete eight General Education Honors courses (four per year) within their first two years in residence. Students admitted to General Education Honors with Advanced Placement credit(s) fulfill the general education course requirement(s) but not the requirement to take a minimum of six to eight general education courses as honors.

Students who complete all requirements of the Honors Program graduate with a University General Education Honors notation on their transcript. They also receive a special honors certificate of graduation signed by the president of the University. In the year of their entrance to the Honors Program, the General Education Honors students receive special recognition and certificates at the University's annual Honors Convocation.

Admission Process: Freshmen are invited to join the Honors Program based on their high school average (3.3 GPA and above) and their SAT I scores (1000 and above). Sophomores and transfer students who have a minimum of six general education courses to complete and a minimum 3.0 GPA and above may also apply for admission.

Scholarship Availability: The General Education Honors Program offers scholarships for entering freshmen and continuing students. First-Time Freshmen Scholarships that carry a stipend of $1000 per year for four years are available. Entering freshmen with at least a 3.6 high school GPA and a score of at least 1080 on the SAT I are encouraged to apply. One to two scholarships per quarter that carry a stipend of $500 are awarded to students continuing in the GE Honors Program. Applicants must apply directly through the General Education Honors Program. Recipients of the scholarships are required to join the General Education Honors Program and complete eight General Education Honors courses within their first two years at the University. They must maintain a minimum cumulative 3.0 GPA and complete at least 36 quarter units of course work in each academic year.

The Campus Context: California State University, Los Angeles, is a comprehensive University that was founded in 1947 by action of the California State Legislature. It is one of twenty-three California State University campuses. It is located at the eastern edge of Los Angeles and adjacent to the western San Gabriel Valley cities of Alhambra and Monterey Park. Cal State LA occupies nearly 200 acres on a hilltop site that once housed one of California's thirty-six original adobes, built in 1776 by Franciscan missionaries and destroyed by fire in 1908. Cal State LA overlooks mountains to the north, the San Gabriel Valley to the east, metropolitan Los Angeles to the west, and the Palos Verdes Peninsula and Catalina Island to the south.

The Los Angeles Civic Center is 5 miles west of the campus. Cal State LA comprises six colleges: the College of Business and Economics; the College of Arts and Letters; the Charter College Education; the College of Engineering, Computer Science, and Technology; the College of Health and Human Services; and the College of Natural and Social Sciences. Cal State LA is distinguished by having the largest number of system-wide Outstanding Professors of the Year. Cal State LA boasts more alumni in the California Legislature than any other California State University; 5 alumni are members of the United States Congress. More than fifty degree programs are offered.

Student Body Undergraduate enrollment is 19,000 students (62.2 percent women). The ethnic distribution of the student body is 0.5 percent Native American, 21.6 percent Asian American/ Pacific Islander, 8.4 percent African American, 53.2 percent Latino, and 16.4 percent white. There are more than 1,500 international students who come from 125 countries around the world. Approximately 88 percent of students are commuters. Approximately 49 percent of students receive financial aid. There are six active sororities, three active fraternities, and twenty-three honors societies.

Faculty Of the 1,031 faculty members, 633 are full-time and 98–99 percent hold terminal degrees. The student-faculty ratio is 30:1.

Key Facilities Campus facilities include the Harriet and Charles Luckman Fine Arts Complex, which was opened in 1994 and houses a large theater and visual arts gallery; the Royal Center of Applied Gerontology; the Anna Bing Arnold Child Center; and the Edmund G. "Pat" Brown Institute of Public Affairs, a prestigious center that focuses on major issues facing the region and the state. The School of Engineering and Technology is particularly proud of its three world-class solar electric vehicles—the Solar Eagle I, II, and III. The Roger Wagner Center for Choral Studies, the Southern California Ocean Studies Institute (SCOSI), and the World Trade Center are also well-known.

The library houses 1 million books and periodicals. There are over eight open-access, self-instructional, and specialized computer technology labs on campus that include IBM-compatible and Macintosh computers. Informational services available through these labs include Netscape, the World Wide Web, and online educational information resources such as LEXIS-NEXIS, Legislate, and FEDIX. In addition to these information resources, the University also provides access to online card catalogs of various educational sources such as Melvyl (UC libraries card catalog), the Library of Congress, OPAC (in-house library card catalog), and LIBS (U.S./World Libraries).

Athletics More than 300 of the University's undergraduates are enrolled in the intercollegiate athletics program. In athletics, the Cal State LA Golden Eagles compete in eleven intercollegiate sports. The University fields six men's teams (cross-country, soccer, basketball, baseball, track, and tennis) and five women's teams (volleyball, cross-country, basketball, track, and tennis). At the national level, the Golden Eagles compete in Division II of the National Collegiate Athletic Association (NCAA). Locally,

Cal State LA is a member of the California Collegiate Athletic Association (CCAA). Since 1990, Cal State LA has produced 18 national champions and 98 All-Americans as part of a total intercollegiate athletics program, which includes 18 Olympians (4 gold medalists, 2 of them in the 1984 Olympic Summer Games).

Study Abroad Cal State LA offers numerous opportunities for students through exchange and study-abroad programs. These include periods of study from a semester to a full academic year through such programs as the California State University International Programs, the International Student Exchange program, Fulbright and Rotary fellowships, and short-term language and cultural study programs. The University's students are provided opportunities to study at more than 100 universities across the United States. The international programs serve the needs of students in more than 100 designated academic majors. The CSU International Programs are affiliated with thirty-six recognized universities and institutions of higher education in sixteen countries.

Support Services There are a number of support services available at Cal State LA through the Office for Students with Disabilities. This office supports and assists students from admissions to graduation. Specific services include disability-related advisement, priority registration, handicapped parking, faculty liaison, and coordination of readers, note takers, sign language interpreters, test proctors, and tutors (disability specific).

Job Opportunities Work-study and student assistant positions are available through the campus Center for Career Planning and Placement.

Tuition: None for state residents, $7872 for nonresidents, per year (2001–02)

Mandatory Fees: Full-time, $1778.25 per year; part-time, per quarter, $392.75 for the first 6 units, $592.75 for 6.1 units or more

Contact: Director: Professor Diane Vernon, Library Palmer Wing 1040A, 5151 State University Drive, Los Angeles, California 90032-8165; Telephone: 323-343-4960; Fax: 323-343-6311; E-mail: dvernon@calstatela.edu; Web site: http://web.calstatela.edu/academic/gehp/

California University of Pennsylvania

4 Pu G M Sc Tr

▼ Honors Program

The Honors Program has a flexible curriculum, which allows students in any major to participate and complete both their individual major and their Honors Program. The specific mission of the Honors Program is to help students prepare for the next phase in their lives after graduation. The Honors Program provides an enhanced educational experience for the most talented students and faculty members in small courses and a personalized environment. Each spring, the Honors Program sponsors a grouping of courses from several academic disciplines arranged to give students a truly interdisciplinary experience. The spring curriculum is rotated each year through a varying emphasis on science, arts and humanities, and social sciences. The program includes an extended field trip experience at significant locales.

The Honors Program has existed since 1980, admits approximately 75 students each year, and has 190 students currently enrolled in the program.

Participation Requirements: The Honors Program is a four-year program that culminates in the writing and oral presentation of a thesis project. Typically, first-year students take two semesters of honors composition courses (6 credits) and the Honors Program orientation course, which functions as a first-year seminar. The Honors Program minimally requires the successful completion of 24 honors credits (eight courses), which includes the senior thesis project. Honors Program students are required to maintain at least a 3.25 (Dean's list) overall cumulative GPA. The transcript of the Honors Program is imprinted with a special indication and designation upon granting of the degree. Honors Program students are given special recognition similar to graduate students in the commencement booklet, and they receive a specific and special recognition on their University transcript.

Admission Process: Program participation is by invitation only. Generally, all incoming students to the University are screened on the basis of their SAT I or ACT scores as well as their high school GPA, which generates the invitation. The minimum SAT I score is 1100 and must be accompanied by a high school cumulative GPA of at least 3.0. An SAT I score of at least 1200 requires no specific high school GPA. A student who achieves a GPA of 3.75 or higher after accruing 30 University credits may seek admission to the program.

Scholarship Availability: The Honors Program receives one annual scholarship, although nearly all academic scholarships at the University are awarded to Honors Program students. Each summer, California University of Pennsylvania participates in the Pennsylvania Summer Honors Program, which provides two Honors Program students the opportunity to study at one of the State System of Higher Education's institutions. Frequently, the scholarship provides a rewarding experience.

The Campus Context: California University of Pennsylvania is a member institution of the Pennsylvania State System of Higher Education with a special mission to develop programs in science, technology, and applied engineering. In addition, California is a comprehensive public institution offering thirty baccalaureate degree programs as well as master's degrees in many disciplines. Its location, along the bend of the Monongahela River, is only 35 miles from downtown Pittsburgh.

Student Body The undergraduate student body is 48 percent men and 52 percent women. The ethnic distribution is 93 percent white, 5 percent black, and 1 percent international. Seventy-one percent of the students receive financial aid.

Faculty The total number of faculty members is 338, of whom 293 are full-time. Fifty-eight percent of the full-time faculty members have terminal degrees. The student-faculty ratio is 19:1.

Key Facilities Manderino Library is a first-rate undergraduate facility containing 413,300 volumes, with an online catalog and many items and indices available on CD-ROM. The Honors Program maintains a small computer facility of its own equipped with Pentium II computers (300 MHz) and laser printers (HP 6M and 5M). Honors Program computers are fiber-optically wired to the University servers, which provide up-to-date computer software and Internet access.

Athletics California offers a wide variety of sports and intramural activities for its students, competing at the NCAA Division II level in both men's and women's athletics. California is a member of the Pennsylvania State Athletic Conference.

Job Opportunities The Honors Program provides several work-study opportunities for its students.

Tuition: $2008 for state residents, $5020 for nonresidents, per semester (2001–02)

Room and Board: $3066 per semester

Mandatory Fees: $593.80 per semester

Contact: Director: Dr. Edward J. Chute, Box 100, California University of Pennsylvania, 250 University Avenue, California, Pennsylvania 15419-1394; E-mail: chute@cup.edu

CALVIN COLLEGE

4 Pr M Tr

▼ Honors Program

The Calvin College Honors Program, first introduced in 1969 and greatly expanded since 1993, is a four-year program of special courses and opportunities intended to help students of outstanding academic ability and motivation develop their gifts so that they will be equipped for leadership in service to God, their communities, and the world at large.

The curriculum of Calvin's Honors Program annually includes special sections of ten to fifteen core courses, which are generally taken in the students' first two years at Calvin. In these honors courses, students are encouraged to develop greater than average initiative and independent study skills while working in greater than usual depth and closer collaboration with their professors. At the junior and senior levels, honors work is generally done by contract in each student's major discipline. Honors students receive special advising, orientation, and assistance in scheduling their classes; may contract to take regular courses for honors credit; are offered special opportunities for research and subsidies for participating in academic conferences; and they are invited to various cocurricular activities for honors students, including the Pew Younger Scholars program for students who are considering careers in academic life.

In recent years, approximately 500 students (about 12 percent of the student body) have been involved in the program annually, along with about 20 faculty members in eleven disciplines.

Participation Requirements: To remain in the Honors Program, students must maintain a GPA of at least 3.3 and take at least one honors course per year. To graduate with honors from Calvin College, students must complete at least six honors courses overall (at least two of these in their major), maintain a GPA of at least 3.3, and fulfill any other departmental requirements for honors in their major discipline, which generally means at least a senior-level research project and a thesis or public presentation. Honors graduates are presented with commemorative medallions at the annual Honors Convocation, and they wear their awards at Commencement. Their achievement is also noted on their transcript and diploma.

Admission Process: Calvin's Honors Program is open to students of all majors and class levels. Incoming students are invited to participate in the Honors Program if they have an ACT composite score of 28 or higher or an SAT I combined score of 1240 or higher. Transfer and continuing students who have a college GPA of at least 3.3 are also eligible for the program.

Scholarship Availability: Virtually all of Calvin's honors students receive merit-based scholarships awarded by the College for academic performance in the highest 15–20 percent of their cohorts. While participation in the Honors Program is not a condition for these awards, a high percentage of the top scholarship groups are active in honors work.

The Campus Context: Calvin College is a four-year liberal arts College founded in 1876 and affiliated with the Christian Reformed Church. It occupies a campus of 370 acres in southeast Grand Rapids. Campus facilities include a Service Learning Center, which coordinates academically based service programs in which about 1,500 students participate annually, and a 174-acre ecosystem preserve adjacent to campus used for recreation as well as scientific research. Rated ninth among 122 regional (Midwest) universities by *U.S. News & World Report* in 1996, Calvin is also highly ranked in the *Fiske Guide*, *Barron's Best Buys*, and *The Princeton Review*. Students may enroll in eighty academic majors or degree programs.

Student Body Total enrollment for fall 1998 was 4,073 undergraduates and 48 graduate students; 44 percent are men, 56 percent are women. The ethnic distribution of the student body is 90 percent white, 1 percent African American, 1 percent Hispanic, 2 percent Asian American, and .2 percent Native American. International students include 136 Canadians and 164 students from forty-two other countries. Fifty-six percent of the students live on campus in fifteen dormitories and eleven apartment complexes; 44 percent commute. Ninety-one percent receive financial aid (80 percent need-based, 20 percent other).

Faculty There are 261 full-time faculty members, of whom 83 percent have their terminal degrees. There are 62 part-time additional faculty members. The student-faculty ratio is 17:1.

Key Facilities Calvin's main library houses 413,000 books, 116,000 bound volumes of periodicals, 132,000 government documents, and 725,000 microforms (volume equivalent). Computer facilities include about 1,300 terminals on campus (Sun, Macintosh, and PC), 450 of them in open computer labs. There is e-mail and Internet access for all students and faculty and staff members.

Athletics Calvin College is a member of the Michigan Intercollegiate Athletic Association, with an extensive Division III program of nine women's sports (soccer, cross-country, golf, volleyball, basketball, swimming, softball, tennis, and track) and eight men's sports (soccer, cross-country, golf, basketball, swimming, baseball, tennis, and track). There are also men's club sports in volleyball, ice hockey, and lacrosse and extensive intramurals.

Study Abroad Study abroad includes programs in Britain, China, Honduras, Hungary, and Spain; affiliated programs in Austria, Egypt, France, Germany, the Netherlands, and Russia; and annual three-week January-term courses in several international locations.

Support Services Disabled students will find all buildings accessible and special housing reserved. The Academic Services Department has a full-time coordinator of services for students with disabilities.

Job Opportunities There are on-campus work opportunities, including about 250 part-time student positions.

Tuition: $12,915 per year (1998–99)

Room and Board: $4500

Contact: Director: Dr. Kenneth Bratt, 365 Hiemenga Hall, 3201 Burton SE, Grand Rapids, Michigan 49546; Telephone: 616-957-6296; Fax: 616-957-8551; E-mail: br_k@calvin.edu; Web site: http://www.calvin.edu

CARROLL COMMUNITY COLLEGE

2 Pu G S Tr

▼ Honors Program

The Honors Program at Carroll Community College is designed for enrichment and flexibility. The program centers around a series of interdisciplinary seminars intended to encourage students to broaden the scope of their thinking, look for interconnectedness, and explore a wide variety of topics from both academic and personal perspectives. Classes are small, generally fewer than 15 students; discussion based; and reading and writing intensive. Each class culminates with student presentations of capstone semester projects. Classes are generally taught by full-time faculty members from a variety of disciplines and are sometimes team-taught. A different course is offered each semester, including one during the summer. Carroll's Honors Program students form a diverse close-knit, but inclusive, group.

Interpreting the symbols: **2**=two-year college, **4**=four-year college; **Pu**=public or state college, **Pr**=private college; **G**=general honors program; **D**=departmental honors program; **S**=small program (fewer than 100 students), **M**=midsize program (100 to 500 students), **L**=large program (more than 500 students); **Sc**=scholarships available in honors program; **Tr**=transfer students accepted into honors program; **HBC**=historically black college; **AA**=academic advisors; **GA**=graduate advisors; **FA**=fellowship advisors.

Students have use of the Honors Lounge, which is shared with Phi Theta Kappa and Psi Beta. The program sponsors First Monday, a monthly discussion group coordinated by Honors Program students, and will begin publishing a newsletter this year. A Web page is available (listed below). Students and the Honors Program Director regularly attend the Maryland Collegiate Honors Council Conference. Carroll's Honors Program students consistently have been nominated to the Phi Theta Kappa/*USA Today* All American Team and have won awards for Outstanding Honors Student, evaluated and presented annually by the Maryland Collegiate Honors Council. The program was founded in 1989, revised in 1994, and currently enrolls 43 students.

Participation Requirements: Students must complete 12 credits at the honors level with a grade of B or better to successfully complete the program. At least 3 of these credits must be from an honors seminar. Remaining credits may be earned through Honors Contracts (individually designed projects in other classes), independent study, or by completing additional honors seminars. Honors Program students must maintain a GPA of 3.25 or higher. Honors courses taken and completion of the Honors Program are indicated on the students' transcripts and in commencement materials.

Admission Process: A GPA of at least 3.25, a teacher recommendation, and a completed application (including application essay) are required for admission of students with 12 or more completed credits at Carroll. Students seeking admission directly from high school need two recommendations, a completed application, and evidence of strong verbal skills. There is rolling admission.

Scholarship Availability: There are currently no dedicated Honors Program scholarships; however, the possibility is being explored. Program graduates have received scholarships to Western Maryland College, University of Baltimore, and Hood College.

The Campus Context: Carroll Community College, located approximately 30 miles from Baltimore in the town of Westminster, Maryland, is an innovative center for learning. Etched over the entrance to the College's Great Hall is the invitation "Enter to Learn." Providing opportunities for learning is central to the mission of the College, and this mission is carried out through a variety of credit and extended learning programs. The College's credit programs not only prepare students for the work world but also prepare students to transfer to four-year institutions. The College has formalized arrangements with many of the four-year institutions located in the Baltimore/Washington metropolitan area, which facilitate the transfer of credits taken at Carroll Community College. As it has grown, the College has continued to expand its facilities and recently opened the Random House Learning Resources Center, which houses the library and academic support services as well as classrooms, offices, and the College mailroom.

The College's modern facilities serve not only the student body but also the surrounding community. The Langdon Family Art Gallery, located off the Great Hall, and the Great Hall itself house exhibits throughout the year. The facilities are also used for monthly concerts, and new Rotary Amphitheater provides a venue for outdoor performances.

Student Body In fall 1998, 2,435 students attended Carroll Community College. The student body is predominantly part-time (1,622 part-time students attended in fall 1998, 66.6 percent of the total enrollment) and predominantly women (62 percent of the fall 1998 enrollment, 1,509 students). Two percent of Carroll's fall 1998 students were African American (52 students), 1 percent (23 students) were Hispanic, and less than 1 percent were Asian/Pacific Islander (15 students) or Native American (7 students). More than 40 percent of the fall 1998 student body was aged 25 or older, with a mean age of 27 years old.

Faculty Carroll Community College employs 45 full-time and 119 part-time faculty members. More than half of the full-time faculty members are women (28 faculty members, 62 percent).

Key Facilities The new Random House Learning Resources Center houses the College library, with a collection of 26,859 books, serial backfiles, and government documents. The College has 314 current serial titles, 2,441 microform titles, and 1,201 video and audio titles. The College owns more than 350 computers for student use, both IBM PCs and Macintoshes, which students may access in the library, computer classrooms, and computer laboratories.

Honorary Societies Phi Theta Kappa

Support Services Carroll Community College offers a variety of services for students with all types of physical and learning disabilities, including individualized instructional support, assistance with learning skills, note-taking, personal counseling, and special testing arrangements. The state-of-the-art facilities are wheelchair accessible.

Tuition: $67 per billable hour in county, $120 per billable hour out of county, $185 per billable hour out of state, 1998–99

Mandatory Fees: 10 percent of the tuition rate plus $2 per billable hour

Contact: Director: Jody Nusholtz, 1601 Washington Road, Westminster, Maryland 21157; Telephone: 410-386-8221; Fax: 410-876-8855; E-mail: jnusholtz@carroll.cc.md.us; Web site: http://www.carroll.cc.md.us/honors

CARTHAGE COLLEGE

4 Pr G S Sc Tr FA

▼ Honors Program

The Honors Program at Carthage College offers students with excellent high school or transfer records a program of study that is tailored to their individual needs. Anyone admitted into the program may take advantage of any or all of the extra academic challenges and support the program offers, and those who complete all requirements graduate with All-College Honors.

Students in the Honors Program encounter a variety of classes. All students enroll in honors sections of Carthage's required first-year seminar courses. They may also receive honors credit for a variety of introductory-level courses by completing the requirements on enhanced honors syllabi for those courses. In advanced courses in their majors, students work closely with their professors to design and complete honors contracts that allow students to examine more closely aspects of that topic that are of greatest interest to them. The honors experience also includes an interdisciplinary Senior Honors Colloquium, in which students from a variety of disciplines gather to examine a common question using the lenses they have developed in their majors. By teaching and learning from each other in this colloquium, students gain a greater understanding not only of the course's central question, but also of the ways in which different individuals and different disciplines might approach such questions and of possible connections between disciplines. Honors courses rarely have more than 16 students and often have between 5 and 10.

Small class size, honors sections, and honors contracts foster close contact between students and professors, one of the hallmarks of the Honors Program. Outside of class, students regularly attend national and regional conventions with their professors to share their work and to learn from others. Students and faculty members also cooperate in several groups to select honors courses and to plan events and activities for students in the program. Because of this contact, professors are better able to identify highly motivated and qualified students and help prepare them for careers, graduate school, and competitive scholarships. In addition, this contact allows students insight into the work and thought of scholars in various academic disciplines.

A student-run Honors Council acts as the students' voice in planning and revising aspects of the Honors Program. The Honors Council also helps plan extracurricular events both on campus and in the Chicago-Milwaukee corridor. These events include speakers, workshops, and visits to museums, plays, operas, and concerts. The Honors Council organizes a peer mentoring program and a yearly forum at which students present their senior theses.

The Carthage Honors Program was originally founded in 1970 and currently has approximately 90–100 students.

Participation Requirements: Students admitted into Carthage's Honors Program may take advantage of any or all of the program's offerings. All requirements for honors (except for the Senior Honors Colloquium) parallel regular college requirements, and students may move into and out of the honors track as they wish.

The full honors curriculum includes three components. The Foundation Component (four courses) includes honors sections of the first-year seminars and enhanced honors syllabi in introductory-level courses. The Concentration Component includes two honors contracts in advanced courses in the major and an exemplary senior thesis in the major presented to an audience outside of the major department. The Integration Component of the Carthage Honors Program asks students to make connections between disciplines by taking a three-course Honors Junior Symposium and by completing the Senior Honors Colloquium.

Students must maintain a cumulative GPA of at least 3.5 to graduate with Honors. Those who complete all requirements earn All-College Honors, but others may choose to earn Honors in the major.

Admission Process: Each year, after examining the ACT scores and GPAs of the incoming class, Carthage sends students from approximately the top 10 percent of that group invitations to the Honors Program. In addition to test scores and grades, the College may also consider performance in its Lincoln Scholarship Competition, which consists of an interview with faculty members and an essay. Both first-year and transfer students are considered for admission into the Honors Program.

Scholarship Availability: Carthage College offers substantial scholarships totaling more than $1 million to incoming and transfer students through its Lincoln Scholarship and Transfer Scholarship Competitions, with awards ranging from full tuition to full tuition with room and board. Most winners of these awards are in the Honors Program, although the program itself does not offer any scholarships of its own.

The Campus Context: Established in 1847, Carthage is a four-year, private, coed, residential college accredited by the North Central Association of Colleges and Schools. One of the premier liberal arts colleges of the Midwest, Carthage is consistently ranked as a "Top Tier" Midwest Regional University by *U.S. News & World Report*. Technology and a focus on active learning are integrated across the curriculum. Innovative academic offerings include an interdisciplinary first-year seminar emphasizing critical thinking, analytical reading, and persuasive writing; January term, when traditional teaching and learning yield to alternative approaches; and senior thesis, which demonstrates mastery of the student's area of study. Close relationships with faculty members lead to research opportunities, internships, great jobs, and graduate school admission. Carthage's 84-acre, parklike suburban campus is located on the shore of Lake Michigan in Kenosha, Wisconsin, which has a population of 80,000. Easy access to Chicago (65 miles south) and Milwaukee (35 miles north) provides social, cultural, and internship opportunities. In addition to recently renovated residence halls, the campus features two new facilities: the $15-million, 65,000-square-foot Hedberg Library with cyber café and the $23-million, 155,000-square-foot N. E. Tarble Athletic & Recreation Center, with a fitness center, indoor track, climbing wall, racquetball courts, and pool area. Carthage is affiliated with the Evangelical Lutheran Church in America and welcomes students of all faiths.

Student Body Undergraduate enrollment at Carthage is 1,725: 52 percent women and 48 percent men. Approximately 10 percent of the students are members of minority groups. Nearly 80 percent of students live on campus. Carthage has a full range of Greek and other social organizations, and there are more than eighty student groups on campus. More than 90 percent of students receive financial aid.

Faculty Of the 148 faculty members, 101 are full-time. Ninety percent of the faculty members have the highest degrees in their fields. The student-faculty ratio is 15:1, and the average class size is 19 students.

Key Facilities The Hedberg Library circulating collection contains more than 130,000 carefully selected books, video recordings, CD-ROMs, and other materials, as well as more than 600 print periodical titles. In addition, Hedberg Library offers an extensive array of electronic information, including a new, Web-based library catalog; electronic indexing and abstracting services of journal literature; news and current events files; an electronic reference desk; subject guides to World Wide Web sites; and full-text computer access to more than 3,000 journal titles. The library has more than fifty computers and more than 400 Ethernet stations. Campuswide computer facilities include a fiber-optic network and T1 Internet access for all residence hall rooms and staff offices. There are computer labs in each residence hall and academic building. Specialized labs are available for graphic design, math, natural sciences, geographic information systems, computer science, and education/curriculum resources.

Honorary Societies Alpha Chi, Alpha Lambda Delta, Omicron Delta Kappa, and Sigma Xi

Athletics Carthage is an NCAA Division III participant and is a member of the College Conference of Illinois and Wisconsin (CCIW). Intercollegiate athletics for men include baseball, basketball, cross-country, football, golf, soccer, swimming, tennis, and track and field. Intercollegiate athletics for women include basketball, cross-country, golf, soccer, softball, swimming, tennis, track and field, and volleyball. Four club sports are also offered: bowling (women), ice hockey (coed), volleyball (men), and water polo (women). There is an active intramural program.

Study Abroad Carthage students often study abroad as a way to experience other cultures and master language skills. Opportunities are available for January-term, semester, and yearlong programs abroad. Recent destinations for study abroad include Argentina, Canada, Colombia, Costa Rica, Cuba, Ecuador, England, France, Germany, Greece, Ireland, Italy, Japan, Mexico, Puerto Rico, Spain, Tanzania, Thailand, and Turkey.

Support Services The campus facilities are accessible to students with physical disabilities. Support is available for students with learning differences. A professionally staffed writing center and individual tutoring are available to all students at no cost.

Job Opportunities Wide arrays of work opportunities are available both on and off campus.

Tuition: $19,150 per year for residents and nonresidents (2002–03)

Room and Board: $5750 per year

Contact: Director: Dr. Gregory Baer, Carthage College, 2001 Alford Park Drive, Kenosha, Wisconsin 53140; Telephone:

Interpreting the symbols: **2**=two-year college, **4**=four-year college; **Pu**=public or state college, **Pr**=private college; **G**=general honors program; **D**=departmental honors program; **S**=small program (fewer than 100 students), **M**=midsize program (100 to 500 students), **L**=large program (more than 500 students); **Sc**=scholarships available in honors program; **Tr**=transfer students accepted into honors program; **HBC**=historically black college; **AA**=academic advisors; **GA**=graduate advisors; **FA**=fellowship advisors.

262-551-5742; Fax: 262-551-6208; E-mail: gbaer@carthage.edu; Web site: http://www.carthage.edu/honors

Catawba College

4 Pr C S Tr

▼ Honors Program

The Catawba College Honors Program offers academically gifted students the opportunity to pursue their interests in company with their intellectual peers and outstanding faculty members. In small classes, often team-taught by 2 or more professors, students explore such topics as Native American Religion and Literature, Man's Place in Nature, and The American Character. The emphasis is interdisciplinary, encouraging creative thinking, productive dialogue, and personal growth. Honors courses frequently carry general education credit so that a student may fulfill general education graduate requirements by taking these courses.

In addition to course work, participation in the Catawba Honors Program brings the opportunity to attend state and national honors conferences and take part in trips to such events as the North Carolina Shakespeare Festival.

Participation Requirements: Students who qualify for the Honors Program may take as few or as many honors courses as they choose. To graduate with College Honors, students must maintain at least a 3.0 GPA and complete 18 hours of honors courses, including a required freshman-level course and a senior honors seminar. Students who complete the requirements have the designation College Honors added to their diplomas and wear a special honor cord during the Commencement ceremonies.

Admission Process: Approximately 35 of the entering freshmen are invited to be in two honors advisory groups and are thus eligible to take honors courses. In addition, any student with at least a 3.0 GPA, including transfer students, may apply to the director for permission to join the program and take honors courses.

The Campus Context: Catawba College, established in 1851, has a beautiful 210-acre campus on the edge of the small historic town of Salisbury, North Carolina. Another 189 acres are devoted to an outstanding ecological preserve.

Student Body Catawba is a four-year liberal arts college with an enrollment of nearly 1,300 students, evenly distributed between men and women. Over twenty-five states and several other countries are represented in the student body. The majority of students reside on campus. Financial aid goes to 82 percent of the students.

Faculty Of the 117 faculty members, 66 are full-time, with 76 percent possessing a terminal degree.

Key Facilities The Corriher-Linn-Black Library resources include over 300,000 volume-equivalents in a wide array of print and nonprint formats. The library is connected to the Internet and thus provides access to library and information resources around the world.

Athletics Catawba is a member of the South Atlantic Conference. Teams are fielded in baseball, men's and women's basketball, men's and women's cross-country, field hockey, football, golf, men's lacrosse, softball, men's and women's soccer, women's swimming, men's and women's tennis, and volleyball. National competition is available for qualifying teams through the NCAA Division II.

Tuition: $12,134 per year (1998–99)

Room and Board: $4650

Contact: Director: Dr. Bethany Sinnott, Salisbury, North Carolina 28144-2488; Telephone: 704-637-4452; Fax: 704-637-4444; E-mail: bsinnott@catawba.edu

Centenary College

4 Pr G S Tr

▼ Honors Program

The Centenary Honors Program is a four-year interdisciplinary academic enrichment program. Consistent with the College's mission, the Honors Program ensures a global perspective within the student's liberal arts experience by focusing on issues of multiculturalism and diversity.

"Intensive Study in Cultural Diversity" is the annual highlight of the Centenary Honors Program. Each year Honors Program students have the opportunity to enroll in this 3-credit course and participate in a one- to two-week study tour. The trips are within the United States and other countries and are offered during intercession or over the summer. Honors Program students receive a stipend to help defray the costs of the trip. Recent trips have been planned for Spain and Ireland. In order to remain eligible for the stipend, students must maintain a GPA of at least 3.2, make appropriate progress in the honors curriculum, and attend at least one Honors Program lecture per semester.

The Centenary College Honors Program enhances the academic opportunities of promising and motivated undergraduates. It enables such students to pursue more effectively, more freely, and more creatively their individual academic aims within the overall mission of the College.

Participation Requirements: Students must take eight honors-level courses. Students must maintain a minimum GPA of 3.2 and complete one honors course per semester. Successful completion of the program is noted on the diploma and official College transcript, and each student is individually recognized at commencement.

Admission Process: For entrance to the program, freshman students who are in the top 10 percent of the incoming class are invited to join the Honors Program. International students must have a TOEFL score of at least 550 or a score of at least 250 on the computer-based test. Transfer students with a college GPA of at least 3.2 are also eligible to enter the program. There is rolling admission to the program.

The Campus Context: Centenary College is an independent coeducational college offering bachelor's degree programs and associate degree programs in the liberal arts and career areas and master's degree programs in education, counseling, counseling psychology, business, and accounting. Centenary College has been affiliated with the United Methodist Church since its founding in 1867. Today, Centenary enjoys a student body rich in diversity in religious and ethnic backgrounds. The 42-acre campus is located in Hackettstown, a residential community in northwestern New Jersey. The College's 65-acre equestrian center is located 8 miles from the main campus on scenic Schooley's Mountain. New York City, the Pocono Mountains, and the New Jersey shore are an easy commute. The offerings of the Centenary Performing Arts Guild and other arts organizations add an important cultural dimension to student life.

Student Body The undergraduate enrollment is 30 percent men and 70 percent women. Ten percent of the full-time undergraduate students are members of minority groups, and 13 percent of the full-time undergraduate population is international. Sixty percent of the full-time population lives in campus housing. Eighty-eight percent of the students receive financial aid.

There are clubs representing many interests, a literary magazine, a newspaper, the Centenary College Fashion Group, an arts guild, and SIFE (Students in Free Enterprise). There are concerts, parties, dances, movie nights, and trips to New York City cultural attractions and to the Poconos for skiing. A fraternity and two sororities sponsor other events. On campus is the Centenary Stage Company, the only theater in northwest New Jersey recognized by Actors Equity. The Centenary Performing Arts Guild sponsors concerts and dance and theater programs.

Faculty The total number of faculty members is 106, of whom 42 are full-time. Fifty percent hold a terminal degree in their field.

Key Facilities The Taylor Memorial Learning Resource Center (LRC) houses a print and audiovisual collection of 92,205 items, including 67,890 items in print, 4,820 audiovisual tapes, 19,481 microforms, and fourteen electronic databases (several that provide full text) and Internet access. The LRC has databases on CD-ROM, workstations for online bibliographic searching, and the Patron Access Catalog.

The computer lab is located inside the LRC, and there are additional microcomputers available on campus for students. Centenary's telecommunications infrastructure can service more than 1,100 voice/data and video connections. Students have available within their residence rooms a private telephone line, voice mail, and Internet access. All resident students are issued a computer.

Honorary Societies Phi Theta Kappa, Alpha Chi, and Kappa Delta Epsilon

Athletics Centenary students enjoy a full range of extracurricular activities, including varsity NCAA Division III intercollegiate athletic teams for men and women as well as an assortment of intramural athletic events. Men compete in basketball, cross-country, golf, soccer, lacrosse, and wrestling, while women compete in basketball, cross-country, soccer, softball, volleyball, and lacrosse. The men's soccer team won the 1995 NSCAA National Championship. Both men and women compete in ISHA equestrian competitions.

Study Abroad Centenary College encourages juniors who are in good academic standing to pursue a Semester Abroad option.

Support Services Through the campus Academic Support Center (ASC), students can receive tutoring by both professionals and peer tutors. Students may request tutoring themselves or may be referred to the ASC by their instructors. The staff counsels students with their academic concerns and aids students seeking academic enrichment and excellence. For the college student with learning disabilities, Centenary offers an individual approach, stressing learning strategies. Project Able at Centenary College is a comprehensive assistance program designed to provide an environment for students with mild to moderate learning disabilities who desire a college education.

Job Opportunities Further professional preparation is provided through internships developed by the College in cooperation with business firms, agencies, and schools. Internship programs are carefully selected to provide specific career-oriented experiences and fulfill certain goals outlined in advance. The Career Center, a multiuser resource and guidance facility, features employment and internship opportunities, career counseling, resume assistance, direct employer referrals, and an annual career fair.

Tuition: $15,100 (2001–02)

Room and Board: $6400

Mandatory Fees: $930

Contact: Director: Ginny Elsasser, Centenary College, 400 Jefferson Street, Hackettstown, New Jersey 07840; Telephone: 908-852-1400 Ext. 2262; Fax: 908-813-1984; E-mail: elsasser@centenarycollege.edu

Central Michigan University

4 Pu G L Sc Tr

▼ University Honors Program

Graduates of the Central Michigan University Honors Program are found in every walk of professional life. Since its founding in 1961, the program has produced a growing community of leaders who serve in important positions around the state and country.

The CMU honors program promotes development of the important skills of inquiry, analysis, synthesis and critical evaluation. Honors students are encouraged to reach beyond the classroom into the realm of research, self-direction, creative innovation, and discovery.

Honors professors provide broad yet personalized instruction in the classroom and act as advisers for students' individualized study and research projects.

The Honors Program offers many benefits, including small classes with enrollment limited to 20 students, University Program (general education) honors course selections each semester, eligibility to reside in a designated honors residence community in either Larzelere or Trout Hall, priority registration, access to specialized academic counseling and mentoring by honors program and residence hall advisers, recognition as an honors program graduate on the official transcript, membership and involvement in Honors Outreach Network (HON), the student organization for honors program members, involvement in honors activities such as an annual trip to Stratford, Ontario, for the Shakespeare Festival and an annual honors program talent show.

Participation Requirements: Honors program requirements are specified in the honors protocol and include 12 credit hours of honors course work, one year of a single foreign language taken at the university level or an approved alternative (retroactive credits do not apply), 6 credit hours of seminar classes, completion of 30 hours of community/volunteer service per year, completion of a senior project approved by the Honors Program Director. Note: Protocol subject to change.

Admission Process: Any incoming freshman with a cumulative high school GPA of 3.5 or higher and a cumulative ACT score of 24 or higher is invited to apply to the honors program. With a 3.75 GPA, the ACT qualifier is waived. Current CMU undergraduate students and transfer students who have earned cumulative GPAs of 3.5 or higher also are invited to apply. To remain active and graduate from the honors program, students must fulfill all protocol requirements and maintain a minimum cumulative GPA of 3.25.

Scholarship Availability: Up to forty Centralis Scholarships are awarded each year to high school seniors who have been accepted for admission to Central Michigan University. The Centralis Scholar Award covers the full cost of tuition, fees, room, and board and provides $500 for general expenses. The award pays for up to 36 credit hours per academic year, including summer sessions. The 2001–02 value for four years was $42,720, or $10, 680 per academic year. Up to twenty of these scholarships are awarded annually. The Centralis Gold Award covers the full cost of tuition, up to 36 credit hours per academic year, including summer sessions. The 2001–02 value for four years was $17,120, or $4280 per academic year. Up to twenty of these scholarships are awarded each year. Students are invited to compete for the Centralis Scholarship in the fall of their senior year provided they have at least a 3.5 cumulative high school GPA. Scholarship information may be obtained by calling 989-774-3076 or 888-292-5366 (toll-free).

During 2000–01, CMU distributed more than $112 million in financial aid and scholarships. More than 17,321 students received aid, and the average award was $6476. All CMU freshmen who graduate from a Michigan High School with a 3.5 or higher high school GPA receive a Board of Trustees Scholarship valued at 12 credit hours per academic year for four years.

The Campus Context: Founded more than a century ago (in 1892) as a teacher's college, Central Michigan University has

Interpreting the symbols: **2**=two-year college, **4**=four-year college; **Pu**=public or state college, **Pr**=private college; **G**=general honors program; **D**=departmental honors program; **S**=small program (fewer than 100 students), **M**=midsize program (100 to 500 students), **L**=large program (more than 500 students); **Sc**=scholarships available in honors program; **Tr**=transfer students accepted into honors program; **HBC**=historically black college; **AA**=academic advisors; **GA**=graduate advisors; **FA**=fellowship advisors.

evolved into a doctoral/research public university that is ranked among the best in the Midwest. CMU provides its growing student population with modern facilities and technology, faculty members who are dedicated to student-centered teaching and research, and a selection of more than 200 programs at the bachelor's, master's, specialist, and doctoral levels.

The University's academic reputation is complemented by opportunities for experiential learning and scholarship. Classified as a Doctoral/Research-Intensive University by the Carnegie Foundation, Central Michigan University supports knowledge development and active learning at undergraduate, graduate, and faculty levels. Students are prepared for careers through internships, real-world research, and experiences with advanced technology.

Central Michigan University offers its student population a broad selection of more than 3,000 individual courses and their choice of twenty-five degrees. CMU offers more than 150 undergraduate and sixty graduate programs through six academic colleges. *U.S. News & World Report* magazine ranked CMU among the top fifteen "best value" universities in the Midwest. This value ranking results from CMU's efforts to provide modern programs, resources, and facilities while working to keep attendance costs lower. CMU is committed to making a college education affordable and helping students who need financial aid.

The Central Michigan University main campus is located in Mt. Pleasant, a progressive city of about 25,000 residents in Michigan's scenic Lower Peninsula. To the north and west are lakes, streams, ski resorts, beaches, and magnificent wilderness areas. To the south and east lie rich farmland and larger metropolitan areas with numerous museums, theaters, art fairs, and shopping opportunities.

Student Body Enrollment on the Mt. Pleasant campus for fall 2001 was about 18,000 undergraduate students and more than 2,000 graduate students. Off campus, through its College of Extended Learning, CMU delivered academic programs and degrees to 8,827 students. CMU students come from all eighty-three counties in Michigan as well as from forty-seven other states and seventy-three other countries. CMU's 140,000 alumni include noted business professionals, educators, broadcasters, legislators, judges, entertainers, medical professionals, athletes, and community leaders.

Faculty CMU's more than 900 full- and part-time faculty members are noted for their research and the personal attention they give to students. CMU faculty members hold strong credentials, including degrees earned at more than 150 institutions. In addition to schools such as CMU, Michigan State University, and the University of Michigan, some studied at Harvard, Yale, Johns Hopkins, Massachusetts Institute of Technology, Princeton, Howard, and Cambridge. CMU faculty members have distinguished themselves in many areas, including cancer research, agricultural policy, and education.

Honorary Societies Phi Beta Kappa, Mortar Board, Golden Key, Phi Kappa Phi, and Alpha Lambda Delta

Athletics CMU's Division I-A athletics program, a part of the Mid-American Conference (MAC), offers seven intercollegiate sports for men and nine for women. CMU is the only school in the MAC to win the prestigious MAC Academic Achievement Award three consecutive times.

Study Abroad CMU has approximately 200 approved programs in more than fifty countries. Students may study for just a few weeks in summer, for one semester, or for one full academic year. There are study-abroad programs for students in almost all courses of study. Financial aid is available for students who study abroad. The cost of study-abroad programs varies from as little as CMU tuition, room, and board on up.

Extracurricular Opportunities CMU students can get involved in more than 225 organizations, including more than thirty award-winning student honor societies. CMU has one of the highest percentages of student participation in intramural sports in the country. Students are strongly encouraged to participate in Leadership Institute–sponsored programs such as Leadership Camp, Leadership Safari, and the Alpha Program.

Tuition: Tuition is $3882 for Michigan residents and $9232 for non-Michigan residents, based on 31 credits taken per year (2001–02).

Room and Board: $4828 per semester

Mandatory Fees: $302.50 per semester (2001–02)

Contact: Director: Edgar Long, University Honors Program, Central Michigan University, 112 Larzelere Hall, Mt. Pleasant, Michigan 48858; Telephone: 989-774-3902; Fax: 989-774-2335; E-mail: longlec@cmich.edu; Web site: http://www.cmich.edu/~honors/

Chaffey College

2 Pu M Sc Tr

▼ Chaffey College Honors Program

The Chaffey College Honors Program offers a rich and varied curriculum for honors students in three different modes. One is the stand-alone class, in which one section of a course is designated as honors. All students in these sections who receive a grade of B or better receive honors credit. A second option is the piggyback mode, in which students enroll in any section of a core course, such as English 1, and gather together 1 hour a week for an honors seminar. The third option is the Honors Program contact, in which students may work on a project of their choice in any transfer-level class. All honors classes are limited to 20 students, and every class includes extracurricular activities, such as a visit to the J. Paul Getty Museum, the Museum of Tolerance, or the California Stock Exchange. Honors faculty members take pride in working closely with honors students to enable them to fulfill their potential and transfer to four-year institutions of higher learning. Community service is an integral part of the program. Students participate in tutoring at the elementary, junior high, and high school levels; buy clothing for underprivileged children; raise money to support the American Cancer Society and other charities; show foreign films for free to the public; and honor the faculty with an end-of-the-year faculty reception. The program was founded in 1993 and currently enrolls 120 students.

Participation Requirements: Students must complete at least 18 semester units of honors course work with a minimum GPA of 3.0 and 54 hours of community service to graduate from the program. Honors Program graduates receive special certificates and a beautiful pin with the Honors Program logo; all honors courses are designated on students' transcripts along with the notation that they are graduates of the Honors Program.

Admission Process: Admission to the Chaffey College Honors Program is based on three criteria: a high school GPA of 3.25 or higher or a college GPA of 3.0 or higher after a minimum of 12 transferable units and two essays. In addition, one of the following criteria must be met: two letters of reference from high school or college faculty members, nomination by a Chaffey College faculty member, combined SAT I scores of 1000 or above or an ACT score of 26 or higher, successful completion of two honors courses at Chaffey College with a grade of B or better or three Advanced Placement classes in high school with grade of B or better, or evidence of special competence or creativity.

Scholarship Availability: Chaffey College is a member of the California Honors Transfer Council, which has developed articulation agreements with UCI, UCLA, UCR, UCSC, USC, Chapman, Pepperdine, and Pomona. Graduates of the Chaffey College Honors Program not only have guaranteed admission or priority consideration at all these schools but also have the opportunity to access scholarships that range from small prizes to full tuition.

In house, many scholarships are available to transferring students that range from $100 to $500. Students may earn more than one scholarship, and many honors students receive $2000 at graduation from various Chaffey scholarships.

The Campus Context: Chaffey College, one of the first colleges to be established in California, is a two-year public community college situated in an area of natural and tranquil beauty in southern California. Its campus occupies 200 acres of rolling lawns and native foliage in the foothills of the majestic San Gabriel Mountains. Founded in 1883 as a private college, Chaffey has been a publicly funded college since 1916. The primary mission of the College is to provide comprehensive, student-centered community college education to the diverse population it serves. It prepares students for transfer programs that ensure their access to upper-division education at the University of California, the California State University, and other public and private universities. Chaffey also prepares students for access to employment in the community. Students who successfully complete the requirements for graduation are awarded Associate in Arts and Associate in Science degrees. Designed to expand educational and cultural experience through visual means, the Wignall Museum/Gallery is a fully equipped facility that offers four exhibitions a year, which are varied in theme and content. Many Honors Program functions take place within the museum/gallery or outside in a beautifully enclosed patio.

Student Body The student population of more than 15,000 reflects the rich diversity of the surrounding community. The largest single ethnic minority group is Hispanic. Two percent of the study body are international students. Women comprise 61 percent of the student population and men, 39 percent. Fifty percent of the students receive financial aid, and 75 percent are nontraditional. All students are commuters; Chaffey has no dormitories.

Faculty Full-time faculty members number 171; 35 have terminal degrees. In addition, the College employs 421 part-time faculty members.

Key Facilities The Chaffey College Library contains more than 73,000 volumes in the circulating and reference book collection and more than 250 different magazines and journals in the periodical wing. The Infotrac Academic Index provides access to the periodical collections, with full text for many titles. SIRS databases provide full text from a large number of publications. Thirty-two computers are available for student use, with Internet access through the Netscape browser. The library also provides video player/monitors to view videos in the library collections, word processing with venda card printers, microfilm readers/printers, copy machines, and a reserve desk for instructor-provided material.

Honorary Societies Alpha Gamma Sigma

Athletics Playing under the name of the Panthers, the men's and women's teams compete in the Foothill Athletic Conference. The men's athletic program offers competition in football, basketball, baseball, swimming, and water polo. The women's athletic program includes competition in basketball, softball, swimming, and volleyball.

Study Abroad Chaffey has no study-abroad programs specifically for honors students, but honors students may participate in foreign language study-abroad programs as well as programs sponsored by the National Collegiate Honors Council.

Support Services Chaffey College maintains a strong commitment to serving people with developmental, learning, physical, communicative, and psychological disabilities and acquired brain injuries who desire postsecondary academic or vocational education. The College has a learning resource program, physically limited student services, and a learning development center.

Job Opportunities Student Employment provides work-study opportunities, job referral, internship referral, cooperative education referral, and personnel services to current and former Chaffey College students.

Tuition: $12 per unit for state residents, $144 per unit for nonresidents (1998–99)

Mandatory Fees: $11

Contact: Chair, Honors Program Committee: Peggy Stiffler, 5885 Haven Avenue, Rancho Cucamonga, California 91737-3002; Telephone: 909-941-2111; Fax: 909-941-2783; E-mail: pstiffler@chaffey.ca.cc.us; Web site: http://www.chaffey.cc.ca.us/

Chattanooga State Technical Community College

2 Pu M Sc Tr

▼ Honors Program

The Chattanooga State Honors Program is an offering of courses and related educational activities designed to provide an enriched collegiate experience for able and highly motivated students. Sections are smaller, offering more individual attention from instructors and more opportunities for independent and original work by students. Class offerings represent a variety of disciplines and areas of focused study: engineering, statistics, English composition, English literature, American literature, world literature, Shakespeare, calculus, leadership development, world history, U.S. history, general psychology, sociology, creative writing (fiction and poetry sections), creative writing on line, Southern culture, folklore, public speaking, religions of the world, Western philosophy, contemporary women artists and writers, and others.

An atmosphere of camaraderie is promoted within the Honors Program; thus, faculty members and students attend local cultural events, such as concerts, operas, and theater productions, or they may visit art museums, historical sites, and other related sites. These events are coordinated with the classroom experience and enhance the development of the student both academically and socially. Students may also be eligible to present outstanding papers or projects at Honors Conferences or participate in conference activities. As with all reputable Honors Programs at other community colleges, universities, and four-year colleges in Tennessee, the Honors Program at Chattanooga State is a member of the National Collegiate Honors Council, the Southern Regional Honors Council, and the Tennessee Honors Council.

Honors students have priority enrollment in the annual spring break trip to Europe. Sponsored by the Honors Program, this trip provides an exceptional learning experience for honors students, who visit London, Paris, Rome, Amsterdam, Athens, and many other European cities. Students may receive up to 6 hours of credit in honors course work during the trip.

Chattanooga State is one of seventeen community colleges in the country to be selected as a site of the Phi Theta Kappa Leadership Development Program. The program's central focus is on the development of skills that aid students in increasing their understanding of themselves and of the theories and techniques of leadership and of group processes. The key course in this program, Leadership Development, is offered through the Chattanooga State Honors Program.

Interpreting the symbols: **2**=two-year college, **4**=four-year college; **Pu**=public or state college, **Pr**=private college; **G**=general honors program; **D**=departmental honors program; **S**=small program (fewer than 100 students), **M**=midsize program (100 to 500 students), **L**=large program (more than 500 students); **Sc**=scholarships available in honors program; **Tr**=transfer students accepted into honors program; **HBC**=historically black college; **AA**=academic advisors; **GA**=graduate advisors; **FA**=fellowship advisors.

The Chattanooga State Honors Program has been in existence for twelve years.

Participation Requirements: To graduate with an honors diploma and to have the honors designation on the transcript, students must complete a total of four honors classes and satisfy the other course requirements of their respective majors. In the process, they must maintain a minimum 3.5 GPA.

Admission Process: To be eligible for the Honors Program, presently enrolled students must have completed 15 semester hours of course work (excluding transitional studies) and have a GPA of at least 3.5, unless granted conditional acceptance by the coordinator. Incoming freshmen must have an ACT composite score of 25 or higher or a high school GPA of 3.5 or greater, unless they have been granted conditional acceptance by the coordinator. In addition to meeting the eligibility requirements, prospective honors students must complete each element of the honors application and secure two letters of recommendation for their entry into the program.

Scholarship Availability: A number of Honors Program Scholarships are available to eligible full-time honors students (both incoming students and those currently enrolled). These scholarships cover full tuition and $150 of book expenses for up to four semesters (fall and spring). To retain an Honors Scholarship for the four semesters, recipients must maintain a minimum 3.5 GPA, must maintain full-time status, and must be enrolled in at least one honors course per semester.

The Campus Context: Chattanooga State Technical Community College has been providing high-quality programs in Tennessee for more than thirty years. When the College began operating in September 1965 in downtown Chattanooga, it was the first technical college in the state as well as the first public institution of higher education in southeastern Tennessee. In 1967, the technical institute moved into a one-building structure at its present location on the banks of the Tennessee River. Since then, it has grown into a multimillion-dollar complex of buildings. Chattanooga State serves a six-county area of southeast Tennessee with a population exceeding 300,000, meeting the needs of area citizens by providing associate degrees and certificate career programs, by offering a wide range of transfer curricula, and by opening pathways to personal enrichment. The College offers Associate of Applied Science degrees and technical certificates in more than fifty career areas and the Associate of Arts and Associate of Science degrees for transfer students.

Student Body Total enrollment is 8,359. The ethnic distribution is 14 percent African American, .003 percent American Indian, 2 percent Asian, 1 percent Hispanic, and 83 percent Caucasian.

Faculty There are approximately 200 full-time faculty members.

Key Facilities The Augusta R. Kolwyck library holdings consist of 73,500 books, 700 magazine subscriptions, 5,200 videotapes, 1,000 audiocassettes and phonograph records. The library staff provides both formal classroom instruction on how to do specific kinds of research and individual point-of-use instruction to students needing assistance in finding materials. Students can print or download from any of the library's computerized information databases. These include the Intelligent Catalog, *The New York Times,* magazine and journal databases, and the Internet. The Internet address for the library is http://www2.cstcc.cc.tn.us/library. The catalog and other curriculum-related resources can be searched through that site.

Honorary Societies Phi Theta Kappa

Study Abroad Honors students have priority enrollment in the annual spring break trip to Europe. Sponsored by the Honors Program, this trip provides a unique learning experience for honors students, who visit London, Paris, Rome, Amsterdam, Athens, and many other European cities. Students may receive up to 6 hours of credit in honors course work during the trip.

Support Services Chattanooga State's Disabilities Support Services ensures that all students with documented disabilities receive the support services needed for academic success when these services are reasonable and do not incur undue hardship on the College. Services include guidance related to matters of disability to faculty and staff members and outside agencies; assistance to students with disabilities with class registration and parking permits; arrangements for testing, if required; tutoring services; academic and auxiliary aids such as readers, scribes for dictation and note-taking purposes, interpreters in the classrooms, captioned TV services, assistive listening systems, and TTY loans to students; coordination of advising and career and personnel counseling services; Vocational Rehabilitation referrals; a support group for students with disabilities; and community education. Furthermore, the Adaptive Computer Lab provides assessment of the needs for adaptive computer assistance of persons who are blind, deaf and hard of hearing or learning disabled or who have mobility problems. It provides training and equipment for students with disabilities who need to use adaptive computer equipment.

Job Opportunities The Federal Work-Study Program at Chattanooga State is a program designed to assist students in meeting their cost of education by providing part-time work opportunities. At Chattanooga State, work-study positions are on and off campus. Hours worked per week are determined by the student's Federal Work-Study award and class schedule for a particular semester. Chattanooga State also offers 18 hours in Cooperative Education Work Experience courses. Cooperative Education Work Experience is a course designed to allow the student to explore a career, work in a structured environment while acquiring marketable job skills, and develop interpersonal skills and self-confidence. This is accomplished by combining on-campus study and off-campus work, lectures, guest speakers, discussion of work experiences, and a written report.

Tuition: $50 per credit hour for part-time residents, $198 per credit hour for part-time nonresidents; $1130 for full-time residents, $4516 for full-time nonresidents (1998–99)

Mandatory Fees: $46

Contact: Coordinator of the Honors Program: De'Lara Khalili, Humanities 232, 4501 Amnicola Highway, Chattanooga, Tennessee 37406; Telephone: 423-697-2449; Fax: 423-697-4430; E-mail: dkhalili@cstcc.cc.tn.us

CHRISTIAN BROTHERS UNIVERSITY

4 Pr G M Tr

▼ Honors Program

The Christian Brothers University (CBU) Honors Program offers an enriched academic experience to gifted and highly motivated students in all disciplines. Members of the Honors Program take a series of special-topics courses with limited enrollment, usually about 20 students. These courses are offered in a variety of disciplines and fulfill general education requirements for all majors. The program offers students the opportunity to explore challenging topics in small groups led by faculty members chosen for their interest in developing courses especially designed for the Honors Program and for their commitment to teaching honors students. The program offers special-topics courses in English, history, philosophy, political science, psychology, and religion as well as a senior research seminar. The Honors Program Director assists honors students and their academic advisers in planning each student's course of study. Program-sponsored social and cultural events provide opportunities for extracurricular enrichment and create a sense of community among honors students and faculty members.

The CBU Honors Program is now in its tenth year. Currently, there are 120 students in the Honors Program.

Participation Requirements: Students participate in the program at two levels. Some students earn Honors Program Diplomas by taking at least six honors courses, including the senior seminar, and maintaining at least a 3.2 GPA. Others take fewer honors courses, selecting those most closely related to their academic interests.

Admission Process: First-year students are invited to apply for admission to the Honors Program during the spring before they enroll at CBU. Invitation to the program is based on high school grades and ACT or SAT I scores. A personal interview is also part of the selection process. Transfer students and students who are not initially selected for membership may also apply for admission, usually after completing one semester at CBU.

The Campus Context: Christian Brothers University (originally Christian Brothers College) was founded in 1871 by members of the Institute of the Brothers of the Christian Schools, a Roman Catholic religious teaching congregation. The 70-acre campus is located in the Midtown section of Memphis, about 4 miles east of downtown Memphis. Students may enroll in twenty-four undergraduate majors leading to Bachelor of Arts or Bachelor of Science degrees from the schools of business, engineering, liberal arts, and science. Master's degrees are offered in business, education, and engineering.

Student Body The University has an enrollment of 1,900 full-time students representing thirty-five states and nineteen other countries; the men-women ratio is about 1:1. Students may participate in more than thirty clubs, groups, and organizations, including theater, art and musical productions; publications; and academic societies as well as national sororities and fraternities.

Faculty There are 109 full-time faculty members, 78 percent with doctorates or other terminal degrees. The student-faculty ratio is 14:1.

Key Facilities Plough Memorial Library has more than 150,000 volumes, periodicals, and microfilms. Computer facilities include 250 computers for student use, located in the library and in labs across campus.

Honorary Societies Alpha Chi

Athletics CBU began competing in the NCAA's Division II in 1996. Sports include basketball, soccer, tennis, cross-country, softball, and volleyball for women and baseball, basketball, soccer, cross-country, tennis, and golf for men. There are fourteen intramural sports.

Study Abroad Study abroad is coordinated through the CBU Registrar's Office.

Tuition: Full-time, $12,400 per year; part-time, $365 per semester hour for day classes, $245 for evening classes, $195 for summer classes (1998–99)

Room and Board: $4080

Fees: $330

Contact: Director: Dr. Tracie Burke, 650 East Parkway South, Memphis, Tennessee 38104-5581; Telephone: 901-321-3343; Fax: 901-321-4340

Cincinnati State Technical and Community College

2 Pu G S Sc Tr

▼ The Honors Experience

The Cincinnati State Technical and Community College Honors Experience is designed to provide academically talented, highly motivated students the opportunity to reach their potential by offering enhanced learning opportunities. The Honors Experience emphasizes a broad-based foundation of educational disciplines with the goal of enabling the student to transfer to a senior institution or enter a professional field at a high skill level with the capacity for continuous learning and responsible citizenship. The Honors Experience values creativity and intellectual curiosity; establishes a community among students and faculty; provides unique course work, enrichment activities, and honors advising; and nurtures individual development and leadership.

The Honors Experience is dedicated to providing students challenging alternatives to completing core courses, as well as specialized courses in both academic and technical fields. All students participate in Honors Orientation and timely multidisciplinary colloquia. Honors course design favors creative approaches to problem-solving, meaningful research and communication, and appreciation of cultural diversity and the arts. The Honors Experience, started in 1999, currently offers sixteen core curriculum courses, with new offerings constantly being added.

Participation Requirements: Honors scholars must meet all requirements of the College and degree program, maintaining a GPA of 3.25 or better. In order to graduate as an Honors Experience Scholar, students must complete 30 credit hours of honors courses, including Honors Orientation, and at least one honors colloquium. Any Cincinnati State student may take an honors course with the permission of the instructor or the Honors Chair.

Admission Process: Incoming students are identified through admissions testing, a high school GPA of 3.25 or better, high school class rank in the top 20th percentile, and SAT or ACT scores. Existing or transfer students may be considered for admission with 18 credit hours of work and a GPA of 3.25 or better. Two letters of recommendation and a personal essay are required with an application to the Honors Experience.

Scholarship Availability: Approximately 18 full merit scholarships are available to Honors Experience scholars. Recipients must meet all College requirements for academic scholarship and complete a separate honors scholarship application in order to be considered for scholarship.

The Campus Context: Chartered by the Ohio Board of Regents in 1969, Cincinnati State is an urban campus accredited by the North Central Association of Colleges and Schools. Cincinnati State has more than seventy associate degree programs and majors, and more than forty certificate programs. The school has a six-year graduate placement rate of 97 percent, a 91 percent pass rate on required licensing/registry exams, and was the only two-year college to win the Ohio Board of Regents Program Excellence Award in all competitions. Thirty percent of students continue their education at other colleges and universities.

Student Body Cincinnati State annually enrolls 12,000 students in credit and noncredit classes; 54 percent are women. The average age is 27. Ethnic distribution is 64 percent white, 26 percent African American, and 10 percent are members of other minorities.

Tuition $62.50 per credit for Ohio residents, $125 for nonresidents (2001–02)

Contact: Honors Chair: Marcha L. Hunley, Cincinnati State, Humanities and Sciences Division, 3520 Central Parkway, Cincinnati, Ohio 45223-2690; Telephone: 513-569-1732; E-mail: hunleym@cinstate.cc.oh.us

The Citadel

4 Pr G S Tr

▼ Honors Program

The Citadel's Honors Program is a specially designed educational experience meeting the needs of students with an outstanding

Interpreting the symbols: **2**=two-year college, **4**=four-year college; **Pu**=public or state college, **Pr**=private college; **G**=general honors program; **D**=departmental honors program; **S**=small program (fewer than 100 students), **M**=midsize program (100 to 500 students), **L**=large program (more than 500 students); **Sc**=scholarships available in honors program; **Tr**=transfer students accepted into honors program; **HBC**=historically black college; **AA**=academic advisors; **GA**=graduate advisors; **FA**=fellowship advisors.

record of academic achievement and a sense of intellectual adventure. While pursuing any one of seventeen degree programs offered by The Citadel, honors students take a series of Core Curriculum Honors Courses—for example, studies based in literature and writing, history, and mathematics—concentrated in their first two years, and an occasional Honors Seminar or Honors Research Project in their third and fourth years.

There are approximately 65 students in the 9-year-old program.

Although The Citadel's Honors Program has many facets, the essential character of our program can be found in three aspects. First, there is a tutorial foundation. All honors courses, from freshman-level courses through senior-level seminars, have attached to them a regularly scheduled, one-on-one meeting between the student and the professor. These are not just check-in meetings to see if the student has any problems; rather, the professor and the student prearrange to work together on one of the assignments of the course.

Second, there is preprofessional counseling. All honors students take a three-semester sequence of courses entitled Personal and Professional Development. Taught entirely in tutorial, it directs students in a three-year period of research, reflection, and writing on the subject of their professional goals, encouraging them to envision their leadership in their future profession and guiding them in exploring, through research and writing, the ideals as well as the facts of that profession.

Finally, there is leadership. The Citadel encourages students to take full advantage of the many leadership opportunities afforded by the military environment of the school. Year after year, the chain of command at The Citadel is heavily populated from top to bottom by Honors Program students. The Citadel has an honors brand of leadership based on the concept of service, which has enabled honors students to consistently earn positions of leadership. The deadline for applying to the program is January 15.

Participation Requirements: Students majoring in one of the sciences or engineering will be required to complete the following honors courses: Honors Personal and Professional Development I, II, and III; Honors English I, II, III, and IV; Honors History I and II; Honors Social Science Project; and one Honors Seminar or Research Project. Students majoring in one of the liberal arts or social sciences will be required to complete the following honors courses: Honors Personal and Professional Development I, II, and III; Honors English I, II, III, and IV; Honors History I and II; Honors Social Science Project; and two Honors Seminars or Research Projects (or one of each). Students who complete all Honors Program requirements are recognized as Honors Program Graduates in the College Commencement ceremony. They receive an Honors Program certificate as well as a gold honors seal on their diploma. A notation is added to the official College transcript to indicate that they have completed the requirements of the Honors Program and to explain what those requirements are. This note comes at the very beginning of the transcript to assist future employers or graduate/professional school admissions committees in understanding what the Honors Program means at The Citadel.

Scholarship Availability: No scholarships are awarded through the Honors Program, although the Honors Director is a member of the College Scholarships Committee.

The Campus Context: Founded in 1842, The Citadel is a state-assisted, comprehensive, liberal arts college in a military environment. The College has two diverse, but equally important, goals. One is to graduate young men and women with alert minds and sound bodies who have been taught the high ideals of honor, integrity, loyalty, and patriotism; who accept the responsibilities that accompany leadership; and who have sufficient professional knowledge to take their places in the competitive world. The second goal is to serve the citizens of the Lowcountry and the state of South Carolina through its coeducational College of Graduate and Professional Studies and a broad range of noninstructional activities and services. In 1995, the College was ranked in the top 10 percent of regional colleges and universities, eleventh overall in the South.

Characteristic of its unique environment, the Citadel Museum displays military, academic, social, and athletic aspects of life on campus. Handsome exhibits trace the history of the College from 1842 to the present. There are regular Dress Parades: South Carolina Corps of Cadets parade on Friday afternoons during the academic year. Featured in these parades are the world-renowned Citadel Regimental Band and the Pipe band.

There are two colleges at The Citadel: The Corps of Cadets (the undergraduate College) and the College of Graduate and Professional Studies. There are seventeen degree programs for the undergraduates and ten for the graduates.

Student Body There are 1,847 students (almost all men) in the Corps of Cadets. The ethnic breakdown of the student body is 88 percent Caucasian, 8 percent African American, 2 percent Asian, and 2 percent Hispanic. Currently, there are 43 international students. All cadets are required to live on campus for all four years. Currently, 54 percent of the members of the Corps of Cadets receive financial aid. There are no fraternities or sororities.

Faculty Of the 244 total faculty members, 163 are full-time and 95 percent hold terminal degrees. The student-faculty ratio is 16:1.

Key Facilities The Daniel Library holds 182,000 volumes. Free writing, learning, and word processing strategies are provided to all segments of The Citadel community. The Citadel computer facilities consist of nine labs holding fifty Macintosh computers, seventy IBM-PCs, and twenty DEC terminals.

Honorary Societies Phi Kappa Phi

Athletics Intercollegiate athletics include football, basketball, track, soccer, tennis, golf, and wrestling. The Citadel also offers a wide range of intramural sports.

Study Abroad A summer study-abroad program exists for students studying French, German, and Spanish in the countries where the language is spoken.

Job Opportunities Students are offered a range of work opportunities on campus, including assistantships and work-study.

Tuition: $3499 for state residents, $8142 for nonresidents, per year (1997–98)

Room and Board: $3950

Fees: A deposit is required to defray the cost of uniforms and supplies: $3900 for freshmen, $1200 for upperclassmen

Contact: Director: Jack W. Rhodes, 171 Moultrie Street, Charleston, South Carolina 29409; Telephone: 843-953-3708; Fax: 843-953-7084; E-mail: rhodesj@citadel.edu

City College of San Francisco

2 Pu G M Sc Tr AA

▼ City College of San Francisco Honors Program

Located in a city whose name alone invites reverie, the City College of San Francisco Honors Program offers students, at modest cost, a place to excel and prepare for transfer to selective universities. City College is one of the largest community colleges in the United States, and its size is mirrored in the honors program with its large range of classes from anatomy to Spanish and including such fields as Chinese and Asian-American studies, archaeology, political science, and ecology, as well as art history, Japanese, Russian, and French courses. The College offers more than fifty academic majors.

Students in the honors program benefit from evenings at the Fine Arts Museums of San Francisco, the American Conservatory Theater, and the San Francisco Ballet and Opera. The College offers an extensive network of student clubs, extracurricular activities, and performing and creative arts events.

Recent alliances make the City College of San Francisco Honors Program a priority starting point for transfer to UCLA; California, Irvine; and San Francisco State. City College also has transfer agreements with a number of first-tier historically black colleges and universities, Hispanic universities, and Tribal colleges. Students have also gone from the honors program to a number of excellent private schools such as Penn State and Stanford.

The program currently enrolls about 300 students.

Participation Requirements: Students may enter the honors program through one of the following criteria: SAT scores of 1100 or higher, ACT scores of 24 or higher, TOEFL score of 650 or higher, scores of 4 or 5 in Advanced Placement (AP) courses, or City College GPA of 3 or higher. Students must then maintain a GPA of 3.0 or higher.

Admission Process: Request or download an application from the Honors Program, City College of San Francisco and return it with required documentation.

Scholarship Availability: Completion of the honors program make students eligible for certain multiple honors scholarships given by the Honors Transfer Council of California; UCLA; and California, Irvine. Students may also apply for Cal Grants and other financial aid while at City College through the Financial Aid Office.

The Campus Context: City College is a large, urban community college, with eight campuses and more than 100,000 students, all in San Francisco. Within the College there are five schools: Liberal Arts, Social and Behavioral Sciences, Science and Math, Applied Technology, and Health and Physical Education.

Student Body Reflecting the diversity of San Francisco, the student body is about 40 percent Asian, 29 percent Caucasian, 15 percent Hispanic, 8 percent African American, and 1 percent Native American. There are about 1,500 international students.

Faculty The 2,000 faculty members reflect the diversity of San Francisco. More than 300 of the faculty members hold doctorates. Many are recognized experts in their field. All classes are taught by faculty members, none by teaching assistants.

Key Facilities The recently constructed Rosenberg Library provides comfortable study areas, computer labs, and language study and tutorial centers. More than $200,000,000 in campus renovations are scheduled for the next several years, thus making City College a more enhancing place to study.

Athletics City College has a full athletics program from baseball to fencing, and it has the number one ranked community college football team in the United States.

Study Abroad City College has a wide range of study abroad activities.

Support Services City College provides disabled students facilities and support services, as well as tutoring, which is often a source of employment for honors students. The College also has an extensive network of counselors and a Transfer Center to help students plan for transferring to other institutions.

Job Opportunities Many work opportunities are available both on and off campus; advising and job placement assistance are available from the Career Center.

Tuition: Tuition is $11 per unit for state residents; $141 per unit for nonresidents; $147 per unit for international students.

Room and Board: City College does not have dorms, but apartments and rooms are available in the city.

Contact: Director: Dr. Tom Blair, Honors Program, Box A-99p, City College of San Francisco, 50 Phelan Avenue, San Francisco, California 94112; Telephone: 415-239-3542; Fax: 415-452-5110; E-mail: tblair@ccsf.org; Web site: http://www.ccsf.org/

The City College of The City University of New York

4 Pu G M Sc Tr AA

▼ Honors Program

The College-wide Honors Program at City College offers selected high-achieving students in all disciplines a particularly challenging academic program. Small classes are designed and taught by an outstanding faculty. The centerpiece of the program is the honors liberal arts core, an enhanced and enriched curriculum that includes interdisciplinary courses in the humanities, sciences, and social sciences and provides an excellent academic base, regardless of a student's eventual specialization. Most courses in the honors curriculum are special sections of required courses, but several innovative alternatives designed particularly for honors students are offered each semester. Most students enter the program as freshmen, but transfer and continuing students are welcome at the discretion of the director.

City College is a home campus for the university-wide CUNY Honors College: University Scholars Program, which accepts new first-year students with outstanding academic records. CUNY Honors College students at City are enrolled in the College-wide Honors Program and take special interdisciplinary seminars using New York City as a resource and text. They receive a "cultural passport" that provides entrance to concerts, theater, art, science, and history museums and galleries.

Honors students take a special section of new student orientation and have access to early registration and special advising. The Honors Center, a suite including a conference room where students have access to computers and current newspapers, provides a place for honors students to study and meet in a supportive atmosphere. The honors staff is also available in the center to advise and assist students.

Depending on their academic interests, honors students may also apply to join a variety of honors-level programs that provide curricular, advising, and/or scholarship enhancement. Among these programs are the Engineering Leadership Program, the City College Fellows Program (for students pursuing the Ph.D. degree), Isaacs Scholars Program (English and languages), Irani-Summerfield Fellows Program (humanities or arts), Minority Access to Research Careers (MARC) Program (biomedical research), and the Rosenberg-Humphrey Program in Public Policy.

Upperclassmen with acceptable GPAs may choose to pursue honors in a particular department. Departmental honors is usually research-oriented, with a sequence of courses or independent study that culminates in research such as a thesis or laboratory research project.

Founded more than thirty years ago, City College's College-wide Honors Program includes approximately 175 students.

Participation Requirements: All students in College-wide Honors take five prescribed core courses. Additional required courses vary depending on the student's degree objective. The total number of credits in the program varies from 21 to 34. Retention in the program requires a cumulative 3.0 GPA. Upon completion of the Honors Program, the designation "Liberal Arts Honors" is entered on the student's record. To remain in the

Interpreting the symbols: **2**=two-year college, **4**=four-year college; **Pu**=public or state college, **Pr**=private college; **G**=general honors program; **D**=departmental honors program; **S**=small program (fewer than 100 students), **M**=midsize program (100 to 500 students), **L**=large program (more than 500 students); **Sc**=scholarships available in honors program; **Tr**=transfer students accepted into honors program; **HBC**=historically black college; **AA**=academic advisors; **GA**=graduate advisors; **FA**=fellowship advisors.

CUNY Honors College: University Scholars Program, students must have a 3.5 GPA by the time they have completed 60 credits. Successful completion of departmental honors is noted on the student's record.

Admission Process: To be admitted to the College-wide Honors Program as an entering freshman, students must have a high school average of at least 85 percent and the appropriate performance on standardized tests. Continuing and transfer students are also eligible at the discretion of the Director and must present similar academic records. Eligible students are invited to apply and must interview for the program. The CUNY Honors College: University Scholars Program admits only new freshmen, who must submit a special application, an essay, and recommendations and be interviewed. The profile of the first Honors College class included a mean SAT I of 1250 and GPA of 92.

Scholarship Availability: The College-wide Honors Program is not a scholarship program, but many honors students receive merit awards. CUNY Honors College: University Scholars students receive full tuition, fees, and a book allowance for four years and an academic expense account to use for educationally enriching experiences such as study abroad. Information about merit scholarships for honors eligible students is available from the Honors Center.

The Campus Context: The City College of New York is the oldest of the colleges which make up the City University of New York. Since its founding in 1847, the College has prepared alumni for success in graduate and professional school and for leadership in business and government. Eight alumni have won the Nobel Prize and nine faculty members are currently members of the prestigious National Academies of Science and of Engineering. The College ranks eleventh nationally in the number of alumni who have gone on to become America's leading business executives. In recent years, City College has ranked in the top 3 percent nationally in the number of graduates who have gone on to earn Ph.D.s. The College prides itself on the large number of undergraduate research opportunities and internships available to its students.

The College includes five schools: the College of Liberal Arts and Science (offering twenty-eight majors); the School of Architecture, Urban Design and Landscape Architecture; the Sophie Davis School of Biomedical Education (a seven-year B.S./M.D. curriculum); the School of Education (offering four majors); and the School of Engineering (offering seven majors).

City College is internationally known for the research activity of it faculty members. The College houses several institutes, including the Institute for Ultrafast Spectroscopy and Lasers and the CUNY Institute for Transportation Systems.

The campus of 35 acres is in the area known as St. Nicholas Heights, in Manhattan. Among its twenty buildings are a landmarked complex of neo-Gothic buildings, Aaron Davis Hall for the Performing Arts, and the Herman Goldman Center for Sports and Recreation.

The College offers students a wide variety of social activities, with more than ninety clubs organized on campus. Students can participate in numerous intercollegiate and intramural sports.

Student Body In 2001, undergraduate enrollment was 8,067; there were 10,483 students enrolled overall. Fifty-three percent of the students are women. The racial/ethnic distribution of the undergraduate student body is 13.5 percent Asian/Pacific Islander, 29.6 percent black, 26 percent Hispanic, and 8.7 percent white.

Faculty The faculty includes about 450 full-time members, 85 percent of whom hold Ph.D. degrees. The student-faculty ratio is 15:1.

Key Facilities The City College libraries include more than 1.4 million volumes, which are housed in the Morris Raphael Cohen Library and three branch libraries. Computer facilities are extensive with student-access workstations located in all of the academic buildings.

Athletics There are fourteen NCAA Division III varsity teams for men and women on campus and seven intramural sports activities.

Study Abroad City College students may study abroad through programs offered by any unit of the City University of New York.

Special Services The College's Office for Student Disability Services coordinates services for students with special needs.

Job Opportunities Many students work on campus as student aides, administrative staff members, laboratory assistants, and tutors. In addition, many students have the opportunity to do undergraduate research.

Tuition: Full-time, $3200 for state residents ($6800 for nonresidents); part-time, $135 per credit for state residents ($285 per credit nonresidents)

Mandatory Fees: $118.70 per year, full-time; $86.70 per year, part-time

Room and Board: City College is a commuter school

Contact: Director: Robin Villa, The City College of New York, Honors Center Room R 6/293, New York, New York 10031-9160; Telephone: 212-650-6917; Fax: 212-650-7337; E-mail: honorscenter@ccny.cuny.edu; Web site: http://www.ccny.cuny/honorscenter

Clarion University of Pennsylvania

4 Pu G S Sc Tr

▼ Honors Program

Clarion University's Honors Program is a "close knit" group of talented students preparing for the future. Honors courses satisfy general educational requirements and include field experiences. The twenty-one-course curriculum promotes development of essential life skills targeted for successful career outcomes. The honors experience extends beyond the walls of the traditional classroom and has included visits with archaeologists in Italy, with psychologists and anthropologists at a primate center, with large corporate firms and small businesses, and with molecular biologists in laboratories. Honors students have studied twentieth-century music, learned the art of problem solving, and pondered the ethical implications of research. In addition, curricular and cocurricular themes prepare Clarion Honors Program students to assume leadership roles. The program has formed learning partnerships with high school programs for the gifted. Academically talented students from these high schools visit the campus for theater performances, environmental science field trips, and debate tournaments. The Honors Program is not for all students—it's only for those individuals who desire professional success, demand academic excellence, and expect to create the future.

The program, which has been in existence since 1986, selects 50 freshmen each year. Currently, there are 100 students who major in the program. Honors students major in every department and college within the University and participate in preprofessional planning.

Participation Requirements: The Honors Program is a four-year program. In the freshman year, students take a 6-credit modes of discourse (linked English and speech class) and a 3-credit humanities course in the spring semester. In the sophomore year, students take a 3-credit mathematics or science class and a 3-credit social sciences course. In the junior year, students take a junior seminar that develops a project (typically within the major) for the senior presentation. Honors 450 is the capstone experience that culminates in a University-wide presentation. This senior project is developed individually with a faculty adviser. Honors courses are taught as special topics and faculty instructors are recruited for their scholarly expertise.

To remain in the program, students must maintain at least a 3.4 cumulative GPA. Successful completion of the program is recognized at commencement and is also noted on the official transcript.

Admission Process: High school students are recruited on the basis of applications. Application sets require SAT I scores of 1150 or higher or equivalent ACT scores, graduation in the top 15 percent of the high school class, activities, a short written statement, and an interview with the Program Admissions Committee. Students may apply for admission to the Honors Program after the first or second semester of the freshman year. Students may major in any discipline within the University.

Scholarship Availability: Scholarships of various amounts are awarded based on academic performance while in high school. Sophomores, juniors, and seniors may receive renewable awards based on academic performance and service. Most honors students are recipients of academic scholarships.

The Campus Context: Clarion University of Pennsylvania and the town of Clarion are located just off Interstate 80, an easy 2-hour drive from Erie, Pittsburgh, and Youngstown. The peaceful wooded countryside and surrounding hills offer a visually pleasing and serene atmosphere, most spectacularly in the autumn. Located within a few blocks of Clarion campus is downtown Clarion, with stores, restaurants, churches, pharmacies, and all necessary services. A hospital, shopping mall, and several hotels are only 2 miles away. Majors are divided among four colleges and one school, including the College of Arts and Sciences, College of Education and Human Services, College of Business Administration, and the School of Nursing. Students may also choose preparatory professional or allied health and health services studies. Clarion University is a member of the State System of Higher Education.

A farsighted building program has transformed Clarion into one of the most up-to-date campuses in Pennsylvania. However, many of the older, ivy-covered buildings remain to preserve the historical beauty. Campus facilities include state-of-the-art Smart classrooms with large-screen computer monitors that are linked to the Internet; a communications center with a TV studio, radio station, new cross-platform, and high-end computer lab for multimedia graphic design and illustration; a science center with fully equipped laboratories, a planetarium, a greenhouse, and a weather station; a fine arts center that houses a theater, an auditorium, music practice rooms, art studios, and an art gallery; the business administration building that houses case-study classrooms, a computer center, and an auditorium; two libraries with computer labs; and a physical education complex, including swimming and diving pools, a gymnasium-auditorium, racquetball courts, and weight training and fitness rooms. Clarion opened a $5.8-million student recreation center in 1999. The Chandler Dining Hall has recently been renovated to make the dining experience similar to that of a food court.

Student Body The undergraduate enrollment is 5,812 students from thirty-three states and forty-two countries. Thirty-eight percent of the students are men and 62 percent are women. Eighty-five percent of the students receive financial aid. The ethnic distribution is 92 percent white (non-Hispanic) and 8 percent black, Asian, and Hispanic. The campus has 104 international students. Thirty-four percent of the undergraduates reside on campus. The membership of the ten national sororities and nine national fraternities at Clarion University totals more than 1,000 men and women.

Faculty The total number of faculty members is 378, of whom 90 percent are full-time. Of the full-time faculty members, 74 percent have terminal degrees. The student-faculty ratio is 19:1 and average class size is 22 to 25 students.

Key Facilities The Rena M. Carlson Library is a new, state-of-the-art $15-million facility. The library offers a broad range of electronic and print information resources and 130 public access computers to support curricular and research needs. The library's collection consists of more than 1.5 million items. It offers access to more than 6,000 full-text periodicals online to faculty members and students on campus and in distance learning programs.

Honorary Societies Alpha Mu Gamma, Alpha Psi Omega, Beta Beta Beta, Kappa Delta Pi, Kappa Kappa Psi, Lambda Sigma, Omicron Delta Epsilon, Phi Alpha Theta, Phi Eta Sigma, Psi Chi, Society for Collegiate Journalists, and Tau Beta Sigma

Athletics The athletic program offers a wide variety of sports and intramural programs for the Clarion University community. Clarion is a member of the NCAA and facilities are available for major sports including baseball, basketball, football, golf, swimming and diving, wrestling, tennis, cross-country, track and field, soccer, and volleyball.

Study Abroad The Honors Program and the Office of International Programs collaborate in providing students with study-abroad opportunities. Students can participate in exchanges, study-abroad programs, internships, and other learning opportunities in most countries around the world. Two full scholarships are available annually for a summer program abroad in collaboration with Honors Programs from the State System of Higher Education.

Support Services Students with disabilities have access to University student support resources, including counseling services and career services.

Job Opportunities Work opportunities are available on and off campus, including the Honors Program Office.

Tuition and Fees: $4016 for residents, $6024 for nonresidents

Room and Board: $4048

Mandatory Fees: $1179

Contact: Director: Dr. Hallie E. Savage, 840 Wood Street, Clarion Pennsylvania 16214-1232; Telephone: 814-393-2585; Fax: 814-393-2430; E-mail: hsavage@clarion.edu; Web site: http://www.clarion.edu/honors

CLARKE COLLEGE

4 Pr G S Tr

▼ Honors Program

The Clarke College Honors Program is designed to enhance the educational experience of Clarke's superior students. The objectives of the Honors Program are to provide intellectual stimuli and challenges for students with superior academic ability, to provide opportunities for these students to interact with each other and build intellectually satisfying and supportive relationships with peers and faculty and staff members, and to deepen the love of learning, understanding of great issues, and independent scholarship among these students.

Honors classes are part of the General Education program and provide academic rigor suitable to challenge and encourage honors students to excel. Course variety is extensive and represented by departments in the humanities, religious studies, social sciences, natural sciences, and fine arts. The honors curriculum engages students in writing, thinking, speaking, reading, listening, and researching topics across the curriculum. These courses are open to honors students only.

Students are given the opportunity to explore topics of interest through extracurricular activities and national competitions. Extracurricular activities are arranged to provide intellectual

Interpreting the symbols: **2**=two-year college, **4**=four-year college; **Pu**=public or state college, **Pr**=private college; **G**=general honors program; **D**=departmental honors program; **S**=small program (fewer than 100 students), **M**=midsize program (100 to 500 students), **L**=large program (more than 500 students); **Sc**=scholarships available in honors program; **Tr**=transfer students accepted into honors program; **HBC**=historically black college; **AA**=academic advisors; **GA**=graduate advisors; **FA**=fellowship advisors.

stimulation by exposing honors students to a variety of interdisciplinary activities outside the traditional classroom. Honors students are encouraged to compete and/or collaborate with the best students from other colleges and universities for academic recognition.

The annual Clarke College Undergraduate Research Conference provides a forum for students to present research conducted at Clarke. The conference features students from the Honors Program who are preparing to present their research at the National Conference for Undergraduate Research (NCUR). Other presenters include students from the Honors Program as well as students who have completed research in other academic departments.

Participation Requirements: The Clarke College Honors Program consists of three components: Curriculum Component, Extracurricular Component, and Academic Excellence Component. The Curricular Component comprises two semesters of Honors Colloquium, the introductory course for first-year students in the Honors Program, plus an additional 9 credits of honors-designated courses. Each student must participate in six extracurricular activities each semester. Finally, each student must participate in at least one external activity that recognizes academic excellence and may include, but is not limited to, submission of a piece of writing for publication or presentation or application for a competitive research assistantship.

Admission Process: Incoming first-year students are admitted to the Honors Program by invitation only. Selection is based on academic factors such as ACT/SAT I scores, GPA, and class standing. Continuing Clarke students with a cumulative GPA of 3.5 or higher may apply for admission into the Honors Program. Applications are reviewed by the Honors Committee. Students must maintain at least a 3.5 cumulative GPA to remain in the program. Successful completion of the program is recognized at commencement and is also noted on the official transcript and diploma.

Scholarship Availability: Honors students are eligible for academic scholarships that are offered to all Clarke students. Clarke College does not offer a scholarship specifically designated for students in the Honors Program.

The Campus Context: Clarke College is a growing four-year, coeducational, Catholic, liberal arts institution. It was founded in 1843 by Mary Frances Clarke, foundress of the Sisters of Charity of the Blessed Virgin Mary (BVM). Clarke is the only BVM college in the U.S. The College's 55-acre tree-filled campus rests on a bluff in a peaceful residential area that overlooks the city of Dubuque (population 60,000) and the Mississippi River. Clarke offers more than forty undergraduate liberal arts fields and preprofessional programs and four graduate programs in education, management, nursing, and physical therapy.

Building on the history and tradition of the BVMs, Clarke will enter the twenty-first century as a distinguished, student-centered, Catholic, liberal arts college recognized throughout the United States for graduating students who are prepared academically, morally, and spiritually to become leaders in a rapidly changing workplace and an evolving, diverse society.

Student Body Clarke College's total enrollment for the fall 1998 semester was 1,279, a 10 percent increase from the previous fall. This marks the eleventh consecutive year for enrollment growth, with a 59 percent increase since 1987. Ninety percent of Clarke students receive some form of financial aid. Sixty-eight percent of Clarke's students are women, while 32 percent are men. Seven percent of the student body are American minority or international students.

Faculty Clarke College has 142 faculty members, of whom 81 are full-time. Approximately 75 percent of Clarke's faculty members hold the highest degrees available in their respective fields. These degrees come from some of the most prestigious colleges and universities, including Duke, University of Chicago, Penn State, Notre Dame, and numerous state institutions.

Key Facilities The Nicholas J. Schrup Library at Clarke College contains more than 129,000 volumes and features an instructional resource center, art slide collection, music materials collection, media center, two-way interactive video/audio fiber-optic classroom, writing lab, and academic support center. Computers are available for student use campuswide, from the residence halls to the library to the computer center and classroom buildings. There are fifteen computer labs on campus, and Clarke's student-to-computer ratio is 8:1. Residence halls are fiber-optic wired for access to the Internet.

Athletics The Clarke Crusaders compete in NCAA Division III. Clarke is a member of the Northern Illinois-Iowa Conference. Intercollegiate teams include men's and women's alpine skiing, basketball, cross-country, golf, soccer, tennis, and volleyball; as well as men's baseball and women's softball. Clarke also offers cheerleading, pompons, and a wide variety of intramural sports.

Study Abroad Clarke College offers study-abroad opportunities for students to study in other countries while earning credits for their Clarke degree. Such opportunities are offered through a consortium of colleges and universities, which increases the number of options and allows students to use a large part of their financial aid to pay for the cost of tuition and other expenses while studying abroad.

Job Opportunities Clarke College offers students federal, state, and campus work-study job opportunities both on and off campus. These opportunities are coordinated by the financial aid office. The career services office works with students to secure internship and cooperative education placements locally, nationally, and internationally.

Tuition: $12,688 full-time, $315 per credit hour part-time (1998–99)

Room and Board: $4886

Mandatory Fees: $240

Contact: Director: Dr. Kent Anderson, 1550 Clarke Drive, Dubuque, Iowa 52001; Telephone: 319-588-6562; Fax: 319-588-6789; E-mail: kanderso@keller.clarke.edu

---

Clarkson University

4 Pr G M Sc Tr

▼ Honors Program

The Honors Program focuses on current and emerging programs in science, technology, and society. It offers special academic challenges and opportunities for Clarkson University's most promising students. The program enables students to take full advantage of their intellectual gifts by providing a first-rate, problem-based curriculum; develops creative problem-solving and leadership abilities; strengthens communication skills, including those required by the new information technologies; and explores the connections between students' engineering, science, liberal arts, or business majors and American society.

The core of the program is its thematic sequence of courses: first year, The Computer and the Age of Information; second year, The Contemporary World: Its Problems and Their Origins; third year, Science: Problems and Possibilities; and fourth year, Research and Modernity. While the topics for these courses change every year, the goal of the sequence is to bring the viewpoints of different disciplines to bear on current problems. Recent problem-based classes have included a sophomore course in which the students built a computer simulation game to model economic and environmental issues associated with the Adirondack Park and a junior seminar, Chaos and Coherency, in which students studied the mathematics of chaos theory and its implications for the stock market.

The program admits 30 first-year students annually and adds approximately 5 students to each class via internal admission or external transfer. Class size is small, typically 13 to 18 students per section, and total honors membership varies between 120 and 140 students.

Participation Requirements: Students take one honors course per semester. First-year students take The Computer as an Intellectual Tool I and II. The first course helps to prepare them for using the computer at a technological university like Clarkson and in their careers; the second explores the social impact and ethical issues associated with new information technologies. Second-year students take a contemporary problem sequence. Their first-semester course focuses on a contemporary problem or issue, then in the second semester they investigate the intellectual or historical roots of that same problem. As currently projected, the fall 1999 course will focus on disaster and will result in the creation of a disaster relief plan; the fall 2000 course will involve designing toys for children with disabilities; and the fall 2001 course will be a green engineering project on recyclable cars. Third-year students take a science seminar with a different topic each year and begin their honors thesis. Fourth-year students complete their thesis and close the Honors Program with a seminar on modernity.

To remain in the program, students, except for those in their first year, must maintain at least a 3.25 cumulative GPA. Successful completion of the program is recognized at commencement and is also noted on the official transcript and diploma.

Admission Process: The Honors Program invites applications from students who have 1350 and above SAT I scores and graduate in the top 10 percent of their class or who have outstanding academic or leadership achievements. An honors application consists of an essay, letter(s) of recommendation, and an interview as well as the student's completed Clarkson application form. In evaluating candidates, the admissions committee looks at the applicant's love of learning, intellectual curiosity, initiative, degree of motivation, ability to handle uncertainty, work ethic, and ability to work with others. Admission to the program is by rolling admission; qualified students who apply after the thirty slots in the entering class are filled are placed on a wait list.

Scholarship Availability: All students accepted into the Honors Program receive an Honors Scholarship as part of their Clarkson University financial assistance package.

The Campus Context: Clarkson University, founded in 1896, offers professional programs in engineering, science, business, liberal arts, and the health sciences as well as distinctive interdisciplinary programs. Preprofessional programs are available in law, medicine, physical therapy, dentistry, and veterinary sciences, and the University has a comprehensive Graduate School. The campus is located on 640 wooded acres in the northern New York village of Potsdam (population 10,200), in the Adirondack foothills near the St. Lawrence River. Major international cities of Montreal, Quebec, and Ottawa, Ontario, are within a 2-hour drive.

Key facilities on the technology-rich campus include the Center for Advanced Materials Processing (a New York State Center for Advanced Technology), with seventy state-of-the-art research labs. Facilities in engineering and science include a Multidisciplinary Engineering and Project Laboratory for team-based projects, such as the Sunrayce or Mini-Baja competitions; a wide variety of other labs equipped for a range of specializations, such as robotics, high voltage, electron microscopy, polymer fabrication, crystal growth, structural testing, virtual reality, molecular design, and human brain electrophysiology; and a Class 10 clean room. In August of 2000, a spectacular new academic building will open with state-of-the-art technology for the Schools of Business and Liberal Arts, along with three multidisciplinary Centers for Communication and Media, Leadership and Entrepreneurship, and Global Competitiveness, accessible to all students.

Student Body Students come predominately from the northwestern United States but also from many other states and countries. About 23 percent of the approximately 2,220 undergraduates are women. There are about 300 graduate students. More than 90 percent of the undergraduates receive some form of financial aid.

Faculty A faculty of 174, including 151 full-time members, serves both the undergraduate and graduate programs. Ninety-five percent of the faculty members have earned doctorates. Courses are taught by faculty members, while graduate students assist in laboratory and recitation situations. The faculty-student ratio is 1:16.

Key Facilities The fully networked campus has more than 3,500 computers and high-end workstations, including more than 200 RS/6000 workstations outfitted for fast, high-resolution 3-D graphics. The library houses more than 500,000 print and microform items and subscribes to 900 journals. All residence rooms, classrooms, labs, and offices have full Internet access.

Honorary Societies Phi Kappa Phi, Tau Beta Pi, and Phi Theta Kappa

Athletics More than 80 percent of the students participate in recreational or intramural sports. Among the athletic facilities are a field house and a gymnasium with racquetball courts, a new 3,000-square-foot fitness center, a swimming pool, and a student center/hockey arena. The campus also has many miles of trails for hiking, cross-country skiing, and biking. Varsity sports programs include an NCAA Division I team in men's hockey and Division III varsity teams in men's and women's basketball, cross-country, golf, lacrosse, alpine and Nordic skiing, soccer, swimming, and tennis; men's baseball; and women's volleyball. Clarkson is a member of the NCAA, ECAC, UCAA, Empire Athletic Association, and the NYSWCAA.

Study Abroad Clarkson provides excellent opportunities for students who wish to study abroad for a semester or a year, through agreements with the City University of London, England; Lulea University, Sweden; Universität Potsdam, Germany; Monash University and Newcastle University, Australia; and Queen's University in Ontario, Canada.

Support Services For students who qualify under the Department of Education criteria, federally funded Student Support Services offers consultation on academic concerns and academic accommodative services for individuals with disabilities. The Office of Accommodative Services assists in areas that include campus access, diet, health, housing, and transportation and arranges for provision of special academic services, ranging from videotaped lectures to counseling.

Job Opportunities The Career and Professional Development Center administers a cooperative education program with industry, which offers students the opportunity to spend from four to eight months working full-time with professionals in a chosen field of interest. The co-op program is structured so that participating students may graduate in four years. Summer internships in industry are also popular. In recent years, more than 95 percent of Clarkson graduates have taken career positions or pursued advanced degrees in their field.

Tuition: $19,825 (1999–2000)

Room and board: $7484

Mandatory Fees: $380

Contact: Director: David Craig, P.O. Box 5755, Potsdam, New York 13699-5755; Telephone: 315-268-2320; Fax: 315-268-2344; E-mail: dcraig@clarkson.edu; Web site: http://www.clarkson.edu/honors/

Interpreting the symbols: **2**=two-year college, **4**=four-year college; **Pu**=public or state college, **Pr**=private college; **G**=general honors program; **D**=departmental honors program; **S**=small program (fewer than 100 students), **M**=midsize program (100 to 500 students), **L**=large program (more than 500 students); **Sc**=scholarships available in honors program; **Tr**=transfer students accepted into honors program; **HBC**=historically black college; **AA**=academic advisors; **GA**=graduate advisors; **FA**=fellowship advisors.

CLEMSON UNIVERSITY

4 Pu G D L Tr

▼ Calhoun Honors College

Established in 1962, Calhoun Honors College strives to enrich the educational experience of highly motivated, academically talented students by providing unique opportunities for scholarship and research. The purpose of honors at Clemson is not to reward past achievement, but to foster continued intellectual growth, to cultivate a lifelong love of learning, and to prepare students for lives as leaders and change agents.

More than 1,100 students participate in the honors program, including approximately 300 freshmen who join the program each year. Thirty percent of Clemson's Calhoun Scholars graduated from high school first in their class; thirty-seven percent scored over 1400 on the SAT I.

The philosophy of Calhoun Honors College is that honors should provide opportunities not just to dig deeper within the student's comfort zone, but also to explore the uncharted territory of new and different subjects. In other words, honors entails excellence outside as well as inside the student's major field of study. To this end, Calhoun Scholars are expected to complete two academic programs, General Honors and Departmental Honors.

In addition to the intellectual challenge of the Calhoun Honors College, some of the advantages of membership are early course registration, extended library loan privileges, and the option of honors housing in Holmes Hall. The Calhoun Honors College also sponsors an annual lecture series that brings to the campus scholars of national and international acclaim. Under a special ticket-voucher system, honors students are provided admission to concerts, plays, and other cultural events at Clemson's Brooks Center for the Performing Arts.

Students with the academic ability and leadership potential to compete for major fellowships such as the Rhodes, Marshall, and Truman Scholarships are provided guidance under the auspices of the Dixon Fellows Program. Admission to this program is highly selective and requires the submission of a personal statement, curriculum vitae, and other written materials.

Participation Requirements: The academic program consists of two components. To earn General Honors, students must complete at least six honors courses of no less than 3 credits each. Most of the courses that honors students take for General Honors also satisfy Clemson's General Education requirements. Among the courses students may take for General Honors are the interdisciplinary Calhoun Honors Seminars. These seminars, which satisfy general curricular requirements in humanities and social sciences, feature such exciting topics as the Art, Politics, and Technology of Food; Plants in Medicine, Magic and Murder; and the Lure and Fear of Biotechnology. The Calhoun Seminars are taught in a specially designed classroom equipped with advanced multimedia technology. The average enrollment in all General Honors courses, including the Calhoun Honors Seminars, is 19.

Normally undertaken in the junior and senior years, Departmental Honors provides opportunities for advanced, in-depth study and research within the student's major field. Although specific requirements are set by individual departments, all students are expected to complete a thesis or similar capstone project over two semesters. Students engaged in Departmental Honors may receive funding for their projects from the Calhoun Honors College. Departmental Honors theses and research projects of Clemson's honors students have resulted in prestigious awards and recognition, including publication, postgraduate grants, and even patents.

Students who successfully complete General and Departmental Honors are recognized at a special awards ceremony on the eve of spring commencement and fall graduation. At this ceremony, graduates are awarded the B.C. Inabinet Memorial Honors Medallion as a lasting symbol of their excellent achievements. Completion of Departmental Honors is recognized on the student's transcript and diploma as well as in the printed graduation program.

To receive credit for General and Departmental Honors, all honors courses, except for those few offered only on a pass/fail basis, must be completed with a grade of A or B.

Admission Process: For entering freshmen, admission to the Calhoun Honors College is by invitation, based on a combination of academic performance indicators, including high school GPA, class rank, and SAT or ACT score. No one factor alone is sufficient for admission. In considering candidates for admission, the Honors Office extends invitations to those students who show promise of meeting the high academic standards of the Calhoun Honors College. In general, honors freshmen rank in the top 5 percent of their high school class, have a GPA of 3.75 or higher, and present SAT scores of 1350 and higher. Clemson students who are not admitted to the program as entering freshmen may become members by earning a cumulative GPA of at least 3.4, provided that they have at least four semesters remaining to complete degree requirements. Continuous membership in Calhoun Honors College requires a cumulative GPA of 3.4 or higher.

Scholarship Availability: Scholarships for Clemson University are administered through the Office of Student Financial Aid. Various types of undergraduate financial aid are offered, such as scholarships, loans, grants, and part-time employment. Except for the Clemson University National Scholarship, there are no specific scholarships associated with membership in the Calhoun Honors College. However, many honors students receive scholarships because of their superior academic qualifications.

The Clemson National Scholarship is the University's most prestigious undergraduate award and is based exclusively on merit and awarded through a competitive evaluation process that considers proven academic excellence and a record of leadership and service. This premier scholarship program provides all-inclusive costs, including tuition, fees, room, board, books, and incidental expenses, and it is renewable for four years. It also includes a waiver of the out-of-state tuition and fee differential if applicable. Clemson National Scholarships are awarded without regard to place of residence or academic major.

The Campus Context: Established in 1889 as Clemson Agricultural College, the college was an all-men military school until 1955, when the change was made to civilian status and the institution became coeducational. In 1964, the college was renamed Clemson University. The 1,400-acre campus is located on the former homestead of statesman John C. Calhoun. Nestled in the foothills of the Blue Ridge Mountains and adjacent to Lake Hartwell, the campus commands an excellent view of the mountains to the north and west. In 2 hours, one can drive either to Atlanta, Georgia, or to Charlotte, North Carolina.

Clemson University's real estate holdings consist of more than 32,000 acres of forest and agricultural lands located throughout South Carolina. The majority of these lands are dedicated to Clemson's research and public-service missions. Fort Hill, the former home of John C. Calhoun and inherited by Thomas Clemson, and the Hanover House are listed on the National Register of Historic Places and are open to the public. The campus also has two recognized historic districts containing the Strom Thurmond Institute, which houses the institute offices and Senator Thurmond's papers and memorabilia, and the Cooper Library which has an area of special collections. The Institute is a part of an instructional and public-service district that includes the Brooks Center for the Performing Arts and a continuing education/conference center.

Clemson University offers seventy-four undergraduate degree programs under the Colleges of Agriculture, Forestry, and Life Sciences; Architecture, Arts, and Humanities; Engineering and

Science; Business and Public Affairs; and Health, Education, and Human Development.

Student Body The total undergraduate enrollment is 13,975 students, of whom 45 percent are women. The ethnic distribution of the student body is fewer than 1 percent international students, 7.9 percent African American, fewer than 1 percent Native American, 1.5 percent Asian American, fewer than 1 percent Hispanic, and 86 percent Caucasian. Of all the students, 49 percent live on campus. Fifty-four percent of the undergraduates receive financial aid. There are twenty-six men's general fraternities and fifteen women's sororities.

Faculty The total number of faculty members is 1,291, of whom 1,147 are full-time. Of the full-time faculty members, 1,033 have a terminal degree. The student-faculty ratio is 17:1.

Key Facilities The Robert Muldrow Cooper Library houses more than 1.6 million items, including books, microforms, periodicals, governmental publications, and electronic materials. The Clemson University Division of Computing and Information Technology (DCIT) supports the computing activities of students and employees with an extensive network of computers. DCIT maintains forty-one computer labs throughout the campus, thirteen of which are public-access. The labs contain high-end PCs and laser printing equipment. Students have access to the Internet, e-mail, and Microsoft Office Professional software, which includes word processing, Excel, and PowerPoint.

Honorary Societies Phi Kappa Phi, Golden Key, and Mortar Board

Athletics Clemson had eleven of its nineteen athletic teams rank in the top twenty-five of their respective polls in 2001, its highest figure since the 1991–92 academic year. Clemson also had 31 all-Americans in 2001, its second-highest figure on record. Twelve of the nineteen programs competed in postseason play, led by both soccer programs, which finished in the top ten in the nation. The Clemson golf team has been the most successful in recent years, posting five straight top ten national rankings between 1997 and 2001. That includes a program best, number two national finish in 2001. The Clemson baseball team has been to the NCAA Tournament every year since 1987, and the women's basketball team has been to NCAA play all but one season since 1988. The Clemson women's track program ranked in the top ten in the nation indoors and outdoors in the 2000–01 academic year, a first in that program's history, while the men's program has won eighteen ACC championships since 1988. Football has a strong tradition of excellence, reaching a bowl game in fourteen of the last seventeen years, while the men's basketball team has been to postseason play in seventeen of the last twenty-four seasons, including 1997, when it was ranked eighth (a program best) in the final *USA Today* coaches' poll.

Study Abroad Through the Office of International Services and Diversity Programs, students can choose from a variety of programs offered overseas. Programs are varied to fulfill the needs of most students and include the Agriculture Exchange Program in Aberdeen, Scotland; the Engineering Exchange and Summer Program at the University of Bristol in England; and the Language and International Trade Exchange and Summer Programs in Mexico, Ecuador, France, Germany, and Spain. Exchange and summer programs abroad are offered in Australia, Belgium, Chile, the Czech Republic, Ecuador, England, France, Germany, Japan, Mexico, Scotland, Spain, and more. With the International Student Exchange Program (ISEP), students can study for a semester or an academic year at one of more than eighty institutions world-wide. Transfer credit usually applies within the major with prior academic department approval. Financial aid and scholarships may also transfer for many of the programs abroad.

Support Services Tutoring services are available through academic departments or through the Academic Services Center. Counseling and Psychological Services provides individual and group counseling, workshops, and psychological testing. Student Disability Services coordinates the provision of reasonable accommodations for students with disabilities. Accommodations are individualized, flexible, and confidential based on the nature of the disability and the academic environment.

Job Opportunities Employment opportunities exist in academic departments, the Athletic Department, the Career Center, dining halls, the Financial Aid Office, the Personnel Office, and residence halls. The Cooperative Education Program is a planned program in which students combine alternate periods of academic study and periods of related work with a participating business, industry, agency, or organization. Work periods normally take place during the sophomore and junior years (including summers), while the freshman and senior years are spent in full-time study.

Tuition: $4886 for state residents, $11,080 for nonresidents, per year (2001–02). This includes the mandatory technology fee of $100 and the mandatory student activity fee of $40.

Room and Board: $4434 minimum

Mandatory Fees: $204 (medical fee only)

Contact: Director: Dr. Stephen H. Wainscott, Clemson, South Carolina 29634; Telephone: 864-656-4762; Fax: 864-656-1472; E-mail: shwns@mail.clemson.edu

---

COASTAL CAROLINA UNIVERSITY

4 Pu G S Sc

▼ Honors Program

The Honors Program at Coastal Carolina University aims to develop the reasoning and articulate student. This significant goal is advanced through a challenging and adventurous curriculum that joins intellectually accomplished and motivated students and faculty members. Honors Program courses provide for enriched study of a carefully focused, often multidisciplinary, subject matter. To ensure participation by students from all disciplines, the Honors Program is designed in accord with the academic requirements of the major areas of study at Coastal Carolina University.

Currently enrolled honors students have major areas of concentration in art studio, biology, business administration, computer science, education, English, finance, marine science, mathematics, physical education, political science, and psychology. The program has approximately 75 students.

Participation Requirements: Course work is recognized on the students' diploma. Honors Program students are required to maintain at least a 3.0 GPA to remain in good standing. Students are expected to complete one honors course each semester for a total of twelve honors courses. Before graduation, each student is required to complete a thesis in their major and give a public presentation.

All students in the Honors Program are encouraged to be active in the Honors Program Council (HPC), which serves as a representative body for students enrolled in the Coastal Honors Program.

Admission Process: Admission into the Honors Program is by invitation. Students are evaluated on the basis of SAT I scores, ACT scores, high school class rank, and their honors program application. Applications are received from January to May.

Scholarship Availability: There are a limited number of $1000 scholarships available.

Interpreting the symbols: **2**=two-year college, **4**=four-year college; **Pu**=public or state college, **Pr**=private college; **G**=general honors program; **D**=departmental honors program; **S**=small program (fewer than 100 students), **M**=midsize program (100 to 500 students), **L**=large program (more than 500 students); **Sc**=scholarships available in honors program; **Tr**=transfer students accepted into honors program; **HBC**=historically black college; **AA**=academic advisors; **GA**=graduate advisors; **FA**=fellowship advisors.

The Campus Context: Coastal Carolina University is located 10 miles from Myrtle Beach. The University offers twenty-two degree programs on campus.

Student Body Undergraduate enrollment is 4,200, of whom 58 percent are women. The ethnic distribution of the student body is 86 percent white, 1 percent Hispanic, 9 percent African American, .5 percent Native American, and 1 percent Asian. There are 75–80 international students. Fourteen percent of the students are residents and 86 percent are commuters. Fifty-nine percent of the students receive financial aid.

Faculty There are 177 full-time teaching faculty members, 76 with terminal degrees. The student-faculty ratio is 18:1.

Key Facilities The library holds 215,475 volumes. Approximately 700 computers are located in the library and academic buildings.

Honorary Societies Phi Eta Sigma

Athletics Coastal Carolina University fields fourteen intercollegiate teams. The men's program includes cross-country, tennis, basketball, soccer, baseball, golf, and track and field. Women compete in cross-country, tennis, basketball, volleyball, golf, softball, and track and field. The teams are named after the Coastal Carolina University mascot, the Chanticleer. The University is affiliated with the National Collegiate Athletic Association (NCAA) Division I and is a member of the Big South Conference.

Study Abroad Coastal Carolina University provides a number of study-abroad opportunities.

Support Services All of the University's facilities are handicapped-accessible.

Job Opportunities Coastal Carolina University employs approximately 400 students on campus.

Tuition: $3150 for state residents, $8720 for nonresidents, per year (1998–99)

Room and Board: $4800

Contact: Director: Dr. Denvy Bowman, P.O. Box 1954, Conway, South Carolina 29528; Telephone: 843-349-2298; Fax: 843-349-2914; E-mail: bowman@coastal.edu

Cochise College

2 Pu G S Sc

▼ Honors Program

The Cochise College Honors Program is designed to provide intellectual challenge and stimulation for motivated, creative, and academically talented students. A prime purpose of this program is to foster the lifelong love of scholarly inquiry, open-mindedness, and independent thinking. Meeting the challenges afforded by the program leads to confidence in intellectual ability and enhances the academic potential of all participants. Cochise College honors students create their own projects with the guidance of faculty mentors, within the context of established college courses. Honors contracts are available for courses in every academic, vocational, and technical discipline. The Cochise College Honors Program began in February 1996 and continues to evolve. As of January 2002, 202 students had successfully completed honors contracts and had taken Eng 102H.

Participation Requirements: At present the Cochise College Honors Program consists of individual 1- to 4-unit contracts between instructors and students. Students must have a minimum 3.5 cumulative GPA, must have completed 12 credits in courses from the General Education curriculum leading to a degree, must be full-time and enrolled in a degree program, and must be approved by the Honors Committee. In addition, students must demonstrate the ability to initiate and follow through with a creative project above and beyond traditional classroom activities. In fall 2001 the following curriculum was available for honors students at Cochise College: Eng 102H (3 credits), Hon 251 Honors Seminar (1 credit), Hon 255 Leadership/Service (3 credits), and Hon 260 The Human Quest for Utopia (3 credits). Another 3-credit class is planned for fall 2002.

Scholarship Availability: The Honors Program offers scholarships for the honors contracts. Cochise College grants a variety of need- and merit-based scholarships to exceptional students in all fields of study. Incoming students are advised to contact the Financial Aid Office. In addition to participation in the College Honors Program, outstanding students are eligible to join Phi Theta Kappa, the international honors society for community college students.

The Campus Context: Cochise College was established in 1961 as the second community college in Arizona. The College is located near the city of Douglas in the southeast corner of the state. From the first semester, the College has been committed to serving citizens throughout the more than 5,000 square miles of Cochise County, an area rich in history and cultural diversity. The growth of Fort Huachuca and Sierra Vista and the increased interest in higher education created a need for a second campus in the southwestern part of the county. The Sierra Vista Campus evolved from a few temporary buildings at Buena High School in the early 1970s to a full-fledged separate campus that opened in 1978. The Willcox Center, located in a historic ranching and farming area in northern Cochise County, offers classes under the supervision of the Community Campus, which provides a variety of programs and services throughout the county and region. The Benson Center opened in summer 2000.

The College offers general Associate of Arts, Associate of Science, Associate of Business, and Associate of General Studies degrees to prepare students for transfer to a four-year institution; the A.A.S. degree, which prepares graduates for employment in a specific career; and numerous vocational certificate programs. The College's Career Action Center integrates the academic experiences with the world of work in its three programs: Cooperative Education, Student Job Placement, and Career Placement. An education at Cochise College provides students with knowledge, information, and technical skills essential for a successful life.

Student Body The enrollment of Cochise College for the academic year 2000–01 was 6,011, with women making up 57 percent of the student body and men, 43 percent. The ethnic distribution is Caucasian, 57.11 percent; Hispanic, 25.8 percent; African American, 7 percent; Asian and Pacific Islander, 3.74 percent; and Native American and Native Alaskan, .98 percent. There are approximately 47 international students. Most of the students are commuters; however, there are 166 students in dormitory rooms and 5 students living in family apartments on the Douglas Campus. Seventy-eight percent of Cochise College students receive some form of financial aid.

Faculty Of the 406 faculty members, 25.8 percent are full-time. Nine percent of the full-time faculty members have terminal degrees. The student-faculty ratio is 15:1.

Key Facilities The Cochise College libraries combine traditional library services with new technologies, which include CD-ROM references, faculty/student access to the Internet, a computerized catalog on CD-ROM, laserdisc technology, and interactive teleconferencing classrooms. The three libraries have in excess of 60,000 volumes, 1,200 video titles, and 300 periodical subscriptions. Students have access to the catalog and periodical indices on CD-ROM as well as to a full range of instructional and media software and hardware.

Honorary Society Phi Theta Kappa

Athletics Cochise College competes with other community colleges in women's soccer, men's and women's basketball, men's and women's rodeo, and men's baseball. The Apache Stonghold Gymnasium on the Douglas Campus is the center for intercollegiate sports, concerts, and a variety of intramural activities.

Support Services Cochise College provides accommodations for students with a documented physical, emotional, or learning disability through the office of the ADA Coordinator.

Tuition: $31 per unit for residents, $45 per unit (1 to 6 units) for nonresidents (2001–02)

Room and Board: $1564 (Douglas Campus)

Mandatory Fees: $20

Contact: Director: Fred Close, 901 Colombo, Sierra Vista, Arizona 85635; Telephone: 520-417-4093; Secretary-Treasurer: Robert Atkinson; Telephone: 520-515-5409; E-mail: atkinson@cochise.cc.az.us; Web site: http://www.cochise.org/honors

COLBY-SAWYER COLLEGE

4Pr G S Tr

▼ Honors Program

The Colby-Sawyer College Honors program is designed to provide highly motivated students with an optional intensive experience in the liberal arts. By creating academic, cultural, and social opportunities for integrative and interdisciplinary intellectual discovery, the program challenges students to not only widen their own avenues of intellectual exploration but to take leadership in a community of scholars and participate as catalysts for inquiry and discussion across the College. The academic courses in the program introduce students to a rich body of interdisciplinary knowledge and the process of interdisciplinary thinking. Small seminar class meetings encourage lively exchanges between students and professors. A four-year program of courses, honors contracts, honors research, and honors internships, begins with an introductory honors seminar or "pathway" to be supplemented with related courses from the regular curriculum, and culminates in the second year with a concluding seminar. The College recognizes honors students by permitting them to study in the reading room of the Cleveland, Colby, and Colgate Archives, by sponsoring monthly out-of-class discussion groups often involving meeting visiting speakers and scholars, and by the award at the time of graduation of an honors certificate. The Honors Program is also a valuable source of information and advice for students wishing to pursue graduate study and graduate fellowships.

Faculty members who teach honors courses are drawn from across the College and represent a broad range of academic disciplines. Founded in 1994–95, the Honors Program has offered courses including the following: History of East Asian Art; Environmental Ethics; Native American Literature and Culture; Myth and Folklore; Gender and Science; Voices of Islam; Leadership Without Leaders; The Science of Science Fiction; The City and Town in American Culture; Many Mansions: Religion in the Americas; Society and Disease; and Performing Shakespeare.

Participation Requirements: The honors curriculum is based on the completion of elective courses with an honors designation, beginning with the honors "pathway" that initiates the general liberal arts program sequence at the College. Each semester, faculty members across the College offer at least two interdisciplinary courses for students in the Honors Program, designating at least one of the courses for first-year students only. These courses may be offered for 1 to 3 credits.

Students participate in the Honors Program in addition to their work in the College's Liberal Education Program and their chosen majors, although some honors courses may satisfy part of the College's Liberal Education requirements. On completion of five honors courses, graduating students receive an Honors Certificate and an Honors designation is added to their diploma and transcript.

Admission Process: Incoming students are invited to apply for admittance to the Honors Program based on superior prior academic performance in high school or at another college. Either a cumulative GPA of 3.5 or an SAT score of 1150 in addition to a letter of application describing an example of independent intellectual or creative exploration or a proposal for future exploration form the basis for evaluation of students' acceptance into the program. Once at the College, a student may apply for application to enter the program after having achieved Dean's List status and a similar letter of application to the Coordinator of the Honors Program.

The Campus Context: Colby-Sawyer College had its origins in the founding of the New London Academy in 1837. In 1928, after ninety years as a coeducational school, the Academy became the Colby Junior College for Women. Baccalaureate programs were introduced in the 1940's, leading to the College's renaming in 1975 as Colby-Sawyer College, a four-year institution. In 1990, Colby-Sawyer once more admitted men, returning the College to its coeducational roots.

Colby-Sawyer College is located on the crest of a hill in New London, New Hampshire, in the heart of the scenic Dartmouth–Lake Sunapee region. A splendid environment for learning is created by the spacious, well-maintained campus and stately buildings that range in style from classic Georgian to the innovative architecture of the Susan Colgate Cleveland Library/Learning Center. Other special campus facilities include Baker Communications Center, Sawyer Fine Arts Center, Windy Hill Laboratory School (preschool, K–3), and the Hogan Sports Center. Colby-Sawyer is widely recognized as one of the most vital small residential colleges in the Northeast. The College offers twelve undergraduate majors. Teacher certification is also available in five subject areas.

Student Body Undergraduate enrollment is 901 students, of whom 64 percent are women. The ethnic distribution of the student body is 90 percent white and 5 percent minority-international (5 percent not reported). There are 26 international students, which constitutes 3 percent of the student body. Of the total student population, 87 percent are resident and 13 percent commuter. Approximately 3 out of every 4 Colby-Sawyer students receive some college grant or scholarship.

Faculty There are 49 full-time faculty members (supplemented by adjunct faculty members), 78 percent with terminal degrees. The student-faculty ratio is 12:1.

Key Facilities The library houses 92,116 volumes. Three computer laboratories create a student:College-provided computer ratio of 7.5:1.

Athletics In athletics, Colby-Sawyer is NCAA Division III in a variety of team and individual sports. Varsity competition for women is offered in Alpine ski racing, basketball, lacrosse, riding, soccer, swimming, tennis, and track and field. Varsity competition for men is offered in Alpine ski racing, baseball, basketball, riding, soccer, swimming, and track and field. The Alpine ski racing team is a member of the United States Collegiate Snowsport Association. Colby-Sawyer College maintains a high-quality program of club, intramural/recreational, and varsity athletics and has a reputation for success in sports throughout the state and region.

Job Opportunities Part-time on-campus employment during the academic year is usually awarded as part of a financial aid package. Campus jobs are assigned by the staff of the Harrington Center for Career Development, and payment is at hourly rates established by state and federal legislation.

Tuition: $20,130 per year (2001–02)

Room and Board: $7720

Interpreting the symbols: **2**=two-year college, **4**=four-year college; **Pu**=public or state college, **Pr**=private college; **G**=general honors program; **D**=departmental honors program; **S**=small program (fewer than 100 students), **M**=midsize program (100 to 500 students), **L**=large program (more than 500 students); **Sc**=scholarships available in honors program; **Tr**=transfer students accepted into honors program; **HBC**=historically black college; **AA**=academic advisors; **GA**=graduate advisors; **FA**=fellowship advisors.

Contact: Coordinator: Professor Ann Page Stecker, Department of Humanities, Colby-Sawyer College, 100 Main Street, New London, New Hampshire 03257; Telephone: 603-526-3644; Fax: 603-526-3452; E-mail: astecker@colby-sawyer.edu; Web site: http://www.colby-sawyer.edu

College Misericordia

4 Pr G S

▼ College Honors Program

The honors program at College Misericordia is an interdisciplinary learning community of students and faculty members working together to create an intellectually stimulating and challenging environment for learning. The academic portion of the honors program consists of three components: alternative courses, monthly Explorations Seminars, and the Capstone Seminar. The first is a sequence of core courses in the humanities and social sciences designed specifically for honors students. Honors classes are small (usually less than 15 students), emphasize discussion and critical analysis of material, use primary sources in addition to traditional textbooks, and focus on developing students' communication skills, particularly in writing. In addition, honors courses are linked by common principles and ideas so that they are strongly interdisciplinary. The program also offers elective honors courses in math, science, and the health sciences. The second academic component of the honors program requires student participation in the Honors Explorations Seminar, which usually meets three times each semester. The seminar takes many different forms, including debates, roundtables, or guest lectures, but it always involves discussion among students and faculty members on a topic of general interest. The final academic component of the honors program is the required Honors Capstone Seminar. Within this seminar, students are guided through a process of self-directed research and writing and produce a professional-quality research paper that is presented to the College community and published in the College Misericordia honors journal, *Honorus*.

The honors program also sponsors a variety of additional academic and social programs and opportunities for honors students. Field trips to local and regional historical and cultural venues are often incorporated into honors classes, as are service-learning opportunities. Annual honors trips are planned in consultation with students and have included trips to Philadelphia; Washington, D.C.; and Montreal. Interested honors students are also encouraged to participate in conferences sponsored by the National Collegiate Honors Council and other colleges and universities. Honors students are integrally involved in making program-related decisions and in planning honors activities and events. This is accomplished primarily through the College Misericordia Honors Student Council, which consists of student representatives from each of the classes.

The College Misericordia Honors Program was founded in 1999 and currently enrolls 60 students.

Participation Requirements: Honors students must complete an alternative 36-credit core sequence of honors courses in the humanities and social sciences similar to the College's required core sequence. Each semester, honors students must successfully participate in the Honors Exploration Seminar. They must also complete the Honors Capstone Seminar, which is usually taken in the senior year.

To remain in the program, honors students must achieve at least a 3.0 GPA in their freshman and sophomore years and a 3.25 GPA thereafter; they must also receive grades of C or better in all honors classes.

Graduating honors students who have fulfilled the requirements of the program receive recognition on their diploma, at College awards ceremonies, and at commencement.

Admission Process: Students are admitted to the honors program by application only. Admissions decisions are based on evidence of intellectual curiosity, which can be reflected in a number of different ways, including high school academic record, SAT scores, writing ability, interest in current events, and involvement in extracurricular activities. Students should contact the directors to request application materials. Applications are generally due in late April, and admissions decisions are made shortly thereafter.

Scholarship Availability: College Misericordia offers a variety of academic scholarships to qualified students. There are no scholarships specifically reserved for students in the honors program.

The Campus Context: Founded in 1924 as Luzerne County's first four-year college, College Misericordia is dedicated to the values of the Sisters of Mercy: mercy, service, justice, and hospitality. The College is located in Dallas, Pennsylvania, on a beautiful, 120-acre suburban campus, yet it is just 9 miles from the city of Wilkes-Barre and near the Pocono Mountains.

Misericordia's hallmark is dedicated faculty members and a high-quality core liberal arts and sciences curriculum. A College Misericordia education uniquely combines high-quality academics, professional preparation, and service leadership.

Misericordia offers twenty-five majors in four academic divisions: behavioral sciences, education, and business; health sciences; humanities; and mathematical and natural sciences. The occupational therapy, speech-language pathology, and physical therapy programs are five-year, entry-level Master of Science degree programs. Misericordia also offers Master of Science degrees in nursing, education, and organizational management. The innovative Choice Program assists students who are interested in college but have not yet chosen a major.

Student Body As of fall 2001, there were 1,202 full-time undergraduate students studying at College Misericordia. Of those, 869 were women and 333 were men. Home to 638 residents, the campus features a vibrant college atmosphere. More than 600 part-time and nontraditional learners also study at College Misericordia. The College offers the lowest tuition of any private college in the area, and nearly 95 percent of students receive financial aid.

Faculty The faculty at College Misericordia is made up of 86 full-time members and 76 part-time instructors. Seventy-six percent have a Ph.D. or other terminal degree. (In some areas of the health sciences, the Ph.D. is not the required terminal degree.) All health science faculty members are fully credentialed in their respective disciplines.

Key Facilities The three-story Mary Kintz Bevevino Library, dedicated in 1999, covers 37,500 square feet and houses stacks for 90,000 volumes. Materials include state-of-the-art information and communication technology and a reference section that offers books, serials, and a variety of periodicals as well as reference search tools, CD-ROMs, an electronic database, and microfilm. The Bevevino Library is a member of the Northeastern Pennsylvania Library Network, which provides access to the 1.5-million-volume collection of participating libraries via its new virtual online catalog.

All residence halls are computer-ready and fully wired for Internet access. College Misericordia maintains one computer for every 10 full-time students. There are four main computer laboratories that offer all students access to e-mail and the World Wide Web, as well as to the latest software, programming languages, and applications for their academic departments. Every residence hall has its own six-station computer lab and study area. In addition, the Bevevino Library and the Banks Student Life Center have more than 200 ports where students can plug in their own or College-owned laptops and access the Internet. This year, the College established a customized NewMedia computer lab where students can study Web site design and other Internet applications.

Honorary Societies All College Misericordia students are eligible for membership in Delta Epsilon Sigma (National Scholastic Honor Society).

Athletics College Misericordia competes in the NCAA Division III, the Eastern College Athletic Conference, and the Pennsylvania Athletic Conference. There are eighteen intercollegiate sports for men and women as well as a popular intramural program. Women's sports include basketball, cheerleading, cross-country, field hockey, lacrosse, soccer, softball, swimming, track and field, and volleyball. Men's sports include baseball, basketball, cross-country, golf, lacrosse, soccer, swimming, and track and field.

Study Abroad College Misericordia has cooperative arrangements with several other colleges for study-abroad opportunities. The College also sponsors its own credit-bearing service-learning opportunities, including the six-week Guyana Experience held every summer.

Support Services In addition to a wide array of counseling and career support services, College Misericordia is a pioneer in helping the learning disabled achieve success at the college level. Since 1979, College Misericordia's Alternative Learners Project (ALP) has provided support to students with disabilities. With a full-time professional staff of 4 and cooperation and support from an excellent faculty and administration, ALP serves about 50 students per year. The first program of its type in Pennsylvania, ALP provides students the means to succeed in their courses by proactively providing training in learning strategies developed by Kansas University's Center for Research in Learning to help adolescents and adults with disabilities become more effective and efficient learners. To the degree that the learning strategies are not sufficient, ALP provides an array of accommodations that students can use to bypass problems produced by their disabilities.

Job Opportunities College Misericordia coordinates internships through its Insalaco Center for Career Development. Misericordia also offers a popular work-study program for qualified students. Funded by the federal government and the College, this work-study program provides part-time jobs for students during the academic year and the summer. Jobs are available on campus and in the local community. Students must document financial need to be eligible. Whenever possible, students are assigned jobs related to their educational interests. The Insalaco Center for Career Development also offers this guarantee to students who choose to participate in their program: if not employed in the chosen field or enrolled in graduate school six months after graduation, Misericordia will offer the student a paid internship in that career.

Tuition: $15,800 per year or $390 per credit hour (2001–02)

Room and Board: Approximately $6730 (varies based on meal plan and room selections) (2001–02)

Mandatory Fees: $850 per year (2001–02)

Contact: Directors: Dr. Marnie Hiester, College Misericordia, Lake Street, Dallas, Pennsylvania 18612; Telephone: 570-674-6316; E-mail: mhiester@misericordia.edu; Dr. Cathy Turner, College Misericordia, Lake Street, Dallas, Pennsylvania 18612; Telephone: 570-674-6777; E-mail: cturner@misericordia.edu; Web site: http://www.misericordia.edu

COLLEGE OF CHARLESTON

4 Pu G M Sc Tr

▼ Honors Program

The Honors Program at the College of Charleston was created in 1978 to provide a program and a community for talented and motivated students who enjoy active participation in small stimulating classes and like to investigate ideas. The Honors Program is dedicated to providing these students with a place where they can flourish and grow; it is a real learning community of teachers and students. In addition to receiving exciting and unique educational experiences, students can participate with their fellow Honors Program students in social, cultural, and intellectual events on the campus and in historic Charleston, South Carolina.

The Honors Program challenges intellectually talented students to make the most of the opportunities available to them and to become actively involved in their own education. In honors classes, students take responsibility for their own learning through class discussions, interaction with faculty members and fellow students, and independent research. Honors students are advised by specially chosen faculty advisers, receive priority registration, and have the opportunity to room with other honors students in special honors residence halls. Classes, seminars, and student gatherings are held in the Honors Center, the historic William Aiken House built by Governor William Aiken in 1839.

Participation Requirements: All students take Honors English, the Colloquium in Western Civilization, and at least three other honors courses, one of which must be interdisciplinary. They also take one semester of calculus and a math course at the 200-level or above. Each student undertakes an independent study under the supervision of a faculty tutor and a senior research project, which culminates in a written paper (the Bachelor's Essay). A student must have a GPA of 3.4 or higher to graduate from the program.

Admission Process: There are about 500 students in the program. Approximately 150 entering students are accepted each year by a faculty/student committee on the basis of applications submitted directly to the program. The successful candidate is typically in the top 10 percent of his/her class, has taken numerous honors and/or AP courses, and is active in extracurricular activities. While there is no minimum SAT I score required, the SAT I scores of entering freshmen average above 1300 or 29 on the ACT. A student may apply for admission to the program at any time but is encouraged to apply to both the College of Charleston and the Honors Program (separate applications) before December 15 to maximize the possibility of being accepted to the program and being considered for all available scholarships. Transfer students and currently enrolled students with a GPA of 3.5 or greater may also apply to the program.

Scholarship Availability: The vast majority of the students in the Honors Program receive some form of academic scholarship. More than 75 percent of the honors students who enrolled in fall 2000 and 2001 received merit scholarships, including the Presidential Honors, Founders, Academic Merit, and other named scholarships. Students are considered for all available College of Charleston merit scholarships on the basis of their admission application credentials, provided they are admitted before January 15 preceding the fall term of freshmen enrollment.

The Campus Context: Situated in the midst of a vibrant, culturally rich city that treasures its past while promoting its future, the College of Charleston is one of the nation's most beautiful and historic campuses. Founded in 1770 and chartered in 1785, the College is the oldest institution of higher education in South Carolina and the thirteenth oldest in the United States. In 1836 it became the nation's first municipal college, and in 1970 the College joined the state's higher education system. There are five undergraduate schools: Arts, Business, Education, Humanities and Social Sciences, and Science and Mathematics. Forty-three undergraduate majors, seventeen interdisciplinary minors, and sixteen graduate programs are offered.

Interpreting the symbols: **2**=two-year college, **4**=four-year college; **Pu**=public or state college, **Pr**=private college; **G**=general honors program; **D**=departmental honors program; **S**=small program (fewer than 100 students), **M**=midsize program (100 to 500 students), **L**=large program (more than 500 students); **Sc**=scholarships available in honors program; **Tr**=transfer students accepted into honors program; **HBC**=historically black college; **AA**=academic advisors; **GA**=graduate advisors; **FA**=fellowship advisors.

The campus consists of more than 100 buildings ranging from historic residences to high-tech classrooms. In addition to the main campus, the College includes a classroom facility in North Charleston, Grice Marine Biological Laboratory on James Island, and a 20-acre outdoor sports complex and recreation and sailing area in Mt. Pleasant.

Student Body There are 9,812 undergraduates of whom 60 percent are women, 10 percent are African American, 5 percent are other minorities, and 2 percent are international students. Seventy percent of the students are South Carolina residents. There are 2,100 students who are housed in six main residence halls and twenty-five houses. Many more rent apartments near campus. Sixty-five percent of undergraduates receive financial aid.

Faculty There are 456 full-time faculty members, 85 percent with terminal degrees. The student-faculty ratio is 18:1.

Key Facilities The library contains 578,492 volumes. The College has two high-end computer centers with more than 100 Mac and PC computers each, plus smaller centers located in classroom buildings and dorms.

Honorary Societies Phi Kappa Phi, Golden Key, and ODK

Athletics The College of Charleston is a member of the NCAA's Southern Conference. Intercollegiate athletic teams include basketball, soccer, sailing, swimming, tennis, golf, equestrian, baseball (men), volleyball (women), and softball (women). The equestrian team rode to a third place finish in the Twenty-Eighth Intercollegiate Horse Show Championship, and they are regularly ranked in the top five in the nation. The men's basketball team has gone to post-season play in five of last six years, and, under Coach Kresse, the Cougars have 534 wins against 134 losses.

Study Abroad Direct international exchange programs link the College with universities in Austria, Chile, Cuba, England, France, Japan, Korea, the Netherlands, Spain, and the Virgin Islands. Study-abroad courses are offered every semester, and other exchange opportunities exist through independent study-abroad programs and the National Student Exchange Program.

Tuition: $3780 for state residents, $8540 for nonresidents, per year (2001–02)

Room and Board: $4570 per year (2001–02)

Contact: Director: Dr. John H. Newell, Honors Program, College of Charleston, Charleston, South Carolina 29424; Telephone: 843-953-7154; Fax: 843-953-7135; E-mail: newellj@cofc.edu; Web site: http://www.cofc.edu/~honors

College of DuPage

2 Pu G M Sc Tr

▼ Honors Program

Honors courses at the College of DuPage offer additional challenges and depth to students' college experience and more opportunities to use their minds well. Students who love to learn, are willing to work, and enjoy bringing their imagination and originality to class should consider applying to honors.

Honors courses are enriched versions of regular courses, designed to help academically talented and highly motivated students achieve their maximum potential. Each year, a range of courses in the liberal arts and sciences is offered, consistent with the emphasis on general education in the first two years of college. Honors classes are characterized by small class sizes and a seminar format, which encourage extensive interaction among students as well as between students and the professor. Many students especially appreciate this opportunity to get to know other students better and to feel more like a part of the academic environment of the College.

Each honors course offers an in-depth treatment of course content; emphasizes the development of such intellectual skills as analysis, synthesis, critical inquiry, application, and discussion; and contains a significant writing component.

Additional program benefits include the opportunity to select an honors mentor among faculty members who teach in the Honors Program, assistance with transfer and scholarship applications, and participation in special honors-related activities.

The program began in 1984 and currently has approximately 400 students taking honors courses each quarter. There are currently more than 550 students in the Honors Scholar Program. Three Honors Program students have been awarded scholarships (ten are awarded nationally each year), and in 1998, one graduate was awarded a Rhodes Scholarship.

Participation Requirements: Students may participate in honors in one of two ways: by taking individual honors courses or by participating in the Honors Scholar Program. To participate by way of individual honors courses, students who meet the general eligibility criteria may apply to the honors coordinator for a permit to register for individual honors courses. Entering freshmen may apply after achieving one of these two criteria: a cumulative high school GPA of at least 3.5 (on a 4.0 scale) or a composite ACT score of 25 or higher. Current College of DuPage students must meet these two criteria: completion of 12 or more college-level credits and a cumulative GPA of at least 3.2. To participate by way of the Honors Scholar Program, students who meet the eligibility criteria may apply for admission to the Honors Scholar Program at any time, though first-year entrance is preferred. Admissions requirements for entering first-year students are a cumulative high school GPA of at least 3.5 (on a 4.0 scale) or a composite ACT score of 25 or higher. Current College of DuPage students must have a minimum cumulative GPA of 3.5 in addition to having completed 12 credits.

Students who complete the Honors Scholar Program receive special recognition at Commencement, at the Celebration of Academic Excellence, and on their transcripts and diplomas.

Scholarship Availability: Those who are admitted to the program are entitled to a waiver of in-district tuition on all honors courses as long as they maintain a minimum cumulative GPA of 3.5 and make satisfactory progress toward completing other program requirements (a minimum of 22 hours of honors courses, including an honors seminar). Special transfer programs and scholarships are also available to students seeking a baccalaureate degree.

The Campus Context: The College of DuPage is the largest single-campus community college in the nation. Located in Glen Ellyn, Illinois, it is about 25 miles west of Chicago and serves nearly all of DuPage County and parts of Will and Cook counties. Degrees offered include Associate in Arts, Associate in Science, Associate in Applied Science, Associate in General Studies, Associate in Engineering Science, and Associate in Fine Arts.

Facilities at the College include the McAninch Arts Center, the Berg Instructional Center, and the Physical Education Building. Cooperative education internships, a theater program, and a number of musical opportunities are available.

Student Body The College enrolls approximately 34,000 students. It receives students from twenty-three public and eight parochial high schools in fifty municipalities. The Honors Program is fortunate to draw students from a strong socioeconomic base that supports education. In fact, nearly 20 percent of the students at the College possess a bachelor's degree. A number of student clubs and organizations are available.

Key Facilities There is an Academic Computing Center, and the library contains approximately 150,000 books and thousands of films, videotapes, compact discs, and microfiche.

Honorary Societies Phi Theta Kappa, Psi Beta, Alpha Mu Gamma

Athletics The College has had one of the most successful community college athletic programs in the nation over the last twenty years, winning several national championships and many regional championships in various sports.

Study Abroad The College of DuPage offers myriad study-abroad opportunities.

Tuition: $37 per quarter hour of credit for area residents, $120 per quarter hour of credit for state residents, $163 per quarter hour of credit for nonresidents, per year (2001–02).

Contact: Honors Coordinator: Alice Snelgrove, 425 Fawell Boulevard, Glen Ellyn, Illinois 60137-6599; Telephone: 630-942-2749; Fax: 630-942-3295; E-mail: snelgrov@cdnet.cod.edu.; Web site: http://www.cod.edu/Academic/AcadProg/Hon_Prog/Honors.htm

College of Mount St. Joseph

4 Pr G S

▼ Honors Program

The Honors Program is designed to meet the needs and interests of highly motivated students who are able to take responsibility for their own learning under the guidance of experienced faculty members. The program stresses the relatedness of the various disciplines and challenges students to make connections among them and between these learnings and life in society as they gain an integrated view of the world around them. Classes are limited to 15 to 20 students and are conducted in a seminar format. All courses have an interdisciplinary focus while at the same time fulfilling in part the core liberal arts and sciences component of the College's curriculum. The program is, therefore, compatible with all undergraduate majors. Faculty members who teach in the Honors Program come from a variety of departments and disciplines and are selected because of their demonstrated excellence in teaching as well as their interest and expertise in interdisciplinary study. In addition to a departmental academic adviser, honors students receive additional advising and consultation from the Director of the Honors Program. Students are encouraged to participate in service learning opportunities and other community service projects on and off campus as a means of developing a global perspective and of seeing connections among cultures, people, and nations.

A comfortable study/lounge area adjacent to an open computer lab is provided for honors students. There is space for quiet study as well as for conversation and group work.

There are approximately 60 students enrolled in the Honors Program, which was founded in 1994.

Participation Requirements: Students must complete a Freshman Seminar, at least five honors courses, and a Senior Seminar, which includes a capstone project of the student's design. Honors students must maintain a GPA of 3.2 or higher. Upon completion of the requirements, students are listed in the graduation program as graduates of the Honors Program. This designation is also noted on their diplomas.

Admission Process: Admission to the Honors Program requires that students score in the 75th percentile or above on the SAT I or ACT, that they be in the upper 25 percent of their high school graduating class, and that they be recommended by a teacher or counselor. Students must also submit a personal essay before they are admitted to the Freshman Seminar. Final admission to the program is contingent upon successful completion of this seminar.

Scholarship Availability: Several categories of scholarships are available to students who quality for the Honors Program. Administration of these is through the College Office of Admission.

The Campus Context: The College of Mount St. Joseph is a Catholic coeducational college founded by the Sisters of Charity in 1920. A liberal arts college emphasizing career preparation, the Mount is dedicated to the individual development of students—intellectually, morally, and spiritually.

The Mount offers forty-three degree programs for its more than 2,300 students, with a faculty commitment to teaching and class sizes small enough to provide the personal attention most students want. Students can gain practical work experience before graduation through the cooperative education program. A warm, close-knit campus community encourages students to exercise their talents to their fullest potential in academic, athletic, and leadership activities. Nestled in the hills overlooking the Ohio River, just 15 minutes from downtown Cincinnati, the Mount's location blends the security of a small-town atmosphere with the excitement and career opportunities of a cosmopolitan city.

The Mount's 75-acre campus features modern buildings, all constructed since 1962. The new Harrington Center expands fitness, recreation, and student activities for the entire campus.

Student Body Undergraduate enrollment is 2,307; graduate enrollment is 178. Of the total, 73 percent are women. Eighty-one percent of undergraduates receive financial aid. There are 58 international students from fifteen countries.

Faculty Of the 111 full-time faculty members, 59 percent hold doctoral or terminal degrees. There are also 108 part-time faculty members, 23 percent of whom hold doctoral or terminal degrees.

Key Facilities The library houses 96,694 volumes. There are nine computer laboratories housing 185 computers, which includes twenty-seven Macintosh and 158 Windows based.

Athletics In intercollegiate athletics, the College of Mount St. Joseph is in NCAA Division III. Men's sports include football, basketball, baseball, wrestling, and tennis. Women's sports include volleyball, basketball, soccer, softball, cross-country, and tennis.

Study Abroad Study-abroad programs London, England, and Seville, Spain, and through the Congress/Bundestag program in Germany are available to all students in art, business, and the liberal arts.

Support Services Project EXCEL is a comprehensive support program at the College specifically designed to assist students with learning disabilities who are enrolled in a regular academic program. Program services include academic advising regarding students' specific needs, instruction related to academic skills development, learning strategies, coping skills, supervised instruction and support by professional tutors, audiotaped texts, note-taking support, a writing lab, assistance with word processing, accommodated testing, monitoring of student progress, and academic/support counseling as needed.

Job Opportunities A variety of on-campus employment opportunities exist for qualified students. In addition, the Office of Cooperative Education administers a program of work opportunities that also provides academic credit to students in all majors.

Tuition: $14,200, $363 per credit hour (2001–02)

Room and board: $2700–$14,450

Mandatory Fees: $45 activities fee, $250 per semester technology fee (student is provided with a wireless, hand-held computer)

Contact: Director: Dr. Alan deCouey, Department of Religious and Pastoral Studies, 5701 Delhi Road, Cincinnati, Ohio 45233-1670; Telephone: 513-244-4937; E-mail: alan_decouray@mail.msj.edu; Web site: http://www.msj.edu/honors

Interpreting the symbols: **2**=two-year college, **4**=four-year college; **Pu**=public or state college, **Pr**=private college; **G**=general honors program; **D**=departmental honors program; **S**=small program (fewer than 100 students), **M**=midsize program (100 to 500 students), **L**=large program (more than 500 students); **Sc**=scholarships available in honors program; **Tr**=transfer students accepted into honors program; **HBC**=historically black college; **AA**=academic advisors; **GA**=graduate advisors; **FA**=fellowship advisors.

College of New Rochelle

4 Pr G S Sc Tr

▼ School of Arts and Sciences Honors Program

The School of Arts and Sciences Honors Program is designed to foster intellectual independence and initiative, leadership abilities, and appreciation of the value of collaboration and community involvement in talented motivated students. To that end, it offers a variety of challenging interdisciplinary seminars, an annual Honors Colloquium, independent study through contract, and opportunities for leadership and community activity.

Freshmen are enrolled in honors sections of the freshman requirements Self in Context and Critical Research Essay, where they explore self, texts, and contexts through group and individual projects that interrelate individual and community. Seniors conclude their course of study with Senior Symposium, a semester of student-led, issue-based seminars emanating from a disciplinary perspective but set in an interdisciplinary forum. Honors students are closely advised in the selection of appropriate honors learning options, seminars, colloquia, and contract learning, all of which are open to students above the freshman level. Honors faculty members are selected on the basis of their creative, student-centered teaching.

Seminars are expressly designed for nonmajors as core alternatives or electives. They are interdisciplinary, issue-based, and involve primary-source readings, discussion, projects, experiential learning environments, and extensive writing. Class size is limited to 15 students.

Honors Colloquia are one-year, 6-credit experiences offered annually to all students above the freshman level and consist of a fall seminar and a spring independent study. Cycled according to student choice, the topics are: New York City: Anatomy of a Metropolis; Democracy in America; Twentieth-Century Global Issues; Science, Technology, and Values; and the Human Drive for Community.

Students above the freshman level are free to develop an independent study contract with a faculty mentor as either a research project or an internship. On Honors Conference Day students present the results of their research to the College community.

There are approximately 45 active full-time student members.

Founded in 1974, the program marked its twenty-fifth anniversary with a series of lectures, readings, films, and fora that examined the perception of women and their role in society and diverse cultures.

Participation Requirements: Students are required to engage in a minimum of two honors academic studies a year and are strongly encouraged to build honors portfolios that reflect program, College, and NCHC activities.

The Honors Diploma is awarded to graduating seniors who have a minimum 3.5 GPA; eight honors options, including one Colloquium and Senior Symposium; and a consistent record of leadership. The Honors Certificate is awarded to graduating seniors who have achieved at least a 3.5 GPA in the honors program, completed five honors options, and participated in honors activities.

Admission Process: Academic scholarship recipients who exhibit both promise for academic achievement and leadership potential are invited into the program directly from high school. Enrolled and transfer students below the junior level who have a 3.3 GPA or higher are also invited into the program. Juniors and seniors are required to maintain a minimum 3.5 GPA.

Scholarship Availability: Presidential Scholarships (full tuition), Honors Scholarships ($7500), and Academic Scholarships ($5000) are awarded to academically qualified applicants during the admission process. Students selected for scholarships generally rank in the top 20 percent of their high school graduating class, have SAT I scores above 1000, and have high school scores above 90 percent. Applicants must file the Free Application for Federal Student Aid (FAFSA). There is no application deadline for entering freshman and transfer students; all financial aid is renewed annually.

The Campus Context: The College of New Rochelle is located on a beautiful 20-acre campus, 1 mile west of the Long Island Sound and 16 miles north of mid-Manhattan. In addition, it has six satellite campuses for adult learners in the metropolitan area. One of the oldest colleges in Westchester County, it was founded in 1904 by the Ursuline order as the first Catholic liberal arts college for women in New York State. Today it is an independent institution with a Catholic tradition, consisting of four regionally accredited Schools: Arts and Sciences (for women only), Nursing, New Resources (for adult learners), and Graduate. The College offers twenty-five programs leading to several baccalaureate degrees.

Student Body Approximately 566 undergraduates are enrolled in the School of Arts and Sciences, 80 percent of whom receive financial aid. A majority of students are from the Northeast. Of these, 2 percent hold student visas. The ethnic distribution of the student body is 38 percent Caucasian, 23 percent Hispanic, 36 percent African American, 3 percent Asian, and 1 percent Native American. The New Rochelle Campus has four residence halls, which house 55 percent of enrolled students.

Faculty There are 81 faculty members; 43 are full-time, 90 percent of whom hold doctorates or terminal degrees. The student-faculty ratio is 11:1.

Key Facilities The College library contains more than 200,000 volumes. Students have access to IBM and Macintosh computers in the several computer labs, Learning Support Services, and the Honors Center.

Athletics The College has a sports program and tennis courts. It participates in NCAA Division III, offering intercollegiate basketball, volleyball, tennis, softball, and swimming teams for women.

Study Abroad College credit for study abroad is available through the International Studies Program. Special competitive scholarships are available for study abroad. The Science Division sponsors a math-science course in England. The Modern and Classical Languages Department has offered Bridging Cultures travel-study courses in Italy, Mexico, Puerto Rico, Egypt, and Greece.

Support Services The Learning Support Services provides professional and peer tutoring for students needing academic assistance in any area of the curriculum. Disabled students find approximately 80 percent of the campus accessible by wheelchair ramps, electronic doors, elevators, special parking, equipped restrooms, and lowered drinking fountains.

Job Opportunities Opportunities for local and New York City internships, co-op work placements, work-study and campus employment jobs, and career explorations are provided by individual departments and the Center for Counseling, Career Development and Placement.

Tuition: $12,320 minimum per year (2001–02)

Room and Board: $6550

Fees: $100

Contact: Dean: Dr. Rosemarie Hurrell, 29 Castle Place, New Rochelle, New York 10805; Telephone: 914-654-5248; Fax: 914-654-5554; E-mail: rhurrell@cnr.edu

College of Notre Dame of Maryland

4 Pr S Tr

▼ The Elizabeth Morrissy Honors Program

Founded in 1981, the Elizabeth Morrissy Honors Program, named to honor the memory of an outstanding Notre Dame professor, meets the needs and interests of students with high ability and motivation. Several honors seminars are offered each semester. There are currently 75 students in the program.

Participation Requirements: Students in the Morrissy Honors Program may major in any area that the College offers and take the same number of credits for graduation as every other student. A student must take at least one Morrissy seminar a year and complete a minimum of 18 credits of honors course work to receive an honors diploma.

Scholarship Availability: Morrissy students hold several kinds of scholarships offered by the College as well as outside scholarships.

The Campus Context: The College of Notre Dame of Maryland, founded in 1873 by the School Sisters of Notre Dame, is situated on 58 wooded acres in a residential neighborhood 10 minutes from downtown Baltimore. The College opened as a collegiate institute and in 1895 began offering a four-year college program of study. In 1896, the state of Maryland authorized Notre Dame to grant degrees. The College offers the Bachelor of Arts degree through its day program. The Continuing Education Program is designed for women over 25, and the Weekend College Program is designed for employed women and men. In addition, a coeducational Graduate Studies program offers the M.A. in several fields. There are twenty-seven degree programs.

Student Body The undergraduate enrollment in the traditional day program is 100 percent women; 6–7 percent are international students. Sixty percent of the women are residents. Eighty-five percent of the students receive financial aid. While there are no social sororities, there are many honors societies.

Faculty There are 233 faculty members; 88 are full-time, 145 are part-time (including adjunct faculty members), and more than 70 percent have terminal degrees. The student-faculty ratio is 13:1.

Key Facilities The Sister Kathleen Feeley International Center houses the English Language Institute and the Office of International Programs. The library contains 424,685 bound volumes, 326,236 microform units, 9,245 video/DVD units, and 2,163 periodicals. Technology-rich facilities are available around the campus, supporting more than 125 student-accessible computers. Two high-technology classrooms, four multimedia facilities, four academic labs, and three student collaboration rooms allow students to access the Internet and run the latest software to support instruction, research, and general use. Each student is issued an Internet-accessible e-mail account and may access a large library of software, including Microsoft Office, OWA, SPSS, Photoshop, Illustrator, Quark, Dreamweaver, Windows 98 and 2000, Mac OS/9, and much more. Facilities also include and English Writing Center, Digital Writing Lab, Faculty Resource Center, and Digital/Multimedia Language Lab and the ability to access the campus's Blackboard Course Management System, which is used to support both local and remote education needs. New systems that will enhance student life and facilitate collaboration and independent research as well as provide access to a growing number of digital library materials are under development, and students may gain access to a myriad of scanners, network printers, and RW-CD and Zip drives from locations around the campus.

Honorary Societies Beta Beta Beta, Delta Mu Delta, Eta Sigma Phi, Kappa Mu Epsilon, Phi Alpha Theta, Phi Lambda Upsilon, Psi Chi, Sigma Tau Delta, and Association for Women in Communications

Athletics The Marion Burk Knott Sports and Activities Complex features an NCAA-regulation gymnasium for basketball and volleyball, glass-backed racquetball courts, dance and exercise rooms, and a fully equipped training room. There is also a game room with a pool table, Foosball, Ping-Pong, and shuffleboard. A walking track overlooks the gym, racquetball courts, and game room. Students also have access to four tennis courts. Two natural grass athletic fields are used for intercollegiate soccer, lacrosse, and field hockey as well as other intercollegiate and intramural athletic activities. Joggers and bikers enjoy the network of paths that crisscross the campus.

Study Abroad The College is committed to providing as much international experience as possible for each student. Through the Office of International Programs, study is offered at international academic institutions during regular semesters or the summer months. In addition, Notre Dame faculty members regularly lead study tours during Winterim and summer terms.

Support Services Residence halls and classrooms are accessible to disabled students.

Job Opportunities Students may work on campus up to 10 hours per week with College approval.

Tuition: $16,600 per year, full-time; $270 per credit, part-time for nursing program (2001–02)

Room and Board: $7200

Mandatory Fees: $300

Contact: Director: Alison Dray-Novey, 4701 North Charles Street, Baltimore, Maryland 21210-2476; Telephone: 410-532-5372; Fax: 410-532-5798; E-mail: adraynov@ndm.edu

College of Saint Benedict/St. John's University

4 Pr G Tr S

▼ Honors Degree Program

The Honors Program at the College of Saint Benedict and St. John's University comprise a small group of students exploring the world of ideas together. These honors students pride themselves on their shared love of learning and an exciting exchange of ideas that rarely ends when the class period is over. The honors program is integrated into the common liberal arts core curriculum, enabling honors students to take honors core curriculum classes in place of classes in the general core curriculum. These courses focus on an interdisciplinary approach to ways of knowing and feature small class sizes (15 to 20 students maximum, frequently fewer than 10) built around lively discussion. In this way, completing the honors program does not interfere with either study-abroad opportunities or the pursuit of single or even double majors.

The program features small out-of-class reading and film discussion groups with professors, service opportunities, and cultural enrichment activities.

The program admits approximately 95 students each year.

Participation Requirements: In the first year, students take either the honors first-year symposium or great issues in philosophy. The honors symposium is centered on one of two broad topic areas: cultural heritages or social justice. Great issues in philosophy

Interpreting the symbols: **2**=two-year college, **4**=four-year college; **Pu**=public or state college, **Pr**=private college; **G**=general honors program; **D**=departmental honors program; **S**=small program (fewer than 100 students), **M**=midsize program (100 to 500 students), **L**=large program (more than 500 students); **Sc**=scholarships available in honors program; **Tr**=transfer students accepted into honors program; **HBC**=historically black college; **AA**=academic advisors; **GA**=graduate advisors; **FA**=fellowship advisors.

examines some of the most challenging questions surrounding the human condition. In the sophomore year, students take either one or two honors courses that serve as lower-division requirements in the core curriculum: natural science, social science, theology, or general humanities. In the junior year, students have the opportunity to take a yearlong course entitled Great Books. This course features the reading and discussion of a large corpus of the world's finest learning and literature. In the senior year, students research and write the honors thesis. For their thesis, students work closely with faculty members from their major field of study to produce high-quality independent undergraduate research.

To remain in good standing, students must maintain at least a 3.0 cumulative GPA in their first year of study and garner a minimum 3.4 cumulative GPA upon graduation. Students who complete the program receive special recognition at graduation along with final transcripts marked All College Honors.

Admission Process: High school students are offered admission to the Honors Program on the basis of college board scores, high school rank, and GPA. Students not admitted in the first term of freshman year may apply for admission to the Honors Program upon the completion of one full term of study. Transfer students may also apply based upon previous academic work.

Scholarship Availability: St. John's University and the College of Saint Benedict have Regents and Trustees merit scholarships not explicitly linked to admission in the honors program. All Regents and Trustees scholarship holders are offered admission to the honors program.

The Campus Context: The College of Saint Benedict and St. John's University are two liberal arts colleges located 4 miles apart in the rolling hills and woods of central Minnesota. Saint Benedict is a college for women, and Saint John's is a college for men. The students of these two colleges share in one common education as well as coeducational social, cultural, and spiritual programs. The colleges share a common curriculum, identical degree requirements, and a single academic calendar. All academic departments are joint, and classes are offered throughout the day on both campuses. The two campuses are linked by free bus service throughout the day and late into the night.

The liberal arts education provided by the College of Saint Benedict and Saint John's University is rooted in the Catholic university tradition and guided by the Benedictine principles of the colleges' founders and sponsoring religious communities. These principles stress cultivation of the love of God, neighbor, and self through the art of listening, worship, and balanced, humane living. The liberal arts, valuable in themselves, are the center of disciplined inquiry and a rich preparation for the professions, public life, and service to others in many forms of work. Graduates of the two colleges have a distinguished record in each of these areas. While the College of Saint Benedict and Saint John's University have historically served first their own region, they welcome growing numbers of students and faculty members from diverse cultures and regions and increasingly serve a national and international community.

Student Body Women are admitted to the College of Saint Benedict. Men are admitted to St. John's University. Each college enrolls approximately 1,800 students from forty-three states and twenty other countries and trust territories.

Faculty The total number of faculty members is approximately 270.

Key Facilities Libraries on each campus hold a combined total of 547,532 volumes and 1,587 active periodical subscriptions along with 255,201 government documents and 110,214 microforms. Online catalogs, linked to seventy-five other libraries in Minnesota, allow searching from anywhere on the campuswide computer network. The two campuses are served by a single computer network. Computer facilities consist of four multimedia computer classrooms, twelve computer access lab facilities, and twenty-nine residence hall computer clusters. There are more than 350 workstations available in addition to network links provided in each campus dorm or apartment.

Athletics Students enjoy some of the finest athletic facilities in Minnesota. The Warner Paelestra (St. John's) and Claire Lynch Field House (St. Benedict) provide for indoor swimming, track, and tennis as well as other indoor sports. Both facilities include state-of-the-art exercise facilities. St. John's and the College of Saint Benedict are members of NCAA Division III and sponsor teams in all major sports. There is a large intramural sports program on both campuses.

Study Abroad St. John's University and the College of Saint Benedict are nationally recognized for their study-abroad programs. The colleges have on-site programs in eleven countries around the world.

Support Services St. John's University and the College of Saint Benedict provide a wide range of support services for students with learning disabilities and physical challenges.

Job Opportunities There are approximately 850 part-time positions available on each campus along with a limited number of positions also available off campus. Student employment is awarded on the same basis as other types of financial aid.

Tuition: $18,015 per year (2001–02)
Room and board: $5606
Mandatory Fees: $300

Contact: Director: Dr. Richard M. White, Department of Chemistry, CSP/SJU, St. Joseph, Minnesota 56334; Telephone: 320-363-5894; Fax: 320-363-5582; E-mail: rwhite@csbsju.edu; Web site: http://www.csbsju.edu/honors

College of St. Catherine

4 Pr G S Tr

▼ Antonian Scholars Honors Program

The objectives of the Antonian Scholars Honors Program are to attract and provide a challenge for women of superior ability; to provide an opportunity for these women to interact with each other and build intellectually supportive relationships with peers and faculty members; to deepen their love of learning, understanding of great issues, and independent scholarship; and to clarify and emphasize the College's commitment to the liberal arts and academic excellence.

A student will have completed the Honors Program provided she maintains a minimum 3.5 GPA overall and in her major and completes the six components of the program, including a Senior Honors Project. Each student must complete a minimum of two Honors Seminars, which may be team taught, are interdisciplinary, and focus on the liberal arts; a minimum of two Honors Contracts, work that is broader in scope and/or showing greater depth than that required in a course; and a third Honors Seminar, Honors Contract, or foreign study during the regular academic year (not including January term or summer). As a senior, the student undertakes a major piece of research or creative work under the guidance of a faculty member, which is publicly presented.

The privileges of membership include the opportunity to travel to regional and national conferences and the opportunity to register on the first day of registration.

The Honors Program began in 1986 and currently has 65 members.

Participation Requirements: To maintain eligibility, a student must be registered in the Honors Program each year, unless she is away from campus (e.g., abroad). A student must complete at least one Honors Seminar or Honors Contract within the first two semesters after being admitted to the program. She may complete at most three components in her senior year, one of which is the Senior Project. A student must earn a grade of B or higher in the honors courses. Successful completion of the Honors Program is noted at graduation and is recorded on the student's transcript. A special diploma is awarded.

Admission Process: Any student who has completed at least three courses at the College but no more than fifteen courses while enrolled at the College may apply. Admission is determined by student interest as reflected in the application, a faculty member recommendation, and a minimum 3.5 GPA. In addition, a limited number of entering first-year and transfer students are offered membership.

Applications are due in December and February.

Scholarship Availability: The College of St. Catherine offers the Presidential Scholarships to students of exceptional ability. Many students receiving these scholarships are also in the Honors Program.

The Campus Context: The College of St. Catherine is a Catholic college with campuses in St. Paul and Minneapolis. It was founded in 1905 as a women's college by the Sisters of St. Joseph of Carondelet. The St. Paul campus provides undergraduate baccalaureate programs for women in the liberal arts disciplines and several professions. The Honors Program is designed for students on the St. Paul campus. There are thirty-eight undergraduate majors and eight master's programs offered on campus. Thirty additional undergraduate majors are available to College of St. Catherine students through affiliation with the Associated Colleges of the Twin Cities consortium.

Student Body Undergraduate enrollment is 2,682 students; 100 percent are women. The ethnic distribution of the student body is 1 percent American Indian, 7 percent Asian, 3 percent African American, and 2 percent Hispanic. There are 81 international students. Of the total student population, 75 percent are commuters and 25 percent are resident. Eighty-seven percent of all students receive financial aid.

Faculty There are 148 full-time faculty members; 70 are ranked part-time, 93 are adjunct, and 83 percent have terminal degrees. The student-faculty ratio is 14:1.

Key Facilities Among distinguished facilities on campus, Our Lady of Victory Chapel is the embodiment of the College's Catholic nature and its close relationship to the Sisters of St. Joseph of Carondelet. Built in the 1920s, it was placed on the National Register of Historic Places in 1986. The O'Shaughnessy Auditorium is a major Twin Cities professional arts and entertainment stage. The Catherine G. Murphy Gallery focuses on women artists and their work.

The library has a total of 390,613 volumes. There are 275 laptop computers leased by students. There are approximately 250 computers available for students in computer labs, academic departments, and residence halls. The Honors Lounge provides computer access to students in the program.

Honorary Societies Phi Beta Kappa

Athletics The College of St. Catherine participates in NCAA Division III intercollegiate athletics. The College offers nine varsity sports: basketball, cross-country, ice hockey, soccer, softball, swimming/diving, tennis, volleyball, and track and field. Also available are intramural and recreational sports opportunities. The Aimee and Patrick Butler Center for Sports and Fitness, which opened in May 1995, is a 56,000-square-foot facility containing training equipment and workout spaces designed with the needs of women athletes in mind. The center includes an eight-lane, 25-yard indoor swimming pool; a sauna and spa; a suspended indoor jogging track; a weight room and cardiovascular workout area; and a gymnasium with courts for volleyball, basketball, and tennis.

Study Abroad The College of St. Catherine actively encourages students to consider incorporating study abroad into their academic curriculum. A wide variety of semester, yearlong, and January-term programs are available each year. The Honors Program supports this opportunity to study abroad as an option for fulfilling one of the components of the program.

Job Opportunities The Student Employment Program assists students in securing part-time positions on campus to meet a portion of their education expenses. All new students who wish to work on campus are guaranteed a job. On-campus jobs include computer consultant, library aide, clerical worker, tutor, dining service worker, lab assistant, and receptionist.

Tuition: $17,280 per year (2000–01)

Room and Board: $4922

Mandatory Fees: $122

Contact: Director: Dr. Suzanne M. Molnar, 2004 Randolph Avenue, St. Paul, Minnesota 55105; Telephone: 651-690-6633; Fax: 651-690-6024; Web site: http://www.stkate.edu/Scholars

College of Saint Elizabeth

4 Pr C S Tr AA

▼ Honors Program

The Honors Program is an integral part of the College of Saint Elizabeth, whose mission is to be a community of learning in the Catholic liberal arts tradition for students of diverse backgrounds and cultures. The Honors Program is offered to the full-time students of the women's college and seeks to promote an intellectual and social environment that challenges students to strive for the highest success academically and culturally. The program encourages leadership that is self-motivated and cooperative. The Honors Program, through its three-pronged goal of scholarship, leadership, and service, endeavors to challenge students to become more responsible, productive, and well-rounded members of society.

Students displaying superior scholarship, leadership, and service are accepted into the program and offered their own curriculum that supplants the general education requirements of the College. Students in the Honors Program are offered two seminars as well as honors sections of already-existing courses and special-topics courses in order to provide them with a broad base of knowledge in the liberal arts and to challenge and enhance their special interests and abilities. The honors curriculum has fewer requirements than those of general education for the College at large, allowing for greater flexibility in curriculum design for the Honors Program student.

In addition, each student in the Honors Program prepares a faculty-mentored honors independent research project that is presented publicly to the College community. This experience, which offers students the opportunity to plan, execute, and present a substantive research or creative project, increases students' ability to organize their work, expand their problem-solving abilities, and practice a variety of leadership skills.

To complement their academic scholarship, Honors Program students exercise their leadership qualities and give service through the various clubs and organizations and in their local communities. Students in the Honors Program are a highly visible and vital presence on campus, where they participate in

Interpreting the symbols: **2**=two-year college, **4**=four-year college; **Pu**=public or state college, **Pr**=private college; **G**=general honors program; **D**=departmental honors program; **S**=small program (fewer than 100 students), **M**=midsize program (100 to 500 students), **L**=large program (more than 500 students); **Sc**=scholarships available in honors program; **Tr**=transfer students accepted into honors program; **HBC**=historically black college; **AA**=academic advisors; **GA**=graduate advisors; **FA**=fellowship advisors.

special workshops, panels, and lectures as well as volunteer work in conjunction with the Volunteer Center. Honors Program students are encouraged to develop their whole person through a responsible giving and sharing of their talents and gifts.

Students are initiated into the program and awarded an honors pin after the successful completion of one honors seminar or two honors sections of courses, usually in October of the sophomore year. All honors courses are labeled as such on the transcripts, and successful completion of the program is also noted on the final transcript. At graduation, honors students who have successfully completed the program wear an honors medallion.

The Honors Program at the College of Saint Elizabeth was initiated in 1961 and has grown steadily to incorporate 90 full-time students at present.

Participation Requirements: Students are expected to complete an honors curriculum of 18 credits, made up of two honors seminars and an additional four honors sections of courses across the liberal arts. These courses are capped at 20 students. In addition, honors students must fulfill the requirements of their major(s) as well as First Year Seminar, English composition I and II, fitness/wellness, and foreign language. Generally during the senior year, students in the program take an honors independent study for 1 to 4 credits in order to work with their mentors on the independent research project, a presentation of which is given at the end of the spring semester of the student's last year of study. The student must maintain at least a 3.5 average and participate in a variety of leadership/service activities in order to remain in the Honors Program.

Admission Process: All students entering the College who have combined SAT scores of 1000 or more are invited into the Honors Program on a provisional basis. After a student fills out an Admittance Request that chronicles the leadership and service activities as well as scholarly awards, the director of the program evaluates the content listed and accepts or denies the applicant. At the end of each semester, the director of the program evaluates the cumulative averages of the Honors Program students to ensure that a minimum 3.5 average is being maintained. If it is not, a student is given one semester in which to reestablish that average. There is rolling admission into the Honors Program. Transfer students are welcome.

Scholarship Availability: While there is no particular scholarship offered by the Honors Program itself for entering students, the College at large offers a number of scholarships based on academic excellence, including Presidential Scholarships (full tuition), Elizabethan Scholarships ($7000–$11,000), Seton Scholarships ($5000), Hispanic Leadership Program Scholarships ($2000), International Student Scholarships (full tuition), and a host of endowed scholarships. Many of the students who are awarded scholarships become members of the Honors Program.

The Campus Context: One of the leading Catholic colleges for women in the United States, the College of Saint Elizabeth is recognized for its long tradition of developing the leadership skills of its students. Because the College maintains a 10:1 student-faculty ratio, students and faculty members enjoy a personal relationship that is marked by mutual respect. A growing international student population affords American students a firsthand experience of interacting with individuals from other cultures and countries and forms a basis for global understanding and friendships. Since 1996, the College has attracted students from more than twenty-three different countries.

Founded by the Sisters of Charity in 1899, the College of Saint Elizabeth was quickly recognized for the quality of its academic programs and drew to its student body young women who were eager to enhance their own lives and to pioneer in fields still closed to women at the turn of the century. The College today has a coeducational School of Graduate and Continuing Studies. Situated on 200 acres of landscaped grounds in historic Morristown, the College of Saint Elizabeth is an education complex that includes twelve buildings. Its library, laboratories, and studios are modern facilities that contain state-of-the-art technology supporting the technological requirements of today's students.

With a railroad stop at the campus entrance and direct access to major highways, the College is ideally situated for both resident and commuting students who wish to take advantage of the entertainment, cultural, and business opportunities of the New York metropolitan area.

Student Body Total undergraduate enrollment at the College of Saint Elizabeth is 1,251. The College's student body is reflective of a diverse population, including 8.5 percent international, 0.2 percent American Indian, 5.4 percent Asian/Pacific Islander, 16.9 percent black, 14.6 percent Hispanic, and 53.6 percent white. Residents comprise 73 percent of the full-time undergraduate enrollment.

Faculty The total number of faculty members is 166. Full-time faculty members numbers 57. Seventy-seven percent of all faculty members have terminal degrees.

Key Facilities Mahoney Library contains 110,272 volumes and 104,965 microforms. The library is a member of VALE, the Virtual Academic Library Environment of New Jersey academic libraries. VALE provides catalogs of New Jersey academic libraries and an array of carefully selected Internet sites. The library also supports DIALOG, online database searching. The audiovisual collections include 3,428 sound recordings, films, filmstrips, and videotapes. The College has a state-of-the-art Academic Computer Center with five large microcomputer laboratories and seven smaller, specialized labs with 152 computers for classes and general student use. In addition to the twelve laboratories available on campus, all students living in the dorms have network connections in their rooms for access to network services.

Athletics The College is a member of the NCAA Division III. Varsity sports include basketball, cross-country, equestrian, soccer, softball, swimming, tennis, and volleyball.

Study Abroad Well-qualified students in good academic standing at the College may choose to study abroad. This is generally done during the junior year. Students have studied in Australia, Spain, Eastern Europe, and England.

Support Services Students with learning disabilities are encouraged to meet with the Director of the Learning Center each semester to discuss their specific needs. Among the accommodations offered to help these students meet their academic requirements are individual support from the Learning Center, advocacy with members of the College community, tutoring, note-takers, use of tape recorders in classes, and alternate forms of assessment (untimed, take-home, or oral tests).

Job Opportunities Internships are offered and encouraged by all academic departments in order to provide students with short-term, professional-level work experience with an employer in a student's field of interest. Students are placed in internships that serve to enhance interpersonal, communication, technical, and field-specific skills and allow a student to gain a greater understanding of a future career.

Tuition: Tuition for full-time students enrolled in the Women's College (2001–02) is $14,700 per academic year.

Room and Board: $7200; part-time students pay $440 per credit hour.

Mandatory Fees: Mandatory fees are estimated at $610 per year.

Contact: Dr. Margaret Roman, Honors Program Director, College of Saint Elizabeth, 2 Convent Road, Morristown, New Jersey 07960; Telephone: 973-290-4313; Fax: 973-290-4389; E-mail mroman@liza.st-elizabeth.edu

College of St. Scholastica

4 Pr G S Tr

▼ Honors Program

Begun in 1995, the Honors Program at the College of St. Scholastica was created to provide an environment for honors students to have enriched learning experiences and to provide a community of support for learners devoted to a vigorous life of the mind. Students who become involved in the Honors Program should strive to love ideas and the discussion of them, not fearing intellectual debate; be able to listen to the ideas of others with respect, no matter how much those ideas might conflict with personal sentiments; be willing to risk the analysis of an idea for its improvement and for the individual's greater understanding; and desire a life of learning.

Approximately 85 students participate in the program each year.

Participation Requirements: Students are required to complete five honors courses, at least two of which are upper level. The Honors Colloquium is strongly recommended for freshmen honors students. Transfer students may satisfy the requirements of the Honors Program by completing three honors courses, at least two of which are upper level, with the permission of the Honors Director.

Admission Process: To be accepted into the program, students must first meet two of the following three guidelines: be in the top 15 percent of their high school class, have a minimum ACT score of 26 or minimum SAT I score of 1100 (PSAT score of approximately 105 is sufficient to apply), and/or a GPA of 3.5 on a 4.0 scale. All applicants must interview with the Honors Director prior to admission to the program. Students must earn a minimum grade of B in all honors courses and have an overall GPA of at least 3.5 to graduate from the Honors Program.

Scholarship Availability: Exceptional students may apply for a Benedictine scholarship through the Admissions Office.

The Campus Context: The campus sits atop a hill overlooking Lake Superior and the cities of Duluth, Minnesota, and Superior, Wisconsin. The facilities include the new Mitchell Auditorium, a 500-seat music hall, a newly expanded Science Hall, Our Lady Queen of Peace chapel, and black box theater as well as the Reif Recreation Center, Somers Residence Hall, the College Library, and a series of apartment complexes for on-campus students. Tower Hall is the center of campus activity. St. Scholastica offers approximately thirty degree programs, six preprofessional programs, and a variety of education and health-care licensure programs as well as a number of free-standing minors.

Student Body The current enrollment is 2,069 students. More than 90 percent of full-time students receive financial aid. The average award is $14,000.

Faculty More than 125 faculty members hold degrees from all over the country. The student-faculty ratio is 12:1, with an average class size of 16.

Key Facilities The library houses about 120,000 volumes, 9,500 microform titles, and 800 periodicals as well as tapes, records, CDs, and online services. On-campus computers include both IBMs and Macs. There are more than 165 terminals with access to the Internet.

Athletics Twelve intercollegiate sports teams exist at CSS. Both men and women can participate in cross-country, soccer, basketball, baseball/softball, and tennis. In addition, a women's volleyball team and a men's hockey team are available. Intramural activities also exist.

Study Abroad There are two study-abroad programs. Spring semester brings the possibility of studying in Ireland. Every spring, professors from the College of St. Scholastica travel with students to live and study in the cottages at Louisburgh. Through the College's sister college in Petrozavodsk, Kerilia, students can also study the Russian language. This exchange program is one of the most active on campus.

Support Services All buildings are handicapped accessible. Services are available for special-needs students.

Job Opportunities Several work opportunities exist for students on campus. The College has a large work-study program for students who meet the financial aid requirements.

Tuition: $17,080 per year (2001–02)

Room and board: $5108

Mandatory Fees: $100

Contact: Director: Dr. Tammy Ostrander, 1200 Kenwood Avenue, Duluth, Minnesota 55811; Telephone: 218-723-6046 (Admissions), 800-447-5444 (toll-free); Fax: 218-723-5991; E-mail: tostrand@css.edu; Web site: http://www.ccs.edu/admiss/honors.html

The College of Staten Island

2 4 Pu S Sc Tr AA

▼ Honors College

The College of Staten Island's (CSI) Honors College provides highly motivated students with a special curriculum of innovative and challenging courses during the first and second years of study that provide a broad yet coherent foundation for the baccalaureate degree. Third- and fourth-year students take up their fields of study in a wide range of majors in which they are encouraged to pursue departmental honors.

The special courses of the CSI Honors College are taught by selected faculty members, who combine outstanding qualifications and scholarship with a strong commitment to teaching. Faculty members and students in the Honors College work together to build a cohesive intellectual community, teaching and learning in classes of 20 or fewer students. The classes include field trips, as well as independent and collaborative research and other creative activities that students may present at undergraduate research conferences on the CSI campus. Students often continue to work with their Honors College faculty mentors throughout their college experience. The Honors College lounge and computer lab provide comfortable spaces in which students can work together, socialize, and meet with faculty members. Honors students are often invited to work with the College's Discovery Institute as tutors in local high schools, assistants to high school teachers, or laboratory assistants and tutors on campus. Seventy students currently participate in CSI's Honors College.

Students who qualify for the CUNY (City University of New York) Honors College: University Scholars Program may participate through the Honors College at the College of Staten Island. Eligible students follow CSI's Honors College curriculum but replace one course per term for the first two years of study with a special CUNY honors seminar, in which students attend special events and participate in exciting cross-campus projects with CUNY University Scholars from all over New York City. CSI's Honors College was founded in 1997; the CUNY Honors College: University Scholars Program was founded in 2001.

Interpreting the symbols: **2**=two-year college, **4**=four-year college; **Pu**=public or state college, **Pr**=private college; **G**=general honors program; **D**=departmental honors program; **S**=small program (fewer than 100 students), **M**=midsize program (100 to 500 students), **L**=large program (more than 500 students); **Sc**=scholarships available in honors program; **Tr**=transfer students accepted into honors program; **HBC**=historically black college; **AA**=academic advisors; **GA**=graduate advisors; **FA**=fellowship advisors.

Participation Requirements: The curriculum for the CSI Honors College follows two main plans: one for students intending to pursue a Bachelor of Arts (B.A.) degree and one for those intending to pursue a Bachelor of Science (B.S.) degree. Students pursuing a B.A. degree enroll in six paired courses in the humanities and social sciences, organized under the headings of American, Western, and non-Western cultures, as well as a humanities/social science capstone seminar. They also take a one-year sequence of biology, chemistry, or physics and one semester each of math, the arts, and computer science. Students pursuing a B.S. degree enroll in four paired courses in the humanities and social sciences, organized under the headings of American, Western, and non-Western cultures. They also take a one-year sequence of biology, chemistry, or physics; a capstone seminar in writing for the sciences; two semesters of calculus; and one semester each of the arts and computer science. The requirements range from 42 to 46 credits.

In addition to the Honors College courses, B.A. students must fulfill a language requirement and B.S. students must take a second year of science courses. CSI Honors College students must maintain at least a 3.0 average; they graduate with the designation of honors on their transcripts.

Admission Process: Students may apply to the CSI Honors College from high schools or from colleges (including CSI) as transfer students. Applicants from high school must have a 90 or higher GPA in academic subjects and demonstrate a record of high SAT scores, Advanced Placement courses, and extracurricular achievement. Students seeking to transfer to the Honors College must have between 12 and 24 college credits and an excellent college GPA. In addition to attending an admissions interview, each applicant must submit an essay and letters of recommendation.

Scholarship Availability: All CSI Honors College students who have attended high school in New York City are eligible for a New York City Merit Scholarship of $1400 per year. All students admitted with a high school average of 90 or above are eligible for a CSI Presidential Scholarship, which ranges from $1000 to $3200 for their first year. Students must reapply for scholarships each year that they attend CSI. Other financial assistance, including scholarships, loans, and part-time employment, is available to qualified students at the College of Staten Island.

The Campus Context: The College of Staten Island is a senior college within the City University of New York. CSI offers a full range of baccalaureate degree programs, a selection of master's degree programs, and, in conjunction with the CUNY Graduate Center, doctoral degrees in selected areas. As a comprehensive college, CSI also offers a select set of associate degree programs.

Located on a 204-acre, parklike campus, CSI features state-of-the-art facilities such as the Astrophysical Observatory; the Biological Sciences/Chemical Sciences Building; the Campus Center; the Center for the Arts, housing undergraduate and graduate programs in the arts as well as superb public spaces; the library, enhanced by computer data–based operations and Media Services, a concentration of pedagogical multimedia materials made accessible throughout the campus via a fiber-optic network; and the outstanding Sports and Recreation Center and athletic fields. As part of CUNY and situated in one of the world's most distinguished cities, CSI provides students the opportunity to establish professional and academic contacts, as well as to study in a vibrant international capital of finance, entertainment, communications, and the arts.

Student Body Total enrollment is 11,115: 9,746 undergraduates and 1,369 graduates, 62 percent women and 38 percent men. Ethnic distribution is 71 percent white, 10.3 percent African American, 9.4 percent Hispanic, 9.1 percent Asian/Pacific Islander, and 0.2 percent American Indian/Native American. All students live off campus. The campus offers close to forty clubs to enhance student life.

Faculty CSI's faculty consists of 320 full-time and 415 part-time members; 48 percent have terminal degrees. The student-faculty ratio is 17:1.

Key Facilities The library houses 212,554 volumes, 877,357 microforms, 14,500 audiovisual materials, and 1,664 other resources. It also provides access to more than 10,000 journal titles, which are available in full text. Computer facilities include a fiber-optic network and wireless Internet access.

Athletics CSI is a member of NCAA Division III. The College has ten teams: basketball, softball, swimming, tennis, and volleyball for women and baseball, basketball, soccer, swimming, and tennis for men. CSI athletics won the first-ever CUNY Athletic Conference Commissioner's Cup in 2000–01.

Study Abroad CSI offers year-round programs in China, Ecuador, Greece, and Italy. Overseas programs in more than twenty countries are open to CSI students through membership in the College Consortium for International Studies.

Support Services All campus buildings are accessible. Special services are also available.

Job Opportunities CSI's students have opportunities for jobs with the Discovery Institute, tutoring in high schools and at the College and working with high school teachers. The College offers paid internships in laboratories on campus and with local institutions such as newspapers and museums. Paid summer internships with nonprofit organizations and businesses are available in New York City and abroad through the competitive Jeannette K. Watson Fellowship.

Tuition: In the 2000–01 academic year, full-time tuition for undergraduates was $1600 per semester for New York State residents and $3400 per semester for nonresidents. Part-time undergraduates paid $135 per credit (resident) and $285 per credit (nonresident).

Room and Board: All students live off campus; housing services are available.

Mandatory Fees: $74 for all full-time students, $48 for part-time students

Contact: Director: Ellen Goldner, Room 206E, Building 1A, CSI, 2800 Victory Boulevard, Staten Island, New York 10314; Telephone: 718-982-2664; Fax: 718-982-2675; E-mail: goldner@postbox.csi.cuny.edu

College of the Redwoods

2 Pu G S Tr AA

▼ Honors Program

College of the Redwoods' Honors Program was created to foster the growth of students who are dedicated, imaginative, and excited about learning. The program nurtures students' self-esteem while encouraging them to stretch to their full potential. It is a selective, challenging program designed for students' successful transfer to competitive four-year schools. Honors classes differ from regular classes in content, creativity, and preparation by both students and faculty members. Each honors course is developed by an experienced, dedicated faculty member and then scrutinized by the college curriculum committee to ensure that it offers an opportunity for active rather than passive learning significantly different from the mainstream counterpart course. Each honors course has met the transfer general education requirements for full articulation with both the University of California and California State University system. Admission to these courses is limited to honors students, and class size averages fewer than 20. Outstanding members of College of the Redwoods' faculty can work closely with students and incorporate innovative approaches to learning not possible in traditional classrooms. Students are subsidized to participate in out-of-town field trips each semester. Planned to complement the course material, this travel also promotes camaraderie among students and faculty members. Recent trips have ranged from a visit with a Yurok elder in his village at the mouth of the Klamath River to an avant garde play in San Francisco.

Additional benefits also available to honors students include priority registration, a partial fee waiver, special academic advising, and library privileges at nearby Humboldt State University. The College of the Redwoods' Honors Program is seventeen years old and currently has 50 students.

Participation Requirements: The honors curriculum is a program of eleven classes selected from those required to transfer to either a California State University or a University of California. These classes are upgraded to honors-level rigor and are offered in a two-year cycle, three classes each semester. The curriculum has been carefully designed to provide a high-quality, well-integrated program of stimulating classes that satisfy general education transfer requirements. To remain a member of the program, a student takes at least one honors course each semester. Honors students are free to select their remaining general education classes and those that fulfill their major requirements. Each honors course completed is noted on the student's transcript, as is successful completion of the program. To graduate as an Honors Program Scholar, a student must complete 15 honors units and have a minimum 3.0 overall GPA. Each spring, the program acknowledges its incoming students and graduates with a dinner. Students receive certificates of completion, and graduates receive special honors medallions to distinguish them at commencement.

Admission Process: An invitation to apply is sent to college students and to local high school seniors whose GPAs are 3.5 or higher. College students' applications are accepted with a minimum GPA of 3.3. Applicants submit recommendations from two of their teachers as well as an essay, which is evaluated as a writing sample. High school students also submit SAT I or ACT scores. A selection committee made up of honors faculty members reviews these materials from high school students in the spring for acceptance the upcoming year and from college applicants both in the fall for spring semester and in spring for the fall semester.

Scholarship Availability: Scholarships of various amounts are awarded through the College Scholarship Office based on academic performance and other criteria. Honors students are among the most frequent recipients of scholarships.

The Campus Context: Five hours north of San Francisco, the College lies between redwood forests and the Pacific Ocean. Founded in 1964, it is a fully accredited two-year college located near Eureka, California, and has approximately 7,500 full- and part-time students. There are also centers in Del Norte and Mendocino Counties. College of the Redwoods offers a variety of lower-division courses transferable to both the University of California and California State University. The campus offers a variety of learning facilities, including diverse computer instruction centers, nursing and dental assisting programs, a police academy, a child development lab, and a number of acclaimed vocational programs. A.A. and A.S. degrees are granted in sixty-four majors.

A number of students continue their education at nearby award-winning Humboldt State University. Others successfully transfer to some of the finest universities in the nation. The opportunity to earn a degree from such a university at a fraction of the full cost is one reason students choose to complete their lower-division work at the College of the Redwoods (CR). Another is that CR students receive excellent preparation for pursuing academic work at the university level. Year after year, GPAs from Redwoods' transfer students show that they outperform students from other community colleges and students who started as freshmen at a California State University.

In addition to unparalleled natural beauty, the local area offers the College community a surprisingly rich combination of recreational and cultural opportunities. These range from kayaking and whale watching to theater and galleries.

Student Body Total enrollment is 7,651; of those students, 59 percent are women. Ethnic distribution of the student population is 75 percent Caucasian, 6 percent Native American, 2 percent African American, and 6 percent Hispanic. Japanese, Pacific Islander, Filipino, and Central American students are also represented. There are 138 international students. Thirty-five percent of students receive financial aid. The majority of students commute, but College of the Redwoods is one of the few community colleges that offer campus housing. Subsidized child care is available for student parents. In addition to Redwoods' chapter of Phi Theta Kappa, a wide range of extracurricular activities are offered by special interest clubs, student government, and athletics.

Faculty There are 104 full-time and 285 adjunct faculty members. Approximately 14 percent of full-time faculty members have terminal degrees, but all faculty members are selected with particular emphasis on their expertise in and dedication to teaching undergraduate students. The student-faculty ratio is estimated at 20:1.

Key Facilities Library holdings include approximately 50,000 volumes in Eureka, with 15,000 more available through the centers, as well as subscriptions to 969 magazines and newspapers. The media collection includes more than 500 videotapes and 1,000 audiocassettes. Also available are the resources of the Online Computer Library Center, the world's largest bibliographic computer database. Librarians are ready to assist students searching for information. The Learning Assistance Center has microcomputers with a growing selection of computer-assisted instruction programs and word processing capabilities for student use: Macintosh, DOS, Windows, and Windows 95. Students have access to the Internet in the library, in the Learning Assistance Center, and at other sites on campus. Other computer facilities include the Writing Center, the Math Lab, and the CIS labs as well as a multimedia lab.

Honorary Society Phi Theta Kappa

Athletics The College boasts competitive athletic teams for both men and women. It is a member of the California Association of Community Colleges and participates in the Golden Valley Conference. Intercollegiate competition is offered in basketball, cross-country, and track and field. In addition, intercollegiate volleyball and softball are offered for women, while baseball and football are offered for men.

Support Services The campus is accessible to physically disabled students. Disabled Student Programs and Services provides assistance, equipment, and services to students with physical impairments. Individualized assessment and instructional support are available for students with learning disabilities.

Job Opportunities Student employment information is available in the Career Center, and a job board is maintained with listing/referrals for local and out-of-the-area job openings. A limited number of part-time work-study positions are awarded on campus, including the position of honors intern.

Tuition: None for state residents, $133 per unit for nonresidents (1999–2000)

Room and board: $5120

Mandatory Fees: $12 per unit

Contact: Coordinator: Pat McCutcheon, 7351 Tompkins Hill Road, Eureka, California 95501; Telephone: 707-476-4327; Fax: 707-476-4422; E-mail: mccutcheon@mail.redwoods.cc.ca.us; Web site: http://www.redwoods.cc.ca.us

Interpreting the symbols: **2**=two-year college, **4**=four-year college; **Pu**=public or state college, **Pr**=private college; **G**=general honors program; **D**=departmental honors program; **S**=small program (fewer than 100 students), **M**=midsize program (100 to 500 students), **L**=large program (more than 500 students); **Sc**=scholarships available in honors program; **Tr**=transfer students accepted into honors program; **HBC**=historically black college; **AA**=academic advisors; **GA**=graduate advisors; **FA**=fellowship advisors.

Colorado State University

4 Pu G L Sc Tr

▼ University Honors Program

The University Honors Program at Colorado State University is committed to the holistic education of its students and develops their intellectual capabilities and personal talents through curricular and cocurricular learning experiences. In 1998, Colorado State University President Albert C. Yates named the University Honors Program one of the University's top priorities as part of an effort to enliven and enrich the undergraduate experience. This designation led to exciting initiatives in the University Honors Program such as the new Honors Core Curriculum and the creation of the Honors Living and Learning Community.

The foundation of the University Honors Program is the Honors Core Curriculum, which offers students an enriched program of humanistic and scientific studies. The core fulfills the majority of Colorado State's general education requirements and includes four interdisciplinary honors seminars, two honors courses in the major, and a faculty-mentored senior honors thesis. The University Honors Program also provides special honors sections of regular courses that students may take as electives or use to satisfy other academic requirements. Honors seminars and classes range from 19 to 25 students and are taught by the University's best teachers.

The senior honors thesis guarantees that all honors students have the opportunity to perform undergraduate research. Students work one-on-one with faculty mentors to complete original research, create artistry, or design projects in an area of their choice. The senior honors thesis is the culminating learning experience of the honors curriculum and is commonly cited by honors graduates as the most rewarding experience of their academic careers.

A unique feature of the University Honors Program is the Honors Living and Learning Community (LLC) located in Newsom Residence Hall. In addition to housing more than half of the honors first-year students, the Honors LLC is home to the University Honors Program offices, two honors seminar rooms, and the honors study lounge. Honors resident assistants live on each of the honors floors, and honors faculty and peer mentors teach classes in the residence hall. Many special events take place in the Honors LLC, including the Faculty Fireside Program where faculty members join students for dinner and discussion, peer advising sessions, social activities like Halloween Karaoke Night, and Honors Student Association meetings.

The University Honors Program enrolls between 225 and 250 first-year students (approximately 5–6 percent of Colorado State's first-year class) who have outstanding records of academic achievement, special talents, and cocurricular accomplishments. Applications are mailed to students admitted to Colorado State who have strong records of academic performance as evidenced by high school GPA, standardized test scores, and class rank. In addition, any interested student may apply to the program.

Participation Requirements: To continue participation in the program, students must make satisfactory progress in completing the Honors Core Curriculum and maintain a minimum 3.0 cumulative GPA their first year and at least a 3.25 cumulative GPA every year thereafter. Students who fulfill the Honors Core Curriculum and achieve a minimum 3.5 GPA are recognized at graduation as University Honors Scholars.

Admission Process: Prospective students are invited to join the program based on high school GPA, SAT I or ACT scores, and class standing. Students already at Colorado State University may seek admission to the University Honors Program if their GPA is 3.5 or better.

Scholarship Availability: Students are eligible for the full range of the University's scholarships if they apply to Colorado State by December 1. More information is available at the University's financial aid Web site (http://www.sfs.colostate.edu). The University Honors Program also offers scholarships to outstanding junior and senior honors students who uphold the ideals of the program.

The Campus Context: Colorado State University has been designated as one of the nation's leading higher education institutions that encourage student character development through service and leadership by the *Templeton Guide,* a top forty-eight ranking by *Kiplinger's Personal Finance* magazine in its "Summa Cum Laude: 100 Best Values in Public Colleges" report, and the top four-year educational institution in Colorado by the Colorado Commission on Higher Education.

Colorado State University has eight colleges: Agricultural Sciences, Applied Human Sciences, Business, Engineering, Liberal Arts, Natural Resources, Natural Sciences, and Veterinary Medicine and Biomedical Sciences. Sixty-five degree programs are offered.

All first-year students are required to live on campus and have the opportunity to choose a Community Living Option Hall based around themes such as alcohol free, engineering, freshman experience, global opportunities, honors, leadership, natural resources, natural sciences, pre–veterinary medicine, and wellness.

Student Body The undergraduate enrollment is 19,899, almost evenly divided between men and women. About 11.5 percent of the undergraduate students are members of ethnic or racial minority groups (1.8 percent African American, 2.6 percent Asian American, 5.8 percent Hispanic, 1.1 percent Native American). There are 243 international students. Seventy-nine percent of the students are residents.

Faculty Of the 1,555 faculty members, 1,120 are full-time and 96 percent hold the Ph.D. or other terminal professional degree. The student-faculty ratio is 18:1.

Key Facilities The library houses approximately 1.8 million volumes. The campus has extensive computer facilities and was recognized by *Yahoo! Internet Life* magazine as one of the "most wired" universities in the nation.

Study Abroad The Study Abroad Office advises students on exchanges and study opportunities. In some cases, scholarships provide support for study abroad.

Tuition: $3252 for Colorado residents, $11,694 for nonresidents, per year (2001–02)

Room and Board: $5040 minimum

Mandatory Fees: $750.44

Contact: Director: Dr. Robert Keller, Newsom Hall E 203, Fort Collins, Colorado 80523; Telephone: 970-491-5679; Fax: 970-491-2617; E-mail: honors@colostate.edu; Web site: http://www.honors.colostate.edu

---

Columbia College

4 Pr G S Sc Tr AA

▼ Honors Program

The Honors Program at Columbia College is designed to enhance the educational opportunities of academically gifted students who seek to participate in analytical, synthetic, and creative study. The program welcomes students who are eager to accept academic challenges and to become creatively involved in their own pursuit of educational excellence. Honors students explore classical works and contemporary thought across the academic disciplines.

Through multidisciplinary and collaborative course work, honors students respond to the significant challenges confronting the next generation of scholars. The honors courses, both within the General Education curriculum and beyond it, are consistent with the students' academic abilities, preparation, and goals. The courses resonate with any academic major or minor and provide opportunities for students to discover their intellectual curiosities, to engage in community service, to develop critical thinking skills, and to excel in oral and written expression.

The program was created through faculty governance in 1997. Although faculty members may propose to teach a special topic course or to designate a General Education course, favorable consideration is given to courses that cohere to one or more of the following descriptions: multidisciplinary, collaborative teaching; travel/cocurricular activities; and reading and writing intensive. The classes range in size from 10 to 20 students. Under the direction of a faculty mentor, honors students are encouraged to complete an honors distinction project during their final year. During fall 2001, approximately 50 students enrolled in the various honors courses, seminars, and colloquia.

Participation Requirements:

To graduate with honors, a student completes at least 21 academic hours in the Honors Program. Entering freshmen who qualify for the Honors Program are strongly encouraged to enroll in HNRS 110 Introduction to Honors and HNRS 111 Introduction to Honors II. These courses, worth 1 and 2 academic credits respectively, are intended to foster a sense of community within the group of honors students and to prepare those students for success as honors students during their next three years. A 1-credit-hour community service project for Honors 310 must be completed prior to graduation. Students may enroll in a maximum of 9 hours of honors credits designated for General Education and may be eligible to enroll in a maximum of 3 hours of honors credits for an honors distinction project. An honors student may apply no more than 6 hours of honors credits transferred from accredited institutions toward the completion of the Honors Program. No honors courses may be taken with the pass/fail option. A minimum 3.25 GPA overall and a 3.0 GPA in honors courses is required to remain qualified for graduation from the Honors Program. Graduation from the Honors Program is recognized during the graduation ceremony and indicated on the final transcript.

Admission Process: Eligible students must demonstrate academic achievement meeting at least two of the following minimum standards: a high school GPA of 3.5; 78th or higher percentile on ACT or SAT; a Columbia College GPA of 3.5.

Eligible students are entered into the Honors Program automatically. Home-schooled or other nontraditionally schooled students are eligible for admission to the Honors Program upon presentation of an ACT, SAT, or GED score at or above the 78th percentile and demonstration of scholarship in high school–level academic course work. Any student may petition for admission to the Honors Program if he or she has completed a minimum of 30 hours of academic credit at Columbia College with a cumulative GPA of 3.6. Transfer students with prior college experience must have 30 semester hours of credit with a minimum GPA of 3.6 or higher on a 4.0 scale and submit a petition to the Honors Program director for admission. To petition for admission, a student must complete a petition form and write a letter to the Honors Program Director including the reasons for desiring admission and the anticipated benefits to the student. The student must also have two Columbia College faculty members submit letters to the Director supporting the petition. The Director grants admission to the program.

Scholarship Availability: Columbia College offers competitive scholarships to honors students of high academic ability. Five freshman students are selected at Scholarship Day to receive the Columbia College Scholarship, which includes full tuition, room, and board. In addition, 5 freshman students are selected at Scholarship Day to receive the Presidential Scholarship, which includes a full-tuition award. To participate in Scholarship Day, applicants must complete the admission process, submit two letters of recommendation and a resume of school/community activities. Scholarship Day activities include a written essay and an interview with Columbia College faculty members and administrators. The deadline to apply for the Columbia College and Presidential Scholarships is February 15. Additional scholarships are available for honors students with high academic ability and are awarded based on specific criteria of academic performance.

Interdisciplinary Honorary Societies include Alpha Chi, Alpha Lambda Delta, Psi Chi, and Who's Who Among Students in American Universities and Colleges.

The Campus Context: Columbia College is located in the city of Columbia, halfway between Kansas City and St. Louis. Columbia, also home to Stephens College and the University of Missouri, has a population of approximately 85,000 and another 25,000 college students. Social, cultural, and academic opportunities abound. The Katy Trail and several state and municipal parks are within proximity, as are great restaurants, coffee shops, shopping areas, and movie theaters. Columbia is perennially ranked as one of "America's Most Livable Cities."

Columbia College is a private, coeducational institution with a tradition steeped in the liberal arts and sciences. The College offers undergraduate degrees in twenty-seven academic fields and three graduate degrees.

Student Body Approximately 850 students attend Columbia College, of whom 20 percent are ethnic minorities and 60 percent are women. Approximately 65 percent of the students receive financial aid. The College also has an evening and an extended studies adult learning program.

Faculty The College employs 50 full-time faculty members, with more than 80 percent holding terminal degrees. The student-faculty ratio is 14:1.

Key Facilities The J. W. and Lois Stafford Library contains more than 70,000 books, subscribes to more than 500 periodicals, and has a sizable collection of microfilm and audiovisual materials. Students have access to the holdings of MOBIUS libraries, a consortium of fifty-three institutions of higher education in Missouri, with a union catalog of more than 14 million items. The Daniel Boone Regional Library is also available to Columbia College students.

The Technology Services Center, which is open seven days per week, provides access to the Internet and provides e-mail access for students. Computer labs are also available in residence halls.

Athletics Columbia College sponsors five intercollegiate sports, including volleyball, basketball, soccer, and softball. The women's volleyball team is the 2001 NAIA National Champion. The College is a member of the American Midwest Conference and The National Association of Intercollegiate Athletics. A wide variety of intramural sports is available as well as an indoor fitness center.

Support Services The Center for Academic Excellence, located in Missouri Hall, offers a variety of educational support services to students at no additional cost. Services include study sessions in almost all academic areas, note-taking and test-taking workshops, sessions developing research skills, and help with documentation or other problems related to research papers.

Job Opportunities Several academic disciplines sponsor both paid and unpaid internships. The College also offers Federal Work-Study on and off campus.

Tuition: $10,506 per year for full-time students (2001–02); $225 per credit hour for part-time students. There are several standard miscellaneous fees.

Interpreting the symbols: **2**=two-year college, **4**=four-year college; **Pu**=public or state college, **Pr**=private college; **G**=general honors program; **D**=departmental honors program; **S**=small program (fewer than 100 students), **M**=midsize program (100 to 500 students), **L**=large program (more than 500 students); **Sc**=scholarships available in honors program; **Tr**=transfer students accepted into honors program; **HBC**=historically black college; **AA**=academic advisors; **GA**=graduate advisors; **FA**=fellowship advisors.

Room and Board: $4576 (2001–02)

Contact: Dr. Brad D. Lookingbill, Assistant Professor of History and Honors Program Director, Columbia College, 1001 Rogers Street, Columbia, Missouri 65216; Telephone: 573-875-7621; E-mail: bdlookingbill@email.ccis.edu.

Columbia College (South Carolina)

4 Pr G M Sc Tr

▼ Honors Program

For more than fifteen years, the Columbia College Honors Program has provided an enriched academic experience for the outstanding student committed to excellence. The fundamental assumption of honors education is that honors students should continually challenge their intellectual limits, working creatively and seriously to reach their highest potential as scholars, individual thinkers, and leaders. The program emphasizes independent learning and a spirited exchange of ideas in a stimulating classroom environment that encourages students to develop their own ideas in a knowledgeable and reasoned framework.

The Honors Program Center offers an attractive and appropriate place for students to study and relax as a collaborative community of learners. The center includes computers fully networked to campus technology, printers, copy and fax machines, a library of honors materials, a seminar table, and comfortable furniture. In addition, new and continuing students may choose honors residential opportunities in selected residence halls.

Approximately 120 students are currently enrolled in the program.

Participation Requirements: Each student must complete 24 hours in honors courses, including the honors seminar and project. A student may enroll in up to 3 hours of honors independent study courses and one honors choice up to 4 hours. Students must maintain at least a 3.4 GPA in the cumulative average. Failure to maintain at least a 3.4 GPA results in one semester of academic probation. Only two semesters of probation are permissible in a student's undergraduate career.

Seniors are honored with a reception prior to graduation at which time they present their honors projects and receive their honors medallions to be worn at graduation. Seniors who complete the honors requirements graduate *cum honore* with an achievement noted on their diplomas.

Admission Process: Students are invited into honors in the freshman year based on their high school GPA, level of courses taken (AP and honors), SAT I or ACT score, class rank, leadership experience, extracurricular involvement, and application essay. Recently, GPAs have averaged above 3.8 and SAT I scores have averaged above 1250, but any motivated, capable student is encouraged to apply. Students may petition for admission past the freshman year with recommendations from College faculty members.

Scholarship Availability: The outstanding rising senior honors student is awarded the prestigious Tull Scholarship. A select group of outstanding honors students from each class also receive honors scholarships. These scholarships are based on GPA, involvement in the Honors Program, and leadership in the College and community.

The Campus Context: Since its founding in 1854, Columbia College has emphasized the value of a liberal arts education rooted in a strong commitment to the education of women. Columbia College is a beautiful, 33-acre campus located just minutes from downtown Columbia, South Carolina. Columbia College is affiliated with the United Methodist Church and has been recognized for nine consecutive years by *U.S. News & World Report* as being among the top ten liberal arts colleges in the South. Only a couple of hours' driving distance from Charleston, Greenville, Myrtle Beach, Charlotte, and Asheville, Columbia College is located in the center of the state. The B.A., B.F.A., B.S., and B.M. degrees are offered in more than thirty areas.

Student Body The total undergraduate enrollment is 1,252 students. The ethnic distribution of the student body is 30 percent African American, 1 percent Hispanic, less than 1 percent Asian, and less than 1 percent Native American. International students constitute less than 1 percent of the total undergraduate population. Ninety percent of freshmen receive financial aid; the average package is $17,057 per year.

Faculty There are 97 full-time faculty members and 55 part-time faculty members. Seventy-six percent hold the Ph.D. or equivalent. The student-faculty ratio is 12:1.

Key Facilities The library houses 170,000 volumes, 650 periodical subscriptions, microfilm, and microfiche. There are a media center and open stacks for easy access. There are five computer labs on campus equipped with e-mail and Internet access. Most classrooms and all residence hall rooms are wired for computer and Internet access.

The Columbia College Leadership Institute for Women coordinates internal and external leadership programs for women. The Barbara Bush Center for Science and Technology is a state-of-the-art complex with complete computer network facilities, including hundreds of ports for laptop access in classrooms and laboratories. The Academic Skills Center provides academic assistance in the form of study skills, writing skills, and peer tutoring. The Collaborative Learning Center facilitates collaboration between and among faculty members and students. The Career Center offers a four-year career planning program, which includes advising, counseling, career planning, and placement.

Honorary Societies Omicron Delta Kappa, Alpha Lambda Delta, and various disciplinary honor societies.

Athletics Intercollegiate competition exists in tennis, volleyball, cross-country, and soccer. Intramural athletics are sponsored by the athletic department and organized by interested students.

Study Abroad Many honors students elect to participate in the study-abroad programs in France and Spain. In addition, honors provides opportunities for travel/study in other countries through distinctive programs such as the NCHC Honors Semester.

Support Services All campus buildings are handicapped-accessible.

Job Opportunities The Office of Student Employment coordinates the numerous work opportunities that are available on and off campus. Honors also helps students to arrange exciting collaborative research fellowship opportunities that carry stipend awards.

Tuition: $15,570 per year (2001–02)

Room and Board: $5240

Mandatory Fees: $300

Contact: Director: Dr. John Zubizarreta, E-mail: jzubizarreta@colacoll.edu; Columbia, South Carolina 29203; Telephone: 803-786-3014; Fax: 803-786-3315; Web site: http://www.colacoll.edu/academic/honors/index.html

Columbus State University

4 Pu G S Sc Tr AA

▼ Honors Program

The Columbus State University (CSU) Honors Program (HP) began in fall 1998 and now has 70 students in the program. Honors students can major in every department and college at CSU and, in most cases, can do so without incurring additional credit hours for their degree. The HP provides significant challenges and opportunities to enrich an exceptional student's education, taking the educational experience beyond the ordinary. The HP strives to create a community of outstanding scholars and to stimulate involvement in campus and community activities. Special funding is provided for select students to study abroad. Special features include a special luncheon with a guest speaker each semester, small classes (15 students maximum), special access to distinguished visitors on campus, waiver of out-of-state tuition for select students, and early registration before all other categories of students.

Participation Requirements: The honors curriculum includes three core curriculum honors courses, three upper-division honors courses in the major, and a thesis. The program also requires participation in four campus events and an off-campus enrichment activity. In most majors, the HP is accomplished in the same number of credit hours as nonhonors programs. To graduate from the HP, students must have a minimum 3.4 overall GPA. Before graduation, the HP awards graduates with a special dinner. Completion of the HP is noted on the transcript.

Admission Process: Entering freshmen may apply to the HP if they have applied for admission to CSU and have a high school GPA of 3.5 or higher and a combined SAT I score of 1200 or higher (with a 550 minimum in each subscore). Students must also supply a letter of recommendation and transcripts. The final selection is made by interview. Transfer and international students are admitted on an individual basis after eligibility has been determined. Students already at CSU may seek admission to the HP if their college GPA is 3.5 or better, they have a combined SAT I score of 1200, and if they have taken fewer than 30 semester hours of core curriculum courses.

Scholarship Availability: At least fifteen honors scholarships are available annually, totalling $13,200 each. The $10,000 awards include an additional guaranteed $3200 to be used toward study-abroad programs. Many other scholarships and grants are also available, including the HOPE scholarship for Georgia residents.

The Campus Context: Columbus State University is situated on a 132-acre campus that includes twenty buildings, student housing in both dormitory and apartment-style arrangements, and state-of-the-art technology facilities. CSU offers fifty-five undergraduate majors and degrees. CSU is a center of excellence in the fine and performing arts; science, mathematics, and technology education; regional economic and community development; and international education and exchange. CSU field research, performing arts, preprofessional experiences, off-campus centers, distance learning and online courses, study-abroad opportunities, and partnerships with regional concerns have made CSU a university without boundaries. Two off-campus facilities provide unusual learning environments for students: the Oxbow Meadows Environmental Learning Center, which is a living laboratory where students can observe and study nature, and the Coca-Cola Space Science Center, which houses a Challenger Learning Center, a planetarium theater that is technologically one of the best in the nation, and the Mead Observatory. The new River Center for Performing Arts serves both CSU's nationally renowned Schwob Department of Music and the surrounding community.

Student Body Undergraduate enrollment is about 5,500 students; 63 percent of the students are women. The minority ethnic distribution is 3 percent Asian, 25 percent African American, 3 percent Hispanic, and 1 percent multiracial (1997 figures).

Faculty Instructional faculty members number 221. Sixty-six percent have terminal degrees.

Key Facilities The Simon Schwob Memorial Library, open more than 90 hours a week, provides online access to more than 100 databases and electronic full text of more than 500 journals.

Honorary Societies Phi Kappa Phi

Tuition: $938 full-time, $78 per credit hour for residents; $3752 full-time, $313 per credit hour for nonresidents (2001–02)

Room and board: $2238–$2438 (available for full-time students only)

Mandatory Fees: $134–$197

Contact: Dr. Barbara Hunt; Telephone: 706-568-2054; E-mail: hunt_barbara@colstate.edu

Community College of Baltimore County Essex Campus

2 Pu G S Sc Tr

▼ Honors Program

The Community College of Baltimore County (CCBC) Essex Honors Program is intended to promote academic excellence in students who are both intellectually gifted and highly motivated. The program aims to enrich the educational experience of the exceptional student and seeks to admit students who have the ability, interest, and initiative to be successful in such a program. Honors students are distinguished by their pursuit of challenge and their willingness to question, and the Honors Program is designed to meet the special needs of these students.

The Honors Program seeks students with outstanding academic records. However, students who are highly capable but who have not previously performed up to their potential are encouraged to apply as well, provided they can demonstrate that they have now found the motivation to excel. Any full- or part-time Essex student may apply for admission to the Honors Program.

Honors courses are designed to foster collaboration and inquiry through an emphasis on student involvement. Honors courses are not designed simply to require more work; rather, they require work at a more sophisticated level. Students are encouraged to think analytically and creatively and are taught to communicate their thoughts effectively in both oral and written projects. Honors courses at Essex can take several forms. There are honors sections of existing courses as well as specially designed honors seminars that examine a wide variety of topics, often from an interdisciplinary perspective. Enrollment in honors courses is limited to 15, and as a result, students have a greater opportunity for interaction with their instructors and with each other.

Regardless of the format, honors courses have in common their emphasis on originality and critical thinking. There is extensive opportunity for open discussion, and collaborative learning rather than individual competition is encouraged. The common focus of all honors courses is on the expansion of the students' ability to learn and the students' ability to use that learning to make discriminating, intellectual choices.

The program is fourteen years old, and current enrollment is 188.

Participation Requirements: Once students are admitted to the program, they are members literally forever. But in order to complete the program and earn an honors certificate, honors students must maintain a minimum overall 3.5 GPA and must complete a minimum of 15 honors credits. When members of the Honors Program graduate, they are recognized at commencement.

In addition, those students who complete the program are guaranteed admission to the College of Notre Dame, Coppin State College, Goucher College, Johns Hopkins School of Continuing Studies, Loyola College, Morgan State University, Towson State University, University of Baltimore, University of Maryland

Interpreting the symbols: **2**=two-year college, **4**=four-year college; **Pu**=public or state college, **Pr**=private college; **G**=general honors program; **D**=departmental honors program; **S**=small program (fewer than 100 students), **M**=midsize program (100 to 500 students), **L**=large program (more than 500 students); **Sc**=scholarships available in honors program; **Tr**=transfer students accepted into honors program; **HBC**=historically black college; **AA**=academic advisors; **GA**=graduate advisors; **FA**=fellowship advisors.

Baltimore County, University of Maryland College Park, and Western Maryland College.

Admission Process: In order to apply to the Honors Program, students must complete an application form, submit three letters of recommendation, and write two brief essays. Students who are interested in honors are interviewed by three members of the Honors Committee, generally 2 faculty members and a student. The Honors Committee meets eight times a year to review applications. While the committee reads transcripts and acknowledges SAT I scores, emphasis is placed less on past grades and test scores than on current performance and level of motivation. The committee has decided that it is generally not interested in the students' past but rather in their present and future; students who are able to demonstrate academic ability and enthusiasm for learning are likely to succeed in honors and will be accepted.

Scholarship Availability: Each member of the Honors Program receives a scholarship for one honors course per semester, provided that the student has earned an A or a B in the honors course and a minimum overall GPA of 3.0 for the semester.

The Campus Context: CCBC Essex is northeast of Baltimore City and is one campus of a three-campus community college system located in Baltimore County. The College was founded in 1957 and sits on 147 wooded acres.

Student Body CBCC Essex serves more than 11,000 day and evening students. The average student age is 27. The student population is 12 percent African American, 3 percent Asian, 1 percent Hispanic, and 84 percent Caucasian.

Faculty There are 142 full-time faculty members and 242 part-time faculty members. Twenty-eight percent have terminal degrees.

Key Facilities The library houses 85,000 printed volumes, 50,000 nonprint volumes, and more than 400 periodicals. There are eight computer labs on campus.

Honorary Societies Phi Theta Kappa

Athletics The College is a charter member of the Maryland JUCO Conference and a member of the National Junior College Athletic Association (NJCAA). Sports available for women include field hockey, soccer, volleyball, softball, basketball, lacrosse, cross-country, indoor track, and track and field. Sports available for men are soccer, basketball, baseball, lacrosse, cross-country, indoor track, and track and field.

Support Services The Office of Special Services provides support services and reasonable accommodations for students with documented disabilities. The office offers an array of services that are geared to the individual's unique needs and disability. Students with disabilities should contact the Office of Special Services for an appointment, allowing ample opportunity to respond to the special service needs of the individual. Services include sign language interpreters; readers; notetakers; braille, taped, or large-print materials; adaptive equipment and assistive technology; study assistance; wheelchair and access assistance; academic advising; career planning assistance; information on tuition waivers; and liaison with outside agencies.

Tuition: $68 per credit for Baltimore County residents, $121 per credit for Maryland residents, $176 per credit for nonresidents (2001–02)

Contact: Director: Rae Rosenthal, 7201 Rossville Boulevard, Baltimore, Maryland 21237; Telephone: 410-780-6880; Fax: 410-682-6871; E-mail: ecchonors@essex.cc.md.us

CONCORDIA UNIVERSITY

4 Pr G S Sc Tr

▼ Honors Program

Designed to enhance a student's overall college career, the Honors Program offers academically successful students the opportunity to broaden and enrich their undergraduate education at Concordia University in River Forest, Illinois. The current focus of the program is the intentional cultivation, development, and application of critical-thinking skills across the curriculum.

All honors classes are limited to honors students and have smaller enrollments than general education classes. Taught by talented faculty members who develop courses in their areas of expertise, honors seminars in particular offer professors opportunity to examine cutting-edge scholarship that might otherwise not be covered in standard courses. Alternative approaches to learning and attention to academic excellence are regular features of honors courses, with special emphasis given to student presentations. The introductory courses—one on perceptions and realities of the American West and one on the history and literature of the Holocaust—each semester prepare an exhibit for the campus community as their culminating class project.

Concordia's campus is only 10 miles from the Chicago Loop, which offers a full range of cultural experiences and events. Honors students have attended plays, performances, and sporting events off campus and the program has in turn brought speakers and performers to campus. Plans for a dedicated study/community space for honors students await completion of current campus building projects and reallocation of facilities.

The Honors Program, founded in 1990, has an average participation of 65 students.

Participation Requirements: Students must complete 12 hours or the equivalent of four courses, beginning with an initial honors experience, Introduction to Honors: Critical Thinking (3 hours), an interdisciplinary humanities-based course. Subsequently, students design their own program, choosing from several flexible options including midlevel Honors Seminars in the Disciplines (topics and readings courses in four discipline areas: social and behavioral sciences, humanities and the arts, theology and philosophy, and math and the sciences), study abroad/semester away opportunities, and independent senior honors projects. In addition, honors students contribute 30 service learning hours to church or community. Program expectations add no additional burden to graduation requirements, but students must maintain a minimum 2.75 GPA to remain in the program. Students successfully completing the course work and service requirements are recognized at commencement as Concordia Scholars.

Admission Process: Incoming students meeting the minimum admission profile—26 ACT and 3.7 high school GPA—receive an invitation to apply to the Honors Program following acceptance to the University, and do so by submitting an application form, essay, and teacher recommendation. In addition, freshman students with a minimum 3.5 GPA after their first semester at Concordia are invited to make application under the same process but must be supported by faculty nominations.

Scholarship Availability: All honors students are eligible for presidential scholarships.

The Campus Context: Concordia University is a four-year, residential private Lutheran university. Concordia is a member institution of the Concordia University System affiliated with The Lutheran Church–Missouri Synod. The University is accredited by the Commission for Higher Learning, North Central Association, National Council for the Accreditation of Teacher Education, and National League for Nursing. Rated in the Top Tier of Midwestern Regional Universities by *U.S. News & World Report,* Concordia offers thirty-three majors in the liberal arts and sciences, fifteen degree options and a four-year nursing program. The 40-acre campus is located in River Forest, Illinois, an affluent suburban neighborhood just 10 miles west of downtown Chicago. All first-year students participate in the First Year Experience, Freedom and Responsibility, a core freshman course designed to acclimate students to the rigors of college learning in a diverse Christian academic community.

Student Body: Approximately 1,400 undergraduate students and 500 graduates are enrolled at Concordia University. Sixty-six percent of undergraduate students are Caucasian (non-Hispanic), 9.2 percent are African American; 4.6 percent are Hispanic, and 2.5 percent are Asian or Pacific Islander. Sixty percent of undergraduates live on campus. The average financial aid package including, need-based, merit, and loan assistance is $10,500. Approximately 90 percent of students receive financial assistance.

Faculty: There are 159 faculty members; 88 are full-time and 72 percent have terminal degrees.

Key Facilities: Klinck Memorial Library houses 167,500 volumes and more than 640,000 microforms, including ERIC documents. The library is open 88 hours per week, providing reference assistance and an excellent interlibrary loan system. Special facilities include the Ferguson Art Gallery, Human Performance Laboratory, and Center for Social Research in the Church. Six residential halls are equipped with cable TV and individual Internet hookups, phone numbers, and voice mailboxes for each student. There are five computer labs on campus with one open 24 hours a day. The new Christopher Center for Learning and Leadership, open fall 2002, will house the College of Education and Early Childhood Center.

Athletics: The Concordia Cougars compete in the NCAA Division III. Men's sports include baseball, basketball, cross-country, football, tennis, track and field, and soccer. Women's sports include basketball, cross-country, softball, tennis, track and field, volleyball, and soccer. Eleven intramural sports are offered. A new track and field, soccer, and football stadium facility opened fall 2001.

Study Abroad: Study abroad opportunities exist in conjunction with other local area private universities.

Support Services: Support services include academic, career, personal, and spiritual counseling. Peer tutoring through the learning assistance program is available for students seeking assistance with study skills and writing. The Writing Center is newly remodeled.

Job Opportunities: Many options for on-campus employment are available. Many opportunities exist for College-sponsored internships or applied learning experiences. Career services workshops coach students in employment interviews, resume writing, and career planning.

Tuition: $16,900 per year or $490 per semester hour (2002–03)

Room and board: $5100 or for room only, $2050

Contact: Director: Dr. Mary Todd, Concordia University, 7400 Augusta Street, River Forest, Illinois 60305-1499; Telephone: 708-209-3036; Fax: 708-209-3176; E-mail: mary.todd@curf.edu

CONVERSE COLLEGE

4 Pr C M Sc Tr AA

▼ Nisbet Honors Program

The Nisbet Honors Program began in 2000 through an endowment from alumna Marian McGowan Nisbet, '62, and her husband, Olin. The program seeks to offer the academically gifted student the challenge and community in which she may grow to her full potential. The Honors Program includes opportunities to do independent research with faculty mentors, to take honors courses with other academically gifted students, to meet nationally known visiting scholars, and to meet socially to discuss intellectually challenging topics.

One of the most unusual features of the program is its emphasis on interdisciplinary learning. The interdisciplinary seminars have 2 faculty members from different fields in the classroom throughout the entire course, and students learn how different branches of learning approach the tasks of collecting and interpreting evidence and of making sense of the complex world. Topics for interdisciplinary seminars over the past few years have included the history of disease, with a historian and a biologist teaching together; human sexuality and the literature of love, marriage, and birth, with a biologist and an English professor, the new South in history and literature, with a historian and an English professor; and psychological and political aspects of American musicals, with a political scientist and a psychologist.

More than 100 students are currently enrolled, and the program continues to expand.

Participation Requirements: To graduate from the program, students must successfully complete a freshman honors seminar (or another honors course if they enter after the fall of the freshman year), one interdisciplinary honors seminar, a 1-credit junior honors seminar, a 1-credit senior honors seminar, and either two more honors experiences (such as two additional honors courses, a yearlong honors course, an honors-directed independent study, or some combination of these) or a senior honors thesis in their major. Students must maintain a GPA of at least 3.0 and receive at least a B- in honors courses to continue in the program.

The senior honors thesis represents a substantial independent research or creative project. Students may begin preparing for this project by applying for summer research grants as early as the summer after the freshman year. With faculty member and peer support, sophomores and juniors explore areas for independent research. They work closely with a faculty mentor during the junior and senior years. The senior honors seminar provides a forum in which students can share their work with others doing honors theses.

Students who complete a thesis and other program requirements graduate with honors in their field and with the designation Graduate of the Nisbet Honors Program. Students who complete the program only through course work graduate with the latter designation alone.

Admission Process: To be invited into the Honors Program as incoming freshmen, students must have applied to and been admitted to the College. A select number of entering freshmen are invited into the program based on their outstanding high school performance and their potential for success in college. To be considered, students generally must have SAT scores of at least 1250 and comparably strong high school records. Students who do well once they have begun their studies at Converse are also considered for the program; freshmen and sophomores must earn at least a 3.3 GPA after taking 12 hours at the College to be invited to apply.

Scholarship Availability: Most students invited into the Honors Program as incoming freshmen are eligible for the College's top scholarships, which range up to full comprehensive fee coverage (tuition, room, and board).

The Campus Context: Founded in 1889, Converse College is a four-year, private, residential, liberal arts college for women that *U.S. News & World Report* consistently rates as a top Southern college. The College draws much of its identity from its Christian heritage while welcoming students of all faiths. The honor tradition remains a vital force on the campus, as students seek to grow in knowledge, personal integrity, and service to the community and to the world. The College also values student governance, allowing trained students to administer the honor code. Students

Interpreting the symbols: **2**=two-year college, **4**=four-year college; **Pu**=public or state college, **Pr**=private college; **G**=general honors program; **D**=departmental honors program; **S**=small program (fewer than 100 students), **M**=midsize program (100 to 500 students), **L**=large program (more than 500 students); **Sc**=scholarships available in honors program; **Tr**=transfer students accepted into honors program; **HBC**=historically black college; **AA**=academic advisors; **GA**=graduate advisors; **FA**=fellowship advisors.

also lead all of the sixty student organizations, gaining valuable leadership experience.

Located in Spartanburg, South Carolina, the College offers many different programs and facilities to help students excel academically and lead balanced lives. The Petrie School of Music at Converse is the nation's only comprehensive professional school of music at a liberal arts college for women. A new athletics facility and an expanded art building allow students to develop their abilities in physical education and in the visual arts. Groundbreaking for a new science building is scheduled for fall 2002, and planning for a renovated student center has also begun. In addition, programs in leadership development, service learning, and study-travel help students learn to lead and serve.

Student Body Total undergraduate enrollment is 732 women, of whom 77 percent are Caucasian, 12 percent members of minority groups, and 2 percent international. Sixteen percent of undergraduates are nontraditional students. Eighty percent of full-time undergraduate students receive financial aid from the College. Ninety percent of students live on campus.

Faculty The College has 86 instructional faculty members; 71 are full-time faculty members, of whom 89 percent hold terminal degrees. The ratio of undergraduate students to faculty members is 9:1 (total ratio of students to faculty members is 13:1).

Key Facilities The library contains 200,000 items, not including periodicals (140,000 cataloged volumes, 60,000 other). Students can access 4,200 periodicals electronically and more than 600 periodicals in print or microform. Computer facilities include a general-purpose computer lab, a general teaching lab, and two special teaching labs for music and for art and interior design. Most classrooms have Internet access, and all student rooms in residence halls have unlimited Internet access, cable, and voice mail.

Honorary Societies Interdisciplinary honor societies available to students in the program: Alpha Lambda Delta (national honor society for freshmen), Mortar Board, Gamma Sigma

Athletics Students participate on NCAA Division II teams in basketball, cross-country, soccer, tennis, and volleyball. An equestrian team also competes regularly in regional competitions, and club sports include dance and synchronized swimming.

Study Abroad Study-abroad opportunities include a regular winter-term study in London, a monthlong study in Rome, a summer archaeological study in Israel, and semester-long or yearlong cooperative programs in France, Spain, and Costa Rica. The College also provides opportunities for shorter study-travel experiences with Converse faculty members. Some scholarships through a college endowment are available for study abroad.

Support Services The Academic Support Center is available not only to help students with documented disabilities receive academic accommodations but also to provide all students with academic counseling. The Writing Center, staffed by peer tutors and directed by an English professor, offers students one-on-one help with the writing process.

Job Opportunities All departments accept internships in a field related to a student's major for academic credit. The Office of Career Services works to tailor individual internships for the honors student to help prepare for graduate school or for a career. Opportunities for employment also exist on campus, and area businesses frequently hire students.

Tuition: $16,850 for full-time undergraduate tuition, $540 per credit hour for part-time traditional undergraduate tuition, $220 per credit hour for part-time nontraditional undergraduate tuition (2001–02)

Room and Board: $5140

Contact: Dr. Laura Feitzinger Brown, Assistant Professor of English and Nisbet Honors Program Co-director; Telephone: 864-596-9115; E-mail: laura.brown@converse.edu; Dr. John Theilmann, Professor of History and Politics and Nisbet Honors Program Co-director; Telephone: 864-596-9703; E-mail: john.theilmann@converse.edu; Web site: http://www.converse.edu/Academics/NisbetHonorsProgram.html

Coppin State College

4 Pu C S Sc Tr

▼ Honors Program

Coppin State College offers an Honors Program for outstanding students who have demonstrated exceptional ability. The primary focus of the Honors Program is to provide academic preparation, character development, and cultural enrichment to the College's high-ability students. Through the offering of honors courses, community-service experiences, and exposure to cultural activities, the program strives to prepare academically outstanding students for progression to graduate and professional schools as well as for employment. In addition, the Honors Program provides students with unique opportunities to hone their analytical and leadership skills.

There are two different categories within the Honors Program to accommodate high-ability students in all majors who desire an honors experience and are at various stages of their college careers. The Four-Year Honors Program is designed for incoming freshmen and the Upper-Division Honors Program is for transfer students.

The first student began in honors in 1981–82. On average, 65 students are enrolled in the program yearly.

Participation Requirements: Students entering the Four-Year Honors Program are required to complete the following courses to earn an honors citation: five honors versions of General Education Requirement courses, HONS 150 (Honors Community-Service Seminar), HONS 380 (Honors Introduction to Research I), and HONS 490 (Honors Thesis). Additionally, students must complete one of the following courses: HONS 381 (Honors Introduction to Research II), HONS 390/391 (Interdisciplinary Honors Seminar), HONS 470 (Honors Field Practicum I), HONS 480 (Honors Research Assistantship), EDUC 460 (Teaching Assistantship Seminar), or MNSC 150 (Computer Literacy). Students who complete the required honors courses and maintain a GPA of at least 3.0 overall and in their honors courses receive honors citations on their academic records and honors program graduation medallions. Prior to graduation, these students receive completion certificates from the Four-Year Honors Program.

Students participating in the Upper-Division Honors Program complete HONS 380 (Honors Introduction to Research I) and HONS 490 (Honors Thesis). Additionally, they are required to complete two of the following courses: HONS 381 (Honors Introduction to Research II), HONS 390/391 (Interdisciplinary Honors Seminar), HONS 470 (Honors Field Practicum I), HONS 480 (Honors Research Assistantship), EDUC 460 (Teaching Assistant Seminar), or MNSC 150 (Computer Literacy). Participants in the Upper-Division Honors Program who complete the required honors courses and who maintain a GPA of at least 3.0 overall and in their honors courses receive honors citations on their academic records. Prior to graduation, these students receive completion certificates from the Upper-Division Honors Program.

Admission Process: The four-year Honors Program offers three scholarships to high school seniors: the Golden Eagle Scholarship, the Eagle Scholarship, and the Opportunity Scholarship. The admission criteria for the Golden Eagle Scholarship are a high school GPA of 3.2 and a combined SAT score of 1200; for the Eagle, a GPA of 2.0 and SAT score of 1000; and for the Opportunity, a GPA of 2.0 and SAT score of 1100. The Upper-Division Honors Program applicant must have completed 45 graduation credits, including English Composition I and II, and obtained a transfer GPA of 3.5.

Scholarship Availability: The Golden Eagle Scholarship provides tuition, fees, and room and board for a maximum of eight semesters. The Eagle Scholarship provides tuition and fees for a maximum of eight semesters. The Opportunity Scholarship provides one-half of tuition and fees for one semester. The Upper-Division Scholarship provides provides $500 each semester for a maximum of four semesters. All scholarship recipients are required to maintain a GPA of 3.0 overall and in their honors courses, and to earn at least 12 graduation credits each semester they receive scholarship support.

The Campus Context: Coppin State College is located on a 38-acre site on West North Avenue in Baltimore, Maryland. There are five divisions on campus: Arts and Sciences, Education, Graduate Studies, Honors, and Nursing. There are fifteen undergraduate degree programs.

Student Body The fall 2001 enrollment total was 4,003. The ethnic distribution of the student body was 95 percent African American, less than 1 percent Asian, less than 1 percent Hispanic, and less than 1 percent Native American. Two percent of the population was international. Eighty percent of students receive aid. There are four fraternities and five sororities.

Faculty There are a total of 106 full-time faculty members and 85 adjunct faculty members, with 64 percent of all faculty members holding terminal degrees. This gives Coppin State College a 15:1 student-faculty ratio.

Key Facilities The library holds 125,000 volumes and 654 serial subscriptions. The Honors Division at Coppin State College also houses the Ronald E. McNair Postbaccalaureate Achievement Program, which is designed to prepare low-income, first-generation, and underrepresented undergraduates for the graduate school experience. The program provides all participants with research courses; seminars on graduate education; graduate school visits; workshops on financial support and graduate admissions; academic, career, and personal counseling; tutoring; and mentoring. Additionally, the program provides summer research experiences to selected students. Each McNair Program participant who satisfies program requirements receives a McNair Scholarship equal to the cost of in-state tuition and fees. There are ninety-five DOS computers and five Macintosh computers located in the library, residence hall, classroom building, science building, Division of Education, and Honors Division.

Athletics Coppin State College is a member of the National Association of Intercollegiate Athletics; the National Collegiate Athletic Association, Division I; and the Eastern Collegiate Athletic Association. The College offers a variety of varsity and intramural activities.

Support Services The Disabled Student and Referral Services Coordinator provides a variety of services to students with disabilities, including making referrals and special arrangements for on- and off-campus services such as counseling, academic advisement, and assistance with registration, financial aid, and library acquisitions. Readers, note-takers, interpreters, and other special aids can be provided if requested at least six weeks prior to the beginning of the semester.

Job Opportunities The Federal Work-Study program makes jobs available to undergraduate and graduate students with demonstrated financial need. These jobs are usually assigned as part of the financial aid package.

Tuition: $3453 for state residents, $8610 for nonresidents, per year (2001–02)

Contact: Assistant Dean: DeChelle Forbes, 2500 West North Avenue, Baltimore, Maryland 21216; Telephone: 410-957-3388; Fax: 410-951-3389; E-mail: dforbes@wye.coppin.edu

CORNING COMMUNITY COLLEGE

2 Pu G S

▼ Honors Program

In 1976, the Council of Full Professors of Corning Community College, under the aegis of the Faculty Association, developed an honors program that would attract and provide an enriched academic experience for high ability and curious students in all academic programs, both technical and transfer, offered by the college. The faculty members, however, were concerned that the honors students should not be segregated from the general student body.

In order to achieve these primary goals, Corning Community College established a unique Honors Program in that there is not a separate honors curriculum or a series of honors courses that a student must take to earn an honors degree. There are no special honors sections that segregate honors students from the general student body. Rather, all academic courses the College offers may be taken at an advanced or honors level by any qualified student in any academic program offered by the College. The program was designed to be interdisciplinary and to give honors students control and responsibility for their own learning and discovery, which very seldom occurs in traditional courses.

An integral part of Corning Community College's Honors Program is the Honors Forum, which is a 3 credit-hour interdisciplinary seminar. The Forum is similar to a graduate seminar. The average size of the Forum is 12 students and 3 faculty members representing the Social Sciences, Humanities, and the Sciences. The Forum faculty members function as guides as well as participants, learning along with the students. The Honors Forum serves several vital functions. It provides honors students with a venue for the exchange and testing of ideas and theories derived from their honors projects, provides students with the opportunity to analyze and synthesize information from students representing a wide variety of disciplines, and allows the students to develop critical-thinking, argumentative, and oral presentation skills usually reserved for upperclassmen or even graduate students.

There are approximately 15–20 students involved in the Honors Program working either in the Honors Forum or independently with their mentor and not enrolled in the Forum.

Corning Community College Honors Program celebrated its twentieth anniversary in 1996, making it the oldest continuous Honors Program in the SUNY College system.

Participation Requirements: A student who has a GPA of 3.5 or better and who is curious as well as highly motivated may take any course at an advanced or honors level by developing an honors project for that course. The honors project or topic to be explored is mutually agreed upon by the student and his/her mentor, who is usually the instructor of that course. The mentor serves as a guide for the honors student, who bears complete responsibility for his/her honors project. The faculty member mentor awards an H (honors designation) for the relevant course.

Honors projects have included the writing of short stories and poems, building and repair of robots, and offering of music recitals as well as the more traditional research projects. Several students have had their honors projects published in professional journals of their chosen field.

Upon successful completion of 12 credit hours of honors-level work, which usually entails two or three honors projects as well as

Interpreting the symbols: **2**=two-year college, **4**=four-year college; **Pu**=public or state college, **Pr**=private college; **G**=general honors program; **D**=departmental honors program; **S**=small program (fewer than 100 students), **M**=midsize program (100 to 500 students), **L**=large program (more than 500 students); **Sc**=scholarships available in honors program; **Tr**=transfer students accepted into honors program; **HBC**=historically black college; **AA**=academic advisors; **GA**=graduate advisors; **FA**=fellowship advisors.

Honors Forum and a cumulative GPA of at least 3.5, the student qualifies for an Honors diploma. Students who successfully complete honors projects also receive individualized letters from faculty member mentors as well as honors faculty members describing their projects and indicating the skills and abilities each student demonstrated throughout the semester. These letters are attached to the student's transcripts and are sent out to potential transfer colleges and/or employers.

The Campus Context: Corning Community College is located on Spencer Hill in Corning, New York. This geographic location is reflected in two distinguished facilities on campus, the Spencer Crest Nature Center and an observatory. Corning is located in upstate New York and is the home of the national and international corporate headquarters of Corning, Inc.

All Honors students are encouraged to participate in a wide range of cultural and civic activities sponsored by the College as well as the local community. Students attend such activities as storytelling festivals, midday concerts, sleeping bag seminars, or an occasional trip to a major metropolitan area for a visit to a museum.

The College offers forty degree programs.

Student Body Undergraduate enrollment is 46 percent men and 54 percent women. Members of minority groups account for about 5 percent of the student population, and international students represent less than 7 percent of the student body. All of the students are commuters. Seventy-five percent of all students receive financial aid.

Faculty Of the 187 faculty members, 107 are full-time. Thirty percent of the faculty members have terminal degrees. The student-faculty ratio is 18:1.

Key Facilities The library houses 68,944 volumes. There are approximately 600 PCs on campus linked to a computer network.

Honorary Societies Phi Theta Kappa

Athletics The Athletic Program at Corning Community College is a three-way program of intramurals, recreation, and intercollegiate sports. The College believes that athletics are a part of the total educational thrust of the College. The Intramural Program allows students to participate in a wide range of competitive/noncompetitive, indoor/outdoor, and day/evening/weekend activities, including badminton, basketball, cross-country, bowling, volleyball, golf, tennis, and wrestling. The Recreation Program is provided for the enjoyment of the community as well as the students. A range of activities, including open gymnasium, open weight rooms, bowling, ice skating, movie discounts, swimming, and table tennis are illustrative examples.

The Intercollegiate Sports Program is offered at the Division III level within the National Junior College Athletic Association (NJCAA). In addition, the College is a member of the Mid-State Athletic Conference (MSAC) and Region III (NJCAA). Eleven sports are offered: women's soccer, men's soccer, cross-country (coed), volleyball, women's basketball, men's basketball, wrestling, cheerleading, softball, baseball, and lacrosse. The College hosts many conference, regional, and national events highlighted by the Division III Women's National Basketball Championship. The College will host this event through 1999.

Study Abroad Corning Community College belongs to the College Consortium for International Studies and is a member of International Studies Association. Through these affiliations, students at Corning Community College can enroll in summer-long, semester-long, or yearlong study-abroad programs in some forty different countries around the globe and receive Corning Community College academic credit.

Support Services Disability services are housed with the Student Support Services Office. Adaptive equipment is housed in the library. The campus is equipped with electronic door openers, curb cuts, ramps, and Braille in elevators.

Job Opportunities Student work-study, tutors, and hourly employment are on an as-needed basis in clerical, buildings and grounds, laboratories, and technical-area positions.

Tuition: $2500 for state residents, $5000 for nonresidents, per year (1999–2000)

Mandatory Fees: $166

Contact: Director: Mr. Joselph J. Hanak, 1 Academic Drive, Corning, New York 14830; Telephone: 607-962-9208; Fax: 607-962-9456 E-mail: hanak@sccvc.corning-cc.edu

Crown College

4 Pr G S Sc Tr

▼ Honors Program

The mission of the Crown College Honors Program is to further the overall mission of the College by offering superior students who seek a greater academic challenge enhanced educational opportunities in order to increase their understanding of what it means to be a Christian intellectual, integrating faith with learning, through the development of critical-thinking and writing skills and interaction with the great ideas that have formed world culture. The Honors Program seeks to achieve this through special courses, involvement in cultural and intellectual activities outside the classroom, and the development of a sense of community among honors students.

Honors students have the opportunity to take small seminar-style classes in which the focus is on student interaction with each other and the ideas they are studying. The professors in the program are taken from among those who are skilled in promoting this type of collaboration and who are willing to allow students the freedom for true intellectual exploration. The Honors Program consciously attempts to create a space where students can voice ideas, test hypotheses, and challenge one another in a supportive and demanding environment.

The Honors Program also provides opportunities for cultural and intellectual enrichment outside the classroom. Whether by sponsoring colloquia or speakers or by providing access to cultural resources in the Twin Cities metropolitan area, the Honors Program helps students connect the ideas they have been discussing and thinking about with the wider culture in which they find themselves.

The program is beginning in the 1999–2000 academic year. Enrollment will be capped at approximately 45 students.

Participation Requirements: There are three elements to the Honors Program. First, students take a series of six honors courses. Five of the six courses are seminars with limited enrollment that are focused on reading, discussing, and writing about great works of world culture. The sixth course is an honors science course. Honors courses generally require more reading, writing, and student involvement than regular courses.

The second element of the program is the fulfillment of various departmental requirements for honors based on the student's major. Most departments currently require students to take three or four contracted honors courses in their major. In a contracted honors course, students sign up for any course as they normally would, but once the course begins, they arrange with the professor the work that is required to have the course accepted for honors credit. Such work might include additional reading or writing. When that work is completed, the student receives an honors grade for the course.

The third element of the program is participation in various cultural and intellectual life events sponsored by the College or the Honors Program. For each semester they are in the program, students attend five such events and write a one-page reflection on each event.

Upon completion of the program, students receive an honors designation on their degree, indication as an honors graduate on their transcript, and special recognition at graduation.

Admission Process: Students who achieve at least a 25 on the verbal ACT or 600 or better on the verbal SAT or who are in the top 15 percent of their high school or Crown College freshman class are automatically eligible to apply to the Crown College Honors Program. Students who do not meet one of these criteria may apply to the program but must show evidence of their potential for success in the program.

Scholarship Availability: Academic performance is taken into account in scholarship determination at Crown College. In addition, an Honors Scholarship of $500 per semester is offered to honors students.

The Campus Context: Crown College is located on a beautiful 193-acre campus about 10 minutes west of the Minneapolis suburbs near the communities of Waconia and St. Bonifacius, Minnesota. The institution was founded in 1916 by Reverend J. D. Williams for the purpose of educating men and women for Christian ministry. The College resided in St. Paul, Minnesota, for more than fifty years, first in a private home, later on Sherburne Avenue, and for many years at 1361 Englewood Avenue. In 1970, the College was moved to its present campus. Today it is nestled among the rolling hills of one of the most lake-dotted regions of Minnesota, west of popular Lake Minnetonka. Just minutes from the bustling Twin Cities of Minneapolis and St. Paul, Crown College offers a place of retreat for learning and growth on a beautiful campus. Crown College offers a variety of majors in the liberal arts and social sciences as well as professional majors in business, teacher education, and Christian ministries.

Student Body Crown College currently enrolls about 800 students. This includes 421 traditional four-year students and 250 adult degree-completion students as well as 97 extension students and 14 graduate students. Enrollment among traditional four-year students is almost equally divided between men and women.

Faculty There are 25 full-time faculty members, of whom 16 hold earned doctorates. The 17:1 student-faculty ratio allows personal attention from professors, which is one of the strengths of the educational program at Crown.

Key Facilities The library at Crown contains more than 100,000 volumes in print as well as another 100,000 items in nonprint formats (microform, electronic titles, audiovisual materials, etc.). The College provides three computer labs, one Macintosh and two PC, with full Internet and World Wide Web access available from all computers.

Athletics Crown College participates in the National Christian College Athletic Association (NCCAA) and fields teams in football, basketball, soccer, cross-country, volleyball, and baseball.

Study Abroad Crown College students have ready access to study-abroad opportunities through the Coalition of Christian Colleges and Universities. Many students also participate in intercultural experience trips organized by the College. Recently, students have traveled to Latvia, China, England, Indonesia, and elsewhere as a part of this program.

Support Services Crown College's Learning Assistance Program and its lab offer help to students who need tutoring or other assistance in order to succeed in college. The College also owns a reading machine for blind students.

Job Opportunities Work-study is available in most areas of the College for many students who qualify for financial aid. Non-work-study positions are also available.

Tuition: $288 per credit, $8640 full-time (30 credits) (1998–99)

Room and board: $4020

Mandatory Fees: $200

Contact: Director: Dr. James Lanpher, 6425 C. R. 30, St. Bonifacius, Minnesota 55375; Telephone: 612-446-4100; Fax: 612-446-4149; E-mail: honors@gw.crown.edu

DAVIS & ELKINS COLLEGE

4 Pr G S Sc AA

▼ Honors Program

The Honors Program at Davis & Elkins College courts philosophers in the root sense of that term: lovers of learning. In an atmosphere of inquiry, the program offers intellectual challenges, depth of investigation into chosen subjects, and an opportunity to integrate thinking across disciplines. It demands active learning in the form of discussion, writing, and oral presentation. While the program is college-wide rather than departmental, its courses satisfy the curricular requirements of the regular academic program either as general education requirements or as electives. Founded in 1984, the Honors Program involves approximately 30 students who meet both in classes and for cultural events.

Participation Requirements: Supervised by their mentors on the honors committee, students must sustain their academic performance. Freshman honors students are expected to earn at least a 3.0 GPA. From their sophomore year on, they must maintain a 3.2 cumulative GPA. Under exceptional circumstances, the honors committee may permit students not fully meeting these criteria to remain in the program on a semester-by-semester basis. In addition, in order to graduate with distinction, students must achieve a 3.0 average within the honors curriculum.

Students devote 18 hours of their undergraduate studies to honors courses. In their first year, they enroll in a writing-intensive English seminar. Over the next three years, they take four 3-credit-hour seminars. These classes, occasionally team-taught and interdisciplinary, bring students into close contact with the fundamental texts in various fields and with their intellectual peers. This group includes their instructors, who are often learning an unfamiliar subject along with the students. To remain in good standing in the program, students take at least one (and no more than two) of the seminars every year. Their honors experience culminates in a senior thesis, typically more than thirty pages in length, or a comparable project within their major or across departments.

The program's curriculum is not confined to the classroom. Honors seminars travel to cultural events and host visiting scholars. Mentors encourage their charges to expand their learning in other ways, such as studying abroad or conducting part of their course work in a second language. At graduation, honors students are eligible for the Purdum-Goddin Distinguished Graduate Award. All who have completed the requisite honors courses and projects with the specified GPA receive the distinguished citation, a sign of their intellectual odyssey.

Admission Process: Admission to the Honors Program is based on academic performance in high school and standardized test scores. Students should have a minimum GPA of 3.0 (on a 4.0 scale) and an ACT score of 25 or higher or SAT score of 1200 or higher. Students who do not meet all of these requirements may be considered for provisional admission based on a review of their academic background by the Enrollment Management Committee.

Scholarship Availability: The College offers substantial academic scholarships, including a scholarship to all students enrolled in the Honors Program. The scholarship amount for Honors Program participants is based on the student's overall high school academic performance and is determined by the Enrollment Management Committee after the student has been admitted.

The Campus Context: Davis & Elkins College is a private liberal arts institution affiliated with the Presbyterian Church U.S.A.

Interpreting the symbols: **2**=two-year college, **4**=four-year college; **Pu**=public or state college, **Pr**=private college; **G**=general honors program; **D**=departmental honors program; **S**=small program (fewer than 100 students), **M**=midsize program (100 to 500 students), **L**=large program (more than 500 students); **Sc**=scholarships available in honors program; **Tr**=transfer students accepted into honors program; **HBC**=historically black college; **AA**=academic advisors; **GA**=graduate advisors; **FA**=fellowship advisors.

and committed to excellence of education in liberal arts and sciences. Located in Elkins, West Virginia, a few hours from Pittsburgh, Pennsylvania, and Washington, D.C., the College combines access to cultural centers with an impressive natural setting in the Appalachian Mountains. In the years since its founding in 1904, the physical plant of Davis & Elkins has expanded to include twenty-two major buildings on a 170-acre campus. The College is accredited by the Commission on Institutions of Higher Education of the North Central Association of Colleges and Schools and offers a range of baccalaureate and associate degree programs.

Student Body Undergraduate enrollment is 610; 41 percent men, 59 percent women. Ethnic distribution is 90 percent white, 3 percent African American, 1 percent Hispanic, 3 percent Asian, 1 percent Native American/Eskimo; 4 percent of the student body is international. Ninety-nine percent of first-year students and 96 percent of continuing students receive financial aid.

Faculty The total number of faculty members is 68 (45 full-time); 80 percent of full-time teachers have terminal degrees. The student-faculty ratio is 10.5:1.

Key Facilities The Booth Library, opened in October 1992, is a state-of-the-art building designed to house 300,000 volumes, 450,000 microforms, and 8,500 pieces of nonprint material accessible through an online catalog. The facility includes archives, a media center, a community room, and a student lounge. Campus computer facilities include labs in the library and two classroom buildings and a fiber-optic network supporting residence halls, offices, and labs.

Honorary Society Alpha Chi

Athletics Davis & Elkins is in Division II NCAA for women in basketball, cross-country, soccer, softball, tennis, and volleyball. Men participate in baseball, basketball, cross-country, golf, soccer, and tennis. In addition, women's and men's ski teams compete under the auspices of the USCSA.

Study Abroad The College participates in a program in London and assists students in planning independent study abroad.

Support Services The College meets all legal requirements for ADA and 504 and has a widely recognized Learning Disabilities program. Information on admission to and costs of the LD program can be obtained through the program director.

Job Opportunities Work opportunities on campus and around town are listed in the Career, Academic and Personal Services Center, which also assists students nearing graduation.

Tuition: $13,324 per year ($445 per credit hour)

Room: $2532

Board: $3094

Mandatory Fees: $420

Contact: Director: Dr. Robert McCutcheon, Davis & Elkins College, 100 Campus Drive, Elkins, West Virginia 26241-3996; Telephone: 304-637-1216; Fax: 304-637-1413; E-mail: mccutchr@dne.edu; Web site: http://www.DnE.edu.

Delta State University

4 Pu G S Tr

▼ University Honors Program

The Delta State Honors Program offers to especially capable and motivated students a challenging program that fosters independent thought and emphasizes critical analysis, stressing intellectual rigor and curiosity as well as advanced scholarship. Students cultivate the ability to express their ideas clearly and effectively, both orally and in writing. The Honors Program also fosters the notion of a community of learners who take an interdisciplinary approach to knowledge and scholarship. The ultimate purpose of the Honors Program is to produce enlightened individuals who are able to think for themselves and make a significant contribution to the larger society.

The Delta State Honors Program begins in fall 1999.

Participation Requirements: Students take six of their required core classes in honors sections and fulfill special honors requirements in their junior and senior years, which include an honors thesis.

Admission Process: Entering students and transfers with a GPA of at least 3.0 may apply for admission to the Honors Program.

The Campus Context: Delta State University is located in Cleveland, Mississippi, a community of 15,000 in the heart of the Mississippi Delta. The University provides a comprehensive education, offering fourteen baccalaureate degrees in forty-four majors, eight master's degrees, the educational specialist degree, and a doctorate in education.

Student Body Undergraduate enrollment is 3,915. Twenty-nine percent of the students are African American. Seventy-five percent attend full-time; 40 percent live in university housing. There are six national fraternities and seven national sororities on campus.

Faculty The total number of faculty members is 275, of whom 181 are full-time and 94, part-time. Fifty-two percent of the faculty members have doctoral degrees.

Key Facilities The W. B. Roberts Library collection consists of 214,489 bound volumes, 774,169 microfilms, 117,420 U.S. government documents, and 1,194 subscriptions. Seven computer labs have thirty microcomputers.

Athletics The University is a member of the National Collegiate Athletic Association at the Division II level, the Gulf South Conference, and the new South Intercollegiate Swim League. Men compete in intercollegiate football, basketball, baseball, swimming, diving, tennis, and golf. Women compete in intercollegiate basketball, tennis, fast-pitch softball, cross-country, swimming, and diving.

Support Services For students with disabilities, the Academic Support Lab ensures program accessibility and compliance with the Americans with Disabilities Act.

Job Opportunities A wide range of work opportunities exist, including work-study positions.

Tuition: $4708 for residents, $7302 for nonresidents per year (1998–99)

Room and board: $4800 minimum

Contact: Director: Dr. Miriam C. Davis, Department of History, 216D Bailey Hall, Cleveland, Mississippi 38733; Telephone: 601-846-4174; E-mail: mdavis@dsu.deltast.edu

Denison University

4 Pr G L Sc Tr

▼ Honors Program

The Denison University Honors Program is designed especially for outstanding students in the college. It consists of seminars and courses intended to meet the intellectual aspirations and expectations of highly motivated and academically gifted students. Working closely with the Director of the Honors Program and a faculty adviser, an honors student may enroll in a select list of course and seminar offerings during the student's Denison career. Special academic events take place each semester for students in the Honors Program. Most honors seminars meet a general education requirement of the college. The honors quarterly newsletter, *Arete*, keeps honors students abreast of current activities in honors work. An Honors Symposium is held annually, and visiting scholars meet regularly with honors students.

The Honors Program is located in Gilpatrick House, the Honors Center for the college. This restored Victorian house is centrally located on the Denison campus and serves as the locus for Honors Program activities. The ground level contains a seminar room modeled after Brasenose College, Oxford; a commons for discussion groups and informal seminars; and the administrative offices for the Honors Program. The upstairs serves as a residence area for 10 students in the Honors Program. The Gilpatrick Fellow assists in planning extracurricular events for students in the Honors Program. A popular event is the Gilpatrick Chowder Hour. This faculty-prepared luncheon for 20 students and faculty members, which is followed by discussion on a current topic, takes place six times during term.

The program was established in 1965 and revitalized in 1986. As of 2001, 580 students are enrolled in the Honors Program. Upperclass students with a minimum 3.4 GPA are eligible to participate in the program. The number of upperclass students averages between 350 and 400 per semester.

Participation Requirements: Denison students with a minimum 3.4 GPA are eligible to register for seminars in the Honors Program. To be a member of and to graduate from the Honors Program, a student needs to complete the following requirements: achieve and maintain at least a 3.4 GPA by the end of the sophomore year, declare intention to the director of the program to complete the requirements in the Honors Program no later than preregistration time in the fall of the junior year, complete at least two honors seminars during the first four semesters, complete at least four honors seminars during the Denison career, and complete a two-term research and senior honors project in the department or program of the student's major. Students wishing to declare the intention to complete the Honors Program requirements should discuss this option with the Director of the Honors Program no later than the end of the sophomore year.

Students who complete the requirements to graduate as a member of the Honors Program are recognized in several ways. On the Friday prior to Commencement, the Honors Program sponsors a special graduation ceremony and reception to honor these seniors. Attended by faculty members and relatives, the ceremony consists of the presentation of a bronze medal and Latin certificate to each student by the Honors Program director and the president of the college. These students also receive a special designation on their college transcript and in the Commencement program indicating that they have graduated as a member of the Honors Program.

Eligible students may participate in the seminars without completing the specific requirements to graduate in the Honors Program.

Scholarship Availability: Denison University is committed to enrolling academically talented individuals, which is evidenced by its comprehensive scholarship program. More than 500 merit scholarships and awards are offered. Entering, first-year students invited to participate in the Honors Program are eligible for Denison's full range of academic scholarships. For the class of 2005, the college offered twenty full-tuition Faculty Scholarships for Achievement, ten full-tuition Mary E. Carr Scholarships, twenty three-quarter–tuition Trustee Awards, eighteen three-quarter–tuition University Scholarships, and more than 400 half-tuition Heritage Scholarships. There is no special application for these awards. To be assured of consideration, the complete Denison application must be received by the admissions office by January 1 of the applicant's senior year of high school.

To receive the Faculty Scholarship for Achievement, the Mary E. Carr Scholarship, the Trustee Award, or the University Scholarship, students must interview with a Denison representative any time prior to March 9 of their senior year. Applicants invited to compete for these awards are also contacted in February of their senior year and asked to submit a scholarship essay.

One renewable full-tuition award is the Jonathan Everett Dunbar Scholarship in the Humanities, awarded annually to 1 outstanding student in the humanities. Interested students must submit a Dunbar application by January 1 of their senior year. Another renewable full-tuition Wells Scholarship in Science is awarded to 1 outstanding science student each year. Interested students must submit a special Wells application by January 1 of their senior year.

Information on all awards is available from the Denison Admissions Office. Notification of the Faculty Scholarship for Achievement, the Mary E. Carr Scholarship, the Trustee Award, and the University, Dunbar, and Wells scholarships winners takes place in March. The profile for students receiving award offers in recent years has been a class rank in the top decile, strong test scores, and evidence of significant extracurricular achievement and essay writing ability. It is advisable to pay particular attention to the preparation of the Denison essay as well as the scholarship essay.

The Campus Context: Denison University is an independently supported coeducational college of liberal arts and sciences that is steeped in tradition and responsive to curricular innovation and creativity in the classroom. The University was founded in 1831 in Granville, Ohio. Granville is a picturesque New England–like village nestled near the Welsh Hills of Licking County and the area has early connections with Native Americans as evidenced by one of the largest collections of burial mounds in the United States. Historically rooted, the village of Granville contains a five-block area that is on the National Registry of Historic Places. Large segments of the Denison campus are also on the National Registry.

Denison has earned a national reputation as an energetic academic community. Students participate actively in their education, work with a faculty committed to teaching and to scholarship, learn to make informed choices, and develop the skills to become tomorrow's leaders.

Denison offers three undergraduate degrees—the Bachelor of Arts, the Bachelor of Science, and the Bachelor of Fine Arts. Forty-two majors and nine preprofessional programs are offered. Special or distinguishing facilities on campus include the Olin Planetarium, the Polly Anderson Field Station in a 350-acre biological reserve, the Swasey Observatory, a high resolution spectrometer lab, a nuclear magnetic resonance spectrometer, economics computer laboratories, and the Burmese art collection. Denison students actively publish seven on-campus disciplinary and interdisciplinary journals.

Student Body Undergraduate enrollment is approximately 2,000, of which women comprise 57 percent. Ninety-eight percent of the students reside on campus. The ethnic distribution is approximately 85 percent Caucasian, 6 percent African American, 2 percent Hispanic, 5 percent Asian-American, and 2 percent other. There are also 101 international students enrolled at Denison. Approximately 95 percent of enrolled undergraduates receive some form of aid. There are eight national fraternities and seven national sororities; all are nonresidential.

Faculty Of the 187 faculty members, 179 are full-time, and 97 percent have terminal degrees. The student-faculty ratio is 11:1.

Key Facilities The library houses 370,000 volumes, 340,000 government documents, 1,200 periodical subscriptions, 20,000 sound recordings, and 4,100 videocassettes. Denison also offers a combined catalog to a collection of more than 1 million volumes as a member of the Five Colleges of Ohio consortium and is a member of the OhioLINK state consortium. Computer facilities include 200 PC and Macintosh microcomputers in twelve student clusters, 252 computers in twenty-nine department labs, and network outlets available to every student living in a residence hall.

Honorary Societies Mortar Board, Phi Beta Kappa, and Phi Society

Interpreting the symbols: **2**=two-year college, **4**=four-year college; **Pu**=public or state college, **Pr**=private college; **G**=general honors program; **D**=departmental honors program; **S**=small program (fewer than 100 students), **M**=midsize program (100 to 500 students), **L**=large program (more than 500 students); **Sc**=scholarships available in honors program; **Tr**=transfer students accepted into honors program; **HBC**=historically black college; **AA**=academic advisors; **GA**=graduate advisors; **FA**=fellowship advisors.

Athletics Denison is a member of North Coast Athletic Conference (NCAA Division III). Denison students may also participate in intercollegiate and intramural sports. There are eleven men's and eleven women's intercollegiate sports, and thirteen men's and thirteen women's intramural sports. Denison has won the NCAC All Sports Championship trophy for four consecutive years (1997–98 through 2000–01).

Study Abroad Study abroad is encouraged as is domestic off-campus study in the Washington Semester, Sea Semester, Arts Program in NYC, Newberry Library Program in Humanities in Illinois, Oak Ridge Science Semester in Tennessee, and Philadelphia Urban Semester. Denison is affiliated institutionally with the Advanced Studies in England Program.

Job Opportunities Work opportunities on campus are available. Approximately 44 percent of full-time undergraduates work on campus. The average amount undergraduates may expect to earn per year from part-time, on-campus work is $2025.

Tuition: $22,550 per year (2001–02)

Room and Board: $6550

Mandatory Fees: $540

Contact: Director: Dr. Anthony J. Lisska, Granville, Ohio 43023; Telephone: 740-587-6573; Fax: 740-587-5688; E-mail: sunkle@denison.edu; Web site: http://www.denison.edu/honors/

DePaul University

4 Pr M Tr AA

▼ College of Liberal Arts and Sciences Honors Degree Program

The DePaul College of Liberal Arts and Sciences Honors Degree Program offers challenging courses for well-prepared, serious students majoring in any discipline. The Honors Degree Program seeks to widen students' perspectives beyond their academic majors and foster critical thinking, self-reflection, and an examination of values. In addition, the Honors Degree Program works to foster active participatory learning, promote interdisciplinary and cross-cultural studies, encourage students to develop facility in a second language, develop the skills necessary for pursuing independent research, help student see themselves as members of larger communities in which they can be leaders through service work and other means, and assist interested students in thinking about and preparing for postgraduate education. The program offers two capstone experiences, the senior seminar and the senior thesis. Whichever of the two options a student chooses, he or she will be engaged in a dialogue about how to become a lifelong learner.

In order to meet these goals, the program offers small classes (usually 20 students), organized in a seminar format and taught by faculty members committed to realizing the program's goals. All core courses emphasize honing students' skills in writing and research, reading, and analysis through carefully structured exercises. In addition, the Honors Degree Program requires intensive language training; encourages self-directed learning through third-year elective courses that include the requirement of a research project; offers a lecture and film series, a study-abroad program, field trips, and opportunities for public service; and provides information and counseling regarding admission to graduate schools and applications for fellowships.

Faculty members teaching in the program are among the most talented and committed faculty members at DePaul. They teach their areas of expertise to students who are excited and enthusiastic to actively engage in the learning process.

The current College of Liberal Arts and Science Honors Degree Program was founded in 1987, and there are currently 375 students enrolled in all four years.

Participation Requirements: The Honors Degree Program consists of twenty courses representing 80 credit hours. These include a ten-course core (core courses include World Literature, History of the Pre-Modern World, Enduring Themes in History, Religious Worlds and Worldviews, Philosophical Inquiry, States Markets and Societies, Art Artist and Audience, and the Urban Experience), a three-course science sequence, a three-course modern language sequence beyond the College requirement, two junior-year approved courses, one junior seminar, one free elective, and either the senior thesis or the senior seminar. To graduate from the Honors Degree Program, students must have attained at least a 3.2 GPA by the last quarter of their senior year. Students who successfully complete the program have their transcripts stamped Honors Program Graduate.

Admission Process: Students are invited to join the Honors Degree Program when they apply for admission to their first year at DePaul. Invitations are issued on the basis of high school GPA, class rank, or ACT scores. In addition, students submit an essay that is evaluated by the Director and the Associate Director. Students whose numerical profile does not match the honors profile but who exhibit a special quality based on the evaluation of the Honors Program Director and Associate Director may be invited for an interview. Some of these qualities may include extensive travel abroad, a keen interest in literature and the arts, or intense engagement with the community throughout high school. In some cases, DePaul students and transfer students may be considered for the Honors Degree Program through the first quarter of their sophomore year.

Scholarship Availability: Scholarships of various amounts are awarded through the Office of Admissions, based on academic performance or financial need. Scholarships are not offered through the Honors Degree Program. Most honors students are recipients of academic scholarships.

The Campus Context: Situated in a beautiful residential neighborhood of historic brownstones and tree-lined streets, DePaul's 30-acre Lincoln Park campus is home to the College of Liberal Arts and Sciences. Three miles to the south of Lincoln Park, the Loop campus is located in the heart of Chicago's financial, legal, corporate, and governmental districts. Chicago is the nation's third-largest city and one of the richest industrial, commercial, and cultural centers in the country. DePaul, a Catholic, Vincentian, and urban university, takes its name from St. Vincent dePaul. The College of Liberal Arts and Sciences was the first college founded by the Vincentian fathers in 1898. DePaul's distinctive spirit seeks to foster in higher education a deep respect for the dignity of all persons, especially the materially, culturally, and spiritually deprived, and to instill in educated persons a dedication to the service of others. In each succeeding generation, the women and men of DePaul have pursued learning in the spirit of Vincent dePaul.

Student Body The undergraduate enrollment is 55 percent women. The ethnic distribution is 65 percent white, 11 percent African American, 9 percent Hispanic, 8 percent Asian/Pacific Islander, 0.3 percent Native American, and 6.7 percent unknown or other. Sixty-two percent of all undergraduate students receive financial aid. There are several national fraternities and sororities active on campus.

Faculty First and foremost, DePaul's faculty is committed to teaching. There are 563 full-time faculty members and 630 part-time faculty members at DePaul. The ratio of students to professors is 15:1. Ninety percent of faculty members hold terminal degrees in their fields.

Key Facilities Each campus houses important library facilities. The most extensive is located on the Lincoln Park campus, the John T. Richardson Library. Collection areas of particular strength are religion, philosophy, and Irish studies. Facilities include a media area for audiovisual materials and the Education Resource Center, with curriculum materials for elementary and secondary school teaching, a slide library, a Career Information Center, and a collection of music recordings and scores. Rare book collections include the Napoleon Collection, the Dickens Collection, and the sporting collection as well as numerous titles dealing with nineteenth century literature and book illustration. The University Archives houses materials documenting the growth and development of DePaul. There are approximately 600 workstations in the Microcenters and computer classrooms through DePaul, which make IBM and Mac computers available to students and provide Internet access. The Student Center, completed in January 2002, is a state-of-the-art facility for student and faculty activites.

Honorary Societies Golden Key and Gamma Kappa Alpha

Athletics When students think of DePaul sports, Blue Demon basketball probably comes to mind. In fact, the Demon's 1998 recruiting class was voted second best in the nation. Other NCAA Division I intercollegiate varsity sports include soccer, cross-country, golf, tennis, and track for men and basketball, cross-country, softball, tennis, track, and volleyball for women. An active intramural program offers everything from floor hockey to co-recreational volleyball. The Ray Meyer Fitness Center, a state-of-the-art facility that provides students a place to practice virtually any sport they desire, was completed in June 1999.

Study Abroad The Foreign Study Program adds an international dimension to students' education. The College has academic programs for college credit in Italy, Germany, England, Hungary, Japan, Mexico, France, Spain, and the Soviet Union. In each case, students take a rigorous course of study that is supplemented by the exciting experience of making their way among people whose customs are quite different from their own.

Support Services DePaul University is committed to providing opportunities to students regardless of their disabilities. Classrooms are wheelchair accessible. The College provides reasonable auxiliary aids and services to students with disabilities. In addition to providing legally mandated services for persons with disabilities who voluntarily seek additional services, the Disabled Student Services Office provides support services for students with disabilities. The Honors Degree Program provides mentors to assist first-year students in honors through their first quarter at DePaul.

Job Opportunities Work-study, undergraduate assistantships, internships, and cooperating learning are available.

Tuition: $16,500 (2001–02)

Room and Board: $6000 average (2001–02)

Mandatory Fees: $25

Contact: Director: Dr. Clara Orban, McGaw Hall 303, 802 West Belden, Chicago, Illinois 60614; Telephone: 773-325-1880; Fax: 773-325-7303; E-mail: corban@depaul.edu; Web site: http://www.depaul.edu/~honors

DePauw University

4 Pr G M Sc Tr

▼ Honor Scholar Program, Management Fellows Program, Media Fellows Program, and Science Research Fellows Program

DePauw University offers four challenging and rewarding honors programs so that high-achieving students with specialized interests can benefit even more from their undergraduate education. A student may apply to and enroll in more than one of these programs.

The purpose of the Honor Scholar Program is to provide a rigorous interdisciplinary experience to academically talented students within a liberal arts educational philosophy. Students selected for the program must not only demonstrate a level of academic achievement that predicts their ability to handle academic content, but also have the ability to generalize from specifics and to apply these generalizations to new and seemingly unrelated knowledge. The Honor Scholar Program complements the required academic courses with discussion-based classes containing 10 to 12 students and a senior thesis through a process similar to a master's thesis. The discussion-based seminars are taught by faculty members recruited for expertise in their own discipline and for competence in facilitating participatory learning among students. The Honor Scholar Program was founded in 1979 and presently has 90 students enrolled.

The DePauw Management Fellows Program is an honors program for students interested in business, management, and entrepreneurship. This four-year learning experience integrates the study of management and entrepreneurship with a liberal arts education. Students complete courses in business ethics, quantitative analysis, economics, and accounting. Management Fellows also participate in a semester-long, credit-bearing, paid internship. Students have interned all over the world in the private, public, and not-for-profit sectors. Past internship sites include Eli Lilly and Co., Indianapolis; Goldman Sachs and Co., Chicago; and Ernst & Young International in London. The Management Center Lecture Series relates practice to theory and is an integral part of the program. Students interact and network with business leaders in a wide variety of industries through the lecture series.

The Media Fellows Program combines analytical and critical study with hands-on media experience within the Eugene S. Pulliam Center for Contemporary Media, a state-of-the-art media facility that is unique to a small liberal arts college. It is intended for students who plan careers in media and for students who want to know how media operate to help them perform effectively in other careers. The first year of the Media Fellows Program lays a philosophical base for media study and an introduction to media in their various forms. During the sophomore year, Media Fellows attend a luncheon discussion series with faculty members and senior Media Fellows. During the junior year, students participate in a semester-long, professional internship in a media setting such as a television network, newspaper, public relations office, or entertainment program. In the senior year, Media Fellows take part in a capstone seminar that includes media projects and extensive reading and discussion. Throughout the four years, students are expected to complete four semesters of work in one of the student media and attend special lectures, luncheons, and seminars featuring media experts. The Media Fellows Program was founded in 1992 and currently has 81 students enrolled.

The Science Research Fellows Program is an honors program for science students. Although the program places an emphasis on science, it maintains a liberal arts focus. There are four major components to the program: a first-year seminar, a student-faculty summer research collaboration, a semester internship, and a capstone seminar. Science Research Fellows have the advantage of getting hands-on research experience during their first year. They are given the opportunity to work in small groups to develop their technical and communication skills. They are also granted the unique opportunity to perform summer research with a science faculty member to more fully develop their investigative ability. The program is excellent preparation for graduate and professional schools.

Interpreting the symbols: **2**=two-year college, **4**=four-year college; **Pu**=public or state college, **Pr**=private college; **G**=general honors program; **D**=departmental honors program; **S**=small program (fewer than 100 students), **M**=midsize program (100 to 500 students), **L**=large program (more than 500 students); **Sc**=scholarships available in honors program; **Tr**=transfer students accepted into honors program; **HBC**=historically black college; **AA**=academic advisors; **GA**=graduate advisors; **FA**=fellowship advisors.

Participation Requirements: Honor Scholars are required to enroll in two full-credit seminars during their first year. Three additional interdisciplinary seminars are required: one each in the social sciences, the humanities, and the sciences. These classes also fulfill certain general education requirements. During the senior year, Honor Scholars may enroll in independent-study classes to generate their thesis. Students must maintain a cumulative GPA of at least 3.2 to graduate from the program.

Management Fellows must complete course requirements in the major of their choice and the Management Fellows core curriculum. To remain a Management Fellow in good standing, a student must attend at least four lectures from the McDermond Center Lecture Series each semester, participate in a paid internship that lasts a minimum of fifteen weeks, and earn at least a 3.2 GPA each semester.

Media Fellows must complete two courses, one emphasizing the process side of media, the other analytical. Media Fellows have a list of courses to choose from, but only one of the two courses can be in their major. Members of the program have three semesters to achieve at least a 3.1 GPA, which they must maintain to remain in good academic standing. By the second semester of the senior year, Media Fellows must complete 7 credits and achieve at least a 3.2 GPA to graduate.

Science Research Fellows are required to enroll in an interdisciplinary, introductory seminar their first year. During the following summer, students participate in a paid, on-campus research project. During their junior or senior year, students have a semester-long internship in a major research setting, such as Harvard Medical School or the National Institutes of Health. The program culminates with a capstone seminar in which students present their off-campus research. Students must achieve a minimum 3.1 GPA by the end of the second year.

Admission Process: Students are invited to join the Honor Scholar Program through a tiered application process. Prospective students submit essay responses to posed questions, which are evaluated by 2 faculty members. Based on the ranking of the essays, a select group of students are invited to interview on campus. During the interview, the student's ability to articulate thoughts, to grapple with indicated inconsistencies in logic, and to incorporate new information is evaluated. From this interviewed pool, a percentage of students are invited to join the program.

Admission to the Management Fellows Program is based on superior academic ability, a high degree of intellectual curiosity, leadership potential, and an interest in a management career. Most students apply to the Management Fellows Program during their high school senior year, although students may be admitted in their first year of college. Admission decisions are based on SAT and/or ACT scores, high school GPA and rank, a written essay, and a formal interview.

Students must complete a special application to the Media Fellows Program in addition to the DePauw University application. Decisions on admission are made based on the quality of the application, which consists of three essay questions, SAT or ACT scores, class rank, and an interview with a member of the faculty governing board for Media Fellows. The program admits approximately 25 students per class.

Students must complete a special application to the Science Research Fellows Program in addition to the regular application to DePauw. Admission decisions are made on the basis of SAT or ACT scores, class rank, quality of the essays on the application form, and a personal interview. The program admits only 18 to 20 students per class.

Scholarship Availability: Students applying to any of the four programs are eligible for merit scholarships. To be considered a candidate for one of the four merit scholarships available to Management Fellows, a student must demonstrate evidence of superior academic performance, leadership abilities, and other personal characteristics necessary for success both at DePauw and after graduation. Selection is made from among those high school seniors who have been admitted to the Management Fellows Program for the following fall. Scholarships are renewable, provided the recipient remains a member in good standing of the Management Fellows Program.

The Campus Context: DePauw University is nationally recognized for a distinctive liberal arts approach that links intellectual rigor with life's work, leading to uncommon success for graduates. Founded in 1837, DePauw is a four-year, private, selective, coeducational, residential, undergraduate liberal arts college and School of Music, located in Greencastle, Indiana. Its student population of 2,200 may choose from more than forty areas of study in the College of Liberal Arts or the School of Music. The academic program is enhanced by meaningful student-professor relationships, extensive internship and study-abroad programs, and a January Winter Term. Greencastle, a town of approximately 10,000 residents, has been recognized as one of the 100 best small towns in America and is located about 45 miles from Indianapolis.

Student Body Total enrollment is 2,202 undergraduates: 43 percent men, 57 percent women. Ethnic distribution is 84 percent white, 6 percent African American, 2 percent Asian, 3 percent Hispanic/Latino, 1 percent Native American, 2 percent multiracial, and 2 percent international. The student body includes residents of forty-three states, the District of Columbia, Puerto Rico, the Virgin Islands, and seventeen countries. Ninety-four percent of students live on campus in residence halls and fraternity and sorority houses. Twelve national fraternities and nine national sororities have chapters at DePauw, where Greek life has been a tradition for nearly 150 years.

Faculty The total number of faculty members is 254 (208 full-time), of whom 92 percent have terminal degrees. The student-faculty ratio is 10:1.

Key Facilities DePauw's three libraries house 318,627 book volumes, 12,126 audiovisual titles, 1,581 print periodical titles, more than 475 electronic titles, and 451,000 government documents. All campus offices and residence hall rooms are wired for Internet access, with computer labs located in all residence halls and most academic buildings. More than half of all classrooms will be equipped for multimedia and Web-based presentations by fall 2003.

Athletics DePauw competes in the NCAA Division III Southern Collegiate Athletic Conference. Men's teams include baseball, basketball, cross-country, football, golf, soccer, tennis, and track and field (indoor and outdoor). Women's teams include basketball, cross-country, field hockey, golf, soccer, softball, swimming, tennis, track and field (indoor and outdoor), and volleyball. There is also an active intramural sports program at DePauw.

Study Abroad More than 80 percent of DePauw students study abroad on Winter Term service or study trips, Winter Term internships, or semester-long enrollment programs. There is a broad range of off-campus study sites on six continents. In 2000, DePauw was ranked sixth among top liberal arts colleges in the percentage of students who studied off campus.

Support Services The Academic Resource Center offers workshops, review sessions, and individual or group tutoring to all students. DePauw is committed to providing reasonable and appropriate accommodations to enrolled students with disabilities to ensure equal access to academic programs and University-administered activities. A student with a disability is encouraged to contact the ADA coordinator upon admission to the University. Services and accommodations for students are provided on an individualized basis. Students with physical disabilities can be accommodated in academic buildings and some residence halls.

Job Opportunities Work opportunities on campus are available through the work-study program. Eighty percent of DePauw students complete at least one internship, often during the Winter Term. The Career Services Office assists students with career placement following graduation.

Tuition: $21,100 per year (2001–02)

Room and Board: $6500 (residence halls)
Mandatory Fees: $400
Contact: Honor Scholar Program Director: Dr. Bruce Serlin, Senior House, DePauw University, Greencastle, Indiana 46135; Telephone: 765-658-6260; Fax: 765-658-6262; E-mail: honorscholar@depauw.edu; Web site: http://www.depauw.edu/honors/index.asp; Management Fellows Program Director: Dr. Gary Lemon, Robert C. McDermond Center for Management and Entrepreneurship, DePauw University, Greencastle, Indiana 46135; Telephone: 765-658-4024; Fax: 765-658-4856; E-mail: garylemon@depauw.edu; Web site: http://www.depauw.edu/honors/index.asp; Media Fellows Program Director: Dr. David Bohmer, Pulliam Center for Contemporary Media, DePauw University, Greencastle, Indiana 46135; Telephone: 765-658-4467; Fax: 765-658-4455; E-mail: dbohmer@depauw.edu; Web site: http://www.depauw.edu/honors/index.asp; Science Research Fellows Program Director: Dr. Bridget Gourley, 310 Julian Science Center, DePauw University, Greencastle, Indiana 46135; Telephone: 765-658-4607; E-mail: bgourley@depauw.edu; Web site: http://www.depauw.edu/honors/index.asp

DICKINSON STATE UNIVERSITY

4 Pu G M Sc Tr AA

▼ Theodore Roosevelt Honors/Leadership Program

Dickinson State University is committed, through the establishment of the Theodore Roosevelt Honors/Leadership Program, to recruiting and retaining outstanding students in the region as well as attracting a more diverse student population by recruiting nationally and internationally. This innovative honors program seeks academically gifted students who will pursue their chosen careers. The program's emphasis on scholarship and leadership is designed to challenge the participants with a curriculum that goes beyond the expectations of their major.

Dickinson State University's unique scholars program has its foundation in the leadership and service exemplified by historical links with President Theodore Roosevelt and his experiences gained when ranching near Medora, North Dakota, during the 1880s. Students study the qualities and practices of effective organizational leadership, which facilitate a unique understanding of leadership and change.

The Theodore Roosevelt Honors/Leadership Program provides additional rigor and intellectually stimulating experiences in addition to leadership training, seminar classes, interdisciplinary study utilizing Internet resources, and special field trips. The program develops leadership skills, broadens perspectives, enhances potential, and prepares students to live, learn, and lead in the new millennium.

Founded in August 2000, the Theodore Roosevelt Honors/Leadership Program currently enrolls approximately 75 students with anticipated growth to roughly 150 students in the coming years.

Participation Requirements: Qualifications for prospective candidates for the Theodore Roosevelt Honors/Leadership Program are: incoming freshmen must have a 3.5 GPA in high school or a minimum ACT score of 26; college transfer students must have completed a minimum of 60 credit hours with a minimum GPA of 3.25, or college transfer students who have completed less than 60 credit hours must meet the freshman requirements plus have a 3.25 cumulative GPA in their college work.

In order to maintain their status as a Theodore Roosevelt Scholar students must complete at least 24 semester hours per academic year, maintain at least a 3.25 cumulative GPA, and be an active participant in the Theodore Roosevelt Honors/Leadership Program.

Beginning with the 2001–02 academic year, participants may receive the scholarship for a maximum of ten consecutive fall and spring semesters.

Graduates of this program have a distinct advantage as they pursue graduate school options or enter the work force. Students completing this program receive a special notation on their transcript signifying they were Theodore Roosevelt Scholars.

Admission Process: Applicants must complete and submit by December 1 the Dickinson State University Scholarship Form along with a one-page essay outlining their career aspirations of the academic year and how a Dickinson State University education can assist them in achieving these goals. Students are also encouraged to describe their participation in school activities and community involvement.

Scholarship Availability: All freshmen admitted into the program are awarded the Theodore Roosevelt Honors/Leadership Scholarship. The current value of the scholarship is $2000 per year. In addition, Dickinson State University's Global Awareness Initiative (GAI) Scholarship is available for many students. Its current value is $500 per year. Coupled with the Center for Multicultural Affairs, the GAI serves to expand the institution's cultural diversity, increase informal learning experiences related to cultural diversity and global awareness, and increase contact with Native American colleges.

More than 80 percent of Dickinson students qualify for financial aid. This year more than $600,000 was awarded in the form of scholarships and awards.

The Campus Context: Dickinson State University is an outstanding four-year college with a solid academic foundation. Having been accredited since 1946 by the Higher Learning Commission of the North Central Association of Colleges and Schools (NCA), DSU is currently enjoying ten years of full accreditation by NCA, granted. DSU's Teacher Education Program also renewed its accreditation by the National Council for the Accreditation of Teacher Education (NCATE), and both levels of the nursing program, associate and bachelor's degrees, are accredited by the National League of Nursing (NLN).

Students may enroll in forty major and forty-four minor programs. Graduating classes average a 98 percent placement rate in either employment or graduate school. Dickinson State students are sought after nationwide and many preprofessional students attend some of the most prestigious graduate schools in the nation. The campus has fifty different organizations and campus activities.

Dickinson, North Dakota, population 17,000, is a pleasant, safe, regional center, located near the scenic Badlands of North Dakota and the Theodore Roosevelt National Park.

Student Body Since 1995, Dickinson State University has experienced a continued growth in its enrollment. Undergraduate enrollment is 2,100 students representing nineteen different countries.

Faculty More than 65 percent of the faculty members have doctorate or terminal degrees with credentials from major universities across the nation. Three-fourths of the classes have fewer than 30 students in them.

Athletics The athletic teams are affiliated with the Dakota Athletic Conference (DAC-10), the National Association of Intercollegiate Athletics (NAIA), and the National Intercollegiate Rodeo Association (NIRA).

Study Abroad Dickinson State University has a cooperative agreement with the Kazakhstan Institute of Management, Economics, and Strategic Research and Planning (KIMEP) and participates

Interpreting the symbols: **2**=two-year college, **4**=four-year college; **Pu**=public or state college, **Pr**=private college; **G**=general honors program; **D**=departmental honors program; **S**=small program (fewer than 100 students), **M**=midsize program (100 to 500 students), **L**=large program (more than 500 students); **Sc**=scholarships available in honors program; **Tr**=transfer students accepted into honors program; **HBC**=historically black college; **AA**=academic advisors; **GA**=graduate advisors; **FA**=fellowship advisors.

in a Study Abroad Program with Wroxten College located in a suburb of London, England.

Tuition and Fees: For 2001–02, tuition was $2463 per academic year for residents of North Dakota, $2607 for residents of Minnesota, $2980 for residents of Montana and South Dakota, $2980 for residents of Manitoba and Saskatchewan (Canada), $3497 for residents of the Western Undergraduate Exchange Program (WUE) states (Alaska, Arizona, California, Colorado, Hawaii, Idaho, Nevada, New Mexico, Oregon, Utah, Washington, or Wyoming) and the Midwest Student Exchange Program (MSEP) states (Kansas, Michigan, Missouri, and Nebraska), and $5915 for all nonresidents.

Room and Board: Fees are $1092 per year for double occupancy in all residence halls and $1524 per year for single occupancy (if space is available). Meal plans are available ranging from $1580 to $1940 per year.

Contact: Director, Dr. David A. Meier, 291 Campus Drive, Dickinson, North Dakota, 58601-4896; Telephone: 800-279-HAWK; Fax: 701-483-2537; E-mail: David.Meier@dickinsonstate.com; Web site: www.dickinsonstate.com.

DILLARD UNIVERSITY

4 Pr G S Tr HBC

▼ Daniel C. Thompson/Samuel DuBois Honors Program

The Honors Program at Dillard University takes as its motto: *non scholae sed vitae discimus* or "we learn not for school, but for life." The Honors Program seeks to nurture and enhance the full potential of highly motivated academic achievers. The honors curriculum is student-centered and stresses the attainment of communicative, analytical, creative, technological, and leadership skills. Through an interactive, interdisciplinary program, students supplement their regular undergraduate curriculum by participating in innovative seminars. Honors students graduate with an increased knowledge of the historical roots of contemporary global and local issues with an emphasis on independent scholarship, problem-solving, and social responsibility. In the process, students acquire critical-thinking skills, ethical values, aesthetic appreciation, and technological expertise that prepares them for the twenty-first century.

Honors students are involved in individual and group activities on and off campus, ranging from tutoring fellow students and organizing campus academic and social activities to interviewing Dillard alumni for the Dillard History Project and serving in the Dillard University Community Development Corporation. The mentorship component exists primarily to allow honors students to identify faculty members who will supervise a senior-year research project. It also seeks to create a peer mentorship network to fortify the honors academic community. The Honors Program has plans to extend the peer network to include the larger University community, in which honors students could serve as role models for non-honors students. The Honors Program also envisions the creation of a community mentorship network that will match honors students with local or regional professionals whose careers correspond to honors students' majors.

Approximately 90 students are enrolled in the Honors Program. Honors students major in every area and division at Dillard University. The program was founded in 1978 and was originally named for the eminent black sociologist Daniel C. Thompson and former president Samuel DuBois Cook.

Participation Requirements: The honors curriculum is a four-year program. Honors students are required to take honors sections of designated core courses. They must also take an additional 15 hours of honors seminars. Beginning in the junior year, honors students conduct work within their respective majors, which culminates with the completion of a thesis or special project during the senior year. Honors students must maintain an overall GPA of at least 3.6. If a student's GPA falls in the range of 3.2–3.59, then they are placed on conditional status for one academic year, during which the student has an opportunity to regain a GPA of 3.6. If the student's GPA falls below 3.2, then they are expelled from the program and lose their University Scholarship.

Each spring, the Honors Program sponsors two major events: a Spring Symposium and an Honors Day Convocation. The symposium provides an opportunity for honors students to give presentations about their work and to interact with faculty members from the larger Dillard community and elsewhere. The convocation features a keynote address by a prominent scholar or public figure and the presentation of certificates and awards. Graduating seniors are permitted to wear special honors cords at graduation and an Honors Program seal is added to their diplomas. Successful completion of the Honors Program is also noted on students' transcripts.

Admission Process: The majority of the students admitted to the Honors Program enter as first-semester freshmen. There are two modes of admission: designation as a University Scholar and by special permission of the Honors Steering Committee. University Scholars compose the core of the Honors Program. Chosen as the outstanding entering first-year students, they are required to participate in the Honors Program to maintain their scholarships. The selection process and criteria for entering students are established by the Office of Enrollment Management and Admissions are as follows: a 24 or higher on the ACT or 1200 or higher on the SAT I and a high school GPA of at least 3.5. Presidential and Merit Scholars are allowed to enter the Honors Program on a voluntary basis, where enrollment permits, but still have to petition for admission into the Honors Program by the end of the spring semester of the freshman year. A complete petition includes a nomination by a member of the honors faculty or an adviser, the submission of high school and college transcripts, and the submission of a writing sample for review by the Honors Program Steering Committee. Second-semester freshmen and first-semester sophomores who have attained a GPA of 3.5 or higher are invited to submit a petition to enter the Honors Program. Petitions for admission will not be granted after the second semester of the third year of enrollment.

Scholarship Availability: The Honors Program does not administer any scholarship funds. The Office of Enrollment Management and Admissions and the Office of Financial Aid have complete jurisdiction in this area.

The Campus Context: Dillard University began as two distinct institutions, Straight College and New Orleans University, both of which were founded in 1869. Initially, both institutions offered instruction on the elementary level, then expanded to include the secondary, collegiate, and professional levels. On June 6, 1930, New Orleans University and Straight College merged to form Dillard University, which is named in honor of philanthropist and educator James Hardy Dillard. The new University elected to follow the practices of the two parent institutions in making no distinction as to race, religion, or sex in the admission of students or in the selection of faculty members. In September 1935, on a new site with a new physical plant, Dillard University began instruction.

The University is located on a 55-acre tract in a lovely residential section of New Orleans, one of the most historic and interesting cities in the nation. At Dillard, the atmosphere of learning is quietly conveyed by oak-shaded walkways, handsome white buildings, and green landscaped lawns. The main campus now consists of twenty-one buildings.

Dillard offers thirty-eight degree programs under six academic divisions: business, education and psychological studies, humanities, natural sciences, nursing, and social science.

The Albert W. Dent Hall is the current home of the Honors Program. Dent Hall is named for the university's third president.

The Honors Program is the sole occupant of the second floor of Dent Hall with administrative offices, a conference facility and state of the art computer laboratory. The division of educational and psychological studies, the athletic department, classrooms, computer labs, a dance studio, weight center and swimming pool are also housed in Dent Hall. The Will W. Alexander Library is the current home of the African World Studies Institute, the first of its kind at a historically black college or university. The Samuel DuBois Cook Fine Arts and Communications Center contains teaching facilities for art, music, drama, and communications. The building also contains a 250-seat multipurpose complex with a stage, a fly loft and orchestra pit, art studios, work rooms and galleries, a TV studio, a radio station, classrooms, seminar rooms, and the National Black-Jewish Relations Conference Center. In keeping with its philosophy that learning is a lifelong process, Dillard University, through its Center for lifelong learning-evening and continuing education programs, offers an extension of the University curriculum that serves adult students of all ages. Four-year degree programs and continuing education studies are available to nontraditional students.

Student Body As of February 2001, undergraduate enrollment was 1,953. Seventy-eight percent of the students are women. Approximately 99 percent of the students are African American. Hispanics (.23 percent), European Americans (.23 percent), and Pacific Islanders (.05 percent) compose just over one half of 1 percent. Sixty percent of the students live on campus. Eighty-eight percent of students receive financial aid. The campus has four national sororities and four national fraternities.

Faculty There are 165 instructional faculty members and 127 full-time faculty members. Sixty-four percent of the faculty members have terminal degrees. The student-faculty ratio is 15:1.

Key Facilities The Will W. Alexander Library houses approximately 135,000 volumes and the main undergraduate computer laboratory.

Honorary Societies Alpha Chi, Beta Beta Beta, Psi Chi, Beta Kappa Chi, National Institutes of Science Honor Society, Alpha Kappa Mu and Omicron Delta Kappa

Athletics Dillard is a member of the Gulf Coast Atlantic Conference and the NAIA. It offers basketball, tennis, and cross-country at the varsity level.

Study Abroad The Office of Global Studies and the Dillard University International Center for Economic Freedom (DUICEF) offer information on a variety of exchanges, study-abroad programs, internships, and service learning opportunities in most countries around the world. The Honors Program also maintains its own extensive file of such opportunities.

Support Services Eight-five percent of the campus is accessible to physically disabled students. The Student Support Services Academic Enhancement Programs Office provides assistance to eligible students who have a need for academic and/or counseling support services.

Job Opportunities Work opportunities are available on and off campus.

Tuition: $9660 per year full time (2001–02) and $6150 per year lifelong learning (2001–02)

Mandatory Fees: Fees total $100 for freshman week and $100 for graduation.

Room and Board: $6586 per year (2001–02)

Contact: Interim Dean: Dr. Rita McMillan, Albert W. Dent Hall, Room 206, 2601 Gentilly Boulevard, New Orleans, Louisiana 70122-3097; Telephone: 504-816-4788; Fax: 504-816-3235; E-mail: rmcmillan@dillard.edu

Dominican University of California

4 Pr G S Sc Tr

▼ Honors Program

The Dominican University of California Honors Program is designed to provide enhanced and alternative modes of education for excellent and highly motivated students throughout the University. It encourages the growth of intellectual independence and initiative, offers special opportunities for independent study and research under faculty mentors, and supports the pursuit of scholarly interests in a broad range of disciplines. It aims to bring together enthusiastic students and faculty members to further the Dominican ideal of intellectual excellence. The program is directed toward students who seek the responsibility of determining the pace, organization, and development of their academic experience by electing to take special honors seminars and/or various forms of independent honors work. Students receive academic advisement from both their major adviser and the honors director to help them set and achieve their own educational goals. The Honors Program provides students with the opportunity to enroll in honors seminars or graduate courses and to do an honors course conversion, course expansion, an honors independent study, or an Honors Study Abroad Experience. The program began in 1989 and currently enrolls approximately 100 students.

Participation Requirements: Honors students must maintain a minimum 3.3 cumulative index in order to remain active in the program. Honors-related financial awards are in jeopardy if the index slips below 3.1. To become an Honors Program graduate, a student must maintain at least a 3.5 cumulative index while completing either 21 units of honors work or a combination of honors seminars and honors contracts that totals seven courses/projects. Transfer students are expected to complete a portion of this requirement depending on their academic standing upon entrance to Dominican University of California. For example, a sophomore transfer student would be expected to complete five courses/projects. The minimum requirements for graduation from the Honors Program by a transfer student are four semesters of residence and four honors projects while maintaining the minimum 3.5 index. For students who successfully complete the Honors Program requirements, the title of the honors thesis and honors program graduation is noted on the official University transcript.

Scholarship Availability: A number of academic scholarships are available at Dominican University of California. Those of interest to honors students include a Presidential Merit Scholarship and a Dean's Merit Scholarship. These are available for entering freshmen with a strong academic record.

The Campus Context: Dominican University of California is composed of the following schools: the School of Arts and Sciences, the School of Business and International Studies, the School of Education, and the School of Nursing and Allied Health Professions. There are eighteen undergraduate and five graduate programs offered on campus.

Student Body Undergraduate enrollment is 949 of which 77 percent are women. The ethnic distribution is approximately 7 percent African American, 10 percent Hispanic, 12 percent Asian, 1 percent Native American, and 4 percent international students. Commuters make up 75 percent of the school's population. Seventy percent of students receive financial aid. Dominican University has no fraternities or sororities.

Interpreting the symbols: **2**=two-year college, **4**=four-year college; **Pu**=public or state college, **Pr**=private college; **G**=general honors program; **D**=departmental honors program; **S**=small program (fewer than 100 students), **M**=midsize program (100 to 500 students), **L**=large program (more than 500 students); **Sc**=scholarships available in honors program; **Tr**=transfer students accepted into honors program; **HBC**=historically black college; **AA**=academic advisors; **GA**=graduate advisors; **FA**=fellowship advisors.

Faculty Of the 200 faculty members at Dominican University, 60 are full-time. The student-faculty ratio is 13:1.

Key Facilities The library houses 100,132 volumes and subscribes to more than 4,000 periodicals. The computer labs house seventy workstations.

Athletics In athletics, Dominican University of California plays NAIA division men's and women's soccer, basketball, and tennis and women's volleyball.

Study Abroad The University currently offers twenty-six study-abroad programs in twenty-two locations in Africa, Australia, Asia, Europe, Central America, and South America. As part of the University's mission to foster an appreciation of cultural diversity and global interdependence, students are encouraged to consider this option. These programs are administered through the International Studies Program.

Support Services There is a disabled-student coordinator on campus. Facilities for disabled students include the Academic Support Department and the Peer Counseling Department.

Job Opportunities Dominican University provides a campuswide work-study program.

Tuition: $18,648 per year (2001–02)

Room and Board: $8900

Mandatory Fees: $350

Contact: Director: Dr. Patricia Dougherty, 50 Acacia Avenue, San Rafael, California 94901-2298; Telephone: 415-257-0154; Fax: 415-459-3206; E-mail: dougherty@dominican.edu

Drexel University

4 Pr G L Tr

▼ University Honors Program

The Drexel University Honors Program enriches the university experience for students of superior intellect and demonstrated academic achievement. The Honors Program is in its seventh year of operation. In the Honors Program, students from all majors receive individual attention throughout their academic progress and participate in a variety of courses that engage small groups of students with Drexel's best faculty members, special trips and cultural events, and social gatherings. The program offers the advantages of an elite liberal arts college within a major technological university. Incoming students are selected for admission based upon their superior intellectual strengths, accomplishments, and motivation. Current students who meet these criteria are also invited to apply.

The following three types of courses carry honors credits: honors sections of courses offered by various departments; interdisciplinary Honors Colloquia, sponsored by the Honors Program; and Honors Options, the individual enrichment of nonhonors courses for particular students, which must be approved in advance by the instructor and program director.

Currently, there are approximately 700 students in the Honors Program. About 120 entering freshmen are admitted each year, which represents about the top 8 percent of the entering class.

Participation Requirements: Flexibility is the hallmark of the Drexel Honors Program. Students may elect as many courses and events as they wish. To remain in the Honors Program, students must maintain a GPA of 3.0 or higher. Qualified honors students may graduate with distinction from the Honors Program. These students must complete 32 credits of honors courses and projects, maintain an overall GPA of 3.5 or higher, and complete a senior project judged worthy of honors. Students aiming for this distinction normally meet with the program director in their junior year to ensure that they understand these requirements and are prepared to meet them.

Admission Process: Students apply directly to the director of the program. The application requires standard information and includes a brief essay. The progress of all students in the University is monitored, and accomplished Drexel students not currently in the program are invited to apply.

Scholarship Availability: Need-based and merit scholarships as well as grants, loans, and work-study programs are available through the Admissions Office. Some co-op positions and faculty research assistant positions are also available to students. The University makes approximately $40 million available annually for scholarship aid. In addition, a six-month co-op typically pays a Drexel student an average of $12,000. The Honors Program itself does not offer scholarships.

The Campus Context: Drexel University is Philadelphia's second-largest private university. It is also the second-oldest—and largest—university in the nation dedicated to cooperative education. Founded in 1891, the University comprises six colleges: Arts and Sciences, Business and Administration, Engineering, Information Science and Technology, Nesbitt College of Design Arts, and Evening College. Forty-six bachelor's, thirty-nine master's, and seventeen doctoral degree programs are offered. Drexel was the first university in the nation to require that each undergraduate have access to a microcomputer, and the campus offers full networking, extensive integration of computers in the instructional program, and access to the Internet across the campus and in the dormitories. Drexel's location in the historic city of Philadelphia also provides diverse cultural sites and activities.

Student Body Of the 8,000 undergraduates, most come from the Northeast. The distribution is 40 percent women, 7 percent international undergraduates, and 25 percent commuters. Residents live in one of five residence halls, apartments, or one of four sororities or twelve fraternities on campus. Eighty percent of students receive financial aid; the total aid package equals $40 million annually.

Faculty There are 450 full-time faculty members. Ninety percent hold terminal degrees in their field. The student-faculty ratio is 13:1.

Key Facilities The Hagerty Library contains 400,000 volumes. The 10,000 computers on campus include Apple and PC machines. Forty-five buildings on campus offer a full range of activities and services.

Athletics The Drexel Dragons compete in NCAA Division I in the following sports: men's and women's basketball, lacrosse, swimming and diving, cross-country, and tennis; men's baseball, crew, golf, soccer, and wrestling; and women's field hockey, softball, and volleyball. Club sports include cheerleading, chess, women's crew, fencing, ice hockey, in-line skating, karate, men's volleyball, riflery, rugby, sailing, skiing and snowboarding, and volleyball. Ten different sports are offered as more informal intramural activities.

Study Abroad Drexel Abroad Programs in Brussels, Bonn, London, Madrid, and Paris combine internships with intensive study of the politics and culture of the host country or, in Brussels, of the European community. Open to students throughout the University; students enroll under Drexel course numbers and receive course credit. Financial aid and merit scholarships travel with the student.

Tuition: $13,472 to $18,406 per year (full-time) or $346 per credit hour for day classes and $185 per credit hour for evening classes (part-time) (1998–99)

Room and Board: $8433

Mandatory Fees: $944

Contact: Director: Mark L. Greenberg, Dean, Honors Center, 5016 MacAlister Hall, Philadelphia, Pennsylvania 19104; Telephone: 215-895-1267; Fax: 215-895-6813; E-mail: mcmenaab@mail.drexel.edu; Web site: http://www.honors.drexel.edu

DUQUESNE UNIVERSITY

4 Pr G M

▼ The Honors College

The Honors College is a select group of students who enjoy living and learning together. These students share a commitment to their studies and come from all of Duquesne University's many schools, from Pharmacy to Business Administration to Liberal Arts, Music, Health Sciences, Natural and Environmental Sciences, and Education. Students in the Honors College constitute a select learning community, as the Honors College students share special CORE curriculum classes, but the social, service, and living dimensions of the Honors College are as important as the academic component. Students in the Honors College find wonderful opportunities of all sorts: for learning, for making friends, for contributing to the University and the community, and for forming lifelong bonds with one another.

Honors College students share a CORE curriculum of seven courses that are required of all students. These courses are distinguished by their small size (20–30 students), their outstanding faculty members, and their interactive character. Learning is lively, personal, stimulating, and enriching in Honors CORE courses. Honors students are also encouraged to engage in special research and study projects under the guidance of their faculty members.

Honors College students can live in the Assumption Living-Learning Center, where the rooms are spacious and each floor has a lounge, a kitchen area, and a computer facility specifically for the use of Honors College students. At the heart of the Honors College experience lies the opportunity for students to become good friends with their classmates. This is particularly important during those first difficult weeks of college, and the Honors College creates a stable base that supports students as they create friendships, academic connections, and lasting memories.

Honors College students have their own Integrated Honors Society, an organization that arranges social outings and activities and identifies and coordinates service projects in the local community. While Honors College students enjoy each other's company and provide service in the community, the students also have the opportunity to learn the leadership skills of running their own organization.

There are many benefits to being in the Honors College: students learn through extraordinary teaching; get early, preferred registration status; live in special quarters that provide academic and social advantages; and receive a special designation on their transcript that identifies them as Honors College students. This designation may enhance employment opportunities and admission to graduate schools.

The Honors College, founded in 1997, grew out of the Integrated Honors Program, which was started in 1984. The program currently enrolls almost 400 students.

Participation Requirements: Honors College students must maintain a minimum GPA and complete the Honors CORE curriculum. The final or capstone course in the Honors CORE sequence is an Honors Seminar.

Admission Process: High school students with strong academic records (minimum 3.5 GPA) and combined SAT scores of 1200 (minimum 620 verbal) or an ACT score of at least 28 are invited to join the Honors College.

Scholarship Availability: Duquesne University offers a full range of competitive merit scholarships. While no scholarships are tied directly to the Honors College, many Honors College students are recipients of merit-based scholarships.

The Campus Context: The secret of Duquesne University is the spirit of Duquesne. It is academic excellence for the mind, but it is also education for the heart and the soul. Duquesne University has been consistently ranked among America's top ten Catholic universities in the annual *U.S. News & World Report* survey. It is rated as very competitive by *Barron's Profile of American Colleges* and as one of Barron's 300 Best Buys in American higher education. Duquesne is nationally and internationally renowned for its historic commitment to teaching, scholarship, and personal attention to students' needs. This unique spirit pervades every corner of Duquesne's ten schools: Liberal Arts, Law, Business Administration, Pharmacy, Music, Education, Nursing, Health Sciences, Natural and Environmental Sciences, and Leadership and Professional Advancement. Students at Duquesne discover all the amenities of a great city, including a magnificent symphony orchestra, opera center, theaters, and major-league teams in football, baseball, and hockey. It is rare to discover a beautiful campus that is recognized as one of the safest campuses in America in the heart of a city.

Student Body Undergraduate enrollment is 5,500; 42 percent are men and 58 percent are women. International students from more than 100 countries attend Duquesne University. There are five living-learning centers, and 50 percent of undergraduate students live on campus. There are nine national sororities and seven national fraternities. Fourteen percent of undergraduates join sororities or fraternities.

Faculty Duquesne has 408 full-time and 444 part-time faculty members.

Key Facilities The Gumberg Library holds an extensive collection of books, journals, electronic resources, microprint, and audiovisual resources. Fully networked and automated, the library offers both on-site and remote access to more than 100 online databases and more than 2,000 electronic journals.

Athletics Duquesne University is a member of Division I of the NCAA, the Atlantic 10 Conference, and the MAAC Football League and has a wide range of men's and women's intercollegiate and intramural sports.

Study Abroad Duquesne University offers a range of study-abroad opportunities for Honors College students and all students, including the University's own campus in Rome, Italy, as well as study-abroad affiliations with universities in twenty countries around the world.

Tuition: $17,478 to $22,309, includes fees

Room and Board: $6764 (based on a double room)

Contact: Director: Roberta C. Aronson, 212 College Hall, Duquesne University, Pittsburgh, Pennsylvania 15282; Telephone: 412-396-1818; E-mail: aronson@duq.edu; Web site: http://www.honorscollege.duq.edu

---

DUTCHESS COMMUNITY COLLEGE

2 Pu G S Sc Tr

▼ Honors Advisement Track

The Dutchess Community College (DCC) Honors Advisement Track provides academically able students an enriched liberal arts education by means of correlated courses and an upper-level interdisciplinary seminar. The track is designed for students who, upon completing the program, intend to continue to work toward a bachelor's degree.

Interpreting the symbols: **2**=two-year college, **4**=four-year college; **Pu**=public or state college, **Pr**=private college; **G**=general honors program; **D**=departmental honors program; **S**=small program (fewer than 100 students), **M**=midsize program (100 to 500 students), **L**=large program (more than 500 students); **Sc**=scholarships available in honors program; **Tr**=transfer students accepted into honors program; **HBC**=historically black college; **AA**=academic advisors; **GA**=graduate advisors; **FA**=fellowship advisors.

The honors experience features small classes, including a freshman seminar that familiarizes students with campus life and provides a forum for questions and answers.

Each semester's course offerings emphasize a central theme. The first semester focuses on global intellectual and cultural traditions; later semesters emphasize American political, historical, and literary development and the complexities and richness of the contemporary world.

Eleven students currently participate fully in the Honors Advisement Track, which was established twenty-five years ago, and 20 more students have been admitted into individual honors courses.

Participation Requirements: Students in the Honors Advisement Track pursue the Associate in Arts degree in liberal arts and sciences: humanities and social sciences. Up to 36 of the 64 credits required for the completion of this degree may be taken as honors courses. These include three sets of content-correlated courses: Global History and Global Literature (ancient), American History and American Literature, and Global Politics and Global Literature (contemporary).

Honors students have the opportunity to participate in out-of-the-classroom activities such as attending lectures, films, and plays and visiting the campuses of four-year colleges. They are also made aware of off-campus study opportunities, internships, and academic competitions.

Admission Process: Students are selected for the Honors Advisement Track on the basis of high school achievement, standardized test scores, and an individual interview. High-ability students identified during the registration process are invited to apply for admission to honors.

Scholarship Availability: New President's Scholarships available for the first time in 1999–2000 year offer free Dutchess Community College tuition to any student in the top 10 percent of his or her high school class. Students must file for financial aid through the traditional channels in order to be eligible for the Presidential Scholarship.

The Campus Context: Dutchess Community College (DCC), a part of the State University of New York, was founded in 1957. The College serves the citizens of Dutchess County and northern Putnam County in the mid-Hudson Valley. It is a comprehensive public open-enrollment college that offers the first two years of a baccalaureate education and prepares students for occupational/technical degrees and certificates for direct entry into career fields. DCC enjoys an outstanding reputation for excellence in teaching, highly qualified and caring faculty members, a visually pleasing environment, fine technology facilities and equipment, and extensive student support services.

Student Body Enrollment is approximately 2,750 full-time students (53 percent women) and 3,470 part-time students (64 percent women).

Faculty There are 121 full-time faculty members (25 percent of whom hold terminal degrees) and 240 adjunct lecturers at the College.

Key Facilities The library holds 99,093 volumes and increasingly extensive electronic information-gathering resources. There are eighteen computer labs for student use on the campus.

Honorary Societies Phi Theta Kappa

Athletics The College is a member of the National Junior College Athletic Association, the Mid-Hudson Athletic Conference, and the National Intramural Association. A variety of intramural sports and men's and women's intercollegiate sports are offered each year.

Study Abroad Students have the opportunity to study abroad during winter or spring break in connection with credit courses in, for example, history or Caribbean literature.

Tuition: $2300 for residents per year (1998–99)

Mandatory Fees: $95

Contact: Directors: Anne Landry or Beth Kolp, 53 Pendell Road, Poughkeepsie, New York 12601; Telephone: 914-431-8560; E-mail: landry@sunydutchess.edu (Professor Landry); Telephone: 914-431-8433; E-mail: kolp@sunydutchess.edu (Professor Kolp)

East Arkansas Community College

2 Pu G S Sc Tr

▼ Honors Program

The Honors Program at East Arkansas Community College (EACC) is designed to attract liberal arts students in the three-county service area who wish to complete a two-year course of study before continuing their education at a four-year school. The program emphasizes enriched core courses, engaging teaching styles, a low student-teacher ratio, and the nurturing of academic camaraderie among participants. Student admission to the program is based on a competitive application process.

The curriculum of the Honors Program at EACC was designed with the transfer student in mind. The four-semester program includes the core courses required by most four-year colleges and universities in Arkansas. Incoming honors students enroll together in a total of 10 semester hours of honors courses, which include a one-hour seminar. Each semester, those students who enter the program are enrolled together in the required honors courses. Each student may elect to take an additional course or two outside of the Honors Program to supplement the core curriculum at any time.

While the core courses do not necessarily demand more of honors students in the way of workload, they differ from the College's usual offerings in approach. Each teacher plans his or her course for the student who has demonstrated an unusual tendency to excel academically. Because of this, the teacher is able to offer more suitable strategies for exposing those students to the subject matter at hand. These possibilities are often absent from regular classes.

Another instructional feature of the program is the opportunity for team-teaching. Especially with the Interdisciplinary Seminar (IDS), which is offered each semester, teachers may work together to design a course that bridges different areas of study. For example, a course based on the interplay of musical and theatrical style in history might be taught by faculty members from the music and drama departments. The possibilities for such collaboration are endless, and such interaction can only improve the entire college.

In the same way that student admission to the program is competitive, teachers in the program are also selected on the basis of application. Instructors who wish to teach in the program must submit a completed application, a sample syllabus, and a budget for the intended course. It is anticipated that the existence of such a program on campus will raise teaching standards across the board.

Most honors classes consist of 15 students. A spirited learning atmosphere is further fostered through group field trips. Each semester, faculty members incorporate into their syllabi an outing to a cultural site that augments the course in some way. These trips may be to museums or exhibits in the nearby cities of Memphis and Little Rock, but they are as likely to include a day trip to a university campus or a Civil War battlefield.

Participation Requirements: All students who are admitted to the Honors Program at East Arkansas Community College receive a full two-year scholarship that includes tuition and books. The scholarships are renewable each semester providing the student has maintained a GPA of 3.2 or greater while enrolled in the program. Participation in the program also includes provisions for all program-related travel and field trips.

Admission Process: Admission to the Honors Program at East Arkansas Community College is competitive. Student enrollment in the program is limited to 15 in each class. Each spring, applications are accepted from students at area high schools. Qualified applicants must meet at least one of the following criteria: a high school GPA of 3.5 or greater, inclusion among the top ten percent of the graduating class, a minimum ACT composite score of 23 (SAT I 1050), or a GPA of 3.5 or greater on 15 transferable college credit hours. Along with the completed application form, the students must submit a 200-word essay and arrange for two letters of recommendation and an official transcript to be sent to the committee. Students may request an application interview as well. Upon acceptance, students are assigned advisers from the Honors Program to help with registration and counseling.

Scholarship Availability: East Arkansas Community College offers full tuition, including books, supplies, and travel, to all students accepted into the Honors Program.

The Campus Context: The 70-acre campus of East Arkansas Community College is located atop Crowley's Ridge just off Highway 284. The campus lies within the limits of Forrest City, which is considered a business and transportation hub of the east central portion of the state. The two-year institution of higher education provides a high-quality educational experience for individual development and improves the general community. The Associate of Arts (A.A.) and Associate of Applied Science (A.A.S) degrees are offered. Degree programs include emergency medical technical paramedic studies, business administration, information systems management, criminal justice, drafting and design, nursing, and administration office technology.

Student Body There are approximately 1,300 undergraduates, of whom 69 percent are women. The ethnic distribution of undergraduates is approximately 46 percent African American, 1 percent Asian or Pacific Islander, 1 percent Hispanic, and 52 percent Caucasian. There are no international students. Sixty-four percent of students receive financial aid.

Faculty Of the 85 faculty members, 39 are full-time and 46 are adjunct. Seven percent of the faculty members hold terminal degrees. The student-faculty ratio is 13:1.

Key Facilities The Learning Resource Center houses 21,942 volumes of books. Computer Education Center facilities include six computer rooms and one large open lab containing sixty-two computers with 486 CPu, fifty-nine computers with 386 CPu, and twenty-eight computers with 8088 CPu. The Learning Center is equipped with up-to-date computers, printers, and educational software to assist students with challenging objectives. Students also have access to the Business and Industry Training Center and the Multimedia Lab.

Honorary Societies Phi Theta Kappa, Gamma Beta Phi

Support Services All academic buildings, the library, the student center, and the Computer Education Center are completely handicapped-accessible. Handicapped parking is available, and restrooms are specially equipped for the convenience of disabled students.

Job Opportunities East Arkansas Community College cooperates with the Department of Health and Human Services to provide employment to students with financial need.

Tuition: $864 for area residents, $1032 for state residents, $1272 for nonresidents, per year (2001–02)

Contact: Chairman of Honors Committee, Forrest City, Arkansas 72335; Telephone: 870-633-4480; Fax: 870-633-7221

East Carolina University

4 Pu G L Tr

▼ Honors Program

The University Honors Program at East Carolina University (ECU) provides special classes with an average size of 18 students and a sense of community for academically superior students. Each semester the program offers four or five honors seminars on different, often interdisciplinary, and frequently controversial topics and some forty honors sections of regular departmental courses. Most of these meet general education requirements, and all seminars help satisfy the University requirement for writing-intensive courses. Seminars have covered a wide range of topics in the humanities, fine arts, sciences, and social sciences. Some of these seminars include "The Voices of Generation X," "Gay Literature," "Writing Poems and Making Drawings," "The Music of Latin America," "The Geology of the National Parks," "Chemistry Behind the Headlines," and "Poverty, Discrimination, and Public Policy." Classes emphasize discussion rather than lecture, essay rather than short-answer exams, and active involvement in the education process.

Students who complete 24 semester hours of honors courses with A's or B's and a GPA of 3.3 or higher earn General Education honors. Upperclass students with at least a 3.5 GPA are invited to complete a 6-semester-hour senior project, which may take the form of a thesis, field experience, public service, portfolio, coteaching, or creative work, and earn University honors in their major or minor.

To foster a sense of community of scholars on the larger campus, the program offers students an honors residence hall, a library study room, their own state-of-the-art computer lab, an active student group, a student newsletter, a fall picnic, a spring Honors Recognition Day, representation on the Honors Program Committee, special lectures and trips, occasional teleconferences and seminars, special honors advising and registration assistance, opportunities for exchange and study abroad, and financial assistance in making presentations at regional and national conferences.

Each semester the program sponsors an Honors Recognition Day, at which students make presentations before the honors student body, graduating seniors are presented certificates, and awards are made. The meeting is followed by a reception at the chancellor's house. The names of graduating students are listed in the honors newsletter, the campus newspaper, and the commencement program. The honors notation becomes a permanent part of the student's transcript as soon as it is earned.

The program is more than thirty years old. In the mid-sixties, the University began offering seminars for selected students by request. In 1978, the current Honors Program was created on a two-year, university-wide format. In 1993, it became a four-year program, with all senior-level departmental honors work being coordinated through the Honors Program. Approximately 750 students are currently enrolled in the program. Fifty-five students graduated from the program in spring 2000. Invitations to participate in the program are issued from October to April.

Participation Requirements: Entering freshmen who present SAT I scores of 1200 or higher, at least a 3.5 GPA, and a top 10 percent high school ranking are invited into the program during their senior year in high school; some freshmen who meet two of these criteria receive provisional invitations. During freshman

Interpreting the symbols: **2**=two-year college, **4**=four-year college; **Pu**=public or state college, **Pr**=private college; **G**=general honors program; **D**=departmental honors program; **S**=small program (fewer than 100 students), **M**=midsize program (100 to 500 students), **L**=large program (more than 500 students); **Sc**=scholarships available in honors program; **Tr**=transfer students accepted into honors program; **HBC**=historically black college; **AA**=academic advisors; **GA**=graduate advisors; **FA**=fellowship advisors.

orientation, students are given academic counseling and are registered for courses. Current ECU students and transfer students with a 3.3 GPA or better also qualify to take honors courses. Students who drop below a 3.0 at the end of the school year are not eligible for courses until they again have a minimum 3.3 GPA.

Scholarship Availability: All merit scholarships are handled by the Office of Admissions, not by the Honors Office, but a large number of honors students hold scholarships. Chancellor's Scholars receive $20,000, University Scholars $12,000, and Alumni Honors Scholars $6000 for the four years. Many special scholarships for in-state, out-of-state, minority, transfer, and other distinct groups of students are available.

The Campus Context: ECU, a constituent institution of the University of North Carolina, is a public doctoral university consisting of twelve colleges and schools: the College of Arts and Sciences and the Schools of Allied Health Sciences, Art, Business, Education, Health and Human Performance, Human Environmental Sciences, Industry and Technology, Medicine, Music, Nursing, and Social Work. It awards the bachelor's, master's, Ph.D., D.Ed., and M.D. degrees. On campus, there are 102 degree programs. The 109 buildings on the main, medical, and allied health campuses are valued at $308 million and include a newly enlarged library and recreation center.

Student Body ECU enrolls 18,900 students, of whom 57 percent are women and 13 percent are members of minority groups. There are more than 150 international students. Of the student population, 85 percent are residential students. Approximately 35 percent of students receive financial aid. There are twenty-three fraternities and fourteen sororities on the main campus.

Faculty The faculty numbers 1,400, of which 88 percent hold terminal degrees. The student-faculty ratio is 15:1.

Key Facilities The newly enlarged central campus library contains more than 1 million books, more than 1 million pieces of microform, and holdings in various other media. There are nearly 2,500 microcomputers and 130 special application terminals throughout the campus. Support for education and research is provided through an IBM ED 900/260 mainframe, SunSparc 20, UNIX and DEC Vax 4000, and 3,400 minicomputers. A fiber-optic network installed in 1995 links the computers with other universities, the NC SuperComputer Complex, and the online library catalog and bibliographical retrieval system. Computer stations are located across campus and in the residence halls. The honors computer lab is one of the most up-to-date on campus.

Athletics ECU plays Division I intercollegiate sports, including men's football (Conference USA), tennis, track, soccer, basketball, diving and swimming, baseball, and golf and women's volleyball, tennis, track, soccer, basketball, diving and swimming, and softball. Students also participate in an elaborate system of intramural sports. A new recreation center provides up-to-date facilities for minor sports and individual workouts.

Study Abroad The ECU Office of International Affairs is a member of several consortia, which promote the exchange of students in the U.S. and 130 institutions abroad for the modest tuition they pay at home. It also sponsors several study-abroad programs in the summer. Some honors credit is given for study abroad. Financial assistance is available.

Support Services Disability Support Services meets the needs of most individuals by offering academic support, attendant services, barrier-free buildings, and adaptive transportation. Full services for the deaf are available, and students may earn a minor in Sign Language Studies. In 1996, the School of Medicine graduated the only profoundly deaf medical student in the nation (a graduate of the Honors Program).

Job Opportunities Work-study and self-help programs assist students with work opportunities on campus. Cooperative education places students in both for-pay and for-credit positions across the country. Other financial aid is available.

Tuition: $2566 for state residents, $10,821 for nonresidents, per year (2001–02)

Room and Board: $4760

Contact: Director: Dr. Michael F. Bassman, Brewster D-107, Greenville, North Carolina 27858-4353; Telephone: 252-328-6373; Fax: 252-328-0474; E-mail: bassmanm@mail.ecu.edu; Web site: http://www.ecu.edu/honors

---

East Central University

4 Pu G D M Tr

▼ Scholastic Honors Program

The East Central University (ECU) Scholastic Honors Program embodies high ideals of academic excellence through which students are provided challenging college experiences and enriched opportunities. Honors students are nurtured through vibrant and distinctive seminar-type classes that are mature in scope, content, and student application. An honors course does not accomplish this by simply increasing the quantitative workload beyond that expected of a nonhonors student but by establishing an environment of scholarly interchange between students and faculty members. Small class size, flexible teaching and learning styles, independent research and presentation, critical-thinking skill development, community involvement, and student collaboration are essential in the honors student's growth and degree progress. There are approximately 250 active honors students in the program.

Participation Requirements: The Honors Program consists of honors courses offered throughout the student's college career. A student who wishes to graduate with University Honors completes a minimum of 26 hours of honors-designated course work as follows: a 1-hour freshman colloquium required during the first semester at ECU and essential in the preparation of honors study, 6 hours from Honors General Humanities I and II or Early and Modern Western Civilization, 9 or more additional hours in honors general education course work, 6 hours contracted in the student's specialized major or senior thesis, and a 3-hour senior interdisciplinary capstone experience. Specialized honors courses are offered in the fields of communication, Western literature, philosophy, critical thinking, and ethics. Students wishing to have the honors designation on their diploma and transcript must maintain at least a 3.0 throughout their college career, and a completed portfolio of the student's research must be on file in the Honors Office.

Transfer students or upperclass students may be admitted to honors and graduate with Departmental Honors. This 9-hour minimum option requires students to complete honors research in their major field and the senior capstone course. Transfer students may include in their degree plan honors courses taken at other institutions but must be approved by the Honors Board.

Students completing all honors degree requirements are recognized at commencement, and final transcripts note their graduation with scholastic honors. The Honors Student Association, a student-led service organization on campus, provides monetary awards each year for the best original research. This student organization participates in many community service projects, funds student presentations at professional conferences, and chaperones and advises incoming freshman scholarship students as they are oriented and enrolled on campus.

Admission Process: Incoming freshmen with a high school GPA of at least 3.5 and a composite ACT score of 24 (with a letter of recommendation) or a composite ACT score of 26 or higher are invited by the Honors Board to apply for admission to the program. Admission is based on academic experience, a demonstration of writing skills, and extracurricular activities. Any continuing or transfer students may petition for admission if their GPA is 3.5 or greater or if they are recommended by other faculty members.

Scholarship Availability: Scholarships of various amounts are awarded through the Office of Student Services based on academic performance and include the Regents, Presidential, Dean's, Academic, and Human Diversity Scholarships. While scholarships are not directly offered through honors, most honors students are recipients of academic scholarships, and participation in honors enhances the student's ability to obtain financial assistance.

The Campus Context: East Central University was established in 1909 and is a part of the Regional Oklahoma University System. The 130-acre urban campus is located in the city of Ada, a community with a population of approximately 18,000. Ada, 90 miles southeast of Oklahoma City, is the commercial, industrial, service, and medical center for a substantial metropolitan and rural area. The Kerr National Environmental Research Laboratory and headquarters of the Chickasaw Nation are found in Ada alongside thriving cement, plastic, petroleum, cattle, and service industries. Ada rests in Oklahoma's Lake Country, which offers many interesting state parks, lakes, and hiking trails. East Central offers thirty-two baccalaureate and seven master's degree programs at four separate campus schools.

Student Body There are 4,400 undergraduates enrolled; 54 percent are women. Although the majority of students are from Oklahoma, the current student body represents seventeen states and sixteen countries. Students participate in more than seventy clubs, and many are members of the four fraternities or three sororities on campus.

Faculty More than 150 full-time faculty members and many adjunct instructors facilitate course work at East Central. Most full-time faculty members have completed terminal degrees and provide outstanding instruction within small-sized classes.

Key Facilities All buildings and computer centers are linked to Internet services, and the University is a transmitter and receiver of OneNet two-way audio and video instructional classrooms. Within the past two years, ECU has opened a new multistory central library and the University Center, both of which have become centers of academic activity on campus.

Athletics ECU competes in the NCAA Division II and is a member of the Lone Star Conference. Intercollegiate sports include baseball (men), basketball, cross-country, football (men), golf (men), soccer (women), softball (women), and tennis. Intramural sports, a vital part of the University's social life and the student's well-being, are available for both men and women in flag football, soccer, basketball, volleyball, softball, and tennis.

Study Abroad A member of the National Student Exchange Program, ECU encourages its students to exchange semesters with students from more than 200 international schools. Through these experiences, individuals gain insight into today's multicultural world and are exposed to different ethnic groups, philosophies, and cultural traditions.

Support Services East Central seeks to maximize the educational opportunities available to students with a variety of educational support services, including state-of-the-art library facilities, a well-staffed student support center for learning-disabled students, several computer laboratories, and a child development center. All academic buildings and resident halls are fully accessible to handicapped students.

Job Opportunities Many students work on campus either as regular student employees or as participants in the Federal Work-Study Program. The University assists students in securing work both on and off campus. The honors office employs student workers who are members of the Scholastic Honors Program.

Tuition: $1800 for state residents, $2077 for nonresidents, per year (1998–99)

Room and board: $2068

Mandatory Fees: $46.50

Contact: Director: Dr. Dennis L. Boe, Box W-3, Ada, Oklahoma 74820; Telephone: 580-332-8000 Ext. 599; Fax: 580-332-1623; E-mail: dboe@mailclerk.ecok.edu; Web site: http://www.ecok.edu/acaddept/honors/

East Stroudsburg University

4 Pu G M Sc Tr

▼ University Honors Program

The Honors Program at East Stroudsburg University (ESU) offers the superior student an opportunity to be challenged beyond the ordinary university education.

At the center of the program are special honors general education courses that feature small class size (15 to 20 students), close student-faculty interaction, and expanded activities outside the classroom, allowing time for creativity and explorations of intellectual depth and breadth. These classes introduce the honors students to various aspects of social, cultural, and scientific heritage and encourage the students to draw connections between the different fields and perspectives studied as well as between the academy and the greater world in which they live.

The classroom experiences are enriched by a variety of field trips and opportunities to attend summer seminars abroad as well as regional and national conventions. Finally, the honor students are encouraged to engage in independent learning and research.

ESU provides an Honors Floor in one of the residence halls for those who choose to reside there. The floor includes kitchen and lounge areas as well as free Internet access from the student rooms.

The program has been in existence since 1989 and admits approximately 30 freshmen and transfer students each year. There are approximately 100 students currently enrolled in the program.

Participation Requirements: In their freshman year, honors students are encouraged to participate in a learning community of two or three honors classes. All honors students are expected to complete a minimum of 18 credits in honors general education classes followed by a multidisciplinary upper-level seminar. After successful completion of their course work, the students choose a thesis adviser in their major, develop a prospectus, and complete an honors thesis in their major.

To remain in the program, students must maintain a minimum 3.3 cumulative GPA and participate in enrichment and service activities. Successful completion of the program is recognized at commencement and is also noted on the official transcript.

Admission Process: Admission to the program is by recruitment from admissions, invitation from the Honors Director, or student-initiated application via the Internet or other media.

Freshmen or transfer students with fewer than 30 credits are expected to place in the 85th percentile of their high school class and achieve 1150 or higher on the SAT I. Transfer students with more than 30 credits may be eligible on the basis of a minimum GPA of 3.3.

Scholarship Availability: Scholarships of various amounts are awarded each spring based on academic performance and active participation in the Honors Program. There are also scholarships each year for 2 students to participate in a special Pennsylvania State System of Higher Education summer honors seminar abroad. A variety of other University scholarships are

Interpreting the symbols: **2**=two-year college, **4**=four-year college; **Pu**=public or state college, **Pr**=private college; **G**=general honors program; **D**=departmental honors program; **S**=small program (fewer than 100 students), **M**=midsize program (100 to 500 students), **L**=large program (more than 500 students); **Sc**=scholarships available in honors program; **Tr**=transfer students accepted into honors program; **HBC**=historically black college; **AA**=academic advisors; **GA**=graduate advisors; **FA**=fellowship advisors.

also available to Honors Students; approximately 65 percent of ESU full-time students receive scholarship aid.

The Campus Context: East Stroudsburg University is one of fourteen institutions in the Pennsylvania State System of Higher Education. The fifty-nine campus buildings are located in eastern Pennsylvania in a small-town setting in the foothills of the Pocono Mountains but less than a 2-hour drive to either Philadelphia or New York City.

The University consists of three colleges, offering sixty undergraduate and fifteen graduate majors. The School of Arts and Sciences offers Bachelor of Science and Bachelor of Arts degrees in twenty-eight majors and four cooperative professional degree programs with other institutions, as well as numerous minors and concentrations. The School of Professional Studies offers Bachelor of Science and Master of Education degrees in various areas and levels of education (the secondary education degree is offered in conjunction with the School of Arts and Sciences). The School of Professional Studies offers Bachelor of Science degrees in recreation and leisure services management and in hotel, restaurant, and tourism management. The School of Health Services and Human Performance offers five majors with five concentrations.

Student Body There are 5,800 students enrolled in the various undergraduate and graduate degree programs. Although the majority of students are from Philadelphia and rural and small towns in Pennsylvania, the University also draws students from neighboring New York and New Jersey. ESU also supports an active international program, drawing students from around the globe.

Faculty Instructional faculty members number 265, and more than 70 percent have terminal degrees. The student-faculty ratio is 19:1.

Key Facilities The Kemp Library houses more than 437,977 books and periodical volumes and 1,290,824 pieces of microform material. It is also a depository for various special collections, most noteworthy being the U.S. government documents and Pennsylvania state publications, with 76,620 documents in the collection. The library uses an integrated online system that may be accessed from the library and computer labs and by modems from home or dorm rooms. The University computing system encompasses a UNYSIS mainframe with thirty systems and an academic computing system spread through faculty offices and 350 PCs in twelve campus computer laboratories.

Athletics The Athletic Department offers a wide variety of intercollegiate and intramural programs. ESU hosts nineteen intercollegiate sports teams for men and women. Facilities include eight athletic fields, track and tennis courts, a field house, and a gymnasium. A student recreation and fitness center has been approved and will shortly be under construction. A 119-acre off-campus student recreation center nearby complements the campus areas.

Study Abroad ESU encourages its students to broaden their educational experiences through study and travel abroad. In addition to opportunities for individual students, several faculty members in the School of Arts and Sciences offer summer courses at Oxford, England; the University of Nancy, France; and the Cultural Studies Academy in Salzburg, Austria. The International Study Program is currently in the process of expansion, and ESU is working toward an NGO affiliation with the UN.

Support Services The University is committed to ensuring equal educational opportunities for students with disabilities. The Center for Educational Opportunity offers a comprehensive program including counseling services, the Learning Center provides individual and group tutoring, and the Speech and Hearing Center provides evaluation and therapy to members of the University and the community.

Job Opportunities Part-time work-study positions are available to students who demonstrate financial need. Further job opportunities are available in the community and the numerous resorts in the area.

Tuition: $4984 for state residents, $11,008 for nonresidents, per year, including mandatory fees (2001–02)

Room and board: $4170–$4224, depending on the meal plan

Contact: Director: Dr. Marcia V. Godich, 212 Fine Arts Building, East Stroudsburg, Pennsylvania 18301; Telephone: 570-422-3743; E-mail: mgodich@p-obox.esu.edu; Web site: http://www.esu.edu/honors

EAST TENNESSEE STATE UNIVERSITY

4 Pu G/D S Sc Tr

▼ University Honors Programs

East Tennessee State University (ETSU) offers a variety of honors programs designed to provide special educational opportunities for academically talented students. Within this mission, the goals focus on recruiting exceptional students; nurturing their intellectual growth through challenging curricula; promoting their commitment to active lifelong learning, leadership, and service; and instilling in them a desire to advance knowledge in their chosen fields. In order to accomplish these goals, honors programs enlist exceptional faculty members who promote innovative and creative approaches to teaching in their classrooms and laboratories. Honors courses are small and provide special enrichment opportunities. Honors Scholars collaborate with professors in research and scholarly activities and receive assistance in the pursuit of fellowships, awards, and access to continued studies in graduate and professional programs. Honors programs are offered in the University Honors Scholars Program and a variety of honors-in-discipline programs in colleges and departments. Discipline-specific programs are designed for students majoring in a specific area and currently are available in the Colleges of Applied Science and Technology, Business, Education, and Nursing (junior admission only) and in the Departments of Biological Sciences, Chemistry, Criminal Justice and Criminology, English, Environmental Health, History, Mathematics, and Physics and Astronomy. New honors-in-discipline programs are added each year. The four-year University Honors Scholars Program is specially designed for incoming freshmen who desire an interdisciplinary approach to general education in addition to their chosen fields of interest. This program was founded in 1993 and currently enrolls 80 students (20 in each class). University Honors Scholars may major in any of the 115 academic programs available at ETSU. Most general education requirements in this program are provided by yearlong interdisciplinary seminars with limited enrollments that emphasize active learning through writing, discussion, and service-learning projects. Students take each honors general education seminar with their own honors class. Faculty teams from different disciplines, each with established teaching and scholarly reputations, design these courses to integrate information across traditional academic boundaries. For their senior thesis, students work in their major or minor interest in collaboration with a faculty member in a significant creative research project. University Scholars have unlimited access to Honors House, including computer facilities and study and meeting rooms. Special workshops assist students with applications to named scholarships and fellowships and graduate and professional schools. Students are encouraged to participate actively in the Honors Student Council and Honors Advisory Committee in addition to other campus organizations. A variety of social and cultural events are arranged each year for University Honors Scholars.

Participation Requirements: University Honors Scholars must successfully complete a minimum of 15 hours per semester. Required honors courses include a semester of calculus, a year of U.S.

history, 24 hours of honors general education seminars, and an honors thesis in their major or minor discipline. University Scholars must attain a GPA of at least 3.0 by their second semester and maintain a minimum 3.25 GPA for their fourth and all remaining semesters. Probationary status may be granted for one semester only before scholarship support is withdrawn. University Honors Scholar is designated on all diplomas and transcripts; special regalia and ceremonies also are provided. College and departmental honors programs include a minimum of 12 credits of honors courses in the discipline plus the capstone senior honors thesis. GPA requirements vary, but graduates must have a 3.2 or better.

Admission Process: The University Honors Scholars Program admits 20 incoming freshmen each year; transfers are not currently accepted in this program. Candidates must submit a special application, usually due before the end of January for admission the following fall. Scholarships are awarded on a competitive basis. For consideration, students should have at least a 29 ACT/1280 SAT I and a minimum high school GPA of 3.5 (4.0 scale). High school curriculum, extracurricular activities, scholastic honors, letters of recommendation, and a personal essay are evaluated by a team of faculty members and advisers. Students that do not meet minimum test scores, but with unique qualifications in other areas, may be considered for admission. Honors-in-discipline programs often require special application, either for incoming freshmen, transfer students, or students already enrolled. Minimum qualifications include at least a 3.2 high school GPA and 25 ACT/1160 SAT or a minimum 3.2 college GPA for transfer students.

Scholarship Availability: All students accepted in any ETSU honors program receive out-of-state tuition. Additional scholarships for honors-in-discipline students are available in some disciplines. University Honors Scholars receive full tuition and fees, costs of standard room and board, and a book allowance; support is available for eight regular semesters. University Scholars are expected to live on campus for their freshman and sophomore years.

The Campus Context: East Tennessee State University is located along the western edge of the Blue Ridge Mountains in northeastern Tennessee. The TriCities (Johnson City, Kingsport, and Bristol) Tennessee/Virginia area is consistently rated by national publications as one of the most desirable places to live and one of the safest regions in America. Just a short drive from the beautiful campus, there are TVA lakes, the Appalachian Trail, ski slopes, mountain rivers, and abundant opportunities for outdoor activities and visiting historic places. On campus, lectures, plays, films, recitals, and concerts are common evening and weekend activities. The faculty and staff members and students take pride in creating an extended family and a learning environment responsive to ETSU's mission of educating students to become responsible, enlightened, and productive citizens. Faculty members are accomplished and practicing scholars who incorporate the products of their scholarship in teaching. Senior faculty members teach a significant number of general education and freshman courses. ETSU offers more than 115 programs of study in nine different colleges. Among these are several distinctive options, including a premedicine program that provides qualified students with early admission to the Quillen College of Medicine, a 4–1 program that enables students to obtain a B.A./M.B.A. in five years, the nation's only four-year blue grass and country music degree program, and Centers of Excellence in Appalachian Studies and Early Childhood Learning and Development. ETSU's Advanced Visualization Laboratory is recognized as the premier academic partner by Alias/Wavefront, placing it above Centers of Excellence in Helsinki, London, Hong Kong, Toronto, and others.

Student Body Overall enrollment is approximately 12,000 students, with 10,000 undergraduates; 59 percent are women. The minority ethnic distribution is 0.5 percent Native American, 1.1 percent Asian American, 4.5 percent African American, and 0.8 percent Hispanic. There are 155 international students representing forty-two countries. Approximately 25 percent of the students live on campus, and more than 50 percent receive some form of financial aid. More than 215 campus organizations are active, including sororities, fraternities, and honorary societies and political, service, academic, and special interest groups.

Faculty Instructional faculty members number 660, and more than 75 percent hold terminal degrees; all honors faculty members hold terminal degrees. The student-faculty ratio is 28:1 in undergraduate classes; in the honors programs, the student-faculty ratio averages 10:1.

Key Facilities The University has a new astronomy observatory and a new $28-million main library, which opened in January 1999 and has a combined storage capacity of more than 800,000 volumes. The library is fully accessible for those with disabilities and includes ample individual and group study areas, special teaching laboratories, and abundant computer facilities, including laptops. The Quillen Medical Library, on the nearby Veterans Affairs campus, houses special biomedical collections. All library systems are fully electronic and Web based. Computer access includes nine open computer labs across campus and specialized computer teaching laboratories in some departments. Multimedia classrooms are used for instruction in many departments.

Honorary Societies Phi Kappa Phi, Alpha Lambda Delta, Gamma Beta Phi, Omicron Delta Kappa, Golden Key, and Who's Who Among Students in American Universities and Colleges.

Athletics ETSU is a member of the NCAA Southern Conference, participating in sixteen major sports, including football, basketball, soccer, tennis, golf, swimming, cross-country, track and field, volleyball, and baseball. A variety of intramural sports are available, including basketball, flag football, volleyball, softball, soccer, tennis, golf, and racquetball, and student interest groups are active in aerobics, skiing, mountain biking, and martial arts. A new Center for Physical Activity, which will offer an indoor track, climbing wall, swimming pool, basketball, racquetball and squash courts, martial arts studio, and many other facilities dedicated exclusively to student use, will open February 2002.

Study Abroad A number of exchange programs are available, including national and international study experiences. An exchange visit with the University of Edinburgh in Scotland occurs annually, and other exchange agreements are in place with universities in Germany, China, and Ecuador and are in negotiation with Hungary and Russia.

Support Services ETSU acknowledges the particular needs of academically qualified students with disabilities and recognizes their right to an education. The University makes every effort to provide an accessible environment and appropriate accommodation. Ninety-five percent of the campus is accessible to physically disabled students. Special computer facilities, document conversion services, sponsored note-takers, readers, and tutors are made available in addition to other measures of accommodation needed.

Job Opportunities Work opportunities are available on and off campus. The Career Development Office advises students on career choices and manages a large number of internships and cooperative work experiences for students.

Tuition: $1278 for state residents and honors students (2001)

Room and board: $1819

Mandatory Fees: $381.50 per semester

Contact: Director: Dr. Rebecca Pyles, 914 West Maple Street, Box 70294, Johnson City, Tennessee 37614-0294; Telephone: 423-439-6456; Fax: 423-439-6191; E-mail: honors@etsu.edu; Web site: http://www.etsu.edu/honors

Interpreting the symbols: **2**=two-year college, **4**=four-year college; **Pu**=public or state college, **Pr**=private college; **G**=general honors program; **D**=departmental honors program; **S**=small program (fewer than 100 students), **M**=midsize program (100 to 500 students), **L**=large program (more than 500 students); **Sc**=scholarships available in honors program; **Tr**=transfer students accepted into honors program; **HBC**=historically black college; **AA**=academic advisors; **GA**=graduate advisors; **FA**=fellowship advisors.

Eastern Connecticut State University

4 Pu G S Sc Tr

▼ University Honors Program

Founded in 1973 and recognized regionally and nationally, the University Honors Program is among the most active in New England. It offers full in-state tuition scholarships to all freshmen. Honors courses are frequently team-taught and involve off-campus experiences, and they all substitute for general education requirements. The goal of the University Honors Program is to provide academically talented and venturesome students with an intellectually stimulating alternate course of study. Small classes, interdisciplinary topics, and professors dedicated to teaching create an atmosphere conducive to the open discussion of ideas and active learning.

In addition to their academic pursuits, honors scholars become involved in a variety of leadership roles and rewarding activities. Many of these, such as the weekend in April when prospective freshmen are invited to visit the campus and stay over in dorms or apartments, are entirely planned and carried out by students. The Honors Club sponsors trips to cultural events, including the NE-NCHC conference each spring, at which more than a dozen students regularly participate as presenters. The Student Honors Council makes recommendations concerning the honors curriculum and requirements and organizes social and cultural events on campus, including the activities of Honors Week in the spring. Students also publish an *Honors Newsletter* each month, continue to construct and upgrade the site on the World Wide Web, and communicate with each other on the honors listserv. Everyone connected with the program gets together twice a year at the director's home for a back-to-school party welcoming freshmen in the fall and a picnic-barbecue during Honors Week in the spring. Honors students are encouraged to take part in exchange programs with universities throughout the United States and abroad.

Participation Requirements: Honors courses are designed to be different from most other courses used to complete General Education Requirements.

Entering freshmen take HON 200, a course taught by the program director with the assistance of honors students as interns and best described as a freshman seminar and writing course, featuring Campus as Text, small-group discussions of reading and writing assignments, and debates. In their second semester, freshmen take HON 201, Reading Across the Curriculum, a course focused on the family and featuring guest professors from four departments: history, sociology, psychology, and economics. The program director introduces and coordinates this course, again, with the assistance of honors students who serve as interns.

During their sophomore and junior years, students take three honors colloquia (HON 360-362), innovative interdisciplinary courses designed specifically for the program by outstanding scholars and respected teachers. Topics recently covered include New England and the Sea, Ethnicity in Canada and the United States, The Museum and Society, and Culture Across the African Diaspora. Many students volunteer for HON 490, a teaching internship, which fulfills a colloquium requirement.

In the spring of their junior year, students take Directed Honors Research with a mentor, ordinarily a professor in their major department, and write a thesis proposal. Working with their mentors both semesters of the senior year, students complete an honors thesis, a creative, scholarly, or scientific project—the program's capstone experience.

Admission Process: Freshmen are admitted to the program by the University Honors Council on the basis of their high school standing, accomplishments, and recommendations, only after they have been accepted into the University. Guidelines include graduation in the top 20 percent of the high school class and a minimum combined SAT I score of 1150. The Honors Council is particularly interested in students who have participated in educational, social, cultural, or other extracurricular projects or activities and whose applications suggest enthusiasm, a willingness to get involved, and leadership. Although the Admissions Office selects promising applications for review by the Honors Council, candidates may apply directly to the Honors Program.

Scholarship Availability: All entering freshmen receive full in-state tuition scholarships, renewable for a total of eight semesters. In addition, supplementary scholarships, for either merit or financial need, and jobs on campus are often available through the Financial Aid Office, which works closely with the Honors Program.

The Campus Context: Founded in 1889, Eastern is located on a beautiful 175-acre campus on the edge of Willimantic, a New England mill town that produced internationally famous cotton thread and textile products in its heyday. A comprehensive university, Eastern offers twenty-five undergraduate majors, including professional studies and education, as well as arts and sciences. Eastern has been designated Connecticut's public liberal arts university.

Student Body Eastern is a largely residential arts and sciences institution with approximately 4,600 full- and part-time students from every region of Connecticut, more than half of the states, and thirty other countries. This multicultural community thrives in Eastern's small college atmosphere in which students readily get to know each other and their faculty.

Key Facilities Facilities include a state-of-the-art library and e-mail and Internet access for all students.

Honorary Societies Omicron Delta Kappa

Athletics Eastern has a wide range of sports programs and facilities, and both the men's baseball and women's softball teams have won Division III NCAA national championships.

Tuition: \$2142 for state residents, \$6934 for nonresidents, per year (2001–02)

Room and Board: \$5510, per year (2001–02)

Mandatory Fees: \$1769 for state residents, \$2730 for nonresidents, per year (2001–02)

Contact: Director: Dr. Jim Lacey, Eastern Connecticut State University, Willimantic, Connecticut 06226; Telephone: 860-465-4317 or 4577; Fax: 860-465-4580; E-mail: lacey@easternct.edu; Web site: http://www.ecsu.ctstateu.edu/depts/honors/

Eastern Illinois University

4 Pu G/D L Tr AA

▼ Honors Programs

Eastern Illinois University offers superior students the opportunity to take part in two honors programs—University Honors, a lower-division program, and Departmental Honors, an upper-division program. Both University and Departmental honors programs offer students of superior academic ability an unusual opportunity to develop their potential for intellectual achievement. These programs are intended to aid students in developing qualities such as independence of mind by undertaking an enriched curriculum that provides in-depth studies.

The University Honors Program is designed for those who begin as freshmen at Eastern. It provides honors sections of required general education courses and upper-division colloquia. Students must take a minimum of 25 hours in honors courses, which will substitute on a one-for-one basis for current general education courses.

The Departmental Honors Program permits all eligible students, including transfer students, to participate in this division of the honors program. All Departmental Honors Programs require a minimum of 12 hours of departmental honors credit. A senior thesis written under the supervision of honors faculty members is required.

Honors faculty members are devoted and experienced professors who enjoy their subjects and care about teaching talented students. Their teaching methods foster inquiry with an emphasis on undergraduate research. Honors faculty members grade students against norms established in regular classes. Students are aware that, as a result of this arrangement, they will not be penalized for taking classes with other superior students. Further, the intellectual stimulation of excellent teachers and outstanding classmates, together with smaller classes, tends to be reflected in good grades. Honors courses emphasize quality rather than quantity. However, they do cover more material in less time. Assignments are not merely more of the same, but encourage students to think, write, and express themselves with clarity. The excitement of exchanges within smaller classes and the stimulation of intellectual challenge make the question of workload irrelevant.

There are 725 students in the program. Students who join benefit from a centrally located honors residence hall, priority registration, priority textbook pickup, extensive scholarships, limited class size, active student-driven Association of Honors Students organization, and individualized attention.

Participation Requirements: University and Departmental Honors Programs are open to students who meet at least two of the following criteria: ACT composite of 26 or higher or SAT I of 1100 or higher, upper 10 percent of high school graduating class, or a minimum 3.5 GPA on a four-point scale for at least 12 hours of course work undertaken at Eastern Illinois University.

The Campus Context: Eastern Illinois University, with a student population of 10,500, is the smallest of the residential state universities. It is situated in Charleston, a town of 20,000 people, and is 180 miles south of Chicago. The location is rural, nestled between glaciated and nonglaciated land.

The University has expanded to more than fifty-five majors and 100 options within those majors. The University is organized into four colleges: the College of Sciences, the College of Arts and Humanities, the College of Education and Professional Studies, and the Lumpkin College of Business and Applied Sciences. Eastern's strength lies in teaching and in professor-student contact. Class size generally runs from 25 to 40 students and, while Eastern does have a Graduate School, rarely do graduate students do the actual teaching of classes. The student-computer ratio is 13:1.

Faculty The faculty members total 639. Seventy-four percent have doctoral or other terminal degrees. The student-faculty ratio is 16:1.

Key Facilities Student housing consists of modern residence halls, University apartments, and newly built sorority and fraternity houses. Nearly 6,000 students live in University housing. After the freshman year, on-campus housing is optional. Students who choose to live off-campus do so in nearby private apartments. The campus itself is 360 acres, with buildings arranged in an easy-to-find manner. No classroom building is more than a 5-minute walk from any other.

Honorary Societies Phi Eta Sigma, Mortar Board, and many others

Athletics Eastern Illinois is NCAA Division I in all sports except football, which is Division I-AA. Men's sports include baseball, basketball, cross-country, football, golf, soccer, swimming, tennis, track and field, and wrestling. Women's sports include basketball, golf, soccer, softball, swimming, tennis, track/cross-country, volleyball, and rugby.

Study Abroad The Honors Programs offer Eastern honors students and students from NCHC member schools the opportunity to participate in the summer Archaeology Course and Field School in Europe. Based at the Universite Catholique de Louvain in Louvain-la-Neuve, Belgium, the program combines archaeology, history, and culture. Students work for part of each day on the excavation of a medieval castle in the heart of the French-speaking region of Belgium. Eastern honors faculty members oversee the students' experiences, and, in tandem with local professors, teach the classes and guide the educational direction of the term.

Students can participate in exchanges and study-abroad programs in many countries around the world through Eastern's Office of International Programs.

Tuition: $2992 for state residents, $8977 for nonresidents, per year (2001–02)

Room and Board: $4654

Mandatory Fees: $1297

Contact: Director: Dr. Herbert Lasky, Booth House, Charleston, Illinois 61920; Telephone: 217-581-2017; Fax: 217-581-7222; E-mail: cfhxl@eiu.edu; Web site: http://www.eiu.edu/~honprog

---

EASTERN KENTUCKY UNIVERSITY

4 Pu G M Sc Tr

▼ Honors Program

The Eastern Kentucky University (EKU) Honors Program has been designed especially for those intellectually promising students who seek a strong grounding in the liberal arts along with their more specialized major. Such students may be most at home in an intellectually intense, small-college atmosphere within the context of the larger University. Small class sizes of no more than 20 students per class allow for individualized attention and for one-on-one dialogue with the instructors. A distinctive feature of the Honors Program is that many courses are team-taught by professors from different disciplines. Such an approach contributes to the integration of knowledge, and the program as a whole provides students with a necessary model of civilized intellectual interaction and allows students to see how ideas become enriched when approached from two different perspectives.

Students share with one another and with the faculty the pleasure and stimulation of outside speakers, films, suppers, trips to historical sites and cultural events, retreats, and state, regional, and national conferences. They have the opportunity of living in an honors hall and making use of an honors common room for study, informal meetings, classes, and programs they plan themselves. A computer network for working on class assignments is also available for students in the program.

The 28-credit-hour program offers courses that emphasize the development of skills in effective communication, critical thinking, and the integration of knowledge from various disciplines. All course work in the EKU Honors Program meets University general education requirements. Therefore, regardless of major, any qualified student can participate in the program.

Fourth-year honors scholars complete a senior-level thesis and seminar. This thesis project can take whatever form suits the subject (e.g., a research paper, a creative composition or art

Interpreting the symbols: **2**=two-year college, **4**=four-year college; **Pu**=public or state college, **Pr**=private college; **G**=general honors program; **D**=departmental honors program; **S**=small program (fewer than 100 students), **M**=midsize program (100 to 500 students), **L**=large program (more than 500 students); **Sc**=scholarships available in honors program; **Tr**=transfer students accepted into honors program; **HBC**=historically black college; **AA**=academic advisors; **GA**=graduate advisors; **FA**=fellowship advisors.

work, a performance or recital). Each student works with a faculty mentor who offers guidance and support throughout the development of the thesis project.

Students who successfully complete the EKU Honors Program curriculum are designated Honors Scholars when they graduate, and the phrase appears on their diplomas and on their official transcripts from the University.

There are currently 300 students in the program.

Admission Process: Students with strong academic backgrounds are invited to apply to the Honors Program. National Merit Finalists and Semi-Finalists are automatically accepted. Beyond these, students with high school GPAs of 3.5 or better on a 4.0 scale and with a score of at least 26 on the ACT are given priority. Other students who demonstrate the potential for outstanding academic performance are considered.

Scholarship Availability: Abundant opportunities for scholarships exist under Eastern's academic scholarship program, and students interested in scholarship aid should apply directly to that program. All students in the Honors Program receive at least a Presidential-level scholarship as well as a Books-on-Loan Award for eight semesters.

The Campus Context: EKU is situated in Richmond, an urban college community of about 25,000 people within a rich farming area. Interstate and intrastate highway systems enhance Richmond's accessibility. Interstate 75 passes within a mile of campus, and Interstate 64 is only 30 minutes away. The Blue Grass and Mountain Parkways are also less than an hour's drive from Richmond. Places of historic and scenic interest surround the University. Richmond, 20 miles south of Lexington on I-75, is within easy driving distance of Boonesborough State Park, Kentucky Horse Park, Herrington Lake, Cumberland Falls, the State Capitol at Frankfort, Natural Bridge State Park, and My Old Kentucky Home in Bardstown. Students are enrolled in twenty-one associate degree programs, eighty-two baccalaureate programs, and thirty master's degree programs.

Student Body There are 12,795 undergraduates, of whom 59 percent are women. The student body includes 4 percent African American, 1 percent Asian, and less than 1 percent Hispanic and American Indian/Alaskan students. One hundred eighty international students complete this diverse population. Seventy-five percent of students receive financial aid.

Faculty There are 628 full-time faculty members; 68 percent hold doctorates or other terminal degrees.

Honorary Societies Lambda Sigma, Phi Kappa Phi, Golden Key, and Mortar Board.

Key Facilities The library contains 900,000 volumes. Computer labs are available in most academic buildings, and PCs are available in dorm lobbies, the library, and the student center.

Athletics Eastern is a member of the Ohio Valley Conference and supports eight varsity sports for men (football in Division I-AA, basketball, baseball, tennis, golf, cross-country, and indoor and outdoor track) and eight varsity sports for women (volleyball, basketball, softball, tennis, golf, cross-country, and indoor and outdoor track). A wide range of intramural sports are offered for both men and women.

Study Abroad Students may study in Europe through the Kentucky Institute for International Studies (KIIS), a consortium of Kentucky colleges and universities. KIIS operates a network of summer programs in Munich, Germany; Salzburg and Bregenz, Austria; Nimes and Paris, France; Florence, Italy; Madrid, Spain; and Mexico. Each of these programs offers a variety of academic courses, which students may take for University credit. Students may study in Britain through the Cooperative Center for Study in Britain (CCSB), a consortium of Kentucky colleges and universities. Students may take courses during Christmas vacation in London, a two-week course in May in Ireland, and a five-week course in the summer in England. They may also enroll in a junior-year-abroad program or enroll for a semester in Oxford. Costs vary according to program.

Job Opportunities Students are offered a range of work opportunities on campus, including federal and institutional work-study and graduate assistantships.

Tuition and Fees: $2706 for state residents, $7374 for nonresidents, per year (2002–03)

Room and Board: $3176 minimum

Mandatory Fees: $300

Contact: Director: Dr. Bonnie J. Gray, 168 Case Annex, Richmond, Kentucky 40475; Telephone: 859-622-1403; Fax: 859-622-5089; E-mail: bonnie.gray@eku.edu; Web site: http://www.honors.eku.edu

EASTERN MICHIGAN UNIVERSITY

4 Pu G D L Sc Tr

▼ University Honors Program

Students with special academic ability and ambition for excellence have the opportunity to match their talents with the high standards of the University Honors Program. They find the small classes, select faculty, supportive atmosphere, and special programming that make for a distinct scholarly community in a large campus setting. Those arriving as freshmen can qualify for general education honors. Students at upper levels, including transfers, may complete departmental honors in a specific major or minor.

Honors students enjoy various advantages, including class sections with enrollment limited to 20 of their academic peers and specially chosen faculty members, priority registration each semester, the possibility of tailoring honors work to their goals through contracts, opportunities for research and conference attendance, excursions and other special programming, and, eventually, the distinction of an honors designation on the official record.

The honors residence hall provides a center for honors activities. It accommodates one third of the program members; furnishes space for meetings, special lectures, receptions, and some classes; and houses the Honors Office.

The program, founded in 1984, enrolls about 900 students.

Participation Requirements: First- and second-year students work on honors in general education, which requires that they complete 18 semester credit hours in honors sections. These sections have limited enrollment; professors selected are among the best in the University and are evaluated each semester. Student recommendations are often used to identify new honors faculty members. Juniors and seniors pursue honors in a major or minor, for which they need to complete 12 semester credit hours, including a 3-credit capstone thesis or project. At all levels, honors students must enroll regularly in honors sections and maintain a GPA of 3.3. They must also complete a total of 30 hours of community service.

Admission Process: To be eligible (with some flexibility) from high school, students need a minimum GPA of 3.7, a minimum ACT score of 25 or SAT score of 1250, and excellent recommendations. To be eligible from a community college, students need a minimum GPA of 3.5 (a minimum of 15 credit hours) and excellent recommendations; from a four-year institution, they need a minimum 3.3 GPA. Students must submit a completed application form, including a 500-word essay, transcripts, and recommendations. Applications are received on a rolling-admission basis, and replies are made promptly.

Scholarship Availability: Fifteen Presidential Scholarships (tuition, fees, room, and board; eight consecutive semesters), fifteen

Regents' Plus Scholarships ($3100 per year, eight consecutive semesters), fifteen Regents' Scholarships ($2600 per year, eight consecutive semesters), and several hundred Recognition of Excellence Scholarships ($500) are offered to prospective freshmen based on a competition held in December. Twenty Honors Undergraduate Fellowships ($1200) are offered each semester to juniors and seniors for research/creative activity in their major or minor.

The Campus Context: The 460-acre campus is located in the highly diverse metropolitan corridor of southeast Michigan. It offers more than 150 undergraduate and graduate programs in five colleges: Arts and Sciences, Business, Education, Health and Human Services, and Technology.

The University also offers the following: the Halle Library, which features high-speed Internet connections; radio stations; an astronomical observatory; TV studios; special education classrooms; the Children's Institute; outdoor recreation; a conservatory for relics from the Titanic; the Marshall Building; automated retrieval; Polymers and Coatings; summer institutes; forensics; Close-Up Theater; science and technology labs; up-to-date computing and communications infrastructure; and high-speed Internet access across campus.

Student Body The co-ed undergraduate enrollment is 18,131; 69 percent are full-time and 60 percent are women. The student body includes 87 percent from Michigan and the balance from forty-three states and sixty-two other countries. Cultural diversity is a highlight: 15 percent of the student body is either African American, Hispanic, Asian, or Native American. There are 150 groups on campus; about thirty are sororities and fraternities, which draw 4 percent of the student population.

Faculty Of the more than 1,200 faculty members, 700 are full-time and 38 percent are women. Of the full-time faculty members, 80 percent have a doctoral or other terminal degree in their discipline. The student-faculty ratio is 20:1.

Key Facilities Fully equipped labs support science and technology programs. An up-to-date computing and communications infrastructure features high-speed Internet access across campus, dedicated computerized classrooms, and open computer commons. A vibrant arts and cultural life is provided in various locations, including a convocation center, two theaters, a recital hall, a concert hall, art galleries, and a public radio station.

Athletics There are twenty-one intercollegiate (Division I) teams and fifteen club and fifty intramural sports, equally divided among men and women. Sports facilities include a football and track stadium, a baseball stadium, a convocation center for basketball and special events, a golf course, two swimming pools, and a five-floor recreation/intramural building with facilities for indoor and outdoor sports, training, fitness, and fun.

Study Abroad The Academic Programs Abroad Office coordinates twenty programs on five continents. Programs offered include foreign languages, cultural history, art, ecology, and education. Some include tours of various countries, while others provide in-country residencies.

Support Services The campus is 93 percent accessible to disabled students. Counseling, information, and tutoring services are available.

Job Opportunities A broad variety of employment opportunities are available both on and off campus. The Career Services Center helps find placements, including co-op internships, on and off campus.

Tuition: $5935 per year for state residents, $13,792 per year for nonresidents (2002–03, estimated)

Room and Board: $5200

Contact: Director: Dr. William A. Miller, Margaret E. Wise Honors Residence, Eastern Michigan University, Ypsilanti, Michigan 48197; Telephone: 734-487-0341; Fax: 734-487-0793; E-mail: emuhonors@emich.edu; Web site: http://www.emich.edu/public/uhp/

EASTERN OREGON UNIVERSITY

4 Pu S Tr AA

▼ Honors Program

The pursuit of an Eastern Oregon University (EOU) honors baccalaureate degree can enrich the educational opportunities available to EOU students and promote an environment for intellectual and personal achievement. EOU's Honors Program is designed to nurture talent by providing opportunities to go further in an academic discipline and broaden or deepen an education beyond the usual required work. EOU's program was founded in 2001 and averages 50 students.

Participation Requirements: The student submits all the honors contracts, with endorsing faculty members' signatures, before being identified as an honors student. In addition to all regular degree requirements, required components for completion of the honors baccalaureate degree include the following: three academic projects, campus leadership, community service learning, and one preprofessional conference presentation/participation, such as the spring symposium. A total of five contracts that outline the degree requirements are to be submitted. Honors seminars are also offered.

An academic honors project should cover the material in greater depth than in regular class assignments. The student is responsible for the greater share of learning and discovery and should have unusual opportunities to explore the subject matter in exciting ways.

The honors student completes three contracts for three academic projects that are to be submitted in the format that is most appropriate to the discipline and subject matter–for example, art, a research paper, an experiment, a performance, or multiproject.

The three academic project contracts can comprise an expanded project based on an upper-division course's content. For example, a student may write a 25-page paper for a course that requires a 15-page paper of all students. Extra course credits will not be awarded for this extra honors effort. The second project choice involves students who choose to work on a unique project in their field of specialization. Field research is strongly encouraged. If the discipline is not a research-oriented area, then a unique project that is not normally carried out in EOU's regular offerings is recommended. The project should be conceptualized by the student in consultation with faculty members. The honors student may receive upper-division credits for their work, which is to be determined by endorsing faculty members. The final project choice is an interdisciplinary project that incorporates the student's major field and one other discipline. The honors student may receive upper-division credits for their work, which is to be determined by endorsing faculty members.

The campus leadership component requires substantial involvement in any aspect of campus service, which demonstrates individual initiative on the part of the student. For example, a regular tutoring assignment through the Learning Center does not fulfill this requirement, even if it is performed without pay. However, a tutoring assignment combined with the production of a supplement to course materials, such as a collection of original study aids to be kept on hand for future use, or a tutoring assignment combined with the offering of extra sessions

Interpreting the symbols: 2=two-year college, 4=four-year college; **Pu**=public or state college, **Pr**=private college; **G**=general honors program; **D**=departmental honors program; **S**=small program (fewer than 100 students), **M**=midsize program (100 to 500 students), **L**=large program (more than 500 students); **Sc**=scholarships available in honors program; **Tr**=transfer students accepted into honors program; **HBC**=historically black college; **AA**=academic advisors; **GA**=graduate advisors; **FA**=fellowship advisors.

that demonstrate a commitment and effort beyond what is normally expected of tutors, does fulfill this requirement.

The community service learning project requires that the student seek out, independently or with the help of the Cornerstones Office, a service opportunity. This opportunity is preferably not directly related to the student's major and takes place in the community beyond the EOU campus. This is not an internship; it is engagement in service to others. Also, the student must complete at least 40 hours of unpaid service of any nature appropriate to the agency and complete two brief papers or projects in other formats to be approved in advance with the Cornerstones Office, including a "preflection," and a final "reflection" linking the service experience with the academic experience.

Admission Process: An honors scholar may be any individual possessing motivation to nominate himself or herself. All students are encouraged to consider the prospect of earning an honors baccalaureate degree. To apply to the program, students must have completed a minimum of 44 credits with a minimum 3.25 GPA. Students submit five honors contracts with endorsing faculty members' signatures that outline the academic, leadership, and service learning components of their program. EOU's Honors Program does accept transfer students. Early admission is offered to outstanding incoming freshmen.

Scholarship Availability: EOU does not offer scholarships for honors scholars.

The Campus Context: Eastern Oregon University is a four-year public university. It was rated as one of America's top colleges in the West by the *U.S. News & World Report* and was praised in another college guide entitled *Cool Colleges: For the Hyper-Intelligent, Self-Directed, Late Blooming, and Just Plain Different*, by author Donald Asher. EOU is located in La Grande, Oregon, which is 4 hours east of Portland and 3 hours west of Boise, Idaho. The University offers baccalaureate degrees in twenty-five programs, including art, biology, agriculture, business, chemistry, computer science, electrical engineering, nursing, English, history, liberal studies, music, mathematics, physics, psychology, theater, fire service administration, multidisciplinary studies and philosophy, politics, and economics. A master's degree is offered in teaching, and associate degrees are offered in general studies and office administration.

Student Body Enrollment is 1,917 students: 835 men, 1,082 women. Ethnic minorities make up 11 percent of the enrollment and 66 percent of the students are from Oregon. Eighty-eight international students represent sixteen countries. Financial aid was given to 1,518 students (78 percent). There are more than fifty student clubs and organizations.

Faculty The total number of facuty members is 111, and 87 work full-time. The percentage of faculty members who hold doctorates or terminal degrees is 94. The student-faculty ratio is 14:1.

Key Facilities The library houses 135,000 books and 1,300 periodical titles, with extensive holdings in maps, U.S. government publications, Oregon documents, audiovisuals, and microforms. Library computer facilities include Internet access. Computer labs are available, featuring both IBMs and Macs.

Athletics EOU participates in NAIA Division II and NCAA Division II in baseball, basketball, cross-country, football, rodeo, soccer, softball, track and field, and volleyball. Club sports include golf, men's volleyball, rugby, skiing, and tennis. Intramural sports feature basketball, flag football, softball, and volleyball.

Support Services The University is handicap accessible with elevators and ramps located throughout campus.

Job Opportunities A variety of work opportunities are available both on and off campus. Listings are provided in the Career Services Center.

Tuition: $3621 per year, in-state or out-of-state (2001–02)

Room and Board: $4750 minimum; $3450 room only

Mandatory Fees: $404 (per term)

Contact: Director: Dr. Elizabeth Boretz, Chair, EOU Honors Committee, One University Boulevard, Ackerman 204C, La Grande, Oregon, 97850; Telephone: 541-962-3599; E-mail: eboretz@eou.edu; Web site: http//www.eou.edu/honors/

EASTERN UNIVERSITY

4 Pr G S Sc Tr

▼ Templeton Honors College

The Templeton Honors College (THC) at Eastern University is a college within the University, offering a classically oriented curriculum to the most academically gifted students. The THC is built around a core studies program that involves seminar and tutorial classes that give full play to intensive reading, writing, and debate. Each cohort of the Templeton Honors College is limited to no more than 24 students. The curriculum functions as an alternative to Eastern University's existing core curriculum and general education requirements. THC scholars take at least one THC seminar or tutorial each semester while concurrently majoring in any of the regular majors and programs of Eastern University.

The principal concentrations of the THC curriculum focus, in the first year, upon the reading of the great books and upon integrative reading in the nature of the liberal arts and the open society. Subsequent seminars are devoted in the second, third, and fourth years to geopolitics, the philosophy of leadership, American intellectual history, evangelical theology, and moral philosophy. The members of the THC's Advisory Council function, in the third and fourth years, as mentors in career and graduate educational development. Articulation agreements in the fourth year permit cross-registration with regional graduate schools. It is the aim of the program to train for leadership in public policy, business, and the natural sciences and to stress interrelationships between these pursuits. The THC participates in Alpha Chi and is a member of the National Collegiate Honors Council.

The Templeton Honors College has been made possible by the generosity of Drs. John M. and Josephine Templeton, who remain integrally involved in the development of the program.

Participation Requirements: THC scholars register for two Honors College seminars/tutorials in each semester of their first year and one each in every subsequent semester. Entering students participate in the Adirondacks natural sciences trip the week before commencing classes; at the end of the first year, students in the entering cohort produce and participate in an Oxford-style debate, open to the entire campus community. THC scholars must maintain a minimum 3.2 GPA throughout their first year and at least a 3.4 GPA in subsequent years to remain in good standing in the THC. In the junior year, THC scholars satisfy their THC requirements by participating for one semester in the THC study outside program, offering off-campus study either abroad in Salzburg, Oxford, or Hong Kong or domestically in Washington, Gettysburg, New York, or Boston. In the senior year, a senior honors thesis is submitted in the context of the senior capstone course in moral philosophy.

Admission Process: Admission to the Templeton Honors College is based on acceptance into the overall undergraduate program at Eastern University, a combined SAT I score of 1350 or higher or an English ACT score of 30 or higher, graduation in the top 9 percent of one's high school class, or extraordinary leadership abilities. Students who transfer to Eastern with a GPA of not less than 3.4 and with not more than 36 hours of undergraduate credit are eligible for admission to the THC with the permission of the Dean. The admissions process involves two stages: a written application and a formal interview with the Dean.

Scholarship Availability: All THC scholars are awarded an Honors Grant of $3000. Separate endowed scholarships provide tuition for students majoring in specific disciplinary areas (e.g., the A. Gilbert Heebner Scholarship for a THC scholar majoring in the University's business programs).

The Campus Context: Eastern University is located in St. Davids, Pennsylvania, along Philadelphia's Main Line, 12 miles from the center of the city of Philadelphia. Its location offers intellectual and professional opportunities among the cultural and corporate institutions of the nation's first capital and easy access to the entire Northeast Corridor. The University offers forty-seven undergraduate majors plus graduate programs in business, education, and counseling.

Student Body The undergraduate student body numbers approximately 1,750, and there are more than 750 students in the graduate programs. The ethnic distribution is 72 percent white, 14 percent black, 3 percent Hispanic, 2 percent nonresident aliens, and 1 percent Asian/Pacific Islander, for an overall minority population of 23.3 percent.

Faculty The total number of faculty members is 75, of whom 64 are full-time. Ninety percent of the full-time faculty members have terminal degrees. The student-faculty ratio is 13:1.

Key Facilities The Warner Library contains 130,000 volumes, 1,200 periodicals, and 700,000 microforms.

Athletics The University offers a wide variety of sports and intramural programs and competes in NCAA Division III.

Tuition: $13,200 (1999–2000)

Room and Board: $5654

Contact: Dean: Dr. Allen C. Guelzo, 106 Heritage House, 1300 Eagle Road, St. Davids, Pennsylvania 19087; Telephone: 610-341-5880; Fax: 610-341-1790; E-mail: aguelzo@eastern.edu; Mrs. Gerri Wissinger, Assistant to the Dean; Telephone: 610-225-5022; Fax: 610-341-1790; E-mail: gwissin2@eastern.edu

---

EDINBORO UNIVERSITY OF PENNSYLVANIA

4 Pu C M Sc Tr

▼ Honors Program

The two-part academic program introduces the core curriculum through general education honors, and concludes with upper-division honors and the departmental senior honors project. The comprehensive program offers motivated students ample opportunities to develop independence and initiative, as well as enabling them to work closely with outstanding University professors. In general education honors, students pursue their chosen academic course of study while completing a series of core honors courses. Of the total required number of credit hours in general education, 25 percent of the total are taken as honors courses. Honors students who complete general education honors receive an award for excellence in general education. Upper-division honors link general education to the more specialized areas of study and culminates with a departmental senior honors project. Senior projects are designed in consultation with academic departments as the most appropriate culminating experience in the individual majors. As a final step in upper-division honors, the senior project is presented in an appropriate public forum, such as journal publication, academic conference, online journal, art gallery, or recital hall. With the successful completion of upper-division honors, including the senior project, the honors student receives the Upper-Division Honors Award.

Honors students attain honors credit hours by taking courses designated as honors courses. Students may also contract courses. A contract is an agreement between an honors student in good standing, a faculty member, and the honors director. In a contracted course, the honors student agrees to do additional course work for honors credit. New in 2001–02 is the curricular link contract. In this type of contract, the honors student initiates a project that links two courses from different departments that are not in themselves interdisciplinary. One of the two courses serves as the contract course of record with that professor issuing the course evaluation. The professor of the other course serves as a reader of the final project. The curricular link contract is particularly appropriate to the student nearing the end of general education honors or at the beginning of upper-division honors. Honors Program students may also attain honors credits by taking courses that are designated as graduate courses.

Honors students enroll in independent study to work on projects that are not in topic areas typically offered in the undergraduate curriculum. For example, the senior honors project is a 6-semester hour project, consisting of two 3-hour independent studies that encourages honors students to develop expertise on a specific topic and to gain research and practical experience. Under the guidance of a faculty mentor, the student is responsible for researching, experimenting, documenting, and presenting in public various components of the chosen project.

Honors students are encouraged to study abroad and are given opportunities that are not available to other university students. There are three major awards in the Honors Program: the General Education Honors Award, the Upper-Division Honors Award, and the Honors Program Diploma.

Students qualify for admission to general education honors based on academic achievement, aptitude test scores, class rank, and teacher recommendations. Historically, entering freshmen honors students have averaged 1225 on the Scholastic Aptitude Test (SAT) or 27 on the American College Test (ACT) and have ranked in the top 10 perecnt of their graduating classes. Students interested in the challenges and rewards of an Honors Program and near or above the historical averages may apply for admission.

A student already attending Edinboro University must be a full-time student with a GPA of 3.5 or higher. As part of the application process, the student must register for an honors course. During the semester of that course, the application semester, the student must provide letters of support from two faculty members, secure the approval of the academic adviser, and complete a plan-of-study in consultation with the honors director and academic advisor. Students qualify for admission to upper-division honors based on academic achievement at Edinboro University of Pennsylvania. Application may be made by any full-time Edinboro University student who has completed 63 credit hours with an overall GPA of 3.4 or higher.

Participation Requirements: An honors student must complete a minimum of 6 honors credits each academic year with a grade of A or B to remain in good standing. To receive the General Education Honors Award, a student must complete 15 honors credit hours. Upper-division honors requires the completion of 9 honors credit hours, including 6 credit hours for the senior honors project. To receive an Honors Program diploma, an honors student must complete both portions of the Honors

Interpreting the symbols: **2**=two-year college, **4**=four-year college; **Pu**=public or state college, **Pr**=private college; **G**=general honors program; **D**=departmental honors program; **S**=small program (fewer than 100 students), **M**=midsize program (100 to 500 students), **L**=large program (more than 500 students); **Sc**=scholarships available in honors program; **Tr**=transfer students accepted into honors program; **HBC**=historically black college; **AA**=academic advisors; **GA**=graduate advisors; **FA**=fellowship advisors.

Program, a total of 24 credit honors. To remain eligible for scholarships, a student must maintain a GPA of 3.5.

Scholarship Availability: Edinboro University has developed a sizable scholarship program to assist students in the University Honors Program. Students entering the Honors Program as freshmen may make application for scholarships at the time of application to general education honors. In 2001–02, more than thirty partial scholarships were awarded to entering freshman and fifty scholarships were awarded to continuing honors students. To be eligible for a scholarship after the freshman year, a student must be in good standing with a GPA of 3.5.

The Campus Context: Edinboro University of Pennsylvania is one of the fourteen universities in Pennsylvania's state system of higher education. The campus is located in northwestern Pennsylvania in a rural setting with lakes, open fields, and woods. There are forty-three buildings and eight are residence halls. The University offers more than 100 degree programs, including fifty-seven minors programs. The degrees offered include: associate of arts, associate of engineering technology, associate of science, bachelor of arts, bachelor of fine arts, bachelor of science, bachelor of science in education, bachelor of science in nursing, bachelor of science in art education, master of arts, master of fine arts, master of education, master of science, and a master of science in nursing.

Student Body The University has an enrollment of 7,200 undergraduate and graduate students. There are international students representing forty-one countries. Ten living-learning communities in the residence halls house some of the University's best students, including honors, international, and social work students.

Faculty There are 408 full- and part-time faculty members, representing a student-faculty ratio of 18:1.

Key Facilities The library is a modern seven-story library with more than 440,000 bound volumes. The University has networked the complete campus, including residence halls. Students have direct-access Internet and may subscribe to cable TV through the NextiraOne Student Technology Center. On campus today, there are thirty-six computer labs; some for training and others are open labs, with 689 computer systems. More than 94 percent of those computers are connected to the Internet and the campus network. Honors students also have a computer lab and private study-library.

Honorary Society Students at Edinboro University are active participates in Alpha Chi National Honor Society.

Athletics In athletics, Edinboro participates in the Pennsylvania Conference. The Fighting Scots compete in the National Collegiate Athletic Association, Divisions I and II.

Study Abroad Honors students are encouraged to study abroad, and are given opportunities that are not available to other university students. Each year, two full scholarships are available for the state system of higher education summer Honors Program. In addition, other programs in Scotland and Italy are available for honors credits.

Support Services The Office of Disabled Student Services administers a program dedicated to enhancing the University's commitment to equal opportunity for the severely physically disabled. The campus supports the largest residency program of its kind in the commonwealth of Pennsylvania, and the disabled population is one of the largest in the entire United States. Edinboro's disabled students and many visitors benefit from a campus that is almost completely accessible to the handicapped. Edinboro University has a national reputation for its services for students with disabilities. Services are provided by the Office for Students with Disabilities (OSD).

Job Opportunities A comprehensive work-study program is in place, and other employment opportunities are available on campus, including assistantships for graduate students.

Off-campus jobs are assigned in public or private nonprofit organizations. To work under this program, students must be enrolled or be accepted for enrollment as full-time students at Edinboro University. Eligibility depends upon their need for employment to defray college expenses, with preference given to applicants from low-income families. The Pennsylvania State Grant and Federal Aid Application and the Edinboro University Financial Aid Application are required.

Tuition: $4016 tuition for state residents, $6024 per year for nonresidents (2001–02)

Room and Board: $4384

Mandatory Fees: $700

Contact: Director: Dr. Tim Cordell, University Honors Program, 715 Baron-Forness Library, Edinboro University of Pennsylvania, Edinboro, Pennsylvania 16444; Telephone: 814-732-2981; Fax: 814-732-2982; E-mail: cordell@edinboro.edu; Web site: honors.edinboro.edu

El Camino College

2 Pu G M

▼ Honors Transfer Program

The El Camino College (ECC) Honors Transfer Program (HTP) offers highly motivated students the opportunity to participate in an academic community where they interact with outstanding faculty members and other students who have the goals to obtain a quality education, be better prepared to transfer to a four-year university, and pursue a bachelor's degree. The HTP is a college-wide program appropriate for all eligible students taking transferable courses.

Twelve to fourteen sections of honors courses are offered each semester. These are primarily general education courses in the fields of art, astronomy, economics, English, history, music, philosophy, and political science. The enrollment in honors classes is limited to about 75 percent of the enrollment for other classes. On rare occasions, honors contract courses are allowed to accommodate special academic needs. The HTP, in conjunction with the Study Abroad Program, allows interested students to do honors work while studying abroad. The College typically runs either two or three study-abroad programs each year.

A cornerstone of the program is the high level of support it receives from several major universities; they offer priority admission guarantees to students who complete the requirements of the HTP. These honors transfer agreements have been established between the HTP and the California State University at Dominguez Hills; Chapman University; Occidental College; Pepperdine University; Pomona College; the University of California at Irvine, Los Angeles, Riverside, and Santa Cruz; and the University of Southern California.

The HTP has an excellent track record for transferring students to the university of their choice. Over the past several years, almost 100 percent of students who completed the program and applied to the universities listed above were accepted.

In addition to the priority admission guarantees offered by the universities listed above, students who complete the HTP have graduation with honors designated on their associate degrees and completion of honors designated on their transcripts. These students have increased chances of receiving scholarships. Some universities offer transfer scholarships designated only for students who have completed community college honors programs, while others offer priority consideration for their regular transfer scholarships.

Benefits offered to HTP members prior to their completion of the program include honors membership designated on transcripts each semester and priority registration in all El Camino College classes. Students have opportunities to serve on HTP student committees such as the Newsletter Committee and the Activities Committee. Special privileges are offered by the universities with which ECC has honors transfer agreements. Examples include an organized Honors Transfer Day visit to campuses, use of libraries, priority scholarship consideration, and complimentary opportunities to attend academic, cultural, and athletic events.

The HTP is twelve years old and has a membership of approximately 250 students. Each academic year begins with a welcome reception for new members and their families.

Participation Requirements: Each semester students are required to complete at least one honors course, maintain a minimum 3.0 cumulative GPA, and attend at least four honors enrichment seminars. New students must complete English 1A their first semester in the program.

To complete the HTP, students must complete at least six honors courses, maintain a minimum 3.0 cumulative GPA, be a member of the HTP for a minimum of three semesters, and complete the requirements necessary to transfer as a junior.

A reception at the end of each academic year is held to honor students completing the program and transferring to a university. At this reception, students receive a certificate of completion. Special certificates and plaques are given to selected students to recognize outstanding academic achievement in honors and outstanding contributions to the honors program.

Admission Process: The requirements for admission to the HTP are a minimum 3.0 cumulative GPA from high school or from at least nine academic units in college and eligibility for English 1A Freshman Composition.

The Campus Context: El Camino College is a public two-year community college in the state of California. Founded in 1947, ECC is located in a suburban setting about 15 miles southwest of Los Angeles. In its mission to offer high-quality, comprehensive educational opportunities to its diverse community, the College offers a wide variety of vocational and academic programs leading to an Associate of Science or an Associate of Arts degree. A certificate of completion or a certificate of competence may be obtained in many vocational areas. El Camino offers the A.S. transfer (twenty-eight majors), A.S. vocational (thirty-five majors), and A.A. transfer and/or vocational (thirty-four majors).

El Camino was fully accredited in 1996. The accreditation evaluation team wrote that the College was commended for its demonstrated and continuing commitment to being a College that is "of" and "for" its community, not just "in" the community. The College presents students and citizens with a constellation of cultural, educational, and activity experiences, which are increasingly responsive to a diverse community. Among special facilities, the campus has an excellent planetarium, an Anthropology Museum giving students hands-on curating experience, and a Child Development Center.

Student Body Undergraduate enrollment is 22,700, of whom 7,300 (26 percent) are full-time-equivalent students. Men comprise 45 percent of the student body. Students have an average age of 27, and all students are commuters. The ethnic distribution at ECC is 28 percent Caucasian, 21 percent African American, 25 percent Hispanic, 15 percent Asian, and 11 percent other. International students comprise 2 percent of the student population. Ten percent of students receive financial aid. While there are no fraternities or sororities on campus, there are more than fifty active academic, service, social, cultural, and religious clubs.

Faculty Of the 805 faculty members, 310 are full-time, and 495 are part-time. Twenty percent of the faculty members hold terminal degrees. The student-faculty ratio is 28:1 or 15:1 if based on full-time-equivalent faculty and students.

Key Facilities The library houses 112,000 volumes. Computer facilities include about thirty labs of varying size that contain a total of about 850 computers.

Honorary Societies Alpha Gamma Sigma

Athletics El Camino College offers an extremely wide variety of athletic programs, including many adaptive physical education programs and a fully equipped exercise laboratory and wellness center for student, faculty, and staff training and testing. Intercollegiate athletics for men include baseball, basketball, cross-country, football, golf, soccer, swimming, tennis, track and field, volleyball, and water polo. Intercollegiate athletics for women include basketball, cross-country, soccer, softball, swimming, tennis, track and field, volleyball, and water polo.

Support Services The El Camino College campus is totally accessible to disabled students. The Special Resources Center provides comprehensive individual need-based assistance (services, equipment, and/or instruction) for students with any physical or learning disability. The High Tech Center provides alternative input/output devices and instruction enabling students to access computers regardless of their disability.

Job Opportunities Work opportunities on campus range from $5.25 to $20 per hour. The Job Placement Center assists students in finding both on- and off-campus positions.

Tuition: None for state residents, $3540 for nonresidents, per year (1997–98)

Mandatory Fees: $410

Contact: Director: Dr. Jean M. Shankweiler, 16007 Crenshaw Blvd., Torrance, California 90506; Telephone: 310-660-3815; Fax: 310-660-3818; E-mail: jshankwe@elcamino.cc.ca.us; Web site: http://www.elcamino.cc.ca.us

Elgin Community College

2 Pu G S Tr

▼ Honors Program

Elgin Community College's (ECC) Honors Program provides academically talented students a coherent set of challenging, enriched course sections that meet general education core requirements for baccalaureate degrees in the areas of communications, mathematics, physical sciences and life sciences, humanities and fine arts, social science, and behavioral sciences. Emphasis is on small class size and innovative learning experiences, including interdisciplinary approaches to common topics, service learning, and specific real-world applications of classroom concepts.

The emphasis for second-semester students is on building a cohort of adventurous students and teachers who get to know each other and learn with one another better than is possible with regular community college scheduling. Options include dual enrollment in subjects linked across disciplines that meet on and off campus, fine arts appreciation courses focused on live performance and gallery-based experiences, and major-related, faculty-mentored, independent study. The 15-year-old program currently has 75 participating students.

Participation Requirements: All students can sample honors sections of core courses and may later choose to commit to the Honors Program. Program enrollees must complete a minimum of 15 hours of honors course work distributed across at least three of the five categories in the general education core for transfer degrees with an A or B.

Interpreting the symbols: **2**=two-year college, **4**=four-year college; **Pu**=public or state college, **Pr**=private college; **G**=general honors program; **D**=departmental honors program; **S**=small program (fewer than 100 students), **M**=midsize program (100 to 500 students), **L**=large program (more than 500 students); **Sc**=scholarships available in honors program; **Tr**=transfer students accepted into honors program; **HBC**=historically black college; **AA**=academic advisors; **GA**=graduate advisors; **FA**=fellowship advisors.

In addition to course work, Honors students must meet participation and service requirements in Phi Theta Kappa or one of five major-related honors societies. A minimum 3.5 GPA at graduation leads to the Honors Scholar designation on the transcript and diploma for the Associate in Arts, Associate in Science, or Associate in Fine Arts degrees.

The Honors Program accepts honors course work from other NCHC member schools. The College offers dual admission and enrollment in four-year institutions, which has led to awarding Honors Scholar status on the transcripts of students who complete all program requirements and successfully transfer to an upper-division program without graduating.

Admission Process: New students are identified and counseled at orientation as potential Honors Program students, while continuing students are identified by College faculty members and screening of student records. To participate in the Honors Program, a student must have met at least two of the following criteria: graduation in the top 10 percent of the high school class, a cumulative high school GPA of at least 3.5 on a 4.0 scale, submission of a composite ACT score of 25 or higher or an SAT I combined score of at least 1000, completion of at least 12 credit hours of articulated college-level course work with a cumulative GPA of 3.25 or higher on a 4.0 scale, submission of written recommendations from 3 high school or college faculty members in at least two disciplines, and approval of the Honors Coordinator.

Scholarship Availability: Trustee Scholarships are available in the categories of academic excellence and leadership in one of ten specific areas. Academic scholarships are noncompetitive awards to students graduating in the upper 10 percent of their high school class who present evidence of rank the semester after high school graduation. Leader scholarships are awards available to current students based on excellence in a particular major or activity. All students who earn an A or B in an honors course and maintain a 3.25 or higher GPA receive credit in the number of those credit hours toward in-district tuition in future semesters.

The Campus Context: Elgin Community College is celebrating its fiftieth anniversary of providing excellence in education and enriched quality of life for residents in the nine diverse constituent communities making up Illinois Community College District 509. The 145-acre main campus is located in the rolling, wooded Fox River Valley southwest of Elgin, 35 miles northwest of Chicago. The downtown Elgin campus, several off-campus sites, and distance learning further extend access to district residents. The eleven main campus buildings are set beside a lake surrounded by restored prairie and total 614,500 square feet of excellent classroom, student resource, and community service space. The Visual and Performing Arts Center, with two state-of-the-art theaters and ample rehearsal and studio and gallery space as well as classrooms, and the Business Conference Center are unusually rich resources for the academic programs housed in them and for outreach to the public.

Student Body The student body is made up of 55 percent women. The ethnic distribution is 59 percent white, 33 percent Hispanic, 4 percent Pan-Asian, 4 percent African American, and less than 1 percent international. The College provides no housing. There are thirty clubs, professional and student performing groups, a writer's center, a forensics team, and a literary magazine. Primary activities for honors students are Phi Theta Kappa and five major-related honors clubs.

Faculty There are 499 faculty members, of whom 118 are full-time. Twenty percent of the full-time faculty members hold doctorates, and more than 50 percent hold terminal degrees within their area of study.

Key Facilities The Learning Resources Center has more than 59,000 print titles, 450 subscriptions, 56,000 microforms, and 4,400 audiovisual holdings. There are more than fifteen instructional computer labs.

Honorary Societies Phi Theta Kappa

Athletics The ECC Spartans participate in the NJCAA Skyway Conference. Men's sports are baseball, basketball, soccer, tennis, and track. Women's sports are basketball, softball, tennis, track, and volleyball. Golf is a coeducational intercollegiate athletics team.

Study Abroad Study-abroad opportunities are available.

Support Services Services are consistent with ADA and Section 504 of the Rehabilitation Act of 1973. The campus is accessible via ramps, braille signage, motorized doors, lifts, and elevators. Academic accommodations include, but are not limited to, tutoring, note-taking, books on tape, advocacy, and testing modifications.

Job Opportunities Work-study positions are available. The Career Center posts positions in the area.

Tuition: $52 per credit hour for District 509 residents, $230.26 per credit hour for out-of-district students, $278.70 per credit hour for out-of-state students (2001–02)

Mandatory Fees: $.50 per credit hour

Contact: Director: Honors Program Coordinator, 1700 Spartan Drive, Elgin, Illinois 60123-7193; Telephone: 847-697-1000 Ext. 7577; Fax: 847-888-5570; E-mail: abiggers@elgin.cc.il.us

ELIZABETHTOWN COLLEGE

4 Pr G S Tr

▼ Hershey Foods Honors Program

The Hershey Foods Honors Program of Elizabethtown College reflects the College's commitment to providing customized learning opportunities for its students. In the case of the Honors Program, the focus of this customization is on students with excellent academic records, superior academic abilities, intellectual promise, and demonstrated initiative. Consistent with the mission of the College, the Honors Program seeks to promote high standards of scholarship and leadership among those students selected for the program. Excellence has been identified as a core value of the College and is a hallmark of the Honors Program. In general, class size is deliberately kept small at Elizabethtown; this is universally so in the Honors Program. Rarely, if ever, do honors classes exceed 15 students.

The opportunity to work closely with faculty mentors from the freshman to the senior year is an explicit goal of everyone associated with the program. In order to foster even greater involvement between faculty-scholars and honors students, cocurricular activities are planned on a regular basis. Events such as field trips to nearby cultural sites (such as Gettysburg, Philadelphia, and Washington, D.C.) are routine. In addition, international travel is both encouraged and valued. Semester-long study-abroad opportunities are expected, but there also are opportunities for students to visit another country in an annual intersession trip (e.g., Austria, Ecuador, and Iceland).

To facilitate such experiences, the Honors Program annually provides each qualified student with a discretionary fund of $500 that can be used in support of these trips or put to such other uses as book and software purchases. In order to help foster a deeper sense of community within the students in the program, an honors office, a reserved lounge, and access to state-of-the-art computer labs are planned as integral parts of the program's facilities.

The Honors Program was established in 1999 and has enrolled more than 90 students into the program over two years.

Participation Requirements: Students entering the program in the freshman year take a two-course sequence of freshman seminars focusing primarily on critical-thinking and foundational skills. The second of these team-taught courses includes perspectives from different disciplines. In the sophomore and junior years, two additional honors sections of courses within the College's core curriculum (or courses from a list of department offerings) are taken. In the junior/senior year a junior-senior colloquium and a capstone thesis requirement must be completed. The first of these is a team-taught course in the model of the freshman seminar. At any time, students may upgrade a regular course to an honors course on the basis of a written contract with a professor and the Honors Director. A total of 24 credits must be acquired in honors courses in order to fulfill the requirements and graduate as a recognized honors scholar. In order to remain in good standing within the program, students must maintain a GPA of at least 3.5 overall.

Admission Process: Admission to the Honors Program is normally at the beginning of the freshman year, although a small number of sophomores may be admitted to the extent that they can be accommodated. Sophomore admission comes upon demonstrated excellence in the first year, the recommendations of at least 2 professors, and the concurrence of the honors committee. For freshmen, the minimum standard for admission is a combined score of at least 1200 on the SAT (with neither the verbal nor the math score below 550) or other standardized test, rank in the top 10 percent of one's high school graduating class, and review by the honors committee acting on the recommendation of the admissions office. Application to the Honors Program must be received by January 15.

Scholarship Availability: Scholarships are routinely offered to Honors Program students. These scholarships currently range between $6000 and $11,000 annually. Normal progress within the program permits the student to retain this grant every year for four years.

The Campus Context: Elizabethtown College, located in south-central Pennsylvania near world-famous Hershey, is ranked second in the most recent *U.S. News & World Report* among Comprehensive Colleges–Bachelor's in the North. Elizabethtown College is a liberal arts college with a strong core program of study. This core program exposes students to the arts, sciences, and humanities, and its purpose is to complement the more intensive study of the academic major. The College offers well-established programs in the physical and natural sciences (biology, chemistry, computer science, mathematics, physics/engineering, and psychology), the humanities (English, fine and performing arts, history, modern languages, philosophy, and religious studies), and social sciences (political science, sociology, and anthropology). Students graduate with degrees in these areas, as well as from professional programs, including business, communications, education, music therapy, occupational therapy, and social work. Faculty members promote real-world experience through collaboration and research with their students. The breadth of its curriculum and the emphasis on experiential learning enable Elizabethtown College students to graduate with the resources to be leaders and critical thinkers.

Student Body The College enrolls 1,750 students, 85 percent of whom live on campus. Average SAT scores for the most recent entering honors class was nearly 1300. Students come from more than two thirds of the United States; Washington, D.C.; and the U.S. Virgin Islands, as well as nearly forty different countries. Approximately one quarter of new students enter the College with advanced standing as a result of AP examination results.

Faculty With 110 full-time faculty members and approximately 30 FTE in part-time instructors, the College has an attractive student-faculty ratio of 12:1. Intimacy and accessibility are hallmarks of the Elizabethtown experience. Nearly 95 percent of faculty members have earned the Ph.D. or equivalent degree. They are teacher-scholars, and many are active in professional development efforts and research programs.

Key Facilities One of the most prominent buildings on campus is the Leffler Chapel and Performance Center, a 900-seat venue for cultural events and formal College assemblies. The High Library, a modern and centrally located structure, contains almost 236,000 books and other items, including a substantial periodical collection. Equipped with one of the College's new "smart classrooms," the library is a focal point for students. Elizabethtown is also home to the Young Center for Anabaptist and Pietist Groups, a research facility that promotes the study of such groups as the Amish (quite prominent in south-central Pennsylvania) and the Church of the Brethren (the body that founded the College in 1899).

Honorary Societies Delphi and Alpha Lambda Delta

Athletics Elizabethtown College has the first women's basketball team in the country to have accumulated more than 800 victories and the most winning men's soccer team in the nation (more than 600 wins). Twenty Division III varsity athletic programs are available at the College. Men's programs include baseball, basketball, cross-country, golf, soccer, swimming, tennis, track and field, wrestling, and lacrosse. Women's programs include basketball, cross-country, field hockey, soccer, softball, swimming, tennis, track and field, volleyball, and lacrosse.

Study Abroad For many years, Elizabethtown has actively participated in the Brethren Colleges Abroad (BCA) program. Through this consortium, the College is able to send qualified students to exceptional programs in Dalian, China; Cheltenham, England; Quito, Ecuador; Strasbourg and Nancy, France; Marburg, Germany; Athens, Greece; Sapporo, Japan; Xalapa, Mexico; Barcelona, Spain; and Cochin, India. In addition, Elizabethtown regularly sends students to Herstmonceux Castle in England through a cooperative arrangement with Queen's University (at Kingston, Ontario, Canada). Students can also participate in a summer study-abroad program in Oxford, England. Honors Program students are strongly encouraged to take advantage of the opportunities provided for international travel and study.

Support Services The campus operates a Learning Center and provides tutorial and other forms of academic assistance for students with learning differences. Any honors student who may be in need of such assistance is free to use the services of the Learning Center at no charge.

Job Opportunities The College operates a career service out of the Counseling Center. In addition, because there is an emerging emphasis within the College on experiential education, there is a growing interest in internship and externship programs. The College's motto (Educate for Service) suggests the focus of campus programs. Students graduating in liberal arts and in professional studies programs are assisted in their job search by the Director and by faculty affiliates of the Hershey Foods Honors Program.

Tuition: $20,200 (2001–02)

Room and Board: $5800

Contact: Director: Dr. Conrad L. Kanagy, One Alpha Drive, Elizabethtown, Pennsylvania 17022; Telephone: 717-361-1416; Fax: 717-361-1149; E-mail: honors@etown.edu; Web site: http://www.etown.edu

Emerson College

4 Pr G S Tr AA

▼ Honors Program

The Emerson College Honors Program is a community of undergraduate scholars who pursue interdisciplinary study in the liberal arts and in the fields of communication and the performing arts. The four-year Honors Program is available to 50 entering students a year and a small number of transfers with outstanding academic ability. All students in the program

Interpreting the symbols: **2**=two-year college, **4**=four-year college; **Pu**=public or state college, **Pr**=private college; **G**=general honors program; **D**=departmental honors program; **S**=small program (fewer than 100 students), **M**=midsize program (100 to 500 students), **L**=large program (more than 500 students); **Sc**=scholarships available in honors program; **Tr**=transfer students accepted into honors program; **HBC**=historically black college; **AA**=academic advisors; **GA**=graduate advisors; **FA**=fellowship advisors.

receive a Trustee Scholarship. Honors Program students enjoy early registration privileges. Honors Program faculty members excel in teaching and are active researchers, artists, and professionals across the disciplines.

Three first-year honors courses fulfill general education requirements and are team-taught in small discussion-based classes comprising 17 students and 2 professors. The First-Year Honors Seminars and Writing Symposia introduce Emerson students to the interdisciplinary study of literature of the Americas, with an emphasis on writing and research skills. The seminars address the relationship between language, power, and social action in various multicultural contexts and from various theoretical perspectives. The Sophomore Honors Seminar acquaints students with the methods of scientific reasoning and the philosophy of science and addresses issues of ethics and values in an interdisciplinary manner.

The Junior Seminar consists of an upper-division course in interdisciplinary studies, a directed independent study, or additional work in the theories and methodologies inherent in the student's chosen concentration. It encourages students to work closely with a professor in their field in preparation for the senior thesis/project. The Honors Program Director and each student's faculty adviser work with seniors in the completion of their year-long concentrated research or creative project. Seniors meet in colloquia where they critique each other's work. Just before graduation, they present their completed work in a Senior Thesis/Project Showcase before the entire community. Each year one student is granted the Outstanding Honors Thesis/Project Award.

Participation Requirements: Honors work includes the year-long first-year and sophomore seminars, a one-semester junior seminar, and a senior thesis/project. Students fulfill six general education requirements upon the completion of four semesters of interdisciplinary work. To graduate from the Honors Program, students must have at least a 3.3 GPA overall, at least a 3.0 GPA in honors seminars, and must complete the senior thesis/project. Successful completion of the Honors Program requirements is noted at graduation and is recorded on the student's transcript.

Admission Process: High school seniors who maintain outstanding academic records and achievement in school and/or community affairs and seek an additional intellectual challenge at the college level may be invited to participate in the Emerson College Honors Program. To be considered, applicants must complete the regular application procedures listed for first-year students by February 1, including the honors essay. Transfer students may enter the program no later than the first term of their sophomore year.

The Campus Context: Founded in 1880 by noted orator Charles Wesley Emerson and located in the urban setting surrounding the Boston Common, Emerson has grown into a comprehensive college offering its more than 2,600 students undergraduate and graduate curricula in the communication arts and sciences and the performing arts. The original concentration on oratory has evolved into specialization in such fields as visual and media arts (radio and television broadcasting, film, and new media), theater arts, journalism, marketing communication, communication studies, communication disorders, and writing, literature, and publishing.

Student Body Full-time undergraduate enrollment is 2,949. Fifty-six percent of the students are women. Ethnic minorities, including African American, Hispanic, Asian, and Native American students, constitute 9 percent of the student population. There are also 158 international students currently attending Emerson. The College is composed of 45 percent resident students. Seventy percent of students receive financial aid.

Faculty There are 95 full-time faculty members and 181 adjunct faculty members. Seventy-six percent of all faculty members have terminal degrees. The student-faculty ratio is 17:1.

Key Facilities The library houses 190,000 print and nonprint items and is a member of the Fenway Library Consortium. The Media Center includes 9,000 films, videotapes, phonodiscs, compact disks, phonotapes, and other media. Two academic computer centers contain both Macintosh and IBM PC/compatible microcomputer labs with direct access to a DEC VAX 4500 time-sharing system.

Honorary Societies Gold Key

Athletics Men's intercollegiate sports include baseball, basketball, golf, lacrosse, soccer, and tennis. Women's intercollegiate sports include basketball, cross-country running, golf, soccer, softball, tennis, and volleyball. Intramural programs for both men and women include basketball, football, tennis, and volleyball.

Study Abroad Students may study overseas at Kasteel Well, located in eastern Holland near the German border. Study is combined with extensive travel and exploring the cultural and historical offerings in several major cities of Europe.

Tuition: $20,224 per year (2001–02)

Room and Board: $9620

Mandatory Fees: $450

Contact: Director: Dr. John D. Anderson, 120 Boylston Street, Boston, Massachusetts 02116; Telephone: 617-824-7872; Fax: 617-824-7857; E-mail: john.anderson@emerson.edu; Web site: http://www.emerson.edu/undergraduate_admission.cfm

EMPORIA STATE UNIVERSITY

4 Pu G S Tr

▼ University Honors Program

The Honors Program at Emporia State University (ESU) offers the best students a challenging academic program to achieve their full potential. The program supplements the regular curriculum at Emporia State University and prepares students for success by encouraging broad reading, individual thinking, creative problem solving, intellectual growth, and personal commitment. The courses within the Honors Program seek to provide a common intellectual experience for students from a variety of disciplines and degree programs. The program is very flexible and can accommodate students from a wide variety of majors.

In addition to the honors courses offered, Honors Program students get to meet and work individually with faculty members, attend special presentations, meet distinguished visitors to the University, travel to special lectures, and attend national and regional honors conventions. Members of the University Honors Program can also elect to stay on the Honors Floor as first-year students or in one of the scholarship residence programs as more advanced students.

Established in 1983, the University Honors Program currently enrolls about 100 students per semester in honors courses.

Participation Requirements: To remain in the Honors Program, students must maintain a minimum GPA of 3.5. In addition to summa, magna, and cum laude recognition, students who complete six honors courses or activities, one of which must be the Freshmen Honors Seminar, graduate "with honors," and students who complete six honors activities or courses and do a public presentation of a senior thesis graduate "with high honors." With completion of the program, graduates have "with honors" or "with high honors" entered on their diploma and transcript.

Admission Process: Students must apply to the program and submit two essays with the application. Admission to the University Honors Program requires a minimum composite ACT score of 26 and a cumulative high school GPA of at least 3.5. Students who do not meet both of these requirements may be admitted to the program after careful review of high school performance and commitment to excellence. Transfer students must have a cumulative GPA of 3.5 or above to apply.

Scholarship Availability: The University Honors Program does not administer its own scholarships. However, the University offers a number of scholarships to academically talented students. Emporia State University also offers Presidential Academic Achievement Awards to outstanding first-year freshmen. These are based on high school GPA and ACT scores.

The Campus Context: Emporia State University offers undergraduate and graduate degrees through the School of Business, the College of Liberal Arts and Sciences, the Teachers College, and the School of Library and Information Management. The University is located in the heart of the Bluestem Region of the Flint Hills and sits on more than 200 acres. There is easy access to the three major metropolitan areas of Kansas—Wichita, Topeka, and Kansas City.

Student Body ESU currently serves more than 5,800 students, with approximately 4,300 undergraduate students. Sixty-four percent of the students are women. The ethnic distribution of students is 85 percent Caucasian, 3.5 percent African American, 0.9 percent Asian American, 3.8 percent Latino/Hispanic, 0.6 percent Native American, and 6.2 percent other. Currently, there are 212 international students on campus. There are more than 130 student organizations, including six fraternities and three sororities.

Faculty The faculty at Emporia State University consists of 240 full-time teaching members who are highly qualified in their respective fields. Eighty-two percent of these faculty members have terminal degrees, and all have considerable teaching experience. The student-faculty ratio is 18:1.

Key Facilities The University Libraries and Archives, housed in William Allen White Library and Anderson Library, respectively, contain more than 733,000 books, government documents, periodicals, microforms, CD-ROMs, and a number of special collections. The library's collection of media resources includes videos, compact discs, sound recordings, audiocassettes, films, laser discs, and slides. In addition, the library subscribes to a wide variety of online databases, some featuring full-text materials, which are accessible to students and faculty members both on and off campus.

Honorary Societies Phi Kappa Phi, Sigma Xi, Cardinal Key, Phi Eta Sigma, and many departmental societies

Athletics Thirteen varsity sports are included in the Department of Intercollegiate Athletics. The varsity sports offered for men include football, cross-country, basketball, baseball, tennis, and track and field. The sports offered for women are basketball, volleyball, tennis, track and field, cross-country, softball, and soccer. Emporia State University is a member of the MIAA and the NCAA Division II. There are also many intramural sports programs and clubs.

Study Abroad The Office of International Education offers many opportunities for studying abroad. There are chances for international exchange year-round with a variety of countries. In addition, several academic departments incorporate travel abroad into departmental offerings. A study-abroad semester can be used to fulfill some of the requirements for the University Honors Program.

Support Services ESU's Office of Disability Services provides and coordinates services to students in order to accommodate their disabilities and promote equal educational opportunities. All buildings have elevators, accessible entrances, and electric door openers.

Job Opportunities There are many opportunities for employment in on- and off-campus jobs. Career Services provides information to students while in school and after graduation. Ninety-nine percent of ESU's May 2000 bachelor's degree graduates were either employed or enrolled in graduate or professional school within six months of graduating from ESU.

Tuition: $2284 for residents, $7138 for nonresidents, per year (2001–02)

Room and Board: $3914 per year

Contact: Director: Dr. Dwight Moore, University Honors Program, Box 4073, Emporia State University, 1200 Commercial Street, Emporia, Kansas 66801-5087; Telephone: 620-341-5899; Fax: 620-341-5607; E-mail: honors@emporia.edu; Web site: http://www.emporia.edu/honors or http://www.emporia.edu

Erie Community College

2 Pu G M

▼ Honors Program

Erie Community College (ECC) is a three-campus SUNY community college. The Honors Program, which has members on each campus, is designed to enhance the education of students showing particular academic ability and interest. It is open to students in all majors, but is most accessible to students in the liberal arts and sciences and other programs that are specifically designed for transfer to four-year institutions, because honors courses are liberal arts and science electives.

Honors courses are either selected from general course offerings or represent a special interest topic of a faculty member. Four interdisciplinary honors seminar courses have been developed and are offered on a rotating basis. The Honors Colloquium, which is a 1-credit course and must be taken for three semesters, is really the central focus of the program. Each semester, a theme is selected and lectures, tours, and other activities related to the theme are planned. Since there is an honors group at each of the three college campuses, activities that bring the groups together are planned each semester. These include a talent show and the Honors Great Debates, where the campuses debate each other. As part of the colloquium, students are committed to 10 hours of community service per semester.

While all classes at ECC are small, honors courses are limited to 25 students. Faculty members attempt to make the courses more student-oriented. Students are asked to do more writing and to be more self-directed in their studies. Students in the program are required to take a minimum of six honors courses during their time at the College, plus three semesters of honors colloquium. The honors coordinator at a student's campus acts as that student's adviser, ensuring that the requirements are met for honors, the student's degree, and transfer. The relationship among the students in the program and between the students and the coordinator is very close. The students feel very much a part of a learning community and report that, rather than a sense of competition, there is a sense of cooperation that helps them succeed.

Graduates receive special recognition at an awards banquet, wear gold braids at Commencement, and have annotated transcripts.

Instituted in 1987, there are currently nearly 100 students in the program. The Honors Program maintains a maximum of only 35 students per campus.

Interpreting the symbols: **2**=two-year college, **4**=four-year college; **Pu**=public or state college, **Pr**=private college; **G**=general honors program; **D**=departmental honors program; **S**=small program (fewer than 100 students), **M**=midsize program (100 to 500 students), **L**=large program (more than 500 students); **Sc**=scholarships available in honors program; **Tr**=transfer students accepted into honors program; **HBC**=historically black college; **AA**=academic advisors; **GA**=graduate advisors; **FA**=fellowship advisors.

Participation Requirements: In order to graduate from the Honors Program, students must complete six honors courses, three semesters of colloquium, maintain a minimum 3.25 overall GPA and at least a 3.0 GPA in honors courses, and complete 10 hours of community service per semester.

Admission Process: Students may apply to the program at the time of admission. Placement test scores are used to invite students to apply at admission, and faculty recommendations are used to invite students in their first or second semester. An interview is required.

Scholarship Availability: There are no scholarships specifically designated as honors scholarships.

The Campus Context: Erie Community College is a three-campus community college in the State University of New York system, offering sixty-nine registered degree programs. The City Campus is located in downtown Buffalo, New York, and serves the urban population of the city. North Campus is a suburban campus, located north of Buffalo in Williamsville, and South Campus is a suburban/rural campus south of Buffalo in Orchard Park.

Student Body Of the 13,000 students, nearly half attend the North Campus and one-fourth attend each of the City and South Campuses. Fifty-four percent of the students are women. The ethnic distribution of the student body is 84 percent Caucasian, 11 percent African American, 3 percent Hispanic, 1 percent Asian, less than 1 percent Native American, and less than 1 percent are international students. All students are commuters, and 55 percent of students receive financial aid. There are eighty-seven clubs and organizations across the three campuses.

Faculty There are 419 full-time and 989 part-time faculty members. The student-faculty ratio is 22:1.

Key Facilities Three learning resource centers contain a total of 145,000 volumes, 1,100 periodical subscriptions, and 12,000 videocassettes, slides, and computer disks. ECC also has academic computing facilities, computer teaching labs, student tutoring stations, and computer-integrated manufacturing.

Athletics Athletics on campus include nationally recognized teams in basketball, softball, hockey and bowling. There are collegiate, extramural, and intramural teams. The City Campus Burt Flickinger Athletic Center, which opened in June 1994, was built to house swimming and other events for the World University Games. It houses an Olympic-size swimming pool with a movable floor, a 25-meter warm-up pool, three regulation basketball courts, a large field house that seats 3,000, an indoor jogging track, and a wellness center. The other campuses also have outstanding athletic facilities.

Support Services There are extensive facilities available for disabled students through the Disabled Students Services Office.

Job Opportunities Work-study opportunities are available through the financial aid office. There are also employment opportunities as student assistants and tutors.

Tuition: $2500 for state residents and $5000 for nonresidents, per year (1998–99)

Mandatory Fees: $100

Contact: Coordinator, South Campus: Donna M. Allen, 4041 Southwestern Blvd., Orchard Park, New York 14127; Telephone: 716-851-1716; Fax: 716-851-1629; E-mail: allendm@ecc.edu; Coordinator, City Campus: Willard Flynt; Telephone: 716-851-1071; Coordinator, North Campus: Dr. Jacqui Bollinger; Telephone: 716-851-1342

EVERGREEN VALLEY COLLEGE

2 Pu G S Sc Tr AA

▼ Honors Institute

Nestled in the beautiful foothills of southeast San Jose is a center for learning—where students can create a work of art or a computer program, study the natural sciences or a foreign language, examine world culture and explore the world of philosophy, improve the quality of communication—and of life—by discovering the value of learning.

The honors program at Evergreen Valley College (EVC) takes community college education a step further by bringing together selected students and distinguished faculty members who share a demonstrated commitment to academic excellence.

The honors courses intensify the educational experience of the exceptional student and facilitate a program of general transfer studies. Smaller classes encourage discussion, promote the exchange of ideas and values, and involve the students in active questioning. A special camaraderie also develops between students as they advance through the honors courses.

Honor students participate in special activities designed to enrich the educational experience and to enhance the sense of belonging to a community of honor students. These activities may include field trips, study groups, visits to museums, attending performances, guest lectures, book discussion groups, poetry readings, forensics forums, and social activities.

The honors programs at EVC invites high-achieving, talented, and motivated students to take their community college education to a higher level of achievement, while finding challenge, excitement, and fulfillment in the experience.

Participation Requirements: To receive the full benefits of the honors program, a student must complete the application process and be an active member of the EVC Honors Institute. To be active, a student must be enrolled in at least one honors course per semester and attend one or more honors-sponsored or sanctioned activities per semester (such as an orientation, field trip, study group, high school outreach, or social activity).

Students completing a minimum of 18 units of honors courses with at least a grade of B on each course attempted and a cumulative 3.25 GPA (GPA) receive an Honors Certificate upon graduation. The levels of honors recognition at graduation are the following: College Honors Scholar, 18 units; Distinguished Scholar, 21 units; and Distinguished Scholar with Highest Honors, 24 units plus service. To qualify for the highest honors designation, honors students must show leadership and/or community/campus service commitment. This can be shown by participation in the Evergreen Valley College Associated Student Body, work on the EVC campus newspaper, volunteer service on the EVC campus or in the community, or involvement in drama, dance, or music extracurricular activities. The activity must be presented to the Honors Advisory Council for award approval.

Admission Process: New students must have a minimum 3.25 cumulative GPA or have a placement test score in the honors range to qualify for the honors program. EVC continuing students who have a minimum 3.25 cumulative GPA also qualify. EVC faculty recommendations may also be used for admission to the program. Honors students also receive specialized individual counseling for course selection and timely transfer to four-year institutions.

Scholarship Availability: Each year, the Honors Institute offers two competitive $1000 scholarships in memory of the Gullo family. Applicants must be active member of the Honors Institute and meet certain eligibility requirements.

The Campus Context: Evergreen Valley College is an established energetic institution located on a picturesque 175-acre site in the eastern foothills of San Jose. The mission of Evergreen Valley College is to prepare and empower students for success in a global multicultural society. The College, as its primary charge, provides continuous access to a wide range of comprehensive and flexible postsecondary academic and occupational programs that prepare Silicon Valley residents of all ages for balanced and productive lives and successful careers. To reach these education goals, the College provides the appropriate support services to meet the needs of an increasingly diverse student population.

In fulfilling this mission, the College assists students in achieving their educational and employment goals including, but not limited to, lower-division transfer and general education, certificates, distance learning opportunities, basic skills instruction, English as a second language, economic development, adult noncredit courses, targeted career training, two-year college degrees, and community services courses.

Honorary Societies Evergreen Valley College is a charter member of Phi Theta Kappa National Honor Society.

Contact: Program Coordinator: Walter Soellner, 3095 Yerba Buena Road, San Jose, California, 95135; Telephone: 408-274-7900, Ext. 6566; Fax: 408-223-9291; E-mail: walter.soellner@sjeccd.cc.ca.us

Fashion Institute of Technology

2&4 Pu G M

▼ Presidential Scholars Program

The Presidential Scholars Program at the Fashion Institute of Technology (FIT) provides academically gifted students an opportunity to have a dialogue with exceptional students from all majors in the college and to discuss ideas and theories in the liberal arts. While pursuing their chosen majors, students participate in challenging liberal arts courses and stimulating colloquia and experience the entire landscape of New York City as their campus as they visit cultural institutions and attend arts performances. The program enrolls approximately 150 students per semester.

Participation Requirements: Each semester students choose from more than a dozen honors liberal arts courses, ranging from Greek mythology to the Bauhaus. Students also participate in four semesters of honors colloquia addressing ideas relating to contemporary cultural, social, political, and economic thought. Students undertake two honors contracts in their major, participate in special projects designed by students and selected faculty members, and engage in cultural outings in New York City. Students must maintain an overall GPA of at least 3.5 to graduate with honors. Benefits include a merit stipend of $500 annually, recognition as a Presidential Scholar on college transcripts and diplomas, priority registration for honors and nonhonors courses, guarantee of a dormitory room, and the ability to substitute honors classes for required introductory liberal arts courses.

Admission Process: Students admitted to FIT are eligible to apply to the Presidential Scholars Program. For the associate degree Presidential Scholars Program, competitive admission is based on SAT I scores, class rank, and high school GPA. For the bachelor's degree Presidential Scholars Program, students need a GPA of at least 3.5 in their A.A.S. program.

The Campus Context: The college occupies a $115-million campus in the Chelsea district of Manhattan where the worlds of fashion, art, design, communications, technology, and manufacturing converge. There are thirty-one degree programs offered. Many majors offer internships in their courses of study. The Museum at FIT is the repository of the world's largest collection of costumes, textiles, and accessories of dress.

Student Body The number of full-time students is 6,408; the number of part-time students is 4,378. Of the total number, 82 percent of the students are women. Twenty-two percent of students live on campus, and 64 percent receive financial aid.

Faculty There are 913 faculty members, of whom 213 are full-time. The student-faculty ratio is 13:1.

Key Facilities FIT houses facilities that mirror those of the fashion and related industries, including a state-of-the-art computer center, TV studios, a toy design workshop, and the only fragrance laboratory located on a college campus. The library contains more than 115,000 titles, including books, periodicals, and nonprint materials.

Study Abroad FIT offers numerous study-abroad programs.

Support Services FIT provides support services for learning disabled students.

Job Opportunities The Federal Work-Study Program and institutional employment provide opportunities for work on campus. Off-campus part-time employment opportunities are excellent.

Tuition: $2622 minimum (A.A.S.) and $2985 minimum (B.F.A. and B.S.) for state residents, $5850 minimum (A.A.S.) and $6800 (B.F.A. and B.S.) for nonresidents, per year (2001–02)

Room and Board: $5685

Mandatory Fees: $270

Contact: Director: Dr. Irene Buchman, Seventh Avenue at 27th Street, New York, New York 10001-5992; Telephone: 212-217-8660; Fax: 212-217-7192; E-mail: buchmani@fitsuny.edu; Web site: http://www.fitnyc.suny.edu

Felician College

4 Pr G S Tr

▼ Honors Program

The Felician College Honors Program is open to all academically superior students in all majors who are pursuing associate or baccalaureate degrees. The Honors Program began in January 1991 and is currently in its eleventh year. There are 60 students in the program.

Participation Requirements: Students take the honors sections of the required English courses Rhetoric and Composition I and II, honors sections of core courses, and honors courses within the discipline. All of the core courses are interdisciplinary and focus on content as well as the competencies of critical thinking, written and verbal communication, and social interaction. The honors sections emphasize an extensive use of primary sources and the study of specialized topics.

One-credit honors seminars are offered each semester. They are interdisciplinary in nature and are frequently team-taught. Examples include "The French Revolution," "The United States in the 1960s," "Biotechnology," "The Evolution of Language," and "Teleology and Human Existence."

Community-based learning, consisting of 15 hours of volunteering each semester, is required for honors graduation.

In their junior or senior years, honors students who have completed 9 or more credits of honors courses may apply to the College's Honors Advisory Board, which meets monthly, to take a nonhonors course for honors credit. The instructor gives a description of how the student's syllabus will reflect the honors-caliber work that would merit the receipt of honors credit.

All graduating seniors in the arts and sciences division complete a senior research project and present it orally before the College community. Honors students may opt to work with a professor and produce an original work of research of honors quality, which is read before presentation by a faculty member in two disciplines outside of the major.

Interpreting the symbols: **2**=two-year college, **4**=four-year college; **Pu**=public or state college, **Pr**=private college; **G**=general honors program; **D**=departmental honors program; **S**=small program (fewer than 100 students), **M**=midsize program (100 to 500 students), **L**=large program (more than 500 students); **Sc**=scholarships available in honors program; **Tr**=transfer students accepted into honors program; **HBC**=historically black college; **AA**=academic advisors; **GA**=graduate advisors; **FA**=fellowship advisors.

Each spring, honors students receive certificates at the annual Honors and Service Learning Dinner. All graduating seniors who complete the program are designated as honors scholars and receive a trophy and certificate at the Graduation Dinner, which is held the evening before commencement. They wear a gold medallion inscribed with the word honor and attached to a ribbon with the College's colors. The words "honors scholar" appear in calligraphy on the diploma near a specially embossed gold College seal.

Admission Process: Newly admitted students to the College are eligible to enter the Honors Program based on their high school averages, SAT I scores, and their rank in their graduating class. Transfer students with 36 or fewer credits from other institutions of higher learning may enter the program using the same criteria as well as an evaluation of their other college grades. Current freshmen and first-semester sophomores may be accepted into the program upon application and interview or if placed on the Dean's List for two semesters. Students in the Honors Program are expected to maintain a 3.2 GPA or higher each semester and achieve at least a "B" in all honors courses.

Scholarship Availability: A variety of scholarships are available for students who meet the criteria for each award. Many of the recipients of scholarships offered by the College are in the College's Honors Program.

The Campus Context: Felician College is a four-year, Catholic, coeducational, liberal arts college located in northern New Jersey. There are three academic divisions—arts and sciences, health sciences, and teacher education. The College offers the following degree programs: one master's degree (M.S.) in nursing, one master's degree (M.A.) in education, two master's degrees (M.A.) in English and Catechesis, thirteen bachelor's degrees (B.A.) in liberal arts and education, three bachelor's degrees (B.S.) in business administration and health sciences, two associate degrees (A.A.S.) in health sciences, and one associate degree (A.A.) in liberal arts.

Felician College is situated in Lodi on the banks of the Saddle River, which winds through the College's beautifully landscaped campus of 27 acres. Located near New York City and other cultural centers in New Jersey and Connecticut, the College is easily accessible and offers students a variety of educational and cultural resources. A second campus opened in fall 1998 in Rutherford, New Jersey.

Student Body Felician College currently enrolls 1,200 undergraduates. The majority of these students are from northern New Jersey. Eighty-four percent of the students are women. The ethnic distribution of the students is 6 percent Asian/Pacific Islander, 8 percent African American, 14 percent Hispanic, and 72 percent Caucasian. International students comprise 12 percent of the College's population. Residential facilities are available for all students and are located on the Rutherford campus. Approximately 50 percent of students receive financial aid.

Faculty There are 60 full-time faculty members, 55 percent of whom hold doctoral or terminal degrees. There are also approximately 49 adjunct faculty members and 15 half-time faculty members. The student-faculty ratio is 15:1.

Key Facilities The College library houses 115,000 books, 795 periodical subscriptions, 149 microforms, and 2,979 video and audio tapes. Ninety PC computers are available on campus in three computer labs, the biology lab, the writing lab, the business lab, the psychology lab, the nursing skills lab, the Center for Learning, and the library. There are ten Macintosh computers available in the art room.

Honorary Societies Kappa Gamma Pi

Athletics The College participates in Division II of the National Association of Intercollegiate Athletics in men's and women's basketball, soccer, and softball.

Study Abroad The Felician College Honors Program offers study-abroad opportunities through the Office of Study Abroad. That program offers accredited education opportunities in the United Kingdom or Australia and additional summer trips for credit to Japan, France, or the United Kingdom.

Support Services A "504 Coordinator" is ensuring that the College is up to the standards of the Americans with Disabilities Act. A Center for Learning and Writing Lab provides support services to all students. The library is outfitted with wheelchair ramps.

Job Opportunities The College offers work-study opportunities and part-time staff positions on campus.

Tuition: $5730 per semester for full-time (12 or more credits) or $382 per credit for part-time (less than 12 credits), undergraduate; $415 per credit, graduate.

Room and board: $4688 per semester, single; $3125 per semester, double; $2604 per semester, triple.

Comprehensive Fees: $475 per semester, residents; $310 per semester, nonresidents; $125 per semester, part-time students.

Contact: Director: Dr. Maria Vecchio, 262 South Main Street, Lodi, New Jersey 07644; Telephone: 201-559-6017

FERRIS STATE UNIVERSITY

4 Pu G M Sc Tr AA FA

▼ Honors Program

The Honors Program at Ferris State University provides intellectual challenges, resources, and support to the University's most able and highly motivated students while encouraging them to serve and lead in local and global communities. To support this mission, stipends are available for national and international travel, and a strong community service component impacts this college town.

In addition to the honors classes, peer advisers, faculty mentors, symposia, study groups, and excellent residence hall computer labs support the educational process. Many of those in honors form strong ties to the honors community for their entire college career. One student remarked, "In honors you're with a group of people who all want to succeed and do their very best. You never know how it may help you. My employer was impressed that I was in honors and on the Dean's list, and that prompted him to call me and offer me an internship."

Honors at Ferris State features general education courses with 15 to 22 students per class; opportunities to do research with professors; and an orientation to arts and culture class in which the students attend plays, concerts, ballets, symphonies, and gallery openings, compliments of the Honors Program. The Honors Senior Symposium, held each spring for the graduating seniors, caps off the honors experience.

The honors halls offer premier living space in the heart of the campus. The upscale, carpeted private rooms with ceiling fans are wired for Internet access and voice mail. Lounges and meeting rooms in the halls are used for study sessions, student gatherings, and seminars.

Founded in 1997, the Honors Program has 331 members in seventy-one different majors. During its short history it has produced a Bread Loaf Scholar and won second prize in a national contest for honors newsletters.

Participation Requirements: Students are required to maintain a minimum 3.25 GPA, take 12 honors credits in general education classes (5 credits freshman year, 6 credits sophomore year, and 1 credit during the junior or senior year), commit to 15 hours of community service per semester, attend three cultural events per semester (tickets are provided by the Honors Program), join an organization or group on campus and assume a leadership position in it by junior or senior year, and submit a poster for the Honors Senior Symposium.

Admission Process: Honors Program students are selected through a special application process. Minimum entrance requirements are a 3.4 high school GPA and 24 on the ACT. However, since the program's inception in 1997, the average high school GPA of entering honors freshmen has been 3.8, and the average ACT score has been 27–28.

Selection is fairly competitive, since the number of freshman places is set at 180. The factors that affect selection are three recommendation forms, ACT score, GPA, and a writing sample that is produced on campus at the Honors Invitational Competition during the last Saturday in February each year. (For those students who are unable to attend this competition due to circumstances beyond their control, other arrangements are made.)

Applications received by the priority deadline of February 8 are given first consideration. After that date, applications are considered on a space-available basis until March 30. All applicants must also file the standard Ferris State University application by the February 8 deadline.

Internal and external transfer students may also qualify for honors, but only if they have freshman or sophomore standing and apply by February 8. For these candidates, the criteria for selection are a minimum 3.25 college GPA, three recommendation forms, and a writing sample.

Scholarship Availability: All students who are admitted to honors receive a $2000 Honors Residential Life Scholarship, which can only be used to defray costs of living in an honors residence hall. This scholarship is renewable for four years and can be added to other existing scholarships, with awards totaling more than $8000 annually. Also, there are stipends awarded annually for national and international travel.

The Campus Context: There are eight colleges at Ferris State University: Allied Health, Arts and Sciences, Business, Education and Human Services, Optometry, Pharmacy, Technology, and University College. The 9,200 students on the Big Rapids campus may enroll in one of 150 majors. A state-of-the-art, new (March 2001), $43,000,000-digital library is the jewel of the campus. Ferris State is part of the Michigan Art Walk, in which various artists from throughout the country are commissioned to create public art within the campus space. A recently renovated Arts and Science Commons, a new Rubber/Elastomer Center, and an outstanding Student Recreation Center also support student life, while the town of Big Rapids offers a full range of amenities. In addition, there is extensive off-campus housing available to students after the sophomore year. The surrounding countryside is excellent for outdoor activities during all four seasons ranging from hunting, fishing, and tubing down the Muskegon River to skating at the ice arena or on the nearby lakes and ponds.

Student Body Undergraduate enrollment is 10,092 (54 percent men and 46 percent women), 838 students are enrolled in graduate school, and there are seven graduate programs. The ethnic distribution is 78 percent Caucasian, 9 percent African American, 6 percent unknown, 3 percent international, 2 percent Asian American, 1 percent Hispanic, and 1 percent Native American. Thirty-eight percent of the students live on campus. Eighty-two percent of the students receive financial aid. There are six sororities, eleven fraternities, and more than 200 student organizations on campus.

Faculty Of the 510 faculty members, 465 are full-time. The student-faculty ratio is 20:1.

Key Facilities The new (March 2001) library occupies 173,484 square feet and houses 341,132 volumes. Computer facilities include a fiber-optic network and Internet access for all nineteen residence halls; there is a computer lab in each residence hall.

Athletics FSU sponsors fifteen intercollegiate varsity sports. Men's sports are basketball, cross-country, football, golf, hockey (Division I), tennis, and track. Women's sports are basketball, cross-country, golf, soccer, softball, tennis, track, and volleyball. Admission to all sports, except for hockey, is free with a valid student ID. A wide range of club and intramural sports for men and women is also available. In the Student Rec Center, there are handball, racquetball, and basketball courts; a swimming pool; and weight rooms. In the tennis facility, there are indoor clay and hard courts.

Study Abroad Study-abroad opportunities are coordinated through the International Affairs Office on the campus.

Support Services Disability Services supplies test readers/writers, note takers, sign-language interpreters, adapted computers, classroom equipment, Kurzweil-JAWS for the blind, the Arkenstone Reader, and special parking. One hundred percent of the buildings are handicapped-accessible.

Job Opportunities Work-study is available in most of the offices and departments on campus, and there are also non-work-study jobs available.

Tuition: Approximately $4413 per year for full-time state residents, $9348 for full-time nonresidents (2002–03)

Room and Board: Approximately $5416 per year (2002–03)

Mandatory Fees: $250 nonrefundable, $102 refundable

Contact: Coordinator: Maude Bigford, HFE 129, Ferris State University, 809 Campus Drive, Big Rapids, Michigan 49307; Telephone: 231-591-2216; Fax: 231-591-5948; E-mail: bigfordm@ferris.edu; Web site: http://www.ferris.edu/htmls/academics/honored

FLORIDA A&M UNIVERSITY

4 Pu G M Sc Tr

▼ Honors Program

The Florida A&M University (FAMU) Honors Program, which is now in its eleventh year of operation, offers students a challenging experience. The approaches to learning in the program are stimulating, and the professors are dedicated. The program's small classes allow for lively and in-depth discussion of topics, and both professors and students benefit from these discussions. Students in the program also enjoy personalized advising and, when necessary, scheduling priority that allows them access to appropriate professors and courses. There are currently 452 participants in the program.

The Honors Program offers special sections of required courses. These special sections permit students to fulfill requirements in areas such as composition, speech, computer programming, and math in small and exciting classes. The honors seminar encourages students to delve more deeply in specific areas, and honors students believe that the personal attention they receive in these smaller classes greatly enhances their learning.

The program offers a wide variety of experiences for its students. Among its activities are the publication of newsletters, internships to the Washington Center, limited internships at the White House, and attendance and participation in community outreach programs. Successful completion of the program is noted on the students' transcripts.

Students also plan and participate in the Bernard Hendricks Undergraduate Honors Conference, an honors retreat, visiting

Interpreting the symbols: **2**=two-year college, **4**=four-year college; **Pu**=public or state college, **Pr**=private college; **G**=general honors program; **D**=departmental honors program; **S**=small program (fewer than 100 students), **M**=midsize program (100 to 500 students), **L**=large program (more than 500 students); **Sc**=scholarships available in honors program; **Tr**=transfer students accepted into honors program; **HBC**=historically black college; **AA**=academic advisors; **GA**=graduate advisors; **FA**=fellowship advisors.

lectures, and Honors Convocation, which is held on the campus during Honors Week. They present research papers and projects and participate in panel discussions.

Participation Requirements: To graduate from the Honors Program, students are required to have at least a 3.2 cumulative GPA. They must also have accumulated a total of 18 hours of honors credit for courses taken at the honors level and are required to have completed a community service component. Juniors and seniors are encouraged to participate in the Honors in the Major section. Students work under the directorship of a major professor on a thesis or project, which is begun during the junior year and completed before graduation. Transfer students who have a GPA of at least 3.2 are also encouraged to become involved in this aspect of the program. The Honors in the Major section helps to prepare students for graduate or professional school.

Admission Process: The Honors Program recruits capable students who thrive in an atmosphere in which the motto is "Excellence with caring." The students are interested in challenging academic activities and intellectual exploration. At the beginning of each school year, new honors students are chosen from among the freshman class. These students meet the following qualifications: a 3.5 high school GPA plus a score of 1100 on the SAT I or 27 on the ACT. In exceptional circumstances, promising students who may not meet the above criteria are given consideration. FAMU's Honors Program welcomes applications from interested students in all disciplines. Students in the Honors Program come from a variety of backgrounds and have diverse academic and social interests. The common thread linking the students in the program is their desire for an innovative and challenging education.

Scholarship Availability: Many of the students coming into the program are presidential scholars who have a full scholarship. The Honors Program also assists qualified participants in obtaining scholarships and fellowships. The Harry S. Truman Scholarship and the Woodrow Wilson Fellowship are two of the most prestigious awards students have received to date. In addition, some program participants have received scholarships and internships at the Washington Center and the White House.

The Campus Context: There are five colleges and seven schools at FAMU. The colleges are the College of Arts and Sciences, the College of Education, the College of Engineering Sciences Technology and Agriculture (CESTA), the College of Pharmacy and Pharmaceutical Sciences, and the FAMU/FSU College of Engineering. The schools are the School of Allied Health Sciences; the School of Architecture; the School of Business and Industry; the School of Journalism and Graphic Communication; and the School of Nursing.

Student Body Total undergraduate enrollment at FAMU is currently 12,100. Approximately 59 percent of the students are women. The ethnic distribution of the student population is 92 percent African American, 5 percent Caucasian, 1 percent Hispanic American, 1 percent Asian, and 1 percent resident alien. There are more than 200 international students. Seventy-six percent of the students live off campus, and approximately 80 percent of the students receive some kind of financial aid. There are numerous honorary and religious societies on campus as well as a tremendous diversity of clubs to meet every student's interests. The campus is home to numerous fraternities and sororities.

Faculty The total number of full-time faculty members is 510. Seventy-two percent of the faculty members hold doctoral or other professional terminal degrees.

Key Facilities The library has 575,732 bound volumes, 19,002 periodicals, and 145,567 microfilms. Audio/video equipment and facilities include videotape monitors, tape players and recorders, film projectors and screens, overhead projectors, a fully equipped television studio, and a photography laboratory. The Florida Black Archives Research Center and Museum is located on the campus. This facility, which complements academic studies in history, has become a popular tourist attraction. The University has several computer labs for use by faculty members and students. There are approximately fifteen computer sites available to students.

Athletics Athletic competition is available for men in baseball, basketball, football, golf, swimming, tennis, and track. Women's athletics include basketball, softball, swimming, tennis, track, and volleyball.

Study Abroad Study-abroad opportunities are available to both students and faculty members; opportunities include exchange visits to China by selected students and faculty members and travel abroad to the Caribbean, South and Central America, and Spain. Students majoring in Spanish have the opportunity to spend the summer in a Spanish-speaking country and earn credit for attending classes in that country while learning the language.

Support Services The Learning Development and Evaluation Center (LDEC) provides individualized supportive services to students with learning disabilities. Disabled-student facilities at Florida A&M University cater to the needs of the students who are physically challenged by providing facilities such as ramps, specially designed rest rooms, and vehicles specially designed to transport the students. Students who have special needs because of a physical or mental handicap should contact the Special Programs and Services Office as soon as they arrive on campus. This office has been established to assist handicapped students attending the University.

Job Opportunities Work opportunities are available on and off campus.

Tuition: In 2001, undergraduate tuition was $81.96 per credit hour for residents and $344.88 per credit hour for nonresidents; graduate tuition was $164.14 per credit hour for residents and $571.30 per credit hour for nonresidents.

Room and Board: $3896

Mandatory Fees: $222

Contact: Director: Dr. Ivy Mitchell, Modular Unit 1, Orr Drive, Tallahassee, Florida 32307; Telephone: 850-599-3540; Fax: 850-561-2125; E-mail: imitchel@famu.edu

FLORIDA ATLANTIC UNIVERSITY

4 Pu G M Sc Tr

▼ Honors College

The Harriet L. Wilkes Honors College of Florida Atlantic University is the first public honors college to be built from the ground up. It is a four-year residential college located on the John D. MacArthur campus in Jupiter, Florida. The Honors College, with its attractive student-faculty ratio, provides the highest quality liberal arts education. Environmental studies and international studies, interdisciplinary courses, and an emphasis on writing are all strong features. Tutorials, one-on-one learning, small classes, and affordable tuition distinguish the Honors College at Florida Atlantic University from all others.

Participation Requirements: The Honors College is a stand-alone college within Florida Atlantic University and is therefore not simply an honors program. It is best compared to a small, private, liberal arts college. Students complete the majority of the 120 credit hours required for graduation within the Honors College. A senior-year thesis is also required of each student. All concentrations in the Honors College lead to a Bachelor of Arts degree in liberal arts and sciences.

Admission Process: The Honors College admits students who benefit from the small liberal arts college experience. Selection decisions are based on the academic record in a college-preparatory curriculum, SAT I or ACT scores, liveliness of intellect, school and community involvement, and the capacity for leadership. Applicants must submit a State University System of Florida Application; an Honors College supplementary application; official transcripts; official SAT I or ACT test scores; a graded writing sample from an English, social studies, or natural sciences class; and three letters of recommendation. The early decision deadline is November 15, early action is January 31, and the regular decision deadline is May 1.

Scholarship Availability: Both academic and need-based financial aid are available to Honors College students. Students must apply for need-based aid. Academic scholarships may be awarded to students who demonstrate the potential to make an outstanding contribution to the Honors College community. Every student applying to the Honors College is reviewed for an academic scholarship. Among the academic scholarships available are the Henry Morris Flagler Awards, worth more than $55,000 over four years and given to 5 incoming freshmen (Florida residents only) each year.

The Campus Context: The Honors College is located on the newest of Florida Atlantic University's seven campuses. Opened in the fall of 1999, the 135-acre John D. MacArthur Campus in Jupiter, Florida, is part of a unique 2,000-acre mixed-traditional community setting that contains housing; a town square with shops, restaurants, and a multi-theatre movie complex; an 18-hole public golf course; and the spring training facilities of two major league baseball teams.

Florida Atlantic University is a member of the State University System of Florida. The University is organized into nine colleges: the Dorothy F. Schmidt College of Arts and Letters; the Colleges of Business, Education, Engineering, and Liberal Arts; the Christine E. Lynn College of Nursing; the Charles E. Schmidt College of Science; the College of Architecture, Urban and Public Affairs; and the Harriet L. Wilkes Honors College. The University's original campus is in Boca Raton, a suburban residential community midway between Fort Lauderdale and West Palm Beach, 45 miles south of Jupiter. The John D. MacArthur Campus is the home of several upper-division and graduate programs from the other colleges in the University.

Student Body The Honors College will serve 500 students upon its completion. Florida Atlantic University as a whole enrolls more than 25,000 students. Students in the Honors College thus have the benefits of a small liberal arts college setting and the advantages of the resources of a large state university.

Faculty The Honors College will have 55 full-time faculty members when maximum enrollment is reached. All of the faculty members hold doctorates or appropriate terminal degrees and have an exceptional ability to educate honors students.

Key Facilities The Honors College library holds a growing collection of books and periodicals. As a member of the State University System of Florida, the library shares loan privileges with other universities throughout the state. The library also has an extensive electronic collection. The campus contains a state-of-the-art PC computer lab and all residence halls offer single-bedroom suites and are hardwired for high-speed Internet connection. There is also special multimedia classroom space available.

Athletics Florida Atlantic University joined NCAA Division I in 1993 and is a member of the Atlantic Sun Conference. Men's sports include baseball, basketball, cross-country, golf, soccer, swimming, and tennis. Women's sports include basketball, cross-country, golf, soccer, softball, swimming, tennis, track and field, and volleyball. FAU also fields a I-AA football program that plays in Pro Player Stadium. All other intercollegiate sporting events take place on the central campus located in Boca Raton. The John D. MacArthur campus in Jupiter offers a variety of recreational facilities for students to enjoy, including a pool, tennis courts, and an all-purpose field.

Study Abroad The Honors College encourages all students to study abroad. Opportunities are offered through the Florida Atlantic University Office of International Programs.

Support Services The Honors College offers a broad range of support services through Florida Atlantic University, including those available through the Students with Disabilities Office, Financial Aid, University Counseling Center, and Minority Student Services.

Tuition: $2850 for Florida residents, $10,540 for nonresidents, per year (2002–03)

Room and Board: $8218 (students are required to live within the campus community)

Contact: Dean: William P. Mech, Harriet L. Wilkes Honors College, Florida Atlantic University, John D. MacArthur Campus, 5353 Parkside Drive, Jupiter, Florida 33458; Telephone: 561-799-8578, 561-799-8646, or 800-920-8705; E-mail: wmech@fau.edu or hcadmissions@fau.edu; Web site: http://www.honorscollege.edu

FLORIDA ATLANTIC UNIVERSITY

4 Pu G S

▼ Lower Division Honors Program

Since 1992, through its Lower Division Honors Program, Florida Atlantic University (FAU) has offered highly motivated and well-prepared students a unique educational experience that goes well beyond the normal course requirements for freshmen and sophomores.

There are currently 60 students enrolled in the program.

Participation Requirements: The program consists of a minimum of 16 honors course credits. The core of the program is four 3-credit honors seminars taken during the freshman year. These seminars, developed and taught by highly experienced faculty members, are limited to 15 students. They substitute for required core-curriculum courses and topics are drawn from the humanities, social sciences, and the sciences. Because of the small size and individual attention, students typically do as well, if not better, academically in these courses than in the normal core-curriculum courses

In addition to the core seminars, students are required to take a 1-credit honors colloquium during the fall semester of the freshman year. This colloquium includes lectures by distinguished faculty members, outside speakers, and performances. Students also take 4 additional credits comprising honors sections of college writing and of the core curriculum courses, upper-division honors equivalences of core courses, elective honors seminars, and a 2- to 3-credit honors-directed independent study.

To successfully complete the program, a student must fulfill all the course requirements and maintain a minimum overall GPA of 3.5 and an honors GPA of at least 3.0

Admission Process: Minimum requirements for acceptance into the honors program are SAT I scores of 1180 or higher or ACT scores of 26 or higher and a GPA of at least 3.5. To apply, students must submit an application, a personal statement, and a letter of recommendation. Because of the limited number of spaces in the program, admission is selective; the application deadline is in mid-May. The program accepts 35 entering freshmen each year. Freshmen enrolled in the Lower Division Honors Program are housed in a special dormitory reserved for honors students. A number of classes are conducted in the dorms.

Scholarship Availability: Although the honors program does not award scholarships, a large number of University scholarships are available; many of them are based solely on academic merit. The FAU Presidential Scholarship, for example, awards $2000 per year for four years to students with a high school average of

Interpreting the symbols: **2**=two-year college, **4**=four-year college; **Pu**=public or state college, **Pr**=private college; **G**=general honors program; **D**=departmental honors program; **S**=small program (fewer than 100 students), **M**=midsize program (100 to 500 students), **L**=large program (more than 500 students); **Sc**=scholarships available in honors program; **Tr**=transfer students accepted into honors program; **HBC**=historically black college; **AA**=academic advisors; **GA**=graduate advisors; **FA**=fellowship advisors.

at least 3.5 on a 4.0 scale and an SAT I score of 1200 or higher or ACT score of 27 or higher. It is renewable up to four years based on academic achievement.

The Campus Context: Florida Atlantic University is a doctoral-degree-granting research institution that is one of the ten universities comprising the State University System of Florida. The main campus is located on an 850-acre site in Boca Raton Florida, a coastal residential community located near West Palm Beach, Fort Lauderdale, and Miami. Additional campuses are located in Davie, Ft. Lauderdale, and North Palm Beach.

The University offers fifty-one bachelor's, forty-three master's, and fourteen doctoral degree programs.

Student Body The University has approximately 19,000 students.

Faculty There are 700 full-time faculty members, of whom 95 percent hold terminal degrees.

Honorary Societies Phi Theta Kappa, Phi Eta Sigma, Phi Kappa Phi, and Golden Key

Tuition: $1900 for state residents, $7200 for nonresidents, per year

Room and Board: $4365

Contact: Director: Dr. Fred Fejes, Boca Raton, Florida 33431; Telephone: 561-297-3858; Fax: 561-297-3132; E-mail: fejes@acc.fau.edu; Web site: http://www.fau.edu/academic/freshman/honors.htm

Florida Community College at Jacksonville

2 Pu G M Sc Tr

▼ Honors Program

The Honors Program at Florida Community College at Jacksonville (FCCJ) offers gifted students unique learning opportunities in specific sections of the associate degree curriculum. The program philosophy is three-fold. It is designed to encourage students to become independent learners capable of critical thinking and self-expression, enable students to see connections in learning that allow them to integrate their classroom learning into a common whole, and allow students to explore facets of learning and materials that are not available in traditional curricula.

There are currently two options available for student participation. The first is to enroll in specific designated honors courses. These courses encompass unique, nontraditional methods of exploring a variety of topics and issues, including United States history, art appreciation, and precalculus. The second option is the Honors Contract. This option provides some flexibility to students if they have already completed the designated honors courses. Students work with a chosen faculty member, usually within their major. The pair determines a specific assignment or project. Honors credit for the course is awarded upon completion of the contract requirements.

A student's participation in the program is recognized upon successful completion of the program requirements. Students receive an Honors Program seal on their diploma, and their transcripts reflect the completion of honors courses.

The program began in 1981 and currently has more than 300 participants.

Participation Requirements: Because FCCJ offers the opportunity for all of its qualified students to participate in the Honors Program, there are two components to the program. Entering freshman students are required to complete a minimum of 18 hours of honors course work over two years. Students who entered FCCJ but did not initially participate in the program and have earned at least 12 college credit hours can graduate from the Honors Program by completing 12 honors credit hours.

Admission Process: Students wishing to participate the honors program must enroll in a degree program and have a GPA of at least 3.25.

Scholarship Availability: Scholarships are available in the amount of $2000 to qualified students who have a GPA of 3.5 or higher. Students who have a GPA between 3.25 and 3.49 and corresponding SAT I or ACT scores may qualify as well. For specific requirements and application materials, prospective students may contact Ms. Gwen Thomas (telephone: 904-632-3108, e-mail: gthomas@fccj.org). The application priority deadline is February 28.

The Campus Context: Florida Community College at Jacksonville consists of four main campuses (Kent, North, South, and Downtown) and houses many centers at various locations in the Jacksonville area. FCCJ offers the Associate of Arts and the Associate of Science degrees. The average age of the traditional undergraduate is 29.

The Center for Academic Excellence and Leadership (CAEL) is new to FCCJ and is located at the Kent campus. It is a gathering place where honors students, Phi Theta Kappa members, Brain Bowl participants, Forenics Team members, and others can meet, interact, and coordinate collaborative activities.

Student Body Florida Community College is a two-year community college with an enrollment of 94,601, with 31,649 college-credit students and 62,952 continuing education students. Approximately 58 percent of the students are women. The ethnic distribution of the total undergraduate population is 18.4 percent African American, 72.1 percent Caucasian, and 9.5 percent other. There are also 213 international students. College-credit students who receive financial aid total 8,707.

Faculty There are 397 full-time faculty members and 1,098 adjunct faculty members.

Key Facilities The library contains 193,585 volumes, and there are fifty-nine computer labs collegewide. The student–personal computer ratio is 15:1.

Honorary Society Phi Theta Kappa

Support Services Disabled students find all academic buildings completely handicapped-accessible. Wheelchair ramps, automatic door openers, and equipped restrooms are available.

Tuition: $1329 for state residents, $4526 for nonresidents, per year (1998–99)

Contact: Director: Dr. Jim Mayes, 3939 Roosevelt Blvd., Jacksonville, Florida 32205; Telephone: 904-381-3451; Fax: 904-381-3462; E-mail: jmayes@fccj.org

Florida International University

4 Pu G L Sc

▼ The Honors College

Talented students are often forced to choose between the exciting opportunities and challenges available at large, research-oriented universities and the close, personal environment offered by small liberal arts colleges. Florida International University (FIU) offers the best of both worlds. The Honors College is a small community of outstanding students, committed teachers, and dedicated scholars who work together in an atmosphere usually associated with small private colleges but with all of the resources of a major urban university.

The College provides an important foundation for students who want to get the most out of their undergraduate years. The transition into higher education is made easier by the student's immediate association with a small group of students and teachers with similar capabilities and aspirations. The undergraduate experience is significantly enhanced by the interdisciplinary focus of the curriculum and the opportunity to work closely with experienced faculty members. Opportunities for graduate and professional study or employment are greatly expanded because of the range of activities and experiences made available to students in the College. The Honors College at FIU offers some of the very best experiences in undergraduate education.

The 12-year-old College currently enrolls 600 students from fifty-seven countries and twenty-one states.

Participation Requirements: Students in the College possess dual academic citizenship. They pursue almost any major available in the University and at the same time complete the honors curriculum. In most cases, participation in the College does not increase the number of credits required for graduation. During each term, students enroll in one honors seminar that is designed to stimulate thoughtful discussion and creativity and to develop communications skills. Honors seminars are limited to a student-faculty ratio of 20:1 and are taught by some of the best teachers in the University. All classes are interdisciplinary, and many are team-taught.

The first two years are structured similarly. All students and faculty members at each level meet in a large-group session one day each week for activities such as lectures, panel discussions, case studies, and student presentations; another class meeting each week is spent in small-group preceptorials. Professors meet with the same small groups throughout the year. Junior seminars meet as independent classes with an emphasis on synthesizing the students' experiences during the previous two years. Many are introduced to graduate-level research activities.

During the senior year, students may choose to continue the sequence of honors seminars, complete a research-based honors thesis, or participate in one of the Honors College study-abroad programs in Italy, Spain, or the Caribbean.

The unique nature of the College extends far beyond the classroom door. The Honors College Society organizes social and community service activities. The faculty and staff members of the Honors College make every effort to ensure that students are aware of the many opportunities available to them, such as fellowships, internships, and summer-study programs. Every year, as the result of this mentoring, many students win national awards and travel throughout the country for funded activities, and teams of students and faculty members travel to regional and national conferences to make presentations.

Students who complete all graduation requirements receive special recognition at commencement and a notation on their transcripts indicating that they graduated through the Honors College.

Admission Process: Admission to the Honors College is selective and limited. Students are admitted only at the beginning of each academic year (fall term). Freshmen with at least a 3.5 overall high school GPA and commensurate scores on the SAT or ACT are eligible for admission to the College. Transfer and continuing FIU students who have maintained a minimum 3.3 GPA in all college-level work and have at least two full academic years remaining in their undergraduate programs are eligible for admission to the College.

Scholarship Availability: Various private and institutional scholarships are available at both the freshman and transfer levels.

The Campus Context: Florida International University, Miami's public research university, is one of America's most dynamic institutions of higher learning. Since opening in 1972, FIU has achieved many benchmarks of excellence that have taken other universities more than a century to reach. The University has nationally renowned full-time faculty members who are known for their outstanding teaching and cutting-edge research and students from throughout the U.S. and more than 130 other countries. Its alumni have risen to prominence in every field and are a testament to the University's academic excellence.

A member of the State University System of Florida, FIU is a research university offering a diverse selection of undergraduate, graduate, and professional programs. Through its sixteen colleges and schools, FIU offers more than 180 baccalaureate, master's, and doctoral degree programs in more than 280 majors; conducts basic and applied research; and provides public service. Committed to both quality and access, FIU meets the educational needs of traditional students as well as an increasing number of part-time students and lifelong learners. Interdisciplinary centers and institutes at the University conduct research and teaching that address economic and social concerns.

Florida International University has two main campuses, University Park and Biscayne Bay Campus. The Honors College operates at both campuses.

Student Body There are more than 32,000 students, including 2,982 international students. Financial aid is received by 43 percent of the students. Fifty-seven percent of the students are women. The ethnic distribution of the student population is 3.4 percent Asian, 14.2 percent African American, 21 percent Caucasian, and 51.4 percent Hispanic. Most students commute. There are nine fraternities and seven sororities on campus.

Faculty The total number of faculty members is 1,400, of whom 1,033 are full-time. Eighty-five percent of the faculty members have terminal degrees. The student-faculty ratio is 27:1.

Key Facilities FIU offers the complete array of student services and activities one would expect at a major state university, with several recently constructed facilities, including a performing arts complex, a student center, athletic facilities, and a library. Volumes in the library total more than 1.1 million. Students have use of a full range of computer facilities, including mainframe and Internet access, free of charge. Honors Place at Panther Hall offers a living and learning housing experience for Honors College students.

Honorary Societies FIU has chapters of more than fifteen honorary societies, including Phi Beta Kappa, Phi Eta Sigma, Phi Kappa Phi, Golden Key, and Mortar Board.

Athletics FIU is a member of the NCAA Division I and the Sun Belt Conference. In recent years, teams have participated in NCAA tournaments in many sports, including baseball and women's and men's soccer and basketball. Intercollegiate football begins in fall 2002.

Study Abroad The University offers more than forty study-abroad programs in many countries, including Bulgaria, Brazil, China, Costa Rica, the Czech Republic, England, France, Haiti, Italy, and Spain. Students may also attend one of more than 150 other U.S. institutions for up to one academic year through the National Student Exchange.

Support Services All facilities are fully accessible by students with disabilities, and the Office of Disabled Student Services provides academic support.

Job Opportunities Work opportunities on campus are numerous and include work-study, part-time employment, and assistantships.

Tuition: $2241.60 for state residents, $9579.30 for nonresidents, per year (30 semester hours, 2001–02)

Room: $2600 minimum

Contact: Dean: Dr. Ivelaw L. Griffith, University Park, DM 233, Miami, Florida 33199; Telephone: 305-348-4100; Fax: 305-348-2118; E-mail: griffiti@fiu.edu

Interpreting the symbols: **2**=two-year college, **4**=four-year college; **Pu**=public or state college, **Pr**=private college; **G**=general honors program; **D**=departmental honors program; **S**=small program (fewer than 100 students), **M**=midsize program (100 to 500 students), **L**=large program (more than 500 students); **Sc**=scholarships available in honors program; **Tr**=transfer students accepted into honors program; **HBC**=historically black college; **AA**=academic advisors; **GA**=graduate advisors; **FA**=fellowship advisors.

Florida Southern College

4 Pr G S Tr

▼ The Honors Program

The Honors Program at Florida Southern College encourages students more to develop a wisdom about life than to increase knowledge about any particular subject area. The College believes that the truly educated sense the beauty, drama, and meaning of life in addition to knowing factual information about their major fields of study. To that end, every course in the Honors Program is interdisciplinary, prompting students to experience the subtle yet dynamic ways that all knowledge is interconnected.

Florida Southern was established in 1998 and has grown consistently, with a 2001–02 enrollment of 40 students. The Honors Program continues to create an environment where creativity, open discussion, a dynamic community of bright students, great ideas, and mentoring relationships with members of the faculty combine to help students comprehend the art of life.

At the freshman and sophomore levels, honors students enroll in seminars of no more than 15 students. These seminars are team-taught by faculty members from different disciplines who invite participants to read, research, and discuss topics of a critical and controversial nature. Recent seminars include Dialogues in Science and Religion, taught by faculty members from the biology and religion departments; From Reflection to Revolution: The Lightning Changes from Classical to Romantic Culture, taught by faculty members from English and music; The Florida Environment: Place, Ecology, and Culture, taught by faculty members from chemistry and English; and Political/ Economic Studies: A Comparison of Developing and Developed Nations, taught by faculty members from economics and political science departments. In these courses, students often take field trips, have guest speakers, and attend lectures and performances to augment the classroom experience. The intimate nature of these seminars promotes close relationships among students and between students and faculty members.

At the junior and senior levels, honors students participate in colloquia, which are courses that allow the students to pursue topics more of their own choosing while still maintaining the interdisciplinary focus. The junior colloquium invites students to interact with the artistic and scholarly world around them; they individually choose the cultural and intellectual events to attend and share their observations with the class as a whole. The senior colloquium calls for honors students to take an active role in solving a problem in the community, giving the students not only a better sense of their place as citizens, but also the real-world experience of confronting a critical issue. In this capstone course, the students work as a group, with each contributing their specific talents, skills, and specialized knowledge. For example, a recent senior colloquium instituted a more comprehensive recycling program on campus, with a biology major helping with the scientific research, a business major preparing the budget, a communications major developing an ad campaign, and a music major and a history major recruiting volunteers.

Outside of the classroom, honors students have developed a camaraderie through a mentoring program for first-year students that pairs them with a junior or senior. Camaraderie is also established through the Association of Honors Students, a campus-recognized club that sponsors trips to plays and performances off the Florida Southern campus, including sending students to the meeting of the Florida Collegiate Honors Council.

In terms of admission to the program, the Honors Committee reviews the records of all high school students accepted to Florida Southern College. Admission to the program is guaranteed for those students who will be graduating with an international baccalaureate diploma, or who have a combined SAT I score of 1250 or above or ACT composite score of 28 or above. Those students with an SAT I score of 1160 to 1249 or an ACT of 26 or 27 will be sent a brief application and will be encouraged to apply. Students who do not meet either of these requirements and are still interested in the Honors Program should contact the director of the program for more information at the address listed below.

Participation Requirements: To earn the distinction of being an Honors Scholar at Florida Southern College, students must take six semesters of honors courses, with a minimum of 18 semester credit hours, and at least three semesters of both seminars and colloquia. By the end of their junior year, students must have a cumulative GPA of at least 3.5 and they must maintain this minimum average through graduation. Students are also expected to uphold the highest standards of academic integrity. Those students who have earned the distinction of Honors Scholar will have that accomplishment noted both on the graduation program and on their transcript and they will be allowed to wear special insignia at graduation.

Scholarship Availability: Florida Southern College gives substantial academic scholarships, but none specifically through the Honors Program.

The Campus Context: Florida Southern College is a four-year, private, coeducational liberal arts college that is affiliated with the United Methodist Church. Located in Lakeland, Florida, a pleasant community of 90,000, the campus consists of approximately 100 acres on the shore of Lake Hollingsworth, and is home to the largest single-site collection of Frank Lloyd Wright architecture in the world. The College offers more than forty undergraduate majors and a master of business administration degree accredited by the Commission on Colleges of the Southern Association of Colleges and Schools. Preprofessional programs are offered in dentistry, law, engineering, medicine, physical therapy, theology, and veterinary medicine; professional programs include accounting, business management, citrus marketing, and education, among others. Less than an hour from both Tampa and Orlando's cultural and recreational opportunities, the College is ideally situated for internships and job opportunities with leading corporations.

Students enjoy state-of-the-art facilities on campus, including the renovated and updated science laboratories, the enhanced computer classrooms across campus, the new music instruction and performance building, and the outstanding wellness center with its pool, gymnasium, aerobics/dance studio, and weight/training room.

Student Body Florida Southern College has an enrollment of approximately 1,750 students. Approximately 60 percent of the students are women, 11 percent represent minorities, and 5 percent are international students. Seventy-seven percent of students receive some form of financial aid. There are six national fraternities and five national sororities on campus.

Faculty Of the 108 full-time faculty members at Florida Southern College, 83.5 percent have their terminal degree. The faculty is primarily a teaching faculty, with members selected not only for their teaching ability, but also for their ability to relate to the needs and concerns of college students. The student-faculty ratio is 16:1.

Key Facilities The Roux Library has more than 140,000 volumes, more than 400,000 microform pieces, more than 7,000 video and audio titles, and more than 700 periodical subscriptions. There are approximately 250 IBM-compatible computers available in nine computer labs, and 75 Macintosh computers available in five laboratories.

Honor Societies Phi Eta Sigma (interdisciplinary)

Athletics Florida Southern College competes in the following NCAA Division II sports: baseball (men only), basketball, cross-country, golf, soccer, softball (women only), tennis, and volleyball (women only). Florida Southern is a member of the Sunshine State Conference.

Study Abroad More students, approximately 100 each year, are taking advantage of the varied study abroad opportunities at Florida Southern. A range of semester-long programs is available through the Study Abroad Office, and the College's affiliations with colleges in England and Mexico facilitate study abroad in those countries. Each summer, faculty members take groups of students to study abroad in England, Spain, and throughout Europe.

Support Services All campus buildings are wheelchair accessible. There are several residence hall rooms specifically reserved for students in wheelchairs, and bathrooms and drinking fountains across campus are appropriately designed to accomodate students.

Job Opportunities The Financial Aid Office assists students with work-study placement. The Career Services Office maintains a listing of jobs available on and off campus and also assists students with finding full-time employment upon graduation. Also, most departments offer an internship program for students.

Tuition: Full-time costs are $6850 per semester; $13,700 per year (2001–02)

Room and Board: $2650-$2800, depending upon meal plan (2001–02)

Mandatory Fees: Activities and technology fees of $115 per semester; $230 per year

Contact: Dr. Alexander M. Bruce, Assistant Dean for Academic Affairs, Florida Southern College, 111 Lake Hollingsworth Drive, Lakeland, Florida 33801; Telephone: 863-680-4124; Fax: 863-680-3088 Web site: http://www.flsouthern.edu/Honors/index.htm

Florida State University

4 Pu G L Sc Tr

▼ University Honors Program

The Florida State University (FSU) Honors Program is nourished by deep liberal arts roots planted in the 1850s. Florida State University is the home of the first Phi Beta Kappa chapter in Florida, and the University Honors Program supports the University's tradition of academic excellence by offering two intellectually challenging curricula—the Liberal Studies Honors Program and the Honors in the Major Program. The University broadly supports the honors program, with more than 300 Florida State faculty members teaching honors courses and serving on honors thesis committees each year.

Florida State offers the University Honors Colloquium and three types of liberal studies honors courses. The Honors Colloquium is a 1-credit-hour weekly forum featuring lectures by distinguished FSU faculty members from across the scholarly and creative arts spectrum, as well as informative presentations from directors of academic programs of interest to honors students. The colloquium is a required course for entering freshman honors students, and the ongoing theme "Art and Inquiry in the Modern University" provides a common intellectual experience for new honors students and also introduces students to the culture and opportunities of a modern research university. Honors seminars are special-topics courses in the humanities, natural sciences, and social sciences, limited to 15 students per course. Honors-only courses are special sections of regular courses that are offered only to honors students. Enrollment is typically limited to 25 students. Students have a choice of thirty to forty honors sections each fall and spring. Honors-augmented courses are regularly scheduled classes in which selected faculty members agree to supervise special projects or additional assignments to enable honors students to earn credit toward the program.

More than sixty departments offer the Honors in the Major Program for students pursuing independent research or creative expression thesis-writing projects. Guided by an honors committee of 3 faculty members, the student carries out the research, creative work, and writing during the junior and senior years. Upon successfully defending the thesis before the supervisory committee, the student receives the designation of having graduated with honors in their major at commencement. Students do not have to be in the Liberal Studies Honors Program to participate in the Honors in the Major Program.

The Honors Council is an elected board of honors students, who act as liaison between honors students, administration, and student government. They represent the program at state and national conferences and plan extracurricular and social events for students in the program.

There are approximately 2,600 students in the program, with roughly 10 percent in the Honors in the Major Program.

Participation Requirements: Students must maintain at least a 3.2 cumulative GPA and complete 18 credit hours of honors classes in order to finish the program. To participate in the Honors in the Major Program, upper-level students (60 or more credit hours) must have completed at least 12 credit hours at FSU, have a cumulative GPA of at least 3.2, and have a project and major professor.

Admission Process: Students must have at least a 3.9 weighted high school GPA (as calculated by the FSU Office of Admissions) and either a minimum 1300 SAT I or a minimum 29 ACT score to be invited into the Liberal Studies Honors Program. Additional information can be found at the University's Web site listed below.

Scholarship Availability: Academic scholarships are awarded by the FSU Undergraduate Admissions Office. Honors students are also eligible for Bess Ward Scholarships administered by the program to help support study abroad.

The Campus Context: Florida State University is located on 463.4 acres in Tallahassee, the Florida state capital. At FSU, emphasis is placed upon advanced-degree programs entailing extensive research activities and preparation for careers in science, the arts, the humanities, the professions, and technological fields. FSU is ranked by the Carnegie Foundation as a Category I research institution and has an established international reputation. It provides for undergraduate students a strong liberal arts–based baccalaureate experience. There are sixteen colleges on the FSU campus, including colleges of engineering, law, and theater, with the latest addition being the College of Medicine—the first new U. S. medical school in more than twenty years. The University currently offers ninety bachelor's degree programs, 100 master's degree programs, thirty advanced master's/specialist degree programs, seventy-two doctoral degree programs, and one professional degree program.

Student Body Of the undergraduates enrolled at FSU, 54.6 percent are women, 72.5 percent are Caucasian, 11.9 percent are African American, 8.1 percent are Hispanic, and 2.7 percent are Asian.

Key Facilities FSU has numerous computer labs open to students, with high-speed access to the Internet and a wide range of Web-based resources (e.g., registration, fee payment, online journals, and course Web sites). Many individual departments also have separate computer labs for students within those majors.

Interpreting the symbols: **2**=two-year college, **4**=four-year college; **Pu**=public or state college, **Pr**=private college; **G**=general honors program; **D**=departmental honors program; **S**=small program (fewer than 100 students), **M**=midsize program (100 to 500 students), **L**=large program (more than 500 students); **Sc**=scholarships available in honors program; **Tr**=transfer students accepted into honors program; **HBC**=historically black college; **AA**=academic advisors; **GA**=graduate advisors; **FA**=fellowship advisors.

Landis-Gilchrist, the University's honors residence-hall complex, is the focal point for a variety of extracurricular activities sponsored by the Honors Council and provides a living environment that facilitates interaction among honors participants. Honors students are not required to live in the honors residence complex. FSU has twelve residence halls accommodating approximately 4,000 undergraduates. These halls have varied visitation policies and special programs.

Study Abroad The FSU Honors Program strongly encourages study abroad and each semester offers merit-based scholarships to honors students participating in FSU's international programs in London, Florence, Moscow, Dublin, and many other locations. For more information on FSU's international programs, including a current list of program sites, students should visit the University's Web site listed below.

Tuition: $2513 for state residents and $10,402 for nonresidents, per year (2001–02)

Room and Board: $5322

Contact: Director: Dr. Kenneth A. Goldsby, 3600 UCA, Florida State University, Tallahassee, Florida 32306-2380; Telephone: 850-644-1841; Fax: 850-644-2101; Web site: http://www.fsu/~honors

Foothill College

2 Pu G M Tr

▼ Honors Institute

The Foothill College Honors Institute offers an extensive program designed to prepare academically talented students for transfer to selective colleges and universities. As a two-year California community college located in the educationally rich Bay Area midway between San Francisco and San Jose, Foothill provides an ideal environment for the first two years of undergraduate education. Special courses and cocurricular activities help prepare honors students for transfer to some of the nation's finest universities.

Honors courses offer a stimulating opportunity to study with other highly motivated students who seek a more rigorous academic experience. These courses are taught by outstanding members of the Foothill College faculty who hold master's or doctoral degrees in their subject of expertise. There is an emphasis on critical-thinking and writing skills, on participating in lively discussions and collaborative work with other students, and on self-directed learning. Honors students work closely with an Honors Institute academic adviser.

Some benefits offered to honors students include priority registration, transfer seminars, quarterly newsletters, scholarship information, and complimentary tickets to cultural events. The Honors Institute offers transfer incentives in the form of partnership agreements with several universities that enable honors students to receive priority admission consideration.

Foothill College's Honors Institute was established in 1983. There are currently 150 students enrolled.

Participation Requirements: Honors sections of general education courses are offered each quarter. Students select the honors courses that meet the needs of their major and transfer program. A minimum GPA of 3.5 must be maintained in order to continue in the program. Each course taken in the Honors Institute carries an "Honors" notation on the transcript. Any student who completes six designated honors courses with a grade of A or B earns the Honors Scholar distinction, which is recognized with a certificate, honored at graduation with a medal, and noted on the transcript.

Admission Process: Students are invited to apply for the Honors Institute based on admission test scores, high school or college scholastic performance (a minimum of 3.5 GPA on a 4.0 scale), an autobiographical essay, and a letter of personal recommendation.

Scholarship Availability: The Honors Institute currently does not offer scholarships to its members. Information about statewide and national scholarships is broadly publicized to honors students throughout the year. Past graduates of Foothill College have received awards at these levels.

The Campus Context: The Foothill College campus offers an impressive array of learning facilities, including large and diverse computer instruction centers, a dental hygiene clinic, animal health technology and ornamental horticultural complexes, a student-operated radio station, and the new Center for Innovation. The campus also houses the Japanese Cultural Center, a large performance theater, a fitness center, and an Olympic-size swimming pool.

The unique award-winning Pacific-style architecture creates an elegant but energizing setting on 125 picturesque acres in the coastal range foothills. This area, located just 45 minutes south of San Francisco in the heart of Silicon Valley, is rich in cultural, educational, and recreational opportunities. A.A. and A.S. degrees are granted in seventy majors.

Student Body Undergraduate enrollment is 18,600, of whom 49 percent are women. The ethnic distribution of the student body is 3 percent African American, 1 percent Native American, 20 percent Asian, 2 percent Filipino, 1 percent Pacific Islander, 11 percent Hispanic, 49 percent Caucasian, and 13 percent other. International students number 600. All students commute to campus, and 14 percent of students receive financial aid. A broad range of extracurricular activities, such as special interest clubs, scholastic and service organizations, sports, and student government, offer students a chance to expand their education beyond the classroom. Foothill College is not a residence school, hence there are no fraternities or sororities.

Faculty There are 191 full-time and 433 part-time faculty members. Approximately 21 percent have doctoral degrees and 63 percent have master's. The student-faculty ratio is estimated at 29:1.

Key Facilities The library houses 75,000 volumes. Students have access to numerous computer facilities. The library has fifteen computers linked to the Internet, with full access to libraries nationwide. Other facilities include the Math Computer Lab, the new Center for Innovation, the Open Computer Lab, the Language Arts Writing Computer Lab, and the IDEA Lab, which is used for fine arts and multimedia. The CTIS Division has four computer labs and a Business Computer Lab.

Honorary Societies Phi Theta Kappa and Alpha Gamma Sigma

Athletics A full schedule of athletic programs is available for men and women interested in competitive team sports, including basketball, golf, soccer, swimming, track and field, water polo, women's volleyball, men's football, and tennis.

Study Abroad Participants in the Campus Abroad Program enjoy an exceptional opportunity to immerse themselves in international cultures while enrolled in regular Foothill courses for credit. Field trips enhance the classwork taught by Foothill faculty members at the campus sites in England, France, Italy, Germany, Mexico, Costa Rica, and Vietnam.

Support Services The Special Education Division offers courses and services on campus and in the community designed to help physically, communicatively, developmentally, and psychologically disabled adults. A full range of support services is available on campus, including testing, tutoring, counseling, and computer training.

Job Opportunities Work opportunities on campus are available.

Tuition: $7 per unit for state residents of California, $89 per unit for nonresidents, and $96 per unit for international students, per year (2002–03). Basic fees total $28.50, which include a student identification card, health services, campus center use, student representation, and a registration support fee.

Contact: Director: Janice Carr, Honors Institute, 12345 El Monte Road, Los Altos Hills, California 94022; Telephone: 650-949-7638; Fax: 650-949-7594; E-mail: honors@fhda.edu; Web site: http://www.fhda.edu/hon/index.html

FORDHAM UNIVERSITY

4 Pr S Sc Tr

▼ Fordham College at Rose Hill Honors Program

The Fordham College at Rose Hill Honors Program is distinguished by its comprehensive and integrated approach to learning. The heart of the program is a sequence of courses taken during the freshman and sophomore years. These courses work together to provide a comprehensive overview of the intellectual and social forces that have shaped the modern world. Each semester in this sequence is devoted to an integrated study of the art, history, literature, music, philosophy, and religion of a particular period. In addition, special courses in mathematics and the sciences for nonscience majors help to bring out these disciplines' important role in contemporary society. This sequence is followed by two courses in the junior year that focus on different social and ethical problems of the modern world. The capstone of the honors curriculum is the senior thesis, an extended research project prepared under the individual guidance of a faculty mentor in one's major field.

The Honors Program is not intended for passive students who are satisfied simply to accept and give back the contents of their professors' lectures. Instead, the program offers an environment where students are able to take the initiative in their own education. In order to foster such active learning, most honors classes are seminars of 12 to 14 students that take place around the long wooden table in Alpha House, the program's own building on campus.

A distinctive curriculum and an ideal learning environment are obviously important elements of the Fordham College Honors Program. What really makes the program special, however, is the community of exceptional students who are its members. Such students come from a wide variety of backgrounds and have a number of different majors and career goals. Recent graduates are indicative of this diversity and include students who went on to attend the Johns Hopkins Medical School, the University of Chicago Law School, and Yale Law School. Another recent graduate had to defer her acceptance to Harvard's graduate program in biology in order to study at Oxford on a Fulbright Scholarship. The Honors Program regularly includes among its membership campus leaders in journalism, politics, drama, sports, and community service.

The Honors Program provides an opportunity for such diverse students to get to know each other outside, as well as inside, the classroom. A number of extracurricular activities bring honors students together throughout the year, and these often give students the chance to meet informally with the honors faculty as well. Every honors student has his or her own key to Alpha House, a facility that is available for either private study or meetings with other students 24 hours a day.

The small size of honors classes makes it impossible to invite every qualified student into the program.

Participation Requirements: The honors curriculum takes the place of the regular Fordham College core curriculum, with the exception of the language requirement. Credit is, of course, granted for Advanced Placement courses taken in high school and for college courses taken elsewhere. Successful completion of the program entitles the student to the designation *in cursu honorum* on the diploma and the transcript.

Admission Process: Admission into the program is quite competitive, with usually no more than 25 to 28 incoming students entering the program each year. A limited number of first-year students with strong academic records are invited to join the program during their freshman year.

Scholarship Availability: Honors students usually receive Presidential or Dean's Scholarships in addition to their regular financial aid.

The Campus Context: Founded in 1841, Fordham University is New York City's Jesuit university, attracting more than 14,000 students annually to its ten undergraduate, graduate, and professional schools. The campus offers undergraduates thirty-five majors plus the possibility of designing an individualized major. Fordham College at Rose Hill is a four-year liberal arts college for full-time students. Located on 85 acres in the North Bronx, next to the New York Botanical Garden and the Bronx Zoo, Rose Hill is the largest "green campus" in New York.

Student Body There are approximately 3,000 undergraduates at Fordham College at Rose Hill. Fifty-five percent of the students are women. The 2,000 resident students live in two residential colleges offering programs that integrate academic and social life under the guidance of a resident "master."

Faculty Of the 224 full-time faculty members, 98.6 percent have terminal degrees. The student-faculty ratio is 17:1.

Key Facilities The campus has a 1.6-million-volume library.

Honorary Societies Phi Kappa Phi, Phi Beta Kappa, and Alpha Sigma Nu

Athletics Intercollegiate athletics include baseball, basketball, cross-country, football, golf, soccer, softball, swimming and diving, tennis, volleyball, and water polo. Fordham participates in the Atlantic 10 Conference for all sports except football, which participates in the Patriot League. A wide range of intramural opportunities is also available.

Study Abroad Study abroad is encouraged for all honors students. Fordham maintains its own study-abroad programs at University College, Dublin; Sogang University in Seoul, South Korea; Blackfriars College, Oxford; Westcott House, Cambridge; Iberoamericana University, Mexico City; and Beijing Institute of Language and Culture, China.

Tuition: Full-time: $18,875 per year; part-time: $629 per credit (1999–2000)

Room and Board: $7720 minimum

Mandatory Fees: $570

Contact: Director: Dr. Harry P. Nasuti, Bronx, New York 10458; Telephone: 718-817-3212; Fax: 718-817-4720; E-mail: ss_nasuti@lars.fordham.edu

FRAMINGHAM STATE COLLEGE

4 Pu G S Sc

▼ Honors Program

The Framingham State College Honors Program is designed to provide academically talented students with the opportunity to enrich their college experience. Courses bearing the honors designation are designed to be intensive experiences that are intellectually challenging and emphasize creativity and analytical thinking.

Honors courses are designed for a maximum enrollment of 15 to 20 students to foster in-depth class discussion and a close

Interpreting the symbols: 2=two-year college, 4=four-year college; **Pu**=public or state college, **Pr**=private college; **G**=general honors program; **D**=departmental honors program; **S**=small program (fewer than 100 students), **M**=midsize program (100 to 500 students), **L**=large program (more than 500 students); **Sc**=scholarships available in honors program; **Tr**=transfer students accepted into honors program; **HBC**=historically black college; **AA**=academic advisors; **GA**=graduate advisors; **FA**=fellowship advisors.

student-instructor relationship. All honors courses may be applied to the general education requirements specified by the College. Honors courses may be taken by students who are not participating in the program on a space-available basis with the permission of the instructor.

Upon their arrival on campus, honors students receive a special orientation to the College and its Honors Program. Thereafter, these students convene regularly to share information, exchange ideas, and discuss topics of interest. Each honors student has a special Honors Program adviser who assists in course selection. Residents may choose to live in a special residence hall reserved for honors students. Because the program is available to majors from every department on campus, the Academic Vice-President, the Director of the Honors Program, the Honors Program Advisory Committee, and the department chairs make a special effort to develop and offer a wide variety of challenging courses.

In addition, funds are regularly set aside for honors field trips in order to engage guest speakers and performing artists and for other activities intended to enrich learning. In certain courses and in the senior seminar, the team approach is used so that students receive an extra measure of instruction and mentoring en route to meeting their objectives. In essence, the program seeks to expose participants to the best the College has to offer.

Founded in 1990, the program currently enrolls approximately 60 students.

Participation Requirements: Freshmen entering the Framingham State College Honors Program must complete the core courses entitled "Expository Writing" and "The Comparative History of World Civilizations." During the remaining three years, participants are required to complete a minimum of four more courses bearing the honors designation, including the honors senior seminar.

Course topics and information about honors courses to be offered can be found in the *Schedule of Classes Bulletin* or through the program administrator's office. During their senior year, participating students must enroll in the honors senior seminar. As a condition of continued enrollment in the Honors Program, a freshman or sophomore must maintain a GPA of at least 3.0 overall and in honors courses. Students falling below these requirements are allowed to continue in the program for a probationary period of one semester. Subsequent continuance is at the discretion of the Honors Program Committee.

Honors students have priority in course registration, special advising, and a customized program of extracurricular enrichment activities. Participation in the Framingham State College Honors Program is noted on the students' transcripts. Students who complete the program also receive a certificate of recognition. The notation of honors student is made on the transcript and the diploma, and students are recognized at graduation.

Admission Process: Entering freshmen are invited to participate in the Framingham State College Honors Program based on a weighted composite of their combined SAT I scores, class rank, and demonstrated potential for superior work at the college level. Any student admitted to the College who was not initially invited to participate in the program may apply directly to the Honors Program Committee for admission. Students may also apply for admission to the Framingham State College Honors Program as sophomores. A minimum GPA of 3.25 together with two letters of recommendation from faculty members and a brief statement of intent should be submitted to the Honors Committee for evaluation before October 1 of the student's sophomore year.

Scholarship Availability: Scholarships are awarded annually to the top 5 honors students who have taken at least three honors courses and are in good standing. Scholarship recipients are recognized at the annual awards assembly of the College.

The Campus Context: Framingham State College is a one-college institution offering ninety-two degree programs.

Student Body Framingham State has an undergraduate enrollment that is 63 percent women. The ethnic distribution of students is 81 percent Caucasian, 2.3 percent African American, 1.8 percent Hispanic, 2 percent Asian or Pacific Islander, 0.4 percent Native American, and 12.7 percent other. There are 66 international students. Forty percent of the students are residents, and 55 percent of students receive financial aid. There are no fraternities or sororities on campus.

Faculty Of the 228 faculty members, 175 are full-time; 77.33 percent have terminal degrees. The student-faculty ratio is 15:1.

Key Facilities The library houses 200,000 print volumes, 1,600 periodical titles and 60,000 volume equivalents in microform. Computer facilities include four general purpose computer labs (130 PCs), four PCs with network access in the Center for Academic Support and Advising, twenty Macs in the Communication Arts Department Lab, fifteen Macs in the Computer Graphics Laboratory in the Art Department, twenty PCs in the Multimedia Laboratory for student and faculty member use in the Media Center of the library. Wiring in the residence halls allows each student to have network access from his or her room.

Athletics Framingham State College offers twelve intercollegiate NCAA Division III sports in addition to coed equestrian and cheerleading. The programs for men include football, basketball, soccer, ice hockey, baseball, and cross-country track. The programs for women are field hockey, soccer, volleyball, basketball, softball, and cross-country track. In addition to the varsity and club offerings, intramural athletics involve more than 2,000 students in seventeen different sports. Through student government, women's and men's rugby are offered at the club level.

In order to ensure that the athletic needs of students are met, an interest survey is administered to each entering class. The commonwealth of Massachusetts has approved $6.2 million to cover half the cost of the proposed human-performance and wellness center. The facility will house varsity, intramural, and recreational sports for men, women, students, and faculty and staff members. It also will accommodate disabled athletes and spectators.

Study Abroad There are many study-abroad opportunities available for students. The Modern Languages Department offers study abroad in Spain, Mexico, Latin America, France, and the Province of Quebec. By arrangement, students in other departments may spend as many as two semesters in foreign study.

Support Services Disabled students find that Framingham State College is an institutional member of Recording for the Blind and Dyslexic and a network member of the Massachusetts Radio Reading Service. The campus provides note takers and custom recorded books for its disabled students in addition to a variety of accommodations available at the Center for Academic Support and Advising.

Job Opportunities On-campus student employment falls into the categories of work-study and student payroll. For work-study, a student must be eligible for financial aid. About 1 percent of the financial aid given to students is in the form of compensation for work-study. Among the other employment opportunities for students on campus are employment by the Residence Life Office to staff the desks at the entrances to six of the seven residence halls. Desks are staffed 24 hours per day throughout the academic year in order to ensure that regulations regarding parietal hours are enforced. Desk workers also sort mail.

Food services employs students to work in the three dining facilities on campus. The College Center maintains a large student payroll to help with student activities and college functions. Students are hired as building managers, information booth attendants, gameroom attendants, set-up crews, and pub workers. These students undergo an extensive training program.

The Student Government Association employs students as escorts to accompany students around campus after the college shuttle bus stops operating at 9:30 p.m. This service runs seven days per week until 3 a.m. The College Library employs non-work-study students. Lastly, the athletic department hires students to assist with keeping statistics at home and away games, running the time clocks, refereeing intramural games, and providing additional office support. The College sponsors a job fair for students interested in on-campus employment. Both work-study and student-payroll employers attend.

Tuition and Fees: $3156 for state residents, $8396 for nonresidents, per year (1998–99)

Room and Board: $3999

Contact: Director: Dr. Nicholas S. Racheotes, c/o the Dean of Undergraduate Education, P.O. Box 9101, Framingham, Massachusetts 01701-9101, Telephone: 508-626-4810; Fax: 508-626-4022; E-mail: nracheo@frc.mass.edu; Web site: http://www.framingham.edu

Francis Marion University

4 Pu G M Tr AA

▼ Honors Program

The Honors Program at Francis Marion University offers higher education that includes extra value. It gives gifted and ambitious students in all majors the opportunity to work with the University's most challenging faculty members in small but stimulating classes, engage in interdisciplinary study that synthesizes knowledge from different disciplines, and achieve their full intellectual potential in preparation for careers and/or graduate or professional school. Participants in the Honors Program are encouraged to take an active role in the learning process and to enter into dialogue with their professors and classmates.

Most honors classes at Francis Marion University are chosen from basic courses that meet general education requirements but employ different, more collaborative, interactive, and interdisciplinary methods and are limited to an enrollment of 15 students per course. Fifteen honors courses (some including labs) are usually offered each fall and spring semester. There are always some upper-division courses. Three special classes, the Core Concepts Continuum for freshmen and the Honors Colloquium and the Honors Independent Study for upperclassmen, are exciting and engaging offerings available only to Honors Program students. Many honors classes meet in the Honors Room, a pleasant seminar-style space, with room to lounge and study when classes are finished. Coffee and hot chocolate are provided, and the room is decorated with framed posters from past fall honors trips. Honors classes often incorporate field trips, dinners, or other special events, and the Honors Program itself offers periodic receptions and other opportunities for honors students and faculty members to meet.

An important feature of the Honors Program is the Honors Student Association (HSA). Membership is open to all honors-eligible students but is optional. HSA coordinates social and academic activities, including receptions, Play Nights, visits with state legislators in Columbia, fund-raising and service activities, and social events. Since 1996, the Honors Program and HSA have sponsored an annual fall trip in November. Groups of 35 students, accompanied by 6 faculty members, have enjoyed fall trips to Washington, D.C.; New York City; Boston; and Orlando (to attend an NCHC Conference). The cost of the fall trips for students is minimal, thanks to University subsidy.

Honors students in their junior year can apply for admission to the Washington Semester Program coordinated by the University of South Carolina's Honors College. Students accepted as fellows live and work in Washington, D.C., for a semester while earning 15 hours of honors credit.

Plans are currently under way to create special honors housing opportunities within the existing residence facilities. Of the approximately 500 honors-eligible students, 150 are usually enrolled in one to three honors classes in a given semester. The Honors Program was founded in 1985.

Participation Requirements: Initial eligibility for the Honors Program is determined by SAT or ACT scores. A minimum score of 1100 on the SAT or 24 on the ACT qualifies an entering student for the Honors Program. Second-semester freshmen must earn an overall GPA of 3.0 or better in order to become or remain eligible for the Honors Program. Sophomores, juniors, and seniors must earn an overall GPA of 3.25 or better in order to become or remain eligible for the Honors Program.

To graduate "With University Honors," students must complete 21 semester hours of honors classes with a minimum GPA of 3.25. Courses taken for at least 9 of these 21 semester hours must be numbered 300 or above. In addition, students must achieve a grade of B or higher in the Honors Colloquium, which deals with a special topic from an interdisciplinary perspective, and successfully complete an Honors Independent Study project. Students graduating "With University Honors" are awarded a gold Honors Cord at commencement, and each year the University gives a cash prize to the recipient of the Duane P. Myers Honors Award.

Admission Process: Students applying to Francis Marion University with a minimum SAT score of 1100 or a minimum ACT score of 24 are automatically eligible to participate in the Honors Program. The Honors Director and faculty members advise these students as a group, with assistance from current honors students, at their orientation and registration sessions. Students may earn or lose honors eligibility, as described in the section above, while enrolled at Francis Marion University.

Scholarship Availability: Francis Marion University gives substantial academic scholarships, but none through the Honors Program. The honors budget provides funding to support students' research projects and student travel to present papers or panels at conferences.

The Campus Context: Francis Marion University, named for General Francis Marion (the "Swamp Fox") of Revolutionary War fame, was established by the South Carolina legislature in 1970 and is a public four-year coeducational comprehensive institution with a growing number of graduate programs.

Located on a beautifully landscaped 300-acre tract of land, Francis Marion University is 7 miles east of Florence (population 125,000), an hour's drive from Myrtle Beach, and 4 hours from the Blue Ridge Mountains.

Francis Marion, which is accredited by the Southern Association of Colleges and Schools (SACS), offers four undergraduate degrees (Bachelor of Arts, Bachelor of Business Administration, Bachelor of General Studies, and Bachelor of Science) with more than thirty areas of study available, including majors, cooperative programs with other institutions, preprofessional programs, and teacher certification options. There are graduate programs in business administration, education, and applied psychology.

Francis Marion has the look and feel of a small liberal arts college with all the benefits of a state-supported comprehensive university.

Student Body Enrollment is approximately 2,800 undergraduate students and 800 graduate students. Ninety-three percent are in-state students, but thirty-two states and thirty-four countries are represented. Undergraduate enrollment is approximately 61 percent women and 39 percent men; the ethnic breakdown is 63 percent white, 31 percent African American, and 6 percent other.

Interpreting the symbols: **2**=two-year college, **4**=four-year college; **Pu**=public or state college, **Pr**=private college; **G**=general honors program; **D**=departmental honors program; **S**=small program (fewer than 100 students), **M**=midsize program (100 to 500 students), **L**=large program (more than 500 students); **Sc**=scholarships available in honors program; **Tr**=transfer students accepted into honors program; **HBC**=historically black college; **AA**=academic advisors; **GA**=graduate advisors; **FA**=fellowship advisors.

Approximately 1,100 students live in on-campus residence halls or apartments. There are eight national fraternities and seven national sororities represented on campus.

Faculty Francis Marion employs 165 full-time faculty members, about 84 percent of whom hold doctoral degrees, and 42 part-time faculty members. Sixty percent of the faculty members are tenured; professors, not graduate students, teach classes. The student-faculty ratio is 15:1, and the average class size is 20.

Key Facilities The James A. Rogers Library is the state's sixth-biggest academic library and the largest in northeastern South Carolina. Its holdings include more than 370,000 volumes, 430,000 microforms, and numerous electronic databases to access information from almost anywhere. Academic Computing Services provides information technology resources and services; in addition, there are eleven distributed student computer labs across the campus, as well as more than thirty terminals in the library. All residence halls have Internet access.

Honorary Societies Phi Kappa Phi and Omicron Delta Kappa

Athletics Francis Marion is in the NCAA Division II Peach Belt Conference, with seven sports each for men and women: men's baseball, men's and women's basketball, men's and women's cross-country, men's golf, men's and women's soccer, women's softball, men's and women's tennis, men's and women's track and field, and women's volleyball.

Study Abroad Francis Marion has exchange programs with universities in Australia, Germany, Mexico, and Switzerland. Exchanges are being developed with universities in France and Great Britain.

Support Services Francis Marion is committed to making programs and activities available to qualified students with disabilities. The University grounds, major buildings, and classes are accessible to individuals with disabilities. Reasonable accommodations (including but not limited to notetakers, interpreters, extended time for examinations, and arrangements for taped books) are coordinated for students with appropriately documented physical and learning disabilities. Several students in the Honors Program are in this category.

Job Opportunities There are several programs offered that enable students to work part-time in various departments on campus, including the Federal Work-Study Program. Information concerning part-time off-campus employment is available from the Office of Career Development, which also provides career counseling.

Tuition: In 2001–02, tuition for a full-time undergraduate resident student was $1810 per semester; a full-time undergraduate nonresident student paid $3620 per semester. A part-time resident student paid $181 per hour; a part-time nonresident student paid $362 per hour.

Room and Board: Charges for different types of housing are Type A (4 students), $951 per semester; Type B (2 students), $1006 per semester; Type C (residence hall, including meals), $1946 per semester; and private room (including meals), $2422 per semester. Available meal plans are the fourteen-meal plan for $925, the nineteen-meal plan for $995, and a debit plan in any amount.

Mandatory Fees: In 2001–02, a full-time undergraduate resident student paid $95 per semester in mandatory fees; a full-time undergraduate out-of-state student paid $120 per semester in mandatory fees.

Contact: Director: Dr. Pamela Rooks, Professor of English, Francis Marion University, Post Office Box 100547, Florence, South Carolina 29501-0547; Telephone: 843-661-1526; Fax: 843-661-4676; E-mail: prooks@fmarion.edu; Web site: http://www.fmarion.edu/honors

Franciscan University of Steubenville

4 Pr C M Tr

▼ Great Books Honors Program

Cicero on old age, Aristotle on friendship and politics, the early Church fathers on justice. Franciscan University students take on these and many other timeless works through the Great Books Honors Program. The program familiarizes students with the great writings of Western civilization, which have been gradually disappearing from much of American higher education. This four-year-long series of eight 4-credit seminars offers an alternative way for top students to satisfy the University's core requirements.

The seminars are presented in chronological sequence, starting in the freshman year with the first written works of man (Early Classical Thought) and ending in the senior year with the influential writers of the twentieth century. The curriculum exposes students to the works of such writers as Homer, Plato, St. Augustine, St. Thomas Aquinas, Shakespeare, Jefferson, C. S. Lewis, John Paul II, and others.

Guided by the teaching authority of the Catholic Church, the honors program calls students to answer moral and ethical questions about the very meaning of life: who God is; what their place in the world is; the just war theory; honesty; friendship; love; heaven, hell, and purgatory; the role of music and education in society; and other timeless virtues and values.

The seminar approach teaches students the art of analysis and discussion, how to defend their position with reasoned arguments, and how to develop critical-thinking skills that can carry over to their major course of study and everyday life.

Faculty members from as many as eight academic departments teach in the program, including Classics, Theology, Philosophy, Psychology, English, and History. This provides a rich variety of perspectives as professor and students immerse themselves in the best recorded works on human and Christian wisdom.

Participation Requirements: To graduate as an honors scholar, students must successfully complete 32 credit hours of honors work or the equivalent of eight, 4-credit-hour honors seminars. For the beginning freshman, this requirement is met by taking one 4-credit-hour honors seminar each semester for eight semesters. The honors program satisfies the entire humanities and social science core and most of the courses required in the communications core.

Honors students are required to maintain an overall cumulative quality point average (QPA) of 3.0. and a 3.0 QPA in all honors program course work. Honors students who complete their honors course work with a QPA below 3.0 receive credit for each course but do not receive the "honors scholar" notation on their diploma.

Admission Process: In addition to completing an application, students interested in the Great Books Honors Program normally must have a cumulative average for high school course work of B+ or its equivalent and a score of 1200 on the SAT or 26 on the ACT. However, all admissions are subject to the judgment and discretion of the Honors Program Admissions Committee.

Scholarship Availability: Through a combination of grants, scholarships, loans, and student-worker opportunities, 85 percent of Franciscan University students receive financial aid. This is offered to needy students as well as to students with high academic achievements. The goal is to provide maximum financial aid from federal, state, private, and institutional sources.

The Campus Context: Ever mindful of the spirit of St. Francis of Assisi, Franciscan University of Steubenville, Ohio, takes to heart the divine directive given to St. Francis to "rebuild my Church"

by integrating strong academics with a lively faith environment. This "faith and reason" combination has been hailed by graduates, Church leaders, and educators for providing an invigorating Catholic liberal arts experience. The University is located in southeastern Ohio, 50 minutes from Pittsburgh. It offers more than thirty undergraduate programs, including eight preprofessional programs such as predentistry and premedicine and seven graduate programs. Programs unique to Franciscan University, in addition to the Great Books Honors Program, include the nation's only human life studies minor, which teaches students to think, speak, and act intelligently on human life issues, and a humanities and Catholic culture major. The undergraduate theology program, the largest in the country, allows students to learn from professors whose writings and presentations on the Catholic faith are known worldwide.

Student Body The University attracts students from all fifty states and twenty-six countries. Despite the recent enrollment growth to more than 2,200, the school maintains a 15:1 student-professor ratio.

Faculty There are 169 full-time and part-time faculty members, both lay and religious. Professors, not teaching assistants, teach at all class levels. Professors of all disciplines are committed to presenting Christian truths based on the teachings of the Roman Catholic Church and often present their material within a Catholic perspective.

Key Facilities The newest building on campus, Saints Cosmas and Damian Science Hall, offers state-of-the-art technology for science and math majors. The John Paul II Library collection includes nearly 230,000 books, 30,000 bound periodicals, and more than 700 current periodicals. The OPAL catalog and OhioLINK network provide access to countless Web sites and databases and more than 6.4 million books and journals.

Study Abroad A highlight of the Franciscan University experience for many students is spending a semester abroad, studying and living in a renovated fourteenth-century monastery near the Austrian Alps. The Austrian program features a four-day class schedule so students may spend extended time visiting religious shrines and cultural and historical sites throughout Europe.

Tuition: For the 2001–02 academic year, tuition and fees for full-time students were $13,900. Room and board costs were $5200.

Contact: Dr. Stephen Miletic, Dean of Faculty, Franciscan University of Steubenville, 1235 University Boulevard, Steubenville, Ohio, 43953; E-mail: smiletic@franuniv.edu; Admissions Department telephone: 800-783-6220; Admissions Department e-mail: admissions@franuniv.edu.

Freed–Hardeman University

4 Pr M Tr

▼ Honors College

The Freed-Hardeman University (FHU) Honors College seeks to provide the optimum educational experience for the talented student in the setting of a Christian university. In honors, attention is given to oral and written communication skills and to the ability to think and respond quickly under pressure. The program blends a strong emphasis on a liberal arts education with the opportunity to pursue guided, independent study in technical or specialized areas. Graduates of the program not only have the necessary theoretical knowledge for success in their field, but also possess problem-solving and communication skills.

Since 1974, the program has served to enhance the undergraduate experience of Freed-Hardeman's best students. Students in honors represent every department in the University having earned H grades (A with honors) in 250 different courses. The Honors Student Association has approximately 110 members.

Participation Requirements: Continued participation in the program or association requires that students maintain at least a 3.3 GPA.

Admission Process: Entry into the program is by invitation after an application process for incoming freshmen or by invitation based on GPA for students with more than 30 semester hours of completed work at FHU. Students transferring from honors programs at accredited colleges and universities are welcomed into honors at Freed-Hardeman and their prior honors work may count as much as 40 percent of the total requirements for graduation with honors. Honors College admission requires success in honors course work at FHU, appropriate GPA, letters of recommendation, and a personal interview.

Scholarship Availability: Freed-Hardeman offers a number of scholarships to students of exceptional ability. Many students receiving these scholarships are also in honors. The Joe and Malinda Ivey College Scholarship provides special assistance to students who are members of minority groups.

The Campus Context: Freed-Hardeman University traces its origin to the 1869 charter of a private high school and college for Henderson, Tennessee. The University is located in a clean, quiet, west Tennessee county-seat town of approximately 6,100 citizens. The campus consists of about 120 acres with twenty-five main buildings. Supplementing the cultural, entertainment, medical, and shopping facilities of Henderson are those of the regional center of Jackson, which is 17 miles north of campus.

The twelve academic departments at Freed-Hardeman University are grouped into six schools: Arts and Humanities, Biblical Studies, Business, Education, Honors College, and Sciences and Mathematics. Students may pursue the Bachelor of Arts, Bachelor of Science, Bachelor of Business Administration, or Bachelor of Social Work degrees. Approximately thirty majors with twenty-five different concentrations within those majors are available. Students may earn a Master of Education, Master of Ministry, Master of Arts in New Testament, or Master of Science in Counseling degree.

Student Body Undergraduate enrollment is 1,414; 52.5 percent of the students are women. The minority ethnic distribution of the total undergraduate population is 6 percent African American and less than 1 percent for all other minority groups. Eighty-seven percent of the students receive financial aid. Social clubs encourage spiritual growth, provide opportunities for social interaction, and present service projects.

Faculty There are 149 faculty members, of whom 93 are full-time and 73 percent have terminal degrees. The student-faculty ratio is 18:1.

Key Facilities Loden-Daniel Library holdings include more than 155,000 volumes, 234,000 microforms, and 1,600 periodicals. The catalog of the library's collection (LIONET) is automated and may be accessed remotely through the Internet. Information technology is an integral part of the library's services, and computer workstations are readily available to students and faculty members wishing to search the Internet. In addition, the library provides access to many online databases such as Ebscohost and ERIC.

Freed-Hardeman University has advanced voice, data, and video networks connecting twenty-five major buildings. Triplex outlets in offices, classrooms, laboratories, and residence hall rooms provide access to these networks. Four major student computer laboratories, smaller department laboratories, and library microcomputers are available each day and most evenings dur-

Interpreting the symbols: **2**=two-year college, **4**=four-year college; **Pu**=public or state college, **Pr**=private college; **G**=general honors program; **D**=departmental honors program; **S**=small program (fewer than 100 students), **M**=midsize program (100 to 500 students), **L**=large program (more than 500 students); **Sc**=scholarships available in honors program; **Tr**=transfer students accepted into honors program; **HBC**=historically black college; **AA**=academic advisors; **GA**=graduate advisors; **FA**=fellowship advisors.

ing school terms. Students may access the campus computer network from any residence hall room by using a personal computer.

Honorary Societies Phi Eta Sigma and Alpha Chi

Athletics Intramural competition between the social clubs includes events in basketball, softball, volleyball, tennis, flag football, and small games such as badminton and racquetball. Intercollegiate sports are played and attract student support. Students compete in basketball, baseball, cross-country, golf, soccer, and tennis for men and basketball, golf, soccer, softball, tennis, and volleyball for women. The University is affiliated with the TranSouth Athletic Conference and the National Association of Intercollegiate Athletics (NAIA).

Study Abroad The University sponsors a program of international studies during the summer semester in Verviers, Belgium. The program provides students an opportunity to earn credits and to travel while experiencing life in an international setting.

Support Services The University is committed to providing equal opportunity in education to qualified students. Disabled students find several buildings totally handicapped-accessible. Modifications or adjustments are made for qualified students with disabilities. Special parking, equipped restrooms, and lowered drinking fountains are also available on campus. The Office of Disability Services assists with the development of an accommodation plan.

Job Opportunities The Federal Work-Study Program is available to students with established financial need. Other campus jobs required by the programs of the University, such as those of teaching assistant or pool lifeguard, may be assigned without regard to the financial need of the student. Off-campus employment during a summer, fall, or spring semester may be sought through the Career Resource Center.

Tuition: $8080 per year (2001–02)

Room and Board: $4710

Mandatory Fees: $1500

Contact: Dean: Dr. Rolland W. Pack, 158 East Main Street, Henderson, Tennessee 38340; Telephone: 731-989-6057; Fax: 731-989-6065; E-mail: rpack@fhu.edu; Web site: http://www.fhu.edu

FROSTBURG STATE UNIVERSITY

4 Pu G M Sc Tr

▼ University Honors Program

The Honors Program at Frostburg State University (FSU) prides itself upon blurring boundaries traditionally found in academia. These boundaries include the authority divide between faculty members, students, and administrators; the boundaries between academic disciplines; and the boundaries between the classroom and the other arenas.

In FSU's Honors Program, students cofacilitate the freshman orientation course, participate in faculty development workshops, serve on the honors program governing committee, and function as equal partners in the redesign of the program's curriculum and requirements. Administrators from diverse sectors of the University routinely teach honors courses and seminars. An Undergraduate Research Opportunity Program pairs honors students with faculty mentors. There are social activities, such as picnics, film discussions, and field trips. Throughout the program, students, faculty members, and administrators operate as collaborators in the learning process.

Honors courses, even if they are housed in a particular discipline, are expected to incorporate material from multiple disciplines and encourage critical thinking. Specially designed interdisciplinary seminars are offered each semester. These seminars are often team taught. Recent topics have included Women, Science, and Society; The Sixties in America; Myths of America and the Ecological Dilemma; Political Psychology; The American South; Native Peoples of North America; Asian Culture; Physics and Metaphysics; The Literature of the Other; The African-American Experience; Self and Other; and The Holocaust. Some of the seminars, such as The Holocaust, are intense, 6-credit experiences.

The Honors Program at Frostburg State offers more than merely a set of traditional courses. Travel/study experiences are offered as honors seminars. Since May 1995, the following honors-sponsored travel/study experiences have been offered: International Politics in Ireland, Mythology as Sacred Geography in Greece, Art and the Social World in New York City, and Environmental Issues in Ecuador. Honors/international housing in Cambridge and Westminster Halls offers students the opportunity to live in a learning community with special programming to complement their honors courses. Honors Learning Communities (Culture, Communication, and Community) offer integrated courses and cocurricular activities. Students and faculty members are active participants in state, regional, and national collegiate honors councils. FSU's Honors Program students are campus leaders active in student government, campus publications, Greek life, and other cocurricular organizations.

The FSU Honors Program is 21 years old and currently enrolls 200 students.

Participation Requirements: Most of the students in the Honors Program are pursuing the distinction of graduating with honors in general education. This requires completion of 24 credits of honors course work, including liberal arts courses and interdisciplinary seminars. Courses taken for honors credit at a community college or another university may be used to complete these requirements.

Students who complete the 24-credit requirement for graduating with honors in general education receive a certificate and recognition at the University's Honors Convocation. In addition, they are recognized at Commencement and their transcript notes the distinction of graduated with honors in general education.

Admission Process: Incoming first semester students are invited to join FSU's Honors Program on the basis of their high school GPA and SAT I scores. Transfer students and others joining the program after their first semester are expected to have a 3.5 college GPA or above.

Scholarship Availability: The Nelson Guild Scholarship is available for juniors participating in the Honors Program. Students are nominated by the Honors Program director based upon their GPA, their involvement in the Honors Program, and their leadership activities.

Meritorious Achievement Awards are available for entering first-year students and transfer students. In addition, more than 137 departmental and interest-related scholarships are available for first-year and continuing students.

The Campus Context: Frostburg State University offers more than thirty-six degree programs. In addition, FSU has a number of programs in cooperation with other Maryland universities, such as the dual degree in engineering offered with the University of Maryland at College Park and the bachelor's/Juris Doctor program offered with the University of Baltimore. A state-of-the-art Performing Arts Center opened in 1995 with a recital hall, drama theater, studio theater, three rehearsal halls, electronic music and piano labs, teaching studios, and practice labs. A state-of-the-art science building opens in 2002.

Student Body The student population at FSU is 53 percent women. The ethnic distribution of the student body is 1 percent Asian, 9 percent African American, 2 percent Hispanic, 1 percent Native American, and 86 percent Caucasian. International students constitute 1 percent of the population. Thirty-two percent of the students live on campus and 85 percent of the students receive some financial aid. There are seven fraternities and seven sororities on campus.

Faculty Of the 326 faculty members, 238 are full-time and 85 percent have terminal degrees. The student-faculty ratio is 16:1.

Key Facilities The library contains 522,000 volumes. FSU has campus and USM access to more than twenty databases and periodical literature, including full-text articles. Computers available for student use include a high-end graphics workstation lab, Macintosh labs, IBM-compatible labs, a robotics and computer interface lab, a Geographic Information Systems/Computer Aided Design lab, writing labs, and residence hall labs.

Honorary Societies Phi Eta Sigma, Pinnacle, and more than thirty honoraries in specific majors.

Athletics FSU's athletic program supplements, but does not overshadow, the academic program. No preferential admission or financial aid is given solely on the basis of athletic talent. FSU is a Division III school, which recruits scholar-athletes and competes in twenty sports. Men compete in basketball, football, soccer, swimming, tennis, baseball, indoor and outdoor track, and cross-country. Women compete in basketball, field hockey, lacrosse, softball, soccer, swimming, tennis, volleyball, outdoor track, and cross-country.

Study Abroad The University sponsors a variety of international opportunities. Frostburg is one of two institutions of higher learning in Maryland participating in the International Student Exchange Program (ISEP). There are more than 100 institutions abroad from which students can make their selections. FSU has official agreements with several universities throughout the world. In addition, individual departments have ties to other universities. The Honors Program has offered travel/study opportunities to Greece and Ecuador and plans one to Japan.

Support Services Disabled Student Services provides accommodations to disabled students, which increase their independence in gaining an education. In addition, Student Support Services helps low-income, first-generation, and disabled students achieve their personal and academic goals.

Job Opportunities Work opportunities are available through the Federal Work-Study Program. Students are also employed by academic and administrative departments on campus, the catering company, and faculty-directed research projects.

Tuition: $4256 for state residents, $9754 for nonresidents, per year (2001–02)

Room and Board: Varies from $4832 to $5964

Contact: Director: Maureen Connelly, 101 Braddock Road, Frostburg, Maryland 21532; Telephone: 301-687-4998; Fax: 301-687-7964; E-mail: mconnelly@frostburg.edu

FULLERTON COLLEGE

2 Pu G S Sc Tr

▼ Honors Program

The Fullerton College Honors Program was established to serve motivated students who want to transfer to highly competitive and respected four-year public and private universities. Transfer is strongly supported to partner institutions belonging to the Honors Transfer Council of California, and these include several campuses of the University of California as well as Chapman University, Occidental College, Pepperdine University, Pitzer College, Pomona College, and the University of Southern California. Honors courses at Fullerton College are designed to appeal to the imagination and challenge the intellect. The philosophy of the Honors Program is to offer an enriched educational experience that challenges first- and second-year college students to explore their ideas under the guidance of experienced teachers who are themselves scholars active in their fields.

The Honors Program offers sixteen courses in the humanities, fine arts, natural sciences, social sciences, and mathematics that satisfy the general education requirements of most majors. Class sizes are small (20–25 students), and many courses incorporate interdisciplinary activities, off-campus experiences, and service learning projects. Honors classes are conducted as seminars, and students are encouraged to participate actively in their own learning through expanded projects and presentations. While the course work is more challenging, most students discover that honors classes stimulate them to do extra work, to be more creative, and to achieve academic excellence. The Honors Program actively recruits students who are stimulated by ideas, who tend to be skeptical of easy solutions, and who are in pursuit of an education, not just a degree.

The Honors Program was established in 1996. Approximately 150 students enroll in six or seven honors courses offered each semester, and 60 to 70 students are actively enrolled in the Honors Program every year.

Participation Requirements: In order to be eligible for transfer certification by the Honors Program, students must complete at least 18 units in honors course work. Honors students must also enroll in at least one honors course each semester while fulfilling additional requirements for transfer or graduation (a one-semester leave of absence may be granted under special circumstances). Honors students must maintain a cumulative GPA of at least 3.0 in transferable courses. All honors classes are noted on transcripts, and students who complete the Honors Program requirements receive a special diploma and are recognized at an Honors Program graduation ceremony.

Admission Process: Honors courses at Fullerton College are open to all interested students. Admission to the Honors Program can be achieved in three ways. New students are automatically accepted with SAT I scores of 1175 or above, ACT scores of 27 or above, or a high school GPA of 3.25 or above. Continuing students must have a GPA of 3.25 or above in at least 9 transferable courses. A third way of gaining admission is for ongoing students to complete two honors courses with a grade of B or above. All students accepted to the Honors Program must have taken or be eligible to take freshman composition (ENGL 100). All interested students are encouraged to enroll in honors courses before seeking admission to the Honors Program.

To apply to the Honors Program, students must complete an application form, submit transcripts, and write an application essay. The selection process evaluates the applicant's expressed motivation and interest in an honors education, the record of achievement, and the applicant's educational goals. Students may apply to the Honors Program at any time during the academic year.

Scholarship Availability: Each year two scholarships are made available to Fullerton College honors students through the Honors Transfer Council of California. In addition, the Honors Program works closely with other honors organizations, including Alpha Gamma Sigma and Phi Theta Kappa, to inform students enrolled in honors courses about scholarship opportunities available to honors transfer students through four-year colleges and universities. Although the Honors Program does not directly award scholarships, many students enrolled in the Honors Program receive academic recognition through financial awards.

The Campus Context: Fullerton College, which is adjacent to the historical district of the city of Fullerton, is the oldest community college in continuous operation in the state of California. The college is situated on a beautifully landscaped 63-acre campus, and many of the mission-style buildings erected in the 1930s

Interpreting the symbols: **2**=two-year college, **4**=four-year college; **Pu**=public or state college, **Pr**=private college; **G**=general honors program; **D**=departmental honors program; **S**=small program (fewer than 100 students), **M**=midsize program (100 to 500 students), **L**=large program (more than 500 students); **Sc**=scholarships available in honors program; **Tr**=transfer students accepted into honors program; **HBC**=historically black college; **AA**=academic advisors; **GA**=graduate advisors; **FA**=fellowship advisors.

reflect the heritage of Southern California. Easy access to recreational facilities at beaches and mountains is provided by two freeways and a Metrorail station that is within walking distance of the campus. Fullerton College is located near several campuses of the University of California and the State University of California as well as private universities. Cultural venues and entertainment facilities are also in the vicinity.

Student Body The total enrollment is approximately 19,000 students, with 52 percent women and 48 percent men. The median age is 25, and the ethnic distribution is 46 percent white, 27 percent Hispanic, 15 percent Asian/Pacific Islander, 3 percent African American, and 3 percent Filipino. More than half the students enrolled at Fullerton College have transfer to a four-year college or university as their main educational goal.

Faculty The total number of the teaching faculty is approximately 700, 285 of whom are full-time. The ethnic diversity of the student population is reflected in the faculty, and the gender ratio of men to women faculty members is also about 50 percent. Approximately 40 percent of the faculty members have terminal degrees.

Key Facilities The William T. Boyce Library has a book collection of almost 100,000 volumes and subscribes to more than 400 periodicals and newspapers. There are twenty-two terminals available in the library for accessing periodical databases and online materials, and the library subscribes to an online provider of scholarly publications and the Encyclopedia Brittanica Online. Fullerton College students also have access and borrowing privileges at CSU and UC libraries. The College also has several classrooms for computer-aided instruction as well as several computer laboratories on campus; some are dedicated to music, graphics, and business activities, and three are available for writing, research, and e-mail.

Athletics Fullerton College has developed an overall sports and intercollegiate athletic program that ranks with the very best nationwide community college circles. Every year, many Fullerton College graduates are offered scholarships to complete their education and continue their athletic careers at four-year colleges and universities throughout the country. Fullerton College is a member of the Mission Football Conference and competes in the Orange Empire Conference in basketball, baseball, softball, cross-country, soccer, tennis, track, and volleyball as well as the South Coast Conference in water polo and swimming.

Study Abroad Each semester, the Semester Abroad Program provides students with an opportunity to enrich their educational experience while receiving Fullerton College units. The foreign locations and courses offered differ from semester to semester. In the past decade, Fullerton College has offered programs abroad in Austria, Costa Rica, England, France, and Italy.

Support Services Fullerton College offers a variety of support services for all students. The Skills Center and Writing Center provide academic support and assistance. A Disabled Students/Learning Resources Center coordinates assistance for students who request their aid.

Job Opportunities The College offers a variety of work opportunities on campus. Many positions are funded through the work-study program, and students need to demonstrate financial need in order to qualify for this support. In addition, other part-time employment opportunities are available in food services, through department labs, and in the writing and tutoring centers.

Tuition: $12 per unit for residents ($360 per year for an average full-time load); $121 per unit for nonresidents; $126 per unit for international students (1998–99)

Mandatory Fees: $42

Contact: Coordinator: Dr. Claudia Stanger, 321 E. Chapman Avenue, Fullerton, California 92832; Telephone: 714-992-7370; Fax: 714-447-4097; E-mail: stanger999@aol.com; E-mail: honors@fullcoll.edu

Gainesville College

2 Pu G S Tr AA

▼ Honors Program

The Gainesville College Honors Program offers academically talented and motivated students classes designed to challenge and stimulate. Scholars may take individual honors courses or join the Honors Scholars Program, which offers a full range of courses, extracurricular activities, and financial assistance. Outside the classroom, the Honors Program provides special trips to cultural events, museums, social events, and visiting speakers. Travel grants help qualified students participate in Gainesville College study-abroad programs. Students also have the opportunity to work closely on a one-to-one basis with faculty mentors. Tuition waivers are available.

Participation Requirements: To maintain their status in the Honors Program, a student must maintain a minimum GPA of 3.2 (in honors and regular courses) and make satisfactory progress toward accumulating a minimum of 12 semester credit hours of honors courses. Upon graduation, honors courses are specified as such on the transcript. Honors scholars are so recognized on their diploma and transcript.

Admission Process: Entering first-year students must meet two of the following criteria: a minimum high school GPA of 3.4 on a 4.0 scale, based on academic courses only; minimum SAT scores of 1100; or a ranking in the top 10 percent of their high school graduating class. Students at Gainesville College may enter if they meet these three criteria: a minimum GPA of 3.2 at Gainesville College, in academic courses only; 15 or more college-level credits; recommendation by a Gainesville College professor. Students meeting these requirements may register for honors classes after receiving an invitation from the honors director.

Scholarship Availability: There are no scholarships available; however, there is a travel grant that allows students to participate in "GC on the Go" trips. Candidates are asked to submit a transcript, a written essay describing how the trip will enhance their educational experience at Gainesville College, and a statement of financial need.

The Campus Context: Gainesville College is a two-year, nonresidential unit of the University System of Georgia located within easy reach of the amenities of a big city (Atlanta), the beauties of nature (Lake Lanier and the Appalachian Mountains of northeast Georgia), and the advantages of a university town (Athens). The main campus, located in Oakwood near Lake Lanier, offers easy access to Atlanta and Gainesville; a satellite campus is maintained at Athens, where the University of Georgia is also located. For its 3,700 students, the College offers Associate of Arts, Associate of Science, and Associate of Applied Science degrees in addition to certificate programs in information technology, geographic information systems and personal fitness training. North Georgia College and State University and Southern Polytechnic State University also offer upper-division courses at the University Center on the Oakwood campus. A strong proponent of teaching the "whole student," faculty and staff members provide a great deal of individual attention to students inside the classroom and out. A broad range of generously supported extracurricular activities include intramurals, clubs, organizations, and performing arts groups, many of which have won awards for their work in national and regional competitions.

Student Body Total enrollment at Gainesville College is approaching 3,700 students: 2,133 women and 1,559 men. The ethnic distribution is 4.5 percent African American, .3 percent American Indian, 2.2 percent Asian, 3.4 percent Hispanic, .9 percent multiracial, and 88.7 percent white. There are 38 international students.

Faculty The total number of full-time faculty members is 99, 43.4 percent of whom have terminal degrees. Including the part-time faculty members, the student-faculty ratio is 20:1.

Key Facilities The John Harrison Hosch Library houses more than 68,000 volumes plus a collection of audiovisual materials and equipment. Various types of student areas—individual study carrels, conference rooms for group study, a large multipurpose room, and the honors classroom—are found in the library. Major emphasis is placed on supporting the curriculum by providing basic works in all subject areas and by subscribing to periodicals, newspapers, indexes, bibliographies, and similar tools of scholarship. There are more than forty computers on the first floor for students' use as well as for use by library instruction classes. These computers allow easy access to GALILEO, the widely acclaimed collection of online databases provided by the state, and GIL, the online catalog for Gainesville College and other University System of Georgia libraries. Around campus, computer labs are numerous, open to the student body, and often upgraded. "Smart" classrooms with the latest computer equipment are plentiful. Gainesville College has been a leader in the state in integrating computer technology into its educational programs.

Honorary Society Phi Theta Kappa

Athletics Gainesville offers a comprehensive intramural program.

Study Abroad Gainesville College offers at least one study-abroad opportunity each year. In the past five years, these trips have included a study of theater in England, a study of the roots of psychology in Austria, a study of rhetoric in Greece, a study of Native American culture in Vancouver, and a study of international business in France. Students participating in such trips integrate their travel into a course they are taking as well as taking part in the educational opportunities offered through the instructors who are leading the trip. They also receive an introduction to the target culture. Gainesville College Honors Program funds up to four travel grants a year, depending on the cost of the trip and the number of applicants. Many of those grants pay the full cost of participation in the "GC on the Go" experience.

Support Services Facilities for disabled students are plentiful. All buildings are wheelchair accessible; all restrooms and drinking fountains are accessible. In addition, there is a coordinator for special programs on campus to help each disabled student obtain all requisite special services.

Job Opportunities On average, the College employs approximately 45 to 65 students each semester in most of the offices and departments on campus. It also participates in the Federal Work-Study program. Students who are eligible work in various campus offices, labs, and the library.

Tuition: For Georgia residents enrolled for 12 or more semester hours, tuition is $640; for nonresidents with 12 or more semester hours it is $1920. In addition, for in-state and out-of-state full-time students, there are the following mandatory fees: a $39 activity fee, a $25 activity fee, and a $2 auto fee.

Room and Board: Gainesville College is a nonresidential college. For a nine-month academic year, room and board for students living with parents and commuting from home is approximately $1800 to $2000. For students living in off-campus housing, the cost rises to $4000 to $8000.

Contact: Director: Dr. Glenda McLeod, Humanities Department, P.O. Box 1358, Gainesville, Georgia, 30502; Telephone: 770-718-3871; Fax: 770-718-3832; E-mail: gmcleod@gc.peachnet.edu

GALLAUDET UNIVERSITY

4 Pr G S Sc Tr

▼ Honors Program

The Gallaudet University Honors Program, established in 1981, is a program of general study designed to provide an alternative liberal arts curriculum for the motivated and talented learner regardless of major. Course offerings include separate honors sections, honors seminars, and honors options or individual honors contracts in nonhonors sections. Courses are discussion based and encourage student-teacher interaction. Approximately 10 percent of entering first-year students are admitted to the Honors Program. There are currently 100 students enrolled in the program.

Participation Requirements: Students in the Honors Program can major in any area and take the same number of credits for graduation as every other Gallaudet University student. Honors Program students must complete a total of 37 credit hours at the honors level with a grade of B or better to qualify for University Honors. Six of these hours are for a senior honors project. Advanced Placement courses fulfill honors course requirements.

Students graduating with University honors are recognized at graduation. Graduation with University honors is recorded on the student's transcript. In addition, the student receives a plaque that is engraved with their name, the University seal, and the signature of the president of the University.

Admission Process: In all cases, admission depends on an interview with the honors director and in some cases, high school or college transcripts are considered. Students qualify for the program in one of three ways: They may qualify for admission directly based on SAT or ACT scores, the reading and writing test scores during New Student Orientation (or before if the student visits campus), or they may qualify based on a GPA of 3.2 or better, an essay on honors education that is evaluated by the director, and three letters of recommendation from their professors.

The Campus Context: Gallaudet University is located in Washington, D.C. In 1864, President Abraham Lincoln signed the charter establishing what is now Gallaudet University. The presidents of the United States sign the diplomas of Gallaudet's graduates. The historical front part of the 99-acre campus was designed by Frederick Law Olmsted, who also designed the United States Capitol grounds in Washington and Central Park in New York City.

The mission of Gallaudet University is to serve as a comprehensive, multipurpose institution of higher education for persons who are deaf or hard of hearing. Gallaudet University is the only liberal arts university in the world designed exclusively for deaf and hard of hearing students. Communication among the faculty and staff members and students, whether in or out of the classroom, is through the use of both sign language and written and spoken English. The University offers twenty-nine undergraduate majors.

Gallaudet University is a member of the Consortium of Universities of the Washington Metropolitan Area. Degree-seeking students can enroll in courses through the consortium if those courses are not available at Gallaudet. Other consortium members are American University, the Catholic University of America, George Mason University, the George Washington University, Georgetown University, Howard University, Marymount University, the University of the District of Columbia, the University of Maryland at College Park, Mount Vernon College, and Trinity College.

Student Body There are 2,243 undergraduate students and 517 graduate students at Gallaudet University. Fifty-two percent of undergraduate students are women, 11 percent are African American, 5 percent are Asian American, 7 percent are Hispanic, 1 percent is Native American, and 4 percent other. International students from approximately fifty countries make up 12 percent of the total enrollment.

Faculty Gallaudet has 222 full-time teaching faculty members.

Key Facilities The library contains 239,433 book volumes, 455,930 titles on microfilm, and approximately 7,000 audiovisual media

Interpreting the symbols: **2**=two-year college, **4**=four-year college; **Pu**=public or state college, **Pr**=private college; **G**=general honors program; **D**=departmental honors program; **S**=small program (fewer than 100 students), **M**=midsize program (100 to 500 students), **L**=large program (more than 500 students); **Sc**=scholarships available in honors program; **Tr**=transfer students accepted into honors program; **HBC**=historically black college; **AA**=academic advisors; **GA**=graduate advisors; **FA**=fellowship advisors.

and videotape titles. It has an internationally renowned special collection of materials on deafness covering the period from 1546 to the present. There are 288 computers in fifteen computer labs. All students, faculty members, and staff members have access to e-mail and the Internet.

Study Abroad Since 1974, Gallaudet University has offered study-abroad programs. Participants usually spend three to six weeks studying and traveling in England, France, Costa Rica, Canada, Mexico, Italy, Switzerland, Germany, or Spain. Courses are offered for credit by various academic departments.

Support Services The campus is completely accessible for students with disabilities.

Job Opportunities Students are offered a range of work opportunities on campus, including work-study and internships.

Tuition: $7870 per year (2001–02)

Room and Board: $7564

Mandatory Fees: $810

Contact: Director: Dr. Shirley Shultz Myers, 800 Florida Avenue, NE, Washington, D.C. 20002-3695; Telephone: 202-651-5755; Fax: 202-651-5065; E-mail: shirley.myers@gallaudet.edu

Gannon University

4 Pr G M Tr

▼ University Honors Program

The student-centered and student-governed Gannon University Honors Program is designed to provide a challenging educational experience to talented and highly motivated students willing to accept the challenge. The program is open to students of all majors and consists primarily of honors sections of courses that are required of all students. The honors courses are limited to 15 students, are conducted as seminars, and are highly interactive. The faculty members who teach in the program are encouraged to be creative in the content discussed as well as in the manner in which it is presented. A hallmark of the program is the community that exists—students with students, as well as faculty members with students. The program is governed by a 15-member Student Advisory Board that is responsible for suggesting courses and faculty members as well as for planning cultural, social, and intellectual outside-the-classroom activities. The Gannon program is a member of the National Collegiate Honors Council, the Northeast Region of the National Collegiate Honors Council, and the Mid-East Honors Association, and students are encouraged to attend conferences sponsored by each of the associations. The Honors Program at Gannon began in 1989 and is now in its thirteenth year. There are 165 students in the program.

Participation Requirements: To graduate as Honors Scholars, students must take 24 credits of honors courses and 6 credits of a foreign language. To graduate as honors associates, they must take 18 credits of honors courses. They must also achieve an overall GPA of 3.25 or above. Honors students complete the same number of credits for graduation as any other Gannon student. Honors students receive special recognition at graduation and their honors courses are documented on their transcripts.

Along with the academic requirements for the program, students are expected to participate in social, cultural, and intellectual activities provided by the program. They are also expected to be involved in some service activity.

Admission Process: Entering freshmen are selected on the basis of their SAT I scores, class rank, GPA, and extracurricular activities. Students already attending Gannon and transfer students must have at least a 3.5 GPA to be considered.

The Campus Context: Gannon University is a private, Roman Catholic, comprehensive university located on the bayfront in Erie, Pennsylvania's third-largest city and one of the busiest ports on the Great Lakes. There are two colleges on campus: the College of Sciences, Engineering, and Health Sciences and the College of Humanities, Business, and Education. Gannon offers seven associate degree programs, fifty bachelor's degree programs, ten preprofessional programs, and eighteen graduate degree programs. Gannon's noteworthy facilities include a Computer Integrated Manufacturing Center, the Metalliding Institute, the Schuster Theater, the Schuster Gallery, and WERG Radio.

Student Body There are approximately 3,400 students enrolled, of whom 59 percent are women. Resident students make up 41 percent of the student body.

Faculty Out of the 282 faculty members, 168 are full-time and 55 percent hold terminal degrees. The student-faculty ratio is 13:1.

Key Facilities The library holds 342,721 bound volumes. There are 341 computers available through several general use and departmental labs.

Honorary Societies Phi Eta Sigma, Lambda Sigma, and Omicron Delta Kappa

Athletics Gannon offers eighteen NCAA Division II sports. Men's sports include baseball, basketball, cross-country, football, golf, soccer, swimming and diving, water polo, and wrestling. Women's sports include basketball, cross-country, lacrosse, soccer, softball, swimming, diving, water polo, and volleyball. Fourteen of the seventeen teams compete in the Great Lakes Intercollegiate Athletic Conference.

Study Abroad The University offers several courses abroad each year. In addition, Gannon cooperates with study-abroad programs offered by other colleges and universities to provide its students with an opportunity to internationalize their education.

Support Services Approximately 85 percent of the campus is accessible to the physically disabled. Wheelchair ramps, elevators, specially equipped restrooms, special drop-off points, lowered drinking fountains and lowered telephones are available, as is a program for students with learning disabilities.

Job Opportunities In addition to the Federal Work-Study Program, approximately 100 part-time job opportunities are available on campus.

Tuition: Full-time: $14,440 (minimum) through $15,380, depending on program, per year (2001–02); part-time: $450–$480 per credit, depending on program

Room and Board: $5700

Mandatory Fees: $446

Contact: Director: Rev. Robert Susa, Gannon University, University Square, Erie, Pennsylvania 16541; Telephone: 814-871-5628; Fax: 814-871-5662; E-mail: susa001@mail1.gannon.edu

Gardner-Webb University

4 Pr G M Sc Tr

▼ Honors Program

The Gardner-Webb University (GWU) Honors Program seeks to nurture academically qualified students in all majors by providing a program of enriched learning experiences in courses taught by an honors faculty. Honors students are inquisitive people, excited by the challenge of scholarship and comfortable in an environment that demands the acquisition of knowledge and the need to think critically about what is learned. Regardless of their majors, honors students are interdisciplinary in their approach. They are able to synthesize their studies and learn from varied cultures and from each other. The Honors Program encourages the highest standards in its students who should exert leadership through their academic and cocurricular accomplishments.

GWU provides an Honors House residence hall for honors students who choose to reside there. The house maintains online capabilities in each room, a computer lab, classroom space, a lobby, and a kitchen. Approximately 30 students may reside in GWU's Honors House.

The GWU Honors Program has been in existence for ten years. There are 100 to 130 students in the program each year.

Participation Requirements: The Honors Program requires the completion of a minimum of 24 hours of course work designated as honors. A minimum of 15 hours of course work should be completed in the first two years of study. Honors courses in the first two years may be selected from honors sections (restricted to honors students) of core curriculum offerings or through honors contracts with faculty members teaching regular sections of the University's overall curriculum.

To receive Honors Program recognition during commencement exercises, a student must meet the following requirements: maintain at least a 3.0 GPA; successfully complete a minimum of 24 hours in honors courses, including HONR 395, 400, and 401; initiate, prepare, present, and defend a senior honors thesis of at least forty pages in length; complete a minimum of 80 hours of community service that contributes to the welfare of the community; and receive the recommendation of the Honors Committee.

Admission Process: Fifty to 80 students are selected to receive Honors Program application materials each year. This initial selection is based on SAT I scores and class ranking. Applications are reviewed by the Honors Committee. Selection is based on academic achievement, potential for leadership, extracurricular activities, and a written statement of personal goals.

Scholarship Availability: Gardner-Webb offers several scholarships, which are available to students in the Honors Program. These include Academic Fellows, University Fellows, and Presidential Scholarships. Some of these provide for full-tuition assistance.

The Campus Context: Gardner-Webb University is a private, coeducational university affiliated with the Baptist State Convention of North Carolina. The University is often referred to as an emerging regional university. The main University campus is situated on 200 rolling, wooded acres in the small town of Boiling Springs in the Piedmont section of western North Carolina. The campus is 60 miles from Asheville and Charlotte. Gardner-Webb students enjoy the lifestyle of a relatively small institution yet have the advantage of being centrally located near major urban resources. Gardner-Webb also offers classes in fifteen other regional facilities through its Greater Opportunities for Adult Learners (GOAL) Program. Students and faculty and staff members are part of a community of learning, and Gardner-Webb seeks to prepare and encourage students to make meaningful contributions to the global community in which they live. The University offers forty-one undergraduate majors leading to the baccalaureate degree, including liberal arts and sciences, business, education, and nursing.

Student Body Undergraduates enrolled on the main campus total in excess of 1,400. Fifty-six percent of the students are women. The ethnic distribution of the student population is 1 percent Asian, 13 percent African American, 1 percent Hispanic, and 1 percent Native American. There are 25 international students. Ninety-three percent of students receive some form of financial aid.

Faculty Of the 115 full-time faculty members (supplemented by 54 adjunct faculty members in the off-campus centers), 70 percent have doctoral or other terminal degrees. The student-faculty ratio is 12:1.

Key Facilities There are approximately 205,000 volumes in Dover Library, plus microforms and other materials for a total item count of more than 740,000. Seven computer labs located throughout campus form the core of the campus computer network. Offices and residence halls are wired into the campus computer network.

Athletics Students may participate in nineteen NCAA Division I sports, including football, soccer, cross-country, basketball, wrestling, golf, tennis, outdoor track and field, and baseball for men and volleyball, soccer, cross-country, basketball, softball, swimming, golf, outdoor track and field, and tennis for women. All of these, with the exception of football, swimming, and wrestling, are Atlantic SUN Conference sports. In addition, men and women can participate in cheerleading and athletic training. Each year the athletic department schedules and participates in more than 300 events.

Study Abroad Study-abroad programs are provided by the Broyhill School of Management and the Departments of Fine Arts, Foreign Languages and Literature, and Religious Studies. Additional travel/study opportunities are available to individual students through a cooperative-study program with CIEE (Council on International Educational Exchange) and AIFS (American Institute for Foreign Study), which permit study in more than thirty countries in Asia, Europe, South and Central America, Africa, and the Caribbean.

Support Services The Noel Program for the Disabled coordinates academic support services for students with disabilities. Accommodations provided for students with disabilities are based on current disability documentation. Accommodations may include specialized educational equipment, adapted computer technology, testing accommodations, books on tape, readers, note takers, tutors, counselors, interpreters for the deaf/hard of hearing, and braille/large print for the blind/visually impaired. Residence halls are equipped with visual fire alarms and visual doorbell lights. All students with disabilities are fully mainstreamed into classes and participate in extracurricular activities sponsored by the University.

Job Opportunities Students are offered a range of work opportunities through work-study programs.

Tuition: $12,520 per year (2001–02)

Room and Board: $4880

Contact: Director: Dr. Tom Jones, Box 7264, Boiling Springs, North Carolina 28017; Telephone: 704-406-4369; Fax: 704-406-3917; E-mail: tjones@gardner-webb.edu; Web site: http://www.gardner-webb.edu

GENEVA COLLEGE

4 Pr G S Tr

▼ Honors Program

The Honors Program at Geneva College has been established to encourage students who want to attain academic excellence. In the document "Foundational Concepts for Christian Education" Geneva College holds to the ideal of academic excellence as a part of its goal of developing the God-given potential of its students. This ideal directs the whole program of the College, but certain parts of the academic program have been designated as honors because they offer special opportunities for greater in-depth scholarly work and research. Each honors student must complete six honors courses during their time at Geneva and complement their scholarship with an honors research project their senior year.

Another component of membership in the program is the attendance at cultural events throughout the academic year. Some of these events are attended on campus, but others are

Interpreting the symbols: **2**=two-year college, **4**=four-year college; **Pu**=public or state college, **Pr**=private college; **G**=general honors program; **D**=departmental honors program; **S**=small program (fewer than 100 students), **M**=midsize program (100 to 500 students), **L**=large program (more than 500 students); **Sc**=scholarships available in honors program; **Tr**=transfer students accepted into honors program; **HBC**=historically black college; **AA**=academic advisors; **GA**=graduate advisors; **FA**=fellowship advisors.

attended in Pittsburgh at the ballet, symphony, plays, operas, and lectures. Students must attend six cultural events each year. Students are also encouraged to attend professional conferences in their own academic disciplines at least once in their four years as students.

Membership in the Honors Program brings both opportunities and responsibilities. The chief aim is to encourage and reward academic excellence as well as to equip leaders for service to God, their communities, their place of employment, and the world. To that end, the program is designed to promote excitement, growth, and challenge. The program has grown significantly since its inception in the 1994–95 academic year. That year, 13 students entered the program, and in 2001–02, 61 students populated the program.

Participation Requirements: The Geneva College Honors Program is open to qualified students in all majors and programs. Participants in this program must be full-time undergraduate students in the College's traditional program.

Admission Process: Incoming freshmen are nominated to the program by the Admissions Office on the basis of GPA and standardized test scores. For students who have completed a year's study at Geneva (30 credits or more), a minimum 3.8 GPA entitles them to apply for honor status.

The Campus Context: Geneva College is located in the town of Beaver Falls, Pennsylvania. Beaver Falls is 40 miles northwest of Pittsburgh, Pennsylvania. The campus occupies 55 acres in a residential setting.

Student Body The undergraduate enrollment at Geneva College is 1,352 students. The student body is represented by students from thirty-seven states and twenty-one other countries. The campus population is primarily residential—75 percent of the students live on campus. Students are able to participate in numerous extracurricular activities.

Faculty The student-faculty ratio is 18:1. Geneva College employs 73 full-time and 69 part-time undergraduate faculty members, 73 percent of whom have terminal degrees.

Key Facilities The main library is McCartney Library, with two smaller curriculum libraries located elsewhere on campus. Books and other holdings number 165,442 in addition to 24,593 audiovisual units.

Athletics Geneva College is represented by the NAIA by thirteen varsity sports. Men participate in football, basketball, baseball, track and field, cross-country, and soccer. Women participate in basketball, softball, soccer, track and field, cross-country, volleyball, and tennis. Intramural activities are also available as are fifty different clubs.

Study Abroad Geneva College is a member of the Coalition for Christian Colleges and Universities, which entitles Geneva's students to participate in its study-abroad programs. The locations of these programs include Moscow, Cairo, Oxford University, Jerusalem University, Costa Rica, and China. Programs in the United States include the American Studies Program in Washington, D.C.; the Los Angeles Film Studies Program; and the Contemporary Music Center on Martha's Vineyard. All these programs entail a semester away from campus.

Contact: Program Director: Mrs. Jerryn S. Carson, 3200 College Avenue, Beaver Falls, Pennsylvania 15010; Telephone: 724-847-6510; Fax: 724-847-6776; E-mail: jscarson@geneva.edu; Web site: http://www.geneva.edu; Admissions Office: Telephone: 724-847-6500 in Pennsylvania, 800-847-8255 (toll-free); E-mail: admissions@geneva.edu

The George Washington University

4 Pr G L Sc Tr

▼ University Honors Program

The University Honors Program enhances the education of undergraduate students at The George Washington University by offering a series of special, limited-enrollment courses that are designed to build intellectual skill and promote student-faculty contact. For entering students, the program offers a year-long seminar on the western intellectual tradition. Freshman and sophomore students also choose from a series of small seminar courses with some of the top faculty members at the University. For juniors, the program offers the University Symposium, a special weekend seminar with world-renowned authors and scholars. All seniors complete a thesis, either through the honors program or through their major department.

The University Honors Program provides extracurricular activities such as student retreats and student-faculty dinners, and offers special housing for its students.

Established in 1989, the program currently enrolls more than 600 students.

Participation Requirements: Students in the University Honors Program must maintain a minimum 3.4 cumulative GPA, take one honors course each semester, and complete a senior thesis. Students who meet these requirements graduate with Latin honors (Cum Laude, Magna Cum Laude, or Summa Cum Laude) and are identified as graduates of the University Honors Program. Students whose cumulative GPA falls below 3.4 may remain in the program as long as it is possible for them to graduate with a 3.4 cumulative GPA at 120 hours.

Admission Process: All applicants must complete the University's Admissions Applications, parts 1 and 2. Students must also complete the supplemental honors application and essays. All materials must be received by January 15.

Scholarship Availability: All students in the University Honors Program receive a Presidential Academic Scholarship of $10,000.

The Campus Context: The George Washington University is a private, independent university located in downtown Washington, D.C., at Foggy Bottom—five blocks west of the White House. The new Mount Vernon campus is also located in the District, and shuttle buses are available for travel between the two campuses. Five schools offering undergraduate degrees: the Columbian School of Arts and Sciences, the School of Business and Public Management, the Elliott School of International Affairs, the School of Engineering and Applied Sciences, and the School of Medicine and Health Science. Seven schools offer graduate degrees—the previous five plus the School of Education and Human Development and the Law School.

Student Body The undergraduate enrollment is 6,600. Fifty-six percent are women; ten percent are international students. Fifty-six percent of the undergraduate students live on campus. There are more than 270 student organizations on campus. Graduate enrollment is 10,000 students.

Faculty Of 600 full-time faculty members, 92 percent have terminal degrees. The student-faculty ratio is 10:1.

Key Facilities The University's libraries house 1.5 million volumes. The Washington area offers extensive additional research facilities. The University belongs to a consortium of other university libraries and is also linked to the National Academy of Science, the World Health Organization, and the State Department. Adjacent or close to campus are the Smithsonian, the National Gallery, the Kennedy Center, the Library of Congress, the National Archives, and the Federal Judicial Center.

Honorary Societies Phi Eta Sigma and Phi Beta Kappa

Athletics The George Washington University is an NCAA Division I School and is a member of the Atlantic 10 Conference. Varsity men's and women's basketball, track, cross-country, swimming, and tennis are available as are men's baseball and golf and women's volleyball and gymnastics. There are also a number of intramural and club sports.

Support Services The Disabled Student Services Office provides many services necessary for disabled students to participate fully in the academic programs and the extracurricular life of the University.

Tuition: $20,370 per year (1998–99)

Room and Board: $7325 minimum

Mandatory Fees: $990

Contact: Director: Dr. David Alan Grier, 2138 G Street NW, Washington, D.C. 20052; Telephone: 202-994-6816; Fax: 202-994-8042; E-mail: uhp@gwu.edu; Web site: http://gwis.circ.gwu.edu/~uhpwww

GEORGIA COLLEGE & STATE UNIVERSITY

4 Pu G M Sc Tr

▼ Honors and Scholars Program

The Georgia College & State University (GC&SU) Honors and Scholars Program is an integral program of learning that presents challenging opportunities for students with proven academic strength. The program promotes student interaction with faculty members through small group discussion, supervised projects, internships, interdisciplinary studies, and service learning projects. This format is designed to facilitate closer student-faculty relationships than most classroom settings permit. Through scholars capstone experiences, such as a senior thesis, a creative project, or an internship, these relationships can continue beyond the foundational (freshman-sophomore) years and into the student's academic major.

The small-group learning that characterizes the Honors and Scholars Program fosters stimulating interaction with some of the best students and most talented faculty members of GC&SU. Emphasis on close, less formally structured relationships and individualized instruction enhances students' capacity for rigorous thinking and provides them with a culturally literate, broadly humanistic intellectual framework for their lives.

Twelve semester hours are required for completion of the Honors and Scholars Program. Honors Seminar I (3 semester hours) is offered each fall semester and is required of all honors students. Discussion of selected readings in this course enhances critical thinking, integrative learning, formulation of thought processes, and oral and written expression. This course also prepares students to assume a more active role in the Honors II Seminars that are offered each spring semester. These seminars center around particular themes or issues of current interest. Students are required to participate in at least one Honors II seminar in order to fulfill the 6 semester hours required for completion of the honors component of the program. These courses are not a part of the core curriculum and are required as additional hours.

Students who complete 60 hours of lower-level courses with a GPA of at least 3.5 are eligible to participate in the Scholars program. This program involves work in the major area and may consist of a research project and senior thesis, study-abroad experiences, or internships as well as other opportunities for expanded study in a specific area. Transfer students as well as students who did not complete the Honors Program but meet the academic criteria are also eligible to participate in the Scholars Program.

The 30-year-old program currently enrolls 160 students.

Participation Requirements: Students must maintain at least a 3.3 GPA in order to remain in the Honors Program. A minimum 3.5 is required for the Scholars Program. If the average falls below the minimum, students have one semester to return to good standing. Honors students may continue to take seminars but are not eligible for recognition unless their average returns to at least 3.3. Students who do not have the minimum required 3.5 GPA are not eligible to participate in scholars experiences. Those who complete the program are recognized with a certificate at graduation, and they also wear special cords and a pin. Recognition on Honors Day is given to all students who take any honors courses during the year.

Admission Process: Admission of first-year students is by invitation and selection. Students who have at least a 3.3 overall high school GPA (GPA) and who have SAT I scores of at least 1100 or ACT scores of at least 24 receive an application for the Honors and Scholars Program with their admission to the University. The application requires a letter of recommendation from a high school teacher or counselor and a short student essay that addresses expectations and why the student wishes to participate. Transfer students and international students who meet the admission criteria may also apply to the program.

With this information, and in some cases an interview, the admission committee selects students for the program. The small-group focus limits the Honors Program to 35 new students per year. Therefore, admission is highly competitive. Although grades are important, other factors, such as extracurricular activities, are also considered. Ultimately, the committee attempts to select the students who have the most potential, who will add diversity to the program through their special interests and other characteristics, and who will benefit from the program. Upon selection, students must maintain at least a 3.3 GPA in order to remain in the program.

Scholarship Availability: Presidential Scholarships for $2100 a year are available for a limited number of entering students. If the student receives the state of Georgia HOPE Grant, the presidential award is adjusted to $600 per semester. Outstanding Student Scholarships, available for entering students and two-year college transfer students, pay for matriculation and fees of $400 per semester for students receiving the HOPE Grant.

The Campus Context: Georgia College & State University, the public liberal arts university of Georgia, was chartered in 1889. Many of the buildings on campus are Georgian style red brick with Corinthian columns and limestone trim. The University comprises a College of Arts and Sciences and Schools of Business, Health Sciences, and Education. Sixty-three degree programs are offered.

Student Body Undergraduate enrollment is 4,086, and 94 percent of the entering freshmen receive the Hope Grant. There are five sororities and seven fraternities on campus. All students in the Honors and Scholars Program belong to the University's student honor society, Eta Sigma Alpha.

Faculty There are 235 full-time faculty members. The ratio of students to full-time faculty members is 22:1.

Key Facilities The Ina Dillard Russell library collection totals more than 500,000 items, and the state library computer system, GALILEO, connects all of the libraries in the University System of Georgia. The Flannery O'Connor collection houses O'Connor's personal collection of more than 700 books, manuscripts, and journals. The Museum and Archives of Education houses the

Interpreting the symbols: **2**=two-year college, **4**=four-year college; **Pu**=public or state college, **Pr**=private college; **G**=general honors program; **D**=departmental honors program; **S**=small program (fewer than 100 students), **M**=midsize program (100 to 500 students), **L**=large program (more than 500 students); **Sc**=scholarships available in honors program; **Tr**=transfer students accepted into honors program; **HBC**=historically black college; **AA**=academic advisors; **GA**=graduate advisors; **FA**=fellowship advisors.

memorabilia of the honorable Carl Vinson, a Milledgeville Native who served Georgia in the U.S. House of Representatives for fifty years. There are ample computer labs, academic computing support for students and faculty members, and video-conferencing classrooms that allow interactive communication with more than 400 sites throughout Georgia. Through the use of this technology, some of the University faculty members also teach classes for servicemen aboard the U.S.S. Carl Vinson.

Athletics Intercollegiate athletics for men include basketball, baseball, tennis, cross-country, and golf. Intercollegiate athletics for women include basketball, fast-pitch softball, tennis, and cross-country. The Office of Intramural Sports and Recreation provides team and individual sports, including fencing, water skiing, and soccer. GC Centennial Center is a 97,000-square-foot multipurpose center that facilitates a comprehensive health/physical education and intercollegiate athletic program.

Study Abroad Georgia College & State University has developed a program that enables students to study abroad for one or for part of one academic year while earning academic credit in their major field. An academic year abroad is currently offered at DeMontfort University, Leicester, the United Kingdom, and Universide de Valladolid, Spain. Summer study-abroad programs are available in Western Europe, the Pacific, Canada, and Mexico.

Support Services All buildings are handicapped-accessible to handicapped students, and the University provides full and equal access to academic and cocurricular programs and activities for physically handicapped students or students with learning challenges.

Job Opportunities The Federal Work-Study Program provides jobs for students who show financial need and who must earn a part of their educational expenses. The Georgia College & State University Student Employment program provides additional opportunities to secure campus employment. Students are interviewed and hired by the various administrative offices, department offices, and other offices at the University.

Tuition: $2136 for state residents, $7356 for nonresidents, per year (1998–99)

Room and board: $4086

Mandatory Fees: $406

Contact: Director: Doris C. Moody, Campus Box 082, Milledgeville, Georgia 31061; Telephone: 912-445-4025; Fax: 912-445-1092; E-mail: dmoody@mail.gcsu.edu; Assistant Director: Robert Viau; Telephone: 912-445-5564; E-mail: rviau@mail.gcsu.edu

GEORGIA PERIMETER COLLEGE

2 Pu G M Sc Tr

▼ Honors Program

The Georgia Perimeter College Honors Program is an academic and student services program for students in any area of study who have demonstrated outstanding achievement and motivation. The Honors Program offers intellectually challenging courses taught by dedicated faculty members, interaction with other students, and opportunities for recognition and service. The courses are primarily core courses in the humanities and social sciences. The purpose of the Honors Program is to encourage students to achieve excellence in all aspects of their experience at Georgia Perimeter College.

Enrollment in honors courses is typically 12 to 15 students. Courses often have a seminar format and emphasize communication skills. Some classes, such as honors composition, meet in fully equipped computer classrooms. Interdisciplinary options are available in a number of courses.

Students in the Honors Program enjoy a number of important benefits, including priority registration, membership in the Honors Program Student Association, and opportunities to travel to various honors conferences. Travel by students to attend and present at state, regional, and national honors conferences is funded by the school. The Honors Program and the Honors Program Student Association also sponsor literary, cultural, and academic programs throughout the year.

Students may join the Honors Program at any point in their academic career at Georgia Perimeter College. The Honors Program began in 1983 and currently enrolls 350 students.

Participation Requirements: Open to students majoring in any discipline, the Honors Program welcomes qualified students at any juncture in their tenure at Georgia Perimeter College. To earn an Honors certificate, the student must have completed at least 45 semester hours of college work with a cumulative GPA of at least 3.3. Of these 45 semester hours, 15 semester hours must have been earned in honors courses in which the student received a grade of B or higher. All classes taken through the Honors Program appear on a student's transcript with an honors designation.

Admission Process: The following eligibility requirements are considered for acceptance into the Honors Program: a composite SAT I score of at least 1200, a minimum 650 SAT I verbal score, or at least a 590 SAT I math score; ACT scores of at least 30 in English or at least 27 in math; National Merit Semi-Finalist status; eligibility for Phi Theta Kappa, the national honorary society for two-year colleges; 9 or more college-transfer credit hours and a minimum 3.5 GPA from another college; at least a 3.5 GPA in academic courses taken at Georgia Perimeter College; and a recommendation from a faculty member and approval of the Honors Program Coordinator.

Scholarship Availability: Each campus of Georgia Perimeter College has several academic scholarships designated for students in the Honors Program; students who have completed at least two honors courses are eligible to apply. Priority is given to those students who have completed the most honors courses and have the highest cumulative GPA.

The Campus Context: Established in 1964, Georgia Perimeter College was formerly DeKalb College. It is a regional, multicampus, two-year institution in the greater metropolitan Atlanta area. With more than 16,000 students enrolled at its four campuses and two centers, Georgia Perimeter College comprises the third-largest institution in the University System of Georgia. Thus, Georgia Perimeter offers its students the resources of a large state university and the intimacy of a small college because of its multiple locations: the Alpharetto Center, the Clarkston Campus, the Decatur Campus, the Dunwoody Campus, the Lawrenceville Campus, and the Rockdale Center. Each of the campuses has a fully equipped distance-learning room.

One of the special features at the College is a botanical garden that contains a remarkable collection of plants native to the southeast. Two of the campuses have large auditoriums and a thriving theater program.

Georgia Perimeter College is primarily a liberal arts transfer institution offering the Associate of Arts degree and Associate of Science degree in a variety of areas appropriate to baccalaureate majors at senior institutions.

Student Body Undergraduate enrollment is 16,000, of whom 60 percent are women. The minority ethnic distribution of the student body is 6 percent Asian, 30 percent African American, and 2 percent Hispanic. Almost 2,000 international students from 120 countries. Georgia Perimeter College offers a supportive environment, including a Second Wind organization, for nontraditional students. The average age of the student body is 25.4 years. The College is nonresidential; however, a wide variety of clubs and organizations offer students a rich cultural and intellectual environment.

Faculty There are 286 full-time faculty members (supplemented by adjunct faculty members); 95 percent have doctorates or other terminal degrees.

Key Facilities The libraries house more than 220,000 volumes. The campus libraries are connected to the GALILEO system, which links all of the libraries in the University System of Georgia. Instructional Support Services and its staff of professional tutors maintain four math and writing tutorial facilities that house sixty computers. The College has seven open computer labs and forty computer classrooms. The Pentium PC stations in these classrooms and labs include full Office Professional Suite and full communications software and world wide web access.

Honorary Societies Phi Theta Kappa

Athletics Georgia Perimeter College fields teams at the intercollegiate level in men's and women's tennis, men's baseball, women's softball and volleyball, men's basketball, and men's and women's soccer. Georgia Perimeter is a member of the National Junior College Athletic Association and the Georgia Junior College Athletic Association. The College also offers an intramural and recreational program for students and faculty members that includes tennis, soccer, softball, basketball, swimming, table tennis, volleyball, and other activities.

Study Abroad The International Center supplies students with updated information about the study-abroad programs in the University System of Georgia as well as programs throughout the country, helps students with applications, and conducts predeparture orientation programs and re-entry programs for those studying abroad. In addition, the University System of Georgia offers a centralized listing of study-abroad programs at each of its thirty-four colleges and universities, including Georgia Perimeter College's own programs. Students register for these programs at their home institution, which facilitates the process of transferring credits and arranging for financial aid.

Support Services The Center for Disability Services coordinates support services provided to students identified as disabled, deaf or hard of hearing, learning disabled, physically disabled, visually impaired, or disabled due to illness. Services include sign-language interpreters, tutors, note takers, specialized advisers, and classroom modifications. Specialized equipment, including portable reading machines, TDDs, and assistive listening devices, is also available to students.

Job Opportunities The Federal Work-Study program is available to qualified students. Selection for the program is made on the basis of need as determined by federal guidelines. In addition, Georgia Perimeter College provides, through its own resources, a limited number of other student assistantships involving part-time work on campus.

Tuition: $53 per semester hour for state residents, $160 per semester hour for nonresidents, per year (2001–02)

Mandatory Fees: $107 per semester

Contact: Director, Clarkston Campus: Dr. Susan McGrath, 555 North Indian Creek Drive, Clarkston, Georgia 30021-2396; Telephone: 404-299-4154; Fax: 404-298-3834; E-mail: smcgrath@gpc.peachnet.edu. Director, Decatur Campus: Marissa McNamara, 3251 Panthersville Road, Decatur, Georgia 30034-3897; Telephone: 404-244-5044; Fax: 404-244-3392; E-mail: mmcnamar@gpc.peachnet.edu. Director, Dunwoody Campus: Dr. Thomas Graham, 2101 Womack Road, Dunwoody, Georgia 30338-4497; Telephone: 770-551-3083; Fax: 770-604-3791; E-mail: tgraham@gpc.peachnet.edu. Director, Lawrenceville Campus: Dr. Jeffrey A. Portnoy, 1000 University Center Lane, Lawrenceville, Georgia 30043; Telephone: 678-407-5324; Fax: 678-407-5273; E-mail: jportnoy@gpc.peachnet.edu.

Georgia Southern University

4 Pu G S Sc

▼ Orell Bernard Bell and Sue Floyd Bell Honors Program

The Bell Honors Program (BHP) is designed to serve the undergraduate educational needs of exceptionally gifted, well-prepared, highly motivated, and creative students. For BHP scholars, an interdisciplinary and team-taught core curriculum employing seminar methods of instruction replaces the standard core curriculum required of other Georgia Southern University (GSU) students. Classes are small and taught by faculty members chosen from among the University's best professors.

The BHP core emphasizes development of critical-thinking skills, active student participation in their own learning, and extensive use of primary materials rather than conventional textbooks. Weekly seminars and colloquia at the freshman, sophomore, junior, and senior levels offer additional enrichment of the education of BHP scholars. BHP scholars who are undecided as to their majors are advised by the program director; other BHP scholars are advised by faculty members of the Honors Council in the appropriate fields.

BHP scholars enjoy special access to faculty members, including opportunities for undergraduate research in their major fields of study. The special BHP core curriculum is recognized by all programs and majors offered at GSU and BHP scholars may major in any field. The special core curriculum is designed for entry at the first-term freshman level and transfer students normally cannot be accepted into the program. The Bell Honors Program offers the atmosphere of a small and highly selective liberal arts college within the context of a University that is large and diverse enough to offer a wide array of strong major programs. The program reflects the central priority of undergraduate instruction, which lies at the core of Georgia Southern University's mission.

BHP scholars enjoy exclusive 24-hour access to Honors House for study and informal social activities. Honors House contains computers and printers for use of BHP scholars, a reference library, study lounges, and a full kitchen.

The program currently has 70 students enrolled.

Participation Requirements: Graduation with BHP scholar status requires completion of the special Bell Honors Program core curriculum (60 quarter hours), completion of 12 quarter hours of BHP seminars and colloquia, and satisfactory performance in all academic work in the judgment of the faculty members of the Honors Council, which conducts a systematic quarterly review of the academic work of each BHP scholar. BHP scholars completing all requirements are, with their parents, guests of honor at an annual dinner hosted by the University president on the evening prior to the June graduation. At this dinner, each BHP scholar graduate is presented with an individually cast and crafted engraved medallion, which is worn at graduation and becomes a permanent memento of the special experience of participation in the program.

BHP scholars are accorded special recognition in graduation ceremonies, graduating first among undergraduate degree recipients. The diploma of each BHP scholar carries a special seal denoting his or her status. The transcripts of BHP scholars include special materials describing the selectivity of the program, the special requirements completed, and descriptions of the special program courses.

Admission Process: The first freshman class entered the BHP in 1982 and the first senior class of BHP scholars graduated in

Interpreting the symbols: **2**=two-year college, **4**=four-year college; **Pu**=public or state college, **Pr**=private college; **G**=general honors program; **D**=departmental honors program; **S**=small program (fewer than 100 students), **M**=midsize program (100 to 500 students), **L**=large program (more than 500 students); **Sc**=scholarships available in honors program; **Tr**=transfer students accepted into honors program; **HBC**=historically black college; **AA**=academic advisors; **GA**=graduate advisors; **FA**=fellowship advisors.

1986. A maximum of 18 new BHP scholars are accepted as entering freshmen annually. The new class is chosen from among high school senior applicants on the basis of SAT and/or ACT scores, high school grades and curricula, extracurricular activities, a required essay, letters of recommendation from teachers, and, for finalists, an individual interview with the Honors Council. Applications from nontraditional students are welcome. The annual deadline for submission of written applications is March 1, and selection decisions are made prior to May 1.

Scholarship Availability: Each BHP scholar is awarded an academic scholarship from the Georgia Southern University Foundation, which covers the cost of tuition and, where applicable, out-of-state fees. This scholarship is renewable for up to four years. BHP scholars who are National Merit Scholars or National Merit Scholarship finalists qualify for an additional scholarship from the GSU Foundation of $1500 per year.

The Campus Context: Georgia Southern University was founded in 1906 as a district agricultural and mechanical school. GSU advanced to become a teacher's college, then a senior college, and in 1990 earned its status as one of five state universities in Georgia. Located 60 miles west of the historic city of Savannah, the University is based in Statesboro, which is a rapidly developing regional trade and manufacturing hub.

Georgia Southern is the most comprehensive university in the southern half of the state. Its more than 600 acres are lush with the traditional oaks, magnolias, pines, and azaleas of the American South. The University is composed of five colleges—Liberal Arts and Social Sciences, Science and Technology, Education, Business Administration, and Health and Professional Studies. In addition, 150 baccalaureate, master's, and doctoral programs are offered.

There are several points of general public interest on the campus that also contribute to the academic experience of students. The University Museum features permanent and visiting exhibits that highlight the culture and history of South Georgia. It is home to a 40-million-year-old mosasaur fossil and the 80-million-year-old Vogtle whale, which is the oldest fossil whale skeleton in North America. The University Planetarium offers periodic shows by a nationally renowned astronomer and faculty member affiliated with the Hubble Space Telescope project. The National Tick Collection is a global clearinghouse for the identification and study of ticks and the diseases that they transmit. The Tools for Life Center provides information, services, and equipment for the disabled. Magnolia Gardens, the University's botanical garden, is a haven for plants and wildlife native to the region. It is frequently used by students to further their studies in biology.

Student Body The total enrollment at GSU is 14,157: 12,477 undergraduates and 1,680 graduates. Although 89 percent of the students are Georgia residents, forty-seven states are also represented in the student body. Fifty-six percent of the students are women. The ethnic distribution among students is 73 percent Caucasian, 24 percent African American, and 3 percent Asian, Hispanic, or other ethnic origin. There are 358 international students from sixty-seven nations. Extracurricular activities include twenty-three social fraternities and sororities, academic clubs relating to fields of study, and nationally affiliated political organizations.

Faculty Georgia Southern University has 600 full-time faculty members and 65 percent have terminal degrees. In addition, there are 70 part-time faculty members. The student-faculty ratio is 24:1.

Key Facilities The library contains 1.9 million volumes and has LEXIS-NEXIS access. The library also houses more than 300 DOS- and MacIntosh-based computers for student use in its Learning Resources Center.

Athletics In athletics, Georgia Southern has NCAA Division I affiliation (I-AA football). Men's sports include football, baseball, basketball, soccer, cross-country, golf, tennis, and swimming. Women's sports include softball, soccer, volleyball, basketball, tennis, swimming, and cross-country. Intramural athletic teams compete in flag football, basketball, softball, volleyball, and other sports. Club intercollegiate teams include rugby, fencing, and horseback riding.

Study Abroad Study-abroad opportunities are sponsored by some academic departments. Other programs are available through shared opportunities at other University System of Georgia schools.

Job Opportunities Many students may supplement their incomes with part-time employment in campus departments or through the Office of Financial Aid as part of an overall assistance package or acquire employment in local retail or service businesses.

Tuition: $1584 for state residents; $5463 for nonresidents, per year

Room and Board: $3675

Mandatory Fees: $471

Contact: Director: Dr. G. Hewett Joiner, Landrum Box 8036, Statesboro, Georgia 30460; Telephone: 912-681-5773; Fax: 912-681-0377; E-mail: hewjoiner@gsvms2.cc.gasou.edu

Georgia Southwestern State University

4 Pu G S Tr

▼ University Honors Program

The University Honors Program (UHP) at Georgia Southwestern State University (GSW) offers outstanding students an enriched environment for learning through enhancement of and alternatives to the general curriculum requirements. The UHP aims to promote lifelong learning, to assist and guide students interested in graduate studies, and to encourage a study-abroad experience. The UHP also attempts to enhance and challenge the education of regularly enrolled students through contact with honors students as well as the experience of participating faculty members.

The types of honors courses include clustered courses of the current curriculum (two faculty members coordinate their respective courses and cosupervise a course project for honors students), which also have nonhonors students enrolled; honors enrichment of a regular course, also with nonhonors students enrolled; special seminars for honors students only; and honors assistantships.

The fall semester of 1999 will mark the inception of the UHP at GSW; a regular enrollment of approximately 100 students is anticipated.

Participation Requirements: The UHP requires honors students to take at least two honors courses each year (a cluster represents one honors course) and maintain a minimum 3.2 overall GPA. Each student will complete an honors project/thesis and a service requirement. Students who complete the program requirements will be hosted at a pregraduation banquet and receive medallions; a special designation will appear on their transcripts at graduation.

Admission Process: First-year students are admitted to the UHP by invitation. The Honors Program Committee will extend invitations to students based upon their SAT I scores, high school GPA and rank in class, and recommendations when available. Transfer students, international students, and students already at GSW may seek admission with a 3.4 minimum GPA and referral by a faculty member. Rolling admissions apply.

Scholarship Availability: The University has a considerable endowment for an institution of its size, particularly the Charles H. Wheatley Scholarship fund for outstanding students (National Merit Scholars with 1100 SAT I and 3.0 or above high school GPA). Others include J. C. Roney Scholarships (National Merit Semifinalists and STAR students), 10 various alumni scholarships, and many other academic scholarships in specific disciplines. Though none of these scholarships has been designated specifically for honors students at present, the UHP will aggressively support its honor students by awarding them scholarships from these resources on an individual basis.

The Campus Context: Georgia Southwestern State University is a senior unit of the University System of Georgia. Founded in 1906 as the Third District Agriculture and Mechanical School, it became Georgia Southwestern College in 1932. In 1964 the College became a senior unit of the University System, and in 1973 added graduate work to the curriculum. In July 1996, the Board of Regents authorized state university status and the institution became Georgia Southwestern State University. The educational experience at GSW is characterized by small class sizes, technology-enhanced instruction, and opportunities to work closely with faculty members. The University, noted for its classical buildings arranged in a crescent, is located on an attractive 187-acre residential campus in the lovely historic town of Americus, 135 miles south of Atlanta and 135 miles north of Florida's Gulf Coast. Americus also boasts of its partnership with Habitat for Humanity, founded and headquartered here, as well as the Jimmy Carter National Historic Site and the Andersonville National Prisoner of War Museum and Cemetery in surrounding Sumter County.

Student Body Undergraduate enrollment is 2,200 (2,600 total), and 67 percent of the students are women. The minority distribution is 26 percent African American, 3 percent Asian, and 3 percent other. Seventy percent of students receive financial aid, and 33 percent of students live on campus. The campus has four fraternities and four sororities.

Faculty There are 147 faculty members, 117 full-time, of whom 78 percent have terminal degrees.

Key Facilities The James Earl Carter Library on the campus of GSW houses 180,000 bound volumes plus 850,000 microform volumes. Ten computers are available in the library with public use of Galileo, Georgia Library Card, and the Internet. Many other computer labs are located in departments across the campus.

Honorary Societies Alpha Chi, Gamma Beta Phi, and Blue Key

Athletics GSW is a member of the NAIA's Georgia-Alabama-Carolina Conference with men's and women's basketball, men's and women's tennis, men's baseball, and women's softball and volleyball. There are many opportunities for student participation in club-level and intramural athletics as well.

Study Abroad Through the UHP office, students can participate in exchanges and study-abroad programs. The University also offers a once-yearly course that includes a two-week work-abroad experience coordinated through Habitat for Humanity's International Headquarters.

Support Services Eighty percent of the campus is accessible to disabled students.

Job Opportunities Job opportunities are available both on and off campus.

Tuition: $1730 for state residents, $6950 for nonresidents, per year (1998–1999)

Room and board: $3120

Mandatory Fees: $501

Contact: Director: Dr. Jeff Waldrop, 206 Administration Building, Americus, Georgia, 31709-4693; Telephone: 912-931-2720; Fax: 912-931-2059; E-mail: mjw@canes.gsw.peachnet.edu

Georgia State University

4 Pu G M Sc Tr

▼ Honors Program

The Honors Program at Georgia State University (GSU) provides a place for high-achieving students to obtain many of the benefits of a small liberal arts college while also receiving the advantages of attending a comprehensive university. It provides small discussion-oriented classes at the core level as well as the upper division. The program provides a natural home for both multicultural and interdisciplinary courses, and it offers some of the most innovative courses in the University. Students are given opportunities to propose and complete a senior thesis and to participate in the design and coordination of colloquia.

Students have the option of residence on an honors floor in dormitory housing. A special community assistant provides programming and guidance for these students.

Approximately 450 students are enrolled in the Georgia State University Honors Program, which was founded in 1975.

Participation Requirements: Students must maintain at least a 3.3 GPA to graduate with an Honors Recognition. Although there is no minimum number of courses required to remain enrolled in the honors program, students who are in good academic standing in the program and who have taken at least one honors course in the past three semesters are considered active in the program. Active students are eligible for priority registration and Honors Program Scholarships. Each spring, the Honors Program presents medallions to any student who has completed the requirements for General, Advanced, or Research honors at an awards ceremony. This recognition is also noted on the student's diploma and transcript.

Admission Process: Students may be admitted to the Honors Program at any stage of their academic careers. Freshmen admitted to the University with a high school GPA of 3.3 or higher and an SAT I of at least 1180 are eligible to apply to the program. Transfer students should have completed 10 hours of transfer credit with a GPA of 3.3 or above. Georgia State students who are already matriculated may also apply to the program if they have completed 10 hours at GSU and have a GPA of 3.3 or better. Students complete an application that requests basic academic data and a short writing sample. Upon receipt of the application, an interview is held and a decision is made at that time.

Scholarship Availability: The Honors Program awards ten Alumni Association Scholarships once a year. Students need to have completed at least two honors courses to be eligible to apply. Recipients are selected by a faculty committee on the basis of academic achievement. The University awards a number of Presidential Scholarships each year to incoming freshmen. These stipends include a cash allowance of $4000 per year for four years plus a grant of $1500 to be used for a summer study or a research project. Applications for these highly competitive awards are usually due by March 1 each year.

The Campus Context: Georgia State University is located in downtown Atlanta, two blocks from the state capitol in the center of the city's financial district and one block north of Underground Atlanta, a popular entertainment and shopping complex. The campus is adjacent to the Georgia State MARTA Station, part of the metropolitan area's extensive public transportation system, and is located two blocks from the central Five Points Station.

The Honors Program occupies facilities in the University Center. Students have the use of a computer/research room, with online access and printing capabilities, as well as a student lounge. Classrooms are adjacent.

Interpreting the symbols: **2**=two-year college, **4**=four-year college; **Pu**=public or state college, **Pr**=private college; **G**=general honors program; **D**=departmental honors program; **S**=small program (fewer than 100 students), **M**=midsize program (100 to 500 students), **L**=large program (more than 500 students); **Sc**=scholarships available in honors program; **Tr**=transfer students accepted into honors program; **HBC**=historically black college; **AA**=academic advisors; **GA**=graduate advisors; **FA**=fellowship advisors.

Student Body Total enrollment is about 26,000. Undergraduate enrollment is about 18,000. Sixty percent of the students are women. The minority ethnic distribution is 28 percent African American, 11 percent Asian American, 3 percent Hispanic, and 0.3 percent Native American. Nine percent of students live on campus, and 50 percent of the students receive financial aid. Students from more than 140 countries are enrolled in the University.

Faculty Instructional full-time faculty members number 988. Eighty-nine percent have terminal degrees. The student-faculty ratio is 15:1.

Key Facilities The GSU main library houses 1.2 million volumes. There are three open-access computer labs on the main campus.

Athletics GSU is a member of the Trans America Athletic Conference (TAAC) and is an NCAA Division I team. GSU has teams in women's basketball, golf, softball, soccer, volleyball, cross-country, and tennis. Men's teams include basketball, golf, baseball, soccer, cross-country, and tennis.

Study Abroad Through the Office of International Services and Programs students can participate in exchanges and study-abroad programs.

Job Opportunities Work opportunities are available on and off campus.

Tuition: $2622 for state residents, $10,528 for nonresidents, per year (2001–02)

Room and Board: $4500 per year for housing

Contact: Director: Dr. Grant Luckhardt, Honors Program, Georgia State University, University Plaza, Atlanta, Georgia 30303; Telephone: 404-651-2924; Fax: 404-651-4890; Web site: http://www.gsu.edu/honors

Goucher College

4 Pr G S Sc Tr

▼ General Honors Program

The General Honors Program at Goucher offers students the chance to examine unusual subjects from complex, multicultural perspectives. It seeks to encourage students to cross boundaries and use problem-solving methods from a variety of fields. In most honors classes, students have 2 professors, each from a different academic specialty. Social science and humanities courses are interdisciplinary and team taught. Science courses focus on research in the laboratory.

While team taught, interdisciplinary courses form the core of the General Honors Program. The Making of the Modern World is the theme for the program. Honors students participate in the Freshman Honors Seminar their first semester. All second-semester freshmen in the General Honors Program take the Modern Condition, an examination of Western civilization between 1890 and 1945.

From the beginning of the first year through the fall semester of the senior year, honors students choose three interdisciplinary electives. Recent honors offerings include Philosophy and the Sciences: The Origin of Time, Shakespeare: Stage and Page, Vietnam: A Fateful Encounter, Film and Modern Japan, and African-American Female Voices. In addition, honors sections are offered in biology, chemistry, and physics and honors students may begin taking these freshman year. All honors students must take at least one science honors elective and at least one non-science honors elective. Students may also pursue independent honors study with individual faculty members.

The capstone experience is the Senior Honors Seminar, which is a course in imaginative problem-solving that offers students the opportunity to investigate a problem and write a research paper combining two disciplinary approaches. The most recent seminar explored the boundaries between nature and culture.

Besides taking honors courses, students attend plays, concerts, lectures, and other cultural events on and off campus. Each semester the Honors Program holds dinners to allow the faculty and students to exchange ideas and enjoy each other's company. General honors is noted on the student's diploma and transcript.

The program is more than 10 years old and currently enrolls 75 students.

Participation Requirements: General honors students must maintain a minimum 3.25 GPA in honors work. An overall GPA of 3.5 or higher, with at least 80 percent of the credits taken in residence on a graded basis, and no fewer than 60 total graded credits are also required for general honors.

Admission Process: Incoming freshmen must have a combined SAT I score of at least 1350 (with neither math nor verbal score below 600) and a ranking in the upper 10 percent of their high school class. There is also an on-campus interview during Scholar's Day. Other students who excel during their first year at Goucher and outstanding transfer students are also invited to join the program.

Applications must be received by February 1.

Scholarship Availability: Numerous merit awards are available to honors and nonhonors students, including Dean's Scholarships (full tuition for four years), Marvin Perry Scholarships (partial tuition for four years), and Rosenberg Scholarships in the Arts ($5000 one-year scholarships).

Scholars must maintain full-time status and remain in good academic and disciplinary standing with the College. Scholars must complete a minimum of 24 graded credits and a total of 30 credits per year and maintain the following GPAs throughout their matriculation at Goucher: Dean's Scholars, 3.0 cumulative GPA throughout freshman year and 3.25 cumulative GPA in subsequent years; Marvin Perry Scholars, 3.0 semester GPA throughout the four years.

The Campus Context: Goucher College offers eighteen majors for the Bachelor of Arts degree and five degrees in interdisciplinary areas. On the graduate level, Goucher offers master's degrees in arts administration, creative nonfiction, education, historic preservation, and teaching, as well as a postbaccalaureate premedical program. Among the distinguished facilities on campus are the Robert and Jane Meyerhoff Arts Center, the Thormann International Technology and Media Center, the Kraushaar Auditorium (seats 1,000), the Mildred Dunnock Theatre (black-box theater), the Todd Dance Studio, the Computer Music Studio, and the Huges Center for Public Affairs.

Student Body The student body at Goucher is 73 percent women. The ethnic distribution of the students is 8 percent African American, 3 percent Asian, 3 percent Hispanic, 4 percent nonresident, 75 percent Caucasian, and 9 percent other. There are 45 international students currently attending Goucher. Residents constitute 68 percent of the student body. Nearly 77 percent of students receive financial aid. There are no fraternities or sororities at Goucher.

Faculty Of the 147 total faculty members, 78 are full-time and 76 percent have a terminal degree. The student-faculty ratio is 10:1.

Key Facilities The Julia Rogers Library houses 292,318 volumes. There are a number of computer facilities on campus, including the Thormann International Technology and Media Center, which has approximately thirty computers; the Hoffberger 117, which has approximately fifteen computers; the Advanced Technology Lab, which has approximately fifteen computers; the Julia Rogers Library, which has approximately ten computers; and various terminals in areas such as the student center and dormitories

Athletics Goucher is an NCAA Division III competitor and a member of the Capital Athletic Conference. The Gophers, as the teams are called, compete in eight varsity sports for women (cross-country, field hockey, basketball, volleyball, lacrosse, swimming, tennis, and soccer) and six for men (cross-country, tennis, soccer, swimming, basketball, and lacrosse), as well as an equestrian intercollegiate program for both men and women.

Study Abroad Goucher's study-abroad programs include a junior year in Exeter, England; the Goucher College-Roehampton Institute Dance Exchange in London; a junior year at Glasgow School of Art, Scotland; a semester abroad in Salamanca, Spain; study-abroad in France (a semester or a year at the Sorbonne); The Politics of Great Britain (January); British Literary Study Tour (January or May); Tropical Marine Biology in Honduras (January); a Summer at London/Cambridge Institute; Summer Study in Greece; European Community Tour (January or summer); a semester/year in Tubingen, Germany; a semester/year in Jerusalem, Israel; a semester/year in Mexico; and the Instep Summer Internship Program (various locations).

Support Services Disabled students find that all programs are handicapped accessible. Students with special needs can be accommodated. Handicapped-accessible parking is available in all lots and near most buildings. Equipped bathrooms and lowered drinking fountains are available in nearly all campus buildings.

While Goucher does not have a separate program for students with learning disabilities, the College does offer a variety of academic support services to all students through the Writing Center and the Academic Center for Excellence (ACE). Services offered through ACE include a mathematics lab, supervised study groups, academic skills peer tutoring, and content area peer tutoring for most courses.

Job Opportunities Eligible Goucher students may work on campus in federally funded work-study positions; non-work-study jobs are also available. In addition, students may receive payment through the Federal Work-Study Program for community service work. For those choosing employment outside of the campus community, many job opportunities are available in and around the Towson and Baltimore areas.

Tuition: $19,415 per year (1998–99)

Room and Board: $7130

Mandatory Fees: $250

Contact: Director: Dr. Laurie Kaplan, 1021 Dulaney Valley Road, Baltimore, Maryland 21204-2794; Telephone: 410-337-6253; Fax: 410-337-6405; E-mail: lkaplan@goucher.edu; Web site: http://www.goucher.edu

Governors State University

Pu G S Sc Tr AA

▼ University Honors Program

While recognizing academic excellence, the University Honors Program is designed to give students an opportunity to pursue an enriched education while attending Governors State University. In so doing, honors students pursue greater depth within their academic major by completing advanced work within their existing curriculum. In addition, honors students obtain greater breadth by taking an interdisciplinary honors seminar in which guest speakers from across the University's campus address a common integrative theme. Having been exposed to a rich diversity of academic perspectives, students then complete a project relevant to their academic major in cooperation with a faculty mentor.

The curricular components of the University Honors Program include one course in the students' major in which they contract with the instructor to do advanced work, one advanced interdisciplinary Honors Seminar, and an honors thesis/project/internship that is completed under the supervision of a faculty mentor.

The curricula of the University are offered through four colleges: the College of Arts and Sciences, the College of Business and Public Administration, the College of Education, and the College of Health Professions.

Beyond the above enriched academic program, honors students also have the combined benefits of a speakers series, the support and guidance of a faculty mentor, participation in special social events, and membership in a community of scholars and learners. Participation in honors is reflected on the student's transcript and with a letter of commendation from the president of the University.

Participation Requirements: The University Honors Program is open to all students who are interested and who expect to be able to meet the graduation requirements for the program. At the beginning of the students' participation in the program, advisement takes place with the Honors Director. At this time, the student signs a letter of agreement that acknowledges the major curricular requirements of the program. Transfer students and students nominated by faculty members are highly encouraged to register with the program.

Admission Process: Students not yet admitted to the University should contact the Admissions Office. Since Governors State University is an upper-divisional university, students need a minimum of 60 hours of college credit to be admitted.

Scholarship Availability: Governors State University offers an array of different scholarships and work-study opportunities. In particular, there is a community college (transfer) scholarship available to students. Community college honors students who are in the process of completing their program successfully can receive a letter of scholarship recommendation from the Honors Program Director.

The Campus Context: Governors State was chartered by the General Assembly in 1969. It is designed to serve undergraduate transfer students and those seeking master's degrees.

The University's main campus is located in University Park, 35 miles south of Chicago and easily accessible by car or commuter train. The campus is located on 750 acres of wooded landscape with several lakes and nature trails and includes the nationally renowned Nathan Manilow Sculpture Park.

Governors State University's primary mission is teaching. It provides an affordable and accessible undergraduate and graduate education to its culturally and economically diverse lifelong learners. The liberal arts and sciences are the foundation of the University's academic programs, which generally emphasize professional preparation.

Governors State University has a strong commitment to cultural diversity in every facet of University life. The University values its multicultural community of students, faculty members, and staff members as they learn together throughout their lives. It addresses the needs of the traditional and nontraditional learners through the breadth of its curriculum, through flexible teaching strategies, and through advanced instructional technologies.

Governors State University is an active partner in the economic and social development of the surrounding metropolitan regions, preparing informed and concerned citizens and providing them a global perspective in an interdependent world.

Tuition: $1176 for state residents, $3528 for non-Illinois residents (2001–02)

Interpreting the symbols: **2**=two-year college, **4**=four-year college; **Pu**=public or state college, **Pr**=private college; **G**=general honors program; **D**=departmental honors program; **S**=small program (fewer than 100 students), **M**=midsize program (100 to 500 students), **L**=large program (more than 500 students); **Sc**=scholarships available in honors program; **Tr**=transfer students accepted into honors program; **HBC**=historically black college; **AA**=academic advisors; **GA**=graduate advisors; **FA**=fellowship advisors.

Contact: Director: Dr. Larry Levinson, University Honors Program, Governors State University, University Park, Illinois 60466; Telephone: 708-534-4578; Fax: 708-534-7895; E-mail: l-levinson@govst.edu

GRAMBLING STATE UNIVERSITY

4 Pu G M Sc Tr HBC AA

▼ Earl Lester Cole Honors College

The Earl Lester Cole Honors College is a non-degree-granting unit in the academic structure at Grambling State University, a level five institution. It was established in 1990 for the purpose of enhancing the development of scholars for service, to provide additional opportunities for academically talented students and to enable them to take responsibility for broadening their education. The goal is to make it possible for bright, determined students to make choices to extend their horizons while earning a degree. The unique academic support program provides a plan that ensures the advanced performance expected of graduates now and in the twenty-first century.

The nontraditional Honors College program is designed to lead to the development of scholars, effective leaders, and dedicated, service-oriented workers. A basic feature of the program is the students' freedom to make choices that enrich their grasp of their chosen majors and enhance sociocultural understandings and global perspectives. Members of the Honors College are challenged to think about this reality: "Where will they be as competent, humane citizens and leaders at the end of four years?" Based on choices made, they ask themselves these questions: "What kind of person will they be when they get their degrees?" "Will they be service-oriented graduates eager to face challenges or persons bound by the limits of their major?" Participants understand that their choices determine the quality of the education they will have gotten when they graduate and what has been gained or lost by virtue of those choices. They recognize the importance of choices, attitudes, affirmations, and visions and understand that participation in the Honors College enhances total self-development. Through extra effort and diverse comrade activities, they become empowered workers and leaders who understand that they receive more immediate attention for interviews and more positive consideration in the market place when applying for jobs or for graduate school. They have a sense of serenity that makes them see that what they have gained in the Honors College empowers them to serve and gives them the desire to serve.

Participation Requirements: Participation in the Honors College focuses on "Making A Difference" in academic performance, in the respective major, and in the specific program thrust of the Honors College. The program consists of a number of Interdisciplinary Seminars, a thesis, projects, and activities. A minimum of 9 semester hours in Interdisciplinary Seminars and a thesis or a special project are required. The minimum requirements are a minimum GPA of 3.2 with 9 to 12 semester hours earned in the total Honors College program.

Students in the Honors College provide individual and group support. They volunteer as supplemental academic helpers for fellow students who have specific subject matter or other problems. Academic supplemental assistance and other types of help are coordinated by leadership in the Honors College Laboratory Center. Students are active throughout the University providing individual and group support by serving on debate teams, SGA Boards, and the University Ambassador Corps and by serving as mentors, class leaders, SGA presidents, internship representatives for major companies, GSU representatives in student research at NAFEO, and project coordinators for Gates Scholars.

Added advantages for members of the Honors College include notation on the transcripts stating that the graduate was a member of the Honors College, preference for housing in Honors Dorms, and a special Medallion Luncheon in recognition of graduating seniors with medallions presented that represent distinction in academic honors attained: Bronze, Silver, and Gold.

Admission Process: Since the Earl Lester Cole Honors College has a high stimulus rating at GSU, throughout the state, and beyond, students and parents make direct contacts for admission. Participation in the Freshman Honors Seminar, Honors 110, is the path to admission in the Honors College. Beginning freshman students with a designated ACT/SAT I score and a required minimum GPA enroll in Freshman Honors Seminar 110. They take general education courses that are designated as honors courses by the Colleges of Liberal Arts and Science and Technology: English, history, mathematics, and the sciences. The courses are taught in the respective colleges by designated professors. The admissions process involves assessment of performance in Honors Seminar 110, a completed application with two letters of recommendation, and a clearance report from the Office of Student Affairs followed by a satisfactory interview and approval by the Honors Committee. Accepted applicants are inducted into the Honors College each October. This is a formal induction ceremony to which parents are invited. They may pin the inductee with the beautiful Honors College badge.

Scholarship Availability: Scholarship availability for the Honors College is related to the scholarship plan of GSU. The University offers scholarships to top ranking students from high schools throughout the state and nation. These students comprise the majority of students who enroll in the Freshman Honors Seminar, Honors 110. Most of these students apply for the Honors College. There is a special Dan/Jan Fulmer scholarship provided by two professors.

The Campus Context: Grambling State University welcomes students to a place where the prevailing spirit emphasizes change and growth that result from involvement, outreach, and diversity, which undergirds the belief that "everybody is somebody." However "somebody" results from self-actualization, which is largely an individual matter. "You make the difference." At GSU, it is believed that the quality of life results from learning, responsibility, relationship, and involvement and that happiness and success depend on outreach: GSU to students and students to GSU.

GSU is located in a small, rural community, easily accessible to I-20, which leads to major cities, including Shreveport and New Orleans. They are approximately 60 miles west and 320 miles south, respectively. There is air service and bus service available.

The University celebrated is Centennial, 1901–2001, using the theme "A Century of Excellence." Throughout its 100 years, Grambling has had as its focus its motto: "The College where everybody is somebody."

During the early years, Charles P. Adams, the founder; Ralph Waldo Emerson Jones, the builder; and Earl Lester Cole, the curriculum engineer, laid the academic and spiritual foundation for Grambling State University, which is a student-centered institution. GSU is proud of its outstanding programs that have and are producing master teachers, writers, poets, scientists, nurses, social workers, business executives, doctors, lawyers, mathematicians, and musicians, including its world-famous Tiger Marching Band that is joining bands from three other institutions to feature the filming of "The Life of a Band Student." In the NCAA College Hall of Fame, the Grambling Drum Major, in uniform, represents all collegiate bands. The Tiger Marching Band was second in line in the inauguration of President Bush.

At GSU, basic areas for student activities and services are provided. Some designated areas include the Floyd L. Sandle Little Theater, Favrot Student Union, Intramural Center, and a central Student Computer Center that is available day and night. Other Computer

Centers are designated in major buildings including the business building, the library, the College of Liberal Arts, and the School of Nursing.

Over the years Grambling State University has maintained a tradition of excellence in its exemplary academic programs, exceptional reputation in extracurricular activities, challenging student-centered activities, wholesome environment for learning, and extraordinary graduates whose excellent performance in major areas of work give them an edge in employment, particularly in teaching, business, computer science, nursing, and social work.

Student Body: GSU students are academically motivated, serious, caring, and diverse, and they enjoy themselves in and out of the classroom. At GSU, there are students from the major cities, states, and countries. They help each other in the computer, language, and science labs. Many students receive financial aid, others have band, choir, dance, academic, writing, athletic, and other scholarships, while some participate in work-study. A number earn funds on internships (summer or semester with IBM, Disney World, State Farm, etc.).

The diversity of the student body at GSU is, in a sense, a microcosm. Through the extensive undergraduate programs and graduate offerings from the master's through the doctoral level, GSU provides, effectively, for 4,600 full-time students. Students participate in college activities including membership in the Honors College, international honor societies and sororities and fraternities, which include Alpha Kappa Alpha, Delta Sigma Theta, Sigma Gamma Rho, Zeta Phi Beta, Alpha Phi Alpha, Omega Psi Phi, and Phi Beta Sigma.

Faculty: The faculty is, in a sense, like the student body in cultural and racial differences. Its members are dedicated and concerned and chiefly full-time, with tenure. They are published, direct major grants, and hold membership in professional organizations.

Key Facilities: The updated library in terms of staff, technology, organization, personnel, and holdings will match any library in a college the size of GSU. The students, faculty, and community are proud of the library. There are 306,023 print resources, 691 paper and microform subscriptions, 108,772 electronic subscriptions, 121,954 microform units, and 8,282 audiovisual materials.

Honorary Societies: Alpha Mu Gamma; Alpha Phi Omega Sigma; National Service Fraternity, Inc.; Alpha Phi Sigma; Delta Psi Kappa; Gamma Beta Phi; Golden Key; Groove Phi Groove; Iota Epsilon Rho; Phi Beta Lambda Business Organization; Sigma Alpha Iota International Music Fraternity for Women; Sigma Tau Delta; Tau Beta.

Athletics: Grambling has been and is a powerhouse in athletics, with Dr. Eddie G. Robinson, the winningest coach in the nation, plus the nationally televised Bayou Classic played annually at Thanksgiving in New Orleans. Its teams are SWAC, National Black College, and Bayou Classic Champions. It is to be noted that GSU produces scholars who are outstanding athletes. GSU is competitive in varsity sports. They are football, basketball, baseball, track and field (includes cross-county and indoor/outdoor teams), tennis, and golf for men and women's basketball, track and field, tennis, golf, softball, volleyball, and bowling. Many students who are involved in various sports, both men and women, are members of the Honors College and remain on the honor roll.

Study Abroad: There is a limited study-abroad program. Students have the option to study abroad as part of an exchange agreement through the NSE program. The interest is great and conferences with international faculty members helps.

Support Services: Provisions are available for the educationally challenged—largely, the mild cases.

Job Opportunities: At GSU, students participate in financial aid work programs that are offered as work-study and undergraduate assistantships. Internship opportunities are good, with effective preparation through Career Awareness Seminars in the Honors College. In addition, students work off campus in local areas, which include the local village and the town of Ruston, 5 miles east. The Honors College at GSU empowers minds and spirits to lead and serve.

Tuition: These tuition figures for the academic year 2001–2002 include all fees and, for on-campus figures, room and board. On campus (in state) $2662.50; off campus (in state) $1294.50. On campus (out-of-state) $5337.50; off campus (out-of-state) $3969.50.

Contact: Dean: Dr. Helen Richards-Smith, Honors College, or Ms. Ellen D. Smiley, Associate Dean, Grambling State University, P.O. Box 326, Grambling, Louisianna 71245; Telephone: 318-274-2114 or 274-2286. World Wide Web: http://www.gram.edu

Grand Valley State University

4 Pu G L Sc Tr AA

▼ Grand Valley State University Honors College

Grand Valley State University (GVSU) offers academically talented students an opportunity to participate in an exclusive community of scholars exemplifying intellectual achievement. The GVSU Honors College is an alternative form of general education that integrates courses and disciplines, offers a variety of team-taught courses, and maintains small class size. Professors give individual attention to each student and expend extra time and energy to help students progress. The Honors College chooses faculty members who are experts in their fields and who are excited about working with undergraduates. The Honors College prepares students to be competitive nationally for graduate and professional programs. Honors students develop high levels of proficiency in research, writing, and critical thinking, synthesizing material from multiple disciplines and often applying analytical skills to primary sources.

All students enrolled in the Honors College are required to take an integrated arts and humanities sequence consisting of four 3-credit courses. This arts and humanities experience serves as a gateway for all subsequent honors education and comprises the honors core. Good performance in these classes satisfies all University writing requirements. The Honors College is flexible in permitting course selection in the sciences and social sciences to accommodate requirements of specific majors or programs. The required Honors Senior Project ensures that all students engage in original work; many students choose to join faculty research projects.

Honors students may live in the same building where they attend their honors classes, the Glenn A. Niemeyer Living Center, which incorporates state-of-the-art thinking in communal living and classroom instruction. The Niemeyer Living Center fosters a close-knit community that shares goals and experiences specially designed to foster academic excellence and the joy of learning. The Honors Office and faculty offices located in the Living Center provide maximum opportunity for faculty-student interaction.

An honors education extends beyond the classroom. Students can take advantage of travel opportunities, entertainment offerings, social events, and service projects. Participating in student organizations helps honors students develop leadership skills to complement their academic skills.

Students share in the governance of the Living Center. The Honors Council, the student governance organization, provides

Interpreting the symbols: **2**=two-year college, **4**=four-year college; **Pu**=public or state college, **Pr**=private college; **G**=general honors program; **D**=departmental honors program; **S**=small program (fewer than 100 students), **M**=midsize program (100 to 500 students), **L**=large program (more than 500 students); **Sc**=scholarships available in honors program; **Tr**=transfer students accepted into honors program; **HBC**=historically black college; **AA**=academic advisors; **GA**=graduate advisors; **FA**=fellowship advisors.

all honors students a voice in their honors experience, not just those residing in the Living Center. Through Honors Council, students attend faculty meetings, make recommendations to the program director, and assume responsibility for the Honors Code.

Honors College students may establish a cocurricular transcript to document their extracurricular activities, which are designed to promote development of leadership skills and appreciation of the richness and diversity of university life.

Participation Requirements: All students who are admitted to GVSU and who have a high school GPA of 3.5 or better and an ACTE composite score of 28 or better are invited to join the Honors College. The decision about admission depends on the review of the applicant's file by a committee of faculty members. In order to continue in the program, students must maintain a minimum GPA of 3.2 and make adequate progress toward the degree requirements. Students who earn a GPA of less than 3.2 but above 2.8 are placed on probation for a period of one year, after which they either return to good standing or are dropped from the program.

Admission Process: All applicants for admission to GVSU who meet the honors criteria of a GPA of 3.5 or better and an ACTE composite of 28 or better receive a mailing with information about the Honors College and instructions about how to apply. Participants in the scholarship competition are also presented with information about the Honors College from faculty members and students. Prospective students who qualify for the Honors College may use the online application process. Qualified applicants are admitted directly into the program and receive information about orientation/registration sessions held during the summer and the special fall honors orientation. Students may wait until they arrive at the summer orientation/registration to apply. Once students apply and are admitted to the Honors College, the honors staff members work closely with housing staff members to facilitate placement in honors housing, the Glenn A. Niemeyer Living Center.

Scholarship Availability: GVSU offers renewable Faculty Scholarships (up to $4000 per year) and renewable Presidential Scholarships (up to $7000 per year) to incoming first-year students as part of an on-campus scholarship competition. To be considered for a Faculty Scholarship, a student needs an ACTE score of at least 29 and a high school GPA of at least 3.5; for the Presidential Scholarship, the minimum ACTE score needed is 32, and the minimum high school GPA is 3.8. These scholarships are not based on need. National Merit Finalists are awarded up to $2000 in additional funds. The Arend D. and Nancy Lubbers Endowment provides additional funding for students in the Honors College.

The Campus Context: GVSU is a comprehensive public university located in Allendale, Michigan, 12 miles west of urban Grand Rapids and 15 miles east of Lake Michigan's sandy beaches. Situated on a wooded ravine and surrounded by meadows and the University golf course, the campus presents opportunities for outdoor learning and recreation. Complementing the bucolic Allendale campus, the Robert C. Pew campus is nestled against the Grand River in the heart of downtown Grand Rapids. Together, the campuses offer first-rate science and engineering labs, a state-of-the-art graduate and law library, art museums with extensive collections, and new dance, art, and design studios.

Rated among "America's 100 Most Wired Universities," GVSU is well-known for innovative technology, including in-class computer stations, Web-based instructional activities, online course postings, and chat groups that may include not only fellow students but also students and faculty members from around the world.

Grand Valley values excellent teaching enhanced by active scholarship, encouraging students to work with faculty mentors. Opportunities for research and internships exist through GVSU's own programs, such as the Robert B. Annis Water Resources Institute and the Hauenstein Center for Presidential Studies. The University has also nurtured strong ties with community institutions, including the Gerald R. Ford Museum, the Van Andel Research Institute, the Grand Rapids City Historian's Office, and private industry.

Student Body For 2001–02, total enrollment was 19,762, including 16,385 undergraduate students. The student profile includes 40 percent men and 60 percent women. Approximately 9 percent of the students are of ethnic minority groups. Seventy percent of the students receive financial aid. There are eleven sororities and twelve fraternities. The number of residents living on campus is 4,054. An additional 2,000 live in nearby privately owned apartments. Thirty-five percent of the students are residential and 65 percent are commuters.

Faculty The total number of faculty members is 575. Eighty percent of the faculty members have a terminal degree. The student-faculty ratio is 22.3:1.

Key Facilities James H. Zumberge Library, the University's main library, is located on the Allendale campus. The library houses more than 672,000 volumes, 3,422 periodicals, 6,200 electronic journals, and 21,639 reels of microfilm along with many other resources, including U.S. government documents. The library has reading and study areas throughout. The GVSU Library Voyager catalog is online and can be accessed from off campus via the World Wide Web. There are more than 100 online databases to search for journal articles and other types of information in many subject areas.

The Steelcase Library is located on the first floor of the DeVos Center on Grand Valley's downtown Pew Campus. The library's circulating collection features an automated retrieval system. The library holds more than 100,000 volumes and can accommodate up to 250,000 volumes. The reading room offers a quiet study area with connections for laptop computers. The Grand Rapids Bar Association's law collection is also housed here.

Grand Valley is one of *Yahoo! Internet Life* magazine's "100 Most Wired Universities" in the nation, recognizing the University's commitment to integrating the latest technology into all aspects of student life. Grand Valley's computer laboratories are well equipped with the latest Intel Pentium and Power PC Macintosh computers. The laboratories also have access to laser printers and image/OCR scanners. High-end computing laboratories allow for specialized applications, such as AutoCAD, Geographical Information Systems, statistical programs, SAP, and multimedia applications. The computer laboratories are open throughout the school year and up to 20 hours a day. The laboratories provide access not only to computers and printers, but also to the full range of software on the network. There are forty computers available in the common areas of residence halls. Campuswide high-speed network and Internet connections are provided in all rooms. Adaptive technology workstations are available.

Honorary Societies Chapter 217 of the National Honor Society of Phi Kappa Phi, Kappa Beta Chapter of Beta Alpha Psi, Beta Chapter of Michigan/Lambda Alpha, Tri Beta, Beta Gamma Sigma, Alpha Phi Sigma, Tau Beta Pi, Sigma Tau Delta, Phi Alpha Theta, Pi Mu Epsilon, Pi Delta Phi, Dobro Slovo, Sigma Delta Pi, Phi Epsilon Kappa, Kappa Epsilon, Pi Sigma Alpha, Psi Chi, Pi Alpha Alpha, Phi Alpha, Alpha Kappa Delta

Athletics GVSU competes in nineteen sports at the NCAA Division II level and is a member of the Great Lakes Intercollegiate Athletic Conference (GLIAC). The school has won GLIAC's all-sports trophy, the President's Cup, eight times in twenty-nine years, including the past three. In 2001, the women's volleyball team won the NCAA Division II Great Lakes Championship, and the women's cross-country team finished fifth in the nation in the NCAA Division II level. The GVSU football team had a 13-1 season, winning the GLIAC Conference and the NCAA Division II Northeast Regional Championship. The Lakers football team finished 2001 as the runner-up in the NCAA Division II National Championship.

GVSU students are admitted free to all home events. GVSU is known for its excellent student support of sports teams and conducts many promotions geared specifically to students during athletic events. Intercollegiate sports teams include men's baseball, basketball, cross-country, football, golf, swimming, tennis, and track and women's basketball, cross-country, golf, soccer, softball, swimming, tennis, track, and volleyball. There are twenty-six club sports, including a rowing/crew team that competes internationally.

GVSU provides the opportunity for everyone to participate in athletics through intramural activities and personal fitness activities. The Student Fitness and Recreation Center offers a wide range of activities and plenty of equipment. Students may work at their own pace or sign up for instructor-led sessions at a variety of intensity levels. In addition, the Field House complex has a Wellness Center, which provides a variety of services, ranging from health screenings and fitness appraisals to exercise and diet counseling.

Study Abroad Students in every major have opportunities to study in another country. The Padnos International Center sponsors summer, semester, and yearlong study-abroad programs through partnerships with universities throughout Europe, Asia, South America, and Australia. GVSU offers study-abroad opportunities in Australia, Barbados, Brazil, Canada, China, Costa Rica, Egypt, El Salvador, England, France, Germany, Hungary, Ireland, Jamaica, Japan, Mexico, New Zealand, Nicaragua, Poland, South Africa, Spain, Sweden, Taiwan, Trinidad, and Tobago.

Support Services Support services for students with disabilities on GVSU's campus include accessible facilities and curricula. The campus provides state-of-the-art assistive technology hardware and software with training from knowledgeable faculty and staff members.

Job Opportunities Most campus jobs are funded under the Federal Work-Study Program. Preference is given to students who have the greatest financial need, who meet the academic progress requirements of Grand Valley, and who are enrolled for a full program of courses. Students usually work an average of 10 to 15 hours a week. Attempts are made to find jobs in line with the students' class schedules and job skills; however, employment is not guaranteed.

The Career Services Office provides extensive services to students as they prepare for postgraduation employment. The staff members assist students in preparing resumes and credentials and in developing interviewing skills. The Web-based system provides an electronic resume database available to employers and a national job listing of opportunities. The office coordinates eight annual career fairs that have company representatives who provide information and interview GVSU students. In addition, the office provides internship listings and assistance in locating internships for students.

An internship is a supervised work experience directly related to an academic discipline. The internship may be full- or part-time and may or may not be a paid work experience. An internship typically lasts for one semester and is available in most GVSU majors. Internships and co-ops may be initiated by the faculty adviser, the employer, the student, or the Career Services Office. The faculty adviser within each academic department is responsible for final approval of internships and co-ops to ensure that the experience meets specific departmental criteria. Students are required to comply with academic departmental GPA requirements for internships or co-ops. The work setting must provide an opportunity for learning that is relevant to the intern's academic field. The employer provides a field supervisor, and the academic department provides a faculty member to direct the experience. Field supervisors evaluate the student before completing the work experience.

Tuition: Tuition is $4920 per year. This covers two semesters of 12 to 16 credits each. Out-of-state tuition for two semesters of 12 to 16 credits each is $10,344 (2001–02).

Room and Board: For 2001–02, Honors Living Center costs were $1815 per semester (not including meal plan); traditional living centers were $2690 per semester (including meal plan); suite-style living centers were $2915 per semester (including meal plan).

Mandatory Fees: There is a $20 nonrefundable application fee.

Contact: Director: Dr. Johnine Callahan, 181 Niemeyer Living Center, One Campus Drive, Allendale, Michigan 49401; Telephone: 616-895-3219; Fax: 616-895-3413; E-mail: honors@gvsu.edu; Web site: http://www.gvsu.edu/honor

GREENSBORO COLLEGE

4 Pr G S Sc Tr

▼ George Center for Honors Studies

The George Center for Honors Studies, the honors degree program at Greensboro College, is designed to challenge and reward students who have a high level of intellectual ability and motivation. One of the program's goals is to build a community of scholars on campus. The program begins developing community among honors students in the freshman year, with a common freshman block composed of two linked honors courses. There are also several extracurricular activities for honors students, such as dinner at the dean's house and "pizza with profs" - an informal monthly gathering of honors students and professors.

The program is not inward-looking by any means, however. It offers students significant opportunities to integrate scholarship and service through its Collaborative Service Learning Program (CSLP). The CSLP invites honors students to spend four weeks in a different culture where they engage in community service and a variety of other learning experiences. The George Center has sponsored CSLP projects in Trinidad, Alaska, and England.

The George Center believes that the ability to view issues from multiple disciplinary perspectives is crucial to intellectual development. Interdisciplinary thinking starts in the freshman year, when professors coordinate the material so that honors students have an opportunity to study the same work or theme in two "linked" courses (e.g., English and history). Later in the curriculum, honors students take special topics seminars that are team-taught by professors from different disciplines. The topics for the interdisciplinary seminars vary from year to year and are based on professors' interests and suggestions from incoming honors students. Recent seminar topics have included Advertising as Art, and Vietnam and the Media.

Greensboro College has had an honors program for more than fifteen years. The program became the George Center for Honors Studies in 1996 when it was endowed by a gift from alumna Eleanor George. There are approximately 70 students enrolled in the program.

Participation Requirements: Freshman honors students take a 6-hour honors block each semester. The block consists of honors English and one other general education course, e.g., history or religion. Sophomores take two honors seminars that are team-taught by professors from different disciplines. The topics for these interdisciplinary seminars vary from year to year and are chosen based on student requests and faculty interests. Honors juniors enroll in a research methods seminar and an independent study. The seminar covers research models, methods, and skills.

Interpreting the symbols: **2**=two-year college, **4**=four-year college; **Pu**=public or state college, **Pr**=private college; **G**=general honors program; **D**=departmental honors program; **S**=small program (fewer than 100 students), **M**=midsize program (100 to 500 students), **L**=large program (more than 500 students); **Sc**=scholarships available in honors program; **Tr**=transfer students accepted into honors program; **HBC**=historically black college; **AA**=academic advisors; **GA**=graduate advisors; **FA**=fellowship advisors.

The independent study is taken under the guidance of a faculty member in the student's major in order to prepare the research plan for the senior honors thesis. Senior honors students enroll in another independent study to carry out the research plan and complete the thesis. Honors students present the results of their senior theses to the campus at the end of the fall or spring semester.

To remain in the program, students must maintain a 3.0 cumulative GPA. Successful completion of the program is recognized at commencement and is also noted on the official transcript and diploma.

Admission Process: Entering freshmen who have an SAT I score of 1100 or higher and a high school GPA of 3.0 or higher are invited to participate in the program. Students transferring into Greensboro College with fewer than 30 hours of college credit who meet the preceding criteria for freshmen and have a college GPA of 3.25 or higher may participate in the program by contacting the program director. Students transferring in with 30 or more hours who have a college GPA of 3.25 or higher may participate in the program by contacting the program director. All students who enter the program without the benefit of the freshman honors block must demonstrate writing proficiency.

Scholarship Availability: Scholarships of various amounts are awarded through the Office of Admissions based on academic performance. Most honors students are recipients of academic scholarships. In addition, students who successfully complete the honors requirements each year are given a $500 participation scholarship for the next academic year. Honors students may enroll in more than 18 hours per semester without paying an overload fee.

The Campus Context: Greensboro College is situated on 40 acres of rolling lawns and trees in a historic district bordering downtown Greensboro, North Carolina. Greensboro has a population of more than 220,000 people and is one of three cities that form the Triad, a major metropolitan area that is home to 1.13 million people. Located 3 hours from the beach and 2 from the mountains, Greensboro offers an array of cultural, educational, and recreational opportunities. The College, founded by the Methodist church in 1838, offers degrees in twenty-three academic disciplines.

Student Body The enrollment at Greensboro College is 1,051. Approximately 73 percent of the students are enrolled as traditional students and 27 percent as adult education students. The College serves a diverse population, attracting students from twenty-nine states and eight countries.

Faculty The total number of faculty members is 101, of whom 53 are full-time. Ninety percent of the full-time faculty members hold the highest degree in their academic discipline.

Key Facilities The James Addison Jones Library houses a collection of more than 102,000 volumes and over 650 periodical and newspaper subscriptions as well as sound recordings, scores, video recordings, and computer software. The library is open more than 80 hours a week, and staff members are available to help with reference services, small group and individualized instruction, locating and obtaining books and journal articles from other libraries, and other information needs. The library offers up-to-date technology in an online catalog shared with other area libraries, automated circulation and interlibrary loan services, CD-ROM and online search services, library-to-library facsimile transmission, the Internet, the World Wide Web, and NC LIVE.

Jones Library also houses the George Center seminar room. All interdisciplinary honors seminars, which are limited in enrollment to 12 students, are held in the seminar room, which has comfortable seating for informal discussion. When seminars are not being held, the room is available as an honors study room. It is equipped with a slide projector, TV/VCR, portable CD player, and computer projection equipment. The George Center has a laptop computer for use by honors students in presentations on campus and at conferences.

The Cowan Humanities Building houses the Computer Lab and the Writing Center. Each has twenty Pentium computers with CD-ROM and sound capability. All are attached to the campus network and allow access to e-mail, the World Wide Web, and scholarly resources. There are two networked high-speed laser printers in each facility, and a variety of software packages are available on the computers and Novell server. A campus fiber-optic backbone supports connections to the network from faculty offices, classrooms, and residence hall rooms. Students are provided with e-mail and Web accounts.

Honorary Societies Alpha Chi

Athletics Greensboro College competes in fifteen intercollegiate sports and sponsors a coed cheerleading program. Greensboro is a member of NCAA Division III and the Dixie Intercollegiate Athletic Conference. The College fields teams in men's and women's basketball, cross-country, lacrosse, soccer, and tennis; men's baseball, football, and golf; women's swimming and volleyball; and a full range of men's and women's intramural and recreational sports. The College's James G. Hanes gymnasium houses an indoor pool, weight-training room, dance gymnasium, athletic training room, and basketball court. In addition, all full-time Greensboro College students have free access to the YMCA, located just two blocks from campus.

Study Abroad Honors students have an opportunity to study diverse cultures, both domestically and abroad, through the George Center's Collaborative Service Learning Program (CSLP). The CSLP is designed to give honors students an opportunity to integrate scholarship and service in another culture. Students who participate in the CSLP take a preparatory seminar in the spring to learn the history and culture of the place they will be visiting, then spend four weeks on location during the following summer. The on-site experience involves some form of service to the community as well as a variety of other learning experiences. Themes and sites for the CSLP have included "Education and Culture" in Trinidad and Tobago; "Environment and Culture" in Cordova, Alaska; and "Eighteenth Century England: Observation and Change in the Age of John Wesley" in London, England.

Support Services Students with varied special needs, physical and academic, have graduated from Greensboro College by fulfilling all essential academic requirements with individualized attention and instruction. Students should submit detailed documentation of their needs to the Director of Academic Development.

Job Opportunities The College offers work-study employment on campus to students who demonstrate financial need. In addition, the Greensboro metropolitan area offers students many internship and job opportunities.

Tuition: $10,800 per year (1998–99)

Room and board: $4700

Contact: Director: Dr. Cynthia B. Hanson, Odell Building, 815 West Market Street, Greensboro, North Carolina 27401; Telephone: 336-272-7102 Ext. 349; Fax: 336-271-6634; E-mail: hansonc@gborocollege.edu; Web site: http://www.gborocollege.edu/admissions/george.htm.

GREENVILLE COLLEGE

4 Pr G S Tr

▼ Honors Program

The Greenville College (GC) Honors Program seeks to identify, encourage, and serve students who desire an enhanced academic experience in keeping with the institution's commitment to the development of excellence in character and service. This selective program provides a value-added academic experience for a select number of students who have demonstrated exceptional academic performance and involvement. It offers recognition of academic achievement, creates opportunities for social interaction among its members, and encourages service. Founded in 1995, the program annually enrolls approximately 20 students. The number admitted each year is determined by graduation and attrition.

Participation Requirements: In the freshman year, students are to enroll in honors English (unless exempt), honors speech communication, honors foundation in the liberal arts tradition, and honors Christian thought and life. The curriculum also includes honors sections of psychology, sociology, literature, biblical studies, and social science courses. During the course of their tenure in the program, members are also to earn 4 credits in HON 110 or 310, Selected Topics, an intensive 1-credit course that combines experiential and theoretical components to study a particular topic. The program curriculum culminates with a required departmental honors thesis. Junior students may earn 2 credits in honors thesis research; senior students may earn up to 4 credits while completing the thesis during their final year.

To remain in the program, freshman students must maintain a cumulative GPA of 3.25 or higher. Others must hold a 3.5 GPA or higher at the end of each academic year. Successful completion of the program is recognized at commencement and is noted on the official transcript and diploma.

Admission Process: Admission to the Greenville College Honors Program is highly competitive and based on a limited number of openings each year. To apply, students entering their first year of college must have an ACT score of 27 or higher or an SAT I score of 1200 or higher, must be in the upper 10 percent of their graduating class, must hold a minimum cumulative GPA of 3.5, must complete a series of essay questions describing their relevant leadership and service experiences, and must submit two letters of endorsement. Returning and transfer students must have a minimum college GPA of 3.5, must complete a series of essay questions describing relevant leadership and service experiences, and must submit two letters of endorsements from college professors. Selection is made by the 9-member Honors Council composed of faculty members and students associated with the Honors Program.

Scholarship Availability: At the present time there are no scholarships awarded expressly for participation in the Honors Program. However, most members hold academic scholarships awarded by Greenville College, and 94 percent of Creenville College students receive financial aid. For information regarding scholarships, students should contact the Office of Admissions.

The Campus Context: The College is located in the town of Greenville, a community of 7,000 residents. The main academic campus is located three blocks from the town square and sits on an 8-acre plot with several of the fifteen buildings arranged in a quad configuration around a grassy open space. All academic and residence halls are within a few minutes' walk of the center of campus. Athletic fields, a sports annex, and a small theater are located further away. Students wishing to participate in the cultural and shopping opportunities of a metropolitan area enjoy visiting nearby St. Louis and its suburbs. Here they find shopping malls; historic sites; museums; live theater; symphony and ballet; major league football, baseball, and ice hockey; ethnic restaurants; an art institute; the zoo; botanical gardens; a science center; and a planetarium.

Established in 1892 by the Free Methodist Church, Greenville College still adheres to the basic Wesleyan principles even though it attracts faculty members and students of diverse religious backgrounds who value the liberal arts tradition. The College is accredited by the North Central Association of Colleges and Schools and several other professional associations and organizations. Three baccalaureate degrees are offered by the College, and students may choose a major from the forty offered. In addition, there are preprofessional studies in eleven career fields, such as engineering, nursing, and architecture.

Student Body Greenville College enrolls approximately 1,100 students. The student body is composed of 48 percent men and 52 percent women. The ethnic distribution is 87 percent Caucasian, 6 percent African American, 3 percent Hispanic, and 1.5 percent Asian/Pacific Islander.

Faculty The faculty members total 145, of whom 59 are full-time. Sixty-three percent of the full-time faculty members have terminal degrees. The student-faculty ratio is 13:1.

Key Facilities The library, which was renovated and enlarged in 1991, contains more than 125,000 books, 494 subscriptions in paper, 1,500 full-text journal titles available online, and more than 4,000 audiovisual materials. The library is a member of a consortium of forty-five Illinois academic libraries that share their resources. Thus, Greenville students not only may access books in person, but may also borrow them from the major universities in Illinois. In the library, there are forty-one computers and thirty-five study carrels wired for laptops, all of which are Internet-accessible. In addition, the library has several computers with online subscriptions to reference sources such as *Encyclopedia Britannica Online* and *Bowker's Books in Print.* In addition to the library computers, there are several other labs on campus containing a total of approximately fifty computers (both PC and Macintosh platforms) to which students have access. Since 1998, the College has had a voluntary program whereby students can rent a laptop computer for use during their stay at Greenville. In 1999, a campuswide wireless network was added which gives all laptop users access to the campus network and the Internet from anywhere on the campus, including the dorm rooms. Students now have access to the Internet, their personal files, and printing services regardless of where they are on the GC campus. A fee is assessed for this service.

Athletics Greenville College offers a wide variety of intramural and intercollegiate sports for men and women. An NCAA Division III institution, Greenville College fields teams in both the St. Louis Intercollegiate Athletic Conference and the Illini-Badger Conference. The team sports are basketball for men and women, soccer for men and women, baseball (men), softball (women), volleyball (women), tennis for men and women, cross-country for men and women, track and field for men and women, and football (men). The Crum Recreation Center is a multipurpose indoor facility containing courts for basketball, volleyball, and badminton; a walking track; and net cages for batting and soccer practice. The Sports Annex located about a mile from campus houses a lap swimming pool, whirlpools, and a weight room featuring free weights and Nautilus-like exercise machines and stationary bikes. The College has a football field, baseball and softball fields, soccer fields, lighted tennis courts, and an outdoor track.

Study Abroad Greenville College encourages students to spend at least one semester in an off-campus program. In cooperation with the Council of Christian Colleges and Universities, overseas study programs are available in Africa, China, Costa Rica, Egypt, England (Oxford Honors Program), and Russia. During the three-week January Interterm, faculty members often sponsor out-of-country travel-study courses. Recent offerings included travel to London, Paris, Hawaii, Germany, Ireland, the Dominican Republic, Puerto Rico, Russia, and the Caribbean.

Support Services The Academic Enrichment Center (AEC) offers academic support services to all students on campus. These include tutoring, supplemental instruction, writing lab tutoring, academic counseling, reading assessment, and study skill seminars. The AEC also assists persons with disabilities in obtaining special equipment or services.

Interpreting the symbols: **2**=two-year college, **4**=four-year college; **Pu**=public or state college, **Pr**=private college; **G**=general honors program; **D**=departmental honors program; **S**=small program (fewer than 100 students), **M**=midsize program (100 to 500 students), **L**=large program (more than 500 students); **Sc**=scholarships available in honors program; **Tr**=transfer students accepted into honors program; **HBC**=historically black college; **AA**=academic advisors; **GA**=graduate advisors; **FA**=fellowship advisors.

Job Opportunities Each year many students are hired by the College through the campus employment or Federal College Work-Study programs. Types of jobs include lab assistants, secretarial/clerical, technology assistants, custodial, and food service. Many students are employed as residence assistants in campus housing. The Career Services Office provides information and assistance to students who seek off-campus employment. Internship placements are handled through the various academic departments.

Tuition: $13,490 full-time, $283 per credit part-time (2001–02)

Room and board: $5186

Mandatory Fees: $510

Contact: Director: Dr. Gene A. Kamp, 315 East College Avenue, Greenville, Illinois 62246; Telephone: 618-664-6610; Fax: 618-664-6610; E-mail: gkamp@greenville.edu; Web site: http://www.greenville.edu/honors

GREENVILLE TECHNICAL COLLEGE

2 Pu D S Sc Tr

▼ University Transfer Honors Program

The University Transfer Honors Program is designed to enhance the Greenville Tech experience for bright, highly motivated students. It is designed for students who want the most out of college. The program's faculty members welcome the opportunity to help these students stretch their intellectual limits.

The honors classes are modeled after graduate seminars. They are small, allowing maximum interaction between the students and the instructor. Lecturing is minimal. Instead, students are expected to be well-prepared for class to encourage a highly participatory process.

Central to the University Transfer Honors Program's philosophy is the idea that honors education does not mean more work for students; it means different work. Different in this case means more give and take between the student and the instructor, greater opportunities for independent research, more difficult materials, and enhanced opportunities for creativity and meeting individual goals.

Participation Requirements: A University Transfer honors graduate must maintain a 3.0 GPA or higher, complete a service requirement, complete at least one seminar course, and complete at least six courses with honors designation.

Admission Process: Current Greenville Tech students and students transferring to Greenville Tech Honors from other colleges must have a GPA of at least 3.4, no less than 9 transferable credit hours, and two letters of recommendation from individuals familiar with their academic performance, at least one of whom is an instructor at the college level. In addition, the honors applicant must submit an essay and have an interview.

High school students entering Greenville Tech Honors must have a high school GPA of at least 3.5 or a score of 1050 or above on the SAT I or a score of 26 or above on the ACT. In addition, high school students must submit two letters of recommendation from individuals familiar with their academic performance, at least one of whom is a high school teacher. Students must also interview with Dr. P. K. Weston, the Honors Program Director.

Scholarship Availability: Many honors students qualify for the LIFE Scholarship (Legislative Incentives for Future Education), recently established by the South Carolina General Assembly and available to students attending South Carolina colleges in the amount of $1000 each year for students in a two-year college. In addition, scholarships are available to honors students based on academic performance. To apply for these scholarships, students should contact Greenville Tech's Financial Aid Office at 864-250-8128.

The Campus Context: Located midway between Charlotte and Atlanta, Greenville offers the best of both worlds—fast-paced opportunity and small-town charm. Students choose from a wide range of activities to suit almost any interest, including festivals such as River Place and Fall for Greenville; golf at many area courses; parks, bike trails, and community centers; the Greenville Braves baseball team; the Grrreenville Grrrowl hockey team; the South Carolina Shamrocks soccer team; auto racing at the Greenville-Pickens Speedway, dirt tracks, and drag racing; college sports; Main Street Jazz, West End Thursday, Downtown Alive, and other weekly events; the Bi-Lo Center; the Peace Center for the Performing Arts; and much more.

Student Body Enrollment is 57 percent women and 43 percent men. Forty percent of the students are enrolled full-time, and 60 percent are enrolled part-time. Thirty-eight percent receive financial aid.

Faculty Within the University Transfer division, there are 83 full-time faculty members. Twenty-two percent of these instructors have terminal degrees.

Key Facilities The library contains more than 56,327 volumes and 730 subscriptions. In addition to a main campus, Greenville Tech maintains the Greer Campus, the Brashier Campus in Simpsonville, and the Northwest Campus in Berea. Computer labs for student use are available on all campuses, with labs in most classroom buildings on the main campus.

Honorary Societies Phi Theta Kappa

Support Services Services are available to help students find the right program for their talents and interests, succeed in their studies, and move on to good jobs. From writing and math centers, offering one-on-one help with questions and problems, to computer labs and the library, which provide access to the best resources available to any college student, the support services help every step of the way.

Job Opportunities The Federal Work-Study Program is designed to help students who would be unable to pursue or continue their studies unless they earned part of the expenses. Enrollment in at least 6 credit hours is required.

Tuition: Full-time: $1700 for county residents, $1850 for state residents, $3750 for nonresidents, per year; part-time: $71 per credit hour for county residents, $78 per credit hour for state residents, $157 per credit hour for nonresidents (1998–99)

Contact: Director: Dr. P. K. Weston, P.O. Box 5616, Greenville, South Carolina 29606; Telephone: 864-250-8786, 800-922-1183 Ext. 8786 (toll-free in South Carolina), 800-723-0673 Ext. 8786 (toll-free out-of-state); E-mail: westonpkw@gvltec.edu; Web site: http://www.greenvilletech.com

GUILFORD COLLEGE

4 Pr G M Sc Tr

▼ Honors Program

The Guilford College Honors Program provides a sequence of classes and independent study options designed to reward and intellectually challenge students seeking superior educational opportunities. Honors classes are small and usually taught as discussion-style seminars, which allow intensive learning in a close and supportive instructional relationship.

Students must take a minimum of five courses during their academic career. Students choose from a variety of team-taught, codisciplinary courses, and specially designed departmental offerings. Under the individual supervision of a faculty adviser, each student completes a senior thesis or project. The program is open to students majoring in all departments of the College. Successful completion of the Honors Program requirements is noted at graduation and on the student's transcript.

In addition to classwork and independent study, students in the Honors Program are encouraged to attend professional and undergraduate research conferences. The Honors Program offers generous travel support to students who present papers, research, or creative projects.

In keeping with the College's Quaker heritage, honors students at Guilford participate fully in the larger campus community. They live in residence halls and take most of their courses with the full student body. Honors students are active in a full range of campus activities, including athletics, student government, campus publications, choir, theater, community service projects, and special interest clubs.

Guilford College, a founding member of the North Carolina Honors Association, participates in the National Collegiate Honors Council and Southern Regional Honors Council. Students, faculty members, and administrators from the College attend the conferences of all three organizations.

There are currently 170 students in the Honors Program.

Admission Process: Most students are admitted to the Honors Program as entering first-year students, and approximately 10–15 percent of the freshman class is accepted into honors. Based on standardized test scores, high school achievement, writing samples, and recommendations, students are invited to attend Spring Interview Day. On that day, prospective honors students are interviewed by faculty members and current students. In addition, first-year and sophomore students who have earned a cumulative GPA of 3.5 or higher are invited to join the program.

Scholarship Availability: Guilford College has allocated substantial funds for honors scholarships, which are awarded without regard to financial need and are currently held by two-thirds of the students in the program. Scholarships are normally awarded when students are admitted to the College.

The Campus Context: Guilford College is a private liberal arts college founded by the Religious Society of Friends (Quakers) in 1837. It is located in Greensboro, North Carolina, on a wooded 340-acre campus that contributes to a serene and friendly atmosphere. Its outstanding faculty is dedicated to undergraduate teaching and views learning as a collaborative venture between students and faculty members. The College offers twenty-nine academic majors plus five cooperative preprofessional programs and eight concentrations. In addition, students can study abroad in six College-sponsored locations, including London, Ghana, Mexico, and China. There is also a domestic program in Washington, D.C.

Student Body The undergraduate enrollment at Guilford is 1,400 students. Women comprise 52 percent of the student body. Students are drawn from forty states and thirty-five other nations.

Faculty There are 89 full-time faculty members supplemented by a number of qualified part-time lecturers. Eighty-six percent of the full-time faculty members have terminal degrees. The student-faculty ratio is 13:1.

Key Facilities The library houses more than 250,000 volumes, and there are more than 1.3 million volumes in the consortium libraries data base. The DEC ALPHA 2100 computing facilities have terminals in ten campus buildings and eight residence halls. There are four student computer labs on campus.

Athletics Athletic activities include seven men's varsity sports and five women's varsity sports as well as an intramural program and club sports. The campus has a Physical Education Center.

Study Abroad Study abroad is available in semester or year programs in Africa, China, England, France, Germany, Italy, Japan, and Mexico.

Tuition: $15,550 per year (1999–2000)

Room and Board: $5610

Mandatory Fees: $570

Contact: Director: Dr. Robert B. Williams, 5800 W. Friendly Ave., Greensboro, North Carolina 27410; Telephone: 336-316-2218; Fax: 336-316-2950; E-mail: bob_williams@guilford.edu

GWYNEDD-MERCY COLLEGE

4 Pr G S Tr

▼ Honors Program

The Honors Program at Gwynedd-Mercy offers excellent students in baccalaureate degree programs enhanced educational opportunities through an integrated curriculum, combining an enriched general education in liberal studies with study in the major. Honors program courses are taught by teams of faculty members who have a strong commitment to interdisciplinary and collaborative teaching and learning. Classes are small, 8 to 10 students on the average, and are conducted in a seminar style.

The Honors Program at Gwynedd-Mercy consists of a series of liberal arts courses that are interdisciplinary in nature. Linked through the exploration of a very broad master theme, The Quest for Community and Freedom: The Individual and Society, the courses examine and explore the contributions made by the Western Tradition and the American experience to people's understanding of human freedom, responsibility in the community, and their relation to nature, giving attention as well to cross-cultural comparisons to these traditions. A capstone course, Towards Global Community, integrates liberal studies with the student's major field through a guided research project. Aimed toward developing a shared intellectual experience, the program seeks to foster the collegiality and community of learning crucial to intellectual growth and encourages students to reflect on the values and principles central to the visions of civility and community of Western democratic, Judaeo-Christian, and other traditions.

Courses are writing-intensive and concentrate on close readings of primary texts. They are enriched by field trips to museums, theaters, and spots of historical and cultural interest.

Founded in 1995, the program currently enrolls 30 students.

Participation Requirements: Students admitted to the program complete six honors courses. With the exception of transfer students, program participants tend to take one course per semester, following a prescribed sequence through the program: three courses in the Western tradition, two in the American Experience, and a capstone course, Towards Global Community, at the conclusion. To remain in the program, students must maintain a minimum 3.0 GPA in honors courses. Upon completion of the six courses, students are awarded a Certificate of Completion that goes into their academic record. Achieving at least a 3.0 GPA in the six honors courses and a minimum 3.35 GPA overall for the bachelor's degree entitles students to their degree with honors, with recognition at commencement and a special diploma.

Admission Process: Enrollment in the Honors Program is by invitation only. For entering freshmen it is based on SAT I or ACT scores, rank in class, faculty member/guidance counselor recommendations, a personal interview, and high school average. For transfer students, GPA from transfer institution(s), letters of recommendation from faculty members at previous institution(s), an interview, and SAT I scores are evaluated. Admission is on a rolling basis.

Interpreting the symbols: **2**=two-year college, **4**=four-year college; **Pu**=public or state college, **Pr**=private college; **G**=general honors program; **D**=departmental honors program; **S**=small program (fewer than 100 students), **M**=midsize program (100 to 500 students), **L**=large program (more than 500 students); **Sc**=scholarships available in honors program; **Tr**=transfer students accepted into honors program; **HBC**=historically black college; **AA**=academic advisors; **GA**=graduate advisors; **FA**=fellowship advisors.

Scholarship Availability: Merit-based academic scholarships of various amounts are awarded through the Admissions Office. The Honors Program does not award scholarships as such. However, most participants in the program are recipients of academic awards.

The Campus Context: Gwynedd-Mercy is an independent Roman Catholic institution for men and women. Founded in 1948 by the Sisters of Mercy, the College is located on a 170-acre suburban campus with easy access to Philadelphia. Well-known for its programs in nursing, education, and business, the College offers associate, baccalaureate, and master's degrees in more than forty fields of study.

Student Body The undergraduate enrollment is 1,521 students from nine states and territories and thirty countries. Eighty-two percent are women, 18 percent are men. Sixty-one percent are part-time, 95 percent are state residents, and 8 percent live on campus. Eighty percent are transfers, 5 percent are international students, and 67 percent are 25 or older. One percent are Native American, 2 percent are Hispanic, 6 percent are black, and 6 percent are Asian or Pacific Islander.

Faculty Faculty members number 181 (93 full-time, 39 percent with terminal degrees, 88 part-time).

Key Facilities Lourdes Library contains 100,000 books, 900 periodicals, and 10,000 media titles. The collection may be identified in the computerized catalogue, and a local area network in the library provides access to CD-ROM–based journal indexes. The library also provides access to the Internet for research and information gathering. More than 110 computers are available on campus for general student use. Computer purchase/lease plans are available.

Honorary Societies Kappa Gamma Pi and Alpha Sigma Lambda

Athletics Gwynedd-Mercy is a member of NCAA Division III. The College offers intercollegiate baseball (M), basketball (M/W), cross-country (M/W), field hockey (W), golf (M), lacrosse (W), soccer (M/W), softball (W), tennis (M/W), and volleyball (W).

Support Services Within the bounds of its resources, the College seeks to meet the needs of students with disabilities. Requests for specific accommodations are processed on an individual basis through the Student Services Division. At the time of acceptance (or anytime thereafter) a request can be made in writing to the Director of Counseling, allowing sufficient time for administrative processing.

Job Opportunities A limited number of work-study opportunities are available on campus to students who demonstrate financial need.

Tuition: Full-time $12,775–$13,710, part-time $290–$325 per credit hour (1998–99)

Room and board: $6000

Mandatory Fees: $275

Contact: Director: Dr. Carol Breslin, Gwynedd-Mercy College, Gwynedd Valley, Pennsylvania 19437; Telephone: 215-646-7300 Ext. 136; E-Mail: breslin.c@gmc.edu

---

Hampden-Sydney College

4 Pr G/D M Sc Tr

▼ Honors Program

The Honors Program at Hampden-Sydney College is designed specifically for the student who gives evidence of intellectual curiosity, independence of thought, excitement in learning, and appreciation of knowledge. It is for young men who spark the enthusiasm of fellow students and challenge the best in their teachers.

Participants in the program are encouraged to take an active role in the learning process, entering into dialogue with their professors and classmates, rather than just listening to lectures. The size of Hampden-Sydney and its excellent faculty make it well-suited to provide a learning environment for such motivated students.

Hampden-Sydney is proud that 16 percent of its students are honors scholars, young men who are recognized for distinguished achievement in secondary school and for their promise of successful careers both in college and in life. Honors scholarships are awarded in four categories. Stipends vary, but all four categories provide a scholarship to meet the recipient's College-determined need.

For such men, Hampden-Sydney has created its Honors Program, which gives participants in the program latitude for intellectual challenge and independent study, broadening their perspective and complementing their formal academic pursuits. Special courses for honors scholars boost curricular breadth. Honors scholars also receive tickets and transportation to attend plays, concerts, and other performances in Richmond, Virginia. On campus, honors scholars occasionally have dinner with visiting dignitaries and are invited to special colloquia. They may themselves hold symposia for other honors students in the region. In addition, participants in the Honors Program at Hampden-Sydney may attend the annual conventions of the Virginia Collegiate Honors Council or the National Collegiate Honors Council.

The Honors Program at Hampden-Sydney was founded in 1978 and admits more than 50 freshmen each year. Other students join the Honors Program as sophomores, juniors, or seniors. There are approximately 170 students currently enrolled in the program.

Participation Requirements: Freshmen honors scholars are invited to participate in a two-semester interdisciplinary seminar that is team taught by two faculty members from different academic divisions of the College. Honors scholars and other strong students are encouraged to apply to participate in the College's Summer Research program during at least one of the summers of their college years. Finally, honors scholars and other qualified students are encouraged to pursue Departmental Honors during their senior year. This program, available in each academic department of the College, includes a semester or yearlong independent research project under the supervision of a faculty mentor. Students who successfully complete the Departmental Honors project graduate with honors in their field of study.

Admission Process: High school students are recruited for the Honors Program on the basis of their high school class rank, their SAT I or ACT scores, their application essay, their letters of recommendation from college counselors and teachers, and, in some instances, a personal interview. The Honors Council also looks closely at the range of activities in which applicants to the program have been involved during their high school years and is particularly impressed by those applicants who have had leadership roles in their extracurricular activities. The application deadline is March 1.

Sophomores and transfer students who perform well during their first year at Hampden-Sydney are eligible to compete for an in-course honors scholarship during the fall of their second year at the College. Other qualified students who are not honors scholars may participate in the summer research and the departmental honors programs.

Scholarship Availability: The Honors Program, with the help of the College's admissions office, awards honors scholarships of various amounts to incoming freshmen based on their academic performance during high school. The Honors Program also awards competitive academic scholarships in course to sophomores and transfer students who perform well during their first year at the College.

The Campus Context: Hampden-Sydney College, founded in 1775 and the tenth oldest college in the country, is located in the heart of southside Virginia, 70 miles west of Richmond, Virginia, and 50 miles east of Lynchburg. The campus consists of 820 acres, much still in woodland, and part of the campus has been designated a National Landmark Preservation Zone.

Hampden-Sydney College, a fully accredited, four-year liberal arts college for men, seeks to "form good men and good citizens in an atmosphere of sound learning," as the original college announcement stated. Students are graduated with either a B.A. or a B.S. in one or more of twenty-seven majors. The newly formed Center for Leadership in the Public Interest provides students who are interested in a career in government with an opportunity to earn a concentration in public service.

Student Body Total enrollment in fall 2001 was 1,025 students. The campus has ten fraternities.

Faculty The total number of faculty members is 106, of whom 78 are full-time. Ninety percent of the full-time faculty members have terminal degrees. The student-faculty ratio is 11:1.

Key Facilities The Eggleston Library contains more than 212,000 volumes. The Fuqua International Communications Center houses an extensive collection of sound and video resources, including equipment for digital image scanning, multimedia production, and satellite video-conference reception. The John Brooks Fuqua Computing Center houses a variety of computer systems for students to use during their stay at Hampden-Sydney. An integrated data switching center handles network traffic over fiber-optic cabling that reaches most of the buildings on campus. All students can access the network from the dormitory rooms and connect to the Internet and the World Wide Web. In addition, there are a variety of computer labs that are available for student use.

Honorary Societies Phi Beta Kappa, Omicron Delta Kappa, and Chi Beta Phi

Athletics The Athletic Department offers a wide variety of programs for varsity and intramural athletics. Hampden-Sydney competes in NCAA Division III and is a member of the Old Dominion Athletic Conference. Hampden-Sydney fields intercollegiate teams in football, lacrosse, basketball, baseball, soccer, cross-country, tennis, and golf and club teams in rugby, fencing, wrestling, bicycling, and lacrosse. Almost 80 percent of the student body participates in the College's intramural athletic program.

Study Abroad The Honors Program at Hampden-Sydney College encourages students to enrich their education by studying abroad for a summer, a semester, or a full year. Each year a number of honors scholars study outside the United States in such places as England, France, Spain, Germany, the Czech Republic, China, Australia, and Mexico. Financial aid is available for honors scholars who wish to study abroad and credits earned at a college-approved program can be transferred to Hampden-Sydney as long as prior permission is obtained.

Support Services The Office of the Associate Dean of Academic Support, which is wheelchair accessible, works with students who have disabilities. In addition, this office administers an extensive system of peer tutors in the academic disciplines. The Writing Center provides both peer and professional tutoring for students who desire help with their writing.

Job Opportunities The Office of Financial Aid maintains extensive lists of part-time jobs that are available on campus and helps place interested students in these jobs.

Tuition: $17,524 (2001–02)

Room and board: $6386 (average)

Mandatory Fees: $627

Contact: Director: Alexander J. Werth, Box 162, Hampden-Sydney, Virginia 23943; Telephone: 434-223-6326; Fax: 434-223-6374; E-mail: awerth@hsc.edu; Web site: http://www.hsc.edu/academics/honors/

Hampton University

4 Pr G M Tr HBC

▼ Honors College

Honors College (HC), the primary component of Hampton University's Honors Program, is a special honors track for motivated, high-achieving students who are willing to seek success rather than avoid failure, who have the courage to take intellectual risks, and who are able to see the world in a "grain of sand." Honors College, established on Hampton University's campus in fall 1986, is designed to promote the development of intellectual, ethical leadership skills while fostering excellence in education, commitment to the learning process, experimentation, and a sense of a learning community. Honors College involves all academic units of the University and includes experiences from the freshman through the senior years. It includes an innovative curriculum; individualized advising and support services; special options, opportunities, and financial incentives; and extracurricular activities.

The honors faculty is made up of teachers who have demonstrated excellence in teaching, who are interested in interdisciplinary applications, who are committed to working with students to facilitate learning and discovery, and who are willing to work with other faculty members to improve the academic environment of the University as a whole.

In addition to participating in enriched courses with others of a similar scholastic aptitude, the student may receive or take advantage of Honors College perquisites, which include the HC pin; priority in course selection at each semester's registration; individualized advising; eligibility for scholarships and internships; participation in special events, field trips, and social activities; a fee waiver for transcripts; individualized assistance in preparing resumes and/or applications for fellowships and postgraduate study; special recognition during Honors Day Convocation; the honors designation on transcripts, Commencement certificates, and the Commencement programs; special honors cords to be worn with graduation regalia; subsidized honors program and honors conference expenses; and the honors newsletter, *Word of Honor.* There are currently 187 students enrolled in Honors College.

Participation Requirements: The Honors College requires students to complete 12 hours of honors credit in the general education courses and 12 hours of honors credit in the major, usually by contract. In addition, the Honors College student must take Argumentation and Debate or Logic and Ethics plus four University honors seminars, including UNV 200 Honors Service Learning Seminar, UNV 290 and 390 University Honors Seminar I and II, and UNV 400 Honors Independent Study Capstone Seminar. For the independent study, students are encouraged to choose a topic of interest that is not directly related to their major.

Admission Process: Entering freshmen, transfer students, and other students who are interested in pursuing an honors experience must apply for admission to Honors College after completing at least 15 hours of course work at the University. A student in Honors College is required to maintain a minimum GPA of 3.2. Other additional requirements are to perform at least 150 hours of community service, serve on an HC Committee for at least one semester, participate in a conference experience, and take the appropriate exam for graduate study.

Interpreting the symbols: **2**=two-year college, **4**=four-year college; **Pu**=public or state college, **Pr**=private college; **G**=general honors program; **D**=departmental honors program; **S**=small program (fewer than 100 students), **M**=midsize program (100 to 500 students), **L**=large program (more than 500 students); **Sc**=scholarships available in honors program; **Tr**=transfer students accepted into honors program; **HBC**=historically black college; **AA**=academic advisors; **GA**=graduate advisors; **FA**=fellowship advisors.

Scholarship Availability: Hampton University offers a number of Presidential and Merit Scholarships. Many students who receive these scholarships are in the Honors College program.

The Campus Context: Hampton University is a privately endowed, coeducational, nonsectarian, comprehensive institution of higher learning with accreditation by the Southern Association of Colleges and Schools and the Department of Education of the Commonwealth of Virginia. A historically black institution, the University serves students from diverse national, cultural, educational, and economic backgrounds. Its curricula emphasis is scientific and professional with a strong liberal arts undergird. The University offers the bachelor's degree in forty-seven areas, the master's degree in eighteen areas, and a Ph.D in physics, physical therapy (DPT), nursing (Ph.D.), and pharmacy (Pharm.D.).

A picturesque campus, surrounded on three sides by water, comprises fifty main buildings and seventy-five auxiliary structures spread out over 204 acres. Five buildings on campus are registered as National Historic Landmarks. The Emancipation Oak, 95 feet in diameter, is designated by the National Geographic Society as one of the ten great trees in the world. This live oak earned its name because the Emancipation Proclamation was read to Hampton residents there in 1863. The shade of the oak served as the first classroom for a newly freed people seeking the blessings of education.

Student Body There are 4,500 undergraduate students, of whom 61 percent are women. There are six fraternities and sororities and fourteen active honor societies on campus.

Faculty A faculty of 300 members plus adjunct faculty members afford a student-teacher ratio of 16:1.

Key Facilities The William R. and Norma B. Harvey Library is a major focal point of the academic and intellectual environment of Hampton University. This 125,000-square-foot, five-story facility has the capacity for more than 600,000 volumes. The fifth floor houses the Academic Technology Mall, which features state-of-the-art technology for student and faculty use.

The Hampton University Museum is the oldest African American museum in the United States and one of the oldest museums in Virginia. The Museum sponsors exhibitions, lectures, symposia, and art workshops and publishes the *International Review of African American Art.* The University Museum has holdings of more than 9,000 objects, including the following: traditional art from Africa, Native America, Asia, and Oceania; African American fine arts; and artifacts that depict the University's history. Located in the newly renovated Huntington Building, the University Museum is a regal, beaux-arts style building that is in the heart of the historic campus.

Honorary Societies Golden Key and Alpha Kappa Mu

Athletics Athletics play an important role in college life at Hampton. These activities offer every student a chance to take part in a sport of his or her choice. There is a program of intramural and recreational activities and intercollegiate athletic sports (NCAA Division I). Teams are fielded in football, basketball, tennis, track, volleyball, softball, golf, and sailing.

Study Abroad Hampton encourages study abroad. The Office of International Programs coordinates activities in fulfillment of the University's special emphasis in international affairs, culture, and global education. This office administers and oversees the development of cooperative agreements and exchange programs that provide mutually beneficial exchanges of scholars, students, and staff members as well as collaborative research projects.

Tuition: $9966 per year

Room and Board: $5090

Mandatory Fees: $1144

Contact: Director: Dr. Freddye Davy, Box 6174, Hampton, Virginia 23668; Telephone: 804-727-5076; Fax: 757-728-6711

Harding University

4 Pr G L Tr

▼ Honors College

The Harding University Honors College was established in 1989 to better serve some of the University's many talented students. It provides opportunities for these students to enrich and broaden their academic experiences. Honors courses stimulate and challenge promising students to develop their scholarship and leadership skills as fully as possible. In particular, this program encourages students to develop high intellectual standards, independent thought, logical analysis, and insight into the nature of knowledge while building their faith in God.

Harding University's Honors College features a three-tier approach to honors education. The Honors Scholar tier serves 40 of Harding's top incoming students each year. Recruited from National Merit Finalists and Trustee Scholars in the freshman class, these students earn some of their general education credits in five honors classes that are limited to 20 students each and are based on discussion and student participation rather than lecture. The classes involve more written and oral work from the students, but they also allow exceptionally close relationships with the teachers. Honors 201 deals with communication and critical-thinking skills. Honors 202 replaces the New Testament survey for freshmen. Honors 203 fits in the humanities area of general education, focusing on the big questions that man has always asked. Honors 204 deals with man and society, covering issues that range from twin studies to chaos theory. Honors 205 addresses the issues of man and his environment.

The Honors Student tier offers students the opportunity to take one or more honors sections of general education classes such as speech, English, art, music, and Bible. To qualify, students must score 27 or above on the ACT or 1200 or above on the SAT. The courses emphasize student responsibility and participation more than rote memorization. Most classes limit enrollment more than the regular sections do, and all are taught by faculty members selected and trained especially for honors education. Great care is taken that the courses are neither more difficult nor easier than the other general education offerings; instead, the focus in on different teaching styles and critical thinking. By following an honors track, students are preparing for their future careers in courses geared more to their academic preparation and ability.

Upper-level students who have completed the general education curriculum in either tier and upper-level and transfer students who qualify can participate in honors contract courses. Individual students and teachers collectively rewrite the syllabus of a course in the student's major, thereby turning it into an honors course. By exchanging some course requirements for other options that fit more with the ideals of honors education, the students can enhance the benefits they receive from courses that they take to complete their majors. The flexible nature of these contracts allows students to go into greater depth in some classes, to explore some supplementary topics in others, and to fine-tune their educational experiences within the limitations of their major and the honors program.

The Honors College is administered by a dean and the Honors Council, which consists of faculty members, administrators, and students. The students elect an executive council that participates on the Honors Council and organizes various activities, including speakers, retreats, picnics, and other social and cultural events. There are currently 620 students enrolled in the Honors College.

Participation Requirements: To remain eligible for the Honors College, students must maintain a minimum 3.25 GPA. Transfers and other students may petition for acceptance by submitting an application and two letters of recommendation from faculty members. To graduate from the Honors College, students must earn 20 hours of honors credits, including at least four courses in the Honors Scholar tier or the Honors Student tier. Those who earn at least 26 hours of honors credits, including at least four courses in the Honors Scholar tier or the Honors Student tier, four honors contract classes, and an honors capstone project, while maintaining a GPA of at least 3.5 are identified at graduation as Honors College graduates with distinction.

Scholarship Availability: Although most honors students receive University scholarships, the Honors College itself does not award scholarships. Eighty percent of Harding University students receive some type of financial aid.

The Campus Context: Harding University is a private Christian institution of higher education committed to the tradition of the liberal arts and sciences. In addition to the Honors College, it is composed of the following academic units: a College of Arts and Humanities; a College of Sciences; a College of Bible and Religion; a School of Business, Education, and Nursing; and graduate programs in religion, education, and nursing. Harding University has seventy-five undergraduate and three graduate degree programs on campus.

Student Body Harding enrolls approximately 5,015 students. Women constitute 55 percent of the student body. The ethnic distribution of students is 3 percent African American, 1 percent Native American, 1 percent Hispanic American, 5 percent foreign national, 88 percent Caucasian, and 1 percent other. There are 165 international students. Sixty percent of the students are residents. Social clubs involve a large majority of Harding students. Fourteen women's clubs and fifteen men's clubs provide students with a variety of club interests and sizes.

Faculty There are 233 faculty members, of whom 219 are full-time. Seventy percent of the faculty members have terminal degrees. The student-faculty ratio is 18:1.

Key Facilities The library's collections include 407,000 volumes and other media, including records, videos, kits, and maps. Harding's Ethernet local area network connects campus computer and information resources and also provides access to global facilities via the Internet. Campus labs, which are open to all students, provide access to DOS/Windows applications and Macintosh applications. These public facilities are complemented by a diverse collection of departmental equipment, which addresses the unique needs of the various disciplines.

Honorary Societies Phi Eta Sigma, Alpha Chi, Omicron Delta

Athletics Athletics play an important role in Harding's educational and recreational life. Harding competes in NCAA Division II. Men's teams are fielded in football, baseball, basketball, track, cross-country, tennis, and golf. Women's teams include basketball, cross-country, tennis, track, and volleyball. Harding's outstanding intramural program involves about 70 percent of men and 55 percent of women. The program includes both team and individual sports, with competition among social clubs and teams organized by the program directors.

Study Abroad The Harding University International Programs, academic programs based in Florence, Italy (HUF); London, England (HUE); Brisbane, Australia (HUA); Viña del Mar, Chile (HULA); and Athens, Greece (HUG), provide unique opportunities for study and travel abroad. No attempt is made to provide a complete curriculum; rather, courses are offered that may be studied with profit in an international setting. Serious involvement in classes, combined with the experience of international living, furnishes students with insights and perspectives that can be gained in no other way. Applications are accepted from students of Harding University and other institutions. Only students with a minimum GPA of 2.0 on at least 27 semester hours are considered. Formal acceptance occurs during the last full semester prior to the semester chosen for attendance.

Support Services Harding complies with the Americans with Disabilities Act of 1990. Most campus buildings are equipped for and accessible to handicapped persons. Class schedules are arranged and other measures taken to provide reasonable accommodations when necessary. New construction is in full compliance with the act.

Job Opportunities Work on campus is a source of financial aid to students, some of whom work up to 20 hours a week and earn more than $1400 per semester. Many, of course, work fewer hours and earn less. There are two work programs: the Federal Work-Study Program, funded by the federal government, and the Harding Program. To qualify for either program, students must complete an approved need-analysis application and the Harding Student Data Form. Students are paid minimum wage on the Federal Work-Study Program and are switched to the Harding Program when work-study funds are expended. The Harding Program rate of pay is 85 percent of minimum wage.

Tuition: $8730 per year (2001–02)

Room and Board: $4498

Mandatory Fees: $300

Contact: Dean: Jeffrey T. Hopper, Box 10898, Searcy, Arkansas 72149-0001; Telephone: 501-279-4056; Fax: 501-279-4184; E-mail: honors@harding.edu; Web site: http://www.harding.edu/

HARTWICK COLLEGE

4 Pr G M Sc Tr AA

▼ Hartwick College Honors Program

Hartwick College Honors Program provides outstanding students diverse opportunities to broaden and deepen their liberal arts and sciences education, enhance the intellectual rigor of their curriculum, and participate in a community of scholars within the greater College community. The Honors Program encourages students from all majors to set high standards for themselves that reflect their commitment to academic excellence. The program is flexible enough so that each participant experiences a broad range of academic challenges. The privilege of becoming an honors student is matched by the responsibility the student assumes in designing and carrying out a demanding and coherent program of study.

Key components of the program are the five student-designed Honors Challenges (scholarly projects pursued in regularly offered courses or through independent collaboration with faculty members or other honors students) and an optional, interdisciplinary Honors Seminar that brings honors students together during the junior or senior year to explore an issue of contemporary significance. Students who successfully complete these elements of the program, earn Distinction in their major, and maintain a cumulative GPA of at least 3.5 (out of 4.0) graduate with College Honors.

Honors Challenges encourage students to connect their intellectual passions with other academic disciplines to make greater sense of their liberal arts education. Working closely with a professor on traditional or research Honors Challenges, an honors student learns how to propose an individualized intellectual project, see the project through to completion, and summarize it

Interpreting the symbols: **2**=two-year college, **4**=four-year college; **Pu**=public or state college, **Pr**=private college; **G**=general honors program; **D**=departmental honors program; **S**=small program (fewer than 100 students), **M**=midsize program (100 to 500 students), **L**=large program (more than 500 students); **Sc**=scholarships available in honors program; **Tr**=transfer students accepted into honors program; **HBC**=historically black college; **AA**=academic advisors; **GA**=graduate advisors; **FA**=fellowship advisors.

in an abstract. These abstracts, which record the student's achievements in the program, can be valuable additions to a student's college portfolio.

Honors students may have the opportunity to live in an honors house and to participate in various honors activities, such as cardboard boat regattas, pizza parties, and trips to Boston or New York City. Honors students also enjoy preregistration for courses and discounts on books (other than required) ordered through the College bookstore. They are eligible to participate in National Collegiate Honors Council conventions, Honors Semesters Abroad, and weekend seminars with honors students at other colleges. Students who complete the program are recognized on their transcripts and at commencement as graduating "With College Honors." Founded in 1982, the program currently has 70 honors students.

Participation Requirements: The Honors Program Co-Directors monitor each student's progress toward meeting the standards for graduating with College Honors and advise any student who is falling behind in meeting those requirements. Students admitted to the program at any time prior to their sophomore year are expected to show progress by completing at least one Honors Challenge during the sophomore year. Normally, students who have completed fewer than three Honors Challenges or have a GPA below 3.4 at the end of the junior year are dismissed from the program. The Honors Program Committee recommends to the faculty members that those honors students who have completed the Honors Program be awarded College Honors upon graduation. To earn that special recognition of achievement, honors students must successfully complete the requirements for departmental distinction in a major field of study or in an Individual Student Program (ISP); five Honors Challenges, distributed across the three academic divisions of Hartwick College (one of the Challenges to be presented at an honors forum); and a minimum of 36 credit units, with a GPA of at least 3.5. Students expected to graduate with College Honors are entitled to wear an honor cord in the Hartwick College colors at commencement.

The Honors Program Committee consists of 4 elected members of the faculty, with at least 1 member representing each division of the College. The Honors Committee also includes as voting members the Honors Program Co-Directors (appointed by the Vice President for Academic Affairs) and 4 honors students (elected by the Student Senate). The committee, with the assistance of the Honors Program Co-Directors, is responsible for programmatic changes, reviewing Honors Proposals, and monitoring all elements of the program.

Admission Process: Incoming students who have been awarded Oyaron or Abraham L. Kellogg Scholarships are, upon admission, invited to apply to the Honors Program. The Hartwick College Admissions Office may also nominate exceptional transfer students to the Honors Program Committee. Matriculated students are invited to apply to the Honors Program if they have completed a minimum of five college-level courses with a cumulative GPA of 3.5 or better, and have attained Level IV in the Writing Program. Advanced Placement courses prior to matriculation at Hartwick do not count toward the five college-level courses. In some cases, the Co-Directors extend the deadline for Level IV writing competence for those pursuing work in the major that makes timely completion of this requirement impossible or to those whose first language is not English. Students invited to apply to the Honors Program are asked to submit a statement of their academic objectives and the place of the Honors Program in their academic plans, as well as a sample of work showing honors potential.

Scholarship Availability: The College awards several academic scholarships.

The Campus Context: Hartwick's purpose as a liberal arts and sciences college is to educate people who will thrive in and contribute to the world of the future; people who are prepared to meet the personal, intellectual, and social challenges of a rapidly changing and increasingly interdependent world. Hartwick holds accreditation from Middle States Association of Colleges and Schools, National Association of Schools of Art and Design, National Association of Schools of Music, National League for Nursing Accrediting Commission, and New York State Board of Regents.

Academic programs offered are accounting, anthropology, art, art history, biochemistry, biology, chemistry (B.A., B.S.), computer science, economics, English, environmental studies, French, geology, German, history, information science, management, mathematics, medical technology, music, music education, nursing, philosophy, physics, political science, psychology, religious studies, sociology, Spanish, and theater arts. An ISP is offered for students whose interests lie outside an established major. Special programs include secondary education, graphic communications minor, Latin American and Caribbean studies minor, museum studies program, U.S. ethnic studies minor, women's studies program, off-campus study, and internships. Preprofessional programs include engineering, health professions, and law.

Hartwick's main campus is on 425 acres in Oneonta, New York, 75 miles from Albany. Hartwick's Pine Lake Environmental Campus is on 918 acres in West Davenport, 8 miles from the main campus. The academic year is a 4-1-4 plan.

Faculty The student-faculty ratio at Hartwick is 11:1, with a total of 151 faculty members, 105 of whom are full-time; 86 percent hold the highest degree in their discipline.

Student Body Hartwick has 1,446 students, who come from thirty states and thirty-five countries. Forty-four percent of the students are men and 56 percent are women. Ethnic distribution is 8 percent ALANA (students of African, Latino, Asian, and Native American descent), with 4 percent international and 64 percent New York State residents. Eighty-six percent of students reside in campus housing. Seventy-eight percent of first-year students receive financial aid. Students are engaged in more than sixty student campus organizations.

Key Facilities Students receive notebook computers, printers, and software. The campus network provides everyone with voice mail, phone, and video and Internet access via the campus network from residence halls, classrooms, and computer labs in Clark Hall, the library, and the Science Facility. The language lab has multimedia stations. The library houses more than 300,000 volumes and currently receives more than 3,000 electronic journals, 2,500 electronic books, 56,000 microforms, and 1,400 audiovisual materials.

Honorary Societies Alpha Psi Omega (dramatics), Beta Beta Beta (biology), the Hartwick College Honor Society, Kappa Mu Epsilon (mathematics), Lambda Alpha (anthropology), Omicron Delta Epsilon (economics), Phi Alpha Theta (history), Pi Delta Epsilon (journalism), Pi Sigma Alpha (political science), Psi Chi (psychology), Sigma Beta Delta (management), Sigma Pi Sigma (physics), Sigma Tau Delta (English), Sigma Theta Tau (nursing)

Athletics Hartwick is in NCAA Division I for men's soccer and women's water polo; NCAA Division III and ECAC for women's basketball, cross-country, field hockey, golf, lacrosse, soccer, softball, swimming and diving, tennis, track and field, and volleyball; and NCAA Division III for men's baseball, basketball, cross-country, football, golf, lacrosse, soccer, swimming and diving, tennis, and track and field. Non-NCAA-affiliated varsity sports include cheerleading for men and women and equestrian for women.

Study Abroad Hartwick's goal is to increase international/intercultural experiences for all students and create an enhanced pluralism context on campus. The curriculum, programs, and forums are designed to help students learn from the ethnic, racial, and national differences represented within the College and Oneonta communities and in various off-campus programs. Off-campus study programs are available during the January

Term, for a semester, or for a full year. Study-abroad opportunities include programs in Thailand, England, Russia, South Africa, and Germany.

Job Opportunities Work opportunities on campus are available. The Trustee Center for Professional Development coordinates extensive career preparation programs, including workshops, internships, and shadow and interview experiences.

Tuition: $25,715

Room and Board: $7050 (room only is $3660 and board only is $3390)

Mandatory Fees: $325

Contact: Hartwick Honors Program Co-Directors: Dr. Eric L. Johnson and Dr. Margaret Schramm, 5th Floor, Yager Hall, Hartwick College, Oneonta, New York 13820; E-mail: honors@hartwick.edu; Web site: http://www.hartwick.edu/honors/

HEIDELBERG COLLEGE

4 Pr G M Tr

▼ Honors Program

The Heidelberg College Honors Program, Life of the Mind, is designed to challenge exceptional, highly motivated students to reach their potential. Life of the Mind is a comprehensive approach to reaching the brightest students by empowering them to explore their abilities within a supportive community of scholars and learners. The program comprises four intellectual areas that are each complemented by an honors seminar. They are the Scholar, the Scientist, the Artist, and the Citizen. Typically, the first year emphasizes the skills needed by the emerging scholar; the second year stresses the scientific method and empirical processes of inquiry; the third year focuses on the aesthetic experience and creative endeavors; and the fourth year requires participants to reflect on the meaning of citizenship and underscores the values of participation in local, national, and global issues.

Recognizing a need for involvement in the greater community, the Honors Program expects students to share their time and talents. A service-learning seminar and 40 hours of service placement are required. Students are also required to compose and present a senior project. After the approval of the Honors Committee and with the guidance of a faculty mentor of the student's choice, a senior project is developed and the results are presented in a public forum. The topic may be related to the student's major or in an area of special interest.

There are many benefits to being in Life of the Mind. The program provides a separate, 24-hour-access study center that includes a lounge, Computer Lab, seminar room, and program office. The honors students also have priority registration each term. In place of approximately 40 hours of general education requirements, the students complete the required seminars along with ten self-selected support courses. The increased flexibility of requirements enables students to more easily engage in additional educational opportunities, such as the completion of a second major, study abroad, or an internship. During the four years, the honors students also compile a portfolio that provides documentation of distinguished accomplishments and credentials.

The Heidelberg College Honors Program, Life of the Mind, was established in 1994. There are approximately 100 students currently enrolled.

Participation Requirements: To graduate from the Honors Program with an Honors Diploma, a student must successfully complete a senior project, four honors seminars, a portfolio, and the service learning component. In addition, each student must complete the requirements of a major and support courses as well as earn a minimum cumulative GPA of 3.3. Graduates of the program are designated by distinctive academic regalia at graduation and receive an Honors Diploma that notes honors courses taken.

Admission Process: First-year entering students are invited to join the Honors Program on the basis of a minimum high school cumulative GPA of a 3.5 or ranking in the top 10 percent of their graduating class and a minimum ACT score of 27 or a minimum SAT I combined score of 1210. Entering first-year students who do not meet the above criteria may apply for admission to the program after completing 15 semester hours while achieving a minimum GPA of 3.5. Transfer students must meet the above high school requirements and have at least a 3.3 cumulative GPA from an accredited college or university or have at least a 3.5 college GPA based on a minimum of 15 semester hours or 22.5 quarter hours and permission of the Program Director.

Scholarship Availability: Scholarships of various amounts are awarded through the Office of Admissions based on academic performance and a scholarship competition held on campus in February. Most honors students are recipients of academic scholarships.

The Campus Context: Heidelberg's 110-acre campus is located in Tiffin, Ohio, a town of 20,000. It is the center of a prosperous agricultural and business area. Heidelberg College, founded in 1850, is a selective, private coeducational liberal arts college that is affiliated with the United Church of Christ. Believing that a liberal education is the best career preparation a person can have to confront the challenges of the future creatively, Heidelberg College offers students a solid base on which to grow in their professional and personal lives. Heidelberg's dynamic community maintains a touch of its Old World heritage yet continually brings innovative ideas into the classroom.

Student Body The undergraduate enrollment is approximately 1,400 men and women. Students come to Heidelberg from more than twenty states and several other countries. This cross-cultural mix helps to keep the campus diverse and to broaden students' knowledge and understanding of ethnic and cultural differences. Ninety-five percent of the student body at Heidelberg receive financial aid.

Faculty The campus has an undergraduate faculty of 125, with 79 full-time professors, of whom 72 percent hold doctoral degrees in their disciplines. The student-faculty ratio is 13:1.

Key Facilities There are 260,055 volumes in the campus library. Beeghly Library also holds a seventy-seat audiovisual room, a seminar and computer room, the Rickard-Mayer Rare Books Room, and the Besse Collection of Letters. The computer facilities located in many areas around campus provide students with a connection to a campuswide network providing e-mail, file transfer, and full access to the Internet. All resident halls have computer jacks in the students' rooms.

Athletics The Athletic Department offers a wide range of sports and intramural programs. Heidelberg offers nine varsity men's sports: baseball, basketball, cross-country, football, golf, soccer, tennis, track, and wrestling. The women's varsity sports program fields seven intercollegiate teams: basketball, cross-country, soccer, softball, tennis, track, and volleyball. The College offers NCAA Division III sports.

Study Abroad Students interested in studying abroad may participate in Heidelberg's own programs in Germany (at Heidelberg University) and Spain, in a program at Oxford University (with the Oxford Study Abroad Program), or in programs

Interpreting the symbols: **2**=two-year college, **4**=four-year college; **Pu**=public or state college, **Pr**=private college; **G**=general honors program; **D**=departmental honors program; **S**=small program (fewer than 100 students), **M**=midsize program (100 to 500 students), **L**=large program (more than 500 students); **Sc**=scholarships available in honors program; **Tr**=transfer students accepted into honors program; **HBC**=historically black college; **AA**=academic advisors; **GA**=graduate advisors; **FA**=fellowship advisors.

arranged cooperatively with other colleges and universities in such locations as Sweden, Latin America, Africa, and the Far East.

Job Opportunities There are work-study opportunities on campus as well as an internship program designed to give students valuable practicum experiences in actual work settings.

Tuition: $12,850 (2002–03)

Room and Board: $5748

Mandatory Fees: $275

Contact: Dean of Honors Program: Dr. Jan Younger, 310 E. Market Street, Tiffin, Ohio 44883-2462; Telephone: 419-448-2157 or 800-434-3352 (toll-free); Fax: 419-448-2124; E-mail: jyounger@mail.heidelberg.edu; Web site: http://www.heidelberg.edu

Henderson State University

4 Pu G M Sc Tr

▼ Honors College

The Honors College provides special attention, support, and opportunities for those students of the highest academic achievement and potential. The curriculum, which is planned and delivered primarily by a select honors faculty, comprises honors general education courses, upper-level interdisciplinary honors seminars and colloquia, independent- and directed-study opportunities, and honors work in each student's major field of study. The curriculum is arranged so that Honors College students do not need to earn more credits for graduation than their contemporaries who are not in the Honors College.

As a complement to its academic program, the Honors College promotes a strong sense of community among students through an emphasis on University service, as well as on cultural and social activities. The new Honors College Hall is the hub of community for students. Honors students also have their own organization, the Areté Society, which is administered by the Honors College Council and composed of 12 students, 3 from each academic classification. The Council members are representatives for, and leaders among, their honors classmates. Among its many accomplishments, the Areté Society numbers the establishment and staffing of an award-winning journal, which includes some of the best scholarly and creative work submitted by Henderson students.

The seed of Henderson's Honors College was a single course, the Honors Colloquium, first offered in the spring of 1979. From that course, the honors effort developed into a program by 1982 and a college by 1992.

Currently, 200 students are members of the Honors College.

Participation Requirements: Once admitted to the Honors College, a student remains in good standing by taking at least one honors class each fall and spring, and by maintaining a cumulative GPA of at least 3.25. To graduate as Honors College scholars, students must complete at least 24 hours of honors-designated work and earn a cumulative GPA of at least 3.25. In order to satisfy the 24-hour requirement, each Honors College scholar must complete 12 hours of honors general education courses and 12 hours of upper-division credit, which includes 6 hours designated by the student's major department. At Commencement, Honors College scholars lead the procession of graduates, are the first to receive their diplomas, and are presented with commemorative medallions. The designation Honors College Scholar is recorded on the diploma and the official transcript of each Honors College graduate, as well as in the Commencement program.

Admission Process: High school students are invited to apply for admission to the Honors College based on their ACT scores. They are selected on the basis of these scores, high school GPA, rank in class, a brief essay, and recommendations.

Scholarship Availability: A limited number of Honors College stipends are available on a competitive basis and are renewable as long as students remain in good standing. Any freshman who is accepted into the Honors College without a stipend may be eligible for one at the beginning of the sophomore year. Freshmen eligible for the Honors College are also eligible to compete for University scholarships, which are awarded on the basis of ACT composite scores at three levels, covering either tuition alone, room and tuition, or room, board, and tuition.

The Campus Context: Henderson State University's overarching mission is to serve as "Arkansas's public liberal arts university." Founded in 1890 as a private liberal arts institution, Henderson remains dedicated to providing excellent undergraduate education in the arts and sciences. Through a common core of courses in the liberal arts, as well as through more specialized curricula in a variety of major disciplines, the University fosters the maximum growth and development of each student. Henderson State University offers forty-nine degree programs on campus.

Henderson State is in Arkadelphia, a progressive city of 10,000 people set among forested hills, lakes, and rivers. The University is 67 miles southwest of Little Rock, the state's capital and largest city, and about 35 miles south of Hot Springs, home of America's oldest state park.

Student Body Undergraduate enrollment is 3,288; 1,828 of the students are women. The ethnic distribution of the student body is 80.9 percent Caucasian, 15.9 percent African American, and 3.2 percent other. There are 57 international students. Thirty-three percent of the students are residents, while the remaining 67 percent commute to campus. Seventy-four percent of undergraduates receive financial aid. There are seventeen sororities and fraternities at Henderson.

Faculty Of the 231 total faculty members, 163 are full-time and 68 are adjunct. Terminal degrees are held by 64.4 percent of the faculty. The student-faculty ratio is 19:1.

Key Facilities Among its special buildings and facilities are the Martin Garrison Activity and Conference Center, which serves as the student center and houses the Reddie Café; the student gymnasium; the game room; racquetball courts; a weight room; and student organization offices, as well as the radio station, the *Oracle* newspaper, and the *Star* yearbook. The Roy and Christine Sturgis Foster Hall houses the Honors College Student Center, student residential suites, classrooms, administrative offices, and the *Arete* magazine office.

Henderson's Huie Library is one of the foremost research libraries in Arkansas, housing a collection of nearly half a million items. The library subscribes to more than 1,500 periodicals as well as more than fifty periodical indexes, including several computerized indexes. The library is a member of AMIGOS, a regional bibliographic network, and OCLC, an international bibliographic network, which give patrons access to more than 25 million items from more than 13,000 libraries worldwide.

Honorary Societies Alpha Chi and Gamma Beta Phi

Athletics Henderson belongs to NCAA Division II. Women's athletics are basketball, cross-country, softball, swimming, tennis, and volleyball; men's athletics are baseball, basketball, football, golf, swimming, and tennis.

Study Abroad Honors College students may take advantage of the British Studies Program, a residential summer session conducted annually at the University of London. The five-week sessions offer study for transfer credit in a variety of disciplines.

Tuition: $2736 for state residents, $5472 for nonresidents, per year (2001–02)

Room and Board: $3400

Mandatory Fees: $196.50

Contact: Director: Dr. David Thomson, 1100 Henderson Street, Arkadelphia, Arkansas 71999-0001; Telephone: 501-230-5192; Fax: 501-230-5144; E-mail: thomsond@hsu.edu

HENRY FORD COMMUNITY COLLEGE

2 Pu G S Sc Tr

▼ Honors Program

The Honors Program (HP) at Henry Ford Community College (HFCC) underwent major reorganization in 1997. Since its inception in 1978, the program had been largely unstructured; the only requirements were that students enroll in the Honors Colloquium, a 2-credit-hour humanities course, in their first semester and then sign-up for an honors option or directed study in the three subsequent semesters. The Honors Colloquium is organized by a member of the honors faculty around a humanities theme. Typically, the convener enlists the participation of other faculty members from across the College to present guest lectures on an overarching theme. Students are exposed to a wide variety of faculty members and diverse topics as well as teaching styles.

The hallmark of the Honors Program at HFCC remains the honors directed study. Students and faculty members alike praise the one-on-one contact they experience in honors directed studies. In the new curriculum, faculty members agree to meet with an honors student at least 1 hour per week outside of the classroom to direct a student project. Faculty members meet three times per semester to discuss students' progress. At the end of the semester, HP faculty members and students convene to hear oral presentations by the students. Students are encouraged to submit their best work for publication and present their work at academic conferences.

With the appointment of a new director, the Honors Program added greater structure to its curriculum, with the addition of core courses aimed at strengthening the writing and research skills of its students. In addition to the Honors Colloquium and directed studies, the program also requires students to take a series of core courses in English composition, speech, computer literacy, social science research methods, foreign language, and math statistics. Nonscience majors are also required to take two semesters of science (with a minimum of one lab science) in their second year, while science majors are required to take two courses in literature, social science, or humanities to qualify for an honors concentration in their degree.

Henry Ford's Honors Program provides full tuition scholarships for its 60 to 70 students. Students are assigned HP faculty mentors.

Participation Requirements: Successful high school applicants should have a GPA of at least 3.5 and/or should have scored in the 80th percentile (composite) or above on the ACT or SAT I. Internal applicants must have completed 12 credit hours of courses that are above the 100 level and must have a GPA of at least 3.5. Honors students must maintain a GPA of at least 3.5. Students receive an honors designation on their transcript denoting courses taken as honors directed studies.

The Campus Context: Henry Ford Community College was established in 1938 as the Fordson Junior College. Classes were suspended for two years during World War II. In 1952, the College adopted its current name. In 1956, the Ford Motor Company donated 75 acres for use by the College not far from the company's world headquarters. The College offers Associate in Arts, Associate in Business, and Associate in Science degree programs. A state-of-the-art robotics lab and a Ford-UAW national training institute are located on campus. There are no fraternities or sororities on campus, although there is an active Phi Theta Kappa chapter.

Student Body There are about 16,000 full- and part-time students on two campuses (a main campus in Dearborn and another in nearby Dearborn Heights). The College currently enrolls 82 international students (F-1 visa holders) from thirty-three countries in Europe, the Middle East, Africa, Asia, and Latin America.

Faculty The faculty consists of approximately 220 full-time and 530 adjunct faculty members; 19 percent hold doctorates, 78 percent have a master's degree or higher, and 3 percent hold bachelor's degrees. The student-faculty ratio 22:1 (actually smaller due to the high turnover of students from one semester to the next).

Key Facilities The library houses 89,000 volumes. There are approximately twelve computer labs, and additional labs are being planned.

Honorary Society Phi Theta Kappa

Athletics Athletics include four women's sports (volleyball, softball, basketball, and tennis) and four men's sports (golf, baseball, basketball, and tennis). The athletic program is in the top five annually in the MCCAA competition for the All-Sports Trophy. Henry Ford has fielded a number of state, regional, and national championship teams and has produced several Academic All-Americans. Last year, 2 student athletes were named Distinguished Academic All-Americans with GPAs of 3.9 or better, and another student was named to the Academic All-American Team with a GPA of 3.6 or better.

Study Abroad The College offers a European Study Abroad program in the summer semester. Students may arrange part of their study abroad by registering for study courses under the direction of faculty members in various departments. The work is planned and evaluated on campus but carried out overseas.

Support Services The College maintains an Office of Special Needs, a comprehensive facility serving students with physical and mental needs and learning handicaps. The Office of Special Needs assists about 300 students a semester. The College also provides special computer labs to assist visual- and learning- impaired students.

Job Opportunities Three types of work opportunities for students are available: co-op education programs, college work-study, and employment by individual departments.

Tuition: $752 for Dearborn residents, $1168 for nonresidents, per 16 credit hours (1998–99)

Mandatory Fees: $53 per semester

Contact: Director: Dr. Nabeel Abraham, Honors Program, A-150 Administration Building, 5101 Evergreen Road, Dearborn, Michigan 48128; Telephone: 313-845-6460; Fax: 313-845-9778; E-mail: nabraham@mail.henryford.cc.mi.us

HERITAGE COLLEGE

4 Pr C S Sc Tr AA

▼ Heritage College Honors Program

The Heritage College Honors Program is designed for students who wish to advance in their educational experience beyond traditional course work by undertaking additional challenges within their classes and their community. Students in this program undertake a rigorous direction of study that includes not only

Interpreting the symbols: **2**=two-year college, **4**=four-year college; **Pu**=public or state college, **Pr**=private college; **G**=general honors program; **D**=departmental honors program; **S**=small program (fewer than 100 students), **M**=midsize program (100 to 500 students), **L**=large program (more than 500 students); **Sc**=scholarships available in honors program; **Tr**=transfer students accepted into honors program; **HBC**=historically black college; **AA**=academic advisors; **GA**=graduate advisors; **FA**=fellowship advisors.

course work but also opportunities to develop cross-cultural awareness and perspective in a variety of forms and through community service.

The program was founded in 2000 and currently enrolls 15 students.

Participation Requirements: In the first two years of the program, students take honors courses in their general college requirement courses. A typical first semester consists of honors courses in English, mathematics, integrated studies (global fine arts and literature), and the Heritage College Core course. During their junior and senior years, honors students take selected honors courses from their major department and honors seminars. The honors seminars provide a unique opportunity for honors students to interact with Heritage College faculty members, scholars from other academic institutions, and/or community leaders to make academic presentations, develop and implement strategies for community improvement, and participate in cultural events.

Admission Process: To qualify for the Heritage College Honors Program, students must have a high school diploma and a minimum 3.3 GPA on a 4.0 scale. To apply, students must submit a supplementary application for the Honors Program along with their application to the College. They must supply letters of support from two high school or college instructors. The admission process also includes an interview with a panel of Heritage College faculty members and a spontaneous writing sample.

Scholarship Availability: There are a limited number of honors scholarships available for incoming students. These scholarships are based upon financial need as determined by the student's financial aid application. They range from $1000 to $3000 per academic year. The Heritage College Honors Program also serves as a conduit to several fellowship programs for upper-level and graduate study.

The Campus Context: Heritage College was founded in 1981 to serve the multicultural populations located in central Washington, populations that have traditionally been underrepresented in American higher education. From its founding, Heritage College has been inspired by a vision of education that embraces issues of national and international significance. These issues revolve around the realization that cooperation across cultural boundaries—whether these boundaries are geographic, ethnic, religious, or economic—is vital to human survival. Heritage College has a student body with substantial diversity, which creates an effective learning community where no single cultural group is a majority. Because the majority of Heritage's students are first-generation college students, the College, within its liberal arts curriculum, offers strong professional and career-oriented programs designed to enrich the quality of life for its students and their communities.

Student Body Undergraduate enrollment is 725. Of these students, 74 percent are women and 26 percent are men. Ethnic distribution is 1 percent African American, 2 percent Asian, 54 percent Hispanic, 16 percent Native American, and 27 percent white. The College has no residential facilities. Approximately 70 percent of undergraduate students receive financial aid.

Faculty The full-time faculty members number 35. Because of the professional and career-oriented curriculum, adjunct faculty members drawn from professions in the community teach in most of the programs. Of the full-time faculty members, 42 percent have terminal degrees. The student-faculty ratio is 11:1.

Key Facilities Heritage College's Donald K. C. North Library was built in 1993. A T-1 line for Internet access was installed in 1994. In 1999, a library automation system, Endeavor Voyager, was purchased. There are four computer labs with twenty workstations in each lab. Computers for student use are located in the library, the Academic Skills Center, the Writing Lab, and the science and math labs as well as the four computer labs.

Support Services: Disabled-student facilities include accessible buildings, and special services are available for disabled students. A full-service Academic Skills Center provides free tutoring, computer-based self-instruction, and peer study groups.

Job Opportunities: Federally funded work-study opportunities and salaried internships in the community are available on and off campus.

Tuition: $6000 per academic year, $250 per semester credit (2001–02)

Contact: Director: Dr. Loren Schmidt, Heritage College, 3420 Fort Road, Toppenish, Washington 98948; Telephone: 509-865-8542; Fax: 509-865-7976; E-mail: lschmidt@heritage.edu

High Point University

4 Pr G M Sc Tr

▼ University Honors Program

The purpose of The University Honors Program at High Point University is to provide an element to the undergraduate curriculum that will intellectually stimulate and provide a social community for those students with exceptionally strong academic abilities and interests. The program is responsible for honors sections of freshman and sophomore university core courses as well as upper-division electives in special topics. It culminates in a senior honors seminar in which students combine a study of central texts with research in their respective chosen fields. Any honors course differs from its nonhonors counterpart by providing one or more of the following: historical context, theoretical background, research activity, and real-world application. Classes are in seminar format, so student discussion is expected. The Odyssey Club is a student organization affiliated with the University Honors Program. The Odyssey Club is responsible each year for a variety of honors student activities, ranging from College Bowl tournaments and student-faculty debates to holiday readings, field trips, and a club retreat. Spring always culminates in Honors Day, featuring the program's annual Student Research Symposium, an opportunity for students to present faculty-mentored research in a conference-session format. Each year, approximately 40 new freshmen enter the University Honors Program through its Presidential Scholarship competition. Those who are not members as entering freshmen can apply through the University Honors Office. There are currently more than 150 members. The program was founded in 1984.

Participation Requirements: Every semester approximately fifteen courses in the schedule, ranging from freshman to senior level, are designated as honors. Members of the University Honors Program must take at least 30 hours of those courses in order to complete the program. Since scheduling conflicts arise as students progress into their major, nonhonors courses may be contracted for honors credit for as many as 9 of the required 30 hours of credit. Honors credit is also available to students involved in study-abroad programs. In order to remain in the program in good standing, students must maintain a G.P.A. of at least 3.2. Completing the 30 hours of honors course work, including the senior seminar, and achieving a G.P.A. of at least a 3.5, students earn the award of All University Honors, recognized in the students' transcripts, and by a gold medallion worn at graduation.

Admission Process: Admissions to the Honors Program is offered to any participant in the Presidential Scholarship competition who places in the top two tiers of awards. Otherwise, the admissions process includes a written application (four topic-focused essays to be reviewed by the University Honors Committee), an interview before the University Honors Committee, an established or (if the applicant's a first-semester freshman) predicted G.P.A. of 3.25 or higher, and two strong faculty member recommendations. Admission occurs on a rolling schedule. Applications are accepted and processed as soon as they are complete.

Scholarship Availability: The Presidential Scholarship competition provides financial awards to academically gifted prospective students each spring. This competition offers a small number of top awards of full tuition and a second tier of awards of $5500. The University Honors Program recruits a large number of its new members each year from those scholarship recipients (as stated above, all winners in these two tiers of the award are offered program membership as entering freshmen). There is also program money available for funding student activities and course development.

The Campus Context: A four-year liberal arts university founded in 1924 by The United Methodist Church, High Point University is located in High Point, North Carolina, a city famous for the manufacture of furniture and hosiery and the world's largest furniture exhibition. High Point is also the home of the North Carolina Shakespeare Festival and is a close neighbor of two other lively cities—Greensboro (a 20-minute drive to the north) and Winston-Salem (a 30-minute drive to the northwest). High Point itself has a population of about 70,000 and is in the Piedmont region of the state, halfway between the Atlantic Ocean to the east and the Blue Ridge Mountains to the west. With thirty-one buildings on 80 acres, the University is located in a quiet residential area a mile from downtown High Point. Interstate Highways 40 and 85 are easily accessible from the campus, and Piedmont Triad International Airport is a few miles north of the campus. The mission of High Point University is to provide vital and distinguished undergraduate and graduate programs for the development of the students' powers of inquiry, command of language, and insight into ethical thought—in the belief that these qualities will best equip its graduates for enterprising and constructive lines. The University offers thirty-nine different majors, ranging from such traditional areas as math, history, and English to such emerging fields as furniture marketing and sports medicine.

Student Body The total enrollment at High Point University is approximately 2,850 students. Approximately fifteen percent of those students are African American (425 total) and 2.5 percent (71 total) represent other members of minority groups, including Native American, Asian, and Hispanic. Approximately 2.25 percent (64 total) are international students, and 60 percent of the total student body is from out-of-state. Approximately 1,500 students commute, and approximately 1,200 are enrolled in the University's Evening Degree program. Four national fraternities and four national sororities are active on campus. Campus life is also supported by a variety of activities, including student government, service organizations, and special interest clubs.

Faculty There are 140 full-time members of the High Point University faculty. Approximately 77 percent hold doctoral degrees. While the faculty members are involved in a variety of professional and civic responsibilities, their primary aim is excellence in teaching.

Key Facilities The University's library holdings include 157,000 print volumes. In addition, the library has thirty-five work stations that are connected to the World Wide Web and operate on an NT local area network. The library also holds 1,400 print subscriptions to journals and has full text access to more than 5,000 journals electronically. On the main campus there are eight computer labs; at the University's satellite campus there are four. All operate Intel-based PC's. Some of the labs serve particular academic departments, and some are open for general access.

Honorary Societies Alpha Chi, The Order of the Lighted Lamp, and Phi Theta Kappa

Athletics High Point University is a member of the Big South Conference and NCAA Division I. Intercollegiate athletic teams for men include basketball, baseball, golf, tennis, soccer, cross-country, and track; women's teams include basketball, cross-country, soccer, tennis, track, and volleyball. In addition, all students have the opportunity to participate in intramural sports.

Study Abroad While there is no study-abroad program specifically associated with the Honors Program, the University provides programs for semester-long study in France, Spain, and Great Britain. Honors students also regularly participate in individually developed faculty travel projects and in collaborative study-abroad programs through other universities. Study-abroad honors credit is available for students who have arranged in advance with the Honors Committee to incorporate an honors project into their travel.

Support Services The University Counseling Office and the Learning Assistance Center help support students with special learning needs.

Job Opportunities All students have the opportunity to participate in the University's Student Career Intern Program (SCIP). The internships arranged through this program vary according to the student's academic major and/or career goals. The Honors Program also sponsors the Student Research Symposium each year, a program of concurrent presentations of student research. In addition, many honors courses include a real-life component that provides practical applications of classroom concepts.

Tuition: $10,040 full-time; $173 per semester credit hour, part-time, up to 11 semester hours (1998–99)

Room and board: $5300

Mandatory Fees: $1080

Contact: Director: Dr. Thomas Albritton, High Point University, Montlieu Avenue-University Station, High Point, North Carolina 27262-3598; Telephone: 336-841-9284; Fax: 336-841-4599; E-mail:talbritt@acme.highpoint.edu

HILBERT COLLEGE

4 Pr G S Tr AA

▼ Honors Program

The Honors Program at Hilbert College, which is contract-based, offers students an opportunity for academic enrichment and personal development. The program allows students to enroll in regular classes and fulfill honors credit requirements by completing advanced work—called in lieu of projects—that is designed by the faculty members teaching those classes. These special projects allow students to have the experience of working one-on-one with the highly credentialed honors faculty members, both within and outside the student's major, from the first semester that the student enrolls.

In addition to the special attention honors students receive at Hilbert College, participants in the program have senior student mentors for the first semester and personal advisement by members of the honors faculty and by faculty members within the student's major.

Started in 2000, the program currently enrolls approximately 20 students, with plans to expand.

Participation Requirements: Students are required to complete 24 credit hours of honors-related course work over four years. (Requirements for transfer students are adjusted accordingly.) These courses are divided equally between lower- and upper-level courses within the major and between lower- and upper-level liberal arts elective courses.

In their first year in the program, students enroll in an Honors Colloquium. The course content is multidisciplinary, and the course structure is discussion-oriented. Each semester, the course

Interpreting the symbols: **2**=two-year college, **4**=four-year college; **Pu**=public or state college, **Pr**=private college; **G**=general honors program; **D**=departmental honors program; **S**=small program (fewer than 100 students), **M**=midsize program (100 to 500 students), **L**=large program (more than 500 students); **Sc**=scholarships available in honors program; **Tr**=transfer students accepted into honors program; **HBC**=historically black college; **AA**=academic advisors; **GA**=graduate advisors; **FA**=fellowship advisors.

focuses on the examination of three important and sometimes volatile issues within the contemporary intellectual community. Through the examination of these issues, the course introduces students to the nature and rigors of intellectual investigation and debate both between and within disciplines.

In their senior year, students participate in a Capstone Colloquium, a culmination of their honors experience, in which they present a version of one of their in lieu of projects to an audience composed of the Honors Council and other interested members of the College community.

Students must also complete 20 hours of community service per academic year and maintain a minimum GPA to remain in good standing in the program.

Students who complete all of the requirements for the program are recognized at the annual academic honors banquet and at commencement and with an indication of honors status on their transcripts.

Admission Process: Eligible students for the program must have the equivalent of at least a 3.5 cumulative average, must be enrolled as full-time day students, and must apply before the first semester of their junior year. The application, which is reviewed by the Honors Council, includes a personal essay and a letter of recommendation. There is a rolling admission process.

Scholarship Availability: Various private benefactors and Hilbert College provide funding for grants and scholarships that are need-based or merit-based. Merit-based aid is given to students in recognition of special skills, talent, or academic ability. Non-need-based aid may also be awarded based on other criteria, such as field of study, ethnicity, or class level.

The Campus Context: Hilbert College is an independent, coeducational four-year institution offering baccalaureate degrees in accounting, business administration, criminal justice, economic crime investigation, English, human services, liberal studies (law and government), paralegal studies, and psychology. Hilbert College encourages personal and organizational change through vision and hope and creates a meaningful, unique undergraduate educational experience based in the liberal arts that enables graduates to impact positively their professions and communities.

Student Body Undergraduate enrollment is approximately 960 students.

Faculty The total number of faculty members is 98. The student-faculty ratio is 16:1.

Key Facilities McGrath Library houses 38,302 titles, 3,337 serial subscriptions, and 724 audiovisual materials. Several computer labs are available for student use.

Athletics Hilbert's sports teams participate in NCAA Division III.

Support Services The Academic Services Center provides services to students with special needs.

Job Opportunities Student work programs are available.

Tuition: $11,600 per semester or $277 per credit hour (2001–02)

Room and Board: $4090 minimum, depending on room type and meal plan.

Mandatory Fees: $500

Contact: Dr. Amy Smith, Director of the Honors Program, Hilbert College, 5200 South Park Avenue, Hamburg, New York 14075; Telephone: 716-649-7900 Ext. 354; Fax: 716-649-0702; E-mail: asmith@hilbert.edu; Web site: http://www.hilbert.edu/academics/honors.asp

HILLSBOROUGH COMMUNITY COLLEGE

2 Pu G M Sc Tr AA

▼ Honors Institute

Hillsborough Community College's (HCC) Honors Institute is designed to provide an intellectually stimulating academic program for exceptionally talented and motivated students. The overall goal of the program is to provide an academic atmosphere in which students learn to think critically, to grow intellectually, and to mature as responsible citizens and leaders. Academic emphasis is on encouraging students to present scholarly papers and projects, to use primary sources, to participate in alternative learning strategies, and to experience related cultural and social activities.

Known and respected for their excellence in teaching, the honors professors are dedicated to inspiring and challenging the students to make the most of their educational experiences. The majority of the honors professors have designed the honors courses that they teach. Currently, twenty-eight honors courses have been developed across the curriculum. As risk takers, the honors professors experiment with alternative learning strategies to foster an environment that results in creative interaction and intellectual flexibility for both professors and students. Cultural excursions and other extracurricular activities within the courses are always encouraged and subsidized by the Honors Institute. Honors courses are offered on all four campuses. Under a special articulation agreement with the University of South Florida, international students can be admitted to the honors international 2+2 program.

In addition to enhanced educational opportunities, honors students have other advantages that help them develop individually and as members of the honors group. All four campuses have fully equipped honors study lounges that are accessible only to honors students. These gathering places provide an atmosphere for healthy competition and camaraderie among the students. The rooms provide seclusion for studying and comfortable areas for socializing. Each fall, the Honors Institute generously subsidizes a state-side trip. The trip is designed around a particular theme, with an honors professor serving as the expert on the topic and traveling with the students. In February of each year, a select honors delegation travels to Boston to participate in the Harvard National Model United Nations. This activity is fully funded by the Honors Institute. Also funded by the Institute, the Brain Bowl Teams compete with other college Brain Bowl Teams. The Honors Institute sponsors student trips to state, regional, and national honors conferences each year. Every spring, the Honors Institute subsidizes a trip to another country so that the students can experience the world beyond the textbook.

The program began in fall 1996 and currently enrolls 220 students.

Participation Requirements: Students must take a minimum of eight honors courses. The College president hosts a special luncheon for the honors graduates. At the College commencement ceremony, the honors graduates are presented with honors medallions and receive diplomas with the Honors Institute seal. Students who do not fulfill all Honors Institute requirements but complete at least 12 hours of honors credit with a minimum overall GPA of at least 3.0 earn the HCC Honors Institute certificate. Each year, 100 percent of the Honors Institute graduates transfer to the universities of their choice. A majority of the students transfer to prestigious institutions on full or partial scholarships.

Admission Process: Students must complete the HCC application forms for admission and the HCC Honors Institute application forms, which include high school or college transcripts and a written recommendation from a high school or college faculty member. Applicants must meet a least one of the following criteria to qualify for the Honors Institute: a minimum high school GPA of 3.5 on a 4.0 scale; a minimum high school GPA of 3.4 on a 5.0 scale; a minimum SAT I combined score of 1160 or ACT composite score of 26; a minimum SAT I combined score of 1050, ACT composite score of 25, CPT writing score of 90 or higher, or CPT reading score of 92 for students who graduated in the top 10 percent of their class; a minimum GPA of 3.3 for 12 hours of dual enrollment; or a minimum cumulative GPA of 3.3 or higher with a minimum of 6 semester hours of college credit. For the fall term, the application deadline with scholarship consideration is April 20. Students should apply by December 1 for the spring term.

Scholarship Availability: There are forty-nine tuition scholarships available on a competitive basis.

The Campus Context: Hillsborough Community College has four campuses: the Dale Mabry Campus, the Ybor Campus, the Brandon Campus, and the Plant City. The College offers fifty-seven associate degree programs.

Student Body Undergraduate enrollment is 17,215, and 58 percent of the students are women. The ethnic distribution for the student body is 2 percent international students and resident aliens, 3 percent Asian, 1 percent Indian, 14 percent African American, 15 percent Hispanic, and 65 percent Caucasian. All students commute to campus, and 29 percent of the students receive financial aid. While there are no fraternities or sororities, students find at least twenty-nine student organizations on the several campuses.

Faculty Of the 708 faculty members, 245 are full-time. The student-faculty ratio is 21:1.

Key Facilities The library houses 170,615 volumes. There are fourteen computer labs on campus, including a Developmental English Lab, an ESL Lab, a Graphics Lab, a Word Processing Lab, and a Project Literacy Lab.

Honorary Society Phi Theta Kappa

Athletics The varsity sports program consists of volleyball, basketball, and softball (fast-pitch) for women and basketball and baseball for men. The Hawks are members of the Florida Community College Activities Association, Suncoast Conference (Division III), and Region VIII of the National Junior College Athletic Association. Tennis and racquetball courts are available for educational and recreational use by HCC students and the community. The gymnasium, which serves as the home court of the Hawks basketball and volleyball teams, also houses faculty offices and classrooms. The weight training room and gymnasium are open for student use free of charge at designated times. The HCC cheerleading squad performs at many athletic events and represents HCC at parades and other community events.

The Athletic Division sponsors intramural programs in the fall and spring semesters. The program includes club activities, league and tournament play, open recreation, and special events.

Support Services Disabled-student accommodations include tutors/notetakers/readers, an LD specialist, adjustable tables and chairs, Braille writers and printers, wheelchairs on every campus, tape recorders, talking scientific calculators on each campus, and visual techs.

Job Opportunities Work opportunities include college work-study and student assistantships.

Tuition: $52.70 for state residents, $196.36 for nonresidents, per credit hour (2001–02)

Contact: Director: Dr. Lydia Daniel, HCC Honors Institute, 10414 E. Columbus Drive, Tampa, Florida 33619; Telephone: 813-253-7894; Fax: 813-253-7940; Web site: http://www.hcc.cc.fl.us/honors

Hinds Community College

2 Pu G M Sc

▼ Honors Program

The mission of Hinds Community College Honors Program (HCCH) is to provide an enhanced and supportive learning environment for outstanding students. The honors program curriculum features designated core-curriculum honors course sections, seminars, interdisciplinary studies, independent study, research opportunities, international study, and leadership development. Special cocurricular activities and field trips are also part of the honors program. Individual and group counseling are provided through the College Counseling Offices and the HCCH Center. HCCH students are given priority in scheduling courses at HCC. The program also helps honors students locate and apply for scholarships at four-year institutions and schedules campus visits and introductions to honors programs at four-year institutions. The HCCH program works closely with Phi Theta Kappa and other honorary scholastic societies with HCC chapters to encourage and reward academic excellence.

Honors courses are offered in the core curriculum areas of art, biology, education, English, history, humanities, math, psychology, and speech. In addition, courses are offered in career exploration, leadership development, and improvement of study. Classes typically have 15–20 students. This allows for collaborative and experiential learning, an assortment of hands-on activities, and more opportunities to read and write at advanced levels. Students are encouraged to become outstanding, independent learners capable of critical thinking and self-expression. Honors courses are taught by experienced members of the Hinds teaching faculty who are known for excellence in the classroom as well as in their academic fields. Students have frequent interaction with other honors students and faculty members help to build a community spirit. The HCCH Center provides a location for students to gather and visit or study. The center has a library, computer lab, group study area, and lounge for both faculty member and student use. The Honors Forum, a weekly seminar for all honors students, provides an opportunity for intellectual discussion on the issues facing society today. Honors advisers in the HCC counseling offices and HCCH Center provide students with personalized attention. Students' individual needs and interests are given priority in all advising.

Students also enjoy picnics, lectures, special presentations, workshops, and field trips. Special events are also scheduled for those students living in Main Hall and Virden Hall on the Raymond Campus.

The first year of a comprehensive program was 1995. Courses have been taught on the Raymond Campus for 20 years. There are now 150 students enrolled in the program. For priority, students should apply no later than March 1.

Participation Requirements: Students are eligible to receive all of the HCCH benefits and fringe benefits as long as they are registered participants. Honors scholarship students must undertake at least 7 hours of honors work during a semester and must enroll in the Honors Humanities Forum each semester (1 semester-hour credit). To graduate from Hinds Community College Honors Program with honors, the HCCH student must complete 26 hours of honors study and maintain a minimum overall GPA of 3.0. Students who accomplish this receive an Honors Program medallion at the graduation ceremonies and an honors seal on the diploma. Honors certificates are given to those graduating students who complete 18–25 honors credits with an overall GPA of 3.0.

Scholarship Availability: The following scholarships are contingent on criteria in parenthesis: Faculty Scholarships (ACT 21–24); Dean's Scholarships (ACT 25–28); Presidential Scholarship (ACT 29+); and Development Foundation Scholarships (criteria vary). HCCH scholarships are available for a maximum of four consecutive fall and spring semesters. Applicants must be Mississippi

Interpreting the symbols: **2**=two-year college, **4**=four-year college; **Pu**=public or state college, **Pr**=private college; **G**=general honors program; **D**=departmental honors program; **S**=small program (fewer than 100 students), **M**=midsize program (100 to 500 students), **L**=large program (more than 500 students); **Sc**=scholarships available in honors program; **Tr**=transfer students accepted into honors program; **HBC**=historically black college; **AA**=academic advisors; **GA**=graduate advisors; **FA**=fellowship advisors.

residents and must be enrolled in 12 or more semester hours, 7 of which must be in honors studies. Scholarship recipients must maintain full-time student status and a minimum 3.0 GPA. Applicants must complete an HCC Financial Aid /Scholarship Application and an HCCH Application and must submit both forms to the HCCH Center. Recipients must be registered with the HCCH Program. The deadline for application is March 1 of each year for the following school year.

The Campus Context: Hinds Community College is composed of six campuses, including the Academic/Technical Center, the Nursing and Allied Health Campus, the Rankin Campus, the Raymond Campus, the Utica Campus, and the Vicksburg Campus. The Raymond Campus offers twenty-eight degree programs.

Student Body On the Raymond Campus, the chief location of the Honors Program, undergraduate enrollment is almost equally divided between men and women. The ethnic distribution of students on campus is 34.5 percent African American, 60.9 percent Caucasian, and about 4.5 percent representing other groups. There are 2 international students. Residents make up 23.7 percent of the Raymond population. Approximately 52 percent of students on campus receive financial aid. There are thirty-four student clubs and social organizations on the Raymond Campus.

Faculty Of the 237 faculty members teaching on the Raymond campus, 178 are full-time. The student-faculty ratio is 16:1.

Key Facilities Noteworthy facilities on campus include the One-Stop Career Center, the Learning Assistance Center, the Resource and Coordinating Unit for Economic Development, the Video Production Studio, the Interactive Classroom, the Deaf and Hard of Hearing Services, the Eagle Ridge Conference Center, the Eagle Ridge Challenge Course, and the Eagle Ridge Golf Course.

The Raymond Library houses 92,325 volumes. The existing library system is currently an online catalog only and interconnects each of the libraries on all six campuses, which contain a composite collection of 164,084 volumes.

Computer facilities include the state-wide Community College Network (CNN) that is available at Hinds only on the Raymond campus. Eighteen other universities and schools of higher education are connected to this network, which provides two-way audio and video for conferences, and/or distance learning as may be required.

There are 1,127 PCs available for student use, including 880 modem units (IBM 386s and 486s and Macs), which attach to the collegewide network. The largest and latest computer facility on the Raymond Campus is Moss Hall and there are plans to open further facilities in the Media Center. The Raymond Campus currently has a total of fifteen instructional networks.

Honorary Societies Phi Theta Kappa, Psi Beta, Alpha Beta Gamma

Athletics Hinds Community College is a member of the Mississippi Junior College Athletic Association and National Junior College Athletic Association. Varsity athletics at the Raymond Campus include football, baseball, golf, softball, track, and soccer.

Study Abroad Hinds Community College is a member of an academic consortium of several colleges and universities in the southern and southwestern United States, supporting an international study program entitled The British Studies Program. This program is a residential summer session offered annually during July and August in London, England. While allowing participants ample free time for independent travel, the session offers upper-division undergraduate and graduate course work. Students can earn up to 8 semester hours in on-site lecturing coordinated by local British scholars who are experts in their fields.

Three- and five-week courses in a wide range of academic disciplines, including humanities, business, education, and fine arts, are offered through the British Studies Program. A mini-break is also scheduled to allow time for personal travel outside of London, along with low-cost optional day tours to general places of interest. Paris, Scotland, Cambridge, Dover, Canterbury, Bath, and Stonehenge are often included.

Support Services Facilities include wheelchair ramps, elevators, and restrooms in instructional buildings, libraries, and residence halls; telecommunications devices (TDD); decoders for closed captioned TV viewing; and flashing fire alarms and doorbells. Interpreters are provided for the deaf and hard of hearing students. Special assistance is given to the visually impaired by the provision of readers, part-time guides, and library visual aid interpreting equipment, including Braille textbooks, tape textbooks, visual tech and Braille typewriters. The Disability Support Services Department provides tutorial and other support services for students who qualify through federal guidelines for Student Support Services for Disadvantaged Students.

Job Opportunities Work opportunities on campus include student worker and work-study positions.

Tuition: $1020 for state residents, $3226 for nonresidents, per year (1998–99)

Room and Board: $1070

Mandatory Fees: $50

Contact: Director: Kristi Sather-Smith or Associate Director: Dr. Lura Scales, P.O. Box 1292, HCCH, 212 Administration Building, Raymond, Mississippi 39154; Telephone: 601-857-3531 or 800-HINDSCC Ext. 3531; Fax: 601-857-3392; e-mail: kasather-smith@hinds.cc.ms.us

Hofstra University

4 Pr G M Sc Tr AA GA FA

▼ Hofstra University Honors College

Hofstra University Honors College (HUHC) provides a rich academic and social experience for students who show both the potential and the desire to excel. Each year, HUHC invites more than one hundred new students to join our growing scholarly community. HUHC students can elect to study in any of the University's more than 100 major programs; students are involved in all fields of advanced study, including premedical, prelaw, engineering, business, communications and media, arts, humanities, and social sciences.

HUHC takes full advantage of the uniqueness of Hofstra University, the wealth of opportunity associated with large universities combined with the personality and individual attention one seeks in a small college. The Honors College curriculum begins with a carefully coordinated sequence of courses, Culture and Expression, that introduces students to college-level intellectual inquiry and provides an arena where the humanities and social science disciplines interact and illuminate one another. Taught by some of Hofstra's most distinguished teacher-scholars, Culture and Expression is the common focal point of the first-year student's experience in HUHC. In addition to Culture and Expression, first-year students may choose to do honors work in science, mathematics, and other areas such as calculus and chemistry.

After the first year, students pursue honors work via honors seminars, honors-only sections of departmental courses, and honors options. The honors seminars and sections are deliberately small, consisting of 15–20 students, and designed to maximize student involvement. Honors-options are tutorial-based enhancements to regular Hofstra classes. As they progress in their fields of specialization, students are encouraged to work one-on-one with faculty members to create an individualized honors curriculum. This structure encourages motivated and talented students to do honors-level work in the fields of study to which they are most deeply committed.

Outside the classroom, HUHC has built a welcoming and supportive social structure for its students, both those who choose to reside on the Hofstra campus and those who commute. Resident students may live in Honors House, a residential complex with social and community-building programs specifically designed for high-achieving students. Each year, specially chosen faculty serve as Honors House mentors. They maintain regular hours in the residence hall, organize social and recreational activities, and offer counsel and help to honors students, accomodating those who are both resident and commuting.

With Manhattan only a half hour away by train, Hofstra's honors students do not need to choose between the comforts of campus life and the vibrancy of New York City. HUHC sponsors regular trips to museums, concerts, plays, professional sports, and other events in Manhattan and elsewhere, usually with discounted or free tickets. Even closer to home, the Hofstra campus hosts over five hundred cultural events each year, including professional quality theater and music events, master classes, lectures by prominent scholars and cultural figures, parties, movies, and other fun events.

Participation Requirements: The 30-credit HUHC curriculum is fully compatible with all Hofstra majors. The first 15 credits consist of the 12-credit first-year course Culture and Expression, and one 3-credit HUHC seminar. All Culture and Expression credits are counted toward fulfillment of the university's core curriculum requirements. The remaining 15 honors credits can be earned through any combination of HUHC seminars, sections and honors-option courses that are consistent with the student's own academic objectives. All HUHC students are encouraged to undertake a senior honors thesis/project as a capstone to their honors experience at Hofstra.

Students must maintain a GPA of 3.4 and make timely progress toward completing both their major and honors requirements to remain in good standing in HUHC. Those who fall below these standards are given time and mentoring to help them return to good standing.

The designation "Honors College Graduate with Distinction" is affixed to the transcript and diploma of students who earn 30 honors credits, including 12 from Culture and Expression, complete a senior honors thesis/project and maintain a minimum GPA of 3.6.The designation "Honors College Graduate" is affixed to the transcript and diploma of students who complete all of the above requirements except the senior honors thesis/project. For transfer and continuing Hofstra students there is an abbreviated "Honors Associate" designation that is added to the transcript upon completion of 18 honors credits, which does not include Culture and Expression.

Admission Process: To be considered for admission to HUHC, students should have achieved a minimum of 1250 on the SAT or 28 on the ACT and graduate in the top 20 percent of their high school class. Accepted students with distinguished high school records who fall below these levels are urged to express their interest in HUHC so that their applications can be considered in light of their overall academic records. HUHC also welcomes Hofstra students and transfers from accredited colleges. These students are eligible for admission to HUHC with a GPA of 3.5 or higher.

The average HUHC student in the fall 2001 entering class had 1320 combined SAT. Fifty-seven percent of this class graduated in the top 10 percent of their high school class. Seventy-eight percent were members of the National Honors Society; 94 percent were members of other honor societies, such as math, Latin, and French; 30 percent were varsity athletes; and 62 percent have substantial community or volunteer work.

Scholarship Availability: Every entering Hofstra student who accepts the invitation to join HUHC receives a merit-based financial award. These awards have ranged from $2500 to $16,000. All awards are guaranteed for up to four years as long as the student remains a member of HUHC and maintains at least the minimum GPA required by the University for scholarship recipients.

The Campus Context: Hofstra University is traditional, contemporary, and innovative. Hofstra is a young university, but in its sixty-seven years it has shown extraordinary vigor and growth. The University offers the student with ability a good education and unusual opportunities for choice. In many fields, special facilities–clinics, Hofstra's Television Institute, the radio station, a reading center, and a playhouse–enrich the curriculum. Hofstra's philosophy is to provide a strong foundation in the liberal arts and sciences. The University's ultimate goal for its students is "the pursuit of knowledge, understanding, and wisdom upon which a good life can be built." The extracurricular program is full and varied.

Hofstra University offers students the opportunity to major in more than 100 areas in the Hofstra College of Liberal Arts and Sciences, the School of Communication, the Zarb School of Business, the School of Education and Allied Human Services, and New College.

Hofstra's 37 residence halls offer a variety of modern living options for the 4,100 resident students. Single, double, and triple rooms are available as well as suites that include two or three bedrooms with a private bath and living room, accommodating four or five roommates.

Other University facilities include the Hofstra Museum, Career Development Center, Psychology Evaluation and Research Center, Speech and Hearing Center, Physical Fitness Center, Hofstra Stadium, and the Hofstra Arena.

A nationally accredited arboretum, Hofstra's campus covers 243 acres and is situated 25 miles east of New York City. The surrounding Long Island area offers recreation of all kinds and includes boating facilities, beaches, golf courses, and theaters. Cultural and educational facilities in New York City are readily accessible by car or railroad.

Student Body Students attending Hofstra come from forty-four states and sixty-seven countries. The freshman class numbers nearly 2,000. The total enrollment at Hofstra is approximately 13,400, consisting of 8,400 full-time undergraduates and 1,200 part-time undergraduates.

Faculty Hofstra's faculty numbers 1,271 members, including 489 full-time members. Ninety percent of the full-time faculty members hold the highest degree in their field. The faculty consists of exceptionally talented men and women who are dedicated to excellence in teaching, as well as scholarship and research. The faculty members, many of whom are nationally known in their disciplines, make it a point to be accessible to their students outside the classroom. The student-faculty ratio is 13:1. The average class size is 24.

Key Facilities Hofstra's fully computerized library has seating for 1,200 students and contains more than 1.6 million volumes, which includes law, as well as special units for periodicals, reserve books, documents, curriculum materials, special collections, and microfilm. The University's computing facilities are designed to provide the latest in time-sharing capability in a multiprogramming environment for both academic and administrative purposes. The Hofstra computer network provides individual accounts for all students for Internet, e-mail, and more than 250 networked software programs. More than 750 PC, Macintosh and UNIX workstations are available to students in the various labs and classrooms on campus. The labs are staffed and one computer lab is open 24 hours a day and seven days per week. All campus workstations have high speed (OC3) Internet access. All resident students are provided with Internet and e-mail access from their dorm rooms. The Language Laboratory has modern facilities for perfecting foreign language skills.

Interpreting the symbols: **2**=two-year college, **4**=four-year college; **Pu**=public or state college, **Pr**=private college; **G**=general honors program; **D**=departmental honors program; **S**=small program (fewer than 100 students), **M**=midsize program (100 to 500 students), **L**=large program (more than 500 students); **Sc**=scholarships available in honors program; **Tr**=transfer students accepted into honors program; **HBC**=historically black college; **AA**=academic advisors; **GA**=graduate advisors; **FA**=fellowship advisors.

Honorary Societies In addition to chapters of Phi Beta Kappa, Phi Eta Sigma, Golden Key National Honors Society, and Alpha Sigma Lambda, Hofstra also has chapters of twenty-seven additional honors societies dedicated to specific majors.

Athletics Hofstra sponsors eighteen intercollegiate athletic programs that compete at the NCAA Division I level. Hofstra's I-AA football team competes in the eleven-school Atlantic ten Football Conference. All other Hofstra teams compete in the ten-university Colonial Athletic Association, with league members from North Carolina to New York. Eight Hofstra teams, including six conference champions, competed in NCAA Championship Tournaments last year. Hofstra also sponsors a full, four-season schedule of intramural sports including basketball, flag-football, indoor and outdoor soccer, volleyball, Ultimate Frisbee, and many more. The Hofstra Recreation facilities include a multipurpose gymnasium, an indoor running track, a complete Universal and free-weight exercise room, an aerobics room, and an Olympic-size indoor swimming pool.

Study Abroad Hofstra sponsors summer study-abroad programs in such places as China, England, France, Germany, Italy, Korea, the Netherlands, and Spain. Other overseas courses are organized by faculty members as part of credit-bearing courses. Recent courses have been held in Mexico and Egypt and similar courses are being planned for India and China.

Support Services As a result of the Program for the Higher Education of the Disabled, Hofstra is 100 percent accessible to persons with disabilities. Necessary services are provided for wheelchair-bound and other disabled students who meet all academic requirements for admission.

Job Opportunities Considered the world capital in everything from finance and accounting to advertising and TV news, New York City and Long Island offer the perfect place to start a career or just sample what's out there. No other place on earth offers this much opportunity. At Hofstra, students intern at a variety of New York City companies, including American Express, Goldman, Sachs & Co., Merrill Lynch, Ralph Lauren, and the New York Stock Exchange. Cablevision, Estée Lauder, Canon USA, and many other Long Island companies are also part of the internship network.

Tuition: In 2001–02, tuition per semester for 12–17 credits was $7460. Tuition and fees totaled $15,722 per college year. New College tuition was approximately $435 more per semester for 12-20 credits. These costs are subject to change for 2002–03.

Room and Board: Room and board averages $7530. A one-time tuition deposit of $250 and room reservation fee of $100 is required.

Mandatory Fees: A University fee of $292 per semester covers certain University services, such as campus activities, admission to theatrical productions, and publication subscriptions. Off-campus housing is also available.

Contact: Dean Warren G. Frisina and Dean J. Stephen Russell, Honors College, Hofstra University, Hempstead, New York 11549-1000; Telephone: 516-463-4842; Fax 516-463-4782; E-mail: Honors@Hofstra.edu; Web site: http://www.hofstra.edu

---

HOLYOKE COMMUNITY COLLEGE

2 Pu G S Sc Tr

▼ Honors Program

The Honors Program at Holyoke Community College (HCC) offers a challenging and rigorous program of study that can be individually designed to fit a student's interests and curriculum. The Honors Program provides a chance to obtain an excellent education at a very low cost with unequaled opportunities for transfer.

The Honors Program consists of a variety of components. During the first year, the program offers an honors learning community that is team taught, integrating the arts and sciences. Students have the opportunity to work closely with faculty members, a reference librarian, and with each other. The Honors Learning Community is limited to 20 students per semester. Learning communities promote multidisciplinary learning experiences that emphasize student seminars, collaborative research projects, and an introduction to scientific and humanistic intellectual history while completing required courses (English 101 and 102 and two lab sciences). Learning communities at HCC have been supported by grants from the National Endowment for the Humanities, the National Science Foundation, the Fund for the Improvement of Post-Secondary Education, and the National Collegiate Honors Council.

Honors students may generally take one honors colloquium during the second year. Honors colloquia are designed to bring students from all academic disciplines together to confront a theme or issue of current concern from the variety of perspectives that the different disciplines represent. Honors colloquia are multidisciplinary seminars (e.g. Infinity, Monsters, Mind, Reality, Gaia, Holocaust: Paradigm of Genocide) that are competitively enrolled and limited to 15 students who are selected each semester by the Honors Committee. The Honors Program awards a colloquium textbook scholarship to all colloquium students. Colloquia generally offer field trips and a series of expert guest speakers. An Honors Colloquium is strongly recommended to those students who wish to transfer to more selective colleges and universities. A colloquium is offered each semester during the day and in the fall semester at night through continuing education. A letter of invitation to apply is mailed to all eligible students.

Students may also complete an honors project (sometimes called a component), which consists of additional, independent work that a student chooses to undertake in conjunction with a professor in most HCC courses. Such work may consist of an extra paper, a paper of greater length or complexity, a research project in a practical setting such as a lab or darkroom, or creative work such as painting, sculpture, writing, or performance. An honors project may be suggested by either the student or a professor. Project topics are limited only by the student's imagination or ability, the professor's course guidelines, and a regard for the degree of academic rigor that is expected by the HCC Honors Program. Upon successful completion of an honors project, the student receives an additional credit for the course, and the student's transcript shows that the course was taken with honors. Projects must receive initial and final approval from the Honors Committee.

Students may also elect to fulfill the honors curriculum option, which amounts to choosing honors as a major. This option is similar to the arts and sciences transfer option but requires the completion of four semesters (or the equivalent) of a foreign language, an honors project, an honors colloquium, and a graduating GPA of 3.5 or better. Students who do not meet these criteria can still graduate in the arts and sciences transfer option. In the near future, students who complete the honors curriculum option will be granted Commonwealth Scholar distinction upon graduation.

The Honors Program was founded in 1984 by Dr. Marion Copeland. The program averages about 100 students per year who are generally expected to maintain a GPA of at least 3.5.

Participation Requirements: Entrance into the program is flexible. Usually, a student must either enter the College as an honors student or achieve a GPA of at least 3.5 after earning 12 credit hours. All courses within the program emphasize writing, critical and creative thinking across disciplines, and analysis.

Students may elect to fulfill the honors curriculum option, which amounts to choosing honors as a major. This option is similar to the arts and science transfer option, but requires completion of an honors learning community, an honors colloquium, and a foreign language.

Students who achieve a GPA of at least 3.5 after 30 hours earned at HCC are invited to be inducted into the international honor society of Phi Theta Kappa. Members are eligible for scholarships and other benefits. They may also wear the society's gold stole and tassel at commencement.

Scholarship Availability: Several scholarships are awarded each year to entering students. Four Honors Program scholarships (one for a Continuing Education student) of $500 each are given annually to graduating or returning students, and the College offers several larger scholarships that are frequently awarded to Honors Program students. Additional scholarship opportunities are also available.

The Campus Context: Holyoke Community College was founded in 1946 but moved into its modern, 135-acre facility in 1974. HCC is located in the Connecticut River Valley of western Massachusetts, close to the Massachusetts Turnpike (I-90) and just off I-91. HCC is located in the region of Springfield, Northampton, and Amherst and is in the heart of the Five College Area (Amherst College, the University of Massachusetts at Amherst, Hampshire College, Mount Holyoke College, and Smith College). A.A. and A.S. degrees and certificates are offered.

Student Body There are 3,350 Day Division students and 1,900 Continuing Education students.

Faculty The student-faculty ratio is 17:1.

Honorary Societies Phi Theta Kappa

Athletics Intercollegiate soccer, baseball, tennis, basketball, softball, and golf are available. There are twenty-nine clubs and student organizations.

Support Services Facilities for disabled students are excellent, as are services for learning assistance.

Tuition: $2240 for state residents (including insurance), $6920 for nonresidents (including insurance), per year

Mandatory Fees: included in the tuition figures above

Contact: Director: Dr. James M. Dutcher, 303 Homestead Avenue, Holyoke, Massachusetts 01040; Telephone: 413-552-2357; Fax: 413-534-8975; E-mail: jdutcher@hcc.mass.edu; Web site: http://www.hcc.mass.edu

---

HOOD COLLEGE

4 Pr G S Sc Tr AA

▼ Honors Program

The Hood College Honors Program, open to students of all majors, offers challenging and rewarding opportunities for academically exceptional students. All courses in the Honors Program have been specifically designed for honors—all are interdisciplinary and many are team-taught. The program provides an exciting learning experience for students who like the challenge of small, discussion-based classes and look forward to the stimulation of teacher-student interaction.

Students take one course a semester designated as honors in their first and second years at Hood (12 hours) and then take two electives and a senior seminar in the final two years at Hood (9 hours). Students in the program may substitute these courses for some requirements in the College's Core Curriculum. In the first year, the Honors Colloquia are designed to refine skills in critical thinking, writing, and speaking. In the second year, honors students have a seminar and experiential learning project.

Transfer students from a recognized community college honors program may transfer with ease into Hood's program. Transfer students who have not completed a community college honors program may, if invited, join the Hood program in the sophomore year.

Participation in the Hood College Honors Program means becoming part of a learning community. Students in the program often room with other participating students. The program offers dinners, trips, and other social events. Honors students have specially selected faculty advisers.

There are 100 students currently enrolled in the program.

Participation Requirements: To graduate from the Honors Program, students must maintain a 3.25 overall GPA. Successful completion of the Honors Program requirements is recorded on the student's transcript and recognized at Commencement.

Admission Process: Students are invited into the Honors Program on the basis of their GPA, SAT I scores, recommendations, and extracurricular activity experience.

Scholarship Availability: Hood College offers a number of Beneficial Hodson Scholarships to students of exceptional ability. Many students receiving these scholarships are also in the Honors Program. In addition, the College offers Trustee Scholarships to students with excellent academic records.

The Campus Context: Hood College is a beautiful 50-acre Georgian campus located in the tree-filled residential section of Frederick, Maryland, and is only an hour from either Baltimore or Washington. Degree programs offered are the Bachelor of Arts (twenty-four majors), Bachelor of Science (one major), Bachelor of Business Administration, Master of Business Administration, Master of Science (seven programs), and the Master of Arts in human sciences (two concentrations).

Student Body Hood is a four-year liberal arts college and has 800 undergraduates: 12 percent men and 88 percent women. The ethnic distribution of the total undergraduate population includes 12 percent African American and 3 percent Hispanic. International students comprise 7 percent of the total population. Seventy percent of graduating students received financial aid.

Faculty There are 72 full-time faculty members, 21 part-time continuing faculty members, and approximately 85 adjunct faculty members. Ninety-two percent of full-time faculty members have terminal degrees.

Key Facilities The library houses 164,000 volumes. There are 222 computer available on campus.

Honorary Societies Phi Kappa Phi, Mortar Board, and twelve other honor societies

Study Abroad Study abroad is encouraged by eliminating one elective requirement in the Honors Program if an honors student studies abroad. Hood runs an excellent Junior-Year Abroad program in Strasbourg, France.

Support Services Students with disabilities find that the main academic building, the library, the dining hall, the student center, and one of the residence halls are totally accessible. Special parking, equipped restrooms, and lowered drinking fountains are also available on campus. The Academic and Career Center provides academic and career support services for any student on campus.

Tuition: $18,795 per year (2001–02)

Room and Board: $6700 (fifteen-meal plan), $6900 (nineteen-meal plan)

Interpreting the symbols: **2**=two-year college, **4**=four-year college; **Pu**=public or state college, **Pr**=private college; **G**=general honors program; **D**=departmental honors program; **S**=small program (fewer than 100 students), **M**=midsize program (100 to 500 students), **L**=large program (more than 500 students); **Sc**=scholarships available in honors program; **Tr**=transfer students accepted into honors program; **HBC**=historically black college; **AA**=academic advisors; **GA**=graduate advisors; **FA**=fellowship advisors.

Mandatory Fees: $325

Contact: Director: Dr. Emilie Amt, 401 Rosemont Avenue, Frederick, Maryland 21701; Telephone: 301-696-3937; Fax: 301-694-7653; E-mail: eamt@hood.edu

ILLINOIS STATE UNIVERSITY

4 Pu G L Sc Tr

▼ Honors Program

The nationally recognized Honors Program at Illinois State University provides enriching educational opportunities for academically talented students. Excellent students committed to their own personal development and to rewarding professional careers find that their Illinois State Honors education prepares them well for professional schools, graduate schools, and for satisfying employment after they graduate. Honors students enjoy the benefits of a small college in the rich context of a large multipurpose university. The University offers them among other benefits early registration; special courses, taught by distinguished teachers and scholars; close, caring personal advisement by Honors Program advisors; unique opportunities for undergraduate research/scholarship with world-class faculty scholars; and special living accommodations that bring them into close acquaintance with other honors students in academic and social programs. Successful graduates of the Honors Program attend law schools, medical schools, and graduate schools. They also obtain outstanding employment with national corporations, both within Illinois and in other states.

Honors students enjoy special sections of regular University courses, including courses in the general education program. They may also enroll in special courses taught by the University's distinguished scholars and faculty members, including advanced colloquia on various topics, independent honor study, and honors.

The Honors Program sponsors several programs designed to help students pursue research and scholarship as undergraduates. This is an especially important opportunity for students aiming for advanced study in graduate or professional schools. Honors students have used such research opportunities as a basis for publishing articles, networking with professors in their disciplines, and receiving national scholarships and academic prizes.

Honors students may, with the advice of select faculty members and Honors Program advisers, participate in the design of their own educational curricula, reflecting their special interests and goals. This option, called the Faculty Colleague Program, includes individualized curricula for academic majors and minors and for general education. It allows outstanding students the ability to shape for themselves useful curricular options that might not be available in any other university.

All honors course work and honors academic designations are recorded on student transcripts. Students may earn certificates in University honors, may become University honors scholars, and may become departmental honors scholars. There are in addition other academic honors at Illinois State, including traditional Latin-named honors, and special scholarships for outstanding students. The program was established in 1964 to meet the needs of academically talented and motivated students. It currently enrolls 1,400 students, which is nearly 8 percent of the undergraduate student enrollment.

Participation Requirements: Students in the program are expected to complete a minimum of 3 credit hours of honors course work per semester. Students taking more than 3 credits of honors work can have these hours banked against future semesters. Once students have accumulated 24 credit hours, they have met the participation requirements.

Admission Process: The program admits new freshmen, transfer students, and current students eligible for the program. All students must apply for admission to the Honors Program, and must complete a personal statement designed to give the admissions committee a sense of how motivated an applicant is to pursue academic work. Students admitted usually have at least an ACT composite score of 27 and a GPA of at least 3.5. Applying high school students are usually in the top 10 percent of their graduating class.

Scholarship Availability: Incoming students are eligible to apply for various merit scholarships, including Presidential Scholarships, Provost's Scholarships, Dean's Scholarships, and Honors Merit Scholarships. These scholarships are valued at from $1000 for one year to $8000 for each of four years. National Merit Finalists may receive additional scholarship funding if they list Illinois State as their university of choice with the NMS Corporation. Current honors students may apply for tuition scholarships, honors research mentorships, and undergraduate research scholarships.

The Presidential Scholars Program is an exclusive and unique academic program that offers students holding presidential scholarships special curricula, both in general education and in their major courses of study; opportunities for study abroad; and select internship and service learning experiences. Presidential scholars in this program enjoy special social activities, such as dinners with the president and special advisement.

The Campus Context: Illinois State University was founded in 1857 as the first public institution of higher learning in Illinois. It is a multipurpose University committed to providing the best undergraduate education among state-supported universities in Illinois, and to offering high-quality selected graduate programs. There are 160 programs of study offered through the Colleges of Applied Science and Technology, Arts and Sciences, Business, Education, Fine Arts and Nursing. The University's academic programs are supported by the services and collections of Milner Library, which maintains more than 3 million books, documents, and items in special collections. Illinois State is fully accredited by the Commission on Institutions of Higher Education of the North Central Association of Colleges and Schools. The teacher preparation programs are accredited by the National Council for Accreditation of Teacher Education.

Students in the Honors Program may choose to live in Honors House, along with international students. Honors House, staffed by student honors assistants serving as liaisons to the Honors Office, offers select social, cultural, and intellectual programs for students. Honors students living in Honors House may also move in several days before students moving into other residence halls each fall, enabling them to avoid long lines and crowds often associated with moving in the fall. The sense of community found in Honors House makes it a popular residence for honors students. Honors House is fully wired for Internet access.

Student Body The University currently enrolls 20,100 students, of whom 17,500 are undergraduates. The undergraduate population is 57 percent women and 43 percent men. The ethnic composition of the undergraduate enrollment is as follows: white/non-Hispanic, 86.4 percent; African American/non-Hispanic, 7.9 percent; Hispanic, 2.3 percent; Asian/Pacific Islander, 1.5 percent; American Indian/Alaska Native, 0.3 percent; and not reported/nonresident alien, 1.6 percent. Included in this number are 321 international students, of whom 120 are undergraduates. Seventy percent of all students receive some form of financial aid. There are twenty-five fraternities and seventeen sororities on campus.

Faculty There are 1,019 instructional faculty members.

Key Facilities The campus has a fiberoptic network, and all classroom buildings and residence halls are on ISU Net, the campus network. There are computer laboratories in all of the classroom buildings and the library.

There are 8,000 spaces on campus in twelve residence halls. University apartment housing is also available. In addition, a relatively large number of upperclassmen live in apartments in Bloomington/Normal. The actual number of commuter students is fewer than one third of the total enrollment.

Athletics The University competes at the I-A level in fifteen sports (men's and women's) and I-AA in football.

Study Abroad The University offers both study abroad and exchange programs through its Office of International Studies and Programs. Honors students play a prominent part in its activities.

Support Services The University is committed to providing access to students with disabilities and has a very active Office of Disability Concerns.

Job Opportunities There are many work opportunities in virtually all areas of the campus.

Tuition: $3037 for state residents; $9112 for nonresidents, per year (1998–99)

Room and Board: $4116

Mandatory Fees: $1047

Contact: Director: Dr. Stephen Rosenbaum, Normal, Illinois 61790-6100; Telephone: 309-438-2559; Fax: 309-439-8196; E-mail: serosen@ilstu.edu; Web site: http://www.ilstu.edu/depts/honors/

Illinois Valley Community College

2 Pu G S Sc Tr

▼ Honors Program

Illinois Valley Community College (IVCC) has established the Honors Program to recognize those students who have demonstrated or who evidence the potential for demonstrating consistent academic excellence. The program is limited to 50 participants selected by a faculty/staff/student committee from among currently enrolled full-time or part-time Illinois Valley Community College students who apply. Honors students are eligible to apply for designated scholarships, honors courses appear on student transcripts, and the honors degree is clearly indicated on transcripts, diplomas, and certificates.

The Honors Program offers three distinct choices to students: at least a three-semester commitment to honors across the general education curriculum, honors in a specific discipline or "major" (to include A.A., A.S., A.A.S., and certificate program areas), and honors experiences limited to specific courses. Opportunities exist for participation in colloquia and special projects.

Begun in fall 1991, the program is limited to 50 students.

Participation Requirements: A degree with honors involves required enrollment and participation each semester in the honors colloquium for 1 semester hour of credit and recommended enrollment in no more than two honors courses per semester. The required honors project is a one-time separate course (1–3 semester hours of credit), to be completed by the end of the final semester of study and to be designed by the student under advice of and consultation with an instructor and approved by the honors committee. Such projects include (but are not limited to) a research essay/report, exhibition, or recital. Students must have a required minimum of 18 semester hours (including the colloquium and honors project) and have completed at least four honors courses. The term "Degree with Honors" appears on the student's transcript and diploma (or certificate).

Honors in the discipline introduces the possibility of honors work in a specific area of study (e.g., art, history, music, biology, economics, or physics) as determined by the faculty of the particular academic discipline. This involves recommended enrollment in no more than two honors courses per semester from among those designated by the faculty of the particular academic discipline; recommended participation in the honors colloquium as determined by consultation among the student, faculty, and counselor; and a required honors project as a one-time separate course (1–3 semester hours of credit), to be completed by the end of the final semester of study and to be designed by the student under advice of and consultation with an instructor and approved by the honors committee. Such projects include (but are not limited to) a research essay/report, exhibition, or recital. There is a required minimum of 12 semester hours (including the colloquium and honors project), and students must have completed at least three honors courses. The term "Honors in the Discipline" appears on the student's transcript and diploma (or certificate).

Honors Courses Only: Students may enroll in individual honors courses (as many or as few as they desire) without necessarily participating in the Degree with Honors or Honors in the Discipline programs.

In the most general sense, an honors course allows students to explore new ideas suggested by a recognized area or discipline of study; expand their knowledge on topics not considered (or merely alluded to) in their regular classes; attempt skills learned in a class, but for which there appears little or no time for application; and enjoy opportunities to originate and develop talents in a recognized area or discipline.

One type of available honors course is that developed by a faculty member, in which the substance, methodology, and form extend beyond a course offered within the regular curriculum. To facilitate articulation and transfer, this course is offered (and appears on the student's transcript) under the prefix, number, and title of a regular course but designated as "Honors." There are also regular courses offered with an honors contract, in which the student pursues the requirements of the course content under advice and guidance from the instructor and completes such enrichment activities and exercises as (but not limited to) additional essays, experiments, fieldwork, readings, discussions, research, presentations to the class, production of work for publication and performance, research into original sources or reviews of current literature, or group projects with other honors students. The designation "Honors" identifies each appropriate course on the student's transcript.

The Honors Colloquium is a requirement for all students pursuing the Degree with Honors and is recommended to students pursuing Honors in the Discipline. It is also available to students pursuing honors courses only. In the colloquium, enrolled students meet regularly, as determined by the structure and content for discussion among themselves and with those faculty members involved with the various honors options. Invited guest specialists may attend, which includes participation of the general public and members of the College community. The content and structure of the colloquium are determined by the Honors Committee and the faculty.

To remain in the program, the honors student must maintain a minimum GPA of 3.5 for all courses in which he or she is enrolled. A student dismissed from the program may petition the Honors Committee for readmission. All honors work is listed as such on transcripts. Students receive a certificate upon completion of the program and recognition at Commencement.

Admission Process: To be considered for admission to any aspect of the Honors Program, students must meet all of the criteria of the category into which they qualify: high school students must

Interpreting the symbols: **2**=two-year college, **4**=four-year college; **Pu**=public or state college, **Pr**=private college; **G**=general honors program; **D**=departmental honors program; **S**=small program (fewer than 100 students), **M**=midsize program (100 to 500 students), **L**=large program (more than 500 students); **Sc**=scholarships available in honors program; **Tr**=transfer students accepted into honors program; **HBC**=historically black college; **AA**=academic advisors; **GA**=graduate advisors; **FA**=fellowship advisors.

have an ACT score of 26 or above (an equivalent SAT I score) or be in the upper 10 percent of their high school graduating class. A high school transcript and letters of recommendation from 2 members of the high school faculty must be presented, along with results of IVCC placement tests demonstrating that the student reads, writes, and reasons at levels appropriate for honors work.

Currently enrolled IVCC students must have a minimum GPA of 3.5 at Illinois Valley Community College and present an IVCC transcript for review, along with letters of recommendation from at least 2 members of the College faculty. Transfer students must have a GPA of 3.5 at the institution(s) from which they transfer. In addition to the review of college transcripts, letters of recommendation are required from at least 2 members of the faculty at the institution(s) from which the student transfers. Students who do not fall into the above categories may also be reviewed for admission.

The Campus Context: The Illinois Valley Community College offers thirty-two baccalaureate transfer degree programs, thirteen vocational programs, and twenty-four certificate programs.

Student Body IVCC has an undergraduate enrollment of 4,400: 45 percent men and 55 percent women. The ethnic distribution is 95 percent Caucasian and 5 percent members of minority groups. There are 9 international students on this 100-percent commuter campus. Forty-nine percent of all students receive financial aid.

Faculty There are 211 faculty members, of whom 140 are part-time. Five percent of the faculty members have terminal degrees. The student-faculty ratio is 17:1.

Key Facilities The library contains 57,000 volumes; 58,000 federal documents and 24,000 Illinois documents; and microfiche and many electronic databases. There are four computer labs with 300 stations on campus. There is also an automated manufacturing center.

Athletics Athletics include men's basketball, baseball, golf, and tennis and women's volleyball, basketball, golf, tennis, and softball.

Study Abroad Illinois Valley Community College is a member of the Illinois Consortium for International Studies and Programs, offering students opportunities to spend a semester in England (Canterbury) or Austria (Salzburg) or a summer session at Costa Rica (San Jose).

Support Services The College offers full academic support for all special-needs students, including an assessment center, peer and professional tutoring, extended testing, and notetaking. In addition, the College is in complete compliance with the Americans with Disabilities Act.

Job Opportunities IVCC employs more than 300 students in clerical, tutorial, and custodial positions.

Tuition: $576 for area residents, $1933 for non-district residents per year (1998–99)

Mandatory Fees: $84

Contact: Director: Giacomo R. Leone, Division of Humanities and Fine Arts, 815 North Orlando Smith Avenue, Oglesby, Illinois 61348; Telephone: 815-224-0491; Fax: 815-224-3033; E-mail: leone@ivcc.edu

INDIANA UNIVERSITY BLOOMINGTON

4 Pu G L Sc Tr

▼ Honors College

The Honors College represents a commitment made by Indiana University (IU) to broaden and enrich the college experience of bright, highly motivated, and creative students. For the University, the Honors College is a way to coordinate honors programs on campus and provide special services for honors students. For faculty members serving in the Honors College, the program means the opportunity to teach bright students in inventive, interdisciplinary, and small-class settings and advanced or intensive classes devoted to particular disciplines. For the prospective honors student, participation in the Honors College can mean opportunities for scholarships, additional housing options, access to special extracurricular programs, study abroad, opportunities to participate in faculty research projects, or a chance to spend a semester or summer pursuing research interests or gaining teaching or other professional experience through internships.

Begun in 1965, the Honors College currently accepts approximately 650 incoming freshmen.

Participation Requirements: Honors students normally take one honors course each semester. It's a challenging experience, but it's also fun. Right from the start, students get to know their fellow students in a small-class environment as they begin the process of expanding each other's minds under the tutelage of an outstanding teacher.

Admission Process: Students interested in the Honors College should obtain and file the freshman application for admission with the IU Office of Admissions. Freshman applicants with combined SAT I scores of 1300 or above (recentered) or an ACT composite score of 30 or above and who rank in the top 10 percent of their graduating class automatically receive an invitation to join the Honors College.

The program encourages other highly motivated students interested in the academic opportunities provided by the Honors College to apply directly after they have been accepted to IU. Students who do not meet initial criteria may have their high school English teacher send a letter of recommendation attesting to their ability to do honors work. Applicants should also send a copy of their high school transcript and write a brief letter explaining why they wish to join the program. The program is especially interested in candidates who have taken either Advanced Placement, accelerated, or honors courses in high school.

Students who do not enter the Honors College as incoming freshmen but show outstanding academic performance in the first semester or year of college may ask to participate in the program at the end of the first or second semester.

Scholarship Availability: The Honors College gives more than 125 scholarships each year to entering freshmen. Honors College Scholarships are competitive merit scholarships that range in value from $1000 to $6000 per year and are awarded solely on the basis of high school achievement. The application requires information about test scores (SAT I and ACT), class rank, and academic and extracurricular involvement; a short essay; and a brief personal statement. Honors College faculty members carefully read each application and select the award recipients.

The Wells Scholars Program offers a unique educational opportunity to a select group of young scholars. The program emphasizes closer interaction with faculty members, an individually tailored curriculum, and special opportunities for internships and study abroad. The full four-year Wells merit scholarships include tuition and room and board. They may also be used to pursue any course of undergraduate study at Indiana University. Applicants must be nominated by their high school to compete for a Wells scholarship.

The Campus Context: Indiana University at Bloomington is composed of the following colleges and schools: College of Arts and Sciences, School of Informatics, the Kelley School of Business, School of Continuing Studies, School of Fine Arts, School of Education, School of Library and Information Science, School of Journalism. School of Music, School of Nursing, School of Allied and Health Sciences, School of Social Work, School of Optometry, School of Law, School of Physical Education, and School of Health, Physical Education, and Recreation. There are ninety-six degree programs offered on campus.

Distinguished campus facilities are the Mathers Museum of World Cultures, Indiana University Art Museum, Indiana University Musical Arts Center, Elizabeth Sage Historic Costume Collection, Glenn A. Black Laboratory of Archaeology, Kinsey Institute, and many laboratory facilities.

Student Body Of the 29,125 undergraduate students in attendance, 52.5 percent are women. Members of ethnic minority groups constitute 19 percent of the student population. Sixty-four percent of students are residents. Fifty percent of students receive financial aid.

Faculty There are 1,614 full-time and 215 part-time faculty members. Ninety-three percent of faculty members hold terminal degrees. The student-faculty ratio is 21:1.

Key Facilities The Lilly Library houses 400,000 books and 7 million manuscripts. It has a collection of rare books and special collections of film and television scripts, sheet music, and children's books.

Throughout the campus, including the main library and student union building, there are twenty-six staffed computer labs. All schools have both staffed and unstaffed computer facilities. All dormitories have computer labs and computer access.

Honorary Societies Phi Eta Sigma, Golden Key, Mortar Board, Phi Beta Kappa, and Alpha Beta

Athletics In athletics, Indiana University has consistently been one of the nation's premier programs, participating in the NCAA and the Big Ten Conference. In addition to winning twenty NCAA team championships in men's basketball (five), men's swimming and diving (six), men's soccer (three), men's cross-country (three), wrestling (one), men's outdoor track and field (one), and women's tennis (one), Hoosier student-athletes have won a total of 122 individual NCAA crowns. The Athletics Department at IU is committed to academic integrity and compliance with NCAA regulations.

Study Abroad At Indiana University, students can make overseas study part of the regular degree program, whatever the major. Students have the opportunity to spend a full academic year, semester, or summer abroad earning IU credit while enrolled in outstanding international universities or classes specially designed for international students. IU's programs abroad are intensive educational experiences that combine academic excellence with cross-cultural learning. IU offers more than sixty overseas programs in sixteen languages (including English) in twenty-seven countries and nearly every field of study. For example, students can study Renaissance Art in Florence, French media in Strasbourg, the European Union in Maastricht, international marketing in Finland, tropical biology in Costa Rica, intensive Russian in St. Petersburg, Japanese in Nagoya, aboriginal culture in Wollongong, or African history in Ghana.

Support Services Disabled students find the campus accessible and special facilities available.

Job Opportunities Work opportunities on campus are available.

Tuition: $4412 for state residents, $13,416 for nonresidents, per year (2000–01)

Room and Board: $5608

Mandatory Fees: $712

Contact: Dean: Lewis H. Miller Jr., 324 North Jordan Avenue, Bloomington, Indiana 47405; Telephone: 812-855-3550; Fax: 812-855-5416; E-mail: millerl@indiana.edu; Web site: http://www.indiana.edu/~iubhonor

INDIANA UNIVERSITY OF PENNSYLVANIA

4 Pu G M Sc Tr

▼ Robert E. Cook Honors College

The Robert E. Cook Honors College at Indiana University of Pennsylvania (IUP) is a residential Honors College designed to give talented students a graduate student atmosphere during their undergraduate education. Students engage in a learning community that blends their academics, social service learning, and residential lives.

The curriculum focuses on critical thinking, communication skills, and problem solving as a group. An interdisciplinary core course serves as the backbone of the curriculum, with other honors courses available in the humanities, sciences, education, and fine arts. This is supplemented through a Social Service program coordinating social service activities with each student's education. Further, a strong study-abroad and internship program provides real settings for further study.

Participation Requirements: Entering freshmen complete a minimum of 23 honors credits. There are two required courses: Honors College Core Course (14 credits, three semesters, HC101, 102, and 201) and an honors section of Senior Synthesis (3 credits). In addition, 3 honors credits must be in a non-humanities course and 3 honors credits must be taken during the junior year. All students have the option to complete an undergraduate thesis.

Sophomore transfer students complete a minimum of 18 honors credits. There are two required courses: Honors College Core Course III (4 credits, one semester, HC 201) and an honors section of Senior Synthesis (3 credits). In addition, 3 honors credits must be in a non-humanities course, and 3 honors credits must be taken during the junior year. All students have the option to complete an undergraduate thesis.

Honors students must maintain a minimum 3.25 QPA, but are granted one semester probation. Successful completion of the College is recognized at commencement and is also noted on the official transcript and diploma.

Admission Process: High school students are admitted on the basis of an application, essays, teacher recommendations, social service, high school average, and SAT I or ACT scores. Transfer students may apply during the first or second semesters. Students may select from any of the more than 100 majors at IUP. There are two decision timelines for applying. The early decision deadline is November 15; regular decision is March 1.

Scholarship Availability: Scholarships of various amounts are reserved specifically for honors students based on application merit and academic performance. Scholarship competition is heavy; however, many students receive some form of support.

The Campus Context: The Robert E. Cook Honors College is located in Whitmyre Hall on the IUP campus in Indiana, Pennsylvania. The town of Indiana is located in Western Pennsylvania, approximately 50 miles east of Pittsburgh. It is a small city of 30,000 residents. Popularly known through the fame of its favorite son, Jimmy Stewart, Indiana houses the Jimmy Stewart Museum, local theater, and government as the county seat of Indiana County.

IUP is a Doctoral I university with more than 100 different majors in six different colleges (Business, Education, Health and Human Services, Humanities and Social Sciences, Natural Science, and Mathematics). Members of the Robert E. Cook Honors College may participate in any major or combination of majors, programs, and/or minors. Honors College students are also

Interpreting the symbols: **2**=two-year college, **4**=four-year college; **Pu**=public or state college, **Pr**=private college; **G**=general honors program; **D**=departmental honors program; **S**=small program (fewer than 100 students), **M**=midsize program (100 to 500 students), **L**=large program (more than 500 students); **Sc**=scholarships available in honors program; **Tr**=transfer students accepted into honors program; **HBC**=historically black college; **AA**=academic advisors; **GA**=graduate advisors; **FA**=fellowship advisors.

actively advised toward the benefits of study abroad, internships, social service, and other experiential learning opportunities.

Student Body The Robert E. Cook Honors College enrolls 100 freshman each fall with a total of 400 students combining the freshman through senior classes. Thirty percent of Honors College students are men. Seventy-five percent of Honors College students receive some form of financial aid.

In the 1998–99 academic year, IUP enrolled 13,736 students: 12,158 undergraduates and 1,578 graduate students. Approximately 6 percent of the students are members of minority groups; 43.4 percent of the population is men. More than four out of five IUP students receive some form of financial aid.

Faculty All honors faculty members have their terminal degrees. There are 743 full-time and 92 part-time faculty members at IUP, with 85 percent being tenure or tenure-track faculty members.

Key Facilities Honors College students who live in Whitmyre Hall, the residence hall for the Honors College, are provided with a PC in their residence room. (All freshman are required to live in Whitmyre Hall for their first year.) Residence PCs carry current software, are linked to the IUP mainframe, have access to the IUP libraries, and have an Internet connection. Access to the campus network is provided through ethernet connections utilizing the campus fiberoptic backbone.

IUP has multiple strategically placed computer laboratories across campus. In addition, many departments maintain their own computer facilities of a focused nature geared toward the specializations of the department.

The IUP Library system combines Stapleton Library, Stabley Library, the Cogswell Music Library, the University School Library, and the branch campus libraries. The book collection surpasses 775,000 volumes. In addition, there are 1.7 million microforms, more than 100,000 bound periodicals, and more than 24,000 volumes of governmental publications.

Honorary Societies Phi Kappa Phi, Mortar Board, Sutton Society, and Phi Eta Sigma

Athletics IUP men's varsity sports include cross-country, football, basketball, swimming, track and field, golf, and baseball. Women's varsity sports include tennis, cross-country, soccer, volleyball, field hockey, basketball, swimming, softball, track and field, and lacrosse. Varsity sports are National Collegiate Athletic Association Division II and part of the Pennsylvania State Athletic Conference.

Study Abroad The Robert E. Cook Honors College strongly encourages students to take advantage of the benefits of a study-abroad experience. The Honors College works with the IUP Office of International Affairs (OIA) to secure the best placements for its students. IUP is a member of the International Student Exchange and has established sites in more than twenty countries on six of the seven continents throughout the world. Students have choices involving duration of stay (academic semester, academic year, or other), time the visit (summer, fall/spring academic semesters), and many other facets of the program. Overseas internships and student teaching are available. In addition, where appropriate, the Honors College and OIA work with students to secure study-abroad opportunities through independent organizations as well.

Support Services Faculty and staff members within the Advising and Testing Center serve to ensure IUP's program access compliance with Section 504 of the Rehabilitation Act of 1973 and the Americans with Disabilities Act. Services provided include, but are not limited to, early registration, assistance in locating accessible housing, equipment loan, test proctoring and reading, notetaking, recording of books, NCR paper, liaison with faculty, OVR, BVS, and general advising and counseling.

Job Opportunities A limited number of federal and state work-study positions are available on campus. Federal and state work-study qualifications are based on financial need. Internships are available through both the Robert E. Cook Honors College and the student's individual department.

Tuition: \$3468 per year for residents, \$8824 per year for nonresidents, \$5202 per year for Ohio and West Virginia residents attending the main campus (1998–99)

Room and board: \$3632

Mandatory Fees: \$756

Contact: Director: Dr. Janet E. Goebel, 136 Whitmyre Hall, Indiana, Pennsylvania 15705; Telephone: 800-487-9122; Fax: 724-357-3906; E-mail: honors-college@grove.iup.edu; Web site: http://www.iup.edu/honors

---

Indiana University–Purdue University at Indianapolis

4 Pu G M Sc Tr AA

▼ Honors Program

The Honors Program was developed in 1979 to enhance the evolvement of Indiana University–Purdue University at Indianapolis (IUPUI) as a national leader among urban institutions, with its mission to promote excellence in research, teaching, and service. The Honors Program is located in University College, the academic unit that serves all incoming students. In emphasizing honors programming, IUPUI demonstrates its conviction that the creation of knowledge through research, the dissemination of knowledge through teaching, and the cultivation of knowledge through student learning are its principal values. Students are not required to pursue their degree with honors in order to participate in honors courses. To optimize opportunities for academic achievement, the Honors Program offers courses designed specifically for honors students, departmental courses for honors and highly motivated students in their majors, and honors independent research papers or projects. Students are also encouraged to participate in international study, field study, and the National Collegiate Honors Council (NCHC) Honors Semesters. Outstanding undergraduates, with the permission of their department, may earn honors credit by enrolling and successfully completing graduate course work.

In addition to academic enrichment, honors students, through the University College Reading Room, can access their personal e-mail and all of the research opportunities available in the University library. The room is equipped with an electronic scanner and software, enabling honors students to enhance their papers and presentations. It is also the meeting area for members of the Honors Club, who use it as a base for campus/club activities and personal socialization. Because the campus is located only six blocks from downtown Indianapolis, students have excellent opportunities for internships and partnerships with the city. The Honors Club annually cosponsors two campus blood drives with the Central Indiana Regional Blood Bank for the benefit of central Indiana citizens.

Upon completion of the honors requirements, Honors Program participants are awarded the following: mention at graduation, a medallion on a neck ribbon that is worn during graduation ceremonies, honors notations placed on the transcript and diploma, and certificates for outstanding service to Honors Club members.

Participation Requirements: All students graduating with general honors degrees must earn a minimum of 24 honors credit hours, an overall GPA of at least 3.3, and a minimum 3.3 GPA in all honors work. The overall requirement is reduced to 21 honors credit hours for those completing a 6-credit–hour Honors Senior Thesis. Students earning Departmental Honors must meet the additional requirements prescribed by their department. A third option, graduation with honors from one's school, is available to students in the Schools of Business, Nursing, and Public and Environmental Affairs.

Admission Process: Acceptance into the Honors Program is based on meeting one of the following qualifications: SAT I scores of at least 1180 (ACT scores of at least 26) and rank in the top 15 percent of one's high school class; a 3.0 or higher GPA earned in a minimum of 12 credit hours of course work; or transferring from another university with a 3.3 or higher GPA or from another university's Honors Program. Application to enroll in specific honors courses or independent study is also available to students with a strong interest or demonstrably high ability in a specific area or study. Academically gifted high school students who are admitted to IUPUI through the SPAN Program (based on high SAT I scores and part-time non-degree-student status) may apply to the program for permission to enroll in honors courses.

Scholarship Availability: The Honors Program offers a number of scholarships for incoming freshmen and continuing students. Some of these scholarships are renewable for one or three years, depending upon the student's continuing academic performance. Entering freshmen who score at least 1180 on the SAT I (26 on the ACT) and are in the top 15 percent of their class automatically receive an IUPUI Academic Excellence Scholarship of $1000 that is renewable for three years if the student attends full time and maintains a GPA of at least 3.0. The Honors Program also offers support for competitive student- and faculty-initiated undergraduate research proposals across the campus. Support is also available for students who are invited to present their research at local, state, or national conferences.

The Campus Context: IUPUI is an urban campus that offers students the dynamic spirit that characterizes a metropolitan city. As a twenty-first-century model for American public higher education, the campus thrives on a fast pace and connections with Indianapolis and its people. It serves more than 27,000 students who may earn degrees from either Indiana or Purdue University. Twenty schools offer a total of 180 degree programs. Although a growing number of its students enter IUPUI immediately following high school graduation, 53 percent return to or start college after working and beginning a family. To better accommodate the student body, IUPUI offers flexible scheduling options, including night, weekend, Web-based, and televised courses.

The University comprises twenty colleges on campus, including Allied Health Sciences, Art, Business, Continuing Studies, Dentistry, Education, Engineering and Technology, Journalism, Law, Liberal Arts, Library and Information Science, Medicine, Music, Nursing, Physical Education, Public and Environmental Affairs, Science, Social Work, and IU and Purdue Graduate Schools.

Student Body Of the undergraduates, 57.7 percent are women. Of the ethnic population, 11 percent of the students are African American, 2.1 percent are Asian, 1.3 percent are Hispanic, and .02 percent are Native American. Nine percent of the students are residents; 91 percent commute. Ninety-six percent receive financial aid.

Faculty Of the 2,400 total faculty members, 1,370 are full-time. The student-faculty ratio is approximately 17:1.

Key Facilities Some of the distinguishing features on campus are a Child Care Center, a Counseling Center, the Indiana University Medical School, the Natatorium (Olympic-size swimming facility), the National Institute for Fitness and Health, a state-of-the-art lecture hall, the Undergraduate Education Center, and an excellent library. The library holds 570,000 volumes and 4,500 current periodicals and 120 computer workstations. There are thirteen computer learning centers.

Honorary Societies Phi Eta Sigma, Alpha Lambda Delta, and Alpha Sigma Lambda

Athletics In athletics, IUPUI is NCAA Division I; men's sports include baseball, basketball, golf, soccer, and tennis, and women's sports include basketball, softball, tennis, and volleyball.

Support Services Disabled-student facilities include the Office of Adaptive Education, sign-language interpreters, note-takers, readers, exam proctors, classroom aides, an active Disabled Students Organization, a special registration process that includes information about campus facilities and parking privileges, computer reading systems, large-print video, and voice character generators.

Job Opportunities Work-study and part-time employment are available.

Tuition: $127.95 for state residents, $398 for nonresidents, per credit hour (2001–02)

Room and Board: $3000 minimum

Mandatory Fees: $500

Contact: Director: E. Theodore Mullen Jr., UC3140, 815 West Michigan Street, Indianapolis, Indiana 46202-5164; Telephone: 317-274-2660; Fax: 317-274-2365; E-mail: emullen@iupui.edu; Web site: http://www.iupui.edu/~honors

---

Indiana University South Bend

4 Pu G M Sc Tr AA

▼ Honors Program

Through its Honors Program, Indiana University South Bend (IUSB) provides a special intellectual challenge for its keenest and most highly motivated undergraduates. Drawing upon the full range of resources that a large university can offer, this program encompasses a broad variety of classes, tutorials, and independent study opportunities. The program expects its most talented students to respond by engaging in academic pursuits that encourage them to strive for individual excellence in their University course of study.

Approximately 50 incoming freshmen annually and approximately 200–225 students participate in the program.

Participation Requirements: Classes in the arts and humanities, business and economics, education, nursing, social and behavioral sciences, and science are offered. An Honors Program certificate is granted to students who have taken a minimum of 18 hours of credit in at least five honors-qualified courses, have completed the Freshman Honors Colloquium, and have completed an honors-qualified project under the individual mentoring of an IUSB faculty member.

Offered for the first time in fall 1996, the Freshman Honors Colloquium consists of lectures by distinguished faculty members from across the University and a weekend symposium spearheaded by a noted scholar. The faculty members chosen to make these ten presentations include the best teachers and scholars on the campus. Each honors student then prepares a 250–500 word response to the lecture/discussion and turns in a paper at the next lecture. Graduate students grade the papers and return them to the students on a weekly basis.

A weekend symposium led by a well-known scholar serves as the capstone event of the Colloquium. One week before the symposium, each honors student turns in a five-page opinion paper based on materials written by the scholar. After the weekend of presentations by the scholar, each honors student submits a twelve- to twenty-page research paper that examines a topic or issue generated by the symposium. All incoming freshman honors students are required to take this class. Although the 2 credit hours earned count toward the student's completion of the honors certificate, the course ordinarily does not fulfill the require-

Interpreting the symbols: **2**=two-year college, **4**=four-year college; **Pu**=public or state college, **Pr**=private college; **G**=general honors program; **D**=departmental honors program; **S**=small program (fewer than 100 students), **M**=midsize program (100 to 500 students), **L**=large program (more than 500 students); **Sc**=scholarships available in honors program; **Tr**=transfer students accepted into honors program; **HBC**=historically black college; **AA**=academic advisors; **GA**=graduate advisors; **FA**=fellowship advisors.

ment that all students who receive an Honors Scholarship take at least one honors class during the year.

Admission Process: Admission to the Honors Program and its classes is open to all qualified students (those with an overall GPA of 3.3 or higher), including part-time students and those who enter the University several years after leaving high school, without restriction with regard to school, major, or class standing.

Scholarship Availability: Several scholarships available only to Honors Program participants are awarded each year. A few particularly promising incoming honors students receive IUSB Alumni Association Scholarships, which cover the students' tuition and mandatory fees during the freshman year. These scholarships, as well as the IUSB Honors Scholarship, are awarded to entering freshmen who fulfill at least two of the following three criteria: a score of 1200 or above on the SAT, a class rank in the top 10 percent of their high school graduating class, and the attainment of an overall high school GPA of at least 3.5 (on a 4.0 scale). These scholarships also are available to transfer students who enter with a cumulative GPA of 3.5 or higher. Annual continuation of these scholarships is based on students' attaining a cumulative GPA of 3.5 or above and the completion of at least one honors course during the academic year. To remain in the program, nonscholarship recipients must maintain at least a 3.3 cumulative GPA. Because the Honors Scholarships are tuition-specific, the University administration requires the filing of the Free Application for Federal Student Aid (FAFSA) and the IUSB Financial Aid forms as a condition precedent for receiving (and then retaining) these scholarships.

The Campus Context: Indiana University South Bend, one of the eight campuses of Indiana University, offers an exceptional education to students of north central Indiana and southwestern Michigan. Overlooking a picturesque stretch of the St. Joseph River and east of downtown South Bend, IUSB is centrally located in the Michiana area. IUSB's buildings contain modern classrooms and science laboratories, spacious auditoriums and studios for the fine arts and the performing arts, a library, a student activities building, extensive audiovisual facilities, and links to computer and instructional television networks that serve the entire IU system. The University offers 100 majors leading to the associate, baccalaureate, or master's degree.

Student Body There are 6,070 undergraduates and 1,347 graduate students. Of the undergraduates, 64 percent are women. Minority ethnic distribution is 6.2 percent African American, 2.3 percent Hispanic, and 1.3 percent Asian. International students constitute 3.1 percent. Most students commute to campus; however, nearby housing can be arranged. Fifty-three percent of students (defined as full-time undergraduates receiving need-based aid) receive financial aid. The campus has one national sorority and one local fraternity.

Faculty There are 264 full-time faculty members, 78 percent of whom have earned the highest degrees within their discipline. Another 246 associate (i.e., adjunct) faculty members teach on campus. The student-faculty ratio is 14:1.

Key Facilities The 476,000-volume library houses several special collections. The twelve computer labs located in classroom buildings and the library are available for student use.

Athletics IUSB offers opportunities in men's and women's basketball, as well as several intramural sports. The recently constructed, 100,000-square-foot student activities center has two gymnasiums, student government offices, a Panhellenic room, conference rooms, a café, a dance studio, a running track, locker rooms, and state-of-the-art exercise equipment.

Study Abroad Many opportunities for study-abroad programs are available through IUSB and through the IU system.

Support Services By coordinating such services as providing texts for students with vision impairments and students with hearing impairments, the Office of Disabled Student Services, which acts as a liaison between the students, instructors, and other University resources, supports disabled students in achieving their academic potential to the greatest extent possible. Other commonly offered services include assistance in scheduling and registering for classes, obtaining books and handicapped parking permits, and arranging for alternative testing and referral to and from Vocational Rehabilitation and other community agencies.

Job Opportunities Work opportunities vary on campus. The World Wide Web (http://www.iusb.edu/~human/) contains a list of current job postings.

Tuition: $2622 for state residents, $7318 for nonresidents, per year (2001–02) (figures are based on a 12-credit-hour load for each of two semesters and exclude laboratory fees)

Mandatory Fees: Full-time: $118.50 per semester; part-time: $46.75 to $118.50 per semester (according to course load and class level)

Contact: Director: Dr. Brenda E. Knowles, 1700 Mishawaka Avenue, P.O. Box 7111, Administration Building 206(a), South Bend, Indiana 46634-7111; Telephone: 574-237-4355; Fax: 574-237-4866; E-mail: bknowles@iusb.edu

Iona College

4 Pr G S Sc Tr

▼ Honors Degree Program

The Iona College Honors Degree Program is designed to meet the educational needs of the most able and highly motivated students at Iona. Grounded in a challenging curriculum, the program offers gifted students the resources and opportunities to develop their talents and to perform at the peak of their capabilities. The course of study is designed to develop intellectual curiosity, analytical abilities, and awareness of ethical and civic responsibilities. The program encourages the development of a small nucleus of independent learners able to inspire each other academically and fosters a sense of self-respect in students, encouraging them to stretch their abilities in pursuit of lifelong learning, independent thinking, and personal fulfillment.

The curriculum promotes an appreciation and understanding of the interrelatedness of knowledge and culture by providing a wide range of interdisciplinary courses and opportunities to study abroad. Students in the program take specially designed honors course offerings, advanced courses, and engage in independent research under the guidance of faculty mentors. Small class sizes of approximately 15 encourage student participation and promote a close student-faculty relationship. Students are offered close individual guidance, both academically and in terms of career preparation. There is a faculty committee that works with students who are interested in applying for competitive grants and fellowships. The committee also advises them regarding graduate and professional studies. A career mentoring program affords students a unique chance to explore career opportunities by matching them with appropriate alumni/alumnae or corporate liaison. Students may major in any discipline in the School of Arts and Science or the Hagan School of Business.

Participants in the Honors Degree Program enjoy other significant privileges. Students receive two tuition-free courses per academic year that may be taken in the winter of summer sessions or as sixth courses during the fall and spring semesters. These free courses can facilitate double majors, accelerate graduation, or broaden the educational experience with no financial burden. Honors students have priority registration, thereby assuring their ability to receive class preferences. A student representative from each year is elected to serve, along with faculty members and administrators, on the Honors Council, which is the policy-making body for the Honors Degree Program.

Honors students have the use of an honors study house on campus that is equipped with computers with Internet access. The facility is a comfortable place that can be used for individual work, group study, or socializing with honors students and faculty members. Students are responsible for running the house and elect representatives to serve on a house governance committee. The Honors Degree Program publishes its own newsletter, which is edited by students and contains articles of interest authored by contributing members of the program.

The program has been in existence for more than twenty years, and admits 30 freshmen each year. There are approximately 100 students currently enrolled in the program.

Participation Requirements: During freshman and sophomore years, students are required to take the Honors Humanities Seminar. Offered as four 3-credit courses, the seminar introduces students to the central concepts of philosophy, history, literature, and religious studies in an interdisciplinary fashion. In the first year, students also take Honors English Composition and Honors Logic and Critical Thinking; in the sophomore year, they also take Honors Speech. The Honors Lecture and Seminar course is required for juniors in the program. The junior seminar focuses on a specific topic and is coupled with a series of public lectures, many delivered by visiting scholars. Students meet in small groups to discuss each lecture with a faculty facilitator. The culmination of the program is the completion of a senior thesis undertaken with a faculty mentor. Seniors present the results of their research in a conference setting open to the College community. Students complete the humanities core curriculum by taking upper level courses in philosophy, literature, history, and religious studies. To fulfill the science and mathematics core, honors students are expected to take calculus and a lab science (biology, chemistry, or physics).

To remain in the program, students must maintain at least a 3.5 cumulative GPA. Students who complete the Honors Degree Program are awarded honors medals at the end of senior year. Honors students receive special recognition during commencement exercises, and an honors seal is affixed to their diplomas. Completion of the program is noted on official transcripts.

Admission Process: High school students are recruited for the Honors Degree Program, and those admitted must have completed an Iona College admissions application. Specific requirements for the program include a minimum high school GPA of 90, minimum combined SAT I scores of 1200 or higher (or a comparable ACT score), a completed Honors Degree Program application and essay, and a personal interview. Students may apply for admission after the first or second semester of freshman year. The deadline for applying to the honors program is February 1; interviews are held in March.

Scholarship Availability: The Honors Degree Program does not directly award scholarships, but scholarships of various amounts are awarded through the Office of Admissions. Because of their high academic achievements, candidates for the Honors Degree Program qualify for Iona College scholarship assistance, which may extend to full tuition Dean's Scholarships.

The Campus Context: Iona College is located in the gracious Beechmont section of New Rochelle. A city of 72,000 people on the Long Island Sound in Westchester County, New Rochelle offers the sophistication of an established suburb and easy access to New York City by automobile or public transportation. Founded by the Christian Brothers in 1940, Iona has grown to be an institution recognized for innovative scholarship, distinguished faculty, and successful alumni. The College offers forty-four baccalaureate degree programs. There are three schools on campus: the School of Arts and Science, the Hagan School of Business, and the Columba School.

Student Body The undergraduate enrollment is 57 percent women. The ethnic distribution is 66 percent white, 19 percent black, 13 percent Hispanic, and 2 percent Asian/Pacific Islander. Ninety-four percent of the students receive financial aid.

Faculty The total number of faculty members is approximately 370, of whom 170 are full-time. Seventy-eight percent of the full-time faculty members have terminal degrees. The student-faculty ratio is 16:1.

Key Facilities The library contains more than 235,000 volumes. The Helen Arrigoni Library/Technology Center houses all materials for the disciplines of mass communications, computer science, education, and management information sciences. In addition to Internet access, the center is equipped with CD-ROM capabilities and headphone and speaker connections that allow for small-group projects on the multimedia systems. About 300 microcomputers (Pentium 486 systems and 386 systems) are available for student use at the New Rochelle, Rockland, and New York City campuses.

Honorary Society Delta Epsilon Sigma

Athletics The athletic department offers a wide variety of sports and intramural programs for all members of the Iona community to enjoy. Iona competes in the Metro Atlantic Conference and fields twenty-one Division I teams. Iona supports a Division I-AA non-scholarship football team and plays traditional rivals St. John's, Georgetown, and Wagner. An extensive intramural program allows up to 1,200 students per year to engage in athletic activities. The John A. Mulcahy Center houses the athletic staff and provides recreational swimming in an Olympic-size pool, a full Nautilus fitness center, men's and women's saunas, and a gymnasium for basketball and volleyball. The Mazella multi-sports field is also available for recreational use.

Study Abroad Iona College encourages students to broaden their educational experiences and gain cultural perspectives through study and travel abroad, especially in areas less affluent than the United States. Iona College has sponsored summer and intercession programs in Ireland, Belgium, France, England, Spain, Italy, Mexico, and Morocco. Full-time students may enroll for a semester-long program in Dublin, Ireland; at St. Mary's College, a constituent part of the famed Trinity College; and at the Irish Institute in Louvain, Belgium. Students enrolled in this program may take Iona courses in Irish history and culture, philosophy, the industrial revolution, peace and justice, and literature. Arrangements can also be made for students to pursue a selected major and foreign language courses. Students may also spend a semester or a year studying independently at an international university. Earned credits may be transferred to Iona College with prior approval.

Support Services The Samuel Rudin Academic Resource Center, which is wheelchair-accessible, provides reasonable auxiliary aids and services to students with disabilities. In addition to providing legally mandated services for persons with disabilities who voluntarily seek additional services, the College Assistance Program provides professional tutoring, academic advisement, and other support services.

Job Opportunities A limited number of part-time positions on campus are available to students who demonstrate financial need. The wage rate varies depending upon skills required and experience.

Tuition: $14,100 per year (1998–99)

Room and Board: $7520

Mandatory Fees: $320

Contact: Director of Honors: Dr. James Carroll, Iona College, New Rochelle, New York 10801; Telephone: 914-633-2694; Fax: 914-633-2019; E-mail: jcarroll@iona.edu

Interpreting the symbols: **2**=two-year college, **4**=four-year college; **Pu**=public or state college, **Pr**=private college; **G**=general honors program; **D**=departmental honors program; **S**=small program (fewer than 100 students), **M**=midsize program (100 to 500 students), **L**=large program (more than 500 students); **Sc**=scholarships available in honors program; **Tr**=transfer students accepted into honors program; **HBC**=historically black college; **AA**=academic advisors; **GA**=graduate advisors; **FA**=fellowship advisors.

Iowa State University of Science and Technology

4 Pu G L Tr AA

▼ University Honors Program

The Iowa State University (ISU) Honors Program is a University-wide program that provides opportunities for students who want to achieve academic excellence, get ahead of the competition, and have a great time in college. It allows students the option of taking introductory courses with smaller enrollments and top-notch instruction. It also assists honors students in creating their own degree programs and working closely with faculty members through a research mentor program and honors project.

Honors courses offer small class sizes and stress more student interaction than lecture. Most students find that taking honors courses does not hurt their GPAs. In fact, students often do their best work in these classes.

Honors seminars give students the opportunity to explore topics not offered to the larger University population. Seminars are offered for 1–2 credits on a pass/fail basis. Students are encouraged to take seminars outside of their major field. Recent popular seminar topics have included emerging infectious diseases, symbiotic relationship between sports and business, apocalypse now and then, and leadership development and team building.

Honors projects give students the opportunity to choose a topic for in-depth study. Many times, students decide to work on projects completely outside of their major. Research grants are awarded to students to help defray the cost of their projects.

The Freshman Honors Program introduces a limited number of qualified and motivated students to the advantages of an honors education, emphasizes learning in small groups, and fosters a sense of community among students with similar abilities and interests.

An honors English composition class, a special freshman honors seminar, and an honors section of the required University library course form the academic core of the program during the fall semester. During spring semester, students may opt to participate in the Mentor Program, a program that places the freshmen with faculty members in a research environment.

Iowa State has offered University Honors since 1960 and Freshman Honors since 1973. There are approximately 900 students in the seven-college Honors Program and 400 students in the Freshman Honors Program. The notation "Graduated in the University Honors Program" is entered on the permanent record, diploma, and in the Commencement program. A certificate is also awarded at the convocations preceding the University Commencement ceremony.

Participation Requirements: Students must submit a program of study approved by the college's Honors Committee. Graduation in the University Honors Program requires a minimum GPA of 3.35, completion of the required number of honors courses and honors seminars, and completion of the honors project.

Admission Process: For the Freshman Honors Program, invitations are sent to students who meet one of the following categories: they are in the upper 5 percent of their high school class, have an ACT composite score of 30 or above, or are a National Merit or National Achievement finalist. Admission is competitive and the program size is limited to 400 students.

Scholarship Availability: There are five competitive scholarships based on the activity level of Honors Program membership.

The Campus Context: Iowa State University, which has aspirations to become the best land-grant university in the nation, offers degree programs in nine colleges: agriculture, business, design, education, engineering, family and consumer sciences, liberal arts and sciences, veterinary medicine, and graduate. Students can choose from more than 100 undergraduate degrees. The University is one of only thirty-two public universities who are members of the prestigious Association of American Universities and is ranked among the nation's top fifty public universities by *U.S. News & World Report.*

Ranked as one of the twenty-five most beautiful campuses in the nation, Iowa State offers students top-rated educational, research, and recreational facilities. In the last two years, the University has completed construction of the first phase of a $61-million engineering teaching and research complex, with the second phase to begin soon; a new family studies and human development building that houses a family development lab; and a very popular student apartment complex. Current projects include the Martin C. Jischke Honors Building, which is located near central campus and is scheduled to open in fall 2002. In addition, the College of Business building and continued improvements to the residence system are underway. The University's Lied Recreation/Athletic Center boasts the nation's longest indoor track and has dozens of sport courts for the University's large intramural program. The Iowa State Center offers students the opportunity to watch Big 12 Conference basketball and wrestling and major concerts at Hilton Coliseum, internationally renowned orchestras and theater performances at Stephens Auditorium, and University-produced plays at Fisher Theater.

Student Body The undergraduate enrollment is 22,087: 56 percent men and 44 percent women. The ethnic distribution is as follows: African American, 2.5 percent; American Indian/Alaskan Indian, 0.4 percent; Asian/Pacific Islander, 2.5 percent; Hispanic, 1.6 percent; and international students, 4.8 percent. Seventeen percent of the University's graduates are from states other than Iowa. Iowa State ranks sixth in the nation for the number of National Merit Scholars enrolled at a public university. Thirty-five percent of undergraduates live in University residence halls, and 65 percent either live off campus or commute. There are thirty-three fraternities and nineteen sororities.

Fifty-six percent of the students received need-based financial aid and 34 percent received merit-based financial aid in 2000–01, including 6,936 merit-based scholarships.

Faculty The total number of faculty members is 1,779, of whom 1,527 are full-time. The student-faculty ratio is 12:1.

Key Facilities The University library system houses more than 2 million volumes and bound serials. A campus telecommunications system allows students to use their personal computers to connect with the University system, Project Vincent, which allows them access to the Internet. With more than 16,000 computer workstations, Iowa State is among the nation's university leaders in access to computers. Students have their own free e-mail addresses and the opportunity to create their own Web pages. *Yahoo: Internet Life!* magazine lists Iowa State as one of the top 100 "Most Wired" universities in the nation.

Honorary Societies: Phi Eta Sigma, Phi Kappa Phi, Golden Key, Mortar Board, Phi Beta Kappa, Alpha Lambda Delta, and Cardinal Key

Athletics Iowa State's Division I intercollegiate athletic teams compete in the Big 12 Conference. There are seven competitive sports for men (basketball, cross-country, football, golf, indoor track, outdoor track, and wrestling) and eleven for women (basketball, cross-country, golf, gymnastics, indoor track, outdoor track, soccer, softball, swimming, tennis, and volleyball). Over the past two academic years, Iowa State's women's basketball, men's basketball, gymnastics, and wrestling teams have ranked among the top ten teams nationally in their respective sports. Iowa State was one of five schools nationally to have ranked teams in women's basketball, men's basketball, and football. In addition, a record 189 student athletes earned Big 12 Conference recognition for posting a minimum of a 3.0 GPA during the 2001 spring semester.

Study Abroad For students who wish to study abroad, there are more than 170 study or work-abroad programs in fifty countries. Programs range from one week to one year. More than 700 Iowa State students annually study or work abroad.

Support Services The Dean of Students' Office offers a variety of student services, ranging from disability assistance programs to academic and personal counseling services. Residences halls can accommodate wheelchairs, and there is a residence apartment for a student that is quadraplegic. There are hearing-impaired accommodations as needed and accommodations for guide dogs.

Job Opportunities Iowa State offers students more than 900 college work-study jobs each year. An Undergraduate Research Assistant Program places 150 high-achieving upperclass students with financial need with faculty researchers. More than 23 percent of Iowa State's full-time undergraduates worked on campus in the 2001–02 school year.

Tuition: $2906 for state residents, $9748 for nonresidents per year (2000–01)

Room and Board: $4432 (2001–02)

Mandatory Fees: $226; additional computer fees: engineering majors, $350 per year; MIS and computer science majors, $280 per year; all other computer fees, $108 per year.

Contact: Director: Elizabeth C. Beck, Martin C. Jischke Honors Building, Ames, Iowa 50011-1150; Telephone: 515-294-4371; Fax: 515-294-2970; E-mail: lcbeck@iastate.edu; Web site: http://www.public.iastate.edu/~honors/homepage.html

ITHACA COLLEGE

4 Pr G S Tr

▼ Honors Program

Based upon a spirit of inquiry, the Ithaca College Honors Program in Humanities and Sciences seeks to build an interdisciplinary academic community both in and out of the classroom. Each year, exceptionally qualified applicants to the College's School of Humanities and Sciences will be invited to apply to the honors program. Accepted students will be eligible for a series of special seminar courses and an array of program-financed, out-of-class activities.

Honors courses are imaginative, intensive seminars in which students accept a great degree of responsibility for their own learning. The courses center on a problem or theme that can be looked at from multiple or even conflicting perspectives: recent topics include the American frontier, the "cultural brain," and the concept of nationhood in the twenty-first century. In the process of exploring this subject, honors students read important and original texts, test time-honored theories, and engage in an active and ongoing exchange of ideas. Dedicated to interdisciplinary education and designed to help students fulfill the general education requirements in the School, the honors program provides the Ithaca College student with the very best the campus has to offer.

Coordinated with the required honors seminars are various out-of-class activities, including pre-semester honors orientation, an honors film series, honors-financed trips to cultural events, and informal get-togethers with fellow students and faculty members. Incoming students are sent two books over the summer, compliments of the program, and encouraged to read them before the first honors gathering in fall.

All honors students are encouraged to partake in the administration of the honors program itself. A student advisory committee will provide crucial input on the current needs of the program, and students are invited to play a major role in matters of publicity, recruitment, and cocurricular activities.

Participation Requirements: An entering student will take an honors first-year seminar in the fall semester. Before graduation, the student will take a total of seven other honors courses: five intermediate seminars, a junior year cultural themes seminar, and a senior year contemporary issues seminar.

Honors students of nearly any major in humanities and sciences can complete the program. Honors requirements are designed to complement departmental requirements, including departmental honors requirements. Qualified students can complete both the school-wide honors program as well as honors within a specific major.

Students successfully completing the full sequence of course work will graduate with Honors in Humanities and Sciences on the official college transcript.

Admission Process: Launched in fall 1996, the honors program now has a full complement of 150 students. Based on information from the Admissions Office, the honors program invites exceptional applicants to the School of Humanities and Sciences to apply to the program. The application process involves two writing samples, such as graded high school essays, and a letter of recommendation from a high school teacher. Qualified students not originally invited into the program may apply after they have completed a semester of work at Ithaca College. Transfer students may apply and will be considered on a case by case basis. Transfer students with associate honors degrees will, if admitted, have a slightly different set of requirements to complete.

Scholarship Availability: Ithaca College offers different levels of merit-based scholarships to qualified applicants. Many students in the honors program are recipients of these merit scholarships.

The Campus Context: Ithaca College is a fully accredited, coeducational, private institution in upstate New York offering a broadly diversified program of professional and liberal arts studies. Founded as a music conservatory in 1892, Ithaca now has four professional schools (Music, Business, Communications, and Health Science and Human Performance) in addition to the School of Humanities and Sciences. Enrolling an undergraduate population of 6,209 and a graduate population of 274, Ithaca College occupies the natural beauty of a hillside location overlooking the city of Ithaca, Cayuga Lake, and Cornell University. Ithaca College offers more than ninety different courses of study across its five schools, including fifty-two possible B.A., B.S., and B.F.A. majors in humanities and sciences. The Center for Natural Sciences, with state-of-the-art undergraduate research facilities, attracts future science majors from all over the country. The Dillingham Center for the Performing Arts, with its modern architectural design and spacious stage, houses the nationally renowned theater arts program.

Student Body The undergraduate student population is 56 percent women, 44 percent men. The ethnic distribution is 88 percent white or Caucasian, 2 percent black or African American, 3 percent Hispanic or Latino, 3 percent Asian or Asian American, 3 percent nonresidential alien, and less than 1 percent Native American. There are 167 international students. Seventy percent of students reside on campus. There are no nationally affiliated social fraternities on campus; there are three professional music fraternities (two are coed, one is comprised of women) and one coed professional performing arts fraternity.

Faculty There are 587 faculty members, 418 full-time. Eighty-eight percent of faculty members have terminal degrees. The student-faculty ratio is 13:1.

Key Facilities The Ithaca College library holds 353,210 volumes. There are thirty computer laboratories across campus, with more

Interpreting the symbols: **2**=two-year college, **4**=four-year college; **Pu**=public or state college, **Pr**=private college; **G**=general honors program; **D**=departmental honors program; **S**=small program (fewer than 100 students), **M**=midsize program (100 to 500 students), **L**=large program (more than 500 students); **Sc**=scholarships available in honors program; **Tr**=transfer students accepted into honors program; **HBC**=historically black college; **AA**=academic advisors; **GA**=graduate advisors; **FA**=fellowship advisors.

than 685 computers available for general student use. Macintosh and DOS capabilities are regularly updated.

Honorary Societies Phi Kappa Phi, Oracle Society

Athletics Ithaca College is a Division III school, offering twelve varsity athletic programs for men and thirteen varsity programs for women. Its athletic teams have enjoyed great success, with twelve national championships in women's soccer, football, baseball, wrestling, field hockey, and gymnastics. In addition to varsity athletics, there is an active intramural program.

Study Abroad The Office of International Programs offers a number of study opportunities throughout the world, and provides advice on both affiliated and nonaffiliated study abroad programs. The College also administers its own program in London, England, where students may take courses in the liberal arts, business, communications, music, and theater arts for a semester or for a year.

Support Services Ithaca College seeks to ensure that all students, including students with disabilities, have equal access to its programs and activities. The Office of Academic Support for Students with Disabilities assists students with appropriate classroom accommodations.

Job Opportunities Ithaca College provides a wide variety of work opportunities—ranging from employment in the dining halls to the college library—as part of its financial aid support. In addition, the Dana Internship Program provides educationally relevant opportunities for highly qualified students with financial need. As Dana interns, students may work during the academic year with faculty on special projects or in the local community in not-for-profit organizations.

Tuition: $20,104 per year (2001–02)

Room and Board: $8615

Contact: Director: James Swafford, School of Humanities and Sciences, Ithaca, New York 14850-7270; Telephone: 607-274-3540; Fax: 607-274-3474; E-mail: swafford@ithaca.edu; Web site: http://www.ithaca.edu/honors/

Jackson State University

4 Pu G L Sc Tr

▼ W.E.B. Du Bois Honors College

The W.E.B. Du Bois Honors College at Jackson State University has graduated more than 1,000 students since its inception in 1980. Graduates of the Honors College have a 100 percent admission rate to graduate and professional schools and an equally successful record of employment.

Designed to provide its participants with an enriched, rigorous, and challenging curriculum, the W.E.B. Du Bois Honors College aims to foster the intellectual development of students; to encourage creative and analytical thinking, critical inquiry, and scholarship; to nurture intellectual independence; and to prepare students well for graduate and professional schools.

Assistance in securing admission to research programs and graduate and professional schools is available. Smaller classes, honors floors for freshmen in two of the dorms, and honors dorms for upperclassmen are offered. Scholarships are available. Current enrollment is 500 students. All majors at the University are represented in the enrollment.

Participation Requirements: Honors sections of the University's general education core curriculum constitute the basis of the Honors College requirements at Jackson State University. In addition, students may take honors courses offered by their departments or by other departments. Weekly meetings for freshmen, special lectures, and individualized advice and guidance throughout the students' tenure are aspects of the program.

Certificates of participation are awarded to students after graduation, and all honors classes taken are recorded on student transcripts as such.

Admission Process: Selection of incoming freshmen to the Honors College is based on ACT/SAT I scores, high school GPA, and rank in class. Transfer students may join the Honors College during their freshman or sophomore year.

The Campus Context: Located in Jackson, capital city of the state of Mississippi, Jackson State University is a public, historically black, multiracial, multiethnic, multicultural, coeducational institution that offers forty bachelor degree, thirty-seven master's degree, six educational specialist degree, and nine doctoral degree programs.

Founded in 1877, Jackson State University has a distinguished history, rich in the tradition of educating young men and women for positions of leadership.

Student Body The University has an overall enrollment of 6,118 students.

Honorary Societies Phi Kappa Phi, Alpha Lambda Delta, Alpha Chi, Alpha Kappa Mu

Tuition: $2688 for state residents, $5546 for nonresidents, per year (1999–2000)

Room and Board: $3460

Contact: Dean: Maria Luisa Alvarez Harvey, P.O. Box 17004, Jackson, Mississippi 39217-0104; Telephone: 601-968-2107; Fax: 601-968-2299

Jacksonville State University

4 Pu C M Sc Tr

▼ College of Arts and Sciences Honors Program

In keeping with the University's mission of serving the academic needs of a diverse student population, the Jacksonville State University College of Arts and Sciences Honors Program was established to provide academically gifted students with the opportunity to fully develop their intellectual potential. The Honors Program provides an enriched educational experience by fostering a strong grounding in the liberal arts and sciences, small classes, interaction with other outstanding and motivated students, instruction from some of JSU's most innovative and engaging faculty members, special activities, and special recognition for students successfully completing 18 hours or more of honors courses.

Participation Requirements: JSU offers honors courses in the arts, humanities, sciences, social sciences, and mathematics, which fulfill freshman and sophomore general studies requirements. Eligible students may take as many or as few honors classes as they wish.

Admission Process: Incoming students who score 25 or higher in the English and math sections of the enhanced ACT or 610 or higher in the verbal and quantitative sections of the enhanced SAT are eligible for the Honors Program. Since test scores may not always provide a complete picture of ability, students may consult with the department head about enrolling in honors classes.

Scholarship Availability: JSU offers scholarships to academically gifted students through its Faculty Scholars program. Alabama residents who score a minimum of 28 on the ACT or 1230 on the SAT may apply for a Faculty Scholarship. This scholarship pays full tuition and is renewable if the recipient maintains the necessary grade requirement. Students awarded this scholarship must reside in campus housing. Entering freshmen with an ACT score of 31 or above or SAT score of 1360 or above are eligible for an Elite Scholars award, which provides full tuition and housing. These scholarships are limited to Alabama residents. McGee Scholarships and Leadership Scholarships are available for non-Alabama residents. For a complete scholarship listing, students should call the Financial Aid Office at 256-782-5006 or consult the scholarship guide on the Web at http://www.jsu.edu.

The Campus Context: Jacksonville State University, located in Jacksonville, Alabama, is a state-supported, regional, coeducational institution. Since its founding in 1883 as an institution to prepare teachers, the University's primary mission has been to provide quality education to the citizens of Alabama by integrating traditional academic pursuits with career-oriented programs at reasonable costs. Drawing students primarily from northeast Alabama, the University is committed to providing a wide variety of undergraduate programs to a diverse population that includes many first-generation college students. In addition to making higher education accessible to diverse segments of society, the University provides the supporting services that students need to achieve a quality education experience.

Student Body Undergraduate enrollment is 6,648: 42 percent men and 58 percent women. The ethnic distribution is 77 percent white, 20 percent African American, 1 percent Hispanic, 1 percent Asian, and 1 percent other ethnic groups. There are eleven fraternities and nine sororities. JSU's chapters of interdisciplinary honors societies are vibrant elements of campus life.

Faculty The number of full-time faculty members is 260, 74 percent of whom have terminal degrees.

Key Facilities The library houses more than 640,000 bound volumes plus numerous periodicals, microforms, and audiovisual materials. The library is a depository for government publications and United States Geological Survey maps. There are seven open computer labs available to students. Dial-up Internet service is available in all dorm rooms, and five dorms have DSL capability.

Honorary Societies Phi Eta Sigma, Omicron Delta Kappa, and Order of Omega

Athletics JSU a Division I member of the Trans America Athletic Conference (TAAC), competing in fourteen sports: seven for men (baseball, basketball, cross-country, football, golf, rifle, and tennis) and seven for women (basketball, cross-country, golf, soccer, softball, tennis, and volleyball).

Study Abroad Study-abroad programs are in the planning stage.

Support Services Disability Support Services (DSS) provides academic support services as required by Section 504/ADA, removing unfair barriers and equalizing opportunities to otherwise qualified students. It provides additional programming for students who have sensory disabilities and works with the faculty and staff to facilitate the student's integration into the academic community.

Job Opportunities Work-study employment, administered through the Financial Aid Office, is available on campus for qualified students. Students desiring to find part-time work in the local area may use the services of the Office for Off-Campus Employment. Counseling and Career Services provides employment assistance to graduating seniors and coordinates programs for part-time off-campus employment, internships, and cooperative education experiences.

Tuition: $2940 for state residents, $5880 for nonresidents per year (2001–02).

Room and Board: $3138 per year (estimated)

Contact: Director: Dr. John H. Jones, English Department, Jacksonville State University, 700 Pelham Road, North, Jacksonville, Alabama 36265; Telephone: 256-782-5537; Fax: 256-782-5441; Web site: http://www.jsu.edu/depart/cas/honorsclasses.html

JACKSONVILLE UNIVERSITY

4 Pr G M Tr

▼ University Honors Program

The Jacksonville University Honors Program is entering its thirteenth year and incorporates a variety of special courses. Some of these courses are honors sections of the core courses. Core courses are courses required of all students graduating from Jacksonville University. The Honors Colloquium is a 1-credit course that explores and defines personal values and goals within a framework of American values. Other honors courses are primarily upper-level and often interdisciplinary in nature. The honors sections of core courses and some of the other honors courses are offered on a regular basis. The course offering varies from time to time, depending upon student demand and faculty interests. There is at least one upper-level honors seminar course offered each semester.

Approximately 100 students are participating in the Honors Program at Jacksonville University this year.

Participation Requirements: Students in the University Honors Program can major in any area the University offers. They may take as many or as few honors courses as they desire. However, to graduate with University Honors, a student must complete at least 25 credits of honors courses, including the Honors Colloquium and at least one upper-level honors seminar. Moreover, students must maintain an overall GPA of 3.5 or better and have a 3.5 or better GPA in the honors courses as well. AP credit for a course may be included as an honors course if the AP score is greater than the minimum score needed for credit at Jacksonville University. Many honors students also achieve departmental honors by completing significant research theses or creative productions as evidence of advanced attainment in addition to maintaining a GPA of 3.5 or better in their major fields.

Admission Process: To be eligible for honors, an entering freshman must have a GPA of 3.2 or better and a combined SAT I score of 1220 or a minimum ACT score of 27. Returning students and transfer students must have earned a cumulative GPA of 3.2 or better.

The Campus Context: Jacksonville University, located amid magnificent oak trees on the banks of the St. John's River in northeastern Florida, was founded in 1934 as a junior college and became a four-year university in 1956. Currently, Jacksonville University is composed of four colleges: the College of Arts and Sciences, the College of Fine Arts, and the College of Business, and the College of Lifelong Learning. There are forty different undergraduate majors in seven undergraduate degree programs.

Student Body Of the 1,858 undergraduates enrolled, 52 percent are women. Fifty percent are housed in the eight residence halls and 50 percent commute. The ethnic distribution is .6 percent Native American/Alaskan, 13.1 percent black, 2.9 percent Asian/Pacific Islander, 4.6 percent Hispanic, 68.6 percent white, 4.6 percent international (92 international students representing forty-eight countries), and 5.7 percent unknown. Seventy-seven percent of undergraduates receive financial aid. Jacksonville University hosts seven fraternities and six sororities.

Faculty Of the 213 faculty members (151 full-time-equivalent faculty members), 113 are full-time faculty members and 100 are adjunct faculty members. Seventy-two percent of the full-time faculty members have terminal degrees. The student-faculty ratio is 14:1.

Key Facilities The University Library contains more than 500,000 volumes. There are more than 200 personal computers on campus

Interpreting the symbols: **2**=two-year college, **4**=four-year college; **Pu**=public or state college, **Pr**=private college; **G**=general honors program; **D**=departmental honors program; **S**=small program (fewer than 100 students), **M**=midsize program (100 to 500 students), **L**=large program (more than 500 students); **Sc**=scholarships available in honors program; **Tr**=transfer students accepted into honors program; **HBC**=historically black college; **AA**=academic advisors; **GA**=graduate advisors; **FA**=fellowship advisors.

for student use located in the dormitories, the library, and in classrooms throughout the campus.

Honorary Societies: Phi Kappa Phi

Athletics Intercollegiate athletics for men include baseball, basketball, crew, cross-country, football, golf, sailing, soccer, tennis, and track and field. Intercollegiate athletics for women include basketball (starting fall 1999), crew, cross-country, golf, soccer, tennis, indoor and outdoor track, sailing, and volleyball. Active intramural and club sport programs are available to all interested students.

Study Abroad Jacksonville University recognizes the general educational value of travel and study abroad and cooperates in enabling students to take advantage of such opportunities. JU is affiliated with the American Institute of Foreign Study and will accept courses in the French language offered at the Ecole Superieure de Commerce in Nantes, France. In recent years JU students have studied in Mexico, Spain, Syria, France, England, Australia, Guatemala, and Costa Rica.

Job Opportunities Students are offered a wide variety of work opportunities on campus. All work programs originate in the Financial Aid Office.

Tuition: $13,360 per year (1997–98)

Room and Board: $4900

Mandatory Fees: $540

Contact: Director: Dr. Robert A. Hollister, 2800 University Boulevard North, Jacksonville, Florida 32211; Telephone: 904-744-3950 Ext. 7310; Fax: 904-745-7573; E-mail: bhollis@ju.junix.edu

JAMES MADISON UNIVERSITY

4 Pu G L Sc Tr

▼ Honors Program

The James Madison University (JMU) Honors Program enhances the intellectual, cultural, social, and career opportunities for the most motivated, enthusiastic, and curious students. It offers rigorous and creative courses and interdisciplinary seminarsthat are taught by outstanding professors in small classes to facilitate discussion and critical thinking. In addition, the program organizes outside lectures, field trips to galleries, concerts and theater, and other special events to stimulate and challenge intellectual and social development. The University also provides opportunities for significant independent research and creative work with faculty mentors. First- and second-year honors students enjoy priority registration.

The Honors Program began in 1961 as 6 hours of independent study culminating in a senior thesis. In 1975 it offered honors sections and seminars to highly qualified first- and second-year students. The first program director was named in 1982, and 50 honors scholars were admitted. The current three-mode structure was instituted in 1986. Today, academically talented JMU students may participate in one of three honors programs: the Honors Scholars, Subject-Area Honors, or the Senior Honors Project. There are 600 students in the program, which is approximately 5 percent of undergraduates.

Participation Requirements: Honors scholars participate in four years of honors study in a bachelor's degree program in any major. They complete 27 hours of honors work—a combination of honors courses, seminars, and independent study—and earn fifty points as a part of the Honors Opportunities Program, which is designated to encourage first-year honors students to get involved in learning outside the traditional classroom setting. They are also required to maintain a 3.25 cumulative GPA. Subject-area honors students enter the program in their second, third, or fourth semesters at JMU. They complete 24 hours of honors work—a combination of honors courses, seminars, and independent study—and maintain a 3.25 cumulative GPA or higher. Senior honors project students enter the program in the second semester of their junior year and complete 6 hours of independent study over three semesters, culminating in documents of significant research or creative work. Each program is designed to prepare students for graduate or professional schools, enhance their opportunities for a rewarding career, and expand their knowledge of themselves, others, and the world.

Honors organizations provide activities and support. The Honors Student Advisory Council advises staff members on the program, policies, and student needs. Honors Publications oversees the publication of the *Honors News* and the *FUGUE*, which is an annual journal of the arts. The Honors Scholars Society plans social activities building community and providing a support network. The Madison Honors Club provides opportunities for honors students to build community and develop leadership while serving others. The student-led organization provides service to at-risk children, families in need, the sick, and the elderly in the community.

Junior and senior honors students in good standing receive honors pins at an annual awards ceremony. Seniors completing the honors scholars or subject-area honors programs receive a medallion to wear at Commencement. All seniors completing a senior honors project and, thus, graduating with distinction, receive a certificate and have their names, project titles, and project directors listed in the Commencement program. The most coveted awards are the Phi Beta Kappa Award for the most outstanding honors project and the Service Award for exceptional service to the program.

Admission Process: To participate in the Honors Scholars Program, a student must apply and be invited to join the program during the senior year in high school. Applicants are evaluated on SAT I scores (the minimum combined score is 1300); unweighted GPA and strength of high school program; participation in school and community activities; two letters of recommendation; and an analytical essay in response to a common text. Admission is competitive; approximately 200 entering freshmen are admitted as Honors Scholars.

To apply for Subject-Area Honors, a student must have earned at least a 3.25 GPA at JMU and must submit a recommendation from a faculty member and an application, including a personal statement. All qualified applicants are accepted. To qualify for participation in the Senior Honors Project, a student must have a cumulative GPA of at least 3.25 and submit a project proposal with the approval of a project director; two readers; the department head and dean; and the director of the Honors Program. Transfer students from recognized honors programs are admitted as subject-area or senior honors project students.

Scholarship Availability: Honors students are eligible to apply for all scholarships and grants offered by the University. Most of these are need-based (FAFSA required). A limited number of merit-based awards are available. These include departmental awards and the James Madison Scholar Awards, which are three four-year awards to National Merit finalists. The Honors Program has very limited scholarship funds. Honors Scholarships, typically $500, are awarded to returning students to assist in foreign study. Edythe Rowley scholarships, typically $1000, are awarded to returning students to meet unanticipated financial needs.

The Campus Context: Founded in 1908, James Madison University has grown from a state normal and industrial school for women to a coeducational comprehensive university. The 486-acre campus is located in Harrisonburg, a progressive city of 30,000 people, in the heart of Virginia's historic Shenandoah Valley. Flanked by the Blue Ridge Mountains on the east and the Alleghenies on the west, Harrisonburg is at the intersection of three major highways: Interstate 81, U.S. 33, and U.S. 11, and is only a 2-hour drive from Washington, D.C.

The University offers small-college friendliness in a large-campus setting. It includes five undergraduate colleges: arts and letters, business, education and psychology, integrated science and technology, and science and mathematics. Undergraduate degree programs include B.A., B.B.A., B.F.A., B.I.S., B.M., B.S., B.S.N., and B.S.W. degrees.

Student Body The undergraduate student body numbers 14,961; 58 percent are women. Eleven percent of the student body are members of minority groups, including 5 percent African-American students. There are 527 international students. Residence halls house 42 percent of undergraduates; 58 percent commute, a majority of those from non-University-sponsored, off-campus student housing apartment complexes. City bus service is convenient and free to JMU students. Forty-five percent of students receive scholarships and grants; 45 percent receive loans. There are 260 student clubs and organizations, including nineteen fraternities and thirteen sororities.

Faculty There are 685 full-time and 533 part-time faculty members; 84 percent hold terminal degrees. The student-faculty ratio is 17:1.

Key Facilities The library offers more than 1,000,000 paper and electronic titles, excluding microforms; 13,726 serial subscriptions (paper, microform, and electronic); 1,060,265 microform units; and 29,000 audiovisual units. It provides access to the Virtual Library of Virginia (VIVA), and to additional resources worldwide through the Internet.

Computer facilities include seventeen technology classrooms and twelve computer labs, including two 24-hour labs. The labs have 327 computers that contain a mix of PCs and Macs, which are open to all students. Honors students have their own computer lab that is equipped with nine computers, as well as a lounge with audiovisual equipment. In addition, some academic departments such as art and art history, computer science, English, foreign languages and literatures, and music have specialized labs for majors. All residence hall rooms are wired for campuswide network access. Students have access to the library's on-line computer, e-mail, and the Internet from labs and from their own personal computers in residence hall rooms or off-campus housing.

Honorary Societies Phi Kappa Phi, Golden Key, and Mortar Board

Athletics More than 500 student athletes compete in NCAA Division I sports (NCAA I-AA football) in CAA, Atlantic 10, ECAC, IC4A, and NIWFA conferences. Women's teams include archery, basketball, cheerleading, cross-country, fencing, field hockey, golf, gymnastics, track and field, lacrosse, soccer, swimming and diving, tennis, and volleyball. Men's teams include archery, baseball, basketball, cheerleading, cross-country, football, golf, gymnastics, track and field, soccer, swimming, diving, tennis, and wrestling.

Study Abroad JMU offers students the opportunity to study for a semester or year anywhere in the world. The University oversees semester-abroad programs in Italy, England, France, Spain, Ghana, and Malta. Students may participate in international exchange or consortium programs in Africa, Asia, Australia, the Caribbean, Europe, Latin America, and the Middle East. Travel programs are also available during the summer.

Support Services The Office of Disability Services ensures that the University complies with Section 504 of the Rehabilitation Act of 1973. Individuals eligible for services include, but are not limited to, those with mobility, orthopedic, hearing, vision, or speech impairments as well as those with learning disabilities. Documentation of the disability is required so that appropriate accommodations may be negotiated. Services include priority registration, course scheduling information, and advising in relation to the disability; interpreters for the deaf; support lab providing equipment for students with visual impairments and learning disabilities; assistance in procuring auxiliary aids and equipment such as taped books; classroom accommodations; and other assistance as needed.

Job Opportunities Work opportunities on campus include federal work-study in administrative and academic offices (FAFSA required), institutional employment by individual departments and service agencies, dining services, campus cadet program, and residence hall advisers and directors. Most on-campus jobs average 10–15 hours per week. Many students also find part-time jobs off campus in Harrisonburg.

Tuition: $4000 for state residents, $9850 for nonresidents, per year (1998–99)

Room and Board: $5290

Contact: Director: Dr. Joanne V. Gabbin, Hillcrest House, MSC 1501, James Madison University, Harrisonburg, Virginia 22807; Telephone: 540-568-6953; Fax: 540-568-8079; E-mail: honors@jmu.edu; Web site: http://www.jmu.edu/honorsprog

JOHN BROWN UNIVERSITY

4 Pr G M Sc Tr

▼ University Honors Program

The John Brown University (JBU) Honors Program, begun in 1987, includes a core of enriched courses that have been developed for gifted, highly motivated students. Participants must complete at least 21 honors hours to receive a University Honors degree. Courses emphasize the development of analytical skills, scholarly growth, and intellectual curiosity. The classes replace regular general education courses. Perhaps more important, the program is the impetus for continued development of JBU as a community of scholars. Many of the courses are experiential, with collaborative and integrative elements that cross disciplinary lines and narrow the gap between school and community by way of projects, field trips, guest speakers, and multimedia experiences. Some courses are modeled on NCHC's Honors Semesters, highlighting Native American and Ozark Mountain cultures, local businesses, and regional arts. The Honors Program emphasizes the exchange of ideas in a variety of settings: in the classroom, in the Honors Center, on field trips, and in the homes of professors.

The Honors Program attempts to recruit successful, innovative professors and serves as a laboratory for the development of pedagogical techniques and courses for the nonhonors curriculum.

JBU honors students are strongly encouraged to model Judeo-Christian principles and good stewardship of their academic gifts through serving in leadership positions on campus and participating in service activities both on and off campus. The Student Honors Organization promotes scholarly presentations and service by the student body as a whole and serves as a peer support group for honors students. The Honors Center, available to honors students 24 hours a day, provides an attractive location for studying, cooking, watching television, and tutoring. Some classes are held in the center.

The total program has approximately 160 students.

Participation Requirements: To continue to the junior and senior levels of the program, a student must have an overall GPA of at least 3.6 at the end of the sophomore year and must submit an outline of honors plans. Successful completion of the program is highlighted at an Honors Convocation and by the presentation of a special honors degree diploma at graduation. Courses are designed at "Honors" on the transcript.

Admission Process: Fifty to 60 entering freshmen are selected by application each June from a large and well-qualified pool of applicants. Transfer students and currently enrolled JBU students

Interpreting the symbols: **2**=two-year college, **4**=four-year college; **Pu**=public or state college, **Pr**=private college; **G**=general honors program; **D**=departmental honors program; **S**=small program (fewer than 100 students), **M**=midsize program (100 to 500 students), **L**=large program (more than 500 students); **Sc**=scholarships available in honors program; **Tr**=transfer students accepted into honors program; **HBC**=historically black college; **AA**=academic advisors; **GA**=graduate advisors; **FA**=fellowship advisors.

who have enough general education courses remaining to be taken for the honors degree may also apply. Eligibility for admission is based on high school GPA and class rank, SAT I or ACT scores, a letter of application, and an interview by the Honors Committee.

Scholarship Availability: Each year, JBU awards eight 4-year, $9000 scholarships (Presidentials) to incoming freshmen who have met the following requirements: scored in the 95th national percentile or above on the ACT or SAT I, graduated with a 3.9 cumulative high school GPA or above (on 4.0 scale), ranked in the top 5 percent in the high school class, demonstrated leadership abilities, written an outstanding letter of application, and successfully completed an interview process. Presidential scholars may also receive other scholarships to cover room and board. The University also awards ten Provost's Scholarships of $5000 each. Recipients must have scored in the 95th national percentile or above on the ACT or SAT I, had a GPA of at least 3.8 in high school, and ranked in the top 5 percent of their high school graduating class.

A large number of JBU honors participants come from the remaining scholarship pool. The institution awards ten $3000 divisional scholarships, numerous academic achievement scholarships ranging from $1000 to $3000 per year, named scholarships donated by individuals and organizations, scholarships in the majors, and various leadership scholarships.

The Campus Context: Founded in 1919 as a nondenominational Christian liberal arts university, John Brown University is located in the foothills of the Ozark Mountains on the Arkansas-Oklahoma border. The campus is surrounded by rural and small-town scenic beauty. Major libraries, theaters, and museums are available with a short drive to Tulsa, Oklahoma.

Recent awards indicate JBU's growing reputation for excellence. For example, John Brown University has been ranked as one of the top 10 regional liberal arts colleges in the South by *U.S. News & World Report's America's Best Colleges* for the past few years and by the Templeton Foundation's "Honor Roll for Character Building Colleges" since that award's inception in 1988. Cancer and DNA research conducted by JBU science faculty members and students has been supported and recognized by the NSF, the National Cancer Institute, and the Radiation Research Institute. JBU is the only undergraduate institution in Arkansas approved to use human cadavers. JBU is in a major capital campaign, the first stage of which is to endow faculty chairs, increase programs, and add a new state-of-the-art computer and science facility and a living-learning campus center. John Brown offers forty-nine majors leading to five baccalaureate degrees in the liberal arts, science, engineering, communications, business, and education.

Student Body JBU has an undergraduate population of approximately 1,400, 53 percent of whom are women. Three hundred are nontraditional students already in the workplace who are seeking degrees through the University's Advanced Degree Completion Program. The remaining 1,100 traditional students come from forty-four states and thirty-four other countries; 20–25 percent are either international or foreign-born U.S. students. Seventy percent of students live on campus. Eighty percent receive financial aid either by scholarship or work-study.

Faculty Students are taught by 89 faculty members (64 full-time). Seventy percent have doctorates or other terminal degrees. The student-faculty ratio is 16:1.

Key Facilities The campus has four public computer labs (seventy computers) and several departmental labs. All have Internet and network capacity. All students have network accounts. The library has 100,000 volumes.

Athletics Varsity teams include basketball, swimming, soccer, tennis, and volleyball. The University also offers a wide range of intramural sports.

Study Abroad JBU offers opportunities for study abroad through its Irish Studies Program and through affiliated programs, such as Latin American Studies, Holy Land Studies, Russian Studies, Medieval and Renaissance Studies (Oxford), and Cambridge Semester. Honors students regularly participate in NCHC's Semesters Program.

Support Services The Office of the Advocate for Students with Disabilities meets the needs of disabled students on an individual basis.

Tuition: $9482 per year (1998–99)

Room and Board: $4478

Contact: Director: Dr. Shirley Forbes Thomas, Honors Center Box 3074, Siloam Springs, Arkansas 72761; Telephone: 501-524-7426 or 7459; Fax: 501-524-9548; E-mail: sthomas@acc.jbu.edu; Web site: http://www.jbu.edu

JOHN CARROLL UNIVERSITY

4 Pr M Tr

▼ Honors Program

The Honors Program at John Carroll University provides exceptional students the opportunity to expand and amplify their educational experience during college. The Honors Program, in conjunction with the Liberal Arts Core, seeks not only to prepare students for a lifetime of learning and to provide them with specific academic content, but also to foster in students a love of learning and the problem-solving and critical-thinking abilities essential for excellence.

The John Carroll University Honors Program is a University-based honors program, rather than a departmentally based honors program or a separate honors college. Thus, students take honors courses as part of the basic Liberal Arts Core. The University, as well as the Honors Program, believes a strong liberal arts background is essential for all bachelor degrees, so students take a selection of courses from different discipline areas designed to provide such a broad base to the undergraduate educational experience. The Honors Program is integrated into the University Core Curriculum and allows honors students to satisfy the core curriculum in ways consistent with their academic abilities and preparation.

In concert with the tradition of Jesuit education, the goal of the Honors Program is to pursue excellence in an environment that promotes the development and understanding of values and emphasizes freedom of inquiry, integration of knowledge, and social responsibility. These themes manifest themselves not just in the academic arena, but also in the development of the whole person.

Through small classes and close contact with faculty members, the Honors Program provides opportunities for greater depth and mastery in a student's education. Through interdisciplinary classes and the cross-disciplinary study of topics and issues, the Honors Program builds a broader perspective out of which a student can reflect on the world and its needs. Through the latitude to construct self-designed majors, the program encourages students to be creative in their college program. Through foreign language study and honors seminars, the Honors Program fosters a better understanding of a global society. Finally, through the community of honors students, who meet together and share social, cultural, and artistic events and have continual contact in classes, the Honors Program develops a camaraderie that strengthens students' ability to participate in the world.

The Honors Program endeavors to prepare a person to be a constructive, thoughtful, and active participant in the local and world communities. An honors graduate is one who values learning, service, and excellence, and thus will continue to learn, serve, and excel in whatever he or she does in life. The modern Honors Program at John Carroll was instituted in 1989–90. The first Honors Program began in 1963. There are approximately 200 students participating in the program.

Participation Requirements: Requirements include competency in English composition, demonstrated by one year of English Composition, or, if a student is exempt through AP credit or testing, one additional course in English that emphasizes writing; competency in oral communication as demonstrated by a one semester course specially designed for honors students or by testing out; competency in foreign language or calculus, demonstrated by two years of a language or by one year of calculus; six H or HP courses that fulfill portions of University Core Curriculum (H courses are honors sections of regularly taught courses; HP courses are special interdisciplinary or team-taught courses designed for honors students); participation in the First-Year Honors Seminar, which uses an interdisciplinary approach to explore a general topic (this seminar is team-taught by 3 faculty members, with each faculty member bringing his or her expertise to bear on the topic); and participation in a Senior Honors Seminar or Senior Honors Project. The seminar uses an interdisciplinary approach to explore a specific topic. This course is jointly taught and usually continues the topic from the First-Year Honors Seminar taken by these students. The Senior Honors Project requires at least 3 hours of independent research under the direction of an adviser.

Honors participants must maintain a minimum 3.5 GPA, and must have a GPA of at least 3.5 at graduation. Students who graduate from the Honors Program are identified by the words Honors Scholar on their transcripts and by a special gold seal on their diplomas. In addition, at graduation, Honors Students are recognized by a gold cord worn with their academic gown.

Admission Process: Entering freshmen seeking admission to the Honors Program should normally have a minimum combined score of at least 1270 on the SAT I or at least a 28 composite score on the ACT, rank in the top 10 percent of their high school class, and have at least a 3.5 GPA in their high school college-preparatory courses. In short, the program is seeking students who rank above the 90th percentile of freshmen throughout the nation. Students in their sophomore and junior years, transfer students, and nontraditional students are also welcome to apply to the program. Currently enrolled students should have a minimum 3.5 GPA in college prior to applying to the Honors Program.

Scholarship Availability: The Honors Program does not administer any scholarships or financial aid. However, the University provides solid financial assistance to honors students. As an indication of that support, virtually all first-year honors students who entered between 1990 and 2001 and who requested financial assistance received merit and/or need-based scholarships. These grants included such awards as American Values Scholarships ($1000–$3000 per year, renewable, based on merit and/or demonstrated leadership or volunteerism, consideration given to need), President's Honor Awards (amounts vary up to $10,000, renewable, merit-based), Mastin Scholarships in the sciences ($10,000 per year, renewable, merit-based), John Carroll scholarships and grants (amount varies, renewable, merit- and need-based), National Merit Scholarships (sponsored by John Carroll, merit-based, up to full tuition, for National Merit Finalists).

The Campus Context: John Carroll University is characterized by several distinguished facilities, including the Breen Learning Center, a recent $6.8-million addition to the Grasselli Library, which has doubled the capacity of the building and has enhanced accessibility of electronic databases; the O'Malley Center for Communications and Language Arts, which features a television studio and newsroom, computer-assisted and audio language laboratories, and a center for writing instruction; and the Boler School of Business's Bruening Hall, which houses high-tech presentation classrooms featuring computerized audio/visual technology. The 263,700-square-foot Charles & Helen Dolan Center for Science and Technology will become the home for the departments of biology, chemistry, mathematics and computer science, physics, and psychology. The building will contain a new science library, shared classrooms, a 250-seat auditorium, teaching and research space, faculty offices, faculty and student research spaces, student meeting and study spaces, as well as a central atrium and interior-light courts to connect departments and promote interdepartmental interaction. The new center will also include a lower-level garage providing 105 parking spaces, a sky-viewing area on the roof, a central receiving area, materials distribution areas, and a vivarium. The University offers thirty-five bachelor's degrees.

Student Body There are 2,799 full-time and 79 part-time students in the College of Arts and Sciences, plus 77 full- and part-time nondegree students. The School of Business enrolls 526 students full-time and 27 part-time. The total enrollment is about 3,500 students. Fifty-five percent of the population are women. The ethnic distribution is 4.4 percent African American, 2.3 percent Hispanic, 0.2 percent members of other minority groups, 87.5 percent white, 2.8 percent Asian or Pacific Islander, and 2.7 percent unknown. There are 19 international students, and 58.5 percent of students reside on campus. Seventy-two percent of students receive need-based financial aid. There are four fraternities and five sororities, all of which have gone national.

Faculty The total number of faculty members is 417, of whom 246 are full-time. Eighty-nine percent of faculty members hold terminal degrees. The student-faculty ratio is 15:1.

Key Facilities The library holds 632,000 volumes. Nearly 1,000 microcomputers are available for student use, and students have access to the Internet.

Honorary Societies Alpha Epsilon Delta, Alpha Kappa Psi, Alpha Sigma Nu, Lambda Iota Tau, Phi Alpha Theta, Phi Eta Sigma

Athletics The University is a member of the National Collegiate Athletic Association Division III and the Ohio Athletic Conference. Men compete in baseball, basketball, cross-country, football, golf, soccer, swimming, tennis, track, and wrestling. Women compete in basketball, cross-country, golf, soccer, softball, swimming, tennis, track, and volleyball. The Don Shula Sports Center, natatorium, tennis courts, weight-training room, racquetball courts, and gymnasium are available for student use.

Study Abroad Study abroad opportunities are coordinated through the Center for Global Education. Highlights include JCU semesters in Beijing, Berlin, and London plus affiliated programs in Austria, Denmark, Italy, and El Salvador. Offerings include short-term study programs, spring semester courses with an abroad component, and service-learning immersion programs. There are long-standing relationships with Japanese universities in Nagoya and Tokyo, ISEP exchanges, and interdisciplinary programs in East Asian studies, Latin American studies, modern European studies, international studies, and international economics and modern languages.

Support Services Ninety-six percent of the campus and 100 percent of the academic programs and services are accessible to physically disabled people.

Job Opportunities The University participates in the Federal Work-Study Program.

Tuition: $17,478 per year (2001–02)

Room and Board: $6300

Contact: Director: Dr. John R. Spencer, 20700 North Park Boulevard, University Heights, Ohio 44118; Telephone: 216-

Interpreting the symbols: **2**=two-year college, **4**=four-year college; **Pu**=public or state college, **Pr**=private college; **G**=general honors program; **D**=departmental honors program; **S**=small program (fewer than 100 students), **M**=midsize program (100 to 500 students), **L**=large program (more than 500 students); **Sc**=scholarships available in honors program; **Tr**=transfer students accepted into honors program; **HBC**=historically black college; **AA**=academic advisors; **GA**=graduate advisors; **FA**=fellowship advisors.

397-4677; Fax: 216-397-4478; E-mail: honors@jcu.edu; Web site: http://www.jcu.edu

Johnson & Wales University

4 Pr G L Sc Tr

▼ Honors Program

The Johnson & Wales University Honors Program is designed to provide scholarly challenges for academically talented students. The university-wide program allows students to enroll in honors sections of their freshmen courses and to make various other courses Honors Options (H-Option) by completing additional assignments, such as papers, presentations, research, or multi-media projects, in addition to their required course work. Honors students culminate their senior year by completing a scholarly paper in their major, community leadership, or another School of Arts and Sciences topic.

The benefits available to honors students are numerous. These students are eligible for membership in the Chancellor's Circle and Collegiate Honors Society (CHS), and they have the opportunity to receive Presidential and Chancellor Scholarships. Honors students are involved in leadership activities and community service learning opportunities. In addition, they may attend presentations by visiting speakers, participate in social events sponsored by CHS, be invited to the annual Honors Banquet, take advantage of the benefits of living in the wellness dorms, and graduate early by taking accelerated courses.

The Johnson & Wales University Honors Program was established in 1994. It currently enrolls 475 students and is still growing.

Participation Requirements: Students within the Honors Program must maintain a minimum 3.4 GPA and complete the required number of honors courses and projects for their respective schools and degrees. Those within the Colleges of Business, Hospitality, and Technology are required to complete a minimum of six courses within the Honors Program for an associate-level degree and twelve courses within the program for a bachelor's-level degree. Students within the Culinary College are required to complete nine honors-level courses and/or labs for an associate degree and sixteen honors-level courses and/or labs for a bachelor's degree. Students in all colleges must complete a final honors project under the guidance of a faculty adviser and submit that project at least one term prior to graduation in order to fulfill the bachelor's degree requirements.

All students meeting these requirements receive the Honors Program designation upon graduation.

Admission Process: Admissions to the Honors Program is offered to entering first-year students and to transfer students who have earned fewer than 30 credits or were enrolled in an Honors Program at the college they previously attended. Eligibility is based on graduation within the top 25 percent of the high school class, minimum scores of 500 on both math and verbal sections of the SAT I, and a minimum GPA of 3.4 for transfer students. The Admissions Office also takes into consideration the strength of the secondary school curriculum, letters of recommendation, leadership activities, and school or community involvement.

Scholarship Availability: Honors students are eligible to receive Chancellor's Scholarships ranging from $10,000 to full tuition or Presidential Scholarships ranging from $2500 to $5000. Both scholarships are renewable for up to four years for continuous, full-time, day-school students, provided the recipient's GPA does not fall below 2.75 for the Presidential Scholarship or 3.4 for the Chancellor's Scholarship. All other requirements for the scholarship must also be met.

The Campus Context: Johnson & Wales University, located in downtown Providence, Rhode Island, is a private coeducational institution that offers students an opportunity to pursue practical career education in business, food service, hospitality, or technology. Named "America's Career University," Johnson & Wales University gives students the traditional classroom education integrated with a unique hands-on learning curriculum that prepares graduates for employment. The University's student-centered, employment-focused perspective stresses personal development as well as career management skills.

Students at Johnson & Wales University enjoy the benefits of a trimester schedule, a four-day week, the ability to earn two degrees in four years, and an "upside-down" curriculum that allows them to begin taking courses in their major beginning in the freshman year. In addition, students are given the opportunity to take advantage of an extensive practicum program, including work at internships, externships, career co-ops, and computer, culinary arts, baking and pastry arts, culinary nutrition, and technology laboratories. Graduates of Johnson & Wales University experience a 98 percent job placement rate in their chosen fields within sixty days of earning their degrees.

In addition to the university experience, students at Johnson & Wales University can also take advantage of Providence's many cultural and historical opportunities and trips to nearby Newport, Rhode Island, and Boston.

Student Body: Undergraduate enrollment at Johnson & Wales University is 8,566 (9,192 total student enrollment): 51 percent men, 49 percent women. Of total undergraduate enrollment, the student population is 72 percent white non-Hispanic, 13 percent black non-Hispanic, 6 percent international, 6 percent Hispanic, and 3 percent Asian. Johnson & Wales has over twenty Greek organizations and social fellowships and more than sixty clubs and organizations. Eighty-two percent of full-time, first-time students receive financial aid from the institution.

Faculty: Johnson & Wales University employs a diverse faculty. Of the 440 faculty members, 61 percent are full-time, 39 percent are part-time, and 23 percent have attained terminal degrees.

Key Facilities: Johnson & Wales University library is located in University Hall. This state-of-the-art facility features a library classroom with a multimedia technological presentation system, Web-based databases and home pages, membership in two library consortia, and up-to-date business resource guides. Along with the numerous technological resources, the library contains more than 85,000 volumes. The College of Culinary Arts also has a library. The Culinary Library contains a noncirculating reference collection of up-to-date holdings in the field of culinary arts.

Accessible through the library computers are 19 electronic computerized databases. The Higher Education Library Information Network (HELIN), one of the two library consortia, allows students to access resources from eight academic libraries. Through the many other databases, students can gain access to thousands of magazines, newspapers, and journals, many offering full text retrieval.

The University houses three student computer facilities, all of which feature IBM-compatible computers, Internet access, translation software to print Macintosh-based files, MS Office Suite, free black and white printing, and color printing for a nominal fee.

Athletics: Johnson & Wales' intercollegiate athletic teams compete against NCAA Division III schools and are members of the Great Northeast Athletic Conference and the Eastern College Athletic Conference. Women's sports include soccer, volleyball, basketball, softball, tennis, and cross-country. Men's sports include soccer, volleyball, ice hockey, basketball, baseball, tennis, cross-country, and wrestling. There are also co-ed golf and cheerleading teams. In addition to its intercollegiate teams, Johnson & Wales also has a variety of recreational and intramural sport programs, two fitness facilities staffed with fitness professionals, and a commitment to health and wellness.

Study Abroad: Numerous study-abroad opportunities are offered through the School of Global Management. Students may participate in either of two international programs conducted during June or July summer sessions. The School of Arts & Sciences also offers a three-week program that starts in late July.

The Business Summer Abroad program is a three- to four-week experience in which students, in teams of 15 to 20, join 2 faculty members plus business partners to investigate business practice, politics, and the culture of various international settings. Recent programs have been held in the Netherlands, Belgium, and Germany; Italy; Czech Republic, Hungary, and Poland; Russia; and Australia, to name a few. The program combines classroom time with case studies and partner visits.

The Arts & Sciences Summer Abroad program is a three-week experience where 15 students study with 3 faculty members at Cambridge University in England and visit Canterbury, London, and Edinburgh.

The Summer Work Abroad program is conducted under the sponsorship of a key business partner. Spring-term seminars prepare teams of 10 students for an intense, two-week visit to the partner's overseas site. There, students work as a continuous improvement consulting team, in areas such as operations or human resources, on important company projects. Recent key business partners have included Textron in England and France and Texas Instruments in Brazil.

Support Services: Johnson & Wales University is dedicated to providing reasonable accommodations to allow learning disabled, physically disabled, and other challenged students to succeed in academic pursuits. Such accommodations include, but are not limited to, supplemental instruction; writing and academic support groups; workshops in stress management, time management, substance abuse awareness, wellness, and learning strategy instruction; note-taking accommodations; oral/extended time exams; decelerated course loads; academic counseling; personal counseling; and tutorial assistance.

Job Opportunities: Johnson & Wales University has an extensive job opportunity network. Students can take advantage of work-study grants, career co-ops, internships, externships, career counseling, an Annual Career Conference, and the Summer Work Experience Program.

Tuition: College of Business: $13,740 (except Equine Business Management/Riding and Equine Studies majors: $16,893); Hospitality College: $14,661; School of Technology: $14,661; College of Culinary Arts: $16,893. (All figures based on 2001–2002 tuition fees)

Room and Board: standard residence halls: $6150; premium residence halls: $7506; weekend meal plan (optional): $762

Mandatory Fees: $600

Contact: Director: Dr. Jim Brosnan, 10 Abbott Park Place, Providence, Rhode Island 02903; Telephone: 401-598-1796; Fax: 401-598-1821; E-mail: pvd.honors@jwu.edu

Johnson County Community College

2 Pu D S Sc AA

▼ Honors Program

The Honors Program curriculum at Johnson County Community College is designed to stimulate and challenge academically talented students. Enrolling in the Honors Program will help students develop their intellectual potential as college students and as members of the academic community. While a part of the Honors Program, students receive a newsletter every three weeks, keeping them informed of campus activities, scholarships, and study-abroad programs. Students are also offered tickets to selected cultural events on campus and invited to participate in the National Collegiate Honors Council and Great Plains Honor Council conferences. Graduates are recognized at graduation and at a special ceremony.

The number of students in the program varies each semester from approximately 100 in the fall semester to approximately 150 students in the spring.

Participation Requirements: Students may elect to participate in any part of the Honors Program, but to graduate from the program students must take an interdisciplinary course that emphasizes inquiry, discovery, and critical thinking and discussion methods that stress student participation; the Honors Forum class, which focuses on a current issue that affects the local, national, and global communities; four honors contracts, which are 1 hour of additional credit extensions to the regularly scheduled courses throughout the curriculum; and perform some volunteer community service.

Admission Process: Students wanting to take an honors contract must have a high school or college cumulative GPA of 3.5 or higher, a minimum composite score of 27 on the ACT, or a score of at least 1340 on the SAT.

Scholarship Availability: Johnson County Community College offers a number of scholarships to students who plan to graduate from the Honors Program and the College. Students submit an application form and are interviewed. Awards are made of up to $900 per semester.

The Campus Context: There are seventeen buildings on campus, including the Cultural Education Center, housing Yardley Hall, which seats 1,300; the Theatre, which seats 400; the Black Box Theatre for academic productions; and the Recital Hall. The College offers more than forty career and certificate programs, eight selective admission programs, and eight selective admission cooperative programs with the Metropolitan Community College District.

Student Body More than 15,000 students enroll in 34,000 credit and continuing education classes each semester. Of these students, 44.2 percent are men and 55.8 percent are women. Members of minority groups account for 8.7 percent of the enrollment. Almost 78 percent of students are Johnson County residents, 16.8 percent are other Kansas residents, and 5.9 percent are out-of-state residents.

Faculty There are 870 full-time and 1,800 part-time faculty and staff members.

Key Facilities The library houses 92,000 bound volumes; 600 periodical subscriptions; 400,000 titles on microfilm; 3,000 records, tapes, and CDs; and twenty-five online bibliographic sources.

Honorary Society Phi Theta Kappa

Study Abroad Through the College Consortium for International studies, JCCC students have an opportunity to study in any one of nineteen countries for a semester or a year. Programs that focus on liberal arts, language and culture, business, and performing and visual arts are available in countries in Europe, Latin America, the Middle East, and Asia.

Support Services Students with disabilities have access to a variety of support services, including reading, notetaking, tutoring, and other services that allow equal access to courses. Assistive computer equipment especially designed for students with disabilities (such as speech synthesizers, screen readers, scanners, adjustable tables, and Braille printers) are also available. Campus buildings are equipped with ramps, elevators, and restrooms designed to accommodate wheelchairs. Parking areas convenient to the buildings are reserved for students with disabilities. In addition, an orientation for students with disabilities is held at the beginning of the fall and spring semesters.

Interpreting the symbols: **2**=two-year college, **4**=four-year college; **Pu**=public or state college, **Pr**=private college; **G**=general honors program; **D**=departmental honors program; **S**=small program (fewer than 100 students), **M**=midsize program (100 to 500 students), **L**=large program (more than 500 students); **Sc**=scholarships available in honors program; **Tr**=transfer students accepted into honors program; **HBC**=historically black college; **AA**=academic advisors; **GA**=graduate advisors; **FA**=fellowship advisors.

Tuition: $60 for county residents, $130 for nonresidents, per credit hour (2001–02)

Contact: Director: Ruth Fox, 12345 College Boulevard, Overland Park, Kansas 66210-1299; Telephone: 913-469-2512; Fax: 913-469-2564

Joliet Junior College

2 Pu G S Tr AA

▼ Honors Program

The Joliet Junior College (JJC) Honors Program, currently in its fourteenth year, is designed to intellectually stimulate and challenge students striving for the utmost in their college education. It consists of a select group of students and faculty members from all disciplines and a core of courses in which the material is covered in greater depth and breadth than in regular courses. Writing and critical thinking are stressed, and because honors classes are small (15 students maximum), many teaching and learning approaches are used.

As their adviser, the coordinator of the Honors Program assists all honors students during their careers at Joliet Junior College and thereafter in, among other things, transferring, seeking scholarships, and gaining employment.

There are currently 60 students in the program.

Participation Requirements: To graduate from the Honors Program students must satisfy all college requirements for graduation, complete 15 credit hours of honors course work, participate in at least one half of all honors colloquia (lecture-discussion sessions run by guest scholars) and honors forums (biweekly discussion sessions run by honors students), and earn a 3.5 or better GPA. All honors courses are designated as such on student transcripts, as is successful completion of the program.

Admission Process: Entering freshmen must satisfy one of the following requirements: graduation in the top 10 percent of the high school class, an ACT composite score of 25 or better, or membership in the National Honor Society. Joliet Junior College students must have a GPA of 3.5 or higher for 15 or more credit hours or two letters of recommendation from college faculty members. An interview with the Honors Program Coordinator is required of all applicants.

Scholarship Availability: Joliet Junior College offers a number of endowed scholarships to qualified applicants. In some cases, participation in the Honors Program may be a factor.

The Campus Context: Joliet Junior College, America's oldest public community college, began with 6 students in 1901 as an experimental postgraduate high school program. Today, JJC serves about 12,000 students in credit classes and another 5,000 students in noncredit courses. JJC is a comprehensive community college that offers prebaccalaureate programs for students planning to transfer to a four-year university, occupational and technical education programs leading directly to employment, adult education and literacy programs, work force and workplace development programs, and academic support services to help students succeed. A total of thirty-four two-year transfer degree programs and thirty-three two-year terminal degree programs are offered.

Student Body Undergraduate enrollment is approximately 12,000. The student population is 60 percent women. Ethnic distribution is .5 percent Native American/Alaska Native, 8 percent black/African American, 7 percent Hispanic, .5 percent Asian/Pacific Islander, and 83 percent white. There are 7 international students. All students are commuters. Fifty percent of students receive financial aid.

Faculty Of the 500 total faculty members, 150 are full-time. Seventy-five percent have an M.A. or the equivalent, 20 percent hold a Ph.D., and 5 percent hold other degrees. The student-faculty ratio is 20:1.

Key Facilities The library has 70,000 volumes and is a member of ILCSO (Illinois Library Computer Systems Organization). Computer facilities include more than 2,000 computers on campus, more than twenty-five networked computer labs, Internet access, free student e-mail, and a Technology Planning Committee, which has an annual budget of nearly $1 million for upgrades and expansion.

Honorary Society Phi Theta Kappa

Athletics Joliet Junior College has the following intercollegiate athletic teams: men's baseball, football, soccer, and tennis; women's softball, soccer, tennis, and volleyball; and men's and women's basketball. These teams are nonscholarship and compete in Divisions II and III of the NJCAA.

Study Abroad A member of the Illinois Consortium for International Studies and Programs (ICISP), Joliet Junior College currently offers students opportunities to study in England, Austria, the Netherlands, Costa Rica, Mexico, and France. In addition, College staff participate in the ICISP faculty exchange program.

Support Services The Joliet Junior College Special Needs Department provides qualified students with assistance ranging from adaptive testing to notetaking assistance, signers, and a special learning resources room.

Job Opportunities Numerous part-time jobs are available on campus to qualified students.

Tuition: $44 for area residents, $171.78 for out-of-district students, $210.47 for out-of-state students, $242.42 for out-of-country students, per credit hour

Mandatory Fees: $10 per credit hour

Contact: Coordinator: Peter L. Neff, 1215 Houbolt Road, Joliet, Illinois 60431-8938; Telephone: 815-729-9020 Ext. 2731; E-mail: pneff@jjc.cc.il.us

Kean University

4 Pu D S Sc Tr

▼ Honors Program

The Honors Program at Kean University offers a personalized program of study to challenge and reward students who display exceptional ability and motivation. Presently, there are Departmental Honors Programs in biology, Earth science, English, political science, and public administration and course offerings in psychology, philosophy, sociology, and music. These offerings provide an exceptional opportunity to work closely with distinguished faculty members and peers and to conduct independent research. Students have an opportunity for advanced scholarship in a supportive, yet challenging environment. Kean honors graduates have gained admission to some of the nation's most prestigious master's and doctoral programs; others have launched successful careers in a variety of fields. The Honors Program at Kean University has been in existence since 1978 and presently enrolls approximately 100 students.

Participation Requirements: Departmental Honors Programs are offered in biology, Earth science, English, political science, and public administration. Each department has its own eligibility standards. Generally, it is expected that all students, regardless of their major, will complete a major research project, a portfolio of creative works, or similar capstone achievement. Generally, it is necessary to complete a minimum of 12 honors credits in order to obtain an honors certificate. However, most honors courses are open to eligible students, both majors and nonmajors, to be taken on an individual basis.

Honors enrollment does not require taking additional courses or credits, rather it involves taking honors sections of some required or elective courses.

Admission Process: Admission to honors programs and individual courses are based on overall GPA, GPA within the discipline, SAT I scores, and high school class rank (usually in the top 25 percent). Departmental interviews may be necessary.

Scholarship Availability: There are a number of undergraduate honors scholarships, which the University awards each spring for use the following year. Financial need is a factor in the awards as are other criteria. Applications are available in the Office of the Director of Scholarships.

The Campus Context: Kean University is an interactive, metropolitan institution of higher learning serving students from the communities of New Jersey and its neighboring states.

There are more than sixty-five academic degree programs on the graduate and undergraduate levels that students may pursue on either a full-time or part-time basis.

The University is located in Union and Hillside townships. The campus is quiet and spacious, spread over 150 acres of woods and lawns, bordering a Union County park and the Elizabeth River. Traffic is restricted to the perimeter of the campus. Only walkways and footbridges transverse the broad interior mall. A total environment has been created in which both esthetic and functional concepts are carefully integrated. Access to the University is excellent with its proximity to major networks of transportation. This, in turn, makes the continuous cultural and intellectual interchange between the cities and the University possible. On campus parking is provided for visitors, faculty members, and students.

Student Body There are 9,510 enrolled undergraduates, 6,312 full-time and 3,198 part-time. There are 1,199 resident students and 8,311 commuter students. The undergraduate enrollment comprises 36 percent men and 64 percent women. The undergraduate and graduate enrollment totals 13,216 students. Asian students comprise 7 percent, African American 17 percent, Hispanic 17 percent, and Caucasian 55 percent of the student body. International students make up 2.6 percent. Fifty-nine percent of the students receive some form of financial aid. There are 14 fraternities and 17 sororities on campus.

Faculty Kean University faculty members are outstanding teachers, accomplished researchers, and active practitioners. They bring to the classroom a wealth of academic knowledge and contemporary experience. Professors are very interested in the growth and development of students. They are not only teachers, but also mentors. Teaching is the primary emphasis of the 357 full-time faculty members.

More than 88 percent of the faculty members hold terminal degrees in their fields with relevant experience in both teaching and research.

Key Facilities The Nancy Thompson Library is a comprehensive learning center holding more than 270,000 volumes of books and 14,200 bound periodicals and microforms and 1,350 subscriptions, CD-ROMs and online databases. The library serves as a regional repository for selected New Jersey publications. Rapid bibliographic retrieval capability is available through online service from several computerized national databases. Kean University participates in an interlibrary loan system through which books and other materials can be borrowed. There are also thirty-six computer labs located around campus.

Honorary Societies Alpha Delta Mu, Alpha Kappa Delta, Alpha Kappa Psi, Beta Beta Beta, Epsilon Pi Tau, Omicron Delta Epsilon, Phi Alpha Theta, Phi Epsilon Kappa, Phi Mu Alpha, Pi Alpha Alpha, Pi Sigma Alpha, Pi Mu Epsilon, Psi Chi, Sigma Alpha Iota, Sigma Phi Omega, Sigma Tau Delta, Sigma Theta Tau, Sigma Xi (club)

Athletics Kean University sponsors sixteen varsity sports teams on the NCAA Division III level with plans to expand the program in the immediate future. A charter member of the New Jersey Athletic Conference, Kean also is affiliated with the Eastern College Athletic Conference (ECAC). Construction of a new multipurpose outdoor athletic facility is completed, and there is a planned overhaul of all athletic facilities as part of a campuswide renewal.

Men at Kean compete in football, soccer, basketball, lacrosse, baseball, and cross-country track. Women compete in field hockey, softball, swimming, basketball, volleyball, soccer, lacrosse, tennis, cross-country, and indoor/outdoor track.

Study Abroad Kean University offers overseas studies programs to eligible matriculated students. At present, students may select from approximately twenty host countries. All overseas students carry a full-time course load and are eligible to apply those credits to meet Kean University degree requirements. Participants are also eligible to apply financial assistance toward the cost of the program.

Support Services Kean University is committed to affirmative action in its admissions and employment practices. Furthermore, the University encourages participation of the disabled and provides support systems to facilitate their access to live and work within the institution.

Job Opportunities The Federal Work-Study Program, maintained with federal funds, provides part-time and summer jobs both on campus and in off-campus agencies for matriculated students with demonstrated need who are registered on at least a half-time basis.

Within the limitations of individual need and employment funding, students may work an average of 20 hours per week while classes are in session or up to 40 hours during vacations and holidays.

Tuition: $3213 for residents, $4829 for nonresidents, per year (1998–99)

Room and board: $4116

Mandatory Fees: $740.50

Contact: Director: Dr. Carole L. Willis, 1000 Morris Avenue, Union, New Jersey 07083; Telephone: 908-527-2539; Fax: 908-629-7068; E-mail: cwillis@turbo.kean.edu; Web site: http://www.kean.edu

KENT STATE UNIVERSITY

4 Pu G L Sc Tr

▼ Honors College

Honors at Kent State University began in 1933–34 when the first senior honors thesis was written. In 1960 the program attained University-wide status and in 1965 became a collegial unit headed by a dean.

The Honors College, open to students of all majors, is at the center of Kent State University's long tradition of providing special attention to undergraduates with outstanding intellectual and creative ability. Within the framework of the larger University, with its diverse academic programs and excellent research and library facilities, the Honors College offers students enriched and challenging courses and programs, opportunities for close relationships with peers and faculty members, and careful advising to meet their interests and goals.

The Honors College is guided by two basic principles. The first is a responsibility to provide academic work that offers intellectual challenge to the best students in the University and demands of

Interpreting the symbols: **2**=two-year college, **4**=four-year college; **Pu**=public or state college, **Pr**=private college; **G**=general honors program; **D**=departmental honors program; **S**=small program (fewer than 100 students), **M**=midsize program (100 to 500 students), **L**=large program (more than 500 students); **Sc**=scholarships available in honors program; **Tr**=transfer students accepted into honors program; **HBC**=historically black college; **AA**=academic advisors; **GA**=graduate advisors; **FA**=fellowship advisors.

them the best effort of which they are capable. To this end courses are designed to stretch the mind, sharpen skills, and encourage high standards of performance.

The second principle is the belief that regardless of degree program, students should be liberally educated. That is, they should understand and appreciate the language, literature, and history of cultures; the social, political, and economic structure of societies; the creative achievements that enrich lives; and the basic assumptions and substance of the natural sciences. In keeping with this belief, the College provides honors sections of many of the University's Liberal Education Requirement courses. Honors students are also encouraged to enrich their major programs by enrolling in related courses across disciplinary boundaries, e.g., studying foreign languages to complement degree programs in business. In addition, honors students pursue double majors in unusual combinations such as mathematics and theater, physics and English, and elementary education and dance.

Honors courses are available throughout the undergraduate years and can be used to meet requirements in all the degree-granting colleges and schools of the University.

All honors freshmen are enrolled in the year-long Freshman Honors Colloquium. The colloquium is a rigorous course in reading, thinking, and writing about literature and ideas. The goal of the course is to develop habits of inquiry, understanding, and communication that will serve the student through the college years and beyond.

In addition to the Freshman Honors Colloquium, many honors courses are taught each semester by distinguished faculty members throughout the University. Although these courses differ in content from art to zoology, they share a common form. Class enrollments are small (no more than 20), and students get to know each other and their professors in an environment that encourages learning through discussion, reading, individual work, and writing.

Honors students are also encouraged to study on a one-to-one basis with members of the faculty. The Individual Honors Work course is available from the freshman through senior years and can take many forms. For example, it has been used by students to create a course not available in the regular curriculum, to intern off campus, or to undertake a specialized scholarly or creative project. Seniors are strongly encouraged to complete the Senior Honors Thesis/Project.

Honors students are advised by the dean and a professional advising staff and by collegial and faculty advisers in their majors. Honors students must meet with their honors adviser at least once each semester in order to register for the following term. Honors students then have priority registration.

Enrollment is currently more than 1,000, with an additional 200 students at the regional campuses.

Participation Requirements: Two categories of graduation recognition are possible: one with a thesis (graduation with honors) and one with course work only (graduation as a member in good standing of the Honors College). Graduation with honors exists in three categories—University, General, and Departmental—and includes a certificate announcing Distinction in the student's major. Each category carries specific course and GPA requirements. The normal expectation is that students complete eight honors courses, with adjustments made for entrance after the freshman year. Students graduating from the Honors College are recognized at commencement and the Senior Honors Brunch; in addition, thesis students are recognized at the annual University-wide Honors Day Convocation and the Senior Thesis Forum.

Admission Process: Students apply directly to the Honors College by having guidance counselors send a copy of their high school transcript (showing class rank, GPA, ACT/SAT scores, and senior courses). Admission and scholarship decisions are made on an ongoing basis. Students who apply after the freshman year are evaluated on the basis of actual college performance. Students may apply as late as the end of the junior year.

Scholarship Availability: The Honors College directly distributes renewable merit scholarships ranging from $1200 to full in-state tuition, room, and board to approximately 65 percent of the freshman honors class. Also included are some discipline-specific awards. Minimum requirements are usually the top 10 percent in both class rank and national test scores.

The Campus Context: Located in Kent, Ohio (population 30,000), Kent State University was founded in 1910 as Kent Normal School and became a university in 1935. It is an eight-campus system serving the needs of the northeast Ohio region. Regional campuses include Ashtabula, East Liverpool, Geauga, Salem, Stark, Trumbull, and Tuscarawas. The centrally located Kent campus lies approximately 35 miles south of Cleveland and 11 miles east of Akron. There are 113 buildings on the 826-acre Kent campus. These include a twelve-story research library with more than 2 million volumes, which also houses the executive offices; a student center, which includes a bookstore, food court, cafeteria, restaurant, ballroom, music listening center, governance chambers, cybercafe, and auditorium; an ice arena, athletic and convocation center, stadium, field house, and recreation center; and numerous classroom buildings and residence halls. There is a campus bus service.

The Kent campus provides baccalaureate, master's, and doctoral degrees.

In addition to traditional collegial and departmental areas, the campus has institutes for liquid crystals, applied linguistics, bibliography and editing, computational mathematics, and water resources and centers for applied psychology, Conrad studies, counseling and human development, employee ownership, international and comparative studies, literature and psychoanalysis, world musics, Pan-African culture, NATO and European community studies, urban design, and the study and prevention of violence.

Student Body Of the 18,382 undergraduate and 4,446 graduate students enrolled on the Kent campus, the majority are from northeast Ohio.

Key Facilities The library houses more than 2 million volumes. There is a also a state-of-the-art recreation and wellness center.

Honorary Societies Alpha Lambda Delta, Golden Key, Mortar Board, Phi Beta Kappa

Job Opportunities Students are offered a range of work opportunities on campus, including work-study, assistantships and fellowships, and University-funded employment.

Tuition: $5600 for state residents, $11,100 for nonresidents, per year (2001–02)

Room and Board: $5150 for a double room; various plans available

Contact: Dean: Dr. Larry R. Andrews, P.O. Box 5190, Kent, Ohio 44242; Telephone: 330-672-2312; Fax: 330-672-3327; E-mail: landrews@kent.edu; Web site: http://www.kent.edu/honors

---

Kentucky State University

4 Pu G S Sc Tr HBC

▼ The Whitney Young College of Leadership Studies

The Whitney Young College of Leadership Studies (WYC) is named after the late Whitney M. Young, Jr., Executive Director of the National Urban League from 1961 to 1971. He was one of the most distinguished leaders of the American Civil Rights movement and a graduate of Kentucky State University (KSU). The mission of the College is to develop in students the qualities of leadership that were demonstrated by Mr. Young. Such leadership qualities and skills include the development of intellectual skills that help students deal with fundamental questions of human existence and make them better able to guide their own lives. WYC is an integrated liberal arts program. It emphasizes student participation in classroom discussion, small classes of 15 or fewer students, a challenging interdisciplinary curriculum with multicultural components, a faculty devoted to undergraduate education, and a community spirit among faculty members and students.

The WYC program is an integrated sequence of seminar, math/science, and language courses and preceptorials according to faculty member and student interest. It is a great books program in which students develop the precision and power of their minds by reading and discussing some of the world's best books.

In addition to the honors program, WYC also administers the Institute for Liberal Studies, the integrative studies courses of the University's liberal studies requirements, and the newly designed international studies program minor. The University Endowed Chair in the Humanities is also housed in the College.

Several program options are available to WYC students. These include a bachelor's degree with a major in liberal studies; pursuit of a double major, one in liberal studies and the other chosen from the traditional disciplines; students may complete a major in liberal studies and a minor in any other discipline; or students may elect to complete only an Associate of Arts degree at WYC.

WYC offers opportunities for study abroad as well as paid summer internships in Washington, D.C. Students gain automatic membership in the National Collegiate Honors Council, with opportunities to attend regional and national conferences. The Whitney Young College Student Council organizes social activities, engages in public service, and participates in field trips.

Approximately 65 students are enrolled in WYC. Honor students major in every department and college at KSU.

Participation Requirements: To earn a Bachelor of Arts degree in liberal studies, a minor is required and students must complete a minimum of 128 credit hours. To earn an Associate of Arts degree in liberal studies, a total of 67 credit hours for the seminar-based option or 65 credit hours for the general liberal studies core option is required. A minor in liberal studies requires the completion of 18 credit hours.

Admission Process: Admission of first-year students to WYC is by special application. After students have applied and been admitted to KSU, prospective students must apply to WYC. Students applying for admission to WYC must possess a strong academic background in high school, a minimum ACT composite score of 21 or the SAT I equivalent, and have a strong desire to learn. Transfer students are also considered and may pursue a student-designed major or minor in liberal studies.

Scholarship Availability: WYC administers its own scholarship program. Application must be made to the Dean of the College. In addition, KSU has a merit-based institutional scholarship program.

The Campus Context: Kentucky State University was founded in 1886 as a normal school for the training of African American teachers for the black schools in Kentucky. Today, KSU is the only historically black institution of higher education and the only HBCU 1890 land-grant institution in the commonwealth. KSU offers six associate degree programs, twenty-nine bachelor's degree programs, and master's degree programs in public administration and aquaculture. The 309-acre campus is located in the state's capital, Frankfort, which is approximately 25 miles from Lexington and 50 miles from Louisville. Campus facilities include an $11.5-million Health, Physical Education, and Recreation complex and 6 residence halls with computer labs as well as in-room telephone and cable TV services.

Student Body KSU is the smallest of Kentucky's public universities with an enrollment of approximately 2,300 students. Seventy-two percent are full-time and 75 percent are Kentucky residents. The ethnic distribution is 59 percent African American, 36 percent white, and 5 percent other. Student organizations range from Greek fraternities and sororities, honor societies, academic clubs, literary groups, art/music clubs, and special interest organizations (nursing, international students, chess, debate, etc.).

Faculty Full-time instructional faculty members number 130. More than two thirds hold the Ph.D. or the highest appropriate degree in their field. The student-faculty ratio is 14:1.

Key Facilities KSU's Blazer Library has 350,000 volumes. There is a campuswide network of mainframe and desktop computers.

Honorary Societies Alpha Kappa Mu

Athletics Varsity athletics competes in NCAA Division II and the Southern Intercollegiate Athletic Conference. There are seven teams for men (baseball, basketball, cross-country, football, golf, tennis, and track) and six for women (basketball, cross-country, softball, tennis, track, and volleyball). KSU also sponsors numerous intramural sports and recreational activities.

Study Abroad KSU offers opportunities for international study to qualified students. The University is a member of the Cooperative Center for Study in Britain. There are also opportunities to participate in student exchanges, internships, and service-learning programs around the world.

Support Services The campus is accessible to physically disabled students.

Job Opportunities Work opportunities are available on and off campus.

Tuition: $2278 for state residents, $6838 for nonresidents, per year (2001–02)

Room and board: $3920

Mandatory Fees: $370

Contact: Dean: Dr. Sam Oleka, Carver Hall, Room 133, Frankfort, Kentucky 40601; Telephone: 502-597-6411; Fax: 502-597-6041; E-mail: soleka@gwmail.kysu.edu

KING'S COLLEGE

4 Pr S

▼ The Honors Program

The Honors Program at King's College allows serious undergraduate scholars the opportunity to pursue their intellectual interests in a way that, while being strongly grounded in the humanities, tailors students' programs to their major field of study. In the freshman and sophomore years, students are exposed to "foundation" honors seminars in history, literature and the arts, and philosophy. Four advanced Honors Seminars in the student's major field are completed at the junior level. Seniors enrolled in the Honors Program spend their final year on campus researching and writing an Honors Thesis in their particular field, under the mentorship of a qualified faculty member. Honors sections are capped at 15 students so as to maximize individual attention and high-quality classroom interaction. Many courses are interdisciplinary, and all honors courses foster the student's active role in the learning process. Honors students at King's College also take part in a number of extracurricular programs specially designed for them, such as noncredit reading groups and informal

Interpreting the symbols: 2=two-year college, 4=four-year college; **Pu**=public or state college, **Pr**=private college; **G**=general honors program; **D**=departmental honors program; **S**=small program (fewer than 100 students), **M**=midsize program (100 to 500 students), **L**=large program (more than 500 students); **Sc**=scholarships available in honors program; **Tr**=transfer students accepted into honors program; **HBC**=historically black college; **AA**=academic advisors; **GA**=graduate advisors; **FA**=fellowship advisors.

Honors Thursday gatherings, at which they share their achievements with their peers. The Honors Program at King's College works hard to integrate study-abroad experiences and experiential learning (such as internships in Washington, D.C., and London) into the student's plan of study.

Participation Requirements: Incoming freshmen graduating in the top 20 percent of their graduating class, with an overall SAT score greater than 1100 and a minimum score of 550 on the verbal portion, are invited by the director to participate in the Honors Program. King's College students who have at least a 3.25 GPA may apply for admission to the program. Students outside the program may register for honors courses, with the permission of the director, if they maintain a minimum GPA of 3.0. Honors certificates are only awarded to those graduating seniors who finish with a GPA of at least 3.4 and have completed all of the required course work in the program.

Scholarship Availability: More than 100 scholarships are available to King's College students. The most prestigious of these are Presidential Scholarships (full tuition) and Moreau Scholarships (combined with Federal Pell Grant and any state grants; the aggregate may not exceed the cost of annual tuition). For more information, students should contact the financial aid office.

The Campus Context: King's College is a four-year college founded in 1946 by priests and brothers from the University of Notre Dame. Like Notre Dame, it is affiliated with the Congregation of the Holy Cross. Graduate study is available in several academic fields. King's College is located in Wilkes-Barre, Pennsylvania, just over 2 hours from both New York City and Philadelphia.

Student Body The student population of King's College, which is coeducational, is roughly 2,500. The population is fairly evenly divided between commuter students and dorm students (mostly from the New York and Philadelphia metropolitan areas). King's College also has a vibrant community of students from many other countries.

Honorary Societies A number of national interdisciplinary honor societies, both Catholic and lay, are present on campus. The annual Honors Convocation celebrates the achievement of student members of these organizations.

Tuition: Basic fee per semester: $8360 (standard course load, 12–17 credits)

Room and Board: $1710 per semester (double room), $2075 per semester (single room, limited availability)

Contact: Dr. Charles S. Kraszewski, Director, Box 37, King's College, Wilkes-Barre, Pennsylvania 18711; Telephone: 570-208-5900 Ext. 5706; E-mail: cskrasze@kings.edu

Kingsborough Community College of the City University of New York

2 Pu G M Sc Tr

▼ Honors Option Program

The Honors Option Program at Kingsborough Community College of the City University of New York was designed to offer a select group of able and motivated students the opportunity for a more challenging and stimulating education. To achieve this purpose, the College offers each semester a series of courses open only to students in this program. Thus, eligible students are given the option to take one or more courses each semester with other students of similar ability and motivation, designed to stimulate thinking, creative endeavor, and intellectual curiosity. Some of the courses are interdisciplinary in nature and are team taught by professors from various academic disciplines. All classes are small enough to facilitate faculty-student interchange and to encourage discussion. The students are also encouraged to become actively involved in the initiation and development of courses and in the evaluation of the program.

In addition to being provided with the option of taking the enriched and horizon-broadening courses scheduled specifically for the program, students are also provided with the opportunity of designing independent study courses or research projects with the assistance and under the supervision of a faculty mentor. In this manner, students may explore topics in a given discipline, or of an interdisciplinary nature, from a variety of perspectives, with creative initiative and in greater depth. The close relationship usually established between students in this program and members of its faculty greatly facilitate such arrangements for the highly motivated and intellectually curious student. The completion of at least 12 honors credits is so noted on the students' transcripts and on the annual graduation program.

Kingsborough encourages its students to participate in student government and a large variety of cocurricular activities, to enrich the students' total college experience, enhance interpersonal relationships, and develop leadership skills. Students in the Honors Option Program are eligible to join the Corporate Career Honors Club, which offers them the opportunity to meet other students of similar interests and abilities, to conduct stimulating programs, and to promote their educational and vocational objectives. The club sponsors lectures, discussions, workshops, social and recreational functions, and various modalities for career exploration and ongoing career development assistance, based on the needs and interests of its members.

There are 175 students currently enrolled in the program.

Admission Process: Students admitted to the College and completing 12–28 credits with a cumulative index of 3.20 (on a scale of 4.0) or better, are eligible to apply for acceptance to the program. A special screening committee reviews and acts on these applications.

Applications must be submitted in January and June.

The Campus Context: Kingsborough Community College, a unit of the City University of New York and accredited by the Middle States Association of Colleges and Schools, is located in Manhattan Beach and has a beautiful 67-acre campus bordered on three sides of the waters of Sheepshead Bay, Jamaica Bay, and the Atlantic Ocean. The ultramodern campus of interconnected buildings is situated in a setting that is convenient to public transportation and provides supervised on-campus or nearby free municipal parking.

Within the framework of the liberal arts curriculum leading to the Associate in Arts (A.A.) degree, students may choose to take the appropriate foundation courses in preparation for professional careers such as medicine, dentistry, pharmacy, law, and education. They receive specific guidance from counselors and faculty advisers concerning the course of studies most suitable for transfer and the achievement of professional objectives. Students may also opt to work toward the Associate in Science (A.S.) degree in the areas of mathematics, computer science, the biological and physical sciences, fine arts, music, and theater arts.

They may also choose from a large variety of career programs, leading to Associate in Applied Science (A.A.S.) degrees. These programs enable students to commence a career upon the completion of the two-year sequence, while leaving open the option of continuing their education toward a higher degree at a senior college.

The College offers high-quality educational programs with a unique and exclusive academic calendar that alternates required twelve-week fall and spring semesters with two optional winter and summer six-week modules at no additional tuition for full-time students. To accomplish its goals, Kingsborough Community College offers a wide range of personalized services such as freshman orientation, academic advisement, free tutoring, career counseling, job placement, and supervised field experience within one's major concentration. The College facilities include an art gallery, a performing arts center, and Olympic-size swimming pool, a private beach, library, and computer and media centers.

Student Body Enrollment is 15,175 students; 63 percent are women. The ethnic distribution is 30 percent black/African American, 8 percent Asian American, 48 percent white, and 14 percent Hispanic. There are 388 nonresident aliens.

Faculty Of the 961 faculty members, 219 are full-time. Eighty-two percent of full-time faculty members have terminal degrees.

Key Facilities The library houses 134,670 volumes. Computers number more than 1,000 PCs in thirteen labs and at other sites.

Honorary Society Phi Theta Kappa

Athletics Major intercollegiate athletics include baseball, basketball, and tennis for men and volleyball, softball, and basketball for women. Intramural sports include football, basketball, softball, soccer, volleyball, and Ping-Pong.

Support Services The College buildings are equipped to be accessible to disabled students. Mathematics and English Skills Laboratories and a Speech, Language and Hearing Center offer support to students in need of remediation or special assistance. The College is also equipped with a Center for the Learning Disabled.

Tuition: $2500 for area residents, $3076 for state residents, $3076 for nonresidents, per year (1998–99)

Mandatory Fees: $100

Contact: Director: Dr. Eric Willner, 2001 Oriental Boulevard, Brooklyn, New York 11235; Telephone: 718-368-5365; Fax: 718-368-4836

KINGWOOD COLLEGE

2 Pu G S Sc

▼ Community of Scholars

The Community of Scholars and Kingwood College take pride in their values-centered curriculum, a highly accessible faculty, and commitment to community. The Mission Statement identifies knowledge as the result of a lifelong pursuit of learning, wisdom as the result of the integration of reflection and action, justice as the promotion of the values that seek a better world, and association that promotes the development of a community of learners. Kingwood believes that these components create an excellent environment for teaching and learning. These components complement the aims of the Community of Scholars program, which are to foster the academic life and liberal education of intellectually able students, to give recognition to outstanding students, and to enhance the intellectual and academic life of the College for the benefit of all students and the College.

The Community of Scholars offers its members excellent instruction and preparation for transfer to a four-year institution. Community of Scholars courses are kept small in size (maximum of 15 students) to ensure close contact with the instructor and a ready exchange of ideas. All Community of Scholars courses are designed to promote knowledge acquisition through reading and discussion rather than by rote learning.

The Community of Scholars program fosters an approach to learning that it labels the Community of Scholars Mentality. The Community of Scholars Mentality includes the following characteristics, among others: a curiosity about the world and a desire to study it in the spirit of critical inquiry, an interest in the academic organization and presentation of knowledge, a willingness to lay the foundations for lifelong learning, an appreciation for the transforming power as well as the practical uses of the liberal arts, an eagerness to understand and improve upon one's own learning styles, and an ability to work independently as well as collaboratively with student scholars and Community of Scholars faculty members.

Community of Scholars faculty members model the characteristics of the liberally trained and educated person who is curious about the world, committed to lifelong learning, respectful yet critical of tradition, and tolerant of the opinions of others while possessing firm convictions based on study and experience. They personally demonstrate and foster in others the ability to take multiple perspectives on an issue and to make connections creatively across disciplines. They create the conditions in which students feel enough trust to take risks as they engage in analytical thinking and creative activity that may be unfamiliar to them. Creativity occurs best when teachers place an emphasis on student autonomy and encourage student experimentation. Creativity serves to reinvent, transform, and regenerate the person. Faculty members are also student centered. In addition to teaching course content, they are interested in teaching students certain ways of knowing (e.g., thinking skills, political awareness, intellectual empathy, value identification, and experimentation that links thinking with acting) that are transferable to other learning situations. They believe in values-centered education.

Participation Requirements: Students who complete 12 hours of honors credit with A's or B's are awarded the Kingwood College Honors Certificate. Students who complete 9 hours of honors credit with a minimum overall 3.5 GPA and 25 hours of community service receive the designation of Honors Scholar. Students who complete 15 hours of honors credit with a minimum overall 3.5 GPA are recognized at commencement and receive the designation of Honors Program Graduate on their diplomas and transcripts. Students who complete 15 hours of honors credit with a minimum overall 3.5 GPA and 25 hours of community service are recognized at commencement and receive the designation of Honors Scholar with Distinction.

Admission Process: Any student can register for an honors course. Students may apply for admission into the Community of Scholars program after the first semester of the freshman year. To qualify for admission, a student must have at least a 3.5 overall GPA and take at least one honors course per semester.

Scholarship Availability: Scholarships (ten per full semester) of $250 each are offered through the Community of Scholars program based on academic performance. High school seniors are eligible, as are currently enrolled Kingwood College students.

The Campus Context: Kingwood College, one of four colleges in the North Harris Montgomery Community College District, is located on 264 beautifully landscaped, heavily wooded acres approximately 25 miles north of Houston in Kingwood, Texas. By offering academic transfer courses, sixteen career programs, community education, and community service, the College enhances the quality of life throughout the area. State-of-the-art technology in both PC and Macintosh environments offers desktop publishing and computer graphic arts students highly marketable job skills. Only Novell-certified computer classes are offered in the district. The College offers the only International Business Practicum in the district. Students set up and operate a business, buying and selling with other U.S. and European college students. The e-business consortium includes 126 U.S. colleges and more than 3,000 European universities.

Interpreting the symbols: **2**=two-year college, **4**=four-year college; **Pu**=public or state college, **Pr**=private college; **G**=general honors program; **D**=departmental honors program; **S**=small program (fewer than 100 students), **M**=midsize program (100 to 500 students), **L**=large program (more than 500 students); **Sc**=scholarships available in honors program; **Tr**=transfer students accepted into honors program; **HBC**=historically black college; **AA**=academic advisors; **GA**=graduate advisors; **FA**=fellowship advisors.

Student Body The enrollment is 38 percent men and 62 percent women. The ethnic distribution is 79 percent white, 6 percent African American, 10 percent Hispanic, and 3 percent Asian/Pacific Islander.

Faculty The total number of faculty members is 216, of whom 63 are full-time. Twenty-four percent of the full-time faculty members have terminal degrees. The student-faculty ratio is 20:1.

Key Facilities The College's technologically advanced Learning Resource Center offers students a world of information through thousands of books as well as through access to the Internet. Student labs with multiple microcomputers are available for student use in the Academic Support Center.

Support Services In addition to providing legally mandated services for persons with disabilities who voluntarily seek additional services, the College Assistance Program provides professional tutoring, academic advisement, and other support services.

Job Opportunities A limited number of part-time positions on campus are available to students who demonstrate financial need. The wage rate varies depending upon skills required and experience.

Tuition: The rate of $41 per credit hour includes a $4-per-credit-hour technology fee and a registration fee of $12 for in-district residents. A full-time student (12–16 credit hours) can expect to pay approximately $348–$460 per semester, excluding book fees (1998–99).

Contact: Co-coordinators: Dr. Dan Coleman and Dr. Dom Bongiorni, Kingwood College, 20000 Kingwood Drive, Kingwood, Texas 77339; Telephone: 281-312-1623 or 1481; E-mail: daniel.coleman@nhmccd.edu or bongiorni@nhmccd.edu; Web site: http://kcweb.nhmccd.edu/employee/bongiorni/hon_prg.htm

Kutztown University of Pennsylvania

4 Pu G S Sc Tr

▼ Honors Program

Founded in 1986, the Kutztown University Honors Program is designed to provide academic and leadership opportunities for the University's most proficient and highly motivated students. The undergraduate program is open to full-time students. It requires a minimum of 21 credits in honors courses that stress in-depth study, research, and challenging exploration of various areas of study. The 21 honors credits also count toward the 120 credits for graduation. Students may earn these honors credits through a variety of methods, including honors courses, internships, course by contract, and by independent study (thesis).

In addition to honors course work, students in the Honors Program also complete two units of service, which do not carry academic credit allocation (one for the community and one for the University). Service opportunities in the community will be offered through a variety of official University sources under the auspices of the off-campus Student Life Center, and an agreement to serve a minimum of 30 hours of service, approved by the Honors Director and the Honors Council, will be established between the student and the community agency in advance of the term that the service is to be completed. For the second unit, students may select from a variety of services to the University, approved by the Director and Honors Council in advance of student participation. The service component of the Honors Program should begin in the student's sophomore year at Kutztown University.

There are currently 225 students enrolled in the program.

Participation Requirements: An honors diploma is awarded to those students in the program who have met all college requirements, completed at least 21 credits in honors course work through any variety of the methods described above, have attained a minimum cumulative quality point average of 3.25, and have completed a two-unit service component.

Admission Process: Freshmen who have been identified as potential honors students based on their high school record and SAT I scores, transfer students from other honors programs, and incumbent students who have earned a cumulative QPA of 3.25 or higher are invited to join the Honors Program. Undergraduate students who are not members of the Honors Program may take an honors course if they have a quality point average of 3.0 or higher in 15 credits taken at the University. These students will not receive honors credits for the course. Permission of the Honors Program Director is required.

Applications must be submitted in the spring semester.

Scholarship Availability: Scholarships based upon merit are available to entering freshmen and to upperclassmen who participate in the Honors Program.

The Campus Context: Kutztown University, a member of the Pennsylvania State System of Higher Education, was founded in 1866 as Keystone State Normal School, became Kutztown State Teachers College in 1928, Kutztown State College in 1960, and achieved university status in 1983. Kutztown University is on a picturesque 326-acre campus located in Pennsylvania Dutch community mid-way between Allentown and Reading, with easy access to Philadelphia and New York City. There are forty-seven undergraduate and fourteen graduate degree programs offered.

The University consists of five colleges: the College of Business, the College of Education, College of Liberal Arts and Sciences, the College of Visual and Performing Arts, and the College of Graduate Studies. Special facilities on campus include an art gallery, planetarium, observatory, weather station, full TV production studios, state-of the-art computer labs, cartography lab, daycare center, and the Pennsylvania Heritage Center. Students also have access to the Wallops Island marine science consortium facility in Virginia.

Student Body Undergraduate enrollment is 40 percent men and 60 percent women. The ethnic distribution is 89.2 percent white, 7.3 percent African American, 2.4 percent Latino, 0.5 percent Asian, 0.4 percent nonresident international, and 0.2 percent Native American. There are 72 international students. Forty-two percent of students are residents, and 58 percent commute to campus. Eighty percent of students receive financial aid. There are six fraternities and five sororities at the University.

Faculty There are 389 instructional faculty members; 361 are full-time and 76 percent hold doctoral degrees. The student-faculty ratio is 17:1.

Key Facilities The library holds 497,752 volumes. The University supports more than 2,700 micros, terminals, and printers for students, faculty members, and administrators. Additionally, there are two terminal rooms and seventeen microcomputer labs on campus.

Athletics Athletics include ten men's intercollegiate sports and eleven women's sports and an extensive intramural program. Modern athletic facilities include a football stadium, a field house, a gymnasium, playing fields, a track, cross-country course, pool, tennis courts, a street hockey court, fitness center, weight room, and a rifle range.

Study Abroad There are eleven international exchange and study-abroad programs.

Support Services Disabled students will find handicapped parking, curb cuts, ramps, electronic doors, and specialized equipment such as Kurzueil Reading Edge, CCTV, scanning software, and zoumtext, extra test time, readers, and scribes.

Job Opportunities Work opportunities are available in most departments.

Tuition: $4016 for state residents, $10,040 for nonresidents, per year (2001-02)

Room and Board: $4426
Mandatory Fees: $465 in-state; $931 out-of-state
Contact: Director: Dr. Guiyou Huang, P.O. Box 730, Kutztown, Pennsylvania 19530; Telephone: 610-683-1391; Fax: 610-683-1393; E-mail: vigoda@kutztown.edu

LaGuardia Community College

2 Pu G M Tr

▼ The Honors Experience

The LaGuardia Honors Experience is dedicated to providing an enriched education to highly motivated students interested in transferring to four-year institutions. The ultimate aim is to equip honors students with the academic competencies and personal confidence needed for success at demanding public and private four-year colleges and universities. Honors students enroll in special sections of regular courses. These sections provide additional instruction in reading complex texts, thinking critically, and writing gracefully and analytically. Students are guided in independent research, oral debate, and the creative examination of ideas. Class sizes are kept small to emphasize discussion and active learning.

Approximately 130 students enroll in honors courses each fall and spring semester.

Participation Requirements: Each semester, approximately eight honors courses are offered in a variety of disciplines. In past semesters, they have included The Novel, American History, Pre-Calculus and Calculus, Sociology, Introduction to Poetry, Principles of Management, and Exploring the Humanities. Students are free to take one or several honors courses in any semester as long as they meet the course prerequisites and honors student prerequisites.

Honors students receive an honors designation on their transcripts and they are invited to attend special transfer information sessions, honors receptions, and guest lectures.

Admission Process: Students are not chosen on the basis of SAT I scores or high school grades, but are recruited from enrolled students who have completed a minimum of 12 credits with a cumulative GPA of at least 3.2. Students are sought for honors who are strong in potential and ambition and who have a desire to engage in challenging academic work.

The Campus Context: Fiorello H. LaGuardia Community College, one of the seventeen undergraduate colleges of the City University of New York, is a vibrant community of teachers and learners. Founded in 1970 and admitting its first class of 540 students in 1971, the College has continually supported the principles of open access and equal opportunity for all. The College serves almost 11,000 students in growing neighborhoods of western Queens as well as the larger New York metropolitan area. It ranks fourth in the nation in the number of degrees granted to minority students and offers the following degree programs: A.A.S. (twenty majors), A.A. (six majors), and A.S. (seven majors).

Student Body There are 10,925 students enrolled in degree programs; 28,000 are enrolled in nondegree programs. Sixty-five percent are women. The ethnic distribution is 37 percent Hispanic, 20 percent black, 16 percent white, and 13 percent Asian. Students are drawn from more than 100 countries. Fifty percent of students are eligible for federal or state financial aid.

Faculty Of the 234 full-time faculty members, the majority possess terminal degrees. An additional 408 adjunct faculty members are employed.

Key Facilities The library houses 65,000 books and 800 journals. Through an electronic network connected to the entire collection of the City University of New York, students have access to 5 million books and 25,000 journals.

Job Opportunities LaGuardia, the only community college with a required co-op ed program for day students, is the second-largest cooperative education college in the country. Each year, 2,200 full-time students are placed in internships at 400 companies, including many of the larger corporations in New York City.

Tuition: $2500 for area residents, $3076 for state residents, $3076 for nonresidents, per year (1998–99)
Mandatory Fees: $110
Contact: Coordinator: Dr. Mohammad-Reza Fakhari, 31-10 Thomson Avenue, Long Island City, New York 11101; Telephone: 718-482-5218; Fax: 718-482-2058; E-mail: mohammad@lagcc.cuny.edu

La Salle University

4 Pr G M Sc Tr AA GA FA

▼ University Honors Program

The pedagogical philosophy of La Salle University emphasizes the need for a strong basis in the humanities for all undergraduates and, for this reason, requires everyone to complete a set of courses that focus on these humanities. Individual academic departments offer students a more intensive study in a specific discipline, but only after the majority of the requirements in this humanistically based core have been completed.

The curricular structure of the honors program follows this general University model, but with modifications that recognize the needs and abilities of the highly motivated and intellectually gifted student. These modifications are primarily in the manner in which the honors program student satisfies these essential University-wide requirements.

In the first year of studies, the honors program student completes three honors courses each term. These courses are in the disciplines of history, literature, and philosophy, and over the course of the year, take the student from the ancient world to the contemporary period. The professors teaching this first-year program make every attempt to coordinate their readings and assignments so that at any particular time during the academic year, the students are viewing the same period of civilization through the perspective of three different disciplines.

A typical week has the student spending 3 hours of class time in each of the three disciplines and 3 hours of time in a special situation in which an attempt is made to integrate the three seemingly distinct disciplines. This last 3-hour period of time brings together all of the first-year students in the program and their professors in a variety of experiences. Some of the sessions are held on campus, and others make use of the many museums and resources of the Philadelphia area. In recent years this has meant afternoons or evenings spent at the Academy of Music with the Philadelphia Orchestra, at the Philadelphia Museum of Art with the curator of the medieval collection, at the Arden Theater with the artistic director, or at the Franklin Institute. Each activity is designed to complement and supplement the work of the classroom—a humanities lab, in effect.

Total enrollment in the honors program is approximately 210 students from the four class years.

Interpreting the symbols: **2**=two-year college, **4**=four-year college; **Pu**=public or state college, **Pr**=private college; **G**=general honors program; **D**=departmental honors program; **S**=small program (fewer than 100 students), **M**=midsize program (100 to 500 students), **L**=large program (more than 500 students); **Sc**=scholarships available in honors program; **Tr**=transfer students accepted into honors program; **HBC**=historically black college; **AA**=academic advisors; **GA**=graduate advisors; **FA**=fellowship advisors.

Participation Requirements: The total number of courses required in honors is a minimum of fourteen, including the independent project. One of the courses must be an ethical issues seminar in the student's major. In addition to the curricular requirements, students are required to maintain a cumulative GPA of 3.0 and a GPA of 3.0 in honors courses to remain active in the honors program.

After having successfully completed the first year of studies, the honors program student is then offered a wide variety of seminars in honors. These seminars allow the student to study topics, time periods, and areas of interest in considerably more depth, using the broad overview of the first year as a solid foundation upon which to build. Serving as the substitutes for the regular core requirements of the University, these seminars are often cross-disciplinary. They can be single course offerings or multiple course offerings (e.g., with teachers team teaching a course). In addition, each honors program student is required to complete an independent study project that is the equivalent of one 3-credit course. This is done on a topic of the student's choosing (not necessarily in the major) and is directed by a faculty member.

Students who complete all of the requirements of the honors program are graduated from La Salle with the special distinction of General University Honors. This distinction is noted on the official transcript, on the diploma, and in a special listing in the Commencement program.

Admission Process: Each year approximately 60 students are admitted to the honors program (from a freshman class of approximately 800 students). Invitations are extended to students who have been accepted for admission by the University, who have combined SAT I scores of approximately 1250, and who rank in the first quintile of their graduating class.

The application deadline is May 1.

Scholarship Availability: Each year La Salle awards approximately thirty full-tuition scholarships to high school seniors. The Scholarship Selection Committee looks for students with a combined SAT I score of approximately 1300 or higher and who rank in the top 10 percent of the graduating class. A separate application for a scholarship must be submitted in addition to the application for admission to the University. Scholarship applications may be obtained by contacting the office of the director of the honors program or through the Office of Admissions.

The Campus Context: La Salle University is a private institution under the auspices of the Brothers of the Christian Schools. Located on a 100-acre campus in the historic Germantown section of Philadelphia, the University is composed of a School of Arts and Sciences, a School of Nursing, and a School of Business Administration. Current undergraduate enrollment is approximately 3,200 full-time students with a faculty of approximately 200 full-time professors. The average class size is 20 students. The graduate division offers advanced degrees in nine areas and currently enrolls approximately 2,500 students.

Tuition: $19,740 per year (2001–02)

Room and Board: $6680

Mandatory Fees: $75

Contact: Director: John S. Grady, 1900 West Olney Avenue, Philadelphia, Pennsylvania 19141-1199; Telephone: 215-951-1360; Fax: 215-951-1488; E-mail: grady@lasalle.edu

LA SIERRA UNIVERSITY

4 Pr G M Tr

▼ La Sierra University Honors Program

The Honors Program at La Sierra University seeks to provide intellectual excellence in the context of a learning community. A community of scholars, involving honors students and faculty members, centers on the series of interdisciplinary courses making up the core curriculum. These courses focus on three themes, drawn from the University's mission: knowing—developing an understanding of the perspectives of different groups (ranging from prophets in the Hebrew Scriptures through twenty-first-century scientists) and how these perspectives interrelate; serving—encouraging students to engage in their communities (civic, professional, religious, cultural, and global) to transform and build them with integrity, courage, openness, and compassion; and seeking—enabling students to contribute to the definition of their own education as they develop excellence in scholarship in a manner and with a subject that is uniquely their own and facilitating the development of students' worldviews as they begin a lifelong process of seeking truth through religious understanding, spiritual contemplation, and moral courage.

Since its inception in 1983, the Honors Program has grown to approximately 110 students. The diversity of the student body, including gender diversity, international diversity, ethnic diversity, and disciplinary diversity (a significant number of students come from the sciences and professional programs, as well as the humanities students typical of almost any honors program), allows for challenging interactions between students as they seek to understand each others' perspectives.

Under the supervision of a faculty mentor, honors scholars plan and carry out a program of original scholarly or creative work. During the sophomore or junior year each student selects a mentor and develops a project proposal. During the senior year the project is completed and culminates in a paper, production, or exhibition including a presentation in an on- or off-campus forum. Every spring, honors research presentations are at the heart of the University Research Emphasis Week.

As part of the senior capstone year, students complete a course examining the religious, moral, and social aspects of their disciplines. This gives them a chance to integrate what they have learned in their majors, their theses, and the core curriculum.

As a community of scholars, students participate in cultural activities throughout the year. In addition to this, the Honors Residence Hall, housing approximately 22 students, allows for a deeper level of interaction and support for students at the sophomore level and higher as they create a community that values scholarship and study.

The program is currently undergoing significant review and revision; for further information, students should visit the program's Web site, listed below.

Participation Requirements: Students complete a series of interdisciplinary courses focusing on the themes of knowing, serving, and seeking. In addition to these courses, students complete an honors scholarship project, in which they conduct an original research or creative project that culminates in a written thesis, production, or exhibition, as well as an oral presentation in an on- or off-campus forum. Community involvement, in which students work to improve and transform a civic, professional, religious, or cultural community, is also integrated into the program. Students must maintain a 3.5 GPA and complete a thesis to graduate with honors, but those who do not complete the thesis requirements may still participate in the program in order to fulfill their general education requirements. The curriculum is currently undergoing significant revision; students should visit the Web page for current details. Students completing the program receive an "Honors Program" designation on their diplomas and on the graduation program; the graduation program also lists the title of the students' theses.

Admission Process: First-year honors scholars are selected based on a separate application process from regular University admissions. To apply to the Honors Program, students must first be accepted into the University. Selection is based on high school GPA, SAT/ACT scores, a letter of recommendation, and an essay.

Applicants are evaluated by a committee consisting of the Honors Director, 2 faculty members, and a senior about to graduate from the program.

Preference is given to students with a 3.5 cumulative GPA and SAT or ACT verbal and math scores above the 60th percentile. Applicants whose scores are lower may on occasion be granted entrance on the basis of other evidence of high motivation and ability.

Applications are accepted at any time, but preference is given to applicants who apply by March 20 (for fall admission).

Transfer students may apply for entry into the Honors Program at any time. These applicants should have a 3.5 cumulative GPA, submit an application essay, and supply a letter of recommendation from a faculty member.

Scholarship Availability: The University gives substantial academic scholarships based on academic merit and need; none of these are currently tied to membership in the Honors Program (this is currently under review).

The Campus Context: La Sierra University is four-year private university accredited by the Western Association of Schools and Colleges and sponsored by the Seventh-day Adventist Church. Rooted in the southern California city of Riverside, the campus is approximately 1 hour from the cultural centers of Los Angeles, the beach, the mountains, and the desert. The University is comprised of four schools: the College of Arts and Sciences, the School of Business and Management, the School of Religion, and the School of Education. Particular campus strengths include involving undergraduate students in original research and scholarship, the integration of religion throughout the curriculum, a particularly strong music program, and a great deal of student diversity. There is no ethnic majority on campus, and approximately 65 percent of the student body is Seventh-day Adventist Christian, 12 percent Catholic, and 12 percent other Protestant, with the remaining students identifying with other religions. In this context, students are encouraged to explore their own identities while coming to understand and respect others.

Student Body Undergraduate enrollment is approximately 1,500, with 52 percent women and 48 percent men. Ethnic minorities comprise 61 percent of the student population, and 60 percent of enrolled students live on campus. Students have the option of being involved in any of the thirty-five student-run clubs and organizations available on campus.

Faculty The student-faculty ratio is 13:1. The 110 full-time faculty members, nearly all with terminal degrees, allow for a great deal of personal interaction between faculty and students.

Key Facilities The library has more than 200,000 volumes in its book collections, plus about 46,000 bound journal volumes representing more than 1,300 currently received journal titles. Extensive microfilm and microfiche collections augment the printed resources of the library and extend the total holdings to more than 640,000 volumes. Online databases and indexes provide full-text access to more than 7,000 current periodical titles. Computer facilities include a campuswide PC and Macintosh computer lab; an additional computer lab is available for students in the Honors Residence Hall.

Athletics La Sierra University has an active intramural program in addition to a competitive varsity program. for basketball and volleyball. The fitness center houses a variety of up-to-date exercise equipment, as well as a climbing wall, outdoor pool, and tennis courts.

Study Abroad Through its affiliation with colleges in France, Germany, Italy, Spain, and Argentina, students may fulfill their foreign language requirements through a summer abroad or may elect to study abroad for a full year.

Support Services The Learning Support Center coordinates services for those with physical or learning disabilities to facilitate educational access to all students.

Job Opportunities Work opportunities on and off campus are available through the Office of Human Resources.

Tuition: $14,940 per year, $415 per quarter hour (2001–02)

Room and Board: $2505 per year minimum (based on double occupancy in the general residence halls or single occupancy in the honors residence hall) for room and $1689 per year minimum for board

Mandatory Fees: $345 per year (2001–02)

Contact: Director: Paul Mallery, Ph.D., South Hall #100, La Sierra University, 4700 Pierce Street, Riverside, California 92515; Telephone: 909-785-2310; E-mail: honors@lasierra.edu; Web site: http://www.lasierra.edu/honors

LAKE LAND COLLEGE

2 Pu G S Sc Tr

▼ Honors Program

In 1978, Lake Land College began its Honors Program. Since that time, 122 students have completed the requirements and have graduated as Lake Land College honors students. The purpose of the program is to provide enriched learning opportunities for superior students through special honors classes and through optional honors independent study and in-course honors independent study in specialized areas. The focus in on the students' academic talents and career goals.

There are currently 43 students enrolled in the program.

Participation Requirements: Program requirements include a minimum 3.5 overall GPA, graduation from a transfer program, and completion of four honors courses (specific classes or independent study—two of the four required honors courses may be independent study) for full-status graduation.

The Honors Program has many advantages, including attending class with other academically talented students. In addition to enriched learning opportunities, honors students may receive special scholarship aid (monetary awards have been made to approximately 15 students per term in this program, in which scholarship is the primary basis for the award); may be recognized by the *National Dean's List, Who's Who In American Junior Colleges*, or *All American Scholars;* will carry an honors designation on their transcripts for each honors course or honors independent study successfully completed; are guests at the annual honors banquet; and receive honors recognition at Commencement.

Admission Process: Students who apply must plan to pursue a college-transfer major at Lake Land College and they must have graduated in the top 10 percent of their high school class or have a composite ACT of 25 or more or have a GPA of 3.5 or above in transfer classes after the completion of at least 12 semester hours of transfer classes.

The Campus Context: Lake Land College is a public community college. Lake Land is located near Mattoon, Illinois, about 45 miles south of Urbana-Champaign and 180 miles south of Chicago. It was founded in 1966. The 308-acre campus hosts seven major buildings plus seven supportive buildings, two campus ponds, a 160-acre agriculture land laboratory, a center for agricultural industries, the 30,000-volume Virgil H. Judge Learning Resource Center, computer labs, a CAD lab, a GIS lab, a child-care lab, a cosmetology clinic, and a dental clinic.

Student Body Lake Land has 5,000 students from across east central Illinois; 49 percent are women.

Interpreting the symbols: **2**=two-year college, **4**=four-year college; **Pu**=public or state college, **Pr**=private college; **G**=general honors program; **D**=departmental honors program; **S**=small program (fewer than 100 students), **M**=midsize program (100 to 500 students), **L**=large program (more than 500 students); **Sc**=scholarships available in honors program; **Tr**=transfer students accepted into honors program; **HBC**=historically black college; **AA**=academic advisors; **GA**=graduate advisors; **FA**=fellowship advisors.

Faculty Seventy-eight percent of full-time faculty members hold master's degrees or higher in their teaching fields. The student-faculty ratio is 21:1.

Honorary Society Phi Theta Kappa

Athletics Lake Land is a member of the National Junior College Athletic Association. Men's sports include baseball, basketball, and tennis. Women's sports include basketball, softball, and volleyball.

Support Services Lake Land College employs a Special Needs Counselor and a Special Populations Coordinator to provide support services to students with a variety of special needs. The architectural design of the campus and buildings is such that Lake Land College has been deemed very accessible by the Illinois Department of Rehabilitation Services.

Tuition: $1296 for area residents, $3336 for state residents, $6852 for nonresidents, per year (1998–99)

Mandatory Fees: $272

Contact: Director: Harold Strangeman, 5001 Lake Land Boulevard, Mattoon, Illinois 61938; Telephone: 217-234-5279; Fax: 217-258-6459; E-mail: hstrange@lakeland.cc.il.us; Web site: http://www.lakeland.cc.il.us/honors/

Lake Superior State University

4 Pu G M Sc Tr

▼ University Honors Program

The Lake Superior State University (LSSU) University Honors Program provides an important dimension of the University's commitment to excellence in teaching and learning. The Honors Program seeks to create a community of scholars characterized by strong student and faculty interaction around the world of ideas. This community fosters an approach to education that incorporates the qualities of self-directed learning, a positive response to demanding work, and an appreciation of knowledge for its own sake.

Classes are limited to 15–18 students, and active participation of students is considered essential to the development of a scholarly community. In addition, an interdisciplinary focus is promoted by the inclusion of students and faculty members from all majors as well as in the course design of the honors core curriculum. Excellence in teaching is emphasized in the selection of faculty members, as is a commitment to working with students in and out of the classroom setting.

Honors students are advised by the Honors Director and by faculty members in their major course of study. They are eligible for advanced scheduling and extended library privileges, opportunities for supportive living and learning arrangements, and an enriched educational experience.

Participation Requirements: The Honors Program student completes 21 credit hours of honors-designated courses. About half of these designated credits may satisfy requirements for General Education and the student's major. The remaining 10 credits meet core requirements for the Honors Program, namely a sophomore- and junior-year seminar as well as the completion of a senior project for honors credit. To remain eligible for participation the Honors Program, students must achieve at least a 3.3 GPA at the end of the sophomore year and a 3.4 GPA at the end of the junior year. Only those students who achieve a 3.5 overall GPA and are active participants in the Honors Program receive an honors degree upon graduation.

Admission Process: Students are invited to become honors candidates as freshmen, based on a combination of ACT scores, high school GPA, essay, and/or an interview. Honors candidates and other full-time students who achieve a GPA of 3.5 for their first two semesters at LSSU are then invited to apply for full admission to the Honors Program.

The Campus Context: LSSU is composed of four schools: the School of Arts, Letters, and Social Sciences; the School of Business and Economics; the School of Engineering Technology and Mathematical Sciences; the School of Health and Natural Sciences. There are sixty-five degree programs offered. Special facilities on campus include a planetarium and a physical education complex with an ice arena, pool, and aquatics laboratory.

Student Body Undergraduate enrollment is 3,400: 52 percent men and 48 percent women. The minority ethnic distribution is .5 percent black, 5.4 percent Native American, .6 percent Asian, and .5 percent Hispanic. International students number 553. The student population is 27 percent resident and 73 percent commuter. Seventy percent of students receive financial aid. There are six fraternities/sororities.

Faculty Of the 175 faculty members, 110 are full-time and 65 percent have terminal degrees. The student-faculty ratio is 19:1.

Key Facilities The library houses 155,000 volumes. Computer facilities include 250 PC stations with Internet and LAN access.

Athletics Lake Superior State offers NCAA Division I men's hockey. All other sports are Division II. Sports offered include men's and women's basketball, men's and women's golf, women's volleyball, men's and women's track, women's softball, men's and women's tennis, and men's and women's cross-country.

Support Services Disabled-student facilities are available.

Job Opportunities Students will find many work opportunities on campus.

Tuition: $4334 for state residents, $6948 for nonresidents, per year

Room and Board: $5231

Contact: Director: Dr. Diana R. Pingatore, 234 Library, Sault Ste. Marie, Michigan 49783; Telephone: 906-635-2101; Fax: 906-635-6678; E-mail: dpingatore@lakers.lssu.edu; Web site: http://www.lssu.edu

Lamar University

4 Pu G M Sc Tr

▼ University Honors Program

The University Honors Program at Lamar is designed to bring out the best in academically talented students and to serve as a core of academic excellence within the University community. Lamar's honors students enjoy the privilege of small classes taught by some of the best professors Lamar has to offer. Students also have opportunities to work with these professors on special projects and independent study. Lamar's honors students are encouraged to do research—including an honors thesis—and to publish and present their work regionally and nationally. Scholarships and grants support students in off-campus internships, field study, and study-abroad programs. Most recently, honors students have participated in internships in Washington, D.C., and at NASA. Through the Honors Student Association, students engage in service projects and are active in campus life. Students also have the opportunity to associate with other Honors Program students in Lamar's newest residence hall, Cardinal Village, which opened in fall 2001. On the Lamar campus, the University Honors Program is housed in the ROTC Building. Facilities include offices (Rooms 102 and 106), as well as a student lounge (103) and a conference room (104). The Honors Program also has access to a large meeting/classroom in the ROTC Building. The Honors Program is governed by the University Honors Council, which has faculty representatives from all colleges of the University. The Executive Council of the

Honors Student Association serves as an advisory board to the Honors Program Director.

The Honors Program has served the needs of Lamar's intellectually gifted students since the mid-1960s. More than 180 students are active participants in the Honors Program.

Participation Requirements: Honors Program students should take one or more honors classes each semester during their first two years at Lamar. The majority of the University's core curriculum requirements may be completed as honors, and advanced interdisciplinary seminars are available. Many students also choose to take an Honors Independent Study class, which enables them to conduct research or engage in creative activity under the supervision of a faculty member of their choice. Continued enrollment in the Honors Program requires that the student maintain at least a 3.1 GPA.

All students entering the University Honors Program are encouraged to work toward becoming Honors Program graduates. There are two ways to achieve this distinction. The student may complete 24 hours of honors classes, including 6 hours of the Honors Thesis. The thesis represents original research or creative work produced by the student under the direction of a faculty supervisor. Alternatively, the student may complete 27 hours of honors classes, at least 9 hours of which are upper-level honors classes.

Special recognition is given to Honors Program graduates at University commencement, including the opportunity to wear the Honors Program medallion. The status of Honors Program Graduate is also permanently affixed to the individual's official University transcript.

Admission Process: Incoming freshmen desiring to participate in the University Honors Program at Lamar must complete an application form and forward it, along with an official copy of the high school transcript indicating class rank and SAT or ACT score, to the Director of the Honors Program. The application must be accompanied by two letters of recommendation from the student's teachers, counselors, administrators, or supervisors and a brief resume of the student's high school activities and achievements. Entering freshmen must have an SAT score of 1100 (ACT 24) or above and exhibit a record of academic achievement and community involvement.

To be considered for scholarships, students must submit their applications for admission to the Honors Program by the last day of February in the year the student expects to enter Lamar in the fall semester. Others seeking participation in the program may apply at any time. Application forms are available from the Honors Program offices.

Scholarship Availability: The McMaster Honors Scholarships at Lamar were instituted in 1976 in memory of Mr. and Mrs. M. W. McMaster of Beaumont. This fund now has an endowment of $2.5 million. The program offers financial support to students both in the form of McMaster Honors Scholarships and in the form of grants to facilitate student participation in research and other enriching educational experiences. McMaster Scholarships range from $500 to $1250 per semester and may be received in combination with other scholarships from the University or the student's major department. In addition, the Tom Jones Memorial Fund provides more than $5500 yearly for two or more honors scholarships. In fall 2001, the Honors Program disbursed more than $60,000 in scholarships to 68 students.

Both incoming freshmen and honors students already enrolled at Lamar may apply for McMaster Honors Scholarships. Eligibility for Honors Scholarships requires an SAT score of 1200 (ACT 27) or above for incoming freshmen and a GPA of 3.2 or higher for current Lamar Honors Program students. Recipients of the scholarships must complete at least one honors class each semester, maintain a minimum 3.2 GPA, perform at least 12 hours of volunteer service per semester, and participate in Honors Program activities, including the Honors Student Association.

Incoming freshmen must submit a McMaster Scholarship application in addition to the Honors Program application, including an official high school transcript. The scholarship application must be supplemented by a letter or essay as described on the application form. Current Lamar students must submit two faculty member recommendation forms. All materials must be postmarked no later than the last day of February. Scholarships are allocated by the Lamar University Honors Council, and notification letters are mailed out before the end of March. Application forms for the McMaster Honors Scholarships are available from the Honors Program Office. Receiving an Honors Program scholarship does not prevent students from applying for other Lamar University scholarships. Students should contact the Scholarships Office at 409-880-1714.

The Campus Context: Lamar University, established in 1923 and commissioned by the Texas Legislature, provides an educational, scientific, technical, and cultural resource center committed to the threefold mission of teaching, research, and service. The University, which is a member of the Texas State University System, emphasizes general education, student access to faculty members, and careful counseling of students. Lamar University creates a liberating educational experience for each student by expanding knowledge, awakening new intellectual interests, examining values, developing talents, providing new skills, and preparing each student to assume an effective role as a citizen.

The University's major divisions are five colleges: Arts and Sciences, Business, Education and Human Development, Engineering, and Fine Arts and Communication. An additional division is the College of Graduate Studies. A health center, religious centers, and recreational centers provide for students' needs. The Setzer Student Center offers facilities for leisure-time recreation and houses the offices of the Setzer Student Center Council, Student Government Association, and student publications.

Lamar University is accredited by the Commission on Colleges of the Southern Association of Colleges and Schools to award associate, bachelor's, master's, and doctoral degrees and is approved by the Texas Education Agency.

Student Body Lamar enrolls more than 8,000 students each semester. The student body is ethnically diverse (74 percent white, 15 percent black, 4 percent Hispanic, 3 percent Asian). Lamar provides opportunities for academic achievement and campus involvement regardless of race, gender, ethnicity, or religion.

Faculty Lamar's faculty is composed of 366 outstanding teacher-scholars, with a classroom student-teacher ratio of 22:1. Most faculty members have terminal degrees in their field and contribute to research, academic writing and publishing, and professional and community services.

Key Facilities The Mary and John Gray Library houses more than a million volumes and provides electronic access to many times that. A media center on the seventh floor provides computers for student use. Many departments, including the University Honors Program, also maintain computer labs and libraries for students.

Honorary Societies Phi Kappa Phi, Alpha Lambda Delta, Phi Eta Sigma, Blue Key

Athletics Lamar athletic teams compete in NCAA Division I intercollegiate athletics in baseball, basketball, golf, tennis, track, and volleyball.

Study Abroad Several international study opportunities are available to Lamar University students. Scholarship support is available through the University Honors Program.

Interpreting the symbols: **2**=two-year college, **4**=four-year college; **Pu**=public or state college, **Pr**=private college; **G**=general honors program; **D**=departmental honors program; **S**=small program (fewer than 100 students), **M**=midsize program (100 to 500 students), **L**=large program (more than 500 students); **Sc**=scholarships available in honors program; **Tr**=transfer students accepted into honors program; **HBC**=historically black college; **AA**=academic advisors; **GA**=graduate advisors; **FA**=fellowship advisors.

Support Services Through the Office of Services for Students with Disabilities, Lamar University makes education and campus life available to all students. Lamar has an internationally known program in deaf studies and deaf education and offers signers and other support for deaf students.

Job Opportunities Lamar students may qualify for work-study or apply for jobs in many of the departments and programs on campus. Internships and cooperative programs are available in many major departments.

Tuition: In-state tuition for an academic load of 15 hours is $1080 per semester in 2002–03. Out-of-state students pay $4245 for tuition per semester for a 15-hour course load. Certain students receiving competitive academic scholarships may be exempt from the payment of out-of-state tuition rates.

Room and Board: Costs of room and board vary depending on location. At Lamar's newest facility, Cardinal Village, students pay $1525 per semester for a suite that includes a private bedroom and a living room and full bath shared with a suite-mate. At Brooks-Shivers Hall, students pay $931 for a shared room. A typical meal plan costs $830 per semester.

Mandatory Fees: Fees assessed by Lamar for all students include a student services fee, a Setzer Student Center fee, a property deposit, a charge for the student ID, a computer use fee, a library use fee, and a health center fee. The parking fee is optional. With the addition of these standard fees and an estimated expenditure for books, the cost of a semester at Lamar University is $1378 in 2002–03 for a Texas resident. Some additional fees are assessed for specific courses.

Contact: Dr. Donna Birdwell-Sykes, Director, University Honors Program, Lamar University, P.O. Box 10968, Beaumont, Texas 77710; Telephone: 409-880-8648; Fax: 409-880-2325; E-mail: birdwell@hal.lamar.edu; Web site: http://hal.lamar.edu/~honors

LAREDO COMMUNITY COLLEGE

2 Pu G S Sc AA

▼ Laredo Community College Honors Program

The Laredo Community College (LCC) Honors Program serves academically gifted students from the Laredo area. The program is unique in that it provides full scholarships covering tuition, fees, and books to 25 freshman students based on merit. Students who maintain eligibility continue to receive the scholarship their sophomore year.

The LCC Honors Program is guided by its mission to encourage students to become outstanding independent learners, capable of critical thinking and self-expression; provide students with opportunities to engage in meaningful teamwork; allow students to explore facets of learning and materials that are usually unavailable in regular courses; increase opportunities for reading and writing at an advanced level; enhance mathematical, scientific, and technological skills; provide for a higher degree of student participation and involvement; and increase the opportunity for academically gifted students to transfer to a major university.

The honors curriculum includes all component areas of the core. It offers designated courses in the humanities, social and behavioral sciences, and mathematics, with contract courses available in the natural sciences and other disciplines. Honors classes are taught by faculty members who are dedicated to presenting students with the most stimulating educational experience and environment possible. Small classes (10–25 students) allow optimum interaction between faculty members and students.

In addition to their classroom experiences, honors students participate in a variety of student development activities. The Honors Student Council meets regularly to plan distinguished-speaker programs, leadership seminars, field trips, community service activities, fund-raisers, and other social events. Each year two sophomore students recognized for their outstanding achievement by honors faculty members are provided with funding to attend the National Collegiate Honors Council (NCHC) national conference. Also, sophomore students (on a rotation basis) have the distinction of serving as student representatives at the College's Board of Trustees meetings. An honors lounge located adjacent to the Honors Office in the Kazen College Center is a gathering place for students to study or just relax and socialize.

Founded in 1988, the program has a maximum enrollment of 50 students.

Participation Requirements: Honors students must successfully complete a minimum of 24 semester credit hours of honors courses. Students take designated honors courses and contract courses to fulfill this requirement. They must maintain an overall GPA of 3.0 and earn no grade lower than C in any course. All honors classes are indicated on official transcripts. Honors program graduates receive a special diploma, wear the honors stole, and are personally recognized during the graduation ceremony by the College president who dons each student with the honors medallion.

Admission Process: To qualify for the honors program, a student must meet at least one of the following requirements: ACT composite score of 23, SAT composite score of 1070, academic recognition on TAAS, or rank in the top 10 percent of the high school class. Final selection is based upon an interview with the Honors Selection Committee. Application forms are available at all area high school counseling centers or at the LCC Honors Office. Each year, the deadline for submitting applications is February 15. A current high school transcript and two letters of recommendation must be included with the application.

Scholarship Availability: The honors program provides full scholarships covering tuition, fees, and books. Scholarships are limited to fall and spring semesters, up to 66 semester credit hours.

The Campus Context: Laredo Community College, located on 200 acres along a scenic bend of the Rio Grande, is a comprehensive institution of higher education, leading the region with innovative instruction. LCC was established in 1946 on the grounds of historic Fort McIntosh. Through its unique blend of modern and historic structures and with caring faculty members recognized nationwide for its focus on student success, LCC provides more than fifty programs of study.

Students attending LCC have many educational options—Associate of Arts, Science, and Applied Science Degrees; technical/vocational certificates leading to immediate employment; course work leading to a bachelor's degree; courses for personal enrichment; noncredit community-interest courses; and adult education and GED training.

LCC is a leader in the region for delivering educational services through distance learning technology, offering courses through video conferencing and the Internet. The College's cable channel provides 23,000 households with educational programming.

Located on the north side of the campus, the Lamar Bruni Vergara Environmental Science Center is a learning laboratory for college students and local school children. A second LCC campus opens its doors in 2004.

Student Body In the fall of 2001, 7,493 students enrolled for college credit courses at Laredo Community College. Statistics show that 93 percent of these students were Hispanic, and 59 percent were women. Approximately 6,000 additional students attended adult education, continuing education, and specialized training programs offered by LCC on the campus and at locations throughout the community.

Faculty Of the 327 faculty members employed at Laredo Community College, 185 are full-time and 142 are adjuncts.

Key Facilities The Harold R. Yeary Library houses approximately 96,500 bound volumes and receives 390 current periodical subscriptions. It is equipped with a comprehensive automation system that offers enhanced access and research capabilities. The Yeary Library also manages the Corral, a high-technology study center that features sixty computers for student use.

Honorary Society Phi Theta Kappa

Athletics Laredo Community College belongs to the Region XIV Athletic Conference and NJCAA, fielding men's baseball, women's volleyball, and coed tennis teams. Intramural activities in all seasonal sports are also available to students.

Study Abroad Some departments and programs sponsor study abroad, but trips are organized individually and are not subsidized by the school.

Support Services The Student Support Services Program at LCC is designed to enhance academic skills, increase retention and graduation rates, facilitate entrance into four-year colleges, and foster a climate that supports the success of low-income/first generation college students and students with disabilities. Specialized support services are available to meet the needs of special populations, such as disabled students, nontraditional students, single parents, returning older students, or retrained workers.

Job Opportunities Both federal and institutional funds are available for student workers on campus.

Tuition: For the 2000–01 academic year, a full load of 15 semester credit hours costs $315 for in-district students, $630 for out-of-district students, and $1050 for out-of-state and foreign students. Cost includes tuition only.

Room and Board: The cost for a standard dorm room per semester is $1010 and $340 per summer session. For rooms with a full-size kitchen, the rent is $1070 per semester and $360 per summer session.

Mandatory Fees: For the 2000–01 academic year, mandatory fees for all students included $18 for health services and matriculation plus a $13 per hour general fee and a $1 per hour activity fee. There are additional fees for classes with labs.

Contact: Honors Coordinator: Anna Maria G. Mendiola, Honors Program, Box 226, West End Washington Street, Laredo, Texas 78040; Telephone: 956-764-5956; Fax: 956-764-5923; E-mail: amendiola@laredo.cc.tx.us; Web site: http://www.laredo.cc.tx.us (Students should select Instructional Departments to navigate to the honors program section of the site.)

Lasell College

4 Pr G S Tr

▼ Honors Program

The Honors Program emphasizes the Lasell hallmarks of student-centered teaching, connected learning, and social responsibility in creating an environment that meets the needs of highly motivated, enthusiastic students. The Program encourages students to explore broadly across disciplines and probe deeply in their chosen field of study. Students gain facility with synthesis of complex ideas, application of knowledge to problems in the professional world, and collaboration with peers and faculty. Students participate in community service to build leadership skills and responsibility. Through a mix of discussions, field explorations, independent and collaborative projects, and personal attention, the program strives to foster a lifelong love of learning and independent thinking. Designation as a Lasell Honor Student represents a high level of academic achievement and unique accomplishments that demonstrate initiative and responsibility.

The objectives of the Honors Program are consistent with the educational objectives of the College but are designed for highly motivated students to work more intensively and creatively to achieve the following: improvement of their writing skills, improvement of their oral communication and presentation skills, learning to work in collaboration with peers, learning to approach issues from an interdisciplinary perspective, connecting theory to practice by completing a community-based project, and demonstration of leadership skills through community service.

Participation Requirements: Students are required to complete eight courses in the Honors Program to be awarded the honors designation on their transcript. The eight courses include four required courses and four honors electives or directed studies. Required honors courses include Honors Colloquium (1c) 100 level, first year (topic for fall 2001: Building Community); Honors Seminar I (3c) 200 level, second year (topic for fall 2001: Change); Honors Seminar II (3c) 300 level, third year (topic for fall 2001: Leadership); Honors Capstone Course (3c) 400 level, fourth year (linked to major). The specific topics of these courses may change every year.

In addition to the above required courses, students must choose four honors courses, two of which must be at the 200 level or higher and have an honors designation. Possible options for honors-level courses include honors writing I, honors writing II (students must place into honors writing classes independently of admission into Honors Program), special topics seminar, honors colloquium II and III (1c offered as needed), leadership II (offered as needed).

Each spring semester there will be different honors courses. Honors students are notified of options through the College Registrar and the Honors Program Director.

Specified courses across the college curriculum are identified that have an additional honors component. Students do not receive additional credit for an honors component, but the honors component is designated as such on their transcripts. Honors component courses count as electives towards the honors distribution requirement.

Students must maintain a 3.3 overall cumulative average to stay in the Honors Program or otherwise demonstrate their continuing eligibility through faculty recommendations and in consultation with the Honors Program Director. If they are unable to do this, they may be asked to take a leave of absence from the program and may request readmission to the Honors Program after one semester. They are required to demonstrate eligibility at that time in consultation with the Honors Program Director.

Students who graduate having completed the Honors Program are acknowledged as Honors Program graduates in the printed commencement program and when called up to receive their diplomas; completion of the Honors Program is also indicated on their transcripts (and they receive an Honors Program completion diploma).

Admission Process: Admission requirements for first-year student admissions during the first semester include a combination of high school GPA, SAT scores, and demonstrated ability to engage in challenging learning experiences (as indicated in admissions application folder). Requirements for admission in the second semester include recommendation of a faculty member, a written statement, and demonstrated ability to engage in challenging learning experiences. For sophomore admission requirements include recommendation by a faculty member, a written

Interpreting the symbols: **2**=two-year college, **4**=four-year college; **Pu**=public or state college, **Pr**=private college; **G**=general honors program; **D**=departmental honors program; **S**=small program (fewer than 100 students), **M**=midsize program (100 to 500 students), **L**=large program (more than 500 students); **Sc**=scholarships available in honors program; **Tr**=transfer students accepted into honors program; **HBC**=historically black college; **AA**=academic advisors; **GA**=graduate advisors; **FA**=fellowship advisors.

statement, and demonstrated ability to engage in challenging learning experiences.

Admission requirements for transfer students (sophomore year only) include a combination of GPA, written statement, and demonstrated ability to engage in challenging learning experiences.

Students in the junior and senior year are not eligible for entry into the Honors Program due to the limited time students would have to complete the requirements. Students are allowed to take an honors course and should refer to the petition policy.

Students not in the Honors Program may petition to take an honors course. Students must complete and submit an Honors Course Request Form in writing to the Honors Director. The requests are reviewed by the Honors Program Director.

The Campus Context: Founded in 1851, Lasell College is a four-year, coeducational, independent, nonsectarian institution of higher education organized around a central educational purpose called "connected learning." Predominantly a residential college with an emphasis on teaching and lifelong learning, Lasell seeks to provide a stimulating environment for the intellectual and personal growth of students in its degree and nondegree programs. In spring 2000, the College opened Lasell Village, the nation's first educational continuing care retirement community. Lasell College is located in Auburndale, Massachusetts, which is a village of Newton, a residential suburb bordering Boston. The "T," Boston's mass transit system, is conveniently located within walking distance of the campus. Spacious lawns and varied foliage provide an attractive setting for the forty-five College buildings, which range in style from Victorian to modern. Distinctive facilities include the Yamawaki Art and Cultural Center, the Athletic Center, and the Winslow Academic Center, which houses state-of-the-art, high-technology classrooms. Tree-lined streets, two athletic fields, the Charles River, and five tennis courts provide abundant opportunity for outdoor activities.

Student Body Lasell's full-time enrollment is at a twenty-eight-year high, with approximately 900 students. The ethnic distribution of students is 10 percent African American, 5 percent Asian American, 6 percent Hispanic, 73 percent white, and 3 percent international. Approximately 50 percent of the students are out-of-state students, and approximately 80 percent live on campus.

Faculty The faculty members total 130, of whom 44 are full-time. Thirty-five percent of the faculty members have terminal degrees. The student-faculty ratio is 11:1.

Key Facilities The Brennan Library houses a collection of more than 55,000 books, more than 70 electronic databases, and hundreds of periodicals. The library is a member of the Minuteman Library Network, which provides access to more than 5 million volumes from more than forty libraries. The Brennan Library provides access to the Internet as well as many electronic databases, print, and nonprint material. There is a state-of-the-art library lab with computers for hands-on library instruction. All of Lasell's academic and residential buildings are networked with fiber-optic cable, providing high-speed access to the Internet and the College Intranet. There are five state-of-the-art computer labs with a wide assortment of software, including graphics software, business applications, statistical packages, experimental programs, tutorials, and Microsoft Office.

Athletics Lasell College holds membership in the NCAA Division III and competes in a total of twelve varsity sports. Women's teams are fielded in basketball, cross-country, field hockey, lacrosse, soccer, softball, and volleyball. Men's teams are fielded in basketball, cross-country, lacrosse, soccer, and volleyball. Intramural and noncredit activities are also offered throughout the academic year.

Study Abroad In 1988, the College established a sister-college relationship with Yamawaki Gakuen Junior College in Tokyo. Faculty members and students from each college participate in monthlong visits, combining lectures with extensive field experience. Independent-study credit may be arranged with permission of the College. Other study abroad opportunities are also available.

Support Services The Lasell Learning Center offers academic support services to assist students in building stronger foundation skills and in further developing their potential, strengths, and confidence. The Center conducts workshops and study groups throughout the academic year.

Job Opportunities The Lasell curriculum, built on the concept of "connected learning," combines breadth in the arts and sciences, professional arts courses, and educational projects that tackle real issues. All of Lasell's degree-granting programs include practical experience through course-based projects, internships, practicums, clinical affiliations, and on-site training, including two on-campus child-care centers, an on-campus inn, and Lasell Village. Work-study opportunities are available on campus.

The Office of Career Services is available to assist students with career preparation (e.g., resume writing and interviewing skills) throughout their undergraduate years.

Tuition: $15,300 per year (2001–02)

Comprehensive Fee: $800

Room and Board: $8000

Contact: Director: Steven F. Bloom, Dean, School of Arts and Sciences and Director of General Education and the Honors Program, Lasell College, 1844 Commonwealth Avenue, Newton, Massachusetts, 02466; Telephone: 617-796-4695; Fax: 617-243-2480; E-mail: sbloom@lasell.edu; Web site: http://www.lasell.edu/html/honors.html

Le Moyne College

4 Pr G S Tr

▼ Integral Honors Program

The Integral Honors Program at Le Moyne College offers the exceptional student an outstanding educational opportunity. While all students are required to balance courses in a major area with core humanities requirements, the Integral Honors Program student participates in an interdisciplinary sequence designed to encourage learning at an advanced level. The students enjoy the challenge presented by their peers in these honors classes. Both current students and alumni/ae cite the atmosphere of warmth, support, collegiality, and intellectual excitement among participants as one of the chief benefits of the Integral Honors Program. All honors courses are team-taught by faculty members from different disciplines, so that students develop an appreciation for the complexity of the issues and texts studied. The capstone experience of the Integral Honors Program is the senior project, which each student initiates and pursues under the direction of a faculty mentor. A public defense of each project in the spring of senior year is a suitable finale to the student's distinguished undergraduate career.

Le Moyne College recognizes Integral Honors students by according them distinctive privileges. For example, although participants in the Integral Honors Program pay regular tuition, they have the privilege of taking extra courses without charge. (These added hours, however, may not be applied to early graduation.) From the spring of junior year through senior year, Integral Honors students enjoy extended borrowing privileges at the Noreen Reale Falcone Library. An Honors House reserved for the use of participants in the Integral Honors Program offers students a place to study, meet, or just relax.

The program serves all majors, and all are represented in its enrollment. Although the program is challenging, members find time to participate in such campus activities as student government, the performing arts, journalism, varsity and intramural athletics, campus ministry, and community service. In addition, the Integral Honors student has opportunities to participate in special curricular and cocurricular activities. In recent years,

Integral Honors students have traveled to New York and Boston to visit museums and to participate in conferences, planned trips to the theater, and sponsored major lectures as well as informal discussions. Each Integral Honors class elects representatives to serve on the Student Honors Council, which has primary responsibility for initiating and planning activities for the program. The Student Honors Council also serves as an advisory body to the Director of the Integral Honors Program for the governance of the program.

A number of departments at Le Moyne offer departmental honors to qualified students, usually through the submission of a senior thesis. The departmental honors option is designed for the student who excels chiefly in the major or for the transfer student who enters Le Moyne too late to participate in the Integral Honors Program. The Integral Honors degree remains the highest distinction conferred by Le Moyne, and includes departmental honors.

The Integral Honors Program was founded in 1982, although a version of an honors program had existed since 1961. The current enrollment is 66 students.

Participation Requirements: In the freshman, sophomore, and senior years, the Integral Honors student enrolls in the honors humanities sequence, which covers developments, ideas, controversies, and classic works from antiquity to the present. This 21-hour series of courses replaces as many hours of general education (core) requirements in the humanities. Along with some lectures, the honors humanities sequence builds on discussions and student presentations, so that students become increasingly responsible for their own learning. In the junior year, the Integral Honors student takes Interdisciplinary Approaches to Knowing: Theory and Applications. One of the goals of this course is to prepare the student for the challenges of the senior project. The senior project, completed under the guidance of a professor-mentor, is the capstone of the Integral Honors Program and allows the student to demonstrate his or her scholarly or creative abilities. The program offers a music elective in alternate years that takes advantage of the rich variety of live performances of music in the area. A student must earn a grade of at least B in each Integral Honors course to maintain Integral Honors status. Although Integral Honors students typically place on the Dean's List (minimum GPA 3.5), a GPA of at least 3.25 is required for graduation with the Integral Honors degree.

Admission Process: The honors humanities sequence does not begin until spring of freshman year, so that students have an opportunity to adjust to campus life before entering the program. In October, all first-year students are invited to a meeting to learn more about the Integral Honors Program and to pick up an application for the program. Outstanding students nominated by the faculty, along with recipients of academic scholarships, receive special invitations and encouragement to apply. Recipients of Presidential scholarships, the most prestigious academic scholarships at Le Moyne, are guaranteed placement in the program should they choose to participate; many of them do. A Faculty Honors Committee comprising representatives from all academic divisions reviews the applications, including high school records, SAT I and other standardized test scores, AP and other college-level work, past and current activities, midsemester grades, a writing sample, a brief statement explaining the candidate's interest in the program, and any other material the candidate may wish to supply. Although the majority of each class begins the program in the spring of freshman year, qualified students, including transfer students, are considered for admission to the sophomore class. Students who enroll at Le Moyne after completing the sophomore year are not eligible for participation in the Integral Honors Program but may be eligible for departmental honors.

Scholarship Availability: Le Moyne offers a generous array of merit-based academic scholarships, along with other forms of financial aid, through the Admissions Office. Although most students admitted to the Integral Honors Program are recipients of merit-based scholarships, Le Moyne does not require those who hold such scholarships to participate in the program.

The Campus Context: Le Moyne College is a four-year Jesuit college that balances a comprehensive liberal arts education with preparation for specific career paths or graduate study. Le Moyne is primarily an undergraduate institution. Average class size is 21 students. No teaching assistants instruct students in any department. The campus environment is one of a closely knit community. Le Moyne's personal approach to education is reflected in the quality of contact between students and faculty members. Student organizations plan concerts, dances, a weekly film series, student talent programs, and special lectures as well as off-campus excursions. The quiet 150-acre tree-lined campus is located in a residential setting 10 minutes from Syracuse, the heart of New York State, whose metropolitan population is about 240,000. Theaters, museums, and other cultural attractions are easily accessible via the public transportation service, which schedules regular stops at the campus; just a few miles outside the city are rolling hills, picturesque lakes, and miles of open country.

Student Body The undergraduate population of Le Moyne includes approximately 2,150 full-time students and 295 part-time students. Undergraduate enrollment is 59 percent women. The ethnic distribution is 88 percent white, 4 percent black, 3 percent Hispanic, 1 percent Asian, 1 percent Native American, and 3 percent other. Eighty percent of full-time undergraduates live in residence halls and townhouses on campus. Financial aid is offered to 95 percent of Le Moyne's students through scholarships, grants, loans, and work-study assignments. A wide range of student-directed activities, athletics, clubs, and service organizations complement the academic experience.

Faculty The Le Moyne full-time faculty numbers 139 men and women; 90 percent have earned the highest degree in their fields. The student-faculty ratio is 14:1.

Key Facilities The Noreen Reale Falcone Library has 215,395 volumes in open stacks. The extensive campus computing system is constantly being upgraded; many classrooms have multimedia capabilities.

Athletics Le Moyne has sixteen NCAA intercollegiate teams, eight for men and eight for women. Men's baseball and women's lacrosse are Division I; other sports are Division II. Intramural sports are also popular; altogether, three quarters of the student body participates in athletics.

Study Abroad The study-abroad program allows students to spend semesters in Australia, Japan, Italy, Spain, France, England, Ireland, and a variety of other countries. Le Moyne is a participant in the sixty-member New York State Visiting Student Program. The Integral Honors Program encourages participants to take advantage of study-abroad and other off-campus opportunities, such as externships. The Honors Program also offers a Le Moyne course in Guatemala during the late summer and early fall. This course is taught by Le Moyne's honors faculty in Guatemala City and Antigua, Guatemala. It is an interdisciplinary study of the contemporary world, and it has been specially designed for Le Moyne's Honors Program's students.

Support Services The Academic Support Center provides services for students with special needs, including those with physical handicaps and learning disabilities.

Job Opportunities Le Moyne administers an AmeriCorps grant that subsidizes students who work in community service positions. Work-study jobs are available on campus. In addition, many depart-

Interpreting the symbols: **2**=two-year college, **4**=four-year college; **Pu**=public or state college, **Pr**=private college; **G**=general honors program; **D**=departmental honors program; **S**=small program (fewer than 100 students), **M**=midsize program (100 to 500 students), **L**=large program (more than 500 students); **Sc**=scholarships available in honors program; **Tr**=transfer students accepted into honors program; **HBC**=historically black college; **AA**=academic advisors; **GA**=graduate advisors; **FA**=fellowship advisors.

ments and programs support students who seek to gain experience through internships.

Tuition: $16,350

Room and Board: $6990

Mandatory Fees: $470

Contact: Director: Mario Saenz, 1419 Salt Springs Road, Syracuse, New York 13214-1399; Telephone: 315-445-4470; Fax: 315-445-6017; E-mail: saenz@mail.lemoyne.edu

LEE COLLEGE

2 Pu G S Sc Tr

▼ Honors Program

The Honors Program at Lee College serves academically talented and highly motivated students. Honors at Lee College reflects the College's mission statement by providing high-quality instruction for its students and preparing them for success in higher education or employment. The program also promotes the College's goals of continued review and revitalization of existing curricula, academic programs, and course offerings while improving recruitment and retention.

Historically, the program has been faculty and student inspired with individual faculty members or students proposing courses. The Honors Program presently consists of team-taught interdisciplinary courses in American studies (offering credit in American history and American literature), environmental science and chemistry, and freshman composition and humanities. Honors contracts, which provide students the opportunity to work on a one-to-one-basis with faculty members, are presently available in eighteen disciplines including accounting, allied health, applied music, biology, chemistry, English, environmental science, government, history, humanities, journalism, kinesiology, literature, philosophy, physics, psychology, sociology, and theater arts. The nature of the contractual arrangements varies from course to course according to the characteristics of the discipline involved.

In addition to the intellectual challenge, honors offers students the following educational advantages: scholarship opportunities, classes limited to 14 students, an honors study suite with computers dedicated exclusively to honors, participation in the governance of the Honors Program, counseling and transfer advisement, college financial support for student travel for presentations at scholarly conferences and conventions, and opportunities to publish. Students enrolled in honors belong to the Student Honors Council, which serves to support the Honors Program and sponsors a fall retreat to promote esprit de corps among honors students. A spring lyceum offers honors students the opportunity to present their work to the College community. Students also participate in the spring and fall symposiums of the Gulf Coast Intercollegiate Honors Conference (GCIHC) and the annual meeting of the Great Plains Honors Conference. Students who present papers at symposiums and conferences or who publish have it so noted on transcripts. The Lee College Honors Program publishes *Touchstone,* the Texas State Historical Association's journal of undergraduate research. Lee College has articulation agreements in honors with a number of public and private universities throughout the state of Texas.

Honors at Lee College began thirty-six years ago with a team-taught, interdisciplinary American studies course. However, the program has recently undergone considerable expansion as the consequence of the appointment of an honors coordinator in 1994. Currently, approximately 70 students are either enrolled in interdisciplinary honors courses or are pursuing honors contracts.

Participation Requirements: The Lee College Honors Program is designed to be an open-ended program that offers students the option of pursuing either full participation or a limited number of hours. Each honors course or contract completed with a grade of B or better is designated honors on transcripts; "completed Honors Program" is noted on the permanent transcript of students who earn 15 hours of more in honors with a cumulative GPA of at least 3.25 on a 4.0 scale.

Admission Process: Students desiring to enroll in honors must meet any two of the following requirements: minimum ACT scores of 26, SAT I scores of 1100 and above (for English honors, must also have a verbal score of 500 and above), 9 or more hours of college-level work with a GPA of 3.5 or better, a minimum score of 6 on the Lee College English placement test and 13 on the reading test (or CPT 82 or above), rank in top 10 percent of high school class, interview with and approval of the honors instructor teaching the class or offering the contract, and recommendation(s) from previous instructor(s).

Scholarship Availability: There are fifteen scholarships available in general honors and six in American Studies. Honors students are also eligible for other scholarships offered by the Lee College Foundation.

The Campus Context: Lee College is a public community college located in Baytown on the Texas Gulf Coast, approximately 30 miles east of Houston. The College is situated on an attractive and well-maintained 37-acre campus that is undergoing a $20-million renovation. This includes construction of a new library/technical center as well as a state-of-the-art gymnasium and health center.

The College offers students two-year Associate of Arts, Associate of Science, and Associate in Applied Science degrees that encompass thirty-four disciplines and twenty-seven technical areas as well as transfer programs that prepare students for baccalaureate degrees at public and private colleges across the state and nation.

One of Lee College's proudest claims is its sixty-eight-year history, the second longest for community colleges in the state of Texas. It has, over the years, consistently been one of the premier community colleges in the state, with an excellently credentialed and long-tenured faculty, financial stability founded on the excellent tax base of the area and the fiscal wisdom of its elected Board of Regents, and the growth of enrollments in its programs.

Student Body The Baytown campus has slightly fewer than 12,000 students per year. In the 1999–2000 school year, 62 percent of students were white; 20 percent, Hispanic; 14 percent, African American; and 3 percent, other. Fifty-five percent of all campus students were women.

Faculty The College has about 150 full-time faculty members, with a varying number of part-time instructors. The percentage of class sections taught by full-time faculty members is approximately 60. The faculty is long-tenured and well-credentialed, but due to the large number of vocational programs offered, only about 30 percent have terminal degrees.

Key Facilities The Library houses approximately 100,000 volumes and 98,000 microforms, has access to several electronic databases, and is a selective federal documents depository, which makes federal agency publications available to the public. The library is a member of TexShare, which allows students, with their TexShare Borrower's Card, to borrow materials from other academic libraries across the state. The library has twenty-one Internet workstations and a staffed twenty-four-station computer lab. Including those in the Library, the College has more than 800 computers in thirty-two labs available to students across the campus.

Honorary Societies Alpha Beta Gamma, Phi Theta Kappa, and Psi Beta

Athletics As an integral part of the College, the Athletic Program promotes and develops athletic excellence, sound academic standards, principles of sportsmanship, educational values, and ethical conduct in accordance with the constitution and by-laws of the National Junior College Athletic Association (NJCAA) and the Region XIV Athletic Conference. Three programs comprise the interscholastic Athletic Program at the College: men's basketball, women's tennis, and women's volleyball. All of these programs compete as Division I full-scholarship programs. The College also sponsors intramural competitions.

Support Services Lee College works closely with the Texas Rehabilitation Commission to aid students with disabilities and encourages students with disabilities to participate fully in campus life. The College designates a member of the Counseling Center staff as the Counselor for Students with Disabilities. The counselor provides personal and academic counseling, tutoring, and loan of equipment and works with students on advocacy issues. Interpreters make it possible for students with hearing impairments to access all areas of college life. Facilities include wheelchair ramps, elevators, and restrooms in instructional buildings.

Job Opportunities Lee College participates in the Federal Work-Study Program. In addition, there are numerous student assistant jobs available on campus. The Counseling Center includes a job placement office that functions as an equal opportunity employer-reference service for students and alumni.

Tuition: $14 per semester credit hour with an $84 minimum for in-district students, $14 per semester credit hour with an $84 minimum plus a surcharge of $18 per semester credit hour for out-of-district students, $40 per semester credit hour with a $200 minimum for nonresidents (2001–02)

Mandatory Fees: $73–$181

Contact: Honors Coordinator: John C. Britt, Lee College, P.O. Box 818, Baytown, Texas 77522; Telephone: 281-425-6375; Fax: 832-556-4023; E-mail: jbritt@lee.edu

Lehman College, City University of New York

4 Pu C M Tr AA

▼ The Lehman Scholars Program and the City University of New York Honors College: University Scholars Program

The Lehman Scholars Program (LSP) is designed for capable and highly motivated students who have the desire and ability to pursue a somewhat more traditional liberal arts course of study. The program offers the advantages of a small, intimate college, including special courses, seminars, and individual counseling. LSP was founded in 1980 and currently has more than 200 students.

Participation Requirements: Students are exempt from all degree requirements. The Lehman Scholars Program has its own requirements. Students must fulfill a one-semester honors course in English composition and stylistics; two years of a language other than English at the college level or its equivalent; four honors seminars, which include three at the 100-level and one at the 300-level from any of four different academic areas (fine and performing arts, humanities, natural science, and social science); and a senior honors essay. There is one exception to these requirements. Students who enter the program with more than 30 credits may be considered for exemption from one of the 100-level seminars after consultation with the program's director.

Students entering the program are paired with a faculty mentor in her or his field of interest. The mentor advises the student in areas of program planning and academic and career goals.

Admission Process: Students who have earned 60 or fewer credits, may apply for either September, June, or January admission. They will be notified about their acceptance in time for the following semester's registration. The application is available in the LSP Office, 128 Carman Hall.

All students are required to have a GPA of at least 3.5 and are expected to maintain it while in the program. Students must supply two letters of recommendation and submit a writing sample. LSP admits very few students directly from high school; most enter in the second semester of their freshman year or during their sophomore year.

Scholarship Availability: There are no scholarships specifically available for LSP.

The Campus Context: Lehman has a 37-acre sylvan campus located in the West Bronx, bordering on the Jerome Park Reservoir. Adjacent to Bronx Science, De Witt, and Walton High Schools, Lehman has its own athletic fields and state-of-the-art athletics facility—the Apex. Lehman's outstanding art gallery and concert hall are known throughout the city's five boroughs. Lehman offers the B.A., B.S., B.F.A., and the B.A./M.A. degrees.

Student Body: The Lehman student body is about 65 percent Hispanic, 25 percent African American or African Caribbean, and 15 percent other students. Undergraduate enrollment is more than 7,000 students. The vast majority of students receive financial aid.

Faculty: Eighty-five percent of the faculty members hold the doctorate or the highest degree in their field.

Key Facilities: The campus has a state-of-the-art information and technology center. The Lehman Library excels in electronic media information research.

Honorary Societies: Golden Key, Phi Beta Kappa, Sigma Xi

Athletics: Lehman has a wide variety of men's and women's intercollegiate and intramural teams.

Study Abroad: The College has an active and effective Study Abroad Office.

Support Services: Lehman has a health center and counseling services on campus.

Job Opportunities: The Career Services Office has information for students regarding employment.

Tuition: $3200 per year for in-state students; $7600 per year for out-of-state and international students

Room and Board: N/A

Mandatory fees: $55 student activity fee

Contact: Director of Honors Programs: Professor of Classics Gary Schwartz, 128 Carman Hall, Lehman College, City University of New York, 250 Bedford Park Boulevard West, Bronx, New York 10468-1589; Telephone: 718-960-8667 or 8968; Fax: 718-733-3254; E-mail: schwartz@lehman.cuny.edu; Web site: http://www.lehman.cuny.edu

LeTourneau University

4 Pr G S

▼ Honors Program

The Honors Program at LeTourneau University challenges academically talented and highly motivated students to reach their full intellectual, social, spiritual, and leadership potential in a global society. Within an active learning environment, the Honors Program fosters ingenuity in independent and collective problem solving, enabling the students to relate learning to experiential practice. The Honors Program offers opportunities to integrate faith and learning; to analyze, synthesize, and evaluate ideas; to express concepts and research effectively; to

Interpreting the symbols: **2**=two-year college, **4**=four-year college; **Pu**=public or state college, **Pr**=private college; **G**=general honors program; **D**=departmental honors program; **S**=small program (fewer than 100 students), **M**=midsize program (100 to 500 students), **L**=large program (more than 500 students); **Sc**=scholarships available in honors program; **Tr**=transfer students accepted into honors program; **HBC**=historically black college; **AA**=academic advisors; **GA**=graduate advisors; **FA**=fellowship advisors.

broaden intellectual horizons through interdisciplinary collaboration; and to explore their major fields with greater depth.

Participation in and completion of the Honors Program require no additional fees, and the program is available to qualified students regardless of their chosen major. In addition to the academic challenges, Honors Program students participate in various social events and community service opportunities. Honors Program students may also become involved with the University's Center for the Development of Christian Leadership. The purpose of the Center is to prepare students to lead transformational change in their local and global communities.

Following two years of careful planning by a University-wide committee, the Honors Program was initiated in 2001. Approximately 25 students are admitted to the program each fall.

Participation Requirements: LeTourneau University Honors Program participants must complete at least 17 credits of honors courses. During the freshman year, students must enroll in three honors courses: Honors Seminar, Biblical Worldview, and either Communication in the Information Age or Creativity: Birth of a Notion.

Students must take two 3-hour honors courses and two 1-hour honors seminars during the sophomore and junior years. The Honors Program student and his/her academic adviser choose from honors courses offered each semester.

During the senior year, two 1-hour seminar honors classes serve as capstone experiences for the students. The courses move the student into dealing with postgraduation issues and life and are required of all Honors Program students.

Upon completion of the Honors Program, students receive an honors degree, wear an honors cord, and are recognized at commencement. Additionally, the students' permanent academic records at LeTourneau University reflect participation in the program.

Admission Process: Participants in the LeTourneau University Honors Program are selected through a specific application process. Students with outstanding academic achievement (ACT/SAT scores, high school GPA) and a record of extracurricular involvement are invited to apply. Selection is highly competitive. The initial cohort of honors students at LeTourneau had average ACT, SAT, and high school GPAs of 31, 1410, and 3.99 respectively.

Scholarship Availability: Honors-caliber students may apply for one of several academic scholarships that are awarded on the bases of standardized test scores and high school cumulative GPAs. Early application is encouraged. These scholarships include Heritage Scholarships, Presidential Scholarships, and Dean's Scholarships.

The Campus Context: LeTourneau University is a coeducational, interdenominational Christian university built upon a foundation of Biblical authority, which seeks to glorify God by integrating faith, learning, and living. LeTourneau is a comprehensive academic institution that offers undergraduate, graduate, and continuing education and sets standards of excellence in aeronautical science, arts and sciences, business, education, kinesiology, and engineering and engineering technology. These programs are distinguished by an approach that provides students with the pure intellectual excitement of learning, coupled with real-life problem-solving opportunities. At the core of all programs is an emphasis on developing communication and critical-thinking skills. LeTourneau University's 162-acre main campus is located in Longview, Texas, amongst beautiful pine tree forests and hills. The progressive city is within a metropolitan statistical area serving 150,000 people and is located on Interstate 20 between Shreveport, Louisiana, and Dallas. LeTourneau also offers adult degree programs and maintains educational centers in Austin, Dallas, Houston, and Tyler.

Student Body LeTourneau University has a total enrollment of more than 3,000. Students come from twenty-five nations and nearly every state, with approximately 50 percent from Texas.

Faculty The student-faculty ratio at LeTourneau University is 16:1. The University employs 150 faculty members (69 full-time).

Key Facilities The Margaret Estes Library provides a gateway to a variety of electronic databases. Students have access to collections listed in more than 35,000 library catalogs. The Paul E. Glaske Center for Engineering, Science, and Technology contains state-of-the-art labs and classrooms for programs in engineering and science. Aeronautical science students operate and maintain the University's modern and well-equipped fleet of aircraft located at the Gregg County Airport. Computer facilities are housed in the Glaske Center, the Margaret Estes Library, and Longview Hall. LeTourneau provides students and faculty and staff members with a superior link to the globe through LeTNet, the LeTourneau network. Access to LeTNet is provided on and off the campus. There are dedicated network connections in residence halls and high-speed modem connections for off-campus students.

Athletics The University fields teams in men's baseball, basketball, cross-country, golf, soccer, and tennis as well as women's basketball, cross-country, golf, soccer, softball, tennis, and volleyball. LeTourneau is a member of the American Southwest Conference, NCAA Division III, and the National Christian College Athletic Association (NCCAA). Intramural sports also contribute to LeTourneau's commitment to developing the whole person—mind, body, and spirit.

Study Abroad LeTourneau University participates in a variety of international study programs, including the following programs sponsored by the Council of Christian Colleges and Universities: China Studies Program; Honors Programme, Oxford; Jerusalem University College; Latin American Studies Program; Middle East Studies Program; Russian Studies Program.

Support Services Impaired students have access to all of the facilities and services at LeTourneau University.

Job Opportunities On-campus job opportunities are listed in the Student Employment Center, which is located in the Financial Aid Office. The Office of Career Development handles all incoming requests for part-time employment off campus.

Tuition: $12,670 per year (2001–02)

Room and board: $5420 per year (2001–02)

Contact: Dr. J. Dirk Nelson, Assistant Vice President for Academic Affairs, LeTourneau University, P.O. Box 7001, Longview, Texas 75607-7001; Telephone: 903-233-3230; Fax: 903-233-3259; E-mail: dirknelson@letu.edu.

Lewis-Clark State College

4 Pu G S Tr

▼ LCSC Honors Program

The Honors Program systematically offers integrated course work and supportive interaction among honors students and faculty mentors to provide students with the skills and experiences necessary to produce meaningful research and scholarship within their disciplines. The introductory course is ID289—Knowledge and Values. This experiential course challenges students to apply and to react to the views about knowledge and values examined by such thinkers as Plato, Descartes, Hume, Mead, Kuhn, Gilligan, and Perry. Following the successful completion of ID289, students work with a faculty mentor to develop a course plan for one of the three curricular paths tailored to their specific major and interests. The remaining courses in the program reside largely within the specific academic majors. Honors students receive special recognition at the graduation ceremony, special notation as an honors student on their final transcripts, and a special honors seal on their diploma.

The LCSC Honors Program is now in its fourth year. A total of 54 students are in the Honors Program.

Admission Process: If students are seriously interested in developing their capacities for critical thinking and research within their major, they enroll in the introductory course (ID289) in the Honors Program. While most honors students have a strong history of excellent academic performance, there is no minimum test score or GPA requirement to enroll in honors. The completion of ID289 with an A or B is the entrance into the Honors Program.

Scholarship Availability: No special scholarships are available for honors students. Most receive financial aid through the campus financial aid office.

The Campus Context: Lewis-Clark State College is a regional undergraduate institution offering an alternative learning environment. It offers programs in the liberal arts and sciences; professional programs in education, nursing, business, and criminal justice; and technical programs. The College is located in an attractive residential area of Lewiston, Idaho, a city of approximately 30,000 located at the confluence of the Snake and Clearwater Rivers. Across the Snake River in Washington is Clarkson, estimated population of 12,000. Within a 50-mile radius is the point at which Idaho, Oregon, and Washington join. The new library and the Centennial Mall provide a positive focal point to the center of campus with statues depicting the travels of Lewis and Clark through the region. The College offers thirty-nine majors for the baccalaureate degree.

Student Body There are 3,000 undergraduate students from two thirds of the United States and approximately twenty-five other countries. Fifty-six percent of students are women and 44 percent are men. The ethnic distribution is 90 percent white American, 3 percent Native American, 2 percent members of American minority groups, and 5 percent international students. Ninety percent of students are commuters; 10 percent are residential. More than 70 percent of students receive financial aid.

Faculty The College employs more than 118 full-time faculty members and a similar number of adjunct members. More than 80 percent of the academic faculty have doctorates or other terminal degrees in their disciplines. The student-faculty ratio is 16:1.

Key Facilities The campus has a 255,000-volume library. There are three computer labs (Mac and DOS platforms) and three computer classrooms.

Athletics Lewis-Clark State College, home of the Warriors, competed in the National Association of Intercollegiate Athletics' Pacific Northwest Division until 1998 and then moved to NCAA Division II status. The College fields nationally competitive teams in baseball, men's and women's basketball, men's and women's cross-country, men's and women's golf, men's and women's tennis, and men's and women's rodeo.

Study Abroad Study-abroad programs are offered throughout the world.

Support Services Disabled students will find classrooms, faculty offices, the student union building, and other campus buildings accessible.

Job Opportunities Students are offered a range of work-study, assistantships, and other employment possibilities on campus.

Tuition: $1102 for state residents, $3738 for nonresidents, per semester (1998–99)

Room and Board: $3130

Mandatory Fees: $1626

Contact: Director: Dr. Kurt Torell, 500 8th Avenue, Lewiston, Idaho 83501; Telephone: 208-799-2385; Fax: 208-799-2820; E-mail: ktorell@lcsc.edu

LEWIS UNIVERSITY

4 Pr G M Sc Tr

▼ Scholars Academy

The Lewis University Scholars Academy is guided by the mission of the University, the pillars of the program, and by the characteristics of quality undergraduate education as defined by the National Survey of Student Engagement.

The University's mission places an emphasis on five essential qualities of Catholic higher education: faith, justice, knowledge, wisdom, and association.

The pillars of the Scholars Academy are dialogue, holism, creativity, experimentation, value inquiry, and political and social awareness. In their various activities both inside and outside the classroom, scholars are expected to participate in dialogue with faculty members and peers. It is through this dialogue that students will find common ground. Honoring the pillar of holism, scholars are encouraged to explore interdisciplinary relationships and to make connections between academic subjects and personal concerns. Scholars are also stimulated to be bold in their intellectual explorations, for it is only through risk-taking and experimentation that creativity can be developed. The Scholars Academy invites students to become deeply engaged in an exploration of personal values and to develop the human characteristics of caring and compassion. Finally, the Scholars Academy promotes awareness of the world beyond the classroom through an emphasis on global perspectives.

The Scholars Academy is also mindful of the characteristics of an engaged university and student body. As defined by the National Survey of Student Engagement, the qualities of a superior undergraduate education include a high level of academic challenge, numerous opportunities for active and collaborative learning, plentiful interactions between students and faculty members, opportunities for enriching out-of-classroom experiences, and an overall supportive campus environment. Through its program of course contracts and out-of-class activities, the Scholars Academy promotes an engaged education.

The scholars participation within the Academy is of two kinds: the course contract and scholars activities. Unlike many honors programs, the Scholars Academy offers very few "scholars only" courses. Instead, it asks its student members to contract with faculty members on course enhancement projects. Scholars are encouraged to take the initiative in defining the course project, finding the intersection between the domain of the course and their own particular interests. Since the inception of the program in 1996, more than 800 contracts have been completed. Out of a total faculty of 170, nearly 100 faculty members have offered contracts. Currently, there are 200 courses listed in which contracts are available.

The out-of-class activities take a variety of different forms. There are on-campus colloquia that explore a theme, such as the concept of time or an aspect of local history, or an academy pillar, such as the colloquium on homelessnes . There are "city-as-text" experiences that give scholars the opportunity to explore the cultural and social variety of the Chicago region and other great American cities. There are opportunities to do small-scale explorations through attendance at events on the University's

Interpreting the symbols: **2**=two-year college, **4**=four-year college; **Pu**=public or state college, **Pr**=private college; **G**=general honors program; **D**=departmental honors program; **S**=small program (fewer than 100 students), **M**=midsize program (100 to 500 students), **L**=large program (more than 500 students); **Sc**=scholarships available in honors program; **Tr**=transfer students accepted into honors program; **HBC**=historically black college; **AA**=academic advisors; **GA**=graduate advisors; **FA**=fellowship advisors.

Arts and Ideas program and through participation in the Scholar in Residence for a Day program. In addition, students may fulfill the activities requirements through participation in service outreach programs, through study abroad experiences, and by attendance at meetings of the Honors Council of the Illinois Region and the National Collegiate Honors Council. The Academy creates its learning community mainly through these activities, but also through several social events each semester.

Student scholars ars honored through recognition at the University graduation and on the final transcript. Additional honors are given at the annual end-of-the-year-symposium. Distinguished student scholars in individual departments are honored as are students who provide considerable service to the program. In addition, recognition is given to outstanding faculty participation in the program and to distinguished faculty scholars.

The director and associate director of the Academy are assisted in the creation of policy and program direction by a 20-member Scholars Council, made up primarily of faculty members and by the nine-member Student Caucus. There is also some student representation.

Participation Requirements: The student scholar earns a scholars diploma by fulfilling the defined requirements for number of course contracts and for participation in out-of-classroom activities throughout their academic career at Lewis. Currently there are three levels of distinction that the scholar can aspire to: the scholars diploma, the distinguished scholars diploma, and the exemplary scholars diploma. Each plateau is characterized by a set number of contracts and activity units. Students are obligated to have at least one audit meeting per year, as well as an exit interview with the director. Currently, the director advises first year students and the associate director works with all other students.

Admission Process: For first-year students, a 3.25 GPA or above and a 24 ACT or above is required for full admission. For transfer students, a 3.25 GPA or above is required for full admission. Provisional admission requirements are the same for all students: a minimum 3.0 GPA and at least a 21 ACT. Provisionally admitted students gain full admittance once they attain a 3.25 GPA or above at Lewis University.

Students may apply for admission to the Scholars Academy at any time, but they will be officially admitted twice annually: August 15 and January 15. As part of the application form, students are required to write a short essay and to provide the Academy with a portfolio of their best work. All must take the orientation colloquium, Becoming a Scholar, at the beginning of the semester.

Scholarship Availability: Student scholars with at least a 24 ACT score are eligible for the $6500 Founders Scholarship. Those with an ACT score of 26 or above are eligible for the $7000 Founders Scholarship.

The Campus Context: Located only 35 miles southwest of Chicago in a picturesque suburban setting, Lewis University offers students the best of all possible worlds. The University is located near the excitement of one of the world's great cities, yet offers a beautiful and peaceful campus conducive to contemplation and the rigor of thought.

Lewis University is an independent Catholic institution of higher learning, sponsored by the (La Salle) Christian Brothers. Lewis is diversified and coeducational, served by more than 405 dedicated lay and religious faculty and staff members. In addition to valuing friendliness, flexibility, and community, LaSallian philosophy emphasizes service to the poor and marginalized, global links, and teaching learning as a call from God.

The University confers undergraduate and graduate degrees in more than fifty programs. Three colleges (Arts and Sciences, Business, and Nursing) offer bachelor's degrees in liberal, scientific, professional, and technical subjects. Master's degrees may be earned in business administration, counseling psychology, criminal/social justice, education, leadership studies, nursing, and school counseling and guidance. Associate degrees are available in aviation. An M.S.N./M.B.A. and a Certificate of Advanced Study in Education are also offered. Certificate programs are also offered in aviation, business, education, and nursing.

In addition to its main campus in Romeoville, Lewis offers programs and/or courses in Oak Brook, Naperville, Hickory Hills, Homewood, Schaumburg, Chicago, Orland Park, Oglesby, and other city and suburban locations. Lewis is accredited by the North Central Association of Colleges and Schools, the National League for Nursing Accrediting Commission, and the Illinois Department of Education.

Student Body Of the 2,948 undergraduates, 55 percent are women and more than 900 are residents. Students who are members of minority groups account for more than 27 percent of the student population.

Faculty Approximately 100 full-time faculty members from more than thirty disciplines in the academic departments of the University participate in the Scholars Academy by teaching courses, offering contracts, or coordinating colloquia. More than 20 faculty members serve on the Scholars Council, the legislative body of the Scholars Academy and the director's advisory board.

Key Facilities In addition to books and periodicals, the library also houses a curriculum collection, a government depository, materials on microform, microreaders/printers, and a full array of indixes and abstracting services, many of which are computerized. Online public access terminals are accessible and user friendly. Computerized access is available for the card catalog of the library. In addition, more than 50 different periodical databases are available through computer access, including many that are full text. Nearly 20 of these databases, including the card catalog, are available through home, office, or residence hall computer access. Internet access is also available. The library is carpeted, air conditioned, and equipped with study carrels, group study rooms, copying facilities, typewriters, word processors, and a media classroom. Audiovisual services are available for library patrons, and bibliographic tours and specialized computer searches may be arranged via the reference department.

The library is a member of several library consortia groups. This allows students access to the University of Chicago libraries, the LIBRAS Group (a consortium of eighteen private academic institutions in the southwest Chicago area), and SMRHEB (seventeen private institutions). In addition, the University library card catalog is part of ILLINET/ONLINE, allowing access to the book collections of more than forty-five major academic libraries throughout the state of Illinois.

Honorary Society Delta Epsilon Sigma

Athletics The University participates in NCAA Division II, Great Lakes Valley Conference. Men's sports include baseball, basketball, cross-country, golf, soccer, swimming, tennis, track and field, and volleyball. Women compete in basketball, cross-country, golf, soccer, softball, swimming, tennis, track and field, and volleyball.

Study Abroad The Scholars Academy offers study-abroad opportunities through the LaSallian Christian Brothers Consortium with institutions of higher education in Central and South America, Europe, and Asia.

Support Services Students with disabilities may be eligible for the services of the State of Illinois Department of Rehabilitation. These services include vocational counseling and training; payment of tuition, fees, and books; and job placement.

Job Opportunities Federal Work-Study is awarded to students based on their financial need. Part-time employment at the University is not exclusively based on financial need.

Tuition: $407 per credit hour (1998–99)

Room and Board: $5030–$7680

Mandatory Fees: $65

Contact: Director: Dr. George David Miller, Box 1030, Romeoville, Illinois 60446; Telephone: 815-836-5864; Fax: 815-838-9456; E-mail: millerge@lewisu.edu; Web site: http://www.lewisu.edu

Lincoln Land Community College

2 Pu G S Sc Tr

▼ Honors Program

The Lincoln Land Community College Honors Program provides unique educational experiences for academically superior students in order to challenge, educate, and reward them at a level consistent with their intellectual needs and abilities. The Honors Program, initiated in fall 1985, offers opportunities for critical thinking, greater student/teacher interaction, in-depth reading and discussion, smaller classes, and contact with other high-ability students.

Each honors student is assigned an administrator or faculty person as a mentor. The mentor advises the student on such matters as Honors Program requirements, scheduling, transferability, and career opportunities.

Students who complete the program are awarded a medallion to wear at graduation. Nominated on the basis of high scholarship, evidence of leadership, and Honors Program participation, one student, upon program completion, is selected as the outstanding honors student. Students who serve on committees are given certificates of appreciation.

There are currently 28 students enrolled in the program.

Participation Requirements: To successfully complete the program and receive special recognition at commencement, students must have successfully completed 15 credit hours of honors course work maintaining a minimum cumulative GPA of 3.25. Successful course completion is defined as receiving a grade of C or higher in all honors courses. Honors courses are enhanced sections of current courses, interdisciplinary courses designed specifically for the Honors Program, and special honors courses. Honors students must register for Leadership (SOC 299). This course is an interdisciplinary course based on the PTK leadership model. Students are also strongly encouraged to attend an orientation program. Monthly student meetings are an integral part of the program.

Admission Process: Students may be admitted to the Honors Program at any time. However, the deadline for scholarship applications is March 1. Transfer students can be admitted to the program; however, as most honors classes offered are general education courses, the student may have already completed some of these courses. Therefore, it is more difficult for transfer students to complete the program.

Scholarship Availability: The LLCC Foundation has established ten $1200 renewable Honors Program scholarships. Scholarships are available to entering freshmen or LLCC students who have earned fewer than 12 semester hours of college credit. Applications must be sent to the Honors Program Director by March 1. Applicants should return the application form and submit high school and college transcripts, two letters of recommendation, and an essay before the applicant can be considered for a scholarship. The committee meets in mid-March to review applications for scholarships and admission to the program.

The Campus Context: Established in 1967 as a community college district, LLCC formally opened its doors on September 23, 1968. The college district has grown steadily and serves more than 16,000 students annually from a 4,007-square-mile district, the largest geographical community college district in Illinois, serving all or parts of fifteen counties. In addition to offering courses during days, evenings, and Saturdays on the 441-acre main campus on the south edge of Springfield, LLCC offers courses at more than ninety-five locations in thirty-one off-campus communities throughout the district. Degree programs include Associate in Arts, Associate in Science, Associate in Applied Science, Associate in General Education, Associate in Engineering Science, and Associate in Fine Arts.

LLCC strives to provide, at an affordable cost, educational, cultural, social, and economic development opportunities for all citizens of District 526. The College guarantees open access, quality education, and the opportunity for success to the student who invests effort, demonstrates ability, and achieves competency. The College recognizes the worth of all individuals and is committed to providing opportunities for them to learn and develop as contributing members of society.

Student Body Undergraduate enrollment is 12,400 students; 40 percent are men. The ethnic distribution is 1 percent Asian/Pacific, .1 percent Native American, 4.3 percent black, 1 percent Hispanic, and 95 percent white. There are 17 international students, .1 percent of the student population. All of the students are commuters. Twenty percent of all students receive financial aid. There are twenty-nine clubs and organizations at LLCC.

Faculty The total number of faculty members is 428; 125 are full-time and 303 are adjunct. Thirty percent of the faculty have terminal degrees.

Key Facilities The library houses 55,000–60,000 volumes. There are twenty-three classroom computer labs plus an open lab in the library.

Honorary Societies Phi Theta Kappa and Alpha Beta Gamma

Athletics Athletics is one part of the many-faceted experiences a student may enjoy in receiving a total education at LLCC. A wide variety of intercollegiate athletic team offerings is available for the aspiring student athlete. Highly competitive schedules are arranged for each team, enabling the athletes to test their athletic skills against other community college athletes. In addition to regular season play, each team plays in post-season tournaments leading to the NJCAA championships. LLCC is a member in good standing of the National Junior College Athletic Association and abides by its rules of eligibility for student participation.

Study Abroad LLCC students have the opportunity for the first time to earn 3 hours of college transfer credit in an overseas immersion study program in London, England, which features fully articulated courses in history, humanities, and political science. The curriculum is innovative and interdisciplinary and features the study of British and American cultures. A second opportunity for study abroad is provided during the spring break period. Home-based study on the Springfield campus begins with an orientation on March 3 and extends to study abroad in Ireland. The program concludes on campus March 13. This experience provides students with an opportunity to study Irish social justice, with particular focus on similarities and differences between the American and Irish social justice systems. Students earn 4 college credits in SCJ 251 (Crime, Justice and Social Diversity) and 3 credits in HUM 165 (British Culture).

Job Opportunities Funds are provided by the federal government and matched partially with College funds to provide part-time jobs for students who have financial need. Jobs are available in almost every campus department. The program is open to students enrolled in a minimum of 6 credit hours.

Tuition: $42 per credit hour (1999–2000)

Mandatory Fees: $5–10 lab fees plus $.75 activity fee per credit hour; $3 technology fee per credit hour

Interpreting the symbols: **2**=two-year college, **4**=four-year college; **Pu**=public or state college, **Pr**=private college; **G**=general honors program; **D**=departmental honors program; **S**=small program (fewer than 100 students), **M**=midsize program (100 to 500 students), **L**=large program (more than 500 students); **Sc**=scholarships available in honors program; **Tr**=transfer students accepted into honors program; **HBC**=historically black college; **AA**=academic advisors; **GA**=graduate advisors; **FA**=fellowship advisors.

Contact: Director: Dr. Ray Huebschmann, Shepherd Road, Springfield, Illinois 62794-9256; Telephone: 217-786-2276; Fax: 217-786-2468; E-mail: ray.huebschmann@llcc.cc.il.us

Lindenwood University

4 Pr G/D M Sc Tr

▼ Honors Program

The Lindenwood Honors Program is designed to encourage high intellectual achievement by providing academic opportunities that emphasize analytical thought, creativity, and cross-disciplinary instruction. There are a number of ways this Honors Program stands apart from many others. The program draws from the existing curriculum. Courses come from all areas of the liberal arts, so courses for honors not typically seen in traditional programs, such as physics, computer science, and mathematics, can be offered. Initial entry into the program is determined by fairly typical criteria: class rank and scores on standardized tests.

A student may be certified as an honor graduate in general education, their major, or both. A distinctive aspect of the program is the service component. This component seeks to round out the academic portion and at the same time keep the student involved with, as opposed to set apart from, the University experience. This service component may take a number of forms, including leadership in the Honors Program, tutoring/mentoring, involvement as a research assistant, or recruitment/retention.

Rather than creating a separate honors college, this system exists within the University curriculum. Under a contract model, students wishing to take a course for honors credit agree to meet certain other conditions in addition to regular classwork. These conditions, left to the discretion of the instructor, have taken the form of extra reading, individual or small group discussions, take-home exams, and papers. This system allows those students not pursuing honors certification an opportunity to complete honors course work. Since honors courses at Lindenwood do not constitute a separate curriculum, they are potentially open to anyone. This means the student who is a late-bloomer or whose abilities may not be reflected by traditional measures has the chance to excel. In all cases, students who successfully complete courses under the conditions of honors have their efforts noted on their transcripts.

Participation Requirements: In order to receive a certificate in General Education in the Honors Program, the student is required to take at least eight courses within the general education curriculum under the conditions of honors. As these courses represent the liberal arts, they would have to be taken from at least three separate areas. The appropriate department would determine requirements for an honors certificate in a given major. In both cases, the student is expected to take part in a service component. These may consist of service to both the University and the surrounding community.

To remain in the program, students must maintain at least a 3.3 cumulative GPA. Successful completion of the program is recognized on the student's official transcript and by certification.

Admission Process: High school students are recruited into the program if they meet one of the following criteria: a minimum composite of 28 on the ACT, a minimum of 1200 on the SAT I, or a high school rank in class equal to the top 5 percent of the graduating seniors. Other students may be admitted into the program if they are sponsored by a Lindenwood faculty member and meet the GPA requirements.

Scholarship Availability: Although not offered through the Honors Program, a number of scholarships of various amounts are available.

The Campus Context: Lindenwood University is located in St. Charles, Missouri, a fast-growing city and county in the greater St. Louis metropolitan area. Founded in 1827, it is one of the oldest institutions of higher learning in the country and the second-oldest west of the Mississippi River. The lovely main campus occupies 268 wooded acres. Lindenwood has experienced dramatic growth in enrollment, programs, and facilities during the last decade. During the fall of 1998, there were nearly 10,000 undergraduate and graduate students enrolled at Lindenwood. Approximately 1,600 students reside on campus. New construction includes a completed performance arena, and new dorms and a student center are soon to be completed.

Student Body The undergraduate enrollment is 63 percent women and 37 percent men. Students come from thirty-seven states and forty-eight countries.

Faculty The total number of faculty members is 278, of whom 124 are full-time. Approximately two thirds of the faculty members hold terminal degrees. The student-faculty ratio is 17:1.

Key Facilities The library contains 222,710 volumes. Computers are available at several campus locations.

Athletics Lindenwood is currently a member of the NAIA and fields teams in twenty-two sports.

Job Opportunities Students living on campus may take part in the Work and Learn Program. Payments take the form of reduced tuition costs.

Tuition: $10,150 per year

Room and board: $5000 per year

Contact: Director: Dr. Michael Stein or Dr. Mary Utley, 209 South Kingshighway, St. Charles, Missouri 63301-1695; Telephone 314-949-4733; E-mail: stein@lindenwood.edu

Lock Haven University of Pennsylvania

4 Pr G S Sc Tr

▼ Honors Program

The Honors Program expresses Lock Haven University's commitment to academic excellence by providing faculty members and students alike with challenging opportunities for creative intellectual growth. The honors curriculum combines a rigorous subject matter grounded in the broad sweep of human civilization and an integrated four-year program for the development of sophisticated intellectual abilities. A spirit of inquiry in the tradition of the liberal arts inspires the program and fosters in each student the capacity for independent learning. Honors courses share an interdisciplinary approach, heavy reliance on classic sources, intensive writing, small size (usually 15–20 students), and active student involvement.

The Honors Program began in 1988 with an entering freshman class of 20 students. The program's growing reputation made possible an expansion to 40 freshmen for fall 1996. Total enrollment is expected to increase gradually from 75 to 100. This expansion has been carefully designed to ensure that the small learning communities of 20 freshmen will remain intact. With the expansion will come a greater variety of honors courses and cocurricular activities.

Participation Requirements: The heart of the Honors Program is a 30-hour program of studies providing students with a uniquely challenging and rewarding educational experience while meeting University requirements both in general education and in the student's major. The particular strength of the honors curriculum lies in its integration of these courses into a cohesive and developmentally sequenced program of study culminating in a senior project and the oral presentation of that project in the honors colloquium.

Honors freshmen form learning communities of 18–20 students and take two classes together each semester: Honors Composition and Literature I and II and Honors Historical and Philosophical Studies I and II. Navigating the sometimes difficult transition from high school to university is made easier by 4 hours per week of cocurricular activities that provide the supportive mentoring of upperclass honors students and faculty members who show freshmen the way to success and helps them develop their own voices as adult learners.

After the freshman year, students take one course for honors credit each semester, either an honors course that satisfies a general education requirement or an honors augmentation of a nonhonors course, usually in the student's major. Augmentation projects are planned to build a foundation for the honors senior project, the culmination of the student's academic program. These projects provide excellent preparation and credentials for graduate and professional schools. Honors students are also encouraged to take advantage of the University's many study-abroad and internship opportunities.

Cocurricular activities are an important part of the honors experience throughout the four years, although the minimum requirement drops to 2 hours per week after the first year. However, many honors students decide to work more hours, assuming responsibility for programs such as freshmen study groups, weekly faculty member and student discussion groups, and service programs, such as tutoring in the local schools.

Honors students may earn official recognition in one of three categories: honors in general education (completed in the sophomore year), university honors (completed in four years), and upper-division honors (completed in five to six semesters by students entering the program as sophomores or second-semester freshmen). Honors graduation in each of the three categories requires completion of honors curricular requirements with a minimum GPA of 3.2 in honors courses and overall as well as active participation in honors cocurricular activities.

Admission Process: Entering freshmen are selected on the basis of high school grades, SAT I scores, essays, recommendations, and high school activities. Continuation in the Honors Program requires a 3.0 GPA (overall and in honors) at the end of the first year and a 3.2 GPA thereafter. Lock Haven University students may also enter upper-division honors after one to three semesters of study; a 3.2 GPA is required.

Scholarship Availability: Three forms of merit-based financial aid are available to honors students. The Lock Haven University Foundation currently awards five Presidential Scholarships of $2000 and twenty Academic Honors Scholarships of $1000 to entering freshmen enrolling in the Honors Program. The Presidential Scholarships are renewable for up to three years. A limited number of Academic Honors Scholarships are awarded to continuing students on a competitive basis. All scholarship renewals and awards after the first year require a minimum GPA of 3.2. Continuation in the Honors Program is optional. In addition to these scholarships, many honors students are employed in the Honors Center for 2–5 hours per week.

The Campus Context: Located in beautiful central Pennsylvania on the banks of the Susquehanna River, Lock Haven University is one of fourteen institutions that make up the commonwealth's State System of Higher Education. This central location combines the benefits of a rural area and bountiful outdoor activities with quick access to Philadelphia, Pittsburgh, and New York City in about 4 hours. Lock Haven University is primarily an undergraduate institution with Colleges of Arts and Sciences and Education and Human Services. The Lock Haven University faculty concentrates on teaching and working closely with students even while finding time to publish best-selling textbooks and conduct groundbreaking research. Classes are never taught by graduate assistants or lab assistants.

The University offers seventy-five degree programs, including nineteen teacher certification programs and preprofessional preparation for law, dentistry, medicine, veterinary science, and physical therapy. Degrees include Associate of Science, Associate of Applied Science, Bachelor of Science, Bachelor of Arts, Bachelor of Fine Arts, Master of Education, Master of Liberal Arts, and Master of Health Science in physician assistant in rural primary care. General education requirements provide a liberal arts background for every undergraduate degree.

Student Body There are 3,795 undergraduates at the main campus and 163 at the Clearfield campus. Forty percent are men. The student body includes 103 international students, primarily residential, and 4.8 percent of students are members of minority groups. Forty-three percent of students are residential; 65 percent of students receive financial aid. Students are offered nine honorary societies, six nationally affiliated fraternities, and five nationally affiliated sororities.

Faculty There are 247 faculty members; 231 are full-time. Faculty members who hold doctoral or terminal degrees number 135. The student-faculty ratio is 18:1.

Key Facilities The Stevenson Library collection contains 361,447 volumes. Student computer laboratories located in all residence halls and most classroom buildings are connected via a high-speed fiber-optic network to the University's full-range of information resources and applications and to electronic services worldwide.

Athletics Lock Haven fields Division I men's wrestling and fifteen men's and women's Division II sports.

Study Abroad Honors students are encouraged to take advantage of the University's many study-abroad and internship opportunities.

Tuition: $4016 for state residents, $8040 for nonresidents, $10,040 of international students, per year (2001–02)

Room and Board: $4520

Contact: Director: Dr. James T. Knauer, 401 North Fairview Street, Lock Haven, Pennsylvania 17745; Telephone: 570-893-2491; Fax: 570-893-2711; E-mail: jknauer@lhup.edu; Web site: http://www.lhup.edu/honors

Long Island University, Brooklyn Campus

4 Pr G M Sc Tr AA FA

▼ University Honors Program

The University Honors Program at the Brooklyn Campus is a liberal arts program for students in all disciplines at the University, designed to assist them to become critical and independent thinkers. This is accomplished through an enriched core curriculum in the liberal arts, with courses usually interdisciplinary in nature, limited to 16 students, stressing student participation and independent study. The Honors Program also gives students freedom to design their own majors. The honors student body reflects the rich cultural and ethnic diversity of New York City, and the cultural advantages offered by New York are incorporated both formally and informally into every facet of the honors experience. Within the University, the Honors Program develops an active community of learners, providing opportunities for intellectual support and social interaction. Most University Honors Program students go on to graduate school or take advanced professional degrees.

The Honors curriculum is divided into three components: the freshman sequence, the sophomore sequence, and advanced

Interpreting the symbols: **2**=two-year college, **4**=four-year college; **Pu**=public or state college, **Pr**=private college; **G**=general honors program; **D**=departmental honors program; **S**=small program (fewer than 100 students), **M**=midsize program (100 to 500 students), **L**=large program (more than 500 students); **Sc**=scholarships available in honors program; **Tr**=transfer students accepted into honors program; **HBC**=historically black college; **AA**=academic advisors; **GA**=graduate advisors; **FA**=fellowship advisors.

electives. The freshman sequence is taken by all freshmen and newcomers to honors who have not fulfilled their core requirements. It is a year-long course cluster of history, English, and philosophy in which students study a selected theme that allows the work of each discipline to be interrelated. The sophomore sequence enables students to complete their requirements in speech, psychology, social science, fine arts, and foreign languages in an honors environment. The advanced electives are interdisciplinary courses designed specifically for honors students. Offered in seminar format, the electives encourage student involvement through an emphasis on field experience, the development of original research or arts projects, and other experiential activities. In order to graduate with honors, students must complete the core courses and three advanced electives.

Transfer students who have completed their core requirements can graduate with honors by completing four advanced electives.

Distinction in honors is granted to students who complete an advanced project expanded from a paper or project originally written for an advanced honors elective. These expanded projects are developed under the guidance of a faculty mentor and a two-member committee. Distinction in honors projects that meet with the approval of the committee and faculty mentor are presented prior to graduation in the annual distinction in honors forum, open to the campus community.

The Honors Program stresses experiential education by drawing on the wealth of opportunities provided by resources throughout New York City. Students are assisted in gaining internships and volunteer placements in major corporations and conduct original research projects in which the city is used as a laboratory for testing theory against practice. The Honors Program also encourages students to participate in NCHC international and national honors semesters and offers funding to support students in these semesters.

Participation in the Honors Program gives students membership in two governance boards: The Honors Advisory Board and the Student Activities Board. The Honors Advisory Board determines the Honors Program curriculum, its instructors, electives, and other Honors activities. It draws its members from the faculty and students in all disciplines across the University. The Student Activities Board, a student club, sponsors activities such as poetry readings, faculty and student presentations, as well as sponsoring honors students' attendance to the National Collegiate Honors Council national and regional conferences and other NCHC events.

Students in the Honors Program can also participate in *Spectrum,* the literary journal of the Honors Program. Edited by honors students, it accepts fiction, poetry, essays, photographs, and art work from students, faculty members, and administrators across the campus.

There are 340 students in the program.

Participation Requirements: Students are required to have a minimum 88 percent high school average and a minimum combined score of 1100 on the SAT I. Students meeting these criteria may apply for admission and are interviewed after submitting an application. A minimum GPA of 3.0 is required for participation.

Scholarship Availability: The University Honors Scholar Award is granted, in addition to any University or departmental scholarships, to new Honors students who have exhibited extraordinary merit. Honors also grants some book voucher awards for incoming freshmen and some residence hall awards for those who wish to live on campus. Long Island University offers generous academic scholarships to incoming students who have already distinguished themselves in the classroom—in high school or at another college. There is also a competitive Continuing Student Study Grant for students who have exhibited extraordinary academic performance while at the University. Student Activity Grants are available for those with outstanding records who wish to work on campus to earn up to 6 tuition credits free each semester. Generous alumni donations to the program help support student participation in NCHC honors semesters, provide additional assistance for students interested in study abroad, and support independent projects.

The Campus Context: The 22-acre urban campus, founded in 1926, is 10 minutes from Manhattan, on Flatbush and Dekalb Avenues. Long Island University is a four-year private coeducational campus with regional accreditation. University Honors students come from all seven schools and colleges of the University: the College of Liberal Arts and Sciences; the School of Business, Public Administration, and Information Sciences; the School of Education; the School of Nursing; the School of Health Professions; and the College of Pharmacy and Health Sciences. The campus has fifty programs leading to the baccalaureate, including liberal arts and sciences, accounting, business, education, pharmacy, nursing, physician's assistant, media arts, and art.

Student Body There are 5,509 undergraduates enrolled; 30 percent are men and 70 percent are women. The majority come from New York City and surrounding areas. The campus has an average of 300 international students (international students are required to have a minimum score of 500 on the TOEFL). Ninety-five percent of students receive financial aid. There are four fraternities and four sororities with no chapter houses.

Faculty Of the 741 total faculty members (289 full-time), 85 percent have doctorates or other terminal degrees. The student-faculty ratio is 19:1.

Key Facilities There are 300,000 volumes in the campus library, which is also connected to the 2.1-million-volume University system.

Honorary Societies Alpha Lambda Delta and Alpha Chi

Athletics Intercollegiate sports for men include baseball, basketball, cross-country, soccer, track (indoor and outdoor), and golf. Intercollegiate sports for women are basketball, tennis, softball, volleyball, cross-country, and track (indoor and outdoor). The University offers NCAA Division I sports.

Study Abroad Study abroad is available through LIU's Friends World Program in England, Kenya, India, China, Japan, Israel, and Costa Rica. Other opportunities exist by department.

Support Services Disabled students find 95 percent of the campus accessible. Features include wheelchair ramps, electronic doors, elevators, special parking, and specially equipped restrooms.

Job Opportunities Internships, co-op work placements, work-study jobs and career placement services are provided through the University's Career Planning and Placement Center.

Tuition: $17,184 per year (2001–02)

Room and Board: $6050

Mandatory Fees: Full-time: $405; part-time: $185 (average cost per year)

Contact: Director: Dr. Bernice Braid, Brooklyn Campus, 1 University Plaza, Pratt 514, Brooklyn, New York 11201; Telephone: 718-488-1657; Fax: 718-488-1370; E-mail: rwheeler@liu.edu

LONG ISLAND UNIVERSITY, C.W. POST CAMPUS

4 Pr G M Sc Tr

▼ Honors Program and Merit Fellowship

The C.W. Post Honors Program is open to students of all majors. It offers a 30-credit course of study designed to cultivate open-mindedness, adventure, and a progressive deepening of purpose. Focused on the individual honors student as a unique intellectual personality, the discussion-style classes encourage writing and oral presentation. Class size is limited to 20, and the curriculum emphasizes a balance between traditional and innovative studies. There are 485 students in the program (9.6 percent of undergraduate students).

Participation Requirements: Students take approximately 18 credits of Honors Program core courses (available in anthropology, art/music, biology, cinema, communications, dance, economics, English, geology, geography, history, math, philosophy, physics, political science, psychology, sociology) and 6 credits of advanced electives. These are invented specifically for the program and are chosen by a student-faculty advisory board. Advanced electives reflect current issues or faculty research and expertise. Recent courses to attract an enthusiastic following include The Cathedrals of France, The Tango, Advertising and Gender, and Marketing in the Age of the Internet. At the most advanced level, students work privately with professors in their major on a 6-credit tutorial and thesis project of their own creation. Honors credits are generally completed within the 128-credit bachelor's degree. To remain in the program students must maintain a 3.2 GPA in the freshman year and a 3.4 GPA every year thereafter. Completion of the 30 credit Honors Program is indicated on the diploma.

Transfer students may become junior/senior participants by maintaining an 3.4 GPA and completing 12 credits in the Honors Program, consisting of two courses, tutorial and thesis. These members also receive an Honors Program diploma citation.

All Honors Program participants are recognized at Commencement. Each year the top scholars receive the Charles Garrett Honors Award at Recognition Day. Other awards for service to the program, for outstanding thesis and for junior-senior participation, are also given.

Participation in the Honors Program means membership in a decision-making community that is both academic and social. The diverse group of students, from all disciplines and many countries, joins with faculty to choose Honors Program curriculum. Members of the program may participate in the National Collegiate Honors Council annual conference as well as the NE-NCHC regional meeting.

Freshmen are introduced to the program in special orientation sections of College 101. The Honors Program Director serves as a general mentor to students who are also assisted by departmental advisers.

All students in the Honors Program participate in the extracurricular Merit Fellowship, which offers several different noncredit series of lectures, cultural events, and an opportunity to perform community service. At the beginning of each semester, students contract to attend five events in Visual and Performing Arts, Media Arts, Education, Humanities, Aspects of Business, or Natural and Social Sciences. Community Service is a commitment of 20 hours per term.

Admission Process: Entering freshmen with a high school average of 90 and combined SAT scores of 1200 (minimum 550 verbal) or above are advised to apply for admission to the Honors Program. Admission is based on high school credentials, including extracurricular activities and other evidence of particular talents and interests, which are discussed in an interview with the director.

Transfer students and continuing C.W. Post students with a GPA of at least 3.4 (freshmen 3.2) are also eligible to apply and request an interview.

Scholarship Availability: There are three important categories of scholarship awards for students in the Honors Program: University Scholar Award ($13,000) requires a 92 HS average and 1300 SAT. Students must maintain 3.5 GPA all years to retain the scholarship. Academic Excellence Award ($8000) requires an 88 HS average and 1200 SAT. Students must maintain 3.2 GPA as freshmen, 3.4 GPA as upperclassmen. Transfer Excellence Award ($9000) is based on a 3.5 GPA transfer credits and maintenance all years. The Transfer Scholar Award ($11,000) requires a 3.9 GPA and completion of an A.A. degree program. The Post Outstanding Scholars Award ($5000) is based on an essay contest and may be held in conjunction with other awards (not to exceed full tuition).

Students receiving other University aid or currently attending C.W. Post without aid may apply for admission to the Honors Program and be considered for scholarships up to $2000/year from the Honors Program and Merit Fellowship. Students must file a Free Application for Federal Student Aid (FAFSA) by March 15. Scholarships are renewed for the length of student participation in the Honors Program/Merit Fellowship (up to four years).

Students who do not wish scholarship consideration are also eligible for the Honors Program with a 90 HS average and 1200 SAT (550 minimum verbal score) or 3.2 college transfer credit. Exceptions are always welcome and encouraged.

The Campus Context: Founded In 1954, the C.W. Post Campus of Long Island University is a wooded, 305-acre campus 25 miles from New York City on Route 25A. The four-year, private, coed campus, with regional accreditation, includes the College of Liberal Arts and Sciences, College of Management, School of Education, School of Visual and Performing Arts, and the School of Health Professions. There are eighty-four programs leading to the baccalaureate, including liberal arts and sciences, accounting, business, education, and media and performing arts. The Tillis Center offers concerts (with inexpensive students tickets) by international symphonies and ballet and opera companies touring the New York area. The Hillwood Museum features major exhibitions of historic and contemporary world art. A student-run radio station, WCWP, state-of-the-art television studio, and computer graphics laboratory are among the facilities that attract students.

Student Body There are 4,676 undergraduates enrolled: 34 percent men, 66 percent women, the majority from the Northeast. The ethnic distribution is 81 percent white, 8 percent African American, 7 percent Hispanic, 3 percent Asian-Pacific, and 1 percent Native American. There are 307 international students. Eighty-five percent of the students receive financial aid. There are ten fraternities and twelve sororities with no chapter houses. There are seventy student clubs on campus as well as academic honorary societies.

Faculty Of the 311 full-time faculty members, 90 percent hold doctorates or other terminal degrees. The undergraduate student-faculty ratio is 19:1.

Key Facilities The University library houses 2.5 million volumes as well as an extensive academic computing center. There are more than 400 microcomputers for student use located in dormitories, classroom buildings, and the computer center. Students may also be linked to the UNIX system, with Internet usage.

Honorary Societies Phi Eta Sigma, Alpha Sigma Lambda

Athletics C. W. Post's varsity teams play in NCAA Division II, except men's baseball, which is Division I. Intercollegiate sports for men include baseball, basketball, cross-country, football, lacrosse, soccer, and track (indoor). Intercollegiate sports for women are basketball, cross-country, field hockey, lacrosse, soccer, softball, tennis, and volleyball. The women's lacrosse team captured the NCAA Division II national championship in 2001. Club sports and intramurals are widely available. The North Shore Equestrian Center housed on the campus presents an opportunity for students interested in boarding their own horses or riding and jumping to participate in Equestrian Team competitions.

Study Abroad Unique study-abroad opportunities exist through LIU's Friends World Program in England, India, China, Japan,

Interpreting the symbols: **2**=two-year college, **4**=four-year college; **Pu**=public or state college, **Pr**=private college; **G**=general honors program; **D**=departmental honors program; **S**=small program (fewer than 100 students), **M**=midsize program (100 to 500 students), **L**=large program (more than 500 students); **Sc**=scholarships available in honors program; **Tr**=transfer students accepted into honors program; **HBC**=historically black college; **AA**=academic advisors; **GA**=graduate advisors; **FA**=fellowship advisors.

and Costa Rica. Students who go abroad with Friend's World design their own independent study programs and participate in active community field work in the host country. Comparative world religions, alternative medicine, global ecology, and the status of women are some of the threads of study that students develop through Friend's World. An exchange program also exists with Keimyung University in South Korea. Other opportunities are available by department.

Support Services Disabled students will find 75 percent of the campus accessible by wheelchair ramps, electronic doors, elevators, special parking, equipped rest rooms, and lowered drinking fountains. The Academic Resource Center provides support for learning-disabled students.

Job Opportunities Internships, co-op work placements, work-study jobs, and career placement services are provided through the University's Center for Professional Experience and Placement (PEP).

Tuition: Approximately $17,220 per year (2001–02); add 6 percent for approximate increase in 2002–03 for all categories of projected costs

Room and Board: $7010 based on double room (2001–02)

Fees: $870

Contact: Director: Dr. Joan Digby, C.W. Post Campus, 201 Humanities Hall, Brookville, NY 11548; Telephone: (516) 299-2840; Fax: (516) 299-4180; E-mail: jdigby@liu.edu; Web site: http://www.cwpost.liunet.edu/cwis/cwp/honors/honors.html

Long Island University, Southampton College

4 Pr M Sc Tr

▼ Southampton College Honors Program

The central goal and philosophy of the Southampton College Honors Program is the stimulation and encouragement of academic activity at the highest level. The program strives to bring together a community of dedicated faculty members and highly motivated students who share a commitment to the finest qualities of scholarship and research. It endeavors to recognize, recruit, reinforce, and retain the most academically and intellectually motivated students in all disciplines at the College and offers an exciting and challenging supplement to the undergraduate experience.

The Honors Program serves as the locus for both traditional and innovative studies and enables the individual honors student to engage in an expanded spectrum of creative endeavors, independent research within a discipline, seminars, and greater interaction with the honors faculty. The Honors Office serves as a repository for information regarding professional and graduate schools, international fellowships (Fulbright, Marshall, Rhodes, Udall, Truman, and Goldwater), and various study-abroad programs.

The Honors Program began in 1984, and there are approximately 260 students in the program.

Participation Requirements: There are four basic components of the Honors Program: participation in a total of seven honors courses (21 credits) for incoming freshmen (proportionally fewer for upperclassmen and transfer students); maintenance GPA of at least 3.25; attendance at the Merit Fellows Lecture Series (involves registering for LECT 201H each semester); attendance at five of the nine lectures each semester; and participation in the honors thesis (for students seeking an Honors Diploma), which can be satisfied either through an internship (490) in conjunction with honors research (492H) or independent study/research (minimum 3-credit course) with a faculty member.

There is an Honors Society that sponsors a variety of social and cultural activities during each semester. In the fall semester, there is an Honors Banquet, held in conjunction with one of the Merit Fellows Lectures. The Honors Society also sponsors trips to New York City to attend Broadway plays, museums, and other cultural venues.

Admission Process: Students are invited to join the Honors Program either as entering freshmen, on the basis of combined SAT I scores (minimum of 1230) or high school averages (minimum of 90 percent), or as transfer students (3.25 GPA or better). Students who do not enter the Honors Program upon entry to the College may, upon completion of at least 15 credits with a GPA of at least 3.25, enter the program at a later date.

Scholarship Availability: On the basis of their academic record, honors students may be offered partial to full tuition scholarships, which may be in addition to need-based financial aid.

The Campus Context: Southampton College is the smallest of the three main campuses of Long Island University and is situated in a rural setting on the East End of Long Island. The others are the C.W. Post campus (approximately 65 miles west—a suburban campus) and Brooklyn campus (another 20 miles west—an urban campus). The College offers thirty-five degree programs. Among these is an internationally known program in marine biology with facilities that include an on-campus Marine Station, with six outboard boats and two larger vessels for both local estuarine studies and oceanographic research. Other notable programs include those in psychobiology, environmental sciences, writing, and fine arts.

The College has had a noteworthy record in the competition for international fellowships, with a total of 33 Fulbright winners, 1 Marshall winner, and 1 Udall winner. Twenty-four of the Fulbright winners, since 1984, were members of the Honors Program, including 15 in the last four years.

Student Body The undergraduate enrollment of about 1,450 full-time students is approximately 60 percent women, with student members of minority groups comprising between 10 and 15 percent of the population. Approximately half of the students live on campus, with the remainder commuting or living in plentiful off-campus housing during the academic year (Labor Day through Memorial Day). Southampton is a popular resort community with a large summer population, and students taking summer courses generally live on campus. About 85 percent of the undergraduates are traditional students (i.e., between the ages of 17 and 23). Approximately 75 percent of the students receive some kind of scholarship and/or need-based financial aid. There are no fraternities or sororities.

Faculty The total number of faculty members is 206. There are 67 full-time members (who teach 65 percent of the courses) and 139 adjuncts. Ninety-three percent have terminal degrees. The student-faculty ratio is 17:1.

Key Facilities The campus library houses 150,000 volumes, but students may access more than 2.4 million volumes through the University collection. Computer facilities include eight laboratories and 150 IBM-compatible and Macintosh computers. A new Technology Center supports the new Theoretical and Computational Studies Group and has superb computational facilities, with twenty powerful Silicon Graphics workstations and a rich array of peripheral devices and software that provide for image editing and graphics manipulation. The College Web Studio has a Silicon Graphics 02 workstation and its own Origin200 server as its authoring tools.

Study Abroad Study-abroad opportunities include internships, co-op placements, a variety of travel courses, and the Friends World Program, with programs in China, India, Costa Rica, Israel, England, Japan, and Kenya. The College has an exchange program with the University of Southampton in the United Kingdom.

Support Services Disabled-student facilities are minimally compliant.

Job Opportunities Work opportunities on campus include tutoring, lab assisting, college work-study, and cafeteria employment. The local East End community provides many jobs in the service areas.

Tuition: $17,220 per year (2001–02)

Room and Board: $4560 (double occupancy), $3590 (fifteen-meal plan)

Mandatory Fees: $900

Contact: Honors Program, Southampton College, 139 Montauk Highway, Southampton, New York 11968; Telephone: 631-287-8396; Fax: 631-287-8419; E-mail: honorsprogram@southampton.liu.edu; Web site: http://www.southampton.liu.edu

Longview Community College

2 Pu G S Sc Tr

▼ Honors Program

The Honors Program at Longview provides an enriched experience for the exceptional student. The programs, courses, and activities promote creative and analytical thinking and aim to foster the development of intellectual skills and interests. The program features small classes, an emphasis on participatory classroom experiences, regular contact with highly stimulating faculty members, an interdisciplinary approach to learning, and elements of independent study.

Honors seminars are restricted to no more than 15 students, while honors sections are typically small but may have as many as 20 students enrolled. The program is small, usually including about 30–40 students each semester, 20 of whom will be eligible to receive honors scholarships. The program was started in 1991.

Participation Requirements: The program requires students to complete at least 18 credit hours of honors course work as part of their associate degree program. Each semester, honors sections of regular courses are offered. These courses are restricted to students eligible for honors work. In addition, one-credit-hour honors seminars are offered. The honors seminars are topical with new topics appearing each semester. Finally, students may take almost any regularly scheduled course for honors credit by contract. In order to be eligible for honors scholarships, a student must be enrolled at least half-time and take at least 4 credit hours of honors courses each semester, chosen from either special sections or by contract, but always including a seminar.

Admission Process: Students may qualify for enrollment in honors courses by submitting composite ACT scores at the 85th percentile, documenting a high school GPA of at least 3.5 (on a 4.0 scale), earning qualifying scores on the reading portion of the new student placement test, or by submitting writing samples along with recommendations from other teachers.

Scholarship Availability: Twenty honors scholarships in the amount of at least $500 are awarded in the fall semester of each year. Successful recipients will have earned a cumulative 3.5 GPA, be at least a half-time student, and be enrolled in at least 4 credit hours of honors course work, including a seminar. Scholarships are renewable for up to two years.

The Campus Context: Longview Community College is the southernmost member of a four-campus community college district that serves a seven-county area near Kansas City, Missouri. The campus is located on 146 acres of rolling hills in the suburban community of Lee's Summit. The College awards the Associate in Arts degree, the Associate in Applied Science degree, the Associate in Computer Science degree, the Associate in Science degree, and a number of certificate programs in business and technology.

Student Body There are approximately 6,000 students, two thirds attending day classes and the rest enrolled in evening and weekend classes. The student body is about 55 percent women, and members of minority groups comprise about 15 percent of the students. Some 45 percent of students receive some form of financial assistance. There are no fraternities or sororities, but a comprehensive program of student activities and campus life enhancement is offered.

Faculty There are 72 full-time faculty members and about 195 adjunct faculty members. Twenty-eight percent of the faculty have earned their Ph.D degrees. The student-faculty ratio (with adjunct faculty included) is approximately 20:1.

Support Services The campus is fully accessible and offers a number of services and programs for disadvantaged and disabled students, including a nationally recognized bridging program for students with head injuries and brain damage.

Tuition: $1710 for area residents, $2940 for state residents, $4050 for nonresidents, per year (2001–02)

Contact: Director: W. Andrew Geoghegan, 500 Longview Road, Lee's Summit, Missouri 64081-2105; Telephone: 816-672-2258; Fax: 816-672-2078; E-mail: geoghega@longview.cc.mo.us

Longwood College

4 Pu G M Sc Tr

▼ Honors Program

Initiated in 1983, the Longwood Honors Program offers courses in a wide variety of majors to academically oriented students seeking intellectual challenge. Honors courses emphasize discussion and writing, regardless of discipline. The small classes (no more than 18 students) encourage teacher-student interaction and opportunities for hands-on learning. For example, the honors section of Introduction to Anthropology includes a three-day dig, allowing students to apply the principles and terms learned in the classroom. Currently 150 full-time undergraduates participate in the Honors Program.

In addition to honors sections of general education courses, classes of general interest (e.g., The Old South, Hitler and the Holocaust, Issues of Sex and Gender) and independent study in a student's major are available.

Honors students are usually housed on two floors of a centrally located dorm. Other benefits include priority registration and travel to regional and national honors conferences.

Participation Requirements: To graduate from the Honors Program, students complete eight honors courses (three at the 300 level or above) with a minimum 3.25 cumulative GPA average in honors and overall. Students successfully completing the Honors Program are recognized at graduation and on their transcripts.

Admission Process: Incoming students are offered admission to the Honors Program based on a review of their high school records, including an unweighted average of their core academic courses; a profile of their college-credit courses, especially through AP and I.B.; and SAT or ACT scores. Successful honors applicants in the class of 2005 had median SATs in the mid-1200s and a median unweighted GPA of more than 3.8. Transfer students with a minimum cumulative 3.25 GPA are also eligible. Freshmen with a Longwood GPA of at least 3.25 after the first semester are also encouraged to apply.

Interpreting the symbols: **2**=two-year college, **4**=four-year college; **Pu**=public or state college, **Pr**=private college; **G**=general honors program; **D**=departmental honors program; **S**=small program (fewer than 100 students), **M**=midsize program (100 to 500 students), **L**=large program (more than 500 students); **Sc**=scholarships available in honors program; **Tr**=transfer students accepted into honors program; **HBC**=historically black college; **AA**=academic advisors; **GA**=graduate advisors; **FA**=fellowship advisors.

Scholarship Availability: Twenty merit-based renewable scholarships of $1000 each are available, five to each class. In addition, two Advanced Honors Program Scholarships of $3000 each are awarded annually, one to a rising junior and one to a rising senior. These are renewable and merit based.

The Campus Context: Longwood College is a residential coeducational comprehensive state college of 3,300 offering programs leading to both the bachelor's and master's degrees. Located in south-central Virginia in a town of 7,000, Longwood is 1 hour from Richmond, Charlottesville, and Lynchburg, and 3 hours from Tidewater and northern Virginia. Twenty-two undergraduate majors with eighty-nine minors and concentrations are offered.

Student Body Longwood enrolls 3,500 undergraduates, the majority from Virginia. Thirty-five percent are men, and 65 percent are women. The ethnic distribution is 2 percent Asian, 9 percent African American, 1 percent Hispanic, 87 percent white, and 1 percent other. Sixty percent of students receive financial aid; work-study is widely available. The campus has nine national fraternities and twelve national sororities. Longwood has 125 clubs and student organizations, including a campus radio station.

Faculty There are 190 faculty members, 69 percent with doctorates or other terminal degrees. The student-faculty ratio is 14:1.

Key Facilities The library houses 400,000 volumes and nearly 700,000 nonprint holdings.

Honorary Societies Phi Kappa Phi, Mortar Board, Alpha Lambda Delta

Athletics Longwood has NCAA Division II membership in men's sports, including baseball, cross-country, golf, basketball, soccer, and tennis and in women's sports, including cross-country, golf, field hockey, lacrosse, soccer, softball, tennis, and basketball. Club sports include riding, volleyball, men's and women's rugby, and synchronized swimming.

Study Abroad Longwood is affiliated with thirteen study-abroad programs for students in any major. Programs are located in England, France, Spain, Martinique, Venezuela, Austria, and Germany. Students may study for a summer, a semester, or a year and have credits earned apply to their Longwood degrees.

Tuition: $9032 for state residents, $14,752 for nonresidents, per year (2002–03), including room and board (fourteen-meal plan)

Contact: Director: Dr. Geoffrey Orth, Honors Program, Longwood College, Farmville, Virginia 23909; Telephone: 434-395-2789 or 434-395-2157; E-mail: honors@longwood.edu

Loras College

4 Pr G S Tr

▼ Honors Degree Program

The Loras College Honors Degree Program is designed to offer a coherent sequence of courses to academically superior students who wish to pursue a broadly based, comprehensive liberal arts education. The program emphasizes a humanistic and synoptic approach to the various academic disciplines that comprise the liberal arts. Each semester the Honors Degree Program sponsors two or three intra- or inter-divisional courses that explore themes central to the study of the liberal arts. The courses are interdisciplinary in approach, employ a variety of learning styles, have enrollments of 15 to 20 students, and are offered in a seminar format.

By completing courses sponsored by the Honors Degree Program and also through independent learning opportunities, service activities, and research projects, students become more active learners better able to synthesize information from their various College courses and construct for themselves a complete learning experience. Finally, by integrating its in-class and cocurricular activities within the larger framework of students' lives, the Honors Degree Program underscores the necessary connection between academic experience and the world beyond the academy in the development of principled thinkers. In recognition of their accomplishments in a variety of courses and a senior capstone experience students earn the Honors Degree.

In addition to its purpose to attract and retain highly motivated and academically superior students, the Honors Degree Program serves to attract excellent teachers. The Honors Degree Program enriches the academic experience of all students at Loras by providing an opportunity for innovative course development.

The current version of the Loras College Honors Degree Program was introduced in 1989. Annually 20 first-year students begin the first course in the program. There are approximately 70 students currently enrolled in the program.

Participation Requirements: In their first three semesters, students in the Honors Degree Program complete several foundational courses: a Modes of Inquiry course in which students employ a holistic critical-thinking approach to explore a seminal event in the Western cultural tradition; a Democracy and Global Diversity course in which students use primary texts to explore both Western and non-Western cultures at a movement of historical crisis; a Catholic Traditions course in which students develop an awareness of the religious dimensions of human experience either by exploring the lives of several significant Catholic figures or by contrasting Catholicism and another religious tradition. During the following five semesters, students complete honors courses in three of the following general education categories: Humanity in the Physical Universe, Foundations for Values and Decisions, Identity and Community, The Aesthetic Dimension of Human Experience, and Cultural Traditions Across Generations. These honors courses are distinguished from their general education counterparts by their strong emphasis on interdisciplinary content and their enhanced opportunities for participation in field trips, conferences, and collaborative research. Representative Advanced Honors courses include Contested Conceptions of Political Economy, Native American Literature, The Vietnam War and American Culture, The Holocaust and Resistance, Great Ideas in Physics, Slavery and Democracy, and Aldo Leopold and the Land Ethic. During their junior year, honors students complete a 1-credit course for the honors dimension of their general education portfolio in which they propose a paper or presentation to an appropriate undergraduate journal or conference. In the senior year, honors students participate in a 3-credit Service Learning course in which they spend 50 hours at a local community organization developing a project that addresses a significant organizational need.

Students are expected to maintain a minimum GPA (GPA) of 3.35 and complete a total of 22 credits in honors courses or projects. The completion of these requirements results in the awarding of the Honors Degree on the official transcript, presentation of a special plaque, and a notation in the commencement program in addition to the degree(s) in an academic major.

Admission Process: On the basis of ACT scores, high school average, and a review of the college preparatory courses on their high school transcript, students are invited to apply to the Honors Degree Program. Final placement in the program is based on the recommendation of the Honors Director and a personal interview between the student and a faculty member who serves as the student's summer registration counselor. A key factor in admission to the program is the individual student's desire to follow the course of studies. Annually a small number of students may be placed in the program after the first or second semester of the first year. Students may major in any discipline in the College.

Scholarship Availability: Scholarships of various amounts are awarded through the Office of Admissions and Financial Aid. These scholarships are based on academic performance and financial need. Scholarships are not offered through the Honors

Degree Program. Almost all honors students are recipients of academic scholarships.

The Campus Context: Loras College, the Archdiocesan College of Dubuque, is a premier, Catholic liberal arts institution whose mission is educating principled thinkers. Located on the bluffs of the Mississippi River in Dubuque and founded in 1839, Loras is Iowa's oldest private college. Only seven other Catholic colleges existed when Loras was founded. With 1,636 students, Loras offers students fifty-four majors, twelve preprofessional programs, and a 96 percent job placement rate. Loras was named to the Top Tier of Midwest Regional Liberal Arts Colleges by *U.S. News & World Report;* is among *Barron's Top 300 Best Buys in Education;* and was named in *Ruggs' Recommendations.*

All full-time students at Loras receive a laptop computer. The entire campus is wired for Internet access, with wireless connections available in common areas.

Loras offers a variety of services and programs for students, including health clinic, personal-psychological counseling, English as a second language program (ESL), advanced placement, writing and mathematics labs, intercultural programs, and an experiential learning/study abroad program.

Student Body The undergraduate enrollment of 1,636 is 51 percent women. Students come from twenty-seven states and thirteen countries. Sixty-six percent of undergraduate students live in campus housing. The average GPA of entering students is 3.26, and 78 percent of students return for their sophomore year. Eighty-six percent of the 2001 entering class received some type of financial aid, including scholarships, grants, loans, and work-study. Fifty-nine student organizations are active on campus.

Faculty The outstanding Loras faculty comprises 123 full-time and 65 part-time members. Seventy-one percent of the full-time faculty members hold the highest degree in their field. Ten faculty members (7 currently teaching) and 10 students have received Fulbright Scholar awards. The student-faculty ratio of 12:1 ensures students individual attention from instructors in an open, friendly, and responsive atmosphere. All students are taught by Loras teaching faculty members.

Key Facilities The Wahlert Memorial Library is one of the three largest private collections in Iowa, with holdings of 431,903 volumes. The library is a depository for state and federal documents, a collection of maps, and an outstanding rare book room that includes a manuscript collection dating back to the twelfth century and sixty-one incunables printed through the year 1500. These holding will move in 2002 into a new state-of-the-art Academic Resources Center.

Honorary Societies Alpha Phi Omega, Alpha Psi Omega, Delta Epsilon Sigma, Kappa Delta Pi, Phi Alpha Theta, Psi Chi, Sigma Tau Delta

Athletics Loras is a member of the NCAA Division III and the Iowa Intercollegiate Athletic Conference. The Duhawks compete in twenty-one sports (eleven for men and ten for women). More than half of all first-year students participate in at least one intercollegiate sport. Loras has produced 163 All-American winners and fifty-three Academic All-America and Scholastic All-American winners. With an extensive intramural program, 80 percent of students and 45 percent of the faculty and staff members participate in more than 100 activities.

Support Services The College offers a learning disabilities program and Partners In Education (PIE) program.

Job Opportunities Campus employment is available to those students demonstrating financial need.

Tuition: $15,980 per year (2001–02)

Room and Board: $5733

Contact: Director: Dr. Andrew Auge, Loras Mail #166, Dubuque, Iowa 52004-0178; Telephone: 563-588-7218; E-mail: aauge@loras.edu; Admissions Office: Telephone: 800-245-6727; Fax: 563-588-7964; E-mail: adms@loras.edu; Web site: http://www.loras.edu

Los Medanos College

2 Pu G S Tr

▼ Honors Program

The Los Medanos College Honors Program offers a rigorous and innovative curriculum that prepares the highly motivated student for transfer to selective colleges and universities. By choosing to complete the first two years of undergraduate study at a community college, students can guarantee themselves small class size, one-on-one interaction with their professors, and a high-quality education that cuts the cost of the bachelor's degree in half.

Honors Program graduates have access to priority transfer agreements and special scholarships with the College's eleven transfer partners, including the University of California, Los Angeles; the University of California, Santa Cruz; the University of Southern California; Pitzer College; and Pomona College. The Honors Counselor and faculty members work one-on-one with students, helping them apply for admission to prestigious transfer universities and scholarships.

In addition to these benefits, students are challenged in dynamic courses taught by outstanding faculty members. Honors courses offer students the opportunity to study more advanced topics and are limited to 25 students, guaranteeing personalized attention and stimulating discussion. Students also have the opportunity to develop Honors Contracts (individual research projects) with their professors. Honors course work is available in more than sixteen departments, including music, chemistry, history, nursing, philosophy, business, and mathematics.

Finally, honors students have opportunities to participate in cultural activities, field trips, conferences, and social events. Los Medanos College is located in the beautiful San Francisco Bay area close to many museums, theaters, and prestigious universities, such as the University of California, Berkeley, and Stanford University.

The Los Medanos College Honors Program is newly designed; the first students will begin honors work in the fall of 1999.

Participation Requirements: Honors course work of general education courses are offered each semester. Students select the honors courses that meet the needs of their major and transfer program. Each course taken in the Honors Program is listed on the student's transcript as honors, and graduates receive special recognition at the commencement ceremony. To be an honors graduate, students must complete their A.A./A.S. degree with five honors courses/contracts plus the Honors Seminar with a GPA of at least 3.25. These five courses or contracts must include at least one from each of the following three areas: humanities and fine arts, social and behavioral sciences, and natural sciences and mathematics.

Admission Process: To be eligible for admission to the Los Medanos College Honors Program students must have completed Freshman English Composition with a grade of A or B or received a 4 or 5 on the AP English exam. In addition, students must either have a high school or college GPA of at least 3.25 or have a letter of recommendation from a Los Medanos professor plus the approval of the Honors Program Advisory Board.

Interpreting the symbols: **2**=two-year college, **4**=four-year college; **Pu**=public or state college, **Pr**=private college; **G**=general honors program; **D**=departmental honors program; **S**=small program (fewer than 100 students), **M**=midsize program (100 to 500 students), **L**=large program (more than 500 students); **Sc**=scholarships available in honors program; **Tr**=transfer students accepted into honors program; **HBC**=historically black college; **AA**=academic advisors; **GA**=graduate advisors; **FA**=fellowship advisors.

Scholarship Availability: Currently, no scholarships are available through the Honors Program.

The Campus Context: Los Medanos College is located on a 120-acre site near the boundary of Pittsburg and Antioch on the beautiful San Francisco Bay Delta, giving students immediate access to watersports such as jetskiing, sailing, windsurfing, and waterskiing. The East Bay is a vibrant community with mild weather. It is close to beaches, ski resorts, nature preserves, wilderness areas, the Silicon Valley, and prestigious universities such as the University of California, Berkeley, and Stanford. Connecting all of this is BART—Bay Area Rapid Transit. Using this system, students have easy access to the funky intellectual life of Berkeley and the iconoclastic sophistication of San Francisco as well as two world-renowned research institutes: the Lawrence Livermore National Laboratory and the Lawrence Berkeley Laboratory. Nearby performing groups and museums include the American Conservatory Theatre, the Dean Lesher Regional Center for the Arts, the San Francisco Opera, the Contra Costa Wind Symphony, and the Lindsay Wildlife Museum. The Bay Area is also one of the most diverse food cultures, with restaurants ranging from Tibetan to French to Cuban cuisine.

Los Medanos College was founded in 1975 and offers A.A. and A.S. degrees in twenty-nine majors.

Student Body Undergraduate enrollment is 7,152, of whom 61 percent are women. The ethnic distribution of the student body is 11 percent African American, .01 percent Native American, 5 percent Asian, 5 percent Filipino, 19 percent Hispanic, 51 percent Caucasian, and 7 percent other. All students commute to campus, and 40 percent receive financial aid. There are no fraternities or sororities. However, a comprehensive student life is an important element of the educational experience at Los Medanos College. A broad range of extracurricular activities, such as special interest clubs, sports, and student government, offer students a chance to expand their education beyond the classroom.

Faculty There are 106 full-time and 117 part-time faculty members. Approximately 20 percent have terminal degrees. The student-faculty ratio is estimated at 30:1.

Key Facilities Students have access to all of the Contra Costa Community College District's libraries, which contain 115,000 volumes. In addition, students have access to seven databases, which includes access to the full text of more than 2,000 magazines and periodicals. There are twenty-six library computer research stations with full access to the Internet, and complete computer classrooms are available in the business, computer science, and English departments.

Honorary Societies Alpha Gamma Sigma

Athletics Los Medanos College offers eight varsity teams competing against colleges throughout Northern California. Men's and women's basketball, football, and women's volleyball participate in conference play in the fall. Baseball, women's softball, and men's volleyball teams compete in the spring. Facilities include a fitness center, an Olympic-size swimming pool, lighted tennis courts, a track, and soccer and baseball fields.

Study Abroad Participants in the Study Abroad Program enjoy an outstanding opportunity to immerse themselves in international cultures while enrolled in regular Los Medanos courses for credit. Field trips enhance the classwork taught by Los Medanos faculty members at the campus sites in England, France, and Italy.

Support Services The Disabled Students Program and Services offers academic support for students who are physically, developmentally, or psychologically disabled. A full range of support services are available on campus including testing, tutoring, counseling, and computer training.

Job Opportunities Work opportunities on campus are available. In addition, the Cooperative Work Experience Program grants college credit for what students learn and accomplish on the job.

Tuition: None for state residents. $3750 for nonresidents per year (1998–99)

Mandatory Fees: $360

Contact: Director: Jennifer Saito or Counselor: Marie Karp, 2700 East Leland Road, Pittsburg, California 94565-5197; Telephone: 925-439-2181 Ext. 810; E-mail: jsaito@ccnet.com or mkarp@ccnet.com; Web site: http://www.losmedanos.net

Louisiana State University and A&M College

4 Pu C L Tr AA FA

▼ Honors College

The Louisiana State University (LSU) Honors College provides opportunity and challenge for academically able and intellectually motivated undergraduate students. Honors students pursue a rigorous academic program that satisfies all requirements of their major and goes beyond those requirements to provide the basis for outstanding achievement and appropriate recognition for that achievement. From small-enrollment interdisciplinary seminars in the freshman year to independent research activities in preparation for the senior honors thesis, honors students work closely with selected members of the LSU faculty.

The Honors College is housed in the magnificent and elegant French House, a French chateau listed on the National Register of Historic Places and located in the center of the campus. The French House provides the College with administrative and faculty offices, seminar rooms, student lounges, a grand salon, and a New Orleans–style café.

LSU honors students and faculty members make up a close-knit community of scholars, epitomized by the residential college located in residence halls that are immediately adjacent to the French House. As many as 700 first-year and upper-division honors students experience the collegiate way of life in a coed residence shared with faculty offices, study halls, and seminar rooms. It is a living environment that fosters academic excellence and close personal interaction between students and faculty members.

In existence for more than thirty years, the LSU honors program became the Honors College in 1992. Currently, the College enrolls approximately 1,300 students, including about 350 first-year students. The facilities, curricula, and programs offered by the LSU Honors College create a small-college atmosphere while still providing students with all the academic, research, and cocurricular advantages of a major research university.

Participation Requirements: During the first two years of study, the Honors College offers students four interdisciplinary courses for a total of 20 credit hours. These courses in humanities and liberal arts form the core of the students' general academic program. The classes are small and presented in a seminar format that encourages interaction with the professors and the other students. The faculty members are carefully selected for their skills in teaching and in developing the intellectual curiosity and problem-solving abilities of students. Students who meet the requirements for credit hours in honors courses and have at least a 3.5 GPA receive sophomore honors distinction.

In their junior and senior years, honors students usually become more focused on a particular academic discipline. Intense intellectual involvement, rigorous standards, and a high level of increasingly independent achievement characterize upper-division honors work. Upper-division honors work typically culminates in a senior honors thesis or project, under the direction of a faculty member from the student's major department. Completion of an upper-division honors program leads to graduation with upper-division honors distinction. Students who achieve both the sophomore and upper-division honors awards graduate with College Honors.

The University confers a sophomore honors distinction certificate, an upper-division honors distinction certificate, and a College Honors diploma citation.

As a coordinating college, the Honors College works with all of the University's academic units to foster the development of undergraduate students. Rigorous academic programs are tailored to students' individual capabilities and to the variety and depth of resources available at a major research university. Graduates receive degrees in their major fields plus honors recognition that enhances their credentials for graduate or professional school admission or for entry into the most attractive job markets.

Admission Process: Entering freshmen with certain minimum ACT or SAT scores and a minimum 3.5 high school GPA are invited to apply for admission to the Honors College. The recommended minimum test scores are 28 composite and 28 English or 27 composite and 30 English on the ACT and 1240 combined and 630 verbal on the SAT. Students who approach but do not attain these qualifications may also apply. Transfer or continuing students who have completed at least their first semester of college with a minimum 3.5 GPA are also invited to apply.

The application deadline is April 15; however, students should apply by December 1 for priority consideration.

Scholarship Availability: Application for admission to LSU constitutes an application for scholarships. Louisiana residents also qualify for state TOPS scholarships.

The Campus Context: Louisiana State University and A&M College is the state's flagship university. Located in the capital of Louisiana, Baton Rouge, LSU is situated on the banks of the Mississippi River 70 miles north of New Orleans and in the center of the rich and colorful culture of southern Louisiana. LSU is a Research I university and one of only twenty-five universities nationwide holding both land-grant and sea-grant status. The University conducts two semesters, a summer term, and a three-week intersession each year. Curricula leading to bachelor's degrees are offered in seventy-one major fields, master's degrees are offered in seventy-five fields, and there are fifty-four Ph.D. programs. The University consists of nine academic colleges: the College of Agriculture, the College of Art and Design, the College of Arts and Sciences, the College of Education, the College of Basic Sciences, the E. J. Ourso College of Business Administration, the Honors College, the College of Engineering, and the College of Music and Dramatic Arts. There are also five schools: the Manship School of Mass Communication, the School of Library and Information Sciences, the School of Social Work, the School of the Coast and Environment, and the School of Veterinary Medicine.

Student Body Enrollment is about 31,500 students: 26,500 undergraduates and 5,000 graduate students. For the undergraduates, 47 percent are men and 53 percent are women. The ethnic distribution of undergraduates includes African-American students (10 percent), Asian students (4 percent), and Hispanic students (3 percent). There are also approximately 700 international undergraduates. Eighty-nine percent of the undergraduate students receive scholarships or grants. Student organizations number more than 300, including twenty-three national fraternities and fifteen sororities.

Faculty The total number of faculty members is 1,451. Of the 1,299 full-time faculty members, 83 percent have terminal degrees. The student-faculty ratio is 20:1.

Key Facilities With a total 19,000 linear feet of manuscripts, the University libraries offer students and faculty members support for instruction and research through collections containing more than 3 million volumes, microform holdings of more than 5 million units, and 25,000 periodical subscriptions.

LSU maintains one of the largest computing facilities in the country. The Office of Computing Services provides computing resources and services 24 hours per day in support of instruction, research, and administrative data processing. In addition to instructional labs, more than thirty common-use computer labs are accessible to students. These resources are integrated with the campuswide, fiber-optic backbone, which provides data ports in classrooms, offices, and residence hall rooms. Computing Services provides all students with online access to instructional, registration, financial, and research services, as well as their own e-mail and Web pages.

Honorary Societies Phi Kappa Phi, Phi Beta Kappa, Phi Eta Sigma, Golden Key, Mortar Board, and Omicron Delta Kappa plus about thirty discipline-specific honorary societies

Athletics The Director of Athletics manages a broad spectrum of intercollegiate sports programs for men and women. Louisiana State University is a charter member (1932) of the Southeastern Conference. LSU meets teams from other major universities in NCAA Division I-A competition in football, basketball (men's and women's), baseball, indoor and outdoor track (men's and women's), cross-country (men's and women's), golf (men's and women's), tennis (men's and women's), swimming (men's and women's), women's gymnastics, women's volleyball, women's soccer, and women's softball.

Study Abroad Through the Office of Academic Programs Abroad, honors students are encouraged to travel and study worldwide for a summer, semester, or academic year. Students select from a wide variety of options for international study. Many join programs led by LSU faculty members, such as summer schools in London, Paris, Spain, and Africa. Others participate in exchange programs, which place students directly in overseas universities, where they study with students in the host countries, or they may enroll directly in an international university. Participating students earn credit toward their LSU degrees and may apply for scholarships or financial aid designated specifically for studying abroad.

Support Services The Office of Disabilities Services assists students in identifying and developing accommodations and services to help overcome barriers to the achievement of personal and academic goals. The office provides services to students with temporary or permanent disabilities. Specialized support services are based on the individual student's disability-based need.

Job Opportunities Through the Federal Work-Study Program, jobs are provided to full-time students who show financial need. Students earn an hourly wage and are paid every two weeks. Those students who want to work on campus but do not qualify on the basis of financial need may seek regular student employment on campus.

Tuition: $3368 for state residents, $8668 for nonresidents, per year (2001–02)

Room and Board: Varies from $3040 to $5990 per year, depending on the plan selected. The average expenditure for a campus residence and meal plan is $4546 per year.

Contact: Perry H. Prestholdt, Honors College, 205 French House, Louisiana State University, Baton Rouge, Louisiana 70803; Telephone: 225-578-8831; Fax: 225-578-8828; E-mail: honors@lsu.edu

LOYOLA COLLEGE

4 Pr G M Sc AA FA

▼ Honors Program

The Honors Program at Loyola brings together students and faculty members with various interests, aiming for academic

Interpreting the symbols: **2**=two-year college, **4**=four-year college; **Pu**=public or state college, **Pr**=private college; **G**=general honors program; **D**=departmental honors program; **S**=small program (fewer than 100 students), **M**=midsize program (100 to 500 students), **L**=large program (more than 500 students); **Sc**=scholarships available in honors program; **Tr**=transfer students accepted into honors program; **HBC**=historically black college; **AA**=academic advisors; **GA**=graduate advisors; **FA**=fellowship advisors.

achievement and intellectual challenge and growth. The program offers students who are serious about their intellectual growth a specially designed series of classes and activities in the humanities.

Because it is committed to the tradition of the liberal arts, the program places special emphasis upon ideas—specifically, those ideas that have shaped the world in which we live. Students in honors engage in a dialogue with the great thinkers of the Western world, both in order to see how essential questions of human existence have been asked over and over again and in order to learn to what extent we are all products of our own historical age.

Courses in the Honors Program enrich and complement the academic experience inherent in a Loyola education. All honors classes are small, and many are conducted as seminars. They contain a judicious combination of lecture, discussion, and student presentation, and, no matter the subject, they always emphasize effective speaking and writing.

The Honors Program offers a wide range of activities in addition to its academic curriculum. The program sponsors a variety of events on campus and makes numerous cultural experiences available off campus. All these activities are designed to demonstrate that the ideas honors students study in the classroom are alive in the culture at large.

The Honors Program has existed for sixteen years and currently serves 216 students; 54 are admitted each year.

Participation Requirements: The Honors curriculum replaces humanities requirements in the College-wide core. Students in honors are free to major in any department at the College. At the heart of the curriculum is an eight-course sequence. Five of these are interdisciplinary explorations of Western intellectual history, moving from the ancient, through the Medieval and Renaissance, to the modern world. The other three courses are seminars and have a more contemporary focus. The remaining courses in the honors curriculum are electives, taken from upper-division offerings in the departments of English, history, philosophy, and theology. At graduation, honors students are given certificates, and the notation Honors Program Participant appears on their transcripts.

Admission Process: Admission to the Honors Program is by invitation only, and students are invited to enroll as incoming freshmen. Prospective students should indicate their interest in honors by checking the appropriate box on the College's Application for Admission. They must have scored above 1350 on the SAT I and maintained a high school GPA of at least 3.7 on a 4.0 scale. They then are sent a separate application for admission to the Honors Program. Students are accepted into honors on a rolling basis. Admission is extremely selective, and neither acceptance by the College nor an award of an academic scholarship is a guarantee of admission to honors.

Scholarship Availability: Loyola offers an extensive merit scholarship program. Presidential Scholarship awards range from $3000 to full tuition. General guidelines for scholarship eligibility are a combined SAT I score of at least 1350 and a high school GPA of at least 3.7. Students admitted to the Honors Program are not automatically awarded an academic scholarship; however, more than 90 percent of the current students in the Honors Program have received scholarship awards.

The Campus Context: Loyola College in Maryland is composed of the College of Arts and Sciences and the Sellinger School of Business. The College offers thirty-two majors and five bachelor's degree programs (B.A., B.S., B.B.A., B.S.E.E., and B.S.E.S). Special facilities include an art gallery, the world's fifth-largest artificial turf athletic field, and multimedia classrooms.

Student Body Total undergraduate enrollment is 3,224 (45 percent men and 55 percent women). The ethnic distribution is 87 percent white, 5 percent African American, 2 percent Asian, 2 percent Hispanic, and 4 percent other. There are 70 international students. Seventy-five percent of the students are residents, 25 percent are commuters. Sixty-five percent of students receive financial aid. There are no fraternities or sororities.

Faculty Of the 452 faculty members, 225 are full-time. Ninety-three percent have terminal degrees. The student-faculty ratio is 14:1.

Key Facilities There are 349,238 volumes in the Loyola/Notre Dame Library. Loyola has fourteen computer labs with IBM and Macintosh computers. On-campus housing is available.

Honorary Society Phi Beta Kappa

Athletics The Loyola College Greyhounds compete at the NCAA Division I level. Twelve of Loyola's fourteen teams compete in the Metro Atlantic Athletic Conference. Men's lacrosse plays an independent schedule, while the women's lacrosse program competes in the Colonial Athletic Association. Loyola fields teams for both men and women in basketball, crew, cross-country, lacrosse, soccer, swimming and diving, and tennis, as well as men's golf and women's volleyball. Loyola also has an extensive club sports program, fielding teams in thirteen different sports for both men and women. The thriving intramural sports program offers an opportunity for friendly competition on campus. Among the many sports offered are flag football, basketball, softball, soccer, volleyball, tennis, racquetball, and squash. There are three fitness centers on campus equipped with weight training machines, Lifesteps, Lifecycles, NordicTracks, ergometers, and fitness testing equipment.

Study Abroad More than 30 percent of Loyola's junior class studies abroad. Students can study in one of Loyola's fourteen programs and exchanges. Loyola sponsors five study-abroad programs: Loyola at Bangkok, Thailand; Loyola at Leuven, Belgium; Loyola at Newcastle, England; Loyola at Alcalá, Spain; and Loyola at Melbourne, Australia. Loyola is also affiliated with exchanges in Montpellier, France; Rotterdam, the Netherlands; La Rochelle, France; Koblenz, Germany; Hirakata City, Japan; Buenos Aires, Argentina; Jönköping, Sweden; Wernigrade, Germany; and Florence, Italy.

Support Services Disability support services, adaptive computer equipment, and accessible facilities are available for students with disabilities. Campus work-study positions are available.

Tuition: $18,200 per year (1998–99)

Room and Board: $6810–$7750

Mandatory Fees: $510

Contact: Director: Dr. Brennan O'Donnell, 4501 North Charles Street, Baltimore, Maryland 21210; Telephone: 410-617-5017; Fax: 410-617-2702; E-mail: bodonnell@loyola.edu; Web site: http://www.loyola.edu

LOYOLA MARYMOUNT UNIVERSITY

4 Pr G M Sc Tr AA GA FA

▼ University Honors Program

The University Honors Program at Loyola Marymount University is for students who value and want to be challenged by an exceptional education through interdisciplinary studies. By teaching several fields of knowledge simultaneously, the program creates and supports an academic environment of intellectual adventure. Taking advantage of its freedom from some of the restrictions involved in the structure of regular core courses, the Honors Program attempts to challenge as well as to inform and to ask hard questions as well as to examine tested solutions. Class sizes in the Honors Program range from 10 to 15 in the lower-division offerings and from 5 to 10 in the upper-division seminar courses. The goal is to provide a carefully integrated and demanding curriculum for the exceptional student.

The honors core curriculum is predicated on an intensive undergraduate experience that combines interdisciplinary core courses with a yearlong tutorial in writing. HNRS 120, On Human Dignity, is concerned with the forces that shape personal identity. By reading and examining works from the classical to the contemporary period, the course considers society's identity as it is reflected in and fashioned by a variety of discourses on what it means to be human. HNRS 130, Society and Its Discontents, introduces students to the construction of social relations in the modern world, in particular as they are viewed from the perspective of critical thinkers after the industrial revolution. HNRS 140, Methods in Science and Engineering, is an experiential course that employs the use of scientific and engineering methods to study the environment and solve technical problems.

Two history courses, HNRS 220 and HNRS 230, span the development of human civilization from its beginnings to the present day. These courses examine the past in its original setting, contextualizing history amid the texts, artworks, philosophies, and social practices of both Eastern and Western cultures. HNRS 240, Natural Philosophy, examines the historical and philosophical nature of scientific discovery, theory, and practice.

HNRS 320, Ethics and Social Justice, explores the complications involved with moral choice as articulated by great traditional and nontraditional thinkers and social activists. Students also take an interdisciplinary seminar, HNRS 398, for an in-depth analysis of a particular theme, problem, or period.

The program culminates in the writing of an honors thesis on a topic within the student's major. The material is presented orally and submitted for publication as a bound thesis. HNRS 495 and 496 are 1- to 2-unit senior seminars designed to help with the writing and presentation of the thesis in HNRS 497.

The Office of Beyond LMU works closely with honors students, helping them pursue scholarships, graduate placement, internships, awards, grants, and study-abroad opportunities. LMU also provides honors housing options on campus. Honors facilities include a dedicated study room with computers, a conference room, a designated classroom, and an outdoor courtyard for social gatherings.

The program was founded in 1958 and currently enrolls 115 students.

Participation Requirements: The honors curriculum takes the place of the Loyola Marymount University core and is made up of nine courses, including an upper-division interdisciplinary seminar. There is a foreign language proficiency requirement as well as an honors thesis. Those students accepted into the program must maintain a minimum GPA of 3.5. Successful completion of the Honors Program is announced at the annual commencement ceremonies and noted on the student's transcript. This recognition is of lasting personal and academic value, identifying the students who are among the very best Loyola Marymount has to offer.

Admission Process: Each year, the Honors Program carefully selects a limited number of incoming first-year students to join the program. In addition, any freshman or first-semester sophomore may apply personally to the directors for admission to the program. To qualify for the Honors Program at LMU, students should have at least a 3.6 unweighted high school GPA and a minimum score of 1300 on the SAT. Before final acceptance into the Honors Program, students are interviewed by either the Director or Assistant Director and possibly members of the Faculty Committee on Honors. A writing sample and letter of reference are also requested. Materials are available February 1, and application review begins on May 1.

Scholarship Availability: Honors students usually receive Trustee or Presidential Scholarships in addition to regular financial aid. Students in the Bellarmine College of Liberal Arts are eligible for additional Cahn Scholarships, which support students during both the regular year and Summer Study Abroad Programs.

The Campus Context: Loyola Marymount University—with one window on the Pacific Ocean and another on the sprawling dynamic complexity of cultures, ages, industries, and images that constitute Los Angeles and southern California—is one of twenty-eight Jesuit universities in the United States and one of five Marymount institutions of higher education. The names Loyola and Marymount have long been associated with Catholic higher education in countries around the globe. LMU shares in these international networks in providing instruction to undergraduate, graduate, and professional students who seek an ethnically diverse university dedicated to the highest academic standards, the education of the whole person, and faith-inspired concern for justice. The city of Los Angeles is Loyola Marymount's laboratory; the vistas of the Pacific its challenge for the future; the glory of God as reflected in the fully human its highest aim.

The University has four colleges: the Bellarmine College of Liberal Arts, the College of Science and Engineering, the College of Business Administration, and the College of Communications and Fine Arts (including the School of Film and Television).

Student Body There are a little more than 5,000 undergraduate students at Loyola Marymount University. Fifty-eight percent of the students are women, and thirty-seven percent represent students from African, Hispanic, Asian, and Native American descent. On-campus residents include 57.2 percent of total undergraduates and 91.9 percent of first-year students.

Faculty Of the 311 full-time faculty members, 69 percent are tenured. The University's student-faculty ratio is 13:1.

Key Facilities The University Libraries hold 899,186 volumes and 10,318 subscriptions. Several computer labs and facilities are available on campus, with both PC and Macintosh capabilities. In addition, all campus dormitories and rooms are wired for Internet and cable access.

Honorary Societies Alpha Sigma Nu Jesuit Honor Society, Alpha Kappa Delta Sociology Society, Beta Beta Beta Biology Society, Beta Gamma Sigma Business Honor Society, Gamma Kappa Alpha National Italian Honor Society, Kappa Delta Pi International Education Society, Phi Alpha Theta History Society, Phi Sigma Tau Philosophy Society, Pi Delta Phi French Society, Pi Mu Epsilon Mathematics Society, Pi Sigma Alpha National Political Science Honor Society, Psi Chi Psychology Society, Sigma Delta Pi Spanish Society, Sigma Tau Delta English Society, Sigma Xi International Scientific Society, Tau Beta Pi Engineering Society, Theta Alpha Kappa Theology Society

Athletics LMU is a member of NCAA Division I. Intercollegiate sports include baseball, basketball, cross-country, crew, soccer, golf, swimming, tennis, volleyball, and water polo. Lacrosse and rugby are intercollegiate club sports, and a variety of intramural opportunities are offered.

Study Abroad LMU offers semester-abroad programs in Beijing, China; Bonn, Germany; and Washington, D.C., and at Biosphere II Center in Arizona. Summer study-abroad programs are available in Kenya; Oxford, England; Paris, France; Spetses Island, Greece; Roatan Island, Honduras; Dublin, Ireland; Rome, Italy; Cuernavaca, Mexico; and Washington, D.C.

Support Services The Office of Disability Support Services provides service to students with special needs.

Job Opportunities LMU offers a variety of job opportunities, both on and off campus, including work-study, undergraduate teaching assistantships, research fellowships, and internships.

Tuition: $20,342 (2001–02)

Interpreting the symbols: **2**=two-year college, **4**=four-year college; **Pu**=public or state college, **Pr**=private college; **G**=general honors program; **D**=departmental honors program; **S**=small program (fewer than 100 students), **M**=midsize program (100 to 500 students), **L**=large program (more than 500 students); **Sc**=scholarships available in honors program; **Tr**=transfer students accepted into honors program; **HBC**=historically black college; **AA**=academic advisors; **GA**=graduate advisors; **FA**=fellowship advisors.

Room and Board: $7100

Mandatory Fees: $352

Contact: Dr. James Landry, Director, or Dr. Kelly Younger, Assistant Director, Loyola Marymount University Honors Program, North Hall MS 8160, One LMU Drive, Los Angeles, California 90045-2659; Telephone: 310-338-1780; Fax: 310-338-7882; E-mail: jlandry@lmu.edu or kyounger@lmu.edu; Web site: http://www.lmu.edu

LOYOLA UNIVERSITY CHICAGO

4 PR G M Sc

▼ Honors Program

Since 1936, the Honors Program has served the most intellectually talented and highly motivated students at Loyola University Chicago. In an atmosphere charged with challenging teaching methods and enthusiastic student participation, professors and students work together in small, stimulating honors classes, exploring critical issues in each discipline.

The intimate, collegial atmosphere helps develop a close working relationship among honors students and faculty members. The most motivated students capitalize on this relationship by becoming involved with independent faculty research projects and by attending a multitude of "brown bag" colloquia by resident and visiting scholars.

While honors students and faculty members come from all across the country and from all walks of life, they share a common bond—the search for truth and meaning through analysis, discussion, and research. Collaboration and individual attention are the hallmarks of the program. As a result, honors students experience a unique sense of community even within the context of the larger university community.

This sense of community is manifest outside the classroom as well. Honors students enjoy social and intellectual interaction in the honors common rooms. They plan social and cultural events as members of the Honors Student Association. Lively classroom discussion, close faculty-student working relationships, a strong sense of community, and intellectual rigor combine in the Honors Program to create the best atmosphere for students wanting to take full advantage of the educational opportunities at Loyola University Chicago.

There are 900 students in the program, which represents 20 percent of each class.

Participation Requirements: Designed for flexibility, the Honors Program curriculum provides an opportunity for in-depth exploration of critical issues within Loyola's Core Curriculum. No additional courses are required to earn the honors degree. Approximately one third (42 semester hours) of an honors student's courses must carry honors credit. Honors credits can be earned by taking special honors sections in core courses, by contracting with a professor in a regular course, or by taking graduate-level courses. Students who fulfill the course requirements of the Honors Program with a GPA of 3.3 receive the honors degree. This distinction is noted at graduation and is recorded on transcripts.

Admission Process: Students who have a weighted GPA of at least a 3.5 and an ACT score of 27 or higher or an SAT score of 1200 or higher are automatically admitted to the Honors Program when they apply for admission to the University. If a student does not meet these initial criteria, he or she is welcome to apply for admission to the Honors Program. The completed Honors Program application includes an essay, one faculty recommendation, and a current high school transcript. Completed applications must be received by March 1.

Scholarship Availability: Students who are admitted to the Honors Program are invited to apply for one of three full-tuition scholarships. The completed Ignatian Scholarship application includes an essay, one faculty recommendation, and a current high school transcript. Candidates are selected for a faculty interview on campus in April. Recipients of this award traditionally have a GPA of 3.7 or higher (on a 4.0 scale) and an ACT score of 29 or SAT score of 1300. Extracurricular involvement, leadership experience, and service are important as well.

In addition, Loyola University Chicago provides scholarships, grants, loans, and work-study jobs for those students who qualify.

The Campus Context: Loyola University's traditional undergraduate liberal arts campus is located on a 45-acre site of large trees and open green space along the shore of Lake Michigan on Chicago's far north side. Nearly 2,000 students reside in on-campus housing. The Lake Shore campus is also home to the Marcella Niehoff School of Nursing. In addition, Loyola University has Schools of Business, Social Work, Law, Education, and Medicine. Degree programs include the B.A., B.S., B.S.Ed., B.A. (Classics), B.B.A., and B.S.N.

Student Body There are approximately 1,432 freshmen and a total of 7,500 undergraduates. Students come from all fifty states and eighty-two other countries. Approximately 30 percent of the student body are African American, Asian-American, Latin American, or Native American. The student-faculty ratio is 13:1. More than seventy-five percent of students receive financial aid.

Faculty Of the 421 full-time faculty members, 96 percent have terminal degrees. Of the 275 part-time faculty members, 49 percent have terminal degrees.

Key Facilities There are 1.3 million volumes in the combined university libraries and open computer labs on all campuses.

Athletics Loyola participates in NCAA Division I in eleven sports, as well as having many intramural team and individual sports. Large fitness and recreational sports facilities are available on several campuses.

Study Abroad Through Loyola's Rome Center Campus, students in all majors have the opportunity to earn Loyola credit while studying in Rome for a semester, a year, or a summer.

Tuition: $18,814 per year (2001–02)

Room and Board: $7400

Mandatory Fees: $588 per year

Contact: Director: Dr. Joyce Wexler, 6525 North Sheridan, Chicago, Illinois 60626; Telephone: 312-508-2780

LOYOLA UNIVERSITY NEW ORLEANS

4 Pr G S Tr

▼ University Honors Program

The Loyola University Honors Program offers the opportunity for academically superior, highly motivated students to take challenging honors courses and to participate in special cultural and intellectual enrichment activities.

Honors students also participate together in such cultural activities as trips to the opera, theater, and art museums, and they attend special seminars and lectures. These supplemental activities are optional but are usually very popular and well-attended. Honors students also have the use of a University honors center as a place to study, relax, and discuss. In addition, students in the full University Honors Program have priority registration with seniors. An active student University Honors Association plans social activities and programming and works with the Honors Director and the University Honors Advisory Board on developing curriculum and policy for the program.

In addition to the University Honors Program and Honors Certificate Program, several departments at Loyola have departmental honors programs, which usually consist of special research projects in the senior year and require GPAs of 3.5 in the major. Students can participate in both the University Honors Program and the honors program of their major.

University Honors graduates wear a white stole at graduation, and their achievement is noted in the graduation program and on their diploma and transcript. Honors Certificate Students are so designated in the graduation program and on their transcripts. A University Honors Program Outstanding Student Award is presented annually to the graduating senior with the highest GPA in honors classes, and a University Honors Association Award is presented to the graduating senior who has the most outstanding record of community service to the Honors Program, Loyola University, and the larger community.

The 16-year-old program currently has an enrollment of 140. About 5–8 percent of the entering first-year students are in the Honors Program.

Participation Requirements: The Honors Program is open to qualified students of all undergraduate colleges and majors. Students in the University Honors Program take a total of 48 credit hours of honors courses throughout the four undergraduate years. These honors courses replace the required common-curriculum courses and therefore do not add to the number of requirements for graduation. In addition to the full University Honors Program, qualified students may choose to participate in the Honors Certificate Program, which consists of 24 credit hours of honors courses. Honors certificate students complete their common-curriculum requirements from the regular nonhonors offerings. Students in the University Honors Program and the Honors Certificate Program are required to maintain a 3.3 overall GPA.

The Honors curriculum includes courses in literature, philosophy, history, religious studies, art, economics, political science, math, and sciences. In their senior year, honors students in the College of Arts and Sciences write a thesis based on original research and students in the Colleges of Business Administration and Music take specially designed honors courses in their major. The honors classes, which are taught by the most outstanding faculty members, are usually smaller than the regular classes, and emphasize active student participation, extensive readings in primary sources, and challenging writing assignments.

Admission Process: Incoming freshmen with high SAT I (1300) or ACT (29) scores and high school GPAs of 3.5 or better are invited to apply to the University Honors Program. The application consists of an essay and a teacher recommendation. The University Honors Advisory Board, consisting of faculty members and Honors students, evaluates the applications and selects the participants. In addition, students with outstanding academic records (3.5 GPA or higher) in their freshman year at Loyola, as well as qualified transfer students, are invited to apply to the Honors Program. If accepted, they are given Honors credit for previous work that was equivalent to the Loyola freshman honors courses. Qualified students who want to enter the Honors Program after the beginning of their sophomore year usually enter the Honors Certificate Program.

The deadline for applying to the program is March 10.

Scholarship Availability: Although many students in the University Honors Program receive full or partial University scholarships, the scholarships are not tied to participation in the University Honors Program.

The Campus Context: Loyola University New Orleans is a coeducational Jesuit university in historic uptown New Orleans. Founded by the Society of Jesus in 1912 as a Catholic and Jesuit institution, Loyola is committed to providing a rigorous value-centered liberal arts education to all qualified persons without regard to race, ethnicity, creed, age, or sex. Loyola is composed of five colleges: the College of Arts and Sciences, the College of Business Administration, the College of Music, the School of Law, and the City College for evening students. Loyola University New Orleans has been listed among the top 10 regional colleges and universities in the South by *U.S. News & World Report* and has been rated as one of the nation's best opportunities for affordable quality education in *Barron's 300: Best Buys in College Education* and *America's 200 Best Buys in College Education.* The University offers ninety-five undergraduate, graduate, and law degree programs.

Student Body The undergraduate enrollment is 3,583—38 percent men and 62 percent women. The ethnic distribution is 3.4 percent Asian, 13 percent African American, 13 percent Hispanic, .6 percent Native American, 64 percent white, .5 percent other, and 5.5 percent unspecified. There are 233 international students. Thirty-four percent of the students are residents; 66 percent are commuters. A dedicated honors living unit in Buddig residence hall houses 40 freshmen and upperclassmen. Sixty-four percent of students receive financial aid. There are three fraternities and six sororities.

Faculty The faculty numbers 251 full-time and 171 part-time. Eighty-six percent have terminal degrees. The student-faculty ratio is 11.9:1.

Key Facilities Loyola University New Orleans has outstanding facilities for its nationally renowned College of Music, including a 600-seat performance hall with excellent acoustics, a music recording studio, and a computerized piano laboratory. The Department of Communications has one of the most highly equipped facilities in the South, with television and radio studios, graphic arts studios, an engineering shop, darkrooms, and a news bureau with national wire service. Writing labs are in all major buildings, equipped not only with computers but also with skilled writing tutors. Academic enrichment provides special facilities for students who need extra help with academic work. There are eleven computer labs in instructional buildings, plus computer clusters in the three residence halls. The new Edgar S. and Louise Monroe Library opened in February 1999. It has a capacity of 500,000 volumes; some of its computer facilities are open 24 hours per day seven days per week. The University Honors Program serves as a clearinghouse for information on prestigious fellowships such as the Rhodes, British Marshall, Truman, and Hertz Foundation and offers support for students applying for these awards.

Athletics Intercollegiate sports (NAIA Division 1) include men's basketball, baseball, golf, tennis, and cross-country and women's basketball, golf, soccer, tennis, cross-country, and volleyball. In addition, students can join many intramural sports clubs. The Recreational Sports Complex includes an Olympic-size pool, handball courts, indoor tennis courts, a state-of-the-art weight room, an indoor track, and a basketball court.

Study Abroad The University Honors Program encourages students to participate in study-abroad programs. Loyola sponsors summer programs in Mexico, Italy, Belgium, Greece, and London. The program in Mexico is also available for a semester and a year. The College of Business Administration also sponsors various international internships.

Support Services The University is fully accessible to disabled students.

Job Opportunities Work-study is awarded through the financial aid process; student assistantships are available through each department and are not contingent on being eligible for financial aid. Positions are available in the residence halls as resident assistants and desk assistants. In addition, the Counseling and Career Development and Placement Center maintains listings of employment opportunities in the local community as well as nationally.

Interpreting the symbols: **2**=two-year college, **4**=four-year college; **Pu**=public or state college, **Pr**=private college; **G**=general honors program; **D**=departmental honors program; **S**=small program (fewer than 100 students), **M**=midsize program (100 to 500 students), **L**=large program (more than 500 students); **Sc**=scholarships available in honors program; **Tr**=transfer students accepted into honors program; **HBC**=historically black college; **AA**=academic advisors; **GA**=graduate advisors; **FA**=fellowship advisors.

Tuition: $12,948 per year (1997–98)
Room and Board: $5830
Mandatory Fees: $316
Contact: Director: Dr. Ted Cotton, Monroe 537M, Box 75, 6363 St. Charles Avenue, New Orleans, Louisiana 70118; Telephone: 504-865-2708; Fax: 504-865-2709; E-mail: honors@loyno.edu or cotton@loyno.edu

LUBBOCK CHRISTIAN UNIVERSITY

4 Pr G S Sc

▼ University Honors Program

The University Honors Program provides students of high academic ability an opportunity to enhance their college educational experience with challenging and stimulating courses. Although it does not require its students to take any more courses or hours than they would take otherwise, the program provides more depth and breadth of study within the courses they do take. The emphasis is on quality and not quantity—that is, honors classes, capped at a maximum of 15 students each, typically are discussion-based and student-centered, dealing with meaningful ideas rather than just adding extra volumes of work to the course load.

Honors faculty members, the Honors Director, the University's Academic Vice President, and honors student representatives comprise the Honors Advisory Council, which makes policy and offers guidance to the program. Students also participate in monthly informal luncheons with the Director and honors faculty members; occasional dinners in faculty members' homes; various service projects; and excursions to concerts, theatrical performances, and museums and other field trips relevant to honors classes.

Benefits of the program include honors academic scholarships, preferred dorm placement, interesting and challenging courses, small class size, the collegiality of like-minded students and professors in academic as well as social settings, the distinction of an honors designation on the transcript, honors recognition at graduation, enhanced marketability of being an honors graduate, study-abroad opportunities, travel scholarships to regional and national conferences, and affiliation with the National Collegiate Honors Council and the Great Plains Honors Council.

The program began in fall 2000 with its first cohort of 15 students with plans to add one or two new cohorts each fall.

Participation Requirements: The University Honors Program is open to students of any major. The program consists of 30 hours of required honors credit. Twelve of these 30 semester hours are taken in an honors core of four courses. These core courses are English, Bible, history, and science, and they satisfy either University or departmental core requirements. All honors students take these courses as the foundation of the honors experience.

An additional 18 hours of the 30 required are courses designated for honors credit. The University presently offers an additional 12 hours of honors courses on a variety of topics, and it plans to continue to add courses as the program grows and develops. Included in these 12 hours is a senior capstone course, HON 4399, Writings and Research, designed to give honors students an opportunity to engage in an extensive research project on an issue or problem in their major field of study. Students fulfill the remaining 6 hours of required honors credit by entering into honors contracts with instructors of a variety of primarily upper-division classes, usually in their majors. In these classes, faculty members give honors students more challenging work to earn the honors designation.

Continuation in the honors program is based on a 3.5 or higher GPA in all honors courses and a 3.25 or higher GPA in all courses. Honors students who successfully complete the 30 hours of honors course work and maintain the GPA requirements receive honors recognition at graduation as well as the distinction of an honors designation on their transcripts and diplomas.

Admission Process: Acceptance in the honors program is based on an ACT composite score of 27 or higher or SAT I composite score of 1210 or higher and a high school transcript with a GPA of 3.5/4.0 or higher or a ranking in the top 10 percent of the graduating class.

Scholarship Availability: Lubbock Christian University offers significant scholarship assistance to deserving students, including an annually renewable $1000 Honors Scholarship to students whose ACT/SAT I and high school GPA scores qualify them for the University Honors Program. This Honors Scholarship is in addition to other academic scholarships awarded by the University. Continuation of the Honors Scholarship is based on students successfully meeting the honors program's GPA and course requirements.

The Campus Context: Lubbock Christian University (LCU) is an institution of higher learning that works to prepare men and women for professional roles and to function effectively in society and in lifelong Christian service. The school is a residential university that grants baccalaureate degrees and master's-level graduate degrees. LCU is divided into three separate colleges: the J.E. and Eileen Hancock College of Liberal Arts, the College of Professional Studies, and the College of Education. Graduate programs in biblical studies and education serve to achieve the goal of preparing leaders for both church and community. There are some features about Lubbock Christian University that set it apart from other colleges. Along with academic training, values related to integrity, truthfulness, morality, family, work ethic, respect of people, and respect of property are taught in light of the Bible. LCU has been named to the Templeton Honor Roll of Character Building Colleges. This honor roll is a listing of schools that encourage the development of strong moral character among students. Character development is a part of campus life and training and is offered to schools and communities across the U.S. and in many other countries. The unique combination of academic training, Christian values, and character training allows graduates to be exceptionally prepared for all walks of life.

Student Body Total enrollment is 1,823: 44 percent men, 56 percent women. Ethnic distribution is 82 percent Caucasian, 10 percent Hispanic, 5 percent African American, 1 percent Asian and Native American, and 2 percent other international ethnicities. Religious affiliations include 50 percent Church of Christ, 17 percent Baptist, 5 percent Catholic, 4 percent Methodist, 5 percent nondenominational, and 19 percent other religions. The campus has social organizations for men and women, mission/Bible gatherings, professional organizations, service organizations, and honors societies.

Faculty The total number of faculty members is 146 (82 are full-time, of whom 52 percent have terminal degrees). The student-faculty ratio is 16:1.

Key Facilities The University Library, located in the east wing of the Administration Building since 1959, was renovated in 1991 with a grant from the Mabee Foundation. The renovation provided a new addition, the Mabee Learning Center with the Pioneer Gallery. The library provides academic support with more than 110,000 books plus periodicals and microforms. The library has electronic databases, Internet access, and an online public-access catalog.

An Information Services computer lab for student use is located in the James and Eva Mayer Multimedia Center. The Morrison Distance Learning Center opened in January 2001 and offers the latest technology for online and distance courses. An interactive television (ITV) classroom is scheduled for completion in May 2002. There are thirteen other computer labs across campus for more discipline-specific instruction, including a visual communications design studio, a lab for CIS majors, a networked computer classroom/lab for humanities, and labs for business, the sciences, agriculture, and education. In addition, all classrooms on campus have Internet access.

Athletics As a participant in the NAIA, LCU provides junior varsity and varsity intercollegiate athletics for both men and women. Women can compete in volleyball and basketball. Basketball and baseball are available for men. Students can participate in an intramural program and have access to the Ramona Perrin Fitness Center.

Study Abroad LCU has two study-abroad programs. There are LCU faculty-led courses taught in various international locations during the summer (for example, London and Mexico City in recent summers) and semester-long programs under the direction of LCU faculty members but taught on location by faculty members from other universities in locations such as Uruguay, Italy, and Mexico.

Support Services The Academic Support Center (ASC) provides students, at their request or with a referral from a faculty member, peer tutoring services for academic courses. Students may also request assistance in improving study skills, time management, note taking, and other appropriate skills to enhance their academic abilities. There are no charges for ASC services.

Job Opportunities The Career Planning and Placement office provides information on part-time and full-time positions for current LCU students and recent alumni. The office houses resources to compose and edit resumes, research businesses or organizations, choose a graduate school, and find a summer job or internship as well as offering other services. Career Services coordinates job fairs, workshops/seminars, and a career evaluation program. Many academic degrees require practicum/ internships with local businesses or organizations.

Tuition: $9784 per year; $306 per semester hour (2000–2001)

Room and Board: $3950 per year

Mandatory Fees: $334 per year

Contact: Director: Dr. Jim Bullock, 5601 19th Street, Lubbock, Texas 79407-2099; Telephone: 806-720-7603; Fax: 806-796-8917; E-mail: jim.bullock@lcu.edu; Web site: http://www.lcu.edu/honors/

Lynchburg College

4 Pr G S Tr AA

▼ Westover Honors Program

The Westover Honors Program offers exceptional undergraduates an alternative to the College's traditional general education curriculum. The honors curriculum makes heavy use of the seminar format and places strong emphasis on collaborative learning and problem solving. The multidisciplinary curriculum is designed to break down intellectual barriers and expose students to new ways of looking at old problems. The faculty members strive to build bridges across the curriculum in order to facilitate the integration of ideas from a variety of disciplines and to form a coherent body of knowledge.

Because of their maturity, self-discipline, and heightened intellectual ability, Westover Fellows take on a significant share of the responsibility for their own education. The seminar format requires high-quality student participation in the classroom and considerable preparation before class. Group projects, research papers, and oral presentations are required in most honors courses. As active members of a vital learning community, students and faculty members engage one another in open discussion as they explore new avenues of inquiry together. The program's maxim is "Question. Doubt. Challenge."

Recognizing that the sharing of ideas and potentially unpopular opinions is a risky endeavor, participants and leaders of the program make every effort to promote a classroom environment characterized by trust and mutual respect. A freshman orientation retreat allows incoming fellows to develop strong bonds before the academic year begins. A freshman seminar introduces students to basic principles of interpersonal communication, conflict resolution, critical thinking, and argumentation. Weekly lunches (attended by honors faculty members and students), freshman honors housing, membership in the Society of Westover Fellows, student representation on the program's advisory council, and a variety of social and educational activities all help to forge a true sense of community.

The program, established in 1987, seeks to admit 20 freshmen annually. There are approximately 50 students currently enrolled.

Participation Requirements: In their freshman year, fellows take 16 credits in honors (Advanced English Composition, Mathematics Seminar, Social Science Seminar, a two-semester Humanities Seminar, and the 1-credit Freshman Seminar), which constitute approximately half of their academic course load. Fellows take 17 credits of honors courses in their sophomore year and an additional 15 credits over the next two years. Examples of recent junior/senior colloquia include America in Vietnam, Manifestations of Anger in Contemporary Society, and Heroes as Persuasive Figures. All students must satisfy the College's foreign language and wellness requirements.

During the first two years in the program, students acquire and refine the essential skills and competencies needed to complete the required Senior Honors Project. This project, normally in the student's major concentration and guided by a faculty committee, culminates in a formal defense that is open to the entire Westover community.

To remain in the program, fellows must maintain both a semester and cumulative GPA of at least 3.0. Successful completion of the program is recognized at commencement, and the designation of Westover Honors Graduate is noted on the diploma.

Admission Process: To be eligible for participation as a freshman, students must have a combined SAT score of at least 1200 and a cumulative high school GPA of at least 3.5. Eligible students are invited to join the program upon their acceptance to the College. Others may contact the Director for special consideration of their qualifications. While most students enter the program as freshmen, some students are invited to enter as sophomores. Invitations are based on the student's freshman year academic performance, recommendations from faculty members, and a personal interview.

Scholarship Availability: Lynchburg College offers academic (merit) scholarships on the basis of high school GPA and SAT scores. For the 2002–03 academic year, scholarships for freshmen in the Westover ability group are $10,000. High school class valedictorians or salutatorians receive an additional $2000. Students may qualify for additional aid based on need and other criteria.

The Campus Context: Lynchburg College, founded in 1903, is located in Lynchburg, Virginia, about 180 miles southwest of Washington, D.C. Its 214-acre campus, with the Blue Ridge Mountains forming the western skyline, has a view and landscape of exceptional beauty. The campus features thirty buildings, predominantly of Georgian style, grouped around the main campus oval. Nearby are the athletic fields, tennis courts, and a small lake. Special facilities include a theater, an art gallery, a

Interpreting the symbols: **2**=two-year college, **4**=four-year college; **Pu**=public or state college, **Pr**=private college; **G**=general honors program; **D**=departmental honors program; **S**=small program (fewer than 100 students), **M**=midsize program (100 to 500 students), **L**=large program (more than 500 students); **Sc**=scholarships available in honors program; **Tr**=transfer students accepted into honors program; **HBC**=historically black college; **AA**=academic advisors; **GA**=graduate advisors; **FA**=fellowship advisors.

ballroom, a chapel, a computer center, a writing center, language labs, technology classrooms, an arboretum, and the 470-acre Claytor Nature Study Center, overlooking the Peaks of Otter, in nearby Bedford County. A state-of-the-art academic and conference complex, featuring a performance auditorium, videoconferencing spaces, a television studio, and a model stock exchange facility, is under construction.

Lynchburg College is a coeducational, nonsectarian liberal arts college related to the Christian Church (Disciples of Christ). Accredited by the Southern Association of Colleges and Schools (SACS), the College offers undergraduate programs in the liberal arts, sciences, and professional disciplines (business, communications, education, and nursing) and graduate programs in business and education.

Student Body Total full-time undergraduate enrollment is 1,680 (40 percent men and 60 percent women). Students come from thirty-seven states and eleven other countries; 45 percent are from out of state. Seven percent are black, 2 percent are Hispanic, 1 percent are Asian, and 1 percent are international. Unless they are living with a family, freshmen, sophomores, and juniors are required to live in College housing. There are four national service fraternities and four national service sororities on campus.

Faculty The total number of full-time faculty members is 109 (68 men and 41 women); part-time faculty members number 82. The student-faculty ratio is 13:1.

Key Facilities To support student and faculty learning and research, the Knight-Capron Library maintains a collection of traditional print and media resources as well as a continuously evolving variety of electronic information resources. Information technology resources include a campuswide network connecting all campus buildings, offices, classrooms, and dormitory rooms to the Internet. All students are provided an e-mail account and shared file space for course work and personal Web pages. Sixteen computer laboratories designed to give students ready access to course-related software and the campus network are available.

Honorary Societies Phi Kappa Phi, Phi Eta Sigma, Alpha Psi Omega, Kappa Delta Pi, Lambda Pi Eta, Omicron Delta Kappa, Phi Alpha Theta, Phi Sigma Iota, Pi Sigma Alpha, Psi Chi, Sigma Tau Delta, and Sigma Theta Tau

Athletics Lynchburg College offers twenty-one intercollegiate sports that compete at the NCAA Division III level in the Old Dominion Athletic Conference. Varsity athletics integrates academic rigor with enthusiastic competition in ten women's sports: basketball, cross-country, field hockey, lacrosse, soccer, softball, tennis, indoor track, outdoor track, and volleyball; nine men's sports: baseball, basketball, cross-country, golf, lacrosse, soccer, tennis, indoor track, and outdoor track; and two coed sports: cheerleading and equestrian.

Study Abroad Lynchburg College encourages its students to spend some time studying abroad. In recent years, the College has offered study-abroad opportunities in languages, literature, art, and international relations in Spain, France, Argentina, Costa Rica, England, and Australia. Students may also consider study-abroad programs offered by AustraLearn, AIFS, ISA, IUS, and other college and university programs.

Support Services Health and counseling services are offered to individuals or groups to promote the emotional, mental, and physical well-being of students. The Career Development Center offers resources, services, and counseling to assist students in internship and career planning. Both the Director of the Honors Program and a professor in the fellow's major serve to advise on academic matters.

Job Opportunities The College offers work opportunities funded by the Federal Work-Study Program and the College Work Program. A job fair is held during orientation, and applications are made directly to Personnel Services–Student Employment.

Tuition: $18,880 per year (2001–02)

Room and Board: $4400 to $5000 (depending on choice of meal plan)

Mandatory Fees: $125 per year (Student Activities Fee)

Contact: Dr. Richard Seymann, Director, or Ms. Rita Detwiler, Vice President for Enrollment Management, 1501 Lakeside Drive, Lynchburg, Virginia 24501; Telephone: 434-544-8100; E-mail: seymann@lynchburg.edu; Web site: http://www.lynchburg.edu/public/westover/

MANCHESTER COLLEGE

4 Pr G M Sc Tr AA

▼ Honors Program

Manchester College has developed the Honors Program to encourage and stimulate students who are seriously interested in expanding their educational opportunities. Currently, more than 10 percent of the student body participates in the Honors Program. Those involved say they enjoy the freedom to study in their own style. At Manchester College, those who become honors students often share common traits. They are self-disciplined, creative, and organized. They are motivated, with a strong desire to learn. They want to do their best. They know that when they expand their minds and move beyond the norm, they expand their opportunities. Unlike some honors programs at other colleges, Manchester honors students aren't set apart from other students. On Manchester's campus, honors students are involved in many campus activities. One current student participates in the Accounting Club, Hispanos Unidos, Modern Languages Club, and is on the women's golf team. Another is a member of the Student Education Association, the Honors Organization, and the cross-country and track teams. A third student worked with the Manchester College Mediation and Reconciliation Team, Manchester Activities Council, and founded TUNSIS, a residential theme unit in Oakwook Hall for students interested in the relationships between science and society. Participants in the Honors Program may sign up for honors courses offered each year; convert regular courses for honors credit; choose to write an Honors Thesis, earning 6 credits toward graduation and public recognition at commencement; earn an Honors Diploma; show graduate schools and employers their accomplishments, because all honors courses are marked on their transcripts; and participate in off-campus cultural events sponsored by the Student Honors Organization. In the 2001–02 academic year, 130 students participated in the program.

Participation Requirements: Honors program participants must maintain a GPA of 3.5 or higher and complete at least 5 semester hours of honors work per academic year. Honors status is maintained for up to a full year for students participating in an approved off-campus program. A small percentage of honors students choose to complete the Honors Diploma. This diploma testifies to the student's ability both to do broad-based study and to plan and complete a significant project associated with the student's major. Requirements for the diploma include a distribution of honors courses and an Honors Thesis.

Admission Process: There are two ways to be admitted to the Honors Program. First, students can be admitted as first-year students. Highly qualified students automatically receive an application for the Honors Program. Such students typically have excellent standardized test scores (an SAT I of 1200 or above, for example) and class rank (generally in the top 5 percent) or other qualifications that indicate strong academic potential. Second, students can apply after starting at Manchester College. Current students can qualify once they have accumulated 28 semester hours of Manchester College credit and have a cumulative GPA of at least 3.5. Transfer students with sophomore standing and a cumulative GPA of at least 3.5 after 12 semester hours of Manchester College credit may also apply.

Scholarship Availability: Nearly all Manchester College Honors Program students receive merit-based scholarships that are awarded through the Offices of Admissions and Financial Aid. While participation in the Honors Program is not a condition for these awards, most of the College's top scholars actively pursue honors work.

The Campus Context: Manchester College seeks to graduate persons of ability and conviction. Grounded in the liberal arts, Manchester offers Bachelor of Science and Bachelor of Arts degrees in thirty-five areas. Manchester is especially known for its programs in accounting, premedicine, education, psychology, and communication studies. Distinctive programs include the nation's first peace studies major and programs in small business administration and nonprofit management.

Manchester College is located in North Manchester, a rural community just 30 minutes from Fort Wayne, Indiana's second-largest city.

Student Body With a student body of approximately 1,200 students, Manchester offers close personal attention, small classes, and a faculty dedicated to teaching. About 85 percent of the student body comes from Indiana, with the balance coming from twenty-three states and twenty-nine countries. Enrollment is nearly equally divided between men and women. International students constitute about 7 percent of the student body, and students of color about 8 percent. Fully 98 percent of Manchester's students received financial aid in 2001–02, with more than $7.1 million in institutional funds awarded.

Faculty Manchester's 72 full-time faculty members are dedicated to teaching and academic advising. Nearly 93 percent hold the Ph.D. or terminal degree in their field. First-year students receive academic advising from primary advisers, full-time faculty members especially trained to address the needs and questions of first-year students.

Key Facilities More than 175,000 volumes fill Manchester's Funderburg Library. Extensive collections are available through interlibrary loan, and databases are available on line. More than 170 computers give students access to a campuswide network and the Internet and are available to students in the Clark Computer Center lab, in residence hall computer labs, and in various departmental labs.

Athletics Manchester College is a member of the NCAA Division III Heartland Collegiate Athletic Conference (HCAC). Athletic opportunities are offered in baseball (men), basketball (men and women), cross-country (men and women), football (men), golf (men and women), soccer (men and women), softball (women), tennis (men and women), track and field (men and women), volleyball (women), and wrestling (men).

Study Abroad Students can study abroad for a semester or a full year in Ecuador, Mexico, China, Japan, India, France, Spain, Greece, England, and Germany. Many students travel abroad during Manchester's three-week January session.

Support Services The Learning Center provides support services for all students. Tutors; study groups; workshops and seminars on time management, study skills, and other success skills; and designated advising are all available through the Learning Center.

Job Opportunities Students are able to work up to 20 hours per week in a wide variety of jobs on campus, from student assistantships in academic and administrative offices to jobs in the library and custodial and food services.

Tuition: $15,230 per year full-time, $505 per credit part-time (2001–02)

Room and Board: $5550

Contact: Director: Dr. Diane Monaco, 604 East College Avenue, North Manchester, Indiana 46962; Telephone: 260-982-5301; Fax: 260-982-5043; E-mail: dkmonaco@manchester.edu; Web site: http://www.manchester.edu/

MANSFIELD UNIVERSITY OF PENNSYLVANIA

4 Pu G S Sc Tr

▼ Honors Program

The Mansfield University Honors Program is a multidisciplinary academic program that features innovative course work and challenging subjects. This program is designed for students with a strong record of academic achievement and desire for new learning experiences. The Honors Program enables students to explore subjects that interest them in greater depth than may be possible in traditional courses and to apply their learned knowledge across traditional academic subjects. It is the goal of the Honors Program to provide students with the knowledge, skills, and opportunities to achieve their full potential during their academic career at Mansfield University. To ensure that this objective is met, the Honors Program offers a dynamic learning environment that includes small classes, unique courses, collaborative and individual research projects, and field-based educational experiences.

All honors students are required to complete a core of honors courses that expose them to the arts, humanities, and sciences. These courses are designed to promote creativity, critical thinking, coherent expression, and a more keen awareness of the world. Honors students are also required to complete honors course electives, the content of which varies each semester. Finally, all honors students are required to complete a capstone Senior Honors Research Project and present their work to the campus community.

Mansfield University's Honors Program is administered by a director and an Honors Council. The Honors Program Director is responsible for the day-to-day operation of the program. The Honors Council consists of faculty members who regularly teach honors courses. The council members share the responsibility of advising honors students. Approximately 70 students are currently enrolled in the Honors Program.

Participation Requirements: All honors students are required to complete five specially-designed core courses, two honors electives, and a Senior Honors Research Project. The Senior Honors Research Project is an independent study experience that is initiated by the student to explore an area of interest. To remain in good standing in the Honors Program, students must maintain at least a 3.0 cumulative GPA in their honors courses and overall. Successful completion of the program is recognized at the annual University-wide honors banquet and is also noted on the official transcript.

Admission Process: Enrollment in Mansfield's Honors Program is by invitation. Incoming freshmen with high class rank and board (SAT I) scores are invited to accept early admission into the Honors Program. Freshman students who exhibit strong academic potential during their first semester are invited to join the program on the basis of faculty recommendation and an interview with the Honors Program Director. Freshmen who have completed their first semester and who have demonstrated excellence in their academic course work are invited to apply for admission into the program. Finally, any first-year student can forward a

Interpreting the symbols: **2**=two-year college, **4**=four-year college; **Pu**=public or state college, **Pr**=private college; **G**=general honors program; **D**=departmental honors program; **S**=small program (fewer than 100 students), **M**=midsize program (100 to 500 students), **L**=large program (more than 500 students); **Sc**=scholarships available in honors program; **Tr**=transfer students accepted into honors program; **HBC**=historically black college; **AA**=academic advisors; **GA**=graduate advisors; **FA**=fellowship advisors.

written request to the Honors Program Director to be considered for admission into the program.

Scholarship Availability: More than sixty scholarships of varying amounts and duration are available for incoming and returning students. These scholarships are awarded by the Mansfield University Financial Aid Office. Four Honors Program Scholarships are awarded each fall to students who are excelling in the Honors Program and at the University. Full scholarships are also provided for the 2 students selected to attend the Summer Honors Program.

The Campus Context: The borough of Mansfield is located in rural North Central Pennsylvania, approximately 30 miles south of Corning, New York, and 50 miles north of Williamsport, Pennsylvania. Founded in 1857, Mansfield Classical Seminary had the shortest life span of any college on record. Four months after it opened, it burned to the ground. The area people believed so strongly in their dream of having a higher education institution that they built it again. This time it remained. Today, Mansfield University is one of fourteen public universities in the Pennsylvania State System of Higher Education. Mansfield offers seventy-seven four-year baccalaureate programs, forty-three academic minors, thirteen two-year associate degree programs, and six master's degree programs. Mansfield University is a place where students and faculty members have the opportunity to get to know each other. Many students embark on research projects with faculty members.

Student Body There were 2,907 students enrolled during the fall of 1997 (2,483 full-time and 424 part-time). Of these, 58 percent were women and 42 percent were men. Forty-five percent of the students come from more than 150 miles away. Nearly 90 percent of the students receive financial aid. Most students participate in one or more of the nearly seventy clubs, fraternities, sororities, and organizations on campus.

Faculty Of the 190 faculty members, 174 are full-time. Approximately 80 percent of the faculty members have terminal degrees. The student-faculty ratio is 16:1, with about 80 percent of the classes having fewer than 30 students.

Key Facilities Renovated in 1996 into a state-of-the-art library, North Hall houses approximately 250,000 volumes and has nearly 500 networked ports to which lap tops can connect to the campus network. Shared catalog and databases throughout the State System of Higher Education provide access to millions of items, many of which are full text. A campuswide network can be accessed from student dorms and off campus. Public labs with access to the Internet, e-mail, and locally served applications are accessible throughout the campus.

Honorary Societies Lambda Sigma

Athletics Mansfield University is a member of the Pennsylvania State Athletic Conference, the largest NCAA Division II conference in the country. Varsity sports available to students include field hockey (W), football (M), baseball (M), softball (W), basketball (M/W), swimming and diving (W), track and field (M/W), and wrestling (M). In addition to varsity sports, a host of intramural sports are offered throughout the year, many taking place in the recently completed Rod C. Kelchner Recreation Center.

Study Abroad Mansfield University has established direct student exchange programs with Charles Sturt University in Australia and Volgograd State University in Russia. Other exchange programs can be arranged through the Office of Cross-Cultural Studies. Selected honors students have the opportunity for study abroad in conjunction with the State System of Higher Education Summer Honors Program.

Support Services The University provides developmental services to students for the successful pursuit of their academic program and personal development. Assistance is available through the Academic Advising Center, Academic Success Center, Athletic Mentoring Program, Counseling Center, Writing Center, and Career Planning and Placement Services.

Job Opportunities Limited employment is available at the University through state and Federal Work-Study programs for students who have shown an evidence of financial need.

Tuition: $3468 for residents, $5202 for good neighbor residents (New York residents from the counties of Broome, Cayuga, Chemung, Cortland, Livingston, Monroe, Onondaga, Ontario, Oswego, Schuyler, Seneca, Steuben, Tompkins, Tioga, Wayne, and Yates), $8824 for nonresidents, per year (1998–99)

Room and board: $3770

Mandatory Fees: $1000 approximately

Contact: Director: Dr. Michael J. Chester, 121 Grant Science, Mansfield, Pennsylvania 16933; Telephone: 570-662-4753; E-mail: mchester@mnsfld.edu

Maricopa Community Colleges

2 Pu G L Sc Tr

▼ District Honors Program

The mission of the Honors Program at Maricopa Community Colleges is to foster a climate of excellence in the colleges and the surrounding communities, to recognize and reward the talent and motivation of outstanding community college students and faculty members, to promote a sense of scholarship and community among program participants and among the colleges, and to raise the awareness of the high quality and variety of educational opportunities and services.

The Honors Program of Maricopa Community Colleges was initiated in January 1981 with an internal grant.

The initial grant allowed a faculty committee to investigate the initiation of a community college honors program and to determine factors that were crucial to the design of such a program. In June 1981, the Governing Board allocated funds for the development and implementation of honors programs at each of the Maricopa Community Colleges. The Office of the Vice Chancellor for Student and Educational Development was assigned to provide coordination of the colleges' programs. Since 1981, the Governing Board has approved funds each year to support the colleges' programs. The Honors Committee at each campus is free within district guidelines to administer these funds according to its needs.

The Honors Forum Lecture Series features nationally known speakers who address specific issues related to an annual theme. The theme is generally adapted from the annual study topic and materials developed by Phi Theta Kappa, the two-year college honorary society.

An Honors Forum course offered at the colleges explores in greater depth the theme and issues discussed throughout the year. The Forum activities provide the opportunity for all honors students throughout MCCCD to have common learning experiences based on the topic chosen for the year. Honors students may be required to attend the lecture and write a synopsis for the honors forum class.

Three times each fall and spring semester, a guest speaker visits two of the ten colleges for informal discussion and a question-and-answer period. A third college hosts dinner with the distinguished visitor. College faculty members and students are invited, as well as the Chancellor, Vice-Chancellors, and Governing Board members. All honors students, faculty members, staff, administrators, and Governing Board members are invited to "Applaud and Celebrate" the activities and accomplishments of the year at an annual convocation held in the spring. Students are recognized and rewarded with special scholarships. This is also an opportunity to recognize and reward faculty members who have taught honors courses for three, five, eight, and twelve years.

Approximately 2,250 students and 400 faculty members participate.

Participation Requirements: Students who are Honors Fee Waiver Scholars and President's Scholars must complete a minimum of 12 hours (100 level and above) of course work each semester. This includes the completion of one honors course each semester. A GPA of 3.25 must be maintained and students must remain in good standing at one of the colleges/centers.

Awards, certificates, and diploma citations conferred upon program completion are issued under the individual jurisdiction of the ten colleges which comprise the Maricopa Community Colleges. These colleges include Chandler-Gilbert Community College, Estrella Mountain Community College, GateWay Community College, Glendale Community College, Mesa Community College, Paradise Valley Community College, Phoenix College, Rio Salado College, Scottsdale Community College, and South Mountain Community College.

Admission Process: In the President's Scholar category, a student must be graduated (within the top 15 percent of the class at the end of the sixth, seventh, or eighth semesters) from a North Central Accredited (NCA) high school in Maricopa County and apply within one academic year from high school graduation. Enrollment in an MCCCD college/center must include at least one honors course per semester. The applicant may not be enrolled in another postsecondary institution, summer school excluded. College-preparatory schools are not included in this restriction. President's Scholars may enroll in the Honors Program at any MCCCD college/center. Enrollment must be for at least 12 credit hours per semester (fall/spring). The scholarship will not cover the cost of course work below 100 level and/or pass/fail classes (P/Z option). Remedial and/or pass/fail-option classes may be included in a student's schedule to meet the 12-credit-hour minimum requirement, but the award will be prorated for the semester.

Scholarship Availability: A number of scholarships are available to honors students, including the President's Scholarship ($570 per semester for up to four semesters), the Honors Fee Waiver (up to $200 per semester, not to exceed four semesters), the Betty Heiden Elsner Scholarship ($100 per semester for two semesters), Chancellor's Scholarship (full tuition and fees for one year plus $150 per semester for books/supplies), and the Foundation Scholarship ($1000 annually per college to be distributed at the discretion of the college).

The Campus Context

Honorary Society Phi Theta Kappa

Tuition: $922 for area residents, $1522 for state residents, $4210 for nonresidents, per year (1998–99). Residents of participating Arizona counties pay area-resident tuition rates.

Mandatory Fees: $300

Contact: Coordinator: Loman B. Clark Jr., 2411 West 14th Street, Tempe, Arizona 85281-6941; Telephone: 602-731-8026; Fax: 602-731-8786; E-mail: clark@maricopa.edu

Marquette University

4 Pr G M Tr

▼ University Honors Program

The Marquette University Honors Program brings together intellectually gifted students and dedicated faculty members from all academic areas of the University and endeavors to provide an environment conducive to the exchange of ideas and the pursuit of excellence and creativity. The University Honors Program offers its students specially designed courses with limited enrollments, interdisciplinary seminars, and the opportunity to pursue independent study in close cooperation with faculty members. Beginning in the fall of 1999, entering first-year students will be expected to live in the Honors Program Residence Hall.

In the Jesuit tradition of *cura personalis,* the University Honors Program offers personal as well as professional support to its students and encourages them to develop their skills and integrate the knowledge they acquire into their daily lives. The requirements in English, history, philosophy, and theology demonstrate the commitment of the University Honors Program to education grounded in the humanities. Through its students the University Honors Program promotes the University's engagement with contemporary problems and its dedication to a life of service to others. Established in 1963, the University Honors Program currently enrolls 250 students.

Participation Requirements: The Marquette University Honors Program is structured around seven honors courses or sections of courses taken in the freshman and sophomore years: English 005 and 006 (World Literature); History 001 and 002 (Western Civilization); Philosophy 050 (Human Nature) and Philosophy 104 (Theory of Ethics); and Theology 001 (Introduction to Theology). During their junior and senior years, as students concentrate on their majors, they earn honors credit through independent study (contracts) in upper-division courses. A limited number of upper-division courses, as well as all senior-level seminars and graduate courses, are designated for automatic honors credit each semester. In order to earn honors credit in a course, students must receive a grade of A, AB, or B.

The Honors Bachelor of Arts or Honors Bachelor of Science degree programs require completion of 15 honors credit courses. The Honors Certificate requires completion of at least 8 honors credit courses. Students in the University Honors Program are required to maintain a semester and overall GPA of at least 3.2.

Admission Process: The Marquette University Honors Program is open to students from all colleges in the University. Each fall semester, 65 freshmen are admitted; 5 to 10 students (transfer or other) are admitted in spring. Admission criteria include strong English skills as evidenced by writing samples and, on average, an ACT English score of at least 30 or SAT I verbal score of at least 620 and senior class ranking in the upper 10 percent. The deadline for application is March 15.

Scholarship Availability: All scholarships are awarded by application to the Financial Aid Office.

The Campus Context: Marquette University, a Jesuit, Catholic institution, stretches across a beautiful 80-acre campus in downtown Milwaukee. With 10,765 undergraduate, graduate, and professional students, Marquette offers a high-quality education. Undergraduates choose from sixty majors in seven colleges and one school—Arts and Sciences, Business Administration, Communication, Education, Engineering, Health Sciences, and Nursing. Each undergraduate program incorporates a strong liberal arts core curriculum, a foundation of the Jesuit, Catholic tradition. Marquette maintains a 15:1 student-faculty ratio. Its faculty is committed to a teacher-scholar model and stresses educating the whole person. Within a year of graduation, 67 percent of Marquette's undergraduates are employed full-time, and 30 percent are enrolled in graduate or professional schools. Marquette's undergraduates consistently perform 100,000 hours of community service each year—an achievement that has earned national recognition. The Graduate School offers forty graduate programs with a wide range of degrees and certificates. One-on-one attention and small class sizes allow graduate students to tailor the academic programs to their own needs and goals. The skilled faculty provides the scope of knowledge, analytical skills,

Interpreting the symbols: **2**=two-year college, **4**=four-year college; **Pu**=public or state college, **Pr**=private college; **G**=general honors program; **D**=departmental honors program; **S**=small program (fewer than 100 students), **M**=midsize program (100 to 500 students), **L**=large program (more than 500 students); **Sc**=scholarships available in honors program; **Tr**=transfer students accepted into honors program; **HBC**=historically black college; **AA**=academic advisors; **GA**=graduate advisors; **FA**=fellowship advisors.

imagination, and commitment that students need in academia and beyond. Marquette offers degrees at five levels: associate, bachelor's, master's, doctoral, and professional.

Student Body The total undergraduate enrollment for Marquette is 7,320 students. Fifty-three percent of the undergraduate students are women and 47 percent, men. The ethnic distribution is 5 percent black, less than 1 percent American Indian, 4 percent Asian/Pacific Islander, 4 percent Hispanic, and 81 percent white.

Faculty The total number of faculty members is 984, of whom 553 are full-time. Ninety-five percent of faculty members have doctoral, first-professional, or appropriate terminal degrees in their field. The student-faculty ratio is 15:1.

Key Facilities There are three libraries on Marquette's campus, a main library, the Memorial Library, and two specialized libraries, the Law Library and the Science Library. Marquette has 1,154,337 books, serial backfiles, and government documents. In addition, there are 9,225 current serial publications, 1,127,091 microform units, 7,276 audiovisual materials, and 60 commercial online services. There are 1,000 computers (Macintosh and IBM compatibles) available to students for general use throughout the campus.

Honorary Societies Phi Beta Kappa and Alpha Sigma Nu

Athletics The NCAA Division I sports at Marquette are men's and women's basketball, men's and women's cross-country, men's golf, men's and women's soccer, men's and women's tennis, men's and women's track and field, women's volleyball, and men's wrestling.

Study Abroad Marquette offers an array of study-abroad and exchange program opportunities on six of the world's seven continents in a variety of nations, including Mexico, Japan, France, Great Britain, Germany, China, Russia, Denmark, Australia, Chile, and many others.

Support Services Marquette strives to integrate qualified students with disabilities as fully as possible into all aspects of university life. The Office of Disability services, located within Student Educational Services, has been designated to coordinate this process in accordance with the University's compliance responsibilities under the law. Accommodations determinations for all students with identified and documented disabilities is made on case-by-case basis. Examples of possible accommodations include taping of textbooks; locating interpreters, note takers, or attendants; orientation to campus; informal counseling; arranging for alternative tests; and advocacy.

Job Opportunities There are many job opportunities, on and off Marquette's campus, available for students. These include work-study, internships, and co-op programs.

Tuition: $16,280–$17,180 per year, $335–$490 per credit hour (1999–2000)

Room and board: $5900 (approximately)

Mandatory Fees: $256

Contact: Director: Dr. Albert J. Rivero, Coughlin Hall 001, P.O. Box 1881, Milwaukee, Wisconsin 53201; Telephone: 414-288-7516; Fax: 414-288-1957; E-mail: albert.rivero@marquette.edu; Web site: http://www.Marquette.edu/as/honors.html

Marshall University

4 Pu G M Sc Tr

▼ Honors Program

The Honors Program at Marshall University, which is open to students of all majors, was established in the early 1960s to provide maximum educational opportunities for students of high ability. Honors students are encouraged to raise their expectations of themselves by pursuing enriched courses within and beyond the regular curriculum. The centerpiece of the program is the team-taught, interdisciplinary seminar that brings together outstanding, motivated students and stimulating professors, usually some of the best teachers on campus. The program typically offers three or four of these 4-hour seminars per semester; they are limited to 15 students.

The mission of the Honors Program is to offer an enhanced educational experience to academically talented and highly motivated students; to design, in collaboration with faculty members who are recognized for excellence in teaching, an innovative, interdisciplinary, and multidisciplinary curriculum that emphasizes critical thinking, communications skills, and collaborative learning; and to supplement that curriculum with enriched academic opportunities that consist of outside lectures, fieldwork, or course-related travel. To this end, students participating in the Honors Program develop confidence in their abilities to understand and discuss complex ideas and texts, as well as to engage in problem solving and research design; learn to apply this new knowledge in meaningful ways that will help them to succeed in their professional and personal lives following college; strengthen their written and oral communication skills; master an ability to work effectively in groups of diverse people; make connections between disciplines; and enjoy a range of supplemental experiences of an academic and social nature with similarly motivated and talented students.

The Honors Program is housed in the John R. Hall Center for Academic Excellence (CAE), which brings together all Honors and Scholarship Programs at Marshall. The facilities include a computer lab, scholarship library, reading room, student lounge, and two seminar classrooms. The CAE also contains the offices of the Executive Director of the CAE, the Chair of Honors, and two administrative assistants. In 1995, honors students formed the Marshall University Honors Student Association (MUHSA), which is open to all eligible students. MUHSA sponsors academic and social events on campus and it advises the faculty committee that oversees the Honors Program through its three seats on that committee, ensuring honors students a voice in deciding the direction of the program.

The number of students in the program is approximately 300.

Participation Requirements: Students who wish to graduate with University Honors on their diplomas must complete 24 hours of honors classes, consisting of HON 101 (the freshman year orientation class), 4 hours of a 100-level seminar, 8 hours of upper-level seminars, and 11 hours of honors credit made up of departmental honors classes or independent study in honors. They must do this while maintaining at least a 3.3 GPA in all courses and a minimum cumulative 3.3 GPA in honors courses. In the past, interdisciplinary seminars have included topics such as "Poetry and the Condition of Music," "War in the Twentieth Century," "Plagues and Epidemics," and "Primatology and Human Evolution." Honors students are advised by the Honors Director and by faculty members in the student's major field of study.

Admission Process: Students may begin honors work at any stage in their college careers, although many begin as freshmen. Entering freshmen with an ACT minimum composite score of 26 (or SAT I equivalent) and at least a 3.3 GPA can enroll in any honors course. Transfer students or students already enrolled with a minimum 3.3 GPA can enroll in any honors course.

Scholarship Availability: Superior high school or transfer students (minimum 3.5 GPA and minimum ACT composite score of 25) can apply for academic scholarships or tuition waivers, the John Marshall Scholarship Program (minimum 30 ACT), the Erma Byrd Scholars Program, the Charles and Mary Jo Locke Hedrick Scholarship (minimum 28 ACT), and the Society of Yeager Scholars Program (minimum 28 ACT). The Honors Program also offers an annual $1000 travel-abroad scholarship and a $500 award for domestic study.

The Campus Context: Marshall University is one of West Virginia's two state universities. Founded in 1837, it is located on a 65-acre urban campus that houses seven different colleges—Business, Liberal Arts, Fine Arts, Science, Education, Community and Technical College, Information Technology and Engineering—and three schools: Nursing, Medicine, and the Graduate School. Marshall University has forty different bachelor's degree programs and seventeen different associate degree programs.

The University has a 30,000-seat football stadium, 10,000-seat basketball stadium, and a state-of-the-art 543-seat theater facility with main stage and experimental stage. The University has also just opened a new, state-of-the-art, $30-million library. Academic facilities include the Birke Art Gallery, H.E.L.P. Center for those with learning disabilities, Center for International Programs, Psychology Clinic, Speech and Hearing Clinic, and the WPBY-TV and WMUL-FM studios.

Student Body Undergraduate enrollment is approximately 16,000 students; 56 percent are women. The ethnic distribution is 93.1 percent white, 4.2 percent black, less than 1 percent Hispanic, 1 percent Asian, and less than 1 percent Native American. There are approximately 100 international students. Fifty-five percent of undergraduates receive financial aid. There are more than 100 social organizations on campus, including ten national fraternities and eight national sororities.

Faculty The total number of faculty members is more than 1,000 (excluding the Community College, Medical School, and library). Of the more than 600 full-time faculty members, 80 percent hold the highest degree in their fields of specialization. The student-faculty ratio is 22:1.

Key Facilities The Library contains 423,000 bound volumes. The main campus maintains more than 1,500 computers for student use in computer centers, labs, classrooms, and the library. The campus network supports nearly 4,000 total high-speed connections. All residence hall rooms are provided with direct Ethernet connections in every room to allow students computer connections to the campus network and full Internet access.

Honorary Societies Phi Theta Kappa, Phi Eta Sigma, and Omicron Delta Kappa

Athletics The University is a member of the NCAA and participates in Division I-A athletics in men's football, men's and women's basketball, men's and women's indoor and outdoor track and field, men's and women's cross-country, men's and women's soccer, men's golf, men's baseball, women's tennis, women's softball, and women's volleyball. The University also has more than twenty intramural programs.

Study Abroad Marshall University has various study-abroad programs, including formal exchange programs with two universities in England and programs in Spain and Mexico. The University is also a member of National Student Exchange, which allows students to attend college in another state, Puerto Rico, Guam, or Canada.

Support Services All campus buildings are accessible for the mobility-impaired student, while two residence halls have been fully renovated and modified extensively for disabled students. Separate programs for learning-disabled students are also available.

Tuition: $2620 for state residents, $6824 for nonresidents, per year (2002–03) (For Kentucky residents of Boyd, Carter, Greenup, and Lawrence Counties and Ohio residents of Lawrence County: $4646 full-time per year)

Room and Board: $5598

Contact: Director: Dr. Evelyn Pupplo-Cody, Chair, University Honors Council, Huntington, West Virginia 25755; Telephone: 304-696-6405; Fax: 304-696-7102; Web site: http://www.marshall.edu/cae/

MARYMOUNT COLLEGE

4 Pr G M Tr

▼ Honors Program

Marymount College offers an Honors Program with breadth and diversity. Specially designed seminars and unique research studies in any discipline give academically strong students the opportunity to challenge themselves, to work closely with professors and other skilled students, and to gain special recognition for their talents.

The Honors Program offers a set of opportunities in which eligible students may participate. Consistently high achieving students are able to select the particular combination of Honors Seminars, Honors Contracts, and Honors Research Mentorships that fit their interests and academic programs. An Honors Floor, with special activities, is available in one of the residence halls. Honors students who maintain their status may register for up to 36 credits each year (18 credits per semester) without extra cost. Payment plans are available through a commercial firm.

Honors seminars are interdisciplinary courses that offer the opportunity to develop intellectual connections among disciplines and topics. These courses are specially developed by the faculty and often include students in final development of the readings and assignments. Each semester, a variety of topics are offered as seminars that are generally limited to 15 students; in the fall, one seminar is reserved for incoming freshmen. The faculty members who develop these special courses are among the best teachers in the College, people who are devoted to challenging and eliciting the best from every student.

In an Honors Contract, students may convert any course into an "honors course" by working out with the faculty member what kind of enrichment and more advanced work will be accomplished. The student stays registered for the course, but the section number is changed so that the designation "Honors" appears on the transcript.

As a college for women, Marymount is committed to fostering research skills so that graduates are able to enter competitive graduate and professional programs. The College is presently in the middle of a second grant from the National Institutes of Health to foster a research environment at a women's college. The Honors Research Mentorship meets very high standards. As to honors, the project should be aimed at publishable quality, understood as up to the standards of professional or student research journals in the discipline, acceptable for presentation at a professional or student conference, and having an exhibitable portfolio or public performance. Publication is not required; rather, quality is the goal. As to research, like independent study, this involves a topic not available in the course catalog, one that is of greater depth. However, it differs in having an active component. A purely research project has the student formulating a hypothesis or thesis of her own and testing or arguing it. For the arts, there is in-depth background research that informs the performance or project. As to mentorship, the professional relationship with a faculty member is a key component. The student becomes, in effect, a junior member of the profession. Students have generally earned junior status before undertaking the mentorship.

Participation Requirements: Entering honors students are strongly encouraged to take the sections of core courses that are reserved for them, as well as to participate in any other honors opportunities that are appropriate. To remain eligible for the Honors

Interpreting the symbols: **2**=two-year college, **4**=four-year college; **Pu**=public or state college, **Pr**=private college; **G**=general honors program; **D**=departmental honors program; **S**=small program (fewer than 100 students), **M**=midsize program (100 to 500 students), **L**=large program (more than 500 students); **Sc**=scholarships available in honors program; **Tr**=transfer students accepted into honors program; **HBC**=historically black college; **AA**=academic advisors; **GA**=graduate advisors; **FA**=fellowship advisors.

Program, students must maintain a cumulative GPA of at least 3.6. A student who falls below that is invited back into the program when she achieves the requisite cumulative GPA. Students who satisfactorily complete the requisite number of honors seminars and other honor opportunities receive an Honors Program Certificate at graduation.

Admission Requirements: Freshmen are invited into the Honors Program based on a combination of high school GPA and SAT scores. Because Marymount College has been increasing admissions requirements over the past few years, the prerequisite changes annually. The goal is to invite about 15 percent of the entering class. Transfer students who have earned a 3.6 cumulative GPA in at least 15 credits are invited to join the program.

Scholarship Availability: Marymount College has an extensive range of merit-based scholarships for both entering and transfer students. Entering freshman and transfer honors students are awarded a President's Scholarship of $10,000 for residents and $8000 for commuters.

The Campus Context: Marymount is an independent liberal arts college whose mission is to prepare women for work in the twenty-first century. Having been a leader in women's education for more than ninety years, the College's academic and cocurricular programs especially address women's needs and goals, their particular concerns, and their special contributions to the world, while promoting understanding and appreciation of diversity. True to its Catholic tradition, Marymount places emphasis on ethical, religious, and spiritual values. Students in all majors are additionally prepared for work through internships in businesses and organizations among a wide network in the New York City metropolitan area. More than 70 percent of students participate in this program, which very often leads to offers of a future position.

The College is situated on a pleasant suburban campus. Many rooms in the residence halls offer stunning views of the Hudson River. There is easy access to New York City by commuter train (30–35 minutes). The College offers morning and late afternoon van service to the station when classes are in session.

On July 1, 2002, Marymount College becomes the fifth undergraduate college of Fordham University. Marymount students will be able to benefit from the academic and social resources of a major Catholic university, while maintaining the character of a small residential college, with its own curriculum, faculty, and student body, committed to the education of women.

Student Body The Women's College is 100 percent women. Adult women and men study in Fordham University's College of Liberal Studies on the weekend. More than 700 women of highly diverse backgrounds study in the Women's College, including 14 percent black, 16 percent Hispanic, 9 percent international, and 7 percent Asian American. While students come from thirty-nine states and twenty other countries, 90 percent are from the twelve Northeast states, from Maine to Virginia. Those receiving financial assistance from any source make up 90 percent of the student body, with 65 percent receiving College scholarships and grants ranging from $2000 to $10,000. Of freshmen entering in fall 2001, 95 percent received some financial assistance, with 91 percent awarded College scholarships. Twelve percent are over the age of 24.

Faculty There are 57 full-time faculty members, of whom 93 percent hold the terminal degree in the discipline. The student-faculty ratio is 9:1.

Key Facilities The Gloria Gaines Memorial Library houses more than 130,000 volumes on campus. Through the Fordham University libraries' terminals on campus, Marymount students have easy access to more than 1.8 million volumes, over 14,000 periodicals and serials, and more than 200 online databases.

Honorary Societies Delta Epsilon Sigma and Phi Beta Delta

Athletics The College is a member of the Hudson Valley Women's Athletic Association and competes in basketball, riding, softball, swimming, and volleyball. In addition, Marymount students are eligible to try out for Fordham University teams.

Study Abroad Marymount has exceptional study-abroad programs open to both matriculated and nonmatriculated students. Marymount sponsors its own programs in England, Ireland, and Scotland. Students may study in other countries through arrangements with Fordham and external programs.

Support Services The Office of Learning Services makes all necessary arrangements for documented handicapped students, including requisite adaptations for the visually and hearing impaired. Tutoring is available to all students through the office, as well as through the Writing Center and Math Lab.

Job Opportunities The College employs a significant percentage of students through both Federal Work-Study and cash lines. Part-time positions in such places as stores, banks, and restaurants are plentiful in the village of Tarrytown and can be reached by a short walk.

Tuition: full-time tuition (24–32 credits), $15,300; part-time tuition, $495 per credit (2001–02)

Room and Board: $8100 (includes computer connectivity fee)

Mandatory Fees: $450 per year for full-time students; $150 per semester for part-time students

Contact: Program Director: Dr. Jordy Bell, Associate Academic Dean, Marymount College, 100 Marymount Avenue, Tarrytown, New York 10591-3796; Telephone: 914-332-8241; Fax: 914-631-8586; E-mail: bellj@mmc.marymt.edu

---

MARYVILLE UNIVERSITY OF SAINT LOUIS

4 Pr G M Sc Tr

▼ Bascom Honors Program

The Bascom Honors Program is named for Marion R. Bascom, a professor who was instrumental in establishing the Honors Program at Maryville University in 1939. Intellectually vital and dynamic, the program has evolved from its original format, modeled after England's Oxford University tutorial system. Today it is a core honors program that recognizes the individual gifts and talents of each student in the program and encourages their maximum development.

Core Honors Program classes are small, usually fewer than 15 students, and are conducted in a seminar-like atmosphere of intellectual sharing. Students' perspectives on the subject help shape and enhance those of their classmates. As a core program, the Bascom Honors Program allows participants to interact with students in all majors offered at Maryville.

Honors Program classes are not designed to be harder than nonhonors classes, but different. Designed for talented students who are capable of independent study, the Honors Program maintains small and challenging classes that encourage discussion, exploration of ideas, and interaction with outstanding faculty members known for their excellence in teaching. Because classes are small and are based mostly on discussion, faculty members almost always know honors students in multiple dimensions rather than just the academic. This makes a real difference when it comes to recommendations to employers or graduate schools.

In Honors Program classes, students take an in-depth approach to the subject matter. For instance, instead of the broad survey of American government, honors students might study the Atomic Age. Rather than the traditional historical chronology of art, a recent Honors Art Seminar sought to design a museum exhibit.

In addition to the core seminars, another highlight of the Bascom Honors Program is the monthly Honors Colloquium. These Sunday evening gatherings provide an opportunity for a social gathering and for stimulating discussions among students and faculty members on a range of important issues. Recent colloquia titles have included Trade and Culture; Gender in the Developing World; and Spiritual Dimensions of the Natural World. The colloquia expose students to totally new ideas not necessarily related to their major. Choosing the Bascom Honors Program adds a depth of experience and involvement to students' Maryville experience.

The Bascom Honors Program currently registers 200 honors students.

Participation Requirements: Bascom Honors Program graduates are required to have completed seven Honors Seminars, two semesters of the same foreign language, two semesters of the Honors Colloquium, and 8 to 15 core elective credits. These requirements produce a total of 52 credit hours, identical to the standard core credit hour requirements for any Maryville graduate.

Upon completion of the requirements for graduation, students receive bachelor's degrees as Bascom Honors graduates in their respective majors and have this noted on their diplomas and in the graduation program. At Maryville University, graduating summa cum laude, with highest honors, is reserved for Honors Program students. Not every honors student receives it, but the summa cum laude degree is valued as something so distinctive that it is only achievable by students who successfully complete the Honors Program, regardless of their grade point average.

Admission Process: Freshmen entering Maryville with an ACT of 25 or above are invited to join the Bascom Honors Program. Currently enrolled Maryville students with GPAs of 3.60 or higher may apply. Those Maryville students with GPAs of 3.0-3.59 may also apply but must have the recommendation of a faculty member. The Director of the Bascom Honors Program accepts students into the program.

Scholarship Availability: The University Scholars Program provides recognition and financial support for outstanding undergraduate students who enter Maryville directly from high school. University Scholars are invited to participate in Maryville's Bascom Honors Program, although all academically eligible prospective undergraduate students are encouraged to apply. Applicants with at least a 3.5 (on a 4.0 scale) high school GPA and at least a 28 ACT composite score (or comparable SAT I combined score) will be considered for these scholarships. Final candidates are selected on the basis of their academic credentials (high school grades and recommendations from high school teachers, counselors, or administrators). Finalists are invited to participate in Scholarship Day Competition, during which each candidate completes an essay based on one of several selected topics, and an interview with a Maryville faculty member. In addition, the Scholarship Day program includes a general information session, a campus tour, and lunch with faculty members and current students. The selection committee considers the results of the essays, interviews, academic credentials, and recommendations in selecting scholarship recipients. Applicants should contact Maryville's admissions office for deadlines and other specific information.

The Campus Context: Maryville University of Saint Louis is an independent coeducational university with an enrollment of over 3,000 undergraduate and graduate students. The quality and variety of its curriculum—solid liberal arts studies and professional programs in business, education, and health professions covering more than forty fields—have attracted an increasing number of students in recent years. A special feature is the large measure of personal concern for each student demonstrated by everyone on campus, from the faculty through the administrative staff to the president.

The University was founded in 1872 by the Religious of the Sacred Heart, moved to its present site in suburban St. Louis in 1961, became an independent college in 1972, and became a university in 1991. On-campus living accommodations are available in two residence halls, which house more than 300 students.

Maryville University is committed to the education of the whole person through its programs, which are designed to meet the needs of traditional and nontraditional students in day, evening, and weekend formats. Primarily an undergraduate teaching university, Maryville offers select, high-quality graduate programs in professional fields where there is evidence both of need and corresponding institutional strength.

The University offers undergraduate programs leading to the B.A., B.S., B.S in clinical laboratory science, B.S. in nursing, B.S. in occupational therapy, B.S. in Physical Therapy, and B.F.A. degrees. Course study includes, in the College of Arts and Sciences, actuarial science, art-studio, biology, chemistry, clinical laboratory science, communications, English, environmental sciences, environmental studies, graphic design, history, humanities, interior design, liberal studies, mathematics, music, organizational leadership, paralegal studies, philosophy, political science, psychology, psychology/sociology, religious studies, science, and sociology and preprofessional studies in dentistry, engineering, law, and medicine; in the John E. Simon School of Business, accountancy, accounting information systems, business administration, information systems, management, and marketing; in the School of Education, art education, and early childhood, elementary, and middle-level education; and in the School of Health Professions, health-care management, music therapy, nursing, occupational therapy, and physical therapy. At the graduate level, an M.A. in education and the M.B.A. are offered.

Student Body Total enrollment is 3,057. Undergraduate enrollment is 2,547; graduate enrollment is 510. Of the total undergraduates, 28 percent are men and 72 percent are women. Racial/ethnicity characteristics of undergraduates are 5 percent nonresident aliens, 5 percent black, non-Hispanic, 2 percent Asian/Pacific Islander, 1 percent Hispanic, 81 percent white, non-Hispanic, and 6 percent not reported. Twelve percent of undergraduates live on campus. Of the current full-time freshman class, 62 percent reside in the University residence halls. Sixty-four percent of undergraduates received some type of financial aid. There are more than 150 international students from forty countries.

Faculty Of 272 total faculty members, 91 are full-time, of whom 85 percent have a terminal degree in their field.

Key Facilities The University Library contains 204,703 volumes (including government documents), 445,000 microform units, 1,558 periodical titles (including electronic subscriptions), 9,596 audiovisual material units, and other library materials. Maryville is a member of OCLC, a bibliographic database that provides access to more than 39 million records for interlibrary loan; the Missouri Library Network Corporation; and the St. Louis Regional Library Network, which allows use of the InfoPass Program. The University is a depository for federal and Missouri documents. The library has access to the Internet and more than seventy databases. The library catalog and a majority of the databases are available through the Internet.

Maryville has more than 200 networked microcomputers available to students. All computers are connected to the Internet and World Wide Web resources. There are ten instructional technology labs and classrooms spread across three campuses. An extensive array of instructional software offerings is available in both Windows and Macintosh environments. A faculty multimedia resource center is available for development of electronic learning materials. Maryville conducts classes using videoconferencing facilities at each campus. The University has constructed three smart multimedia classrooms, where instructors and students can easily use a variety of technologies controlled via an electronic podium.

Interpreting the symbols: **2**=two-year college, **4**=four-year college; **Pu**=public or state college, **Pr**=private college; **G**=general honors program; **D**=departmental honors program; **S**=small program (fewer than 100 students), **M**=midsize program (100 to 500 students), **L**=large program (more than 500 students); **Sc**=scholarships available in honors program; **Tr**=transfer students accepted into honors program; **HBC**=historically black college; **AA**=academic advisors; **GA**=graduate advisors; **FA**=fellowship advisors.

Honorary Societies Alpha Lambda Delta, Delta Epsilon Sigma, Omicron Delta Kappa, and Pinnacle Society

Athletics In intercollegiate athletics, Maryville is NCAA Division III and a charter member of the St. Louis Intercollegiate Athletic Conference. Men's sports include baseball, basketball, cross-country, golf, soccer, and tennis. Women's sports are basketball, cross-country, golf, soccer, softball, tennis, and volleyball. A variety of intramural sports are offered throughout the year tailored to students' interests.

Study Abroad Maryville University encourages students in good standing to expand their perspectives about themselves and about the world through numerous study-abroad opportunities for a summer, a semester, or a year. With adequate planning, the study-abroad experience can be integrated with the academic program in such a way that the student can progress toward graduation. Most financial aid (except work-study) is usually applicable to study abroad.

The International Programs Office has resources available to assist students in planning a study-abroad experience in many parts of the world. In addition, Maryville has affiliations with several colleges and universities outside the United States.

Support Services Students with disabilities have a right to participate in or benefit from programs offered at the University. Maryville is committed to providing reasonable accommodations for students with special needs. Services available include readers; notetakers; free peer tutors in selected subjects; tape recorders; quiet, distraction-free testing environments; allowance of extra time to complete examinations; and liaison with faculty members.

Job Opportunities Comprehensive theory grounded in the real world—that's the essence of Maryville's internship, cooperative education, and service learning opportunities. Students benefit from a wide variety of work-place settings in the metropolitan St. Louis area and beyond. Federal Work-Study and campus employment are among other job opportunities available.

Tuition: $13,650 full-time per year, $389 per credit hour part-time (2001–02)

Room and Board: $6000

Mandatory Fees: $120 full-time, $60 part-time

Contact: Director: Dr. Linda Pitelka, 13550 Conway Road, St. Louis, Missouri 63141-7299; Telephone: 314-529-9621; Fax: 314-529-9925; E-mail: pitelka@maryville.edu

MASSACHUSETTS COLLEGE OF LIBERAL ARTS

4 Pu G S Tr

▼ Honors Program

The Honors Program at Massachusetts College of Liberal Arts (Mass. College) concentrates on two primary goals: offering courses that meet the demands of talented students and fostering a supportive community that places a high value on scholarly and creative achievement. The courses all explore interdisciplinary questions that bring into common focus several different dimensions of life, such as ethical standards, scientific exploration, social policy, personal beliefs, and the natural environment. Recent offerings have included such courses as Ethics and Animals, Math and Social Justice, Botany and Society, The Romantic Movement, The Holocaust and the Nature of Prejudice, and Art and Society. A complete list is available on the Web site listed below. The courses are all taught in small sections with a discussion format by the most stimulating faculty members at the College. Groups of students are encouraged to engage the faculty in discussions about developing fresh course topics.

To promote a community of inquiry, honors students are invited to meet regularly together for informal discussions on subjects of current interest, and they hold discussions with visiting scholars over meals. The Honors Center is stocked with a reference library, computers, artistic supplies, and study spaces that are all reserved for use by honors students. The Honors Program promotes a spirit of intellectual adventure for the entire campus and not just for a select group of students, and everyone who takes an interest in honors events is encouraged to participate in them.

There are currently more than 130 students in the program.

Participation Requirements: To remain in the program, students need a minimum 3.2 overall GPA. To earn the All College Honors notation on the diploma and the transcript, students must complete six honors courses with an overall GPA of 3.4. By completing a thesis or capstone project, students can graduate as a Commonwealth Scholar, a recognition granted by the statewide Commonwealth Honors Program

Admission Process: Entering students with at least a 3.2 GPA are invited to become honors students, and currently enrolled students receive similar invitations every term. Students may also join on their own initiative or be recommended by faculty members.

Scholarship Availability: While the Honors Program administers no scholarships directly, there are a number of generous scholarships available through the Admissions Office to students with high academic performance. Scholarships are awarded on admission.

The Campus Context: Located in the Berkshire hills of western Massachusetts adjacent to both New York and Vermont, Massachusetts College of Liberal Arts is the public liberal arts college for the Commonwealth. Surrounded by spectacular natural beauty, the College is not only near major ski areas, but it is a cooperating neighbor with the major sites of the "cultural Berkshires": the Clark Art Institute, the Massachusetts Museum of Contemporary Art, the Tanglewood Music Festival, Jacob's Pillow Dance Theatre, the Rockwell Museum, Williams College Art Museum, the Bennington (Vermont) Museum, and many similar musical and artistic venues. Boston, New York, and Montreal are all destinations for field trips and personal exploration.

Founded as a normal school in 1894, Mass. College has developed into a coeducational, residential college with an academic program of fourteen majors, twenty-seven minors, and thirty-one different concentrations. In addition, the College has a concert hall for musical performances and lectures, two gymnasiums, a fitness center, sports fields, and its own ice rink for hockey and skating.

Student Body The student body of about 1,500 is 60 percent women. About 70 percent of the student body receives financial aid.

Faculty The faculty totals 105 full-time members, 78 of whom hold terminal degrees in their field. The student-faculty ratio is 14:1.

Key Facilities Freel Library has 167,765 volumes and a series of computer-assisted research tools. As a participant in the state college library consortium, the library quickly obtains materials from throughout the Northeast. The Computer Center has four different studios with both PC and Macintosh capacity. The library and the Computer Center, as well as the dorms, are all connected to the Internet, and the campus has a complete distance learning facility.

Athletics The College participates in NCAA Division III athletics for both men and women in soccer, basketball, softball, baseball, hockey, cross-country, golf, tennis, and volleyball. It also has a vigorous intramural program in basketball, skiing, golf, equestrian sports, broomball, water polo, tennis, and other sports, and it sponsors recreational physical activity in related areas.

Study Abroad A number of students study abroad every year in a range of affiliated programs, and the College sponsors its own travel courses to Europe, Asia, and Australia. A faculty adviser for international study assists students in making arrangements in the program that best matches their interests and ambitions.

Support Services A well-supported Learning Services staff offers professional tutorials and other assistance to students who experience academic difficulties. Every summer, the College sponsors an enrichment program for entering students who will benefit from special preparation for college-level work. The entire campus meets the state regulations on handicapped accessibility.

Job Opportunities The Career Center administers a full battery of on-campus employment through the work-study and other programs. It further supports students in launching their careers through resume workshops and sponsoring on-campus visits by prospective employers.

Tuition and fees: $3597 for Massachusetts residents, $4112 for qualifying residents of New York and southern Vermont, and $11,957 for nonresidents (2001–02)

Room and board: $5493

Contact: Director: David J. Langston, 375 Church Street, North Adams, Massachusetts 01247; Telephone: 413-662-5371; Fax: 413-662-5010; E-mail: dlangsto@mcla.edu; Web site: http://www.mcla.mass.edu/academics/honorsprog/

McHenry County College

2 Pu G S Sc

▼ Honors Program

The Honors Program is devised to attract and retain academically talented students. Its curriculum is structured to help students develop a strong foundation in academic skills such as critical thinking, problem solving, reading, and writing within a small-class environment. Students in the program have an opportunity to participate in NCHC activities, including honors semesters. They are also supported in research projects through the Honors Council of the Illinois Region. Honors at McHenry provides students with local recognition of their academic achievement and then assists them in making a link to the honors programs at four-year/senior institutions through transcript notation and individual articulation.

Founded in 1987, the program currently enrolls 55 students per semester.

Participation Requirements: Honors Program members must maintain a 3.5 GPA. Students in the program complete 16 to 20 hours of honors courses, which are separate sections of existing courses and are identified on the transcript. At graduation, honors graduates have a special tassel to identify them and a special gold seal on their diplomas.

Admission Process: Students may gain admission to the Honors Program based on any two of the following criteria: a high school GPA of 3.5; a minimum composite ACT score of 24 or minimum combined SAT I score of 1000; college-transfer GPA of 3.5 for a minimum of 12 hours; MCC GPA of 3.5 for a minimum of 12 hours; membership in good standing of Phi Theta Kappa; two academic letters of recommendation; and a personal interview with the Honors Coordinator or appointed representative. Any student with a 3.2 GPA can enroll in an honors course.

Scholarship Availability: The Honors Program offers thirteen scholarships per semester. These generally are for tuition in honors courses, although they can be applied to books if the student already has other tuition scholarships.

The Campus Context: Located on a 110-acre campus in a suburban setting, McHenry County College offers three transfer degree programs: the Associate in General Education, the Associate in Science, and the Associate in Arts degrees.

Student Body Full-time enrollment is 2,268: 42 percent men and 58 percent women. Five percent of the student body are members of minority groups: 1 percent Asian, less than 1 percent African American, and the remainder Hispanic. Fifty-three percent of students receive some financial aid. All students commute to campus. While there are no social fraternities or sororities on campus, there is a chapter of Phi Theta Kappa. The average age is 29.8 years.

Faculty Of the 232 faculty members, 86 are full-time and 12 hold doctorates. The student-faculty ratio is 10:1.

Key Facilities The library houses 39,089 volumes. Computer facilities include academic computing labs, classroom support labs, and approximately fourteen computer classrooms with a minimum of twenty-four computers per room.

Honorary Society Phi Theta Kappa

Athletics In athletics, McHenry offers women's softball, basketball, and tennis and men's baseball, soccer, basketball, and tennis. The fitness center, open to students and the community, has multipurpose facilities for indoor and outdoor activities.

Study Abroad Study abroad is available with honors credit for participation in the Illinois Consortium for International Studies and Programs (ICISP) with sites in Canterbury, England, and Salzburg, Austria.

Support Services Disabled students will find an excellent special needs program to accommodate them.

Job Opportunities There are numerous opportunities for student employment on campus

Tuition: $1170 for area residents, $5342 for state residents, $6123 for nonresidents, per year (1996–97)

Mandatory Fees: $14

Contact: Directors: Dr. Carol E. Chandler and Dr. Dora M. Tippens, 8900 U.S. Highway 14, Crystal Lake, Illinois 60012-2761; Telephone: 815-455-8691 or 8692; Fax: 815-455-3762; E-mail: cchandle@pobox.mchenry.cc.il.us

McKendree College

4 Pr G S

▼ Honors Program

The McKendree College Honors Program is designed to enhance the undergraduate educational experience of exceptionally able students. It is a four-year interdisciplinary program for the talented student—a challenging, unified, but diverse curriculum offering an opportunity to do independent work in one's major field. The program has five main goals. The first is to provide special opportunities to explore the liberal arts in greater depth and variety than is currently available in the core curriculum, to investigate the connections among the various disciplines, and to make the liberal arts an integral part of students' development into thinking, feeling, knowledgeable, and morally aware critical thinkers. The second is to provide an environment that increases the quantity and quality of interaction with intellectual peers and faculty members and to stress the sharing of talents with all peers. The third is to ensure that the atmosphere created ultimately benefits the entire College community through a revitalization of interest in the liberal arts, in learning for its own sake, in infusing knowledge and ideas into the everyday life of the College, and in sponsoring and attending cultural activities that can help enrich the education of all McKendree students. The fourth is to provide the opportunity to engage in independent research to better prepare students for graduate study or employment in their major fields. The fifth is to develop leadership skills

Interpreting the symbols: **2**=two-year college, **4**=four-year college; **Pu**=public or state college, **Pr**=private college; **G**=general honors program; **D**=departmental honors program; **S**=small program (fewer than 100 students), **M**=midsize program (100 to 500 students), **L**=large program (more than 500 students); **Sc**=scholarships available in honors program; **Tr**=transfer students accepted into honors program; **HBC**=historically black college; **AA**=academic advisors; **GA**=graduate advisors; **FA**=fellowship advisors.

that will enhance the campus community and prepare students to assume leadership roles as interested and involved citizens of the local, state, national, and world communities.

Participation Requirements: The McKendree College Honors Program comprises two parts. The first is an integrated, interdisciplinary series of courses organized around a broad theme. The second is a thesis based on research activity or a creative product in the student's major field, completed during the junior and senior years. All students in the program are required to enroll in the honors courses each semester, except in unusual circumstances as approved by the Honors Council. The Honors Council comprises a representative from each of six divisions and 2 student members. The council serves to review curricular matters as well as to assist the Director in matters of policy, planning, recruitment, and retention. Each honors seminar requires extensive outside reading coupled with frequent writing assignments and active discussion participation. Students in the program are expected to maintain a GPA of 3.0 or better to remain in the program. Students who successfully complete all requirements in the program and who meet all other graduation requirements of McKendree College are identified on their transcripts and diplomas as graduates of the McKendree College Honors Program.

Admission Process: To qualify for admission to the McKendree College Honors Program, applicants must meet three criteria. They must have a cumulative high school GPA of 3.6 or better (on a 4.0 scale), rank in the top 10 percent of their high school graduating class, and have a composite ACT score of 27 or better or a combined SAT I score of 1200 or better.

High school seniors who meet all three of these criteria and who are interested in participating in the program must submit a completed application for admission to the College; the application must include an official high school transcript and official test scores for the ACT or SAT I. Students will then receive an invitation from the program in the spring of their senior year in high school. Included in that invitation will be a response card indicating the student's interest in joining the program as well as the deadline for returning the card, normally by March 31. Only 18 students are admitted per year.

Scholarship Availability: Presidential Scholarships are awarded to qualified freshman students, who must be enrolled full-time. No distinctions are made for those students enrolled in the Honors Program.

The Campus Context: Established in 1828 by pioneer Methodists, McKendree is the oldest college in Illinois and the oldest in the nation with continuous ties to the United Methodist Church. The College is located in Lebanon, Illinois, a quiet community of about 3,700 people with a downtown business district in easy walking distance of the campus.

McKendree's location is a blend of the rural and the urban. The 80-acre main campus is within 25 minutes of downtown St. Louis to the west and is equally close to the popular Carlyle Lake outdoor recreation area to the east. The College takes seriously its responsibility as a liberal arts institution. It is dedicated to preparing purposeful, effective adults whose intellectual, career, and social skills will make them able contributors in the workplace—persons filled with a spirit of free inquiry and a moral commitment to truth. To these ends, McKendree offers twenty-six academic majors and several professional programs, with numerous academic and job-related support facilities designed to make each student's learning experience successful and enriching. The College serves students from many backgrounds and has a special mission of service to the southern Illinois region and the metropolitan area adjacent to St. Louis.

Student Body Total enrollment at the College is 1,200 on the main campus in Lebanon, including 55 percent women. In terms of ethnicity, 4 percent are Native American; 1 percent, Hispanic; 9 percent, African American; 1 percent are Asian American or Pacific Islander; and 1 percent are international. Eight percent are transfer students.

Of those who applied for financial aid, 69 percent had their need fully met. The average percent of need met is 63 percent. The average amount awarded is $8844.

There are 615 college housing spaces available. Freshmen are guaranteed college housing. There are two national fraternities, four national sororities, and three local sororities.

Faculty There are 60 full-time faculty members and 97 part-time instructors. Eighty-two percent of the faculty members have terminal degrees.

Key Facilities Holman Library houses a growing collection of more than 76,000 volumes in open stacks along with approximately 75,000 other resource items—government documents, audiovisual materials, microforms, computer software, and at least one online service. Access to the collections of Illinois libraries is available through a statewide computer network. The College has four computer labs with 325 computers available for student use. A campuswide network can be accessed from student residence rooms and from off campus. Students can contact faculty members and/or advisers through e-mail. There are computers for student use in the computer center, computer labs, classrooms, library, and dorms, where students' rooms provide access to the Internet/World Wide Web and on- and off-campus e-mail addresses. A staffed computer lab on campus provides training in the use of computers, software, and the Internet.

Honorary Societies Alpha Psi Omega, Kappa Delta Pi, Lambda Pi Eta, Phi Alpha Theta, Pi Gamma Mu, Sigma Beta Delta, Sigma Delta Tau, and Sigma Zeta

Athletics The College is a member of NAIA. Intercollegiate competition is offered in men's baseball, men's and women's basketball, men's and women's cross-country, men's football, men's and women's golf, men's and women's soccer, women's softball, men's and women's tennis, men's and women's track and field, and women's volleyball.

Study Abroad The College encourages students to broaden their educational experiences and opportunities at Harlaxton in the United Kingdom and Queen's College in Belfast.

Support Services Holman Library, Voigt Science Center, Ames Dining Hall, and the first floors of dormitories are wheelchair-accessible as are the new academic center and Bothwell Chapel. The Learning Resource Center provides reasonable auxiliary aids and services to students with disabilities. In addition to providing legally mandated services for persons with disabilities who voluntarily seek additional services, the Learning Resource Center provides tutoring and other academic support services.

Job Opportunities A limited number of part-time positions on campus are available to students who demonstrate financial need.

Tuition: $10,400 full-time, $325 per credit hour (1998–99)

Room and board: $4600 (approximately)

Mandatory Fees: $100 (approximately)

Contact: Director: Dr. Michele Stacey-Doyle, Honors Program, 701 College Road, Lebanon, Illinois 62254-1299; Telephone: 618-537-6903; Fax: 618-537-6259; E-mail: mstacey@atlas.mckendree.edu; Web site: http://www.mckendree.edu.

McNeese State University

4 Pu G S Sc AA

▼ Honors College

The establishment of the Honors College at McNeese strengthens the University's commitment to "Excellence with a Personal Touch" in undergraduate education. The program is designed for outstanding students with strong academic records who desire an alternative course of instruction at the college level. Twenty-five students are selected by the Honors College Admission

Committee for entrance into the Honors College for the fall semester each year. The Honors College provides unique courses taught by exemplary professors, providing intellectual stimulation, opportunities for interdisciplinary experiences, and enhanced probability for success in a career or in graduate and professional schools.

The elements of McNeese's honors program include unique core courses that satisfy general education requirements. Communications, humanities, natural sciences, and applied sciences courses are designed to stimulate thinking, improve written and oral communication skills, and promote classroom discussion. The average class size of a core honors course is 25. Students are required to earn 12 hours of credit in freshman and sophomore core honors courses. During the junior year, students can investigate a special topic through independent reading and writing, in-depth scholarly research, or completion of a creative project under the guidance of an honors professor. They may also choose an honors option contract for traditional courses by adding independent elements (e.g., a research paper/project, presentation at a regional or national meeting, volunteer service project) as decided by the professor of the course, department head, and Director of the Honors College. Seniors are required to conduct undergraduate research and present their findings in a seminar and write a Senior Honors Thesis. Students must complete 25 hours of honors courses as well as service and leadership requirements in order to earn the Honors College Distinction on their diplomas and official transcripts.

The quality of the teaching in core honors courses is superb, and the professors are highly acclaimed for their teaching styles. These professors have been selected for their expertise in their academic fields, excellence in the classroom, and enthusiasm for teaching. All honors professors and academic advisers of Honors College students are committed to the academic and personal development of students and work diligently to encourage their growth.

The four-room Honors Suite is conveniently located on the first floor of Drew Hall. The Honors Student Center, adjacent to the Director's office, provides a spacious room for honors students to study, discuss issues, and exchange ideas, as well as to socialize. Students gather there for the initial meeting for honors seminars, a 1-hour required course for freshman- and sophomore-level honors students. Students also conduct some of the work and the planning for service activities in the Honors Student Center. The Honors College Office and a small reading room are also located in the Honors Suite.

Students participate in various leadership positions, and honors officers have attended the NCHC national conferences in Chicago and Washington, D.C. They are actively involved in service projects, including tutoring at the women's shelter, painting ceramic butterflies, bowling for the homeless, and participating in science shows at local elementary schools and CHEM EXPO. They fraternize at the honors' socials, such as honors picnics, pizza parties, barbecue by the lake, and supper with professors. The Honors College sponsors 3 guest lecturers annually, including prestigious speakers from the Welch Foundation and Fortune 500 companies. The Honors College at McNeese was founded in fall 2000 and currently has 46 students enrolled.

Participation Requirements: Students enrolled in the Honors College at McNeese must earn at least 24 credit hours each year with an overall 3.0 average and volunteer 50 hours of service during their freshman and sophomore years in order to renew their Honors College Scholarships. They must earn 25 credit hours in honors courses, including the core honors courses; maintain an overall 3.0 average; and complete the service and leadership requirements in order to graduate with the Honors College Distinction.

Admission Process: High school seniors and early admission students having excellent academic records and college preparatory backgrounds, as well as a desire to excel, are encouraged to apply for the Honors College Scholarship at McNeese. The minimum scores for consideration are an ACT of 27 or an SAT of 1210 and a cumulative GPA of 3.4 on a 4.0 scale. Other considerations are leadership and service activities during high school and a personal or telephone interview with the Honors College Admissions Committee. Students must send an application packet that includes a completed application, two copies of their high school transcript, a written essay, and three letters of recommendation to the admissions committee before the priority deadline of February 1, 2002. (The second deadline is April 1, 2002.)

Scholarship Availability: The Honors College Scholarship pays for all tuition and other required fees for registration. It pays for a dormitory room and provides $1000 in Cowboy Cash toward meals and $1000 for purchasing books and other instructional items per year. All students accepted into the Honors College are given a full scholarship that is renewable for three years, providing the student earns at least 24 credit hours each year and meets the service and leadership requirements for the Honors College Scholarship.

The Campus Context: McNeese State University is located in southwest Louisiana in Lake Charles, which has a population of 175,000. Lake Charles, situated along the I-10 corridor between Houston, Texas, and Baton Rouge, offers a variety of outdoor activities, cultural events, festivals, and entertainment opportunities. The McNeese campus consists of a 99-acre main campus, 402-acre farm, and 65-acre athletic plant and student apartment complex, golf driving range, and coliseum. McNeese is a comprehensive university that offers a wide range of baccalaureate and graduate degrees through its six colleges and the Dore School of Graduate Studies. As a public institution, McNeese is committed to the principles of equal opportunity and nondiscrimination.

Student Body Undergraduate enrollment is 6,845: 59 percent women and 41 percent men. Ethnic minorities, including African American, Hispanic, Asian, and Native American, constitute 21.8 percent of the student population. There are 82 international students, and there are thirteen social fraternities and sororities and thirteen honor societies.

Faculty There are 300 full-time faculty members, and 60 percent of all faculty members have terminal degrees. McNeese has an outstanding faculty. One professor's work has been identified as among the most influential of 400 persons in the century. Some have been highly productive in their research efforts, garnering millions of dollars in grants; others serve as editors of international journals. A number of the professors have extensive publications. Some have been recognized for their contributions to music, art, and theater, and several have been appointed as Fulbright scholars. Although they are involved in research and other scholarly work, faculty members are willing to work with students in small groups and individually to enhance their learning environment.

Key Facilities The Lether E. Frazar Memorial Library has 546,183 holdings, including more than 300,000 volumes, microfilm, and unbound documents. Students may use any of the seventy computers housed in the Holbrook Student Union TASC lab and the Memorial Library lab or any of the sixty computers in the Academic Computing Center. Many of the departments at McNeese also have computer labs.

Interpreting the symbols: **2**=two-year college, **4**=four-year college; **Pu**=public or state college, **Pr**=private college; **G**=general honors program; **D**=departmental honors program; **S**=small program (fewer than 100 students), **M**=midsize program (100 to 500 students), **L**=large program (more than 500 students); **Sc**=scholarships available in honors program; **Tr**=transfer students accepted into honors program; **HBC**=historically black college; **AA**=academic advisors; **GA**=graduate advisors; **FA**=fellowship advisors.

Honorary Societies Phi Kappa Phi International, Alpha Lambda Delta, Delta Tau Alpha, Sigma Tau Delta, Kappa Kappa Psi, Kappa Omicron Nu, Blue Key National (men), Epsilon Alpha Epsilon Local (women), Lambda Alpha Epsilon, Pi Sigma Alpha National (political science), Psi Chi (psychology), Sigma Tau Theta (nursing), and Tau Beta Sigma National (band)

Athletics McNeese participates in Division I-AA football, while all other varsity sports are categorized as Division I in the NCAA. The University is also a member of the prestigious Southland Conference and competes for championships in football, baseball, basketball, golf, cross-country, and indoor and outdoor track for the men and in soccer, volleyball, baseball, softball, tennis, cross-country, and indoor and outdoor track for the women. Intramural contests are held in fifteen sports, with awards and recognition being given to winners. Students enter into competition representing fraternities, sororities, dorms, school clubs, organizations, religious student centers, and independents.

Study Abroad Students successfully completing the first two years in the honors program have the option to study abroad in established programs. McNeese belongs to a consortium for studies in classics, history, and art history at the Intercollegiate Center for Classical Studies in Rome. In addition, McNeese offers international study courses in art and art history through the art department during the summer semester.

Support Services McNeese has an office for students with disabilities that is open full-time and operates according to ADA guidelines.

Job Opportunities Students are offered a wide range of work opportunities, including work-study, peer tutoring, and other campus employment.

Tuition: The Honors College Scholarship pays for all fees not covered by TOPS (Tuition Opportunity Program for Students) for Louisiana students and for all out-of-state student tuition and fees.

Room and Board: Freshman students choosing to live in a residence hall are required to pay a minimal amount above the $1000 per year covered by the Honors College Scholarship for a meal ticket.

Mandatory Fees: Fees are covered by the Honors College Scholarship.

Contact: Director: Joan E. Vallee, McNeese State University, P.O. Box 93430, Lake Charles, Louisiana 70609-3430; Telephone: 337-475-5456 or 800-622-3352 Ext. 5456 (toll-free); Fax: 337-475-5950; E-mail: jvallee@mail.mcneese.edu; Web site: http://www.mcneese.edu

MEDAILLE COLLEGE

4 Pr G S Sc AA

▼ The Theodore Roosevelt Scholars Program at Medaille College

The Theodore Roosevelt Scholars Program at Medaille College is an innovative learning community in which students of demonstrated academic ability can enhance their skills for thinking critically and creatively about challenging ideas. The program combines honors-level general education courses with special mentoring activities that, in the tradition of Theodore Roosevelt, seek to develop the student's mind, body, and spirit while encouraging intellectual rigor, physical vigor, and moral and social commitment. Roosevelt was not only a renowned U.S. President inaugurated in Buffalo, a governor of New York State, and a Police Commissioner of New York City, but also a Nobel Peace Prize–winning statesman, a recipient of the Congressional Medal of Honor, and a prominent orator, historian, conservationist, rancher, naturalist, and explorer. His energetic and complex life thus inspires the program, which challenges its students to engage wholeheartedly in the exhilarating pursuit of excellence.

The heart of the Scholars Program is a set of nine honors-level liberal arts and sciences courses developed and taught by dedicated and enthusiastic faculty members. These courses are part of Medaille's general education core and fulfill requirements for all of the school's baccalaureate programs. This means that students from any major can participate in the program without having to take extra courses beyond the regular graduation requirements.

Without question, the honors-level sections of these courses are challenging; they are designed to fulfill the needs of students with the ability and the motivation to thrive in such demanding academic environments. They are also designed to connect important topics and skills that are not just introduced once and forgotten, but reinforced in multiple courses. Close faculty member collaboration has produced a unique, integrated sequence of courses aimed at developing a deep understanding of the general education core's leading ideas. Students seeking entry into demanding career fields or selective graduate schools find these critical-thinking and communication skills crucial to their success.

Medaille College is proud of its reputation for having small classes and a low student-faculty ratio. As Medaille students, it is natural for Theodore Roosevelt Scholars to maintain close contact with their professors. They also receive formal and informal mentoring through a variety of special events intended to bring faculty members and students together outside the classroom. Receptions, presentations, and other activities are all planned to foster a true learning community whose members share academic and nonacademic interests; for instance, the faculty includes individuals who are passionate not only about the arts and sciences, but also about physical and outdoor pursuits, such as martial arts, fencing, fly fishing, and cycling.

In addition to these classroom and mentoring opportunities, students participating in the Theodore Roosevelt Scholars Program are eligible for special honors scholarships and other scholarship aid they may qualify for. Furthermore, Scholars Program students have access to distinguished guests and speakers during on-campus visits. They also benefit from a flexible registration procedure that ensures their enrollment in honors courses on schedule and in sequence. Finally, students in the Scholars Program receive special library benefits to support intensive, honors-level study, and they earn official recognition of their achievements at graduation.

The Theodore Roosevelt Scholars Program was founded in 2001.

Participation Requirements: Students in the Theodore Roosevelt Scholars Program take special honors sections of nine general education courses in a prescribed sequence. They also participate in a variety of formal and informal mentoring activities designed to bring students and faculty members together outside of the classroom. In addition, Scholars Program students earn official recognition of their achievements at graduation.

Admission Process: Incoming Trustee and Presidential Scholarship recipients with strong SAT scores receive automatic invitation into the program. Other students with academic records or SAT scores indicative of honors potential receive automatic consideration for the program by a faculty committee. Students who do not receive automatic invitation or consideration need not be discouraged, though, as the program also welcomes applications from other interested and qualified students. Those who wish to apply should write to the Director at the address below to explain their qualifications and make their strongest case for admission into the program. Upon receiving such applications, the College reviews the pertinent academic records and test scores before making the program admission decisions.

Scholarship Availability: As first-time freshmen, students participating in the Theodore Roosevelt Scholars Program are eligible for special honors scholarships in addition to other scholarship aid they may qualify for. Many also receive Trustee Scholarships of $6000 per year, Presidential Scholarships of $3000 per year, or Dean's Scholarships of $2000 per year. Returning students are also eligible for a variety of scholarships; applications for these scholarships are available in the Financial Aid Office in the spring semester of each academic year.

The Campus Context: Medaille College is a private, nonsectarian, coeducational institution committed to serving the educational needs of the region's diverse population with an expanding set of undergraduate and graduate degree programs. The attractive 13-acre campus is located in the heart of Buffalo at Agassiz Circle (Parkside Avenue and Route 198), adjacent to the Frederick Law Olmsted–designed Delaware Park and just a short walk or drive from the wonderful museums, shopping districts, and homes of the Elmwood, Parkside, and North Buffalo neighborhoods. Medaille concentrates on excellence in teaching, with an emphasis on personal attention to its diverse student body. Its curriculum provides a solid liberal arts and sciences foundation and early access to career-oriented education through the most comprehensive internship program in the area.

Student Body For the fall 2001 semester, total undergraduate enrollment at Medaille College was 1,512 students, with 71 percent women and 29 percent men. Resident students constituted 10 percent of the student body and commuters 90 percent; 42 percent of the students were nontraditional students. Approximately 80 percent of students at Medaille receive financial aid.

Faculty The total number of faculty members at Medaille is 123 (62 full-time). The student-faculty ratio is 17:1, and the average class size is 15 students.

Key Facilities The Medaille College Library, a New York State Advanced Level Electronic Doorway Library, is located in Alice Huber Hall; many library services, including the automated catalog and online periodicals, are accessible through Medaille's Web site at http://www.medaille.edu.

The Academic Computing Center (ACC) is located on the second floor of Huber Hall. The complex holds two computerized classrooms and an open lab. The New Media Institute (NMI), located in the Main Building, is dedicated to teaching and training students in the trends of multimedia technologies. Students use NMI resources to create interactive CD-ROMs, design World Wide Web pages, create professional presentations, and compile digital and printed senior portfolios. All NMI and ACC computers are networked via a fiber-optic backbone accessing the Internet through T1 lines.

Honorary Societies Alpha Chi, Phi Theta Kappa

Athletics Medaille College sponsors a Division III athletic program through the National Collegiate Athletic Association and is a founding member of the Upstate Athletic Alliance. Medaille also holds membership in the National Small College Athletic Association and has sent teams to the national championship tournament for three of the past four years. Intercollegiate sports include baseball, basketball, cross-country, lacrosse, soccer, softball, and volleyball; in addition, a variety of sports are available at the intramural and extramural levels of competition.

Support Services Medaille College's Office of Disability Services works to assist students with disabilities in all aspects of their college life; students requesting services and/or accommodations must contact the office directly.

Job Opportunities Medaille College participates in the Federal Work-Study Program, which allows students with financial need to work in jobs on campus to earn part of their educational expenses. In addition, Medaille's Career Planning and Placement Center posts notices of part-time and full-time job openings outside the office and on the Medaille Job Beat Web site. There are also many other off-campus student employment opportunities in the surrounding metropolitan area.

Tuition: Full-time tuition was $12,240 per academic year; part-time tuition was $408 per credit hour (2001–02 academic year).

Room and Board: Room and board fees totaled $5800 per year, assuming double occupancy (2001–02 academic year).

Mandatory Fees: Full-time mandatory fees totaled $280 per academic year; part-time mandatory student fees totaled $40 plus $8 per credit hour (2001–02 academic year).

Contact: Dr. A. Lee Nisbet, Director of the Theodore Roosevelt Program or Dr. Gerald J. Erion, Honors Coordinator, Medaille College, 18 Agassiz Circle, Buffalo, New York 14214; Telephone: 716-884-3281; Fax: 716-884-0291

MERCY COLLEGE

4 Pr D S Sc Tr

▼ Honors Program

The Honors Program at Mercy College is open to all motivated day students who have General Education requirements to fulfill or room in their programs for electives. Some major courses may also be taken as an honors option.

Honors classes are conducted as seminars that emphasize a spirit of inquiry in an atmosphere of collegiality between students and faculty members. The stimulating environment encourages students to raise their academic expectations while the supportive community offers opportunities to develop new leadership capacities. Trips, special events, and service projects provide cultural experiences outside of the classroom.

Students who have taken three or more honors courses and have maintained a GPA of 3.2 or greater receive a Certificate of Membership. Students who have taken nine of more honors classes receive the Christie Scholar Award. Awards are given for scholarship, academic development, and leadership. Outstanding student papers are presented in an annual symposium to which the entire campus is invited.

The twenty-year-old program currently enrolls 75 students.

Participation Requirements: To be an official member of the Honors Program, a student must have taken at least three honors courses and must maintain a GPA of 3.2 or above. Members of the Honors Program are also expected to be active in the community life of the honors club. Community meetings are held at least bimonthly in the Honors Student Center.

Scholarship Availability: Mercy College offers many scholarships to exceptional students. Many students in the Honors Program take advantage of these scholarships.

The Campus Context: Mercy College is a comprehensive college offering both undergraduate and graduate degrees. Founded in 1950 by the Sisters of Mercy, the College became independent in 1969. Set on the spectacular Hudson River in Westchester County, just 35 minutes from the heart of New York City, Mercy College is one of the largest independent and coeducational four-year colleges in New York State. The main campus is located in Dobbs Ferry, with branch campuses situated in Yorktown Heights, White Plains, and the Bronx.

The College offers twenty-nine undergraduate majors leading to baccalaureate degrees and four graduate majors leading to master's degrees.

Interpreting the symbols: **2**=two-year college, **4**=four-year college; **Pu**=public or state college, **Pr**=private college; **G**=general honors program; **D**=departmental honors program; **S**=small program (fewer than 100 students), **M**=midsize program (100 to 500 students), **L**=large program (more than 500 students); **Sc**=scholarships available in honors program; **Tr**=transfer students accepted into honors program; **HBC**=historically black college; **AA**=academic advisors; **GA**=graduate advisors; **FA**=fellowship advisors.

Student Body There are more than 7,000 undergraduate enrollees and 850 graduate students. Thirty-five percent of the population are men and 65 percent are women. The ethnic distribution is .16 percent Native American, 1.6 percent Asian, 7.8 percent black, 17.3 percent Hispanic, 25.15 percent white, and .4 percent other. Two hundred students live in the Residence Hall. There are 189 international students.

Faculty Mercy has 157 full-time faculty members and 485 part-time adjunct faculty members, with more than 60 percent of the full-time faculty members holding doctorates. The student-faculty ratio is 17:1.

Key Facilities The library holds 293,000 volumes. There are more than 500 microcomputer systems available, both IBM-compatible and Macintosh.

Honorary Societies Alpha Chi

Athletics Intercollegiate athletics in men's soccer, basketball, baseball, and tennis are offered, and women's intercollegiate athletics include volleyball, basketball, softball, and tennis. Golf and cross-country teams exist for both men and women.

Study Abroad Mercy College encourages students to enrich their educational experience by spending some time studying abroad in approved programs. Academic credit is given for satisfactory foreign study.

Job Opportunities Students are offered work opportunities on campus that include work-study and campus employment.

Tuition: $7800 per year (1998–99)

Room and Board: $7600 minimum

Contact: Director: Dr. Nancy A. Benson, 555 Broadway, Dobbs Ferry, New York 10522-1189; Telephone: 914-674-7432; Fax: 914-674-7542; E-mail: nbenson@mercynet.edu

Mercyhurst College

4 Pr G M Sc Tr AA

▼ Honors Program

The Mercyhurst College Honors Program (MCHP) has a rich assortment of curricular and extracurricular opportunities for academically accomplished students who seek extraordinary intellectual stimulation. Selected entering freshmen and transfer students are invited to participate in the Honors Preparation Year (HPY). In this trial year, the HPY students have the opportunity to sample the MCHP before formally joining in the spring term. During the HPY, students take at least one honors course, attend intellectual and/or cultural events on campus, and perform service learning. They are invited to numerous out-of-classroom events such as meals, hikes, and coffeeshop gatherings with honors faculty members. At the end of the HPY, students who wish to join the MCHP must submit an admission portfolio to the director. Students must have a minimum QPA of 3.0 at the College, attend at least ten events that are intellectual or cultural in nature, perform 10 hours of community service, and secure two letters of recommendation from faculty members at the College as part of the admission process. In the spring, students are officially inducted into the MCHP. MCHP students continue attending intellectual and cultural events on campus; by their junior and senior years, they are often creating and/or participating in these events. MCHP students also continue taking honors courses. By graduation, they have taken at least nine honors courses. At least six of these courses must be honors classes that also satisfy the Collegewide Liberal Studies Core requirement, while the others may be courses in which the student completes an "honors contract." Honors courses offered at Mercyhurst are lively and small (fewer than 20) and often feature student-led discussions; they are more student centered and student driven than non-honors courses. The courses are often designed to allow students more freedom in their education; this format is outstanding preparation for graduate school. Honors students have input into the creation of honors courses at the College. All honors students must write a senior thesis if their major does not require one.

Extracurricular activities and professional development are major components of the MCHP experience. Honors students at Mercyhurst College create many of the events that define the intellectual and cultural life of the College, from discussion on timely issues to performing arts presentations. In addition, MCHP students play a prominent role in national, regional, and Collegewide conferences, symposia, shows, and performances. Honors students at Mercyhurst College have read papers at national professional meetings, been successful in major national scholarship competitions, had their papers published in a variety of journals, and had their work shown in regional exhibits. MCHP graduates study at some of the most prestigious graduate and professional schools. The College works with advisers and students to prepare them for candidacy for graduate school.

Approximately 90 honors students are in the MCHP. There are an additional 100 students who are eligible to enroll in honors courses despite not being in the program.

Participation Requirements: To graduate with College Honors, students must maintain a 3.35 QPA, complete a total of nine honors courses (three of which may have been honors contracts), attend fifteen events of intellectual or cultural interest each year, perform 15 hours of service each year, and write an approved senior thesis (in chosen major) or an honors thesis.

Admission Process: Participating in the MCHP requires an invitation from the Director. Each year about 120 entering freshmen are invited to join the program. Invitations are based on SAT I or ACT scores, high school records, and recommendations. Transfer students are eligible to join the MCHP and invitations are based on former college or university performance. Students already at Mercyhurst who have a record of academic achievement are also encouraged to consider the MCHP, particularly if recommended by a faculty member.

Scholarship Availability: While the MCHP Director supervises the awarding of just one academic scholarship, many are available through the College's Office of Financial Aid.

The Campus Context: Mercyhurst College, in Erie, Pennsylvania, is located on 75 acres of orchards, lawns, and gardens overlooking Lake Erie. Erie, located in the rolling hills and vineyards of Pennsylvania, is the state's only port and home to the famous beaches and nature preserves of the Presque Isle peninsula. Founded in 1926 by the Sisters of Mercy, the College is a vibrant, coeducational institution of more than 3,000 students, the majority of whom are campus residents. The B.A., B.S., and M.S. are offered in 120 different academic programs.

Numerous certificate programs are also available. The Mercyhurst College campus includes a student union, an ice center, a performing arts center/opera house, an apartment complex, and a town-house village. Other features include an observatory, a theater, a language laboratory, and a food lab/restaurant. To be completed by the fall of 2002 is a new, $7-million academic building. This three-story, 45,000-square-foot building will serve as Mercyhurst's new academic hub, with "smart" classrooms, seminar rooms, lab spaces, and faculty offices. Included in the building will also be a new suite of rooms for the Honors Program (seminar room, staff office, director's office, and student center).

Student Body The student body of more than 3,000 is composed of 55 percent women, with 63 students from eight other countries. Eighty-seven percent are campus residents and nearly 90 percent of students receive financial aid.

Faculty A faculty of more than 200 includes 117 full-time faculty members, 60 percent of whom have a Ph.D. or other terminal degree. The student-faculty ratio is 17:1.

Key Facilities The College library owns 160,000 volumes and uses CD-ROM and Internet access to utilize the world's great libraries and databases. There are approximately 200 PCs available to students in several locations, including a sophisticated science computing center that offers five UNIX machines. Students may use e-mail and access the Internet in many computer centers.

Honorary Society Phi Eta Sigma

Athletics The athletics program offers a multitude of fitness and sports activities to the Mercyhurst community. The College offers twenty-five varsity intercollegiate sports, including men's and women's crew, volleyball, basketball, golf, soccer, cross-country, lacrosse, rowing, tennis, water polo, field hockey, and ice hockey. Football, baseball, and wrestling for men and softball for women are also offered at the College. Most of the sports are NCAA Division II affiliated, with the exception of men's and women's ice hockey, which compete at the Division I level. Mercyhurst also participates in a number of athletic conferences. Affiliations include the Eastern College Athletic Conference (ECAC), the Great Lakes Intercollegiate Athletic Conference (GLIAC), the Midwest Intercollegiate Volleyball Association (MIVA), and the NCAA Division I Metro Atlantic Athletic Conference's (MAAC) Hockey League. The seventeen intramural sports include football, golf, volleyball, basketball, hockey, soccer, softball, badminton, bowling, and tennis. In addition, Mercyhurst provides access to a full-service, on-campus fitness center that features all the latest in aerobic and strength-conditioning physical fitness equipment; the fitness center is open to all Mercyhurst students.

Study Abroad Many study-abroad opportunities exist through the academic departments and the Honors Program.

Job Opportunities A wide variety of job opportunities exist in work-study and assistantship positions.

Tuition: $13,940 per year (2001–02)

Room and Board: $5694

Mandatory Fees: $1050

Contact: Director: Dr. Candee C. Chambers, 501 East 38th Street, Erie, Pennsylvania 16546; Telephone: 814-824-2383; Fax: 814-824-2188; E-mail: hondir@mercyhurst.edu; Web site: http://www.mercyhurst.edu

MESA STATE COLLEGE

4 Pu G S Sc Tr

▼ Honors Program

The Honors Program at Mesa State College offers promising and motivated students enhanced opportunities for academic growth. All aspects of the program are focused on exciting learning experiences, an emphasis on developing intellectual skills rather than collecting facts, close relationships with the honors faculty members and with other honors students, and the assistance of the Honors Program Director in accessing the academic, administrative, and personal support that will allow students to make the most of their college careers.

Lower-division honors courses consist of specially designed sections of general education courses, taught by faculty members recruited for their expertise and teaching excellence. By varying the offerings from semester to semester, students are able to fulfill the general education requirement in small, discussion-based classes instead of large lecture classes. Upper-division honors courses are interdisciplinary, focused around themes or issues that can be illuminated from various perspectives.

Honors students also have the option of producing an honors thesis on some topic within their major. Under the guidance of an adviser they pursue a line of research/inquiry culminating in a written work that will be bound and included in the College library's holdings. Such projects are especially valuable in preparing students for graduate work, and the successful completion of an honors thesis is cited at graduation and on students' transcripts. The program is still growing, having begun in 1993. It will be capped at approximately 125 students. There are currently 70 students enrolled in the program.

Participation Requirements: Students selected for enrollment must maintain a GPA of at least 3.0 and must take at least one honors course a year to be retained in the program. If students accumulate an average of at least 3.0 in 18 hours of honors courses, 6 of which are upper-division, they are cited at graduation and on their transcripts as having earned academic honors.

Admission Process: Students must submit an application to the Honors Program separate from the application to the College. The exact application package depends on whether the applicant is an incoming freshman or a current student at the College.

Entering freshmen should apply by May 1. Currently enrolled students may apply each semester.

Scholarship Availability: Mesa State College offers a large number of scholarships for exceptional students.

The Campus Context: Mesa State College is an architecturally pleasing, beautifully planted, 42-acre campus bordered by a residential neighborhood. The town of Grand Junction is located in the western part of the state of Colorado. Both the location of the College and its spreading reputation as providing a top-notch education at a public college price has made it the fastest-growing college in Colorado. Its twenty-five degree programs lead to the B.A., B.S., B.B.A., or B.S.N.

Student Body There are 5,300 undergraduates enrolled, 44 percent are men and 56 percent are women. These include 67 international students. Sixty-three percent of all students receive financial aid.

Faculty Of the 192 full-time faculty members, 88 percent have terminal degrees. The part-time faculty numbers 100. The student-faculty ratio is 21:1.

Key Facilities The library houses 205,000 volumes. Many computer labs are located in the library and academic buildings. The Tutorial Learning Center provides learning support. A new science building was completed in 1997, a new art and communication building in 2001, and a new music and theater building in 2002.

Honorary Society Alpha Chi

Athletics Mesa State has NCAA Division II teams for men in baseball, basketball, tennis, and football and for women in soccer, softball, basketball, golf, cross-country, tennis, and volleyball. In addition, there are many intramural sports. The campus has a new 32,000-square-foot Recreational Center.

Support Services All buildings are handicapped-accessible.

Tuition and Fees: $2185 for state residents, $6800 for nonresidents, per year

Room and Board: $5700

Mandatory Fees: $433

Contact: Director: Dr. L. Luis Lopez, 1100 North Avenue, Grand Junction, Colorado 81502; Telephone: 970-248-1646; Fax: 970-248-1199

Interpreting the symbols: **2**=two-year college, **4**=four-year college; **Pu**=public or state college, **Pr**=private college; **G**=general honors program; **D**=departmental honors program; **S**=small program (fewer than 100 students), **M**=midsize program (100 to 500 students), **L**=large program (more than 500 students); **Sc**=scholarships available in honors program; **Tr**=transfer students accepted into honors program; **HBC**=historically black college; **AA**=academic advisors; **GA**=graduate advisors; **FA**=fellowship advisors.

MESSIAH COLLEGE

4 Pr G M Sc

▼ Honors Program

The Messiah College Honors Program was inaugurated in the fall of 1998. The mission of the Honors Program is to foster academic excellence and to cultivate an intellectually rigorous Christian world view, thus equipping young men and women for lives of leadership and service.

Students in the Honors Program take several interdisciplinary honors courses beginning in their freshman year and continuing through their junior year. These small, seminar-type courses are taught by senior faculty members and cover topics such as Art of the Ancient Americas, Darwin and Darwinism, and The Writer's Call to Fidelity: Wallace Stegner's Example. In their fourth year, students participate in a two-semester Senior Honors Project and Colloquium, culminating in a public presentation. In addition to these credit-bearing experiences, students meet each semester outside of the classroom in the Honors Congress to discuss timely issues. Throughout the academic year students also have opportunities to interact with special campus guests as part of the Honors Discourse. The College's proximity to the academic and cultural centers of Washington, Philadelphia, Baltimore, and New York provide additional opportunities for students in the Honors Program.

Students from all of the college's applied and liberal arts majors are eligible to participate in the Honors Program. Moreover, in keeping with College's commitment to educating the whole person, students in the Honors Program are strongly encouraged to participate in the college's many cocurricular opportunities, including those in athletics, music, theater, student government, campus publications, and off-campus ministries.

Program enrollment is 140 students.

Participation Requirements: Students in the Honors Program must take an honors section of First Year Seminar, honors sections of three other interdisciplinary general education courses, and complete a two-semester Senior Honors Project. Students in the Honors Program must maintain a minimum cumulative 3.3 GPA as first-year students and at least a 3.6 GPA for each following year. Upon graduation, recognition of the student's completion of the Honors Program is noted at commencement and on the student's college transcript.

Admission Process: No special application is required. As part of the regular college admissions process, students who meet minimum eligibility requirements are considered for the program. Minimum requirements for the Honors Program are an SAT I score of at least 1300 and graduation in the top 10 percent of the student's high school class. From the eligible pool of candidates, 100 students are selected for on-campus interviews. After the on-campus interview and evaluation of all other application materials, approximately 32 students are selected each year for the Honors Program.

Scholarship Availability: All students who are selected for the Honors Program receive scholarship aid. Each year, four freshman students are awarded a full-tuition Trustees Scholarship, while all other freshman in the Honors Program receive scholarships covering at least one-third tuition.

The Campus Context: Messiah College was founded in 1909 by the Brethren in Christ Church. The College is located in Grantham, Pennsylvania, which is 15 minutes south of Harrisburg, the state capital. Facilities have grown from a single building to a campus of 400 acres, with buildings valued at more than $100 million. The College also has an urban center located on the campus of Temple University in Philadelphia.

Since its founding, Messiah College has been committed to an embracing evangelical spirit rooted in the Anabaptist, Pietist, and Wesleyan traditions of the Christian Church. The College's motto, Christ Preeminent, guides the College's mission, which is to educate men and women toward maturity of intellect, character, and Christian faith in preparation for lives of service, leadership, and reconciliation in church and society.

As a Christian college of the liberal and applied arts and sciences, Messiah is a residential undergraduate college with an enrollment of 2,600 students. The College endowment is in excess of $100 million.

Student Body Approximately 60 percent of the College's 2,600 students are women, and nearly 6 percent are ethnic minorities. Most students are of traditional college age, and 90 percent live in College residences. More than 50 percent of the College's students come from more than forty states and several other countries. The student body represents more than forty religious denominations.

Faculty The College's full-time faculty members number approximately 150, with 75 percent holding terminal degrees. Coming from a multitude of backgrounds, they represent nearly 150 graduate schools and many denominational affiliations.

Key Facilities The Murray Library provides a wide variety of learning resources in an architecturally striking atmosphere. The library houses more than 300,000 items, including books, media, periodicals, and microfilm. The library houses a computerized library management system that enables students to search library holdings, either on-site or through the College's computer network. The library provides access to hundreds of databases, including connection to more than 10,000 libraries and more than 40-million bibliographical sources. College librarians support an active instructional program that assists students in learning how to make the best use of the technology and resources available through the library.

The college provides an impressive variety of computing facilities. Students have access to more than 200 microcomputers located in eight computer labs. All labs are connected to the campus network. In addition, all student rooms in campus residence halls and townhouses are wired for computer access.

Athletics Messiah College is a member of the NCAA Division III. The College fields eighteen intercollegiate sports teams, including men and women's soccer, cross-country, lacrosse, tennis, and basketball. The College participates in the Middle Atlantic Conference, and several of Messiah's teams enjoy national rankings every year.

In addition to intercollegiate athletics, Messiah College's campus provides opportunities for many indoor and outdoor activities. Besides outdoor track facilities, tennis courts, athletic fields, and hiking trails, the Sollenberger Sports Center is an exceptional indoor facility containing a pool, racquetball courts, an indoor track, and four basketball courts.

Study Abroad Significant numbers of Messiah College students from nearly all disciplines participate in a wide variety of overseas programs lasting from three weeks to a full semester. Students in the College Honors Program are strongly encouraged to take advantage of overseas study opportunities. These opportunities include College-sponsored programs in Russia, China, France, Spain, and Kenya as well as many other countries.

Support Services Messiah College provides support services for handicapped and learning disabled students through the College's Office of Disability Services. The College's Writing Center and Learning Workshop provide additional assistance with writing and study skills.

Job Opportunities Students are offered a variety of work opportunities. These include work-study and the College's Scholar-Intern Program.

Tuition: $16,860 per year (2001–02)

Room and board: $5500

Mandatory Fees: $175

Contact: Director: Dr. Dean C. Curry, Grantham, Pennsylvania 17055; Telephone: 717-766-2511; E-mail: dcurry@messiah.edu; Web site: http://www.messiah.edu

MIAMI UNIVERSITY

4 Pu G L Tr

▼ University Honors Program

As an integral part of Miami University, the University Honors Program offers students a learning community that consciously supports the University's goals for liberal education: thinking critically, understanding contexts, engaging with other learners, and reflecting and acting. The program's mission is to support and provide opportunities for individuals who are strongly motivated academically and who desire a highly challenging and intellectually enriched learning environment. Through a rigorous curriculum, vibrant cocurricular experiences, and close advising and mentoring, the University Honors Program is committed to nurturing the intellectual and personal development of its students.

The honors program empowers students to see themselves as generators of knowledge rather than as passive transmitters of wisdom; moves students to greater self-reflection about pragmatic and value issues surrounding responsible participation in a community; increases students' awareness of their relation to populations and global issues beyond those in which they are immediately and locally involved; increases students' abilities to communicate with others, both verbally and in writing; increases students' appreciation of the enriching visions of human possibility offered by artistic and aesthetic expression; enhances students' abilities to contextualize the events and milestones of their lives; and broadens students' abilities to learn from experiences different from their own.

Miami's University Honors Program, established in 1984, enrolls approximately 750 students.

Participation Requirements: Honors students are required to complete ten Honors Experiences in order to graduate with University Honors. Honors Experiences encompass a broad array of learning opportunities. They consist of honors courses as well as other experiences such as study abroad, independent undergraduate research with a faculty mentor, selected internship experiences, and graduate courses. Of the required ten Honors Experiences, eight must be honors courses. In addition to program requirements, students may elect to complete an honors thesis. These students graduate with the notation University Honors with Distinction on their transcripts. Students completing program requirements but selecting the no-thesis option earns the notation University Honors.

First-year students participate in a faculty mentor program that gives them the opportunity to interact closely with faculty members outside the classroom. This program encourages students to engage in intellectual inquiry by providing a variety of venues for discussions and reflection.

Admission Process: Admission to the University Honors Program is highly selective. In 2001–02, students were automatically offered admission if they had an SAT score of 1360 (or better) or an ACT score of 31 (or better) and were in the top 5 percent of their high school graduating class. High-ability students whose scores do not meet the admission requirements for the honors program may be selected to participate in Miami's Oxford Scholars Program. These students may apply to the honors program after completing 15 Miami credit hours with an earned GPA of 3.5 (or better). Applications are considered on a space-available basis.

Scholarship Availability: All students admitted to the University Honors Program receive an annual renewable scholarship of $1250. In addition, awards are available to assist students with research expenses, travel to professional conferences, and other academic endeavors. All honors students have the opportunity to earn up to 8 free-tuition credits that can be used for summer study at Miami or in one of Miami's many international study-abroad programs.

Honors students are also eligible to apply for one of the largest undergraduate awards in the nation—Miami's Joanna Jackson Goldman Memorial Prize. This award annually supports a graduating Miami senior for a year of independent scholarship or creative activity. The amount of the prize is approximately $25,000. Eligibility for the award includes an outstanding academic record, demonstrated capacity for independent work, and creative initiative in some field of scholarship or the arts. The application deadline for this annual award is mid-November.

The Campus Context: Miami is known as one of the nation's top public undergraduate universities and as one of the best educational values in America. Miami has seven divisions or colleges, the College of Arts and Science, the School of Engineering and Applied Science, the Richard T. Farmer School of Business Administration, the School of Education and Allied Professions, the School of Fine Arts, the School of Interdisciplinary Studies (Western College Program), and the Graduate School. There are nearly 100 undergraduate majors to choose from, plus preprofessional programs in law, medicine, and other disciplines.

Student Body There are 15,014 undergraduate students; 45 percent are men and 55 percent are women. The ethnic distribution of students is 4 percent African American, 2 percent Asian, and 2 percent Hispanic. There are approximately 112 undergraduate international students. Commuters account for 55 percent of the students. Forty percent of the undergraduates receive some form of financial assistance. There are twenty-seven fraternities and twenty-one sororities on the campus.

Faculty The total number of faculty members is 975. Full-time faculty members number 787. Eighty-nine percent of the full-time faculty members have terminal degrees. The student-faculty ratio is 17:1. All honors courses are taught by full-time faculty members.

Key Facilities According to *Yahoo! Internet Life,* Miami is one of the country's 100 most wired colleges. The rankings are based on infrastructure, student resources, Web portal, e-learning, technical support, and wireless access. Miami has spent $23.3 million to provide high-speed computer access to offices, labs, classrooms, and each residence hall room. One hundred percent of Miami's residence hall rooms are wired for computer access (and cable TV), as are 100 percent of the offices and labs. Miami also provides wireless computer access in several locations, including the libraries, Shriver Center, and various academic centers. Four libraries on the Oxford Campus contain more than 2 million cataloged volumes and offer computer-based searching.

Special facilities of importance to honors students include Bishop Hall, a centrally located upperclass residence hall, and the first-year Honors and Scholars Living Learning Community residence hall. Two research scholar rooms are available each year to upperclass honors students conducting research. Applications for these rooms are due in mid-October.

Athletics All athletics are NCAA Division I. These include women's sports in basketball, cross-country, field hockey, soccer, softball, swimming and diving, synchronized skating, tennis, track and field, and volleyball. Men's sports include baseball, basketball,

Interpreting the symbols: **2**=two-year college, **4**=four-year college; **Pu**=public or state college, **Pr**=private college; **G**=general honors program; **D**=departmental honors program; **S**=small program (fewer than 100 students), **M**=midsize program (100 to 500 students), **L**=large program (more than 500 students); **Sc**=scholarships available in honors program; **Tr**=transfer students accepted into honors program; **HBC**=historically black college; **AA**=academic advisors; **GA**=graduate advisors; **FA**=fellowship advisors.

cross-country, football, golf, ice hockey, swimming and diving, and track and field.

Study Abroad Miami consistently ranks among the top ten universities in the nation for the number of students studying abroad. Miami's Luxembourg Campus, set in the heart of Europe, provides an opportunity for students from any major to study for a semester or a year. In addition, there are exchange programs in five countries and access to more than 130 universities worldwide through the International Student Exchange Program. The University Honors Program administers a unique program that allows students to study at the prestigious Cambridge University in England. This rigorous 16-credit semester exposes students to the British "supervision" method of highly individualized study.

Support Services For students with physical disabilities, the Office of Disability Resources ensures program accessibility and compliance with Section 504 of the Rehabilitation Act of 1973 and the Americans with Disabilities Act. Miami provides such aids as sound amplifiers; adapted computing equipment; reading machines; and services such as sign language interpreters as requested, closed-caption television on the campus, and a network of telecommunication devices for the deaf throughout various University offices, as well as volunteer reading programs for students who require taped textbooks.

Job Opportunities The Office of Student Financial Aid coordinates all student employment on the campus. Students who do not qualify for work-study jobs may seek paying jobs on the campus. An all-University student job fair, offered each fall, provides an opportunity for students to learn about different kinds of on-campus employment as well as submit applications for available positions. A brochure, *Working on Campus,* provides information about campus employers, job classifications, and wage rates.

Tuition: $5796 for state residents and $13,470 for nonresidents per year (2001–02)

Room and Board: $5970

Mandatory Fees: $1119

Contact: Director, University Honors Program, Bishop Hall, Oxford, Ohio 45056; Telephone: 513-529-3399; Fax: 513-529-4920; E-mail: honors@muohio.edu; Web site: http://www.muohio.edu/honors

MICHIGAN STATE UNIVERSITY

4 Pu G L Sc Tr AA

▼ Honors College

The Honors College (HC) serves academically talented, committed students who wish to pursue and achieve academic excellence. The College strives to ensure an enriched academic and social experience for its members and create an environment that fosters active, innovative learning.

Members of the Honors College design their own individualized programs of study in the fields of their choice, enroll in dynamic honors classes and seminars, participate in faculty-led research projects, and join other Honors College students who share curiosity, concern, and enthusiasm in an environment brimming with outstanding social and community activities. Honors College members are not constrained by standard curricular requirements; they are committed instead to academic work enriched by honors courses, research experiences, and graduate course substitutions.

Honors College members can choose to live with other honors students on one of the honors floors in Bryan, Case, Gilchrist, Holmes, or Mason halls. Students seek advising and can use the computer lab and honors lounge in the newly renovated Honors College facility, Eustace-Cole Hall. The Honors College also supports honors student organizations, including the Honors College Programming Board, the Honors College Student Advisory Committee, the Honors College Service Corps, and MOSAIC (the HC's minority student association).

As one of the first and most distinctive honors programs, the Honors College at Michigan State University (MSU) was founded in 1956. Approximately 2,200 students are currently enrolled in the Honors College.

Participation Requirements: In fulfilling the requirements for an enriched program of study, a student may use a combination of the various types of honors opportunities available. Honors College members are not required to take a specific set of classes, freeing them to select from among the University's vast advanced course offerings. Members major in any area; honors experiences are a way to enhance all components of their college education.

Members are required to complete eight honors experiences by the time of graduation, averaging one honors course, section, or option every semester. Honors courses, honors sections of regular courses, honors work in nonhonors classes, graduate courses, honors research, and honors theses are considered appropriate honors experiences.

To remain a member in good standing, an Honors College student must establish a cumulative GPA of at least 3.2 during the freshman year and maintain a GPA of at least 3.2 until graduation. At graduation, the distinction of membership in the Honors College is noted on a student's diploma and transcript. It is also reflected in the commencement gown, which includes the respected honors stole.

Admission Process: Students interested in becoming members of the Honors College should first apply for admission to Michigan State University. A completed application serves as an application for Honors College membership; there is no separate application process.

Membership in the Honors College is by invitation only. Invitations are extended to high school students who rank in the top 5 percent of their high school graduating class and have an ACT composite score of at least 30 or an SAT I total score of at least 1360. For those students who have outstanding records and are close to the criteria, the Honors College may request additional information before extending an invitation for membership.

Freshmen who establish excellent records at MSU (normally a 3.5 cumulative GPA or higher) may apply for membership after their first semester. Students are also asked to write an essay outlining their interests and aspirations and propose a detailed program of honors study for the sophomore year.

Scholarship Availability: The Honors College sponsors several scholarships for its incoming students. Professional Assistantships, Honors College Tuition Grants, Honors College STATE scholarships, and Honors College National Scholarships are available for exceptional in- and out-of-state students invited to join the HC. HC invitees are candidates for the University's largest merit awards and National Merit scholarships.

Continuing students enjoy access to other significant HC scholarships, including study-abroad scholarships, academic excellence scholarships, and independent research awards. MSU Honors College members also have an exceptional record of achievement in attaining major national and international scholarships and fellowships, including Rhodes, Marshall, and Truman scholarships and National Science Foundation graduate fellowships.

The Campus Context: Founded in 1855 as one of the nation's pioneer land-grant institutions, Michigan State University has a rich history of providing exceptional educational opportunities to undergraduates of diverse interests, abilities, and backgrounds. Academically ambitious students discover a comprehensive education with more than 150 programs of study offered by twelve undergraduate degree–granting colleges: Agriculture and Natural Resources, Arts and Letters, Business, Communication Arts and

Sciences, Education, Engineering, Human Ecology, James Madison, Natural Science, Nursing, Social Science, and Veterinary Medicine. In addition, students can pursue preprofessional studies in human, osteopathic, and veterinary medicine.

MSU's campus, located 1 mile from the state capital in a residential suburb, is a distinctive blend of the traditional and innovative within a park-like landscape. Known as one of the most beautiful campuses in the nation, MSU is home to Spartan Stadium, the world's most powerful superconducting cyclotron, a medical complex, and sophisticated scientific research laboratories. Students also have access to a wide range of facilities to enhance their college experiences, including the Jack Breslin Student Events Center, the Wharton Center for Performing Arts, and two intramural buildings devoted to student sports activities.

Student Body MSU's undergraduate enrollment is 34,342; total enrollment is 43,366. Fifty-two percent of the students are women. The minority ethnic distribution for undergraduates is 0.5 percent Native American, 2.3 percent Hispanic, 4 percent Asian American, and 8.6 percent African American. There are 2,798 international students from more than 110 countries attending MSU. More than 50 percent of students live on campus in the largest on-campus residence hall system in the United States. The campus has twenty-nine fraternities, sixteen sororities, and eight historically African-American Greek letter organizations.

Faculty There are 2,535 teaching faculty members at MSU; 95 percent of all faculty members hold the highest degrees awarded in their fields. The undergraduate student-faculty ratio is approximately 10:1.

Key Facilities MSU libraries house approximately 4.5 million volumes. There are more than thirty-five computer laboratories across campus in residence halls and classroom buildings.

Honorary Societies Golden Key, Mortar Board, and Phi Beta Kappa

Athletics MSU is a member of the NCAA Division I Big Ten and competes in thirteen intercollegiate sports for men and thirteen intercollegiate sports for women. MSU also provides a wide program of intramural sports for students.

Study Abroad Through the Office of Study Abroad, MSU students can participate in more than 150 academic programs in countries around the world. MSU is currently top among individual research institutions in the total number of students studying abroad each year. Honors College students have special scholarships to support their international endeavors and can earn honors credit while studying abroad.

Support Services OPHS-Disability Resource Center (517-353-9642) facilitates accommodations for all persons with disabilities at MSU.

Job Opportunities Work-study, undergraduate assistantships, internships, and cooperative education experiences are available to students on and off campus.

Tuition: $4972.50 for state residents, $13,320 for nonresidents, per year (2001–02)

Room and Board: $4678

Mandatory Fees: $654

Contact: Director: Professor Ronald C. Fisher, Eustace-Cole Hall, East Lansing, Michigan 48824; Telephone: 517-355-2326; Fax: 517-353-4721; E-mail: honors@msu.edu; Web site: http://www.msu.edu/unit/honcoll/

Middle Tennessee State University

4 Pu G M Tr

▼ Honors College

The 26-year-old MTSU Honors College is a 36-semester hour integrated enrichment program offering courses in all five of the University colleges.

The Honors College's commitment to enrichment extends beyond the classroom. The Honors Student Association hosts faculty firesides, a special invitation to HSA members to a faculty member's home for an evening of informal discussion and social interaction. In addition, there are Honors Lyceum events—Poetry Slams, Song Slams, Celtic music, and Blues concerts—to showcase the talent of the University and the community. Also offered is the Honors Lecture Series, an interdisciplinary approach to a single topic where faculty members, administrators, and guest speakers lecture from their discipline's perspective. In addition, the Honors College features an Honors Living and Learning Residential center.

Outstanding class recognition, a 12-hour certificate after meeting the general studies requirement, and an Honors Medallion awarded to graduating seniors are several ways superior students are recognized. To graduate with University Honors, students must achieve at least a 3.25 GPA.

There are more than 700 students enrolled in the college.

Participation Requirements: The first 18 hours of the Honors curriculum consist of lower-division/general studies courses. Enrollment is limited to 20 or fewer students. The 18 hours of upper-division requirements include 8 hours of specially crafted upper-division courses, a 6-hour interdisciplinary colloquia requirement, a thesis tutorial, and the capstone honors thesis. These courses are limited to 15 or fewer students. The final requirement for graduation with University Honors is an honors thesis/creative project. Each thesis writer selects an adviser and is assigned committee members. After the thesis defense and public presentation, theses are bound and become part of the permanent holdings of the MTSU library. The University is very proud of its emphasis on undergraduate research as it prepares seniors for advanced study.

Admission Process: Entering freshmen must have a minimum ACT composite score of 26 or higher or a high school GPA of at least 3.5 on a 4.0 system. Returning students and transfers must have a minimum 3.0. Students whose GPA falls below a 3.0 will be unable to register for honors classes.

Scholarship Availability: Scholarship opportunities exist for in-state entering freshmen and those who have achieved outstanding academic records while participating in the Honors College. In particular, three academic achievement scholarships ($1000) are awarded by the Honors scholarship committee.

The Campus Context: Middle Tennessee State University is located in Murfreesboro, less than a mile from the exact geographic center of the state. Murfreesboro, a historic city of about 50,000, is 32 miles southeast of Nashville via I-24 and is easily accessible from any direction. MTSU students and personnel can enjoy the advantages of a metropolitan atmosphere without the impersonalization associated with a big city. The five academic colleges include Basic and Applied Science, Business, Education, Liberal Arts, and Mass Communication. The University offers a total of nine undergraduate degrees.

Student Body The total undergraduate enrollment is approximately 18,000. Ethnic distribution is 16,000 white students, 1,900 African-American students, 200 Hispanic students, 300 Asian students,

100 Native American students, and 46 unclassified students. There are 208 international students. Students receiving financial aid number 11,000. There are twenty-six fraternities and fifteen sororities.

Faculty There are 739 faculty members, 71 percent have terminal degrees. The student-faculty ratio is 22:1.

Key Facilities The new library holds more than 600,000 volumes. Computer facilities include more than forty computer labs on campus. All full-time faculty members have PCs in their offices. Fiber optics connect all buildings and departments.

Honorary Societies Alpha Theta, Hampton Society, Order of Omega, Phi Eta Sigma, Phi Sigma Pi, Tau Omicron, Golden Key

Athletics The University is a member of the Ohio Valley Conference and National Collegiate Athletic Association. MTSU is represented annually in athletics by baseball, basketball, cross-country, I-A football, golf, and tennis, as well as a women's program that includes basketball, tennis, cross-country, softball, track, and volleyball.

Study Abroad The International Programs and Services Office (IPSO) is the clearinghouse for study-abroad and exchange program development and information for MTSU students and faculty members. IPSO facilitates study-abroad and exchange opportunities by advising students on study, travel, and work programs; advertising departmental programs; joining institutional study-abroad consortia; holding special events and presentations; and maintaining reference books, videos, and informational catalogs on study, travel, and work programs overseas.

Job Opportunities A work-study program is established on campus.

Tuition: $1906 for state residents, $6732 for nonresidents, per year (1998–99)

Room and Board: $3382

Mandatory Fees: $243

Contact: Dean: John Paul Montgomery, 106 Peck Hall, Murfreesboro, Tennessee 37132; Telephone: 615-898-2152; Fax: 615-898-5455; E-mail: honors@frank.mtsu.edu; Web site: http://www.mtsu.edu/~honors

Midland College

2 Pu G S Sc Tr

▼ Honors Program

The Midland College Honors Program is designed to offer a set of stimulating courses to academically talented students. It was inaugurated in fall 1995 to give the College's highest achieving students a chance to challenge their abilities with more rigorous course requirements than those expected of the mainstream two-year college student. The program develops students' critical thinking, writing, and speaking skills through advanced projects and discussion groups that involve research as well as oral and written presentations. Students work closely with instructors to complete a series of independent-study assignments that require time and effort beyond the standard course criteria. These may include extended biology research projects, analytical theme reports, and small-group participatory sessions with other honors students.

Participation Requirements: Students take one honors course per semester throughout the two-year college curriculum to satisfy the 12-hour requirement for honors students. These are built around a core of two humanities courses. Additional honors credit is earned from among elective courses in such fields as biology, economics, or literature. Courses are offered for vocational-technical as well as academic credit.

Admission Process: Students must demonstrate any one of the following to meet admission criteria: inclusion in the top 20 percent of the high school graduating class, TAAS scores high enough for exemption from the TASP exam, a combined score of 1050 or above on the SAT I (with a minimum of 500 on both parts of the exam), a composite score of 23 or above on ACT (with a minimum of 19 on either math or English), membership in Phi Theta Kappa, or standing on the Dean's List or the President's List at Midland College.

Scholarship Availability: Midland College offers a variety of privately funded sources of financial aid such as the Abell-Hanger and Fasken Scholarships, in addition to public sources of assistance.

The Campus Context: Midland College is a beautiful 115-acre campus with a series of easily accessible one- and two-story buildings designed with a southwestern appearance. The institution is a comprehensive two-year college offering students the resources of a privately funded endowment of more than $6 million. The College is located in Midland, which has a population of about 95,000 people who are primarily employed in white-collar jobs provided by the oil industry. The sister city of Odessa, 20 miles away, combines with Midland to offer a metropolitan statistical area of almost 250,000 residents.

The College is divided into six instructional divisions: Business Studies, Health Sciences, Technical Studies, Communications/Fine Arts, Math/Sciences, and Social/Behavioral Sciences. Midland offers five degrees at the associate level in forty-nine fields of study.

Student Body The student body consists of 4,700 credit students and 10,000 noncredit students; 41 percent are men, 59 percent are women. Ethnic distribution is 75 percent white, 17 percent Hispanic, 5 percent African American, and 3 percent other. There are 40 international students. All students commute except resident athletes who are housed in on-campus dorms. Forty-eight percent of students receive financial aid. There are twelve social and special interest clubs.

Faculty Eighty-seven faculty members are full-time; 26 instructors possess doctoral degrees and 59 possess master's degrees. There are 198 adjunct faculty members. The student-faculty ratio is 31:1.

Key Facilities The library houses 50,293 volumes. Computer facilities include eight computer labs, including a writing lab, a multipurpose lab, a journalism lab, a math lab, and an office studies and computer instruction lab.

Athletics In athletics, men's and women's varsity basketball and golf teams are active and available. Women's softball is also available.

Study Abroad International study is available in individual course trips to such destinations as Central America, Europe, Asia, and the Middle East.

Support Services Disabled-student services include complete counseling and support for studies and job placement.

Job Opportunities Work-study is available on campus (15 hours a week) and part-time employment is available as well.

Tuition: $632 for area residents, $680 for state residents, $974 for nonresidents, per year (1996–97)

Contact: Director: Dr. Russell H. Goodyear, 3600 North Garfield, Midland, Texas 79705; Telephone: 915-685-4605; E-mail: rhgoodyear@midland.cc.tx.us

Midwestern State University

4 Pu G S Sc Tr

▼ Honors Program

First established in 1964 and developed upon Midwestern State University's (MSU) Tradition of Excellence, the University Honors Program offers high-achieving MSU students a challenging premier undergraduate learning experience. From the Honors Introductory Seminar at the beginning, through honors designated classes taught by outstanding faculty members, to the Honors

Capstone Course and graduation with honors at the end, the MSU Honors Program serves as a powerful program from start to finish.

Midwestern State University is a member of the National Collegiate Honors Council and the regional Great Plains Honors Council. These affiliations broaden the scope of opportunities available for honors students. By enriching the educational experience of MSU's honors students, the MSU Honors Program creates an atmosphere of intellectual fellowship that enhances the University-wide quality of education and promotes Midwestern State University as the center of intellectual growth and development in north central Texas.

Participation Requirements: Participation in the Honors Program recognizes the student's potential to work in a more challenging educational framework, guided by some of Midwestern's most outstanding faculty members. In order to graduate with Honors Program distinction, students are required to successfully complete twelve honors designated courses. The selection of honors designated courses includes an honors introductory seminar at the beginning and an honors capstone course at the end. In order to remain in good standing in the program, honors students must take at least one honors designated class each fall and spring semester and maintain a minimum cumulative GPA of 3.25 at all times. In addition to these curricular requirements, the Honors Program requires participation in a variety of enriching, extracurricular components, such as a guest speaker series, participation in professional conferences, faculty mentoring, field trips, opportunities for community service and leadership, and a choice of undergraduate research projects, internships, or study abroad. Honors housing offers students a supportive living/learning environment. Finally, honors experiences and achievements will better prepare students for success and leadership in graduate and professional schools, in the job market, and as citizens of the global community.

Admission Process: Admission to the Honors Program is by application and is based upon a minimum composite SAT score of 1200 or an ACT of 27, a written essay, and a faculty letter of recommendation. Individuals may under special circumstances be granted provisional status based on alternate requirements. Students, including transfer students, may not enter the Honors Program later than their sophomore year.

Scholarship Availability: Honors Students in good standing receive a yearly honors scholarship until graduation. Participation in the Honors Program is also an important consideration for selection of Midwestern's coveted Clark and Hardin Scholars, MSU's highest undergraduate honors.

The Campus Context: Midwestern State University is accredited by the Commission on Colleges of the Southern Association of Colleges and Schools (1866 Southern Lane, Decatur, Georgia 30333-4097; telephone: 404-679-4501) to award baccalaureate and master's degrees. The campus is located in the heart of Wichita Falls, Texas, a town of approximately 103,000, situated midway between the Dallas–Fort Worth Metroplex and Oklahoma City, Oklahoma. Wichita Falls is the retail, industrial, and recreational center of the region and is home to Sheppard Air Force Base and a NATO training center. MSU offers forty-seven different undergraduate degree programs as well as opportunities for graduate studies in various fields. More than ninety-five different campus organizations represent the wide-ranging interests of our student body. The Artist-Lecture Series brings prominent speakers to campus.

Student Body The student body population stands at approximately 6,000 students, of whom 55 percent are women. More than 300 international students are currently enrolled at Midwestern State. Financial aid programs are available through the University, including merit- and need-based scholarships and work-study programs.

Faculty Midwestern has 200 full-time and 115 adjunct faculty members. More than 95 percent of all classes at MSU are taught by professors, not graduate students. The faculty-student ratio is 1:20 and the average undergraduate class has fewer than 30 students

Key Facilities The Moffett Library includes more than 700,000 volume equivalents, including periodicals, microforms, and government publications, as well as a variety of nonprint materials. Since 1964, Moffett Library has been a partial U.S. government depository, as well as a depository for state publications. The library is a member of OCLC through its regional network, AMIGOS. It offers online public access catalogs and lets users search journal and newspaper indexes, government information, and the Internet. Computer labs are available for student use in the academic buildings and the student center. All students have a personal e-mail account and access to the Internet whether they are on or off campus. The computer-student ratio is 1:15. Bolin Science Hall houses state-of-the-art scientific instrumentation including a nuclear magnetic resonance spectrometer. J.S. Bridwell Hall provides actual clinical settings for dental hygiene, respiratory care, nursing and radiologic sciences. The MSU Health and Wellness Center offers free weights and nautilus machines for every fitness level.

Honorary Societies Alpha Chi, Alpha Lambda Delta, Mortar Board, and Phi Eta Sigma

Athletics The University is a member of Division II of the National Collegiate Athletic Association and the Lone Star Conference. Most major sports are established at Midwestern, including football, volleyball, basketball, soccer, and tennis. The University also has an extensive intramural program. Activities are provided for both men and women as well as coed sports.

Study Abroad The University sponsors study abroad opportunities in England, Mexico, and France.

Support Services The Career Management Center introduces and guides students through the professional development process. The Academic Support Center offers classes and services to maximize the students' academic potential at MSU. The Counseling Center helps to coordinate accommodations for students with disabilities. All buildings on campus are accessible to students with physical disabilities.

Job Opportunities Work opportunities are available on and off campus.

Tuition and Fees: $1532 for residents, $4667 for nonresidents, per semester (fall 2002)

Room and Board: $2064–$2756 per semester, depending on choice of residence and meal plan.

Contact: Midwestern State University Honors Program: 3410 Taft Boulevard, Wichita Falls, Texas 76308; Telephone: 940-397-4534; Fax: 940-397-4042; E-mail: honors@mwsu.edu

---

Millersville University of Pennsylvania

4 Pu G M Sc Tr

▼ University Honors College

The University Honors College provides challenging and enriching educational experiences for Millersville University's most talented and motivated students. Those who elect to join the College are encouraged and guided by their faculty mentors to fully realize their academic and professional potential and to

Interpreting the symbols: **2**=two-year college, **4**=four-year college; **Pu**=public or state college, **Pr**=private college; **G**=general honors program; **D**=departmental honors program; **S**=small program (fewer than 100 students), **M**=midsize program (100 to 500 students), **L**=large program (more than 500 students); **Sc**=scholarships available in honors program; **Tr**=transfer students accepted into honors program; **HBC**=historically black college; **AA**=academic advisors; **GA**=graduate advisors; **FA**=fellowship advisors.

raise their sights and ambitions beyond what they felt was possible for them to accomplish. The College is designed to give the students the knowledge, skills, and self-confidence they need to prosper in graduate and professional school as well as in the world of business.

Designed to fulfill the University-wide general education requirements, the College is open to undergraduate students in all majors. It provides honors students with a core of stimulating and demanding liberal arts courses. These courses are intended to introduce honors students to the intellectual underpinnings of Western culture while developing their ability to think critically, do independent research, and write in a style that is both lucid and analytical. The core requirements explore the evolution of the Western intellectual and literary traditions, mathematical theory and applications, scientific methods in theory and practice, and multicultural/interdisciplinary studies. These requirements include an honors composition course and an advanced writing experience in the form of a senior thesis. The core courses are intended to encourage a commitment to academic pursuits while providing a common intellectual bond. The core is augmented with a variety of honors general education electives from which the student may choose. The majority of these courses put emphasis on research and writing.

Honors courses have limited enrollments. This creates an intimate and stimulating learning environment where students from varied backgrounds and disciplines can develop a sense of intellectual camaraderie. While honors courses involve both depth and breadth of study and stress independent research and writing, the workloads required are manageable. The primary concern of the faculty members who teach in the College is the cultivation of the academic talents of the honors students. Through formal study and informal advisement, the University Honors College prepares and encourages Millersville University's finest students to continue their education in graduate and professional schools. Honors graduates compete for entrance into the nation's finest graduate programs.

The University Honors Program was founded in 1980. The Honors Program became the Honors College in 2001. There are approximately 300 students enrolled in the College.

Participation Requirements: Completion of the program requires that students achieve a grade of B– or better in a minimum of 30 hours of honors credits; write and submit a thesis, which must be approved by the Honors Program Committee; and attain a final GPA of 3.35 or higher. Students graduating in the program receive the University Honors Baccalaureate and normally graduate with departmental honors in their respective majors.

Admission Process: Students must apply separately to the University Honors College. A one-page essay on one of a number of designated topics must accompany the application. A letter of recommendation is also required. Admission is rolling. Entering freshmen who have combined SAT I scores of 1200 or better and are in the top 10 percent of their high school graduating class are eligible to join the University Honors College. As motivation, enthusiasm, and commitment to learning are often better predictors of success than test scores, students who do not meet these formal criteria but who are seriously interested in participating in the program are encouraged to apply to the Director for admission.

Scholarship Availability: The University Honors College administers a limited number of four-year scholarships restricted to students enrolled in the University Honors College. These scholarships can be combined with scholarships awarded by both admissions and academic departments.

The Campus Context: Millersville University of Pennsylvania, located in scenic Lancaster County, is one of the fourteen state-owned institutions of higher education that make up Pennsylvania's State System of Higher Education. The primary mission of Millersville University is to promote intellectual development through an exemplary liberal arts–based education. The University is committed to the proposition that a thorough broad-based foundation in the arts and sciences is a necessary condition for the development of the whole person. It embraces the conviction that all of its degree programs must maintain a strong liberal arts component while preparing students to engage in productive and contributive lives as professionals.

Many cultural opportunities are available in the nearby cities of Philadelphia, Baltimore, Wilmington, and Washington, D.C. Lancaster, Pennsylvania, is the home of the Lancaster Symphony Orchestra and the Fulton Opera Theater. The Millersville University campus has its own theater, music hall, and art gallery, all of which exhibit the artistic creations of the students and faculty members.

Many of the University's buildings have been recently renovated and/or expanded. The newly enlarged science center is one of the finest and most up-to-date science facilities in the region. The University has two athletic buildings, a fitness center, and a sports stadium.

Bachelor's and associate degrees are awarded in sixty-one areas.

Student Body There are approximately 7,500 students enrolled at the University, more than 70 percent of whom are undergraduates. Sixty percent of the undergraduates are women.

Faculty Of 325 full-time faculty members, 70 percent hold doctoral or terminal degrees.

Key Facilities The Helen A. Ganser Library houses more than 1 million books, periodicals, microfilms, and audiovisual materials and approximately 2,750 magazine subscriptions. The library has an online catalog, electronic periodical indexes, and full-text databases that are remotely accessible. The University maintains more than thirteen computer laboratories across campus.

Honorary Societies Phi Kappa Phi and Phi Eta Sigma

Athletics The University is NCAA Division II for all major men's and women's sports.

Study Abroad Millersville University students may study abroad in nearly every country worldwide for a summer, a semester, or an academic year.

Support Services The University admits students without regard to disability. Where physical barriers exist, accessibility is accomplished by reasonable accommodations and equipment.

Job Opportunities Students are offered a wide range of employment opportunities on campus. A strong co-op/internship program is also in place.

Tuition: $3468 for residents, $14,266 for nonresidents, per year (1999–2000)

Room and Board: $2255 per semester

Mandatory Fees: $466 per semester

Contact: Dr. Steven Miller, University Honors Program, Millersville University, P.O. Box 1002, Millersville, Pennsylvania 17551-0302; Telephone: 717-872-3571; Fax: 717-871-2216; E-mail: steven.miller@millersville.edu; Web site: http://www.millersv.edu/~honors/

MINNESOTA STATE UNIVERSITY, MANKATO

4 Pu G M Tr

▼ Honors Program

The mission of the Honors Program at Minnesota State University is to provide a challenging interdisciplinary program of study for a highly motivated group of undergraduates and to function as an alternative to the traditional general education curriculum. By providing opportunities for students to meet weekly with professors in small, personalized classroom settings, the Honors Program allows participants to become part of a community of scholars that includes experienced faculty members who share a commitment to the program's goals. Honors Program participants have opportunities to attend special lectures, go on field trips, and work at one's own pace in a setting that encourages goal setting, perspective taking, and independence. The Honors Program is designed to help ensure a successful undergraduate experience, to foster creativity and self-direction, and to prepare students for future professional and postgraduate work.

The program consists of three main components. The first is seminars, meeting once weekly. These seminars are taken each semester, with varied topics. Honors sections of general education courses are another component. These are sections of regular general education courses that are taken only by honors students. These classes are often much smaller than regular sections and offer students a chance to work more closely with faculty members. Topics courses are the third component. These consist of classes taught in a discussion/seminar format, offered through different disciplines. The topics courses are taken by upper-level students. The final requirement is a senior project, completed in the student's major discipline with a faculty member as adviser.

A new and exciting feature of the Honors Program is the Honors Learning Community, in which 15 entering honors students are enrolled. This honors cohort takes a group of courses together during the first year on campus and is housed on the same floor of a University residence hall. The Honors Club plans activities such as trips to the Twin Cities area for plays, pizza parties, and discussions on courses to be offered.

The flexible course requirements of the Honors Program at Minnesota State University allow many students to graduate with a double major or to graduate early. The combination of small classes and top students and faculty members allows students to actively learn and interact. The Honors Club provides for social interaction for honors students. The combination of these features makes the Honors Program at Minnesota State University a unique opportunity for students to get all that they can out of their college experience.

Upon graduation from the University, the Honors Program student is designated a University Scholar. This distinction is noted upon the transcript and in a certificate presented to the student. Honors stoles are worn by graduates at the graduation ceremonies.

Students in the program number approximately 250.

Participation Requirements: In order to graduate as part of the Honors Program, a student must maintain a minimum 3.3 GPA and manifest high competency in communication skills. Those students pursuing a B.A. degree are also required to complete at least one year of a foreign language.

Admission Process: Students must first apply and be admitted to Minnesota State University. If they meet the requirements, they may then apply for admission to the Honors Program. Qualifications for entering the program are graduation in the upper 10 percent of the high school class and a minimum composite score of 25 on the ACT test or its equivalent.

Scholarship Availability: No scholarships are offered strictly to Honors students. However, Minnesota State University offers a variety of scholarships to both incoming freshmen and transfer students and students in their major disciplines. Students are urged to contact either their major department or the Admissions Office for further details on these scholarships.

The Campus Context: Minnesota State University is located in Mankato, Minnesota, in the Minnesota River valley. The University was founded as a Normal School in 1867. In 1921 it became a state teachers college, and in 1957 broadened its mission and became Mankato State College. In the 1970s the College was granted university status and began moving to its current location on the hill overlooking Mankato. Mankato is located approximately 70 miles south of the Minneapolis/St. Paul metropolitan area. Programs are available leading to baccalaureate degrees, master's degrees, and specialist degrees.

Student Body Undergraduate enrollment is 13,000. Students from more than sixty countries make up an international student enrollment. A wide variety of activities are available for students. The Student Development Programs and Activities Office coordinates many groups and provides on-campus movies, speakers, and other entertainment. Fraternities and sororities involve many students in activities both on and off campus.

Faculty There are 600 full-time faculty members, supplemented by adjunct faculty members and graduate teaching assistants.

Key Facilities The Memorial Library has approximately 1 million volumes and 3,200 current periodicals. The library features an on-line catalog access system.

The Academic Computer Center (ACC) is a centralized computer lab available for students. Equipment includes Macintosh and PC computers, e-mail and World Wide Web access, and laser printers. The lab is open for all students to use. Students with their own personal computers and modems may access the campus computer network via telephone lines.

Three housing complexes on campus offer rooms for single, double, and triple occupancy. Choices available include quiet study floors, coed floors, intercultural floors, and others. The residential complexes house approximately 2,800 students each year.

Honorary Societies Phi Kappa Phi, Golden Key, Alpha Lambda Delta

Athletics Intramural sports are available in all seasons and students may sign up to play volleyball, softball, basketball, and floor hockey.

Study Abroad Students have the opportunity to study abroad. Minnesota State University offers regularly scheduled programs in Mexico and France, various foreign study tours, and the opportunity to share other universities' study-abroad programs.

Job Opportunities Students are offered a range of work opportunities on campus, including assistantships, work study, and non-need-based employment.

Tuition: $3050 for state residents, $6468 for nonresidents, per year, banded tuition (12–18 credits)

Room and Board: TBA

Mandatory Fees: $300

Contact: Director: Suzanne Bunkers, 203 Morris Hall, MSU, Mankato, Minnesota 56001; Telephone: 507-389-5056; E-mail: suzanne.bunkers@mnsu.edu

Minot State University

4 Pu G S Tr

▼ Program in Honors

The Program in Honors at Minot State University has been in existence for seven years and is intended to provide an opportunity for students who have a desire to reach beyond the normal bounds of their university curriculum and attain broader yet more intensive educational goals. Small classes and the development of individual analytical skills are emphasized throughout the honors classes. Students are drawn to the program from all majors available on campus and thus bring a variety of skills and insights to the honors experience. This is augmented

Interpreting the symbols: **2**=two-year college, **4**=four-year college; **Pu**=public or state college, **Pr**=private college; **G**=general honors program; **D**=departmental honors program; **S**=small program (fewer than 100 students), **M**=midsize program (100 to 500 students), **L**=large program (more than 500 students); **Sc**=scholarships available in honors program; **Tr**=transfer students accepted into honors program; **HBC**=historically black college; **AA**=academic advisors; **GA**=graduate advisors; **FA**=fellowship advisors.

by a strong representation of nontraditional students within the program. Outstanding teaching faculty at the University who desire to work with students seeking greater intellectual heights comprise the honors faculty and serve as honors advisers together with the Director and the students' major advisers.

The 43 students currently enrolled in the Honors Program not only have full access to all of the University's facilities, they are granted early registration, extended library privileges, and the use of a well-appointed Honors Center with its own bank of computers connected to the Internet.

Participation Requirements: The Honors curriculum consists of two freshman seminars, three underclass courses chosen from a broad range (one each from the areas of humanities/fine arts, natural sciences/mathematics, and social sciences) and at least one year of a foreign language. This is followed by two seminars during the junior year and a capstone project or essay.

Admission Process: Students are selected for the Honors Program in one of two ways. Incoming freshmen with a high school GPA of 3.7 and/or a minimum cumulative ACT score of 25 are invited to join the honors seminar and from there pass into the program. Transfer students and students who do not meet the initial requirements but who demonstrate the ability to do honors work based on their university performance are recruited for application.

The Campus Context: Minot State University was founded in 1913 as the North Dakota Normal School and became a state university in 1983. The campus is located in Minot, North Dakota, situated near the geographical center of North America, 50 miles south of the Canadian border. As a land-grant public institution, Minot State's mission is dedicated to the education of all inhabitants of the state and larger community. The University offers forty-seven undergraduate majors leading to baccalaureate degrees in arts and sciences, business, and education/social sciences.

Student Body Enrollment currently is approximately 3,700, including some 600 international students, principally from Canada. The majority of the student population is from North Dakota.

Faculty There are 235 full-time faculty members in addition to adjunct members. Sixty-five percent of full-time faculty members have terminal degrees. The student-faculty ratio is 16:1.

Key Facilities The campus library houses 350,000 volumes. There are two on-campus computer labs with Macintosh and DOS computers plus Internet connections for all faculty offices.

Athletics Men's athletics include football, basketball, track, tennis, and cross-country; women's athletics are available in basketball, track, tennis, cross-country, and volleyball.

Study Abroad Minot State University is a member of ISEP (International Student Exchange Program) providing its students with study-abroad opportunities around the world. Institutional exchange programs with Keele University in England and Kyushu University in Japan provide additional possibilities.

Support Services The North Dakota Center for Disabilities serves the upper Midwest in providing outreach programs and services in special education, communication disorders, and speech pathology.

Job Opportunities Work-study is available on campus in a variety of areas.

Tuition: $2241 for state residents, $2731 full-time for residents of Manitoba, Montana, Saskatchewan, and South Dakota, $5515 for nonresidents, per year; $113.78 per semester hour part-time for residents of Manitoba, Montana, Saskatchewan, and South Dakota

Room and Board: $2360

Mandatory Fees: $180

Contact: Director: Robert J. Scheeler, 208 Model Hall, MSU, Minot, North Dakota 58707; Tel: 701-858-3014; Fax: 701-839-6933; E-mail: bradleyd@warp6.cs.misu.nodak.edu

Mississippi State University

4 Pu G L Sc Tr

▼ University Honors Program

The University Honors Program is a challenging variation of the standard curriculum, through which students in all academic majors enrich their undergraduate study. The University-wide program that relies on the Giles Distinguished Professors and the elected Honors Council as its faculty and student advisory groups serves departmental majors in all colleges and schools by tailoring programs for talented students.

Freshmen and sophomores meet institutional core curriculum requirements by choosing from among forty departmental courses in five colleges; juniors and seniors earn elective credits, conduct independent research, formulate special projects, adapt advanced courses for honors credit, or utilize internships, study-abroad, honors seminars, or thesis options. Credits offered through the Honors Program support a unique honors design sequence in the School of Architecture; the preparatory programs for Presidential Endowed, Schillig, Hearin-Hess, Stennis, and Truman scholars; and the early admissions program of the College of Veterinary Medicine.

Individual small-enrollment courses taught by carefully selected outstanding members of the professorial teaching faculty are enhanced by field trips, guest lecturers, and innovative experimentation as expansions of challenging and interesting study that students elect to pursue without adding to degree requirements.

Honors Forum is an emblem of the focus of the program on expanded exposure and experience. The weekly session has consistently relied on co-sponsorship with such units as the Cultural Diversity Center, the Women's Study Program, the Center for International Security and Strategic Studies, and colleges, schools, and departments to host participants of international reputation in diverse fields. Forum also coordinates instructive and analytical programming with the University performing arts and lecture series to ensure students' insight into formal presentations, performances, and exhibitions.

The UHP also provides access to experiential study programs, including a summer archaeological dig in LaHav, Israel, open to students in all disciplines; geology/geography study on San Salvador Island in the Caribbean; and core-level courses and internships through study abroad.

Confidence in the ability of capable students to select options that reflect their interests and concerns is central to the philosophy of a program that presents diverse options for an undergraduate experience. The MSU Honors Program does not impose requirements for particular courses; instead it attempts to present both breadth and depth of options for study and experience that will contribute equally to academic and personal development.

The University Honors Program celebrated its thirty-third anniversary in 2001. The liberal arts Stephen D. Lee Honors Program, established in 1968, was expanded into a University-wide program in 1982 and has grown to a 2001 enrollment of 1,010 students who have an average ACT composite of 28.8 and an average GPA of 3.7. Annual enrollments of 900 to 1,000 in forty rotated honors courses in five colleges/schools reflect a breadth of institutional commitment to the Honors Program as a named MSU priority for undergraduate education.

Participation Requirements: UHP students who complete 12 hours of graded honors course work and 2 pass/fail credits for Forum receive Phase I certification; those who complete a total of 24 hours of graded course work, including internship, independent research, and/or study-abroad credits, and 4 Forum credits receive Phase II certification and distinction as an Honors Scholar. The distinctions are noted on the official transcript and are recognized at an annual awards ceremony, at which students with 4.0 averages, selected outstanding students from each class, and elected outstanding honors faculty members are also identified.

Admission Process: Admission for entering freshmen is determined by two categories: unconditional admission with a minimum composite score of 28 on the ACT and/or a minimum combined score of 1240 on the SAT I, a ranking in the upper 20 percent of one's class, and correlative high school grades; and conditional admission for those who do not meet the primary standard directs advisement for specific courses based on standardized test subscores and evidence of academic strength in a subject matter area. After earning a minimum of 15 hours, at MSU or elsewhere, any student with a 3.4 cumulative average has full privileges, including priority preregistration. Transfer students may apply honors credits earned elsewhere to UHP requirements.

Scholarship Availability: Fifty competitive $800 Honors Program Scholarships for 2001 entering freshmen were awarded to recipients with an average ACT composite of 30; University Freshman Academic Scholarships range from $2000 (minimum composite score of 26 on the ACT or minimum combined score of 1160 on the SAT I) to $10,000 (minimum ACT composite score of 32 or minimum combined SAT I score of 1390). National Merit awards may be added with an MSU award for another $20,000. Recipients of the Schillig Leadership Scholarships ($30,000) and Hearin-Hess ($20,000) engineering awards are named Honors Scholars without additional MSU funding other than National Merit awards. All of these awards carry a waiver of out-of-state tuition; Eminent Scholar awards from the Mississippi Legislature may add from $4000 to $10,000 for Mississippi residents. College and departmental scholarships may be added after the freshman year.

The Campus Context: Mississippi State University, established in Starkville, Mississippi, under the auspices of the Morrill Act in 1878, is a comprehensive Research I land-grant institution. Its students and alumni define the excellence of its achievements in learning, research, and service, notably in the selection of 15 Truman Scholars, 3 Goldwater Scholars, and a Udall Scholar and through alumni such as noted author John Grisham, past president of Dow Chemical Hunter Henry, former editor of the *New York Times* Turner Catledge, gourmet Craig Claiborne, professional baseball star Will Clark, and Von Graham, former CEO of Arthur Andersen.

There are eleven colleges/schools: Accountancy, Agriculture and Life Sciences, Arts and Sciences, Architecture, Business and Industry, Continuing Education, Education, Engineering, Forest Resources, Veterinary Medicine, and the Graduate School. In addition, the Mississippi Agricultural and Forestry Experiment Station with ten branches and the Mississippi Cooperative Extension Service are located at MSU.

Degree programs offered include eighty-three bachelor's, sixty-four master's, one education specialist, twenty-eight doctoral, and one professional, including 113 majors at the B.A./B.S. level.

The grounds of the University comprise approximately 4,200 acres, including the central campus that typifies the geographical beauty of the South, in part because of academic emphasis of landscape architecture and horticulture. Among more than fifty academic buildings, the notable structures around an open central quadrangle include Lee Hall, Montgomery Hall (National Register), Colvard Union, and McCool Hall, a gift of the founder of Holiday Inn Corporation to house the College of Business. McComas Hall houses the University Theater and the University Gallery.

Among more than 325 buildings valued at $450 million, the Honors House is unique as a facility for the Honors Program—a 3,500-square-foot 1898 home converted to create a library, a computer laboratory, a student lounge, a student council office, and well-appointed reception rooms widely utilized by the entire University community. Honors students have access to photocopiers, monitors with VCRs, and personal computers.

The current University bulletin lists forty-four special units supporting teaching, research, and service. The University Honors Program heads an entry that includes Army and Air Force military programs, the Institute for the Humanities, the Division of Business Research, one of eighteen National Science Foundation Engineering Research Centers, the Research Center of the John C. Stennis Space Center, the Raspet Flight Research Laboratory, the Center for Robotics, Automation, and Artificial Intelligence, the *Mississippi Quarterly* literary journal, the Social Science Research Center, the State Chemical Laboratory, the Center for International Security and Strategic Studies, and the Cobb Institute of Archaeology, housed in a teaching, research, and museum facility that focuses on both Middle Eastern and Native American concerns.

Student Body Mississippi State University, frequently having the largest enrollment in the state, has a current enrollment of 16,878 students, including an undergraduate enrollment of 13,604. Men comprise 52 percent of the student body, while 48 percent are women. The ethnic distribution is 18 percent African American, .24 percent Native American, 1 percent Asian American, .8 percent Hispanic, and 71.8 percent white. International students represent 5.1 percent of the student population. There are 12,659 in-state residents (75 percent of the student body) and 4,219 out-of-state and international residents (25 percent of students). Approximately 80 percent of undergraduate students receive some form of financial aid. Mississippi State University has eighteen national social fraternities and ten national sororities, which have approximately 17 percent of the student body as members. MSU also has 300 registered organizations. *The Reflector* (newspaper) and *The Reveille* (yearbook), as well as a student-operated radio station WMSV, unite service and experiential learning.

Faculty MSU has a full-time instructional faculty of 924. Of these, 81.6 percent are in the tenure-track professorial rank, 8 percent are at the rank of instructor, and 3 percent are at the rank of lecturer. Ninety-three percent hold terminal degrees appropriate to their disciplines. Only professorial-rank faculty members teach honors courses, having been selected by agreement of the department, the Honors Program administrator, and the Honors Council, which conducts a separate student evaluation of all honors classes.

The undergraduate student-faculty ratio is 15:1, an interesting ratio in relation to usual enrollments of 10 to 20 in honors courses.

Key Facilities The University Libraries house 1.5 million volumes and more than 16,202 periodical subscriptions, including the collections of Mitchell Memorial Library, the School of Architecture Library, and the College of Veterinary Medicine Library, all of which offer online computer access. Special collections and archives include extensive Mississippiana and contributions of such notables as U.S. Senator John C. Stennis, U.S. Representative G. V. Montgomery, and Turner Catledge, former editor of the *New York Times.* A central library of 235,000 square feet was completed in 1995 at a cost of $14.6 million.

Computing access is a priority at Mississippi State University, as represented in full online access in all residence halls, as well as through major computing centers and laboratories available to undergraduate students in Butler Hall, McCain Engineering, Hilbun Hall, and Mitchell Library, as well as large multiuser UNIX systems in Allen Hall. Academic and research computing is facilitated by a large, rapidly expanding campus network that

Interpreting the symbols: **2**=two-year college, **4**=four-year college; **Pu**=public or state college, **Pr**=private college; **G**=general honors program; **D**=departmental honors program; **S**=small program (fewer than 100 students), **M**=midsize program (100 to 500 students), **L**=large program (more than 500 students); **Sc**=scholarships available in honors program; **Tr**=transfer students accepted into honors program; **HBC**=historically black college; **AA**=academic advisors; **GA**=graduate advisors; **FA**=fellowship advisors.

links dozens of mainframe computer systems and departmental servers with thousands of workstations.

Network access to remote branches of the University, as well as to the Internet, is provided through high-speed wide-area connections through the campus network. MSU is eleventh among American universities in supercomputing power and the only SEC institution on the top 500 list. The Engineering Research Center's cluster is the fifteenth-largest cluster at any site classified as academic and twenty-third worldwide.

Among twenty on-campus residence halls, Hull Hall is designated as a freshman and upper-division co-residential facility to accommodate men and women honors students.

Honorary Societies Phi Theta Kappa, Phi Eta Sigma, Lambda Sigma, Phi Kappa Phi, Golden Key, Mortar Board

Athletics Intramural sports utilize four basketball courts, three volleyball courts, a fitness machine circuit, an outdoor swimming pool, a fitness/jogging trail, and playing fields for softball and flag football. Other organized programs having facilities include racquetball, tennis, and soccer. The Sanderson Center, a 146,000-square-foot indoor facility, was opened in 1998. This facility includes a swimming pool, a weight room, eight racquetball courts, a track, three aerobics studios, two gymnasiums, a climbing wall, and a café.

Intercollegiate efforts under the auspices of the 12-member Southeastern Conference include football, basketball, baseball, cross-country, track, tennis, and golf for men and basketball, volleyball, tennis, golf, cross-country, track, and soccer for women. Campus facilities include Scott Field (52,000-person capacity), the M Club (400-person capacity), a multipurpose coliseum (10,500-person capacity), four practice football fields, a six-court tennis complex, Noble (Baseball) Field (6,700-person capacity), an all-weather running track, a soccer field, and a physical fitness complex.

Study Abroad Study abroad is advocated as one the institutional priorities for undergraduate education and supported through academic exchanges with institutions in Italy, England, Holland, Germany, Spain, Quebec, Mexico, Costa Rica, Japan, and Korea. Mississippi State University is a member of the Cooperative Center for Study Abroad, a consortium of American colleges and universities with study-abroad programs and internships in English-speaking regions. A growing program is the International Business Program that conjoins business and language study culminating in an internship while living with a host family.

Support Services Mississippi State University has gained national recognition for its commitment to accommodation of physically disadvantaged or learning-disabled students. Virtually all major classroom and laboratory buildings are accessible, but priority registration and focused advising ensure students' full advantage of every University function.

The Office of Student Support Services provides numerous services for special needs students, including orientation and academic advising for new students, financial aid advising, arrangement of classroom accommodations, special services of note-takers and readers, and special equipment and resources such as adapted examinations. Academic support is designed for those with learning disabilities; access to appropriate housing is ensured. Extensive handicapped parking and widespread sidewalk access distinguish the institutional commitment to accommodation.

Job Opportunities Work opportunities transcend the level of being simply sources of income. Work-study and wages employment opportunities exist in all divisions. Particularly valuable is the Cooperative Education Program, which combines practical experience with formal education in a five-year program of alternating semesters. Co-op students earn competitive salaries as reflected in the $8 million earned by 1,000 MSU students who were employed by major businesses in 2001.

Tuition: $3592 for state residents, $8128 for nonresidents, per year (2001–02)

Room and Board: $5198

Mandatory Fees: $595

Contact: Director: Dr. Jack H. White, Post Office Box EH, Mississippi State, Mississippi 39762; Telephone: 662-325-2522; Fax: 662-325-0086; E-mail: jwhite@honors.msstate.edu; Web site: http://www.msstate.edu/dept/uhp/

MISSISSIPPI UNIVERSITY FOR WOMEN

4 Pr G

▼ Honors College

The Honors College at Mississippi University for Women (MUW) provides opportunities for academically advanced and motivated students to participate in a learning experience that is intensive and innovative. The Honors College encourages and nurtures intellectual curiosity and advanced scholarship. The college meets the unique learning needs of academically capable students by offering advanced sections of core requirements, interdisciplinary studies, independent research, and training in leadership. The ultimate purpose of the Honors College is to produce students who are exceptionally well educated, who serve as intellectual catalysts on campus, and who, through their success, help ensure the continuing legacy at MUW.

Participation Requirements: Honors students enroll in one of two honors core sequences or at least three honors courses within the core curriculum: Humanities Sequence: English Composition and History of Civilization I and II; Science and Mathematics Sequence: Biology with Lab I and II and a mathematics course more advanced than college algebra. In addition, honors students complete the following courses during the first two years: two semesters of a foreign language and four semesters of Honors Forum (HO 101), a bimonthly lecture series. A special program is scheduled for each session, and at least once a month, students are addressed by a guest speaker. Honors students enroll in Honors Forum for each semester of their freshman and sophomore years.

During their junior year, honors students enroll in two Special Topics Seminars (HO 303), which are interdisciplinary and sometimes team-taught. As one of the unique features of the Honors College, the seminar offers educational opportunities in a nontraditional, undergraduate instruction format modeled on the graduate seminar. The students contribute substantially to the course material and the instructional process. Often, grades are assessed on the basis of participation and a single substantial research project. The seminar is intended to make the most academically advanced students comfortable with the structure of graduate courses in order to encourage them to continue their studies beyond the undergraduate level. Some examples of interdisciplinary topics have included Socio-Biology; Post-Modernism in Art, Film, and Literature; Seminal Texts; and Hitchcock and Freud.

Two semesters of Independent Study (HO 401/402) are required during the senior year. The Independent Study program gives students the opportunity to work closely with faculty advisers on a two-semester project that is modeled on the master's thesis.

Admission Process: The recipients of Centennial, University, and McDevitt scholarships are automatically members of the Honors College. Other students with excellent high school records or proven success in college courses are encouraged to apply and may request an application from the Director of the Honors College.

Scholarship Availability: The University offers substantial academic scholarships, but not through the Honors College, although participation in honors may be a requirement for the scholarship.

Campus Context: MUW has a total enrollment of around 2,300 students and a student-faculty ratio of approximately 16:1. Columbus-Lowndes County has a combined population of approximately 75,000 and is home to the state's third-busiest airport. The community is conveniently located 2 hours from Birmingham, 3 hours from Memphis, and 4–5 hours from New Orleans and Atlanta.

Contact: Director: Dr. James R. Keller, Honors College, Mississippi University for Women, Box W-1634, Columbus, Mississippi 39701; Telephone: 662-329-3792; E-mail: jrk@muw.edu; Web site: www.muw.edu/honors.

Mississippi Valley State University

4 Pu G S Tr HBC

▼ Honors Program

Mississippi Valley State University's (MVSU) Honors Program enhances the University's academic offerings and fosters an intellectual campus climate. Honors Program goals are to provide educational opportunities and support activities to a core group of students capable of moving at an accelerated pace, to promote enhanced educational opportunities to students capable of excelling in particular disciplines of study, and to promote all-campus events and activities aimed at developing and maintaining an inviting and invigorating intellectual and cultural atmosphere.

The Honors Program at MVSU challenges high-potential students to do their best in the company of their peers. Honors sections of core curriculum courses motivate freshman and sophomore honors students to get a good start in their college careers. Honors courses throughout the University program provide a motivating atmosphere through a student's senior year.

Students enrolled in the Honors Program are given special opportunities, including easy access to computers, special dormitory accommodations, and diverse travel opportunities.

The 13-year-old program enrolls 85 students.

Participation Requirements: To remain active in the Honors Program, students are required to enroll in a minimum of 12 credit hours each semester. Students should maintain a cumulative GPA of 3.0 or better.

Admission Process: Freshman applicants must achieve a minimum ACT composite score of 20 (or the SAT I equivalent) with no subscore below 16 and meet the general admission requirements of the University. Graduating high school seniors with an ACT composite score of 20 or above and a GPA of at least 3.2 in College Preparatory Curriculum (CPC) courses are extended an invitation to join the program upon their acceptance into the University. An information sheet and application form are enclosed in the letter, and students are required to complete the application form and write an essay. Once the information is in the Honors Program's office and evaluated/documented, a letter of acceptance is sent to admitted students. Sophomore/transfer students whose cumulative GPA is at least 3.2 and whose candidacy for admission into the program is supported by recommendations from two college teachers will be considered for admission.

Scholarship Availability: Scholarships that are offered are mainly academic or athletic in nature.

The Campus Context: MVSU offers a choice of twenty-seven degree programs.

Student Body Ninety-eight percent of students receive some form of financial aid. There are a total of eight fraternities and sororities on campus.

Faculty The student-faculty ratio is about 25:1. There are 199 faculty members, 10 part-time and 189 full-time; 47 percent have terminal degrees.

Key Facilities The library holds 200,000 volumes. Internet accessibility is available there. Other departments also offer computer availability.

Honorary Societies Alpha Kappa Mu and Alpha Chi

Athletics Athletics for men and women are offered; the University is a member of the Southwestern Athletic Conference.

Support Services Disabled students find the buildings on campus accessible.

Job Opportunities Work opportunities include work/study and work aid.

Tuition: $2646 for state residents, $5546 for nonresidents, per year (1998–99)

Room and Board: $2584

Contact: Director: Barbara J. P. Washington, 14000 Highway 82 West, Itta Bena, Mississippi 38941; Telephone: 601-254-3642; Fax: 601-254-3667/3452

Missouri Southern State College

4 Pu G M Sc Tr AA

▼ Honors Program

The Honors Program at Missouri Southern State College is intended to encourage academic excellence by providing special opportunities and challenges for exceptional students.

Entrance into the program is by invitation. Because admission is selective and competitive, classes normally are smaller than regular classes, with no more than 25 students, permitting honors students to enjoy interaction with other outstanding students in an informal atmosphere conducive to exciting and challenging discussions.

Honors courses put our best students in small classes with our best teaching professors from the freshman year onward. Working together, distinguished professors and honors students have opportunities to expand the educational experience beyond that available in regular courses. Students receive personal attention and special guidance and the program is flexible to permit students to pursue particular scholarly interests and to engage in innovative and creative approaches to learning in depth.

The core of the Honors Program experience at Missouri Southern State College is the Developing Scholars Program. In addition to providing specific challenges and opportunities, the Honors Program is designed to help the brightest and best students mature as scholars. The features of the program address specific areas of intellectualism and scholarship, developing self, cognitive, and cultural awareness from the first year onward.

Students in the Honors Program are required to complete an international study experience, highlighting their further development as scholars by observing or studying a culture other than their own. Following the experience, the students will be guided through a reflective analysis.

Honors students have many opportunities for extracurricular and cocurricular activities, including Epsilon Mu Sigma, the Honors Program student organization, as well as many discipline-specific organizations. In addition, upperclass honors students mentor first-year students in the program. The Honors Program at Missouri Southern also encourages academic learning outside the classroom, through service-learning and study abroad.

Interpreting the symbols: **2**=two-year college, **4**=four-year college; **Pu**=public or state college, **Pr**=private college; **G**=general honors program; **D**=departmental honors program; **S**=small program (fewer than 100 students), **M**=midsize program (100 to 500 students), **L**=large program (more than 500 students); **Sc**=scholarships available in honors program; **Tr**=transfer students accepted into honors program; **HBC**=historically black college; **AA**=academic advisors; **GA**=graduate advisors; **FA**=fellowship advisors.

The Honors Program at Missouri Southern was founded in 1986 and currently enrolls approximately 160 students.

Participation Requirements: Honors students at Missouri Southern are required to complete 26 semester credit hours in honors courses, including Honors Forum, a discussion-based course; Service-Learning, a course that emphasizes hands-on experience in the community; international study or travel, with an eye toward developing an appreciation of other cultures; and a senior thesis, in which the student develops an original idea, using primary research in their discipline. In addition to taking other honors courses in their disciplines, students can enhance existing upper-division courses for honors credit.

To maintain honors eligibility, students must have a minimum of a 3.0 GPA their first semester, a 3.25 GPA their second semester, and a 3.5 GPA for the remainder of their time at Missouri Southern. Students successfully completing the requirements of the Honors Program will have a special notation appear both on their diploma and on their transcripts.

Admission Process: All students who wish to participate in the Honors Program must be admitted to Missouri Southern. Incoming freshmen with a composite score on the ACT of at least 28 or with a GPA of at least 3.5 on a 4.0 scale in high school course work are invited to apply for admission to the program. Two letters of recommendation, one from the student's high school principal and one from a high school teacher, are required. In addition, an essay assigned by the Honors Program directors may be required. International students must also score a minimum of 535 on the paper-based TOEFL or a minimum of 200 on the computer-based TOEFL. The Honors Program office will evaluate all student applications and selected students will be invited to complete a personal interview with one of the honors directors.

As part of the admissions process, the Honors Committee will evaluate all application materials and the results of the personal interview. The deadline for completing all formalities is March 1 of the year prior to fall admission.

Students who have already completed between 15 and 30 hours of course work with a GPA of 3.5 at Southern, or any other accredited college or university, are also invited to apply for admission into the program.

Scholarship Availability: Once admitted to the Honors Program at Missouri Southern, students will receive the Walter and Fredrica Evans Scholarship. The Evans is a four-year renewable scholarship that covers tuition, book rental fees, and student activity fees for fall and spring semesters. Additional scholarship funds to cover on-campus room and board are available for Evans Scholars who are National Merit Semi-Finalists or who have an ACT Composite score of 31 or better. This scholarship is the finest Southern offers.

The Honors Program will offer special admission to Missouri's associate degree graduates who hold the CBHE Bright Flight Scholarship. Those with at least a 3.5 GPA will be eligible for a scholarship that covers the full cost of tuition, room and board, activity fees, and textbook rental. Other financial aid is available to students through the Office of Financial Aid.

The Campus Context: Missouri Southern State College is a four-year institution that specializes in undergraduate university education with an international perspective. The College focuses on classroom teaching, resulting in a tradition of small classes and close, personal interaction between faculty members and approximately 5,900 students. This approach is maintained through a low student-teacher ratio of 18:1. Southern's faculty members come from all over the world, with degrees from prestigious universities and professional experience in the disciplines they teach. Missouri Southern is made up of four schools (arts and sciences, business, education, and technology) with more than 100 degree options. Special features of Missouri Southern include the Institute of International Studies; the Bud Walton Theatre, an experimental black box performance space; and a new multipurpose 80,000-square-foot athletic center, with seating for approximately 3,500.

Student Body Undergraduate enrollment in 2001–02 was 5,899 students: 3,365 women and 2,534 men. Ethnic distribution is 91 percent white, 3 percent American Indian, 2 percent African American, 1 percent Latino, and 1 percent Asian. International students make up 2 percent of the student body. Non-traditional students make up 33 percent of all students. Approximately 600 students live on campus. Almost 50 percent of students live within 20 miles of campus.

Faculty Of 261 faculty members, 208 are full-time and 61 percent have terminal degrees in their respective fields.

Key Facilities The campus library houses more than 238,000 books and 1,200 periodicals. A state and federal government documents collection, a law library, and a 584,000-item microform collection provide additional reference materials for student research. Additional materials and services are available through the library's link with a nationwide computer network of libraries and on CD-ROM. State-of-the-art computer labs are located in the library and throughout the campus for student use.

Athletics Missouri Southern is home to eleven varsity teams in NCAA Division II that include baseball, basketball, football, golf, soccer, softball, track and field, tennis, and volleyball.

Study Abroad Through its Institute of International Study, Missouri Southern has study-abroad opportunities via the International Student Exchange Program in more than 100 countries. Bilateral exchange programs are also available in eleven countries, including Chile, China, Costa Rica, France, India, Sweden, and Switzerland. In addition, students have opportunities for international internships.

Support Services Appropriate accommodations are provided for students with documented disabilities. Students needing such accommodations should contact the Coordinator of Disability Services.

Job Opportunities Students have a wide range of work opportunities available, including work-study, internships, and cooperative education.

Tuition: $90 per credit hour for Missouri residents and $180 per credit hour for out-of-state students, which is the lowest in the state of Missouri in 2001–02.

Mandatory Fees: Equipment fee, $40 (full-time), $20 (part-time); student activity fee, $25 (full-time), $15 (part-time); parking fee, $15.

Room and Board: Residence halls cost $2100 per semester, including twenty meals per week.

Contact: Dr. Patricia P. Kluthe, Director, Honors Program, Missouri Southern State College, 3950 East Newman Road, Joplin, Missouri 64801-1595. Telephone: 417-625-3005; Fax: 417-625-3168; E-mail: kluthe-p@mail.mssc.edu; Web site: http://www.mssc.edu/honors

Monmouth University

4 Pr G M Sc Tr

▼ Honors Program

The goal of the Honors program at Monmouth University is to present a curriculum with courses that provide a unique learning experience. Group identity materializes among those participating. From the outset of the freshman experience, students see themselves as contributors to an especially dynamic community. A sense of freedom of expression develops inside the classroom and is often carried on outside of class.

Courses in the Freshman Honors Program are clustered together, with faculty members developing common themes and assignments, enhancing the opportunity for students to make connections and to see issues from different points of view. Every course in each cluster is limited to 20 students, fostering a classroom environment of diversity, discussion, and debate. Honors students annually produce a journal, *Crossroads,* whose purpose is not only to involve the students in the creative process of a journal, but also to help them gain professional experience publishing their honors theses and projects.

Faculty members are selected for their breadth of learning and multidisciplinary expertise and are distinguished contributors in their respective fields. Students in the honors community are encouraged to develop a special rapport with their professors. Such rapport is important not only in the classroom, but also during extracurricular activities scheduled to enhance the material and theme of the program. These activities include free trips to some of the great Broadway shows, visits to New York museums, a film series, three annual honors parties, and a series of guest lectures.

The Honors Program at Monmouth was established in 1979 and was reconceptualized ten years later, with the cornerstone of the program being the Freshman Honors Cluster. Enrollment in the Honors Program is currently about 350 students, including 130 new freshmen. The four-year program at Monmouth is growing steadily, having tripled in size over the last five years.

Participation Requirements: Beyond the freshman year, a student can take one or more honors courses or pursue the entire Honors Program. Students in the program must complete the requirements of their major and maintain a GPA of 3.2. In addition, to graduate from the program and have the diploma so noted, a student must successfully complete 19 credits (if English 151H is taken) or 22 credits (if the English 101H-102H sequence is taken) as follows: English 151H, Writing and Research (3 credits) or English 101H-102H, College English I & II (6 credits); at least one honors seminar from humanities, social sciences, mathematics/ natural sciences, or business (3 credits); HO 498H, Senior Honors Thesis Proposal (2 credits) and HO 499H, Senior Honors Thesis (2 credits). Students in the Honors Program are advised by specially designated honors advisers and the department in which the student's major is housed.

Admission Process: Students eligible for the Honors Program are those who enter the University on academic scholarship or are admitted to the University with a high school rank in the top 20 percent and a total combined SAT I score of 1100 or better, have a cumulative GPA of at least 3.2 after taking 12 credits at Monmouth University, or transfer to Monmouth University with at least 30 credits in an acceptable program and a cumulative average of at least 3.2 in all previous college-level work.

Scholarship Availability: Many students in the program hold academic scholarships from the University. The Honors Program promotes the Truman, Rhodes, Carnegie, Mellon, and Roosevelt scholarships and fellowships. The program also awards monetary prizes for the best scholarly paper, best scholarly group project, best non-paper project, and for the highest GPA. Graduates of the Honors Program have their transcripts and diplomas duly noted.

The University utilizes institutional resources (academic grants and scholarship programs) and is a participant in all major state and federal aid programs.

The Campus Context: The 138-acre Monmouth University campus is located in a quiet, residential area 2 miles from the Jersey Shore and about 90 minutes from both New York City and Philadelphia. The campus includes among its fifty buildings a pleasant blending of old and contemporary architectural styles. Monmouth University is an independent, comprehensive institution of higher learning comprising six schools: the School of Humanities and Social Sciences; the School of Science, Technology and Engineering; the School of Education; the School of Business Administration; the Edward G. Schlaefer School; and the Graduate School.

Student Body The total number of undergraduates at Monmouth is 3,880 (3,147 full-time and 733 part-time); 42 percent are men and 58 percent are women. The ethnic distribution of undergraduates is .2 percent Native American, 1.5 percent Asian-American, 4.5 percent African American, 4 percent Hispanic/Latino, and 77 percent white. There were 62 (1.7 percent) international students registered in fall 1995. Approximately 55 percent of undergraduate students receive financial aid. Monmouth University has eight fraternities and six sororities. There are also a number of Honors Societies on campus.

Faculty There are 179 full-time faculty members at the University, 71 percent of whom hold terminal degrees. Full-time faculty members are supplemented by adjuncts. The average institutional class size is 23 (the honors classes have a maximum capacity of 20).

Key Facilities The Guggenheim Memorial Library has 248,000 volumes on the shelves and subscribes to 1,300 periodicals. Extensive back files of periodicals are maintained in bound form and on microfilm. The Library's automated resources include GOALS (Guggenheim On-Line Automated Library Services), a public access catalog, and a circulation and library management system (which may be reached from public terminals within the building and across Monmouth's campus). GOALS may also be accessed from off-campus with a modem-equipped personal computer. The Library recently created an Information Commons of twelve networked computers capable of accessing all campus computer resources and the Internet.

The academic programs are supported by state-of-the-art computer hardware, software, and facilities. The major components include five UNIX and nine Novell server systems connected by a sophisticated campus Ethernet network spanning twenty-three buildings and encompassing more than 750 workstations campus-wide. More than 320 workstations distributed among seventeen laboratories are specifically dedicated to student use. The University provides each student with a personal account for electronic mail, production tools such as word processing, spreadsheet, database, and presentation software, World Wide Web browsing tools, and electronic access to the Library's catalog. The University maintains campus network connections in the residential halls.

About 34 percent of the undergraduates live in the eleven residence halls; the University opened a residence hall in fall 1996, and further building is planned.

Athletics Athletics constitute an integral part of a Monmouth University education. The NCAA Division I athletic program offers excellent opportunities for qualified athletes who wish to participate. Both the men's and women's programs compete on the Division I level, and are members of the Northeast Conference. The athletics program fields men's varsity teams in baseball, basketball, cross-country, football, golf, indoor track, soccer, tennis, and outdoor track and field. Women's varsity teams participate in basketball, cross-country, indoor track, lacrosse, soccer, softball, tennis, and outdoor track and field. Women's field hockey began in fall 1997.

Study Abroad Monmouth is a member of the College Consortium for International Studies, through which most students enroll in programs located in Spain, Ireland, France, and England. Monmouth is also a member of the Partnership for Service-Learning, an organization that combines academic study and community service in several countries including England, Jamaica, and the Philippines.

Interpreting the symbols: **2**=two-year college, **4**=four-year college; **Pu**=public or state college, **Pr**=private college; **G**=general honors program; **D**=departmental honors program; **S**=small program (fewer than 100 students), **M**=midsize program (100 to 500 students), **L**=large program (more than 500 students); **Sc**=scholarships available in honors program; **Tr**=transfer students accepted into honors program; **HBC**=historically black college; **AA**=academic advisors; **GA**=graduate advisors; **FA**=fellowship advisors.

Support Services The Office of Students with Disabilities serves those students who have special needs, whether they are the result of a permanent disability or a temporary condition. It provides information, guidance, and referrals in working with students and faculty members in supporting academic needs. It also assists in locating interpreters, notetakers, readers, and writers, as well as coordinating housing accommodations and arranging for special parking. All buildings on campus have wheelchair access.

Job Opportunities The Federal Work-Study Program provides on-campus and off-campus employment in a variety of settings to eligible students. Currently, the University provides employment for more than 300 students in the program. There are also a number of part-time, on-campus jobs during the school year. In general, students in this non-need-based employment program are limited to a maximum of 20 hours per week.

Tuition: $13,270 per year (1998–99)

Room and Board: $5808

Mandatory Fees: $530

Contact: Director: Dr. Brian T. Garvey, West Long Branch, New Jersey 07764-1898; Telephone: 908-571-3620; Fax: 908-263-5293; E-mail: garvey@mondec.monmouth.edu; Web site: http://www.monmouth.edu/monmouth/academic/honors.html

Montana State University–Bozeman

4 Pu G M Sc Tr

▼ University Honors Program

The University Honors Program provides academically motivated students with outstanding opportunities to undertake interdisciplinary course work and undergraduate research leading to a University honors degree. Such studies, in addition to disciplinary course work, provide extraordinary preparation for professional careers or graduate and advanced studies. Honors Seminars constitute the heart of the program and are characterized by individualized instruction and class interaction. Faculty members and students together engage in critical discussions of issues that cut across the diverse range of traditional departmental subjects. Teaching is primarily Socratic: emphasis is placed upon informed class discussion rather than lectures. Considerable attention is given to the development of analytic and critical skills and expression of them through speaking and writing. Texts and Critics is a two-semester course taught by faculty members representing every college at the University. Serving as a University core in oral communication and the humanities, the course addresses fundamental issues through critical reading and analysis of seminal books that are the foundation texts of advanced studies in all major discipline fields.

The Honors Program annually offers a variety of seminars for sophomores and upperclass students. These upper-division seminars may also earn University core credit in each of the major discipline categories. The seminars are interdisciplinary and are typically taught by the most respected and stimulating faculty members on campus. Honors sections of chemistry, physics, math, English, music, and economics are also offered. Limited enrollments in seminars and sections permit intensive study and discussion. Opportunities for independent study are available through honors contracts that are taken only at the upper-division level. Contracts permit students to work with a specific faculty member on Oxford-style reading tutorials or research projects.

Extracurricular, outdoor, and social activities are an important feature of the daily life of the program. In order to provide an ideal blend of living and learning, special on-campus housing is also available to honors students.

The Honors Program was founded in 1983, and 550 students are currently enrolled.

Participation Requirements: Graduates of the program receive an Honors Degree in addition to their departmental degree. Graduation in honors requires 16 to 28 credits in honors courses, most of which can be core curriculum honors courses; a minimum 3.5 overall GPA; and one year or its equivalent of a foreign language. To graduate with highest distinction, a thesis and a minimum 3.7. GPA is required. Students with energy, self-reliance, and imagination are encouraged to discuss their interests with the director or assistant director. To maintain good standing in the program, students must demonstrate significant and continuing progress toward their specific degree in addition to satisfying the particular standards of honors course work and research.

Admission Process: Admission to the program is determined by its director according to guidelines approved by the University Honors Program Advisory Committee. Admission is by application and includes an essay along with supporting letters and evidence of standing in the upper 10 percent of the applicant's high school class. Applicants are expected to have high ACT or SAT I scores. Transfer students or those already enrolled in the University are expected to have demonstrated high academic achievement and personal initiative.

Scholarship Availability: Twenty Presidential Scholarships are awarded to first-year students. Presidential Scholars are recipients of the University's most prestigious award. Scholarships provide annual tuition and fee waivers for four years as well as a financial merit grant for each of the same four years. Numerous merit-based departmental and outside scholarships are also available to qualified applicants.

The Campus Context: Bozeman, a city of 30,000, lies in the heart of the Gallatin Valley, a rich farmland of scenic grandeur in mountainous southwestern Montana. The 1,170-acre campus comprises more than forty classroom and administrative buildings, including ten residence halls, four cafeterias, a Health and Physical Education Complex, Museum of the Rockies, and the Strand Union Building, which serves as the center of campus activities and a convention center. The campus is spacious but not sprawling. A landscaped mall serves as the heart of the campus. Shopping centers, restaurants, and theaters are all within walking distance. Undergraduate instruction at Montana State University–Bozeman is administered through the Colleges of Agriculture; Arts and Architecture; Business; Education, Health and Human Development; Engineering; Letters and Science; and Nursing. The University currently offers bachelor's degrees in forty-seven fields with many diverse options, the master's degree in forty-one fields, and the doctorate in thirteen. Programs particularly appropriate for students in applied research or teaching are available.

Student Body More than 11,700 students attend MSU–Bozeman, 10,254 of whom are undergraduates. Fifty-five percent are men and 45 percent are women. The University enjoys the presence of nearly 500 international students. Approximately 80 percent of undergraduates receive some form of financial aid. There are thirteen national sororities and fraternities active on campus.

Faculty Of the 650 resident faculty members, three fourths have terminal degrees in their fields and more than two thirds hold doctorates. Because of the nature of a land-grant university, many of the faculty members hold joint appointments with affiliated research organizations on campus. The student-faculty ratio is approximately 19:1.

Key Facilities Renne Library is a multistory building centrally located on campus. An experienced library faculty provides information services. Computerized, online information searching using DIALOG, CAS, and MEDLINE is offered as well as CD-ROM offline searching of selected heavily used information databases. Interlibrary loan and document delivery are also offered to users. Internet access and online catalog and circulation is available. The collection of print materials is particularly strong in science, technology, and the health sciences. A Special Collections section provides resources on Montana and its history. Cheever Hall also houses a Creative Arts Library as a primary resource center for Schools of Art and Architecture. Within departmental and campuswide facilities, students have ready access to more than 800 microcomputers, seventy-eight Macs, and more than 200 distributed minicomputers and workstations. A state-of-the-art, campuswide fiber-optic network affords more than 3,200 locations in the residence halls with access to the network.

Honorary Societies Phi Kappa Phi, Alpha Lambda Delta, Mortar Board, and Golden Key

Athletics MSU–Bozeman is a member of the NCAA Division I Big Sky Conference. Men compete in football (I-AA), basketball, indoor and outdoor track, cross-country, and tennis. Women compete in basketball, volleyball, indoor and outdoor track, cross-country, tennis, alpine and Nordic skiing, and golf. Rodeo competition for men and women is conducted through the Big Sky Region of the National Intercollegiate Rodeo Association.

Study Abroad The Office of International Education provides high-quality educational opportunities abroad for MSU–Bozeman students at 220 universities in fifty countries.

Support Services Disabled Student Services provides services for students with physical or learning disabilities. The campus is also readily accessible to physically disabled students.

Job Opportunities The Student Employment Center assists students in locating part-time jobs on or off campus. There are a number of employment opportunities available in residence halls, at reception desks, and with the various food services on campus. Work-study/financial aid status is available but not necessary to qualify for student employment. A variety of undergraduate research assistantships are available through individual colleges.

Tuition: $3400 for residents, $10,150 for nonresidents per year (2002–03)

Room and Board: $5050

Contact: Director: Dr. Victoria O'Donnell, Bozeman, Montana 59717-2140; Telephone: 406-994-4110; Fax: 406-994-6747; E-mail: honors@montana.edu; Web site: http://www.montana.edu/honors

MONTCLAIR STATE UNIVERSITY

4 Pu G M Sc Tr

▼ Honors Program

Conceived in 1985 by faculty who relish the stimulation of working with exceptional students, the Honors Program at Montclair State University (MSU) has produced graduates who succeed in every field of endeavor. Some of its alumni have gone on to study for doctorates at Temple, Yale, Boston, and New York Universities, while others have graduated from medical school. It is worth noting that as of fall 1998, every one of its students who has applied to law school has been admitted. Among program graduates who have not yet gone on to advanced study are members of major accounting firms, artists, writers, musicians, social workers, business executives, researchers, and master teachers.

Throughout the undergraduate experience, the Honors Program emphasizes interdisciplinary study. It is the University's belief that new insights and understandings are gained outside the artificial boundaries imposed by subject areas. This approach creates a climate that fosters creativity and original thinking, for faculty members and students alike. For those admitted into the Honors Program, the undergraduate experience offers an opportunity to work intensively with a distinguished member of the faculty on advanced curricular, extracurricular, and individual projects. It means greater opportunities for achievement, recognition, and leadership, not only during undergraduate studies but in the years to follow.

There are currently 205 students in the program.

Participation Requirements: During the freshman year, honors students take two year-long seminars: Great Books and Ideas and Twentieth Century Civilization. Great Books and Ideas focuses on seminal thinkers from Plato to Nietzsche as they reveal themselves through their own writings. Twentieth Century Civilization concentrates on profound ideas and issues of our own time; in this interdisciplinary course, students explore twentieth-century revolutions that range from the political to the artistic. In the sophomore year, honors studies may include a year's seminar on interdisciplinary science, a semester on the foundations of the creative process, or a seminar on social analysis. Juniors prepare for advanced work as they immerse themselves in courses centered on ways of knowing and modes of inquiry.

Honors students take eight honors courses during their first three years. Most of them can be applied toward fulfillment of the University's general education requirement. Students who complete the honors sequence and maintain at least a 3.2 GPA receive an honors certificate, which is conferred at a special ceremony.

Admission Process: To be eligible for the Honors Program, students must meet at least two of the following criteria: a rank in the top 10 percent of their high school class, a score of at least 600 on either the verbal or the math sections of the SAT I, a combined SAT I score of at least 1200, and an unusual ability in the creative arts, exceptional leadership, or other extraordinary accomplishment. Those who qualify for consideration will be asked to complete an application that includes a brief essay. In addition, some students may be interviewed by a member of the Honors Program advisory board as part of the admission process.

Scholarship Availability: There are currently about 205 students in the Montclair State University Honors Program and to varying degrees all of them are supported by scholarships, ranging from the full tuition and fee waivers offered to all of New Jersey's Bloustein Scholars; to endowed Honors Program awards of $1250, $1000, and $750 per year; and finally to book scholarships of up to $250 per year awarded to all students enrolled in honors seminars.

The Campus Context: Established in 1908, Montclair State University is a state-assisted, coeducational, comprehensive public teaching university with a wide range of undergraduate and graduate programs and a commitment to excellence in instruction and research. MSU is located on a beautiful 200-acre campus in a leafy suburb in northern New Jersey, 12 miles west of midtown Manhattan. The University offers forty-three undergraduate degree programs.

Student Body There are a total of 9,742 undergraduates; 7,166 are full-time. Sixty-two percent are women, 38 percent men. The ethnic distribution is 64 percent white, 15 percent Hispanic, 10.3 percent African American, 5.4 percent Asian/Pacific Islander, and .3 percent Native American. Seventy percent of the full-time students are commuters; 30 percent are residents. Sixty percent of students receive financial aid. There are forty fraternities and sororities.

Interpreting the symbols: **2**=two-year college, **4**=four-year college; **Pu**=public or state college, **Pr**=private college; **G**=general honors program; **D**=departmental honors program; **S**=small program (fewer than 100 students), **M**=midsize program (100 to 500 students), **L**=large program (more than 500 students); **Sc**=scholarships available in honors program; **Tr**=transfer students accepted into honors program; **HBC**=historically black college; **AA**=academic advisors; **GA**=graduate advisors; **FA**=fellowship advisors.

Faculty Of the 442 full-time faculty members, 91 percent hold terminal degrees. Including the supplementary adjunct faculty, the student-faculty ratio is 15:1.

Key Facilities The library houses 439,880 books, 2,800 periodical subscriptions, and more than 1 million nonprint items. The University has extensive and growing computer facilities, including computer laboratories, computer classrooms, and a campuswide microcomputer network. All students are provided the opportunity to maintain a user account on the central system.

Athletics The athletic program features a full range of intercollegiate sports for men and women, and a major athletic facilities program has been launched, with the completed construction of a new fieldhouse and baseball stadium. MSU's athletic program is in the New Jersey Athletic Conference, in NCAA Division III.

Study Abroad There is an active and comprehensive international study program; many students in the Honors Program have taken a semester abroad, and several have participated in the Oxford University International Summer School. Full transfer credit is available for approved study-abroad programs.

Job Opportunities Student assistantships and work-study opportunities exist widely, and there are internships and cooperative education programs available to most majors.

Tuition: $4120 for state residents, $5861 for nonresidents, per year, including fees (1998–99)

Room and Board: $5802

Contact: Director: Dr. Tom Benediktsson, Upper Montclair, New Jersey 07043; Telephone: 973-655-7374; E-mail: benediktsson@saturn.montclair.edu

Montgomery College

2 Pu G S Sc

▼ Honors Program

The mission of the Montgomery College Honors Program is to stimulate and challenge academically talented students. This experience helps students develop critical thinking skills, leadership skills, and their intellectual potential. The Honors Program also strives to create a challenging environment for the student to achieve academic excellence through enriched course material and innovative research. It offers students the freedom to work independently with faculty members to promote personal growth and lifelong learning.

The program is contract based; students work with a faculty mentor to design a project that is an in-depth investigation of a topic related to the course content. The projects may include laboratory or fieldwork, reading and writing assignments, or other assignments as deemed appropriate by the mentor. At the end of the semester, students are required to make an oral presentation of their project.

One of the goals of the Honors Program is to build a sense of "community" among the honors students. To that end, the students attend and participate in a student retreat, a mid-semester get-together, and an end-of-semester honors luncheon. The student retreat is held at the beginning of the semester to serve as an Honors Program orientation. It is also an opportunity for the students to get to know each other through team building activities. The other activities allow for the social interaction among the honors students. In addition, students have the opportunity to attend local, regional, and national honor conferences.

The program provides honors students with the opportunity to do community service by volunteering their time in a number of places throughout the community. Students who plan to complete at least 9 hours of honors credit are eligible to participate in this activity.

The Montgomery College Honors Program began in spring 2000 and has approximately 60 students currently enrolled in the program.

Participation Requirements: Upon successfully completing 15 hours of honors contract credit with a GPA of 3.5 or better, students receive the designation of Honors Program Graduate on their diploma and transcript, special recognition at graduation, and a medallion commemorating the event.

To graduate as an honors scholar, a student must complete at least 9 honors credit hours with at least a 3.5 GPA as well as 25 hours of community service; students receive a silver cord as recognition at graduation. With the completion of 15 honors credit hours with a minimum 3.5 GPA and completion of 25 hours of community service, a student may qualify to graduate as an Honors Scholar with Distinction; these students receive a gold cord and a medallion as recognition at graduation.

Admission Process: High school graduates enrolling at Montgomery College for the first time must meet at least one of the following criteria: graduate in the top 10 percent of the graduating class; have 1000 or higher on the SAT, or 25 or higher composite score on the ACT within the past five years; or have ASSET scores of 45 or higher in reading, 50 or higher in writing, and 45 or higher in intermediate algebra.

Students enrolled at Montgomery College who have completed a minimum of 9 hours or more of college-level courses must have a minimum 3.5 GPA in order to participate in the Honors Program. Any student who does not have at minimum 3.5 GPA may still participate in the program with permission of the instructor in his or her regularly scheduled class.

Scholarship Availability: Any student in the Honors Program who is carrying 12 or more college credit hours, has a minimum GPA of 3.5, and is attempting at least one honors contract, is eligible for available Honors Program scholarships after the completion of 9 hours of college credit. The scholarships are awarded to the top students based on their overall GPAs, letters of recommendations, and a short essay. The scholarship is used for tuition, books, or fees for the following semester. The scholarship is nonrenewable.

Honors Program scholarships are available for top high school graduates from select high schools from the surrounding area serviced by Montgomery College. These are two-year scholarships, renewable each year if the student completes 12 hours of college credit each semester, maintains a minimum 3.5 GPA, and completes an honors contract each semester. The scholarship is used for tuition, books, or fees.

Other scholarships are available through the Financial Aid Office.

The Campus Context: Montgomery College is one of five colleges in the North Harris Montgomery Community College District (NHMCCD). It is located approximately 35 miles north of downtown Houston on 100 acres of pine forest. Completed in 1995, it offers more than thirty career programs as well as academic transfer courses in a variety of subjects. Programs of note include biotechnology, computer information technology, criminal justice, human services, management, physical therapy assistant studies, and vocational nursing. It prides itself in having a guaranteed annual schedule and provides an array of services to demonstrate that it is a truly student-centered college.

Montgomery College is in proximity to the biotechnology sector located in the Woodlands. The College has a Biotechnology Institute that uses partnerships with local schools and businesses to help prepare a wide range of students for entry into the biotechnology industry.

The University Center (TUC) is a partnership with NHMCCD and six Texas universities. It is located adjacent to Montgomery College. It provides the opportunity for students to continue their college education by completing a bachelor's or master's degree. TUC provides programs in fifty areas of study and offers the latest in high-tech education and a variety of formats, including distance learning, and times for students to complete their education.

The Center for Business and Technology Training (CBTT) in Conroe serves as a satellite center for individuals and employers to develop the skill training needed to be competitive in the workplace. CBTT offers career advancement in areas of manufacturing, computers, and other high-tech or business-related areas.

Student Body: The total enrollment is approximately 5,900 students (fall 2001), 40 percent men and 60 percent women. The average class size is 21 students. Ethnic distribution is 83 percent white, 8.3 percent Hispanic, 5.1 percent African American, and 3.5 percent other. The average age of the student population is 28.

Faculty: There are 48 full-time faculty members, of whom 43 percent have master's degrees and 23.4 percent have Ph.D.'s.

Key Facilities: The state-of-the art resource center helps promote advanced, computerized learning for the student population. Students and faculty members have access to on-line books and periodicals as well as to more than 27,000 books. The library also has both Macintoshes and PCs for use by student and faculty members. The Extended Learning Center provides tutoring and facilitated study groups for various disciplines of study. There are 5 full-time librarians; the library is open seven days a week for more than 80 hours per week.

Honorary Societies: Phi Theta Kappa

Study Abroad: Students have an opportunity to travel to Guadalajara, Mexico in the summer. The students study, live, work, and explore in an intense "emersion" experience as part of a partnership between the College and the Universidad Autonoma de Guadalajara (UAG), one of the finest private universities in Mexico.

Support Services: Montgomery College's Student Development Division is a service-oriented unit with a professionally trained team dedicated to providing quality support assistance to students with disabilities. Reasonable accommodations are based upon the individual needs of each student.

Job Opportunities: The College work-study programs are need-based programs. On-campus employment is open to credit students with a desire to work on campus.

Tuition: $26 per credit hour for district residents; $66 per credit hour for state residents; $81 per credit hour for nonresidents (2001–02)

Mandatory Fees: $5 per credit hour technology fee plus $12 registration fee.

Contact: Gayle LoPiccolo, Montgomery College Honors Director, Office B200C, 3200 College Park Drive, Conroe, Texas 77384; Telephone: 936-273-7445; Fax: 936-273-7362; E-mail: mchonors@nhmccd.edu or lopiccolo@nhmccd.edu; Web site: http://wwwmc.nhmccd.edu/students/life/honorsprogram.html

MOREHOUSE COLLEGE

4 Pr D M Tr HBC

▼ Honors Program

Morehouse College offers a four-year, comprehensive Honors Program providing special learning opportunities for students of superior intellectual ability, high motivation and broad interests. Faculty members in the program nurture the student throughout his college life, in the areas of scholarly inquiry, independent and creative thinking, and exemplary scholarship. Honors Program students take special sections of regular Morehouse courses, taught by honors faculty members who are chosen on the basis of their reputations as outstanding teachers. Course enrollment is limited to 20 students. The program is open to all students in all academic disciplines.

The Honors Program Club, one of the College's chartered student groups, elects its officers and sponsors activities for HPC members and for the College community. Morehouse is actively involved in the state, regional, and national Honors organizations; Georgia State Honors Council affords students a chance to try out their leadership skills and to be elected to offices.

The Honors Program at Morehouse College was established in 1981 and restructured in 1987. It currently enrolls 200 students, 65 of whom are freshmen.

Participation Requirements: Students in lower-division honors (freshmen and sophomores) are enrolled in special sections of English, foreign languages, world history, mathematics, philosophy, political science, and sociology. Other freshman and sophomore courses are chosen by the student and are taken with members of the student body in the regular program. On the basis of his status as an Honors Program freshman and sophomore, a student is expected to earn honors on the departmental level as a junior and senior. In upper-division honors there are no Honors Program courses; rather, the student completes special course-related assignments, makes presentations, participates in seminars, and focuses on departmental research.

The honors senior thesis is a staple of honors programs across the country. Currently under study at Morehouse, the senior thesis (or project) component of the HP degree will provide excellent preparation for students desiring to do graduate or professional study or to enter high-level jobs upon graduation. Also being considered is a community service component that will enable talented, concerned students in the HP to help persons in Atlanta neighborhoods and to receive recognition for this kind of work.

Honors Program students must maintain a GPA of at least 3.2 during the freshman and sophomore years. The minimum for juniors and seniors is 3.25. Any student falling below the minimum has the next semester to raise his GPA and to resume his good standing in the program. If he does not attain the minimum, he will be dropped from the program. Students below the minimum 3.2 will have until May to improve their GPAs. No first-semester freshman below 2.7 is dropped from the program or put on probation unless he falls so low that he cannot reach the minimum cumulative GPA by May.

Admission Process: Admission to the Honors Program is based on SAT I scores and high school GPA. Second-semester freshmen and first-semester sophomores may apply to the program if they are not admitted as incoming freshmen, but the most desirable time to join is at the start of the freshman year. Generally, students with combined SAT I scores of at least 1160 or an ACT composite of 27 or above are eligible for the program. The deadline for applying to the program is April 18.

Scholarship Availability: The Morehouse Honors Program does not award scholarships to its students. More than 90 percent of HP students receive full or partial awards from the College's scholarship pool. Morehouse College Honors Program students have been recipients of the following national competitive scholarships: the Rhodes Scholarship (1994), Marshall Scholarships (1994 and 1996), and the UNCF Mellon Scholarship (1991, 1994, and 1996).

The Campus Context: Morehouse College offers three degree programs and is a men's school with a population of 2,970.

Student Body Ninety-five percent of students are African American, and 5 percent are international students. Approximately 55

Interpreting the symbols: **2**=two-year college, **4**=four-year college; **Pu**=public or state college, **Pr**=private college; **G**=general honors program; **D**=departmental honors program; **S**=small program (fewer than 100 students), **M**=midsize program (100 to 500 students), **L**=large program (more than 500 students); **Sc**=scholarships available in honors program; **Tr**=transfer students accepted into honors program; **HBC**=historically black college; **AA**=academic advisors; **GA**=graduate advisors; **FA**=fellowship advisors.

percent of the students are residents, 45 percent commuters. Eighty percent of students receive financial aid.

Faculty Of the 231 faculty members, 179 are full-time and 70 percent hold terminal degrees. The student-faculty ratio is 16.7:1.

Key Facilities The library houses approximately 1.5 million volumes. Seven computer facilities on campus are located in the Academic Computing Center, Electronic Classroom, Mathematics Lab, Writing Skills Lab, Computer Science Labs, Biology Lab, and Business Department Lab. There are five fraternities.

Athletics The intercollegiate athletics program is recognized by the College as a valuable asset in developing campus spirit. Morehouse College athletic teams are known as the Maroon Tigers. College colors are maroon and white. Teams compete with those of similar-sized institutions in football, basketball, tennis, and track and field sports. Morehouse College is a member of the Southern Intercollegiate Athletic Conference (SIAC) composed of sixteen colleges and universities in five states, and the National Collegiate Athletic Association (NCAA), Division II. This affiliation permits all Morehouse College athletes to receive regional and national recognition for their accomplishments. The intercollegiate athletic program is under the direction of the Director of Athletics.

A member of an athletic team must maintain good academic and social standing and may not represent the College if he is on athletic, academic, or disciplinary probation. All students who meet association eligibility regulations may become candidates for athletic teams.

Study Abroad Study-abroad programs are available in every discipline, including the business programs of the renowned London School of Economics. There are also two Morehouse-based programs: the Summer Program in Oaxaca, Mexico, which has attracted Morehouse participants since the early 1980s, and the Summer Program for French students on the island of Martinique. Both programs begin immediately after final examinations and last four weeks. Each offers 6 hours of credit with optional internships. To facilitate study abroad, certain financial aid scholarships are available to students, including the Merrill Scholarship. All students who wish to study abroad for a semester or a year and receive Morehouse credit must submit appropriate applications to the Director of Study Abroad and International Exchanges.

Support Services International students who are admitted to Morehouse College are provided with various services at the Center for International Studies. These include nonacademic advising, immigration matters, host-family opportunities, and other services that help make their experience at Morehouse successful.

Job Opportunities Students can find employment through the work-study program, as well as mentoring and assignments/internships in scientific and computer laboratories.

Tuition: $8480 per year (1998–99)

Room and Board: $3291

Mandatory Fees: $1554 per year (full-time), $777 per semester (part-time), $53 technology fee

Contact: Director: Jocelyn W. Jackson, 830 Westview Drive, SW, P.O. Box 140141, Atlanta, Georgia 30314; Telephone: 404-215-2679; Fax: 404-215-2679

Morris College

4 Pr G S Sc

▼ Morris College Honors Program

The Morris College Honors Program is a college-wide academic unit that operates within the framework of the Division of General Studies. It was established in 1983 and is currently undergoing organizational change. From its inception, the program has provided opportunities for academically talented, highly motivated, and determined students to enrich and broaden their college experience. The primary goal of the Morris College Honors Program is to ensure that students develop strong oral and written communication and critical-thinking skills. Faculty members associated with the Morris College Honors Program are expected to nurture students toward attaining this goal.

The Morris College Honors Program is implemented through five components, each of which is designed to enrich the students' learning in a supportive environment. The first component consists of honors sections of regular courses. The second component is an extracurricular "bridging" experience for freshmen and first-semester sophomores who have been identified by faculty members or honors students as potential candidates for the Morris College Honors Program. This experience offers the students opportunities to participate in various field trips, community service projects, special programs, and retreats, culminating in a report to the Honors Council and the honors student organization. The third component, the core of the honors curriculum, consists of four required interdisciplinary honors seminars at the junior and senior levels. The capstone of this experience is the Senior Honors Seminar that requires students to complete a thesis, under the supervision of a faculty adviser, and to present their work in an Honors Colloquium. The Honors Module, the fourth component, consists of a variety of social, cultural, and educational events that include informal discussions with faculty members and distinguished campus visitors, visits to museums and art galleries, and attendance at concerts, plays, and colloquia. The fifth component is the student organization Reinforcers, Achievers, and Representatives of Excellence (RARE), which emphasizes the development of leadership skills and a sense of community. In keeping with the Morris College philosophy, RARE is devoted to service-learning and involvement in community service projects. There are approximately 25 to 30 students in the Morris College Honors Program out of a campus population of 986 students. Morris is affiliated with honors organization at the state, regional, and national levels. Students are actively involved in the National Association of African American Morris College Honors Programs (NAAAHP) and the Southern Regional Honors Council (SRHS).

Participation Requirements: Honors students may be enrolled in any undergraduate curriculum. To remain in good standing in the program, a student must maintain at least a 3.4 GPA. Honors students whose GPA drops below this level are allowed a probationary period to continue the program and raise their cumulative average. All honors students are required to complete a research course prior to enrolling in the specially designed honors seminars. A student who successfully completes all the requirements of the Morris College Honors Program is awarded the honors medallion and wears the honors stole at commencement. Successful completion of the Morris College Honors Program is designated on the official transcript.

Admission Process: Second-semester freshmen with 3.4 GPAs are invited to complete applications for admission to the program. References from two professors are required, followed by an interview process initiated by the Honors Director. Honors students participate in this process and make their recommendations to the director.

Scholarship Availability: Morris College offers a number of presidential, endowed, and United Negro College Fund scholarships. Ninety percent of students receiving these scholarships are in the Morris College Honors Program.

The Campus Context: Morris College, located in Sumter, South Carolina, was founded in 1908 by the Baptist Educational and Missionary Convention of South Carolina. Morris College is fully accredited by the Southern Association of Colleges and Schools. On January 1, 1982, Morris College became a member of the

United Negro College Fund. The College offers twenty undergraduate majors leading to the B.A., B.S., and B.F.A. degrees.

Student Body Undergraduate enrollment is 986 students. More than 65 percent are women. Ninety-four percent of students receive financial aid. The campus has eight fraternities and sororities.

Faculty There are 60 full-time faculty members; 65 percent have doctorates. There are also 20 adjunct faculty members. The student-faculty ratio is 16:1.

Key Facilities The library houses more than 95,000 volumes. There are seven network computer facilities.

Athletics Athletics include intercollegiate basketball and cross-country for women and men. There are women's softball and men's baseball teams.

Job Opportunities Students are employed as tutors in the Student Support Services Program and in other programs, including work-study.

Tuition: $6482 per year (2001–02)

Room and Board: $9995

Mandatory Fees: $154.50

Contact: Director of Honors, 100 West College Street, Sumter, South Carolina 29150; Telephone: 803-934-3180; Fax: 803-775-5669

MOTT COMMUNITY COLLEGE

2 Pu G L Sc Tr AA

▼ Honors Program

The Mott Community College (MCC) Honors Program is designed to provide a more stimulating and rigorous option for academically talented and motivated students in all majors. Although the emphasis lies in enhancing scholarship opportunities for students whose goals include transferring to a four-year institution, the program also provides a competitive edge to students seeking immediate employment. Honors Program participants have garnered transfer scholarships from prestigious colleges and universities across the nation. A Transfer Alliance Agreement with the University of Michigan–Flint (UM–F) ensures that MCC Honors Program graduates are given first priority for the UM–F Junior/Senior Honors Program.

Two of the program's hallmarks are diversity and flexibility. Because MCC serves a wide range of traditional and nontraditional students, the College offers participation in an honors experience to some students who would otherwise not have such an opportunity. The College serves dually enrolled high school students, traditional high school graduates, those who have a lapse in attendance between high school and college, and those retraining for a second career. This brings a rich blend of experience and interests to the honors discourse. Students select from a rotating schedule of honors courses that either meet a general education requirement or are electives recommended for several majors. The capstone experience is the Honors Colloquium, which focuses on an interdisciplinary topic. The honors topic, selected annually by the Honors Steering Committee, becomes a catalyst for all the honors courses each year and provides opportunities for guest lectures and extracurricular activities. Honors classes are intimate (usually 15–25 students), stress participative learning, and provide opportunities for research, publication, oral presentations, and community service.

Biannual honors retreats provide leadership training and transfer scholarship preparation. A special honors adviser, in conjunction with an adviser in a student's major, helps coordinate the student's long-range goals. Dedicated honors faculty members have a strong mentoring relationship with students as well. Students are expected to prepare an honors portfolio that demonstrates measurable outcomes to meet stated Honors Program objectives. Honors students have produced College and regional award-winning essays and have placed on All-Michigan and All-America Academic Teams.

Participation in the Honors Program is rewarded with a partial tuition scholarship and special recognition, such as the honors diploma and medallion at graduation. Academic enrichment, such as participation in local, regional, and national conferences, and cultural experiences, such as trips abroad, also prepare MCC honors students for transfer to a four-year institution. Currently, 120 students participate in the Honors Program, which was established in 1988.

Participation Requirements: Students must be enrolled in at least 6 credit hours to qualify for the Honors Program Scholarship. To receive an Honors Program diploma upon graduation, a student must complete at least 12 credit hours in honors course work. At least 3 of these credits must be from the course designated as the Honors Colloquium. In addition, a student must have a minimum cumulative GPA of 3.5 at the time of graduation and must meet all the requirements for an established associate degree at MCC (Associate of Arts, Science, Applied Science, or General Studies). Honors Program participants who choose to transfer early, but who have maintained a minimum GPA of 3.5 or higher and have completed at least 9 credit hours in honors courses, receive an Honors Certificate of Achievement. Both honors diploma and honors certificate recipients and their guests participate in an honors graduation dinner and medallion ceremony. In addition, honors diploma recipients are distinguished at commencement by the wearing of medallions and being the first to receive their degrees. Honors designations for all honors courses are noted on the students' transcripts.

Admission Process: Invitations to apply to the Honors Program are sent to all MCC students who are enrolled in a minimum of 6 credit hours and who have a cumulative GPA of 3.5 or higher after completion of 12 MCC credit hours in 100- or 200-level courses. Transfer students with the same academic profile from other accredited colleges may apply. High school students with a cumulative GPA of 3.5 or higher at graduation are also encouraged to apply. Dual-enrolled high school students with a GPA of 3.5 or higher may be provisionally admitted to the Honors Program, with full admission after one semester at MCC if they meet the standard criteria for all applicants. Dual-enrolled students must have permission from their high school administrator. The Honors Program Coordinator (or, for unusual circumstances, the Steering Committee) determines membership acceptance from the pool of minimally qualified applicants on the basis of high school or college transcripts, evaluation of an original essay, evaluation of two letters of recommendation, and an interview. This is a rolling admissions process.

Scholarship Availability: Students admitted to the MCC Honors Program are eligible for the Honors Program Scholarship, which is awarded purely on academic merit. This scholarship can only be applied to honors-designated sections for a maximum of two courses per semester and up to 32 credit hours total. The scholarship amount is based on in-district tuition and fees and must be used for the semester of application. Other financial assistance, including scholarships, grants, loans, and work-study employment, is available to qualified students who are admitted to MCC.

The Campus Context: Established in 1923 as Flint Junior College, the College was renamed Charles Stewart Mott Community College in 1973 in tribute to its benefactor. MCC is fully accredited

Interpreting the symbols: **2**=two-year college, **4**=four-year college; **Pu**=public or state college, **Pr**=private college; **G**=general honors program; **D**=departmental honors program; **S**=small program (fewer than 100 students), **M**=midsize program (100 to 500 students), **L**=large program (more than 500 students); **Sc**=scholarships available in honors program; **Tr**=transfer students accepted into honors program; **HBC**=historically black college; **AA**=academic advisors; **GA**=graduate advisors; **FA**=fellowship advisors.

by the Higher Learning Commission of the North Central Association. Today, more than 17,000 students are enrolled on the main campus in Flint, Michigan, or at extension sites in Genesee and Lapeer Counties. As of fall 2002, the new Regional Technology Center is expected to serve east-central Michigan with cutting-edge modularized instruction, emphasizing simulation technology. The College's Divisions of Business, Fine Arts, Health Sciences, Humanities, Information Technology, Science and Math, Social Sciences, and Technology offer academic and vocational programs that prepare students for transfer or employment. Many courses are now taught online or via distance learning, adding convenience for working students and allowing the College in the Workplace Program to serve students even outside the state. In addition, several universities are represented at the University Center, providing students with the opportunity to complete the final two years of certain bachelor's degrees and master's degrees on the MCC campus.

Student Body Enrollment for academic year 2000–01 was 17,299 combined credit- and noncredit-seeking students. MCC's 2000 Self-Study for Accreditation reported 29.5 percent full-time and 70.5 percent part-time students, with 59.8 percent women and 40.2 percent men. Ethnic distribution was 77.3 percent white, 18.8 percent African American, 2 percent Hispanic, 1 percent Native American, and 0.9 percent Asian American. The average age of the MCC student is 27 years.

Faculty There are approximately 450 faculty members, of whom 155 are full-time. Seventeen percent have Ph.D. degrees, and 75 percent have M.A. degrees or higher.

Key Facilities Library services and resources include facilities for individual and group study, print and nonprint materials for circulation or reference, and the Flint Area Library Cooperative Online Network (FALCON), which is an automated network of more than 500,000 books and other materials. Links with the Online Computer Library Center, Inc. (OCLC), allow access to myriad databases. The library also houses the Learning Center and Tutorial Services, the Viewing/Listening and Testing Center for distance learning courses, and a suite of TV production and editing studios that enable the College to create its own distance learning courses. Computer labs that are primarily DOS-based are readily available.

Honorary Society Phi Theta Kappa

Athletics MCC is a member of the Michigan Community College Athletic Association and the National Junior College Athletic Association. In recent years, nearly 100 student athletes have produced outstanding intercollegiate teams. For example, the men's varsity basketball team ranks second in the nation for Division II, and the women's basketball team finished fourth nationally in 2001. Other varsity sports include baseball, cross-country, golf, softball, and volleyball. Many campus recreational activities, such as swimming, tennis, weight training, and aerobics, are also available.

Study Abroad Study-abroad opportunities are available in foreign language, art, and international business.

Support Services Learning/DisAbility Services offer centralized, free, academic assistance, such as peer and professional tutoring for handicapped and/or learning-disabled students and for students with limited English proficiency. The Special Populations/Perkins, Student Support Services (TRIO), and Upward Bound grant projects are also administered by the Learning Center staff. Every attempt has been made to maintain a barrier-free environment in all campus buildings.

Job Opportunities Career and job placement services consist of a Career Resource Center used by students and community members and a Student Employment Center that places students in work-study positions within the College and in community service. Mott graduates enjoy a 91 percent job placement rate, based on a five-year average.

Tuition: Tuition was $1467.60 per year ($61.15 per contact hour) for in-district residents, $88.25 per contact hour for out-of-district residents, and $117.70 per contact hour for out-of-state residents (for 2001–02).

Mandatory Fees: Registration/student services fee: $43.50 per semester or session; lab fee: $5–$150 per course for selected classes; late registration fee: $25.

Contact: Heather Sisto Collins, Honors Program Coordinator, PCC-218, Mott Community College, 1401 East Court Street, Flint, Michigan 48503-2089; Telephone: 810-232-3058; E-mail: hcollins@mcc.edu; Web site: http://www.mcc.edu/honors

Mount Mary College

4 Pr G S Sc Tr

▼ Honors Program

The purpose of the Mount Mary College Honors Program is to reward superior scholarly achievement and to provide special challenges to serious students who wish to achieve maximum benefits from their college education. Honors seminars are interdisciplinary courses offered each semester and taught by faculty members from various departments. Classes are small and offer students and faculty members opportunities for discussion, thought, and reflection in the exploration of ideas. Each professor teaches one of the classes during the semester, offering students a range of viewpoints on the semester's topic. The course focus varies but has consistently considered a topic from multiple perspectives. For example, recent course topics that have enlightened students and faculty members include Ethics for a New Millennium and the Shifting Paradigm: Art Meets Science and Spirituality in a Changing Economy. Each professor teaches from her or his area of expertise, research, and scholarship. Students select a professor/mentor and meet several times throughout the semester while preparing a final project/essay.

The program began in 1962 with a multidisciplinary seminar in contemporary French existentialism. The Honors Program has 25 students currently enrolled.

Participation Requirements: Students in the program are expected to achieve a cumulative GPA of at least 3.5 at the time of graduation; to accumulate 6 academic points in honors seminars, independent study, internships, and a thesis/project; and to accumulate 4 nonacademic points in nonpaid, noncredit activities that promote personal growth, such as presenting a paper at a convention, participating in a Wingspread conference, studying abroad, or offering service (tutoring and/or other noncurricular activities that fulfill this requirement). Students completing the program receive the diploma citation Graduation in the Honors Program.

Admission Process: Incoming first-year students fulfilling at least two of the following criteria are invited to join the Honors Program: a high school GPA of 3.5 or higher, rank in the upper 10 percent of their high school class, and a score of 28 or above in the ACT or 600 or above in at least one area of the SAT. Freshman students not initially invited may apply for admission to the program. Freshman students achieving at least a 3.5 GPA upon completion of the first semester also may apply for admission to the program. Transfer students who come to Mount Mary with a 3.5 GPA or better from their previous college may join the program. Returning students need to complete 12 credits with a minimum 3.5 GPA before applying for admission to the program.

The Campus Context: Mount Mary College is a four-year urban Catholic college for women sponsored by the School Sisters of Notre Dame that provides an environment for the development of the whole person. The College encourages leadership, integrity, and a deep sense of social justice arising from sensitivity to moral values and Christian principles. The Honors Program is small, accepts transfer students, and has an Honors Program Director who oversees students' progress in the program.

Contact: Mount Mary College, 2900 North Menomonee River Parkway, Milwaukee, Wisconsin 53222

MOUNT ST. CLARE COLLEGE

4 Pr G S Sc Tr

▼ Mount St. Clare Scholars' Institute

The Mount St. Clare Scholars' Institute offers an enhanced undergraduate experience for able and highly motivated students in any of the College's majors. At the heart of the curricular experience is a series of limited-enrollment interdisciplinary honors courses taught by selected faculty members. In addition, Scholars' Institute members have opportunities to work closely with senior Mount St. Clare faculty members in joint research projects, participate in distinctive cocurricular and extracurricular activities, and have access to enhanced internships and capstone courses. Participants also have opportunities for international study.

The Scholars' Institute is a new program and is scheduled to be implemented in the 2002–03 academic year. It replaces the College's former Bonaventure Scholars program, founded in 1991.

Participation Requirements: Participants take one interdisciplinary honors course per semester. These courses may, in some cases, also be applied to general education or major requirements. Students must meet higher expectations in capstone courses. Cocurricular requirements are currently under development. Students sign a contract that requires them to maintain a minimum 3.5 GPA and to meet program requirements.

Students have a notation of successful completion of the program placed on their transcripts and are recognized at Commencement.

Admission Process: Admission to the Scholars' Institute is by application to the faculty steering committee. New freshmen with an ACT composite score of at least 26 (or at least 1160 on the SAT I) or a minimum high school GPA of 3.5 may apply. Applicants should also submit a substantial example of written work (such as a research paper). Transfer students who have at least 60 semester hours of college-level work with at least a 3.5 cumulative GPA may apply. They should also submit a substantial example of written work. Current Mount St. Clare students may apply after completion of at least 30 semester hours with a minimum cumulative GPA of 3.5 and submission of a substantial example of written work. The program features rolling admissions.

Scholarship Availability: Scholars' Institute participants are eligible for financial aid based on need and merit.

The Campus Context: Mount St. Clare College (MSC) is a coeducational liberal arts college that takes pride in its Franciscan heritage and commitment to the cornerstones of concern, compassion, respect, and service. The College is located on a scenic bluff in the Mississippi River town of Clinton, Iowa, which has a population of 28,000 and is located midway between Chicago and Des Moines. MSC students report a high level of satisfaction with the personalized education they receive and the family-like atmosphere on campus. The College offers B.A., B.S., B.G.S., and B.A.S. degrees in twenty-two major programs and more than fifty submajor specializations. The 100-acre campus includes two residence halls, classroom and laboratory facilities, a library, and a new general-purpose facility, the Durgin Educational Center, which houses state-of-the-art classrooms and athletic facilities.

Student Body Mount St. Clare had a total enrollment of 519 in fall 2001, of whom 401 were undergraduates (184 men and 217 women). Approximately 36 percent live on campus, and 28 percent are nontraditional students. MSC students come from twelve states and ten countries. Thirteen percent of students belong to minority groups and 4 percent are international students. Approximately 93 percent of full-time MSC students receive financial aid. There are a variety of student groups and associations on campus but no fraternities or sororities.

Faculty In fall 2001, the total number of faculty members was 53 (23 full-time). Forty-eight percent of full-time faculty members have terminal degrees. The student-faculty ratio is 14:1.

Key Facilities The library houses 158,374 items (80,759 books and government documents, 73,405 microforms, and 4,210 other), as well as a wide range of online databases and electronic books and full-text items. It is an OCLC member library and a member of Quad-LINC, a regional library consortium. There is one main computer lab as well as four smaller labs, including labs in each residence hall. Individual rooms in the residence halls are wired for the Internet. The College is also part of the Iowa Communications Network, a statewide fiber-optics system. A major upgrade of campus information technology is in progress.

Honorary Societies Lambda Sigma, Alpha Tau Omega (local junior/senior honor society)

Athletics Mount St. Clare College is a member of the National Association of Intercollegiate Athletics (NAIA) Division II and of the Midwest Classic Conference. The College fields teams in fourteen sports: baseball, basketball, cross-country, golf, soccer, track, and wrestling for men and basketball, cross-country, soccer, softball, tennis, track, and volleyball for women.

Study Abroad The College sponsors summer study in Assisi and Perugia, Italy, and a London theater tour during the spring semester. Other international study experiences may be arranged.

Support Services The campus is handicapped accessible. A limited range of support services are available for learning-disabled students.

Job Opportunities MSC offers College work-study, and internships are available in many academic programs.

Tuition: For 2001–02, full-time tuition was $13,800. The part-time rate was $405 per semester hour.

Room and Board: For 2001–02, room and board ranged from $4950 to $6125, depending on single or double occupancy.

Mandatory Fees: For 2001–02, mandatory fees for full-time students amounted to $250.

Contact: Dr. Curt Lowe, Academic Dean, Mount St. Clare College, 400 North Bluff Boulevard, Clinton, Iowa 52732; Telephone: 563-242-4023 Ext. 1301; Fax: 563-242-2003; E-mail: willow@clare.edu

MT. SAN ANTONIO COLLEGE

2 Pu G M Tr

▼ Honors Program

Mt. San Antonio College's Honors Program provides an enhanced curriculum for highly motivated students. To help students reach their full academic potential and to facilitate transfer to highly competitive universities, the College has developed twenty-eight honors courses from the Humanities and Social Sciences Division, the Natural Sciences Division, and the Business Division. These course are designed to foster not only mastery of content but also advanced critical thinking, analysis, discussion, and writing skills. Classes are designed to maximize student participation through group and individual presentations of course material.

Interpreting the symbols: **2**=two-year college, **4**=four-year college; **Pu**=public or state college, **Pr**=private college; **G**=general honors program; **D**=departmental honors program; **S**=small program (fewer than 100 students), **M**=midsize program (100 to 500 students), **L**=large program (more than 500 students); **Sc**=scholarships available in honors program; **Tr**=transfer students accepted into honors program; **HBC**=historically black college; **AA**=academic advisors; **GA**=graduate advisors; **FA**=fellowship advisors.

Classes range from 10 to 20 students, offering a full range of courses throughout the disciplines, from biology to art history, from statistics to world religions, from micro economics to literary genres. The Honors Program encourages its participants to join Phi Theta Kappa and take advantage of leadership opportunities and the annual honors topic teleconference. Honors Program students help coordinate and implement the honors topic seminars and related field trips.

The Honors Program includes summer honors study-abroad opportunities. Two honors courses (6 units) are offered each summer in London or Paris for an accelerated four-week semester.

The Mt. San Antonio College Honors Program accepted its first students in 1995 and currently has 386 students actively pursuing Honors Certification. Approximately 50 to 75 students a year are certified as Honors Program Graduates.

Participation Requirements: Students are required to take any six honors courses. They must attend the Honors Topic Teleconferences each fall and maintain a minimum 3.2 GPA for Honors Certification. Successful completion of the Honors Program is recognized at commencement and is also noted on the official transcript and the graduation diploma.

Admission Process: High school and college students are recruited on the basis of their high school or college GPAs, SAT I scores, an application, and a teacher/professor recommendation. Students may apply for admission directly from high school or after having completed 12 transferable college units. In addition, for admission into the program, all students must be eligible for Freshman Composition. Students may major in any discipline. Application to the program is open throughout the year. Students with lower than a 3.5 GPA may be waived into the program based on faculty recommendations and personal interviews.

Scholarship Availability: Scholarships of various amounts are awarded through the Financial Aid Office based on academic performance and financial need. Scholarships are not offered through the Honors Program. Most Honors Program students receive the major scholarships on campus each year.

The Campus Context: Mt. San Antonio College is a public community college located on 422 acres in the San Gabriel Valley, 23 miles east of the Los Angeles Civic Center. The College's central location affords extensive cultural and recreational opportunities in major theater, music, and sports venues as well as mountain and ocean resorts within an hour's drive.

The College extends its opportunities to both academic and vocational students through a Child Development Center, a farm, a Performing Arts Center, planetarium, radio station and cable TV station, and a ten-acre Wildlife Sanctuary. The College also has an International Student Programs Center, a Job and Career Placement Center, a Re-Entry Center, a Small Business Development Center, and a Veterans' Affairs Center (only a few of the many resources available to students and the community).

Student Body Mt. San Antonio College is the largest single-campus community college in California, with a student population of more than 35,000. The enrollment is composed of 46 percent men and 54 percent women. The ethnic distribution is 39 percent Hispanic, 26 percent white, 20 percent Asian and Pacific Islander, 7 percent black, 6 percent Filipino, and 2 percent "other non-white." More than ninety languages are represented on campus.

Faculty Instruction is organized under a divisional structure with departments within each division. The College has five instructional divisions that house thirty-six departments and 937 full- and part-time faculty members.

Key Facilities The library contains more than 60,000 volumes and subscribes to 747 magazines and periodicals. In addition to Internet access, students may access over 1,700 full-text magazine and journal articles on the library's local area network. More than 300 microcomputers are available in the Learning Assistance Mega lab located on the first floor of the library building. In addition, there are six other student computer labs located throughout the campus.

Athletics Mt. San Antonio College has one of the most extensive community college athletic programs in the country, offering a comprehensive program with twenty-two sports. The athletic facilities include an Olympic-size pool, a 15,000-seat football stadium, a 1,470-seat gymnasium, a wrestling gym, strength-training facilities, an Exercise Science/Wellness Center, and an Olympic quality track. Mt. San Antonio College hosts the largest track and field event in the nation, with more than 50,000 participants. The College is especially proud of its 1997 National Football Championship and the fact that it is the number one community college in California for articulating football players into four-year college football programs.

Study Abroad Mt. San Antonio College offers students a wide range of study-abroad options. The Work and Study in London Program enables students to study international business and marketing while working in Britain. Eligible students may also participate in any of the programs offered by the Council on International Educational Exchange at study centers around the world. In addition, the College's membership in the California Consortium for International Education permits students to participate in study-abroad programs sponsored by other colleges throughout California. Finally, its participation in the Foothills Consortium for Study Abroad also provides program opportunities for students with other local community college students.

Support Services Disabled Student Programs and Services offers special programs and services for students with disabilities. Extended Opportunity Programs and Services offers academic and financial opportunities for educationally disadvantaged students.

Tuition: $12 per unit for California residents, $121 per unit for nonresidents, $138 per unit for F-1 Visa Foreign Students (1998–99)

Contact: Dr. Mary Brackenhoff, 1100 North Grand Avenue, Walnut, California 91789; Telephone: 909-594-5611, ext. 4665; Fax: 909-468-3999; E-mail: mbracken@mtsac.edu; Web site: http://www.mtsac.edu/

MT. SAN JACINTO COLLEGE

2 Pu G S Tr

▼ Honors Enrichment Program

The mission of the Honors Enrichment Program is to create, promote, and sustain a learning community of highly motivated and capable students and faculty members that enhances the College and the greater community. Currently, the College offers thirty-four courses across the curriculum in an honors component format. The honors component is taught concurrently with the regular section of the class and, in addition, meets independently with the instructor to conduct discussion sections, research projects, or field experience. Up to 5 honors students may enroll in an honors component. Faculty members are committed to the success of honors students and create components that enhance the students' critical thinking and creativity. The capstone of the Honors Enrichment Program is an interdisciplinary honors seminar that explores a contemporary issue such as children and violence or immigration and its impacts.

Founded in 1996, the Honors Enrichment Program's current enrollment is 65.

Participation: Honors students must complete 12 honors semester units in three disciplines and the Honors Seminar for certification. Student must have a minimum GPA of 3.0 in honors course work. Depending upon level of admission, students must maintain either a cumulative GPA of 3.5 or a cumulative GPA of 3.0 with 3.5 semester GPAs for each semester the student is enrolled in the program.

Upon certification, students receive a seal for their diploma, a plaque, and transcript recognition.

Admission Process: New students, who have completed no college work, must have a 3.7 on a 4.0 scale high school GPA or a 1200 SAT I score. They also need a letter of recommendation from the principal of their school attached to the application. For returning or transfer students, 12 or more degree applicable semester units should be completed with a minimum cumulative GPA of 3.0 and 3.5 in the last 12 degree-applicable units completed. These students also need faculty recommendations. Applications are available from the HEP coordinator or at Admissions and Records and Counseling offices and are accepted on a rolling admission basis.

Scholarship Availability: While the institution offers no honors scholarships, students are eligible to compete for honors scholarships from the Honors Transfer Council of California, of which the College is a member. These are $100 scholarships given to students who have completed a member college's honors program and are transferring to a four-year institution. Two essays from the College may be submitted to this competition.

The Campus Context: The Mt. San Jacinto Community College District covers 1,700 square miles in central and southwestern Riverside County, one of California's fastest-growing and most dynamic regions.

The San Jacinto Campus is centrally located on State Highway 79 in the northern end of the San Jacinto Valley and serves residents of the eastern portion of the college district. The Menifee Valley Campus, opened in the fall of 1990, is located approximately 25 miles to the southwest, strategically located to serve the growing communities along the Interstate 215–Interstate 15 corridor.

Student Body Total enrollment in credit, noncredit, and community-services classes exceeds 9,000 students.

Key Facilities The San Jacinto campus has been master-planned and essentially will be rebuilt over the next fifteen to twenty years to accommodate 12,000 to 15,000 students. In 1993, the Alice P Cutting Business & Technology Center opened to students with new laboratories for business, computer information science, engineering technologies, electronics, and photography. In 1995, a state-of-the-art music building opened on the San Jacinto Campus. The 1995–96 year saw a vast increase in classroom space on the Menifee Valley Campus with the opening of the Allied Health and Fine Arts buildings. Construction plans also call for the first phase of a new library facility on this campus.

Honorary Societies Phi Theta Kappa

Support Services The Board of Trustees, the Superintendent/President, and all of the faculty and staff members of Mt. San Jacinto College have made a commitment to provide the highest quality transfer and occupational education programs and services in a supportive teaching and learning environment.

Tuition: $118 per unit for nonresidents

Mandatory Fees: $12 per unit enrollment fee

Contact: Dr. Bea Ganim, Honors Enrichment Program Coordinator, Mt. San Jacinto College, 28237 La Piedra Road, Menifee, CA 92584; Telephone: 909-672-6752 ext. 2713; Fax: 909-672-0454; E-mail: bganim@msjc.cc.ca.us.

MOUNT VERNON NAZARENE COLLEGE

4 Pr G S Sc Tr

▼ Honors Program

The Honors Program at Mount Vernon Nazarene College (MVNC) is designed to provide rewarding challenges for high achievers in the way of specific courses, seminars, and other out-of-the-ordinary experiences both on and off campus. Honors students have access to exceptional learning opportunities that strengthen competence in liberal arts subjects as well as the students' major fields. The mission of the MVNC Honors Program is to develop within academically advanced students a greater understanding of what it means to be a Christian intellectual, integrating faith with learning through the development of critical-thinking skills. In the end, the goal of the program is to produce servant leaders driven by a reasoned application of Scripture to their chosen field.

The Honors Program facilitates exploration of issues of interest with other academically motivated students as well as senior faculty members in small class settings that are discussion and participation oriented and intellectually stimulating. What sets the MVNC program apart from other Honors Programs is the Honors Seminar, which provides a forum for all four classes of honors students to interact on the basis of presentations in various fields of the liberal arts. In addition, students are required to complete an Independent Research Project by their fourth year. The participation with other academically advanced students in the seminar as well as an independent study project creates a balance that provides the student with a challenging and well-rounded education experience.

Although the program is only in its fourth year, it has experienced tremendous success each year and has developed the needed foundation for a high-quality program. Approximately 50 students are enrolled in the MVNC Honors Program.

Participation Requirements: Students must be involved in the Honors Seminar each semester they are on campus. They are expected to achieve at least 4 credit hours of honors work in general core courses either in honors sections or through a system of contracting to complete extra or advanced work by agreement with the professor. They must also complete an Independent Research Project (IRP), which comprises 4 credit hours of research within the major field of the student. The student working on an IRP is mentored by a faculty member within the major department and the final work is examined by a committee of three faculty members.

To remain in the program, students must maintain a minimum 3.5 GPA. Upon completion of all the requirements, the student graduates with College Honors and Departmental Honors, which is noted on the diploma, transcript, and graduation program.

Admission Process: First-time freshmen may apply with two letters of recommendation attesting to the student's academic ability, an interview with the Honors Program Committee either in person or on the telephone, a score of at least 27 on the ACT, a minimum high school GPA of 3.4 (on a 4.0 scale), and any other information the applicant or committee deems necessary or helpful. Students applying after their second semester at the College must have completed 26 credit hours with at least a 3.6 cumulative GPA, two letters of recommendation from college professors, and an interview with the Honors Committee. Transfer students must have at least a 3.6 GPA, an ACT composite score of 27 or above, letters of recommendation from two professors, and an interview with the Honors Committee. The deadline for application is March 1.

Interpreting the symbols: 2=two-year college, 4=four-year college; **Pu**=public or state college, **Pr**=private college; **G**=general honors program; **D**=departmental honors program; **S**=small program (fewer than 100 students), **M**=midsize program (100 to 500 students), **L**=large program (more than 500 students); **Sc**=scholarships available in honors program; **Tr**=transfer students accepted into honors program; **HBC**=historically black college; **AA**=academic advisors; **GA**=graduate advisors; **FA**=fellowship advisors.

Scholarship Availability: An annual scholarship of $250 is awarded to all honors students. In addition, significant scholarships are awarded through the Office of Admissions based on academic performance and can be renewed over the course of a four-year degree program.

The Campus Context: The campus is located on the outskirts of Mount Vernon, Ohio, a charming town known as Ohio's Colonial City, and named Ohio's Most Livable Community in *Ohio Magazine.* The town of 15,000 is only 45 miles northeast of Columbus, Ohio's largest city, and is within a short drive of four other metropolitan areas. The College's 210 beautifully landscaped acres provide a serene and secure atmosphere for learning and social life. The College offers more than sixty academic programs and a full range of preprofessional programs. There are more than thirty academic and residence buildings, including computer labs, an art gallery, a nearly 2,000-seat chapel/auditorium, performance hall, The Den, Hyson Campus Center, Visual Arts Center, Thorne Library/Learning Resource Center, Free Enterprise Business Center, and an AM-FM radio station. Academic degrees offered are associate, Bachelor of Arts, Bachelor of Science, Bachelor of Business Administration, Master of Ministry, and Master of Education degrees.

Student Body Total enrollment is 1,876, 58 percent women and 42 percent men, representing thirty-two states and six other countries. Traditional students number 1,352, and there are 986 students living on campus. Approximately 89 percent of all returning students receive financial aid.

Faculty The total number of faculty members is 139; 74 of them are full-time. Fifty-six faculty members hold doctoral degrees. The student-faculty ratio is 17.4:1. Average class size is 22.

Key Facilities Thorne Library/Learning Resource Center, built in 1996, contains 90,045 volumes, 3,382 microfiche, 560 periodicals (titles), and 5,989 nonprint items. Also available through the library is access to OhioLink, which provides electronic access to 24 million volumes. MVNC is committed to providing students with high-quality computing and technology platforms. MVNC maintains a high-speed communication network throughout the campus with direct access to the Internet and World Wide Web as well as to the most current computer technology, operating systems, application software, and state-of-the-art multimedia facilities. Students can access the Internet and e-mail from residence halls and apartment complexes. There are five general-use computer labs on campus as well as an academic support computer lab and a computer science lab. There are a total of 140 IBM and MacIntosh computers in the general-use labs.

Honorary Societies Alpha Chi and Phi Delta Lambda

Athletics MVNC offers a total of nine intercollegiate sports to students. Men participate in baseball, basketball, golf, and soccer, and women participate in basketball, soccer (1999–2000), softball, and volleyball. MVNC is a member of the American Mideast Conference and competes in the NAIA Division II and the NCAA Division I. Along with intercollegiate athletics there are nine intramural sports for students to enjoy. The Donoho Recreation Center offers basketball and volleyball courts and a weight room for student use. Also available to all students are aerobics classes, sand volleyball courts, tennis courts, and softball fields. Over the years, MVNC has established a winning tradition in many sports, most notably winning nine conference titles and going to the NAIA college world series once in baseball, having a 91-8 home record in the 1990s in volleyball, and advancing to the quarterfinals in the NAIA Division II national tournament in men's basketball.

Study Abroad The MVNC Honors Program offers the opportunity for students to study in England in conjunction with the Oxford Honors Program. There are also numerous other opportunities to study abroad that are not limited to honors students. There are occasions in which students are able to enroll in courses in other countries by studying independently and then transferring the credits back to MVNC. There are many opportunities to travel abroad as part of the curriculum of MVNC courses that are designed to expand personal and intellectual boundaries. MVNC's relationship with the Coalition of Christian Colleges and Universities opens doors for semesters abroad in China, Russia, Hungary, Latin America, England, and the Middle East.

Support Services The office of Academic Support and Retention provides support in the way of tutoring and academic counseling services for all students, as well as accommodation for students with learning and physical disabilities. Qualified tutors are made available to students in core courses as well as by appointment through the Academic Support Lab. Services for students with specific disabilities include special administration of tests, books on tape, note takers, special tutoring, personal academic counseling, and supplemental instruction.

Job Opportunities The Student Employment Office coordinates approximately 500 on-campus jobs for students along with community work opportunities. A portion of the earnings are generally applied to the student's college bill.

Tuition: $10,792 (1999–2000)

Room and board: $4041

Mandatory Fees: $430

Contact: Director: Dr. Thomas Mach, 800 Martinsburg Road, Mount Vernon, Ohio 43050; Telephone: 740-397-9000 Ext. 3711; Fax: 740-397-2769; E-mail: tmach@mvnc.edu; Web site: http://www.mvnc.edu

MOUNT WACHUSETT COMMUNITY COLLEGE

2 Pu G S Sc Tr

▼ Honors Program

The Honors Program at Mount Wachusett Community College provides an intellectually challenging academic experience, emphasizing stimulating courses, a high degree of student-faculty interaction, and an interdisciplinary perspective. Consequently, students who have demonstrated substantial potential in prior high school or college-level study are exposed to a highly individualized experience. As a result of the program, honors graduates will be better prepared to continue their advanced studies at colleges and universities throughout the country and to bring their academic talents to the attention of future employers.

The College's Honors Program is twelve years old, has an enrollment of about 40 students, graduates 12 to 16 students per year, and has been designated Commonwealth Honors Program status by the Massachusetts Board of Higher Education.

Participation Requirements: Participation in the program requires a 3.3 GPA. Honors students whose GPA drops below the required 3.3 will be allowed on probationary semester to continue the program and raise their cumulative average. All honors students are required to participate in certain classes, including an honors college–level English course, an honors college–level math course, and a lab science as well as two honors courses. These may be component courses based upon courses already required by a student's degree program or specially designed honors courses. A component course is any course already required by a student's degree program that has been deemed suitable as an honors component by the respective division. A component course is designed to require such additional activities as independent research, one-on-one tutorials, and/or a special project. Any particular component course is the result of a written agreement between a faculty member and a student that receives approval by the respective Division Dean. An Honors Colloquium is also required. Interdisciplinary in nature and team taught, past titles of these classes have been Gender Issues in American Society, Literature and Culture, Perspectives on Leadership, and Critical Thinking.

Students completing the Honors Program receive special recognition at graduation, and the title of Commonwealth Honors Scholar is designated on their official transcripts.

Scholarship Availability: Mount Wachusett Community College provides a tuition waiver to all honors students during their final semester, when they are completing both their honors and degree requirements with a minimum 3.3 average.

The Campus Context: Founded in 1963, Mount Wachusett Community College is located on a scenic 269-acre campus in north-central Massachusetts and is one of fifteen state-supported community colleges in Massachusetts. It has an enrollment of 2,000 students plus 1,400 in continuing education. There are twenty-four degree programs and twenty-five certificate programs.

Student Body Sixty-two percent of enrollees are women, and 13 percent of the students belong to ethnic minority groups. Thirty international students attend. All students commute, and 56 percent receive financial aid.

Faculty There are 71 full-time faculty members supported by a large number of adjunct faculty members. Eleven percent of full-time faculty members have doctoral degrees, and 87 percent have master's degrees.

Key Facilities The library contains 55,000 volumes and an adaptive computer center. There are sixty-two open-access computers for student use and a total of 524 desktop computers distributed throughout the campus.

Honorary Societies Phi Theta Kappa and Alpha Beta Gamma

Athletics The College does not have an intercollegiate sports program, but there is a fitness and wellness center located in a large athletic facility that is open to the community as well as the campus.

Study Abroad An International Education Committee has initiated overseas exchanges and study for college credit.

Support Services All facilities are fully wheelchair-accessible, and there is a disabilities counselor.

Job Opportunities The work-study program is available to all students.

Tuition: $25 for state residents, $230 for nonresidents, per credit (2001–02)

Mandatory Fees: $85 per semester plus $62 per credit

Contact: Coordinator: Dr. Thomas Malloy, 444 Green Street, Gardner, Massachusetts 01440-1000; Telephone: 508-632-6600; Fax: 508-630-3211; E-mail: t_malloy@mwcc.mass.edu; Web site: http://www.mwcc.mass.edu

---

Murray State University

4 Pu G M Sc Tr AA

▼ Honors Program

The Murray State University Honors Program is designed to enrich the educational experience of highly motivated students by increasing the opportunity for interacting with outstanding research faculty members, both in small class settings such as honors seminars and in ongoing research experiences.

The Honors Program seminars are courses specially designed to meet the needs of the most able students. Instruction takes various forms, but interactive learning is stressed. The honors seminars are distributed among the social sciences, fine arts, humanities, literature, natural sciences, and international affairs. Students typically enroll in one of these seminars throughout their college experience or until the honors sequence is completed.

There are approximately 212 students in the Honors Program out of a campus population of 9,100 students.

Participation Requirements: Honors students may be enrolled in any undergraduate curriculum. To remain in good standing in the Honors Program, a student must maintain a GPA 3.2 (on a 4.0 scale). A student who successfully completes all the requirements of the Honors Program (course sequence, language and mathematics competencies, travel abroad, senior thesis) is awarded the honors medallion, which is worn at Commencement. The honors diploma is also awarded at graduation and a citation on the academic transcript indicates successful matriculation in the Honors Program.

Admission Process: The program accepts entering first-year students who are National Merit Semifinalists or have a composite ACT score of 28 or above and rank in the top 10 percent of their high school class.

Scholarship Availability: Ten Presidential Scholarships are awarded annually to entering freshmen who generally have a composite ACT score of 28 or above and rank in the top 7 percent of their high school class. The award covers in-state tuition, fifteen meals per week, and a semiprivate dormitory room. Numerous departmental scholarships are also available.

The Campus Context: Murray State University was founded in 1922 and is located in the Jackson Purchase lake area of western Kentucky. The University's 232-acre main campus is in Murray, a city of 17,000, which has been highlighted as Kentucky's safest college town. The University is composed of five colleges: Business and Public Affairs; Education; Humanities and Fine Arts; Health Sciences and Human Services; and Science, Engineering, and Technology. The University also has a School of Agriculture. Eighty-five undergraduate majors are offered, leading to a Bachelor of Arts or Bachelor of Science degree.

Murray State houses a Center of Excellence for Reservoir Research and the Mid-America Remote Sensing Center, which studies satellite-generated data for resource management. Murray State has consistently been ranked among the top 25 percent of southern regional and liberal arts colleges in *U.S. News & World Report's* annual issue of "America's Best Colleges".

Student Body About 9,100 undergraduates and graduates are enrolled, the majority from the mid-central states of Kentucky, Illinois, Tennessee, Indiana, and Missouri. The campus has nine fraternities and six sororities.

Faculty There are 350 full-time teaching faculty members; 80 percent hold doctoral or terminal degrees. The student-faculty ratio is 24:1.

Key Facilities The University libraries contain approximately 850,000 resource materials, including 460,000 bound volumes, and subscribe to approximately 3,000 periodical and serial titles annually. Computer labs and terminals are located in each of the college's buildings and libraries as well as in the residential hall areas.

Honorary Societies Phi Eta Sigma and Alpha Chi

Athletics Murray State is a charter member of the Ohio Valley Conference and is a Division I member of the National Collegiate Athletic Association. There are eight men's and seven women's sports. Riflery is sponsored as a coeducational sport. Sponsored sports for men include football, basketball, baseball, golf, cross-country, tennis, indoor track, riflery, and outdoor track and field. Competition is available for women in cross-country, tennis, basketball, riflery, softball, and indoor and outdoor track and field. The Murray State rifle team has won three

Interpreting the symbols: **2**=two-year college, **4**=four-year college; **Pu**=public or state college, **Pr**=private college; **G**=general honors program; **D**=departmental honors program; **S**=small program (fewer than 100 students), **M**=midsize program (100 to 500 students), **L**=large program (more than 500 students); **Sc**=scholarships available in honors program; **Tr**=transfer students accepted into honors program; **HBC**=historically black college; **AA**=academic advisors; **GA**=graduate advisors; **FA**=fellowship advisors.

national championships, and one of its members won a gold medal at the 1984 Olympic Games.

Study Abroad The mission of Murray State University includes as a priority the commitment to international education in order to prepare students to function in an increasingly interdependent world. Murray State is the headquarters for the Kentucky Institute for International Studies, offering programs during the academic year and each summer in Austria, Ecuador, France, Germany, Italy, Mexico, and Spain. It is a member of the Cooperative Center for Studies in Britain, offering programs in the English-speaking countries of the British Commonwealth.

Support Services The Services for Students with Disabilities Program is located in the Learning Center. Services include securing textbooks on cassette tapes, test proctoring, tutorial assistance, guidance, and counseling.

Job Opportunities The University offers a wide variety of financial aid programs. The Financial Aid Office handles all requests for student employment.

Tuition: $1377 for state residents, $3711 for nonresidents, per semester (2001–02)

Room and Board: $3100

Contact: Director: Mark Malinauskas, 708 Fine Arts Building, Murray, Kentucky 42071; Tel: 502-762-3166; Fax: 502-762-3405; E-mail: mark.malinauskas@murraystate.edu

Nassau Community College

2 Pu G M Sc Tr

▼ Honors Program

Nassau's rigorous Honors Program, now in its twenty-third year, has about 250 students in the program. Students at the College who have a GPA of 3.4 or better are also invited to take some honors classes if seats are available, bringing the number of students taking honors to about 500. The program appeals to the many talented and highly motivated students who want to develop their potential more fully as they study for the associate degree. The transfer-oriented curriculum features at its core enriched work in English, history, calculus, foreign language, philosophy, computers, and the humanities and social sciences.

More than fifty sections of challenging honors classes are offered each term in addition to several special seminars of an interdisciplinary and/or multicultural nature. This umbrella program accommodates all majors at the College and enhances transferability. All students in the program are personally advised by the Coordinator of the Program who also writes all their letters of recommendation. In addition to the excellent honors faculty, consisting of almost all award-winning instructors for Excellence in Teaching, honors classes, because of their small size (no more than 22 students per class), allow for a great deal of personal interaction and discussion.

Over the years, as the program has continually grown and expanded, participants have the opportunity to supplement their academic work with honors-sponsored extracurricular activities such as the Adopt-A-Class Program, the Writing Literacy Project, the Selected Scholars Program, and the Honors Club and Journal, which provide creative outlets.

Another special feature of Nassau's Honors Program is its Honors Connection Program, an outreach vehicle to the high schools. The Connection Program provides a unique opportunity to highly motivated high school juniors and seniors to take college courses for credit on campus.

There are currently 471 students enrolled in the program.

Participation Requirements: To maintain membership in the program, students must keep up a 3.3 GPA each semester. The average GPA of each graduating class has been 3.6 or above. Students usually graduate with a minimum of 35 to 55 honors credits out of the mandatory 64 to 66 credits necessary for a degree. An H designation is noted on the transcript next to each honors course taken.

Admission Process: Freshmen are selected for the program based on their high school transcripts, which must reflect a 90 average in English, social studies, math, and science. Students already in attendance at Nassau can enter the program after their first semester if they have achieved a GPA of 3.4 or better and have been recommended by an instructor.

Scholarship Availability: For four graduating Honors Program participants, a scholarship, based on academic abilities and service to the program and community, is available. A special Honors and Awards Ceremony to honor graduates is held each May. At this time all honors graduates receive special certificates and the winners of the two Honors Program Scholarships are announced. Two scholarships are also available for incoming freshmen.

The Campus Context: Nassau is the largest of SUNY's thirty community colleges and enjoys a nationwide reputation for academic excellence and ease of transferability to four-year schools. Located in the heart of Nassau County, Garden City, the 225-acre campus is approximately 20 miles from New York City. The Commission on Higher Education of the Middle States Association of Colleges and Schools describes Nassau's faculty as "perhaps without rival across the community colleges of the nation." Nassau offers three degree programs: the A.A. in liberal arts; the A.S. in liberal arts and sciences, business and accounting, nursing, computers, and allied health science programs; and an A.A.S. degree in twenty-seven different areas. Also, Nassau offers fourteen different certificate programs.

Over the years the campus has expanded physically. In 1978, two new academic wings, a modern library, a physical education complex, and an administrative tower were added to the existing classroom and administrative buildings. To meet current demands, a third academic wing, including a new student center, theater, and art facilities, has been built and opened in 1996.

Student Body Since Nassau opened its doors in 1960, its enrollment has increased from 632 to the current figure of 22,500. It still maintains an attractive student-faculty ratio of 21:1. Of the 22,500 students, approximately 55 percent are women and 45 percent are men. More than a quarter of the student population is over the age of 25. All students commute to campus. Nassau does not have a formal fraternity/sorority system. It does, however, have a full range of clubs and organizations.

Faculty There are more than 700 full-time faculty members, the majority of whom have doctorates or terminal degrees in their fields.

Key Facilities The library houses approximately 180,000 volumes. College facilities include a general-purpose facility that is available to all members of the academic community and a state-of-the-art Academic Computer Center in the library. In addition, there are a variety of learning or help centers to assist students in all curricula available.

Honorary Society Phi Theta Kappa

Athletics Nassau has men's and women's teams in every sport. Expert coaching in some of the finest indoor and outdoor athletic facilities has made the men's and women's varsity teams dominant forces in the National Junior College Athletic Association. Individual athletes have gone on to prominence at senior colleges and universities, as well as in professional sports as coaches and physical education teachers.

Support Services A full range of services is available for disabled students, including full access to all classroom buildings, bus service, special counselors, and tutors.

Tuition: $1200 per semester (full-time) or $100 per credit (part-time) for (2001–02)

Mandatory Fees: $85

Contact: Coordinator: Professor Carol Farber, 1 Education Drive, Garden City, New York 11530; Telephone: 516-572-7194

Neosho County Community College

2 Pu G S Sc

▼ Honors Leadership Academy

The Neosho County Community College (NCCC) Honors Leadership Academy challenges students to take honors level courses, practice leadership skills, and experience being a member of an exciting learning community. The program, started in 2000, offers a unique and challenging learning experience to students with the desire to excel. Members of the Academy have the opportunity to enroll in special sections of select general education courses that provide a stimulating learning experience. Members are also encouraged to realize their full potential and responsibility for leadership by studying leadership skills that use current research and classic examples. They share these experiences as a member of an exciting and committed learning community. The Honors Leadership Academy is a member of the National Collegiate Honors Council and the Great Plains Honors Council.

To be accepted by the Academy, students must have a high school or college cumulative GPA of 3.5 or higher and an ACT score of 25 or above or an SAT score of 700 or above. To begin the admissions process, students must complete the general admissions requirements. Students must then fill out an Honors Leadership Academy application and write an essay that includes a biographical sketch with educational and personal goals, along with what the student feels they offer the Academy. A copy of ACT or SAT scores, high school and/or college transcripts, and three letters of recommendation must accompany the application and essay.

Participation Requirements: Members of the Academy must maintain a 3.5 GPA, enroll full-time in honors core courses, participate in Academy activities, and volunteer 20 hours of community or school service each semester. To graduate from NCCC as an Honors Scholar, students must complete 21 or more hours of honors courses, have a 3.5 GPA, and fulfill all other requirements of the Honors Leadership Academy.

Scholarship Availability: Neosho County Community College offers a variety of scholarships, as well as federal financial assistance. The College awards more than $1 million of assistance each year to help students fund their educational expenses. Students are encouraged to inquire about federal financial aid, academic scholarships, in-district scholarships, and endowment scholarships. Talent and program scholarships are available from one of the following areas: academic excellence challenge team, art, athletic training, baseball, basketball, coed cheerleading, dance, cross-country/track and field, debate, forensics, golf, Honor's Leadership Academy (Honors Program), music (vocal and instrumental), nursing, senior citizen, soccer, softball, sports information, technical and industrial, theater, volleyball, and wrestling.

The Campus Context: Neosho County Community College is a full-service community college located in the heart of Southeast Kansas. In 1936, NCCC opened its doors to 192 students in Chanute, Kansas, as a junior college. Today, NCCC serves more than 1,500 students each semester between the main campus in Chanute and the branch campus in Ottawa. As a full-service campus, NCCC students enjoy the convenience of on-campus housing, food service facilities, and a comprehensive student life program.

Student Body Student enrollment for fall 2001 was 1,519. Of these students, 30 percent were men and 70 percent were women. Members of minority groups account for 13 percent of the enrollment. Thirty-six percent of students are Neosho County residents, 53 percent are other Kansas residents, 6 percent are from out-of-state, and 5 percent are international students. Eighty-six percent of NCCC students are Caucasian, 6 percent African American, 1 percent Asian-Pacific, 2 percent Hispanic-Latino, 1 percent Native American, and 1 percent have other backgrounds.

Faculty There are 122 full and part-time faculty members. Ninety-six percent of full-time instructors hold a master's degree or higher. The student-teacher ratio is 16:1

Key Facilities The library houses 37,045 bound volumes; 118 periodical subscriptions; 3,668 titles on microfilm; 734 records, tapes, and CDs; and 3 online bibliographic sources. Computer facilities include more than 220 computers on campus and more than 138 networked computers housed within 10 computer labs. The CAVE (Center for Academic and Vocational Excellence) houses a top-of-the-line I-Mac lab with the latest in publishing and graphics software.

Honorary Society Phi Theta Kappa

Athletics NCCC offers a variety of collegiate athletic programs for men and woman and some have received state and national recognition. These programs include athletic training, baseball, basketball, coed cheerleading, dance, cross-country/track and field, golf, soccer, softball, volleyball, and wrestling. NCCC is a member of the Kansas Jayhawk Community College Conference.

Support Services NCCC's Center for Academic and Vocational Excellence (CAVE) is designed to help students achieve their educational goals. The CAVE provides many free services, including academic advising; career counseling; computer access, including Internet and e-mail; developmental, supplemental, and computer-aided instruction; GED and ABE instruction and testing; job posting and placement services; placement testing; pre-employment training; study areas; and tutoring. Many students qualify for NCCC's STARS program. This federally funded Student Support Services program helps participants who are first generation college students or have a disability meet federal income guidelines. The services include access to STARS computer lab; campus visits to universities; exposure to cultural activities; free tutoring; personal, career, and academic counseling; and workshops.

Tuition: $31 per credit hour for Kansas residents, $45 per credit hour for non-Kansas residents, and $100 per credit hour for international students (2001)

Room and Board: Campus housing with 19 meals per week was $3400 per year maximum (2001)

Mandatory Fees: $17 per credit hour for Kansas residents; $5 extra per credit hour for out-of-district students (2001)

Contact: Coordinator: Sara Harris, Honors Leadership Academy, 800 West 14th Street, Chanute, Kansas 66720; Telephone: 620-431-2820 Ext. 239

Neumann College

4 Pr S Sc Tr

▼ Honors Program

Founded in 1989, the Honors Program is two-tiered, including a Freshman Honors and a College Honors Program. There are 40 students currently enrolled in the program.

Interpreting the symbols: **2**=two-year college, **4**=four-year college; **Pu**=public or state college, **Pr**=private college; **G**=general honors program; **D**=departmental honors program; **S**=small program (fewer than 100 students), **M**=midsize program (100 to 500 students), **L**=large program (more than 500 students); **Sc**=scholarships available in honors program; **Tr**=transfer students accepted into honors program; **HBC**=historically black college; **AA**=academic advisors; **GA**=graduate advisors; **FA**=fellowship advisors.

Freshman Honors consists of two 6-credit multidisciplinary seminars that are team-taught, one in the fall and the other in the spring semester. The seminars incorporate aspects from the disciplines of philosophy, history, political science, psychology, literature, and communication arts. In addition, there is an emphasis on the integration of computer skills during both seminars. College Honors consists of a series of three multi-disciplinary seminars that are offered to sophomore, junior, and senior students. The seminar topics are selected primarily through student input.

The focus of the Honors Program is on innovative, experimental methodologies that seek new ways to develop critical thinking and communication skills. All honors seminars are discussion-oriented with small group work and in-class exercises devoted to critical thinking skill development. There are no lectures and no essay examinations, but rather students are evaluated on the development of strong oral and written communication and critical-thinking skills. The Director of Honors is also the adviser to honors students during their first year.

Participation Requirements: Completion of the College Honors Program requires an overall GPA of 3.6 or above in 9 credits of honors seminars. Those who successfully complete the program are awarded a certificate of completion at the Honors Convocation.

Admission Process: Freshman Honors usually consists of 20 students selected for their academic, extracurricular, and leadership achievements in high school; candidates must also be interviewed by the Director of Honors. While SAT I scores and class rank are considered, emphasis is given to those students who have demonstrated a potential for leadership and academic excellence. Entrance into College Honors requires an overall GPA of 3.4 or above and an interview with the Director of Honors. College honors seminars are limited to 20 students.

Scholarship Availability: Neumann College offers scholarships to students based on merit. All Honors students are on scholarship.

The Campus Context: Founded by the Sisters of St. Francis of Philadelphia, Neumann College is a small suburban campus in Delaware County, Pennsylvania, near Philadelphia, Pennsylvania, and Wilmington, Delaware. With a curriculum that balances the liberal arts and the professions, it now serves not only the community of the Delaware Valley but also a more diverse demographic population. Neumann offers the Bachelor of Arts degree, Bachelor of Science degree, and Liberal Studies degree. Neumann's most distinguished facility is the Living and Learning Complex. This brand-new, fully wired complex can house up to 500 students. It includes a fitness center with locker rooms, meeting rooms, and study rooms.

Student Body Undergraduate enrollment is 1,264; 368 (29 percent) are men. While 1,019 students are white, diversity comes from the 2 American Indian/Alaskan, 17 Asian/Pacific Islander, 150 African American, and 33 Hispanic students. Twenty-eight percent of students are residents, while 72 percent commute. Seventy-five percent of students receive financial aid. There are no fraternities or sororities.

Faculty Of the 146 faculty members, 51 are full-time. Sixty percent of full-time faculty members hold terminal degrees. The student-faculty ratio is 8:1.

Key Facilities The library houses 95,167 volumes and 1,695 periodical subscriptions. Computer facilities include seventy-five PCs.

Athletics The Neumann College intercollegiate athletic program provides students with the opportunity to compete with other colleges in eastern Pennsylvania, New Jersey, Delaware, and Maryland. The level of competition falls within the framework of Division III of the National Collegiate Athletic Association (NCAA). Varsity sports are offered to both men and women who compete in the Pennsylvania Athletic Conference and the Eastern College Athletic Conference.

Study Abroad Qualified students may study abroad by obtaining permission of the division chairperson to join a program sponsored by a regionally accredited American college or university. Such programs are offered as summer institutes and academic year programs.

Support Services Disabled students find all facilities handicapped accessible.

Job Opportunities There is a federally funded work-study program and direct employment by units of the College.

Tuition: $12,960 per year (full-time), $310 to $515 per credit according to program (part-time) (1998–99)

Mandatory Fees: $490

Contact: Director: Robert P. Case, One Neumann Drive, Aston, Pennsylvania 19014-1298; Telephone: 610-558-5578; Fax: 610-459-1370; E-mail: bcase@smtpgate.neumann.edu

New College of Florida

4 Pu C L Sc Tr

▼ Honors Program

New College professors advise and guide their students within a highly flexible program that emphasizes active learning and individual responsibility. Rather than follow a rigid standardized curriculum, each student works with a faculty sponsor to negotiate academic contracts. These contracts outline the student's choice of courses and design of independent work based primarily on individual goals and major requirements within the context of the liberal arts curriculum.

Professors provide students with direct advice for individual improvement by assessing course work and independent study projects through written evaluations rather than letter grades. Faculty sponsors receive these evaluations as well, enabling them to advise their students according to their specific strengths and needs.

The College builds independent work into each year of the academic program. Students pursue additional individualized research through tutorials, which are independent undertakings that are counted as courses. Each year, nearly 240 classroom courses are offered and 500 independent study projects are arranged. In addition, faculty members approve nearly 700 individual and small group tutorials.

Fourteen students were selected for research experiences for undergraduates programs sponsored by the National Science Foundation in 2001. In that same year, 9 students were selected for other summer funded research projects and 25 presented papers at the National Conference on Undergraduate Research. The program's focus on research has made New College a leading per capita producer of alumni who go on to obtain doctoral degrees. Graduates include William Thurston (winner, Fields Medal in mathematics), Esther Barrazone (President, Chatham College), and Anita Allen (Professor of Law and Philosophy, University of Pennsylvania).

Concentrations include anthropology, art history, British and American literature, biology, chemistry, classics, economics, environmental studies, French language and literature, German language and literature, history, humanities, international and area studies, literature, mathematics, medieval and Renaissance studies, music, natural sciences, philosophy, physics, political science, psychology, public policy, religion, Russian language and literature, social sciences, sociology, Spanish language and literature, urban studies, and visual arts. Partial concentrations are available in theater and gender studies. With faculty permission, students also may design special topic and interdisciplinary majors.

Campus activities are chiefly initiated by students. Student government funds more than 90 groups and functions per year, including social justice events, hobby clubs, parties, concerts, religious organizations, and informal athletic teams. Sports tend to be inclusive. With the exception of the men's league softball team, anyone may play regardless of athletic talent.

New College was founded in 1960 as a private liberal arts college for the academically talented. It joined Florida's State University System in 1975. As a public honors college, it continues to offer the rigorous program and intimate environment of a highly competitive private college, but at the modest cost of attending a state-sponsored university. Current student enrollment is 634 and the student-faculty ratio is 11:1. Classes are generally quite small and 60 percent of classes are less than 20 students.

Participation Requirements: Requirements for a student's area of concentration and general breadth of curriculum are individually negotiated with the faculty sponsor, as are the requirements for successful completion of each academic contract and independent study project.

In order to graduate, each student must successfully complete at least seven semester-long academic contracts, three independent study projects, and a senior thesis with an oral baccalaureate examination before a faculty committee and interested members of the campus community. The examination represents the collegial responsibility of the faculty that no student may graduate until the quality of their educational achievement has been closely examined and approved by three faculty members.

The state of Florida additionally requires successful completion of the College Level Academic Skills Test (CLAST). Most students are exempted from this requirement on the basis of college entrance exam scores.

The New College faculty, in executive session at the last faculty meeting of the academic year, votes conferral of the Bachelor of Arts degree for each member of the graduating class.

Admission Process: For freshman admission, the factors in descending order of importance are as follows: the level of difficulty of courses, grades, application essays, exam scores (SAT I or ACT), letters of recommendation, and activities. Rank in class, if provided, is considered to provide context for the student's record. An interview is encouraged but optional, with the exception of early admission candidates.

For transfer applicants, recommendations are more important than the exam scores. Additional TOEFL scores are required for international applicants for whom English is not the first language (computer-based test minimum score of 220; paper-based test score of 560).

For the middle 50 percent of the freshman class of 2001, SAT I scores were 1270–1410, ACT scores were 27–31, and the weighted GPA, as calculated by New College, was 3.6–4.1.

Students are admitted on a rolling basis, beginning in September. The deadline to apply for spring semester entry for transfer students only is December 1. The College reserves the right to cancel the spring admission cycle in order not to exceed enrollment goals. The deadline to complete the admission application for fall semester entry is May 1.

Scholarship Availability: The application deadline for priority scholarship consideration for fall applicants is February 1. Scholarships are for four years, minus any transfer credit assigned, and contingent upon continued funding and compliance with academic renewal criteria. A list of the scholarships and their qualification criteria is as follows: To qualify for the New College Excellence Award, a National Merit finalist or National Achievement finalist must select New College as the first-choice school according to NMSC procedures. The NMSC stipend will be supplemented to guarantee a scholarship of $30,000 ($7500 per year). To qualify, a National Hispanic Scholar must be recognized through the College Board National Hispanic Scholar Recognition Program. Applicants must be entering freshmen only. The New College Heritage Award amounts to $20,000 ($5000 per year). Heritage Scholars are selected for excellence in community citizenship. An additional application and interview process are required for this award. The Partial Out-of-State Tuition Exemption has a minimum of $12,000 ($3000 per year) and is contingent upon funding by the Florida Legislature. The New College Admissions Committee Award offers a minimum of $4000 ($1000 per year). The New College Foundation Scholarship provides a minimum of $4000 ($1000 per year). The IB Scholar Award is for $10,000 ($2500 per year). Twenty scholarships are reserved for international baccalaureate students who received the New College Junior Scholar Award in the junior year of high school. Applicants must be entering freshmen only.

The Campus Context: New College's home is a 144-acre bayfront campus. The College lies within a public educational, cultural, and historic district that includes the John and Mable Ringling Museum of Art and the Asolo Theatre. The district's four Gilded Age mansions, three on the campus and one on the adjoining museum grounds, are listed in the National Register of Historic Places. The campus mansions are in regular use as classrooms, offices, and reception areas. *Money* magazine has named New College's hometown one of the six Best Places to Live in America, as well as the Best Small City in America. Sarasota has many fine cultural institutions, including the Florida West Coast Symphony, an opera company, a ballet company, and Van Wezel Performing Arts Hall. Downtown has an art cinema and a 20-screen megaplex, and is studded with restaurants, art galleries, antique stores, and consignment shops.

Student Body New College's enrollment is strictly full-time and undergraduate. Roughly 60 percent of the 634 students live on campus. There are no fraternities or sororities.

Faculty The total number of full-time faculty is 58. Ninety-eight percent hold a Ph.D. or terminal degree in their field.

Key Facilities The Jane Bancroft Cook Library, completed in 1986, has been honored by the American Institute of Architects for its outstanding design. Its diverse resources, congenial atmosphere, and distinguished collections and programs have all been structured to foster independent work. More than 500 students can study in Cook Library at the same time. Facilities include classrooms, lounges, display areas, research carrels, a special collections room, two group study rooms, and the Thesis Room (the College's archive that holds each graduate's senior project). The Media and Educational Technology Center, located on the second floor, houses a language lab with computerized, interactive language learning stations; a production lab; music listening labs; preview rooms for small group conferences and media review; and an electronic classroom with interactive live teleconferencing.

The campus also has new science facilities–the Heiser Natural Sciences Complex and the Pritzker Marine Biology Research Center were designed to enhance collaborations between faculty members and students. The Pritzker Center's saltwater tank effluent is cleaned by means of an artificial wetland, planned and constructed as part of a senior thesis project by Trina Hofreiter '01.

Free Internet access, e-mail accounts, and software training workshops are provided for all students. Each residence hall room has Ethernet access to the campus network. There are six computer labs on campus and two are student-run, student-funded labs with Macintosh computers available for 24-hour student use. computers in the Macintosh lab have a few basic

Interpreting the symbols: **2**=two-year college, **4**=four-year college; **Pu**=public or state college, **Pr**=private college; **G**=general honors program; **D**=departmental honors program; **S**=small program (fewer than 100 students), **M**=midsize program (100 to 500 students), **L**=large program (more than 500 students); **Sc**=scholarships available in honors program; **Tr**=transfer students accepted into honors program; **HBC**=historically black college; **AA**=academic advisors; **GA**=graduate advisors; **FA**=fellowship advisors.

applications that most users should need, which include Appleworks 6, Internet Explorer, other Internet applications, and games. In addition, some computers also have Microsoft Word. The Publications Office computers have desktop publishing and graphics software (Quark, Adobe Photoshop, and Illustrator). The standard applications of the other four computer labs include the Microsoft Office package (Word, Excel, Access, PowerPoint, FrontPage) and Internet services (Internet Explorer, FTP, Telnet). Two of these labs are reserved for classes and workshops.

Study Abroad New College students have studied in Africa, Asia, and Latin America with the School for International Training; at the University of Glasgow and University of Newcastle; in London and Florence with Florida State University's study centers; in Budapest with the Budapest Mathematics Seminar; in the study-abroad programs of other U.S. universities through New College's membership in the National Student Exchange; and in many other locations through a variety of additional institutions and programs.

Support Services Support services for students with disabilities are facilitated and arranged through the Office of Student Affairs.

Job Opportunities The Career Center lists details on job opportunities in the area and facilitates links with local organizations and the alumni mentoring network for internships. The Career Center holds an annual job fair and an annual volunteer/internship fair, as well as workshops on interviewing, writing resumes, and applying to graduate or professional school. Students are sometimes hired by the academic divisions for assistance in the labs or to provide help with study sessions.

Tuition: The 2001–02 tuition and fees for Florida residents total $2863. For out-of-state residents, the total was $12,329.

Room and Board: The 2001–02 standard room and board fees totaled $5184. Off-campus residents are required to participate in a reduced cafeteria plan that totals $283.

Contact: Provost: Dr. Charlene Callahan, Cook Hall, 5700 North Tamiami Trail, Sarasota, Florida 34243-2197; Telephone: 941-359-4320; Fax: 941-359-4655; E-mail: callahan@ncf.edu; Web site: http://www.ncf.edu

New Jersey Institute of Technology

4 Pu G L Sc Tr AA

▼ Albert Dorman Honors College

The Albert Dorman Honors College at the New Jersey Institute of Technology (NJIT) prepares exceptional students to become leaders in the fields of engineering, architecture, management, medicine, science, and government. Students are offered special honors classes and seminars taught by dedicated faculty members, a wide array of research opportunities, a special lounge, separate study and computing areas, guaranteed on-campus housing, and a series of colloquia at which speakers and panels discuss current scientific and social issues of the day. All students, from both in and out of the state, receive merit-based scholarship packages, which are often supplemented by university, corporate, or endowed grants. Classes are small (generally 20 to 30 students) and are taught by professors chosen for their ability to work especially well with the most talented students.

In the first year, each student creates an Individual Education Plan in a Freshman Seminar and meets with an honors adviser. Starting in the second year, each student is advised by a professor from his or her major department. Special honors courses, approximately one fourth of each student's degree program, are offered both in the specific curricula required by each of the five degree-granting colleges and the courses required university-wide. An important component of many students' development is provided by research done with professors at NJIT or the University of Medicine and Dentistry, by hands-on internships either at major corporations (including Exxon, IBM, Allied Signal, and Merck) or at smaller but important specialized firms, or by student-designed and implemented grants. In addition to conventional programs, students may be admitted to accelerated programs in medicine, dentistry, optometry, and law or to a special five-year bachelor's/master's program that includes up to two summers of paid internship experience.

Growing from the Honors Program founded in 1985, the Honors College (1994) now numbers 525 students. More than 110 first-year students and 50 transfer or second-/third-year students are enrolled each year. Approximately 1 in 6 new first-year students at NJIT is a member of the Albert Dorman Honors College.

Participation Requirements: Each student selects eight lower-division honors courses from offerings in mathematics, science, computer science, and the liberal arts and three upper-division honors courses—an honors humanities seminar; an honors course in either management or science, technology, and society (STS); and an honors capstone course in the student's major. Architecture students and all students who enter after the first year take a slightly modified program. All students are required to maintain at least a 3.2 GPA (3.4 for the accelerated medical program) and to attend sixteen colloquia.

Each student's membership in the Honors College is recognized at graduation and noted on his or her diploma.

Admission Process: In addition to completing the NJIT application, students must file a one-page honors application. All qualified candidates are interviewed by the Honors College. Applicants are asked to have a minimum combined SAT I score of 1250 (1400 for the accelerated medical program), to rank approximately in the top 15 percent of their class (top 10 percent for all accelerated programs in medicine, dentistry, optometry, and law), and to have participated in activities in or out of school. Exceptions to the required rank and SAT I scores are sometimes made for students who have attended exceptional high schools or have participated in especially noteworthy activities. Admission is not automatically granted to those who meet the minimum requirements. In 2001, first-year students on average had combined SAT I scores of 1315 and ranked in the top 7 percent in their high schools. Transfer students who have been members of honors programs/colleges or who have a GPA of at least 3.5 and have engaged in extracurricular/leadership activities are encouraged to apply. For such students, college performance outweighs SAT I scores and high school class rank.

Scholarship Availability: All Honors College students receive a supplementary merit scholarship package. Awards depend on SAT I scores and class rank and may include a partial room grant.

The Campus Context: NJIT is New Jersey's public technological university. Located 10 miles from Manhattan near the transportation hub of the nation's largest urban region, it shares the University Heights section of Newark with three other educational institutions: Rutgers University, Essex County College, and the University of Medicine and Dentistry of New Jersey.

Founded in 1881, NJIT today has a student enrollment of more than 8,800; of these, about 5,800 are undergraduate students in six academic divisions: Newark College of Engineering (1919), the School of Architecture (1975), the School of Management (1998), the College of Science and Liberal Arts (1982), the College of Computing Sciences (2001), and the Albert Dorman Honors College (1994). The Rutgers-Newark campus, with more than 10,000 students, is adjacent to NJIT, allowing the development of jointly sponsored academic programs that draw upon the faculty and facilities of both universities. This close relationship has created many other benefits, including online cross-registration, mutual library privileges, and shared cultural and social activities.

NJIT awards bachelor's degrees in applied physics; architecture; biology; biomedical engineering; chemical engineering; chemistry; civil engineering; computer engineering; computer science; electrical engineering; engineering science (pre-optometry, pre-medicine, predentistry); engineering technology (transfer only, concentrations in computers, construction/contracting, electrical, manufacturing, mechanical, surveying, and telecommunications); environmental engineering; environmental science; geoscience engineering; history; human-computer interaction; industrial engineering; information systems; information technology; management; mathematics; mechanical engineering; professional and technical communication; science, technology, and society (interdisciplinary course work in humanities, social and natural sciences, and engineering or architecture); and statistics and actuarial science.

Known for the quality of its academic programs, NJIT has become a leader in interdisciplinary applied research. Research expenditures, funded by leading corporations, foundations, government agencies, and other organizations, now exceed $50 million annually. At NJIT, research and public service centers are an essential part of education in such fields as environmental science and engineering, manufacturing, electronics and communications, information technology, material science and engineering, transportation, infrastructure, and architecture and building sciences.

Student Body Of NJIT's 5,800 undergraduates, 4,000 are full-time day students. Of these, 1,100, including half of the freshman class, live on campus in the University's four residence halls. Nineteen fraternities and eight sororities are active on campus. Ranked fourth in the nation by *U.S. News & World Report* for campus diversity, NJIT has a student body that is 22 percent women, 11.5 percent African American, 11.4 percent Hispanic, 22.1 percent Asian/Pacific Islander, and 14.5 percent international.

Faculty The University has a full-time faculty of 404 and an adjunct staff of 200. Ninety-eight percent of faculty members have the highest academic degree attainable in their field. The student-faculty ratio is 15:1.

Key Facilities The University's Robert W. Van Houten Library houses a collection of 160,000 books and 1,000 journal subscriptions and provides electronic access to more than 10,000 journals.

Ranked as a "perennially most wired" university by *Yahoo! Internet Life,* NJIT is one of the most computing-intensive campuses in the nation. NJIT has constructed its own information superhighway comprising 400 miles of fiber-optic cable and 651 miles of twisted pair cables that reach every office, classroom, and laboratory on the University's 45-acre campus. All on-campus student housing is hard-wired. Each new full-time freshman receives a computer to use throughout his/her undergraduate years, and all students and faculty members have access to the University's virtual private network, providing access to e-mail, the Internet, and NJIT's online resources from any location at any time.

Athletics NJIT offers thirteen NCAA Division II varsity sports: basketball, fencing, soccer, swimming, tennis, and volleyball for men and women and baseball for men. All students can participate in club sports and an extensive intramural program. The Fleisher Athletic Center includes three gymnasiums; a fitness center containing computer-controlled biking equipment, Cybex resistance units, and an indoor track; a weight room; four racquetball/squash courts; a martial arts center; a six-lane swimming pool; and an aerobics/dance studio. Facilities also include four outdoor, lighted hard-court tennis courts and the soccer/baseball field, a lighted natural-grass facility with seating for 1,000 spectators.

Support Services At the University Learning Center, trained undergraduate and graduate tutors and professionals provide a wide array of academic support services, including one-on-one and small group tutoring and study skills and test-taking workshops. The Instructional Video Resource Room allows students to receive hands-on tutoring in computer science courses.

Additional support for students is provided by the Constance A. Murray Women's Center, the Counseling Center, the student-run Stop-In Center, and the Office of Career Development Services.

Job Opportunities NJIT is located at the hub of the nation's most vibrant and active corporate environment. The headquarters and facilities of many leading companies of the world, including AT&T, Exxon, Merck, Prudential, and Nabisco, are located nearby. This provides significant opportunities for cooperative education, internships, and part-time employment. NJIT's cooperative education programs are among the most active in the nation. A total of 449 students worked in cooperative education positions and internships during 2001, earning more than $4.8 million with 350 employers. Another 2,600 students earned $4.7 million in student employment on and off campus.

Tuition: $6158 for residents, $10,810 for nonresidents per year (2001–02)

Room and board: $7490

Mandatory Fees: $1042

Contact: Director: Dr. David Reibstein, Associate Dean, University Heights, Newark, New Jersey 07102-1982; Telephone: 973-642-4448; E-mail: honors @njit.edu; Web site: http://honors.njit.edu

New Mexico State University

4 Pu D L Tr

▼ University Honors Program

The University Honors Program provides motivated undergraduate students with opportunities to broaden and enrich their academic programs. In small classes taught by master teachers, honors students engage in lively discussion and collaborative investigation of interdisciplinary topics. By taking honors courses, students also work toward completing general education requirements and disciplinary requirements in their majors. Honors courses are challenging, but the individual attention students receive makes the honors experience worthwhile.

Approximately 1,000 students are enrolled in the program each year.

Participation Requirements: After completing the 18 required credits of honors work with an overall GPA between 3.5 and 3.74, students earn the right to graduate with University Honors. If students attain an overall average of 3.75 or better, including the required honors credits, students are eligible to graduate with Distinction in University Honors. Both forms of recognition are noted on diplomas and transcripts, as well as in Commencement programs. Each student is also awarded a certificate of distinction. Upon completion of two upper-division courses, students receive recognition on the Commencement program along with a certificate of distinction.

Admission Process: An entering freshman must have a minimum composite ACT score of 26 to qualify; other students need a 3.5 GPA to enroll. For new freshmen, continued participation is contingent on maintaining a GPA of 3.3; sophomores, juniors, and seniors must maintain a GPA of at least 3.5. Students who do not meet minimum eligibility requirements may petition the Honors Director for admission to the program. A student may enter the program from the first semester of freshman year until the beginning of the second semester of the sophomore year.

Interpreting the symbols: **2**=two-year college, **4**=four-year college; **Pu**=public or state college, **Pr**=private college; **G**=general honors program; **D**=departmental honors program; **S**=small program (fewer than 100 students), **M**=midsize program (100 to 500 students), **L**=large program (more than 500 students); **Sc**=scholarships available in honors program; **Tr**=transfer students accepted into honors program; **HBC**=historically black college; **AA**=academic advisors; **GA**=graduate advisors; **FA**=fellowship advisors.

Scholarship Availability: New Mexico State University administers an extensive program of grants, scholarships, and loans. The awarding of grants and loans is based on need, while the awarding of scholarships is based mainly on academic ability and, in some cases, need.

The Campus Context: New Mexico State University is a campus of several colleges: Agriculture and Home Economics, Arts and Sciences, Business Administration and Economics, Education, Human and Community Services, and the Graduate School. A total of 149 degree programs are offered.

Student Body Of the 15,643 students, 7,847 are men and 7,796 are women. Diversity is demonstrated by the 4,901 Hispanic, 499 Native American, 327 African American, and 145 Asian-American students. The University enrolls 743 international students. About 14 percent receive graduate assistantships; 20.2 percent of the students receive various grants; 18 percent receive scholarships, graduate fellowships, waivers, and child care; 4.6 percent participate in work-study; and 7.2 percent engage in on-campus employment.

Faculty There are a total of 656 faculty members, making the student-faculty ratio 18.6:1. Approximately 50 faculty members from all of the colleges teach in the Honors Program.

Honorary Societies Phi Kappa Phi and Golden Key

Key Facilities The library houses 1 million volumes. There are five computer facilities operating both DOS-based and Macintosh computers.

Tuition: $1503 for state residents, $5007 for nonresidents, per semester (2001–02)

Room and Board: $2148 minimum

Contact: Director: Dr. William Eamon, Las Cruces, New Mexico 88003; Telephone: 505-646-2005; Fax: 505-646-1755; E-mail: weamon@nmsu.edu; Web site: http://www.nmsu.edu/~honors

NEWBERRY COLLEGE

4 Pr S Sc Tr

▼ Summerland Honors Program

At Newberry College, students and faculty members walk together on the path of knowledge and along the way they bring to life a distinctive learning community. The Summerland Honors Program accentuates all that is best about living and studying at Newberry College, a place where people are willing to seek innovative and memorable educational opportunities and experiences by taking risks inside and outside of the classroom. The Summerland Honors community is a perfect haven for students to search for understanding and to consider a myriad of questions old and new.

In many ways the human story has been and will continue to be a quest for identity. How have we understood what it means to be human? The Summerland Honors Program is structured upon the theme, Quest for Identity, and will afford opportunities to explore this essential question from a number of vantage points. Indeed, each of the three years of paired, interdisciplinary, and team-taught seminars focuses on a particular perspective concerning this quest for identity. Year one studies the question from the perspective of the arts and humanities. Year two examines the question through the lens of the natural sciences. The third year probes the quest for identity from the perspective of the social sciences.

In each of the six honors seminars, students will also participate in enrichment activities designed to engage them actively in their learning and to provide opportunities for them to apply their knowledge in service to the campus and the local community. Finally, an integrative capstone course in the senior year will ask students to reflect and build on the preceding three-year experience. Courses taken in the honors program will fulfill core requirements in the humanities, natural sciences and social sciences, as appropriate.

Members of the Summerland Honors community learn to weave a tapestry of understanding around any topic and to layer insight upon insight thereby achieving a breadth and a depth of understanding. Participants become independent learners who take responsibility for leading and sustaining study and discussion on any topic. The service-learning component provides even greater opportunities for growth and rewards. Summerland Honors Program graduates are prepared and motivated for active citizenship, empowered and ready to assume positions of advocacy for social change as a way to make life more productive and meaningful.

An innovative curriculum and a spirited learning community enable participants to realize Newberry College's institutional goals. While educating the whole person, the Summerland Honors Program promotes the development of communication skills (oral and written), the development of critical-thinking skills, and emphasizes an awareness of ethical concerns.

Fall 1996 marked the inaugural year of the program, which is limited each year to 20 participants in the freshmen class. There are a total of 45 to 50 students currently enrolled in the program.

Participation Requirements: In order to graduate from the Honors Program, a student must hold a cumulative 3.25 GPA in the Honors Program and in the general curriculum. Six Summerland Honors Seminars are required to graduate from the program. Students must also complete the Senior Capstone Experience. Successful completion of the Honors Program requirements is noted at graduation, is recorded on the student's transcript, and is designated on the student's diploma.

Admission Process: Admission to the Summerland Honors Program is based on multidimensional criteria, including high school GPA, high school class rank, SAT I/ACT equivalent scores, and interviews with members of the Newberry College community. Applications are received from February to May.

Scholarship Availability: Most Summerland Honors students receive Founder Scholarships and Presidential Scholarships; however, they are eligible for other Newberry College scholarships.

The Campus Context: A private undergraduate liberal arts institution established in 1856, Newberry College is affiliated with the Evangelical Lutheran Church in America. With a mission focused on educating the whole person, Newberry epitomizes the typical small-college amenities of personal attention, easy rapport between students and faculty, and a supportive environment for academic, personal, and social development. Degree programs include the B.A. (seventeen majors), B.S. (thirteen majors), B.M., and B.M.E.

Student Body There are 731 undergraduates enrolled; 48 percent are women. International students account for 2 percent of total undergraduates. Ninety percent of students receive some form of financial aid. There are three social sororities, six social fraternities, two academic sororities, and five academic fraternities.

Faculty There are 41 full-time faculty members (supplemented by adjunct faculty members); 65 percent have doctoral degrees. The student-faculty ratio is 11:1.

Key Facilities The library houses 100,000 volumes. The campus has one computer lab with thirty units that have Internet and e-mail access.

Athletics Intercollegiate athletics for men include baseball, basketball, football, golf, soccer, and tennis. Athletics for women include basketball, golf, softball, tennis, and volleyball. Newberry College also has intramural football, baseball, and softball.

Job Opportunities Students are also offered a variety of work-study opportunities on campus.

Tuition: $15,000 per year (2001–02)

Room and Board: $4470 for a double-occupancy room, $5470 for a private room

Mandatory Fees: $400

Contact: Director: Dr. Jesse L. Scott, 2100 College Street, Newberry, South Carolina 29108; Telephone: 803-276-5010; Fax: 803-321-5627; E-mail: honors@newberry.edu; Web site: http://newberry.edu

Newbury College

2+2 Pr G S Sc Tr

▼ Honors Program

The Newbury College Honors Program is open to the top 10 to 15 percent of students enrolled in the College, regardless of major. Admission to the program is available to entering students or students who have completed one semester at Newbury.

Students take one course per semester (3 or 4 credit hours) as an honors course, although they may elect to take more than one course per semester and a seminar in their final year. Honors sections are integrated into the regular course offerings, and in addition to regular course work, students are expected to produce a significant report or presentation on a topic of their choice, growing out of the course work and prepared throughout the semester in close cooperation with the mentoring faculty member. The Honors Project must contain significant creative and critical aspects and, where appropriate, a self-reflective component.

The Honors Seminar is a multidisciplinary seminar with a different area of focus each session. Students may be required to undertake off-campus visits as part of the seminar, which culminates in a final project designed to incorporate all honors work done during the student's career at Newbury.

The emphasis of the program is on participation in a learning community of closely connected students and faculty members working together.

The first students were admitted for the fall 1996 semester. Currently, there are 25 students in the program. Expected enrollment is approximately 70 students (about 8 percent of the total full-time student enrollment).

Admission Process: Entering students are invited to join the program after a review of their admission application by the Honors Committee. Students who have completed a semester at Newbury may be recommended by a faculty member.

Scholarship Availability: Many honors students typically receive one or two substantial merit-based scholarships.

The Campus Context: Newbury College is located in Brookline, a largely residential suburb of Boston. It is within walking distance of mass transit service to Boston. Newbury offers both associate and bachelor's degree programs.

Student Body Undergraduate day enrollment is 912 students, 51 percent of whom are women. The ethnic distribution is 57 percent white, 22 percent international, 13 percent African American, 4 percent Hispanic, and 4 percent Asian/Pacific Islander.

Faculty There are 47 full-time and 64 part-time faculty members.

Key Facilities Five computer labs on campus offer both Mac- and IBM-based platforms. The Academic Resource Center provides learning support for all students on campus.

Tuition: $12,300 per year (1998–99)

Room and Board: $6750 minimum

Mandatory Fees: $600

Contact: Coordinator: Roberta Allison, 129 Fisher Avenue, Brookline, Massachusetts 02445; Telephone: 617-730-7086; Fax: 617-738-2497

Norfolk State University

4 Pu G M Tr HBC

▼ Honors Program

The Honors Program, now in its second decade, offers an enriched and challenging program of study for full-time students who show exceptional academic potential. All students taking special Honors (H) courses are considered part of the program, which is open to all majors. Students completing 15 or 30 hours of honors courses receive special diplomas inscribed "Parsons Vice Presidential Scholar" and "Parsons Presidential Scholar," respectively.

Benefits of the program include the following: small enriched courses taught in-depth; the opportunity to work closely with top faculty members; seminars and lectures given by visiting scholars; opportunities to present original research at state, regional, and national collegiate honors council meetings; invitations to civic and cultural events, with opportunities to meet famous leaders and artists; recognition of work at the annual Honors Luncheon; a computer lab; and rewards in employment and graduate school.

Honors courses are generally taught seminar-style in the Parsons Honors Center. Most require more independent work from students and all offer participation in cocurricular and extracurricular trips and activities.

The program currently enrolls about 200 students.

Participation Requirements: Most honors courses are core curriculum offerings required for all majors (e.g., English 101 H). There are also major courses in specific departments (e.g., Accounting 201 H) and interdisciplinary seminars (e.g., GST 345/346 H and 445/446 H), with topics that change each semester. Students graduating as Parsons Vice Presidential Scholars (15 hours) or Parsons Presidential Scholars (30 hours) must take at least one such seminar and have a minimum 3.0 GPA upon graduation (with no grade lower than a C in an honors course and at least a 3.0 GPA for all honors courses taken). Parsons Presidential Scholars are also required to participate in community service for academic credit. Parsons Vice Presidential Scholar and Parsons Presidential Scholar are both diploma citations.

Admission Process: Students may be invited to enter the Honors Program in the following circumstances: upon admission as freshmen according to high school records (3.0 GPA minimum and at least 900 combined SAT I score) and other indicators of academic proficiency (these students are expected to complete the 30-hour sequence of courses and required seminars) or as sophomores, juniors, or seniors having achieved a 3.5 or above GPA for all courses completed in the curriculum (or 3.0 by permission of the instructor).

Scholarship Availability: The Honors Program currently offers $250 per semester to eligible students. Students who participate in the program also have an advantage in competing for regular University scholarships. Students accepting Presidential Scholarships or Board of Visitor Scholarships from the University are required to participate in the Honors Program. For complete information, students should contact the Financial Aid Office directly.

The Campus Context: Norfolk State University (NSU) is composed of the following five colleges: the School of Liberal Arts, the School of Business and Entrepreneurship, the School of Educa-

Interpreting the symbols: **2**=two-year college, **4**=four-year college; **Pu**=public or state college, **Pr**=private college; **G**=general honors program; **D**=departmental honors program; **S**=small program (fewer than 100 students), **M**=midsize program (100 to 500 students), **L**=large program (more than 500 students); **Sc**=scholarships available in honors program; **Tr**=transfer students accepted into honors program; **HBC**=historically black college; **AA**=academic advisors; **GA**=graduate advisors; **FA**=fellowship advisors.

tion, the School of Social Work, and the School of Science and Technology. Associate, baccalaureate, master's, and doctoral degrees are offered in more than sixty areas. Among the distinguished facilities are the L. Douglas Wilder Performing Arts Center (a 1,900-seat state-of-the-art theater), the Center for Materials Research Lab, the Brambleton Community Outreach Center, and nationally ranked ROTC and NROTC programs and facilities.

Student Body Undergraduate enrollment is approximately 37 percent men and 63 percent women. The ethnic distribution is 89 percent black, 8 percent white, and 3 percent other. There are 89 international students. Residents make up 34 percent of the student population and commuters, 66 percent. Eighty-eight percent of the students receive financial aid. There are nineteen fraternities/sororities, sixteen honor societies, four literary societies, and three military societies.

Faculty Of the 466 faculty members, 300 are full-time. The student-faculty ratio is 15:1.

Key Facilities The University computer system consists of an campus area network (NSULAN), which is an Ethernet-based LAN using DECNET, TCP/IP, NT, and PATHWORKS. There are approximately 300 access stations in nine student laboratories on campus. There are seven dial-in telephone lines. All students and faculty and staff members are provided free and unrestricted access to all academic computing resources.

Honorary Societies Golden Key, Alpha Kappa Mu

Athletics The Department of Athletics is currently a member of the National Collegiate Athletic Association (NCAA) and the Mid-Eastern Athletic Conference (MEAC). There are varsity teams in baseball (men), softball (women), basketball (men and women), football, cross-country (men and women), track and field (men and women), indoor track (men and women), volleyball (women), tennis (men and women), bowling (women), and wrestling (men). Women's soccer was added in fall 2000.

Support Services The University has an Assistive Technology Lab for students with disabilities and those who wish to learn more about assistive technology products and applications. Resources and equipment include Zoomtext, Naturally Speaking, a Duxbury Braille Translator and Braille printer, talking calculators, and voice-activated recorders. Accommodations can also be made through Disability Services with instructors of disabled students.

Job Opportunities Work-study opportunities are available.

Tuition: $2814 (12 hours) for state residents, $8262 (12 hours) for nonresidents, per year (2001–02)

Room and Board: $5466

Contact: Director: Dr. Page R. Laws, 700 Park Avenue, Norfolk, Virginia 23504; Telephone: 757-823-8208 or 757-823-2303; Fax: 757-823-2302; E-mail: honors@nsu.edu; Web site: http://www.nsu.edu/programs/honors/

North Carolina Agricultural and Technical State University

4 Pu G M Sc Tr HBC AA

▼ Honors Program

The Honors Program of North Carolina Agricultural and Technical State University (A&T) exemplifies the institution's commitment to excellence in teaching and learning. The program offers high-achieving students a challenging but supportive academic, cultural, and leadership environment that stimulates them to reach their full potential as independent learners and future decision makers. Its approach to education stresses close interaction between faculty members and students, supports intellectual experimentation, raises students' commitment to demanding work, provides opportunities for leadership development, and stimulates cross-cultural awareness and appreciation. The Honors Program also provides a stimulus for faculty members who teach honors courses to rethink old approaches and experiment with new ones, thus contributing to improved instruction across the curriculum. The program currently has nearly 400 members.

Participation Requirements: There are two tracks that students can pursue in the A&T Honors Program. The Honors in General Education track requires at total of 24 hours of classes. Of these, a minimum of 9 hours must be earned in low-enrollment honors sections of regular general education classes. Students may take a maximum of 9 hours in regular general education classes for honors credit by making arrangements with the instructor to carry out additional activities that enrich the academic experience beyond that of a non-honors student taking the same class. These enrichment activities must be identified in an Honors Contract. Finally, students must take 6 hours of low-enrollment honors seminars that are usually interdisciplinary in nature and always approach topics from a broad viewpoint. Students must maintain a 3.5 cumulative GPA to remain in and graduate from the Honors in General Education track.

The second track is Honors in the Major. It, too, is a 24-hour program. Students are required to take 18 hours of major classes for honors credit, either by enrolling in low-enrollment honors courses or by earning honors credit through the contract process. Students in the Honors in the Major track must also take 6 hours of honors seminars. Finally, they must complete a senior thesis or creative project and present their work in a public setting. To remain in and graduate from the Honors in the Major track, students must maintain a 3.5 cumulative GPA.

Students who complete both tracks of the Honors Program are required to take only 6 hours of honors seminars, which may be earned while enrolled in either or both honors tracks.

Students who join the Honors Program as incoming freshmen must complete 12 hours of honors courses by the end of their first year in order to remain in the program. Likewise, a student in the program must pursue a minimum of one course for honors credit each semester to remain in the program. A minimum cumulative GPA of 3.5 is also required at all times. Students who fall below a 3.5 have one semester to bring their grades back up. Students whose cumulative GPA falls below 3.5 for two semesters in a row are dismissed from the program.

Admission Process: Entering freshmen are invited to join the Honors Program if they have a cumulative weighted GPA of at least 3.7 on a 4.0 scale and an SAT combined score of at least 1050 or an ACT composite score of 22. Some entering students, including high school valedictorians and salutatorians, National Merit and Achievement Scholarship finalists, and graduates of the North Carolina School of Science and Mathematics, are automatically invited to join the program. Students who score a 1200 on the SAT or 29 on the ACT are also automatically eligible to join the Honors Program. Students already at A&T are eligible to join the Honors Program once they have compiled a cumulative GPA of 3.5 and completed a minimum of 12 hours of classes. Transfer students who were members of the honors program at another accredited institution are immediately eligible to join the A&T Honors Program. Transfer students who were not in an honors program can join the A&T Honors Program as soon as they complete a minimum of 12 A&T hours of classes with a cumulative GPA of 3.5.

Scholarship Availability: The University awards a wide range of Chancellor and other merit-based scholarships. Many of the awardees are members of the Honors Program.

The Campus Context: North Carolina Agricultural and Technical State University was founded in 1891 as one of two land-grant institutions in the state. Originally, it was established to provide postsecondary education and training for black students. Today, A&T is a comprehensive institution of higher education with an integrated faculty and student body and is a constituent institution of the University of North Carolina. It offers degrees at the baccalaureate, master's, and doctoral levels. There are eighty-three degree programs at the undergraduate level offered by A&T's five schools and two colleges, including the Schools of Agriculture, Business and Economics, Education, Nursing, and Technology and the Colleges of Engineering and Arts and Sciences. Among its distinguished facilities are a new state-of-the-art library, the Fort Interdisciplinary Research Center, the Mattye Reed African Heritage Center, and the Taylor Art Gallery. The 200-acre campus is just nine blocks from downtown Greensboro, a thriving city of about 200,000 located midway between Washington, D.C., and Atlanta. Well-known for its quality of life, the city's mix of industry, cultural activities, and institutions of higher learning contributes to the vibrant intellectual life on the A&T campus.

Student Body Undergraduate enrollment was 6,850 in 2000–01. Slightly more than half of the students are women. Ninety-two percent of the student body is African American and 5 percent is white. About one third of the undergraduate student body lives on campus. Nearly 90 percent of all undergraduates receive financial aid. There are four sororities and five fraternities at A&T.

Faculty There are 461 full-time faculty members, of whom 80 percent have terminal degrees. The student-faculty ratio is 15:1.

Key Facilities The new high-tech Bluford Library houses almost 500,000 volumes plus nearly a million microforms and extensive collections of government documents and audiovisuals. The library subscribes to more than 4,000 periodicals. In addition, the library is aggressively expanding its electronic resources, many of which are accessible through the campus computer network. There are eight University-operated computer labs as well as many others located in departments and colleges around the campus. The Computer Center provides numerous training programs for students throughout the year.

Honorary Societies Alpha Lambda Delta, Golden Key, Alpha Chi, and Alpha Kappa Mu

Athletics A&T is a member of the NCAA Division I and the Mid-Eastern Athletic Conference (MEAC). It fields teams in nine major sports, including football, basketball, baseball, volleyball, bowling, softball, swimming, track, and tennis. The University also sponsors a large intramural program.

Study Abroad The University encourages students to travel and study abroad. The Honors Program awards up to 6 hours of honors credit for course work completed overseas. Study abroad is coordinated through the Office of International Programs.

Support Services The Office of Disability Support Services ensures ready accessibility to all academic programs, services, and activities to all A&T students. The office arranges for any needed support services, reasonable accommodations, or academic adjustments to ensure that disabled students may succeed in their chosen field of study.

Job Opportunities A&T aggressively pursues opportunities for student internships and co-ops with major companies and government agencies. The Office of Career Services holds a nationally recognized career fair each fall that attracts recruiters from more than 200 companies and government agencies seeking students for permanent, internship, summer, and co-op positions. It also sponsors additional job fairs for students interested in careers in nursing, teaching, or state government agencies. There are also many on-campus job opportunities, often funded by research grants or federal work-study aid.

Tuition: $1222 per year for North Carolina residents, $9354 per year for out-of-state students (2001–02)

Room and Board: $4250

Mandatory Fees: $1017

Contact: Director of the A&T Honors Program: Dr. Peter Meyers, 329 Gibbs Hall, North Carolina Agricultural and Technical State University, 1601 East Market Street, Greensboro, North Carolina 27411; Telephone: 336-256-0277; Fax: 336-334-7837; E-mail: peterm@ncat.edu; Web site: http://www.ncat.edu/~honors

North Carolina State University

4 Pu G D L Sc Tr

▼ University Honors Program

The University Honors Program at North Carolina State University (NC State) is the program of opportunity for high-achieving students who wish to make the most of their undergraduate educational experiences. The University Honors Program enables students to develop an exceptionally rich college curriculum that opens up new possibilities for active, innovative learning and for engagement in the full work of a major research university.

The University Honors Program emphasizes student initiative, cross-disciplinary approaches to learning, and creative problem solving. Honors students achieve these goals through participation in small classes, small Honors Seminars, common housing opportunities, honors advising, a four-year Honors Plan of Study, cultural events, research opportunities, study abroad, and other honors support services.

Students invited into the University Honors Program at NC State have a full four years of honors opportunities open to them. In the first two years, students participate in Honors in General Education, taking the Honors Colloquia, Honors Seminars, and honors sections of regular classes. Students take at least three Honors Seminars, participate in a research experience under close faculty supervision, and complete at least four honors sections of regular classes. Students in the junior and senior years get more deeply into the subject of their major by participating in Honors in the Discipline, leading to a degree with honors and other special recognition.

At the heart of the honors academic experience are interdisciplinary honors seminars and opportunities for research. The seminars are unique, special topic courses available only to students in the University Honors Program. The seminars, which promote active and engaged learning, are small and often team-taught by nationally recognized senior faculty members. Students explore how knowledge is discovered, created, valued, and put to use. Honors students at NC State also engage in the research mission of the University from the very beginning, working with faculty members in labs and on research projects of their own design. The University Honors Program provides substantial grants so that students may continue their research over the summer months.

In addition, University Honors Program students have access to special honors sections of courses that meet general education requirements in nineteen academic departments across the University. Students may also develop special contracts for honors credit to earn honors recognition in any academic course offered by the University.

The University Honors Program also houses the Office of Undergraduate Fellowship Advising, which supports students competing for nationally competitive scholarships and fellowships, including the Rhodes, Marshall, Mitchell, and Gates

Interpreting the symbols: **2**=two-year college, **4**=four-year college; **Pu**=public or state college, **Pr**=private college; **G**=general honors program; **D**=departmental honors program; **S**=small program (fewer than 100 students), **M**=midsize program (100 to 500 students), **L**=large program (more than 500 students); **Sc**=scholarships available in honors program; **Tr**=transfer students accepted into honors program; **HBC**=historically black college; **AA**=academic advisors; **GA**=graduate advisors; **FA**=fellowship advisors.

Scholarships. Special funds, advising, and other incentives are available so that students will have an undergraduate experience that is as broadening and enriching as it is challenging and engaging.

NC State's University Honors Program has been in existence since 2000 and currently involves 800–1,000 students.

Participation Requirements: The University Honors Program sponsors Honors in General Education (typically in the first two years) and Honors in the Discipline (typically in the junior and senior years). Students in Honors in General Education are expected to develop and pursue an Honors Academic Plan of Study, complete at least 24 hours of honors course work including three or more Honors Seminars and a Research or Independent Study project, and complete Honors 101 and 102: Introduction to Honors at NC State University, while maintaining a GPA of 3.25 or higher. Students in Honors in the Discipline complete an additional 9 or more hours of honors course work in the discipline of their major, while maintaining a GPA of 3.25 or higher.

Admission Process: Applicants for freshman admission to NC State University are invited to participate in the University Honors Program after they have been accepted to the University, based on an assessment of their potential for exceptional academic performance and success in the University Honors Program. Students are chosen for admission based on a review of six criteria: 1) the rigor of the high school curriculum, 2) high school GPA, 3) high school class rank, 4) writing skills, 5) background or interest in research, and 6) evidence of initiative and creativity. Priority in admission is given to students who have pursued a challenging high school curriculum, who show evidence of being creative and able to thrive in an environment that stresses opportunity and challenge, who show potential and interest in research, who rank in the top 10 percent of their classes, and whose SAT scores are in the top 10 percent of test takers. While there are no fixed standards for admission, recently, the average total SAT score for students accepted into the University Honors Program has been higher than 1375 and the average high school GPA has been higher than 4.5 (weighted grades). Students admitted to the freshman class at NC State who are not accepted into the University Honors Program through the regular process of admission are invited to submit applications for admission. Undergraduate students who prove their academic ability by performance during their first or subsequent semesters at NC State University may also apply for admission to the University Honors Program.

Scholarship Availability: North Carolina State University offers a competitive scholarship program for entering freshmen to recognize and encourage exceptional academic ability and talent. The NC State Merit Scholarship Competition includes both University-wide (noncurriculum specific) scholarships and merit scholarships given by the individual colleges and academic departments for students planning to enter their specific majors. In addition, the Park Scholarship Program, supported by the Roy Park Foundation, awards at least sixty full scholarships to North Carolina State University each year. These four-year awards cover tuition and fees, room and board, textbooks, academic supplies, and living expenses, plus a stipend for a personal computer and other enrichment activities. For all honors students, the University is committed to meeting the demonstrated financial need of all incoming freshmen who participate in honors and who meet the Financial Aid Preference deadline.

The Campus Context: North Carolina State University, located in the Research Triangle of piedmont North Carolina, is one of the nation's premier research universities. Building on its land-grant heritage, NC State has emerged as a national leader in science, engineering and technology while developing outstanding programs in the humanities, education, business, and design. NC State's library system has been named a research library of the future for its innovative use of technology at the service of learning and is rated thirty-fifth among research university libraries nationwide. The University also supports a thriving arts community, with award-winning theater, music, dance, and arts programs. The University's Centennial Campus is a national leader in developing partnerships between education and industry, providing students with unique opportunities to combine academic learning with engagement in current issues and opportunities.

NC State is located 1 mile from North Carolina's state capitol in Raleigh, a city recognized for its quality of life, economic vitality, and cultural richness. The home of North Carolina's symphony orchestra and state art, history, and science museums, Raleigh provides NC State's students with a wide variety of enrichment opportunities. Set amid the rolling hills of the Piedmont, Raleigh is almost equidistant from the state's historic and scenic Outer Banks and the Great Smoky Mountains.

NC State is composed of twelve colleges: the College of Agriculture and Life Sciences, the College of Design, the College of Education, the College of Engineering, the College of Natural Resources, the College of Humanities and Social Sciences, the College of Management, the College of Physical and Mathematical Sciences, the College of Textiles, the First-Year College, the Graduate School, and the College of Veterinary Medicine.

More than 100 baccalaureate degree programs are offered, providing the University's diverse student body with a wide array of curricular opportunities. Cooperative relationships with other colleges and universities in Raleigh, Durham, and Chapel Hill contribute to NC State's position at the center of one of the nation's richest and most diverse academic communities.

Student Body Undergraduate enrollment is approximately 22,500 students, 57 percent of whom are men. The ethnic distribution is approximately 80 percent white, 10 percent African American, 5 percent Asian/Pacific Islander, 2 percent Hispanic, and 1 percent Native American. There are about 335 international students who make up 2 percent of the population. Approximately 40 percent of the students are residents; the remaining 60 percent are commuters. There are twenty-three fraternities and six sororities.

Faculty Of the more than 1,700 faculty members, 1,604 are full-time, and 97 percent have terminal degrees.

Key Facilities The library houses approximately 2.9 million volumes, more than 3.7 million microform titles, 37,000 serial subscriptions, and a large and growing array of online bibliographic services. Computer facilities are numerous. All student residential rooms are linked to a campus network, and there is a computer purchase plan available. There are more than 5,000 computers available for student use in the computer center, computer labs, research center, learning resources center, classrooms, library, student center, and dorms; all provide access to the main academic computer, off-campus computing facilities, e-mail, online services, and the Internet. The campus is rapidly becoming wireless-accessible to the Internet. Staffed computer labs on campus are open 24 hours a day and provide training in the use of computers and software.

Honorary Societies Phi Beta Kappa, Phi Eta Sigma, Phi Kappa Phi, Sigma Xi, and numerous departmental and disciplinary honor societies

Athletics In athletics, NCSU belongs to Atlantic Coast Conference and competes in NCAA Division I (except football, which is I-A). NC State's athletic teams have been successful over the years, winning numerous conference championships and the NCAA Championship in men's basketball in 1974 and 1983. There are twelve varsity sports for men, eleven for women, plus cheerleading and dance team. Men's varsity sports include soccer, cross-country, football, basketball, swimming, riflery, indoor track, wrestling, golf, tennis, track, and baseball. Varsity sports for women are soccer, cross-country, golf, riflery, volleyball, basketball, indoor track, swimming, gymnastics, track, and tennis. The University also maintains an extensive program of intramural-recreational sports administered by the Department of Physical Education; more than seventeen intramural sports and thirty sports clubs/activities are supported.

Study Abroad NC State sponsors a variety of study abroad programs, including Semesters in Ghana and Spain and Summer Programs in Oxford, London, Vienna, Prague, Berlin, Florence, New Delhi, Ghana, Tanzania, Guatemala, Mexico, Peru, and Japan. In addition, NC State participates in ISEP and programs sponsored by other institutions.

Support Services The Office of Disability Services (DSS) provides assistance based on each student's particular needs and circumstances. Students may receive priority scheduling, tutors, priority housing, test accommodations, reader/typing services, van transportation, note takers, interpreters, tapes of lectures, parking, and additional learning resources. The Student Organization for Disability Awareness meets periodically to provide mutual support and suggestions to the DSS office.

Job Opportunities Hundreds of work-study opportunities are available on campus: many academic departments provide paid research and other work opportunities to students and service units (University Housing, University Dining, Campus Student Center) also provide numerous opportunities for employment. In addition, NC State supports a special Honors Co-operative Education program, enabling students to work in career-related sites with minimal disruption of their academic progress. Also, many students readily find work opportunities in the Raleigh area.

Tuition: $2328 for state residents, $12,320 for nonresidents, per year (2001–02)

Room and Board: $5700

Mandatory fees: $947 (2001–02)

Contact: Interim Director: John N. Wall, Campus Box 8610, Raleigh, North Carolina 27695; Telephone: 919-513-4078; Fax: 919-513-4392; E-mail: university_honors@ncsu.edu; Web site: http://www.ncsu.edu/university_honors/

North Central College

4 Pr G M Sc Tr AA FA

▼ College Scholars Program

The College Scholars Program was created to attract students capable of superior work and to provide them with the opportunity to have a challenging and broadening intellectual experience. Course work emphasizes interdisciplinary study, individualized research, and other special projects. The five-course History of Ideas seminar series is of particular interest to freshmen and sophomores. The seminar format encourages lively discussion of intellectually engaging issues ranging from the classical era through the twentieth century. College Scholars are advised by specially selected honors advisers, usually in their major, and are encouraged to develop independent studies and take designated honors courses. Members of the College Scholars Program are encouraged to become involved in Wingspread Scholars (a regional conference program) and the Richter Fellowship Program (funding for independent study work). Social activities throughout the academic year encourage contact with professors and other students to provide intellectual stimulation and support.

The College Scholars Program at North Central College (NCC) was established in 1982. There are approximately 200 members.

Participation Requirements: To sustain membership in the program, a student must maintain a minimum GPA of 3.0 and earn at least 3 hours of honors work each year.

College Scholar is a title bestowed upon graduating students who have completed 30 hours of honors work, including at least one Honors Seminar at the 300 or 400 level and a Senior Honors Thesis (which is hardcover bound and shelved in the College library). College Scholars Participant is a title bestowed upon graduating students who have completed at least 18 hours of honors credit, including one Honors Seminar at the 300 or 400 level. A grade of A or B must be earned for honors credit to be awarded. All honors course work is noted on the student's transcript.

Admission Process: Admission to the program is by invitation (entering freshmen) and by application (throughout the academic year). Acceptance of entering freshmen is based on the student's ACT/SAT I score, high school record, NCC Admission Counselor's recommendation, and results of a personal interview. Other applicants are selected using demonstrated interest in the program, ACT/SAT I scores, high school and/or college GPA, and a recommendation from an NCC professor.

Transfer students who participated in an honors program at another institution are admitted to the College Scholars Program upon submission of an application. They may bring honors credit to NCC from a similar program, provided they were in good standing at the institution from which they are transferring.

Scholarship Availability: Freshmen applying to North Central College may qualify for Presidential Scholarships (academic) in amounts from $3000 to $16,000; transfer students may qualify for renewable academic scholarships of up to $10,000 and/or one of ten Phi Theta Kappa (a community college honor society) scholarships of $2000 awarded each year. Performing arts scholarships are awarded in amounts up to $4500. Endowed departmental scholarships are available.

The Campus Context: Founded in 1861, North Central College is an independent, comprehensive college of the liberal arts and sciences known nationally for excellence in teaching and for the quality of its faculty and students. The 54-acre campus is located in a beautiful old residential area of Naperville, a city of more than 130,000. Naperville is located in the heart of the rapidly growing high-technology Illinois Research and Development Corridor that is bounded by Argonne National Laboratory on the east and Fermi National Accelerator Laboratory on the west and is 29 miles from downtown Chicago.

The College awards Bachelor of Arts and Bachelor of Science degrees in fifty majors from twenty-two academic departments and offers preprofessional programs in engineering, law, and medicine in cooperation with major research universities. The College offers master's degrees in five areas.

Student Body North Central enrolls nearly 1,800 full-time undergraduates. About 1,000 live in College-owned housing, and about 900 live off campus or commute. An additional 350 undergraduates are enrolled part-time in day, evening, and weekend classes. Of the undergraduate students, 45 percent are men; 12 percent are members of minority groups. There are 36 undergraduate (2 graduate) international students representing twenty-one countries. More than 450 students are enrolled in graduate programs. Ninety-four percent of freshmen receive financial aid. North Central College does not have social fraternities or sororities; however, there are more than forty student organizations and performing groups active on campus. NCC also maintains an award-winning student-staffed radio station and several student publications.

Faculty Eighty percent of the 119 full-time teaching faculty members have a doctorate or highest degree in their field, and faculty members also serve as the academic advisers to students. There are 26 half-time faculty members, most of whom have a long-standing relationship with the College. The student-faculty ratio is 14:1.

Key Facilities Oesterle Library offers students and faculty members ready access to more than 23 million items in forty-five college

Interpreting the symbols: **2**=two-year college, **4**=four-year college; **Pu**=public or state college, **Pr**=private college; **G**=general honors program; **D**=departmental honors program; **S**=small program (fewer than 100 students), **M**=midsize program (100 to 500 students), **L**=large program (more than 500 students); **Sc**=scholarships available in honors program; **Tr**=transfer students accepted into honors program; **HBC**=historically black college; **AA**=academic advisors; **GA**=graduate advisors; **FA**=fellowship advisors.

and university libraries in Illinois, in addition to more than 142,000 volumes in the stacks. The library also provides access to numerous information resources via its Web site and each term offers a full schedule of library instruction, classes, and orientations.

All students and faculty and staff members have access to a voice, video, and data network, including full Internet access from their residence halls, classrooms, computer laboratories, and offices. Recently, 10 MB of Web space was made available to every enrolled students for personal pages, and 5 MB of hard drive space for classes. In the sciences, students can use molecular modeling software, a 300-MHz magnetic resonance spectrometer, a gas chromatograph/mass spectrometer, a liquid chromatograph, a pulsed nitrogen laser, a phase-constant video microscope, PCR thermal cyclers, and an environmental chamber to pursue laboratory research. A few years ago, the College raised funds to complete a $2-million challenge to purchase and create an endowment for scientific equipment, supported by a $500,000 commitment from the Kresge Foundation. North Central also has state-of-the-art language and market research laboratories.

Athletics North Central College is a member of the NCAA Division III and the College Conference of Illinois and Wisconsin (CCIW). Student athletes participate in nineteen intercollegiate sports. Men compete in baseball, basketball, cross-country, football, golf, soccer, swimming, tennis, track and field, and wrestling; women compete in basketball, cross-country, golf, soccer, softball, swimming, tennis, track and field, and volleyball.

Study Abroad International study is encouraged at North Central. Through its association with the Institute of International Education, the College maintains current information concerning at least 200 domestically accredited programs in more than sixty countries. Formal study-abroad programs exist with Imperial College at the University of London, England, and with Asesoria Gerencial in San Jose, Costa Rica. Students are encouraged to apply for a Richter Fellowship to fund international study. This is a distinctive program that grants up to $5000 for independent study projects of unusual merit and scope. Smaller grants are available for projects on or off campus.

Support Services North Central College has made and continues to make modifications to its facilities and programs so as to provide access for those individuals with disabilities.

Job Opportunities Students are employed on campus in a variety of areas, including academic offices, the business office, residence halls, food service, maintenance, the activity center, and the library.

Tuition: $16,995 per year (2001–02)

Room and Board: $5724

Contact: Director: Dr. Thomas F. Sawyer, College Scholars Program, 30 North Brainard Street, Naperville, Illinois 60540; Telephone: 630-637-5330; Fax: 630-637-5121; E-mail: tfs@noctrl.edu

NORTH DAKOTA STATE UNIVERSITY

4 Pu G S Sc Tr

▼ Scholars Program

An interdisciplinary alternative for highly motivated students, the North Dakota State University (NDSU) Scholars Program provides an opportunity for the lively exchange of ideas within and outside the classroom. Scholars enroll in a colloquium (small discussion class) each of the first three years. Though the themes vary, the basic structure and format of the colloquia in all three years remain the same: discussion, reading, and writing focused on themes and ideas that can be explored through several different disciplines. During the fourth year, scholars complete an independent study project or senior thesis, usually in their major field, with the guidance of a faculty member in the discipline and a Scholars Program adviser.

Although the program is housed in the College of Humanities and Social Sciences, scholars have primary majors in the range of disciplines offered at North Dakota State, such as engineering, chemistry, computer science, pharmacy, and architecture. The program also has a Student Council that organizes a variety of cocurricular and social activities, including a series of lectures by faculty members outside the Scholars Program, trips to galleries and theatres, volunteer activities, and informal social activities.

Begun in 1969, the program currently has 60 active students.

Participation Requirements: Students must take one 3-credit colloquium each of the first six semesters of the program. A senior thesis is required in the fourth year.

Admission Process: First-year scholars are selected on the basis of high school grades, a writing sample, and/or recommendations and interviews. After the first semester, students from any college within the University may apply to join the program. The deadline for applying to the program is April 1.

Scholarship Availability: Two $1000 scholarships are available to scholars having majors within the College of Humanities and Social Sciences. Several annual awards ($300–$400), regardless of major, are granted based on academic performance.

The Campus Context: North Dakota State University is composed of seven colleges: Agriculture, Business Administration, Engineering and Architecture, Human Development and Education, Humanities and Social Sciences, Pharmacy, and Sciences and Mathematics. The University offers twenty-one doctoral programs, forty-eight master's programs, and eighty-one bachelor's programs. There are noteworthy research facilities in chemistry, biochemistry, pharmacy, psychology, and plant sciences. The Institute for Regional Studies is also well known.

Student Body The student population is 57 percent men and 43 percent women. International students constitute 4 percent of the total student body. Sixty-five percent of the students receive financial aid.

Faculty Of the 404 faculty members, 88 percent hold terminal degrees. The student-faculty ratio in undergraduate classes is 19:1.

Key Facilities The library houses 450,000 bound volumes and 3,450 serials. Information Technology Services provides a complete range of computer services (UNIX/DOS/Macintosh).

Athletics In athletics, North Dakota State University is in the NCAA Division II and also participates in the North Central Intercollegiate Athletic Conference. Men's sports include baseball, basketball, football, cross-country, gold wrestling, and indoor/outdoor track; women's sports are basketball, cross-country, indoor/outdoor track, softball, and volleyball.

Study Abroad Study abroad is available through direct exchange programs in Mexico, the Netherlands, and Australia. Many other arrangements are available through individual departments.

Tuition: $2566 for state residents, $6300 for nonresidents, per year; tuition for nonresidents eligible for the Western Undergraduate Exchange and Western Interstate Commission for Higher Education programs and residents of Manitoba, Montana, Saskatchewan, and South Dakota: $3684 per year full-time, $153 per credit part-time; Minnesota resident tuition: $2752 per year full-time, $114 per credit part-time

Room and Board: $3246

Mandatory Fees: $330

Contact: Director: Paul Homan, P.O. Box 5075, Fargo, North Dakota 58105; Telephone: 701-231-8852; Fax: 701-231-1047; E-mail: phoman@plains.nodak.edu; Web site: http://www.acm.ndsu.nodak.edu/~nuschlrs/index.html

North Harris College

2 Pu G S Sc Tr

▼ Honors Program

The mission of the North Harris College Honors Program is to augment existing programs and to reaffirm the College's commitment to excellence by identifying, recruiting, and challenging academically motivated students, providing enrichment and flexibility to develop full student potential while offering faculty members the opportunity for renewal and innovation. The Honors Program offers enrichment of course materials and the freedom to work independently and collaboratively with faculty members who encourage lively, engaging discourse and activity outside the classroom.

Honors credit is earned through special contracts and classes with a coordinator who is committed to an open-ended approach to learning. Students are encouraged to contribute extensively and creatively through small group interaction, seminars, laboratories, oral reports, special research projects, informal discussions, and both individual and group projects.

The Honors Student Organization (HSO) is in charge of workshop presentations, debates, and seminars each semester. The organization selects and coordinates presentations for Honors Day each semester. In addition, its members operate the Honors Program booth at Oktoberfest and Spring Fling and write the honors newsletter, *The Honors Scholar.* Representatives from the organization serve on the honors committee.

In addition to the Honors Student Organization's activities, interaction among honors students is promoted through attendance at honors conventions and the pizza luncheon each midsemester.

The Honors Scholar Community Service Program provides an opportunity for honors students to make a difference in their communities by volunteering their time in a community service activity. Any honors student who has or plans to complete at least 9 hours of honors credit is eligible to participate in the program.

The program began in 1993 and averages approximately 80 students each semester.

Participation Requirements: Upon successfully completing 15 hours of honors contract credit with a GPA of 3.5 or better, students receive the designation Honors Program Graduate on their diploma and transcript, special recognition at graduation, and a medallion commemorating the event.

To graduate as an honors scholar, a student must complete at least 9 honors credit hours with at least a 3.5 GPA as well as 25 hours of community service. With the completion of 15 honor credit hours with a minimum 3.5 GPA and completion of 25 hours of community service, a student may qualify to graduate as an Honors Scholar with Distinction.

Admission Process: The Honors Program is open to all students. Any student may attempt an honors contract or class any semester they are enrolled at North Harris College with permission of the instructor in his or her regularly scheduled class and acceptance by the honors coordinator for that contract.

Scholarship Availability: Any student in the Honors Program who is carrying 6 or more college credit hours, has at least a 3.5 GPA, and is attempting at least one honors contract is eligible for the Honors Program scholarship after the completion of 12 hours of college credit. The scholarships are awarded to the top students who apply, based on their GPAs. The scholarship may be used for tuition, books, or fees and related educational expenses for the following semester. The Honors Program scholarship is renewable for an additional two semesters with reapplication.

The Campus Context: North Harris College, nestled on more than 200 acres of piney woods, is the original and largest North Harris Montgomery Community College District campus. Founded in 1973, it offers more than sixty programs of study, including university transfer and numerous education courses and programs. North Harris College is keenly focused on leading-edge technology in emerging technical job fields. The College is also north Houston's center for the arts, including a juried art gallery and a comprehensive fine arts curriculum with a calendar of free and low-cost theater, music, arts events, and exhibits. In addition, North Harris College has opened two full-service satellite centers serving as community outreach sites that help students start a degree or certificate program they can finish at the main campus.

Student Body The total enrollment is 9,171 students, 40 percent men and 60 percent women. The ethnic distribution is 54 percent white, 16 percent black, 19 percent Hispanic, and 9 percent Asian. The average age of the students is 26.8. Out-of-state and international students account for 3 percent of the population.

Faculty The total faculty numbers between 500 and 525, with 178 full-time faculty members. More than 92 percent of the full-time faculty members have advanced degrees.

Key Facilities The library holds more than 65,000 books, approximately 101,700 government documents, 247,500 microfilm units, 3,000 audiovisual units, and more than 700 periodical subscriptions. The business division has 200 computers in nine labs.

Honorary Societies Phi Theta Kappa

Athletics North Harris College's men's and women's club soccer teams compete with other colleges and universities that are members of the Texas Collegiate Soccer League. This program is organized and financed by the students who participate, with some support from the Recreational Sports Department. Recently, a women's basketball club (called the Rimshakers) was started that has been competing with other schools on a competitive but informal basis. The main emphasis at the College is on intramurals and informal recreation. Leagues, tournaments, fun runs, and other special events are offered.

Support Services North Harris College is committed to providing quality services for students with disabilities. Reasonable accommodations are prescribed through the Disability Services Office, based upon the individual needs of each student. The College offers a variety of accommodations and support services, including interpreting services, diagnostic services, counseling services, modified testing, etc. The College has an excellent Assistive Technology Lab, where students receive training in the use of the technology as well as access to the equipment, both in the lab and in class. Some equipment is available for students to check out. Types of technology include a scanner/reader, Braille translation, voice activated computer, screen readers, personal amplification systems, closed-circuit televisions, refreshable Braille as well as tape recorders, magnifiers, and writing devices. Appointments may also be scheduled through the lab for readers, scribes, and student assistants. The lab is responsible for converting print text into alternate format, as needed.

Job Opportunities The North Harris College business and applied technology departments offer more than twenty coop programs. Internships are available in biology, child development, emergency medicine, management, and office administration. Capstone experiences are offered in art, biology, criminal justice, drama, electronics, and government. On-campus employment is open to credit students who are enrolled for at least 1 credit hour and who have a desire to work on campus. College Work-Study

Interpreting the symbols: **2**=two-year college, **4**=four-year college; **Pu**=public or state college, **Pr**=private college; **G**=general honors program; **D**=departmental honors program; **S**=small program (fewer than 100 students), **M**=midsize program (100 to 500 students), **L**=large program (more than 500 students); **Sc**=scholarships available in honors program; **Tr**=transfer students accepted into honors program; **HBC**=historically black college; **AA**=academic advisors; **GA**=graduate advisors; **FA**=fellowship advisors.

programs are need-based programs, including the Federal Work-Study and Texas College Work-Study programs.

Tuition: $26 per credit hour for district residents, $66 per credit hour for state residents, $217 per credit hour for nonresidents (2001–02)

Mandatory Fees: $5 per credit hour plus $12 registration fee

Contact: Chair: Sandy Deabler, North Harris College Honors Office A-168, 2700 W. W. Thorne Drive, Houston, Texas 77073; Telephone: 281-618-5528; Fax: 281-618-5574; E-mail: sandy.deabler@nhmccd.edu; Web site: http://www.northharriscollege.com/admissions/honors/index.cfm

North Hennepin Community College

2 Pu G S

▼ Honors Program

The North Hennepin Community College (NHCC) Honors Program is designed to give the College's top students a way to increase their academic abilities. Two honors seminars, limited to 20 participants, offer students the opportunity to hear and interact with speakers from the community and from the College. The seminars also provide students the opportunity to get to know and work with other students in the program. While the College does not have specific honors courses, students are able to work one-on-one with faculty members who offer Honors Option contracts in their courses. Individual scholarship advising and help is offered to students through the Honors Coordinator and through a special scholarship seminar. At the end of spring semester, a special reception, attended by members of the faculty and administration, friends, and family, is held for those who have completed the program. Since its beginning in 1989, more than 60 students have completed the program. Each year, 25 to 50 students contract to take Honors Option credits. Of those students, an average of 8 to 10 enroll in the program annually.

Participation Requirements: Students take two 1-credit seminars taught by the Honors Coordinator and successfully complete three Honors Contracts offered by Honors Program faculty members. They must maintain a 3.3 GPA in order to complete the program. The notation "Honors Program" appears at the top of their transcripts. At graduation they lead the procession of graduates. Their names appear first on the graduation program, designating that they are graduates of the Honors Program, and they are called up to the podium where the Vice President presents them as the school's premier students and awards each a special certificate.

Admission Process: Students must complete 15 credits and obtain a 3.3 GPA. They must also be recommended by an instructor, write a 500-word essay explaining why they wish to be a part of the Honors Program, and have an interview with the Honors Coordinator.

Scholarship Availability: The Presidential Scholarship ($3000) is for high school seniors who graduate in the top 15 percent of their high school class. Selection criteria include academic achievement, extracurricular activities, a written statement describing the importance of the scholarship to the applicant and the importance of higher education to the applicant's goals, and academic need.

The Barbara Mantini Phi Theta Kappa Scholarship ($1000) is awarded to an outstanding student (cumulative GPA of 3.5 or better) who is a PTK member and has given exceptional service to PTK, either as an officer or as an active member. Selection criteria (in order of importance) include 40 PTK or more service points or equivalent academic performance, a written statement describing the importance of the scholarship to the applicant in meeting academic or career goals, an NHCC faculty member's written reference, and financial need.

The Baccalaureate Scholarship ($5000) is given annually to encourage and support an NHCC student who continues to pursue higher education after graduation or transfer from North Hennepin Community College. Application is open only to students currently enrolled at the College who complete their studies in the academic year the scholarship is offered. Eligibility requirements include earning at least 30 credits with a minimum GPA of 3.0 at North Hennepin through the spring semester in which the student plans to graduate. Selection criteria include academic achievement, a demonstrated strong belief in the value of a liberal arts education, qualities of thoughtfulness and creativity demonstrated through the essay and an interview, and a demonstrated concern for the future, which extends beyond oneself.

The Campus Context: Established in 1966, North Hennepin Community College is part of the Minnesota State Colleges and Universities System. NHCC is located in Brooklyn Park, Minnesota, a rapidly growing suburb northwest of Minneapolis–St. Paul. The College primarily serves the communities of Brooklyn Park, Maple Grove, Brooklyn Center, Plymouth, Champlin, and Osseo. The College's 84-acre campus is composed of nine 1-story brick buildings, a central courtyard, accessible parking lots, athletic fields, hiking trails, and a nature preserve area.

Accredited by the North Central Association of Colleges and Schools, NHCC is a comprehensive community college offering course work and preprofessional programs for transfer to baccalaureate programs or immediate entry into careers. The business program is accredited by the Association of Collegiate Business Schools and Programs, the nursing program is accredited by the National League for Nursing Accrediting Commission and approved by the Minnesota Board of Nursing, the medical laboratory technician program is accredited by the National Accrediting Agency for Clinical Laboratory Science, the legal assistant program is approved by the American Bar Association, and the peer tutor program is accredited by the College Reading and Learning Association.

Student Body North Hennepin enrolls approximately 7,680 students, 3,300 of whom attend full-time. Approximately 75 percent of the students who complete an Associate of Arts degree transfer to four-year schools. Students who complete an Associate of Science degree also transfer to four-year institutions. More than 700 international students attend the College.

Faculty Of the 188 faculty members, 97 are full-time instructors and 22 percent have terminal degrees.

Key Facilities The NHCC library has 40,558 volumes and 15,672 other holdings. The library is part of the PALS network, which connects students to all community college and state university libraries in Minnesota.

Honorary Society Phi Theta Kappa

Athletics North Hennepin students participate in varsity baseball and softball and in intramural sports.

Study Abroad Study-abroad options include a semester in Costa Rica and various study options in other countries.

Support Services The College offers Disability Access Services, counseling services, and tutoring services in nearly all academic areas, including a Writing Center run by the English Department.

Job Opportunities Work-study is available to all students who qualify.

Tuition: $2874.50 full-time per academic year, plus $200–$400 for books (2001–02)

Mandatory Fees: $5 Student Life fee, $4 technology fee, and a $3 parking fee, per credit

Contact: Honors Coordinator: Sandra Hofsommer, Honors Program, North Hennepin Community College, 7411 85th Avenue, North, Brooklyn Park, Minnesota 55445; Telephone:

763-424-0856; Fax: 763-493-0531; E-mail: sandra.hofsommer@nhcc.mnscu.edu

Northeast Community College

2 Pu G S Tr

▼ Honors Program

Northeast Community College's (NECC) Honors Program permits academically talented students to go above and beyond the normal course of studies demanded by their individual degree requirements. A wide variety of program courses are offered on an individual basis as well as team-taught classes and forums, with service learning and leadership components required of many of the classes. The College's Honors Programs course offerings are all-inclusive and campuswide and include distance-learning possibilities for students living a great distance from campus. Students have the opportunity to work closely with honors faculty members in classroom and mentor contexts and receive their help and guidance in selecting courses that ensure their eligibility to graduate from the Honors Program.

Northeast Community College's Honors Program is in its fifth year of existence, having been initiated in the fall semester of the 1997–98 school year. The program presently enrolls about 25 students.

Participation Requirements: To graduate from the Honors Program, students are required to maintain a minimum 3.5 GPA and take a minimum of 12 credit hours of honors classes above and beyond the requirements specific to their degree. This must include at least four Honors Contracts. These students must also satisfy service learning and leadership components. Honors Program graduates are honored by receiving a diploma bearing a gold Honors Program seal, by being announced as Honors Program graduates, and by being the first graduates to cross the stage.

Admission Process: Students are identified as potential Honors Program participants when they fill out the Honors Program Application Form. In an interview, the Honors Program Director informs students that some specific information is needed to verify their eligibility. This could include a GPA of at least 3.5, an ACT score of 15 or higher or an SAT I of 1230 or above, recommendations, portfolios, and information about any special talents or abilities. If a college student's GPA is 3.5 or above, he or she is admitted to the program without further investigation. If a student is admitted for any other reason, he or she is considered a probationary honors student and must show that he or she can attain and maintain at least a 3.5 GPA. All first-time freshmen Honors Program applicants are accepted as probationary students, no matter what their high school GPA. The deadline to apply and register for Honors Program classes or contracts is the end of the third week of the fall or spring academic term.

Scholarship Availability: No scholarships specific to Northeast Community College's Honors Program are available at this time. However, many on- and off-campus organizations as well as foundations and businesses have scholarships available to qualified students. The College's Board of Governors and the Northeast Community College Foundation also award grants and scholarships.

The Campus Context: Northeast Community College is located at the northeast edge of Norfolk, Nebraska, one of the fastest-growing cities in the state. Northeast is the only community college in Nebraska that offers vocational, liberal arts, and adult education programs on one main campus. The College, established in 1973, is accredited by the North Central Association of Colleges and Schools and offers A.A., A.A.S., and A.S. degrees, diplomas, and certificates in more than eighty-five programs of study.

Student Body Approximately 4,200 students attend on-campus classes, with another 3,500 attending classes at satellite locations or through distance-learning systems. Of NECC's on-campus student body, 54 percent are men and 46 percent are women. The ethnic distribution is 97.6 percent white, 6 percent Hispanic, 4 percent American Indian, 2 percent Asian, and 2 percent black. About 350 students live on campus while the rest commute.

Faculty Of the 175 on-campus instructors, 105 are full-time and 70 are part-time. Four percent have terminal degrees. The student-faculty ratio is approximately 22:1.

Key Facilities The library houses 32,000 volumes, 320 magazine and 69 newspaper subscriptions, and 2,500 audio/visual titles and provides five online databases and Internet access. There are several other computer facilities on campus.

Honorary Societies Phi Theta Kappa.

Athletics Northeast Community College is a member of the Nebraska Community College Athletic Conference and the National Junior College Athletic Association. NECC teams compete in women's volleyball, men's and women's basketball, and men's golf.

Support Services Student Services provides support and auxiliary services to students with documented physical and/or mental disabilities. Qualified students may request special support services such as interpreters, note takers, tutors, and testing accommodations. Student Services administers funds and coordinates support services with area agencies and college departments.

Job Opportunities Students may qualify for a wide range of work opportunities on campus including work-study and tutoring.

Tuition: $45 per credit hour for residents, $56.25 per credit hour for nonresidents (2001–02)

Room and board: $2962–$3516 per year

Mandatory Fees: $6.25 per credit hour

Contact: Director: Dr. Linda Boullion, 801 East Benjamin, Norfolk, Nebraska 68701; Telephone: 402-844-7354

Northeast State Technical Community College

2 Pu G S Sc Tr AA

▼ Honors Program

The Northeast State Technical Community College (NSTCC) Honors Program offers honors sections of regular courses in English composition and literature, U.S. history, speech, computer science, psychology, philosophy, biology, history, and women's studies. These classes offer challenging, stimulating opportunities for increased knowledge and personal growth for students as they are small, discussion- and writing-based classes with a high level of teacher-student interaction.

Students must fulfill a requirement to attend and write about one Lyceum lecture per semester. These lectures, presented by both program faculty members and guests, are designed to not only impart information but also generate critical thinking and discussion on campus about important issues.

The Honors Program was implemented in 1991–92 and has a current enrollment of 40 students.

Participation Requirements: To receive an honors diploma, students must complete 18 hours of honors courses. Successful

Interpreting the symbols: **2**=two-year college, **4**=four-year college; **Pu**=public or state college, **Pr**=private college; **G**=general honors program; **D**=departmental honors program; **S**=small program (fewer than 100 students), **M**=midsize program (100 to 500 students), **L**=large program (more than 500 students); **Sc**=scholarships available in honors program; **Tr**=transfer students accepted into honors program; **HBC**=historically black college; **AA**=academic advisors; **GA**=graduate advisors; **FA**=fellowship advisors.

completion of Honors Program requirements is noted on the student's diploma and transcript.

Admission Process: Students may enter the program in one of two ways: they may enter as first-semester freshmen with an ACT composite of 25 or better or an SAT I combined score of 1140 and an acceptable writing sample, or transfer/returning students may be enrolled after completion of 12 hours of college-level course work with a minimum 3.25 GPA and an acceptable writing sample.

Scholarship Availability: There are scholarship opportunities available to NSTCC honors students through the NSTCC Foundation. Book scholarships of $200 are awarded to honors students each semester. All students enrolled in the program full-time who meet the minimum GPA requirement and fulfill the Lyceum requirement are eligible to receive the scholarship until graduation.

The Campus Context: Northeast State Technical Community College is a two-year technical community college located in Blountville, Tennessee, about 2 hours' drive northeast of Knoxville, Tennessee. The school offers a university parallel transfer curriculum and a variety of technical terminal degrees in such fields as drafting, electrical technology, emergency medical technician studies, and business.

Tuition: $744 for Tennessee residents, $2973 for nonresidents, per semester

Mandatory Fees: $80

Contact: Coordinator: James Whorton, Assistant Professor of English, P.O. Box 246, Blountville, Tennessee 37617-0246; Telephone: 423-323-3191; Fax: 423-323-3083; E-mail: jwhorton@nstcc.cc.tn.us; Web site: http://www.nstcc.cc.tn.us

Northeastern Illinois University

4 Pu G M Sc Tr

▼ University Honors Program

Motivated students. Great teachers. Challenging classes. Special opportunities. The University Honors Program at Northeastern Illinois University (NEIU) offers an outstanding educational experience for undergraduate students in all colleges and majors who have a commitment to excellence. The program provides a nurturing environment for qualified students to take the long-term view, look beneath the surface, and to probe issues in depth. The program serves as a laboratory for academic innovation that seeks to improve undergraduate education and provides a place for students to discover the best in themselves. The University Honors Program does not replace a regular program of study, but enhances it by encouraging students to build strong relationships with faculty members and their fellow honors students in small, innovative classes emphasizing analytic writing and communication and critical-thinking skills.

The University Honors Program encourages students to enhance their undergraduate experience with out-of-classroom academic experiences. Honors students are active participants in NEIU's Annual Student Research and Creative Activities Symposium. They also present papers at other academic conferences. The University Honors Program is an integral part of the NEIU community, and its students are active campus leaders. It helps students to reach their full potential as undergraduates and prepares them for the challenges of graduate education or employment.

Founded in 1986, the University Honors Program currently enrolls 150 full- and part-time students.

Participation Requirements: The University Honors Program offers an unusual two-tier program that allows transfer students to join the program easily. Freshmen and sophomores (Level I) take seven of their thirteen required general education courses in special honors sections. Juniors and seniors (Level II) take two honors electives in their major or minor, the Honors Seminar, and the Honors Colloquium. Level II culminates with the Honors Thesis, an independent research or creative project.

Students must maintain a cumulative GPA of at least 3.25 in their honors and nonhonors work to remain in good standing. All students completing Level I or Level II receive a certificate at NEIU's annual Student Awards Ceremony. Completion of Level I is noted on the official transcripts. Students completing Level II are designated as Honors Scholars, which is marked on the official transcript and diploma.

Admission Process: To be eligible for the University Honors Program, entering freshmen must have a minimum ACT score of 26 or have an ACT score of 23-25 and rank in the top 10 percent of their high school graduating class. Transfer students must have a GPA of 3.25 or above. Students already enrolled at NEIU may seek admission if they have a GPA of 3.25 or above. All applicants must complete an University Honors Program application, which includes an essay. Two letters of recommendation are required.

Scholarship Availability: Students enrolled in the University Honors Program are eligible to apply for Honors Merit Tuition Awards. The program has designated Tuition Awards for transfer students and members of minority groups. In addition, NEIU has merit scholarship programs at the university, college, and departmental levels. Honors students are frequent recipients of these awards.

The Campus Context: Northeastern Illinois University is a comprehensive public commuter university located in a residential neighborhood on the northwest side of Chicago. Dedicated to excellence and access, NEIU offers high-quality undergraduate and graduate programs to a highly diverse student body. Because of its urban location, the University serves a population that is diverse in age, culture, language, and race. This diversity is a major asset, allowing academic programs to utilize a variety of perspectives to enrich the teaching and learning experience. NEIU's location also provides students with many opportunities to integrate field-based learning, research, and community service with classroom instruction.

NEIU offers thirty-seven undergraduate majors through the three Colleges of Arts and Sciences, Business and Management, and Education as well as nontraditional degree programs. The University also has three off-campus centers: El Centro de Recursos Educativos serving the westside Latino community; the Center for Inner City Studies on Chicago's south side; and the multi-university center in Lake County. Students at all locations may enroll in the honors program.

Student Body The undergraduate enrollment is 7,500; 62 percent of students are women. Minority enrollment is 25 percent Hispanic/Latino, 13 percent African American, and 12 percent Asian American. Fifty-five percent of students receive financial aid.

Faculty The total number of faculty members is 530, of whom 331 are full-time. Seventy-eight percent of the full-time faculty members have doctoral or equivalent degrees. The student-faculty ratio is 19:1.

Key Facilities The library contains more than 650,000 volumes and more than 850,000 additional educational support items, such as recordings, microfilms, documents, and maps. The library subscribes to more than 3,800 periodicals and is a repository for federal and Illinois state documents. There are four University-operated computer labs on campus with more than 300 microcomputers with Internet access.

Athletics The physical education complex, open to all students, contains a pool, two gyms, racquetball courts, running track, weight room, fitness center, tennis courts, and athletic fields. The Intramural and Recreation Program provides a wide-variety of organized sport opportunities. NEIU does not compete in intercollegiate athletics.

Study Abroad NEIU students are encouraged to take full advantage of the study-abroad opportunities sponsored by the University.

Study-abroad experience helps students focus their academic goals and augments their employment prospects. Currently these study-abroad opportunities include summer programs in Mexico and South Africa and short-term trips to Belize, India, England, Puerto Rico, and Germany. Semester and year-abroad programs are also available. In most cases, financial aid may be applied towards study-abroad programs. Some scholarship funds are also available.

Support Services The Handicapped Educational Liaison Program works with University, city, state, and federal agencies to help physically or learning-disabled students to obtain assistance that enables them to compete with their nondisabled peers. Ninety-five percent of the campus is accessible to physically disabled students. Other University support services include the Returning Adult Program (RAP), Women's Services, tutoring, counseling, and academic advising.

Job Opportunities Work opportunities are available on and off campus.

Tuition: $2084 for state residents, $6552 for nonresidents, per year (1998–99)

Mandatory Fees: $602

Contact: Coordinator: Ricki J. Shine, 5500 North St. Louis Avenue, Chicago, Illinois 60625; Telephone: 773-794-6277; E-mail: r-shine@neiu.edu; Web site: http://www.neiu.edu/Honors.htm

Northeastern State University

4 Pu G S Sc Tr

▼ Honors Program

The Honors Program at Northeastern State University (NSU) is a challenging educational option for academically talented students who enjoy learning. Honors students work with distinguished faculty members and peers in enhanced courses, pursue independent research, and participate in cocurricular cultural experiences.

Benefits of being an honors student include academic scholarships through the Academic Scholars Program, Baccalaureate Scholars Program, or selected Collegiate Scholars; special honors courses; priority enrollment; enrichment activities, cultural events, and field trips; faculty mentorship on individual research projects; use of exclusive honors facilities; Honors Scholar recognition at graduation; and designation on the diploma.

The Honors Program at NSU offers a unique opportunity for gifted students to grow academically in an intellectually stimulating student-friendly environment.

Participation Requirements: To maintain honors eligibility, students must maintain a minimum GPA and follow the approved Honors Program contract.

Admission Process: Students must have an ACT composite score of 30 or higher with a high school GPA of 3.5 or higher, an ACT composite score of 29 with a high school GPA of 3.65 or higher, or an ACT composite score of 28 with a high school GPA of 3.8 or higher; a high school ranking within the upper 10 percent; and a written essay read and approved by the Honors Committee. Students must also complete and submit an approved Application for Admission to Northeastern State University and the Northeastern State University Honors Program.

Scholarship Availability: One goal at NSU is to seek the best and brightest students. Each year NSU awards many of these students scholarships based on merit and talent. All freshmen that meet the ACT score and/or GPA criteria are eligible to be considered for admission in the Honors Program. Students must remain in good academic standing to receive the eight-semester scholarship.

The Campus Context: NSU is located in the beautiful Ozark Mountains. A comprehensive regional university, NSU implements a mission of excellence in teaching, research, and service. The campus covers an area of approximately 200 acres. The native trees and the natural elevation of the grounds have been preserved through the years to make the campus outstanding for natural scenic beauty.

There are six colleges at NSU: Arts and Letters, Business and Industry, Education, Social and Behavioral Sciences, Optometry, and Mathematics, Science, and Nursing.

Contact: Director: Dr. Karen Carey, Northeastern State University, 600 North Grand, Tahlequah, Oklahoma 74464; Telephone: 918-456-5511 Ext. 2236; E-mail: careyka@nsuok.edu; Web site: http://nsuok.edu/admissions/honors.html or http://araaho.nsuok.edu/~honors

Northeastern University

4 Pr G L Sc Tr AA

▼ University Honors Program

The University Honors Program at Northeastern University offers outstanding students academic and extracurricular opportunities to enhance their university experience. Honors students complete the requirements of their major and college, but they also participate in honors courses as part of their curriculum.

The honors curriculum consists of separate honors offerings of selected courses as well as single-credit add-ons to an existing course, referred to as an honors adjunct. Separate honors courses are four credits and feature small class sizes with extensive faculty-student interaction. Honors adjuncts are additional meetings and assignments that involve a faculty member and the honors students in a regular class. In addition, many honors students complete a two-course junior/senior honors project as the capstone experience of their undergraduate career. While taking an honors course, students are eligible for an overload privilege, which allows them to take an additional course without a tuition charge.

Offices of the Honors Program include a student lounge and computer lab. Most freshmen and a small number of upperclass students in the Honors Program live in Kennedy Residence Hall, which features suite living arrangements and various activities for honors students. All honors students can participate in social activities sponsored by the Honors Program, including discounted tickets to cultural and sports events in Boston.

The University Honors Program began in 1986 and currently includes 1,750 students. Each year, approximately 200 students enter the program as freshmen and a number of other students join from the upper classes.

Participation Requirements: Honors students who begin during their freshman year complete six honors courses their first year, two courses in each of their sophomore and middler years, one course in their junior year, and the junior/senior honors project. Completion of all these courses earns a student the University Honors Program Distinction. For students who enter the program after the freshman year, completion of the junior/senior honors project results in the College Honors Program Distinction. Students must maintain a 3.25 GPA to remain in the Honors Program.

Interpreting the symbols: **2**=two-year college, **4**=four-year college; **Pu**=public or state college, **Pr**=private college; **G**=general honors program; **D**=departmental honors program; **S**=small program (fewer than 100 students), **M**=midsize program (100 to 500 students), **L**=large program (more than 500 students); **Sc**=scholarships available in honors program; **Tr**=transfer students accepted into honors program; **HBC**=historically black college; **AA**=academic advisors; **GA**=graduate advisors; **FA**=fellowship advisors.

Admission Process: Incoming freshman are admitted to the Honors Program based upon their high school GPA and SAT scores. Students who have already attended Northeastern may enter the Honors Program if they have a cumulative GPA of 3.4 or higher.

Scholarship Availability: Scholarships are available specifically for honors students. In the winter of each year, honors students can apply for a scholarship if they have completed or registered for the requisite number of honors courses during that year. The amount of the award depends upon a student's financial need and GPA. In addition, honors students are eligible for a number of other scholarships available to all students at the University.

The Campus Context: Founded in 1898, Northeastern University is a national research university that is student-centered, practice-oriented, and urban. Most students participate in the co-operative education model, which alternates professional studies and liberal arts coursework on campus with paid professional work in the student's area of interest. Students in the co-op program typically complete their Northeastern degree in five years, creating a new class of middlers between the sophomore and junior years.

Northeastern University consists of six colleges: Arts & Sciences, Business Administration, Computer Sciences, Engineering, Bouve College of Health Sciences, and Criminal Justice. The university also includes a law school and numerous graduate programs.

The University is located in the city of Boston, which is the state capital of Massachusetts, a major urban area, and the home to a large number of other educational institutions. The University's campus is close to numerous attractions, including the Museum of Fine Arts and Fenway Park, the home of the Boston Red Sox. With quick access to the city's subway system, students at Northeastern can travel throughout the metropolitan area to enjoy other cultural and social activities.

Student Body In 2000, undergraduate enrollment was 13,800 full-time students and 5,900 part-time students. In addition, there were approximately 4,200 graduate and law students on the Northeastern campus.

Faculty The University employs 770 full-time faculty and 1,600 full-time staff members. Thirty percent of faculty members are at the full professor rank, and thirty-six percent are women.

Key Facilities Snell Library on the Northeastern campus includes over 900,000 bound volumes, two million microforms, and a large collection of serial titles, audio and video materials, and government documents. The library includes three computer labs, a language lab, a new cybercafe with Internet connections, and membership in the Boston Regional Library System, which provides access to other college and university libraries in the Boston area. There are 40 computer labs and classrooms on campus and an Intranet system with e-mail addresses for all Northeastern students.

Athletics University athletic teams participate in ten intercollegiate sports, primarily at the Division I level and football is Division IAA. There also are numerous intramural leagues.

Study Abroad Study abroad opportunities are available through some colleges and include academic studies at sites around the world.

Support Services Support from the Disability Resource Center allows students with disabilities to participate in all activities on campus. In 2000, approximately 500 students received support services from this center.

Job Opportunities Co-operative work experience, as well as internships, provide excellent opportunities for students to develop workplace skills and connect with possible employers. In 2000, 7,900 undergraduate students participated in co-op work experiences at 2,700 employers in 33 states and 29 countries. Many students find jobs with their co-op employers after graduation.

Tuition: Tuition for full-time undergraduate freshmen is $20,535 for three quarters or a full year of classes. Upper-class students are charged approximately $17,250 for two quarters. Most students are on co-op in the third and fourth quarters.

Mandatory Fees: Fees for undergraduate students are $66 per quarter for nonresidents and $83 per quarter for residents, exclusive of health care. The waivable health center fee is $901 per year.

Room and Board: Room rates at campus residence halls range from $1085 to $2645 per quarter. Board per student ranges from $610 to $1445 per quarter, depending upon the number of meals purchased.

Contact: Director: John Portz, 1 Nightingale Hall, Northeastern University, Boston, Massachusetts 02115; Assistant Director: Faith Crisley; Administrative Assistant: Christina Ventresca, Telephone: 617-373-2333; Fax: 617-373-5300; E-mail: j.portz@neu.edu, f.crisley@neu.edu, or c.ventresca@neu.edu; Web site: http://www.honors.neu.edu.

Northern Arizona University

4 Pu G L Sc Tr AA

▼ Honors Program

The Northern Arizona University (NAU) Honors Program is the oldest in Arizona, having begun in 1955. NAU's Honors Program provides many opportunities for academically motivated students to succeed by offering a challenging set of seminar-style courses that encourage the free exchange of ideas. Classes are small and interactive, and students and faculty members work closely together. Honors students are members of a close, supportive community of scholars and benefit from one-on-one advising with professional academic advisers, priority registration, and specialized scholarship opportunities.

Honors students are encouraged to live in the Cowden Learning Community, a 24-hour, quiet, substance-free residence hall providing a free 24-hour computer lab, on-site tutoring, Honors Program classrooms, and access to honors offices. Because it is close to the Cline Library, the University Union, and other residence halls, Cowden is the ideal location for students dedicated to their studies. There are currently more than 600 students enrolled in the growing program.

Participation Requirements: At the core of the honors program is a formal curriculum aimed at helping students acquire and refine skills while focusing on a range of topics, ideas, and problems. The Liberal Studies Honors curriculum is designed to meet the University's liberal studies requirements without infringing on the opportunity to pursue a major and minor field of course work.

Opportunities and experiences outside the classroom contribute significantly to students' learning. Through service learning activities, study abroad, exchange and immersion experiences, internships, and undergraduate research, program participants are encouraged to apply what they have learned in the classroom and to learn while working with individuals in the many sectors of society. Students are encouraged to participate in these activities as well as the many educational, cultural, and social events coordinated and supported by the Honors Program.

The University honors curriculum is an option for students who have completed the liberal studies honors curriculum and wish to complete a senior thesis during their final year. The thesis involves a two-semester effort of research guided by a faculty adviser.

AP, I.B., and transfer credit is considered on an individual basis, but is generally accepted. To graduate "with liberal studies honors," students must graduate with a cumulative GPA of 3.5 or higher (on a 4.0 scale). The "with liberal studies honors" designation is in addition to the "cum laude" notation.

Admission Process: Through an application process, incoming students who have fewer than 30 transferable credit hours need to meet one of the following: achieve a composite ACT score of 29 or higher, achieve a combined SAT score of 1290 or higher, or graduate in the top 5 percent of their high school class. Students who have participated in honors courses/AP classes in high school but do not meet these requirements may petition to join the Honors Program. To petition, students must include with their completed application a copy of their high school transcript, one letter of recommendation, and a 500-word essay on why being a part of the program is important.

Transfer students (30 or more transferable hours) are admitted if they have a cumulative GPA of 3.5 or higher from their former institution. These students must include a copy of their transcript with their application.

A student who does not meet any of the above entrance criteria can still join the Honors Program after they complete 12 semester hours of course work that leads to an undergraduate degree at NAU. A student who earns a 3.5 or higher cumulative GPA can apply to this program based on their NAU course work.

Scholarship Availability: More than 2,000 scholarships are available; awards range from several hundred to several thousands of dollars. Awards are made on the basis of financial need, academic qualifications, and evidence of student involvement. Applications for scholarships are due in mid-February, with awards announced in mid-March of each year.

The Campus Context: Northern Arizona is the smallest of three state-supported universities in Arizona and emphasizes excellence in undergraduate instruction. It was founded in 1899 and enrolls approximately 14,000 students at the Flagstaff campus, with another 6,000 enrolled through distance education options that include satellite branches, interactive instructional television, and Web courses. NAU offers more than 100 undergraduate degrees, including all of the liberal arts and sciences and professional degrees in health sciences, nursing, business, forestry, hotel and restaurant management, education, communication, and engineering.

NAU is located in Flagstaff in north-central Arizona. Flagstaff is a city of about 55,000; its elevation is approximately 7,000 feet on the high Colorado Plateau. The area is surrounded by ponderosa pine forests. Six miles to the north, the extinct volcanoes of the San Francisco Peaks rise to nearly 13,000 feet; both downhill and cross-country skiing are excellent.

The Grand Canyon is a 90-minute drive to the north, and six other national parks and monuments are within a similar radius. The area contains many geological, astronomical, and biological sites of interest; five major astronomic observatories are within a 15-minute drive, including Lowell, where the planet Pluto was discovered. Also nearby is the U.S. Geologic Survey's Center for Astrogeology.

Student Body Among the 14,000 students, the ratio of men to women is roughly 40:60, and about 23 percent of students are members of ethnic minority groups, primarily Hispanic American and Native American. International students comprise 4 percent of the student body. More than half of all students choose to live in residence halls on campus; all halls are wired for direct access to the Internet and most contain computer laboratories. There are about a dozen fraternities and sororities active on campus.

Faculty There are approximately 800 faculty members on campus, with more than 85 percent holding the earned doctorate or other terminal degrees. There are about forty master's programs and nine doctoral programs on campus. The student-faculty ratio is 22:1, with more than three quarters of NAU classes taught by full-time faculty members.

Key Facilities The 203,000-square-foot Cline Library contains more than a 1.3 million volumes. The library subscribes to about 6,000 current periodicals, including more than seventy local, national, and international newspapers.

Athletics The varsity athletic programs meet NCAA standards for gender equity, compete in Division I, and include six men's and nine women's sports, including basketball, cross-country, football, golf, tennis, track and field, soccer, swimming and diving, and women's volleyball. NAU is a member of the Big Sky Conference, and many of the teams—including both men's cross-country and women's volleyball—earned Big Sky Conference championships in the 2000–01 season. There is a wide range of intramural sports and sports clubs ranging from soccer and racquetball to table tennis and rugby as well as most winter sports. Year-round active participation in outdoor sports of all kinds is common for students.

Study Abroad Through its National Student Exchange and international education programs, NAU honors students typically spend a semester or two at either another U.S. university or in Australia, France, Germany, Great Britain, Mexico, Spain, and other countries. Many of these programs allow the student to pay regular NAU tuition in place of the tuition at the host institution.

Job Opportunities More than half of all honors students currently work part-time; there are a wide range of both on-campus and off-campus work and co-op and internship opportunities. Both federally funded work-study postions and student wage positions are available. There are also specialized programs for members of the Navajo, Apache, and Hopi tribes and students with disabilities. All campus buildings are handicapped-accessible.

Tuition: $2412 for state residents, $10,278 for nonresidents, per year (2001–02)

Room and Board: $4956 for a freshman residence hall room with traditional meal plan

Mandatory Fees: Approximately $76

Contact: Director: Professor Pamela Eibeck, (pamela.eibeck@nau.edu); Program Coordinator: Glenn Hansen (glenn.hansen@nau.edu); P.O. Box 5689, Northern Arizona University, Flagstaff, Arizona 86011-5689; Telephone: 520-523-3334; Fax: 520-523-6558; Web site: http://www.nau.edu/honors

Northern Illinois University

4 Pu G L Sc Tr

▼ University Honors Program

The University Honors Program at Northern Illinois University (NIU) serves to provide a special educational experience for academically talented students with a commitment to the pursuit of knowledge and understanding. Honors courses provide the opportunity for greater intellectual interaction among faculty members and students and among students themselves. The classes are usually special sections of regular courses with smaller enrollments, taught by faculty members who have demonstrated exceptional ability to teach undergraduate students. The University Honors Program is broad and inclusive enough to provide this opportunity to students pursuing any undergraduate major. The curriculum of the Honors Program provides students the opportunity to participate in the design of their own educational study and research in their chosen discipline. All honors credit applies toward the University graduation requirements, and therefore the program may be completed without any extra time requirements. Credit earned toward a departmental honors degree automatically becomes a component of the University Honors degree. There is no loss of credit or time as a result of withdrawal from the Honors Program.

All incoming freshmen honors students are required to attend the Taft Retreat, an overnight orientation program held at NIU's Lorado Taft field campus (35 miles west of DeKalb). It is designed

Interpreting the symbols: **2**=two-year college, **4**=four-year college; **Pu**=public or state college, **Pr**=private college; **G**=general honors program; **D**=departmental honors program; **S**=small program (fewer than 100 students), **M**=midsize program (100 to 500 students), **L**=large program (more than 500 students); **Sc**=scholarships available in honors program; **Tr**=transfer students accepted into honors program; **HBC**=historically black college; **AA**=academic advisors; **GA**=graduate advisors; **FA**=fellowship advisors.

to introduce new honors students to NIU and the Honors Program, and it is conducted by upper-division honors students and honors staff and faculty members.

Honors Residence Floors provide a coed, quiet lifestyle environment for like-minded and academically motivated students. Students participating in the Honors Residence Program are required to participate in educational, cultural, and/or community/campus programs while in residence.

There is no limit placed on the number of honors-eligible students admitted to the program. Approximately 1,000 students are active in the University Honors Program at NIU. These students may represent any major and any class level. All honors students are strongly encouraged to be active on and off campus in educational, cultural, social, and service programs. Honors students may receive personalized academic advising at the Honors Center.

Participation Requirements: Students may be admitted as new freshmen, transfer students, or continuing NIU students. The four-year program is divided into Phase I (primarily freshmen and sophomores) and Phase II (primarily juniors and seniors). Phase I of the program requires students to complete 15 credit hours of honors course work over approximately four semesters. Based on a 4.0 scale, students must maintain a minimum 3.0 cumulative GPA and a minimum 3.2 honors GPA while in Phase I. Students who complete Phase I with the minimum GPAs are awarded Lower Division Honors, which appears only on the transcript. In order to continue to Phase II, students must have at least a 3.2 cumulative GPA and at least a 3.2 Honors GPA. Phase II requires 12 credit hours of honors course work over approximately four semesters. All courses in Phase II must be at the 300–400 level and include an Honors Seminar (taken outside the student's major) and a Capstone (senior independent study). Students who complete both phases with a minimum 3.2 cumulative GPA and a minimum 3.2 Honors GPA are awarded University Honors, which appears on the transcript and diploma and allows the student to wear a gold cord at graduation. An additional certificate is awarded to graduates with Upper Division Honors or University Honors at the Excellence in Undergraduate Education Ceremony shortly before graduation.

Admission Process: Incoming freshmen graduating in the top 10 percent of their high school class with an ACT composite of 27 or better are encouraged to participate in the University Honors Program. Freshmen applicants are also required to submit an essay and two teacher/counselor evaluations. Students who have already earned college credit, either as a transfer student or as a continuing NIU student, must have at least a 3.2 GPA on a 4.0 scale. A brief essay is also required as part of the transfer/continuing student application. Any applicant who is slightly below the requirements may be admitted on a provisional basis. New honors-eligible freshmen and transfer students who have not applied to the Honors Program prior to summer orientation may be invited to visit the Honors Center on that day. Admission is rolling.

Scholarship Availability: Through the University Scholarships Committee, the Honors Program offers numerous, highly competitive, merit-based scholarships for both incoming freshmen and transfer students. The awards are University Scholar/Academic Finalist: freshmen (6–7), transfers (1–2); Faculty Fund Academic Finalist: freshmen (2); Phi Theta Kappa: transfers (1); Academic Finalist: freshmen (10–15), transfers (4–8); and Phi Kappa Scholarship: transfers (4). For continuing honors students, there are six peer adviser, three community leader, and four honors house leader positions, with availability varying depending on current recipient graduation rates. Numerous other scholarships are disseminated through the Honors Program but may be open to any qualified applicants.

The Campus Context: Northern Illinois University was originally founded as Northern Illinois State Normal School in 1895 to meet the increased demand for public school teachers. NIU is located on the 514-acre main campus in DeKalb, Illinois, a community of 40,000 people 65 miles west of Chicago. It offers the advantages of ease in daily living associated with a medium-sized town while at the same time providing the cultural advantages of a major urban center. In addition, many of the NIU's programs are enhanced by the University's proximity to high-technology research in the Chicago and suburban area as well as a variety of opportunities for clinical experience necessary in certain fields. NIU offers approximately seventy fields of study for undergraduate students in the Colleges of Business, Education, Engineering and Engineering Technology, Heath and Human Sciences, Liberal Arts and Sciences, and Visual and Performing Arts.

The Honors Center is located in the Campus Life Building and houses the administrative offices, a computer lab, seminar rooms, and Capstone Library. The Campus Life Building is located near the center of campus, providing easy access to other programs on campus.

Student Body Undergraduate enrollment at NIU in fall 2001 was 17,468 undergraduates, with 53 percent women and 47 percent men. Ethnic distribution is 75.4 percent Caucasian, 10.7 percent African American, 5.7 percent Hispanic, 6.7 percent Asian, 0.3 percent American Indian, and 1.2 percent nonresident alien. Thirty-five percent of students live on-campus, 7.9 percent have a permanent address in DeKalb, 16.2 percent have a local address in DeKalb, and 40.5 percent commute. Seventy-three percent of students receive financial aid. Nine national sororities and sixteen national fraternities associate with NIU.

Faculty NIU faculty consists of 1,249 total individuals, with 1,012 being full-time. Eighty-two percent of NIU's full-time faculty members hold doctoral or terminal degrees in their fields. The student-faculty ratio is about 17:1.

Key Facilities The University Libraries consist of Founders Memorial Library, five branch libraries (including the Map and Music Libraries), and the Regional History Center/University Archives. More than 770,000 people use these facilities each year. Founders Memorial Library has five levels with 290,000 square feet of space and seating capacity for 1,600 students. NIU library holdings total 1.4 million books, 1.1 million government publications, 2.4 million microforms, 214,000 maps, and 43,800 audiovisual materials, and it maintains subscriptions to approximately 8,000 periodicals and newspaper titles. Approximately ninety computer labs exist throughout campus and may be located in academic buildings, residence halls, and individual programs. Students may also use dial-in facilities from their own personal computer.

Athletics NIU is a NCAA Division IA school and a member of the Mid-America Conference (MAC). Men's varsity sports include football, swimming and diving, soccer, golf, basketball, baseball, tennis, and wrestling. Women's varsity sports include volleyball, tennis, soccer, swimming and diving, gymnastics, basketball, golf, softball, and cross-country. Sixteen sports clubs are also available at NIU.

Study Abroad NIU is nationally known for the extensive study-abroad program opportunities offered to its undergraduate students. Approximately 600 students from NIU and other colleges and universities enroll in forty-five semester/academic-year programs, in twenty-two short-term programs, and in student exchanges and internships each year. The semester/academic-year programs are located in all regions of the world and meet a wide range of student interests. The topical short-term programs range from three to nine weeks, and most are directed by NIU faculty members. Various financial aid programs, including scholarships, grants, and student loans, may be available. The University Honors Program offers the Excellence in Education grants for studies in research and artistry.

Support Services The Center for Accessibility Resources offers a wide range of services to students with disabilities, including assistance with admissions, registration, housing, and advocacy with the faculty and supporting staff members. Other services provided to persons with visual, physical, learning, hearing, or other disabilities include, but are not limited to, special parking arrangements; books and exams in adapted media; assistance in obtaining readers, writers, and typists; adapted testing arrangements; specialized transportation; interpreters for the deaf; assistive listening devices; and assistance in finding note takers. Through Educational Services and Programs (ESP), students whose precollege education may not fully enable them to take maximum advantage of their potential and the opportunities of higher education may receive a comprehensive, coordinated collection of counseling, academic preparation, and support services designed to assist them in gaining entry into and ultimately graduating from college.

Job Opportunities Work/job-related programs at NIU include work-study, cooperative education, internships, and employment in food service, the library offices, residence hall, and the Holmes Student Center. Opportunities also exist in film projection, data entry, life guarding, piano accompaniment, tutoring, and recreation. The Student Employment Office may be contacted for information, applications, and referrals. In addition, the Job Location and Development program (JLD) is designed to aid all eligible NIU students in finding part-time and vacation off-campus employment.

Tuition: $3000 full-time for residents (1999–2000)

Room and board: $4000–$5600 (1998–1999)

Mandatory Fees: $920 (1999–2000)

Contact: Director, University Honors Program, DeKalb, Illinois 60115; Telephone: 815-753-0694; Web site: http://www.niu.edu/honors

NORTHERN KENTUCKY UNIVERSITY

4 Pu G M Sc Tr

▼ Honors Program

The Honors Program offers interdisciplinary seminars in its own campus building, which includes student facilities, such as a lounge, reading room, and computer room. At the core of the honors experience, the seminars emphasize discussion and discovery of ideas, almost always with an interdisciplinary emphasis. Seminars are organized on a topical basis, fulfilling the overall framework of four general areas: Humanity and Nature, Humanity and Society, Humanity and the Imagination, and Humanity and the Machine. In addition to an interdisciplinary focus, seminars are also available in a World Cities/World Cultures series, designating specific cities and regions for intensive study. Students may also substitute or use designated international study opportunities for honors credit. A number of seminars are cross-listed with disciplines when appropriate (e.g., a World Cities course about the Caribbean is cross-listed with the French major). Faculty members noted for their excellence in teaching are recruited from all University departments to participate in the program. An annual Visiting Professorship in Honors offers additional opportunities for student course work and projects.

All students must complete a Senior Honors Thesis (often but not necessarily in their majors), which gives them the opportunity to research and write about topics of significance, conduct original research, or develop creative projects. The thesis may be completed in written form or it may document a creative project (such as a photography exhibition).

In addition, cocurricular activities sponsored by both the program and the student Honors Club are available. These include campus events, lecture series, field trips, and other activities that integrate learning and experience. Students may choose to be active in state or national associations of honors students.

The 17-year-old program currently enrolls 350 students.

Participation Requirements: The Northern Kentucky University Honors Program provides qualified students with 15 semester hours of seminars, each having a maximum enrollment of 15 students, and 6 hours of Senior Honors Thesis credit. Those students who successfully complete the 21 hours become designated "University Honors Scholars" and fulfill the requirement of a minor towards graduation.

Admission Process: Entering freshmen with a composite ACT score of 26 or an SAT I score of 1180 (or significant achievement in high school), already enrolled students with a minimum GPA of 3.25, and transfer students from other honors programs are eligible for the program.

Scholarship Availability: Scholarships are offered for the outstanding junior honors student and outstanding honors students majoring in business; students who do individual research projects or international study are eligible for Zalla Fellowship monies.

The Campus Context: Northern Kentucky University is composed of four colleges: the College of Arts and Sciences, the College of Business, the College of Education, and the College of Professional Studies. Among the distinguished facilities on campus is the collection of public sculptures by internationally recognized artists such as Red Grooms and Donald Judd and the historic Kentucky one-room log schoolhouse.

Student Body Undergraduate enrollment is 13,000; 42 percent of the students are men. Three percent of the student body is African American. There are 225 international students. Ninety-three percent of the students are commuters, and 7 percent are residents. Forty-five percent of the students receive financial aid. There are seven fraternities and six sororities.

Faculty Of the 764 faculty members, 373 are full-time; 82 percent hold terminal degrees. The student-faculty ratio is 17:1.

Key Facilities The library houses 285,000 volumes. Computer facilities include dual platform (Apple and IBM) computer labs in all major buildings.

Honorary Societies Golden Key and Alpha Chi

Athletics The NKU Norse play NCAA Division II games in the Great Lakes Valley Conference. On the varsity level, there are six men's sports (baseball, basketball, cross-country, golf, soccer, and tennis) and six women's sports (basketball, cross-country, fast-pitch softball, tennis, soccer, and volleyball).

Study Abroad Study abroad for honors students is offered summers (in odd-numbered years) in London; other study-abroad opportunities are available in Europe, Latin America, and Australia.

Support Services Disabled students find the entire campus wheelchair-accessible.

Job Opportunities Work opportunities on campus exist as federal and other work-study opportunities.

Tuition: $2460 for state residents, $6708 for nonresidents, per year (2001–02)

Room and Board: $3316 minimum

Contact: Director: Tom Zaniello, Honors House, Highland Heights, Kentucky 41099; Telephone: 859-572-5400; Fax: 859-572-6093; E-mail: tzaniello@nku.edu; Web site: http://www.nku.edu/~honorsprgm

Interpreting the symbols: **2**=two-year college, **4**=four-year college; **Pu**=public or state college, **Pr**=private college; **G**=general honors program; **D**=departmental honors program; **S**=small program (fewer than 100 students), **M**=midsize program (100 to 500 students), **L**=large program (more than 500 students); **Sc**=scholarships available in honors program; **Tr**=transfer students accepted into honors program; **HBC**=historically black college; **AA**=academic advisors; **GA**=graduate advisors; **FA**=fellowship advisors.

NORTHERN MICHIGAN UNIVERSITY

4 Pu G S Sc Tr

▼ Honors Program

Opening in 1998, the Honors Program at Northern Michigan University provides academically motivated students with the opportunity to work toward their undergraduate degrees by taking specially designed departmental and interdisciplinary courses taught by highly skilled faculty members who are eager to work with talented students. The Honors Program exists to encourage excellence for undergraduate students of exceptional academic promise by providing enhanced opportunities for individual learning, collaborative innovation, and close cooperation with faculty members. In addition to taking honors courses, students complete University graduation requirements, including those of their selected majors, and finish as honors seniors completing a senior capstone directed study.

Participation Requirements: The Honors Program offers academically talented students an alternative curriculum to the required liberal studies program. To graduate from the Honors Program, students must complete 24 credits of core courses, 12 credits of honors contract courses, and 4 credits of honors capstone; demonstrate proficiency in precalculus or a higher level and the fourth semester of a foreign language; and maintain a minimum 3.0 overall GPA. Completion of the Honors Program is noted on students' transcripts and by recognition at campus ceremonies.

Admission Process: Admission of first-year students to the Honors Program is by invitation. After students have applied and been admitted to NMU, the Honors Program sends applications, reviews those submitted, and admits students to the program based on their high school GPA (3.5 minimum), test scores (27 ACT or SAT I equivalent minimum), applicants' personal essays, and letters of recommendation from high school teachers, counselors, and principals. Students already at NMU and transfer students are admitted on an individual basis after eligibility has been determined.

Within NMU and Honors Program guidelines, the program accepts Advanced Placement credits.

Scholarship Availability: The Honors Program recommends qualified students for the Mary L. Campbell Scholarships each year. In addition, Honors Program students often qualify for other merit-based scholarships.

The Campus Context: Northern Michigan University was established in 1899 as the Northern State Normal School. Today almost 200 academic programs in twenty-nine departments are offered in the Colleges of Arts and Sciences, Business, Professional Studies, and Technology and Applied Sciences. The campus is centrally located on the south shore of Lake Superior in Michigan's scenic Upper Peninsula.

Currently, the Honors Program is housed in the University Center and conducts its classes in buildings across campus. Some of the campus facilities of special interest include the Seaborg Science Center, which includes the recently completed New Science Facility; the renovated West Science Building; and the Superior Dome, one of the largest wooden domes in the world. NMU is designated as the only United States Olympic Education Center by the U.S. Olympic Committee.

Student Body Undergraduate enrollment is 7,672; 54 percent are women, and 7 percent are non-Caucasian. There are 1,182 out-of-state students and 107 international students. Thirty-four percent of students live on campus, and 80 percent of NMU undergraduates receive financial aid.

Faculty Instructional faculty members number 298. Eighty-six percent hold either doctorates or the highest degrees in their fields. The student-faculty ratio is 21:1.

Key Facilities The NMU Lydia Olson Library holds 521,280 books and journals and is the center for electronic research services. There are four University-operated computer labs; other computer labs are located in departments and residence halls.

Athletics NMU is a member of the NCAA, GLIAC, and the CCHA. Varsity teams for women include Alpine skiing, basketball, cross-country, Nordic skiing, soccer, swimming and diving, and volleyball and for men, basketball, football, hockey, Nordic skiing, and golf.

Study Abroad Through NMU's International Affairs Office, students can participate in exchanges and study-abroad programs in more than thirty-five countries around the world. All programs are coordinated through international program consortia agreements, and financial aid can be applied in most cases.

Support Services The Office of Disability Services provides accommodations for students with documented disabilities.

Job Opportunities Work opportunities are available on and off campus through the JobSearch Center.

Tuition: $3192 for state residents, $5976 for nonresidents, per year (2001–02)

Room and Board: $5436, per year (2001–02)

Mandatory Fees: $1064.60, per year (includes a $100 athletic events fee for first-time students and a $770 computer fee)

Contact: Dr. William Knox, University Center, Room 2306, 1401 Presque Isle Avenue, Marquette, Michigan 49855; Telephone: 906-227-2380; Fax: 906-227-1235; E-mail: honors@nmu.edu

NORTHERN STATE UNIVERSITY

4 Pu G S Sc Tr

▼ Honors Program/Honors Society

Northern State University (NSU) has developed two tracks in its approach to honors education. The first is the traditional, small-college approach: a requirement of 18 credit hours of honors classes, including an honors project or thesis supervised by a faculty committee. This is called the Honors Program. The second track is the Honors Society, which is separate yet interwoven with the Honors Program. These two tracks allow students maximum involvement in intellectual experiences and also the ability to choose how deeply to become involved with the honors concept.

Courses available to students in the Honors Program include English Composition, Literature, The Physics of Music, History, Political Science, Economics, Environmental Photography, and honors seminars for first- and third-year students. Courses are developed by interested faculty members and cover a wide range of topics.

The honors thesis or project is begun in the junior year and completed (ideally) in the first semester of the senior year. The student is responsible for forming a faculty committee and proposing the project to the committee. The student then prepares and defends the thesis or project under the supervision of the committee. Approximately 25 students are active in the program.

The Honors Society is a student-run and student-funded organization that is deeply involved in the intellectual life of NSU. The society publishes *Shelterbelt,* an anthology of student literature and art in full color. Over the years the society has purchased a collection of international films, both modern and classic. These films are available to all members to borrow or view in the Honors Center lounge. The society sponsors a Quiz Bowl for high school students attending the Northern South Dakota Science Fair that is held annually on campus. Teams of faculty members, administrators, and students test their wits and reflexes in a campuswide quiz show produced by the society. The society has a lounge area with a TV, a VCR, and a computer lab. Approximately 100 students are active in the society.

Participation Requirements: Students in the Honors Program must maintain a 3.25 GPA. Students who successfully complete the Honors Program graduate in their chosen majors, but their degree is designated *In Honoribus,* this being the highest academic honor granted by NSU. The diploma itself is oversized, and the honors graduates are singled out at Commencement and are awarded their diplomas before all other undergraduate degrees. The first *In Honoribus* degree was awarded by NSU in 1988.

Admission Process: Invitations to join the Honors Program are determined by ACT scores and high school class rankings, but self-nominations are accepted.

In contrast to the selectivity of the Honors Program, the NSU Honors Society is open to all students, without regard to grades or test scores, and is funded primarily by general activity fees. There is a high correlation of membership between the Honors Program and the Honors Society, as might be expected, but many students enjoy membership in the society without being members of the Honors Program.

Scholarship Availability: Students interested in the Honors Program/Honors Society should apply to the Office of Financial Assistance to be considered for a range of scholarships. The recommended deadlines are important and should be carefully followed.

The Campus Context: Northern State University, located in northeastern South Dakota, began life as the Northern Normal and Industrial School in 1901 and continues as a regional (South Dakota, North Dakota, Minnesota) university of 2,900 students. The compact campus of large trees and well-maintained buildings is located in South Dakota's third-largest city, Aberdeen (population 25,000). The nearest metropolitan area is the twin-city area of Minneapolis and Saint Paul, about a 5-hour drive. Airline connections are frequent. NSU plays a major role in the life of the community and enjoys widespread support from fans of athletics and the arts. The campus has five art galleries, a performing arts center, and a multiuse sports center.

NSU is comprised of the College of Arts and Sciences, the School of Business, the School of Education, and the School of Fine Arts. In support of both NSU and the state business community is the South Dakota International Business Institute (SDIBI). An English as a second language program is provided by the SDIBI. There are forty-nine majors and forty-one minors available.

The Regents of Education of South Dakota have designated NSU as the Center of Excellence for the state in the field of international business. This interdisciplinary major is administered by the School of Business and combines business, language, and cultural studies.

Student Body Sixty percent of the students are women. Eighty-nine percent are white, 2 percent are foreign nationals, 6 percent are American Indian, and 1 percent are black. Thirty-seven percent of the students live on campus, and 10 percent commute. Eighty percent receive financial assistance. There are no social fraternities and sororities, but there are numerous departmental and honorary organizations.

Faculty The faculty numbers 119, of whom 98 are full-time. Seventy-six percent have terminal degrees. The student-faculty ratio is 24:1.

Key Facilities The library has just undergone a major building project, doubling in physical size. Holdings are about 225,000 volumes, plus considerable electronic capability. More than 700 personal computers are available in twenty-three labs on campus. Student labs have access to the Internet and the World Wide Web.

Honorary Society Phi Eta Sigma

Athletics NSU is affiliated with the NCAA Division II and the Northern Sun Intercollegiate Conference. NSU competes in men's and women's basketball, golf, cross-country, indoor track and field, outdoor track and field, and tennis; men's football, baseball, and wrestling; and women's softball, volleyball, and soccer.

Study Abroad Study abroad opportunities include formal arrangements with the University of Warsaw (Poland); the University of Sichuan (China); Fachhochschule Magdeburg (Germany); Tec de Monterrey, Campus Sonora Norte (Mexico); and the National Student Exchange, as well as short trips organized by individual faculty members to various European countries.

Support Services The campus is being converted, with additional ramps and elevators, to full access for the physically disabled.

Job Opportunities Nearly 300 work-study positions are funded each year through the Office of Financial Assistance, and many departments also have budgets for direct payment for student labor.

Tuition: $1796 for state residents, $2130 for residents of Minnesota, $2696 for residents of Western Undergraduate Exchange states, $5716 for all other nonresidents, per 33 credit hours

Room and Board: $2492 per year

Mandatory Fees: $1236 per year

Contact: Director: Mark McGinnis, 12th Avenue and South Jay Street, Aberdeen, South Dakota 57401; Telephone: 605-626-2515; Fax: 605-626-3022; E-mail: mcginnim@wolf.northern.edu; Web site: http://www.northern.edu

Northwest College

2 Pu G S Tr

▼ Honors Program

The Northwest College (NWC) Honors Program creates, identifies, and enhances opportunities (academic, cultural, and social) responsive to the needs of highly motivated undergraduate students. It strives to maintain a balance between tradition and innovation, between established values and emerging insights.

For students with an enthusiasm for learning, the Northwest College Honors Program offers an opportunity of a challenging experience in core courses, to confront complex issues in honors seminars, to participate in extracurricular honors activities, and to receive special recognition on transcripts and at graduation ceremonies. In addition, graduates of the program have an excellent opportunity to transfer into an honors program at a four-year college or university. Honors degree students will join a nationwide network of their peers in similar programs. In addition, an honors degree from Northwest College may enhance students' chances to earn additional scholarships.

Honors seminars are small, team-taught by members of the outstanding Northwest faculty, and designed to bring together talented students from all majors across campus. The seminars are innovative, interdisciplinary, and intended to encourage a sense of close community among participants. In years past, the honors seminars included Voices of Science, Holocaust, Ethics, Nuclear Century, and The Sixties. In addition to enrolling in the seminars, students can also elect to receive honors credit for work in any regular college-level class offered at Northwest. Students choosing this approach to earning honors credit fulfill advanced course requirements developed by the instructor.

Participation Requirements: Students must maintain a minimum 3.5 GPA to stay in the program. To graduate with an honors

Interpreting the symbols: **2**=two-year college, **4**=four-year college; **Pu**=public or state college, **Pr**=private college; **G**=general honors program; **D**=departmental honors program; **S**=small program (fewer than 100 students), **M**=midsize program (100 to 500 students), **L**=large program (more than 500 students); **Sc**=scholarships available in honors program; **Tr**=transfer students accepted into honors program; **HBC**=historically black college; **AA**=academic advisors; **GA**=graduate advisors; **FA**=fellowship advisors.

designation, students must complete at least 30 credit hours from NWC and have earned at least a 3.5 GPA for NWC college-level credits.

Admission Process: Students must have a minimum 3.5 GPA or 25 ACT or better when entering from high school to be admitted to the Honors Program. Students must submit an Honors Program application, high school and college transcripts, and a narrative.

The Campus Context: Northwest College is a two-year, residential college offering transfer programs based upon the traditional arts and sciences and occupational programs that include strong general education requirements. Northwest prepares students to transfer anywhere in the nation to continue their education or to join the work force.

Northwest's modern 124-acre campus has fifty-seven buildings, including five residence halls and eighty apartments for 825 students. The campus is often described as one of the most beautiful in Wyoming. It is located in northwest Wyoming about 70 miles from Yellowstone National Park and 90 miles south of Billings, Montana. The campus, which is surrounded by three mountain ranges, is perfectly located for outdoor classes and recreational activities such as mountain climbing, kayaking, skiing, and spelunking.

Student Body There are more than 1,700 full-time students with an average age of 21.2. Thirty-five states and ten other countries are represented on campus.

Faculty There are 88 full-time and 77 part-time faculty members.

Key Facilities Library holdings include 37,500 volumes, 400 periodicals, and 52,000 pieces of microfiche. Windows and Mac labs are accessible as are the Internet and e-mail accounts. The library is a government documents depository and offers users electronic access to more than 4 million titles.

Athletics The College is a member of NJCAA. Men's basketball, wrestling, and rodeo are offered as are women's basketball, volleyball, and rodeo.

Support Services The Learning Skills Center provides free tutoring and services for students with a disability.

Job Opportunities Northwest College offers cooperative education and work-study opportunities.

Tuition: $1452 per year (1998–99)

Room and Board: $2932

Contact: Director of Admissions: Tom Herzog, 231 West 6th Street, Powell, Wyoming 82435, Telephone: 800-560-4NWC (4692) (toll-free); E-mail: herzogt@mail.nwc.whecn.edu; Web site: http://www.nwc.whecn.edu

Oakland University

4 Pu G M Sc Tr AA GA FA

▼ Honors College

Oakland's Honors College is designed for highly motivated students seeking a rich, valuable, and challenging undergraduate education. Honors College students are typically high achievers who want to think and question. Small classes that average 10 to 20 students allow for more interaction between the professor and other students in an intimate and intellectually friendly atmosphere. It offers a specially designed core of general education courses in art, literature, Western civilization, international studies, social science, mathematics, logic and computer science, and natural science and technology. A new set of courses is offered each semester, providing students with multiple chances to select courses of specific interest in different disciplines over a four-year period. All Honors College courses satisfy the University's general education requirements. Honors College students work toward completion of the Honors College requirements in conjunction with a departmental major. Honors College students also benefit from priority (first-day) registration beginning in the second semester of their freshman year.

Participation Requirements: In addition to achieving a GPA of at least 3.3 to graduate from the Honors College, students take four Honors College core courses in four general education categories. They achieve second-year foreign language proficiency by completing the two-year sequence of courses for the respective foreign languages. Students may take a foreign language placement test to determine where in the sequence they should start. Honors students also must produce an independent project (thesis). Every student must complete a work of substantial scholarly or creative achievement, which can be carried out in the student's major area of study. The student, together with a faculty sponsor/mentor, develops a proposal for the project, submits it to the Honors College Advisory Council for approval, and carries out the work. The end result is almost always a written thesis (it could be, however, a creative performance, a dance recital, or another type of creative activity), which must be approved by the mentor and the Advisory Council. In addition, honors students must take the Senior Colloquium, the fifth required course from the Honors College. This is the capstone course in the program, which is designed to explore a topic of current interest in the world. It is open only to juniors and seniors.

Admission Process: Admission to the Honors College is open to any student with an excellent academic record, including first-year students (high school applicants), transfer students, and currently enrolled students. Students are accepted into the Honors College throughout the year. Transfer students and currently enrolled Oakland students are evaluated primarily on the basis of their GPA (minimum of 3.3), recommendations, and an on-site interview. High school seniors must first apply to and be accepted by Oakland University. To be eligible for automatic admission to the Honors College, these students should have a GPA of at least 3.6 and a minimum composite ACT score of 25. Students whose GPA is higher then 3.6 may be admitted with a slightly lower ACT score. Students whose ACT score is higher than 25 may be admitted with a slightly lower GPA. Students who are eligible for automatic admission receive a letter from the Honors College indicating they have been admitted to the program.

Scholarship Availability: Several types of scholarships specifically for Honors College students are available. The David and Marion Handleman Scholarship provides half-tuition scholarships and is targeted to students who are demonstrated leaders and who have performed well academically. The J. Alford Jones Memorial Scholarship is awarded to an entering Honors College student. Applicants must have a minimum GPA of 3.5 and a composite score of 25 or above on the ACT. The Honors College Alumni Affiliate Scholarship provides support annually for a full-time student in the program. Additional Honors College scholarships are awarded to upper-level students to assist them in carrying out their independent projects.

The Campus Context: Oakland University (OU) is a growing, top-rated academic institution located in Rochester Hills, Michigan. OU offers students a personal, high-quality education through flexible class schedules and new facilities, student services, classroom technologies, labs, internships, co-ops, research opportunities with corporate partners, and degree and certificate programs.

Last year, *U.S. News & World Report* ranked Oakland University among the top national public universities. The Carnegie Foundation for the Advancement of Teaching recognized OU as one of the country's 110 doctoral research-intensive universities, giving graduate and undergraduate students the opportunity to work directly on research projects with expert faculty members.

With a record-breaking 15,875 students in fall 2001, Oakland is exploring new ways to prepare leaders through work-based learning and emerging technologies. New laboratories challenge students with real-life business problems. Oakland collaborates with business and industry to meet the demands of a highly educated workforce in southeastern Michigan and the world. To keep pace with OU's growing student population, Oakland University is enhancing its campus. In fall 2002, Oakland University is scheduled to open its new Education and Human Services Building and a student housing apartment complex. In fall 2000, Oakland opened the new R. Hugh and Nancy Elliott Hall of Business and Information Technology.

Student Body Oakland University offers a diverse range of programs for its students. A visit to OU's campus shows the many different types of students who live and go to school there. About 59 percent of students attend OU full-time, while the remaining 41 percent are part-time students. The majority (64 percent) of OU's undergraduate students are between the ages of 17 and 22. Fifteen percent of undergraduates are between 25 and 34 years old. About six percent are 45 to 55, and .5 percent are 55 or older.

Each year, Oakland University welcomes a more diverse student population. In 2001, minorities made up 13.5 percent of the total population, while about 3 percent of students claimed foreign nationalities. The minority breakdown is as follows: African American, 7.5 percent; Asian/Pacific Islander, 3.9 percent; Hispanic, .6 percent; American Indian/Alaskan Native, 0.5 percent; and foreign nationalities, 3 percent.

Faculty Oakland University has more than 400 full-time faculty members, 98 percent of whom hold Ph.D.'s from prestigious universities around the world. Nearly all of OU's classes are taught by faculty members; less than 1 percent are taught by teaching assistants.

Key Facilities Oakland University students receive a free OU e-mail account. That account gives them access to OU dial-up modem pools and MichNet modem pools to connect to OU computers and the Internet free of charge. The University offers e-mail training to new students. Computer labs throughout the campus contain PC and Macintosh computers, which are equipped with MS Office, Web browsers, and class-specific software. Wireless Internet access is available from the Oakland Center, OU's student union, and residence halls. Many classrooms also have technology-based features to enhance instruction.

Oakland University also offers many courses (or components of courses) online. In addition, students may register and pay for classes through the Internet.

Oakland's Kresge Library is conveniently located at the center of the campus and includes more than 654,000 books and audiovisual items, 2,000 journal and newspaper subscriptions, 215,000 federal and state documents, and more than 1.1 million microforms. The library also has a collection of electronic full-text journals and electronic books. To provide even greater resources to students, Kresge Library subscribes to many online services, such as FirstSearch, Infotrac, Web of Science, LEXIS-NEXIS, and MathSciNet. Students can access these services at the library or through its Web site at no charge. The library also houses a computer lab equipped with PC and Macintosh computers.

Honorary Societies Golden Key International Honour Society and National Collegiate Honors Council

Athletics As a member of NCAA Division I athletics and the Mid-Continent Conference, Oakland University's Golden Grizzlies compete in men's and women's basketball, cross-country, golf, soccer, and swimming and diving. Women's teams also play softball, tennis, and volleyball, while the men also compete in baseball. In its first two years competing in Division I athletics, OU's Golden Grizzlies won eleven conference titles, an unprecedented accomplishment.

Study Abroad Oakland University and the University of Detroit Mercy are proud to cooperate with Corpus Christi College to offer the British Studies at Oxford Program. It gives vital, firsthand exposure to the historical, artistic, political, cultural, and commercial milieu that informs literary and political works, business management, communication, educational theories, and fine arts studied in OU's courses.

All courses consist of a combination of lecture and tutorial, many of them with course-related excursions. Each course meets for a minimum of 10 hours of lecture a week in addition to individual and group tutorials. Tutors require either tests or essays, sometimes both.

Most courses are open to graduates and undergraduates as well as to those who can demonstrate university-level academic proficiency. All courses may be taken for University credit or may be audited, but auditors are expected to take seriously the academic responsibilities of the program.

Support Services Through the Office of Equity, OU works to increase recruitment, retention, and graduation of students, particularly underrepresented racial and ethnic groups such as African American, Latino, and Native American. The office also offers programs and services to ensure academic and social success, such as peer mentoring, leadership development, and academic and peer counseling.

Through Oakland's Academic Skills Center, students can get the support they need to excel in classes and college life. Here, students can take advantage of individual and group tutoring, training in study skills and strategies, supplemental instruction, self-paced instructional materials, and more. These services are available free of charge to OU students.

Job Opportunities Oakland University offers students many opportunities to help pay for their college education. Through the government-funded Federal Work-Study Program, undergraduate and graduate students with financial need can get part-time jobs on campus. Many other on-campus jobs are available without demonstrated financial need.

In addition, Oakland's Placement and Career Services office provides direct access to career-related full-time, part-time, and seasonal job opportunities through on-campus interviews, job referrals, posted job notices, and a job vacancy bulletin.

Graduate students may be appointed to assistantships in schools and departments. Departments that offer assistantships nominate graduate students for these positions. Stipends depend on assignment, hours of work required, and qualifications.

Tuition: Oakland University is committed to keeping costs as low as possible, giving students an excellent education at an affordable price. The following estimated costs are for the 2001–02 academic year and are based on full-time (12 credits for undergraduates, 8 credits for graduates) attendance for one semester. The semester costs for on-campus room and board, based on double occupancy, are also included. In-state costs are $1587 for tuition, $236 for fees, $280 for books and supplies, and $2489 for room and board, for an estimated total of $4592 per semester. Tuition for out-of-state students costs $4368. All other in-state costs apply, so out-of-state students pay an estimated total of $7373 per semester.

Contact: Interim Director: Barry Winkler, 409 Dodge Hall of Engineering, Oakland University, Rochester, Michigan 48309; Telephone: 248-370-2398; E-mail: winkler@oakland.edu; Web site: http://www2.oakland.edu/hc/index.cfm

Oakton Community College

2 Pu G M Tr

▼ Honors at Oakton

Honors at Oakton offers academically talented students all the advantages of a traditional liberal arts college education: small

Interpreting the symbols: **2**=two-year college, **4**=four-year college; **Pu**=public or state college, **Pr**=private college; **G**=general honors program; **D**=departmental honors program; **S**=small program (fewer than 100 students), **M**=midsize program (100 to 500 students), **L**=large program (more than 500 students); **Sc**=scholarships available in honors program; **Tr**=transfer students accepted into honors program; **HBC**=historically black college; **AA**=academic advisors; **GA**=graduate advisors; **FA**=fellowship advisors.

classes, distinguished faculty members, and challenging courses. It is a program designed for students who have the ability to succeed anywhere but who choose to remain close to home and obtain a high-quality education at an affordable cost. Through participation in the student-centered, writing-intensive program, students are prepared to face the challenges of further education and competitive career markets.

Honors students themselves are the best advocates of Honors at Oakton. These comments are typical of those found on students' evaluations of their courses: "There is a closeness established among a smaller group, and I felt more at ease." "Honors students were really excited about the class and challenges. They were trying to achieve something extra for themselves, which impressed me." Honors classes feature discussions and student involvement and independent and collaborative work. One student wrote: "We were guided into an understanding of the whys rather than just bone dry facts."

Honors at Oakton features interdisciplinary, team-taught seminars, honors sections of general education courses, and the opportunity to pursue honors contract work in regular courses. Honors classes are usually composed of about 15 students, and they are taught by the best faculty members in the College. Oakton honors students have won a Truman Fellowship and a place on the Phi Theta Kappa All-American team; they have given papers at the National Undergraduate Research Conference, the annual conference of the National Collegiate Honors Council (NCHC), and the conference of the Society for Ecological Restoration.

Honors at Oakton sponsors a student organization and a variety of out-of-classroom activities, including trips to the theatre, symphony, and Chicago area museums; such guest speakers as Scott Turow, Tim O'Brien, Leon Lederman, and Frances Fitzgerald; an off-campus leadership workshop; and an annual banquet. Personalized counseling assists students at every step with academic choices, and when the time comes to transfer, students are able to attend workshops on choosing a transfer institution, finding and applying for financial aid, and completing the application. An annual luncheon brings transfer admission directors from Northwestern University, the University of Chicago, Loyola University, DePaul University, and other Chicago-area colleges and universities to campus to meet with honors students. Oakton honors students have transferred successfully to such institutions as these, as well as Cornell University, Oberlin College, Grinnell College, the University of Notre Dame, and many other outstanding colleges.

Honors at Oakton enrolls between 150 and 200 students every year.

Participation Requirements: Students must take 18 hours of honors courses to graduate as an Honors Program Scholar, but many students take fewer than 18 hours, and some take many more. All honors courses are specially designated on the transcript. To graduate as an Honors Scholar, students must maintain a minimum 3.25 GPA, and honors program graduates are specially noted at graduation.

Admission Process: To be admitted to Honors at Oakton, a student must have an ACT score of at least 25 or an SAT score of at least 1150 and be in the top 20 percent of the high school class. Students are also admitted to Honors at Oakton based on a minimum 3.5 GPA at Oakton or a transfer school or a GED score of at least 300. Students with a bachelor's degree or higher are automatically eligible for Honors at Oakton. Students must maintain a minimum 3.25 GPA to continue in the program.

The Campus Context: Oakton Community College has two campuses, one in Des Plaines and the other in Skokie, Illinois. Among special services, a modern child-care center is available for children of students and staff and faculty members. Tutoring is available for all subjects, as are support services for students with physical and learning disabilities. Other features include media-based courses, adult student services, and international student services. The College offers three baccalaureate degrees and thirty-five vocational degrees and certificates.

Student Body The total enrollment at Oakton is 10,400: 44 percent men and 56 percent women. All are commuter students, with an average age of 30. Approximately 6 percent of students receive financial aid.

Faculty Of the 600 faculty members, 152 are full-time and 448 are part-time. The student-faculty ratio is 17:1.

Key Facilities The library houses 70,000 volumes and has immediate access to material from Illinois libraries. There are fourteen computer labs housing 600 computers. A full array of constantly updated courses is available in computer science, applications, and technology.

Honorary Society Phi Theta Kappa

Athletics Oakton has ten intercollegiate athletic teams competing in the Skyway Conference: golf, cross-country, women's volleyball, and tennis; men's soccer in the fall; men's and women's basketball in the winter; and baseball, women's softball, and men's tennis in the spring.

Study Abroad Students have opportunities for study abroad in Canterbury, England; Salzburg, Austria; San Jose, Costa Rica; and Diemen and Hertogenbosch, the Netherlands. There are also study-abroad and NCHC-sponsored semesters for honors students.

Job Opportunities Students find opportunities for employment on campus as 15-hour-per-week student aides.

Tuition: $1260 for area residents, $3780 for state residents, $5040 for nonresidents, per year (1999–2000)

Mandatory Fees: $48

Contact: Director: Dr. Richard Stacewicz, 1600 East Golf Road, Des Plaines, Illinois 60016; Telephone: 847-635-1914; Fax: 847-635-1764; E-mail: rstacewi@oakton.edu

---

The Ohio State University

4 Pu L Sc Tr

▼ University Honors Program

Within the context of a major research university, the Ohio State University Honors Program offers outstanding students a variety of exciting learning opportunities, including more than 185 honors courses each year. Honors classes have an average size of 18 students, are taught by members of the faculty with a strong commitment to undergraduate education, and can only be taken by honors students.

Honors students have many opportunities for research and scholarship under the guidance of a faculty member. Typically, this culminates in a senior honors thesis and graduation with distinction. Grants and scholarships are available on a competitive basis to students involved in their own research projects. Each spring selected students present their research at the Denman Undergraduate Research Forum.

Four honors living centers provide on-campus housing for honors students. They provide rooms in a variety of sizes and configurations, comfortably furnished study areas, a fully equipped kitchen, game areas, and television lounges. Personal computer centers are located within or near all four honors residence halls.

An active program of cocurricular activities is associated with the University Honors Program, including the Honors Peer Mentor Program, which matches first-quarter honors students with upperclass honors students, and the Honors Cultural Program Board, which plans and stages a variety of cultural and educational programs, service projects, and student-faculty events.

The 14-year-old program currently enrolls 4,000 students.

Participation Requirements: To maintain honors eligibility, students must maintain a minimum GPA and in the Colleges of Arts and Sciences follow an approved honors contract.

In addition to Summa, Magna, and Cum Laude recognition awarded to students graduating in the top 10 percent of the class, graduation with honors is awarded to students completing an honors contract. Graduation with distinction is given to students successfully completing a thesis project.

Admission Process: To join the program, students must have graduated in the top 10 percent of their high school class and have either an ACT score of 30 or above or a SAT score of 1300 or above. Outstanding students who do not meet these criteria are encouraged to submit an essay with their applications.

Scholarship Availability: The Ohio State University offers a competitive merit aid program, with scholarships awarded based upon a student's high school record, ACT or SAT scores, and the results of an on-campus scholarship program. These scholarships include University Scholarships, $1200 per year awards for four years; Tradition Scholarships, half in-state tuition for four years; Medalist Scholarships, full in-state tuition for four years; and Presidential Scholarships, which provide full in-state tuition, room and board, book allowance, and miscellaneous expenses for four years.

National Merit and National Achievement Scholarships are awarded to National Merit/Achievement finalists who designate Ohio State as their first-choice institution of attendance by February 15. Such students may also receive a Distinguished Scholarship. Taken together, these scholarships cover full in-state tuition plus $4500 per year for four years.

Other financial assistance, including scholarships, research support, grants, loans, and part-time employment, is available to qualified students at the Ohio State University.

The Campus Context: There are nineteen colleges at the Ohio State University: Arts; Biological Sciences; Business; Dentistry; Education; Engineering; Food, Agricultural, and Environmental Sciences; Human Ecology; Humanities; Law; Math and Physical Sciences; Medicine and Nursing; Optometry; Pharmacy; Social and Behavioral Sciences; Social Work; University College; and Veterinary Medicine. Students may enroll in 215 majors in 104 academic departments. Distinguished facilities on campus include the Ohio Supercomputer Center, Wexner Center for the Arts, and the James Cancer Research Center and Hospital.

Student Body Undergraduate enrollment is 40,993: 21,320 men and 19,673 women. The ethnic distribution is 87 percent white, 6.7 percent African American, 4.4 percent Asian-American, 1.6 percent Hispanic, and 0.3 percent Native American. There are 3,827 international students. About 18 percent of students live on campus, and another 21.6 percent live in the area adjacent to campus. There are thirty fraternities and twenty sororities.

Faculty Of the 4,310 faculty members, 3,909 are full-time, 95 percent of whom have terminal degrees. The student-faculty ratio is 14:1.

Key Facilities The library houses 4.7 million volumes. Extensive computer facilities include two Cray supercomputers.

Athletics In athletics, Ohio State has thirty-two Division I intercollegiate varsity teams, seventy sports clubs, and sixty-two intramural sports programs.

Study Abroad Study-abroad opportunities are coordinated through the Office of International Education.

Support Services Disabled-student facilities include accessible buildings and special services.

Job Opportunities A wide array of work opportunities are available both on and off campus.

Tuition: $3879 for state residents, $10,869 for nonresidents, per year (1998–99)

Room and Board: $4907

Contact: Director: Dr. Mabel Freeman, Kuhn Honors and Scholars House, 220 West Twelfth Avenue, Columbus, Ohio 43210; Telephone: 614-292-3135; Fax: 614-292-6135; E-mail: osuhons@osu.edu; Web site: www.osu.edu/units/honors/honors.html

The Ohio State University at Newark

2 Pu G S Sc Tr AA

▼ Honors Program

Housed within a regional campus of a major research university, the Ohio State University at Newark (OSU-Newark) Honors Program attempts to cultivate excellence in students who demonstrate an outstanding commitment to academic achievement. The program does this by creating opportunities for students to enhance their thinking skills, pursue deep questions, try new things, and change the world. Honors courses are small classes with more student discussion and less lecture than in some other courses. They usually require an independent research project, and students teach each other on the basis of their research. Students usually can fulfill the requirements for freshman composition, history, humanities, math, science, and social science by taking honors courses. In addition, a 1-credit-hour honors seminar is offered on a different topic every quarter. It typically meets for one day, all day, on a holiday and is graded pass/non-pass. Honors courses are more informal than other courses, and students get to know the instructor very well. Often, they meet in the Honors Apartment, which provides space for classes, meals, meetings, hanging out, or studying. The Honors Apartment is furnished with computers, a fully equipped kitchen, and seminar tables. Honors students receive a key that allows them to use the apartment during regular hours. Laurel, OSU-Newark's honors society, meets in the apartment regularly, as do individuals and several classes.

One corridor of Campus View Village is set apart for honors students. Here, high-ability students study, work, and play together. Honors students compete for the privilege of living in the Honors Corridor. Students are selected on the basis of their potential leadership in the Honors Program, on the campus, or in the community. Those who are chosen are designated LeFevre Fellows. All honors-eligible students are encouraged to apply.

Limited to 15 students, honors courses are taught as seminars and, yet, count toward the general education curriculum required of all Ohio State graduates. Students can take one or two courses or a full two-year honors sequence. Honors students are the first to be enrolled in their chosen courses.

Participation Requirements: To maintain honors status, students must maintain a minimum 3.4 GPA and take one honors course per year.

Admission Process: The criteria for incoming first-year students are an ACT score of at least 26 or an SAT score of at least 1170 and a ranking in the top 10 percent of the high school class or an ACT score of at least 24 or an SAT of at least 1100 and a ranking in the top 5 percent of the high school class. To attain honors affiliation, students who meet these criteria must take an honors course.

Interpreting the symbols: **2**=two-year college, **4**=four-year college; **Pu**=public or state college, **Pr**=private college; **G**=general honors program; **D**=departmental honors program; **S**=small program (fewer than 100 students), **M**=midsize program (100 to 500 students), **L**=large program (more than 500 students); **Sc**=scholarships available in honors program; **Tr**=transfer students accepted into honors program; **HBC**=historically black college; **AA**=academic advisors; **GA**=graduate advisors; **FA**=fellowship advisors.

A student already at OSU-Newark must have a minimum GPA of 3.4 (not including remedial courses) with a minimum of 15 credit hours. Transfer students must complete one quarter on campus and achieve a minimum 3.4 GPA to become eligible. To attain honors affiliation, students who meet these criteria must take an honors course.

OSU-Newark honors students lose their "H" status when they move to the Columbus campus. To regain honors status, students must apply to the honors program in their college.

Scholarship Availability: OSU-Newark awards a number of full and partial tuition scholarships to new honors students. The criteria for consideration include completion of the high school college preparatory curriculum and strong academic performance as evidenced by rank in class, GPA, and standardized test scores. To qualify, students must either be in the top 10 percent of their class with an ACT score of at least 26 or SAT score of at least 1170 or be in the top 5 percent of their class with an ACT score of 24 or 25 or SAT of 1090 to 1150. These Honored Scholar scholarships are renewable for a second year to students who have at least a 3.5 cumulative GPA and 45 credit hours at the end of spring quarter of their first year.

OSU-Newark selects a number of honors students to be LeFevre Fellows. Some recipients receive monies toward tuition and books. The others live in the Honors Corridor at Campus View Village at a reduced rent. Applicants must be honors students who complete a project to benefit the campus or the community. These awards are for one year only, but students may reapply in subsequent years.

The Campus Context: Ohio State's regional campuses are not separate institutions; rather, they are geographical extensions of a single university. Courses offered at OSU-Newark are the same as those taught in Columbus and appear on students' transcripts exactly as they would at the main campus. The faculty members are hired, promoted, and tenured according to the same guidelines as their colleagues at other campuses. So OSU-Newark offers students all the conveniences and advantages of a small campus without the hassle of transferring credit when moving to the main campus.

OSU-Newark is also more than simply a transfer campus. Students earn both bachelor's and master's degrees in elementary education at OSU-Newark and can complete all the course work necessary for bachelor's degrees in English, history, and psychology. Other Ohio State majors require at least some courses that are available only in Columbus.

Student Body Undergraduate enrollment is 2,079, including 1,260 women and 819 men. Commuter students comprise 92.8 percent of the undergraduate population. OSU-Newark's racial and ethnic composition is 92 percent white, 3.4 percent African American, 1.7 percent Asian American, 0.7 percent Native American, and 0.6 percent Hispanic. International students comprise approximately 0.2 percent of the student population. No national sororities or fraternities are present at OSU-Newark.

Faculty Of the 110 faculty members at OSU-Newark, 57 are full-time, 79 percent of whom have terminal degrees.

Key Facilities The Newark Campus Library subscribes to more than 400 periodicals, houses about 45,000 volumes, and has more than 500 videos along with several hundred CDs and audio books. In addition, by virtue of being part of both the Ohio State University library system and OhioLINK (the statewide consortia of about eighty academic libraries), the Newark Campus Library has access to nearly 100 databases, several thousand full-text journals, and borrowing privileges from all OhioLINK members via daily courier service. OSU-Newark's computer facilities feature an open lab for all students, as well as labs for writing, math, and psychology.

Honorary Society Laurel

Athletics The Newark Campus Athletic Department provides athletic, recreation, and fitness opportunities for both OSU-Newark students and students at Central Ohio Technical College, which shares the facilities with OSU-Newark. Newark Campus student-athletes participate in competition through the Ohio Regional Campus Conference on six club sport teams. The teams involve approximately 85 students in intercollegiate athletic activities annually.

Study Abroad Study-abroad programs are coordinated through the Columbus campus of OSU.

Support Services The Learning Assistance Center and Disability Services (LAC/DS) is the academic support unit in Student Support Services. LAC/DS provides free programs and services designed to help students sharpen skills necessary to succeed in college.

Job Opportunities Work opportunities are available both on and off campus.

Tuition: $3606 per year for in-state students (2001–02)

Contact: Director: Dr. William L. MacDonald, 1179 University Drive, Newark, Ohio 43055; Telephone: 740-366-9330; Fax: 740-366-5047; E-mail: macdonald.24@osu.edu; Web site: http://www.newark.ohio-state.edu/~osuhonor

---

Ohio University

4 Pu M Sc Tr

▼ Honors Tutorial College

Ohio University's Honors Tutorial College is based on the tutorial model of collaborative learning found at Oxford and Cambridge Universities, in which each student meets in individual sessions with faculty members to discuss and explore content assigned, researched, and examined.

The College was founded in 1972 after nearly ten years of departmentally based honors programs. The Honors Tutorial College is a full degree-granting college in twenty-six academic disciplines ranging from biological sciences to physics and journalism to dance. A Secondary Education Certificate is also available for Honors Tutorial students. These programs are separate and distinct from the traditional undergraduate degrees, although the honors student's curriculum may include traditional course work as well as tutorials.

Each program has a core curriculum, and students enroll in at least one tutorial each term. Additional collateral course work is selected with the help of an adviser in a fashion that permits tailoring of each student's total college curriculum. There is no hour minimum for graduation; students must demonstrate competencies through high-quality writing, thinking, and a research thesis or project that is defended before graduation.

Honors Tutorial students are the only students who are not responsible for the University's general education requirements, save freshman English and junior composition, which may be waived. Some programs are three years in duration, and students sometimes remain a fourth year and complete the requirements for the master's degree in their discipline.

Approximately 200 faculty members participate as tutors each year, giving service, in most cases, to the College in addition to their normal academic loads. Tutors are full-time faculty members with outstanding teaching and research credentials.

Admission Process: Students are selected on the basis of SAT I and ACT scores, rank in their high school class, achievement, academic discipline, and a personal interview by the Director of Studies in the academic program of choice. Although some programs require higher scores and indications of achievement, the minimums for consideration (not admission) are 1300 on the SAT I, 30 on the ACT, and a rank in the top 10 percent of the student's high school class. Significant scholarly, literary, artistic, and community experiences are also considered in the determination of the student's application. A very limited number of openings are available for transfer students from both within and outside the University.

The College currently has a ceiling of 225 students. Each year, the College receives more than 400 applications, from which it selects approximately one third for on-site personal interviews and traditionally admits 100 for a yield of 55 to 65.

Applications for the following fall quarter are due by December 15.

Scholarship Availability: Scholarships and grants are available from full tuition, room, and board to smaller grants and awards. Research apprenticeship programs provide, on a competitive basis, salary for student researchers to work with faculty members on significant projects.

The Campus Context: Ohio University, a Research II university, is the oldest university in the Northwest Territory, having been founded in 1804. It offers academic programs on five regional campuses in addition to the main campus at Athens. The Honors Tutorial College programs are only available on the Athens campus. The University is located on a residential campus in southeast Ohio.

There are ten colleges on campus: Arts and Sciences, Business, Communication, Education, Engineering, Fine Arts, Health and Human Services, Honors Tutorial, Osteopathic Medicine, and University. In addition, the University offers certificate programs in many areas, most notably women's studies and international studies. Students are enrolled in 269 baccalaureate, 153 master's, forty-seven doctoral (including osteopathic medicine), and twenty-four associate degree programs.

The University has excellent science laboratories, including an accelerator facility, and state-of-the-art electronic media facilities, including public television and radio stations, film facilities, and digital photojournalism labs.

Student Body Of the 19,327 students enrolled at the Athens campus, about 54 percent are women and 46 percent are men. Minority distribution is 6 percent, and there are more than 1,096 international students from more than ninety-seven countries. For the academic year 2000–01, more than 5,000 institutional scholarships were awarded. There are thirty-four sororities and fraternities on the Athens campus with strong student support.

Faculty There are more than 900 full-time faculty members on the Athens campus, nearly all with appropriate terminal degrees; 90 percent have attained the rank of full or associate professor. The ratio of students to faculty members in non-tutorial classes is 21:1.

Key Facilities The University library has Association of Research Libraries (ARL) status and contains more than 2 million volumes. The library system is part of OhioLink, a computer network of university libraries. The University has many mainframes and specialty mini-mainframes for specific departments and research. Every residence hall room is equipped with a computer and printer. Each student is given an e-mail address and is able to access University, library, and Internet facilities. In addition, the Honors Tutorial College supports an excellent computer laboratory in Hoover Hall, the residence hall in which most honors students live.

Athletics The 13,000-seat Convocation Center is the site of sporting events, and the Ping Recreation Center is one of the finest multipurpose facilities in the nation. The University offers a full range of athletics and is a member of the Mid-American Conference.

Study Abroad The University has a full-time Education Abroad Office, helping students take advantage of programs at more than 100 universities around the world. In addition, the Honors Tutorial College has special exchange agreements with a number of universities abroad, and students are encouraged to participate.

Support Services The University is in full compliance with the Americans with Disabilities Act (ADA) and has available administrative, instructional, and other appropriate support, including specialty technologies, for students needing such assistance.

Job Opportunities The University offers work-study programs and an advanced career exploration work program. In addition, the Athens business community offers a number of work opportunities for students.

Tuition: $5493 for state residents, $11,562 for nonresidents, per year (2001–02)

Room and Board: $6276

Contact: Dean: Dr. Joseph H. Berman, 35 Park Place, Athens, Ohio 45701; Telephone: 740-593-2723; Fax: 740-593-9521; E-mail: berman@ohio.edu; Web site: http://www.ouhtc.org

OKLAHOMA BAPTIST UNIVERSITY

4 Pr G S Tr AA

▼ Honors Program

The Oklahoma Baptist University (OBU) Honors Program offers academic enhancement and opportunities for independent study and fellowship with other academically outstanding students in all majors. The Honors Program curriculum includes some common classes and multiple opportunities for independent study, service, and travel. Students in the Honors Program are asked to complete two of three capstones—extended volunteer service, study abroad, and a senior thesis. Additional costs and course requirements above those required for normal graduation are minimal.

It is also possible to complete an honors degree by writing a thesis under the guidelines and direction of the University honors committee.

In the freshman year, Honors Program students complete a 3-hour Introduction to Honors (Critical Skills) course and a 3-hour honors version of Composition and Classical Literature in lieu of normal freshman English requirements. After the freshman year, students complete at least four honors colloquia (0–1 hour each), an honors biblical ethics course (in lieu of another required course in religion), a contracted study course in the major (1–2 hours), and two of three capstone experiences. Service internship requires a minimum of 80 clock hours on an approved project. Travel/study abroad requires at least four weeks of immersion in a non-U.S. cultural setting. The thesis requires an extended research and independent writing project completed under direction of a faculty adviser; thesis completion involves registration for a 3-hour independent study course. Students must maintain a 3.25 GPA overall to remain active in the program.

Students inside or outside of the Honors Program may elect to complete only the thesis for honors graduation. They must have a 3.5 GPA overall and in the major at the time of application (mid-junior year) and at completion. Students work with a faculty adviser, an off-campus reader, and the University honors committee, presenting several progress reports and eventually a public presentation/defense and a final document.

Participation Requirements: Participation is offered to all entering freshmen with a high school GPA of 3.5 or higher and scores of 29 (composite) on the ACT or 1300 (combined) on the SAT. Students with slightly lower test scores and high motivation are encouraged to apply as space is available. Occasionally other highly successful and motivated freshmen are allowed to join the

Interpreting the symbols: **2**=two-year college, **4**=four-year college; **Pu**=public or state college, **Pr**=private college; **G**=general honors program; **D**=departmental honors program; **S**=small program (fewer than 100 students), **M**=midsize program (100 to 500 students), **L**=large program (more than 500 students); **Sc**=scholarships available in honors program; **Tr**=transfer students accepted into honors program; **HBC**=historically black college; **AA**=academic advisors; **GA**=graduate advisors; **FA**=fellowship advisors.

program after the first semester of the freshman year. Transfer students who come to OBU after having been active in an honors program are admitted, but their experiences are assessed and requirements are adjusted individually.

Scholarship Availability: Many OBU students are awarded academic scholarships, but no scholarship aid is given simply for participation in the Honors Program. Some awards are made by the program to assist honors students to complete study abroad or thesis research.

The Campus Context: Oklahoma Baptist University is a senior-level coeducational institution with a curricular emphasis in the liberal arts. It is located in Shawnee, a city of 28,000 residents, which is 30 miles east of Oklahoma City, near the geographical center of the state. The 189-acre campus is just 2 miles south of Interstate Highway 40.

OBU utilizes the semester calendar plan with a four-month fall term, a four-week January term, a four-month spring term, and 2 four-week summer terms. The University is composed of the College of Arts and Science, the Warren M. Angel College of Fine Arts, the Paul Dickinson School of Business, the School of Nursing, and the Joe L. Ingram School of Christian Service. All students complete strong general studies requirements in what is referred to as the Unified Studies program, which includes requirements in communications, English, math, philosophy, religion, science, social sciences, and western civilization. There are more than seventy-five areas of concentration and majors in various departments of instruction. Students may also design their own interdisciplinary majors.

The campus is known by students and alumni as Bison Hill, a reflection of the school's mascot but also of the historic sense of place in what was Indian Territory until Oklahoma statehood in 1907, the same year in which the first board of trustees for the college was named. The present campus site, chosen in 1915, today includes twenty-six major buildings. Among the more recent additions are the Bailey Business Center, the W. P. Wood Science Building, and the renovated Sarkey's Telecommunications Center.

Students at Oklahoma Baptist University are encouraged to pursue development in the academic, physical, and spiritual dimensions of their lives, and many participate in programs of public service and/or ministry, even while enrolled in classes. A large number of OBU students participate in summer missions and/or study programs, both in the U.S. and abroad. Graduates in recent years have found entry-level occupations in business, communications, education, fine arts, recreation, religious ministry, scientific and technical areas, and social services. Many, including graduates of the Honors Program, have also continued their education in some of the nation's finest graduate programs (e.g., Illinois, Columbia, Princeton). An unusually high percentage of premedicine majors gain acceptance to medical studies programs (graduates are currently at Duke, Mayo, Oklahoma, and Kansas).

Student Body Total enrollment for fall 2001 was 2,017, including off-site students. On-campus students totaled 1,610, 60 percent of whom were women. Ethnic distribution is 87 percent white, non-Hispanic; 3 percent African American; 5 percent Native American; 2 percent Asian American; and 2 percent Hispanic American. Eighty-seven percent of students received financial aid; the average award was $7800 per year. Sixty-six percent of students live in campus housing; of these, 95 percent are freshmen.

Faculty Full-time faculty members total 118; of these, 81 percent hold terminal degrees.

Key Facilities Library holdings include 230,000 books, serials, government documents; 1,800 serial subscriptions; 315,000 microform items; and 7,600 audiovisual items. The library also contains special research collections and a listening and audiovisual center. There are eight computer labs containing more than twenty workstations each, plus additional labs in dorms and multiple computer accessibility in the library for catalog and World Wide Web access; in addition, all dorm rooms are wired for Web access.

Athletics All sports are NAIA Division I, including men's and women's basketball, golf, tennis, and track; men's baseball; and women's softball. In recent years, teams have been nationally ranked in most sports, and there have been numerous academic all-American awards.

Study Abroad OBU maintains a full-time staffed international study office to assist students planning to travel and/or study abroad. The University does not maintain any international campus, but does have regular programs: TESOL at Xinjiang University in Urumqi, China, during summers, and full-year student exchange with Seinan Gaukuin in Fukuoka, Japan. Many students study abroad through individually arranged programs.

Honorary Societies Phi Eta Sigma, Mortar Board, Omicron Delta Kappa

Support Services Campus facilities are currently 95 percent handicapped-accessible. The University testing office assists students with academic handicap identification and accommodation. Two percent of students currently receive some sort of academic accommodation.

Job Opportunties Institutional work-study is available through various campus departments; some student employment requires work-study qualification. Several departments maintain internship and cooperative education programs.

Tuition and Fees: In 2001–02 tuition was $9500 per year; mandatory fees were $740 per year.

Room and Board: $3470 per year (including fourteen meals per week)

Contact: Director: Dr. Doug Watson, OBU Box 61244, 500 West University, Shawnee, Oklahoma 74804; E-mail: doug.watson@mail.okbu.edu; Web site: http://www.okbu.edu/academics/honors.html.

Oklahoma City University

4 Pr G M Tr

▼ University Honors Program

Oklahoma City University (OCU) established the University Honors Program in 1990 to meet the special interests and needs of intellectually gifted students. Open to qualified undergraduates of all majors, the University Honors Program offers honors sections of Foundation Curriculum (general education) courses. Honors students may choose from a wide variety of these courses, which include psychology, computers and artificial intelligence, literature and philosophy, history, and many others. During their first semester in the Honors Program, all new students enroll in the 1-hour Honors Colloquium, a course designed to help each class of honors students become better acquainted with each other and the Honors Program. The capstone honors course is the Junior-Senior seminar, which is offered with varying topics each semester.

At Oklahoma City University, an honors course generally covers the same material as a traditional course, but honors sections are smaller and more often use a seminar format. The requirements differ from those of regular classes, not so much in the amount of work demanded as in the type of work. Honors classes typically involve extensive class participation, and written work is often in the form of essays or individual research projects.

In addition to the academic advantages of the University Honors Program, OCU honors students enjoy other benefits as well. Honors students have the benefit of priority semester enrollment and an additional .25 added to each credit hour of honors courses. Honors students have opportunities to meet with visiting scholars and attend special events, both social and academic. As part of a network of the National Collegiate Honors Council,

OCU honors students may present papers at regional and national conferences and participate in exciting summer and semester programs.

There are 120 students in the program.

Participation Requirements: In order to be a University Honors Program graduate, students must complete 25 hours in honors sections of Foundation Curriculum courses while maintaining at least a 3.5 cumulative university GPA and a 3.25 cumulative GPA in honors courses.

Two courses, the Honors Colloquium and the Junior-Senior Seminar, are required for all students in the program. Students may select from a variety of courses, including independent research, to complete the balance of the 25-hour requirement. Upon successful completion of the requirements, honors students receive special recognition upon graduation, a gold stole to wear at the Commencement ceremony with their cap and gown, and a special designation on their diplomas.

Admission Process: The University Honors Program welcomes applications during the fall semester from all interested OCU first-year and sophomore students. To be eligible, a student must have a 3.5 GPA in a minimum of 12 OCU hours. The application process includes documentation of previous University midterm grades, written recommendations from 2 OCU faculty members, and a brief essay describing why the student wishes to join the program.

Currently enrolled students should apply no later than October 15.

Scholarship Availability: OCU offers a wide variety of scholarships, both academic and need-based, to students of exceptional ability and promise.

The Campus Context: Oklahoma City University is a campus of seven colleges and schools: Petree College of Arts and Sciences; Margaret E. Petree College of Music and Performing Arts, which houses the School of Music and the School of American Dance and Arts Management; Kramer School of Nursing; Meinders School of Business; Wimberly School of Religion and Graduate Theological Center; and the Law School. Nine bachelor's degrees with seventy majors and eleven master's degrees are offered on campus.

Distinguished campus facilities include the Petree College of Arts and Sciences Building, a two-story structure featuring classrooms, offices, a learning center, seminar and meeting rooms, and a mass communication center that houses the campus newspaper and OCU-TV2 station. OCU-TV2 is a wireless cable television station that provides students with hands-on production experience and access to a professionally designed studio and two control rooms. The Sarkeys Law Center, opened in spring 1994, houses classrooms, seminar rooms, moot courtrooms, the Native American Legal Resource Center, administrative offices, and student organization offices. The Gold Star Building, renovated in 1996, which houses the law library, faculty offices, and the offices of the OCU Law Review, contains four floors of library space and offices and is crowned by a tower that has become an Oklahoma City landmark. The Kramer School of Nursing building is a state-of-the-art newly constructed facility. The Noble Center for Competitive Enterprise building houses the Meinders School of Business, the B.D. Eddie Business Research and Consulting Center, the Jack Conn School of Community Banking, offices, and classrooms.

The Kirkpatrick Fine Arts Center, which houses the School of Music, offices, classrooms, and practice rooms, contains the Kirkpatrick Theater, a 1,119-seat facility with a fully equipped proscenium stage; Burg Theater, a 255-seat auditorium with a three-quarter round stage used for dramatic productions, lectures, and other special presentations; dance studios; costume and scene shops; dressing rooms; and the recently constructed 500-seat Petree Recital Hall, which is designed to offer the finest facilities for large and small instrumental and vocal ensembles and solo recitals and audio and television recording of performances and is equipped with two 9-foot Steinway Concert Grand pianos.

The Bishop W. Angie Smith Chapel is home to the Wimberly School of Religion and Graduate Theological Center, classrooms, and offices. In this building, designed by Pietro Bulluschi, the main chapel seats 650 and features four large German stained glass windows depicting the seasons. The Norick Art Center, designed to be as functional, comfortable, and safe for students as possible, contains the Hulsey Gallery, designed by specifications from the Smithsonian Institute.

Student Body Undergraduate enrollment is 2,229: 41 percent are men. The ethnic distribution is as follows: white, 57 percent; Asian/Pacific Islander, 2 percent; black, 5 percent; American Indian, 3 percent; and Hispanic, 2 percent. Twenty-six percent (580) of the students are international. Eighty percent of the students are commuters, while the other 20 percent are campus residents. Sixty-four percent of all undergraduates receive financial aid, and 88 percent of all domestic undergraduate students receive financial aid. There are three social fraternities and three social sororities.

Faculty Of the 341 faculty members, 174 are full-time. Seventy-seven percent of full-time faculty members have terminal degrees. The student-faculty ratio is 14:1.

Key Facilities The Dulaney-Browne Library houses 419,329 volumes, 5,509 current serials, 878,988 microforms, 9,649 audiovisual materials, and five online services. Library resources also include archives for the Oklahoma Conference of the United Methodist Church, the University Archives, the Foundation Center collection, the Shirk History Center, the Rapp Language Laboratory, the Listening Library, the children's literature collection, and the reference collection. The campus has 218 computers, ten in each residence hall and the others located in on-campus labs.

Honorary Societies Phi Eta Sigma and Alpha Chi

Athletics OCU is a member of the Sooner Athletic Conference and National Association of Intercollegiate Athletics (NAIA), offering nine men's and women's sports. Men's sports include basketball, baseball, soccer, golf, and tennis. Women's sports include basketball, softball, soccer, and tennis. Men's basketball has won four national championships, women's basketball has won one national championship, softball has won three National Championships, and a member of the men's tennis team has won the national singles championship. All teams have been participants in post-season championship competition, and individual members of the various teams have been named All-Americans and Academic All-Americans.

Study Abroad OCU is a member of the Council on International Education, offering opportunities for students to study and do internships in England, Germany, Mexico, and China. OCU has existing relationships with various colleges and universities throughout the world. Academic departments offer a range of international study opportunities each year, and the University sponsors overseas trips for performing arts majors.

Support Services The Office for Disability Concerns meets each semester to review requests for special accommodations and make recommendations as to what services are appropriate and available. Ninety-nine percent of the campus is accessible to the physically disabled.

Job Opportunities Numerous work opportunities for students are available through the Federal Work-Study Program, University Work Studies Program, and contract labor.

Tuition: $8880 per year (1998–99)

Room and Board: $4248

Interpreting the symbols: **2**=two-year college, **4**=four-year college; **Pu**=public or state college, **Pr**=private college; **G**=general honors program; **D**=departmental honors program; **S**=small program (fewer than 100 students), **M**=midsize program (100 to 500 students), **L**=large program (more than 500 students); **Sc**=scholarships available in honors program; **Tr**=transfer students accepted into honors program; **HBC**=historically black college; **AA**=academic advisors; **GA**=graduate advisors; **FA**=fellowship advisors.

Mandatory Fees: $85

Contact: Director: Dr. Virginia McCombs, 2501 North Blackwelder, Oklahoma City, Oklahoma 73106; Telephone: 405-521-5457; Fax: 405-521-5447; E-mail: vmccombs@frodo.okcu.edu; Web site: http://frodo.okcu.edu/www/departments/honors/honors.html

Oklahoma State University

4 Pu G D L Tr AA FA

▼ The Honors College

The Honors College provides many opportunities and challenges for outstanding undergraduate students in a supportive learning environment. Special honors sections of general education courses, interdisciplinary honors courses, and special honors projects allow students to enhance their learning experience. Classes are small (typically 20–22 students, but frequently smaller), and a wide range of honors courses is offered each semester. Honors courses are taught by members of the faculty who are experienced and known for excellence in the classroom and in their academic fields. Frequent interaction with other honors students and faculty members helps honors students develop a "sense of belonging" in the small-college atmosphere of the Honors Program while being able to take advantage of the opportunities offered by a comprehensive research university.

Active participants in the Honors College (6 honors credit hours per semester during the freshman and sophomore years, 3 hours per semester thereafter) earn use of the Honors College Study Lounge and computer lab in the Edmon Low Library, early enrollment for the following semester, and extended semester-long library checkout privileges. They also have the option to live in Parker Honors Hall on a space-available basis.

Special honors advising is provided by Honors Advisors, who themselves have earned honors program or Honors College degrees.

Honors College students regularly participate in conferences of the Great Plains Honors Council and the National Collegiate Honors Council, as do members of the faculty and professional honors staff. Opportunities for community service are available, as are research opportunities with faculty members that lead to the senior honors thesis or senior honors report.

In the past five years, Honors College students have won Rhodes, Marshall, Truman, and Fulbright Scholarships. Honors College students work closely with the OSU Office of Scholar Development and Recognition for fellowship advice. Approximately two thirds of Honors College degree students continue their education in graduate and professional schools, including some of the most prestigious in the nation, while others seek immediate entry into their chosen career fields.

In the 1995 decennial accreditation review of Oklahoma State University by the North Central Association of Colleges and Schools, the University Honors Program, which is currently known as The Honors College, was found to be one of the major strengths of the university. The OSU Honors Director is a past President of the National Collegiate Honors Council.

Honors opportunities have been in existence since 1965 in the College of Arts and Sciences and since 1989 on a University-wide basis. There are currently 718 active participants.

Participation Requirements: The Honors College degree is the highest distinction that may be earned by an undergraduate student at Oklahoma State University (OSU). Requirements include completion of the General Honors Award (21 honors credit hours with a distribution requirement over four of six broad subject-matter areas and including a minimum of two honors seminars or special interdisciplinary honors courses), completion of the Departmental or College Honors Award (12 upper-division honors credit hours, including a senior honors thesis or senior honors project), a total of 39 honors credit hours, and an OSU cumulative GPA of at least 3.5. Transfer students may count up to 15 transfer honors credit hours toward the General Honors Award. The honors hood is conferred on Honors College degree recipients at Commencement, along with a special Honors College degree diploma.

Admission Process: Freshmen are eligible for admission to the University Honors College on the basis of an ACT composite score of 27 or higher (SAT I 1200 or higher) and a high school GPA of 3.75 or higher. Continuing students are eligible according to the following OSU and cumulative GPAs: 0–59 credit hours, 3.25; 60–93 credit hours, 3.37; 94 or more credit hours, 3.5.

Scholarship Availability: The Honors College does not award scholarships. For information about scholarships, interested students should contact the Office of Financial Aid at OSU.

The Campus Context: Oklahoma State University is a campus of nine colleges: Agricultural Sciences and Natural Resources; Arts and Sciences; Business Administration; Education; Engineering, Architecture, and Technology; Human Environmental Sciences; Graduate College; Osteopathic Medicine (in Tulsa); and Veterinary Medicine. There are seventy-nine bachelor's, sixty-two master's, one specialist, and forty-four doctoral degree programs offered. Among the unique facilities on campus are an Advanced Technology Center, a Center for International Trade Development, a Food Processing Center, the Noble Research Center, the Old Central (Oklahoma Museum of Higher Education), the Seretean Center for the Performing Arts, the OSU Telecommunications Center, and the Center for Laser Technology.

Student Body Undergraduate enrollment is 17,211; 52.1 percent are men. The ethnic distribution of students is Caucasian, 80.2 percent; international, 4.7 percent (1,001); Native American, 8.3 percent; African American, 3.3 percent; Hispanic, 1.9 percent; and Asian, 1.7 percent. Approximately 76 percent of all students receive financial aid. There are twenty-three fraternities and thirteen sororities on campus.

Faculty The faculty totals 1,370. Of the 1,183 full-time faculty members, 87 percent have terminal degrees. The student-faculty ratio is 15:1.

Key Facilities The OSU library houses nearly 2.2 million volumes. In addition to the University mainframe computer, there are computer labs maintained by Computing and Information Services in the following locations: Bennett Hall (fifty-one systems), Wilham Hall (eighty-eight systems), Student Union (sixty-two systems), Classroom Building (seventy-eight systems), Engineering South (fifteen systems), Mathematical Sciences (fifty-nine systems), and the College of Business Administration (seventy-six systems). Some individual colleges and departments also have computer laboratories. All students automatically receive an e-mail address. The Edmon Low Library is computerized, and the Honors Program Study Lounge and computer facility are now located in the Library.

Honorary Societies Phi Eta Sigma, Phi Kappa Phi, Golden Key, and Mortar Board

Athletics OSU is a member of the new Big 12 Conference, one of the most competitive NCAA conferences in the nation.

Study Abroad Study-abroad opportunities are handled by the OSU Office of International Programs, which should be contacted directly. Bailey Family Memorial Trust scholarships for study abroad are frequently received by Honors Program students.

Support Services Facilities for disabled students include computer labs with adaptive technology. A list of full services is available from the Student Disabilities Services Office.

Job Opportunities There is a campus work-study program and employment with various campus units.

Tuition: Full-time: $1566 minimum for state residents, $5123 minimum for nonresidents, per year; part-time: $65.50 minimum for state residents, $213.45 minimum for nonresidents, per credit hour

Room and Board: $4856 minimum

Mandatory Fees: Full-time: $642.32 minimum per year; part-time: $35.68 minimum per semester

Contact: Director: Robert L. Spurrier Jr., 510 Edmon Low Library, Stillwater, Oklahoma 74078-1073; Telephone: 405-744-6799; Fax: 405-744-6839; E-mail: spurbob@okstate.edu; Web site: http://www.okstate.edu/honors

Oklahoma State University–Oklahoma City

2 Pu G S Sc Tr

▼ Honors Program

The Honors Program at Oklahoma State University–Oklahoma City (OSU–OKC) is in the developing stage. Because of an intensive promotional effort and a change in the requirements to participate, the program has established itself on campus and in the metro area of Oklahoma City. Since 1998, any student who wants to enroll in an honors course or complete an honors contract in a college course can do so, regardless of GPA. To get the honors credit on their transcripts, students have to earn an A or B in the course. Opening the Honors Program in this way to all interested students has resulted in increased numbers of active students and a greater awareness of the Honors Program on the campus and in the community. In the past two years, the number of students enrolled in honors courses and those who have contracted for honors projects has increased every semester. Currently, there are over 50 active honors students, and this number is expected to grow to 100 by the next year.

The Honors Program at OSU–OKC, a two-year college, is concerned with preparing students to transfer to four-year institutions with credible academic records. Participation helps students in raising their GPAs, and students meet other honors students at area and regional honors conferences. The Central Oklahoma Two-Year College Honors Council's Colloquium every fall and the Great Plains Honors Conference every spring have become popular and well-attended opportunities for students to present their projects. They gain confidence in their own scholarship and look forward to being a part of a university honors program or honors college when they graduate from OSU–OKC.

Honors students work closely with faculty sponsors. Most projects are presented to the class and provide research and study beyond the scope of the course, which benefits all students enrolled. Since OSU–OKC is a commuter campus and most students have families and jobs, it is not possible to hold regular meetings. However, along with the conferences, students are recognized each semester and they receive certificates, pins, and awards, and they share with faculty members and other students the types of projects they have done in the past semester. These events have brought about a sense of community and continuity among honors students and their faculty sponsors.

Participation Requirements: Honors hours are earned by enrolling in an honors course, usually English, humanities, or math, or contracting for individual honors projects in a college course of the student's choice. There is no specific GPA required, but in order for the honors credits to appear on the student's transcript, a grade of A or B must be earned in the course. The first 3 hours of honors credit earn a certificate; pins showing total hours earned are given for 6, 9, and 12 hours; and a student receives the Graduate Honors Scholar award for 15 hours of honors credit and a GPA of at least 3.5.

Admission Process: Students are considered members of the OSU–OKC Honors Program upon completion of their first 3 hours of honors work. Honors contracts are prepared by providing a description of the project and submitting it for approval to the honors committee by the end of the fourth week of the semester. After approval, the contracts are returned to the sponsors to be completed by the fourteenth week. Many honors students are members of the Alpha Pi Nu chapter of Phi Theta Kappa.

Scholarship Availability: Fee waiver scholarships are awarded each semester to applicants who have earned 6 hours of honors credit, hold a GPA of at least 3.5, and are active students in the current semester.

The Campus Context: OSU–OKC is a branch campus of Oklahoma State University in Stillwater, Oklahoma. OSU–OKC is a North Central Association–accredited, state-assisted, public two-year college. Located in the heart of Oklahoma City at the crossroads of Interstates 44 and 40, the campus enrolls approximately 4,500 full- and part-time students each semester. OSU–OKC has grown from a campus of one building with fewer than 100 students in 1961 to a campus that today consists of 80 acres, nine modern buildings, 227 full-time and adjunct faculty members, and a staff of 153 caring and committed people.

Offering more than twenty-five Associate in Applied Science degree programs with numerous areas of emphasis, eight Associate of Science degree programs, a variety of certificate programs, and developmental education courses, the Oklahoma City campus takes pride in its student-centered approach to collegiate education. The curriculum is designed in response to local employment needs and input from professionals who serve on OSU–OKC advisory committees.

State-of-the-art training facilities for firefighters and police officers attract students from the area; the horticulture division offers full nursery, gardening, and golf course programs. In addition, a two-year nursing degree program, a drug and alcohol counseling program, and a business technology degree program are developing extensive distance education courses. The comprehensive Learning Center, which attracts visitors from across the country, provides a model of tutoring in all disciplines and multimedia instruction and facilities for students.

The mission of OSU–OKC is to provide collegiate-level career and transfer educational programs and supportive services that will prepare individuals to live and work in an increasingly technological and global community.

Student Body Total enrollment is approximately 4,000 students per semester, of whom 54 percent are women. Ethnic percentages are 11 percent black, 5 percent Native American, 4 percent Asian, 3 percent Hispanic, 1 percent nonresident alien. Fifty-six percent of the students are under 24 years of age, and 44 percent are over 24 years of age.

Faculty Full-time faculty members number 62, and 15 percent have terminal degrees.

Key Facilities The library at OSU–OKC contains 14,000 print and audiovisual holdings as well as a growing collection of electronic databases and subscriptions. There are eleven computer lab/classrooms on campus.

Job Opportunities Work-study programs and internships are available on and off campus, and there is a job placement service.

Tuition: $61.35 per credit hour (2002)

Mandatory Fees: $40

Interpreting the symbols: **2**=two-year college, **4**=four-year college; **Pu**=public or state college, **Pr**=private college; **G**=general honors program; **D**=departmental honors program; **S**=small program (fewer than 100 students), **M**=midsize program (100 to 500 students), **L**=large program (more than 500 students); **Sc**=scholarships available in honors program; **Tr**=transfer students accepted into honors program; **HBC**=historically black college; **AA**=academic advisors; **GA**=graduate advisors; **FA**=fellowship advisors.

Contact: Honors Committee Co-Chair: Janeen Myers, 323 Learning Resource Center, 900 North Portland, Oklahoma City, Oklahoma 73107; Telephone: 405-945-8694; Fax: 405-945-9141; E-mail: janeenm@osuokc.edu

Old Dominion University

4 Pu G L Sc Tr

▼ Honors College

Established in 1986, the Academic Honors Program was renamed the Honors College in 1996. It administers the Undergraduate Research Program, the award-winning President's Lecture Series, degrees with honors for the academic departments, and a program of study for honors students. This four-year program offers specially designed, low-enrollment courses exclusively to honors students. In the first two years, the majority of these courses is used to fulfill the University's lower division General Education requirements. To complete the course of study in the Honors College, students must take a minimum of six general education honors courses, two upper-division courses as honors, a junior tutorial, and a senior colloquium. Academic degrees are earned in any of the six colleges of the University.

With an emphasis on teaching, innovation, and small classes, the Honors College offers the experience of a small liberal arts college within the framework of a large university. After four years of such an experience, students are better equipped to structure their lives and careers to meet their individual needs and strengths. A program that offers the best of both a small college and a large university naturally promotes greater sensitivity to self and society.

There are approximately 525 students in the Honors College.

Participation Requirements: Currently enrolled students and transfer students who have completed their lower-division general education requirements may participate in the honors experience by taking upper-division courses as honors (open to any student with a GPA of 3.25), earning a degree with honors in their major, or competing for a $1000 undergraduate research grant (open to all juniors and seniors with minimum GPAs of 3.4). Students must maintain an overall GPA of 3.25. Each spring at the Honors College awards banquet, graduates receive a certificate, a medal to wear on their gown, and a silver tassel for their mortar board. Their names are listed separately in the graduation program, and note of their accomplishment is made on their student transcripts.

Admission Process: Criteria used to select the 150 first-year students admitted annually include high school GPA and curriculum, SAT scores, class rank, and a written personal statement. Other students are admitted on the basis of a 3.5 college GPA, completion of at least four remaining general education courses as honors courses, and two letters of recommendation from University faculty members.

Scholarship Availability: All Honors College students receive an annual $500 stipend. The College also has an endowed scholarship, the Cranmer/Skinner Scholarship, which provides two awards each year. The Claire Nesson Academic Honors Scholarship and the Brock Foundation Honors Scholarship fund an additional 3 honors students each year. Students who opt for the dual-degree program between the College of Arts and Letters and the College of Engineering and Technology are eligible to apply for the endowed Sumitoma Scholarship. This scholarship also requires that the student study Japanese and do an internship at the Sumitoma Corporation in Japan (expenses paid). Honors College students are eligible to receive a $500 travel grant for study abroad.

The Campus Context: Old Dominion University had its formal beginning in 1930 as the Norfolk Division of the College of William and Mary. It gained its independence in 1962. Currently, the University has seven colleges: the College of Arts and Letters, the College of Business and Public Administration, the Darden College of Education, the College of Engineering and Technology, the College of Health Sciences, the Honors College, and the College of Sciences. Old Dominion University has sixty-five baccalaureate programs, sixty-eight master's programs, two certificates of advanced study, and twenty-two doctoral programs.

Student Body Of the 19,000 students, 57 percent are women, 22 percent are African American, 6.5 percent are Asian American, and 3.5 percent are Native Americans and Hispanics. About 80 percent of the entering freshmen come from Virginia. At present, 1,500 international students from more than 100 countries are in residence. About 2,500 students live on campus in residence halls, while another 3,500 live adjacent to the campus in a variety of private apartments and a number of special houses. There are seventeen fraternities and ten sororities on campus.

Faculty The full-time faculty numbers 607. All tenured and tenure-track faculty members must hold the doctorate or the terminal degree in their field. The student-faculty ratio is 17:1.

Key Facilities The library holds more than 2 million items. The University has an IBM 3090 mainframe and UNIX platform and four public networked labs; the dorms and campus buildings are also networked. In all, there are 1,600 computer workstations.

Distinguished facilities include TELETECHNET—in partnership with several community colleges, military installations, and private corporations, Old Dominion delivers upper-division undergraduate courses to place-bound students throughout the Commonwealth of Virginia. Other facilities of note include the Child Study Center, the Applied Marine Research Facility, and the close research connections with NASA (Langley) and the Continuous Electron Beam Accelerator Facility in Hampton, Virginia.

Honorary Societies Phi Eta Sigma, Phi Kappa Phi, and Golden Key

Athletics The athletic teams have won twenty national championships since 1975, including three in women's basketball, eight in field hockey, eight in sailing, and a Division II men's basketball crown in 1975. Teams have competed on the Division I level within the NCAA since 1976 and currently belong to the Colonial Athletic Association. The University sponsors sixteen intercollegiate sports, including eight men's sports (soccer, wrestling, basketball, swimming, tennis, baseball, golf, and sailing) and eight women's sports (soccer, basketball, cross-country, field hockey, swimming, tennis, lacrosse, and sailing).

Study Abroad Study abroad is available in every discipline and ranges in length from short summer group programs to individual exchanges lasting for a semester or a full academic year. Currently, study abroad is offered at eighty universities worldwide, including direct exchanges with England and Australia.

Job Opportunities A substantial number of jobs are available for students on campus, including work-study opportunities.

Tuition: $129 for state residents, $408 for nonresidents, per credit hour (2000–01)

Room and Board: $3024–$5000 per year

Mandatory Fees: $96

Contact: Dean: Dr. Louis H. Henry, 218 Education Building, Norfolk, Virginia 23529-0076; Telephone: 757-683-4865; Fax: 757-683-4970; E-mail: lhhenry@odu.edu; Web site: http://www.odu.edu/ao/honors

Oral Roberts University

4 Pr G M Sc Tr AA

▼ Honors Program

The purpose of ORU's Honors Program is to provide academically gifted students an educational experience at a level that both transcends the rigor and scope of the general curriculum and integrates the ethical responsibilities of using God's intellectual gifts for the healing of humanity into the concept of the "whole person" education. The program is designed for students and faculty members who possess the mental resources to plan, create, and implement strategies and programs that further fulfill the University's Statement of Purpose. This program continues the University's tradition of instilling character in students and preparing them for a lifetime of leadership and service to their community and world.

Successful, innovative faculty members are actively recruited to teach honors classes. These courses are designed to promote classroom discussion and allow opportunities to continue the learning process outside of class through field trips and extracurricular activities. Class enrollment is normally limited to 18 to 24 students. Social events are planned monthly, beginning with an orientation reception at the start of the year and a luncheon with the President of ORU. Honors dormitory housing is available, which promotes quiet hours and a high-quality academic atmosphere.

Founded in 2000, the program currently includes 70 students, with plans of reaching more than 300 students by 2004.

Participation Requirements: ORU's Honors Program is two-tiered, with 16 to 18 Fellows and 60 to 100 Associate Fellows accepted each year. Fellows must have exceptionally high academic credentials (e.g., National Merit Scholars) and outstanding application packets. Associate Fellows have high academic credentials and strong application packets. All Honors Program students must complete a minimum of 24 hours of honors courses at the 100 to 200 level plus any unique requirements within selected majors. Fellows take one special interdisciplinary honors seminar during each of the first six semesters. Each of these seminars is taught by 2 faculty members from separate departments to promote interdisciplinary exchange. Senior Papers that display outstanding academic scholarship are required as the capstone course for all Honors Program students. Graduating students who fulfill these requirements and have a cumulative GPA of at least 3.45 receive special recognition at an honors reception, during their department's hooding ceremony, and during commencement. Transcripts designate whether they graduated with honors as a Fellow or as an Associate Fellow.

Admission Process: Honors-caliber high school students who have strong test scores (at least 1280 on the SAT or 29 on the ACT), excellent academic records (minimum 3.45 GPA), demonstrated leadership skills and church and community service, and supportive letters of recommendation are encouraged to apply to the Honors Program by the deadline in early March. Students from this pool are selected by the end of March as either Fellows or Associate Fellows. Transfer students and current ORU students can apply to be Associate Fellows if they meet the above requirements.

Scholarship Availability: All of ORU's Honors Program students receive merit-based scholarships. ORU offers Presidential Awards by invitation only to students who have a minimum unweighted GPA of 3.45 and minimum scores of 31 on the ACT or 1360 on the SAT. Academic tuition scholarships are awarded automatically to students scoring at least 24 on the ACT or 1100 on the SAT.

The Campus Context: ORU was founded as a result of evangelist Oral Roberts' decision to obey God and fulfill His mandate to build a university "on God's authority and the Holy Spirit." God's commission to Oral Roberts was to "Raise up your students to hear My voice, to go where My light is seen dim, My voice is heard small, and My power is not known, even to the uttermost bounds of the earth. Their works will exceed yours, and in this I am well pleased." ORU is a charismatic university, founded in the fires of evangelism and upon the unchanging precepts of the Bible.

ORU is a four-year, residential, private university accredited by the North Central Association of Colleges and Schools. ORU is a member of the Council for Christian Colleges and Universities. The University offers sixty-five undergraduate majors, ten master's degree programs, and two doctoral degree programs. Twenty-four major buildings grace the ORU campus, located on 263 acres of scenic, rolling countryside in suburban Tulsa, 1 mile from the Arkansas River. Tulsa, which has been called "one of America's most beautiful cities," offers many cultural opportunities for students.

Student Body Undergraduate enrollment is 3,536; 41 percent are men and 59 percent are women. The student body is made up of students from more than forty denominations who represent all fifty states. Ethnic distribution is 74 percent white, 17 percent African American, 5 percent Hispanic, 3 percent Asian American, 1 percent Native American/Eskimo, and 4 percent international. The 194 international students come from fifty-three countries. Seventy-four percent of the students are full-time and 26 percent are part-time. Residential students constitute 52 percent, commuters 48 percent. Ninety-four percent of first-year students and 85 percent of continuing students receive financial aid.

Faculty The total number of faculty members is 289 (197 full-time), of whom 55 percent have terminal degrees. The student-faculty ratio is 17:1.

Key Facilities The library contains a collection of approximately 400,000 volumes in print, electronic, microform, and audiovisual formats. The collection is searchable through an online catalog available on the library's integrated online library computer system. Networked resources are available on forty-five workstations in the library and on thousands of computers located throughout the campus. The library's Electronic Resources Center is a collection of online and CD-ROM electronic databases that provide full text, abstracts, and indices of periodicals and other literature. Other special service areas within the library include the Curriculum Media Center, the music listening room, and the Holy Spirit Research Center.

The University services about 2,000 campus computers, which include computer labs in each dormitory and at least ten computer labs in academic hubs throughout the campus. Dormitory rooms are wired for individual student computers, and more than 1,500 students currently have personal computers on the network.

Honorary Societies Honors students may choose to join ORU's chapter of Gamma Beta Phi. Many academic disciplines also have local chapters of their honor societies.

Athletics Oral Roberts University is an NCAA Division I member of the Mid-Continent Conference. ORU sponsors sixteen varsity sports (eight men's and eight women's). The Golden Eagles field men's teams in baseball, basketball, cross-country, golf, soccer, and tennis as well as indoor and outdoor track and field. For women, ORU sponsors basketball, cross-country, golf, soccer, tennis, indoor and outdoor track and field, and volleyball. Since joining the Mid-Continent Conference on July 1, 1997, ORU has won several men's and women's all-sports awards. ORU has also captured three Mid-Con Commissioner's Cup titles, awarded to the league's most outstanding all-around athletics program.

Study Abroad Study-abroad opportunities include all student programs of the Council for Christian Colleges and Universities (http://bestsemester.com). ORU occasionally offers its own off-campus programs. In addition, a student may design a personalized study-abroad program but must work closely with an academic adviser to develop the program at least one year in advance of

Interpreting the symbols: **2**=two-year college, **4**=four-year college; **Pu**=public or state college, **Pr**=private college; **G**=general honors program; **D**=departmental honors program; **S**=small program (fewer than 100 students), **M**=midsize program (100 to 500 students), **L**=large program (more than 500 students); **Sc**=scholarships available in honors program; **Tr**=transfer students accepted into honors program; **HBC**=historically black college; **AA**=academic advisors; **GA**=graduate advisors; **FA**=fellowship advisors.

studying aboard. Prior to going abroad, a student's proposal must be approved by ORU's International Study Committee.

Support Services The Student Resources Office at ORU, in compliance with Section 504 of the Rehabilitation Act of 1973 and the Americans with Disabilities Act, ensures that no qualified individual with a disability is denied reasonable accommodation in modification of policies, practices, and procedures. The Comprehensive Advisement Center helps first-time freshmen and transfer students make a smooth transition to college life at ORU. The Cooperative Learning Center provides academic tutoring services on an individual basis. Each dormitory wing has an Academic Peer Advisor, a Resident Advisor, and a Wing Chaplain. The Counseling Center is also available to meet students' individual needs.

Job Opportunities Work opportunities on campus and around town are listed in the College and Career Guidance Center. Honors students are actively recruited to work with faculty members as teaching assistants and office help and in other areas. The College and Career Guidance Center assists students nearing graduation.

Tuition: $12,600 per year or $525 per semester hour (2002–03)

Room and Board: $5570

Mandatory Fees: $525

Contact: Director: Dr. John Korstad, Professor of Biology, Oral Roberts University, 7777 South Lewis Avenue, Tulsa, Oklahoma 74171; Telephone: 918-495-6942; Fax: 918-495-6297; E-mail: jkorstad@oru.edu; Web site: http://www.oru.edu/university/departments/admissions/honors

Oregon State University

4 Pu G L Sc Tr AA

▼ University Honors College

The University Honors College (UHC) is a campuswide degree-granting college, one of twelve at Oregon State University (OSU). It awards the Honors Baccalaureate of Science, Arts, or Fine Arts in the academic discipline, designating one of two tracks within the UHC. Students may major in any academic discipline and complete either the 30-credit "Honors Scholar" or the 15-credit "Honors Associate" track. The goal of the UHC is to provide a small college environment within a larger university and to stress education that focuses on relationships rather than subjects or disciplines. UHC classes are limited to 20 at the lower division and 12 at the upper division, and a writing-intensive skills requirement is included in the "Honors Scholar" track.

UHC courses are transcript visible and denoted by a departmental prefix and an H suffix or HC prefix. All courses are proposed by interested faculty members or by other nomination and are screened by the UHC Council. UHC courses are not automatically renewed and are assumed to be taught on a one-time-only basis that requires a renewal application. UHC courses may be regular quarter-length classes or offered in a compressed, weekend, or evening-course format. About three quarters of UHC offerings parallel the general education requirement of the institution; the remainder are UHC colloquia designed especially for UHC students. A study-abroad option is available, either independently or as part of OSU's unique concurrent degree requirements for an International Degree.

The University Honors College at OSU currently has more than 500 students (80 percent are from Oregon, and 22 percent are members of minority groups). The program draws students from across the country and around the world. Honors students may elect to live in the Honors Residence Hall.

Participation Requirements: Once admitted, UHC students must maintain a minimum GPA of 3.25 to remain in good standing. Sub-par performance results in a probationary window to improve academic performance prior to dismissal from the UHC portion of OSU.

Admission Process: Applicants to the UHC must be admitted or applying to OSU. An application form is available upon request from the UHC or via its Web site. The deadlines are as follows: fall term admission only, February 1; early admission, November 1. Admission criteria are flexible and include an opportunity to "write in" thorough responses to a series of essay questions. Transfer students in good standing in their honors unit (also students participating in the National Student Exchange) from a recognized program may be admitted on a space-available basis.

Scholarship Availability: UHC students are supported by scholarships from their academic colleges or by Presidential, Achievement, and Provost (merit-based) Scholarships. Additional scholarship support is being developed, and other decentralized support is available.

The Campus Context: The main OSU campus consists of more than 265 buildings spread across 420 wooded, sylvan acres in the mid-Willamette Valley on the banks of the Willamette River, about 85 miles south of metropolitan Portland and equidistant from the Pacific Ocean and the Cascade Mountains (1-hour driving time). Among the "off-site" holdings are the Hatfield Marine Science Center, a Portland Center, the McDonald/Dunn Forests, and a number of distant learning sites.

Oregon State University is a member of the PAC-10 Conference and is one of eighty-eight Carnegie Research I institutions in the country. In addition to the UHC, OSU has eleven undergraduate degree-granting colleges. There are eighty-one bachelor's programs, seventy-eight master's programs, fifty-seven doctoral programs, and two professional degree programs.

Student Body With nearly 17,500 students (37 percent women), OSU enrolls students from every state in the country and approximately 100 other countries (more than 1,150 students). Members of American minority groups comprise approximately 13 percent of the overall student body. UHC students have the option of living in the UHC Residence Hall (McNary Hall) or any other campus facility. The majority of the students live on or near campus. There are thirteen sororities and twenty-six fraternities that provide live-in opportunities.

Faculty OSU has 2,900 faculty members (2,800 full-time). Eighty-four percent hold their field's highest degree.

Key Facilities The library houses approximately 2 million volumes and provides outstanding computer connectivity to all electronic databases. OSU is known for extensive student access computing facilities, including five general student access areas with 445 machines and 1,807 other machines, including a twelve-station UHC student access lab/instructional facility. All students are given Internet addresses upon enrolling at OSU, and all residence halls have computer jacks in student rooms. UHC uses weekly e-mail messages to share information with and communicate with its students.

Honorary Societies Phi Eta Sigma, Phi Kappa Phi, Mortar Board, Cardinal, Blue Key, and Alpha Lambda Delta

Athletics Athletics includes fifteen sports recognized at NCAA Division I and plentiful intramural and informal opportunities.

Study Abroad Coordinated by the Office of International Education, OSU offers fifty-eight programs in more than thirty countries and includes a concurrent International Degree option to be awarded in conjunction with another baccalaureate degree. All UHC students are eligible and may earn credit for study abroad.

Support Services Coordinated by Services for Students with Disabilities, services for disabled students include note takers, sign language interpreters, books on tape, alternative testing, etc.

Job Opportunities Through Student Employment Services, various employment opportunities exist on campus, including work-study and study employment.

Tuition: $3700 for state residents, $13,500 for nonresidents, per year (2001–02)

Room and Board: $5250–$5950 (2001–02)

Mandatory Fees: $450

Contact: Dean: Dr. Jon Hendricks, 229 Strand Hall, Corvallis, Oregon 97331-2221; Head Advisor: Jane Siebler; Telephone: 541-737-6400; Fax: 541-737-6401; E-mail: honors.college@orst.edu

PACE UNIVERSITY

4 Pr G M Tr AA FA

▼ Honors Degree Program

The Pace University Honors Program promotes the intellectual growth of outstanding students in all majors. The program consists of a sequence of honors courses as well as lectures, social events, and cultural activities, drawing on the varied resources of New York City and Westchester, including the Metropolitan Museum of Art, the Cloisters, and Ellis Island. Students are also involved in completing a senior honors project, which may be related to their major field of inquiry. The goals of the Pace Honors Program are to deepen the intellectual experience of highly motivated, gifted students, encouraging them to enlarge their scope of knowledge on several levels, and to continue to build a vibrant, close-knit community of students and faculty members who are engaged in the process of learning and teaching.

Through specialized course work, extracurricular activities, and research, students develop relationships with professors and their contemporaries in a stimulating, challenging environment over four years of college. Students have the opportunity to work independently while shaping their own education. Honors courses are offered in a variety of fields, including literature, history, philosophy, business, religion, mathematics, theater, fine arts, language, science, and computer science. These courses are taught by a distinguished faculty and are offered at core and advanced levels. The program is a model program within the University community and is dedicated to nurturing and challenging students. Lectures and events both compliment and enhance works studied more formally in class. Pace honors students win awards and grants both within and outside of the University, and alumni often go on to pursue graduate degrees in a variety of fields, such as business, law, and history.

The program has been in existence for more than twenty years and admits approximately 70 freshman students on the New York City campus and 40 on the Pleasantville campus each year. There are more than 500 students currently enrolled in the programs on both campuses.

Participation Requirements: Entering freshmen are required to take a total of eight honors courses. These usually include a sequence of courses in the humanities and sciences; in addition, in Pleasantville, one course must be an honors seminar. Students who enter the Honors Program at the beginning of the sophomore year must take six honors courses. Those who enter at the beginning of the junior year must take four honors courses. One or two of these may be honors option courses, in which honors students develop a contract with a professor that involves completion of an extra project (such as a significant additional paper or report) to earn honors credit. Honors credit may also be given for supervised internships that are discussed with and approved by the Director. Students are also required to attend various honors-related lectures and events. A minimum GPA of 3.3 must be maintained to remain in the program and receive the Honors Certificate and medallion upon graduation. Students' transcripts indicate all honors course work and completion of the honors thesis.

Admission Process: To be eligible for membership in the Honors Program, entering freshmen must have a minimum high school average of at least 90 or the equivalent and a minimum score of 550 on the math section and 550 on the verbal section of the SAT I. Students who transfer to Pace and enter in the sophomore or junior year must have achieved a minimum GPA of 3.3 (B+) at their prior college or university. Current Pace students in their sophomore or junior year who have achieved a minimum GPA of 3.3 are also eligible.

Scholarship Availability: Pace University's financial aid policy is to provide the maximum financial aid available to qualified students to make their attendance at Pace a reality. To this end, the University administers a wide range of scholarship and financial aid programs designed to enable students to pursue their studies to graduation. The basis of selection is ability and/or need. Most financial aid is renewable on a yearly basis, provided there is adequate funding and the student remains eligible. Financial aid offered through Pace University includes President's and Deans' Scholarships, the Trustee Recognition Award, Pace Incentive Awards, the Pace Grant, athletic scholarships, and student employment.

The Campus Context: Pace University is a cohesive institution that offers undergraduate students a choice of locations at which to study. Each campus has a distinctive atmosphere, ranging from the quintessential urban campus (New York City) to the suburban/rural campus (Pleasantville).

Student Body As of fall 2001, both campuses combined serve a total of 8,913 undergraduate students. Of these, 43 percent are self-identified as white, 11 percent are black, 13 percent are Asian, 11 percent are Hispanic, fewer than 1 percent are Native American, and 22 percent are "other" or nonreported.

Faculty There are 444 full-time faculty members in the University. Approximately 82 percent hold the Ph.D. As of fall 1997, the student-faculty ratio is 15:1.

Key Facilities University libraries contain more than 410,500 volumes and subscriptions to more than 800 magazines and newspapers. In addition, there are special collections of domestic and international corporate reports, clipping files on current topics, and children's books. The library is automated through the INNOPAC Integrated Library System, making the holdings of the library searchable via the Internet. In addition, access to approximately thirty other libraries in the New York City and Westchester vicinities is available. Items not contained in the in-house collections can be obtained for students through interlibrary loan or commercial document delivery services.

Pace University has several Computer Resource Centers that are open for student use. They are equipped with networked PCs and peripherals and support the software suite Microsoft Office Professional as well as Netscape Communicator. Each dormitory room is equipped with data, cable, and voice jacks. Dorm students have direct computing access to the data network, cable television, and voicemail.

Athletics Pace is NCAA Division II, except men's baseball, which competes in the NCAA Division I. Intercollegiate sports include men's baseball, basketball, tennis, cross-country, lacrosse, football, indoor track, and outdoor track. Women participate in basketball, tennis, volleyball, cross-country, softball, soccer, equestrian, indoor track, and outdoor track.

Job Opportunities The University has an outstanding co-op program that arranges paid employment for eligible students beginning at the end of their freshman year. Because of Pace New York's prime location, employment opportunities and internships are

Interpreting the symbols: **2**=two-year college, **4**=four-year college; **Pu**=public or state college, **Pr**=private college; **G**=general honors program; **D**=departmental honors program; **S**=small program (fewer than 100 students), **M**=midsize program (100 to 500 students), **L**=large program (more than 500 students); **Sc**=scholarships available in honors program; **Tr**=transfer students accepted into honors program; **HBC**=historically black college; **AA**=academic advisors; **GA**=graduate advisors; **FA**=fellowship advisors.

readily available with major corporations and leading cultural institutions and government agencies.

Tuition: $16,650 per year (2001–02)

Room and Board: Room, $4720–$6860; board, $1500 (average)

Mandatory Fees: $430

Contact: New York City campus: Dr. William Offutt, Honors Program, Pace University, One Pace Plaza, New York, New York 10038; Telephone: 212-346-1697; Fax: 212-346-1217; E-mail: woffutt@pace.edu. Pleasantville campus: Dr. Janetta Rebold Benton, Honors Program, Pace University, Mortola Library, 861 Bedford Road, Pleasantville, New York 10570; Telephone: 914-773-3848; Fax: 914-773-3967; E-mail: jbenton@pace.edu.

Pacific University

4 Pr G S Tr

▼ University Honors Program

The Honors Program at Pacific University offers exceptional students the opportunity to define excellence as they explore the many ways of perceiving and thinking that have shaped the world. Interdisciplinary and innovative, honors seminars allow gifted students to satisfy College core requirements in the company of others who approach their education creatively and energetically as they pursue high standards and new experiences. These honors courses enable students to build a powerful foundation for work in their majors by challenging them to integrate approaches from several disciplines as they strengthen their abilities as writers, critical thinkers, and imaginative problem solvers.

In the first semester, honors students meet the College's writing requirement; in the next three, they exercise their skills as writers and thinkers as they work toward satisfying requirements for work in the natural and social sciences, the arts and humanities, and in cross-cultural studies. In the fifth honors seminar, which is taken in the spring term of junior year, students prepare for independent capstone projects within their disciplines as they consider the meaning of work, the significance of entering a profession, the obligations that accompany education, and the exercise of power. In the senior year, all honors students design and complete a capstone project or thesis that demonstrates academic excellence and creativity and meets both the program's and the departmental criteria for honors work: all honors theses and capstone projects are assessed by an Honors Review Board and presented to the community.

The University Honors Program also sponsors cocurricular events that complement the seminars and support the development of a community of learners both within and beyond the program. The Honors Chautauqua Program, endowed by the Merles Bryan Fund, brings a scholar-in-residence to campus each semester. These visiting scholars and performers meet with honors students in various settings and present their work to the Pacific community in lectures or performances. The Student Honors Council advises the Director of Honors in selecting the Chautauqua Scholars and coordinates its own cocurricular programming, also underwritten by the Merles Bryan Fund, which supports honors students both on and off campus by defraying registration and travel costs for students to present their work at conferences. In celebration of achievement in honors, juniors and seniors in the program enjoy a spring-term retreat at the Oregon coast, gathering around a set of common questions to seek uncommon answers. The 35-year-old program currently enrolls 85 students.

Participation Requirements: To graduate with University Honors, students must complete Honors 100 and three sections of Honors 200, as well as Honors 350. Honors students must also complete a senior thesis or capstone project that satisfies departmental criteria for honors work and passes the Honors Review Board, which is composed of the Director of Honors and the faculty members teaching in honors. All honors students must participate in the cocurricular activities supported by the University Honors Program, including the Honors Chautauqua Program and the Junior/Senior Year Retreat. Honors students who wish to study abroad are encouraged to do so in either the second semester of sophomore year or the first semester of junior year. Students choosing to study abroad in the sophomore year may either double enrollment in honors in a semester before they leave or take a 200-level honors seminar in the spring term of junior year, concurrently with Honors 350. Students who are studying for a full year as juniors are expected to take Honors 350 in the spring term of the year they return. The University Honors Program supports study abroad as an important complement to its offerings.

First-year students may continue with a 3.2 GPA or better but must achieve a 3.5 cumulative GPA by the end of the sophomore year and then maintain a 3.5 cumulative GPA to complete the program. Honors students must also meet all College of Arts and Sciences graduation requirements unless an exception is approved by the Honors Committee. No courses in the University Honors Program may be taken pass/fail. Honors students are recognized at commencement, and the transcripts and diplomas of honors students denote Graduation with University Honors.

Admission Process: Prospective students are invited to apply to the University Honors Program when they apply for admission to the College of Arts and Sciences. University Honors admission decisions are based on GPA, SAT I or ACT scores, and an essay that reveals the student's background, interests, and motivations. University Honors students entering Pacific generally have a high school GPA of 3.7 and SAT I scores of 1200 or ACT scores of 26, but applications from other interested students are considered. Students enrolled at Pacific are invited to apply after their first and second semesters. First-year students are invited to apply to the University Honors Program for admission in the second semester on the basis of faculty recommendation. All students with a Pacific GPA of 3.5 or higher at the end of their second semester are invited to apply for admission in the third semester. Interested and qualified transfer students should consult with the Director of Honors to discuss options for entering and completing the program.

Scholarship Availability: No particular scholarships are reserved for honors students, although many receive residential awards.

The Campus Context: Pacific University is composed of seven colleges and schools: College of Arts and Sciences, College of Optometry, School of Occupational Therapy, School of Physical Therapy, School of Professional Psychology, School of Education, and School for Physician Assistant Studies. There are twenty-six undergraduate degree programs.

Among the noteworthy facilities on campus are the Strain Science Center, the Taylor-Meade Performing Arts Center, and suite-living.

Student Body The undergraduate enrollment is 63 percent women. The ethnic distribution is 18 percent Asian/Pacific Islander, 2 percent Hispanic, .4 percent black, and 1.5 percent American Indian/Alaska Native. There are 110 international students, including those registered in the English Language Institute and in graduate programs. Sixty-four percent of the students are residents on campus. Eighty-two percent of students receive institutional aid. There are three fraternities and three sororities on campus.

Faculty Of the 86 full-time undergraduate faculty members, 73 have terminal degrees. The student-faculty ratio is 11.1:1.

Key Facilities The library houses 99,558 catalogued volumes, 30,218 periodical volumes (with 1981 periodical titles in the collection), and a total of 117,546 government documents in paper, microfiche, and electronic formats. Students have access to 145 Apple Power

Macintosh computers and fifty-one PCs through lab, library, and classroom facilities, as well as to two video-editing systems, laptop computers, digital cameras, and data projectors for student projects and presentations. All residence hall rooms are wired for free 10 Base T Ethernet access to the campus network and the Internet. Nonresident students have free access to the modem pool for e-mail and library catalog access. Students can access e-mail and other resources from any location on the Internet, provided they have completed the proper paperwork.

Athletics Pacific University is an NCAA Division III school. The sporting events at Pacific University include baseball, men's and women's basketball, men's and women's cross-country, men's and women's golf, men's and women's soccer, softball, men's and women's tennis, men's and women's track and field, volleyball, and wrestling.

Intramural activities include flag football, volleyball, and 3-on-3 basketball in the first semester, 5-on-5 basketball in the winter, and softball in the spring. Additional activities are announced yearly.

Study Abroad All students at Pacific are encouraged to consider overseas study as an educational experience. Pacific offers a variety of international study programs that incorporate most academic disciplines. Depending on the particular program, students may study abroad for either a semester or full academic year and do not necessarily need foreign language competency. Financial aid and other scholarship awards are applicable to overseas study. For Pacific's Modern Language and International Studies majors, study abroad is a requirement. Pacific has twenty-eight different programs in fourteen countries, including Australia, Austria, China, Ecuador, England, France, Germany, Ireland, Japan, Mexico, the Netherlands, Scotland, Spain, and Wales.

Support Services The Office of Services for Students with Disabilities exists to serve students who qualify for special services under federal law. Pacific University provides the same educational opportunities for students with disabilities that it provides for all students, unless undue burden would result. The University maintains academic standards that apply to all students.

Students with disabilities may require additional or specialized services to meet academic standards. If it is determined that a student does fit the criteria for having a learning disability, the following accommodations may be available: tutoring, special classroom and housing accommodations, permission to tape lectures and/or discussions, books on tape, note takers, advance copies of syllabi and lecture notes, access to voice activation and speech synthesis software, extra time for exams, space with minimal distraction for exams, reduced class load, and resource materials.

Job Opportunities Work opportunities are available on campus as teaching and research assistants, clerical workers, groundskeepers and recyclers, statisticians, team managers, field crew helpers, and community service-related jobs.

Tuition: $18,800 per year (2001–02)

Room and Board: $4809 minimum

Mandatory Fees: $450

Contact: Director: Dr. Sarah Phillips (on sabbatical); Acting Director: Dr. Pauline Beard, 2043 College Way, Forest Grove, Oregon 97116; Telephone: 503-359-2989; Fax: 503-359-2775; E-mail: beardp1@pacificu.edu; Web site: http://www.pacificu.edu

Palm Beach Atlantic College

4 Pr G S Sc Tr AA

▼ Frederick M. Supper Honors Program

The Frederick M. Supper Honors Program at Palm Beach Atlantic College (PBA) provides motivated students from all majors with the opportunity to participate in a community of scholars. Members of this community share a genuine passion for intellectual contemplation and discussion, and they encourage, challenge, and support one another in the endeavor to seek wisdom.

To develop a thoughtful and insightful Christian worldview, honors students take seminar classes based on reading and discussing the great works of human civilization. These works, referred to as the Great Conversation, integrate literature, history, religion, philosophy, art, and science, and they address timeless questions and issues that continue to shape society's worldviews. These works serve as a core curriculum to educate students broadly for any vocation. Because of the focus on character formation, honors courses help students prepare for any career and, more importantly, for life. The program is intended to produce servant leaders who glorify God in word, thought, and deed.

Honors courses are kept small to encourage students to interact with one another and to develop relationships with honors faculty members. Faculty members embrace the opportunity to serve as academic role models who mentor students inside and outside the classroom. Likewise, students in the Honors Program learn a great deal from one another and provide leadership for the greater campus community. Members of the Honors Program form a cohesive group of scholars on campus, and they often establish friendships that last a lifetime.

Located in the heart of downtown West Palm Beach, Florida, PBA affords excellent opportunities for honors students to attend and participate in cultural and social events. These activities are often integrated into the classroom experience. Palm Beach Atlantic also requires its students to give time in service to the community. There are countless ways that students can serve, and these activities often become important social and intellectual experiences for honors students.

Graduates of the program have been very successful in graduate school, law school, medical school, and seminary. They have also had successful careers in business, education, communication, politics, law, and other areas.

Founded in 1989, the program enrolls an average of 80 students.

Participation Requirements: Honors students take worldview courses that integrate various disciplines from the humanities, including history, philosophy, literature, art, and religion. These courses substitute for a significant portion of the College's general core curriculum. Students also take honors versions of core courses, including public speaking and composition. In addition, honors students take seminar courses exploring issues in Christianity, non-Western civilizations, economics, political science, and the philosophy of science. Honors students also complete a senior project in their major or some other area of interest.

To remain in good standing, students must maintain a minimum 3.5 cumulative GPA and may not receive more than one C in honors course work.

Students who successfully complete the program and graduate from the College are recognized by a note on their transcript, a seal on their diploma, and special recognition at commencement. Honors alumni maintain ties to one another and the program through several communication channels, including a newsletter.

Admission Process: Acceptance is based on high performance on the ACT (29 or above) or SAT (1300 or above) and on outstanding high school grades (minimum 3.5 GPA on a 4.0 scale or a ranking in the top 5 percent of their class). Students also write an essay expressing their understanding of and desire to participate in the Frederick M. Supper Honors Program. An

Interpreting the symbols: **2**=two-year college, **4**=four-year college; **Pu**=public or state college, **Pr**=private college; **G**=general honors program; **D**=departmental honors program; **S**=small program (fewer than 100 students), **M**=midsize program (100 to 500 students), **L**=large program (more than 500 students); **Sc**=scholarships available in honors program; **Tr**=transfer students accepted into honors program; **HBC**=historically black college; **AA**=academic advisors; **GA**=graduate advisors; **FA**=fellowship advisors.

interview may also be scheduled with members of the honors committee. Students not meeting these requirements may be considered on a case-by-case basis by the honors committee.

Scholarship Availability: All students who enroll in the Frederick M. Supper Honors Program receive an honors scholarship. This scholarship covers approximately one half of the Palm Beach Atlantic tuition for every semester the student is enrolled in the program. This scholarship can be received for four years. Other financial assistance, including scholarships, grants, loans, and part-time employment, is available to honors students at Palm Beach Atlantic.

The Campus Context: Palm Beach Atlantic College is a comprehensive Christian college. Founded in 1968, PBA offers high-quality education with a distinctive Christian emphasis for students of all faiths. Palm Beach Atlantic is accredited by the Southern Association of Colleges and Schools (SACS) to award associate, bachelor's, master's, and doctoral degrees. More than seventy programs of study are arranged into seven academic schools: Arts and Sciences, Education and Behavioral Studies, Rinker School of Business, Music and Fine Arts, Ministry, Pharmacy, and MacArthur School of Continuing Education. PBA is rated as one of America's Best Colleges by *U.S. News & World Report* and has been recognized in *The Templeton Guide: Colleges That Encourage Character Development.* PBA offers excellent modern facilities on a 25-acre campus in downtown West Palm Beach, Florida, directly across the Intracoastal Waterway and only minutes from the Atlantic Ocean. PBA's urban location puts entertainment, restaurants, shopping, internships, and service opportunities within easy walking or bicycling distance. With the temperature usually in the 70s or 80s, PBA students can enjoy outdoor activities year-round.

Student Body Undergraduate enrollment is 2,225. Graduate enrollment is 375. Nearly 1,000 students live on campus.

Faculty The number of full-time faculty members is 100, 74 percent of whom have terminal degrees. The student-faculty ratio is 19:1.

Key Facilities The library houses 157,000 volumes. PBA has more than 850 computers on campus. It was the first college in Florida to offer wireless Internet connections campuswide. PBA also offers PalmNET, a campuswide network that gives students and faculty and staff members access to each other via e-mail and to the Internet, World Wide Web, library databases, and more. A Windows-based computer and printer are in every student residential room as well as on the desk of every full-time faculty member.

Athletics Palm Beach Atlantic competes in fourteen men's and women's sports at the NAIA level and offers an active intramural program.

Study Abroad International study programs are available in China, England, Latin America, the Middle East, and Russia.

Tuition: $13,040 per year (2001–02)

Room and Board: $5301.08

Contact: Dr. Thomas St.Antoine, Director of Honors Program, Palm Beach Atlantic College, P.O. Box 24708, West Palm Beach, Florida 33416-4708; Telephone: 561-803-2279; Fax: 561-803-2280; E-mail: stantoit@pbac.edu; Web site: http://www.pbac.edu

Palm Beach Community College

2 Pu G M Tr

▼ Palm Beach Community College Honors Program

Honors at Palm Beach Community College (PBCC) pursues a more active and interactive learning environment in which students and faculty members share responsibility for attaining a more creative and comprehensive understanding and deeper analytical interpretation of course concepts and their applications in an interdisciplinary and global context.

PBCC's Honors Program serves approximately 150 students each term. PBCC students can participate in honors by enrolling in honors courses or through the completion of honors project contracts in any credit course.

Honors classes are offered for many general education courses. Honors class sizes at PBCC are smaller, from 5 to 20 students, thus allowing for more discussion, presentations, and in-depth learning. Students develop critical-thinking and research skills in collaborative learning environments that may include field trips, field experiments, and guest speakers. Students learn to use discipline-specific research methodologies and primary resources as they collect, analyze, and evaluate data. If the student chooses to complete an honors project, the student and faculty member sign a contract in which the student agrees to complete a research paper in the course with the guidance of the faculty member.

Participation Requirements: Students are eligible to participate in honors with a minimum cumulative GPA of 3.0. No previous course work is required. To enroll in ENC 1121 Honors College Composition I, an ACT score of 27 or higher in English or an FCELPT score of 87 or higher in reading and sentence structure is also accepted. Students must maintain at least a 3.5 GPA to continue honors course work. Upon completion of 12 credit hours of honors course work while maintaining a minimum 3.5 GPA, students become eligible to apply for honors graduation. Honors graduates receive an honors graduate notation on their transcript and an honors seal on their diploma.

Admission Process: There is no application process for the Honors Program. Students must meet the eligibility requirements to enroll in classes or complete honors projects.

Scholarship Availability: PBCC does not offer an honors scholarship; however, transfer scholarships to universities are available.

The Campus Context: The mission of Palm Beach Community College is to provide an accessible and affordable education through dedicated and knowledgeable faculty and staff members, a responsive curriculum, and a strong community partnership, which together enable students to think critically, demonstrate leadership, develop ethical standards, and compete effectively in the global workplace.

Palm Beach Community College became Florida's first public community college in 1933. A richly diverse, comprehensive two-year institution, PBCC is dedicated to serving the educational needs of the residents of Palm Beach County, Florida, by providing Associate in Arts, Associate in Science, and Associate in Applied Science degrees; professional certificates; workforce development; and lifelong learning. PBCC's four campuses are located in Belle Glade, Boca Raton, Lake Worth, and Palm Beach Gardens. Classes are also held at local high schools, hospitals, and other off-campus sites.

Palm Beach Community College is accredited by the Commission on Colleges of the Southern Association of Colleges and Schools (SACS) to award the Associate in Arts and Associate in Science degrees.

Student Body PBCC enrolls approximately 20,000 credit students. Approximately 78 percent are enrolled in Associate in Arts degree programs, and 22 percent are enrolled in Associate in Science degree programs. PBCC has nearly 400 international students. Twenty-one percent of all students receive financial aid.

Faculty PBCC employs 232 full-time faculty members and 1,161 part-time faculty members. Part-time faculty members include those who may teach as little as one class in the noncredit areas of career and technical education, criminal justice, and workforce development.

Key Facilities Library services and resources support the curriculum, faculty members, and students at all four PBCC locations. Campus libraries maintain a diverse collection of materials that includes books; periodicals; local, state, and national newspapers; microforms; and reference materials. Access to all library materials and electronic collections of books, periodicals, and journals is available through LINCC (Library Information Network for Community Colleges), the online catalog. More than 2,000 journals and periodicals are available online and in full text, and electronic books add more than 10,000 volumes to the collection. Computer facilities include more than 2,800 computers used in libraries, labs, classrooms, and offices.

Honorary Societies Each of PBCC's four campus locations has a chapter of Phi Theta Kappa, the Honors Society.

Athletics PBCC has varsity intercollegiate athletic teams for women (basketball, softball, and volleyball) and for men (baseball and basketball). The program provides an opportunity for students to experience competition, skill development, self-discipline, and cooperation.

Intramural and recreational activities are sponsored by Student Services. These activities represent a broad selection of individual and team sports. Opportunities are available for students to participate in all phases of the intramural program, including planning, organizing, competing, and officiating.

Study Abroad International field trips and summer study-abroad courses vary from year to year and are based on interest and demand.

Support Services Palm Beach Community College is committed to providing full access to all programs, services, and facilities to qualified individuals with disabilities as mandated by Section 504 of the Rehabilitation Act of 1973 and by the Americans with Disabilities Act of 1990. Students with disabilities are encouraged to meet with the disability service representative at their campus before registration. This adviser assists with course selection and accommodation needs and also coordinates other campus resources to best meet the educational needs of students with disabilities.

Job Opportunities PBCC offers many on-campus job opportunities for students, including work-study, student ambassadorships, and customer service representatives.

Tuition: Tuition for state residents is $50 per credit hour; tuition for out-of-state residents is $187.22 per credit hour.

Mandatory Fees: A nonrefundable $20 fee is charged for processing applications, and a one-time $5 fee is charged each term for registration. Some limited-access programs charge an additional application fee.

Contact: Susan Caldwell, Academic Coordinator, 3000 Saint Lucie Avenue, Boca Raton, Florida 33431; Telephone: 561-862-4652; Fax: 561-862-4406; E-mail: caldwels@pbcc.cc.fl.us; Web site: http://www.pbcc.cc.fl.us/honors/

PARADISE VALLEY COMMUNITY COLLEGE

2 Pu G M Sc

▼ Honors Program

At Paradise Valley Community College (PVCC), honors courses are offered as single courses, as concurrent sections with regular sections, and as project courses. With the latter two, honors students are expected to do additional, in-depth work that will enhance their classroom experiences.

During the school year, honors students participate in several programs designed to build a learning community among Maricopa Community College District (MCCD) honors students. They may attend special programs, concerts, theater events, and guest lectures each semester. The Maricopa district brings six nationally prominent guest speakers for the honors program each year; they visit with students at several of the campuses during their stay. All honors students from the ten MCCD colleges also have the opportunity to take an annual honors trip to a different site each year. In addition, honors students are recognized each spring at a district-wide Honors Convocation and receive special recognition at graduation. Honors course work receives an honors designation on college transcripts.

The fourteen-year-old program currently enrolls nearly 150 students.

Participation Requirements: In order to remain eligible for this program, students must enroll in a minimum of 12 hours per semester and maintain a 3.25 GPA. Students must also enroll in and complete at least one honors course each semester.

Admission Process: The Paradise Valley Community College Honors Program is open to all students who graduate in the top 15 percent of a Maricopa County high school class or who have earned a 3.25 GPA in at least 12 credit hours from any of the Maricopa Community Colleges. All students who apply and who qualify are accepted.

Scholarship Availability: The Presidents' Scholarship program is open to all Maricopa County high school graduates who are in the top 15 percent of their high school classes. Students may apply as early as the end of their junior year and remain eligible for two semesters following graduation, provided they do not attend any other college or university during that time. The scholarship is renewable for up to four consecutive semesters, provided students continue to meet the requirements of the Honors Program. This portion of the program is designed to attract top area high school students to Maricopa colleges.

Returning students may be eligible for the fee waiver portion of the program if they have earned a 3.25 GPA in at least 12 credit hours at any of the Maricopa Community Colleges. Fee waivers are awarded depending on the number of credits students are taking. There is no time limit on the number of semesters of eligibility, within reason, as long as students maintain a 3.25 GPA and take one honors course per semester.

The Campus Context: The PVCC story began in the late 1970s amid the rapid growth of the Greater Paradise Valley area. As the population north of the Phoenix Mountains expanded, community advocacy for a higher educational facility to serve the area grew as well. In 1983, following a request by the Paradise Valley Community Council, the Maricopa Community College District Governing Board created the Northeast Valley Task Force to study the feasibility of such a facility. Funding for the first phase of this new facility was provided by a countywide bond election in September 1984. In early 1985, Dr. John A. Córdova, then Dean of Instruction at Phoenix College, was selected Provost of the Northeast Valley Education Center (NVEC), as the facility was then named. NVEC began operations as an extension of Scottsdale Community College in offices on Bell Road.

On December 5, 1985, a "groundlifting" ceremony for the new campus was held at its present location. In November 1986, the Governing Board changed the name to Paradise Valley Community College Center in anticipation of opening the new campus. PVCC was dedicated on May 2, 1987, and classes at the new campus began that fall with more than 4,000 students. Paradise Valley Community College began offering classes from temporary offices near 30th Street and Bell Road in northeast Phoenix in the fall of 1985. In the fall of 1986 the College moved to its present campus on the southeast corner of 32nd Street and Union Hills Drive.

Today, enrollment totals more than 6,000 full- and part-time students. An additional 1,000 students are enrolled in noncredit

Interpreting the symbols: **2**=two-year college, **4**=four-year college; **Pu**=public or state college, **Pr**=private college; **G**=general honors program; **D**=departmental honors program; **S**=small program (fewer than 100 students), **M**=midsize program (100 to 500 students), **L**=large program (more than 500 students); **Sc**=scholarships available in honors program; **Tr**=transfer students accepted into honors program; **HBC**=historically black college; **AA**=academic advisors; **GA**=graduate advisors; **FA**=fellowship advisors.

community education programs that include the PVCC Chamber Orchestra, Flute Choir, and Women's Chorus and watercolor, drawing, and money management classes. PVCC's students come primarily from the north Phoenix, Scottsdale, Cave Creek, Carefree, and Paradise Valley areas and represent the diversity of the College's service area. Students include recent high school graduates, working adults, and active senior citizens. The average age is around 30.

Paradise Valley Community College is one of Arizona's newest community colleges, receiving its first accreditation in 1990 from the North Central Association of Colleges and Schools. Following full accreditation in 1990, the Governing Board designated PVCC an independent college within the Maricopa Community College District.

The curriculum focuses on transfer to four-year institutions and offers a range of undergraduate courses in fall, spring, and summer terms. New offerings include degree and certificate programs in international business and hazardous materials technology.

Today, Paradise Valley Community College, led by President Gina Kranitz, enjoys an international reputation for excellence. The College was recently named a Regional Center for Asian Studies by the East-West Center of Honolulu, Hawaii. PVCC is a member of the World Trade Center of Arizona. The College is proud of its 1,000-piece Buxton Collection of American Indian and Western Arts and Crafts, which was dedicated during PVCC's tenth anniversary celebration. The Buxton collection contains religious or quasi-religious art from the American Southwest as well as from Spain, Mexico, and Central and South America. The pieces were acquired at art shows and sales conducted by the Heard Museum, the Friends of Mexican Art, various art galleries, and, in many cases, from the artists themselves.

In 1995, PVCC received a ten-year reaccreditation from the North Central Association, which called the College a "premier" institution. It offers the associate degrees in arts, general studies, applied science, and business.

Student Body Of the more than 7,000 undergraduates enrolled, the majority are from the southwest; 37 percent are men and 63 percent are women. The ethnic distribution of students is Caucasian, 81 percent; Hispanic, 6.9 percent; other, 6.6 percent; Asian, 2.9 percent; African American, 1.4 percent; and American Indian, 1.2 percent. There are more than 100 international students. All students are commuters. Twenty-five percent of the students receive financial aid.

Faculty There are 84 full-time faculty members and 300 part-time faculty members. More than 35 percent of full-time faculty members have their doctorates or other terminal degrees. The student-faculty ratio is 21:1.

Key Facilities The library houses more than 30,000 volumes. Computer facilities include an IBM Lab and Macintosh Apple Lab. Other facilities include 278,000 square feet of classrooms, laboratories, offices, public meeting rooms, and a state-of-the art Fitness Center on a 90-acre site. The Student and Community Services Center building houses the Phoenix office of Northern Arizona University, which offers classes on the PVCC campus.

Honorary Society Phi Theta Kappa

Athletics Paradise Valley Community College is currently participating in its first year of competition in intercollegiate athletics. Cross-country is offered for both men and women as a fall sport, while men's and women's tennis and men's golf are offered as spring sports. As one of the colleges in the Maricopa Community College District, PVCC is a Region 1 member of the NJCAA. Athletic teams at PVCC compete in tennis and cross-country at the Division II level, while golf is a Division I sport. Any student interested in athletics at PVCC should contact Cindy Shoenhair, Assistant Athletic Director, for more information.

Study Abroad Paradise Valley Community College does not offer study abroad at this time. However, it does offer an International Internship, which is a 3-credit course (IBS122).

Support Services For disabled students, the Paradise Valley Community College Special Services Office provides reasonable accommodations, classroom accessibility, resources, support services, and auxiliary aids to assist students in a successful college career.

Job Opportunities Students can find a variety of work on campus. Work-study jobs are available to students who show financial need. Tutoring opportunities are available through the Learning Support Center.

Tuition: $1270 for area residents, $5400 for nonresidents, per year (2001–02)

Mandatory Fees: $10

Contact: Director: Dr. Linda Knoblock, 18401 North 32nd Street, Phoenix, Arizona 85032; Telephone: 602-787-7244; Fax: 602-787-7250; Web site: http://www.pvc.maricopa.edu/

Passaic County Community College

2 Pu G S Sc Tr

▼ Honors Program

The Honors Program at Passaic County Community College (PCCC) offers highly motivated, academically accomplished students an environment designed to enrich their college experience. Challenging seminars, special classes, and independent research projects further develop students' analytical skills and creative abilities. Distinguished faculty members representing a comprehensive range of disciplines work closely with and encourage students participating in this rigorous and rewarding program.

The benefits of the Honors Program are both immediate and long lasting. Students in the program attend many exciting and enjoyable events, including guest lectures, visits to museums, art exhibits, concerts, theatrical productions, opera, and dance presentations. This balance of stimulating creativity and enhanced intellectual exploration provides successful students with powerful advantages in future efforts, whether in pursuit of career opportunities or transfer options to four-year colleges and universities.

Participation Requirements: Students in the Honors Program must complete four honors studies by any of the following methods: honors courses or core courses with honors section designation or honors contracts or independent study. All students are required to attend a one-semester interdisciplinary seminar.

Students must maintain a minimum GPA of 3.5.

Admission Process: Recent high school graduates may apply for admission into the Honors Program if they have scored at least 1,000 on the SAT I or have ranked in the top 20 percent of their high school graduating class. Currently enrolled college students can apply for admissions to the program when they have completed 12 college-level credits with a GPA of 3.5 or above.

All students must complete an honors application, which includes an essay and a letter of recommendation.

All applicants must be approved by the honors committee, which is composed of the Honors Director and honors faculty members.

Scholarship Availability: Honors students who express a need and meet the criteria are eligible for a variety of scholarships, including the Educational Opportunity Fund, instituted and sponsored by the state of New Jersey; Garden State Scholars Program; Passaic County Community College Foundation Scholarships; Federal Pell Grant; Federal Stafford Loans; Federal Supplemental Educational Opportunity Grants; and Tuition Aid Grant.

The Campus Context: Passaic Community College was established in 1971 and serves more that 4,000 full- and part-time students. It is located in Paterson's downtown Urban Enterprise Zone, 15 miles west of New York City. Students choose from among forty associate degree and certificate programs. The College maintains articulation agreements with nearly all of New Jersey's major colleges and universities. PCCC continues to enjoy record enrollments. To meet these needs, the College is in the midst of a comprehensive expansion project. The main campus in Paterson's historic district is doubling the size of its library and building a child-care center. The College will soon occupy the historic Hamilton Club, where it will unveil a new art gallery and a conference and technology center. In Wanaque, the College is building a new academic center to provide rural residents with increased access to higher education. The College is accredited by the Middle States Association of Colleges and Schools.

Student Body Undergraduate enrollment is 38 percent men and 62 percent women. The College serves a culturally and ethnically diverse population. Three fourths of the students come from a minority background. The ethnic distribution is 51.7 percent Hispanic, 21.2 percent black, 18.5 percent white, 6.6 percent Asian/Pacific Islander, 0.2 percent Native American, and 1.7 percent other. Fifty-two percent are foreign born. They represent seventy-three countries and all of the world's major religions. The average age of a PCCC student is 28 years old. All students commute to campus. There are no traditional fraternities or sororities.

Faculty Of the 270 faculty members, 76 are full-time and 20 percent have terminal degrees.

Key Facilities The library houses more than 46,000 volumes and 240 periodicals. The electronic resource subscriptions include ProQuest, ABI Inform, Psych Info, CINAHL, Encyclopedia Americana, and EBSCO. There are sixty-five computers with Internet access. In the fall of 1999, the library will add fifty Internet connected computers at the main campus and the same number in the electronic resource center and flex lab at the Wanaque site.

Honorary Societies Phi Theta Kappa

Athletics The College varsity athletic program competes in men's and women's basketball and men's soccer. The College is a member of the National Junior College Athletic Association, Region XIX, and the Garden State Athletic Conference.

Support Services At PCCC, students who present documentation of a disability are eligible for services through the Counselling Department's Office of Special Needs Services. Services take the form of accommodations to regular college program, the use of adaptive aids, and, in some cases, individual or small group tutoring. Students with hearing impairments can request an interpreter for class lectures. Notetaking devices or notetakers are available to those students with fine motor disabilities. Special registration to accommodate mobility difficulties or to assist students with visual disabilities can be arranged.

Job Opportunities Students are offered a range of work opportunities on campus, including tutoring, laboratory assistantships, and work-study.

Tuition: $65.75 per credit for residents, $131.50 per credit for nonresidents (1998–99)

Mandatory Fees: $11.60 per credit; additional fees for some courses may not exceed $215 per semester

Contact: Director: Dr. Esther Hager, 1 College Boulevard, Paterson, New Jersey 07505; Telephone: 973-684-5213: Fax: 973-684-5843; E-mail: ehager@pccc.cc.nj.us: Web site: http://www.pccc.cc.nj.us

PELLISSIPPI STATE TECHNICAL COMMUNITY COLLEGE

2 Pu G S Sc Tr

▼ Honors Program

Pellissippi State Technical Community College instituted an honors program in fall 1995 to offer academically able and highly motivated students the opportunity to participate in courses designed to provide an enhanced college experience.

There are currently 75 students enrolled in the program.

Participation Requirements: Students may participate in honors by taking one course or by taking several. Honors Program students take the same number of hours for graduation as other students. Enriched sections of the general university parallel courses are offered in such subjects as Western Civilization and General Biology. The courses are open to any student who meets the entry-level criteria for the particular course. Thirty-five students enrolled in four courses during the inaugural term. All graduating students who complete 12 hours of honors courses and maintain a 3.0 GPA are given special recognition on their diploma.

Scholarship Availability: Designed for students who meet certain criteria and participate in the Honors Program, up to twenty scholarships are available for Pellissippi Scholars. In order to apply for the scholarship, a student must have a 25 or higher composite ACT score and a minimum 3.5 GPA in high school or previous college work. The student must complete an application and write an essay. Recommendations are required for students who do not have an ACT score. A committee then evaluates the applications and selects the recipients.

Pellissippi Scholars are required to take at least one honors course each semester, maintain a 3.0 GPA, and complete 12 hours of honors courses by the time they graduate.

The Campus Context: Pellissippi State Technical Community College was founded as State Technical Institute at Knoxville, Tennessee, and became a community college offering university-parallel courses in 1988 while still maintaining its emphasis on technology. A Tennessee Board of Regents institution, the College serves Tennessee's third-largest metropolitan area. Pellissippi State grants A.A. and A.S. degrees for university-parallel students; the A.A.S degree in seventeen technical career programs such as chemical and environmental engineering technology, communications graphics technology, and video production technology; and five certificate programs.

The College recently completed a new 500-seat performing arts center and an Educational Resources Center that contains the library, study areas, computer classrooms, and a Learning Center for tutoring in math and English. In fall 1996 the College developed Weekend College, a series of classes that allows students to complete certain degrees in four years by attending classes on the weekends.

In 1998, Pellissippi State initiated Fast Track courses to enable students to complete their associate degrees more quickly. Fast Track courses condense regular sixteen-week courses into intensive five-week minisessions.

Student Body There are 8,058 students enrolled, including 91 international students; 45.1 percent are men and 54.9 percent are women. Almost 30 percent receive financial aid.

Faculty Of the 480 total faculty members, 161 are full-time, approximately one fourth of whom have doctorates or other terminal degrees. The student-faculty ratio is 18:1.

Key Facilities The library houses 43,000 volumes. About 675 IBM-compatible computers are located in twenty-four labs on three

Interpreting the symbols: **2**=two-year college, **4**=four-year college; **Pu**=public or state college, **Pr**=private college; **G**=general honors program; **D**=departmental honors program; **S**=small program (fewer than 100 students), **M**=midsize program (100 to 500 students), **L**=large program (more than 500 students); **Sc**=scholarships available in honors program; **Tr**=transfer students accepted into honors program; **HBC**=historically black college; **AA**=academic advisors; **GA**=graduate advisors; **FA**=fellowship advisors.

campuses, and 104 Macs are located in six Macintosh labs on the main campus. All students have computer accounts with access to the Internet.

Honorary Societies Phi Theta Kappa, Lambda Sigma

Study Abroad City of Bath College (England) has entered a collaborative agreement with Pellissippi State to develop academic exchanges and course projects.

Job Opportunities A small number of work-study positions are available on campus.

Tuition: $1274 for state residents, $4660 for nonresidents, per year (1998–99)

Mandatory Fees: $144

Contact: Director: Dr. Carol Luther, 10915 Hardin Valley Road, P.O. Box 22990, Knoxville, Tennessee 37933-0990; Telephone: 423-694-6439; E-mail: cluther@pstcc.cc.tn.us

PENNSYLVANIA STATE UNIVERSITY

4 Pu G L Sc Tr

▼ Schreyer Honors College

The Schreyer Honors College is Penn State's University-wide undergraduate honors program. Selected students in all of Penn State's academic colleges may simultaneously be members of the Schreyer Honors College and pursue a broad range of opportunities for study, research, and scholarly exploration. The goal of the Schreyer Honors College is to provide an environment in which students of high ability can achieve their academic potential, while they develop as responsible civic leaders and global citizens. In short, the Schreyer Honors College has a three-part mission: achieving academic excellence, building a global perspective, and creating opportunities for leadership and civic engagement.

The Schreyer Honors College's hallmark is flexibility in accommodating the diverse intellectual interests of highly talented students. The curriculum is designed to challenge, enrich, and broaden students' general education and to deepen their preparation for graduate study or a profession. Schreyer Scholars may choose from a wide variety of special honors courses and sections to satisfy their degree requirements. A Scholar's progress in his or her field of specialization is enhanced by honors courses, independent study and research, access to graduate-level courses, and honors-option work in regular courses. The Schreyer Honors College encourages and facilitates the creation of individualized programs by providing maximum flexibility to students and advisers.

A fundamental element of the best undergraduate education is the interaction between outstanding faculty members and motivated students. The Schreyer Honors College fosters such interaction through courses of reduced size (usually 15–25) and extensive non-classroom programming in its two residence halls. An honors thesis is the capstone experience for Schreyer Scholars and leads to an honors diploma from Penn State. The College thus provides students with the advantages often identified with small liberal arts colleges along with the libraries, laboratories, and research opportunities of one of the world's great universities.

The Schreyer Honors College was founded as the University Scholars Program in 1980 and became a College in 1997. It currently has approximately 1,800 students, of whom 300 are first-year students.

Participation Requirements: Schreyer Scholars must take at least three honors courses or sections during their first year (one of which must be Honors First-Year Composition) and at least three honors courses or sections during the sophomore year. During their remaining time at Penn State, they must complete at least 14 credits of honors work. The Schreyer Honors College expects that Scholars will take their honors work in both general education and the major(s), but there are no requirements about the precise distribution of honors work. Scholars who enter after the first year are subject to these requirements from the time they join the Schreyer Honors College. Scholars must maintain at least a 3.2 cumulative average each semester and must file an Annual Academic Plan.

All Scholars must complete an honors thesis in order to graduate with an honors diploma from Penn State. Before each commencement, graduating Schreyer Scholars receive the Scholars medal at a special awards ceremony.

Admission Process: First-year Schreyer Scholars are selected through a special application process. Students with exceptional high school records and excellent SAT I scores are encouraged to apply. Selection is highly competitive as the number of first-year places is set at a maximum of 300. While many factors weigh heavily in the selection process, including essays and teacher recommendations, first-year students entering in 2001 had an average SAT I score above 1415 and an average high school GPA of 4.08. The College is looking for students who will thrive as members of an intellectual community: students who will be active participants in all their courses (including those outside their major) and who are interested in the range of opportunities offered by the Schreyer Honors College.

Applications received by the priority deadline of November 30 are given first consideration. After that date, applications are considered on a rolling basis until March 30. All applicants must also complete the standard Penn State application, which has the same priority and final deadlines.

Penn State students may be nominated for entry into the Schreyer Honors College by their major department after the fourth semester, based upon outstanding academic performance and research potential. Junior-year entrants to the Schreyer Honors College do not receive the Academic Excellence Scholarship, but they receive all other benefits of the program from the time they enter. Transfer students can be evaluated for membership in the Schreyer Honors College after their complete academic record from their previous institution is available.

Scholarship Availability: All first-year entrants to the Schreyer Honors College are awarded the Academic Excellence Scholarship (AES), renewable for eight semesters provided they remain Scholars in good standing. The current value of the AES is $2500 per year. In addition, many Scholars receive merit scholarships from their Penn State major or academic college.

The Campus Context: Penn State is one of the world's great teaching, research, and service institutions. The University Park campus is located at the geographical center of Pennsylvania, with easy access to Philadelphia; Pittsburgh; Washington, D.C.; and New York. With more than 40,000 undergraduate and graduate students in more than 180 fields distributed among eleven academic colleges, the campus provides endless curricular and extracurricular opportunities. Distinctive facilities at University Park include the Palmer Museum of Art, the Applied Research Laboratory, Eisenhower Chapel, and the Penn State Creamery. The town of State College offers a full range of amenities, and there is extensive off-campus housing available to students after their first year. The surrounding countryside is ideal for outdoor activities year-round.

For Penn State students who choose to begin their studies at another location, including Schreyer Scholars, the University has eighteen campuses throughout the state.

Student Body Undergraduate enrollment at University Park is approximately 24,000, of whom around 6,500 are first-year students. Another 20,000 undergraduates are enrolled at other Penn State locations. The University attracts more than 2,500 undergraduate and graduate international students each year. There are more than 500 student groups and organizations at the University Park campus.

Faculty Penn State employs more than 4,000 faculty members and researchers, and each year many distinguished visiting faculty members come to Penn State from all over the world. Virtually all faculty members at the University Park campus hold a terminal degree. There are more than 250 endowed and distinguished professorships. Penn State is ranked third nationally in the number of faculty members and students who win Fulbright Fellowships to teach and conduct research abroad.

Key Facilities The newly renovted Pattee and Paterno Libraries and the network of department libraries at University Park collectively rank among the top twenty academic libraries in the United States, and library users at other locations have unlimited access to University Park collections. All campuses have extensive computer labs, and at University Park all dormitories have network connections. Penn State is a leader in the development of the new Internet II high-speed academic computing network.

Athletics Penn State is an NCAA Division I participant in a full range of men's and women's sports in the Big Ten Conference. Many programs, including women's volleyball and men's football, have consistently achieved national prominence. The University Park campus also has an extensive array of intramural and club sports.

Study Abroad Penn State offers more than 130 summer, semester, and yearlong programs abroad, including those offered through consortial agreements with other institutions. Each year, more than 1,500 undergraduates study abroad. The Schreyer Honors College places great emphasis on education abroad and offers several distinctive short-term programs each year. Recent programs include a Theatre Arts program in London and an Agricultural and Rural Sociology program in Peru. The College supports more than 170 Scholars per year in their study, research, service, and internships abroad through the Schreyer Ambassador Travel Grant program.

Tuition and Fees: $7396 for residents, $15,520 for nonresidents per year (2001–02 at University Park). These costs do not take Academic Excellence Scholarships or any other merit or need-based aid into account.

Room and Board: $5310 (approximately)

Contact: Schreyer Honors College, 10 Schreyer Honors College, The Pennsylvania State University, University Park, Pennsylvania 16802-3905; Telephone: 814-865-2060; E-mail: scholars@psu.edu; Web site: http://www.shc.psu.edu

Philadelphia Biblical University

4 Pr G S Sc Tr AA

▼ Honors Program

The Honors Program at Philadelphia Biblical University (PBU) seeks to develop Christian scholars who integrate their biblical studies with their general and professional education. With the study of the Bible at the center of all University education, the Honors Program is, accordingly, interdisciplinary in nature.

The Honors Program emphasizes the conversation between the Bible and the Great Books that has shaped the Western tradition. Through reading and studying foundational texts in Western philosophy, political science, church history, and literature, students develop their skills of reasoning and shaping oral and written arguments. The approach is text centered, student focused, and writing intensive. In the four honors courses, with enrollment in each limited to 15 students, classes consist of discussion-based seminars complemented by tutorials that present the historical-cultural-intellectual context for the texts read. Essay examinations ascertain the student's development in the course.

In addition to the honors courses, the honors community of faculty members and students meets biweekly for a meal and a colloquium. Honors colloquia include student or faculty presentations and open discussion of selected topics under the direction of the honors faculty. Each semester, one of the colloquia is designated a university-wide forum. The honors forums cover a broad range of interdisciplinary topics and foster intellectual stimulation and collegiality within the larger university community. To provide the students with extracurricular learning experiences, the Honors Program plans special activities twice per semester. These educational opportunities open the student to the historical, cultural, artistic, and academic world of Philadelphia and the surrounding region.

The capstone of the Honors Program is the honors project. The students choose a research topic designed to bring together all of their education. Working closely with an adviser, the students learn and apply the fundamentals of researching and writing a thesis.

The honors faculty members are aggressively involved in mentoring the students from their freshman year to graduation. The development of student-faculty relationships provides an important scaffolding for the student's intellectual development. Faculty members advise students in course work, colloquium topics, and the honors project. They also teach courses, plan colloquia and activities, and accompany the students on extracurricular activities.

Participation Requirements: Students must take the four designated honors courses (philosophy, history of Christianity, political science, and literature), participate in the honors colloquia and special activities every semester in the program, and submit a thesis or special project at the end of their senior year. The honors student must maintain a cumulative GPA of at least 3.5 to continue in and graduate from the program. Successful completion of the program requirements is recognized with a special seal on the diploma and notation on all official transcripts.

Admission Process: The honors committee selects from each entering class up to 10 students who have proven their ability to participate in study and dialogue requiring advanced levels of critical thinking. Students with SAT scores of 1250 or higher (or the ACT equivalent) and with a cumulative GPA or 3.5 or higher (on a 4.0 scale) have a higher probability of being admitted into the program, but no applicant is accepted or refused solely on the basis of these scores. With the application to the program the student must submit an essay, which is evaluated by the whole committee. Applicants must have a formal interview with the committee during the summer or early in the fall semester. The application deadline for incoming freshman students is April 1. It is customary for the honors committee to reserve room in the program for transfer students or other exceptional students who may not have had the opportunity to submit their applications as incoming freshmen or who may not have been ready for the program's intellectual rigor right out of high school. These applicants are reviewed by the committee, and the applicants are invited to an interview. Underclassmen not initially accepted into the Honors Program may reapply during a subsequent semester if they feel that the merit of their application has been enhanced since their previous attempt.

Scholarship Availability: Students with at least a 3.6 GPA and an SAT score of 1350 (30 on the ACT) or higher are eligible for consideration for the Honors Academic Scholarships of $8000 per year.

The Campus Context: Situated on a 110-acre wooded campus just 30 minutes north of Philadelphia, the University provides an ideal location in which to study. Accredited undergraduate and graduate programs are offered in a variety of subjects. Undergradu-

Interpreting the symbols: **2**=two-year college, **4**=four-year college; **Pu**=public or state college, **Pr**=private college; **G**=general honors program; **D**=departmental honors program; **S**=small program (fewer than 100 students), **M**=midsize program (100 to 500 students), **L**=large program (more than 500 students); **Sc**=scholarships available in honors program; **Tr**=transfer students accepted into honors program; **HBC**=historically black college; **AA**=academic advisors; **GA**=graduate advisors; **FA**=fellowship advisors.

ate programs include Bible, business, education, music, and social work; graduate programs include Bible, Christian counseling, education, educational leadership and administration, and organizational leadership. Eighteen social, professional, and theological organizations are open to undergraduate students.

Notable University facilities include the Mason Activity Center (containing the dining commons, gymnasium, student lounges, and bookstore), Masland Learning Resource Center/Library, and the 48,000-square-foot Biblical Learning Center, which, when complete, will provide nineteen state-of-the-art classrooms that enhance the learning experience.

As its name indicates, Philadelphia Biblical University is committed to applying biblical truth in all spheres of human activity, including spiritual development, intellectual inquiry, personal relationships, and professional training. The University seeks to graduate leaders whose lives are distinctly biblical in thought and action and who possess the skills necessary to fulfill their God-given callings.

Student Body Undergraduate enrollment is 1,070 (45 percent men, 55 percent women). Ethnic distribution is 81 percent white, 12 percent African American, 2 percent Asian, 2 percent Hispanic, and 3 percent international. More than half of the full-time traditional undergraduates are in dual-degree programs, earning both a baccalaureate degree in Bible and a baccalaureate degree in either business, education, music, or social work. More than 90 percent of all full-time traditional undergraduates receive financial aid (83 percent of first-time students).

Faculty The total number of faculty members is 169. Of the 62 full-time faculty members, 57 percent have terminal degrees. The student-faculty ratio is 15:1.

Key Facilities The library has more than 225,000 volumes (150,820 books, 63,503 microforms, 13,577 other). Computer facilities include a fiber-optic network backbone, Internet access for all on-campus residence halls and offices, two computer labs in the library, and an e-mail lab in the student lounge. The new classroom building offers network ports at all student desks in each classroom.

Athletics PBU is Division III in the NCAA and Division II in the NCCAA for basketball, cross-country, soccer, tennis, volleyball, men's baseball, women's softball, and women's field hockey. There is an active intramural program.

Study Abroad Third-year students may elect to spend a semester at Jerusalem University College. Other study-abroad opportunities may be approved.

Support Services All academic buildings and two dormitories are wheelchair accessible.

Job Opportunities Work opportunities are plentiful both on and off campus. Work-study is available. Internships can be either paid or volunteer. Career Counseling offers a wide range of services to all students.

Tuition: Full-time tuition is $11,700 per year; part-time tuition is $352 per credit for 1 to 7 credits and $451 per credit for 8 to 11 credits (2002–03)

Room and Board: $5405 per year (2002–03)

Mandatory Fees: $290 per year (2002–03)

Contact: Dr. Samuel Hsu, Chair, Honors Program, Philadelphia Biblical University, 200 Manor Avenue, Langhorne, Pennsylvania 19047-2990; Telephone: 215-702-4321 or 800-366-0049 (toll-free) Ext. 4321; Fax: 215-702-4342; E-mail: shsu@pbu.edu; Web site: http://www.pbu.edu/academic/honors/index.htm

Philadelphia University

4 Pr G S Tr

▼ Honors Program

The Honors Program at Philadelphia University was established in 1985 to bring together highly motivated students and dedicated faculty members in a program that is both challenging and supportive. Overall, the program aims to reach beyond professional or specialized training and to inspire students to a full lifetime of broad and intellectual curiosity, self-sustained inquiry, and personal growth. It attempts to develop critical thinking and leadership skills and widen awareness of global issues.

The program is a combination of accelerated, enriched courses and cocurricular activities designed to challenge selected students at the University. The program's core of 22 credits is composed of honors work in both College Studies and career-specific courses. There are an optional community service learning component and opportunities for enrollment in graduate-level courses. Honors credit is available during study abroad and through co-op and internship programs.

Participating faculty members from across campus often teach enriched sections of existing courses or supervise independent study or research projects. These faculty members are dedicated teachers and scholars respected for their effectiveness in the classroom and for original contributions to their field of specialty. The Honors Program not only challenges students, but also demands an extension of faculty roles beyond customary professional expectations. These are the roles of the catalyst and mentor as well as of one who perceives and understands shifting pressures on students and student energies as the term progresses.

The 10-year-old program enrolls approximately 150 active students.

Participation Requirements: Students are expected to maintain a B/B+ average and enroll in at least one honors course per year. Students are recognized at graduation if they have maintained a 3.0 GPA and taken at least three honors courses. Students receive the full honors awards if they have a 3.3 or better GPA and have completed the required 22 honors credits.

Transfer students who enter the University with more than 45 credits may waive all or some of the lower-division honors requirements and satisfy all of the required 22 honors credits with upper-division honors courses. Transfer students who have participated in an Honors Program at another institution may transfer lower-division honors credits.

Any student enrolled at the University may enroll in honors courses as a noncertificate honors student if their overall GPA is above 3.0. Honors courses are noted on student transcripts, and completion of the program is cited on the diploma at Commencement.

Admission Process: The program is offered each year, by invitation, to a select number of qualified students. Admission to the Honors Program is based upon proof of a student's potential for high academic achievement. A majority of honors students are identified by their high school performance. The University may evaluate the student's GPA, class rank, SAT/ACT scores, and extracurricular activities. All entering freshmen and/or transfer students may apply for admission to the Honors Program. Although there is an attempt to identify eligible students before admission to the University, students who have demonstrated academic excellence during their first and second term may also be invited to join the program.

A student may be admitted to the Honors Program at one of the following times in their baccalaureate experience: prior to matriculation as either a freshman or a transfer student, if admission criteria for the Honors Program have been met (based on high school rank, standard test scores, interviews, etc.) or after one term of work at the University, with a faculty recommendation and GPA above 3.1.

Scholarship Availability: The University offers a number of faculty grants and scholarships to freshmen and transfer students, based on academic merit. Many students receiving these scholarships and grants are also in the Honors Program.

The Campus Context: Philadelphia University is composed of five schools: the School of Architecture and Design, the School of Business Administration, the School of Science and Health, the School of Textiles and Materials Technology, and the School of General Studies. Thirty-two undergraduate and nine graduate programs are offered on campus. The University is well-known for its Design Center.

Student Body There are 2,181 full-time undergraduates: 37 percent men and 63 percent women. The ethnic distribution is Caucasian, 82 percent; African American, 8 percent; Asian/Pacific Islander, 3 percent; and Spanish/Hispanic, 3 percent. International students represent 3 percent of the student body. Of the total student population, 60 percent are residents and 40 percent are commuters. Ninety-five percent of full-time students receive financial aid. There are four fraternities and two sororities.

Faculty The total number of faculty members is 399; 25 percent are full-time, and 75 percent have terminal degrees. The student-faculty ratio is 12:1.

Key Facilities There are 85,700 volumes in the library. The campus has 300 computers, Macintosh and IBM. There are multiple labs in the computer center, library, learning center, and architecture and design center (CAD lab/studios).

Athletics The University has NCAA Division II teams in women's basketball, field hockey, lacrosse, soccer, softball, tennis, and volleyball. For men, the University has an NCAA Division I soccer team and Division II teams in basketball, baseball, golf, and tennis.

Study Abroad Study-abroad options are available in Austria, Australia, England, France, Germany, Ireland, Italy, Mexico, Scotland, and Spain.

Support Services The University offers academic support for all special-need students; this support includes a learning center and services such as peer tutoring, extended testing, and note taking.

Job Opportunities A variety of work opportunities is available on campus in administrative and academic offices and labs.

Tuition: $17,600 minimum per year full-time, $310–$586 per credit part-time (2001–02)

Room and Board: $8466

Contact: Director: Dr. Abigail Lee Miller, School House Lane and Henry Avenue, Philadelphia, Pennsylvania 19144-5497; Telephone: 215-951-2906; Fax: 215-951-2652; E-mail: millera@philau.edu

PIEDMONT COLLEGE

4 Pr S Tr

▼ Piedmont Honors College

The Piedmont Honors College provides a select group of qualified students the opportunity to pursue their college studies in a tutorial setting with a designated professor. Using the Oxford tutorial model, the Honors College encourages self-regulated learning that develops intellectual independence, improves critical thinking, and emphasizes oral and written communication skills. Taught by carefully chosen faculty members, honors courses are designed to build intellectual skill and promote faculty-student contact. As a result, the course work is generally more integrative, more analytic, and more interactive than some non-honors courses. However, honors courses are not designed to create more work than what is expected in the traditional lecture setting. Enrollment in honors sections is generally limited to 10 students. The Honors College sponsors, from time to time, colloquia on a variety of topics. In addition, the Honors College may sponsor Dinner with the President, Pizza with the Profs, theater and museum trips, and other activities. Honors College students are expected to attend all Honors College events. The Piedmont Honors College was established in 1996 and currently enrolls 20 students.

Participation Requirements: Students must take at least four honors courses (typically, two in the freshman and two in the sophomore year) in addition to completing a junior and senior thesis requirement. To remain in the program, students must maintain a cumulative GPA of at least 3.25. Successful completion of the program is noted on the official transcript and diploma.

Admission Process: Students must submit the following to be considered for admission to the Honors College: a letter stating why they would like to enter the Honors College, a writing sample, two letters of recommendation from current teachers (or current employer), high school transcripts, and SAT I or ACT results. In addition, an interview may be required with the Piedmont Honors College Admissions Committee. Application to the Piedmont Honors College cannot be considered until a student has completed an application for admission to the College.

Scholarship Availability: Scholarships of various amounts are awarded through the Office of Financial Aid. Scholarships are not offered through the Honors College. Most honors students are recipients of academic scholarships.

The Campus Context: Affiliated with the Congregational Christian Churches, Piedmont is a private, nonprofit college with a 100-year history of providing higher education. Located in Demorest, Georgia, Piedmont College is in the northeastern portion of the state, 75 miles from Atlanta, resting in the foothills of the southern Blue Ridge mountains. Piedmont students enjoy numerous opportunities for cultural, recreational, and social activities, including special lectures, exhibits, music programs, and drama productions. Many students also participate in the Piedmont College Praxis program as volunteers for community service. In 2000, the College will complete a new 40,000-square-foot science building for biology, chemistry, physics, and mathematics. The College also houses National Public Radio (NPR) station WPPR 88.3 FM.

The College offers twenty-four baccalaureate degree programs. There are four schools on campus: the School of Arts and Sciences, the School of Business, the School of Education, and the R. High Daniel School of Nursing.

Student Body The undergraduate enrollment is 39 percent men and 61 percent women. The ethnic distribution is 90 percent white, 7 percent black, 1 percent Hispanic, and 1 percent Asian/Pacific Islander. Twenty-six percent of the undergraduate enrollment is over the age of 25. Ninety-five percent of undergraduate students receive financial aid.

Faculty The total number of faculty members is 169, of whom 90 are full-time. Seventy-seven percent of full-time teaching faculty members have terminal degrees. The faculty-student ratio is 1:11.

Key Facilities The Piedmont College Library presently has more than 100,000 volumes, a fully automated books catalog, Internet connections to more than forty remote databases, individual seating for more than 100 library users, three group study rooms, a public-access computer lab, and meeting rooms. The building also meets ADA codes. There are also three other computer labs on campus. All faculty and staff members have networked computers. All students have T1 Internet access, e-mail, and cable television. Off-campus users have dial-in access to the campus network.

Athletics Piedmont College's program of intercollegiate and intramural athletics is designed to promote student interest in athletics, to foster sound physical development, and to teach

Interpreting the symbols: **2**=two-year college, **4**=four-year college; **Pu**=public or state college, **Pr**=private college; **G**=general honors program; **D**=departmental honors program; **S**=small program (fewer than 100 students), **M**=midsize program (100 to 500 students), **L**=large program (more than 500 students); **Sc**=scholarships available in honors program; **Tr**=transfer students accepted into honors program; **HBC**=historically black college; **AA**=academic advisors; **GA**=graduate advisors; **FA**=fellowship advisors.

good sportsmanship. Athletic facilities include the College gymnasium, eight tennis courts, and athletic fields. A new gymnasium, which will feature weight rooms and an exercise track, is currently under construction. Intercollegiate sports include men's and women's basketball, men's and women's soccer, men's baseball, women's softball, and women's volleyball. The College also sponsors several sports at the club level, including tennis, golf, crew, running, cheerleading, and mountain biking. Piedmont College is a member of the NAIA Division I and a provisional member of NCAA Division II. Piedmont plays in the Georgia Alabama Carolina Conference (GACC).

Study Abroad Piedmont College encourages students to broaden their educational experience and gain cultural perspective through study and travel abroad. Piedmont has recently organized student trips to England, Italy, Russia, and Egypt.

Support Services The Academic Support Office offers free services to all students. These services include individual and small group tutoring, computer-assisted study, academic counseling, and assistance with learning and study strategies. The office also provides reasonable and appropriate accommodations to students with disabilities.

Job Opportunities A limited number of part-time positions on campus are available to students who demonstrate financial need. The wage rate varies depending upon skills required and experience.

Tuition: $8700 per year (1999–2000)

Room and board: $4350

Contact: Director: Dr. Cynthia L. Vance, P.O. Box 10, Demorest, Georgia 30535; Telephone: 706-778-8500, Ext. 241; Fax 706-776-2811; E-mail: cvance@piedmont.edu; Web site: http://www.piedmont.edu/honors

PIMA COUNTY COMMUNITY COLLEGE

2 Pu G M Sc Tr

▼ Honors Program

The Pima County Community College (PCCC) Honors Program provides a supportive environment in which academically exceptional students can meet their potential and excel. Founded in 1973, the program brings together highly motivated students and outstanding instructors in small course sections that feature an intensified approach to the traditional academic or occupational disciplines. The program is designed to allow students in all majors to participate without adding to overall course load.

Students begin with the Honors 101 Colloquium, a dynamic, interdisciplinary course in which they practice creative and critical reflection; engage in scholarly research, writing, and collaboration; debate social issues in relation to history, science, politics, economics, technology, psychology, and the arts; and explore their understandings of cultural diversity in local and global contexts. Students subsequently enroll in Honors Program sections of general education courses to fulfill the requirements for their degrees. They may also choose to develop an honors contract with an instructor of a class that is not being offered as part of the Honors Program in order to receive honors credit for the class. Honors contracts must be approved by the Honors Program Council.

In addition, students may elect to enroll in Honors 210, which involves them as members of the Advisory Student Planning Board for the Honors Program; Honors 296, Independent Study; and/or Honors 298, Advanced Topics. All Honors Program courses also have an optional service learning component.

Participation Requirements: In order to remain in the Honors Program, a student needs to be actively pursuing a degree, taking courses, and maintaining a GPA of 3.5. If a student's GPA falls below 3.5, he or she will have a one-semester probationary period during which to improve. In order to graduate with the Honors Program distinction, students must complete a minimum of 15 honors credits and finish with an overall GPA of 3.5.

Admission Process: Students new to higher education must meet one of the following criteria: a high school GPA of at least 3.5 and membership in a high school honor society, Advanced Placement (AP) credit and a GPA of at least 3.5, an ACT score of at least 29 or an SAT score of at least 1290, a high school GPA of 3.5, and placement into Writing 101 and Reading 112. Continuing education and transfer students must meet one of the following criteria: a GPA of 3.5 for all courses 100 level and above and a minimum of 12 credits completed at or above the 100 level; or a GPA of 3.5 and placement into Writing 101 and Reading 112. Applications for the Honors Program can be obtained from the Honors Coordinator or Advising Office of any Pima College campus.

Scholarship Availability: Every year, the Honors Program offers scholarship support to its students through the Scholar Award and the Scholar Competition. In addition, the campus Honors Coordinators work with individual students to identify additional local and national scholarships for which they may qualify.

The Campus Context: Pima County is located in Tucson, Arizona, a thriving multicultural city surrounded by a lush desert valley and four spectacular mountain ranges. Through its five campuses, the College offers degrees and certificates in seventy-three distinct program areas, including university transfer in science, liberal arts, or business; occupational specialties; general studies; developmental education; and customized training for corporate and nonprofit organizations. Pima's strengths include small classes, quality instruction in a caring environment, respect for diversity, responsiveness to local and global communities, and a commitment to continual growth in vision, leadership, and service to students.

Student Body The fifth-largest multicampus community college in the nation, Pima County Community College opens its doors each year to more than 65,000 credit and noncredit students. Twenty-eight percent of Pima College students are Hispanic, 3 percent are Native American, 4 percent are Asian, 4 percent are African American, and 61 percent are Anglo or other. More than 600 international students from eighty countries attend PCCC. Women comprise 56 percent of the student body. All students commute, and 26 percent are enrolled full-time. The average age of students is 28 years.

Faculty Pima College's top priority is excellent instruction. The 1,577 faculty members (359 full-time and 1,218 adjunct) bring a rich array of advanced degrees, professional expertise, and teaching experience to their work.

Key Facilities Four libraries at four campuses make available more than 200,000 multimedia resources and offer connections to a variety of electronic databases as well as to the World Wide Web. Students and members of the local community enjoy cultural enrichment at the College's Center for the Arts. More than thirty-five intramural and campus recreation programs, in addition to intercollegiate athletics for men and women, meet a wide range of student interests. Services for students include financial aid, academic advising and assessment, career counseling, disabled student resources, minority education programs, and women's reentry programs. Each campus has a computer laboratory with personal computers available for student use.

Honorary Society Phi Theta Kappa

Tuition: $822 (state residents) or $4932 (nonresidents) for two semesters of 15 credit hours each (1998–99)

Mandatory Fees: $5 (once per semester for registration processing fee)

Contact: Director: Director of Honors Program, Pima County Community College, 4905B East Broadway Boulevard, Tucson, Arizona 85709-1100; Telephone: 520-206-4986; Fax: 520-206-4788; E-mail: mfoster@pimacc.pima.edu; Web site: http://pima.edu/

PITTSBURG STATE UNIVERSITY

4 Pu G & D M Sc Tr

▼ Honors College and Departmental Honors Program

Pittsburg State University offers two types of honors programs: The Honors College and the Departmental Honors Program.

The primary mission of the Honors College is to provide a more meaningful educational experience for select superior students. The Honors College curriculum at the freshman-sophomore level offers intellectually stimulating general education courses. The junior-senior level Honors College students become integrated into the Departmental Honors Program.

Established in 1986, the Honors College currently enrolls approximately 190 students.

Participation Requirements: To graduate from the Honors College program, entering freshmen must complete a minimum of 12 hours of general education honors courses and honors orientation. A minimum 3.4 GPA must also be maintained. Presidential and transfer scholars must also complete the Departmental Honors Program with a minimum of 9 credit hours. Departmental Honors offers the opportunity for mentored research above normal requirements for designated upper-level course work. Other Honors College scholars are also encouraged to complete Departmental Honors. A 3.5 GPA is required to enter Departmental Honors course work, which is open to any qualified campus student.

Admission Process: Honors College members are a carefully screened and select group of scholarship recipients. Most enter the program their freshman year after formal application and acceptance. A small number of junior-level transfer students, screened international students, and high-achieving freshmen are also admitted. To be eligible, freshmen must have a 28 composite ACT, a minimum 3.7 high school GPA (on a 4.0 scale), and/or provide proof of adding multicultural diversity to the honors program. Transfer scholars must have completed 40 semester hours with a minimum GPA of 3.75 on a 4.0 scale. A transcript verifying class standing and course preparation, a letter of activities and awards, and recommendations comprise the application package. The deadline for high school applicants is March 1 and for transfers is April 1.

Scholarship Availability: The Honors College has 12 Presidential Scholars, 20 University Scholars, 6 Transfer Scholars, and an additional group of select scholars admitted annually. Presidential Scholars receive fall and spring tuition, room and board, and a book allowance. University and Transfer Scholars receive fall and spring in-state tuition and are eligible for other awards.

The Campus Context: Pittsburg State University is one of six Kansas Regents institutions. It is located 120 miles south of Kansas City. Honors College students can enroll in any of more than 100 majors in the College of Arts and Sciences, the College of Business, the College of Education, and the College of Technology.

Student Body University enrollment is approximately 7,000.

Key Facilities Library, computer, and other academic resources are readily available.

Honorary Societies Lambda Sigma, Phi Kappa Phi, Pinnacle, Omicron Delta Kappa, Rho Lambda

Athletics Pittsburg State is in the NCAA Division II, with a long tradition of "Gorilla" pride in the sports programs, most notably football. Other sports include men's and women's basketball, track, and cross-country; men's baseball and golf; and women's volleyball and softball.

Tuition: $2100 for state residents, $6464 for nonresidents, per year (1998–99)

Room and Board: $3544

Contact: Director: Dr. Christine E. Fogliasso; Assistant Director: Dr. Bradley P. Cameron, 1701 South Broadway, Pittsburg, Kansas 66762; Telephone: 316-235-4329

PORTLAND STATE UNIVERSITY

4 Pu G M Sc Tr

▼ University Honors Program

The Honors Program at Portland State University (PSU) is a small, degree-granting program primarily meant for students who intend to go on to graduate or professional school. It is therefore the faculty's intent to shape an environment and culture like that of a small liberal arts college within the larger university. Once admitted to the program, students in honors are excused from general University requirements and instead work toward the undergraduate degree by means of a combination of courses within the honors college and work within the departmental major. Students may choose any of the departmental majors offered at Portland State.

Students in honors at Portland State come from a diverse range of backgrounds and pursue a wide variety of majors. While most (better than 80 percent) of students come directly from high school, honors at Portland State also admits a number of "returning" students and transfers (although applications are generally not accepted from students with more than about 60 quarter hours of credit). What students in the honors college share is a commitment to learning and an equal commitment to excellence, which is reflected in their achievements. They are active in a wide variety of campus and extracurricular activities. In one recent year, program students were chairing the student senate, serving as editors of the newspaper and literary magazine, and chairing not only the history and business, but also the foreign language honor societies.

Students from the program share, as well, a record of achievement. The program is extremely proud of the level of success of the graduates: a recent survey indicated that better than 80 percent of Honors Program graduates had gone on to one or more advanced degrees, whether a professional degree (e.g., M.D., J.D., or M.B.A.) or one of the academic degrees (e.g., Ph.D.). The program was begun in 1969, and enrollment is limited to 200.

Participation Requirements: After the core courses of the first and second years, course work in the honors college falls into one of two kinds: courses in the "middle tier" and the upper-division seminars (called colloquia) connected with the Visiting Scholars' Project. The middle tier and colloquia courses are generally small—never more than 15 students—and interdisciplinary in nature.

Each year the program brings to campus a number of noted American and international scholars to work with program students in the upper-division seminars. Visiting lecturers (numbering at this point nearly 200) have included the noted French historian, member of the College de France, and Director of the Bibliotheque Nationale, Emmanuel Le Roy Ladurie; Nobel laureates Sir Peter Medawar and Gunther Stent; feminist philosopher, playwright, and novelist Helene Cixous; and economist Robert Heilbroner.

Interpreting the symbols: **2**=two-year college, **4**=four-year college; **Pu**=public or state college, **Pr**=private college; **G**=general honors program; **D**=departmental honors program; **S**=small program (fewer than 100 students), **M**=midsize program (100 to 500 students), **L**=large program (more than 500 students); **Sc**=scholarships available in honors program; **Tr**=transfer students accepted into honors program; **HBC**=historically black college; **AA**=academic advisors; **GA**=graduate advisors; **FA**=fellowship advisors.

In 1985, the University Honors Program began a unique internship program for its students in Washington, D.C. That project began with one student working for an academic quarter in the Smithsonian's Archives; since that beginning the project has grown substantially, both in number of students and in their success. Sixteen to 20 students each year are now placed in internships covering a wide range of possibilities: the entire array of Smithsonian-associated institutions, carefully selected nongovernmental organizations such as Common Cause, many federal offices and agencies in the capital, and, for premedical students, valuable internships in the National Institutes of Health and the National Institute of Mental Health. Students completing the program receive an honors diploma.

Applications are accepted on a rolling basis. Students should contact the Admissions Office for further information.

Scholarship Availability: Some limited tuition-remission scholarships are available.

The Campus Context: There are seven major academic units: the College of Liberal Arts and Sciences, the School of Business Administration, the School of Education, the College of Engineering and Computer Science, the School of Fine and Performing Arts, the College of Urban and Public Affairs, and the Graduate School of Social Work. Thirty-five bachelor's, forty-three master's, and ten doctoral programs are offered.

Student Body Total enrollment, including graduate level, is 20,185. Forty-seven percent of the population is men and 53 percent is women. Ethnic distribution is as follows: 68.1 percent white, 8.6 percent Asian/Pacific Islander, 5.3 percent international students, 2.9 percent Hispanic, 2.8 percent black, 1.2 percent Native American, and 11 percent other/no response. Almost 45 percent of the students receive some form of financial aid. The campus has three fraternities and three sororities.

Faculty There are nearly 600 full-time faculty members.

Key Facilities The library houses more than 1 million volumes. There are ten computer labs, including a special Honors Program computer lab.

Honorary Societies Phi Kappa Phi, Golden Key

Athletics PSU sponsors sixteen intercollegiate varsity sports. Men's sports are football, basketball, cross-country, golf, outdoor and indoor track (Big Sky Conference), baseball, and wrestling (PAC 10). Women's sports are cross-country, basketball, soccer, tennis, outdoor and indoor track, volleyball (Big Sky Conference), and softball. Admission to athletic events is free with a valid University ID card. A wide range of intramural and club sports for men and women is also offered. Recreational hours for the gymnasium, handball court, swimming pool, and weight rooms are available.

Study Abroad The Office of International Education Services sponsors a wide variety of study-abroad programs year-round, including opportunities in Europe, Eastern Europe, Russia, China, Southeast Asia, Australia, Africa, South America, and Central America. Residence credit and home campus registration are offered, as is financial aid.

Support Services Disabled Services for Students offers a wide range of services and assistance, including note takers, test readers/writers, sign-language interpreters, priority registration, adapted computers, and classroom equipment. Most buildings are fully accessible.

Job Opportunities PSU participates in the Federal Work-Study Program for students demonstrating a need for part-time employment to pursue a college education. The Student Employment Office manages other student employment opportunities.

Tuition: $3525 for state residents, $12,291 for nonresidents, per year

Room and Board: $5500

Mandatory Fees: $486

Contact: Director: Professor Lawrence P. Wheeler, P.O. Box 751, Portland, Oregon 97207; Telephone: 503-725-4928; Fax: 503-725-5363; E-mail: hon@pdx.edu; Web site: http://www.honors.pdx.edu

PRAIRIE STATE COLLEGE

2 Pu G S Tr

▼ Honors Program

The Prairie State College (PSC) Honors Program offers to good students an opportunity to fulfill standard requirements in a more stimulating and personalized environment than that of regular classes. The program was founded in 1991 and has tripled in size since then. Eligible students may enroll in honors sections of first-year required courses in the areas of English, biology, history, humanities, philosophy, psychology, social sciences, and speech. Classes are limited to 18 students and are taught by full-time instructors who are interested in complementing or replacing lectures and tests with in-depth, project-oriented activities. Courses include at least one field trip or visiting speaker. Some honors classes have been scheduled to fit together into a single, 6-credit-hour unit.

Participation Requirements: Students may enter the program at any time that they become eligible; most eligible students are informed by letter. Eligibility is based on at least college-level placement scores in reading, writing, and math or a minimum 3.5 GPA in 12 hours of college-level course work.

Admission Process: Students may enroll in as many or few honors courses as they wish. At least a 3.5 GPA must be maintained. Honors courses are designated on the students' transcripts.

The Campus Context: Founded in 1958, Prairie State College is a public two-year college that serves Illinois Community College District 515. It is located in Chicago Heights, Illinois, approximately 35 miles south of Chicago. The College services nineteen surrounding communities: Beecher, Chicago Heights, Crete, Flossmoor, Ford Heights, Glenwood, Homewood, Matteson, Monee, Olympia Fields, Park Forest, Richton Park, Sauk Village, South Chicago Heights, Steger, University Park, and portions of Country Club Hills, Hazel Crest, Lynwood, and adjacent unincorporated areas of Cook and Will Counties. The College awards Associate of Arts, Associate of Science, Associate of Applied Science, and Associate of General Studies degrees as well as short-term and long-term technical certificates. Programs include curricula in the occupational and technical fields as well as courses in the liberal arts, general education, and preprofessional programs. Prairie State College also provides courses in general studies, both credit and non-credit, to meet cultural, vocational, and avocational need of the community.

Student Body In fall 1998, there were 5,275 total students (credit and noncredit) enrolled as of the tenth day. Of the degree-seeking students, 52 percent are white non-Hispanic, 29 percent are black non-Hispanic, 7 percent are Hispanic, 1 percent are Asian or Pacific Islander, and less than 1 percent are Native American or Alaskan Native. Ten percent of the total number of degree-seeking students were categorized as unknown.

Faculty At Prairie State College in fall of 1998, there were 315 faculty members, both full-time and adjunct. Of those, 85 were considered full-time. Fifteen percent of the full-time faculty members have doctoral degrees, first-professional degrees, and/or the appropriate terminal degrees in their field. (All honors classes are taught by full-time instructors, about fifty percent by those with terminal degrees.)

Key Facilities At the Learning Resource Center (LRC) at Prairie State College, students have access to 45,000 books, serial backfiles, and government documents. It carries 515 serial subscriptions, including periodicals, newspapers, and government documents. The LRC maintains an Online Public Access Catalog, which is accessible from computers other than the ones located in the LRC. Students can also access other library catalogs through its system.

Students have 300 computers available for their use through computer labs, student labs, and the Learning Resource Center. The Internet/World Wide Web can be accessed through most of these computers. In the computer lab, there is assistance and training available for the computer, software, and the Internet.

Honorary Society Phi Theta Kappa

Athletics Various men and women's sports are made available for student participation. For men there is intramural basketball, soccer, and volleyball as well as intercollegiate baseball, golf, and soccer. For women, intramural basketball, soccer, and volleyball are also available as well as intercollegiate golf, soccer, softball, and tennis.

Study Abroad Students who maintain a high GPA at Prairie State College are eligible to apply for the Study-Abroad program. There are currently four different programs available to students, a summer semester in San Jose, Costa Rica; a fall or spring semester in Canterbury, England; a fall or spring semester in Salzburg, Austria; and a spring semester in the Netherlands.

Support Services There are many services provided for special needs students at Prairie State College once students are identified as having a handicap or learning disability. There are tutors available to work extra hours with the students, opportunities to take untimed tests, note-takers for courses they are registered in, readers for testing, and different equipment and software available. Equipment available for special needs students includes The Reading Edge, LP Windows, WindowEyes, and Optelec Enlargers.

Job Opportunities Prairie State College offers many different job opportunities, such as work-study programs and internships. In addition, counselors and advisers are available for help with choosing careers as well as job placement services.

Tuition: $1404 for in-district residents, $4092 for residents, $4932 for nonresidents, $5412 for international students, per year (1999–2000)

Contact: Director, Enrollment Development: Rich Kiefer; Telephone: 708-709-3512; E-mail: rkiefer@prairie.cc.il.us; Honors Coordinator Maurine Stein; Telephone: 708-709-3771; E-mail: mstein@prairie.cc.il.us

Prairie View A&M University

4 Pu M Tr HBC

▼ University Scholars Program

The University Scholars Program responds to the need for more highly competent leaders and practitioners in all fields. Selection of students for the Scholars Program is based on outstanding academic achievement, participation in extracurricular activities and/or community-based outreach programs, expressed interest in eventual pursuit and completion of the doctorate or other professional degree, and a commitment to fulfilling a service-learning project as part of degree-completion requirements.

Advanced Placement credit in core courses, especially English and mathematics, is awarded to qualified scholars. Each scholar is assigned a faculty mentor who may or may not be in the student's academic major. Students enroll in a freshman-level colloquium or seminar, attend intellectually challenging seminars and workshops, travel to special culturally enriching events, and begin a research project no later than the junior year, completing it by the end of the senior year. Scholars are provided broad options in selecting elective courses. Students are encouraged to participate fully in the life of the campus and to seek opportunities to develop strong leadership and communication skills.

Upon completion of the program, students receive a University Scholars Program cord and pendant in a formal ceremony. The expectation is that students who remain in the program until graduation should graduate at least *cum laude*. A notation of University Scholars Program completion is indicated on the transcript.

Admission Process: Students are required to have the following high school qualifications in order to be eligible to participate: a minimum 3.5 GPA on a 4.0 scale; an SAT I score of at least 1200 or an ACT score of at least 25; a strong college-preparatory background in mathematics, science, and English; recommendations from high school teachers, including rating of academic performance, motivation, and self-discipline; and passage of any state-mandated examination used as a high school exit examination. Transfer students with a college GPA of 3.5 or higher may apply for admission to the University Scholars Program.

Scholarship Availability University Scholars Program applicants are encouraged to apply for the Presidential Scholarships and/or the Regents Scholarship by April 1. Employment opportunities, primarily of the work-study variety, are available.

The Campus Context: Prairie View A&M University is a member of the Texas A&M University System. Its academic organization consists of six colleges and three schools. The units include the College of Agriculture and Human Sciences; the College of Arts and Sciences; the School of Architecture; the College of Business; the College of Education; the College of Engineering; the School of Juvenile Justice; the College of Nursing; and the Graduate School. More than eighty academic degree programs are available. Some instruction is provided at sites in Houston, at Fort Hood/Killeen, and at Bryan–College Station.

Student Body The undergraduate enrollment (fall 2000) was approximately 5,300 students: 44 percent men and 56 percent women. Students come from thirty-six states and thirty-three other countries. The ethnic distribution is 93 percent black, 3 percent white, 2 percent international, 2 percent Hispanic, and 1 percent Asian or Pacific Islander. The resident population is 91 percent. About 85 percent of the students receive financial aid.

Faculty Of the 388 faculty members, 282 are full-time.

Key Facilities The library houses 322,306 volumes.

Tuition: Approximately $1008 for state residents, approximately $6072 for nonresidents per year (fall 2001 semester, based on 12 semester credit hours per semester)

Room and Board: $5665 per year (based on a 21-meal plan)

Mandatory Fees: Approximately $1000

Contact: Director: Wash A. Jones, Ph.D., P.O. Box 2879, Prairie View, Texas 77446; Telephone: 936-857-2851; Fax: 936-857-2994; E-mail: wash_jones@pvamu.edu

Prince George's Community College

2 Pu G M Sc Tr AA

▼ Honors Program

The mission of the Honors Program at Prince George's Community College (PGCC) is to promote the intellectual growth and enrichment of academically outstanding students. Founded in 1981 as a single seminar course with a few students, the program now offers more than twenty-four honors sections each semester

Interpreting the symbols: **2**=two-year college, **4**=four-year college; **Pu**=public or state college, **Pr**=private college; **G**=general honors program; **D**=departmental honors program; **S**=small program (fewer than 100 students), **M**=midsize program (100 to 500 students), **L**=large program (more than 500 students); **Sc**=scholarships available in honors program; **Tr**=transfer students accepted into honors program; **HBC**=historically black college; **AA**=academic advisors; **GA**=graduate advisors; **FA**=fellowship advisors.

to more than 300 students. In addition, the Honors Program offers an interdisciplinary honors colloquium each semester in a variety of areas.

The Honors Program emphasizes small classes (usually 10 to 15 students) that offer unique opportunities in participatory learning, interaction, and faculty mentoring. Most honors classes are seminar-style and seek to help the student become an independent learner and critical thinker. The honors faculty consists of more than 40 senior faculty members and master teachers, many of whom are actively involved in professional development in their fields.

Members of the College's Honors Program enjoy many unique opportunities. Some of the benefits include access to the honors student lounge, which houses computers, desks, a phone, a study area, and meeting space to socialize. In addition to a full-time Honors Coordinator, the Honors Program employs 2 part-time Assistant Faculty Coordinators in Marketing and Recruitment and in Activities to work with honors students. The honors society provides many cocurricular activities for students, including the College Bowl, the Model United Nations club, and Tau Pi, the College's chapter of Phi Theta Kappa. Honors students also can earn credit for internships related to their majors through the College co-op education program.

Students who graduate from the honors program transfer to many top four-year institutions locally and nationwide, including Georgetown, Johns Hopkins, American, Catholic, George Mason, and Howard Universities, the University of Maryland, and Goucher and Washington Colleges, to name a few.

In 2000, the Honors Academy was introduced into the Honors Program. The Honors Academy is designed for academically outstanding students who are interested in a rigorous program of academic excellence, intellectual development, leadership, and community service. Benefits of the academy include dual admission to selected four-year academic institutions; full tuition while at PGCC and scholarship upon transfer through completion of the B.A. degree; and seamless transfer from Prince George's Community College to the partnering institutions. Eligibility for the academy is competitive; students must have and maintain a GPA of 3.5 or above, have a combined SAT score of 1050 or higher, complete at least seven honors courses, perform 15 hours of community service each semester, and assume a leadership role within the honors program.

Participation Requirements: Students in the honors program may take as many or as few honors courses as they choose. However, to graduate with a Citation in Honors, students must take a minimum of five honors courses with a cumulative GPA of 3.25 or higher. Each May, students are recognized for high academic achievement and excellence in research, writing, or a particular discipline or for overall merit at the Honors Convocation, which is followed by a reception for the students, faculty, and family members.

Admission Process: To be admitted into the Honors Program, incoming and currently enrolled students must meet the following criteria: a high school GPA of 3.0 or higher and a score of 550 or higher on the SAT verbal test or scores of 95 or higher on the Accuplacer Reading test and 108 or higher on the Accuplacer Sentence Structure test administered by the College testing center. To remain eligible for the Honors Program, students must maintain a 3.0 cumulative GPA in the College.

The Campus Context: Prince George's Community College was founded in 1958. Last year, the College was chosen as one of sixteen schools nationwide to earn the designation "Leadership Institution" from the Association of American Colleges and Universities. The College is housed primarily on the main campus in Largo, Maryland, but opened two satellite campuses during the 2000–01 academic year. The College offers more than fifty academic degree programs and hundreds of continuing education and workforce education programs, including a distance learning program.

Student Body More than 13,000 students representing more than ninety countries are enrolled at Prince George's Community College. Approximately two thirds of the student body are women. Nearly 75 percent of the students attend school part-time, or less than 12 credit hours. A total of 645 students graduated with associate degrees in 2001.

Faculty A total of 641 faculty members teach at the College, 45 percent of whom are full-time and 55 percent of whom are adjunct faculty appointments.

Key Facilities The College features a library/media center, a television and recording studio, photography and graphic production facilities, and a computer center.

Honorary Societies Phi Theta Kappa and Psi Beta, the national honor society for psychology

Job Opportunities Through its cooperative education program, students have an opportunity to earn college credits for work-related internships. Many internships turn into paid employment. In addition, students are offered a variety of employment opportunities on campus.

Tuition: For full-time Prince George's Community students tuition is $2400 per year, for Maryland residents tuition is $3900, and for out-of-state residents tuition is $5900 per academic year.

Contact: Dr. Melinda Frederick, Coordinator, Honors Program and Honors Academy, Marlboro 1087, 301 Largo Road, Largo, Maryland 20774; Telephone: 301/322-0433; Fax: 301/808-0960; E-mail: fredermj@pg.cc.md.us; Web site: http://academic.pg.cc.md.us/honorsprogram/

PURDUE UNIVERSITY

4 Pu L Sc Tr

▼ Honors Programs

Purdue University offers a wide range of honors experiences, and its two largest schools, the School of Engineering and the School of Liberal Arts, offer many varied opportunities for honors work. Many departments throughout the University also have special honors tracks of their own, so that some students at Purdue are able to graduate with departmental, School, and University honors.

The School of Liberal Arts Honors Program is designed to foster excellence and intellectual curiosity and to provide a rich, stimulating, and challenging educational experience for creative and highly motivated students throughout the University. The program offers both Honors Only courses (courses with limited enrollment, stressing close student-faculty interaction) and Honors Option courses, in which students enroll in regular courses but are provided with special honors experiences. Advanced students in the program design their own honors work through Honors by Special Arrangement, through which they arrange individual honors projects with professors and tailor their honors experiences to their particular personal and professional interests. Many students become part of their professors' research teams, refining their skills by participating in major research projects and contributing to their field long before graduation. Each year, the program sponsors an Honors Colloquium, featuring outstanding undergraduate work in the School, and students often go on to present their work at regional and national professional conferences.

Students in the Liberal Arts Honors Program also enjoy a wide range of supplementary activities through the Honors Experience. These include special information sessions, often led by members of the Honors Council; meals with visiting speakers; and reduced-price tickets to a wide variety of concerts, plays, films, lectures, special exhibitions, and other experiences on and off campus. Members of the Honors Council help to determine the program's activities and events each year and sponsor numerous opportunities for community service work in the greater Lafayette area.

Founded in 1979, the School of Liberal Arts Honors Program involves more than 800 students, with approximately 500 students actively taking courses each semester.

The Freshman Engineering Honors Program is designed to provide the highly motivated and academically successful student with a broader and more enriched educational experience during his or her freshman year. The program is intended to cultivate the inquisitive nature of its participants by allowing them to explore, expand, and excel in a curriculum, which promotes both scholastic achievement and breadth of knowledge.

Begun in 1958, the Freshman Engineering Honors Program traditionally enrolls approximately 160 students each year.

Both programs provide students with a small-school environment while enjoying the resources of many of the nation's top programs. Honors students in these programs have the opportunity to enroll in smaller classes, to form relationships with other high-achieving students, and to develop strong, personal relationships with faculty members and advisers. Students in the Freshman Engineering Honors Program are also able to interact with professional engineers in industry, both on campus and during visits to industrial sites. The Freshman Engineering Honors Program stresses team-based learning, an approach that presents students with hands-on projects that allow application and demonstration of knowledge. All courses taken for honors are noted on the students' transcripts.

Entering students at Purdue also have the opportunity to join various learning communities, which provide unique opportunities to learn with small groups of students, often with a particular academic focus, theme, or interest. In addition, the Lilly Endowment has funded a number of special topics courses specifically designed for adventurous and highly self-motivated first-year students.

Participation Requirements: Students in the School of Liberal Arts Honors Program may take as many honors courses as they wish. To maintain honors eligibility, students must maintain a minimum 3.0 GPA. For Full Honors, students must graduate with a 3.3 GPA, take a minimum of 24 hours of honors credit, and fulfill the distribution requirements of the School honors degree.

Students in the School of Engineering Honors Program must successfully complete the following requirements: enroll in and complete 7 credit hours of honors and/or honors-designated courses each semester of the freshman year, earn a 3.4 cumulative GPA at the end of that year, and be active in at least one student organization throughout the year.

Admission Process: To take honors courses in the School of Liberal Arts, entering students must have graduated in the top 10 percent of their high school class or have a composite ACT score of 27 or above or a combined SAT I score of 1150 or above. No special application is required. Students arrange to enroll in honors courses through their counselors.

Students interested in the Freshman Engineering Honors Program must meet one of the following eligibility requirements: be a Merit Scholarship recipient (which includes but is not limited to National Merit Finalist or Scholar Award, Beering Scholar Award, Dean's Engineering Scholar Award, Minority Engineering Program Honors Merit Award, or Women in Engineering Program Honors Merit Award); or have an SAT of 1360 (or an equivalent ACT of 31) or above and be in the top 10 percent of their high school class (or have a GPA of 3.8 or above at schools that do not provide rankings).

Scholarship Availability: Most honors students receive one of the many academic or talent scholarships offered by the Division of Financial Aid. Purdue grants an Academic Success Award, which is based solely on the SAT or ACT score and class rank and is automatically awarded with admission. There are also major scholarships ranging from the Beering Scholars Program for the 80–100 top high school seniors who have been admitted by the first week in December (full financial support through graduate school at Purdue), the Indiana Resident Top Scholar Award (150 awards covering eight semesters of undergraduate study), National Merit Finalist Scholarships, and Valedictorian Scholarships.

Three specific scholarships are dedicated to beginning engineering students: the Dean's Engineering Scholarship, the Women in Engineering Scholarship, and the Minority Engineering Scholarship. These scholarships require a separate application, including essays. All Dean's Engineering Scholarship winners are also automatically eligible for additional merit scholarships, often dependent upon the student's chosen specialty.

In addition, the School of Liberal Arts offers approximately forty merit-based scholarships for entering students in the Dean's Scholar Program, which offers students the opportunity to work one-on-one with professors in various departments while earning $1000 stipends. These awards require a separate application, including essays and recommendations. The Honors Program also offers limited additional merit-based scholarships for upper-level students in the program.

The Campus Context: Purdue University is one of America's premier research universities, one of sixty-eight land-grant institutions, and one of the twenty-five largest universities in the country. Founded in 1869, the main campus at West Lafayette is located on a nearly 1,600-acre site not far from the Wabash River. Students may pursue more than 200 specializations organized under the Schools of Agriculture, Consumer and Family Sciences, Education, Engineering, Health Sciences, Liberal Arts, Management, Nursing, Pharmacy and Pharmacal Sciences, Technology, and Veterinary Medicine.

Purdue Convocations annually bring to campus dozens of theatrical productions, jazz and popular music groups, touring opera and musical companies, symphony orchestras, and chamber music groups. The greater Lafayette community of about 70,000 (not including Purdue students) also provides numerous cultural activities, including a symphony orchestra, civic theater, numerous choral organizations, and ballet. The West Lafayette campus is about an hour's drive from Indianapolis and approximately a 2-hour's drive from Chicago, with all the attractions.

Student Body More than 38,000 undergraduate and graduate students from across the nation and more than a 100 other countries are enrolled on the West Lafayette campus and extension campuses.

Undergraduate enrollment at West Lafayette is more than 30,000 students, of whom approximately 7,000 are first-year students. Most undergraduates are from Indiana (71 percent), and more than 6,000 undergraduates are currently enrolled in programs in the liberal arts. Purdue has been coeducational since its second year of operation, and today about 42 percent of the students on the main campus are women. The ethnic distribution is 6 percent African American, 3 percent Hispanic, 3 percent Asian American, 84 percent Caucasian, and 2 percent international students. About 85 percent of first-year students live in University housing, but almost 24,000 undergraduate and graduate students live in rental housing off campus. The Greek system is strong at Purdue. About 20 percent of Purdue's undergraduates belong to the forty-one fraternities and twenty-five sororities on campus. There

Interpreting the symbols: **2**=two-year college, **4**=four-year college; **Pu**=public or state college, **Pr**=private college; **G**=general honors program; **D**=departmental honors program; **S**=small program (fewer than 100 students), **M**=midsize program (100 to 500 students), **L**=large program (more than 500 students); **Sc**=scholarships available in honors program; **Tr**=transfer students accepted into honors program; **HBC**=historically black college; **AA**=academic advisors; **GA**=graduate advisors; **FA**=fellowship advisors.

are also five cooperative houses for men and seven for women. Most students belong to at least one of the more than 600 official student organizations on campus, and more than thirty leadership and honorary programs and societies are active on the West Lafayette campus.

Faculty There are approximately 2,200 faculty members on the West Lafayette campus. The great majority of them hold the terminal degree for members in their fields. The student-faculty ratio is 16:1.

Key Facilities The Purdue libraries house more than 2.5 million volumes, almost 20,000 journal subscriptions, and more than 9,000 audiovisual materials. The online catalog offers access to all the materials housed in the main collection and the fourteen divisional libraries. Computer facilities include fiber-optic networks for all residence halls and offices. There are also numerous computer labs across campus. All students are given e-mail addresses and access to the World Wide Web. The Purdue Writing Lab offers one-to-one assistance with writing, as well as online assistance to all students within the University.

Honorary Societies Phi Beta Kappa, Golden Key, Mortar Board, Alpha Lambda Delta, and Phi Eta Sigma

Athletics Purdue is an NCAA Division I School, offering eighteen varsity sports. The football team has been ranked nationally among the top twenty-five during each of the past three years, and the Boilermaker men's and women's basketball teams won seven of the fourteen Big Ten titles in a span of seven years (1994–2000), plus a women's national championship. The West Lafayette campus also provides an extensive range of intramural and club sports.

Study Abroad Purdue University offers summer, semester, and yearlong study-abroad programs for every major at more than forty countries around the world. There are 168 exchange and Purdue-administered programs, and Purdue also provides sixty additional educational opportunities through affiliation with other institutions.

Support Services Facilities for disabled students are plentiful. Seven of the largest housing facilities are accessible to students who use wheelchairs. Additional services for students with disabilities include a note-taking service, class-taping service, and alternative testing conditions and methods.

Job Opportunities Work-study, undergraduate assistantships, internships, and cooperative educational experiences are all available. The Division of Financial Aid maintains a student employment database for numerous part-time jobs on and off campus and is available to students whether or not they receive financial aid. Each student's academic adviser can also arrange time blocks to schedule classes and allow time for employment.

Tuition: $4164 for residents, $13,872 for nonresidents per year (2001–02)

Room and Board: $6120 (average)

Contact: Director: Dr. Clayton D. Lein, School of Liberal Arts Honors Program, 1289 LAEB, Purdue University, West Lafayette, Indiana 47907; Telephone: 765-494-6296; Fax: 765-494-3660; E-mail: clein@sla.purdue.edu; Web site: http://www.sla.purdue.edu/honors/; Freshman Engineering Honors Program, 1286 Engineering Administration, Purdue University, West Lafayette, Indiana 47907; Telephone: 800-440-9885 (toll-free); Fax: 765-494-5819; E-mail: frehonor@ecn.purdue.edu; Web site: http://Engineering.Purdue.edu/FrE/programs/honors/

Queens College of the City University of New York

4 Pu G M Sc Tr

▼ Honors Programs

Queens College offers a variety of honors sequences. High-achieving students selected to join Honors College University Scholars Program participate in challenging honors programs. They attend the Honors College Seminar, which integrates cultural experiences with academic study. The seminar focuses on the arts, history, citizens, and vast resources of New York City. The Honors College Cultural Passport provides an introduction to the great cultural institutions of New York, including museums, theater, and concerts. University Scholars participate in a wide range of activities with Honors College students from other City University of New York (CUNY) campuses. They meet leaders in the arts, government, business, and science and have opportunities to pursue internships and mentoring experiences.

Honors in the Humanities (HTH) is an 18-credit honors minor with a sequence of courses in literature and thought. The upper-level courses are weekly seminars around a large table in the HTH library; they are usually led by 2 faculty members. The lively, far-ranging discussion is centered on great works of drama, fiction, history, philosophy, poetry, and religion. The program encourages students to think critically, to read carefully and analytically, and to articulate and defend ideas both orally and in writing. To participate in HTH is to be challenged toward self-realization by professors, books, and other students. HTH has its own reference library with more than 4,000 volumes.

Honors in the Mathematical and Natural Sciences is designed to enhance research skills and opportunities for students interested in a career in the mathematical and natural sciences. An initial interdisciplinary Science Honors Seminar is followed by research courses and opportunities for mentoring, fellowships, and assistantships. Science honors students become participating members of a community of scientific scholars that includes students and faculty members.

The Business and Liberal Arts (BALA) program is a rigorous, interdisciplinary 24-credit minor that connects liberal arts students to the world of business. It was designed in consultation with leaders of the corporate world who said their greatest need was for the thinking, writing, and speaking skills of liberal arts graduates to fill managerial positions. BALA reaffirms the importance of the liberal arts while offering a series of courses designed to bridge study in the traditional liberal arts with a business career. The program features internships in New York's exciting business community and mentoring by business leaders. Journalism at Queens College is a broad-based 21-credit minor designed in partnership with distinguished leaders of the New York media. Leading New York journalists teach in the program and serve as mentors. The program emphasizes writing and critical thinking and teaches students how to report the news and how to function in a media environment. It provides opportunities for internships with major news organizations. The journalism minor enhances any major, from English to economics to science. Incoming freshmen may apply to all these programs. Departmental honors concentrations are offered by some departments; for example, the Financial Economics Honors Program is an option available to majors within the College's Department of Economics.

The Office of Honors and Scholarships provides special opportunities for academically strong students. Incoming freshmen with outstanding high school records may apply to participate in these activities, including a freshman colloquium, an honors writing and literature course satisfying a number of College requirements, and specially designated sections of courses that meet liberal arts requirements. The weekly freshman colloquium is designed to introduce students to the College's outstanding faculty and to diverse fields of study.

All of these honors programs promote cohesive academic and social communities within the larger Queens College community. Most have their own student lounges. Most have program completion noted on transcripts. Students may participate in more than one program.

The Freshman Year Initiative (FYI) Program offers first-semester students the resources to guide them through their first academic experiences here. Through FYI, students are able to register for classes that may otherwise be unavailable to first-year students. Classes in FYI communities are taught by some of the best, most experienced and sought-after professors at Queens College. Being part of an FYI community ensures that students get to know a small group of fellow first-year students and become resources for each other in the transition from high school to college.

Admission Process: Applications for these programs may be made through the Office of Undergraduate Admissions in conjunction with completion of the Queens College Scholars Application. Students may also apply directly to these programs, preferably before the start of their freshman year.

Scholarship Availability: Scholarships are awarded on the basis of a student's high school record, letters of recommendation, SAT I scores, and a personal essay. Approximately 40 incoming first-year students are accepted into the Honors College University Scholars Program. University Scholars receive a special funding package that includes full tuition scholarships, stipends, an academic expense account to pay for enriching experiences such as study abroad and to use for living expenses during unpaid internships, and a free laptop computer. The University Scholars Program awards full tuition and partial two-year scholarships to academically outstanding incoming freshmen. The College awards scholarships to academically strong incoming transfer students who hold an A.A. or A.S. degree. Renewal of scholarships is contingent on a student's maintenance of a high standard of academic performance.

The Mellon Minority Undergraduate Fellowship offers financial support, opportunities for summer research, and close faculty mentoring to highly qualified students in core fields in arts and sciences. Designed to address the underrepresentation of black, Latino, and Native American people in higher education, it is open to juniors and seniors who have a commitment to attending graduate school and attaining a Ph.D. Students in the program normally receive two years of support, including a tuition fellowship, a stipend during the academic year (offered in compensation for research assistance the student undertakes), and a grant each summer for study or academic travel.

The Campus Context: Queens College is one of the senior colleges of the CUNY system, and like the CUNY campuses, Queens is a commuter school. Queens College was cited by the *New York Times Selective Guide to Colleges* as the strongest college within the CUNY system. Funded by the state of New York, Queens College serves all the people of the state, but most of the College's students live in New York City's five boroughs or the counties of Nassau, Suffolk, or Westchester. Students from other states and other nations also attend Queens College. The campus is located off the Long Island Expressway in the urban/suburban area of Flushing, Queens.

The College has four academic divisions: Arts and Humanities, Mathematics and Natural Sciences, Social Sciences, and the School of Education. There are fifty-three undergraduate majors leading to the baccalaureate degree, which includes the Bachelor of Arts, Bachelor of Fine Arts, Bachelor of Music, and Bachelor of Science.

Student Body The student population is achievement oriented and diverse—sixty-seven native languages are spoken here, providing an extraordinary environment.

There are approximately 12,000 undergraduate students enrolled in all divisions. Sixty-three percent are women. The ethnic distribution of the total undergraduate population is 55 percent white, 16.1 percent Asian-Pacific Islander, 15.6 percent Hispanic, 9.8 percent African American, .1 percent American Indian/Alaskan Native, and 3.3 percent other. More than 39 percent of the students receive financial aid. In addition to various academic honor societies, including Phi Beta Kappa, there are three social fraternities and two social sororities on campus.

Faculty Of the more than 1,000 total day and evening faculty members, including adjuncts, nearly 550 are full-time, including more than 95 percent with doctoral degrees.

Key Facilities Among the College's facilities is the Aaron Copland School of Music, which, in addition to its academic programs, provides the College community with the opportunity to attend musical and performing arts events by students and distinguished faculty members. The 490-seat LeFrak Concert Hall is noted for its tracker organ. The campus also has the 2,143-seat Golden Center auditorium, which presents outstanding professional productions for the general public and also serves as a College resource.

The landmark Chaney-Goodman-Schwerner clock tower at the Rosenthal Library is dedicated to the memory of three civil rights workers who were murdered in Mississippi during the Freedom Summer of 1964. One of them, Andrew Goodman, was a Queens College student.

The library contains print and nonprint material, including approximately 752,900 books, 3,260 current print and electronic periodicals, a growing collection of multimedia in its Media Center, and an extensive collection of microform material. In addition, the library is a selected depository for many United States government publications. The College's library also provides Internet access through computer labs and public access workstations, offering online databases, electronic journals, reference sources, and a collection of electronic books.

In addition to courses offered by the Department of Computer Science, students are provided access to the College's computer systems. Students and faculty and staff members use the College facilities that provide more than 600 College-owned computer workstations for students and compatible microcomputers for classroom and open laboratory use.

Athletics The intercollegiate program provides students with the opportunity to compete on the varsity level and includes basketball, baseball, cross-country, golf, swimming, tennis, track, volleyball, and water polo. The recreational program is made up of two components: organized intramural activities and informal open recreation.

Study Abroad Students are invited to participate in study-abroad programs, which include semester and yearlong programs to China, Denmark, Ecuador, England, Greece, Italy, and Paris. Students are able to participate in programs offered by any of the CUNY campuses. Queens College sponsors the New York/Paris exchange program and study-abroad programs to England and Italy.

Support Services Disabled students find most of the academic and administrative buildings accessible, including the library, dining hall, and student union. Special parking is available. Only restrooms in the newer buildings on campus are handicapped equipped and have lowered drinking fountains. Some of the

Interpreting the symbols: **2**=two-year college, **4**=four-year college; **Pu**=public or state college, **Pr**=private college; **G**=general honors program; **D**=departmental honors program; **S**=small program (fewer than 100 students), **M**=midsize program (100 to 500 students), **L**=large program (more than 500 students); **Sc**=scholarships available in honors program; **Tr**=transfer students accepted into honors program; **HBC**=historically black college; **AA**=academic advisors; **GA**=graduate advisors; **FA**=fellowship advisors.

buildings have been equipped with automatic doors. The Office of Special Services provides a full range of services to enhance educational and vocational opportunities for students at Queens College with disabilities.

Job Opportunities Students eligible for federal financial aid may elect on- or off-campus work-study. In addition, the College hires a limited number of college aides to assist in department and administrative offices and in the library.

Tuition: $3200 for state residents, $6800 for nonresidents, per year (2001–02)

Mandatory Fees: $187

Contact: Director: Professor Sue Goldhaber, Office of Honors and Scholarships, B Building, Room 310, 65-30 Kissena Boulevard, Flushing, New York 11367; Telephone: 718-997-5502; Fax: 718-997-5498; E-mail: honors@qc.edu; Web site: http://www.qc.edu

RADFORD UNIVERSITY

4 Pu G M Tr

▼ Honors Academy

The Honors Academy provides academic enrichment opportunities for talented students and recognizes outstanding student achievement. The Academy includes the honors curriculum and a residential component, Floyd Hall, that has been designated as the honors living and learning community. As a designated Center of Excellence, the Honors Academy is a focal point for the promotion and recognition of academic excellence at Radford University (RU), and it provides a stimulating academic environment and intellectual challenges for students and faculty members. Campus projects sponsored by the Honors Academy include the campus College Bowl tournament, the Undergraduate/Graduate Forum, the Senior Academic Recognition Banquet for members of academic honor fraternities and leadership organizations, and the Highlander Academy, a summer academic enrichment experience for middle and high school students that also provides leadership experience for Honors Academy members, who serve as teaching assistants.

Through participation in the Honors Academy, students can customize and enhance their undergraduate experience as they interact with peers who are motivated to achieve academic excellence and with faculty members whose professional passions are teaching and learning. Honors Academy members who fulfill an Honors Plan of Study (HPS) and maintain required GPAs are designated as Highlander Scholars. New Highlander Scholars are inducted and graduating Highlander Scholars are recognized at the Spring Honors Banquet every April. Highlander Scholars complete honors course work in three areas: general education honors-designated courses, their academic major, and a capstone project that they present at the RU Undergraduate/Graduate Forum. General education honors-designated courses emphasize the development of critical-thinking skills, as well as excellence in written and oral communication, and have 20 or fewer students enrolled. These courses are enhanced with interactive, seminar-style teaching; field trips; guest speakers; and enrichment assignments that allow students to take more responsibility for their own learning.

Honors courses in a major are accomplished through an honors contract and mentoring with a faculty member. The honors contract customizes a course based on the specific interests and academic aspirations of the student. Highlander Scholars accomplish a senior capstone project with the supervision of a faculty adviser. Examples of capstone projects include original laboratory research, a thesis, a portfolio of creative works, international travel, an internship, student teaching, and a clinical experience. The Honors Academy Student Organization is the social component for Honors Academy members, and it provides opportunities for leadership as well as campus and community service.

The Radford University Honors Academy is affiliated with the National Collegiate Honors Council (NCHC), the Southern Regional Honors Council (SRHC), and the Virginia Collegiate Honors Council (VCHC). These affiliations allow Highlander Scholars the opportunity to participate in conferences and events with other honors students from across the United States.

The Honors Program at Radford University was founded in 1980, and the transition to the Honors Academy was completed in 1998. Currently there are 264 Honors Academy members; 111 of them have earned the coveted title of Highlander Scholar. More information about the Radford University Honors Academy is available at the Web site at http://www.radford.edu/~honors.

Participation Requirements: The following minimum GPAs are required for Honors Academy membership: 3.0 for freshman class standing, 3.3 for sophomore class standing, 3.4 for junior class standing, and 3.5 for senior class standing. To retain membership in the program, Highlander Scholars must continue to meet these GPA eligibility requirements and make progress toward completing their HPS.

To graduate from the Honors Academy as a Highlander Scholar, students must have a minimum 3.5 overall GPA and complete at least 27 hours of honors course work from the following three areas in accordance with their HPS: 6–12 hours of general education honors-designated courses, 12–15 hours of honors courses in the academic major or related courses, and 3–6 hours in a capstone project. All Highlander Scholars are required to present the results of their capstone project at the Undergraduate/Graduate Forum. Highlander Scholars who fulfill all requirements necessary to graduate from the Honors Academy are awarded a certificate and a Distinctive Honors stole at the Spring Honors Banquet and are recognized in the Honors Academy newsletter and by the University President at the commencement ceremony.

Admission Process: High school students who possess two of the following three credentials are invited to join the Honors Academy at the time they are admitted to Radford University: SAT scores of 1100 or above or an ACT score of 24 or above, a high school GPA of 3.5 or above, and a rank in the top 20 percent of their graduating class.

Highlander Scholars are members of the Honors Academy who have an approved HPS, which is the agreement that outlines how the student will satisfy the curriculum requirements of the Honors Academy. Students who were not invited into the Honors Academy as entering students are invited to join and may apply to become Highlander Scholars after they have completed at least one semester at Radford University and meet the eligibility requirements.

Scholarship Availability: The Radford University Foundation awards full and partial Presidential Scholarships to new students based on high school credentials, an application process, and competitive interviews held during the spring. Recipients of these scholarships are invited to join the Honors Academy. The RU Foundation also awards approximately 400 partial scholarships to students enrolled at Radford University based on an application process during the spring. The Honors Academy office nominates all interested and qualified Honors Academy members for prestigious national scholarships and awards, such as the Rhodes, British Marshall, Goldwater, and Truman Scholarships, and mentors those nominees through the application process.

The Campus Context: Radford University, founded in 1910, is located in the city of Radford along the New River in southwest Virginia between the Blue Ridge and Allegheny Mountains in the southern Appalachian Mountains. Radford is located 20 miles from Blacksburg, home of Virginia Tech, and 45 miles south of

Roanoke on Interstate 81. In addition to its 177-acre campus, the University owns the 376-acre Selu Conservancy.

RU is a coeducational, comprehensive public university with highly diverse curricula for undergraduates and selected graduate programs. It has six undergraduate colleges: Arts and Sciences, Business and Economics, Education and Human Development, Information Science and Technology, Health and Human Services, and Visual and Performing Arts. Within these colleges, 112 undergraduate programs are offered. The University environment is residential, with most students living in University residence halls or within walking distance of the campus. The Radford University Art Museum offers a full schedule of exhibits; music, dance, and theater department productions allow students to attend, as well as participate in, numerous performances throughout the year. The Dedmon Center houses a natatorium with an eight-lane swimming pool; basketball, handball, racquetball, and volleyball courts; a weight room; a steam room; and a jogging track.

Student Body There are 7,589 undergraduates enrolled, 87 percent of whom are from Virginia, with the remaining 13 percent from forty-five other states, the District of Columbia, and sixty-five other countries. The RU student body is 61.5 percent women and 38.5 percent men. Approximately 73.5 percent of the students receive financial aid.

Faculty The full-time faculty members total 356, and 82 percent of faculty members hold doctoral degrees. The faculty-student ratio is 1:19.

Key Facilities The McConnell Library houses a collection of more than 300,000 books and bound periodicals. A full-time staff of 28, including 12 librarians, provides a variety of library and instructional services. Radford University establishes computer accounts for all faculty members, staff members, and registered students, which allow them to develop personal Web pages, use e-mail, and have modem access from off campus. The Walker Technology Center is a general-purpose computer lab facility with more than 100 PC and Macintosh workstations available for use by all students and faculty and staff members. Many academic departments also maintain computer labs equipped with software specific to their needs.

Honorary Societies The following academic honor fraternities are available to Radford University students: Alpha Lambda Delta, Alpha Psi Omega, Alpha Sigma Lambda, Beta Beta Beta, Beta Gamma Sigma, Chi Sigma Iota, Kappa Delta Pi, Kappa Mu Epsilon, Mu Phi Epsilon, Phi Alpha, Phi Delta Phi, Phi Kappa Phi, Phi Sigma Iota, Phi Theta Kappa, Pi Delta Phi, Pi Gamma Mu, Pi Omega Pi, Psi Chi, Sigma Delta Pi, Sigma Gamma Epsilon, Sigma Tau Delta, Sigma Theta Tau, and Upsilon Pi Epsilon. The following leadership organizations are available to Radford University students: National Residence Hall Honorary, Omicron Delta Kappa, Order of Omega, Phi Sigma Pi, and Rho Lambda.

Athletics The campus has eight intercollegiate sports for men (baseball, basketball, cross-country, golf, indoor track, outdoor track, soccer, and tennis) and eleven for women (basketball, cross-country, field hockey, golf, indoor track, outdoor track, soccer, swimming and diving, tennis, softball, and volleyball). All compete in the Big South Conference, NCAA Division I. The University also offers numerous intramural athletic programs.

Study Abroad Radford University sponsors study-abroad opportunities in Austria, Brazil, China, England, France, Germany, Greece, Ireland, Italy, Japan, Mexico, Scotland, Spain, and Venezuela. Other opportunities are available through academic departments. For more information, students should visit the Web site of the International Education Center at http://www.radford.edu/~intlprog/.

Support Services Assistance for students who have a documented disability is offered through the Disability Resource Office (DRO). For more information, students should visit the DRO Web site at http://www.radford.edu/~dro-web.

Job Opportunities Work-study and work-scholarship programs are provided through the Office of Financial Aid. For more information, students should visit the Office of Financial Aid Web site at http://www.radford.edu/~finaid. Internships and service-learning experiences are coordinated through the Center for Experiential Education. For more information, students should visit the Center for Experiential Education Web site at http://www.radford.edu/~intern.

Tuition: Full-time tuition and fees for in-state residents were $3070 per academic year. Part-time tuition and fees for in-state residents were $128 per semester hour. Full-time tuition and fees for out-of-state residents were $9208 per academic year. Part-time tuition and fees for out-of-state residents were $384 per semester hour. These expenses were accurate for the 2001–02 academic year.

Room and Board: The annual cost of room and board was $5234 for the 2001–02 academic year.

Mandatory Fees: Required fees are included in the cost of tuition as indicated above.

Contact: Director: J. Orion Rogers, Ph.D., Honors Academy, Box 6971, Radford, Virginia 24142; Telephone: 540-831-6125; Fax: 540-831-5004; E-mail: honors@radford.edu; Web site: http://www.radford.edu/~honors. Individuals with disabilities needing accommodations should call 540-831-5128 or 540-831-6125 (voice).

RAMAPO COLLEGE OF NEW JERSEY

4 Pu S Tr

▼ College Honors Program

The Ramapo College Honors Program is designed for students who desire a scholarly environment and an opportunity to interact with challenging faculty members and like-minded students. The Honors Program provides expanded opportunities for learning and reflection. Graduation from the College Honors Program is one indicator of a highly motivated, highly skilled, self-initiating individual.

There are currently 25 students enrolled in the program.

Participation Requirements: Students may participate in College Honors Program by completing three H-option courses and receiving an Honors Certificate or by completing three H-option courses and completing a senior project.

H-Option courses are those in which students, in consultation with their instructors, do additional, in-depth work. The H-Option is not simply an add-on to the given course requirements; it requires students to perform more extensively and more intensively. The number of H-Option courses required for graduation with College Honors varies from two (for students who transfer into honors courses) to three (for all other students). Each H-Option course must be at the 200, 300, or 400 level and carry at least 3 credits. Students are encouraged to make experiential education (co-op, service-learning, fieldwork) a component of one of their H-Option courses.

During the first four weeks of the semester, the student designates one or two of the courses in which he or she is registered as an "H-Option" course. This designation is accomplished by completing the H-Option contract form with the course instructor and filing that form with the Director of the Honors Program in the Office of Academic Affairs. At the end of the semester, if the student successfully completes the honors work and attains a

Interpreting the symbols: **2**=two-year college, **4**=four-year college; **Pu**=public or state college, **Pr**=private college; **G**=general honors program; **D**=departmental honors program; **S**=small program (fewer than 100 students), **M**=midsize program (100 to 500 students), **L**=large program (more than 500 students); **Sc**=scholarships available in honors program; **Tr**=transfer students accepted into honors program; **HBC**=historically black college; **AA**=academic advisors; **GA**=graduate advisors; **FA**=fellowship advisors.

grade of A- or A in the course, he or she is awarded an H or an H+ grade. In the event that the student does not successfully complete the honors work or does not earn a grade of at least A- in the course, he or she receives only a letter grade; no honors credit is earned. One 3- or 4-credit course at the 200 level and two 3- or 4-credit courses at the 300 level or higher can be taken for an H-Option as long as the faculty member and the student are in agreement about the contract.

The H-Option contract provides explicit provision for periodic consultation between the student and instructor for both project design and implementation, the description of work to be completed, and the description of the evaluation procedure.

The Honors Project is the culmination of the student's honors work at the College. The project is proposed and approved in the junior year and undertaken in the senior year as an independent study under the guidance of a faculty member. Students earn 3 credits for the completion of the proposal and an additional 3 credits for the completion of the project. Projects may result in research monographs, screenplays, performances, and installations. Students must receive a grade of A- or better for the proposal and the project in order to earn honors credits.

The benefits of the Honors Program are numerous. Graduate and professional schools regard enrollment in honors as one indicator of excellence. Students are encouraged to take part in nationwide conferences and are eligible for financial support so that they may attend. Successful completion of the Honors Program is indicated on the student's official transcript. Students are recognized for their accomplishments at the annual Honors Convocation.

Admission Process: Students are encouraged to apply to the Honors Program during their first semester at the College. Admission is based on the following criteria: grade point index, SAT I scores, extracurricular/leadership activities, and recommendations. Transfer students are also invited to seek admission to the program. Students who were enrolled in an honors program at another institution may receive honors transfer credits. Evaluation is made on a case-by-case basis.

The Campus Context: Established in 1969, Ramapo College is a four-year state college of liberal arts, sciences, and professional studies offering twenty-six academic majors. The 300-acre campus is only 25 miles from New York City. More than 600 courses are offered days, evenings, and Saturdays each semester. The Bachelor of Arts, Bachelor of Science, Bachelor of Social Work, Master of Arts in Liberal Studies, and Master of Science in education technology degrees are offered. Joint programs offered are the Bachelor of Science in Nursing, Allied Health, and Clinical Lab Science with the University of Medicine and Dentistry of New Jersey and the Master of Science in Management with the New Jersey Institute of Technology.

The campus is built around four academic buildings, a student center, a library, a gymnasium, playing fields, an administration building, the International Telecommunications Center, and the Angelica and Russ Berrie Center for Performing and Visual Arts.

Student Body There are 3,527 full-time and 1,672 part-time students from twenty-two states, the District of Columbia, Puerto Rico, and sixty-four other countries. About 1,200 students are housed on campus.

Faculty Of the 170 full-time faculty members, 95 percent have the doctorate or other terminal degree. The faculty is supplemented by adjunct specialists and other visiting scholars.

Key Facilities There are 145,413 volumes in the library.

Support Services The barrier-free campus is accessible to disabled students.

Tuition: $4416 for state residents, $7802 for nonresidents, per year (2001–02)

Room and Board: $7372

Contact: Director: Dr. Martha Ecker, 505 Ramapo Valley Road, Mahwah, New Jersey 07430; Telephone: 201-684-7530; Fax: 201-684-7697

Randolph–Macon College

4 Pr G S

▼ Honors Program

The Randolph–Macon Honors Program, established in 1982, is designed to challenge and stimulate superior students by allowing them to substitute for regular collegiate requirements special courses, specifically designed for the program, that are unique, low-enrollment, and high-participation and developed and taught by excellent teachers. Honors students are expected to take at least four of these courses during their first three years at the College.

In addition, the program requires an honors student to complete at least two departmental honors units. These may take the form of a senior thesis, independent study or research, or an individualized honors contract in a regular course offering. Students normally take these units in their major or minor department during their junior and senior years.

Honors students also have the advantage of the use of a former faculty home that was dedicated to the use of the program. It contains a seminar room; a library; a living room area for meetings, programs, and sociability; a fully equipped kitchen; several personal computers; study space; and a room where two honors students may live.

The Student Honors Association provides programming for cultural and social events.

There are currently about 100 students in the program.

Participation Requirements: Students must maintain a cumulative GPA of 3.25 (3.0 for freshmen) and make no grade lower than B- in an honors course to continue as members of the program.

Admission Process: Students gain entrance to the program by invitation before they enroll at the College if specific criteria are met (top decile of graduating class and 1250 or better on combined SAT I verbal-math scores) and by academic performance during their first year in residence at the College.

The Campus Context: Randolph–Macon College is a coeducational, liberal arts, undergraduate institution located in Ashland, Virginia, a town of about 7,000 located 15 miles north of Richmond, Virginia.

The January term (students normally enroll in one 4-week course) also provides opportunities for courses off campus and allows nearly 100 students to enroll for credit in academic internships in a variety of departments. The College offers Bachelor of Arts and Bachelor of Science degrees. There are thirty majors available.

Student Body Total enrollment is 1,150, currently evenly divided between men and women. Financial aid is primarily awarded on the basis of need. More than half of the student body receives financial aid. Interested students should contact the Admissions Office. A variety of extracurricular activities exist, ranging from publications to drama to service organizations. Ninety percent of students live on campus. There are seven chapters of national fraternities and five chapters of national sororities on campus.

Faculty The faculty includes 84 full-time faculty members plus 18 full-time–equivalent instructors. Most full-time faculty members have terminal degrees.

Key Facilities Computer facilities are available to students in three large laboratories. In addition, dormitories are wired so that students, using their own PCs, have access to e-mail and the World Wide Web.

Honorary Society Phi Beta Kappa

Athletics The College participates in NCAA Division III athletics and fields eight teams for men and eight for women. In addition, an extensive intramural program is available. The Brock Sports and Recreation Center, a state-of-the-art athletic facility, opened in 1998.

Study Abroad The Study Abroad Program offers opportunities to enroll in courses in colleges and universities in the United Kingdom, France, Spain, Germany, Italy, Greece, Japan, Mexico, and South Korea.

Tuition: $18,570 per year (2001–02)

Room and Board: $5300

Mandatory Fees: $525

Contact: Director: Dr. Arthur Conway, Telephone: 804-752-3720, E-mail: aconway@rmc.edu; Assistant Director: Dr. David Brat, Telephone: 804-752-7353, E-mail: dbrat@rmc.edu; Fax: 804-752-7231, Ashland, Virginia 23005; Web site: http://www.rmc.edu/academics/honr/

RARITAN VALLEY COMMUNITY COLLEGE

2 Pu G/D S Sc Tr

▼ Honors Program

The Honors Program at Raritan Valley Community College is an outstanding opportunity for students to engage in advanced study. It features eighteen honors courses, six honors options in nine academic disciplines, and, by special permission, independent study tailored to a student's individual interests. Students may enroll in individual honors courses, departmental honors, or the full program. Honors courses enrich and challenge students beyond a course's regular scope and curriculum. Depending on the discipline, many courses are conducted in seminar fashion at the College's exclusive Seminar Center, a private retreat specifically designed for honors teaching. All provide individualized attention, sophisticated use of research, and intellectually stimulating readings; most also offer field trips, distinguished guest lectures, and opportunities for service learning. Overall, an honors course is a privileged domain where each student's creativity and the free exchange of ideas are nurtured along with those of other, like-minded students.

Students may take individual honors courses without having to enroll in the full program or departmental honors, where they enroll in at least two honors courses in a given department. In both cases, Honors or Departmental Honors appear on the student's transcript. Students who wish to enroll in the entire program take five honors courses and participate in the Community of Scholars, a common forum fashioned for honors students and faculty members that meets at least once each semester.

The Community of Scholars features a noncredit series of lectures or presentations by honors students, honors faculty members, or invited scholars. Students enrolled in the full program must attend a minimum of two colloquia and offer one presentation emanating from an honors course that need not be tied to the same semester. The colloquium invites students to share ideas, participate in panel discussions, and/or present papers or projects formulated by or designed for a given honors course. Faculty members or invited scholars present pedagogical approaches or current scholarship in various fields. The underlying philosophy of the Community of Scholars, an integral component of the Honors Program, is the mutual fostering and encouragement of an open exchange of ideas, enhancing scholarship and academic inquiry.

Participation Requirements: All students, whether they are taking one honors course, departmental honors, or are enrolled in the complete program must have completed a minimum of two credit-bearing courses (6 credits) and have a GPA of 3.5 or higher, earned either at Raritan Valley or at another institution of higher learning. Visiting or transfer students require a letter of recommendation from a previous instructor. Recent high school graduates or those currently enrolled seeking advanced placement must hold a high school GPA of at least 3.5 and provide a letter of recommendation from either a faculty member, a principal, or a guidance counselor. In some instances, permission to enroll may be granted at the discretion of the Honors Director or the professor, upon submission of a writing sample.

Students wishing to enroll in the complete program, in addition to meeting the minimum criteria, must enroll in five honors courses with total honors credit of between 15 and 18, one of which must be either English I, Honors—Composition and Controversy, or English II, Honors—Literature and Analysis, unless the student has already completed a version of these courses at another institution, in which case another English course may be substituted in consultation with the Honors Director; maintain a GPA of at least 3.5 as they continue in the program; and participate in the Community of Scholars. Course selection shall be spread over more than two disciplines with no more than two courses being introductory level; at least one must be an upper-level course, one must be in the student's field of study, and one must require a major research component.

Admission Process: Each semester the Honors Director asks department chairs to submit a list of honors courses to be offered for the upcoming term, after which a course offering sheet is distributed college-wide, posted at major locations of student interest, including all student clubs and activities, and mailed to all current, past, and potential honors candidates based on eligibility requirements. The current honors brochure is also mailed to every area high school principal, guidance counselor, and honors society adviser to attract academically talented high school students wishing advanced placement. In addition, the director circulates a Recommendation for Honors form college-wide so that individual faculty members may recommend students for honors work within and across disciplines. Students are also identified as honors candidates by the counseling department and by the registrar based on their meeting basic eligibility requirements.

Scholarship Availability: The Honors Program, in conjunction with the Morris and Dorothy Hirsch Holocaust and Genocide Studies Scholarship fund, sponsors an essay competition each year to foster sensitivity toward issues relating to genocide studies, including but not limited to attitudes on race, culture, gender, and ethnicity. The judges comprise of a member of the Holocaust committee, a faculty member, and a member of the Honors Council. The winner is showcased at the Spring Community of Scholars colloquium, at which portions of the essay are featured. The essay is also made part of the permanent collection of holdings in the College's Holocaust Library and Center and is featured on its Web page. The winner receives a $500 scholarship; an honorable mention, if one is awarded, receives $250. Further merit scholarships for deserving honors students who demonstrate a serious commitment to academic study are being created in the next academic year.

The Campus Context: Located on 240 acres of farmland in rural North Branch, and originally founded as Somerset County College in 1965, Raritan Valley Community College became the first bi-county college in the state in 1987 when Hunterdon and Somerset Counties agreed to share in its sponsorship. A comprehensive two-year college, Raritan Valley offers three types of associate degrees, Associate of Arts (A.A.), Associate of Science (A.S.), and Associate of Applied Science (A.A.S.), together with certificates in more than seventy areas of academic study. Students have easy access to numerous modern facilities, including the Centers for Advanced Teaching and Technology, a state-

Interpreting the symbols: **2**=two-year college, **4**=four-year college; **Pu**=public or state college, **Pr**=private college; **G**=general honors program; **D**=departmental honors program; **S**=small program (fewer than 100 students), **M**=midsize program (100 to 500 students), **L**=large program (more than 500 students); **Sc**=scholarships available in honors program; **Tr**=transfer students accepted into honors program; **HBC**=historically black college; **AA**=academic advisors; **GA**=graduate advisors; **FA**=fellowship advisors.

of-the-art Planetarium, and a new Advanced Technology Communication Center. A Holocaust Center will be dedicated in 1999, and construction of a new Science Center will begin next year. In 1995 the Center for International and Business Education was the only U.S. College to receive President Clinton's prestigious E award, recognizing contributions in helping businesses to promote United States trade. More than 400 courses are offered each semester in day and evening sessions and via the Web. Programs of study include career programs (designed to prepare students for entry-level positions) and transfer programs (designed for transfer to four-year institutions). In addition to the latest in classroom and laboratory technology, the main campus features a 1,000-seat theater, library, swimming pool, gym, fitness center, planetarium, and cafeteria. Comprehensive support services include child care, counseling, tutoring, and job placement.

Student Body Total enrollment is 12,700 per year, which includes about 3,800 part-time students. The population is 56 percent women, 44 percent men. In addition, several thousand more enroll in noncredit courses, seminars, and other forms of customized training through the Institute for Business and Professional Development. The ethnic distribution is 59.2 percent Caucasian, 4.6 percent African American, 5.9 percent Asian, 4.6 percent Hispanic, 0.2 percent Native American, and 25.6 percent not reported. Thirty-three percent are full-time students, 67 percent are part-time, 85 percent work outside of the classroom, and 63 percent transfer to four-year institutions. The average age is 28; all students commute to campus.

Faculty Of the 326 faculty members, 98 are full-time and 228 are part-time; 28 percent of full-time faculty members have terminal degrees. The student-faculty ratio is 18:1.

Key Facilities The 80,000-volume Evelyn S. Field Learning Resource Center offers online computer searching with full access to the Internet and CD-ROM indexes. The center is open to all students as well as to the community. In addition, the center houses the Morris and Dorothy Hirsch Research Library of Holocaust and Genocide Studies, which has also sponsored the essay competition for the Honors Program each year. This research library features computerized, audio-visual, and traditional book materials as well as a dedicated computer that connects via the Internet to all of the major Holocaust research centers worldwide, including the National Holocaust Museum in Washington. Centers for Advanced Teaching and Technology (CATT classrooms) bring vast multimedia resources into designated classrooms via fiber optics. Raritan Valley was the first community college in the state to offer this state-of-the-art technology, receiving the coveted IBM/American Association of Community Colleges 1995 Network Distributed Education award for this innovation. The CATTs feature high resolution video projectors as well as audio-visual consoles with remote controls and computers. Professors can uplink VCR tapes, video discs, and software from the College's Media Center without leaving the classroom.

Honorary Societies Alpha Epsilon Pi

Athletics The College is a member of the National Junior College Athletic Association (Region XIX) and the Garden State Athletic Conference. The College engages in varsity competition in golf, baseball, basketball, tennis, softball, and soccer. Represented at the state and national levels in many sports, the College enables students to compete for athletic scholarships at four-year colleges and universities. Students are encouraged to use the fitness lab, pool, track, tennis courts, and gymnasium.

Study Abroad Through Global Visions, a 3-credit course featuring classroom presentations followed by a two-week trip to various destinations of educational interest, students have the opportunity to engage in a rare melding of regional interdisciplinary study. The countries that have been explored include Ecuador, Peru, Chile, and Bolivia.

Support Services The Educational Opportunity Fund (EOF) program offers assistance to students who have limited educational opportunities and who are financially unable to attend college. Tutoring is also available for students who need academic assistance and General Educational Development (GED) testing is available for those seeking to obtain a high school diploma. Raritan Valley also accommodates students with physical or learning disabilities. Physically disabled students complete an Auxiliary Aid Survey; assistance is then granted based upon need. For learning-disabled students, the College offers alternate testing procedures, extended time for tests, note-taking assistance, and tape recording of lectures.

Job Opportunities Students are offered a range of work opportunities on campus including tutoring and work-study. Within the Honors Program, honors students have undertaken private tutorials to assist students with writing and researching skills. In addition, Cooperative Education is a college experience in which students work part-time, acquire academic credit along with on-the-job training, and are paid for the work they perform. For students in the liberal arts, Cooperative Education provides a sampling of various professional and vocational environments, while for career students, it offers the chance to gain experience in a chosen field and to audition for a potential full-time employer. Cooperative Education courses are available in the following academic programs: business, criminal justice, computer information systems, early childhood education, fitness specialist studies, legal assisting, liberal arts, office administration, management information systems, real estate, retailing, science, and mathematics.

Tuition: $60 per credit for county residents (Hunterdon or Somerset County), $120 per credit for state residents, $240 per credit for nonresidents (1999–2000)

Mandatory Fees: $9 per credit registration fee, $25 per semester technology fee

Contact: Director: Dr. Lynne M. DeCicco, Lamington Road and U.S. Route 28, P.O. Box 3300, Somerville, New Jersey 08876; Telephone 908-526-1200 Ext. 8384; E-mail: ldecicco@rvcc.raritanval.edu; Web site: http://www.rvcc@raritanval.edu

Redlands Community College

2 Pu S Tr

▼ Honors Program

The Redlands Community College (RCC) Honors Program consists of course work that offers academically talented students stimulating class experiences and interaction with other exceptional students. The benefits that the students receive are recognition by faculty members and administrators of their academic abilities and achievements, enhanced opportunities for acceptance in honors programs at four-year institutions, participation in a challenging and enriching curriculum, interaction with other honor students, and special recognition at their graduation ceremonies.

The designated honors courses, the interdisciplinary seminars, and the contracted courses are taught by faculty members who have exhibited excellence in teaching and who have shown a distinct interest in working with honors students. The honors faculty and the Honors Directors are available to the students to aid them in their research and presentations at the Great Plains NCHC Regional Conference and the University of Oklahoma Undergraduate Research Day.

Because Redlands Community College is a small school, honors students have access to all campus facilities and an honors study room with a reference library, a multimedia computer, and access to the Internet. Students graduating with honors must have a 3.25 GPA. In addition to being recognized at their graduation ceremonies, honors students have their accomplishment noted on their transcripts.

In existence for twelve years, the program currently enrolls 30 students.

Participation Requirements: After acceptance, honors students must successfully complete 15 credit hours of honors work to graduate with honors. Twelve of the hours may be completed through a contract with an individual instructor or by taking designated honors courses. Three credit hours must be earned through interdisciplinary honors seminars. Honors students are also encouraged to participate in the Great Plains NCHC Regional Honors Conference and in the Central Oklahoma Two-Year College Honors Council's annual colloquium. In order to get honors credit for a contracted course, honors students must complete an honors project and receive at least a B in the course. The honors project does not affect the student's grade in a contracted course. Students who graduate with honors are given special recognition at the graduation ceremony and receive a medallion at an honors dinner.

Admission Process: Students applying to the RCC Honors Program for the first time as freshmen must meet requirements based on ACT scores and high school GPAs. Other students may rely on their college GPAs and a successful interview with an Honors Director.

Scholarship Availability: Incoming freshmen are eligible for tuition waiver scholarships, and all other honors students may apply for the Faculty Honors Scholarships, which are given at the end of every fall term. These are based on the number of honors credit hours, GPA, and participation in honors activities on campus.

The Campus Context: Redlands Community College offers forty-seven degree programs.

Student Body The College has an undergraduate enrollment of 778 men and 1,159 women. The ethnic distribution of students is 83 percent white, 6 percent American Indian, 4.5 percent black, 3 percent nonresident alien, 2 percent Asian, and 2 percent Hispanic. All of the students are commuters. Seventy-one percent receive financial aid.

Faculty Of the 112 faculty members, 24 are full-time. Ten percent have terminal degrees. The student-faculty ratio is 24:1.

Key Facilities There are five computer facilities in classrooms and the student commons. Among other special facilities are the Multimedia Building, Equine Center, the Cultural Center, and the Olympic-size pool.

Honorary Society Phi Theta Kappa

Athletics RCC sponsors four intercollegiate athletic teams, which compete in women's volleyball, women's basketball, men's basketball, and men's baseball. All four teams are members of the National Junior College Athletic Association and the Bi-State conference. The volleyball team is a member of the NFCAA Division I, and each of the other teams is a member of the NJCAA Division II. Books, tuition, and fee scholarships are available in each of the intercollegiate sports. As a member of the NJCAA Division II, RCC may award no housing assistance. Each team at RCC has had the enviable opportunity to compete in its respective national tournaments many times.

Support Services All buildings meet the requirements for accessibility. In addition, there are special services and equipment for the deaf and blind.

Job Opportunities Usually, twenty work-study positions are available, and approximately 40 students are working on E&G money. In addition, the RCC Cooperative Education program offers numerous opportunities for students to supplement their incomes.

Tuition: $1387.50 for state residents, $3277.50 for nonresidents, per year (1998–99)

Contact: Director: Linda Hasley, 1300 South Country Club Road, El Reno, Oklahoma 73036; Telephone: 405-262-2552 ext. 2308; Fax: 405-422-1200

RHODE ISLAND COLLEGE

4 Pu G M Sc Tr

▼ College Honors Program

Designed for motivated students with superior academic records, the College Honors Program offers opportunities for individualized study, special classes, and extracurricular intellectual and social activities. The College Honors Program has two parts: General Education and Departmental Honors.

Students admitted to the program take the majority of their General Education requirements in specially designed honors sections. Those sections are limited to about 15 students in order to promote class participation and to encourage relationships among students and between students and teachers. Honors classes are taught by professors chosen for their commitment to undergraduate education, their abilities in the classroom, and their scholarly credentials. While the honors sections normally do not demand a greater amount of work and are not graded on a higher scale than nonhonors sections, they are meant to be more intellectually challenging and often make use of innovative pedagogical methods.

Students who complete General Education Honors have the option of doing honors in a particular academic major. Such Departmental Honors experiences involve the completion of a Senior Honors Project in which students work one-on-one with a professor of their choice on a topic of their choice. The Senior Honors Project is especially important for students who plan to go on to graduate or professional school.

Honors students have access to an honors lounge and are encouraged to participate in various extracurricular activities, both social and cultural. Those who live on campus may opt to reside in special quiet suites reserved for students in the program. The College Honors Program was founded in 1982. It admits about 50 freshmen each year and currently has about 220 active students.

Participation Requirements: Students take at least six of their ten required general education classes in honors sections, normally including the four core courses on culture and critical thinking. They must maintain a minimum 3.0 cumulative GPA to remain in the program. Those choosing to stop with General Education Honors are so recognized at commencement and on their official transcripts. Students choosing to go on to a Senior Honors Project in a department are recognized for General Education Honors, Departmental Honors, and College Honors. Senior Honors Projects may be done in virtually any academic area and may be of different kinds, e.g., research, critical, creative, or performative. They are normally done over the two semesters of the senior year and are awarded 6 credit hours toward graduation.

Admission Process: Students are invited into the program as freshmen on the basis of high-school records, SAT I scores, personal essays, and other supporting materials. There is no special application form for honors, only a box to check on the regular college application. Applications are reviewed individually on a rolling basis by a faculty honors committee. Students may also apply to the program after their first semester at the college.

Scholarship Availability: The College Honors Program awards the only merit-based academic scholarships at the College. There are

Interpreting the symbols: **2**=two-year college, **4**=four-year college; **Pu**=public or state college, **Pr**=private college; **G**=general honors program; **D**=departmental honors program; **S**=small program (fewer than 100 students), **M**=midsize program (100 to 500 students), **L**=large program (more than 500 students); **Sc**=scholarships available in honors program; **Tr**=transfer students accepted into honors program; **HBC**=historically black college; **AA**=academic advisors; **GA**=graduate advisors; **FA**=fellowship advisors.

several types of honors scholarships, ranging from about one-third to full in-state tuition. Honors scholarships are renewable for a total of eight semesters. Honors students who live on campus are also eligible for special residential scholarships. In addition, the College makes every effort to meet the financial need of students in the program with nonrepayable grants.

The Campus Context: Rhode Island College is the state's oldest public institution of higher learning. For the last four decades, it has been located on a 170-acre campus that combines the relaxed atmosphere of the suburbs with the convenience of a metropolitan location—only 10 minutes from downtown Providence. Students often take advantage of the busy cultural and social calendars that characterize the lively arts scene in Providence and its many colleges and universities. In addition, Boston and Cambridge are 1-hour north, Cape Cod, 1 hour east, and Newport, 1 hour south. The area is served by frequent bus and train transportation. The College is made of four divisions: the Feinstein School of Education and Human Development (which includes the Henry Barnard Laboratory School), the School of Social Work, the Center of Management and Technology, and the Faculty of Arts and Sciences, which provides the General Education Program and thirty-eight academic majors of its own. A new performing arts center will be completed in 1999. The College has a distinguished record in both the performing and visual arts—both academic programs and regular musical and theatrical series. It also is the site of eight exhibitions a year at the Bannister Art Gallery.

Student Body Undergraduate enrollment includes 4,351 full-time students and 2,465 part-time students. The minority ethnic distribution is 6 percent Hispanic, 4 percent Asian-American, 3 percent African American, and 3 percent Native-American. There are about 20 international students each year. Seventy percent of the students are women. Ninety-five percent of the students are Rhode Islanders. There are also 1,806 graduate students. Five residence halls accommodate 830 students. A significant percentage of the students are nontraditional students who may be returning to school after years of work or military experience or years of raising a family. Seventy-two percent of freshman financial aid applicants receive need-based financial aid, with an average award of about $4760 per year including grants, work-study, and loans.

Faculty There are 375 full-time faculty members, with 83 percent holding terminal degrees in their areas of specialization. Forty-four percent are women.

Key Facilities The Adams Library has 400,000 volumes, 1,500 periodical subscriptions, CD-ROM databases, and major collections on microfilm and microfiche. HELIN system provides World Wide Web links to a shared catalog of college libraries in Rhode Island. There are some 250 IBM PC and Macintosh microcomputers available for academic users, located in laboratories in several buildings across the campus. A campuswide Ethernet network connects most of these labs, allowing access to the Internet and World Wide Web. Videoconferencing and streaming video labs are being created. There is a college television studio that also serves as a video editing area. Several of the labs are geared exclusively to interactive multimedia usage.

Athletics The College participates in NCAA Division III baseball, basketball, cross-country, indoor track, outdoor track, soccer, tennis, and wrestling for men and basketball, cross-country, gymnastics, indoor track, outdoor track, soccer, softball, tennis, and volleyball for women. The College holds membership in the National Collegiate Athletic Association, Eastern Collegiate Athletic conference, Little East Conference, New England College Athletic conference, National Collegiate Gymnastic Association, and New England College Wrestling Association. Many intramural and recreational opportunities are also available.

Study Abroad There are special summer programs at the South Bank University in London; the Language Center in Cuernavaca, Mexico; and in Cape Verde. A winter intercession program in Cuernavaca, Mexico also operates. The Feinstein School of Education and Human Development has a semester-long program at the University College of Saint Martin in Lancaster, England. In addition, the College participates in the New England-Quebec exchange program, enabling students to study at any university in this Canadian province. The Study Abroad Office assists students in making other overseas study arrangements, and the Shinn Study Abroad Fund assists several students each year in semester and year-long study abroad.

Support Services Tutorial services for mathematics, writing, and other selected subjects are offered.

Job Opportunities Work opportunities are available on and off campus. Internships in Rhode Island and Washington, D.C., are also available as are graduate assistantships.

Tuition and fees: $3149 for residents, $7929 nonresidents, $4459 MTP for specified Massachusetts communities, $4459 NEBHE for New England residents in certain programs (1998–99)

Room and Board: $5250–5850 per year

Contact: Director: Dr. Spencer Hall, English Department, Providence, Rhode Island 02908; Telephone: 401-456-8671; Fax: 401-456-8379; E-mail: shall@ric.edu; Web site: http://www.ric.edu/fas

Richmond, The American International University in London

4 Pr G S Tr

▼ Honors Program

The Richmond Honors Program is designed to provide its international students with a variety of challenging learning opportunities both inside and outside the classroom. Intercultural analysis, intellectual curiosity, and independent research are three key factors that shape the variety of creative and interactive courses offered. At the heart of the Honors Program are the interdisciplinary core seminars, which focus on a different topic every semester. To date, the topics have included Globalization and Internationalism; The Body, Metaphor and Identity; Ethics and Values; and The Creative Impulse. Guest speakers are invited to examine a topic from a particular angle, and these lectures are open to the community at large.

The specially selected faculty members who run the small honors classes of up to 12 students encourage both group work as well as individual projects that use London as a resource. Courses are designed in the upper division to allow honors study-abroad students from other institutions who come to Richmond for a semester or a year to study with Richmond's own honors degree students. Guest lectures, field trips, and other special activities create an exciting cross-cultural learning environment that is central to the University's mission.

There is a student-led Honors Society that serves as a forum for academic leadership. Student benefit from priority registration and are given invitations to selected cultural events. A special residence, put aside for honors students, is available. Each semester, students are awarded a stipend of $150 to cover the cost of textbooks.

There are currently 50 students in the Honors Program, which was founded in 1996.

Participation Requirements: Students must complete a minimum of 24 credits of honors courses. These include the interdisciplinary core seminars, honors sections of courses that satisfy general education requirements, a junior/senior honors course in their major, and the final honors capstone course, London as Text, in which an independent research project is undertaken connected to their major and supervised by an appropriate faculty mentor. The course is structured around interdisciplinary London themes and invited speakers. Students must present their research to their peers and invited faculty members.

A cumulative GPA of at least 3.4 is needed to remain in the program. Students are recognized annually at the Awards Ceremony and at commencement, and successful completion of the program is noted on students' transcripts.

Admission Process: New students, including those with fewer than 45 transfer credits, are recruited on the basis of their previous grades, their test scores, an essay, and, if possible, an interview. Students already at the University with a cumulative GPA of 3.4 or higher are invited to join. Students generally may not enter the program if they have accumulated more than 45 credits.

Scholarship Availability: Scholarships based on academic performance and financial need can be obtained through the Office of Admissions and Financial Aid. Scholarships are not offered through the Honors Program, although many honors students receive scholarships and financial assistance of various amounts.

The Campus Context: Richmond is located in one of the world's major cultural, political, and financial centers. London as a global city is a key attraction for both students and faculty members and remains one of the most important learning resources for the institution. First- and second-year students attend the Richmond Hill campus, situated near the River Thames in southwest London, whereas the third-year, fourth-year, and graduate students attend the central London Campus in Kensington. The University offers A.A., B.A., B.S., M.B.A., M.S., and M.A. programs in more than twenty subject areas and has a joint program in engineering with the George Washington University. It has an extensive internship program, study centers in Florence, Italy, and Shizuoka, Japan, and an international field study project that is based in a different country for five weeks every summer. The faculty and programs are organized into two schools: the School of Arts and Sciences and the School of Business.

Student Body There are approximately 1,200 students who come from more than 100 countries. There is no dominant national group. Thirty-three percent hold European passports.

Faculty There are 130 faculty members, full- and part-time. Seventy-two percent of the full-time faculty members have terminal degrees. The average class size is 17, and the student-faculty ratio is 12:1.

Key Facilities The library contains more than 57,000 volumes, 220 newspapers/periodicals, and extensive CD-ROM and online databases. There are extensive interlibrary loan arrangements with the University of London and other specialist libraries. The computer network links 300 PCs and connects to the Internet. Applications include Microsoft Office, e-mail, and instructional software. Six computer labs include PCs, and a Macintosh-based lab offers a collection of graphics software. The Center for New Media is equipped with multimedia authoring and digital video editing equipment.

Athletics A range of sports and recreational activities are organized by the University. These include soccer, basketball, tennis, cricket, and tae kwon do. University sports teams participate in a number of regional leagues. The Hill campus houses a few facilities, but generally students join local clubs or, for a modest fee, the Kensington-based students enjoy the athletic facilities of the nearby Imperial College, University of London.

Study Abroad Since the vast majority of students at Richmond are not British, they basically spend their whole time at the University "studying abroad." Students are encouraged to attend the study center in Florence, Italy, particularly if they are studying art history, or the one in Shizuoka, Japan, which features an internship in a Japanese company. Some students go to the U.S. for a semester abroad.

Richmond offers honors students from U.S.-based institutions an opportunity to come to London for a semester and participate in Richmond's Honors Program. Students are required to take the London as Text class and are given priority registration for their other courses. Although faculty members in London supervise the research, the U.S. home institution may choose to be involved in the choice of topic or grading of the project in order for the course to count toward honors credit at the home campus.

Support Services The University offers special support services for learning disabled students and provides for students with special needs.

Job Opportunities A limited number of part-time positions on campus are available to students who demonstrate financial need.

Tuition: $13,410 per year (1999–2000)

Room and Board: $7970

Mandatory Fees: $1020

Contact: Director: Dr. Sara Chetin, Queens Road, Richmond, Surrey TW10 6JP, England; Telephone: 171 368 8411; Fax: 181 332 3050; E-mail: chetins@richmond.ac.uk; Web site: http://www.richmond.ac.uk

ROANOKE COLLEGE

4 Pr G M Sc Tr AA

▼ Honors Program

The Roanoke College Honors Program provides distinctive educational opportunities and challenges for students who possess a strong academic background, broad extracurricular interests, and leadership abilities. Superior faculty members, engaged students, and outstanding curricular and cocurricular programs all contribute to an environment in which students can realize their full personal, moral, and intellectual potential. The program also encourages service to the community and active involvement in the life of the College.

The honors curriculum consists of a sequence of dynamic interdisciplinary courses that substitute for the College's general studies requirements throughout the four years. Students begin with a freshman seminar that provides a foundation in critical thinking and written and oral communication. As sophomores, they take a two-semester sequence that focuses on the central themes and issues in human civilization. Juniors select from topical courses in the humanities, sciences, and social sciences that emphasize diverse cultures and perspectives. Seniors bring all the fields of study to focus on selected contemporary issues in a capstone course. Students also work closely with one or more faculty members to complete an honors project, usually a research project or artistic creation related to their major field of study.

The outside of class and service components of the Honors Program are as enriching as the curriculum. Through the Plenary Enrichment Program (PEP), students attend a range of events, such as plays, concerts, operas, films, lectures, and discussions, both on and off campus. Students also participate in service activities each semester, donating time and energy to the campus and local communities. These events give students a broader view of intellectual life outside the classroom and provide wonderful opportunities for discussions and thought. An annual reflective paper completes the PEP requirement.

Interpreting the symbols: **2**=two-year college, **4**=four-year college; **Pu**=public or state college, **Pr**=private college; **G**=general honors program; **D**=departmental honors program; **S**=small program (fewer than 100 students), **M**=midsize program (100 to 500 students), **L**=large program (more than 500 students); **Sc**=scholarships available in honors program; **Tr**=transfer students accepted into honors program; **HBC**=historically black college; **AA**=academic advisors; **GA**=graduate advisors; **FA**=fellowship advisors.

Participation Requirements: To graduate with the Honors Program designation, students must complete the honors curriculum and an honors project; complete distribution requirements in mathematics, foreign language, and the social, physical, and life sciences; and participate in the Plenary Enrichment Program each semester they are studying on campus. Students may major in any discipline and participate in the Honors Program, but must maintain at least a 3.2 cumulative GPA to remain in the program and to graduate with the honors designation. Successful completion of the program is recognized at commencement and is noted on the diploma.

Admission Process: Most students enter the Honors Program as freshmen, and students should apply to the program when applying for admission to the College. Applications are considered on the basis of academic performance, extracurricular interests, and leadership abilities as evidenced by high school grades and course work, class rank, SAT I or ACT scores, extracurricular activities, and responses to questions on the application form. Letters of recommendation and a personal interview are recommended. The application deadline is March 15.

It is also possible to enter the Honors Program at the beginning of the sophomore year; transfer students who will be entering their sophomore year are encouraged to apply.

Scholarship Availability: Honors students receive a Davis Honors Scholarship of $2000 each year they participate in the program. The Davis Honors Scholarship is in addition to other aid or scholarships they may receive.

The Campus Context: Roanoke College strives to provide a high-quality education for students interested in their development and potential as citizen leaders. Access to faculty members granted by a low student-teacher ratio enables personalized education to occur for Roanoke students. Opportunities for independent study and advanced research in modern facilities are widely available and strongly encouraged. Situated in a spectacular natural setting 15 minutes from the metropolitan resources of Roanoke city and within easy travel distance from Atlanta, New York, and Washington, D.C., this small Lutheran college offers a top-notch education enhanced by recreational, intellectual, social, and cultural opportunities. Students pursue a Bachelor of Arts, Bachelor of Science, or Bachelor of Business Administration degree, selecting from thirty-three majors, thirty-one minors, and thirteen concentrations.

The College supports the Cabell Brand Center for International Poverty and Resource Studies, the Olin Fine Arts Library, the Center for Community Research, the Center for Community Service, and the Center for Church and Society. The Belk Fitness Center, completed in 1998, is considered to be among the best of any small college in the United States. The Sutton Student Center currently houses the Commons (student dining hall), student lounges, a big-screen television room, a game room, the Bookstore, and the Cavern, a popular campus snack shop. Construction of a new campus center will commence in May of 1999. Other notable campus features include state-of-the-art scientific equipment such as a Fourier Transform Infrared Spectrometer, a Gas Chromatograph-Mass Spectrometer, a High Performance Liquid Chromatograph, and a Nuclear Magnetic Resonance (NMR).

Student Body The student population at Roanoke exceeds 1,700, with more than thirty-nine states and territories and fifteen other countries represented. Enrollment is 40 percent men and 60 percent women, and the ethnic distribution is 94 percent white, 2.7 percent black, 1.5 percent Asian, 1.2 percent Hispanic, and 6 percent Native American. Approximately 91 percent of Roanoke College students receive some form of financial aid, and more than 25 percent of the College's alumni seek postgraduate study.

Faculty More than ninety percent of the 100 full-time faculty members at Roanoke College hold the highest degree in their field. These faculty members represent such universities as Chicago, Yale, Amerien, Cornell, Pennsylvania, Duke, Stanford, Harvard, Princeton, Colorado, Oxford, John Hopkins, Virginia, North Carolina, Minnesota, Berkeley, Vanderbilt, and Denver.

Key Facilities The renovated Fintel Library contains more than 436,716 bound volumes and non-book pieces, subscribes to more than 742 periodicals, facilitates interlibrary loans for students and faculty members, and also houses the Henry H. Fowler Collection, the James Olin Congressional Papers, the Howard Hammersley Photographic Collection, and other special collections containing rare religious and historic works. The College's Information Services department supports eight networked computer labs (100 percent Pentium computers) linked to the campus network, the World Wide Web, Internet, and e-mail services.

Honorary Societies Alpha Chi, Alpha Lambda Delta, and Omicron Delta Kappa

Athletics Roanoke College has excellent facilities to support every phase of a well-rounded athletic program. There is an athletic field and all-weather track with seating for 1,400 and playing and practicing fields for soccer, lacrosse, and field hockey. Tennis courts are located near the gymnasium. The physical education and recreation center includes two basketball courts, a state-of-the-art Fitness Center, classrooms, an athletic training room, offices, and locker rooms. The College is a member of the National Collegiate Athletic Association Division III and the Old Dominion Athletic Conference. Men compete with other colleges in soccer, cross-country, basketball, track and field, tennis, golf, and lacrosse. Women's varsity sports include soccer, field hockey, volleyball, cross-country, basketball, softball, tennis, lacrosse, and track and field. The intramural and recreational programs provide a wide variety of team and individual activities. Additional sports and games are played as coed teams or on an individual basis. Club sport activities include men's volleyball, baseball, cheerleading, and ice hockey.

Study Abroad Through membership in several exchange programs, Roanoke College provides study options in diverse global locations and in all disciplines. ISEP offers study at 100 sites in thirty-eight countries where the language of instruction may be in English or in a foreign language. The CREPUQ Exchange brings study opportunities at most universities in Quebec, Canada. Study in all disciplines is available with instruction in English, French, or both. At the University of East Anglia in Norwich, England, Roanoke College students continue to earn credit while studying with British students. Opportunities to study in Asia include a semester program in China as well as an exchange program with Kansai Gaidai University in Japan. Individual students may also participate in approved junior-year abroad and semester-abroad programs of other colleges through the cooperation of accredited colleges and universities. Summer study abroad has long been a tradition at Roanoke College. Students may spend five weeks in the Virginia Program at Oxford or may participate in May travel courses offered by Roanoke College faculty members.

Support Services A nationally acclaimed Office of Academic Services provides professional academic advice to all students, along with peer tutoring, career planning, and placement.

Job Opportunities Approximately 600 work-study positions exist for qualified students.

Tuition: $16,655

Room and Board: $5450

Mandatory Fees: $750 and a one-time orientation fee of $125

Contact: Admissions: Telephone: 540-375-2270; Fax: 540-375-2267; E-mail: admissions@roanoke.edu; Web site: http://www.roanoke.edu

Robert Morris University

4 Pr G S Sc AA

▼ International Honors Program

The Robert Morris University International Honors Program is the University's niche honors program, providing students with an opportunity to study abroad and to complete specialized course work geared toward multicultural and international understanding. The program accepts students from all majors offered by the school. The International Honors Program allows students the opportunity to distinguish themselves as scholars.

The International Honors Program is a four-year program designed to enhance the student's understanding of and ability to deal with the increasingly global environment that exists today. Students who have strong academic records and who have demonstrated leadership ability and a strong interest in the international arena are recruited for the program. Students enter the program as freshmen.

The benefits for students in the International Honors Program include priority scheduling, a minor in intercultural communications, the opportunity to study abroad for either one or two semesters, more challenging course work, the experience of completing a senior thesis/project, and many other benefits.

The International Honors Program is an active and dynamic organization. It has a mission and it works hard to achieve that mission. International Honors Program students plan projects and carry out activities that bring an important international dimension to Robert Morris University and to the surrounding communities. Through service to others, International Honors Program students not only work hard to begin now to make the world a better place, but they also learn international leadership skills in the process.

Participation Requirements: Students in the program must maintain and graduate with a minimum cumulative GPA of 3.0 on a scale of 4.0 during the years of undergraduate study. The study-abroad experience must be completed by the beginning of the senior year. Students may fulfill this requirement during the summer or by participating in a preapproved work experience in another country. Students in the program are expected to consistently exhibit character qualities in accordance with the policies and procedures defined in the Robert Morris University handbook and the International Honors Program Handbook. Students in the program must show consistent progress toward completion of the program, including completing course work and remaining active participants in the program.

Admission Process: To be admitted to the program, incoming freshmen must have serious interest in international topics and issues, a minimum of two years of high school foreign language study, a high school GPA of 3.5 or higher (on a 4.0 scale), and an SAT score of 1100 or higher or an ACT score of 27 or higher.

Scholarship Availability: Robert Morris University extends academic scholarships to all students who achieve the criteria necessary to be admitted to the program. In addition, opportunities exist for international and honors students to receive additional scholarships based on academic merit.

The Campus Context: The 230-acre Moon Township campus is a living-learning center for nearly 1,000 resident students and 2,166 off-campus students. Twenty-two buildings are in use, including classrooms, a library, residence halls, a cafeteria, and a student center with a multipurpose ballroom and student offices. The Pittsburgh Center of the University features a university atmosphere in a business setting. Facilities include an eight-story, air-conditioned classroom building featuring an academic and student services annex, the Visual Communications Department, and the Center for Non Profit Management.

Student Body Undergraduate enrollment is 3,813: 1,950 men and 1,863 women. The ethnic distribution is 83 percent white, 8.4 percent African American, 1.2 percent Asian American, 0.6 percent Hispanic, and 0.2 percent Native American. There are 72 international students. About 23 percent of the students live on campus. Robert Morris has five fraternities and two sororities.

Faculty The school employs 302 instructional faculty members; 106 are full-time, and 75 percent hold a terminal degree. The student-faculty ratio is 19:1.

Key Facilities The school includes a new student center, Sewall Center, and Hale and Franklin Centers. The Patrick Henry Building houses the extensive library. Other key facilities include the Learning Factory, which is dedicated to engineering, and the Academic Media Center.

Athletics Robert Morris currently has fourteen NCAA Division I varsity athletic teams, five club sports, and several intramural sports programs.

Study Abroad The Study Abroad Program Office facilitates all of the students who hope to complete an international study-abroad experience.

Support Services Robert Morris offers students the opportunity to use both the Center for Student Success and Career Services. About 35 percent of the campus is handicapped accessible.

Job Opportunities A variety of job opportunities are available through the school for student workers.

Tuition: $6000 per semester

Room and Board: $3290

Contact: Director: George Semich, Ed.D., 451 Student Center, 881 Narrows Run Road, Moon Township, Pennsylvania 15108; Telephone: 412-262-8665; E-mail: honorsprogram@robert-morris.edu or semich@robert-morris.edu; Web site: http://www.robert-morris.edu

Rochester Community and Technical College

2 Pu G S Tr

▼ Honors Program

Honors at Rochester Community and Technical College (RCTC) offers challenge, recognition, and a myriad of other opportunities through several avenues.

First, the Honors Program curriculum offers special honors courses to provide students with a strong grounding in primary texts and critical thinking.

Second, the Honors Program offers mentoring and help in transferring. Students work closely with the RCTC Honors Program Coordinator, who serves as a personal academic mentor, often with the help of a faculty member in the major field. Working with the Coordinator on schedule set-up also earns them the right to priority registration. In addition, to help take the mystique out of the transfer process, Honors Program students are able to participate in "Bridging the Transfer Gap," a workshop designed specifically to address the transfer needs of highly motivated Honors Program students. The Coordinator also writes recommendations and calls transfer institutions.

Third, the RCTC Honors Program offers camaraderie and activities meant to stimulate the intellect. Students can attend special Honors Program SALON sessions throughout the year, have the option of working with GATE (Gifted and Talented) children in the Rochester Public Schools, develop special events for the University Center-Rochester (UC–R) campus, have a "big brother" or "big sister" to help them with various aspects of college life, and have the opportunity to attend conferences with other honors program students from the state, Midwest, and/or nation.

Interpreting the symbols: **2**=two-year college, **4**=four-year college; **Pu**=public or state college, **Pr**=private college; **G**=general honors program; **D**=departmental honors program; **S**=small program (fewer than 100 students), **M**=midsize program (100 to 500 students), **L**=large program (more than 500 students); **Sc**=scholarships available in honors program; **Tr**=transfer students accepted into honors program; **HBC**=historically black college; **AA**=academic advisors; **GA**=graduate advisors; **FA**=fellowship advisors.

Fourth, students who qualify can also become a member of Phi Theta Kappa (PTK), an international two-year college academic honor society that provides educational and cultural programs and scholarships. The 3-year-old program currently enrolls 60 students (PTK membership is not included in that number).

Participation Requirements: To earn an Honors Diploma, students must apply to the program, be accepted, take honors credits as listed below, and maintain a GPA of 3.3 or above. At graduation, students who have at least a 3.3 GPA and who have completed the appropriate number of honors credits receive a certificate, receive and wear a golden medallion at the graduation ceremony, are identified on the graduation program, and are named as Honors Program graduates as they walk across the stage. The transcript also clearly identifies honors credits. The Honors Diploma necessitates 18 credits, with a minimum of three disciplines, for the A.A. degree; 15 credits, with a minimum of two disciplines, for the A.S. degree; and 12 credits, with a minimum of two disciplines, for the A.A.S. degree.

Admission Process: Interested individuals may apply anytime during the year by filling out an application form. Honors Program students are selected on the basis of GPA, school and/or community experiences, and other life experiences. For the English Honors sequence, the students must also score above 90 percent on the college writing placement test.

Scholarship Availability: Presidential Scholarships are available to all entering freshmen in the top 5 percent of their high school graduating class. RCTC offers a number of other scholarships for both incoming, returning, and outgoing students, and many students who receive scholarships are also in the Honors Program.

The Campus Context: The 4,000 members of the diverse student body of Rochester Community and Technical College, founded in 1915, can choose from sixty-four areas of study, including both transfer and technical majors. Students can attend RCTC full-time, part-time, days, evenings, or weekends, and RCTC offers some classes via computer modem and television.

The campus (University Center–Rochester) also houses students at the University of Minnesota–Rochester Center (UMN–RC) and Winona State University–Rochester Center (WSU–RC), institutions that collaborate with RCTC to offer four-year and graduate degrees to approximately 6,000 students. For example, the University Center at Rochester has more than a dozen "2 plus 2" programs with Winona State University—Rochester Center that allow students to take the first two years of a four-year degree at RCTC and then transfer to WSU–RC for the final two years.

There are also twenty-four master's-level programs available in Rochester, more than half of which are offered by WSU–RC and the UMN–RC. The UMN–RC now also offers a Bachelor of Arts degree in English.

Student Body The student profile includes 60 percent women; 43 percent of students are 25 and older. About half of the students are from Rochester, while 40 percent come from elsewhere in Minnesota.

Faculty There are 100 full-time RCC faculty members who are supplemented by adjunct faculty members.

Key Facilities The Goddard Library houses 65,000 books, 650 periodical titles, and a variety of microforms, CD-ROMs, and electronic databases. The library catalog (PALS) is computerized. The campus has numerous computer and ITV labs. All students have access to e-mail addresses.

Athletics Diverse offerings are available, including intramurals.

Support Services Facilities for disabled students are available.

Job Opportunities Work-study is available.

Tuition: $2264 for state residents, $4305 for nonresidents, per year (1998–99)

Contact: Coordinator: Dr. Lynette Reini-Grandell, 851 30th Avenue SE, Rochester, Minnesota 55904-4999; Telephone: 507-285-7244; Fax: 507-285-7496; E-mail: lynette.reini-grandell@roch.edu; Web site: http://www.acd.roch.edu/honors/

Rochester Institute of Technology

4 Pr C M Sc AA

▼ Rochester Institute of Technology Honors Program

The Rochester Institute of Technology (RIT) Honors Program features seminar-style classes and individualized research and study options and provides a supportive and encouraging environment for students with intellectual curiosity and academic distinction. Students benefit by working closely and sharing academic experiences both in and out of the classroom with other honors students and faculty members.

The Honors Program is designed for students who seek to challenge themselves in exemplary learning experiences such as undergraduate research projects, honors seminars, and study abroad; who wish to extend and share their knowledge through participation in professional associations and conferences; and who hope to join other outstanding students and faculty members in a wide range of special activities throughout the year, including field trips, social events, and community-service projects.

One of the distinguishing features of the RIT Honors Program is its career-oriented focus. Honors activities and courses are designed to enhance the professional dimension of the collegiate experience. The major components of the Honors Program include professional opportunities within the student's college, enhanced general education courses, and specially designed experiential education activities.

Honors students have access to special courses, seminars, projects, and advising in their home college. The honors-level general education curriculum, which provides extracurricular opportunities for learning outside the classroom, brings all honors students together. Capitalizing on RIT's assets as one of the nation's foremost career-oriented universities, the Honors Program offers opportunities for students to work with faculty members on applied and interdisciplinary research projects as well as enhanced cooperative education experiences and internships. Each college has designated an experienced faculty member to serve as its Honors Program advocate. Advocates work with students one-on-one to develop educational and career plans and professional and experiential learning opportunities such as research placements, co-ops, internships, and study abroad. Honors students are encouraged to pursue study abroad to add an international perspective to their education. They work with the Honors Program director for guidance on how to add study abroad to their academic plans. The Honors Program in RIT's Kate Gleason College of Engineering also provides extensive international opportunities. Whether a first-year or upperclass student, honors students can choose to live in honors housing within the residence halls. This option increases the chances for interaction with other honors students outside the classroom.

Participation Requirements: Students in the Honors Program are expected to participate in the honors courses and cocurricular activities in their college and replace approximately half of their liberal arts requirements with honors courses. Honors students are also required to participate in two cocurricular learning experiences per year. All students who wish to continue in the program are subject to an annual review by the Honors Advisory Committee. Program continuation is subject to GPA and other requirements.

Admission Process: Applicants who submit the RIT Application for Undergraduate Admission by February 1 are invited to apply for Honors Program admission if their high school grades, rank, and test scores place them among the top five percent of the applicants to the University. This normally requires grades and a ranking of at least 95 percent and an SAT I score of 1350 or higher. Students who are invited to apply for admission to the Honors Program are asked to submit supplemental application materials, including a teacher recommendation, two admission essays, and a listing of academic awards, college-level courses, and special enrichment programs they have participated in.

Scholarship Availability: All students accepted into the RIT Honors Program receive an Honors Program Scholarship. In addition, RIT has a generous merit scholarship program for all qualified students regardless of financial need (Presidential Scholarships). Renewal criteria are provided with award notification.

The Campus Context: As one of the nation's premier career-oriented universities, RIT's goal is to prepare students for the future, wherever it may lead. RIT offers high-quality programs for successful careers, respected and accessible faculty members, sophisticated academic facilities, and an active campus life. There is also a special emphasis on learning through experience. RIT has been recognized by *U.S. News & World Report* as the number one comprehensive university in the North for academic reputation and as one of America's best college values.

Few universities provide RIT's variety of career-oriented studies. The eight colleges offer more than 200 programs of study in business, engineering, art and design, science and mathematics, liberal arts, photography, hotel management, computer science, information technology, and other areas. As a major university, RIT offers academic opportunities that extend far beyond science and technology, including more liberal arts courses and faculty members than are at most liberal arts colleges. With a strong foundation in the humanities and social sciences, RIT students understand both technological developments and the larger philosophical and ethical issues presented by technology.

Student Body Enrollment consists of approximately 9,500 full-time and 2,300 part-time undergraduate students and 2,300 graduate students. Enrolled students represent all fifty states and more than ninety countries. Deaf students number approximately 1,200.

Faculty There are 832 full-time, 31 part-time, and 484 adjunct faculty members. Eighty-five percent have terminal degrees. RIT's student-faculty ratio is 13:1, and 91 percent of the classes have fewer than 40 students.

Key Facilities Wallace Library is a multimedia resource center with a collection of more than 750,000 items. Resource materials include 15,000 journal subscriptions, 380,000 microforms, 3,100 audio cassettes and recordings, 6,700 film and video titles, and more than 350,000 books. Specialized academic facilities include dozens of "smart" classrooms, computer centers and microcomputer labs, computer graphics and robotics labs, microelectronics and computer engineering facilities, more than 150 color and black-and-white photography darkrooms, digital and traditional printing presses, ceramics kilns, glass furnaces, a blacksmithing area, art galleries and performance auditoriums, a laser optics laboratory, a greenhouse, an animal-care facility, a student-run hotel and restaurant, and a computer-controlled observatory.

Honorary Societies Alpha Sigma Lambda (National Service and Leadership Honor Society), Golden Key International Honor Society, Order of Omega (National Fraternity and Sorority Honor Society), Phi Alpha (National Social Work Honor Society), Phi Kappa Phi Honor Society, Pi Kappa Gamma (National Packaging Science Honor Society), Tau Alpha Pi (National Engineering Technology Honor Society), Tau Beta Pi (National Engineering Honor Society)

Athletics RIT's intercollegiate teams include men's baseball, basketball, crew, cross-country, ice hockey, lacrosse, soccer, swimming, tennis, track, and wrestling and women's basketball, crew, ice hockey, lacrosse, soccer, softball, swimming, tennis, track, and volleyball. Extensive intramural sports programs are offered. Facilities include five multipurpose courts, eight racquetball courts, a fitness center, a dance/aerobics studio, an indoor track, two gymnasiums, a swimming pool, a wrestling room, a weight room, an ice arena, and outdoor facilities that include tennis courts, an all-weather track, and numerous athletics fields.

Study Abroad To prepare students for success in an increasingly global society, RIT offers a range of study-abroad opportunities. Summer programs are available in more than a dozen regions, including Western Europe, Australia, Japan, Russia, Singapore, China, South America, and the Caribbean. During the academic year, programs in Florence, London, Strasbourg, Madrid, and Hong Kong are popular destinations for RIT students, who can study abroad for up to a full academic year.

Support Services A full range of support services is available through the Learning Development Center, including academic accommodations and disability services. RIT is home to the National Technical Institute for the Deaf (NTID), the nation's largest technical college for deaf and hard-of-hearing students.

Job Opportunities Cooperative education provides paid, career-related work experience in many degree programs. RIT has the fourth-oldest and one of the largest cooperative education programs in the world, annually placing 2,600 students in co-op positions with 1,300 employers. More than 600 companies visit RIT annually, conducting more than 6,500 employment interviews. Internships and clinical field experiences are built into other RIT academic programs, including the allied health and social work programs, and provide valuable work experience in real-world settings.

Tuition: $18,633 (2001–02)

Room and Board: $7,266 (2001–02)

Mandatory Fees: $333 (2001–02)

Contact: Director: Dr. Catherine Hutchison Winnie, 21 Lomb Memorial Drive, Rochester, New York, 14623-5603; Telephone: 585-475-7634; Fax: 585-475-7633; E-mail:honors@mail.rit.edu; Web site: http://www.rit.edu/~620www/honorsprogram/

ROCKFORD COLLEGE

4 Pr G S Tr

▼ Honors Program in Liberal Arts

The purpose of the Honors Program in Liberal Arts is to encourage excellence through a program of special courses, broad distribution requirements, and extracurricular events.

The four special courses, which introduce students to the development of Western civilization from the ancient Greek and Hebrews down to the present, are developed and taught by a course director and another faculty member from a complementary discipline. Each course approaches its period of study through broad, interdisciplinary historical studies of art, literature, philosophy, science, religion, and politics. Guest lectures and other presentations by visiting scholars are scheduled frequently.

The broad distribution requirements encourage contact with as many departments as possible outside students' majors. Extracurricular events, both academic and social, extend students' studies beyond the classroom and enable them to form friendly relationships with faculty members that characterize liberal studies at their best.

There are 20 students currently enrolled.

Interpreting the symbols: **2**=two-year college, **4**=four-year college; **Pu**=public or state college, **Pr**=private college; **G**=general honors program; **D**=departmental honors program; **S**=small program (fewer than 100 students), **M**=midsize program (100 to 500 students), **L**=large program (more than 500 students); **Sc**=scholarships available in honors program; **Tr**=transfer students accepted into honors program; **HBC**=historically black college; **AA**=academic advisors; **GA**=graduate advisors; **FA**=fellowship advisors.

Participation Requirements: One liberal arts course is offered each semester, beginning with Liberal Arts 201 and proceeding in chronological order. These four 4-credit courses cover the ancient world, the Middle Ages, the Renaissance and Reformation, and the Enlightenment and the modern world. Students must take all four to complete the program (though not necessarily in order) and must achieve an average of at least 3.0 in all four with no grade below C in any one.

Distribution requirements involve 8 credits of arts (at least on studio course) and 12 credits each in language and literature, science and mathematics, and social sciences. All students in the Honors Program must also take 12 credits (two years) of a foreign language (French, German, Greek, Latin, or Spanish) or demonstrate by examination that they have attained that level.

Admission Process: To be invited to participate in the program as entering freshmen, students should have a composite score of at least 27 on the ACT or appropriate scores on the SAT I, have graduated in the top 10 percent of their senior class in high school, or merit special consideration.

New transfer students must have had at least a 3.35 GPA (B) in the two most recent college semesters; students with only one semester of college work must have had at least a 3.35 GPA during that semester.

To enter after one semester or more at Rockford College, students must have a minimum cumulative 3.0 GPA. If they do not meet the ordinary standards, students may apply for special consideration and may be admitted at the discretion of the Chair of the Honors Program in Liberal Arts. To continue in the program and complete it successfully, students must maintain a cumulative GPA of at least 3.0.

Scholarship Availability: A Socratic Society Scholarship is offered.

The Campus Context: Rockford College is located in Rockford, Illinois, a city of approximately 140,000 about 60 miles west of Chicago's O'Hare Airport. The College is a coeducational, private, nondenominational liberal arts college with strong professional programs in business, education, and nursing.

Student Body Rockford College has approximately 800 full-time and 700 part-time students.

Faculty There are 85 full-time faculty members.

Honorary Societies Phi Beta Kappa

Study Abroad Rockford College regularly sends students to study for a semester at Regent's College in Regent's Park, London, England. It also participates in several other study-abroad programs and has sent students to study in Greece, Australia, Spain, and Japan as well as other countries.

Tuition: $15,500 (1998–99)

Room and board: $4750–$5450

Contact: Director: Professor Stephen Hicks, 5050 East State Street, Rockford, Illinois 61108; Telephone: 815-226-4078; Fax: 815-394-5171; E-mail: stephen-hicks@rockford.edu; Web site: http://www.rockford.edu/

ROGER WILLIAMS UNIVERSITY

4 Pr G M Sc AA

▼ University Honors Program

The University Honors Program, established in 1994, enrolls approximately 5 percent of the freshman class. There is a total annual participation of nearly 200 full-time students, representing the breadth of the University's undergraduate programs. The University Honors Program holds an institutional membership in the National Collegiate Honors Council. Learning on the collegiate level encourages independent and original thinking in all course work. These qualities are particularly characteristic of the University Honors Program. Students and faculty members in the program share a passion for learning. The University Honors Program supplements a student participant's undergraduate education, distinguishing them as superior scholars and active participants in the University community.

Participation Requirements: The University Honors Program curriculum is writing intensive. It consists of six prescribed courses in the first two years of study, including special sections of the University core course requirements; a community service or leadership experience in the junior year; and a final major-related project for performance or presentation in the student's year of graduation. They usually engage the student in research and written assignments. The University Honors Program includes a service or leadership and a major-related presentation, in addition to the core curriculum courses. These requirements provide opportunities for students to mentor freshman in the University Honors Program while conceiving and implementing a leadership or service project with the support of the Honors Advisory Council and the Feinstein Service Learning Program. Drawing upon major-related interests (and, if required in the major, the senior thesis), graduating honors students will be able to share some aspect of their undergraduate study and research with the academic community.

Admission Process: SAT, ACT, TOEFL scores are used as admissions criteria. High school average, strength of high school curriculum, rank in class, academic recommendations, personal essay, extracurricular activities, are all factors considered by the honors admissions committee. For maximum consideration for merit-based scholarships and those particularly for honors scholarships, applications should be received on or before February 1.

Scholarship Availability: Maintain a cumulative 3.3 GPA to maintain annual scholarship for consecutive years (full-time day status) of undergraduate study and remain active in the Honors Program. In addition, all academic requirements of the Honors Program must be achieved.

The Campus Context: Roger Williams University is an independent, coeducational institution, accredited by the New England Association of Schools and Colleges. The 140-acre waterfront campus in the historic seacoast town of Bristol, Rhode Island provides an ideal setting for learning and teaching. In 1999 and again in 2000, *U.S. News & World Report's* Best Colleges Guide listed Roger Williams University in tier one of regional liberal arts colleges in the Northeast.

Student Body The University's student body of more than 3,700 men and women includes traditional and nontraditional, full- and part-time students. Students come from 26 states and 45 countries, and are commuters as well as on-campus residents. More than 2,500 men and women are enrolled as full-time undergraduates at Roger Williams University; 1,700 are enrolled as part-time students. The University is dedicated to creating a challenging and supportive learning environment for every student. Full-time undergraduates take classes on the Bristol campus and the majority live on campus. The ratio of men to women is 1.3 to 1. Most students hail from the Northeast, primarily Connecticut, Massachusetts, New Jersey, New York, and Rhode Island. International students represent an increasingly significant part of the student body.

Key Facilities The University library system contains a book collection of more than 175,000 volumes and is growing at the rate of nearly 5,000 volumes a year. An integrated library system and an online Web-based catalog facilitate research. The collection includes more than 1,000 periodical titles, an extensive backfile in bound volumes and on microfilm, and online access to thousands of more materials. A computer link further expands research capabilities, providing instant access to the library collections of Rhode Island colleges and universities. The Main Library, open 92 hours a week, and the Architecture Library, open 83 hours a week, ensure full service in both facilities for students and faculty members. An after-hours study room is located in the main library. A library facility at the Metropolitan College in Providence provides weekday evening services. The libraries supplement resources by affiliating with statewide and national professional and academic groups and associations.

Tuition: $18,360 (2001–02)

Mandatory Fees: $1090 (2001–02)

Room and Board: $8510 (2001–02)

Contact: Director: Dr. Peter Deekle, Telephone: 401-254-3063; E-mail: pdeekle@rwu.edu

Rollins College

4 Pu C S Tr AA

▼ Honors Degree Program

Rollins College offers a special program in the liberal arts for students with exceptional abilities. The Honors Degree Program provides unusual breadth in the liberal arts and exceptional depth in the student's chosen major. Successful completion of the Honors curriculum leads to a distinct and separate undergraduate degree, Artium Baccalaureus (A.B.) Honoris—the Honors Bachelor of Arts degree.

Honors students complete a core of interdisciplinary courses designed to provide an integrated understanding of the liberal arts. A series of four team-taught seminars during their first and second years introduces students to the various methods of inquiry in the liberal arts. These courses substitute for some of the general education requirements of the regular A.B. program and are designed to teach students to think and write critically across a broad range of disciplines, to encourage a synthetic interdisciplinary understanding of the liberal arts, and to encourage and prepare students to be independent thinkers. Honors seminars in the third and fourth years support significant independent research projects that represent the culmination of students' careers at Rollins.

Participation Requirements: Honors degree students must take a special team-taught honors seminar in each of their first four semesters at the College. These seminars are designed to encourage students to think across traditional disciplinary boundaries. Adventurous students are encouraged to spend a semester away from the campus (usually during the junior year) pursuing experiential learning, study abroad, or some other exceptional educational opportunity. Seniors engage in a two-term independent research project in their major fields. Honors degree students are expected to maintain a cumulative GPA of at least 3.33 at all times. Successful graduates receive special recognition at Commencement and are awarded a distinctive degree—the Artium Baccalaureus Honoris.

Admission Process: Entering first-year students are invited to join the Honors Degree Program only if their high school records show evidence of a special scholastic aptitude and attitude. Candidates for admission are evaluated by reference to their high school grades, standardized test scores (SAT or ACT), and quality of application essay. Honors students normally constitute the top 10 percent of the Rollins entering class. Invitation to join the program is extended at the time of notice of admission to the College.

Students who transfer to Rollins at or prior to the beginning of their sophomore year may be considered for admission to the Honors Degree Program as well.

Scholarship Availability: There are no scholarships specifically related to the Honors Degree Program, though most honors students receive merit-based and need-based financial aid for attending Rollins.

The Campus Context: Rollins College is a small private liberal arts college located on the shores of Lake Virginia in beautiful Winter Park, Florida. The oldest institution of higher learning in Florida, Rollins maintains focused emphasis on quality liberal education in an atmosphere of innovation and experimentation.

Rollins ranks high for the rigor and quality of the undergraduate education that it provides. Home to the Annie Russell Theatre, the Cornell Art Museum, and annual Bach Festival and the "Spring Term with the Writers" program, Rollins is known as a home for the lively arts.

Student Body Rollins College of Arts and Sciences has about 1,600 full-time undergraduate students. The diverse student body comes from forty-nine states and twenty-five other countries. The geographically diverse mix, which is represented also in terms of cultures, languages, and ethnicity, forms the basis for a cosmopolitan community of learners on Rollins' beautiful lakeside campus.

Most full-time students reside on campus. There are more than seventy student organizations of various kinds, from traditional Greek organizations to political, artistic, and intellectual groups.

Faculty In the arts and sciences program at Rollins College there are 185 faculty members, of whom 141 are full-time; 92 percent of the full-time faculty members have terminal degrees.

Key Facilities Holdings in Olin Library include 295,000 volumes. Other library holdings include 1,546 periodical subscriptions and 50 online databases. Computer facilities include sixteen public terminals (OPAC) for library use (Dell Pentium) and two labs with thirty computers each for student computer work.

Athletics Rollins boasts men's and women's varsity teams in basketball, cross-country, golf, rowing, sailing, soccer, swimming, tennis and waterskiing. In addition, there are teams in men's baseball and women's softball and volleyball. Rollins belongs to the NCAA Division II and to the Sunshine State Conference.

Study Abroad Adventurous Honors Degree Program students are encouraged to study abroad at some point (usually in the junior year). Rollins has extensive international programs, including semester programs in Australia; London, England; Germany; and Asturias and Madrid, Spain.

Support Services Facilities for disabled students are plentiful. The library, campus center, athletic building, dorms, and office buildings are wheelchair accessible. Accessible restrooms and drinking fountains are readily found.

Job Opportunities Many students are engaged in work-study. In addition, there are some employment opportunities on campus and around town (listed in the Human Resource Office). The Career Planning and Placement Office assists students nearing graduation in their search for employment.

Tuition: $11,602.50 per semester (2001–02)

Room and Board: Room (based on double occupancy), $2114.50 per semester; board, $1556 per semester (2001–02)

Mandatory Fees: $338.50 per semester (2001–02)

Contact: Director: Professor J. Thomas Cook, Honors Degree Program, Rollins College, Box 2659, 1000 Holt Avenue, Winter Park, Florida 32789-4499; Telephone: 407-646-2518; Fax: 407-646-2517; E-mail: tcook@rollins.edu

Roosevelt University

4 Pr G S Sc Tr

▼ Roosevelt Scholars Program

The Roosevelt Scholars Program is designed to train the future leaders of the Chicago metropolitan area. The program attracts

Interpreting the symbols: **2**=two-year college, **4**=four-year college; **Pu**=public or state college, **Pr**=private college; **G**=general honors program; **D**=departmental honors program; **S**=small program (fewer than 100 students), **M**=midsize program (100 to 500 students), **L**=large program (more than 500 students); **Sc**=scholarships available in honors program; **Tr**=transfer students accepted into honors program; **HBC**=historically black college; **AA**=academic advisors; **GA**=graduate advisors; **FA**=fellowship advisors.

some of Roosevelt's most talented undergraduate students who wish to prepare for a career and also to explore the world of ideas. By bringing students and professors together in small classes and individual research settings, the Scholars Program fosters a strong feeling of community.

The Scholars Program offers an enriched academic program that combines courses in a student's area of interest with interdisciplinary courses that address issues facing metropolitan Chicago. Faculty mentors help students shape their academic programs. Professional mentors—accomplished Chicago-area leaders—help keep students on the paths to success. There are internships and research opportunities at leading business, cultural, and governmental organizations. Roosevelt Scholars receive generous merit scholarship support (as well as need-based financial aid).

The courses include honors sections of the University General Education curriculum in the humanities, social sciences, and sciences. In addition, students take other honors-level studies in urban and metropolitan issues. The curriculum culminates in an Honors Thesis.

Besides taking honors courses, students attend lectures, plays, concerts, and other cultural events on and off campus.

The Roosevelt Scholars Program began in September 1998. There are 120 students currently enrolled in the program. Plans call for there to be 200 students participating in the program by September 2004.

Participation Requirements: For students entering the Scholars Program as freshmen, the Scholars Program curriculum is a ten course sequence culminating in an Honors Thesis, in which students pursue original research under the guidance of a faculty mentor. Students who enroll in the Scholars Program after their freshmen year are not required to take the full ten-course sequence. The program is tailored specifically for each student depending upon their previous academic course work taken at Roosevelt or another institution.

Admission Process: Admission to the Roosevelt Scholars Program is competitive. The program is open to entering freshmen with strong high school academic records, class ranks, and ACT or SAT I scores. Roosevelt students already enrolled or transfer students who have demonstrated outstanding academic achievement are also eligible. To be considered for the program, students must fill out an application form requiring three short essays. Finalists are invited for personal interviews.

Scholarship Availability: All participants in the Roosevelt Scholars Program receive merit scholarship support ranging from partial to full tuition over four years. Need-based financial aid is also available for those who qualify.

The Campus Context: Roosevelt University was founded in 1945 to provide equal educational opportunity to students of all racial, ethnic, and religious backgrounds. A commitment to academic excellence and social justice characterizes Roosevelt's curriculum and the University's involvement in the Chicago metropolitan area.

The University has two campuses that bridge metropolitan Chicago: one in downtown Chicago on Michigan Avenue in the heart of Chicago's cultural and political center and one in the northwest suburb of Schaumburg near O'Hare International Airport and numerous corporate headquarters.

Roosevelt University is composed of five colleges: College of Arts and Sciences, Walter E. Heller College of Business, College of Performing Arts, College of Education, and the Evelyn T. Stone University College. The academic programs include more than 100 undergraduate majors plus preprofessional programs in medicine, law, dentistry, and veterinary medicine. Roosevelt also offers sixty-seven master's degree programs and two doctoral programs. Roosevelt schedules day, evening, and weekend classes so that students may work while attending school.

Student Body The 4,628 undergraduates come from thirty states and sixty-two other countries; 62 percent are women. Approximately 90 percent of Roosevelt's undergraduate students are residents of the greater Chicago metropolitan area. The ethnic distribution of undergraduate students is 47 percent white, 27 percent African American, 12 percent Hispanic, 5 percent Asian, and 9 percent not listed. There are 182 international students.

Eighty-five percent of undergraduate students receive financial aid. Roosevelt's policy is to provide maximum financial assistance for students who demonstrate financial need. There are also scholarships awarded to entering freshmen and transfer students on the basis of academic ability. Many are renewable up to the completion of the bachelor's degree program. The University also has a limited number of Music Performance Awards for music majors. Talent awards are also available for theater majors.

Faculty The faculty includes 640 members, 198 of whom teach full-time. Eighty-five percent of the full-time faculty members hold terminal degrees. The student-faculty ratio is 16:1.

Key Facilities The collection of the main library exceeds 350,000, including 63,000 microfilm titles. The Music Library houses an additional 228,713 books, 12,000 sound recordings, and 10,000 pieces of sheet music and is furnished with audio equipment for individual listening. Roosevelt students also have access to more than 25 million additional volumes through the University's membership in the Chicago Academic Library Council and the Illinois Library Network. Materials in libraries all over the country can be located quickly by means of the University's Online Computer Library Center (OCLC) computer terminals.

The University has new IBM microcomputer laboratories. There are 180 computers in the University computer centers.

Support Services A special support program is available for learning-disabled students.

Job Opportunities There is a campus work-study program. Because of Roosevelt's prime location in Chicago, internships are available with major corporations and leading cultural institutions and governmental agencies.

Tuition: $459 per semester hour or $13,770 (for 30 hours) per year (2001–02)

Room and board: $6270

Mandatory Fees: $200

Contact: Director: Dr. Samuel Rosenberg, School of Policy Studies, 430 South Michigan Ave., Chicago, Illinois 60605; Telephone: 312-341-3697; Fax: 312-341-3680; E-mail: srosenbe@roosevelt.edu

Rose State College

2 Pu S Sc Tr

▼ Honors Program

The Honors Program at Rose State College (RSC) offers all students an opportunity to experience an intellectual and cultural enrichment of the college environment. Students may elect to be involved in any part of the Honors Program. Each semester, honors-designated sections or regular courses, primarily those that satisfy General Education degree requirements, are offered, along with special topics and interdisciplinary courses in most semesters. A third option is the contract for honors credit, which students may arrange on an individual basis with mentoring professors. Students admitted to the Honors Program become eligible to apply for Honors Scholarships.

There are currently 40 students enrolled in the program.

Participation Requirements: To graduate from the program, students must meet all requirements for a two-year degree with a 3.5 or higher GPA; earn at least 12 honors credit hours at RSC; earn A's or B's in all classes taken for honors credit; and submit an annotated résumé of all honors work to the Honors Committee. Those who successfully complete the Honors Program receive appropriate notations on diplomas and transcripts.

Admission Process: Although any RSC student may take offered honors classes, those who wish to enter the Honors Program must have a 3.5 GPA in high school and an ACT score of 27 or above, complete two RSC honors classes with an A or B, or demonstrate a special skill or talent to the Honors Committee.

The Campus Context: Rose State College is a two-year college located on 100 acres in Midwest City, Oklahoma, a suburb of Oklahoma City. Forty-six degree programs are offered leading to the Associate in Arts, Associate in Science, and Associate in Applied Science degrees.

Student Body Approximately 8,000 students enroll in the fall and spring semesters, 41 percent men and 59 percent women. Sixty-six percent of the student body is full-time; the remaining 34 percent is part-time.

Faculty There are 139 full-time faculty members (supplemented with adjunct faculty), 24 percent with doctorates or other terminal degrees. The student-faculty ratio is 21:1.

Key Facilities The library houses 80,000 volumes. There are eight computer labs with PCs.

Support Services Disabled students have access to all buildings (with electronic doors) and special tables/chairs in classrooms.

Tuition: $914.50 for state residents, $2867.50 for nonresidents, per year (1998–99)

Mandatory Fees: $387.50

Contact: Director: Claudia Buckmaster, Humanities 113, Midwest City, Oklahoma 73110-2799; Telephone: 405-733-7506; Fax: 405-736-0370; E-mail: cbuckmaster@ms.rose.cc.ok.us

Rowan University

4 Pu G Sc Tr AA

▼ University Honors Program

The Rowan University Interdisciplinary Honors Program is open to students in every academic major. Emphasis is placed on interdisciplinary study and active learning. The program's smaller classes nurture development of student writing, speaking, and critical-thinking skills. Connections among ideas and disciplines are enriched by encouraging students to question, study, and analyze primary texts.

Students take the initiative in their own learning and work in collaboration with peers. They may join in selecting texts, nominating faculty members for the program, and creating curriculum. The concentration provides the space for students to take up different points of view outside any single discipline. Students think critically about the interplay between liberal learning and career preparation within and beyond academic fields.

Participation Requirements: Students must complete three lower-level and three upper-level courses in the concentration. An independent honors project may be substituted for one upper-level course. All honors courses fulfill general education requirements. They may also be applicable to writing intensive and multicultural–global requirements. A minimum of 18 credit hours in interdisciplinary studies and a 3.5 GPA are required for completion of the concentration.

Admission Process: Applications for admission are reviewed by the Honors Program Coordinator. Criteria for freshmen acceptance rests on a combination of scores on standardized tests (AP exam scores and 1200 on the SAT I), letters of recommendation, and high school rank. Students with a 3.5 GPA at the end of their first year are invited to apply for admission to the program.

Scholarship Availability: More than 70 percent of Rowan University students receive financial aid through an assortment of grants, scholarships, loans, and part-time employment. Last year's grant and loan programs totaled more than $8 million. Each year, alumni, private groups, and individuals also provide more than $120,000 in scholarships to incoming students.

The Campus Context: After 70 years as Glassboro State College, a $100-million gift from Henry and Betty Rowan provided the means to transform the College. The Rowan University vision is to become a regional university that emphasizes undergraduate programs. A new $18-million library, funded by the state, opened in spring 1995. The 200-acre campus is only 30 minutes from Philadelphia and 55 minutes from Atlantic City.

Six colleges form the University: Liberal Arts and Sciences, Communication, Education, Business, Fine and Performing Arts, and Engineering.

Student Body About 7,500 undergraduates enroll in thirty-one undergraduate degree programs. Rowan University has more than 150 chartered student organizations. Clubs, honor societies, fraternities, and sororities work in the framework of an elected Student Government Association. Homecoming, Family Weekend, and Project Santa offer community-wide activities. The Glassboro Center for the Arts and the Annual Jazz Festival provide part of the wide range of cocurricular cultural activities available to enrich student life.

Faculty Of the 324 full-time faculty members (supplemented by an adjunct faculty), 80 percent have doctorates or appropriate terminal degrees. The student-faculty ratio is 16:1, and the average class size is 23.

Key Facilities The 350,000-volume library is networked to computer labs. There are eight residence halls and three apartment complexes. Twenty-one IBM and Macintosh labs are located in academic buildings.

Athletics Rowan has had ten NCAA Division III championships in basketball, baseball, soccer, and track and field, and more than 100 All-American athletes have attended Rowan. The intramural program is extensive and complements the intercollegiate competition. The Recreational Center and Student Center offer a full range of activities.

Study Abroad Qualified undergraduates earn 15–30 credits in overseas programs in Europe, Latin America, Australia, Asia, and Africa. Programs are coordinated with all academic majors as integral components of the degree models.

Job Opportunities Federal Work-Study (no more than 20 hours per week) is available to students who qualify for federal financial aid. Institutional Work-Study offers opportunities for students who are not eligible for need-based financial aid.

Tuition: $5779 for state residents, $10,279 for nonresidents, per year (2001–02)

Room and Board: $6586

Contact: Director: Virginia Brown, Ph.D., Savitz Building, Third Floor, Glassboro, New Jersey 08028-1701; Telephone: 856-256-4775; E-mail: brown@rowan.edu; Web site: http://www.rowan.edu

Interpreting the symbols: **2**=two-year college, **4**=four-year college; **Pu**=public or state college, **Pr**=private college; **G**=general honors program; **D**=departmental honors program; **S**=small program (fewer than 100 students), **M**=midsize program (100 to 500 students), **L**=large program (more than 500 students); **Sc**=scholarships available in honors program; **Tr**=transfer students accepted into honors program; **HBC**=historically black college; **AA**=academic advisors; **GA**=graduate advisors; **FA**=fellowship advisors.

RUSSELL SAGE COLLEGE

4 Pr S Tr

▼ Honors Program: "Honoring Women's Voices Through Academic Achievement"

The Honors Program at Russell Sage College (RSC) honors women's voices in all fields and endeavors, offers sustained opportunities for cross-disciplinary study through multidisciplinary approaches, and supports students in directing their own learning. Three options are available to students: General Honors, Advanced Honors, and Honors Affiliate. Students in General Honors enroll in a 12-credit program of honors courses and graduate with distinction as Honors Scholars. With the exception of Founder's Seminar, all credits "double count" as general education courses. Students must earn a B or better in each honors course for it to count toward their overall honors credits. Junior and/or senior students may enroll in Advanced Honors where they work in a one-to-one relationship with a faculty member on an Advanced Honor Project (6 credits). Students may design and carry out their own research projects in their majors or in other areas of interest (such as a project related to ITD 420). Finally, students may enroll in one or more honors course in areas of particular interest without having to complete the 12-credit requirement. Students who choose to be Honors Affiliates receive honors designation on their official transcript. These courses are open to affiliates on a space-available basis.

Class size is limited to 18, and all classes are taught by full-time faculty members. Faculty members address both the content and pedagogical issues that are indicated by the theme of the honors seminar, and each provides an out-of-class experience. Faculty members are encouraged to conduct their courses in such a way as to promote self-discovery.

Admission Process: Admission to the program is automatic for interested students who have a high school average of 92 or better or who have maintained a college GPA of at least 3.4. Transfer students who meet the GPA requirements and who are currently enrolled in an honors program are accepted into the program. The director of the honors program may also admit motivated students who do not yet meet those standards but show special ability or promise.

Scholarship Availability: There are no honors scholarships at this time.

The Campus Context: Russell Sage College is open to women only, while Sage Evening College, Sage Graduate School, and the affiliated Junior College of Albany are coeducational. RSC offers thirty-five degree programs. Among special facilities on campus are the Allies Center for the Study of Difference and Conflict, the Allies Center for Conflict Mediation Information and Education, the Center for Citizenship, the Center for the Exploration of International Issues, a First-year Mentoring Program, the Helen M. Upton Center for Women's Studies, and the Social Policy Research Center.

Student Body Undergraduate enrollment is 100 percent women and includes 12 percent historically underrepresented groups and 2 international students. Forty-nine percent of students reside on campus. RSC has no sororities.

Faculty Of the 160 faculty members, 120 are full-time. Eighty-five percent have terminal degrees. The student-faculty ratio is 9:1.

Key Facilities The library houses 230,000 volumes. Computer facilities include five classrooms, with two more in development. The Computing Center has multiple Sun SPARCserver 1000s.

Honorary Society Phi Kappa Phi

Athletics In athletics, the College is NCAA Division III in basketball, tennis, soccer, volleyball, and softball.

Study Abroad Study abroad is available at Oxford University and Shanghai Institute, as are programs in Puerto Rico, Spain, and the Bahamas.

Support Services Many of the buildings are handicapped-accessible.

Job Opportunities Work-study grants are available.

Tuition: $14,920 per year (1999–2000)

Room and Board: $6020 minimum

Mandatory Fees: $580

Contact: Director: Dr. Julie Ann McIntyre, 405 Gurley Hall, Russell Sage College, Troy, New York 12180; Telephone: 518-244-2255; Fax: 518-244-4545; E-mail: mcintj@sage.edu

RUTGERS, THE STATE UNIVERSITY OF NEW JERSEY, CAMDEN COLLEGE OF ARTS AND SCIENCES

4 Pu L Sc Tr AA GA FA

▼ Rutgers College Honors Program

The Rutgers College Honors Program (RCHP) offers academically talented undergraduates the best resources of a nationally recognized major public research institution and the advantages of a smaller college atmosphere. Members of the Honors Program have a wide variety of intellectual and cocurricular interests, but also belong to a community of scholars—faculty and staff members and peers—who share an enthusiasm for the life of the mind. The program fosters that enthusiasm by inviting students to take part in the development of an individualized honors experience. Because the College believes that students should take an active role in shaping their education, there are no requirements, with the exception of the College's degree requirements, imposed upon all members of the program. The Rutgers College Honors Program challenges students to explore the intellectual and social diversity of the campus and to seek ways to put theory into practice beyond the campus.

Members of the Honors Program may choose not only from the thousands of regular undergraduate and graduate course offerings, but also from a wide variety of honors courses, including small interdisciplinary colloquia on nontraditional topics, enhanced sections of traditional courses that explore the disciplines in greater depth with the some of the best faculty members, and nontraditional departmentally based seminars that provide a richer perspective on traditional disciplines. Enrollment in most honors courses is limited to between 15 and 30 students and the environment of these courses is one in which both faculty members and students consider themselves learners. Many students incorporate internship opportunities and study abroad into their honors experiences.

Rutgers College Honors Program students are invited to take advantage of an extensive mentoring and advising support network. A peer mentoring program helps ease the transition between high school and college by matching each incoming student with an Honors Program member in advanced standing. The Faculty Mentor Program places students in close and continuing contact with an experienced faculty member in the student's discipline of choice as early as the first year; students often develop lasting friendships with faculty mentors and may pursue research projects with their guidance during the course of their college careers. Dedicated Honors Program staff members provide academic and personal advising to students throughout the four years, in addition to running workshops on topics such as getting involved in the research life of the University, admission to graduate school, securing major fellowships, and choosing a career path. With this guidance and support from a community of scholars, students in the Honors Program actually create new knowledge. Faculty members actively seek out program members for participation in research and students are encouraged to design their own research projects; funding is available from the freshman through senior years. Students who take advantage of this opportunity have commented on the fact that it prepares them to do well in their graduate work and to enter the professional world. Each year, the program sponsors a Student Research Day, an event that allows recipients of research funding to present their work to the University community. A Student Lecture Series fosters discussion about research in an informal setting throughout the year. Many students go on to write senior theses or take graduate courses as an outgrowth of their research.

A shared residential community is also an important aspect of the Rutgers College Honors Program. In two honors residence halls, students participate in a wide variety of cocurricular and social experiences. Incoming students may elect honors housing upon matriculation.

The program also often sponsors cultural outings to New York and Philadelphia and purchases tickets for members at performances and screenings in the area. Twice yearly, early in the fall and at the end of the academic year, the entire membership gathers for social events, and smaller gatherings take place throughout the year.

The Rutgers College Honors Program was established in 1980. Approximately 800 of the most talented undergraduate scholars in a college of 11,000 students are members of the program.

Participation Requirements: In order to take an active role in defining their own honors experience, RCHP students are not required to fulfill a set of requirements. Students who participate in other programs (departmental honors programs, the Henry Rutgers Scholars Program, or the Interdisciplinary Honors Option [see below]) in the sophomore through senior years complete requirements of those programs.

Honors Program students are expected to maintain a semester GPA of at least 3.25 in each term of the first year and 3.5 in each term thereafter at Rutgers. Students whose semester average is below the required average in any one semester are placed on probation. If a student's semester average is below the required average for two semesters in a row, that student is dismissed from the program. Advising is available to Honors Program students who have been placed on honors probation or dismissed from the program. Any student who has been dismissed from the Rutgers College Honors Program is eligible to request readmission to the program after attaining the required term average in a subsequent semester.

Students looking for an additional challenge or a unique way to bridge disciplines may complete the Interdisciplinary Honors Option. This option requires submission of a proposal in the second term sophomore or first term junior year outlining the interdisciplinary study to be undertaken; at least one interdisciplinary honors course outside the major concentration category (for example, a major in English [humanities] must take at least one social science or math/science interdisciplinary seminar/course); 60 hours of community service, either through a campus organization, through the University's Civic and Service Education (CASE) program (1 credit community service associated with a specific academic course), or a combination thereof; a one-term interdisciplinary junior project, which may be either independent study (with faculty readers from at least two different departments) or study abroad; a two-term interdisciplinary senior thesis project, requiring faculty committee members from at least two different departments; and continued membership in the Rutgers College Honors Program and achievement of its academic standards. Students who have completed all components of the Interdisciplinary Honors Option are awarded Interdisciplinary Honors upon graduation.

Admission Process: Only students who have applied and been admitted to Rutgers College through an application submitted to the Office of Undergraduate Admissions are considered for the Rutgers College Honors Program. Application to Rutgers College by the Office of Undergraduate Admissions' priority application date of December 1 is encouraged to ensure full consideration for the Honors Program.

Admission to the Rutgers College Honors Program is based upon two components: SAT score and rank in class. Both of these components must fall within the following eligibility guidelines in order for a student to be admitted to the program: for SAT scores of 1350 to 1390, class rank must be in the top 5 percent; for SAT scores of 1400 to 1490, class rank must be in the top 10 percent; and for SAT scores of 1500 to 1600, class rank must be in the top 15 percent. No offers of admission are mailed after March 15.

Each year approximately 50 students who have completed the first year at Rutgers College are invited to become members of the RCHP, based on the cumulative GPA in June. Actual admission is based on a review of their record and RCHP application materials, including an essay. Transfer students who have completed less than 40 credits at another institution are considered for admission on an individual basis.

Scholarship Availability: There are no scholarships offered directly through the Honors Program. There are, however, many University and Rutgers College merit-based scholarships available to high-achieving students.

The Campus Context: Rutgers University's New Brunswick campus boasts a broad array of academic, cultural, and social opportunities. Rutgers College is the largest of the undergraduate schools on the New Brunswick campus and offers more than 100 major options. Rutgers is an active research university and a member of the American Association of Universities, to which only sixty-three of the almost 4,000 colleges and universities in the United States and Canada belong. Undergraduate students have access to the most current academic innovations and the chance to work closely with renowned professors. New Brunswick's urban setting provides students with leisure options for all tastes, including numerous downtown theaters, restaurants of every variety and price range, and Rutgers' own Zimmerli Art Museum. New York City and Philadelphia are each only a 45-minute train ride away. The residential character of the city offers many off-campus living options that are popular with upperclassmen.

Student Body Rutgers College is an undergraduate college within Rutgers, the State University of New Jersey. Approximately 11,000 students are enrolled at Rutgers College. The College is situated on the New Brunswick campus, which has a total enrollment of approximately 28,000 undergraduate students and 7,500 graduate students. Of the approximately 28,000 undergraduate students on the New Brunswick campuses, approximately 56 percent are white, 18 percent are Asian, 8 percent are African American, 8 percent are Latino, and 3 percent are international.

Faculty There are a total of 2,600 faculty members at Rutgers University's three regional campuses, 98 percent of whom hold terminal degrees. There are 800 full-time Faculty of Arts and Sciences members in New Brunswick alone. These faculty members provide approximately 75 percent of all undergraduate instruction on the New Brunswick campus.

Key Facilities Ranked among the top twenty-five research libraries in the United States, the Rutgers University Library system is

Interpreting the symbols: **2**=two-year college, **4**=four-year college; **Pu**=public or state college, **Pr**=private college; **G**=general honors program; **D**=departmental honors program; **S**=small program (fewer than 100 students), **M**=midsize program (100 to 500 students), **L**=large program (more than 500 students); **Sc**=scholarships available in honors program; **Tr**=transfer students accepted into honors program; **HBC**=historically black college; **AA**=academic advisors; **GA**=graduate advisors; **FA**=fellowship advisors.

comprised of twenty-six libraries on the three regional campuses. These libraries contain more than 3.7 million volumes and an online digital library that are available to all Rutgers students. Computing facilities located on each Rutgers campus include Apple Macintosh and DOS/Windows personal computers and X-terminals. Residence halls on all New Brunswick campuses are wired for the Internet. A technology initiative currently underway, called RUNet 2000, is a $100-million project to install a University-wide data, voice, and video network (the largest undertaking of its kind at a major public university). RUNet 2000 will transform the University's teaching, research, and public outreach missions by connecting all residential, academic, and administrative buildings.

Honorary Societies Phi Beta Kappa, National Society of Collegiate Scholars, Golden Key

Athletics From the first intercollegiate football game in 1869 to the present, Rutgers has a rich tradition of athletic competition. Over the years Rutgers has produced dozens of sport professionals, including players and coaches in the NBA, the WNBA, the NFL, Major League Baseball, and Major League Soccer. Today, the University sponsors about fifty intercollegiate teams on the Division I and III levels, along with cheerleading and dance teams.

Study Abroad Rutgers Global Programs offers study abroad opportunities in more than eighteen countries. There are full–academic year programs, single-semester programs, summer programs, and programs that focus on special topics and issues.

Support Services Rutgers College offers academic and other support and counseling services (both peer and professional) for all students. The Office of Disabled Students provides information and support for disabled students.

Job Opportunities The Rutgers University Career Services Office provides information and support to all students as they search for summer, academic-year, and post-graduation employment. The Student Employment Office provides information to all students about on-campus employment opportunities. New Brunswick and the surrounding communities offer extensive job placement opportunities.

Tuition: $5250 for New Jersey residents, $10,688 for nonresidents per year (2001–02)

Room and board: $6676

Mandatory Fees: $1172

Contact: Director: Dr. Muffin Lord, 210 Milledoler Hall, 520 George Street, New Brunswick, New Jersey 08901-1167; Telephone: 732-932-7964; Fax: 732-932-8418; E-mail: rcghp@rci.rutgers.edu; Web site: http://rchonors.rutgers.edu

SACRED HEART UNIVERSITY

4 Pr G S Sc Tr

▼ Honors Program

The Honors Program at Sacred Heart University is organized around those ultimate questions about reality and human life that are an unavoidable part of the human experience and are at the heart of the human puzzle. The program stands firm in the conviction that the honors experience should offer gifted students the opportunity to confront these questions, explore the answers that have been offered throughout the history of human thought and reflection, and test these answers in the light of their own experience. Honors students are offered, through the University's core requirements, the opportunity to confront the questions of meaning and orientation, of suffering, and of the reality of death and questions of freedom, responsibility, morality, justice, hope, God, and the nature of the physical world and to understand and appreciate themselves as the historical beings that they are. In providing this opportunity, Sacred Heart University believes that it is fulfilling in a special way for its most gifted students its commitment to a liberal arts education—an educational experience that is truly liberating from ignorance, prejudice, and unexamined opinions. As expressed in the University's mission statement, "the University aims to assist in the development of people knowledgeable of self, rooted in faith, educated in mind, compassionate in heart, responsive to social and civic obligations, and able to respond to an ever changing world."

Participation Requirements: The Honors Program at Sacred Heart University is a University Honors Program, as opposed to a college- or department-based honors program. The honors curriculum consists of at least thirty credits in courses that fulfill the University's liberal arts core requirements. Some of these courses may be interdisciplinary, and some may be team taught; all challenge, enrich, and expand the understanding of the honors student.

The liberal arts core program is divided into two parts: the required core and the elective core. The required core consists of 18 credits, 15 of which the honors student takes in honors sections. The elective section of the core consists of 30 credits taken from four areas. The honors student takes at least 15 of these credits in honors sections, with at least one course from each of three areas—humanities, social sciences, and the sciences—along with honors sections of Philosophy 101 and Religious Studies 101. Honors courses transferred into the University are considered for honors credit at the discretion of the Honors Committee. Honors credits are made up in the elective core for nonhonors transfer courses counted toward the required core.

Those honors students who complete the honors core may also apply for honors in their major. The specific requirements for honors in a major field of study are determined by the specific academic department awarding honors. However, all students working for honors in their major are required to register for an honors tutorial in the first term of their senior year and for an honors thesis or project in the second term of their senior year.

Admission Process: Admission to the Honors Program is competitive, with no more then forty incoming students admitted to the program each year. An invitation to join the Honors Program is extended on the basis of the following criteria: SAT I scores totaling at least 1200, high school transcripts that indicate a cumulative GPA of at least 3.2 on a 4.0 scale, graduate in the top 10 percent of the high school class, and an interview with the Director of the Honors Program and the Honors Committee. Only students who meet all of these criteria are considered eligible to receive an invitation to join the Honors Program. Students who are accepted must maintain a minimum GPA of 3.4 to remain in the program. Some students may apply and be admitted to the Honors Program as sophomores on the basis of having achieved a GPA of at least 3.4 in their freshman year, the recommendation of instructors in their freshman courses, and an interview with the Honors Committee.

Scholarship Availability: The University offers an academic scholarship program that is available to qualified students. These students must meet two of the following criteria: a 3.2 cumulative high school GPA in English, math, science, social studies, and foreign language; a high school ranking within the top 20 percent of the class; and/or SAT I scores of 1100 or better. The amount of the scholarship is awarded on a sliding scale, with points being given according to GPA rank and SAT I scores. The amount of the scholarship, which is based solely on academic merit, ranges from $3000 to $7000 a year. There is no separate application procedure necessary. The student is recommended for the scholarship through the admission process. The scholarship committee notifies in writing students who have received this scholarship. Students who apply for another scholarship, the University's Scholars, must meet the following criteria: a minimum 1200 SAT I score; valedictorian or salutatorian of their high school graduating class; and a minimum 3.4 cumulative high school GPA. This scholarship is worth $10,000.

The Campus Context: Sacred Heart University is a coeducational, independent, comprehensive Catholic university offering twenty-nine undergraduate degree programs, with combined undergraduate/graduate degrees in business, chemistry, computer science, nursing, physical and occupational therapy, and religious studies. Certification programs in education, preprofessional health and law advising programs, and NATA–accredited athletic training internships are available.

Founded in 1963, the University has experienced unprecedented growth over the past six years, making it the third-largest Catholic university in New England. Recent improvements to the suburban 56-acre campus have included new academic and student life programs and six new residence halls, new athletic fields, and the William H. Pitt Health and Recreation Complex. Committed to technology, the University requires entering students to have a computer.

Student Body There is a full-time undergraduate enrollment of 2,300 and a part-time undergraduate enrollment of 1,700. There are 1,600 graduate students. Together, these students represent eighteen states and fifty-five countries. Twenty-four percent are from multicultural backgrounds. Sixty-five percent of the population lives in residence halls on campus. Eighty-five percent of the students receive financial assistance.

Faculty There are 135 full-time faculty members and 267 adjunct members. Eighty-one percent of the faculty members have terminal degrees.

Key Facilities The library houses 177,000 volumes. The University's computer network includes five computer classrooms, a multipurpose lab, and more than 120 IBM-compatible and Macintosh computers. All incoming students are required to purchase University-approved laptop computers. Six residence halls were built between 1992 and 1994. Other new construction includes a $1.2-million synthetic-surfaced multipurpose athletic field and extensive renovations to the main academic buildings, including state-of-the-art science labs, faculty offices, and renovations to existing classrooms and the dining hall.

Study Abroad The opportunity to live and study abroad is an essential component of the Honors Program.

Support Services The University's facilities are accessible to all students.

Job Opportunities Students are offered a range of work-study positions. Some non–work-study positions are also available.

Tuition: $7000 per year (full-time)

Room and Board: $7938

Contact: Director: Dr. Walter Brooks, 5151 Park Avenue, Fairfield, Connecticut 06432; Telephone: 203-371-7730; Fax: 203-371-7731; E-mail: brooksw@sacredheart.edu

---

SAGE JUNIOR COLLEGE OF ALBANY

2 Pr G S Sc Tr

▼ Honors Program

The Sage Junior College of Albany (JCA) Honors Program offers challenging, liberal arts honors courses in which students exercise personal creativity and initiative. Maximum class size is 15. Interdisciplinary and team-taught seminars and honors contract courses provide opportunities for both collaborative and independent student inquiry. Recent course offerings have included American Ethnic History; Environmental Science, which combines biology and American environmental literature; Art History, which combines classical art and literature; Humanities Seminar in Creative Process; and Humanities Capstone Seminar, an investigation into the impact of technology on such disciplines as biology, mathematics, communications, literature, philosophy, art, and music. For the Honors Capstone Seminar, students work on a term project with a personal faculty mentor, learning to seek out contacts and resources in the larger community. Projects are presented at a year-end Honors Symposium.

Founded in 1993, the Honors Program has grown from an initial 10 scholars to a current enrollment of 46.

Participation Requirements: Honors Scholars must complete at least 12 credits in honors courses. Of these credits, 3 must be in Honors Humanities Seminar III and 3 in Honors Capstone Seminar: Technology and Humanities. The remaining 6 credits must be taken in natural science and social science honors courses. Students must maintain a minimum 3.0 GPA in honors courses and a cumulative GPA of at least 3.25 in order to graduate as designated Honors Scholars.

Honors Affiliates, students who do not choose to complete the Honors Scholar program but who have demonstrated a high degree of academic achievement and creative ability, may enroll in one or more honors courses.

All successfully completed honors courses receive an (H) designation on official transcripts.

Admission Process: Entering students who wish to enroll as Honors Scholars must have achieved a high school cumulative GPA of 85 or better in college preparatory courses and SAT I scores of 1100 or better, with no score less than 500, or an ACT score of 25, with no subscore below 21. Additional consideration is given to the student's personal essay, personal interview, and record of demonstrated creativity, leadership, and service. Transfer students who have achieved at least a 3.0 GPA at their previous institutions may also enroll.

Scholarship Availability: Presidential Honors Scholarship, a $4000 tuition award, is an academic merit scholarship awarded to full-time first-year students who have met the Honors Program admission requirements. An interview is required. The application deadline is May 1. The award is renewable for the second year for students who have completed 30 credits at the conclusion of their first year and have maintained at least a 3.0 GPA.

The Campus Context: Established in 1957, Sage JCA is a private, two-year, coeducational college offering associate degrees in such fields as art, business, communications, humanities, legal studies, liberal arts, math and science, and health and human services. Nationally respected for its programs in fine arts, graphic design, interior design, and photography, Sage JCA has the distinction of being one of a few two-year private colleges accredited by the National Association of Schools of Art and Design (NASAD). Special programs offer opportunities for short-term study and travel in England, Italy, Puerto Rico, and Jamaica in the areas of art, literature, languages, and science. Geographically located in the area of Albany known as University Heights, the campus is the platform for innovative academic collaboration and resource sharing with other nearby institutions. Rolling lawns and mature trees enhance the charm of the traditional brick residence hall and classroom buildings. Settled within a friendly and well-maintained neighborhood, the campus is close to the Capitol and downtown theaters, museums, and shops.

Student Body Enrollment is 631, with 568 full-time and 63 part-time students. Of these, 65 percent are women. Commuters comprise 82 percent and residents 18 percent of the population.

Faculty Full-time faculty members number 36, adjuncts, 26. Fifty-six percent of the full-time faculty members have terminal degrees.

Key Facilities Students have access to the libraries on both campuses of The Sage Colleges. Combined library holdings are 357,573 bound volumes, 1,336 periodical subscriptions, 3,304 microform

Interpreting the symbols: **2**=two-year college, **4**=four-year college; **Pu**=public or state college, **Pr**=private college; **G**=general honors program; **D**=departmental honors program; **S**=small program (fewer than 100 students), **M**=midsize program (100 to 500 students), **L**=large program (more than 500 students); **Sc**=scholarships available in honors program; **Tr**=transfer students accepted into honors program; **HBC**=historically black college; **AA**=academic advisors; **GA**=graduate advisors; **FA**=fellowship advisors.

titles, thirty-six CD-ROM titles, and 12,680 audio-visual items. The Albany campus has 123 computers in eight computer labs and its own art gallery.

Athletics Sage JCA is a member of the National Junior Collegiate Athletic Association and offers competition in men's basketball and women's volleyball.

Support Services The Academic Support Center offers a full range of counseling and tutoring services as well as support for students with documented physical disabilities and learning disabilities.

Job Opportunities Experiential learning is central to the career development program at Sage JCA. Cooperative education and work experiences provide students with paid positions related to their field of study. Credit-bearing internships are also arranged. Alumni connections and linkages to the World Wide Web also provide current job access and information.

Tuition: 8580 per year full-time, $285 per credit hour, part-time (1999–2000)

Room and board: $5950

Mandatory Fees: $230 per year plus $100 technology fee for commuters, $300 for residents per year

Contact: Coordinator: Judy Waterman, 140 New Scotland Avenue, Albany, New York 12208; Telephone: 518-292-8608; Fax: 518-292-1910; E-mail: waterj@sage.edu

SAINT ANSELM COLLEGE

4 Pr G S Tr

▼ Honors Program

The Saint Anselm College Honors Program offers outstanding students a challenging and exciting blend of enhanced core courses, honors electives, independent research projects, thesis development, and enriched interaction with faculty members and fellow honors students. Grounded firmly in the belief that a truly liberal education combines breadth and depth, the Honors Program draws highly motivated students and faculty members from all disciplines to work closely together in intensive critical thinking, research, and cultural experiences. The Honors Program enables students to derive the most from their college education, deepen their mastery of the liberal arts, and distinguish themselves as they pursue graduate and professional schools and employment.

The Honors Program encourages students to shape their research and course selection around their interests. The College makes every effort to be flexible regarding study abroad, internships, and independent study requests. Honors classes are typically capped at 15 students. They tend to be interactive seminars, emphasizing individual initiative in research and reading.

As part of their honors experience, students enjoy social and cultural events, such as the yearlong series of honors suppers with faculty members, trips to theaters and museums in nearby Boston, and film discussions with faculty members. The Honors Student Advisory Council provides a forum for student planning and communication and the Honors Room is a place to congregate, study, and meet with faculty members.

Founded in 1995, the program involves an average of 90 students

Participation Requirements: Requirements for the Honors Program include enhanced core courses, honors electives, advanced foreign language/literature, and an honors thesis. Students take four semesters of honors humanities courses during their freshman and sophomore years, honors ethics, and two additional honors core courses selected from theology, philosophy, and English. Two semesters of advanced-level foreign language or literature and four honors electives complete the curricular requirements. Students may substitute an honors contract for one of the honors electives. All Honors Program participants write an honors thesis under the direction of a faculty adviser. The language requirement often serves as the basis for a language certificate; the requirement can be fulfilled abroad or through independent study. Students choose to follow one of three honors tracks: arts and sciences, social sciences, or nursing. Students who complete the program receive an Honors Bachelor of Arts degree or an Honors Bachelor of Science in Nursing.

Admission Process: Admission to the Honors Program is obtained either by invitation or by application. Invitations to participate in the Honors Program are sent to incoming students whose high school records and SAT I or ACT scores demonstrate superior academic ability. Highly motivated students who have demonstrated academic success may also apply to the Honors Program. Application is made to the Director of the Honors Program. Admission to the College is rolling, with an early decision deadline of December 1.

Students must maintain a GPA of 3.0 (B) or better to remain in the program.

Scholarship Availability: Saint Anselm College offers a merit aid program, awarding Presidential Scholarships on the basis of a student's high school record and ACT or SAT scores. All Presidential Scholars are invited to join the Honors Program, although no financial aid is attached to the program itself.

The Campus Context: Founded in 1889, Saint Anselm College is a four-year Catholic, coeducational liberal arts college in the Benedictine tradition. Centrally located in southern New Hampshire's largest city, an hour from the Atlantic coastline, Boston, Massachusetts, and the White Mountain National Forest, the College occupies a wooded campus of more than 400 acres.

Distinctive features of the campus include the Abbey church; Dana Humanities Center, which houses the Koonz Theater; Goulet Science Center; the Chapel Arts Center; and the New Hampshire Institute of Politics at Saint Anselm College, which has received nearly $10 million dollars of federal funding for renovation and programming within the past two years.

Saint Anselm College offers 28 majors, including nursing and a cooperative engineering program, and 11 certificate programs. The heart of the core curriculum is the two-year humanities program, Portraits of Human Greatness, which includes a full roster of cultural events to complement the multidisciplinary course. Support for academic programming includes two student computing centers, an academic resource center, and a visual resource study center.

More than sixty clubs and student organizations offer a wide variety of activities. Some of the major activities are the Abbey Players (theater), the Saint Anselm Chorus, the Thomas More Debate Society, the *Saint Anselm Crier* (student newspaper) and the Saint Anselm Jazz Band. The Center for Volunteers involves students in a range of community service opportunities in the greater Manchester area, serving the homeless, the elderly, and children. Campus Ministry offers Urban Immersion and Spring Break Alternative programs in a variety of locations and countries.

Student Body The College enrolls approximately 1,900 students representing twenty-seven states and sixteen other countries. Approximately 88 percent of the students live on campus in college-owned or affiliated housing.

Faculty Of the 122 full-time faculty members, 116 hold Ph.D. or the highest degree in their discipline. The faculty-student ratio is 1:14.

Honor Societies Delta Epsilon Sigma, Delta Sigma Rho, Pi Gamma Mu, Phi Alpha Theta, Omicron Delta Epsilon, Sigma Theta Tau, Sigma Delta Pi, Pi Delta Phi, Psi Chi, Pi Sigma Alpha, Beta Beta, Beta

Key Facilities The Geisel Library houses more than 215,000 bound volumes and maintains a collection of 4,000 periodical titles,

8,000 audiovisual units, and more than 65,000 microforms. All academic and residential facilities are linked to high-speed access to the Internet.

Athletics Nineteen men's and women's intercollegiate athletic teams compete and the Division II level in the Northeast 10 Conference. Facilities include fields for baseball, football, lacrosse, and soccer, as well as the Carr Activities Center and Stoutenburgh Gymnasium. Intramural activities include basketball, hockey, women's field hockey, cross-country skiing, tennis, soccer, softball, volleyball, and others.

Study Abroad Study-abroad opportunities include semester or yearlong programs in England, Scotland, Ireland, France, Germany, Spain, Italy, and Australia.

Job Opportunities A wide array of work opportunities are available both in Manchester and on campus through work-study and student payroll. The Office of Career and Employment Services assists students as they approach graduation.

Tuition: $19,460 (2001–02)

Room and Board: $7350

Mandatory Fees: $665 for first-year students and $520 for other undergraduates.

Contact: Director: Dr. Denise T. Askin, Saint Anselm College, P.O. Box 1725, Manchester, New Hampshire, 03102-1310; Telephone: 603-641-7092; E-mail: daskin@anselm.edu; Web site: http://www.anselm.edu/academics/

St. Cloud State University

4 Pu G L Sc Tr

▼ University Honors Program

The St. Cloud State University Honors Program is a unique alternative to the University's general education program. Established more than thirty years ago, the program has a feeling of community fostered among the students that is part of what makes the program so successful. The program begins by accepting about 120 students each year. These diverse students from a variety of backgrounds are pursuing a wide range of academic interests. These students are active participants in small classes of fewer than 25 students. Most classes are topical, so new course titles are offered every semester and seldom repeated unless popularity necessitates offering it more than once. There are currently 460 students enrolled in the program.

The Honors Program also offers an honors residence hall to further create an atmosphere of community. W. W. Holes Hall is generally reserved for incoming freshmen and offers traditional residence hall living for men and women.

In addition, the opportunity to become involved in the Honors Club allows the students to have a direct voice in how the program is run and any changes that are made. A student committee reviews applications and selects new, incoming students. They also select course topics and recruit the professors to teach those classes. Committees meet to discuss any changes in the program. The students also have the opportunity to represent the program at the regional and national conventions. In addition, students become actively involved with each other while enjoying a multitude of social events and by volunteering in the community.

Honors students don't just limit themselves to the honors community, though; they become leaders in all of their disciplines and actively participate in a multitude of clubs, programs, and organizations. Many of the Excellence in Leadership awards given out across campus annually are given to honors students, even though honors students make up only 3 percent of the seniors on campus.

In addition to the unique variety of innovative courses, there are many benefits from being in the program. Honors students are given priority registration, beginning with the first semester of their second year. Students are given honors class listings in advance, making it easier to plan their schedules. They also have the opportunity to take advantage of the many international studies programs that St. Cloud State offers, and they have the special opportunity to study at Oxford University in England. At graduation, students are given honors distinction on their transcript.

Participation Requirements: Students must complete 36–39 semester credits of honors courses to fulfill their general education requirements. The required core includes three interdisciplinary courses, English composition and literature, two mathematics and natural science courses, and a speech course. The remaining credits are elective credits from honors courses. Also required is 1 year of a foreign language. New topics are offered each semester, and students can take the ones that interest them most. Students must maintain an overall GPA of 3.25 to graduate with Honors Program distinction.

Admission Process: Students can apply at the end of the junior year in high school in order to ensure admission to the honors program in their freshman year of college. High school students living near SCSU or staying in a residence hall can take honors courses in the Post-Secondary Enrollment Options (PSEOA) program in order to experience honors prior to college enrollment.

Applying to honors and applying to the University are separate processes. Students must submit ACT scores in order to be admitted to the University. Honors applications are reviewed weekly or biweekly. The University accepts some credits from general education, transfer, and AP, CLEP, and IB tests.

Scholarship Availability: Honors students are eligible for many general University freshman scholarships. Their Honors Program application doubles as their scholarship application simply by checking a box on the program application. This saves time and paperwork.

The Campus Context: St. Cloud State University has been in existence for more than 125 years. The University was founded originally as a teaching school, and superior education has been its priority in all disciplines ever since. St. Cloud State University is composed of five colleges: the College of Social Science, the College of Fine Arts and Humanities, the College of Business, the College of Education, and the College of Science and Technology. A total of 130 degree programs are offered on campus.

Student Body Undergraduate enrollment is approximately 14,000; graduate enrollment is approximately 1,200. Women make up 54 percent of the enrollment, and men 46 percent. Of the total population, about 91 percent are Minnesota residents. Approximately 1,000 international students attend full-time.

Faculty Of the 739 faculty members, 76 percent have terminal degrees. The student-faculty ratio is 22:1.

Key Facilities A new state-of-the-art Learning Resource Center houses 704,922 volumes in print, with more than 2 million print and nonprint items (film, microfiche, audiovisual, etc.). All computer labs on campus offer students a wide variety of computer programs with both Macintosh and IBM computers. "The Beehive" offers flexible hours, allowing students to work until 1 a.m. on school nights. Internet, e-mail, and World Wide Web access is available from all computers and dormitory rooms.

Honorary Societies Lambda Sigma, Tau Kappa, Phi Kappa Phi

Interpreting the symbols: **2**=two-year college, **4**=four-year college; **Pu**=public or state college, **Pr**=private college; **G**=general honors program; **D**=departmental honors program; **S**=small program (fewer than 100 students), **M**=midsize program (100 to 500 students), **L**=large program (more than 500 students); **Sc**=scholarships available in honors program; **Tr**=transfer students accepted into honors program; **HBC**=historically black college; **AA**=academic advisors; **GA**=graduate advisors; **FA**=fellowship advisors.

Athletics St. Cloud University participates in eighteen sports for men and women, all NCAA Division II, except hockey, which is Division I.

Study Abroad St. Cloud State encourages students to enhance their education by taking advantage of one of the many study-abroad programs offered through the University. Aside from airfare cost, these overseas programs are usually offered at the same cost of tuition as St. Cloud State. During their time abroad, students have the opportunity to live and study in another culture while completing many of their honors and major requirements.

Students are also given ample time for independent travel and exploration. One of the most popular destinations is St. Cloud State's campus in Anwick, England, where students live and study in the Duke of Northumberland's castle. Other campuses include those in China, Costa Rica, France, Germany, and the Czech Republic. Honors students have the special opportunity of studying abroad at Oxford University in England.

Support Services The Office of Student Disability Services offers a wide range of assistance, including priority registration, sign language and oral interpretation, note taking, alternative testing, and referrals to support services.

Job Opportunities Work-study is available in most of the offices and departments on campus for the many students who qualify for financial aid. In addition, non-work-study positions on campus can be acquired by many students who do not qualify for financial aid.

Tuition: $3290 for state residents, $6632 for nonresidents per year, including fees (2001–02)

Room and Board: $3445

Contact: Director: Dr. Beverly Stadum, 229 Centennial Hall, St. Cloud State University, 720 Fourth Avenue, South, St. Cloud, Minnesota 56301; Telephone: 320-255-4945; E-mail: honorprg@stcloudstate.edu; Web site: http://stcloudstate.edu/~honors

Saint Francis University

4 Pr G S Tr AA

▼ Honors Program

The Saint Francis University (SFU) Honors Program is designed to challenge highly motivated students. It offers innovative course work, extensive faculty-student interaction, individualized honors advising, and additional opportunities for tutorial and independent study. The Honors Program curriculum affords many choices so that honors students may design a personal program of study.

One clear differentiation between this program and virtually all others is the Semester of Service. All SFU Honors Program students are required to undertake a service project to benefit specifically the University or the local community. The reason for requiring the service semester is simple: the truly well-educated student shares his or her talents. The Semester of Service project reflects the Franciscan ideal of concern for others above self and the Honors Program's commitment to that ideal. Founded in 1984, the program currently enrolls 80 students.

Participation Requirements: All courses completed for honors credit are duly designated on the student's transcript. Those who complete all honors curricular requirements and who have achieved at least a 3.25 cumulative GPA receive the Honors Program diploma—a large, hand-lettered parchment diploma presented in traditional rolled fashion at commencement. Honors Program graduates receive special velvet diploma bags during the annual awards convocation hosted by the President. The notation "Honors Program Graduate" appears on the transcript and in the commencement program.

Admission Process: Enrollment is by application. Applicants must place within the first quintile of their high school graduating class with at least a 3.25 GPA and SAT I scores of 1100 or above with emphasis on the verbal score. An interview with a member of the Honors Program Committee is not required but highly recommended. The deadline for application is March 1.

Scholarship Availability: Although there are no scholarships tied directly to the Honors Program, because eligibility guidelines are similar, all Honors Program members are scholarship recipients. Most scholarships awarded by the University are based on academic accomplishment, not on financial need. Some are based on service to the University or on other criteria determined by the donors.

The Campus Context: Saint Francis University is the oldest Franciscan university in the country. Located on 600 wooded acres, the mountaintop campus is a half hour from the cities of Altoona and Johnstown and less than a 2-hour drive from Pittsburgh.

In addition to twenty-six majors—seven in the health sciences—the University also offers a nationally recognized general education program designed to cultivate the knowledge, skills, and values that students will use and live by the rest of their lives. It includes interdisciplinary freshman seminars, linked courses, thematic minors and clusters, a convocation program, a special freshman advising program, senior capstones, service learning, a summer reading program for freshmen, and emphasis courses in values and ethics, multiculturalism and global awareness, communications, creative and critical thinking, and primary source materials.

The University is justly proud of its academic reputation. Students have won prestigious academic All-American honors, graduate fellowships, and numerous other national awards. The campus is also distinguished by the Southern Alleghenies Museum of Art, Dorothy Day Center for Social Justice, Center for Global Competitiveness, Center of Excellence for Remote and Medically Underserved Areas (CERMUSA), and Mount Assisi Monastery and Gardens.

Student Body The 1,250 undergraduates enrolled at Saint Francis come primarily from the Northeast. Approximately 85 percent of those who enroll receive financial aid. There are two national sororities, one local sorority, two national fraternities, one service sorority, and one service fraternity.

Faculty A 15:1 student-faculty ratio ensures personal attention from 80 full-time professors, nearly 75 percent of whom hold doctoral or terminal degrees.

Key Facilities Three fully equipped computer labs provide Internet and e-mail access for all students. A state-of-the-art electronic/multimedia classroom and a distance learning/teleconferencing studio provide interactive learning opportunities. Beginning in fall 2001, all new students entering SFU receive wireless laptop computers.

The Pasquerilla Library contains more than 170,000 volumes, more than 900 periodical subscriptions, and nearly 2,000 non-print materials. Facilities within the library include a typing room, seminar rooms, an electronic classroom, a microform area, and a computer lab that features ten workstations equipped with full campus network and Internet access.

Honorary Society Delta Epsilon Sigma

Athletics The University sponsors a twenty-one-sport NCAA Division I program for both men and women and a full student-directed intramural program for all students. The Maurice Stokes Athletics Center features an indoor swimming pool, racquetball courts, indoor tennis and volleyball courts, a suspended running track, a weight room, and a 3,500-seat basketball arena. Other facilities include a nine-hole golf course, outdoor tennis courts, and soccer and softball fields.

Study Abroad Study abroad is encouraged for all honors students. A semester (or more) of study abroad may substitute for a required upper-level honors colloquium. The University is a member of the Cooperative Center for Study Abroad (CCSA). All of the credits earned through CCSA are Saint Francis University credits and do not have to be transferred. In past CCSA programs, Honors Program students have studied at Oxford University, the University of Heidelberg, the University of Cork, and Richmond College in London.

Support Services For students with learning disabilities, the University offers many opportunities for assistance, including tutoring and academic advisement.

Job Opportunities Both internships and work-study are available for qualified students.

Tuition: $16,512 per year (2001–02)

Room and Board: $6974

Contact: Director: Donna M. Menis, 117 Evergreen, Loretto, Pennsylvania 15940; Telephone: 814-472-3065; Fax: 814-472-3937; E-mail: dmenis@francis.edu; Web site: http://www.francis.edu

SAINT JOSEPH COLLEGE

4 Pr G S Tr AA

▼ Honors Program

The Honors Program at Saint Joseph College offers highly motivated students the opportunity to excel in a challenging academic environment. Students join a community of learners in a sequence of stimulating classes and independent studies that culminate in a capstone team-taught interdisciplinary seminar. They participate in honors courses drawn from a wide array of academic disciplines, as well as broadening their intellectual and cultural horizons through diverse extracurricular activities. Trips to major museums in Boston and New York City are often planned in conjunction with academic topics. The program also provides low-cost tickets that encourage students to sample the rich cultural opportunities of nearby Hartford (e.g., theater at the Hartford Stage Company and intellectual conversations at the Connecticut Forum). The interdisciplinary honors curriculum draws from outstanding faculty members who work closely with students to develop fully their individual talents. In a program that promotes self-reliance and initiative, students work with a faculty mentor to explore an area of academic interest through an in-depth independent study project. Honors students present these projects at the College's annual Undergraduate Research Symposium, as well as at regional and national conferences.

Participation Requirements: Honors students complete four honors classes designed to help them meet their general education and liberal arts requirements. These courses include Introduction to Astronomy: Astrophysics and Cosmology; fine arts electives such as Art of Egypt: Ancient to Coptic, History of Greek Art, and French and American Impressionism; Honors Problems of Philosophy; Human Heredity and Birth Defects; Systems Thinking; and Honors Thematic Approaches to Literature. During their junior year, honors students work with a faculty mentor on an independent study or service-learning course. As their capstone honors experience, seniors participate in a team-taught, interdisciplinary course. Topics include Writing Women's Lives: The Construction of Self; Political Psychology; and Native American Literature and History.

Honors students are expected to maintain a minimum 3.25 GPA, complete the honors course sequence, and participate in the intracurricular and extracurricular enrichment opportunities. Students completing the honors sequence graduate with "In Honors" on their transcript.

Admission Process: Incoming first-year students with strong SAT scores (minimum combined scores of 1100) and excellent high school records are identified by the College's Admissions Office. Students meeting honors criteria are invited into the program by the Honors Director. The Director and an honors student worker provide additional information about the program upon request.

Transfer students with GPA scores of 3.5 and outstanding Saint Joseph College student identified by advisers or faculty members may also be nominated for the program. Interested students write a letter of interest and are interviewed by the Honors Director and a member of the Honors Council.

Scholarship Availability: The College provides numerous merit scholarships. A majority of the incoming honors students benefit from these awards. The program provides stipends to students participating in regional or national academic conferences.

The Campus Context: For more than sixty years, Saint Joseph College, a four-year private institution, has been combining excellence in liberal arts with professional education. Founded in 1932 by the Sisters of Mercy, the original women's college has expanded to include a coeducational graduate school and a weekend/evening college for men and women. It is accredited by the New England Association of Schools and Colleges. Saint Joseph College is a community that promotes the growth of the whole person in a caring environment that encourages strong ethical values, personal integrity, and a sense of responsibility to the needs of society. The College offers thirty-four majors as well as teaching certification in early childhood education, elementary education, middle school education, secondary education, and special education. Small classes and close faculty-student relationships ensure individual attention and mentoring.

The College is located in suburban West Hartford, within easy access of its consortium schools, Trinity College and the University of Hartford, as well as Hartford's arts and entertainment district. Nearby attractions include the Meadows Music Theatre, which features indoor and outdoor concerts; the Wadsworth Atheneum, the oldest public art gallery in the United States; and the Bushnell Memorial, which frequently features touring Broadway shows.

The College has thirteen Georgian brick buildings arranged around two tree-lined quadrangles on an 84-acre campus. Recently, the College constructed the new Carol Autorino Center for the Arts and Humanities, which includes an art gallery, a bistro, practice rooms, and an auditorium.

Saint Joseph College alumni have had considerable impact on the welfare of their communities. They are leaders in many fields, including aerospace research, business, medicine, education, social work, environmental science, law, and politics.

Student Body There are 1,185 undergraduates in the Women's College. The combined graduate and undergraduate colleges have a total of 1,740 full-time students.

Faculty The College employs 74 full-time faculty members and 4 librarians. Of the total faculty members, 75 percent are women. Currently, 85 percent have a doctorate or terminal degree in their field. There is a 1:11 faculty-student ratio.

Key Facilities Pope Pius XII Library has a collection of more than 134,000 volumes including computer databases, periodicals, microfilms, and audiovisuals; OPAC, and a Web site. Access to many databases and full-text articles was recently significantly expanded with the connection to I-CONN.

Athletics In the decade since the constuction of a state-of-the-art athletics center, the College has become competitive in seven NCAA Division III sports: basketball, cross-country, softball, soccer, swimming, diving, tennis, and volleyball. The athletics center features a six-lane pool, gymnasium, suspended jogging track, dance studio, and fitness center.

Interpreting the symbols: **2**=two-year college, **4**=four-year college; **Pu**=public or state college, **Pr**=private college; **G**=general honors program; **D**=departmental honors program; **S**=small program (fewer than 100 students), **M**=midsize program (100 to 500 students), **L**=large program (more than 500 students); **Sc**=scholarships available in honors program; **Tr**=transfer students accepted into honors program; **HBC**=historically black college; **AA**=academic advisors; **GA**=graduate advisors; **FA**=fellowship advisors.

Study Abroad The Office of International Studies and the Director of International Studies work closely with students interested in study abroad. Experiences are tailored to individual interests and can be pursued through summer or semester programs in a wide variety of countries. Cultural exchange programs with institutions in Japan, England, and Denmark are also available. Periodically, the program offers a summer-service experience in Guatemala.

Support Services An Americans with Disabilities Act (ADA) director is available to work with handicapped and learning-disabled students. The director works with the students and faculty members to develop appropriate accomodations.

Job Opportunities The College has numerous work-study opportunities for eligible students. Most majors encourage field-study placements as an integral part of the program. Students can also take advantage of a variety of internship opportunities coordinated by the Office of Career Services.

Saint Joseph College students may take consortium classes at nearby Trinity College and the University of Hartford. They may also take language or women's studies classes at the University of Connecticut, Central Connecticut State College, and the Hartford College for Women.

Tuition: Tuition and mandatory fees for first-year students entering in 2001 were $16,930. Part-time enrollment costs were billed at $435 per credit hour.

Room and Board: Annual room and board costs for 2001 were $7140.

Contact: Dr. Elizabeth C. Vozzola, Honors Director, Saint Joseph College, 1678 Asylum Avenue, West Hartford, Connecticut 06117; Telephone: 860-231-5545 or 860-231-5409 (Honors Lounge); E-mail: evozzola@sjc.edu

SAINT JOSEPH'S COLLEGE

4 Pr G S Tr

▼ Honors Program

The Saint Joseph's College Honors Program is a four-year core curriculum for students of high academic achievement. The arts and sciences are integrated in a specially tailored curriculum that includes in-depth research in primary materials, writing-intensive courses, continued interaction among students and faculty members, and ongoing opportunities for students to discover and express their unique talents. Through their courses, extracurricular activities, and a range of enrichment opportunities, Honors Program students encounter exciting challenges and grow intellectually, aesthetically, and spiritually while at the same time earning a major and preparing for graduate school or a profession. Students also may participate in service-learning activities in the surrounding community. A semester abroad, preferably in the junior year, is strongly encouraged for honors students. The curriculum builds beyond the classroom in other ways, as well, leading students to explore the roles of the arts and sciences in the world. During the senior year, honors students share with the College community examples of their creative expression. The curriculum concludes with a capstone course in which students prepare individual growth plans for the future, outlining how they plan to make the arts and sciences part of their lifelong learning experiences and how they may incorporate the arts and sciences into their careers.

The Honors Program is open to students regardless of major. Students from the various arts and sciences as well as students majoring in the professional arts share the same honors curriculum. Classes are small, usually no larger than 20 students, to maximize interaction through discussion and ensure that faculty members and students come to know each other well.

The Honors Program has been created to help fulfill the Mission of the College, especially by fostering a strong academic community in which honors students develop the full range of their talents and learn to work together for the mutual benefit of each other and for a better world.

The program was implemented in 1998 with incoming freshmen. Approximately 20 freshmen will be admitted to the Honors Program each year, so the program will include about 80 students when fully implemented.

Participation Requirements: Students take Honors Humanities I and II during the freshman year. The curriculum continues in the sophomore year with two additional courses, Scientific Inquiry (combining the sciences, mathematics, and philosophy) and Social Inquiry (integrating the social sciences). Later courses include a research project, a creative-expression project, and a capstone course in which students plan future experiences in the arts and sciences. Students are encouraged to study abroad during one of the junior semesters. The total honors curriculum consists of 30 credits.

Successful completion of the Honors Program is recognized at commencement and on official transcripts.

Admission Process: High school students are admitted to the Honors Program based on SAT I scores, high school GPA, class rank, student essay, recommendations, extracurricular activities, and a thorough review of past academic accomplishments. Admission is on a rolling basis until all honors slots are filled.

Scholarship Availability: College scholarships are awarded through the Office of Admissions in cooperation with the Office of Financial Aid, but the Honors Program does not offer separate scholarships.

The Campus Context: Saint Joseph's College of Maine, the only Catholic college in Maine, offers a liberal arts education to men and women of all ages and faiths. Founded in 1912 and sponsored by the Sisters of Mercy, the College's mission focuses on the intellectual, spiritual, and social growth of its students within a values-centered environment. Special emphasis on internships and career-oriented majors, such as communications and nursing, complement the traditional curriculum.

The sustained growth in student population has led to the opening of a new residence hall, Carmel Hall, which houses 90 students. The Harold Alfond Student Center is scheduled for completion in summer 1999. It will house a swimming pool, basketball courts, an elevated jogging track, a rock climbing wall, weight rooms, and a dance/aerobics studio. Future construction plans include a new academic building.

The 331-acre campus is located on the shore of Sebago Lake and offers students a rural setting 3 miles from the town of Windham, 16 miles from Portland, and 125 miles from Boston. The Sebago Lake region, one of Maine's most beautiful spots, is also well known as one of the state's premier four-season recreational areas. The Greater Portland community has many cultural, artistic, social, and recreational facilities and events. Portland is served by six airlines and two major bus companies.

Student Body Full-time undergraduate enrollment averages 750 students annually. Overall student enrollment in the traditional undergraduate program numbers 1,300. Sixty percent of the students are women. The geographical distribution shows twelve states and three countries represented, with most students coming from the Northeast. More than 75 percent of full-time students live on campus. As a small school, Saint Joseph's College of Maine looks to its students to take an active role in campus leadership. Opportunities to get involved in student government, athletics, cultural, and social organizations are numerous.

Faculty The faculty is an outstanding group of professional educators; 95 percent have an earned doctorate or another appropriate terminal degree. The student-faculty ratio is 16:1.

Key Facilities The Margaret H. Heffernan Center (1983) complements the distinguished original estate buildings and the other campus facilities that were added when the College moved to its present location in 1956. The library/learning center is located in the Heffernan Center. Mercy Hall, the main academic building, houses the computer center. All student residence hall rooms are networked to accommodate e-mail and Internet access.

Honorary Societies Delta Epsilon Sigma

Athletics Intercollegiate athletic competition for both men and women is actively sponsored by the College. Teams compete in baseball, basketball, cross-country, field hockey, golf, soccer, softball, and volleyball. Recreational facilities include tennis courts, a multipurpose gymnasium with an addition for dance and weight lifting, a private sandy beach on Sebago Lake, a skating pond, and cross-country running and ski trails as well as the new Alfond Center.

Study Abroad For students who seek an international program, the College participates in both ISEP, the International Student Exchange Program, through the local area consortium, and the Nova Scotia Exchange Program. With ISEP, students may study for up to one year in one of fifty countries worldwide. As part of the Nova Scotia Exchange Program, students may select one of several universities located in the Canadian maritime province.

Job Opportunities Saint Joseph's participates in the Federal Work-Study program.

Tuition: $13,240 (1999–2000)

Room and board: $5950

Mandatory Fees: $495

Contact: Director: Dr. Edward J. Rielly, 278 Whites Bridge Road, Standish, Maine 04084-5263; Telephone: 207-893-7930; Fax: 207-893-7866; E-mail: erielly@sjcme.edu

SAINT JOSEPH'S UNIVERSITY

4 Pr G M Sc Tr

▼ Honors Program

The Saint Joseph's University (SJU) Honors Program seeks to produce well-educated, articulate citizens who exemplify the highest standards of academic, professional, and personal achievement. It offers an enriched general education curriculum that broadens cultural interests, integrates knowledge, sharpens writing skills, and encourages student involvement in the learning process.

The curriculum is composed of intellectually rigorous courses that satisfy both general education and major requirements. The honors core consists of a group of yearlong, interdisciplinary, team-taught courses in arts, sciences, and business that appear in a regular cycle. These sequence courses are complemented by one-semester courses in a wide range of disciplines at various levels of entry.

There are distinctive benefits attached to belonging to the Saint Joseph's Honors Program. Team-taught courses allow distinguished faculty members to share their knowledge and expertise with students in a challenging academic environment. Individual honors courses stress a detailed and thoroughly scholarly exploration of different fields of knowledge. The student-faculty ratio in the Honors Program is 10:1. Honors students register ahead of other students.

Honors suites in the residence halls allow like-minded students to live together, even as freshmen. Honors students are provided with free tickets and transportation to concerts and performances by world-renowned institutions such as the Arden Theater Company, the Curtis Institute of Music, the Philadelphia Orchestra, the Pennsylvania Ballet, the Academy of Vocal Arts, the Philadelphia Museum of Art, and the Franklin Science Institute. Receptions, concerts, and lectures are regularly sponsored by the Honors Program for honors students.

Student peer mentors report to the program directors about social activities, class work, registration, and other student concerns. Students have access to Claver House, a quiet retreat where honors students can study, work with personal computers, and attend receptions. Students have opportunities to present research and creative work at national conferences and seminars; they are also kept informed about scholarship and funding opportunities for graduate and professional work.

Participation Requirements: Students may enroll in General Honors, which is awarded upon successful completion of eight honors courses. Because all honors courses fulfill other curricular requirements of the University, the Honors Program imposes no courses over and above those required of non-honors students. Students are required to maintain a cumulative average of 3.5 or better in order to graduate with the General Honors Certificate.

Students may also participate in Departmental Honors, which is awarded upon successful completion of the general curriculum and a two-semester research project in their senior year. Students of exceptional caliber may apply for the University Scholar designation. Those who qualify are freed from four to ten of their senior-year course requirements in order to complete an independent project of unusual breadth, depth, and originality.

General Honors Certificate is noted on the student's permanent record and is awarded upon successful completion of General Honors. An Honors Degree, noted on the permanent record and acknowledged on a distinctive diploma, is awarded to students who have completed General Honors and the Departmental Honors project. University Honors, noted on the permanent record and acknowledged on a distinctive diploma, is awarded to students who have completed General Honors and the University Scholar research project.

Admission Process: Incoming students are invited into the Honors Program if their SAT I combined score is above 1350 and they have a high school grade average of at least 3.75. Freshmen who achieve a GPA of 3.5 or better in their first semester at SJU are also invited to join the Honors Program.

Scholarship Availability: Each year, Saint Joseph's University awards merit-based scholarships to freshman candidates who have outstanding academic and achievement records. Students are selected by a scholarship committee. A formal application is not required for merit-based scholarships; however, for any additional assistance, candidates must apply. Instructions are given in detail at the time of the candidate's application. Students who are awarded these scholarships are automatically invited to join the Honors Program. Board of Trustees' Scholarships are awarded to freshman recipients who have superior academic records. Candidates typically rank at or near the top of their high school class, have an "A" GPA, and SAT I scores in the 1400 and above range. These scholars must maintain a 3.2 GPA in order to retain their scholarship each year.

Presidential Scholarships are awarded to candidates who achieve significant results in their high school class and have SAT I scores of 1300 and above. The value of this scholarship ranges from one-half to three-quarter tuition. These scholars must maintain a 3.2 GPA in order to retain their scholarship each year.

University Scholarships are awarded to incoming freshmen who rank in the top 10 percent of their high school graduating class and have SAT I scores in the 1200 and above range. The value of this scholarship ranges from one-fourth to one-half tuition.

The Campus Context: The University offers forty degree programs.

Interpreting the symbols: **2**=two-year college, **4**=four-year college; **Pu**=public or state college, **Pr**=private college; **G**=general honors program; **D**=departmental honors program; **S**=small program (fewer than 100 students), **M**=midsize program (100 to 500 students), **L**=large program (more than 500 students); **Sc**=scholarships available in honors program; **Tr**=transfer students accepted into honors program; **HBC**=historically black college; **AA**=academic advisors; **GA**=graduate advisors; **FA**=fellowship advisors.

Student Body Saint Joseph's University has a full-time undergraduate enrollment of 3,500: 45 percent men and 55 percent women. The ethnic distribution of students is 83 percent white, 9 percent black, 3 percent Hispanic, and 2 percent Asian/Pacific Islander. There are 83 international students. Fifty-four percent of the students are residents; the remaining 46 percent commute. Eighty-five percent of the students receive financial aid.

Faculty Saint Joseph's University has 194 full-time faculty members; 98 percent hold terminal degrees. The student-faculty ratio is 17:1.

Athletics Saint Joseph's University is a member of NCAA Division I in twenty varsity sports (ten men's, ten women's). In addition, there are more than thirty intramural sports and a variety of recreational and fitness programs.

Support Services In accordance with the Americans with Disabilities Act (ADA) guidelines, students with disabilities are ensured equal educational opportunities, counseling services, and access to facilities and programs.

Job Opportunities Saint Joseph's University participates in the Federal Work-Study program. Students may work up to 8 hours per week. The number of jobs is contingent upon government allocations.

Tuition: $21,700 minimum per year (2001–02)

Room and Board: $6450

Mandatory Fees: $300

Contact: Director: Dr. Sandra Fillebroun, 5600 City Avenue, Philadelphia, Pennsylvania 19103; Associate Director: Dr. David R. Sorensen, Telephone: 610-660-1795; E-mail: sfillebr@sju.edu or dsorense@sju.edu; Web site: http://www.sju.edu/honors

SAINT LEO UNIVERSITY

4 Pr G S Sc Tr

▼ Honors Program

The Saint Leo University Honors Program consists of an integrated sequence of six interdisciplinary courses that are spread over the first three years of college. In addition, there is an extensive senior-year honors project that is carried out under the supervision of a distinguished faculty mentor.

Honors courses focus on the reading, interpretation, and assimilation of great books in the liberal arts and sciences. Informed absorption of great ideas, rather than mere acquaintance with them, is the goal of the program. The Honors Program does not seek to provide a comprehensive treatment of world intellectual achievement or to undertake a survey of Western civilization. Its purpose is to probe in depth the original minds of a few significant thinkers, doers, and dreamers.

Honors courses are small in size and emphasize responsive writing, discussion, and collaborative learning. Each course has its own theme or focus supplied by the instructor, but the entire sequence of honors courses is carefully integrated so that knowledge obtained in one course applies directly to the next one. The Honors Program strives to reinforce the notion that a liberal arts education furnishes a coherent body of knowledge that serves the whole human being.

The Honors Program provides an alternative means of satisfying the general education requirements that all Saint Leo University students must fulfill. Students are therefore encouraged to apply regardless of their major. In the Honors Program, students representing a wide variety of intellectual perspectives meet on common ground, frequently debating controversial subjects and exploring personal concerns and interests.

The Honors Program, which has been in existence since 1982, admits 40 to 50 freshmen each year. There are approximately 100 students enrolled in the program.

All freshmen honors students are provided with free state-of-the-art computers and high-speed access to the Internet. Each honors class uses a Web site to supplement classroom learning and every student is expected to maintain a personal Web site as an academic portfolio. Students are frequently involved in activities that explore the boundaries of computer-enhanced learning.

Participation Requirements: In the freshman year, students take The Classical World View and The Christian Vision. The two freshmen English composition courses are linked to these core courses, so that learning and assignments are frequently shared. In the sophomore year, students take The Humanistic Tradition, which covers the period from the Renaissance to the Enlightenment and scientific revolutions. In the junior year, students take The Human Condition, which details the founding of the social sciences in the eighteenth and nineteenth centuries, and The Modern World View. Junior-year courses are taught in the Oxbridge tutorial style of small groups working quasi-independently. In the spring of the junior year, students take a 1-credit Honors Research Methods course to assist them in developing their senior-year honors project. During the entire senior year, students work independently on a research or creative project of their choice under the supervision of a faculty member. Seniors present the results of their projects in an evening forum open to the University community.

Students arriving from junior college honors programs may elect to join the Saint Leo University Honors Program in its third year. Students wishing to study abroad at the Saint Leo University Madrid campus may substitute a directed study abroad course for either of the junior year core courses.

To graduate from the program, students must complete the honors core requirements (18 credit hours for freshmen, 6 credit hours for transfer students), the research methods course, and the senior research project, 4 credit hours. In addition, students must maintain a minimum 3.0 GPA and have not received less than a B in two honors courses.

Upon graduation from the program, honors students receive a medallion to be worn during graduation ceremonies and an Honors Program Graduate distinction on their transcripts and diplomas.

Admission Process: To be eligible for participation in the Honors Program, freshman students must have at least a 3.25 GPA with a score of 1100 on the SAT I or 24 on the ACT. Transfer students must have 60 to 75 credit hours with a minimum 3.5 GPA or a minimum 3.25 GPA if they have been involved in honors courses at their previous college. All students must also submit a letter of recommendation from a teacher or instructor as well as a letter to the honors program director stating why they wish to participate in the Honors Program and what they feel they will add to the program. All students wishing to participate in the Honors Program must first complete the standard admission process and be admitted to Saint Leo University before applying to the Honors Program.

Scholarship Availability: Academic scholarships are available for both freshmen and transfer students entering the Honors Program. Freshmen receive a $3000 annual, renewable scholarship and a Pentium computer, which is theirs to keep after completing 60 credit hours and two years in the Honors Program. Freshmen who complete the Honors Program with a GPA of at least 3.5 also receive tuition remission worth approximately $6000 for their final semester.

Transfer students entering the Honors Program are awarded either a $3000 or $4000 annual, renewable scholarship that depends on their cumulative college GPA, but do not receive a computer. A $4500 scholarship is awarded to transfer students who are members of the Phi Theta Kappa Honor Society.

The Campus Context: Saint Leo University is a four-year, private University affiliated with the Catholic Church. Saint Leo is committed to giving its students an education that prepares them for the future. The goal of Saint Leo University is to develop the whole person, both academically and personally, through the Catholic tradition. Located just 25 miles north of downtown Tampa, Florida, and 60 miles west of Orlando, the campus occupies 170 acres of rolling hills and wooded grounds. The rural setting is conducive to academic success, but it is located near enough to metropolitan areas to give students the advantage of a number of social and professional options, including access to internships.

Saint Leo University offers nearly forty traditional majors, preprofessional programs, specializations, and career-oriented studies. Degrees offered are the Bachelor of Arts, Bachelor of Science, Bachelor of Social Work, Master of Business Administration, and Master of Education. The School of Business offers majors in accounting, business administration, computer information systems, health-care administration, human resource administration, and sport management. There are specializations in management, marketing, hospitality and tourism, and international business. The School of Arts and Sciences offers majors in biology, English, environmental science, history, international studies, medical technology, political science, psychology, and religion. The School of Education and Social Services offers majors in criminology, elementary and secondary education, health services management, and social work. Preprofessional programs in dentistry, law, medicine, and veterinary science are also offered.

Student Body Saint Leo University has an enrollment of approximately 1,500 full- and part-time students on the main campus and 7,000 students in extension programs located on eleven military bases and six community colleges stretching from Virginia to Key West. The student body represents thirty-four states and twenty-seven countries: 60 percent of students are from Florida, 21 percent from the Northeast, 6 percent are from the Midwest, and 6 percent are international. Of the students at the main campus, approximately 500 live on campus.

Faculty There are a total of 117 faculty members, 42 full-time and 75 part-time. Most courses are taught by full-time faculty members. In some cases, part-time faculty specialists are employed to provide students with real-world experience in their classes. Seventy-eight percent of all full-time faculty members hold a doctorate. The student-faculty ratio is 15:1.

Honorary Societies Delta Nu and Phi Theta Kappa

Athletics Saint Leo competes in NCAA Division II sports for men in baseball, basketball, soccer, tennis, cross-country, and golf. Women compete in basketball, softball, tennis, volleyball, cross-country, and golf. Students can also participate in a variety of intramurals as well as sailing. On the campus there are lighted racquetball and tennis courts and football, soccer, baseball, and softball fields. A 154-acre lake with sailing facilities, a weight room, and outdoor Olympic-size swimming pool and two eighteen-hole golf courses adjacent to and immediately across from the campus provide numerous options for student recreation.

Study Abroad Special opportunities are available at Saint Leo University's Center for International Studies in Madrid, Spain. Students take liberal arts courses from full-time faculty members and live with specially selected families. Students are immersed in the Spanish culture; travel throughout Spain is a part of the curriculum. An academic semester or a summer program may be chosen. Saint Leo University also works closely with other institutions to provide additional study-abroad opportunities in Europe, Asia, Latin America, and Africa, including an agreement with John Cabot University in Rome, Italy, that offers special educational opportunities to Saint Leo University students. Institutional financial aid is available to be used for these study-abroad experiences.

Support Services The Office of ADA Student Support Services assists students with disabilities in achieving access to higher education and promotes their ongoing personal and educational success. The office provides reasonable accommodations to students with documented disabilities as well as tutoring to all students.

Job Opportunities Student employment opportunities are available on campus for all students who wish to work. Employment runs the gamut from working in University administrative offices to refereeing for intramural sports. Unpaid internships are also offered through many of the undergraduate programs.

Tuition: $11,450 per year (1999–2000)

Room and board: $5400–$6530

Mandatory Fees: $200 student activity fee and a one-time $200 orientation fee

Contact: Director: Dr. Hudson Reynolds, MC 2127, P.O. Box 6665, Saint Leo, Florida 33574-6665; Telephone: 352-588-8340; E-mail: reynolds@saintleo.edu; Web site: http://www.saintleo.edu/honors

---

St. Louis Community College at Florissant Valley

2 Pu M Sc

▼ Honors Program

The Honors Program at St. Louis Community College at Florissant Valley encourages students to work up to their capacity. This allows them to be recognized as achievers by both employers and educational institutions. This program has been serving honors students for more than eleven years. Honors credit gives students an edge in the job market and in scholarship awards. Honors students are often eligible to receive full and partial scholarships both at this college and transfer institutions. Florissant Valley is fully accredited by the North Central Association of Colleges and Universities. With few exceptions, honors courses are transferable to other colleges and universities.

The program emphasizes small classes and lively discussion in the classroom. Students are expected to complete honors-quality work and are given one-on-one attention from their honors instructors and the honors office staff. Upon successful completion of honors classes, students are given certificates of recognition. In addition to regular honors courses, selected seminars are also offered for honors credit. Each seminar focuses on a particular theme or topic. It has a limited enrollment and usually two faculty members or several guest speakers. It requires participation, close attention to detail, solid research, and a love of discussion. The atmosphere is exciting as students and faculty members learn from each other. The annual fall satellite seminar is taught in cooperation with the National Collegiate Honors Council and broadcast via satellite to more than sixty colleges nationally.

The Honors Program currently enrolls 100 students per semester.

Admission Process: In order to qualify, students must have a score of 1100 or above on the SAT I, a composite score of 25 on the ACT, scores on the Accuplacer that correlate with the above, graduate with a cumulative high school GPA of 3.5 or above on a 4.0 scale, or have completed at least 12 college credits in courses numbered 100 and above with a cumulative GPA of 3.5 on a 4.0 scale.

The Campus Context: St. Louis Community College at Florissant Valley awards the Associate in Arts, Associate in Applied Science, and General Transfer Study degrees as well as Certificates of

Interpreting the symbols: **2**=two-year college, **4**=four-year college; **Pu**=public or state college, **Pr**=private college; **G**=general honors program; **D**=departmental honors program; **S**=small program (fewer than 100 students), **M**=midsize program (100 to 500 students), **L**=large program (more than 500 students); **Sc**=scholarships available in honors program; **Tr**=transfer students accepted into honors program; **HBC**=historically black college; **AA**=academic advisors; **GA**=graduate advisors; **FA**=fellowship advisors.

Specialization and Certificates of Proficiency. One of the distinguished facilities on campus is the Child Development Center, a lab school for the child development program that serves students and other people in the community. This program also serves four-year colleges. State and national accreditation are expected within the year.

Student Body The College has an undergraduate enrollment of more than 7,000 students. The student body is diversified, consisting of 37 percent men and 63 percent women. Sixty percent are white, 31 percent are African American, and 9 percent are other nationalities, including American Indian, Asian, and Hispanic, among others. Eighty-nine percent of the students are local residents, and the remaining 11 percent are commuters. Twenty-eight percent of students receive financial aid. There is an active chapter of the Phi Theta Kappa honor society on campus that serves students, the campus, and the community in a variety of ways. Currently, there are 373 members.

Faculty With more than 385 part-time and 142 full-time faculty members, students benefit from a student-faculty ratio of 13:1. Terminal degrees for faculty members include twenty-three Ph.D.s, three Ed.D.s, and five M.F.A.s.

Key Facilities There are more than 87,000 volumes in the campus library. There are computer labs at five different locations on this campus.

Honorary Society Phi Theta Kappa

Athletics Florissant Valley offers more than forty-five activities through its physical education department. Professional (pre-teaching) courses and continuing education courses are also offered. The nine fitness/wellness-related courses, centering in the Fitness Center, are the most popular. An athletic scholarship fund benefits approximately 100 team members each year.

Study Abroad Throughout the year, various study-abroad opportunities are offered in several locations around the world, including Canterbury, England.

Support Services The College recognizes that some students have special needs and has an office that provides services for students with documented disabilities.

Job Opportunities Students often have the opportunity to work on this campus through the work-study program and other occasional jobs.

Tuition: $1344 for area residents, $1696 for state residents, $2144 for nonresidents, per year (2001–02)

Contact: Director: Mary Seager, 3400 Pershall Road, St. Louis, Missouri 63135; Telephone: 314-595-4461; Fax: 314-595-2143; Web site: http://www.stlcc.cc.mo.us/fv/honors

St. Mary's College of Maryland

4 Pu G S Sc Tr

▼ Scholars Program

The St. Mary's College of Maryland Scholars Program was created in 1998. The program is designed to provide exceptional opportunities for students who have demonstrated their commitment to the liberal arts and sciences through their outstanding academic success and their commitment to the improvement of society, especially through leadership and service roles. By combining academic excellence with a leadership and service orientation, the Scholars Program aims to develop in students an understanding of leadership and leaders, especially those individuals who can inspire others to subordinate narrow self-interest for a greater good.

Scholars Program participants are exempt from some of the requirements for the general education program. Instead, they complete an alternative curriculum that is designed as an enriching and challenging means of attaining a liberal arts education of high quality, combining academic rigor and scholarship with an understanding of the importance of leadership and service.

Students take interdisciplinary seminars and a tutorial that focus on the themes of leadership and service in the first two years of the program. In addition to the seminars, students must obtain advanced proficiency in two of three proficiency areas (writing, mathematics, and a foreign language) and complete a leadership/service portfolio. Moreover, in the senior year, each Scholars Program student completes an 8-credit original project, guided by a faculty mentor with expertise in the subject matter of the project.

In addition to the special curriculum and individualized attention from scholars administrators and faculty members, the Scholars Program also sponsors extracurricular events, both on and off campus, for Scholars students. These events frequently take advantage of the College's proximity to Washington, D.C., and Baltimore and the extraordinary cultural events that these cities offer.

Participation Requirements: Students are required to attain and maintain a minimum 3.5 cumulative GPA to be eligible for graduation with Latin honors. Furthermore, all required courses must be completed with a grade of C or better.

Admission Process: About half of the students in the Scholars Program are selected directly from high school based on their cumulative GPA, the rigor of their course work, their combined SAT I scores, an application essay, and special talents and activities related to leadership and service. The other half of the students in the program are selected after they have completed at least a semester of college work, either at St. Mary's or elsewhere. Most of those students join the program at the beginning of their sophomore year. Around 20 students join the program each year.

The Campus Context: St. Mary's College of Maryland is a state-supported, undergraduate, coeducational, residential college located in southern Maryland, 70 miles southeast of Washington, D.C., and 95 miles south of Baltimore, on beautiful Chesapeake Bay waters. The campus of 275 acres consists of rolling meadows, lawns, and woodland along the shores of the St. Mary's River. Founded in 1840 as a women's seminary, St. Mary's has evolved into a four-year institution that in 1991 was designated by the state of Maryland as its public honors college. It is described by many of the college guides as a public Ivy and a best buy. It offers twenty-one majors, including an independent, student-designed major.

Student Body There are approximately 1,600 students enrolled.

Faculty There are 113 full-time faculty members, 95 percent with doctorates or other terminal degrees, supplemented by more than 60 part-time faculty members. The student-faculty ratio is 13:1.

Key Facilities The library houses a collection of more than 190,000 items, including books, bound periodicals, microforms, and media, with extensive interlibrary loan and online services available. The College provides extensive computer services, including an open-access forty-eight-station computing facility in the library.

Honorary Societies Phi Beta Kappa

Athletics Athletics include fifteen intercollegiate sports, twelve club sports, and a diverse intramural athletic program. Sailing teams receive national rankings.

Study Abroad Many study-abroad options exist. In recent years, students have studied in Chile, China, Costa Rica, Czechoslovakia, Ecuador, England, France, Germany, Russia, Senegal, and Spain.

Tuition: $6100 for state residents, $10,800 for nonresidents, per year (1999–2000)

Room and Board: $5970

Mandatory Fees: $1075

Contact: Director: Dr. J. Roy Hopkins, Academic Services, St. Mary's City, Maryland 20686; Telephone: 301-862-0388; E-mail: jrhopkins@osprey.smcm.edu.

St. Mary's University of San Antonio

4 Pr G S Sc

▼ Honors Program

The St. Mary's University Honors Program is a special course of study designed to challenge academically gifted undergraduates. The program's curriculum ("the academic marathon") is a sequence of eight enriched courses, commencing with philosophy and culminating in a senior thesis in the student's major field. Honors courses normally meet general core curriculum requirements, and participation in the program is compatible with all majors.

In addition to the academic curriculum, the program offers a rich variety of social and cultural opportunities ranging from concerts and theater performances to campouts and community service projects. Through both curricular and cocurricular offerings, the program seeks to nurture the intellectual, moral, and cultural talents of the students as they prepare for lives of leadership and service to their communities. Successful completion of Honors Program requirements is announced at graduation and is indicated on the student's transcript. Graduates typically go on to pursue graduate and professional studies in medicine, law, and a host of other disciplines. Many graduates eventually go on to earn doctoral degrees.

Founded in 1985, the program currently serves more than 100 students.

Participation Requirements: Students must maintain a 3.25 (B+) to remain in the program.

Admission Process: Although admission is selective, the program actively seeks a community of students who are diverse in their backgrounds and interests. From among more than 100 students invited to apply each year, the program enrolls approximately 20–25. Students are normally recruited directly from high school and usually rank in the top 5 percent of their classes, with commensurate scores on their college admission exams (currently an average SAT I score of 1300 and an average ACT score of 29). Students may join the program in their sophomore year if they have earned a 3.8 or above GPA in their first year at St. Mary's.

Applications must be submitted by March 15.

Scholarship Availability: While there are no honors scholarships per se, students admitted to the program who remain in good standing are guaranteed not less than $12,500 per year in scholarship or grant support administered through the University. Students who would otherwise have received less than $12,500 are automatically raised to this level. Members are also guaranteed the option of a campus work-study position, either federal or institutional, if they desire it. Engineering majors may qualify for a fifth year of guaranteed support.

The Campus Context: St. Mary's University, founded in 1852 by Marianist brothers and priests, is the oldest university in San Antonio and the oldest and largest Catholic university in Texas and the Southwest. A historic and culturally diverse city of more than 1 million residents, San Antonio is an important gateway to Latin America and a major center of international trade and commerce. St. Mary's University encompasses three undergraduate schools offering more than forty degree programs, a graduate school, and a school of law.

Student Body The total enrollment exceeds 4,200 students, including 2,600 undergraduates. Undergraduate enrollment is 57 percent women. With respect to ethnic distribution, 63 percent of undergraduates identify themselves as Hispanic, 26 percent as Anglo, 3 percent as African American, 2 percent as Asian or Pacific Islander, and fewer than 1 percent as Native American. International students number 115. About 87 percent of undergraduates receive financial aid. More than 40 percent live on campus. More than seventy student organizations offer opportunities for campus involvement, including twenty-nine academic and professional organizations, five honors societies, four service organizations, nine social fraternities and sororities, and a variety of religious, political, cultural, and special interest organizations.

Faculty A faculty of more than 300 includes 176 full-time members. Nearly 90 percent of full-time faculty members hold the doctoral degree or its equivalent in their fields. The student-faculty ratio is 14:1.

Key Facilities Library resources include more than 200,000 books, more than 1,000 periodical titles, a media center, and a government documents depository containing more than 185,000 items. Computer facilities include four computer labs (academic library, biology, mathematics, and engineering) as well as tutoring computers in the Learning Assistance Center. Selected classrooms are enhanced with computer and multimedia facilities.

Honorary Society Delta Epsilon Sigma

Athletics In athletics, St. Mary's now competes in the NCAA Division II, having previously captured national championships in women's softball (NAIA) and men's basketball (NAIA) and baseball (NCAA). Men's and women's teams compete in ten varsity sports. In addition to its intramural programs, the University sponsors an active intramural program.

Study Abroad The University actively encourages study abroad, operating its own programs in London, Madrid, Innsbruck (Austria), Mexico, Chile, and Brazil.

Support Services Virtually all facilities on campus are accessible to disabled students.

Job Opportunities Work opportunities on campus include not only Federal Work-Study but also a special honors work-study option for those who qualify.

Tuition: $7,100 per semester (2001–02)

Room and board: $2768 per semester

Mandatory Fees: $300 per semester

Contact: Director: Dr. Daniel Rigney, Reinbolt 302/Box 47, One Camino Santa Maria, San Antonio, Texas 78228; Telephone: 210-436-3201; Fax: 210-436-3500; E-mail: drigney@stmarytx.edu

St. Philip's College

2 Pu G S Sc

▼ GIVE Honors Program

The St. Philip's College GIVE (Great Ideas, Visions and Experiences) Honors Program, open to students of all majors, offers challenging and rewarding opportunities for academically exceptional students. The program provides an exciting learning experience for students who like the challenge of small, discussion-based classes and who look forward to the stimulation of teacher-student interaction. Unlike traditional courses, which present material from a single field of study, Honors Program courses draw ideas and information from many fields,

Interpreting the symbols: **2**=two-year college, **4**=four-year college; **Pu**=public or state college, **Pr**=private college; **G**=general honors program; **D**=departmental honors program; **S**=small program (fewer than 100 students), **M**=midsize program (100 to 500 students), **L**=large program (more than 500 students); **Sc**=scholarships available in honors program; **Tr**=transfer students accepted into honors program; **HBC**=historically black college; **AA**=academic advisors; **GA**=graduate advisors; **FA**=fellowship advisors.

addressing concerns common to all disciplines and recognizing that there are no boundaries to thought and inquiry. Honors Program courses examine the historical and intellectual origins, the growth, and the development of today's issues, the connections among them, and their consequences for tomorrow. Throughout the courses, the Honors Colloquia are designed to refine skills in critical thinking, writing, and public speaking. Honors Program students are advised by the Honors Director and by faculty members in the student's major field of study. Students enjoy a close relationship with honors faculty members and with each other in a network of academic and personal support.

Honors Program students have access to all of the resources at St. Philip's College, San Antonio College, Palo Alto College, Northwest Vista College, and the University of Texas at San Antonio. While students enjoy the advantage of a small, challenging program, they have access to all the resources of four community colleges and a major university, including an internationally respected faculty, fully equipped computer labs, four libraries with well over a million holdings, and a wide range of student services.

Participation Requirements: Students in the GIVE Honors Program are required to take the same number of credits for graduation as every other St. Philip's College student. Honors Program students take the Interdisciplinary Honors Seminar [Humanities I & II (HUMA 1301 & HUMA 1302), Western Civilization I & II (HIST 2311 & HIST 2312), World Civilization I & II (HIST 2321 & HIST 2322), and Interdisciplinary Studies I & II (IDST 2372 & IDST 2373)] and courses in foreign language, lab science, English, and mathematics.

Admission Process: To apply for the Honors Program, students must first be enrolled at St. Philip's College and then apply to the GIVE Honors Program. The application process includes a formal application, two letters of reference from instructors, and a statement written by the student describing his or her interests, academic goals, and future plans. In addition, students must supply a certified copy of their college transcripts, showing a cumulative GPA of at least 3.3 (on a 4.0 scale) and proof that they passed (or are exempt from) the TASP (Texas Academic Skills Program) exam.

Scholarship Availability: Accepted students are awarded a full scholarship that pays all fees and tuition to St. Philip's College. They also receive a voucher for books and supplies for each semester that they are in the Honors Program.

The Campus Context: St. Philip's College is located on the east side of San Antonio, 2 miles from the center of town and easily accessible from all parts of San Antonio and its surrounding areas. St. Philip's College, founded in 1898, is a comprehensive, public community college whose mission is to provide a high-quality educational environment that stimulates leadership, personal growth, and a lifelong appreciation for learning. As a historically black college, St. Philip's College strives to be an important force in the community, responsive to the needs of a population rich in its ethnic, cultural, and socioeconomic diversity.

St. Philip's College seeks to create an environment fostering excellence in academic and technical achievement while expanding its commitment to opportunity and access. The College takes pride in its individual attention to students in a flexible and sensitive environment. As a dynamic and innovative institution, St. Philip's College values the role of creative and critical thought in preparing its students, campus, and community to meet the challenges of a rapidly changing world.

The College offers seventy-two associate majors, including liberal arts and sciences, business, and education.

Student Body Undergraduate enrollment is 8,000.

Faculty There are 206 full-time faculty members (supplemented by 260 adjunct faculty members), 30 percent with doctorates or other terminal degrees. The student-faculty ratio is 13:1.

Key Facilities The library houses 866,874 volumes. There are twenty computer labs located in the library and academic buildings.

Honorary Society Phi Theta Kappa

Job Opportunities Students are offered a wide range of work opportunities on campus, including assistantships and work-study.

Tuition: $732 for area residents, $1380 for state residents, $2760 for nonresidents, per year (1997–98)

Contact: Director: Dr. J. Paul De Vierville, 1801 Martin Luther King Drive, San Antonio, Texas 78235; Telephone: 210-531-3491; Fax: 210-531-4760; E-mail: jdevierv@accd.edu

SAINT XAVIER UNIVERSITY

4 Pr G S Sc Tr

▼ Undergraduate Honors Program

Saint Xavier University's Undergraduate Honors Program offers an enriched academic experience to talented and highly motivated students. The distinctive feature of the program is collaborative student and faculty member research and creative projects. The program is designed to nurture skills and habits of mind that enable students to become independent thinkers and learners and leaders in their chosen fields.

Honors at Saint Xavier features interdisciplinary seminars designed around themes of compelling interest. Because of the interdisciplinary focus of the seminars, students gain an understanding of the types of questions posed and the methodologies employed in a range of fields in the arts and sciences, preparing them for more independent research. Students also engage in junior-year field work that provides hands-on experience to enrich learning in the students' areas of interest. Field work activities are designed to help generate ambitious proposals for senior-year independent or group research under the direction of faculty mentors. The fruits of these senior projects are presented at University-wide forums, and students are encouraged to submit them to regional and national undergraduate conferences and journals. The program also provides ongoing cultural and social activities to stimulate thinking and to foster community.

Small class sizes encourage student participation and promote close student-faculty relationships. An Honors Student Center centrally located on campus is designed to reinforce a strong sense of intellectual and social community among program participants.

Participation Requirements: In their first two years, students take five Honors Seminars that satisfy 27 semester hours of University core requirements. These seminars include Honors English, Honors Humanities, Honors Social Science, Honors Science, and Honors Computers/Technology. The interdisciplinary seminars each year are designed around broad themes that also are explored in guest lectures and cultural activities. Upcoming themes include The Idea of America and The Good Life.

In their junior year, honors students engage in 6 semester hours of field work that might include local internships, an apprenticeship at a research laboratory, on-campus research under faculty direction, study abroad, or group creative or research activities. By the end of their junior year, honors students, working in collaboration with faculty mentors, have formulated fairly detailed proposals for senior-year research or creative projects. Throughout their field work year, students continue to meet periodically as a group, sharing their progress and discoveries and critiquing one another's proposals.

Working collaboratively with their faculty mentors, senior-year students receive 6 semester hours of credit for conducting, completing, and presenting their research and creative projects.

Students must maintain at least a 3.2 cumulative GPA to remain in the program. Successful completion of the program is noted on the student's official transcript and diploma.

Admission Process: High school students are invited into the program on the basis of their high school averages, ACT or SAT I scores, and other credentials that they supply in their applications to Saint Xavier. Students may pursue any major offered by the University.

Scholarship Availability: All honors students are considered for Presidential Scholarships. In addition, students are awarded up to $500 in each of their first two years and up to $1000 in their junior and senior years for learning and research technology, supplies, or travel. Students must submit an itemized request for these funds, explaining how they will be used.

The Campus Context: Founded by the Sisters of Mercy in 1846, Saint Xavier University is a coeducational, private, Catholic university on a 55-acre campus in a residential neighborhood in southwest Chicago. It offers the advantages of a supportive campus community in proximity to a rich urban culture. The campus contains modern classroom buildings, including the Graham School of Management and the Andrew Conference Center, an art gallery, a radio/TV studio, and a new Athletic/Convocation Center. It serves a diverse student population of more than 4,100 and offers thirty-five undergraduate majors and twenty-seven graduate degree programs in the Schools of Arts and Sciences, Management, Education, and Nursing. The Career and Personal Development Center offers a broad range of life/career services delivered by a highly trained counseling and placement team. Child-care service is provided for the children of students staff and faculty members.

Student Body The undergraduate enrollment is 74 percent women, and 23 percent of the students are members of minority groups. Eighty-five percent of the matriculated undergraduate students qualify to receive financial aid.

Faculty The total number of faculty members is 279, of whom 149 are full-time. Of the full-time faculty members, 82 percent have terminal degrees. The student-faculty ratio is 14:1.

Key Facilities The library contains 170,000 volumes and 899 current periodical subscriptions and offers a program of service that provides access to other library collections in the area as well as nationwide through an interlibrary loan service. Access to thirty-six electronic databases is also available. The University is connected to the Internet and a collection of statewide, regional, and national computer networks covering most of the industrial world. Internet access is available in five of the ten computer labs available for hands-on instruction as well as course work.

Athletics Saint Xavier University participates in a competitive intercollegiate program. Women compete in soccer, cross-country, volleyball, and softball while men participate in football, baseball, basketball, and soccer. The entire Saint Xavier athletic program belongs to the National Association of Intercollegiate Athletics.

Support Services The University supplies a wide range of tutoring and academic support services through its Learning Assistance Center and its Student Success Program.

Job Opportunities Work opportunities are available in the work-study program on campus. The Cooperative Education program provides experiential learning in the form of internships and part-time employment in the region.

Tuition: $500 per credit hour

Room and board: $5974

Contact: Director: Dr. Judith R. Hiltner, 3700 West 103rd Street, Chicago, Illinois 60655; Telephone: 773-298-3230; Fax: 773-799-9061; E-mail: hiltner@sxu.edu; Web site: http://www.sxu.edu/honors

SALEM STATE COLLEGE

4 Pu G M Sc Tr

▼ The Honors Program

The Honors Program of this state-supported College provides motivated and talented students with the stimulating and challenging educational opportunities typically found at name-brand private campuses. The academic program features small-sized, discussion-based classes that fulfill core and distribution requirements. Interdisciplinary honors seminars orient students toward a senior-year capstone project, typically a research project or academic thesis conducted in close affiliation with a faculty mentor. The program enables students to present research at a variety of conferences, to undertake internships, and to study and travel abroad.

The Honors Program at Salem functions as a community within the College, and events include large and small dinners, speakers, social events, and outings (e.g., whale watches, apple picking, etc.). Students have access to an Honors Center in the library and to honors housing. Honors students run their own undergraduate organization.

Founded in 1983, the Salem State College Honors Program is an active participant in Massachusetts' Commonwealth Honors Program as well as in the National Collegiate Honors Council. Of 4,800 students at the College, 140 are in the Honors Program.

Participation Requirements: The Honors Program is appropriate for students in all majors. Students satisfy all College core requirements by taking required a 3-credit honors freshman writing class, a 6-credit honors literature sequence, a 6-credit honors history sequence, and a 3-credit honors speech course.

Honors Program students may also elect to satisfy all College distribution requirements through honors electives in biology, philosophy, political science, psychology, and sociology. As juniors and seniors, students in the program participate in 2 one-semester interdisciplinary seminars. Senior honors projects are generally conducted through departmental honors courses. Students maintain a 3.2 or higher cumulative average.

Participation in the Honors Program is highlighted in the Commencement program and indicated on students' permanent transcripts.

Admission Process: Applicants to the program are evaluated on the quality of their responses to a prompt that asks the student: to attach a statement about himself or herself and the student's outlook on college; what makes the Honors Program a good fit for the student; and assuming that the student is more than his or her GPA and SAT scores, what can the student tell Salem to fill in the picture. While applicants are expected to score above 600 on either the verbal or the quantitative scales of the SAT and to have high school GPAs at or above 3.3, the program coordinator may take other factors into account in deciding admissions. Currently enrolled students and transfer applicants should have an overall college GPA of 3.5 or better and fewer than 35 college credits.

Scholarship Availability: The great majority of students receive scholarships from funding sources that are restricted to members of the Honors Program. The Senator Paul Tsongas Scholarship, for qualified in-state students, covers tuition and fees for four years. Presidential Honors Scholarships cover the cost of tuition for four years. Charlotte Forten Scholarships provide tuition and fees for students from underrepresented groups. Salem State College Foundation Grants provide grants of varying amounts.

Interpreting the symbols: **2**=two-year college, **4**=four-year college; **Pu**=public or state college, **Pr**=private college; **G**=general honors program; **D**=departmental honors program; **S**=small program (fewer than 100 students), **M**=midsize program (100 to 500 students), **L**=large program (more than 500 students); **Sc**=scholarships available in honors program; **Tr**=transfer students accepted into honors program; **HBC**=historically black college; **AA**=academic advisors; **GA**=graduate advisors; **FA**=fellowship advisors.

Students also may receive stipends for study abroad and Washington internships.

The Campus Context: Salem Normal School was started in 1854 as part of the reform movement associated with educator Horace Mann. In its evolution into a State Teachers College (1932) and then a liberal arts college with graduate programs (1968), Salem State has maintained its regional leadership for preparing teachers. But its reputation has grown to encompass noteworthy programs in thirty-four areas including marine biology, cartography, geology, communications, social work, business, nursing, Spanish, and all the creative and performing arts.

Nicknamed the "Witch City," Salem has a rich history that shows in its architecture, libraries, museums, and harborside restaurants and shops. A short walk from campus is a waterside park with a secluded beach and a reconstructed seventeenth-century village. Boston, 20 miles away, is accessible by MBTA bus and by a commuter-rail line that, in the other direction, extends to picturesque Gloucester and Rockport on Cape Ann.

The campus has grown with the recent acquisition of neighboring acreage. Plans are in the works for a new state-of-the-art theater and business center. Recent renovations have included both the main dining commons and the campus center.

Student Body Salem's undergraduate (day) enrollment is 4,600 students, with 954 living on campus. (Housing priority is given to Honors Program students.) While the overwhelming majority come to the campus from towns and communities within a 40-mile radius, students, particularly in the Honors Program, come from most regions of the country as well as from Europe, Asia, Africa, the Caribbean, and Central America. Extracurricular opportunities abound on our campus, from the student-run radio station to the newspaper, from the literary magazine to the student Historical association, from the multicultural student association to the gay-straight student alliance—and Honors Program students are frequently in leadership positions. The typical Salem State student juggles a busy campus life with the demands of a part-time off-campus job. The College's Student Life staff works hard to keep the campus lively on weekends, when commuter students are away.

Faculty Of 375 full-time faculty members, more than 75 percent hold terminal degrees. The College also employs 107 part-time faculty members.

Key Facilities The library has kept up with the recent revolution in information technology, making an antique of the old card catalogue. Online resources are fully supported, and the College is a member of area and regional library consortia. The study facilities are comfortable and quiet. Honors Program students have access to reserved study carrels.

Exercise facilities in the new Wellness Center are also state of the art. The campus is expanding the number of so-called "smart classrooms," and computer workstations are available in labs in many campus buildings. Teleconferencing facilities are available.

The marine station at nearby Cat Cove provides hands-on access to marine biology projects.

Honorary Societies The College hosts active chapters of both Alpha Lambda Delta and Phi Kappa Phi, national interdisciplinary academic honor societies.

Athletics Salem State is a powerhouse within the Massachusetts State College Athletic Conference (MASCAC). The College holds memberships is the National Collegiate Athletic Association (NCAA) Division III, the Eastern Collegiate Athletic Conference (ECAC), the New England Collegiate Athletic Conference (NECAC), and the Massachusetts Association of Intercollegiate Athletics for Women (MAIAW). The College fields twenty-two varsity teams, many of which include students from the Honors Program.

Study Abroad Salem State College offers its own study-abroad programs in both France and Spain. In addition, the Office for Study Abroad enables students to participate individually in programs all over the world. Honors Program students have in recent semesters studied in Ireland, Great Britain, and Spain.

Support Services Salem State College is committed to meeting the needs of disabled students. Its disabilities office is an active presence on campus (telephone, 978-542-6217). Renovations have improved campus accessibility. The College also maintains academic support services, including a writing center that serves all ability levels.

Job Opportunities The student employment office serves as a clearinghouse for jobs both on and off campus. Work-study opportunities are common, and Honors Program students are eagerly sought after. The College has recently initiated an on-campus enterprise zone for business start-ups, affording many students with employment opportunities within their fields. Several departments enable students to have appropriate off-campus internship opportunities.

Tuition and Fees: $2928 for in-state students; $9178 for out-of-state students.

Room and Board: $5038

Contact: Coordinator: Professor Rod Kessler, Honors Program, Salem State College, 352 Lafayette Street, Salem, Massachusetts 01970; Telephone: 978-542-6247; Fax: 978-542-6753; E-mail: honors@salemstate.edu; Web site: http://www.salem.mass.edu/honorsprogram/index.html

Salisbury University

4 Pu G M Sc Tr

▼ Thomas E. Bellavance Honors Program

The Thomas E. Bellavance Honors Program at Salisbury University (SU) is designed to bring together superior students and dedicated faculty members in a small University environment within the diversity of opportunity of the larger University community. It offers motivated students who are serious about their intellectual growth a variety of special classes enhanced by many cultural events and activities. The program fosters close individual contact between students and faculty members and brings together talented students with many interests.

Honors courses and extracurricular activities are intended to enrich and complement other educational opportunities and programs available to Salisbury students. The overarching goal of the Honors Program is to give high-achieving students intense and exciting educational experiences to enhance their development as independent thinkers and learners who are able and eager to take an active role in their own intellectual development. Real learning involves exploration and discovery, and the Honors Program gives students the opportunity and encouragement to be Columbuses of the intellectual life.

There are currently 205 students enrolled in the program.

Participation Requirements: To begin their intellectual journey, Honors Program students are required to take a sequence of four honors core courses: Critical Thinking and Writing, Issues in Social Science, Issues in Humanities, and Issues in Natural Sciences. These are designed to give students in the Honors Program a shared intellectual experience in the arts and sciences in order to develop a community of learners and to encourage a spirit of collegiality in pursuit of knowledge, a spirit that is essential for intellectual growth and personal fulfillment.

Core courses and honors electives satisfy both general education and honors requirements so that students need not take these courses in addition to those required for graduation in their majors.

Those students who finish the four-course sequence with a 3.0 GPA in the core and in their courses overall are also invited to graduate with honors by taking two additional honors courses and writing an honors thesis in their major or by taking three additional honors courses. The additional honors courses are in a variety of disciplines that are designed to augment the core experience, covering topics such as non-Western cultures, mathematical reasoning, art and music histories, and others.

The honors thesis is the capstone intellectual experience for students in the Honors Program and is a valuable opportunity to do independent research with a faculty mentor on a topic of personal interest in one's major field. Clearly, the thesis experience is excellent preparation for graduate or professional school. Students who fulfill these requirements and receive an overall GPA of 3.35 are recognized on their transcript and diploma as having graduated with "Bellavance Honors—With Distinction." Students who take three additional courses in lieu of two courses and a thesis graduate with "Bellavance Honors."

Tangible benefits of the Honors Program include small, stimulating classes taught by creative, supportive faculty members; recognition on transcripts and diplomas of participation in the Honors Program; use of the Honors Center, a lovely nine-room house adjacent to campus with lounges, a computer room, study areas, a kitchen, and a recreation room; participation in a variety of cultural, social, and public-service activities; and scholarships and small monetary awards to recognize outstanding scholars in the program. But even more important are the intangible benefits the students have received. As one honors graduate stated, "The Honors Program provided me with a nurturing environment in which to develop a higher level of thinking skills which I will use throughout college and throughout my life."

Admission Process: Incoming freshmen with superior academic records (minimum 3.25 GPA/combined SAT I scores of 1250) are invited to join the program prior to arriving at Salisbury. Current undergraduates with University GPAs of 3.25 or better are also invited to apply for admission.

The Campus Context: Salisbury University, formerly Salisbury State University, is a rarity among public institutions in Maryland—all of its four schools are endowed. These multimillion-dollar gifts have expanded scholarships and other opportunities for students, including those in the Honors Program.

With an emphasis on active learning, including undergraduate research, internships, community service, and travel abroad, SU is earning a national reputation for undergraduate excellence. According to the Maryland Higher Education Committee, Salisbury has the highest four-, five-, and six-year graduation rate of any campus in the University System of Maryland. For the fifth straight year, SU has been ranked by *U.S. News & World Report* as one of the top ten public regional universities in the North. *Kiplinger's Personal Finance Magazine* ranks SU among the top public universities nationally, and Princeton Review ranks SU among the nation's 331 best campuses, both private and public.

The key to SU's success is the significance placed on the relationship between students and professors. Full professors, including those in the Honors Program, serve as undergraduate advisers. They often teach freshmen courses and routinely lead students on trips and retreats, from exploring the Chesapeake Bay to touring Europe and beyond.

The SU campus is situated among some of the loveliest neighborhoods in the city of Salisbury, the hub of the Eastern Shore. Greater Salisbury, with a population of some 85,000, makes up for its lack of size with a strategic location. The city's airport and port are the second busiest in Maryland, after Baltimore. The city is 30 minutes from the beaches of Ocean City, Maryland, and less than 2 hours from the urban excitement of Baltimore and Washington, D.C. It is within easy driving distance of New York, Philadelphia, and Norfolk.

Comprising 144 acres, the SU campus is a compact, self-contained community. A cross-campus walk takes 8 minutes. Friendly, convenient, safe, and beautiful are just a few of the adjectives used to describe it.

Student Body In this close-knit community, there are some 6,100 undergraduates from thirty-eight states and thirty-seven other countries.

Faculty Students are taught by 291 full-time professors. Some 90 percent of the tenure-track faculty members have the highest degree in their field and include National Endowment for the Humanities scholars and Fulbright professors. The student-faculty ratio is 18:1.

Key Facilities Blackwell Library, with some 1.2 million bound volumes, microforms, and other printed collections, is the main campus research center. The library is a member of the University System of Maryland Interlibrary Loan Program. Seven campus computer labs with Macintosh and IBM personal computers are part of the campus Novell network. The Edward H. Nabb Research Center for Delmarva History and Culture is earning a national reputation for historical research of the Middle Atlantic region. The Communications Center has fully equipped television and recording studios. Fulton Hall is home to the fine and performing arts. In fall 2002, a $37-million state-of-the-art science education and research building opens. At 145,500 square feet, it is one of the largest in Maryland.

Athletics Salisbury University has one of the most distinguished NCAA Division III athletic programs in the nation. In 2001, it was fifteenth in the Sears Director's Cup rankings among all 395 Division III institutions. SU participates in nineteen NCAA sports: women's basketball, cross-country, field hockey, lacrosse, soccer, softball, swimming, tennis, track and field, and volleyball and men's baseball, basketball, cross-country, football, lacrosse, soccer, swimming, tennis, and track and field. SU's twenty-two intramural sports and sixteen sports clubs are immensely popular.

Study Abroad International experiences vary, from short-term study/travel tours to yearlong stays in the country of the student's choice. The Office of International Education Programs provides guidance and information on a variety of international experiences, from study abroad to internships and work and volunteer opportunities.

Job Opportunities Salisbury University commits $2.1 million of its operating budget to student employment. Almost 30 percent of undergraduates work on campus. The Center for Career Services and Professional Development also coordinates internships in government, nonprofit service agencies, and business.

Tuition: $4486 for state residents, $9942 for nonresidents, per year, including fees (2001–02)

Room and Board: $6090

Contact: Director: Dr. Tony Whall, Bellavance Honors Center, Salisbury University, Salisbury, Maryland 21802; Telephone: 410-546-6902; Fax: 410-677-5019; E-mail: rawhall@salisbury.edu; Assistant Director: Dr. Richard England; Telephone: 410-546-6943; E-mail: rengland@salisbury.edu; Web site: http://www.salisbury.edu/schools/honors/

SAM HOUSTON STATE UNIVERSITY

4 Pu G M Sc Tr

▼ Elliott T. Bowers Honors Program

The Honors Program at Sam Houston State University was initiated in 1990 to attract highly motivated and academically talented students. Based on the active involvement of highly select faculty members, the program seeks to create an intellectual and social climate that encourages students to develop their potential both in and out of the classroom. To this end, the

Interpreting the symbols: **2**=two-year college, **4**=four-year college; **Pu**=public or state college, **Pr**=private college; **G**=general honors program; **D**=departmental honors program; **S**=small program (fewer than 100 students), **M**=midsize program (100 to 500 students), **L**=large program (more than 500 students); **Sc**=scholarships available in honors program; **Tr**=transfer students accepted into honors program; **HBC**=historically black college; **AA**=academic advisors; **GA**=graduate advisors; **FA**=fellowship advisors.

program creates a community of scholars, wherein both students and professors interact and challenge each other in developing their abilities. Specifically, the program provides personalized instruction and mentorship opportunities in supporting the University's overall mission of maintaining high academic standards and fostering community service.

The Honors Program provides these achievement-oriented individuals, through financial support, an opportunity to interact with other similarly motivated students, special course offerings leading to an unusually broad educational experience, limited enrollment classes, closer contact with the faculty, the opportunity to participate in early registration, and access to distinctively designed facilities, including Spivey House, the honors residence hall.

Approximately 110 students are actively involved in the Honors Program. Honor students are found in every department and college at Sam Houston State University.

Participation Requirements: The honors curriculum is a four-year program that requires the same number of credits as the general educational program. To remain in the Honors Program, students must maintain at least a 3.25 GPA. To graduate with the Honors Program designation, students must complete at least 24 hours of honors credit, including two multidisciplinary seminar classes. To graduate with highest honors, students must complete an additional 6-hour honors thesis. The designation With Honors in the Honors Program or With Highest Honors in the Honors Program is recorded on the student's transcript and is noted during the graduation ceremony. Honors graduates are also provided with a distinctive honors medallion for the graduation ceremony.

Admission Process: To be considered for admission to the Honors Program, students must submit a special application. Incoming freshmen are considered eligible for consideration if they have a composite SAT I score of 1200 or above or a composite ACT score of 28 or above or if they have graduated in the top 10 percent of their high school class. For transfer or continuing students, eligibility is based upon a college cumulative GPA of 3.4 or better. All applicants must submit transcripts, a written essay, and letters of reference. Admission is competitive. A panel of faculty members reviews all applications to determine which students will be invited to participate in the program.

Scholarship Availability: The Honors Program administers two scholarship programs. The Elliott T. Bowers Scholarship provides at least $200 per semester to every student for a total of eight semesters. Junior and senior honors students are also eligible to compete for four Augusta Lawrence Scholarships (each valued at $1000). In addition, Sam Houston State University has other scholarships at the departmental, college, and university levels. Typically, honor students compete quite well for these scholarships.

The Campus Context: Sam Houston State University (SHSU), named after Texas' greatest hero, General Sam Houston, was founded in 1879. SHSU offers ninety-one undergraduate degree programs, seventy-seven master's programs, and doctoral programs in criminal justice, educational leadership, and forensic clinical psychology. SHSU's College of Business is fully accredited by the AACSB–The International Association for Management Education. The College of Criminal Justice ranks as one of the premier criminal justice institutions in the nation.

Located on 1,256 acres (211 on the main campus), SHSU offers three recreational sports fields; an indoor running track; racquetball, basketball, volleyball, aerobics, and weight rooms; two outdoor pools; a fully staffed University Health Center; thirty-six residence halls; married and sorority housing; two agricultural complexes; and a rodeo arena.

Sam Houston State University is located in Huntsville, Texas, a city of 34,500 residents between Houston and Dallas. Although only 70 miles from downtown Houston, Huntsville is surrounded by forests, lakes, and ranch land. The Huntsville State Park is nearby.

Student Body Enrollment is 12,205; 56 percent of the students are women. The minority ethnic distribution is 1 percent Native American, 1 percent Asian American, 8 percent Hispanic, 12 percent African American, and 1 percent international.

Faculty Instructional faculty members number 530. Sixty-six percent hold doctoral or terminal degrees. The student-faculty ratio is 21:1.

Key Facilities The Newton Gresham Library contains approximately 810,551 books and bound periodical volumes and maintains approximately 3,191 periodical and subscriptions. The University has developed a state-of-the-art fiber-optic network connecting all major campus buildings. Attached to this network are servers for administrative functions, academic computing, and research computing. This network is also connected to the Internet, providing all students access to Internet mail, Web servers, GOPHER servers, BBSs, IRC servers, and many other valuable network resources. Open VMS, Windows NT, and UNIX servers are available for use.

Athletics SHSU, a member of the NCAA's Southland Conference, competes in football, basketball, baseball, softball, tennis, track and field, and golf. SHSU also fields club teams in a variety of sports, including soccer, cycling, lacrosse, rugby, and in-line rugby.

Study Abroad Sam Houston State University sponsors summer programs in Florence, Italy, and Puebla, Mexico.

Support Services SHSU provides assistance for physically disabled students and academic assistance for students with disabilities. Services include magnification equipment and the Open Book, a reading system for the visually impaired.

Job Opportunities Work opportunities are available on and off campus.

Tuition: $2384 for residents, $8554 for nonresidents, per year (1999–2000)

Room and board: $2490–$3590

Contact: Director: Dr. Richard Eglsaer, P.O. Box 2479, Huntsville, Texas 77341; Telephone: 409-294-1178; Fax: 409-294-3798; E-mail: psy_rfe@shsu.edu

San Diego City College

2 Pu G M Tr

▼ Honors Program

In keeping with the mission statement of San Diego City College, the Honors Program was conceived as a means to enhance both the transferability of students to four-year institutions and the employability of students enrolled in occupational/vocational curricula. By employing multiple measures of prior achievement as well as an interview component and an extensive faculty referral system, program coordinators recruit a broad range of motivated and talented students, many who have never recognized their own honors potential. Sixteen years of experience have proven that honors students are not found, but made.

Three distinct program strands can be distinguished in the honors curriculum. The official class schedule for each semester lists twelve departmental honors courses from all across the college, selected through a faculty proposal process. Several of these are linked thematically within a general education core curriculum, A World of Ideas. A flexible, student-driven honors contact component extends the reach of the program into departments and time periods that could not support full honors sections. Contracts are signed agreements between students and professors committing both to an enriched experience of a regular course with additional honors-level objectives specified beyond the regular ones. This is euphemistically called "the people's honors program," since it is predominantly student driven.

Honors offerings are distinguished from their mainstream counterparts by their rigor, depth, intensity, interdisciplinary or cross-disciplinary content, and innovation in the modes of classroom teaching and learning. Students can expect smaller, more interactive classes with an extra measure of faculty member and counselor consultation and much more collaborative work, including research and class presentation. Transfer-level skills in critical thinking, writing, and general communication are emphasized, and development of motivation and self-confidence are of prime importance. Social and cultural events, either planned or purely spontaneous, are an important part of the student and faculty experience.

The City College Honors Program has been recognized by a number of major universities through formal transfer alliances, which prioritize (sometimes even guarantee) acceptance of program graduates into upper-division studies. Among these partners are the University of California at Irvine, Los Angeles (UCLA), Riverside, San Diego, and Santa Cruz; University of Southern California (USC); San Diego State University; Pomona College; Pitzer College; Whitman College; Chapman University; and Occidental College.

Participation Requirements: Generally speaking, individual City College honors courses are open to all qualified students. However, the thematically linked pairs of courses taught within the honors core curriculum, A World of Ideas, are core requisite and also require that students first indicate their commitment to complete the 15-unit graduation requirement of the Honors Program, generally using core classes to do so. For these core students, the advantage of sharing the challenges and rewards of participation with the same group of peers over several semesters quickly becomes evident. All Honors Program graduates, either core students or those accumulating individual departmental honors courses and honors contracts to total at least 15 units, must maintain an overall GPA of at least 3.25, with no honors grade less than B.

Admission Process: To enroll in individual departmental honors sections or to qualify for an honors contract attached to a regular nonhonors course, students with no previous college work must satisfy at least one of the following criteria. They must have a high school GPA of at least 3.5, a minimum SAT I score of 1100, a minimum ACT score of 25, a City College placement score of R5W5, or permission of the honors course instructor with concurrence of an Honors Program coordinator.

Students with previous college experience must satisfy at least one of the following criteria. They must have a minimum cumulative GPA of at least 3.25 in 12 or more baccalaureate-level units or a minimum GPA of 3.50 in the field of the selected honors class or permission of the honors course instructor with concurrence of an Honors Program coordinator.

For admission to the honors general education core curriculum, A World of Ideas, honors core students must submit a personal essay and a transcript and participate in an orientation interview with program coordinators. Most students apply during the summer months for startup core classes in the fall semester, although it is possible to join the core on a space-available basis at later dates.

To arrange honors contracts: Within the first two weeks of the semester students and professors, in close consultation with an Honors Program coordinator, formulate honors objectives to append to the curriculum of a regular, nonhonors course. Signoffs by the department chair and honors dean then extend authority to the College Records Office to administratively transfer students into newly created honors contract courses, which are noted on the final transcript exactly as honors sections are.

Scholarship Availability: All City College students are eligible for scholarships made available through the college foundation, which distributes nearly half a million dollars every year to deserving students. Honors Program students (those who, like the honors core cohort, have committed to completion of at least 15 units of transferable honors courses) may compete for several City College Presidential Honors Scholarships. The same group is also eligible for the San Diego Scholarship Foundation Book Awards, which pay for all books and supplies for up to four semesters and may be continued after a student transfers to a local university.

The Campus Context: San Diego City College is the flagship campus of the three-college San Diego Community College District, with an eighty-five-year history of distinguished service to America's Finest City. Its classic red brick buildings, accented by modern gray concrete colonnades and full-glass walls, are set in a beautifully landscaped campus less than a mile from San Diego Bay at the southern edge of Balboa Park, around which modern San Diego took form at the beginning of the century. From its walkways and plazas, one's gaze finds wonderful natural vistas in virtually every direction. Within walking distance are the businesses, library, and cultural venues of the city core; the lush gardens, museums, and playing fields of the park; and world-class institutions, such as the Fleet Science Theater, the Old Globe Theater, and the San Diego Zoo. Three freeways and a light rail trolley system at the College's doorstep whisk passengers to and from destinations all across the county.

As a comprehensive community college, City College offers instruction to several distinct populations: transfer students moving toward four-year institutions, occupational students preparing for the job market, individuals or business/industry workgroups intent on retraining or skill building, and lifelong adult learners. Associate degrees, certificates, and diplomas are offered in more than fifty majors. Of special note are instructional and enrichment programs in radio/television, biotechnology, nursing, gender studies, international perspectives, distance learning, alcohol/drug studies, and world cultures. The College is also deeply involved in regional economic development, serving as home to the Center for Applied Competitive Technologies (CACT) and the San Diego Business Incubator for fledgling businesses.

Student Body More than 14,000 students attend City College; about 3,500 are full-time, including 57 percent women, and 10,500 are part-time, including 52 percent women. Just under 50 percent are in degree programs. The average age of the students is 29, and all are commuters to the campus. More than seventy countries are represented among the student body. The race/ethnicity distribution is 30.4 percent white non-Hispanic, 23.1 percent Hispanic, 22.8 percent black non-Hispanic, 13.2 percent Asian/Pacific Islander, 1.2 percent Native American/Alaska Native, 1.6 percent nonresident alien, and 7.8 percent unknown.

Faculty Of the 525 faculty members, 200 are full-time, 50 (25 percent) of whom have terminal degrees.

Key Facilities The library houses 73,000 volumes and 337 current serial subscriptions in both print and electronic formats. A commercial online service affords Internet/World Wide Web access to student users, and basic training is provided. There are 400 computers available for student use in a large computer center, several instructional labs, a learning resource center lab, the library, and a graphics/multimedia center. A discount computer purchase plan is available at the College bookstore.

Honorary Societies Alpha Gamma Sigma, Phi Theta Kappa

Athletics City College offers a wide range of intramural activity classes for all students. Intercollegiate competition is offered in

Interpreting the symbols: **2**=two-year college, **4**=four-year college; **Pu**=public or state college, **Pr**=private college; **G**=general honors program; **D**=departmental honors program; **S**=small program (fewer than 100 students), **M**=midsize program (100 to 500 students), **L**=large program (more than 500 students); **Sc**=scholarships available in honors program; **Tr**=transfer students accepted into honors program; **HBC**=historically black college; **AA**=academic advisors; **GA**=graduate advisors; **FA**=fellowship advisors.

men's and women's basketball, cross-country, golf, soccer, tennis, track and field, and volleyball; men's baseball; and women's softball.

Support Services The Disabled Students Programs and Services (DSPS) Office provides programs, services, and auxiliary aids for students with disabilities in compliance with state and federal legislation. The office also coordinates the disbursement of special state funding and the support services offered by community agencies and College departments. Services available to qualified students may include priority enrollment, note takers or note-taking materials, test-taking accommodations, reader/signer/interpreter services, use of special equipment and adaptive devices, and specialized counseling and referrals. The campus is compliant with regulations regarding accessibility of handicapped students to all buildings and rooms.

Job Opportunities The City College Career Center is staffed by 2 full-time and 2 part-time employees. Services to students include career counseling and planning, individual job placement, maintaining a job bank and career library, and sponsoring on-campus job fairs and employer recruitment visits. An extensive work-study program administered by the financial aid office arranges on-campus jobs with specific departments.

Tuition: $11 per semester unit for residents, $130 per semester unit for nonresidents (2001–02)

Mandatory Fees: $22

Contact: Coordinators: Dr. Herald Kane, Dr. Kelly Mayhew, or Dr. Candace Waltz, 1313 12th Avenue, San Diego, California 92101; Telephone: 619-388-3642 or 3512; Fax: 619-388-3931; E-mail: hkane@sdccd.net, kmayhew@sdccd.net, or cwaltz@sdccd.net

San Diego Mesa College

2 Pu G M Sc Tr

▼ Honors Program

San Diego Mesa College's Honors Program serves self-motivated and qualified students by providing exceptional and intense learning experiences in classes that are usually highly interactive. Topics are explored in depth; typical assignments emphasize critical thinking, extensive reading and writing, and student presentations and critiques. Activities may also include opportunities for individual research projects, close interaction with faculty members and participation in community and cultural events.

The Honors Program is open to all students (part-time or full-time, day or evening) and can be found in all disciplines (liberal arts, fine arts, sciences, business, vocational, etc.).

Participation Requirements: Mesa College offers a variety of honors courses on a semester-by-semester basis. Students may graduate with honors by completing 15 hours of honors course work with a minimum 3.25 cumulative GPA. Core honors courses currently include English 101 (Reading and Composition), English 205 (Intermediate Composition and Critical Thinking), Music 110 (Music for Elementary School Teachers), Music 125 (Creativity, Diversity, and Esteem), Art History 110 (Prehistoric to Gothic), and Art History 111 (Renaissance to Modern). The range of core courses is currently under expansion.

Students may create Honors Contracts for all transferable non-honors sections. The Honors Contract allows a student to enhance the classroom experience and obtain honors credit in the course. The contract requires participation from both the student and the faculty member. The result is a course-within-a-course in which the honors student completes both the regular course material and the agreed upon honors-level work within that course.

Honors students have the opportunity to work closely with honors faculty members both in and out of the classroom. The Honors Campus Coordinators help students choose courses, design Honors Contracts, and pursue transfer to four-year institutions.

Admission Process: Students with no previous college work must satisfy one of the following: high school GPA of at least 3.5 or SAT I minimum score of 1100 or ACT minimum score of 25 or honors instructor recommendation.

Students with previous college work must satisfy one of the following: at least a 3.25 overall GPA in 12 or more units or a minimum 3.5 GPA in the field of the selected honors class or honors instructor recommendation.

Transfer students should note that honors courses at Mesa College may qualify them for early registration at San Diego State University and for its Honors Program. In addition, honors transfer agreements are in effect at Chapman and Pacific Universities; Pitzer, Pomona, Occidental, and Whitman Colleges; University of California campuses Irvine, Riverside, and Santa Cruz; and California State University campuses Dominguez Hills and Fullerton. University of California, San Diego, and Brigham Young University are pending, and UCLA and other campuses are under negotiation.

Besides the honors class sections, the Honors Program at Mesa College also encompasses Honors Contracts. These are individual agreements between a student and an instructor that enable a student to do honors-level work and receive honors credit within a regular nonhonors section. Contracts are established and processed within the normal drop/add period with all paperwork completed by the fourth week of the semester.

Scholarship Availability: In the fall 1998 semester, Mesa College, through the generosity of the San Diego Scholarship Foundation, began offering a Book Scholar Award. Criteria include honors participation, financial need, and full-time status. This scholarship, for qualifying honors students, pays for textbooks (250 maximum per semester) for up to four semesters. The scholarship may transfer to four-year institutions in California, as well.

The Mesa College Scholarship Foundation offers a host of scholarships, which are available to honors students as well as the general student body.

The Campus Context: San Diego Mesa College opened in 1964 as the second campus in the San Diego Community College District (following San Diego City College, established in 1916). Today, Mesa College, along with City College, Miramar College, and the Educational Cultural Complex comprise the second-largest community college district in California, offering a choice of educational programs unparalleled in the region.

Student Body Mesa College's diverse enrollment exceeds 24,000 students. All students commute to campus. Mesa's student demographics break down as follows: Native American 1.3 percent, Asian/Pacific Islander 14 percent, Latino 3.1 percent, African American 6.5 percent, Filipino 5.9 percent, white 51.9 percent, and other 2.7 percent. There are no traditional fraternities or sororities on campus.

Faculty There are 726 faculty members at Mesa College. Full-time faculty members total 255, and there are 471 adjunct faculty members. Amongst the full-time faculty members, there are fifty-two terminal degrees, forty-seven of which are doctoral degrees and five of which are M.F.A.s.

Key Facilities The new Learning Resource Center opened in April 1998. The $20-million state-of-the-art facility occupies 107,000 square feet in four stories. Situated at the center of the campus, the LRC offers expanded library holdings, an enormous computer lab for student use, and advanced media facilities.

Honorary Societies Phi Theta Kappa, Alpha Gamma Sigma, and Psi Beta

Athletics San Diego Mesa College provides intercollegiate competition for students in the following sports: men's and women's cross-country, basketball, volleyball, soccer, water polo, tennis, swimming, and track and field; men's football and baseball; and women's softball.

Support Services Through Disabled Students Programs and Services (DSPS), San Diego Mesa College provides programs and services for students with disabilities in compliance with state and federal legislation, including Section 504 of the Rehabilitation Act of 1973 and the Americans with Disabilities Act (ADA). Student participation in the program is voluntary.

Specialized classes for students with disabilities are available to support the college academic and vocational programs through DSPS, Physical Education, and the English Departments. Services provided include priority enrollment, readers, interpreters for deaf students, note takers and/or note taking materials, test-taking modifications, tape recorders, braillers, use of special equipment and adaptive devices, and specialized counseling and referral. Liaison with community agencies is also an important component of the program. The campus is physically accessible.

Job Opportunities A range of on-campus work opportunities is available, including tutoring and work-study.

Tuition: $11 per unit for residents, $120 per unit for nonresidents (2001–02)

Mandatory Fees: $12 per semester

Contact: Coordinators: Dr. Allison Primoza and Sondra Frisch, G103, 7250 Mesa College Drive, San Diego, California 92111; Telephone: 619-388-2351 (Primoza); Telephone: 619-388-2989 (Frisch); E-mail: aprimoza@sdccd.net or sfrisch@sdccd.net; Honors Counselor: Anthony Reuss; Telephone: 619-388-2674, E-mail: areuss@sdccd.net; Web site: http://teachers.sdmesa.sdccd.cc.ca.us/~aprimoza/honors/index.html

SAN DIEGO STATE UNIVERSITY

4 Pu G M

▼ University Honors Program

The University Honors Program at San Diego State University (SDSU) has been established to serve the needs of students whose academic potential has already been demonstrated and who wish to challenge that potential in special classes and through other opportunities designed for very capable students.

Students are encouraged to contribute and develop in an active way and to get to know the instructors personally. To ensure this, honors classes are smaller than the average, and the course work is developed to appeal to the superior student. Classes emphasize uniqueness in organization, method, and approach; they do not simply demand greater quantity of work. Lower-division classes provide 4, rather than the usual 3, units to acknowledge special readings and projects to permit individual response to the subject matter of the course.

Because of the general nature of the program, students in all majors are encouraged to apply. One of the strengths of the program is the opportunity to be in an intellectual peer group involving students from a wide variety of backgrounds who express a diversity of points of view and perspectives shaped by their different fields of study. Students apply to the Honors Program because they value intellectual growth. They enjoy learning and like to grapple with ideas, understanding that definitive answers or resolutions to problems are often elusive.

In addition to the opportunities in conjunction with the classes, honors students are encouraged to develop original projects and research inspired by their personal interests. The work may culminate in a senior thesis during the final year, and it provides valuable preparation for careers in many fields, both academic and nonacademic. Projects may involve students in off-campus internships if they so desire.

The Honors Director meets personally with each student to help in identifying special interests and talents and in defining the student's future plans.

Honors students receive privileges in registration to facilitate choice of classes and are encouraged to seek satisfaction of some basic course requirements through waivers, challenge exams, and advanced placement.

There are currently 250 students enrolled in the program.

Admission Process: Entering freshmen should have an SAT I score of 1100 or above (minimum ACT score of 26), a GPA of 3.5 or above, or a successful record of advanced classes in high school. The selection committee is guided in its decision by the student's motivation and interest in the program and by high school records, test scores, and other evidence of a commitment to learning.

Students may also apply before the start of their third semester in college if their SDSU GPA is 3.5 or above. Upperclass students should write a letter describing in detail their general academic and related interests (including possible choice of major) and their plans, however tentative, for a future career. A transcript and a sample of the student's work must accompany the application. Any original or photocopied (not retyped) essay written within the past year, whatever the subject, is acceptable. Generally, receipt of applications is required the semester prior to admission.

The Campus Context: San Diego State University encompasses 4.5-million square feet in forty-four academic buildings. It offers bachelor's degrees in seventy-six areas, master's in fifty-five, and doctorates in nine.

Student Body Enrollment is roughly 41,000, divided almost equally between men and women. Ethnic distribution is 53 percent white, 12 percent Mexican-American, 5 percent black, 5 percent Filipino, 4 percent other Hispanic, 3 percent Southeast Asian, 1 percent Pacific Islander, 1 percent American Indian, 2 percent nonresident, and 10 percent other/not listed. There are thirty-one fraternities and sororities on campus.

Faculty The total number of faculty members is 2,953, of whom 1,216 are full-time.

Key Facilities The library houses more than 1 million volumes.

Support Services Disabled Student Services offers accessibility information, orientation for students, reader services, and assistance with books on tape, etc.

Tuition: $927 for state residents, per semester; $246 for nonresidents, per unit (1998–99)

Room and Board: $5556 minimum

Contact: Director: Dr. Thomas J. Cox, 5500 Campanile Drive, San Diego, California 92182-1623; Telephone: 619-594-1261; Fax: 619-594-7934; E-mail: tjcox@mail.sdsu.edu

SAN FRANCISCO STATE UNIVERSITY

4 Pu G S Sc

▼ Presidential Scholars Program

The San Francisco State University (SFSU) Presidential Scholars Program is available to a select group of 20 to 25 new freshmen each fall following an application process that takes place in February and March. Those selected for the Presidential Scholarship receive automatic payment of registration fees for the freshman year, renewable for as many as three additional years if renewal criteria are met. Scholars take an orientation seminar

Interpreting the symbols: **2**=two-year college, **4**=four-year college; **Pu**=public or state college, **Pr**=private college; **G**=general honors program; **D**=departmental honors program; **S**=small program (fewer than 100 students), **M**=midsize program (100 to 500 students), **L**=large program (more than 500 students); **Sc**=scholarships available in honors program; **Tr**=transfer students accepted into honors program; **HBC**=historically black college; **AA**=academic advisors; **GA**=graduate advisors; **FA**=fellowship advisors.

and two general education courses as a group and share in periodic cocurricular, cultural, and social events.

The Presidential Scholars Program was initiated in 1995–96. It includes a total of approximately 80 continuing students.

Participation Requirements: In order to continue in the program, students must complete at least 24 units per year, take no more than 3 units per year on a credit/no-credit basis, maintain a cumulative GPA of at least 3.25, and participate in all required activities, including the scholars orientation and seminar plus one or two meetings and two special events per semester.

Admission Process: Applicants for the Presidential Scholarship must be California residents who have applied as first-time freshmen for the fall semester, have a high school GPA of at least 3.8, and complete an application showing evidence of academic and personal achievement, extracurricular contributions to school and/or community, and the ability to express oneself effectively.

The Campus Context: San Francisco State University is located in the city of San Francisco, the hub of the San Francisco Bay Area. Founded in 1899, SFSU is now a comprehensive university, one of twenty-three campuses of the California State University (CSU) system. SFSU's eight colleges include Behavioral and Social Sciences, Business, Creative Arts, Education, Ethnic Studies, Health and Human Services, Humanities, and Science and Engineering. SFSU offers 115 bachelor's and ninety-three master's degree programs.

Student Body Undergraduate enrollment is approximately 21,000 students; 60.6 percent are women. The ethnic distribution includes 30.5 percent non-Hispanic white, 30.8 percent Asian, 14.3 percent Hispanic, 10.7 percent Filipino, 7.5 percent African American, .9 percent American-Indian, .8 percent Pacific Islander, and 4.6 percent other/not specified. There are 1,122 international students. About 1,450 students are campus residents. Forty-six percent of students receive financial aid. SFSU has sixteen fraternities and eleven sororities.

Faculty SFSU has 1,570 faculty members, 792 of whom are tenured or on tenure track.

Key Facilities The library holds more than 3.5 million books, periodicals, microform, and CD-ROM materials. Internet accounts are available free of charge to all faculty members, staff members, and students. All permanent faculty members have Internet-capable computing equipment. All rooms in the residence halls are wired for Internet access. In addition to one 24-hour computer lab in the residence halls, the University has three central computer labs (one of which is open 24 hours), college-housed computer labs in each of the eight colleges, a faculty and staff computer training center, and multimedia computing equipment and training through the Center for the Enhancement of Teaching.

Honorary Societies Golden Key and Phi Beta Kappa

Athletics SFSU is a member of the California Collegiate Athletics Association, a Division II conference in the NCAA. The athletics program offers fifteen varsity teams. Men's teams include baseball, basketball, cross-country, soccer, swimming, track and field, and wrestling. Women's teams include basketball, cross-country, soccer, softball, swimming, track and field, tennis, and volleyball. Athletic facilities include two gymnasiums, an indoor pool, a weight room, a conditioning center, a wrestling room, a 6,500-seat stadium, an all-weather track, a softball field, a baseball field, and fourteen tennis courts.

Study Abroad California State University International Programs provide numerous opportunities for students to earn residence credit at their home CSU campus while pursuing full-time study at a host university or special study center abroad. CSU International Programs serve the needs of students in more than 100 designated academic majors and are affiliated with thirty-six recognized universities and institutions of higher education in sixteen countries, offering a wide selection of study locales and learning environments. Additional study-abroad opportunities are available for study in each of seven foreign languages.

Support Services With few exceptions, the campus is completely accessible to persons with disabilities. Additionally, the Disability Resource Center provides support services for a broad range of students with disabilities. Services include registration assistance and priority registration, classroom accommodations, mobility services, deaf services, print access, and learning disability services.

Job Opportunities Numerous student assistantships and work-study opportunities are available through the Career Center.

Tuition: None for state residents, $246 for nonresidents, per unit (2002–02)

Room and Board: $7360

Mandatory Fees: $1826

Contact: Director: Dr. Gail Whitaker, ADM 447, 1600 Holloway Avenue, San Francisco, California 94132; Telephone: 415-338-2789; Fax: 415-338-1814; E-mail: whitaker@sfsu.edu; Web site: http://www.sfsu.edu/~scholars

San Jacinto College South

2 Pu G M Sc Tr

▼ Honors Program

The San Jacinto College South Honors Program offers academically talented and highly motivated students special opportunities for enriched learning and recognition. The program provides a stimulating range and depth of scholarly pursuits within an interdisciplinary context.

The program offers three types of academic experiences. First is the interdisciplinary course, which combines freshman English and History courses for two semesters. Combining writing, literature, and history, these two courses, one offered in the fall semester and one offered in the spring semester, challenge students to blur the lines of distinction between academic fields. This course is limited to 15 students. Next, the honors program offers honors courses in other specific departments, including psychology, sociology, economics, and speech. These courses are also limited to 15 students. Finally, the program offers Honors by Contract in virtually every other academic department, where students work on independent projects with selected faculty members.

Approximately 100 students have accepted the San Jacinto College South Honors Program challenge.

Participation Requirements: Members are expected to enroll in at least 3 hours each semester they are in the Honors Program. In addition, members are encouraged to participate in the campus Honors Program retreat and in the Annual Gulf Coast Intercollegiate Honors Council Retreat as well as in local, state, and national research and writing contests.

Admission Process: Graduating high school seniors, returning students, and transfer students can are recruited based on their SAT I or ACT scores, TAAS scores, San Jacinto College GPA, or high school GPA.

Scholarship Availability: Each year the Honors Program awards more than $7000 in scholarships to entering and returning students based on their academic potential and achievements.

The Campus Context: San Jacinto College South is located in suburban Houston, approximately halfway between downtown and Galveston Island. Nearby communities include Southbelt, Pearland, Friendswood, Pasadena, and the Clear Lake City area (which includes NASA's Johnson Space Center). Founded in 1961 by several local school districts, its service area includes most of eastern and southeastern Harris County—an area of more than 800,000 people and home to the largest concentration of petrochemical plants in the world. San Jacinto College South is proud of its academic reputation, particularly the fact that for ten of the past eleven years its students have performed at a higher level at upper-level institutions than those from any other of the other nine Gulf Coast Consortium Community Colleges. San Jacinto College South also has a large campus spread out more than 181 acres.

Student Body With more than 5,000 students, San Jacinto College South has approximately 40 percent men to 60 percent women. More than 400 international students are enrolled, making the campus much more diverse and cosmopolitan in its outlook.

Faculty With more than 100 full-time members, the faculty has one of the highest percentages among community colleges in Texas for instructors with earned doctorates. Most classes are limited to 36 students, with honors classes limited to 15 students.

Key Facilities The new Parker Williams Library was completed in 1997. With a fine collection, the library is well-known for its Texana Collection, housed in the Robert Merrifield Texana Room, which has more than 5,000 print items available for research. In addition to the numerous computers located for student use in the library, open labs can be found in several buildings. The College is preparing to build a new technology center to consolidate the many computer labs.

Athletics San Jacinto College South offers varsity men's soccer and women's softball. Both programs are affiliated with the NJCAA. Both teams have been ranked in the top fifteen in the nation since their inauguration in the mid 1990s.

Support Services San Jacinto College South offers a full range of support services, most of them housed in the J. D. Bruce Student Center. All of the buildings on campus are ADA accessible. In addition, there are writing and math labs to help students in their courses.

Job Opportunities Students may apply for a number of campus jobs as well as community opportunities through the Job Placement Center, located in the J.D. Bruce Student Center.

Tuition: $16 per hour for in-district students, $30 per hour for out-of-district students, $60 per hour for out-of-state students (1998–99)

Mandatory Fees: $212 per year (approximately)

Contact: Director: Dr. Eddie Weller, 13735 Beamer Road, Houston, Texas, 77089-6099; Telephone: 281-929-4614; Fax: 281-929-4615; E-mail: ewelle@south.scjd.cc.tx.us; Web site: http://www.sjcd.cc.tx.us/

SANTA CLARA UNIVERSITY

4 Pr G M Tr

▼ University Honors Program

Inspired by Santa Clara's Catholic, Jesuit tradition, the University Honors Program pursues academic excellence enlightened by ethical reflection and openness to the spiritual dimensions of human experience. It seeks to educate especially talented students for responsible leadership in their professions and communities.

The program gives selected students an opportunity to combine the breadth of liberal learning with the depth achieved through specialization in a major field. Students take part in small, seminar-style classes marked by close faculty-student interaction, student participation, and a focus on written expression. Students may specialize in any of the majors offered in the humanities, natural and social sciences, business, and engineering.

An Honors Program seminar enrolls from 10 to 16 students. Students blend honors courses with regular classes as they pursue undergraduate degrees in their major fields. Most Honors Program classes fulfill core requirements required of every student. These include distinctive, cross-disciplinary Western Culture seminars as well as special courses in writing, mathematics, chemistry, and religious studies. Most freshmen reside on campus, where they are placed in proximity groups that encourage both mutual support and interaction with the general student body.

The University Honors Program is divided into two stages. Level I accepts students arriving for their first year of university study. After completing Level I, most students qualify to continue to the University Honors Program, Level II. Level II also accepts students who did not begin at the first level but qualify after starting college.

Special features include a senior thesis in each student's major. A University scholarship annually sponsors one junior honors student for a year of study at the University of Oxford in England. The Santa Clara University School of Law guarantees admission to Honors Program students who meet specific requirements while completing the program.

The University Honors Program was founded in 1963. It accepts 45 to 50 students a year and has a four-year enrollment of about 180.

Participation Requirements: Level I requires that students complete six designated Honors Program courses during their first two years. These courses include the Western Culture, religious studies, and writing seminars. For students who start at Level I, Level II requires an additional three courses plus a thesis or capstone project. Those entering at Level II must complete five designated honors courses and a thesis project. Study abroad brings Honors Program credit. The minimal GPA is 3.0. Successful completion of either or both levels is noted on a student's permanent transcript.

Admission Process: High school seniors interested in admission to the University Honors Program (UHP) should first complete the application process for the University. Admission to the program itself may occur either through invitation or application. Invitations are issued on the basis of scores, grades, and other information in the University admissions file. Freshman students typically present a verbal SAT I above 620, a combined score in the mid-1300s or higher, and a correspondingly high GPA in college-prep courses. In 1998, UHP freshmen showed a median unweighted GPA of 3.94 and a median combined SAT I of 1420. Submitting an application guarantees review of a student's academic record by the program director. An application is available at the program's Web site.

Enrolled students who apply for Level II should have a Santa Clara GPA of at least 3.5 and submit two letters of recommendation from Santa Clara faculty members. Transfer students should complete 32 quarter units at Santa Clara or a similar four-year institution before applying to the program.

Scholarship Availability: Santa Clara bases financial aid primarily on demonstrated need. All candidates are advised to file FAFSA and Profile forms as required by the Office of Financial Aid. Students invited to the University Honors Program are automatically considered for available merit grants, that is, Academic Deans' Scholarships and Honors Awards. Merit scholarships usually, but not necessarily, supplement need-based awards.

The Campus Context: As the oldest institution of higher learning in California (established in 1851), Santa Clara University is one of the nation's most respected Jesuit universities. It was established on the site of the Mission Santa Clara de Asis, the eighth of the original twenty-one California missions. Roses, palm trees, lush lawns, and clay-tile roofs are what immediately strike visitors to Santa Clara. The 104 acres of lush gardens are accented by authentic Spanish architecture, with the Mission Church as the visual focal point of Santa Clara's campus, creating a beautiful,

Interpreting the symbols: **2**=two-year college, **4**=four-year college; **Pu**=public or state college, **Pr**=private college; **G**=general honors program; **D**=departmental honors program; **S**=small program (fewer than 100 students), **M**=midsize program (100 to 500 students), **L**=large program (more than 500 students); **Sc**=scholarships available in honors program; **Tr**=transfer students accepted into honors program; **HBC**=historically black college; **AA**=academic advisors; **GA**=graduate advisors; **FA**=fellowship advisors.

peaceful, safe environment in which students take great pride. Santa Clara, located in the heart of Silicon Valley, blends a sense of history and tradition with a vision that values innovative and deep commitment to social justice.

Santa Clara University offers forty-five bachelor's degree programs on one campus composed of three colleges: Arts and Sciences, Business, and Engineering. In addition to the academic resources available, students may enjoy visiting the historic Mission Church, which is surrounded by beautiful gardens; the de Saisset Museum, which features a year-round display of early California artifacts; a new fitness and tennis complex; the Ricard Observatory; the KSCU radio station; and the Mayer Theatre, offering quarterly student theater productions. The campus is also close to shops and restaurants.

Student Body Undergraduate enrollment is 4,332; 52 percent of the students are women. The ethnic composition of the degree-seeking undergraduate student body is 2.6 percent African American, .01 percent Native American, 19.5 percent Asian American, 14.1 percent Hispanic, 53.9 percent white, 6.6 percent are of unknown ethnicity, and 2.9 percent are international. Forty-one percent of students live on campus, and 69 percent of SCU undergraduate students receive financial aid. Ten percent of men and 15 percent of women join one of the four fraternities or four sororities on campus.

Faculty Instructional faculty members number 335. Ninety-two percent of full-time faculty members have terminal degrees. The student-faculty ratio is 15:1.

Key Facilities There are two libraries on campus. Orradre, the main library, contains more than 450,000 bound volumes, 150,000 more in microform and video format, and multiple online subscriptions to electronic research resources. The Heafey law library is also available to undergraduate students. All dorms, lounge, and study areas are wired for network access. Ten on-campus computer labs provide 525 computer terminals for student use.

Honorary Societies Alpha Sigma Nu, Beta Gamma Sigma, Phi Beta Kappa, Order of Omega, Sigma Xi, and Tau Beta Pi

Athletics SCU is a member of the NCAA's Division 1. On-campus facilities are available for intercollegiate sports such as baseball, softball, basketball, volleyball, soccer, tennis, and water polo. Off-campus facilities for golf, crew, and cross-country are also available. SCU also sponsors intramural and club athletic programs in such sports as football, lacrosse, racquetball, weight lifting, and rugby.

Study Abroad Santa Clara University takes part in cooperative study-abroad programs at more than seventy-five sites in Europe, Central and South America, the Caribbean, Canada, Africa, Asia, and Australia. In addition to traditional study abroad, Santa Clara offers international internship and volunteer opportunities through experiential and service learning partnerships. An endowed scholarship sponsors 1 honors student for a junior year at Mansfield College, Oxford University.

Support Services More than 60 percent of the campus is accessible to physically disabled students.

Job Opportunities Work opportunities are available on or off campus. Students may visit the on-campus career center for assistance in internship or job placement at any Silicon Valley company.

Tuition: $17,442 (1998–99)

Room and board: $7323

Mandatory Fees: $180

Contact: Director: Rev. Arthur Liebscher, S.J., Santa Clara University, Santa Clara, California 95053-0638; Telephone: 408-554-4439; Fax: 408-554-2340; E-mail: aliebscher@scu.edu; Web site: http://www.scu.edu/SCU/Programs/Honors/honors.htm

SANTA FE COMMUNITY COLLEGE

2 Pu G M Tr

▼ Honors Program

Santa Fe Community College's (SFCC) Honors Program offers academically talented and motivated students a wide variety of special-topic 3-credit seminars and 1-credit colloquia, most of which are elective. All courses stress creative thinking, and many are interdisciplinary. The seventeen-year-old program enrolls about 140 students and has recently been expanded to include honors sections or options for general education courses.

Participation Requirements: Students must take 12 hours of honors courses and maintain a GPA of at least 3.5 to graduate with an Honors Certificate. Students who have completed these requirements receive special recognition at graduation and an Honors Program designation on their transcript.

Admission Process: Students are eligible for honors courses after completing at least 12 hours of college credits at SFCC with a minimum 3.5 GPA, and they are invited into the program. Transfer students and those who do not meet these criteria may be enrolled in specific courses with special permission from the Honors Coordinator.

Scholarship Availability: Honors students can apply for special Honors Program scholarships and can also receive Board of Trustees scholarships available to the top 10 percent of the high school graduates from Bradford and Alachua Counties. Other scholarships for students who meet the criteria are available from the SFCC Endowment Corporation and the Florida Bright Futures Program.

The Campus Context: Santa Fe Community College was established in 1965 to provide high-quality higher education to the citizens of Alachua and Bradford Counties. The main campus is set on 175 acres in northwest Gainesville. A Downtown Center, opened in 1990, is near the University of Florida, while the Andrews Center in Starke serves Bradford County. The College's Art Gallery, which offers exhibitions of contemporary art, is a teaching gallery for students and the public. The SFCC annual Spring Arts Festival is a nationally recognized event that attracts exhibitors from all over the country, and the College also sponsors prize-winning dance, theater, and debate groups. SFCC is a comprehensive community college that offers an Associate of Arts degree, twenty-eight Associate of Science degrees, and community education classes.

Student Body The College enrolls more than 13,700 students, including 52 percent women. The ethnic distribution is 76.4 percent white, 11 percent African American, 7 percent Hispanic, 2.7 percent Asian, 0.7 percent Native American, and 2.2 percent other. There are more than 400 international students from eighty countries.

Faculty There are 559 faculty members, of whom 264 are full-time; 19.2 percent have terminal degrees.

Key Facilities The new library houses 100,00 volumes, 5,015 microform units, and ninety-two electronic titles, and a cyberspace cafe. Paper and microform periodicals number 500, and there are sixty-six online databases. Forty-five rooms are equipped with computers, and students have access to 850 computers at the main campus and other centers.

Honorary Societies Phi Theta Kappa

Athletics Santa Fe Community College is a member of the Florida Community College Activities Association, the governing organization for intercollegiate sports competition for Florida's junior colleges. The College competes in softball, baseball, and basketball.

Support Services The student-centered learning environment at SFCC is supported by the Disabilities Resource Center, which provides services and accommodations for students with documented disabilities. These include interpreters, note-takers, special equipment, and alternative testing arrangements.

Job Opportunities Many different work opportunities exist on campus, including work-study, tutoring, and clerical positions.

Tuition: $151.35 per 3-credit course for residents, $563.85 for nonresidents (2002)

Contact: Coordinator: Dr. Barbara Oberlander, 3000 North West 83rd Street, Gainesville, Florida 32606; Telephone: 352-395-5330; Web site: http://www.santafe.cc.fl.us

SAUK VALLEY COMMUNITY COLLEGE

2 Pu G S Sc

▼ SVCC Honors Program

In 1977, a steering committee met to study the feasibility of establishing an honors program. Their planning resulted in the start of the SVCC Honors Program in the fall semester of 1978. The infant program experienced the struggles associated with all new programs. Perhaps the most fundamental issue was the selection of the method by which the student would experience honors work. Both separate honors courses and honors work integrated into the regular course structure were used and evaluated. The latter method evolved as the method of choice.

The student and the course teacher establish a contract detailing the honors work that extends beyond the normal course requirements. The experience of working individually with a subject area expert is learning at its best. Beyond the obvious benefit of increased learning, the student's transcript displays the selected course as an honors course, and today more than ever superior transcripts lead to superior opportunities. Membership also provides the student with the opportunity to compete for SVCC Honors Scholarships. The supervision of the honors students often brings renewed professional vitality to the individual teacher.

Providing opportunities for our most talented students to interact with our instructional staff leads to greater student satisfaction and success. The program provides the College with excellent PR and generates several news releases each year. The program provides an excellent basis for contact with area high school educators and is an important part of SVCC's overall recruitment effort. Successful students are the best recruiters the College can have.

The program is administered by the honors program director with the assistance of the honors committee. The committee is chaired by the honors director and consists of 1 delegate from each of the instructional divisions. The committee provides advice in all areas of program operation with the primary functions of screening candidates for admission and selection of scholarship recipients.

Participation Requirements: To be an honors graduate, the student must complete a minimum of 12 semester hours of honors course work. The student must have a GPA of 3.5 or greater on a 4.0 scale.

Admission Process: Potential members must complete a request for admittance form which includes an essay detailing their academic goals and how the honors program relates to those goals. The essays are reviewed and evaluated by the honors committee. The student must also meet at least one of the following criteria: ACT score of 27, graduation in the upper 10 percent of their high school class, membership in their high school's National Honor Society, or have been named an Illinois State Scholar. Students who do not meet any of the criteria may apply after completion of 12 semester hours of SVCC course work with a GPA of 3.5 or greater. Such students must also obtain a faculty member referral.

Scholarships Availability: The honors program provides scholarships based on academic excellence. Each semester the membership competes for the awards, which currently are valued at a total of $2000.

The Campus Context: Sauk Valley Community College is located in the heartland of the midwest near Dixon, Illinois, the boyhood home of President Ronald Reagan. The College serves a population of about 105,000 and provides opportunities for students to complete the first two years of a bachelor's degree, improve employability through career education, achieve competence in essential skills, continue learning on a lifelong basis, and enhance the cultural and economic climates of our communities.

SVCC fulfills the mission of a "community" college by relying on a democratic philosophy and the implementation of multiple roles. The College was founded in 1965.

Student Body Approximately 3,000 students register for classes at Sauk each semester. There is nearly a 50/50 split between transfer and career programs. In addition, hundreds of area residents participate in workshops and seminars each semester.

Faculty The College has about 120 faculty members, about 40 percent of whom are full-time.

Key Facilities More than 150 computers are employed in labs, classrooms, and offices. The College has a learning assistance center providing free student tutoring in a number of academic areas.

Honorary Society Phi Theta Kappa

Job Opportunities Students are offered a range of internships and work opportunities, including work-study programs.

Tuition: In-district tuition is $48 per semester hour; out-of-district tuition is $171.74 per semester hour; out-of-state tuition is $221.57 per semester hour.

Contact: Dale Heuck, Honors Program Director, SVCC, 173 IL Rte 2, Dixon, Illinois; Telephone: 815-288-5511 Ext. 416; Fax: 815-288-1880; E-mail heuckd@svcc.edu.

SCHREINER UNIVERSITY

4 Pr G S Sc Tr

▼ Schreiner University Honors Program

The Schreiner University Honors Program values its members' unique histories and recognizes each individual in the quest to interpret his or her place in this world. The program intends to provide personalized learning experiences to meet the needs and interests of academically aggressive college students by offering honors courses designed to engage students in a dynamic liberal arts education; cocurricular opportunities to develop academically, socially, and spiritually; recognition of such students as "Schreiner Honors Scholars"; and standards advantageous for graduate school admission.

Students are provisionally accepted into the program. At the end of their fall semester, students who persist in their desire to become Schreiner University Honors Program members and who fulfill the expectations of honors students will, by full faculty vote, be nominated for formal induction into the program during its annual January ceremony. Seniors are honored with their honors rings during this ceremony.

Interpreting the symbols: **2**=two-year college, **4**=four-year college; **Pu**=public or state college, **Pr**=private college; **G**=general honors program; **D**=departmental honors program; **S**=small program (fewer than 100 students), **M**=midsize program (100 to 500 students), **L**=large program (more than 500 students); **Sc**=scholarships available in honors program; **Tr**=transfer students accepted into honors program; **HBC**=historically black college; **AA**=academic advisors; **GA**=graduate advisors; **FA**=fellowship advisors.

Schreiner University expects its honors students to be actively involved in the program by taking ownership of it through planning and engaging in program activities and by exploring avenues for experiential learning. In addition, honors students should strive toward these ideals: exercising greater initiative and independence in order to foster a community of scholars; displaying an eagerness to learn in and out of the classroom; exhibiting integrity and ethical conduct; being willing to accept intellectual risks; and acknowledging an Aristotelian treatise which asserts happiness is achieved through contemplation of philosophic truth rather than through the pursuit of pleasure, fame, and wealth.

Each semester, the Schreiner University Honors Program sponsors excursions designed to provide personal, social, and/or cultural enrichment for its students. In the past, these activities have included private luncheons with distinguished guests such as Joy Harjo, poet; Millard Fuller, founder of Habitat For Humanity; star gazing at a local observatory; overnight excursions to the Renaissance Festival and the Seminole Canyon area to view ancient rock art; and cultural events in San Antonio and surrounding areas.

Honors students have priority class registration, monthly luncheons focused on a group activity, and the above-mentioned opportunities for extracurricular involvement.

Each year, the program reserves a moderate portion of its budget to fund scholarship opportunities such as presenting papers at regional and national conferences. A written proposal requesting funds for such scholarship are considered each semester at midterm by the Honors Committee.

The University provides opportunities to spend a semester, a year or a miniterm in a structured program at a college or university abroad and/or in the United States. A written proposal due the year prior to the intended study experience is required of all students seeking study outside of the campus.

Founded in 1989, the program involves an average of 60 students.

Participation Requirements: All honors students enroll in one honors course each semester. An interdisciplinary sequence beginning with the First-Year Honors Seminar comprises the mandatory honors-designated courses with these sections offering enhanced curriculum and experiential learning opportunities. Such curricula may require students to complete up to 7 more credit hours beyond the requirements for their degree plans. By their senior year, most honors students have completed this sequence and contract an honors course within their major to satisfy their honors course requirement.

To remain in good standing in the Schreiner University Honors Program, students must meet minimum cumulative GPA requirements based on the following sliding scale. Freshmen must maintain a minimum cumulative GPA of 3.25; sophomores, 3.35; juniors, 3.45; and seniors, 3.5. Students must also exhibit academic and social integrity. A breach in acceptable conduct will, upon the recommendation of the Honors Committee, be cause for dismissal from the program. Examples of such cause for dismissal: academic dishonesty, i.e., plagiarism, cheating, or serious violations of state or federal law. In addition, students must complete honors courses. Either a grade of F for an honors-designated course or failure to complete the honors component of contracted course is grounds for probation or dismissal.

To be recognized as a Schreiner Honors Scholar, a student must have a minimum cumulative GPA of 3.5, have participated in the honors program for at least the last four consecutive semesters, and have completed one semester in the Honors Colloquium.

Admission Process: The Admissions Office automatically notifies the Honors Program Director of all first-year freshmen and transfer students who meet the quantitative standards noted below. Through written correspondence, the director invites qualified candidates to apply. The final deadline for honors application process is June 10.

Students are invited to become first-semester provisional honors candidates based on the following criteria: a high school GPA of at least 3.5; the level of courses taken, including AP and honors; class rank; SAT/ACT score (minimum 1100/25); leadership experience; extracurricular activities; and a Presidential essay.

If applicants believe their scores and GPA do not reflect their abilities well, they may present other indicators of their promise such as recommendations from teachers or creative work, or they may request a personal interview.

Each spring, the Schreiner University Honors Program invites current students who have proven to be aggressive learners and who have yet to complete four consecutive, full-time semesters at Schreiner University to be considered for admission into honors. The deadline for application is February 28.

Current students and transfer students are invited to become first-semester provisional honors candidates based on the following criteria: a cumulative GPA of at least 3.25; leadership experience; extracurricular activities; a Presidential essay; and an interview with the Honors Committee.

Scholarship Availability: The University offers substantial academic scholarships through its Schreiner Scholars Competition each February. Students who meet the above-mentioned honors criteria compete for $9000 scholarships guaranteed for four years. This competition requires an application, an essay, and a faculty interview.

The Campus Context: Approximately 60 miles northwest of San Antonio, Kerrville is the home of Schreiner University. A resort community nestled among the hills of south central Texas and along the Guadalupe River, its nearly 25,000 citizens enjoy generally dry weather, cool nights, and sunny days. As a small, primarily residential liberal arts university affiliated with the Presbyterian Church (U.S.A.), Schreiner carries out its education purpose in the conviction that the pursuit of knowledge is integral to the Christian mission of worship and service and is undertaken in the context of thoughtful interactions among a diverse community of faculty and staff members and students, a process that empowers students to discover and assimilate knowledge in personalized learning experiences.

Student Body: Undergraduate enrollment is 800; graduate enrollment is 25.

Faculty: The total number of faculty members is 77 (56 full-time), of whom 55 percent have terminal degrees. The student-faculty ratio is 17:1.

Key Facilities: The library houses more than 83,000 volumes, 300 journal subscriptions, 109 online databases, 10,000 online journals, 12,000 e-books, 800 video and sound recordings, thirteen public terminals with a access to the Internet and electronic resources, the Sun Porch Electronic classroom, a Multimedia Production Center, an Archival Digitizing Center, and ten group study rooms. With one distance-learning classroom, a computer lab housed in the Teaching and Learning Center, and wireless Internet access, Schreiner continues to move forward with offering students technology to support their academic needs.

Athletics: The athletic program is an integral part of the whole person development program of the University whose basic components are intercollegiate sports and intramural sports. In each, the objective is to provide both men and women opportunity for participation in organized athletic competition. With teams for baseball, basketball, golf, soccer, softball, tennis, and volleyball, the University competes in the American Southwest Conference of the National Collegiate Athletic Association (NCAA) in Division III and also competes in the National Association of Intercollegiate Athletics (NAIA).

Study Abroad: In 2001, Schreiner marked the first year of a generous University commitment to international study with the aid of substantial scholarships available to qualified candidates.

Through Eckerd College of St. Petersburg, Florida, Schreiner partners to offer semesters in London. The international study coordinator also assists students in locating a suitable program to match an individual's needs. Summer travel trips to San Miguel de Allende, Mexico, and London, England, remain the staples of Schreiner study abroad.

Honorary Societies: Alpha Chi, Alpha Lambda Delta, Kappa Mu Epsilon, and Sigma Tau Delta

Support Services: The Teaching and Learning Center provides free academic assistance to all students whereas the Learning Support Service (LSS) Office is separately dedicated to assisting students who have documented learning disabilities. To date, 2 honors students have been LSS students, and honors students are typically employed by LSS as note-takers.

Job Opportunities: A comprehensive student-employment program exists, offering Federal Work-Study, Schreiner work-study, and community internships.

Tuition: $6059 (fall or spring term)

Room and Board: Room charges vary depending on facilities (central campus residential facilities or Pecan Grove apartment facilities) averaging $1965 per semester. Dining charges vary depending on the chosen meal plan with a nineteen-meal plan plus $50 snack bar credit at $1705 and an eleven-meal plan plus $50 snack bar credit at $1000.

Contact: Honors Program Director: Ms. Jacqueline M. Burton, CMB# 5943, 2100 Memorial Boulevard, Kerrville, Texas 78028; Telephone: 830-792-7254; Fax: 830-792-7442; E-mail: jmburton@schreiner.edu

Scottsdale Community College

2 Pu G M Sc Tr

▼ College Honors Program

The Honors Program at Scottsdale Community College (SCC) provides general education for students who seek challenges in learning, who are curious, who question, and who are eager to test assumptions. The program offers a series of specially designed courses for transfer and two-year students. The purpose of the Honors Program is to foster greater depth of thought in reading, writing, and discussion with faculty members and guest lecturers that will better prepare honors students to complete baccalaureate degrees or begin their careers.

The 17-year-old program enrolls 170 students.

Participation Requirements: Honors students can be enrolled full- or part-time, are expected to enroll in at least one honors course each semester, and must maintain a GPA of 3.25.

Admission Process: Recent high school graduates must rank in the top 15 percent of their graduating class or qualify through placement tests; continuing or transfer students must have completed 12 credit hours of college classes with a 3.5 or better.

Scholarship Availability: Scottsdale Community College offers a variety of stipends for honors students in addition to scholarships that are available to all students. The Chancellor's, Maricopa Foundation, and Betty Elsner Scholarships are Maricopa College District awards for continuing honors students. For recent Maricopa County high school graduates in the upper 15 percent of their graduating class, Presidents' Scholarships are available from the District. Partial fee waivers are awarded to all honors students who do not receive any of the above awards.

The Campus Context: Scottsdale Community College is one of ten colleges in the Maricopa Community College District. It was founded in 1971 and is located on the Pima/Salt River Reservation just east of the city of Scottsdale, Arizona. There are three degree programs at the College, the Associate of Arts degree for transfer students, the Associate of Applied Science degree for students in occupational programs, and an Associate of General Studies degree for students whose educational goals require flexibility. Several of the occupational programs are unique; the School offers degree programs in tribal management, equine science, interior design, and hotel and restaurant management in addition to the usual programs.

Student Body Spring enrollments for the College were 10,400 total. The breakdown is 87 percent first-year and 56 percent women. The ethnic distribution is as follows: 81 percent Caucasian, 4.1 percent American Indian, 5.5 percent Hispanic, 1.5 percent African American, 2.7 percent Asian, and 4.8 percent international. Thirty-one percent are between the ages of 20 and 25. While there are no sororities or fraternities, there are twenty-eight officially recognized clubs and organizations for students interested in the arts, environment, ethnic groups, and community service.

Faculty There are 135 full-time and 319 part-time faculty members, with a student-faculty ratio of 17:1. Sixty-eight percent of the faculty members have terminal degrees, and 26 percent have doctorates.

Key Facilities The library at SCC has 46,000 volumes; however, students have ready access to the more than 500,000 volumes available in all of the Maricopa College libraries. Computers are available to all students in the library, the computer lab, the Writing Center, and the Independent Study Lab in the Social and Behavioral Sciences Division.

Honorary Society Phi Theta Kappa

Athletics The athletic program has a strong intramural program emphasizing lifelong sports (golf, handball, jogging) and intercollegiate competition in baseball, basketball, cross-country, football, golf, soccer, tennis, and track and field. Students in the intercollegiate program must conform to the eligibility rules established and maintained by the National Junior College Athletic Association.

Support Services The Office of Disability Resources and Services assists all students with disabilities through a variety of social and academic services. All buildings are in compliance with the Americans with Disabilities Act, and special parking permits are available.

Tuition: $1100 for area residents, $5250 for state residents, $5250 for nonresidents, per year (1999–2000)

Mandatory Fees: $5 registration fee

Contact: Coordinator: Harry Hude, 9000 East Chaparral Road, Scottsdale, Arizona 85250; Telephone: 480-423-6525; Fax: 480-423-6200; E-mail: hude@sc.maricopa.edu; Web site: http://www.sc.maricopa.edu

Seattle Pacific University

4 Pr G M AA

▼ University Scholars

The University Scholars program at Seattle Pacific University (SPU) is an alternative general education program for selected students who are highly motivated to pursue an intense academic program studying great works of art, literature, philosophy, social science, and natural science in their historical contexts. In their first three years, students are part of a cohort that progresses through a curriculum of great works, examines the relationship of science and faith, and considers the West's relationship to the world. In their senior year, students work individually with faculty mentors to produce an honors paper or project in a discipline.

Interpreting the symbols: **2**=two-year college, **4**=four-year college; **Pu**=public or state college, **Pr**=private college; **G**=general honors program; **D**=departmental honors program; **S**=small program (fewer than 100 students), **M**=midsize program (100 to 500 students), **L**=large program (more than 500 students); **Sc**=scholarships available in honors program; **Tr**=transfer students accepted into honors program; **HBC**=historically black college; **AA**=academic advisors; **GA**=graduate advisors; **FA**=fellowship advisors.

University Scholars courses are team-taught and rigorously interdisciplinary and offer intensive peer discussion. The program's goal is to create a faithful community of self-motivated scholars engaged in thoughtful cross-disciplinary conversation, writing, and action on issues facing the church and the world. Scholars gather for social events several times a year, including presentations and a celebration of the senior honors projects each spring.

Founded in 1970, the program enrolls a maximum of 40 students in each cohort, for a total of approximately 150–160 University Scholars.

Participation Requirements: During their first two years, University Scholars take the Honors University Seminar and then a sequence of courses called Texts and Contexts. In their junior year, they take a sequence of courses in Faith and Science, and their capstone experience begins with a seminar on Christianity and Scholarship, followed by 4 credits of work in an honors project or thesis. A total of 36 credits in University Scholars courses is required for graduation, and students must maintain a minimum 3.2 cumulative GPA in order to remain in the program. At commencement, University Scholars receive special recognition and an indication on their transcripts that they have completed the University Scholars program.

Special service to the University community is a high priority for University Scholars. Each year, the graduating senior who most exemplifies the high ideals of the program is honored with the Wesley E. Lingren Award in honor of the founding director.

Admission Process: University Scholars are selected through a special application process. Students with excellent SAT or ACT scores and exceptional high school GPAs are invited to apply by writing an honors entrance essay. The average high school GPA of entering freshmen is 3.58. Students who are highly motivated or who are specially gifted in a particular field are urged to contact the director if they find they have not received an invitation to apply. While many factors contribute to the selection process, most first-year students entering in 2001 had an SAT (or ACT equivalent) score of above 1300.

Scholarship Availability: The University gives substantial academic scholarships, but they are not directly tied to the University Scholars program.

The Campus Context: SPU is a flourishing Christian university of the arts, sciences, and professions serving 3,600 students. Founded in 1891 by the Free Methodist Church of North America, it is recognized both for academic excellence and the efforts of its graduates to engage the culture to bring about positive change in the world. SPU has been designated one of America's best colleges by *U.S. News & World Report* and has been included on the John Templeton Foundation Honor Roll for Character-Building Colleges.

Seattle Pacific's beautiful 45-acre, tree-lined city campus lies in a residential area just 7 minutes from downtown Seattle, the business and cultural heart of the Pacific Northwest. A gateway to Canada and the Pacific Rim, Seattle offers easy access to a wide variety of outdoor recreation, such as sailing, skiing, hiking, and camping. The city also offers world-class fine arts, including opera, theater, symphony, and ballet. Seattle Pacific takes advantage of its urban setting by providing hundreds of internship and service experiences in the city's hospitals, schools, businesses, and churches.

In addition to its bachelor's degrees, SPU awards Master of Arts (M.A.), Master of Business Administration (M.B.A.), Master of Education (M.Ed.), Master of Science (M.S.), Master of Arts (TESOL), Master of Science in Nursing (M.S.N.), Doctor of Education (Ed.D.), and Doctor of Philosophy (Ph.D.) degrees.

Student Body Students come to SPU from thirty-nine states and twenty-six countries, representing more than fifty different Christian denominations. More than half of Seattle Pacific's undergraduate students live on campus in five residence halls and several apartment complexes. The University's unique leadership program encourages students to cultivate their individual talents by putting them to work in student government, ministries, performing groups, publications, clubs, and organizations.

Faculty The full-time faculty at Seattle Pacific is composed of 166 members, who are committed to the highest academic standards. Ninety-four percent of SPU's full-time faculty members hold the Ph.D. or an equivalent terminal degree. Seattle Pacific professors are experts in their fields; they publish, speak, and conduct research throughout the world. Their first priority, however, is teaching.

Key Facilities At the heart of the Seattle Pacific campus is the spacious, 62,000-square-foot library. It provides learning resource services, the latest technology, space for study and research, and approximately 150,000 volumes, arranged on open shelves for easy access. The library collection is accessible online in the library and through the campus computer network via its automated catalog. The library's Instructional Technology Services Department offers media production, satellite downlink, and duplication services. All Seattle Pacific residence halls have been wired to give students dedicated online connections to e-mail, the Internet, and the campus computer network.

Honorary Societies Ivy Honorary (affiliated with Mortar Board) and Alpha Kappa Sigma

Athletics Seattle Pacific's intercollegiate athletic program fields NCAA Division II teams in men's and women's basketball, crew, cross-country, soccer, and track and field and women's gymnastics and volleyball. All students have access to intramural sports as well as extramurals, special events, and health and fitness activities. The University's Royal Brougham Pavilion is one of the premier sports and recreation arenas in the Puget Sound area.

Study Abroad Seattle Pacific students have many opportunities to enhance their education with off-campus study. Each year, approximately 65 Seattle Pacific students participate in overseas study programs: the European Quarter, the Normandy (France) Studies Program, and the Salamanca (Spain) Program. Biennially, 30–35 students travel and study in Britain during British Isles Quarter. During quarter and summer breaks, students have the opportunity to join Seattle Pacific Reachout International (SPRINT) teams that travel to countries such as Northern Ireland, Russia, Nicaragua, Uganda, and Romania for a short-term mission experience.

Support Services Accommodations and support related to learning, physical, or psychological disabilities are arranged through the professional staff in Seattle Pacific's Center for Learning.

Job Opportunities A prime benefit of Seattle Pacific's location is the opportunity for internships in businesses, schools, hospitals, and other organizations. Research has shown that students who participate in internships find jobs more quickly after graduation and find jobs that are well suited to their interests and skills. To help students locate part-time jobs, the Office of Student Employment maintains a Job Board and Web page that list open positions for students. The Office of Student Employment also coordinates the Federal Work-Study, Community Service, and State Work-Study programs.

Tuition: $16,335 per year, full-time; $454 per quarter credit, part-time (2001–02)

Room and Board: $6249 per year (2001–02)

Mandatory Fees: $90 technology fee per year (2001–02)

Contact: Director: Dr. Susan VanZanten Gallagher, Marston Hall, Seattle Pacific University, 3307 Third Avenue West, Seattle, Washington 98119; Telephone: 206-281-2152; Fax: 206-281-2335; E-mail: gallaghe@spu.edu; Web site: http://www.spu.edu/acad/univ-scholars

SEMINOLE COMMUNITY COLLEGE

2 Pu G S Sc Tr

▼ Honors Seminar Program

The Honors Seminar Program at Seminole Community College (SCC) is a 22-credit curriculum that offers all qualifying students a unique academic opportunity to broaden and enrich their college experiences. The primary goal is to provide an atmosphere in which talented students can learn to think critically, grow intellectually, and expand their education beyond the classroom and into the public arena. The Program offers enriching classes in all areas of the general education requirements. Several classes are built around common themes so that the content is intertwined in various ways to enhance learning. In addition, students are encouraged to attend conferences to present scholarly papers as well as experience and participate in related cultural and social activities offered within the college and the community.

Upon completing a minimum of 22 honors credits, students in the program graduate with an Associate of Arts Honors Diploma. The Honors Seminar Program also offers an Honors Certificate Program. Students who qualify for the Honors Seminar Program may elect to earn a minimum of 12 credit hours in honors classes to receive a certificate upon graduation. This allows students whose majors require a strict course of study to take some of their general education courses, such as English, speech, and humanities, within the Honors Program.

Respected for their excellence in teaching as well as ability to motivate students, the honors professors are committed to building and expanding the program. They enjoy the challenge and the opportunity to develop courses that include alternative teaching and learning strategies that result in creative interaction for both students and teachers. Moreover, the Honors Seminar Program Coordinator works closely with each student to give personal advisement for classes as well as scholarship and transfer guidance and information.

SCC Honors students traditionally excel. Many have earned prestigious scholarships, such as the Woodrow Wilson Scholarship, upon transferring to four-year institutions in Florida, the United States, and abroad. In addition, they earn places on the All-USA Academic Teams sponsored by USA Today and *Who's Who in American Colleges and Universities.*

Honors classes typically have 16 to 20 students. Consequently, ample opportunity is available for students to bond with each other as well as the professors. Small class size allows for intellectual growth through collaborative and experiential learning, hands-on activities, and intellectual interaction.

Participation Requirements: SCC Honors Seminar Program welcomes any student who meets the following qualifications: high school seniors must have an GPA of at least 3.2 and a score of 1050 or higher on the SAT I or 23 or higher on the ACT. Those who take the College Placement Test must have minimum scores of 95 in reading and sentence skills and a minimum of 75 in math skills. Higher scores than minimums are preferred on all entrance tests. In addition, students are required to submit letters of recommendation, come for an interview, and prepare and submit a writing sample on campus. Once admitted to the Honors Seminar Program, students must maintain a 3.0 in honors classes and a 3.2 in non-honors classes. Students are required to complete a minimum of 22 credit hours of honors classes to graduate with an Honors Diploma. Those who wish to earn the Honors Certificate must complete a minimum of 12 credit hours in honors classes. Students are expected to volunteer their time and talent for activities sponsored by the College and the campus Phi Theta Kappa chapter.

Because SCC is a community college, many nontraditional students attend. Those who are uncertain of their qualifications as previously explained are still urged to apply or call for more information. Questions and concerns can be discussed in an interview.

Admission Process: Students who wish to apply to the Honors Seminar Program must have an interview with the Honors Coordinator and provide transcripts, previously written work, and letters of recommendation. The admission process is further explained in Honors brochures, which are available upon request.

Scholarship Availability: Honors students who have financial needs can receive scholarships funded by the Academic Improvement Trust Fund established by the Florida State Legislature. These merit scholarships were created to provide money for academically talented students and to expand diversity among community college students. In addition, Seminole Community College hosts a Dream Auction and other fund-raising events whose proceeds are matched by the state. Most of the monies go into scholarship funds that qualifying students may be eligible for. Currently, about 85 percent of all honors students receive some kind of scholarship aid.

The Campus Context: Established in 1965, Seminole Community College has been providing high-quality educational opportunity to residents of Seminole County and beyond for more than thirty-five years. The main campus is on a 200-acre site in beautiful, lake-dotted country southwest of Sanford, near Lake Mary. SCC has two additional campuses. The Hunt Club Campus opened in 1987 to serve residents of western Seminole County. Located in eastern Seminole County within five miles of the University of Central Florida, the Oviedo Campus opened in 2000. The College has been accredited since 1966 by the Commission on Colleges of the Southern Association of Colleges and Schools to award Associate of Arts and Associate of Science degrees as well as various other certificates and diplomas.

Student Body Undergraduate enrollment for fall 2001 was 10,565 students. SCC has a diverse population: 1,108 are African Americans, 254 are Asian, 1,255 are Hispanic, 37 are Native Americans, 7,176 are White, and 201 are other. All students commute to one of the three campuses. Student associations, business organizations, and clubs, such as Student Government Association, Brain Bowl, Hispanic Society, African-American Society etc., are well-established on campus to reflect the varied interests and diversity of the student body population. There is also a chapter of Phi Theta Kappa, the National Community College Honor Society.

Faculty 115 full-time instructors teach college credit classes; 15 percent have terminal degrees.

Key Facilities The Learning Resource Center (library), located on the main campus as well as the Oviedo Campus, houses 94,355 print and nonprint materials as well as computer facilities.

Honorary Society Phi Theta Kappa

Athletics Seminole Community College is a member of the Florida Community College Activities Association, the governing body for intercollegiate sports competition for junior college participation within the state. SCC teams compete in basketball, baseball, and softball.

Study Abroad Students have the opportunity to combine preparation on campus, international travel, and study abroad in the several disciplines through through Travel Study in British Literature (ENL 2950), Summer Semester in Cambridge, and

Interpreting the symbols: **2**=two-year college, **4**=four-year college; **Pu**=public or state college, **Pr**=private college; **G**=general honors program; **D**=departmental honors program; **S**=small program (fewer than 100 students), **M**=midsize program (100 to 500 students), **L**=large program (more than 500 students); **Sc**=scholarships available in honors program; **Tr**=transfer students accepted into honors program; **HBC**=historically black college; **AA**=academic advisors; **GA**=graduate advisors; **FA**=fellowship advisors.

Travel Study in Anthropology (ANT 2950). Content varies depending on the program in which students enroll. Students must be 18 years of age on or before departure. Permission of instructors or the department chair is required. Destinations vary dependent on the content to be covered.

Support Services Disabled Student Services provides grant-funded support services and auxiliary aids to students with documented physical or mental disabilities. Through this office, qualified students with disabilities may request course substitutions, special support services such as interpreters, note-takers, and tutors and testing accommodations. Disabled Student Services administers state auxiliary aid funds, coordinates support services with area agencies and College departments, and conducts workshops to help faculty members and students creative a positive learning environment for students with disabilities.

Job Opportunities Students are offered a range or work opportunities on campus, including tutoring and work-study.

Tuition: $52.43 for state residents, $194.03 for nonresidents, per credit hour (2001–02)

Contact: Beverly Bailey, Honors Seminar Program Coordinator, Seminole Community College, 100 Weldon Boulevard, Sanford, Florida 32773; Telephone: 407-328-2458 or 2355 (Honors Center); Fax: 407-328-2201; E-mail: honors@scc-fl.com or baileyb@scc-fl.com.

Shepherd College

4 Pu G M Sc Tr

▼ Honors Program

The mission of the Honors Program at Shepherd College is to create an academic environment in which gifted students can experience education in a dynamic and interactive way. Through seminars that promote active engagement in the subject area, independent research, a student-centered curriculum, and innovative teaching techniques, students in the Honors Program have the opportunity to become more self-directed in their learning. In the Honors Program, education does not simply take place in the classroom or through texts. Students become directly involved in the area of study through international and domestic travel, field trips, one-to-one interaction with professors and classmates, and a variety of activities outside the classroom that enhance the learning experience.

In addition to expanding the students' academic horizons, the Honors Program encourages student leadership and service to the community. The aim is to create graduates who are independent thinkers, insatiable learners, and responsible, socially conscious citizens. Honors students will leave Shepherd equipped to attend the finest graduate schools in the country and to be successful as solid contributors in their chosen professional careers. Graduates of the Honors Program are given recognition at graduating ceremonies.

The Honors Center at Shepherd College is located on the first floor of the Thacher Hall residence building. The Center includes the Office of the Director, the newly redecorated study lounge, and a computer lab. The Honors Residence Wing is also located on the first floor, allowing students to take full advantage of these facilities.

The 7-year-old program currently enrolls 130 students.

Participation Requirements: During the freshman year, honors students must participate in the honors core: Honors Written English and Honors History of Civilization. This two-semester, team-taught seminar introduces freshman honors students to major types of expository and critical writing in conjunction with the study of Western civilization. Topics focus on philosophical thought throughout history with emphasis on changes in government, economics, arts, science, and literature.

After completing the freshman core seminar, honors students may choose an honors course in a specific discipline or a special topics course. Special topics courses are team-taught seminars that cover interdisciplinary studies. In the past, these courses have included analysis of environmental issues; an exploration of the arts through theater, fine art, music, and dance; and the study of the history and culture of regions both within the United States and on an international level.

During their junior year, honors students begin research toward a major thesis to be completed as a graduation requirement. Each student chooses a mentor from the faculty and begins to formulate a reading list that would contribute to a thesis proposal. In collaboration with his/her thesis director, the student develops an original idea about the chosen topic and then analyzes the information using research to substantiate this idea.

Scholarship Availability: Shepherd College Presidential Scholarships are awarded to freshmen who have demonstrated outstanding academic potential based on both their high school grades in a college-preparatory program and their scores on either the ACT or the SAT I. The quality of high school courses as well as extracurricular activities both within and outside of high school are also considered. Scholarships may also be awarded to transfer students who have demonstrated outstanding academic progress based on their previous college work and grades.

The Honors Program awards several Presidential Scholarships to candidates who stand out for their high academic achievements, leadership in high school activities, and community service. These $1500 scholarships may be renewed yearly for a total of four years as long as the recipient maintains a cumulative yearly Shepherd GPA of at least 3.2 and completes at least 15 semester hours of course work per semester. For consideration for the Presidential Scholarships, students must complete the admissions application process by the stated application deadlines.

The Rubye Clyde Scholarship has been set up by the Shepherd College Foundation in recognition of Rubye Clyde McCormick and is designed for outstanding West Virginia students with solid academic credentials. Full tuition and fees as well as room and board for one year (about $5000) are provided through the scholarship. This scholarship is renewable if the student meets academic criteria established by the Shepherd College Foundation. In order to renew the scholarship, the student must have a 3.5 GPA or above with a course load of 15 credit hours per semester. This scholarship is open to a student in any major or field of study.

One Ralph and Margaret Burkhart Scholarship is awarded to an Honors Program candidate each year. This scholarship provides $5000 per academic year for tuition and fees, room and board, and books and supplies. Minimum selection criteria include a high school GPA of 3.5, a score of 1270 on the SAT I or 30 on the ACT, a personal interview with the Director of the Honors Program, and an essay that is part of the honors admission process. This scholarship is renewable each year based on the following criteria: enrollment in and completion of a minimum of 15 credit hours per semester and a GPA of at least 3.5.

The Hearst Foundation, Inc., was founded in 1945 by publisher and philanthropist William Randolph Hearst. In 1948, Mr. Hearst established the California Charities Foundation. Soon after Mr. Hearst's death in 1951, the name was changed to the William Randolph Hearst Foundation. Both foundations are independent private philanthropies operating separately from the Hearst Corporation. The charitable goals of the two foundations are essentially the same, reflecting the philanthropic interests of William Randolph Hearst—education, health, human services, and culture. Any student applying to the Honors Program is eligible for an award from these foundations. Potential recipients are judged on leadership, community service, and a superior academic record.

The Campus Context: Shepherd College is an institution offering fifty-six major degree programs. Among its notable facilities are the Civil War Center and the Sara Cree Wellness Center.

Student Body The Shepherd College student population consists of approximately 40 percent men. The minority ethnic distribution is about 7.4 percent, with about 4.3 percent black, 1.5 percent Hispanic, 1 percent Asian, and 1 percent Native American and international students. There are eleven professional fraternities, five social fraternities, and four sororities.

At Shepherd College, more than 90 percent of financial aid is awarded to students who have, through application, shown that they need additional money to meet college expenses.

Faculty There are 257 faculty members; of the 119 full-time faculty members, 87 percent hold terminal degrees. The student-faculty ratio is 19:1.

Key Facilities The library houses 195,000 volumes and 428,000 total items and is a Selective Federal Depository. There are a number of computer facilities on campus, including microclassrooms, with fifty computers that run Windows 95 or 98, and a lab, with twenty-three computers that run Windows 95. Internet access is available in the library, White Hall, and most labs, with dial-in access available in the residence halls.

Athletics Shepherd College is a member of the National Collegiate Athletic Association (NCAA) and the West Virginia Intercollegiate Athletic Conference (WVIAC). Varsity sports for men are soccer, football, basketball, baseball, tennis, golf, and cross-country; varsity sports for women are volleyball, basketball, tennis, softball, and cross-country.

Study Abroad Study-abroad opportunities at Shepherd College can take two forms. Through classes, student trips have included travel to Hungary and Senegal. Independent travel is also encouraged and arrangements can be made with the director.

Support Services The College counselor has been designated as the staff member to assist students with disabilities.

Job Opportunities Work-study is available to students who qualify for financial aid. For those who do not qualify, individual departments do budget money for student assistants. The Residence Life Office offers positions as Resident Assistants and Hall Security.

Tuition: $2228 for state residents, $5348 for nonresidents, per year (1998–99)

Room and Board: $3984

Contact: Director: Dr. Patricia Dwyer, 199 Thacher Hall, Shepherdstown, West Virginia 25443; Telephone: 304-876-5244; Fax: 304-876-3101; E-mail: pdwyer@intrepid.net

Shippensburg University of Pennsylvania

4 Pu M Tr

▼ Honors Program

The Honors Program at Shippensburg University is designed for academically motivated students who thrive in an atmosphere of creative learning and intellectual exploration. The program, which is open to all majors, offers courses within the general education curriculum. Honors courses differ from regular offerings by their small enrollment and emphasis on student participation. First semester students generally enter the program through a group of general education courses that might include World History I, Honors English, and a social science course, such as World Geography or Cultural Anthropology. Second semester students might take World History II, Basic Oral Communication, and a humanities course in music or literature. At the sophomore and junior levels, there are course offerings such as Justice in America and Chemistry in the Modern World. Other honors elective courses often develop around topics to encourage in-depth examination of a central theme or concept. The Honors Program offers experimental courses, such as Exploring Innovation and Invention, that provide students with the opportunity for independent application of their academic background.

Honors students also receive special advising and priority scheduling to ensure them access to appropriate courses and professors. To broaden professional experiences, many honors students volunteer time to a variety of campus and community organizations. Some honors students organize a Saturday school for middle school students. Honors students have the opportunity to meet in small discussion groups with internationally known figures. The state system also offers a 6-credit honors summer program with a thematic focus. Shippensburg University provides 2 students with a full scholarship to participate in this special, intensive program.

To ensure student involvement in the direction of the program, two honors students serve on a faculty steering committee. There is also a student steering committee, which is open to all honors students and plans social events, supports discussions with distinguished speakers who visit the campus, coordinates the volunteer program, and helps provide mentors for incoming students. *Honorable Intentions* (the program newsletter) and regularly scheduled meetings keep participants informed and allow for discussion of issues that relate to the program.

The program began in 1984 and currently enrolls 150 students.

Participation Requirements: To graduate from the Honors Program, students must complete 24 credit hours of honors general education courses. Students are expected to maintain a minimum 3.25 overall QPA and a 3.25 QPA in honors courses. Successful completion of the Honors Program is noted at graduation and is recorded on the student's transcript. Students also receive a Certificate of Graduation from the Honors Program.

Admission Process: Shippensburg University's Honors Program accepts 50 students for each entering class from those who formally apply. Entering University students should have a minimum SAT I score of 1150 (25 on the ACT), be in the upper-fifth of their high school class, and have participated in a variety of extracurricular activities. If an entering freshman is not admitted to the program because of limited space, but obtains a QPA of 3.25 the first semester, the student is encouraged to reapply for acceptance. The Director of Honors interviews interested, currently enrolled students to determine if they meet the criteria for admission and are able to complete 24 credits of general education honors courses. Interested high school seniors, transfer students, and undergraduates enrolled at Shippensburg University may obtain an application form from the Honors Program.

Applications must be submitted by March 1.

Scholarship Availability: The University does not offer scholarships designated specifically for honors students. However, it does offer a number of scholarships for qualified students.

The Campus Context: Founded in 1871, Shippensburg University is a member of the Pennsylvania State System of Higher Education. It is a comprehensive university offering both undergraduate and graduate degree programs. Shippensburg University is conveniently located in the Cumberland Valley of south central Pennsylvania, overlooking the Blue Ridge Mountains. The campus is situated on 200 acres of rolling land and is surrounded by a vast array of cultural and recreational sites.

Interpreting the symbols: **2**=two-year college, **4**=four-year college; **Pu**=public or state college, **Pr**=private college; **G**=general honors program; **D**=departmental honors program; **S**=small program (fewer than 100 students), **M**=midsize program (100 to 500 students), **L**=large program (more than 500 students); **Sc**=scholarships available in honors program; **Tr**=transfer students accepted into honors program; **HBC**=historically black college; **AA**=academic advisors; **GA**=graduate advisors; **FA**=fellowship advisors.

Shippensburg is a small university with a faculty dedicated to teaching. The emphasis on academic excellence has helped graduates to be recruited by businesses, government agencies, and educational institutions. Shippensburg graduates are regularly selected for admission to the finest graduate and professional programs. Small classes and a friendly campus make it easy to make friends, get involved, and receive the most from a university education. Visitors to the campus can see why a small university with a broad curriculum and diverse activities can start them on their way to success.

Fifty-two undergraduate programs are offered in the College of Arts and Sciences, the John L. Grove College of Business, and the College of Education and Human Services. A Division of Undeclared Majors offers students undecided about their majors a chance to earn credits.

Sixteen graduate degree programs are also offered. Special or distinguishing facilities on campus include fashion archives; an art gallery; a vertebrate museum; an on-campus elementary school; public service centers in arts/humanities, government, and management; a planetarium; and the Women's Center.

Student Body Undergraduate enrollment is approximately 6,200. There are more than 350 students who are members of minority groups on campus. Sixty-six percent of the freshmen receive financial assistance. Students belong to one local fraternity, twelve national fraternities, three local sororities, and eight national sororities.

Faculty Of the 320 full-time-equivalent faculty members, more than 85 percent are full-time; 85 percent have doctorates or terminal degrees. The student-faculty ratio is 20:1. All classes are taught by faculty members, not graduate assistants.

Key Facilities Ezra Lehman Memorial Library provides Web access to the following materials: its holdings, the holdings of the state library and twenty-four other academic libraries, a variety of full-text databases, electronic books, and Internet sites. The collection includes more than 2 million items, including bound volumes, microform pieces, periodicals, audiovisual titles, government documents, and University archives. The Information and Computing Technologies Center maintains a campus network, with a number of computer labs for student use. Each student receives an e-mail account and access to the Internet.

Honorary Societies Phi Kappa Phi and Phi Sigma Pi

Athletics Shippensburg University competes in Division II of the NCAA, offering eight men's and ten women's sports. In addition, there are many intramural sports and recreational activities.

Study Abroad Shippensburg University encourages students in all majors to consider the value of a semester or year of study in another country. The Study Abroad Program is designed to assist students in deciding if study abroad is appropriate and then helps students select a country, choose a program, complete the application process, and support participants while they are abroad. The University has educational agreements with universities in the United Kingdom, Canada, Denmark, and other countries. Because of its membership in the Pennsylvania State System of Higher Education International Studies Consortium, Shippensburg enables students to study abroad in each member's programs. In addition, the University has access to more than 4,500 other international programs. These experiences allow students to gain cultural knowledge and social skills that enhance their opportunities for advanced study and careers.

Support Services Learning and/or physically disabled students attend regular classes and receive scheduling preferences if registered with the Office of Social Equity. Most buildings are completely or partially accessible. Accommodations such as note takers, audio-aids, readers, and tutors can be obtained through the Office of Social Equity. Specialized equipment includes a Xerox Kurweil personal reader, a Comtek Telecaption 4000 closed caption decoder, VTEK viewing machines to magnify print, and phones with a TDD for the hearing impaired.

Job Opportunities There are opportunities for part-time employment on and off the campus through federal and campus work programs. Students with demonstrated financial need are given priority in job placement, but an effort is made to place as many students as possible who have desired work skills. These positions include work in administrative and faculty offices, the library, classes, University residence halls, and on the campus grounds. Additional employment opportunities are available through the campus food service and the Student Association. Students should apply for jobs through these organizations directly.

Tuition: $4016 for state residents, $10,040 for nonresidents, per year (2001–02)

Room and Board: $4642 for a room and 15-meal plan. Additional optional meal plans are available.

Mandatory Fees: $988

Contact: Director, Honors Program, 1871 Old Main Drive, Shippensburg, Pennsylvania 17257; Telephone: 717-477-1604; Fax: 717-477-1389; E-mail: clyoun@ark.ship.edu; Web site: http://www.ship.edu

---

SINCLAIR COMMUNITY COLLEGE

2 Pu G S Tr

▼ Honors Program

The Sinclair Honors Program is designed to meet the needs of academically superior students who seek intellectual challenge and are willing to assume more responsibility for the learning experience. The aim of the program is to identify, stimulate, and recognize Sinclair's best students. Honors courses cultivate critical-thinking skills, encourage individual inquiry, and demand high-quality performance and responsibility. Honors works closely with Phi Theta Kappa and the Ohio Fellows Program. The Honors Director presides over an Honors Council made up of faculty members, students, and counselors.

Started in the 1980s, the program enrolls about 100 students each quarter in honors classes, and about 20 honors scholars are currently active. It is affiliated with the National Collegiate Honors Council and the Mid-East Honors Association.

Participation Requirements: Any Sinclair student may take an honors course with permission from the instructor or Honors Director. Honors scholars must maintain a minimum 3.25 GPA or a 3.5 to be eligible for quarterly $500 scholarships. Honors scholars must complete five honors courses in three different disciplines, and one of those courses must be interdisciplinary. They must also complete a service learning project, a requirement that may or may not earn credit.

Admission Process: Students are identified through admissions testing as possible honors participants and are invited to apply. However, any student who meets the criteria may apply at any point while at Sinclair. Two letters of reference and a personal essay are required in addition to at least a 3.25 GPA and an interview with the Honors Council.

Scholarship Availability: Honors scholars with a GPA of 3.5 or better are eligible to apply for Honors Scholarships up to six times (six quarters) while attending the College. These scholarships, provided by the Sinclair Foundation, are for $500 maximum per quarter and may be used for tuition, fees, and bookstore charges. An application with letters of reference is required, and students must apply in writing for renewal each quarter.

The Campus Context: Sinclair was founded as a YMCA-related institution in 1887 and became the public community college for Montgomery County in 1959. The present large, modern campus in downtown Dayton was designed by Edward Durrell Stone and opened in 1972. It enrolls nearly 20,000 students each quarter and offers a broad variety of university parallel, certificate, and vocational degree programs. The student body is highly diverse. Sinclair is accredited by the North Central Association of Colleges and Schools. It is rated the best community college in Ohio and also has the state's lowest tuition.

Student Body Sinclair enrolls about 20,000 students each quarter; 66 percent are women. The ethnic distribution is 80 percent white, 17 percent African American, and 3 percent other minorities, primarily Asian.

Faculty Of the 306 full-time faculty members, 60 have earned a terminal degree. The College employs about 600 part-time instructors, some of whom also have terminal degrees.

Key Facilities The Learning Resources Center owns about 139,000 volumes and subscribes to 621 periodicals. The campus has more than 1,400 computers, many of which are available to students in seventy-three different labs and other locations. The new Center for Interactive Learning (CIL) is one of the most advanced distance-learning facilities in the nation.

Athletics Sinclair offers a full range of varsity athletics and facilities for students and faculty and staff members in the Physical Activities Center. Teams compete in basketball, baseball, tennis, golf, and other sports.

Study Abroad Students who have a GPA of 2.0 or better and meet discipline-specific requirements may apply for the study abroad program.

Support Services Sinclair offers a full range of services for handicapped students, along with a tutorial center, a program for adult college education, a college for seniors, a developmental studies program, credit for lifelong learning, and a large experience-based education department. Scholarships and financial aid are available for most programs, as is work-study. The Distance Learning Division and TV Sinclair, operating out of the new Center for Interactive Learning, are growing rapidly.

Tuition: $31 per credit for Montgomery County residents, $49 for other Ohio residents, $80 for nonresidents (1998–99)

Contact: Director: Dr. Thomas Martin, 444 West Third Street, Dayton, Ohio 45402-1460; Telephone: 937-512-5189; Fax: 937-512-5192; E-mail: tmartin@sinclair.edu; Web site: http://www.sinclair.edu/departments/honors/

South Dakota State University

4 Pu G M Sc Tr

▼ Honors College

The South Dakota State University (SDSU) Honors College is new to South Dakota State University, but the University has offered honors courses since the 1960s and has supported a formal University Honors Program for approximately twenty years. The SDSU Honors College is the newest approach to the University's long-standing commitment to excellence in education. It is an investment in this goal to graduate students who are globally aware and competitive, gifted in communication skills, exceptionally knowledgeable in their disciplines, active in community affairs, and motivated to excel in their professional pursuits.

Students participating in the SDSU Honors College benefit in many ways. Learning is enhanced when students form communities and complete limited-enrollment honors courses together. Students grow intellectually as a result of their relationships with faculty mentors on campus and with external mentors drawn from a variety of professions and enterprises. On-campus students have the opportunity to be grouped in a shared housing area, making it easier to form student support and study groups. Students may participate in sponsored undergraduate research under the supervision of University faculty members and are required to participate in a variety of course-centered and Honors College-sponsored enrichment programs. Students receive faculty guidance in seeking highly competitive international, national, and institutional fellowships or scholarships for graduate or professional studies. Graduate study and career opportunities are broadened through the Honors College networking with other universities and public and private-sector employers.

Honors College courses have limited enrollments of no more than 25 students. The courses emphasize student responsibilities for course quality and outcomes and further emphasize active student participation in the learning process. Honors College courses are dedicated to developing the highest level of proficiency in communication skills, critical-thinking skills, and creativity. The Honors Colloquium and the directed study requirement place special emphasis on integration and synthesis of ideas.

Honors College enrichment opportunities, an integral part of Honors College courses, are required beyond academic expectations. These enrichment opportunities are designed to contribute to the social and cultural maturity of students as well as to serve as an alternative means of teaching and learning. Participation in enrichment programs is required in some instances and encouraged in other instances. Enrichment opportunities take many forms, including campus lectures, theater performances, field trips, conference attendance, social gatherings, and study abroad.

Campus residential hall space is dedicated to a residential life program for freshman and sophomore Honors College students on a request basis. Honors College programming, computer usage, and study areas are included. The residential life program seeks to promote a sense of unity among Honors College students and seeks to facilitate the promotion of Honors College academic and enrichment objectives.

Current student enrollment in honors courses is approximately 180 students.

Participation Requirements: The Honors College curriculum is a four-year program. The curriculum includes 15 credit hours of honors general education courses, 3- to 6-credit courses of Honors Colloquium, 3 to 6 credit hours of honors directed study, and 6 credit hours of honors contract course work. Participation in enrichment opportunities is also required. A total of 27 honors course credits and a minimum cumulative 3.4 GPA are required to graduate with Honors College distinction.

Admission Process: Incoming freshmen with an ACT score of 27 or above or the equivalent SAT I score and/or rank in the upper 10 percent of their high school class are invited to enroll for general education honors sections. Exceptions are made for other students who have demonstrated high academic ability, exceptional motivation, or extraordinary talents. Eligible students who wish to continue in the Honors College must apply for full admission toward the end of their first year. Admission exceptions are made for transfer students. Once accepted for continued enrollment, students must earn a minimum 3.0 GPA for a given semester, complete at least one honors course each academic year, complete minimum enrichment opportunities, and receive a positive recommendation from their faculty mentor to maintain the continued enrollment status. There is no additional cost for initial or continued Honors College enrollment.

Scholarship Availability: Honors College students are eligible to apply for one or more of the nearly 2,000 achievement-based University, college, and departmental scholarships.

The Campus Context: South Dakota State University was founded in 1881 as the state's land-grant university. SDSU is a comprehensive

Interpreting the symbols: **2**=two-year college, **4**=four-year college; **Pu**=public or state college, **Pr**=private college; **G**=general honors program; **D**=departmental honors program; **S**=small program (fewer than 100 students), **M**=midsize program (100 to 500 students), **L**=large program (more than 500 students); **Sc**=scholarships available in honors program; **Tr**=transfer students accepted into honors program; **HBC**=historically black college; **AA**=academic advisors; **GA**=graduate advisors; **FA**=fellowship advisors.

four-year university offering more than 200 majors, minors, and options in the eight colleges, which include the Colleges of Agriculture and Biological Sciences, Arts and Science, Education and Counseling, Engineering, Family and Consumer Sciences, Nursing, Pharmacy, and General Registration. SDSU is located in Brookings, a town of more than 18,000 on the east-central edge of South Dakota. SDSU students enjoy an open, relaxed, and safe campus environment. The campus is the site for the South Dakota Agricultural Heritage Museum, the South Dakota Art Museum, and the Northern Plains Biostress Laboratory, in addition to more than fifty academic, athletic, performing arts, and residential life buildings.

Student Body South Dakota State University is South Dakota's largest university, with an enrollment of 9,300. The student body is predominantly white/Caucasian. The Asian/Pacific minority constitutes 2.4 percent of the student body and Native American, 1.3 percent. There are approximately 180 international students representing twenty-seven other nations on campus. Three fourths of the students are South Dakota residents. Women constitute 51 percent of the student body. Students between 18 and 23 years of age make up 85 percent of the student body. Ninety percent of the students receive financial aid.

Faculty Seventy percent of SDSU's 514 full-time faculty members hold terminal degrees in their disciplines. The average class size at SDSU is 25 students, and the student-teacher ratio is 15:1.

Key Facilities Library services and collections are housed in the spacious three-level Briggs Library. Library collections consist of more than 540,000 bound volumes, 350,000 government documents, and additional holdings of microtext, maps, newspapers, and pamphlet materials. More than 3,000 journal titles are received currently, with another 800 titles available electronically in full-text format. For students, SDSU provides five general-access computer labs plus a computer design lab with eighteen to thirty-two IBM-compatible machines in each lab. Many individual departments and colleges provide separate labs for special needs. All residence halls offer direct Internet connection. E-mail services are free for students, and the opportunity is provided for students to create their own World Wide Web home pages.

Honorary Societies Alpha Lambda Delta, Golden Key, Mortar Board, Phi Kappa Phi, Pi Gamma Mu, Sigma Xi

Athletics SDSU competes in the NCAA Division II North Central Conference and fields teams in ten men's sports and ten women's sports. Nearly 6,000 students participate in more than forty intramural and club sports offered each year.

Study Abroad SDSU does sponsor a formal study-abroad program. There is a formal agreement for student exchange with Manchester Metropolitan University in Manchester, England, and formal travel study programs with Chungnam National University in Taejon, South Korea. Other travel-study courses are arranged in Spain, Mexico, Costa Rica, Bolivia, and France.

Support Services SDSU reaffirms that it is committed to a policy of nondiscrimination on the basis of physical or mental disability/impairment in the offering of all benefits and services and educational and employment opportunities. Services include assisting in acquisition of taped materials, facility accommodations, course scheduling assistance, classroom accommodations, and referral to other service agencies.

Job Opportunities The Career and Academic Planning Center provides students assistance in their search for part-time, summer, intern, or full-time employment. The Federal Work-Study financial aid awards are based on financial need and SDSU award policy. Many jobs are on campus, and the local business and industrial community offers many other opportunities for part-time employment, internships, and community service jobs.

Tuition: $1996 for residents, per year; $6352 for nonresidents for 32 credit hours; $62.40 per credit hour for residents, $198.50 per credit hour for nonresidents (2001–02). Special rates apply to residents of Minnesota, Iowa, Nebraska, Wisconsin, and states that are members of the Western Interstate Commission for Higher Education (WICHE).

Room and Board: $3040 for two semesters (2001–02)

Mandatory Fees: $1812 (2001–02)

Contact: Director: Distinguished Professor Robert Burns, SDSU Admin. 315, Box 2201, Brookings, South Dakota 57007; Telephone: 605-688-4913; Fax: 605-688-6540; E-mail: robert.burns@sdstate.edu.

South Florida Community College

2 Pu G S Sc Tr

▼ Honors Program

The Honors Program at South Florida Community College (SFCC) invites academically talented students to engage in a rigorous and self-directed educational experience. Students who complete 15 honors credits receive recognition at graduation. Their classes are smaller with increased student involvement, which makes this program challenging and exciting. Students master and document such skills as critical thinking and writing, verbal presentations, and rhetorical and logical analysis, and such attributes as leadership and service. Courses are currently provided in the humanities, social/behavioral sciences, and the sciences. A dental assistant program is being planned.

SFCC instituted its Honors Program in order to offer less expensive and more challenging learning experiences to the best students in the district. The main focus is on transferring students into honors programs at Florida's four-year colleges and universities and on making sure that students can compete for scholarship money that is available only to honors program graduates.

Courses that meet the general education requirements are offered in a variety of formats to fit students' schedules and learning styles. Examples of courses include an honors symposium for groups of speakers or a series of presentations on campus, an honors seminar for an interdisciplinary study of a theme or subject, and an honors section of a course for learning the subject matter via interactive and self-directed teaching methods. In the past, the program has used the honors topics and televised broadcasts produced by the National Collegiate Honors Council.

The Honors Program offers a variety of extracurricular activities, including service learning and several clubs and student organizations dedicated to motivated students. The program requires that students document at least 25 hours of service learning in the communities and offers many opportunities each semester for meaningful volunteer work. Under consideration is the idea of allowing students to earn honors credit for participating in SFCC's Jazz Ensemble. Moreover, SFCC offers internship opportunities.

The Honors Program also requires that each student take a capstone course, The Competitive Edge. This course is designed to familiarize students with two subjects: success in a four-year college and success in the business world. The course involves leadership skills and professional standards as well as study skills and academic planning. Speakers from the professional community address key issues in this course, and faculty members work closely with Career Center staff members to make sure that students are ready for professional challenges. In addition, speakers from nearby colleges and universities are invited to participate.

Participation Requirements: In order to receive recognition from the Honors Program with a gold seal on the diploma and a pin, students must complete 15 or more honors credit hours with a cumulative GPA of 3.3 or higher; a major research project that indicates critical, independent thinking and the ability to present in-depth, authoritative research, both verbally and in a well-written and well-documented paper; and at least one honors seminar. In addition, students' computerized records must indicate the proper documentation for rhetorical analysis, logical analysis, critical-thinking skills, writing skills, 25 logged hours of service learning, at least one major verbal presentation with visual aids (at least 10 to 15 minutes), and completion of the course, The Competitive Edge.

Admission Process: There are several paths into the Honors Program at South Florida Community College. A student wishing to enter the program must provide proof of one of the following to be accepted automatically: SAT I score of at least 1100, ACT score of at least 25, top 5 percent of high school class or minimum cumulative GPA or 3.65 out of 4.0, minimum cumulative GPA of 3.3 in at least 12 hours of college credit courses, 111 or higher on sentence skills component of Computerized Placement Test (CPT), or at least 111 on sentence structure component of the Florida College Entry-level Placement Test. Should a student wish to be accepted into the Honors Program but not meet any of the above criteria for automatic acceptance, the student may appeal directly to the Honors Council with a letter of application. The student must also submit either two letters of recommendation from college instructors or a research proposal. The Honors Council, after reviewing all of the applications, will schedule an interview with the student. The Honors Program will have a form for students to fill out to request permission to enter the program. The South Florida Community College Admissions office will process the paperwork and verify the student's proof.

Scholarship Availability: There are three ways that graduates of the Honors Program can receive scholarships for their four-year programs. There are scholarships for transfer students with a good academic record, Phi Theta Kappa scholarships, and honors program scholarships to students with an A.A. degree with recognition from the Honors Program. Furthermore, the South Florida Community College Foundation is prepared to provide some level of assistance to each student selected for the SFCC Honors Program as an incentive to participate.

The Campus Context: Since 1965, South Florida Community College has provided a very inexpensive, high-quality, local education. It was established in 1965 when the legislature authorized a state-supported two-year college to serve Highlands and Hardee Counties. DeSoto County joined the College District in 1984. The local area includes small business and service industries, especially citrus, and several growing towns, including Sebring, home of the 12 Hours of Sebring race. The College is nicely situated equidistant from Orlando and Tampa, and the local area remains quiet and comfortable, with a small-town friendliness. As one of the most comprehensive community colleges in the state, SFCC offers instruction in many different areas, including college credit, vocational noncredit, adult and community education, and workforce development. The College grants the Associate of Arts degree, eighteen Associate of Science degrees, and Associate of Applied Science degrees.

Student Body Undergraduate enrollment is 39 percent men and 61 percent women. The ethnic distribution is 76.4 percent white, 11.9 percent black, 10 percent Hispanic, .86 percent Asian, .3 percent Native American, and .5 percent other. Limited off-campus housing is offered at the Hotel Jacaranda in Avon Park. Although there are no traditional fraternities or sororities, South Florida Community College sponsors the Tau Epsilon chapter of Phi Theta Kappa as well as many other clubs and student organizations.

Faculty Of the 21 relevant faculty members, all are full-time and have terminal degrees. The student-faculty ratio in honors classes is 15:1.

Key Facilities The library houses 44,000 books and periodicals. There are two computer labs and several computerized classrooms on campus. The Citrus Center and the Public Service Academy are located on campus. A University Center is under construction.

Honorary Societies Phi Theta Kappa

Athletics South Florida Community College is a member of the Florida Community College Activities Association, which is the governing body for intercollegiate sports competition for junior college participation within the state. SFCC teams compete in women's volleyball, women's tennis, and men's baseball.

Study Abroad South Florida Community College sponsors trips abroad through EF Educational Tours. While destinations may vary from semester to semester, students may receive college humanities credit through HUM 2701, Humanities Overseas Study Program.

Support Services Disabled Student Services (DSS) is a unit of SFCC Student Services, in compliance with Section 504 of the Rehabilitation Act of 1973, as amended, and the Americans with Disabilities Act of 1990. The purpose of DSS is to provide services to students with disabilities. The program of services for qualified students includes but is not limited to admission and registration assistance, special campus, orientation, notetaking, tutoring, alternative testing, audiovisual aids, readers, scribes, and mobility aids. These services permit students access to the same educational opportunities as their nondisabled peers and are offered within the institution's philosophical framework that stresses student independence and self-reliance. DSS operates in cooperation and conjunction with other units in Student Services (Assessment Center and Student Support Services) to ensure continuity of services. In addition, DSS works closely with other public and private rehabilitation agencies to facilitate the coordination of services.

Job Opportunities Students are offered a range of work opportunities on campus, including tutoring and work-study. Internships with businesses in the surrounding community are encouraged.

Tuition: $51.31 per semester hour for state residents, $192.39 per semester hour for nonresidents (2001–02)

Contact: Director of the Honors Program, 600 West College Drive, Avon Park, Florida 33825; Telephone: 863-453-6661; Fax: 863-784-7229; Web site: http://www.sfcc.cc.fl.us

South Mountain Community College

2 Pu G S Sc Tr

▼ Honors Program

The philosophy of the Honors Program at South Mountain Community College is consistent with that of the Maricopa Community College District: to provide education for the diverse interests, needs, and capacities of the students it serves. The Honors Program exists to enhance the academic preparation of exceptional students in their initial college years. The aim of the Honors Program is to promote a sense of scholarship and community among its participants.

The Honors Program is designed to enhance students' intellectual growth by offering challenging courses and increased contact with other honors students. The program includes honors sections of general education classes, honors contract options, faculty mentors, special activities, and forum presentations that permit students to hear and talk with prominent lecturers. Each year the Maricopa District Honors Program presents an Honors Forum Series based on an honors study topic selected in conjunc-

Interpreting the symbols: **2**=two-year college, **4**=four-year college; **Pu**=public or state college, **Pr**=private college; **G**=general honors program; **D**=departmental honors program; **S**=small program (fewer than 100 students), **M**=midsize program (100 to 500 students), **L**=large program (more than 500 students); **Sc**=scholarships available in honors program; **Tr**=transfer students accepted into honors program; **HBC**=historically black college; **AA**=academic advisors; **GA**=graduate advisors; **FA**=fellowship advisors.

tion with Phi Theta Kappa, the international honor society for two-year colleges. The Honors Forum course (HUM 190) is offered to prepare students for concepts discussed at the lectures. Finally, each honors course is designated HONORS on the student's official transcript.

Honors students enjoy a sense of community, an environment of excellence, and greater depth in their academic experience under the guidance of faculty mentors. In addition to honors sections of general education courses, special seminars, and the contract option, students are able to participate in honors-sponsored cultural, social, and educational events, including opportunities for travel to honors conferences and Phi Theta Kappa activities.

The program, which began in 1981, currently enrolls 50 students per academic year.

Participation Requirements: To graduate as a South Mountain Community College Honors Program scholar a student must complete a total of 15 credits in course work designated as Honors. The course work must include 3 credits of HUM 190 (Honors Forum) and 12 credits selected from at least three different course prefixes. Students who complete the above distribution of courses with grades of A or B and an overall GPA of 3.25 or higher receive special designation as Honors Program Graduates at the annual College award program and on the graduation program. The Honors designation indicates excellence and commitment both to prospective employers and to the admissions offices at other colleges and universities.

Admission Process: Any student may enroll in a specific honors section with the instructor's approval. Recent high school graduates who are in the top 15 percent of their high school class from a Maricopa County high school should apply for the President's Scholarship, which will also give them standing in the Honors Program. Continuing students should submit an Honors Program application to the Honors Coordinator.

Scholarship Availability: Honors Program students have several opportunities for scholarships and fee waivers. Graduates of a Maricopa County high school who have ranked in the top 15 percent at the end of the sixth, seventh, or eighth semester and who have not attended another college or university are eligible for the President's Scholarship. Continuing students who have completed 12 or more credits of college-level work at SMCC or another college or university with a cumulative GPA of at least 3.25 are eligible to apply for fee waiver status. All continuing members of the SMCC Honors Program who plan to return for the following academic year are considered by the Honors Committee for the Chancellor's Scholarship, Honors Foundation Scholarship, and the Betty Hedin Elsner Scholarship. In addition, applications for the All-USA Academic Team and the Guistewhite Scholarship are available through the Honors Office.

The Campus Context: South Mountain Community College, a member of the Maricopa County Community College District, was founded in 1979. The College is located in the shadow of South Mountain Park, the largest municipal park in the United States. Near both downtown Phoenix and Tempe, just minutes from the I-10 and Superstition freeways and Arizona State University, South Mountain Community College is served by the Phoenix Transit Bus System. Known as the "College with the Personal Touch," South Mountain is one of the smaller of the Maricopa colleges. The College offers three degrees—Associate of Arts, Associate of General Studies, and Associate of Applied Science—as well as several certificate programs. Among the campus facilities is a child-care center licensed by the Arizona Department of Health Services and Department of Economic Security.

Student Body Of the 2,500 enrolled students, the majority are from the Phoenix area. All students commute to campus.

Faculty There are 40 full-time faculty members, 28 percent with doctorates.

Key Facilities The Learning Resource Center includes the MCCCD Online Public Access Catalog, Eureka, InfoTrac, and EVIN, in addition to standard library materials. Computer facilities house Macintosh, IBM, and Digital computers.

Honorary Society Phi Theta Kappa

Athletics Men's sports are basketball, baseball, soccer, and cross-country; women's sports are softball, volleyball, basketball, soccer, and cross-country.

Support Services The campus is handicapped accessible.

Job Opportunities Opportunities for work-study jobs exist in most departments.

Tuition: $40 for area residents, $63 (1–6 credits) or $75 (7 or more credits) for state residents, $65 (1–6 credits) or $177 (7 or more credits) for nonresidents, per credit hour (1999–2000)

Mandatory Fees: $5 per semester and college

Contact: Coordinator: Helen J. Smith, 7050 South 24th Street, Phoenix, Arizona 85040; Telephone: 602-243-8122; Fax: 602-243-8306; E-mail: smith_h@smc.maricopa.edu; Web site: http://www.smc.maricopa.edu (under construction)

SOUTHEAST MISSOURI STATE UNIVERSITY

4 Pu G M Tr

▼ Honors Program

The Honors Program at Southeast Missouri State affords its students a great deal of flexibility in determining how to best make use of program resources and fulfill program requirements. Students select from a variety of honors sections of courses in the University's nationally recognized University Studies liberal education curriculum. In addition, students can design their own projects to earn honors credit by contract in nonhonors sections of courses. The Senior Honors Project can also be tailored to their individual interests and needs. Given this freedom, former honors students have created senior projects as diverse as original laboratory and/or literature research in a wide variety of disciplines, comparisons of American and Welsh educational practices based on a study-abroad experience, musical and literary analyses based on a senior voice recital, preparation of a one-women exhibition by an fine arts major, and development of an elaborate program for educating junior high students about Shakespeare.

The creativity and exuberance of the honors students is matched by the skill and love of teaching of the honors faculty members. Most honors faculty members are recruited on the basis of student recommendation as one of the best teaching faculty members on campus. The honors faculty members enjoy working closely with students in the classroom as well as on extracurricular projects. Most honors classes are kept to between 15 and 25 students to facilitate the type of interactive learning environment the honors faculty members consider most appropriate for achieving a true honors educational experience. In addition to being successfully involved in their individual disciplines, honors faculty members demonstrate their creativity in the original courses they design. Honors sections have been offered in courses as diverse as Victorian Studies, Science and Religion, North American Indians, and The History of the Future.

Service learning has been an integral part of the Honors Program for the past seven years. Freshmen are encouraged to participate in modest service activities. Opportunities for much more extensive service involvement are available for all students in the program. All service activity is coordinated by the Learning in Volunteerism committee that is composed of honors students exclusively.

The Honors Program offices are located in a comfortable house situated on one corner of the campus. In addition to work space, the house contains a nice living room for informal gatherings and a handy kitchen, making the honors house a relaxing home-like gathering place for the members of the honors community. The Southeast Honors Program was established in 1984. It currently has about 500 students.

Participation Requirements: To remain in the Honors Program, students must maintain a minimum GPA of 3.25 and maintain active involvement in the program. A minimum of 24 hours of honors credit must be accumulated to complete the program. Students are also required to complete a senior honors project. Students who complete the Honors Program requirements are designated Honors Scholars and receive highest recognition at both the Honors Convocation and the Commencement Ceremony. They receive a certificate of completion and a medallion to be worn at the commencement exercises. Notification of completion of the Honors Program requirement is added to their academic transcript.

Admission Process: Admission to the Honors Program requires a cumulative high school GPA of at least 3.4 on a 4.0 scale and an ACT composite score of at least 25. Students who do not meet these standards may be admitted to the program by petition if, at the end of 12 semester hours of college work, they have earned a cumulative GPA of at least 3.25.

Scholarship Availability: The Honors Program does not administer its own scholarships. However, the University has a generous merit scholarship program, and the vast majority of honors students hold one of the four top merit scholarships: the Governor's, Regents', University, and President's Scholarships. For the 2001–02 academic year, these scholarships held values as follows. The Governor's scholarship covers incidental fees (tuition), general fees, and textbook rental for the equivalent of up to 32 hours per academic year at Southeast and residence hall fees in a standard, double-occupancy room with fifteen meals per week. National Merit/Achievement Finalists may receive additional allocations. The Regents' scholarship covers incidental fees (tuition) for the equivalent of up to 32 hours per academic year. The University Scholarship provides $2500 per academic year for out-of-state students. The President's Scholarship provides $1500 per academic year for in-state students. For further information on scholarships, students should contact the Admissions Office at 573-651-2590.

The Campus Context: Southeast Missouri State University is situated on more than 200 acres on a hill overlooking Cape Girardeau, a city of 40,000 citizens, and the Mississippi River. Southeast was established in 1873 as the Southeast Missouri Normal School, and its current title was approved on August 24, 1972. Southeast offers close to ninety degrees through its six colleges: the Donald L. Harrison College of Business; the Colleges of Education, Health and Human Services, Liberal Arts, and Science and Technology; and the Polytechnic Institute.

The Southeast campus is pretty, friendly, and safe even as the University is aggressively transforming itself into a twenty-first century educational center. The recently completed College of Business building and the newly remodeled College of Liberal Arts building are state-of-the-art classroom, office, and conference centers. The newly expanded Student Recreation Center is one of the finest facilities of its kind at a school the size of Southeast. A new facility for the Polytechnic Institute that opened in fall 2001 has won an award for its innovative design. Efforts are currently underway to secure funding to convert a historic former seminary overlooking the Mississippi River into a beautiful River Campus, which will include magnificent centers for the visual and performing arts.

Cape Girardeau is the largest hub for retailing, medicine, manufacturing, communication, and cultural activities between St. Louis, Missouri, and Memphis, Tennessee. It offers many of the commercial resources of bigger cities while retaining a more relaxed atmosphere. Favorite student points include the beautiful city parks, several picturesque spots on the Mississippi River, and the nearby Trail of Tears State Park. The Show Me Center, a joint venture between the University and the city, is a very versatile exhibition hall that has played host to such diverse attractions as Bob Hope; Garth Brooks; Aerosmith; the St. Louis Symphony; the traveling company of *Jesus Christ, Superstar;* and the Monster Truck Rally.

Student Body Approximately 8,500 undergraduates are enrolled in the University. Sixty-five percent of enrolled undergraduates and 60 percent of enrolled freshmen receive financial aid.

Faculty Southeast employs more than 350 full-time faculty members, with a student-faculty ratio of 18:1.

Key Facilities Kent Library houses approximately 408,875 volumes accessible on open shelving. The periodicals collection contains 2,400 subscriptions. The microform collection contains 804,000 items. The library has been a selective depository for United States government publications since 1916, and in 1977 it was designated a depository for Missouri state documents. It holds about 287,366 items in this collection. The Rare Book Room contains more than 800 rare and unusual books and manuscripts. Southeast has six University-operated computer labs, with other computer labs located in departments within the University.

Honorary Societies Phi Eta Sigma and Phi Kappa Phi

Athletics Southeast's sports are classified at the NCAA Division I level. The University is a member of the NCAA and the Ohio Valley Conference. It offers seven sports for men and eight sports for women. Men's sports include football, cross-country, basketball, indoor and outdoor track, baseball, and golf. Women's sports include volleyball, cross-country, basketball, indoor and outdoor track, gymnastics, softball, and tennis.

Study Abroad Students are afforded the opportunity to travel abroad through a number of University department-sponsored programs. The International Exchange Program extends these opportunities to such countries as Great Britain, the Netherlands, Sweden, and Mexico. A catalog of available programs is available through the Office of Extended Learning.

Support Services Most facilities are fully accessible to disabled persons. Furthermore, the University has committed itself to take the appropriate measures to accommodate any disability. Reassignment of classes or other services to accessible locations, redesigning equipment, assignment of aides, alterations of existing facilities, and construction of new accessible facilities are all means of accommodation provided by Southeast.

Job Opportunities Work opportunities are available on and off campus.

Tuition: Approximately $3234 for residents, $6069 for nonresidents, per year (2001–02)

Room and Board: $4380–$5649

Mandatory Fees: Approximately $440

Contact: Director: Dr. Larry Clark, MS 2050, Cape Girardeau, Missouri 63701; Telephone: 573-651-2513; E-mail: lclark@semo.edu

SOUTHEASTERN LOUISIANA UNIVERSITY

4 Pu G M Sc Tr

▼ University Honors Program

The University Honors Program (UHP) at Southeastern Louisiana University is designed to prepare students to recognize and be

Interpreting the symbols: **2**=two-year college, **4**=four-year college; **Pu**=public or state college, **Pr**=private college; **G**=general honors program; **D**=departmental honors program; **S**=small program (fewer than 100 students), **M**=midsize program (100 to 500 students), **L**=large program (more than 500 students); **Sc**=scholarships available in honors program; **Tr**=transfer students accepted into honors program; **HBC**=historically black college; **AA**=academic advisors; **GA**=graduate advisors; **FA**=fellowship advisors.

conversant with significant ideas, deeds, and events that have shaped the world and will shape the future; to have confidence in their abilities to think for themselves, write clearly, and speak effectively; and to be leaders in their communities and professions. It aims to prepare responsible individuals to be perpetual learners who realize their potential for a fully human, ethical, and prosperous life.

The University Honors Program offers integrated sequences of courses that provide highly motivated students a strong foundation in liberal education and career preparation. In small classes (the average class has 15 students), honors students enjoy conditions for learning at the peak of their abilities. Four honors curriculum options, distinguished by comprehensive and in-depth coverage of the material in a learning community environment, facilitate discussion, debate, and intellectual friendship among students and with professors. Special scholarships, travel opportunities, extracurricular events and lectures, an honors residence hall, and achievement awards round out the benefits of honors education at Southeastern. The honors learning-community experience is centered in two sequences of four courses, taught by professors recognized for their excellence in the classroom. The Freshman Honors Seminar, a constellation of two English and two history honors courses, provides an excellent foundation of knowledge through study of some of the most influential books written and the major historical events that have shaped Western civilization. In English, students read and discuss the culture-creating epics of Homer, Virgil, Dante, Milton, and selected modern authors. In history, with the aid of primary sources, they learn about the intellectual, political, religious, artistic, social, scientific, and technological changes that have made our world possible. A sequence of four "Ideas in Conflict" courses familiarizes advanced students with great books written by thinkers whose ideas have sharpened human understanding of such central issues as the nature of justice, claims of truth, the structure of nature, the meaning of political right and obligation, and the forces of modern social, psychological, and cultural development. Honors courses are also available in math, biology, economics, interdisciplinary arts, U.S. history, dramatic literature, and modern fiction as well as in the curricula of the different majors that Southeastern offers.

Many alumni have reported that their honors program experience at Southeastern made a transformative difference in their undergraduate education and strengthened their credentials for graduate, law, and medical schools and for careers in education, government, business, research, and the health fields.

In addition to foundational courses in the core of the University Honors Program, Southeastern also offers upper-division honors tracks in its four colleges of Arts and Sciences, Education and Human Development, Business and Technology, and Nursing and Health Sciences. A standard of participation in the UHP must be met to qualify for entry into one of the college honors tracks, which are designed to provide the most dedicated students special course and research opportunities for enhancing their preparation for success in their professions and careers.

Participation Requirements: Four curriculum paths eventuating in appropriate graduation awards are open to students: (1) 16 hours in UHP courses plus 9 to 15 hours in a track offered in a college to earn an Honors Diploma in a discipline in one of the colleges; (2) 25 hours in UHP courses plus a senior thesis in the major to earn an Honors Diploma in the University Honors Program; (3) meeting the requirements of (2) above plus 9 to 12 hours in a college track to earn an Honors Diploma in a discipline in a college and the University Honors Program; or (4) 28 hours in UHP courses, 12 additional nonhonors hours, and 12 hours of foreign language to earn an Honors Diploma in Liberal Studies. Every honors path requires foreign language study and a senior thesis in the student's major. Students meeting a threshold of early progress in the University Honors Program earn a Sophomore Honors Distinction award in addition to graduation awards.

Admission Process: A composite score of 21 on the ACT and a 3.0 high school GPA qualify an entering freshman to join; a cumulative GPA of 3.0 in 12 or more hours of university credit qualifies an advanced student to join. Traditional and nontraditional students in every major are encouraged to participate. Each college may have special criteria for accepting students into its upper-division honors track. Transfer students, to earn awards, must meet minimum participation requirements proportioned to their point of entering Southeastern.

Scholarship Availability: On a competitive basis, the Honors Program offers Presidential Honors Scholarships valued at $1000 per semester to entering freshmen and advanced students making outstanding progress. Information regarding many other available scholarships may be obtained by calling the Financial Aid Office (985-549-2244 Ext. 2245).

The Campus Context: Southeastern Louisiana University was founded as a junior college in 1925, and in 1928 was established as a four-year curricula college. In 1946 SLU became an accredited university and now consists of five colleges: the College of Arts and Sciences, College of Basic Studies, College of Business and Technology, College of Education and Human Development, and College of Nursing and Health Sciences. Southeastern has sixty-six degree options available on the associate, bachelor's, and master's level in business, education, liberal arts and sciences, and nursing.

Student Body There are approximately 15,000 students enrolled at Southeastern; about 13,050 are undergraduates. Of the undergraduates, approximately 40 percent are men. The undergraduate population has an ethnic makeup of 89 percent white and 11 percent minority students. There are about 50 international students. The majority of students enrolled are commuters. The nine fraternities and sororities on Southeastern's campus have more than 560 student members.

Faculty Of the 606 faculty members, 435 are full-time (63 percent with a doctorate) and 171 are part-time.

Key Facilities There are approximately 330,000 bound volumes in Sims Memorial Library along with more than 3,700 titles on microfilm, 2,300 periodical subscriptions, and national online catalog utilities. There are approximately 500 computers on campus that are available for general student use with access to the main academic computer, off-campus computing facilities, and the Internet.

Athletics In athletics Southeastern is a member of the Southland Conference, offering men's golf; women's soccer and volleyball; and baseball, basketball, cross-country, tennis, and track and field for both men and women.

Study Abroad Students may enroll for credit in study-abroad courses in Canada, England, France, Italy, Mexico, and Spain.

Support Services The Office of Student Life works with students with disabilities to help them adjust to campus life.

Job Opportunities A work-study program is available.

Tuition: $2030 for state residents, $4296 for nonresidents, per year (1998–99)

Room and Board: $2400 minimum

Mandatory Fees: $125

Contact: Director: Dr. Jim Walter, Director, SLU Honors Program, 611 North Pine Street, SLU Box 10489, Hammond, Louisiana 70402; Telephone: 985-549-2135; E-mail: jwalter@selu.edu; Web site: http://www.selu.edu/Academics/Honors/

SOUTHEASTERN OKLAHOMA STATE UNIVERSITY

4 Pu G M Sc

▼ Southeastern Honors Program

The Southeastern Honors Program has been built on the foundation created by the Parsons Scholars Program, which has a long and honorable tradition at Southeastern. The Parsons Scholars Program was established in 1978 by Dr. David L. Parsons, who earned a Bachelor of Arts degree from Southeastern in 1928.

Today, the Southeastern Honors Program is an academic honors program that provides distinctive educational experiences for students with special talents and outstanding academic abilities. The program also offers cocurricular enrichment experiences and challenges high-caliber students to achieve their academic potential.

Southeastern honors students are enrolled in honors sections of liberal arts courses as part of their general education curriculum. Honors courses are designed to provide an opportunity for honors students to take a more in-depth study of the subject. To make this possible, enrollment in each course is limited. The courses are generally more discussion oriented, and, in some instances, attendance at campus cultural events is included as a requirement of the course. In addition to honors courses, honors students receive numerous other special benefits, including access to specially designated housing, priority enrollment, field trips, cultural events, and enrichment activities as well as faculty mentorship in individual scholarly projects, opportunities to attend honors conferences, and recognition upon graduation and notation on the transcript.

More than 100 students are currently enrolled in the Southeastern Honors Program.

Participation Requirements: The honors curriculum consists of nine general education honors courses scheduled over the four-year period. Program graduates receive special recognition upon graduation, and completion is noted on the transcript.

Admission Process: Honors applicants must have an ACT composite of 25 or higher from a National Test Date. Applicants must submit a letter of recommendation from a high school faculty member or administrator who is familiar with the student's character, accomplishments, and potential. They must also submit an original, typed, single-page letter addressed to the Honors Committee stating why they that would be a good candidate for the Southeastern Honors Program and what an honors scholarship would mean to them. All applications must include an approved Application for Admission to Southeastern Oklahoma State University as well as a completed Application for the Southeastern Honors Program. All applicants who fulfill the preceding requirements are eligible to participate in interviews and tests on Honors Program/Scholarship Finalists Day, after which scholarships are awarded.

Scholarship Availability: The Honors Program administers six types of scholarships, which vary in requirements and awards. The Academic Scholars award is available to applicants with ACT scores within the 99.5 to 100 percentile levels in Oklahoma. Recipients must maintain a cumulative GPA of 3.25 or higher and complete 24 hours per year. The Regional University Scholars award is available to Oklahoma applicants with an ACT composite of 30 or higher. Recipients must maintain a cumulative GPA of 3.25 or higher and complete 24 hours per year. The Parsons Scholars award is available to Oklahoma applicants with an ACT composite of 25 or higher. Recipients must maintain a cumulative GPA of 3.0 or higher and complete 30 hours per year. The Presidential Honors Scholars and the University Honors Scholars awards are available to applicants with an ACT composite of 25 or higher. Recipients must maintain a cumulative GPA of 3.0 or higher and complete 25 hours per year. Various Academic Achievement Awards are also available.

The Campus Context: Southeastern is linked by tradition to the geographic region of southeastern Oklahoma and north-central Texas. Although new programs have produced many changes in the geographic origins and the ethnic backgrounds of the students, they are still primarily products of small towns and rural communities in Oklahoma and Texas. Located in the southeastern part of Oklahoma in the city of Durant, the University is 15 miles from the Oklahoma-Texas border; 90 miles north of Dallas, Texas; 160 miles southeast of Oklahoma City; and 15 miles east of Lake Texoma (one of the largest man-made lakes in the world, with approximately 580 miles of shoreline). Durant is a city of in excess of 13,500 people. It is surrounded by productive farm land, three rivers, and a state park. The economy of Durant is changing from one that has been primarily agricultural to one that is more diverse. This change has been influenced by the recreational opportunities at nearby Lake Texoma, which serves more than 5 million visitors annually, and by the presence of approximately fifty business and industrial firms.

More than eighty years have passed since Southeastern first opened its doors. The 20 acres and no buildings of 1909 have expanded to 176 acres and forty-six buildings. The 30 faculty members and 324 students have increased to approximately 200 faculty members and 4,000 students.

Student Body Undergraduate enrollment is approximately 4,000; 56 percent of the students are women. The minority ethnic distribution is 30 percent Native American, 4.3 percent African American, 1 percent Hispanic, and .6 percent Asian American. The campus has three national social fraternities and two national social sororities.

Faculty Southeastern's faculty numbers 211 members, 160 of whom are full-time instructors. Sixty-nine percent of Southeastern's faculty members hold doctoral degrees.

Key Facilities The Henry G. Bennett Memorial Library houses more than 178,000 volumes, 398,000 microforms, and 1,241 current periodical titles as well as 76,000 government documents. The library also belongs to the AMIGOS Bibliographic Network and OCLC, through which it has access to more than 28,000,000 titles for interlibrary loan and cataloging purposes. Both IBM and Apple computer labs are located in various buildings as well as in some of the dorms.

Athletics Southeastern is an NCAA Division II school and participates in the Lone Star Conference. Southeastern offers baseball, basketball, cross-country, football, softball, tennis, and volleyball.

Job Opportunities Southeastern participates in the Federal Work-Study Program and offers other student employment on campus. Off-campus employment is also available.

Tuition: Approximately $1104 for residents, $2988 for nonresidents, per year (1998–99)

Room and Board: $2038

Mandatory Fees: $411

Contact: Director: Dr. Lisa Hill, Station A Box 4066, Durant, Oklahoma 74701; Telephone: 580-924-0121 Ext. 2724; E-mail: lhill@sosu.edu; Web site: http://csclub.sosu.edu/~honor/

Interpreting the symbols: **2**=two-year college, **4**=four-year college; **Pu**=public or state college, **Pr**=private college; **G**=general honors program; **D**=departmental honors program; **S**=small program (fewer than 100 students), **M**=midsize program (100 to 500 students), **L**=large program (more than 500 students); **Sc**=scholarships available in honors program; **Tr**=transfer students accepted into honors program; **HBC**=historically black college; **AA**=academic advisors; **GA**=graduate advisors; **FA**=fellowship advisors.

SOUTHERN ILLINOIS UNIVERSITY EDWARDSVILLE

4 Pu G L Sc Tr AA

▼ Deans' Scholars Honors Program

With the help of distinguished faculty mentors, Deans' Scholars Honors Program students can choose a self-designed curriculum to explore their intellectual interests. Deans' Scholars seminars are small and restricted to Scholars only. Students can study one or two academic areas in-depth or a variety of courses outside their major. New freshmen with a combined score of 180 for high school class rank and ACT composite percentile are invited to become Deans' Scholars. In addition, any Southern Illinois University Edwardsville (SIUE)–admitted freshman-, sophomore-, or junior-level student with a GPA of at least 3.5 is eligible to apply. Selection is based on academic history and letters of recommendation from at least 3 instructors familiar with the student's high school or university course work.

SIUE honors students actively learn and network in a chosen field through one of the national honorary organizations and societies represented on campus. The University has developed a number of programs to recognize academic excellence among students. These include the Honor Society of Phi Kappa Phi, the Deans' Scholars Honors Program, Deans' College Honors Club, the Chancellor's Scholars Program, and special recognition of outstanding students at the annual Honors Day Convocation.

Other opportunities for high-achieving students include the Presidential Scholarship (up to 11 incoming freshmen are selected annually) and the Chancellor's Scholars Program (up to 20 incoming freshmen are selected annually), both of which include automatic admission to the Deans' Scholars Honors Program. The SIUE Undergraduate Research Academy encourages students to pursue self-designed research typically available only at the graduate level. Working with faculty mentors, students explore far-reaching, progressive areas of study that stimulate their individual intellect. Any junior- or senior-level student may compete for this opportunity.

Chancellor's Scholars and Presidential Scholarship recipients live in Prairie Hall during their freshman year. Students who wish to network with other high achievers may request to live in the Scholars Focused Interest Community (FIC). FIC residents share the same major and/or interests and can participate in a variety of special programming sponsored by University Housing. Focused Interest Communities include Scholars, Emerging Leaders, Healthful Lifestyles, Business, Technology/Computers, Nursing, Education, Creative Arts (music, art, theater, and dance), and Engineering.

Participation Requirements: To fulfill the General Education requirement, Deans' Scholars take at least 33 semester hours. Of these, a minimum of three courses (at least 9 credits) must be in each of the three general education areas: fine arts and humanities, natural science and mathematics (one of which must emphasize scientific inquiry), and social sciences. No more than 9 hours may be taken at the 111 level. Questions as to whether certain courses count toward the fulfillment of area requirements are resolved by the Deans' Scholars Coordinator in consultation with the student's adviser. Included in social sciences are the disciplines of anthropology, history, economics, geography, political science, psychology, and sociology. Students can fulfill 3 hours of the requirements of one general education area with courses from their major.

To complete their 33 hours, Deans' Scholars are required to take 3 semester hours of a Deans' Scholars Seminar (DS 120), which includes work on composition and oral communication and is required of all entering Deans' Scholars freshmen. Deans' Scholars students also are required to take 3 semester hours of an interdisciplinary seminar, DS 320 or an IS course offered as a seminar. Deans' Scholars are required to complete one course exploring intergroup relations and one course exploring either international issues or international culture. These courses are allowed to fulfill the appropriate general education area requirements. The above requirements cannot be satisfied by skills courses.

The IS Seminar is required of all students accepted as Deans' Scholars. Transfer students accepted as Deans' Scholars must meet the requirements outlined above through courses accepted for transfer or through University courses approved by the College or School Deans' Scholars Coordinator or the Deans' Scholar Program Coordinator. This stipulation also applies to SIUE students accepted as Deans' Scholars after their first semester at SIUE.

Admission Process: As a rule, freshman-, sophomore-, and junior-level students who have been admitted to the University and who have a GPA of at least 3.5 on a 4.0 scale are eligible to apply. Letters of recommendation are required from at least 3 instructors familiar with the student's high school or university work. High-ranking high school seniors are encouraged to apply for admission to the Deans' Scholars program upon matriculation at SIUE.

Selection of Deans' Scholars students is made on the basis of candidates' previous academic work, together with the letters of recommendation from instructors. Candidates complete the admission requirements by filing a program responsibility form showing courses they have already taken and those they plan to take. Upon approval of the program of study, students are formally designated as Deans' Scholars.

Scholarship Availability: On the basis of admission credentials, the Presidential Scholarship Program admits up to 11 entering freshmen who are Illinois high school graduates, have achieved a 29 or above on the ACT or 1280 or above on the SAT, and have a GPA of 3.75 on a 4.0 scale. The award is $5000 per year, renewable for eight semesters. Recipients are also offered at least $1500 toward their first year's housing costs.

On the basis of admission credentials and a Chancellor's Scholars application submitted by December 15, up to 20 entering freshmen are selected for this four-year award. The Chancellor's Scholars Program is offered to students with strong academic ability and a record of personal achievement, leadership, and service. Minimum requirements for consideration are a 26 or above on the ACT and be in the upper 10 percent in class rank. The award covers in-state tuition and fees and also provides $1500 toward first-year housing costs.

The Johnetta Haley Scholars Program encourages minority students to enter engineering, sciences, nursing, and education. Scholarships are awarded on the basis of admission credentials. Minimum requirements are a 22 or above on the ACT and be in the upper 25 percent in class rank. The award value ranges from $300 to full in-state tuition and is renewable for four years. Interested students should submit their admission application and credentials by November 15 prior to the academic year for which they are seeking a scholarship.

In addition to the four-year awards described above, Campus Residence Honors, Provost's Scholarships, and Fine Arts Scholarships (one-year awards) also are available on the basis of admission credentials submitted by November 15.

The Campus Context: SIUE is the choice of more than 12,400 students enrolled in forty-three undergraduate programs, fifty-two minors, and fifty-three graduate and professional programs. Accredited by the Higher Learning Commission of the North Central Association of Colleges and Schools, SIUE is committed to excellence in undergraduate education. Regular faculty members teach the vast majority of class hours; graduate assistants teach only 3 percent of SIUE classes. One of the most affordable universities in Illinois, SIUE offers educational grants, scholarships, student employment, and low-interest loans. An unusual textbook rental program helps make college even more affordable, saving students hundreds of dollars per year on textbooks.

The SIUE student body is diverse, ranging from recent high school graduates to seasoned business executives returning for advanced degrees. The University draws students from as near as Edwardsville, from as far as China, and from sixty-five countries in between. These students enjoy the facilities of a young and growing campus, with award-winning faculty members, research laboratories, state-of-the-art equipment, numerous computer labs, spacious classrooms, outstanding recreational facilities, modern residence halls, and lakeside apartments. Centrally located in the semirural setting just outside Edwardsville, Illinois, and just minutes from downtown St. Louis, SIUE gives students access to a vast variety of recreational and employment opportunities.

Student Body Undergraduate enrollment is 9,799; 57 percent are women and 43 percent are men. The ethnic distribution includes nonresident aliens, 1.7 percent; black non-Hispanic, 11.9 percent; American Indian/Alaskan Native, 0.4 percent; Asian/Pacific Islander, 1.4 percent; Hispanic, 1.4 percent; and white non-Hispanic, 83.3 percent. The majority of SIUE students are between the ages of 18 and 24, the average being 21.4 years.

Faculty Total faculty members number 751, including 483 full-time, 84 percent of whom have terminal degrees. The student-faculty ratio is 17:1. SIUE faculty members are leaders in their academic disciplines. Their research, teaching, and publications have earned wide respect and recognition, including Fulbright Fellowships and grants from the National Science Foundation, the National Institutes of Health, the National Endowment for the Arts, and the National Endowment for the Humanities. More than 84 percent have earned the terminal degree appropriate to their field, and all teach at both the undergraduate and the graduate levels.

Key Facilities Lovejoy Library maintains more than 1 million volumes and subscribes to more than 6,500 serials and periodicals. The library's collection includes 1.5 million microform items, 540,000 U.S. government documents, 150,000 maps, 43,000 audiovisual titles, and thousands of special research items. The library's resource-sharing agreements make it possible for SIUE students to use other academic, public, and special libraries in the St. Louis area. Electronic access also is provided to the collections of other libraries in Illinois and throughout the world. Materials from these collections may be obtained through the interlibrary loan service.

Audio Visual Services provides complete audiovisual assistance, including the development of new media using up-to-date technology to meet the needs of University faculty and staff members and students. Audio Visual Services maintains a collection of 3,300 items, including films, CD-ROMs, laser discs, and videotapes. The Self-Help Laboratory is available to students who wish to produce their own instructional materials for classroom presentations. The Self-Instruction Laboratory provides equipment for using materials in the media collection. A small room is available for group viewing. Staff members are available to help with hardware and software.

Academic Computing manages computer laboratories and classrooms for student and instructor use. Hardware and software for curriculum support are purchased in consultation with multidepartmental cluster committees. General-purpose open-access student computer laboratories are located in Lovejoy Library, all residence halls, Cougar Village Commons, Founders Hall, Alumni Hall, Peck Hall, Dunham Hall, the Science Building, and the Engineering Building.

Honorary Societies Beta Alpha Psi, Beta Gamma Sigma, Eta Kappa Nu, Eta Sigma Gamma, Gamma Theta Upsilon, Kappa Delta Pi, Lambda Alpha, Omicron Delta Epsilon, Omicron Kappa Upsilon (Nu Xi Chapter), Phi Alpha Theta, Phi Eta Sigma, Phi Kappa Phi, Pi Kappa Lambda, Pi Mu Epsilon, Psi Chi (psychology), Sigma Lambda Chi, Sigma Theta Tau, Sigma Xi, and Chi Epsilon

Athletics SIUE's athletics program consists of fifteen varsity sports, with seven for men, including baseball, basketball, cross-country, soccer, tennis, track, and wrestling. The eight women's sports include basketball, cross-country, golf, soccer, softball, tennis, track, and volleyball. The University is a member of the National Collegiate Athletic Association (NCAA) Division II and the Great Lakes Valley Conference (GLVC).

Study Abroad Through its study-abroad programs, SIUE complements the work of its academic departments by facilitating the placement of students overseas. Whether studying a foreign language and its culture, researching international business practices, or immersing themselves in nursing practices of another country, study abroad enables students to learn new perspectives and ideas. SIUE offers opportunities for undergraduate study abroad in a variety of countries. These take the form of exchanges, consortia agreements, or travel/study participation. SIUE students have recently participated in programs in Mexico, France, England, Austria, Sweden, the Netherlands, and Haiti. Study abroad fulfills University undergraduate academic requirements and generally qualifies for financial aid.

Support Services The Director for Students with Disabilities in the Office of Disability Support Services is responsible for implementation and coordination of many of the programs, activities, and services for persons with disabilities. The Director offers academic advising and registration, guidance and counseling, referrals to related offices and departments, and assistance in obtaining specialized equipment or supplies, support services, and special accommodations. A Learning Disabilities Specialist also is available.

Job Opportunities Part-time student employment is available at SIUE under both the regular student employment program and the Federal Work-Study Program. SIUE also helps students find off-campus employment through the Job Locator Program. SIUE offers a broad range of part-time student work opportunities in almost every phase of University operation or service. Although many of the positions are in the clerical, maintenance, or food service areas, there are many challenging positions that develop the administrative, research, or technical skills of students. Students usually work 15–20 hours per week as class schedules permit. Generally, students begin working at the federal minimum wage and receive increases as total accumulated hours increase.

Tuition: $3588.60 per year for undergraduate Illinois residents (15 hours; 2002–03)

Room and Board: $2966, room; $1722, board (Meal Plan B)

Contact: Director of Admissions: Boyd Bradshaw, Office of Admissions, Box 1600, Southern Illinois University Edwardsville, Edwardsville, Illinois 62026-1600; Telephone: 618-650-3705; Fax: 618-650-5013; E-mail: admis@siue.edu

---

SOUTHERN NEW HAMPSHIRE UNIVERSITY

4 Pr G S Sc Tr

▼ Honors Program

The Southern New Hampshire University Honors Program, founded in 1992, is dedicated to creating an environment in which unusually motivated students are offered an atmosphere in which excellence is expected, a challenging curriculum that fosters independent thinking in the company of like-minded

Interpreting the symbols: **2**=two-year college, **4**=four-year college; **Pu**=public or state college, **Pr**=private college; **G**=general honors program; **D**=departmental honors program; **S**=small program (fewer than 100 students), **M**=midsize program (100 to 500 students), **L**=large program (more than 500 students); **Sc**=scholarships available in honors program; **Tr**=transfer students accepted into honors program; **HBC**=historically black college; **AA**=academic advisors; **GA**=graduate advisors; **FA**=fellowship advisors.

individuals is offered, and participants are encouraged to be actively involved in their own education.

The honors curriculum, comprising a minimum of 20 percent of the students' course work, consists of three kinds of experiences: Honors Courses that are taught in a seminar environment, with approximately 15 students; Honors Modules that are attached to regular college courses; and two mandatory program courses, Honors 201 and Honors 401.

The Honors Courses are specifically designated courses that are taught by honors faculty members. They are usually designed to offer greater challenge, with experiential learning and either more material or a higher level of material than in regular courses.

An Honors Module is an extra component that is added to a regular college course. The honors student, in consultation with the professor, enters into a contractual agreement to extend the work in the course in order to receive honors credit.

Honors 201 is a yearlong interdisciplinary seminar for honors students in their sophomore year. Each year, the focus of the course changes. Past Honors 201 topics have included such diverse subjects as technology and society, the ideal city, the utopian vision, gender issues of the 1990s, and *Genesis* and *Revelation* and their use and abuse in Western culture. Honors 401, or the Honors Thesis, is the culminating experience of the Honors Program. It is a yearlong project undertaken with the guidance of a faculty member chosen by the student. The student and the faculty mentor design a course of study during the spring semester of the junior year and spend the entire senior year completing it.

In addition to the academic requirements, there are two other program components of character and service. Southern New Hampshire University Honors Program participants are expected to maintain a high level of integrity of character and to endeavor to hold high moral and ethical standards. Students in the Honors Program are also required to offer service to the program and the College as a whole by participating in various honors committee and campus organizations.

The Honors Program is student run. The Honors Board, which is responsible for maintaining the quality of the program, is made up of 2 senior representatives and 1 representative from each of the other classes. These members invite 2 faculty members to join them. There are an additional seven committees that are charged with responsibilities that include facilities maintenance and planning activities. Students are active in every aspect of the program.

The Honors Program curriculum is thus adaptable to each student's individual needs and interests and works with virtually any undergraduate program offered at Southern New Hampshire University. Honors students are also offered opportunities for trips, conferences, participation in the Model United Nations in New York, special programs, volunteerism, retreats, and other enriching activities.

There are 44 students in the program as of February 1, 1999. Fifteen entering freshmen are accepted each year. The maximum number of program members is 60.

Participation Requirements: Once accepted to the program, students must maintain a minimum 3.0 GPA in every semester, as well as grades of B or higher in all honors experiences. Currently, students in all majors are eligible, with the exception of the two-year culinary program and the three-year accelerated program.

A graduating Honors Program student is recognized at the graduation honors ceremonies by receiving an Honors Program Medal and a special honors certificate, having their names listed in the graduation program, and receiving special notation on their transcripts.

Admission Process: Generally, applicants should have combined SAT I scores of at least 1000 (new scaling), high school GPAs of 3.2 or better, outstanding entrance essays, and evidence of interest in learning, character development, and service. Students usually enter the program at the beginning of their freshman year, but transfer students may also be accepted if they offer fewer than 60 transfer credits. Current Southern New Hampshire University freshmen and sophomores are also accepted for entrance into the next year's honors class on a space-available basis.

The Campus Context: Southern New Hampshire University, founded in 1932, is a private, accredited, nonprofit, coeducational, professional and liberal arts college. The campus, on 200 wooded acres, is located on the Merrimack River in Manchester, New Hampshire, and is at the crossroads of northern New England. It is an hour's drive from the best skiing in the East, the beaches of New Hampshire and Maine, and the cultural activity of Boston. There are twenty-two majors leading to baccalaureates in business, liberal arts, and hospitality administration.

Student Body Undergraduate enrollment is 1,400; 60 percent of the students are men. Ethnic distribution of the undergraduate population is 1 percent African American, 1 percent Hispanic, 3 percent Asian American, and 29 percent unknown. Approximately 15 percent of the students are international. Seventy-five percent of students receive financial aid. There are four fraternities and four sororities.

Faculty The College has 62 full-time undergraduate faculty members, 34 full-time graduate faculty members, 96 total undergraduate faculty members, and 137 total graduate faculty members. Sixty-five percent of full-time faculty members have terminal degrees. The student-faculty ratio is 17:1.

Key Facilities In addition to the 109,488-volume library, there are more than 350 IBM-compatible and Apple computers in the campus network.

Athletics Southern New Hampshire University is a member of the National Collegiate Athletic Association, the Eastern College Athletic Association, and the New England Collegiate Conference. All intercollegiate teams compete at the Division II level. Men's teams include basketball, soccer, baseball, ice hockey, and lacrosse. Women's teams include basketball, soccer, volleyball, and cross-country. Athletic scholarships are available for soccer and basketball for both men and women. A strong intramural program is also available.

Study Abroad Students have the opportunity to study abroad during the fall term at the University of London and the University of Greenwich in Woolwich, England.

Support Services Disabled-student facilities include a Learning Center and tutoring services. Most of the campus is accessible for physically disabled students.

Job Opportunities Students are offered a wide range of work opportunities on campus that include work-study and campus payroll positions.

Tuition: $12,990 per year (1998–99)

Room and Board: $5538 minimum

Mandatory Fees: $580

Contact: Director: Dr. Julianne S. Cooper, 2500 North River Road, Manchester, New Hampshire 03106-1045; Telephone: 603-668-2211; Fax: 603-645-9772; E-mail: j.cooper@snhu.edu; Web site: http://www.nhc.edu

SOUTHERN UNIVERSITY AND AGRICULTURAL AND MECHANICAL COLLEGE

4 Pu G L Sc Tr HBC AA

▼ Honors College

The Honors College at Southern University and Agricultural and Mechanical College in Baton Rouge provides an enhanced educational experience for students who have a history of strong academic achievement and motivation and who have shown exceptional creativity and talent. Innovative pedagogy, flexible and competitive curricula, and mentoring relationships with distinguished faculty members and scholars are focal points of the program. The College also provides cultural and intellectual opportunities designed to motivate students to perform at the highest level of excellence that they are capable of and through which they may become knowledgeable and effective leaders. The core curriculum consists of honors colloquia, designated honors courses in the general education curriculum, and honors courses in the student's major area of study. Students pursue Honors Option Contracts from the general education curriculum and the student's major area of study to complete the requirements for the honors degree. Honors core courses are taught in a newly constructed honors building. This complex houses the main office, instructors' offices, classrooms, a media laboratory, a conference room, and a student activity center. Honors housing, equipped with computer laboratories and study rooms, is available for freshmen and upperclassmen. Program enhancements include an Annual Pinning Ceremony; Scholar-in-Residence/Visiting Scholars Program; study-abroad opportunities in Orizaba, Mexico, and Accra, West Africa; scholarship opportunities; co-ops and internships; membership in professional organizations; and service learning opportunities, sometimes associated with the study-abroad programs. In 1987, the Southern University Board of Supervisors designated the honors program as the Southern University Honors College. The current membership is 602 students.

Participation Requirements: Participation in the Honors College is voluntary. However, students must maintain a minimum 3.0 cumulative GPA within a two-semester period. Students who complete the honors curriculum have special designations of honors included on their transcripts and diplomas. In order to achieve this recognition, the following requirements must be met: a cumulative 3.0 GPA in all course work pursued; a cumulative 3.3 GPA in all honors work pursued; at least 32 honors credit hours, including 6 hours of honors colloquia, 2 hours of honors thesis or independent study, and 9 hours in a junior- or senior-level course in the student's major area; and the recommendation of the College Dean that Honors College distinction can be awarded. In addition to the honors diploma, a bronze medallion containing an engraved replica of the Honors College logo attached to a ceremonial ribbon is presented to all students completing the program.

Admission Process: Students must apply for admission to the program. Membership in the Honors College is based on two classification types, General Honors and University Scholars. Students applying for General Honors must have a minimum ACT composite score of 23 or SAT combined score of 1060; a minimum high school GPA of 3.3; an assessment of cocurricular activities; two letters of recommendation from the high school principal, counselor, or instructor; and submission of an essay on a designated topic or a recently corrected writing activity, three to five pages in length. Students applying as University Scholars must have a minimum ACT composite score of 27 or SAT combined score of 1210; a minimum high school GPA of 3.5; an assessment of cocurricular activities; two letters of recommendation from the high school principal, counselor, or instructor; and submission of an essay on a designated topic or a recently corrected writing activity, three to five pages in length.

Other indices evaluated for admission are class rank, interviews, and college preparatory courses. Application deadlines are determined by the Office of the Registrar; these are July 1 for fall semester, November 1 for spring semester, and April 1 for the summer term. Admission to the Honors College for continuing and transfer students is based on a minimum cumulative GPA of 3.5, two letters of recommendation, full-time status, and an interview. Transfer students must have full-time status at the time of their transfer or the last semester of college matriculation.

Scholarship Availability: Scholarships are available in two categories. Tier I, a maximum full scholarship that is available to incoming freshmen, includes tuition with out-of-state fees, room and board, and books and supplies in variable amounts. Applicants must have a minimum cumulative GPA of 3.5, a minimum ACT score of 27 or SAT score of 1260, thirteen college-preparatory courses, and 12 credit hours pursued. Students may also be eligible if they rank first in their graduating class, are National Achievers or National Merit Scholars, and have a GPA of less than 3.4 but an ACT score of 29 or higher or an SAT score of 1300 or higher. Tier I scholarship retention is based on a cumulative GPA of 3.3 and 12 credit hours earned the previous semester. Transfer students must have a minimum cumulative GPA of 3.5 and full-time status the previous semester and may not include any development education courses

Tier II partial scholarships offering tuition or room and board are available to incoming freshmen who have a minimum cumulative GPA of 3.2 and a minimum ACT score of 21 or minimum SAT I score of 990 with thirteen college-preparatory classes and 12 credit hours pursued. Students may also be eligible if they rank first or second in their graduating class or are National Achievers or National Merit Scholars. Tier II scholarship retention is based on a cumulative GPA of 3.0 with 12 credit hours earned the previous semester. Transfer students with a minimum cumulative GPA of 3.5 and 30 credit hours, which may not include developmental education courses, are also eligible.

The following awards, certificates, citations, etc., are also available: graduating senior with the highest average award, student with the highest average in the College award, Straight "A" Student Awards, Chancellor's Scholars/Circle of Excellence, ADTRAN Corporation Scholarships, Georgia Pacific Scholarships, Thurgood Marshall Scholarships, and Honors Medallion Awards.

The Campus Context: Southern University and A&M College is composed of the following colleges and schools, along with their degree programs: College of Agricultural, Family and Consumer Sciences (B.S. in agricultural sciences, agricultural economics, family and consumer sciences, and urban forestry); School of Architecture (B.S. in architecture); College of Arts and Humanities (A.A. in jazz; B.A. in English, fine arts, French, history, mass communications, music, Spanish, speech communications, and theater); College of Business (B.S. in accounting, business economics, business management, and marketing); College of Education (B.A. in elementary education, special education, and music education; B.S. in secondary education and therapeutic recreation and leisure studies); College of Engineering (A.A.S. in electronics engineering technology; B.S. in electrical engineering, civil engineering, electronics engineering, and mechanical engineering); Honors College; Junior Division/General Studies; School of Nursing (B.S. in nursing); School of Public Policy and Urban Affairs (B.A. in political science); College of Sciences (A.S. in law enforcement; Certified Hazardous Material Management; B.S. in biology, chemistry, computer science (scientific option), computer science (business option), criminal justice, mathematics, physics, psychology, rehabilitation services, social work, sociology, and speech pathology and audiology); and the Graduate School (Master of Arts in counseling education, mass communications, mental-health counseling, and social sciences (history, political science, and sociology); Master of Science in biology, chemistry, computer science (operating/information systems, and educational computing), environmental science,

Interpreting the symbols: **2**=two-year college, **4**=four-year college; **Pu**=public or state college, **Pr**=private college; **G**=general honors program; **D**=departmental honors program; **S**=small program (fewer than 100 students), **M**=midsize program (100 to 500 students), **L**=large program (more than 500 students); **Sc**=scholarships available in honors program; **Tr**=transfer students accepted into honors program; **HBC**=historically black college; **AA**=academic advisors; **GA**=graduate advisors; **FA**=fellowship advisors.

mathematics, physics, rehabilitation counseling, therapeutic recreation, and urban forestry; Master of Education in administration and supervision, elementary education, secondary education, and special education; Master of Professional Accountancy; Master of Public Administration in health-care administration, public policy/analysis, midcareer, and generalist; Master of Science in nursing; and Doctor of Philosophy in environmental toxicology, mathematics and science education, nursing, and special education).

Among special campus features and programs are the Southern University African American Museum, the Center for Service Learning, the Division of Continuing Education, the Cooperative Education Program, and the Strengthening Historically Black Colleges and Universities (HBCU) Program.

Student Body Total student enrollment averages 9,300, with a 41:60 ratio of men to women. Enrollment by ethnicity reflects 94.31 percent African Americans, 3.76 percent Caucasians, and 1.93 percent of other races. Seventy-four percent of student enrollment represents Louisiana residents, and 13 percent represents transfer students. Eight national fraternal groups, members of the Pan Hellenic Council, are represented on campus.

Faculty Full-time faculty members number 465, 67 percent of whom have the doctoral degree.

Key Facilities The library houses 106,112 paper volumes, 684,080 paper titles, 586,630 microform units, 946 electronic titles, 1,974 serial subscriptions, and 41,705 audiovisual material units. Computer laboratories are located in the honors dormitories (three); the library, student union, and computer science department (three); and the computer technology center. There are computer systems for each faculty member.

Other distinguishing facilities include a site/sculpture acknowledging the founding of Baton Rouge, Louisiana; a basketball arena/dome; the student union building, with its food court, barber shop, beauty salon, and picnic facilities; and the student outdoor recreation pavilion.

Honorary Societies Alpha Chi (interdisciplinary), Alpha Delta Mu (social work), Alpha Kappa Delta (sociology), Alpha Kappa Mu (interdisciplinary), Alpha Mu Gamma (foreign languages), and Alpha Tau Alpha (agricultural education)

Athletics Southern University and A&M College is a member of the National Collegiate Athletic Association (NCAA) Division I. The athletics program received NCAA certification in 1996. The intercollegiate teams compete in the Southwestern Athletic Conference (SWAC), which is composed of two divisions, the Western and Eastern. Each division supports five teams. Men's sports include baseball, basketball, cross-country and track, football, golf, and tennis. Women's sports include basketball, bowling, cross-country and track, golf, softball, tennis, and volleyball. The athletic facilities include the A. W. Mumford Stadium (football), F. G. Clark Activity Center (basketball), Lee-Hines Field (baseball), a women's softball field, and tennis courts.

Study Abroad Study-abroad opportunities are available through various departments and colleges. In addition, opportunities are also coordinated by the System Office of International Affairs and Development. The University has articulation agreements between the University of Ghana and the Honors College (interdisciplinary) and the Universidad del Valle de Orizaba and Veracruz, Mexico (elementary Spanish course and community service).

Support Services The University has a van that is accessible for transportation of students with disabilities. New buildings are accessible and have accommodations for individuals with disabilities. The University also has designated accessible parking spaces for individuals with documented need. Sidewalks have curb ramps, and street crossings are marked. If a student with a disability enrolls in a class that is scheduled in an inaccessible classroom, the class is reassigned to an accessible classroom. The University makes reasonable accommodations for its students, faculty and staff members, administrators, and visitors at any campus function.

Job Opportunities The University has a Career Services Center that provides comprehensive career services to students to enhance their educational development. The center assist students in choosing their career and college majors, in obtaining appropriate work experience prior to graduation, in obtaining information and skills on how to seek employment, and in furthering their chosen careers by obtaining employment or continuing into graduate or professional schools. Internships and work-study opportunities are available in each department and are assigned according to availability and need. The University also has a Business and Industry Cluster organization that provides leadership in recruiting students through internships into the corporate world.

Tuition: $1341 for state residents per semester, $2896 for nonresidents per semester (undergraduate full-time; part-time is prorated)

Room and Board: $5954–$6726 per year

Contact: Dean: Dr. Beverly D. Wade, Honors College, Southern University and A&M College, P.O. Box 9413, Baton Rouge, Louisiana 70813; Telephone: 225-771-4845; Fax: 225-771-4848; Web site: http://www.suhsa.homestead.com

Southwest State University

4 Pu G M Sc Tr

▼ Honors Program

The Honors Program provides a way for qualified students to design their own general studies requirements by selecting specific courses from the catalog and/or designing specific projects that complement their particular strengths. Honors students are allowed to enroll in classes that are full at the time of registration and may take any class for an extra honors credit. Upon completion of their work, honors students are given special recognition at Commencement and acknowledgment on their transcripts. The program sponsors an Honors Club, which sanctions social events and trips.

The Honors Program was initiated in 1971 and currently enrolls 130 students.

Admission Process: Students wishing to enter the program must have achieved a composite ACT score of at least 26 and must provide a letter of reference from a high school counselor or principal.

Scholarship Availability: Scholarships are awarded on a competitive basis to currently enrolled honors students. Incoming and transfer students are awarded scholarships, when qualified, by the Admissions Office working in conjunction with the President's Office.

The Campus Context: Southwest State University (SSU), one of seven institutions in the Minnesota state university system, opened its doors in 1967 and graduated its first class in 1971.

Southwest State's academic program is administered through the Division of Academic Affairs. The University offers forty-three baccalaureate majors, four associate degree majors, and thirty-three minors. In addition, two master's degree programs and six certifications are offered. Students can enter a four-year bachelor's program (Bachelor of Arts, Bachelor of Science, or Bachelor of Applied Technology), opt for a two-year associate degree (Associate in Science), or enter one of sixteen preprofessional programs.

SSU is fully accredited by the North Central Association of Colleges and Schools. Individual departments hold accreditation from the American Chemical Society, the National Board of Teaching, and the National Association of Schools of Music.

Southwest State's modern campus covers 216 acres and includes twenty-four buildings that incorporate barrier-free architecture to provide maximum accessibility for the University's physically disabled students. All academic buildings are connected by enclosed skywalks and hallways and have ramps and elevators.

Student Body Today the University enrolls more than 2,800 students. Sixty-five percent of SSU's students come from the nineteen-county service area in southwestern Minnesota, while the remainder come primarily from other parts of Minnesota and the Upper Midwest.

Faculty The University has 125 faculty members. Two thirds of the full-time faculty members have earned the highest degree in their discipline.

Tuition: $82.75 for state residents, $180.45 for nonresidents, per credit hour (1998–99)

Room and Board: $1697 per year (double occupancy, nineteen-meal plan)

Mandatory Fees: $73.20 activity fee, plus others

Contact: Director: Dr. Hugh M. Curtler, Marshall, Minnesota 56258; Telephone: 507-537-7141; Fax: 507-537-7154; E-mail: curtler@ssu.southwest.msus.edu.

Southwest Texas State University

4 Pu G M Sc Tr

▼ University Honors Program

The Southwest Texas State (SWT) University Honors Program provides challenges and opportunities for talented students through a curriculum designed to enhance traditional courses of study. In small, seminar-type classes, honors students discuss ideas and raise questions stimulated by readings, field trips, and presentations. Dedicated faculty members provide an atmosphere that promotes curiosity, creativity, and a lifetime love of learning. Although specific topics vary, each course crosses traditional disciplinary boundaries and offers students an opportunity to pursue knowledge in an exciting interdisciplinary atmosphere. Recent course offerings have included Elementary Number Theory; Technology and Gender in Film; Astronomy in Art, Literature and History; and Baseball and the American Experience.

Honors students may opt to live in Butler Residential College, one of two residential colleges at SWT. In addition, the Honors Student Association is an active social and service organization that is open to all honors students.

Established in 1967 by history professor Emmie Craddock, the University Honors Program initially served a handful of students and offered only one course per semester. Today, approximately 430 students are served and the program offers up to sixteen courses each semester.

Participation Requirements: To graduate in the University Honors Program, students must complete at least five honors courses (15 hours), including the Honors Thesis. Honors courses can substitute for general education courses and/or individual school requirements. To remain in the University Honors Program, a student must maintain a minimum GPA of 3.25.

Honors course schedules are made approximately one year in advance, giving students the opportunity to integrate honors courses into their degree plans. While many of the honors courses are advanced offerings, several lower-division courses are offered each year.

Participation in the University Honors Program allows students to become part of a community within the University. Students receive special advising for their honors courses with special emphasis on integrating honors courses into their degree requirements. Honors students have access to two seminar rooms, a student lounge, and a computer lab with Internet capabilities. Honors students are eligible to register early each semester. Many students present their honors thesis research at national conferences and publish work in regional and national publications. Students can apply for an Honors Thesis Grant to fund up to $500 of their thesis research. In addition, they may choose to present their final thesis at the undergraduate Honors Thesis Forum, which is held at the end of each semester.

Admission Process: Entering freshmen with a composite ACT score of at least 27 or SAT I score of 1180 or who are in the top 10 percent of their graduating class are eligible for admission to the program. Currently enrolled and transfer students with a GPA of at least 3.25 are also eligible. Students can submit applications at any time during their college careers and can withdraw from the program at any time without penalty.

Scholarship Availability: All freshman and transfer applicants and currently enrolled students who have completed at least one honors course may apply for the Emmie Craddock Scholarship. Freshman applicants must have a minimum ACT score of 27 or SAT I score of 1150. Transfer and continuing students must have a GPA of 3.5 or above to be eligible. Currently enrolled students who have completed 60 hours and have a GPA of 3.3 or above are eligible to apply for the James and Elizabeth Camp Scholarship. Currently enrolled students of junior or senior standing with a GPA of 3.5 or higher may also apply for the B.F. and Stan Friedman Scholarship. In addition to the Craddock, Camp, and Friedman scholarships, ten University Honors Program scholarships are awarded annually.

The Campus Context: Southwest Texas State University was founded in 1899 as the Southwest Texas Normal School. Located at the headwaters of the San Marcos River, SWT is midway between Austin and San Antonio. Set along the edge of the Texas hill country, SWT offers recreation and beauty. Southwest Texas State is a large, public university that offers small-school advantages, such as one-on-one interaction between students and faculty members. The campus is home to eight colleges: Applied Arts, Business, Education, Fine Arts and Communication, Health Professions, Liberal Arts, and Science and the University College. SWT offers more than 130 different degree plans.

Student Body Undergraduate enrollment is 23,500: 44 percent men, 56 percent women. The ethnic distribution of the undergraduate population is 73 percent Anglo, 18 percent Hispanic, 5 percent African American, 2 percent Asian American, and 2 percent international. More than half of all students receive scholarships, grants, or loans.

Faculty Of the 1,034 faculty members, 764 are full-time. The student-faculty ratio is 20.5:1.

Key Facilities The library houses 3.2 million volumes. There are thirty-three fraternities and sororities on campus.

Honorary Societies Phi Eta Sigma, Phi Kappa Phi, Golden Key, and Alpha Chi

Athletics The Bobcats compete in the Southland Conference in NCAA Division I (I-AA in football). SWT fields teams for NCAA competition in baseball, basketball (men's and women's), cross-country (men's and women's), football, men's golf, softball, tennis (men's and women's), track and field (men's and women's), and women's volleyball. Unofficial teams are everywhere—on a sunny day, they are found in any space big enough to resemble a field. Some teams play in organized intramural leagues, while others fill a free afternoon.

Job Opportunities Students are offered a wide range of work experiences throughout campus, including work-study opportunities. Career Services offers job placement assistance while students attend SWT and after graduation. Many community businesses

Interpreting the symbols: **2**=two-year college, **4**=four-year college; **Pu**=public or state college, **Pr**=private college; **G**=general honors program; **D**=departmental honors program; **S**=small program (fewer than 100 students), **M**=midsize program (100 to 500 students), **L**=large program (more than 500 students); **Sc**=scholarships available in honors program; **Tr**=transfer students accepted into honors program; **HBC**=historically black college; **AA**=academic advisors; **GA**=graduate advisors; **FA**=fellowship advisors.

employ students and offer flexible scheduling to accommodate students' class schedules with their work schedules.

Tuition: $2016 for state residents, $3540 for nonresidents, per year (2001–02)

Room and Board: $4560

Mandatory Fees: $974

Contact: Director: Dr. Timothy L. Hulsey, San Marcos, Texas 78666; Telephone: 512-245-2266; Fax: 512-245-8959; E-mail: th08@swt.edu

Southwestern Illinois College

2 Pu G L S Tr

▼ Honors Program

The Honors Program, currently only offered at the Granite City campus of Southwestern Illinois College, seeks to enrich the experiences of intellectually curious students by providing an academically rigorous learning environment that can offer a challenging academic experience. The intent of the program is to provide a stimulating environment which will expand critical and creative thinking skills as well as enhancing opportunities for intellectual growth. Students in the program have the opportunity to enroll in specified honors courses or the option of honors contracts in disciplines such as literature, music, business, history, political science, psychology, or sociology. In all honors course work, students and faculty members alike seek and expect excellence.

Students who complete the program are awarded a medallion to wear at graduation. The Honors Program, initiated in fall 2001, currently enrolls approximately 20 students.

Participation Requirements: To successfully complete the course of study and graduate from the Honors Program, students must have successfully completed 12 credit hours of honors course work maintaining a minimum cumulative GPA (GPA) of 3.5. Successful course completion is defined as receiving a grade of B or higher in all honors courses. Honors course work includes either enhanced sections of regular courses (honors sections) or individual contracts made within the context of a regular course (honors contracts). Honors sections are kept small and are taught by selected faculty members. Collaborative learning and nontraditional methods of instruction are highly encouraged.

Admission Process: Students may be admitted to the program at any time. Candidates must complete an application, which includes space for students to clarify their reasons for applying to the program, what they hope to accomplish in the program, and what they will contribute to the program. In addition, students must meet one of the following criteria: graduate in the top 10 percent of their high school class and be eligible for placement into ENG 101; graduate from high school with a cumulative GPA of 3.5 or above and be eligible for placement into ENG 101; score 540 on the verbal section of the SAT or have a composite score of 26 on the ACT; earn 12 college credit hours with a minimum cumulative GPA of 3.5 and be eligible for placement into ENG 101; or obtain special permission from the Honors Program Committee.

Scholarship Availability: Any student attending Southwestern Illinois College District 522 public or private high schools and graduating in the top 10 percent of his or her class can apply for the Top 10 Percent Tuition Scholarship. Potential honors students are strongly encouraged to apply for this program which is awarded for up to six continuous semesters.

The Campus Context: Founded in 1946, Southwestern Illinois College is part of the Illinois Community College System. The College has grown steadily to include three campuses in Belleville, Granite City, and Red Bud. All campuses are within easy access to St. Louis. Students come from six states and territories and nineteen other countries. The College employs 791 full- and part-time faculty members with a student-faculty ratio of 16:1. Southwestern Illinois College strives to provide an affordable education to its students while offering a variety of cultural, economic, and social opportunities.

The Granite City Campus is located on 4950 Maryville Road, Granite City, Illinois, which offers the Honors Program. The fall semester enrollment was more than 2,800 students. The campus offers more than forty degree and certificate programs. There are more than 30 full-time faculty members and opportunities for service and social activities for the students.

Tuition: $47 per credit hour (2001–02)

Contact: Honors Program Coordinator: Dianna Rockwell, 4950 Maryville Road, Granite City, Illinois 62040; Telephone: 618-931-0600 Ext. 6685, 800-222-5131 (toll-free in Illinois); E-mail: dianna.rockwell@southwestern.cc.il.us

Spelman College

4 Pr G S Tr

▼ Ethel Waddell Githii Honors Program

Working with all the academic departments and programs, the Ethel Waddell Githii Honors Program of Spelman College seeks to amplify the intellectual opportunities for the students and faculty members of the entire Spelman community. The program identifies students who have a love of learning and equips them to become lifelong learners by granting them the opportunity to participate actively in their intellectual and personal development from the early stages of their college careers. Students are invited to choose from among the more challenging and innovative courses within a wide variety of disciplines, select courses which have been specially designed for the program, and suggest new courses to meet their intellectual curiosity. The Honors Program also sponsors special events, makes arrangements for the students to attend cultural activities in Atlanta, and promotes community service opportunities in keeping with the student's academic explorations.

Participation Requirements: Honors students may major in any traditional department or develop their own major. Honors students take the same number of credits for graduation as all other Spelman students. Honors students take a core curriculum of honors math, honors freshman composition, honors philosophy, and two honors electives. If a student has received AP credits for one of these courses, she may be exempted from the corresponding course. All of the courses may be used to fulfill the College's core curriculum. In addition, all students in the Honors Program write an honors thesis in their major. The thesis might include—for example, in the case of an art student—a portfolio or performance.

To remain in the program, freshmen and sophomores must maintain a 3.1 GPA. Juniors and seniors must maintain a 3.2 GPA. Successful completion of the Honors Program is noted on the transcript and on the graduation program.

Admission Process: Freshmen are selected each April for the Honors Program on the basis of their high school average and SAT scores, as well as by an application process that includes the writing of essays. Application deadlines are January 12 and April 12.

Scholarship Availability: There are no scholarships given for participation in the Honors Program; however, Honors Program students are encouraged to apply for regular scholarships given by the College.

The Campus Context: An outstanding historically black college for women, Spelman strives for academic excellence in liberal education. The College is a member of the Atlanta University Center consortium, and Spelman students have the opportunity to take classes on all of the other members' campuses. The College is located very close to the center of Atlanta, Georgia, on a beautiful 32-acre campus graced with historic nineteenth-century buildings as well as the recently completed, state-of-the-art Cosby Building for the Humanities. Plans are under way for a new science building. The College has, for the last several years, been regularly listed by *Money* magazine as one of the ten best buys in American higher education.

Student Body Undergraduate enrollment is 1,961. Sixty percent of the students are residents on campus.

Faculty There are 134 full-time faculty members, 83 percent with doctorates or other terminal degrees. The student-faculty ratio is 14:1.

Key Facilities The library houses 1.4 million volumes. Computer facilities include sixty IBM-compatible computers located in dormitories and academic buildings.

Study Abroad Spelman students are encouraged to spend their junior year on either domestic or international exchange. The College participates in a wide range of exchange programs and offers some scholarships to students who take advantage of these opportunities.

Job Opportunities Students are offered a range of work opportunities on campus, including work-study and general work programs.

Tuition: $9000 per year (1998–99)

Room and Board: $6560

Mandatory Fees: $1425

Contact: Director: Dr. James J. Winchester, 350 Spelman Lane, SW, Box 1395, Atlanta, Georgia 30314; Telephone: 404-223-7556; Fax: 404-215-7863; E-mail: jwinches@spelman.edu

SPRINGFIELD TECHNICAL COMMUNITY COLLEGE

2 Pu G S Sc AA

▼ Honors Program

Responding to the needs of its many highly motivated and gifted students, the Springfield Technical Community College (STCC) Honors Program offers honors-level courses and an Honors Certificate Program for those students of exceptional ability who are seeking an enriched collegiate experience.

In many departments of the College, honors-level courses are offered to students who wish to pursue a deeper understanding of the course material. Extensive supplemental reading, research, and writing are required of those students in honors add-on courses. Individualized student contracts for research at the honors level may be negotiated with faculty members, offering students closely supervised research and writing opportunities in a discipline of study. A third option for honors course work involves honors colloquia courses, which promote original scholarship and active learning in small, interdisciplinary seminars. Honors colloquia are generally team taught, drawing upon faculty members from disciplines across the arts, humanities, and social sciences. Recent topics for colloquia have included Arts in Action, Self and Society, From Star Gazers to Star Wars, and Contemporary Ethical Dilemmas.

The Massachusetts Board of Higher Education has recognized the program as a Commonwealth Honors Program, providing smoother transfer processes and more scholarship opportunities for students as well as statewide recognition of STCC honors students. Students have access to an Honors Center equipped with Internet-access computer systems, reference library, study desks, and meeting space.

Participation Requirements: Students pursuing the STCC Honors Certificate are required to complete a minimum of 15 credits of honors-level course work. Six of these credits must be taken in colloquia and 3 credits must be in Research Methodology. Honors students must maintain a GPA of at least 3.5 out of 4.0 to qualify for completion of the certificate. Students completing honors courses have these notated on their official transcripts. Students completing the requirements receive certificates at commencement.

Admission Process: Honors Certificate Program participants are selected on the basis of their academic potential and motivation. Entering freshmen with a minimum 3.5 QPA from high school or a minimum 3.0 QPA from a high school honors program or at least a 1000 combined SAT I score are eligible to apply for admission. Currently enrolled students at the College are eligible after competing 12 college-level credits with a QPA of 3.5 or better. Students whose QPAs do not meet the above standards may apply for admission by submitting a letter of recommendation from a recent teacher and either a letter of intent explaining why admission to the program is sought or an original writing sample demonstrating their academic competence.

Scholarship Availability: Students who complete the requirements and receive the Honors Program Certificate are awarded a scholarship of $500 to pursue further educational opportunities.

The Campus Context: STCC, founded in 1967, is the most comprehensive community college in the Massachusetts system, offering sixty-eight associate degree or certificate programs to nearly 7,000 students in business, engineering/science transfer, engineering technologies, health sciences/nursing, and liberal arts transfer.

STCC is located on the 55-acre Springfield Armory National Historic Site that overlooks downtown Springfield. A museum administered by the National Park Service is located on the west end of the former parade ground. Springfield Armory was the nation's first arsenal, established in 1793, and is the subject of the Longfellow poem The Arsenal at Springfield. The Springfield Rifle was developed here, and the Armory was a source of technology transfer for the northeast.

STCC is the only technical institution in the state system and continues the Armory's tradition of technological advances. Nationally known for excellence in technology education, STCC was chosen by Bell Atlantic as the lead college in the $8-million New England Next Step program and by the National Science Foundation as the Northeast Center for Telecommunications Technologies.

STCC has become a force in regional economic development. In 1996, the STCC Technology Park was established on an additional 15.3 acres across the street from the campus. This venture, which reunites two major segments of the Springfield Armory, is the home of a growing number of technology-based businesses that will benefit from the proximity of STCC and provide a place where STCC students may learn, intern, and eventually be employed. The Technology Park will also house the Springfield Enterprise Center and STCC Entrepreneurial Institute.

STCC students enjoy a professional and caring environment, receiving individualized attention from faculty members who have successful real-world experience. The faculty members are involved in the continual improvement of the educational experience, participating in an active quality team for learning and teaching as well as the new Professional Development Center for faculty and staff members. Many faculty members have created

Interpreting the symbols: **2**=two-year college, **4**=four-year college; **Pu**=public or state college, **Pr**=private college; **G**=general honors program; **D**=departmental honors program; **S**=small program (fewer than 100 students), **M**=midsize program (100 to 500 students), **L**=large program (more than 500 students); **Sc**=scholarships available in honors program; **Tr**=transfer students accepted into honors program; **HBC**=historically black college; **AA**=academic advisors; **GA**=graduate advisors; **FA**=fellowship advisors.

their own multimedia productions to assist students in the learning process; others are devising distance-learning versions of appropriate courses.

The Student Success Center, which opened in fall 1998, is a comprehensive academic support facility that coordinates all campus tutorial services, provides assistance and advocacy for returning adult students, offers walk-in academic advising when regular advisers are not available, offers tutorial software, and works with the STCC faculty to provide students with various computer-based learning experiences as part of their course work.

Student Body Approximately 55 percent of STCC's 3,886 day-division students are women; 24 percent are minority, and the average age is 25. There are a small number of international students. STCC is not a residence campus and has no fraternities or sororities. Nearly 55 percent of the day-division students receive some form of financial aid. The School of Continuing Education enrolls an additional 2,776 students whose average age is 34. The overall college ethnicity proportion is 20 percent.

Faculty STCC has 175 full-time faculty members, of whom 16 percent hold terminal degrees in their field, and 72 part-time faculty members.

Key Facilities The library holdings include 63,724 volumes and 15,835 audiovisual items. The library also subscribes to 539 journals, magazines, and newspapers. The STCC community has access to the libraries of the eight Cooperating Colleges of Greater Springfield (1 million volumes) as well as to the forty academic, public, and special libraries that participate in the CW/MARS computer network. The STCC library offers students eleven computer terminals with Internet access, providing online database tools, both full text and in index form.

STCC offers its students nearly 600 workstations in twenty-five computer labs across the campus, with IBM and Macintosh microcomputers. STCC is the only college in the area with two IBM AS/400 minicomputers dedicated to academic use. Staff members are readily available in the computer labs to answer questions and assist students in their use of the college's computers. Campus buildings are connected by fiber-optic cable through Ethernet or token-ring networks.

Honorary Societies Phi Theta Kappa

Athletics STCC is a member in good standing of the NJCAA (Division III) and the Massachusetts Community College Athletic Conference. There are currently eight intercollegiate or club sports teams at STCC, including men's soccer, basketball, and baseball along with women's soccer, basketball, and softball. Golf and tennis are offered in the spring as coed sports. STCC has advanced to the national championship tournaments in men's soccer, women's soccer, and men's basketball, golf, and tennis.

Support Services The STCC Office of Disability Services provides support services, academic accommodations, career development, and job placement for students with documented disabilities. Also available for students is an extensive laboratory of assistive and adaptive technology, including voice input and output, scanners, Braille equipment, and specialized keyboards. Services are provided for students with a wide range of disabilities, including learning disabilities, visual and hearing disabilities, physically challenged, and medical conditions.

Job Opportunities The STCC Office of Cooperative Education/Career Services and Transfer Affairs offers a wide variety of employment-related services to students and alumni. The Cooperative Education program allows student to earn credit for taking advantage of part-time employment in their field while completing degree requirements in twenty-one associate degree programs. Career Services assists students and alumni who are seeking full- or part-time employment after graduation. College Work-Study is administered through the Financial Aid Office and encourages 10 to 20 hours per week of community service and work related to the student's course of study.

Tuition: $25 per credit for residents, $234 per credit for nonresidents, $37.50 per credit for residents of other New England states provided that the program desired is not available in their state or that the community college is closer than that in the home state (2001–02)

Mandatory Fees: $584

Contact: Coordinator: Professor Arlene Rodriguez, Deliso Hall, Room 113, One Armory Square, Springfield, Massachusetts 01105; Telephone: 413-755-4244; Fax: 413-755-6022; E-mail: arodriguez@stcc.mass.edu; Web site: http://www.stcc.mass.edu

State University of New York at Binghamton

4 Pu G M Se AA

▼ The Binghamton Scholars Program

Designed for entering students of exceptional merit, the Binghamton Scholars Program consists of a four-year honors curriculum that provides high-achieving students with an intellectually challenging learning experience. The curriculum emphasizes the development of high-level research and computer skills, communication skills in both spoken and written languages, collaborative learning experiences in project-centered courses, and opportunities to work closely with faculty members from across the disciplines and throughout the professional schools. Students also participate in a variety of experiential learning venues and internships, both on and off the Binghamton campus. As Binghamton Scholars, they have many occasions to showcase their best academic work and forge links between education and career.

Students enrolled in the Binghamton Scholars Program enjoy the following benefits: renewable merit scholarships, travel subsidies and research grants, access to reserved study areas and computer work areas, early registration for classes, a guaranteed double room in a residential college of the student's choice in the first year, special counseling for postgraduate study, and a portfolio of work instead of just a resume. Upon graduation and successful completion of the program, students may earn recognition for All-University Honors and/or as Binghamton Scholars.

The Binghamton Scholars Program admitted its first class in fall 2000; the program currently enrolls 160 students and expects to enroll a total of 320 students by fall 2003.

Participation Requirements: Required scholars courses include one course in each of the first two years, one internship or experiential learning activity in the junior year, and one capstone or departmental honors project in the senior year. These are not additional required courses; they typically fulfill general education requirements and may count toward the student's major.

In addition to their scholars courses, students participate in at least two semester-long Scholars Leadership Forums, one in the student's first two years at Binghamton and a second in the last two years. The forums meet once each week during the semester with a faculty mentor. They have a budget and the freedom to invent, design, and implement a project that will enrich the life of the University or benefit the greater Binghamton community.

Students in the Scholars Program record the progress of their undergraduate education in a portfolio and share it with a faculty/staff portfolio-review committee each year. The experience helps students reflect on where they want to be and provides them with material for their senior resumes.

In order to graduate with the designation Binghamton Scholar, students must achieve a cumulative GPA of at least 3.25. In order to graduate with the designation All-University Honors, students must achieve a cumulative GPA of at least 3.5. In order to receive either designation and remain in the program, students must demonstrate steady progress toward a degree, including timely completion of Scholars Program credit and noncredit requirements; maintain a cumulative GPA of at least 3.25; and abide by the Rules of Student Conduct, the student conduct code of Binghamton University.

Admission Process: The Binghamton Scholars Program is highly selective. Students invited to participate in the program typically have SAT scores in the high 1300 range or better (30+ on the ACT) and average high school grades in the mid- to high 90s. The selection process is designed to ensure representation of students from each school within the University. Selection criteria may vary slightly among candidates from each school. Special attention is paid to students who have overcome adverse circumstances and achieved academic success.

The program requires no special application. Application to the University includes an initial application, a transcript of secondary school course work and grades, a Supplementary Admissions Form (which asks candidates to write an essay and to present information about honors awards earned, work experiences, extracurricular activities, and community service), and SAT or ACT scores. Scores on standardized tests must be received directly from the testing agency. As the Admissions Office reviews applications, it identifies candidates for the Binghamton Scholars Program and invites them to participate. Competition for spaces in the program runs high.

Binghamton makes admissions decisions on a rolling basis. Admission to the Binghamton Scholars Program is limited to 80 students each year. The University considers those who complete their applications for admission early. Therefore, in order to receive full consideration for this program, prospective students should be sure that the University has received their Supplementary Admissions Form and SAT/ACT scores by January 15.

Scholarship Availability: Students accepted to the Binghamton Scholars Program receive either full or partial tuition scholarships.

The Campus Context: Binghamton University is one of the four university centers of the State University of New York. Known for the excellence of its students, faculty and staff members, and programs, Binghamton enrolls nearly 13,000 students in programs leading to bachelor's, master's, and doctoral degrees. The University's curriculum, founded in the liberal arts, has expanded to include selected professional and graduate programs, and its faculty members and students come from many different cultures and backgrounds, representing a wealth of ideas to explore and enjoy. Binghamton has an excellent research library, outstanding computer facilities, a superb performing arts center, and a wide assortment of course offerings. While highly regarded as a research university, Binghamton also offers the comfort and attention of a smaller school. Students in the Scholars Program can choose to reside in one of Binghamton's four residential colleges and communities that integrate living and learning opportunities through the presence of faculty masters drawn from the ranks of tenured faculty members. With offices in the college or community, faculty masters are readily accessible to students for mentoring and academic advising. To enhance this integrated concept, classrooms, libraries, cultural programs, activity space, and faculty offices are housed within the residential settings. A varied program of guest speakers, lectures, films, panel discussions, exhibits, and workshops supplements formal courses.

Student Body Undergraduate enrollment is 10,167: 4,703 men and 5,464 women. The ethnic distribution is 52 percent white, 6 percent African American, 17 percent Asian American, 5 percent Hispanic, and .1 percent Native American. There are 222 international students. About 54 percent of the students live on campus. There are thirty-five fraternities and sororities and more than 150 other student organizations on campus.

Faculty The total number of faculty members is 784 (509 full-time), of whom 96 percent have terminal degrees. The student-faculty ratio is 19:1.

Key Facilities The library collection currently numbers more than 3 million bound volumes and microform, document, and serial holdings and grows at an annual rate of 100,000 total items. Extensive and up-to-date computer support is readily available for research and instruction at every level.

Honorary Societies The campus has chartered chapters of Phi Beta Kappa, the Golden Key National Honor Society, and Phi Eta Sigma, the national freshman honor society. There are, in addition, chapters of eighteen different academic honor societies in the Decker School of Nursing, the Thomas J. Watson School of Engineering and Applied Science, the School of Management, and the Harpur College of Arts and Sciences.

Athletics The intercollegiate athletic program offers nineteen varsity teams (ten men's and nine women's) and competes in the National Collegiate Athletic Association (NCAA) Division I, America East Conference.

Study Abroad The University encourages all of its students to study abroad as valuable preparation for an increasingly interdependent world. Binghamton currently sponsors eighteen study-abroad programs through the Office of International Programs.

Support Services The University provides a range of support services for its students: Academic Advising, a Career Development Center, the University Counseling Center, University Health Service, International Student and Scholar Services, and Services for Students with Disabilities.

Job Opportunities The Federal Work-Study Program (FWS) is offered to those students who are new to the University who are eligible and request the FWS on their FAFSA. Many students also find jobs in offices and departments on campus. Students may find information on part-time off-campus employment in the Student Financial Aid and Employment Office.

Tuition: $1700 for New York residents, $4150 for out-of-state residents, per semester

Room and Board: University housing, $1900 per semester; meals (standard dining plan), $1151 per semester

Mandatory Fees: $583 per semester

Contact: Director: Michael J. Conlon, Binghamton Scholars Program, College-in-the-Woods Library, Box 6000, Binghamton University, Binghamton, New York 13902-6000; Telephone: 607-777-3583; E-mail: scholars@binghamton.edu; Web site: http://scholars.binghamton.edu

State University of New York at New Paltz

4 Pu G S Tr AA

▼ SUNY New Paltz Honors Program

The SUNY New Paltz Honors Program exists to challenge New Paltz students beyond what is normally expected of them. It was designed around the philosophy that intense and rigorous courses taught by outstanding instructors (who offer much encouragement) and filled with motivated, focused students would create the optimal learning environment. The SUNY New Paltz Honors Program is small (around 100 students), so selectivity in acceptance is required. Once students are admitted into the program, they take special honors seminars that are cross-disciplinary and in-depth in scope. The honors seminars emphasize discussion and nonlecture-based learning; students

Interpreting the symbols: **2**=two-year college, **4**=four-year college; **Pu**=public or state college, **Pr**=private college; **G**=general honors program; **D**=departmental honors program; **S**=small program (fewer than 100 students), **M**=midsize program (100 to 500 students), **L**=large program (more than 500 students); **Sc**=scholarships available in honors program; **Tr**=transfer students accepted into honors program; **HBC**=historically black college; **AA**=academic advisors; **GA**=graduate advisors; **FA**=fellowship advisors.

are expected to come to class with something to say and to actively participate in debate and discussion.

Beyond the academic requirements, the SUNY New Paltz Honors Program provides students with the opportunity to meet and work with other like-minded students on class-related projects or extracurricular creative endeavors. These projects can take the form of anything from organizing an academic conference or discussion, to painting a mural, working on the newsletter, running a workshop on yoga, or any other skill, talent, or interest. The Honors Center also organizes several trips per semester, including the very popular biannual weekend retreat to the Ashokan Reservoir in the Catskill Mountains.

The SUNY New Paltz Honors Program is centered in the Honors Center, a building designed especially for honors students. It includes study space, a lounge area, a kitchen, seminar rooms, and a computer center complete with photocopiers, scanners, and other equipment. Best of all, it is open 24 hours a day, seven days a week to honors students.

Ultimately, the honors experience is what the student makes of it. The term itself is inclusive of both the academic and extracurricular aspects of the SUNY New Paltz Honors Program. Basically, it refers to life as a member of the program.

Participation Requirements: Academically speaking, honors students are required to take and actively participate in four honors seminars. Seminars focus on a wide variety of topics and students can begin taking them the second semester of their freshman year. Ideally, a student should only take one seminar per semester and should complete them by the end of the junior year.

An honors student is also required to complete a senior thesis project. The senior thesis allows honors students to explore an area of interest in great detail. The students discusses his or her topic with both the Program Director and another professor who works closely with the student throughout the duration the project. A thesis may be based on a topic within the student's major or on a completely unrelated subject. A thesis written as a requirement for the student's major may also be acceptable. In order to complete the thesis, the student should register for an independent study with his or her advising professor on the topic of the thesis. This should be done the first semester of the senior year. If the student chooses to, he or she may present the thesis in a ceremony held prior to commencement.

One requirement that exists outside of the classroom is the completion of 30 hours of community service. Community service (also known as service learning) allows students to help others while learning about themselves and the world around them.

Admission Process: Prospective freshmen are invited to apply to the SUNY New Paltz Honors Program in the course of the admission process to the University. The following criteria are considered minimal qualifications for acceptance into the program: SAT scores of 1150 or higher; high school average of 90 or higher; two writing samples; and two letters of recommendation.

Students who transfer into New Paltz as sophomores of juniors can apply to the SUNY New Paltz Honors Program in the course of the admission process to the University. The following criteria are considered for acceptance into the program: an overall college GPA of 3.3 or higher; a portfolio, i.e., two or more examples of writing from the past year and/or project or project description (for students in the arts and sciences); and recommendations from at least 2 previous college professors.

All honors students must maintain a minimum semester GPA of 3.3. If two consecutive semesters pass without a student enrolling in a seminar (except in the case of Study Abroad), an assumption is made that the student is no longer interested in being a part of the SUNY New Paltz Honors Program, and his or her name is removed from its roster.

Scholarship Availability: A limited number of merit-based scholarships are offered to entering freshmen each year. Participation in the SUNY New Paltz Honors Program is not a requirement for receipt of any of these scholarships.

The Campus Context: SUNY at New Paltz is the only residential public university in the mid-Hudson region. It is the nation's ninty-ninth-oldest collegiate institution, tracing its heritage to 1828 and the founding of the New Paltz Academy. SUNY at New Paltz offers undergraduate and graduate programs in the liberal arts and sciences which serve as a core for professional programs in the fine and performing arts, education, health care, business, and engineering. SUNY at New Paltz is located in the scenic Hudson Valley, midway between the state capital of Albany and metropolitan New York City. The University provides unique opportunities for enriching its academic programs. SUNY at New Paltz has a diverse faculty of distinguished scholars and artists who collaborate across the disciplines and professional areas to inspire their students to a love of learning, a meaningful engagement with the life of the mind, and an involvement in public service.

New Paltz offers more than 100 undergraduate programs within the College of Liberal Arts and Sciences, School of Engineering and Business Administration, School of Education, and School of Fine and Performing Arts. The Graduate School offers more than fifty master's degree programs and six predoctoral programs. The New Paltz experience is enhanced by such opportunities as the SUNY New Paltz Honors Program, the Model UN Program, the New Paltz Summer Repertory Theater, the Center for International Education, the London Theater Winterim, the Summer Archeological Field School, the UN Semester Program, and the wide variety of field work, internship, and cooperative education opportunities.

Student Body There are 7,838 full-time students at New Paltz. Of these, 6,053 are undergraduates and 1,785 are graduate students.

Faculty There are 288 full-time faculty members, 86 percent of whom hold a Ph.D. or terminal degree. There are 270 part-time faculty members.

Key Facilities The Sojourner Truth library contains more than 550,000 volumes. In addition, there are extensive computer facilities on campus.

Honor Societies Eta Kappa Nu, Kappa Delta Phi, Phi Alpha Theta, Phi Beta Kappa, Phi Delta Kappa, Pi Sigma Alpha.

Athletics New Paltz competes at the NCAA Division II level in men's baseball and men's and women's basketball, cross-country, field hockey, lacrosse, soccer, softball, swimming and diving, tennis, track and field, and volleyball. There are intercollegiate club sports in men's and women's rugby, men's ice hockey, and equestrian competition. There is an indoor and outdoor athletic and recreation complex on campus.

Study Abroad Overseas study is available through the Center for International Education and various SUNY-sponsored programs. New Paltz sponsors programs in Belgium, the Czech republic, Denmark, Ecuador, France, Germany, Greece, India, Ireland, Israel, Italy, Jamaica, Japan, Mexico, the Netherlands, New Zealand, Philippines, Scotland, Spain, the United Kingdom, and Zimbabwe.

Support Services New Paltz maintains offices of Students Advising, Center for Academic Development and Learning, Career Advising and Fieldwork, Disabled Student Services, Student Health Center, and Psychological Counseling Center.

Job Opportunities Employment is available on campus through the College Work-Study, NYS Temporary Service, College Auxiliary Services, SUNY Research Foundation, and the Office of College Activities. Off-campus employment listings are posted by the Office of Financial Aid.

Tuition: $1700 per semester for New York State residents (full-time), $4150 per semester for nonresidents (full-time)

Room and board: $1560 for room and $1084 for food service, per semester

Mandatory Fees: $432.50 (total per semester) for college fee, activity fee, health service fee, athletic fee, technology fee, and health insurance

Contact: Director: Jeff Miller, Honors Program, SUNY New Paltz, 75 South Manheim Boulevard, New Paltz, New York 12561; Telephone: 845-257-3934; Fax: 845-257-3937; E-mail: millerj@newpaltz.edu; Web site: http://www.newpaltz.edu/honors

STATE UNIVERSITY OF NEW YORK AT OSWEGO

4 Pu G S Sc Tr

▼ College Honors Program

The SUNY Oswego Honors Program consists of a core of courses designed to stimulate students' intellectual growth and develop their analytical abilities. Unlike traditional courses, which present material from a single field of study, Honors Program courses draw ideas and information from many fields, addressing concerns common to all disciplines and recognizing that there are no boundaries to thought and inquiry. Honors Program courses examine the historical and intellectual origins, growth, and development of today's issues, the connections among them, and their consequences for tomorrow. The program emphasizes small classes—about 20 students—and the lively exchange of ideas in the classroom. The Honors Program seeks out faculty members who have demonstrated excellence in teaching, who are especially skilled in their fields, who are interested in thinking across disciplines, and who are committed to working with students in a variety of formal and informal settings. Honors Program students are advised by the Honors Director and by faculty members in the student's major field of study. Students enjoy a close relationship with honors faculty members and with each other in a network of academic and personal support.

Honors Program students have access to all of SUNY Oswego's facilities. This is one of the great benefits of the Honors Program; while students enjoy the advantages of a small, challenging program, they have access to all the resources of a major university, including an internationally respected faculty, a library with more than 1 million holdings, fully equipped computer labs, and a wide range of student services.

Participation Requirements: Students in the Honors Program can major in any area the College offers and take the same number of credits for graduation as every other SUNY Oswego student. Honors Program students take 18 hours in the Honors Core (Intellectual Traditions I and II, The Social Sciences, Literature and the Arts, Science in the Human Context, and The Search for Meaning), as well as courses in a language, lab science, English, and math. (If an Advanced Placement course covers the same material as an Honors Program course, the AP course will fulfill the honors requirement. For example, a student with AP credit in calculus or a lab science already will have met those particular requirements.) In addition, students in the Honors Program explore a subject of their choice in depth with a faculty adviser—usually within their major—by writing an honors thesis.

To graduate from the Honors Program, students must have a minimum 3.0 GPA overall, a minimum 3.3 GPA in their major, and a minimum 3.3 in the Honors Core. Successful completion of the Honors Program requirements is noted at graduation and is recorded on the student's transcript.

Admission Process: Freshmen are selected each May for the Honors Program on the basis of their high school average and their SAT I scores. Sophomores and first-year students who are not selected may also apply for admission.

The Campus Context: The State University of New York, College at Oswego was founded in 1861 as the Oswego Normal School and became a SUNY college in 1962. SUNY Oswego is located in Oswego, New York, about 50 miles northwest of Syracuse, and occupies 700 acres right on the shore of Lake Ontario. Oswego offers sixty undergraduate majors leading to the baccalaureate, including liberal arts and sciences, business, and education. In the past decade a number of highly respected national publications, including *U.S. News & World Report, Barron's,* and *Money* magazine, have rated SUNY Oswego's education as outstanding, an "Ivy league education at a state university price." In 1998, *Kiplinger's Personal Finance Magazine* ranked SUNY Oswego among the top 100 state colleges and universities based on its value and quality.

Student Body There are 6,500 undergraduates enrolled; the majority are from the Northeast.

Faculty Of the 300 full-time faculty members, 75 percent have doctorates or other terminal degrees. There are also adjunct faculty members. The student-faculty ratio is 22:1. Most of the Honors Program faculty members are recipients of the SUNY Chancellor's Award for Excellence in Teaching.

Key Facilities The library houses 462,555 volumes. There are 600 Macintosh and DOS computers, located in the library, dormitories, and academic buildings. In addition, every dorm room has high-speed Internet connections.

Athletics Intercollegiate athletics for men include baseball, basketball, cross-country, diving, golf, hockey, lacrosse, soccer, swimming, tennis, and volleyball. SUNY Oswego also offers a wide range of intramural sports and club teams, including crew (rowing) for both men and women.

Study Abroad Through its International Education Program, SUNY Oswego students in all majors have the opportunity to study overseas in England, France, Spain, Mexico, Italy, Germany, Puerto Rico, Australia, Hungary, and Japan. Students may study abroad for a summer, for a semester, or for a year. Credits earned in this way apply to the student's SUNY Oswego degree requirements.

Job Opportunities Students are offered a range of work opportunities on campus, including assistantships and work-study.

Tuition: $3400 for state residents, $8300 for nonresidents, per year (2001–02)

Room and Board: $3890 for a double-occupancy room, $2806 for full board

Mandatory Fees: $760

Contact: Director: Dr. Norman L. Weiner, 105A Mahar Hall, Oswego, New York 13126; Telephone: 315-312-2190; Fax: 315-312-6790; E-mail: weiner@oswego.edu; Web site: http://www.oswego.edu/honors

STATE UNIVERSITY OF NEW YORK AT STONY BROOK

4 Pu G M Sc Tr

▼ Honors College

The Honors College at the State University of New York at Stony Brook is an innovative academic program that promises to challenge, stimulate, and enrich superior students. Each year, a

Interpreting the symbols: **2**=two-year college, **4**=four-year college; **Pu**=public or state college, **Pr**=private college; **G**=general honors program; **D**=departmental honors program; **S**=small program (fewer than 100 students), **M**=midsize program (100 to 500 students), **L**=large program (more than 500 students); **Sc**=scholarships available in honors program; **Tr**=transfer students accepted into honors program; **HBC**=historically black college; **AA**=academic advisors; **GA**=graduate advisors; **FA**=fellowship advisors.

small group of high-achieving students is invited to join the Honors College and take advantage of an exciting curriculum, extraordinary career guidance, an array of cultural activities, and a supportive social environment.

The Honors College has its own interdisciplinary core curriculum, especially tailored to high-achieving students. Students are taught by faculty members with a strong commitment to undergraduate teaching. In 1997, the University at Stony Brook was rated second among all public research universities. All honors students are engaged in research and other creative activities during their years at Stony Brook. The Honors College also sponsors a range of 1-credit courses that engage students in a range of cultural and community activities.

Honors College students receive priority housing in a renovated residence hall reserved for honors students. The hall has its own computer laboratory, lounges, and access to a nearby fitness center. The College sponsors student social and cultural events throughout the year.

Each year, several incoming Honors College students are accepted into the Scholars for Medicine (B.A./M.D.) program, which reserves them a seat in Stony Brook's School of Medicine upon successful completion of the four-year undergraduate program.

The Honors College at Stony Brook was founded in 1988. There are approximately 250 students enrolled in the College.

Participation Requirements: The Honors College curriculum consists of a four-year program that requires the same number of credits as the general education program. Students take 19 credits of courses designed specially for the program as well as 6 credits of departmental honors courses. Students can major in any field.

To graduate from the Honors College, students must maintain a minimum cumulative GPA of 3.0. Honors College members also complete a senior project that represents the culmination of their honors experience at Stony Brook.

Admission Process: Students must file a general application for the University at Stony Brook as well as a specific application for the Honors College. Students applying for freshmen admission are expected to have minimum SAT I scores of 1250 as well as an unweighted high school average of 93 percent. Transfer students must have compiled a minimum GPA of 3.5 in their college-level work. Special attention is also paid to students' writing ability, as demonstrated through their personal essay and other application materials. Applications from students who have demonstrated leadership in extracurricular activities and/or excellence in visual, performing, or literary arts are particularly encouraged. Students who wish to apply for the Scholars for Medicine program must have minimum SAT I scores of 1350. They also write a second essay that is included with every Honors College application.

Admissions folders are initially read by members of the Honors College Advisory Board. The board consists of faculty members from the College of Arts and Sciences, the College of Engineering and Applied Sciences, and the Marine Sciences Research Center as well as members of the Honors College administration. Final decisions are made by the Chair and Assistant to the Chair of the Honors College. The Dean of Admissions for the Medical School chooses candidates for Scholars for Medicine from a group recommended by the Honors College.

The deadline for freshmen admissions is January 15. The deadline for transfer admissions is May 1.

Scholarship Availability: All members of the Honors College receive at least a $2000 scholarship in their first year. Many four-year scholarships are also available. To retain four-year scholarships, students must remain members of the Honors College.

The Campus Context: The State University of New York at Stony Brook (USB) was founded in 1956; in 1960, a report prepared for the State Board of Regents declared that Stony Brook's destiny was to become a major research university to "stand with the finest in the country." Today the early vision of Stony Brook has been realized. It is one of only eighty-eight public and private colleges and universities nationwide to be classified as a Research I institution by the Carnegie Foundation.

Stony Brook is situated on 1,100 acres midway between New York City and the resort area of the Hamptons on Long Island's East End. Major facilities include the five-theater Staller Center for the Arts and the 4,000-seat Sports Complex.

Stony Brook has exceptional strength in the sciences, mathematics, humanities, fine arts, social sciences, engineering, and health professions. Major academic units of the University include the College of Arts and Sciences, College of Engineering and Applied Sciences, the W. Averell Harriman School for Management and Policy, and Health Sciences Center, which is made up of the Schools of Medicine, Health Technology and Management, Dental Medicine, Nursing, and Social Welfare. Some of Stony Brook's research units include the Marine Sciences Research Center, Institute for Theoretical Physics, Institute for Mathematical Sciences, Center for Biotechnology, Howard Hughes Medical Institute, and the Center for Regional Policy Studies.

Student Body Undergraduate enrollment is 11,267; graduate enrollment is 6,609. Of that total, 50 percent are women and 50 percent are men. The ethnic population is 9 percent African American, 21 percent Asian American, and 7 percent Hispanic. Forty-seven percent of students live on campus, and 72 percent of students receive financial aid. The campus has fifteen fraternities and fifteen sororities.

Faculty Instructional faculty members number 1,610. Ninety-five percent hold doctoral or terminal degrees. The student-faculty ratio is 17:1.

Key Facilities The Frank Melville Jr. Library holds more than 1.9 million volumes and 3 million publications in microformate. Instructional computing facilities include more than 300 computers and terminals that are distributed over ten sites.

Honorary Societies Phi Beta Kappa, Golden Key, and Sigma Beta

Athletics In intercollegiate athletics, USB is NCAA Division I and a member of the ECAC. Men's sports include baseball, basketball, cross-country, football (Northeast Conference), indoor/outdoor track and field, lacrosse, soccer, swimming and diving, and tennis. Women's sports include basketball, cross-country, golf, indoor/outdoor track and field, soccer, softball, swimming and diving, tennis, and volleyball.

Study Abroad The State University system sponsors numerous academic programs throughout Western Europe, the Middle East, the Far East, Canada, and Latin America. Stony Brook also sponsors programs in Bolivia, France, Germany, Great Britain, Italy, Jamaica, Korea, Poland, and Spain.

Support Services The Disabled Student Services office assists students with disabilities in accessing the many resources of the University.

Job Opportunities Students are offered a range of work opportunities on campus, including assistantships, research positions, work-study, student employment, and internships.

Tuition: $3400 for state residents, $8300 for nonresidents, per year (2001–02)

Room and Board: $5558

Mandatory Fees: $532

Contact: Director: Honors College, Ward Melville Library N3071, Stony Brook, New York 11794-3357; Telephone: 631-632-4378; Fax: 631-632-4525; E-mail: honorscollege@notes.cc.sunysb.edu

---

State University of New York College at Brockport

4 Pu G M Sc Tr

▼ College Honors and Upper-Division Honors Program

Brockport's Honors Program sponsors two unique programs, the College Honors Program and the Upper-Division Honors Program, for students with strong academic records. These programs allow students to enrich their college experience, maximizing both the breadth and the depth of their academic study. Honors students select courses from the College's wide variety of course offerings and also undertake in-depth research in a specific area of their academic major. Both programs allow students to satisfy the College's general education requirements, enroll in special honors seminars of approximately 15 students taught by SUNY Brockport's most distinguished faculty members, and to complete an honors thesis or project under the personal supervision of a faculty member in their major.

College Honors is designed for students entering the Honors Program in their freshman year. Students in College Honors complete their general education breadth requirements with a flexible mixture of honors seminars and conventional courses. Students take four honors courses in their first two years and they may select these courses on the basis of their academic strengths, personal interests, academic major, or even create their own courses. In the last two years of college, students in the College Honors Program take three honors courses, including the Junior Research Colloquium and an independent research course for the senior honors thesis.

Upper-Division Honors is designed especially for transfer students and SUNY Brockport students who have shown significant academic achievements during their first two years of college courses. Students in this program complete the three Upper-Division Honors courses required in the College Honors Program. SUNY Brockport's 20 year-old Honors Program admits more than 130 new students each year, and approximately 450 students are enrolled in the program.

Participation Requirements: Honors students must maintain a 3.25 GPA and take at least one honors course each year to participate in the programs. College Honors students must complete seven honors courses, including the honors thesis. Upper-Division honors students complete three Upper-Division honors courses, including the honors thesis. The completion of College Honors or Upper-Division Honors is noted on the students' transcripts.

Admission Process: Students must apply and be accepted in order to enroll in honors seminars and participate in Honors Program activities. Entering freshmen should have a high school GPA of at least 90.0 and SAT total scores of at least 1150 or the equivalent. Transfer students and current SUNY Brockport students should have a GPA of at least 3.30.

Scholarship Availability: SUNY Brockport's wide-ranging program of scholarships make it possible for all entering students in the Honors Program to qualify for financial assistance. In addition, the Honors Program has supplemental scholarships for eligible entering freshmen.

The Campus Context: Founded in 1835 as the Brockport Collegiate Institute, the State University of New York College at Brockport is a coeducational comprehensive college that places student success as its highest priority. The College lies along the historic Erie Canal, 20 miles west of Rochester, New York, in the village of Brockport (pop. 9,800). The College also offers courses at a variety of Rochester-area locations, including the Metro Center classroom/computer lab complex and the prestigious Visual Studies Workshop, both in downtown Rochester. A broad offering of liberal arts and professional academic programs lead to BA, BS, BFN, BSN, MFA, MA, and MS degrees and 17 teacher-certification programs. An extensive selection of co-op and internship opportunities match students with many of Rochester's top employers, providing invaluable real-world experience. SUNY Brockport is an integral part of the Village of Brockport, providing students with easy access to unique shops, eateries, theater and other activities.

Student Body SUNY Brockport enrolls 6,264 undergraduate and 1,870 graduate students, most of whom are New York State residents.

Faculty The SUNY Brockport faculty includes 23 Distinguished Professors, SUNY's highest academic ranking; 71 Chancellor's Award for Excellence in Teaching recipients; 13 Fulbright Scholarship Awardees; and 2 Guggenheim Awards.

Key Facilities The online catalog and research tools of The Drake Memorial Library put accurate and up-to-date information at students' fingertips. In addition to the 20 computer labs across campus there is the Dailey Computer Center, the hub of campus technology, with PC, Macintosh, and SUN Workstation labs, while the computational science department houses Intel and Silicon supercomputers. Lennon Science Center reopened the fall of 2001 after a $14-million renovation.

Athletics SUNY Brockport students participate in twenty-three Division III varsity sports as well as an extensive intramural sports program. The Tuttle Athletic Complex houses an ice arena, Olympic-sized pool, gymnasiums, and a state-of-the-art workout facility.

Study Abroad SUNY Brockport has the largest study-abroad program in the SUNY system and is one of the top ten programs in the nation, providing students with a wide variety of overseas study opportunities.

Support Services The Student Learning Center helps students improve study skills and offers tutoring in a variety of academic subjects. The Counseling Center is available to help students deal with stressful situations that can arise as part of the college-adjustment process. The Academic Advisement Office helps students plan and monitor their progress toward degree completion.

Job Opportunities The Office of Career Services helps students explore a range of employment opportunities with more than 700 internships, 50 paid internships, 500 community service jobs, and more than 5,000 student employment jobs. Its Web-based JobShop also helps students find jobs while still in college and after graduation.

Tuition: $3400 for state residents; $8300 for nonresidents, per year (2000–01)

Room and Board: $6110

Mandatory Fees: $727

Contact: Director: Dr. Mark A. Anderson, 219 Holmes Hall, SUNY College at Brockport, 350 New Campus Drive, Brockport, New York 14420; Telephone: 716-395-5400 or Ext. 5054; Fax: 716-395-5046; E-mail: honors@brockport.edu

State University of New York College at Cortland

4 Pu G M Tr

▼ SUNY Cortland All-College Honors Program

The State University of New York College at Cortland (SUNY Cortland) All-College Honors Program provides students with

Interpreting the symbols: **2**=two-year college, **4**=four-year college; **Pu**=public or state college, **Pr**=private college; **G**=general honors program; **D**=departmental honors program; **S**=small program (fewer than 100 students), **M**=midsize program (100 to 500 students), **L**=large program (more than 500 students); **Sc**=scholarships available in honors program; **Tr**=transfer students accepted into honors program; **HBC**=historically black college; **AA**=academic advisors; **GA**=graduate advisors; **FA**=fellowship advisors.

demonstrated academic excellence the opportunity for continued intellectual challenge in a rigorous, coherent, and integrative program. Honors students participate in courses with an emphasis on student-faculty interchange and community building. The program provides a mechanism for students to distinguish themselves and also enhances the general learning environment for all students and faculty members, the College, and the community.

Honors classes are small, generally no more than 20 students, providing an opportunity for greater interaction among students and faculty members. Most honors courses are taken in conjunction with the College's general education program, but there are some opportunities to take honors courses in the student's major. All honors program students are required to complete an honors thesis for credit in their junior or senior year. In addition, all honors program students must complete 40 hours of community service.

Beginning in fall 2002, all honors program freshmen will be housed in the same residence hall.

Honors program students are encouraged to participate in a variety of programs, including an annual retreat at the College's outdoor recreation facility in Raquette Lake, New York, and trips to various cultural events in the region. The honors program also sponsors student participation in the annual conference of the Northeast Regional Honors Council. The student honors journal, *Parnassus,* normally includes a number of honors program students among its contributors and editorial board members.

The honors program is staffed by a coordinator (who functions as an unofficial adviser for honors program students) and a student assistant. The honors program office, centrally located in the College's main academic building, includes a meeting room/study lounge for students and a small computer lab in addition to the coordinator's office. The SUNY Cortland All-College Honors Program is affiliated with the National Collegiate Honors Council (NCHC) and is a member of the Northeast Regional Honors Council. The program was founded in 1982, and there are 120 students currently enrolled in it.

Participation Requirements: To complete the honors program, students must take at least 24 credit hours of honors-level courses. Students fulfill this requirement by taking a combination of specially designated honors courses, contract courses, and a course in which they complete the required honors thesis. Students may also use a maximum of two writing intensive (WI) courses beyond the all-College requirements toward the completion of the honors program. Specially designated honors courses are offered in a variety of general education categories. In addition, a few majors now offer honors sections of their courses. Some of the courses offered through the general education program and in the majors are unique to the honors program and others are special honors sections of courses offered to the general student population.

Students in the honors program are expected to maintain a 3.2 cumulative GPA. Honors program students who are in the top 5 percent of their respective classes are recognized each year at Honors Convocation. Students who complete the honors program requirements earn an honors designation on their diplomas and their transcripts and they are recognized in the commencement program.

Admission Process: Students seeking to be admitted to the honors program as freshmen must indicate early in April that they would like to be considered for the program. The Honors Program Coordinator then reviews their admissions files and takes into consideration their high school GPAs (unweighted), SAT and/or ACT scores, class rank, extracurricular activities, and admissions essays in making decisions about accepting students for the program. Students are also admitted to the program as sophomores. Students who are applying to be admitted as sophomores must be in the top 5 percent of the freshman class in order to be considered. About 40 students are admitted each year as freshmen, and about 10 are admitted as sophomores.

Scholarship Availability: There are no scholarships tied to admission to the honors program. However, SUNY Cortland does offer a number of scholarships that are based on academic merit, and many students who receive these scholarships also participate in the honors program. Examples of these scholarships include the SUNY Cortland Presidential Scholarships, the SUNY Cortland Leadership Scholarships, and the Residential Service Scholarships. For more information about SUNY Cortland's many scholarship opportunities (and other sources of financial aid), students should visit the Admissions Office Web site at http://www.cortland.edu/finaid/scholarships.html.

The Campus Context: The State University of New York College at Cortland traces its beginnings to 1868 and offers programs leading to bachelor's and master's degrees both in the arts and sciences and in professional studies. SUNY Cortland is a moderate-sized institution with approximately 5,700 undergraduate students and 1,300 graduate students. State assisted, Cortland is a charter member of the State University of New York. SUNY Cortland now has more than 50,000 living alumni, and Cortland graduates can be found in each of the fifty states, the District of Columbia, and more than forty other countries.

The campus is located in Cortland, a small city in the geographic center of New York State adjacent to the Finger Lakes and within an hour's drive of Syracuse, Ithaca, and Binghamton. The College campus covers 191 acres located within walking distance of the city of Cortland's business district. The main campus is divided into three distinct areas. Most of the classroom buildings, the Memorial Library, the Miller Building, and the Brockway-Cheney-DeGroat residence and dining hall complex are found on the upper campus. The remaining residence halls, Neubig and Winchell Dining Halls, and Corey Union are at the center of the campus. The Park Center, Lusk Field House, and the athletic fields and track are located on the lower campus. A shuttle bus service is operated between the lower and upper campuses when classes are in session.

Student Body Total undergraduate enrollment for the 2001–02 academic year was approximately 5,800 students. Out of the 5,800 students on campus about 80 percent of them received financial aid. Traditional students make up the majority at SUNY Cortland and they reside on campus. The campus offers the opportunity to be a part of one of five national sororities or one fraternity.

Faculty The total number of faculty members is 469. Of the 469, 252 are full-time and 217 are part-time. Approximately 80 percent have terminal degrees.

Key Facilities The Cortland Memorial Library houses 397,160 volumes, 298,616 titles, and 1,238 periodicals. The Cortland campus includes more than 850 computers in forty labs, and students in all majors increasingly find themselves completing interactive learning exercises, using the latest software and consulting online resources. For example, the International Communications and Culture computer lab is the site of a multimedia materials course taught by a Spanish and a French professor, in which students learn to master presentation software, streaming audio and video, and other high-tech tools. In the Geographic Information Systems laboratory, students create sophisticated computerized maps for a wide range of purposes, from urban planning to environmental conservation.

Honorary Societies Phi Kappa Phi, Phi Eta Sigma, Alpha Sigma Lambda, Alpha Kappa Delta, Beta Beta Beta, Eta Sigma Gamma, Kappa Delta Pi, Omicron Delta Epsilon, Phi Alpha Theta, Pi Delta Phi, Pi Sigma Alpha, Psi Chi, Sigma Delta Pi, Sigma Phi Omega, Sigma Pi Sigma, and Sigma Tau Delta.

Athletics All teams play in NCAA Division III. SUNY Cortland athletic affiliations are as follows: National Collegiate Athletic Association (NCAA) Division III, State University of New York

Athletic Conference (SUNYAC), Eastern College Athletic Conference (ECAC), New York State Women's Collegiate Athletic Association (NYSWCAA), National Collegiate Gymnastics Association (NCGA), New Jersey Athletic Conference (NJAC) (football only), and the Empire Collegiate Wrestling Conference. Men's athletics include cross-country, football, and soccer (fall); basketball, ice hockey, indoor track and field, swimming/diving, and wrestling (winter); baseball, lacrosse, and outdoor track and field (spring). Women's athletics include cross-country, field hockey, golf, soccer, tennis, and volleyball (fall); basketball, gymnastics, ice hockey, indoor track and field, and swimming and diving (winter); lacrosse, softball; and outdoor track and field (spring).

Study Abroad SUNY Cortland has the longest-standing study-abroad program in the SUNY system. Its first program was established in Neuchatel, Switzerland, in 1964. Cortland provides twenty-six different study-abroad opportunities at fourteen locations in ten countries on four continents. The strengths of Cortland's programs include a high degree of integration into the host universities' curriculum, relatively low cost compared to many colleges, a wide variety of locations and curricular choices, and a long tradition and solid reputation.

Support Services SUNY Cortland is committed to upholding and maintaining all aspects of the Americans with Disabilities Act (ADA), approved in 1990, and Section 504 of the Rehabilitation Act of 1973. As an institution, it is dedicated to ensuring reasonable access to its campus programs and facilities and continuously seeks to augment and improve its services. The Office of Student Disability Services has been designated as the office that coordinates services for students with documented disabilities who voluntarily identify themselves to the office.

Job Opportunities Career Services provides assistance and resources for every aspect of career development, from choosing a major or career path to developing the skills necessary to pursue one's goals. Among the many services provided are career counseling, access to career resource materials, workshops, and volunteer, internship, and/or employment opportunities. The internship program combines academic study with career-related work and learning experiences. Students use their talents, skills, and ingenuity in career-related work while earning up to 16 credit hours toward graduation. The internship program is open to Cortland students from all majors who are in good academic standing and have completed their sophomore year.

Tuition: State University of New York tuition for full-time undergraduates who are legal residents of New York State is currently $3400 for the academic year (fall and spring semesters). Tuition for out-of-state undergraduates is currently $8300. Under State University of New York policy, students must have resided in New York State for one year before entering college and satisfy other residency requirements as determined by the State University of New York to qualify for in-state tuition rates. Graduate-level tuition charges are currently $213 per credit hour for New York State residents and $351 per credit for out-of-state residents. This information is based on the 2001–02 school year.

Mandatory Fees: The College Fee is $25 per year or $12.50 per semester. The fee is required under administrative policy of State University of New York and is not refundable. The College's Program Service Charge is required of all students enrolled in credit-bearing course work and is designed to incorporate various normally required fees and charges, including athletic, student health service, transportation, technology, and student activity fees, into one consolidated charge. It is understood that all students do not equally participate in each of the components, but receive equivalent overall benefit from the universally available services enhancing campus life. Certain special and remote site programs are exempt. Total fee costs are about $774. This information is based on the 2001–02 school year.

Room and Board: Room and board expenses vary depending on accommodations and the meal plan chosen by the student. The room charge is $3380 to $5080, depending on room choice. The meal plan charge is $2400 to $2800, depending on plan choice. This information is based on the 2001–02 school year.

Contact: Coordinator: Dr. J. Richard Kendrick Jr., B-13 Old Main, SUNY Cortland, P.O. Box 2000, Cortland, New York 13045-0900; Telephone: 607-753-4827; Fax: 607-753-5989; E-mail: honors@cortland.edu; Web site: http://www.cortland.edu/honors.

State University of New York College at Oneonta

4 Pu G S Tr

▼ Oneonta Scholars Program

The Oneonta Scholars Program is a four-year, 18-credit program designed for students who wish to seek out challenging academic experiences and want to contribute to the intellectual and cultural life of the academic community. Freshman and sophomore course work emphasizes skill development and interdisciplinary perspectives while junior and senior course work emphasizes discipline-based experiences. The courses are designed to fit into the student's program of study. Scholars take the same number of credits as other students and courses taken during the freshman and sophomore years satisfy general education requirements.

The Oneonta Scholars Program is designed to develop and foster the qualities found in an Oneonta Scholar: inquisitive, creative, independent, and critical thinking; strong academic ability; and a high capacity for independent work. Students who participate in the Scholars Program have the opportunity to enjoy exciting and challenging course work in a small-class setting, to develop close working relationships with Oneonta's best faculty members, and to become part of a network of similarly motivated students.

The four-year Oneonta Scholars Program was implemented in the fall of 1996. It is a direct outgrowth of the pilot Freshmen Scholars Program, which was initiated in 1994. There are currently 94 students involved in the new program.

Participation Requirements: During the freshman year, students take the Freshman Scholars Seminar. The Freshmen Scholars Seminar is designed to build critical-thinking, reading, writing, speaking, and listening skills. In addition, freshmen may take general education courses from a selection of courses offered for scholars.

The junior and senior year course work allows the student to specialize in his or her major. Students may contract with a course instructor and the Oneonta Scholars Program office to take any course for scholars credit. Students must complete at least 3 credits of independent work in their major with a faculty mentor. The independent work can take the form of an internship, field experience, a thesis, a research project, or creative work.

Once accepted into the program, the student must maintain a minimum overall GPA of 3.3 and receive no less than a grade of B in any Scholars course in order to maintain eligibility. Successful completion of the program is noted on the student's transcript.

Admission Process: The eligibility process is flexible to ensure that all qualified students have the opportunity to apply. Students may enter the program up to the first semester of their junior year. Entering freshmen are invited to participate based on SAT

Interpreting the symbols: **2**=two-year college, **4**=four-year college; **Pu**=public or state college, **Pr**=private college; **G**=general honors program; **D**=departmental honors program; **S**=small program (fewer than 100 students), **M**=midsize program (100 to 500 students), **L**=large program (more than 500 students); **Sc**=scholarships available in honors program; **Tr**=transfer students accepted into honors program; **HBC**=historically black college; **AA**=academic advisors; **GA**=graduate advisors; **FA**=fellowship advisors.

I scores, high school class rank, and high school GPA. Returning students and transfer students may initiate the application process.

Scholarship Availability: The College at Oneonta has recently established the Mildred Haight Memorial Scholarships. Beginning in 1997, 20 incoming freshmen receive $500 grants each to purchase books and other educational supplies at the College Bookstore. The awards are being made to accepted students early in the admission cycle, and the primary criterion is high school GPA.

The Campus Context: The State University of New York College at Oneonta, a state-supported, comprehensive, coeducational college of the liberal arts, was founded in 1889 and was incorporated into the State University of New York system in 1948. Oneonta State is located in Oneonta, New York (population 15,000), about halfway between Albany and Binghamton, just off Interstate 88 near the western foothills of the Catskill Mountains. In a comprehensive study of academic quality and cost, *Money* magazine's *1996 Money Guide: Your Best College Buy Now* ranked Oneonta seventy-ninth among some 2,000 public and private four-year colleges and universities nationwide, and fifteenth among schools in the Northeast. The College at Oneonta has sixty-five undergraduate degree programs and twenty master's degree programs.

Outstanding facilities include Milne Library, with the largest collection of library materials among all the SUNY colleges, and the nationally recognized Physics and Chemistry Multimedia Laboratory. The campus also features the Goodrich Theatre in the Fine Arts Building, the Hunt College Union, the Electronic Classroom in the Instructional Resources Center, and the Morris Conference Center. In addition, the College owns and maintains a facility on Otsego Lake in Cooperstown, which houses the Biological Field Station and the Cooperstown Graduate Program in History Museum Studies.

Student Body The College at Oneonta enrolls 4,800 full-time students. The student population is 40 percent men. Ninety-seven percent of students are from New York State, 10 percent are 25 years old or older, and 8 percent are students of color. Eighty percent of the students receive financial aid. There are eight sororities and no fraternities.

Faculty The College at Oneonta has 223 full-time and 118 part-time faculty members. Seventy-two percent of the faculty members have earned a doctorate or other terminal degree in their field. The student-faculty ratio is 20:1.

Key Facilities Milne Library houses 537,832 volumes, the largest collection of library materials among all the SUNY colleges. The College at Oneonta has more than 300 PCs for student use, many networked to a central VAX cluster; unlimited campuswide access to the Internet; eighteen computer labs (nine open seven days a week); and eleven specialized labs for computer graphics, geographic mapping, economics and business, and other disciplines. The Chemistry and Physics Multimedia Lab is nationally known.

Construction has begun on the new 91,000-square-foot SUNY-Oneonta Field House. The main area will seat 3,000 people for basketball games and 4,500 people for events that permit seating on the floor, such as lectures or debates. The new Field House will also house a dance studio, two racquetball courts, an indoor track, a weight training/fitness center, and other administrative and support spaces.

Athletics The College at Oneonta competes in the NCAA, ECAC, NYSAIAW, and SUNY Athletic Conference, fielding intercollegiate teams for men in baseball, basketball, cross-country, lacrosse, soccer, tennis, and wrestling, and for women in basketball, cross-country, field hockey, lacrosse, soccer, softball, swimming, tennis, and volleyball. Men's soccer is in NCAA Division I; all other intercollegiate athletic teams compete in NCAA Division III.

Study Abroad Study-abroad programs (some for a full year, some for a semester, and some for the summer) are offered in Japan, Germany, England, Canada, Russia, and India. Oneonta students also participate in the hundreds of other study-abroad programs available each year through other SUNY colleges and universities. The Office of International Education assists students who wish to pursue opportunities for education abroad.

Support Services Through the Office of Services for Students with Disabilities, Oneonta provides a range of educational accommodations unique to individual students. Such provisions include special testing accommodations and classroom services for students with documented need of them. Other available services include placement-testing accommodations during orientation, housing accommodations, assistance with access problems, advisement about particular disability issues, assistance with funding coordinates, and referrals to appropriate resources.

Job Opportunities The College has a professionally staffed Student Employment Service providing students with on-campus and off-campus employment opportunities.

Tuition: $3400 for state residents, $8300 for nonresidents, per year (1997–98)

Room and Board: $5790

Mandatory Fees: $358 to $484

Contact: Dr. Virginia Harder, 332C Netzer Administration Building, Oneonta, New York 13820-4015; Telephone: 607-436-3184; Fax: 607-436-2689; E-mail: harderv@oneonta.edu

State University of New York College at Plattsburgh

4 Pu M Sc Tr

▼ Honors Program

Honors Seminars, Learning Communities, Honors Tutorials, mentoring programs, and research opportunities are just a few of the special teaching/learning opportunities that distinguish SUNY Plattsburgh's Honors Program. All of these relationships are energized by interactions between bright, active, and motivated students and committed teacher/scholars. Intellectual and academic challenges in a supportive and developmental context encourage students to self-discovery and accomplishment beyond what they may believe they can do.

The organization of the Honors Program is fairly simple. It is a four-year program divided between General Honors (primarily for freshmen and sophomores) and Advanced Honors (for juniors and seniors). In the General Honors portion of the Honors Program, students are expected to complete four Honors Seminars. Honors Seminars are highly interactive classes limited to 15 students. Seminar topics change every semester, though all seminars satisfy part of the College's General Education Program. At least one Learning Community is also offered each semester to General Honors students. The Advanced Honors part of the program allows students to undertake research projects of their own design under the guidance of a faculty mentor. Students are expected to make a public presentation of the honors thesis, which is the normal outcome of the research project. Advanced honors students also can pursue Honors Tutorials dealing with a wide range of topics.

The Honors Program at SUNY Plattsburgh is housed in the Redcay Honors Center. Facilities include a large study/lounge, two specially designed seminar rooms, a library, a computer lab, and a kitchenette. On the administrative side of the Honors Center is a reception/secretarial space, the Director's office, and an office for visiting scholars. Students in the Honors Program have direct access to visiting scholars. The distinguished roster of visiting scholars includes a number of Nobel Laureates, such as Joseph Brodsky, Eugene Wigner, and Derek Walcott.

The success rate of students who complete the Honors Program and apply to graduate and professional schools is nearly 100 percent. Honors Program alumni have distinguished themselves in many fields and maintain close contact with currently enrolled students.

The Honors Program is fully integrated into the rest of the College. Virtually every academic program at the College is represented among students in the Honors Program. The Honors Program is a supplement to rather than a substitute for other high-quality academic programs on campus.

The Honors Program was established in 1984. There are currently about 250 students in the program.

Admission Process: Entering freshmen whose high school average is 92 or above and whose SAT I scores are 1200 or above are automatically admitted into the Honors Program. Others may be admitted on the basis of an interview. Currently enrolled students with a 3.5 or higher GPA are automatically admitted.

Scholarship Availability: The College awards a number of full-tuition, four-year renewable Presidential Scholarships through the Honors Program each year to incoming freshmen. Additional Sophomore Presidential Scholarships are usually awarded. The Honors Program itself also awards a number of Redcay Honors Scholarships and Redcay Advanced Honors Scholarships.

The Campus Context: SUNY Plattsburgh is a campus of three schools: the School of Arts and Sciences, the School of Professional Studies, and the School of Business and Economics. Fifty-six undergraduate majors are offered on campus. Among the distinguished facilities are the SUNY Plattsburgh Art Museum including the Winkel Sculpture Garden, Rockwell Kent Gallery, Burke Fine Arts Gallery, and Museum Without Walls. The campus is proud of its Health/Fitness Center, Valcour Conference Center on Lake Champlain, Twin Valleys Outdoor Education/Recreation Center in the Adirondacks, and Miner Center for In Vitro Cell Biology Research.

Student Body Undergraduate enrollment is approximately 5,200: 40 percent men, 60 percent women. International students on campus number about 200.

Faculty There are 270 full-time faculty members, 90 percent with a Ph.D. or other terminal degree. The student-faculty ratio is 21:1.

Key Facilities The Feinberg Library houses more than 350,000 volumes, with computerized indexing and access. There are VAX minicomputers (academically dedicated) and hundreds of microcomputers widely distributed on campus, along with a campuswide optical fiber network with complete Internet access.

Honorary Societies Phi Eta Sigma, Phi Kappa Phi, and numerous disciplinary honorary societies

Athletics SUNY Plattsburgh offers a full range of intercollegiate athletics. The College is committed to the principles of Division III of the NCAA in all intercollegiate athletics. Club sports include rugby, volleyball, and skiing. The College has hosted the World University Games and was the staging site for the U.S. Olympic Team for the 1976 Montreal Olympics, resulting in world-class athletic facilities.

Study Abroad Students will find unlimited opportunities for study in Canada, including placement in Canadian universities, private corporations, and government agencies, through its nationally prominent Center for the Study of Canada. Similar opportunities abound in Central and South America through the College's Southern Cone Program. Opportunities for study abroad in more than 140 countries exist through SUNY. The Honors Program supports and encourages its students to take advantage of these opportunities and many do so.

Support Services The campus is fully handicapped-accessible.

Job Opportunities There are many employment opportunities for students on campus. These include assistantships, work-study and temporary service positions, research positions, and positions with various College services.

Tuition: $3400 for state residents, $8300 for nonresidents, per year (1998–99)

Room and Board: $4250

Mandatory Fees: $437

Contact: Director: Dr. David N. Mowry, 121-123 Hawkins Hall, Plattsburgh, New York 12901; Telephone: 518-564-3075; Fax: 518-564-3071; E-mail: david.mowry@plattsburgh.edu

State University of New York College at Potsdam

4 Pu G M Sc Tr

▼ Honors Program

The SUNY Potsdam Honors Program has three goals. The first is to recognize, reward, and provide enhanced educational opportunities for the College's best students. The second is to prepare students who, upon graduation from SUNY Potsdam, are ready to become highly successful in their pursuits, whether they include graduate school, full-time employment, or other service, research, or creative endeavors. The third is to provide intellectual enrichment for the entire campus community. The program seeks to develop students' scholarship, leadership, and service capabilities, and students with similar inclinations are sought. It is expected that once there is a full complement of honors students enrolled (probably by the fall 2002 semester), there will be approximately 250 honors students in all (roughly the top academic 7 or 8 percent of the College's total undergraduate student population).

The program provides honors students with a strong and distinctive academic experience, which includes qualitatively different and academically strengthening interaction with members of the SUNY Potsdam faculty and staff as well as enriched opportunities for interaction with other honors students. There are tangible benefits as well, which are designed to help honors students meet the program's goals. For example, a brand-new honors lounge, an honors computer lab, and a nearby study room were recently opened. Honors students are also offered priority registration, small enrollment honors sections of courses (average class size of about 15 to 20 students), diverse honors course offerings (including, during a recent academic year, calculus I and II; composition; philosophy; sociology; Spanish I and III; child development; Freud, Film, and Society; American Landscapes; and U.S. History Since 1877), other programming of special interest to honors students, an Honors Student Organization, the opportunity to travel to Northeast Regional and National NCHC conventions, and special mentoring and advising relationships with select members of the SUNY Potsdam faculty, staff, and student body. The program was founded in 1998 and currently has about 230 students enrolled.

Participation Requirements: The Honors Program curriculum is broken into two parts: General Honors, which is intended for freshmen and sophomores, and Advanced Honors, which is intended for juniors and seniors. General Honors students must take at least three honors-level courses, which are offered in a variety of areas, during their first two years at Potsdam. In addition, a required General Honors Colloquium is offered for first-semester freshmen as well as other SUNY Potsdam students who have not yet taken the colloquium. Later in the program, Advanced Honors students take a colloquium on the topic Scholar as Citizen during their junior year and also complete an Advanced

Interpreting the symbols: **2**=two-year college, **4**=four-year college; **Pu**=public or state college, **Pr**=private college; **G**=general honors program; **D**=departmental honors program; **S**=small program (fewer than 100 students), **M**=midsize program (100 to 500 students), **L**=large program (more than 500 students); **Sc**=scholarships available in honors program; **Tr**=transfer students accepted into honors program; **HBC**=historically black college; **AA**=academic advisors; **GA**=graduate advisors; **FA**=fellowship advisors.

Honors thesis or project as they work in close collaboration with an advising team, a personal librarian mentor, and other members of the College's teaching faculty. There are a number of options available through which Advanced Honors students can complete their thesis or project requirement. Students must maintain a minimum cumulative GPA of 3.0 (for all course work) to remain in good standing within the program. Students who complete either General Honors or Advanced Honors will be so recognized at commencement and on their transcripts; anyone completing both the General and Advanced Honors curricula will graduate as a SUNY Potsdam Distinguished Scholar.

Admission Process: In order to qualify for application to the Honors Program, incoming first-year students must have a minimum 93 percent high school GPA. (Exceptions to these qualification guidelines can be made at the discretion of the Honors Program Director on a student-by-student basis.) In addition, certain incoming first-year students automatically qualify for admission to the program. These include high school class valedictorians or salutatorians as well as National Merit Finalists or Semifinalists. Transfer students who have completed an honors program at a two-year college are eligible for automatic acceptance into the SUNY Potsdam Honors Program. In addition, transfer or current students who have at least a 3.25 cumulative GPA are eligible to apply for program admission through the Honors Program Director. Interested students from off-campus can obtain program and application information by contacting the Honors Program Office at 315-267-2966.

Scholarship Availability: Virtually all incoming first-year honors students qualify for four-year renewable scholarship funds ranging upward from $2000 per year. Renewability of this award is contingent on maintenance of at least a 3.25 GPA each year. Students should contact the SUNY Potsdam Office of Admission at 315-267-2180 for more details. Consideration for these scholarships requires no additional application.

The Campus Context: SUNY Potsdam was established in 1816 as the St. Lawrence Academy and, consequently, has the longest history of any SUNY school. Although SUNY Potsdam continues its tradition of teacher preparation, the liberal arts are at the core of the curriculum.

Potsdam is a small Victorian village built in the 1800s on the banks of the Raquette River, about 30 miles south of the Canadian border at Massena, New York, and Cornwall, Ontario, Canada. In addition to the 10,000 people who are permanent residents of the village, about 8,000 students are enrolled at Clarkson University and SUNY Potsdam, which are both located in Potsdam. Potsdam's downtown area has been recently restored and is registered as a National Historic District.

Student Body The undergraduate enrollment is about 3,600 men and women. Students come from throughout New York State, and the College's student body represents the greatest geographical diversity of any four-year college in the SUNY system. There are about 100 extracurricular groups and activities, including fraternities and sororities, student government, yearbook and newspaper staffs, a literary magazine, broadcast FM radio station, and musical performing arts groups.

Faculty The full-time teaching faculty has 199 members, and there are 72 part-time faculty members. Sixty-five percent of the faculty members hold doctorates or terminal degrees in their discipline. Senior faculty members regularly teach beginning courses, as well as more advanced courses, and are available to help students outside of class. The student-faculty ratio is 12:1 in the Crane School of Music and 20:1 in all other areas.

Key Facilities Crumb Library, which seats up to 600 people, is located in the center of the academic quadrangle. It is open 96 hours a week and houses more than 1,030,000 items, including 395,000 bound volumes, 604 microforms and other nonbook materials, 55,000 federal and state documents, and 1,300 active periodicals. The library's online catalog and an array of specialized equipment, such as copiers, microfilm reader-printers, audiovisual equipment, CD-ROM search stations, and aids for physically challenged users, provide access to materials in various formats. The professional staff is dedicated to helping students find and use information sources of all kinds. Also located in the library is the James H. Levitt Memorial Computing Center.

The Crane Music Library maintains the most extensive music collection in northern New York State. The collection includes 16,000 books, 24,000 music scores, 16,000 sound recordings, and tapes of performances at Crane dating back to the late 1940s. The library's audio facilities include ten listening rooms and twenty-nine listening carrels. Also located in the library are computers and printers for patron use.

SUNY Potsdam offers its students and faculty a robust computing environment to support their academic work. In addition to its campus mainframe cluster (DEC Alpha 2100), Potsdam has more than 200 personal computers located in student computing centers around the campus. These centers include the Levitt Memorial Computing Center, a general-use facility; a number of computer classrooms; a student word processing center; and a microcomputer laboratory for educators. All of these personal computers, in addition to those owned by students and faculty members, are tied into centralized computing facilities via a campuswide network. These facilities provide e-mail, conferencing, and Internet access for electronic communication between students and faculty members and other colleges. The purchase of personal computers is strongly recommended at Potsdam because of their increased use in course work research. The campus supports an Apple Macintosh computer purchase program. Workshops and individual assistance in the use of personal computers are available for students.

Honorary Societies Phi Kappa Phi and Phi Eta Sigma

Athletics Approximately 75 percent of the students participate in intramural sports, and there are eight women's and seven men's varsity sports teams.

Study Abroad SUNY Potsdam offers several study-abroad programs for academic credit in Grenoble, France; Potsdam, Germany; Lincoln, Liverpool, and Birmingham, England; Rockhamton, Australia; and Puebla, Mexico. Potsdam students may also choose to participate in any of more than 250 other student-abroad programs offered throughout the SUNY system.

Job Opportunities The College participates in the Federal Work-Study Program. Students not eligible for Federal Work-Study funds can find jobs on campus.

Tuition: $3400 for residents, $8300 for nonresidents (estimated for 2001–02)

Room and board: $6390 (average)

Mandatory Fees: $729

Contact: Director: Dr. David A. Smith, 149 Morey Hall, Potsdam, New York 13676; Telephone: 315-267-2900; Fax: 315-267-2677; E-mail: smithda@potsdam.edu; Web site: http://www.potsdam.edu/SPHP/webpg.html

State University of West Georgia

4 Pu G M Sc Tr

▼ Honors College

The University offers honors distinction in all of its undergraduate degree programs. More than fifty honors courses per year are offered exclusively to honors students on a regular basis in accounting, astronomy, biology, chemistry, economics, English, history, marketing, mathematics, personal wellness, political science, psychology, and other subjects. The average enrollment in the classes is fifteen and students are always taught by full-time faculty members who have a strong commitment to excellence in undergraduate education. Honors work is also available in regular courses.

The hallmarks of West Georgia's honors experience are faculty-directed undergraduate research and preparation for graduate or professional school. Honors students have excelled in research presentations at national, regional and state-wide conferences, and students have had their research published in academic journals. Almost ninety percent of those who complete the Honors College curriculum requirements have gone on to graduate or professional school. In the past few years, West Georgia honors students have been accepted for admission to graduate or professional school at the following institutions: Harvard University, Stanford University, the California Institute of Technology, the Massachusetts Institute of Technology, the Georgia Institute of Technology, the University of California at Berkeley, Cambridge University, Columbia University, the University of Pennsylvania, Vanderbilt University, the University of Indiana, the University of North Carolina at Chapel Hill, Emory University, Georgetown University, the University of Georgia, Mercer University, the State University of West Georgia, and many others.

Honors College administrative offices are located in the Honors House, which also features a computer lab, patio with outdoor grill and picnic tables, and kitchen facilities for student use. The Honors College residence hall has its own computer lab, music practice room, recreation room, kitchen facilities, internet access in each room, and extensive residence hall programming provided by Honors College staff members.

The West Georgia Honors Program was established in 1975. In 1999, the Board of Regents of the University System of Georgia elevated the status of the program to Honors College, thereby creating the first Honors College in the state of Georgia.

Participation Requirements: To graduate with Honors College distinction, students must earn credit for ten or more honors courses, including two seminars at the junior or senior level; complete an honors senior thesis or research project in their major; and maintain a minimum GPA of 3.2 in Honors College courses and in all other academic work. Completion of this distinctive curriculum is a mark of scholarly excellence and is appropriately recognized on all official West Georgia transcripts.

Admission Process: Admission to the Honors College is open to entering freshmen who meet two of the following three criteria: a combined SAT score of at least 1200 or the ACT equivalent, a minimum score of 610 on the verbal portion of the SAT or ACT equivalent, or a minimum high school GPA of 3.5. The Honors College is also open to any student who has completed 15 or more hours at West Georgia with a minimum overall GPA of 3.2.

Scholarship Availability: All Honors College students who are Georgia residents are recipients of HOPE scholarships, which cover all tuition costs and some additional expenses. In addition, the Honors College offers more than forty Presidential Scholarships. Most of these are worth $4000 per year and are good for eight semesters provided that the recipients maintain eligibility for Honors and make progress in completing the Honors College curriculum. There are many other scholarships available through the University for which Honors students are eligible. Finally, the Honors College also offers a number of out-of-state tuition waivers for non-Georgia Honors College students.

The Campus Context: The State University of West Georgia is a co-educational, residential, liberal arts institution located in Carrollton, which is approximately 45 miles west of Atlanta. The University offers a range of disciplinary, interdisciplinary, and professional degrees from fifty-nine fields in these college: arts and sciences, business, and education. Offerings include the engineering studies program, which allows students to complete degrees in physical, chemical, and geologic engineering at the Georgia Institute of Technology. West Georgia offers students opportunities for intellectual and personal development through quality teaching, scholarly inquiry, creative endeavor, and service to the public. The campus supports its students with first class facilities, including the Townsend Center for the Performing Arts, the Thomas B. Murphy Holocaust Teacher Training and Resource Center, the Antonio B. Waring Archeological Laboratory and the New Technology-enhanced Learning Center, which is a $20-million, 110,000-square-foot, state-of-the art academic building featuring "smart" classrooms where every student has a computer at their desk.

Student Body West Georgia enrolls 9,010 students; 64 percent are women and 36 percent are men. Approximately 35 percent of the undergraduates are freshmen. The student body is diverse with 75 percent Caucasian, 21 percent African American, 1.3 percent international students, 8 percent Hispanic, 8 percent Asian, and 2 percent are American Indian students. West Georgia students participate in ninety-four different service organizations, fraternities, student groups, and honors organizations.

Faculty There are 256 full-time and 75 part-time faculty members who are employed at West Georgia. Virtually all full-time faculty have terminal degrees. The student-faculty ratio is 19:1.

Key Facilities The Ingram Library participates in Georgia Interconnected Library and Galileo (Georgia Library Learning Online), which provides automated services and access to catalogs of all Georgia public university libraries, full-text journals, and encyclopedia databases. Located in the heart of the Academic Quad, Ingram Library holds 353,181 bound volumes, 23,526 microfilm, 1,040,266, microform, and 29,990 volumes and pieces of special collection material. West Georgia is committed to providing student access to technology. Computer labs are located in most of the academic buildings on campus. All residence halls are wired to provide Internet access and Honors College students have computer labs in the Honors House and in the Honors residence hall.

Athletics As a member of the Gulf South Conference, the University supports ten intercollegiate athletic programs in NCAA Division II. Women's sports include volleyball, cross-country, basketball, tennis, and softball. Men's sports include football, cross-country, basketball, baseball, and tennis.

Study Abroad A number of study abroad programs are offered during the summer semester or for longer periods. Summer programs include French language, civilization, and literature in Tours, Paris, and Nice, France; Spanish language, culture, and literature in Cuernavaca, Mexico; international business in New York and London; art and art history in Bayeux, France, as well as Paris and London. State-wide programs are also available. For a longer experience, the University has an exchange agreement with the University of Northumbria in Newcastle, England.

Support Services The Student Development Center coordinates special services for disabled students. Services include such aids as note takers, sign-language interpreters, books on tape, readers, special furniture, student aides, hearing- and visual- aids equipment, and other assistance as needed.

Job Opportunities Work opportunities on campus and around Carrollton are available through the Office of Career Services. Numerous cooperative education and internships opportunities are available, including the governor's internship and the United States Senate internship programs. Student employment on campus is available in most academic departments and the Honors House offices.

Tuition: $1234 for residents and $4132 for nonresidents per year (2001–02)

Room and Board: $1030–$1137 double occupancy; private room differential $533

Interpreting the symbols: **2**=two-year college, **4**=four-year college; **Pu**=public or state college, **Pr**=private college; **G**=general honors program; **D**=departmental honors program; **S**=small program (fewer than 100 students), **M**=midsize program (100 to 500 students), **L**=large program (more than 500 students); **Sc**=scholarships available in honors program; **Tr**=transfer students accepted into honors program; **HBC**=historically black college; **AA**=academic advisors; **GA**=graduate advisors; **FA**=fellowship advisors.

Contact: Dean: Dr. Donald R. Wagner, Honors College, State University of West Georgia, 1600 Maple Street, Carrollton, Georgia 30118: Telephone: 770-836-6636; Fax: 770-836-4666; E-mail: dwagner@westga.edu; Web site: http://www.westga.edu/~honors/

STEPHEN F. AUSTIN STATE UNIVERSITY

4 Pu G M Sc Tr

▼ School of Honors

The School of Honors offers no courses of its own. It provides honors sections of many basic courses, and in areas where there are no courses offered, students may complete unique projects and gain special credit through honors contracts. Students must complete 25 hours of honors course work (in any areas) during their four years of college. Those who do so are able to graduate with a separate School of Honors diploma in addition to the regular college diploma. Normally an incoming freshman is expected to take a 1-credit-hour SFA 101 honors course (Introduction to College Life) and 24 additional hours in any areas of their choosing. The SFA 101 course requirement is waived for any transfer student who has amassed at least one semester of college course work.

The average class size for honors sections is fewer than 25, and some classes are as small as 12 students. The courses are usually taught by the most able and distinguished professors at the University, and they are designed to foster independent thinking and comradeship among the participants. Honors students who maintain a GPA of 3.25 or higher are eligible to live at Wisely Hall, designated as the Academic Excellence Dorm for the University. It is centrally located and is provided with several private rooms on the ground floor for students with physical disabilities. Admission to Wisely Hall requires an SAT I score of at least 1220 or an ACT score of at least 27 plus class standing in the top 25 percent. There is also a suite of rooms, conveniently located, that houses the offices of the School of Honors Director and the Honors Administrative Assistant and a meeting and seminar room. This room also contains desktop computers, several laser-jet printers, and a TV-VCR combo with cable and satellite connections.

The program makes available laptop computers that can be checked out during the week or on weekends. There is also a copying machine available for honors student use. School of Honors students have the privilege of registering first at the University, at the same time as graduating seniors. This virtually guarantees that they will get the courses and hours that best suits their schedule. There are currently about 700 students in the program, which was created eight years ago. These students explore extracurricular activities through their own Honor Student Association. They are involved in projects ranging from raising money for impoverished children at winter holiday-time to attending an off-Broadway show at one of Houston's leading theaters. Individual colleges and departments of the University offer membership in local, regional, and national honors programs. The Honor Student Association was named Student Organization of the Year for 2000 by vote of the student government of the University.

Participation Requirements: Students may take their required 24 hours of course work in any area they wish. There are no standard academic courses or capstone courses at this time, although the University Honors Council has been considering this and other ideas to further enrich the program. Continued participation requires that students maintain an overall GPA of at least 3.25 (on a 4.0 scale) plus a 3.0 average or higher in all honors courses. If the student fails to achieve this, they have two semesters to lift their grades back up to standards. After that, they must be inactive in the program. At graduation time, the Registrar stamps the transcripts of all those who successfully completed the program with a statement that the student has earned their degree "through the School of Honors." A separate diploma is presented, signed by the President of the University, the Dean of the appropriate college, and the Director of the School of Honors. All honors courses completed are designated on the transcript with the letter H.

Admission Process: Admission to the program requires an SAT I score of at least 1220 or an ACT score of at least 27. The program also seeks students in the top 15 percent of their graduating class, and consideration is given to students whose national test scores are slightly lower than required, but whose high school grades and class ranking is very high. Those with the appropriate SAT I or ACT scores may rank below the top 15 percent in their graduating class. Some small or private schools do not rank graduates. Class ranking is waived for them and, of course, for home-educated applicants. Extracurricular activities are factored in, as are letters of recommendation. Admission dates are not critical, as this is a state university that has a rolling admission process.

Scholarship Availability: The School of Honors offers numerous major scholarships based solely on achievement. Three Vera Dugas Scholarships are awarded each year. They pay $4000 per semester for a maximum of eight semesters, or a total of $32,000. This should provide complete room, board, tuition, and fees for the winners for their whole college careers. A minimum of eleven University Scholars Awards are made each year. They pay $1000 per semester for a maximum of eight semesters, or a total of $8000. These are divided among the seven colleges of the University. Receipt of scholarship aid of $2000 or more per year entitles recipients to in-state tuition if they are not residents of Texas. Periodically, the School of Honors is also able to provide additional support, known as Hoops for Scholars, through funds made available through the Athletic Program. When sufficient funds are available, they pay $2500 per semester for up to eight semesters, or a total of $20,000. Information and most forms may be downloaded from the Web at the site listed in the Contact section of this description. The absolute deadline for any year's applications is February 1.

The Campus Context: Stephen F. Austin University (SFA) is located 125 miles north of Houston, Texas. It is a coeducational school of approximately 12,000 students. It is located in a town of 35,000 residents in a heavily forested region of East Texas, sometimes known by the people of the area as the Piney Woods. The geography is low rolling hills with numerous lakes and streams. The University is divided into seven colleges: Liberal Arts, Fine Arts, Sciences and Mathematics, Business, Education, Forestry, and Applied Arts and Sciences. SFA is one of the largest teacher training institutions in the state, with special emphasis on early childhood programs and primary education preparation. The Department of Human Services offers extensive programs in speech pathology and orientation and mobility. The Arthur Temple School of Forestry is one of the most prestigious in the country, and its environmental science program has grown into a multidepartmental effort to train students for that specialty. Forestry is one of the two programs to offer training up through the doctoral level, the other being public school administration. The University also has outstanding theater and music training programs and a newly accredited School of Social Work. Most students are required to live on campus during their first two years. Many then move to one of the numerous and easily accessible apartment complexes near the University.

Student Body There were 9,001 full-time undergraduate students enrolled in fall 2001 (3,704 men and 5,297 women). In addition, there were 1,282 part-time undergraduate students. There were 1,286 full- and part-time graduate students enrolled. More than 70 percent of all students receive some form of financial assistance, and more than 80 percent live on campus or in apartments or houses near the campus. The commuter population is relatively small, and more than 80 percent of the undergraduate population is in the traditional age group. There are fourteen pan-Hellenic social fraternities and five sororities that are active on campus.

Faculty Instruction is provided by 419 full-time faculty members and 229 part-time faculty members. The ratio of full-time faculty members to full-time students is 20:1. More than 75 percent of the full-time faculty members hold doctorates or the highest terminal degree in their field.

Key Facilities The holdings of the Ralph Steen Library include more than 500,000 books, 135,000 bound volumes of periodicals, 250,000 documents, and vast holdings on microfilm and microtext. There are more than 200 study carrels available for graduate students and undergraduates, and the library also contains several rooms for joint-study efforts. There is also a very effective interlibrary loan program for books and periodicals. The library has a large microcomputer lab with a variety of desktop computers and printers available for student use. There are also numerous computer facilities available in classroom buildings and in the Boynton Computer Building. Most computers are connected to the Internet via a fiber-optic network.

Athletics The University plays all varsity sports within the Southland Conference (Division I-AA). Men's sports include football, basketball, golf, indoor and outdoor track, and cross-country. Women's sports include basketball, softball, volleyball, tennis, soccer, indoor and outdoor track, and cross-country.

Support Services The Office of Disability Services attempts to make the teaching staff aware of the special needs of students with physical impairments. Normally about 100 to 125 students register with the office, and teachers are contacted about their needs. There are also a number of students registered with the office who have a learning disorder or Attention Deficit Disorder. Next in percentage are those with various degrees of visual impairment. The office informs the faculty members, who are requested to take these impairments into consideration.

Job Opportunities A number of students are able to take advantage of federally funded work-study grants. Some departments do make undergraduate jobs and internships available, but these are normally for those taking upper-division course work.

Tuition: $1728 for residents, $6792 for nonresidents, per year (2001–02)

Room and Board: $4575

Mandatory Fees: $602

Contact: Director: Dr. Allen Richman, Box 6114 SFA Station, Nacogdoches, Texas 75962; Telephone: 936-468-2813; Fax: 936-468-7619; E-mail: arichman@sfasu.edu; Web site: http://www.sfasu.edu/honors

STONEHILL COLLEGE

4 Pr G M Sc AA

▼ Honors Program

The Stonehill College Honors Program is designed to enhance and enrich the educational experience of many of the talented and highly motivated students at the College. The program promotes independent learning and thinking, thoughtful and creative expression in writing, collaborative work with fellow students and faculty members, and vigorous discussion and debate about the issues central to the human experience.

Honors courses are limited to 20 students but are frequently smaller. Honors courses are offered in the humanities, the social sciences, and the natural sciences. In the senior year, honors students enroll in one of several innovative team-taught interdisciplinary capstone seminars that address a selected topic. Honors students who fulfill all the requirements of the program graduate with a special designation.

Throughout the academic year, the Honors Program sponsors a wide variety of cocurricular programs, including lectures, dramatic presentations, and trips to Boston, Providence, and New York City. The program also provides students with a strong social and academic bond during all four years. Honors students are not separated from the rest of the student body, and there is no exclusive honors housing; therefore, program participants interact with the entire campus community. In addition, the Honors Program is compatible with all majors and courses of study and with study-abroad programs.

The Honors Program was founded in 1994. Each year, approximately 60 freshman students are enrolled as honors students; the total enrollment in the program is about 250 students.

Participation Requirements: All honors courses, except the Honors Senior Seminar, meet general studies requirements at the College. In the freshman year, honors students take two honors courses each semester in philosophy and religious studies and in literature and history. In the sophomore and junior years, students take honors courses in the social and natural sciences. In the senior year, honors students take one team-taught, interdisciplinary Honors Senior Seminar. In all, honors students must take a minimum of seven honors courses over four years, but they may take more if they wish.

Honors students who fulfill all the requirements of the program graduate from the College with the special designation Stonehill Scholar and receive recognition and a distinctive medallion at commencement.

Admission Process: Admission to the Stonehill Honors Program is competitive. The committee carefully reviews each student's high school course profile, academic performance, weighted rank, and standardized test scores (SAT I or ACT). The College looks for contributors both in the classroom as well as in the high school community. On average, invited students rank in the top 4 percent of their high school class with combined SAT I scores of 1250. No separate application is required. Students may petition for admission after the first semester of freshman year.

Scholarship Availability: Talented and financially needy students can receive honors scholarships from $3500 to full tuition. Stonehill also awards a limited number of merit-based scholarships to outstanding students who do not demonstrate financial need. No special application is required other than the PROFILE and FAFSA forms.

The Campus Context: Stonehill is a coeducational Catholic college located just 20 miles south of Boston. Founded in 1948, Stonehill continues the rich tradition of a rigorous liberal education based on Catholic values that started when the Holy Cross Fathers established the University of Notre Dame in South Bend, Indiana. As a comprehensive undergraduate college of 2,000 students, Stonehill offers thirty-one major programs in the liberal arts, natural sciences, and business. The College's programs aim to foster effective communication, critical-thinking, and problem-solving skills in all students.

Stonehill provides its students with a powerful environment for learning where its students are safe, known, and valued. The College has a beautiful campus, an enviable location, state-of-the-art facilities, and an involved and engaging faculty. Eighty percent of the students live on campus and take advantage of the more than sixty Stonehill clubs and organizations as well as the wide range of activities offered in nearby Boston.

Interpreting the symbols: **2**=two-year college, **4**=four-year college; **Pu**=public or state college, **Pr**=private college; **G**=general honors program; **D**=departmental honors program; **S**=small program (fewer than 100 students), **M**=midsize program (100 to 500 students), **L**=large program (more than 500 students); **Sc**=scholarships available in honors program; **Tr**=transfer students accepted into honors program; **HBC**=historically black college; **AA**=academic advisors; **GA**=graduate advisors; **FA**=fellowship advisors.

Student Body Stonehill's full-time degree-seeking undergraduate population in fall 2001 numbered 2,167 students (42 percent men, 58 percent women). The student body represented thirty U.S. states and eleven other countries. Ninety-four percent of the 588 freshmen reside on campus. More than 90 percent of the freshmen return to Stonehill in the sophomore year. In 2001, 85 percent of Stonehill students received some form of financial assistance, and the average freshman financial aid award was $11,585.

Faculty Stonehill's faculty is committed to teaching, advising, and working closely with students. The faculty-student ratio is 1:13. Seventy-seven percent of the 127 full-time faculty members have terminal degrees in their respective fields.

Key Facilities A new multimillion-dollar Library and Networked Information Center opened in fall 1998. The MacPhaidin Library provides access to the online Computer Library Center, a CD-ROM network, multimedia computers, and the Internet. The Lockary Computer Center supports Windows, Macintosh, and UNIX operating systems on Intel, Power PC, and SPARC platforms. There are more than 100 machines available for public use. The campus network provides a high-speed Internet connection, and the network may be accessed locally via Ethernet or remotely via modem.

Honorary Societies Lambda Epsilon Sigma

Athletics Stonehill sponsors eighteen varsity NCAA Division II teams in baseball, basketball, cross-country, equestrian, field hockey, football, ice hockey, lacrosse, soccer, softball, tennis, track, and volleyball. Stonehill is a member of the Eastern College Athletic Association (ECAC) as well as the Northeast-10 Conference. A wide variety of intercollegiate club sports and recreational activities are available. The Sally Blair Ames Sports Complex, designed for general student use, houses a weight-training facility, dance and aerobics studio, jogging track, and cardio-vascular/strength-training center.

Job Opportunities Stonehill sponsors a full-time international internship program in London, Brussels, Dublin, Paris, Montreal, and Madrid for students interested in combining a work experience with international travel. Internships are offered in a variety of professions, including advertising, business, education, health administration, law, medical research, sociology, art, theater, and politics.

Exciting on-the-job internships also exist in Boston and Washington, D.C. and other U.S. cities for Stonehill students. A sample of sites include the U.S. Supreme Court, Fidelity Investments, WBZ-TV Channel 4, Massachusetts General Hospital, the Department of Justice, and the New England Revolution. Through participation and observation, Stonehill interns supplement their traditional classroom learning with real-world experience.

The SURE Program affords Stonehill students the opportunity to participate in a paid summer research project. This program provides students with the chance to broaden their research skills and publish in professional journals.

Part-time employment opportunities are available on campus as well as off campus in the local area. Jobs are posted both in the Career Services Office and Student Aid and Finance Office.

Tuition: $17,680 (2001–02)

Room and board: $8,492

Mandatory Fees: $680

Contact: Director: Professor Richard Capobianco, Department of Philosophy, 320 Washington Street, North Easton, Massachusetts 02357; Telephone: 508-565-1037; E-mail: rcapobianco@stonehill.edu

Suffolk County Community College

2 Pu L Sc Tr

▼ Honors Program

The Honors Program at Suffolk County Community College is designed to provide a special challenge to academically talented and highly motivated students. It combines small classes, enthusiastic faculty members, talented students, and rigorous course work to create an environment that nurtures intellectual growth.

The program challenges its students to fulfill their true potential and provides them with an enhanced college experience. Offering priority day classes to full-time and part-time students, the program has consistently attracted a mix of recent high school graduates and returning adult students whose diverse experiences enrich classroom discussions and expand the opportunities for learning.

Honors alumni consistently report that the program has prepared them superbly for the demands of baccalaureate and graduate studies. The program offers special transfer advising assistance; graduates have been admitted to some of the nation's most prestigious colleges and universities.

As a comprehensive community college, Suffolk strives to provide a full spectrum of learning opportunities, reflecting the varied needs of county residents. The Honors Program is an important element of that continuum and exemplifies the College's commitment to academic excellence. Students are encouraged to explore the challenges and rewards of honors classes at Suffolk's three campuses.

The Honors Program at Suffolk County Community College has been in existence for seventeen years; there are approximately 400 students currently enrolled in the program.

Participation Requirements: A minimum of 16 credits in interdisciplinary honors courses and 6 credits in supplementary honors courses satisfies the diverse requirements for the Honors Diploma.

Alternatively, qualified students may enroll in the Honors Certificate of Recognition Sequence as part of their chosen curriculum. High school graduates with a B+ average or better and a minimum score of 1100 (minimum 550 verbal) on the SAT are encouraged to apply. The Honors Recognition Sequence is accomplished by successfully completing a minimum of 12 credits of interdisciplinary honors courses or 8 credits of interdisciplinary courses and 6 credits of supplementary courses.

Students enrolled in the Honors Program are expected to maintain a GPA of at least 3.2 each semester. If a student receives a grade lower than B in an honors course, his/her participation in the program is subject to review. Suffolk County Community College students must maintain a minimum 3.2 GPA to graduate from the program.

Admission Process: Qualified students may enroll in the Honors Diploma Sequence while engaged in a curriculum of their choice. High school graduates with a B+ average or better and a minimum score of 1100 on the SAT are encouraged to apply.

Scholarship Availability: The scholarship program is administered under the auspices of the Suffolk County Community College Foundation. Scholarships are made possible through the generosity of various individuals, student organizations, College faculty and staff members, local and community groups, and business firms and by fund-raising activities of the Suffolk County Community College Foundation.

Scholarships are available to full-time and part-time freshmen and transfer students in virtually all academic career programs.

Awards are based solely on academic merit. The amounts of the awards range from partial to full tuition coverage.

To maintain full-time scholarship eligibility for two years, students must maintain at least a 3.2 GPA and take at least two honors courses each semester. To continue part-time scholarship eligibility for two years, recipients must enroll in at least one honors course per semester and maintain a minimum 3.2 grade point average.

The Campus Context: The Ammerman Campus at Selden encompasses 156 acres and has twelve academic, administrative, and auxiliary buildings. The Western Campus at Brentwood occupies a 207-acre site with eleven academic, administrative, and auxiliary buildings, including a 95,000-square-foot building that houses classrooms, laboratories, the library, and a theater. The Eastern Campus is located on a 192-acre site near Riverhead and contains three academic and two auxiliary buildings. In 1985, the College opened a satellite facility called the TechniCenter, located at 205 Oser Avenue in Hauppauge Industrial Park. The TechniCenter brings the College to the student. Designed specifically for business and industrial training, it offers many options for both management and labor: credit courses, noncredit courses, and specifically tailored technical training. Degree programs offered include A.A. (five majors), A.A.S. (thirty-eight majors), A.S. (nine majors), and fourteen 1-year certificate programs.

Student Body Undergraduate enrollment is 20,745: 40.7 percent men, 59.3 percent women. The minority ethnic distribution of the total undergraduate population is 4 percent African American, 6 percent Hispanic, and 1.6 percent Asian American. Sixty-five percent of full-time students and 50 percent of all students (by head count) receive financial aid.

Faculty There are 401 full-time faculty members and 977 adjuncts.

Key Facilities There are 208,000 volumes in the library. The campus has 250 IBMs and fifty Macs available for student use. Special facilities include the Academic Skills Center, Language Lab, Math Learning Center, Reading Center, and Writing Center.

Athletics Intercollegiate athletic programs are offered at the Ammerman and Western Campuses. Eastern Campus students may participate at the campus of their choice. At the Ammerman Campus, men may compete in baseball, basketball, bowling, cross-country, golf, lacrosse, soccer, tennis, track and field, and volleyball (club). Women may compete in basketball, bowling, cheerleading, cross-country, equestrian, softball, tennis, track and field, and volleyball. The Western Campus offers athletic competition for men in baseball, basketball, bowling, golf, and soccer, while women may compete in bowling and softball.

Support Services The College is committed to maximizing educational opportunities for students with disabilities by minimizing physical, psychological, and learning barriers. Special counseling is available on each campus to help students achieve academic success through the provision of special services, auxiliary aids, and reasonable program modifications. Examples of services/accommodations include registration and scheduling assistance, use of tape recorders, sign language interpreters, special testing conditions, notetakers, reader services, taped texts, and specialized library equipment.

Tuition: $2180 for state residents, $4360 for nonresidents, per year (1998–99)

Mandatory Fees: $106

Contact: Albin J. Cofone, College Honors Coordinator, 533 College Road, Selden, New York 11784; Telephone: 631-451-4335; E-mail: cofone@sunysuffolk.edu

Susquehanna University

4 Pr G M Tr

▼ University Honors Program

The Honors Program at Susquehanna University offers a challenging program of study for the exceptional student interested in a more independent and interdisciplinary approach than that usually offered to an undergraduate. The program is especially well suited to the aggressively curious, active learner who values breadth of study, multiple perspectives, and answers that go beyond the superficial. It has been recognized as a model for other honors programs throughout the country.

Limited to 50 students in each entering class, the program includes a series of special courses and projects throughout all four undergraduate years. Discussion groups, lectures, off-campus visits, and residential programs complement Honors Program courses.

The University's Scholars' House, a small, comfortable residence for students involved in academically challenging projects, serves as the center of many Honors Program activities, including fireside chats, a film series, and practice sessions for the University's College Bowl team. Many of the Scholars' House residents are members of the Honors Program. Some of their projects include the establishment of a campus jazz society, the development of a World Wide Web connection for the Scholars' House, an economic and ecological study of the tradeoffs facing the logging industry in Maine, a comparison of Christianity and Buddhism, and a children's book.

As a member of the National Collegiate Honors Council, Susquehanna regularly participates in or hosts special events for honors program students from throughout the Northeast and other regions. Honors students also have access to a variety of special off-campus projects at locations ranging from the Woods Hole Oceanographic Institution in Massachusetts and the United Nations in New York to Pueblo Indian sites in New Mexico.

The first honors class enrolled in 1982. Approximately 150 students are currently enrolled.

Participation Requirements: Participating students take an honors course during three of their first four semesters. The first course, "Thought," focuses on ideas and their expression. "Thought and the Social Sciences" or "Thought and the Natural Sciences" are cross-disciplinary views of the social and natural sciences. "Thought and Civilization" is an interdisciplinary look at literature and cultures. These Thought courses replace required Core courses.

In the sophomore year, honors students write a research-supported essay developing a topic of their choice. This experience offers students an opportunity to work one-on-one with faculty members early in their undergraduate studies.

As juniors and seniors, honors students select 8 semester hours from a series of 300-level interdisciplinary honors seminars that also fulfill the University's Core requirements or that serve as especially interesting and challenging electives. As seniors they also engage in a senior honors seminar that fulfills the Core requirement for a "Futures" course and a senior research project.

Students normally must maintain a cumulative GPA of 3.3 or higher at the end of each semester to remain in the Honors Program. Candidates who successfully complete all the requirements of the Honors Program graduate with University Honors.

Scholarship Availability: Scholarships are held by many students in the University Honors Program, but are not tied to the program in any way. Honors Program enrollees typically qualify for one of

Interpreting the symbols: **2**=two-year college, **4**=four-year college; **Pu**=public or state college, **Pr**=private college; **G**=general honors program; **D**=departmental honors program; **S**=small program (fewer than 100 students), **M**=midsize program (100 to 500 students), **L**=large program (more than 500 students); **Sc**=scholarships available in honors program; **Tr**=transfer students accepted into honors program; **HBC**=historically black college; **AA**=academic advisors; **GA**=graduate advisors; **FA**=fellowship advisors.

the top scholarships awarded by Susquehanna. A description of these scholarships and their value during the 1999–2000 academic year follows.

University Assistantships, Susquehanna's most prestigious academic scholarships, are awards of $10,500 that include a professional work experience (about 10 hours a week on average) with a member of the University faculty or administrative staff. Recipients typically rank in the top 5 percent of their high school classes and score in the top 10 percent nationally on standardized tests.

The other four scholarships are valued at $8500 annually. Recipients of these scholarships typically rank in the top 10 percent of their high school classes and score in the top 15 percent nationally on standardized tests. Valedictorian/Salutatorian Scholarships are given to students who rank first or second in their high school classes in a demanding academic program. Degenstein Scholarships, funded by the Charles B. Degenstein Scholars Program, are given to exceptionally able students with preference to those intending to major or minor in programs within Susquehanna's Sigmund Weis School of Business. Scholarships for Distinguished Achievement in Science and Mathematics are awarded to students planning majors in the sciences, computer science, or mathematics; recipients are chosen on the basis of outstanding academic achievement. Presidential Scholarships are awarded on a competitive basis to new students who have demonstrated superior academic achievement and personal promise.

The Campus Context: Susquehanna University is organized into three schools: the School of Natural and Social Sciences; the School of Arts, Humanities and Communications; and the Sigmund Weis School of Business. Bachelor of Arts, Bachelor of Science, and Bachelor of Music degrees are offered.

Special care has been taken to maintain the architectural integrity of the campus, especially during recent years of renovation and expansion. Recent projects include a new high-technology center for business and communications, which opened in 1999, and the construction in 1995 of three new residence halls—Shobert Hall, Roberts House, and Isaacs House. The new housing provides a combination of townhouse and apartment-like living spaces for 87 students. Susquehanna is also very proud of its Broadway-caliber Degenstein Center Theater and museum-quality art gallery. Fisher Science Hall has been featured as a model facility for undergraduate science education by Project Kaleidoscope, a national effort to strengthen undergraduate science and mathematics education supported in part by the National Science Foundation.

The Scholar's House was opened in 1994 for members of the Honors Program and other interested students. Adjacent to the Charles B. Degenstein Campus Center, the residence for 24 students has become a stimulating environment for intellectual camaraderie. In 1996, Susquehanna students celebrated the twentieth anniversary of the nationally recognized Project House System, in which groups of volunteers organized and approved as "project houses" live and work together.

Student Body Undergraduate enrollment is 1,657 full-time, 20 part-time; 43 percent men, 57 percent women. The ethnic distribution is 93 percent white, 2 percent African American, 2 percent Hispanic, 2 percent Asian American, and 1 percent other. Approximately 75 percent of the student body receive scholarships and/or need-based financial aid. There are four sororities and four fraternities.

Faculty There are a total of 168 faculty members, 103 full-time. Ninety-one percent have the Ph.D. The student-faculty ratio is about 14:1.

Key Facilities The library houses 252,000 volumes. There are 150 microcomputers available in six computer laboratories. The majority of lab computers are IBM-type, but there is also a small lab with Macs. Thanks to connections in every residence hall room, students have access to the World Wide Web and other Internet functions using Netscape and other browsing software. Students also have access to e-mail both on and off campus and to the library on-line catalog including, First Search, a service that provides access to more than fifty databases on a wide variety of subjects.

Athletics Susquehanna is an NCAA Division III school and a member of the Middle Atlantic Conference. There are twenty-two varsity sports for men and women. Men's teams include baseball, basketball, cross-country, football, golf, indoor track, lacrosse, soccer, swimming, tennis, and track. Women's teams include basketball, cross-country, field hockey, indoor track, lacrosse, soccer, softball, swimming, tennis, track, and volleyball. Rowing, for men and women, is a club sport with a full-time coach. Other club sports include conditioning, cycling, rugby, indoor soccer, and men's volleyball. Susquehanna also sponsors an active intramural sports program.

Study Abroad Susquehanna strongly encourages students to consider study abroad. There are eleven direct exchange programs including the University of Konstanz (Germany), the University of Copenhagen (Denmark), Senshu University (Japan), and many others available through national clearinghouses. Susquehanna also sponsors a semester in London exclusively for junior business majors. Courses are taught by faculty members from the University's Sigmund Weis School of Business and faculty members from leading London universities. There are also a number of opportunities for internships abroad.

Support Services Disabled students will find that all of Susquehanna's classroom buildings, administration buildings, library, chapel/auditorium, campus center, and gymnasium are wheelchair-accessible, as are several of the residence halls.

Job Opportunities Students are offered a range of work opportunities on campus including work-study, assistantships, and cash jobs. A graduated pay scale rewards increased responsibility for second-, third-, and fourth-year students who return to their previous positions.

Tuition: $19,380 per year (1999–2000)

Room and Board: $5550

Mandatory Fees: $290

Contact: Director: Dr. Linda McMillin, 514 University Avenue, Selinsgrove, Pennsylvania 17870-1001; Telephone: 570-372-4193; Fax: 570-372-2722 (Admissions/Financial Aid); E-mail: mcmillin@susqu.edu; Web site: http://www.susqu.edu

SYRACUSE UNIVERSITY

4 Pr G L

▼ Honors Program

The Honors Program is divided into two 2-year sections: General University Honors for students entering the program as freshmen or sophomores and Thesis Project Honors for juniors and seniors. Eligible students may participate in either section or both. A total of 850 students are currently enrolled in the program. The program began in 1965 in the College of Arts and Sciences, but today is an all-University program.

Participation Requirements: General University Honors consists of honors courses and seminars that demand a sincere commitment to learning and scholarship, actively involve students and teachers in joint exploration, and constantly stress scholarly habits and skills of analysis, independent research, and communication. The program provides an exciting and enriching beginning to a student's college career, while also providing an introduction to students who share the desire for a rigorous and engaging intellectual experience. Honors students take four special honors courses, one orientation seminar, and two other lower division seminars during four semesters.

The Freshman Honors Seminar is an ongoing orientation to Syracuse University (SU) that introduces students to the world of ideas, the life of the mind, and the many educational opportunities on campus and in the wider community. The seminar eases the transition from high school to college. Students are assigned to a small group that meets weekly with a faculty member to discuss ideas, explore new ways of thinking, discuss current issues, perhaps think in unorthodox or cutting-edge ways, and reflect on the purpose and goals of a quality undergraduate education. Students are drawn from all the schools and colleges at SU and share this academic diversity in the class. They also get to know a professor and his or her world as a professor.

Honors courses are offered in a wide variety of disciplines. They are specially-designed courses; however, generally they satisfy liberal arts core requirements in the student's home college. These courses are quite different from those offered in the regular curriculum; they are smaller, use different texts, have different assignments, and are led by full faculty members. Discussions are usually spirited and require active participation by the students.

Two lower-division seminars, usually taken during the sophomore year, are intended to expose students to the cultural and civic life in the wider community. In one seminar, students attend the opera, the Syracuse Symphony, the Equity Theatre at Syracuse Stage, exhibits at the Everson Museum of Art, and a performance at Crouse College. Thorough background presentations before each event prepare students for what they are going to see. After viewing the performances, students write their own art critiques. Then, an extensive review and discussion afterwards heightens their appreciation of the event. The Introduction to Political Culture Seminar offers the same experience-based approach to the study of civic life in the local community; students may explore the Islamic community, the Latino community, women's issues, the Jewish community, the Hmong community, the struggle for gay and lesbian rights and culture, the India-Indian community, the Haudenosaunee community, or participate in a community-wide discussion called "Race Dialogues." Alternately, students may take a seminar focusing on scientific issues and practice, such as the natural history of Onondaga County or the weather in upstate New York.

Students may substitute either one honors course or two seminars by participating in a special honors opportunity connected to studying abroad. Students are asked to read and reflect about their impending move overseas, keep a journal and write reflective essays during their study abroad, and reflect upon reentry as they return.

Thesis Project Honors is a program that assists accomplished undergraduates in designing theses in their majors, while providing the structure to facilitate the completion of these theses. Junior seminars assist students in defining their research projects, designing them, identifying faculty members to guide their work, and creating personalized strategies for completion. The senior seminars assist students in refining their research or projects, gathering resources, help keep the plan on track to completion, and help prepare students to consider graduate school. Each student is encouraged to select graduate or advanced upper-level courses to complement the work in his or her thesis. Each thesis project is guided by 2 faculty members. The thesis project may be presented in any appropriate form—research paper, prose, performance, or multimedia—and it always includes a written analysis and/or critique. At the conclusion of senior year, students present their work at an oral defense with their faculty and a representative from the Honors Program.

A student must achieve cum laude distinction in his or her home college to be awarded General University Honors or Thesis Project Honors. A student completing the requirements for General University Honors receives a certificate and the award is noted on the transcript. A student completing the requirements for Thesis Project Honors is awarded a medal at a special graduation ceremony; further, the diploma notes that the student graduated with honors in the major.

Admission Process: The average total SAT score of entering first-year students is 1360 and they rank in the top 5 percent of their graduating high school classes. The deadline for application by incoming students is April 25. First-year students may apply for admission after their first semester on campus. Second semester sophomores with a minimum cumulative GPA of 3.5 on a 4.0 scale are invited to apply to Thesis Project Honors.

Scholarship Availability: Syracuse University provides a generous merit scholarship program for all qualified students regardless of financial need. There are no scholarships associated directly with the Honors Program.

The Campus Context: Syracuse University is set on a beautiful residential campus that encompasses more than 200 acres and 170 buildings. Situated on a hill, overlooking downtown Syracuse, students enjoy the traditional college environment, while realizing the social and recreational opportunities of a medium-sized city. SU has nine undergraduate colleges on campus including the School of Architecture, the College of Arts and Sciences, the School of Education, the College of Engineering and Computer Science, the College of Human Services and Health Professions, the School of Information Studies, the School of Management, the Newhouse School of Public Communications, and the College of Visual and Performing Arts.

Syracuse University strives to be the nation's leading student-centered research university. Unlike most research universities, Syracuse is committed to priorities that place its students first and foremost in importance. Small classes, intensive advising, emphasis on transition to college in the first year, and active learning characterize a systematic approach to assuring a productive teaching and learning environment. Improved classroom opportunities through smaller classes provide students with close attention from faculty members. Most classes average about 30 students.

In virtually every aspect of students' lives at Syracuse, choices abound. The range of courses available, opportunities to study abroad and for internships, the scope of residential living possibilities, the array of cocurricular and extracurricular activities, and most importantly, the choices of more than 200 undergraduate majors make Syracuse University particularly attractive to students who value a range of options. Syracuse combines a campuswide commitment to the finest teaching, advising, and mentoring with the on-going discovery of a respected research institution. Syracuse University has a long history of promoting learning through teaching, research, scholarship, creative accomplishments, and service.

Student Body Undergraduate enrollment is 10,702; graduate enrollment is 3,719. The student population is 54 percent women. Of the main campus undergraduate and graduate students, nearly 16 percent of the students are of ethnic minority groups, and 10 percent are international students. Seventy-five percent of the students receive financial aid. There are twenty-six fraternities and twenty-one sororities.

Faculty Of the 1,404 faculty members, 832 are full-time. Eighty-six percent of full-time faculty members hold terminal degrees. The student-faculty ratio is 12:1.

Key Facilities The library's collections include approximately 3.1 million volumes, 13,500 periodicals and serials, 4.7 million microforms, and 852,900 audiovisual materials. The library's special collections include rare books and manuscripts, and an audio laboratory and archive. Many of the library's electronic databases and resources can be accessed from residence halls and computer clusters. Students may use any of the 1,200 comput-

Interpreting the symbols: **2**=two-year college, **4**=four-year college; **Pu**=public or state college, **Pr**=private college; **G**=general honors program; **D**=departmental honors program; **S**=small program (fewer than 100 students), **M**=midsize program (100 to 500 students), **L**=large program (more than 500 students); **Sc**=scholarships available in honors program; **Tr**=transfer students accepted into honors program; **HBC**=historically black college; **AA**=academic advisors; **GA**=graduate advisors; **FA**=fellowship advisors.

ers available across campus. SU provides Internet access and e-mail accounts/services for all students. Online Web registration is available for both undergraduate and graduate classes.

The academic buildings at Syracuse University span the century, with fifteen listed in the National Register of Historic Places. Other key facilities on campus are the Joe and Emily Lowe Art Gallery, the 50,000-seat Carrier Dome, the Holden Observatory, the Bird Library, the Arthur Storch Theatre, a 200-seat house for drama, and the Schine Student Center. Additional facilities include the Institute for Sensory Research, the Center for Public and Community Service, the Child Care and Child Development Laboratory School, the CASE Center for Research in computer applications and software engineering, a new $4.5 million environmental systems laboratory complex, and the community darkrooms for photography. The Newhouse Communications Center has some of the finest facilities available for journalism and telecommunications. The Global Collaboratory Multimedia Classroom is a high-technology multimedia classroom that links students with the world. The Center for Science and Technology, which is affiliated with the Northeast Parallel Architecture Center, houses dozens of scientific laboratories containing state-of-the-art equipment, including one of the finest laser spectroscopy laboratories in the world. The Gebbie Clinic has clinical and laboratory suites for hearing and speech pathology.

Honorary Societies Phi Beta Kappa, Phi Eta Sigma, Phi Kappa Phi, Phi Sigma Pi, Psi Chi, Golden Key International Honor Society, and the National Society of Collegiate Scholars are a few of the honorary societies on campus. For a current list, students should visit the Honors Web site, listed below.

Athletics In athletics, all women's and men's varsity teams are NCAA Division I, and many are nationally ranked. Men's sports include basketball, crew, cross-country, football, indoor track and field, lacrosse, outdoor track and field, soccer, and swimming and diving. Women's sports include basketball, cross-country, field hockey, indoor track and field, lacrosse, outdoor track and field, soccer, softball, swimming and diving, tennis, and volleyball. A member of the Big East Conference, Syracuse University teams are known as the Orangemen and Orangewomen.

Study Abroad Students can study abroad for a semester, a summer, or a year through the Division of International Programs Abroad (DIPA) without interrupting their degree programs and with or without proficiency in a foreign language. Approximately 800 undergraduate students from all colleges within the University and from universities across the United States study abroad through DIPA each year. The University operates centers in London, England; Strasbourg, France; Florence, Italy; Madrid, Spain; and Hong Kong. DIPA offers additional opportunities to study at an international university in many countries, including Australia, Belgium, Chile, the Czech Republic, Germany, Ireland, Israel, Hungary, Japan, Korea, Poland, and Russia.

Support Services The Office of Disability Services provides support services to students with documented disabilities. Services include tutoring, extended time for tests, reading machines, tape recorders, talking books, oral tests, note-taking services, a learning center, support groups, study circles, and proofreaders. A disability access specialist is available to assist learning-disabled students who apply for assistance.

Job Opportunities Syracuse University offers between 3,700 and 4,000 qualifying students Federal Work-Study employment, including community service positions, both on and off campus and throughout the central New York area. The University also offers non-FWS employment opportunities on campus, and off campus through the JLD program. Interested students may investigate these employment opportunities through JOBNET, located on the University's Web site at: http://sumweb.syr.edu/seo/.

Tuition: $21,500 per year (2001–02)

Room and Board: $8750

Mandatory Fees: $460

Contact: Director: Professor D. Bruce Carter, 306 Bowne Hall, Syracuse, New York 13244-1200; Telephone: 315-443-2759; Fax: 315-443-3235; E-mail: bcarter@psych.syr.edu; Web site: http://www.honors.syr.edu

Tarleton State University

4 Pu G S

▼ Honors Degree Program, Presidential Honors Program

The Honors Degree Program offers honors sections of most core curriculum subjects, including English, history, government, chemistry, biology, and speech. Honors classes present students with intellectually challenging material, innovative approaches to subjects, increased opportunities for honing critical-thinking and writing skills, and the opportunity to interact closely with similarly motivated students. Honors classes—depending on the subject—emphasize discussion and student participation, primary sources and monographs over textbooks, textbooks that emphasize critical thinking over textbooks that emphasize feedback of information, special lab equipment that would not be available to most science students until graduate school, student projects and research, and essay exams over multiple choice tests.

In addition to taking honors sections of the core curriculum courses, students who have completed at least four of these basic honors courses may, with the permission of the department head and the director of the Honors Degree Program, take one upper-level special problems course for honors credit. Plans are in progress for additional honors classes in several areas, as well as an upper-level departmental component.

The 7-year-old program currently enrolls 80 to 100 students each semester in honors classes.

The Presidential Honors Program at Tarleton State University is made up of a select group of students chosen as entering freshmen on the basis of demonstrated excellence in academics as well as leadership, service, and a capacity for intellectual inquiry. The program looks for highly motivated students with a wide range of interests who have a strong desire to further their education—not only toward the end of job security or professional advancement, but with the goals of increasing their knowledge and benefiting their society. Presidential Honors Scholars participate in intellectual and creative activities, both directed and independent.

The 15-year-old program currently enrolls approximately 30 students, with 10 admitted each fall.

Participation Requirements (Honors Degree Program): All Tarleton students who have a GPA of at least 3.0 are eligible for honors classes. Students with a lower GPA may register for an honors class with the permission of the instructor. Any student who completes 18 or more hours of such classes with a minimum 3.0 GPA in honors classes and overall will receive recognition as an Honors Degree Program graduate. Graduation from the Honors Degree Program is indicated on the student's transcript.

Participation Requirements (Presidential Honors Program): In the first two years, students take an annual Honors Seminar, a specially designed course open only to them. Seminar topics have focused recently on a variety of subjects—Issues in Education; Political Leadership; the Development of Scientific Thought; and Philosophy, Sophistry and Democracy. Students also enroll in at least 9 hours of Tarleton's regularly scheduled honors classes offered in the Honors Degree Program, and they must complete a 3-hour senior independent research project. Presidential Honors Scholars must have at least a 3.4 cumulative GPA and must complete a minimum of 15 hours of solid academic courses every semester. PHP students have the opportunity to attend a professional conference in their major field of study. They also provide leadership and service to the University and the community. Graduation from the program is indicated on the student's diploma.

Scholarship Availability: While there is no scholarship directly associated with the Honors Degree Program, students interested in scholarships should pursue the Presidential Honors Program described above.

Students admitted to the Presidential Honors Program receive an annual scholarship of $4000 and priority in dormitory assignments, registration, and other areas of campus life. Presidential Honors Scholars are free to pursue any major course of study offered at Tarleton. The scholarship is renewable for four years, as long as the student meets required standards. Recipients are required to participate in the Honors Degree Program (see above) and maintain a 3.4 GPA in each long semester and an 3.0 overall GPA.

The Campus Context: Tarleton State University is composed of several colleges: Arts and Sciences, Agriculture and Technology, Education and Fine Arts, Business Administration, and Graduate Studies.

Student Body The undergraduate enrollment is 6,369: 47.48 percent men and 52.52 percent women. The ethnic distribution of students is 0.71 percent American Indian/Native Alaskan, 0.57 percent Asian/Pacific Islander, 2.81 percent black, 4.55 percent Mexican American, 91.21 percent white. There are 10 international students. Seventy percent of the students receive some form of financial aid. Students participate in five sororities and six fraternities.

Faculty There are more than 220 faculty members and the student-faculty ratio is 20:1.

Key Facilities The library houses 285,000 volumes. There are numerous computer labs on the campus.

Honorary Societies Phi Eta Sigma, Alpha Chi

Athletics In athletics, Tarleton State is in NCAA Division II, Lonestar Conference.

Study Abroad Some study abroad opportunities are available.

Support Services Disabled students will find wheelchair access to all buildings, a Teaching and Learning Center with special facilities and programs for disabled students, and an in-house training and research facility for exercise physiology for individuals with neurological disabilities. The Disabilities Certification Officer is the Associate Vice President for Academic Affairs.

Job Opportunities Work opportunities on campus include work-study, regular student employment, and graduate assistantships.

Tuition: $960 for state residents, $7380 for nonresidents, per year

Room and Board: $2324 minimum

Mandatory Fees: $978

Contact: Director: Dr. Craig Clifford, Box 0545, Stephenville, Texas 76402; Telephone: 254-968-9423; E-mail: cliffor@vms.tarleton.edu

TARRANT COUNTY COLLEGE

2 Pu G M Sc AA

▼ Cornerstone Honors Program

The Cornerstone Honors Program at Tarrant County College (TCC) offers a two-year, humanities-based core curriculum intended to give the high-ability student an academically rigorous foundation in preparation for transfer to a senior institution. The theme of the program is "Beliefs, Knowledge, Creations, Institutions: Cornerstones of Character and Civilization." Central to this curriculum are the four Cornerstone courses, one taught in each of the four semesters. These courses are team-taught and interdisciplinary, providing an ordered sequence of content considered central to a liberal education. Content relies heavily on readings in the humanities and emphasizes critical thinking expressed in both written and oral forms.

Cornerstone scholars enjoy the benefits of small classes and an integrated curriculum, including interdisciplinary dialogue and research. Service learning is emphasized, with opportunities for off-campus learning experiences made available each semester. Spring projects in political science often culminate in a trip to Austin for dialogue with state lawmakers. History courses require extensive historiography practice—from oral history documentation to local, historical marker reviews. The capstone aesthetics experience includes a weeklong fine arts tour of New York City.

Most graduates of the program transfer to senior institutions in Texas, many of which offer substantial scholarships to Cornerstone scholars. Hailed by these institutions as the "Cadillac honors program," the Cornerstone Honors Program has succeeded in preparing high-ability students in the Fort Worth area for junior transfer since 1991, with approximately 120 new freshman scholars joining each year. Initiated with a grant from the National Endowment for the Humanities, the program is now available on each of the College's four campuses.

Participation Requirements: Cornerstone honors graduates earn a 64-credit-hour Associate of Arts degree that includes 36 hours of Cornerstone honors courses. Nonhonors requirements are fulfilled by taking courses chosen in accordance with individual degree plans and academic interests. Honors courses are preselected and are taken in a particular sequence so as to highlight the four "cornerstones" of the program: beliefs, knowledge, creations, and institutions. Cornerstone scholarships are awarded to all incoming freshmen and are renewed each semester for those who maintain a cumulative GPA of 3.0. Before each commencement, graduating Cornerstone scholars receive the Cornerstone medallion at a special awards ceremony.

Admission Process: Application for admission to the Cornerstone Honors Program is separate from application to Tarrant County College. Admission to the Cornerstone program is based on merit only. Criteria include academic record, recommendations, class standing, SAT or ACT scores, honors and activities, performance on an essay, and an interview with Cornerstone faculty members. Thirty new freshman scholars are admitted on each of the four Tarrant County College campuses each fall semester. Because the Cornerstone courses must be taken in a particular sequence, rolling admission is not available.

Scholarships: All incoming freshmen receive a $500-per-semester scholarship. This scholarship is renewable each semester that the student maintains a cumulative GPA of 3.0. Other financial assistance, including scholarships, grants, loans, and part-time employment, is available to qualified students at Tarrant County College.

The Campus Context: Tarrant County College, a comprehensive two-year public college, is among the ten largest colleges and universities in Texas. It offers courses in approximately thirty university-transfer and fifty career areas. Four campuses, strategically located in Tarrant County, serve the north Texas county's 1.44 million residents: two campuses in Fort Worth, the county's largest city; one in Arlington, the second-largest city; and one in Hurst. Day, evening, weekend, one-day-a-week, short-term, Internet, and instructional television courses are offered. The Associate of Arts degree prepares students to transfer to four-year colleges and universities. Students transferring from TCC frequently outperform all other transfers and students who start their educa-

Interpreting the symbols: **2**=two-year college, **4**=four-year college; **Pu**=public or state college, **Pr**=private college; **G**=general honors program; **D**=departmental honors program; **S**=small program (fewer than 100 students), **M**=midsize program (100 to 500 students), **L**=large program (more than 500 students); **Sc**=scholarships available in honors program; **Tr**=transfer students accepted into honors program; **HBC**=historically black college; **AA**=academic advisors; **GA**=graduate advisors; **FA**=fellowship advisors.

tion at the four-year schools. Associate of Applied Science degree and Certificate of Completion programs prepare students in one to two years for such careers as aviation, automotive, and information technology; nursing and allied health; police and fire; hospitality and dietetics; and semiconductor manufacturing and railroad operations.

Student Body Fall 2001 enrollment was 28,852, of which 57 percent of the students were women. Ethnic distribution is 67 percent white, 12 percent African American, 13 percent Hispanic, 6 percent Asian, and 1 percent unknown. Most students live in Tarrant or surrounding counties. Fourteen percent of students receive need-based financial aid. The College has more than 100 student clubs and organizations. There is no on-campus housing and no national sororities or fraternities.

Faculty The total number of faculty members is 1,245 (468 full-time). Eight percent hold advanced degrees in their respective fields. The student-faculty ratio is 22:1.

Key Facilities Four libraries contain 162,331 volumes and 120 computer workstations, with additional ones being added. All campuses have well-equipped labs and classrooms.

Honorary Society Phi Theta Kappa

Athletics TCC does not have intercollegiate athletics.

Study Abroad Study trips are offered from time to time. Past destinations have included South America, France, and England.

Support Services Disability Support Services offers students with disabilities accommodations that include note takers, readers, tutors, arranged testing accommodations, scooters, motorized wheelchairs, closed-circuit television, tape recorders, talking calculators, adaptive computers, mobility assistance, and interpreters for the hearing impaired.

Job Opportunities Campus work-study jobs are among financial aid programs. Career and Employment Services Offices list on- and off-campus job openings. On-campus employment recruitment and interviews and career development assistance are provided.

Tuition: $997 per year ($29 per semester hour with a minimum of $100 per semester) for full-time, in-district students (2001–02)

Mandatory fees: $10 processing/evaluation; $6 per semester hour for building use; $1 per semester hour for student services, to a maximum of $10 per semester hour; $5 records

Room and board: There is no on-campus housing.

Contact: Northwest Campus Director: Dr. Tony Roberts, Cornerstone Honors Program, 4801 Marine Creek Parkway, Fort Worth, Texas 76179; Telephone: 817-515-7696; E-mail: tony.roberts@tccd.net. Northeast Campus Director: Dr. Tim Gilbert, Cornerstone Honors Program, 828 Harwood Road, Hurst, Texas 76054; Telephone: 817-515-6421; E-mail: timothy.gilbert@tccd.net. South Campus Director: Brian Johnson, Cornerstone Honors Program, 5301 Campus Drive, Fort Worth, Texas 76119; Telephone: 817-515-4709; E-mail: brian.johnson@tccd.net. Southeast Campus Director: David Price, Cornerstone Honors Program, 2100 Southeast Parkway, Arlington, Texas 76108; Telephone: 817-515-3386; E-mail: david.price@tccd.net.

Temple University

4 Pu G M Sc Tr

▼ Temple University Honors Program

The Temple University Honors Program began as the College of Arts and Sciences Honors Program in 1967. In 1988, the program was expanded to include outstanding students enrolled in all fourteen schools and colleges at the University. The honors program offers these academically talented, motivated, and interested students a place of their own in the context of a major research university.

The heart of the program is a set of courses open only to honors students and typically taught by specially selected, full-time faculty members, many of whom have won the Temple University Great Teacher Award. The program features small classes of about 20 students and encourages a lively, seminar-style classroom atmosphere. Students (representing nearly every major in the university) usually complete university CORE requirements through their honors courses. In addition, they take honors lower- and upper-level electives, some created specifically for the program. They may also participate in departmental honors programs. Honors students may apply for the TempleMed and TempleLaw Scholars program. University honors students enrolled in the Fox School of Business and Management participate concurrently in SBM Honors, a four-year program.

The University Honors Program, in collaboration with the Honors Student Council, arranges special lectures, poetry readings, political panels, career talks, and field trips. The students publish a newsletter, manage a Web site, own an honors listserv, and spend time in the honors lounge, where computers and companionship are available. They are eligible to live on the honors floor in the residence halls, where an honors student is the resident assistant.

The program is jointly administered by a physicist and a religionist who serve as academic advisers for honors students. Working closely with departmental advisers, they help students with course selection, decisions about majors, career choices, scholarship and graduate school applications, and job opportunities and internships. The staff also includes 2 graduate students and 2 undergraduate honors students.

Participation Requirements: Honors students receive an Honors Certificate after having passed eight honors courses (six for transfer students), usually after about two years. Students are encouraged to continue taking appropriate honors courses throughout their undergraduate studies. They must maintain a 3.0 GPA overall. Successful completion of the Honors Program is recorded on the student's transcript.

Admission Process: During the normal application process to the University, all students are screened for honors; no separate application is required. Selection criteria include high school credentials, application essay, recommendations, and SAT I scores. About 200 freshmen annually are accepted; most are offered financial aid based on merit and/or need. Transfer students and freshmen or sophomores already at Temple may also be admitted if their college performance is excellent.

The Campus Context: Talented students from the region and from around the world study at Temple University, a major teaching and research university. Temple actively promotes programs that helps students bridge the worlds of academia and work. Degree programs are offered in the college of Liberal Arts; the College of Science and Technology; the College of Engineering; the Fox School of Business and Management; the School of Tourism and Hospitality Management; the College of Education; the School of Communications and Theater; the School of Social Administration; the College of Allied Health Professions; the Tyler School of Art; the Esther Boyer College of Music; the Department of Dance; the Architecture Program; and the Department of Landscape Architecture and Horticulture. There are 118 undergraduate programs of study, 127 master's programs, and sixty-five doctoral programs.

Student Body Temple's enrollment is 27,000, including 18,000 undergraduates of great ethnic diversity; 52 percent are women, 81 percent are state residents, and 2 percent are international students.

Faculty Of the 2,650 faculty members, 1,650 are full-time; 86 percent have terminal degrees. The undergraduate student-faculty ratio is 13:1.

Key Facilities The library houses 2.1 million volumes, 15,600 periodicals, and 70 CD-ROMs. There are 2,000 computers for student use.

Honorary Societies Golden Key, Phi Beta Kappa

Athletics In athletics, Temple is a member of NCAA Division I in all sports except men's football (Division I-A). Intercollegiate sports are men's baseball, football, golf, and tennis; women's fencing, field hockey, lacrosse, softball, and volleyball; and basketball, crew, gymnastics, soccer, and track and field for both men and women. Intramural sports are basketball, bowling, football, rugby, soccer, softball, tennis, and volleyball.

Study Abroad Study abroad is available at Temple's campuses in Rome and Tokyo; there are also exchange programs with several universities in Germany, Britain, France, and Puerto Rico.

Support Services The University has excellent facilities for disabled students.

Job Opportunities There are 610 part-time jobs available on campus.

Tuition: $6098 for state residents, $11,128 for nonresidents, per year (1998–99)

Room and Board: $5506

Mandatory Fees: $280

Contact: Directors: Dr. Dieter Forster and Dr. Ruth Tonner Ost, 1301 Cecil B. Moore Avenue, Philadelphia, Pennsylvania 19122-6091; Telephone: 215-204-7573; Fax: 215-204-6356; E-mail: dieter@vm.temple.edu or rost@vm.temple.edu; Web site: http://www.temple.edu/honors

Tennessee State University

4 Pu G L Sc Tr AA HBC

▼ University Honors Program

The Tennessee State University Honors Program (UHP) promotes positive and lifelong learning, scholarly inquiry, and a commitment to the service of others. From its inception, the primary goal of the program has been to create and maintain a community of academically bright and talented students who serve as campus leaders and role models, impacting positively on the entire University and enhancing the mission of Tennessee State University (TSU). The UHP honors the Tennessee State University motto, "Think, Work, Serve." In addition, the UHP stresses excellence as a way of life for the TSU scholar.

Special challenges and opportunities are offered to some of the most talented and highly motivated of the University's undergraduate students. These students enjoy a close, collaborative relationship with distinguished faculty members, small class sizes, and a chance to work at the cutting edge of an academic discipline. The UHP includes all academic units of the University and covers all four years of the undergraduate experience.

In addition to the stated benefits, a UHP student also enjoys honors scholarships; challenging courses designed especially for UHP students; intellectually oriented faculty members and peers; grant opportunities to fund student research projects during the summer and to support student domestic and international travel; a variety of social and cultural activities; use of the McDonald Williams Honors Center, which offers an atmosphere for study and relaxation; and special internships and graduate study opportunities.

The UHP was established in 1964, which distinguishes it as one of the oldest honors programs in the country. There are currently 650 students in the University Honors Program.

Participation Requirements: The University Honors Program requires students to complete 24 honors credits, which include 12 hours of general education requirements and 12 hours of junior/senior-level courses. Students may contract special courses for honors credit. Each student is required to take the honors senior thesis. Other mandatory courses include honors freshman and sophomore English and the honors junior and senior colloquium. All other honors credits are chosen from honors electives.

Admission Process: Entering freshmen must have a minimum 26 ACT or 1170 SAT and a 3.1 GPA. Transfer students must have a minimum 3.4 GPA. An application process is offered each fall for new and transferring students. The latest a student can be admitted to the UHP is the first semester of the junior year. Students must maintain a minimum 3.4 GPA in order to graduate through the University Honors Program.

Scholarship Availability: Each year, the UHP offers two scholarships through the Joan C. Elliot Memorial Scholarship Fund. Transfer students from community colleges who are members of Phi Theta Kappa Honor Society are eligible to apply for three scholarships awarded each year. TSU offers a number of Presidential and Foundation Honors Scholarships. Many students who receive these scholarships are members of the UHP.

Honorary Societies Golden Key, Phi Kappa Phi, and Alpha Kappa Mu

Contact: Web site: http://www.tnstate.edu

Tennessee Technological University

4 Pu G M Sc Tr

▼ Honors Program

Emphasizing a broad range of cocurricular activities, leadership training, communication skills, preprofessional research, and creative problem solving, the Tennessee Technological University (TTU) Honors Program strives to create an atmosphere in which young scholars can discuss their ideas and experiences in a supportive yet challenging environment. The program encourages students not only to participate in existing activities, but also to create and organize workshops, committees, presentations, and other events that expand their own range of expertise and draw on individual initiative and teamwork.

In addition to offering smaller class sections and greater opportunities for in-depth study, the TTU Honors Program publishes two student-produced newsletters and an annual *Honors Handbook,* offers several annual leadership retreats, participates in community service activities, and maintains a host of student-run committees that plan and facilitate social events, make Honors Program policy decisions, and organize a variety of social service and recreational projects. These include active intramural sports teams, weekly movies and lively discussions, visits to faculty homes, interdisciplinary luncheon forums, jam sessions, reading groups, and daily gatherings in the Honors Lounge.

TTU honors students participate enthusiastically in honors conferences at the state, regional, and national levels, typically sending one of the largest delegations in the nation. Other opportunities for experience in scholarly research and career skills include mentorships with professors in a student's major field, resume building and preparation, and collaborative/interdisciplinary projects in which honors faculty members and students work together. As a result, each year the University is

Interpreting the symbols: **2**=two-year college, **4**=four-year college; **Pu**=public or state college, **Pr**=private college; **G**=general honors program; **D**=departmental honors program; **S**=small program (fewer than 100 students), **M**=midsize program (100 to 500 students), **L**=large program (more than 500 students); **Sc**=scholarships available in honors program; **Tr**=transfer students accepted into honors program; **HBC**=historically black college; **AA**=academic advisors; **GA**=graduate advisors; **FA**=fellowship advisors.

able to prepare and recommend TTU honors graduates successfully for graduate fellowships and competitive graduate school programs.

Participation Requirements: There are three categories of membership in the TTU Honors Program. A full member has a cumulative QPA of at least 3.5 (except first-semester members who may drop to a 3.1) and is making progress toward graduation with honors. An associate member is one who has been admitted to the Honors Program but whose QPA is temporarily lower than 3.5, but remains at least 3.1. He or she continues to be an active participant in the program and must continue to take honors courses. An affiliate member is a student who enrolls in one or more honors courses but who has not yet met full membership requirements. This three-tiered approach encourages students to remain involved in cocurricular activities, academic challenge, and ongoing leadership training.

Honors 1010, a ten-week introductory honors seminar, is required of all full members. The purpose of the course is to promote understanding of diverse views, collaborative learning, collegial exchange, and intellectual and personal growth in the college years.

Honors Colloquia (Honors 4010), often interdisciplinary, address topics that are not offered as part of the regular University curriculum. The colloquia explore relationships among social, cultural, historical, environmental, economic, and other concerns. Recent topics include a team-taught environmental field study; religion in the politics of the Middle East, the U.S., and South America; space-time physics; human rights and the law; a cross-cultural survey of mysticism; the ethnomusicology of China; and recombinant DNA.

Directed Studies, Honors 4020, allows a student, in collaboration with a faculty member, to explore an area of interest not ordinarily covered in regular classes.

In addition to all relevant University, college, and departmental requirements of the student's chosen curriculum, *in cursu honorum* students must successfully complete the following requirements: Honors 1010 (1 semester hour), at least two honors colloquia (Honors 4010) or one colloquium and one independent study (Honors 4020), at least 15 additional semester hours in honors courses in at least three different disciplines, and achievement of a minimum cumulative QPA of 3.5.

Admission Process: Incoming freshmen must have an ACT composite of 26 or higher or the SAT I equivalent of 1170. As full members of the Honors Program, they may attend early registration and are assigned a Big Sibling (an established honors student who serves as a mentor). Transfer students, or students enrolled at Tech more than one semester, may enter the Honors Program by completing one honors course and achieving a cumulative QPA of 3.5 or higher.

Scholarship Availability: The TTU Honors Program does not fund scholarships directly. However, due to an agreement with the Tennessee Board of Regents, the Honors Program provides Enrichment Options (HPEO) in place of the 75 hours of work Financial Aid attaches to its scholarships. Full members of the Honors Program participate in other activities, such as the Big Sibling Program, in which students are trained as mentors for incoming freshmen; service activities; work with a mentoring professor on research or a special project; presentations (both attending and giving); workshops; attending state, regional, and national honors conferences (TTU routinely sends a large delegation); participating in campus clubs and/or interest groups; playing intramural sports; and many other intellectual and social activities.

The Campus Context: The 235-acre main campus of Tennessee Technological University is located on Interstate 40, approximately 75 and 100 miles from Nashville and Knoxville, respectively. Cookeville has a population of more than 25,000 and is located on Tennessee's Highland Rim. There are many parks and natural areas within short driving distance. The campus is compact, and everything is within easy walking distance. Students and faculty members enjoy the lowest crime rate among the state's major colleges and universities.

TTU, part of the Tennessee Board of Regents, is a four-year public coeducational university consisting of the following schools and colleges: Colleges of Agriculture and Human Ecology (5 percent of enrollment), Arts and Sciences (21 percent), Business Administration (16 percent), Education (20 percent), Engineering (25 percent), the School of Nursing (4 percent), and the School of Graduate Studies. Tech is accredited by nine agencies, including the Southern Association of Colleges and Schools. Thirty-eight undergraduate majors are offered, with fifty-four options leading to the B.S. degree and three leading to the B.A. degree. Eight graduate programs lead to the M.S., seventeen to the M.A., one to the M.B.A., sixteen to the Ed.S., and one to the Ph.D. in engineering.

TTU is the only Tennessee public institution with three engineering-related Centers of Excellence: the Center for Electric Power; the Center for the Management, Utilization and Protection of Water Resources; and the Center for Manufacturing Research and Technology Utilization.

TTU has two Chairs of Excellence in the College of Business Administration: the J.E. Owen Chair of Management Information Systems and the William Eugene Mayberry Chair of Production and Operations Management.

Student Body The total enrollment is 8,653, with full-time students numbering approximately 7,500. The population comes from ninety-four of Tennessee's ninety-five counties, forty-one other states, and fifty-seven other countries. Fifty-one percent are men, 49 percent women; 8.3 percent are from racial or ethnic minority groups; and 97 percent are U.S. citizens. Sixty-six percent of the students receive financial aid (approximately $22 million is administered annually). There are five sororities, twelve social fraternities, and chapters of Omega Phi Alpha and Alpha Phi Omega.

Faculty There are 379 faculty members, 77 percent with doctoral degrees. The student-faculty ratio is 12:1 in Honors, 25:1 campuswide.

Key Facilities The 521,900-volume library houses more than 310,000 books, 3,400 periodicals, and 148,000 U.S. government publications. There are thirty-five computer labs, with additional specialized labs in each department, and VAX terminals in dormitories.

Noteworthy facilities include the Bryan Fine Arts Center, Women's Center, University Recreation and Fitness Center, and the Joe L. Evins Center for Appalachian Crafts, which is located on Center Hill Lake.

Honorary Societies Phi Kappa Phi, Mortar Board, Omicron Delta Kappa

Athletics TTU is a member of NCAA Division I and the Ohio Valley Conference. It has sixteen intercollegiate teams, including football, basketball, baseball, and rugby (both men's and women's). The women's basketball team has won eleven OVC championships, including the All Sports Trophy—second place in 1993, first in 1990.

Job Opportunities Students find work on campus in the Computer Center Helpdesk, food services department, campus bookstore, and the Centers of Excellence; many other campus departments look to the student body for employees.

Tuition: $2800 for state residents, $6355 for nonresidents (2001–02)

Room and Board: $3320 (double room and meals)

Mandatory Fees: $2306 (nonresidents only)

Contact: Director: Dr. Connie Hood, Box 5124, TJ Farr 204, Cookeville, Tennessee 38505; Interim Associate Director: Dr. Rita Barnes; Telephone: 615-372-3797; E-mail: honors@tntech.edu; Web site: http://www2.tntech.edu/honors/

Texas A&M University

4 Pu G D L Sc Tr AA

▼ University Honors Programs

The University Honors Program at Texas A&M University (TAMU) offers special opportunities for high-achieving students to pursue academic work that challenges their interests and abilities. The program is campuswide, encompassing all undergraduate colleges within the University. As a result, honors students have access to the entire spectrum of educational resources available at Texas A&M. Honors courses and individualized research programs bring together outstanding students and faculty members in an environment designed to encourage initiative, creativity, and independent thinking.

Taught by some of the University's most distinguished faculty members, honors classes are kept small. Honors students have the opportunity to work one-on-one with leading professors and to receive individual attention and special services typically available only on smaller campuses. At the same time, students enjoy the resources of one of the nation's major research universities, including state-of-the-art laboratory, library, and computing facilities. The University is among the top twenty-five public universities in the nation.

Honors students at Texas A&M pursue regular majors in any one of the 150 degree plans available to undergraduates through the College of Liberal Arts, Geosciences, Agriculture and Life Sciences, Architecture, Education, Veterinary Medicine, the Mays College and Graduate School of Business, and Look College of Engineering. Students customize their honors curriculum by choosing from the more than 300 honors course sections a year, selecting honors studies in their core curriculum requirements and/or within their disciplines. With the help of honors advisers, they are encouraged to pursue honors sequences that may be departmental, college-level, or University-level.

The University Honors Program, in conjunction with its scholarship program, attracts successful, confident, and motivated students from across the nation. Texas A&M is among the top ten institutions enrolling National Merit Scholars and among the top twenty-five in the enrollment of National Achievement Scholars. Scholarships are available for students with a proven academic record who also show promise of leadership. The University has two honors residence halls. Lechner Hall houses freshman Honors and scholarship students, while Clements Hall serves the upperclassmen. Both halls are coed.

Honors students receive multiple services from the Honors Program Office: a special newsletter, freshman college night gatherings, advising on national scholarship competitions, and help in accessing the resources of the University and beyond.

More than 2,500 students enroll in the honors courses each semester.

Participation Requirements: While participation is flexible, students receive University-level honors designation on their transcripts by completing the following requirements: 36 honors hours over a defined distribution requirement for University Honors; 19 honors hours across the core curriculum for Foundation Honors; or 9 honors hours, 6 research hours, and a senior thesis for University Undergraduate Research Fellows. Students completing departmental or collegiate honors tracks receive an Honors Certificate from the corresponding unit. College honors tracks are available through the Dwight Look College of Engineering, the Lowry Mays College of Business, and the College of Liberal Arts. Advantages include interdisciplinary seminars and contact with industry professionals.

Admission Process: No application is necessary to participate in the University Honors Program. Incoming freshmen with a minimum 1250 on the SAT (28 ACT) and who graduated in the top 10 percent of the class are automatically admitted to honors study if they wish. Thereafter, any student who maintains a minimum 3.4 cumulative GPR may take honors courses. Transfer students are admitted on a case by case basis, usually with a minimum 3.5 GPR. Students are free to take as few or as many honors courses as they wish.

Scholarship Availability: The Office of Honors Programs and Academic Scholarships also is responsible for the selection and administration of all the major four-year academic scholarships. Each spring the office makes about a thousand award offers to students with exemplary academic records and a proven record of leadership and community involvement. The average SAT I score of students receiving the top scholarship award is 1460. The Texas A&M Scholarships are for $2500 or $3000 a year and are renewable for four years by meeting specific renewal criteria. Texas A&M University also sponsors any National Merit Finalist with a scholarship through the National Merit Corporation. National Merit Finalist packages can range from $28,600 to $48,600. To encourage study abroad among the honors community, a $1000 award is offered to students who wish to take part in a Texas A&M-sponsored study-abroad program. An additional incentive scholarship program rewards scholarship students after their freshman year to become University Scholars. As ambassadors of the University, University Scholars will have distinguished themselves on campus during their first year with their academic and leadership record. Currently enrolled students who are not on scholarship may compete for one-year scholarship awards of $1000.

The Campus Context: The 5,000-acre campus of Texas A&M University is located in the Bryan/College Station area, a 2-hour drive from Dallas, Houston, San Antonio, and Austin. Texas A&M University is a land-grant, sea-grant, and space-grant university and is the flagship of the Texas A&M University System. Ten colleges make up the main campus at College Station: Agriculture and Life Sciences, Architecture, the Dwight Look College of Engineering, Education, the George Bush School of Government and Public Service, Geosciences and Maritime Studies, Liberal Arts, the Lowry Mays College and Graduate School of Business, Medicine, and Veterinary Medicine. The University offers 151 undergraduate degree programs.

Among distinguished facilities on campus are the George Bush School of Government and Public Policy, the George Bush Presidential Library, the World Shakespeare Bibliography, a cyclotron, the Texas Transportation Institute, and the Nautical Archaeology Program.

Student Body Approximately 36,000 undergraduates comprise 80 percent of the total enrollment at the University. The ethnic makeup is approximately 3 percent Asian-American, 2 percent African American, 9 percent Hispanic, and 82 percent white. The student body is typically of traditional college age with 1 percent nontraditional students and is evenly divided between men and women. More than half of the students enrolled ranked in the top 10 percent of their high school graduating class, and the mean composite SAT I score was 1175. TAMU has the eleventh-largest endowment per student in the nation among public institutions. More than 70 percent of the students usually receive some type of financial aid.

Faculty There are 1,877 full-time faculty members, 80 percent with earned doctorates. The student-faculty ratio is 22:1.

Interpreting the symbols: **2**=two-year college, **4**=four-year college; **Pu**=public or state college, **Pr**=private college; **G**=general honors program; **D**=departmental honors program; **S**=small program (fewer than 100 students), **M**=midsize program (100 to 500 students), **L**=large program (more than 500 students); **Sc**=scholarships available in honors program; **Tr**=transfer students accepted into honors program; **HBC**=historically black college; **AA**=academic advisors; **GA**=graduate advisors; **FA**=fellowship advisors.

Key Facilities The library houses 2.7 million volumes and 4.9 million microforms. There are 25,000 computers connected to the campus network.

Honorary Societies Phi Eta Sigma, Lambda Sigma, Tau Kappa, Phi Kappa Phi, and Golden Key

Athletics Texas A&M University is a member of the new Big 12 Conference. Within that alliance approximately 475 TAMU student-athletes carry the Aggie banner into competition in ten sports, all at the NCAA Division I level. For the academic year of 1995–96, Texas A&M ranked sixteenth nationally in the Sears Cup ratings, the annual review of successful intercollegiate athletic programs sponsored by *USA Today* and Sears, Roebuck Corporation. Highlights of the Aggie athletic facilities are 82,600-seat Kyle Field, a new student recreation center that includes a state-of-the-art natatorium, and the 12,500-seat Reed Arena. While athletics endeavors and facilities are the primary focus of most of the Department of Athletics, Texas A&M's Center for Athletic Academic Affairs has been recognized as providing one of the most comprehensive and successful academic support programs in the country.

Study Abroad There are multiple semester and summer study-abroad programs available to students in all majors. Each summer alone, there are ten to fifteen programs that take Aggies around the world, with special concentration in Texas A&M's areas of geographic priority: Mexico and Latin America, Europe, and Pacific Asia. Texas A&M has two study-abroad centers, one in Castiglion Fiorentino, Italy, and one in Mexico City.

Tuition: $2350 for state residents, $8620 for nonresidents, per two semesters (2002–03)

Room and Board: $6352

Mandatory Fees: $1172

Contact: Executive Director: Dr. Edward A. Funkhouser, 101 Academic Building, TAMU 4283, College Station, Texas 77843-4233; Telephone: 979-845-6774; Fax: 979-845-0300; E-mail: honors@tamu.edu; Web site: http://honors.tamu.edu

Texas Christian University

4 Pr G M Tr

▼ Honors Program

At present, the Honors Program membership numbers approximately 400 from an undergraduate student body of 6,300.

The Honors Council is the Honors Program's primary governing body. It develops program goals and philosophies and approves new honors courses. The council is an official University committee consisting of both faculty members and honors students. The Honors Week Committee is also a University committee consisting of both professors and students. It plans and supervises the activities of Honors Week. The Honors Cabinet is the student governing body of the Honors Program. It serves as an advisory body to the Director by addressing student concerns about program policy, classes, and activities.

One of the Cabinet's primary goals is to build a sense of community in the Honors Program. Cabinet members plan both academic and social extracurricular activities such as the Fall Escape, firesides, trips to museums and plays, and dinners, as well as other activities designed to provide opportunities for students and professors to get to know one another. Cabinet members elect the Cabinet Chair, Vice-Chair, and Secretary at their first meeting in January. The Chair is an ex officio member of the Honors Council and the Honors Week Committee and also serves on Intercom, a committee of TCU student leaders.

Participation Requirements: Students in the Honors Program must remain in good academic standing by meeting certain grade requirements and fulfilling honors curriculum requirements. Freshmen and sophomores are expected to participate in at least one honors class each semester until they have fulfilled the Lower Division honors requirements. They must, however, complete these requirements no later than the end of their sophomore year. Continuance in the program past the freshman year requires a cumulative TCU GPA of 3.0; to continue past the sophomore year requires a cumulative TCU GPA of 3.4. After completing the Lower Division honors requirements, juniors and seniors are eligible to engage in Departmental and University Honors courses. Honors degrees are conferred upon Honors Program graduates who complete the Lower Division requirements, meet the specific Departmental and/or University Honors criteria, achieve an overall TCU and cumulative GPA of 3.5 or higher, and complete at least 60 credit hours at TCU exclusive of credit by examination.

During their freshman and sophomore years, honors students must complete either the Honors Intellectual Traditions Track or the Honors Western Civilization Track to fulfill the Lower Division requirements. Both tracks emphasize the history of Western civilization and are comprised of 15 credit hours.

The Honors Intellectual Traditions Track requires an Honors Freshman Seminar (or another 3-hour honors class) in the first semester of the freshman year, three semesters (9 hours) of Honors Intellectual Traditions (HHIT 1113, 2123, 2133), and an additional honors class (3 hours) of the student's choice. The HHIT sequence explores interrelationships among history, religion, literature, philosophy, and art from the ancient Greek, Hebrew, and Roman worlds through the twentieth century. The Honors Western Civilization Track requires 15 hours of courses, consisting of 6 hours of History of Civilization (HIST 2003, 2013) plus 9 hours of honors classes. The 9 hours of honors classes are chosen from specially designated honors sections of UCR courses offered each semester.

Students who complete the Lower Division honors curriculum requirements and achieve a cumulative GPA of 3.4 by the end of their sophomore year are invited to begin work toward one or both tracks for graduation with honors. The distinctions of University Honors and Departmental Honors are an official part of the student's degree and are listed on the student's academic transcript. University Honors are awarded to students who complete four Honors Colloquia (The Nature of Society, On Human Nature, The Nature of Values, and The Nature of the Universe or Origins). Additionally, students must show evidence of proficiency in a foreign language at the sophomore level either through completion of 6 hours of 2000-level foreign language courses or through credit by examination.

Departmental Honors are awarded to students who engage in honors courses involving significant research in their major. Requirements typically consist of a junior-level seminar and a Senior Honors Project. Since these are research courses, their descriptions are intentionally broad. Although the form of a project is not restricted, and may include compositions, exhibits, or performances, the project must culminate in a document that is housed in the Special Collections Department of the Mary Couts Burnett Library, with its 1.85 million volumes.

Admission Process: Admission to the TCU Honors Program, founded in 1962, is by invitation and is separate from admission to the University. Entering freshmen are invited to join on the basis of criteria set each year by the Director and the Honors Council. Generally speaking, these include both SAT I/ACT scores and graduating rank in class. The goal of the invitational criteria is to produce a program membership of the top 10 to 12 percent of the students entering TCU each fall. Since intellectual motivation is a significant factor in determining academic success, those who fall slightly short of test score criteria, but who wish to undertake the challenge, may be admitted at the discretion of the Honors Program Director. Additionally, freshmen achieving at least a 3.4 GPA at the end of the fall semester are eligible to join the program.

Scholarship Availability: Merit-based scholarships range in value from $1500 per semester to forty-two full-tuition scholarships.

The Campus Context: Texas Christian University, founded in 1873 as AddRan Male and Femen College, has five undergraduate colleges, including the AddRan College of Arts and Sciences, Harris College of Nursing, the College of Fine Arts and Communications, the School of Education, and the M. J. Neeley School of Business.

Student Body There are approximately 6,300 students currently enrolled, 59 percent of whom are women. The ethnic distribution of the student body is as follows: African American, 4.2 percent; American Indian, .6 percent; Asian American, 2 percent; Hispanic, 5.2 percent; Anglo American, 78.2 percent; and unknown, 4.7 percent. There are more than 300 international students enrolled. Of the TCU student body, 52.2 percent live on campus while 47.8 percent prefer to live off campus. Fifty-five percent of the student body receives some type of financial aid. TCU houses nine social fraternities and nine social sororities, as well as numerous service fraternities and honorary societies, including Phi Beta Kappa, Mortar Board, Golden Key National Honor Society, and Alpha Lambda Delta.

Faculty The student-faculty ratio is 15:1, with a faculty of 350, including 338 full-time professors, 93 percent of whom have terminal degrees.

Key Facilities Honors housing is currently available on campus.

Honorary Societies Phi Theta Kappa, Golden Key, Mortar Board, Phi Beta Kappa, and Alpha Lambda Delta

Job Opportunities There is a wide range of work opportunities on campus.

Tuition: $10,350 per year (1998–99)

Room and Board: $4000

Mandatory Fees: $1240

Contact: Director: Dr. Kathryne S. McDorman, TCU Box 297022, Fort Worth, Texas 76129; Telephone: 817-257-7125; Fax: 817-921-7333; E-mail: a.trinkle@tcu.edu; Web site: http://www.tcu.edu

TEXAS LUTHERAN UNIVERSITY

4 Pr G S Sc Tr

▼ Honors Program

To become a member of the Texas Lutheran Honors Program is to become a part of a group of about 70 TLU students who have been selected because of their superior academic achievement. Some highly qualified students are appointed to the program as incoming freshmen. Additional students are appointed at the end of their freshman year. Honors students have new opportunities for liberal learning beyond the general requirements of students, and are permitted greater flexibility in curriculum planning. Academic requirements for Honors Program members are meant to encourage breadth as well as depth of study, interdisciplinary understanding, and the challenge appropriate to high academic standing.

Honors seminars and the directed readings course provide members with the opportunity to work closely with their professors and with students who are their intellectual peers. Members have the option of a senior honors thesis or performance project to fulfill their honors course requirement; this may be coordinated with one's departmental senior seminar. Members can even write their own curriculum if they choose to. Additional benefits of Honors Program membership include reductions in costs of tickets to cultural events on campus and in the surrounding region. The Honors Student Study Grant program provides research and special project funds for members involved in independent study courses or other research. Informal forums for discussion of student/academic issues or for talking with special guest speakers enhance lunch or supper get-togethers.

In existence for more than twenty years, the program now enrolls 71 students.

Participation Requirements: Honors Program members at Texas Lutheran University must fulfill the University's 124-credit hour requirement for graduation as well as the associated 30 upper-division hour requirement. In addition, they must complete the general education core courses, GEC 131-132 and GEC 134, or be exempted from the former by advanced placement examination. Honors applicants are expected to have completed this requirement by the time of application to the program.

Unique to the program is the requirement of 12 upper-division hours in the subject areas, although members are required to take fewer total hours here. Except for theology (where the 6-hour requirement still applies), they need take only a minimum of 3 hours in each of the other seven subject areas, but four courses must be taken at the junior or senior level.

The honors courses are designed especially for Texas Lutheran University honors students, and only they can register for them. These courses were created to provide members with the kind of intellectual discussions appropriate to their level of academic ability; the seminars are generally interdisciplinary in nature. All program members must fulfill 4 to 6 hours of honors course work to graduate as honors students. Courses include a senior-level directed readings course and a sophomore-level course that focuses on arts and ideas.

Members must maintain a 3.25 GPA. The deadline for applying to the program is April 1.

The Campus Context: Texas Lutheran University is located in Seguin, Texas; the campus is 160 acres and is roughly 35 miles from San Antonio. Texas Lutheran has celebrated its 105th year of service to higher education. Texas Lutheran gained college status in 1932; as of August 1996 Texas Lutheran College became Texas Lutheran University. Texas Lutheran is affiliated with the Evangelical Lutheran Church in America. The University offers twenty-seven majors and nine preprofessional programs. Bachelor of Arts, Bachelor of Science, and Bachelor of Business Administration degrees are conferred. In the center of the campus is the Chapel of the Abiding Presence.

In addition, Jackson Auditorium, which seats 1,100 people, is an exciting center for cultural events, and Hein Dining Hall provides both indoor and outdoor ambiance for all meals. There is also the Alumni Student Center (ASC), which is the home of many of the organizations on campus, as well as mailboxes, a bookstore, and a snack bar. Other focal points on campus are the Burton E. Grossman Fitness Center; the Jesse H. Jones Physical Education Center, home to the Texas Lutheran Bulldogs; and the Johnson Health Center. Moody Science has been renovated and a new section of the Krost Building was added in the spring of 1996.

Student Body The student population is 1,512, including the students at Randolph Air Force Base and Guadalupe Valley Hospital. Gender distribution is 62 percent women. Ethnic distribution is 75.2 percent white, 14.0 percent Hispanic, 4.5 percent international, 2.9 percent African American, 1.7 percent Asian American, 6 percent Native American. Seventy percent of full-time students live in University housing.

Ninety percent of students receive financial aid. No student pays the full cost of his/her education. Earnings from a substantial endowment coupled with generous gifts help reduce the expenses

Interpreting the symbols: **2**=two-year college, **4**=four-year college; **Pu**=public or state college, **Pr**=private college; **G**=general honors program; **D**=departmental honors program; **S**=small program (fewer than 100 students), **M**=midsize program (100 to 500 students), **L**=large program (more than 500 students); **Sc**=scholarships available in honors program; **Tr**=transfer students accepted into honors program; **HBC**=historically black college; **AA**=academic advisors; **GA**=graduate advisors; **FA**=fellowship advisors.

so that charges assessed to students represent only about 75 percent of the cost of their schooling.

Faculty The total number of faculty members is 97; 65 are full-time. Sixty-seven percent of the faculty members have terminal degrees. The student-faculty ratio is 13:1, and the average freshman class size is 30 students.

Key Facilities The library houses 143,862 volumes. In addition, an online search system and resources of more than 200,000 volumes in the Council of Research are available. Texas Lutheran has a computer lab open to all students throughout the week.

Athletics Intercollegiate athletics for men include soccer, tennis, basketball, golf, and baseball. Intercollegiate athletics for women include soccer, tennis, volleyball, basketball, and fast-pitch softball. The campus also has intramural softball, football, basketball, and volleyball, all of which are coed.

Support Services Texas Lutheran provides reserved parking spaces throughout the campus for handicapped students. Most classroom buildings, residence halls, and administrative buildings, as well as the library, have access ramps, and some have elevators.

Job Opportunities Part-time campus jobs are available to students who are in good academic standing. Preference is given to students with financial need, but particular job skills and departmental referral occasionally take precedence. Normally students work 6 to 10 hours per week.

Tuition: $11,374 per year (1999–2000)

Room and Board: $4022

Mandatory Fees: $70

Contact: Director: Dr. Peter Ansorge, Seguin, Texas 78155; Telephone: 830-372-6069; Fax: 210-372-8096; E-mail: pansorge@txlutheran.edu

TEXAS TECH UNIVERSITY

4 Pu G L Tr

▼ University Honors College

An element that distinguishes Texas Tech University (TTU) is its University Honors College, which is available to serve the interests of students from all disciplines, as well as students majoring in the honors multidisciplinary natural history and humanities Bachelor of Arts degree. Accepting only the most academically motivated students, the College is dedicated to examining life and society and to broadening its participants through unusual classes, challenging reading, wide-ranging discussions, and stimulating instruction. Moreover, the University Honors College strives to prepare its participants for a lifetime of self-education.

Several features add to the ideal of educating the honors students at Texas Tech University. The University Honors College produces a wide variety of interdisciplinary classes, where professors especially strive to meet the objective of providing the broadest possible undergraduate educational experience. In addition, the University Honors College sponsors and cooperates with an extensive array of undergraduate research initiatives. Honors advisers provide personal counseling for students who are interested in securing national and international scholarships. The program financially supports study abroad and provides students with information and programs of particular interest. It has special entry and early decision programs for undergraduates who are interested in medical school, law school, and graduate business study. It is also through the honors office that incoming students receive scholarship support at the University—a scholarship program that is among the most generous in the region. Finally, there are special and superior residence hall accommodations available to honors participants. In combination with a number of cocurricular activities and University privileges accorded especially to honors students, the University Honors College is recognized as the ideal opportunity on campus for meeting the special needs and providing the special opportunities that high-end students have and want.

Another unique feature of the Texas Tech University Honors College is its extensive student involvement. Students sit on committees, engage in recruiting, help make decisions on course content and textbooks, and evaluate faculty members. Honors students are members of their own student organization, Eta Omicron Nu, which provides social, service, and other extracurricular opportunities. Honors students also represent the University at national and regional honors conventions, and Honors Ambassadors represent the program at a variety of special events.

Currently, there are approximately 1,000 students at the University Honors College.

Participation Requirements: The University Honors College requires that students maintain a GPA of at least 3.25 to remain in good standing and exhibit meaningful progress toward attaining an honors degree. The honors degree requires 24 hours of honors course work to graduate with honors and 30 hours, including a senior thesis, to graduate with highest honors.

Admission Process: There are several different routes to admission into the Honors College, but in the final analysis, students must be formally accepted before they can take advantage of the various benefits and advantages that the program offers. The minimum requirement for application to the University Honors College consists of one or more of the following: a cumulative SAT I score of at least 1200 or a cumulative ACT score of at least 28, graduation within the top 10 percent of the high school class, or submission of a written essay (in addition to the essays required in the application itself) in which compelling reasons are provided for why the above criteria have not been met and an explanation of why the student thinks that he or she would especially benefit by belonging to the University Honors College; continuing Texas Tech students or transfer students must have a GPA of at least 3.4 GPA. Other factors that are considered in the admission process are the nature and extent of extracurricular activities, grades in college-preparatory high school classes, qualities reflected in two letters of recommendation, and a written essay. Complete and current application information and forms are available on the World Wide Web at http://www.honr.ttu.edu.

Because there are limits on the number of students that can be admitted, students must apply to the University Honors College as soon as they are reasonably sure that they will be attending Texas Tech. Applications are accepted each year from about September 1 to April 15. An early decision option allows students to apply by December 15 to receive notice of acceptance by February 1. Students are admitted on a rolling basis as applications are received. Applicants are not admitted outside of these enrollment dates unless there are exceptional circumstances.

Scholarship Availability: A large number of significant scholarships are available; nonresident students who qualify for at least $1000 in scholarship awards from Texas Tech University pay Texas resident tuition, as do students from New Mexico, Oklahoma, and Arkansas who reside in counties bordering Texas. (Residents of New Mexico and Oklahoma from non-bordering counties also pay a greatly reduced rate.) Information and forms are available on the World Wide Web at http://www.fina.ttu.edu.

The Campus Context: Texas Tech University is a comprehensive research institution with nine separate colleges (including the University Honors College), a Law School, and a Health Science Center/Medical School. Founded in 1923, TTU is located in Lubbock, Texas, the premier city of the Southern Great Plains region. With a graduate and undergraduate enrollment of 25,000, Texas Tech is large enough to offer a multiplicity of programs and degrees yet small enough to retain a small-college ambiance.

Texas Tech University has historically offered excellent and highly personalized educational opportunities combined with the advantages of being a major research institution. The University is attractive and spacious, with remarkably congenial personnel. The city of Lubbock, with a population of 200,000, offers a comfortable level of sophistication while remaining small enough to help ease the transition from high school to college life. Lubbock features numerous cultural, professional, and business opportunities as well as convenient access to a variety of recreational activities, including mountain and water sports. Lubbock Lake Landmark is an archaeological preserve that contains evidence of habitation by a variety of ancient peoples on the Southern High Plains. Its record spans at least 11,500 years, and it is listed on the National Register of Historic Places. In addition, the TTU Museum and Ranching Heritage Center offer unique artistic and cultural opportunities.

Honorary Societies Lambda Sigma, Phi Kappa Phi, Golden Key, and Mortar Board

Tuition: $1260 for state residents and bordering counties (as described above), $2160 for non-bordering New Mexico and Oklahoma counties, and $7590 for nonresidents; $900 for books and supplies, per year (2002–03)

Room and Board: $5537

Mandatory Fees: $2424

Contact: Dean: Gary M. Bell or Associate Dean: Kambra K. Bolch, Room 103, Holden Hall, P.O. Box 41017, Lubbock, Texas 79409-1017; Telephone: 806-742-1828; Fax: 806-742-1805; E-mail: honors@ttu.edu

Texas Woman's University

4 Pu G M Sc Tr

▼ Honors Scholar Program

The Honors Scholar Program at Texas Woman's University (TWU) provides talented and motivated students in all majors an enriched academic and cultural environment. The three-fold emphasis upon the development of skills in writing, research, and technology provides students with preparation that will be useful to them throughout their careers.

While its students strive for academic excellence in the classroom, they also enjoy ample cultural and social opportunities throughout the year. Students in the program organize cultural activities that include attendance and theatrical performances, music recitals, dance performances, and tours of various art galleries and museums. The University's proximity to the Dallas–Ft. Worth Metroplex offers program participants a wide variety of cultural and social experiences. Students regularly attend and present at the National Collegiate Honors Council and the Great Plains Honors Council. The program sponsors a trip abroad each year; past destinations included London, northern Spain, and southern Italy.

The program was begun in 2000 and currently has 200 students. The TWU honors program is diverse, with 14 percent Hispanic and 11 percent African-American students. Enrollment is limited to 5 percent of the undergraduate student body in order to provide participants with individualized assistance in areas ranging from advising to career planning to the preparation of scholarship and graduate school applications.

Currently, there are three honors floors in the residence halls, each with a study lounge or kitchenette. Students in the program enjoy membership in the Athenian Honor Society (the cultural, social, and representative organization for participants) and a number of campus privileges, including early registration and extended library privileges.

Upon completion, students graduate as TWU honors scholars and receive recognition at commencement, an honors scholar medallion, a certificate, and an acknowledgment of participation on both the diploma and University transcripts.

Participation Requirements: The Honors Scholar Program accepts students either as new freshmen or as transfer students. All students must complete 24 hours of honors-designated course work, which includes a three-hour capstone project in the senior year. These hours may be fulfilled through a combination of honors course work, honors contract work, or select graduate courses in the student's major field. Students are allowed to select any combination of honors courses being offered and consult with the Director and academic advisers to tailor a program of honors study to their particular major. Students must maintain a minimum GPA of 3.30 throughout.

Admission Process: Students must apply to the Honors Scholar Program for admission. The application requires students to provide basic information about their academic preparation and their leadership, creative, athletic, or service experiences. Applicants are also asked to provide three references and a brief personal statement. Telephone or in-person interviews are conducted by the program's director.

Freshmen are admitted on the basis of SAT I scores, high school grades and rank, and extracurricular activities. While admissions decisions are based on a combination of factors, generally the admissions committee gives preference to students with a minimum SAT score of 1200 and to those who are in the top 10 percent of their high school class. New freshmen seeking admission for the fall semester should submit applications no later than April 1.

Transfer students are accepted on the basis of college GPA and extracurricular activities. As with freshman applicants, the admissions committee considers more than grades alone but gives preference to candidates with a GPA of 3.5 or higher. Students who have completed an honors program at an NCHC-member two-year school are guaranteed admission. Up to 12 hours of honors credit may be accepted from honors programs that are NCHC-member institutions. Transfer students may apply at any time.

Scholarship Availability: Texas Woman's University provides substantial academic scholarship support to qualified candidates, including several scholarships for honors program participants each year. In addition, the Honors Scholars Program provides assistance for all participants in identifying and applying for departmental, university-wide, and external scholarships. The University's new international study scholarships provide assistance for those seeking to study abroad.

The Campus Context: Texas Woman's University is a four-year, coeducational, public university. The main campus is in Denton, a community of almost 80,000, located 35 miles north of the Dallas–Ft. Worth Metroplex, the ninth-largest urban center. Clinical centers are located in Dallas and Houston. TWU was established in 1901 and continues its mission of providing quality education to all students, especially women. Old Main, the University's first building, still stands upon the beautiful 270-acre wooded main campus, along with the historic Little Chapel-in-the-Woods. The undergraduate student enrollment is 4,476, and 106 undergraduate programs are offered. TWU consists of six colleges and schools: the College of Arts and Sciences, the College of Professional Education, the College of Health Sciences, the College of Nursing, the School of Occupational Therapy, and the School of Physical Therapy. There is also a Graduate School.

Student Body The total student enrollment is 7,928, of whom 91 percent are women. The undergraduate enrollment is 4,405, and

Interpreting the symbols: **2**=two-year college, **4**=four-year college; **Pu**=public or state college, **Pr**=private college; **G**=general honors program; **D**=departmental honors program; **S**=small program (fewer than 100 students), **M**=midsize program (100 to 500 students), **L**=large program (more than 500 students); **Sc**=scholarships available in honors program; **Tr**=transfer students accepted into honors program; **HBC**=historically black college; **AA**=academic advisors; **GA**=graduate advisors; **FA**=fellowship advisors.

the undergraduate ethnic distribution is 61 percent white, 21 percent African American, 10.9 percent Hispanic, 4.6 percent Asian/Pacific Islander, .7 percent Native American and Alaskan Native, and 2 percent International.

Faculty The faculty numbers 762, with 52 percent full-time. The student-faculty ratio is 13:1.

Key Facilities TWU's Blagg-Huey Library has holdings of 549,116 print volumes, 10,000 e-book volumes, 8,287 current periodical and serial publications, 1,532,563 microforms, and 84,120 audio visual materials to support all major areas of study. In addition to the standard printed bibliographies, indexes, and abstracts in the Reference Department, the library offers Web-based and local access to literature searches from ninety computer databases. Computer labs are located throughout the campus, including the residence halls, the library, the student center, and a new Technology Center containing eighty computer stations is planned for fall 2002.

Honorary Societies Phi Kappa Phi, Golden Key, Alpha Chi, Mortar Board, Phi Theta Kappa (alumni chapter), Athenian Honor Society

Athletics Texas Woman's University competes in Division II NCAA for women in basketball, gymnastics, softball, volleyball. Women's soccer will be added in 2002. In addition, the Wellness Center offers participation in intramural sports, fitness classes, and access to exercise facilities, including indoor and outdoor swimming pools, tennis courts, an indoor track, and an 18-hole golf course.

Study Abroad The Center for International Education offers study-abroad opportunities for brief field travel, summer sessions, and semester-long and yearlong study. Texas Woman's University is an affiliate of the American Institute for Foreign Study and has a study-abroad program with Harlaxton College in England.

Support Services TWU is committed to providing assistance and accommodation to qualified students with specific disabilities or needs. The Office of Disability Services serves as a liaison for students with disabilities and as a referral resource for support services on campus and in the community.

Job Opportunities Many jobs are available to students both on- and off-campus. Employment is coordinated through the Career Services Office.

Tuition: Yearly tuition is $2340 for state residents and $8790 for nonresidents.

Mandatory Fees: Yearly fees are estimated at $790 per student.

Room and Board: $4428

Contact: Director: Dr. Guy Litton, P.O. Box 425678, Texas Woman's University, Denton, Texas 76204-5678; Telephone: 940-898-2337; Fax: 940-898-2835; E-mail: alitton@twu.edu; Web site: www.twu.edu

THIEL COLLEGE

4 Pr G S Sc Tr

▼ Honors Program

The purpose of the Thiel College Honors Program is to provide an integrative education designed to enhance the student's critical thinking, to enable the student to make connections among disciplines, and to promote the student's understanding of cultures around the world. In order to provide a sound educational structure within which honors students may exercise significant choice, the Honors Program requires completion of a separate Honors Core as a substitute for the college's general education requirements. Distinctive to this core are interdisciplinary courses that emphasize multiple ways of seeing and knowing, the complex interrelatedness among elements in the cultural and natural worlds, techniques of information gathering, gaining skill in problem solving, gaining experiences in the process of making value choices among alternatives, and openness to accepting the criticism of ideas.

In addition to the course work, participation in the Honors Program includes a number of special opportunities and activities, all of which are intended to encourage growth in an environment of small classes and meetings, free intellectual inquiry, and close association with professors and other members of the college community. These activities include discussion sessions with visiting artists, scholars, and public figures; travel to cultural events in Cleveland and Pittsburgh as well as annual trips to such sites as Toronto or Washington, D.C., and to the Mid-East Honors Association conference; and social events that bring together all participants in the program, including an annual dinner at the home of the President of the College. In addition, students enjoy the benefits of an honors center for study or small group meetings and honors housing.

The program was founded in 1981, and there are approximately 60 current student participants.

Participation Requirements: The Honors Program core consists of 36 to 48 credit hours, depending upon the student's foreign language placement. Requirements include a yearlong sophomore interdisciplinary course and a yearlong junior capstone course in which the student completes an original creative or problem-solving project under the direction of a faculty mentor. These courses are distinctive to the Honors Program, having no equivalents elsewhere in the curriculum. The student also completes a year each of Western Humanities and Science and Global Heritage with honors discussion sections and distinctive honors sections of freshman composition and religion. Each student must demonstrate language competency at the intermediate level.

To remain in the program, a student must maintain at least a 3.0 cumulative GPA with no more than one semester below 3.0. Successful completion of the program is recognized in the commencement program and by the wearing of an honors cord at graduation. It is also noted on the student's official transcript and by a gold seal attached to the diploma.

Admission Process: Applicants to the College who have an 1140 or higher SAT I, a 25 or higher ACT, or rank in the upper 5 percent of their high school graduating classes are automatically invited to join the program. There are no deadlines for application, since all students are admitted to the College on a rolling basis. Students may also apply for admission during the spring semester of their freshman year if they earned at least a 3.0 in the fall term and have a faculty member's recommendation. All students may participate in the program regardless of their majors or fields of study. All decisions about admission or retention within the program are subject to review by the Honors Program Committee.

Scholarship Availability: Freshmen entering the program are eligible to compete for a variety of academic scholarships. Upperclass students are eligible to apply for a number of endowed scholarships, one of which is restricted to Honors Program students and provides several awards each year. Most program participants receive academic scholarships.

The Campus Context: Thiel College is located in the western Pennsylvania community of Greenville, a town with a population of approximately 6,000. Although the immediate area is semi-rural, Greenville enjoys easy highway access to the museums, libraries, and other cultural institutions and recreational opportunities to be found in Pittsburgh and Cleveland (each 75 miles away), Erie (65 miles), and Youngstown (35 miles). Thiel was founded in 1866 and is affiliated with the Evangelical Lutheran Church in America. The College offers the B.A. degree in the various fields of the humanities, arts, social sciences, natural sciences, and preprofessional disciplines as well as a B.S.N. The College houses The Haller Enterprise Institute, The Thiel Center for Women's Leadership, and The Institute for Science and Religion in a Global Context.

Student Body The undergraduate enrollment is approximately 1,000, made up of 53 percent women and 47 percent men. About 87 percent of the students are white, 8 percent are African American, and 5 percent are international, coming primarily from countries in Asia and Africa. About 70 percent of the students are residential, while about 20 percent are nontraditional. Approximately 96 percent of the students receive some form of financial aid. There are four national social fraternities and four national social sororities with chapters on campus.

Faculty There are 90 faculty members, of whom 56 are full-time. Ninety-three percent of full-time faculty members have terminal degrees in their fields. The student-faculty ratio is approximately 12:1.

Key Facilities Langenheim Memorial Library contains more than 155,000 volumes and receives more than 1,200 journals in addition to serving as a federal depository library—the number of government documents now numbering more than 290,000. The library has been a part of the OCLC computer network since 1983 and also subscribes to a number of other online services. There are presently four computer labs on campus providing Internet and e-mail access for students. Beginning in 1999–2000, the campus will be fully wired for computer access, including each residence hall room, and a 24-hour computer lab will be available in the newly remodeled and expanded student center.

Honorary Societies Alpha Chi, Lambda Sigma, and Les Lauriers

Athletics Thiel is a member of the NCAA Division III Presidents' Athletic Conference in which it competes in eighteen men's and women's sports. The College's Rissell-Beeghley Gymnasia provide facilities both for intercollegiate competition and for a full range of intramural sports. In addition, the College has just completed construction of new tennis courts and is planning to build its first on-campus football stadium.

Study Abroad Study abroad is required of international business and modern languages majors. Colleges and universities with which Thiel has articulation agreements, including in some cases student exchange programs, are located in South Korea, Japan, and Malaysia, with new initiatives underway with institutions in China and Russia. The College has also sponsored summer travel for students to Europe, Central America, and South America.

Support Services The Academic Resource Center and Writing Lab provide advising and tutoring services staffed both by a professional staff and by students. The Language-Media Lab and Audio-Visual Services make available a full range of instructional media and equipment. Services for students with disabilities are arranged through the Academic Resource Center Director. The College also has a part-time professional counseling service in affiliation with Sharon Regional Health Systems.

Job Opportunities More than half of Thiel students have work-study positions as part of their financial aid packages. Most academic departments include internships and cooperative education among their options for majors, and the College maintains a full-time Cooperative Education Office to assist students in making arrangements. Many of these placements include both academic credit and compensation.

Tuition: $9990 full-time, $260–$433 part-time (1999–2000)

Room and board: $5374 (1998–99)

Mandatory Fees: $170 minimum

Contact: Director: Dr. Margarita E. Garcia Casado, Assistant Professor of French, 75 College Avenue, Greenville, Pennsylvania 16125-2181; Telephone: 724-589-2081; Fax: 724-589-2021. NCHC Small College Committee Representative: Dr. Jay A. Ward, Professor of English and Former Honors Program Director; Telephone: 724-589-2161; E-mail: jward@thiel.edu; Web site: http://www.thiel.edu; (click on Academics)

TOWSON UNIVERSITY

4 Pu D C S Sc

▼ Honors Programs

Honors programs at Towson University include the Honors College and the Departmental Honors Program.

The Honors College at Towson University is a community of scholars interested in intellectual interaction, academic achievement, and leadership opportunities. Students may major in any field at Towson and be part of the Honors College. Established in 1969, the Honors College includes more than 800 students who take exclusive honors classes, live in honors residence halls, conduct research with faculty members, and participate in special honors study-abroad programs. Honors College classes are small (usually enrolling 18 or fewer students) to facilitate discussion and collaborative learning.

Honors College students are required to complete 18 credits of Honors College courses. Honors College courses are offered in a variety of disciplines and the majority of them satisfy the University's general education requirements. Honors seminar courses on various topics are offered as well. In addition, leadership courses in Community Service and Community Building provide an opportunity for honors students to integrate service-learning into their class schedules.

Getting involved and connecting with the campus are also part of the Honors College experience. Honors students are invited to join Excelsior, the Honors Student Association, which organizes activities such as barbecues, trips to Baltimore theaters, and volunteer opportunities with groups like Habitat for Humanity. The Honors College also offers guidance and support to students applying for fellowships and grants for advanced academic work, such as the Fulbright or Marshall Scholar awards.

The Honors College is headquartered on the fifth floor of Cook Library. The Honors College Lounge is a convenient place to study or relax, with computers available for e-mail, research, and word processing. Another center of Honors College activities is the Lieberman Room in the Lecture Hall, which houses an extraordinary collection of contemporary paintings, drawings, and sculptures. The Richmond Hall Commons Room is a fully equipped, high-tech classroom used for a number of honors courses. It also serves as a meeting place for special Honors College functions and as a study lounge for honors students.

The Departmental Honors Program is distinct from the Honors College. It represents intensive, individualized, and directed education beyond the normal course of instruction. The program includes 6 to 9 credits in seminars, directed readings, and research projects in the major. A senior thesis is required, as is an oral defense of the thesis.

To be admitted to the program, students must present a cumulative GPA of at least 3.25 and a minimum GPA of 3.5 in their major, or have the consent of their faculty adviser. Students who complete an approved program receive a diploma and transcript with the designation Bachelor of Science or Bachelor of Arts with honors. Currently, the departments of art; biological sciences; computer and information sciences; economics; electronic media and film; English; history; mass communication and communication studies; mathematics; modern languages; kinesiol-

Interpreting the symbols: **2**=two-year college, **4**=four-year college; **Pu**=public or state college, **Pr**=private college; **G**=general honors program; **D**=departmental honors program; **S**=small program (fewer than 100 students), **M**=midsize program (100 to 500 students), **L**=large program (more than 500 students); **Sc**=scholarships available in honors program; **Tr**=transfer students accepted into honors program; **HBC**=historically black college; **AA**=academic advisors; **GA**=graduate advisors; **FA**=fellowship advisors.

ogy; physics, astronomy, and geosciences; political science; psychology; and sociology, anthropology, and criminal justice offer Departmental Honors Programs.

Students interested in Departmental Honors should meet with their faculty adviser and the chairperson or honors coordinator of their major department to discuss their plans at the beginning of their sophomore year.

Participation Requirements: To graduate from the Honors College, students must maintain a minimum cumulative GPA of 3.5 and complete 18 credits of Honors College courses. It is recommended that students take at least one Honors College course each semester until completion of the 18 credits.

To be eligible for Departmental Honors, students must have a minimum GPA of 3.25 and a GPA of at least 3.5 in those courses. To graduate with departmental honors, the student must complete and successfully defend a research thesis or a creative project (depending on the major) and maintain at least a 3.25 overall average and a minimum 3.5 average in required courses in the major.

Admission Process: Incoming freshmen are considered for admission to the Honors College if they meet one or more of the following criteria: a minimum SAT I score of 1180 with a minimum 620 verbal; placement in the top 10 percent of their high school graduating class or a high school GPA of at least 3.5, with an SAT I minimum of 550 verbal and 500 math; or special permission of the Honors Program Director after review of the student's academic record. Students transferring from another college or university must have a minimum GPA of 3.50 in order to be considered for participation in the Honors College.

Scholarship Availability: Honors College scholarships are awarded on a competitive basis to incoming students admitted to the Honors College. An application and essay are required. Recipients are required to remain in good standing in the Honors College to continue to receive the scholarship.

In addition, Towson University awards a limited number of academic scholarships to qualified incoming freshmen and transfer students each fall. Candidates who are selected as admissions applications are received from academically gifted high school seniors and from Maryland community college transfer students with an A.A. degree. Priority is granted to the earliest admission applicants. No separate application for these scholarships is needed, but an admission application, transcripts, and test results should be filed and completed by December 1. Academic scholarships can only be applied toward educational expenses at the University.

The Campus Context: Founded in 1866, Towson University is nationally recognized today for its excellent and affordable programs in the arts, sciences, business, communications, health professions, education, and computer science. Towson offers a student-centered learning environment that encourages the development of the whole person. Academic programs are offered though eight colleges: the College of Business and Economics, the College of Education, the College of Fine Arts and Communication, the College of Health Professions, the College of Liberal Arts, the College of Science and Mathematics, and the College of Graduate Education and Research, and the College of Extended Programs. Students may choose from sixty undergraduate majors and thirty-five graduate programs.

The second-largest institution in the University System of Maryland, Towson enrolls nearly 17,000 students, including more than 800 international students. The University is located on a beautiful rolling campus in the northern suburbs of Baltimore, convenient to the amenities of both the Baltimore and Washington metropolitan areas. Because of its location, Towson is able to place students in internships in many state and federal government agencies.

The general education curriculum at Towson stresses contexts for learning that include the impact of science and technology on all dimensions of experience; American social, political, economic, and cultural history and how it shapes choices for the future; cultural legacies from the Western heritage and how they predicate, advance, or impede contemporary understanding and choices; and global awareness and recognition of the role of human diversity in a rapidly evolving world order. The general education curriculum also stresses the development of skills for gathering and evaluating information, analyzing and interpreting, weighing alternatives, forming and expressing opinions and conclusions, appreciating diverse points of view, and moving comfortably in the realm of ideas and values.

Student Body In fall 2001, Towson University enrolled 13,959 undergraduates, including 11,757 full-time and 2,202 part-time students. Sixty percent of the students are women. The ethnic distribution of the student body is 10 percent African American; 5 percent Native American, Asian, and Hispanic; 77 percent Caucasian; and 3 percent international. Resident students make up 31 percent of full-time undergraduates. Approximately 66 percent of students receive financial assistance. There are thirteen fraternities and ten sororities.

Faculty Of the 1,219 total faculty members, 571 are full-time. Eighty-four percent of full-time faculty members hold terminal degrees. The student-faculty ratio is 18:1.

Key Facilities The Albert S. Cook Library, located near the center of the campus, contains more than 580,000 books, more than 2,180 periodicals, and a variety of other media, including microforms, audiocassettes, videos and DVDs. In addition to Towson's library, the online catalog gives Towson students access to the collections of all the other University System of Maryland campus libraries. The more than 75 online databases and 400 electronic journals provide indexing to thousands of periodical articles, many of which are full text.

Towson has thirty-five computer labs throughout the campus. Some are maintained centrally as general computer labs, but most are equipped to meet the specific needs of students in the departments that maintain them. For instance, the sociology/ anthropology/political science computer lab includes network software for complex analysis and communication software for an interinstitutional course in international negotiation.

Athletics An NCAA Division I program since 1979, Towson University fields intercollegiate athletic teams in twenty-three sports. The Tigers have twelve sports for women and eleven sports for men. The Tigers compete in the Colonial Athletic Association in twenty-one of those sports, joining CAA rivals Delaware, Drexel, Hofstra, George Mason, James Madison, North Carolina at Wilmington, Old Dominion, Virginia Commonwealth and the College of William and Mary. In addition, the nationally recognized Tiger gymnastics team competes in the East Atlantic Gymnastics League while the Tiger football squad is a member of the Patriot League. The University's 24-acre sports complex includes Minnegan Stadium, home of the Tiger football, field hockey, track, and lacrosse teams. With a seating capacity of 5,000, the Towson Center is the home of the Tiger basketball teams as well as the volleyball and gymnastics squads. The University's athletic facilities include an NCAA-regulation swimming pool, gymnasiums, weight-training rooms, a sand volleyball court, tennis courts, fitness centers, and racquetball and squash courts. Towson also offers a comprehensive intramural program for men and women.

The Tigers field men's teams in baseball, basketball, cross-country, football, golf, indoor track, lacrosse, outdoor track and field, soccer, swimming and diving, and tennis. Women's teams are fielded in basketball, cross-country, field hockey, gymnastics, indoor track, lacrosse, outdoor track and field, soccer, softball, swimming and diving, tennis, and volleyball. Both men's and women's teams compete for state, regional, and national honors under the guidance of an outstanding coaching staff.

Study Abroad Towson offers opportunities for study in more than forty countries in Asia, Australia, Canada, Central and South

America, Europe, and the Middle East. More than 180 students from a variety of disciplines participate in study-abroad and exchange programs each year.

The Honors College offers special study-abroad programs during the summer and minimester. The honors programs of the University of Maryland College Park; The University of Maryland, Baltimore County; and Towson University offer a joint study-abroad program for honors students at all Maryland colleges and universities each summer.

Support Services Towson University provides services and accommodations to students with documented disabilities to ensure that its programs and activities are fully accessible. The University does not have a specially designed program for students with disabilities, but instead offers an array of support services and accommodations that are coordinated by the Disability Support Services (DSS) office. Students seeking accommodations and services must identify themselves to DSS and request an appointment to discuss their needs and requests. Students are encouraged to register with DSS as soon as possible after admission to the University to ensure timely provision of services. Up-to-date documentation of a disability is required for services, and accommodations are provided on the basis of individual needs and circumstances. Services include: preadmission counseling; priority registration; authorization of accommodations and assistance with implementing them; arrangements for readers and recorded texts, note-takers, and sign language interpreters; access to assistive technology; short-term instructional support; orientation and mobility services; and liaison with and referral for additional services available on campus and in the community.

Job Opportunities The Career Center is a resource for jobs and internships on- and off-campus. Many undergraduates find part-time jobs at Towson in clerical positions, tutoring, ushering at sports events, managing recreational facilities, graphics production, monitoring computer labs, and technical work.

Tuition: $5189 for state residents, $12,368 for nonresidents, per year (estimated 2002–03); additional academic fees may be incurred based on the courses taken.

Room and Board: $6322

Contact: Honors College, Towson University, 8000 York Road, Towson, Maryland 21252-0001; Telephone: 410-704-4677; Fax: 410-704-4916; E-mail: honors@towson.edu; Web site: http://www.towson.edu/honors

TRINITY CHRISTIAN COLLEGE

4 Pr G S Tr

▼ Honors Program

The Honors Program of Trinity Christian College provides a community of challenge and support for academically gifted students. These students take delight in learning and discovery both inside and outside of the classroom. The program began in the fall of 1998 and includes 75 students. Because Trinity's Honors Program is driven by the conviction that effective education must involve learners as whole persons, the program situates its academic, curricular components within a rich context of cocurricular opportunities. These opportunities include exploring and enjoying the cultural resources of Chicago, cultivating friendships with fellow students and faculty members through social interaction, spiritual growth, and service through projects on Trinity's campus and in the surrounding community.

The curriculum of the Honors Program is designed to foster the development of intellectual responsibility, encouraging students to become responsible for their own ideas and intellectual growth. They are also responsible to their fellow students through participating in a collaborative approach to learning. In addition, students are responsible to society through discovering, articulating, and beginning to implement a personal vision for Christian intellectual leadership in their vocations and in public life. This emphasis on the development of intellectual responsibility is evident in the structure and content of honors courses. These courses range in size from 5 to 15 students and are conducted in a seminar style, which offers intensive, personal engagement with faculty members and fellow students. The focus of honors courses is on foundational issues approached through primary texts, with constant attention to the relevance of these texts and issues to life today.

Participation Requirements: During their freshman year, students take an honors writing course, which substitutes for the required writing course in the college core. During their sophomore year, students take an honors philosophy course; this course substitutes for one of the required philosophy courses in the college core. During their sophomore, junior, or senior year, students take at least one interdisciplinary honors seminar course centered around a specific topic. During their junior or senior year, students complete at least 2 semester hours of honors work in their major discipline. In addition, each student in the Honors Program has two of their Interim courses designated for honors credit by arrangement with the Honors Program Director Interim is a two-week, 2-credit term in January and all Trinity students are required to take courses in at least two Interim terms.

To remain in the Honors Program, students must have a minimum 3.3 cumulative GPA at the end of each academic year. To graduate from the Honors Program, students must complete the honors curriculum and have at least a 3.5 cumulative GPA upon graduation. Successful completion is recognized at the College's Honors Convocation and is noted on the student's official transcript.

Admission Process: Incoming freshmen are invited to apply for admission to the Honors Program if they have a minimum ACT composite score of 28 and are either in the top 10 percent of their graduating class or have at least a 3.5 GPA on a 4.0 scale. Students who do not meet these criteria or who are not formally part of the program may apply to the Director of the Honors Program for permission to enroll in honors courses.

Trinity students may apply for admission to the Honors Program after the freshman year if they have a cumulative GPA of at least 3.5. Transfer students who transfer fewer than 33 credits and have a minimum ACT composite score of 28 and at least a 3.5 GPA in college-level course work may also apply. The deadline for prospective new students to apply to the program is March 1.

Scholarship Availability: Scholarships of various amounts, based on academic performance, leadership (in athletics, music, journalism, or student organizations), or demonstrated need, are awarded through the Office of Admission and Financial Aid. No scholarships are directly administered by the Honors Program. All entering students are automatically considered for honors scholarships when their applications are reviewed. Most students in the Honors Program are recipients of academic or leadership scholarships.

The Campus Context: Trinity Christian College is a liberal arts college committed to developing and articulating a vision of Christ's lordship over all of life, building a community distinguished by Christian integrity and love, and equipping servants of Jesus Christ for lives of meaningful action. Trinity is located in Palos Heights, Illinois, which is a suburban community of 12,000 people nestled among thousands of acres of forest preserves just half an hour's drive southwest of the heart of Chicago. The 50-acre campus offers tangible evidence of the College's recent growth

Interpreting the symbols: **2**=two-year college, **4**=four-year college; **Pu**=public or state college, **Pr**=private college; **G**=general honors program; **D**=departmental honors program; **S**=small program (fewer than 100 students), **M**=midsize program (100 to 500 students), **L**=large program (more than 500 students); **Sc**=scholarships available in honors program; **Tr**=transfer students accepted into honors program; **HBC**=historically black college; **AA**=academic advisors; **GA**=graduate advisors; **FA**=fellowship advisors.

and bright future. The College has a national reputation for providing high-quality, reasonably priced Christian liberal arts education. Trinity graduates are known for their integrity, intelligence, and conscientiousness.

Trinity offers major courses of study in accountancy, art, biology, business, business communication, business education, chemistry, church education, communication arts, computer science, elementary education, English, exercise science, history, information systems, mathematics, music, nursing, philosophy, physical education, psychology, sociology, science education, Spanish, special education, and theology. Professional programs include accounting and business, education and special education, nursing, pre–physical therapy, allied health services, predentistry, prelaw, premedicine, and preseminary.

Student Body In fall 2001, 794 students were enrolled at Trinity, 61 percent of whom were women. About two thirds live on campus in one of five residence halls. The Molenhouse Student Center serves as the focal point for student services and activities. The Student Association supervises student organizations and promotes student involvement at Trinity through its committees on student activities, academic affairs, student publications, and student ministries.

Faculty The total number of faculty members is 108. Forty-nine are full-time faculty members, of whom 62 percent have their terminal degree. All full-time faculty members teach classes and advise students. The average class size is 31 students for core classes and 10 students for upper-division courses. Small class size allows students to receive individual attention and meaningful feedback from professors. The faculty-student ratio is 1:13.3.

Key Facilities The Jennie Huizenga Memorial Library contains 71,816 volumes. There are four labs equipped with computers for student work. The labs, computers in the library, and all residence-hall rooms have Internet access.

Athletics Trinity supports varsity sports in men's soccer, basketball, volleyball, and baseball and in women's soccer, volleyball, basketball, and softball. Opportunities for participation at the club level are available in women's tennis and men's and women's track and field.

Trinity competes in the Chicagoland Collegiate Athletic Conference (CCAC) and is a member of the National Association of Intercollegiate Athletics (NAIA) and the National Christian College Athletic Association (NCCAA).

Study Abroad Trinity offers an outstanding program for studying beginning, intermediate, or advanced Spanish in the ancient city of Seville, Spain. The semester in Spain program offers courses of study for a semester; Trinity's Interim term, which is two weeks in January, or an entire year. Students may also participate in an in-depth study of the history and culture of the Netherlands in association with Dordt College.

Trinity is also a member of the Council for Christian Colleges and Universities, which is an association of more than 100 Christ-centered institutions of higher education. The council offers students programs in Hollywood, California; San Jose, Costa Rica; Cairo, Egypt; Oxford, England; Shanghai, China; Nizhni Novgorod, Russia; and Washington, D.C.

Support Services Trinity's academic services coordinator can arrange for tutoring or other support services as requested by students. The College also provides legally mandated services for persons with disabilities who voluntarily seek additional services.

Job Opportunities Under the Federal Work-Study Program, eligible students may obtain on-campus employment by which they can earn up to $1400 per academic year. In addition, a number of on-campus positions are available for interested students. Many students find jobs off campus in the Chicagoland area in a variety of businesses and services.

Tuition: $13,470 per year; approximately $465 per semester hour (2001–02)

Room and board: $5445

Contact: Director: Aron D. Reppmann, 6601 West College Drive, Palos Heights, Illinois 60463; Telephone: 708-239-4750; Fax: 708-597-5858; E-mail: aron.reppmann@trnty.edu; Web site: http://www.trnty.edu/depts/honors/

Truman State University

4 Pu G S Tr

▼ General Honors in Arts and Sciences

Truman State University's General Honors Program is not the usual honors program. With its outstanding student body (Truman is a highly selective institution), highly qualified faculty and staff members, small class sizes, interdisciplinary seminars, and Residential College Program, Truman already gives every student the benefits many universities can only give to their honors students. All Truman State University students are eligible to pursue general honors by taking the courses designated by the respective disciplines as being those courses whose successful completion by a nonmajor is especially noteworthy. These courses explore in-depth topics or encourage a more sophisticated viewpoint than the general requirements.

Participation Requirements: General Honors in Arts and Sciences is awarded to graduating seniors who have completed five approved courses, with at least one course from each of the areas of mathematics, science, humanities, and social science and with a cumulative GPA of at least 3.5. Only grades of A and B count toward the general honors GPA requirement of at least 3.5 in those five courses. Only courses with 3 or more hours of credit count toward general honors. Students who complete a single undergraduate major may not satisfy general honors requirements with any course in their major field. Students who complete two or more majors may use any approved courses to satisfy general honors requirements.

Admission Process: There is no formal admissions process for Truman's General Honors Program. Students are encouraged to attend information sessions and other general honors events and declare their intention to pursue general honors. All students who meet Truman's highly selective admission standards qualify for participation in this program.

Scholarship Availability: Truman State University has a nationwide reputation for providing a high-quality education at an affordable price. In fact, 95 percent of the incoming freshmen receive some form of financial assistance. Currently, there are no scholarships available through the General Honors Program.

The Campus Context: At Truman State University, students have an honors college experience in every classroom. They enjoy smaller classes taught by professors instead of graduate students. With a 15:1 student-faculty ratio and an average class size of 22, students get personal attention from Truman's world-class faculty members. Both in and out of the classroom, professors are committed to the students' success. In an age when most colleges put a premium on faculty research, at Truman, student success is the top priority. Truman students have had exciting internships as early as their freshman year while working with government leaders, business executives, broadcast and print media professionals, accountants, archeologists, marine biologists, advertising agents, doctors, musicians, and artists.

Truman also participates in the Washington Center internship program and sponsors the Missouri Government Internship Program. There are many opportunities for research. Research at Truman spans all disciplines, and each year Truman awards approximately forty institutional grants to undergraduates pursuing research projects. Last year, more than 675 students participated in undergraduate research. These types of real-life experiences can open windows of opportunity and provide a link between the classroom and the world beyond the campus. Truman is proud to showcase the newly renovated Ophelia Parish building. This building houses Truman's Fine Arts Department and includes a state-of-the-art courtyard theater and a blackbox theater; brand-new ceramics, sculpture, printmaking, and fibers studios as well as visual communication and digital computer labs; and a large recital hall, separate rehearsal rooms for band and chorus, and many practice rooms with pianos. Along with the renovations to Ophelia Parish, renovations are scheduled for Magruder Hall (the science building).

Student Body Truman has an undergraduate enrollment of approximately 6,000 students, with about 150 international students from fifty different countries. There are approximately 43 percent men and 57 percent women, and approximately 20 percent of women and 35 percent of men are involved in Greek sororities and fraternities. The list of available cocurricular activities is also extensive. Truman offers general honors, as well as honors in individual disciplines, many professional societies, and diverse opportunities to provide service to both the campus and the community around it. Truman also supports forensic activities, in which intercollegiate speech and debate mixes psychology, critical thinking, research, current events, and communication—truly a liberal arts activity.

Faculty The philosophy of the faculty members at Truman promotes one-to-one interaction and an open-door office policy. Truman's faculty members display a strong commitment to high-quality teaching and to serving as positive role models in and out of the classroom. The limited enrollment allows for an approximate 15:1 student-teacher ratio; 75 percent of the full-time faculty members hold doctorates or terminal degrees. Approximately 95 percent of the freshman classes are taught by regular faculty members who represent most major graduate institutions in the United States and several graduate institutions abroad.

Key Facilities Pickler Memorial Library supports faculty and student research, with a collection of 427,286 volumes, 1,509,988 microforms, and 3,700 serial subscriptions; interlibrary loan services; and access to bibliographic databases online and on compact disc. Truman State University provides many computing resources for students. Whether students use computers available in the computer labs or they bring their own computers, the following resources are available: a Truman State University e-mail account, an account on IBM RS/6000 server running AIX (UNIX), 10 MB of drive space for personal Web sites, and access to campus computer labs, including labs located in each residence hall.

Honorary Societies Phi Beta Kappa, Phi Kappa Phi, Alpha Phi Sigma, Blue Key National Honor Fraternity, Cardinal Key National Honor Society, Omicron Delta Kappa, Phi Eta Sigma, Phi Theta Kappa

Athletics Truman is an NCAA Division II participant in the Mid-America Intercollegiate Athletics Association. Truman offers a wide variety of sports for men and women and is especially well known for women's soccer, swimming, and volleyball.

Study Abroad Study-abroad opportunities are coordinated through the Center for International Education Abroad. International study provides a cross-cultural learning experience that affects students in ways that no classroom can. Each year, more than 300 Truman students study abroad in programs offered around the world. Summer, semester, and yearlong programs are offered, as are internships abroad. Truman is a member of the College Consortium for International Studies (CCIS), the Council on International Educational Exchange (CIEE), Australearn, and the International Student Exchange Program (ISEP). When these programs are combined with ones directly sponsored by Truman, students have access to programs in nearly fifty countries, and the opportunities keep growing.

Support Services The Services for Individuals with Disabilities office coordinates services for students with learning disabilities and physical challenges. Special adaptive equipment is available in Pickler Memorial Library. Several apartments and residence hall rooms have been modified to accommodate students with disabilities. Students and faculty and staff members are encouraged to call the office to make arrangements for special assistance.

Job Opportunities Numerous job opportunities are available to students both on and off campus.

Tuition: $3800, resident; $6928, nonresident (2001–02 academic year)

Room and Board: $4736

Mandatory Fees: $32 activities, $50 parking (optional), $150 freshman orientation

Contact: Dr. Patricia Burton, Director of General Honors Program and Professor of Philosophy, Division of Social Science, McClain 234, 100 East Normal, Kirksville, Missouri 63501; Telephone: 660-785-4636; E-mail: ss84@truman.edu

TULSA COMMUNITY COLLEGE

2 Pu S Sc Tr

▼ Honors Program

The TCC Honors Program offers honors courses to curious and self-motivated students who wish to grow personally and academically. The goal of the program is to provide students with an enriched academic environment through more direct involvement in their own learning experience. Classes are smaller, interaction with peers and professors is lively, and opportunities for independent study are provided. The Honors Program was developed in 1985. TCC currently has 70 Honors Scholars.

Admission Process: All students are welcome to take honors courses; however, a 3.0 GPA is recommended. In order to become an Honors Scholar, the student must meet two of the following criteria: combined score of 1100 on the SAT I or composite ACT score of 25 or above; high school GPA of at least 3.5, ranking in the upper 10 percent of the high school graduating class, or GED score of at least 310, or membership in high school honor society; 3.5 GPA on a minimum of 12 credit hours; demonstration of special abilities or awards in writing or other significant projects; completion of two honors credit courses at TCC with a grade of B or A. Students must also submit a writing sample and a letter of recommendation from a qualified instructor and must be approved by all honors coordinators.

Scholarship Availability: Honors Scholars qualify for the TCC Honors Scholar State Regents Tuition Waiver; the University of Tulsa also offers partial scholarships to TCC Honors Scholar graduates. Also, the TCC Honors Program awards "Talentships" each year to Honors students—honors faculty members recommend students for the award. Academic Scholars Scholarships, which provide eight semesters of support, are awarded to five Honors Scholars each year.

The Campus Context: Tulsa Community College is composed of four campuses: Metro, Northeast, Southeast, and West. Among the distinguished facilities available to students are international language labs, a Disabled Student Center, a Center for the Hearing Impaired, nurseries for horticulture, a performing arts center, a Computer Integrated Manufacturing Center, specialized medical labs, and Career Assessment Centers.

Student Body The student population is 41 percent men and 59 percent women. The ethnic distribution of students is 79 percent white, 8 percent African American, 3 percent Asian American, 6

Interpreting the symbols: **2**=two-year college, **4**=four-year college; **Pu**=public or state college, **Pr**=private college; **G**=general honors program; **D**=departmental honors program; **S**=small program (fewer than 100 students), **M**=midsize program (100 to 500 students), **L**=large program (more than 500 students); **Sc**=scholarships available in honors program; **Tr**=transfer students accepted into honors program; **HBC**=historically black college; **AA**=academic advisors; **GA**=graduate advisors; **FA**=fellowship advisors.

percent Native American, 3 percent Hispanic, 1 percent other. There are 77 international students from forty-eight different countries.

Faculty Of the 1,175 faculty members, 255 are full-time. Fifteen percent of the full-time faculty members hold doctorates. The student-faculty ratio is 21:1.

Key Facilities Library holdings include 114,602 volumes. The Computer Instructional Labs are designed to provide many services to students. These services include microcomputers to support courses where microcomputer technology is used, computer- aided instruction packages to supplement classroom work for certain courses, program construction for computer language courses, instructional assistance for equipment and software usage, and a centralized workspace for students. The labs are staffed with personnel to assist in these areas.

Honorary Society Phi Theta Kappa

Study Abroad Study abroad is encouraged. The International Campus allows students to earn credit for TCC course work taught in another country by TCC faculty members.

Support Services Disabled students will find computer and adaptive equipment, tape recorders and tapes, academic counseling, extended test time, reserved classroom seating, accessible bathrooms, and reserved parking.

Job Opportunities There is a Federal Work-Study program offering approximately 100 positions, with a 20-hour work week.

Tuition: $1237 for state residents, $3117 for nonresidents, per year (1998–99)

Contact: Director: David Lawless, 909 South Boston MC510, Tulsa, Oklahoma 74119-2095; Telephone: 918-595-7378; Fax: 918-595-8378; E-mail: dlawless@tulsa.cc.ok.us

Tyler Junior College

2 Pu G S Sc Tr

▼ Scholars' Academy

"The Scholars' Academy at Tyler Junior College provides a variety of enriched academic experiences for talented and motivated students. Within a system that combines rigorous course work with creative interaction, Scholars' Academy students are challenged to become responsible leaders in their community." This mission statement summarizes the intent of this new program at Tyler Junior College. High school seniors with excellent records and potential are encouraged to consider this new option on their way to a four-year degree. The Scholars' Academy features small classes of core curriculum courses and occasional electives. While all academic disciplines can be involved in the program, most of the honors curriculum will be liberal arts oriented.

Faculty members involved in the program will not only teach the separate honors classes, but will also be involved in extracurricular enrichment activities. Students will be required to take part in special learning opportunities, which include speakers, short trips, and a service learning component.

The Scholars' Academy has its own lounge/study area that houses a classroom as well as offices for the director of the program and a faculty adviser. The lounge is equipped with computers for student use.

Each student will be given special attention in planning their two-year curriculum and in registering for classes each semester. In addition, the director and faculty advisers will assist the student in securing admission and seeking scholarships for further study.

The Tyler Junior College Scholars' Academy will receive its first students in fall 1999.

Participation Requirements: Students in the Scholars' Academy must complete 21 hours of honors courses to qualify for recognition at graduation. A 3-hour leadership seminar is a required part of this program. To continue in the program, students must maintain at least a 3.2 GPA. In addition, 12 clock hours of community service are required of each student in the program. Both the transcript and the diploma will indicate that the student has graduated from the Scholars' Academy.

Admission Process: Admission to the Scholars' Academy is determined by a variety of factors. They are a minimum 3.5 GPA on high school work, a minimum ACT of 23 or SAT I of 1070, extracurricular/leadership activities, recommendations from 2 teachers, and an essay. Transfer students are encouraged to apply to the program once they are accepted by the College.

Scholarship Availability: Scholarships are available for all academy students. As the program grows, the level of scholarship aid may vary and be competitive.

The Campus Context: Tyler Junior College was founded in 1926 and is the largest single-campus community college in Texas. Its many educational and cultural activities have engendered a close relationship with the community and the surrounding East Texas area. Opportunities in music, theater, and athletics are a regular and outstanding feature of community life in Tyler. Through programs initiated by the business, science, and liberal arts schools, the College reaches out to students and adults in the region.

Tyler Junior College, with a student body of approximately 8,000, offers the Associate in Arts and Associate in Applied Science degrees plus technical certificates.

Honorary Societies Phi Theta Kappa

Contact: Interim Director: Dr. Gene Kirkpatrick, Box 1090 TJC, Tyler, Texas 75711; Telephone: 903-510-2439; Email: gkir@tjc.tyler.cc.tx.us.

University at Buffalo, The State University of New York

4 Pu G L Sc Tr

▼ University Honors Program

The University Honors Program at the University at Buffalo, The State University of New York (UB), provides academically talented students with the opportunity to pursue a rigorous and challenging intellectual experience within their undergraduate studies. In bringing to UB some of the brightest high school students in the United States, the honors program creates a small-college atmosphere within a large university setting. Here, each honors scholar has the opportunity to create a program of study that fits his or her unique interests.

The honors program encompasses all undergraduate divisions. Approximately 250 students are admitted each year. Included in this number are 10 students who enter as performing and creative arts scholars and who major in art, dance, media study, music, and theater. Honors scholars receive merit-based scholarships, participate in small honors seminars, are provided with a faculty mentor upon entrance to UB, attend Evening with Faculty programs, and work on major research projects early in their college careers.

In addition, each semester the honors program accepts highly qualified current University students into the Advanced Honors Program. Students are eligible to apply once they have completed 45 credit hours and have a minimum overall GPA of 3.5. Transfer students are eligible to apply and should contact the honors program office for transfer student admissions criteria.

The 20-year-old program currently enrolls more than 900 students.

Participation Requirements: To maintain their status in the University Honors Program, entering freshman honors scholars participate in the Freshman Honors Colloquium during their first semester. In addition, they complete four honors seminars within their first two years of study at UB. Freshmen must maintain a minimum GPA of 3.2. Sophomore, junior, and senior honors scholars must maintain a 3.5 GPA each semester and cumulatively to graduate as honors scholars. Students in the program receive the following transcript notation: University Honors Scholars, University Honors Program.

Admission Process: Freshmen entering the honors program are selected on the basis of their high school average and SAT scores. University at Buffalo applications are due by the end of December. Additional applications are required for Distinguished Honors Scholarships and Performing and Creative Arts Scholarships.

Scholarship Availability: Students who qualify for the honors program receive one of three scholarships: the Distinguished Honors Scholarship, which covers the entire cost of attending UB for four years (including tuition, room, board, fees, and expenses), a $4000-per-year scholarship for four years, or a $2500-per-year scholarship for four years. Students selected for the Performing and Creative Arts Program receive $2500 per year for four years. Distinguished Honors Scholarship applicants must submit a separate application, including an essay, a resume, and letters of recommendation. Performing and Creative Arts applicants must submit a separate application to the program; auditions, portfolios, and a personal interview are required. Advanced honors scholars are selected on the basis of their college performance, a written personal statement, and letters of recommendation from their professors. Scholarships are not available to advanced honors students.

The Campus Context: The State University of New York at Buffalo is composed of many schools and faculties offering more than 100 undergraduate majors and sixty-four minors: the School of Architecture and Planning, College of Arts and Sciences, School of Engineering and Applied Sciences, School of Health Related Professions, School of Informatics, School of Management, School of Medicine and Biomedical Sciences, School of Nursing, and School of Pharmacy and Pharmaceutical Sciences. Those with graduate programs only are the School of Dental Medicine, Graduate School of Education, School of Law, and School of Social Work.

The University at Buffalo is the largest of SUNY's sixty-four units and the largest public university in the Northeast. It is a member of the Association of American Universities, the most prestigious academic organization in the country. The University is located on two campuses. UB's original campus, located in the northeast corner of Buffalo, houses the Schools of Dentistry and Medicine and Biomedical Sciences. Three miles away in the town of Amherst is the 1,200-acre North campus. Highlights of this campus include the Center for the Arts, which contains three theaters, two dance studios, a University gallery, and an art department gallery; the Center for Computational Research, which houses one of the leading academic supercomputing sites in the United States; and the National Center for Earthquake Engineering Research.

Student Body Undergraduate enrollment is 17,290, 54 percent of whom are men. The ethnic distribution of students includes 21 percent minority students (8 percent African American, 4 percent Hispanic American, 9 percent Asian American, and less than 1 percent Native American). There are 848 international students. Twenty-one percent of undergraduate students live on campus. Eighty-two percent of students receive financial aid. There are twenty-seven Greek-letter social organizations with campus recognition, fifteen sororities, and twelve fraternities.

Faculty Of the 1,932 faculty members, 1,236 are full-time; 97 percent hold terminal degrees. The student-faculty ratio is 14:1.

Key Facilities The campus has nine libraries containing more than 3.2 million volumes and 26,400 serials. There are seven public computing sites on campus, all with laser printing available. All of these sites are staffed by computer consultants. The University contains more than 700 mainframe terminals and more than 700 microcomputers for student, faculty, and staff use. All students are issued computer accounts at orientation. The University supports IBM and Macintosh computers and uses UNIX systems.

Honorary Societies Phi Eta Sigma, Golden Key, Mortar Board, and Phi Beta Kappa

Athletics UB participates in NCAA Division I varsity athletics. Varsity athletics for men include baseball, basketball, cross-country, diving, football, soccer, swimming, tennis, track and field, and wrestling. Varsity athletics for women include basketball, crew, cross-country, diving, soccer, softball, swimming, tennis, track and field, and volleyball. UB also offers a wide range of intramural activities in team and individual competition, as well as corecreation and club teams.

Study Abroad Students are able to take any study-abroad program offered through UB, the SUNY system, or any other accredited school in the United States.

Support Services The Office of Disability Services provides and coordinates services for people with disabilities. It helps to support the educational and social objectives and goals of individuals with disabilities at the University.

Job Opportunities Students on Federal Work-Study can often find part-time jobs in offices and laboratories on campus. Students can also work for the libraries, computing services, and food service or in the Commons plaza, which is located on campus.

Tuition: $3400 for state residents and $8300 for nonresidents, per year (2001–02)

Room and Board: $6209

Mandatory Fees: $1330

Contact: Administrative Director: Dr. Josephine Capuana; E-mail: capuana@buffalo.edu; or Academic Director: Dr. Clyde Herreid, Distinguised Teaching Professor of Biology, 214 Talbert Hall, Buffalo, New York 14260; Telephone: 716-645-3020; Fax: 716-645-3368; Web site: http://buffalo.edu/honors/

THE UNIVERSITY OF AKRON

4 Pu G L Sc Tr AA FA

▼ University Honors Program

Since its beginning in 1975, the University Honors Program has supported high-achieving and highly motivated students with its special curriculum opportunities. More than 1,000 students have achieved graduation as University Scholars during the twenty-five-year history of the program. Challenging curricular options, honors classes, scholarships, and priority registration are only a few of the many benefits honors students receive.

The University of Akron honors program spans the entire University. Students complete the requirements for a major in one of more than 200 bachelor's degree programs across campus. A faculty adviser, the Honors Preceptor, from each of the majors is assigned to an incoming student and works closely with the student as an adviser throughout his or her course of study. Honors sections of courses are provided in many areas in order to ensure an enriching experience of studying and interacting with other high-achieving students. In place of the General Education requirements of the University, honors students complete an individually selected set of courses to meet the honors distribu-

Interpreting the symbols: **2**=two-year college, **4**=four-year college; **Pu**=public or state college, **Pr**=private college; **G**=general honors program; **D**=departmental honors program; **S**=small program (fewer than 100 students), **M**=midsize program (100 to 500 students), **L**=large program (more than 500 students); **Sc**=scholarships available in honors program; **Tr**=transfer students accepted into honors program; **HBC**=historically black college; **AA**=academic advisors; **GA**=graduate advisors; **FA**=fellowship advisors.

tion requirements. The 38-hour requirement (including physical education) incorporates course work in humanities, languages and the arts, social sciences, and natural sciences and mathematics.

Honors program students participate in three 2-credit colloquia during their sophomore, junior, and senior years. These interdisciplinary seminars are open only to honors students and they provide a small class size for increased discussion and interaction among students. The three colloquia are topical courses in humanities, social sciences, and natural sciences.

Students are required to complete a Senior Honors Project. This capstone experience begins during the junior year with a student selecting a sponsor, topic, and committee and developing a proposal. The student's completion of the Senior Honors Project is considered to be a unique opportunity to apply their learning and test their abilities. Students are encouraged to focus on an interdisciplinary topic for their study and then present their research in the annual Undergraduate Student Research Poster Session sponsored by the honors program. Upon completion of the Senior Honors Project and course work requirements while maintaining a GPA of at least 3.4, students are recognized at graduation with the designation of University Honors Scholar.

Scholarship opportunities are abundant within the honors program and across the University. The program provides ongoing academic and career counseling to students in all disciplines of study. Gallucci Hall is the special residence hall for honors students and houses computer labs for honors students, classrooms, and the honors program offices. The program is currently increasing in size as seen by the doubling of honors students in the 2001 incoming class. Approximately 550 students are in the honors program, representing a range of local, national, and international students.

Participation Requirements: Students who are accepted as honors students complete an individually designed course of study in collaboration with their faculty preceptor. Students are required to complete a minimum of 128 credits, including major requirements, honors distribution requirements, colloquia, and their Senior Honors Project. The project, an integral part of the honors experience, may take the form of a research report, a senior thesis, or an artistic or creative work.

GPA levels must be maintained to be an honors scholarship recipient. These levels are: two semesters or 32 credits, 3.25; four semesters or 64 credits, 3.3; and six semesters or 96 credits, 3.4. In order to complete the undergraduate degree with the University Honors Scholar designation, the final GPA must be 3.4 or higher.

Admission Process: A special application process is required for honors students. High school performance criteria, as well as standardized test scores, are considered. Students must achieve two of the three following criteria for admission to the program: ACT composite score of at least 27 or SAT combined score of at least 1200, GPA of 3.5, and rank in top 10 percent in class. Essays are required for admission as is an invited interview on campus. Students who qualify are invited for an interview by University faculty members and administrators. This experience provides an opportunity for the student to come to campus and meet with faculty members while applying for acceptance into the program. For students entering as transfer students, as continuing students at the University of Akron, or as students who have delayed the start of their college studies, similar evidence of academic excellence and potential is required. The application deadline for the honors program (and scholarship support) is February 1, although students are encouraged to apply earlier.

Scholarship Availability: Honors program students are eligible for generous academic scholarships awarded for merit. The Lisle M. Buckingham Scholars are guaranteed sufficient funds to cover tuition and fees, residence hall costs, and meal plans. Two levels of honors scholarships are the Honors Merit Scholarship (approximately half tuition and fees) and the Honors Recognition Scholarship (approximately one quarter tuition and fees). Other generous scholarship opportunities are available to high-achieving students. Additional information on scholarships, deadlines, and qualifications is available from the Office of Student Financial Aid.

The Campus Context: The University of Akron is the public research university for northern Ohio. Founded in 1870, it is the only public university with a science/engineering program ranked among the nation's top five by *U.S. News & World Report.* For 130 years, the University of Akron has been an active participant in Akron's renaissance of commercial and artistic endeavors.

The University of Akron excels in such areas as polymer science, global business, marketing, dance, and intellectual property law. Servicing approximately 24,358 students, the University offers more than 350 associate, bachelor's, master's, doctoral, and law degree programs. The University of Akron is an educational community of diverse peoples, processes, and programs. Alumni of the University number more than 115,000. They include scientists, engineers, artists, lawyers, educators, and other professionals in every state and eighty-four other countries.

The 180-acre campus includes seventy-nine buildings. The new initiative, Landscape for Learning, has committed more than $200 million to construct six new buildings and renovate many more. An additional 30 acres of green space is also included in this plan. Residence halls and a large dining facility serve more than 2,000 students. The recreational facilities include the Ocasek Natatorium and the Gardner Student Center. The Akron Symphony and Ohio Ballet perform in the University of Akron's E. J. Thomas Performing Arts Hall.

Student Body Undergraduate student enrollment at the University of Akron is 18,905. The diverse student body is from forty-one states in the U.S. and eighty-three countries. There are more than 200 majors and areas of study. Various student services are available including the Counseling, Testing, and Career Center; the Office of Accessibility; and the Student Employment Services as well as the new Career Advantage Network that offers students practical experience in their chosen field prior to graduation. More than 200 student organizations are on campus serving a wide variety of purposes for students, and there are 22 fraternities and sororities registered at the University.

Faculty The University of Akron has more than 788 full-time faculty members, many of whom are renowned in their fields of study. More than 72 percent of the full-time faculty members hold the highest degree recognized for instruction in their field.

Key Facilities Library facilities are housed in three separate locations: Bierce Library, the science library, and the Archival Services. The library collection contains more than 2.8 million items, including books, periodicals, and government and archival documents. Library services are extensive, providing reference and research assistance, user education, and computer-based information searching.

Many computer facilities are found throughout the campus. Technology-enhanced classrooms are growing in number, high-speed wireless networking across campus has been completed, and 150 wireless laptop computers are available to use at Bierce Library.

Honorary Societies Beta Gamma Sigma (business), Golden Key National Honor Society, Mortar Board, Phi Sigma Eta, and Tau Beta Pi (engineering)

Athletics The University offers a complete sports program, competing in Division I A and belonging to the Mid-American Conference (MAC). A wide variety of men's and women's sports are available, including men's baseball, basketball, and football and women's basketball, soccer, and softball. A broad array of intramural sports is offered throughout the year for University students.

Study Abroad The University of Akron, in conjunction with the Office of International Programs, encourages students to participate in study-abroad opportunities. There are study-abroad affiliations with many universities throughout the world, and the programs are open to students regardless of major or language training. Recent honors students have studied in Korea, Ghana, Australia, and Italy.

Support Services The University welcomes students with disabilities. The mission of the Office of Accessibility is to provide equal access opportunities to students with disabilities and coordinate academic accommodations, auxiliary aids, and programs to enable students with disabilities to maximize their educational potential.

Job Opportunities A variety of employment opportunities are provided at the University. The Office of Student Employment assists students in finding part-time employment both on and off campus. The Federal Work-Study Program is available for those students who qualify.

The Career Advantage Network is a new program at the University of Akron offering experiential learning opportunities for all undergraduate students entering after summer 2001. These experiences may include cooperative education, internships, clinical work and fieldwork, and student teaching.

Tuition: The full-time tuition at the University of Akron is $4567.20/year for Ohio residents; nonresident tuition is $10,768.20/year. There are tuition adjustments for academically qualified nonresidents that are $100 per credit hour above in-state tuition. These tuition rates are effective spring 2002.

Mandatory Fees: The General Service Fee for all University students is $241.20 per semester ($482.40 per year). Other mandatory fees include the Facilities Fee ($120), the Technology Fee ($5.50 per credit), and the Career Advantage Network Fee ($2 per credit).

Room and Board: The Housing Fee schedule for the academic year 2001–02 was $3550. There is a range of meal plan options, from the nineteen-meal Gold Plan option ($2328 per year) to the ten-meal plan ($1896 per year).

Contact: Dr. Dale H. Mugler, Director, University Honors Program, Gallucci Hall 155, University of Akron, Akron, Ohio 44325-1803; Telephone: 330-972-5365; E-mail: dmugler@uakron.edu; or Dr. Karyn Bobkoff Katz, Associate Director, University Honors Program, Gallucci Hall 155, University of Akron, Akron, Ohio 44325-1803; Telephone: 330-972-8679; E-mail: kkatz@uakron.edu; Web site: http://www.uakron.edu/honors.

THE UNIVERSITY OF ALABAMA

4 Pu G S Sc Tr

▼ Computer-Based Honors Program

Whether one wants to be an English professor, a marketing executive, or an electrical engineer, not being able to apply computer technology to one's career field is a lot like not being able to read. The Computer-Based Honors Program (CBHP), a department of New College at the University of Alabama, is looking for 40 students who want to approach their fields of study, whatever they may be, with the best tools the Information Age has to offer. The CBHP, cited by the National Institute of Education as one of the six most intriguing honors programs in the United States, gives students opportunities to learn how to use computing technology in their major field of study. The program also gives 6 members of each entering class the chance to earn while they learn—six fellowships of $3000 per year, renewable for four years, are awarded on a competitive basis to CBHP students.

At the beginning of the freshman year, students take a highly accelerated course to introduce them to basic concepts of computing, to at least two computer languages, and to practical uses of the computer in problem solving. Although this course advances rapidly, it does not require any prior experience with computers.

When students are proficient in using the computer, they work as computer-oriented research assistants with faculty members or industry associates whose interests coincide with theirs. Projects in which CBHP students are involved usually entail researching a particular subject or experimenting with the computer as an instructional tool. The student participates in planning the project, in preparing the computer programs needed to complete the project, and in interpreting the results.

During the sophomore, junior, and senior years, students meet with other CBHP students in a weekly seminar with the program director. This systematic, long-term contact with students whose abilities are comparable to their own provides students with a forum for satisfying social and intellectual exchanges not readily available anywhere else.

The Computer-Based Honors Program was founded in 1968 with a National Science Foundation grant. There is a maximum of 160 students in the program. The desingation Computer-Based Honors Program appears on the honors student's diploma and transcript.

Participation Requirements: The average ACT score is 32; the average SAT I score is 1350. The average high school GPA is 3.9 to 4.0. The application, transcript, and essay are due by January 15. Twenty students are admitted based on their applications and are invited for a two-day visit to the campus.

Scholarship Availablility: Six scholarships are awarded. Twenty-five total scholarships of $3000 are awarded per year, renewable based on continued superior performance. Three endowed scholarships from $2600 to $3000 are available to CBHP students on a competitive basis.

The Campus Context: The University of Alabama consists of twelve colleges and schools: Arts and Sciences, Commerce and Business Administration, Communication, Community Health Sciences, Continuing Studies, Education, Engineering, Graduate School, Human Environmental Sciences, Law, Nursing, and Social Work. The University offers 275 degrees in more than 150 fields of study, providing its students a wide range of choices, and offers courses of study at the bachelor's, master's, specialist, and doctoral levels.

Student Body Of the roughly 15,000 undergraduate students on campus 48 percent are men, 52 percent women; 80 percent are white, 12 percent African American, 1 percent Hispanic, and 5 percent international; 61 percent receive financial aid. There are forty-eight fraternities and sororities and more than 300 student organizations.

Faculty Of the 995 faculty members, 805 are full-time, with 97 percent holding terminal degrees. The student-faculty ratio is 18:1.

Key Facilities There are more than 2 million volumes in the libraries and state-of-the-art computing facilities in every major building.

Athletics The Crimson Tide sponsors eleven women's and nine men's sports, competing at the NCAA Division I level as a participant in the twelve-school Southeastern Conference. The University of Alabama is home to twelve national football championships, three gymnastics championships, and a host of national and SEC individual champions in other sports.

Study Abroad The Capstone International Program Center offers a large number of study-abroad opportunities.

Interpreting the symbols: **2**=two-year college, **4**=four-year college; **Pu**=public or state college, **Pr**=private college; **G**=general honors program; **D**=departmental honors program; **S**=small program (fewer than 100 students), **M**=midsize program (100 to 500 students), **L**=large program (more than 500 students); **Sc**=scholarships available in honors program; **Tr**=transfer students accepted into honors program; **HBC**=historically black college; **AA**=academic advisors; **GA**=graduate advisors; **FA**=fellowship advisors.

Support Services The campus provides unrestricted access for disabled students.

Job Opportunities Nineteen percent of the students work part-time on campus with average annual earnings of $2000.

Tuition: $3292 for state residents, $8912 for nonresidents, per year (2000–01)

Room and Board: $4910

Contact: Director: Dr. Cathy Randall, Maxwell Hall, P.O. Box 870352, Tuscaloosa, Alabama 35487; Telephone: 205-348-5029; Fax: 205-348-2247; E-mail: cbhp@bama.ua.edu; Web site: http://www.cbhp.ua.edu

The University of Alabama

4 Pu G L Sc Tr

▼ University Honors Program

Qualified students seeking a special academic challenge in their undergraduate work can find it in the University Honors Program (UH) at the University of Alabama (UA). More than 1100 students from all schools and colleges in the University participate in the program. The University Honors Program gives outstanding students the opportunity to work with their peers and with outstanding faculty members in an enriched academic environment. It also offers students the opportunity to combine some of the benefits of a small-college experience with the advantages of a major research university.

Honors courses have limited enrollment in order to facilitate interaction between students and faculty members. Honors courses often parallel regular University courses, but they offer enriched content and provide for more student input and creative writing. The University Honors Program fulfills core curriculum and other requirements, allowing students to pursue their own specific degree and study objectives within the honors framework. Students in the program do not take a full schedule of honors courses. Most students take perhaps two honors courses each semester. However, all students are expected to take at least one honors course during each academic year of their first two years of the program in order to retain the privilege of priority registration. The evaluation of student work in honors courses neither penalizes nor unduly rewards students for their honors course work. Most students perform well in classes they find to be interesting and challenging.

Founded in 1987, the program now enrolls 1150 students.

Participation Requirements: Students complete a total of 18 hours of honors credit, 3 to 6 of which may include an honors thesis. Students must choose two UH courses at the 100- 200-, or 300-level in order to graduate with the Honors designation; they must also write an honors thesis in order to graduate with the Honors with Thesis designation.

The official transcript identifies honors courses, thereby enhancing an honors student's position in competing for employment or admission to professional schools. The University diploma indicates Honors status, with that distinction noted at graduation ceremonies. Each year the Honors Program Student Association, a body of students who are also members of the Honors Program, gives the Outstanding Honors Program Graduate Award to a senior who has served the honors community faithfully and well over her or his undergraduate career at the University.

Admission Process: Students with an ACT score of at least 28 or an SAT I score of at least 1240 are automatically admissible to the program. National Merit Finalists, National Achievement Finalists, National Hispanic Finalists, and UA Presidential Scholars are automatically admissible. Students not admitted to the program as freshmen may apply after they have earned a GPA of 3.3 or higher for a semester's work at UA. Transfer students with at least a 3.3 GPA on courses transferred to UA are also automatically admissible. All participants must maintain at least a 3.3 GPA and give evidence of actively pursuing the honors requirements to remain a member in good standing in the program.

Scholarship Availability: The Barrett C. and Tally Gilmer Shelton Scholarship and the Jo Nell Usrey Honors Scholarship are available to entering freshman who are participating in the University Honors Program and who are receiving no other financial aid from the University. Other scholarships include seven John K. McKinley Student Excellence Awards and the Alton C. and Cecile C. Craig Scholarship. Support for research and study abroad is available form the McWane Endowment.

The Campus Context: The University of Alabama at Tuscaloosa consists of twelve colleges and schools: Arts and Sciences, Commerce and Business Administration, Communication, Community Health Sciences, Continuing Studies, Education, Engineering, Graduate School, Human Environmental Sciences, Law, Nursing, and Social Work. The University offers 275 degrees in more than 150 fields of study, giving students a wide range of choices at the bachelor's, master's, specialist, and doctoral levels.

Student Body Of the total student body, 48 percent are men and 52 percent women. The ethnic distribution of minority students is 14 percent African American; 1 percent Hispanic-American; and 5 percent international. There are forty-eight fraternities and sororities as well as more than 300 student organizations on campus.

Faculty Of the 995 faculty members, 805 are full-time, with 97 percent holding terminal degrees. The student-faculty ratio is 18:1.

Key Facilities There are more than 2 million volumes in the libraries and state-of-the-art computing facilities in every major building.

Honorary Societies Phi Eta Sigma, Lambda Sigma, Phi Kappa Phi, Golden Key, Mortar Board, Phi Beta Kappa

Athletics The Crimson Tide sponsors eleven women's and nine men's sports, competing at the NCAA's Division I level as a participant in the twelve-school Southeastern Conference. The University of Alabama is home to twelve national football championships and three national gymnastics championships. The University is also the home of many other national and SEC individual champions in other sports.

Study Abroad The Capstone International Program Center and the International Honors Program offer a large number of study abroad opportunities.

Support Services The campus provides unrestricted access for disabled students.

Job Opportunities Nineteen percent of the students work part-time on campus with average annual earnings of $2000.

Tuition: $3292 for state residents, $8912 for nonresidents, per year (2000–01)

Room and Board: $4910

Contact: Director: University Honors Program, Box 870169, Tuscaloosa, Alabama 35487-0169; Telephone: 205-348-5500; Fax: 205-348-5501; E-mail: uhp@bama.ua.edu; Web site: http://www.uhp.ua.edu/

The University of Alabama at Birmingham

4 Pu G M Sc Tr

▼ University Honors Program

Combining cultural diversity with high academic standards, the UAB Honors Program provides an innovative, interdisciplinary curriculum designed for bright, motivated students of all disciplines, backgrounds, and ages. The 33-hour honors curriculum, which replaces the core curriculum at UAB, offers courses that are team-taught by scholar/teachers in disciplines as diverse as engineering, English, theology, biochemistry, business, and psychology; the study of a single subject—such as the environment—from these multiple perspectives generates critical thinking, mutual understanding, and teamwork. In addition, the curriculum is perpetually innovative, with no course offered more than once, so that students are introduced to the latest information, methodologies, social trends, and technologies.

The intensive extracurricular focus of the Honors Program extends the undergraduate experience beyond the course work to a way of life. The faculty and staff members and students of the Honors Program comprise a close community of active teachers and learners who share their energy and commitment not only with each other but with the larger community, where honors students provide services to local public school students, homeless women and children, and the elderly.

The Spencer Honors House, a magnificent old church on the UAB campus that was built in 1902, houses a number of computers that are wired through the Ethernet to Internet 1 and 2. All entering students receive an e-mail account, and computer workshops familiarize students with the newest technologies. All the honors course work takes place in the Honors House, as do more than fifty lectures, films, social gatherings, and discussion groups each year. The Honors House is available to honors students at all times, and the facilities include a kitchen, a pool table, computers, a copy machine, a stereo, a television, and lots of space for studying and relaxing.

During the past eighteen years, hundreds of students in the Honors Program have attended state, national, and regional honors conferences, given formal academic presentations, served in regional and national elected offices, and/or attended honors semesters in the Czech Republic, Greece, Spain, New York, or El Paso. UAB has hosted a regional conference and three state conferences, and it has also sponsored numerous field trips for its students, from ski trips to museum visits.

The 18-year-old program currently enrolls a maximum of 200 students; an additional 125 students are enrolled in departmental honors programs.

Participation Requirements: In order to remain in the program, students must maintain a GPA in their honors course work of at least 3.0. During each year of participation in the program, honors students are included in the University Honors Convocation and receive the notation "University Honors Program" on their transcripts. Students who complete the program graduate "With University Honors" and—in addition to being acknowledged in the Commencement program—are honored at a special graduation ceremony for honors students.

Admission Process: Students are selected for the program on the basis of national test scores, GPA, two letters of recommendation, an essay, a personal interview, and any special evidence a student chooses to submit. There are no numerical minimums for scores or GPAs, but the program seeks students with academic ability, creativity, intellectual promise, and competence in basic skills. The program admits a maximum of 50 students per year.

Application before January 15 is strongly encouraged.

Scholarship Availability: While most honors students are awarded scholarships by the University, the program awards twenty-one scholarships of five kinds: 1) five University Scholarships (full tuition and fees plus $1000 per year for four years) for students with a minimum 28 ACT and 3.5 GPA; 2) five Hess-Abroms Honors Scholarships ($4000 per year for four years) for students who best meet the general program criteria indicated above; 3) three Juliet Nunn Pearson Scholarships ($1000 each) for promising incoming students; 4) four named scholarships ($1500 each) for students already in the program, on the basis of need and merit; and 5) five Spencer Scholarships ($2000 each) on the basis of need and merit.

The Campus Context: The University of Alabama at Birmingham is composed of twelve schools (undergraduate enrollment in parentheses): Arts and Humanities (1,025), Natural Sciences and Mathematics (1,406), Social and Behavioral Sciences (1,683), Education (799), Engineering (485), Business (1,650), Medicine (10), Nursing (217), Optometry, Dentistry (12), Health-Related Professions (340), and Public Health. Special features include a major academic health center; Reynolds Historical Library; and Alabama Museum of Health Sciences. The University offers 136 degree programs.

Student Body Undergraduate enrollment is 9,954; 58 percent are women; 25 percent are African American, 62 percent white, and 11 percent other. There are 335 international undergraduate students. Thirty-four percent of undergraduates receive financial aid. There are eleven fraternities and eight sororities.

Faculty The faculty members total 1,934, with 1,727 full-time and 91 percent with terminal degrees. The student-faculty ratio is 18:1.

Key Facilities The two libraries house more than 1.5 million volumes. Most residence halls are fully wired for the Internet, and computer clusters are widely available throughout the campus for student use.

Honorary Societies Phi Kappa Phi, Golden Key, Alpha Lambda Delta, Omicron Delta Kappa, and numerous disciplinary honorary societies

Athletics In athletics, the University is NCAA Division I in men's and women's basketball, soccer, golf, and tennis; men's football and baseball; and women's cross-country and track, rifle, softball, synchronized swimming, and volleyball.

Study Abroad Study-abroad programs are available in Mexico, France, the Bahamas, Costa Rica, and Italy; there are eight additional UAB exchange programs with other universities.

Support Services There is a Disability Support Services (DSS) Program, and the DSS Office ensures that all UAB programs and services are accessible to students with disabilities. UAB offers a full-service Career Center, Retention Office, TRIO Academic Services Program, and Counseling and Wellness Center and a full range of other student services.

Job Opportunities Work opportunities include work-study, co-op, and numerous research and lab positions.

Tuition: $2970 for state residents, $5940 for nonresidents, per year (2001–02)

Room and Board: $6714

Mandatory Fees: $670

Contact: Director: Dr. Ada Long, Spencer Honors House, 1530 3rd Avenue South, Birmingham, Alabama 35294-4450; Telephone: 205-934-3228; Fax: 205-975-5493; E-mail: adalong@uab.edu; Web site: http://www.hp.uab.edu

---

THE UNIVERSITY OF ALABAMA IN HUNTSVILLE

4 Pu G M Tr AA

▼ University Honors Program

The Honors Program at the University of Alabama in Huntsville enhances the opportunity for academic excellence. It offers study of the scientific and humanistic accomplishments of the past and

Interpreting the symbols: **2**=two-year college, **4**=four-year college; **Pu**=public or state college, **Pr**=private college; **G**=general honors program; **D**=departmental honors program; **S**=small program (fewer than 100 students), **M**=midsize program (100 to 500 students), **L**=large program (more than 500 students); **Sc**=scholarships available in honors program; **Tr**=transfer students accepted into honors program; **HBC**=historically black college; **AA**=academic advisors; **GA**=graduate advisors; **FA**=fellowship advisors.

present in order to increase knowledge of the self and of the world. It provides academically talented undergraduate students with opportunities to develop their special talents and skills within an expanded and enriched version of the curriculum. Students in the Honors Program participate in structured enrichment activities that include honors course work parallel to regular offerings, special interdisciplinary seminars, field trips, and the option of independent study and research. First- and second-year students take Honors Forum, a course designed to introduce the multidisciplinary focus of the honors education. Seniors complete an Honors Senior Project directed by an adviser in their major and formally present their research findings in a public forum. In all of these specially designed classes and activities, students are assured an exciting academic career that will also nurture their special talents. The Honors Program offers personalized academic guidance and counseling for all honors students, but especially for first- and second-year participants. The UAH Honors Program provides a path to a unique education.

The Honors Program is housed in a small complex that includes the director's and assistant's office and two comfortably outfitted study and lounge rooms. These rooms also include computers, basic reference books, and selected journals, newspapers, and other print media. This setting provides the opportunity for academic and social interaction among students, special campus guests, the director, and honors faculty members.

The 11-year-old program currently enrolls 130 students.

Participation Requirements: An honors student is required to maintain a cumulative GPA of 3.3 or above. Graduation from the program requires 28 hours of honors course work. Graduating honors students are awarded University Honors recognition at Honors Convocation and at Commencement. The title of the senior project is printed in the Commencement booklet and "University Honors" is printed on the diploma.

Admission Process: All academically eligible students are urged to participate in the Honors Program. The minimum requirement for first-year students is a high school GPA of 3.5. Minimum test scores for admission are as follows: ACT composite, 28: English 29; math 26. SAT I composite, 1200: verbal 610, math 590. Enrolled UAH students who complete 12 hours of course work with a GPA of 3.3 or higher may be invited to join the program based on outstanding performance.

Scholarship Availability: Scholarships are handled through the Financial Aid Office. Although no funds are designated specifically for honors students, many of them receive scholarships based on academic merit.

The Campus Context: The University of Alabama at Huntsville offers a considerable number and variety of degree programs: thirty-eight bachelor's degrees (B.A., B.S., B.S.B.A., B.S.E., B.S. N.), fifteen master's degrees (M.A., M.S., M.S.E., M.S.N.), and ten doctorates (Ph.D). UAH is home to the following research and development centers: Aerophysics Research Center, Center for Applied Optics, Center for Automation and Robotics, Center for Management and Economic Research, Center for the Management of Science and Technology, Center for Microgravity and Materials Research, Center for Space Plasma and Aeronomic Research, Consortium for Materials Development in Space, Earth Systems Science Laboratory, Information Technology and Systems Laboratory, Johnson Research Center, Propulsion Research Center, and the Research Institute.

Student Body Undergraduate enrollment is 51 percent men and 49 percent women. The ethnic distribution is: 79 percent white (non-Hispanic); 11 percent black (non-Hispanic); 2 percent Hispanic; 3 percent Asian/Pacific Islander; 1 percent American Indian/Alaskan Native; 4 percent nonresident aliens. Forty-five percent of undergraduates receive financial aid. There are six fraternities and five sororities on campus.

Faculty The total number of instructional faculty members is 469; 283 are full-time and 93 percent have terminal degrees. The student-faculty ratio is 10:1.

Key Facilities In addition to the 426,344 books, serial backfiles and government documents, the library houses 413,909 titles on microfilm, 3,105 current serial subscriptions, and 1,835 sound recordings. Approximately 250 personal computers are available for student use. They are located in the computer center, the student center, the library, and computer labs. Students have access to the campus mainframe computer (DEC 7000/910), the Alabama Super Computer (CRAY X-MP 24), and the Internet.

Honorary Societies Phi Kappa Phi, Phi Beta Kappa

Athletics UAH is a member of the NCAA and the Gulf South Athletic Conference and offers the following Division II intercollegiate sports: men's baseball, ice hockey, and soccer; women's softball and volleyball; and basketball, cross-country, and tennis for both men and women. The men's hockey team won the Division II National Championship for 1996 and all 6 starters were All-Americans. UAH finished the season with a record of 26-0-3. UAH offers the following intramural sports: basketball, bowling, crew, flag football, golf, racquetball, softball, swimming, table tennis, volleyball, and weightlifting.

Study Abroad Study-abroad opportunities exist.

Support Services All University buildings are accessible for the physically disabled. Note-taking and reader services are available. The following services are available for learning-disabled students: note-taking, readers, remedial courses, study skills courses, tutors, tape recorders, and oral and untimed tests.

Job Opportunities UAH offers part-time on-campus student employment and Federal Work-Study.

Tuition: $3692 for state residents, $7772 for nonresidents, per year (2000–01)

Room and Board: $4000

Contact: Director: Dr. Richard F. Modlin, Honors Program, Huntsville, Alabama 35899; Telephone: 256-824-6450; Fax: 256-824-7339; Web site: http://www.uah.edu/honors

University of Alaska Anchorage

4 Pu G S Sc Tr AA

▼ University Honors Program

The University Honors Program of the University of Alaska Anchorage (UAA) allows outstanding students from all disciplines to interact with one another through an interdisciplinary core curriculum and informal social activities. Honors classes have an intimate feel, generally range between 12 and 20 students, and are taught by faculty members with a strong commitment to innovative undergraduate education. All honors freshmen and sophomores take courses that allow them to participate in community service projects and heighten community and cultural awareness. University Honors also offers students the opportunity to participate in guided individual research within their chosen course of study. Honors seniors can choose from a variety of senior-year capstone experiences.

Outside of classes, Honors Program students receive a weekly honors newsletter and participate in various social events, including retreats, game nights, visiting speakers, and other functions. A wing in the campus residence halls is reserved for honors students. All students in the program have access to an honors computer lab, where they can study and socialize.

Founded in 1998, the program currently enrolls approximately 80 students.

Participation Requirements: Students admitted into baccalaureate degree programs can participate in the program. Students must complete 9 credits of honors course work as freshmen and sophomores, a 1-credit thesis-preparatory course in the junior year, and a 6-credit senior capstone thesis, project, or seminar. Students who complete the required course work with a cumulative GPA of at least 3.5 have University Honors Scholar noted on their transcript, receive special recognition at commencement, and receive a certificate of achievement.

Admission Process: To join the program, students must have achieved a high school or college GPA of at least 3.0 and show strong evidence of ability to reach and maintain at least a 3.5 GPA level at UAA. Applications are judged based on the student's letter of application, writing sample, high school or college transcripts, SAT and/or ACT scores, and references.

Scholarship Availability: The University of Alaska system offers scholarships to the top 10 percent of all Alaska high school graduates (the University of Alaska Scholars Program, worth $1375 per semester in 2001–02). The UAA Honors Program also offers a limited number of full and partial tuition waiver scholarships to incoming freshmen and continuing students in the program, available to both resident and nonresident students. Other tuition waiver scholarships are available through the University of Alaska President's Office and the University of Alaska Anchorage Chancellor's Office. Other financial assistance, including scholarships, research support, grants, loans, and part-time employment, is available to qualified students at UAA.

The Campus Context: UAA is a comprehensive university offering a full range of program options, from one-year certificates to associate, bachelor's, and master's degrees. The University Honors Program is housed on the Anchorage campus in a culturally diverse city of approximately 260,000. The attractive wooded campus serves as a cultural hub for the city, providing theater, music, arts, and sports events. Careful development has left the campus an urban oasis with resident populations of moose, waterfowl, and birds.

Student Body The UAA campus serves approximately 13,000 full- and part-time students.

Faculty At the Anchorage campus, there are 385 faculty members (2001). The student-to-faculty ratio is 14.2:1, with an average class size of 19.4.

Key Facilities The UAA library includes more than 735,000 volumes, 500,000 microform units, subscriptions to 3,400 journals, and an extensive sheet-music collection. Computer facilities include fiber-optic network and Internet access for all residence halls and offices. There are computer labs in the residence hall commons as well as many other buildings on campus. Special computer labs are also available in many schools, colleges, and programs.

Honorary Societies Phi Kappa Phi, Beta Gamma Sigma, Golden Key

Athletics UAA is in the NCAA Division I for ice hockey and Division II for basketball, cross-country, gymnastics, and skiing.

Study Abroad UAA is a member of the National Student Exchange Program and the Northwest Council on Study Abroad (NCSA). NCSA programs are available in London, England; Siena, Italy; and Angers, France.

Support Services Facilities for students who experience disabilities are plentiful. Services provided by the Office of Disability Support Services include ASL interpreters, note-taking assistance, textbooks in alternative formats, testing accommodations, and access to adaptive computer technology.

Job Opportunities A wide variety of work opportunities for students are available both on and off campus. The Career Services Office assists students looking for employment while in school and approaching graduation.

Tuition: $2370–$2700 for residents; $7440–$7770 for nonresidents per year (2001–02)

Room and Board: $5680 minimum per year; room only, $3400 per year (2001–02)

Mandatory Fees: $352 per year (2001–02)

Contact: Director: Ronald Spatz, 3211 Providence Drive, Anchorage, Alaska 99508; Telephone: 907-786-1086; Fax: 907-786-1060; E-mail: afrms1@uaa.alaska.edu; Web site: http://www.uaa.alaska.edu/honors/

UNIVERSITY OF ALASKA FAIRBANKS

4 Pu G M Sc Tr

▼ Honors Program

The University of Alaska Fairbanks Honors Program is open to students in all majors. The program features the personalized attention of small classes with top professors within a larger research university. Specially selected faculty advisers guide honors students through their years as undergraduates.

The Honors Program offers an enriched core curriculum for approximately 200 talented students. Honors courses are offered in all disciplines with the availability of honors contract work in standard University courses. Many of these courses are designed specifically for the Honors Program and are frequently interdisciplinary. Honors students take at least one honors course per semester toward completion of the 27 credits of honors course work required for graduation in the program. Students may also earn honors credit for study abroad and internships.

The program emphasizes undergraduate research. In their senior research projects, all honors students have the opportunity to work directly with faculty members. All honors students must complete a senior honors thesis in their major discipline.

The Honors Student Advisory Committee organizes social events and fundraising activities that contribute to a sense of community within the University.

Currently, there are 200 students in the program.

Admission Process: Students apply first to the University, then make application to the Honors Program. Students from other recognized college and university honors programs are welcomed as transfer students. There is no formal deadline.

Scholarship Availability: The Donald R. Theophilus Fund for Scholars, the Howard and Enid Cutler Scholarship, the Pat Anderson Scholarship, and the Helen Walker Memorial Scholarship are designated for honors students; the Usibelli Coal Mine Honors Scholarship, which is also designated for honors students, is awarded to 20 students. Many general University scholarships (that range from $500 to $4000) are awarded to honors students.

The Campus Context: The University of Alaska Fairbanks offers a once-in-a-lifetime opportunity to experience the adventure of Alaska at the nation's farthest-north university. Situated in the Tanana Valley, between the Alaska Range to the south and the Brooks Range to the north, UAF offers many opportunities for outdoor activities and observation of wildlife and scenic beauty. UAF is a four-year university that is home to the University of Alaska Museum and the Geophysical Institute. UAF is the national leader in National Science Foundation-funded arctic research. The University offers degrees in 103 majors.

Student Body The undergraduate enrollment is approximately 8,000 (this figure includes the rural campuses); 55 percent are women, 45 percent men. Eighty-six percent are Alaska residents, 11 percent are from other states, and 3 percent are from other

Interpreting the symbols: **2**=two-year college, **4**=four-year college; **Pu**=public or state college, **Pr**=private college; **G**=general honors program; **D**=departmental honors program; **S**=small program (fewer than 100 students), **M**=midsize program (100 to 500 students), **L**=large program (more than 500 students); **Sc**=scholarships available in honors program; **Tr**=transfer students accepted into honors program; **HBC**=historically black college; **AA**=academic advisors; **GA**=graduate advisors; **FA**=fellowship advisors.

countries. Ethnic minorities comprise approximately 25 percent of the total student body. Ninety-one percent are undergraduates, 9 percent are graduate students. The average age is 30.

Faculty There are 433 full-time and 222 part-time faculty members. The student-faculty ratio is approximately 13:1.

Key Facilities The University's Rasmuson Library houses 1,030,120 volumes, not counting government documents and materials on microfilm and microfiche. It has the world's most extensive arctic and circumpolar archives. IBM and Mac computers are available in the Honors House. An honors dorm is available.

Honorary Societies Phi Kappa Phi, Golden Key

Athletics The University of Alaska Fairbanks offers intercollegiate athletics in several sports, including skiing, volleyball, hockey, basketball, and marksmanship.

Study Abroad The University is affiliated with several study abroad and student exchange programs. UAF students may enroll at one of 115 NSE colleges and universities throughout the U.S. and pay the in-state tuition rate. UAF also has student exchanges or study abroad programs with universities in Australia, Austria, Canada, Denmark, Ecuador, England, Finland, France, Germany, Ghana, Greece, Italy, Japan, Mexico, Norway, Russia, Spain, Sweden, Taiwan, and Venezuela. Honors students are encouraged to participate in such programs.

Support Services Almost all academic buildings are accessible to disabled students. Special parking, equipped restrooms, and lowered drinking fountains are also available throughout campus.

Tuition: $3000 for state residents, $9000 for nonresidents, per year (2001–02)

Room and Board: $5060

Mandatory Fees: $500

Contact: Director: Dr. Roy K. Bird, P.O. Box 756282, Fairbanks, Alaska 99775; Telephone: 907-474-6612; Fax: 907-474-5559; E-mail: honors@uaf.edu; Web site: http://www.uaf.edu/honors/index.html

The University of Arizona

4 Pu G L Sc Tr

▼ Honors College

The Honors College at the University of Arizona is a community of scholars. The program draws on the resources of one of the top fifteen public universities in the country and adds the benefits of an innovative, personal, and challenging learning community. It is no wonder that more than 1,000 new students (including 59 National Merit Scholars) decide to join the ranks each year.

UA Honors students have the option of enrolling in University-wide offerings of more than 200 honors courses each semester. The average class size is 15 students. There are no required honors courses; students work with their adviser to decide which honors course opportunities are most appropriate for their curriculum. Honors courses emphasize the development of written and verbal skills, as well as research and problem-solving techniques. The atmosphere in the courses is one of interaction and challenge, but not competition.

The UA Honors College offers a full complement of benefits to round out students' educational experiences. There are four honors residence halls, each equipped with a computer lab, to house 700 students. Students may apply for $40,000 in research grants awarded annually. They may wish to attend one of the monthly Forum Luncheons, where they can meet other honors students and faculty members in an informal setting. There is a network of more than 100 honors advisers throughout the campus to assist students in reaching their personal and academic goals. Finally, many students appreciate the extended library privileges and early registration opportunities that are a part of the program. The Honors College was founded in 1962 and currently has 3,920 students actively participating in the program.

Participation Requirements: To graduate with honors, students complete between 18 and 30 units of honors course work, including a senior thesis in their major area of study. Students who complete the requirements for graduation with honors (unit requirement, senior thesis, and maintenance of a cumulative GPA of 3.5 or higher) have that distinction indicated on their diploma. The degree would read, for example, "Bachelor of Arts with Honors" or "Bachelor of Science with Honors". All students who graduate with honors receive a gold cord to wear with their graduation cap and gown. Those honors students who complete requirements and maintain a 4.0 GPA receive a silver bowl inscribed with their name, "Academic Award of Excellence," and their year of graduation. Students are also eligible to qualify for academic distinction (cum laude, magna cum laude, summa cum laude) based on their cumulative GPA.

Honors graduates go on to win national awards, such as the Truman, Marshall, and Rhodes scholarships. UA honors students are placed into medical and law school at twice the national average, and they receive fellowships and grants to continue their education at top-ranked graduate programs throughout the U.S.

Admission Process: Honors admission is offered to a select group of students each year. To be considered, the University of Arizona's general application for admission must be completed. Strength of curriculum, test scores, GPA, and class rank are all part of the consideration process. To remain active members of the Honors College, students must maintain a cumulative GPA of 3.5 or greater.

Scholarship Availability: The University of Arizona awards over $16 million in scholarships each year. One of the strongest programs, for National Merit Finalists, provides scholarships of at least $4300 for Arizona residents and $6500 for nonresidents. The Honors College works with the Office of Scholarships and Financial Aid to identify and target outstanding students for University awards. The best advice for those students who are interested in receiving scholarship assistance is to apply early and send test scores. The University begins making scholarship offers in the winter before a student's anticipated enrollment (i.e., December for August enrollment).

The Campus Context: The University of Arizona, founded in 1888, is located in Tucson and offers a top-ranked education on a 343-acre, resort-like campus. The University has been designated by the Carnegie Commission as a Research I institution, the highest ranking, since 1976. With 133 different degree programs, the University is also one of fifty-eight institutional members of the Association of American Universities. The UA is ranked thirteenth among public universities in research and development, and undergraduate students benefit from funding brought in by research grants. The faculty members, technology, and equipment available, in all disciplines, are simply among the best in the country. Special facilities on the campus include the Center for Creative Photography, the Arizona Cancer Center, the Arizona State Museum, the Udall Center for Studies in Public Policy, and the Optical Sciences Center. Independent sources consistently rank UA among the nation's top schools: *U.S. News & World Report* listed UA in the top 5 up-and-coming U.S. universities, UA was named in the 1994 edition of *The Guide to 101 of the Best Values in American Colleges and Universities*, and Barron's lists UA among its recommended colleges.

Student Body Undergraduate enrollment is 48 percent men, 52 percent women; 14 percent Hispanic, 5 percent Asian, 3 percent African American, 2 percent Native American, and 69 percent Anglo. There are more than 1,000 international undergraduate students. Sixty-eight percent of freshmen live on campus (4,836 total spaces in the residence hall system). More than two thirds of the students receive $170 million in financial aid each year. The campus has nineteen sororities and twenty-seven fraternities.

Faculty There are 1,627 faculty members, 97 percent with doctoral degrees. The student-faculty ratio is 20:1.

Key Facilities The library holds 4 million volumes. There are seven open-access computer labs and many departmental specialty labs. Labs contain a combination of Windows/DOS, Macintosh, and UNIX-based machines. Each residence hall room provides a free direct link to UAInfo, the World Wide Web, and the Internet for students bringing personal computers to campus.

Honorary Societies Phi Eta Sigma, Golden Key, Mortar Board, Phi Beta Kappa

Athletics UA participates in NCAA Division I, Pac-10 athletics. The University maintains the nation's fourth-ranked all-around sports program, with six teams ranked in the top 10 nationally. The women's softball team has won the national championship twice in the last three years. Eight sports are available to men (baseball, basketball, football, tennis, golf, swimming/diving, cross-country, and track and field) and ten sports are available to women (basketball, golf, tennis, softball, volleyball, swimming/diving, cross-country, track and field, gymnastics, and soccer). Students also participate in intramural and club sports, which attract more than 20,000 students annually. On a day-to-day basis, students pursue their personal best in the Student Recreation Center, an $11-million building, created in response to student requests, that has won national awards for design and program quality.

Study Abroad The UA's Study Abroad Office has information about hundreds of program opportunities throughout the world. Students may choose to participate in UA-sponsored programs in Mexico, Europe, the Mediterranean, Russia, and Taiwan, or join another university program as a transfer student for a summer, semester, or academic year. Study-abroad scholarships are available to help support program costs.

Support Services The Center for Disability Related Resources assists students with physical, developmental, and learning disabilities.

Job Opportunities Students are offered a range of work opportunities on campus, including assistantships and 2,313 work-study positions.

Tuition: $2264 for state residents, $9416 for nonresidents, per year (1999–2000)

Room and Board: $5548

Mandatory Fees: $69

Contact: Dean: Dr. Patricia MacCorquodale, Slonaker House, Room 107, Tucson, Arizona 85721-0006; Telephone: 520-621-6901; Fax: 520-621-8655; E-mail: pmac@arizona.edu; Web site: http://www.honors.arizona.edu/

UNIVERSITY OF ARKANSAS

4 Pu C L Sc Tr AA FA

▼ Fulbright College of Arts and Sciences Honors Studies Program

The Fulbright College Honors Studies Program was created in 1956. Initially, though many core honors courses were offered, the focus was mainly departmental. In 1986, a four-year honors core was developed. Now students are able to participate in honors studies in one of two ways—The Four-Year Scholars Program or the Departmental Honors Program. Both programs are designed to provide bright, energetic students with a deeper understanding of their fields and to place that understanding in the context of a broad liberal arts education.

Participation Requirements: The Four-Year Scholars program offers an honors core curriculum as an alternative to the regular core. An NEH-sponsored four-semester humanities course has been designed to combine world literature, world civilization, and fine arts requirements. Students also have the opportunity to choose among a wide variety of colloquia. Departmental honors students must complete 12 hours of honors classes. Both groups complete an honors research or terminal project in the field of study.

Students who successfully complete required honors course work and a research project in their field of study graduate with honors. Cum laude, magna cum laude, or summa cum laude—depending on the quality of the work completed—are noted on transcripts and diplomas. Students graduating with honors wear stoles and medals at graduation marking their outstanding accomplishments.

Admission Process: Students are admitted on several criteria: high school records, class rank, ACT or SAT I scores, academic awards and prizes, and participation in special programs or institutes. Students entering the Four-Year Scholars Program usually have a high school GPA of 3.5 or better and a score of 28 on the ACT (1240 on the SAT I) or higher. Students entering the Departmental Honors Program usually have a current college GPA of 3.25 and must be recommended by a member of the student's department. These guidelines are flexible. A student who does not meet the basic requirements should schedule an interview with the director.

Scholarship Availability: The University of Arkansas awards numerous academic scholarships. Most of the students participating in Honors Studies have been awarded one of these scholarships. Only the Sturgis Fellowships are directly awarded by the Honors Studies Office. The Sturgis Endowment for Academic Excellence funds eleven fellowships ($43,000 for four years) each year. In addition to room, board, and tuition, Sturgis Fellowships can be used to pay for travel abroad or for equipment, such as computers and musical instruments.

The Campus Context: The University of Arkansas (Fayetteville) is made up of six colleges: Fulbright College of Arts and Sciences, School of Architecture, College of Business Administration, Dale Bumpers College of Agriculture and Food and Life Sciences, College of Education, and College of Engineering.

Student Body The undergraduate enrollment totals 11,973. Forty-seven percent are women, 53 percent men. African Americans make up 6.02 percent of the population, Asians 2.5 percent, Hispanics .9 percent, and Native Americans 1.82 percent. Eighty percent of the students live off campus. There are 285 international undergraduate students at the University of Arkansas.

Study Abroad The Fulbright Institute at the University of Arkansas houses the Study Abroad Program. Many campus scholarships (up to $8000 each) specifically for study abroad are available. The University has a variety of exchange programs.

Tuition: $3116 for state residents, $8674 for nonresidents, per year (2001–02)

Room and Board: $4454 minimum

Fees: $764

Contact: Professor Sidney Burris, Old Main 517, Fayetteville, Arkansas 72701; Telephone: 501-575-2509; Fax: 501-575-2491; E-mail: sburris@uark.edu

Interpreting the symbols: **2**=two-year college, **4**=four-year college; **Pu**=public or state college, **Pr**=private college; **G**=general honors program; **D**=departmental honors program; **S**=small program (fewer than 100 students), **M**=midsize program (100 to 500 students), **L**=large program (more than 500 students); **Sc**=scholarships available in honors program; **Tr**=transfer students accepted into honors program; **HBC**=historically black college; **AA**=academic advisors; **GA**=graduate advisors; **FA**=fellowship advisors.

UNIVERSITY OF ARKANSAS AT FORT SMITH

4 Pu G S Sc Tr

▼ Honors Program

The University of Arkansas (UA) at Fort Smith Honors Program provides a variety of activities and options to enrich and broaden the educational experience of highly motivated and talented students. The program provides opportunities for diverse educational activities, such as discussion groups, forums, and mentor relationships, that help the students grow both academically and personally. Honors classes at UA Fort Smith present a challenging learning environment where ideas and concepts are examined in seminar formats with small numbers of students. Honors classes explore topics in greater depth and focus on the development of fundamental abilities beyond the basic general education competencies.

The Chancellor's Scholars Program is the UA Fort Smith's premier merit-based award for high school seniors. Chancellor's Scholars are among the top students in their graduating classes, have a proven record of academic and leadership excellence, and show potential for continued growth in an academically challenging environment. The students benefit from honors seminar courses that are exclusive to the Chancellor's Scholars Program and work with distinguished faculty members. Students not accepted into this program may take honors courses and apply for acceptance to the University Honors Program. To receive a bachelor's degree with honors from the UA at Fort Smith, a student must complete a minimum of 24 credit hours of honors courses, including a junior honors seminar and a senior honors project.

The University of Arkansas at Fort Smith honors courses challenge students with a different type of learning experience. The honors courses focus on primary source materials rather than rely on textbook information. Field trips to archeological sites and museums allow honors students to gain firsthand knowledge in subject areas.

Other advantages for honors program students include an honors lounge and media center that is equipped with its own computer, free interlibrary loans at Boreham Library for honors course study, and participation in the community service arm of the UA Fort Smith Honors Program.

Participation Requirements: For a bachelor's degree with honors, students must complete 24 hours of honors credit, achieve mastery in all general education competencies, and maintain a minimum 3.25 GPA in all course work.

Graduating Chancellor's Scholars and University Honors students are given special recognition at the spring honors convocation and receive special medallions to wear at graduation. In addition, an honors seal is placed on the diploma and the honors degree is noted on the student's official transcript.

Admission Process: Applicants for the Chancellor's Scholars Program should demonstrate evidence of high motivation, leadership, and academic skills. An application for the program includes recommendations from high school instructors, an on-campus interview and writing sample, and an ACT composite score of 27 or higher. Applications for the Chancellor's Scholars Program must be submitted by February 15. Annual renewal of the scholarship requires maintenance of a minimum 3.25 GPA and completion of 30 hours or more during the freshman year.

Applicants for the University Honors Program may be submitted at any time and must include recommendations from instructors, a minimum 3.25 GPA in UA Fort Smith classes, or an ACT score of 25 or higher.

Scholarship Availability: The Chancellor's Honors Program awards a full tuition scholarship and $500 toward books and supplies each semester. Other students may qualify for merit-based scholarships and a University Honors book scholarship.

The Campus Context: From its inception in 1928 as Fort Smith Junior College, the University of Arkansas at Fort Smith has existed to serve the educational, training, and cultural needs of the area. In 1952, the junior college moved to the current campus, and in 1965, it became a state-supported community college under the name Westark Junior College. Through several name changes, the college grew as a two-year school and opened a University Center in 1990 to offer bachelor's degrees from other institutions. On January 1, 2002, the school merged with the University of Arkansas system as a university campus, offering bachelor's degrees. With these changes, UA Fort Smith has experienced substantial growth in enrollment, faculty, facilities, and curricula.

The University of Arkansas at Fort Smith confers bachelor's degrees in selected majors and specialty area such as the Bachelor of Manufacturing Technology. It continues to offer two-year degrees to meet the needs of area residents, including the Associate of Applied Science, the Associate of General Studies, the Associate of Arts, and various certificates.

Student Body Enrollment at UA Fort Smith in fall 2001 was 5,746. Of that total, 43 percent were men and 57 percent were women.

Faculty Of the 16 faculty members teaching honors courses, 50 percent hold doctorate or other terminal degrees.

Key Facilities Boreham Library has holdings of approximately 65,000 books and a growing collection of audiovisual items, including videotapes, cassettes, CDs, and DVDs. The library subscribes to approximately 600 periodicals and eight newspapers, some of which are available on microfilm or microfiche.

In efforts to keep pace with emerging technologies, the library makes available several databases on compact disk. It also has access to online databases from vendors such as American Psychological Association, Health and Wellness Resource Center, MLA, ERIC, LEXIS-NEXIS, First Search, and Expanded Academic Index. Through membership in Online Computer Library Center (OCLC), the largest online bibliographic utility in the world, the library's interlibrary loan service is capable of accessing library collections both nationally and internationally.

Reciprocal borrowing privileges among UA Fort Smith, Fort Smith Public Library, and Scott-Sebastian Regional Library entitle current UA Fort Smith students to library privileges at any of these three institutions.

The new 80,000-square-foot campus center includes a 500-seat multipurpose ballroom, a cafeteria and dining room, a food court, offices and workrooms for student organizations, the campus bookstore, student lounges and game rooms, a copy center, a career center, conference rooms, and student services offices.

Athletics UA Fort Smith teams engage in intercollegiate competition in men's basketball and baseball and women's basketball and volleyball. The University is a member of the National Junior College Athletic Association Region II and the Bi-State East Conference.

Support Services UA Fort Smith seeks to provide reasonable accommodations and services to students who are physically and learning disabled. The underlying philosophy of the Americans with Disabilities Act (ADA) program, which is under the direction of the Dean of Student and Academic Support Services, is to provide support, where possible, that will facilitate the academic progress of each individual student.

Job Opportunities Qualified students are offered a range of work opportunities on campus, including work-study and scholar-preceptor positions.

Tuition: $1470 for Sebastian County residents, $1740 for other Arkansas residents and residents of Sequoyah or LeFlore Counties in Oklahoma, $3420 for nonresidents, per year (2001–02)

Mandatory Fees: $15 registration fee per semester

Contact: Director: Dr. Henry Q. Rinne, 5210 Grand Avenue, P.O. Box 3649, Fort Smith, Arkansas 72913-3649; Telephone: 479-788-7545; E-mail: hrinne@uafortsmith.edu; Web site: http://www.uafortsmith.edu/academic/uho

University of Arkansas at Little Rock

4 Pu G S Sc Tr

▼ Donaghey Scholars Program

The Donaghey Scholars Program, though fairly young and fairly small (20 to 25 new Scholars are admitted each year), has matured into a distinctive and distinguished honors program.

It is distinctive in part because of its smallness (the program's size fosters intimacy and a genuine sense of community). The program's distinctiveness also derives from its curriculum. The Donaghey Scholars Program curriculum is comprehensive and highly structured; it features an interdisciplinary core of team-taught seminar-format courses that replaces the University's general education core. These core courses emphasize primary texts, critical thinking, active debate, and lots of writing (and rewriting). In addition to the core, Donaghey Scholars take seminars on special topics, develop competence in a foreign language, and do a final project. By the time a Scholar graduates, he or she should be both a good generalist and someone ready to contribute to his or her own field.

The Donaghey Scholars Program is also distinctive in linking participation in the program to financial aid. All Donaghey Scholars receive generous scholarships.

The Donaghey Scholars Program began in 1984; currently 80 scholars are enrolled.

Participation Requirements: To complete the program, Donaghey Scholars must complete a core of interdisciplinary courses totaling 35 hours (Colloquium I and II; Rhetoric and Communication I and II; Science and Society I and II; History of Ideas I, II, and III; Individual and Society I and II; and Creative Arts I and II). In addition, scholars must take a math course (3 hours) and a course in American history or American national government (3 hours). Scholars also develop competence in a foreign language and study abroad. They must also take three seminars (totalling at least 5 hours), complete a final project, and do an exit interview. To remain in good standing, scholars must maintain a minimum 3.25 GPA. Upon graduation, scholars receive a certificate indicating they have completed the program, and they wear distinctive maroon robes at commencement.

Admission Process: Since only 20 to 25 new scholars can be admitted each year, admission to the program is highly competitive. The program's admissions committee proceeds holistically. It weighs several factors, including test scores, aptitude for foreign languages, genuine interest in other cultures, letters of recommendation, writing samples, extracurricular and service activities and other evidence of leadership, an interview, and academic record (this last is the most important factor). Highly motivated, broadly curious, articulate, imaginative, and well-organized students who can contribute to and profit from the program (and the University) are sought. Students with previous college work as well as those who have just finished high school are eligible. The students are diverse; they represent a good mix of backgrounds, abilities, and interests. The program has always welcomed nontraditional and international students.

Scholarship Availability: Donaghey Scholars receive the University's most generous academic scholarships. All Donaghey Scholars receive tuition and fees, a generous stipend (currently $3250, $5750, or $8250 each year), and support for study abroad—the Donaghey Scholars Program is one of only a handful of programs in the United States that requires its students to study abroad and subsidizes that study.

The Campus Context: The University of Arkansas (UALR) was founded in 1927 as Little Rock Junior College and was housed in public school buildings. In 1949, the college moved to its current location in southwest Little Rock on land donated by Little Rock businessman, Raymond Rebsamen. In September, 1969, the University merged with the University of Arkansas System and became one of the eight campuses.

Taking advantage of its metropolitan location, the University offers programs and services that respond to the special needs and interests of individuals, the community, business, and government. UALR offers certificates and degree programs at the associate, baccalaureate, master's, specialist, and doctoral levels. Disciplines in which degrees are offered include the arts; business, health, and public administration; communication; education; engineering technology; the humanities; instrumentation; law; social, physical, and life sciences; and social work. Beginning with the 1999–2000 academic year, UALR will offer its new minor in information technology, followed by degree programs in telecommunications systems engineering and computer systems engineering within the newly formed College of Information Science and Systems Engineering.

Student Body Undergraduate enrollment at the University of Arkansas at Little Rock for fall 1998 was 8,383 students; graduate and law school students totaled 2,158. The minority ethnic distribution of students is 0.6 percent Native American, 1.3 percent Hispanic, 3.4 percent Asian American, and 22.8 percent African American. There are approximately 370 international students representing more than forty countries at UALR. The overall average age of students is 27 years old.

There are more than 100 student organizations and clubs registered at UALR. These groups offer opportunities for leadership and student development experiences, they recognize scholarship and leadership achievements, and they provide social experiences and opportunities to promote common interests in areas such as religion, philosophy, ethics, social action, politics, recreation, and hobbies.

Faculty The student-faculty ratio at UALR in fall 1998 was 14:1. UALR has 369 full-time and 332 part-time faculty members; 333 faculty members have terminal degrees and approximately 43 percent of all faculty members are tenured or on tenture-track.

Key Facilities UALR has one library on the main campus, the Ottenheimer Library, which is a selective depository for federal documents; the Ottenheimer Library is also a depository for the European Communities and the State of Arkansas. The UALR School of Law has its own library, offering a strong current collection in U.S. law and emphasizing academic and practitioner needs. The Ottenheimer Library's 1997–98 holdings were as follows: 297,500 book titles; 336,000 book volumes; 103,250 bound periodicals; 311,900 government documents; and 268,800 microfiche titles.

UALR provides students with e-mail, World Wide Web, Telnet, and gopher access and has approximately 500 PCs and Macs available for general student use. A total of 2,000 PCs and Macs are available for faculty and staff member and student use.

Honorary Societies Phi Kappa Phi and Golden Key

Athletics The UALR men's athletic program is a member of the National Collegiate Athletic Association Division I and abides by NCAA rules and regulations. Men's and women's teams compete

Interpreting the symbols: **2**=two-year college, **4**=four-year college; **Pu**=public or state college, **Pr**=private college; **G**=general honors program; **D**=departmental honors program; **S**=small program (fewer than 100 students), **M**=midsize program (100 to 500 students), **L**=large program (more than 500 students); **Sc**=scholarships available in honors program; **Tr**=transfer students accepted into honors program; **HBC**=historically black college; **AA**=academic advisors; **GA**=graduate advisors; **FA**=fellowship advisors.

in the Sun Belt Conference. Men's sports include baseball, basketball, cross-country, tennis, and water polo. Women's sports include cross-country, soccer, swimming, tennis, track, and volleyball.

Study Abroad Working through UALR's Programs Abroad Office, students can take advantage of language-based summer programs and semester or yearlong exchanges in Austria, France, Mexico, and Spain. In addition, students may participate in individualized programs to countries such as Egypt, Costa Rica, Slovenia, and the Netherlands.

Tuition: $2328 for residents, $6000 for nonresidents (1998–99)

Room: $2500–$3750

Mandatory Fees: $12 per credit hour

Contact: Director: Dr. C. Earl Ramsey, 2801 South University, Little Rock, Arkansas 72204; Telephone: 501-569-3389; Fax: 501-569-8185; E-mail: ceramsey@ualr.edu; Web site: http://www.ualr.edu/~dsp

University of Arkansas at Monticello

4 Pu G S Sc Tr

▼ Honors Program

The UAM honors curriculum consists of four core colloquia for freshman and sophomore students and independent work at the junior and senior levels, leading to a senior thesis. The core courses are interdisciplinary and are unique in the University curriculum. Colloquia topics vary and are related closely to the annual theme around which cocurricular and extracurricular activities are designed. These four courses may substitute for general education requirements in the humanities, social science, and math or science. Class size is limited to facilitate discussion.

Faculty members are invited to participate in the Honors Program, both as colloquia instructors and as mentors for the upper-level students working toward theses. Preferred faculty members are engaged actively in research and have a demonstrated interest in sharing enthusiasm for intellectual inquiry.

Cocurricular and extracurricular activities are vital elements in the program. From the informal Brown Bag Friday talks in the Honors Center each week to Sunday in the City, a monthly excursion to Little Rock for events such as symphony performances, IMAX films, and traveling exhibits at the Design Museum to satellite programming through NCHC and travel to research conferences, UAM Honors Program students are offered a rich variety of intellectual stimulation. In addition, students have exclusive, 24-hour access to the Honors Center, which includes multiple computers with Internet access, a full kitchen, activity room, and study lounge.

The 4-year-old program has 55 participants.

Participation Requirements: Graduation as a University Honors Scholar requires completion of 18 hours of honors courses and two Honors Options courses in the major, maintenance of a minimum 3.0 GPA, and completion of a senior thesis.

Admission Process: High school students with ACT composite scores of 24 and above are recruited directly for the program. Students must apply to the program, providing transcripts and letters of recommendation, and are invited to the campus for an interview that includes attending a Brown Bag Friday presentation; writing a brief, extemporaneous essay; meeting faculty members in an interview setting; and touring campus facilities. Rising sophomores and transfer students may apply for fall admission to the program when vacancies are available and all admission criteria are met.

Scholarship Availability: The Honors Program includes full-tuition four-year scholarships, a book credit of $250 per semester, payment of all fees, and credit toward a double-occupancy dorm room for entering freshmen. Entering sophomores are offered three years of full tuition and the book allowance.

The Campus Context: The University of Arkansas at Monticello is situated in the pine forests of southeast Arkansas on the edge of the rich Mississippi Delta and is the home of the state's only school of forestry. UAM was established in 1909 as the Fourth District Agricultural School, and 300 acres of University land are still devoted to agricultural teaching and research. The campus is located 100 miles southeast of Little Rock and became part of the University of Arkansas system in 1971.

Student Body There are 2,370 undergraduates, primarily from southeast Arkansas: 41 percent men, 59 percent women. The ethnic distribution is 85 percent Caucasian and 15 percent African American. Eighty-five percent of the students are commuters.

Support Services Some facilities are accessible for the disabled on the lower floors. The Office of Special Student Services coordinates the needs of disabled students.

Tuition: $1906 for state residents, $4114 for nonresidents, per year (1996–97)

Room and Board: $2400 minimum

Contact: Director: Dr. Linda J. Webster, Monticello, Arkansas 71656; Telephone: 870-460-1232; Fax: 870-460-1961; E-mail: webster@uamont.edu; Web site: http://cotton.uamont.edu/~webster/webster.html

University of Arkansas at Pine Bluff

4 Pu G M Tr HBC

▼ Honors College

The Honors College at the University of Arkansas at Pine Bluff (UAPB) is designed for academically oriented and motivated students. Its overall goal is to identify and recruit students of superior academic ability and potential performance and students who have a commitment to challenge, toward the end of developing the Honors College as a standard of excellence and a paradigm for all UAPB students. The program embraces the concept that it is a planned set of arrangements to serve the needs of talented, gifted, and committed students so much so that the general student population will benefit from the leadership of these students and from interaction with them in classes and forums. In addition, the faculty will be challenged to provide for those students the kinds of experiences that will motivate them to work to their potential. Ultimately, the community, state, and nation will receive the benefit of a group of leaders and citizens who will be willing, capable, and able to have a positive impact on the quality of life for all citizens. The program utilizes current faculty members to develop and implement challenging courses; it recruits bright, energetic young people; and it exposes them to activities that increase their probabilities of success in their chosen fields.

The plan of the Honors College corresponds to the mission of the University, part of which is to create a "culturally enriching environment for disadvantaged students" and to provide "specialized research, education, public service, and human resources to the state . . ." One of the University's specific goals is to increase the institution's capability for meeting the needs of both the superior and the inadequately prepared student, and this program targets those superior students.

The Honors College is a participation program that is open to any serious student who wants to respond to the challenge of honors courses and other honors experiences. Admission requirements are not so rigid that a desire to participate is ignored if a student exhibits potential, simply because that student does not meet the established ACT score requirement. This policy is commensurate with the general admission policy adhered to by the University.

The Honors College does not directly offer honors classes; it is an interdisciplinary unit that collaborates with all disciplines in developing either honors sections of existing courses, new honors courses, or contractual honors work in existing courses. Honors sections usually have an average of 15 students; however, students who contract for work in other sections may be in classes of 25 or more. To do this, students must communicate with instructors who agree to assign more challenging course work, and they both sign the contract, which is returned to the Honors College and then submitted to the registrar's office. Honors suites have been established in the dorms for upperclassmen, and there is an honors floor for incoming freshmen, one for men and one for women.

Participation Requirements: Members of the Honors College are required to maintain at least a 3.25 GPA. Students who fail to maintain the required GPA are placed on probation and given one semester in which to raise their averages. They are suspended from the program if they fail to comply. Suspended students may apply for readmission, and each case is considered individually.

Honors College students are encouraged to participate in the UAPB Research Forum either individually or collaboratively with faculty. In order to qualify as an Honors College graduate, students must enroll in and complete a minimum of 15 credit hours and complete each course with at least a B. Having satisfied all Honors College requirements—GPA, community service, maintenance of an acceptable portfolio, accumulation of the required number of hours in honors, and involvement in honors activities—the student will have Honors College Graduate indicated on his or her transcript and will be so recognized at commencement.

Admission Process: The Honors College administration collaborates with high school counselors and staff members of the University's basic and academic services to recruit incoming freshmen. Though the Honors College caters to freshmen, other students, sophomores, juniors, and transfer students are accepted. Entering students must apply for formal admission to the Honors College by obtaining an application for admission from the Honors College. Entering freshmen must have an ACT score of 21 or above, must rank in the top 25 percent of their graduating class, and must have a firm commitment. Students already enrolled in the University who can demonstrate that they have made a commitment to the objectives of the Honors College may also apply.

Students admitted into the Honors College are advised to visit with the Dean to discuss desires and expectations and to inquire about scholarships, internships, and other perks of membership. Honors College students form the Honor Student Association, which has scheduled meetings each second and fourth Tuesday. Students are required to attend scheduled meetings and participate in Honor Student Association activities.

Scholarship Availability: The Honors College supervises three scholarship per year: The Thurgood Marshall Scholarship, the Rouse Family Scholarship, and the USDA Scholarship. The Thurgood Marshall and the USDA scholarships are offered to incoming freshmen only. Students applying for these scholarships must obtain a formal application packet, have a cumulative GPA of at least 3.0 on a 4.0 scale and an ACT score of 25 or higher, and submit the completed packet to the Dean of the Honors College, who sits on the scholarship advisory committees.

Thurgood Marshall Scholarship recipients are allowed to enter into any of the academic disciplines; however, the USDA Scholarship recipients must enter into a discipline related to agriculture. Students who receive these scholarships are required to maintain a minimum 3.0 GPA each semester in order to retain their scholarship. Any student who fails to maintain the appropriate GPA automatically loses his or her scholarship privilege.

The Rouse Family Scholarship is available to any upperclassman enrolled at the University. Students interested in receiving the Rouse Family Scholarship must obtain and submit a completed application form and demonstrate financial need. Students applying for this scholarship must be enrolled as full-time students and have a cumulative GPA of at least 3.25. This scholarship is given in the spring semester of each year in amounts ranging from $250 to $1000 and may be used for the purpose of paying the balance of tuition, the purchase of books and/or supplies, or to supplement other educational costs.

The Campus Context: The University of Arkansas at Pine Bluff is a land-grant residential institution founded in 1873 as Branch Normal College, a branch of the University of Arkansas. The University opened to students on September 27, 1875. UAPB is also the second-oldest public institution in Arkansas and the oldest institution with black heritage. Since 1873, the institution has grown and changed its official name on two occasions: in 1927 to Arkansas Agricultural, Mechanical and Normal College (Arkansas AM&N) and in 1972 to University of Arkansas at Pine Bluff.

UAPB's vast campus, located in northeast Pine Bluff, is a blend of oak and pine trees that comprise 318 acres of forty-one major buildings and agriculture and aquaculture research farms. UAPB is multicultural, with a diverse student population that includes people just out of high school, professionals improving their qualifications, and nontraditional students.

The University's academic offerings comprise forty-two bachelor's degree programs, sixty-one concentrations, two associate degree programs, and more than 700 courses. In 1990–91, the UA Board and Arkansas Department of High Education granted approval for UAPB to offer graduate classes and two graduate degree programs in elementary education and secondary education. A third graduate degree in aquaculture/fisheries was recently approved and implemented.

The Honors College, re-established in 1985 and located in room 202 of the newly renovated Research Center, offers a rigorous academic challenge to high-achieving students. Being located in the Research Center allows its 160 members computer labs and research accessibility.

The L.A. Davis Student Union houses student government offices, a recreation center, a conference room, the student cafeteria and snack bar, and a ballroom that holds an approximate capacity of 250 people.

The Kenneth L. Johnson Health, Physical Education and Recreation Complex is equipped not only with physical education facilities but also has classrooms, an indoor heated swimming pool, a lecture hall, and an arena.

The Hathaway/Howard Fine Arts Center houses the University's Music, Theater, and Art Departments and is the site for the art exhibitions of past and present administrators, emeriti, and professionals.

Corbin Hall, which was named after the school's first chief administrator, J. C. Corbin, houses the institution's School of Education.

Student Body As of fall 1998, the University of Arkansas at Pine Bluff had an enrollment of 3,100, 35.22 percent of whom live on campus. The number of white, non-Hispanic students is 177; the number of Hispanic students is 9, the number of Asian or Pacific

Interpreting the symbols: **2**=two-year college, **4**=four-year college; **Pu**=public or state college, **Pr**=private college; **G**=general honors program; **D**=departmental honors program; **S**=small program (fewer than 100 students), **M**=midsize program (100 to 500 students), **L**=large program (more than 500 students); **Sc**=scholarships available in honors program; **Tr**=transfer students accepted into honors program; **HBC**=historically black college; **AA**=academic advisors; **GA**=graduate advisors; **FA**=fellowship advisors.

Islander students is 13; the number of Native American/Alaskan students is 0; and the number of unknown students is 2 with the remainder of the population being African American or black. The number of students who reside in the University's dormitories is 1,081, which is 35 percent of the total student population.

Faculty Because the Honors College does not have its own faculty, it utilizes the faculty members of the different disciplines throughout the entire University.

Key Facilities The University's library, the Watson Memorial Library, has recently been completely renovated and is now equipped with 257,007 volumes and sixteen computers with Internet access. It also has a small lecture room and office space.

Athletics UAPB is a member of the Southwest Athletic Conference (SWAC), and facilities are available for all major sports, including baseball, basketball, football, golf, swimming, tennis, and track and field. There is a large University-sponsored intramural program.

Job Opportunities Work opportunities are available through the University's offices of Career Planning and Placement and Cooperative Education. There are also opportunities for students to work on and off campus.

Tuition: $900 full-time (14–18 credit hours) for residents, $2268 for nonresidents (1998–99)

Room and board: $1670

Mandatory Fees: $263

Contact: Dean: Dr. Carolyn Blakely, 1200 North University Drive, P.O. Box 4931, Pine Bluff, Arkansas 71611; Telephone: 870-543-8065; Fax: 870-543-8063; E-mail: blakely_c@vx4500.uapb.edu

UNIVERSITY OF BALTIMORE

Pu G S Sc Tr AA GA FA

▼ Helen P. Denit Honors Program

The University of Baltimore's Helen P. Denit Honors Program was developed in 1978 with a unique mandate to serve the last two years of undergraduate education to a broad mix of students majoring in business, the liberal arts, and law.

Known as the "career-minded university," the University of Baltimore (UB) provides professionally oriented students an opportunity to continue their education with an array of flexible programs and schedules.

UB's Honors Program emphasizes the notion that "career" involves the lifelong pursuit of learning, excellence, and intellectual satisfaction. The academic curriculum, taught by faculty members from all areas of the University, is designed to engage, challenge, and enrich students' professional study by offering innovative honors classes and interdisciplinary seminars. Students are encouraged to become involved in independent study and research opportunities with faculty members who share their same interests. There are also opportunities for students to present their ideas at local, regional, and national conferences and to travel and study abroad.

Because of the University's downtown location, the Honors Program is able to take advantage of the cosmopolitan nature of Baltimore by offering an array of enrichment opportunities at no cost to students. These opportunities include enjoying opera next door at the Lyric Theatre, listening to the Baltimore Symphony Orchestra at the nearby Meyerhoff Symphony Hall, and viewing exciting theater at Center Stage. Because of its location close to Annapolis and Washington, D.C., there are numerous museums and other attractions of historical and cultural interest within a short driving distance.

The Honors Program has a lounge in the Merrick School of Business on the fourth floor, room 425. There, students find an excellent place for hanging out, with comfortable chairs, computers, printers, snacks, a refrigerator, and a microwave. Students should visit http://www.ubalt.edu/honors to learn more about the Honors Program and staff members.

Participation Requirements: Students are expected to achieve and maintain at least a 3.5 GPA to be eligible for participation in the Helen P. Denit Honors Program. Students are expected to take a minimum of four honors courses (12 credit hours), one of which should be a capstone project. These capstone projects are archived at the Langsdale Library and may be displayed, with permission of the student, on the Honors Program's Web site.

Students in good standing are eligible to participate in the cultural and social activities that the Honors Program has to offer. Limited funds are available to carry out research toward the completion of the capstone project, field trips, and attendance at conferences.

Successful completion of the program is noted on the diploma as graduating cum laude, magna cum laude, or summa cum laude and on the transcript as graduating from the University of Baltimore's Helen P. Denit Honors Program.

Admission Process: Students transferring to UB with a GPA of 3.5 or higher are invited to apply for the Honors Program. Students who complete their A.A. degree with honors at a community college with which UB has an articulation agreement are automatically admitted into the Honors Program. Current undergraduate students in both the Yale Gordon College of Liberal Arts and the Merrick School of Business whose GPA is 3.5 or above or who have been nominated by a professor are encouraged to apply. Students should submit a personal statement as to why they wish to participate in the Honors Program and submit two academic letters of recommendation.

Given the complexity and diversity of the student body and the large number of older students returning to school, students not meeting the GPA requirement may petition for provisional acceptance into the Honors Program. Decisions are made on a case-by-case basis.

UB has a rolling admissions policy, and applications are accepted until the last day of registration each semester, space permitting. However, the earlier an application and credentials are received, the earlier an admission decision can be made. It is recommended that students file an application by July 1 for the fall semester, November 1 for the spring semester, and April 1 for the summer session. A nonrefundable $20 application fee is required at the time of application. An online application is available at http://www.ubalt.edu/admissions, or students may request an application by calling or writing to Admissions Office, University of Baltimore, 1420 North Charles Street, Baltimore, Maryland 21201-5779; Telephone: 410-837-4777 or 877-ApplyUB (toll-free).

Scholarship Availability: Although the Honors Program does not offer scholarships, UB funds a number of merit scholarships for outstanding transfer students. For example, the Wilson Scholarship offers Maryland residents 100 percent of in-state tuition; for nonresidents, it offers 100 percent of in-state tuition plus an additional award of $1500 per year. To qualify for this scholarship, the student must have an entering cross-institutional GPA of at least 3.5, be enrolled full-time, be nominated by a community college, qualify for the Maryland State Distinguished Scholarship, or have an application to UB.

The Dean's Scholarship covers 50 percent of in-state tuition for Maryland residents; for nonresidents, it covers 50 percent of in-state tuition plus an additional award of $1500 per year. To qualify for this scholarship, the student must have an entering cross-institutional GPA of at least 3.25 and be enrolled full-time.

The Phi Theta Kappa Scholarship is available for Phi Theta Kappa members designated by community colleges. The scholarship covers 75 percent of in-state tuition for Maryland residents; for nonresidents, it covers 75 percent of in-state tuition plus an additional award of $1500 per year. To qualify for this scholarship, the student must have an entering GPA of at least 3.5 and be enrolled full-time.

Part-Time Scholars Program Scholarships covers 50 percent of in-state tuition (6 to 11 credits per semester) for Maryland residents; for nonresidents, it covers 50 percent of in-state tuition (6 to 11 credits per semester), plus an additional award of $750 per year. To qualify for this scholarship, the student must have an entering GPA of at least 3.5.

The Campus Context: UB is situated downtown in the historical and cultural center of the city, next door to the Lyric Opera House, and within a short walk of the Meyerhoff Symphony Hall and the Maryland Institute College of Art. Delightful architectural structures surround the University, leading the students to discovery during walking tours. The Dime Museum and the Great Blacks in Wax Museum are within walking distance, as are the Walters Museum of Art and the Peabody Music Institute.

The Baltimore Museum of Art, the American Visionary Art Museum, and the Baltimore Aquarium are all within a mile of UB. For the sports enthusiast, Oriole Park at Camden Yards and PSINet (Ravens) Stadium are approximately 3 miles south of the campus. Annapolis, the capital of Maryland, located on the beautiful Chesapeake Bay, is a 45-minute drive away, and Washington, D.C., is a 1-hour commute from the University.

UB has a recreational center with a gymnasium, racquetball courts, and a fully equipped exercise room complete with treadmills, stationary bikes, StairMasters, free weights, and weight machines. The Athletic Club, located on the third floor of the Academic Center, is free to students, faculty members, and staff members.

Bachelor of Science degrees are offered in applied information technology; business administration, with specializations in accounting, computer information systems, economics, entrepreneurship, finance, human resource management, international business, jurisprudence, and marketing; corporate communication; criminal justice; forensic studies; government and public policy; and management information systems. Bachelor of Arts degrees are offered in history, interdisciplinary studies, human services administration, jurisprudence, and psychology. New and exciting programs are constantly being developed to serve the career and intellectual needs of the diverse body of students.

Student Body The undergraduate student population of the University, including part-time students, is 2,016 students. There are 901 full-time students and 1,115 part-time students. Students come from seven states and territories and represent sixty countries.

UB is a coed institution, with 59 percent women and 41 percent men; 45 percent attend school full-time. Seventy-three percent of the students are 25 years old or older. The average age is 32. The graduate student population is 947, and the professional student population is 1,711.

UB has a diverse student population—30 percent African Americans, 2 percent Asian Americans, 2 percent Hispanic Americans, and 1 percent Native Americans.

Faculty There are 332 faculty members: 49 percent full-time, 70 percent with terminal degrees. The student-faculty ratio is 14:1, making a high-quality education available to all and a particularly easy way to have a natural mentoring process. The faculty members come from a great variety of backgrounds, and many are consultants, bringing a wealth of experience and connection to the outside world. Students have the opportunity to engage in dialogue with faculty members and business leaders on the cutting edge of their disciplines and benefit from their mentorship.

Key Facilities The Langsdale Library has 258,747 titles, 10,738 serial subscriptions, and 883 audiovisual materials. The library participates in the State of Maryland system and provides easy access to materials held at other institutions through electronic databases and interlibrary loan.

UB prides itself on the availability of computers throughout the institution. The Honors Program has a student lounge where computers and printers are located for the exclusive use of honors students.

Athletics UB has a recreational facility with treadmills and other exercise machines, a full-size gymnasium, and a sauna open to students, faculty members, and staff members. UB has intramural sports, badminton, basketball, golf, racquetball, table tennis, tennis, volleyball, weight lifting, women's club crew, and men's crew, soccer, and softball.

Study Abroad UB encourages and facilitates study-abroad programs through the International Office, the College of Liberal Arts, and the School of Business. A limited number of scholarships are available for students who wish to enhance their educational experience by studying abroad. UB students have studied in Albania, China, England, Europe, Holland, Jamaica, and Latin America. The University has an exchange program with Rotterdam Ichthus Hogeschool for corporate communication students.

Support Services The Academic Resource Center offers free services to all students. These services include individual and small-group tutoring, computer-assisted study, academic counseling, and assistance with learning and study strategies. Preparation for the GMATs and mini-computer workshops are offered, and a small fee is charged. Honors students can find employment opportunities at the Academic Resource Center.

The Office of Disability Support Services provides assistance to students with a wide range of visible and nonvisible disabilities. The office works closely with the Academic Resource Center and with faculty members and staff members to make sure that accessibility and accommodations are provided.

Job Opportunities UB graduates are sought for employment by a wide range of companies and organizations, including state and federal government, as well as private organizations. During 1998–99, 128 organizations recruited on campus. The Career Center assists students in their job searches and career choices. The Career Center employs 6 full-time and 2 part-time professionals. Their services include job fairs, resume preparation, interview workshops, resume referral, career/interest testing, career counseling, careers library, job bank, job interviews, employer site visits, internships, networking events, career programs, and individualized assistance as required by the student.

This comprehensive program's success is reflected in the fact that 88 percent of the class of 1999 had job offers within six months of graduation.

Tuition: Part-time in-state tuition is charged at $169 per credit for undergraduates; full-time in-state tuition is charged at a flat rate of $1842 for undergraduates. Part-time out-of-state tuition is charged at $491 per credit for undergraduates; full-time out-of-state tuition is charged at a flat rate of $5887 for undergraduates.

Room and Board: There are no residence halls at UB. Students find apartments nearby, and there are listings of housing choices at the Center for Student Involvement.

Mandatory Fees: Additional mandatory fees are $150 for 3 credits, $240 for 6 credits, $324.50 for 9 credits, $224 for 12 or more credits for in-state students, and $405 for 12 or more credits for out-of-state students.

Contact: Edward R. Kemery, Ph.D., Director of the Helen P. Denit Honors Program, Associate Professor of Management, 1420 North Charles Street, Baltimore, Maryland 21201-5779; Telephone: 410-837-6583; Fax: 410-837-5722; E-mail: honors@ubalt.edu

Interpreting the symbols: **2**=two-year college, **4**=four-year college; **Pu**=public or state college, **Pr**=private college; **G**=general honors program; **D**=departmental honors program; **S**=small program (fewer than 100 students), **M**=midsize program (100 to 500 students), **L**=large program (more than 500 students); **Sc**=scholarships available in honors program; **Tr**=transfer students accepted into honors program; **HBC**=historically black college; **AA**=academic advisors; **GA**=graduate advisors; **FA**=fellowship advisors.

UNIVERSITY OF CALIFORNIA, DAVIS

4 Pu G L AA FA

▼ Davis Honors Challenge

The Davis Honors Challenge (DHC) is an open-application, campuswide honors program designed for highly motivated students who want more challenging course work, closer contacts with faculty members, and dynamic interaction with similarly motivated peers.

The goals of the DHC are to foster students' critical-thinking and analytic interpretation skills, improve communication and research skills, provide experience in group dynamics and collaborative exploration of problems, and develop familiarity with electronic communication and visual presentation methods. These goals are realized through the DHC course offerings that include lower-division departmental honors courses, special DHC sections of regular courses, DHC seminars, and special study opportunities.

The Davis Honors Challenge, now in its sixth year, is steadily growing and currently enrolls 600 students.

Participation Requirements: First- and second-year students participating in the DHC take two honors courses and one problem-oriented interdisciplinary seminar per academic year. Second-year students have the option to substitute an honors contract for an honors course. Third-year students are required to complete two honors contracts and one upper-division honors seminar. Fourth-year students participate in a yearlong team honors project. All students who complete the program receive transcript notation for each year of participation.

Admission Process: Incoming and continuing UC Davis students apply in the spring quarter for places in the Davis Honors College for the following year. Prospective students complete a short essay application. Rather than GPA or SAT scores, DHC uses a nontraditional approach and bases admission on the following qualities: demonstrated evidence for enthusiasm, commitment and leadership, a desire to take an active role in one's education, a willingness to learn in new and different ways, an ability to function effectively in a group-learning environment, and an understanding of the goals of the program.

Scholarship Availability: DHC does not control any scholarship funding nor the scholarship selection process.

The Campus Context: The University of California (UC) began in 1868. Today the University is one of the largest and most renowned centers of higher education in the world. Its ten campuses span the state, from Davis in the north to San Diego in the south. In between are the Berkeley, San Francisco, Santa Cruz, Santa Barbara, Merced, Riverside, Irvine, and Los Angeles campuses. All UC campuses adhere to the same admission guidelines and high academic standards, yet each has its own distinct character, atmosphere, and academic individuality. Together, the ten campuses have an enrollment of more than 173,000 students, 90 percent of them California residents.

Founded in 1905 as the University Farm and designated as a general campus in 1959, UC Davis offers a full range of undergraduate and graduate programs, as well as professional programs in law, management, medicine, and veterinary medicine. With approximately 6,000 acres, UC Davis is the largest of the ten University of California campuses and second-largest in budget, total expenditures, and enrollment. UC Davis stands twenty-second in research funding among universities in the United States according to recent information from the National Science Foundation. *U.S. News & World Report* ranked UC Davis twelfth among public universities nationally. UC Davis is one of only sixty-two universities admitted to the prestigious Association of American Universities. The campus' unusual resources include a 150-acre arboretum, seven natural reserves, more than twenty research institutes or centers, five museums, and three galleries.

The University's reputation for excellence has attracted a distinguished faculty of scholars and scientists in all fields of scholarship. UC Davis faculty members rank sixteenth in quality among comprehensive public universities nationwide, according to a multiyear study of U.S. doctoral programs reported in 1995 by the National Research Council. Creative teaching and academic innovation are encouraged by several programs, including the $30,000 Prize for Teaching and Scholarly Achievement, believed to be the largest award of its kind in the country.

Ecologically aware and socially innovative, Davis has a small-town friendliness and spirit of volunteerism that distinguishes it from cities of similar size. Residents are active in local, national, and international political causes; in the arts; and in community organizations. Students compose a large portion of the city's population of 58,000, making Davis one of the state's few remaining "college towns."

UC Davis has three colleges: Letters and Science, Agricultural and Environmental Sciences, and Engineering. The biological sciences program is administered through the intercollegiate Division of Biological Sciences. In addition, UC Davis has four professional schools: Law, Management, Medicine, and Veterinary Medicine. Altogether, 150 undergraduate majors and seventy-nine graduate degree programs are offered.

Student Body Undergraduate enrollment is 20,388: 44 percent men, 56 percent women. The ethnic distribution is 43 percent Caucasian, 2.8 percent American Indian/Alaskan Native, 2.8 percent black/African American, 7.4 percent Chicano/Mexican American, 2.6 percent Latino/other Spanish American, 4.5 percent Filipino/Philipino, 15.4 percent Chinese/Chinese American, 1.9 percent Japanese/Japanese American, 2.5 percent Korean/Korean American, 1.3 percent Pacific Islander, 2.4 percent other Asian, 2.4 percent East Indian/Pakistani, and 2.4 percent other or no data. Most of the students are residents. There are twenty-five fraternities and eighteen sororities.

Faculty Of the 2,030 faculty members, 1,694 are full-time; 98 percent hold terminal degrees. The student-faculty ratio is 18.7:1.

Key Facilities The UC Davis Library System contains more than 3 million volumes and receives 44,614 periodical and journal titles annually. The thirteen on-campus computer labs include six Macintosh and five PC facilities, as well as a media distribution facility and a new media laboratory.

Athletics In 2000–01, UC Davis received the prestigious Sears Directors Cup signifying the best NCAA Division II intercollegiate athletics program in the country—for the fourth time in six years. UC Davis began to give athletics scholarships in 1998. Intramural sports programs serve 15,000 of the 20,388 undergraduates, and sports clubs serve another 1,200 students.

Study Abroad Through the Education Abroad Program, the University offers study in cooperation with more than 100 institutions in thirty-six different countries. Approximately 1,000 UC Davis students study abroad each year.

Support Services The Disability Resource Center offers students full services and accommodations.

Job Opportunities The Student Employment Center assists students and student spouses in obtaining on-campus positions.

Tuition: None for state residents, $10,244 for nonresidents per year (2001–02)

Room and Board: $5438

Mandatory Fees: $4072 (2001–02)

Contact: Director Kenneth L. Verosub, 162 Kerr Hall, University of California, Davis, One Shields Avenue, Davis, California 95616-8518; Telephone: 530-754-4098; Fax: 530-754-8311; E-mail: verosub@honors.ucdavis.edu; Web site: http://www.honors.ucdavis.edu

UNIVERSITY OF CALIFORNIA, DAVIS

4 Pu G M

▼ Integrated Studies

Integrated Studies (IS) is an invitational, residential honors program for 70 first-year students. Its goals are to help students integrate ideas from humanities, natural sciences, and social sciences and correlate information from self-contained disciplines through interdisciplinary or multidisciplinary approaches to learning; to provide excellent teaching for first-year students in small, highly personalized situations; to provide an academic residential community, similar to the best small-college communities, within a large research university; to provide students with challenging, participatory approaches to learning to encourage student-faculty interactions on a more personal level than that realized in the large classroom situation common to public research universities; and to provide effective, personalized advising on academic matters.

Integrated Studies faculty members are disciplinary specialists with proven excellence in teaching who have a particular interest in how their research and discipline are related to other disciplines, to contemporary society, and to philosophical issues of the day.

The Integrated Studies program is 33 years old and currently enrolls 70 students.

Participation Requirements: Integrated Studies students are required to take three specially designed, 4-unit IS courses and two 1-unit IS seminars during the academic year. All students who complete the program receive transcript notation.

Scholarship Availability: Regents Scholars, selected by an independent faculty committee, are guaranteed places in Integrated Studies. IS does not control any scholarship funding or the scholarship selection process.

The Campus Context: The University of California began in 1868. Today the University is one of the largest and most renowned centers of higher education in the world. Its ten campuses span the state, from Davis in the north to San Diego in the south. In between are the Berkeley, San Francisco, Merced, Santa Cruz, Santa Barbara, Riverside, Irvine, and Los Angeles campuses. All UC campuses adhere to the same admission guidelines and high academic standards, yet each has its own distinct character, atmosphere, and academic individuality. Together, the ten campuses have an enrollment of more than 165,000 students, 95 percent of them California residents.

Founded in 1905 as the University Farm and designated as a general campus in 1959, UC Davis offers a full range of undergraduate and graduate programs, as well as professional programs in law, management, medicine, and veterinary medicine. With approximately 6,000 acres, UC Davis is the largest of the ten University of California campuses and second-largest in budget, total expenditures, and enrollment. UC Davis stands twenty-second in research funding among universities in the United States, according to recent information from the National Science Foundation. *U.S. News & World Report* ranked UC Davis tenth among public universities nationally. UCD is one of only sixty-two universities admitted to the prestigious Association of American Universities. The campus' unusual resources include a 150-acre arboretum, seven natural reserves, more than twenty research institutes or centers, five museums, three galleries, and a major performing arts venue, the Robert and Margrit Center for the Performing Arts.

The University's reputation for excellence has attracted a distinguished faculty of scholars and scientists in all fields of scholarship. UC Davis faculty members rank sixteenth in quality among comprehensive public universities nationwide, according to a multiyear study of U.S. doctoral programs reported in 1995 by the National Research Council. Creative teaching and academic innovation are encouraged by several programs, including the $30,000 Prize for Teaching and Scholarly Achievement, believed to be the largest award of its kind in the country.

Ecologically aware and socially innovative, Davis has a small-town friendliness and spirit of volunteerism that distinguishes it from cities of similar size. Residents are active in local, national, and international political causes; in the arts; and in community organizations. Students comprise a large portion of the city's population of 60,000, making Davis one of the state's few remaining "college towns."

UC Davis has three colleges: Letters and Science, Agricultural and Environmental Sciences, and Engineering. The biological sciences program is administered through the Intercollegiate Division of Biological Sciences. In addition, UC Davis has four professional schools: Law, Management, Medicine, and Veterinary Medicine. Altogether, 150 undergraduate majors and seventy-nine graduate degree programs are offered.

Student Body Undergraduate enrollment is 20,444, with 46 percent men and 54 percent women. The ethnic distribution is 42.6 percent Caucasian, 1.1 percent American Indian/Alaskan Native, 3.1 percent black/African American, 6.8 percent Chicano/Mexican American, 3.4 percent Latino/other Spanish American, 4.1 percent Filipino/Philipino, 14.9 percent Chinese/Chinese American, 2.1 percent Japanese/Japanese American, 2.4 percent Korean/Korean American, 0.8 percent Pacific Islander, 3.9 percent other Asian, 2.2 percent East Indian/Pakistani, and 7.7 percent other or no data. Most of the students are residents. There are twenty-five fraternities and eighteen sororities.

Faculty Of the 1,894 faculty members, 1,634 are full-time; 98 percent hold terminal degrees. The student-faculty ratio is 18.7:1.

Key Facilities The UC Davis Library System contains more than 2.8 million volumes and receives 41,000 periodical and journal titles annually. The thirteen on-campus computer labs include six Macintosh and five PC facilities, as well as a media distribution facility and new media laboratory.

Athletics UC Davis has four times been awarded the Sears Directors Cup for its successful participation in nonscholarship Division II intercollegiate athletics. Intramural sports programs serve 13,000 of the 20,000 undergraduates, and sports clubs serve another 1,000.

Study Abroad Through the Education Abroad Program, the University offers study in cooperation with more than 100 institutions in thirty-five different countries. Approximately 400 UCD students study abroad each year.

Support Services The Disability Resource Center offers students full services and accommodations.

Job Opportunities The Student Employment Center assists students and student spouses to obtain on-campus positions. During 2001–02, 6287 students completed internships on campus, in outlying areas, and abroad.

Tuition: None for state residents, $10,245 for nonresidents, per year (2001–02)

Room and Board: $5438

Mandatory Fees: $4072

Contact: Director: James F. Shackelford, 2292 Social Sciences/Humanities, One Shields Avenue, Davis, California 95616-8715; Telephone: 530-752-9906; Fax: 530-752-8964; E-mail: jfshackelford@ucdavis.edu; Web site: http://www.ucdavis.edu/honors

Interpreting the symbols: **2**=two-year college, **4**=four-year college; **Pu**=public or state college, **Pr**=private college; **G**=general honors program; **D**=departmental honors program; **S**=small program (fewer than 100 students), **M**=midsize program (100 to 500 students), **L**=large program (more than 500 students); **Sc**=scholarships available in honors program; **Tr**=transfer students accepted into honors program; **HBC**=historically black college; **AA**=academic advisors; **GA**=graduate advisors; **FA**=fellowship advisors.

UNIVERSITY OF CALIFORNIA, IRVINE

4 Pu G M Sc Tr

▼ Campuswide Honors Program

Located on 1,500 acres of beautiful coastal foothills 5 miles from the Pacific Ocean, the University of California, Irvine (UCI), offers its most talented students the opportunities of its Campuswide Honors Program. UCI, known for research and teaching excellence, has a lively student body with an international background and a casual lifestyle. The Campuswide Honors Program is dedicated to promoting high standards of scholastic excellence and personal growth by combining the best of an excellent liberal arts college with the broad range of opportunities offered by a major research university.

The Campuswide Honors curriculum features interdisciplinary and discipline-based classes designed to challenge and introduce talented students to important topics, issues, and methods of inquiry. Honors students gain from the dynamic and creative spirit that has led to 2 UCI faculty members receiving the Nobel Prize in different disciplines (physics and chemistry). All honors students pursue research in their individual academic disciplines under the supervision of faculty members. Research grants, summer research programs, and research symposia are part of the Campuswide Honors Program experience as well.

The Campuswide Honors Program enrolls approximately 600 students from the freshman through senior years (about 3 percent of the undergraduates) and represents every major on campus.

Honors advising by faculty members, professional staff, and peers provides program participants with assistance in planning their course of study and applying for scholarships, graduate and professional schools, internships, and education abroad programs.

One hundred and forty Campuswide Honors students live in honors houses on campus. Honors students also have the privilege of special reading rooms in the UCI libraries; extended library privileges; participation in many social and cultural activities, including weekly coffee hours, beach bonfires, poetry readings, visits and informal lectures in faculty members' and students' homes; and annual camping retreats.

Participation Requirements: To graduate from the Campuswide Honors Program, students complete sequences of honors classes, finish a research thesis project, and achieve a minimum cumulative GPA of 3.2 (most honors students have GPAs above 3.5). Successful completion of the Campuswide Honors Program is noted at the annual Honors Convocation and appears on the diploma and final transcript.

Ninety percent of Campuswide Honors graduates pursue graduate or professional degrees within two years of graduation from UCI. Recent graduates are attending Harvard, Princeton, Cornell, Stanford, Berkeley, UC San Diego, and UCLA; the Universities of Chicago, Oxford, and London; and other excellent schools.

Admission Process: Admission is competitive, with most students invited while in high school. About half of the incoming freshmen in 2001 had SAT scores higher than 1400 and high school GPAs of more than 4.2 (honor-course weighted). Transfer students and continuing UCI students apply for entry to the program.

Scholarship Availability: A majority of Campuswide Honors Program students are awarded Regents' Scholarships, the most prestigious University of California award. Regents' Scholars are selected for outstanding scholastic achievement and leadership potential and in recent years have received more than full in-state fees for four years plus funding for summer school. A few Distinguished Honors Scholarships that pay all expenses associated with a UCI education are awarded to outstanding honors students who require financial assistance.

The Campus Context: Founded in 1965, UCI ranks among the leading research universities in the United States. UCI offers fifty-seven bachelor's degree programs; forty-two master's degree programs; thirty-nine Ph.D. programs; M.B.A., M.D., and Ed.D. programs; and teacher credential programs.

Student Body There are 17,865 undergraduates enrolled: 49 percent men, 51 percent women. The ethnic distribution of undergraduates is 2.2 percent African American/black, 23.7 percent Caucasian/white, 8.6 percent Chicano/Mexican American, 3 percent Latino/other Spanish American, 17 percent Chinese/Chinese American, 3.6 percent East Indian/Pakistani, 7.8 percent Filipino/Philipino, 3 percent Japanese/Japanese American, 9.1 percent Korean/Korean American, 8.8 percent Vietnamese/Vietnamese American, 3.3 percent other Asian, 0.4 percent Native American, 0.3 percent Pacific Islander, and 9 percent unlisted. There are 496 international students. Approximately one third of UCI undergraduates reside on campus, one third live off campus, and one third live at home. Sixty percent receive some form of financial aid. There are 268 student organizations registered on campus, including thirty-four sororities and fraternities.

Faculty Of the 1,428 faculty members, 1,178 are full-time equivalent and 98 percent have Ph.D.'s or M.D.'s. The student-faculty ratio is 18:1.

Key Facilities The UCI libraries house 2.2 million volumes as well as provide print and online journal, microform, cartographic/graphic materials, audio and video recordings, and film access. Most books and periodicals are on open shelves and are easily accessible, a rarity in libraries today. Network computer access is easily available to students on campus. Every classroom, library, and residence hall has high-speed Internet connection activity and wireless network access is available throughout the campus; some are configured to meet the specific needs required by some majors. A number of computer labs are open 24 hours a day.

Honorary Societies Phi Beta Kappa, Alpha Epsilon Delta, Alpha Kappa Delta, Chi Epsilon, Golden Key International Honour Society, Lambda Alpha Kappa, Omega Chi Epsilon, Omicron Delta Epsilon, Phi Alpha Theta, Phi Lambda Upsilon, Pi Gamma Mu, Pi Sigma Alpha, Pi Tau Sigma, Psi Chi, Sigma Delta Pi, Sigma Pi Sigma, Sigma Xi, Tau Beta Pi

Athletics UCI's intercollegiate athletic program features nineteen sports. Men's and women's teams compete in NCAA Division I in the Big West Conference. The men's teams include basketball, cross-country, track and field, golf, swimming, diving, and tennis. Men's soccer, volleyball, and water polo teams compete in the Mountain Pacific Sports Federation; the coed sailing team competes in the Intercollegiate Yacht Racing Association; and crew in the Pacific Coast Championships. UCI women's teams compete in basketball, crew, cross-country, soccer, swimming, diving, tennis, track and field, volleyball, and water polo.

Study Abroad Students may participate in the Education Abroad Program (EAP) of the University of California, which operates in cooperation with about 140 host universities and colleges in thirty-three countries throughout the world. UCI's International Opportunities Program helps students take advantage of worldwide opportunities for study, work, internship, volunteering, research, and noncredential teaching.

Support Services Disabled students receive assistance from admission through graduation from the Disability Services Office. Specialized services and equipment include assistance in the classroom, a computing lab for disabled students providing special computer technology and training, and a van that can be used for off-campus transportation for medically and academically related purposes.

Job Opportunities Students are assisted in finding jobs on campus and in the community by the Career and Life Planning Center.

Room and Board: $6268 minimum

Fees: $4555.50 for state residents, $15,629.50 for nonresidents (fees are subject to change)

Contact: Director: Dr. Roger McWilliams, Division of Undergraduate Education, 1200 Student Services II, Irvine, California 92697-5680; Telephone: 949-824-5461; Fax: 949-824-2092; E-mail: honors@uci.edu; Web site: http://www.honors.uci.edu/~honors

University of California, Santa Barbara

4 Pu C L Tr

▼ College of Letters and Science Honors Program

The College of Letters and Science Honors Program provides a four-year educational experience designed to challenge the University's most motivated students, encourage them to their finest efforts, and stimulate them to assume their place in the world of ideas. The Honors Program attracts students who wish to take full advantage of the resources of a research university. Typically, they enter the University already thinking of themselves as scholars. Their aim is to leave the University of California, Santa Barbara (UCSB), with an education, not just a degree. They are not afraid to seek out their professors; they thrive in an intimate collegiate atmosphere where they can participate in a long tradition of intellectual inquiry, working closely with peers and professors in small classes, research laboratories, and special programs. Because the Honors Program is open to qualified students in all majors, it provides a cross-disciplinary meeting place for students with wide-ranging interests.

The College Honors Program is committed to the creation of a vital, richly textured community both on and off campus. In the spirit of shared governance, students in the Honors Program work with the College Provost and deans, the faculty, and the honors adviser to ensure that the program is responsive to the needs of today's undergraduates. Housing is available to interested students in the Scholars Floors, which are designated floors of University-owned residence halls for high-achieving students, with special interdisciplinary programming that brings students together with their faculty mentors. Juniors and seniors in the Honors Program complete a minimum of 10 hours of community service each year, and lower-division students are encouraged to prepare themselves for the service requirement by exploring the many opportunities for volunteerism at UCSB's Community Affairs Board, one of the largest student volunteer organizations in the nation. Through the Honors Program's Isla Vista Tutoring Program, students mentor sixth graders in the local elementary school, assisting them with math and English and providing academic encouragement and support. Honors students are eligible for numerous internships that supplement their regular course work. They also work as program coordinators, peer advisers, mentors, and proctors in the honors study lounge. Many honors students find positions assisting the faculty members on research items.

Participation Requirements: To complete the College Honors Program and earn the Academic Excellence Award at commencement, students must take at least 36 honors-designated units during their years of undergraduate study and fulfill the service requirements. At least 20 of these units must be upper division. Transfer students admitted to the College Honors Program upon entrance to UCSB only need to complete the 20 upper-division, honors-designated units. More flexible rules apply to students who participate in the yearlong University of California Education Abroad Program. Students who complete the College Honors Program are acknowledged at commencement by a special reception and are entitled to wear special regalia. Completion of the College Honors Program is noted on the final transcript.

Admission Process: The College Honors Program is open to any student with an overall UCSB GPA of at least 3.5 on a minimum of 12 graded baccalaureate units. Entering first-year students are invited into the College Honors Program based on high school GPA and SAT I (or ACT) and SAT II scores. In the typical entering freshman class, 10 percent of students are in the College Honors Program. Transfer students with a minimum 3.6 GPA when they enter UCSB are eligible and are encouraged to apply. Once accepted, students may continue as program members as long as they maintain the required GPA and complete honors courses. Eligibility criteria are subject to change at any time.

Scholarship Availability: Many students in the College Honors Program receive Regents scholarships at the time of admission. Regents Scholarship recipients are selected from among the top student scholars applying for admission to the University. Selection criteria include academic excellence, depth and breadth of academic preparation, and potential for success at UC Santa Barbara. Financial aid is awarded on the basis of financial need as well as scholastic merit. In a typical year, nearly 60 percent of UC Santa Barbara's students receive some form of financial aid.

The Campus Context: The University of California, Santa Barbara sits at the edge of the Pacific Ocean and is backed by the Santa Ynez Mountains, providing a picturesque setting for an academic community made up of 901 faculty members and 18,000 students. The school moved to this 989-acre site on a promontory 10 miles north of downtown Santa Barbara in 1954, a decade after joining the University of California system. The stunning physical environment of UC Santa Barbara and the research facilities of a world-class institution create an outstanding learning environment. UCSB's 300 buildings house three undergraduate colleges, a graduate division, two professional schools, and seven national research centers. Storke Tower, a 175-foot bell tower, distinguishes the spacious grounds. UC Santa Barbara, one of sixty-five members of the prestigious Association of American Universities (AAU), is recognized as a premier research institution ranking in the top two in research excellence and productivity among public institutions in the nation. Students in the College of Letters and Science Honors Program enjoy the advantages of this top-notch research institution with the additional benefits of smaller classes and special programs.

Student Body Undergraduate enrollment is 17,379 and 54 percent of the students are women. The ethnic distribution is 1 percent Native American/Alaskan, 3 percent black/African American, 56 percent Caucasian, 11 percent Chicano, 4 percent Latino, 13 percent Asian/Pacific Islander, 2 percent Filipino, 1 percent East Indian/Pakistani, and 2 percent other. There are 119 undergraduate international students. More than 80 percent of UCSB students live on campus or within a 1-mile radius of campus. Nearly 60 percent of UCSB undergraduate students receive some form of financial aid. There are fourteen national sororities and twelve national fraternities.

Faculty Of the 901 faculty members, 172 are part-time and ninety-eight percent hold doctoral degrees. The student-faculty ratio is 18:1.

Key Facilities The UCSB libraries house more than 2.6 million volumes and receive more than 17,000 journals and periodicals annually.

Honorary Societies Alpha Lambda Delta, Golden Key, Mortar Board, National Society of Collegiate Scholars, and Phi Beta Kappa

Athletics UCSB's intercollegiate athletic program features twenty-one sports. UCSB's men's and women's teams compete in NCAA Division I, Big West Conference, and Mountain Pacific Sports

Interpreting the symbols: **2**=two-year college, **4**=four-year college; **Pu**=public or state college, **Pr**=private college; **G**=general honors program; **D**=departmental honors program; **S**=small program (fewer than 100 students), **M**=midsize program (100 to 500 students), **L**=large program (more than 500 students); **Sc**=scholarships available in honors program; **Tr**=transfer students accepted into honors program; **HBC**=historically black college; **AA**=academic advisors; **GA**=graduate advisors; **FA**=fellowship advisors.

Federation. The men's teams include baseball, basketball, cross-country, golf, swimming, tennis, and track and field. Men's gymnastics, soccer, volleyball, and water polo compete in the Mountain Pacific Sports Federation. UCSB's women's teams include basketball, cross-country, gymnastics, soccer, softball, swimming, tennis, track and field, and volleyball. Women's water polo competes in the Mountain Pacific Sports Federation. Approximately 80 percent of UCSB students participate in either club or intramural sports.

Study Abroad The University of California offers overseas study programs in cooperation with more than 100 host universities and colleges in thirty-four countries throughout the world.

Support Services The Disabled Students Program works to increase the retention and graduation rate of students with temporary and permanent disabilities, ensure equal access to all educational and academic programs, and foster student independence. The University is strongly committed to maintaining an environment that guarantees students with disabilities full access to educational programs and activities.

Job Opportunities Career and Counseling Services offers career and major planning, a career resources library, a campus interview program, and an internship program. The UCSB Washington Center awards academic credit for internships based in Washington, D.C.

Tuition: None for state residents; $10,704 for nonresidents, per year (2001–02)

Room and Board: $8042

Mandatory Fees: $4301 for state residents; $4671 for nonresidents

Contact: Alan J. Wyner, Dean, Division of Student Academic Affairs; Regina Fletcher, Honors Coordinator; College of Letters and Science, University of California, Santa Barbara, Santa Barbara, California 93106; Telephone: 805-893-3109; Fax: 805-893-7654; E-mail: rfletcher@ltsc.ucsb.edu; Web site: http://www.honors.ltsc.ucsb.edu

University of Central Arkansas

4 Pu G M Sc Tr

▼ Honors College

The University of Central Arkansas (UCA) Honors College has offered a minor in honors interdisciplinary studies for students in all majors since 1982. UCA established the Honors College to heighten the educational experience for intellectually gifted students with demonstrated records of achievement. It provides a structured setting within which the student is encouraged to test varied skills by subjecting them to the give and take of dialogue with other students and faculty members.

The program is divided into two parts: the Honors Program for freshmen and sophomores and the Honors College for juniors and seniors. The Honors Program consists of a two-semester Freshman Honors Seminar and a two-semester Sophomore Honors Seminar. This four-course sequence is entitled The Human Search. The Honors College consists of interdisciplinary seminars, an Oxford tutorial, and the completion of an honors thesis project. This 30-hour curriculum stresses the arts of inquiry, conversation, and collaboration. Dr. Terrel Bell, former U.S. Secretary of Education, called the program "an Ivy League education at a bargain basement price." UCA has been cited by the Carnegie Foundation for having a "creative and innovative program."

Students who graduate from the Honors College receive a hand-crafted medallion worn at commencement, a special certificate that includes printing of the thesis title, and acknowledgment of honors category on the diploma. There are currently about 450 students in the program.

Participation Requirements: Students enrolled in the Honors Program must maintain a minimum 3.25 GPA. To be admitted into the Honors College, the student must have completed at least one course in the Honors Program and must have an overall GPA of at least 3.5. Sophomores deliver a sophomore lecture as part of the College application process, and seniors give an oral presentation of their honors thesis project.

Scholarship Availability: Nearly all students in the program receive University scholarships. Supplemental honors scholarships are available and are awarded based on merit and need. Funds are also awarded on a competitive basis to students who submit proposals for travel abroad and for undergraduate research or internship programs. Transfer students are accepted if space allows. The requirements vary, depending on the student's year in school, credits earned, and so on.

In 1997, a UCA honors scholar and history major was awarded the prestigious Harry S. Truman Scholarship, a $30,000 award given to only 65 students in the United States each year. That year there were nearly 900 applicants and 175 finalists. In 2001, a UCA Honors Scholar and philosophy major received a Rhodes Scholarship to study classics at Oxford. He was one of only 32 recipients nationwide.

The Campus Context: The University of Central Arkansas is located in Conway, Arkansas, just 30 minutes from Little Rock, and includes the College of Business Administration, College of Education, College of Fine Arts and Communication, College of Health and Applied Sciences, College of Liberal Arts, and College of Natural Sciences and Mathematics.

Student Body Undergraduate enrollment is 7,471, including 61 percent women. The ethnic distribution is 79 percent Caucasian, 14 percent black, 1 percent Native American, 1 percent Asian American, 1 percent Hispanic, and 4 percent other. There are 212 international students. Of the total population, 1,461 students are residents and 6,010 are commuters. Seventy-two percent of the students receive financial aid. There are ten fraternities and nine sororities.

Faculty Of the 382 full-time faculty members, 76 percent have terminal degrees. There are an additional 120 part-time faculty members. The student-faculty ratio is 18:1.

Key Facilities The library houses 1,393,831 items, including 399,636 monographs and 2,600 bound periodicals. UCA's Data Processing Department offers its students and staff members access to the Internet. The Honors College has its own Honors Center located in McAlister Hall. It is generally open from 8 a.m. to midnight while classes are in session. The Honors College has four residence halls that offer private rooms to those individuals who qualify.

Athletics The athletic program at the University of Central Arkansas has been one of the most successful in the state over the past thirty years. UCA teams dominated the Arkansas Intercollegiate Conference for much of the 1970s and all of the 1980s and have been just as successful since moving into the prestigious NCAA Division II and Gulf South Conference in 1993. UCA currently fields intercollegiate teams in ten sports, four for men and six for women. The women's sports include volleyball, basketball, tennis, softball, soccer, and cross-country. The men's sports include football, basketball, baseball, and soccer. The teams compete in the sixteen-team Gulf South Conference, the largest Division II conference in the country and one of the most highly respected athletically.

The UCA women's program finished second overall in 1995–96 for the GSC All-Sports Award, which goes to the school that finishes highest in the final standings in its combined sports. The UCA football team, which has won the most competitions in Arkansas over the last two decades, won nine straight AIC titles and three NAIA national championships from 1983–91. The men's basketball team reached the nationally televised NAIA championship game in Kansas City, Missouri, twice in the early 1990s. UCA is also the alma mater of six-time NBA All-Star and two-time Olympian Scottie Pippen, who was an All-American in 1985–87. UCA placed 30 student athletes on the GSC Honor Roll in 1998–99, with 11 on the All-Academic Team.

The women's cross-country team won the first Gulf-South Championship for UCA, and men's basketball finished runner-up in the Gulf-South Tournament in 1998. Women's soccer completed its first season in the Gulf-South Conference, while the men's soccer team went to the playoffs for the second year.

Study Abroad UCA has established a campus in the Netherlands at Maastricht. Students may spend a semester abroad in Europe or a summer abroad there. UCA also offers several three- to five-week credit-bearing study-abroad opportunities during the summer months. All of the programs are coordinated by specific academic departments in conjunction with the Office of International Programs. UCA students may also choose to participate in a five-week Spanish language and culture program at the University of Guadalajara to earn credit in Spanish. Language training is offered at beginning, intermediate, and advanced levels. To more fully experience Mexico, participants live with local families. In addition to the academic program, creative workshops and guided excursions are also available.

Interested students may travel to England for three weeks every other summer as part of a study trip sponsored by the Department of English. Participants visit London, Stratford-on-Avon, the Lake Country, and other places of literary, theatrical, and historical interest. Credit in English may be awarded.

In addition to opportunities available through the UCA International Programs Office, Honors College students are eligible for grants for study abroad. The Travel Abroad Grants (TAG) program has sent students to China, India, Southeast Asia, Australia, Scotland, France, and Africa, to name just a few destinations. These students did everything from attending universities in these countries to traveling, working in internships, and assisting in local medical care for remote villages. The Honors College has established a relationship with Westminster College at Oxford and the Oxford Summer Seminar Program at Trinity College with the University of Massachusetts Amherst.

Support Services All classroom buildings and facilities are handicapped accessible, complying with Arkansas state law concerning handicapped accessibility.

Job Opportunities Work opportunities on campus exist for undergraduates in two programs: the UCA Student Help Program and the Federal Work-Study Program, which is federally funded. The Career Services/Cooperative Education Center provides assistance for students seeking part-time employment off campus. The center also assists students seeking internships and cooperative education experiences in their particular majors. Besides work-study opportunities, honors scholars are eligible to apply for Undergraduate Research Grants for Education (URGE). These grants give honors scholars the chance to participate in research for their honors theses, departmental theses, internships, and major areas of study. Some examples of recent URGEs are dolphin communication, cancer research, art history, environmental ethics, and foreign language instruction in elementary schools.

Tuition and fees: $3738 minimum for residents, $6798 minimum for nonresidents, per year (2001–02 estimated)

Room and board: $3490

Contact: Director: Dr. Richard I. Scott, P.O. Box 5024/McAlister 306, 201 Donaghey Avenue, Conway, Arkansas 72035; Telephone: 501-450-3198; Fax: 501-450-3284; E-mail: honors@mail.uca.edu; Web site: http://www.uca.edu/honors

University of Central Florida

4 Pu G L Sc Tr

▼ The Burnett Honors College

The Burnett Honors College at the University of Central Florida (UCF) is the center of academic excellence at the University. Its purpose is to enhance and broaden the education of the most talented undergraduate students attending UCF. University Honors is a four-year program that includes intensified course work within the General Education Program (GEP), as well as upper-division interdisciplinary seminars, lectures, and activities beyond the classroom. Honors in the major typically involves two semesters of study at the junior or senior level culminating in the preparation and defense of an honors thesis. Students may participate in both programs.

Honors classes are the main attraction of the University Honors program. Honors GEP classes are limited to 20 students, 15 for composition, and are taught by select faculty members. Interdisciplinary seminars, involving innovative, cutting-edge scholarships, are proposed by faculty members and selected on a competitive basis. Since the University Honors program draws students from across the University, it must maintain strong academic course work tailored to the needs of each student; consequently, the Burnett Honors College values diversity of education and is as responsive to the demands of the psychology student as it is to the demands of the engineer. To that end, the College offers upper-division honors course work for specific majors, including business, engineering, computer science, and molecular biology and microbiology.

Social acclimation of students to the University is an important priority. For honors students, this process begins in the Honors Freshman Symposium, one of the oldest traditions in honors and the premier First Year Experience class at UCF. This 1-credit class is intended to introduce new students to University life and to celebrate the love of learning. Students are divided into teams of about 20 who are mentored by an upper-division honors student. Students receive individual weekly contact from their team leaders in addition to meeting together for the symposium, in which a different faculty member presents a research topic or other informative lecture each week. These faculty members are among UCF's best—world-class scholars who offer exciting and innovative ways of thinking about a subject. Students then have an opportunity to ask questions and participate in discussions about the evening's topic. In addition, students are kept informed of important University information and local cultural events.

The College staff is dedicated exclusively to the needs of its students, who have the opportunity for personal academic advisement at every stage of their University experience, from freshman to senior year. Also housed in the Burnett Honors College is the Office of Student Scholarship and Fellowship Advisement (OSSFA). OSSFA serves all UCF students who apply for prestigious scholarships such as Rhodes, Truman, Hertz, and Marshall, providing guidance throughout the application process.

With the opening of the Burnett Honors College building in spring 2002, students have a state-of-the-art center located in the core of campus. In addition to classroom and meeting space, facilities include an honors reading room with kitchen facilities for between-class breaks, and an honors computer lab, where students use the latest available computer technology for class assignments or Internet access.

Interpreting the symbols: **2**=two-year college, **4**=four-year college; **Pu**=public or state college, **Pr**=private college; **G**=general honors program; **D**=departmental honors program; **S**=small program (fewer than 100 students), **M**=midsize program (100 to 500 students), **L**=large program (more than 500 students); **Sc**=scholarships available in honors program; **Tr**=transfer students accepted into honors program; **HBC**=historically black college; **AA**=academic advisors; **GA**=graduate advisors; **FA**=fellowship advisors.

Student participation in the administration of the Burnett Honors College is integral to its success. The College's vital student organization, Honors Congress, participates in seminar selection and discusses program policy as well as sponsoring educational and social activities for honors students. In addition, the College provides support for educational and cultural events, such as offering reduced-price tickets to museums and local cultural events and sponsoring informal lunches where students can hear from internationally known speakers. The College also supports honors students' participation in national and regional meetings of professional organizations such as the National Collegiate Honors Council.

Graduates of the Burnett Honors College have attended institutions such as Berkeley, Duke, Harvard, UCLA, and the University of Chicago. Since its origin in 1989, the program's enrollment has grown to approximately 1,200 students. In 1998, the Florida Board of Regents conferred college status to the Honors Program. Presently, the Burnett Honors College is a premier program in terms of academic integrity and student support, one that relishes future challenges and changes.

The deadline for applying is March 1.

Participation Requirements: To graduate from the Honors College, students must maintain both a minimum 3.2 UCF GPA and a 3.0 GPA in honors courses and take 12 credit hours of General Education course work in honors, 1 credit hour of Honors Symposium, and a minimum of 9 hours of upper-division honors course work that varies by college, for a total of 22 hours. Honors in the Major students must maintain a minimum 3.2 overall GPA and a 3.5 in the major in addition to successful completion of a thesis or project that is overseen by a 3-member faculty committee. University Honors students may also elect to do Honors in the Major if qualified. All honors course work is undertaken in small classes limited to 20 or fewer students where close student-faculty interaction is essential.

Successful completion of the University Honors and/or Honors in the Major is recorded on the student's transcript and noted at graduation. Graduating honors students receive the Honors Medallion to wear at commencement.

The Campus Context: The University of Central Florida is located in east central Florida, a region with a population of about 2.5 million. Known principally for its tourist attractions, the area is one of the fastest-growing regions in the nation. East central Florida is noted for its many lakes. Atlantic beaches are an easy hour's drive from the main campus. The area offers Broadway productions, pop and classical music headliners, art festivals, a Shakespeare festival of UCF origin, and the National Basketball Association's Orlando Magic.

UCF is a 1,442-acre campus comprised of 113 permanent buildings radiating outward from an academic core, where UCF's colleges, classrooms, and library are located. UCF houses six colleges—College of Arts and Sciences, College of Business, College of Education, College of Engineering, College of Health and Public Affairs, and the Burnett Honors College. Excluding honors, all colleges offer both master's and doctoral programs. More than $300 million in construction is planned over the next five years.

New campus facilities include the 15,000-square-foot Burnett Honors College building and an 84,000-square-foot student Recreation and Wellness Center. Other facilities on campus include the Center for Research and Education in Optics and Lasers (CREOL), the National Center for Forensic Science, the Institute for Simulation and Training (IST), the Center for Discovery of Drugs and Diagnostics, the Space Education and Research Center (SERC), the Center for Applied Human Factors in Aviation (CAHFA), the Florida Solar Energy Center (FSEC), the Small Business Development Center (SBDC), and the Department of Aerospace Studies (Air Force ROTC).

Key Facilities The University Library, housed in a 200,000-square-foot facility, has a collection of more than 1.3 million volumes (books, journals, and government documents) with approximately 8,000 subscriptions (journals, newspapers, and other serials) and more than 32,000 media titles. The library is a partial depository for U.S. and Florida documents and U.S. patents. LUIS, the library's online catalog, is accessed through terminals in the library, at other campus locations, or from off-campus computers. Through LUIS, library users are able to determine whether the UCF library owns a particular item and the location and availability of the item. LUIS also provides online access to catalogs of all state university libraries in Florida and to ERIC, IAC, and other indexes.

UCF has been the only Florida university named one of the nation's "Most Wired Campuses" by *Yahoo! Internet Life* magazine for the last three years. Access to the Internet and campus information servers is available to all students. Computer Services provides central support services for administrative data processing, instruction and research computing, telecommunication networks, e-mail, telephony, information technology, training, user help, and microcomputer technology retail to the University. Computer Services maintains seven public-access labs available to all UCF faculty and staff members and enrolled students for class work or research. Each lab contains from fifteen to 100 computers connected to UCF's LAN. Students may access registration, grades, and financial aid information online.

Honorary Societies Alpha Psi Omega, Eta Kappa Nu, Phi Kappa Phi, Sigma Tau Delta, Golden Key

Athletics The University of Central Florida is a member of the National Collegiate Athletic Association (NCAA) Division I and competes in the Atlantic Sun Conference. UCF's current intercollegiate sports for men include baseball, basketball, cross-country, golf, football, soccer, and tennis. Women's sports include basketball, cross-country, golf, rowing, soccer, softball, track, tennis, and volleyball. Crew and waterskiing are intercollegiate club sports for both men and women. UCF recreational facilities include an 84,000-square-foot student Recreation and Wellness Center, with 10,000 square feet of fitness and cardio space, an indoor track, four basketball courts, three aerobics/group exercise rooms, and a climbing wall. Other facilities include lighted tennis and racquetball courts an outdoor swimming pool, golf driving range, volleyball and basketball courts, and ball fields.

Study Abroad The UCF study-abroad programs are designed and administered by UCF faculty members. Students have a choice of programs that last one year, one semester, or six weeks. Some programs require proficiency in a foreign language, others do not. Prerequisites, length of stay, and academic requirements vary by program. UCF has summer programs in Canada, Germany, Italy, Spain, and Russia. UCF faculty members and students also participate in State University System programs in London, England, and Florence, Italy. The Burnett Honors College awards study-abroad scholarships on a competitive basis to honors students each year.

Support Services Student Disability Services provides information and orientation to campus facilities and services, assistance with classroom accommodations, assistance with course registration, disabled parking decals, counseling, and referral to campus and community services for students with disabilities. Services are available to students whose disabilities include, but are not limited to, hearing impairment, manual dexterity impairment, mobility impairment, specific learning disability (such as dyslexia), speech impairment, visual impairment, or other disabilities that require administrative or academic adjustments.

Tuition: $2400 for state residents, $10,289 for nonresidents, per year (2001–02)

Room and Board: Approximately $4600 (2001–02)

Mandatory Fees: Approximately $180

Contact: Director: Dr. Allyn MacLean Stearman, PO Box 161800, Orlando, Florida 32816-1800; Telephone: 407-823-

2076; Fax: 407-823-6583; E-mail: honors@pegasus.cc.ucf.edu; Web site: http://honors.ucf.edu

University of Cincinnati

4 Pu G L Tr AA

▼ University Honors Scholars Program

The University Honors Scholars Program (UHS) is an all-University program open to academically talented and motivated students enrolled in any of the University of Cincinnati's (UC) colleges. The mission of the Honors Scholars Program is to help academically talented students tap their academic and leadership potential, foster their personal growth, increase their satisfaction, engender a love of learning, facilitate graduation with University Honors, and equip them for further study and successful careers, primarily through enriching their educational experience and secondarily by enhancing their cocurricular involvement.

Honors students can select honors sections of existing courses to fulfill both major and elective credits. Specialized-topics courses allow students to earn elective credit in interdisciplinary-focused courses. All honors courses have a limited enrollment of 25, though many of the topics courses are much smaller. Students also have the option of earning credit for nonhonors courses by preparing a contract to complete a special learning project.

Honors students also have access to a broad range of social and cultural events sponsored by the Honors Program. These events provide students the opportunity to interact with honors students from different colleges and majors. Students in the program have access to specialized honors housing, with honors students as resident assistants, social and service programming, and computer labs located on the floor. A student computer lab is also located in the honors suite.

The Pre-Professional Advising Center offers specialized advising and assistance to preprofessional students and is part of the Honors Program. This office oversees Connections and Connections-E, programs that offer guaranteed admission to UC's prestigious Medical College to select incoming freshmen.

Honors-PLUS is a demanding undergraduate business honors curriculum operating in cooperation with the Honors Program. By combining academic and work experiences, the program integrates the resources of the UC, the College of Business Administration, and greater Cincinnati's businesses to provide graduates with the knowledge and skills necessary for immediate productive employment and position them for advancement as business and community leaders.

The Honors Scholars Program, formerly located in the College of Arts and Sciences, became a University-wide honors program in 1991. Currently in a growth phase, enrollment is 1,400 students, with an anticipated enrollment of 1,700 in 2003.

Participation Requirements: Students must earn 24 credit hours to earn a lower-division honors distinction. Students who wish to earn full University Honors must earn 36 honors credits prior to graduation. Of the 36 credits, 9 must come from specially designated honors topics courses. Students can earn credit in the following ways: honors sections of introductory or intermediate courses, honors special-topics courses, honors contracts for nonhonors courses, honors individually guided study, departmental honors courses, and departmental senior capstones/theses. In order to maintain membership in the program, students must maintain a minimum 3.2 cumulative GPA and make reasonable progress toward completion of the hours requirements. Upon graduation with 36 hours of honors credit, students receive special recognition at an honors graduation ceremony. Students who graduate with a GPA of 3.2 to 3.74 receive special notation on both the transcript and diploma as an Honors Scholar. Students who graduate with a GPA of 3.75 or higher receive special notation as a Distinguished Honors Scholar.

Admission Process: Applicants are evaluated using the following criteria: test scores, high school rank, high school GPA, writing skills, strength of the high school schedule (AP, honors classes, etc.), academic awards or honors, leadership, activities, and service. The typical honors student has an SAT score of 1300, an ACT composite of 29, and a high school GPA of 3.8. Applications are accepted at any time; however, for priority consideration, application materials must be received by March 15. Students already at UC may apply after accumulating 12 hours of credit with a minimum GPA of 3.2.

Scholarship Availability: Financial aid is administered through the Office of Financial Aid. Of special interest to potential honors students is the Cincinnatus Scholarship Competition, which is open to prospective students who apply to the University of Cincinnati and meet eligibility criteria similar to admission to the Honors Program, including academic excellence, community service, and performance during the competition itself. Four-year awards range from $6000 to $60,000. On average, 90 percent of honors students receive Cincinnatus scholarship awards.

In addition, many colleges offer specific college-based scholarship funds. For example, the College of Business Administration provides scholarship funds to students under the Honors-PLUS program. It offers total financial support, co-op experience, and a personal mentor.

Honors Undergraduate Awards are given to promote research and scholarly or creative activity among honors students at UC. These awards enable honors students to undertake projects of an original nature within their major field of study.

The Campus Context: The University of Cincinnati is a state-supported research institution located in southwest Ohio. UC includes a main academic campus often called West Campus, a medical campus known as East Campus, a branch campus in suburban Blue Ash, and a rural branch campus in Clermont County, just east of Cincinnati.

Student Body Total student enrollment for the 2001–02 academic year was 33,180, of whom there were 18,094 full-time undergraduate students, 4,496 full-time graduate and professional students, 10,590 part-time undergraduate students, and 2,796 part-time graduate and professional students. About 89 percent of the University's total enrollment are Ohio residents. Women constitute 52.7 percent of UC's student population and men 47.3 percent. Approximately 3,600 students live on campus, and another 750 live in fraternity and sorority housing.

Faculty A faculty of 2,366 full-time members, plus adjunct faculty members, affords a student-teacher ratio of 18:1.

Key Facilities University libraries hold more than 1.6 million books, 20,000 journal and serial subscriptions, and more than 3 million microforms in eleven locations on the central campus. Separate libraries serve music, law, art, engineering, science, mathematics, and classics students. OhioLINK, an online catalog, connects students to the holdings of Ohio's academic libraries and gives students access, via their computers, to 31 million resources.

Eight West Campus microcomputer laboratories are provided and maintained by the University for use by UC students and faculty and staff members. These labs offer access to popular word processing, database, graphics, spreadsheet, and other applications on both Windows and Macintosh computers plus access to UCnet, the UC network. Lab users can access their

Interpreting the symbols: **2**=two-year college, **4**=four-year college; **Pu**=public or state college, **Pr**=private college; **G**=general honors program; **D**=departmental honors program; **S**=small program (fewer than 100 students), **M**=midsize program (100 to 500 students), **L**=large program (more than 500 students); **Sc**=scholarships available in honors program; **Tr**=transfer students accepted into honors program; **HBC**=historically black college; **AA**=academic advisors; **GA**=graduate advisors; **FA**=fellowship advisors.

accounts on the Bearcat® Online–dedicated e-mail server, as well as accounts on the Student Access Network. Honors students also have access to a computer lab housed in the honors suite. Honors students living in honors housing have computer access on their floors.

Honorary Societies Alpha Lambda Delta, Beta Alpha Psi, Chi Epsilon, Golden Key, Mortar Board, Order of Omega, Phi Beta Kappa, Pi Chi Epsilon, Sigma Sigma, Tau Beta Pi

Athletics The University of Cincinnati competes in seventeen Division I intercollegiate sports and is a member of Conference USA. A well-developed intramural sports program offers UC students an opportunity to participate in a wide range of sports and activities. The Honors Program offers students the opportunity to participate in honors-designated leagues structured within the framework of the intramural program. The Laurence and Shoemaker Centers provide students access to swimming pools, weight-lifting equipment, exercise rooms, and other facilities. An indoor track and outdoor all-weather track are also available.

Study Abroad The University of Cincinnati is committed to attaining worldwide recognition as a center for international activities and research. To achieve this goal, the University has developed the Institute for Global Studies and Affairs. The institute serves students, faculty members, members of the administration, and alumni by providing leadership for the University's globalization initiatives, including international curriculum, research efforts, programs, projects, and activities. Building on these activities, the University attracts ever-increasing numbers of highly qualified international students and scholars. The Honors Program offers students an opportunity to earn a Global Studies Certificate by combining structured course work and travel-abroad experiences.

Support Services The Educational Services Office serves as a major source of freshman information and referral. Tutorial services help students with specific academic troubles through one-on-one tutoring. Learning skills assistance and programs for undeclared majors and on-campus transfers plus academic skills seminars and personal development workshops are offered. The Office of Disabilities Services certifies students with disabilities to receive services such as counseling, reader referral, recording/reading rooms, interpreters, special parking, and elevator keys.

Job Opportunities UC has co-op programs in seven colleges, including the oldest co-op program in the country. In 1999–2000, co-op students earned a total of $27 million. Typical UC co-op students earn $8600 annually from their assignments. In addition to UC's outstanding cooperative education program, students work at numerous on- and off-campus positions. In addition, six colleges offer internships and field or clinical experiences.

Tuition: $5169 for residents, $14,652 for nonresidents, per year (2001–02)

Room and Board: $6498

Mandatory Fees: $332 per quarter

Contact: Director: David Meredith, Director of Enrollment Management, University Honors Scholars Program, University of Cincinnati, P.O. Box 210007, Cincinnati, Ohio 45221-0007; Telephone: 513-556-6274; Fax: 513-556-2890; E-mail: honors@uc.edu; Web site: http://www.honors.uc.edu

UNIVERSITY OF CONNECTICUT

4 Pu G D L Sc Tr

▼ Honors Scholars Program

The Honors Programs enable intellectually gifted and highly motivated students to receive the richest possible education at the University of Connecticut. Enthusiastic and energetic students who are looking for smaller classes, extensive discussions with professors, more individual attention, special projects, and research opportunities recognize that the Honors Programs are outstanding opportunities. The Honors Programs at the University of Connecticut provide talented students with an enhanced undergraduate experience through a number of opportunities.

Freshman and sophomore students who are enrolled in the Honors Scholar Program typically enroll in one or two honors courses each semester. These special sections are smaller in size and provide an enhanced learning experience through the more in-depth discussions and varied perspectives that typically come out of this learning format. Students who actively participate in honors courses during their first two years may be eligible for the Honors Certificate Award.

Upper-division honors study is specific to each student's major. Because each discipline is different, the specific junior/senior-level requirements are at the discretion of the academic departments. Typical honors work in the major may involve special projects in major courses, departmental seminars, independent study, and graduate courses. The Honors Programs Office sets the minimum University-wide requirements for graduation as an Honors Scholar, which include the participation in special honors projects, course work, and the completion of an honors thesis as defined by the major department. Students should consult with their departmental honors advisers regarding specific or additional major requirements.

Honors students also participate in learning experiences outside the classroom through Mini-Courses, Conversations, and Journeys Seminars. Through Mini-Courses, guest speakers lecture on specific topics dealing with current events or topics. Journeys Seminars and Conversations provide a smaller group setting for students to learn from an individual's interesting life story and discussions on hot topics.

Other opportunities available to Honors Program students include the Washington, D.C., internship program for students who would like to spend a semester with a U.S. congressman. Students who are interested in research may apply for the summer research fellowships to obtain support for collecting data for or presenting research or displaying their research in poster format at the annual Frontiers in Undergraduate Research-Arts, Sciences, and Humanities (FUR-ASH).

Social amenities of the Honors Scholars Program include a student-run literary magazine, an ad hoc music group and film club, picnics and parties each term, and a nineteenth-century house that provides rooms for studying, practicing music, chatting, and holding classes. A student organization, the Honors Council, allows students to plan honors scholars activities at the Storrs campus and has representatives who sit at faculty meetings. Honors Scholars also have the option of living in designated honors floors in a residence hall. Honors South, a specially designated building in the state-of-the-art residence hall complex, is open to honors upperclassmen. The complex has classrooms, computer labs, and multipurpose event rooms.

The Honors Scholars Program is diverse in terms of students' ethnic and racial backgrounds. An Honors Program for upper-division students in the humanities and social sciences is available at the Stamford regional campus. The Stamford Honors Program features interdisciplinary seminars, an evening lecture series, and a senior-year thesis component.

The Honors Scholars Program, which began its pilot program in 1964, currently enrolls more than 1,000 students.

Participation Requirements: To remain in good standing in the Honors Scholars Program, students must take at least one honors course per academic year. In addition, first-year students must earn a total GPA of at least 3.0 and sophomores and juniors a total GPA of at least 3.1. To graduate with the title "Honors Scholar" on one's official transcript and diploma, a student at minimum must complete 12 credits of upper-division honors course work, complete a senior thesis, and have a total GPA of at least 3.2. Departments sometimes add further requirements for the Honors Scholar designation.

The Honors Programs also offer an honors certificate to students who have been unusually active in the Honors Scholars Program during their first two years of study. Although the Honors Scholars Program is the core of the Honors Program, the University offers two additional programs for highly motivated students.

Each fall, a maximum of 30 students are selected for the prestigious University Scholar Program based on the rigor and imagination of a proposed plan of study. Graduation as a University Scholar is the highest academic honor bestowed to undergraduates at the University of Connecticut. Students may combine the University Scholar and the Honors Scholar designations. Students wishing to pursue a challenging program that is less intensive than either the University Scholar or Honors Scholar designations may instead opt to fulfill the requirements for the Degree with Distinction Program, if offered by the major department. As part of the requirements of this program, students must complete a distinction project, which demonstrates a high level of mastery of the discipline.

Admission Process: High school seniors should have a combined SAT I score of at least 1320 and be in the top 8 percent of their graduating class. Case-by-case decisions are made for students who have overcome unusual challenges or who have demonstrated outstanding ability in particular fields of study. Transfer students must have earned, at their previous institution, a total GPA of at least 3.4. Any first-year student or sophomore at the University of Connecticut who earns a total GPA of 3.2 while at the University is eligible to join the program, regardless of high school record or SAT scores.

Scholarship Availability: The University's Undergraduate Admissions Office awards a number of four-year, merit-based scholarships to incoming students. These scholarships are renewable for up to four years, provided that students meet the minimum grade requirement. The Admissions Office awards these scholarships according to a mixture of the following criteria: class rank, high school GPA, rigor of curriculum, extracurricular activities, and SAT I scores. Further information regarding scholarships for incoming freshmen is available via the Web at http://www.admissions.uconn.edu/schlprog.htm.

The Campus Context: The University of Connecticut has eleven schools and colleges offering 101 degree programs on the Storrs campus: the College of Agriculture and Natural Resources, College of Continuing Studies, School of Allied Health Professions, School of Business Administration, School of Education, School of Engineering, School of Family Studies, School of Fine Arts, College of Liberal Arts and Sciences, School of Nursing, and School of Pharmacy. Distinguished facilities on campus include the William Benton Museum of Art, the Museum of Natural History, Thomas J. Dodd Research Center, Harry A. Gampel Pavilion, and the Jorgensen Center for the Performing Arts.

Student Body There are 13,251 students on the Storrs campus with almost an equal balance of men and women. The ethnic distribution is 4.9 percent African American, 5.9 percent Asian American, 4.5 percent Latino American, .3 percent Native American, 83.4 percent Caucasian, and 1.1 percent international. Residents make up 67 percent of the student population, commuters 33 percent. Sixty-eight percent of the students receive financial aid. There are fourteen fraternities and nine sororities.

Faculty Of the 1,121 full-time faculty members, 95 percent have terminal degrees. The student-faculty ratio is 12:1.

Key Facilities The library houses 2.1 million volumes. Computer facilities include more than 1,800 terminals on campus located in the Computer Center, the Babbidge Library, various schools and colleges, and some residence halls. The mainframe is an IBM ES 9000.

Honorary Societies Phi Kappa Phi, Golden Key, Mortar Board, Phi Beta Kappa, Alpha Lambda Delta, Lambda Pheta Alpha

Athletics In varsity athletics, Division I sports at the University of Connecticut are baseball, men's and women's basketball, men's and women's cross-country and track, women's field hockey, men's golf, men's ice hockey, women's lacrosse, women's rowing, men's and women's soccer, men's and women's tennis, and women's volleyball. Football is a Division II sport. A wide variety of intramural sports is also available.

Study Abroad The University of Connecticut is in the forefront of study abroad programs; not only transfer credit but also grades earned abroad can be applied to degree programs. Through the Study Abroad Office, there are opportunities for study in virtually all countries and there are extensive offerings for students in all colleges.

Support Services Disabled students are assisted by the Center for Students with Disabilities; students with documented learning disabilities are assisted by the University Program for College Students with Learning Disabilities.

Job Opportunities Students interested in employment find work-study opportunities, numerous internship opportunities, and a Student Employment Office on campus.

Tuition: $4282 for state residents, $12,056 for nonresidents, per year (2000–01)

Room and Board: $6062

Mandatory Fees: $1314

Contact: Interim Director: Donna Fournier, 300 Mansfield Road, Unit 1147, South A Room 128, Storrs, Connecticut 06269-1147; Associate Director: Patricia M. Szarek, Telephone: 860-486-4223; Fax: 860-486-0222; E-mail: donna.fournier@uconn.edu or pszarek@uconn.edu; Web site: http://www.honors.uconn.edu

---

University of Dayton

4 Pr G L Sc

▼ Honors and Scholars Programs

The University of Dayton has a University-wide Honors Program restricted to 40 entering first-year University Scholars each year. Only students admitted to the University as beginning University Scholars are eligible to apply to the Honors Program. Honors students are entitled to all the benefits awarded to University Scholars.

The University Honors Program began in 1979 and graduated its first full class of students completing the program in 1983. It currently enrolls 150 honors and approximately 2,000 scholars.

The University of Dayton admits selected beginning and transfer undergraduate students to the University as University Scholars. Students who do not matriculate at the University as Scholars but subsequently earn a cumulative GPA of 3.5 or higher at the end of an academic year are added to the roster of University Scholars. Scholars whose GPA falls below a cumulative 3.0 at the end of an academic year are dropped from the roster of University Scholars.

The only automatic curricular impact of being named a University Scholar is the halving of the usual full-year first-year English composition requirement to a special one-semester course. Con-

Interpreting the symbols: **2**=two-year college, **4**=four-year college; **Pu**=public or state college, **Pr**=private college; **G**=general honors program; **D**=departmental honors program; **S**=small program (fewer than 100 students), **M**=midsize program (100 to 500 students), **L**=large program (more than 500 students); **Sc**=scholarships available in honors program; **Tr**=transfer students accepted into honors program; **HBC**=historically black college; **AA**=academic advisors; **GA**=graduate advisors; **FA**=fellowship advisors.

nected with this course is the visit to campus of the annual Scholars Author, one of whose books the first-year students will have studied in their Scholars English class.

In addition, University Scholars are given automatic permission to enroll in an extensive variety of specially designed Scholars sections of regularly offered courses. Many of these classes satisfy University-wide general education requirements. Registration in Scholars sections is not required of University Scholars, but all Scholars classes are given special designation on University transcripts. Moreover, funding to Scholars for conducting or presenting research is limited to Scholars who have taken two or more Scholars courses.

The Scholars Program also sponsors an annual Scholars Symposium, an annual Scholars Speaker in the Distinguished Speakers Series, an annual Scholars Artist Residency connected with the University Arts Series, and deeply discounted tickets to selected cultural events.

Special Scholars sections of University residence halls are available to limited numbers of first-, second- and third-year students.

The program began in 1979-80; its annual enrollment is 1,200 to 1,300 students, or approximately the top 20 percent of the undergraduate student body.

Participation Requirements: Honors Program students take a series of five semester-long Honors Program Seminars during their first five semesters at the University. Currently in English, history, sociology, philosophy, and engineering systems design, these seminars satisfy University-wide general education requirements. In the final seminar, the entire junior Honors Program class works as a team on a complex project using a systems approach. Students must then complete an acceptable honors thesis and graduate with a 3.0 or higher GPA to be awarded an Honors Program degree. Students graduating from the honors program are recognized at University Commencement.

Admission Process: All prospective Honors students and Scholars should apply no later than April 1.

Scholarship Availability: Many Honors Program students are awarded scholarships as University Scholars. Supplementary scholarships are available to Honors Program students who are not already receiving full-tuition scholarships but are doing commendable academic work and making important contributions to the life of the University community. Honors Program students are also eligible for substantial funding for the required independent research (thesis) project, the culminating stage in the Honors Program degree.

The Campus Context: Founded in 1850 by the Society of Mary, the University of Dayton is a private, coeducational school directed by the Marianists, a Roman Catholic teaching order. It is among the nation's largest Catholic institutions of higher learning. The main campus of more than 100 landscaped acres is on a hill overlooking the city of Dayton, Ohio. Among special facilities are the Language Learning Center, Diverse Student Population Services for African American and Latino students, and the University of Dayton Research Institute.

The University's major academic units are the College of Arts and Sciences, the School of Business Administration, the School of Education, the School of Engineering, and the School of Law. There are more than seventy degree programs on campus.

Student Body Undergraduate enrollment is 7,100: 52 percent women and 48 percent men. The population includes 2.5 percent African American and 1 percent Hispanic students as well as 65 international students. First- and second- year students are 96 percent residents, with only 4 percent commuting to campus. Ninety percent of the students receive some form of financial aid plus nonrepayable grants, scholarships, educational loans, and part-time employment. There are ten sororities and fifteen fraternities.

Faculty Of the 781 faculty members, 404 are full-time; 85 percent have terminal degrees. The student-faculty ratio is 15:1.

Key Facilities The library houses 1.3 million volumes, 701,937 microforms, 3,095 periodical subscriptions, and 1,000 records and tapes, as well as access to on-line bibliographic retrieval services. Computing facilities include access to CRAY-YMP at the Ohio Supercomputer Center, Columbus; PC networks; and access to the Internet.

Athletics In athletics, the University of Dayton is a member of the Atlantic 10 Conference; the football team plays in the Division I-AA Pioneer League. There are seven men's intercollegiate sports: football, soccer, cross-country, basketball, baseball, golf, and tennis. There are nine women's intercollegiate sports: volleyball, soccer, cross-country, basketball, indoor track, softball, golf, tennis, and outdoor track.

Study Abroad The International Education Programs Office can help students find opportunities to study, work, or do service abroad. Students can earn up to a full semester of credit abroad in cities such as Madrid, Dublin, London, Vienna, and Lille. The Department of Languages offers opportunities to earn up to 6 credit hours in Segovia, Spain; Mexico; Marburg, Germany; Quebec; and Paris. The School of Business offers study abroad programs in Augsburg, Germany.

Support Services Disabled Student Services provides assistance and counseling for prospective and enrolled students with physical or learning disabilities. It assists with the identification of special needs and the coordination of special services and related aspects of campus adjustment.

Job Opportunities The Federal Work-Study Program provides on-campus employment opportunities for full-time and three-quarter-time students who demonstrate financial need. University employment opportunities for students who do not qualify for the Federal Work-Study Program are available through the Student Employment Office. Cooperative Educations ("the co-op system") allows students to alternate terms of on-campus study with terms of off-campus work at jobs related to their academic concentration.

Tuition: $16,320 per year (2001–02)

Room and Board: $5280

Mandatory Fees: $530; $1322 (computer)

Contact: Director: Dr. Steven P. Dandaneau, 125 Alumni Hall, Dayton, Ohio 45469-0311; Telephone: 937-229-4615; Fax: 937-229-4298; E-mail: steven.dandaneau@notes.udayton.edu

University of Delaware

4 Pu G L Sc Tr

▼ University Honors Program

The University of Delaware (UD) Honors Program, begun in 1976, combines the considerable resources of a major research university with the small class sizes and the personal attention that are typical of the nation's finest small colleges. After nearly a decade of rapid growth, the program now offers honors degrees in eighty-four (out of 124) majors in all six of the University's colleges, as well as honors residence hall living (required for first-year students and optional for upperclass students) and extensive cocurricular programming. Historically, the program has also functioned as a laboratory for pedagogical innovation, piloting programs such as undergraduate research, which offers students an opportunity to collaborate on research with faculty mentors; problem-based learning in the sciences; and peer tutoring.

Participation Requirements: First-year honors students are encouraged to enroll in a program of studies that can qualify them for the General Honors Award. Requirements include 18 honors credits in the first two years of University study, with 12 in the first year; a 3.0 or higher cumulative GPA; and residence in first-year honors housing). In addition to honors sections of courses that satisfy departmental, college, and University general education requirements, this course work must include a first-year honors colloquium, a small-enrollment (20 students), writing-intensive interdisciplinary seminar.

Upper-division students work toward various forms of recognition in addition to the General Honors Award, including the Honors Foreign Language Certificate, the Honors Degree, the Honors Degree with Distinction, and the Degree with Distinction. Both versions of an honors degree require 30 credit hours of honors course work; the Honors Degree with Distinction and the Degree with Distinction recognize the successful completion of a 6-credit senior thesis. Honors degree tutorials (4 students per section) and interdisciplinary honors degree seminars complement departmental capstone course offerings and discovery-learning experiences for seniors. Honors Program students participate extensively in the full complement of academic enrichment activities available to UD students, including UD's nationally renowned undergraduate research program, study-abroad programs on all seven continents, community service projects, academic internships, and service-learning experiences.

Two unique opportunities within the Honors Program are also of note. The Writing Fellows Program is a service-learning program that trains approximately 40 advanced Honors Program undergraduates to work as writing tutors with first-year honors colloquium students and in a variety of assignments across the University population at large. The Alison Scholars Program provides exceptional arts, humanities, and social science students with an early introduction to academic enrichment and special-event programming. It also allows some flexibility in meeting University general education requirements so that participants can move more quickly into advanced undergraduate (and even graduate) course work or pursue a more creative combination of studies spanning various general education groups.

The Honors Program typically enrolls 500 new freshmen each year, creating a University-wide living-learning community for students in all six undergraduate colleges. Extensive cultural, social, recreational, and academic cocurricular programming reinforces the strong sense of community among students living either in first-year honors housing or in one of several centrally located upper-division honors residence areas.

Admission Process: First-year students apply for admission to the Honors Program when they apply for admission to the University. Other UD students may begin participating in honors courses and enrichment opportunities after they have achieved a 3.0 (B) or higher GPA in courses taken at the University; a formal application process for internal transfer is also available. At present, there are approximately 2,000 students enrolled in the program (about 13 percent of the University's undergraduate population). All students completing applications by January 15 are automatically considered for merit scholarships.

Scholarship Availability: Honors students compete for and receive the lion's share of the University's general pool of merit scholarships, which range from $1000 to complete coverage of tuition, room and board, and a book stipend.

The Campus Context: The University of Delaware serves as the state's public university and is a Research II land-grant, sea-grant, and space-grant institution. Chartered by the state of Delaware in 1833 (but with origins traceable to 1743), its main campus is located in Newark, Delaware, a suburban community of 28,500 located midway between Philadelphia and Baltimore. There are 124 undergraduate majors available.

Research apprenticeships with faculty mentors give talented, motivated University of Delaware undergraduates a chance to see and take part in what is happening on the front lines of discovery at UD today. Every UD college, department, and research center provides opportunities for undergraduate involvement in faculty research activities. Six to 700 hundred students participate each year. For more information, students should consult http://www.udel.edu/ur.

The University has active chapters of Phi Beta Kappa, Phi Kappa Phi, Alpha Lambda Delta, Phi Sigma Pi, and many other academic honor societies; honors students are often their officers.

Student Body There are 15,731 full-time undergraduates, 59 percent of whom are women. Minority groups comprise 12.9 percent of the student population.

Faculty Of the 1,049 faculty members, 88 percent have a doctoral or terminal degree. The undergraduate student-faculty ratio is 14:1.

Key Facilities The library houses 2.4 million volumes; there are twenty public computing sites. Many student musical performance and theatrical groups exist on campus.

Honorary Societies Phi Kappa Phi, Phi Beta Kappa, Alpha Lambda Delta

Athletics UD has twenty-three varsity sports (eleven for men, twelve for women; North Atlantic Conference, Division I; football Atlantic 10 Conference, I-AA) and innumerable intramural and fitness opportunities.

Study Abroad UD has more than sixty study-abroad programs in more than thirty subjects in at least twenty-five countries in Europe, Asia, Latin America, the Caribbean, and Africa. For more information, students should consult http://www.udel.edu/studyabroad/.

Tuition: $4770 for state residents, $13,860 for nonresidents (2001–02)

Room and Board: $5534 minimum

Mandatory Fees: $520

Contact: Director: Dr. Ann L. Ardis, University Honors Program, 186 South College Avenue, Newark, Delaware 19716; Telephone: 302-831-2340; Fax: 302-831-4194; E-mail: aardis@udel.edu or honorsprogram@udel.edu; Web site: http://www.udel.edu/honors/

University of Denver

4 Pr G M Sc Tr

▼ University Honors Program

The University Honors Program combines the individual attention of a small liberal arts college with the resources of a midsized national university. Highly motivated students of proven intellectual ability and curiosity are invited to engage their peers and professors in scholarship and interdisciplinary learning. All majors—arts and humanities, business, natural sciences, social sciences, and performing arts—are represented. Honors students may take advantage of special opportunities on and off campus to enhance their undergraduate education and prepare for graduate work and professional careers. Most important, the University Honors Program cultivates a standard of intellectual excellence applicable to any walk of life and fosters habits of thought and mind that lead to a lifetime of inquiry and liberal learning. Students leave the program with well-developed minds because they are liberally educated persons.

Challenging and interdisciplinary course work together with enriching extracurricular activities allow honors students to excel in the company of intelligent and energetic peers and in close

Interpreting the symbols: **2**=two-year college, **4**=four-year college; **Pu**=public or state college, **Pr**=private college; **G**=general honors program; **D**=departmental honors program; **S**=small program (fewer than 100 students), **M**=midsize program (100 to 500 students), **L**=large program (more than 500 students); **Sc**=scholarships available in honors program; **Tr**=transfer students accepted into honors program; **HBC**=historically black college; **AA**=academic advisors; **GA**=graduate advisors; **FA**=fellowship advisors.

contact with distinguished faculty members. The four-year program affords students the opportunity to complete their university requirements with specially designed honors classes in the Divisions of Arts, Humanities, and Social Sciences as well as in the Division of Natural Science, Mathematics, and Engineering. Approximately half of the first-year honors students elect to take the Coordinated Humanities program, an integrated three-quarter sequence that spans antiquity to the twenty-first century and combines history, literature, religion, art, philosophy, and religious studies. Many departments offer honors sections of introductory and advanced classes. Honors professors teach a wide variety of interdisciplinary upper-level seminars designed to allow students to pursue their majors while expanding and crossing disciplinary boundaries. In all, more than forty honors courses are offered each quarter, and, in most cases, honors classes range from 8 to 15 students.

The University Honors Program fosters a community of conversation—a place to meet other bright and energetic students who want to explore the world of ideas. Activities within and outside the classroom aim not only at the acquisition of knowledge but also at learning through conversation—a two-way engagement with the books of the past and the minds of the present in the company of one's peers. Learning through conversation means more than acquiring a facility in self-expression and the capacity for analysis, argumentation, reflection, and investigation. Conservation cultivates habits of thought and personality in which one learns how best to speak, to listen, and to attend to the voice of the creative imagination. Of course, because the best conservations are frequently those punctuated by laughter and light-heartedness, the Honors Program offers times to get away and enjoy each other's company. The Honors House Living and Learning Community (an optional residential environment), mountain retreats, outdoor activities, and cultural events in the city of Denver provide honors students with opportunities for unstructured time to converse and delight in what nature and civilization have to offer. Honors students are leaders on campus and in the Denver community; they are regularly competitive for the major national and postgraduate fellowships, including the Fulbright, Rhodes, and Marshall Scholarships. University of Denver honors students are those who are willing—and have the courage—to contemplate the past so as to understand the present and form intelligent hopes for the future.

The University Honors Program was founded in 1960 and currently has 450 students.

Participation Requirements: Students must take at least 12 credits of honors courses during their first two years and at least two interdisciplinary honors seminars during their second and third years and complete either a senior honors thesis/project or 6 credits of business honors seminars. Students must maintain a 3.4 GPA or higher to remain in good standing and graduate with University Honors distinction on their transcripts.

Admission Process: Qualified students admitted to the University of Denver are invited to apply to the University Honors Program. High school GPA, class rank, test scores, and the admissions essay are all considered when inviting students to apply. Because numeric records do not always adequately reflect a student's talent and promise, the honors application gives students an opportunity to further demonstrate their intellectual ability and curiosity. Applications are sent directly to the student shortly after the University extends an offer for admission. Most students admitted to the program have at least a 3.85 high school GPA, are in the top 10 percent of their graduating class, and have at least a score of 1290 on the SAT I or 28 on the ACT.

Scholarship Availability: Almost all students admitted to the University Honors Program receive merit awards ranging from $4000 to full tuition. Scholarships are renewable provided that the students meet the academic standards of their respective programs. Sixty-eight percent of undergraduate students receive financial aid; 51 percent of aid distributed to undergraduate students is in the form of scholarship or grants, 36 percent is in student loans, and 13 percent of aid is work-study.

The Campus Context: The University of Denver, the oldest independent university in the Rocky Mountain Region, enrolls 9,385 students in its undergraduate, graduate, and first professional programs. The University was founded in 1864 by John Evans while he was governor of the Colorado Territory. Earlier, Evans had established Northwestern University in Evanston, Illinois. Located just south of downtown Denver in a pleasant residential neighborhood, the University is close to the natural wonders of the Rocky Mountains and to the city's museums, performing arts centers, bookstores, and lively downtown areas. Many students find internships with local business, at the mayor's office, or at the Capitol.

The University offers fourteen bachelor's degrees in more than 100 areas representing a full range of disciplines in the arts, humanities, social sciences, natural sciences, international studies, and business. Honors students often take advantage of graduate courses and faculty members, including programs in art, biology, business, education, English and creative writing, international studies, law, psychology, and public policy. For qualified students, there are several five-year integrated degree programs that combine a B.A. or B.S. with a graduate degree in business (including the M.B.A.). Recent capital improvements for students include new instructional buildings for natural sciences, math and engineering, business, law, and performing arts, as well as a new residence hall and state-of-the-art athletics center.

Five residential Living and Learning Communities (LLCs) are open to students (including honors students): the Honors House LLC, the Environmental Awareness LLC, the Wellness House LLC, the International LLC, and the Pioneer Leadership Program LLC. Each Living and Learning Community offers distinctive residential and curricular programming in a setting that fosters community and conversation around a topic of common interest.

Student Body The total enrollment is 9,385. Undergraduate enrollment is 4,110; graduate enrollment is 5,275. Among the undergraduates there are 686 students who are members of minority groups (17.63 percent) and 207 international students (5.04 percent). The student population is 44 percent men and 56 percent women. Fifty percent are Colorado residents; non-Colorado students hail from all fifty states and many other countries. There are approximately eighty student groups on campus, including department, honorary, minority, and religious organizations; social fraternities and sororities; and hobby, interest, and service groups.

Faculty DU employs 425 full-time appointed faculty members, 92 percent of whom hold the highest degrees offered in their fields. The student-faculty ratio is 13.1.

Key Facilities The library houses 3,051,117 items. It is linked by computer with all major libraries in the region. It is open 100 hours per week.

Laptop computers are required of all first-year students. Computer facilities are available in every residence hall 24 hours a day. Student access labs have been established at several different central locations on campus. Many departments have their own labs. All students are given e-mail addresses and access to the World Wide Web.

Honorary Societies Phi Beta Kappa, Golden Key, Mortar Board, Alpha Lambda Delta, Pinnacle, and SPURS.

Athletics DU's Division of Athletics and Recreation sponsors nineteen Division I varsity sports, twenty-three club sports, and eighteen intramural sports.

Study Abroad The University of Denver encourages undergraduate study abroad and offers a wide range of opportunities in Europe, Africa, Asia, Australia, Canada, and Latin America. Students may go abroad for part of their studies and spend a summer, quarter, semester, or year studying in another country.

Programs overseas can include courses in any of the major fields offered at the University and represent a variety of program types, from direct exchanges that integrate students into the host university to study centers set up for English-speaking students. Financial aid that a student receives can, in many cases, be used to finance overseas study as well. Honors Program students are eligible for special International Service and Research Fellowships of up to $4000 for education abroad.

Support Services Services for students with physical disabilities are coordinated through the Office of Disability Services. Examples of accommodations include readers, peer note-takers, interpreters, testing adaptations, adaptive technology, and advocacy. The University also offers many resources through the Learning Effectiveness Program.

Job Opportunities Students are offered a range of work opportunities on campus, including assistantships and work-study. Off-campus jobs are plentiful and varied because of the University's proximity to opportunities in the city.

Tuition: $21,456 (2001–2002)

Room and Board: $6747

Mandatory Fees: $579

Contact: Todd Breyfogle (Director) or Katy Craig (Assistant Director), University Honors Program, Mary Reed Building 17, 2199 South University Boulevard, Denver, Colorado 80208; Telephone: 303-871-2035; Fax: 303-871-4783; E-mail: tbreyfog@du.edu or kcraig@du.edu; Web site: http://www.du.edu/honors

University of Evansville

4 Pr G M

▼ Honors Program

The University of Evansville (UE) Honors Program admits bright, talented students who have the desire to excel scholastically in a stimulating academic environment. The program challenges students to maximize their potential in all areas of study and offers an enhanced curriculum with the opportunity to share ideas and viewpoints with other outstanding students. The program attracts students from all majors and fosters independent thinking. All honors students seek a significant challenge from their professors as well as from each other. Participation in the Honors Program provides students with a rewarding college experience both in and out of the classroom.

Honors classes are interdisciplinary and are taught across the curriculum. Students in the Honors Program are able to enroll in any honors class regardless of major. The senior project is intended to serve as the capstone of the program and is presented at the University of Evansville, at a regional conference, or at the National Conference for Undergraduate Research.

Currently, 130 students are participating in the program.

Participation Requirements: Honors students are required to complete five honors classes during their tenure at the University and maintain a 3.5 overall GPA. In the senior year, each student completes a research project or performance and presents the project in a public forum.

Admission Process: Entering students who have a minimum high school GPA of 3.75 and an SAT of 1250 or ACT of 28 are invited by letter to apply to the program. Freshman are then selected on the basis of an Honors Program application, which includes such information as class rank, test scores, extracurricular activities, leadership roles, and one or more short essays. Applications are accepted in March each year. Students are notified of acceptance in April. Applications submitted during the freshman year are also considered.

Scholarship Availability: Academic scholarships ranging from $2000 to $8000 are available, although they are not restricted to Honors Program participants. One hundred percent of honors students currently receive merit-based financial aid. The average merit-based scholarship of the freshmen enrolling in 2001 was $7700. (Note: This is only the amount of merit scholarship received and does not include other forms of financial aid.) The average award of aid from all sources was $11,507 in 2001.

The Campus Context: The University of Evansville is a fully accredited, independent, comprehensive, liberal arts- and sciences-centered university with several professional schools. Founded in 1854, the University is affiliated with the United Methodist Church. UE is committed to a broad-based education for its undergraduate students. *U.S. News & World Report* ranks the University of Evansville in the top ten as one of "America's Best Colleges in the Midwest" and number one in percentage of full-time faculty members in the top ten. Located in southwestern Indiana, Evansville is situated within 150 miles of Louisville, Nashville, St. Louis, and Indianapolis. Evansville has a population of approximately 135,000 with a metropolitan-area population of about 300,000. The scenic 75-acre campus includes thirty-one major buildings, sensibly arranged for the convenience of students. There are more than 100 areas of study on campus.

Student Body Approximately 2,400 undergraduate students from across the nation and nearly fifty other countries attend the University. The student body is 60 percent women, with an ethnic distribution of 86 percent white, 5 percent domestic minority, and 9 percent international. There are six fraternities and four sororities on campus.

Faculty There are 222 faculty members, 174 of whom are full-time. Eighty-seven percent hold terminal degrees. The student-faculty ratio is 13:1.

Key Facilities Library holdings total 250,000 volumes. Students have access to a wide variety of services ranging from computers in residence halls and computer labs to Internet access in residence hall rooms. Both Mac and PC labs are available.

Honorary Societies Phi Eta Sigma, Phi Kappa Phi, and Mortar Board

Athletics A member of the NCAA, the University of Evansville competes at the Division I level in all fifteen sports. UE sponsors varsity teams in baseball, basketball, cross-country, golf, soccer, swimming and diving, and tennis for men and in basketball, cross-country, golf, soccer, softball, swimming and diving, tennis, and volleyball for women. UE is a member of the Missouri Valley Conference in all fifteen sports.

Study Abroad Study abroad at the University of Evansville enjoys a high profile, with the Offices of Academic Advising, Financial Aid, and Residence Life joining forces to encourage students to study either at the University's own Victorian manor house in England or in one of the more than 100 approved study-abroad sites. Virtually all majors can study abroad at UE with most of their financial aid intact. UE's Victorian manor house, Harlaxton College, has more than 100 rooms, offering not only UE course credit but also a Meet-a-Family program, optional field trips, and competitive sports against locals. In addition, Harlaxton College is recognized as one of the top twenty-five study-abroad programs in the nation. Thirty percent of the 2001 graduating class studied abroad.

Support Services All campus buildings are handicapped accessible.

Job Opportunities About 550 students are employed on campus. Work-study positions are available through a federally funded program for students who demonstrate financial need according

Interpreting the symbols: **2**=two-year college, **4**=four-year college; **Pu**=public or state college, **Pr**=private college; **G**=general honors program; **D**=departmental honors program; **S**=small program (fewer than 100 students), **M**=midsize program (100 to 500 students), **L**=large program (more than 500 students); **Sc**=scholarships available in honors program; **Tr**=transfer students accepted into honors program; **HBC**=historically black college; **AA**=academic advisors; **GA**=graduate advisors; **FA**=fellowship advisors.

to the Free Application for Federal Student Aid (FAFSA). The average job represents 8 hours of work per week at the current minimum wage for academic-year earnings of $1300.

Tuition: $17,050 per year (2001–02)

Room and Board: $5250 minimum

Mandatory Fees: $345

Contact: Director: Dr. Mary E. Pritchard, 1800 Lincoln Avenue, Evansville, Indiana 47722; Telephone: 812-479-2511; Fax: 812-474-4054; E-mail: mp43@evansville.edu; Web site: http://www.evansvile.edu/honorsprogram/

The University of Findlay

4 Pr G M Sc Tr

▼ Honors Program

The University of Findlay Honors Program provides a challenging educational experience that enriches and accelerates a student's academic growth. The program encourages and stimulates students beyond general academic excellence by providing opportunities for independent research, individual guidance, and specially designed courses and seminars. Students design their own honors curriculum by virtue of the projects they develop and the honors classes they choose.

Admission to the Honors Program requires a certain GPA for semester hours earned. Freshmen, however, may be admitted to the program during the first semester on the basis of their high school GPA and ACT score. Students must also obtain the recommendations of 2 faculty members for admission to the program.

Students who choose to develop their own projects do so through either a 1-hour contract or an independent research project. Both options allow students to pursue individual academic interests in conjunction with a professor who works with the student on the project. The projects are approved by the Honors Advisory Board on the basis of academic scope and depth and creativity. Students may also enroll in Honors Seminars that are developed by faculty members and are offered each semester on a one-time basis. These seminars are intense courses challenging the highest level of academic excellence within various fields of the liberal arts curriculum, offering honors students the opportunity to study beyond the regular curriculum. In addition, honors students may enroll in graduate classes in the Liberal Studies Program for honors credits.

Since its beginning in 1984, the Honors Program has enjoyed continuous growth and currently enrolls 150 students. In March 1995, the faculty adopted new goals for the program. Whereas previous goals emphasized independent study, new goals now include more freshman participation, more opportunities that challenge the highest level of academic excellence, more opportunities for faculty development and collaborative faculty/student research, and an environment that will encourage the aspirations and the achievement of superior students. The Honors Program sponsors Academic Excellence Day each year to give students the opportunity to present papers and projects to the entire campus.

Participation Requirements: In order to graduate as an Honors Scholar in a particular field, a student must have accumulated 16 hours of honors credits, 4 of which are a senior major independent research project, with grades of B or above in all honors endeavors. The student must also have accumulated a 3.5 or higher GPA. Honors Scholars are recognized by designation in the graduation program, the University of Findlay bachelor's hood, and a special diploma from the Honors Program.

Scholarship Availability: The University of Findlay offers numerous scholarships to students of exceptional ability.

The Campus Context: The University of Findlay was founded as Findlay College in 1882 by the Churches of God, General Conference (formerly Churches of God in North America) and the citizens of the city of Findlay. The institution is the only university affiliated with the Churches of God and it acknowledges, preserves, and honors its Judeo-Christian heritage. Its colleges include the College of Liberal Arts, College of Science, College of Education, College of Business, and College of Graduate Studies. There are several distinguished facilities: the Mazza Collection Gallery, a one-of-a-kind collection of illustrator art from children's books; English and Western equestrian farms; a preveterinary facility; the environmental management facility; and the health sciences building.

Student Body Undergraduate enrollment is 3,693, 40 percent of whom are men. The ethnic distribution is 74 percent Caucasian; 5 percent African American; 5 percent Hispanic/Latino; 1 percent Asian/Pacific Islander; 1 percent Native American, and 14 percent international (270 students). The resident-commuter ratio is 1:2. Eighty-five percent of the students receive financial aid. There are four fraternities and two sororities.

Faculty There are 255 full-time faculty members, 53 percent with terminal degrees. The student-faculty ratio is 18:1.

Key Facilities The library houses 122,617 volumes. The University is also a part of OhioLink, a sixteen-school consortium of libraries and resources. Several million dollars have been designated for upgrading equipment and the wiring of the entire campus. The capital improvement has included the installation of fiber optics throughout all the buildings. Computer labs are available and accessible to students for both classroom and individual use. Students have access to the computer system for academic purposes from their individual residence hall rooms. All students have the option of opening an e-mail account and using the Internet.

Honorary Society Tau Omega Pi

Athletics The University of Findlay is affiliated with both the National Collegiate Athletic Association (NCAA) Division II. The University also competes in the Mid-Ohio Conference and the Mid-States Football Association. Varsity teams include men's baseball, basketball, cross-country, football, golf, ice hockey, soccer, swimming and diving, tennis, indoor and outdoor track and field, and wrestling. Women's varsity sports include basketball, cross-country, golf, ice hockey, soccer, softball, swimming and diving, tennis, indoor and outdoor track and field, and volleyball. Equestrian teams and hockey are club sports.

Study Abroad Students may participate in study-abroad programs and experience international living in the International House on campus.

Support Services Individuals who need auxiliary aids for effective communication in programs and services of the University of Findlay are invited to make their needs and preferences known to the ADA Compliance Coordinator.

Job Opportunities Students may apply for many work opportunities and assistantships on campus.

Tuition: $17,088 per year (2001–02)

Room and Board: $6434

Mandatory Fees: $220

Contact: Director: Marjorie M. Schott, 1000 North Main Street, Findlay, Ohio 45840; Telephone: 419-434-4821; Fax: 419-434-4822; E-mail: schott@findlay.edu; Web site: http://www.findlay.edu

University of Florida

4 Pu G L Sc AA FA

▼ University Honors Program

The University Honors Program at the University of Florida (UF) is designed to create opportunities. First among these is a selection of exclusive honors courses with limited enrollment to enhance the general education requirements of the University. Honors courses reflect the academic diversity of UF, with faculty members from almost all colleges participating. Honors courses provide the students with an opportunity to work with outstanding faculty members in a small class environment. Some honors courses are limited enrollment sections of regular courses, such as calculus and Spanish, while others are special interest courses designed by their instructors specifically for the honors program, such as Biology and Natural History of Fireflies and Ancient Greek Literature and Medicine.

In addition, the honors program offers students access to other opportunities. Honors students receive individualized academic advising from senior faculty members and have access to a writing coach assigned to the honors program. Honors students may apply for housing in the Honors Residential College at Hume Hall. This is the first residential college created from the ground up at a major U.S. university. Located in the central part of the campus, this residential facility features suite-type rooms, large commons areas, classrooms, and office space for honors advisers. UF is proud to be a leader in housing and honors among its peer institutions. Space in the Honors Residential College is limited, and requests are accepted on a first-come, first-served basis. Honors students sponsor a variety of extracurricular events and produce an annual literary and arts review. Honors students are encouraged to study abroad, work internships, and participate in service activities.

Honors students should consider dual-degree programs offered by many departments that allow students to double count up to 12 to 15 credits for both the bachelor's and master's degrees, thus decreasing the time it takes to get both degrees by at least one semester. In addition, undergraduates may participate in cutting-edge research through the University Scholars Program. Students selected as University Scholars are awarded $2500 stipends for summer research under the direction of a leading faculty member.

The University of Florida is one of the most comprehensive universities in the U.S., with degree programs in almost every field. The honors program at UF combines the advantages of a large, state university—large libraries, advanced laboratories, big-time athletics, academic diversity, a superior faculty, and low tuition—with the small-class environment of a small college.

The University of Florida is located in Gainesville, Florida, in the north-central part of the state. Known as the "tree city," Gainesville and UF are heavily wooded with majestic oaks and towering longleaf pines. Gainesville is about an hour away from historic fishing villages on the Gulf and endless white beaches on the Atlantic.

The University Honors Program was created in 1985 by expanding a program that had been resident in the College of Liberal Arts and Sciences for many years. There are currently about 1,800 students active in the University Honors Program. They represent students from all colleges that grant the bachelor's degree.

Participation Requirements: In order to remain active in the University Honors Program, students must take at least one honors course during each semester (other than summer) and maintain a GPA of at least 3.0. Participation in the honors program is entirely voluntary and usually lasts for the first two years of a student's program, leading to the completion of the general education requirements. At that time, the successful honors student may apply for the Associate of Arts degree with honors and may request a Certificate of Completion. Individual colleges administer honors in the junior and senior years that can lead to graduation with high, higher, or highest honors at the bachelor's level.

Admission Process: Incoming freshmen are invited to participate in the University Honors Program if they have scored at least 1350 (verbal plus quantitative) on the SAT I or at least 30 on the ACT and have a high school GPA of at least 3.9 as computed by the UF admissions office. For additional information concerning admission to UF, students should visit the admission Web site at http://www.reg.ufl.edu.

A student who does not meet the above criteria for invitation into honors may be considered for admission to the program after completion of the first semester at UF if performance indicates potential benefit from the program.

The University of Florida accepts up to 30 semester credits based on Advanced Placement and/or International Baccalaureate examination scores. UF also accepts credit earned during dual enrollment.

Scholarship Availability: The only scholarships provided by the honors program are to current students in support of study abroad. Students seeking scholarship support should contact the Office of Student Financial Affairs and the Dean's office of the college in which the student wishes to enroll.

The Campus Context: The University of Florida is a public, land-grant research university. As one of the most comprehensive universities in the United States, it encompasses virtually all academic and professional disciplines on a single campus. It is the oldest and largest of Florida's universities and is one of sixty-two members of the Association of American Universities (AAU). Situated on about 2,000 acres, the campus includes classrooms, libraries, laboratories, dormitories, and other facilities in approximately 900 buildings. Some of the more unique facilities are a microkelvin laboratory, capable of producing some of the coldest temperatures in the universe; a 100-kilowatt training and research nuclear reactor; the second-largest academic computing center in the South; and a self-contained intensive-care hyperbaric chamber for treating near-drowning victims.

The University of Florida is accredited to award bachelor's, master's, specialist, and engineering degrees as well as doctoral and professional degrees. It has twenty-one colleges and schools and more than 100 interdisciplinary research and education centers, bureaus, and institutes. Almost 100 undergraduate degree programs are offered. The Graduate School coordinates more than 200 graduate programs throughout the colleges and schools. Professional postbaccalaureate degrees are offered in dentistry, law, medicine, pharmacy, and veterinary medicine.

Student Body The enrollment at the University of Florida is approximately 46,000 in 2002, including more than 4,000 international students from more than 100 different countries. Until 1947, UF was limited to men only, but today the student body has an equal number of men and women. Seventy-six percent of students are undergraduates, 18 percent are graduate students, and 6 percent are in professional programs.

Approximately 2,600 African-American students, 3,800 Hispanic students, and 2,400 Asian American students attend UF. Ninety percent of entering freshmen rank above the national mean on scores on standard entrance exams. In 2001–02 UF ranked third among public universities and sixth among all universities, with 166 National Merit Scholars enrolling.

Faculty The University of Florida has approximately 4,000 distinguished faculty members with outstanding reputations for teaching, research, and service. UF currently has 54 eminent scholars chairs, each funded at more than $1 million to attract nationally and internationally recognized scholars.

Interpreting the symbols: **2**=two-year college, **4**=four-year college; **Pu**=public or state college, **Pr**=private college; **G**=general honors program; **D**=departmental honors program; **S**=small program (fewer than 100 students), **M**=midsize program (100 to 500 students), **L**=large program (more than 500 students); **Sc**=scholarships available in honors program; **Tr**=transfer students accepted into honors program; **HBC**=historically black college; **AA**=academic advisors; **GA**=graduate advisors; **FA**=fellowship advisors.

A small sampling of honors faculty members includes a Nobel laureate, Pulitzer Prize winners in editorial writing and poetry, inventors of Gatorade and Bioglass (a man-made material that bonds with human tissue), one of the four charter members of the Solar Hall of Fame, and an art faculty with 80 percent of its members in *Who's Who in American Art.*

Key Facilities The honors program and the Division of Housing are pleased to announce the completion of the Honors Residential College (HRC) at Hume Hall, an all-new residential facility exclusively for honors students. Patterned after the British model, the HRC combines residential housing and academic space in the same physical facility. Suite-style rooms are clustered around eighteen large commons areas with recreational facilities and a kitchen. Two state-of-the-art classrooms for honors courses are included in the HRC. Office space for honors advisers and honors student organizations is located in the central commons area along with reception areas and a study room. Goverance of the residence is combined with the previously existing Student Honors Organization, a novel approach among housing facilities at UF.

Athletics For each of the last ten years, the University of Florida has ranked among the nation's five best collegiate athletic programs as ranked by the National Association of Collegiate Directors of Athletics. UF is a member of the NCAA and the Southeastern Conference (SEC). It competes in Division I for all of its eighteen athletic teams. The eight men's teams include baseball, basketball, cross-country, football (national champions in 1996), golf, swimming and diving, tennis, and track and field. The women compete in basketball, cross-country, golf, gymnastics, swimming and diving, soccer (national champions in 1998), softball, tennis, track and field, and volleyball.

Study Abroad The Office of International Studies and Programs offers UF students the opportunity to study in a wide range of academic and cultural settings. The office coordinates thirty-two semester-long and yearlong programs and twenty-eight summer programs in twenty-four countries. Subject areas include language, culture, and history; marine, forest, and tropical ecology; environmental engineering; business and public relations; fine arts; journalism; architecture; and wildlife management.

Support Services The Dean of Students Office (DSO) provides individual assistance for students with documented disabilities. Services are based upon student need and the impact of the specific disability. The support services may include but are not limited to campus orientation, registration assistance, approval of reduced course loads, classroom and examination accommodations, course substitutions, course drops when disability related, securing auxiliary learning aids, and assistance in general University activities. In addition, the DSO provides advocacy for all UF students.

Job Opportunities The Career Resource Center (CRC) provides career planning, cooperative education/internship work experience opportunities, and employment assistance to all students at UF. The CRC assists students in developing and exploring career plans related to academic interests, acquiring career-related work experiences, developing personal strategies to ensure successful employment upon graduation, and assisting students in an interview environment that leads to securing employment. Last year the CRC had 138,000 visitors and sponsored numerous career days.

Tuition and Fees: approximately $2500 for residents, $10,400 for nonresidents (2001–02)

Room and Board: $5430

Mandatory Fees: $950

Contact: Director: Dr. Sheila Dickison, Suite 140, Tigert Hall, Box 113260, Gainesville, Florida 32611-3260; Telephone: 352-392-1519; Fax: 352-392-1888; E-mail: honors@ufl.edu; Web site: http://www.honors.ufl.edu

University of Georgia

4 Pu G L Sc Tr

▼ Honors Program

The Honors Program provides participants with special honors classes in the freshman/sophomore core curriculum, honors courses in a variety of majors, the opportunity to design and pursue interdisciplinary majors, more intensive versions of courses required for departmental majors, and independent study under faculty supervision culminating in an honors thesis or project. In addition to individualized advising throughout their education, the program provides students with special support for graduate and professional school application as well as national fellowship and scholarship competitions. The Honors Program is open to qualified undergraduates in all the schools and colleges of the University.

Most honors classes and seminars have enrollments of 20 students or fewer and are taught by specially selected faculty members. Unlike high school honors or advanced placement classes, the University's honors courses do not carry more credit, or offer higher grade points, than regular classes. Rather, they are smaller, enriched in content, and sometimes more specialized. Honors classes provide faculty members with opportunities to introduce their disciplines more deeply, employing innovative and more individualized approaches. Students in the program choose from more than 200 honors classes offered annually. These classes usually fulfill core curriculum requirements. The University of Georgia (UGA) Undergraduate Bulletin lists honors classes under the departments in which they are offered. Honors class course numbers are followed by an H.

Honors students may enroll in upper-division classes in the major with honors option to pursue a subject more deeply within the setting of a regular course. Students arrange additional readings and other assignments with the class instructor and secure honors credit for these classes by filing a form with the Honors Program. Honors students may also enroll in directed-study classes that enable them to work independently on a sustained research project under the guidance of a faculty member. This usually leads to an honors thesis, often comparable to a master's thesis, but the outcomes may take a different form—a recital, exhibition, performance, or some type of internships. Alternatively, honors students may enroll in graduate classes or pursue a joint bachelor's/master's degree program. Honors-directed reading classes and honors theses classes are available in most departments.

Honors students are advised by professional advisers and honors faculty members. In addition, the Honors Program provides graduate and professional school application support and selects and prepares students for national and international fellowships and scholarships. In the past five years, students in honors at Georgia have secured three Rhodes Scholarships, two Mellon Humanities awards, and three Udall, twelve Goldwater, nine Fulbright, one Gates-Cambridge, and three Truman scholarships.

Students may enter the Honors Program as freshmen or by collegiate entry after at least one semester's enrollment. The Honors Program accepts transfer students as well. Transfer students may petition to count honors classes from their previous institutions toward graduation with honors from UGA. In order to make timely progress toward their degrees while registering for honors classes, students in the program are accorded registration priority ahead of all nonhonors undergraduates.

The Honors Program was founded in 1960 and currently enrolls 2,200 students.

Complete information about the University of Georgia Honors Program is available at its Web site, listed below.

Participation Requirements: To graduate with honors, students must complete nine honors classes across a range of subjects with a GPA of at least 3.3 (3.4 in all classes) and an honors thesis or project. Completion results in graduation with honors in the department of the student's thesis or project, as recorded in transcripts and diplomas. Students graduating with a thesis or project and twelve honors classes and at least a 3.6 GPA are accorded high honors.

Admission Process: Admissions is highly competitive and is based on an application, an essay of 250 words on a topic chosen annually, and a description of extracurricular and public service commitments during high school as well as high school grades and SAT I or ACT scores. Applications for admission are sent to students with very strong academic records and high test scores when they are admitted to the University. Others may request an application. While there is no minimum GPA or SAT I score required of admission, in 2001 the average high school GPA was 3.98 and the average SAT I score was 1394.

Students not admitted as first-semester freshmen are eligible for collegiate entry to the Honors Program based on a University GPA of at least 3.7 in 14 semester hours of academic credit.

Transfer students are eligible for admission based on their academic records using the same standards as those for UGA collegiate entry.

Scholarship Availability: Almost all Georgia resident students in the Honors Program receive Georgia HOPE scholarships covering tuition, fees, and book expenses. University of Georgia charter scholarships and a number of out-of-state tuition waivers are awarded on several, mainly academic, criteria.

The University awards approximately twenty-five Foundation Fellowships per year. These four-year scholarships pay the full cost of attendance, provide three summer study opportunities, annual spring travel-study programs, individual faculty mentorships, and a wealth of on-campus academic experiences, cultural and recreational advantages, and public service opportunities. Foundation Fellowships are awarded on the basis of a separate application, due late in November, and an interview process. Successful candidates are required to participate in the Honors Program.

The Honors Program provides a limited number of scholarships for participants in its Academic Scholarship Identification Program, which provides a number of academic enrichment opportunities for honors and nonhonors sophomores and juniors.

All other scholarships are offered through the Office of Financial Aid and the Department of Admissions of the University.

The Campus Context: The University of Georgia is located in Athens, approximately 60 miles northeast of Atlanta. Athens is a medium-sized college town that provides many cultural opportunities both on and off campus. UGA offers undergraduate and graduate education in thirteen schools and colleges.

Student Body There are 23,000 undergraduate and 8,000 graduate students. Approximately 55 percent of undergraduates are women, and minorities represent approximately 15 percent of enrollment. Admission to the University is competitive (in 2001 the average freshman's high school GPA was 3.65, and the average SAT I score was 1205). Approximately 10 percent of entering freshmen are invited to enroll in the Honors Program, representing all thirteen colleges and schools.

Faculty Many of the faculty members are listed in the Honors Program's *Research Opportunities for Undergraduates* handbook, indicating their interest in working with undergraduates on various research projects. The total number of teaching and research faculty members exceeds 2,500.

Key Facilities The University library includes approximately 3.7 million items and is fully computerized. There are more than twenty computer labs on campus, in dorms, departments, libraries, and the student center. In most disciplines, facilities are state-of-the-art and available to honors students conducting research under faculty supervision.

Honorary Societies Phi Beta Kappa, Phi Kappa Phi, Alpha Lambda Delta, Phi Eta Sigma, Mortar Board, Golden Key, and Blue Key

Athletics UGA is a member of the Southeastern Conference and competes in many NCAA varsity sports. There is also an active intramural athletic program. The Ramsey Center for Physical Activities is one of the largest and best facilities of its kind in the country and is available for intramural and recreational use.

Study Abroad The University provides a variety of study-abroad options, including programs at Oxford and in Verona, Tanzania, Zimbabwe, Seville, Lyon, and Avignon. Several of these programs are highly selective, but honors students have the strongest record of participation. Students also enroll in study-abroad programs sponsored by other universities and in the National Student Exchange within the U.S.

Job Opportunities The University has work-study programs and also employs students in many service areas. In addition, Athens has many opportunities for students to find part-time or full-time work, often within walking distance of campus.

Tuition and Fees: $3276 for residents, $10,786 for nonresidents, per year

Room and Board: $5000 (approximately)

Contact: Associate Provost and Director: Jere Morehead, Honors Program, University of Georgia, Athens, Georgia 30602-6116; Telephone: 706-542-3240; Fax: 706-542-6993; E-mail: morehead@uga.edu; Web site: http://www.uga/edu/honors/

UNIVERSITY OF HARTFORD

4 Pr G D M Tr

▼ University Honors Program

The University Honors Program at the University of Hartford is an academic program designed to offer a stimulating, challenging intellectual environment for highly motivated and talented students across campus. Honors courses are kept small to allow for frequent participation and exchanges among students and faculty members. Moreover, faculty members who teach in the Honors Program are among those who have proved themselves both in scholarship and research and in the classroom. Faculty-student interaction is highly prized and cultivated to encourage students to develop their intellectual abilities and talents and their desire to continue lifelong learning and experience personal fulfillment. Many students work along with their professors in the laboratories and studios, honing their skills and contributing to their field long before graduation.

The curriculum is flexible and not only provides special honors sections of courses and honors seminars but also promotes interdisciplinary acquisition of knowledge through the University's nationally acclaimed All University Curriculum, a program that encourages students not only to cross disciplinary lines but to apply their learning and life's experiences in subjects ranging from Epidemics and AIDS to Literature and Films of Other Cultures, the Caribbean Mosaic, Creativity, Hunger: Problems of Scarcity and Choice, A Western Heritage: The Humanities, and Sources of Power. There are twenty-five widely recognized national honors societies at the University and numerous

Interpreting the symbols: **2**=two-year college, **4**=four-year college; **Pu**=public or state college, **Pr**=private college; **G**=general honors program; **D**=departmental honors program; **S**=small program (fewer than 100 students), **M**=midsize program (100 to 500 students), **L**=large program (more than 500 students); **Sc**=scholarships available in honors program; **Tr**=transfer students accepted into honors program; **HBC**=historically black college; **AA**=academic advisors; **GA**=graduate advisors; **FA**=fellowship advisors.

undergraduate scholarships as well as the John G. Martin Scholarship to Oxford for one graduating senior each year. Each year, the Honors Program sponsors the Undergraduate Research Colloquium, which showcases outstanding student research, creative work, and special projects. Some of these students have also presented at national conferences and have had their work published in journals in their fields.

The University believes that the total honors experience involves life outside the classroom. The Honors Residential College provides an atmosphere supportive and conducive to study as well as a cohesive social and intellectual environment. There is one faculty member in residence there at all times. Participation in the University Honors Program is not a requirement to live in the Honors Resident College. The Honors Student Organization sponsors annual cultural, scientific, and social events. Opportunities also exist for volunteer and community service work as well as internships both on campus and in the greater Hartford area.

Participation Requirements: The usual honors load comprises 3 to 9 credits of general education courses, 6 credits in honors seminars, and 6 credits in either Thesis Research/Honors Research Writing, Humanities Center Seminar work, or a University Scholar Project. Eighteen credits of honors course work are required to complete the program. The honors curriculum has been designed both to encourage student interaction across the colleges in honors sections of required general education courses and to provide opportunities for enriched or accelerated work within the curricula of the individual colleges. Each college has defined a special honors experience for its students. Students matriculated in one college may complete all the requirements for honors in another college and thereby earn the University Honors designation. The students' programs must be approved by the Honors Coordinators of both the college of matriculation and the one in which they are completing the honors requirements. Contract honors courses may be taken when students find a particular course that they would like to pursue in-depth that is not offered as an honors section.

Admission Process: Students in all nine colleges of the University may participate. Eligibility is determined upon admission to the University on the basis of SAT I or Act scores and class rank. Approximately 150 incoming freshmen qualified for the University Honors Program last year. Subsequently, students can participate in the program once they have fulfilled the eligibility requirements for honors in their college. Students may continue in the program as long as they maintain the GPA required by their college. To graduate with University Honors, students must have an overall average of at least 3.25 and at least a 3.0 in their honors course work. The designation of University Honors on the diploma is different from Graduation Honors, which is based purely on GPA (Latin honors).

Scholarship Availability: Scholarships of various amounts are awarded through the Office of Admissions and Financial Aid based on academic performance. Scholarships are not offered directly through the University Honors Program. Most honors students are recipients of academic or talent scholarships. There are other scholarships available through the colleges of the University after matriculation.

The Campus Context: University of Hartford has a 320-acre suburban campus divided between two campuses. Its nine colleges and schools offer seventy undergraduate majors. The eight colleges on the main campus are housed in modern buildings constructed since 1960. Recent additions are the Harry Jack Gray Center, which houses the Mortensen Library, bookstore, studios, a museum, conference center, 1877 Club (restaurant), the Communication Department, and the Sports Center. The Hartford College for Women's 13-acre wooded campus, listed on the National Register of Historic Places, is a blend of traditional ivy-covered Georgian buildings and modern classroom buildings. The University and surrounding area offer unmatched cultural and social opportunities. The University itself boasts the Lincoln Theater, site of professional dramatic productions, concerts, and lectures; the Maurice Greenberg Center for Judaic Studies; the Museum of American Political Life; and the Hartt School of Music and the Hartford Art School, with the Joseloff Gallery. Within a short drive are the world-renown Wadsworth Athenaeum; Bushnell Memorial Hall, home of the Connecticut Ballet, the Connecticut Opera, and traveling Broadway shows; the Hartford Civic Center; and the award-winning Hartford Stage Company. Within 2 hours of campus are the cities of Boston and New York City, with all their attractions.

Student Body The undergraduate enrollment is about 4,000; 50 percent of the students are women. The minority ethnic distribution is 7.2 percent black, 3.9 percent Hispanic, and percent 2.1 Asian/Pacific Islander. There are 224 (5.6 percent) international students. Sixty-four percent of the students live on campus, and 85 percent of University of Hartford students receive financial aid. The campus has eight fraternities and seven sororities.

Faculty There are 625 full-time and adjunct faculty members. The undergraduate and graduate faculties are essentially the same group, and 78 percent hold the terminal degree in their field. Each new student is assigned to a faculty adviser during summer orientation. The ratio of full-time faculty members to full-time undergraduate students is 1:13.

Key Facilities The Mortensen and Mildred P. Allen Memorial Libraries, housed in the Harry Jack Gray Center, and the Bess Graham Library at Hartford College for Women collectively have holdings of 600,000 books, journals, microforms, musical scores, sound recordings, and videotapes. Approximately 2,100 periodical and scholarly journal subscriptions are maintained, and they are supplemented by databases accessing more than 17,000 academic journals. An online catalog offers access to the materials housed in these three libraries. There are 380 computers/terminals on campus for general student use, some located in one of the six University-operated computer labs, equipped with microcomputers (PCs and Macintoshes), computer workstations, and terminals that are connected to the campus network and the Internet. In addition to these computer labs, there are specialized computer facilities. Additional facilities and advanced equipment for the study of earth sciences are available at the nearby Talcott Mountain Science Center. The University's Computer Center operates a high-performance campuswide network, which connects all student residential housing, all academic buildings on campus, and the University's remote locations. The library is connected to the campus network and provides network access in study carrels and study rooms.

Honorary Societies Alpha Lambda Delta, Alpha Chi, Phi Theta Kappa, and the Order of Omega

Athletics The Department of Athletics offers Division I varsity competition in sixteen sports, eight for men and eight for women: baseball, basketball, cross-country, golf, lacrosse, soccer, softball, tennis, outdoor track, and volleyball. The University has 253 student-athletes from twenty-one states and thirteen other countries and is a member of the America East Conference. Hartford also offers athletic competition through an intramural and club program. Approximately 1,800 students in twenty sports participate each year in the diverse intramural program. The University Sports Center is a comprehensive athletics complex of 130,000 square feet that provides a home for intercollegiate, intramural, and club sports; fitness and health-related activities; and recreation and socializing for students, faculty and staff members, and alumni. It also features a main arena for the University's basketball teams and other collegiate programs, an NCAA competition-size swimming pool and an outdoor pool, two weight rooms, and courts for volleyball, badminton, squash, and racquetball. Behind the Sports Center there are six lighted tennis courts adjacent to the soccer fields.

Study Abroad The University encourages students to participate in overseas student exchanges and study-abroad programs. Summer, semester, and academic-year programs are available in a number of countries, including Argentina, Australia, Austria, Belgium, Chile, Czech Republic, Ecuador, France, Hungary, India, Ireland, Israel, Italy, Japan, Mexico, the Netherlands, the Philippines, Poland, Russia, Scotland, Spain, Switzerland, and Turkey. In addition, international internships are available through several of the University's affiliated programs. Of particular note are two competitive scholarships for study abroad. The John G. Martin Scholarship, modeled after the Rhodes and Marshall Scholarships, gives one University of Hartford graduating senior the opportunity to study for two years at Oxford University. The second scholarship is the Stephen Joel Trachtenberg Scholarship/Hebrew University of Jerusalem, which annually provides one or more scholarships to exceptional undergraduate students. These scholarships are highly competitive, but University of Hartford students are given preference.

Support Services Learning Plus provides academic support services to any students with diagnosed disabilities through individual tutorials, test accommodations, and letters of disclosure. The Center for Reading and Writing offers one-to-one assistance with academic strategies through professional tutoring in writing, task management, note-taking, organizing and reviewing classroom notes, and preparing for exams. The Math Lab helps students in mastering mathematical and computer concepts.

Job Opportunities The Career Center maintains a listing of on- and off-campus jobs available to students. In addition, Federal Work-Study positions are available, both on and off campus, for those who demonstrate financial need. The University administers a cooperative education program for students who wish to seek employment related to their fields of study. In addition, a full listing of internship opportunities is maintained at the center.

Tuition: $17,180

Room and board: $7230

Mandatory Fees: $1034

Contact: Director: Dr. Jill Dix Ghnassia, 128 A Hillyer Hall, 200 Bloomfield Avenue, West Hartford, Connecticut 08117; Telephone: 860-768-4935; Fax: 860-768-5085; E-mail: ghnassia@mail.hartford.edu; Web site: http://www.hartford.edu (then select "Other Programs" and then "University Honors Program")

UNIVERSITY OF HOUSTON

4 Pu L Sc Tr

▼ The Honors College

Created to serve the intellectual needs of gifted undergraduates in more than 100 fields of study, the Honors College provides the careful guidance, flexibility, and personal instruction that nurture excellence. Members of the College devote a significant portion of their formal course work to a collective examination of the system of values and achievements that form the Western cultural heritage, a knowledge of which has traditionally defined the educated person.

For the 350 students who join each fall, the Honors College offers the advantages of a small college without sacrificing the wealth of resources and rich diversity of a large university. The College offers its students special privileges, facilities, and extracurricular activities that foster an atmosphere of collegiality and a spirit of camaraderie.

The faculty and staff members of the Honors College believe that a university education should offer more than the acquisition of marketable skills and challenge the University's best students to develop qualities of mind and character that foster excellence beyond school and the workplace.

Participation Requirements: Honors students are expected to take The Human Situation, a team-taught course designed to introduce students to great books in the Western tradition. In addition, students are expected to take at least one honors course each semester and to maintain a cumulative GPA of at least 3.25.

Admission Process: The official scholarship/application deadline is April 1, but applications are reviewed as soon as they are received. Each applicant to the Honors College is considered individually; admission is based on academic and extracurricular achievement, standardized test scores, and a student essay. Applications from transfer students are welcome; for such students acceptance is based primarily on prior college work.

Scholarship Availability: Applicants to the Honors College are automatically considered for the sizable number of merit-based scholarships the University awards to new students. National Merit finalists receive all-expense scholarships. Out-of-state students who receive merit-based scholarships worth at least $1000 qualify for in-state tuition (see below). In addition, the Honors College awards smaller scholarships to both entering and continuing students, and need-based financial assistance is also available.

The Campus Context: The University of Houston occupies a spacious campus situated near the central business district, the Museum District, and the Texas Medical Center. The Honors College is housed in the M. D. Anderson Library in the middle of the campus, near the Quadrangle of Honors residence halls. The University offers more than 100 bachelor's degree programs and is distinguished for the English department's creative writing program, the Texas Center for Superconductivity, the Conrad N. Hilton College of Hotel and Restaurant Management, and various programs in engineering and the natural sciences.

Student Body The University's student body is large (about 23,000 undergraduates) and reflective of the diverse population of the city of Houston. While most UH students commute, the Honors College encourages its students to live on campus, and the residential community of 3,400 ensures a vibrant campus life. Various campus activities and student groups, including national chapters of fraternities and sororities, offer students a rich array of cultural and social opportunities.

Faculty The University has almost 2,000 faculty members, most of whom hold the highest degree in their fields. All Honors College faculty members hold terminal degrees.

Key Facilities The campus contains three libraries, which house more than 2 million volumes, 3 million microfilms, and 15,000 journals. Students have access to more than 4,000 computer workstations and are entitled to an e-mail account, Internet access, and technical assistance and training.

Honorary Societies Phi Kappa Phi, Omicron Delta Kappa, The National Society of Collegiate Scholars, Mortarboard, Golden Key International, and other disciplinary honor societies

Athletics The University offers a full range of opportunities for men and women to participate in sports. The gyms, pools, and other facilities are open year-round. Alumni of the track and basketball programs include Olympians Carl Lewis, Hakeem Olajuwon, and Clyde Drexler, and the men's golf program is nationally renowned.

Study Abroad The Honors College encourages its students to participate in travel and study-abroad programs. Opportunities are publicized and encouraged by faculty members, and both the Honors College and the University make grants to underwrite some of the costs. The Honors College administers several travel-

Interpreting the symbols: **2**=two-year college, **4**=four-year college; **Pu**=public or state college, **Pr**=private college; **G**=general honors program; **D**=departmental honors program; **S**=small program (fewer than 100 students), **M**=midsize program (100 to 500 students), **L**=large program (more than 500 students); **Sc**=scholarships available in honors program; **Tr**=transfer students accepted into honors program; **HBC**=historically black college; **AA**=academic advisors; **GA**=graduate advisors; **FA**=fellowship advisors.

abroad programs for credit, including those to France, the United Kingdom, Italy, Greece, and Israel.

Support Services The University provides support for students with health impairments, learning disabilities, mental health issues, and physical limitations. The campus is accessible via ramps, curb cuts, free inner-campus handicapped parking, and Braille signs. Care services are also available through the University Housing Department.

Job Opportunities Work-study, regular employment, and internship opportunities are available on campus, through Student Services, and within the Honors College.

Tuition and Fees: The estimated total of tuition and mandatory fees for a full-time student is $3168 per academic year for state residents and most students with scholarships.

Room and Board: $5000, average per academic year

Contact: Director: Dean Ted Estess, the Honors College, 16 M. D. Anderson Library, University of Houston, Houston, Texas 77204-2001; Telephone: 888-827-0366 (toll-free); Fax: 713-743-9015; Web site: http://www.uh.edu/honors

UNIVERSITY OF IDAHO

4 Pu G M Sc Tr

▼ University Honors Program

Established in 1982, the University Honors Program (UHP) at the University of Idaho (UI) offers a stimulating course of study and the benefits of an enriched learning community for exceptional students from all colleges and majors. The program's diverse curriculum serves a variety of student needs and interests. Beyond the classroom, the program's extracurricular opportunities include concerts, plays, films, lectures, and other excursions that foster cultural enrichment, fellowship, and learning. The great majority of the 650 students currently active in the program are able to participate without adding to the total number of credits needed for graduation.

Honors faculty members support students in developing their initiative and their abilities to think critically and creatively. Most honors classes are small, and honors students thus benefit from close intellectual contact and discussion with their instructors and fellow students. The program director, associate director, and program adviser act as supplemental academic advisers to all students who qualify for honors study. The UHP is devoted to enabling each student to achieve his or her potential.

Many honors students are leaders on campus and in their living groups. Elected members of the Honors Student Advisory Board help to determine innovative honors seminar offerings and take the lead in planning UHP trips and social events. As part of a dynamic, broad-based education, members are also encouraged to participate in either domestic or international exchange programs. Honors advisers work with students individually to determine appropriate credit within the honors curriculum.

Participation Requirements: A member in good standing of the University Honors Program must be registered at UI, take an average of one honors course every second semester, and maintain a minimum 3.2 cumulative GPA. Students who complete 19 credits of required honors courses and achieve a cumulative GPA of 3.0 or higher in those courses earn the University Honors Core Award. Students who complete 29 credits of required honors course work and achieve a cumulative GPA of 3.0 or higher in those courses earn the University Honors Program Certificate. Depending on which courses students select, the 16 to 20 credits that are required for an honors certificate also satisfy the general University core requirements in the humanities, social sciences, and sciences that all students must complete to graduate.

Admission Process: Incoming freshmen are invited to apply to the program on the basis of their high school GPA and standardized test score(s). Criteria for admission are based on a correlation between the student's high school GPA and the ACT composite score or SAT combined score. For example, students who have an ACT composite score of 28 or an SAT combined score of 1250 and a 3.7 high school GPA meet the initial minimum criteria. The correlation, however, is based on a sliding scale so that students with test scores higher than those noted above may have GPAs below 3.7 and still meet the minimum criteria; students with higher GPAs may have test scores lower than the examples offered above and still meet the minimum criteria. Those who do not meet the above criteria but who would like to participate in the honors program are encouraged to apply and may be asked to submit letters of recommendation from two teachers. To be considered for admission, students applying from high school must also submit a two-page essay as part of the application. Students who demonstrate superior performance upon completing their first semester at the University of Idaho (achieving a minimum 3.5 GPA) may also apply for admission. Transfer students are considered for admission on a case-by-case basis; students in good standing in an honors program at their previous school are automatically considered for admission, and their transcripts will be evaluated and appropriate credit given toward the honors certificate.

Scholarship Availability: Each year scholarships are offered to a select number of students entering the program. These non-need-based awards are based on academic merit and are applied to resident fees. No additional application form is required. Likewise, a select number of honors program out-of-state tuition waivers are offered to non-Idaho residents. Both scholarships and tuition waivers are awarded for up to eight semesters for freshmen, six semesters for sophomores, and so on. Renewal of funding is contingent on a student's satisfactory progress toward earning an honors certificate while maintaining an overall GPA of 3.3. In addition, UHP members have been successful in taking advantage of close mentorship and advice regarding prestigious national scholarship opportunities.

The Campus Context: The University of Idaho is the state's comprehensive land-grant institution with primary responsibility statewide for doctoral degrees, research programs, and professional public service. There are 146 on-campus programs leading to the baccalaureate. As the state's premier institution of higher education, UI has a nationally recognized program of general education and ranks nationally as a research university. On campus are the Colleges of Agriculture, Business and Economics, Education, Engineering, Natural Resources, Law, Letters and Science, and Mines and Earth Resources.

Student Body Enrollment is 11,625 students, of whom 45 percent are women. Approximately 10 percent of the students have an ethnic background other than Caucasian; 229 international students represent eighty countries. Seven percent of the students receive work-study, 36 percent are scholarship recipients, and 45 percent receive assistance from long-term or short-term loans. The eighteen fraternities and nine sororities serve 1,600 students.

Faculty There are 1,446 faculty members; 859 are full-time. The student-faculty ratio is 17:1.

Key Facilities The library houses more than 2 million volumes. A new computer backbone with extensive and expanding availability of computer access has recently been installed. The campus has more than twenty student general-use PC and Mac student computer labs, with more than 700 computers available to students. Technical support is provided for the University's twenty media-enhanced classrooms and eight compressed video classrooms.

Honorary Societies Phi Eta Sigma, Phi Kappa Phi, Phi Beta Kappa, Golden Key, Mortar Board

Athletics A strong intercollegiate athletic program is available for both men and women. Men's programs include basketball, cross-country, football, golf, indoor track and field, and tennis. The women's programs consist of basketball, cross-country, golf, indoor and outdoor track, soccer, tennis, and volleyball.

Study Abroad Students may participate in the following study-abroad programs: International Student Exchange Program (ISEP), Council on International Education (CIEE), and University Studies Abroad Consortium (USAC). Students may also participate in UI's direct exchange programs with universities in Denmark, Ecuador, France, Germany, Japan, Mexico, Nepal, Peru, Spain, Sweden, and the United Kingdom.

Support Services The services for students with disabilities provide support for students with temporary or permanent disabilities, in accordance with the Rehabilitation Act of 1973 as amended in 1992, and the Americans with Disabilities Act of 1990. Buildings on campus continue to be brought to code to be handicapped-accessible.

Job Opportunities A student employment program was initiated in fall 1995 and provides student employment in positions covering all aspects of University functions, ranging from trainee levels to coordinator and technical levels. Students gain job experience, references, and additional financial resources while pursuing an academic degree. The Cooperative Education Program assists students in finding and applying for academically relevant work experiences. In 1999–2000, more than 400 students were placed in internships or cooperative education experiences with more than 175 local, state, regional, national, and international organizations and/or employers.

Tuition: None for state residents, $6000 for nonresidents, per year (2001–02)

Room and Board: $4000

Mandatory Fees: $2720

Contact: Director: Stephan Flores, Room 315, Idaho Commons, P.O. Box 442533, Moscow, Idaho 83844-2533; Telephone: 208-885-6147; Fax: 208-885-7722; E-mail: honors@uidaho.edu; Web site: http://www.uidaho.edu/honors_program

The University of Illinois at Chicago

4 Pu G L Sc Tr

▼ Honors College

The Honors College at the University of Illinois at Chicago offers an enhanced academic experience to approximately 1,200 talented and motivated undergraduates. Freshmen enroll in yearlong interdisciplinary honors core course sequences and may also register for departmental honors offerings. Beyond the freshman year, students choose from a variety of other honors options, including honors seminars in a broad range of disciplines, undergraduate research, and the College peer-tutoring program. All these activities are monitored through a mentoring system that is one of the College's strengths.

At the end of the first year, each student is assigned to an Honors College fellow, a faculty member in the student's major interested in working with honors students. The fellows, who include many of UIC's outstanding scholars, act as advisers for the students' honors work and as resources for information on academic opportunities in the major, courses, graduate school, and careers. The Honors College fellow mentoring process allows students a chance to develop contacts with faculty members at an early stage in their university experience.

In addition, the Honors College offers its students personalized attention and advising, as well as dedicated facilities such as a computer lab, a social lounge, and study rooms and events such as student-faculty luncheons, an annual dinner dance, and an honors convocation for graduating seniors. The Honors College sponsors the *Ampersand,* the College newsletter; *Red Shoes Revived,* a student literary journal; and the *Journal of Pre-Health Affiliated Students.* Honors College students also receive extended library privileges.

Students who opt to live on campus may take advantage of special honors housing, where residents enjoy a special living/learning environment and a sense of honors community within the residence halls.

Participation Requirements: All members of the Honors College are expected to fulfill two requirements: students must successfully complete an honors activity each fall and spring terms, and students must maintain a minimum cumulative UIC GPA of 4.25 (on a 5.0 scale). Honors College membership is noted on student transcripts and at the University Honors Day ceremony held each spring.

Admission Process: Honors College students are selected on the basis of their academic achievement. Entering freshmen should have a minimum ACT score of 28 (SAT of 1240) and rank in the upper 15 percent of their high school graduating class. Enrolled students with at least a 4.25 cumulative UIC GPA and transfer students with at least a 4.5 cumulative GPA are also encouraged to apply. Students not meeting the above requirements may request consideration for membership on the basis of other evidence of merit.

Scholarship Availability: The Honors College offers the University Scholar Award, a merit-based scholarship opportunity for beginning freshmen, which covers full or half tuition and fees for up to four years. Only Illinois residents are eligible.

The College also grants a limited number of one-semester tuition waivers to its continuing students based on a combination of merit and need, in addition to the Flaherty Awards for Study Abroad and the Sarah Madonna Kabbes Awards for Undergraduate Research. Phi Theta Kappa scholarships are available for transfer students. The UIC Office of Special Scholarship Programs assists students in applying for nationally competitive scholarships.

The Campus Context: Located in the heart of Chicago within walking distance of the Loop, the University of Illinois at Chicago is a vital part of the educational, technological, and cultural fabric of the metropolitan area. One of the eighty-eight Carnegie Research I universities in the nation, UIC is the largest and most diverse university in the Chicago area, with 105 buildings on 216 acres; another 85 acres are currently being developed for academic, residential, and commercial use. UIC offers bachelor's degrees in eighty-eight academic areas, master's degrees in eighty-six disciplines, and doctorates in fifty-eight specializations. UIC has been named a "best buy" by *Barron's Best Buys in College Education.*

Student Body The total enrollment for 2001–02 was 25,512, including 15,587 undergraduates; 45 percent are men, and 55 are percent women. The minority ethnic distribution is 11 percent African American, 17 percent Hispanic, and 23.5 percent Asian; 295 international students make up another 2 percent. In addition, 13 percent of undergraduates live in campus housing, and 76 percent of students receive financial aid.

Faculty Full-time faculty members number more than 2,000; the student-faculty ratio is 13:1. In 2001, 7 UIC faculty members received National Science Foundation Career Awards, and a professor in the College of Architecture and the Arts received a MacArthur Fellowship, the second such "genius grant" awarded to a UIC faculty member in the past five years.

Interpreting the symbols: **2**=two-year college, **4**=four-year college; **Pu**=public or state college, **Pr**=private college; **G**=general honors program; **D**=departmental honors program; **S**=small program (fewer than 100 students), **M**=midsize program (100 to 500 students), **L**=large program (more than 500 students); **Sc**=scholarships available in honors program; **Tr**=transfer students accepted into honors program; **HBC**=historically black college; **AA**=academic advisors; **GA**=graduate advisors; **FA**=fellowship advisors.

Key Facilities The library houses more than 2 million volumes. There are fifteen public computer labs on campus, with a 10,000-user network. The UIC Medical Center is the largest in the country.

Honorary Societies: Phi Eta Sigma, Phi Kappa Phi, Golden Key, and Phi Beta Kappa

Athletics UIC fields fifteen teams in NCAA Division I intercollegiate athletics, including the UIC Flames basketball team. In addition, many intramural and recreational activities are provided for students, faculty and staff members, and alumni.

Study Abroad UIC offers a wide range of options for international study; students can study abroad for a summer, a semester, or a year from a selection of programs located in thirty countries.

Support Services The UIC Office of Disability Services assists students with documented learning disabilities, vision or hearing impairments, and emotional or physical disabilities. The Academic Center for Excellence (ACE) is an academic support program open to all students, as are the Counseling Center and the Office of Career Services. Minority support services are also available, including the African American Academic Network (AAAN), the Latin American Recruitment and Educational Services (LARES), and the Native American Support Program.

Tuition: $3830 minimum per year full-time for state residents, $10,490 minimum for nonresidents; $638 minimum per semester part-time for state residents, $1748 minimum for nonresidents (2001–02)

Room and Board: $6026 minimum

Mandatory Fees: $552

Contact: Interim Dean: Janet Madia, UIC Honors College, The University of Illinois at Chicago, 828 South Halsted Street (M/C 204), Chicago, Illinois 60607-7031; Telephone: 312-413-2260; Fax 312-413-1266; E-mail: hcinfo@uic.edu; Web site: http//www.hc.uic.edu

---

University of Illinois at Urbana–Champaign

4 Pu G M Sc AA FA

▼ Campus Honors Program

The Campus Honors Program (CHP) offers special challenges and opportunities to a small number of academically talented and highly motivated undergraduate students. It fosters collaborative relationships between students and distinguished faculty members through small intensive classes, a faculty mentor system for introducing students to the intellectual standards and methodologies of academic disciplines, and informal contacts encouraged by cocurricular offerings. CHP sponsors four series of noncredit cocurricular events: a Scholar Adventurers lecture series on faculty research, a Study Abroad at Home series of seminar-workshops centering on other cultures, a series of dress-rehearsal visits at Krannert Center for the Performing Arts, and an International Tasting Club lunch series. The aim is to encourage breadth and excellence from the outset of the student's college career and to facilitate interaction with scholars at the cutting edge of their disciplines.

Approximately 125 new students can be admitted to the CHP each year as first-year students, out of almost 6,000 entering freshmen. A few additional students, however, may join the program on an off-cycle basis at the beginning of the sophomore year. Designated as Chancellor's Scholars, CHP students may be enrolled in any undergraduate curriculum. Those who meet retention requirements continue as Chancellor's Scholars throughout their undergraduate career. Required CHP course work is concentrated in the freshman and sophomore years, when students take intensive and specialized versions of general education courses. At the junior and senior levels, when students are necessarily involved in their majors, they are required to take only one advanced CHP seminar. In short, the emphasis is on fundamental principles and interdisciplinary connections, because the CHP is for students who desire an undergraduate education that is broad and general as well as professionally specialized.

CHP seeks to combine the advantages of a major public institution with those of a small liberal arts college. Opportunities offered by the program include challenging, limited-enrollment courses; summer research and travel grants; social and intellectual activities beyond the classroom; use of Honors House, with computer facilities and an electronic communications bulletin board; access to the University library stacks; priority registration for classes; and interaction with an outstanding group of peers.

CHP courses represent additional opportunities for academically gifted and adventurous students; they are not an alternative curriculum. They provide an honors-quality way of satisfying general education requirements for graduation and of helping students to discover the interrelations between their own discipline and other disciplines. CHP does not supplant or conflict with the University's departmental honors programs. In consultation with their departmental academic advisers, Chancellor's Scholars develop their own combination of regular and CHP courses. Most important, CHP is a challenge. A Chancellor's Scholar must make a commitment to intellectual life and to the dialogue and community in the Honors House.

This is not a "residential" honors program. In their housing and social life, Chancellor's Scholars are not isolated from the thousands of other excellent students on this "public ivy" University campus. The University Housing Division offers a wide variety of theme-oriented and special-interest housing options, and honors students are encouraged to choose options that suit their personal needs and open doors into the larger community.

The Campus Honors Program was established in fall 1986. Its steady-state enrollment is 500 students—125 students at each undergraduate (freshman through senior) class level.

On the University of Illinois at Urbana–Champaign campus, each of the colleges also hosts an honors program called the James Scholar program—named in honor of the fourth president of the University of Illinois, Edmund J. James (1904–20). this honors program, as hosted by individual colleges, recognizes academic excellence, fosters independent study, and encourages research opportunities.

Participation Requirements: Honors students are not required to take specific courses. Students choose from a varied menu of CHP offerings, those which suit their personal interests as well as their college and department curricular requirements. The majority of honors courses satisfy general education requirements (directly or by petition) and are taken during the first two years of undergraduate study. In fact, four of the five CHP courses honors students must take can be either honors versions of general education courses or special topics courses that may be taken as electives.

The fifth course is an interdisciplinary seminar taken either the junior or senior year, when students are occupied with honors programs at the department level; by formal petition, study abroad may be substituted for this seminar. Most majors can accommodate the five-course/15-credit CHP requirement without difficulty.

Chancellor's Scholars must also attend a total of four Scholar Adventurers faculty lectures and one dress rehearsal at the Krannert Center for the Performing Arts and must maintain a minimum cumulative GPA of 3.25 (on a 4.0 scale). All CHP students receive transcript notation of Chancellor's Scholar status. In addition, those who successfully complete the academic challenges and cocurricular participation required by the program receive a special certificate upon graduation.

Depending on the college of matriculation, students enroll in honors courses, complete honors credit learning agreements, and/or meet additional curriculum and grade point requirements to remain eligible for continuation in the program. James Scholars in all colleges receive early registration privileges and may concurrently be recognized by other University and college honors programs or groups.

Admission Process: Entering freshmen with high ACT/SAT I scores and exceptional high school records are invited by CHP to apply for admission to the program, but any incoming or currently enrolled freshman may ask to be considered. Acceptance is based upon such factors as standardized test scores, high school class rank and GPA, evidence of creative and leadership abilities as displayed in extracurricular interests and activities, the strength of the application essays, and evidence of willingness to accept CHP challenges and contribute to the program. The Campus Honors Program is open to students in all majors offered on the Urbana-Champaign campus, and an effort is made to ensure that each incoming class of Chancellor's Scholars is broadly representative of the curricula of the University as a whole. The Campus Honors Program seeks students who are strongly motivated not only to excel but also to make a difference at Illinois.

Interested students should apply for admission to the University of Illinois at Urbana-Champaign (UIUC) by November 15 of their senior year in high school and for admission to the CHP by February 1 for the following fall. Applying to the CHP involves completing a form and writing one or more short essays. Applications mailed after the February 1 deadline will receive secondary consideration.

The admissions process to the individual college James Scholar Programs varies slightly, but active participants represent the top 10 to 15 percent of students at the University of Illinois. Admitted first-year students are characterized by outstanding academic records, high general aptitudes for college work, and reputations for seriousness of purpose, persistence, and self-discipline in educational endeavors.

Scholarship Availability: One of the attractions of the University of Illinois is its low cost, compared to many other top-rated American colleges and universities. Beyond that, CHP can offer a limited number of partial tuition waiver scholarships to accepted students who are not Illinois residents. These waivers defray part of the out-of-state portion of tuition for the first year and may be renewed for the second year if the student meets all requirements for continuance in CHP. First-year Chancellor's Scholars from Illinois receive a $200 scholarship to help with educational expenses.

High-achieving students who can demonstrate financial need have an excellent chance of being granted additional financial aid beyond what the CHP is able to provide. To receive University-awarded financial aid, undergraduate students must be enrolled for at least 12 credit hours and must complete a need-analysis document for the Office of Student Financial Aid. The deadline date for first-priority processing and equal consideration of financial aid applications is mid-March prior to the academic year for which aid is desired.

There are no extra costs or additional fees for applying to CHP or being a student in the Campus Honors Program.

A limited number of merit-based scholarships are available to entering James Scholars in specific colleges.

For further information, students should visit the UIUC Web site at http://www.honors.uiuc.edu/honors-at-illinois/index.html.

The Campus Context: Since its founding in 1867, the University of Illinois at Urbana-Champaign has earned a reputation of international stature, consistently recognized for excellence in both teaching and research. Founded in the tradition of the nation's finest land-grant universities, Illinois has sustained its commitment to an undergraduate education that combines the most advanced technical and professional instruction with a broad-based program in the liberal arts and sciences. Ten undergraduate divisions (colleges, institutes, and schools) offer some 4,000 courses in more than 150 fields of study.

Among the University's most outstanding resources are the University library, which houses the nation's third-largest academic collection; student access to about 4,000 computers campuswide; more than 850 student organizations; a large University residence hall system designed to support each student's academic efforts; and the acclaimed Krannert Center for the Performing Arts (a magnificent showcase for more than 300 music, theater, opera, and dance productions a year).

The campus encompasses about 1,470 acres (200 major buildings) and is located in the twin cities of Champaign and Urbana (combined population 100,000). It is situated about 140 miles south of Chicago, Illinois.

Student Body As of fall 2001, undergraduate enrollment was 28,114. Based on earlier statistics, approximately 53 percent of the students are men and 91 percent are Illinois residents. The ethnic distribution is 12.9 percent Asian/Pacific Islander, 7.3 percent African American, 5.4 percent Hispanic, 0.2 percent Native American, 71.3 percent white, 1.3 percent international, and 1.5 percent other/unknown. There are fifty-two national fraternities and twenty-seven national sororities on campus, with about 17 percent of men undergraduates and 22 percent of women undergraduates as members.

Faculty As of fall 2001, the total number of faculty members was 1,911, more than ninety-one percent of whom have terminal degrees. The undergraduate student-faculty ratio is 15:1.

Key Facilities The University library is the largest public university library in the world, housing more than 9 million items in the main library and in the forty departmental libraries. A pioneer in library automation, the library now has one of the largest online public-access catalogs, serving a network of more than 800 public, private, and academic libraries in Illinois.

Thirteen open-access sites with a variety of personal computer equipment and software are available to students and faculty and staff members. Students may access the Internet and BITNET with e-mail, ftp, gopher, listservs, news groups, telnet, the world wide web, and other available services. Almost 4,000 microcomputers are available for student use. All residence halls have connections to the campus network.

Athletics UIUC participates in Division I athletics in nine sports for men and ten for women. These include basketball, cross-country, golf, gymnastics, tennis, and track for both men and women; baseball, football, and wresting for men; and soccer, softball, swimming/diving, and volleyball for women. Memorial Stadium hosts Big Ten football, and the Assembly Hall is used for NCAA basketball games.

Study Abroad Many undergraduate students study abroad for a summer, semester, or academic year as part of their UIUC degree program. Study-abroad programs are sponsored by colleges and departments as well as the campus Study Abroad Office, which provides information on opportunities available in most parts of the world.

Support Services Nearly every facility on campus is accessible to people with physical disabilities, and the University's programs and services for people with disabilities have served as models worldwide. The Division of Rehabilitation-Education Services

Interpreting the symbols: **2**=two-year college, **4**=four-year college; **Pu**=public or state college, **Pr**=private college; **G**=general honors program; **D**=departmental honors program; **S**=small program (fewer than 100 students), **M**=midsize program (100 to 500 students), **L**=large program (more than 500 students); **Sc**=scholarships available in honors program; **Tr**=transfer students accepted into honors program; **HBC**=historically black college; **AA**=academic advisors; **GA**=graduate advisors; **FA**=fellowship advisors.

provides for the accommodation of students with disabilities, and Beckwith residence hall serves students who need assistance in coordinating personal attendant services. In addition, the University of Illinois Wheelchair Athletics Program has a long tradition of leadership and excellence in wheelchair sports. The athletes receive an outstanding education along with training of Olympic and Paralympic caliber.

Job Opportunities The Office of Student Financial Aid offers employment assistance to University students seeking part-time work; it also administers the Federal Work-Study Program. Some departments have undergraduate assistantships available. Cooperative education programs (i.e., alternating periods of University attendance with periods of employment in industry or government) are open to students in the College of Engineering and the School of Chemical Sciences.

Tuition: $4410 (base rate) for state residents, $13,230 (base rate) for nonresidents (2001–02)

Room and Board: $6090

Mandatory Fees: $1350 (includes fees for which a refund or exemption is available)

Contact: Director: Prof. Bruce F. Michelson, Campus Honors Program, 1205 West Oregon, Urbana, Illinois 61801; Telephone: 217-244-0922; Fax: 217-333-2563; E-mail: chp@uiuc.edu; Web site: http://www.honors.uiuc.edu

University of Kansas

4 Pu G L Sc Tr

▼ University Honors Program

The University Honors Program (UHP) at the University of Kansas (KU) recently celebrated its forty-fifth anniversary. Founded in 1956, the program has grown and evolved over the years. The UHP exists to help provide its students with the intellectually challenging and stimulating courses, the out-of-course experiences, and the personalized advising they need to gain the most from their undergraduate years and to be well-prepared for succeeding years. Honors courses emphasize critical thinking and skill in self-expression and are taught by outstanding faculty members. The UHP encourages students to take advantage of study-abroad programs, internships, scholarships, and fellowships. Honors students have several options for on-campus housing. They can choose from nine scholarship halls or from two honors floors in suite-style or traditional settings.

Participation Requirements: The UHP is a four-year program that does not add extra course hours to degree requirements. Students take a freshman tutorial and complete eight additional honors courses or equivalents to fulfill the program. On average, students enroll in one or two honors courses per semester. Students must maintain a 3.25 GPA. Completion of the UHP is noted on students' transcripts.

Admission Process: Honors staff members consider several aspects in admitting students into the program. Students in the UHP typically qualify through one or more of the following: a strong academic record, a minimum 31 ACT composite score, a minimum 1340 SAT I composite score, a Summerfield or Watkins-Berger Scholarship, or National Merit Finalist standing. Students not accepted before the beginning of their first year may reapply after completing at least one semester.

Scholarship Availability: The University offers nearly $5 million in scholarships to incoming students. Some scholarships are awarded based solely on merit and others on both merit and need. Returning students may compete for nearly seventy Undergraduate Research Awards and twenty University Scholar's Program Awards. There are also the Donna Evans Kingsbury Scholarship, the Sara and Mary Paretsky Award for Creativity, the J. Michael Young Opportunity Award, the College Scholarships, and several other awards and scholarships for graduating seniors. The UHP coordinates the local level of several national scholarships such as the Goldwater, Truman, Rhodes, Marshall, and the Udall. The UHP also provides assistance to applicants of the National Science Foundation, the Fulbright, and the Mellon Fellowships.

The Campus Context: The University of Kansas is a major comprehensive research and teaching university. KU offers seventy-five undergraduate programs. Established in 1866, the University has four locations–the main campus, Lawrence; the Medical Center campus, Kansas City; the School of Medicine Clinical Campus, Wichita; and the Edwards Campus, Overland Park. The Lawrence campus is located in the heart of the city on a ridge called Mount Oread and stretches across 1,000 acres with more than 17,000 trees and 100 major buildings. *National Geographic* named it one of the nation's most attractive campuses. With a population of 80,000, the city of Lawrence offers a wide range of services within walking distance, including downtown shopping, theaters, restaurants, cafes, art galleries, recreational services, and parks. Clinton Lake, 2 miles west of town, provides opportunities for water sports, hiking, and camping. Lawrence is only 30 miles east of Topeka, the state capital, and 40 miles west of Kansas City, a major city offering an international airport and abundant cultural opportunities.

Student Body KU has more than 28,000 students; approximately 20,000 are undergraduates. Fifty-three percent of the students are women. The minority ethnic distribution is 3 percent African American, 3.5 percent Asian American, 2.4 percent Hispanic, and 1 percent Native American. There are more than 1,800 international students. Students come from fifty-three U.S. states and territories and 116 different countries.

Faculty There are 2,154 faculty members and 95 percent have earned a doctorate or terminal degree.

Key Facilities The University has outstanding research facilities. The twelve libraries on campus contain more than 3.8 million volumes. There are more than thirty-seven computer labs available for student use, equipped with 1,054 Macintosh and personal computers.

In addition, other important facilities include the Higuchi Biosciences Center, the Institute for Life Span Studies, the Institute for Public Policy and Business Research, the Dole Center, the Max Kade Center for German-American Studies, the Museum of Anthropology, the Natural History Museum, Spencer Art Museum, The Lied Performing Arts Center, and Wilcox Classical Museum.

Honorary Societies Phi Theta Kappa, Phi Eta Sigma, Lambda Sigma, Tau Kappa Phi, Golden Key, Mortar Board, Phi Beta Kappa, Omicron Delta Kappa, Owl Society, Phi Kappa Phi, Alpha Kappa Delta, Chi Epsilon, Eta Sigma Phi, Kappa Tau Alpha, Order of Omega, Phi Alpha Epsilon, Phi Beta Delta, Phi Delta Kappa, and Phi Sigma Alpha

Athletics The University of Kansas belongs to the Big 12 conference and has Division I teams for all major sports: baseball, basketball, cross-country, football, golf, rowing, soccer, softball, swimming, tennis, indoor and outdoor track, and volleyball. There are also numerous opportunities for intramural sports.

Study Abroad Students at KU may choose from seventy programs that encompass fifty-five different countries. The KU Office of Study Abroad can assist students in obtaining international jobs and internships. The University Honors Program also has special programs in London and Israel.

Support Services The University offers transportation, special equipment, and counseling to students with disabilities through the Student Development Center and through Services for Students with Disabilities.

Job Opportunities There are several work opportunities available on and off campus.

Tuition: Tuition for the 2001–02 year was $78 per credit hour for state residents and $309 per credit hour for nonresidents.

Room and Board: $4348 per year

Mandatory Fees: If enrolled in more than six hours each semester, then students pay a flat fee of $551 for the academic year.

Contact: Dr. Barbara Schowen, University Honors Program, University of Kansas, 1506 Engel Road, Lawrence, Kansas 66045-3854; Telephone: (785) 864-4225; Fax: (785)-864-5178; E-mail: honors@ku.edu; Web site: http://www.ku.edu/~honors/ ~

University of La Verne

4 Pr G S Sc Tr AA

▼ University Honors Program

The University of La Verne (ULV) Honors Program is open to students majoring in all fields of study. For those who demonstrate exceptional academic achievement and motivation, the ULV Honors Program offers increased opportunities for intellectual and personal growth through an interdisciplinary curriculum that emphasizes critical thinking skills and the integration of knowledge from various disciplines. Honors students participate in specially designed seminars and colloquia, receive individualized attention from faculty mentors, and take part in community outreach activities and cultural programs.

There are approximately 75 students in the program.

Participation Requirements: Students receive the designation "Honors Program Graduates" on their diplomas and final transcripts by completing four interdisciplinary seminars (topics vary), a minimum of three colloquia, and a senior capstone seminar that integrates their major field of study with a broadly focused theme. Honors Program participants complete at least 10 semester hours of honors course work, including representative seminars and colloquia. Honors Program graduates and participants are recognized at the Honors Commencement Breakfast, when their graduation medallions and certificates are presented by the Honors Director, the President, and other academic officers.

Honors Program students are given preferential registration schedules, receive individual academic advisement from the Honors Director, and enroll in a special Honors section of University 100, the college orientation course for first-year students.

Admission Process: Candidates must have a combined SAT score of 1100 or above/ACT of 25 and a minimum 3.5 cumulative high school average. Transfer students need a minimum cumulative college GPA of 3.3. Students are encouraged to apply by March 1 for fall admission and by December 1 for spring admission. Candidates for admission after these dates will be considered on a space-available basis. The University of La Verne subscribes to the Candidate's Reply Date of May 1 (for fall semester) and does not require advance payment or confirmation or intent to enroll prior to this date.

Scholarship Availability: The University of La Verne offers Honors Program Scholarships to students who are enrolled in the Honors Program. These renewable annual scholarships of $1000 are offered in addition to the guaranteed scholarships available to all entering students, based on GPA. In 2001–02, entering freshmen with a GPA of 3.5 or higher received a $7500 merit scholarship. Merit scholarships are also available to transfer students. The sum of grant and scholarship funds received by any individual student may not exceed the total cost of tuition.

The Campus Context: The University of La Verne is a comprehensive university offering bachelor's, master's, and doctoral degrees to approximately 6,000 students. Major divisions include the College of Arts and Sciences, the School of Business and Economics, the College of Law, the School of Organizational Management, and the School of Continuing Education. Central campus enrollment is 1,422, while the remainder of the student population studies at centers located throughout California, in Alaska, and in Athens, Greece. An independent, nonsectarian institution of higher learning founded more than 100 years ago by members of the Church of the Brethren, the University of La Verne offers a strong liberal arts curriculum as well as education in selected professional fields for undergraduate students. ULV is located in the San Gabriel Valley, about 30 miles east of Los Angeles. ULV is accredited by the Western Association of Schools and Colleges and is a member of the Association of Independent California Colleges and Universities, the Independent Colleges of Southern California, and AACSB International–The Association to Advance Collegiate Schools of Business. There are forty-six undergraduate, sixteen master's, and three doctoral degree programs. Special facilities include the Dailey Theater for the Performing Arts; the Child Development Center; and the unique Supertents, housing the Student Center, Minority Resource Center, and theater.

Student Body The undergraduate enrollment is 1,422, including 40 percent men. Ethnic distribution is 38 percent Caucasian, 36 percent Hispanic, 1 percent international, 7 percent Asian/Pacific Islander, 9 percent African American, 1 percent Native American, and 8 percent other. Eighty percent of students receive financial aid. Forty-two percent of the students live on campus in three residence halls. There are six fraternities and sororities and more than twenty clubs and organizations.

Faculty There are 97 total full-time faculty members, 81 percent with doctorates or other terminal degrees. The University-wide student-faculty ratio is 11:1.

Key Facilities Library holdings total 436,000 volumes, including 215,000 volumes in Wilson Library and 221,000 volumes in the College of Law. Computing facilities include 150 microcomputers of various models and operating systems, high-power graphics workstations, mainframe access, full Internet and BITNET access, and consultation services.

Honorary Society Alpha Chi, Sigma Lambda Delta

Athletics In athletics ULV offers ten NCAA Division III intercollegiate sports for men: baseball, cross-country, football, golf, soccer, swimming, tennis, track, and water polo; one nonconference men's sport (volleyball); and nine NCAA Division III intercollegiate sports for women: basketball, cross-country, soccer, softball, swimming, tennis, track, volleyball, and water polo.

Study Abroad Study abroad is available through Brethren Colleges Abroad consortium in China, Ecuador, England, France, Germany, Greece, India, Japan, Mexico, and Spain. ULV offers semester-abroad opportunities in China/Hong Kong and Mexico. Travel studies are available through departments, especially during January Interterm.

Support Services Disabled Student Services are coordinated through the Health Center and Office of Student Services. Special parking permits, elevator keys, and other support services are available.

Job Opportunities Student employment is widely available through work-study as well as other opportunities. The Career Development Center provides guidance and assistance in finding employment. Placement services and internships are available through many academic departments.

Tuition: $19,500 per year (2001–02)

Room and Board: $7040

Contact: Director: Dr. Andrea Labinger, University of La Verne, 1950 Third Street, La Verne, California 91750; Telephone: 909-593-3511 Ext. 4357; Fax: 909-392-2714; E-mail: labinger@ulv.edu

Interpreting the symbols: **2**=two-year college, **4**=four-year college; **Pu**=public or state college, **Pr**=private college; **G**=general honors program; **D**=departmental honors program; **S**=small program (fewer than 100 students), **M**=midsize program (100 to 500 students), **L**=large program (more than 500 students); **Sc**=scholarships available in honors program; **Tr**=transfer students accepted into honors program; **HBC**=historically black college; **AA**=academic advisors; **GA**=graduate advisors; **FA**=fellowship advisors.

UNIVERSITY OF LOUISVILLE

4 Pu L Tr AA GA FA

▼ University Honors Program

The University of Louisville has a comprehensive Honors Program for students who have shown promise of sustained, advanced intellectual achievement. Established in 1982, the Honors Program provides the opportunity for students to study in small classes and engage in an intensive and challenging educational experience. Honors classes promote discussion, personalized study, in-depth research, and reading, as well as close relationships with faculty members and peers.

Eligible freshmen are invited to enroll for Honors Campus Culture, an orientation to campus life for new students, presented in a weekend format before the fall semester begins. Honors sections of general education courses are offered each semester. These classes provide a strong foundation for upper-level study and meet requirements across colleges. Honors scholar seminars are interdisciplinary courses open to sophomores, juniors, and seniors. Often team-taught, these seminars tend to focus on topics of immediate interest to students. Some recent courses include Shimmering Words, Flickering Images;, Media in American Society; Sensational Fictions: Scandal and the Nineteenth-century Novel; Religion and Mass Media; Revolutions in Science; and Immigration and Ethenticity. In addition, the Overseers' International Seminars combine semester-long, in-depth study with substantially subsidized travel to locations outside the United States. Seminars have included exploring the rainforests of the Amazon, the culture of Kenya, the art of Rome, and Buddhism in China. Seminar topics change annually, and specific descriptions are mailed to all eligible students each semester.

The Honors Building is a renovated, 100-year-old townhouse that is typical of Victorian Louisville. The second-oldest building on campus, it is now home to a classroom, seminar room, library, computer center, and the administrative offices of the Honors Program. Situated close to commuter parking and residence halls and equipped with kitchen facilities, the Honors Building is a convenient place for honors students to study, relax, and meet for meals. Throughout the year, the Honors Building is also the site of many presentations, receptions, and social events open to honors students.

Redefined in 2001, the Honors Program has been enrolling and tracking increasing numbers of students. Approximately 800 students are currently involved in honors work, a number which represents about one third of all University of Louisville students who are eligible.

Participation Requirements: Honors students may major in any undergraduate program in the University and fulfill the same requirements as all students. Although there are no required honors courses, eligible students are advised by the Honors Program staff and are encouraged to take at least 24 hours of honors-designated course work during their academic career to graduate as an Honors Scholar. In addition, active honors students choose to be involved in many of the extracurricular offerings of the Honors Program, such as peer mentoring, community service projects, career mentoring with experienced professionals in the local area, attendance at regional and national honors conferences, and undergraduate research related to senior honors projects.

All honors course work is noted on a student's transcript, and college honors are awarded on the basis of GPA and other factors determined by each undergraduate unit. Graduation as a University Honors Scholar is noted on students' transcripts and diploma.

Admission Process: New students are eligible to take courses in the Honors Program if they have an ACT composite score of 27 or the equivalent SAT I composite score of 1210. Belated admission to or continuation in the program requires a college GPA of 3.35 or higher. Transfer students are eligible to participate if their transferred GPA is 3.35 or higher. Registration in honors courses requires permission acquired during advising with an Honors Program staff member.

Scholarship Availability: While no admission scholarships are awarded through the Honors Program, many full tuition scholarships are awarded to honors-eligible students through the Office of Admissions. Continuing students may apply for annual scholarships that are awarded solely on the basis of academic performance.

The Campus Context: The University of Louisville is a state-supported, urban university located in Kentucky's largest metropolitan area. The University has three campuses encompassing thirteen graduate and undergraduate colleges, schools, and divisions. These include Arts and Sciences, Business and Public Administration, Music, the Speed School of Engineering, and Nursing. Nationally recognized graduate programs are offered in business, dentistry, education, law, and medicine. The University offers a total of 164 degree programs.

Among the distinguished facilities are the J.B. Speed Art Museum, the Computer-Aided Engineering Lab with Robotics Laboratory, and the Rapid Prototype Facility.

Student Body Undergraduate enrollment is approximately 14,650; 46 percent are men and 54 percent are women. Minority students represent more than 18.6 percent of the undergraduate population; international students make up another 1.5 percent. Ninety-two percent of undergraduates commute to campus; 8 percent live in residence halls. Sixty-two percent of students receive some form of financial aid. Students may participate in sixteen fraternities and ten sororities.

Faculty Of the 2,053 faculty members, 1,469 are full-time, 90 percent with doctorates or other terminal degrees. The student-faculty ratio is 12:1.

Key Facilities The University libraries house a total of 1.3 million volumes. Computer facilities include a campuswide network with more than 3,000 PCs and terminals and resident hall and Internet access. There are many student computer labs.

Honorary Societies Phi Eta Sigma, Phi Kappa Phi, Golden Key, and Mortar Board

Athletics The University fields an outstanding athletics program, providing intercollegiate competition for men and women in seventeen varsity sports.

Study Abroad The International Center organizes study-abroad programs, led by University of Louisville faculty members, to many different countries. The center supports the American International Relations Club, a student organization that encourages interaction among Americans and international students. Many opportunities are available to work or study in Montpellier, France, or Mainz, Germany, through the Sister City program. New initiatives are combining course work at the University with extended overseas experiences.

Support Services The Disability Resource Center provides specialized services to meet the needs of disabled students. Buildings and classrooms are required to be accessible to all students.

Job Opportunities There are many opportunities to work on campus through work-study programs, undergraduate research grants, assistantships, and cooperative education.

Tuition: $3794 for state residents, $8280 for nonresidents, per year (1998–99)

Room and Board: $3330

Contact: Director: Dr. John Richardson, Honors Building, University of Louisville, Louisville, Kentucky 40292; Telephone: 502-852-6293; Fax: 502-852-3919; E-mail: john.richardson@louisville.edu; Web site: http://www.louisville.edu/a-s/honors

University of Maine

4 Pu G M Tr

▼ Honors College

Honors at the University of Maine (UMaine) originated in 1935 and today provides a unique opportunity for a community of 500 motivated students to investigate diverse academic areas of the University, to be challenged in a supportive intellectual environment, and to critically engage fellow students and enthusiastic, distinguished faculty members in thoughtful, provocative discussion. The benefits and rewards are substantial, and the program is flexible enough to be tailored precisely to the individual student's needs and interests. Students enrolled in the Honors College simultaneously complete their degree requirements in one of the five traditional colleges at the University.

The Honors College at UMaine is founded on the belief that genuine excellence in college-level studies means substantial understanding and informed appreciation of areas outside a major field of specialization as well as focused excellence within it. With an emphasis on learning that both broadens and deepens, the College serves to expand students' perspectives by exploring areas of thought not closely related to their disciplines and to allow them to work in their majors with greater intensity than would be possible within a conventional course pattern. Honors study begins with interdisciplinary broadness and concludes with an in-depth thesis project in the major field.

The Campus Context: The University of Maine at Orono, which offers eighty-one degree programs, is composed of the Colleges of Business, Public Policy, and Health; Education and Human Development; Engineering; Natural Sciences, Forestry, and Agriculture; and Liberal Arts and Sciences. Among special facilities on campus are the Maine Center for the Arts, including the Hudson Museum and the Hutchins Concert Hall; The Maine Folklife Center; the Margaret Chase Smith Center for Public Policy; the Senator George J. Mitchell Center for Environmental and Watershed Research; and the Maynard F. Jordan Planetarium and Observatory.

Student Body Of the 8,511 undergraduate students enrolled, 53 percent are women. Students from minority groups represent 4 percent of the student population and international students represent 2 percent. Eighty-five percent of the students receive financial aid. There are thirteen fraternities and six sororities on campus.

Faculty Of the 720 faculty members at the University, 519 are full-time and 86 percent of the full-time faculty members hold terminal degrees. The student-faculty ratio is 13.6:1.

Key Facilities The library houses 1.2 million books, serial backfiles, and government documents. The Department of Information Technologies provides computer services, including public computer clusters, a help center, a computer store and repair facility, Internet and Intranet services, free electronic mail and conferencing, instructional workshops, and remote access.

Honorary Societies Phi Kappa Phi and Phi Beta Kappa

Athletics Through the Departments of Athletics and Recreation, the University offers programs in intercollegiate sports and recreation (intramual sports, open recreation, fitness, sports clubs, and outdoor recreation). Because these activities are recognized as an integral part of the education process, the University supports them with professional staff members, equipment, and facilities. These programs promote education leadership, physical fitness, athletic excellence, community service, healthy life skills, and fun. Students are offered extensive and equal opportunities for participation and achievement.

Study Abroad The University of Maine supports a number of study-abroad opportunities throughout the world. Several of these programs are direct one-to-one exchanges with universities in Canada, Europe, Australia, Asia, and South America. English-speaking programs are widely available, even in countries where English is not the native language. There are opportunities for language immersion programs. Through reciprocal student-exchange programs, students pay tuition, fees, and sometimes room and board to the University of Maine as they would while enrolled at UMaine. They pay no regular fees at the host institution. Financial aid and scholarships may be used as appropriate. Applicants must have a minimum GPA of 2.75. For information, contact the Office of International Programs.

Support Services The Onward Program assists disabled students with academic, physical, and advocacy needs.

Job Opportunities Student employment is available through Federal Work-Study, regular jobs, and the Work Merit Program.

Tuition: $4200 for state residents, $11,940 for nonresidents, $6300 for nonresidents eligible for the New England Regional Student Program, per year (2001–02)

Room and Board: $5728

Mandatory Fees: $870

Contact: Director: Charlie Slavin, 5716 Robert B. Thomson Honors Center, Orono, Maine 04469-5716; Telephone: 207-581-3262; Fax: 207-581-3265; E-mail: slavin@honors.umaine.edu; Web site: http://www.honors.umaine.edu

University of Maine at Augusta

4 Pu G S Sc Tr

▼ Honors Program

The Honors Program at the University of Maine at Augusta (UMA) offers those students who have demonstrated intellectual potential and personal commitment an enriched academic experience. Not only are studies at UMA enhanced socially and intellectually, but the honors student is better prepared to continue his or her advanced studies and bring academic talents and abilities to the attention of prospective employers.

The Honors Program is not a separate degree program, but is designed to augment the course work required for a degree. In most cases, honors courses can be substituted for required or elective credits.

Any student, upon the recommendation of the Director of the Honors Program, may register for an honors course without being formally admitted into the program. However, to graduate from the program with honors designation, a student must meet the specific requirements of the Honors Program.

There are currently 80 students enrolled in the program.

Participation Requirements: The requirements of the Honors Program are flexible to meet the needs of students—part-time, full-time, traditional, and nontraditional.

UMA offers two honors options, one for associate degree students and another for bachelor's degree students. For those students in the Associate Degree Honors Program, 15 credit hours of honors courses are required, and for those in the Bachelor's Degree Honors Program, 21 to 24 hours are required. All Honors Program participants are required to take a foundation course in critical thinking and writing, an interdisciplinary topical seminar (honors colloquium), and a capstone seminar with thesis. The

Interpreting the symbols: **2**=two-year college, **4**=four-year college; **Pu**=public or state college, **Pr**=private college; **G**=general honors program; **D**=departmental honors program; **S**=small program (fewer than 100 students), **M**=midsize program (100 to 500 students), **L**=large program (more than 500 students); **Sc**=scholarships available in honors program; **Tr**=transfer students accepted into honors program; **HBC**=historically black college; **AA**=academic advisors; **GA**=graduate advisors; **FA**=fellowship advisors.

remaining credits may include other topical seminar courses, honors independent studies, or nonhonors courses contracted for honors credit.

In addition, an Honors Program student has the option of completing 45 hours of community service in lieu of an honors elective. Also, upon completion of the associate degree honors requirements, a student may continue in the bachelor's degree honors program. In addition to the requirements for the associate degree program, the continuing student is required to complete 6 additional hours of honors electives and a senior honors thesis.

It is also possible for students at a distance to participate in the UMA Honors Program, since at least one honors course per year is offered over the University of Maine interactive television system.

The UMA Honors Program began offering courses in the spring semester of 1986, with 24 students. All students admitted to the program automatically become members of the Honors Program Student Association. Upon completion of the Honors Program requirements, the student receives a Certificate of Completion and a medallion to be worn at graduation.

Admission Process: To enter the Honors Program, an interview with the Program Director is scheduled, and the student must submit an application form and three letters of recommendation for consideration by the Honors Council. To continue in the program, the student must maintain a minimum GPA of 3.2 and earn a minimum grade of B in honors courses.

Scholarship Availability: The Honors Program administers two scholarships of its own, which are awarded annually to active participants in the program. There are also four UMA Presidential Scholarships that are dedicated to program participants. In addition, there is a Leadership Program Scholarship available to an honors program student who serves as a leadership intern in the Honors Program Director's office. All entering students are eligible for general Presidential Scholarships based on merit.

Tuition: $101 for state residents, $247 for nonresidents, per credit hour; $4230 for nonresidents eligible for the New England Regional Student Program, per year

Mandatory Fees: $11.50 per credit hour

Contact: Director: Jon A. Schlenker, 46 University Drive, Augusta, Maine 04330; Telephone: 207-621-3262; Fax: 207-621-3293; E-mail: jons@maine.edu; Web site: http://www.uma.maine.edu

UNIVERSITY OF MARYLAND, BALTIMORE COUNTY

4 Pu G M Sc Tr

▼ Honors College

The UMBC Honors College seeks to develop the talented and curious individual's faculties of analysis and exposition through an enhanced liberal arts experience, to foster a sense of membership in an intellectual community, and to instill learning as a way of life. The College frequently notes that the English word "school" derives ultimately from the Greek term schole, meaning "leisure," and that the word "liberal" in the phrase "liberal arts" refers to the freedom associated with free time—time away from survival needs and available for intellectual development.

Among the advantages offered by a medium-sized research university, the UMBC Honors College provides the atmosphere of a small community of learning and energetically sponsors a variety of programs and activities that often intentionally blur the distinction between the curricular and the extracurricular. Toward that end, every year the College sponsors a variety of special courses—whether honors versions of regular courses or specially commissioned interdisciplinary honors seminars (such as Methods and Materials of Research, Knowledge and Responsibility, Professional Issues and Decision Making, Paradigms of Belief, and Cultures of Childhood)—and encourages participation in activities ranging from its Visiting Scholar Program (through which College members attend a seminar and dine with such individuals as Carol Moseley-Braun, Robert Coles, Jonathan Kozol, Noam Chomsky, Lani Guinier, and Marge Piercy), community service projects (such as Project Discover, which addresses the needs and outlook of fourth- and fifth-grade students in the inner city), and cultural events (such as trips to New York to see Mary Zimmerman's *Metamorphoses* or the National Theatre of Greece's production of Sophocles' *Electra)* to study-travel programs abroad (to such places as Greece, Turkey, Spain, Portugal, Sicily, Malta, Tunisia, and England).

Membership in the Honors College is intentionally kept small. Limited to a total enrollment of 500, the College seeks to matriculate 125 freshmen each fall. Small classes, with a maximum of 25 students and an average of 17, encourage collaborative learning through dialogue between students and instructors and the involvement of students in research.

Upon completion of the Honors College requirements, members receive the Certificate of General Honors at an annual ceremony. A notation of the award appears on the student's transcript.

Initiated as the Honors Program in 1982, the Honors College was given its present coherence and designation in 1988. The motto of the College is "Learning for living, not only for making a living."

Admission Process: A separate application for admission to the College must be submitted in addition to that submitted for admission to UMBC; the Honors College application requires a composition, answers to background and interest questions, and a letter of reference. The chief criterion for membership in the College is an abiding curiosity and a will and energy during the university years to learn how to satisfy that curiosity. Generally, a minimum combined SAT I score of 1300 and a minimum cumulative high school GPA of 3.5 are expected for consideration for admission as a freshman to the Honors College. In fall 2001, the profile of the Honors College freshmen consisted of an average SAT I score of 1384 and high school GPA of 3.96.

Transfer students or current UMBC students are expected to have established a minimum cumulative college GPA of 3.25 to be considered for membership. Members maintain their eligibility by taking at least one honors course per academic semester and maintaining at least a 3.25 cumulative GPA.

Scholarship Availability: The Honors College offers scholarships for both the regular academic year and special sessions. All prospective freshmen who submit applications by February 1 are considered for academic-year scholarships that are highly competitive. Approximately 15 percent of the freshmen entering the College receive such scholarships, which range from $1000 per year to full tuition, room, and board. Each year, all members of the College are invited to apply for summer- and winter-session scholarships; proposals involving independent research and/or study abroad are particularly encouraged for these awards.

The Campus Context: UMBC opened in 1966 and has grown to become a flourishing mid-sized research university of more than 11,000 students (graduate and undergraduate). A highly selective university in the eleven-campus University System of Maryland, UMBC is situated on 500 acres southwest of the city of Baltimore and affords immediate access both to that city's cultural, social, and commercial benefits (such as the Walters Art Gallery, the Baltimore Museum of Art, the Inner Harbor, Oriole Park at Camden Yards, and the Meyerhoff Symphony Hall) and to those of Washington, D.C. Philadelphia is 2 hours away, and New York is 3½ hours away. There are thirty-seven undergraduate (B.A./B.S.) programs, twenty-nine M.A./M.S./M.F.A/M.P.S. programs, and twenty Ph.D. programs offered on campus.

In addition to an Arts and Sciences Program that offers the opportunity to major in twenty-five different areas, there is the College of Engineering. Students obtaining certification in education must also complete the requirements for one of the academic majors.

Special facilities of particular significance to undergraduates include the Shriver Center, which places students in co-ops and internships in the immediate area and around the world, manages community service projects that bring the resources of the University to the public, and connects students to a wide range of social service projects. Among its special programs are the Student Literacy Corps, a tutoring program for children and adults in Baltimore, and the Shriver Peaceworker Program for returning Peace Corps volunteers. The Howard Hughes Medical Laboratory offers undergraduate students extensive research opportunities in the biomedical field. UMBC also has an imaging resource center, a molecular biology laboratory, and an art gallery.

Student Body A total of 9,328 undergraduates are enrolled at UMBC: 4,634 women (50 percent) and 4,694 men (50 percent). The ethnic distribution is African American, 1,607 (15.1 percent); American Indian, 47 (0.5 percent); Asian American, 1,691 (15.3 percent); Hispanic, 244 (3 percent); white, 5,260 (56 percent); international, 431 (4.6 percent); and other, 148 (1.5 percent). About 38 percent of students are residents. Forty-nine percent of students who applied for aid received some form of financial aid. There are 170 registered organizations on campus, including ten fraternities and eight sororities.

Faculty Full-time faculty members number 446, 86 percent with terminal degrees. Part-time faculty members number 308. The total number of faculty members is 754. The student-faculty ratio is 16:1.

Key Facilities The UMBC library contains 749,619 bound volumes and 4,282 periodicals; electronic resources, including an online catalog, bibliographic and full-text databases, and Internet and World Wide Web access; and special collections, including photography (more than 1.5 million photographs), scientific archives (such as those of the American Society for Microbiology), science fiction, Marylandia, English graphic satire, and Utopian literature. UMBC students have access to 673 microcomputers, either Intel-based PCs or Apple Macintoshes, through which they may access the Internet.

Honorary Societies Phi Beta Kappa, Phi Kappa Phi, and Golden Key as well as discipline-based honor societies

Athletics There are ten men's and twelve women's NCAA Division I sports available on campus. UMBC belongs to the Northeast Conference (NEC) and supports a number of intramural and club sports.

Study Abroad UMBC maintains study-abroad programs in Mexico, Germany, Italy, and the United Kingdom. Students may also receive credit for participation in programs sponsored by other universities. The Honors College sponsors annual study-travel programs.

Support Services The UMBC campus is 95 percent handicapped accessible, and a Director of Support Services is available to coordinate student requests for assistance.

Job Opportunities Twenty-six percent of undergraduates work on campus during the academic year.

Tuition: $4374 for state residents, $9754 for nonresidents, per year (2002–03)

Room and Board: $4998

Mandatory Fees: $1536

Contact: Director: Dr. Jay M. Freyman, Associate Professor of Ancient Studies; Associate Director: Dr. Lawrence Lasher, Associate Professor of English, UMBC, 1000 Hilltop Circle, Baltimore, Maryland 21250; Telephone: 410-455-3720; Fax: 410-455-1063; E-mail: honors@umbc.edu

University of Maryland College Park

4 Pu G L Sc Tr AA GA FA

▼ University Honors Program

The University Honors Program is the long-established program for the most talented students on campus in their first two years and was recently ranked as one of the top nine programs in the nation in *Ivy League Programs at State School Prices* (Prentice Hall). It offers the opportunity to become part of a close-knit community of faculty members and intellectually gifted undergraduates committed to acquiring a broad and balanced education.

The University Honors Program combines the best of a major research institution—preparing the student for up-to-date, productive careers—with the best of a wide-ranging undergraduate program, developing the intellectual breadth necessary for a long, responsible life in a complex, fast-changing world. The honors program challenges the student to explore the full range of the academic and social diversity of the College Park campus and to seek ways to serve the needs of the larger world off campus.

Through an exciting array of small classes taught by experienced faculty members and through contact with other like-minded undergraduates, the honors program provides an intellectual home for the curious, adventuresome, and enthusiastic student. Pleasure in dialogue and debate, involvement in the world of ideas and opinions, and a willingness to experiment with unfamiliar concepts characterize the students involved in the program. Honors housing is available in several residence halls.

The first two years of honors emphasize broadening intellectual horizons through a mix of honors seminars—mostly lively interdisciplinary courses—and "honors-version" courses (these are smaller and more focused versions of regular departmental offerings). In small class settings, faculty members and students explore the major issues, universal themes, and intellectual concepts that enable the various disciplines to do their share of the work of the mind. These courses allow the student to explore or test a commitment to a possible major while meeting the University's distribution requirements—and they open broad new intellectual vistas unavailable in high school.

All honors students take either HONR 100 or 200. HONR 100, "The Responsibilities of a Liberally Educated Person," is a first-semester colloquium that encourages beginning students to think broadly about the personal and social value of education and about what it means to be an educated person. Carefully selected readings, community service projects, and cross-cultural activities are shared with 15 other honors students. HONR 200 introduces students to the world of research. Conversations with selected faculty members in a variety of academic areas, as well as visits to their labs, studios, or field stations, give students insight into the issues of disciplinary method, personal commitment, ethics, and funding of university research and other creative projects.

Honors seminars form the heart of the program. They are limited to 15–20 students and emphasize individual responsibility and lively intellectual exchange. Faculty members are chosen not only for their knowledge and interest in their subject but also for

Interpreting the symbols: **2**=two-year college, **4**=four-year college; **Pu**=public or state college, **Pr**=private college; **G**=general honors program; **D**=departmental honors program; **S**=small program (fewer than 100 students), **M**=midsize program (100 to 500 students), **L**=large program (more than 500 students); **Sc**=scholarships available in honors program; **Tr**=transfer students accepted into honors program; **HBC**=historically black college; **AA**=academic advisors; **GA**=graduate advisors; **FA**=fellowship advisors.

their commitment to undergraduate honors education. HONR 169Z, "Knowledge and Its Human Implications," is a wildly interdisciplinary course aimed at second-semester students: it allows the student to study six texts from six different disciplines to see how knowledge is constructed and what the human implications of different kinds of knowledge are.

Approximately 2,000 students are currently enrolled in the program.

Participation Requirements: The 700 most talented new students are invited each year. Students normally complete their Honors Citation in four or five semesters and then may pass on into departmental honors work. Students may continue to take honors seminars and stay involved with the program by teaching in HONR 100 or 200, serving on committees, and so on. The average combined SAT score of admitted students is 1410, and the average GPA is 4.2.

Scholarship Availability: Merit scholarships are independent of participation in honors, though most major scholarship winners are also admitted to honors. There are small scholarships for students in good standing in the program for their second and third years.

The Campus Context: The University of Maryland at College Park is the flagship campus of the University of Maryland system and is located on a traditional campus of Georgian buildings in suburban College Park between Washington, D.C., and Baltimore, Maryland. The exceptional resources of the Washington-Baltimore area provide students with extensive research and internship opportunities to enhance the quality education they receive at UMCP.

The University offers bachelor's degrees in ninety-four academic areas, master's degrees in eighty-nine disciplines, doctorates in seventy specializations, and one first professional degree. It is academically organized into the Colleges of Agriculture and Natural Resources; Arts and Humanities; Behavioral and Social Sciences; Computer, Mathematical and Physical Sciences; and Life Sciences and the School of Architecture; the Robert H. Smith School of Business; the A. James Clark School of Engineering; the Philip Merrill College of Journalism; the School of Public Affairs; the Graduate School; and the College of Veterinary Medicine (Maryland campus of the Virginia-Maryland Regional College of Veterinary Medicine. Thirty-five percent of the University's undergraduate programs and 34 percent of its graduate programs are ranked in the top twenty-five by *U.S. News & World Report.*

Student Body In fall 1998 the undergraduate enrollment was 25,099, including 51 percent men. Ethnic distribution was Caucasian, 59.4 percent; African American, 13.1 percent; Asian, 13.8 percent; Hispanic, 5.1 percent; Native American, .3 percent; and 5.5 percent unknown. Thirty-nine percent of students are residential; 2.9 percent are international. Forty-five percent of students receive financial aid.

Faculty The total number of faculty members is 3,591; 2,749 are full-time, and 96 percent hold doctorates or other terminal degrees (as of fall 2000). The student-faculty ratio is 13:1 (fall 2000).

Key Facilities The library has a collection of more than 2.7 million volumes, with subscriptions to more than 30,000 periodicals, and offers computerized resources, including online cataloging and access to full-text and other databases. The libraries include a number of specialized collections such as the International Piano Archives at Maryland, the Library of American Broadcasting, the East Asia Collections, Marylandia, and rare books. Students have access to more than 760 PCs and 170 Macs in computer labs throughout the campus, including some 24-hour facilities.

Honorary Societies There are more than fifty honorary societies at Maryland for students who excel in scholarship and leadership, including Phi Beta Kappa, Alpha Lambda Delta, Phi Eta Sigma, Golden Key, Phi Sigma Pi, Mortar Board, Phi Kappa Phi, and Omicron Delta Kappa.

Study Abroad Through the Study Abroad Office, students may participate in a wide range of overseas study programs tailored to full-year, semester, summer, winterterm, or spring break time periods in twenty countries, including Britain, Germany, Denmark, Sweden, Israel, Italy, Brazil, Japan, Mexico, Spain, Belgium, Argentina, and the Galapagos Islands.

Support Services The Disablity Support Services Office in the Counseling Center is available to students requesting assistance. The campus is 95 percent handicapped-accessible.

Job Opportunities The campus Career Center assists students in obtaining employment both on and off campus. There is an extensive Federal Work-Study Program on the campus.

Tuition: $4334 for state residents, $12,406 nonresidents, per year (2001–02)

Room and Board: $6740 (2001–02)

Mandatory Fees: $1007 (2001–02)

Contact: Director: Dr. Maynard Mack Jr., Anne Arundel Hall, College Park, Maryland 20742; Telephone: 301-405-6771; Fax: 301-405-6723; E-mail: mmack@deans.umd.edu; Web site: http://www.inform.umd.edu/honors

UNIVERSITY OF MASSACHUSETTS AMHERST

4 Pu G L Sc Tr AA FA

▼ Commonwealth College

Commonwealth College is the honors college at the University of Massachusetts Amherst. Commonwealth College offers academically talented students the advantages of a small honors college and the wide-ranging opportunities of a nationally recognized major research institution. Honors students participate in small classes and colloquia, receive individual counseling, and have outstanding opportunities to conduct significant research while working closely with faculty members. The honors college is a campuswide, comprehensive, four-year program; students from all majors in every college are eligible to join the honors college.

The heart of Commonwealth College Honors is to provide the love of learning. The curriculum of the College emphasizes inquiry and facilitates critical analysis, independent research, collaborative work, and effective communication skills. Consistent with the land-grant mission of the University, Commonwealth College also promotes engagement with society. The College affords its students many opportunities for engagement through a variety of academically based opportunities, including internships, co-ops, experiential learning courses, leadership training, and community service learning courses. The College also promotes student leadership through specific leadership courses, through its speaker series and alumni mentoring/shadowing programs, and by arranging student participation in College activities, including peer mentoring, committee work, and activity planning. The honors curriculum includes entirely enriched honors courses, colloquia, interdisciplinary seminars, service learning, and a culminating experience requirement. The culminating experience is a 6-credit activity that may range in scope from the more traditional thesis to approved capstone courses in academic study, guided reflection, and experience gained through community service, study abroad, or internship. In addition, many junior and senior honors students take graduate-level courses and obtain honors credit. Courses taken through the Five College Consortium (Amherst College, Hampshire College, Mount Holyoke College, and Smith College in cooperation with the University of Massachusetts Amherst) may be petitioned for substitution as honors courses.

Commonwealth College offers a variety of special programs. The college sponsors a lecture series that brings distinguished visitors to campus to speak on selected national issues. Through the Pizza & Prof Night seminar series, students meet outstanding faculty members from across the campus. The Citizen Scholars Program offers scholarships and leadership training for students who engage in challenging work, linking academics to community outreach. The International Scholars Program prepares student for study abroad and provides limited scholarship assistance. The Office of National Scholarship Advisement assists eligible students who are applying for national fellowships, such as the Rhodes, Marshall, Fulbright, and Truman Scholarships.

All incoming first-year students arrive on campus a day early in the fall to participate in a special Labor Day Orientation. First-year honors students may select from several residential options, such as theme-based honors learning communities in the Orchard Hill Residential Area, the Talent Advancement Programs (TAP) in the Southwest Residential Area, and Thatcher Language House.

Commonwealth College encourages students to undertake research and supports their efforts by helping to identify faculty mentors, teaching thesis workshops, offering research fellowships for financial assistance and sponsoring a statewide conference on undergraduate research.

A variety of resources and services are available to students through Commonwealth College. The advising component is both comprehensive and integrative, with individual counseling from faculty, professional, and peer advisers. The College also publishes a newsletter, sponsors service projects and student gatherings, and administers a competitive awards program. Graduating honors students may request a dean's letter of recommendation for prospective employers and graduate schools.

The University Honors Program was established in 1961, and was replaced by the honors college, Commonwealth College, in 1999 and now has a total membership of more than 2,000.

Participation Requirements: All students who complete Commonwealth College requirements will graduate as Commonwealth College Scholars. These requirements include a GPA of 3.2 or better, foundation skills, honors courses, and a culminating experience. To graduate with higher Latin honors, students must attain a minimum GPA of 3.5 for magna cum laude or 3.8 for summa cum laude. Cum laude is determined by GPA and residency requirements alone. To graduate with any level of honors, a student must complete 48 graded credits of residence. Departmental or Interdisciplinary honors are awarded in addition to Commonwealth College and Latin honors. Specific requirements vary depending on a student's major. Foundation requirements include writing, oral communications, and computer literacy. Honors courses must be completed with grades of B or better. Required courses include College Writing; a minimum number of general education courses, one of which must of an Interdisciplinary designation; and the Dean's Book series (students must complete three 1-credit seminars; the 3 credits count as meeting the Commonwealth College requirement for a second interdisciplinary honors course). Three of the required honors courses must be at the 300 level or above, of which two must comprise a 6-credit culminating experience. Accommodations may be made for those entering the college after the freshman year. Under no circumstances shall the Dean's Book requirement or the culminating experience be waived. Students who complete a minimum of 48 graded credits in residence and graduate from the Commonwealth College receive one or more of the following types of honors noted on their diplomas and transcripts, depending on their honors track and GPA: Commonwealth College Scholar; Departmental Honors or Interdisciplinary Honors; and cum laude, magna cum laude, or summa cum laude.

Admission Process: Entering first-year students are admitted to the program by invitation. Each student's application to the University is evaluated on the basis of academic achievement in high school, test scores, and an essay by the student. Average first-year honors students who entered in fall 2001 ranked in the top 5 percent of their high school class, attained a weighted high school GPA of 4.0 in their academic course work, and scored 1315 on the SAT I. Entering transfer students may be admitted either by invitation or by applying to the college during the first month of their entering semester if they have a 3.2 GPA or higher from their previous institution. Others may apply based on their academic record at the University if they have a 3.2 GPA or higher.

Scholarship Availability: The University of Massachusetts Amherst has a variety of merit scholarships available for incoming first-year and transfer students. Selections, which are administered by the Admissions Office, are made during the admission process.

In addition, Commonwealth College has an endowed scholarship fund and several research fellowships. Selection criteria for the David J. Snyder, Rachel and John Morton, Nancy Cullen, and Charles Hoff Scholarships are listed on the College Web site. Sophomore honors students may apply for Sophomore Fellowships of up to $1000 per semester for work done under the direct supervision of a faculty mentor. The Citizen Scholars Program awards scholarships of $1000 per year for two years to a select group of students who wish to serve their community and become active leaders in the commonwealth. The Class of 1991 Public Service Fellowship and the Frank and Helen DiGiammarino Citizen Scholarship support students engaged in community service projects. The International Scholars Program Scholarships and the Oxford Seminar Summer Scholarships support students in study-abroad programs. Fifty Honors Research Fellowships of up to $1000 each are awarded to senior and junior honors students through a competitive application process. Students must submit a proposal outlining their project accompanied by a letter of endorsement from their faculty sponsor.

Commonwealth College also administers a competitive awards program. The deadline for applications is in the spring, generally mid-March. Recipients are announced at the honors graduation and awards ceremony, where they receive a special certificate. For the Honors Dean's Awards, ten annual awards of $500 each are made to senior honors students based on the excellence of their thesis or project. For the Class of 1941 Humanitarian Award, depending on endowment earnings, one or two awards of at least $1000 are made annually. Recipients are chosen from among junior and/or senior honors students in good standing who provide documentation of their community service and submit a written essay.

The Cooke Family Fund Scholarship carries a cash prize of approximately $1000. Selection is made from among senior honors students who have shown outstanding academic achievement, including successful completion of research in the student's major, and have demonstrated significant University or community service. The Howard H. Quint Memorial Prize in Honors was established in memory of Professor Howard Quint, former History Department Chair and a founder of the Honors Program. The prize of approximately $400 is awarded jointly by the history department and Commonwealth College to a senior honors student based on the student's academic record through the junior year. Through the Lawrence Payne Scholarship in Public Service, $1000 is awarded to a senior honors student based on academic achievement and demonstrated commitment to public service.

Interpreting the symbols: **2**=two-year college, **4**=four-year college; **Pu**=public or state college, **Pr**=private college; **G**=general honors program; **D**=departmental honors program; **S**=small program (fewer than 100 students), **M**=midsize program (100 to 500 students), **L**=large program (more than 500 students); **Sc**=scholarships available in honors program; **Tr**=transfer students accepted into honors program; **HBC**=historically black college; **AA**=academic advisors; **GA**=graduate advisors; **FA**=fellowship advisors.

The Campus Context: The University of Massachusetts Amherst is composed of nine colleges: Humanities and Fine Arts, Natural Sciences and Mathematics, Social and Behavioral Sciences, Education, Engineering, Food and Natural Resources, Management, Nursing, and Public Health and Health Sciences. Degree programs on campus include six associate, eighty-nine baccalaureate, sixty-nine master's, and fifty doctoral degrees.

Among special facilities is the Fine Arts Center, complete with concert hall, gallery, Rand Theater, and Bezanson Recital Hall. In addition, the University has six additional galleries, the Mullins Sports Arena, an observatory, and a botanical garden. Through the Five College Consortium, students at the University of Massachusetts Amherst also have direct access to the wide range of courses and faculty at Amherst College, Hampshire College, Mount Holyoke College, and Smith College. Course registration is easy. No fee is involved. Coordinated academic calendars, open library borrowing, and fare-free buses linking the campuses contribute to a strong sense of community among the schools. Lectures, films, concerts, and other events at all five campuses create an exciting and intellectually rich environment.

The Undergraduate Advising and Academic Support Center (UAASC) supports various programs that are designed to meet diverse student needs, including the bachelor's degree with an individual concentration, English as a second language, learning support services, premajor advising services, and psychological counseling, assessment, and testing services. The Career Network offers comprehensive career planning and placement services.

Student Body Undergraduate enrollment is 51 percent women. The ethnic distribution is 8 percent Asian, 5 percent black, 4 percent Hispanic, and 83 percent white. There are 348 international students. Fifty-nine percent of the students live on campus. Sixty-eight percent of degree-seeking students receive financial aid. There are twenty-one fraternities and twelve sororities.

Faculty Of the 1,276 instructional faculty members, 1,151 are full-time; 94 percent hold terminal degrees. The student-faculty ratio is 18.1:1.

Key Facilities The library houses 3 million volumes. Computer facilities are available in the Graduate Research Center, the W.E.B. DuBois Library, selected dormitories, and numerous department-supervised computer rooms. Facilities are available to all students for $30 per semester. If students bring their own computers, Internet and e-mail access is available in all dorm rooms; all dorm rooms have dedicated Ethernet hook-ups allowing access that is 100 times faster than the highest modem speed. Computers are also available at the University Store at a student discount.

Honorary Societies Phi Kappa Phi, Golden Key, Mortar Board, Phi Beta Kappa, Alana, and Alpha Lambda Delta

Athletics Amherst is a member of NCAA Division I and the Atlantic 10 Conference. It offers twenty-nine intercollegiate sports and fourteen intramural sports programs. Outdoor facilities include 120 acres of multipurpose fields and twenty-two tennis courts. In addition, the University has an ice rink, three swimming pools, five handball/squash courts, seven racquetball courts, weight rooms, fitness centers, basketball/volleyball/badminton courts, and indoor/outdoor tracks.

Study Abroad The University has ninety international exchanges with more than forty countries. The International Programs Office (IPO) offers assistance to students interested in arranging a semester or year abroad. IPO keeps on file, by country and subject/major, information on programs available at other institutions. Students are encouraged to meet with a specific resource person regarding the program of interest. In addition, they are encouraged to meet with their faculty adviser to be sure the selected study-abroad program fits well with the curriculum requirements of their individual major. The study-abroad programs are designed to provide international study at a cost comparable to that of the University. Any financial aid, scholarships, or loans that a student receives to attend the University apply while the student participates in an approved study-abroad program.

Support Services Disability Services works to provide accommodations to qualified disabled students, ensuring that the University offers an environment that is accessible and equitable to all students.

Job Opportunities The Office of Financial Aid Services provides current listings of on- and off-campus temporary, part-time, and seasonal job opportunities that can be used to defray educational costs. In addition, the University offers a need-based Federal Work-Study program that provides part-time employment to students in a variety of on-campus departments and off-campus agencies.

Tuition: $1714 for state residents, $9937 for nonresidents, per year (2001–02)

Room and Board: $5115

Mandatory Fees: $3993 minimum

Contact: Dean: Dr. Linda L. Slakey, 504 Goodell Building, 140 Hicks Way, Amherst, Massachusetts 01003-9272; Telephone: 413-545-2483; Fax: 413-545-4469; E-mail: comcol@comcol.umass.edu; Web site: http://www.comcol.umass.edu

University of Massachusetts Boston

4 Pu M Sc Tr AA FA

▼ University Honors Program

The University Honors Program has been designated a Commonwealth Honors Program within the state system. It is open to students from the Colleges of Arts and Sciences, Nursing, and Management.

The Honors Program offers, in part, an accelerated, enhanced, and more rigorous version of the campus's general education program. At its heart is an array of 100- and 200-level courses, of which students select five. These courses—unique to the program and not honors sections of standard courses—are multidisciplinary and involve special enrichments, such as assignments at Boston's Museum of Fine Arts, computerized experiments, and presentations by visiting scholars. Recent offerings include "Shapers of the 17th Century," "Imagining Mars," "Melancholia," and "The History of Eugenics." Honors students are also required to study math and foreign language and must meet a higher standard in these fields than students in general.

The emphasis at the advanced levels of the four-year program falls on independent projects and research. All honors students take a semester of Junior Colloquium, a unique course in the College that attempts to socialize them to the role of the researcher. Under a faculty leader and with the assistance of visiting scholars, the group explores a common topic while each student defines an individual research project. Recent topics include "Media and Cultural Change," "Green Chemistry," "Imagined Selves," and "Humor: Its Many Meanings." All program students are required to complete a senior-year thesis or project. Honors students are also urged to participate in the annual Conference on Undergraduate Research of the Massachusetts Public Higher Education System and in the National Conference on Undergraduate Research.

Since 1999, honors students have won two Fulbright fellowships and qualified as finalists and semifinalists for the Rhodes and Marshall scholarships.

Honors students enjoy priority registration and a lounge and seminar room that are equipped with computers and printers. New students are welcomed at special events: an Honors Orientation in the fall, which centers on a common reading, and a Family Night in the spring, which features a lecture by a faculty member.

The 25-year-old program currently enrolls 165 students.

Participation Requirements: A student who takes the full program completes 21 credits in honors sections, in addition to the requirements in math and language and the senior thesis. Transfer students and late-admitted students take a modified version of the program. Enrollment in honors classes is limited to 20 students; the Junior Colloquium is limited to 12. Students in the program must maintain a minimum 3.2 GPA. The program awards the Robert H. Spaethling Prize to the one or two students who complete the first two years of the program with the highest distinction. Successful completion of the entire program is recognized at the spring honors convocations and is recorded on the student's transcript.

Admission Process: Freshmen and new transfer students for fall term are selected mainly during the summer orientation periods. For spring term, these students are selected during the January orientation periods. Continuing students are selected during preregistration periods in November and April. The program chooses students according to ability, motivation, and excellence of preparation, as evidenced by high school and college records, test scores, and special accomplishments. A personal statement and an interview with the Director are required.

Scholarship Availability: The program awards ten scholarships each year. In addition, the campus offers thirty Chancellor's Scholarships and four Commonwealth Scholarships to incoming students each year; many of these full-tuition grants are awarded to members of the Honors Program. Continuing students with 30 graduation credits may apply for a variety of merit scholarships.

The Campus Context: The Boston campus of the University of Massachusetts was founded in 1964. To the original Liberal Arts College were later added four others: Management, Community and Public Service, Nursing, and Education. Degree programs include the B.A. and B.S., with sixty-one major programs and sixty-five minors, concentrations, and undergraduate certificate programs; twenty-five programs and six additional graduate certificates leading to the M.A.; and nine Ph.D. programs.

Among the special facilities is WUMB-FM, a public radio station staffed in part by students. A new campus center opened in 2001. The Office of Student Life and the Student Senate sponsor nearly fifty organizations as well as the student newspaper, *The Mass Media;* the literary magazine, *The Watermark;* the Harbor Art Gallery; and the Wit's End Cafe.

The campus is situated 3 miles from downtown Boston on a peninsula reaching into Boston Harbor. It shares this site with the John F. Kennedy Presidential Library and the Massachusetts State Archives and Museum. Several works by major sculptors have been installed on the campus under the "Arts on the Point" Project. The University is conveniently located at an exit of the main North-South Expressway and free shuttle buses connect it to the local subway stop. City buses also serve the campus. UMass-Boston is a commuter campus; its Housing Referral Service assists students in finding accommodations and roommates in Boston and its environs.

Student Body Undergraduate enrollment is approximately 9,500. The median age of full-time students is 24; 43.4 percent are men, 56.6 percent women. Thirty-five percent of the students are members of ethnic minorities; the distribution is .5 percent Native American, 12.2 percent Asian American, 14.7 percent African American, 6.7 percent Hispanic, and 1 percent Cape Verdean. International students make up 7.5 percent of the undergraduate population.

Faculty The faculty members include winners of more than forty National Science Foundation grants, thirty-five Fulbright Fellowships, sixteen fellowships from the National Endowment for the Humanities and five from the National Endowment for the Arts, five Ford Foundation Fellowships, eight Guggenheim Fellowships, a special merit grant from the National Institutes of Health, and a Pulitzer Prize. Of the 835 faculty members, 464 are full-time and 89 percent of the full-time faculty members hold terminal degrees. The student-faculty ratio is 16:1.

Key Facilities The Healey Library holds more than 550,000 volumes and subscribes to more than 3,000 periodicals. The University's membership in several library consortia gives students access to other major collections in the Boston area. Computing Services operates three Macintosh labs, five PC labs, and one VAZ lab. In addition to serving as a resource used by students who are learning computer languages, various labs offer World Wide Web access, word processing, and accounting software. All labs are staffed by computer consultants.

Honorary Societies Golden Key, National Honor Society, and Alpha Lambda Delta Freshman Honor Society

Athletics The Clark Athletic Center includes a gymnasium, skating rink, and six-lane, T-shaped pool. A new Fitness Center is fully equipped, and special rooms on campus accommodate dance, wrestling, and other contact sports. Other facilities include an eight-lane, 400-meter track, eight tennis courts, twenty-four sailboats, and football, soccer, and softball fields. There are eighteen varsity teams. UMass-Boston participates in Division II in hockey and Division III in other competitive sports.

Study Abroad There are diverse study abroad opportunities. The University has exchange agreements with nearly forty international universities. Special programs include a winter session program in Cuernavaca and a summer program in Ireland.

Support Services The Lillian Semper Ross Center provides a full range of services to students with physical, emotional, and learning disabilities, including an Adaptive Computer Laboratory. The campus is fully accessible to disabled students.

Job Opportunities The Student Employment Office assists students with placement in work-study and non-work-study positions on campus. The office also maintains listings of nearby off-campus companies and organizations interested in employing students.

Tuition: $1714 for state residents, $9758 for nonresidents, per year (2001–02)

Mandatory Fees: $2585

Contact: Director: Dr. Monica McAlpine, Healey Library, 100 Morrissey Boulevard, Boston, Massachusetts 02125-3393; Telephone: 617-287-5520; Fax: 617-287-3858; E-mail: monica.mcalpine@umb.edu

University of Massachusetts Dartmouth

4 Pu G M Tr

▼ University Honors Program

The University Honors Program reflects the goals of an institution that places emphasis on the quality of its undergraduate teaching, dedicates itself to cultivating excellence across the board, and aspires to make enrichment opportunities available to all its students. It does so by offering opportunities for outstanding and highly motivated students to participate in challenging courses and programs. It promotes close interactions between talented faculty members and students in all disciplines, encourages and supports student growth and development through independent and collaborative thinking and research, fosters a public conscience and service, and provides the support and atmosphere for full development of student potential. A writing

Interpreting the symbols: **2**=two-year college, **4**=four-year college; **Pu**=public or state college, **Pr**=private college; **G**=general honors program; **D**=departmental honors program; **S**=small program (fewer than 100 students), **M**=midsize program (100 to 500 students), **L**=large program (more than 500 students); **Sc**=scholarships available in honors program; **Tr**=transfer students accepted into honors program; **HBC**=historically black college; **AA**=academic advisors; **GA**=graduate advisors; **FA**=fellowship advisors.

fellows program, open by nomination of University faculty members or the director, offers up to 9 credit hours to students who study and conduct research in writing pedagogy, collaborative learning, and peer tutoring and who apply their learning by serving as writing fellows in advanced undergraduate courses across the curriculum.

Limited-enrollment honors courses encourage active student participation in learning and close faculty-student interaction. These courses offer enrichment features, such as distance learning settings that allow interaction among students on different campuses, access to specially designed information sources and databases, individualized lab experiments, field trips, attendance at performances and social events, and research support. Committed faculty members in a variety of fields also foster honors students' growth by agreeing to sponsor honors contracts, student research, creative and public service projects, and participation in professional conferences and by encouraging students to seek challenges within their majors (such as undergraduate TA programs, scholarships, and summer research opportunities).

In addition to a core academic program, the program sponsors a colloquium series and the Margaret Mullaney Panos honors essay contest, an annual honors convocation, and honors undergraduate research grants. Honors students enjoy priority registration, field trips, special library privileges during the senior thesis/project year, and public recognition. The Honors Program offers housing in the Honors Residence area, where the program maintains a satellite office. The University of Massachusetts Dartmouth (UMD) program participates in an annual statewide undergraduate research conference that is sponsored by the Massachusetts public system of higher education and the Commonwealth College at the University of Massachusetts Amherst.

The program is 18 years old and currently enrolls approximately 200 students.

Participation Requirements: The four-year academic honors program requires completion of 30 credits in honors courses. In fulfilling program requirements, students may combine honors courses and contracts with credits from special honors semesters, summer programs, and study abroad. Courses taken outside the major (18 credits) generally fulfill distribution and/or general education requirements. Among their honors credits, students must complete a multidisciplinary research seminar and a 3- to 6-credit capstone project (a thesis or a creative or public service project). A GPA of at least 3.2 is required for continuation in the program; successful completion is recognized at the annual University-wide Honors Convocation and at commencement and on the official transcript and diploma.

Admission Process: Entering first-year students receive invitations to join the program based on high school grades and rank and performance on standardized tests (SAT I). Recommendations of high school teachers and guidance counselors are also considered. Both UMD students and transfer students with a GPA of 3.2 or higher are accepted into the program as long as they have a reasonable possibility of completing it. Honors credits earned at other schools in the Massachusetts system of public higher education and from other four-year institutions are accepted in fulfillment of program requirements as appropriate.

Scholarship Availability: Recipients of UMass System Commonwealth Scholarships are expected to participate in the honors programs on their respective campuses. These scholarships are awarded to entering freshmen who have a combined SAT I score of at least 1400 and a top 5 percent ranking in their high school graduating classes (or a high school GPA of at least 3.85). As many as eight of these scholarships have been awarded to members of an entering class at UMass Dartmouth. Many University Scholarship winners and recipients of Chancellor's Merit Scholarships receive invitations and participate in the University Honors Program. The Director sits on the University's Merit Scholarship Committee, which awards merit scholarships to upperclass students.

The Campus Context: The University of Massachusetts Dartmouth is located in rural southeastern Massachusetts on a 710-acre campus that is 10 miles from the ocean and less than 1 hour from Cape Cod and Boston, Massachusetts, and Providence, Rhode Island. The architecturally innovative campus, designed by Paul Rudolph, opened in 1966. A four-year, comprehensive public university, UMass Dartmouth is one of four undergraduate institutions in the University of Massachusetts system. Special or distinguishing campus facilities include a Center for Marine Science and Technology, located on the New Bedford harbor, and fine arts and artisanry facilities (ceramics, fiber arts, wood, jewelry/metals, printmaking, and sculpture studios) located in University buildings in downtown New Bedford. UMass Dartmouth offers undergraduate and graduate degrees through five colleges: Arts and Sciences, Business and Industry, Engineering, Nursing, and Visual and Performing Arts. The University offers more than forty undergraduate majors, including B.A., B.S., and B.F.A. degrees; eighteen master's degree programs (M.A., M.S., M.F.A., M.A.E., M.B.A., and M.A.T.); and two Ph.D. programs—one in chemistry (joint program with UMass Lowell) and one in electrical engineering.

Campus services include a University Advising Center; premedical, prelaw, and pre-M.B.A. advising; an Academic Resource Center, which offers peer tutoring in three learning centers; a Counseling Center; a Career Resource Office; Health Services; a Woman's Resource Center; and a Child Care Center.

Student Body Undergraduate enrollment was 5,928 in fall 2001; 52 percent of the undergraduate students are women. The ethnic distribution among undergraduates was 3 percent Cape Verdean, 2.9 percent African American, .8 percent American Indian/Alaskan Native, 2.6 percent Asian/Pacific Islander, and 2.1 percent Hispanic; 1.2 percent of the undergraduates were international students. About 40 percent of the students reside on campus in dormitories (first- and second-year students) or town-house apartments (juniors and seniors). Sixty-five percent of undergraduate students receive financial aid. The campus has three fraternities and two sororities.

Faculty The number of full-time instructional faculty members is 358. Eighty-seven percent of the faculty members have terminal degrees. The student-faculty ratio is 14:1.

Key Facilities The University Library houses more than 450,000 books, 18,000 nonprint resources, and 460,000 government documents; it subscribes to more than 2,900 periodicals. The library provides one-on-one instruction with student interns and individualized research assistance from professional librarians. UMass Dartmouth is a member of the Boston Library Consortium, an association of major college and research libraries in Massachusetts and Rhode Island. There are four general-access computer labs, four computer classrooms, and two distance learning facilities. Additional computer labs, such as the first-year English lab, the language lab, and the engineering impulse program labs, are located in departments and colleges. All dormitory rooms are wired to provide Ethernet service, which allows access to e-mail, the library, CyberEd, distance learning, and the Internet.

Athletics UMass Dartmouth is a member of NCAA Division III; teams compete in the Eastern College Athletic Conference (ECAC), the Little East Conference, and various other sport-specific conferences. Intercollegiate teams for men include baseball, basketball, cross-country, football, golf, ice hockey, lacrosse, soccer, swimming and diving, tennis, and track and field (indoor and outdoor). Women's teams include basketball, cheerleading, cross-country, equestrian, field hockey, lacrosse, soccer, softball, swimming and diving, track and field (indoor and outdoor), and volleyball. Athletic facilities include the Tripp Athletic Center, with swimming and diving pools and a fitness center; a running track; a practice soccer field; softball fields; tennis courts; and intramural fields. The athletics department also offers an extensive intramural program and instructional programs in aerobics, jazz dancing, tennis, swimming, life saving, first aid, and CPR.

Study Abroad UMass Dartmouth has formal exchange agreements with Nottingham-Trent University (England), the University of Grenoble (France), Freiburg/Baden-Württemberg Universities (Germany), and Minho University (Portugal), as well as programs in the arts and textiles in Portugal, France, and Canada. The University also offers access to programs for study abroad in most countries throughout the world through a consortium of public higher education institutions in Massachusetts. Students may apply credits from study abroad, NCHC Honors semesters, and other U.S. summer and academic-year honors programs (in the U.S. or abroad) to their UMass Dartmouth honors program.

Support Services The Office of Disabled Student Services offers mobility assistance, reading assistance, note-taking, alternative testing, peer counseling, and advocacy and support.

Job Opportunities Numerous work-study positions are available on campus in offices, including departmental offices, the Honors Program, the library, the laboratories and learning centers, and administrative and student services offices. Resident assistants in campus housing receive annual compensation (worth approximately $5100) as follows: a single room, telephone installation and all local calls, a board allowance of $500 per semester, and $400 per semester applied to fees. A selected number of non-work-study positions are also available. Students have the opportunity to earn credit for experiential learning both on and off campus; some of these positions may be paid as well.

Tuition: $1417 for state residents, $8099 for nonresidents, per year

Room and Board: $5723 (double), $5884 (single), $3544 (town house without board), plus $244 for telephone installations

Mandatory Fees: $2726 for state residents, $4198 for nonresidents

Contact: Director: Dr. Louise Habicht, 285 Old Westport Road, North Dartmouth, Massachusetts 02747-2300; Telephone: 508-999-8277 or Ext. 8820 (Honors Office); Fax: 508-999-9235; E-mail: lhabicht@umassd.edu; Web site: http://www.umassd.edu/SpecialPrograms/Honors/

University of Massachusetts Lowell

4 Pu G S Tr AA

▼ Honors Program

The University of Massachusetts Lowell Honors Program is a University-wide, comprehensive enrichment program of undergraduate studies, including research as a basic component, for outstanding students in all majors. Although departmental honors programs have existed since the start of the 1970s, the consolidation into a full-fledged University Honors Program (which still allows purely departmental honors projects) was undertaken in 1995 with the establishment of a 24-member Honors Council under the aegis of the Provost.

The mission of the Honors Program is "to provide enriched academic opportunities to meet the educational needs of exceptionally talented students and to foster the pursuit of scholarly excellence in undergraduate higher education. By fostering interactions among outstanding, motivated students and outstanding, dedicated faculty, the Honors Program is directed toward the recruitment, development, guidance, retention and professional growth of gifted students in activities designed to enhance their critical, cognitive and creative potential."

Normally, all freshman honors students are placed in special sections of the College Writing two-semester course taught by the English department, and all sophomore honors students are enrolled in the two-semester Honors Colloquium conducted by the Honors Director. Over and above this, they are also free to take additional departmental courses, including core and general education courses, for honors credit as either designated honors courses or "Contract Honors" courses. Many of these are given in seminar format; thus honors students enjoy the benefits of small class size and individualized attention. Any student who attains a GPA of at least 3.5 after the first semester is eligible for initiation into the Freshman Honors Society, the Lowell Chapter of Alpha Lambda Delta.

In general, the program emphasizes personalized advising and guidance, encourages students to use the excellent library and multimedia facilities, and offers a wide range of special services, including an honors residence accommodation for students who wish to live on campus. For all participants, field trips, distinguished guest speakers, cultural events, and undergraduate research opportunities are central features of the honors experience. Trips, conferences, receptions, and informal pizza parties promote close contact with honors faculty members and with the Honors Council.

Among the students, there is a strong sense of community; study groups and peer counseling are encouraged as elements of daily life in the "Honors family." Honors students feature prominently in community service projects and are often approached specifically by local employers or institutions as exemplifying the best of the University's undergraduate scholar resources.

Participation Requirements: Students enrolled in the Honors Program in their freshman year must complete at least 24 credits of honors course work. Students admitted after the freshman year must complete at least 18 honors credits. All Honors Program credits must be completed at a satisfactory level with a grade of B or better. At least 3 of the total required credits must be obtained from satisfactory completion of an honors thesis or project entailing original research or scholarly activity. This is normally undertaken in one or both semesters of the senior year.

All students' academic transcripts show the honors courses taken by that student for honors credits, regardless of whether the above requirements have been met. Students who graduate with a cumulative GPA of at least 3.25 and the requisite number of honors credits will, in addition to the conventional baccalaureate degree (which may be awarded, where appropriate, at the cum laude, magna cum laude, or summa cum laude level) in their major discipline, have an Honors Diploma conferred upon them at Commencement.

Admission Process: To be eligible for admission to the Honors Program, applicants must have achieved a score of at least 1200 combined on the SAT I scale or at least 26 on the ACT; and/or have graduated in the top 15 percent of their high school class; and/or must submit at least two detailed letters of recommendation for honors work from principals, teachers, or guidance counselors. Transfer students must have an overall cumulative GPA of at least 3.25 from an acceptable accredited academic institution of higher learning.

Scholarship Availability: Membership in the Honors Program does not entail any additional fees. On the contrary, many of the available Commonwealth of Massachusetts or University scholarships (as well as those from business, industry, and private donations) are awarded to Honors scholars.

The Campus Context: The University of Massachusetts Lowell was constituted in 1991 as one of the five campuses comprising the

Interpreting the symbols: **2**=two-year college, **4**=four-year college; **Pu**=public or state college, **Pr**=private college; **G**=general honors program; **D**=departmental honors program; **S**=small program (fewer than 100 students), **M**=midsize program (100 to 500 students), **L**=large program (more than 500 students); **Sc**=scholarships available in honors program; **Tr**=transfer students accepted into honors program; **HBC**=historically black college; **AA**=academic advisors; **GA**=graduate advisors; **FA**=fellowship advisors.

UMass system (along with Amherst, Boston, Dartmouth, and the Medical School at Worcester). The campus is situated in the Merrimack Valley, approximately 25 miles northwest of Boston. Its antecedent institutions of higher learning were Lowell State College and Lowell Technological Institute, established respectively in 1894 and 1895. Their merger in 1973 marked the formation of the University of Lowell, conferring baccalaureate and higher degrees. The Lowell campus itself is made up of three campuses (North, South, and West Campus), together with ancillary facilities at, for example, the Wannalancit Mill in central Lowell. Special facilities on campus include Centers for Learning (on the North and South Campus), an Adaptive Computing Laboratory, and a Counseling Center.

At present, the Lowell campus is comprised of four undergraduate colleges, Arts and Sciences, Engineering, Health Professions, and Management, which offer courses at the bachelor's, master's, and doctoral levels, as well as one college, Education, which offers graduate degrees only. There are twenty-nine bachelor's degree programs and ten Bachelor in Continuing Education programs available on the Lowell campus.

Student Body The undergraduate population is composed of 6,000 full-time day students and 4,000 continuing education students. Fifty-seven percent are men and 43 percent are women. The ethnic distribution of students is 62 percent white, 8.3 percent Asian, 3.5 percent Hispanic, 2 percent black, and 0.1 percent Native American, with an additional 21 percent unknown. The 163 international students make up 2.7 percent of the population. Eighty-five percent of the students are from in state, and 15 percent are from out of state. Thirty-three percent live on campus, and 67 percent are commuters. Although there are no fraternities or sororities recognized by the University, at least two have been independently organized.

Faculty There are 405 full-time and 155 part-time faculty members.

Key Facilities The campus has two libraries with an operating budget of approximately $2.7 million. Computer facilities include more than fourteen locations on the North Campus and seven on the South Campus that offer extensive opportunities for computation, word processing, spreadsheets, graphic design, multimedia, tutorials, computer-assisted design, e-mail, and network processing, The libraries and dormitories house some computer facilities and an effort is currently under way to create a separate, special facility for honors students.

Athletics A broad-based program of athletic and recreational opportunities is fostered by the University to promote the general health, welfare, and development of all participants. The Recreational Sports Office provides a comprehensive program for the entire community, including intramural sports, informal recreation, sports clubs, and instructional programs. There are more than thirty intramural sports offered in individual and team formats in a variety of lifetime/leisure sports such as tennis, badminton, and racquetball.

Team sports include soccer, volleyball, basketball, and ice hockey. Sports clubs include bowling, dance, equestrian, cheerleading, karate, lacrosse, outing, rugby, volleyball, skiing, shooting, and swimming. The Department of Athletics currently offers a program of twenty varsity sports. The school is a member of the NCAA and competes primarily at the Division II level (ice hockey is Division I). A gymnasium (including Nautilus facilities and a 25-yard, six-lane swimming pool, together with a wrestling/aerobics room and squash, basketball, volleyball, and racquetball courts) is on the North Campus, adjacent to athletic fields, tennis courts, and a running path. The South Campus also has extensive facilities, and the Tsongas Arena offers ice hockey and recreational ice skating.

Study Abroad Study-abroad opportunities are available to those undergraduate students in their sophomore or later years who have a cumulative GPA of 2.5 or better and faculty recommendations. Through the coordinator of the Study Abroad Office, students can find programs in twenty-two countries, with financial aid if needed.

Support Services The Office of Disability Services offers extensive assistance, counseling, and coordination facilities for disabled students. The following list gives an indication of the scope of such services: adaptations, classroom procedures, housing, individual accommodations, interpreters, note-taking, parking/transportation, personal care attendants, preferential registration, readers/aides/scribes, specialized equipment, adaptive technologies, oral exams, taped books, the Adaptive Computing Lab, the American Sign Language Club, enlarged print literature, and Braille.

Job Opportunities Work-study opportunities for qualified students are manifold and encouraged.

Tuition: $4179 for state residents, $11,816 for nonresidents, per year

Room and Board: $5215

Mandatory Fees: $76

Contact: Director: Dr. Stephen Pennell, University of Massachusetts Lowell, 1 University Avenue, Lowell, Massachusetts 01854-2881; Telephone: 978-934-2798; Web site: http://www.uml.edu/honors

The University of Memphis

4 Pu G D L Tr

▼ University Honors Program

The University of Memphis's University Honors Program, founded in 1975, provides exceptional educational opportunities for highly motivated and able students. The program enables students to take advantage of the more intimate learning environment offered by small classes. Honors faculty members promote active learning and provide excellent teaching, including individualized support and attention.

The program offers special curricular options and the opportunity to earn honors distinction. Classes within the program span the entire range of the University. A general education curriculum is available for freshmen and sophomores, while juniors and seniors may pursue interdisciplinary or departmental honors or may even design their own honors curriculum.

Lower-division students are expected to pursue the Honors Certificate, which is awarded to any honors student who completes a minimum of 12 hours of honors course work (usually general education courses) with a grade of A or B and the 1-credit-hour Honors Forum. Honors sections at the lower-division level are academically challenging, and efforts are made to keep their size considerably smaller than regular sections.

Upper-division students may choose from three tracks leading to graduation with honors. Departmental, Interdisciplinary Liberal Arts, or Individualized Thematic Honors are conferred upon students at graduation who attain overall GPAs of 3.25 or higher and who complete the program requirements. Students also have the opportunity to earn special transcript designations, such as With University Honors or Undergraduate Research Scholar, by completing appropriate program requirements.

The extensive program combines out-of-classroom experiences, such as cultural events or discussions with visiting scholars, with an active social environment in which to meet other honors students, thereby creating an honors community atmosphere. Honors students are expected to participate in community service projects while in the program.

Admission Process: Freshman applicants must complete an Honors Program application and submit an essay and letter of recommendation, have a high school GPA of 3.5 or higher, and have a composite score of 27 or higher on the ACT or 1200 or higher on the SAT I. Provisional admission may be possible for those who do not meet both the high school GPA and the standardized test score criteria. Transfer and continuing students must complete the Honors Program application, submit an essay and letter of recommendation, and have a college GPA of 3.0 or higher for freshmen and sophomores or 3.25 or higher for juniors and seniors. Provisional admission may be possible for those who do not meet the required grade point average.

Scholarship Availability: The University of Memphis provides more than $4 million in scholarships to high-ability students. Many students who receive scholarships are members of the University Honors Program.

The Campus Context: Located on a beautifully landscaped campus in a quiet residential area, the University of Memphis is the largest institution in the Tennessee Board of Regents system. Since its founding in 1912, the University of Memphis has evolved into a distinguished urban university with nationally recognized academic, research, and athletic programs. The University's six colleges offer baccalaureate degrees in fifty-four majors and seventy-two concentrations, master's degrees in forty-five subjects, doctoral degrees in eighteen disciplines, the Juris Doctor (law), and a specialist degree in education.

Student Body A total enrollment of about 20,000 students includes graduate students, law students, and almost 16,000 undergraduates. Approximately 2,500 students live on campus. The student population represents every state and seventy-four other countries. Approximately 40 percent of students are between ages 18 and 22, with students who are members of minority groups accounting for 35 percent of the total enrollment. Fifty-eight percent of the students are women.

Faculty The more than 1,000 full-time faculty members provide a student-faculty ratio of 20:1; 80 percent of the faculty members have doctorates or other terminal degrees.

Honorary Societies Phi Eta Sigma, Phi Kappa Phi, Golden Key, and Mortar Board

Athletics The University of Memphis sponsors teams representing the University in nine intercollegiate sports for men and seven intercollegiate sports for women. The University of Memphis is a member of the National Collegiate Athletic Association (NCAA) Division I-A and the Conference USA, formed in 1995–96.

Study Abroad The University of Memphis offers a British Studies Program each summer in London, England. The University is also a member of the International Student Exchange Program and has sent students to universities in Spain, Argentina, and Canada. Scholarships are available for both programs. The University of Memphis is a member of the National Student Exchange Program, with students participating in domestic exchange opportunities at 160 schools.

Support Services Student Disability Services provides information, guidance, and specialized support services that enable students with disabilities to take full advantage of the educational opportunities at the University. Services include pre-enrollment planning, early registration, coordination of academic accommodations with faculty members, alternative testing service, campus shuttle service, and coordination of adapted campus housing.

Job Opportunities Students are offered a range of work opportunities on campus, including assistantships and work-study.

Tuition: $2562 for state residents, $7434 for nonresidents, per year (1998–99)

Mandatory Fees: $68

Contact: Director, University Honors Program, 404 Jones Hall, University of Memphis, Memphis, Tennessee 38152; Telephone: 901-678-2690; Fax: 901-678-5367; Web site: http://www.people.memphis.edu/~wwwhonors

UNIVERSITY OF MIAMI

4 Pr G L Tr

▼ Honors Program

In 1957, the faculty of the University of Miami (UM) established the General Honors Program to provide an academically challenging course of study for outstanding students. The program was later expanded by the addition of departmental honors. Students who satisfactorily complete the requirements for general and/or departmental honors are graduated with General Honors and/or Departmental Honors; the award is noted on the graduate's diploma and official transcript.

The program now offers approximately 200 courses and sections each semester at the introductory through advanced levels, in a wide variety of fields, in all colleges and schools of the University. In general, honors courses are small classes taught as seminars with emphasis on interactive learning and discussion.

Invitations to General Honors are extended to approximately 10 percent of the entering freshman class on the basis of their outstanding scholastic achievement in high school and their high scores on college entrance examinations. A student of any undergraduate school or college is eligible for consideration as a member of the Honors Program. The program currently enrolls 1,500 students.

Participation Requirements: To remain in the Honors Program, a student must maintain an overall academic average of 3.3 and complete at least two honors courses per academic year. To graduate with General Honors, a student must complete at least 24 credits in General Honors courses and have an overall GPA of 3.3. Twelve of the 24 credits must be in courses at the 200 level or above. No more than 12 credits in the student's major may be counted toward the 24 credits in General Honors.

Admission Process: Freshmen and sophomores may be admitted to the Honors Program if they have achieved a 3.3 or higher cumulative GPA in their college courses and have earned no more than 60 credits. Transfer students may apply if they have a 3.3 or higher cumulative GPA and have earned no more than 60 credits toward graduation. Inquiries should be made directly to the Honors Program office. All applicants should note that admission to the University of Miami must precede admission to the Honors Program.

Students may withdraw from the program at any time at their discretion. They should notify the Honors Office in writing of their intention to withdraw. Honors students' GPA and general performance are reviewed each academic year. Any student who fails to maintain the required cumulative GPA or fails to take the required number of honors credits will be excused from the program. Student may re-enter the program when their GPA has been raised to a 3.3; however, students must inform the Honors Office of the improved average and of their interest in re-entering the program.

The Campus Context: The University of Miami has four campuses: Coral Gables, Medical, Rosenstiel, and South Campuses. They incorporate 161 University-owned buildings totaling approximately 5.2 million square feet on more than 400 acres of land. The University offers 180 bachelor's programs, 125 master's programs, and sixty doctoral programs.

Student Body Undergraduate enrollment is 9,020 (43 percent men). The ethnic distribution is 53 percent white, 29 percent Hispanic, 6 percent Asian, and 11 percent black. International students constitute 8 percent of degree undergraduates. Thirty-eight percent of the students are residents, 62 percent commuters.

Interpreting the symbols: **2**=two-year college, **4**=four-year college; **Pu**=public or state college, **Pr**=private college; **G**=general honors program; **D**=departmental honors program; **S**=small program (fewer than 100 students), **M**=midsize program (100 to 500 students), **L**=large program (more than 500 students); **Sc**=scholarships available in honors program; **Tr**=transfer students accepted into honors program; **HBC**=historically black college; **AA**=academic advisors; **GA**=graduate advisors; **FA**=fellowship advisors.

Seventy-five percent to 80 percent of the students receive financial aid (University and federal funds). There are fifteen fraternities on campus.

Faculty Faculty members total 2,466 (2,044 full-time), 96 percent with terminal degrees. The student-faculty ratio is approximately 13:1.

Key Facilities The library houses more than 2.2 million UM publications and is a Federal Government Documents Depository. The Ungar Computing Center (central facility) is equipped with an IBM 9672-RB6 Enterprise Server, an IBM AS/400-820, an IBM RS/6000-580, an IBM RS/6000-F20, an IBM AS/400-B20, a DEC VMS cluster with two DEC 4100 systems, a DEC 4100, and a DEC 1000A. More than sixty computer labs are located in the residential colleges, libraries, schools, and colleges. The University has a campus network with a gateway to national and international networks, Internet, and Internet2. The University has deployed a wireless network on all three main campuses that complements its extensive wired network.

Honorary Societies UM has more than fifty academic honor societies, including Phi Beta Kappa.

Athletics The Hurricanes compete in Division I of the NCAA with eight men's and ten women's sports. In 1991, UM became a member of the Big East Conference. Men's competition includes baseball, basketball, cross-country, football, swimming and diving, tennis, indoor track and field, and track and field. Women's competition includes basketball, crew, cross-country, golf, soccer, swimming and diving, tennis, track and field, and volleyball.

Study Abroad The University of Miami Study Abroad Program offers an extensive array of overseas programs in more than twenty-one countries. Half of the programs offer course work taught in English. Many departments at UM encourage study abroad options as part of their basic curriculum. Studying abroad is open to sophomores, juniors, and seniors for a semester, a full academic year, or during the summer. Full University credit is awarded for approved courses.

Support Services The Office of Student Disability Services (ODS) coordinates auxiliary aids and services for students with disabilities. ODS receives and verifies documentation of disabilities and serves as a clearing house for information on disability-related matters. Information and services are available to enrolled students, their parents or sponsors, and faculty and staff members.

Job Opportunities Through the Federal Work-Study Program, the University offers on-campus jobs to undergraduate students demonstrating financial need.

Tuition: $23,228 per year (2001–02)

Room and Board: $7948

Mandatory Fees: $419

Contact: Director: Dr. Benjamin D. Webb, P.O. Box 248106, Coral Gables, Florida 33124-5595; Telephone: 305-284-5384; Fax: 305-284-5241; E-mail: bwebb@miami.edu; Web site: www.miami.edu/honors-program/

University of Michigan–Flint

4 Pu G S Sc Tr

▼ University Honors Scholar Program

Founded in 1979, the University of Michigan–Flint Honors Scholar Program offers students of superior ability and demonstrated achievement an opportunity to broaden and enrich their undergraduate education. The program is open to students in all majors.

The program consists of four core courses at the freshman and sophomore levels that stress intensive reading, writing, and the development of papers for undergraduate conferences.

Five honors elections or independent study projects over the course of the four years provide additional enrichment and allow students the opportunity to work one-on-one with specialists in the field.

Unique to the honors program is an off-campus experience that is open to all students. Subsidized by a grant of $3000 to help cover expenses, students travel to another state or country to work with specialists in their field at a university campus, institution, or workplace during the summer of their junior year.

Off-campus study has proven to be a life-changing experience. Over the history of the program, more than 150 students have traveled to more than twenty countries for their off-campus experience. Projects have included chemical ecology: a new discovery about sea spiders off the coast of Tasmania (biology); Native American customs and literature, New Mexico (English and American studies); study of postwar nuclear weapons policies in Auckland, New Zealand (history); development of programmed artificial intelligence for a robot at Carnegie Mellon University (computer science); research in genetics at Australia National University in Sydney (chemistry); cancer research at the University of London Medical Laboratories in England (biology); internship with congressman Dale Kildee in Washington, D.C., for the study of the Endangered Species Act (political science); and science and communication studies at the Rothhamsted Institute in the United Kingdom (communication and biology).

Off-campus study culminates in an Honors Thesis, during which students develop a project based on or associated with the research, internship, or other academic experience completed while off campus.

In their senior year, an interdisciplinary senior seminar allows students to focus on a theme from the perspective of their discipline and to share their off-campus research and experiences.

Students also participate in museum visits and a fall trip to the Stratford Festival in Canada for the performance of a Shakespeare play. Over the past five years, more than 100 students have participated in undergraduate conferences by presenting refereed papers on a wide variety of subjects. The University has an active Student Honors Council, whose members participate in all aspects of the honors program.

Classes in the honors program are small. The program itself generally has from 55 to 65 members, encouraging a friendly and supportive atmosphere. The director knows all of the students personally, and the students get to know the professors in their major, especially their honors adviser, who guides them through their course of study. Numerous students continue these relationships for many years after graduation, attesting to the closeness of the academic and personal relationships formed in the program.

Participation Requirements: Students must be full-time and must maintain a GPA of 3.5 or higher in order to remain eligible for the program. Requirements include a foreign language component.

Admission Process: Students who have been accepted at the University of Michigan–Flint are eligible. At least a 3.5 GPA and a minimum ACT score of 26 are recommended for application to the program. Students fill out an application, and, after an initial screening, about 35 students are selected for interviews by faculty members and honors program students. Application deadlines for rolling admission are February 15, March 15, and April 15. Students who apply early have a better chance of being accepted into the program. Twenty-five students are admitted at the freshman level.

Transfer students are also accepted into the program for a special two-year junior-senior-level transfer program, which includes the off-campus study, senior seminar, and thesis.

Scholarship Availability: Students are eligible for a total of $6600 in scholarships over the course of four years. A tuition scholarship of $300 per semester is awarded during the freshman and sophomore years (tuition at the University of Michigan–Flint is under $2000 per semester). This aid rises to $600 per semester during the junior and senior years for students who remain in good standing. Students receive up to $3000 to cover their expenses for the off-campus study project, and a special endowed scholarship is available for junior and senior students. In addition, the University of Michigan–Flint offers numerous scholarships for students demonstrating a high level of achievement at the high school level.

The Campus Context: The University of Michigan–Flint, a branch Campus of the University of Michigan at Ann Arbor, is a fully accredited university that focuses on undergraduate education. The University has approximately 6,000 students. It has opportunities for a Bachelor of Science in Nursing, a professional doctorate in physical therapy, and a Master of Business Administration. The graduate program is relatively small.

The campus buildings are new (10 to 15 years old at most) and include a well-appointed library with full electronic links to the University of Michigan at Ann Arbor library, one of the largest university libraries in the United States. In addition to the Murchie Science Building and French Hall (humanities and social sciences), the University has a University Center for students, with very active student associations and student government, and a well-equipped recreation center that is free to all full-time students.

Tuition: $4100 per year for Michigan residents, $8200 per year for nonresidents (2002–03)

Room and Board: Varies. Students commute or find apartments in the vicinity of Flint.

Contact: Dr. Maureen Thum, Department of English, University of Michigan–Flint, Flint, Michigan 48502; Telephone: 810-762-2367; E-mail: mthum@umflint.edu (students should use Inquiry, Honors Program as the subject header to identify their request and to ensure prompt response); Web site: http://www.flint.umich.edu

University of Minnesota, Morris

4 Pu G S Tr

▼ Honors Degree Program

The Honors Degree Program of the University of Minnesota, Morris (UMM), is at the core of the University's mission as a public liberal arts college and inspires students to pursue learning for its own sake and to create their own interdisciplinary links between fields of study. Through its courses, mentorship program, participatory events, and individualized research projects, the Honors Program helps build a community of scholars working together in a friendly, supportive atmosphere. The program promotes world citizenship and involvement with communities beyond the University through study abroad and community-based research. Honors students are active in Campus of Difference, a nationally recognized student-faculty working group that studies and promotes diversity.

With a maximum enrollment of 20 students, honors sections allow greater access to faculty members inside and outside the classroom. Honors students complete four honors courses, including a capstone experience: a Senior Honors Project, Undergraduate Research Opportunities Project (UROP), or Morris Area Project (MAP). UROPs and MAPs include a stipend of $1000 and may be used to support research and travel out-of-state and overseas. Through undergraduate research, the Honors Degree Program allows motivated students to begin preparation for employment and postgraduate study. Many students present the results of their research at national conferences and publish their findings.

The program admits approximately 60 students per year and currently has an enrollment of around 100 students.

Participation Requirements: Students are required to complete four honors courses during their four years and participate in the mentoring program. They are encouraged to complete the honors section of First Year Seminar upon admission to the program. In the mentoring program, freshmen and sophomores work with upperclass mentors who meet with them regularly and critique reaction papers written about designated campus cultural events. In their final year, students complete an independent research project under the direction of a faculty sponsor.

To remain in the program, students must earn As in at least one half of their courses. Special recognition is given at commencement to students who complete the honors curriculum; official transcripts and diplomas bear the mention Honors.

Admission Process: High school students are invited to apply to the Honors Program on the basis of class rank and SAT I or ACT scores. The complete application, which includes an essay, must be submitted by August 20. Students may be admitted at the beginning of the second semester of their freshman year or by transfer during their sophomore year upon completion of the necessary requirements.

Scholarship Availability: Campuswide scholarships of different amounts, awarded through the Office of Admissions, are based on financial need and academic performance. Special scholarships and tuition reductions exist for students who are members of minority groups. Native American students are granted a tuition waiver. The Honors Degree Program does not offer scholarships and financial aid; however, most honors students are receipts of awards, such as the Presidential Scholarships that are automatically granted to all entering freshmen who graduate in the top 10 percent of their class.

The Campus Context: The University of Minnesota, Morris, is located in west-central Minnesota, approximately a 2½-hour drive from Minneapolis. It is the only liberal arts college in the Minnesota system, of which it has been called the "jewel in the crown" by successive chancellors for the excellence of its undergraduate education. Located in a rural community of 6,000, the college involves its students in town life through public performances in the arts and humanities, community-based research projects, and student tutoring and teaching in area elementary and high schools. Students find affordable living quarters on and off campus; a local coffeehouse is the focus of music, poetry readings, and other events. A large fleet of University vehicles and generous assistance to student organizations allow campus groups such as the Geology Club, French Club, History Club, Art Club, and Computer Science Club to travel to Alaska, Canada, California, Louisiana, and Washington, D.C. A new science facility opened in January 2000, housing classrooms, offices, and laboratories.

Student Body The enrollment is 60 percent women. The ethnic distribution is 84 percent white, 5.5 percent African American, 6.6 percent Native American, 2.7 percent Asian/Pacific Islander, and 1.2 percent Hispanic. Seventy-nine percent of students receive financial aid.

Faculty The total number of faculty members is 120, all of whom are full-time. Eighty-three percent have terminal degrees. The student-faculty ratio is 16:1.

Key Facilities The Briggs Library contains 328,141 volumes. A new Science and Math Complex, with state-of-the-art laboratories

Interpreting the symbols: **2**=two-year college, **4**=four-year college; **Pu**=public or state college, **Pr**=private college; **G**=general honors program; **D**=departmental honors program; **S**=small program (fewer than 100 students), **M**=midsize program (100 to 500 students), **L**=large program (more than 500 students); **Sc**=scholarships available in honors program; **Tr**=transfer students accepted into honors program; **HBC**=historically black college; **AA**=academic advisors; **GA**=graduate advisors; **FA**=fellowship advisors.

and teaching facilities, has just been completed. The Hasselmo Language Teaching Center, completed in 1998, holds twenty multimedia workstations, tapes, videocassettes, and CD-ROMs. All campus residence rooms are equipped with Ethernet computer connections; computer labs at several campus locations are open 24 hours a day for easy access to new Dell and Apple computers.

Athletics The Athletic Department fields men's Division II teams in football, basketball, baseball, track, wrestling, tennis, and golf and women's teams in basketball, track, wrestling, tennis, and golf. UMM has produced Olympic medal winners in wrestling, and its women's wrestling team is consistently highly ranked nationally. Most Morris students compete in the sport of their choice through the intramural sports program. Students may use the all-new Regional Fitness Center, with an indoor running track, weight rooms, swimming pools, a sauna, and racquetball and multipurpose courts.

Study Abroad UMM encourages all of its students to study, work, and teach abroad through its own English Language Teaching Abroad Program (ELTAP); summer programs in England, France, Italy; and Global Campus program at the Twin Cities campus. ELTAP students teach English in more than thirty countries while earning full credit. Expenses for a semester of the ELTAP program are roughly equivalent to costs for a semester of residency in Morris.

Support Services The Academic Assistance Center provides peer tutoring in all subjects and offers assistance to students with special learning needs.

Job Opportunities The Career Center sponsors numerous job fairs and assists students in obtaining job interviews and internships. Students who are work-study eligible may find part-time positions on campus. A limited number of Morris Area Internships (MAI) are available, which allow students to work in various administrative offices and departments on campus while earning wages.

Tuition: $5548

Room and Board: $4460

Mandatory Fees: $708

Contact: Director: Dr. Matthew Senior, 215 Community Services Building, University of Minnesota, Morris, Morris, Minnesota 56267; Telephone: 320-589-6464; Fax: 320-589-1661; E-mail: ummhonor@mrs.umn.edu; Web site: http://www.mrs.umn.edu/academic/honors/index.html

University of Minnesota, Twin Cities

4 Pu M Tr

▼ Honors Programs

Honors programs at the University of Minnesota are designed to give special recognition to the talents, achievements, and potential of talented and highly motivated students. Honors students enjoy the best of two worlds: the uncommon depth and breadth of study at one of the nation's finest public research universities plus the extra challenge, personal attention, and sense of community often associated with small, highly selective private colleges.

The College of Agricultural, Food, and Environmental Sciences; College of Biological Sciences; College of Human Ecology; College of Liberal Arts; Carlson School of Management; College of Natural Resources; and Institute of Technology admit freshmen to their honors programs. Programs vary, but all share a commitment to scholarship, academic excellence, and personalized learning. Opportunities include research apprenticeships, workshops, and colloquia with outstanding University scholar-teachers; special limited-enrollment courses and seminars; advanced-study opportunities, including internships and independent study; honors housing; study abroad; one-on-one honors advising by professional honors advisers, peer advisers, and honors faculty members; undergraduate teaching and research assistantships; retreats, field trips, and other informal group activities with other honors students and faculty members; social and cultural activities that promote friendship and community among honors students; and honors recognition at special events, culminating in graduation with honors.

Participation Requirements: Honors students who take at least three honors courses and maintain at least a 3.5 GPA during their first two years of study may earn the freshman-sophomore Honors Certificate, which is noted on their transcript. Upperclass students who take at least four more honors courses, maintain at least a 3.5 GPA in their advanced classes, and meet departmental honors requirements may graduate with an honors degree.

Admission Process: New freshmen are admitted by application in the year prior to their arrival on campus. Typically, these new freshmen are in the 90th percentile of their high school class and have a composite score of at least 28 on the ACT or 1260 (verbal and math combined) on the SAT I. The University's Office of Admissions publishes a booklet, *Academic Scholarships & Honors Programs,* which contains an application for all freshman scholarships and honors programs on the Twin Cities campus. Transfer students may apply directly to one of the college honors programs.

Scholarship Availability: Merit scholarships are available to students from the University, from colleges, and from departments. The University awards about $4 million in scholarships each year to incoming freshmen, and colleges and departments award several hundred thousand dollars a year in scholarships both to incoming and continuing students.

The Campus Context: The University of Minnesota, Twin Cities, founded in 1851, bridges both Minneapolis and St. Paul and is one of the largest campuses in the U.S. As a land-grant university, it is committed to teaching and learning, research and scholarship, and public service. Students can choose from 150 majors at the bachelor's degree level in virtually all areas of study, from accounting, aerospace engineering, American Indian studies, and architecture to sales and marketing management, soil science, theater arts, wildlife, and women's studies. Facilities include the University Recreation Center, the celebrated Weisman Art Museum, and the acoustically outstanding Ted Mann Concert Hall. New facilities for students for fall 2002 include the expanded and extensively remodeled student union, architecture building, and digital technology center library.

Student Body Undergraduate enrollment on the Twin Cities campus is approximately 27,000, equally divided between men and women. A magnet for international students, the University attracts more than 3,000 students representing 130 countries.

Faculty There are 2,275 tenured, full professors teaching in 373 fields of study, many of whom participate in the Undergraduate Research Opportunities Program or teach a freshman seminar reserved for 15 first-year students.

Key Facilities The University library system has more than 5 million volumes, with electronic access to libraries worldwide. With more than 20,000 computer workstations for student use throughout campus, each student has an Internet account with access to the World Wide Web.

Honorary Societies Phi Kappa Phi, Golden Key, Mortar Board, and Phi Beta Kappa

Athletics The twenty-three men's and women's teams are major players in Big Ten athletics. Intramural teams number more than 2,500 with another thirty sports clubs (such as Ultimate Disc or the Alpine Ski Club).

Study Abroad With more than 170 programs in eighty countries, the Global Campus is one of the nation's largest study-abroad departments. Honors students earn honors credit through study-abroad experiences.

Support Services The Disablity Services Center is a model for similar programs across the country and provides all of the services that allow students with disabilities to flourish academically.

Job Opportunities Because the campus is surrounded by a vibrant metropolitan area, opportunities for students to work are plentiful. With more than 16,000 jobs to choose from, many students work on campus to help pay for their expenses. College career services provide internship and community service opportunities as well as job placement services.

Tuition: $5282 minimum for state residents, $15,002 minimum for nonresidents, per year (2001–02)

Room and Board: $5382

Mandatory Fees: $734

Contact: Director: Professor Richard W. McCormick, 115 Johnston Hall, Minneapolis, Minnesota 55455; Telephone: 612-624-5522; Fax: 612-626-7314; E-mail: mccor001@umn.edu; Web site: http://cla.umn.edu//honors

THE UNIVERSITY OF MISSISSIPPI

4 Pu G M Sc Tr AA

▼ The McDonnell-Barksdale Honors College

The McDonnell-Barksdale Honors College offers an enriched program of study designed to stimulate the intellectual growth of undergraduate students from all majors while providing them with an entire honors college experience. Originating in 1953 as the Faulkner Scholars Program and existing as an honors program until fall 1997, the College was established through an endowment from two Ole Miss alumni: Netscape Corporation President James L. Barksdale and his wife, Sally McDonnell Barksdale, who made the largest private gift at that time to the University of Mississippi to fund this unique institution. Through an additional gift in 1999, they have provided even more opportunities for honors students. The Honors College brings together select students and distinguished faculty members in an atmosphere of exploration and inquiry.

The honors curriculum begins with four core courses that are taken in the freshman and sophomore years: the Honors Freshman Seminar, interdisciplinary courses divided into units such as "Self and Cosmos" and "Self and Society," and Honors Sophomore English. These courses develop students' critical reading and writing skills and introduce students to various worlds of literature. These courses, usually limited to 15 students, are in a seminar format. Students also take honors sections of departmental courses, which are taught by the University's most outstanding faculty members. The core and departmental courses usually work to fulfill general education requirements. In the junior and senior years, students complete a research project and senior thesis in their majors. A minimum of 29 hours of honors courses (which includes the research and thesis) are required to graduate as an honors student. Honors students also are required to perform community service and attend forums sponsored by various departments on the campus.

Honors College students benefit from small classes in which they can develop a camaraderie with other exceptional students and their professors, 24-hour access to computers in the Honors College computer lab, study-abroad and internship opportunities, honors floors in residence halls, early registration for classes, and special activities at the Honors College's building, which is located in the heart of the Oxford campus. In addition to housing four classrooms and the computer lab, the Honors College offers a living room, kitchen, and study rooms. A large deck behind the building and a courtyard in front offer different environments for class, study, or socializing.

Participation Requirements: To graduate from the Honors College, students must achieve a cumulative GPA of at least 3.5 by their senior year (freshmen must achieve a 3.2) and meet the minimum requirements for community service and the forum series. Students who take honors courses receive a special "H" designation on their transcripts for each course that is satisfactorily completed. All students who successfully fulfill all Honors College requirements graduate with special recognition and receive a special distinction on their transcripts.

Admission Process: The Honors College selects its students based on evidence of distinguished academic performance, significant achievement in scholastic and extracurricular activities, and the potential to make a substantial contribution to the University community throughout their college careers. Each incoming class is limited to 135 students, and, in general, the minimum requirements are at least a 28 ACT (1230 SAT I) score and a 3.5 minimum high school GPA. Students with less than a 28 ACT score may still apply.

Students in incoming classes have an average 31 ACT (1350 SAT I) score and high school GPA of 3.85. Each class has included, on average, 28 National Merit and National Achievement Semifinalists. Students entering the Honors College have had a history of involvement in extracurricular activities, such as student government, the creative and performing arts, academic competitions, athletics, and community service.

Transfer students may also apply for the junior-entry program. To enter as a junior, a student must have at least a 3.5 GPA and the permission of his or her department to do the research and thesis requirements. Junior-entry students also take one additional honors course and fulfill the community service and forum requirements.

Interested students should request an admission packet from the Honors College and submit it by February 1. Students should also submit the University application to the admissions office.

Scholarship Availability: The Honors College awards a total of fourteen scholarships annually, each providing $6000 a year, through three endowments. In addition, the University of Mississippi offers a number of scholarships to students of exceptional ability. The University also participates in a full range of federal and state financial aid programs. Financial aid is available to 80 percent of students through scholarships, grants, loans, and University funds.

The Campus Context: Known around the world as Ole Miss, the University of Mississippi is located in the beautiful and delightfully southern town of Oxford, Mississippi. There are several distinctive facilities on campus, including the Croft Institute for International Studies, the Mississippi Center for Supercomputing Research, the Research Institute for Pharmaceutical Sciences, the National Center for Physical Acoustics, the National Center for Natural Products, the National Food Service Management Institute, the Center for the Study of Southern Culture, and Rowan Oak (William Faulkner's home).

Ole Miss offers more than 100 majors and special programs for undergraduates in six academic divisions: College of Liberal Arts, School of Education, School of Accountancy, School of Business Administration, School of Engineering, and School of Pharmacy. There are seventy-nine bachelor's degree programs, forty-two master's degree programs, twenty-six doctoral programs, three specialist programs, and two first professional programs.

Student Body Founded in 1844, Ole Miss currently serves more than 10,000 undergraduate students. Of these students, 49 percent

Interpreting the symbols: **2**=two-year college, **4**=four-year college; **Pu**=public or state college, **Pr**=private college; **G**=general honors program; **D**=departmental honors program; **S**=small program (fewer than 100 students), **M**=midsize program (100 to 500 students), **L**=large program (more than 500 students); **Sc**=scholarships available in honors program; **Tr**=transfer students accepted into honors program; **HBC**=historically black college; **AA**=academic advisors; **GA**=graduate advisors; **FA**=fellowship advisors.

are men. The ethnic distribution of total undergraduates is 84 percent white, 12 percent black, 1 percent Asian/Pacific Islander, 1 percent Hispanic, and 2 percent non–U.S. citizen. The University has thirty-two nationally recognized social fraternities and sororities. With nearly 200 academic and special interest clubs and honoraries, almost every major field of study has its own professional society.

Faculty The University has 505 full-time faculty members of whom 460 are tenured or tenure-track; 84 percent have terminal degrees.

Key Facilities The John Davis Williams Library, which contains the main collections of books, periodicals, microforms, manuscripts, audiovisual materials, and maps for use by the University community, currently houses more than a million volumes. The University also has four branch libraries on campus: the Blues Archive, the Music Library, the Department of Chemistry Library, and the School of Pharmacy Library. Two autonomous libraries, the James O. Eastland Law Library and the Public Policy Research Center Library, complement the resources contained in the Williams Library and its branches.

The University Information Technology office offers public computing labs, e-mail accounts, space for creating Web pages, and personal computing support. Residence halls, academic and administrative buildings, and many fraternities and sororities are wired for direct network access. In fact, *Yahoo! Internet Life* has ranked the University of Mississippi as one of the 100 Most Wired Colleges in the country.

Athletics Ole Miss offers some of the best action in the Southeastern Conference, including football, basketball, tennis, baseball, track, softball, volleyball, soccer, and golf, which infuse the campus with excitement throughout the year. Intramural sports for both men and women allow students to grow in mind, spirit, and body.

Study Abroad Ole Miss offers study-abroad opportunities to qualified students during the academic year and the summer. Students of all classifications can choose from more than forty countries. Many of the programs are exchange programs that charge the school tuition and apply the student's school scholarships to the cost. Honors students are also eligible to receive study-abroad stipends from the Honors College.

Support Services The University has made numerous changes in the physical environment of the campus to accommodate students with physical disabilities. It continues to work with students on an individual basis to provide reasonable accommodations within the campus environment. The Honors College building is handicapped-accessible.

Job Opportunities Students are offered a range of work opportunities on and off campus, including assistantships and work-study.

Tuition and Fees: $3153.50 for state residents, $6517.50 for nonresidents, per year (2001–02)

Contact: McDonnell-Barksdale Honors College, P.O. Box 1848, University of Mississippi, University, Mississippi 38677; Telephone: 662-915-7294; Fax: 662-915-7739; E-mail: honors@olemiss.edu; Web site: http://www.honors.olemiss.edu

UNIVERSITY OF MISSOURI–COLUMBIA

4 Pu G L Tr AA FA

▼ Honors College

The University of Missouri–Columbia (MU) Honors College is a campuswide program designed to provide talented students with appropriate academic challenges and special opportunities. The Honors College does not offer academic degrees; rather, it serves outstanding students from all of MU's undergraduate colleges by providing a more personalized education and individual attention and support. Honors courses are of two types: honors sections of regularly offered courses and special honors colloquia that are limited to 20 honors students (e.g., Medical Ethics, Theories of Creativity, and Paradigms and Paradoxes: A Brief History of Science).

The academic centerpiece of the Honors College, the four-semester Humanities Sequence, provides an interdisciplinary introduction to Western culture and intellectual history from ancient to contemporary times. A staff of outstanding instructors combines lectures and small discussion groups in this study of the artistic, literary, religious, and philosophical expressions of Western civilization. The Humanities Sequence follows a great books tradition. Students are asked to read original works, in translation, from Plato to Sartre in philosophy and from Homer to Toni Morrison in literature. The Humanities Sequence includes the following courses: the Ancient World, the Middle Ages and the Renaissance, the Early Modern World, and the Modern Era.

The Honors College has recently introduced a Social Science Sequence and a Science Sequence for nonscience majors. As companions to the Humanities Sequence, Asian Humanities and the Emerging Canons of the Americas broaden the curriculum. One-hour Career Explorations in ten different professions are reserved for first-year students.

The Honors College Community Involvement Program (HCCIP) is a nationally recognized outreach program that pairs honors students with at-risk youth from local secondary schools. HCCIP encourages MU's brightest and most energetic students to improve the lives of those around them. As mentors, pals, and tutors, the honors students not only make a difference in the lives of the young people, they also develop leadership and public service skills for themselves as well as a sense of social responsibility.

Primarily designed for first- and second-year students, the Honors College accepts approximately 650 new students each year or about 15 percent of the incoming freshman class.

Participation Requirements: Honors College students must maintain a 3.0 or higher GPA to remain honors eligible. However, students may take as many or as few honors courses per semester as they like. Honors classes receive a "GH" (General Honors) designation on their transcript. If a student completes 20 hours of honors course work and graduates with a 3.3 cumulative GPA or better, he or she can earn an Honors Certificate, which is also noted on the transcript.

Admission Process: Currently, students are automatically eligible for the program out of high school if they have a minimum ACT score of 29 (or its equivalent on the SAT I) and rank among the top 10 percent of their graduating class. Intellectually curious students who are not automatically eligible but who believe they would profit from enrolling in honors courses are encouraged to petition the College by including an essay with their applications. Honors-eligible students will be sent an application to the College shortly after being accepted to MU. Other students may write to the Honors College and request an application. Transfer students and students already attending MU are eligible if they have a 3.5 cumulative GPA and at least 30 college credit hours.

The Campus Context: The University of Missouri–Columbia, established in 1839, is the first public university in the area of the former Louisiana Territory. Rated among the nation's very best by the *Fisk Guide to Colleges* and the *Insider's Guide to Colleges,* Missouri is often called a "public ivy"—academically rigorous, pleasantly affordable, and friendly. Missouri is a place where honors undergraduates can find a comfortable home and combine the advantages of a small college with the resources of an acclaimed research institution. MU offers more than 200 undergraduate and graduate degree programs from the Colleges of Agriculture, Arts and Science, Business and Public Administration, Education, Engineering, Human Environmental Science, Journalism, Natural Resources, Nursing, and Social Work and the School of Health Related Professions. Distinguished campus facilities include a research reactor; the postbaccalaureate Schools of Law, Medicine, and Veterinary Medicine; and the world's first School of Journalism.

Student Body Undergraduate enrollment is 17,700; graduate enrollment is 4,000. The total enrollment includes 48 percent men. The ethnic distribution is 0.5 percent Native American, 7.5 percent Asian American, 6.3 percent African American, 1.4 percent Hispanic American, and 6.4 percent international students. Approximately 73 percent of students receive financial aid. There are thirty-four fraternities and twenty sororities, to which approximately 25 percent of the students belong.

Faculty Of the 1,675 faculty members, 1,603 are full-time. Eighty-eight percent hold a Ph.D. or professional degree. The student-faculty ratio is 19:1.

Key Facilities MU's library consists of seven branches containing more than 10 million bibliographic sources for research, including 2.86 million volumes.

Athletics MU sports include Big 12 basketball, baseball, and football along with diving, golf, gymnastics, soccer, softball, swimming, tennis, track and field, volleyball, and wrestling. The campus also has an extensive range of intramural and club sports.

Study Abroad Through agreements with universities around the world, MU students can study abroad during the summer, for a semester, or for an entire year. Missouri sponsors study-abroad opportunities in Australia, China, Costa Rica, Denmark, France, Germany, Italy, Japan, Mexico, the Netherlands, Romania, Russia, Spain, Taiwan, and the United Kingdom.

Support Services Services for disabled students include alternative testing arrangement, classroom accommodations, and on-campus transportation.

Tuition: $4586 for state residents, $12,468 for nonresidents, per year (2001–02)

Room and Board: $4825–$5746

Contact: Director: Dr. Stuart B. Palonsky, 211 Lowry Hall, Columbia, Missouri 65211; Telephone: 573-882-3893; Fax: 573-884-5700; E-mail: palonskys@missouri.edu; Web site: http://www.missouri.edu/~honorwww/

University of Missouri–St. Louis

4 Pu G M Sc Tr

▼ Pierre Laclede Honors College

Founded in 1989, Pierre Laclede Honors College (PLHC) is an academic division of the University of Missouri–St. Louis that enjoys its own buildings (residential and classroom) and grounds on a wooded site about 1 mile from the main campus. The primary mission of the college is to enrich the intellectual lives of its students by providing a challenging general education curriculum based on the traditional disciplines of the arts and sciences. With this goal in mind, PLHC admits highly motivated undergraduates who have the potential to act as producers, rather than consumers, of their own education. Honors students cultivate their creative capacities through a seminar-based pedagogy where written and spoken arguments are judged not on the status of the producer but on the quality of his or her ideas and the firmness of their foundation in academic study, critical thought, clear expression, and personal and cultural experience. PLHC fosters an intellectual climate in which democracy, diversity, excellence, and civility are fundamental, coequal values and produces graduates whose liberal education readies them for a lifetime of learning in and from a professedly civil, democratic, diverse, and meritocratic society.

Other than a Freshman Symposium on the city of St. Louis as a cultural and educational resource, honors seminars range in size from 5 to 15 students. An Honors Writing Program based on individual consultation runs in tandem with the honors seminar curriculum and aims at the production of a personal Writer's Portfolio at graduation. PLHC students are also encouraged to undertake supervised academic research (normally in their major), and all approved research projects carry special scholarship funding. Additional scholarship support is also normally available for those students who wish to pursue an exchange program at another university, whether abroad or in the United States or Canada. Qualified students may enter a special program with the University's College of Optometry that leads to the Doctor of Optometry degree in seven years, and all students are encouraged to take part in internships that include partnerships with leading St. Louis civic and cultural organizations.

The Pierre Laclede Honors College is expanding in size and now enrolls approximately 300 students, who major in every division and most departments of the University.

Participation Requirements: Most honors students use their honors seminars principally to meet the University's general education requirements, although a number of honors courses may be used to meet major requirements in a variety of departments. Four-year students must take a minimum of 40 credit hours in honors courses, while two-year (transfer) students must take 22 credit hours in honors courses. Both four-year and transfer honors programs include six credit hours of independent study and/or supervised research. Graduation from the honors program requires maintenance of a minimum 3.2 GPA, and honors graduates are recognized at University commencement exercises, on their final transcripts, and by issuance of a special Honors College graduation certificate.

Admission Process: Although admission to the Honors College can be by invitation, applicants are strongly recommended to apply for joint admission to the University and to the Honors College (there is a joint application form). Whether applying or invited, students are assessed by previous educational records, references from teachers, test scores (ACT or SAT I), and writing samples. Applicants are also normally invited to the college for a tour and an interview with the Dean or Associate Dean.

PLHC follows University of Missouri system guidelines on acceptance of advanced-placement credits and, for transfer applicants, adheres to Missouri state (CBHE) guidelines on transfer and articulation.

Scholarship Availability: PLHC scholarships are based on merit. Average academic scholarship support from the Honors College is about $1000 annually, and about sixty residential scholarships ($1000 each) are also available. In addition, honors students may receive (and most do receive) additional scholarship support from the University of Missouri–St. Louis, from special departmental scholarships at the University, and/or from other sources, such as Missouri Bright Flight and special National Access awards (for out-of-state students). Most scholarships are renewable subject to suitable academic performance; for Honors College scholarships, a minimum 3.2 GPA must be maintained.

There is also a range of scholarships available in music and music education. Many Honors College students hold music or sports scholarships in addition to their academic scholarships.

The Campus Context: The University of Missouri–St. Louis was founded in 1963 as an autonomous campus of the University of Missouri system (the others are at Columbia, Rolla, and Kansas City). It has seven colleges: PLHC, the College of Arts and Sciences, the Evening College, the School of Business Administration, the School of Education, the Barnes College of Nursing,

Interpreting the symbols: **2**=two-year college, **4**=four-year college; **Pu**=public or state college, **Pr**=private college; **G**=general honors program; **D**=departmental honors program; **S**=small program (fewer than 100 students), **M**=midsize program (100 to 500 students), **L**=large program (more than 500 students); **Sc**=scholarships available in honors program; **Tr**=transfer students accepted into honors program; **HBC**=historically black college; **AA**=academic advisors; **GA**=graduate advisors; **FA**=fellowship advisors.

and the School of Optometry. Together, these Colleges offer forty-two undergraduate majors, seven preprofessional programs, twenty-six master's programs, ten doctoral programs, and one professional degree program. Established on the site of a former country club in north St. Louis County, the University is surrounded by racially integrated middle- and upper-income housing suburbs on the east, south, and west and bounded by Interstate 70 on the north. I-70 and I-170 afford easy access by car, and the University also has two stations on the Metrolink rapid transit line, which runs from the nearby Lambert International Airport and on to the center of the city, terminating in East St. Louis, Illinois. The Honors College occupies the former Incarnate Word Convent and includes faculty and student offices, seminar rooms, a library and periodicals reading area, a computer lab, a student lounge and kitchen, and a residence hall. The convent chapel is used for social and cultural events, public lectures, and for the Freshman Symposium. The College's outdoor swimming pool looks over a county park, while immediately to the south there is a nine-hole public golf course. A new student center is under construction, and generous Missouri state funding has been approved for a new center for the performing arts.

Student Body Sixty-one percent of the approximately 12,000 students at the University are women. Seventy-seven percent are Caucasian, and 23 percent are members of minority groups (13 percent are African-American students). Full-time students comprise 45 percent of the whole student body; almost all honors students are full-time.

Faculty While enjoying the advantage of a seminar-based, traditional liberal arts education, Pierre Laclede Honors College students share fully in the benefits of being part of a large, public research university, which includes a distinguished faculty. Ninety-three percent of the regular faculty members and about 80 percent of all 520 full-time faculty members hold the terminal degree in their discipline.

Key Facilities There are excellent library facilities. The Thomas Jefferson Library holds nearly 1 million volumes and incorporates the Mercantile Library of St. Louis, the oldest library west of the Mississippi and a superb research facility in itself. State-of-the-art computing and science labs include the recently opened Molecular Biology Laboratory and an expanding number of smart classrooms.

Athletics The University of Missouri–St. Louis athletic program includes sponsored intramural sports and intercollegiate NCAA Division II competition in baseball, basketball, tennis, softball, volleyball, and golf. Scholarships are available for men and women in intercollegiate sports.

Study Abroad The Center for International Studies at the University of Missouri–St. Louis has exchange agreements with more than seventy other universities in Africa, Asia, Australia, Europe, and Central and South America. About 20 honors students participate in such exchanges every year. In addition, the Honors College itself administers exchanges with U.S. and Canadian universities under the auspices of the National Student Exchange (NSE), and typically these involve 10 honors students annually. The Honors College also hosts many incoming exchange students, whether they come under the auspices of International Studies or NSE.

Support Services Students with disabilities are welcome and accorded appropriate support and assistance. Wheelchair access is available to almost all classroom, library, and laboratory space in the Honors College and on the main campus.

Job Opportunities Honors students are eligible and often well qualified for academic- and career-related internships, some of which can be used to meet part of the independent study requirement. Part-time jobs are available on and off campus, including work in the Honors College itself.

Tuition: $4500 per year

Room and Board: $4003–$5234

Contact: Dean: Dr. Robert M. Bliss, Pierre Laclede Honors College, University of Missouri–St. Louis, 8001 Natural Bridge Road, St. Louis, Missouri 63121-4499; E-mail: rmbliss@umsl.edu

THE UNIVERSITY OF MONTANA–MISSOULA

4 Pr G M Sc Tr

▼ The Davidson Honors College

The Davidson Honors College is a campuswide association of faculty and students united by a common concern for academic and personal excellence. Its mission is to foster intellectual and civic values and to support the best possible teaching and learning circumstances for participating faculty and students.

The College offers an academic and social home to motivated and talented students as they pursue their undergraduate education. Students from all major areas in the College of Arts and Sciences and the professional schools are welcome, as are students undecided about a major. Honors is not a major in itself but an enhanced approach to fulfilling General Education requirements. It is compatible with all undergraduate majors.

The Davidson Honors College building is located at the center of the University of Montana–Missoula (UM Missoula) campus. It provides honors students with a large, comfortable lounge area; kitchen space; a multimedia computer lab; and quiet study rooms in addition to classrooms and office space.

The Honors Students' Association sponsors a variety of social activities and community service projects throughout the year. A special honors/international dormitory floor is available. The Davidson Honors College also sponsors the University of Montana Volunteer Action Services, an office coordinating local service agencies with campus resources and supporting the integration of community service experience into the academic curriculum.

There are 475 students in the College.

Participation Requirements: Davidson Honors College students are required to complete a minimum of seven honors courses, including one cluster of lower-division courses, one honors seminar, and an honors thesis or project.

Graduation through the Davidson Honors College requires a cumulative GPA of 3.0 or higher and 3.4 or higher in the major field. Upon completion of the requirements, students receive their bachelor's degrees as University Scholars in their respective majors and have this noted on their diplomas.

Admission Process: Students must apply separately to the Davidson Honors College. Selection is made by the faculty adviser. The priority deadline is February 1.

Scholarship Availability: The Davidson Honors College administers the Presidential Leadership Scholarships, UM's premier academic scholarship program for incoming freshmen. The Davidson Honors College also administers other campus-based scholarship programs for juniors and seniors, as well as several national competitions.

The Campus Context: The University of Montana has provided a high-quality, well-rounded education to students and a wide range of services to Montanans since it was chartered in 1893. UM is the center of liberal arts education in Montana, balancing that core commitment with intensive programs of professional preparation. The University is a major source of research, continuing education, economic development, and fine arts and entertainment, as well as a driving force in strengthening Montana's ties with countries throughout the world.

UM's Missoula campus comprises the College of Arts and Sciences, the Graduate School, the Davidson Honors College, the College of Technology, and seven professional schools, including business administration, education, fine arts, forestry, journalism, law, and pharmacy and allied health sciences. In addition to Missoula, UM includes three affiliated campuses: Western Montana College of the University of Montana, Dillon; Montana Tech of the University of Montana, Butte; and College of Technology of the University of Montana, Helena. The variety and number of degree programs offered are bachelor's, fifty-two; master's, forty-five; doctorate, nine; Associate of Applied Science, thirteen; and Certificate of Completion, fifteen.

Student Body Undergraduate enrollment is 12,000; graduate enrollment is 1,665. Of the total, 48 percent are men. Fifty percent of undergraduates receive financial aid. There are 400 international students from seventy countries. UM has ten national fraternities and four national sororities. Most maintain chapter houses near campus.

Faculty Of the 547 full-time faculty members, 79 percent hold doctoral or terminal degrees.

Key Facilities The library houses 673,852 volumes. There are six computer labs housing 130 computers: twenty-five Macintosh and 105 DOS or Windows-based.

Athletics In intercollegiate athletics, UM is NCAA Division I and a member of the Big Sky Conference. Men's sports include football (I-AA), basketball, cross-country, tennis, and indoor/outdoor track. Women's sports include basketball, cross-country, golf, soccer, tennis, indoor/outdoor track, and volleyball.

Study Abroad The Office of Foreign Languages and Literatures acts as an information and referral center for international study opportunities in a wide variety of countries.

Support Services Disability Services for Students guarantees equal access to the University of Montana–Missoula academic programs by students with disabilities. This is accomplished through the coordination and provision of adjunct services and through responsible advocacy designed to promote a hospitable and accessible learning environment.

Job Opportunities Students are offered a range of work opportunities on campus, including assistantships and work-study.

Tuition: $2318 for state residents, $7656 for nonresidents, per year

Room and Board: $4154

Contact: Dean: Gerald Fetz, University of Montana–Missoula, Missoula, Montana 59812; Telephone: 406-243-2541; E-mail: dhc@selway.umt.edu

The University of Nebraska at Kearney

4 Pu G M Sc Tr AA HBC

▼ The University of Nebraska at Kearney Honors Program

The Honors Program at the University of Nebraska at Kearney (UNK) is a central academic priority within an undergraduate curriculum noted for integrating liberal arts education and disciplinary specialties that is executed by a faculty known for individualized work with students in the classroom and lab. Designed for students of high academic abilities, the UNK Honors Program offers an exciting experience in the liberal arts tradition. Small general studies classes of 18 students or less enhance student-faculty interaction, encourage active engagement in discussion, and increase opportunities for in-depth intellectual exploration. At the same time, this four-year program enriches and supplements all academic majors in the University by including requirements in both general studies and a student's chosen discipline.

Each semester, approximately twelve to fifteen different general studies classes in a wide variety of departments are offered as honors classes. These classes fulfill University general studies requirements as well as honors requirements. The program also offers interdisciplinary seminars that are designed to reveal the relationships between the disciplines. One example is the Human Genome, a class students may take for political science or biology general studies credit. This class explores the scientific, legal, ethical, economic, and social implications and consequences of the mapping of human DNA. Another example is the Search for Myth, which can fulfill psychology or English literature general studies credit. This class explores a wide variety of cultural and historical mythologies and their current significance through readings of literature and nonfiction. The UNK Honors Program also provides an excellent opportunity for independent study at the major level. Students complete 9 hours in their respective majors through Honors Options, through which a major course is chosen and an honors project is created within the confines of the course requirements. The student works side by side with a professor to complete the honors-level work. Through this personal attention, students gain much more knowledge of their disciplines.

An Honors Residence Hall provides both living and social opportunities. Students may live in the Honors Hall to experience the academically oriented atmosphere. Many service and social activities take place during each semester and often originate in the Honors Hall. Students are not isolated; they mix with the larger community and reap the benefits of social and professional variety.

Participation Requirements: Participation in the Honors Program requires a student in the freshman or sophomore year to enroll in one honors class per semester until 15 honors credits have accumulated. In the junior and senior years, students are required to complete 9 hours of Honors Option courses within their chosen discipline. Honors Option courses are usually taken 3 hours at a time and are culminated by a senior study. Honors participation is designated by an honors notation on the student's transcript as well as an honors designation at graduation.

Admission Process: First-time freshmen must normally have a minimum ACT score of 26 or above, rank in the top 25 percent of their high school class, and complete a written essay for admission to the program. Currently enrolled freshman and sophomore students with a cumulative GPA of 3.5 or better are encouraged to apply to the honors program.

Scholarship Availability: The Honors Program offers a variety of scholarships to its students. The Honors Room Waiver Scholarships provide a room in a UNK residence hall for two years. The Honors Silver Scholarship is a $1500 two-year award. The Honors Achievement Scholarship is a one-year $1000 grant. These scholarships are awarded based upon the criteria for acceptance into the program. Two students in each incoming freshman class receive the Omaha World Herald/Kearney Hub Scholarship. This scholarship provides tuition, books, fees, and room and board for four years. To apply for this scholarship, students must have an ACT score of 28 or higher, rank in the top 10 percent of the graduating class, and write an essay. Honors scholarship recipients may hold other scholarships, and students may participate in the program without a scholarship.

The Campus Context: UNK is centrally located within the heart of Nebraska's Platte River Valley. With more than 170 diverse undergraduate degree options, students have many exciting career opportunities to explore. This comprehensive university is noted for smaller class settings and experienced faculty members who are committed to teaching students first. In addition to cultivating a successful academic experience, the University of Nebraska

Interpreting the symbols: **2**=two-year college, **4**=four-year college; **Pu**=public or state college, **Pr**=private college; **G**=general honors program; **D**=departmental honors program; **S**=small program (fewer than 100 students), **M**=midsize program (100 to 500 students), **L**=large program (more than 500 students); **Sc**=scholarships available in honors program; **Tr**=transfer students accepted into honors program; **HBC**=historically black college; **AA**=academic advisors; **GA**=graduate advisors; **FA**=fellowship advisors.

at Kearney also provides a very supportive environment for students to refine leadership skills and creates numerous opportunities for many areas of development. The University of Nebraska at Kearney offers students a university education at an affordable price and provides them with an excellent experience. The community of Kearney is part of an economically diverse and vibrant three-city midstate population center, the largest between Lincoln and Denver, with a multitude of cultural, recreational, and employment/internship opportunities.

Student Body UNK typically draws students from every county in Nebraska, from many states nationwide, and from more than fifty countries abroad. The total enrollment is about 6,500, and the on-campus residential community numbers about 2,000 annually.

Faculty There are 317 full-time faculty members on the UNK campus, with an additional 113 part-time. Of these instructors, 90 percent have terminal degrees. The student-faculty ratio is 16:1.

Key Facilities The Calvin T. Ryan Library carries a comprehensive collection of books, periodicals, volumes, and other forms of media and offers extensive access to online databases and interlibrary loan services. There are a centrally located general-use computer lab that is available 24 hours a day, seven days a week; computer labs in ten residence halls; and Internet access from every room.

Honorary Societies UNK is host to the freshman honorary Phi Eta Sigma and a senior honorary, Mortar Board. In addition, most academic departments have a discipline-specific honorary.

Athletics UNK is an NCAA Division II school and a member of the Rocky Mountain Athletic Conference (RMAC). There are sixteen men's and women's sports, including men's baseball, football, and wrestling; women's softball, volleyball, and swimming; and men's and women's cross-country, basketball, tennis, golf, and track and field. UNK also has an extensive intramural sports program.

Study Abroad UNK is a member of the International Student Exchange Program (ISEP), which is a membership organization of more than 225 higher education institutions around the world that are committed to international exchange. In addition, UNK is the only Nebraska school participating in the National Student Exchange Program, which is a network of 147 colleges and universities across the United States.

Support Services The Office of Student Support Services on the UNK campus offers many one-on-one services to UNK students and works with faculty members to assist students who are first-generation or low-income or have a disability that significantly interferes with academic performance. The University's goal is to participate in creating a community of independent learners who capitalize on academic strength and develop acceptable coping strategies for areas of weakness. A wide variety of student support services are available, including writing and tutoring assistance, academic and career advising, personal counseling, special technologies to assist disabled students, and more than 150 student organizations centered in a newly expanded and renovated student union.

Job Opportunities Students are employed on campus, and jobs are readily available in the Kearney community across the full range of economic/commercial activity.

Tuition: $92.45 per hour (in-state), $172.75 per hour (out-of-state)

Room and Board: $1423 per semester (minimum)

Mandatory Fees: $139 per semester (minimum)

Contact: Dr. Peter Longo, Professor and Honors Director, MSAB 112, University of Nebraska at Kearney, Kearney, Nebraska 68849; Telephone: 308-865-8497; E-mail: longop@unk.edu

Admissions, University of Nebraska at Kearney, Kearney, Nebraska 68849; Telephone: 800-KEARNEY (toll-free); E-mail: admssionsug@unk.edu

UNIVERSITY OF NEBRASKA–LINCOLN

4 Pu G D L Sc Tr

▼ University Honors Program

The University Honors Program provides students of proven ability and distinguished high school record with a challenging academic experience in college. The honors program is a community of scholars—an intense intellectual experience for the most talented and committed students in a major research university setting. The program gives students who strive for academic excellence an opportunity to explore new knowledge through research, actively participate in a process of discovery, and appreciate and respect diversity of opinions.

In honors classes, special seminars, and research opportunities, students enrich their curriculum regardless of the academic major they have chosen. Honors classes are small, generally limited to 20 students (they often have as few as 10 participants), and are taught by faculty members noted for both their teaching and research accomplishments. These classes stress critical thinking and communication skills and involve the student in an active learning environment. The honors course work prepares students for the program's capstone research or creative project, which is undertaken in the senior year under the supervision of a faculty mentor. Many students have considered the senior project the most rewarding intellectual experience in their academic life. Many program students present their research at scholarly conferences and the annual Undergraduate Research Conference, which is held on campus and hosted by the University Honors Program.

Honors program students are invited to live in a community of scholars in the Neihardt honors residence. Intense discussions and debates spill out of classrooms and into hallways, student rooms, and lounges. Faculty members and campus administrators often stop by to talk with students at fireside chats and in more formal settings. Special events and social activities for honors students take place in Neihardt's common areas and courtyards. The residence also houses the honors program office, several classrooms that are used for honors classes, a 24-hour computer lab, study rooms, and student lounge areas.

The honors community is shaped by its students. The Honors Board, 21 elected student representatives, makes a vital contribution to the community by helping develop honors program policies and planning social and cultural events for program members.

Students in the program are encouraged to participate in study-abroad opportunities offered by the University as well as internship and cooperative education programs.

Participation Requirements: The program consists of a minimum of 24 hours of honors course work. Students enroll in a section of the required freshman honors seminar and complete at least 6 honors hours per year and a total of 15 honors hours in the first two years. Juniors and seniors in the program complete at least 3 honors hours per year and a total of 9 honors hours in the final two years, including the required upper-level honors seminar and an honors research or creative project (e.g., thesis).

To ensure that students make proper progress toward completing honors program requirements, they file a Statement of Academic Interest that outlines their educational and professional goals prior to completing 64 hours of college work and a Memorandum of Study in their junior year that identifies the research or creative activity they intend to complete in their senior year. Students must have a minimum 3.5 cumulative GPA at the time of graduation. Completion of the program is recorded on the student's academic transcript and a special notation is made on the diploma and in the University's Commencement Program.

Admission Process: The program is available by application only. A faculty committee reviews applications twice a year, first after the November 15 early notification deadline and again after the March 1 final deadline for application. Four hundred students, approximately 10 percent of the University's freshman class, are admitted annually.

The application requests information about the student's academic performance in high school, including a transcript and letters of recommendation from teachers and counselors, scores earned on the ACT and SAT I tests, and essays on assigned topics. Most students admitted to the program are in the top 10 percent of their high school graduating class, have ACT composite scores of 29 or higher, and have taken full advantage of honors or AP courses, if offered, in their schools.

Scholarship Availability: All honors students benefit from a book scholarship that pays for all their required textbooks in honors and nonhonors classes. Retention of the scholarship requires that students fulfill program participation requirements outlined above and maintain a minimum 3.5 cumulative GPA. The scholarship may be held for up to four years.

The Campus Context: The University of Nebraska–Lincoln (UNL), chartered by the Legislature in 1869, is part of the University of Nebraska system, which serves as both the land-grant and the comprehensive public university for the state of Nebraska. Those responsible for its origins recognized the value of combining the breadth of a comprehensive university with the professional and outreach orientation of the land-grant university, thus establishing a campus that has evolved to become the flagship campus of the University of Nebraska.

Through its three primary missions of teaching, research, and service, UNL is the state's primary intellectual center and provides leadership throughout the state through high-quality education and the generation of new knowledge. UNL attracts a high percentage of the most academically talented Nebraskans, and graduates of the University form a significant portion of the business, cultural, and professional resources of the state.

The University of Nebraska–Lincoln has been recognized by the Legislature as the primary research and doctoral degree–granting institution in the state for fields outside the health professions. UNL is one of a select group of research universities that holds membership in the American Association of Universities (AAU). Through its service and outreach efforts, the University extends its educational responsibilities to the people of Nebraska on a statewide basis. Many of UNL's research and service activities have an international dimension in order to provide its students a significant global perspective.

Student Body Undergraduate enrollment is 17,980; 46.7 percent are women. The ethnic distribution of students is Caucasian, 90.35 percent; African American, 2.15 percent; Native American, 0.3 percent; Asian, 5.4 percent; and Hispanic, 1.8 percent. Approximately 4,300 students live in University residence halls. There are also twenty-four fraternities and fifteen sororities on campus.

Faculty There are 1,519 faculty members at the University. The student-faculty ratio is 15:1.

Key Facilities The University library houses 2.4 million volumes. Students have ready access to computing resources: there are many computer labs on campus and in the residence halls, and all residence hall rooms have computer connections. Upon registering, students are issued an e-mail address.

Honorary Societies Alpha Lambda Delta, Phi Eta Sigma, Golden Key, Omicron Delta Kappa, Mortar Board, Phi Beta Kappa

Athletics The University of Nebraska's Department of Intercollegiate Athletics is a member of the nationally prominent Big 12 Conference. Nebraska offers twenty-four varsity sports for men and women. The Campus Recreation Center, completed in 1992, offers numerous programs in intramural sports, outdoor recreation, and fitness and wellness services.

Study Abroad Through its Office of International Affairs as well as college-based international programs, UNL offers a myriad of study-abroad opportunities. Honors students are strongly encouraged to participate in study-abroad programs that are harmonized with their honors responsibilities on the home campus.

Job Opportunities Work opportunities are available on and off campus.

Tuition: Tuition per credit hour is $101.25 for undergraduate residents and $288 per credit hour for nonresidents. Fees for full-time students are $396 per semester.

Room and Board: Room and board in the residence halls is $4564 for a double-occupancy room and nineteen meals per week for an academic year.

Contact: Director of the University Honors Program: Dr. Patrice Berger, 118 Neihardt Residence Center, 540 North 16th Street, Lincoln, Nebraska 68588-0659; Telephone: 402-472-5425; Fax: 402-472-8204; E-mail: pberger1@unl.edu

---

University of Nebraska at Omaha

4 Pu G M Sc Tr AA FA

▼ University Honors Program

The Honors Program at the University of Nebraska at Omaha (UNO) is for students who want to get the most out of their efforts and who enjoy stimulating experiences. The Honors Program consists of the University's most talented, involved, and exciting students, along with highly qualified and dedicated faculty members.

Honors students participate in special limited enrollment sections of core requirement courses, taught at a level and pace appropriate for honors students. Interdisciplinary colloquia are the core of the Honors curriculum and allow students to see the interaction between disciplines while offering an alternative way of fulfilling University requirements. An important advantage of honors classes is the stimulation able, motivated students offer each other.

Outside of the classroom, the Honors Program Student Advisory Board provides social and cultural activities, including guest speakers, tours, weekend trips, and an annual banquet. During Honors Week, senior honors students offer colloquia for the entire University community on their senior theses/projects. Honors students have their own lounge and study room in the Honors Office where they can visit, share ideas with friends, study, or just relax. A real sense of community exists.

There are many opportunities available to Honors Program participants. Internships and experiential learning opportunities are also available for students. UNO honors students have been recipients of Truman Scholarships and Rotary Scholarships.

All honors courses are noted on the student's transcript. If a student completes the Honors Program and meets all of the criteria, he or she is recognized at graduation, receives recognition in the Commencement Program, has an appropriate notation made on the diploma, and receives a personal letter of recommendation from the Chancellor.

The 22-year-old program currently enrolls more than 400 students.

Participation Requirements: Students meet the requirements of the University Honors Program by successfully completing 30

Interpreting the symbols: **2**=two-year college, **4**=four-year college; **Pu**=public or state college, **Pr**=private college; **G**=general honors program; **D**=departmental honors program; **S**=small program (fewer than 100 students), **M**=midsize program (100 to 500 students), **L**=large program (more than 500 students); **Sc**=scholarships available in honors program; **Tr**=transfer students accepted into honors program; **HBC**=historically black college; **AA**=academic advisors; **GA**=graduate advisors; **FA**=fellowship advisors.

hours of credit in honors courses and by meeting their college's GPA requirements of 3.25 to 3.50 for the Honors Program. The 30 hours are part of a student's overall program, not additional hours. The 30 hours of honors credit are usually met in the following manner: 12–15 hours of honors sections of general education requirements; 6 hours of interdisciplinary colloquia; 3–6 hours of senior thesis or project; and 3–6 hours of special seminars, internships, electives, or experiential classes.

Admission Process: Students are admitted to the Honors Program as entering freshmen if they have minimum ACT scores of 26 or minimum SAT I scores of 1200 or by special recommendation from high school principals or counselors. Students already enrolled are admitted to the Honors Program if their overall GPA ranges from 3.25 to 3.5, depending upon their respective colleges. Transfer students from other honors programs are eligible if they were members in good standing in their previous programs and complete the Honors Program requirements.

Scholarship Availability: The Honors Program offers scholarships designed specifically for honors students. They are the Distinguished Scholarship, World Herald Scholarship, and Scottish Rite Scholarship. In order to receive any of these scholarships a student must participate in the Distinguished Scholarship Competition.

The Campus Context: The University of Nebraska at Omaha is a campus of nine colleges, including the College of Arts and Sciences, College of Business Administration, College of Public Administration and Community Service, College of Continuing Studies, College of Education, College of Information Science and Technology, College of Fine Arts, College of Human Resources and Family Sciences, and College of Engineering and Technology. The type and number of degree programs offered are Bachelor of Arts (twenty-eight majors); Bachelor of Science (fifty-three majors); Bachelor of Fine Arts (three majors); Bachelor of Music (two majors); M.A., M.S., and M.B.A. (fifty-two concentrations); and Ph.D. (six programs, four of which are jointly administered with University of Nebraska at Lincoln).

Student Body The total undergraduate enrollment is 15,106, of whom 47 percent are men. The ethnic distribution of students is 81.6 percent white, 5.9 percent black, 2.6 percent Hispanic, 2.3 percent Asian/Pacific Islander, .5 percent American Indian/Alaskan, and 3 percent nonresident alien. There are 629 international students on campus. Fifty-eight percent of the students receive financial aid. There are seventeen fraternities and sororities. University Village offers apartment-style living for 576 students in 144 suites. Housing is also available in the Scott Residence Halls.

Faculty The total number of faculty members is 871, of whom 494 are full-time. More than 83 percent of the faculty members have terminal degrees.

Key Facilities The library houses 760,000 volumes. There are ten computer labs on campus. Students have access to word processors and the Internet through the computer labs.

Honorary Societies Phi Eta Sigma, Phi Kappa Phi, Golden Key, and Alpha Lambda Delta

Athletics The University of Nebraska at Omaha has a complete intercollegiate athletic program that includes sports for men and women. The University is a member of the NCAA Division II and competes in the North Central Conference. The men's and women's teams have won several NCC championships. In addition, Campus Recreation offers a wide variety of recreational and sports activities to UNO students, faculty and staff members, and their families. Major programs include informal recreation, intramural sports, sport clubs, aquatic activities, outdoor recreation, noncredit instruction, and other special events.

Study Abroad Study-abroad opportunities are offered through the Honors Program and through the Office of International Studies.

Support Services The Office of Services for Students with Disabilities, known as SSD, has a professional special needs counselor available to assist students in determining eligibility and reasonable accommodations. The Disabled Students Agency's (DSA) purpose is to support students with temporary or permanent disabilities and to assist disabled students to assimilate into the University population by providing special resources. The Learning Center provides instruction and services to assist students in the development of skills necessary for effective academic performance and positive adjustment to the college learning environment.

Job Opportunities Help in finding on- and off-campus employment is available in Student Employment Services, located in the Career Planning and Placement Services Office. Job postings are listed in the Campus Wide Information System. Internships are posted in specific categories. Weekly employment lists are available in the Career Planning and Placement Office.

Tuition: $2783 for state residents, $7830 for nonresidents, per year (2001–02)

Mandatory Fees: $442

Contact: Rosalie C. Saltzman, Omaha, Nebraska 68182-0218; Telephone: 402-554-2598; Fax: 402-554-4963; E-mail: rosalie_saltzman@unomaha.edu

UNIVERSITY OF NEVADA, LAS VEGAS

4 Pu G L Sc Tr

▼ Honors College

The Honors College (HC) provides a dynamic, diverse, and inclusive learning community for all qualified high school, transfer, and continuing students who choose to participate. This community is built around a shared commitment to academic excellence that manifests itself in rigorous traditional courses, innovative interdisciplinary seminars, opportunities for research and internships, and other special educational activities that form the nucleus of the honors experience at UNLV.

The HC, by collaborating with UNLV's outstanding faculty and utilizing resources found in the vibrant city of Las Vegas, creates educational opportunities and encourages unique curricular development; this allows students from disparate majors to challenge themselves and enhance their academic and personal growth by working together or independently in traditional and nontraditional formats. Consequently, the HC, in concert with departments, faculty, and students, is determined to be a locus of quality undergraduate education and to augment UNLV's quest to become a premier urban university.

The College offers students two ways to enhance and enrich their undergraduate experience: University Honors (UH) and Department Honors (DH). Both programs are available to all undergraduates regardless of their major. Twenty-four percent of graduates have earned degrees in liberal arts, 20 percent in business and economics, 20 percent in science and mathematics, and 10 percent in engineering. The remaining 26 percent have graduated from other colleges on campus. These statistics demonstrate one of the great strengths of Honors at UNLV—the disciplinary diversity of the students who participate. The first class of 38 students entered the HC in fall 1985. The College now admits approximately 130 freshmen a year and has a total enrollment of 800 students.

Participation Requirements: *University Honors:* Students participating in UH are required to complete a minimum of 30 credits of honors courses graded with conventional letter grades (A,B,C,D,F). Students joining UH directly from high school ordinarily use honors courses to satisfy most of UNLV's general education core requirements. Students joining UH after enrolling at UNLV or who transfer to UNLV may apply some of their regular courses toward the honors core but will still be required to meet the 30-credit minimum and the specific curricular requirements of the honors core.

Participants in UH typically take between one fourth and one third of their courses through the HC; the majority of courses are concentrated in the student's major and related areas.

Department Honors: DH is a two-year program and has two focal points: a senior thesis/project, usually done in the student's major field, and four 400-level honors seminars. Students join this program before the start of their junior year. Students can graduate with UH, DH, or both. DH combines the broadening experience of four upper-division honors seminars with a 6-credit senior thesis/project that functions as the capstone of the undergraduate experience. The honors seminars count as generic core courses and can be used to satisfy the fine arts, humanities, or social science core requirements.

The honors experience provides a small-college atmosphere within the larger university. Students share a common core of classes and have the opportunity of studying together in the Lloyd Katz Honors Lounge, living in honors clusters in the residence halls, and attending special events together. These opportunities are designed to help students reach their academic potential.

Students who complete all curriculum requirements for UH or DH with a UNLV cumulative GPA of 3.3 or higher and a cumulative honors GPA of 3.0 or higher will receive an HC Medallion at graduation and have their successful participation denoted on their final UNLV transcript. Students graduating with honors can also earn the Latin designations cum laude, magna cum laude, or summa cum laude if they satisfy the appropriate HC requirements.

Admission Process: Students can join UH directly from high school, after one or more semesters at UNLV, or when transferring to UNLV from another college or university. High school students in the top 5 percent of their high school class, with an ACT composite score of at least 28, or with a combined Scholastic Assessment Test (SAT I) score of at least 1250 are encouraged to apply. Current UNLV students or transfer students with a 3.5 or higher college GPA are also encouraged to apply. The criteria listed above are guidelines; each student applying for admission to UH will have his or her application carefully reviewed by the Honors College Admission Committee.

To be eligible to participate in DH, students must have a cumulative GPA of 3.5 or higher or be students in good standing in the UH Program.

Scholarship Availability: The HC has approximately $200,000 of scholarship money that is awarded to freshmen and continuing students.

The Campus Context: UNLV is located in the exciting and dynamic city of Las Vegas and is surrounded by picturesque mountains and desert. Its beautifully landscaped 335-acre campus is home to 20,000 students who are enrolled in more than 139 undergraduate, master's, and doctoral degree programs. UNLV has nine academic colleges not including Honors: business, education, engineering, fine arts, health sciences, hotel administration, liberal arts, sciences, and urban affairs.

Student Body Fifty-six percent of the students are women and approximately 16,000 are undergraduates. Almost half of the undergraduates receive some form of financial assistance. The diverse student population includes international (5 percent), black non-Hispanic (6 percent), Hispanic (7 percent), Asian/Pacific Islander (9 percent), and Native American (1 percent). More than 1,000 students live on campus; the remainder of the students either commute or live in one of the apartment complexes near the University.

Faculty UNLV has 632 full-time faculty members. Ninety-three percent have terminal degrees. The student-faculty ratio is 20:1.

Key Facilities The new $50-million Lied Library has more than 700,000 volumes and is home to the HC. The HC space in the library includes the Lloyd Katz Honors Lounge, which has nine computers for student use and a quiet study area. The University has a CRAY Supercomputer and many other computer laboratories and facilities.

Honorary Societies Phi Kappa Phi, Golden Key

Athletics UNLV is a member of the NCAA and Mountain West Athletic Conference and competes in fifteen intercollegiate Division I sports. Men's sports include baseball, basketball, football, golf, soccer, swimming and diving, and tennis, and women's sports include basketball, cross-country, indoor and outdoor track, soccer, softball, swimming and diving, tennis, and volleyball.

Study Abroad The Office of International Programs offers a wide variety of study-abroad programs. Most programs allow students to remain registered at UNLV while studying abroad. Programs are currently available in Australia, Chile, Costa Rica, England, France, Germany, Italy, Mexico, Spain, Switzerland, and Thailand. UNLV also participates in the National Student Exchange (NSE). Scholarships and financial aid are available.

Support Services The Disability Resource Center provides academic accommodations for students with qualified disabilities.

Job Opportunities Employment opportunities exist for students whether or not they qualify for financial aid.

Tuition: $2070 for state residents, $3105 for nonresidents eligible for Western Undergraduate Exchange, $7430 for nonresidents, per year (1998–99)

Room and Board: $5694

Mandatory Fees: $30

Contact: Assistant to the Dean: Susanne Pierce, Box 457003, Maryland Parkway, Las Vegas, Nevada 89154-7003; Telephone: 702-895-2263; Fax: 702-895-2289; E-mail: susanne.pierce@ccmail.nevada.edu; Web site: http://www.unlv.edu/colleges/honors

UNIVERSITY OF NEVADA, RENO

4 Pu G D M Sc Tr

▼ Honors Program/112

The Honors Program of the University of Nevada, Reno, is designed for students who are eager to learn in the environment of intellectual exchange and interaction, who are self-motivated, who are determined to test values and discuss ideas with professors and peers, and who possess strong academic records. The program is open to students in all majors. The program features instruction by carefully selected outstanding faculty members, small classes, honors residences, an honors center, and an active Honors Student Association.

Scholarships, undergraduate research grants, and study-abroad opportunities are available. All students are provided free accounts on the Internet. The program takes particular pride in the success of its graduates in postgraduate fellowship competitions and in admission to graduate/professional schools. The program is rated as one of the nation's best in *Ivy League Programs at State School Prices: The 55 Best Honors Programs at State Universities Nationwide.*

Interpreting the symbols: **2**=two-year college, **4**=four-year college; **Pu**=public or state college, **Pr**=private college; **G**=general honors program; **D**=departmental honors program; **S**=small program (fewer than 100 students), **M**=midsize program (100 to 500 students), **L**=large program (more than 500 students); **Sc**=scholarships available in honors program; **Tr**=transfer students accepted into honors program; **HBC**=historically black college; **AA**=academic advisors; **GA**=graduate advisors; **FA**=fellowship advisors.

The current program began in fall 1989 and now enrolls 400 students.

Participation Requirements: Thirty academic credits are required to complete an honors degree. Honors degrees are assigned traditional Latin designations of achievement according to GPA at graduation. Honors classes are available in the University's core curriculum, in the student's major, and as electives. Students have a wide choice of courses and have latitude in choosing courses to take for honors. The only required course is the Honors Senior Thesis/Project, which is completed in the student's major. The program is designed to fit within a student's educational program without the need for additional time or credits. A 3.25 GPA is required to continue in the program. In addition to course work, a variety of activities are available to students, including the program's Pizza Seminars, in which current topics and issues of general interest (e.g., gender communication, world religions, diversity) are discussed in an informal atmosphere.

Completion of the Honors Program is the only way to graduate with Latin distinction at the University of Nevada, Reno. Distinctions are: summa cum laude (with highest praise), 3.9 or higher; magna cum laude (with great praise), 3.7–3.89; and cum laude (with praise), 3.5–3.69. Students who complete the Honors Program but have a GPA lower than 3.5 graduate with honors recognition.

Admission Process: Participation in the program is by direct application to the Honors Program. The Admission Committee reviews considerable information about the applicant, including the academic record, activities, work experience, teacher recommendations, and an admission essay. Students are encouraged to apply if they meet one of the following criteria: 3.65 GPA (unweighted), 28 ACT or equivalent SAT I score, or top 10 percent of graduation class. Achievement of one or more of these numerical criteria does not itself guarantee admission because the entire application is carefully reviewed. Students should be advised that average and mean scores of admitted students are well above the minimum scores stated in the application criteria. Transfer students are welcome. The Honors Program application deadline is February 1.

Scholarship Availability: Scholarships are available by application to the Scholarship Office. Scholarships are primarily based on academic achievement.

The Campus Context: The University of Nevada, Reno, is a campus of ten colleges: Agriculture, Arts and Sciences, Business Administration, Education, Engineering, Human and Community Sciences, Mackay School of Mines, Reynolds School of Journalism, Graduate School, and the University of Nevada School of Medicine. Seventy-four undergraduate and sixty-one graduate degree programs are offered on campus. The University is home to the unique Basque Studies Program and is headquarters for the University Studies Abroad Consortium.

Student Profile The student population is 47 percent men and 53 percent women. The ethnic distribution is white, 78.6 percent; international, 5.2 percent; Asian/Pacific Islander, 5.1 percent; Hispanic, 4 percent; black, 1.6 percent; American Indian, 1.2 percent; and not listed, 4.3 percent. Twelve percent are resident students; the 88 percent of commuter students includes students living in neighborhoods near the University. Approximately 50 percent of the students receive financial aid. The campus has ten fraternities and four sororities.

Faculty There are 810 faculty members; 696 are full-time and 77 percent have terminal degrees. The student-faculty ratio is 19:1.

Key Facilities The library holds 1 million volumes. There are twenty-two computer labs with PCs/Macs and full Internet access.

Honorary Societies Phi Kappa Phi, Golden Key

Athletics The University is NCAA Division I and a member of the Big Western Conference. Men's programs are maintained in baseball, basketball, football, golf, and tennis. Women's programs are in basketball, swimming, track, volleyball, and tennis. Extensive intramural sports are available to all students.

Study Abroad The headquarters for the University Studies Abroad Consortium (USAC) is located on campus. USAC currently has programs in Australia, Chile, Costa Rica, England, France, Germany, Italy, Spain, and Thailand. Other opportunities exist through department and college affiliations. The University is a member of the National Student Exchange. Honors credit is available for study abroad.

Support Services Disabled students find the campus totally accessible. Academic support services are available.

Job Opportunities Support services are also available for both on-campus and off-campus student employment. Job lists are maintained at both offices. Work-study is encouraged for eligible students.

Tuition: $2490 for state residents, $8612 for nonresidents, per year (2002–03)

Room and Board: $6000

Mandatory Fees: $116

Contact: Director: Francis X. Hartigan, Reno, Nevada 89557; Telephone: 775-784-1455; Fax: 775-784-1756; E-mail: honors@honors.unr.edu; Web site: http://www.honors.unr.edu

The University of New Mexico

4 Pu G L Tr

▼ The University Honors Program

The University Honors Program (UHP) at the University of New Mexico (UNM) originated in 1957 with a group of 30 students. The UHP continues to offer high-achieving students many of the personal advantages of a small liberal arts college within the diversity of a large research university. At the heart of the UHP are small interdisciplinary seminars taught by selected faculty members who are committed to exploring significant ideas while encouraging active student participation. The emphasis in the seminars is on intensive reading and writing and active student participation. The UHP is open to students of all majors. The seminars are specifically designed for honors—all are interdisciplinary and many are team-taught.

The UHP is housed in the Dudley Wynn Honors Center, named after its founder. In addition to housing five classrooms, the center provides a place for informal discussions, student activities, and various group projects. In a warm, friendly atmosphere, UHP students meet to study together, continue seminar discussions, or just relax between classes. The large central area, affectionately known as the Forum, is also used for more formal lectures and receptions.

There are currently 1,112 students participating in the University Honors Program.

Participation Requirements: Admission is by application only, and students must take a minimum of 21 credit hours (seven seminars) in the UHP, with a minimum of one seminar at each level (100–400). They are required to maintain a minimum cumulative GPA of 3.2. Some colleges require that students file a petition for permission to count the seminar toward graduation. Students may enter the UHP at any point, provided they can complete the requirements. Transfer students may be able to transfer up to 9 hours of comparable work.

Three 100-level seminars, Ancient, Medieval, and Modern Legacies, offer a common opportunity for students. They not only learn about significant ideas and traditions beginning with the Greco-Roman and Judeo-Christian, but also learn the process of seminar learning and honors education. Several 200-level seminars examine other legacies and world views: women, Africa, the Far

East, the Americas, and the origins of mathematics, science, and technology. The 300-level seminars are interdisciplinary explorations of specific topics designed to demonstrate the interconnectedness of academic disciplines. Recent seminars have focused on the significance of biomedical ethics, the nature and politics of nuclear energy, the origins of prejudice, arts across cultures, and creative leadership. At the 400 level, seniors are offered a capstone seminar that includes a service-learning component. They may also choose to be student teachers, a unique opportunity for undergraduates, or to research and write a thesis.

In addition to the curriculum, the UHP affords students a variety of other learning opportunities, including field-based language and cultural programs, international and national exchange opportunities, leadership in student organizations, and the opportunity to staff Scribendi: The Western Regional Honors Review, an outstanding literary magazine.

Students who fulfill the requirements of the program become candidates for graduation with an honors designation. Honors distinctions used at UNM are cum laude, magna cum laude, and summa cum laude. Graduation with an honors designation is not automatic. Honors levels are determined by the University Honors Council. Aside from the minimum requirements of the UHP, students are expected to have a reasonably broad liberal arts education. Students should attempt to take course work in the humanities, languages, social sciences, mathematics, physical sciences, and life sciences insofar as it is possible to do so within the restrictions of their majors and minors.

The Campus Context: Founded in 1889, the University of New Mexico occupies a 700-acre campus along the old Route 66 axis of Albuquerque. Albuquerque is defined by the Rio Grande, a river that has supported the life-giving land along its gentle banks since prehistory. The second defining natural monument is the Sandia Mountains, the southernmost shield of the Rockies. The protective wall of the Sandias and the Rio Grande create an inspirational urban setting of great beauty of livability. As the epicenter of one of America's most ethnically diverse populations, UNM serves a broad cross-section of people with different needs, goals, and perceptions. This fact has made UNM a model of the contemporary multicultural institution—a true University for the Americas. The campus is composed of thirteen colleges and schools: Anderson Schools of Management; Architecture and Planning; Arts and Sciences; Education; Engineering; Fine Arts; Graduate Studies; Health Sciences; Law; Medicine; Nursing; Pharmacy; and University Studies. Students may earn bachelor's degrees in ninety-eight majors and master's and doctoral degrees in sixty-nine concentrations.

There are five museums, housing collections from art to natural history, and nine libraries among the more than 170 buildings. Other distinguished facilities include the Learning Resource Center, Planetarium, radio station, TV station, Robotics Laboratory, Microcomputer Laboratories, Photo-history Collection, and a Lithography Institute. Additionally, there are UNM extension campuses located in Los Alamos, Santa Fe, Taos, Gallup, and Valencia County. Faculty members and students number about 40,000 on all campuses. Altogether, the University employs nearly 15,000 people. It functions as the state's largest institution of higher learning and offers more than 170 accredited areas of study.

Student Body There are 24,431 students enrolled (undergraduate enrollment is 15,516): 43.1 percent men and 56.9 percent women. The ethnic distribution is 54.3 percent white, 25.5 percent Hispanic, 10.7 percent Native American, 3 percent African American, 2.6 percent Asian, and 1.1 percent international (505). Commuters make up 92 percent of the student population and residents the remaining 8 percent. Eighty-five percent of the students receive financial aid. Two percent of the men belong to ten national fraternities. One percent of the women belong to the four national sororities.

Faculty The total number of faculty members is 2,901. Of the 1,461 full-time faculty members, 92 percent have terminal degrees. Benchmark accomplishments among the UNM faculty include the development of an entirely new field, high-energy atomic physics, by Professor Howard Bryant. His pioneering work led to the development of the Quantum Theory and the Big Bang Theory. UNM's nationally ranked mathematics department attained worldwide stature when a UNM professor helped provide the solution to a longstanding problem known as the Atiyah-Jones Conjecture. The student-faculty ratio is 13:1.

Key Facilities There are nine libraries containing 1.8 million volumes, 5 million microform items, and 320,034 audiovisual forms and subscriptions to 18,230 periodicals. The campus has seven computer pods and four classrooms in various locations on campus. Computers in use include IBM and compatible microcomputers, Apple Macintosh microcomputers, and X-terminals.

Honorary Societies Phi Eta Sigma, Phi Kappa Phi, Golden Key, Mortar Board, Phi Beta Kappa

Athletics There are thirteen intercollegiate sports for men and eleven for women. There are also thirty-two intramural sports for men and twenty-six for women.

Study Abroad National Student Exchange offers students an opportunity for educational travel and study at 112 participating schools across the U.S. The International Programs provides services for students to travel abroad to England, France, Spain, Mexico, Italy, Germany, and many other countries. Students may also participate in the Honors Semesters Program. The Honors Program offers special programs to Spain, Mexico, and Australia.

Support Services Ninety-five percent of the campus is accessible to disabled students.

Job Opportunities Students are offered a wide range of scholarship and employment opportunities, including assistantships and work-study.

Tuition: $3026 for state residents, $11,424 for nonresidents, per year (2001–02)

Room and Board: $6000 per academic year

Contact: Director: Dr. Rosalie C. Otero, University College 21, The University of New Mexico, Albuquerque, New Mexico 87131-1456; Telephone: 505-277-4211; Fax: 505-277-4271; E-mail: otero@unm.edu and honors@unm.edu; Web site: http://www.unm.edu/~honors

UNIVERSITY OF NORTH CAROLINA AT ASHEVILLE

4 Pu D M Sc Tr

▼ University Honors Program

The University Honors Program offers special educational opportunities to academically talented and motivated students. The college-wide program welcomes freshmen, transfers, and continuing students from all academic departments.

The Honors Program offers courses as well as cocurricular activities designed to extend learning beyond the classroom. Courses include special sections of many general education requirements, such as freshman composition and humanities, and challenging junior and senior honors seminars. The Honors Program emphasizes both breadth and depth in liberal education. The breadth comes through special emphasis on interdisciplinary

Interpreting the symbols: **2**=two-year college, **4**=four-year college; **Pu**=public or state college, **Pr**=private college; **G**=general honors program; **D**=departmental honors program; **S**=small program (fewer than 100 students), **M**=midsize program (100 to 500 students), **L**=large program (more than 500 students); **Sc**=scholarships available in honors program; **Tr**=transfer students accepted into honors program; **HBC**=historically black college; **AA**=academic advisors; **GA**=graduate advisors; **FA**=fellowship advisors.

courses. Depth, or excellence in a particular field, is encouraged through undergraduate research with a faculty mentor in the academic major. Additional educational opportunities include independent study and internships.

The Honors Program also offers a range of extracurricular activities designed to foster community and leadership among participants.

The 14-year-old program currently enrolls 300 students.

Participation Requirements: Students who complete requirements of the Honors Program graduate with Distinction as a University Scholar. Those requirements include completion of 15 hours of honors credit (including the Senior Honors Colloquium and an honors special topics course) with a 3.5 GPA, a 3.5 GPA in the last 60 hours of credit, and completion of a research or creative project.

Admission Process: Freshmen apply directly to the Honors Program. Participants are chosen on the basis of SAT I scores, rank in class, and leadership activities. Transfer students may also apply for admission, provided they have earned a 3.5 GPA on all transfer hours. Continuing UNCA students may apply if they have earned a 3.0 GPA. Students must maintain a 3.0 GPA and must complete at least one 3-hour honors course during their first four semesters in order to remain a member of the Honors Program.

Scholarship Availability: The Honors Program itself does not offer scholarships but cooperates closely with the University Laurels Academic Merit Scholarship Program. Students interested in those academic scholarships apply as part of the UNCA application process. Students identified as merit scholarship candidates are invited to the campus for Interview Day, usually scheduled in February. Many candidates for the University Laurels Academic Merit Scholarships are also considered for admission to the University Honors Program.

The Campus Context: The University of North Carolina at Asheville is the "Public Liberal Arts University" in the state's widely respected system of higher education. As such, UNCA is a place where students, faculty members, and staff members know and interact with each other across departmental and disciplinary lines, where the focus is always upon undergraduates, and where the curriculum teaches students to become their own best and lifelong teachers. Located in the mountains of western Northern Carolina, UNCA offers undergraduate degree programs in the arts and humanities, the natural and social sciences, and selected preprofessional programs firmly grounded in the liberal arts. A total of thirty-seven degree programs are offered on campus.

The University has earned national recognition for its Humanities Program, a four-course sequence of history and world culture that is the core of UNCA's liberal arts curriculum and, according to the National Endowment for the Humanities and the Association of American Colleges, a "model" for other institutions of higher education.

UNCA's Undergraduate Research Program, which provides funding and faculty support for student research projects, trips to conferences, and publication opportunities in all disciplines, has received widespread attention and national acclaim. The National Conference on Undergraduate Research, a multidisciplinary forum founded and hosted by UNCA in 1987, continues to draw thousands of faculty and student participants from around the country every year.

The University's 265-acre hilltop campus, located 1 mile from downtown Asheville, is named one of America's "most livable cities" in Rand McNally's *Places Rated Almanac* and one of the nation's top ten cities in *Outdoor* magazine. The region has the largest concentration of national forest on the East Coast, and the surrounding Blue Ridge and Great Smoky Mountains are the ideal setting for any outdoor enthusiast.

Student Profile The undergraduate enrollment is 3,135: 43 percent men and 57 percent women. The ethnic distribution is 91.6 percent white, 1 percent Asian, 3.4 percent black, 1.4 percent Hispanic, and .3 percent American Indian. There are 39 international students. The resident/commuter ratio is 3.5:6.5. Forty-five percent of students receive financial aid. UNCA has five fraternities and three sororities.

Faculty The total number of faculty members is 287; 161 are full-time, and 87 percent have terminal degrees. The student-faculty ratio is 12:1.

Key Facilities The library houses 251,953 volumes. Computer facilities include two Digital Alphaservers, a VAX 4000, eight multipurpose computer labs, several departmental computer labs, and a high-speed fiberoptic network connecting all buildings on campus to the Internet and World Wide Web. All classrooms have network connections, and each residence hall student is provided with an individual network port to connect a personally owned computer. There are two distance learning facilities on campus that enable students to participate in courses offered over the North Carolina Research and Education Network.

Honorary Societies Phi Eta Sigma

Athletics The Justice Health and Fitness Center houses an indoor swimming pool, basketball court, dance studio, and fully equipped weight room. Outdoor athletic facilities include the recently completed Greenwood Fields (for soccer, baseball, and softball), tennis courts, and a track. A new multimillion-dollar addition to the complex, opened in 1996, adds three indoor courts, an elevated track, racquetball courts, and an extensive weight facility. UNCA is a member of the NCAA's Big South Conference. Division I intercollegiate sports include men's basketball, baseball, cross-country, golf, soccer, tennis, and track and women's basketball, cross-country, soccer, tennis, track, and volleyball.

Study Abroad There are numerous study-abroad opportunities. Students may take part in summer programs sponsored by UNCA at Oxford and Cambridge; study for a semester in Santander, Spain; study at the Universidad del Azuay, a university in Cuenca, Ecuador, with which UNCA has an exchange relationship; and take advantage of summer and academic-year programs abroad at sites ranging from Costa Rica to Poland offered by the North Carolina Consortium for Study Abroad.

Support Services UNCA complies with laws that are designed to protect the rights of disabled persons, including the Americans with Disabilities Act (ADA) of 1990 and Section 504 of the Rehabilitation Act of 1973. UNCA focuses on the students as individuals and works toward equal opportunity, full integration into the campus environment, physical accessibility, and the provision of reasonable accommodations, auxiliary aids, and services to students.

Job Opportunities Work opportunities on campus include federal and institutional work-study.

Tuition: $768 for state residents, $7186 for nonresidents, per year (1998–99)

Room and Board: $4058

Mandatory Fees: $1124

Contact: Director: Dr. Phyllis Lang, 141 Karpen Hall, Asheville, North Carolina 28804; Telephone: 704-251-6227; Fax: 704-251-6614; E-mail:plang@unca.edu; Web site: http://www.unca.edu/factsheets/honors_fact.html/

University of North Carolina at Chapel Hill

4 Pu G L Tr

▼ Honors Program

The Honors Program at the University of North Carolina (UNC) at Chapel Hill offers a challenging curriculum of small classes and seminars at one of the nation's premier research universities. The more than 100 honors courses taught during each academic year are primarily for first-year students, sophomores, and juniors. The senior honors program centers on writing a thesis in a student's major department.

Honors courses are small, usually limited to no more than 15 to 20 students, and they are taught by regular members of the faculty, including many who have won teaching awards. The courses cover a wide variety of topics in the humanities, social sciences, natural sciences, and fine arts. Some of these courses are honors sections of regular courses and others are special seminars especially created for the Honors Program. The Honors Office awards course development grants each year to enable faculty members to create seminars that are interdisciplinary or incorporate new approaches to teaching. Some seminars provide opportunities for service in order to apply classroom principles and theory to real world challenges. One Civic Arts seminar, for example, combines the study of urban education and the policy debates surrounding it with hands-on experience mentoring junior high school students from the nearby city of Durham.

The Honors Program also encourages its students to study abroad and operates four honors semester-abroad programs in cooperation with the University's Study Abroad Office. The Honors Semester in London is the University's academic year-round presence in London, providing 30 students each semester an opportunity to live among Londoners, attend seminars taught by outstanding faculty members drawn from area universities, and take daily advantage of the cultural riches of this unique metropolis. A summer Honors Program in London, led by a UNC professor, gives students a chance to take classes in British literature and culture and to pursue individual research and study interests. Honors and other qualified students may also spend a semester in Prague, exploring this remarkable city and the issues transforming Central and Eastern Europe. The Honors Semester in Australia links UNC–Chapel Hill with two outstanding universities there. Students may spend a semester either at the University of Melbourne or at Murdoch University in Perth.

Honors advisers help students plan their curricula in light of their educational and career goals. The Undergraduate Advisory Board organizes an array of activities outside the classroom. These include service projects, social events, and Food for Thought, a series of informal faculty lectures and discussions with students.

One distinctive feature of the Honors Program at UNC is its accessibility. Indeed, the *1998 Fiske Guide to Colleges* called the Honors Program at Chapel Hill one of the "most accessible in the country." Students not initially invited into the program may apply after arriving on campus. Moreover, students who are not in the Honors Program can take honors courses on a space-available basis if they have at least an overall B average.

During the fall semester of 1999, the Honors Program will move to its new home, the James M. Johnston Center for Undergraduate Excellence. It will feature seminar rooms, offices for distinguished honors faculty members, two state-of-the-art computer classrooms, facilities for lectures and other special events, and a lounge where students can have a cup of coffee, read a newspaper, or converse with other students or a faculty member. The building will also house an Office for Undergraduate Research and the Office for Burch Programs, including the Burch Fellows Program and the Burch Field Research Seminars. Through the former, students can apply for competitive fellowships to pursue independent projects. The Field Research Seminars enable professors to take small groups of students off campus for a semester in order to conduct research on a particular topic.

The Honors Program was created in 1954 and maintains an enrollment of approximately 650 first-year students, sophomores, and juniors as well as approximately 300 seniors working on honors theses in their major departments. More than 300 other students take advantage of honors course offerings each year.

Participation Requirements: After entering the Honors Program, students must maintain a cumulative GPA of at least 3.0 and take at least two honors courses per academic year in order to remain in the program through the junior year. Students receive a notation on their official transcripts for each academic year in which they complete the Honors Program requirements.

In the senior year, the successful completion and defense of an honors thesis under the direction of a faculty mentor qualifies a student for graduation with Honors or Highest Honors and to have this distinction designated on the diploma. To begin work on an honors thesis, a student must have a minimum overall GPA of at least 3.2 and permission of her or his major department. A student may write a thesis without having previously participated in the Honors Program.

Admission Process: There is no separate application for the Honors Program for incoming first-year students. Students are selected for invitation into the program in three separate rounds from the pool of high school seniors admitted to UNC at Chapel Hill: in mid-December, early March, and early April. Two hundred students, about 6 percent of the entire first-year class at the University, join the program each fall. The selection is based primarily on academic criteria, such as a student's course selection, class rank, grades, and SAT I/ACT scores.

First-year students may apply to the program at the start of their second semester, and sophomores may apply at the start of the fall semester. Students who transfer to UNC as sophomores may apply at the start of their first academic year.

Scholarship Availability: The UNC Honors Office has no scholarships to distribute directly to students; however, need-based scholarships and several types of merit-based awards are available through the University's Office of Student Aid and Scholarships. Because of the high academic accomplishment of Honors Program participants, many receive merit awards. In 1998, more than 60 percent of first-year honors students received merit scholarships.

The Campus Context: The University of North Carolina at Chapel Hill was founded in 1789 as the nation's first public university. *U.S. News & World Report's 1999 Annual Guide to America's Best Colleges* ranked UNC–Chapel Hill as the nation's third-best public university and twenty-fourth among all universities. The campus is situated in the heart of Chapel Hill, a community of about 50,000 that is widely considered one of the most appealing college towns anywhere. It is at the western point of the Research Triangle, an area of about 1-million people comprising Chapel Hill, the cities of Durham and Raleigh, and Research Triangle Park, home of many corporate offices and scientific research centers. Chapel Hill has one of the best-known and most exciting live music scenes in the country. Cultural highlights on the historic campus include the Morehead Planetarium, the Ackland Art Museum, the beautiful Coker Arboretum, and indoor and outdoor theaters. UNC Hospital, a leading center for medical research and teaching, is on campus, as are most of the venues for Tar Heel athletic events, including the Dean E. Smith Center, Carmichael Auditorium, Koury Natatorium, and Kenan Stadium.

The University offers more than fifty undergraduate majors in the College of Arts and Sciences as well as undergraduate degree programs in professional schools, such as the Schools of Journal-

Interpreting the symbols: **2**=two-year college, **4**=four-year college; **Pu**=public or state college, **Pr**=private college; **G**=general honors program; **D**=departmental honors program; **S**=small program (fewer than 100 students), **M**=midsize program (100 to 500 students), **L**=large program (more than 500 students); **Sc**=scholarships available in honors program; **Tr**=transfer students accepted into honors program; **HBC**=historically black college; **AA**=academic advisors; **GA**=graduate advisors; **FA**=fellowship advisors.

ism and Mass Communication, Business Administration, Education, Public Health, Pharmacy, and Nursing. UNC also has numerous graduate programs in the humanities, social sciences, and natural sciences as well as in its professional schools, including the ones mentioned above and the Schools of Medicine, Law, Dentistry, Social Work, and Information and Library Science.

Student Body UNC's undergraduate enrollment is 15,400 out of a total enrollment of 24,000. Eighty-two percent of the student body is from North Carolina, and the remaining 18 percent comes from forty-two different states and thirty-seven different countries. African-American students make up 11.2 percent of undergraduates; Asian students, 4.8 percent; Native Americans, approximately 1 percent; and international students, approximately 1 percent. About 61 percent of undergraduates are women. More than one third of undergraduates receive some form of financial aid. Many students participate in the more than 370 clubs and student organizations on campus. There are more than 40 fraternities and sororities, and about 18 percent of undergraduates belong to these organizations.

Faculty The University has 2,420 faculty members, 94 percent of whom hold the terminal degree in their fields.

Key Facilities The 15 on-campus libraries (excluding independent libraries administered by individual departments) have cumulative holdings of nearly 5 million bound volumes, more than 4 million microforms, and more than 44,000 subscriptions to serial publications. In addition to traditional resources, the library system offers a range of powerful electronic research tools, including ninety fully equipped Pentium workstations that permit access to the library's catalogs and the Internet, as well as online indexes, databases, and full-text services.

The many campus computer labs, fifteen of them administered by a central technology office and others by individual departments, give students convenient access to the latest equipment and software. In addition, each dormitory room is hard-wired for Internet access. Beginning with the first-year class entering in the fall of 2000, all incoming students will be required to own laptop computers, which will be offered at a discount price as part of the Carolina Computing Initiative.

Honorary Societies Phi Beta Kappa

Athletics UNC is an NCAA Division I university with twenty-eight varsity teams, including football, fencing, and women's crew as well as men's and women's soccer, basketball, swimming, lacrosse, and track and field. Students can also participate in more than sixty intramural and club sports. Athletic facilities open to students include basketball, tennis, and racquetball courts; indoor and outdoor pools; an outdoor track; a golf course; bowling alleys; low and high ropes courses; general purpose playing fields; and the Student Recreation Center, which operates a well-equipped weight room, cardiovascular machines, and aerobics classes.

Study Abroad Special honors study-abroad programs send more than 100 students to four destinations each year. In addition to these opportunities, the general UNC Study Abroad Program administers more than seventy programs in twenty-eight different nations. Honors students are encouraged to take advantage of either option.

Support Services In addition to tutorial services that may be offered by individual academic departments on campus, the Writing Center and the Learning Center are open to all students. The centers provide consultation on particular assignments and assistance in the development of general skills and strategies for writing, studying, time management, and test taking. Learning Disabilities Services assists students with diagnosed learning disabilities and/or attention deficit disorders and students who have sustained severe head injuries in achieving their academic potential within the regular academically competitive curriculum. Student Health offers basic medical care of all kinds, and the University Counseling Center provides confidential personal counseling and psychological services. Career Services assists students in obtaining internships, in long- and short-range career planning, and in preparing effective job applications.

Student Disability Services works actively with the classroom scheduling office to ensure that classroom accessibility is not a problem for any student. A regular point-to-point shuttle service operates on campus for all students; the shuttle fleet includes three lift-equipped vans that operate by pre-arrangement.

Job Opportunities Many undergraduates hold jobs through campus work-study programs or with the numerous places of business adjacent to campus in downtown Chapel Hill.

Tuition: $1456 for residents, $10,622 for nonresidents, per year (1998–1999)

Room and board: $5500

Mandatory Fees: $403.16

Contact: Associate Dean for Honors: Robert C. Allen; Assistant Dean for Honors: W. Miles Fletcher, 300 Steele Building, CB 3510, Chapel Hill, North Carolina 27599-3510; Telephone: 919-966-5110; Fax: 919-962-1548; Web site: http://www.unc.edu/depts/honors

UNIVERSITY OF NORTH CAROLINA AT CHARLOTTE

4 Pu G M Sc Tr

▼ University Honors Program

The University Honors Program at the University of North Carolina at Charlotte offers a curriculum of study that is creative, imaginative, and challenging. The program's innovative course work focuses on global issues, including war and peace, economics and the international community, science and values, and human rights. Enrichment seminars introduce students to the arts and diverse cultural activities of the Charlotte metropolitan area and the world through an Honors Study Abroad experience.

Beyond the classroom, honors students volunteer in a variety of service projects ranging from delivering food to a soup kitchen in Charlotte to working with children in Scotland. Many honors students choose to live in Poplar Hall, a unique coed, apartment-style residence hall considered to be the most desirable on campus. Features of Poplar Hall include a computer lab devoted exclusively to honors students as well as spacious common areas where students attend lectures, discussion groups, and honors meetings. Other highlights of the Honors Program include an annual retreat to Sunset Beach.

The University Honors Program is more than just rigorous classes. Its goals are to foster creativity, stimulate the imagination, and encourage students to be active in improving the human condition.

The Honors Program has received local and national recognition for its academic excellence and community service. For example, the student-initiated project of delivering leftover cafeteria food to the uptown soup kitchen has been featured in national publications such as *USA Today* and *Ecodemia*.

Honors students have also received National Merit Scholarship awards such as the Phi Kappa Phi Graduate Fellowship.

The University Honors Program at UNCC began thirteen years ago and currently enrolls 205 students.

Participation Requirements: To graduate with University Honors, students must complete a four-course sequence of honors courses, 4 credit hours of enrichment seminars, a 40-clock-hour community service laboratory, and a senior project. Graduates must maintain a 3.0 GPA overall and 3.2 GPA in University Honors courses.

Admission Process: UNCC actively recruits the upper 2–3 percent of entering students into the Honors Program as they apply to the University. The admission criteria are based on high school rank and SAT scores, which results in a predicted GPA. All applicants must submit an essay along with their application. Upper-division students with a GPA above 3.5 are also encouraged to apply to University Honors.

Scholarship Availability: Approximately 40 percent of the full-merit scholars who are enrolled at UNCC participate in the University Honors Program. Although the program actively recruits them, their participation is by their election. The Honors Program also awards small study-abroad scholarships to all active honors students who choose to study abroad.

The Campus Context: As the fourth-largest member of the University of North Carolina system, UNC Charlotte combines state-of-the-art facilities with 1,000 acres of landscaped grounds, forests, and streams. Located in the leading urban center of the Carolinas, the campus is easily accessible from major interstates and highways. The University, neighboring University Research Park, and new residential communities make up the rapidly growing University City area of north Charlotte.

UNC Charlotte offers its 16,370 students eighty-one undergraduate and graduate degree programs. In addition, the city of Charlotte, located in the Southern Piedmont of North Carolina, is one of the fastest-growing urban centers in the nation and offers a diversity of cultural and educational opportunities.

Student Body Undergraduate enrollment is 49 percent men and 51 percent women. The ethnic distribution includes 16.7 percent African Americans and 2.7 percent international students. Twenty-seven percent of the population are out-of-state students; 27 percent of students live on campus. Approximately 6,400 students received financial aid in 1997–98. There are twenty-three fraternities and sororities and a new student center for campuswide activities.

Faculty The total number of full-time faculty members is 655. Faculty members hold their highest degrees from U.S. graduate schools and thirty international universities. The student-faculty ratio is 16:1, and the average class size is 33.

Key Facilities The library houses 577,386 bound volumes and more than 1 million units in microform. There are more than 200 computers, including Gateway 2000 and Macintosh machines, available in student labs on campus. Internet access is provided.

Honorary Societies Phi Eta Sigma, Phi Kappa Phi, Golden Key

Athletics UNC Charlotte offers fourteen intercollegiate sports for men and women on the varsity level, including baseball, basketball, cross-country, golf, softball, soccer, tennis, track, and volleyball.

Study Abroad Numerous study-abroad opportunities exist, ranging from ten-day trips to various countries around the world to full academic years spent abroad.

Support Services Disability Services assists students with academic and physical accommodations based on documentation of disability. Services include, but are not limited to, priority registration assistance; orientation to available services; development of individualized educational plans; special testing accommodations; taped textbooks, Braille, and/or large print services for visually impaired students; assistive technology loans; referrals to tutoring and other campus support services; interpreting services for students who are deaf; individual counseling and advising; and referrals to human services agencies.

Job Opportunities Work opportunities on campus are available, ranging from cooperative education with multinational corporations to working in the campus bookstore, library, or an academic department. UNC Charlotte has its own Student Employment Office to aid interested students in finding a job.

Tuition: $1800 for state residents, $9320 for nonresidents, per year (1997–98)

Room and Board: $3800 minimum

Contact: Director: Dr. Al Maisto, Macy 101, 9201 University City Boulevard, Charlotte, North Carolina 28223-0001; Telephone: 704-547-4824; Fax: 704-547-3116; E-mail: amaisto@email.uncc.edu

UNIVERSITY OF NORTH CAROLINA AT GREENSBORO

4 Pu G M Tr FA

▼ Honors Program

The mission of the University of North Carolina at Greensboro (UNCG) Honors Program is to enrich the intellectual lives of able and highly motivated undergraduate students, to create a community of students and faculty members who love learning, and to celebrate the outstanding achievements of students. To accomplish these goals, the Honors Program sponsors honors courses, provides advising about how to take advantage of the program and other academic opportunities, administers awards that recognize academic excellence, presents special programs, and organizes extracurricular activities.

The Honors Program is the program of choice for students who have the talent and determination to take full advantage of their time at UNCG. Through special courses and research projects, a variety of extracurricular activities including study abroad, and the camaraderie of top students and faculty members, the Honors Program provides students with opportunities and challenges that enhance their education at UNCG. Along the way, the Honors Program staff stands ready to provide guidance, support, and encouragement to help students craft a program of study that meets their individual needs and interests and opens up new possibilities for the future.

Teachers of honors courses are deeply engaged with their disciplines and dedicated to helping students achieve their greatest potential. Courses are typically small (20–22 students) and foster discussion, collaboration, and mutual discovery among students and faculty members. Many of the advanced honors courses, such as the Senior Honors Project, allow students to do original and sophisticated work and are an excellent preparation for graduate school, professional training, and other postgraduation endeavors.

The Honors Program also sponsors a number of extracurricular events, many of which are created and run with the help its students. Among these events are weekly coffees, the annual Raft Debate, the annual Student Symposium, lectures and special performances, field trips, pizza parties, and community service projects.

In collaboration with UNCG's Office of International Programs, the Honors Program provides interested honors students with the chance to have more than the usual study-abroad experience. Before going abroad, students meet together with a UNCG faculty member to discuss background readings and the character of the country they are about to visit. Once abroad, students and the UNCG faculty member spend a week exploring and taking in cultural activities before classes begin. During their semester, students take classes, travel, and engage in a variety of writing assignments that allow them to reflect on their experience.

Participation Requirements: The Honors Program is divided into two components: a general education component (12 semester hours of honors courses) to be completed by the end of the sophomore year and a discipline-based component (12 semester

Interpreting the symbols: **2**=two-year college, **4**=four-year college; **Pu**=public or state college, **Pr**=private college; **G**=general honors program; **D**=departmental honors program; **S**=small program (fewer than 100 students), **M**=midsize program (100 to 500 students), **L**=large program (more than 500 students); **Sc**=scholarships available in honors program; **Tr**=transfer students accepted into honors program; **HBC**=historically black college; **AA**=academic advisors; **GA**=graduate advisors; **FA**=fellowship advisors.

hours, including a senior honors project) to be completed by graduation. Students must maintain a GPA of at least 3.3 to participate in the program. However, they may complete either component or complete both of the components as their interest, abilities, and circumstances allow. Students who complete the Honors Program are recognized at a banquet held at the end of the spring semester. Students who complete the requirements for General Education Honors receive a Certificate of General Education Honors and have that honor noted on their official transcript. Students who complete Disciplinary Honors receive a Certificate of Honors in their major/interdisciplinary studies and have that honor, along with the title of their senior honors project, noted on their official transcript. Finally, students who complete both General Education Honors and Disciplinary Honors receive a Certificate of Full University Honors in their major/interdisciplinary studies and have that honor, along with the title of their senior honors project, noted on their official transcript.

Admission Process: New freshmen must have at least a 3.8 weighted high school GPA, or at least a 1200 SAT score (or ACT composite score of 27 or higher), or be a Merit Award Program finalist, or be the recipient of a Deans' Scholars award, a Superintendents' Scholarship, or a Teaching Fellows Scholarship. Transfer students must have at least a 3.3 GPA from their former school(s). Current UNCG students must have a 3.3 GPA. Eligible students may join the Honors Program by filling out an application form, available on the Honors Program Web site or in the Honors Program Office.

The Campus Context: UNCG is located in a thriving metropolitan area with a population approaching 1 million. Greensboro offers the amenities of a larger city while still affording the charm and comfort of a small-town atmosphere and is located only 2 hours from North Carolina's mountains and only 4 hours from North Carolina's beaches. The UNCG campus itself is located near the center of town, yet its immediate surroundings include the College Hill neighborhood of student and faculty homes, quaint apartment houses, and Tate Street, which is lined with a wide variety of shops, restaurants, and coffeehouses. Academic programs are offered in the College of Arts and Sciences and UNCG's six professional schools: the Joseph M. Bryan School of Business and Economics, School of Education, School of Health and Human Performance, School of Human Environmental Sciences, School of Music, and School of Nursing.

Student Body With approximately 13,000 students, the UNCG student body is diverse in its interests and backgrounds. Of the total University population, 32 percent are men and 68 percent are women. The ethnic distribution of the total UNCG population is 75 percent white and 25 percent minority, including 17 percent African American. Approximately 55 percent of UNCG students receive some type of financial aid.

Faculty Among the 595 full-time faculty members are nationally known scholars whose research and creative work regularly contribute new knowledge to their fields; 87 percent hold terminal degrees in their disciplines. The student-faculty ratio is 14:1.

Key Facilities Jackson Library has more than 2.7 million items, including 703,000 federal and state documents and 970,000 items in microtext. It subscribes to 5,100 printed periodicals, newspapers, and other serials and more than 6,400 electronic journals in full text. The library catalog, electronic reserves, more than 140 online and full-text databases, and other resources are available in the library, on campus (via a personal computer or one of UNCG's many computer labs), and on the Web with a valid UNCG ID. The Weatherspoon Art Gallery houses what is considered to be the most outstanding permanent collection of contemporary art in the Southeast. Its new $25.7-million music building has a 350-seat recital hall, a 130-seat organ recital hall, and numerous other rooms for performance, practice, research, and study. In summer 2002, the newly renovated and expanded student center, the Elliott University Center, is scheduled to open, and the University is eagerly awaiting the completion of its new state-of-the-art science building.

Athletics UNCG has a sixteen-team intercollegiate athletics program that competes in NCAA Division I and the Southern Conference. Student athletes have received thirty All-America awards, fifteen Academic All-America honors, and numerous regional and conference honors, and there have been thirteen team appearances and fifteen individual appearances in NCAA tournaments, including five by the men's soccer team. Students can also participate in a wide variety of intramural sports, fitness programs, informal recreation, club sports, team building, challenge courses, and outdoor recreation. The Rec Center covers 87,000 square feet and includes a 38-foot climbing wall, a three-court gymnasium (for basketball, volleyball, soccer, and badminton), a jogging track, racquetball courts, a weight room with Cybex and free weights, exercise bikes, elliptical trainers, and treadmills. Students may also use the swimming pool, the newly renovated tennis courts, and various athletic fields.

Study Abroad UNCG's International Programs Center is able to place students in any of thirty-five countries overseas. The UNCG Honors Program, in conjunction with the International Programs Center, runs an Honors Abroad Program that provides travel and learning opportunities in addition to the regular study-abroad experience, all at a cost similar to that of a resident student at UNCG.

Support Services The Student Success Center provides tutoring, academic counseling, computer instruction, skills development, and workshops. The Career Services Center provides guidance and resources to students and alumni, including career planning, experiential learning, and student employment. UNCG also offers a variety of support services for the special needs of adult students, disabled students, and international students.

Tuition: $1302 for state residents, $9752 for nonresidents per year (2001–02)

Room and Board: $4998

Mandatory Fees: $1243

Contact: Director: Dennis Patrick Leyden, 112 Foust Building, University of North Carolina at Greensboro, P.O. Box 26170, Greensboro, North Carolina 27402-6170; Telephone: 336-334-5538; E-mail: askhonors@uncg.edu; Web site: http://www.uncg.edu/hss

University of North Carolina at Pembroke

4 Pu G M Tr AA

▼ University Honors College

The University Honors College (UHC) at the University of North Carolina at Pembroke (UNC Pembroke or UNCP) recognizes and promotes the scholarly and personal growth of academically accomplished students in an intellectually stimulating environment with greater curricular flexibility and close interaction with faculty. The UHC learning community includes six interdisciplinary seminars within the General Education curriculum, a leadership program, cultural and service opportunities, and a senior research project. The University Honors College provides opportunities for supplemental cultural experiences and supports student participation in relevant academic conferences within the state, regionally, and nationally. Honors students are encouraged to consider study abroad and to pursue graduate or professional education upon graduation. The University Honors College is located in Old Main, the signature building on campus, and includes a computer lab and lounge for UHC students. University Honors College students may elect to live in shared residential facilities. Graduates receive a special diploma at commencement and the designation of University Honors College graduate on all transcripts. The University Honors College was inaugurated during the 2001–02 academic year. It supplants the longstanding Chancellor's Scholars Program. Currently, 30 freshmen are enrolled in the University Honors College. The goal is 5 percent of the total undergraduate student body or approximately 200 students.

Participation Requirements: Students who enter the University Honors College as freshmen begin with an intensive learning community experience, taking four general education core courses together, to support relationship building and program identification. The UHC curriculum includes a total of four interdisciplinary seminars, of which one is generally taken each semester. A two-semester sequence of guided research, with a faculty member in the major field, provides an opportunity to undertake an independent creative project or research endeavor that is presented to the members of the academic community. Research throughout the collegiate experience is supported through funding and opportunities for participation in conferences and research endeavors.

The University Honors College meets on a monthly basis to support a sense of community. Members of the University Honors College participate in cultural activities on campus and develop a University service project annually. Generally during the freshman year, UHC students are part of LSOP (Leadership and Service Opportunities Program), designed to enhance leadership development and to support community involvement. University Honors College students receive recognition in a number of formal and informal ways including priority registration, honors advising, special encouragement for study abroad programs and graduate study and selected research opportunities. In a relatively small institution, University Honors College students are well known and well regarded.

Continuation in the University Honors College requires a minimum GPA of 3.0 at the end of the freshman year, 3.25 at the end of the sophomore year and 3.50 at the end of the junior year, as well as successful completion of required course work, the research sequence and other program expectations.

Admission Process: University Honors College students are accepted through a special application process. Students are selected based upon documented academic ability and demonstrated leadership. Motivated students with strong SAT (1100) or ACT (24) scores and superior academic records (minimum 3.5 GPA) are invited to submit an application to the University Honors College. Two letters of recommendation should accompany the application as well as a statement written by the student describing his or her interest in participating in an honors program. Admission decisions are made by the program director with the assistance of the advisory committee.

Scholarship Availability: Admission to the UHC is independent of financial assistance. However, fully two thirds of the University student body receives some form of financial assistance and all students admitted to the University Honors College are considered for financial assistance. Sources of aid include need-based grants, federal and state loan programs, and endowed specialized and general scholarships. Some financial assistance programs carry a work/service requirement of 8 hours weekly in a University or community placement.

Campus Context: UNC Pembroke is one of the sixteen campuses in the University of North Carolina system. Founded in 1887 to educate American Indians, the University is now one of the most culturally diverse institutions in the southeast. The 126-acre campus is located on the coastal plains of southeastern North Carolina near I-95 and U.S. Highway 74. The University is approximately 1½ hours south of Raleigh and 1½ hours north of the North and South Carolina beaches and 2 hours east of Charlotte.

A regional public comprehensive university, UNC Pembroke awards a broad range of baccalaureate and master's degrees accredited by the Commission on Colleges of the Southern Association of Colleges and Schools. The University is organized around one college and three schools: the College of Arts and Sciences and the Schools of Business, Education, and Graduate Studies. University Honors College students elect course work from among fifty-five majors and more than 100 concentrations, interdisciplinary programs, and academic minors. The most popular majors among all students are education and business.

Student Body With 3,500 undergraduates and 500 graduate students, UNC Pembroke offers opportunities available in a large institution with the personal attention characteristic of a small college. UNC Pembroke is recognized as one of the most culturally diverse schools in the Southeast. Students are drawn from seventeen nations and twenty states. Participation in athletics, clubs, and organizations of all kinds is enhanced by the size and welcoming environment of the UNC Pembroke. Most departments have clubs for their majors. Other clubs reflect the diversity of the UNCP student body, including the Native American Students Organization, the African American Student Organization, and the International Student Organization. Many cocurricular activities complement academic programs including APPLE Corps (peer leadership), University Marshals, Student Ambassadors, University Band, Pep Band, Chamber Singers, Concert Choir, Jazz Ensemble, Gospel Choir, UNCP Television, the *Indianhead* (yearbook), the *Pine Needle* (student newspaper), and University Theatre. UNC Pembroke has six national and three local fraternities. There are six national sororities and one local sorority. A Leadership and Service Opportunities Program (LSOP) enables students to develop leadership skills through campus and community service as well as cultural activities. All University Honors College students participate in the LSOP program.

Faculty There are 165 full-time faculty members and 82 part-time faculty members. The student-faculty ratio is 16:1. Seventy-one percent of faculty have the terminal degree in their teaching discipline. The average class size is 25 students, with very few classes more than 40. No classes are taught by teaching assistants.

Key Facilities The Sampson-Livermore Library serves a chief information resource center for the University and as a link to other libraries within the University of North Carolina and the nation. The library, with 300,000 volumes and 1,500 periodical subscriptions, is a depository for selected state and federal documents and houses local historical materials. Library services include reference and information consultation and assistance, computerized database searching, interlibrary loan, orientation, and library use instruction. Resources available to patrons include print materials for research and recreational reading, print and online indexes, a computerized catalogue, Internet access, microform and photocopiers, study facilities, a computer laboratory, multimedia equipment, and materials.

The Office of University Computing and Information Services provides infrastructure and support for academic computing services. There are approximately 300 computers on campus that are available for student use, including a 24-hour lab, multiple departmental labs, and general lab facilities. The University provides Internet access, e-mail, Web hosting, and data storage from all labs and dormitory rooms. A Blackboard CMS server supports classroom sites. The University Honors College has a dedicated computer lab within the University Honors College facility available only to UHC students.

Athletics UNC Pembroke competes in NCAA Division II athletics as a member of the Peach Belt Athletic Conference with seven men's varsity sports (baseball, basketball, cross-country, golf, soccer, track and field, and wrestling) and seven women's varsity sports (basketball, cross-country, soccer, softball, tennis, track

Interpreting the symbols: **2**=two-year college, **4**=four-year college; **Pu**=public or state college, **Pr**=private college; **G**=general honors program; **D**=departmental honors program; **S**=small program (fewer than 100 students), **M**=midsize program (100 to 500 students), **L**=large program (more than 500 students); **Sc**=scholarships available in honors program; **Tr**=transfer students accepted into honors program; **HBC**=historically black college; **AA**=academic advisors; **GA**=graduate advisors; **FA**=fellowship advisors.

and field, and volleyball). The team nickname is the Braves and the mascot is the red-tailed hawk. The school colors are black and gold.

Study Abroad The Office of International Programs provides opportunities to students who wish to study abroad. Overseas opportunities are currently available in thirty-five countries worldwide through UNC-EP, the systemwide program that enables students to participate in affordable, high-quality semester or yearlong study abroad programs.

Support Services The Office of Disability Support Services provides services and tools to enable students by the Americans with Disabilities Act and Section 504 of the Rehabilitation Act of 1973 to better accomplish their educational and academic goals.

Job Opportunities A limited number of work-study positions, linked to financial need, are available on campus. Work placements include the library, cafeteria, administrative and departmental offices, and laboratories. The Career Opportunities Center offers a variety of employment and career planning services including internships and co-op experiences during the student's academic career.

Tuition: In-state, $576; out-of-state, $4537 (2001–02)

Room and Board: Residential fees vary according to facility and meal plan selection.

Mandatory Fees: $458.50, plus $45 insurance (2001–02)

Contact: Dr. Carolyn R. Thompson, University Honors College, University of North Carolina at Pembroke, P.O. Box 1510, Pembroke, North Carolina 28272-1510; Telephone: 910-521-6841; Fax: 910-521-6606; E-mail: honors@uncp.edu; Web site: http://www.uncp.edu/honors_college

University of North Carolina at Wilmington

4 Pu G/D M Sc Tr

▼ Honors Scholars Program

The Honors Scholars Program at the University of North Carolina at Wilmington (UNCW) provides academically talented students with a variety of innovative and unique educational experiences both in and out of the classroom. The program seeks to encourage curiosity, critical thinking, and independent work skills by offering exciting academic and cultural activities as well as the opportunity for close working and social relationships with the faculty members. The program includes academics, cocurricular activities, and the opportunity to reside in a designated honors residence.

In fall 2001, there were a total of 330 students in the program, including 90 freshmen, 90 sophomores, and 150 juniors and seniors.

Participation Requirements: Honors students take a 3-credit freshman interdisciplinary honors seminar in their first semester and a 3-credit honors topical seminar in their second year. In addition, students take 2 credits of honors enrichment seminars and 12 hours of honors sections of basic studies in their first two years. Honors classes are small—usually 20 students or fewer—to encourage discussion and independent work. If eligible, students may achieve Departmental Honors in their major in their last two years, culminating in a 6-credit senior project. The University Honors designation requires the full four-year participation, with honors in a discipline.

Admission Process: Students may enter the program as incoming freshmen (by invitation based on high school grades, SAT/ACT scores, and class rank) or as sophomores based on earned GPA. Students enter Departmental Honors based on an earned GPA of 3.2 or better.

Scholarship Availability: A limited number of merit scholarships are available on a competitive basis for students accepted into the Honors Scholars Program. In addition, several academic departments have scholarship funds for majors in their disciplines.

The Campus Context: UNCW is one of the sixteen autonomous campuses of the University of North Carolina. Located on a beautiful 650-acre campus in the historic port city of Wilmington and 5 miles from the Atlantic Ocean, UNCW is composed of the College of Arts and Sciences and three schools—the Cameron School of Business Administration, the Watson School of Education, and the School of Nursing. For the fourth consecutive year, UNCW is ranked among the top ten public regional undergraduate universities in the South by *U.S. News & World Report's America's Best Colleges. Kiplinger's* rated UNCW as one of thirteen public universities that are best for out-of-state students. UNCW offers seventy undergraduate degree programs and twenty-five graduate degree programs, including an undergraduate marine biology program ranked as one of the top five in the nation by the *Gourman Report.* The new $17.5-million Center for Marine Science, on the Intracoastal Waterway, is the region's premier research, education, and public service facility dedicated to the marine sciences. What distinguishes UNCW from many other comprehensive universities is its promise to educate for the twenty-first century students who have a sense of civic responsibility and leadership. This promise is grounded in a unique academic focus that connects student learning in and out of the classroom across four broad themes: regional engagement, natural environment, information technology, and internationalization. Ingrained into the academic program, these themes provide a framework for imparting knowledge so students know that what they learn is connected and how it is relevant to living in the real world.

Student Body Undergraduate enrollment is 9,800. The student population has a minority enrollment of 8 percent and an international enrollment of 1 percent. The campus has a residential quality to it, with 25 percent of undergraduates living on campus and another 50 percent residing within a 1-mile radius of the campus in private apartment complexes. A new 265-bed residence hall is scheduled to open in fall 2003, and a 400-bed apartment complex is under design review. There are twelve fraternities and twelve sororities with no on-campus chapter housing.

Faculty Of the 607 faculty members, 426 are full-time and 181 are part-time. Ninety percent hold a Ph.D. or other terminal degree in their field. The student-faculty ratio is 16:1, and the average class size is 16 students.

Key Facilities The William Madison Randall Library houses 493,784 hardbound volumes, 4,280 subscriptions, 370,175 U.S. government documents, and 759,245 microfilm files. The library's reach is extended through a multiuniversity consortium; more than 100 electronic databases; a fifty-station computer lab open 24 hours a day, seven days a week; and twenty wireless laptop computers available for checkout.

The ninety-six-bed Honors House is a living/learning environment for students enrolled in UNCW's Honors Program. The Honors House features a 24-hours-a-day/seven-days-a-week computer lab, a full kitchen, a TV lounge, a classroom, and meeting space to accommodate a dynamic student population, with members committed to student leadership, scholarship, and service.

The Center for Marine Science at Myrtle Grove is the newest and most technologically advanced coastal ocean science research facility along the eastern seaboard. It supports research in oceanography, coastal and wetland studies, marine biomedical and environmental physiology, marine biotechnology and aquaculture, and marine geology.

The National Undersea Research Center at UNCW is funded by a grant from the National Oceanic and Atmospheric Administration as part of the National Undersea Research Program (NURP). The center at UNCW supports undersea research off the southeastern United States from North Carolina to Texas. The center's facilities and staff members are located at the University's

Center for Marine Science in Wilmington, North Carolina, and in Key Largo, Florida. UNCW's Aquarius, the world's only underwater laboratory, and the National Undersea Research Center received the prestigious 2000 Conservation Award from the Wildlife Conservation Society.

UNCW's 108-acre Ev-Henwood Nature Preserve and Coastal Forest Research Station in Brunswick County is also available for public tours. The $8-million UNCW Student Recreation Facility, funded totally with student fees, opened in 2000. The Herbert Bluethenthal Memorial Wildflower Preserve is a 10-acre tract in the center of the campus and is dedicated to the preservation of the rich and varied flora of southeastern North Carolina.

The Upperman African-American Cultural Center, located in the University Union, offers programs and resources on multicultural diversity issues. Wise Alumni House, a stately historic mansion that serves as the UNCW Alumni Association's headquarters, opened in 1997 after extensive renovation. The Campus Commons, a visually attractive meeting place featuring a three-pronged lake with lighted fountains, a network of sidewalks, and an open-air amphitheater, is a site of outdoor campus activity year-round. The newest addition is the 50-foot Millennium Clock Tower, a gift of the class of 2000.

Honorary Societies UNCW recognizes outstanding scholarship through more than twenty honorary societies and academic achievement awards. A partial listing includes Phi Kappa Phi, Phi Eta Sigma National Honor Society for Freshmen, Phi Alpha Theta International Honor Society in History, Pi Mu Epsilon National Mathematics Honors Society, Psi Chi National Honor Society in Psychology, Sigma Tau Delta International English Honor Society, Upsilon Pi Epsilon International Honor Society for the Computing Sciences, Sigma Theta Tau Honor Society in Nursing, and Sigma Delta Pi National Collegiate Hispanic Honor Society.

Athletics UNCW holds NCAA Division I membership in the Colonial Athletic Association and fields nineteen varsity teams, including men's and women's programs in basketball, tennis, golf, track and field, cross-country, swimming, diving, and soccer. Other varsity programs include volleyball, softball, and baseball. UNCW consistently has one of the highest graduation rates for varsity athletes in the UNC system. The Seahawks' athletics facilities include the 6,000-seat Trask Coliseum, an Olympic-sized natatorium with a diving well, a 1,200-seat baseball stadium, a 2,000-seat soccer stadium, the Harold Greene Track and Field Complex, and the Boseman Softball Field. As part of Project 2002, an 18,000-square-foot sports medicine building is planned. Club and intramural sports include rowing, surfing, sailing, Ultimate Frisbee, and a seasonal schedule of team sports.

Study Abroad The Honors Scholars Program offers an honors semester at the University of Wales in Swansea, plus opportunities for enrichment seminars abroad during the spring break. Recent trips have included Prague, London, Scotland, and the Galapagos Islands. The Office of International Programs is responsible for faculty and student exchange programs and other international activities at the University. Its goal is to expand and strengthen international ties among individuals, units, and programs on the campus and to encourage the exchange and flow of ideas and information, which is crucial for the development of global knowledge and awareness. UNCW is a member of the International Student Exchange Program (ISEP). ISEP offers exchange possibilities for UNCW students in more than 100 universities abroad. In addition, UNCW offers exchange and study-abroad opportunities for students in Australia, Barbados, Belize, Brazil, Chile, China, Costa Rica, Ecuador, Finland, France, Germany, Great Britain, Japan, Jordan, Korea, Spain, Sweden, and Thailand. Summer study-abroad opportunities are also available to UNCW students in many locations.

Support Services Both the Office of Disability Services and the General College Advising Center assist in adapting general University programs and providing necessary services, including tutoring, testing assistance, readers, note-takers, and help with class registration.

Job Opportunities Campus work opportunities include Federal Work-Study, library, work-assistant, recreational facilities, and computer lab jobs.

Tuition and Fees: In-state, $2571; out-of-state, $9921 (per year)

Room and Board: $5506

Contact: Director: Dr. Kate Bruce, University of North Carolina at Wilmington, Wilmington, North Carolina, 28403-3297; Telephone: 910-962-3374; Fax: 910-962-7020; E-mail: deanb@uncwil.edu; Web site: http://www.uncwil.edu/honors/

University of North Dakota

4 Pu G M Tr AA

▼ Honors Program

Students of all majors and interests take part in the Honors Program at the University of North Dakota (UND). By emphasizing small classes (18 students or less), close student-faculty cooperation, and an interdisciplinary approach to learning, the Honors Program provides the opportunity for talented and engaged students to move beyond the traditional college education in pursuit of research, creativity, and academic excellence.

The general education requirements are waived for all honors students, and the program routinely works with students to tailor a program of study that best fits their goals, talents, and aspirations. This flexibility allows students to balance the demands of their more traditional major with the goals they wish to accomplish through honors. A student may combine honors with any major on campus or use the program as a vehicle for designing an individual major. The Honors Program prepares students for graduate school, professional school, or immediate employment.

The classroom is where the true honors experience is fostered. Faculty members design the courses they have always wanted to teach, and students share in that excitement in situations where their opinions and knowledge are respected like never before. Honors students have taken part in and even helped teach such courses as the Sociology of Sport, Approaching the Holocaust, Independent Filmmaking, and the Brain. At least ten special colloquia such as these are offered every semester to ensure that students find honors courses that fit their interests and their schedules. Special events outside the classroom, such as conferences and performances, contribute to the spectrum of ideas already presented in the curriculum. The Senior Thesis project and other independent studies allow for close contact with faculty members and ideas. Honors students have opportunities to have fun, taking trips, dancing at the annual formal, publishing their own magazine, and participating in community service projects. Benefits of membership include special advisement, early registration, and access to a centrally located facility complete with a computer lab, study rooms, and a lounge.

The Honors Program was founded in 1961. It currently has 400 students, who take advantage of a small liberal arts environment inside a large research university complete with schools of engineering, business, aerospace, law, and medicine.

Participation Requirements: Honors students must complete 24 credits of honors course work, including 8 credits of colloquia

Interpreting the symbols: **2**=two-year college, **4**=four-year college; **Pu**=public or state college, **Pr**=private college; **G**=general honors program; **D**=departmental honors program; **S**=small program (fewer than 100 students), **M**=midsize program (100 to 500 students), **L**=large program (more than 500 students); **Sc**=scholarships available in honors program; **Tr**=transfer students accepted into honors program; **HBC**=historically black college; **AA**=academic advisors; **GA**=graduate advisors; **FA**=fellowship advisors.

and 9 credits of the Senior Thesis. Students must complete the Sophomore Honors Portfolio by March of their sophomore year. The Honors Committee, made up of faculty members from a broad range of disciplines, evaluates the portfolio. Successful completion means full membership in the program and designation as a full member on each student's official transcript. Students are then allowed to move on to the Senior Thesis, a 9-credit independent project conducted over at least two semesters, usually during the senior year. A minimum 3.2 GPA must be maintained to graduate from the program.

Upon graduation, an honors student is designated a Scholar in the Honors Program and receives a special seal on his or her diploma and the proper designation on the official transcript.

Admission Process: High school seniors whose ACT or SAT scores, high school records, or other accomplishments constitute a significant record of achievement are eligible to apply to the Honors Program. Students are evaluated on these standards, along with a required essay. Those already enrolled in a college or university are encouraged to set up an appointment with the Coordinator to discuss admission.

Scholarship Availability: Although the Honors Program itself does not offer scholarships, most students receive scholarships through the University of North Dakota.

The Campus Context: The University of North Dakota is a medium-sized, comprehensive liberal arts university in the community of Grand Forks, a classic college town. With 150 programs of study and 11,764 students, UND attracts students from every state in the nation and more than forty countries. They praise UND for offering academic excellence, a wide range of opportunities, and a vigorous, exciting environment with individual attention from professors. Nearly all of the University's new students rank in the top half of their high school classes, with about half in the top quarter. UND graduates are highly regarded by prospective employers and work all over the nation and world. About 200 regional and national companies each year come to the campus to recruit UND students.

The University has ten colleges: Aerospace Sciences, Arts and Sciences, Business and Public Administration, Continuing Education, Education and Human Development, Engineering and Mines, Graduate School, Law, Medicine, and Nursing. It offers majors ranging from aerospace to zoology and is known for its meteorology, business, allied health, and engineering programs, just to name a few. Baccalaureate degree programs number ninety-one, with forty-six master's degree programs, seventeen doctoral programs, one specialist degree, and the only law and medical programs in the state.

The 550-acre campus, known for its beauty, has more than 220 buildings, which range from classic collegiate architecture to ultramodern buildings. The North Dakota Museum of Art is located on campus, along with a fine arts center, theater, concert auditorium, and top-notch athletics facilities. Grand Forks, on the North Dakota–Minnesota border, offers four distinct seasons and a safe, fun atmosphere with plenty of restaurants, shopping, and recreation, as well as a lively arts community.

Student Body UND enrolls 11,764 students, 9,785 of whom are undergraduates. About half are from North Dakota, a quarter from Minnesota, and the rest from every state and forty countries. About a third of the students choose to live in on-campus residence halls or apartments or in the thirteen fraternity and sorority houses. Most students (about 75 percent) receive some form of financial aid. American Indians make up the largest ethnic group at UND, with about 3 percent of the student body. Men slightly outnumber women, 52 percent to 48 percent. The average age of undergraduate students is 22.

Faculty Full-time faculty members and researchers number 582, with about 80 percent holding the highest degree in their field. Part-time faculty members number 153.

Key Facilities The Chester Fritz Library owns approximately 1.3 million items, receives 5,100 journals, and provides access to 2,500 electronic journals and 2,300 electronic books and Web sites. The library also contains extensive special collections and family history documents and serves as a government depository and patent and trademark depository. Branch libraries include the Energy and Environmental Research Library, the F. D. Holland Geology Library, and the Gordon Erickson Music Library. Other major libraries on campus are the Harley E. French Library of the Health Sciences and the Thormodsgard Law Library.

All residence hall rooms have a direct, high-speed connection to the Internet. Most departments have computer labs with specialized software and high-speed connections, and a 24-hour lab is available at the Memorial Union. A laptop program is in place for students enrolled at the Odegard School of Aerospace Sciences.

Honorary Societies Phi Beta Kappa, Phi Eta Sigma, Golden Key, and Mortar Board

Athletics The University of North Dakota fields men's teams in NCAA Division I ice hockey and Division II football, basketball, baseball, cross-country, golf, track and field, and swimming and diving. Women compete at the Division II level in basketball, cross-country, golf, soccer, softball, swimming and diving, track and field, volleyball, and tennis. They have a Division I independent team in ice hockey.

UND athletic teams have won seven national championships in ice hockey and three national championships in women's basketball, as well as a national football championship in 2001. UND athletes have some of the highest GPAs in the NCAA. The University was ranked tenth in the nation in 2001 for its 77 percent athlete graduation rate; the national average is 49 percent.

Athletics facilities include the new $100-million Engelstad Arena, the top college hockey facility in the nation; the new Grand Forks Alerus Center for football; and the Hyslop Sports Center, which houses two basketball courts, an Olympic-size swimming pool, handball and racquetball courts, and more.

Study Abroad Study-abroad opportunities are available through the Office of International Programs. Students can earn credit for studying abroad for a semester, a summer, or an entire year.

Job Opportunities Students have work opportunities on campus through the Federal Work-Study Program. Career Services provides assistance to students seeking internships, cooperative education experiences, and job placement after graduation.

Tuition: $3262 for North Dakota residents, $3582 for Minnesota residents, $4640 for residents from states participating in the Western Undergraduate Exchange or the Midwest Higher Education Consortium, and $7862 for other nonresidents, per year, includes fees

Room and Board: $3805

Contact: Coordinator: Jeanne Anderegg, Honors Program, Box 7187, Grand Forks, North Dakota 58202; Telephone: 701-777-3302; Fax: 701-777-2365; E-mail: jeanne_anderegg@und.nodak.edu; Web site: http://www.und.edu/dept/honors

University of North Florida

4 Pu G&D M Sc Tr

▼ University Honors Program

The University Honors Program provides students with an interdisciplinary educational experience that is dedicated to developing responsible and creative leaders. Students and faculty members form learning communities that connect the classroom to the Jacksonville area as a lab. Both the curriculum and the cocurricular features challenge students to make connections between the University and the world. Student power and responsibility shape every aspect of the program. Freshmen first see this power in action in a five-day Student-Run Orientation, which focuses upon goal setting, leadership, and experiential and service learning. The first-year foundation experience includes 11 hours of active seminars designed to help students learn from different points of view, discover how knowledge connects, and take control of their education. Second-year students continue in seminars that assist them in creating their honors portfolio and in making connections to their major. Second-, third-, and fourth-year students may serve as facilitators for honors colloquia; they also benefit from subsidized programs designed to expand their ability to apply their knowledge to the wider world through international travel, Washington internships, and study-abroad options. The program has subsidized group travel to Argentina, Brazil, China, Costa Rica, and Peru. Trips in the near future include Ireland and West Africa. The cultural learning that takes place during these trips is experiential learning in the richest sense. Students and faculty members form a learning community that explores clashing cultures and radically different natural and urban environments. Every honors student interested in a semester's internship in Washington has been funded and accepted by the Washington Center. Students of every major have been placed in prestigious internships at such places as the National Institutes of Health, the Tribune Company, *Newsweek*, the Kennedy Center, the National Organization for Women, and the Shakespeare Theatre. Student-facilitated service-learning colloquia are offered every term in areas such as refugee services, domestic violence, at-risk youth, HIV/AIDS, and the environment. Students created both a Diversity Retreat and a Teen Leadership Conference for area high school students and facilitate Racial Reconciliation Workshops each term for the campus community in connection with the film *The Color of Fear.* Because of the strength of student commitment to service, the Jacksonville Jaguars Foundation and Nike Corporation have formed a nationally unique partnership with the University of North Florida (UNF) Honors Program. Honors students created and run the Nike/Jaguars Foundation Community Scholars Mentoring Program, which provides precollege mentoring and full academic scholarships to at-risk youth who are admitted to the University. Students take responsibility, under the guidance of the Honors Service Learning Coordinator, for creating the scholarship process, administering the funds, and designing and running a three-year mentoring program. An honors dorm, designated seminar rooms, and computer and community rooms are available for honors students. The University Honors Program was founded in 1990 and enrolls 500 students.

Participation Requirements: Students who complete 17 hours of lower-division honors course work, pass their portfolio, and post a minimum 3.4 GPA but do not continue in the University Honors Program earn the distinction University Honors on their diploma. Those students who meet the above criteria and continue in the program can do so in one of two tracks. Interdisciplinary Honors requires 8 hours of honors work; a junior seminar, which consists of two colloquia in which program participants mentor first-year honors students; and a 3-hour senior thesis or special project. Students apply directly to the University Honors Program. Honors in the Major is the second track at the upper level. A variety of majors throughout the University offer this 8-hour program. GPA requirements vary by department, but all Honors in the Major students write a 6-hour thesis and participate in two colloquia to mentor first-year honors students. At graduation, students who successfully complete University Honors and one of the upper-level tracks earn the highest honors distinction on their diploma: Baccalaureate Honors. Students in Interdisciplinary Honors whose thesis or special project is approved by the Honors Council earn the diploma distinction Interdisciplinary Honors. Departments award Honors in the Major.

Admission Process: The Honors Program Admissions Coordinator works closely with University admissions. To be eligible for the University Honors Program, students must have an SAT I score of at least 1250 or an ACT score of at least 30, be in the top 10 percent of their high school class, and have leadership or service experience. Admission is rolling. Interdisciplinary Honors admits students transferring into the program from UNF or other institutions if they present a minimum 3.5 GPA; GPA requirements vary by department from 3.4 to 3.7 for Honors in the Major students.

Scholarship Availability: The Honors Council awards scholarships in several different categories: four-year University Honors Scholarships ($1200 per year); International Baccalaureate Scholarships ($1200 per year); Washington Center Scholarships ($4000 or $5000 one-term scholarships); and Out-of-State Fee Waivers ($5000 per year). Special Leadership and Cultural Scholarships in honor of Alan Ling reward students for their superior leadership in enriching the Honors Program at the University of North Florida ($1000–$2000 renewable scholarships). Students must maintain a minimum 3.4 GPA and remain enrolled in an honors track to receive an honors scholarship.

The Campus Context: UNF is located in a city of more than one million people. The campus is on a 1,000-acre nature preserve, roughly halfway between downtown Jacksonville and the Atlantic Ocean. Given the experiential nature of the honors curriculum, Jacksonville's varied environments make it ideal as a learning lab. The area is rich in Florida history, with St. Augustine, America's oldest city, less than 1 hour away; Fort Caroline, America's oldest European settlement (1564) is just minutes from campus. North Florida's beaches, the St. Johns River, and barrier islands provide opportunities to discover coastal ecosystems. Students of the arts enjoy museums, art galleries, the symphony, theater, and ballet. The NFL's Jacksonville Jaguars make a big impact on UNF honors students, given the University's close service-learning partnership with them. Business students enjoy the fact that Jacksonville is a major center for manufacturing, insurance, transportation, and finance and is one of the busiest port, trucking, and rail centers of the Southeast. Visitors are struck by the beauty of this relatively young institution (1972). Lakes and nature trails and live oak trees provide an appealing environment. Student dorms and apartments (most built within the past four years) and the dining facilities surround a campus lake. The College of Health and the College of Business enjoy new, state-of-the-art buildings. A new fine arts center is the next major building. The athletic facilities have all been built or renovated within the past ten years. The University's commitment has always been to providing high-quality undergraduate education. Because UNF is one of the smaller universities in the Florida system, students find small classes and a rapport with faculty. Because a significant number of students study part-time at night, the feel of the campus is more like an institution, with 6,000 students.

The College of Arts and Sciences offers the Bachelor of Arts, Bachelor of Fine Arts, Bachelor of Science, and Bachelor of Music degrees. The College of Business Administration offers the Bachelor of Business Administration degree. The College of Computing Sciences and Engineering offers the Bachelor of Science and Bachelor of Science in Electrical Engineering degrees. The College of Education offers the Bachelor of Arts in Education degree. The College of Health offers the Bachelor of Science in Health, Bachelor of Science in Nursing, and Bachelor of Science in Health/Master of Science in Physical Therapy degrees.

Student Body The total campus enrollment is 11,389, 5,370 if whom are undergraduates. Women comprise 59 percent of the student population. There are 4,060 part-time students. Nine percent of the students are from out-of-state. The student body is

Interpreting the symbols: **2**=two-year college, **4**=four-year college; **Pu**=public or state college, **Pr**=private college; **G**=general honors program; **D**=departmental honors program; **S**=small program (fewer than 100 students), **M**=midsize program (100 to 500 students), **L**=large program (more than 500 students); **Sc**=scholarships available in honors program; **Tr**=transfer students accepted into honors program; **HBC**=historically black college; **AA**=academic advisors; **GA**=graduate advisors; **FA**=fellowship advisors.

.4 percent Native American, 4 percent Hispanic, 9 percent black, 5 percent Asian American or Pacific Islander, and 2 percent international. Forty-five percent of the students are 25 or older. Eleven percent live on campus, and 11 percent are transfer students. Of all full-time matriculated undergraduates who enrolled in 1997, 65 percent applied for financial aid, 83 percent of those were judged to have need, and 31 percent of those had their need fully met. The average percent of need met was 73 percent. The average amount awarded was $9123. In 1997, 678 non–need-based awards were made. For financial aid, students must submit the FAFSA and financial aid transcript (for transfers). The priority deadline for financial aid is April 1. There is a deferred payment plan. Waivers are provided for employees or children of employees and senior citizens. There are four national sororities and four national fraternities.

Faculty Of 660 total faculty members, 389 are full-time (75 percent of whom have terminal degrees), and 271 are part-time.

Key Facilities The Thomas G. Carpenter Library contains 661,292 books, 3,000 serials, 57,753 audiovisual materials, an OPAC, and a Web page. Operations spending in 1996–97 totaled $3.2 million.

There are 250 computers available for general student use. A computer is recommended for some students. A campuswide network can be accessed from off campus. Students can contact faculty members and/or advisers through e-mail. Computers for student use in the computer center, computer labs, classrooms, the learning resource center, and the library provide access to the Internet and the World Wide Web. A staffed computer lab on campus provides training in the use of computers and software. Academic computing expenditures in 1996–97 totaled $1 million.

Honorary Societies Phi Theta Kappa, Phi Kappa Phi, and Golden Key

Athletics UNF is a member of the NCAA Division II. Intercollegiate sports include men's baseball, men's and women's basketball, men's and women's cross-country, men's and women's soccer, women's softball, men's and women's tennis, men's and women's track and field, and women's volleyball. Intermural sports include archery, badminton, basketball, bowling, fencing, field hockey, football, golf, lacrosse, racquetball, rugby, sailing, soccer, softball, swimming and diving, table tennis, tennis, volleyball, and weightlifting. Students with questions about athletics should contact Dr. Richard Gropper, Athletic Director (904-620-2833), or Ms. Kathy Klein, Senior Women's Administrator (904-620-2833).

Study Abroad Study abroad programs are available in Belize, England, France, Ireland, and Italy; .2 percent of students participate. There are SUS programs in London and Florence. The University Honors Program offers study-abroad opportunities that are described in the first section.

Support Services The Disabled Student Program Office acts as a liaison between disabled students and the academic community. In compliance with Section 504 of the Rehabilitation Act of 1973 and the Americans with Disabilities Act (ADA) of 1990, the Disabled Services Program provides academic assistance, such as interpreters, notetakers, readers, priority registration for selected disabilities, and test-taking assistance/proctoring. Some specialized equipment also is available, such as tape recorders and tapes, a braille typewriter, Visual-Tek, Zoomtext, a VentPro voice synthesizer, OsCar with Duxbury/PC Braille Translator, Versa Point Braukke Enbisser, Dragon Dictate, Reading Edge, Type 'N' Speak, amplification devices for the hard of hearing, and computers on adjustable-height tables. Disabled students are encouraged to register with the Office of Disabled Services prior to the beginning of each semester.

Job Opportunities Cooperative Education is offered in a variety of formats from which students may choose. Cooperative Education is an experiential learning concept that engages employers in an educational partnership with UNF. Students enter the program as an integral part of their education, experiencing a blend of actual on-the-job work with related classroom study, thus giving them a more complete picture of their chosen career. Internships are available to all students and provide short-term, career-related experiences to enhance their understanding of specific career requirements and to assist in reaffirming their majors. These experiences may be paid or nonpaid, with flexible work hours. The Employment Experience Program is a full- or part-time educational experience in which students may choose to alternate terms of full-time study at UNF with terms of full-time paid employment or part-time work or to work full-time for one or two consecutive semesters in business, industry, government, or human resource agencies. Academic credit up to a maximum of 6 hours may be earned with departmental approval in specific majors, depending upon the feasibility and applicability of the work experience to the degree experience, and may include internships, field experiences, and other directed off-campus activities that are supervised and arranged by the department chair. Student internships are required in both curriculum and instruction and special education programs in the College of Education and Human Services, as well as in the College of Health. Internships also are available in the communications, criminal justice, history, psychology, and public administration programs in the College of Arts and Sciences. Certifications are available, as is VA Work-Study. Federal Work-Study is a program that is supported with matching funds from UNF. This program is designed to assist students by providing employment opportunities and work experience while attending school. Students must demonstrate financial need.

Tuition: $71.89 for state residents, $293.75 for nonresidents, per credit hour (1998–1999)

Room and Board: rates available through the Housing Office (904-620-4663; fax: 904-620-4670)

Mandatory Fees: $15 material fee (may be assessed for certain visual and graphic arts, science, health science, and nursing courses), $25 orientation fee

Contact: Director: Dr. Marnie Jones; Admissions Coordinator: Ali Roberts; University of North Florida, 4567 St. Johns Bluff Road South, Jacksonville, Florida 32224-2665; Telephone: 904-620-2649; Fax: 904-620-3896; E-mail: mjones@unf.edu or aroberts@unf.edu; Web site: http://www.unf.edu/dept/honors/

University of North Texas

4 Pu G L Sc Tr

▼ University Honors Program

The University Honors Program of the University of North Texas (UNT) is committed to the enrichment of the college experience for highly talented and motivated students who want to build an excellent educational and intellectual foundation. Opportunities both within and beyond the classroom are designed to foster intellectual curiosity among members of the community of honors scholars and prepare students for a lifetime of learning. Eligible undergraduate students in any major may participate in the University Honors Program.

Honors students enjoy the flexibility of choosing honors courses that interest them while retaining the freedom to take regular courses whenever they wish. Honors courses of three types are offered: special honors sections of regular courses, specially designed courses that are available only to honors students, and interdisciplinary seminars that are offered under the Honors prefix. Most honors courses meet general education requirements, which all students must satisfy to receive the baccalaureate degree. All honors courses are offered in small sections to foster student involvement and classroom discussion, and every honors course is taught by a University professor who has a strong commitment to undergraduate education. Honors students at UNT appreciate the opportunity to meet and study with distinguished scholars in disciplines across the University while still pursuing a major in the department of their choice.

Beyond the classroom, honors students find many opportunities to enrich and expand their horizons. The University Honors Program sponsors several programs throughout the academic year, including the brown bag lunch series and the afternoon conversation series. In addition, honors students edit and produce their own literary magazine, called *PROCESS,* which is published annually. Individual academic advising and online schedule changes are provided to honors students through the Office of Academic Core Programs. Honors housing is available, and special programming is provided to students who choose to live in the honors residential setting. All students are also invited to visit the Honors Reading Room, which is part of the honors complex, where they may avail themselves of books, daily newspapers, and magazines; they also have the use of a television and VCR to enjoy the program's video library.

The University Honors Program was created in fall 1994 and currently has an enrollment of approximately 725 students.

Participation Requirements: The University Honors Program requires completion of at least 24 honors credit hours, including the capstone seminar or capstone thesis, and maintenance of a GPA of at least 3.0.

Admission Process: A separate application, available from the Office of Academic Core Programs, is required. Freshman applicants are required to submit the completed application form, a high school transcript, a writing sample, and the names and addresses of two teachers or counselors who may be contacted for a reference. Typical applicants have an SAT I score of at least 1150 or an ACT score of at least 27 and are in the top echelon of their high school class. The average SAT I score of honors students is approximately 1275. Beyond those requirements, students may request special consideration on the basis of demonstrated special talent in specific areas, including music, art, theater, dance, and writing. Continuing and transfer students are also eligible to join the program.

Scholarship Availability: The University Honors Program annually awards a number of scholarships to students who are named by the program as Davidson Scholars, Conroy Scholars, or McMurtry Scholars. In addition, Honors students are eligible for many scholarships that are available through the Office of Financial Aid and Scholarships. Honors students are encouraged to apply for prestigious national and international scholarship awards, and assistance is provided to all applicants through the Office of Post-Graduate Scholarships in conjunction with the University Honors Program.

The Campus Context: The University of North Texas is located in Denton, just 35 miles north of Dallas and Fort Worth, a metropolitan area of almost 5 million people. With more than 27,000 students, UNT is the largest university in the region and the fourth-largest university in Texas. There are nine colleges and schools on campus: College of Arts and Sciences, College of Business Administration, School of Community Service, College of Education, School of Library and Information Sciences, School of Merchandising and Hospitality Management, College of Music, School of the Visual Arts, and Toulouse School of Graduate Studies. Ninety-five undergraduate programs are offered.

Student Body The total student enrollment is 27,054, including 21,059 undergraduates and 5,995 graduates. The ethnic distribution is 76.3 percent white, 9.2 percent African American, 7.8 percent Hispanic, 3.8 percent Asian/Pacific Islander, .8 percent Native American and Alaskan Native, and 4.3 percent nonresident alien. The gender distribution is 54 percent women. More than 4,450 students live on campus in ten residence halls.

Faculty The full-time faculty numbers 778. The student-faculty ratio is 17:1.

Key Facilities Library holdings include more than 1.5 million cataloged items in four separate facilities on campus. Computing facilities offer fourteen general access labs in ten buildings on campus supporting PC, Macintosh, and PowerMac platforms.

Honorary Societies Golden Key and Mortar Board

Athletics UNT competes in Division I-A of the National Collegiate Athletic Association in seven men's sports: football, cross-country, basketball, golf, tennis, indoor track, and outdoor track. Women also compete in NCAA Division I-A in volleyball, basketball, tennis, golf, cross-country, indoor track, and outdoor track. In addition, Recreational Sports offer opportunities for participation in intramural sports, fitness classes, or sports clubs and access to exercise facilities.

Study Abroad The Study Abroad Center offers exchange programs in thirty-seven countries; additional opportunities are available through faculty-led, affiliated, and nonaffiliated programs. The National Student Exchange program provides students with the opportunity to study at any of 175 universities in the United States or its territories at in-state tuition rates. Both programs allow exchanges for either a semester or a year, and financial assistance is available.

Support Services The Office of Disability Accommodation furnishes assistance with registration, scheduling, academic access, and certain educational auxiliary aids for students whose disabilities necessitate special accommodations for equality of educational opportunity.

Job Opportunities The Student Employment Service provides a variety of employment opportunities on and off campus to currently enrolled students in order to help them offset their college expenses and develop good work records.

Tuition: $1326 for state residents, $4835 for nonresidents, per semester

Room and Board: $4202 per year

Contact: Director: Dr. Gloria C. Cox, Office of Academic Core Programs, General Academic Building 309A, P.O. Box 305189, Denton, Texas 76203; Telephone: 940-565-3305; Fax: 940-369-7370; E-mail: gcox@unt.edu; Web site: http://www.cas.unt.edu/acadcore

UNIVERSITY OF NORTHERN COLORADO

4 Pu G M Sc Tr

▼ Honors Program

The UNC Honors Program was established in 1958 with the intent of aiding the University's most highly motivated undergraduate students in research and writing a thesis. It became a full four-year program linked to Life of the Mind, an NEH-funded general education program, in 1985. Since then, the Honors Program has grown dramatically to its current membership of 300 students and faculty coordinators in every college. In 1992, Honors and Life of the Mind were recognized by CCHE as co-Programs of Excellence in Colorado. UNC Honors has three principal dimensions: enrichment in general education, enrichment in the major field, and the Student Honors Council.

To satisfy the enrichment in general education dimension, each student in the Honors Program is required to take at least three

Interpreting the symbols: **2**=two-year college, **4**=four-year college; **Pu**=public or state college, **Pr**=private college; **G**=general honors program; **D**=departmental honors program; **S**=small program (fewer than 100 students), **M**=midsize program (100 to 500 students), **L**=large program (more than 500 students); **Sc**=scholarships available in honors program; **Tr**=transfer students accepted into honors program; **HBC**=historically black college; **AA**=academic advisors; **GA**=graduate advisors; **FA**=fellowship advisors.

Life of the Mind courses as enrichment in his or her general education curriculum. These highly interactive and interdisciplinary courses are open to all students and are taught by UNC faculty members who have demonstrated excellence in teaching. In addition, Honors students are required to take a connection seminar during their sophomore year. These team-taught seminars bring together some of UNC's best professors with the intent of connecting disciplines, cultures, and times. The seminars focus on interdisciplinary topics such as science and ethics, the art of film, art and technology, urban development and alternative communities, and issues in multiculturalism.

The enrichment in the major field component of the program allows each UNC honors student to research and write a thesis under the mentorship of a faculty adviser in his or her field. The thesis is the academic capstone of each honors student's college career. Beyond the assistance given to them by their adviser, each honors student is provided with several other opportunities and aids through the Honors Program. Students are given the opportunity to present their theses at Research Day during Academic Excellence Week at UNC and at the National Conference on Undergraduate Research.

Chartered in 1985, the Student Honors Council (SHC) is one of UNC's most active student organizations on campus and in the Greeley community. It comprises 11 elected officers and seeks the involvement of all honors students. Throughout the academic year, the council organizes and coordinates several academic and social activities on campus and in the community. The International Film Series and Fall Film Festival are run by the council. Academic pizza seminars are offered by the council with the intent of gathering students to discuss controversial issues and/or to meet and learn more about a UNC faculty member. SHC also offers an After School Enrichment Program for two of the elementary schools in Greeley. It cosponsors events such as poetry readings with the UNC English Department and academic forums and film discussions with several of the cultural centers on campus. Finally, the council produces and publishes five newsletters a year that are sent to students, faculty, and alumni of the Honors Program.

Admission Process: Students are selected for the Honors Program on the basis of their GPA (3.5 high school, 3.25 college), class rank (top 10 percent), ACT score (composite of 27), a letter of introduction, and letters of recommendation. They may apply for the program as incoming freshmen, transfers, or at any time throughout their University career (as long as they are still able and willing to meet all program requirements before graduation).

Scholarship Availability: Honors students are given the opportunity to apply for a grant for up to $500 from the CCHE Mind/Honors Programs of Excellence fund for research expenses.

The Campus Context: University of Northern Colorado has undergraduate enrollment in six colleges: Arts and Sciences, Education (including a laboratory school with grades K–12), Health and Human Sciences, Business Administration, Performing and Visual Arts, and Continuing Education. There are 107 undergraduate degree programs offered.

Student Body The undergraduate student population is 9,082 (41 percent men). The ethnic distribution is 1 percent Native American, 2 percent African American, 5 percent Asian American, 8 percent Hispanic, and 84 percent white. There are 95 international students. Thirty-one percent of the students live on campus. Seventy-one percent of all undergraduates receive financial aid. There are eight fraternities and four sororities.

Faculty Of the 566 faculty members, 413 are full-time and 153 part-time. Seventy-nine percent of the faculty members have terminal degrees. The student-faculty ratio is 22:1.

Key Facilities The library houses 982,053 volumes. Computer facilities are readily available across campus.

Athletics In athletics, University of Northern Colorado is NCAA Division II. Men's varsity sports include basketball, football, golf, tennis, track, and wrestling, and women's varsity sports include basketball, golf, soccer, swimming, tennis, track, and volleyball.

Support Services Disabled students are assisted by the Disability Access Center.

Tuition: $1967 for state residents, $8997 for nonresidents, per year (1998–99)

Room and Board: $4570 minimum

Mandatory Fees: $684

Contact: Director: Dr. Ron Edgerton, Honors Program, University of Northern Colorado, Greeley, Colorado 80639; Telephone: 970-351-2940; Fax: 970-351-2947; E-mail: rkedger@bentley.univnorthco.edu Web site: http://www.univnorthco.edu/honors

UNIVERSITY OF NORTHERN IOWA

4 Pu S

▼ College of Social and Behavioral Sciences (CSBS) Honors Program

UNI's College of Social and Behavioral Sciences houses seven departments (Design, Family, and Consumer Sciences; Geography; History; Political Science; Psychology; Social Science Teaching; Social Work; and Sociology, Anthropology, and Criminology) and offers more than twenty majors. The CSBS Honors Program is the first of the University's five colleges to establish an honors curriculum. Honors courses consist of honors sections of general education courses and seminars limited to and designed for honors students only. Class sizes are small (15–20 students maximum) and are designed specifically to provide a variety of learning opportunities such as field trips, experiential learning, and guest speakers. Students are encouraged to foster an area of interest for research and individual study under the guidance of CSBS faculty members. Honors students receive personalized academic and career advising; are notified of special research, scholarship, and academic opportunities; and are given access to honors facilities (such as a lounge and computers, among others). Established in 1998, the CSBS Honors Program currently has approximately 60 students.

Participation Requirements: The curriculum requires 15 hours of credit in honors courses: three hours may be taken through honors sections of general education courses, 3 hours of upper division honors seminar, and 3 hours of honors thesis. Students enrolled in the program must also complete 6 hours of honors electives that may include but are not limited to course work, study abroad, internships, and research assistantships. Honors courses are noted on the transcripts as such. To remain in the program, students must maintain a minimum 3.3 semester GPA and major in or intend to major within CSBS. Graduation from the honors program requires that the student complete all 15 hours to receive recognition on the transcript and during the graduation ceremony.

Admission Process: Entering first-year students may apply to the CSBS Honors Program with either a 27 or better on the ACT, a class rank within the top 20 percent of the high school class, or have a high school GPA of 3.65 or better. Current CSBS students may apply if their UNI cumulative GPA is 3.3 or better. Only CSBS majors or intended majors are admitted to the honors program. Students admitted in fall 2001 or later may apply to the University Honors Program.

Scholarship Availability: No scholarships are exclusively offered to honors students. CSBS offers a wide range of scholarships to any majors within the college.

The Campus Context: University of Northern Iowa was established in 1876 as a training ground for teachers and has grown to house five colleges: Business Administration, Education, Humanities and Fine Arts, Natural Sciences, and Social and Behavioral Sciences. More than one hundred majors are offered in a variety of fields. UNI is home to the UNI-Dome, a wellness/recreation center, a museum, and the Gallagher-Bluedorn Performing Arts Center. UNI has more than 180 recognized student groups and organizations.

UNI is located in a metropolitan area of approximately 110,000. Situated on the banks of the Cedar River in northeast Iowa, the Cedar Falls–Waterloo metropolitan area provides benefits of urban life in a small-town setting. Cedar Falls is centrally located and contains miles of bike trails.

Student Body Undergraduate enrollment is approximately 12,475 (58 percent women). The minority ethnic distribution is 1 percent Native American, 1 percent Hispanic American, 1 percent Asian American, and 2 percent African American. There are 191 international students.

Faculty Instructional faculty members number 852. Full-time faculty members number 703. Eighty-nine percent have terminal degrees. The student-faculty ratio is 16:1.

Key Facilities UNI Rod Library houses 886,380 volumes, 720,321 microfiche publications, and subscriptions to 3,358 periodicals and newspapers. Information is available through CD-ROM or off-campus, online services like LEXIS-NEXIS. Computer labs are distributed throughout the UNI campus, in classroom buildings, residence halls, and the library. UNI has full Intranet and Internet access in all residence halls at no charge to access the system.

Athletics Nineteen men's and women's intercollegiate athletics programs compete at the NCAA Division I level in the Missouri Valley Conference. The UNI football team competes at the IAA level in the Gateway Conference. The Panthers have a nationally recognized coaching staff that maintains championship programs in football, basketball, wrestling, volleyball, and track and field. Facilities are available for all major sports, including those previously mentioned, and golf, swimming, tennis, racquetball, and rock climbing.

Study Abroad Students are encouraged to pursue study abroad. UNI's Study Abroad Office offers student exchanges, internships, and service learning experiences.

Support Services Student Disability Services offers academic support services, personal care attendants, and modified residence hall rooms for students with permanent or temporary disabilities.

Job Opportunities Work opportunities are available on or off campus. UNI's Student Employment Center offers assistance in finding work-study or part-time employment.

Tuition: $3116 for state residents, $8438 for nonresidents, per year (2001–02)

Mandatory Fees: Computer fee: $126, health fee: $106, activity fee: $92

Room and Board: $4410

Contact: Rowena Tan, Coordinator of Scholarships and Honors, Sabin 117, University of Northern Iowa, Cedar Falls, Iowa 50614-0403; Telephone: 319-273-7286; Fax: 319-273-2222; E-mail: tan@uni.edu; Web site: http://csbsnt.csbs.uni.edu/honors/index.html

UNIVERSITY OF NORTHERN IOWA

4 Pu G M Sc Tr AA

▼ University Honors Program

The University Honors Program at UNI is a program that allows motivated and interested students to make the most of their collegiate experience. The program offers challenging classroom experiences, interaction with faculty members, and social connections with other capable students. The program includes all five undergraduate colleges, and membership in the University Honors Program is compatible with any of the University's 120 majors.

The University Honors Program provides unique educational opportunities for motivated students. Honors sections of general education and University courses are made up entirely of honors students, with a class limit of 20. Students also choose from Honors Seminars, unique courses developed specifically for the program. Students round out their University Honors Program curriculum by selecting honors electives. These hours can be earned in additional honors sections of general education classes, seminars, or major courses or through independent studies. The culmination of the honors experience comes in the form of the senior thesis/project. This project allows students to independently explore a scholarly area of interest prior to graduation.

Participation in the University Honors Program helps students develop close ties with UNI faculty members. Small honors sections of classes allow for in-depth, one-on-one interaction, and a faculty member guides the honors thesis/project. Small class sizes also allow for considerable interaction with classmates. In addition, honors social events extend the group's connection beyond the walls of the classroom. Out-of-class activities include events like guest speakers, hayrides, and movie nights. Students can also take advantage of group attendance at theater events at the Gallagher-Bluedorn Performing Arts Center or field trips that offer cultural and practical experience. An Honors Student Advisory Board gives students the opportunity to influence the direction of the program, share their ideas on a variety of programming issues, and help plan academic, social, and outreach events.

The program admitted 60 students for its 2001–02 inaugural year. Plans call for a target size of approximately 500 students.

Participation Requirements: The University Honors Program offers two designations for participation, University Honors with Distinction and University Honors. To remain in good standing in the University Honors Program, students are required to maintain a minimum GPA of 3.3. Graduates of the program are honored at commencement and have an honors designation noted on their transcripts.

Students pursuing University Honors with Distinction take 32 hours of honors courses, consisting of 12 hours of general education, 6 seminar hours, 11 hours of honors electives, and a 3-hour senior honors thesis/project. University Honors, designed with transfer students in mind, requires 20 hours of honors courses, made up of 6 seminar hours, 11 hours of honors electives, and a 3-hour senior honors thesis/project.

Admission Process: Entering first-year students may apply if they meet one or more of the following requirements: an ACT composite score of 27 or better (SAT I score of 1210 or better), high school class rank in the top 10 percent, or high school cumulative GPA of 3.65 or better. Plans call for current students with a UNI cumulative GPA of 3.3 or better to be able to apply beginning in fall 2002.

Interpreting the symbols: **2**=two-year college, **4**=four-year college; **Pu**=public or state college, **Pr**=private college; **G**=general honors program; **D**=departmental honors program; **S**=small program (fewer than 100 students), **M**=midsize program (100 to 500 students), **L**=large program (more than 500 students); **Sc**=scholarships available in honors program; **Tr**=transfer students accepted into honors program; **HBC**=historically black college; **AA**=academic advisors; **GA**=graduate advisors; **FA**=fellowship advisors.

Students submit an application, including their activities, achievements, and a short essay, to be considered for admission into the University Honors Program. The Honors Advisory Committee reviews applications and makes admission decisions.

Scholarship Availability: The Nadyne Harris Endowed Scholarship makes funding available to University honors students majoring in the liberal arts. In addition, the University offers a wide range of merit-based scholarships for which many honors students are eligible.

The Campus Context: The University of Northern Iowa was established in 1876 as a training ground for teachers and has grown to house five colleges: Business Administration, Education, Humanities and Fine Arts, Natural Sciences, and Social and Behavioral Sciences. One hundred twenty majors are offered in a variety of fields. UNI is home to the UNI-Dome, a wellness/recreation center; a museum; and the Gallagher-Bluedorn Performing Arts Center. UNI has more than 180 recognized student groups and organizations.

UNI is located in a metropolitan area of approximately 110,000. Situated on the banks of the Cedar River in northeast Iowa, the Cedar Falls–Waterloo metropolitan area provides benefits of urban life in a small-town setting. Cedar Falls is centrally located and has miles of bike trails.

Student Body Undergraduate enrollment is approximately 12,475 (58 percent women). The minority ethnic distribution is less than 1 percent Native American, 1 percent Hispanic American, 1 percent Asian American, and 2 percent African American. There are 191 international students.

Faculty Instructional faculty members number 852, of whom 703 are full-time. Seventy-three percent have terminal degrees. The student-faculty ratio is 16:1.

Key Facilities UNI Rod Library houses 886,380 volumes, 720,321 microfiche publications, and subscriptions to 3,358 periodicals and newspapers. Information is available through CD-ROM or off-campus, online services like LEXIS-NEXIS. Computer labs are distributed throughout the UNI campus—classroom buildings, residence halls, and the library. UNI has full Intranet and Internet access in all residence halls; there is no charge to access the system.

Athletics Twenty men's and women's intercollegiate athletics programs compete at the NCAA Division I level in the Missouri Valley Conference. The UNI football team competes at the Division I-AA level in the Gateway Conference. The Panthers have a nationally recognized coaching staff that maintains championship programs in football, basketball, volleyball, wrestling, and track and field. Facilities are available for all major sports, including those previously mentioned and golf, swimming, tennis, racquetball, and rock climbing.

Study Abroad Students are encouraged to pursue study abroad. UNI's Study Abroad Office offers student exchanges, internships, and service-learning experiences.

Support Services Student Disability Services offers academic support services, personal-care attendants, and modified residence hall rooms for students with permanent or temporary disabilities.

Job Opportunities Work opportunities are available on or off campus. UNI's Student Employment Center offers assistance in finding work-study or part-time employment.

Tuition: $3116 for state residents, $8438 for nonresidents, per year (2001–02)

Room and Board: $4410

Mandatory Fees: Computer fee: $126, health fee: $106, activity fee: $92

Contact: Dr. Harry Brod, Director, 257 Communication Arts Center, University of Northern Iowa, Cedar Falls, Iowa 50614-0355; Telephone: 319-273-3175; E-mail: harry.brod@uni.edu; Web site: http://www.uni.edu/honors

UNIVERSITY OF OKLAHOMA

4 Pu G L Tr

▼ Honors College

The Honors College incorporates a curricular program dedicated to providing academically talented students with the opportunity to develop their intellectual potential to the fullest. The Honors College utilizes the Honors College faculty as well as the best research and teaching faculty members from all undergraduate colleges of the University to offer special honors courses at both the upper-division and lower-division levels. The courses are limited to approximately 22 students, with enrollment restricted to members of the Honors College. This gives each honors course a rich environment of academically talented students. The lower-division honors courses include courses that fulfill the University of Oklahoma (OU) general education requirements. The upper-division courses include special-topic seminars, team-taught colloquia, and independent study and research with faculty members in the student's major discipline. Students in the Honors College may elect to enroll in up to 9 credit hours of honors courses each semester. Honors students must complete a minimum of 20 hours of honors-designated course work: 12 credit hours including a 3-credit-hour freshman seminar, 5 hours of honors reading and research, and a 3-credit–hour honors colloquium.

The program began in 1962, went through a major reorganization in 1987, and became an Honors College in 1997. There are approximately 1,900 students currently enrolled.

Participation Requirements: Continued membership in the Honors College requires both maintaining an OU cumulative GPA of 3.4 and exhibiting continued progress toward completion of the curricular requirements of an honors degree. Progress is defined as completing at least one honors course during every 30 credit hours earned at the University, or approximately one honors course per academic year for full-time students. Most honors students take two or three honors courses per year.

Students successfully completing the honors curriculum with a 3.4–3.59 GPA have a cum laude designation on their diploma, with a 3.6–3.79 GPA a magna cum laude designation, or with a 3.8 GPA or higher a summa cum laude designation.

Admission Process: Freshmen entering the University of Oklahoma are eligible to apply to the Honors College if they have a composite ACT score of 29 or higher or an SAT total of 1230 or higher and they rank in the top 10 percent of graduates in their high school class or they have a high school GPA of 3.75. Transfer students who come to the University of Oklahoma with 15 or more college credit hours and a transfer GPA of 3.4 or higher are eligible to apply. OU students who have earned 15 or more hours of OU credit and have maintained a cumulative GPA of 3.4 or higher are eligible to apply. Final admission into the Honors College is determined by an evaluation of the Honors College application form, which includes a written essay of 400–500 words.

The Campus Context: The University of Oklahoma Norman campus, established in 1890, is composed of thirteen colleges: Architecture, Arts and Sciences, Michael F. Price College of Business, Continuing Education, Education, Engineering, Fine Arts, Geosciences, Graduate, Honors, Gaylord College of Journalism and Mass Communication, Law, and Liberal Studies. There are 103 undergraduate degree programs offered on campus. The Sam Noble Oklahoma Museum of Natural History at OU is the largest University-based natural history museum in the United States, housing more than 5 million natural history artifacts.

Student Body Undergraduate enrollment is 18,675 students, of whom 51 percent are men. There are 1,600 international students. Sixty-one percent of students receive financial aid. There are twenty-five fraternities and sixteen sororities.

Faculty Of the 1,432 faculty members, 1,179 are full-time.

Key Facilities The campus is equipped with PC and Macintosh computer labs in the library, classroom buildings, and some of the dorms.

Honorary Societies Phi Kappa Phi, Golden Key, Mortar Board, and Phi Beta Kappa

Study Abroad Study abroad is available through reciprocal exchange with 129 programs worldwide. Honors credit is given for study abroad. Honors at Oxford, a 6-hour upper-division course, is offered every summer and includes three weeks of study at Oxford University in England. Students experience the tutorial style of learning, which is the dominant method at Oxford and Cambridge.

Support Services The Office of Disabled Student Services provides support services to students with disabilities. The office is committed to the goal of achieving equal educational opportunity and full participation for students with disabilities. OU has adopted the Americans with Disabilities Act Accessibility Guidelines.

Tuition: $2022 minimum for state residents, $6746 minimum for nonresidents, per year (2001–02)

Room and Board: $4903

Mandatory Fees: $691

Contact: Dean: Dr. Steve Gillon, Honors House, 1300 Asp Avenue, Norman, Oklahoma 73019; Telephone: 405-325-5291; Fax: 405-325-7109; E-mail: smgillon@aol.com; Web site: http://www.ou.edu/honors

UNIVERSITY OF OREGON

4 Pu L Sc Tr AA

▼ Robert D. Clark Honors College

Robert D. Clark Honors College, located within the University of Oregon (UO), offers the advantages of a small, liberal arts college and a major research university. Clark Honors College grants both the Bachelor of Arts and Bachelor of Science degrees.

Clark Honors College provides an extensive, balanced curriculum of interrelated courses in the humanities, social sciences, natural sciences, and mathematics, which complements students' work in their chosen majors. This core curriculum is designed to foster creative, critical thinking and accounts for about one third of students' credits toward graduation. Clark Honors College aims to reach beyond professional or specialized training to inspire students to a full lifetime of intellectual curiosity and personal growth. Students work closely with Clark Honors College professors to establish a broad knowledge base and develop skills that cross all boundaries. Each student is an integral part of this exciting learning community with other highly motivated students, award-winning faculty members, mentoring alumni, and a supportive staff. Discussion-centered classes are limited to 25 students and are taught by skilled faculty members. Students also participate in seminars and colloquia that will help them merge education with real-world experiences. Close advising is an important aspect of Clark Honors College, from summer or fall orientation preceding the first year to faculty supervision of the honors thesis in the senior year.

In their senior year, students prepare an advanced research or creative project and present it orally before a faculty committee. Throughout the honors thesis process, students work individually with professors from their major field. As the culminating experience of their undergraduate career, the senior thesis and oral presentation give students an opportunity to demonstrate both the breadth of learning attained at Clark Honors College and the specialized knowledge gained from their major.

Robert D. Clark Honors College, established in 1960, is the oldest Honors College in the United States. About 650 students are currently enrolled, representing interests in all scholarly disciplines. Students come from all over the nation and the world and every year the student body increases in ethnic and geographic diversity.

Admission Process: High school seniors who have demonstrated academic excellence are encouraged to apply to Clark Honors College. A small number of transfer students are also accepted each year. Students must apply both to the University for general admission as well as to Clark Honors College. A complete Clark Honors College application consists of an application form, two teacher recommendations, transcripts, SAT I or ACT scores, and an essay, all of which must be sent in one packet directly to Clark Honors College. Application materials are contained in the Clark Honors College brochure, which is available by contacting the Clark Honors College Office.

The early notification deadline is November 1 and the regular application deadline is February 1. Students who complete their application by November 1 or February 1 are guaranteed full consideration by the Clark Honors College admissions committee. Students who apply by November 1 will be notified of the committee's decision by December 15; students who apply by February 1 will be notified by April 1. Late applications and transfers are considered individually on a space-available basis.

Scholarship Availability: Scholarships are awarded through the University, academic departments, and private sources. Oregon Presidential Scholarships are designated for promising students from Oregon. The University of Oregon is the only public institution in Oregon to sponsor National Merit Scholarships. The general University scholarships application is due February 1. Clark Honors College awards a small number of merit scholarships. All students who complete their Clark Honors College application by November 1 or February 1 are eligible for these awards.

The Campus Context: Located at the southern end of the beautiful Willamette Valley, the University of Oregon in Eugene lies between the Pacific Ocean to the west and the Cascade Mountains to the east. Eugene, a city of more than 120,000, is small enough to be friendly and casual and large enough to offer many cultural opportunities. The city is known for its parks, bike and running paths, outdoor craft and food markets, and performing arts.

Students can spend their weekends immersed in the stacks of the UO library system, which is the largest in the state, or enjoy the white water of the McKenzie River that flows out of the Cascades northeast of town.

Students can participate in more than 270 clubs on campus, including the Honors College Student Association (HCSA), political and environmental groups, professional organizations, cultural heritage organizations, religious groups, and service programs.

More than 250 concerts and recitals are presented annually by visiting artists, faculty members, and advanced students. Three theaters on campus offer a full range of plays produced both by faculty members and qualified students.

Honorary Societies Phi Eta Sigma, Alpha Lambda Delta, Golden Key, Mortar Board, Phi Beta Kappa, and Druids and Friars

Athletics Intercollegiate competition, club sports, and intramurals offer several levels of athletic participation. The University is a member of the Pac-10 Conference (NCAA Division I) and sponsors seven women's teams: basketball, cross-country, golf, softball, tennis, track and field, and volleyball. The seven men's teams are basketball, cross-country, football, golf, tennis, track and field, and wrestling.

Study Abroad Clark Honors College students are encouraged to study abroad and can take advantage of the many programs

Interpreting the symbols: **2**=two-year college, **4**=four-year college; **Pu**=public or state college, **Pr**=private college; **G**=general honors program; **D**=departmental honors program; **S**=small program (fewer than 100 students), **M**=midsize program (100 to 500 students), **L**=large program (more than 500 students); **Sc**=scholarships available in honors program; **Tr**=transfer students accepted into honors program; **HBC**=historically black college; **AA**=academic advisors; **GA**=graduate advisors; **FA**=fellowship advisors.

offered by the University to study all over the world. Programs last from a single term to one full year.

Tuition: $4185 for state residents; an estimated $15,025 for nonresidents, per year (2002–03)

Room and Board: $5900

Contact: Director: David A. Frank, Clark Honors College, 1293 University of Oregon, Eugene, Oregon 97403-1293; Telephone: 541-346-5414; E-mail: honors@darkwing.uoregon.edu; Web site: www.uoregon.edu/~honors

UNIVERSITY OF PITTSBURGH

4 Pu G L Sc Tr

▼ University Honors College

The University of Pittsburgh Honors College (UHC) is dedicated to high attainment among able and motivated undergraduates University-wide. In addition to approximately eighty science and humanities courses each year offering small class sizes with special depth and challenge, UHC's broad portfolio of academic offerings includes concentrated academic advising, undergraduate teaching and research fellowships, a distinguished and demanding degree option, summer research and field programs, and a wide variety of cocurricular activities created and run by students themselves. The latter include an undergraduate string ensemble (The Brackenridge Quartet), a professionally refereed undergraduate scholarly journal (*The Pittsburgh Undergraduate Review*), Pittsburgh's singular undergraduate literary journal (*The Three Rivers Review*), and a College Bowl team.

In effect, UHC provides a rich palette of selections from which discerning students can choose as they please. Its location atop Pitt's historic Cathedral of Learning is also a 24-hour home-away-from-home for quiet study and academic exchange that commands a 50-mile panoramic view of western Pennsylvania.

The availability of a special degree for qualified students—the Bachelor of Philosophy (B. Phil.)—distinguishes UHC from an honors "program." This special competency-based baccalaureate degree is available to students in any undergraduate school of the University. Its general requirements include demonstrated academic performance, completion of degree requirements in the home school of admission, and accomplishment of a distinctive program of study approved by UHC advising that typically reflects broad scope across the disciplines and depth within a discipline. The special requirement of the B. Phil. is the completion and defense of a thesis during the junior and senior years under the tutelage of a faculty adviser. By the last term in residence, the student must publicly present the results of this independent scholarship to a Faculty Examination Committee, including one external examiner from outside the University of Pittsburgh who is selected by the faculty adviser to spend several days on campus.

The University Honors College provides special academic and career advising to complement the formal advising programs offered by schools and departments. Through unlimited individualized advising, UHC brokers the University of Pittsburgh's wealth of resources to the undergraduate level, helping ambitious students network to opportunities and expertise they would otherwise miss. UHC's advising staff is especially experienced in helping talented students combine diverse academic interests into educationally sound and appealing plans of study. Considerations include the University's full range of certificates, majors, and other degree plans as well as national scholarships and fellowships for undergraduates. Due to UHC, Pitt students for over a dozen years have won more of the nation's most prestigious undergraduate awards—the Rhodes and Marshall scholarships—than any other college or university in Pennsylvania, private or public.

The University of Pittsburgh dedicated UHC during its 1987 bicentennial ceremonies. Headcount enrollment in UHC courses now tops 700 students each year, including many students from the College of Business Administration and nearly 100 students from the School of Engineering.

Participation Requirements: UHC is a flexible, nonmembership personalized operation whose many varied offerings respond to the individual initiative of interested students rather than any fixed participation criteria. There is no required level of participation in UHC; qualified students choose involvement in as many or as few opportunities as they wish. In some cases, students may "try out" for the select few positions available in an activity, such as the Brackenridge Quartet or editorial positions on *The Pittsburgh Undergraduate Review* or *The Three Rivers Review.* In other cases, such as open musical performances, poetry readings, and literary discussion groups, space for involvement is not generally a problem. Requirements for course work participation are indicated below.

Admission Process: The University Honors College is not a membership organization. There is no separate application for admission to UHC beyond the student's application to his or her targeted undergraduate college. Permission for involvement in UHC offerings, such as UHC courses, proceeds on the ongoing basis of a student's immediate past achievement. Entering freshmen having a combined SAT I score above 1270 and ranking in the top 10 percent of their high school graduating class are automatically qualified to take any UHC course whose particular prerequisites have been satisfied. The same goes for continuing students having a QPA of at least 3.25 (B+) in their prior term. Students who do not meet this threshold may make their case to a member of the UHC staff or to their academic adviser for qualification to enroll in any particular UHC course.

Scholarship Availability: Freshman applicants for the fall term who file a complete admissions application by January 15 of their senior year are automatically considered for merit-based academic scholarships. These scholarships are based on high school performance, the degree of difficulty of the curriculum, class rank, and college entrance examination test results. Out of a freshman class of about 3,100, close to 600 scholarships are awarded, varying in the amount from $1000 to full tuition, room, and board.

UHC oversees the awarding of the Chancellor's Undergraduate Scholarship, which covers full tuition, room, and board for four and sometimes five years. Competition for the Chancellor's is by invitation following nominations by the Office of Admissions and entails written work as well as a possible interview. UHC also makes available in some cases upper-class merit scholarships from its private endowment.

The Campus Context: The University of Pittsburgh is one of the foremost research institutions in the United States and Canada. At the center of the Pittsburgh campus is the Cathedral of Learning, a Gothic skyscraper, housing classrooms and offices.

Pittsburgh ranks seventh in the nation in the number of Fortune 500 companies with headquarters in the city. Its corporate environment provides many opportunities for internship and career exploration for students. Other attractions are concerts, art festivals, professional sports (the Steelers, Pirates, and Penguins), the Pittsburgh Symphony, opera, ballet, and multiple opportunities for theater.

Among the ninety-six baccalaureate degree programs available at the Pittsburgh campus, the University of Pittsburgh has nationally ranked programs in art, philosophy, history and philosophy of science, Latin American studies, information sciences, nursing, social work, metallurgical engineering, history of art and architecture, economics, and business.

The 132-acre campus is located 3 miles from downtown Pittsburgh in an area noted for parks, galleries, museums, libraries, and concert halls. The campus is easily accessible by car, bus, and plane (the airport is 18 miles away). Students enjoy free public transportation within Pittsburgh and Allegheny County.

Student Body The current Pittsburgh campus undergraduate enrollment is 16,798. Fifty-three percent are women. The ethnic distribution is 84 percent white, 10 percent African American, 1 percent Hispanic, and 4 percent Asian/Pacific Islander. One percent are international students. Seventy percent of the students receive financial aid. There are eighteen national fraternities and fifteen national sororities with a total of 1,366 members. Pittsburgh campus residence halls house 5,200 undergraduate students. Many students choose to live off campus but within walking distance. Students can ride Port Authority Transit (PAT) buses and light-rail vehicles free throughout Allegheny Country 24-hours-a-day merely by showing their Pitt I.D. Card.

Faculty The total number of faculty members at the Pittsburgh campus is 3,468, of whom 2,892 are full-time. Ninety-one percent of the Pittsburgh campus faculty members have a Ph.D. or its equivalent. The student-faculty ratio is 15:1.

Key Facilities There are twenty-seven University library collections on or near the campus that contain more than 7.4 million items (including microforms) and more than 22,000 periodicals. PITTCAT is the University's online catalog, offering author, title, subject, and keyword access to materials in all University libraries. The University was the first to integrate voice, data, and video on a campuswide fiber-optic distribution system. Computing and Information Services operates personal and institutional-sized computing hardware to serve academic, research, and administrative needs. Seven public computing labs are equipped with more than 700 personal computers and workstations [Windows NT 4.0 Workstations, Apple PowerMac PCs (7100, 7200, 7300) and Sun Sparc Ultra UNIX workstations].

Honorary Societies Delta Pi Epsilon, Golden Key, Lambda Sigma, Mortar Board Senior Honor Society, Omicron Delta Kappa, Phi Beta Kappa, Phi Eta Sigma Freshman Honorary, Phi Sigma Pi, Rho Lambda, and Tau Kappa Epsilon.

Athletics Most of the University of Pittsburgh's athletic teams compete in the Big East. Pittsburgh fields eighteen men's and women's varsity teams featuring nearly 250 student athletes. Men's sports include basketball, baseball, cross-country, football, soccer, swimming and diving, track and field (indoor and outdoor), and wrestling. The Panthers sponsor the following women's sports: basketball, cross-country, gymnastics, soccer, swimming and diving, tennis, track and field (indoor and outdoor), and volleyball. The Fitzgerald Field House has four basketball courts, eight squash courts, two handball/racquetball courts, a place for wrestling, a baseball batting cage, and a 220-yard banked indoor track. Trees Hall has eleven racquetball courts, five basketball courts in two huge gyms, superb gymnastic equipment, an Olympic-sized swimming pool, a dance studio, and a weight and exercise room. The Charles L. Cost Sports Center complex features nine tennis courts and an indoor field for intramural sports and recreation. The University has just received state funding to help build a new Convocation Center near the Pitt Stadium that will provide an arena for basketball, track and field, concerts and performing arts, and commencement exercises.

Study Abroad The University of Pittsburgh is affiliated with the Institute for European Studies (IES), the Institute for Asian Studies (IAS), the Council for International Educational Exchange (CIEE), and Tel Aviv University, offering study-abroad opportunities in Great Britain, Europe, the former U.S.S.R., Israel, and Asia. Through the International Student Exchange Program (ISEP) and other University-sponsored interinstitutional exchanges, Pitt students are able to study in Africa, Asia, Central and South America, and Europe. In addition, through Pitt's association with Educational Programs Abroad (EPA), internships are available to students in Europe. Many of these programs are offered at virtually the same price as attending Pitt. The University of Pittsburgh is an academic sponsor of Semester at Sea. The Semester at Sea program is a chance to study the world while traveling by ocean liner. Students spend roughly 40 percent of their time on the ocean and 60 percent in ports of call around the globe. Pitt faculty members join with teachers from other major universities in the United States and abroad to offer more than sixty voyage-relevant courses on each voyage. Credits earned meet the required standards, permitting transfer to students' university or college.

Support Services The University offers services through Disability Resources and Services (DRS). These include exam accommodations, taped textbooks, sign language interpreter/real-time reporting, instructional strategy assistance, disability parking and transportation, and an adaptive computing and training lab. Students with learning disabilities are invited to participate in the First Year Transition Program. The objective of this program is to improve the retention, matriculation, and academic performance of students with learning disabilities by providing the transferable skills necessary for academic work and to foster self-reliance and independence. Participants attend one group session per week to discuss topics such as self-advocacy, rights and responsibilities, and general skills and strategies. Students are also assigned an appointment each week to meet with a DRS learning specialist to focus on individualized learning strategies and skills.

Job Opportunities There are approximately 1,300 students working part-time in work-study positions on campus. These positions are available to students who demonstrate financial need. Internships are available to students in every major. In the past, students have worked at *Pittsburgh Magazine*, the Buhl Science Center, the Pittsburgh Penguins, and KDKA (TV and radio). In addition, the University's Internship Office collaborates with the Washington Center for Learning Alternatives (WCLA) to provide students with Washington-based internships in journalism and communications, the sciences, theater, fine arts, business, political science and urban studies, mathematics and computer science, and engineering.

Tuition: $5884 for residents, $12,918 for nonresidents for the College of Arts and Sciences (1998–99)

Room and board: $5598

Mandatory Fees: $540

Contact: Dean: G. Alec Stewart, University Honors College, University of Pittsburgh, Pittsburgh, Pennsylvania 15260; Telephone: 412-624-6880; Fax: 412-624-6885; E-mail: uhchome@pitt.edu; Web site: http://www.pitt.edu/~uhchome

UNIVERSITY OF PORTLAND

4 Pr G M Sc Tr

▼ Honors Program

The Honors Program was designed for students of exceptional ability who seek an intellectually challenging academic experience. It is open to students with superior high school records who are highly motivated to learn through exposure to stimulating ideas.

Honors students may concentrate their studies in any major field at the University; the honors curriculum fills a portion of the University core requirements for graduation in all majors. Through a combination of seminars and small classes of 10 to 20 students, the program provides an opportunity for in-depth study in the

Interpreting the symbols: **2**=two-year college, **4**=four-year college; **Pu**=public or state college, **Pr**=private college; **G**=general honors program; **D**=departmental honors program; **S**=small program (fewer than 100 students), **M**=midsize program (100 to 500 students), **L**=large program (more than 500 students); **Sc**=scholarships available in honors program; **Tr**=transfer students accepted into honors program; **HBC**=historically black college; **AA**=academic advisors; **GA**=graduate advisors; **FA**=fellowship advisors.

core curriculum. The Honors Program professors are among the best at the University, and they are specifically selected to be part of the program. The students and faculty members form a community that facilitates learning in and out of the classroom.

Freshmen take a one-week early course just prior to their fall semester. This is both an academic course and an introduction to the program. Freshmen and sophomore honors students choose one course each semester from among the honors courses offered that term. In the junior year, honors students participate in a junior seminar. Seniors complete an independent research project or thesis under the supervision of a faculty member in the area of the student's major. Each student who completes all Honors Program requirements has a designation entered on their transcript, wears a bachelor's degree hood during the graduation ceremony, and receives a medallion with their name, year of graduation, and University of Portland Honors Program engraved.

Approximately 25 entering freshmen are accepted each year (about 5 percent of the total entering freshmen) as are 3 or 4 sophomores or transfer students. There are currently 110 students in the program.

Participation Requirements: In addition to the orientation course, four regular honors classes, a junior seminar, and a thesis or project in their major, students are expected to participate in some of the cocurricular activities offered each year, which include trips to plays, symphony, ballet, opera, weekend retreats, and barbecues. In order to continue in good standing in the program, freshmen must earn a minimum GPA of 3.0, sophomores a 3.1, juniors a 3.2, and seniors a 3.3.

Admission Process: Students accepted to the University of Portland may apply for admission to the Honors Program. The Honors Program Advisory Committee composed of students and faculty members review these applications and make recommendations on acceptance to the director. The deadline for application is in March.

The Campus Context: The University of Portland is situated on 130 acres in a quiet residential neighborhood on a bluff overlooking the Willamette River. The campus is 15 minutes from downtown Portland, 90 miles from the Oregon Coast, and 60 miles from the Cascade Mountains. There are six colleges and schools on campus, including the College of Arts and Sciences, Multnomah School of Engineering, Dr. Robert B. Pamplin, Jr. School of Business Administration, School of Education, School of Nursing, and the Graduate School. Forty-nine degree programs are available.

Student Body Undergraduate enrollment is 2400; 41 percent are men. Three percent of the students are international students, 55 percent are campus residents, and 85 percent of students receive financial aid.

Faculty There are 249 faculty members, 166 of whom are full-time. Ninety-three percent have terminal degrees. The student-faculty ratio is 13:1.

Key Facilities The Wilson W. Clark Memorial Library shelves more than 360,000 bound volumes of books and journals. The campus has twelve computer labs and three computer classrooms.

Honorary Society Alpha Kappa Delta, Alpha Kappa Psi, Alpha Lambda Delta, Beta Beta Beta, Beta Gamma Sigma, Blue Key, Delta Epsilon Sigma, Kappa Delta Pi, Lambda Pi Eta, Phi Alpha Theta, Psi Chi, Sigma Delta Pi, Tau Beta Pi

Athletics The University provides a strong intramural and recreational athletics program for students. The intercollegiate program competes at the NCAA Division I level. The men's and women's programs compete in the West Coast Conference in basketball, cross-country, golf, soccer, and tennis. The men's program also offers baseball and track (the track program competes as an independent). The women's program also offers volleyball.

Study Abroad The University provides an academic-year program in Salzburg, Austria, and four summer-study programs in London; Tokyo; Salzburg, Austria; and Morelia, Mexico. The University is also a member of the Independent Liberal Arts Colleges Abroad consortium, which offers two additional study-abroad opportunities: a fall or spring semester in London and a fall or spring semester in Granada, Spain. In conjunction with the Institute of European Studies, the University offers a one- or two-semester program in Paris or Nantes, France, for students interested in advanced studies in the French language and a one- or two-semester program in Freiburg, Germany, for students interested in advanced studies in the German language.

Tuition: $18,930 per year (2001–02)

Room and Board: $5740 minimum

Mandatory Fees: $100

Contact: Director: Dr. James G. Stemler, 5000 North Willamette Boulevard, Portland, Oregon 97203; Telephone: 503-943-7221; Fax: 503-943-7804; E-mail: stemler@up.edu

University of Puerto Rico at Humacao

4 Pu G S Tr

▼ Programa Académico de Honor

The Programa Académico de Honor (PAH, Academic Honors Program) provides students with the opportunity to take full advantage of the university experience at the University of Puerto Rico at Humacao. Since its inception in 1989, the program has aimed to enrich the educational formation/development of the student within an interdisciplinary context/frame. PAH students benefit from academic offerings unique to the honors program, including interdisciplinary seminars, independent studies, a computer room and study area, faculty-level library privileges, and photocopying at no charge. Each student is assigned an academic adviser who helps them plan their program of study and prepare for graduate school. In addition, the program organizes orientation sessions on graduate school admissions requirements, scholarships, and financial aid programs.

There are 80 students in the program.

Participation Requirements: In the first three years of study, students must complete an Independent Study or Introduction to Research course, an honors seminar, and a third language. In their fourth year, students must prepare an honors thesis in their selected area of study under the supervision of a professor. At PAH, there is the belief that the student's learning experience must transcend the classroom. Thus, in order to be considered active members of PAH, students must also participate in cocurricular activities organized by the program. Students who fulfill all the requirements of the program receive a certificate upon graduation and their accomplishment is recorded on their transcript.

Admission Process: Students of all majors with a minimum 3.3 GPA are invited to join the program during their first and second year in college. Admission is contingent upon several factors, including a good GPA, a successful interview, and, most important, the student's willingness to fulfill the requirements of the program. Applications are due in February and March.

Scholarship Availability: Although PAH does not offer any scholarships, students with a high GPA may benefit from tuition exemption offered by the College.

The Campus Context: Thirty-nine years ago, the University of Puerto Rico initiated one of the most innovative projects undertaken for many years—to take the University closer to the people by providing access to secondary education to residents of eastern Puerto Rico. The objective was accomplished with the inauguration of the Colegio Regional de Humacao, now the

University of Puerto Rico at Humacao, a state-funded, four-year, coeducational institution, and one of the eleven units that make up the University of Puerto Rico System. The University is located in the city of Humacao on the eastern coast of the island of Puerto Rico, 35 miles from the San Juan metropolitan area. Ten associate degree programs and eighteen bachelor's degree programs are offered on campus.

Student Body The total undergraduate enrollment is 4,476 students, of whom 71 percent are women and 99.9 percent are Hispanic. All students commute to school as there is no college-affiliated student housing. Seventy percent of the students receive financial aid. There are several fraternities and sororities, but only one sorority is officially recognized by the University.

Faculty There are 321 active faculty members, of whom 295 are full-time; 33 percent have doctorates. The student-faculty ratio is 15:1.

Key Facilities The library houses 109,656 volumes and 10,221 microform holdings. There are 166 computer terminals available for student use at various locations throughout the campus.

Athletics Intercollegiate athletics include baseball (men), basketball, cross-country, soccer (men), softball, table tennis, tennis, track and field, volleyball, and wrestling (men). The University also offers a wide range of intramural sports for both men and women.

Study Abroad Study-abroad opportunities include participation in the Student Exchange Program and special summer courses that include travel to a different country (e.g., Europe). Students can study in the continental U.S. through the National Collegiate Honors Council Exchange Program.

Support Services Most of the facilities in the College are handicapped-accessible.

Job Opportunities Students who are eligible for financial aid may find employment on campus through the work-study program. Other opportunities for employment are available off campus.

Tuition: $550 for residents, per semester. Nonresident students who are U.S. citizens pay an amount equal to the rate for nonresidents at a state university in their home states. $2400 for international students, per year (2001–02)

Room and Board: Not available on campus. For commuters, $6650 (estimated, 2001–02)

Fees: $35 construction per year, $25 per lab. International students pay an additional $940 per year.

Contact: Coordinator: Dr. Maritza Reyes, Oficina de Asuntos Académicos, CUH Station, Humacao, Puerto Rico 00791; Telephone: 787-850-9303; Fax: 787-850-9403; E-mail: ma_reyes@cuhac.upr.clu.edu

University of Puerto Rico Río Piedras Campus

4 Pu L Tr

▼ Honors Program

The Honors Program, established in 1961, answered directly to the Chancellor's Office but has undergone fundamental changes since its inception. Currently, the Honors Program answers to the Office of the Dean of Academic Affairs (Certification No. 122 (1993–94) of the Academic Senate).

The Honors Program offers students the opportunity to achieve an integrated undergraduate education of excellence in an innovative and creative atmosphere. Integrated education provides an open and flexible approach to the learning process, in which not only the incorporation of diverse areas of knowledge is favored, but also the necessary specialization to master a given field. The Honors Program aspires to cultivate an environment in keeping with the dynamic spirit of professors and students interested in exploring new possibilities and new horizons in terms of the content as well as the focus of academic offerings. The Honors Program creates an alternative for those students who wish an individualized study environment and flexible and varied curricular offerings that enrich their majors.

Although the Honors Program does not offer academic degrees, students who have fulfilled all Honors Program requirements receive a Certificate of Recognition. This information is also registered in the academic transcript, where the title of the honors thesis appears.

The Honors Program enriches the University experience and helps integrate knowledge in an interdisciplinary way. The student has access to a series of special academic benefits, namely, small classes, direct contact with professors, independent research, interdisciplinary and research seminars, and association with similarly motivated undergraduate students. Available to the students are seminar and study rooms, as well as a lounge for academic and social interaction.

Participation Requirements: Each student is assigned an academic adviser or mentor who guides and counsels in the formation of a study plan.

In addition to taking the courses required by their respective Colleges, the students must fulfill the following Honors Program requirements: learn a third language in addition to Spanish and English, take a tutorial and a research seminar, and prepare an honors thesis. The Governing Board, in consultation with the student, has the discretion to make adjustments in these requirements through substitutions, equivalencies, or additions. This depends upon a student's particular needs. All of the Honors Program's academic offerings respond to the demands of the highest academic standards.

Admission Process: In order to be admitted to the Honors Program students must have completed at least one semester of University studies with a full-time program; have a 3.5 GPA or higher at the time of applying for admission to the Honors Program; submit two or three letters of recommendation; and demonstrate, through interviews with the Directors of Studies and the Governing Board, the capacity and interest to satisfactorily meet Honors Program requirements. After this process, the Governing Board decides which candidates are accepted into the Honors Program.

The Campus Context: There are eleven colleges and schools at the University of Puerto Rico, Río Piedras Campus: Architecture, Business Administration, Education, General Studies, Humanities, Law, Library Sciences, Natural Sciences, Public Communication, Planning, and Social Sciences. Students may enroll in 132 academic programs. Distinguished facilities on campus include libraries, seminars, laboratories, a museum, and a theater.

Student Body Undergraduate enrollment is 17,787 students.

Faculty Of the 1,444 faculty members, 1,160 (80.3 percent) are full-time, 48.6 percent have a doctoral degree, and 46.8 percent have a master's degree.

Key Facilities The library houses 2,132,882 volumes and each college has extensive computer facilities. There are various research institutes in areas such as tropical ecology, social sciences, and Caribbean studies.

Tuition: $30 per credit for residents plus registration fees; nonresidents of Puerto Rico who are citizens of the United States are charged an additional amount, equal to the minimum tuition that a resident of Puerto Rico would pay at a state institution in the nonresident's place of origin; international students pay

Interpreting the symbols: **2**=two-year college, **4**=four-year college; **Pu**=public or state college, **Pr**=private college; **G**=general honors program; **D**=departmental honors program; **S**=small program (fewer than 100 students), **M**=midsize program (100 to 500 students), **L**=large program (more than 500 students); **Sc**=scholarships available in honors program; **Tr**=transfer students accepted into honors program; **HBC**=historically black college; **AA**=academic advisors; **GA**=graduate advisors; **FA**=fellowship advisors.

$1200 plus registration fees. Nonresident students, participating in exchange programs established between the University System and other institutions of higher education, pay the amount decided upon in the individual exchange program agreements. This amount shall not be less than the amount paid by a resident student.

Mandatory fees: $15 admisistrative fee for admission; graduation candidates and all other undergraduate students enrolled in two or more courses must have health insurance coverage, be it private or the University's. Students who have private health insurance, including those admitted for the summer session, must submit evidence of coverage. All other students except those under visiting status must acquire the University's health plan insurance.

Contact: University of Puerto Rico, Río Piedras Campus, P.O. Box 21847, UPR Station, San Juan, Puerto Rico 00931-1847; Telephone: 787-764-0000 ext. 3288, 2221, and 4945; Fax: 787-764-3044.

UNIVERSITY OF ST. THOMAS

4 Pr G S Sc

▼ Honors Program

The purpose of the Honors Program at the University of St. Thomas (UST) is the creation of virtuous professionals, who are makers and preservers of a culture that is not hostile to the virtuous life. This requires two distinct but related educational activities: the tradition or the handing over of artifacts and archetypes of Western culture to students and an apprenticeship in the redeployment of these cultural instruments in the contemporary world, which ideally will result in their reform and transformation. Established in 1989, the Honors Program currently enrolls 50 to 70 students.

Participation Requirements: The program begins with four interdisciplinary, team-taught seminars that have a two-fold purpose: to connect the study of Western culture with the problem of living one's life and to provide structural principles for understanding culture itself and, therefore, of facilitating understanding of non-Western cultures. Team-teaching both furthers the interdisciplinary nature of the courses and encourages collaboration in learning among students and faculty members.

These four courses are the necessary prologue to a course in reflective practical action. This course combines reading and discussion with individual service projects. In this way, students learn how values become incarnate in the world through work and how self-development is connected with service to others.

An undergraduate research project, which culminates in the presentation of results in a University forum, is designed to foster professional creativity and responsibility as well as collaboration with a faculty mentor.

A final team-taught seminar undertakes an interdisciplinary approach to the analysis and solution of some contemporary problem. As they prepare to leave the University, students discover that their education, liberal and professional, has given them the power to understand and transform contemporary society in the light of their values.

Successful completion of the Honors Program is noted on the student's transcript. Graduates of the Honors Program receive a certificate and medallion at Commencement, and Honors Program is printed on their diploma.

Admission Process: In order to be considered for admission, students must complete the University's general scholarship application and arrange for an interview with the program. Students must have a GPA of at least 3.5 on a 4.0 scale, be in the top 15 percent of their graduating class, and have an SAT I score of at least 1150 (recentered) or an ACT score of at least 26.

Scholarship Availability: All members of the UST Honors Program receive scholarships. These include the President's Scholarship, which is valued between $40,000 and $53,000 and is given to students who are in the top 10 percent of their graduating class and have an SAT I score of at least 1250 (or 27 on the ACT) and a strong recommendation; the St. Thomas Aquinas Scholarship, which is valued at $26,000 and awarded to students who are in the top 15 percent of their graduating class and have an SAT I score of at least 1150 (or 25 on the ACT) or to students who are in the top 20 percent of their class and have an SAT I score of at least 1200 (or 26 on the ACT); and the Scholarship for Excellence, which is valued at $53,000, for students who have achieved national recognition by becoming semifinalists in the National Merit, National Achievement, or National Hispanic Program and who are in the top 25 percent of their class.

The Campus Context: The University of St. Thomas is composed of the School of Arts and Sciences, School of Education, Cameron School of Business, and School of Theology. Among the distinguished facilities are a genetic research facility in the Biology Department. Thirty-two degree programs are offered on campus.

Student Body Undergraduate enrollment is 1,597, with 34 percent men. The student population is 52 percent white, 21 percent Hispanic, 7 percent African American, 9 percent Asian Pacific, 1 percent Native American, and 2 percent other. The 222 international students represent 8 percent of the student body.

Key Facilities The library houses 200,000 volumes. There is a computer facility with forty computers and a writing laboratory with thirteen computers and six portables.

Honorary Societies Delta Epsilon Sigma and Alpha Sigma Lambda

Athletics The John D. Jerabeck Activity and Athletic Center has a basketball/volleyball arena with bleacher seating capacity of more than 800, four racquetball/handball courts, locker rooms for men and women, a weight room, a dance/cardiovascular exercise studio, a sauna, and six large classrooms. Outdoor facilities at the JAAC include two tennis courts, a swimming pool, and a basketball area.

Tuition: $13,050 per year (1998–99)

Room and Board: $5170 minimum

Mandatory Fees: $112

Contact: Director: Dr. Terry Hall, 3800 Montrose Boulevard, Houston, Texas 77006; Telephone: 713-525-3587; Fax: 713-525-2125; E-mail: thall@stthom.edu; Web site: http://www.basil.stthom.edu/honors

UNIVERSITY OF SAN DIEGO

4 Pu

▼ University Honors Program

The University of San Diego Honors Program is designed to provide students of superior ability and accomplishment with challenges and opportunities that allow them to realize their potential more fully. The four-year course of study provides an interdisciplinary curriculum that is integrated with a student's major area of study as well as the University's general education requirements. The program emphasizes teaching excellence, small classes, and a core curriculum of innovative and exciting courses. Honors students have numerous opportunities for individual counseling and discussions with honors faculty members.

In the freshman year, honors students enroll in an honors preceptorial during fall semester and a section of a lower-division general education course in the spring. During their sophomore and junior years, honors students enroll in at least two upper-division, team-taught interdisciplinary courses. These courses, which change yearly, represent the honors core curriculum. In the team-taught courses, students approach traditional topics from a fresh perspective, which cuts across standard disciplinary boundaries. Students come to realize that scholarly work is not restrained or limited by the boundaries of disciplines or areas of study.

The Honors Senior Colloquium, offered each spring, provides honors students with the opportunity to explore a topic that has interested them during their undergraduate work at USD. Students are encouraged to consider topics that have been most engaging and lend themselves to further study. Some students choose to expand work initiated in another class. These students must continue work in which they are already invested, rather than recycle work previously submitted for a grade. All projects include original research, primary sources, an oral presentation, and considerable dedication and time. Each student works under the direction of a faculty adviser in his or her major.

The USD Housing Office began on-campus theme housing for the Honors Program in 1995, open to freshmen and upperclass students. The suite-style apartments offer amenities not available in the regular freshmen dorms, as well as increased opportunities for honors freshmen to get to know each other.

The USD Honors Program was established in 1979. The program admits approximately 80 students per year, and there are 200 students currently enrolled.

Participation Requirements: Students must complete a minimum of 25 honors units for graduation with the honors diploma. This is an average of one honors course each semester. Of these 25 units, students must take at least two upper-division, team-taught interdisciplinary courses. Students studying abroad for one semester receive 4 honors program units toward the required 25 honors units. Honors students must maintain a GPA of at least 3.4.

The curriculum begins with the Honors Preceptorial, which introduces new students to the University and the Honors Program. It ends with a senior capstone experience, which includes an optional independent study, a thesis, and participation in the Honors Senior Colloquium.

Students who complete the 25-unit course of study receive an honors diploma and are the only undergraduate students who wear a gold cord during the spring commencement ceremonies.

Admission Process: Most honors students enter the program at the beginning of their freshman year, although students with excellent academic records may apply for admission at the end of their freshman year. Transfer students are evaluated for admission on an individual basis. In general, students in the program are among those who have the highest high school GPAs and SAT or ACT scores upon entering USD. Invitations to apply to the Honors Program are issued to students on the basis of scores, grades, and personal achievement. In 2001, freshman entering the Honors Program had a 4.09 average weighted GPA and an average combined SAT I score of 1300. Applicants answer a set of four questions that ask students to describe their achievements and their experience in completing a difficult project. Students are expected to have an active interest in their own education and an appreciation for academic challenges. In evaluating the records of high school seniors, the Office of Admissions and the Director of the Honors Program seek to choose those students who have the ability and motivation to achieve in the program. Attention is paid to those who will most benefit from the honors curriculum.

Scholarship Availability: University scholarships are awarded through the Office of Undergraduate Admissions in cooperation with the Office of Financial Aid Services, but the Honors Program does not offer separate scholarships. Most honors students, however, are awarded merit-based scholarships.

The Campus Context: The University of San Diego includes the College of Arts and Sciences, School of Business Administration, School of Education, School of Law, Hahn School of Nursing and Health Science, and the Joan B. Kroc Institute for Peace and Justice.

The 180-acre campus overlooks Mission Bay Aquatic Park, with views of San Diego Bay and the Pacific Ocean. Close to business, cultural, residential, and recreational areas, the campus is near the air and rail terminals, and a city bus line runs right past the campus. Known for many reasons as "America's Finest City," San Diego has an almost perfect climate with warm, sunny days and cool evenings. Throughout the year, students can take advantage of San Diego's many outdoor recreational and cultural opportunities. The museums of Balboa Park, the Old Globe Theater, the zoo, Sea World, the beaches, the opera, and downtown San Diego and La Jolla are only minutes away. The rapidly developing economy of greater San Diego provides varied employment opportunities for the USD graduate.

Student Body Of the 4,400 undergraduate students at the University of San Diego, 58 percent are women and approximately 43 percent live on campus. Thirty percent of students come from underrepresented groups, and 3 percent are international students. Seventy-one percent of students receive financial aid. There are five sororities and five fraternities and more than seventy other academic, professional, cultural, language, ethnic, and recreational organizations on campus.

Faculty The total number of full-time faculty members is 315. Ninety-seven percent of the faculty have terminal degrees. The student-faculty ratio is 18:1.

Key Facilities The University of San Diego has two major libraries: the Copley Library and the Legal Research Center (LRC). The Copley Library houses more than 375,000 volumes and subscribes to 2,200 periodicals. The Legal Research Center houses more than 498,000 volumes. Both libraries have more than 3,000 journals available in electronic form and access to around 60 databases. The Copley Library is also part of the San Diego Circuit, which allows access to the CSUSM, UCSD, and SDSU libraries. The Joan B. Kroc Institute for Peace and Justice is housed in a 90,000-square-foot building where students are prepared for careers in conflict resolution and human rights. A 150,000-square-foot Center for Science and Technology will be completed in 2004, with seventy new laboratory facilities. The Jenny Craig Pavilion is a 5,100-seat arena used to host a range of sporting, educational, and cultural events. The University also has eight computer facilities that house more than 450 computers for student, faculty, and staff use.

Honorary Societies Kappa Gamma Pi, Mortar Board

Athletics The University of San Diego Toreros have Division I NCAA teams in baseball, basketball, crew, cross-country, football (I-AA), golf, soccer, and tennis for men and in basketball, crew, cross-country, soccer, softball, swimming, tennis, and volleyball for women. Approximately two thirds of the University community participate in intramural programs.

Study Abroad Study-abroad opportunities include one semester and yearlong programs in Australia, Austria, Canada, Costa Rica, England, France, Germany, Italy, Japan, Mexico, Spain, and the British West Indies.

Support Services USD provides students with disabilities with accommodations or with modifications to policies and practices in order to ensure that students have an equal opportunity to participate in all USD programs, services, and activities. The purpose of accommodations is not to guarantee success but to provide access and equal opportunity.

Job Opportunities Approximately 21 percent of students are employed by the University during the academic year. Work

Interpreting the symbols: **2**=two-year college, **4**=four-year college; **Pu**=public or state college, **Pr**=private college; **G**=general honors program; **D**=departmental honors program; **S**=small program (fewer than 100 students), **M**=midsize program (100 to 500 students), **L**=large program (more than 500 students); **Sc**=scholarships available in honors program; **Tr**=transfer students accepted into honors program; **HBC**=historically black college; **AA**=academic advisors; **GA**=graduate advisors; **FA**=fellowship advisors.

opportunities on campus and around town are listed in the Student Employment Office. The Career Services Office assists students nearing graduation.

Tuition: undergraduate tuition for 2001–02 is $10,175 per semester or $705 per unit

Room and Board: $3195–$5070 per semester

Mandatory Fees: $108 per semester

Contact: Director: Dr. Noelle Norton, 5998 Alcala Park, San Diego, California 92110; Telephone: 619-260-7847; Fax: 619-260-7880; E-mail: norton@sandiego.edu; Web site: http://www.sandiego.edu/honors

THE UNIVERSITY OF SCRANTON

4 Pr G M AA FA

▼ The Honors Program

The Honors Program at the University of Scranton provides an exceptional opportunity for selected students to receive an education of greater depth and breadth. It is open to full-time students in all majors and requires no extra fees.

The program is carefully designed to lead students to progressively more sophisticated and independent work, both in and out of their majors. Unlike most honors programs, it admits students in their sophomore year and concentrates not on honors sections of courses but on one-on-one work with faculty members. This carefully mentored work provides an exceptional opportunity for honors students to know and work with committed faculty members.

The most distinctive element of Scranton's Honors Program is the tutorials it makes available to upper class students. Honors students satisfy three to five major and nonmajor course requirements with honors tutorials. These provide intensive interaction with faculty members and move the student from participating in carefully designed courses to working under the direction of a faculty member to explore a personally chosen subject. These tutorials are often interdisciplinary and are frequently designed to correlate with other honors work. Their flexibility includes the availability of any subject which a faculty member is willing to teach, such as a tutorial on French philosophy conducted in French, and the possibility of responding to new discoveries or circumstances, such as a tutorial on terrorism, which was reconceptualized after September 11, 2001.

The independent work of the tutorials is extended in the senior honors project. This involves the intensive exploration under a mentor's direction of a specialized topic, which is either academic or professional. The finished projects are defended before a three-person panel, bound, and placed in the library.

In addition to the tutorials and project where the student is the only pupil, the program also includes an interdisciplinary course limited to honors students with an average size of 22 students and two seminars limited to no more than 14 students. Periodic social events provide informal opportunities to extend the friendships formed in the course and seminars.

The Honors Program at the University of Scranton was established in 1966 and currently has an enrollment of 115 students.

Participation Requirements: Admitted as sophomores, honors students must take an interdisciplinary honors course that satisfies a general education requirement. Recent offerings include Victorian Studies, which uses Victorian literature to examine such topics as social class, the role of women, and religion; Elements of Natural Sciences, which examines topics such as light, cosmology, chaos, and pseudoscience; and Science over the Edge, which addresses topics at the boundaries of the natural and social/behavioral sciences such as the human genome project and sociobiology.

As juniors and seniors, honors students must take three tutorials, one of which must be in their major and one in their second major or out of their major. These can satisfy major, cognate, or general education requirements. Honors students must participate in two seminars and one should be based on an interdisciplinary reading list and the second on the senior projects. These semester-long seminars, which each meet for an hour weekly, are free of tuition charge but satisfy only honors graduation requirements. Finally, honors students must complete a two-semester, six-credit project in their major, which ordinarily satisfies a major's elective requirements. They must successfully defend this project before a three-person panel.

Continued participation in the program requires appropriate progress toward completion of the honors curriculum and toward the 3.5 GPA that is required for graduation. Honors students are recognized at graduation and their diploma and transcript note their completion of the program.

Admission Process: Students ordinarily apply to the Honors Program in their sophomore year. The application deadline is October 1. Freshmen or transfer students who expect to graduate in three years may also apply if they have a minimum of 18 credits. Exceptional juniors are occasionally admitted to the program.

Applicants must demonstrate a reasonable possibility of achieving the minimum 3.5 GPA (cum laude) required for honors graduation; ordinarily this means at least a 3.3 GPA. In addition to the GPA, acceptance is based on an application and essay, faculty recommendations, high school and college records, interviews, and SAT or ACT scores.

Scholarship Availability: The University gives substantial academic scholarships, but none through the Honors Program.

The Campus Context: A Jesuit institution in Pennsylvania's Pocono northeast, The University of Scranton is known for many things, especially its outstanding academics, state-of-the art campus and technology, and exceptional sense of community.

Founded in 1888, the University offers more than 80 undergraduate and graduate academic programs of study through five colleges and schools. New majors added in recent years include electronic commerce, enterprise management technology, accounting information systems, exercise science, and media and information technology. Scranton also offers 44 minors, almost 30 concentrations and tracks, and three programs for high-achieving students.

The University of Scranton has constructed twenty-two new buildings and renovated fifteen others in the last twenty years. Recent additions to campus include: Brennan Hall, a five-story, 71,000-square-foot home for the Kania School of Management; McGurrin Hall, a four-story 65,000-square foot home for the Panuska College of Professional Studies; and Mulberry Plaza, a four-building, 40,000-square-foot town-house complex.

For eight consecutive years, *U.S. News & World Report* ranked Scranton among the ten finest master's universities in the North and sixth in the 2002 edition. *Yahoo! Internet Life* has ranked Scranton among the nation's 100 Most Wired Colleges and Universities for the past three years and 39th in the 2001 edition. In addition, Scranton is one of only 100 schools in the nation on Templeton's Honor Role of Character-Building Colleges.

In 2000–01, more than 2,400 Scranton students engaged in more than 144,000 hours of community service. Included in these hours are multiple service-learning projects that integrate volunteer work, course work, and reflection.

The University has a student population of approximately 4,800, including adult, part-time and graduate students. The 3,600 full-time undergraduate students include 43 percent men and 57 percent women, with students from 27 states and more than 10 other countries. Nearly 900 students enroll each year as freshmen. There are no fraternities or sororities.

The University of Scranton's graduation rate for all students is 66 percent for four years (38 percent above national averages) and 78 percent for six years (24 percent above national averages). The University's retention rate, which is the percentage of students continuing their education after the first year of college, is 90 percent.

Faculty With a student-to-faculty ratio of just 13:1 and an average class size of 23 students, professors get to know their students. The total number of faculty members is 388 and 256 work full-time. Members of the faculty hold degrees from 135 different universities in thirty countries on five continents. More than 82 percent of the faculty hold a doctoral or other terminal degree in their field.

Key Facilities The Weinberg Library holds 270,214 books, 63,083 periodicals, and 98,742 microfilm volume equivalents. There are 814 computer workstations available to students and the dormitories are wired so that students can connect their own computers to the University system.

Honorary Societies Honors students are eligible for membership in Alpha Sigma Nu, the National Jesuit Honor Society.

Athletics Men's NCAA Division III varsity teams include soccer, cross-country, lacrosse, wrestling, basketball, ice hockey, tennis, golf, baseball, and swimming. Women's Division III teams compete in soccer, cross-country, lacrosse, field hockey, volleyball, basketball, tennis, softball and swimming. Club sports include men's volleyball, men's and women's track and field, rugby, bowling, cycling, and crew. A campuswide intramural sports program enrolls thousands of participants.

Study Abroad Honors students frequently study abroad for a semester or year. Adjustments are made to their program requirements based upon this experience.

Job Opportunities The University offers many work-study opportunities for eligible students. Individual departments offer internship possibilities, and all students are invited to participate in the Faculty Student Research Program and the Faculty Student Teaching Program.

Tuition: Flat tuition is $19,330 per year (2001–02). For junior and senior honors students, this does not cover the usual 18 credits, but 21 credits per semester.

Mandatory Fees: Mandatory fees are $200 per year (2001–02)

Room and Board: $8434 per year (2001–02)

Contact: Director: Ellen Miller Casey, Ph.D. English Department, University of Scranton, Scranton, Pennsylvannia 18510; Telephone: 570-941-7426; Fax: 570-941-6657; E-mail: caseye1@scranton.edu

UNIVERSITY OF SOUTH ALABAMA

4 Pu G D M Sc Tr

▼ Honors Program

The University of South Alabama (USA) Honors Program offers a curriculum of interdisciplinary excellence designed to stimulate analytical and critical thinking of exceptionally qualified and highly motivated students. In this effort, the USA Honors Program challenges the students with scholarly creative activities, exposes them to cultural enrichment, and requires them to engage in community service. The USA Honors Program aspires to instill in students the intellectual excitement that will better prepare them for productive careers and citizenship. Within the context and diversity of a midsized urban university, the USA Honors Program provides the academic and cultural atmosphere and setting expected of a small, personal campus community of excellence.

The main honors option, the University Honors Program, is a campuswide program that includes honors course work and extracurricular activities throughout the four years of a student's undergraduate career. In addition to general University curriculum requirements and degree requirements of the selected major, University honors students also complete enriched honors general studies courses, honors seminars, and a Senior Honors Project. A cornerstone of the program is that each student is assigned a faculty mentor, chosen from the student's major department or suggested by the Honors Program until a major has been identified, who directs the student through the research and scholarly experience that culminates in an Honors Senior Project. Mentors are outstanding faculty members of the University.

Honors classes are small (usually 20 or fewer students) and are taught by the University's most stimulating faculty members. Specially scheduled scholarly presentations involve honors students and the wider academic community in a format that includes the opportunity to debate various issues and to listen to and interact with invited speakers and performing artists.

In addition to challenging academic opportunities, the University Honors Program offers a variety of activities that extend learning beyond the classroom, including social and cultural activities and community service projects. All University honors students are required to participate on a continuing basis in community and campus service activities. University honors students are encouraged to participate in international programs and off-campus internships and are assisted by the program in applying for national or international scholarships (e.g., Fulbright and Rhodes scholarships and graduate and professional schools). University honors students are also given priority for registration and an option to select honors housing.

A second honors option, Departmental Honors, is available in many majors to transfer and upperclass students who enter with more than 32 semester hours. To receive a designation of With Distinction in the major, Departmental Honors students must complete the Senior Honors Project and meet the specific honors requirements of the major department.

Participation Requirements: Participants in the USA Honors Program take 30 semester hours of honors credit in a combination of special sections of selected general studies courses, honors seminars, and honors electives (often in their major). Only grades of C or better count toward the Honors Program. The culminating experience of the program is the Senior Honors Project, designed and conducted in close collaboration with a faculty mentor from the major field of study. The Senior Honors Project often results in a student-authored publication. Honors students are involved together in community and campus service projects and regularly attend cultural and scholarly events facilitated by the Honors Program Office.

University honors students must maintain satisfactory progress in the honors curriculum to remain in the program. Required overall GPAs for honors students are 3.0 or higher after the freshman year, 3.25 or higher after the sophomore year, and 3.5 or higher after the junior year and through completion of the requirements of the Honors Program. A student may be placed on honors probation for a period of one semester and must attain the required GPA at the end of the probationary semester in order to return to full status in the Honors Program.

Completion of the University Honors Program is signified by the notation of With University Honors on the transcript and special recognition in the graduation program. All honors courses are specifically noted on the transcript.

Interpreting the symbols: 2=two-year college, 4=four-year college; **Pu**=public or state college, **Pr**=private college; **G**=general honors program; **D**=departmental honors program; **S**=small program (fewer than 100 students), **M**=midsize program (100 to 500 students), **L**=large program (more than 500 students); **Sc**=scholarships available in honors program; **Tr**=transfer students accepted into honors program; **HBC**=historically black college; **AA**=academic advisors; **GA**=graduate advisors; **FA**=fellowship advisors.

Admission Process: High school seniors with a minimum 27 composite ACT (or comparable SAT I score) and a minimum 3.5 (of 4.0) high school GPA are invited to apply. USA students and transfer students who have completed no more than 32 semester hours with a GPA of at least 3.5 are also eligible to enter the program. Students without the above qualifications who feel they have strong potential for success in the University Honors Program are encouraged to submit an application package and documentation of evidence of their special qualifications for review by the Honors Admissions Committee. Transfer students applying for admission to the program should indicate any credit earned in other honors programs. An honors application package includes a completed honors application form, two letters of recommendation, and an essay on a topic specified annually by the USA Honors Program, in addition to a USA admission application and high school transcripts and standardized test scores.

Scholarship Availability: The University of South Alabama offers USA Honors Scholarships to qualified participants in the USA Honors Program. Scholarship award amounts are based upon ACT scores and range from $12,000 to $32,000 for four years.

The Campus Context: The University of South Alabama, a comprehensive, coeducational institution, is the only major public institution of higher learning on the upper Gulf Coast. The University is strategically located in Mobile, Alabama, which has a population of more than 1 million within a 100-mile radius. The 1,200-acre beautifully wooded campus boasts more than seventy modern buildings, including the recently dedicated Laidlaw Performing Arts Center, a 40,000-square-foot laboratory addition to the College of Medicine, eight new fraternity and sorority houses, and a new 10,000-seat sports arena. On-campus housing offers diverse options for two or four persons in typical dormitory rooms and efficiencies or apartments in modern coed buildings. The main campus is bordered by the Mobile City golf course and Municipal Park and is about 10 miles from downtown Mobile, 3 miles from the regional airport, and 35 miles from the beaches of the Gulf of Mexico. The moderate climate allows year-round outdoor sports activities.

Undergraduates may select from forty-seven majors in eight academic divisions including, in order of enrollment, Arts and Sciences, Education, Business, Allied Health Professions, Nursing, Engineering, Computer and Information Sciences, and Continuing Education and Special Programs. USA teaches most nursing and professional components of allied health at the USA Springhill Campus located approximately 7 miles from the main campus. Graduate students in medicine and health-related fields are trained in three teaching hospitals and associated clinics and research laboratories operated by the University.

Student Body More than 12,000 students are enrolled annually at USA, comprising 60 percent women and 40 percent men. Approximately 74 percent of students are white, 16.5 percent African American, 3 percent Asian-Americans, 1 percent Hispanic-American, and 1 percent Native Americans. International students comprise about 8 percent of the student population. The diverse student body represents forty-two states and ninety-eight other countries. Eight sororities and twelve fraternities are active at USA. Nine new sorority and fraternity houses are located on campus, and the remainder have facilities near the campus. The average ACT of entering freshmen is 22.4, and the annual graduation class is approximately 2,021.

Faculty The University of South Alabama has 688 faculty members, 82 percent of whom have earned doctorates. Instruction in all majors is by faculty members only, not graduate students. The average class size is 22, with a campus faculty-student ratio of 1:13.

Key Facilities USA libraries consist of the University Library and the Biomedical Library, with a location on the campus and another at the USA Medical Center; the Archives at the USA Springhill Campus; and an extension at the USA Baldwin County Campus. The online catalog, selected periodical indexes, and the catalogs of other Alabama academic libraries are also available remotely through modern connections and a World Wide Web page. Library holdings include 463,784 bound volumes, 861,050 microforms, 3,735 serial titles, and more than 1 million government documents. A newly initiated expansion of the University Library is expected to will double its capacity, provide additional teaching and learning facilities and support services, and include state-of-the-art electronic access and referencing capabilities.

Honorary Societies Abeneefuo Kuo, Alpha Chi, Golden Key, Mortar Board, Omicron Delta Kappa, Phi Beta Delta, Phi Eta Sigma, and Phi Kappa Phi

Athletics USA's NCAA Division I teams compete nationally in a wide range of sports. Men and women each field teams in basketball, cross-country, golf, tennis, and track and field. In addition, women compete in soccer and volleyball and men in baseball. USA is in the Sunbelt Conference. USA also has a very active campus recreation and intramurals sports program in which honors students have a significant involvement.

Study Abroad The USA Office of International Programs coordinates all studies abroad and assists the Honors Program Office in facilitating honors students in locating, applying for, and funding internships and semesters abroad.

Support Services The USA Special Student Services Office provides assistance to students who are physically, emotionally, or learning disabled.

Job Opportunities The USA Career Services Center provides assistance with job searches and training in employability skills and coordinates parallel and alternating co-op employment programs. Additional assistance is available from the USA Student Employment Center. The University participates in the student work-study program. Undergraduate research assistantships are available in several departments.

Tuition: $3230 for residents, $6460 for nonresidents, per year (2001–02)

Room and board: $3746 (2 students per suite and a 12-meals-per-week plan)

Contact: Director: Dr. Judy P. Stout, Administration Suite 300, Mobile, Alabama 36688; Telephone: 251-460-6261; Fax: 251-460-6575; E-mail: honors@usouthal.edu; Web site: http://www.southalabama.edu/honors/

UNIVERSITY OF SOUTH CAROLINA

4 Pu G L Sc Tr AA FA

▼ South Carolina Honors College

South Carolina Honors College represents the University of South Carolina's (USC's) tangible commitment to providing its finest undergraduates with a superlative education consonant with their abilities and potential. The College serves as a visible and vital academic unit intended to attract the best high school students in the state, region, and country and provide them with a firm foundation for their future achievements.

Over the past three decades, the administrations of five University presidents created and sustained the Honors Program and its successor College. Their efforts resulted in an Honors College offering a peerless academic experience unifying the benefits of a small liberal arts college with the opportunities of a comprehensive university. It fuses these qualities in a unique synthesis, offering complementary combinations and counteracting the potential negatives of each academic environment. Everything that is done reflects the integration, not separation, of these educational alternatives.

As in a fine liberal arts college, Honors College classes are limited in size, populated by talented students, and taught by faculty members dedicated to designing courses that involve these students more actively in their own education. Honors students, however, are not set apart from the University but are a part of it. This simple change in preposition makes a world of difference for the students; it opens to them the world of the comprehensive University, with its research resources, diverse programs and curriculum, and rich campus culture.

The goals of the College are best represented by the type of student it hopes to attract and fulfill: leaders who are scholars; young men and women with a love of learning and faith in the role of reason; students who combine those elements common to all educated people, namely, the ability to use language with clarity and grace; appreciation of experimental sciences and scientific method; and insight into their own and other cultures through history, literature, and the arts, as well as the social sciences.

The Honors College sets high standards for its students and, therefore, for itself. Success is measured not only by the quality of the students attracted to the College but by the quality of the academic program the College offers them. Graduation with Honors from the South Carolina Honors College involves more than earning good grades; it stands for a substantive experience that challenges the students across the breadth of their academic endeavors.

Each semester, the Honors College offers approximately 120 courses across the undergraduate curriculum. In addition, the graduate schools of law, medicine, and public health also offer honors courses. In the lower division, the College provides courses that may be used to fulfill the general education requirements of all the undergraduate colleges in the University. In addition, upper-division courses are offered in areas with sufficient majors or general interest. Honors courses consist of honors sections of existing University courses or special classes developed especially for and existing only in the Honors College.

The Honors College office is located on the historic Horseshoe, the antebellum campus of the University. Honors facilities include classrooms, student lounges, and honors housing for up to 600 students.

The College has approximately 1,000 students.

Participation Requirements: Students who wish to earn honors from South Carolina Honors College must complete 45 credits of honors course work, including a 29- to 30-credit core and a 3- to 15-credit senior thesis. Honors core requirements consist of 6 credits of English, 8 of science, 6 of history of civilization, 6 of humanities/social sciences, and at least 3 credits of math/analytical.

Graduation with Honors from South Carolina Honors College is an official University honor that appears on the diploma and the transcript of each student who fulfills the requirements. In addition to formal recognition at each University Commencement, the Honors College holds its own ceremony to recognize those students completing all the requirements.

The College also offers its own interdisciplinary degree, the Baccalaureus Artium et Scientiae. In order to be admitted, applicants must be fourth-semester Honors College students with a minimum GPA of 3.6. They must develop a program of study approved by a panel consisting of the Associate Dean and Dean of the Honors College and 2 faculty advisers. They must take the maximum general education requirements of both the College of Science and Math and the College of Liberal Arts; complete an advanced foreign language course; take at least 69 credits of honors course work, including at least a 9-credit senior thesis; and maintain a minimum 3.5 GPA.

Admission Process: Entering freshmen generally score more than 1300 on the SAT I and rank in the top 5 percent of their high school class. They are selected on the basis of an application that includes both academic and extracurricular criteria. Students who have completed at least one semester of college (at USC or elsewhere) may also apply. To remain in the Honors College, students must maintain a minimum GPA that is set at 3.0 their first semester and rises to 3.3 by their senior year. The deadline for applying is February 1.

Scholarship Availability: Two scholarships, the South Carolina Honors College Scholarship and the William A. Mould Scholarship, are administered through the Honors College. The South Carolina Honors College Scholarship is awarded to out-of-state honors students with no other scholarship support. The Mould Scholarship is awarded to deserving students on the basis of need. Recipients are selected based on their enrollment in the Honors College.

The vast majority of honors students hold scholarships granted by the University of South Carolina. Students complete the same application for the University's major merit scholarships as for the Honors College.

The Campus Context: There are eighteen colleges and schools within the University of South Carolina. They are the College of Applied Professional Sciences, College of Business Administration, College of Criminal Justice, College of Education, College of Engineering, School of the Environment, College of Journalism and Mass Communications, Law School, College of Liberal Arts, College of Library and Information Science, School of Medicine, School of Music, College of Nursing, College of Pharmacy, School of Public Health, College of Science and Mathematics, College of Social Work, and South Carolina Honors College. More than 400 degree programs, including 80 bachelor's degrees, are offered on the Columbia campus.

The University of South Carolina is home to several distinguished facilities, including McKissick Museum, accredited by the American Association of Museums, and the University of South Carolina Press. The Koger Center for the Arts hosts University, local, national, and international performances. In addition, the University has a number of research bureaus and institutes, including Belle W. Baruch Institute for Marine Biology and Coastal Research; Center for Electrochemical Engineering; Center for Mechanics of Materials and Nondestructive Evaluation; Center for Industrial Research; Center for Industry Policy and Strategy; Center for Information Intelligence Technology; Center for Outcomes Research and Evaluation; Center for Retailing; Center for Science Education; Center for the Study of Suicide and Life Threatening Behavior; Division of Research, College of Business Administration; Earth Sciences and Resources Institute; Electron Microscopy Center; Institute for Families in Society; Richard L. Walker Institute of International Studies; Institute of Public Affairs; Institute for Southern Studies; Institute for Tourism Research; the National Resource Center for the Freshman Year Experience and Students in Transition; the Riegel and Emory Human Resource Research Center; South Carolina Institute of Archaeology and Anthropology; Southeast Manufacturing Technology Center; and TRIO Programs.

Student Body Undergraduate enrollment is 15,500 and includes 45 percent men. The ethnic distribution among the student population is 17.7 percent African American, 3 percent Asian/Pacific Islander, 1.4 percent Hispanic, .2 percent Native American, 73.5 percent white, and 2 percent nonresident alien. There are 329 international students. The student body is made up of 39 percent residents and 61 percent commuters. Approximately 55 percent of students receive financial aid. There are twenty-one fraternities and fifteen sororities.

Faculty Of the approximately 1,100 total faculty members, 1,000 are full-time and 90 percent have terminal degrees.

Interpreting the symbols: **2**=two-year college, **4**=four-year college; **Pu**=public or state college, **Pr**=private college; **G**=general honors program; **D**=departmental honors program; **S**=small program (fewer than 100 students), **M**=midsize program (100 to 500 students), **L**=large program (more than 500 students); **Sc**=scholarships available in honors program; **Tr**=transfer students accepted into honors program; **HBC**=historically black college; **AA**=academic advisors; **GA**=graduate advisors; **FA**=fellowship advisors.

Key Facilities The library houses more than 7 million items, including 2.6 million volumes and more than 4 million units in microform. The Computer Services Division (CSD) offers free mainframe and microcomputer application classes. CSD provides a public microlab with laser printing and text/graphics scanning support and a reference room of computer periodicals. CSD also sponsors a public microlab located at the Thomas Cooper Library. Departmental computer labs are located throughout campus, and students and faculty and staff members can access the University mainframe via modem and emulation software.

Honorary Societies Phi Eta Sigma, Golden Key, Mortar Board, and Phi Beta Kappa

Athletics The University sponsors an extensive program in intercollegiate sports that includes nine sports for men and ten sports for women. Baseball, basketball, cross-country, football, golf, soccer, softball, swimming, tennis, track, and volleyball are offered. The University of South Carolina is a member of the Southeastern Conference, and its athletic teams regularly play teams of that conference as well as those of other institutions across the nation. Among the facilities for athletics at the University are Williams-Brice Stadium, with a seating capacity of 80,250; the Coliseum, which seats more than 12,400; and an all-weather track with stands for 2,500. The baseball stadium seats 4,000, and stands with a capacity of 2,000 are located at the Sam Daniel Tennis Center. The University Club provides USC golfers with an excellent course for matches as well as practice. The George Terry Spring Sports Center and an indoor facility, including dressing rooms and a weight room located at Williams-Brice Stadium, provide complete, modern facilities for varsity athletes.

The Sol Blatt Physical Education Center provides extensive indoor space for student sports, including an Olympic-sized swimming pool. Women's basketball locker rooms were completed in 1994, and improvements to the overall women's athletic facilities have been made. Construction has been completed on a basketball practice facility and volleyball competition site adjacent to the Coliseum as well as to new boxes, club seating, a press box, and a football office complex with a departmental video studio at Williams-Brice Stadium. A new wellness center and basketball arena are scheduled to open in 2002–03.

Study Abroad Study Abroad Programs offers a great variety of study-abroad and exchange opportunities for students who wish to study in another country. Overseas study programs are available for both undergraduate and graduate students. The Honors College in particular has special exchange relationships with the Universities of Kent, Hull, and Leeds in England. The length of the study-abroad program may be the academic year, one semester, or a short-term program during the summer. The International Programs Office provides guidance to students considering study abroad and maintains a resource library with information about program offerings and financial aid.

Support Services Disability Services provides assistance to disabled students by operating a transportation service, providing microphones to instructors teaching hearing-impaired students, and serving as a liaison between students and faculty in providing services to accommodate disabled students who meet ADA guidelines.

Job Opportunities The Federal Work-Study Program provides part-time employment for students to meet their educational expenses. To be eligible for employment under this federal program, a student must be enrolled in the University or fully accepted for admission and demonstrate financial need. Students who are enrolled at least half-time work an average of 15 to 20 hours per week. During vacation periods it is sometimes possible to work up to 40 hours per week. Pay rates vary with the job assignment. The Student Employment Office is a source of information about part-time job opportunities in the city of Columbia. Many students also locate employment in one of the academic departments of the University.

Tuition: $4124 for state residents, $11,064 for nonresidents, $6210 for nonresidents with scholarships, per year (2001–02)

Room and Board: $4350 minimum

Contact: Dean: Dr. Peter C. Sederberg, Harper College, Columbia, South Carolina 29208; Telephone: 803-777-8102; Fax: 803-777-2214; E-mail: sederberg@schc.sc.edu; Web site: http://schc.sc.edu

University of South Dakota

4 Pu G M Sc Tr

▼ University Honors Program

The University of South Dakota's (USD) Honors Program provides especially motivated, creative, and thoughtful students an enriched undergraduate experience and prepares them well for life after college. The program is grounded in the liberal arts and promotes lifelong learning, responsible citizenship, and cultural appreciation. Honors students benefit from a special curriculum of smaller, more challenging classes that complements work done in their chosen major field(s). Honors students participate in a wide array of special events and opportunities sponsored by the Honors Program. Many of USD's honors graduates have won prestigious national scholarships, and the majority go on to pursue graduate and professional training at some of the best institutions across the United States.

The heart and soul of the University Honors Program is the special honors curriculum. Students complete an integrated honors core curriculum instead of the University's general core curriculum. The honors core does not add any additional credit hours. During their freshman and sophomore years, students take a course based on a cannon of "great books" and then spend two semesters in an interdisciplinary civilization course taught by at least 4 faculty members from different disciplines. As upperclassmen, honors students complete three honors seminars, courses that join 15 honors students with 1 or more USD professors in a setting that permits intensive interaction on special topics. The seminars promote thoughtful discussion and give students expanded opportunities to exhibit their oral and written communication skills as well as to express themselves in creative projects. Professors from the graduate and professional schools at USD (such as medicine, law, and business) regularly offer honors seminars.

As seniors, honors students choose a committee of professors with whom they design and complete an honors project in an area of personal interest. Honors projects range from original compositions of literature to artistic performances to specialized scientific experiments. Nearly all culminate in a written honors thesis. These projects permit students to enjoy a one-on-one mentoring relationship with professors from all segments of the University.

Honors students come from across the region. They have a wide variety of academic majors. The group makes up about 5 percent of the total student body, but they have a much higher representation in leadership positions across campus. Students have the opportunity to choose to live on the honors floor, a high-energy community of committed scholars. The honors community is further enriched by its student-run Honors Association, which offers fun, yet somewhat educational, programs.

The University Honors Program is housed in three magnificently restored rooms in Old Main—the oldest public higher education building in South Dakota, which was restored and rededicated in 1997. A computerized card entry lock gives Honors Students access to the area after hours. Three desktop computers are available exclusively for use by Honors Students. Students often meet here after classes to check e-mail, chat, or complete papers.

The University Honors Program, which has been open to students in all undergraduate majors since 1968, currently enrolls about 270 students. It is administered by a Faculty Director, a full-time Assistant Director, and a secretary.

Participation Requirements: The honors core curriculum includes both honors classes (specially designed courses only for honors students) and honors requirements (regularly scheduled courses open to all students). Required honors courses include English composition, speech, Ideas in History, interdisciplinary civilization, and three seminars, as well as a thesis. Honors requirements include 1 year of a laboratory science, one semester of calculus (or a semester of trigonometry or precalculus and honors logic), 1 year of a foreign language, and a course in the fine arts. Advanced Placement and transfer credits are usually accepted for all honors requirements and for honors English composition.

Admission Process: Students must submit an application form, high school transcript, ACT or SAT I scores, and a resume of high school awards and activities. The honors staff evaluates the students' test scores, high school grades, class rank, choice of high school courses, and honors/awards/activities. Successful applicants usually have test scores and high school grades in the 90th percentile or above. However, the committee also considers evidence of exceptional ability and/or motivation that may not be shown by test scores or grades.

Most students apply for admission as first-year students, but students in the first two or three semesters of college are encouraged to apply as well. For these students, the committee looks for evidence of undergraduate success. Applications are considered on a rolling basis.

Scholarship Availability: USD offers several major merit-based scholarships for talented students, most of whom participate in the Honors Program. National Merit Finalists who specify USD as their first college of choice are automatically eligible for resident tuition, fees, and room and board for four years. USD's prestigious Presidential Alumni Scholarship provides four years of resident tuition and fees. The USD School of Medicine offers up to six early admissions to the School of Medicine to superior South Dakota applicants who enter the Honors Program, and the Law School has a similar program for up to 5 South Dakota applicants.

The Campus Context: "The University of South Dakota is the comprehensive university within the South Dakota System of Higher Education. The University's mission is to provide graduate and undergraduate programs in the liberal arts and sciences and in professional education. . ." (Mission Statement). It includes the College of Arts and Sciences, College of Fine Arts, Graduate School, and Schools of Business, Education, Law, and Medicine. The University, which began classes in 1882, is located in Vermillion, a community of about 10,000 located on the bluffs of the Missouri River in southeastern South Dakota. It is 60 miles from Sioux Falls, South Dakota; 40 miles from Sioux City, Iowa; 125 miles from Omaha, Nebraska; and 30 miles from Lewis and Clark Lake.

Student Body Total enrollment is 8,161, of whom 5,325 are undergraduates. Of the undergraduates, 59 percent are women and 41 percent are men. Twenty-one percent of undergraduates are from thirty-eight states outside of South Dakota. International students represent forty-two countries. About 20 percent of undergraduates are age 25 or older. USD has nine fraternities and four sororities.

Faculty USD has 430 faculty members. Of the 380 full-time faculty members, 84 percent have terminal degrees.

Key Facilities USD's on-campus library holdings include nearly 1.5 million books, bound periodicals, and government documents. All students can use the Law School and Medical School libraries, as well as the main library. The online catalog, which is accessible through the Internet, includes holdings of all USD libraries and of other colleges' libraries.

About 1,500 computers or terminals are available for general student use in many locations on campus, including dormitories. Students with their own computers can access the campus network (and through it, the Internet) from dormitory rooms and off-campus locations.

All first-year undergraduates and law and medical students at the University of South Dakota were the first in the nation to receive Palm™ handheld computers in fall 2001.

Honorary Societies Phi Beta Kappa, Omicron Delta Kappa, Golden Key, and Mortar Board (among others)

Athletics USD is a member of the North Central Conference, one of the top leagues in NCAA Division II. It sponsors men's baseball, basketball, cross-country, football, swimming, tennis, and track and women's basketball, cross-country, soccer, softball, swimming, tennis, track, and volleyball. Students also participate in these sports and many others as intramural or club activities. All students can use the 145,000-square-foot DakotaDome, with its indoor football field, swimming pool, track, and basketball, racquetball, volleyball, and tennis courts.

Study Abroad The International Studies Program provides opportunities to earn credit at one of seven international campuses. USD departments also sponsor international study tours and internships.

Support Services USD is committed to providing assistance and accommodation to qualified students with specific disabilities or needs. Students seeking to register or to obtain accommodations should contact the Office of Disability Services.

Job Opportunities Many opportunities are available for work-study, other hourly employment (on and off campus), internships, undergraduate research stipends, and other types of employment. Several honors students assist professors who are conducting research.

Tuition: $1997 per year, $62.40 per credit hour for residents; $6352 per year, $198.50 per credit hour for nonresidents (2001–02)

Room and Board: $3151

Mandatory Fees: $1889

Contact: Director: Dr. Karen Olmstead, Old Main 120, 414 East Clark Street, Vermillion, South Dakota 57069; Telephone: 605-677-5223; Fax: 605-677-3137; E-mail: honors@usd.edu; Web site: http://www.usd.edu/honors

UNIVERSITY OF SOUTH FLORIDA

4 Pu G D L Sc Tr AA FA

▼ University Honors

Honors at the University of South Florida (USF) is designed for the academically superior student who wishes to go the extra mile, who embraces challenge, who wants to enhance the University experience, and who is intrigued by alternative approaches to learning. USF offers a four-year honors track for incoming freshmen and a two-year track for qualified transfer and upper-level students. Honors is for motivated students regardless of major. Honors students develop a strong sense of community.

Honors seeks to attract students of superior academic ability and provide them with intellectual challenges and enrichment. The program assists students in developing and refining critical skills in thinking, reasoning, analysis, and writing. These skills prove invaluable as students pursue graduate or professional

Interpreting the symbols: **2**=two-year college, **4**=four-year college; **Pu**=public or state college, **Pr**=private college; **G**=general honors program; **D**=departmental honors program; **S**=small program (fewer than 100 students), **M**=midsize program (100 to 500 students), **L**=large program (more than 500 students); **Sc**=scholarships available in honors program; **Tr**=transfer students accepted into honors program; **HBC**=historically black college; **AA**=academic advisors; **GA**=graduate advisors; **FA**=fellowship advisors.

school and career choices and challenges. Honors' goals are achieved by providing opportunities for students and faculty members to interact closely in a series of liberal arts–oriented, mainly team-taught, interdisciplinary classes of limited size. Subsequently, students work independently on a senior thesis/project under the close supervision of faculty mentors. Many students also participate in undergraduate research.

Honors students are afforded special services within a highly individualized and nurturing environment. This environment fosters a sense of belonging and provides both an academic and social home throughout the USF years. USF Honors is an exciting experience that combines the advantage of a small, highly personalized college with the resources of a major research university. It is a place where students can reach out, learn, and grow. Students in the program receive special recognition at the University's graduation ceremony, and their honors status is noted on the transcript and the diploma.

The program began in 1983 and currently enrolls 1,300 students.

Participation Requirements: The Four-Year Track (28 credits that substitute for the University's liberal arts requirements) encompasses a student's entire college career; the Two-Year Track (13 credits that substitute for an equal number of liberal arts requirements) is for the junior and senior years. Small, intimate classes encourage interaction among students and faculty members.

Admission Process: Students in the Four-Year Track typically have weighted high school GPAs of 3.75 and SAT I scores of 1300 or ACT scores of 29. Two-Year Track students typically have 3.5 transfer GPAs and SAT I scores or ACT scores similar to Four-Year Track students. Students with these credentials are invited to participate in Honors. Students earning the International Baccalaureate (I.B.) diploma or graduating in the top 5 percent of their classes are also invited.

Scholarship Availability: Every student who is enrolled in an Honors course and maintains the required Honors GPA is awarded a scholarship each semester. Scholarships range from $500 to $2000 per year. Non-Florida residents receive scholarships in the form of out-of-state tuition waivers that average about $3000 per year. Students must apply by December 31 to be eligible for other USF scholarships.

The Campus Context: University of South Florida is composed of six undergraduate colleges: Arts and Sciences, Business, Education, Engineering, Nursing, and Visual and Performing Arts. There are three professional schools: Architecture, Medicine, and Public Health. All colleges are located on the Tampa campus, with some degree programs offered at the regional campuses in St. Petersburg, Lakeland, and Sarasota. The University offers more than 200 undergraduate and graduate degree programs (including master's, specialty, doctoral, and M.D. degrees).

The College of Visual and Performing Arts is home to the internationally known Graphicstudio, the only university art program in the country to have its collections archived at the National Gallery of Art in Washington, D.C. The College of Public Health is the only one in the state of Florida. The College of Education, which has a new facility that opened in fall 1997, is the largest urban college of education in the country, with 173 faculty members and more than 23,000 alumni. The College of Engineering, which developed the country's first carport for electric vehicles, hosts the annual Engineering Expo, the largest and oldest exhibition in the country (6,000 participants last year). USF presented about 35,000 student credit hours via distance learning technology last year and supports more than 125 remote distance learning affiliate sites.

Notable facilities include the Sun Dome, an 11,000-seat multipurpose facility; Martin Luther King Plaza, an area at the center of campus dedicated to Martin Luther King that provides students and faculty members with space to gather at events, study, and enjoy the Florida sunshine; and the Phyllis P. Marshall Center, home to many student services. There are more than 300 registered student organizations, including eighteen national fraternities and twelve national sororities.

Student Body The student population is 59 percent women and 41 percent men. The ethnic distribution is 73 percent Caucasian, 10 percent African American, 9 percent Hispanic, 5 percent Asian/Pacific Islander, and .3 percent American Indian. There are 1,493 international students. Fifteen percent of the students reside on campus.

Faculty There are more than 2,300 total faculty members, of whom 2,179 are full-time, 85.4 percent with terminal degrees. Among the faculty members are 73 Fulbright Scholars and 42 endowed chairs. The student-faculty ratio is 22:1. Eighty-four percent of the classes have fewer than 40 students; 2 percent have more than 100 students. Approximately 3,095 classes are offered each semester.

Key Facilities The library houses 1.9 million volumes, 9,950 periodical subscriptions, 4 million microforms, and 154,275 audiovisuals. Students have 34,000 seat hours per week of open computing facilities. Fourteen individual facilities include IBM and Macintosh computers in addition to printing capabilities. Residence halls are wired for direct access to the mainframe, and all students have e-mail addresses, Internet access, and help-desk support upon request.

Honorary Societies Phi Kappa Phi, Golden Key, and Mortar Board, in addition to twenty-six major-specific honor societies

Athletics USF sponsors eighteen intercollegiate sports that compete at the NCAA Division I level, and the Bulls are a charter member of Conference USA. Men and women athletes participate in baseball, basketball, cross-country/track, golf, soccer, softball, tennis, and volleyball. Fall 1997 was the first season of Bulls football. Students can also choose to participate in a wide range of intramural and club sports. All recreational facilities, including six football and soccer fields, twenty-two tennis courts, eight basketball and volleyball courts, a 1.4-mile fitness trail, four pools, twelve racquetball courts, and 6,500 square feet of free weight and cardiovascular equipment, are free to students with their student ID. In addition, USF has a Riverfront Park for canoe rental and picnics and offers many exciting outdoor adventure trips throughout the year.

Study Abroad USF offers the world as a classroom. Most study-abroad programs run four to eight weeks, usually during the summer. Shorter tours are also available. Programs include visits to England, Spain, France, Normandy, Germany, Greece, Italy, Mexico, Russia, Trinidad, and more. There is also an International Exchange Program, which allows students to go on exchange for a term or year to schools in any of a dozen countries at a cost comparable to those of USF.

Support Services Student Disability Services provides resources to students with documented disabilities. In 2000, 720 students received assistance. Some exceptions can be made for students who do not meet the University's admission requirements.

Job Opportunities Students have the ability to work on campus through the Federal Work-Study Program or for an hourly rate in many different departments. Job listings of on- and off-campus employers are posted in the Career Center.

Tuition: $2520 for state residents, $10,410 for nonresidents, per year, based on 15 credit hours per semester (2002–03)

Room and Board: $6110, per year

Contact: Director: Dr. Stuart Silverman, 4202 East Fowler Avenue-FAO 274, Tampa, Florida 33620; Telephone: 813-974-3087; Fax: 813-974-5801; E-mail: silverman@honors.usf.edu

UNIVERSITY OF SOUTHERN CALIFORNIA

4 Pr G S Sc

▼ Baccalaureate/M.D. Program

Students who want to attend the University of Southern California (USC) next year as a college freshman and plan to attend medical school after graduation may apply to enter the Baccalaureate/M.D. Program. Students who earn admission to both the University and the program for the fall of their freshman year also have a space in the entering first-year class at the USC Keck School of Medicine upon completing their undergraduate degree. USC offers the Baccalaureate/M.D. program to students who want to incorporate a broad understanding of human experience alongside their professional expertise. The program does not offer accelerated study to provide a shortcut for students to become younger doctors. Rather, the year program prepares students to be better doctors. The guaranteed space in medical school allows students freedom to explore many academic subjects and student activities. During their first four years, Baccalaureate/M.D. students engage the widest possible range of ideas, faculties, and the community available at one of the nation's largest private research universities. Many of USC's students volunteer, engage in cutting-edge research, and study abroad. The Keck School of Medicine, where Baccalaureate/M.D. students spend their final four years, has meant better health for people around the globe in all fields of medical care. Through fourteen affiliated hospitals in southern California, USC physicians serve more than 1 million patients each year. USC's Health Sciences campus, located 3 miles northeast of downtown Los Angeles, is a major center for basic and clinical biomedical research, especially in the fields of cancer, gene therapy, the neurosciences, and transplantation biology.

Participation Requirements: Once enrolled at USC, Baccalaureate/M.D. students are required to complete the sequence of undergraduate courses considered prerequisites for the nation's best medical schools, including two semesters each of calculus, physics, chemistry, organic chemistry, and biological sciences, and one semester each of microbiology and biochemistry. To retain eligibility for admission to the Keck School of Medicine, students must maintain a 3.3 GPA overall and in their science prerequisite courses. Students must take the MCAT exam and score above average on all sections.

Admission Process: USC selects Baccalaureate/M.D. students through a competitive process. Excellent grades and test scores are important but do not guarantee admission. USC also looks for extraordinary credentials of community involvement, preparation for medicine, and enthusiastic recommendation. From the annual group of 500 or more applicants, USC invites only 100 for an interview. While this number seems a bit daunting, applicants should know that USC accepts into the program not only highly qualified students, but students that represent the diversities of a growing and changing world culture. Final enrollment for the program each year is 25–30 students.

The Campus Context: USC, founded in 1880, is the oldest and largest private research university in the American West and a member of the Association of American Universities—the sixty elite research universities in the United States and Canada. USC ranks as one of the top ten private research universities in the United States, based upon federal research and development support. The University offers bachelor's degrees in seventy-six undergraduate majors as well as master's, doctoral, and professional degrees in 122 fields of study. Approximately 28,000 students attend classes on the University Park campus near downtown Los Angeles or on the Health Sciences campus. More than half of the student body are undergraduates.

Student Body USC recruits nationally and internationally for a selective student body. The University received more than 26,000 freshman applications for the most recent entering class of more than 2,750 freshmen. The class of 2006 boasts average SATs of 1319 and GPAs of more than 3.9. USC consistently ranks in the top three universities in America that enroll international students. Nearly half of the students in the current freshman class are persons of color.

Faculty USC's faculty includes Nobel Prize laureate George A. Olah, Jefferson Lecturer Stephen Toulmin, and 36 National Academy members. More than 200 faculty members have received prestigious academic and professional awards, spanning such institutions as the National Institutes of Health, the National Science Foundation, the Alfred P. Sloan Foundation, the National Endowment for the Humanities, the John Simon Guggenheim Foundation, and the Academy of Motion Pictures Arts and Sciences. The ratio of faculty members to students is 1:14 and the average class size is 26.

Key Facilities USC's information technology environment is rich in resources and opportunities for students. The Information Services Division (ISD) is responsible for serving the University community's information technology needs in networking, library services, academic computing, and telecommunications. USC's libraries are a complex matrix of resources, experts (both human and artificial), and digital tools dedicated to goals of scholarship. At the heart of the matrix is ISD's central research facility, the Doheny Memorial Library. Also, the internationally acclaimed Leavey Library is a magnet for undergraduate teaching, research, and technology-enhanced study. Together, USC's library facilities house 3.4 million books, 5.6 million microforms, 3.1 million photographs, 22,000 journals, and a half million government documents. In addition, with numerous Public Computing Centers across campus, ISD provide the latest technology to ensure that the USC community can take full advantage of the World Wide Web and other Internet resources they need.

Athletics USC has a distinguished record of intercollegiate athletic competition in twenty sports.

Study Abroad The USC Office of Overseas Studies, a part of the College of Letters, Arts, and Sciences, offers thirty-eight study-abroad programs in more than twenty different countries and participation is open to all USC undergraduate students.

Support Services Disability Services and Programs (DSP) provides support services to enable students with disabilities to develop their academic potential while having the dignity of working toward an independent lifestyle. Numerous services are available for students with physical, psychological, and learning disabilities.

Job Opportunities The Career Planning and Placement Center provides exceptional career services to all members of the University family. USC's array of programs includes career counseling, workshops, internships, job listings, Career Days, and USC Resume Day. The newly developed Trojan Network provides additional opportunities to network with alumni in all career fields. The Career Planning and Placement Center is located on two levels in the Gwynn Wilson Student Union.

Tuition: Full tuition for 2001–02: $25,060 (12–18 undergraduate units) or $844 per unit

Room and Board: Annual cost estimate: $8000

Mandatory fees: $236.50 (includes health fee). In addition, all new students (except domestic graduate students) pay an orientation fee of $130.

Interpreting the symbols: **2**=two-year college, **4**=four-year college; **Pu**=public or state college, **Pr**=private college; **G**=general honors program; **D**=departmental honors program; **S**=small program (fewer than 100 students), **M**=midsize program (100 to 500 students), **L**=large program (more than 500 students); **Sc**=scholarships available in honors program; **Tr**=transfer students accepted into honors program; **HBC**=historically black college; **AA**=academic advisors; **GA**=graduate advisors; **FA**=fellowship advisors.

Contact: Jonathan Burdick, Associate Dean, College Admission Office, CAS 100, University of Southern California, University Park, Los Angeles, California 90089-0152; Telephone: 213-740-5930; Fax: 213-740-1338; Web site: http://college.usc.edu/bamd/

UNIVERSITY OF SOUTHERN CALIFORNIA

4 Pr G M Sc

▼ Thematic Option Honors Program

The Thematic Option Program at the University of Southern California (USC) is for serious students who recognize the value of a liberal arts education and are willing to work for it. Thematic Option courses eliminate the barriers that separate disciplines, teaching students to appreciate the relationships between literature, history, philosophy, and science. An interdisciplinary core curriculum, intensive writing seminars, individual advisement, and extensive interaction with faculty members are at the heart of the Thematic Option experience. Professors selected for their commitment to students, scholarship, and teaching foster lively discussions in small classes. Students who enroll in the Thematic Option curriculum explore the diversity of the liberal arts while satisfying the University's general education requirements. The Thematic Option curriculum consists of four core classes taught around distinct themes. In the core classes students ask the big questions: What is human nature? What is justice? How can we know these things? The first two core courses center on broad ethical issues and approaches to historical change. The second two focus on epistemology, representation, and social construction. Linked writing seminars with one-on-one writing tutorials allow students to improve their writing skills through close personal attention. Students round out their general education requirements with two additional courses chosen from a wide array of University offerings—one in either the humanities or the social sciences and the other in the natural sciences.

Thematic Option reaches beyond the classroom, making extracurricular activities an important part of the overall learning experience. These activities, which include films, dinners, and seminars, become the context for an enjoyable and stimulating intellectual community. Each year, Thematic Option hosts a two-day Undergraduate Research Conference in which students present their own academic work in a public forum on panels chaired by USC faculty members. Past conference topics include postmodernism, the millennium, the idea of high/low in contemporary culture, and anarchy. The program also sponsors films, dinners, seminars, and excursions in and around Los Angeles. Students can also unite their academic and residential lives by choosing to live in one of the residential colleges, including the deans' halls, where honors students and faculty-in-residence share a supportive and stimulating environment.

Participation Requirements: The program requires completion of the four core classes, two semesters of writing instruction and two supplemental courses. For most students, a foreign language is also required. Students working toward a B.A. degree usually take two core classes and a writing seminar each semester of the freshman year. Students working toward a B.S. degree in the College of Letters, Arts, and Sciences; the School of Engineering; or the Marshall School of Business usually take one core class and a writing seminar each semester of the first two years. Students working toward bachelor's degrees in architecture, filmic writing, performing arts, public administration, and other selected programs follow course schedules compatible with their major requirements. Thematic Option requirements are typically completed by the end of a student's second year. Upon graduation, students who satisfy all curricular requirements for the program receive a certificate of completion.

Admission Process: Students with a grade average of at least an A- and an SAT score of 1400, with greater weight accorded to the verbal score, are invited to participate in Thematic Option. Those who do not receive an invitation may apply directly to the program after admission to USC is granted. Because the program fills quickly, students interested in securing a place are urged to apply as soon as possible. Students from all majors at the University can participate.

Scholarship Availability: Thematic Option students compete well for all merit scholarships including Trustee (full-tuition), Presidential (half-tuition), and Deans (quarter-tuition). Students who wish to be considered for Trustee and Presidential Scholarships must apply to USC before the scholarship consideration deadline in early December of each year.

The Campus Context: USC, founded in 1880, is the oldest and largest private research university in the American West and a member of the Association of American Universities—the sixty elite research universities in the United States and Canada. USC ranks as one of the top ten private research universities in the United States, based upon federal research and development support. The University offers bachelor's degrees in seventy-six undergraduate majors as well as master's, doctoral, and professional degrees in 122 fields of study. Approximately 28,000 students attend classes on the University Park campus near downtown Los Angeles or on the Health Sciences campus 3 miles northeast of downtown Los Angeles. More than half of the student body are undergraduates.

Student Body USC recruits nationally and internationally for a selective student body. The University received more than 26,000 freshman applications for the most recent entering class of more than 2,750 freshmen. The class of 2006 boasts average SATs of 1319 and GPAs of more than 3.9. USC consistently ranks in the top three universities in America that enroll international students. Nearly half of the students in the current freshman class are persons of color.

Faculty USC's faculty includes Nobel Prize laureate George A. Olah, Jefferson Lecturer Stephen Toulmin, and 36 National Academy members. More than 200 faculty members have received prestigious academic and professional awards, spanning such institutions as the National Institutes of Health, the National Science Foundation, the Alfred P. Sloan Foundation, the National Endowment for the Humanities, the John Simon Guggenheim Foundation, and the Academy of Motion Pictures Arts and Sciences. The ratio of faculty members to students is 1:14 and the average class size is 26.

Key Facilities USC's information technology environment is rich in resources and opportunities for students. The Information Services Division (ISD) is responsible for serving the University community's information technology needs in networking, library services, academic computing, and telecommunications. USC's libraries are a complex matrix of resources, experts (both human and artificial), and digital tools dedicated to goals of scholarship. At the heart of the matrix is ISD's central research facility, the Doheny Memorial Library. Also, the internationally acclaimed Leavey Library is a magnet for undergraduate teaching, research, and technology-enhanced study. Together, USC's library facilities house 3.4 million books, 5.6 million microforms, 3.1 million photographs, 22,000 journals, and a half million government documents. In addition, with numerous Public Computing Centers across campus, ISD provide the latest technology to ensure that the USC community can take full advantage of the World Wide Web and other Internet resources they need.

Athletics USC has a distinguished record of intercollegiate athletic competition in twenty sports.

Study Abroad The USC Office of Overseas Studies, a part of the College of Letters, Arts, and Sciences, offers thirty-eight study-abroad programs in more than twenty different countries and participation is open to all USC undergraduate students.

Support Services Disability Services and Programs (DSP) provides support services to enable students with disabilities to develop their academic potential while having the dignity of working toward an independent lifestyle. Numerous services are available for students with physical, psychological, and learning disabilities.

Job Opportunities The Career Planning and Placement Center provides exceptional career services to all members of the University family. USC's array of programs includes career counseling, workshops, internships, job listings, Career Days, and USC Resume Day. The newly developed Trojan Network provides additional opportunities to network with alumni in all career fields. The Career Planning and Placement Center is located on two levels in the Gwynn Wilson Student Union.

Tuition: Full tuition for 2001–02: $25,060 (12–18 undergraduate units) or $844 per unit

Room and Board: Annual cost estimate: $8000

Mandatory fees: $236.50 (includes health fee). In addition, all new students (except domestic graduate students) pay an orientation fee of $130.

Contact: Robin Romans, Ph.D., Director, Thematic Option Honors Program, CAS 200, University of Southern California, University Park, Los Angeles, California 90089-0153; Telephone: 213-740-2961, 800-USC-2961 (toll-free); Fax: 213-740-4839; Web site: http://www.usc.edu/thematicoption

UNIVERSITY OF SOUTHERN INDIANA

4 Pu G/D M Tr

▼ University Honors Program

The Honors Program at the University of Southern Indiana (USI) is designed to offer expanded opportunities for those students who show promise of outstanding academic achievement. Participation in the program exposes students to a wider range of intellectual and academic experience, provides enriching extracurricular activities, promotes rewarding interaction between students and honors faculty members, and gives students the opportunity to form lasting friendships with other students who are committed to academic excellence. The Honors Program curriculum serves to supplement and enrich the students' overall experience within any of the University's major fields of study. Honors classes are generally smaller in size, providing increased class participation and discussion. Students in the program grow through special classes that stress the interrelatedness of knowledge, skill in oral and written communication of ideas, and methods and techniques for the analysis, synthesis, and evaluation of information. In addition to priority registration, honors students have the opportunity to live in honors housing and make use of an honors common room, which is used for study, informal meetings, classes, and programs the students themselves plan. Participation in honors housing, especially during the freshman year, also facilitates the very helpful mentoring program sponsored by the Student Honors Council. The designation of University Honors Scholar is awarded to those students who successfully complete the honors curriculum, a distinction that is noted on both the diploma and the official transcript.

Some departments offer students the further opportunity to combine Program Honors with Departmental Honors. The course requirements for Departmental Honors are specific to each major that offers this option. Students may choose to complete both Program and Departmental Honors by arrangement with the Director of Honors, the department chairperson, and the individual professor. These students receive a diploma that documents their accomplishment as a University Honors Scholar and designates their graduation with Distinction in the Major.

Participation Requirements: Typically, honors students enroll in specially designated sections of courses taken either from the University Core Curriculum or from the student's major. Students generally take one or two honors courses in a given semester as part of their normal progress toward the baccalaureate degree. To receive an honors diploma, students must complete their undergraduate work with a cumulative GPA of 3.25 or above and complete a minimum of 21 hours of honors credit with grades of A or B—including a 1-hour freshman colloquium and an honors component to their 3-hour senior synthesis course.

Admission Process: Students who have earned an SAT score of 1200 or an ACT composite of 27 or higher are immediately accepted into the Honors Program. Other interested students are encouraged to apply. Evaluations of these students are made on the basis of cumulative GPA, class rank, academic background, and extracurricular activities. Students who have completed a minimum of 15 semester hours at USI or elsewhere with a minimum cumulative GPA of 3.25 may apply as space permits.

Scholarship Availability: USI has numerous merit scholarships at the departmental, college, and University level. As an ongoing service, honors students are provided with assistance in identifying and applying for these scholarships and awards. Most honors students are recipients of scholarships.

Contact: Dr. Phyllis Toy, Director of Honors, University of Southern Indiana, 8600 University Boulevard, Evansville, Indiana 47712; Fax: 812-464-1960; E-mail: ptoy@usi.edu

UNIVERSITY OF SOUTHERN MAINE

4 Pu G S Sc Tr

▼ University Honors Program

Honors at USM is a community-style program in which all students take the same series of courses. These begin with four 4-credit colloquia, taken one per semester, and include Wisdom Stories From Four Worlds, which investigates justice and the relationship of the individual to social institutions in ancient Greece, Rome, the Judaic world, and early Christianity; Truth(s), Lie(s), and Legacy(ies) in a Medieval Mindscape, which focuses on the relationship of religion and political power and the development of the mystical tradition in Christianity and Islam into the later Catholic Church and the Islamic Empire; Scientific Revolutions and Critiques, which traces the structure of science from Aristotle to the modern environmental movement, with particular emphasis on the relationships between science, religion, and magic in Renaissance and Reformation times; and Progress, Process, or Permanence, which deals with alienation and uncertainty, particularly as exemplified in nineteenth- and twentieth-century literature and philosophy. All of the colloquia emphasize readings from original materials, extensive writing, and a discussion format. Classes are limited to 15 students.

Honors faculty members are from departments in various colleges and schools at USM. They are chosen for their excellent teaching records and their desire to teach in an interdisciplinary environment.

The University of Southern Maine enrolls many nontraditional students, and this diversity is reflected in those taking honors courses. An honors class usually includes traditional students

Interpreting the symbols: **2**=two-year college, **4**=four-year college; **Pu**=public or state college, **Pr**=private college; **G**=general honors program; **D**=departmental honors program; **S**=small program (fewer than 100 students), **M**=midsize program (100 to 500 students), **L**=large program (more than 500 students); **Sc**=scholarships available in honors program; **Tr**=transfer students accepted into honors program; **HBC**=historically black college; **AA**=academic advisors; **GA**=graduate advisors; **FA**=fellowship advisors.

just out of high school, part-time students who also work, and older students who are returning to school. Students with many different majors are found in the program.

All honors courses are taught at the Honors House, a converted residential building adjacent to the Portland campus. The building contains offices, seminar rooms, a kitchen, and a student lounge. It is also the editorial headquarters for *The Maine Scholar*, a refereed journal supported by all the Honors Programs in the University of Maine System. The *Scholar* accepts works from students, faculty, and independent writers that are directed toward its yearly theme. Recent thematic issues include the environment, childhood, and diaspora.

There is an active Honors Student Association that sponsors social and cultural events on campus and coordinates volunteer work by members of the program. Student representatives are voting members of the Honors Faculty Board, which governs program operations.

The program was developed in the early 1980s with the help of funding from the National Endowment for the Humanities and accepted its first students in 1986. About 35 students each year are now accepted. The total enrollment is fewer than 100, or approximately 1 percent of the USM undergraduate student body.

Participation Requirements: Besides the four 4-credit colloquia, honors students take an optional 3-credit thinking and writing course plus one required 3-credit honors seminar, with at least two topic choices. Seminars are offered each semester on a different topic. Under the direction of a faculty committee, all students also do a senior thesis project to complete their honors work, beginning with a thesis workshop. Elective honors courses are available in writing and in directed research or reading. Completion of the colloquium sequence and writing course excuses the student from 18 credits of USM core courses; completion of the sequence plus the seminar and thesis allows students to graduate with University Honors.

Admission Process: Students must apply by April 1 to start the program the following fall. There is no GPA requirement for applicants. The application portfolio includes a completed application form, two recommendations, a personal essay, and academic transcripts; the program arranges an interview for the applicant with one of the honors faculty members when the written application materials are complete. Open houses for applicants and their families are held two or three times during the spring, when they can talk to current honors faculty members and students. Applications are accepted from individuals entering the University for the first time or from those who have attended previously. Completion of program requirements normally requires three years, although it is possible to complete them in two.

Scholarship Availability: Honors currently awards five scholarships per year, in amounts from $1000 to $2000, to students in the program. Students must have completed at least one honors course before they can apply. Both academic performance and financial need are considered in scholarship awards. Small grants are also available to assist with thesis expenses. Honors students are usually very successful at competing for University-wide scholarships as well.

The Campus Context: The University of Southern Maine is the second-largest of the seven universities in the Maine public university system. USM has two principal campuses: a city location in downtown Portland and a traditional New England campus in the small town of Gorham, 10 miles inland. Many classes are taught at both campuses, which are connected by free shuttle buses. The school offers approximately forty undergraduate majors and seventeen graduate programs in the College of Arts and Sciences and the Schools of Business, Applied Science, Nursing, Education and Human Development, and Law. Self-designed undergraduate majors are available, and a number of honors students have pursued these.

Student Body USM enrolls about 9,500 students, about 7,800 of whom are in undergraduate degree programs. Approximately 2,000 students are dorm residents. The undergraduate population is 41 percent men and 59 percent women; 2.6 percent are members of minority groups, and 6 percent are international students. Ninety-four percent of students are Maine residents, and 65 percent receive financial aid, the average award totaling about $4300. Thirty-two states and fifteen other countries are represented.

Faculty The University currently has 321 full-time faculty members, supplemented with adjuncts.

Key Facilities The USM library has about 400,000 volumes, with another 200,000 in the law library. There are more than 1 million microform units as well. All Maine system universities participate in an interlibrary loan program. Computer labs, with both IBM and Mac computers and Internet access, are available on both campuses. Internet connections and access to the campus local area network are also available in residence halls.

Athletics USM participates in athletics at the NCAA Division III level and offers fourteen intercollegiate athletic programs, including a baseball team that has won the national championship (1991). There are also extensive intramural activities and clubs for off-campus sports such as skiing and sailing.

Study Abroad The University encourages students to spend a semester or more at a foreign university; students can study in Austria, Canada, England, Ireland, Latvia, the Netherlands, or Ukraine. Scholarships and financial aid are available. In addition, USM is a member of the National Student Exchange program, in which degree students can spend up to a year at one of 120 participating universities in the United States while paying only in-state tuition. Five colleges and universities in the Portland region also participate in the Greater Portland Alliance, allowing students to take courses not offered at USM at other schools.

Tuition: $128.50 for state residents, $259 for nonresidents, $192.75 for nonresidents eligible for the New England Regional Student Program, per credit hour (2001–02)

Room and Board: $5298 (minimum), per year

Contact: Director: Janice L. Thompson or Coordinator of Student and Alumni Affairs: Alexandrea Taylor, 96 Falmouth Street, P.O. Box 9300, Portland, Maine 04104-9300; Telephone: 207-780-4330; Fax: 207-780-4333; E-mail: jthomp@usm.maine.edu or alexet@usm.maine.edu; Web site: http://www.usm.maine.edu/~honors

University of Southern Mississippi

4 Pu M Sc Tr

▼ The University Honors College

The University of Southern Mississippi's Honors College is a comprehensive four-year program that aims to identify, encourage, and reward academic excellence in all fields and to serve students who desire a broadly based undergraduate education. The honors curriculum is designed for students who have intellectual curiosity and the ambition and discipline to master a comprehensive liberal education, whatever major field of study they choose. Students may pursue any undergraduate degree program offered by the University while they are members of the Honors College.

Honors students participate in a range of academic experiences, including interdisciplinary, team-taught classes; smaller sections of core classes, including biology, anthropology, economics, English, music appreciation, and psychology; special-topics seminars, such as Computers and Society, The History of Jazz, Life in the Universe: The Emerging Science of Astrobiology, and Civil Rights and the South); and independent research culminating in a senior thesis. There are also many opportunities to socialize and build camaraderie through events such as the annual Awards Banquet in the spring; activities organized by the Honors College Student Ambassadors, a student recruitment group; and the annual fall picnic and spring semiformal dance, sponsored by the Honors Student Association (HSA). The HSA (Web site: http://honors.pitas.com) also organizes student community service initiatives.

Honors College graduates are well prepared for study in graduate and professional schools that lead to exciting and prestigious careers. Recent graduating honors scholars have entered the following schools, among others: Harvard University Medical School, Stanford University, McGill University, and Georgetown University Law School. Graduates who directly entered the professions or who attained professional positions after graduate school accepted the following positions, among others: acquiring editor, Pearson Custom Publishing; developmental chemist, Ethyl Corporation; cartographer, National Geographic Society; business analyst, Amoco; professional saxophonist, The Rascher Quartet; and director, Roots and Shoots Program of the Jane Goodall Institute.

The Honors College at USM was founded as an honors program in 1965; it was organized as a separate college in 1976, making it one of the oldest honors colleges in the nation. There are approximately 300 students in the program.

Participation Requirements: The program is divided into two parts: General Honors (freshman and sophomore years) and Senior Honors (junior and senior years). The cornerstone of the General Honors program is a four-semester humanities survey entitled World Thought and Culture, better known as Colloquium, which substitutes for the general core requirements in history, literature, and philosophy. These classes are taught by a team of humanities professors who provide an overview of human endeavor from the beginnings of civilization through the twentieth century. The other component of the General Honors curriculum is the departmental honors sections of required general education courses. The honors courses are usually smaller than non-honors courses and therefore allow for more reading, writing, and classroom participation than typically might be required in a lower-division course.

In Senior Honors, students continue with honors course work, but they emphasize independent study and scholarship leading to an honors thesis in their major. During the junior year, students enroll in two honors seminars taught by professors from a wide variety of disciplines; at least seven different seminars are presented each year, including one or more service learning courses. Prospectus Writing, a course taken during the junior year, helps students plan and prepare the bibliography for the senior thesis. During the senior year, honors students undertake the senior thesis, a substantial undergraduate study carried out under the direction of a research adviser from the department of the student's major. Students also must pass a special comprehensive examination in the major, taken in their final semester, and participate in the Senior Symposium, in which students give a public presentation of their thesis.

Students in the Honors College are required to complete 26 hours of honors course work in General Honors as well as maintain a 3.0 GPA in all course work; a GPA of 3.25 is required to continue into Senior Honors. Students in Senior Honors are required to complete an additional 10–12 hours of course work, including the senior thesis.

Students completing Senior Honors receive on their diplomas a Latin designation for graduation with honors and wear the distinctive honors medallion with the academic robe at commencement.

Honors students receive enriched advisement through the Honors College, consisting of scheduled advisement periods each semester along with informal sessions throughout the year. Incoming freshman enjoy priority registration and orientation at an April Honors Preview program.

The Coordinator of General Honors serves as adviser to freshmen and sophomores, while the Coordinator of Senior Honors does the same for juniors and seniors. This is in addition to the advisement students receive through the department of their major. The staff of the Honors College also assists qualified students with graduate school applications and with applications for prestigious national fellowships. In recent years, the Honors College has been proud to claim 9 Barry M. Goldwater scholars, a Mellon fellow, a Truman scholar, 3 Rotary scholars, a Howard Hughes premedical fellow, 3 Phi Kappa Phi national fellows, and 2 finalists in the Rhodes Scholarship competition.

Honors housing is provided in two recently renovated, centrally located residence halls on campus. Residence in honors housing is not required, but many students (especially freshmen) take advantage of this unique opportunity to live and learn with other honors scholars.

Each year, the Honors College sponsors the University Forum lecture series, in which honors students enroll for academic credit. Recent speakers include Supreme Court Justice Antonin Scalia, feminist Gloria Steinem, biologist Edward O. Wilson, and novelist Kurt Vonnegut. Freshmen in the Honors College host receptions after each forum lecture, and honors students are able to talk one-on-one with internationally known speakers at these informal sessions.

Admission Process: Students are admitted as freshmen into the Honors College based on an excellent record of achievement on the ACT/SAT and in high school classes, with attention to honors, AP, and other rigorous courses completed; recommendations from high school teachers and counselors; extracurricular activities, including work experience and community service; and honors, awards, elected offices, and other achievements. The Honors College also accepts transfer students and rising juniors into the Senior Honors program provided that they have a 3.5 GPA on 40 or more hours of course work. Application deadlines are February 1 for students applying for the Presidential Scholarship and March 15 for all other applicants.

Scholarship Availability: The University offers ten or more Presidential Scholarships each year to entering honors freshmen on a competitive basis; these scholarships are worth $29,000 to $47,000 and cover the costs of tuition, room, board, and fees. Other scholarships offered exclusively to Honors College students are the $3000 George R. Olliphant Scholarships and the $1200 Honors College Scholarships, the latter awarded to all students. The Honors College also encourages participation in USM's study-abroad program and offers some scholarship support for students studying abroad.

The Campus Context: The University of Southern Mississippi was founded in 1910 as a state-supported normal (teaching) college and became a comprehensive university in 1962. The University is classified as a Carnegie Doctoral II Institution. The main campus is located in Hattiesburg, the "Hub City" of south Mississippi, with an area population of 100,000. Hattiesburg combines the safety and friendliness of a small town with the diversity and excitement of a larger city and has been designated America's Most Livable Small City by the U.S. Conference of Mayors. The city is located 90 miles south of Jackson, the state capital; 75 miles north of the Gulf Coast; and 100 miles northeast of New Orleans, Louisiana.

The 1,090-acre campus and its 155 buildings provide a convenient and comfortable setting for each student's academic experience.

Interpreting the symbols: **2**=two-year college, **4**=four-year college; **Pu**=public or state college, **Pr**=private college; **G**=general honors program; **D**=departmental honors program; **S**=small program (fewer than 100 students), **M**=midsize program (100 to 500 students), **L**=large program (more than 500 students); **Sc**=scholarships available in honors program; **Tr**=transfer students accepted into honors program; **HBC**=historically black college; **AA**=academic advisors; **GA**=graduate advisors; **FA**=fellowship advisors.

USM's teaching and research facilities stand among beautiful oaks near a magnificent rose garden. The columned buildings of the University's original campus blend comfortably with modern structures such as the state-of-the art, $20-million Polymer Science Research Facility. A 133,000-square-foot student recreation complex, the Payne Center, opened in 1995. Two new buildings, the $11-million Liberal Arts Building and the $14-million Theater and Dance Building, have just been completed and opened. The Honors College will move its offices to the new International Center, scheduled for completion in 2004.

There are ten academic colleges and eight schools: the Colleges of the Arts, Business Administration, Education and Psychology, Health and Human Sciences, Liberal Arts, Nursing, Science and Technology, Marine Sciences, International and Continuing Education, and the Honors College and the Schools of Music, Professional Accountancy, Home Economics, Human Performance and Recreation, Social Work, Communication, Library Science, and Engineering Technology. In addition, the Gulf Coast campus at Long Beach, including teaching centers in Jackson County and Keesler Air Force Base, is the nontraditional, nonresidential campus serving the Gulf Coast metropolitan area. The University offers ninety bachelor's degrees, sixty-one master's degrees, two specialist's degrees, and nineteen doctoral degrees. Programs that have been designated as Centers for Excellence include Polymer Science, English, Music, Nursing, and Accounting.

Student Body The University of Southern Mississippi has an enrollment of 14,510, with 12,819 on the Hattiesburg campus and 1,691 on the Gulf Coast campus. Undergraduate enrollment is 10,792 (60 percent women, 40 percent men). The ethnic distribution among students on campus is 19 percent African American, 2 percent Asian, 1 percent Hispanic, 1 percent Native American, and 78 percent white. International students from more than sixty countries number over 300. Sixty-nine percent of undergraduate students on the Hattiesburg campus receive financial aid. There are thirteen residence halls housing 3,400 students. There are thirteen national fraternities, nine with houses on campus, and twelve national sororities, nine housed in the Panhellenic Residence Hall. USM also has more than 200 student organizations; the most popular are the University Activities Council, the Student Government Association, and residence hall associations. The *Student Printz* (newspaper), *The Southerner* (yearbook), and WMSU (campus radio station) provide students with the opportunity to receive hands-on training while contributing to the campus culture.

Faculty The University has 612 full-time and 95 part-time faculty members. Approximately 94 percent of the full-time tenure-track faculty members hold a doctoral degree, and most others hold the terminal degree in their academic discipline. The student-faculty ratio is 19:1.

Key Facilities Joseph Anderson Cook Library contains the University's principal collections, with 1.8 million volumes, approximately 5,000 periodical subscriptions, and computerized research services. An addition to Cook Library was completed in 1995, enlarging the library by 150 percent. William David McCain Library and Archives houses the University's special collections of rare books, manuscripts, and archives, including the de Grummond Collection of children's books and illustrations.

The Polymer Science Research Center opened in April 1991. In *U.S. News & World Report*'s exclusive ranking of graduate programs, the Southern Miss doctoral polymer program tied for third in the nation.

The Office of Technology Resources coordinates the campus's state-of-the-art technology capabilities. The University is implementing a comprehensive PeopleSoft information system, which includes SOAR Web registration and grade retrieval system (called Eagle Vision). Students can use computer labs (with free Internet access), which are located throughout campus. There is wireless access throughout campus, including all residence halls. OTR also offers discounted Internet service access. The Cook Library card catalog (ANNA) is online, and the library provides a laptop checkout program.

Athletics The University is a Division I-A member of the National Collegiate Athletic Association (NCAA) and Conference USA; it fields teams in ten intercollegiate sports, including baseball, basketball, football, golf, tennis, and track for men and basketball, cross-country running, golf, tennis, track, soccer, softball, and volleyball for women. Athletic facilities include Roberts Stadium (capacity of 33,000), Reed Green Coliseum, Pete Taylor Baseball Park, and Southern Miss Track Facility/Marshall Bell Track.

Intramural sports include badminton, squash, soccer, rugby, fencing, racquetball, softball, and weight lifting.

Study Abroad USM began its many credit-abroad programs in 1976 with the creation of the British Studies Program. In 1995, the University gained the distinction of ranking fourth in the nation among doctoral institutions for its credit-abroad programs. Since 1976, more than 6,700 students have participated in these programs, which now include more than twenty summer, semester, and yearlong study-abroad programs in Britain, Cuba, Jamaica, Mexico, Austria, Germany, Scotland, Wales, Canada, Ireland, Italy, Belgium, Kenya, France, Spain, Australia, and New Zealand. In fall 2002, Southern Miss is scheduled to inaugurate the Abbey Program, a European center offering a sophomore semester-abroad experience in an eleventh-century chateau and abbey in Pontlevoy, a small town in the Loire Valley of France. Honors students are active participants in the University's study-abroad programs.

Support Services All buildings are physically accessible, and there is adequate parking available on campus. The Office of Support Services for Students with Disabilities exists to help disabled students. Federally funded TRIO Programs (Student Support Services and the McNair Scholars' Programs), as well as other campus academic assistance programs, also serve students.

Job Opportunities Work-study, assistantships, and a variety of student employment opportunities are offered on campus. In 1998, the Cooperative Education Program offered 150 students work experience in conjunction with their degree programs. The Office of Career Planning and Placement runs this co-op program and assists students in their postgraduate job searches.

Tuition: $3416 for state residents, $7934 for nonresidents per year (2001–02)

Room and Board: $3910 per year

Contact: Director: Dr. Maureen Ryan, Dean, Box 5162, Hattiesburg, Mississippi 39406-5162; Telephone: 601-266-4533; Fax: 601-266-4534; E-mail: honors@usm.edu; Web site: http://www.honors.usm.edu

---

THE UNIVERSITY OF TAMPA

4 Pr G M Sc Tr

▼ Honors Program

Academic achievement, global perspective, critical thinking and leadership are the cornerstones of The University of Tampa (UT) Honors Program. Honors Program courses and activities build upon these as they encourage participants to challenge mind-sets and aspire to excellence.

The curriculum of The University of Tampa Honors Program centers around an array of courses that encourage students to question conventional wisdom, pursue excellence, and prepare themselves for graduate studies, successful careers and societal leadership. Each year, the courses and many of the activities relate to a particular theme. In 1999–2000, for instance, the theme will be Ideas on the Cutting Edge. Beginning with a 1-credit Gateways to Honors class, most of the Honors Program courses fulfill general education requirements as well as Honors Program requirements. Every year, they include courses from the humanities and fine arts, the natural sciences, and the social sciences; but all courses are linked to the common theme. Honors classes bring the best students together with the best faculty members in stimulating, small-group settings.

In addition to its array of special theme courses that link different fields of study in a common endeavor, the Honors Program offers many outstanding learning opportunities and practical experiences. Each year, 4 University of Tampa Honors Program students receive one-term scholarships to Oxford University in England, where they study in a one-on-one tutorial atmosphere with Oxford faculty members. Another special aspect of the program is its nonfiction journal, *Respondez*, entirely written and edited by Honors Program students. The UT Honors Program also offers a Washington, D.C., Semester; Undergraduate Research Fellowships to undertake research with faculty members; Model United Nations activities (including participation in the Harvard National Model United Nations); College Bowl competition among teams on campus and against other colleges and universities; and special Honors Enrichment Tutorials, modeled on the Oxford system, within upper-level classes. The Honors Council gives students an active role in shaping the program and provides extracurricular activities that support program goals. Honors residence hall areas, an Honors lounge, and an Honors study are available and help foster a sense of community.

Founded in 1983, The University of Tampa Honors Program is a University-based honors program that welcomes and includes students from all majors. In the past three years, it has more than doubled in size. Its current enrollment is 350 students.

Participation Requirements: Freshmen enrolling in the program must complete a one-term, 1-credit Gateways to Honors course designed to introduce them to The University of Tampa and its Honors Program. To graduate with Honors Program Distinction, they must complete at least five Honors Programs courses and earn a cumulative GPA of at least 3.5. Sophomores entering the program must meet the same requirements, with the exception of the Gateways to Honors course. Juniors entering the program who have had previous honors program experience or have graduated from a recognized community college honors program are required to take three Honors Program courses. Two of these may be Honors Thesis, Honors Independent Study, Oxford Term, Washington Semester, or Honors Enrichment Tutorials.

Graduates with Honors Program Distinction are honored at a special dinner each year, receive an Honors Graduate medallion and ribbon, and are given special recognition at the graduation ceremony and in the graduation program. In addition, all Honors Program courses are designated as such on students' transcripts (even if they do not graduate with Honors Program Distinction).

Admission Process: Students are automatically considered for admission to the Honors Program when they are admitted to the University. Last year, 93 percent of those invited to join at entry did so. Freshmen should have an academic GPA of at least 3.5 or an SAT I score of 1180 or higher (ACT score of 26). The cumulative academic GPA must be at least 3.2 and the SAT I score at least 1100 in all cases. Transfer students should have a minimum 3.5 GPA or very strong recommendations. Students from recognized university, college, or community college honors programs will be accepted upon receipt of a letter of recommendation from that institution's Director of Honors.

Scholarship Availability: Full-time Honors Program students who are U.S. citizens or resident aliens receive an academic scholarship: Presidential, Dean's, or Transfer. These vary in amount based on academic qualifications. The Honors Program awards Oxford Term and Study Abroad Scholarships to continuing students on a competitive basis. It also awards Honors Research Fellowships to continuing students on a competitive basis.

The Campus Context: The University of Tampa is a private, comprehensive university in the center of a dynamic urban setting. Plant Hall, the main classroom and administration building, is a national historic landmark and one of the finest examples of Moorish architecture in the Western Hemisphere. It is the jewel in the crown of UT's 75-acre riverside campus. Just across the Hillsborough River is the shimmering skyline of downtown Tampa, one of the fastest-growing cities in the United States. Jobs, internships, and community service opportunities abound. The campus has more than forty buildings, including seven residence halls, a library, art galleries, a theater, a museum, modern science labs, and outstanding fitness and athletic facilities. A 40-foot boat, the BIOS, is for classroom-based research in marine and environmental science. Students enjoy free access to the Internet and E-mail via a new high-speed campus computer network from their residence hall rooms or from numerous computer labs on campus.

More than sixty majors, minors, certificates, and preprofessional undergraduate programs are offered in two colleges: the College of Liberal Arts and Sciences and the College of Business. A Master of Business Administration and a Master of Science of Nursing are also offered. A strong integrated core curriculum centered in the liberal arts is at the heart of UT's learn-by-doing approach. All classes are taught by professors, not graduate assistants. Ninety-five percent of the faculty members have Ph.D.'s.

Student Body With just 2,000 full-time students and a 16:1 student-faculty ratio, students enjoy a close-knit residential campus and a real sense of community. Students represent fifty states and more than seventy-five countries. More than ninety clubs and organizations are open for student participation.

Honorary Societies Phi Eta Sigma, Phi Theta Kappa Alumni Association, Omicron Delta Kappa, Alpha Chi

Athletics The University of Tampa has one of the nation's top NCAA Division II sports programs. Spartan teams have won four national championships in the 1990s. Men's sports include basketball, baseball, crew, cross-country, golf, soccer, and swimming. Women's sports are basketball, crew, cross-country, soccer, softball, swimming, tennis, and volleyball.

Study Abroad International experience is a celebrated focus of campus life and study. UT has exchange programs with universities in Mexico, the United Kingdom, The Netherlands, France, Sweden, and Switzerland for semester or yearlong study. Summer and short-term travel courses are also offered each year. Students study foreign languages using the latest learning technologies, including computerized labs and SCOLA—a satellite providing TV programming in numerous languages from around the world.

Tuition: $14,310 per year (1998–99)

Room and board: $4800

Contact: Director: Dr. Richard Piper, Box 100F, 410 West Kennedy Boulevard, Tampa, Florida 33606-1490; Telephone: 813-253-3333 Ext. 3570; Fax: 813-258-7237; E-mail: rpiper3404@aol.com

THE UNIVERSITY OF TENNESSEE AT CHATTANOOGA

4 Pu G M Sc Tr AA GA FA

▼ University Honors Program

The University Honors (UHON) Program at UTC is a four-year interdisciplinary program that stresses the importance of a global

Interpreting the symbols: **2**=two-year college, **4**=four-year college; **Pu**=public or state college, **Pr**=private college; **G**=general honors program; **D**=departmental honors program; **S**=small program (fewer than 100 students), **M**=midsize program (100 to 500 students), **L**=large program (more than 500 students); **Sc**=scholarships available in honors program; **Tr**=transfer students accepted into honors program; **HBC**=historically black college; **AA**=academic advisors; **GA**=graduate advisors; **FA**=fellowship advisors.

perspective through the study of great literature, fine art, and profound ideas. The UHON seminars are designed especially for small groups of honors students and are intended to encourage intellectual, moral, and social growth. The program's goal is to foster a community of scholars who benefit from each other's work and who provide the University with new ideas and ways to achieve excellence.

In order to achieve this goal, the program provides the honors students with special benefits, including exclusive 24-hour access to a 2,200-square-foot reading room and adjacent computer lab, intensive academic advisement, priority registration for classes, a stipend for local symphony and theater performances, and substantial funding for annual study trips abroad.

The UHON Program was privately endowed in 1977 and expanded to its current size in 1986 through a grant from the National Endowment for the Humanities. The program currently includes about 130 students, 15 select faculty members, and 4 adviser-administrators.

Participation Requirements: The required UHON curriculum consists of 33 semester hours (Humanities I and II; Classical and Medieval Historical and Political Thought; Development of Scientific Thought; Origins of Social Science; Contemporary Social Science; one course from Chinese and Japanese Traditions, Traditions of Latin America, or African Traditions; and two courses from film, music, art, or theater history and aesthetics). During the senior year, each UHON student undertakes an independent departmental honors project with the guidance of a faculty member in the major. The project carries 4 hours of academic credit and usually results in a research paper of substantial length and quality that must be defended before a committee from the major department. All UHON courses replace the University's general education requirements.

Students must maintain at least a 3.5 cumulative GPA for all college course work, earn at least 24 hours toward graduation each academic year, and complete the sequence of UHON seminars. They are also expected to participate in the social, cultural, and service life of the University.

UHON students receive designations on their diplomas and in the commencement program as University Honors Scholars. Students also receive engraved medallions at commencement as recognition of their achievement in completing the program.

Admission Process: Prospective freshmen must submit a separate application, which is available from the UHON Office or Web site, to the UHON Program by February 1. There is no minimum high school GPA or test score required, but successful applicants present average ACT scores of 29 and high school GPAs of 3.8. Applications include a creative essay, a report of extracurricular activities, and recommendations from teachers. Promising candidates are invited for a two-day conference at UTC, where they are able to explore the campus, attend University classes and a special seminar, visit with faculty representatives from various departments, and socialize with current UHON students and other applicants. The visit also gives the UHON staff a chance to evaluate applicants by means of interviews, informal discussions, and observed classroom interaction. Final selections are completed by March 20.

Students not admitted as freshmen may apply to become Associate Honors Scholars if they have completed at least 24 hours of course work at UTC with a cumulative GPA of 3.5 or better. Associate Honors Scholars are eligible for all benefits of the UHON Program except the Honors Program Scholarships.

Scholarship Availability: About twenty new scholarships are awarded each year to freshmen selected for the UHON Program, including sixteen William E. Brock, Jr. Scholarships; two Paul Koblentz Memorial Scholarships; and two Roberta M. "Bobbie" Yates Scholarships. Those students not receiving UHON scholarships are considered for all other merit-based awards offered by the University. Virtually all UHON students receive scholarships. In 2001–02, UHON students received about $250,000 in state scholarship funds and $455,000 in exclusive UHON scholarships—nearly $5000 per year per student.

The Campus Context: The University of Tennessee at Chattanooga began in 1886 as a private liberal arts college and became one of four primary campuses of the University of Tennessee system in 1970. The campus is located on 116 acres in downtown Chattanooga, a city of 150,000.

The University is composed of the Colleges of Arts and Sciences, Business Administration, Education and Applied Professional Studies, Engineering and Computer Science, and Health and Human Services, which includes the Schools of Nursing, Rehabilitation Professions, and Social and Community Services. Degree programs include Bachelor of Arts, Bachelor of Fine Arts, Bachelor of Music, and Bachelor of Science in forty-three undergraduate majors, with eighty-seven program concentrations. Master's degrees are offered in eighteen majors, with fifty-eight program concentrations. The University also offers a Specialist in Education degree program, with three concentrations.

UTC is in a period of growth, with construction under way for a new University Center, a $25-million engineering building, and additional student apartments. Also on campus are WUTC FM 88.1 (Chattanooga's National Public Radio station), the Southeast Center for Education in the Arts, the Archaeology Institute, and Cadek Conservatory.

Student Body Undergraduate enrollment is 7,105 (42 percent men). The student population is 79.2 percent white, 16.2 percent black, 1 percent Hispanic, 3.2 percent Asian/Pacific Islander, and .3 percent American Indian. There are 126 international students. Residents living in campus housing make up 20.8 percent of the population. Sixty-five percent of students receive financial aid. There are nine fraternities and eight sororities.

Faculty Of the 608 faculty members, 343 are full-time. Eighty percent of full-time faculty members hold terminal degrees. The student-faculty ratio is 16:1.

Key Facilities The library houses 486,978 books and 1.3 million microforms. Computer facilities include IBMs and Macintoshes in three large general-purpose labs and twenty-three departmental labs. High-speed Internet access is available in all classroom buildings and every dorm. Students can access both the University library catalog and registration system through the World Wide Web.

Honorary Societies Local chapters of Phi Eta Sigma, Golden Key, Mortar Board, Alpha Society, and Alpha Lambda Delta are available at the University.

Athletics In athletics, UTC is a member of NCAA Division I. Men's sports include basketball, cross-country, football (I-AA), golf, indoor and outdoor track, tennis, and wrestling. Women's sports include basketball, cross-country, indoor and outdoor track, soccer, softball, tennis, and volleyball. Club sports include men's and women's crew (rowing) and men's soccer and rugby. UTC's recreational facilities include an indoor racquet center, a natatorium, and a 12,000-seat arena with specialized areas for dance, gymnastics, and wrestling. A 20,000-seat football stadium was completed in 1998.

Study Abroad UTC maintains bilateral exchange programs with Masaryk University in the Czech Republic, Haifa University in Israel, Lulea University in Sweden, and Nagoya University of Foreign Studies in Japan. The University also participates in the Cooperative Center for Study in Great Britain as well as the International Student Exchange Program (ISEP) and the National Student Exchange (NSE) Program.

Support Services Disabled students find UTC committed to providing equal opportunity for all students. Most buildings are wheelchair accessible, and many projects are under way to enhance accessibility. The College Access Program (CAP) provides support services for students with documented learning disabilities.

Job Opportunities Work opportunities on campus include laboratory and research assistantships for undergraduates, tutoring and work-study programs, and jobs in the bookstore and food service areas.

Tuition: Tuition is $2698 for state residents and $9228 for nonresidents per year (2001–02). Non-Tennessee residents who are members of the University Honors Program are charged in-state tuition rates.

Room and Board: The average dorm fee is $2200 per year, and board is estimated at $2300.

Mandatory Fees: Other mandatory fees (program and service, technology, facilities, and debt service) total $538 annually. Students receiving UHON scholarships have all tuition and fees covered.

Contact: Director: Gavin Townsend, 615 McCallie Avenue, Chattanooga, Tennessee 37403; Telephone: 423-755-4128; Fax: 423-785-2128; E-mail: gavin-townsend@utc.edu; Web site: http://www.utc.edu/univhon/

The University of Tennessee

4 Pu G L Sc Tr

▼ University Honors Program

The University Honors Program at the University of Tennessee (UT), Knoxville, is a campuswide program open to students pursuing any of approximately 120 academic majors in ten colleges. The goals of the University Honors Program are to provide enhanced academic opportunities, to foster intellectual development, and to promote campus and community involvement to high-ability students that are appropriate to their diverse interests. The 16-year-old program currently enrolls a total of 600 students. Other honors opportunities on campus include honors courses and departmental honors programs.

Entering students attend early orientation sessions, are assigned a peer mentor—an honors student of similar interests, and have the opportunity to live in an honors learning community in Morrill Hall. Honors students receive priority in courses and residence hall selection each term and have enhanced library and computing privileges. During the academic year, students have unlimited access to the honors lounges, including computer facilities and study areas. Honors dinners are held on a regular basis each year, and evening information sessions feature a wide range of academic and extracurricular opportunities. Academic and career advising is customized to each student's interests and culminates in the selection of a faculty mentor to provide advice on academic issues, professional opportunities, and the senior thesis.

Honors students are leaders in all areas of campus life, from the classroom to the community. The University Honors Program facilitates their pursuits of challenging curricula, including graduate classes, independent research and creative work, and off-campus study. On campus, they are elected leaders of student government and other campus organizations, appointed members of deans' student advisory committees, and work each year to make improvements to the campus. They are active and creative volunteers in organizations that serve the broader off-campus community.

A distinctive feature of the University Honors Program is its emphasis on original work, demonstrated through opportunities for students to become engaged in faculty-sponsored research. Students are encouraged to participate in professional organizations and activities; the annual Exhibition of Undergraduate Research and Creative Achievement provides a public forum for presentation of original works. The University Honors Program furthermore assists students in the pursuit of major competitive fellowships, scholarships, and internships, and honors students have been recipients of Rhodes, Fulbright, Truman, Goldwater, and National Science Foundation awards.

Participation Requirements: University Honors students complete a 1-credit honors seminar each semester, formal honors courses during the first two years, a contract honors course in the major during the junior year, and a senior thesis under the supervision of a faculty mentor. Students also are eligible to participate in one of the many departmental honors programs on campus. A minimum 3.25 GPA is required to maintain full standing in the program. Honors courses are indicated on transcripts; honors degrees are indicated on the transcript and diploma.

Admission Process: Admission is available to entering students who are recipients of one of the following four-year academic scholarships: Oldham, Whittle, Manning, Bonham, Haslam, Holt, McClanahan, Neyland, Roddy, Tennessee, African American Achiever, Bicentennial, and Presidential (National Merit Finalist). Additional opportunities exist for students transferring from other NCHC-member honors programs. A limited number of students may be admitted each year following completion of the first year at UT with a superior academic record, including honors courses.

Scholarship Availability: Interested students are encouraged to complete the University's Entering Freshman Scholarship Application (November 1 postmark deadline) or the Transfer Scholarship Application (February 1 postmark deadline) to be considered for competitive scholarships. Interviews for selection of the top competitive awards, Oldham, Whittle, and Manning, are held early in the spring semester. Scholarships awarded based upon certified grades and scores (Presidential–National Merit, Bicentennial, African American Achiever) require admission by February 1. University honors students who are not Tennessee residents are exempted from paying out-of-state tuition.

The Campus Context: The University of Tennessee, Knoxville, is composed of twelve colleges (ten offering undergraduate degrees): Agriculture and Natural Resources, Architecture and Design, Arts and Sciences, Business Administration, Communications, Education, Engineering, Human Ecology, Law, Nursing, Social Work, and Veterinary Medicine. There are eighty-three graduate/professional degree programs and 120 undergraduate degree programs, including fourteen interdisciplinary majors and opportunities to completely customize a major.

Student Body Undergraduate enrollment is 20,124, equally divided between men and women. There is a minority enrollment of 12 percent and 972 international students. Thirty-five percent of the students reside on campus, and 33 percent of students receive financial aid. There are twenty-five fraternities and sixteen sororities.

Faculty Of the 1,244 faculty members, 1,217 are full-time. Eighty-seven percent have terminal degrees. The student-faculty ratio is 18:1.

Key Facilities The library system houses more than 2 million volumes, contains an enhanced computer media center, and provides customized research support to students. Computer facilities include a UNIX system and remote labs in residence halls, classroom buildings, and the libraries. Technologically advanced and wireless classrooms in addition to computer connections in all residence hall rooms further facilitate the use of the latest instructional and communication technologies. University Honors has three rooms (two are reservable with PCs and Macs) with a full range of peripherals.

Interpreting the symbols: **2**=two-year college, **4**=four-year college; **Pu**=public or state college, **Pr**=private college; **G**=general honors program; **D**=departmental honors program; **S**=small program (fewer than 100 students), **M**=midsize program (100 to 500 students), **L**=large program (more than 500 students); **Sc**=scholarships available in honors program; **Tr**=transfer students accepted into honors program; **HBC**=historically black college; **AA**=academic advisors; **GA**=graduate advisors; **FA**=fellowship advisors.

Outstanding facilities available to all students include the University Center (study, cultural events, speakers, and cafeterias), Clarence Brown Theatre and Carousel Theatre (campus and professional theatrical productions), Music Hall (faculty, student, and visiting musical productions), International House (cultural programs and study and conference areas, and Black Cultural Center (cultural programs, study facilities, tutoring).

Opportunities for study at other universities are facilitated by membership in the National Student Exchange (coordinated by the Center for Undergraduate Excellence) and the International Student Exchange Program (coordinated by the Center for International Education). The UT/Batelle collaborative management of the Oak Ridge National Laboratory has increased the opportunities for scientific research by students.

Athletics The University of Tennessee, Knoxville, is an NCAA Division I school and a member of the Southeastern Conference. In addition to a wide range of varsity intercollegiate sports, the University hosts several intercollegiate competitive club sports and intramural activities including twenty-two men's and twenty-three women's sports.

Study Abroad The University is a member of ISEP (International Student Exchange Program) and maintains information on numerous academic exchange and study-abroad programs through the comprehensive library of the Center for International Education. Regularly offered programs through the university are Normandy Scholars (intensive study during spring semester, study at Caen during the summer), and Semester in Wales (Swansea each fall). Other opportunities include summer programs in Germany, Italy, Mexico, and Spain.

Support Services The Office of Disability Services coordinates support for students who need assistance, including transportation on campus, handicapped parking facilities, audio taping, and compliance with access to facilities mandated by the Americans with Disabilities Act. Tutoring is available to all students at no charge through the Office of Minority Student Affairs, and employment opportunities exist for students wishing to work as tutors. The Writing Center provides consultation.

Job Opportunities The Office of Financial Aid maintains listings of employment opportunities for students and coordinates the Federal Work-Study Program. Students also may be employed on research contracts and grants through academic departments. The Office of Career Services coordinates information for employment and internships, in addition to providing free consultation concerning resumes and interviewing skills. The University Honors Program actively promotes employment opportunities for students in administrative offices on campus.

Tuition: $3234 for state residents, $7596 for nonresidents, per year (2001–02)

Room and Board: $4342

Mandatory Fees: $550

Contact: Director: Dr. Thomas W. Broadhead, Knoxville, Tennessee 37996-1410; Telephone: 865-974-7875; Fax: 865-974-4784; E-mail: honors@utk.edu; Web site: http://www.acad.utk.edu/honors

The University of Tennessee at Martin

4 Pu G M Sc Tr

▼ Honors Programs

Honors Programs at the University of Tennessee at Martin (UTM) comprise the University Scholars Program and the Honors Seminar Program. Together these programs involve approximately 300 students annually in honors courses, seminars with visiting speakers, independent research and creative projects, cultural activities, and service projects.

The University Scholars Program, founded in 1981, is a sequence of courses and extracurricular activities for a select group of talented and motivated students. The major goal is to provide special academic opportunities that will help these students to perform with distinction in their careers and as citizens. Interdisciplinary inquiry and independent study and research characterize this program. The program currently is limited to 60 undergraduate students at all levels in the University. Scholars students enroll every semester in one University Scholars course, accumulating a four-year total of 10 hours toward graduation with the designation University Scholar.

The Honors Seminar Program, founded in 1984, brings together students and distinguished campus visitors (scholars, leaders, or artists) in seminars to discuss and examine issues and ideas. Approximately 240 students are currently active in the program. Honors Seminar students attend a series of public presentations by visiting speakers. They select one speaker with whom to study in more depth in two special seminars. Up to 4 hours of elective credit toward the degree may be earned.

Admission Process: Students with a minimum ACT composite score of 28 or a minimum SAT I score of 1240 and a minimum high school GPA of 3.5 may apply for University Scholars Program admission prior to their freshman year. A few students with outstanding freshman college records at UTM or who are transferring from another institution may also be invited to apply. A minimum 3.3 GPA is required for good standing. Students qualify for the Honors Seminar Program by having an ACT composite score of 28 or higher or an SAT I score of 1240 or higher and a high school GPA of 3.5 or higher. Students apply for the program by completing the regular applications for admission and financial aid at UTM. A minimum 3.2 GPA is required for good standing.

Scholarship Availability: Students invited into the University Scholars Program are assured of a scholarship package of at least $4000 per year for up to four years of their participation. Honors Seminar students are assured of a scholarship package of at least $3000 per year for up to four years of their participation.

The Campus Context: The University of Tennessee at Martin, located in northwest Tennessee, is a primary campus of the University of Tennessee system. UT Martin offers undergraduate degree programs in more than eighty specialized fields of study through the Colleges of Agriculture and Applied Sciences, Business and Public Affairs, Education and Behavioral Sciences, Engineering and Natural Sciences, and Humanities and Fine Arts.

The University community enjoys a 250-acre campus that features forty-six academic and support buildings. Residence halls house more than half of the student body. The campus is a registered botanical garden and has received the Professional Grounds Maintenance Society's Grand Award for school and university grounds. Honors Programs are housed in the Holland McCombs Center on the quadrangle. The Honors Center portion of McCombs consists of an office, the Tennessee Room, a seminar room, and Honors Study/Computer Laboratory.

Student Body Of the 5,500 undergraduates, 56 percent are women. The ethnic distribution includes 15 percent African American and 0.5 percent Asian.

Faculty There are 260 full-time faculty members, 62 percent of whom have terminal degrees. The student-faculty ratio is 21:1.

Honorary Societies Phi Eta Sigma and Phi Kappa Phi

Key Facilities Paul Meek Library, which was recently expanded from 65,000 to 120,000 square feet, has more than 300,000 volumes. The campus is wired with fiber-optic cables connecting academic, administrative, and residential buildings.

Athletics UT Martin is an NCAA Division I institution and a member of the Ohio Valley Conference. Intercollegiate athletics include basketball, cross-country, indoor and outdoor track, softball, tennis, and volleyball for women and baseball, basketball, cross-country, football, golf, riflery, and tennis for men. There are also several recreational activities and sports for men and women.

Study Abroad Honors Program students are encouraged to study abroad through tours associated with courses and led by University professors. Semester and academic-year fellowships abroad are encouraged. University Scholars students may qualify to apply one semester's scholarship to study-abroad or National Honors Semesters.

Tuition: $3280 for state residents, $9810 for nonresidents, per year (2001–02)

Room and Board: $3820

Contact: Director: Dr. William H. Zachry, 19 Holland McCombs Center, Martin, Tennessee 38238; Associate Director: Dr. Daniel J. McDonough; Telephone: 731-587-7436; Fax: 731-587-1082; E-mail: zachry@utm.edu; Web site: http://www.utm.edu/honors

The University of Texas at Arlington

4 Pu G M Sc Tr

▼ The Honors College

The Honors College is a community of exceptionally able and highly motivated students who want the excitement and stimulation of a major urban university and the individual attention available in an Honors College. Having as its purpose the promotion of a general spirit of inquiry among students and faculty, the Honors College sets standards for academic excellence at The University of Texas at Arlington (UTA). Honors scholars from all disciplines study together in interdisciplinary team-taught core courses, honors sections of lower-division University requirements, advanced honors courses in disciplinary majors, and colloquia and seminars in special topics. Honors Study Abroad Programs offer intensive on-site learning experiences in international settings. Honors Service Learning courses provide community service opportunities and support for student interested in volunteerism. The Honors Senior Research Thesis/Creative Project is the culmination of work in the major and draws on the honors experience. Course work in the Honors College is compatible with any major, and all honors course offerings fulfill core, departmental and/or college requirements. The Honors College is a nondegree-granting unit. All honors degrees are awarded in the disciplines of the academic schools and colleges.

In addition to a challenging curriculum, the Honors College regularly schedules social and intellectual activities that extend learning experiences beyond the classroom: honors symposia, informal gatherings, lecture series, and artistic performances. The Honors College Council (HCC), elected from the honors student body; the Honors Faculty Advisory Council (HFAC); representatives from the Colleges; and the Honors Dean, is responsible for the ongoing operation of the Honors College. Honors College membership now stands at around 600 students.

Participation Requirements: Honors degrees are granted in the disciplines of the University's eight schools and colleges (Architecture, Business Administration, Education, Engineering, Liberal Arts, Nursing, Science, and Social Work) and in the Interdisciplinary Studies Program. To graduate with an honors degree, the student must be a member of the Honors College in good standing (minimum 3.2 GPA) and complete the degree requirements in a disciplinary major.

Honors requirements: at least 24 hours of honors course work (all of which fulfill University core or disciplinary major requirements) to include at least two interdisciplinary seminars or honors special topics courses (6 hours) and 9 advanced honors hours in the major, including Research Methods or the equivalent (3 hours); a senior thesis/research project (3 hours); and a selective course in the major (3 hours).

Remaining honors courses may be chosen from special honors sections of University core requirements, other honors interdisciplinary seminars/special topics courses, Honors Service Learning, Honors Internship, honors electives or honors courses in the major.

Continuing UTA students and transfer students who join the Honors College (with 60 hours or more) must complete only one interdisciplinary seminar. The 24-hour requirement for transfer students may be adjusted in some colleges.

Admission Process: The Honors College seeks students with broad interests, varied talents, and diverse cultural backgrounds. Admission is competitive. Entering freshman honors applicants must have a combined SAT I score of at least 1200 or an ACT score of at least 27 and be in the upper 10 percent of their high school graduating class. Continuing and transfer honors candidates must have a minimum 3.2 GPA. Admission, however, is not based solely on grades or scores; the Admissions Committee (comprised of honors faculty and staff members) also considers faculty recommendations and applicant statements of purpose in the selection of candidates. Applications for admission are available online at the Web site listed below or in the Honors College Office.

Scholarship Availability: The Honors College, in conjunction with the UTA Scholarship Office, annually awards nearly 500 scholarships to honors students each year. Scholarships are renewable for up to three additional years for students who maintain the requisite GPA of 3.2 or higher. The Honors Undergraduate Research Program, in concert with UTA's other schools and colleges, also places students in funded research assistantships in their disciplines. Applications are available in the Honors College Office. Information on departmental and organizational scholarships and financial aid is available online at http://www2.uta.edu/fao/ or in the Scholarship and Financial Aid Offices, 252 Davis Hall.

The Campus Context: The University of Texas at Arlington is a comprehensive teaching, research and public service institution. Located in the heart of the Dallas/Fort Worth metropolitan area, one of the fastest-growing areas in the nation, UTA is organized into eleven units: Honors College, College of Business Administration, College of Engineering, College of Liberal Arts, College of Science, School of Architecture, School of Nursing, School of Social Work, School of Urban and Public Affairs, School of Education, and the Graduate School.

UTA ranks among the nation's top fifty schools in the graduation of engineering professionals, the University's Energy Systems Research Center is consistently rated as one of the nation's top ten, and UTA was chosen as one of NASA's three sites for research in hypersonic aircraft. Eighty-seven percent of the University's applicants are accepted into medical schools. Ninety-six percent of the students in the School of Nursing's Nurse Practioner Program pass the National Certification Exam. UTA's Distance Education Programs rank the highest in Texas, and state-of-the-art computer facilities and services support on- and off-site learning. The *Shorthorn,* the school newspaper, was named best college newspaper by the Rocky Mountain Collegiate Press Association. Out of ninety-three M.S.W. programs nationwide, the School of Social Work was ranked ninth in faculty productivity/

Interpreting the symbols: **2**=two-year college, **4**=four-year college; **Pu**=public or state college, **Pr**=private college; **G**=general honors program; **D**=departmental honors program; **S**=small program (fewer than 100 students), **M**=midsize program (100 to 500 students), **L**=large program (more than 500 students); **Sc**=scholarships available in honors program; **Tr**=transfer students accepted into honors program; **HBC**=historically black college; **AA**=academic advisors; **GA**=graduate advisors; **FA**=fellowship advisors.

publications, and the School of Urban and Public Affairs was rated the fourth-best program of its kind in the nation. The wheelchair basketball team, the Movin' Mavs, holds ten current world records and more than 150 gold medals in international track competitions.

Student Body The second-largest component of the University of Texas system, UTA enrolls about 21,000 students, of whom approximately 16,300 are undergraduate; 52.5 percent are women. Of the students, 56.4 percent are Anglo, 11.7 percent are black, 9.7 percent are Asian, 10 percent are Hispanic, and .7 percent are Native American. The international student population is 2,300 and comes from eighty countries. Approximately 15 percent of UTA's students live on campus. About 30 percent receive financial aid.

Faculty UTA employs 1,216 faculty members, of whom 708 are full-time; 508 are tenure/tenure track. Of the full-time tenure/tenure-track faculty members, 85 percent hold terminal degrees. The student-faculty ratio is 21:1. Faculty members teach in eighty-four baccalaureate, sixty-nine master's, and thirty doctoral programs.

Key Facilities The library contains more than 3 million books, microforms, government documents, maps, and technical reports and subscribes to more than 5,500 current journals and serials. It holds one of the nation's most extensive Texas and Gulf Coast cartography collections and was designated as the depository for more than 1 million U.S. Nuclear Regulatory Commission documents and photos.

Honorary Societies UTA is home to twenty-nine honor societies. The Greek system is composed of twelve national fraternities and ten national sororities.

Athletics All men's and women's intercollegiate teams are members of the Southland Conference. All teams compete in Division I of the National Collegiate Athletic Association. Teams are fielded in men's baseball, basketball, cross-country, golf, tennis, track and field, and wheelchair basketball and in women's basketball, cross-country, softball, tennis, track and field, and volleyball.

Study Abroad The Honors College offers at least two interdisciplinary, team-taught study-abroad programs each summer. UTA offers twenty study-abroad and student exchange programs located in ten different countries worldwide.

Support Services The Office for Students with Disabilities ensures equal opportunity and access to all programs and activities on campus and offers specially designed services for specific disabilities.

Job Opportunities The Offices of Student Employment Services and Human Resources make available to all students current job listings, including work-study and non–work-study positions, internships, and teaching and research assistantships. Through these offices, at least 1,200 work-study and non–work-study students are employed on campus, and 3,426 students are employed off campus.

Tuition: $3750, resident; approximately $8500, nonresident (2001–02)

Room and Board: For residence living, $2080 to $4250 for residence halls and $350 to $561 per month for UTA-owned apartments; UTA meal plan, $1970 per year

Mandatory Fees: $700 (books)

Contact: Dean Carolyn A. Barros, The University of Texas at Arlington, Box 19222, Arlington, Texas 76019; Telephone: 817-272-7215; Fax: 817-272-7217; E-mail: honors@uta.edu; Web site: http://honors.uta.edu

The University of Texas at Austin

4 Pu M Sc Tr

▼ Mitte Business Honors Program

The core of the Mitte Business Honors Program (BHP) consists of twelve courses taught at an advanced level by experienced faculty members. Modeled after graduate business courses, the curriculum emphasizes discussion, case study, and research of actual business situations. Students are exposed to leading-edge theories and examples of best business practices. This hands-on approach utilizes team projects with written proposals and oral and multimedia presentations. Students also have opportunities to represent the University at national conferences and international case competitions. While course size is limited to enhance interaction and cohesiveness, the program has recently grown and currently consists of approximately 120 students in each of the four classes.

Established in 1960, the Mitte Business Honors Program has consistently broadened students' academic experiences while providing preparation for immediate entry into challenging business careers or graduate study. BHP students are able to double major in the Red McCombs School of Business. The second major could include accounting, engineering route to business, finance, international business, management, management information systems, marketing, or the professional program in accounting (a five-year concurrent B.B.A./M.B.A. program). They may also combine business honors with another major outside the McCombs School, such as economics, government, history, or the Plan II Honors program in the College of Liberal Arts.

The BHP is coordinated by a faculty director, an external affairs director, and specially appointed counselors to advise students about degree planning, course scheduling, career opportunities, summer internships, resume writing, and interviewing principles. Students benefit from a growing international network of alumni who hold important positions in areas such as investment banking, management consulting, public accounting, and law. One hundred scholarships are awarded annually to Mitte Scholars, the students of the Mitte Business Honors Program.

Admission Process: Freshman admission is based upon high school ranking, SAT I scores, leadership in organizations, and extracurricular events. A business resume, essays, and current recommendations are required to complete the admission packet. Successful applicants demonstrate the ability to balance outstanding academics with the leadership skills necessary in business. Earned GPA, rigor of course work, and leadership are important factors used to evaluate transfer applicants.

The deadline for admission for freshmen is February 1; the deadline for internal sophomore transfer applicants is April 30.

The Campus Context: Founded in 1883, the University of Texas at Austin has grown into a campus of 350 acres with a student body of 38,000 undergraduate students and 12,000 graduate students. Undergraduates may choose courses from more than 160 fields of study, supported by extensive computer facilities and one of the largest academic libraries in the nation. The city of Austin, with a population of about 500,000, is a green and cosmopolitan setting for the University. Students benefit from both the local communities in arts—dance, music, theater, and the visual arts—and the numerous recreational activities made possible by the temperate climate of the hill country of central Texas.

Tuition: $2016 for state residents, $7080 for nonresidents, per year (2001–02)

Room and Board: $5671

Mandatory Fees: $2400

Contact: Director: Dr. Eli Cox III; External Affairs Director: Mr. Adam Ward, Mitte Business Honors Program, CBA 2.312, Austin, Texas 78712; Telephone: 512-475-6325; Fax: 512-471-9458; E-mail: texasbhp@bus.utexas.edu; Web site: http://www.bus.utexas.edu/~bhp/

UNIVERSITY OF TEXAS AT EL PASO

4 Pu G M Sc Tr

▼ University Honors Program

The University of Texas at El Paso (UTEP) Honors Program, open to students of all majors, is designed for the academically motivated student who seeks an intellectual challenge and a more personal focus in education. The program provides an environment conducive to intellectual growth through honors courses, group activities, and interaction in the Honors Lounge, which is available for study, conversation with other honors students, and Honors Council meetings. The Honors Lounge is a home for honors students and facilitates a sense of community among students and faculty members.

Honors classes are small, theoretically oriented, and taught by outstanding faculty members in a personalized classroom environment. Creative thinking, writing, verbal, and reading skills are emphasized. During the first two years, honors classes encourage students to broaden their academic horizons, while the last two years emphasize depth. For some students, this depth will culminate in an honors senior thesis, a year-long research project that is bound and placed in the library as a permanent record of the student's achievement. Students graduating with the University Honors Certificate, University Honors Degree, and/or a cumulative GPA of 4.0 receive a certificate(s) designating their respective honor or honors. Students who join the Honors Council participate in an induction ceremony and receive a certificate of membership.

Each semester, a variety of honors sections are offered at the lower- and upper-division levels. These courses can be used to meet requirements for the bachelor's degree as well as the University Honors Degree (e.g., English, history, accounting, or biology). Departments offering courses include accounting, anthropology, biological sciences, chemistry, English, finance, geological sciences, history, languages and linguistics, philosophy, physics, political science, sociology, and theater arts. Well before registration, the Honors Program publishes descriptions of honors courses and biographical data on honors faculty members for the students' information. Students may also contract for honors credit in nonhonors courses. All honors courses completed are designated with honors on the student's academic transcript. Students must apply to participate in the program. The program is 20 years old and currently enrolls 400 students.

Participation Requirements: The Honors Program offers two options: the University Honors Degree and the University Honors Certificate. The Honors Degree requires the student to complete a minimum of 30 hours of honors courses and have a minimum GPA of 3.3 upon graduation. These include honors courses in all basic education areas and 6 hours of upper-division honors hours and/or 6 hours of honors thesis. The graduate will have University Honors Degree on the diploma and on the permanent academic transcript. The Honors Certificate requires 18 hours of honors courses, 6 hours of which must be upper-division, and a minimum cumulative 3.3 GPA upon graduation. Such students will have University Honors Certificate recorded on their diploma and permanent transcript. A University Honors Certificate will also be awarded.

All students who satisfactorily complete the Honors Program requirements graduate with special recognition. Graduating with honors adds a special distinction to transcripts and diplomas and therefore, to graduate and/or professional school applications. In addition, honors graduates are publicly recognized at the annual Honors Convocation and at Commencement ceremonies.

The Honors Program hosts faculty and campus visitors to speak on topics of interest to honors students. Such speakers have included judicial persona and journalists as well as mayoral and city council candidates.

Honors students are invited to join the Honors Council and so interact with other honors students and assist in the planning of honors activities according to their interests. Students who join the Honors Council participate in an induction ceremony and receive a certificate of membership.

Admission Process: Freshman students may apply to the program if they have a superior score on the SAT or ACT or rank in the top 15 percent of their high school graduation class. A cumulative GPA of 3.3 is required for admission of current or transfer students. Once admitted to the program, students must maintain a 3.3 GPA.

Scholarship Availability: UTEP offers many scholarships to students of exceptional ability, ranging in amounts of $150 to $4000. In addition, ten Houston Endowment, Inc., scholarships of $5000 each are awarded annually to University Honors Program members.

The Campus Context: The University of Texas at El Paso is composed of six colleges, including Business Administration, Education, Engineering, Liberal Arts, Health Sciences, and Science. The University offers sixty-four bachelor's degree programs, fifty-seven master's degree programs, and eight doctoral degree programs.

The campus has several distinguished facilities. The Sun Bowl, which is the second-oldest college bowl in the U.S., seats 52,000. The Special Events Center, which is used for graduations, basketball games, and concerts, seats 12,222. The UTEP Dinner Theatre is a very successful theater that produced the American premier of Timothy Rice's *Blondel.* In 1989, the Union Dinner Theatre was selected from more than 800 colleges and universities to perform its production of the musical *Chess* at the Kennedy Center for the Performing Arts in Washington, D.C. Over the past eleven years, the Union Theatre has grown to become one of the most successful arts organizations in El Paso.

Student Body Undergraduate enrollment is 13,642. Fifty-four percent of the students are women. The student body is 11.8 percent white, 2.4 percent black, 72.5 percent Hispanic, 1.2 percent Asian American, .3 percent Native American, and 10 percent Mexican. Commuters comprise 84.7 percent of the students; 41 percent of students receive financial aid. There are eight fraternities and six sororities.

Faculty Of the 853 total faculty members, 645 are full-time. Eighty-nine percent have terminal degrees. The student-faculty ratio is 16:1.

Key Facilities The library houses 918,960 books, 3,551 serial subscription titles, and 88,301 documents. Computer facilities include five to six labs with PCs and Macs. An additional twelve labs featuring personal computers are located in various colleges and departments.

Honorary Societies Golden Key, Mortar Board, Alpha Chi, and Alpha Lambda Delta

Athletics The UTEP Miners have a rich sports tradition that includes the 1966 National Basketball Championship, seven Western Athletic Conference basketball championships, twenty national championships in track and field, numerous bowl bids in football, nationally ranked men's and women's tennis teams, a second-place finish in the NCAA Golf Championships, and a rifle team that has become a perennial top 10 squad.

Study Abroad As a member of the Texas Consortium for Study Abroad, UTEP is able to offer qualified students the possibility of

Interpreting the symbols: **2**=two-year college, **4**=four-year college; **Pu**=public or state college, **Pr**=private college; **G**=general honors program; **D**=departmental honors program; **S**=small program (fewer than 100 students), **M**=midsize program (100 to 500 students), **L**=large program (more than 500 students); **Sc**=scholarships available in honors program; **Tr**=transfer students accepted into honors program; **HBC**=historically black college; **AA**=academic advisors; **GA**=graduate advisors; **FA**=fellowship advisors.

an academic year, semester, or summer session at universities in Australia, Austria, Britain, Czech Republic, France, Hong Kong, Italy, Japan, Mexico, Russia, and Spain. Internships are also available in Britain. Study at other universities in the U.S. and its territories and Canada is available through the National Student Exchange.

Support Services The Disabled Student Services Office provides support and advocate services to help mainstream both physically and learning disabled students into the campus community. The office also extends services to students who become temporarily disabled due to injury or recent surgery and to women with at-risk pregnancies. A wide array of support services are available free of charge to assist disabled students in their college career. These services include note-taking, sign language interpreters, a telecommunication device for the deaf, special test accommodations, equipment loan programs, and arranging to have classes moved from inaccessible to accessible locations.

Job Opportunities Part-time job opportunities are posted on the bulletin board outside the Career Services Center Office. After filling out the proper application card, students are referred to the board to check on jobs and obtain a referral from the secretary. The requirements for consideration for part-time campus employment are met with an application along with proof of enrollment.

Tuition: $1485 (15 credits) for residents, $4670 (15 credits) for nonresidents, per year (2001–02)

Mandatory Fees: $560

Contact: Director: Dr. Lillian F. Mayberry, Honors House, El Paso, Texas 79968-0607; Telephone: 915-747-5858; Fax: 915-747-5841; E-mail: mayberry@utep.edu; Web site: http://www.utep.edu/honors/

The University of Texas–Pan American

4 Pu G M Sc Tr AA

▼ University Honors Program

Through its University Honors Program, the University of Texas–Pan American (UT-PA) demonstrates a sincere commitment to provide an exceptional educational experience for academically talented undergraduate students. Small classes, innovative teaching techniques, individualized instruction, research opportunities, academic recognition, and a wide variety of extracurricular activities are just some of the benefits of this outstanding program.

Participants in the University Honors Program are eligible to enroll in honors classes. Because they are typically small in size—usually 20 students or less—these classes provide a comfortable forum for in-depth discussion and interaction among students and faculty members. Enrichment, rather than acceleration, is the main objective. Students find that honors classes are not necessarily more difficult than others, but rather more stimulating and interesting.

During the junior year, University Honors Program students have an opportunity to select a topic that is of particular interest and undertake an independent studies project under the one-on-one guidance of a knowledgeable faculty adviser. This project is designed to offer honors students invaluable experience in the skills of independent research and decision making that prepares them for future graduate and career challenges. Honors faculty members and honors thesis/project advisers are especially selected for their commitment to undergraduate education and for their skills in mentoring students.

The 30-year-old program currently enrolls more than 200 students.

Participation Requirements: All honors students are to complete 13 hours of honors core requirements. The Honors Council, the advisory group that oversees the University Honors Program, has recommended that students complete a minimum of 6 additional honors hours.

Admission Process: Entering freshmen may gain admission to the program in any one of the following three ways: have a composite ACT score of at least 22 (or the SAT I equivalent, 1030); graduate in the top 10 percent of the student's high school class; or graduate from high school with a grade average of 90 or above in academic courses.

Students who have earned 12 or more hours of college credit with at least a 3.0 GPA are also eligible to apply to the program. The applicant's college grades and recommendations from professors determine his or her admission to the program.

In addition to the summa, magna, and cum laude recognition awarded to students by the University, the University Honors Program awards students who successfully complete a thesis/project with certification of honors graduation. The certification also specifies the student's level of distinction.

Scholarship Availability: Currently, there are three competitive scholarship funds administered through the University Honors Program. Interested students first must be accepted into the program. Applications for these scholarships are available by February 1 of each year; deadline for priority consideration is March 1 of each year. These scholarships are awarded for the following academic year. Depending of fund availability, scholarships are also awarded in January. Small research scholarships are also available to assist students with the completion of the thesis/project.

Other financial assistance, including grants, University scholarships, loans, and part-time employment, is available to qualified students through the Office of Student Financial Aid.

The Campus Context: The University of Texas–Pan American is a component of the University of Texas System, serving the south Texas region commonly referred to as the Rio Grande Valley on the U.S.–Mexico international border. UT–Pan American is the only comprehensive university in the state's seventh most populous county and enrolls the highest number and highest percentage of Hispanics among Texas public universities. The University offers fifty bachelor's degree programs through its six colleges. UT-PA is accredited by the Southern Association of Colleges and Schools to award bachelor's, master's, and doctoral degrees (Level V). UT-PA is designated as a Hispanic Serving Institution (HSI) The 220-acre campus consists of forty modern buildings/complexes connected by a covered walkway situated on a beautifully landscaped campus highlighted by palm trees and shaded by live oaks.

Student body Undergraduate enrollment is 11,971. More than 86 percent of these students are Hispanic; 6 percent are white (non-Hispanic); 1 percent are Asian; and 0.42 percent are African American. UT-PA is predominantly a commuter campus. Approximately 2 percent of the population are classified as international students. More than 70 percent of the student body receives financial aid. There are ten national sororities and fraternities on campus as well as more than 100 registered student organizations.

Faculty The total number of faculty members is 601, of whom 419 are full-time and 290 are tenured or are on tenure-track.

Honorary Societies One special benefit for University Honors Program participants is that they become eligible for membership in Gamma Beta Phi, a national honors and service society. Students must have successfully completed 12 semester hours and be in good standing in the University Honors Program. Membership in Gamma Beta Phi is restricted to University Honors Program participants. Other honor societies available to students with the requisite GPA are Kappa Delta Pi, Lambda Delta, Psi Chi, Lambda Alpha, and Golden Key.

Key Facilities The library houses a collection of approximately 437,000 volumes, 300,000 government documents, 4,500 periodical subscriptions, 1 million microforms, and 6,000 audiovisual items. The number of online subscription services available to students is growing rapidly. The Academic Services Building houses more than a dozen computer labs for students. Other smaller computer lab rooms are located in the education, engineering, math, and geology departments and in the library.

Athletics UT-PA competes in NCAA Division I for women in basketball, cross-country, golf, tennis, track and field, and volleyball, and for men in baseball, basketball, cross-country, golf, tennis, and track and field. Currently, UT-PA is not affiliated with an athletic conference, with the exception of the men's and women's tennis teams who compete in the Southland Conference.

Study Abroad No programs exclusively for honors students are available at this time. The campus does have a Center for International Studies that sponsors study-abroad opportunities each year.

Support Services The Office of Services for Persons with Disabilities (OSPD) provides supportive services that meet the educational, career, and personal needs of persons with disabilities who attend UT-PA.

Job Opportunities The Office of Career Placement Services and the Office of Student Financial Aid list work opportunities for students on campus and in neighboring communities. The Cooperative Education Program offers students full-time and part-time internship opportunities.

Tuition: $816, 12 hours, in-state (2001–02)

Room and board: $4417.80 average per year (2001–02)

Mandatory Fees: $ 284.73, 12 hours, in-state (2001–02)

Contact: Director: Dora E. Saavedra, Ph.D., SBSC Building, Room 104, The University of Texas–Pan American, 1201 West University Drive, Edinburg, Texas 78539-2999; Telephone: 956-381-3461; Fax: 956-381-2484; E-mail: honors@panam.edu; Web site: http://www.panam.edu/academic/honors.cfm (under construction)

University of Texas at San Antonio

4 Pu G M Sc Tr

▼ University Honors Program

The mission of the University Honors Program at the University of Texas at San Antonio (UTSA) is to provide enhanced educational opportunities for selected, motivated, enthusiastic, diverse, and inquisitive students and to foster the pursuit of excellence in undergraduate higher education. A second mission of the University Honors Program is to increase the number of outstanding students at UTSA and to assist in retaining those students through all four years of their undergraduate experience. As a result, University Honors Program students make a visible and positive impact on the entire university community.

In order to accomplish its mission, the UTSA University Honors Program (1) creates opportunities for honors students to work closely with faculty members who are dedicated to providing superior instruction for honors students and who attempt to encourage lively and engaging discourse; (2) provides opportunities for honors students to engage in supervised research and other creative work; (3) offers personalized academic advising, guidance, referrals for scholarships and internships, and support to honors students as a manifestation of the interest the University has in their academic progress; (4) provides opportunities for honors students to learn from other highly motivated students in small, interactive classes of 12 to 25 students; and (5) attempts to create a social and cultural environment to support the formation of a well-rounded individual, confident of his or her place in the community and the world.

The University Honors Program is open to students in all academic majors. The program, which was founded in 1985, admits up to 150 students each year. There are approximately 400 students currently enrolled in the program.

Participation Requirements: To graduate with University honors, students must complete a minimum of 24 hours of honors course work, have a minimum GPA of 3.25, and write an honors thesis. The 24 hours of honors course work must include 6 hours of honors seminars and 3 hours of World Civilization. The capstone experience in the University Honors Program is the completion of the honors thesis. The thesis is an independent research or creative project developed with the assistance of a faculty Thesis Advisor. Each semester students working on their honors thesis present the results of their research in an Honors Research Colloquium. Students can receive $300 to $400 in grant assistance to support their thesis work through the UTSA Undergraduate Fellows Program. Successful completion of the requirements for graduation with University honors is recognized at the Student Honors Convocation and is noted on the official transcript.

Students who do not intend to graduate with University honors are welcome to join the honors program, as well. To be considered an active member eligible for preferential honors registration at the library, members of the honors program must complete a minimum of 3 hours of honors course work per year.

Admission Process: Applicants to the program are required to submit an application form, an essay, two letters of recommendation, and high school and/or college transcripts. High school seniors, transfer students, and enrolled UTSA students are encouraged to apply for admission. General guidelines for admission to the program are a class standing in the top 10 percent and a minimum SAT-R score of 1000 or an ACT score of 22; or a class standing in the top 20 percent and a minimum SAT-R score of 1200 or an ACT score of 27; or a college GPA of 3.3 or better for a minimum of 12 hours. The admissions committee evaluates each student individually, weighing intellectual promise, seriousness of purpose, and writing skills, so students who fall close to these guidelines are encouraged to apply.

There is rolling admission to the University Honors Program, but incoming transfer students and new freshman applicants who wish to receive honors scholarships must mail their applications by February 1.

Scholarship Availability: The University Honors Program offers approximately 100 honors scholarships each year. The largest of these scholarships are the twenty Presidential Honors Scholarships ($1500 a year for up to four years) and the three Alliance Capital Management Scholarships ($2500 a year for up to four years) awarded to new UTSA students each year. Out-of-state and international students who receive honors scholarships of $1000 or more are eligible to pay in-state tuition rates. To be eligible for Presidential Scholarships and Excellence in Education Awards, incoming freshmen and transfer students must apply by February 1. Other honors scholarships require no special application and are awarded to students already enrolled and in good standing with the University Honors Program.

The Campus Context: The University of Texas at San Antonio, a comprehensive public university, serves the San Antonio metropolitan area, South Texas, and the Rio Grande Valley. UTSA offers eighty-four bachelor's, master's, and doctoral degrees. Established in 1969 as an academic component of the University

Interpreting the symbols: **2**=two-year college, **4**=four-year college; **Pu**=public or state college, **Pr**=private college; **G**=general honors program; **D**=departmental honors program; **S**=small program (fewer than 100 students), **M**=midsize program (100 to 500 students), **L**=large program (more than 500 students); **Sc**=scholarships available in honors program; **Tr**=transfer students accepted into honors program; **HBC**=historically black college; **AA**=academic advisors; **GA**=graduate advisors; **FA**=fellowship advisors.

of Texas System, UTSA is projected to continue as one of the state's fastest-growing and most diverse universities. UTSA's 600-acre campus on Loop 1604 at the edge of the Texas Hill Country and a new Downtown Campus offer state-of-the-art facilities. Outstanding faculty members recruited from top universities, a rigorous and comprehensive curriculum, accredited professional programs, extensive student support services, and relatively small classes contribute to UTSA's reputation as one of the nation's must innovative metropolitan universities. UTSA provides a full range of student support services, including an Office of Minority Affairs, a Scholarship Office, an Office of New Student Programs, a Career Services Center, a Testing and Assessment Center, and the Tomás Rivera Center for Student Success.

Student Body In fall 2001, 17,392 undergraduate and 2,449 graduate students were enrolled at UTSA. About 55 percent of students were women and 45 percent were men. About 47 percent of all students are Anglo, 43 percent are Hispanic, and 5 percent are African American. Asians, American Indians, and international students account for about 6 percent of all students. Students aged 17 to 22 made up 44 percent of total enrollment; those 23 to 29 accounted for 31 percent; and those over 30, 25 percent. About 2,000 students live on the 1604 campus in a residence hall and apartments, and another 3,000 live in apartments close to campus. There are more than 150 registered student organizations, including national sororities and fraternities.

Faculty UTSA has about 800 faculty members, more than half of whom are full-time, tenured, or tenure-track. Ninety-eight percent of the full-time faculty members hold doctorates or equivalent terminal degrees. About two-thirds of the faculty members hired in the last five years have been women and members of minority groups.

Key Facilities The UTSA Library collections include 500,000 books, 2,300 periodical subscriptions, and 22,500 audiovisual items and provide access to a wide variety of electronic resources. There are four major student computing labs at the two campuses, providing 24-hour access to the Internet, library resources, and University and faculty Web sites. Students may enroll on line.

Athletics UTSA athletic teams compete with NCAA Division I universities. A member of the Southland Conference, UTSA fields teams in fourteen sports: men's and women's basketball, cross-country, tennis, and outdoor track; men's golf and baseball; and women's volleyball and softball. Athletic facilities include the 5,100-seat Convocation Center, new stadiums for baseball and softball, lighted tennis courts, and soccer fields.

Study Abroad UTSA sponsors international programs with Kyoto University, Queensland University (Brisbane, Australia), the University of British Columbia, Keele University (Staffordshire, England), and La Universidad National Autonoma de Mexico. Financial aid for study abroad is available to all UTSA students through the International Education Financial Aid Fund.

Support Services The Office of Disabled Student Services provides tutoring, assistance with test-taking, and special facilities for disabled students. The campus is 100 percent accessible.

Job Opportunities The University Honors Program works closely with the Career Services Center and other UTSA offices to match students with undergraduate assistantships, internships, and cooperative education programs. More than 70 percent of UTSA students work on and off campus.

Tuition: $2010 for residents (30 hours) per year (1998–99)

Room and board: $6500

Mandatory Fees: $740

Contact: Director: Dr. Ann R. Eisenberg, 6900 North Loop 1604 West, San Antonio, Texas 78249; Telephone: 210-458-4106; Fax: 210-458-5730; E-mail: aeisenberg@utsa.edu.

The University of Toledo

4 Pu G L Sc Tr

▼ University Honors Program

The Honors Program at the University of Toledo provides an academically stimulating environment that encourages students to make the most of their University education. Students meet other students with similar interests, become involved in research or creative projects, work with honors faculty members, attend conferences, and receive help in preparing for future career or professional goals.

The University Honors Program is available across all colleges and in all majors, including interdepartmental programs such as Africana studies and women's and gender studies. Honors courses are offered within various departments as well as in the Honors Program itself, providing a wide range of selections for students in the program.

Among the many advantages of honors participation is the option of taking courses designed with honors students in mind. These courses are smaller in size, focus on student-faculty interaction, may be set up as interdisciplinary seminars, and give students an opportunity to get to know their peers and their professors. Honors seminars cover a range of disciplines and issues; recent examples include The Legacy of Vietnam, Archaeology of Ancient Egypt, and Political Leadership.

In addition to a range of stimulating courses, honors students have the chance to meet other honors students through priority housing in the Academic House and International House Residence Halls, participation in the Student Honors Council at UT, attendance at student Brown Bag Presentations, and participation in service learning , as well as through many other intellectual, social, and community events.

The Honors Program also encourages student participation at regional and national research conferences. Many students present their research, read or perform creative work, or exhibit artwork and other projects to academic audiences. Students also receive help and advice in applying for various scholarships, internships, or travel-abroad programs.

Honors students have priority advanced registration when enrolling in their courses, and the honors staff and departmental advisers provide personal attention in academic advising, including advice about overall educational and personal objectives, assistance in graduate and professional school selection, and the preparation of letters of recommendation.

Students graduating from the Honors Program receive a citation on their diplomas. In addition, students are awarded an honors medallion upon graduation.

The 38-year-old program currently enrolls more than 800 students.

Admission Process: Admission to the Honors Program is based on high school GPA, ACT or SAT I scores, an extracurricular résumé, and references. Students entering directly from high school with a 3.75 GPA or higher and an ACT composite of 28 or higher (or SAT I combined score of 1240 or higher) are encouraged to apply. Highly motivated students with at least a 3.5 GPA and an ACT composite of at least 25 (or minimum SAT I combined score of 1140) are also considered for admission to the program.

Scholarship Availability: Many honors students receive University-sponsored scholarships, such as the Founders Scholarship and the Tower Excellence Scholarship. The minimal application standards for many other scholarships are the same as for the Honors Program. The Huebner Scholarship, available through the Honors Program, offers short-term aid to honors students in need. Sullivan Fellowships are available to support honors student research.

The Campus Context: The University of Toledo is a nationally recognized comprehensive public university with a broad range of undergraduate and graduate programs serving students from almost every county in Ohio, all fifty states, and ninety-eight countries. The University of Toledo enrolls approximately 20,000 students and is located in a suburban setting within the metropolitan Toledo area that is home to 600,000 people.

The nine colleges on campus include Arts and Sciences, Business Administration, Education and Allied Professions, Engineering, Graduate School, Health and Human Services, Law, Pharmacy, and University College. The University offers 156 undergraduate majors.

Distinguished features of the campus include the Academic Center complex, which consists of Sullivan Hall, the Honors Center office and classroom building, the Academic House Residence Hall, and the all-suite International House Residence Hall. The three-building Engineering Complex, completed in 1995, houses the Polymer Institute, National Center for Tooling and Precision Components, and the Edison System Facility. The Lake Erie Research Center, located at Maumee Bay State Park, is a cutting-edge soil and water research and education facility. The Art Department is located in the award-winning Center for the Visual Arts designed by Frank Gehry.

Student Body The student body is 52 percent women. In addition, 11.2 percent of the students are African American, .3 percent are American Indian/Alaska Native, 1.7 percent are Asian/Pacific Islander, 2.1 percent are Hispanic, and 73.2 percent are white. There are 5.8 percent international students on campus. Nearly 86 percent of the students are commuters, and 66 percent of the students receive some form of financial aid. There are fourteen fraternities and thirteen sororities at the University of Toledo.

Faculty The total number of faculty members is 961, of whom 678 are full-time and 590 have terminal degrees. The student-faculty ratio is 20:1.

Key Facilities The library houses more than 1.5 million volumes. Computer facilities include twenty-four computer labs and more than 500 units.

Athletics Intercollegiate athletic teams for men consist of baseball, basketball, cross-county, football, golf, swimming, tennis, and track and field. Women's teams consist of basketball, cross-country, golf, soccer, softball, swimming, tennis, track and field, and volleyball. The state-of-the-art Student Recreation Center has been recognized as one of the best in the country.

Study Abroad The Salford study-abroad program is available for majors in biology, chemistry, and physics. Study-abroad opportunities include Costa Rica, France, Germany, Ireland, Japan, Mexico, Malaysia/Singapore, Scotland, and Spain.

Support Services The Office of Accessibility provides a variety of services for disabled students, including note-taking, tutoring, counseling, an adaptive computer room, and intercampus transportation.

Job Opportunities In addition to many work-study opportunities, the Career Services office coordinates and posts information about a variety of part-time jobs and provides students a chance to participate in a career mentor (job-shadowing) program.

Tuition: $4172 for state residents, $11,530 for nonresidents, per year (2001–02)

Room and Board: $6104

Mandatory Fees: $930

Contact: Director: David Hoch, Sullivan Hall, Honors Academic Center, Toledo, Ohio 43606-3390; Telephone: 419-530-6030; Fax: 419-530-6032; E-mail: honors@uoft02.utoledo.edu; Web site: http://www.utoledo.edu/honors/

University of Utah

4 Pu G D L Sc Tr

▼ Honors Program

Through its Honors Program, the University of Utah attracts highly motivated and accomplished students to its more than seventy undergraduate majors, which are housed in fifteen different colleges and schools. Students who start their college work at Utah can satisfy their general education and bachelor's degree requirements through honors classes taught by professors selected because of their success as teachers. Honors courses are taught in groups never exceeding 30, all of whom are honors students. Those who transfer from other institutions or who do not start work in honors immediately can still complete the required seven honors courses and the honors thesis/project to earn an honors baccalaureate degree in their major discipline. In some majors, students can complete all or some of their honors courses through departmental honors tracks that provide honors classes as part of the major program.

The promise of the Honors Program is excellent service to students. Students are encouraged to come into the program offices to select courses and review their program. A prethesis interview is scheduled for students before they start work on their thesis/project. It is common for students still in high school to come in, often with their parents, to learn about the Honors Program as part of their evaluation of possible universities to attend.

The Honors Program provides a separate curriculum of courses in a variety of topics, ranging from lower-division courses such as Intellectual Traditions of the West, calculus, writing, diversity, and American Institutions to upper-division seminars offering a continually changing selection of topics and interdisciplinary studies reflecting a wide variety of academic departments. In the newly developed departmental honors tracks, individual departments schedule honors courses or sections for their own majors. These courses satisfy the requirements for the honors degree as well as for the departmental major. The Department of Mathematics and the School of Computing have been approved for departmental honors tracks. Some departmental honors courses serve majors from other departments. The Departments of Mathematics and Chemistry now have such courses.

As the capstone of their work toward an honors degree, students complete an honors thesis/project in their major department. This work is representative of the research or creative activity typically done in the student's major. The final projects range from traditional research papers to creative writing, films, dances, or other fine art. A departmental honors coordinator helps students refine their project idea and then assigns a faculty member in the department to supervise the work. The supervisor, the departmental coordinator, the department chair, and the Honors Program director approve each honors thesis/project.

The Honors Program administration consists of a director, an assistant director, an academic program specialist, a development director, and 2 part-time students. There are no faculty members housed in the Honors Program. Professors are recruited from the academic departments to teach honors courses. In some cases, adjunct instructors who do not hold tenure-track appointments in an academic department are used when they have given evidence of superior teaching and tenure-track faculty members are not available. In a few instances, distinguished

Interpreting the symbols: **2**=two-year college, **4**=four-year college; **Pu**=public or state college, **Pr**=private college; **G**=general honors program; **D**=departmental honors program; **S**=small program (fewer than 100 students), **M**=midsize program (100 to 500 students), **L**=large program (more than 500 students); **Sc**=scholarships available in honors program; **Tr**=transfer students accepted into honors program; **HBC**=historically black college; **AA**=academic advisors; **GA**=graduate advisors; **FA**=fellowship advisors.

professionals in the community who are accomplished teachers are asked to teach preprofessional courses for law, medicine, and business areas.

Participation Requirements: Students qualify for the Honors Program by earning a prescribed Admissions Index based on their high school grades and their score on standardized tests such as the SAT or ACT. Continuing students qualify by having earned at least a 3.4 GPA in their college work. To remain in the program, students must maintain at least a 3.4 GPA.

The Campus Context: The Honors Program at the University of Utah was founded in 1960 by a Ford Foundation Grant. In 1965, the program became a line item on the University's budget. However, it had never had its own building or center and had very little space to fulfill all of its functions. Just recently, the University's president gave Building 619 to the Honors Program for an Honors Center. This building has three wings. Wing A serves as the classroom wing. Wing B is the administration wing. It houses offices for the director, assistant director, academic specialist, and development director and two stations for part-time employees. This is the area where students register, meet with honors advisers, and meet with an administrator for the prethesis interviews. Wing C has a lounge or meeting room with a table for approximately 15 people, a study room for students, a computer room to be used by students, a kitchen, bathroom facilities, and storage space.

Student Body While numbers vary through ongoing additions and subtractions, there are about 1,500 to 2,000 students in the Honors Program, or a little less than 10 percent of the undergraduate student body.

Faculty Faculty members from more than fifteen academic departments and nine colleges or schools teach in the Honors Program. They typically are active research scholars as well as accomplished undergraduate teachers. Traditional lectures are rare. Instead, courses use highly interactive formats that actively involve students in their own learning. Some courses include a service-learning component.

University of Vermont

4 Pu M Tr

▼ John Dewey Honors Program

A variety of honors options are available at the University of Vermont (UVM). The largest is the John Dewey Honors Program (JDHP), which offers highly motivated students enrolled in the University's College of Arts and Sciences an especially challenging and creative undergraduate experience. Through small writing- and discussion-based seminars and various cultural and social events, John Dewey Scholars work to gain a broad and integrated knowledge of the disciplines included in the liberal arts.

First-year JDHP students take two first-year special topics seminars (one in the fall, one in the spring) designed especially for them. In the sophomore year, students take an interdisciplinary seminar called Knowledge and Theory. This seminar provides the basis for subsequent upper-level seminars, taught by some of the best teachers at UVM, dealing with topics as varied as Twentieth-Century Fascism; the Geography of Wealth and Poverty in the United States; the Ethics, Law, and Science of Death and Dying; and Conceptions of the Good Life in Psychology and Economics. An annual, 1-credit mini-seminar brings outstanding scholars to campus to meet with honors students and speak on their areas of research. A variety of social and cultural events are also offered, including, for example, a group trip to Montreal to explore the art museums. In addition, honors students are strongly encouraged to pursue study abroad and to fulfill the requirements for Phi Beta Kappa.

John Dewey Scholars have a private lounge where they can study or work on a computer. They are granted early enrollment for courses and have graduate student privileges at the library. Discount tickets are available for plays and musical and other cultural events. There is also an honors housing option.

Founded in 1995, the John Dewey Honors Program currently has approximately 175 students. This number is expected to grow to approximately 270 by 2003.

Participation Requirements: John Dewey Scholars satisfy general and college distribution requirements as well as the requirements of their majors and minors. In addition, first-year students take a 3-credit honors seminar in each of their first two semesters. Sophomores take the Knowledge and Theory seminar, juniors take another 3-credit special topics seminar, and seniors complete a 6-credit College Senior Honors Thesis or Creative Project (students must have a minimum overall GPA of 3.2 to be eligible to complete this requirement). The only other program requirements are that each student must take at least one Spring Mini-Seminar for 1 credit, and all students completing the senior thesis/creative project must participate in a zero-credit Senior Thesis Seminar that meets twice a month. Students who fulfill the requirements attend an honors awards dinner. At commencement, they wear special honors medallions and receive certificates recognizing them as John Dewey Scholars.

Admission Process: Approximately 40 of the top students in the incoming freshman class are invited to participate in the John Dewey Honors Program. The same number of positions are reserved for students to join the program in their sophomore year. Any student in the College of Arts and Sciences with a 3.2 or higher GPA may apply to the program at the end of the first year. The Honors Council, which consists of faculty members from all areas of the College, selects students for the sophomore honors class based on a personal essay, two letters of recommendation from UVM faculty members, and academic performance in the first year.

Scholarship Availability: Though no specific scholarships are set aside for JDHP students at this time, a number of scholarships are available for outstanding University of Vermont students, and JDHP students may be considered for these funds. The JDHP Director has a discretionary fund to help students with mini-scholarships to cover the cost of special events and projects.

The Campus Context: Founded in 1791, the University of Vermont is the fifth-oldest university in New England (after Harvard, Yale, Dartmouth, and Brown) and among the twenty oldest institutions of higher education in the nation. Known as UVM, from its Latin name Universities Viridis Montis, the University today offers more than ninety majors in eight undergraduate areas: the Colleges of Arts and Sciences, Agriculture and Life Sciences, and Engineering and Mathematics; and the Schools of Allied Health Services, Nursing, Business Administration, and Natural Resources. UVM also features a Graduate College and a College of Medicine.

Located in Burlington, Vermont, a city of approximately 40,000, the UVM campus sits on a hill nestled between Lake Champlain and the Green Mountains. Burlington has been named one of the nation's Big Ten college towns by Edward B. Fiske in his book *The Best Buys in College Education.*

The John Dewey Honors Program is housed in the top floor of Old Mill, one of the oldest and most prominent buildings on campus. The lounge and program office are on the same floor as the main seminar room used for program classes. The living facilities are in the Living/Learning Center complex nearby.

Student Body UVM's undergraduate enrollment is 7,400; approximately 55 percent women and 45 percent men. ALANA (African, Latino/a, Asian, and Native American) students represent 4.4 percent of the student body. Nearly 60 percent of UVM's students come from outside the state of Vermont, primarily from the other New England and Mid-Atlantic states, although students come from throughout the United States and more than twenty-five other countries. Nearly 50 percent of students live on campus, and over half receive financial aid. Students participate in more than ninety on-campus clubs and organizations; about 9 percent join the Greek system of six sororities and eleven fraternities.

Faculty Instructional faculty members number 919, of whom 89 percent have earned the terminal degree in their field. UVM's student-faculty ratio is 14:1.

Key Facilities Bailey-Howe Library, the largest in the state, holds 1.7 million books, serial backfiles, and government documents; 1.7 million microforms, and 20,000 serial subscriptions. Undergraduates also have access to the Dana Medical Library and the Cook Chemistry and Physics Library. Although most students bring their own computer to campus, 238 university-owned computers are available to students. Extensive academic and research facilities serve undergraduate as well as graduate students. The Fleming Museum, Royall Tyler Theatre, and several other facilities on campus support a wide variety of exhibits and performing arts and other cultural events.

Honorary Societies Phi Eta Sigma, Golden Kay, Mortar Board, and Phi Beta Kappa

Athletics UVM is an NCAA Division I school, with fourteen women's and thirteen men's intercollegiate sports. Facilities at the Patrick Gymnasium complex include facilities for basketball, hockey, swimming, dance, tennis, exercise, and weight training.

Study Abroad UVM's Office of International Educational Services sends approximately 400 students to all areas of the world for a semester, academic year, or summer. UVM participates in exchange and affiliate programs and lists roughly 100 approved overseas programs from other institutions.

Support Services The Office of Specialized Students Services supports students with learning differences. Most buildings are accessible to physically disabled students. Other services include the Office of Career Services, the Counseling and Testing Center, and the Center for Health and Wellbeing.

Job Opportunities Work opportunities are available on and off campus.

Tuition: $8040 for residents, $20,100 for nonresidents, per year (2001–02)

Room and board: $6096

Mandatory Fees: $625

Contact: Director: Professor Bob Taylor, 509 Old Mill, Burlington, Vermont 05405-4110; Telephone: 802-656-4289; Fax: 802-656-1376; E-mail: rtaylor@zoo.uvm.edu.

University of Victoria

4 Pu G M Sc Tr AA GA

▼ Honours Program

The Honours Program at the University of Victoria (UVic) offers academic enrichment for highly motivated students. More than 25 academic units offer Honours Programs with a number of opportunities for combined programs, satisfying the requirements for two departments. More than 200 students are registered in Honours programs.

Participation Requirements: Students must maintain a minimum GPA to continue in the program. Students in an honours program must normally complete an honours thesis or graduating essay to fulfill the requirements of the degree. Each academic unit has an honours adviser. Academic advice is also available from the Faculty Advising Centres. Students who achieve a minimum graduating GPA in required courses graduate with an honours degree "with distinction."

Admission Process: Students normally apply for admission to an Honours Program at the end of their second year of University study. Admission is based on completion of specified prerequisites and a minimum GPA.

Scholarship Availability: The University of Victoria offers a competitive merit aid program with awarded scholarships based on a student's high school record at admission and on course work completed at the University for continuing students. Other financial assistance, including bursaries, loans, and part-time employment, is also available to qualified students. UVic awards more than Can$2 million each year in merit-based scholarships.

The Campus Context: The University of Victoria, one of Canada's leading universities, provides a unique and inspiring learning environment. UVic has earned a reputation for commitment to research, scholarship, and work-integrated learning. The University is widely recognized for its innovative and responsive programs and its interdisciplinary and international initiatives. Here, more than 18,000 students find outstanding social, cultural, artistic, environmental, and athletic opportunities. The stunning UVic campus is located on Canada's spectacular west coast, in British Columbia's capital city.

UVic has 1,576 student residence spaces plus 181 units in the David and Dorothy Lam Family Student Housing Complex.

Academic programs at UVic are constantly evolving to provide education that will equip students to live successful, productive lives in our rapidly changing world. The University is a comprehensive university, with Faculties of Business, Education, Engineering, Fine Arts, Graduate Studies, Human and Social Development, Humanities, Law, Science, and Social Sciences. UVic has Canada's third-largest university cooperative education program, integrating academic studies with relevant paid work experience in forty academic areas. In 2000–01, UVic co-op students completed 2,879 work-term placements across Canada and in thirty-five other countries. UVic is home to interdisciplinary teaching and research centres involved in advanced materials; aging; Asia-Pacific initiatives; automation, communication, and information systems; cooperative studies; dispute resolution; earth and ocean research; environmental health; forest biology; global studies; humanities; integrated energy systems; and religion and society. The University has 102 active exchange programs with institutions in twenty-five countries around the world. UVic's Division of Continuing Studies delivers twenty-one certificate and diploma programs to 14,000 participants annually.

Researchers at the University of Victoria work on the cutting edge of knowledge creation, making major contributions in a wide range of fields, from fuel cells and cancer cells to climate change and cultural change. UVic researchers participate in thirteen of the twenty-two federal Networks of Centres of Excellence, studying applied mathematics, automobiles of the twenty-first century, bacterial diseases, genetic diseases, geomatics, health information science, language and literacy, microelectronics, mechanical wood pulps, protein engineering, robotics and intelligent systems, sustainable forest management, and telecommunications. UVic is home to the Canadian Climate Centre, Canada's national laboratory for computerized climate modeling. UVic professors hold five Natural Sciences and Engineering Research Council industrial research chairs in cryofuels systems, electromagnetic fields and living systems, radio frequency engineering, and environmental management of drinking water.

Student Body The student enrolment, as of November 1, 2001, was 18,195 (including 2,143 graduate students); 59 percent are

Interpreting the symbols: **2**=two-year college, **4**=four-year college; **Pu**=public or state college, **Pr**=private college; **G**=general honors program; **D**=departmental honors program; **S**=small program (fewer than 100 students), **M**=midsize program (100 to 500 students), **L**=large program (more than 500 students); **Sc**=scholarships available in honors program; **Tr**=transfer students accepted into honors program; **HBC**=historically black college; **AA**=academic advisors; **GA**=graduate advisors; **FA**=fellowship advisors.

women, 36 percent are part-time students, and 70 percent come from outside Greater Victoria.

Faculty There are 628 regular continuing faculty members (33 percent are women), 441 sessional instructors, 670 specialist/ instructional staff. A total of 92 percent of the faculty members have terminal degrees.

Key Facilities UVic's Centre for Innovative Teaching is a state-of-the-art classroom building, specially designed and equipped to support the effective use of learning and teaching technologies. The University is home to one of Canada's fastest university-based supercomputers, used to investigate some of the most challenging questions in science and engineering. UVic's Language Centre combines computers, audio-visual equipment, and satellite technology to serve instruction in more than 20 languages. UVic's library houses 1.78 million books.

Athletics UVic teams have won forty-one national Canadian Inter-university Sport (CIS, formerly CIAU) championships: eight in men's basketball, four in men's cross-country, three in men's soccer, eight in women's basketball, nine in women's cross-country, nine in women's field hockey; and eleven other Canadian university championships: four in men's rowing, two in men's rugby, and five in women's rowing.

Support Services A new student orientation program helps make the transition to UVic a positive and exciting experience. Other support services include counselling, health, and career services.

Tuition: Can$2152 for Canadian students, Can$6456 for international students (2001–2002)

Room and Board: Can$5392 for a single room; Can$4736 for a double room (on campus for eight months)

Contact: Assistant Dean and Director: Dr. Michael C.R. Edgell, Advising Centre for Humanities, Science and Social Science, P.O. Box 3045 STN CSC, Victoria, British Columbia V8W 3P4 Canada; Telephone: 250-721-7567; Fax: 250-721-7059; E-mail: dadv@uvic.ca; Web site: http://www.uvic.ca

UNIVERSITY OF WASHINGTON

4 Pu G L Sc Tr

▼ University Honors Program

The University Honors Program was founded in 1961 in the College of Arts and Sciences and subsequently extended to the College of Engineering. Believing in the ancient Greek notion that the goal of education is to prepare citizens for intelligent action in the world, the University Honors Program exists to meet the educational needs of the ablest and most highly motivated undergraduates at the University of Washington. It seeks to identify and recruit exceptional students and to provide them with special academic advising, close contact with honors faculty members, and the opportunity to build a learning community among honors faculty members and students.

The program provides a formal curricular structure that extends across the full span of undergraduate study by combining honors general education with advanced honors courses in the major. The honors interdisciplinary core curriculum brings dedicated students and faculty members together in small classes (average size 30) that address several concerns: methods of inquiry in the natural sciences, social sciences, and humanities; historical and cross-cultural perspectives; and effective communication. Critical-thinking and writing skills are emphasized across the honors curriculum. Research methods and the presentation of individual research findings are particularly emphasized in the final, departmental phase of an honors degree. In all, some 300 honors courses and sections of courses are offered each year. Approximately 1,000 students are enrolled in the honors program, which is housed in Mary Gates Hall, a center for undergraduate education.

Participation Requirements: The honors core curriculum (which replaces the general education/breadth requirement) consists of three-year course sequences, one each in Western Civilization, World Civilization, and Natural Science. In the College of Engineering, two honors science sequences and one of the two civilization sequences may be completed in lieu of the College of Arts and Sciences pattern. Business and Nursing follow the Arts and Sciences model. To maintain good standing in and graduate from the Honors Program, students must achieve a minimum 3.3 overall GPA and are normally required to present a 3.5 or better in their major subject. Completing the honors general education core as well as departmental honors requirements results in the degree With College Honors. Students who enter into and complete the honors requirements in the major only, graduate With Distinction. This option is particularly suited to transfer students and those students who enter the University with a very substantial number of college credits earned while still in high school and through such options as AP examinations.

Admission Process: Students apply for the College Honors Program as part of their application for UW admission, providing an Honors Essay and a school evaluation letter in addition to the regular admissions materials. Admission is competitive and conducted on a rolling basis. Applicants are selected on the basis of several factors, including grades, curriculum, test scores, essay, activities, and school recommendation. Candidates are most apt to be given consideration for one of the 150 entering places if they present grades of 3.8 or better and SAT I scores well above 1300. GPA adjustments are made for schools whose grading practices more closely approximate those of the University of Washington (UW). Freshmen can also apply for late entry into honors based on their academic record after their first two quarters at the University. Advanced undergraduates can enter the Honors Program at the invitation of their major department, normally by the junior year, and become candidates for the degree With Distinction.

Scholarship Availability: The University of Washington offers a number of merit-based scholarships (UW Undergraduate Scholars, for state residents; President's Scholars; and Mary Gates Scholars) and the University Honors Program offers several Mary Gates Endowment Honors Scholarships to entering students. Exceptional students are automatically considered based on their admissions applications and their honors applications. National Merit Scholarships are awarded to the most qualified candidates from among those who have designated the University of Washington as their first-choice institution. A variety of financial aid offers, scholarships, research and leadership grants, and campus employment opportunities are also available to undergraduates.

The Campus Context: Founded in 1861, the University of Washington is the oldest public university on the West Coast. Originally located in the heart of pioneer Seattle, the University relocated in 1895 to its present 700-acre campus situated between Lake Washington and Portage Bay. The University offers more than 130 majors and 1,800 courses each quarter through twelve schools and colleges: Architecture and Urban Planning, Arts and Sciences, Business Administration, Education, Engineering, Forest Resources, Nursing, Ocean and Fishery Sciences, Public Health and Community Medicine, Social Work, Dentistry, and Medicine. Schools and colleges that offer postgraduate studies only include Law, Library Information Science, Pharmacy, and Public Affairs. Additional campuses are located in Tacoma and Bothell, Washington, but do not presently offer an honors program. Significant campus features include Meany Hall Performing Arts Center, the Burke Museum, Henry Art Gallery, and the University Medical Center.

Student Body Undergraduate enrollment at the Seattle campus as of autumn 2001 was 30,005 out of a total enrollment of 37,412.

Thirty one percent of the undergraduates come from African American (3 percent), Asian (22.5 percent), Hispanic (4 percent), and Native American (1.5 percent) backgrounds. Women comprise 51 percent of the total, and 5.5 percent of the enrollment is made up of international students. Forty-one percent of the undergraduates receive need-based financial aid. About 30 percent of undergraduates live on campus or immediately adjacent in fraternities and sororities; 60 percent of undergraduate live within walking distance of campus. Currently, twenty-nine residential fraternities and sixteen sororities are associated with the University.

Faculty Teaching faculty members number 3,527, of whom 2,670 are full time; 97 percent have the terminal degree.

Key Facilities The University Library system includes 5.7 million volumes and 5.9 million serials and other holdings. There are currently seven computing laboratories that provide general access workstations, with another to open in Mary Gates Hall by spring 2000.

Honorary Societies Phi Beta Kappa, Golden Key, Phi Eta Sigma, and Mortar Board

Athletics UW is a member of the Pac 10 conference, and its men's and women's teams compete at NCAA Division 1 level (except for men's crew, a non-NCAA sport). Women's sports include basketball, crew, cross-country, golf, gymnastics, soccer, softball, swimming, tennis, track and field, and volleyball. Men's sports include baseball, basketball, crew, cross-country, football, golf, soccer, swimming, tennis, and track and field.

Study Abroad Study abroad for all UW students is coordinated through the Office of International Programs and Exchanges. Currently, UW participates in some fifty international programs and has exchange arrangements with an additional 100 institutions around the world.

Support Services The Disabled Student Services Office provides services and academic accommodations to students with documented permanent and temporary disabilities.

Job Opportunities A wide variety of job opportunities are available on campus and in the general Seattle area.

Tuition: $3984 for residents, $13,260 for nonresidents, per year (2001–02)

Room and board: $5415

Contact: Associate Director: Dr. Julie Villegas, Box 352800, 211 Mary Gates Hall, Seattle, Washington 98195-4300; Telephone: 206-543-7444; Fax: 206-543-6469; E-mail: villegas@u.washington.edu; Web site: http://depts.washington.edu/uwhonors

THE UNIVERSITY OF WEST FLORIDA

4 Pu G M Tr AA

▼ University Honors Program

At the University of West Florida, the University Honors Program (UHP) is defined by the following words: areté, téchne, and sophía. With a focus on excellence, skill, and wisdom, the UHP engages academically talented students in learning that has breadth, depth, and a richness of texture; provides an expeditious and enriching path to a first degree; and opens the right doors to life beyond the University environment.

Areté, or excellence, is the overarching concept for the University Honors Program. Honors students, as well as the program that serves them, are dedicated to the pursuit of excellence through determination and vitality. Téchne means skill, and it is through pursuing areté in any discipline or art—whether it be computer programming, accounting, marine biology, history, music, psychology, film production, management, or anything else—that one becomes first competent and then expert in that discipline. Sophía means wisdom, which is the knowledge achieved through study, insight attained through experience, satisfaction gained from serving others, understanding that stems from struggling with and then solving a problem, and the sound judgment that comes from being able to see not just two sides, but all sides of an issue.

With students who are enrolled in many different majors, the academic portion of the University Honors Program is centered upon smaller honors sections of general studies courses and special honors seminars. Honors classes are designed to have more depth, not be more difficult. All honors classes are restricted to Honors Program students, and the seminars are usually limited to 15 students. Honors sections of general study courses can be found in everything, ranging from chemistry to religion. Honors seminars are truly unique opportunities. Designed to enrich the academic lives of students with interesting topics, recent seminars have been Bio-Medical Ethics, Great Films, Tolkien, and Passage to India. For students with interests beyond the regularly offered general studies courses and seminars, additional courses of study can be arranged with individual professors to fulfill academic requirements. The culmination of the honors student's experience in the program is the honors thesis, which is a focused research project completed in cooperation with the University's best faculty members.

Beyond the classroom, the program, along with the student-composed Honors Council, seeks to provide enriching and meaningful activities. Service events such as Habitat for Humanity and Make-A-Difference-Day, along with student social gatherings are regular occurrences. The program also strives to couple academic classes with domestic and international travel experiences. Recent trips have been to Honduras, the Great Smoky Mountains, and Italy. The University Honors Program also publishes an award-winning newsletter, *Infinite Wisdom* (first place in the nation, 2001), which can afford writing and publishing opportunities.

The University Honors Program houses a study area, student lounge, computers specifically for use by honors students, and administrative offices. The program also has special honors student housing in new dorm facilities. Honors students have registration priority over other students and receive recognition by the University president at the University's commencement exercises.

Founded in 1989, the University Honors Program currently enrolls 350 students.

Participation Requirements: Once admitted, students in the University Honors Program must maintain a GPA of at least 3.0 (B average). To graduate as a University Honors Scholar, which includes a special Honors Graduation Ceremony and recognition at the University's commencement exercises, students entering as freshmen must complete 24 semester hours of honors course work. This includes four lower division honors courses, three upper division honors seminars or electives, and an honors thesis. The honors thesis should be the culmination of a student's experience in the program. Transfer students and students not admitted as freshmen complete a more concentrated version of these requirements. Upon graduation from the University Honors Program, students receive an annotated transcript asserting their status as an Honors Scholar.

Admission Process: Entering freshmen seeking admission to the University Honors Program are asked to submit an Honors

Interpreting the symbols: **2**=two-year college, **4**=four-year college; **Pu**=public or state college, **Pr**=private college; **G**=general honors program; **D**=departmental honors program; **S**=small program (fewer than 100 students), **M**=midsize program (100 to 500 students), **L**=large program (more than 500 students); **Sc**=scholarships available in honors program; **Tr**=transfer students accepted into honors program; **HBC**=historically black college; **AA**=academic advisors; **GA**=graduate advisors; **FA**=fellowship advisors.

Program application. In general, the applicant must have a cumulative, unweighted GPA of 3.5 or higher or rank in the top 10 percent of their graduating high school class, and must have an ACT composite score of 26 or higher, or a combined 1170 or higher on the SAT. Applicants who do not meet these requirements are encouraged to apply, as some students are admitted on probational status each year. Transfer students seeking admission to the program must submit an Honors Program application, have an overall transfer GPA of 3.25, and submit a letter of recommendation from the Honors Director of their previous institution. UWF students seeking admission to the program who were not admitted as freshmen must submit an application, have an overall UWF GPA of 3.25, and submit a letter of recommendation from a UWF faculty member.

Scholarship Availability: In addition to the state-sponsored scholarship programs for Florida students, the University offers a number of different scholarships designed for many different types of students. Both merit-based and need-based scholarships are offered, as are student loans. There are seven different merit-based scholarships offered by the University to qualified students upon admission. Among these are the following: the Pace Scholars Program, $4000 per year for four years; The John C. Pace, Jr. Scholarship, $1000 per year for four years; and the Presidential Scholarship, $1000 per year for four years. The University Honors Program offers financial assistance to students wishing to pursue international or other alternative educational experiences.

The Campus Context: Located on 1,600 acres of nature preserve, The University of West Florida is nestled in a beautiful section of the Florida panhandle among wide verandas, massive moss-draped oaks, spacious greens, and meandering walkways. Focused on a students first concept, UWF is considered to be one of the 100 best values in public education by Institutional Research & Evaluation, Inc. Students and faculty members enjoy a relationship that is more commonly found at small, private institutions. The University confers bachelor's degrees in more than forty-five different majors with more than 100 specializations, ranging from art to molecular biology.

Among the University's distinguished facilities, UWF operates centers in downtown Pensacola, Eglin Air Force Base and Naval Air Station Pensacola, a branch campus in Fort Walton Beach. The University also owns 152 acres of beachfront property on Santa Rosa Island adjacent to the Gulf Islands National Seashore. The Institute for Human and Machine Cognition, founded by the Florida Legislature in 1990, is an interdisciplinary research institute that concentrates on cognition in humans and machines. Some recent research partners include NASA and the U.S. Department of Defense.

The University also features a natatorium that houses an Olympic size swimming pool that adjoins the Field House, a center for indoor sports, large-group activities, and recreation. The Field House contains a fitness center, combatives room, and group exercise class facilities. Sailing and waterskiing facilities are nearby, and the campus nature trails attract thousands of visitors annually.

Student Body Undergraduate enrollment was 7,422 in fall 2001, of whom 57 percent are women. Ethnic minority students make up 23 percent of the student body, and at any given time there are nearly 125 international students on campus. More than 2,000 undergraduate students were admitted in 2001 and UWF continues to grow. There are twelve nationally affiliated fraternities and sororities on campus.

Faculty The University has a total of 522 faculty members. Of these members, 248 are full-time and 75 percent hold the doctorate or final degree in their specialty. The student-faculty ratio is 20:1.

Key Facilities Computer labs on campus contain both PC and Mac computers dedicated for student use. Access to the campus network, e-mail, and the Internet is provided for on-campus students via a high-speed internal LAN network and off-campus students via dial-up. Student e-mail can be accessed via the Internet and students have storage space for Web pages on the University's servers. The main computer lab is open 24 hours a day. The library contains more than 2 million items and has its own special collections area with items dating back to the fourteenth century, including manuscripts signed by Thomas Jefferson and Albert Einstein. The University Honors Program has its own residence halls, study areas, and lounge.

Honorary Societies Phi Eta Sigma, International Golden Key Honor Society, Alpha Sigma Lamda, Beta Gamma Sigma, Kappa Phi Alpha, Omicron Delta Kappa, Phi Alpha, Phi Kappa Phi, Pi Sigma Alpha, PsyChi, Order of Omega

Athletics UWF participates in NCAA Division II sports. The University has six women's and six men's varsity teams: basketball (men and women), baseball (men), softball (women), soccer (men and women), tennis (men and women), volleyball (women), and golf (men). Intramural sports include sailing, fencing, bowling, swimming, and the ever-popular Ultimate Frisbee.

Study Abroad UWF's Office of International Education and Programs arranges more than twenty study-abroad exchange programs on every continent except Antarctica. However, UWF does have a marine biology professor who conducts research there. The University Honors Program also arranges international travel for Honors Program students. Recent trips have been to Italy, England, Japan, and Honduras.

Support Services UWF is proud of the services provided for students with handicaps or disabilities. Along with fully accessible buildings, classrooms, and lab rooms, the University maintains services that include special computers, note takers and readers, sign-language interpreters, and a tutoring/mentoring program designed to ensure the success of any student.

Job Opportunities There are many job opportunities for students both within the campus community and in the surrounding area. UWF posts job listings weekly and the Career Center is available to students for career counseling, job placement services, or placement as an intern for college credit.

Tuition: $2300 for state residents; $8000 for nonresidents, per year, full-time (2002–03 estimated)

Room and Board: $5500

Contact: Director: Dr. Greg Lanier, University Honors Program, 11000 University Parkway, Building 50, Room 224, Pensacola, Florida, 32514; Telephone: 850-474-2934; Fax: 850-473-7256; E-mail: glanier@uwf.edu; Web site: http://www.uwf.edu/uhp/

University of Wisconsin–Eau Claire

4 Pu G M Sc Tr

▼ University Honors Program

The University Honors Program provides an extra measure of challenge and enrichment for students in any of the colleges at the University of Wisconsin–Eau Claire campus. It strives to enhance their critical thinking and communication skills, capacity for independent learning as well as working in teams, and leadership abilities. Courses are limited to a maximum of 20 students and are highly interactive. Students receive individual attention by faculty members in ways that cannot be done in larger courses. Almost all honors courses apply to credits needed for general education and provide a special means of meeting graduation requirements. The program does not increase the number of courses students are required to take as an undergraduate.

Colloquia courses change from semester to semester, and some are team-taught. They are usually offered during several semesters, but new ones are added each year and some are dropped. Departmental courses are predictably scheduled each semester and include basic courses in accounting, art, biology, chemistry, communications, economics, history, mathematics, music, philosophy, physics, political science, psychology, religious studies, and sociology. The first-year seminar is team-taught by honors seniors who enroll in Mentoring in Honors and are supervised by the director. The course provides an introduction to the baccalaureate degree, the purpose of a liberal education, and the nature of academic disciplines. The senior honors seminar is a retrospective, integrative experience. Most departments offer students the opportunity to earn departmental honors in their majors. Students may pursue departmental honors without being participants in the University Honors Program. Admissions to departmental programs generally require a 3.5 GPA in the major and in total credits.

The physical location of the program provides a classroom; a student study area with computers, a refrigerator, and a microwave; a conference room; a reception area; and the director's office. A student organization arranges trips to museums, theaters, and concerts as well as a variety of social activities. Outside of classes there are weekly Breakfasts with a Profess, monthly Pizzas with a Professor, special speakers, and support for attending state, regional, and national honors conferences.

The University Honors Council establishes policies for the program, approves honors courses, and selects honors faculty. This council consists of faculty representatives from each of the colleges as well as student representatives. More than 135 faculty members have taught honors courses.

The 19-year-old University Honors Program currently enrolls 375 students.

Participation Requirements: To earn University Honors, students must complete at least the following: a 1-credit first-year honors seminar, 12 credits of interdisciplinary honors colloquia (or 9 credits of colloquia if a senior 1-credit Mentoring in Honors is completed), 12 credits of departmental courses limited to honors program students, and a 1-credit senior-level honors seminar. They must have at least a 3.5 GPA at graduation. This totals 24–26 credits of honors courses out of the 120 needed for graduation.

Students completing the requirements for University Honors receive special recognition during the Commencement ceremonies. They wear an honors medallion on a gold ribbon along with gold cord, and they stand to be recognized. Their achievement is noted on their permanent records and transcripts. They each receive a special certificate. *

Admission Process: Students are invited to participate in the honors program in several ways. Most are recruited as incoming first-year students based on two criteria: they must be in the top 5 percent of their high school graduating class and they must have an ACT composite of at least 28 or an SAT I score of at least 1280. Because these criteria miss a number of outstanding students, some are invited based on faculty recommendations and placement test scores. Finally, students are invited after they have completed 15 credits if they have a 3.67 GPA or better and an ACT composite score of at least 26. Transfer students who have been participating in honors programs at other college or universities are admitted and given credit for previous honors courses toward meeting the program's requirements for graduation with University Honors.

Scholarship Availability: Students eligible to participate in the University Honors Program are awarded at least a $500 freshman honors scholarship. Larger scholarships are also available and awarded competitively.

The Campus Context: UWEC is a comprehensive university within the UW System and emphasizes its mission as a liberal arts institution. The University composes the Colleges of Arts and Sciences, Business, and Professional Studies. The College of Professional Studies includes the Schools of Education, Nursing, and Health and Human Services. There are a total of eighty-two degree programs offered.

Special facilities on campus include the Goodner Collections and Owens Collection of Native American Materials, the S. W. Casey Observatory, the L. E. Phillips Planetarium, and the James Newman Clark Bird Museum.

Student Body Undergraduate enrollment is 60 percent women. The ethnic distribution of students that are members of minority groups is .7 percent black, .6 percent American Indian, 2.6 percent Asian, and 1 percent Hispanic. There are 141 international students. Thirty-nine percent of the students live in residence halls, and 60 percent of students receive financial aid. There are seven fraternities and sororities.

Faculty Of the 487 faculty members, 412 are full-time and 87 percent hold terminal degrees. The student-faculty ratio is 20:1.

Key Facilities The library houses 594,979 volumes. There are eighteen general computer labs with Apple Macintosh and PC systems available for students and faculty. The student-to-computer ratio is 11:1.

Honorary Societies Phi Eta Sigma, Phi Kappa Phi, Golden Key, Mortar Board, Alpha Lambda Delta, Omicron Delta Kappa, and Society of Participating Honor Students

Athletics The athletic program for women consists of varsity teams in basketball, cross-country, golf, gymnastics, ice hockey, soccer, softball, swimming and diving, tennis, track and field, and volleyball. The men's program consists of varsity teams in basketball, cross-country, football, golf, ice hockey, swimming and diving, tennis, track and field, and wrestling. Both the men and women compete on the national level as members of the National Collegiate Athletic Association (NCAA) Division III.

Study Abroad The University academic community strongly encourages students to live and study overseas. Students must be in good academic standing to participate and are required to carry a minimum credit load of 12 hours. Programs are offered on a regular basis in Australia, Austria, China, Costa Rica, Denmark, France, Germany, Great Britain, Ireland, Japan, Latvia, Mexico, Poland, Spain, and Sweden. Two percent of students participate in international study programs.

Support Services Services are available to students with disabilities and handicap conditions, including diagnosed learning disabilities. All academic buildings are handicapped-accessible, and students have a choice of accessible residence halls on both upper and lower campus.

Job Opportunities Work opportunities on campus include federal and non-federal work-study.

Tuition: $3471.70 for state residents, $12,111.70 for nonresidents, per academic year (2001–02)

Room and Board: Double room, $2150; food service, $1410

Mandatory Fees: $100

Contact: Director: Dr. Ronald E. Mickel, 209 Schneider Hall, Eau Claire, Wisconsin 54702-4004; Telephone: 715-836-3621; Fax: 715-836-2380; E-mail: mickelre@uwec.edu; Web site: http://www.uwec.edu/Admin/Honors/honors.htm

Interpreting the symbols: **2**=two-year college, **4**=four-year college; **Pu**=public or state college, **Pr**=private college; **G**=general honors program; **D**=departmental honors program; **S**=small program (fewer than 100 students), **M**=midsize program (100 to 500 students), **L**=large program (more than 500 students); **Sc**=scholarships available in honors program; **Tr**=transfer students accepted into honors program; **HBC**=historically black college; **AA**=academic advisors; **GA**=graduate advisors; **FA**=fellowship advisors.

UNIVERSITY OF WISCONSIN–MADISON

4 Pu G/D L Sc Tr

▼ College of Letters and Science Honors Program

The College of Letters and Science (L&S) Honors Program began in 1960 in response to a petition from 172 students asking the faculty to help challenge them more fully. The faculty legislation chartering the program states: "At the heart of our proposals is the creation of more challenge and opportunity, especially in terms of increased depth and breadth, and more freedom of initiative, for the top-notch students at all stages of their career." The profile of honors students is that 71 percent are from in state and 29 percent are from out of state, the average class rank is the 95th percentile, the average GPA is 3.87 on a scale of 4.00, the average ACT is 31.3, and the average SAT I is 1383. Beyond the raw statistics, students have participated in soccer, cross-country, tennis, track, football, basketball, skiing, Tae Kwon Do; have hiked 500 miles of the Appalachian Trail; acted in Shakespeare's plays; sung in musicals; played all the instruments in orchestra and band; performed service in Mexico and the Altiplano of Bolivia; and conducted workshops for SADD. Honors students are represented and led by their official Honors Student Organization, which organizes extracurricular field trips to the theater and to tour Frank Lloyd Wright homes in Oak Park and service activities for disadvantaged and minority students in the community. A weekly e-mail news bulletin apprises students of events and scholastic opportunities, such as funds for sophomore research apprenticeships and senior honors theses. Approximately 1,200 students are enrolled in the Letters and Science Honors Program.

Participation Requirements: Honors students work to complete the requirements for three different kinds of honors degrees that are available to students in the College of Letters and Science: Honors in the Liberal Arts, Honors in the Major, and Comprehensive Honors. Honors in the Liberal Arts is likely to be the primary focus for most first- and second-year students before they begin to concentrate on their majors. Honors in the Liberal Arts requires students to earn at least 24 honors credits (with a GPA of 3.3 or higher) in broadly distributed subjects ranging from the humanities to the social and natural sciences. Honors in the Major is the second type of honors offered by the College of Letters and Science. Its requirements can be completed independently from Honors in the Liberal Arts; neither is a prerequisite for the other. The curriculum for Honors in the Major is established by each academic department and program in the College. Students must apply to their major department for permission to enter this phase of the Honors Program. Requirements vary a great deal from department to department, but all are designed to culminate in a senior-year experience in which students are exposed to the cutting edge of that particular field. Many Honors in the Major students write an original research thesis, but, in some departments, students produce an original work of art, put on a performance, or complete a practicum in which they begin to act as professionals in their chosen field. Finally, Comprehensive Honors is awarded to those students who complete the requirements for both Honors in the Liberal Arts and Honors in the Major. Comprehensive Honors is the highest recognition that the College of Letters and Science can award an undergraduate, and students entering the program are urged to work toward this goal.

Admission Process: Admission to the Honors Program (which, for first-year students, means being admitted to pursue Honors in the Liberal Arts) is highly competitive. To apply, students should submit the L&S Honors application along with a 500-word essay describing the talents, experiences, and special qualities they are most eager to share with this community. Applications are accepted and read on a rolling basis, but there is normally a mid-May deadline. Because positions in the program are limited and the quality of applicants has been rising in recent years, the honors staff carefully considers all aspects of an applicant's record, including extracurricular activities. It is thus not possible to identify any one criterion that ensures admission to the program. In recent years, the average honors student has ranked in the 95th percentile of his or her high school class, has had a GPA of 3.9, and has had standardized test scores of 31 on the ACT and 1410 on the SAT I. Applications are encouraged from students who rank in the top 10 percent of their high school class and who have test scores of at least 30 on the ACT composite score or 1320 on the combined SAT I. Students from unranked high schools should have the appropriate test scores and a minimum high school GPA of 3.6 on a 4.0 scale. Sophomores, juniors, and transfer students with a minimum 3.3 GPA are considered for admission to Honors in the Liberal Arts based on their undergraduate course work, an essay, and a letter of recommendation from an instructor; in some cases, the Honors Dean may grant exceptions to these admissions criteria. Students applying to complete Honors in the Major must consult with the honors adviser in their major department to learn the admissions process and requirements. Students must maintain at least a 3.3 cumulative GPA to remain in the Honors Program.

Scholarship Availability: The Honors Program annually administers a number of awards and scholarships in support of undergraduate research. Burack Scholarships help support honors students in the University of Wisconsin (UW) Academic Year Abroad program, and students can earn honors credit for course work done on UW study-abroad programs. Every summer Sophomore Research Apprenticeship grants support 30 undergraduates who learn how to conduct original scholarly and scientific investigations while working alongside some of UW's outstanding research faculty members. Trewartha and Honors Thesis Research Grants support research during the academic year and also in the summer, when students often have more time to concentrate on their projects. In addition, many honors students win prestigious, University-wide Hilldale Research Fellowships.

The Campus Context: UW–Madison's campus was originally intended by Madison planners in the 1830s to be a municipal cemetery. Now the University claims more than 900 acres of picturesque grounds along Lake Mendota, the largest of Madison's lakes. Bascom Hall, the University's main administrative building, serves as a centerpiece to campus. It sits atop Bascom Hill, exactly 1 mile west, along historic State Street, of the State Capitol. Points of interest on campus include North Hall, the first building on the campus; Carillon Tower in front of the Social Science Building; the Library Mall, with its clock tower and fountain; Picnic Point, a peninsula of woods, trails, and beaches that juts out into Lake Mendota; Science Hall and the Armory-Gymnasium on Langdon Street, both National Historic Landmarks; and the Memorial Union, whose lakefront terrace offers a popular meeting place for students and the community. South of campus and along the shores of Lake Wingra lies the UW Arboretum, which features natural and restored samples of Wisconsin plant and animal life. Before the city of Madison existed, the lakeshore site where UW–Madison is now located was an Indian encampment. Indian effigy mounds—many in the shape of animals—still are evident around the campus. Madison, with a population of 201,786 (1997 estimate), was rated the best place to live in the nation by *Money* magazine's annual survey in 1996. UW–Madison was founded in 1848. The calendar is by semester and current enrollment is 41,219. The Chancellor is John Wiley. The main campus consists of 933 acres. There are also 2,354 acres of off-campus properties, 6,100 acres of experimental research stations, and a 1,262-acre arboretum. Undergraduates have 146 majors to choose from. There are 4,546 courses to enroll in. The University has forty-five libraries with more than 5.4 million volumes.

Student Body Enrollment is 41,219. There are 28,476 undergraduates, of whom 5,919 are freshmen, 6,231 are sophomores, 7,375 juniors, 8,951 seniors, 8,620 graduate students, and 2,374 professional students. There are 1,749 special students. Of the total enrollment, 19,769 are men and 21,450 are women. Wisconsin residents number 26,093.

Faculty UW–Madison has 2,175 faculty members with terminal degrees and 5,918 academic staff members.

Key Facilities Libraries, formerly the exclusive province of page-turners and card-flippers, have now been overrun by keyboard-tappers. Users can now access not only the electronic catalog of UW–Madison holdings but also databases that encompass other galaxies of information. One of the benefits of a large university is the sheer size of its library holdings: UW–Madison offers 5.5 million volumes in more than fifty locations plus access to 30 million citations through databases. In fact, so many people beat a path to the library doors, real and electronic, that UW–Madison is the second-largest interlibrary lender in North America. In recent years the technology of learning at UW–Madison has been transformed with head-spinning speed. With the support of the Division of Information Technology (DoIT), faculty members are creating and using software programs that tangibly improve teaching. Applications range from modeling complex molecular structures to understanding how the inner ear works to composing musical harmonies. E-mail accounts that enable students to communicate via computers with professors and other students are available to everyone on campus. Students are encouraged to access the Internet and cruise for information of all sorts, from the latest physics research done in Denmark to meteorological reports from Alaska. All students who own personal computers, and more than half of them do, can log on to campus network services from home. Students also have access to 16 on-campus labs with 1,000 computers. In addition, all student rooms in residence halls feature computer connections to the campus network and Internet—no modem or trek to a computer lab is necessary.

Honorary Societies Beta Alpha Psa, Golden Key, Mortar Board, National Society of Collegiate Scholars/NSCS (UW), Order of Omega, Phi Eta Sigma, Phi Kappa Phi, Phi Lambda Sigma, and Pi Tau Sigma (Wisconsin Alpha Chapter)

Athletics UW–Madison has more than nine athletic facilities available. Football, basketball, hockey, softball, tennis, swimming and diving, track, and other sports are all professionally played. For details on UW athletics, students should visit http://www.wisc.edu/ath/athdep/index.html.

Study Abroad Each year, through the Office of International Studies and Programs (OISP) alone, about 400 students study abroad at fifty-one sites in thirty-three countries. They can study Chinese in Beijing, Chilean history in Santiago, and French literature in Aix-en-Provence. They can also go abroad by staying home and choosing courses form nine area studies programs or signing up for one of the forty languages offered each semester, from ancient Egyptian to Zulu. In 1993, OISP established an Undergraduate Travel Awards fellowship program for students enrolling in its overseas programs. With additional funds from the College of Letters and Science, OISP granted fifty travel awards of $1500 to students planning to study abroad in 1994–95. The office also coordinates campuswide fellowships for overseas study, including the Fulbright Program and the National Security Education Program (for both graduate and undergraduate students). In 1993, UW–Madison ranked sixth in the nation in its number of Fulbright graduate-student grantees. Although the Office of International Studies and Programs sends the largest number of UW–Madison students overseas every year, there are several other campus programs that serve specialized needs within the professional schools. These programs offer courses, internships, externships, and other practical experiences that are consistent with education and training for their particular fields. The number of study-abroad programs within the professional schools is increasing along with the growing need for international training and experience in the professions.

Support Services The McBurney Center and TRIO Learning Support Services programs offer support and services for handicapped and learning disabled students. Tutoring, access, and many other services are provided.

Job Opportunities UW–Madison offers innumerable research assistantships and job opportunities through departments such as the Career Advising and Planning Service, the Student Job Center, and the Undergraduate Research Scholars Program as well as many online resource listings.

Tuition: $3791 for full-time residents, per year (2000–01)

Room and board: $5470

Contact: Director: Cyrena Pondrom, 415 South Hall, 1055 Bascom Mall, Madison, Wisconsin 53706; Telephone: 608-262-2984; Fax: 608-263-7126; E-mail: honors@lssaa.wisc.edu; Web site: http://www.lssaa.wisc.edu/honors/

University of Wisconsin–Milwaukee

4 Pu G L Sc Tr

▼ University Honors Program

Established in 1960 within the College of Letters and Science, the University Honors Program became University-wide in 1982. It brings together outstanding students and faculty from all University of Wisconsin–Milwaukee (UWM) schools and colleges. Committed to the importance of the liberal arts, the program offers small discussion seminar classes that provide many of the benefits of a small liberal arts college at a large metropolitan university. It attracts some of the most talented students from the University's various schools and colleges.

Honors classes differ from regular classes at UWM in that they are small interactive seminars. With a maximum of about 15 students each, honors seminars are conducted in an atmosphere of openness and intellectual exchange. Exploring fundamental works in the humanities, arts, natural sciences, and social sciences, the seminars generate lively discussion of major issues and problems. No examinations are given. Instead, students are encouraged to think critically about important questions and to explore these questions through writing. Grades are based on the quality of each student's written and oral work.

In 1991, the Honors Program received a Bradley Foundation grant funding 3 visiting assistant professors to teach exclusively in the program for three-year terms. The Bradley Professors have strengthened a strong undergraduate teaching program by providing continuity for the curriculum and personal attention to students. In addition to the Bradley Professors, some of UWM's best teachers and scholars teach regularly in the program, offering undergraduates the opportunity to work with faculty members often available only to graduate students. The Honors Program seeks to bring to a public institution the same level of excellence in liberal arts that is associated with the country's best private colleges.

Approximately 500 students are currently participating in the program.

Participation Requirements: The honors curriculum comprises introductory humanities seminars with variable topics (e.g., The Shaping of the Modern Mind); honors calculus; upper-level

Interpreting the symbols: **2**=two-year college, **4**=four-year college; **Pu**=public or state college, **Pr**=private college; **G**=general honors program; **D**=departmental honors program; **S**=small program (fewer than 100 students), **M**=midsize program (100 to 500 students), **L**=large program (more than 500 students); **Sc**=scholarships available in honors program; **Tr**=transfer students accepted into honors program; **HBC**=historically black college; **AA**=academic advisors; **GA**=graduate advisors; **FA**=fellowship advisors.

seminars in humanities, social and natural sciences, and the arts; independent study; research; study abroad; and an optional senior thesis or project. Students can major in any area. Honors students fulfill many of their general education requirements (GER) through honors seminars. They can also use upper-level honors credits to fulfill major requirements. Students may remain in the program as long as they maintain a strong B average. In order to graduate with an honors degree, students must have a 3.5 GPA overall at time of graduation and complete 21 honors credits.

All students successfully completing the program receive an Honors Degree—a special diploma with "Honors" or "Honors with Thesis" distinction, which is reflected on their transcripts. Finally, they receive a certificate at a formal graduation reception in May.

Admission Process: Students may be admitted as freshmen or continuing students. Freshmen are recruited from students who graduate in the top 20 percent of their high school class and have high scores on the Wisconsin English Placement Test and the ACT. Continuing and transfer students enter the program as freshmen or sophomores based on a college GPA of 3.4 or higher. Because UWM is a commuter campus, many honors students are returning students who work full- or part-time while carrying challenging academic loads. Others are top students from local high schools. This diversity is part of the program's strength.

Scholarship Availability: One or more Honors Program Scholarships of $1000 to $1500 are available to honors seniors. The Milwaukee Braves/Fred Miller Scholarship provides four-year support of $850 per semester. The William F. Halloran Scholarship offers $500 to a freshman in the Honors Program. The Langston Hughes Scholarship provides two awards of $1000 each to support African-American students in the Honors Program. The KleinOsowski Scholarship awards $500 to qualified students in engineering or the natural sciences.

The Campus Context: The University of Wisconsin–Milwaukee is a campus of eleven schools and colleges: School of Allied Health Professions, School of Architecture and Urban Planning, School of Business Administration, School of Education, College of Engineering and Applied Science, School of Fine Arts, College of Letters and Science, School of Library and Information Science, School of Nursing, School of Social Welfare, and Graduate School. Eighty undergraduate majors, forty-six master's programs, and seventeen Ph.D. programs are offered on campus. UWM is the only school in Wisconsin to offer a nationally accredited professional degree in architecture and one of only fifteen schools in North America to offer the Ph.D. program in architecture.

Among distinguished facilities on campus are the School of Business Administration (1995), considered the most technologically advanced building in the University of Wisconsin System; Center for Business Competitiveness; Institute of Chamber Music; Center for Great Lakes Studies; Professional Theatre Training Program; Laboratory for Surface Studies; Center for Teacher Education; Center for Twentieth Century Studies; and the Women's Studies Consortium.

Student Body Undergraduate enrollment is approximately 23,800 and is 55.6 percent women. The ethnic distribution of students is 8.4 percent black, 2.1 percent Asian, .8 percent Indian, 3.8 percent Hispanic, 1.8 percent Southeast Asian, and 80.3 percent white. There are 673 international students (2.8 percent of the population). Of the total number of students, 91.2 percent are commuters, and approximately 55 percent receive financial aid.

Faculty Of the 1,333 faculty and instructional staff members, 784 are full-time. The student-faculty ratio is 19.2:1.

Key Facilities The library contains nearly 5 million bibliographical listings, more than 1 million book titles, and 1.2 million volumes. The Golda Meir Library is the second-largest academic library in Wisconsin and houses the American Geographical Society Collection, the largest privately owned geographical research collection in the Western Hemisphere. Computer facilities include eight general access labs open for student use as well as computer labs within individual schools and colleges with approximately 1,400 student workstations. The labs provide IBM, IBM-compatible, and Macintosh computers. The Sandburg Residence Hall rooms are wired for network access. Campus computers are linked to WiscNet, a statewide higher education network that includes other campuses of the UW System; CICNet, which includes the Big-10 institutions; and the Internet and the National Information Infrastructure.

Honorary Societies Phi Eta Sigma, Phi Kappa Phi, Golden Key, Mortar Board, and Phi Beta Kappa

Athletics UWM students are eligible to participate in sixteen intercollegiate sports, or they can get their exercise in numerous intramural and club sports. UWM is a member of the Midwestern Collegiate Conference, one of the top NCAA Division I athletic conferences in the country. UWM competes in basketball, cross-country, soccer, swimming, track, and volleyball for men and women and in men's baseball and women's tennis.

Study Abroad Students have the opportunity to participate in study-abroad programs coordinated through the Center for International Education. Architecture and urban planning students may attend a spring semester program in Paris or a summer program in Oxford, England. Fine arts students can take drawing and painting during the spring semester in Paris and study in Florence or Paris in the summer.

Support Services The Student Accessibility Center (SAC) promotes access to educational programming for UWM students with disabilities. Services are made available according to the student's individual needs. Students with disabilities are encouraged to contact SAC upon acceptance to UWM. To ensure that appropriate accommodations are provided, SAC relies on the medical and diagnostic reports that students provide.

Job Opportunities There are more than 1,500 student employment positions on campus.

Tuition: $4056 for state residents, $14,868 for nonresidents (2001–02)

Room and Board: $3636 minimum

Mandatory Fees: $594

Contact: Director: Professor Lawrence Baldassaro, 302 Garland Hall, P.O. Box 413, Milwaukee, Wisconsin 53201; Telephone: 414-229-4658 or 414-229-4636; Fax: 414-229-6070; E-mail: honorweb@csd.uwm.edu; Web site: http://www.uwm.edu/Dept/Honors

University of Wisconsin–Oshkosh

4 Pu G M Tr

▼ University Honors Program

The University Honors Program at the University of Wisconsin–Oshkosh offers a challenging and enriching academic experience to undergraduates who have clearly demonstrated their commitment to academic excellence. The curriculum of the University Honors Program has a 19-credit requirement built around several interdisciplinary courses and designated general education courses taught by selected faculty members.

Courses in the University Honors Program are limited to 25 students but average about half that number. About twelve honors courses are offered each semester to University Honors Program students, who have early registration privileges. Special orientation and registration workshops are held for all University Honors Program students.

Honors courses and the faculty members who teach them are selected by the University Honors Program Committee, composed of faculty representatives from the four colleges and students in the University Honors Student Association. All University Honors Program students must also attend a cultural event and file an activities report each semester they are in the program.

In addition to this curriculum, the University Honors Program emphasizes participation in the broader life of the University and community. The University Honors Student Association organizes recreational programs, a lecture series (Pizza with Professors), and field trips to cultural sites in the region. Students in the program are encouraged to participate in the Upper Midwest Honors Conference, held each spring.

The program has been in operation since 1981. There are currently 300 active students in the program. The University limits the number of University Honors Program students to no more than 5 percent of the undergraduate student enrollment.

Participation Requirements: All University Honors Program students enroll in the following courses, a total of 7 academic credits: honors seminar (3 credits), a thematic interdisciplinary seminar for new University Honors Program students; Culture Connection (1 credit), a cultural activities course modeled on a tutorial that involves writing assignments under the direction of honors readers; and either an honors senior thesis (3 credits), a thesis or project unique to the University Honors Program but earning credit in a student's major field of study, or an honors senior seminar (3 credits), an interdisciplinary capstone course. The remaining 12 academic credits are earned in sections of general education courses that are offered exclusively for University Honors Program students.

University Honors Program students must maintain a minimum GPA to remain in good standing: first-year students, 3.2/4.0; sophomores, 3.3/4.0; juniors and seniors, 3.4/4.0; and 3.5/4.0 to receive University Honors. Graduating students present their senior thesis projects at an Honors Thesis Symposium. At an awards ceremony held at the end of each semester, graduates receive a University Honors Program medallion, which they wear at the University's graduation ceremony. The University Chancellor presents the medallion to each University Honors Program graduate in an assembly of University faculty and staff members, administrators, and students' families and friends. The designation of Scholar Graduate—University Honors Program appears on the graduate's official transcript.

Admission Process: All students who are in the top 10 percent of their high school graduating class and who have an ACT composite score of 26 or better are automatically eligible for admission, as are all high school valedictorians and National Merit Scholars. Entering students who meet only one of these criteria may send a letter to the director requesting admission to the program explaining why special consideration is warranted in their case and enclosing a copy of their high school transcript. Second-semester students who achieved a specific GPA requirement during their first semester are invited to participate in the University Honors Program without regard to high school standing or ACT score. Approximately 70 students per year enter the program by means of their grade point averages.

Scholarship Availability: There are no scholarships specifically for University Honors Program students, though University Honors Program students receive a wide range of academic achievement scholarships. As of 2002, the University has increased the number of scholarships.

The Campus Context: The University of Wisconsin–Oshkosh is a campus of four colleges: the Colleges of Letters and Science, Education and Human Services, Business Administration, and Nursing. Fifty-one undergraduate degree programs are offered. One third of the undergraduates live on campus and another one third live independently within walking distance of campus.

Student Body The student body is 59 percent women. European Americans constitute 96 percent of enrolled students; the remaining 4 percent are Hispanic, African American, Asian American, and American Indian. About 80 to 100 international students are enrolled annually. About 85 percent of the students are residents, and approximately 65 percent of undergraduates receive some form of financial aid. There are thirteen fraternities and sororities and numerous student organizations active in the Oshkosh Student Association.

Faculty Of the 529 faculty members, 344 are full-time. Ninety-seven percent of full-time faculty members have terminal degrees. The student-faculty ratio is 18:1.

Key Facilities The library houses 425,000 volumes and has electronic access to 6,000 books. It subscribes to 1,800 current periodicals in paper and has access to 6,000 full-text periodicals. General access computer labs are located in six academic buildings. Many computer labs are available. Four buildings contain IBM computer labs. These labs have a combined total of 390 Windows-based computers and sixty Macintosh computers. Hardware is upgraded every three years; software is upgraded annually. Each residence hall also has computer labs. These labs have a combined total of 120 computers, both Windows-based and Macintosh. The English department has a teaching computer lab, and the library has computers for Web and Internet reference and accessing holdings of the University's library and other libraries in the state.

Athletics For spectators and competitors, the nineteen-sport intercollegiate athletic program offers a wide variety of opportunities to University students. The athletic program is a member of the National Collegiate Athletic Association (NCAA) Division III. The men's and women's sports programs are members of the Wisconsin Intercollegiate Athletic Conference. Men's sports include baseball, basketball, cross-country, football, soccer, swimming and diving, tennis, track and field (indoor and outdoor), and wrestling. Women's sports include basketball, cross-country, golf, gymnastics, soccer, softball, swimming and diving, tennis, track and field (indoor and outdoor), and volleyball.

Study Abroad The University encourages study abroad. The four colleges offer increasing numbers of opportunities to do so and help students arrange study abroad through programs sponsored by UW System institutions and other universities.

Support Features Disabled students will find that the campus is handicapped-accessible. Some residence halls and all classrooms are designed to be accessible. Buildings have a designated entrance with electronic openers for accessibility. Bathrooms are near classrooms. A lounge with computers is designated for students with disabilities.

Job Opportunities Every department is allocated money for student assistants and work-study positions. The University is the largest employer of students in the area. The number of jobs available on campus consistently outnumbers the students available for work.

Tuition and Fees: $6456 for state residents, $23,480 for nonresidents, $3560 compact reciprocity fee for Minnesota residents, per year (2001–02)

Room and Board: $3816

Contact: Director: Dr. William Baurecht, University Honors Program, Polk 8, 800 Algoma Boulevard, Oshkosh, Wisconsin 54901-8654; Assistant Director: Ms. Carey Molinski, Telephone: 920-424-1303; Fax: 920-424-7317; E-mail: baurecht@uwosh.edu, molinski@uwosh.edu; Web site: http://www.uwosh.edu/honors

---

Interpreting the symbols: **2**=two-year college, **4**=four-year college; **Pu**=public or state college, **Pr**=private college; **G**=general honors program; **D**=departmental honors program; **S**=small program (fewer than 100 students), **M**=midsize program (100 to 500 students), **L**=large program (more than 500 students); **Sc**=scholarships available in honors program; **Tr**=transfer students accepted into honors program; **HBC**=historically black college; **AA**=academic advisors; **GA**=graduate advisors; **FA**=fellowship advisors.

UNIVERSITY OF WISCONSIN–STOUT

4 Pu G M Tr

▼ University Honors Program

The University Honors Program (UHP) at the University of Wisconsin–Stout (UW–Stout) aims to enhance the undergraduate experience of highly motivated and talented students. Four Honors Seminars, four Honors Contracts, and biannual Honors Colloquia provide a framework in which students deepen and broaden their general education and their major studies in concert with other engaged students and committed faculty members. In the seminars, students use primary sources to explore fundamental problems in the disciplines; the capstone Seminar in Service explicitly challenges students to connect their learning with their responsibilities as educated citizens. In Honors Contracts, students select a professor with whom they design a project based on their own interest and curiosity. In Honors Colloquia, students and faculty members of the UHP join to study and debate issues that intersect scholarship and civic responsibility. The UHP Student Association conducts social activities and aids in UHP policy formation. Involvement in state, regional, and national honors activities provides students with opportunities to present and discuss their research and to meet other motivated students. UHP students bring diverse personal, intellectual, and professional interests to the program; through their participation in the UHP, they bridge their differences and create a sense of community within the University.

The UHP began in 1994. Approximately 130 students, representing each of Stout's major programs, are enrolled in the University Honors Program.

Participation Requirements: The University Honors Program requires 23 honors credits. Students earn 11 of these credits in Honors Seminars and 12 through Honors Contracts. All but 3 of these honors credits fulfill the University's general education requirements. Students also join with faculty members in Honors Colloquia held each semester. To graduate from the UHP, students must maintain a minimum 3.0 GPA in Honors Seminars and at least a 3.25 overall GPA. UHP graduates are recognized at graduation, and successful completion of the UHP is noted on each student's diploma and transcript.

Admission Process: First-year students who rank in the top 10 percent of their high school class and those who rank in the top 10 percent of Stout's ACT scores are invited to join the UHP upon acceptance to the University. Other first-year, transfer, and nontraditional students may apply for admission. Factors considered in application admissions decisions include the student's special skills and accomplishments, motivation for learning, teacher recommendations, and past academic performance. Applications are considered up to the sixth week of class each semester. Admissions decisions are made by the UHP Director and the UHP Advisory Committee.

Scholarship Availability: The UHP does not administer scholarships. The UW–Stout Foundation does, however, award a number of scholarships for which UHP students are uniquely qualified.

The Campus Context: The University of Wisconsin–Stout was founded in 1891 by the progressive educator and legislator, James Huff Stout. Stout's philosophy of hands-on, minds-on learning is seen today in a curriculum that integrates liberal learning with specialized career preparation as well as in the quality and quantity of student-faculty interaction. The twenty-seven undergraduate programs, many among the largest of their kind, are housed in three colleges. In 2001, UW–Stout became the first university to be awarded the Malcolm Baldrige National Quality Award. Stout becomes a laptop campus in fall 2002.

Stout's hands-on, minds-on approach to learning ensures that students are challenged to apply what they are learning. In addition to traditional research and writing, each Stout student produces class projects every semester, often as a member of a collaborative team. The result is a University that brims with student creativity and productivity and a friendly campus atmosphere grounded in students' shared learning experiences.

Located in Menomonie, on the shores of Lake Menomin and near the banks of the Red Cedar River, the Stout campus is 75 miles east of Minneapolis–St. Paul. Interstate 94 provides easy access to the cultural riches of the Twin Cities, while two-lane country roads lead through the rolling Knapp Hills and the waterways invite exploration of the area's natural beauty. In their free hours, Stout students might be found cross-country skiing, trout fishing, or traveling to a gallery opening in Minneapolis.

The UHP is located at the center of campus in Harvey Hall, the second-oldest building on campus.

Student Body Undergraduate enrollment is 7,162; 49 percent of the students are women. The minority ethnic distribution for the campus is .45 percent Native American, .89 percent African American, .45 percent Hispanic, and 1.65 percent Asian American. Thirty-seven percent of the students live in University housing. Seven percent of students are between 25 and 29 years of age, and 7 percent are 30 years of age and older. Sixty-five percent of students receive financial aid. The campus has 120 student organizations, including five fraternities and five sororities.

Faculty Full- and part-time instructional faculty members number 367. Of the full-time faculty members, 77 percent have the terminal degree in their discipline, and most Stout faculty members bring professional job experience to their work in the classroom. The student-faculty ratio is 21:1.

Key Facilities The Library Learning Center houses 223,000 volumes, 1,022,730 microforms, 15,000 audio and visual titles, and 1,530 journal subscriptions. There are 130 laboratories on campus and more than 400 computer workstations in specialized and open-access laboratories and dormitories. A HELP desk is available for assistance with computer problems. Dorm rooms are wired for Internet access; off-campus students receive free Internet access through the University server.

Athletics Johnson Fieldhouse and the new Williams Stadium are home to fourteen men's and women's intercollegiate sports, club sports, the intramural program, and two climbing walls. Fieldhouse facilities are in use daily from early morning to late night for instruction, intercollegiate and intramural sports, and open recreation. UW–Stout competes in the Wisconsin Intercollegiate Athletic Conference in NCAA Division III.

Study Abroad Through UW–Stout's International Programs office, UHP students participate in study-abroad programs and internships around the world. The University has special programs in Scotland, England, Mexico, Germany, Australia, and Sweden.

Support Services All campus classrooms and offices and two blocks of residence halls are accessible to physically disabled students. The presence of Stout's renowned program in Vocational Rehabilitation has long ensured the participation of disabled students in University activities. The Office of Services for Students with Disabilities provides an array of services and programs for learning disabled students.

Job Opportunities Each of Stout's distinctive major programs strives to integrate the world of work into the undergraduate experience. Work opportunities are available on and off campus. Most Stout students complete an internship or a cooperative learning experience during their undergraduate study; many complete both. For the last eighteen years, more than 90 percent of Stout graduates have found employment in a field related to their majors; in 1999–2000, 269 companies recruited graduating seniors and 327 companies recruited co-op students.

Tuition and Fees: $3502.08 for Wisconsin residents, $3694.08 for Minnesota residents, $12,026 for nonresidents, per year (2001–02)

Room and Board: $2938–$3254

Contact: Director: Dr. Robert Horan, 140 Harvey Hall, Menomonie, Wisconsin 54751-0790; Telephone: 715-232-1476; Fax: 715-232-1346; E-mail: horanr@uwstout.edu

UNIVERSITY OF WYOMING

4 Pu G L Sc Tr AA GA FA

▼ University Honors Program

For students with wide-ranging curiosity and a passion for learning, the University of Wyoming Honors Program offers a sequence of five challenging core courses, a senior independent research project, a variety of extracurricular activities, and optional housing within a campus residence hall or in the newly remodeled Honors House. Additional benefits include substantial scholarships for resident and nonresident students and for study abroad, support for travel to conferences, and special recognition on the transcript and at graduation.

Honors core courses are limited to 18 or 20 students, taught by some of the University's best faculty members, and designed to bring together talented students from all majors. Courses are innovative and interdisciplinary, set up to encourage a sense of community among the participants. Like other UW students, an Honors Program participant follows a course of study leading to a degree in one of the six undergraduate colleges and eighty-five majors. Honors courses count toward general education requirements.

The honors senior research project, initiated in the junior year and developed through the senior year, focuses on a topic chosen by the student and explored with the help of a faculty specialist. Projects in the creative arts, as well as more traditional experiments and analyses, are encouraged. By developing a strong competence in research or an area in the creative arts, an honors student gives his or her undergraduate education a highly individual stamp. The senior project often leads directly into graduate studies or a special career path.

Honors courses and faculty members are selected each year by the student-faculty Honors Advisory Committee from proposals invited from all faculty at the University. Honors faculty members need to demonstrate a strong record of innovative and effective teaching. The Wyoming Honors Program was initiated in 1958 and now enrolls 632 students.

Participation Requirements: In order to graduate with the University Honors Program, a student must maintain a 3.25 GPA and complete five seminars and the senior independent project, totaling 18 semester credit hours. Students who complete the program are recognized at graduation with a gold stole and a designation on their transcript and diploma.

Admission Process: To join the program as a freshman, a student must meet one of three criteria: a composite ACT score of 28, a combined SAT score of 1240, or a high school GPA of 3.7. Strong students who do not meet one of these criteria should write to the program director and explain their reasons for wishing to participate.

Transfer students may join the program if they have two years or more of course work remaining. They must have a transfer GPA of 3.25.

All applications are reviewed, and priority is given to those received before February 10.

Scholarship Availability: Scholar's Stipends in the amount of resident tuition and fees are awarded for four years to 18 incoming freshmen, regardless of residency. Nonresident and nontraditional students may compete for University of Wyoming Dr. Scholl Foundation Scholarships. Boyd Special Academic Opportunities Scholarships assist enrolled students who plan to study in an off-campus setting, such as international exchanges, internships, exchanges at other U.S. universities, and independent research travel. Several other scholarships are awarded every year.

The Campus Context: Founded in 1886, the University of Wyoming is a land-grant institution and the state's only university. The 785-acre campus in Laramie, a town of 27,000, lies at 7.200 feet in the southeastern corner of the state. Located between two mountain ranges and within 2 hours of Denver, the campus and the community offer access to a great many outdoor activities and cultural opportunities. Notable research collections can be found in the Rocky Mountain Herbarium, the Departments of Anthropology and Geology, the Art Museum, the Insect Museum, and the American Heritage Center. Undergraduate research is strongly encouraged and well supported. The Colleges of Agriculture, Arts and Sciences, Business, Education, Engineering, and Health Sciences offer a wide range of liberal arts and professional degrees. Students can also earn degrees through the School of Environment and Natural Resources, create a self-designed major, complete a B.A. and an M.B.A. in a five-year program, or earn a professional pharmacy degree in six years.

Student Body Undergraduate enrollment in 2000 was 8,550 and growing. The student body's ethnic distribution is 92 percent Caucasian, 3 percent Hispanic, 1 percent African American, 1 percent American Indian, 1 percent Asian American, and 2 percent other. International students (2 percent) come from fifty-three countries. Seventy-five percent of freshmen receive financial aid, and that figure rises to 82 percent for continuing students. The large majority of students live on campus or within a 3-mile radius. Ten fraternities and four sororities offer alternatives to the residence halls and housing in the community.

Faculty There are 596 full-time faculty members, of whom 84 percent hold a doctorate, 2 percent a J.D., and 11 percent the master's or other appropriate degree. The student-faculty ratio is 13.7 to 1.

Key Facilities University libraries hold more than 1.2 million volumes, 13,000 periodical and serial titles, an extensive collection of books and documents in microform, and a library of 165,000 maps. Special collections and rare books are housed at the American Heritage Center, with more that 7,000 primary files in the areas of popular culture, western history, transportation, business history, and conservation. Students also have fast access to the world of the Web. Every room in the residence halls and the Honors House provides no-fee access to the Internet, and the Honors Program has two computer labs. In addition, thirty-three other computer pods are available to students.

Honorary Societies Chapters of several general honorary societies recognize academic excellence at the University of Wyoming, including Phi Kappa Phi, Golden Key, Mortar Board, and Phi Beta Kappa.

Athletics Competing in NCAA Division 1-A and the Mountain West Conference, the University of Wyoming supports men's teams in basketball, cross-country, football, golf, swimming and diving, track, and wrestling. Women's teams compete in basketball, cross-country, golf, soccer, swimming and diving, tennis, track, and volleyball.

Study Abroad An extensive roster of exchange programs are available to honors students, including special bilateral exchanges with universities in the United Kingdom, France, Mexico, Germany, Russia, Denmark, and the Netherlands. Every spring the London Semester teams Wyoming and British faculty members for three months of classes and field trips in one of the world's cultural capitals.

Interpreting the symbols: 2=two-year college, **4**=four-year college; **Pu**=public or state college, **Pr**=private college; **G**=general honors program; **D**=departmental honors program; **S**=small program (fewer than 100 students), **M**=midsize program (100 to 500 students), **L**=large program (more than 500 students); **Sc**=scholarships available in honors program; **Tr**=transfer students accepted into honors program; **HBC**=historically black college; **AA**=academic advisors; **GA**=graduate advisors; **FA**=fellowship advisors.

Support Services University Disability Support Service provides a variety of accommodations and services for students with physical, cognitive, and psychological disabilities.

Job Opportunities Many honors students help with educational expenses through Federal Work-Study jobs, other campus employment, undergraduate research assistantships, and internships. Jobs in the community are readily available.

Tuition and Fees: Resident tuition for 2001–02 is $2316; nonresidents pay $7788. Various tuition reduction plans for nonresidents provide benefits up to $4000 and are awarded on the basis of high school GPA.

Room and Board: Room and board rates are flexible, but the standard charge is $4744.

Mandatory Fees: Fees were $49 in 2001–02.

Contact: Director: Duncan Harris, Honors Center, Merica Hall 102, Box 3413, University of Wyoming, Laramie, Wyoming 82071; Telephone: 307-766-4110; Fax: 307-766-4298; E-mail: honors@uwyo.edu; Web site: http://www.uwadmnweb.uwyo.edu.Honors/default.htm

Utah State University

4 Pu G M Sc Tr

▼ Honors Program

Utah State University's Honors Program, established in 1965, provides a distinctive academic environment for highly motivated undergraduates. Honors is not organized as a separate college or department; its members do not take on additional general education requirements; and students do not major in honors. At Utah State, honors is a program woven through the University's colleges and departments that allows students to do enhanced class work in a portion of their general education and upper-division courses.

Honors students work in smaller classes; they pursue their studies in greater depth; and they enjoy closer contact with professors. Members of the program may take intensive seminars, experimental classes, and interdisciplinary courses. They gain honors credit on their transcripts and work toward one of three honors degrees options.

Honors courses feature the University's leading professors, active student participation, and diverse class experiences. The courses emphasize the development of a student's skills in writing, speaking, and critical thinking. Students earn honors credits in honors-dedicated courses, which are composed entirely of honors students and feature small class size, with every class meeting offering accelerated course material. Enrollment for these classes is limited to honors students and honors-eligible students. Upper-division honors students enrolled in a department honors plan may also use honors contracts to earn honors credit in course work leading to an honors degree.

The Honors Program serves students who work hard, who raise questions, and who seek answers. It is designed for those who want to go beyond minimum requirements and narrow specialties. The program benefits students who want to make the most of their University experience. Its members form a community of scholars whose curiosity, creativity, and enthusiasm for learning foster educational achievement and personal growth.

Where students start in the Honors Program depends largely on the status of their general education course requirements. Students who need to complete general education course work begin with the orientation course (1 credit, pass/fail, fall semester), which provides the information students need to start working in honors. Students who have completed their general education course work begin by applying for admission to a department honors plan (in which students will complete a portion of their upper-division course work for honors credit).

The program is 32 years old and currently enrolls 400 students.

Participation Requirements: Students may work toward one of three honors degree options. These are University Honors with Department Honors, which requires 30 total honors credits in lower-division courses selected from the honors course list and upper-division courses within an official department honors plan and includes the creation and presentation of a senior thesis/project and seminar; Department Honors, which requires 15 total honors credits in upper-division courses within an official department honors plan and includes the creation and presentation of a senior thesis/project and seminar; and University Honors, which requires 30 total honors credits in lower-division courses selected from the honors course list and an individually designed upper-division plan and includes the creation and presentation of a senior thesis/project and seminar.

Admission Process: A limited number of entering freshmen are invited to join the Honors Program each year. These are students who have been awarded University Club Scholarships, Quinney Scholarships, Sterling Scholarships, Presidential Academic Scholarships, and those who have been named National Merit Finalists or Semi-Finalists. Students with university transcripts (transfer or re-entry students or students with concurrent enrollment credit) must have a minimum cumulative GPA of 3.5 to join the program. There are no extra fees. Once in the program, honors students must maintain a minimum GPA of 3.5.

Others may join the Honors Program upon completion of 24 graded semester credits with a cumulative GPA of at least 3.5. Credits earned in concurrent enrollment courses or credits transferred from other institutions apply when they have been posted on the Utah State University (USU) record. AP credits do not count toward this requirement. When a student has achieved the necessary number of credits and GPA, she or he should petition to join the program by submitting a personal letter of intent plus a letter of recommendation from a University professor.

Students admitted to the program are eligible to register for honors classes. Those who plan to complete honors degrees should plan to take at least one honors course every semester to fulfill the degree requirements.

Scholarship Availability: The Morse Honors Scholarship, named in honor of the former director of the USU Honors program and the former provost of USU, is a $600 scholarship available to Honors Program students with a minimum 3.5 cumulative GPA who have been accepted into a department honors plan (or an individually designed plan for University Honors). The key criterion is the promise of outstanding academic achievement (as indicated by record in honors courses, proposed honors senior project, and GPA). Financial need is also considered. The application includes a statement of academic objectives, honors program activities, senior project proposal, postgraduation plans, and other scholarship and/or financial aid information. The deadline is mid-April.

The Campus Context: Utah State University was founded in 1888 as the state's land-grant college. The 400-acre campus, with 100 buildings, is located a magnificent valley of northern Utah, in the city of Logan, the county seat of Cache County. USU is made up of a School of Graduate Studies and eight colleges: Agriculture, Business, Education, Engineering, Family Life, Humanities, Arts, and Social Sciences, Natural Resources, and Science. Undergraduates may choose from more than forty-five department majors.

USU sponsors a wide range of cultural activities appealing to the community, including the Performing Arts professional concert series; Arts and Lectures Series; Festival of the American West and Great West Fair; Irving Wassermann Festival; Ronald V. Jensen Living Historical Farm; Nora Eccles Harrison Museum of Art;

Old Lyric Repertory Theatre; USU Theatre; department recitals, concerts, and exhibits in art, dance and music; and Utah Festival Opera.

Student Body Enrollment is approximately 19,900 students. Students are from every county in Utah, all other states, Puerto Rico, and sixty-nine other countries. Eighty-six percent of students are Utah residents. More than 120 organizations offer special interest and social activities and a sense of belonging for USU students, such as preprofessional and honorary societies, residence halls, and eleven fraternities and sororities.

Faculty There are 809 faculty members at USU, creating a 25:1 student-faculty ratio.

Key Facilities Libraries house more than 1.9 million bound volumes and 2.2 million microform items and subscribe to 13,979 periodicals. In addition, the libraries have cooperative agreements with all universities and colleges in Utah. Access to information worldwide is available via electronic technology with delivery available through interlibrary loan.

The campus has eleven computer centers for undergraduate use, with 644 DOS units and 156 Mac units.

Student Services, located in the Taggart Student Center, provides a hub for programs and agencies facilitating academic support services, admissions, career services, Children's House, counseling center, Disability Resource Center, financial aid, high school/college relations, housing, International Student Office, multicultural affairs, parking, Personal Development Center, programs and entertainment, Student Health Services, Student Support Services, substance abuse prevention/education, and Women's Center/Re-entry Center.

Honorary Societies Phi Kappa Phi, Golden Key, and Mortar Board

Athletics USU is a member of the Big West Athletic Conference, where men's teams have competed since 1978 and women's teams since 1990 in all major sports. USU has won ten conference championships, including 1995–96 titles in men's cross-country and basketball and men's and women's track and field. Utah State athletic teams participate at the NCAA Division I-A level in football, women's volleyball and soccer, and men's and women's cross-country, tennis, softball, and track and field. Athletic facilities on campus include the Romney Stadium (30,257); the Dee Glen Smith Spectrum (10,270); the Nelson Recreation Fieldhouse; the Health, Physical Education and Recreation Building; and the Western Surgery Center. A new, multipurpose, indoor practice facility is under construction.

Study Abroad The USU Study Abroad Program offers exchange opportunities in China, Germany, Japan, Korea, and Mexico.

Support Services The Disability Resource Center of Utah State offers campus orientation, building access, registration assistance, technical equipment (such as computers, voice synthesizers, closed captioned decoders, scanners, and enlarged output devices), referral information, taped texts, telephone services, counseling, tutors, interpreters, and readers.

Job Opportunities Students have a number of work opportunities to choose from on campus, including assistantships, work-study, and a Cooperative Education Internship Program.

Tuition: $2246 for state residents, $6802 for nonresidents, per year (1998–99)

Room and Board: $4720

Mandatory Fees: $387

Contact: Director: Dr. David Lancy, 374 Merrill Library, Logan, Utah 84322-3015; Telephone: 801-797-2715; Fax: 801-797-3941; E-mail: honors@cc.usu.edu; Web site: http://www.usu.edu/~honors/index.html

UTAH VALLEY STATE COLLEGE

2/4 Pu G M Sc

▼ Honors Program

The Honors Program at Utah Valley State College is designed to challenge motivated students. Students who enter honors are deeply committed to realizing their academic, professional, and human potential. Honors courses facilitate this goal by providing small classes (no more than 20 students) that encourage an intimate, intensive, and stimulating learning experience. Students interact with each other and distinguished faculty members who have been carefully selected on the basis of scholarship, teaching ability, and rapport with students. The emphasis is on the development of reading, writing, and discussion skills that lead to productive analysis in all areas of the human experience. There are approximately 300 honors students currently enrolled.

Participation Requirements: Honors graduates complete honors courses that fulfill general education requirements and compose a thesis. They must graduate with a GPA of at least 3.5. Upon graduation, an honors seal is placed on the diploma and the transcript.

Admission Process: To enter the Honors Program, a candidate must meet GPA and ACT or SAT requirements and be interviewed by the honors director.

Scholarship Availability: Graduates have preferred transfer and access to scholarships at all Utah universities.

The Campus Context: Utah Valley State College is a beautiful campus surrounded by the Rocky Mountains and situated 40 miles south of Salt Lake City in Orem, Utah. A state college, it is composed of two interdependent divisions. Students are the primary focus and first priority at Utah Valley State College. The lower division embraces and preserves the philosophy and mission of a comprehensive community college, while the upper division consists of programs leading to baccalaureate degrees in areas of high community demand and interest. Most students are commuters. The mean age of students is 22.

Student Body The student enrollment is currently 22,000 and rapidly growing. Ten percent of students are international (most are Hispanic, Asian, Polynesian, and American Indian), and the rest represent all fifty states. All major financial aid programs and a broad variety of scholarships are available. More than 60 percent of students receive financial aid.

Faculty There are 350 contract faculty members and approximately 500 adjuncts.

Key Facilities Computer labs and online services are widely available and provide general or specialized (e.g., math, English) services.

Honorary Society Phi Theta Kappa

Athletics Utah Valley Sate College is a member of the Scenic West Athletic Conference of the NCAA.

Study Abroad There are many study-abroad opportunities available, including Western Europe, Russia, and Asia.

Support Services The campus offers full access to challenged individuals and a comprehensive range of student services.

Tuition: $1682 for state residents, $5262 for nonresidents, per year (2001–02)

Mandatory Fees: $320

Contact: Director: JaNae Brown Haas, History Department, Mailcode 185, 800 West 1200 University Parkway, Orem, Utah 84058; Telephone: 801-764-7013; Fax: 801-226-5207; E-mail: haasja@uvsc.edu; Web site: http://www.uvsc.edu

Interpreting the symbols: **2**=two-year college, **4**=four-year college; **Pu**=public or state college, **Pr**=private college; **G**=general honors program; **D**=departmental honors program; **S**=small program (fewer than 100 students), **M**=midsize program (100 to 500 students), **L**=large program (more than 500 students); **Sc**=scholarships available in honors program; **Tr**=transfer students accepted into honors program; **HBC**=historically black college; **AA**=academic advisors; **GA**=graduate advisors; **FA**=fellowship advisors.

Valdosta State University

4 Pu G M Sc Tr

▼ University Honors Program

The Honors Program at Valdosta State University provides special classes and activities for students who have demonstrated their commitment to academic achievement and who are looking for experiences that will enrich them beyond the scope of the average. Honors courses are not more difficult than non-honors courses, just more enjoyable and rewarding, designed to encourage students to think creatively, foster in them a love of learning, and provide the best possible foundation for their academic careers and personal lives.

The Honors Program offers special sections of classes in a wide variety of disciplines, including the humanities, the sciences, mathematics, fine arts, and the social sciences. Each course satisfies core curriculum requirements while at the same time counting toward completion of the Honors Program. Enrollment is limited to 15 students per section, with each course offering a unique blend of solid content and stimulating format in an enriched environment.

Honors seminars are a special feature of the Honors Program. These seminars are interdisciplinary and discussion based, focused each year on a different timely and interesting topic. Entering students enroll in the Honors Introductory Seminar during their first year. After having completed the requisite number of honors courses, students then finish their honors experience with the Honors Capstone Seminar. These seminars—Myth and Ritual in Modern Society, the Question of Evil, Native American Religions, Cosmology, Modern and Contemporary Views of Human Nature, Society and the Sexes, the Individual and Society, Moving Beyond Hatred, Developing Ethical Decision Making Skills, Geology and Mythology in the Mediterranean, Issues in Science and Religion, the American View of Nature, Women in the Arts, and the Role and Function of a University—are designed to give all students in the Honors Program a shared intellectual experience in order to develop a community of learners and encourage a spirit of collegiality in the pursuit of knowledge, a spirit that is essential for intellectual growth and personal fulfillment.

The Honors Option allows students to continue honors work during their junior and senior years. Through the Honors Option, students may receive honors credit while enrolled in regular course sections by extending class work into new areas or pursuing it in greater depth.

Honors students may also become members of the Honors Student Association and enjoy a variety of special activities and social events. Through participation in the Honors Forum, a series of lectures and discussions led by VSU faculty, visiting scholars, and members of the community, honors students have the opportunity to discuss new ideas and exciting research in a relaxed yet challenging atmosphere. Honors students also engage in public and community service learning projects. Finally, through its membership in the National Collegiate Honors Council, the Southern Regional Honors Council, and the Georgia Collegiate Honors Council, the VSU Honors Program opens the door to numerous conventions, symposia, trips, and study abroad and offers many opportunities to meet and work with other honors students from all parts of the nation and the world.

There are 300 students in the 25-year-old program.

Participation Requirements: To complete the program, students must accrue 24 hours of honors course credit, including two honors seminars, and participate in some form of community service. Students who complete the Honors Program receive an Honors Program diploma, transcript notation, and a gold seal on their University diploma. Students also receive public recognition at the University's annual Honors Day ceremony.

Admission Process: Students with a high school GPA of 3.0 and a verbal or math SAT I score of 550 receive invitations to join the Honors Program. Other students who demonstrate qualities of the superior student are encouraged to apply. Students already enrolled in a university should have at least a 3.0 GPA to seek admittance.

Scholarship Availability: The Honors Program does not offer scholarships itself; however, the University offers a large number of scholarships. Residents of Georgia who have the Hope Scholarship have most of their tuition paid for them.

The Campus Context: Noted for its Spanish Mission architecture, Valdosta State University is composed of five colleges: Arts and Sciences, Business Administration, Fine Arts, Nursing, and Education. The University offers ninety-four degree programs with forty-nine undergraduate majors leading to the B.A. or B.S., ranging from astronomy to sports medicine, including a pre-engineering tandem program with Georgia Tech.

Student Body The University has 9,000 undergraduates enrolled; 59 percent are women. Twenty percent of the student body are African American; 10 percent are from out of state. The campus has twenty-one fraternities and sororities.

Faculty There are 400 full-time faculty members (not including a considerable number of adjunct faculty), 73 percent of whom hold doctorates or other terminal degrees. The student-faculty ratio is 23:1.

Key Facilities The library houses 1.2 million volumes. There are fifteen computer labs scattered across campus housing a total of 1,700 PCs.

Honorary Society Phi Kappa Phi

Athletics VSU has an NCAA Division II athletic program, consisting of baseball, basketball, cross-country, football, golf, and tennis for men and basketball, cross-country, softball, tennis, and volleyball for women. The football team has been especially strong in Division II, coming in second for two years in the national championships.

Study Abroad Numerous study-abroad opportunities exist through the Office of International Programs.

Support Services Much of the campus is accessible to disabled students, and the Special Services Office of the University has a strong presence on campus, ensuring that all special needs students find adequate support.

Job Opportunities Numerous work opportunities exist through the Work Study Program Office.

Tuition: $1263 for state residents, $4161 for nonresidents, per semester (2001–02)

Room and Board: $3300

Contact: Director: Dr. Brian Adler, VSU Honors House, Valdosta State University, Valdosta, Georgia 31698; Telephone: 229-249-4894; Fax: 229-219-1396; E-mail: badler@valdosta.edu; Web site: http://www.valdosta.edu/honors

---

Valencia Community College

2 Pu G L Sc

▼ Honors Program

Valencia Community College inaugurated its Honors Program in January 1990 and now serves more than 1,000 students on four campuses. The program annually attracts dozens of students with SAT I scores in excess of 1400 and ACT scores in excess of 32. There are a number of valedictorians and salutatorians from twenty-two local high schools, and students from several other states and countries have been attracted to Valencia because of its Honors Program. In addition, more than 450 of the 1,000 honors students are currently on full tuition scholarships administered by the Honors Program. The program offers students a choice of more than forty different honors courses across the curriculum. In addition, it offers a four-semester sequence of Interdisciplinary Studies (IDS). Students may choose to take only honors courses or only IDS or to mix and match the two approaches to honors. The Honors Program emphasizes small classes (average size is 15) and participative learning. Most classes are seminar style and seek to help the student become an independent learner. The Honors Program faculty is made up of master teachers, many of whom are noted authors and scholars in their disciplines. There is a close mentoring relationship between honors faculty members and students. Students are advised by 5 special honors counselors and receive preferential early registration for classes.

For the past seven years, virtually 100 percent of Honors Program graduates have transferred as full juniors to upper-division colleges and universities, including many of the nation's most prestigious institutions, such as Duke, Tulane, Emory, Georgia Tech, New College, and Georgetown. Currently, two thirds of the graduates are receiving scholarships to their institutions. In addition, the Honors Program office currently has more than seventy transfer scholarships to colleges and universities, which allow Valencia's Honor Program Director to select the scholarship recipients.

One of the hallmarks of the Honors Program is its holistic approach to developing honors students. This approach seeks to develop students' social and leadership skills in addition to intellectual and academic abilities. Toward this end, the program sponsors numerous field trips, a speakers series, social events, leadership training, and trips to state, regional, and national honors conferences (all at program expense). In addition, the program provides an annual spring break trip to a different country. While this trip is not paid for entirely by the program, it is heavily subsidized so that students pay only a fraction of the cost.

In addition to the resources offered by Valencia and the Orlando area, students in the Honors Program have full check-out privileges at the libraries of Rollins College and the University of Central Florida. Each of Valencia's campuses also offers an Honors Resource Center, where honors students have access to computers, group study areas, and other resource materials in addition to a comfortable and well-appointed room in which to just relax or carry on a conversation.

Participation Requirements: Students in the program may elect to take as many or as few honors courses as they wish. If students have 12 hours of honors course work (out of 60 hours required for an Associate of Arts degrees) and a minimum 3.0 overall GPA at graduation, they receive an Honors Certificate. Students with 24 hours of honors course work and a minimum 3.25 overall GPA at graduation receive an Honors Degree. Both Honors Certificate and Honors Degrees graduates and their guests participate in a special buffet dinner/graduation ceremony. In addition, they are distinguished at the regular college commencement ceremony by the wearing of honors stoles and honors medallions as well as having a special section in the commencement program. Honors Degree graduates also have their transcripts marked with the designation Graduated With an Honors Degree.

Admission Process: To be admitted to the Honors Program, students must meet one of the following requirements: be in the top 10 percent of their high school graduating class; have a cumulative high school GPA of at least 3.5 on a 4.0 scale or 4.3 on a 5.0 scale; have a minimum combined SAT I score of 1170; have a minimum composite ACT score of 26; have a CPT score of 100 or higher in writing and 97 or higher in reading or an 83 or higher in elementary algebra and 44 or higher in college-level mathematics; or have a cumulative Valencia GPA of 3.25 or higher with a minimum of 12 hours of college-level course work completed.

The Campus Context: Valencia Community College was founded in 1967. Valencia is located in Orlando, Florida, and has three campuses ranging from 99 to 180 acres each, as well as two satellite centers and a downtown center housing administrative offices. Valencia is the fourth-largest of twenty-eight community colleges in the Florida higher education system. However, Valencia is now the second-largest producer of Associate of Arts degrees in the United States. Valencia also has the fourth-largest community college foundation in the nation. Its Honors Program has produced a number of award-winning students, including several Academic All-American first- and second-team winners, more first- and second-place Florida Collegiate Honors Council writing contest winners than any other college or university in the state, and a winner of the coveted Portz Award, which is given by the National Collegiate Honors Council. Valencia is fully accredited by the Southern Association of Colleges and Schools.

Student Body Valencia enrolls approximately 28,000 credit-seeking students; 88 percent are enrolled in Associate of Arts degree programs and 12 percent are enrolled in Associate of Science degree programs. Valencia has nearly 500 international students, which is unusual for a community college. Thirty-seven percent of all students receive financial aid.

Faculty Of the total faculty members, 63 percent are full-time and 37 percent are adjuncts.

Key Facilities Computer facilities include more than 2,000 DOS and Macintosh computers located in labs, libraries, and academic buildings.

Honorary Society Phi Theta Kappa

Study Abroad Through its international education program, Valencia students have an opportunity to study abroad for a summer, semester, or year. Credits earned in this way apply toward the student's Valencia degree requirements.

Job Opportunities Students are offered a range of work opportunities on campus, including both Federal and Valencia Work-Study opportunities.

Tuition: $1150 for state residents, $4000 for nonresidents, per year

Contact: Director: Ronald G. Brandolini, Honors Program, 1800 South Kirkman Road, Orlando, Florida 32811; Telephone: 407-299-5000 Ext. 1729; Fax: 407-299-5000 1 1912; E-mail: rbrando@valencia.cc.fl.us; Web site: http://www.gate.net/~valencia/honors/honors2.html

VALPARAISO UNIVERSITY

4 Pr M Tr AA

▼ Christ College, the Honors College

Christ College is the Honors College of Valparaiso University (VU). Established in 1967, Christ College celebrates more than thirty years of providing honors-level, interdisciplinary study to academically talented students. The curriculum, taught by master teacher-scholars, emphasizes the liberal arts and the humanities. The College takes its name from respected colleges established centuries ago. In the tradition of those colleges, Christ College is dedicated to the cultivation of intellectual, moral, and spiritual virtues. The College's name also suggests its accord with VU's goal of academic excellence in a Christian context.

Interpreting the symbols: **2**=two-year college, **4**=four-year college; **Pu**=public or state college, **Pr**=private college; **G**=general honors program; **D**=departmental honors program; **S**=small program (fewer than 100 students), **M**=midsize program (100 to 500 students), **L**=large program (more than 500 students); **Sc**=scholarships available in honors program; **Tr**=transfer students accepted into honors program; **HBC**=historically black college; **AA**=academic advisors; **GA**=graduate advisors; **FA**=fellowship advisors.

All Christ College (CC) students are concurrently enrolled in one of VU's other colleges—Arts and Sciences, Business Administration, Engineering, or Nursing—where they earn their bachelor's degrees. Study in Christ College complements all academic programs, and many CC courses fulfill the University's general education requirements. Christ College honors courses invite the more intellectually curious student into the rigors and rewards of the life of the mind by offering an integrated approach to university studies and subtler methods of independent inquiry.

The Honors College is located in Mueller Hall, a modern building at the center of VU's campus, with a state-of-the-art multimedia lecture hall, newly refurbished classrooms and seminar rooms, faculty offices, presentation space, and a gracious fireside commons/art gallery. The College has its own dean, assistant dean/academic adviser, and 7 full-time faculty members. Direct and personal relationships are promoted between students and faculty members as they create together a distinctive learning community in and out of the classroom.

The nationally respected Christ College Freshman Program is a two-semester study of great works of history, literature, philosophy, and religion, from the earliest writings to the present day. Critical reading, writing, and discussion are emphasized. To balance the critical and literary focus of the discussion classes, the program also meets one evening each week for group activities connected with the fine and performing arts. During the fall semester, these sessions culminate in the Christ College Freshman Production, an original dramatic-musical performance, based on ideas and themes discussed in the program, and written and produced entirely by students. Oxford Union–style debates of significant current issues are the focus of the spring semester.

Typical sophomore courses include study of selected classic intellectual and literary texts and their relationships to works of art and music, an exploration of the nature and purpose of Christian theology, and an introduction to discipline-oriented interpretive skills as students examine primary materials in the humanities, social sciences, or natural sciences, Junior/senior-level students choose from a variety of topical seminars. A senior capstone course provides an integrative experience in which students give shape to the substance of their lives through autobiographical narrative and reflect upon the character and meaning of their future work. Seniors prepare resumes and are closely advised in applying to professional and graduate schools.

Approximately 80 first-year students are accepted for membership in Christ College as they enter Valparaiso University. Total Christ College enrollment is 300 students.

Participation Requirements: Christ College students are concurrently enrolled in one of Valparaiso University's other colleges: Arts and Sciences, Business Administration, Engineering, or Nursing. The Christ College curriculum, which complements all academic programs and meets many general education requirements, extends from freshman year to graduation. The yearlong 16-credit CC Freshman Program meets the University's core requirements for first-year students. CC sophomores, juniors, and seniors typically earn 3 to 7 additional credits in honors courses each year. Undergraduate research, independent study, and the writing of an honors essay or thesis are encouraged. A student who successfully completes 38 credit hours in a sequence of Christ College courses receives the designation Christ College Scholar upon graduation from Valparaiso University. A graduate with 30 credits is designated Christ College Associate. Students are expected to maintain a 3.3 (B+) or better GPA in all University course work and in CC courses. Successful students receive the transcript designation Christ College Scholar or Christ College Associate upon graduation. Seniors are honored at a banquet at which special medallions are presented. Christ College also offers a complementary major in humanities, a minor in humanities, and a joint admissions program with the Valparaiso University School of Law.

Admission Process: Students admitted to Valparaiso University who have demonstrated academic excellence in high school, strong SAT I or ACT scores, intellectual curiosity and creativity, and leadership in extracurricular activities are identified by the Office of Admissions for review by Christ College. A CC faculty committee and the CC Dean review the students' VU applications, giving particular attention to performance in high school AP and honors courses and to the application essay. Qualified students are then invited to apply to Christ College. Decisions on acceptance are made by the CC Dean after reviewing the CC applications. Approximately 80 first-year students are accepted for membership each year. The Christ College freshman class of 2001–02 presented combined average SAT I scores of 1370 and average English ACT scores of 32. Admissions are on a rolling basis. VU upperclass students and transfer students with superior records of academic achievement may be invited to join CC after the freshman year.

Scholarship Availability: Valparaiso University offers merit scholarships and awards for students with special academic talents, interests, abilities, or backgrounds. Christ College does not award regular academic scholarships of its own, though most honors college students are the recipients of academic scholarships. Two Christ College Diversity Scholarships in the amount of full tuition may be awarded each year to academically talented multicultural first-year students who have been admitted to Christ College.

The Campus Context: Valparaiso University was founded in 1859 and purchased by the Lutheran University Association in 1925. An independent, private institution of higher learning distinguished by its Lutheran heritage of scholarship, freedom, and faith, the University provides strong programs of liberal and professional studies that are well-grounded in the arts and sciences. The faculty is dedicated to challenging teaching and care for the individual in a residential setting where students can develop as whole persons, motivated and prepared to serve both church and society. In addition to the College of Arts and Sciences, VU features strong undergraduate Colleges of Engineering, Nursing, and Business Administration as well as Christ College, its nationally prominent Honors College, in which qualified members of the other colleges may be concurrently enrolled. More than sixty academic programs are offered.

VU's location in Northwest Indiana places the campus within an hour's drive of the arts, culture, and excitement of Chicago and about 15 minutes from the beautiful Indiana Dunes National Lakeshore on Lake Michigan. The friendly city of Valparaiso has a population of 26,000. The 310-acre VU campus has sixty modern academic buildings and residence halls, including a well-equipped Athletics-Recreation Center, the spectacular new Center for the Arts, and one of the largest collegiate chapels in America.

Student Body VU's 3,700 students (3,000 undergraduates) come from most states in the nation and more than forty countries around the world. More than 65 percent of the students reside on campus. There are seven national sororities and nine national fraternities. About 35 percent of students affiliate with Greek letter organizations. Students participate in more than 100 extracurricular organizations. Service learning, volunteer, and community service opportunities are abundant.

Faculty Valparaiso University's full-time faculty members number 220, of whom 87 percent hold doctoral or other terminal degrees in their fields. Another 80 adjunct or part-time faculty members also instruct. The student-faculty ratio is 13:1. Class size averages 22 students (Christ College classes are smaller, with an average of 15 students).

Key Facilities Moellering (undergraduate) Library owns 714,657 volumes and subscribes to 16,158 periodicals. Moellering Library was renovated during 1995 to 1997 to create an electronic classroom, group study rooms, a newspaper reading lounge, video viewing room, and an up-to-date music library. The Law Library holds 135,000 volumes and 3,225 current periodical subscriptions. Electronic Information Services provides campuswide voice mail and e-mail as well as access to national and international networks via the Internet and video conferencing. Networks of Windows, Macintosh, and DOS computers are available in student computer clusters that are located in most academic buildings and all residence halls. General applications supported include word processing, spreadsheets, databases, desktop publishing, statistics, and presentation graphics. Peripherals include plotters, CD-ROM drives, laser disk players, laser printers, color printers, and scanners.

Honorary Societies Alpha Lambda Delta and Mortar Board

Athletics The Valpo Crusaders are NCAA Division I in eighteen athletic teams: men's baseball, basketball (Mid-Continent Conference), cross-country, football (I-AA), soccer, swimming, tennis, and track; women's basketball (Mid-Continent Conference), cross-country, soccer, softball, swimming, tennis, track, and volleyball. Personal fitness facilities, a wide range of indoor and outdoor recreational opportunities, and various intramural sports are also offered.

Study Abroad Valparaiso University sponsors fourteen international studies programs. VU faculty-directed study centers in Cambridge, England, and Reutlingen, Germany, are exclusively for VU students. Twelve others are offered in conjunction with host-institution programs: Tubingen, Germany; Puebla, Mexico; Grenada, Spain; two programs in Paris (study or study/internship); two programs in Japan (Osaka/internship or Kyoto/language and East Asian studies); Hangzhou, China; London's Oak Hill College; Anglia Polytechnic University in Cambridge; Athens; and Namibia. Students also participate in semester-long programs in New York, Chicago, and Washington, D.C. Christ College students regularly participate in off-campus study programs.

Support Services Valparaiso University provides a strong academic advisement program for all students. Christ College students have academic advisers in their majors and in Christ College. Other services include a faculty-directed writing center and group study and tutorial assistance for many areas of general education.

Job Opportunities VU has a strong cooperative education program in all colleges. Internship programs are offered by several departments of the Colleges of Arts and Sciences and Business Administration. Campus employment opportunities are abundant. VU's Career Center offers assistance with undergraduate employment as well as postgraduate placement.

Tuition: $18,100 per year (2001–02)

Room and board: $4870

Mandatory Fees: $600

Contact: Dean: Dr. Mark R. Schwehn, Valparaiso, Indiana 46383-6493; Telephone: 219-464-5022; Fax: 219-464-5159; E-mail: mark.schwehn@valpo.edu; Web site: http://www.valpo.edu/christc

VILLANOVA UNIVERSITY

4 Pr G M Sc Tr AA FA

▼ Honors Program

The Villanova University Honors Program is a distinctive academic community comprised of students and faculty members who particularly enjoy the experience of intellectual growth. The program is designed to provide exceptional opportunities for critical and independent thinking, for the creative exchange of ideas, and for the synthesis of intellectual insights into lived experiences. Honors enhances the academic life central to a Villanova education by bringing together talented students and faculty members in challenging seminars, individual research projects, and cocurricular activities. Members of the program enjoy the benefits of a small college environment, while taking full advantage of the many resources of the broader University community.

Through the Faculty Mentors Program, Academic Peer Advisors, and Alumni Network, honors students receive excellent academic advisement throughout their college careers in selecting courses and majors, preparing for summer and postgraduate opportunities, and learning to identify and develop their own intellectual voices. Of special note, the Honors Program coordinates the Bryn Mawr College–Villanova University Exchange and the Connelly-Delouvrie International Scholars Program, which provides funding for overseas study. Villanova Honors Program graduates are frequently elected to Phi Beta Kappa and other prestigious honor societies, often receive the medallions awarded for academic excellence at graduation, and are highly successful in their pursuit of prestigious fellowships, graduate and professional school acceptances, and career opportunities.

Students can major, concentrate, or take individual courses in the Honors Program. An academic division within the College of Liberal Arts and Sciences, the program currently offers courses in the humanities, social sciences, and natural sciences, which are required areas of study for all of the University's majors. The program also offers courses that satisfy some of the core requirements of the College of Commerce and Finance. Honors courses are taught by faculty members who have distinguished themselves as dynamic teachers and scholars. These small seminars emphasize interdisciplinary approaches, extensive reading and writing, and the development of critical skills of judgment and analysis in a climate of mutual respect and cooperation. Innovative courses in the program include team-taught seminars and seminars given by visiting professors. All honors courses are enriched by a variety of lectures, cultural events, and social activities.

Faculty members and students meet outside of class individually, as a class, and as part of larger program events. The student-run Honors Events Committee invites speakers and organizes trips to cultural events in New York and Washington, D.C. Local Philadelphia highlights like the Philadelphia Orchestra, Independence Hall, and South Street are a short train ride away, with a regional rail-line stop on campus. Students present their own research in the informal atmosphere of Friday Colloquia and share their musical and artistic talents in recitals and exhibitions. All students are invited to contribute to *The Polis,* the program's literary magazine. Honors students also coordinate a number of service initiatives, including a sophomore service-learning community, which integrates volunteer experience with academic course work and residence hall community development. In addition, students participate equally with faculty members in setting policy and selecting new courses for the program. Every year is different depending on the special interests and initiatives of students themselves.

Honors students participate actively in all aspects of the Villanova community; honors is only one aspect of their campus life. Averaging two to three courses (the standard course load is five) in the program per semester, honors students bring to the program their own diversity of talents, interests, and experiences. They often hold leadership positions in student government, campus publications, musical and theatrical performance groups, and volunteer service projects, both on and off campus.

Founded 40 years ago, the Villanova Honors Program has grown from a core of interdisciplinary humanities seminars into a four-year curriculum, which serves approximately 500 students

Interpreting the symbols: **2**=two-year college, **4**=four-year college; **Pu**=public or state college, **Pr**=private college; **G**=general honors program; **D**=departmental honors program; **S**=small program (fewer than 100 students), **M**=midsize program (100 to 500 students), **L**=large program (more than 500 students); **Sc**=scholarships available in honors program; **Tr**=transfer students accepted into honors program; **HBC**=historically black college; **AA**=academic advisors; **GA**=graduate advisors; **FA**=fellowship advisors.

from all of the University's colleges: Liberal Arts and Sciences, Commerce and Finance, Engineering, and Nursing. Currently, 450 students are registered with the Honors Program. There are a total of 175 majors and 100 concentrations across the four years (approximately thirty majors and twenty-five concentrations in each graduating class).

Participation Requirements: To remain active in the program, honors students must earn a minimum GPA of 3.33. Students who complete the program requirements may graduate with a Bachelor of Arts, Honors Program (B.A.H.) or Bachelor of Science, Honors Program (B.S.H.). Both the B.A.H. and the B.S.H. degrees may be combined with a second major in another discipline. Each of these four-year comprehensive majors culminates in a year-long senior thesis project. The Honors Program Sequence in Liberal Studies (honors concentration) is another option. All Honors Program certifications require a minimum GPA of 3.33.

Admission Process: Incoming students are invited to apply to the program in the June immediately prior to their enrollment at Villanova based on their SAT I scores (at least 1330, with a minimum of 630 on both math and verbal sections), high school record (rank in the top 10 percent), and/or a previously expressed interest in the program. Current undergraduate students apply upon the recommendation of a faculty member or through their own initiative.

Scholarship Availability: Villanova University offers a number of merit-based scholarships to members of each incoming class. Designed to recognize distinctive achievement and to attract superior students to the University, these scholarships include the four-year full tuition Presidential Scholarship administered by the Honors Program, sizable partial-tuition Villanova Scholar Awards, Commuting Scholar Awards, Augustinian Scholarships, and college-specific scholarships that are administered through the Office of University Admission.

All of the students who receive scholarships to Villanova are invited to participate in the courses and activities of the Honors Program.

The Campus Context: Villanova University is composed of four colleges: the College of Liberal Arts and Sciences, the College of Commerce and Finance, the College of Engineering, and the College of Nursing. Students can choose from more than forty undergraduate majors and forty-seven graduate programs. Special facilities on campus include the St. Augustine Center for the Liberal Arts, an observatory in the renovated Mendel Science Center, the new Center for Engineering Education and Research, and the newly renovated and expanded Bartley Hall, which houses the College of Commerce and Finance.

Student Body Undergraduate enrollment is currently 6,587. The student body is equally divided between men and women. The ethnic distribution of the students is 3 percent African American, 1 percent Native American, 5 percent Hispanic, 5 percent Asian, and 84 percent Caucasian. The population includes 2 percent international students. Resident students comprise 67 percent of the student population. Sixty-two percent of the students receive financial aid. There are eight fraternities and eight sororities.

Faculty Of the 826 faculty members, 517 are full-time, and 90 percent hold terminal degrees. The student-faculty ratio is 12:1.

Key Facilities Falvey Library is the gateway to information resources and services at Villanova, providing the latest in electronic databases and resources as well as nearly 800,000 volumes. There are 400 computers available on campus for general student use. Most computers are IBM or IBM-compatible. There are some Macs on campus. Students have access to the Internet, World Wide Web, and e-mail.

Honorary Societies Phi Kappa Phi and Phi Beta Kappa

Athletics Most sports are Division I, with the exception of football, which is Division I-AA. Women's sports are basketball, field hockey, softball, track and field, cross-country, volleyball, swimming and diving, crew, soccer, tennis, water polo, and lacrosse. Men's sports are basketball, football, baseball, track and field, cross-country, swimming and diving, soccer, tennis, lacrosse, and golf.

Study Abroad Villanova sponsors study-abroad programs in Asia, Western Europe, the Middle East, and Latin America. Students also can enroll for credit in study-abroad programs at other institutions. Approximately 17 percent of Villanova students participate in study-abroad opportunities.

Support Services Learning support services and other offices on campus work with disabled students to meet their individual needs.

Job Opportunities Work-study positions are available as part of financial assistance packages. Other non-work-study jobs are available in offices, laboratories, libraries, and food services.

Tuition: $22,630 minimum per year (2001–02)

Room and Board: $8190

Mandatory Fees: $300

Contact: Director: Dr. Edwin L. Goff, 800 Lancaster Avenue, Villanova, Pennsylvania 19085; Assistant Director: Christine Muller, Telephone: 610-519-4650; Fax: 610-519-5405; E-mail: honorsprogram@villanova.edu; Web site: http://www.honorsprogram.villanova.edu

---

Virginia Commonwealth University

4 Pu G L Sc Tr AA

▼ Honors Program

The Virginia Commonwealth University (VCU) Honors Program is designed to meet the needs of academically talented undergraduate students through a challenging and exciting program with high academic standards. The University Honors Program offers students an opportunity to exchange ideas, ask questions, participate in research, and explore values with fellow students and teachers who have been carefully selected for their scholarship and teaching excellence. The University Honors Program offers the opportunity for students to expand their creative and intellectual horizons and to benefit from small classes in which there is greater interaction between students and faculty members and among students themselves. Some honors courses are special sections of regular classes open only to honors students. Class size is limited (usually to 20 or fewer students) to maximize student participation and interaction with the instructor. In these special sections, subjects are discussed in-depth, and discussions often continue after class.

Other courses are unique to the Honors Program. Of particular interest among these are the modules. These are single-focus courses that occupy only one third of a semester. The modules are often interdisciplinary and strive to connect the student's studies. Honors students receive personal and careful advising from both the Honors Program faculty and faculty members in their major field of study. This allows them to devise courses of study that meet academic requirements while allowing for the development of individual educational objectives.

Honors students, while benefiting from their association with a smaller unit within the University, also have the benefit of the resources of a major research university. Virginia Commonwealth University is located on two Richmond campuses: the Academic Campus and the Medical College of Virginia Campus. The University offers a wide range of academic opportunities and is committed to its mission of excellence in teaching as well as to the expansion of knowledge through research.

The Honors Program offers a variety of intellectual, cultural, and social activities as important supplements to classroom study. Among these are weekly brown bag lunches, honors seminars, an outstanding lecturer series, and the Honors Idea Exchange, which is a registered student campus organization composed of honors students. The center of activities and community for the University Honors Program is the Honors Center at West Grace Street. In the center, students have meeting rooms, quiet study rooms, a computer laboratory, a copy machine, and recreation areas. The Honors Center is open during the day and at night for study. In addition, many honors students are housed in the building containing the Honors Center, and some of the classes are also conducted there.

The Honors Program is committed to enriching the student's academic and personal endeavors. Since those in the Honors Program are serious students, special privileges are provided beyond the vast resources available to all VCU students. These privileges include access to early registration the week before the rest of the student body, graduate student library privileges, and honors housing in specific wings of the residence halls. Guaranteed admission programs with professional-level health sciences programs and graduate programs in basic health sciences, business, education, and others represent other opportunities for qualified honors students.

The Honors Program at Virginia Commonwealth University began in 1983 and has grown over the years to currently serve more than 1,600 students.

Participation Requirements: Successful completion of the Honors Program leads to graduation with University Honors, an accomplishment that is documented on official transcripts and diplomas. Graduation requirements for completing the Honors Program differ according to school or major. In addition to completing at least six module courses and maintaining a minimum cumulative GPA of 3.5 and a minimum 3.2 GPA in honors courses, honors students present a dossier documenting how they have met the University's expectations for an honors education.

Admission Process: The Honors Program is open to entering freshmen with SAT I scores of 1270 or higher who rank in the upper 15 percent of their graduating class and to transfer students and continuing students with an overall GPA of 3.5 or higher with 30 college semester hours. Students may also be admitted on an individual basis with evidence of sufficient personal commitment to do honors-level work.

Scholarship Availability: In addition to a significant number of merit-based scholarships awarded by the University, the Honors Program recognizes continuing VCU students who demonstrate academic achievement in the Honors Program with approximately $60,000 in scholarship aid. Honors Program Scholarships are awarded by the Honor Council, an advisory board to the Honors Program. Honors Program scholarships worth $500–$2500 are open to continuing honors students in all majors.

The Campus Context: Virginia Commonwealth University is a state-aided institution with undergraduate, postgraduate, and health professions programs located on its two campuses in Richmond, Virginia. The Medical College of Virginia Campus is located near the financial, governmental, and shopping areas of downtown Richmond; the Academic Campus is 2 miles west in Richmond's historic Fan District, a residential area that dates from the nineteenth century. Currently, VCU operates a College of Humanities and Sciences, the School of Graduate Studies, and eleven schools, including Allied Health Professions, Art, Business, Dentistry, Education, Engineering, Mass Communications, Medicine, Nursing, Pharmacy, and Social Work. VCU offers more than fifty baccalaureate, sixty master's, twenty-one doctoral, and three first-professional degrees, along with twenty-eight postgraduate certificate programs.

Student Body VCU enrolls approximately 24,000 students in undergraduate and graduate programs on the two campuses. More than 13,000 VCU students are undergraduates. Diversity is thriving on the VCU campus; 36 percent of undergraduates are multicultural students, and 1,554 international students from 125 countries study at VCU. There are twenty-one social fraternities and sororities that serve students.

Faculty The full-time faculty at VCU numbers 1,663; approximately 925 adjunct faculty members supplement the full-time faculty. Of the full-time faculty members, 89 percent hold terminal degrees. The student-faculty ratio is 13:1.

Key Facilities The University libraries house in excess of 1.6 million volumes in the two campus libraries. VCU students and faculty and staff members have access to a wide variety of computing resources, such as electronic library holdings, e-mail, and special databases and programs. These facilities also allow connection to the Internet, including the World Wide Web, the University fiber-optic backbone network, and local area networks on both the Academic and MCV campuses. Local dial-up access is also available to the University network and associated computer resources. Public laboratories with a wide array of hardware and software are located in many locations around the campuses.

Honorary Societies Phi Eta Sigma, Phi Kappa Phi, and Golden Key

Athletics More than 250 student athletes participate in the sixteen athletic programs sponsored by the University. Athletic teams for men include baseball, basketball, cross-country, golf, soccer, tennis, and indoor and outdoor track and field. Women's teams include basketball, cross-country, field hockey, soccer, tennis, volleyball, and indoor and outdoor track and field. VCU also offers a wide range of intramural sports for men and women.

Study Abroad VCU students may extend their educational horizons by studying abroad. The Center for International Education cooperates annually with the Department of Foreign Languages to offer summer study programs in Austria, France, Italy, Russia, and Spain or Guatemala. In addition, it has coordinated topics courses in Brazil, Indonesia, Mexico, and the United Kingdom. The Department of Foreign Languages, in an agreement with EUROCENTRES, offers short-term, semester-long, or year-long culture and language immersion programs in France, Germany, Italy, Japan, Russia, and Spain. VCU students may also participate in the International Student Exchange Program, which allows enrollment in member institutions worldwide.

Support Services The Program of Services for Students with Disabilities provides information and assistance in academic planning and advising to VCU students identified as having a disability.

Job Opportunities Students have access to a variety of work opportunities on campus, including assistantships and work-study.

Tuition: $3675 for state residents, $13,855 for nonresidents, per year, includes fees (2001–02)

Room and Board: $5081

Contact: Director: Dr. John Berglund, 701 West Grace Street, P.O. Box 843010, Richmond, Virginia 23284-3010; Telephone: 804-828-1803; Fax: 804-827-1669; E-mail: jfberglu@vcu.edu; Web site: http://www.vcu.edu/honors

Virginia Military Institute

4 Pu G S Sc Tr

▼ Institute Honors Program

The Institute Honors Program exists primarily to enrich the academic experience of VMI's most outstanding cadets through activities that encourage an affinity for intellectual inquiry and develop the capacity for sophisticated engagement of issues

Interpreting the symbols: **2**=two-year college, **4**=four-year college; **Pu**=public or state college, **Pr**=private college; **G**=general honors program; **D**=departmental honors program; **S**=small program (fewer than 100 students), **M**=midsize program (100 to 500 students), **L**=large program (more than 500 students); **Sc**=scholarships available in honors program; **Tr**=transfer students accepted into honors program; **HBC**=historically black college; **AA**=academic advisors; **GA**=graduate advisors; **FA**=fellowship advisors.

and problems, whether ethical, civic, or professional. In all of its elements, the program stresses peer leadership, strong oral and written communication skills, and the highest standards of academic integrity and excellence.

While several of VMI's academic departments offer programs leading to honors in the major, the Institute Honors Program is intended to recognize a broader range of achievement than honors earned in any particular major. Attainment of Institute Honors is viewed as the highest academic achievement at VMI.

Cadets who are admitted to the program participate each semester in an Honors Forum, where a faculty moderator encourages serious conversation about current events and issues of significance. Sections of the forum meet weekly, and students are provided with free subscriptions to major newspapers and periodicals (e.g., *The Economist*) to stimulate discussion.

Typically offered at the sophomore and junior levels, specially designated honors courses present the opportunity for cadets to broaden their academic and intellectual horizons across the disciplines. These courses are taught as seminars, with much emphasis on student participation. Enrollment is strictly limited, allowing ample time for individual attention from the professor in tutorials, which are required in addition to regular class meetings. Several honors courses are offered each semester on topics such as Literature and Politics in German History; Environmental Myth, Ethics, and Justice; Chemistry in a Cultural Context; Africa in Modern Times; and Paris, a course that included a class field trip to the city during break.

The crowning achievement of the Institute Honors candidate at VMI is the completion of a senior honors project or thesis under the supervision of a faculty member in the major department. The senior honors project/thesis concludes with a public presentation by the cadet, open to faculty members and other students as well as interested members of the college community. A copy of the final document is bound and shelved in a special section of the VMI library.

Participants in the Institute Honors Program are viewed as prime candidates and receive a regular flow of information, encouragement, and assistance in applying for prestigious national awards such as the Rhodes, Marshall, Fulbright, and Goldwater Scholarships. In addition, they are eligible for many special local resources, opportunities, and awards. An ample fund is available to encourage individuals or groups of cadets in the program to plan special projects, trips, and guest speakers. Grants to support research for the senior project/thesis are available through VMI's progressive and well-endowed Undergraduate Research Initiative. Several prizes are given for outstanding papers and other work produced in honors courses.

Each semester, honors cadets are invited to participate in events organized especially for them. Recently, for instance, a group enjoyed breakfast with former Secretary of State Henry Kissinger while he was on the campus for a speech. In addition to the opportunities available at VMI, cadets in the program benefit from programs offered by VMI's close neighbor, Washington and Lee University, and other nearby institutions, such as the University of Virginia and James Madison University, as well as from Lexington's proximity to such major cities as Richmond and Washington, D.C.

Participation Requirements: Honors cadets must participate in a section of the Honors Forum each semester they are enrolled at VMI and have been admitted to the program. The program also requires two honors courses. To provide broad exposure to the disciplines, one course is required in each of two academic groups: engineering/science and liberal arts/leadership. The final requirement is a senior project/thesis, completed under the direction of a faculty mentor and concluding with a public presentation of that project. Cadets must maintain a minimum cumulative GPA of 3.5 in order to remain in the program. Institute Honors Scholars are identified in a special section of the commencement program that includes the titles of their senior projects and names of their advisers. Attainment of Institute Honors is registered on the official VMI transcript.

Admission Process: Admission is guaranteed for all Institute Scholars. On a rolling basis, the program is open by application to other matriculating freshmen whose high school records suggest strong academic potential; those who end the freshman year with a minimum cumulative GPA of 3.5; and others who meet the minimum GPA requirement and who can demonstrate the ability to meet all of the program requirements in a timely, reasonable manner. Applications for admission to the program are evaluated by the Institute Honors Review Committee.

Scholarship Availability: Through the Admissions Office, VMI offers approximately fifteen full academic Institute Scholarships annually to outstanding entering cadets. These scholarships cover all costs of cadetship, including a generous allowance that is deposited in the recipient's account to cover the purchase of books and incidentals. Financial need is not a criterion for selection. Institute Scholars are guaranteed admission to the Institute Honors Program. Scholarships for non–Institute Scholar participants in the program are planned for 2001–02.

The Campus Context: Virginia Military Institute, founded in 1839, has remained true to its mission to produce "educated and honorable men and women" by preparing them with an education for the future. After 162 years of preparing young men for future leadership roles, the Institute made the transition to coeducation in August 1997 and has successfully assimilated women into the Corps of Cadets while maintaining those elements of the VMI experience that have formed the essence of the Institute's traditions. The Institute graduated its first women in May 1999. Located in Lexington, Virginia (population 7,000), VMI is nestled in the historic Valley of Virginia.

A four-year undergraduate college, VMI combines the studies of a full college curriculum within a framework of military discipline, with emphasis placed on the qualities of honor, integrity, and responsibility. Its 1,250 cadets pursue B.A. or B.S. degrees in fourteen disciplines in the general fields of engineering, science, and liberal arts. Undergirding all aspects of cadet life is the VMI Honor Code, to which all cadets subscribe.

Major ratings publications frequently include the Institute in their lists of top undergraduate programs. The 2002 edition of *U.S. News & World Report*'s "America's Best Colleges" ranks VMI as the nation's top national public liberal arts college. The Institute enjoys the highest endowment per student of any public college in the nation.

Student Body The Corps of Cadets includes approximately 1,250 students from forty-five states and nineteen other nations. All cadets at VMI live on campus, attend full-time, wear the historic gray uniform, and participate in corps activities. An applicant must be between the ages of 17 and 22, must be unmarried, and may not be a parent.

Faculty In 2001–02, VMI had at total of 145 faculty members; 100 are full-time and 97 percent of these hold terminal degrees in their fields of expertise.

Key Facilities Preston Library is dedicated to supporting the educational needs of cadets and the instructional and research needs of VMI's faculty and staff members. Holdings include more than 269,000 volumes of print materials and microforms (microfilm and microfiche). In addition, 5,000 nonprint items are housed in the general collection and in the Timmins Music Room. The library receives 730 scientific, literary, and general periodicals and provides access to more than 100 full-text and citation databases purchased through the Virtual Library of Virginia (VIVA) consortium. Preston Library is a selective government documents depository and currently holds 150,000 U.S. government and Virginia state documents, including an extensive number of materials produced by the Department of Defense.

The library collections are housed in a recently renovated building equipped with nearly thirty networked computers for research use. A new computer instruction lab enables librarians to offer hands-on training in the many electronic resources available.

The VMI local area network provides e-mail, word processing, spreadsheets, database management, graphics, writing analysis, compilers, statistical packages, and a variety of other software. VMI currently has twelve microcomputer labs to support instruction. There is a general lab in each of four academic buildings, a CADE and CEC lab to support mechanical engineering, two electrical engineering labs, a civil engineering lab, a Sun Workstation lab to support computer science, a new lab for modern languages, and a newly expanded lab in Preston Library for teaching and training.

The Barracks, where all cadets live, is wired to allow access to the VMI network and the Internet. Computer support for cadet-owned computers is offered through the Information Technology Department. Cadets who purchase the recommended laptop units receive support enabling them to successfully use their laptops on the VMI network. Computer support may also include tutorial sessions, Web page access, and trained cadet technicians for evening support. VMI's presence on its Web site, listed below, is the primary source of centralized current information for the Institute.

Athletics VMI offers conference, independent, and club sports for men in football, basketball, baseball, cross-country, indoor and outdoor track, wrestling, soccer, golf, swimming, and tennis. Women compete in cross-country and indoor and outdoor track, and there are plans to add women's soccer as early as fall 2003. A rifle team includes both men and women squad members.

Study Abroad VMI encourages cadets to engage in a variety of international educational experiences. The Institute maintains a number of international exchange relationships that facilitate this goal. In addition to semester programs, VMI offers a summer-abroad program with broad geographic coverage.

Two scholarship funds, the Ruth Miller Lanford Fund and the Burress Fund, specifically provide financial assistance to cadets for study-abroad or international internship opportunities. The Office of International Programs administers these programs. Approximately 10 percent of VMI's students participate in international study programs each year, and VMI has developed exchange programs with military academies in Britain, Germany, France, Lithuania, Thailand, Taiwan, Mongolia, Hungary, and Estonia. Significant numbers of VMI cadets also study each summer at Oxford University as part of a five-school Virginia consortium.

Support Services Cadets find ready access to faculty members and peer tutors through mentorship and tutoring programs, both formal and informal. In addition, the J. Clifford Miller, Jr. '28 Learning Center helps cadets at all levels to meet a variety of academic goals. The VMI Writing Center is staffed by professional tutors who provide assistance with assignments in composition and writing-intensive courses in the disciplines.

Job Opportunities Students are not permitted to work during the first year, but after that year, jobs are available in libraries, departmental offices, laboratories, the Cadet Center, and the VMI mess hall. In addition, cadets may be paid for work in certain types of undergraduate research, supervised by a faculty mentor.

Tuition: $2924 for state residents, $13,992 for nonresidents (2001–02)

Room and Board: $4838, including required residence in Barracks and twenty-one meals per week

Mandatory Fees: $3370, including Auxiliary Fee (medical services, activities, athletics, etc.), Technology Fee, and Quartermaster Fee (laundry, pressing, haircuts, etc.). Qualified cadets receive ROTC allowances to help defray the Quartermaster Fee.

Contact: Associate Dean for Academic Affairs and Chair: Robert L. McDonald, Institute Honors Advisory Committee, 213 Smith Hall, Virginia Military Institute, Lexington, Virginia 24450; Telephone: 540-464-7212; Fax: 540-464-7779; E-mail: mcdonaldrl@mail.vmi.edu; Web site: http://www.vmi.edu

---

Virginia Polytechnic Institute and State University

4 Pu G L Sc Tr

▼ University Honors Program

While the University Honors Program offers a significant complement of honors core curriculum courses, a colloquia series, and research opportunities, the major focus for the program is to encourage each student to seek a superior education consisting of the following elements: significant accomplishment in the instructional arena, participation in intellectual life beyond the instructional level, leadership/service activity, and extensive interaction with members of the faculty.

To these ends, such activities as a summer reading program leading to student-faculty conversation groups, special classes taught by senior faculty members, special classes concerning research methodologies, participation in major scholarship competitions, and seeking one of three honors degrees become tools students use. Because of the high quality of entering students, freshman honors courses are designed to assist students with Advanced Placement and International Baccalaureate, and other earned college credits link students to the broader curriculum of the University. A personal statement, curriculum vita project, and course of study planner assist students in preparing to use the curriculum to their advantage. Honors students are encouraged to seek diversity, and, as a result, many choose multiple majors and minors, often across college boundaries. The Honors Program and Graduate School maintain a five-year bachelor's/master's program.

The staff consists of a director, an assistant director, and an associate director. The faculty members participating in the program are drawn from the University at large, but the Academy of Teaching Excellence (made up of about 80 faculty members who have won major teaching awards) oversees the program. Faculty participation is both high (typically 200 faculty members participate in some aspect of the program) and enthusiastic. Working with the faculty, honors students have participated in research that has led to participation in professional meetings and publication in academic journals.

Honors provides access to the major facilities of the University, including some (such as graduate library privileges) not open to other undergraduate students. The Honors Program offers special lectures, faculty teas, and special leadership seminars in a not-for-credit environment. These activities are all integral to the education of the whole person.

The University Honors Program also administers advising for students who are planning a career in medicine or dentistry. A full-time faculty member counsels students individually and oversees the preparation and submission of letters of evaluation at the time of their application to professional school. The emphasis in premedical planning is on a broad education combined with a strong foundation in the natural sciences.

Interpreting the symbols: **2**=two-year college, **4**=four-year college; **Pu**=public or state college, **Pr**=private college; **G**=general honors program; **D**=departmental honors program; **S**=small program (fewer than 100 students), **M**=midsize program (100 to 500 students), **L**=large program (more than 500 students); **Sc**=scholarships available in honors program; **Tr**=transfer students accepted into honors program; **HBC**=historically black college; **AA**=academic advisors; **GA**=graduate advisors; **FA**=fellowship advisors.

The University Honors Program is more than 25 years old. The last six have been under the direction of the Academy of Teaching Excellence. There are about 1,500 students in the program.

Admission Process: Entering students must score 1300 or higher on the SAT I (620 verbal, 600 math) and must be in the top 10 percent of their graduating high school class. If the school does not rank, students must have a 3.75 GPA or better for automatic qualification. Students not meeting these criteria are invited to apply upon demonstration of special talent.

Scholarship Availability: The Honors Program offers merit-based scholarships as well as others that are both need- and merit-based. Scholarships range from $1000 to $3000. The honors application serves as the application for these scholarships.

The Campus Context: The seven colleges within the University are the Colleges of Agriculture and Life Sciences, Architecture, Arts and Sciences, Forestry and Wildlife, Human Resources and Education, and Veterinary Medicine and the Pamplin College of Business. Virginia Tech offers 103 degree programs.

Student Body The University enrolls more than 19,000 students. The student body is 42 percent women. There are more than 1,300 international students. Virginia Tech is a residential campus.

Faculty There are more than 1,600 faculty members, 1,430 of whom are full-time. The student-faculty ratio is 17:1.

Key Facilities The library holds more than 1.8 million volumes. Virginia Tech is a national leader in providing students access to the latest in computing facilities. Every dorm room is connected to the World Wide Web through Eudora (hardwired). There are computer labs in several dorms and academic buildings. The environment is very conducive to both DOS and Mac users. Special computer facilities include a multimedia lab, scientific visualization lab, and a new information building. Many departments are experimenting with computerized learning environments.

Honorary Societies Phi Eta Sigma, Phi Kappa Phi, Golden Key, Mortar Board, and Phi Beta Kappa

Athletics Most athletics are NCAA Division I. Virginia Tech is football's Music City Bowl champion and has renowned men's and women's basketball teams.

Study Abroad Virginia Tech owns a villa in Riva St. Vatale, Switzerland. Each semester, 2 faculty members take 25 students for a semester's study. Many other opportunities for study abroad are available in the various colleges.

Support Services Handicapped-accessible facilities are extensive and managed by a special office on campus.

Job Opportunities Work-study and other campus jobs are available. Many other off-campus opportunities exist. Honors students often participate in the co-op program.

Tuition: $3620 for state residents, $11,844 for nonresidents, per year (1998–99)

Room and Board: $3780

Contact: Director: Charles J. Dudley, 1 Hillcrest Hall, Blacksburg, Virginia 24061-0427; Telephone: 540-231-4951; E-mail: honors@vt.edu; Web site: http://www.vt.edu:10021/univhonors/

Wagner College

4 Pr G M Sc Tr

▼ Honors Program

The Wagner College Honors Program offers students in all majors an opportunity for academic enrichment, both inside the classroom and out.

All honors courses at Wagner fulfill the College-wide distribution requirements, and they are designed to provide the College's best students with a challenging, interactive learning environment that will enhance their overall academic experience at the College. The classes are small and taught by Wagner's finest faculty members.

The honors experience at Wagner extends beyond the classroom to a variety of cocurricular activities organized for honors students, ranging from a speaker series, a foreign film series, and other events on campus to trips into Manhattan to visit galleries and museums and attend plays and concerts. This creates a close-knit learning community for honors students that provides them with stimulation, friendship, and support. Many of Wagner's finest honors students also play an important leadership role on campus in student government, athletics, music, and theater. The Honors Program at Wagner is now in its tenth year and has become an important feature of the College's academic program.

There are 150 students in the program.

Participation Requirements: Students must complete five honors courses (out of a total of 36 units required for graduation), usually to meet the College distribution requirements. The final honors course is a Senior Honors Project, which is taken in the first semester of the senior year and gives advanced students an opportunity to work independently with a faculty mentor. Students who complete the program and maintain a minimum GPA of 3.5 receive an Honors Certificate upon graduation.

Admission Process: Students apply first to Wagner, and the Admissions Office decides who will be invited to join the Honors Program. Transfer students who wish to join may apply to the program director at the end of the freshman year or the beginning of the sophomore year. February 15 is the priority deadline.

Scholarship Availability: Wagner awards Presidential or Founders' Merit Scholarships to the best incoming freshmen, who are also invited to join the Honors Program. Scholarship recipients are not required to join the program, however, and students who have not received these prestigious scholarships are permitted to apply for admission to the Honors Program.

The Campus Context: Wagner College is a competitive, four-year private college founded in 1883. It is located on a lovely 105-acre, wooded campus on a hill overlooking New York harbor, only a ferry ride away from Manhattan. Twenty-two degree programs are offered on campus.

Student Body Undergraduate enrollment is 1,900; 52 percent are women. The ethnic distribution includes a minority population of 17 percent and 44 international students. Sixty-five percent of students are residential, and 70 percent receive some form of financial aid. There are five fraternities and five sororities.

Faculty The faculty numbers 182, of whom 95 are full-time; 82 percent hold terminal degrees. The student-faculty ratio is 18:1.

Key Facilities There are 285,000 volumes in the library. Other facilities include a mainframe computer and 150 IBM PC terminal environments, two electron microscopes, an art gallery, and a planetarium.

Honorary Society Omicron Delta Kappa

Athletics Wagner is NCAA Division I-A in all intercollegiate athletics except football, which is Division I-AA. Wagner is one of the five founders of the NIT at Madison Square Garden, and it has a tradition of excellence in baseball, basketball, and football. There is a well-equipped fitness center in the Student Union.

Study Abroad Wagner offers extensive opportunities for study abroad in Asia and Europe as well as other parts of the world. In association with the prestigious Institute for European and Asian Studies, Wagner students may study for a semester or summer in London, Madrid, Paris, Rome, Tokyo, and Vienna, among other locations.

Support Services The campus is partially accessible to disabled students and makes readers available for blind students.

Job Opportunities Work opportunities on campus include Federal Work-Study and non–work-study positions available in most administrative offices, residence halls, and academic departments.

Tuition: $20,500 per year (2001–02)

Room and Board: $7000

Contact: Director: Dr. Miles Groth, Staten Island, New York 10301; Telephone: 718-390-3482; Fax: 718-420-4158; E-mail: mgroth@wagner.edu; Web site: http://www.wagner.edu

WALDORF COLLEGE

4 Pr G S Sc Tr

▼ Honors College

The Honors College at Waldorf provides a rewarding learning environment for highly capable students. The program is distinguished by its select faculty members, interdisciplinary courses and seminars, independent projects, and a culminating world trip.

In addition to special course offerings and the world trip, Honors College students may choose to go on regional cultural trips, usually at no cost, to attend plays, concerts, lectures, and conferences.

There are 60 students currently enrolled in the program.

Participation Requirements: Students may remain in Honors College as long as they meet the 3.25 GPA eligibility requirement. Each semester students may take honors sections of general education courses, honors courses, and/or independent projects in their majors. Honors College students with at least a 3.5 GPA who also take several prescribed courses, undertake a special research project in their major, and give a presentation at Waldorf's annual academic conference are eligible for Waldorf Scholar status. Waldorf Scholars travel for two or three weeks to a global destination with 2 faculty members. Students pay a nominal fee for the trip; the College subsidizes most of the cost in honor of its Honors Scholars.

Entering students take a two-semester freshman seminar that replaces the first-year English requirement, and they may elect to take honors sections of other required courses. Sophomores typically take a philosophy course that is team-taught by selected faculty members, administrators (including the president of the College), and outside resource persons from the community. Honors colloquia, which focus on controversial issues in a seminar setting, are offered each semester.

The Campus Context: Waldorf College is a distinctive residential college affiliated with the Evangelical Lutheran Church of America. It occupies 50 acres and fourteen buildings in Forest City, Iowa, to which it attracts a student body of about 700 students from the region and from twenty states and twenty nations of the world. The College offers a variety of B.A. and A.A. degrees. All entering students are equipped with IBM Thinkpads, and the campus is fully networked. Computer facilities and student access to high-end technology at Waldorf exceed the capabilities of most other institutions in the region. The Honors College, another special offering at Waldorf, is an expansion of the very successful Honors Program that has been a feature at Waldorf for twelve years.

Student Body Of the 700 students, 46 percent are women. Four percent represent ethnic minorities. There are 77 international students. Ninety-five percent of the students receive financial aid.

Faculty The faculty totals 62 members, of whom 42 are full-time, and 43 percent have Ph.D. or other terminal degrees.

Key Facilities The library houses 40,000 volumes. All students are provided IBM Thinkpad laptops; also available are a fourteen-station multimedia lab and two computer labs. Waldorf's business and communications programs offer work in the new multimedia lab that has fourteen PowerMacs. The AVID digital video editing suite is also available to students.

Honorary Society Phi Theta Kappa

Athletics Waldorf has a very successful program of intercollegiate athletics, competing in Region XI of the National Junior College Athletic Association. Sports include baseball, basketball, football, golf, soccer, and wrestling for men and basketball, golf, soccer, softball, and volleyball for women.

Study Abroad Business and communications B.A. students can spend a winter term studying in Oxford, England; humanities B.A. students can spend a spring term in London; and Honors College students may participate in the world trip, a guided study trip abroad.

Support Services The campus is accessible to the physically disabled; support personnel and programs are available to the learning disabled.

Job Opportunities Waldorf offers work-study and other work opportunities on campus.

Tuition: $12,708 per year (2001–02)

Room and Board: $5252

Mandatory Fees: $620

Contact: Director: Dr. Robert Alsop, 106 South 6th Street, Forest City, Iowa 50436; Telephone: 641-585-8225; Fax: 641-585-8194; E-mail: alsop@waldorf.edu

WALSH UNIVERSITY

4 Pr G S Sc Tr AA

▼ General Honors Program

The Walsh University General Honors Program offers motivated and capable undergraduate students the opportunity to broaden and deepen their academic experience. Students participate in an intellectually challenging and innovative curriculum emphasizing interdisciplinary and independent studies. Outside of the classroom, honors students have the advantage of enriching cultural and social activities planned especially for them. As members of the Walsh University Honors Society, honors students join with faculty, administrators, and peers in fostering a community of learners with a shared sense of purpose in the pursuit of academic excellence.

The program began in 1993–94. There are currently 60 students in the program, which can accommodate up to 24 students in each of the freshman, sophomore, junior, and senior classes.

Participation Requirements: In their freshman year, students in the General Honors Program take special sections of history and English. In their sophomore year, they take two special sections of Honors World Literature. Qualified transfer and second-year students can join the honors program under the Track II option with Honors 200.

In their junior year, honors students take two team-taught, interdisciplinary courses with rotating topics and complete a junior honors project in one of their regularly scheduled upper-division courses, usually in their major.

The capstone of the honors program is the senior honors thesis, an independent research project of either 3 or 6 credits that allows students to investigate issues of significance while working closely with a supportive faculty mentor. Honors projects are

Interpreting the symbols: **2**=two-year college, **4**=four-year college; **Pu**=public or state college, **Pr**=private college; **G**=general honors program; **D**=departmental honors program; **S**=small program (fewer than 100 students), **M**=midsize program (100 to 500 students), **L**=large program (more than 500 students); **Sc**=scholarships available in honors program; **Tr**=transfer students accepted into honors program; **HBC**=historically black college; **AA**=academic advisors; **GA**=graduate advisors; **FA**=fellowship advisors.

modeled on the types of research, writing, and creativity typical of graduate schools and are meant to serve as preparation for such study. The project includes an oral presentation in a final celebration with faculty members and peers in fulfilling the final requirements of the program.

All honors courses except the senior thesis fulfill either core or major requirements. Students completing the General Honors Program graduate with 27 to 30 credit hours of honors courses. Track II students graduate with 18 to 21 credit hours.

Admission Process: To be eligible to apply for the General Honors Program, students must meet any two of the following three criteria: a high school GPA of 3.5 or above, a minimum ACT score of 27 or a minimum SAT I score of 1200, and graduation in the top 10 percent of one's high school class. Track II candidates must have completed at least 30 credit hours of undergraduate work with at least a 3.3 GPA. Students remain in good standing in the honors program with a 3.3 cumulative GPA and at least a grade of B in all honors courses.

Scholarship Availability: The University offers a limited number of full tuition Presidential Scholarships to incoming freshmen. Presidential Scholars are automatically part of the honors program. To apply for a Presidential Scholarship a student must meet two of the following three criteria: 4.0 GPA, rank in the upper 1 percent of the graduating class, and a minimum score of 31 on the ACT or 1230 on the SAT I. All other students accepted into the honors program receive a $1000 Honors Program Scholarship in addition to other scholarships they may qualify for. Honors Program Scholarships are renewable each year a student remains eligible for the program.

The Campus Context: Walsh University is an independent, coeducational, Catholic liberal arts institution. Founded by the Brothers of Christian Instruction, Walsh University is dedicated to a values-based education with an international perspective in the Judeo-Christian tradition. Walsh University is located in North Canton, 5 miles north of Canton in northeastern Ohio. Akron is 20 miles away, and both Cleveland and Youngstown are within an hour's drive. Walsh University has nine major buildings on its 60-acre suburban campus. More than forty degree programs are offered.

Among distinguished campus facilities is the Hannon Child Development Center, which provides specialized educational facilities for special-needs and at-risk children ages 2–10 and their families. It has teaching stations for teacher preparation students, a motor development room for physical activities, classrooms for University and early education students, and a computer classroom. The Science Center was recently renovated extensively in support of the University's physical therapy program. The University offers a pre–physical therapy program and is accredited by the Ohio Board of Regents and the American Physical Therapy Association for its five-year bachelor's degree in physical therapy. Renovations have included the creation of a mini-clinic, academic laboratory, conference room, and offices. A large, new student center is scheduled for completion in spring 2002.

Student Body Undergraduate enrollment is approximately 1,400. Fifty-nine percent are women. The ethnic distribution is 0.1 percent American Indian/Alaskan Native, 5 percent black/African American, 0.3 percent Asian American, and 80 percent white. There are 47 international students. Resident students make up 30 percent of the population, and approximately 80 percent of the students receive financial aid.

Faculty There are a total of 125 faculty members, 65 of whom are full-time. Sixty-eight percent hold terminal degrees. The student-faculty ratio is 19:1.

Key Facilities The library houses 130,000 volumes, 750 current periodical subscriptions on paper, and 400 current periodical subscriptions with full text on CD-ROM. There are more than 130 computers on campus available to students, including Macs and PCs. There are large computer labs in the Science Center, Lemmon residence hall, and the Hannon Child Development Center. Computers in other buildings are also available to students. Campus computers are networked with Internet access. Computer hookups with Internet access are located in each residence hall room (student must provide computer).

Athletics Walsh University has eight men's and eight women's intercollegiate athletic teams, which are members of the Mid-Ohio Conference (MOC), National Association of Intercollegiate Athletics (Division II) and the Mid States Football Association. Men's sports include baseball, basketball, cross-country, football, golf, soccer, tennis, and track. Women's sports include basketball, cross-country, soccer, softball, synchronized swimming, tennis, track, and volleyball. In 1995–96, Walsh won the MOC All-Sports Award, becoming the first school to win the award three times.

Support Services Facilities for disabled students include the Lemmon residence hall, which is particularly suited for special-needs students. Most of the campus is accessible to disabled students, and Walsh offers assistance for disabled students on an individual basis.

Job Opportunities With the exception of the summer sessions, work opportunities on campus are offered through the Federal Work-Study Program.

Tuition: $12,760 per year (2001–02)

Room and Board: $6910

Mandatory Fees: $375

Contact: Director: Dr. John Kandl, 2020 Easton, NW, North Canton, Ohio 44720; Telephone: 330-490-7127; Fax: 330-499-8518; E-mail: kandl@alex.walsh.edu

WASHINGTON STATE UNIVERSITY

4 Pu G L Sc Tr

▼ University Honors College

The University Honors College (UHC) at Washington State University is one of the oldest (founded in 1960) and best known honors programs in the nation. A free-standing academic unit, the UHC offers highly motivated and talented students a four-year general education curriculum. The UHC has as its primary goal the fostering of genuine intellectual curiosity and the encouragement of lifelong learning among its students. The UHC aims to support the best possible teaching and learning opportunities for participating faculty members and students. Honors courses are small and are taught by faculty members who have a commitment to teaching undergraduate students. The UHC has a tradition of encouraging students to study a foreign language and to study abroad. Approximately half of the honors students complete a foreign language through the intermediate level; one third study abroad in one of the University's special Honors Exchanges or Education Abroad programs.

Several special programs are available to WSU honors students. These include the Honors/Veterinary Medicine program that enables eligible students to complete a B.S./D.V.M. in six years rather than eight; the 4 & 1 program that allows students to obtain a B.A. in a liberal arts major and an M.B.A. in five years rather than six; special Honors Exchanges to Wales and Denmark; and the opportunity to live in WSU's Scholars Residence Hall or Honors Hall.

Approximately 1,100 students are enrolled in the UHC. Honors students major in every department and college at WSU.

Participation Requirements: The honors curriculum is a four-year program that requires the same number of credits as the general education program. To graduate from the UHC, students must have a minimum 3.2 overall GPA. Each semester, the UHC honors its graduates before Commencement when certificates, awards, and special honors medallions are distributed. Completion of the Honors curriculum also is noted on students' transcripts.

Admission Process: Admission of first-year students to the UHC is by invitation and by application. After students have applied and been admitted to WSU, Honors College faculty members review their files and identify prospective honors students based upon their high school grades, test scores (SAT or ACT), and (if available) recommendations from high school faculty members or counselors. Those who do not meet automatic admissions criteria (a minimum GPA of 3.8 and a minimum SAT of 1280) may submit an application. Transfer and international students are admitted on an individual basis after eligibility has been determined.

Within WSU guidelines, the UHC accepts Advanced Placement, International Baccalaureate, and Running Start credits to fulfill honors requirements.

Scholarship Availability: The Honors College administers many scholarships. In addition, WSU has many merit scholarship programs at the departmental, college, and university level. Honors students are among the most frequent recipients of these awards. Regents Scholars receive a full-ride university scholarship for four years, and are automatically admitted to the UHC.

The Campus Context: Washington State University was founded in 1890 as the state's land-grant university. There are ninety-six degree programs offered in the nine colleges, which include the Colleges of Pharmacy, Liberal Arts, Veterinary Medicine, Agriculture and Home Economics, Business and Economics, Engineering and Architecture, Sciences, Nursing, and Education. The main campus in Pullman is located in the rolling farmlands of southeast Washington. WSU is one of the largest residential campuses west of the Mississippi River. WSU's branch campuses were established in 1989 and are located in major urban areas in the state: Spokane, the Tri-Cities, and Vancouver.

The UHC is housed in Honors Hall. Within Honors Hall are faculty and staff offices, a library, a formal lounge, and three residence floors. There is also access to a state-of-the-art computer lab. At this time, honors programs are available only on the Pullman and Vancouver campuses.

Student Body Undergraduate enrollment is 16,839; 52 percent of the students are women. The minority ethnic distribution is 1.5 percent Native American, 5.3 percent Asian-American, 3 percent African American, and 3.3 percent Hispanic. There are 1,158 international students. Forty-two percent of students live on campus, and 62 percent of WSU undergraduate students receive financial aid. The campus has twenty-five fraternities and fourteen sororities.

Faculty Instructional faculty members number 1,255. Eighty-three percent have terminal degrees. The student-faculty ratio is 13:1.

Key Facilities WSU libraries house more than 2 million volumes. There are seven University-operated computer labs; many other computer labs are located in departments and colleges.

Other special or distinguishing campus facilities include Stevens Hall, on the Historic Register, the oldest and most continuously in-use residence hall West of the Mississippi River; the new Veterinary Teaching Hospital; a new main library; Beasley Performing Arts Coliseum; and art, anthropology, and science museums. The new Student Recreation Center is the largest in the country.

Honorary Societies Phi Eta Sigma, Phi Kappa Phi, Golden Key, Mortar Board, Phi Beta Kappa, National Society of Collegiate Scholars

Athletics WSU is a member of the NCAA's PAC 10, and facilities are available for all major sports, including baseball, basketball, crew, football, golf, swimming, tennis, and track and field. WSU has one of the largest University-sponsored intramural programs in the nation.

Study Abroad Through WSU's Education Abroad Office, students can participate in exchanges, study-abroad programs, internships, and service-learning opportunities in most countries around the world. The Honors College has special exchanges to Wales and Denmark.

Support Services Ninety percent of the campus is accessible to physically disabled students.

Job Opportunities Work opportunities are available on and off campus.

Tuition: $4190 for state residents, $11,355 for nonresidents, per year (2001–02)

Room and Board: $5200

Mandatory Fees: $414

Contact: Dean: Dr. Mary Wack, Honors Hall, Room 130, Pullman, Washington 99164-2012; Telephone: 509-335-4505; Fax: 509-335-3784; E-mail: honors@wsu.edu

Wayne State University

4 Pu G/D M Tr

▼ Honors Program

The Honors Program at Wayne State University (WSU) is designed for highly motivated students with superior abilities who learn in the intimate atmosphere associated with small selective colleges, yet who thrive on being in a leading urban research university with outstanding physical and cultural facilities. Undergraduates in any college or department may, if eligible, take honors courses. There are two honors tracks: students may choose departmental or University honors or do both. Transfer students can complete all requirements in their junior and senior years.

The program is located in its own building; it also has a separate study room in the undergraduate library. A new dormitory facility allots special space to honors students. Currently, approximately 800 students are enrolled, 125 of whom are honors majors or comajors.

Participation Requirements: Students take 15–20 percent of their course work in honors in a variety of settings: exclusive honors classes, honors sections of regular classes, and Honors–Option, which turns a regular course into honors for individual students. Honors classes are limited to no more than 20 students. Each honors student must take an upper-division interdisciplinary seminar offered by the program and complete an honors thesis or project. The Honors Program designation is attached to both the transcript and the diploma upon successful completion of the program.

Admission Process: Entering freshmen must have a GPA of at least 3.5 or a score of at least 1100 on the SAT I (26 on the ACT). Transfer students are required to have a GPA of at least 3.3. All Presidential Scholarship recipients are automatically eligible.

Scholarship Availability: Research grants up to $500 are available. In addition, the University has a Presidential Scholarship Program available to selected Michigan high school and community college students who have demonstrated scholastic ability as they graduate from their educational institutions. The award for high school students provides tuition for a maximum of eight semesters (32 credits per academic year), and the award for Michigan community college graduates offers tuition for a maximum of

Interpreting the symbols: **2**=two-year college, **4**=four-year college; **Pu**=public or state college, **Pr**=private college; **G**=general honors program; **D**=departmental honors program; **S**=small program (fewer than 100 students), **M**=midsize program (100 to 500 students), **L**=large program (more than 500 students); **Sc**=scholarships available in honors program; **Tr**=transfer students accepted into honors program; **HBC**=historically black college; **AA**=academic advisors; **GA**=graduate advisors; **FA**=fellowship advisors.

four semesters (32 credits per academic year). Eligibility requirements for high school graduates include a minimum 3.5 GPA and an SAT I score of 870 or higher or an ACT score of 22 or higher. Eligibility requirements for Michigan community college graduates include an earned associate degree and a minimum 3.75 GPA. For more information, students should contact the University Admissions Office, 3 East, Helen Newberry Joy Student Services Center; Telephone: 313-577-3577.

The Campus Context: The early history of the University is an account of originally unrelated colleges and schools that were united in 1933 into a single institution, Wayne University, under the control of the Detroit Board of Education. In 1956, this institution became Wayne State University. The University makes available more than 600 fields of study or concentration leading to more than 350 different degrees at the bachelor's, master's, and doctoral levels. Wayne State University is a national research university with an urban teaching and service mission. It is in the top 2.5 percent of all universities nationally in the Carnegie Commission rankings. More than 100 buildings provide housing for the service, instructional, and research needs. WSU is an equal opportunity/affirmative action employer.

Student Body Some 70 percent of WSU full-time undergraduates receive financial aid. The University awarded more than $100 million in financial aid to more than 17,000 students in 1999–2000. A substantial number of fraternities and sororities are on the campus.

Faculty Instructional faculty members number 2,705. The student-faculty ratio is 11:1.

Key Facilities The total holdings at the Walter P. Reuther Library exceed 3 million volumes, 18,000 serials, and a broad range of electronic resources accessible on more than 700 public computers.

Athletics Wayne State University sponsors fourteen NCAA Division II teams and Division I men's and women's hockey teams. Plans are under way to raise some other teams to Division I status. The Matthaei Complex offers myriad drop-in activity areas that include courts and fields for basketball, football, jogging, racquetball, soccer, squash, tennis, and volleyball; a weight-training/exercise room; and swimming/diving facilities. A state-of-the-art recreation and fitness center is at the center of the campus. The use of these facilities is free.

Study Abroad WSU sponsors travel-study programs in Ghana and South Africa, Benin and West Africa, Cuba, Haiti, and Greece; an exchange program with the University of Salford in England; and a junior year in Munich, Germany.

Support Services For students with physical or learning problems, there are an Educational Accessibility Services Office and an Academic Success Center, both equipped to provide a wide array of services.

Job Opportunities Work-study arrangements, student assistantships, and internships are plentiful on campus, as are work opportunities off campus.

Tuition: $3888 for residents ($129.60 per credit hour) and $8910 for nonresidents ($297 per credit hour) per year.

Room and Board: Room and board for an independent, full-time student are approximately $6450 for nine months.

Mandatory Fees: Omnibus fee of $11.70 per credit hour up to a maximum of 12 credits per semester.

Contact: Administrative Assistant: Stuart May, 2311 Faculty/Administration Building, Detroit, Michigan 48202; Telephone: 313-577-3030; E-mail: ab1508@wayne.edu

WEBER STATE UNIVERSITY

4 Pu G M Sc Tr

▼ Honors Program

The Honors Program fosters the growth of intellectual independence and initiative, invites a sophisticated level of classroom and extracurricular interaction, and examines complex issues from diverse perspectives. The chief goal of the Honors Program is to help students become competitive with graduates of any undergraduate institution. To do this, the Honors Program believes that each student should be well grounded in the liberal arts, engage in exploration and research, develop and articulate personal perspectives through strong written and oral communication skills, develop an understanding of global issues through travel study opportunities, become an active participant in the campus and local community through community service and volunteerism, and join in the creation of an undergraduate community of scholars.

Honors Program classes are limited to a maximum of 15 students and are taught by a select faculty. Honors faculty members are distinguished by their commitment to academic excellence and for their ability to work and communicate with highly motivated undergraduates. The University's teaching method emphasizes reading original sources, writing essays, and Socratic dialogue. The Honors Program also creates a learning community of students and faculty members through extracurricular social and cultural activities, guest speakers, study groups, participation in national and regional conferences, and travel-abroad opportunities.

There are two honors designations in the Weber Honors Program: University Honors and Departmental Honors. University Honors are available to all Honors Program students graduating with a bachelor's degree. Departmental Honors are available to students majoring in departments with designated Departmental Honors options. The new honors student begins taking University Honors classes to satisfy their general education requirements starting with an introductory honors education class. Established in 1969, the program currently enrolls 166 students (34 seniors, 38 juniors, 32 sophomores, and 62 freshmen).

Participation Requirements: To graduate with University Honors, a student must complete a minimum of 27 University Honors credits, including 21 honors core credits, and can include 6 credit hours of classes with an honors component in their major. The Honors Core classes include Perspectives in the Applied Arts and Sciences: Introduction to Intellectual Traditions (3 credits), choice of at least one West and one East, Intellectual Traditions: Great Ideas of the West in the Classical and Medieval Eras (3 credits), Intellectual Traditions: Great Ideas of the Modern Era (3 credits), Intellectual Traditions: Great Ideas of the East (3 credits), Great Books (3 credits), Honors Colloquium (1–3 credits), and Honors Senior Project (2–8 credits, taken over a two-semester period normally during the last two semesters of the senior year).

The requirements for graduation with Departmental Honors vary depending on the student's departmental major. Most departments require students graduating with Departmental Honors to complete 9 credit hours of University Honors classes, 12 hours of upper-division classes in their major with an honors component, and maintain a cumulative 3.5 GPA.

Students are expected to take an honors class every semester until general education requirements are completed, after which they are expected to take at least one course every other semester. No grades below B will be acceptable for credit toward graduation with University or Departmental Honors. Student progress is reviewed each semester. An honors student having apparent difficulty in maintaining these standards will be offered counseling and assistance from the honors professional staff.

Official recognition is given for the completion of University Honors or Departmental Honors. Notation of these achievements is made on the graduating Honors student's transcript and diploma and entered into Commencement programs.

Admission Process: A student may apply for entrance into the Honors Program anytime after formal acceptance by the Weber State Admissions Office. However, to take advantage of the many options available, early entrance is recommended. An application form is available in the honors office. The applicant is asked to provide evidence of a cumulative GPA of at least 3.5 or an ACT score of 26 or SAT I score of 1150; provide a recommendation from a university professor, a high school teacher or counselor, or another professional educator; give the honors director a writing sample; attend an honors orientation with a member of the Honors Program staff; and register for the honors introductory class. Incoming first-year students may elect to participate in the Honors Bridge Program.

The Campus Context: Weber State University (WSU), established 1889, is a four-year institution of higher education in Ogden, Utah. WSU offers 153 separate degrees and is the largest and most comprehensive undergraduate program in the state of Utah. It has a student body of 14,000 drawn predominantly from the Wasatch Front but also including students from forty-six states and thirty-four other countries. Its forty-eight buildings house abundant classrooms and laboratories, excellent student computing facilities, outstanding performing arts auditoriums, a spacious library, and a well-equipped health and fitness center. There are six colleges on campus: Applied Science and Technology, Arts and Humanities, Business and Economics, Education, Health Professions, and Science and Social and Behavioral Sciences.

WSU is large and complex enough to offer a stimulating educational challenge but small enough to be concerned about the welfare of individual students. WSU works closely as partners-in-learning with communities and organizations.

Student Body Undergraduate enrollment is 13,900; 53 percent are women. Ethnic distribution of the total undergraduate population is 1 percent African American, 1 percent Native American, 2 percent Asian/Pacific Islander, and 3 percent Hispanic. About 55 percent of the students receive financial aid.

Faculty There are 441 full-time faculty members, 80 percent of whom have doctorates or other terminal degrees. The student-faculty ratio is 18:1.

Key Facilities The library houses 407,956 bound volumes; 2,196 periodical subscriptions; 453,388 titles on microform; 12,379 audio, video, and computer titles; and 59,377 maps.

Student computer labs are distributed around the campus and are under the charge of various departments. In addition, academic computing manages fifty-two PC workstations in natural science and nine PC and three Mac workstations in the library. The Honors Center is on the second floor of the library; there are five PC/Windows computers available for student use. There are twenty-five PC and two Mac workstations in the Wattis Lab, fifty-two PC workstations and a classroom with thirty workstations in social science, and forty-three Mac workstations in education.

Honorary Societies Phi Kappa Phi and Golden Key

Support Services WSU is a fully accessible campus for disabled students. Service programs include reading, note-taking, interpreting, scribe service, and campus transportation.

Job Opportunities Cooperative education, internship programs, and on-campus job opportunities, including work-study, are available through the Career Services Office.

Tuition: $2252 for state residents, $6718 for nonresidents, per year (2001–02)

Room and Board: $3198

Mandatory Fees: $426

Contact: Director: Dr. Robert Mondi, 2904 University Circle, Ogden, Utah 84408-2904; Telephone: 801-626-6186; Fax: 801-626-7568; E-mail: rmondi@weber.edu

West Chester University of Pennsylvania

4 Pu G M Sc Tr AA

▼ Honors Program

The aim of the Honors Program at West Chester University (WCU) is to provide an exciting environment for academically gifted and highly motivated students to interact in a learning community of peers, faculty members, administrators, and staff members that will challenge and enrich the students' college experience. Grounded in the liberal arts tradition, the Honors Program seeks cross-disciplinary connections to develop students' natural intellectual abilities and challenge them to employ those gifts on behalf of the larger community. To that end, the Honors Program seeks to build character and foster a commitment to lifelong learning that prepares leaders for the twenty-first century. The program's aim is summarized best in its motto: To be honorable is to serve.

The Honors Program's newly introduced curricular focus fosters this aim. During the first five semesters, a core of nine sequenced courses will familiarize students with defining and addressing leadership challenges facing today's communities. These classes, designed by dedicated, enthusiastic honors faculty members, are usually team-taught and small (10–20 students), thus fostering discussion and opportunities for off-campus learning experiences. Upon completion of the honors core, the culminating experience, a student-designed senior project mentored by a faculty member, provides students with the opportunity to identify, investigate, and address creatively a problem in a community business, nonprofit agency, or research laboratory. Many students have found their senior projects to be effective springboards to future academic or professional aspirations.

Throughout their years in the West Chester Honors Program, students experience many benefits beyond the strictly academic. They receive support from both fellow students and honors faculty and staff members, who are always available for additional advising. WCU honors students also enjoy the substantial benefits of priority scheduling and honors housing in Killinger Hall, which is fully wired for individual computer connection to the University system. Honors students qualify for honors scholarship awards and have the opportunity to participate in the International Summer Honors Program, whose locations rotate annually. Finally, students qualify for membership in the very active Honors Student Association and have the opportunity to serve on the Honors Council and governance committees.

WCU's Honors Program, which was founded in 1978, admits 40 freshmen each year. There are approximately 130 students currently enrolled in the program.

Participation Requirements: By the end of their fifth semester, all honors students must complete a 27-hour honors core that includes 100- and 200-level cross-disciplinary courses. These courses, plus one additional science course, fulfill the University's general education requirements for honors students. The 100-level core courses focus on personal development, including physical and psychological well-being, communication, and ethics and morality in a technological age. Courses at the 200-level build upon the learner's knowledge of self and address broader perspectives of community and social change. Program members are expected to maintain a minimum 3.25 GPA, progress through the honors core, and actively participate in campus community life to remain in good standing with the program. After comple-

Interpreting the symbols: **2**=two-year college, **4**=four-year college; **Pu**=public or state college, **Pr**=private college; **G**=general honors program; **D**=departmental honors program; **S**=small program (fewer than 100 students), **M**=midsize program (100 to 500 students), **L**=large program (more than 500 students); **Sc**=scholarships available in honors program; **Tr**=transfer students accepted into honors program; **HBC**=historically black college; **AA**=academic advisors; **GA**=graduate advisors; **FA**=fellowship advisors.

tion of the honors core, students complete a 3-credit senior project. Each spring, the WCU Honors Program honors its graduates with an Awards Banquet attended by the honors faculty and top University officials; special awards and certificates are distributed at this time.

Admission Process: Membership in honors is competitive, with a maximum of forty seats open each fall. Current membership includes students from forty-four different academic majors; 72 percent women, 28 percent men, and 12 percent multicultural. Incoming freshmen and transfer students are normally invited to apply to the program if they demonstrate at least two of the following: a minimum high school GPA of 3.5; a minimum SAT I score of 1200; rank in the top 20 percent of their graduating class; a record of achievement in high school Honors/AP courses. Invited students are asked to submit an application form, two short essays, and a letter of recommendation. Candidates are reviewed by committee and selected on the basis of commitment to service, leadership potential, and their fit with the program's philosophy. WCU employs a rolling admissions policy.

Scholarship Availability: The Honors Program awards the Mynn Diefendorfer White Honors Scholarship, a $1000 renewable tuition scholarship, to an outstanding junior in the Honors Program. In addition, WCU has many merit scholarship programs at the departmental, college, and University level. Honors students are among the most frequent recipients of these awards.

The Campus Context: A comprehensive, multipurpose institution, West Chester University of Pennsylvania offers high-quality undergraduate and graduate degree programs in more than 100 subject areas as well as certification programs. As the second-largest member of the State System of Higher Education, West Chester is able to provide a full and rewarding educational experience at an affordable cost. With a rich heritage dating back more than 125 years, West Chester University was founded in 1871 as West Chester Normal School. Today, more than 11,400 students, along with 1,500 faculty and staff members, study and work on the picturesque 388-acre campus situated in the Borough of West Chester. Strategically located at the center of the mid-Atlantic corridor, between New York City and Washington, D.C., West Chester is just 25 miles west of Philadelphia and 17 miles north of Wilmington, Delaware.

Student Body Undergraduate enrollment is 9,400 undergraduate students and about 2,000 graduate students. West Chester's student body represents a cross section of many ethnic, racial, and religious groups and includes students from all economic levels.

Faculty The total number of faculty members is 713, of whom 549 are full-time. The number of faculty members holding terminal degrees is 402. The student-faculty ratio is 17:1.

Key Facilities The Francis Harvey Green Library contains more than 874,000 volumes. The centrally located Academic Computing Laboratory provides computer access for all students on campus. In addition, each dormitory and residence hall is computer equipped while each room in the honors dormitory, Killinger Hall, is wired for computer use.

Honorary Societies Delta Kappa Gamma, Kappa Delta Pi, Omicron Delta Kappa

Athletics West Chester University offers a well-balanced program for men and women, with opportunities for competition in its intercollegiate programs. WCU student athletes compete in the PSAC (Pennsylvania State Athletic Conference), recognized as one of the most competitive Division II conferences in the country. The exceptions are men's lacrosse and gymnastics and men's and women's indoor track, which compete as Division II independents, and field hockey, WCU's only Division I program, which has become a member of the Atlantic 10. The Department of Recreation and Leisure Programs provides leisure activities for the entire University community, including competitive intramural sports, sport clubs, informal recreation opportunities, special events, aerobics, wellness and fitness programs, and outdoor recreation. WCU has a multitude of athletic facilities, including the Sykes Union Fitness Center, the Sanderson Court recreation area, and the indoor Hollinger/Ehinger complex on North Campus. South Campus accommodations include the Farrell Football Stadium, baseball and softball diamonds, tennis courts, a quarter-mile track, and fields for football practice, soccer, field hockey, and lacrosse.

Study Abroad While the West Chester Office of International Studies sponsors study-abroad programs to many countries around the world, two WCU honors students are selected each year to participate in a three-week, fully funded study-abroad program with other honors students from across the State System of Education. Past students have studied archaeology in England and Italy. The 2002 trip will focus on conflict in Spanish art and culture, and upcoming trips will focus on the Renaissance and Reformation in Italy, Germany, and England; the Enlightenment in Scotland; and nation building in South Africa.

Support Services West Chester University is committed to compliance with the Americans with Disabilities Act of 1990. In addition to providing legally mandated services for persons with disabilities who voluntarily seek additional services, the Office of Services for Students with Disabilities coordinates tutoring, academic advisement, and other support services.

Job Opportunities Numerous work opportunities are available both on and off campus.

Tuition: $1734 for residents, $4412 for nonresidents, per year (1998–1999)

Room and board: $1430

Mandatory Fees: $385

Contact: Director: Dr. Kevin W. Dean, 131 Francis Harvey Green Library, West Chester, Pennsylvania 19383-2423; Telephone: 610-436-2996; Fax: 610-436-2620; E-mail: dcarney@wcupa.edu; Web site: http://www.wcupa.edu/_ACADEMICS/cae.hon/default.htm

West Liberty State College

4 Pu G S Tr

▼ Honors Program

The West Liberty State College (WLSC) Honors Program offers enrichment courses and programming for honors students in the context of a small state-related college. The program, which is more than 30 years old, was greatly revised in 1991 and 1999 to its present offerings. In a minimum of four semesters, students take a total of four honors courses, either seminars or one-to-one mentoring with a faculty member on a topic of the student's choice. In addition, students complete an independent capstone project. A provision of the Honors Program also permits students to design and carry out independent study courses in any discipline, with the permission of the department. The program provides regular opportunities for cultural and intellectual enrichment activities. The program currently serves 30 students, many of whom reside in Bonar Hall, which is the campus honors residence hall.

WLSC students having a College GPA of 3.5 and minimum of four semesters remaining before graduation may apply for admission the Honors Program at the beginning of any semester. The applications, which include essays and recommendations, are individually considered by the Honors Council that oversees the program and selects candidates for admission.

Participation Requirements: Honors Program students must maintain a GPA of 3.5. They are also required to have a minimum of four semesters of active participation in the program, including monthly meetings and one cultural or intellectual group activity per semester. Students meeting all requirements of participation, courses, and the capstone project receive recognition at the spring Honors Convocation, and at commencement by wearing honors stoles and having a special program designation. Their participation is also noted on their transcripts.

Scholarship Availability: West Liberty State College awards a variety of scholarships for students of exceptional academic merit, including its highest academic scholarship, the Elbin Scholars Award, based on ACT and high school GPA. Elbin Scholars are also eligible for freshman membership in the Honors Program. The Honors Program itself does not provide scholarships.

The Campus Context: West Liberty State College, the oldest institution of higher education in the state, is an accredited, coeducational, state-assisted college in the narrow northern panhandle of West Virginia between southwestern Pennsylvania and eastern Ohio. The rural setting of the hilltop campus provides relative seclusion for study and its proximity to cities gives students ample opportunity for internships, employment, and recreation. The College offers strong liberal arts and professional programs. Nearly 30 percent of the student body are pursuing degrees in elementary or secondary teacher education, while 21 percent are enrolled in business curricula. Notable College facilities include the Academic, Sports, and Recreation Complex with a new state-of-the-art, multipurpose arena, science of exercise suite, wellness/fitness center, conference center, and the Arnett Hall of Natural Sciences that has excellent laboratories and equipment. Seven residence halls on campus, including the honors residence Bonar Hall, serve students.

Student Body Undergraduate enrollment in 2001 was 2,633 students, consisting of 1,172 men and 1,461 women. Resident students make up 45 percent of the population while nontraditional students account for 17 percent.

Faculty Of 166 faculty members, 112 are full-time and 46 have terminal degrees.

Key Facilities The Paul N. Elbin Library houses more than 200,000 print volumes and 800 hard copy periodical and newspaper subscriptions. Computing facilities are located the Main Hall lab and PC labs around campus.

Athletics Intercollegiate athletics offers fifteen men's and women's sports; the college belongs to Division II of the NCAA.

Support Services The College provides both accessible buildings and special services for students with disabilities.

Job Opportunities In addition to the Work-Study Program, the College employs students as assistants to head residents and part-time assistants in certain departments.

Tuition: For 2001–02, semester charges were $1258 for state residents and $3124 for nonresidents.

Room and Board: For 2001–02, semester charges were $1920 for Bonar Hall, honors dorm; $1670 for all other dorms.

Contact: Director: Dr. Linda O. McGinley, Humanities, West Liberty State College, P.O. Box 85, West Liberty, West Virginia 26074; Telephone: 304-336-8203; E-mail: mcginlin@wlsc.edu

West Los Angeles College

2 Pu G S Tr

▼ Transfer Honors Program

The Transfer Honors Program at West Los Angeles College (WLAC) offers academic enrichment courses to highly motivated students. The mission of this program is to better prepare the honors students to transfer successfully. Students also enjoy consideration for special transfer scholarships and housing concessions as honors graduates.

Students who complete the Transfer Honors Program receive priority consideration for transfer admission to major four-year universities. At present, West Los Angeles College has established transfer agreements with the following institutions: the University of California at Los Angeles, Irvine, Riverside, Santa Cruz, Santa Barbara, and San Diego; Pomona College; Chapman University; Pepperdine University; Pacific University; Pitzer College; San Diego State University; Whitman College; and the University of Judaism. When an honors student is ready to transfer, the Director alerts the transfer university that a West Los Angeles College student's Transfer Honors Program certification is being sent for special consideration.

In addition to stimulating and challenging classes with enthusiastic faculty members, honors students enjoy honors social events and special programs and activities such as guest speakers, seminars, conferences, monthly honors workshops, luncheons and dinners with the Director, and field trips. While enrolled in honors classes, students also receive library privileges at the campuses of the University of California.

The Transfer Honors Program was formally reestablished in fall 1999. It has grown from an offering of four honors classes to thirty-five in spring 2002. Currently, there are approximately 75 honors students in the program, and the number is increasing with each semester.

Participation Requirements: Both high school graduates and continuing students can participate in the Transfer Honors Program.

Admission Process: Transfer Honors Program students are selected through a special application process. Students entering this program directly from high school must have a 3.0 GPA, be eligible for English 101, and have a recommendation from a teacher or counselor and a mandatory meeting with the Transfer Honors Program Director or counselor. Continuing WLAC students must have a 3.0 GPA, be eligible for English 101, complete 12 transferable units, and have a mandatory meeting with the Director or counselor. To complete the program, students must maintain a minimum 3.2 GPA and complete 18 honors units and the courses necessary for transfer as a junior in their major.

Scholarship Availability: Each year, West Los Angeles College awards a series of awards and scholarships from on- and off-campus sources. Both honors and non-honors students are eligible to apply. However, starting in 2002, two scholarships of $500 each are awarded only to students in the Transfer Honors Program.

The Campus Context: West Los Angeles College is a two-year, public community college accredited by the Accrediting Commission for Community and Junior Colleges. WLAC is one of nine community colleges within the Los Angeles Community College District. The College offers more than forty associate degrees, sixteen occupational certificates, and twenty-eight transferable programs. The Program for Accelerated College Education (PACE) is a full-time college transfer program for working adults in liberal arts and business or for those who wish to become teachers. The vocational programs prepare students for careers in airplane maintenance technology, business, travel and tourism, digital imaging, dental hygiene, and public safety.

Student Body Undergraduate enrollment is approximately 11,000: 33 percent men and 67 percent women. The ethnic distribution is 50 percent African American, 25 percent Hispanic, 10 percent white, 10 percent Asian American, and 5 percent Native American and others. There are 120 international students. All the students are commuters, since there are no residential halls. There are more than twelve campus clubs, including Alpha Gamma Sigma, Lambda Alpha Epsilon, Black Student Union, Christian Club, Math Club, and Associated Students Organization (ASO).

Interpreting the symbols: **2**=two-year college, **4**=four-year college; **Pu**=public or state college, **Pr**=private college; **G**=general honors program; **D**=departmental honors program; **S**=small program (fewer than 100 students), **M**=midsize program (100 to 500 students), **L**=large program (more than 500 students); **Sc**=scholarships available in honors program; **Tr**=transfer students accepted into honors program; **HBC**=historically black college; **AA**=academic advisors; **GA**=graduate advisors; **FA**=fellowship advisors.

Faculty The total number of full-time faculty members is 115; 30 percent have terminal degrees. The average class size is 28–32 students.

Key Facilities The Heldman Learning Resource Center (HLRC), includes the library (with 100,000 volumes and titles), writing lab, tutoring center, computer lab, and one of the most technically advanced foreign language labs in the country. The state-of-the-art Aviation Technology Complex facility offers instruction in high-demand aviation career skills. The newly opened Fine Arts Complex houses a theater, galleries, recital halls, classrooms for digital imaging, computer graphics, desktop publishing, and art and music classes. The men's gym and the women's gym both have all the latest exercise equipment and machines. The Data Center Lab provides Internet capabilities for all students.

Athletics West Los Angeles College offers some of the finest instruction in ice hockey, as well as other collegiate sports, including track and field, skating, football, and basketball. There is an active intramural program.

Study Abroad Study-abroad opportunities include summer programs in China, Israel, Poland, and Mexico.

Support Services Disabled-student facilities include accessible buildings and special services. The Citizen Program provides education and classes in preparation for U.S. naturalization. The Jump Start Program offers college-level classes at local high schools.

Job Opportunities The Job Placement Office provides employment counseling and job opportunities for students on campus as well as for members of the community.

Tuition: $11 per unit for California residents, $134 per unit plus an enrollment fee of $11 per unit for out-of-state and international students

Mandatory Fees: $11 per semester for Health Fee, $1 per semester for Student Representation Fee

Contact: Director: May Du Bois, Transfer Honors Program, West Los Angeles College, 9000 Overland Avenue, Culver City, California 90230-3519; Telephone: 310-287-4397; Fax: 310-841-0396; E-mail: duboism@wmail.wlac.cc.ca.us; Web site: http://www.wlac.cc.ca.us

---

WEST VIRGINIA UNIVERSITY

4 Pu G L Sc Tr

▼ University Honors Program

The Honors Program incorporates a style of learning and living at West Virginia University tailored to the highly motivated, excelling student's special requirements. Honors courses, designed to stimulate creativity and provoke in-depth discussion, are offered in classes with 20 or fewer students. Faculty members noted for their scholarly achievement and outstanding instruction teach these classes. These same teachers and other faculty members serve as honors advisers, guiding students through their individual academic programs and fostering a philosophy of lifelong learning. Live-and-learn communities in the residence halls give students in the same majors an opportunity to live and take classes together, and a special residence hall is designated for Honors Program students.

Upon graduation, the students' diplomas and transcripts indicate the degree earned and the designation University Honors Scholar. In addition, 2 graduating seniors are chosen each year for the Joginder and Charlotte Nath Award, which is geared toward students doing research. The Dennis O'Brian Award recognizes 2 outstanding seniors who have exemplified service, toward both the community and the Honors Program.

Established in 1981, the Honors Program has graduated more than 1,100 students. Currently, there are approximately 700 students in the program. Generally, the Honors Program accepts the top 5 percent of WVU students.

Participation Requirements: To graduate as a University Honors Scholar (UHS), students must complete a minimum of 24 credit hours of designated honors courses. There are two tracks that a student may follow: a regular track, which requires a minimum of 18 credit hours of honors courses plus a 3-credit senior seminar and 3–6 credit hours in a summer guided reading or research study for a minimum total of 24–27 credit hours; and a thesis track in which students take a minimum of 18 hours of honors courses plus 6–12 hours of independent research. Switching between these two tracks is flexible. To remain in the program, the student must maintain a minimum 3.2 GPA during the freshman year, a 3.3 during the sophomore and junior years, and a 3.4 GPA or better during the senior and subsequent years.

All entering freshmen are required to take a 1-credit honors orientation class, which is taught by upper-class honors students, and to live in the honors section of Dadisman Hall (if they are living on campus). Trips to Washington, D.C., and Pittsburgh, PA, are planned throughout the year, as well other social and cultural activities.

Admission Process: Entering freshmen are considered for admission to the program on the basis of their ACT or SAT composite standard scores and their high school GPAs or their status as National Merit Semifinalists. WVU students with fewer than 34 credit hours and at least a 3.7 GPA with no grades of I or W may also apply. There is no deadline for application to the program. Transfer students who have accrued 34 or fewer college credit hours and have maintained an overall GPA of 3.7 or better with no grades of I or W from an accredited institution may be accepted as a WVU honors student. In addition, honors students with college GPAs that meet WVU standards for regularly admitted honors students will be accepted if the honors admissions standards at the University from which a student is transferring are similar to those at WVU.

Scholarship Availability: Most scholarships are offered through the WVU Scholars Program, a comprehensive awards program ranging from the full cost of an undergraduate education to several hundred dollars. Many students in the Scholars Program are also in the Honors Program, although acceptance into one of the programs does not automatically qualify students for the other. If students have no other aid of any kind (scholarships, grants, or loans), the Honors Program does offer a small stipend for full-time honors students.

The Campus Context: West Virginia University Agricultural College, officially founded in February 1867, was renamed West Virginia University in 1868, and the land-grant mission has shaped the University's overall curriculum ever since. WVU is located in Morgantown, West Virginia, about 70 miles south of Pittsburgh and 200 miles west of Washington, D.C. WVU is a member of the North Central Association of Colleges and Schools and has three branch campuses: Potomac State College in Keyser, West Virginia; WVU–Parkersburg in Parkersburg, West Virginia; and WVU Institute of Technology in Montgomery, West Virginia.

The Morgantown campus contains 158 buildings on 673 acres. Many campus buildings are listed on the National Register of Historic Places. WVU operates eight experimental farms and four forests throughout the state. More than $254 million is being invested in new facilities for the library complex, student recreation center, life science building, and other campus improvements. In addition, the Personal Rapid Transit (PRT) moves students from one end of campus to the other in only a matter of minutes. Built by the U.S. Department of Transportation as a national research project, the PRT consists of computer-directed, electric-powered cars that operate on a concrete and steel guideway.

WVU is composed of seven colleges and six schools. The Colleges are Agriculture, Forestry, and Computer Sciences; Eberly College of Arts and Sciences; Business and Economics; Creative Arts; Engineering and Mineral Resources; Human Resources and Education; and Law. The Schools are Dentistry, Journalism, Medicine, Nursing, Pharmacy, and Physical Education. The University offers a total of 166 degree programs.

Student Body Undergraduate enrollment is 15,175. The ethnic distribution of undergraduates is 91.4 percent white; 3.5 percent black, 2 percent Asian or Pacific Islander, .9 percent Hispanic, and .2 percent American Indian/Alaskan native. There are 286 international undergraduate students. Approximately 68 percent of the students at WVU receive some form of financial aid. There are more than 250 student organizations, from fraternities and sororities to service, recreational, and political clubs.

Faculty Of the 1,617 total faculty members, 1,417 are full time; 85 percent of the full-time faculty members hold doctorates or the highest degree offered in their field. The student-faculty ratio is 18:1.

Key Facilities The University libraries include ten facilities containing more than 3 million volumes and microforms/microfilms and more than sixty electronic databases. The University's Master Plan includes a major, consolidated library complex, including new construction and renovation.

Mainframe computing resources are available to students via campus computer sites maintained by WVU Computing Services. Student sites are located in the Evansdale Library and the Mountainlair (student union). Additional computer sites are located in almost all residence halls. Many academic departments also provide microcomputer and mainframe access in computer labs throughout the campus.

Honorary Societies Phi Kappa Phi, Golden Key, Mortar Board, Phi Beta Kappa

Athletics As a member of the NCAA and Big East conference, WVU competes on the Division I level in twenty varsity sports. Men's intercollegiate athletics include baseball, basketball, cross-country, diving, football, riflery, soccer, swimming, tennis, track, and wrestling. Women's intercollegiate athletics include basketball, cross-country, gymnastics, riflery, soccer, swimming, tennis, track, and volleyball. WVU also offers one of the largest intramural sports and sports clubs programs in the country.

Study Abroad Various opportunities for study abroad are available through WVU's International Studies Office. The Honors Program has a special relationship with the University of Leeds in England.

Support Services All buildings on campus are handicapped-accessible, and special facilities can be found across the campus. Disability Services is a resource center that provides services for individuals with a wide range of disabilities, including those with mobility, sight, or hearing impairments, as well as those with hidden disabilities such as diabetes, cardiovascular problems, learning disorders, asthma, allergies, or epilepsy.

Job Opportunities Students can apply for work-study through the Financial Aid Office. Other work opportunities can be found through the student union and other departments within the University, including the Student Services Center.

Tuition: $2482 for state residents, $7666 for nonresidents, per year (1998–99)

Room and Board: $4832

Contact: Director: Dr. William E. Collins, 248 Stalnaker Hall, P.O. Box 6635, Morgantown, West Virginia 26506-6635; Telephone: 304-293-2100; Fax: 304-293-7569; E-mail: uhp@wvu.edu; Web site: http://www.honors.wvu.edu

Western Carolina University

4 Pu L Sc Tr

▼ Honors College

The Honors College is a fully interdisciplinary undergraduate College designed to enhance the academic and social experience of outstanding students at Western Carolina University (WCU). A chief aim of the program is to connect these students with excellent faculty members. The academic center of the College provides meeting space for students, free copying, and computer access. The honors residence is Reynolds Hall, an air-conditioned facility with seminar rooms and study spaces. The College is student-centered. The Honors Board of Directors is a student organization that advises the dean in setting goals and determining priorities. The Board of Directors organizes College social activities and participates in recruitment. Students also manage the Honors College Web site.

Both honors students and the College administration believe the Honors College should support the efforts of all students at WCU. All honors activities are open events. In addition, the College is responsible for the following activities, which are for all students: an annual Undergraduate Expo where student present results of research or artistic activities, travel to the National Conference on Undergraduate Research, the Undergraduate Research Grant Program, and the Mountain Heritage Day 5-K Road Race. Service activities include participation in the annual Tuckaseegee River Clean-up and sponsorship of campus blood drives.

The WCU Honors College is one of the few that grants its own diploma. This is available for Honors College students in any degree program offered at the University.

There are more than 800 students enrolled in the Honors College.

Participation Requirements: To receive the Honors College diploma, students must complete 30 hours in honors classes and graduate with a minimum cumulative GPA of 3.33. Honors classes include liberal studies classes available only to students enrolled in the College. Students may also earn honors credit through honors contracts or independent projects in upper-level courses.

Admission Process: Students must be accepted to Western Carolina University before applying to the Honors College. To be considered for admission, at least one of the following criteria must be met: 3.5 high school GPA or above, SAT I of 1200 or higher or ACT of 30 or higher, or high school class rank in the top 10 percent. The more of these criteria that are met, the more likely a student is to be accepted. Students who achieve a 3.5 GPA in their first semester at WCU are also eligible. Those currently enrolled at WCU and transfer students must apply to the Honors College for admission consideration.

Scholarship Availability: Several merit-based scholarship programs are administered by the Admissions Office at WCU, including full scholarships for National Merit Scholars. There are also some scholarship funds available through the Honors College.

The Campus Context: Western Carolina University is located in the mountains of North Carolina in one of the most biologically diverse regions of the United States. Within a half-hour's drive are the Great Smoky Mountains National Park, the Blue Ridge Parkway, and the Cherokee Reservation. There are many opportunities for a wide range of outdoor activities, including mountain biking; white-water rafting, canoeing, and kayaking on nearby rivers; and hiking in the nearby Nantahala National Forest. Because of these and similar activities, tourism is a major industry in the area.

Interpreting the symbols: **2**=two-year college, **4**=four-year college; **Pu**=public or state college, **Pr**=private college; **G**=general honors program; **D**=departmental honors program; **S**=small program (fewer than 100 students), **M**=midsize program (100 to 500 students), **L**=large program (more than 500 students); **Sc**=scholarships available in honors program; **Tr**=transfer students accepted into honors program; **HBC**=historically black college; **AA**=academic advisors; **GA**=graduate advisors; **FA**=fellowship advisors.

Founded as a teacher's school in 1889, WCU is part of the sixteen-campus University of North Carolina system. The Colleges of Applied Sciences, Arts and Sciences, Business, and Education and Allied Professions offer fully accredited degree programs in more than seventy fields. The emphasis at WCU is excellence with a personal touch. Close faculty-student relationships result in a considerable amount of undergraduate involvement in research activities. The University features a sophisticated technological infrastructure, and the campus is fully networked. All first-year students are required to bring their own computers.

Student Body There are approximately 5,600 undergraduate students and 1,100 graduate students enrolled at WCU. About 50 percent of the students receive financial aid, and 45 percent live on campus. There are nine social sororities and twelve social fraternities. Extensive outdoor and entertainment programming is provided for students by Last Minute Productions, a student-led organization. WCU also has a very strong intramural programs.

Key Facilities Hunter Library houses more than 590,000 volumes and more than 3,000 periodicals and serials, including regional, national, and international newspapers. Computer classrooms and computer labs are distributed across campus. All residence hall rooms and faculty offices are networked.

Honorary Societies Alpha Lambda Delta, Mortar Board, Phi Beta Lambda, Phi Kappa Pi, and Phi Sigma Phi

Athletics WCU is a NCAA Division I-AA school and a member of the Southern Conference for football. It provides a full program of intercollegiate sports, including football, baseball, men's and women's basketball, men's and women's golf, women's volleyball, men's and women's indoor and outdoor track, men's and women's cross-country, women's tennis, and women's soccer.

Study Abroad The Honors College coordinates the National Student Exchange program at WCU. This program includes many study-abroad options through a consortium of more than 150 universities. The Office of International Programs and Services offers many other study-abroad programs.

Support Services The Office of Student Support Services provides an array of special services for students who need their assistance.

Job Opportunities Employment of various kinds is available on campus, including work-study assignments.

Tuition: $1323 for residents, $9245 for nonresidents (proposed for 2002–03)

Room and board: $3596 (proposed)

Mandatory Fees: $1411 (proposed)

Contact: Dean: Dr. Jill Ghnassia, G-55 Stillwell Building, Cullowhee, North Carolina 28723; Telephone: 828-227-7383; Fax: 828-227-7011; E-mail: Ghnassia@email.wcu.edu; Web site: http://www.wcu.edu/honorscollege

---

WESTERN CONNECTICUT STATE UNIVERSITY

4 Pu G S Tr

▼ University Scholars Program

The University Scholars Program at Western Connecticut State University (WestConn) was founded in 1987 to foster and nurture academic excellence among outstanding students in all of the three schools of the University. The purpose of the program is threefold: 1) to provide an opportunity for academically gifted students to excel in response to the challenge of an honors enrichment program; 2) to offer students the chance to "tailor" their honors work to their own particular interest; and 3) to emphasis the need to bring a holistic, multidisciplinary, and multicultural awareness to the problems and opportunities confronting humanity.

In addition to honors seminars and courses, the Honors Council and honors student group ACCESS (Academic, Cultural and Community Enrichment for Student Scholars) sponsor a variety of cultural and educational programs throughout the academic year. The program is currently limited to a maximum of 35 students. Plans call for the reorganization and expansion of the program over the next few years.

Participation Requirements: Within the structure of current program, students take three honors seminars, three honors or "enhanced" courses, and complete three honors activities in order to finish the program requirements. Outstanding juniors or seniors may opt for the Associate University Scholars Program, which consists of one honors seminar, one honors or enhanced course and one honors activity. Recent honors seminars have been conducted on such topics as "Music as American Social History," "The Family," and "The Idea of the University." Students must maintain at least a 3.2 GPA and make satisfactory progress toward completing the program requirements to remain in the program. Members in good standing are eligible for priority registration, special library privileges, and an honors housing arrangement. Those who successfully complete the program receive a special certificate, notation on their transcript and recognition at graduation.

Admission Process: First-year students must have a minimum SAT score of 1050 or graduate in the top 20 percent of their high school class. Students already in residence at the University must have a minimum GPA of 3.2 to be eligible for admission. Both first-year and continuing student applicants also need references and evidence of significant curricular or extracurricular activity. An application to the program is available through the Director.

Scholarship Availability: The University provides a number of academic scholarships; however, none are given directly through the University Scholars Program.

The Campus Context: Founded in 1903, Western Connecticut State University is dedicated to providing both a high-quality university education and a memorable campus experience at an affordable cost. With programs in the arts and sciences, business and professional studies, WestConn takes pride in providing an outstanding education to its students.

WestConn offers educational programs through four academic units: the Ancell School of Business, the School of Arts and Sciences, the School of Professional Studies, and the Division of Graduate and Continuing Education. The most popular majors include communication and theater arts, education, business, justice and law administration, and nursing. WestConn offers two campuses—in Danbury, in the heart of Western Connecticut, as well as a satellite campus in Waterbury. Danbury is a major city in Fairfield County in the foothills of the Berkshire Mountains, just 65 miles north of Manhattan and 50 miles west of Hartford.

Student Body Total enrollment as of fall 2001 was 5,918 students (5,080 undergraduate, 838 graduate); 48 percent men, 52 percent women. The ethnic distribution was 76 percent white, 10 percent African American, 6 percent Hispanic, 1 percent international, and 7 percent were classified as "other" or unknown. Twenty-three percent of all undergraduates were age 25 or over. Approximately 28 percent of the students lived on campus.

Faculty The total number of faculty members is 442. Eighty percent of full-time faculty members have terminal degrees. The student-faculty ratio is 15:1.

Key Facilities A number of facilities contribute to academic life on campus. The newly renovated and expanded Haas Library holds 144,532 volumes and more than 1,273 serials. Students are encouraged to make use of the campuses cutting-edge computer and laboratory facilities, and they are invited to hone their craft in superior theater and musical facilities.

Athletics There are a variety of NCAA Division III men's and women's sports, intramural sports, and a premier recreation center that includes a swimming pool, indoor track, and weightlifting machines.

Study Abroad WestConn has numerous opportunities for students to study abroad.

Support Services The University provides services for learning-disabled students through the Office of Disability Services. The campus also features a child-care center, counseling center, health services office, career development center, and campus ministries.

Job Opportunities WestConn offers some work-study opportunities to students. Numerous jobs are available in the nearby area.

Tuition, Room, and Board: As part of the Connecticut State System of Higher Education, WestConn offers a high-quality educational program at a reasonable cost. It is estimated that a full-time, in-state undergraduate student who lives and eats on campus will pay $10,961 for 2002-03. This estimate of annual costs includes tuition, fees, room, and board. Books, laboratory fees, health insurance and personal expenses are not included in the estimate.

Contact: Director: Dr. Steven Ward, Department of Social Sciences, 181 White Street, Danbury, Connecticut 06810; Telephone: 203-837-8458; Fax: 203-837-8526; E-mail: wards@wcsu.ctstateu.edu; Web site: www.wcsu.edu/scholars

Western Illinois University

4 Pu G L Sc Tr

▼ University Honors Program

The University Honors Program (UHP) at Western Illinois University (WIU) is a free-standing academic unit committed to providing academically talented and motivated students an enriched academic curriculum and opportunities for leadership, professional growth, and service.

Consistent with its commitment to academic excellence, the Honors Program offers special general honors tutorials and seminar, and honors seminars and in-course and research opportunities within departments and academic areas. The general honors courses are taught by select honors faculty members who foster opportunities for discussion and debate and who promote critical reasoning, cross-disciplinary thinking, and communication skills. These general honors courses count toward the honors student's general education requirements. The honors courses within disciplines and major/specialty areas provide opportunities for in-depth study, research, and professional development. These courses fulfill the student's major or minor requirements.

The UHP also fosters leadership, professional growth, and service. This is accomplished in part through the honors curriculum and in part through activities and events sponsored by the program. A special leadership colloquium enables student to reflect directly on leadership. Research and thesis projects afford students opportunities to form mentoring relationships with faculty members. In-course honors projects promote the development of portfolios to be used at the time of job or graduate school interviews. In addition the UHP encourages students to participate in its governance through representation on the University Honors Council, the Honors Student Advisory Board, the Honors Floor Council, and the Student Honors Association.

Special programs available to Western's honors students include several preprofessional programs. Study in the dual program pre-engineering, pre-architecture, premedicine, prenursing, preoptometry, predentistry, and preveterinary is available. Of particular interest is the UHP's specially developed interdisciplinary prelaw honors minor open to all majors. This minor provides a valuable background for the study and practice of law and emphasizes writing, effective speaking, and critical-thinking skills.

Western Illinois University's University Honors Program was established in 1983 and currently enrolls approximately 550 students from thirty-four academic departments.

Participation Requirements: Students who intend to graduate as Honors Scholars must complete a minimum of 7 hours of general honors seminars, including a 1-hour capstone colloquium, and a variable number of hours within their honors area, including thesis and intern options. They must also have an overall GPA of at least 3.4 as well as a minimum 3.4 in their honors work. A 1-hour general honors colloquium and completion of the requirements in the honors area are required of transfer students from schools with approved honors programs. Students electing to graduate as Transfer Honors Scholars are required to take a 1-hour general honors colloquium and complete the honors requirements in their declared honors area. Upon completion of the program, graduating seniors are recognized at a special honors convocation, awarded a bronze medallion, and have the honors seal stamped on their diplomas and transcripts.

Admission Process: Admission of first-year students to the UHP is based on a combination of each student's ACT scores and class rank; transfer students are eligible for participation in the program if they have a GPA of at least 3.2 for 14 to 44 semester hours (sh), 3.3 for 45 to 59 sh, and 3.4 for 60 sh and above. On-campus students are eligible for participation in the UHP if they have earned a minimum GPA of 3.2 for 14 to 44 semester hours or 3.3 for 45 to 59 semester hours.

Scholarship Availability: The UHP and the Western Illinois University Foundation offer a number of scholarships for first-year students, transfers, and continuing honors students. The program awards four-year WIU Foundation-Honors Scholarships, Sherman Honors Freshman Scholarships, Outstanding New Freshmen Scholars, WIU Transfers Honors Scholarships, and Sophomore, Junior, and Senior Scholarships. The Keith Webb Memorial Scholarship is awarded annually to outstanding students in the prelaw honors minor. In addition, the UHP awards a number of Research Grants, Study Abroad Honors Scholarships, and a Writing Prize Award.

The Campus Context: Western Illinois University is a regional public institution founded in 1899. There are thirty-four degree programs offered in the four colleges of Arts and Sciences, Fine Arts and Communication, Education and Human Services, and Business and Technology. The main campus is situated in the gently rolling farmland of west central Illinois near the Mississippi, and its branch campus is located in one of the state's largest urban areas approximately 70 miles to the north. For students in biology and agriculture, there is a 300-acre farm, the Alice L. Kirbe Life Sciences Station on the Mississippi, and a partnership program with Chicago's Shedd Aquarian. For the arts, there are several theaters and a University art gallery.

At this time, honors is available only on the main Macomb campus. The UHP is housed on the main floor of the University Library. Within the honors center are the offices of the director, associate director, and the staff and a student lounge. In addition to these facilities, the UHP has three honors floors in the residence halls and, in one of the residence halls, a designated honors seminar room.

Student Body Undergraduate enrollment is 10,192; 51 percent of all students are women. The minority distribution is 6 percent African American, 2 percent Hispanic, 1 percent Asian American, and 0.3 percent Native American. There are 350 international students, an active International Friendship Club, and an annual

Interpreting the symbols: **2**=two-year college, **4**=four-year college; **Pu**=public or state college, **Pr**=private college; **G**=general honors program; **D**=departmental honors program; **S**=small program (fewer than 100 students), **M**=midsize program (100 to 500 students), **L**=large program (more than 500 students); **Sc**=scholarships available in honors program; **Tr**=transfer students accepted into honors program; **HBC**=historically black college; **AA**=academic advisors; **GA**=graduate advisors; **FA**=fellowship advisors.

International Bazaar. Forty-seven percent of students live on campus, and 50 percent of undergraduate students receive some kind of financial aid. The campus has thirty-eight Greek-letter social organizations and thirteen national sororities.

Faculty Instructional faculty members number 672, with an on-campus student-faculty ratio of 15:1. Seventy-eight percent of the full-time faculty members hold doctoral degrees or the highest degree in their fields. General honors courses are taught by a select honors faculty.

Key Facilities The University Library anchors the campus visually and academically. Built around a central atrium rising six stories, the central library houses more than 1 million catalogued volumes, 3,300 current journal subscriptions, and twenty-five foreign and domestic newspapers and provides computer access to all state and select private university libraries. There are more than 900 computers in twenty labs and eleven resource centers.

Athletics Western's ten men's and nine women's teams compete in NCAA Division I Mid-Continent Conference. The football team plays at NCAA-AA in the Gateway Football Conference and has advanced to the I-AA national playoffs four times and as won the conference championship in 1988, 1997, and 1998.

Study Abroad Western has more than 100 study-abroad and exchange programs in South America, Europe, and Asia. The Western Illinois Spanish Experience is an intensive program in Spain and Mexico; the Western Illinois Studies Abroad in France offers study at the Institut de Touraine. Western is also a member of the North American Consortium for International Advancement and is affiliated with Educational Programs Abroad and the American Institute for Foreign Study.

Support Services For students with disabilities, WIU provides accessible classrooms, housing, personal care attendants, and parking.

Job Opportunities Work-related programs including college work-study, student employment, internships, and cooperative work plans are offered by the University.

Tuition: $2730 for state residents, $5460 for nonresidents, per year (1999–2000)

Room and board: $4210

Mandatory Fees: $649.95

Contact: Director: Dr. Thomas E. Helm, 1 University Circle, Macomb, Illinois 61455-1390; Telephone: 309-298-2228; Fax 309-298-2791; E-mail: Te-Helm@wiu.edu

---

Western Kentucky University

4 Pu G L Sc Tr

▼ University Honors Program

The University Honors Program challenges Western's most outstanding students to achieve intellectual and personal excellence and to take an active role in their professional training and personal growth. By marrying a community of highly motivated students with the most dedicated and active scholars on campus, the University Honors Program creates an environment centered on self-determined, interdisciplinary, and participatory learning. Honors students and faculty members interact with and learn from one another as peers; as a result, students are contributors to, rather than simply assimilators of, their educational experience. The program also sees community service as an educational benefit, and students participate in (among other things) adult literacy programs and in mentoring at-risk children to enhance student growth and the well-being of the community.

Honors courses stress independent and critical thinking, development of writing and speaking skills, and a broad world view. There is a greater focus on original source material and research methodology than exists in nonhonors courses. Most classes incorporate classroom debates, student-led discussion, and group research projects. This approach facilitates a deeper presentation of course material and freer, more wide-ranging discussion than is possible in nonhonors courses.

The 24-credit honors curriculum includes enriched sections of general education courses as well as interdisciplinary honors colloquia and an honors thesis. Class size in honors courses is limited, and enrollment is restricted to honors-eligible students. With the exception of two 1½-credit colloquia, all honors work can be used to simultaneously fulfill general education or major/minor requirements; as such, the honors program can be completed without increasing the total number of hours required for graduation.

Currently, more than thirty general education courses are available to be taken for honors credit, representing the areas of written and spoken communication, humanities, social and behavioral sciences, natural sciences and mathematics, and cultural diversity. Upper-division honors credit may be earned through either advanced honors courses or honors augmentation of upper-division courses in students' major or minor disciplines. Students find the flexibility of honors augmentation particularly appealing, as it allows them to expand their knowledge and skills in areas of particular relevance to their professional development.

Honors colloquia are offered each semester. These are organized around specific topics, selected by each instructor, within the broad theme of culture, science, and the self. Many focus on contemporary social or ethical issues, while others are devoted to reading and discussing the works of important thinkers. All emphasize self-directed learning, analytical writing, and free discussion of ideas.

The honors experience culminates in the honors thesis, which is a work of sustained original research or creative activity completed under the guidance of one of Western's best scholars. Thesis projects vary widely in both nature and content; students in the humanities, business, and social or natural sciences develop their research skills, while those in creative disciplines enhance their craft. All bring new insight or a novel perspective to the topic at hand. Thesis work requires students to put into practice the analytical and communication skills emphasized throughout the honors curriculum, resulting in concrete evidence of their ability to undertake and complete meaningful scholarly activity.

Students receive a number of tangible benefits from participation in the honors program, including the opportunity to live in honors housing, priority registration, and funding to support thesis research and travel to professional conferences. Honors graduates have their achievement noted on their official transcript and are presented with a bronze medallion carried on a red-and-white–striped ribbon to be worn at commencement. While these features are significant, the greatest benefit of honors participation is the chance to interact on a daily basis with others who are equally committed to learning, inquiry, reflection, and action.

There are currently more than 550 students and 50 participating faculty members in the honors program; approximately 150 first-year students join the program each year.

Participation Requirements: Participants must maintain a college GPA of at least 3.2. However, a one-semester grace period is usually provided for those whose GPA falls below 3.2.

Students recognized as Honors Program graduates must have a final GPA of 3.4 or higher. The designation Graduate of the University Honors Program is added to each graduate's final transcript, as is the title of the student's senior honors thesis. Graduates also receive an Honors Program certificate and medallion in recognition of completion of the program.

Admission Process: Students starting the Honors Program as entering freshmen should have a minimum 3.5 high school GPA and a score of at least 25 on the ACT or 1150 on the recentered SAT I. Those with very strong grades or aptitude scores who do not meet the other standards are considered individually. Students with at least 16 hours of college work are admitted with a minimum 3.2 college GPA.

Scholarship Availability: The Honors Program awards about sixty-five $400 scholarships each year to students in good standing with and making regular progress toward completing the honors program. These scholarships may be added to any other scholarship a student receives. Applications for scholarships are submitted online. Students currently receiving honors scholarships are required to apply for renewal each year. The deadline for submission of both types of applications is April 1.

Honors scholarships are awarded on a competitive basis, and students must be in good standing with the program in order to be considered. To be in good standing, students must have an overall GPA of 3.2 or higher, a minimum of 6 hours of honors credit within the first 30 credit hours after joining the program, a minimum of 12 hours of honors credit within the first 60 hours after joining the program, and have filed a degree program (with honors courses approved by the Honors Director) by the end of the fall semester of the junior year. (The criteria apply as applicable at the time of the application.)

The Campus Context: Western Kentucky University is composed of five colleges: Potter College of Arts, Humanities and Social Sciences; Gordon Ford College of Business Administration; College of Education and Behavioral Sciences; College of Science, Technology and Health; and Community College. Sixteen degree programs are offered on campus. Special facilities include the Kentucky Library and Museum and the Hardin Planetarium.

Student Body Undergraduate enrollment is approximately 60 percent women. The ethnic distribution of students is 7 percent African American, .01 percent Asian, .06 percent Hispanic, .04 percent Native American, and 91 percent white. There are 92 international students. Eighty-six percent of the students are residents. Seventy-five percent of the students receive financial aid. There are fourteen fraternities and eleven sororities.

Faculty Of the 913 faculty members, 559 are full-time; 84.4 percent hold terminal degrees. The student-faculty ratio is 17:1.

Key Facilities The library houses more than 500,000 volumes. The entire campus is networked. More than 660 computers are available in the library, classroom buildings, and student center.

Honorary Societies Phi Eta Sigma, Phi Kappa Phi, and Golden Key

Athletics Western has intercollegiate athletics teams in baseball, basketball, cross-country, football, golf, soccer, swimming, tennis, track and field, and volleyball. The University is a member of and adheres to the regulations of the Sun Belt Conference and the National Collegiate Athletic Association. The intramural-recreational sports program exists to provide all students, and faculty and staff members a setting for constructive participation in recreational activities. It consists of men's and women's competitive sports, coed sports, faculty/staff activities, recreational free-play, instructional programs, organized fitness classes, and sports club activities.

Study Abroad Among study-abroad options are the Western in France Program in Montpelier, France, and Study Tour Programs in Britain, including the Ireland Program, Celtic Program, and King's College Program. Also available are summer terms, special-interest Christmas vacation tours, and Semester in Cambridge. The Kentucky Institute for International Studies offers summer study programs in Austria, Ecuador, France, Germany, Italy, Mexico, and Spain. Study-travel programs are also offered by various University departments.

Support Services The Student Support Services Program provides comprehensive, continuing academic assistance for undergraduate students with academic potential who meet financial guidelines, are from families where neither parent holds a bachelor's degree, or are physically disabled. In coordination with the Office of the Dean of Student Life, the project offers individual assistance to qualified students with disabilities (including learning disabilities) in need of accommodation. Tape recorders, alternative testing procedures, and a support group are available as needed. All services are free of charge to qualified students.

The Office for Disability Services helps students with disabilities experience an adequate academic and social environment while attending the University. The office coordinates its activities through many other campus offices as well as public agencies. Students with disabilities receive priority in academic advising and class selection with particular attention to locations of accessible classes.

Job Opportunities Employment for students is available through the Federal Work-Study Program (FWS), Institutional Work Program, full-time summer employment opportunities, and referral service for off-campus job placement.

Tuition: $1422 for state residents, $3712 for nonresidents, per semester (2001–02)

Room and Board: $3500 per year

Mandatory Fees: $242 per semester

Contact: Director: Dr. Doug McElroy, Honors Center, 1 Big Red Way, Bowling Green, Kentucky 42101-3576; Assistant Director: Patricia Minter; Telephone: 270-745-2081; Fax: 270-745-2081; E-mail: doug.mcelroy@wku.edu or patricia.minter@wku.edu; Web site: http://www.wku.edu/Honors/

Western Maryland College

4 Pr G S Tr

▼ Honors Program

The faculty instituted the Honors Program to challenge academically talented students. Rooted in the liberal arts, the program encourages critical and creative thinking and humane, responsible actions.

The curriculum is composed of specially designed liberal arts courses, often taught in innovative ways. Students meet the College's basic liberal arts requirements through a combination of these special study seminars and courses offered through other departments. Class size is limited to 15, allowing each student to develop a voice and an opinion in classroom discussions and after-class gatherings. The experience culminates with a senior seminar and paper or project presentation. The program also provides for individual study, particularly the Senior Honors project. A College Scholar certificate is awarded upon graduation.

Honor students may deepen their study of the liberal arts while living in an environment that is conducive to the exchange of ideas. They may choose to live and study in honors suite-style housing, where extended quiet hours are respected and students often continue the dialogue begun in class.

Extracurricular activities encourage the development of ideas in other formats. Students may join organized trips to Baltimore and Washington, D.C., (less than an hour's drive from campus) for cultural events or help with various local community service opportunities. There are also leadership opportunities, such as representing one's class on the Faculty Honors Committee; organizing activities; representing the College at state, regional, and national honors conventions; and guiding community service

Interpreting the symbols: **2**=two-year college, **4**=four-year college; **Pu**=public or state college, **Pr**=private college; **G**=general honors program; **D**=departmental honors program; **S**=small program (fewer than 100 students), **M**=midsize program (100 to 500 students), **L**=large program (more than 500 students); **Sc**=scholarships available in honors program; **Tr**=transfer students accepted into honors program; **HBC**=historically black college; **AA**=academic advisors; **GA**=graduate advisors; **FA**=fellowship advisors.

activities. The Honors Program also sponsors an annual lecture series, and students are encouraged to attend regular talks by Phi Beta Kappa scholars.

The program is directed by Nancy Palmer, who specializes in comparative literature and mythology and shares the responsibility of running the program with elected student representatives. Founded in 1986, the Honors Program currently enrolls approximately 100 students.

Participation Requirements: To graduate from the Honors Program, students must complete both semesters of the required Great Works of the Western World course, a choice of three other specially designated honors courses, and the honors senior seminar, a course developed and taught by faculty members at the request of the graduating class. Twenty-four honors credits are required to complete the program. Students must maintain at least a 3.4 GPA to remain in the program. Students who complete the Honors Program with a cumulative GPA of 3.4 or better receive special recognition at commencement and certificates designating them as College Scholars. The Delta Chapter of Phi Beta Kappa at Western Maryland also awards a Writing Award to the graduating senior with the best research paper.

Admission Process: All admissions applicants are reviewed and considered for the Honors Program. Admission to the program is competitive, and approximately 30 first-year students—selected on the basis of outstanding academic records, test scores, and leadership potential—are invited to enter the program each fall. Other first-year students may be selected during their second full semester. Transfer students with outstanding academic records are also encouraged to apply. Upon selection by a faculty committee, candidates receive a letter of invitation from the Director of the Honors Program and must respond by May 1.

Scholarship Availability: The College awards more than $1 million every year to selected entering students who have at least a 3.5 GPA and minimum combined SAT I verbal and mathematics scores of 1100. All students accepted in the Honors Program receive academic scholarships, but must apply as part of the admissions process.

The Campus Context: Western Maryland College (WMC) provides an ideal location for learning, bringing together students from twenty-three states and nineteen countries. Its picturesque campus is situated on a hilltop in historic Westminster, just a short drive from two of the nation's major metropolitan centers, Baltimore and Washington, D.C. Western Maryland was one of the first coeducational colleges in the nation and has been both innovative and independent since its founding in 1867.

The tradition of liberal arts studies rests comfortably at Western Maryland, which has exemplary teaching as its central mission at both the undergraduate and graduate levels. The faculty is engaged in research and professional writing. Its members are involved at the highest levels of their respective professions; they are sought after as consultants in many spheres, but their primary mission is teaching. Enrollment of 1,600 undergraduates enables WMC to care about students in a personal way, to provide individual guidance, and to be responsive to the needs of students. Graduates leave Western Maryland enriched not just because of their classwork, but because of their meaningful interactions with one another.

A flexible liberal arts curriculum stresses the ability to think critically and creatively, to act humanely and responsibly, and to be expressive. WMC is fully accredited by the Middle States Association of Colleges and Secondary Schools and is listed as one of the selective national Liberal Arts Colleges by the Carnegie Foundation for the Advancement of Teaching. WMC is internationally recognized for its graduate program in training teachers for the deaf.

Student Body The College enrolls 1,600 students from twenty-three states and nineteen countries; 45 percent are men. At WMC, the key is involvement. Ninety percent of students live on campus; 40 percent compete on one of twenty-four athletic teams, and 100 percent enjoy activities sponsored by eighty diverse student groups, including an active Greek system of social fraternities and sororities, five with national affiliations. WMC has enrolled international students since 1890; currently more than 14 percent of the total student population are from other countries. The College continues an active commitment to the broadest educational and social experience, particularly in bringing together students from diverse cultures.

Faculty Faculty members, 90 full-time professors, 95 percent of whom hold the most advanced degrees in their fields, devote themselves to classroom, lab, and studio teaching. Many conduct research; most involve students in their work. Professors teach a maximum of three courses each semester, allowing them ample time to spend with students outside of the classroom helping them plan academic programs, arrange internships, and prepare for careers. An average class size of 20 students encourages discussion and learning is collaborative rather than competitive. WMC's president, provost, dean of students, and financial vice president all teach undergraduate courses. Faculty members also serve as advisers to many student organizations.

Key Facilities The new Hoover Library, open 100 hours a week, offers 207,000 bound volumes, 180,965 titles, 842 current journals on standing order, 3,000 online periodicals, 2,315 video cassettes, and 7,811 audio recordings in addition to a selection of daily newspaper and current periodicals, media viewing and listening stations, online databases, personal reference assistance, a 24-hour computer lab, and borrowing privileges in area library systems.

The Science Center, a $13-million facility completed in 1999, features computer-based laboratories.

There are seven computer labs on campus, including a 24-hour lab containing a total of 148 PC and Mac computers.

Honorary Societies Phi Beta Kappa, Omicron Delta Kappa, and Trumpeters

Athletics Athletic teams compete in Division III of the NCAA and the Centennial Conference, a group of eleven national liberal arts colleges and universities. There are twelve sports for men: baseball, basketball, cross-country, football, golf, indoor and outdoor track, lacrosse, soccer, swimming, tennis, and wrestling. There are twelve sports for women: basketball, cross-country, field hockey, golf, indoor and outdoor track, lacrosse, soccer, softball, swimming, tennis, and volleyball. Academics are important to the men and women who participate on WMC's athletic teams. The graduation rate of athletes matches that of nonathletes. The off-the-field success of WMC student-athletes has gained national recognition: more than 27 varsity athletes have been nominated for GTE Academic All-America recognition within recent years.

Study Abroad WMC students may choose from dozens of study-abroad programs to arrange foreign study for either a semester or an entire year. Students elect to study abroad at established study centers that offer English-speaking courses in England, Wales, Mexico, and, since 1993, WMC-Budapest, Hungary, where the College has a branch campus. This special program offers education to young men and women from Europe and other parts of the world who are interested in preparing for careers in the new global marketplace. Located at the crossroads of central Europe, WMC-Budapest offers a four-year undergraduate program in business administration and economics, communication, and political science. Bilingual students may attend programs at study centers in Paris, Granada, and Vienna. Other programs have taken students to Greece, Spain, and Austria.

Job Opportunities Work-related programs include work-study, undergraduate assistantships, internships, and cooperative education.

Tuition: $21,760 per year (2002–03)

Room and board: $5280

Mandatory Fees: $350 (one-time fee)

Contact: Director: Nancy Palmer, 2 College Hill, Westminster, Maryland 21157-4390; Telephone: 410-857-2430; Fax: 410-386-4601; E-mail: npalmer@wmdc.edu; Web site: http://www.wmdc.edu; Honors Program Web site: http://stuser.wmdc.edu/Honors/honors.html

WESTERN MICHIGAN UNIVERSITY

4 Pu L Sc Tr AA FA

▼ Lee Honors College

The Lee Honors College at Western Michigan University was created more than three decades ago for academically talented students and has become an integral part of the University community. Honors students study in every discipline and take advantage of the diverse and rich array of courses to deepen and develop their major and minor fields of study. The goal is to provide an environment where each student will grow through personal relationships with other students and faculty members while engaging in academic challenges with opportunities for leadership.

When students enter the Lee Honors College, they have all of the resources a large, comprehensive university can offer, with the attention and personal care of a small college of 1,200 students. The academic experience is enhanced by opportunities to live in a residence hall with other honors students, pursue international study, set up rewarding internships, and apply for research grants. The honors experience is an inclusionary one.

Participation Requirements: The program consists of two learning communities, or clusters, of honors classes at the freshman/sophomore level (normally 6 to 9 credit hours at the freshman and at the sophomore level), two single courses at the junior/senior level (for a total of 6-8 credit hours), and a senior-level capstone, Thesis Project.

Students must maintain a 3.25 GPA or higher to remain in good standing. The number of credit hours is variable. Students graduate with a transcript notation and diploma that they are graduates of the Lee Honors College. The notation includes the title of their thesis.

Admission Process: Students may be admitted at various stages of their academic career. They may enter as freshmen, as currently enrolled students at WMU, or as transfer students through the junior year. Chief criteria for freshman admission to the Honors College are high school or university academic achievements and aptitude as measured by GPA (in the range of 3.6 or better) and ACT composite scores (in the range of 26 or better). College transfer students should present a cumulative GPA of 3.5 or better. Students are also evaluated by the quality of an academic essay, cocurricular and community activities, and two recommendations from teachers or counselors.

Scholarship Availability: There is a Dean's Summer Research Grant, which is open to students between the junior and senior year who are researching their Thesis Project. The college also administers the Undergraduate Research and Creative Activities Award for junior- and senior-level students.

The Campus Context: Western Michigan University was founded in 1903 and has evolved into a national, student-centered research institution recognized for its academic excellence and accessibility. It is dedicated to advancing knowledge through teaching, research, and service and remains firmly focused on making a positive difference in the lives of those it serves throughout Michigan, across the country, and around the world. *U.S. News & World Report* has ranked WMU among the top 150 national public universities in the United States for nine consecutive years. Two education guidebooks, *America's 100 Best College Buys* and *America's Best College Scholarships,* include WMU in their recent editions. The Michigan Legislature has recognized WMU as one of the state's five graduate-intensive, research-oriented public universities. In fact, nearly one fourth of WMU's students are pursuing graduate degrees. The National Association of State Universities and Land-Grand Colleges, the oldest higher-education association in the United States, includes WMU in its selective roster of members. WMU is one of only ninety-one public universities in the nation, and only four in Michigan, to be granted a chapter of Phi Beta Kappa, the most prestigious national academic honorary society in the United States.

In addition to its Graduate College and Lee Honors College, WMU supports seven degree-granting colleges: Arts and Sciences, The Haworth College of Business, Education, Engineering and Applied Sciences, Fine Arts, Aviation, and Health and Human Services.

WMU's main campus is located just off interstate 94 and U.S. Highway 131 in the Southwest Michigan city of Kalamazoo, which is less than 3 hours by car from Detroit and Chicago.

In addition to WMU, three other higher education institutions are located in the area as are several Fortune 500 firms, including Haworth Inc., the Kellogg Company, Pharmacia & Upjohn Inc., and the Whirlpool Corporation.

Well-known for its involvement in the arts, Kalamazoo County supports theatrical, musical, and dance groups; offers art, aviation, and cultural museums; and boasts a nature center and a five-branch public library system. It plays host to a variety of concerts, shows, and seasonal festivals. The sandy beaches of Lake Michigan are less than an hour's drive away.

Student Body Total enrollment is 28,931 students; 23,156 are undergraduates while graduate enrollment is 5,775. There are 13,501 men and 15,430 women. Financial aid awards in the categories of grants and scholarships, work, and loans went to 17,324 students. There are twenty-two national fraternities and sixteen national sororities on campus.

With more than 26,500 students, WMU ranks among the nation's sixty largest institutions. It enrolls a significant minority student population as well as one of the largest numbers of undergraduate international students among Michigan's public universities. The University attracts international students from almost 100 countries and maintains institutional linkages with universities and agencies in more than twenty-five countries.

Faculty Undergraduate and graduate faculty numbers 952 full-time and 190 part-time members. Ninety-three percent have appropriate terminal degrees in their fields.

Key Facilities There are five divisions of libraries containing 3,651,223 total volumes, 773,036 items on microfilm, 6,676 subscriptions, 195,005 maps, and 74,070 slides. There are four major computer labs, and each residence hall complex has a computer room.

Honorary Societies Phi Beta Kappa, Mortar Board, Golden Key, Phi Kappa Phi, and Alpha Lambda Delta

Athletics WMU is a Division I NCAA school and member of the MAC Conference. Men's sports include baseball, basketball, football, cross-country, soccer, hockey, and tennis. Women's sports include basketball, cross-country, gymnastics, volleyball, and tennis.

Study Abroad Western Michigan University urges all students to include a semester or year abroad in their academic program. The Office of International Affairs/Study Abroad approves programs for credit transfer and assists students through the various steps to ensure full credit transfer and full application of financial aid. While not limited to participation in WMU-sponsored programs, students are encouraged to consider first

Interpreting the symbols: **2**=two-year college, **4**=four-year college; **Pu**=public or state college, **Pr**=private college; **G**=general honors program; **D**=departmental honors program; **S**=small program (fewer than 100 students), **M**=midsize program (100 to 500 students), **L**=large program (more than 500 students); **Sc**=scholarships available in honors program; **Tr**=transfer students accepted into honors program; **HBC**=historically black college; **AA**=academic advisors; **GA**=graduate advisors; **FA**=fellowship advisors.

the programs offered through WMU. These include fall semester in Burgos, Spain, or Beijing, People's Republic of China; winter semester in either Besancon, France; Queretero, Mexico; Saratov, Russia; or Bonn, Germany; or semester/full-year opportunities through exchanges in Japan, Germany, the Netherlands, Norway, and Sweden or through the twinning program in Malaysia. Special need-based grants are available for semester and year-long foreign-language-based study-abroad experiences.

Support Services WMU has programs and services for learning disabled students. The services, available to all learning disabled students, include note-taking services, oral tests, readers, untimed tests, tape recorders, reading machines, talking books, and a writing lab.

Job Opportunities There are job opportunities on campus, which include work-study, auxiliary services employment, and assistantships.

Tuition: $4465 for residents, $9611 for nonresidents, per year (2001–02)

Room and Board: $5528

Mandatory Fees: $602

Contact: Dean: Joseph G. Reish, Kalamazoo, Michigan 49008; Telephone: 616-387-3230; Fax: 616-387-3903; E-mail: joe.reish@wmich.edu; Web site: http://www.wmich.edu.honors

WESTERN WASHINGTON UNIVERSITY

4 Pu G M Sc Tr

▼ University Honors Program

The Western Washington University Honors Program was created in 1962 to offer selected students of high academic achievement the opportunity to participate in a challenging intellectual enterprise. Since then, honors has grown to offer a wide variety of courses in general education, more specialized seminars, and the opportunity to work one-on-one with a faculty member in the completion of a senior project.

Honors courses are rigorous and stress active participation, writing, and independent thinking. Honors faculty members come from programs and departments throughout the University and are known campuswide for their excellence as classroom teachers.

Honors students come from every college in the University, but the largest number major in the natural sciences, including programs such as premedicine and environmental science. Students in honors must fulfill all the requirements set forth in the University's *Bulletin,* including those for general education and the major. Students with AP credit, work in the International Baccalaureate program, or other forms of credit that award them advanced standing may be able to count that work toward completion of the requirements for the program.

The program admits up to 50 freshmen each year and has a total enrollment of about 160.

Graduation through honors is a mark of distinction, and students are recognized at Commencement and receive notations on their transcripts indicating they have completed the program.

Participation Requirements: Students who enter the program as freshmen complete a yearlong sequence of courses that introduces them to the Western cultural tradition and other general education courses and specialized seminars. Seminar topics change annually and cover all the major disciplinary areas (e.g., natural sciences, humanities, and social sciences). Honors classes are always small and are open only to honors students. Sections of the freshman sequence and other general education courses have enrollments of not more than 25 to 30, while seminars enroll 12 or fewer. All students who graduate through the program must complete a senior project, where they work individually with a professor or, in some instances, more than one professor. The project is usually in the major, but in some cases it may be in an auxiliary area. Students are encouraged to think creatively about the project, and while many elect to write a traditional thesis, recitals, shows, and other creative works have all been offered to fulfill this requirement. To graduate through honors, students must maintain a minimum 3.5 GPA for the last 90 graded credits of academic work and fulfill specific departmental requirements where they exist. Students in the program have gone on to graduate and professional programs at the finest institutions in the nation.

Admission Process: Admission to the program is competitive. Entering freshmen, transfer students, and already enrolled Western students may apply directly or answer an invitation from the program. Honors does not use set formulas for admission. Rather, candidates are evaluated according to a number of factors in order to determine the likelihood of their success in the program. When reviewing an applicant, the program considers previous academic achievement, including GPA and class rank; a detailed letter of recommendation; scores on appropriate tests; the applicant's writing; and when possible, an interview. In considering students for admission, the program regards a demonstrated commitment to serious academic work to be at least as important as aptitude. Applications should be received by March 15.

The Campus Context: Western Washington University was founded in 1893 as one of the state's normal schools. It became a college of education in 1937, a state college in 1961, and a university in 1977. The University is located in Bellingham, a community of 50,000 on Puget Sound, about 90 miles north of Seattle, Washington. The 190-acre campus is located on a hill high above Bellingham Bay, an arm of Puget Sound, and in the words of one publication "is a stunning blend of art and nature." Its outdoor sculpture collection is internationally renowned. Almost 200 undergraduate majors are offered leading to baccalaureate degrees in the humanities, social sciences, natural sciences, and many applied and professional programs; students may also design their own majors. Western has been mentioned numerous times in *U.S. News & World Report, Barron's,* and *Money* magazines as an outstanding educational value. Its honors program has been cited in *Money* magazine as one of the twenty-five best in the nation. Outdoor activities are easily accessible and include skiing, boating, and hiking.

Student Body The total enrollment is 11,600, more than 90 percent of whom are undergraduates. Students come primarily from the state of Washington. Women outnumber men by approximately 55 to 45 percent. Members of minority groups constitute approximately 15 percent of enrollment, with those of Asian descent most common. Approximately 50 percent of students receive financial aid. Western does not have fraternities or sororities.

Faculty There are more than 450 full-time faculty members and in excess of 100 adjunct faculty members. Almost all hold doctorates or other terminal degrees. The student-faculty ratio is 24:1.

Key Facilities The Wilson Library holds more than 800,000 volumes and an additional 1 million microform titles. There are networked microcomputing labs across campus available to students with general purpose software for both Macintosh and IBM computers. Students regard computer facilities as easily accessible, but many students bring their own.

Fourteen residence halls house approximately 4,000 students. The campus has a residential character, and most students live within walking or easy driving distance.

Honorary Societies Phi Eta Sigma, Phi Kappa Phi, Beta Alpha Psi, Beta Gamma Sigma, Omicron Delta Epsilon, Phi Alpha Theta, Pi Sigma Alpha, Golden Key, Psi Chi, Sigma Xi, Sigma Pi Sigma, National Society of Collegiate Scholars

Athletics The University offers broadly based intercollegiate sports programs for men and women. Western competes in the National Collegiate Athletic Association's Division II. Approximately two thirds of students participate in intramural sports.

Study Abroad Western students may study abroad through ISEP or other international programs. Study abroad is compatible with most majors, and many honors students elect the option to do academic work in another country.

Job Opportunities A wide variety of on-campus employment opportunities is available.

Tuition: $3015 for state residents, $10,755 for nonresidents, per year (2001–02)

Room and Board: $5271

Mandatory Fees: $274.50

Contact: Director: Dr. George Mariz, 228 Miller Hall, Bellingham, Washington 98225-9089; Telephone: 360-650-3446; Fax: 360-650-7789; E-mail: george.mariz@wwu.edu

WESTERN WYOMING COMMUNITY COLLEGE

2 Pu G S Tr

▼ Honors Program

The Honors Program at Western Wyoming Community College (WWCC) was designed for students with superior academic records, above-average enthusiasm for learning, and intellectual curiosity. The Honors Program's mission is to challenge bright students by encouraging learning communities within the classroom and opportunities for intellectual growth outside the classroom. Through field trips and classroom interaction, students form lifelong friendships with others who share their commitment to learning.

Organized in 1991, the Honors Program accepts 10 incoming first-year students and 10 second-year students, so that each fall a mixed group of 20 students begin the program together. This system allows the program to attract excellent freshmen and to include nontraditional students who have proved themselves to be academically superior in their first year of college. The 20 Honors Program students are chosen each spring through a process of application and an essay. Freshmen must submit an application, an essay, and ACT scores; WWCC faculty members must nominate sophomores, who must submit an essay and a college GPA.

As part of the Honors Program, students participate in two special honors colloquiums in humanities and social science. The humanities course incorporates cultural field trips into the course content, as students examine the role of the arts and humanities in the human experience. Students travel to symphonies, operas, art galleries, plays, and museums at the program's expense as part of this course. The social science colloquium explores issues central to the human experience, along with explorations into the community. Topics vary from year to year.

Honors Program students also pursue an individual research project, working closely with a faculty mentor. This project allows them to investigate a topic of their choice, become familiar with research methods, and develop their own expertise on a topic of personal interest, giving their education a highly individual stamp.

Honors Program students are also eligible to enroll in any of ten honors courses offered yearly. Most of these challenging courses are seminar style, with limited enrollment. Taught by some of Western's most dedicated faculty members, these courses encourage participation and bring together talented students from all majors. While they are intended for academically motivated students, honors courses are not simply more work with stiffer competition. They are innovative, intellectually stimulating, and designed to develop a community of scholars among the participants.

Participation Requirements: Students participating in the Honors Program are expected to maintain a GPA of at least 3.25 in 15 credit hours. They must also enroll in two honors courses per academic year, including the two honors colloquiums in humanities and social science. Students who have participated in the WWCC Honors Program are automatically accepted into the honors programs at the University of Wyoming, Weber State University, and Utah State University. In addition, colleges and universities throughout the nation recognize the Honors Program designation on a student's transcript as a sign of superior work.

Admission Process: To be admitted to the Honors Program, first-year students must have a score of at least 25 on the ACT or 1100 on the SAT, complete the WWCC admissions process, and complete an Honors Program application. To be admitted as sophomores, students must be nominated by a faculty member who has had them in class, have attained at least a 3.75 GPA in their freshman year, submit an Honors Program application in March, and plan to enroll full-time for two more semesters. Twenty students are selected on the basis of academic records, letters of recommendation, and application essays. Honors Program participants are screened and selected during the spring for the following academic year.

Scholarship Availability: Although specific Honors Program scholarships are not offered, most students selected for the program receive some type of scholarship from the College. Institutional scholarships may be awarded for academics, special abilities (art, dance, music, and theater), occupational programs, and athletics. Academic scholarships may be awarded to high school seniors with a minimum 3.1 cumulative GPA on a 4.0 scale and a score of at least 18 on the ACT or 1070 on the SAT. Two continuing students in each of seven WWCC divisions may be selected for academic division scholarships after nomination by each division. Students with a minimum 3.0 cumulative GPA and at least 12 credit hours at WWCC are eligible for consideration. Additional grants may be awarded to students through WWCC's foundation grant program, including Civic Grants, Whisenand II Grants, and Anna Baird Williams Grants, and through the Western Wyoming College Foundation.

The Campus Context: Western Wyoming Community College was founded in 1959. A public, two-year college, WWCC is located in Rock Springs, Wyoming, on a 10-acre campus and has outreach locations in nine western Wyoming communities. A $64-million campus expansion was completed in 1990. The all-enclosed and architectural-award-winning campus provides an attractive and modern environment for student study and recreation. The primary mission at WWCC is to help students meet their education and career goals. At Western, students are able to explore majors while satisfying general education requirements. The average class size is 15, so students benefit from individualized attention. Students have the opportunity to get involved in hands-on activities such as education practicums, internships at the Wyoming State Legislature, archaeology digs, and various opportunities for international travel. Special facilities include a dinosaur museum, a natural history museum, the Weidner Wildlife Exhibit, and excellent theater facilities. The closest cities are Salt Lake City (180 miles) and Denver (350 miles). WWCC welcomes students from all backgrounds and does its best to see that each student succeeds in his or her chosen endeavor. WWCC believes the community college provides opportunities for transfer students as well as skills for those who wish to go directly to work after completing a technical program.

Student Body WWCC enrolls approximately 2,600 students, consisting of 1,000 full-time students and 1,600 part-time students. The

Interpreting the symbols: **2**=two-year college, **4**=four-year college; **Pu**=public or state college, **Pr**=private college; **G**=general honors program; **D**=departmental honors program; **S**=small program (fewer than 100 students), **M**=midsize program (100 to 500 students), **L**=large program (more than 500 students); **Sc**=scholarships available in honors program; **Tr**=transfer students accepted into honors program; **HBC**=historically black college; **AA**=academic advisors; **GA**=graduate advisors; **FA**=fellowship advisors.

full-time enrollment includes students from twenty-five states and territories and more than 40 international students from fifteen other countries. On-campus apartments, semiprivate rooms, and suite units provide housing for 400 full-time students. Seventy percent of the students are enrolled in a transfer program, and 30 percent are enrolled in a vocational program. Seventy-seven percent of all full-time students receive some financial aid. Sixty-nine percent of total college financial aid is awarded as scholarships and grants, 31 percent as loans or jobs.

Faculty There are 73 full-time faculty members and 120 part-time faculty members. Ten percent of the full-time faculty members hold terminal degrees.

Key Facilities Hay Library contains 60,000 volumes, 412 serial subscriptions, and 2,000 audiovisual materials and participates in an interlibrary loan program that provides access to 45 million books. The library is a congressionally designated selective depository for U.S. governmental publications. The library also has unique collections on railroad history, American Indians, antique and collector glass, World War II, and Vietnam. More than 300 up-to-date computers are located in five student-use labs on campus.

Athletics WWCC fields NJCAA teams for women's volleyball and basketball and men's basketball and wrestling. WWCC sponsors a coed cheerleading squad and dance team, and a full intramural program is available to all students and staff members.

Support Services Student services include online registration; personal and career counseling; personalized academic advising; workshops on stress, time management, and social issues; ADA assistance; a children's center; international student support; and a career and placement center. The modern campus, completed in 1988, has won several architectural awards and is fully enclosed and accessible.

Job Opportunities On-campus work-study jobs are available through institutional and federal work-study programs. Internships are available through various departments, particularly in the social science and exercise science programs.

Tuition: Tuition is $1404 for state residents and $3756 for nonresidents per year. Students from Western Undergraduate Exchange schools and Nebraska residents pay $2004 per year. (2001–02)

Room and Board: Room and board cost approximately $2734 per year. Room and board charges vary according to the type of housing and meal plan selected.

Contact: Honors Program Director: Karen Love, 2500 College Drive, Rock Springs, Wyoming 82901; Telephone: 307-382-1733; E-mail: klove@wwcc.cc.wy.us; Director of Admissions: Laurie Watkins, P.O. Box 428, Rock Springs, Wyoming 82902-0428; Telephone: 307-382-1647 or 800-226-1181 (toll-free); Fax: 307-382-1636; E-mail: admissions@wwcc.cc.wy.us; Web site: http://www.wwcc.cc.wy.us

WESTMINSTER COLLEGE

4 Pr G S AA

▼ Honors Program

The Honors Program provides Westminster College students who are academically and intellectually prepared with the opportunity to satisfy their College-wide Liberal Education (LE) Skills and Liberal Education Distribution course requirements in an alternative and unique manner. By completing a seven-course sequence of interdisciplinary, team-taught honors courses, students earn an honors certificate while satisfying these requirements. Moreover, by understanding their historical, scientific, and intellectual heritage, honors students are prepared to be articulate and responsible members of society and defenders of their own ideas. The classes are restricted in size, employ seminar-style approaches, and emphasize study of primary texts.

The Honors Program also provides an enhanced educational experience for students by giving them access to supplementary resources like the "Pizza with Profs" lecture series; the Honors Program resource library; special enriched learning experiences, such as attendance at cultural events and other field study; funding to attend and give papers at academic conferences; leadership training opportunities like the student Honors Council; special recognition opportunities like the honors seminar book awards; and opportunities to participate in special meetings with distinguished visiting scholars and lecturers.

The program was founded in 1987 and currently enrolls approximately 100 students.

Participation Requirements: Students admitted to the program must maintain a GPA of at least 3.25 overall and 3.0 in honors courses. If an honors student falls below these GPA minimums, a probationary semester is used to allow the student to return to the minimum GPA standards for continued participation. Students who complete seven courses in the honors LE sequence are awarded a special certificate recognizing this achievement (contingent on Westminster graduation).

To be awarded the Honors Degree, students must satisfy the following requirements at graduation: maintain a minimum GPA of 3.0 in all honors course work, including those courses listed below for the honors degree, and a minimum GPA of 3.25; complete seven LE courses, with no more than one of these courses taken CR/NC; complete four semesters of college-level instruction in a single foreign language (or the equivalent); complete 6 credit hours of course work in Honors 300 or 400 seminars; and complete a senior project in the student's major for a minimum of 3 credit hours. The nature of this project is determined in conjunction with the Director of Honors and the student's major adviser.

Admission Process: Incoming students expressing a desire to enroll in the Honors Program are ranked according to the following criteria: ACT scores, high school GPA, and the quality of a written statement that explains why the student wishes to participate and why he or she feels qualified for participation in the program. The top 35 students are invited to enroll in honors courses. If accepted students decline the offer, the invitation process continues until a class of 35 students is formed. In the past, a typical incoming honors student has had a 3.8 GPA and a 28 composite ACT score. Students who fall near or above these guidelines and who sincerely wish to be in the program are encouraged to apply by including the written statement described above with their Westminster application.

Since a number of high-achieving, upperclass Westminster College students may not have applied to the Honors Program as incoming freshmen but may still wish to participate in some of its classes, any undergraduate in good standing with a GPA of 3.5 or higher is eligible to enroll in 300- and 400-level honors seminars. The Honors Program is an active part of the larger College community and welcomes the energy, intellect, and diversity that students bring to the Honors Program from different disciplines across the campus.

Scholarship Availability: While the Honors Program itself does not administer any scholarships, the College has a wide range of financial support available. Ninety-six percent of freshmen at Westminster receive financial aid, averaging approximately $11,000 per student annually. Merit-based scholarships are available to incoming freshmen and transfer students as well as to continuing students, thanks to a generous endowment program and institutional aid program. Every full-time student admitted to Westminster is automatically considered for merit-based scholarships awarded by the College, which are based on GPA from previous academic (high school or college) course work. More than $7.9 million was awarded in institutional scholarships in 2000–01.

The Campus Context: Westminster College is the only independent, private liberal arts college in Utah. Westminster has been a vital part of the Intermountain West's history and educational heritage since 1875. Most students are attracted to the College because of its small size and the personal attention students receive, its prime location in a moderately large urban area close to mountain skiing and recreation areas, and its relatively modest tuition and fees.

The College is located in a quiet residential area about 10 minutes southeast of downtown Salt Lake City. On-campus housing consists of residence halls for both men and women, which can accommodate 500 students. Off-campus rental housing is readily available in the neighborhood. Westminster is made up of four undergraduate colleges—Arts and Sciences, Business, Education, and Nursing—that offer approximately thirty different majors. Course work leading to an academic minor is available in the following additional areas: environmental studies, gender studies, French, music, religion, Spanish, and speech and theater arts.

Salt Lake City, home of the 2002 Winter Olympics, is a metropolitan area of approximately 1.3 million people. It is located in a valley (at an elevation of 4,700 feet) between two rugged mountain ranges. Salt Lake City has an international airport and good rail service. Downtown Salt Lake City is easily accessible to students by bus, car, or bicycle. Attractions in the downtown area include professional sports events, ballet, theater, concerts, and shopping to suit all tastes. The area has four pleasant seasons, with limited amounts of rain and snow in the valley and moderate temperatures. The Wasatch Mountains, bordering the Salt Lake Valley on the east, have what has been called "the greatest snow on Earth." These mountains are ideal for the winter sports enthusiast as well as those who enjoy hiking, biking, and camping.

Student Body Undergraduate enrollment is approximately 2,000, of whom women comprise 59 percent. Twenty-four percent of students live on campus. The ethnic distribution is 79 percent Caucasian, 5 percent Hispanic, 3 percent Asian or Pacific Islander, and 13 percent other/unknown. Students come from twenty-eight states and twenty countries.

Student activities include student government, campus publications, choir, intramural sports, honorary societies, the campus ministry council, the ski club, and a variety of special interest groups, including aviation, nursing, science, education, premed, and computer science. Students can participate in the ROTC programs of the U.S. Air Force, U.S. Army, and U.S. Navy through cooperative programs at the University of Utah.

Faculty Westminster has 125 full-time faculty members, approximately 85 percent of whom have terminal degrees in their fields. The student-faculty ratio is 17:1.

Key Facilities Westminster's campus has six major classroom buildings, a science laboratory building, a student computer terminal room, a fine arts building, a nursing laboratory, and a separate building for classes in wheel-thrown and hand-built pottery.

The Giovale Library, erected in 1997, houses 120,000 volumes and contains group-study areas, a multimedia classroom, media viewing areas, and individual study carrels, all with computer network access. The 50,000-square-foot, state-of-the-art building, which has a seating capacity of 290 people, also houses an open computer lab, a faculty Web training lab, and the Department of Information Technology.

Honorary Society Alpha Chi

Athletics Westminster College offers intercollegiate basketball, golf, and soccer for men and basketball, golf, and volleyball for women. There is also an active intramurals program on campus.

Study Abroad Westminster students may participate in travel/study trips (for credit) during May Term and the summer session. Students can also make individual arrangements for international study through advisement from the College's international studies adviser and the Career Resource Center and through a cooperative agreement with the Foreign Study Office at the University of Utah.

Support Services Westminster's START Center provides new student services like orientation, testing, placement, and academic advising, as well as help in other areas, including disability services.

Job Opportunities Many work opportunities exist on and off campus. The Career Resource Center assists students in selecting and preparing for their postcollege professional lives.

Tuition: $15,990 for the academic year (2002–03) for a full-time student (registering for 12 to 16 semester hours). This figure includes costs for the fall semester, spring semester, and May Term.

Room and Board: $4820 (2002–03). Books and supplies are estimated at $900 per year.

Contact: Director: Dr. Richard Badenhausen, Honors Program, Westminster College, 1840 South 1300 East, Salt Lake City, Utah 84105; Telephone: 801-832-2460; Fax: 801-484-5579; E-mail: rbadenhausen@westminstercollege.edu; Web site: http://www.westminstercollege.edu/honors/

WICHITA STATE UNIVERSITY

4 Pu G M Tr

▼ Emory Lindquist Honors Program

The Emory Lindquist Honors Program serves students in all six degree-granting colleges of the University. In 1996, the program inaugurated a new honors curriculum in which students pursue an honors track through the University's general education requirements and complete a senior project in their major field. Additional nonrequired honors courses are also available.

The honors program provides academic advising services and faculty mentoring, actively supports students seeking national postgraduate scholarships and fellowships, and encourages participation in regional and national honors organizations.

The program maintains a popular student lounge, computer room, and an honors residence facility. The student-led Honors Society sponsors a continuing series of lectures, discussions, field trips, and social occasions. The annual freshman retreat orients students to college life and academics.

In addition to recognition awarded by the University to all students achieving outstanding academic records, Honors Program graduates are eligible for additional recognition. Students who satisfy honors graduation requirements receive the notation Honors Program Graduate on their transcripts and are recognized at Commencement. The highest-ranked honors program graduates each year are named Emory Lindquist Scholars and are recognized at Commencement. With departmental approval, Honors Program participants completing a senior project earn departmental honors at graduation.

The program is more than 30 years old and currently enrolls 550 students.

Participation Requirements: The honors track in general education begins with a sequence of three freshman/sophomore seminars. Enrollment in these seminars is limited to 15 students. Seminar topics range widely, but are consistent with the general education program's focus on the traditional liberal arts and sciences. Honors seminars are also designed to develop a student's

Interpreting the symbols: **2**=two-year college, **4**=four-year college; **Pu**=public or state college, **Pr**=private college; **G**=general honors program; **D**=departmental honors program; **S**=small program (fewer than 100 students), **M**=midsize program (100 to 500 students), **L**=large program (more than 500 students); **Sc**=scholarships available in honors program; **Tr**=transfer students accepted into honors program; **HBC**=historically black college; **AA**=academic advisors; **GA**=graduate advisors; **FA**=fellowship advisors.

learning skills by emphasizing writing, oral communication, library research, and mathematics. After completing the seminar sequence, honors students are required to take two upper-division honors courses. Finally, students (along with their department major adviser) design a two-course senior project, typically involving independent research, a senior thesis, and a community project.

Admission Process: Generally, freshmen are admitted to the program if their composite score on the American College Testing's ACT is 26 or higher or if their high school GPA is 3.5 or higher as certified by the University. Transfer and continuing students may enter the program if they have achieved a minimum GPA of 3.25 in university-level studies and if they satisfy the minimum GPA requirements. Those who are not members of the program may enroll in honors courses if they have the permission of the honors director. To be admitted to the program, a student must submit an honors program application and meet with a program representative.

Scholarship Availability: Many participants hold major University scholarships, most of which are awarded through the annual Distinguished Scholarship Invitational. Approximately $3.4 million is awarded annually.

The Campus Context: Wichita State University is composed of six colleges: Barton School of Business, College of Education, College of Engineering, College of Fine Arts, College of Health Professions, and Fairmount College of Liberal Arts and Sciences. There are 113 degree programs on campus. Among distinguished facilities are the National Institute of Aviation Research, Weidemann Hall (Markusson Organ), and the Outdoor Sculpture Collection.

Student Body Undergraduate enrollment is 14,750; 54 percent are women. Members of minority groups make up 15 percent of students, and there are 9 percent international students. Eighty percent of students commute to campus. There are ten fraternities and eight sororities.

Faculty Of the 461 full-time faculty members, 87 percent have terminal degrees. The student-faculty ratio is 18:1.

Key Facilities The library houses 1 million volumes. University Computing provides mainframe computer and PC labs with individual workstations.

Honorary Societies Phi Eta Sigma, Phi Kappa Phi, Golden Key, Mortar Board, Alpha Kappa Delta, Omicron Delta Kappa, Pi Delta Phi, Pi Sigma Alpha, Pi Tau Sigma, Pinnacle, Tau Beta Pi, Senior Honor Men and Women

Athletics Wichita State University is a Division I member of the NCAA, competing in eleven intercollegiate sports (seven men's, eight women's), including men's and women's basketball, baseball, bowling, cross-country, golf, rowing, softball, tennis, track, and volleyball. Both men's and women's bowling teams hold multiple national championships in the past decade; the baseball team is a frequent participant in the College World Series.

Study Abroad The University participates in many cooperative study-abroad programs.

Support Services Wichita State University has one of the most handicapped-accessible campuses in the region. A campus office provides signing services, on-campus transportation, and other enabling assistance to disabled students.

Job Opportunities Special work-study opportunities and many other on-campus jobs are available.

Tuition: $2046.40 for state residents, $7087.60 for nonresidents per year

Room and Board: $2490 minimum

Mandatory Fees: included in tuition

Contact: Director: Almer J. Mandt, III, 1845 Fairmount, Wichita, Kansas 67260-0102; Telephone: 316-978-3375; Fax: 316-978-3234

WIDENER UNIVERSITY

4 Pr G M Sc Tr

▼ Honors Program

Guided by the principle that serious students create opportunities to learn from one another as well as from faculty, Widener's honors classes are limited to a maximum of 15 students and are conducted as seminars. Faculty members encourage student involvement in setting the direction of courses. Participants in Widener's Honors Program also attend a minimum of eight outside-of-class events including performances, lectures, and art museum receptions on campus; cultural events in Philadelphia and Wilmington; presentations at nearby schools and cultural centers; and various social events. Students in the Honors Program find that they have joined a community of mutual support and friendship in which the educational experience is exceptional.

Each year in March, Widener celebrates Honors Week. The purpose of Honors week is threefold: to recognize the members of the eighteen academic honor societies, to foster the spirit of academic achievement, and to engage the campus community in a series of academic lectures and student presentations culminating in an Honors Convocation on Friday evening.

Honors courses are not necessarily more demanding than regular classes in terms of the amount of work required. Rather, they are structured to allow for spirited discussion and interaction. A sampling of the courses that have been offered include the Renaissance, the Psychology of Hypnosis, Impressionism, Race and Ethnicity in American Society, Communism in Theory and Practice, and Children at Risk. Students may also elect to pursue an independent study honors course. The usual course distribution is a freshman honors seminar, freshman honors English, one junior honors colloquium, and at least two other honors courses. However, students are encouraged to take as many additional honors courses as they wish. Honors courses are taught by faculty members selected for their ability to stimulate and challenge inquisitive students.

All honors courses count toward the University's general education requirements, which must be met by all students for graduation. Thus, students enrolled in any of Widener's undergraduate majors may participate in the program. Now in its thirteenth year, the Honors Program in General Education currently has 200 student participants.

Participation Requirements: In order to continue in the Honors Program, each participant must maintain a minimum overall GPA of 3.0 and a minimum GPA of 3.0 in all honors courses taken. A Certificate of Honors in General Education is awarded at graduation to students who successfully complete at least five honors courses. Those who also complete a second junior honors colloquium or an honors independent study earn a Certificate of Advanced Honors in General Education.

Admission Process: High school students who apply to Widener are invited to participate in the Honors Program based on SAT scores and high school records. Traditionally, students who are in the top 10 percent of their graduating classes and have SAT I scores of 1200 or higher are invited to participate. Applicants selected for the Honors Program are given priority consideration for Widener's Presidential Scholarships. After the first and second semesters of the freshman year, other students displaying excellence in college work may apply for admission to the program.

The Campus Context: Widener University is composed of three campuses and eight schools and colleges, including the College of Arts and Sciences, School of Engineering, School of Management, School of Nursing, School of Law, School of Hotel and Restaurant Management, School of Human Service Professions, and University College. All full-time undergraduate programs are offered on the main campus in Chester, Pennsylvania.

Of the 124 degree programs leading to the associate, bachelor's, master's, or doctoral degree, fifty-one are baccalaureate programs for full-time students.

Student Body Within the total enrollment on all three campuses of 8,500 students, 2,300 are full-time undergraduates and, thus, eligible for consideration for the Honors Program. Of the 2,300 undergraduates, 48 percent are women and 61 percent are residential students. The diversified student body includes 11.2 percent African Americans, 3.4 percent Asian Americans, 77.7 percent Caucasians, 2.2 percent Latin Americans, and .5 percent Native Americans. The 3 percent international students come from forty-five other countries. Approximately 66 percent of the full-time undergraduates receive financial aid. Widener offers an active social life and a full range of cocurricular and extracurricular activities. In addition to eight social fraternities and four sororities, all nationally affiliated, there are eighty student clubs and organizations.

Faculty Widener's excellent faculty numbers 692, of whom 283 are full-time. Ninety-two percent hold the doctorate or terminal degree in their field. The student-faculty ratio is 12:1.

Key Facilities The University's library holds 228,000 volumes and numerous computer laboratories with hardware and software appropriate to the courses of study. Academic facilities supporting the courses include the television studio and graphics labs for the communication studies program; kitchens and front-desk labs for the hotel and restaurant management majors; and field-specific laboratories for electrical, mechanical, and chemical engineering for each of the science majors and for nursing, languages, and pre–physical therapy majors.

While neither art nor music are offered as majors, there are excellent facilities for those who wish to pursue these interests. The Widener Art Museum houses a permanent collection of eighteenth- and nineteenth-century American and European art and presents five exhibitions by contemporary artists and a juried student art show each year. The music studio offers lessons by professional musicians and both musicians and engineering students produce compact disks in the state-of-the-art recording studio. Honors students and students not in the program populate the Writing Center, the Academic Skills Center, and the Math Center, where faculty members and outstanding students offer one-on-one assistance with homework, term papers, and research.

Honorary Societies Phi Eta Sigma, Phi Kappa Phi, Alpha Chi

Athletics With a brand-new stadium and full athletic complex, Widener also offers twenty-four NCAA Division III varsity sports for men and women, a cheerleading squad, ROTC rifle and pistol team, and a full range of intramurals.

Support Services Disabled students will find ready access to most buildings and a willingness to accommodate for special needs, coordinated by an on-campus specialist.

Job Opportunities Work-study opportunities and internships are also available.

Tuition: $19,300 minimum per year (2001–02)

Room and Board: $7150

Contact: Director: Dr. Elnora Rigik, One University Place, Chester, Pennsylvania 19013; Telephone: 610-499-4349; Fax: 610-876-9751; E-mail: honors.program@widener.edu

William Jewell College

4 Pr G S Sc Tr

▼ Oxbridge Honors Program

The Oxbridge Honors Program is an adaptation of the tutorial style of learning tradition at Oxford and Cambridge Universities in England (whence the name Oxbridge). Rather than enroll in courses in their majors, Oxbridge students engage in directed, independent reading under the direction of faculty tutors; write and defend essays in weekly tutorial meetings, and prepare for comprehensive examinations over their major field of study. All Oxbridge students spend their junior year studying in either Oxford or Cambridge through a William Jewell College study-abroad program. Oxbridge students complete the College's interdisciplinary general education program and take electives with other William Jewell College students in the familiar American classroom, thereby combining the best of the British and American educational traditions.

Oxbridge offers majors in seven traditional liberal arts majors, several of them interdisciplinary in nature. They are English language and literature, history, history of ideas (an interdisciplinary major tracing the main philosophical ideas of western European culture through a great books curriculum), institutions and policy (a study of the economic and political institutions of today's world and formulation of public policy for them), music (focusing on enriched offerings in music literature and analysis), and two majors in science (molecular biology and ecology and systematics).

The Oxbridge Honors Program and the tutorial style of learning it requires have several educational benefits. Oxbridge students take responsibility for their own learning and education in a way not typically found in American undergraduate programs. The tutorial method (with its emphasis on independent reading and weekly essays) stimulates study of selected topics in depth, rather than superficial coverage of broad fields of study. The comprehensive examinations encourage students to synthesize and integrate their entire undergraduate education, rather than treat each course as a unit unrelated to the whole. The full year of study in England, an integral part of the program, helps students develop self-reliance and work with tutors and students from different cultural and educational backgrounds.

Oxbridge also offers opportunities for undergraduate research. Each summer, 4 Oxbridge honors students receive funding to remain on campus and engage in research under the guidance of a faculty mentor. Some students organize their own research projects, while others act as assistants to faculty members in their ongoing research.

The program has been in existence since 1982 and has graduated more than 125 students. Oxbridge admits 15 to 20 new freshmen each year as well as a few transfer students entering the program as sophomores. There are currently 42 students enrolled in the program.

Participation Requirements: All new Oxbridge students (freshmen and transfer students entering as sophomores) take two classroom seminars (not tutorials) their first semester. These seminars help prepare students for their tutorial work and emphasize critical reading and thinking, evaluation of evidence, and writing of essays. For the remainder of their first year and their sophomore year, Oxbridge students typically enroll in one tutorial course each term. (Their other courses are selected from the general education curriculum and electives.) All Oxbridge

Interpreting the symbols: **2**=two-year college, **4**=four-year college; **Pu**=public or state college, **Pr**=private college; **G**=general honors program; **D**=departmental honors program; **S**=small program (fewer than 100 students), **M**=midsize program (100 to 500 students), **L**=large program (more than 500 students); **Sc**=scholarships available in honors program; **Tr**=transfer students accepted into honors program; **HBC**=historically black college; **AA**=academic advisors; **GA**=graduate advisors; **FA**=fellowship advisors.

students study in Oxford or Cambridge their junior year. In their senior year, they continue to enroll in tutorials, including a synthesis tutorial in the spring semester. All Oxbridge students must pass comprehensive examinations over their major field.

Oxbridge majors are defined by the topics to be addressed on comprehensive examinations rather than by a list of required courses or a particular number of credit hours. To remain in good standing in Oxbridge, students must earn at least a B in each tutorial attempted and maintain an overall minimum GPA of 3.0. Successful completion of Oxbridge is recognized at commencement and on the students' transcripts.

Admission Process: While high standardized test scores (such as ACT or SAT I) and high school GPA are good indicators of success in Oxbridge, admission is not determined on a numerical basis. Applicants for the Oxbridge Honors Program must complete a special application, including several essays, and be interviewed by a faculty admission panel. The reviewers are looking for qualities such as self-motivation, initiative, enjoyment of reading and learning, and perseverance in addition to academic potential as measured by grades and test scores.

Scholarship Availability: Since the Oxbridge Honors Program is endowed, this personalized education is offered at the same cost as other William Jewell programs. All Oxbridge students receive and Oxbridge Scholar Award, a scholarship of $9000 that is renewed annually as long as the student is in good standing at Oxbridge. Students' financial aid awards are applicable to their year of study in England. In addition, each Oxbridge student receives an additional scholarship for that year to help defray some of the extra costs inherent in overseas study.

The Campus Context: William Jewell, established in 1849, blends a rich history with state-of-the-art facilities on 149 wooded acres in the Kansas City suburb of Liberty, Missouri. The College is accredited by the North Central Association of Colleges and Schools and offers both the Bachelor of Arts and Bachelor of Science degrees. Dually aligned with the Missouri Baptist Convention and the American Baptist Churches USA, William Jewell offers a rigorous liberal arts education within a values-centered environment. The curriculum offers extensive programs in business, accounting, music, and nursing and preparation for the state teaching certificate. The general education curriculum focuses on the Responsible Self, an interdisciplinary approach. The flagship Oxbridge Honors Program, funded by The Hall Family Foundation, combines British tutorial methods of instruction with opportunities for a year of study in Oxford or Cambridge, England. The Pryor Leadership Studies Certificate Program teaches personal, vocational, and civic leadership through a combination of seminars, internships, and personal growth experiences. William Jewell's Harriman Arts Program is considered the Midwest's premiere program in the performing arts. Campus facilities include an observatory, an art gallery, and a radio station.

Student Body Enrollment includes 1,089 full-time students and 280 part-time students. Of the full-time students, 60 percent are women. The student body represents approximately thirty states and ten foreign nations. Of the fall 2001 entering class, more than one third graduated in the top 10 percent of their class. The average ACT score was 24.4. More than 90 percent of last year's entering class received some type of financial aid and/or scholarships. Students may opt to join one of four national fraternities or one of four national sororities.

Faculty A faculty of 84 full-time and 49 part-time members gives a student-faculty ratio of 11:1. More than 80 percent of the senior faculty members have doctorates. The average class size is 20 students.

Key Facilities The Charles F. Curry Library houses 265,182 volumes and 819 serial titles. More than 7,000 items are added annually. The library is an active member of local, regional, and national computer-based library networks and offers extensive Internet access. More than 14 million volumes are available through the MOBIUS database. The Learning Resource Center (LRC) offers listening and viewing facilities for individuals and small groups. Housed in the LRC is a collection of 29,000 nonprint materials, such as videotapes and compact discs. The LRC is equipped with a satellite downlink and houses a video conference center. More than 100 IBM-compatible computers are available campuswide to students; all students have e-mail accounts and Internet access.

Honorary Societies Mortar Board

Athletics William Jewell College enjoys an outstanding record of achievement in athletic competition. The men's basketball team is a strong NAIA competitor, having made the Final 4 during the 1990s. The football team made NAIA history by going to national playoffs four consecutive years and by becoming the first college team in NAIA history to win 500 football games. The College is a member of the Heart of America Athletic Conference and competes in baseball, basketball, cheerleading, cross-country, football, golf, soccer, tennis, and track for men and in basketball, cheerleading, cross-country, dance team, golf, soccer, softball, tennis, track, and volleyball for women. The National Association of Intercollegiate Athletics standards of eligibility serve as the guideline for the conference sports activities. A strong program of intramural men's and women's sports is also offered.

Study Abroad William Jewell offers twenty-two different study-abroad programs to its students. All students enrolled in the Oxbridge Honors Program study for their entire junior year in one of three programs in Oxford or in Cambridge: the Oxford Overseas Study Course, a private course of study under the direction of Professor Francis Warner, Dean of Degrees of Saint Peter's College, Oxford; The Centre for Medieval and Renaissance Studies, affiliated with Keble College, Oxford; or Homerton College, Cambridge University.

Support Services The Academic Achievement Center offers assistance in developing study skills and writing proficiency. The Office of Counseling and Testing offers professional services to students making educational, vocational, and personal decisions. Trained counselors are available to administer and interpret various tests helpful in assessing the student's aptitudes and interests.

Job Opportunities Work opportunities are provided through Federal Work-Study, which includes community service positions. A non-Federal work program, Workshop, is available on a limited basis. In addition, the Office of Career Services assists students interested in off-campus employment opportunities.

Tuition and fees: $14,750 full-time per year, $555 per credit hour part-time (2001–02)

Room and board: $4390

Contact: Dr. John Westlie, Senior Tutor, 500 College Hill, Liberty, Missouri 64068. Telephone: 816-781-7700 Ext. 5121; Fax: 816-415-5005; E-mail: westliej@william.jewell.edu; Web site: http://www.jewell.edu/oxbridge/

William Paterson University

4 Pu G S Sc Tr

▼ University Honors Program

The William Paterson University Honors Program offers opportunities for rigorous, in-depth, and cross-disciplinary study that leads to academic performance at the highest level. The program consists of seven distinctive tracks, each with its own coordinator. These tracks are Biopsychology, Cognitive Science, Humanities, Life Science and Environmental Ethics, Music, Nursing, and Performing Arts. The tracks are not a major, but a distinctive set of courses that add breadth to or reinforce a student's chosen major. For example, the Humanities Track is open to students of all majors and provides a cross-disciplinary look at Western civilization. The Nursing Track, on the other hand, is open only to students of nursing and promotes research on issues of public health. While the goals of individual tracks may vary, the overall aim of the program is to enrich the student's experiences and provide unique educational opportunities. In the long run, these experiences enhance the student's success in graduate or professional school, strengthen career prospects, and foster a lifelong commitment to learning.

Each of the tracks can be tailored to fit with the student's major. Since the required courses of most tracks can be incorporated into the student's regular curriculum, honors students generally do not have to take courses beyond the usual University requirements in order to complete the track. For example, behavior genetics is a requirement for the Biopsychology Track, but it is also a major elective for biology and psychology majors. Honors students benefit from smaller classes, more individualized instruction and advisement, increased opportunities for faculty-student research, closer interaction with faculty members and other honors students, and the opportunity to participate in regularly scheduled interdisciplinary events. The capstone experience of each track is a public performance. It may take the form of a recital, the presentation of research results or an internship experience, or the production of a play or musical. Upon completion of the track and graduation from the University, the student is honored at an awards ceremony and receives an Honors designation on the diploma and transcript. There are no additional fees for enrolling in the program.

The University Honors Program also offers several sections of honors general education courses each semester. These courses are available to high-achieving freshmen, sophomores, and transfer students who have not met all of their general education requirements. Honors sections of general education courses enroll 20 or fewer students and are taught by faculty members who have designed the course specifically for highly motivated students. Students in these courses benefit from rigorous course work and smaller class sizes and may or may not choose to apply to one of the University Honors Program tracks.

Two tracks of the program (Biopsychology and Humanities) were begun in 1976. The remaining five tracks were added in 1999, and the seven tracks were then designated the University Honors Program. The program currently enrolls 90 students in tracks and an additional 100 in honors sections of general education courses.

Participation Requirements: At this time, the tracks vary in required credits but range from 14 to 19 credits. It is anticipated that the requirements will increase to 23 to 30 credits when a three-course honors general education requirement is added to the program in the fall semester of 2002. Each track is a vertical progression of courses and experiences. The Humanities Track, for example, requires five courses. One interdisciplinary seminar covers topics in the classical, medieval, and Renaissance epochs, while a second covers the age of revolutions and the twentieth century. An advanced colloquium focuses on a more restricted time period, such as the Enlightenment. With those three courses as a base, students complete a two-semester thesis on a topic chosen with their honors adviser. In each track, this vertical progression in the student's curriculum culminates in a one-on-one intensive interaction with a faculty member in an independent study, thesis, or similar major writing assignment.

As a public institution that sets out to enroll a cross section of students in the region, the Honors Program strives to balance access and excellence. Thus, the entry requirements are modest but the curricular requirements are intense, and only a portion of those students who initially enroll complete the program. To remain in the program, a student must maintain a minimum 3.0 cumulative GPA.

Admission Process: Students with a minimum 3.0 GPA fill out a formal application to apply for a particular track. Depending on the track, an interview, essay, or faculty nomination may be required. In order to enter an honors section of a general education course, students need at least a 1200 SAT score and must rank in the 90th percentile (or its equivalent) in their high school class.

Scholarship Availability: Both the University and the Alumni Association award competitive scholarships based on academic merit to entering freshmen. These are available through a number of federal and state grant, loan, scholarship, and work-study programs. In addition, the Honors Program has the highly selective Rummel Scholars Program, which provides partial support for four years for entering freshmen.

The Campus Context: William Paterson University offers thirty undergraduate and eighteen graduate programs through its five colleges: Arts and Communication, Business, Education, Humanities and Social Sciences, and Science and Health. Certification is available in elementary, secondary, and special education. Preprofessional programs in dentistry, law, medicine, and veterinary medicine are arranged at the request of students.

Founded in the city of Paterson in 1855, William Paterson is one of the nine state colleges and universities in New Jersey. Set on 370 wooded acres, the campus feels a world away from city bustle. Yet New York is just 20 miles east, and the Manhattan skyline is visible from several vantage points.

Student Body The University has nearly 10,000 students: 8,454 undergraduate students and 1,491 graduate students (2000–01 academic year). Of the undergraduate population, 58.2 percent are women and 41.8 percent are men. The ethnic distribution is 66.9 percent white, 11.9 percent African American, 3.7 percent Asian-American, 13.6 percent Hispanic/Latino, and 0.2 percent Native American. Twenty-six percent of undergraduates reside on campus in residence halls or apartment-style facilities that accommodate 2,274 students.

Faculty There are 1,051 full-time employees, 34 percent of whom are faculty members (358). Approximately 82 percent of the faculty members have a doctoral degree. The average undergraduate class size is 21 students; the student-faculty ratio is 12:1.

Key Facilities Key facilities are the recently renovated David and Lorraine Cheng Library; the Ben Shan Center for Visual Arts, which houses art galleries and studios; and the Shea Center for Performing Arts, with its 940-seat theater. The Power Art Building features arts studios and gallery space. Hobart Hall is a state-of-the-art communication facility that houses two broadcast-quality TV studios, a multipurpose computer lab, a film studio, an FCC-licensed FM radio station, one uplink and four downlink satellite dishes, and a cable system and a computerized telephone system for voice and data transmission. The Atrium contains a writing center, multimedia language lab, tutorial center, and computing support facilities. Research facilities include fully equipped biochemistry, molecular biology, and neurobiology laboratories and biotechnology and DNA equipment. William Paterson University is a member of the New Jersey Intercampus Network (NJIN), a nonprofit organization of forty-five colleges and universities fostering the growth of video, voice, and data networking.

Honorary Societies At present, the University has no interdisciplinary honors societies but has a set of sixteen discipline-specific honor societies, including Phi Alpha Theta (history), Alpha Kappa Delta (sociology), and Beta Beta Beta (biology).

Athletics The University has nineteen intercollegiate sports teams: nine for men and ten for women, including successful NCAA teams in men's baseball and women's softball. Campus facilities

Interpreting the symbols: **2**=two-year college, **4**=four-year college; **Pu**=public or state college, **Pr**=private college; **G**=general honors program; **D**=departmental honors program; **S**=small program (fewer than 100 students), **M**=midsize program (100 to 500 students), **L**=large program (more than 500 students); **Sc**=scholarships available in honors program; **Tr**=transfer students accepted into honors program; **HBC**=historically black college; **AA**=academic advisors; **GA**=graduate advisors; **FA**=fellowship advisors.

include a competition-size indoor pool, outdoor tennis courts, and a lighted athletics field complex.

Study Abroad Students at William Paterson University have the opportunity to participate in a study-abroad program under the sponsorship of the New Jersey State Consortium for International Studies (NJSCIS). Programs exist in a great number of institutions in Asia, Africa, Australia, Europe, and Latin America.

Support Services The Office of Disability Services coordinates services, including assistance in registration, advisement, parking, referrals, adapted classroom activities, and other special needs. Adaptive aids and equipment are also available, as are a few specially equipped rooms in the residence life complex.

Job Opportunities A wide array of work opportunities is available both on and off campus.

Tuition: Annual tuition (including fees) is $5700 for full-time (12 credits or more) students who are New Jersey residents and $8880 for full-time nonresident students (2001–02 academic year).

Room and Board: $6680 per year (2001–02 academic year)

Contact: Director: Dr. Martin Hahn, University Honors Program, Hunziker Hall, 105A, William Paterson University, Wayne, New Jersey 07470; Telephone: 973-720-3657; Fax: 973-720-3693; E-mail: hahnm@wpunj.edu; Web site: http://www.wpunj.edu/icip/honors/

William Rainey Harper College

2 Pu G M Sc Tr

▼ Honors Program

The Harper College Honors Program offers a variety of general education courses to all students who have been accepted into the program. Students choose those courses that fit their academic and career needs. Honors courses differ from traditional courses in ways determined by the instructors in consultation with the institutional Honors Committee; in general, students are given greater responsibility for designing projects, taking on leadership roles in class discussions, and planning classroom activities. On occasion, interdisciplinary courses are offered. Small classes are the norm: they usually have between 8 and 15 students. Honors instructors are selected for their demonstrated excellence in teaching and for expertise in their chosen disciplines. Honors students are advised by the Honors Coordinator, honors faculty, and college counselors.

English 101, English 102, and Speech 101 (the communications core) are offered every semester during the regular academic year. A journalism independent study is also offered for those students interested in working on the honors newsletter, *The Challenger.* Other courses in business/social science, the humanities, and mathematics/science are also regularly offered. Summer honors courses are also available.

In addition, honors students at Harper automatically become members of the Honors Society, the social arm of the program. The Honors Society elects its own officers and meets weekly to discuss program plans and conduct wide-ranging, open discussions on topics of current interest. Cultural, social, and community service events are planned and carried forward by members of the society.

Honors students are encouraged to attend and actively participate in honors conferences and conventions.

The Harper College Honors Program has been active since 1989 and currently enrolls 200 students.

Participation Requirements: Honors students must successfully complete four honors courses, including an Honors Colloquium course (Humanities 105, Great Ideas of World Civilizations), and maintain a minimum 3.25 GPA in order to graduate from the Harper College Honors Program. Students who take three or fewer honors courses will have the honors course designation indicated on transcripts but will not qualify for honors graduation. The number and type of honors courses taken is at discretion of the student. Each Honors Program graduate receives a citation on the diploma as well as an Honors Program pin, which is awarded at the annual Honors Convocation.

Scholarship Availability: Students who qualify with a 3.5 or better GPA are encouraged to join Phi Theta Kappa. There are a number of scholarships available only to PTK members.

The Campus Context: William Rainey Harper College in Palatine, Illinois, is a public community college and part of the Illinois system of higher education. The College, established in 1965 by voter referendum, is governed by an elected Board of Trustees. Harper serves high school districts 211 (Palatine and Schaumburg Townships), 214 (Elk Grove and Wheeling Townships), and Barrington United School District 220. The Harper College district covers an area of about 200 square miles. Academic programs are administered primarily through seven divisions: Liberal Arts; Business and Social Science; Life Science and Human Services; Academic Enrichment and Language Studies; Wellness and Human Performance; Technology, Mathematics, and Physical Science; and Student Development. Fifty-five degree programs are offered on campus.

Student Body There are 15,000 undergraduates enrolled (7,600 full-time equivalent); 58 percent are women. The ethnic distribution is 10.3 percent Asian, .3 percent Native American, 3 percent African American, 6.7 percent Hispanic, and 74 percent white; there are 109 international students. About 13–15 percent of students receive financial aid. All students commute to campus.

Faculty Of the 821 faculty members, 221 are full-time. The student-faculty ratio is 18:1.

Key Facilities The library houses more than 100,000 books, 126,000 media items, and 850 magazine titles. There are more than fifty computer labs on campus with more than 850 computers.

Athletics Harper offers varsity baseball, basketball, football, golf, soccer, softball, tennis, track and field, and wrestling, plus a variety of intramural athletic programs. Honors students are counseled and encouraged to participate in competitive sports.

Study Abroad Harper's International Program regularly offers study-abroad opportunities to places such as Canterbury, England; Salzburg, Austria; the Netherlands; Costa Rica; and Mexico. Students who study abroad may have one of the four courses required for Honors Program graduation waived.

Support Services Buildings on campus are disabled-accessible. In addition, Harper offers instructional support services, learning disability testing, tutoring services, testing accommodation, reader and scribe services, TTY (telephones for the deaf), and academic advising. A recent Honors Program graduate is dyslexic; the program welcomes students who face such challenges.

Job Opportunities Students are offered a range of work-study opportunities on campus. The Honors Program student aide is a work-study participant.

Tuition: $1500 for area residents, $6372 for state residents, $7917 for nonresidents per year (1999)

Mandatory Fees: $64

Contact: Coordinator: Dr. Trygve Thoreson, Liberal Arts Division, Palatine, Illinois 60067; Telephone: 847-925-6489; Fax: 847-925-6039; E-mail: tthoreso@harper.cc.il.us

Wilmington College

4 Pr G S Sc Tr

▼ Honors Program

The Honors Program is designed to enrich the academic experience of qualified students with honors sections of English

Composition and the Global Issues Seminar, which is a core curriculum course at the College; interdisciplinary seminars; a senior project; and various noncredit enrichment activities. The program is open to entering freshmen on the Wilmington campus who received a score of 25 or higher on the ACT, had a minimum of a B average in high school, and graduated in the upper one fifth of their high school class. Those who meet requirements are identified when they are admitted and are given an opportunity to enroll in the program. Transfer students who are interested in joining the program should contact the Director of the Honors Program. The program was established by faculty members in 1995 and currently enrolls 55 students.

Participation Requirements: First-year students enroll in special sections of English Composition and the College's core course, the Global Issues Seminar. Sophomores and juniors enroll each term in one-hour seminars directed toward special studies that are not offered as part of the regular curriculum. Seniors take an honors seminar in Global Cultures and Issues and complete an enhanced capstone senior project in their majors. Honors students must maintain a cumulative GPA of 3.3 or above. Field trips, campus speakers, and special events on and off campus are planned for the honors students. Students who compete the program will be recognized at graduation and have their completion of the program noted on their transcripts.

The Campus Context: Wilmington College is a private, career-oriented liberal arts college founded by the Religious Society of Friends (Quakers) in 1870. The main campus is located in Wilmington, Ohio, which is an hour drive from Cincinnati, Dayton, and Columbus, Ohio. The city of Wilmington has been named one of the best small towns in the United States. More than twelve hundred students are enrolled on the main campus in day programs and an Evening College. In addition, there are two branches located in the Cincinnati metropolitan area. As part of the College's Quaker heritage, classes are also offered in three correctional facilities. Wilmington has been profiled twice by the John Templeton Foundation for its character-building initiatives and programs in student leadership development. Wilmington College is accredited by The Higher Education Commission of the North Central Association of Colleges and Schools. The College's close ties to the local community are demonstrated by the 21,000 hours of community service provided each year by faculty, students, and staff members.

Student Body Total enrollment is 1,876 and more than one half of students are women. On the main campus, students are from eleven different states and five countries. Nonwhite students make up 7 percent of the student body. Nearly 70 percent of the full-time students on the main campus reside in College housing, which includes six residence halls that are both women and co-ed, two apartment-style complexes, and special interest housing. More than 95 percent of students on the main campus receive financial aid.

Faculty The total number of faculty members is 71 and 66 percent have terminal degrees. The student-faculty ratio is 16:1.

Key Facilities Four computer labs offer free Internet access, log-ins, and e-mail accounts, and are open 98 hours per week. An academic farm and new equine studies center are within an easy walk of campus. All of the residence halls are wired and provide more than 100 software titles for student use. The library is fully automated and is a member of OhioLink, a statewide consortium of academic libraries, which provides access to the major collections in the state.

Honorary Societies Green Key (general), Sigma Tau Delta (English), Delta Tau Alpha (agriculture), Omicron Delta Epsilon (international economics), and Sigma Delta Pi (Spanish)

Athletics Wilmington College is a member of the Ohio Athletic Conference, which is the oldest NCAA Division III conference in the country. It offers the following sports for women: basketball, cross-country, equestrian, golf, indoor and outdoor track and field, soccer, softball, swimming, tennis, and volleyball. Men compete in baseball, basketball, cross-country, equestrian, football, golf, indoor and outdoor track and field, soccer, swimming, tennis, and wrestling. There is an active intramural program, and the local YMCA is located on the Wilmington College campus.

Study Abroad Study abroad programs are available in Vienna, Austria; Edgehill, England; Macerata, Italy; and Morelia, Mexico. Short-term study programs have included tours in Spain, Italy, Greece, France, Brazil, the Bahamas, and Iceland. In addition, the football team has traveled to Barcelona, Spain and the women's basketball team has traveled to Australia.

Support Services The Academic Resource Center (ARC) provides tutoring and supplemental instruction (SI) at no cost. In addition, the director of ARC coordinates services for disabled students.

Job Opportunities Approximately 350 of the 1,200 main-campus students work on campus. Job openings are readily available in the local community. The Career Center provides assistance in resume writing, job-seeking skills, interviewing techniques, and hosts recruiters on campus. Nearly 50 percent of students take an internship while enrolled.

Tuition: $15,360 per year (2001–02)

Room and Board: $2920 minimum; $3160 for board

Mandatory Fees: $386

WINONA STATE UNIVERSITY

4 Pu G S Tr

▼ Honors Program

The Honors Program provides students with a liberal education tailored to the abilities and interests of talented students. It is a program to which students with high potential can apply as entering first-year students, transfer students, or as enrolled students. The Honors Program offers courses with a multi-disciplinary focus within the framework of humanities, natural sciences, and social sciences. The program keeps class sizes small in order to facilitate learning by participation, discussion, and integration of knowledge from multiple sources. The program represents a community of faculty members and students seeking to develop the potential of honors students. Successful completion of the Honors Program gives graduates enhanced prospects for successful career placement and graduate school admission.

Participation Requirements: Incoming students who are Distinctive Admits meet qualifications for the Honors Program.

Admission Process: Enrolled students can apply for admission to the program if they have a college GPA of 3.25 or above. Transfer students can apply for admission if they meet the GPA criteria for enrolled students.

Scholarship Availability: Winona State University (WSU) has many merit-based scholarship programs at the departmental, college, and University levels. In addition, the University honor associations (Alpha Lambda Delta and Golden Key) each offer a yearly scholarship to their members. WSU offers three types of academic scholarships to outstanding students who come to WSU directly from high school. These scholarships range from $750 to $2500 and are renewable for eight semesters if a minimum 3.5 GPA is maintained. A Resident Tuition Scholarship awards resident rates to nonresident first-year students. The value of this award is $3200, and it is renewable for eight semesters with a minimum

Interpreting the symbols: **2**=two-year college, **4**=four-year college; **Pu**=public or state college, **Pr**=private college; **G**=general honors program; **D**=departmental honors program; **S**=small program (fewer than 100 students), **M**=midsize program (100 to 500 students), **L**=large program (more than 500 students); **Sc**=scholarships available in honors program; **Tr**=transfer students accepted into honors program; **HBC**=historically black college; **AA**=academic advisors; **GA**=graduate advisors; **FA**=fellowship advisors.

3.0 GPA. Applicants should consult the current undergraduate catalog for further details.

The Campus Context: The mission of Winona State University is to educate and enlighten its citizenry at a distinctive institution: a community of learners dedicated to improving the world.

Located in the beautiful bluff country of the Mississippi River Valley, the Winona campus is largely residential and primarily serves a traditional student-age population, while the Rochester campus serves primarily nontraditional students. The Institute for Lifelong Education, headquartered on the Rochester campus, meets the needs of the nontraditional student on each campus and provides the structure for outreach activities compatible with the mission of WSU. Commonly held principles help Winona State University prepare undergraduate and graduate students on both campuses. Differences are valued and everyone works collaboratively, continuing a legacy of a century and a half of service.

Winona State is an exemplary arts and sciences institution with select professional and graduate programs anchored in a general education core. As a midsized public university, it is committed to retaining small class sizes and to challenging students by maintaining rigorous academic standards. Faculty members and members of the administration are involved with students, facilitate cooperative and active learning, provide prompt feedback, emphasize time on task, communicate high expectations, and respect the students' diverse talents and ways of knowing. Faculty members are dedicated to creating an optimal learning environment for students by using contemporary technology and by building learning communities that help students maximize their postgraduation successes. Students acquire the disciplinary expertise enabling them to pursue careers or enter graduate or professional schools. They learn the value of aesthetics and ethical integrity along with the importance of becoming community leaders and furthering the public good.

Winona State University recognizes that many of the learning experiences of college occur outside the classroom. It, therefore, is committed to building and maintaining a caring community. On both campuses, community members strive for amicable relationships based on shared values and an affirmation of the principle of freedom of speech within an atmosphere of civility and mutual respect. Governed by collective bargaining agreements and guided by principled leadership, the University respects diversity and collaborates to resolve issues that affect everyone. Common successes and the University's distinctive heritage is celebrated.

The University is committed to measuring results against self-defined and national standards. Through this ongoing assessment, one in which students and faculty and staff members participate, the University will improve continuously and establish accountability for results. Thus, Winona State University's social contract to provide educational benefits to the people of Minnesota, the nation, and the world will be reaffirmed.

Student Body WSU enrollment for fall semester 2001 was slightly more than 7,000 students, which included 690 graduate students. Of the total student headcount, 6,500 study on the main campus in Winona; another 800 study at the WSU-Rochester Center, located in Rochester, Minnesota; and an additional 200 attend classes in special regional offerings. WSU's student population is approximately 58 percent women. About 3 percent of WSU's student population are members of minority groups.

This fall, Winona State University enrolled the largest number of new international students in the history of the program, as 109 new international students began studying at Winona State in August, at the start of the fall semester. Those students bring WSU's total international student enrollment to 338. These international students represent fifty-three countries.

Last year 72 percent of all WSU students received some form of financial aid, including grants, loans, and work-study programs. The average award was about $3500. Total financial aid awards at WSU last year amounted to $25 million.

There are more than 150 clubs and organizations at Winona State University, allowing students opportunities for fun activities that complement their studies. Among these are eight national fraternities or sororities and a number of national honor societies in specific academic disciplines.

Faculty WSU employs 375 faculty members, 330 of whom are full-time. More than 65 percent of WSU faculty members hold the Ph.D. or other terminal degree in their fields.

Key Facilities The University's latest building, the library, opens in 1999. This exceptional facility holds more than 500,000 volumes and has 800 study spaces available, most of which are wired for network access by laptop computer. Other exciting features include forty multimedia computers for student use as well as sixteen group study rooms. Plans also call for a twenty-eight-seat electronic classroom that is interactive television (ITV) capable. Winona State has made a commitment to its students to ensure advanced technology in a facility that will not only provide great research opportunities but will also provide quiet study space as well as a place to learn and interact with others.

Honorary Societies Alpha Delta Mu, Alpha Lambda Delta, Alpha Upsilon Alpha, Beta Beta Beta, Delta Sigma Pi, Golden Key, Kappa Delta Pi, Phi Alpha Theta, Pi Mu Epsilon, Pi Sigma Delta, Psi Chi, Sigma Theta Tau, and Sigma Theta

Athletics Winona State's athletic and academic programs are built on the principles representing a focus on excellent learning community and placing a high value on the personal development and scholarship of its athletes. The accomplishments of WSU's athletes are visible both on the field and in the classroom. Nearly every sport has received individual and team honors, including conference, district, and national championships, as well as having participants named to All-American and Academic All-American Teams. The Winona State Warriors compete in the Northern Sun Intercollegiate Conference (NSIC) and are NCAA Division II. Membership in the NSIC includes Bemidji, Moorhead, and Southwest State Universities; the Universities of Minnesota–Duluth and Morris; and Northern State University in South Dakota.

Study Abroad A variety of study-abroad options are available for students interested in broadening their university experience and enhancing their resume by including a living and learning experience in another country. In addition to programs sponsored by WSU, students may select programs through other universities. Programs vary in location, length, cost, admission requirements, application deadlines, focus, etc., so it is important to receive the most recent and detailed information. Early and careful planning for study abroad is important; students will want to maximize the academic and cultural benefits of the experience. All WSU-sanctioned programs that are one semester or more carry 12 to 15 credits per semester (short-term study/tours carry fewer credits).

Support Services This is a federally funded program, and students are eligible for its services if they have a low income, are a first-generation college student, or have a physical disability. Services include tutoring, academic, advising, counseling, and help in deciding a major.

Job Opportunities WSU offers work-study positions. Many departments offer internship experiences with credit and, in some instances, with pay. To apply for an internship, students must be fully matriculated with an established cumulative GPA at WSU of 2.0 or higher.

Tuition: $8500 for residents, $12,300 for nonresidents, per year

Room and board: $3900

Mandatory Fees: $100 (at Residential College for new freshmen)

Contact: Director: Dr. Kristi Lane, Phelps Hall, Room 231H, Winona State University, Winona, Minnesota 55987; Telephone: 507-457-5435; Fax: 507-457-2327; E-mail: klane@vax2.winona.msus.edu

Winthrop University

4 Pu G S Tr

▼ Honors Program

The Honors Program at Winthrop University seeks to encourage and enhance the intellectual growth of students through a program of small-enrollment courses taught by high-quality faculty members who prompt active student participation and interaction. The program seeks to capture the imagination and to foster the joy of learning by constructing a challenging, personalized learning environment that facilitates the development of analytic problem-solving skills, promotes both independent and cooperative learning along with presentation skills, integrates knowledge across traditional course and discipline boundaries, and enriches learning opportunities through multicultural and international studies.

Winthrop University's Honors Program encourages learning through a variety of settings, including seminars, independent directed study, interdisciplinary courses, a senior thesis, and a selection of 1-credit intensive symposia centered on great works or current events. The student's course program is constructed by the student with the consultation of his/her adviser and the Director of the Honors Program. After completing the Honors Program at Winthrop, students not only have a deeper, richer understanding of the content studied, they retain the joy of learning, the strength of independent thought, and the ability to direct their own learning.

Participation Requirements: Winthrop University's Honors Program is open to all students after at least a GPR of 3.0 at Winthrop has been achieved. Incoming freshmen are invited to participate in the program based on high school class rank and SAT I or ACT scores. In the first semester of the freshman year, Honors Program students enroll in a cluster of two thematically integrated courses specifically designed for honors students. A student attains a degree with honors through satisfactorily completing 23 hours of course work in honors while maintaining a minimum 3.0 GPR based on his/her total course work. Honors courses must be completed with a B or better to be accepted for honors credit. Twelve hours must be in the student's major. Either a freshman cluster of courses or a 3-hour interdisciplinary seminar must be completed. A senior thesis/project must be completed in the student's major. Two 1-hour symposia must be completed. The student's course plan should be designed with the help of an adviser and filed with the Honors Program Director at the beginning of the junior year. For graduation with an Honors Program degree, the plan must receive the approval of the Honors Director.

In addition to the honors courses offered each semester through the Honors Program Office, students also have the option of taking a course through contracted study, which involves a student contracting with the professor of a regularly scheduled course to take that course for honors credit.

Admission Process: Incoming freshman students are invited by the Honors Program Director to participate based on their SAT I or ACT scores and high school class rank. All other students are eligible for the Honors Program after they have achieved a GPR of 3.0 or higher. The Honors Program is open to students in all majors at Winthrop University.

Scholarship Availability: Scholarships of various types are offered through the Office of Admissions based on academic performance. The Honors Program Office does not offer any scholarships; however, most honors students are the recipients of academic scholarships.

The Campus Context: Winthrop University, founded in 1886, has been an educational leader in South Carolina for more than a century. The University offers a total of fifty-nine undergraduate degree programs through the four academic divisions: College of Arts and Sciences, the College of Business Administration, the College of Education, and the College of Visual and Performing Arts. In 1997, Winthrop achieved 100 percent national accreditation of eligible academic programs. Winthrop University's campus is located in Rock Hill, South Carolina, just 30 minutes away from the Charlotte metropolitan area. The beautiful, tree-lined campus is located in the National Register of Historic Places. The University's original Rock Hill facilities were built in the neo-Georgian architectural style of the early 1900s. Students living on campus are only a short walk away from classes, the cafeterias, Dacus Library, and Dinkins Student Center. Also situated conveniently are a theater, two auditoriums, art galleries, a recital hall, and the largest music conservatory in the Carolinas. The recreational area surrounding Winthrop Lake includes a modern 6,500-seat coliseum and athletic development facilities, numerous sports fields, a golf course, racquetball courts, and the Shack, a popular student gathering spot.

Student Body Undergraduate enrollment in 1998 was 4,340; 2,998 of the students were women. The ethnic distribution was white, non-Hispanic 71.6 percent; black, non-Hispanic 23.9 percent; international 2.0 percent; Native American 0.5 percent; Asian/Pacific Islander 1.1 percent; and Hispanic 0.8 percent. Forty-seven percent of the students live on campus. Sixty-five percent of the students receive financial aid.

Faculty There are 420 full- and part-time faculty members. Of the 290 full-time faculty members, 82 percent hold the terminal degree in their field of study. With a student-faculty ratio of 17:1, Winthrop faculty members are able to take a personal interest in the individual needs and development of every student.

Key Facilities The faculty members and collections of the Dacus Library are an integral part of the University's instruction programs. The Dacus On-line Catalog system provides easy access to the library's collections. The library's holdings total more than 500,000 volumes and volume-equivalents, which are supplemented by resources available through the national interlibrary loan program. Winthrop's academic computing division supports the University's instructional and research functions. Students have access to diverse computing resources, including more than fifteen microcomputer laboratories that support PC and Macintosh platforms for open access and instructional needs in all four major academic areas. Dial-up services provide students and faculty members with 24-hour access to Winthrop's network and computing facilities. All main campus buildings are directly connected to the campus network. Computer needs for visually impaired students and Braille printing services are also provided by the academic computing division. Winthrop is a node on the Internet, which allows students free e-mail accounts and many other informational resources.

Honorary Societies Alpha Lambda Delta, Omicron Delta Kappa, and Phi Kappa Phi

Athletics Winthrop University participates in NCAA Division I intercollegiate competition in men's and women's basketball, tennis, golf, track, and cross-country; women's softball and volleyball; and men's baseball and soccer.

Study Abroad Winthrop University Honors Program students are encouraged to study abroad, and the University has exchange programs in Australia, China, England, and Germany. In addition, Winthrop also participates in the National Student Exchange Program, which allows Winthrop students to study for up to one year at one of the more than 150 colleges and universities throughout the United States while paying Winthrop tuition. In conjunction with the University of South Carolina's Washington

Interpreting the symbols: **2**=two-year college, **4**=four-year college; **Pu**=public or state college, **Pr**=private college; **G**=general honors program; **D**=departmental honors program; **S**=small program (fewer than 100 students), **M**=midsize program (100 to 500 students), **L**=large program (more than 500 students); **Sc**=scholarships available in honors program; **Tr**=transfer students accepted into honors program; **HBC**=historically black college; **AA**=academic advisors; **GA**=graduate advisors; **FA**=fellowship advisors.

Semester Program, Winthrop encourages its Honors Program students to spend a semester in Washington, D.C., working and studying.

Support Services The Counselor for Students with Disabilities acts as a liaison between the student and University community. Since each student has a unique set of special needs, the Counselor for Students with Disabilities makes every effort to work with the student to acquire access to programs and services.

Job Opportunities Work opportunities are available on and off campus. Students who wish to work on campus may review the job opportunities posted in the Financial Resource Center. The office has listings for campus positions that require the Federal Work-Study subsidy and those positions that do not require work-study.

Tuition: $4032 for residents, $7250 for nonresidents, per year (1998–99)

Room and board: $3904

Mandatory Fees: $10

Contact: Director: Dr. Kathy A. Lyon, 206 Tillman, Rock Hill, South Carolina 29733; Telephone: 803-323-2320; Fax: 803-323-2340; E-mail: lyonk@winthrop.edu

Wittenberg University

4 Pr G M Tr

▼ University Honors Program

The Wittenberg University Honors Program, which was created in 1978, heightens and enhances the rich variety of intellectual experiences possible in a liberal arts education. The program provides an academic and social climate in which students of high academic potential can find a community of classmates and teachers engaged in intellectual inquiry at the highest level. The program brings students together in special, often interdisciplinary seminars during the sophomore and junior years and affords mutual support as each student undertakes independent work culminating in a senior honors thesis or project within the major. Housed in the beautiful historic Matthies House, the program invites students to use the study and social facilities in the house.

Participation Requirements: Upon enrollment at Wittenberg, first-year students who are Wittenberg University Scholar Award recipients are granted status as University Honors Program candidates. Students may then apply for admission to the Honors Program in the spring semester of their first year. Membership is also open to other interested students at this time. The program typically serves about 200 members from a student body of more than 2,000. To become eligible for the Wittenberg Honors Program, first-year students who have met the minimum 3.5 GPA must apply to the Honors Program Committee (comprised of the Honors Program Director, 6 faculty members, and 4 current honors students) for permanent entry into the program. Applications include two faculty recommendations, a creative essay, and a short application. Once in the program, students may graduate with Wittenberg University Honors if they maintain a 3.5 cumulative GPA and complete the program requirements. These include participating in at least two honors seminars and completing/defending an honors thesis/project in the relevant department.

Admission Process: No students are automatically admitted to the program but, instead, must apply for admission in January of their first year at Wittenberg.

Scholarship Availability: The University awards substantial scholarships based on academic excellence, but none are awarded through the Honors Program. Small grants help senior honors students with costs of the senior honors thesis/project.

The Campus Context: Wittenberg is a four-year, private, residential, undergraduate liberal arts college affiliated with the Evangelical Lutheran Church in America. It has an enrollment of approximately 2,100 students coming from all fifty states and forty other nations and has a full-time faculty of 150 members. Wittenberg is located in a residential area of Springfield, a city of 65,000 in a metropolitan area of 150,000 in southwestern Ohio. It has a local Phi Beta Kappa chapter and grants a total of forty-two undergraduate majors, as well as a master's degree in education.

Wittenberg University is a nationally recognized college for the liberal arts and sciences, which is distinguished by its strong interdisciplinary programs such as East Asian studies and Russian area studies. Independent evaluators recently found the East Asian studies program to be among the finest of its kind among colleges or universities of any size. Although Wittenberg's traditional strengths have been in the liberal arts, recently the sciences, management, and education have also developed into popular majors for students. One in 4 students choose a science major, designed to emphasize collaborative problem solving among students and collaborative research between students and faculty members. The management department also promotes field study through a program to place students as problem solvers in area businesses. Wittenberg is one of only a handful of colleges to include community service as a graduation requirement. Eight thriving preprofessional programs help contribute to the record of Wittenberg students, in which 70 percent eventually pursue graduate studies.

Student Body Wittenberg enrolls more than 2,000 full-time students, representing all fifty states, the Virgin Islands, Puerto Rico, and forty international countries. The greatest concentration of students is from the Northeastern and Midwestern parts of the United States, although the student body includes students from coast to coast. Wittenberg's student body includes 16 National Merit Scholars, 4 Ohio Academic Scholars, and 153 Lutheran Scholars. More than a third of entering freshman have not yet decided on their major field.

Faculty The faculty consists of 145 full-time teaching members and 9 members of the administrative and professional staff with faculty rank. Of the full-time faculty members, 96 percent hold the Ph.D. degree or other appropriate terminal degree in their field. Wittenberg's academic community encourages frequent dialogue between students and faculty members. Indeed, the mission and size of the school fosters personal contact both in class and in nonacademic settings. The student-faculty ratio is 14:1.

Key Facilities The library houses 360,000 volumes and a University archive of historic books and documents. Wittenberg is also a member of the OhioLink system, which provides students with access to most university libraries in the state. Computer facilities include open labs in the library, residence halls, and classroom buildings, as well as a new classroom building equipped with "smart" classrooms. Honors students have access to their own computer lab with printing capacity in the Matthies House.

Athletics Wittenberg is ranked in the NCAA Division III and is a member of the North Coast Athletic Conference. Varsity sports include men's and women's lacrosse, tennis, cross-country, track and field, swimming, basketball, and soccer; women's field hockey and softball; and men's football and baseball. There is also an active intramural program and several club sports, including rugby.

Study Abroad Study-abroad opportunities exist in Australia, Austria, Great Britain, Ireland, Sweden, Japan, South Korea, China, Mexico, Cuba, and Spain, and approximately 25 percent of students study in an other country for at least a semester.

Support Services The library, Student Center, and most other buildings on campus are wheelchair accessible. The University strives to meet the needs of students with learning disabilities.

Job Opportunities Work opportunities on campus are coordinated by the Office of Student Employment. In addition, the Career Center works with students throughout their time at Wittenberg with job advice, resume writing, and placement.

Tuition: $22,530

Room and Board: $5776; room only, $2984

Mandatory Fees: Student Senate Fee, $150

Contact: Director: Dr. Tammy Proctor, Wittenberg University, P.O. Box 720, Springfield, Ohio 45501-0720; Telephone: 937-327-7841; Fax: 937-327-7991; E-mail: tproctor@wittenberg.edu; Web site: http://www4.wittenberg.edu/academics/honors/

Worcester State College

4 Pu G M Sc Tr AA

▼ Commonwealth Honors Program at Worcester State College

The mission of the honors program at Worcester State College is to offer all qualified students an outstanding undergraduate experience through courses that emphasize innovative pedagogy and the values of liberal learning. Honors classes are small (often fewer than 20 students) and are designed to encourage active and lifelong learning. Small classes and extracurricular programs provide honors students with greater interaction between their peers and a select core of dedicated faculty members. In addition to stimulating classes, honors students also enjoy campus speakers, field trips to cultural centers, occasional luncheons with faculty members, and an annual dinner with the college president. Founded in 1996, the program currently enrolls 150 students and recently earned accreditation as a Commonwealth Honors Program from the Massachusetts Board of Higher Education.

Participation Requirements: The core program requires completion of eight honors courses (24 credits) normally taken during the student's freshman and sophomore years (or two courses per semester). Each course is designed to help fulfill the College's general education requirements and must be passed with a grade of B or better. Students cannot take an honors class on a pass/fail basis. Students can elect to become a Commonwealth Honors Scholar once they fulfill the core requirements of the college-wide program, maintain a minimum GPA of 3.2, and complete a 3-credit capstone course in the junior or senior year. Special accommodations can be made for transfer students and others who have difficulty coordinating honors program requirements with those of their academic major.

Admission Process: Students are invited to join the honors program in one of two ways. The Office of Admissions selects an initial group of roughly 50 students for each fall term based on a series of indicators (primarily SAT scores and high school GPA) that predict a high likelihood of academic success at the College. A second group is selected at the completion of the fall term based on academic performance while at the College. Students interested in becoming an honors student should contact the admissions office directly.

Scholarship Availability: The College awards approximately fifty scholarships for each incoming class of honors students. Scholarships are intended to support a student for four years and must be maintained with a minimum GPA that varies for each type of award.

The Campus Context: Worcester State College was founded in 1874 and enrolls approximately 5,000 full- and part-time students in twenty-four undergraduate and a dozen graduate programs. Located on 58 acres of rolling, wooded land in the quiet residential West End of Worcester, the campus offers a unique blend of suburban and urban amenities. Once a thriving industrial city, Worcester has reemerged as the educational, commercial, and high-technology center of central Massachusetts and is now New England's third-largest city. Located in the heart of central New England, Worcester is home to almost a dozen other colleges and universities, several museums and research centers, and a wide variety of cultural activities. Worcester State College is easily accessible by public transportation from downtown Worcester, conveniently located near the Worcester Regional Airport, and an hour or so by car from Boston and Springfield, Massachusetts; Hartford, Connecticut; and Providence, Rhode Island.

Student Body Enrollment is roughly 2,700 full-time and 1,500 part-time students at the undergraduate level and 75 full-time and 675 part-time students at the graduate level. Two residential living quarters house 688 students, while 84 percent commute. More than 40 percent of the students are over the age of 25, and 95 percent of the students come from Massachusetts.

Faculty The total number of faculty members is 264 (173 full-time), of whom 65 percent have terminal degrees. The average student-faculty ratio is 15:1.

Key Facilities In 2000, the College opened the Kalyan K. Ghosh Science and Technology Center, with state-of-the-art research and teaching laboratories. In addition, honors students have their own computer lab and study lounge located in the center of the College's 160,000-volume library.

Athletics Worcester State is a Division III member of the NCAA, the Massachusetts State College Athletic Conference (MSSCAC), the New England Football Conference (NEFC), the Eastern College Athletic Conference (ECAC), and the Massachusetts Association for Intercollegiate Athletics for Women (MAIAW).

Study Abroad Worcester State is a member of the College Consortium for International Studies (CCIS), with more than thirty-five programs in thirty countries. Worcester State also has direct exchange programs with universities in Worcester, England; Puerto Rico; Portugal; and China. For more information, students should contact the College's International Programs Office.

Support Services Students are encouraged to use the following services on campus: Career Services, the Counseling Center, the Learning Assistance Center (LAC), Alternatives for Individual Development (AID), Disability Services Office (DSO), the Writing Center, and Health Services.

Tuition: For the 2001–02 academic year, full-time in-state tuition was $2573; full-time out-of-state tuition was $7050.

Room and Board: Those living on campus paid approximately $5000 for room and board.

Mandatory Fees: All students paid at least $1603 in additional fees.

Contact: Dr. Steven H. Corey, Professor and Director, College Honors Program, Worcester State College, 486 Chandler Street, Worcester, Massachusetts 01602. Students should note that Dr. Corey will be on leave for the fall 2002 semester; in his absence, they may contact: Admissions Office, Worcester State College; Telephone: 508-929-8710; Fax: 508-929-8174; Web site: http://wwwfac.worcester.edu/honors/

Wright State University

4 Pu G M Sc Tr AA

▼ University Honors Program

The Wright State University Honors Program was created in 1972 to meet the needs of the University's brightest, most ambitious students. It is open to students of all majors and provides a varied curriculum consisting of honors sections of general education courses; service-learning courses; interdisciplinary core

Interpreting the symbols: **2**=two-year college, **4**=four-year college; **Pu**=public or state college, **Pr**=private college; **G**=general honors program; **D**=departmental honors program; **S**=small program (fewer than 100 students), **M**=midsize program (100 to 500 students), **L**=large program (more than 500 students); **Sc**=scholarships available in honors program; **Tr**=transfer students accepted into honors program; **HBC**=historically black college; **AA**=academic advisors; **GA**=graduate advisors; **FA**=fellowship advisors.

courses in the humanities, social sciences, and natural sciences; and broadly interdisciplinary topical senior seminars. Departments are also free to propose honors sections of regular courses both at the introductory and advanced level. First-year students are able to participate in learning communities of linked courses in which the same 20 students enroll. Most majors offer students the opportunity for intense honors work in the major during the senior year. Students may choose from three honors designations, which are noted on the transcript and in the Commencement program: University Honors Scholar, General Studies Honors, and Departmental Honors.

The primary mission of the Honors Program is to produce a body of graduates who are well-educated, socially conscious, and capable of assuming leadership roles in society. The Honors Program is responsible for providing undergraduates with all the tools and every opportunity to create a stimulating, well-rounded, solidly grounded, and socially responsible education. The program currently has approximately 1,160 alumni, disproportionately distributed in the medical, legal, and academic professions, where many of them are beginning to move into leadership roles. Alumni surveys indicate that the program is fulfilling its mission.

The Honors Program encourages diversity in its student body, its faculty members, course content, and extracurricular activities. Transfer students and nontraditional students are particularly welcome additions to the student mix. Students who complete honors work at another NCHC institution receive honors credit at Wright State for those courses.

Honors classes are small—between 15 and 20 students. Faculty members are encouraged to try innovative, student-centered teaching styles. Honors classes usually feature discussion, collaboration, creative projects, or extensive research papers. Most honors courses are writing-intensive. Ongoing assessment indicates that students are happy with their honors courses, often citing them as the only undergraduate courses that challenged them to think analytically. To recognize and encourage outstanding teaching, the students select a faculty member as Honors Teacher of the Year.

About 9 percent (345 members) of each incoming class enter the University as honors students. The overall number of active participants averages about 750. Honors students may elect to live in the Honors House in Boston Hall.

Participation Requirements: To remain active, students must maintain a minimum 3.0 GPA and make progress toward graduation with honors. Approximately 75 students complete one of the honors degree options each year. To meet their requirements, students choose from sixty to seventy courses each year. Students who complete University Honors take a minimum of eight honors courses plus a departmental program. General Studies Honors requires eight courses and a minimum cumulative GPA of 3.4. Many departmental programs also require students to complete at least one University Honors seminar.

Admission Process: Students are admitted to the program based on high school or college performance.

Scholarship Availability: Honors students are supported by a comprehensive scholarship program. Fifteen to 20 incoming students receive substantial Honors Scholarships that commit them to four years of participation in the Honors Program. Continuing students compete for awards of varying amounts. Several modest awards are usually offered each quarter. Upper-division honors students are recognized with Distinguished Senior Awards, research grants, and the Heritage and Salsburg Scholarships. An Honors Program Development Fund exists to help students with travel to conferences, international study, and other extracurricular opportunities.

The Campus Context: Wright State is a comprehensive metropolitan university located 12 miles northeast of Dayton, Ohio. The 557-acre main campus includes twenty-one major buildings and a 200-acre biological preserve.

Student Body Approximately 16,000 students pursue a variety of degrees: more than 100 undergraduate majors and forty graduate or professional programs, including the M.D., Psy.D., Ph.D., and Ed.S. Most students are Ohio residents, with a fairly small international component (1.7 percent). Thirteen percent of students are classified as members of minority groups (mostly African American), and 55 percent are women. Fraternity and sorority life is growing, but still represents a relatively small presence on campus. While Wright State is primarily a commuter school, approximately 2,500 students live on campus.

Faculty On the main campus, excluding the medical school, Wright State has a total of 520 full-time faculty members. At the assistant professor rank and above, 89 percent hold earned doctorates in their field.

Key Facilities The Paul Lawrence Dunbar Library houses more than 520,000 volumes, the Fordham Health Sciences Library, and a music library. Through OhioLINK, students may search all academic libraries in the state. All students are eligible to receive an account for access to a variety of computer systems, thus enabling access to Internet resources. The campus is in the process of becoming networked.

Honorary Societies Phi Kappa Phi, Golden Key, Alpha Lambda Delta

Athletics Playing in NCAA Division I athletics, Wright State emphasizes women's and men's basketball, baseball, and women's volleyball and fields competitive teams in other sports. Wright State competes in the Horizon Leagur.

Study Abroad Students may choose from a variety of study-abroad opportunities. No programs currently require such an experience. Approximately 35 students per year participate.

Support Services Wright State is especially noted for its services to students with disabilities.

Tuition: $4596 for state residents, $9192 for nonresidents, per year (2001–02)

Room and Board: $5700

Contact: Director: Dr. Susan Carrefiello, 3640 Colonel Glenn Highway, Dayton, Ohio 45435; Telephone: 937-775-2660; E-mail: honors@wright.edu

YORK COLLEGE OF PENNSYLVANIA

4 Pr G S Sc Tr AA

▼ York College Honors Program

York College's Honors Program seeks to provide challenging and engaging experiences for academically motivated and accomplished students. The program offers course work, special academic and career advising, and extracurricular enrichment activities to its small group of undergraduate students. Students find that the community of scholars created by the Honors Program stimulates and supports their intellectual growth and interests while providing recognition for their extra efforts. The honors curriculum supplements the student's regular academic program by replacing a portion of the College's general education requirements with enhanced honors courses. The students belong to an Honors Club, in which they enjoy the fellowship of the honors community. The club has a great deal of autonomy in designing the activities of the group, such as overnight trips to New York City and Washington, D.C.; book discussions; and national conference attendance. A key characteristic of the College as a whole, and the Honors Program in particular, is individual attention to students' whole development as a person. Small and innovative classes with enthusiastic and talented faculty members, regular contact with several advisers, and a fun and engaging orientation give the College the opportunity to meet the students' needs for intellectual and personal growth.

The program was developed in 2000 and enrolled its first class of approximately 30 students in the fall of 2001.

Co-Coordinators of the Honors Program for 2001–02 are Dr. Perri B. Druen, Psychology, and Dr. Jim Kearns, Mechanical Engineering.

Participation Requirements: In order to become an Honors Program Graduate and receive special recognition at the Commencement Ceremony, students must complete a minimum of 20 honors credits in such courses as honors core and general education courses, including English and Information Literacy, Critical Thinking, psychology, and history; honors special-topics courses, which may be interdisciplinary or particularly timely, including Elections in America or Youth Violence; and honors-by-contract courses, in which a student may add an honors component to any regular course by working with the instructor of the course to customize projects for the student; complete an honors project, which is typically in the student's major area and may include research studies, performances or recitals, design projects, or works of fine art or poetry; complete a service component, in which students contribute to the academic culture at the College and in the community by organizing activities such as field trips, tutoring services, York College's own student conference, or service learning in courses; and attain an overall GPA of 3.3.

Admission Process: To be eligible for participation, students must apply to and be accepted by York College. The criteria for acceptance into the program are not solely based upon measures of previous academic performance. All interested students are encouraged to apply and are evaluated individually on the basis of their preparedness and motivation for honors study. Preference is given to students who have achieved a combined SAT score of 1200 or higher and who rank in the top 20 percent of their high school graduating class. Interested students who are accepted to the College may request an application at the address listed below. The application includes a list of honors and awards, extracurricular and leadership activities, and a prompted essay. Students who apply early are notified of acceptance in late March or early April; after that, admission is on a rolling basis.

Scholarship Availability: Incoming students with a minimum SAT score of 1200 and a rank in the top 20 percent of their high school class are invited to apply for Trustee and Presidential Scholarships. A competition on campus, held early in the spring semester, determines the winners.

The Campus Context: York College of Pennsylvania is an independent institution of higher education that offers degree programs in both the arts and sciences and professional majors. The 118-acre campus, located in a suburban area 45 miles north of Baltimore, traces its history to the York County Academy, which was chartered in 1787. York College is a comprehensive academic institution offering seventy high-quality academic programs of study. While the overwhelming majority of matriculated students are enrolled in either a Bachelor of Arts or a Bachelor of Science program, the College also offers a Master of Business Administration degree and Associate of Arts and Associate of Science degrees. All undergraduate degree programs at the College require students to complete a foundation of general education course work. Noteworthy learning facilities include a learning resource center, an art gallery, a radio station, a TV station, a telecommunications center, an Abraham Lincoln artifacts collection, a rare-books collection, an oral history room, engineering laboratories, psychology laboratories, and a nursing education center. *U.S. News & World Report* ranks York College of Pennsylvania as a best value among regional universities in the northern United States for offering high educational quality at an affordable price. York College has also been consistently listed as a national best buy in *Barron's Best Buys in College Education.*

Student Body The College draws its 4,000 full-time undergraduate students from thirty states and thirty-eight countries. Typically, 50 percent of York's freshmen hail from Pennsylvania, 20 percent from New Jersey, 10 percent from Maryland and New York, and 2 percent each from Connecticut, Virginia, and Delaware. Fifty-six percent of full-time students are women, and 5 percent are members of minority groups. There are eighty student organizations on campus, including ten fraternities and eight sororities. Freshman-to-sophomore retention is 83 percent, and 76 percent of all full-time undergraduates receive financial aid.

Faculty York College employs 377 faculty members; 136 are full-time, and 78 percent hold doctorates or terminal degrees. The student-faculty ratio is 15:1.

Key Facilities York College offers fourteen computer labs with more than 300 up-to-date computers that are available to all students and faculty and staff members. Every computer is equipped with full Internet access, e-mail, online course registration, library catalog search capability, and remote access to other colleges and sites around the world. All campus residence hall rooms have full network and Internet access. The library contains 300,000 volumes, 500,000 microform items, 11,000 audiovisual items/CDs, and subscriptions to 1,500 periodicals.

Honorary Societies Honor societies such as Alpha Chi, Alpha Phi Sigma, Sigma Theta Tau, Phi Alpha Theta, Phi Sigma Pi, Pi Kappa Delta, and Sigma Iota Epsilon are available to eligible students.

Athletics York College offers an extensive intercollegiate athletics program, consisting of baseball, basketball, cheerleading, cross-country, golf, lacrosse, soccer, swimming, tennis, track, and wrestling for men and basketball, cheerleading, cross-country, field hockey, soccer, softball, swimming, tennis, track, and volleyball for women. York College is a member of NCAA Division III and the Capital Athletic Conference. Most students participate in a diverse intramural program, which features a wide variety of men's and women's sports that are played throughout the academic year. Rugby, women's lacrosse, women's soccer, and men's volleyball are played as club sports.

Study Abroad Study-abroad exchange programs are offered in England (University College of York St. John), Korea (Honam University), Mexico (Cemanahual Educational Community), and Ecuador (Pontificia Universidad Catalica del Ecuador in Quito).

Support Services Seventy-five percent of the campus is handicap-accessible. Wheelchair ramps, elevators, special parking, specially equipped restrooms, special class scheduling, lowered drinking fountains, and lowered telephones are available.

Job Opportunities Internships are available and encouraged for all York College students and are required for some majors. Work-study and work aid positions are available to students with demonstrated need. Cooperative experiences are required in certain majors. On- and off-campus employment opportunities are maintained in the Career Services Office.

Tuition: $7000 (2001–02)

Room and Board: $5128

Mandatory Fees: $422

Contact: Admissions Office, York College of Pennsylvania, York, Pennsylvania 17405; Telephone: 717-849-1600 or 800-455-8018 (toll-free); Web site: http://www.ycp.edu

---

Interpreting the symbols: **2**=two-year college, **4**=four-year college; **Pu**=public or state college, **Pr**=private college; **G**=general honors program; **D**=departmental honors program; **S**=small program (fewer than 100 students), **M**=midsize program (100 to 500 students), **L**=large program (more than 500 students); **Sc**=scholarships available in honors program; **Tr**=transfer students accepted into honors program; **HBC**=historically black college; **AA**=academic advisors; **GA**=graduate advisors; **FA**=fellowship advisors.

YOUNGSTOWN STATE UNIVERSITY

4 Pu G L Sc Tr

▼ University Scholars and Honors Programs

The Honors Degree Program is designed to create a continuing community of intellectual excellence. Exceptional students brought together from diverse disciplines and challenged with extraordinary courses and learning experiences outside the classroom can find in the program opportunities to develop their full cultural and intellectual potential, with their unique academic achievements being recognized with an honors degree. Intended to foster interdisciplinary interaction, self-expression, experimentation, leadership, and academic excellence, the Honors Degree Program serves as a tangible emblem of Youngstown State University's commitment to education, teaching innovation, and cultural enrichment.

The 23-year-old program currently enrolls 600 students.

Participation Requirements: To graduate from the Honors Program, students must have a minimum 3.4 GPA overall and have completed 36 credit hours of honors courses, with 12 hours outside their major, three courses related by department, two courses at the 700-800 level as honors or nonhonors, and a senior thesis. Students wear an honors medal at Commencement, and, upon graduation, students are distinguished by a diploma recognizing their honors degree.

Admission Process: First-quarter students either in the top 15 percent of their high school graduating class or with a minimum ACT score of 26 (or minimum combined SAT I score of 1140) as well as other interested students may apply. University Scholars who have an ACT score of at least 28 or an SAT I score of at least 1260 are automatically enrolled in the program. Students who have completed at least 12 hours with a minimum GPA of 3.4 are also encouraged to join the Honors Degree Program.

Scholarship Availability: The University Scholarship is YSU's most prestigious scholarship. These are awarded to first-year students who have graduated from high school in the same year that they will enroll at YSU as full-time students. Candidates must have, as minimum criteria for award consideration, a score of 28 or better on the ACT or 1220 or better on the SAT I and be recognized as National Merit or Achievement Semifinalist or rank in the upper 15 percent of high school class pursuing a college-preparatory curriculum. The value of the scholarship (estimated at $10,000) includes all fees and tuition for up to 58 hours per year (20 quarter hours for two quarters and 18 quarter hours for one quarter), plus campus room and board fees and a $360 academic-year book allowance. If renewed for four years of study, the estimated value of the scholarship is $40,000.

Forty-five new University scholarships (full cost) are awarded annually for a total of 180. In addition, twenty full-cost scholarships are available to students who have completed Associate Degree program at a community college or technical school.

The Campus Context: Youngstown State University had its beginning in 1908 as the School of Law of the Youngstown Association School. It underwent many changes until 1967, when it joined the Ohio system of higher education and became known as Youngstown State University. The current colleges that are part of the Youngstown State include College of Arts and Science; the Warren P. Williamson, Jr. College of Business Administration; the College of Education; the College of Engineering and Technology; the College of Fine and Performing Arts; and the College of Health and Human Services. There are eighty-one degree programs on campus, some with more than one track or concentration. Among distinguished facilities are the McDonough Museum, Cataro House, Veterans Memorial, and Butler Institute of American Art.

Student Body Undergraduate enrollment is 12,533; 5,646 are men and 6,887 are women. Approximately 9,800 students receive financial aid. There are six sororities and eight fraternities.

Faculty Of the 800 faculty members, 420 are full-time. Seventy-seven percent of faculty members hold terminal degrees. The student-faculty ratio is approximately 18:1.

Key Facilities The library contains 697,212 volumes, more than 1 million microforms, and 201,996 government documents. The library is part of the Online Computer Library Center, which provides reference and interlibrary loan services. It is also a member of OhioLINK, a statewide library and information network linking university, college, and community college libraries as well as the State Library of Ohio.

Fifty-one computer labs housing 1,100 computers are available in several buildings on campus and contain IBM and Macintosh computers. All personal computers are networked to allow access to local software as well as to other facilities on campus such as Maag Library and Internet sites worldwide. The honors residence hall is also equipped to allow students to connect to the network from their rooms with the purchase of an Ethernet card.

Honorary Societies Phi Kappa Phi, Golden Key

Athletics Participation in athletics is open to any student who qualifies under the YSU, NCAA, and conference eligibility regulations. Men's teams compete in intercollegiate baseball, basketball, cross-country, football, golf, tennis, and track and field. Women's intercollegiate teams compete in basketball, cross-country, softball, soccer, tennis, track and field, and volleyball.

Study Abroad Various departments offer study-abroad opportunities for credit. Students interested in international study consult with their major departments and the study-abroad adviser.

Support Services Facilities for disabled students include a lounge, adapted rooms in housing, Archenstone reading machine in the library, a computer for voice input and output at end of year, and a campus escort service.

Job Opportunities There are many opportunities for students to work on campus, including positions in parking services, the library, or computer labs and as resident assistants, peer assistants, research assistants, and office assistants.

Tuition: $2940 for state residents, $4704 for nonresidents within a 100-mile radius, $6936 for nonresidents outside a 100 mile-radius, minimum per year

Room and Board: $4560

Mandatory Fees: $699

Contact: Director: Dr. Nathan P. Ritchey, One University Plaza, Youngstown, Ohio 44555; Telephone: 330-742-2772; Fax: 330-742-4743; E-mail: nate@math.ysu.edu, alcossen@cc.ysu.edu; Web site: http://www.ysu.edu/honors/index.htm

Geographic Index